CRIMINAL PROCEDURES

EDITORIAL ADVISORS

ASPEN CASEBOOK SERIES

CRIMINAL PROCEDURES

Cases, Statutes, and Executive Materials

Fourth Edition

MARC L. MILLER
Vice Dean and Ralph W. Bilby Professor of Law
The University of Arizona James E. Rogers College of Law

RONALD F. WRIGHT
Professor of Law
Wake Forest University School of Law

Published by Wolters Kluwer Law & Business in New York.

Wolters Kluwer Law & Business serves customers worldwide with CCH, Aspen Publishers, and Kluwer Law International products. (www.wolterskluwerlb.com)

To contact Customer Service, e-mail customer.service@wolterskluwer.com, call 1-800-234-1660, fax 1-800-901-9075, or mail correspondence to:

Wolters Kluwer Law & Business
Attn: Order Department
PO Box 990
Frederick, MD 21705

Printed in the United States of America.

1 2 3 4 5 6 7 8 9 0

ISBN 978-0-7355-0720-3

Library of Congress Cataloging-in-Publication Data

Miller, Marc (Marc Louis)
Criminal procedures : cases, statutes, and executive materials / Marc L. Miller and Ronald F. Wright. — 4th ed.
p. cm. — (Aspen casebook series)
Includes bibliographical references and index.
ISBN 978-0-7355-0720-3
1. Criminal procedure — United States — Cases. I. Wright, Ronald F., 1959-II. Title.

KF9618.M52 2011
345.73'05 — dc22

2011018125

SFI label applies to the text stock

About Wolters Kluwer Law & Business

Wolters Kluwer Law & Business is a leading global provider of intelligent information and digital solutions for legal and business professionals in key specialty areas, and respected educational resources for professors and law students. Wolters Kluwer Law & Business connects legal and business professionals as well as those in the education market with timely, specialized authoritative content and information-enabled solutions to support success through productivity, accuracy and mobility.

Serving customers worldwide, Wolters Kluwer Law & Business products include those under the Aspen Publishers, CCH, Kluwer Law International, Loislaw, Best Case, ftwilliam.com and MediRegs family of products.

CCH products have been a trusted resource since 1913, and are highly regarded resources for legal, securities, antitrust and trade regulation, government contracting, banking, pension, payroll, employment and labor, and healthcare reimbursement and compliance professionals.

Aspen Publishers products provide essential information to attorneys, business professionals and law students. Written by preeminent authorities, the product line offers analytical and practical information in a range of specialty practice areas from securities law and intellectual property to mergers and acquisitions and pension/benefits. Aspen's trusted legal education resources provide professors and students with high-quality, up-to-date and effective resources for successful instruction and study in all areas of the law.

Kluwer Law International products provide the global business community with reliable international legal information in English. Legal practitioners, corporate counsel and business executives around the world rely on Kluwer Law journals, looseleafs, books, and electronic products for comprehensive information in many areas of international legal practice.

Loislaw is a comprehensive online legal research product providing legal content to law firm practitioners of various specializations. Loislaw provides attorneys with the ability to quickly and efficiently find the necessary legal information they need, when and where they need it, by facilitating access to primary law as well as state-specific law, records, forms and treatises.

Best Case Solutions is the leading bankruptcy software product to the bankruptcy industry. It provides software and workflow tools to flawlessly streamline petition preparation and the electronic filing process, while timely incorporating ever-changing court requirements.

ftwilliam.com offers employee benefits professionals the highest quality plan documents (retirement, welfare and non-qualified) and government forms (5500/PBGC, 1099 and IRS) software at highly competitive prices.

MediRegs products provide integrated health care compliance content and software solutions for professionals in healthcare, higher education and life sciences, including professionals in accounting, law and consulting.

Wolters Kluwer Law & Business, a division of Wolters Kluwer, is headquartered in New York. Wolters Kluwer is a market-leading global information services company focused on professionals.

About Wolters Kluwer Law & Business

Summary of Contents

Contents

PART FOUR

MEASURING PUNISHMENT AND REASSESSING GUILT 1361

Preface

The American criminal justice system is huge, complex, and varied. Federal, state, and local governments together spend over $200 billion each year on policing, prosecution, trial, and punishment. Well over 2.3 million persons are incarcerated in federal and state prisons, and state and local jails, in the United States at any one time. Another 5 million are on probation or parole.

There are almost 18,000 separate police agencies in the United States, with around 800,000 sworn officers. There are even more "private police" and security agents. In an average year, these officers and agents make more than 14 million arrests.

Criminal cases are prosecuted by more than 2,400 prosecutors' offices, employing about 35,000 attorneys and more than 50,000 additional staff. They obtain about 1 million felony convictions every year, and even more misdemeanor convictions. Thousands of attorneys work as public defenders or as defense counsel in private practice. Thousands of judges hear cases in trial and appellate courts. Lawyers often find their first jobs in the criminal justice system. Some stay for life.

Criminal procedure is the body of law governing this collection of systems. The law of criminal procedure directs — or at least attempts to direct — the actions of police officers, prosecutors, defense attorneys, judges, and other government officials. Criminal procedure limits the way the government may interact with citizens, suspects, defendants, convicted offenders, and victims.

The federal government, every state government, and many local governments operate criminal justice systems. They all spend time, effort, and money each year running and reshaping their respective systems. Although the federal system is one of the largest systems standing alone, the state and local systems collectively are much larger. Virtually all misdemeanors are processed in state courts, along with almost 95 percent of all felony convictions. Criminal justice in the United States is overwhelmingly a state and local function.

There is no one criminal procedure: Each system follows its own set of rules, controlled to different degrees by outside authorities. Procedural rules come from many sources, including constitutions, legislatures, courts, and executive branch agencies. Because the issues of criminal procedure are common and accessible — unlike, say, antitrust law — a wealth of less formal constraints, including community views and the media, also shape procedure. We have titled this casebook "Criminal Procedures" to reflect these multiple layers and sources of law.

The Approach in This Casebook

A criminal procedure casebook must impose some order on the morass of cases, rules, and practices that characterize criminal justice systems. One accepted way to make this material accessible for newcomers is to focus on the role of one important institution, the United States Supreme Court, and on one important source of law, the United States Constitution.

Since the days of the Warren Court, starting in 1953, the Supreme Court has influenced criminal justice systems in profound ways. It made the Bill of Rights in the federal Constitution a shaping force for every criminal justice system. The Warren Court made the story of criminal procedure, told from the point of view of the Supreme Court, compelling. The main topics of controversy were police practices: stops, searches, and interrogations. Other decisions of the Court created a basic framework for providing defendants with counsel and for conducting criminal trials. For years, the focus on the Supreme Court's constitutional rulings guided students through the questions that most concerned judges and lawyers.

But the story of this one institution offers less explanatory power as time passes. Traditional issues on the Court's constitutional criminal procedure docket now occupy less of the attention of judges, attorneys, defendants, victims, and others concerned with criminal justice. Most criminal defendants do not go to trial. Many have no complaints about illegal searches or coerced confessions. These defendants and their lawyers care about pretrial detention, the charges filed, the plea agreements they can reach with the prosecutor, and their sentences.

The central questions have shifted in light of changes in the workload, politics, funding, and structure of criminal justice institutions. For example, the question of *whether* indigent defendants will get counsel has become a question of what counsel they will get. New crime-fighting strategies — such as community policing and curfews — advances in technology, and changes in the political and social order raise new questions and place old questions in a new light. For judges, sentencing questions in particular have attained higher priority: Determining the proper sentence in some systems now requires more time from court personnel than resolution of guilt or innocence.

The U.S. Supreme Court leaves important dimensions of most procedural issues unresolved and thus leaves other institutions free to innovate; they have done so. The issues of current importance in criminal procedure are being shaped in multiple institutions, including state courts, legislatures, and executive branch agencies.

This book adopts a panoramic view of criminal procedure, emphasizing the interaction among, and variety within, criminal justice systems. In our opinion, students in an upper-level course such as criminal procedure can and should move beyond the skills of case synthesis and beyond the ability to appreciate the role of only one institution. Our materials emphasize the following themes and objectives:

- *Procedural variety.* In each area we present competing rules from the federal and state systems. We also occasionally examine procedures from earlier times or from non-U.S. systems. Reviewing different possible procedural rules encourages critical analysis and helps identify the assumptions held and judgments made in the design of each criminal system.
- *Materials from multiple institutions.* In addition to leading U.S. Supreme Court cases, we make extensive use of state high court cases, statutes, rules of procedure, and police and prosecutorial policies, and we encourage readers to consider the interactions among multiple institutions. Examining the efforts of different institutions to achieve similar goals highlights the reality of procedural innovation and reform.
- *Real-world perspective.* We focus on procedures and issues of current importance to defendants, lawyers, courts, legislators, and the public. We devote the most attention to the issues arising in the largest number of cases.
- *Street-level federalism.* Federal law, typically in the form of constitutional decisions by the U.S. Supreme Court, still plays an important role in guiding the investigation and prosecution of high-volume street crimes. The interactions of police with citizens and suspects form the workaday setting for issues of criminal justice. The impact of abstract constitutional doctrine on these daily interactions raises important theoretical questions about federal-state relations and interactions among jurisdictions and governmental institutions.
- *Political context.* Materials trace the political environment surrounding different institutions and issues. We explore the impact of public concerns such as terrorism, drug trafficking, domestic abuse, and treatment of crime victims on procedural rules. Funding decisions with regard to criminal justice systems also offer a window into the political setting.
- *Impact of procedures.* We consider the effects that different procedures have on law enforcers, lawyers, courts, communities, defendants, and victims. We emphasize primary materials but include social science studies as well, especially when they have been the basis for procedural reform. This perspective keeps in mind the managerial needs of criminal justice: Any legal rule must apply to multitudes of defendants in overcrowded systems.

By studying the various ways in which state and local systems have answered crucial procedural questions, students become aware of a broader range of policy alternatives. They form a more complete picture of the complex and interactive workings of the criminal justice system. Our goal in emphasizing the variety within criminal procedure is to produce lawyers who know both the current law and the way to shape better law down the road.

Conceptual Anchors

Our emphasis on variety does not mean that we will survey the practices of all 50 states on each issue; this casebook is not a treatise. Rather, the materials highlight the majority and minority views on each topic, as well as the federal view. The major positions on a topic are usually summarized in the first note following the principal materials. Truly distinctive answers to problems are mentioned occasionally as a point of comparison with the leading approach, but the uniqueness of the position is always highlighted.

The book addresses a wide range of U.S. Supreme Court precedents, including the recognized core of essential cases and many of the most recent important decisions. State supreme court decisions summarizing and critiquing a U.S. Supreme Court decision, or a line of cases, represent effective teaching tools since the state cases tend to highlight the competing doctrinal positions. State supreme court opinions by and large show less interest in the positions of individual justices than do U.S. Supreme Court decisions and devote less attention to questions about consistency with past decisions. State supreme court opinions often provide provocative settings that show how principles operate in practice. They tend to present succinctly the textual and institutional arguments favoring a procedural requirement, the values furthered by the rules, and their likely effects on police, suspects, and communities.

Studying a variety of possible answers to important procedural questions has an unexpected effect: through criticism and contrast it provides students with a firmer grasp of the federal approach, including current federal constitutional criminal procedure, than does presentation of federal law alone. Students become better equipped to understand what is truly important about the current norms. Short "problems" throughout the book also enable readers to apply and integrate basic concepts.

The state cases appearing in this book take every conceivable position with respect to Supreme Court precedent, ranging from total agreement to complete rejection, and encompassing subtle variations in interpretation and emphasis. For a large number of state cases that focus on state constitutional or statutory questions, the position of the U.S. Supreme Court is simply irrelevant. The case selection does not favor decisions merely because they reject the U.S. Supreme Court view — the "new federalism" approach. These materials are not a battle cry for state court independence; they simply reflect the vibrancy of state supreme courts and state law.

The Fourth Edition

The fourth edition of this book is a response to changes in the field, incorporating emerging themes and major issues. Such themes and issues — the turning points in the law — result at least as often from dramatic events outside the courtroom as from blockbuster judicial decisions. Such dramatic and unexpected "drivers" of change in criminal procedure over the years since the first edition of this book appeared include increasing attention to issues of race, especially the so-called DWB (driving while black) stops on American highways and the "innocence" projects that have revealed strings of wrongful convictions. The fourth edition continues to explore the legal echoes within domestic criminal procedure of the attacks on September 11, 2001, and the ongoing war on terrorism.

We have made changes in every chapter. Some of those changes reflect actual shifts in doctrine, while others are the result of suggestions by teachers and students about cases and materials that worked well in the classroom, and others that might be improved.

Our attention to developments in the states provides a large pool of new cases, statutes, and rules to draw from, keeping the discussion anchored to current reality in criminal justice. For example, many of the cases in this book were decided after 2000. Recent federal developments also find their place in these pages. Significant U.S. Supreme Court cases added to this edition include Arizona v. Gant, Berghuis v. Thompkins, Herring v. United States, Maryland v. Shatzer, Padilla v. Kentucky, and Rothgery v. Gillespie County.

The overall goal of these changes has been to produce a book that remains fresh and engaging.

Criminal Procedure Courses

This book covers the full spectrum of procedure, from casual police-citizen interactions to appeals. Part One examines police activities, including stops, investigations, searches, arrests, interrogations, and identifications. This coverage is the heart of the basic criminal procedure course, often labeled the police practices course. It is typically taught in three or four classroom hours.

Most law schools now offer a second procedure course — often called the bail-to-jail course — that focuses on the regulation of prosecutors, defense counsel, and courts before and during trial. Part Two examines procedural issues before trial, including the provision of defense counsel, and Part Three explores adjudication of guilt through both the most common method (the plea bargain) and the most prominent one (the trial). Some survey or advanced courses include an introduction to the new law of sentencing and the procedures governing appeals and collateral review of convictions. Part Four provides a relatively brief introduction to sentencing and post-conviction review.

The materials throughout this volume address interrelated themes; criminal procedure is a relatively coherent field. It is not necessary, however, to study the materials on police practices before those on adjudication, for example. Within each course, the teacher can approach topics from a variety of perspectives and using a number of different doctrinal starting points. Students should not be surprised if their professor presents the chapters in an order different from the one we have used or adds chapters, cases, or other materials to the course.

Procedure, Politics, and Reform

This book reminds readers regularly about the political environment shaping the work of every institutional actor in criminal justice. The materials consider the changing political priorities that make enforcement especially urgent for certain criminal laws — those punishing drug trafficking, environmental crimes, and sexual assault, to name a few. Such high-priority enforcement efforts influence criminal procedure more generally. Terrorism is the newest and most tragic law enforcement priority, and we consider the potential impact of new approaches and doctrines aimed at terrorists on domestic criminal procedure and the implications for more typical crimes.

The theme of jurisdictional and institutional variation draws critical attention to the role of states, whose systems handle 94 percent of the felonies prosecuted in the United States. But while the federal and state systems are the most appropriate levels at which to consider constitutional and statutory constraints, the local level is the true locus of criminal justice power. It is also the place where criminal justice systems in the United States engage most citizens. There are roughly 3,000 counties in the United States, including 254 in Texas and 168 in Georgia.

The local foundations of discretionary power in U.S. criminal justice systems are reflected in the funding for those systems. Just over half of all criminal justice funding comes from the local level, just over 30 percent from the state level, and just under 20 percent from the federal level. But funding is not spread evenly across system components. Police services are primarily funded at the local level, prisons are funded at the state level, and the costs of prosecution and adjudication are funded primarily at both the local and state levels. There has been much legal and public debate over the 30-year expansion in the federal prosecution of what traditionally would have been local drug offenses; today, immigration and drug crimes dominate the federal criminal docket, although the federal courts do continue to handle traditional areas of federal interest such as bank robbery and large-scale fraud.

Students who appreciate the handful of basic political struggles that time and again shape procedural debates will be better able to direct changes in the system and to influence decisions in close cases. The struggles center on questions such as these: What are the purposes of the criminal justice system? In particular, what is the relevance of criminal law and procedure to the social goals of crime control and prevention? How does the theory and practice of federalism inform criminal justice theory and practice? Can we trust the police? How vital is the adversary system and the role of defense counsel to the success of that system? Are we comfortable with the broad discretion exercised on a daily basis by police and prosecutors? How important is it to treat suspects similarly? Should we explicitly consider the costs of procedures?

The priorities inherent in this textbook suggest a return to the study of criminal procedure as a genuine procedure course, not a course in constitutional adjudication. The constitutional component remains an indispensable part of the course but is not the sum total of criminal procedure.

The return to a fuller conception of criminal procedure offers enormous opportunities to those who study the system and to those who will soon participate in its operation and evolution. When many institutions are able to shape a legal system, there are many opportunities for change. We hope each student will leave this course with a sense of the drama and the special challenges of each case and of the entire process. We hope each student will finish school ready to create procedures more sound than those that exist today.

Marc Miller
Ron Wright

Tucson, Arizona
Winston-Salem, North Carolina
February 2011

Acknowledgments

Creating a new edition of this book powerfully reminded us of how communities make work more fun and make final products better. Our debts extend to our friends and colleagues, our institutions, our students, our teachers, and our families.

Some of the teachers who use this book contact us on occasion to suggest improvements for future editions. They include Laura Appleman, Doug Berman, Stephanos Bibas, Frank Bowman, Irus Braverman, Darryl Brown, Jenny Carroll, Steve Chanenson, Jack Chin, Jennifer Collins, Steve Easton, Nancy Gertner, Aya Gruber, Thaddeus Hoffmeister, Jim Jacobs, Sam Kamin, Elizabeth Ludwin King, Tamara Lave, Kay Levine, Dan Markel, Tracey Meares, Alan Michaels, Tommy Miller, Kenneth Nunn, Jenny Roberts, Kami Simmons, Jonathan Simon, Shandrea Solomon, Kate Stith, Paul Stokstad, Andrew Taslitz, Sandra Guerra Thompson, Robert Wagner, Jonathan Witmer-Rich, David Yellen, and Tung Yin. It is a great joy for us as editors to learn from them what is happening in classrooms all over the world.

Scholars who provided wise counsel on earlier editions, which is still very evident in the revised volume, include Albert Alschuler, Akhil Amar, Barbara Babcock, Adolph Dean, Nora Demleitner, George Fisher, Dan Freed, Mark Hall, Mark Harris, Lenese Herbert, Andrew Kull, Gerard Lynch, William Mayton, David Orentlicher, Leonard Orland, Alan Palmiter, Anne Poulin, Aaron Rappaport, Sadiq Reza, Natsu Saito, Stephen Schulhofer, Charles Shanor, Rick Singer, Michael Smith, Charles Weisselberg, Bert Westbrook, and Deborah Young. We have also learned from two extensive published reviews of this book. See Robert Weisberg, A New Legal Realism for Criminal Procedure, 49 Buff. L. Rev. 909 (2001), and Stephanos Bibas, The Real-World Shift in Criminal Procedure, 93 J. Crim. L. & Criminology 789 (2003).

We have both been graced with great teachers, all of whom became friends. We can trace in these pages the influence of Norval Morris, Frank Zimring, Edward Levi, Richard Epstein, Philip Kurland, David Currie, James Boyd White, Owen Fiss, Robert Burt, Peter Schuck, Steven Duke, and Judges Frank Johnson and John Godbold.

Over the years we have worked on this project with many fine students whose energy renewed our own. They include Liz Asplund, Amber Byers, Ryan Carter, Pablo Clarke, Perry Coumas, Don Donelson, Ben Durie, Joseph Ezzo, Heather Gaw, Jennifer Gibbons, Kaitlyn Girard, Elizabeth Goodwin, Whitney Hendrix, Antoine Marshall, Emily Parish, Russ Rotondi, and Rebecca Stahl. Exceptional research help on earlier editions came from Roger Abramson, Nathan Adams, Wes Camden, Sean Monaghan, Tyronia Morrison, Alice Shanlever, and Daniel Terner.

We have made heavy demands on our libraries and technology experts, and owe thanks to Marcia Baker, Terry Gordon, Sarah Gotschall, Will Haines, Deborah Keene, Lori Levy, William Morse, Stuart Myerberg, Holliday Osborne, John Perkins, and Erika Wayne. Steve Turner, the former director of the Wilsonville, Oregon, public library, helped us achieve greater clarity throughout the book. Kristie Gallardo, Barbara Lopez, Beverly Marshall, Radine Robinson, and Marissa White provided timely administrative support for this edition and earlier ones: It is a miracle they did not ask to work with faculty other than us.

We also have debts to many of the hard-working and visionary lawyers and judges in the criminal justice system. A few who provided special assistance are Harry Connick and Tim McElroy of the District Attorney's office in New Orleans; Numa Bertel of the Orleans Indigent Defender Program; Judge Camille Buras of the District Court in New Orleans; Lawson Lamar and William Vose of the State Attorney's office in Orange County, Florida; Russell Hauge of the Kitsap County Prosecutor's Office in Washington; Peter Gilchrist of the District Attorney's Office in Mecklenburg County, North Carolina; Patricia Jessamy of the State's Attorney's office in Baltimore, Maryland; and Chief Judge James Carr of the U.S. District Court for the Northern District of Ohio. We appreciate the willingness of police departments and prosecutorial and defender's offices to give us copies of their policies and manuals. We have also gained insight from our conversations with skilled reporters and criminal justice reformers, including Kevin Corcoran.

Family debts for so consuming a project are hard to recognize in print, and even harder to repay in life. Joanna Wright, ever the curious one, shows an interest in everything from exclusionary rules to font sizes. Andrew Wright keeps reminding us that justice for real people must be the bottom line for any legal procedure. Owen Miller (age 8) is full of questions about everything, starting with the basics: "What is a bad guy?" and "Why do police officers carry guns?" Evelyn Miller (4) wants to know why this book has so many words and so few pictures. Wyatt Miller (2) is still focused on questions of even a more fundamental nature. Conversations with our brothers Travis Wright, who is a police officer, and Craig Miller, who for years worked on justice reform projects and now teaches inner-city high school students history and government, helped us remember that criminal procedure rules guide the behavior of people in very different settings. Other family members (especially Alex Miller, Renata Miller, Katy Miller, Denis Wright, Kyung Ah Wright, and the Ohlingers and Mannings) read parts of the manuscript and forgave us for the piles of papers and disks at every family gathering.

Our parents have been our teachers, our friends, and our models. Ron's father, Ronald F. Wright, Sr., died when Ron was a law student, but his energy and optimism pervade this book. Marc's father, Howard, for many years a law professor, provided steady advice from beginning to end. Our mothers, Marian and Shirley, showed a confidence that helped us keep our destination in mind when work seemed nothing but roads.

This book sits between covers only because of the daily encouragement and advice of Amy Wright and Christina Cutshaw. Putting up with writing projects is not part of the wedding vows; perhaps it should be.

Albert Alschuler, Implementing the Criminal Defendant's Right to Trial: Alternatives to the Plea Bargaining System, 50 U. Chi. L. Rev. 931 (1983). Copyright © 1983 by the University of Chicago Law Review. Reprinted with permission.

Paul G. Cassell & Bret S. Hayman, Police Interrogation in the 1990s: An Empirical Study of the Effects of Miranda, 43 UCLA L. Rev. 839 (1996). Copyright © 1996 by The Regents of the University of California. All Rights Reserved. Reprinted by permission of the authors and the UCLA Law Review.

Erwin Chemerinsky, An Independent Analysis of the Los Angeles Police Department's Board of Inquiry Report on the Rampart Scandal. Copyright © 2000 by the author. Reprinted with permission.

John P. Cronan, Is Any of This Making Sense? Reflecting on Guilty Pleas to Aid Criminal Juror Comprehension, 39 Am. Crim. L. Rev. 1187 (2002). Copyright © 2002 by the American Criminal Law Review. Reprinted with permission.

Frank Easterbrook, Plea Bargaining as Compromise, 101 Yale L.J. 1969 (1992). Copyright © 1992 by The Yale Law Journal Company. Reprinted by permission of The Yale Law Journal Company and Fred B. Rothman & Company.

Richard S. Frase, State Sentencing Guidelines: Diversity, Consensus, and Unresolved Policy Issues, 105 Colum. L. Rev. 1190 (2005). Copyright © 2005 by the author. Reprinted with permission.

David Frisby, Florida's Police Continuum of Force, Trial Advoc. Q. (July 1993). Copyright © 1993 by the Florida Defense Lawyers Association. Reprinted with permission.

John Griffiths, Ideology in Criminal Procedure, or a Third "Model" of the Criminal Process, 79 Yale L.J. 359 (1970). Copyright © 1970 by The Yale Law Journal Company. Reprinted by permission of The Yale Law Journal Company and Fred B. Rothman & Company.

Ralph Norman Haber & Lyn Haber, Experiencing, Remembering and Reporting Events, 6 Psychol. Pub. Pol'y & L. 1057-1091 (2000). Copyright © 2000 by the American Psychological Association. Reprinted with permission.

John Kaplan, Defending Guilty People, 7 U. Bridgeport L. Rev. 223 (1986). Copyright © 1986 by the University of Bridgeport Law Review Association. Reprinted by permission of the Quinnipiac Law Review.

Tracey L. Meares, Norms, Legitimacy, and Law Enforcement, 79 Or. L. Rev. 391 (2000). Copyright 2000 by the Oregon Law Review. Reprinted with permission.

Herbert Packer, Two Models of the Criminal Process, 113 U. Pa. L. Rev. 1 (1964). Copyright © 1964 by the Trustees of the University of Pennsylvania. Reprinted with permission.

Dale Parent, Structuring Criminal Sentences: The Evolution of Minnesota's Sentencing Guidelines (1988). Copyright © 1988 by Butterworth Legal Publishers. Reprinted with permission from LEXIS Law Publishing, Charlottesville, VA (800) 446-3410. All Rights Reserved.

Reena Raggi, Local Concerns, Local Insights, 5 Fed. Sent'g Rep. 306 (1993). Copyright © 1993, Vera Institute of Justice. Reprinted with permission of the author.

Lawrence W. Sherman and Richard A. Berk, The Minneapolis Domestic Violence Experiment. Washington, D.C., Police Foundation, 1984. Reprinted with permission of the Police Foundation.

William J. Stuntz, The Substantive Origins of Criminal Procedure, 105 Yale L.J. 393 (1995). Copyright © 1995 by The Yale Law Journal Company. Reprinted by permission of The Yale Law Journal Company and Fred B. Rothman & Company.

Barbara Underwood, Ending Race Discrimination in Jury Selection: Whose Right Is It, Anyway? 92 Colum. L. Rev. 725 (1992). Reprinted by permission of the author and the Columbia Law Review.

Vera Institute of Justice, Fair Treatment for the Indigent: The Manhattan Bail Project, in Ten-Year Report, 1961-1971. Reprinted by permission of Vera Institute of Justice, Inc.

Ronald Wright & Marc Miller, The Screening/Bargaining Tradeoff, 55 Stan. L. Rev. 29 (2002). Copyright © 2002 by the Board of Trustees of the Leland Stanford Junior University. Reprinted with permission.

PART ONE

GATHERING INFORMATION

I

The Border of Criminal Procedure: Daily Interactions Between Citizens and Police

Criminal procedure shapes the behavior of police, prosecutors, defense attorneys, and courts as they investigate crimes, prosecute, defend, and adjudge defendants, and sentence criminals. Many institutions create procedural rules to regulate the criminal justice process.

Looking at police work, for example, there are rules about when police can stop, search, and arrest suspects. But not all police activities are subject to rules. For example, no state has a body of law telling police officers how they should talk with people on their rounds. Why not? Legal systems are supposed to prevent extraordinary and undesirable police actions. Thus, when a legal system allows some kinds of police activities to fall outside the bounds of formal legal rules, it is an indication of what society considers to be ordinary and desirable policing.

A society's vision of ordinary and desirable police behavior determines the "border" of criminal procedure — that is, the point where the law, in the form of rules from whatever source, starts to guide and limit police activity. This chapter explores that border. It suggests that assumptions about the *ordinary* behavior of the police shape the procedures we will study in later chapters, procedures that govern the *exceptional* confrontations between citizens and officers.

Modern criminal procedure assumes that the police initiate contact with citizens while "engaged in the often competitive enterprise of ferreting out crime." Johnson v. United States, 333 U.S. 10 (1948). But the police do many things in addition to ferreting out crime. The cases in Section A involve police-initiated actions that pursue some purpose other than enforcing the criminal law — actions often referred to as the "community caretaker" function of police. Should police and citizens have different powers and responsibilities when the police act outside their law enforcement mode? In the cases in Section B, citizens initiate the relationship by commenting on police behavior, usually in colorful (though rarely original) terms. In Section C, we consider the power of police to control the movement of kids, gang members, and other people. The chapter concludes with an examination of different philosophies of policing (in particular the currently dominant "community policing" model), asking whether a change in overall philosophy should produce changes in the relevant procedural rules governing the police.

A. POLICE AS COMMUNITY CARETAKERS

Any description of police work (and, therefore, any set of procedural rules to control the police) must reckon with the wide variety of functions that the police perform. Most of the time, police officers interact with citizens without giving a thought to making an arrest or gathering evidence of a crime. It is estimated that police officers devote roughly 70 percent of their time to matters other than criminal enforcement. The following materials — drawn from statutes, police department manuals, and cases — offer concrete images of police trying to accomplish something other than enforcing the criminal law. The police might view their task as defusing domestic disputes, or moving people out of dangerous or unhealthy situations, or offering guidance to young people, or something else. How should procedural rules that apply to the police account for these different functions? Should there be different rules for the police when they pursue "community caretaker" objectives rather than "law enforcement" objectives?

■ OREGON REVISED STATUTES §133.033

(1) [Any] peace officer of this state . . . is authorized to perform community caretaking functions.

(2) As used in this section, "community caretaking functions" means any lawful acts that are inherent in the duty of the peace officer to serve and protect the public. "Community caretaking functions" includes, but is not limited to:

(a) The right to enter or remain upon the premises of another if it reasonably appears to be necessary to:

(A) Prevent serious harm to any person or property;

(B) Render aid to injured or ill persons; or

(C) Locate missing persons.

(b) The right to stop or redirect traffic or aid motorists or other persons when such action reasonably appears to be necessary to:

(A) Prevent serious harm to any person or property;

(B) Render aid to injured or ill persons; or

(C) Locate missing persons. . . .

INDIANAPOLIS POLICE DEPARTMENT JOB DESCRIPTION: PATROL OFFICER

% TIME	*CRITICAL TASKS*
15%	1. Patrols assigned area in vehicle and on foot; maintains high patrol visibility to assist in crime prevention; actively performs routine beat patrol, concentrating on high incident areas, to detect possible criminal activities or needs for service; regularly checks businesses and residential areas; monitors radio broadcasts by Communications and other officers to ensure awareness of activities in area and to provide assistance, if needed; identifies, reports, and responds to suspicious activities or needs for service.
14%	2. Performs variety of police-community relations functions; meets and talks with citizens, providing information and advising of safety measures; visits local businesses to determine needs for service; assists motorists, providing directions; talks with juveniles in district to establish rapport; makes presentations to neighborhood organizations and block clubs. . . .
12%	3. Performs duties relating to service and assistance (lost child, injured persons, walk-aways, prowlers, abandoned vehicles, dog bites, civil law disputes, vehicle inspections, etc.). . . .
10%	4. Receives emergency and non-emergency radio runs and information from Communications; . . . responds to run, using siren and/or red lights in emergencies. . . .
10%	5. Prepares reports (incident reports, capias information sheets, probable cause affidavits, accident reports, arrest slips, [uniform traffic tickets], property slips, inter-departments, etc.) relating to activities in accordance with General Orders/Department Directives; observes and records events. . . .
8%	6. Performs duties relating to criminal investigation and apprehension; responds to scenes of possible criminal activity through radio runs, notification, or observation; assesses scene to determine situation needs (assistance from other officers, ambulance, detective, K-9, etc.); provides assistance to victim(s); searches and secures crime scene; interviews victims and witnesses to determine and verify nature of offense and identify suspect(s); notifies Communications of descriptions for broadcast; assists in pursuit (foot and vehicular) and/or apprehension of suspects; interrogates suspects, advising of Constitutional rights; makes arrests using only that force necessary; conducts search of arrested suspects; ensures suspects are transported to appropriate detention area and evidence is secured; advises victims of procedures to follow in prosecution.

% TIME	*CRITICAL TASKS*
6%	7. Performs duties relating to disturbances and domestic violence; . . . evaluates situation to determine needs (assistance from other officers, ambulance, etc.); administers first aid, if needed; assists in resolution of conflicts; subdues violent subject using only that physical force necessary; makes arrests as needed to preserve peace . . . ; advises victim of possible courses of action.
5%	8. Performs duties relating to traffic enforcement; observes traffic violations; stops vehicles; checks registration and licenses for status; advises driver of violation committed and need to maintain safe driving practices; conducts or requests breathalyzer tests, if indicated; issues citations and makes arrests to enforce law, advising violator of rights. . . .
5%	9. Performs duties relating to accident investigation and assistance; . . . assists in extraction of victims and provision of first aid; secures scene to prevent further incidents; conducts investigation, gathering evidence, taking statements, and preparing diagrams; conducts or requests breathalyzer tests, if indicated; issues citations and makes arrests to enforce law, advising violator of rights. . . .
5%	10. Testifies in court; prepares for testimony, reviewing reports and notes; meets with victims, witnesses, detectives, defense attorneys, and representatives from Prosecutor's Office to review case; . . . presents testimony in accordance with Department policy. . . .

■ STATE v. MICHAEL DUBE

655 A.2d 338 (Me. 1995)

WATHEN, C.J.

Michael Dube appeals from his conviction of endangering the welfare of a child, entered in the District Court following Dube's conditional guilty plea. The defendant challenges the District Court's denial of his motion to suppress [evidence that he claims was] obtained as a result of an illegal search. We vacate the Judgment of conviction.

On July 4, 1993, two officers of the Sanford Police Department responded to a call from the custodian of the apartment building in which defendant lived with his family. Defendant was not at home and the custodian needed to enter the apartment to stop sewage or water from leaking into the apartments below. The custodian had his own key but asked the police officers to accompany him to verify that he was only dealing with the emergency. When they entered the kitchen, the officers were struck with an "incredible smell of urine and feces." There was a puddle of urine on the kitchen floor, and an open diaper containing human feces that appeared to have been walked through by a baby. The feces had been tracked throughout the apartment. The officers watched the custodian [work on toilets on the first and second floors]. From where they stood on the landing, the officers could see into the three bedrooms. In the baby's bedroom and the children's bedroom, they saw clothes strewn on the floor covered with animal and human feces. There were at least 75-100 individual feces "right beside the baby's crib," and a similar number around the bunk beds and more in the hallway.

Officer Beaulieu called the Sanford Police Department to request that the Department of Human Services (DHS) send a caseworker to the apartment. He also radioed for another police unit to bring a camera. The officers asked the custodian to "stand by," and when he finished with the repairs the custodian waited on the sidewalk. About five minutes later, two officers arrived with a camera and Officer Beaulieu took pictures of parts of the apartment, and then went outside to wait with the custodian. When two DHS workers arrived, they were shown around the apartment by Officer Beaulieu. Thereafter, defendant and his family returned home, and he was charged with endangering the welfare of a child. . . .

Defendant argues that the initial entry into the apartment by the police officers was unlawful and a violation of the fourth amendment proscription against unreasonable searches. [We have noted] that a police officer has a legitimate role as a public servant to assist those in distress and to maintain and foster public safety. Local police officers frequently engage in community caretaking functions, totally divorced from the detection, investigation, or acquisition of evidence relating to the violation of a criminal statute.

In this case, the custodian had a statutory right to enter the apartment in response to an emergency, and the court found that it was reasonable for the police to accompany him. During the time that the officers were on the premises performing a lawful police function, their observations, made with their natural senses, without acting to enhance their view, [were proper].

Defendant next argues that even if the officers' initial entry was lawful, their continued presence at some point became unlawful. We agree. Although the officers were lawfully on the premises during the time the custodian was dealing with the plumbing emergency, their continued presence after the repairs were completed was unlawful. [The law required them at that point to leave the apartment and obtain a warrant before proceeding with any further searches. Although the photographs only recorded what was in plain sight,] the photographs were taken after the custodian had finished his repairs. [Once] the repairs were complete, the justification for the presence of the police in the apartment ceased. . . . We are required to vacate the judgment. . . .

STATE v. MICHAEL LOVEGREN

51 P.3d 471 (Mont. 2002)

NELSON, J.

. . . ¶3 On the night of October 31, 1998, Officer Gary Hofer of the Richland County Sheriff's Department was on routine patrol. At approximately 3:05 A.M., he came upon a vehicle parked on the side of Highway 16 South in Richland County between Crane and Sidney. The vehicle's motor was running, but its headlights were off. Officer Hofer stopped to investigate.

¶4 When Officer Hofer approached the vehicle and looked in the window, he saw Lovegren sitting in the driver's seat. Lovegren appeared to be asleep. Officer Hofer knocked on the window and, when Lovegren did not respond, Officer Hofer opened the door. Lovegren suddenly woke up and stated: "I was drinking." Officer Hofer smelled a strong odor of alcohol and he noticed that Lovegren's eyes were bloodshot, so he had Lovegren perform various field sobriety tests. Lovegren failed both the one-legged stand and the heel-to-toe test. Hence, Officer Hofer transported Lovegren to the station, where a breath test was performed. The test results showed that Lovegren's blood alcohol content was 0.115. Officer Hofer read Lovegren his *Miranda* rights and wrote out a citation charging him with driving under the influence of alcohol in violation of §61-8-401, MCA. . . .

¶6 On May 12, 1999, Lovegren filed a motion in the District Court asking the court to suppress all of the evidence obtained in the investigative stop on the grounds that Officer Hofer lacked a particularized suspicion of any wrongdoing on Lovegren's part, thus the stop was not justified. On May 26, 1999, the District Court denied Lovegren's motion, stating that a particularized suspicion was not required in this situation, as Officer Hofer had a duty to investigate for Lovegren's own safety.

¶7 . . . Lovegren was subsequently convicted of the charge and the District Court [fined Lovegren $420 and sentenced him to 60 days in jail with all but one day suspended. The court also suspended Lovegren's driver's license for six months. Lovegren appeals.]

¶10 . . . Lovegren contends that this investigative stop was not justified because Officer Hofer did not have a particularized suspicion that Lovegren had committed, was committing, or was about to commit an offense.

¶11 Lovegren also contends that the District Court overstepped its authority by inferring more from the police reports than what they actually said. Lovegren notes that in the police report, Officer Hofer clearly stated that the driver of the vehicle "appeared to be asleep" and that there were no references in the report to any signs of struggle or trauma to indicate the need of further assistance. Thus, Lovegren argues that the District Court erred in concluding that although the report indicates that the driver appeared to be asleep, the officer could not know whether the driver was asleep, ill, unconscious or even dead.

¶12 The State argues, on the other hand, that the District Court correctly determined that Officer Hofer did not need a particularized suspicion of criminal activity in this situation. The State maintains that the court correctly applied the "community caretaker doctrine" — even though the court did not identify it as such — in determining that Officer Hofer was justified in stopping to check on Lovegren's welfare and that Officer Hofer would have been derelict in his duties had he not done so. . . .

¶16 [Many courts recognize that some of the least intrusive police-citizen encounters do not] involve any form of detention at all and, therefore, [do] not involve a seizure. This category is generally referred to as the "community caretaker" or "public safety" function. . . .

¶18 Because this Court has not squarely addressed the community caretaker doctrine, we take this opportunity to survey the law from other jurisdictions in this area and to set forth our own test for application of this doctrine.

¶19 Of the many jurisdictions that have addressed this doctrine, a majority have adopted it in some form. However, the boundaries of this doctrine that control the judgment exercised by the officers in these situations are not consistent across all of the jurisdictions. Indeed, our review of the cases leads us to conclude that some jurisdictions have expanded the doctrine beyond what would likely be acceptable given the enhanced protection of the right of individual privacy and against unreasonable searches and seizures guaranteed under Article II, Sections 10 and 11 of the Montana Constitution. . . .

¶20 [T]he majority of the jurisdictions that have adopted the community caretaker doctrine have determined that a peace officer has a duty to investigate situations in which a citizen may be in peril or need some type of assistance from an officer. [The opinion cited cases from Minnesota, Alaska, New Jersey, Vermont, and Washington State.]

¶21 [T]he caretaking duties that come under this doctrine are varied and range from assisting a driver slumped over in his car to stopping a man walking alongside a road. [The opinion cited cases from Alaska, Arkansas, Illinois, North Dakota, Virginia, Wyoming, Alabama, and Wisconsin.]

¶22 In addition, many jurisdictions have recognized that the scope of any intrusion following the stop must be limited to those actions necessary to carry out the purposes of the stop, unless particularized suspicion or probable cause subsequently arises. See State v. Dube, 655 A.2d 338 (Me. 1995) (initial entry into apartment by police as they accompanied building custodian so he could make emergency repairs was lawful, but squalid conditions of apartment did not create exigent circumstances justifying officers' continued presence in apartment after repairs were completed). . . .

¶24 [W]hen an officer claims that he or she acted under the community caretaker doctrine, many jurisdictions use a two-step approach to analyze the officer's actions. First, if an officer states that he stopped to assist a person who appeared to be in need of assistance, an objective view of the specific and articulable facts must be examined to determine whether they support the officer's statements. And, second, a determination must be made regarding at what moment the officer "seized" the person and thereby implicated Fourth Amendment protections. . . .

¶25 With this survey of the foregoing case law in mind, we adopt the following test in relation to the community caretaker doctrine. First, as long as there are objective, specific and articulable facts from which an experienced officer would suspect that a citizen is in need of help or is in peril, then that officer has the right to stop and investigate. Second, if the citizen is in need of aid, then the officer may take appropriate action to render assistance or mitigate the peril. Third, once, however, the officer is assured that the citizen is not in peril or is no longer in need of assistance or that the peril has been mitigated, then any actions beyond that constitute a seizure implicating not only the protections provided by the Fourth Amendment, but more importantly, those greater guarantees afforded under Article II, Sections 10 and 11 of the Montana Constitution as interpreted in this Court's decisions.

¶26 Applying this test in the present case, the facts support the conclusion that Officer Hofer had objective, specific and articulable facts suggesting that Lovegren might be in need of assistance. While Lovegren might simply have been asleep, he might just as likely have been ill and unconscious and in need of help. Under these circumstances, Officer Hofer had the right to check on Lovegren's welfare and to open the door of Lovegren's vehicle when Lovegren failed to respond to a knock on the window of his vehicle. As the State points out, it would have been a dereliction of Officer Hofer's duties if, after knocking on the window and obtaining no response, Officer Hofer walked away and continued on his patrol. Thus, under the community caretaker doctrine, when Officer Hofer opened the door to check on Lovegren, Officer Hofer had not yet "seized" Lovegren.

¶27 However, when Officer Hofer opened the door, not only did Lovegren awake, but he voluntarily stated that he had been drinking. At that time, Officer Hofer also noticed other signs of intoxication giving him a particularized suspicion to make a further investigatory stop — i.e., the field sobriety tests — which eventually developed into probable cause for an arrest. This escalation of events leading to Lovegren's arrest is proper. . . .

¶28 Accordingly, we hold that the District Court did not err when it denied Lovegren's motion to suppress.

Problem 1-1. The Right to Be Left Alone?

Officer Gary Taylor of the Olla Police Department responded to a report of an injured person walking along Highway 125. Upon arriving at the scene, Officer Taylor observed two men: Reverend Allen Scott McDowell, who was responsible for placing the call, and Robert Stowe. Stowe, who was intoxicated, had fought with his wife earlier and punched through a window, resulting in a deep cut on his right arm, which was dripping blood. Officer Taylor wrapped a towel around Stowe's arm in an attempt to stop the blood flow. Stowe responded in a belligerent manner, cursing loudly. Officer Taylor tried to take him to get medical attention for his arm. Stowe refused and became increasingly hostile and threatening. Traffic began to back up, because Stowe and the officer were standing in the middle of the highway. Realizing that he was unable to reason with Stowe, Officer Taylor told him that he was under arrest for disturbing the peace. At this point, Stowe hit Officer Taylor in the head, knocking him backward across the road and into a roadside ditch. Eventually, with the assistance of Reverend McDowell and a bystander, the officer handcuffed Stowe and placed him in the patrol car.

Stowe was charged with disturbing the peace, under a statute that prohibits people from acting "in a manner which would foreseeably disturb or alarm the public." Stowe claims that he was minding his own business, disturbing no one. He made it apparent to all of his "rescuers" that he wanted no help and resented their interference in his personal misery. He argues that the police officer's attempt to force medical attention on him was an unconstitutional seizure of his person in violation of the Fourth Amendment of the U.S. Constitution. The Fourth Amendment guarantees a citizen's right to be free from "unreasonable" searches or seizures. How would you rule? Cf. State v. Stowe, 635 So. 2d 168 (La. 1994).

Notes

1. *Community caretakers: majority view.* The majority of the states have applied some form of the community caretaker doctrine to police. As we saw in *Dube* and *Lovegren*, this concept often arises when courts relax the usual restrictions on searches and seizures that apply during a criminal investigation. The community caretaker function has been used to justify entry into homes and stops of automobiles, with police officers pursuing various "caretaker" missions. See Laney v. State, 117 S.W.3d 854 (Tex. Crim. App. 2003) (officer entered trailer after midnight to determine where two young boys lived); State v. Deneui, 775 N.W.2d 221 (S.D. 2009) (during investigation of theft of natural gas, officers noticed ammonia fumes emanating from home and entered based on concern that potential occupants may have succumbed to fumes). Does an energetic community caretaker function provide a convenient after-the-fact rationale for searches that would not otherwise be legal?

Does the community caretaker function interfere with a citizen's right to be let alone, perhaps by sleeping in a car? Is it built on a faulty premise, "We're from the government, and we're here to help you"? One way to think about these questions is to identify the precise crime that should form the basis for charges against Stowe in Problem 1-1. Is it fair to say that Stowe's only crime was "bleeding in public" after he made it "apparent to all of his 'rescuers' that he did not require their assistance, and resented their intrusion into his personal misery"? See State v. Stowe, 635 So. 2d 168 (La. 1994) (Ortique, J., dissenting).

The U.S. Supreme Court has also recognized the community caretaking function. In Brigham City v. Stuart, 547 U.S. 398 (2006), the Court held that the Fourth Amendment does not bar law enforcement officers from entering a residence without a warrant if they have "an objectively reasonable basis to believe that an occupant is seriously injured or imminently threatened" with a serious injury. See also Colorado v. Bertine, 479 U.S. 367 (1987) (noting community caretaker value of inventory searches, which are not subject to the warrant requirement because they are "totally divorced from the detection, investigation, or acquisition of evidence relating to the violation of a criminal statute") (quoting Cady v. Dombrowski, 413 U.S. 433 (1973)).

2. *Distinguishing community caretaker functions from criminal enforcement.* As suggested by the Oregon statute, the Indianapolis job description, and the *Dube* and *Lovegren* cases, the community caretaker function of the police can cover a wide variety of activities. As explained in *Dube,* a community caretaker function can change to a crime control function. What factors might identify such a shift in function? See Williams v. State, 962 A.2d 210 (Del. 2008) (officer who stopped person who appeared to need assistance did not convert the stop into an illegal detention by asking for person's name and date of birth; officer must have record of who receives assistance to respond to later claims of officer wrongdoing or to further later criminal investigations). If a police department receives a 911 call reporting unusual noises behind the neighbor's house, should that be treated as a "crime control" or a community caretaker episode? What if a patrol officer responds to a burglar alarm? What if 95 percent of burglar alarm calls are false calls? Review the job description of a patrol officer in Indianapolis, and attempt to sort the various duties into the community caretaker or the crime control category. Courts usually declare that the officer's subjective intent when performing an action does not determine whether the courts will treat it as community caretaking or a criminal investigation. See State v. Kramer, 759 N.W.2d 598 (Wis. 2009).

There is debate among courts about whether the community caretaker doctrine should apply to the entry of homes, or whether it should remain limited to police encounters with individuals inside vehicles. For a survey of this debate about the proper boundaries of the community caretaker doctrine and a description of the related concept known as the "emergency aid" doctrine, see the web extension for this chapter at *http://www.crimpro.com/extension/ch01*.

Should statutes or ordinances, rather than judicial decisions, define the boundaries of community caretaker authority? Would the Oregon statute provide a different outcome in *Dube*?

3. *Adjusted procedural controls for different police roles.* The *Dube* court suggests that it is appropriate to have higher procedural requirements for police officers who are investigating a crime, and to apply more lax requirements to officers acting in a community caretaker function. What features of community caretaker functions

might justify this different treatment? Are caretaker functions less intrusive for citizens? Do those activities produce less severe consequences than a criminal investigation? Do police encounter a greater variety of situations during community caretaking, making it less amenable to general rules than the conduct of a criminal investigation? Could a legal system subject all police activity — whether or not directed toward criminal law enforcement — to the same procedural requirements? See Debra Livingston, Police, Community Caretaking and the Fourth Amendment, 1998 U. Chi. Legal F. 261; Michael R. Dimino, Sr., Police Paternalism: Community Caretaking, Assistance Searches, and Fourth Amendment Reasonableness, 66 Wash. & Lee L. Rev. 1485 (2009).

B. POLICE ENFORCEMENT OF CIVILITY

Police and citizens have very many exchanges that do not enter the casebooks and that are not governed by statutes or other rules. Because of the informal and personal nature of many of these exchanges, they will often be resolved in the streets, or in police precincts and prosecutors' offices, without ever becoming a source of formal (or traceable) conflict. But the lack of formality in day-to-day exchanges between police and citizens does not mean the exchanges are unimportant. These low-level interactions — at the border of criminal procedure — may be the place where trust and distrust, abuse and respect, are firmly established in the public mind.

■ STATE v. SHARON MATSON
818 A.2d 213 (Me. 2003)

CALKINS, J.

Sharon Matson appeals from a judgment of conviction of obstructing government administration. . . . On appeal, Matson argues that there was insufficient evidence that her rude and disruptive conduct toward a police officer who was in the process of arresting her companion constituted "intimidation" within the meaning of section 751. We agree and vacate the judgment.

At approximately 2 A.M. on December 7, 2001, Rockland Police Officer Finnegan stopped a car for having a license plate light out, illegal attachment of plates, and suspicion of operating under the influence (OUI). Finnegan testified that he smelled alcohol on the breath of the driver, Gifford Campbell, and Finnegan asked Gifford to step out and walk to the front of Finnegan's cruiser for field sobriety tests. Campbell's passenger, Sharon Matson, came out of the car yelling, "No, no fucking way. You're not doing to him what you did to me," a reference to the fact that Finnegan had arrested her for OUI a few months before. Finnegan told Matson to sit in the car, to calm down, and not to interfere, but she refused and kept shouting. Finnegan performed a horizontal gaze nystagmus test on Campbell but did no additional field sobriety tests because Matson continued yelling at him and no back-up officers were available. As Finnegan told Campbell he was under arrest for operating after suspension, Matson "charged forward," saying, "No, no fucking way. You're not arresting him." Matson stepped to within a couple of feet of Finnegan; as he began walking Campbell to the cruiser, she stepped in his way and refused to move, shouting all the while. Finnegan warned her she could be arrested for obstructing government administration and told her to step back, get out of the way, and stop interfering. She responded by saying, "Arrest me." He moved her out of the way with his left hand while holding Campbell with his right and walked past her to the cruiser. She followed, shouting. Finnegan stopped to search Campbell, and then moved him toward the rear door of the cruiser. Matson stepped in front of them, stood with her back against the door, spread her arms, and said, "No, no way, you're not taking him to jail." Finnegan told her to get out of the way, and she refused and again told him to arrest her. He moved her aside again, this time with his right hand, put Campbell in the cruiser, and arrested her. Matson said, "Good, I wanted you to arrest me." On cross-examination, Finnegan stated that he was not in fear of Matson at any time and that she never struck him, threatened him, or called him names.

The court took judicial notice of the file in Matson's OUI case, which indicated that she had been released on bail, with conditions, in May 2001, and that the conditions remained in effect until the court found her not guilty in January 2002. Campbell and Matson testified to a story different from Finnegan's, in which Finnegan used excessive force against Matson. In its closing, the State noted that it did not allege disorderly conduct and that Matson had a right to say what she said, but it argued that Matson had interfered with Finnegan's arrest of Campbell by intimidation and force. The court found that Finnegan's testimony was credible, that Matson's testimony was inconsistent, and that it was unlikely that the events transpired as she had described them. The court found that Matson's conduct involved intimidation but not force and found her guilty of obstructing government administration. . . . The court sentenced Matson to pay fines. . . .

Title 17-A M.R.S.A. §751(1) provides: "A person is guilty of obstructing government administration if the person uses force, violence or intimidation or engages in any criminal act with the intent to interfere with a public servant performing or purporting to perform an official function." Because the court based its determination of guilt on a finding that Matson had used intimidation, not force, and because there is no doubt that, in arresting Campbell, Finnegan was a public servant performing an official function and that Matson intended to interfere with that arrest, the issue on appeal is whether the evidence supports a finding that her conduct involved intimidation within the meaning of the statute.

We have interpreted the intimidation provision in section 751 once, in State v. Janisczak, 579 A.2d 736 (Me. 1990). The defendant in that case interfered with an arrest by yelling profanities at officers, who were struggling with a large, violent suspect. We adopted a definition of intimidation as "unlawful coercion, extortion, duress, or putting in fear." We then applied that definition to hold that

> no reasonable trier of fact could find on the evidence presented that Janisczak's actions constituted unlawful coercion, extortion, or duress. Further, although all five of the officers who were present at the scene testified at trial, none stated that he was put in fear by the defendant. Nor did any officer present testimony from which a jury reasonably could infer that one or more of the officers was afraid of Janisczak or his actions.

The State attempts to distinguish *Janisczak* on the basis that the defendant's conduct there consisted solely of speech, whereas Matson physically interfered with the arrest here. This argument is unconvincing. In holding in *Janisczak* that the evidence was insufficient to prove intimidation, we focused not on the lack of physical interference, but on the fact that the officers were not actually intimidated by the defendant's conduct. That analysis is controlling here. Finnegan admitted that he was not put in fear by Matson's conduct, and there is no basis for concluding that her actions constituted coercion, much less duress or extortion. The State presented no evidence that Finnegan was intimidated.

The State seems to suggest that Matson must have been guilty of obstructing government administration because she physically interfered with an arrest. However, physical interference without the use of force, violence, or the commission of a crime and which does not actually intimidate the police officer has not been made a crime. The Legislature could have drafted section 751 to prohibit any physical interference with a public servant performing an official function, but it chose not to do so. Cf. Model Penal Code §242.1 ("A person commits a misdemeanor if he purposely obstructs, impairs or perverts the administration of law or other governmental function by force, violence, physical interference or obstacle.").... Instead, 17-A M.R.S.A. §751-A only prohibits refusal to submit to arrest by the arrestee himself, and then only if it involves physical force or substantial risk of bodily injury. The Legislature chose to draft section 751 narrowly, and we have construed it narrowly.

The evidence was insufficient to support Matson's conviction for obstructing government administration....

SAUFLEY, C.J., dissenting.

I respectfully dissent. In reviewing a sufficiency of the evidence challenge to a criminal conviction, we must view the evidence and any inferences that can be drawn from the evidence most favorably to the result reached by the trial court.... The Court's opinion does not directly address the defense evidence. However, that evidence, interpreted most favorably to the trial court's result, suggests a considerably more violent and forceful confrontation between the defendant and the police officer than is suggested by the State's evidence which is the focus of the Court's discussion....

As the officer was moving the arrested driver towards the cruiser, Matson blocked his way and his entrance to the cruiser door. She refused the officer's request to move out of the way at which point, according to the defense evidence, the officer had to forcibly push or pull Matson to the side, causing her to fall down. According to the defense evidence, Matson then got back up and came at the officer again, either as he was placing the arrestee in the cruiser or after he had placed the arrestee in the cruiser. Again, the officer had to push Matson back.... Further shouting then occurred with Matson swearing at the officer and inviting him to arrest her. Matson was arrested at about the same time as a back-up officer arrived on the scene.

The sum of this evidence indicates that Matson obstructed the officer's efforts to conduct field sobriety tests and take the driver into custody. The evidence indicates, essentially without dispute, that the officer was sufficiently intimidated by Matson's actions that he ceased doing field sobriety tests before he otherwise would have done so and he called for back-up assistance. Further, as the officer was attempting to put the arrestee into his vehicle, Matson physically obstructed the officer's efforts, leading to a physical confrontation between Matson and the officer requiring him to use force — Matson's evidence indicates considerable force — to move her out of the way and place the arrestee in the police cruiser. . . .

The Court's opinion indicates that there was insufficient evidence to support a finding that Matson used "force, violence or intimidation." Certainly, the officer's ceasing field sobriety tests and calling for back-up as a result of Matson's shouting, swearing, insults and confrontational behavior can reasonably be construed to support a finding of at least some degree of intimidation. Further, Matson's physical blocking of the officer's efforts to place the arrestee in his cruiser required the officer to deviate from what otherwise would have been his normal practice and to forcibly move Matson aside so he could complete his arrest. The evidence indicates that Matson then came at the officer a second time and again had to be restrained as she was objecting to the arrest.

The Court cites State v. Janisczak, 579 A.2d 736 (Me. 1990), to suggest that this evidence is insufficient to support a finding of fear, violence or intimidation. However, *Janisczak* must be distinguished from this case. The Court's opinion in *Janisczak* indicates that the confrontation there involved five officers and the one defendant and that no officer stated that he was "put in fear by the defendant." Here, a lone officer was faced with two people, one who he was arresting and another who was completely out of control, combative and physically attempting to prevent the officer from performing his function. The officer certainly had sufficient concerns about the safety of the situation to deviate from his normal practice, suspend field sobriety tests, call for back-up and forcibly move Matson aside to terminate her physical obstruction of his arrest. These circumstances demonstrate sufficient force and intimidating behavior by Matson to support the conviction beyond a reasonable doubt. Accordingly, I would affirm the judgment of conviction on the charge of obstructing government administration. . . .

Notes

1. *Police enforcement of civility: majority view.* Appellate cases involving arrests for incivility toward police officers are rare. One reason might be that citizens are rarely uncivil toward police, though this seems unlikely. Sometimes police arrest citizens for direct interference with their duties and charge them with obstruction or interfering with an arrest or assault, but in the absence of physical contact police more often respond with the indirect charge of disorderly conduct. Prosecutors refuse to charge some of these arrests, and trial courts dismiss others.

Most state appellate decisions reverse disorderly conduct convictions based solely on profane insults directed toward police officers. See Jones v. State, 798 So. 2d 1241 (Miss. 2001). But a few sustain such convictions. In City of St. Paul v. Morris, 104 N.W.2d 902 (Minn. 1960), two officers entered a restaurant at 1:30 A.M. and arrested three people (including the half brother of the defendant, Robert Morris) for consuming liquor in a restaurant not licensed for such consumption. As the officers left the restaurant, Morris walked behind them asking the officers why they were arresting his brother. The defendant then said to the officers two or three times, "You white motherfuckers, what are you picking on us for, why don't you pick on the white people?" The officers then arrested Morris. Other patrons of the restaurant were close enough to hear what Morris said, but he used a normal tone of voice and there was no noise, fighting, violence, or threats among the other patrons. The ordinance in question made it a misdemeanor for a person to make "any noise, riot, disturbance or improper diversion." The appellate court upheld Morris' conviction because the ordinance "embraces acts which corrupt the public morals or outrage the sense of public decency." The officers had no special duty to tolerate such verbal abuse: "there is no sound reason why officers must be subjected to indignities such as present here, indignities that go far beyond what any other citizen might reasonably be expected to endure." Although the dissenting opinion stressed the racial tension evident in the conflict, the majority believed that the case raised no racial issue: "under the particular facts involved, we have no doubt that the expression would be equally provocative and offensive to any citizen, regardless of race." For a more recent example of a court sustaining a conviction based on abusive language directed at a police officer, see Spry v. State, 396 Md. 682 (Md. 2007) (affirming arrest for disturbance of the peace one day after Spry initially refused an officer's request to leave the scene of a fight and said to the police officer, "Fuck you, bitch").

What differences might explain the different outcomes in *Matson* and *Morris*? Could you imagine a court today not seeing a racial issue involved based on facts like those in *Morris*? What has changed?

2. *Nonjudicial procedural rules for enforcing civility.* Were the officers in these cases really concerned with "disorderly conduct," or were they concerned with something else? If you were responsible for training police, would you recommend that officers enforce civility, both among citizens and toward officers? Would you draft a policy that offers guidance on this question?

3. *The capacity of the police to tolerate abuse.* How does the Maine court in *Matson* view the need for police officers to tolerate abusive outbursts by citizens? Does the court hold police officers to higher standards of tolerance than might be expected of ordinary citizens? Should the tolerance expected of an officer depend on rank and experience?

4. *The capacity of the police to impose punishment.* How upset do you think Officer Finnegan was after the appellate court reversed Matson's conviction for resisting arrest? Appellate courts often dismiss charges of disorderly conduct or resisting arrest after a citizen directs profanity toward an officer. Why might such decisions not deter officers from making such arrests? Perhaps the answer comes from the observation made by some police officers that "If you can't give 'em a rap, you can still give 'em a ride."

C. CONTROL OF GANGS AND KIDS

Not everyone will respond civilly to police requests, and the police often desire more formal control than the combination of words, fear, and respect allow. Laws such as gang and loitering ordinances and curfews provide a more formal and enforceable basis for control of citizens by police. These laws exist not only at the border of criminal procedure, but at the borders of government powers and individual rights more generally. These cases raise the most basic questions of our government: What powers *must* government have? What powers *may* government have? What powers must government *not* have?

In 1992, the city of Chicago passed an ordinance, §8-4-015 of the Municipal Code, giving police authority to disrupt loitering by gang members.

(a) Whenever a police officer observes a person whom he reasonably believes to be a criminal street gang member loitering in any public place with one or more other persons, he shall order all such persons to disperse and remove themselves from the area. Any person who does not promptly obey such an order is in violation of this section. . . .

(c) As used in this section:

(1) "Loiter" means to remain in any one place with no apparent purpose.

(2) "Criminal street gang" means any ongoing organization, association in fact or group of three or more persons, whether formal or informal, having as one of its substantial activities the commission of one or more [enumerated] criminal acts . . . , and whose members individually or collectively engage in or have engaged in a pattern of criminal gang activity. . . .

(e) Any person who violates this section is subject to a fine of not less than $100 and not more than $500 for each offense, or imprisonment for not more than six months, or both. In addition to or instead of the above penalties, any person who violates this section maybe required to perform up to 120 hours of community service. . . .

In 1997 the Illinois Supreme Court held that the ordinance violated the U.S. Constitution. City of Chicago v. Jesus Morales, 687 N.E.2d 53 (Ill. 1997). The city petitioned the U.S. Supreme Court for certiorari. The Supreme Court's decision follows.

■ CITY OF CHICAGO v. JESUS MORALES

527 U.S. 41 (1999)

STEVENS, J.*

In 1992, the Chicago City Council enacted the Gang Congregation Ordinance, which prohibits "criminal street gang members" from "loitering" with one another or with other persons in any public place. The question presented is whether the Supreme Court of Illinois correctly held that the ordinance violates the Due Process Clause of the Fourteenth Amendment to the Federal Constitution.

I.

Before the ordinance was adopted, the city council's Committee on Police and Fire conducted hearings to explore the problems created by the city's street gangs, and more particularly, the consequences of public loitering by gang members. Witnesses included residents of the neighborhoods where gang members are most active, as well as some of the aldermen who represent those areas. . . . The council found that a continuing increase in criminal street gang activity was largely responsible for the city's rising murder rate, as well as an escalation of violent and drug-related crimes. It noted that in many neighborhoods throughout the city, "the burgeoning presence of street gang members in public places has intimidated many law abiding citizens." Furthermore, the council stated that gang members "establish

* [Justices O'Connor, Breyer, and Kennedy joined Parts I, II, and V of the opinion. Justices Souter and Ginsburg joined the opinion in its entirety. — EDS.]

control over identifiable areas . . . by loitering in those areas and intimidating others from entering those areas; and [m]embers of criminal street gangs avoid arrest by committing no offense punishable under existing laws when they know the police are present. . . ."

Two months after the ordinance was adopted, the Chicago Police Department promulgated General Order 92-4 to provide guidelines to govern its enforcement. That order purported to establish limitations on the enforcement discretion of police officers "to ensure that the anti-gang loitering ordinance is not enforced in an arbitrary or discriminatory way." The limitations confine the authority to arrest gang members who violate the ordinance to sworn "members of the Gang Crime Section" and certain other designated officers, and establish detailed criteria for defining street gangs and membership in such gangs. In addition, the order directs district commanders to "designate areas in which the presence of gang members has a demonstrable effect on the activities of law abiding persons in the surrounding community," and provides that the ordinance "will be enforced only within the designated areas." The city, however, does not release the locations of these "designated areas" to the public.

II.

During the three years of its enforcement, the police issued over 89,000 dispersal orders and arrested over 42,000 people for violating the ordinance.[7] . . .

III.

The basic factual predicate for the city's ordinance is not in dispute. As the city argues in its brief, "the very presence of a large collection of obviously brazen, insistent, and lawless gang members and hangers-on on the public ways intimidates residents, who become afraid even to leave their homes and go about their business. That, in turn, imperils community residents' sense of safety and security, detracts from property values, and can ultimately destabilize entire neighborhoods." The findings in the ordinance explain that it was motivated by these concerns. We have no doubt that a law that directly prohibited such intimidating conduct would be constitutional,[17] but this ordinance broadly covers a significant amount of additional activity. Uncertainty about the scope of that additional coverage provides the basis for respondents' claim that the ordinance is too vague. . . .

Vagueness may invalidate a criminal law for either of two independent reasons. First, it may fail to provide the kind of notice that will enable ordinary people to understand what conduct it prohibits; second, it may authorize and even encourage arbitrary and discriminatory enforcement.

7. City of Chicago, R. Daley & T. Hillard, Gang and Narcotic Related Violent Crime: 1993-1997, p.7 (June 1998). The city believes that the ordinance resulted in a significant decline in gang-related homicides. It notes that in 1995, the last year the ordinance was enforced, the gang-related homicide rate fell by 26%. In 1996, after the ordinance had been held invalid, the gang-related homicide rate rose 11%. However, gang-related homicides fell by 19% in 1997, over a year after the suspension of the ordinance. . . .

17. In fact the city already has several laws that serve this purpose. See, e.g., Ill. Comp. Stat. ch. 720 §§5/12-6 (1998) (Intimidation); 570/405.2 (Street gang criminal drug conspiracy); 147/1 et seq. (Illinois Street Gang Terrorism Omnibus Prevention Act); 5/25-1 (Mob action). . . .

IV.

[The] term "loiter" may have a common and accepted meaning, but the definition of that term in this ordinance — "to remain in any one place with no apparent purpose" — does not. It is difficult to imagine how any citizen of the city of Chicago standing in a public place with a group of people would know if he or she had an "apparent purpose." If she were talking to another person, would she have an apparent purpose? If she were frequently checking her watch and looking expectantly down the street, would she have an apparent purpose? . . .

The city's principal response to this concern about adequate notice is that loiterers are not subject to sanction until after they have failed to comply with an officer's order to disperse. "[Whatever] problem is created by a law that criminalizes conduct people normally believe to be innocent is solved when persons receive actual notice from a police order of what they are expected to do." We find this response unpersuasive for at least two reasons.

First, the purpose of the fair notice requirement is to enable the ordinary citizen to conform his or her conduct to the law. No one may be required at peril of life, liberty or property to speculate as to the meaning of penal statutes. Although it is true that a loiterer is not subject to criminal sanctions unless he or she disobeys a dispersal order, the loitering is the conduct that the ordinance is designed to prohibit. If the loitering is in fact harmless and innocent, the dispersal order itself is an unjustified impairment of liberty. . . . Because an officer may issue an order only after prohibited conduct has already occurred, it cannot provide the kind of advance notice that will protect the putative loiterer from being ordered to disperse. Such an order cannot retroactively give adequate warning of the boundary between the permissible and the impermissible applications of the law.

Second, the terms of the dispersal order compound the inadequacy of the notice afforded by the ordinance. It provides that the officer "shall order all such persons to disperse and remove themselves from the area." This vague phrasing raises a host of questions. After such an order issues, how long must the loiterers remain apart? How far must they move? If each loiterer walks around the block and they meet again at the same location, are they subject to arrest or merely to being ordered to disperse again? . . .

The Constitution does not permit a legislature to set a net large enough to catch all possible offenders, and leave it to the courts to step inside and say who could be rightfully detained, and who should be set at large. This ordinance is therefore vague not in the sense that it requires a person to conform his conduct to an imprecise but comprehensible normative standard, but rather in the sense that no standard of conduct is specified at all.

V.

The broad sweep of the ordinance also violates the requirement that a legislature establish minimal guidelines to govern law enforcement. . . .

It is true, as the city argues, that the requirement that the officer reasonably believe that a group of loiterers contains a gang member does place a limit on the authority to order dispersal. That limitation would no doubt be sufficient if the ordinance only applied to loitering that had an apparently harmful purpose or effect, or possibly if it only applied to loitering by persons reasonably believed to be criminal gang members. But this ordinance, for reasons that are not explained in the findings of the city council, requires no harmful purpose and applies to non-gang members as well as suspected gang members. . . .

VI.

. . . We recognize the serious and difficult problems testified to by the citizens of Chicago that led to the enactment of this ordinance. We are mindful that the preservation of liberty depends in part on the maintenance of social order. However, in this instance the city has enacted an ordinance that affords too much discretion to the police and too little notice to citizens who wish to use the public streets. . . .

O'CONNOR, J., concurring in part.

[The ordinance] fails to provide police with any standard by which they can judge whether an individual has an "apparent purpose." Indeed, because any person standing on the street has a general "purpose" — even if it is simply to stand — the ordinance permits police officers to choose which purposes are permissible. Under this construction the police do not have to decide that an individual is "threaten[ing] the public peace" to issue a dispersal order. [The] ordinance applies to hundreds of thousands of persons who are not gang members, standing on any sidewalk or in any park, coffee shop, bar, or other location open to the public. . . .

Nevertheless, there remain open to Chicago reasonable alternatives to combat the very real threat posed by gang intimidation and violence. For example, the Court properly and expressly distinguishes the ordinance from laws that require loiterers to have a "harmful purpose," from laws that target only gang members, and from laws that incorporate limits on the area and manner in which the laws may be enforced. In addition, the ordinance here is unlike a law that "directly prohibit[s]" the "presence of a large collection of obviously brazen, insistent, and lawless gang members and hangers-on on the public ways" that intimidates residents. Indeed, as the plurality notes, the city of Chicago has several laws that do exactly this. . . .

BREYER, J., concurring in part.

[The ordinance does not] limit in any way the range of conduct that police may prohibit. . . . Since one always has some apparent purpose, the so-called limitation invites, in fact requires, the policeman to interpret the words "no apparent purpose" as meaning "no apparent purpose except for. . . ." And it is in the ordinance's delegation to the policeman of open-ended discretion to fill in that blank that the problem lies. To grant to a policeman virtually standardless discretion to close off major portions of the city to an innocent person is, in my view, to create a major, not a "minor," limitation upon the free state of nature. . . .

The ordinance is unconstitutional, not because a policeman applied this discretion wisely or poorly in a particular case, but rather because the policeman enjoys too much discretion in every case. [The] city of Chicago may no more apply this law to the defendants, no matter how they behaved, than could it apply an (imaginary) statute that said, "It is a crime to do wrong," even to the worst of murderers. . . .

SCALIA, J., dissenting

The citizens of Chicago were once free to drive about the city at whatever speed they wished. At some point Chicagoans (or perhaps Illinoisans) decided this would not do, and imposed prophylactic speed limits designed to assure safe operation by the average (or perhaps even subaverage) driver with the average (or perhaps even subaverage) vehicle. This infringed upon the "freedom" of all citizens, but was not unconstitutional.

Similarly, the citizens of Chicago were once free to stand around and gawk at the scene of an accident. At some point Chicagoans discovered that this obstructed traffic and caused more accidents. They did not make the practice unlawful, but they did authorize police officers to order the crowd to disperse, and imposed penalties for refusal to obey such an order. Again, this prophylactic measure infringed upon the "freedom" of all citizens, but was not unconstitutional.

Until the ordinance that is before us today was adopted, the citizens of Chicago were free to stand about in public places with no apparent purpose — to engage, that is, in conduct that appeared to be loitering. In recent years, however, the city has been afflicted with criminal street gangs. . . . Once again, Chicagoans decided that to eliminate the problem it was worth restricting some of the freedom that they once enjoyed. The means they took was similar to the second, and more mild, example given above rather than the first: Loitering was not made unlawful, but when a group of people occupied a public place without an apparent purpose and in the company of a known gang member, police officers were authorized to order them to disperse, and the failure to obey such an order was made unlawful. The minor limitation upon the free state of nature that this prophylactic arrangement imposed upon all Chicagoans seemed to them (and it seems to me) a small price to pay for liberation of their streets. The majority today invalidates this perfectly reasonable measure . . . by elevating loitering to a constitutionally guaranteed right, and by discerning vagueness where . . . none exists.

[The ordinance is not vague.] The criteria for issuance of a dispersal order under the Chicago Ordinance could hardly be clearer. . . .

The Court [argues] that the "apparent purpose" test is too elastic because it presumably allows police officers to treat de minimis "violations" as not warranting enforcement. But such discretion . . . is no different with regard to the enforcement of this clear ordinance than it is with regard to the enforcement of all laws in our criminal-justice system. Police officers (and prosecutors) have broad discretion over what laws to enforce and when. . . .

The fact is that the present ordinance is entirely clear in its application, cannot be violated except with full knowledge and intent, and vests no more discretion in the police than innumerable other measures authorizing police orders to preserve the public peace and safety. [The] majority's real quarrel with the Chicago Ordinance is simply that it permits (or indeed requires) too much harmless conduct by innocent citizens to be proscribed. . . .

But in our democratic system, how much harmless conduct to proscribe is not a judgment to be made by the courts. So long as constitutionally guaranteed rights are not affected, and so long as the proscription has a rational basis, all sorts of perfectly harmless activity by millions of perfectly innocent people can be forbidden — riding a motorcycle without a safety helmet, for example, starting a campfire in a national forest, or selling a safe and effective drug not yet approved by the FDA. All of these acts are entirely innocent and harmless in themselves, but because of the risk of harm that they entail, the freedom to engage in them has been abridged. The citizens of Chicago have decided that depriving themselves of the freedom to "hang out" with a gang member is necessary to eliminate pervasive gang crime and intimidation — and that the elimination of the one is worth the deprivation of the other. This Court has no business second-guessing either the degree of necessity or the fairness of the trade. . . .

THOMAS, J., dissenting.

. . . Gangs fill the daily lives of many of our poorest and most vulnerable citizens with a terror that the Court does not give sufficient consideration, often relegating them to the status of prisoners in their own homes. The city of Chicago has suffered the devastation wrought by this national tragedy. Last year, in an effort to curb plummeting attendance, the Chicago Public Schools hired dozens of adults to escort children to school. The youngsters had become too terrified of gang violence to leave their homes alone. The children's fears were not unfounded. In 1996, the Chicago Police Department estimated that there were 132 criminal street gangs in the city. Between 1987 and 1994, these gangs were involved in 63,141 criminal incidents, including 21,689 nonlethal violent crimes and 894 homicides. Many of these criminal incidents and homicides result from gang "turf battles," which take place on the public streets and place innocent residents in grave danger. . . .

As part of its ongoing effort to curb the deleterious effects of criminal street gangs, the citizens of Chicago sensibly decided to return to basics. The ordinance does nothing more than confirm the well-established principle that the police have the duty and the power to maintain the public peace, and, when necessary, to disperse groups of individuals who threaten it.

[It] is important to note that the ordinance does not criminalize loitering per se. Rather, it penalizes loiterers' failure to obey a police officer's order to move along. A majority of the Court believes that this scheme vests too much discretion in police officers. Nothing could be further from the truth. Far from according officers too much discretion, the ordinance merely enables police officers to fulfill one of their traditional functions. Police officers are not, and have never been, simply enforcers of the criminal law. They wear other hats — importantly, they have long been vested with the responsibility for preserving the public peace.

In order to perform their peace-keeping responsibilities satisfactorily, the police inevitably must exercise discretion. Indeed, by empowering them to act as peace officers, the law assumes that the police will exercise that discretion responsibly and with sound judgment. That is not to say that the law should not provide objective guidelines for the police, but simply that it cannot rigidly constrain their every action. By directing a police officer not to issue a dispersal order unless he "observes a person whom he reasonably believes to be a criminal street gang member loitering in any public place," Chicago's ordinance strikes an appropriate balance between those two extremes. Just as we trust officers to rely on their experience and expertise in order to make spur-of-the-moment determinations about amorphous legal standards such as "probable cause" and "reasonable suspicion," so we must trust them to determine whether a group of loiterers contains individuals (in this case members of criminal street gangs) whom the city has determined threaten the public peace. . . . Today, the Court focuses extensively on the "rights" of gang members and their companions. It can safely do so — the people who will have to live with the consequences of today's opinion do not live in our neighborhoods. Rather, the people who will suffer from our lofty pronouncements are people . . . who have seen their neighborhoods literally destroyed by gangs and violence and drugs. They are good, decent people who must struggle to overcome their desperate situation, against all odds, in order to raise their families, earn a living, and remain good citizens. As one resident described, "There is only about maybe one or two percent of the people in the city causing these problems maybe, but it's keeping 98 percent of us in our houses and off the streets and afraid to shop." By focusing exclusively on the imagined "rights" of the two percent, the Court today has denied our most vulnerable citizens the very thing that Justice Stevens elevates above all else — the "freedom of movement." And that is a shame. I respectfully dissent.

TRACEY L. MEARES, NORMS, LEGITIMACY AND LAW ENFORCEMENT

79 Or. L. Rev. 391 (2000)

Why do some communities exhibit high crime rates while others do not? As an answer, I have looked to social disorganization theory. This is a theory developed by Clifford Shaw and Henry McKay to explain why juvenile delinquency remained high in certain areas of central cities over time despite population turnover. In Shaw and McKay's classic work, they maintained that low economic status, ethnic heterogeneity and residential mobility led to the disruption of community social organization, which, in turn, accounted for variation in crime and delinquency rates in a given area. See Clifford R. Shaw & Henry D. McKay, Juvenile Delinquency and Urban Areas (rev. ed. 1969). To support this theory, the researchers demonstrated that high rates of juvenile delinquency were specific to certain areas in the cities they studied and that these rates persisted over time despite population turnover. This finding motivated the researchers to reject individual-level explanations of delinquency and focus instead on the features of the communities in which the juveniles lived in order to explain the high crime rates.

Contemporary researchers have applied Shaw and McKay's insights to the longstanding problematic observation that African-Americans are under criminal justice system control out of proportion to their representation in the general population. . . . [They] have documented that major differences often exist between the ecological contexts in which poor African-Americans typically reside on the one hand, and those in which poor whites typically reside on the other. Poor white families tend to reside in communities that feature more family-stable contexts than poor black families. . . . Indeed, Professors Robert Sampson and William Julius Wilson have noted, "[R]acial difference in poverty and family disruption are so strong that the 'worst' urban contexts in which whites reside are considerably better than the average context of black communities." Robert J. Sampson & William Julius Wilson, Toward a Theory of Race, Crime, and Urban Inequality, in Crime and Inequality 37, 42 (John Hagan & Ruth D. Peterson eds., 1995).

In terms of social organization theory, these different contexts translate into different levels of capacity of neighborhoods to resist and reduce crime. This is in large part because ecological contexts affect the extent to which neighborhood residents exert social control — informal mechanisms rather than formal regulation imposed by police and courts — to achieve public order. . . .

Norm enforcement is easier when individuals in a community have social linkages and trust one another. Individuals who reside in communities in which there are few social linkages and where distrust is rampant will have difficulty exerting social control over one another. Empirical work bears this out. While ecological factors such as poverty, joblessness and family disruption are associated with crime, criminologists have shown that such factors are mediated by community-type social capital factors such as prevalence of friendship networks, participation in formal and informal organizations like churches and PTAs and the like. Such social structural factors provide the linkages along which norms of law abidingness can travel. They are "norm highways."

It is critical to understand, however, that the norms on social highways can travel in any direction. There is no necessary reason why community norms must be directed toward the project of crime control. In fact, one can easily imagine tight social networks supporting criminogenic conduct on a community-wide basis. . . .

Because social capital factors appear to matter more to explaining high crime rates in communities than individual-level factors, it makes sense to engineer crime policy that takes account of this reality. The social capital thesis calls into question policies that attempt to control crime simply by manipulating an individual's calculus regarding whether "crime pays" in the particular instance. In fact, deterrence-based strategies directed toward individual law breakers may even exacerbate the very activity the strategy purports to curb. For example, if lawmakers choose to address illegal drug selling by increasing the number of those convicted for drug selling and by increasing prison sentences for those convicted of such activity (which is basically the current American approach to drug crimes), then one expected consequence is that more individuals will be imprisoned for longer periods of time. Although the standard economic conception of crime suggests that this strategy should make a dent in the level of illegal drug activity, social organization theory's emphasis on social capital and norms suggests that this strategy will backfire. The highest numbers of those caught under this approach will tend to be street-level dealers, who are not evenly distributed throughout a city, but who are geographically concentrated in disadvantaged, minority neighborhoods. . . . Removal of these individuals in large numbers from their communities will be associated with higher levels of joblessness, low economic status, and family disruption, which in turn will disrupt the social structural and cultural determinants of community-based social control. . . .

The best norm-based strategies will maximize social organization benefits without visiting as high a cost on disadvantaged communities as high rates of imprisonment do. Drug enforcement strategies, such as reverse drug stings, redistribute enforcement costs to communities that have the capacity to absorb the consequences of possible imprisonment. These, and strategies that attempt to disrupt illegal drug markets without relying at all on imprisonment, such as using loitering ordinances to make it difficult for drug buyers to find street sellers, can address illegal drug markets without concentrating the costs of imprisonment on the communities least prepared to absorb those costs. . . .

Norms and Compliance

Do people obey the law because they fear the consequences if they do not? Or, do they obey the law for other reasons? Focusing on the former question, economists have looked primarily to deterrence theory to explain compliance. The foundations of this theory are well-known. People rationally maximize their utility, and they, therefore, shape their behavior in response to incentives and penalties associated with the criminal code. . . . This view suggests that compliance is instrumental. This view also fuels the current trend toward "get tough on crime" approaches, which feature policies such as truth-in-sentencing, long sentences for drug offending, and so-called "three-strikes-and-you're-out" sentences.

Social psychologists have offered another view of compliance with the law. By pointing to normative bases for compliance rather than instrumental ones, these researchers have connected voluntary compliance with the law to the fact that individuals believe the law is "just" or because they believe that the authority enforcing the law has the right to do so. See Tom R. Tyler, Why People Obey the Law 3-4 (1990). . . . In contrast to the individual who complies with the law because she is responding to externally imposed punishments, the individual who complies for normative reasons does so because she feels an internal obligation. [There] is empirical work demonstrating that legitimacy matters more to compliance than instrumental factors, such as sanctions imposed by authorities on individuals who fail to follow the law or private rules.

[This is good news] because relying only on carrots and sticks to produce compliance can be a costly strategy. [Instrumental] means of producing compliance are not self-sustaining. Authorities must be willing to maintain mechanisms of instrumental compliance. For example, if deterrence is to be produced by maintaining a certain probability of detection of rule-breakers, then authorities must be willing to devote resources to maintenance (or increase) of the desired level of police to ensure that the requisite probability of detection is met. Therefore, instrumental means of producing compliance always depend on resource limits.

Legitimacy . . . can be acquired simply by changing procedures and practices of current officials in ways that require almost no additional resources. For example, some research indicates that police who regularly treat arrestees with courtesy are more likely than those who do not to be viewed as legitimate. While police officers may not like to be told to be more polite to arrestees, this research suggests that law enforcement gains could be achieved more cheaply than through more instrumental means simply by telling officers to "be nice." . . .

A legitimacy-based program of law enforcement will focus more on persuasion than it will focus on punishment. And, in order to persuade, authorities will have to pay attention to the creation of the necessary social capital that engenders trust relationships between governors and the governed. . . .

Community Participation in Policing

Generation of participation by stakeholders in criminal justice processes is a feature of . . . law enforcement that should enhance legitimacy of government. [A key aspect of creating participation is] the leveling of authority between government officials and the governed. [The process described here] requires government officials to cede some of their exclusive power to enforce laws.

In an attempt to address the complaints of residents concerned about gang violence and open-air drug selling, the City of Chicago has recently adopted an ordinance that empowers police officers to approach groups of people involved in gang loitering or narcotics-related loitering, inform those individuals that they are engaged in prohibited loitering, order the individuals to disperse from within sight and hearing of the place which the order was issued, and inform the individuals ordered to disperse that they will be subject to arrest if they fail to obey the order or return to the area during the next three hours. This ordinance is a revised version of another anti-gang loitering ordinance adopted by Chicago. The original ordinance was struck down by the Supreme Court as unconstitutionally vague. While the original ordinance defined loitering as staying in one place "with no apparent purpose," the revised ordinance defines gang loitering as "remaining in any one place under circumstances that would warrant a reasonable person to believe that the purpose or effect of that behavior is to enable a criminal street gang to establish control over identifiable areas, to intimidate others from entering those areas, or to conceal illegal activities." Similarly, narcotics-related loitering means "remaining in any one place under circumstances that would warrant a reasonable person to believe that the purpose or effect of that behavior is to facilitate the distribution of substances in violation of the Cannabis Control Act or the Illinois Controlled Substances Act." The definitions of both types of loitering incorporate specific language from both Justice Stevens' opinion for the plurality and Justice O'Connor's concurrence, which was joined by Justice Breyer.

[The] revised ordinance contains language that has both social organization benefits and legitimacy benefits. Consider social organization first. The sociology explained above suggests that law enforcement strategies that depend on imprisonment of a large number of geographically concentrated individuals should be avoided if possible. Of course, some criminal offenses demand imprisonment, such as murder or robbery. But other offenses likely are better dealt with through norm-focused strategies. Open-air drug selling is an example. The anti-gang, anti-narcotics loitering ordinance adopted by Chicago empowers police officers to disrupt drug markets without arresting large numbers of low-level dealers who retail in open areas and who are concentrated in minority, poor areas of the City. These dealers depend on confederates to stand in strategic areas to advertise the drugs they are selling to the many buyers who come from outside the particular community in which the drugs are sold — often the suburbs. Without the "advertisers" these outsiders cannot find the dealers. So, enforcement of the anti-narcotics provision of the ordinance can disrupt the market without arrest and potential subsequent conviction and imprisonment of the dealer. This is a social organization benefit. . . .

The City Council recognized that drug selling and gang clashes are intimately bound up in place. Therefore, the ordinance provides that the Superintendent of Police shall designate areas of the city for enforcement by written directive. In order to make this designation, the ordinance also provides that the Superintendent "shall consult as he or she deems appropriate with persons who are knowledgeable. . . . Such persons may include . . . elected and appointed officials of the area [and] community-based organizations . . . who are familiar with the area." . . .

The consultation provision provides a key opening for increased perceptions of legitimacy of Chicago police among the communities in which this ordinance will be enforced. By its very structure the ordinance reduces the hierarchy inherent to municipal policing. This ordinance creates a partnership in the law enforcement process, and through that process creates greater accountability of the police to the members of affected communities. . . . [This] process provides both invitations to participation as well as meaningful signals to community members that their opinions count.

Cooperation Between the Church and the Police

. . . There has been an ongoing effort in Chicago to create more ties between the pastors of African-American churches on Chicago's impoverished West side and the police. To create these bonds the commander of Chicago's highest-crime Police District tried an extremely innovative strategy. Three years ago, he facilitated a community-wide prayer vigil. In groups of ten, the participants stood on designated corners — the same corners where lookouts often hawked their wares by calling out, "Rocks and Blows!" — and prayed. Following the prayer vigil, the whole group and over 7,000 more community residents went to a large park for a "praise celebration," where there was music provided by a 400-member gospel choir, food, and inspirational speeches.

Importantly, it is not the vigil itself that creates the legitimacy benefits; rather, it is the organization process — the monthly meetings in the police roll call room and regular contact between ministers and police officials — that generated the social capital that drives assessments of trust. Of course, there would have been no meetings but for the prayer vigil, so the vigil is a necessary component. [But] the process of putting on the vigil was an opportunity for both the police and the ministers to begin to see themselves as part of the same group — a necessary component to trust generation. . . .

Our current approach to crime control is basically inconsistent with the project of improving community capacity for social control — especially the capacity of those communities that possess the highest crime rates. The United States imprisons more people than any other country in the world, and the bulk of those imprisoned are African-American males, who likely come from urban areas. Social organization theory tells us that this approach is dangerously counterproductive.

Notes

1. *Order maintenance.* Is order maintenance (or as Justice Thomas labels it, "peace-keeping") a crime control function or a community caretaker function? Should police have the general authority to ask citizens to "move on"? If you were a member of the Chicago City Council, could you draft a constitutional gang ordinance that would serve similar purposes to the ordinance struck down in *Morales*? State and federal cases on gang and order maintenance provisions are uncommon. Why?

As Professor Meares points out, the city of Chicago amended its anti-loitering ordinance to address the Court's concerns as expressed in *Morales.* The ordinance itself now requires the police superintendent to designate "hot zones" of gang or narcotics activity, where the police may enforce the ordinance. The superintendent must consult community groups (along with various law enforcement officials) when designating the hot zones. See Chicago Police Department General Order No. 00-02. Would the amended ordinance survive a constitutional challenge? (No challenges have succeeded so far.) Does it reinforce community crime control efforts?

2. *Community control of police.* The opinions of the Justices in *Morales* reveal different visions of "ordinary" policing and the ordinary methods of controlling police. For the plurality and concurring justices, pre-announced rules of law are necessary to hold police discretion to an acceptable minimum; legislators and judges control

the police through formal sources of law. For the dissenting justices, police discretion is perfectly ordinary, even desirable. Control of the police comes from political pressure on elected officials at the local level rather than from pre-announced rules. Are these visions realistic about the power of legal rules or political pressure to influence police operations? Professors Dan Kahan and Tracey Meares argue that doctrines granting broad discretion to police officers (including loitering laws) are more defensible today than in the 1960s because of the rising political power of African Americans in the nation's inner cities. Techniques formerly used to harass and exclude African Americans from public life could now become the tools of minority communities to free themselves from rampant criminality. Kahan & Meares, The Coming Crisis of Criminal Procedure, 86 Geo. L.J. 1153 (1998); see also Debra Livingston, Police Discretion and the Quality of Life in Public Places: Courts, Communities, and the New Policing, 97 Colum. L. Rev. 551 (1997). Is their vision of democratic accountability realistic?

3. *Social norms and the sources of crime.* As the excerpt above implies, Meares assigns only a secondary role to the police in the prevention of crime. The police (and the criminal procedure rules that structure their behavior) can contribute best to the control of crime if they ultimately strengthen the *community's* own ability to control crime. Thus, the "disorganization" of a community is the most salient source of crime, and the best rules for the police are built around an awareness of that source.

What are some other accounts of the sources of crime, and how might those accounts change your views on the proper role of the police? Several criminological theories over the years have emphasized the genetic and biological components of crime. (Sometimes this leads to searches for identifiable traits among a criminal "type," an enterprise that too often has degenerated into racial stereotyping or other unsound generalizations.) If you believe that some individuals have a biological or psychological predisposition to commit crimes, how might that affect the rules you would expect the police to follow? If the causes of female crime are different from the causes of male crime, does that have implications for policing?

Other criminological theories emphasize various aspects of the criminal's social environment. For instance, according to "strain theory," unemployment, poverty and other sources of stress induce many people to commit crimes. "Social learning" theory suggests that many criminals learn to commit their crimes because the people around them reinforce criminal actions and attitudes. The influence of these theories and many other explanations for crime have waxed and waned among criminologists over the years. See Robert Agnew, Crime Causation: Sociological Theories, in Encyclopedia of Crime and Justice (Joshua Dressler ed., 2002). For each of these accounts of the sources of crime, how might the police best contribute to the control of crime? For a survey of the leading criminological accounts of crime, see the web extension for this chapter at *http://www.crimpro.com/extension/ch01*.

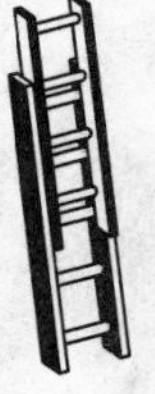

4. *Community crime control antecedents.* There are historic antecedents for today's forms of community crime control. Professor Jonathan Simon describes the thousand-year-old tradition of "frankpledge" in England, where each frankpledge group (originally 100 households) was held collectively responsible for crime control. From the tenth through the fifteenth centuries, free adult males had a legal obligation to "report offenses committed by other members of the group and to be financially obligated for any failure to produce the offender at presentment." During the "view of the frankpledge," the male population gathered before representatives

of the crown and local elites. The officials collected taxes and fines, registered newcomers, and took reports on crime. In this way, the frankpledge system "integrated crime control into the everyday lives of the common people and local government." Simon, Poor Discipline: Parole and the Social Control of the Underclass 18-20 (1993). The frankpledge system created strong incentive for private social control of criminal behavior. Does it resemble crime control in small towns in the United States today? Is the frankpledge compatible with a mobile society? How does the relationship between citizen and police officer in a community policing model resemble the frankpledge?

Problem 1-2. Juvenile Curfews

At 10:35 P.M., 15-year-old David Simmons and a friend were skateboarding in a Panora, Iowa, shopping center. A police officer issued citations to them for violating a Panora juvenile curfew ordinance, which provided as follows:

1. It is unlawful for any minor [under 18] to be or remain upon any of the alleys, streets or public places or places of business and amusement in the city between the hours of 10 P.M. and 5 A.M. of the following day.
2. The curfew shall not apply to any minor who is accompanied by a guardian, parent or other person charged with the care and custody of such minor, or other responsible person over 18 years of age, nor shall the restriction apply to any minor who is traveling between his home or place of residence and the place where any approved place of employment, church, municipal or school function is being held.
3. It is unlawful for any parent, guardian or other person charged with the care and custody of any minor to allow or permit such minor to be in or upon any of the streets, alleys, places of business or amusement, or other public places within the curfew hours except as provided in subsection 2.
4. It is unlawful for any person, firm or corporation operating a place of business or amusement to allow or permit any minor to be in or upon any place of business or amusement operated by them within the curfew hours except as provided in subsection 2.
5. Any peace officer of this city while on duty is hereby empowered to arrest any minor who violates the curfew. Upon arrest, the minor shall be returned to the custody of the parent, guardian or other person charged with the care and custody of the minor.

Simmons was found guilty of violating the curfew ordinance. The penalty imposed was a $1 fine plus surcharge and costs. Simmons appealed the conviction, with strong support from his parents. The Simmons family also asked the city council to repeal or amend the curfew ordinance.

As an appellate court judge, how would you rule on his appeal? Is the ordinance constitutional? As a member of the city council, would you vote to repeal or amend the ordinance? Compare City of Panora v. Simmons, 445 N.W.2d 363 (Iowa 1989).

Notes

1. *Juvenile curfews: majority position.* Many state and local governments have passed laws empowering the police to enforce a "curfew" on persons less than 18 years old. The practice is now commonplace: A 2005 survey by the National League of Cities showed that over half of the cities surveyed had enacted juvenile curfew laws, and two-thirds of the cities with curfew laws passed them within the last 20 years. Children and parents who challenge the validity of these laws argue that the curfews are unconstitutionally vague and interfere with fundamental rights such as the "right to travel" or the right of parents to make basic parenting decisions without governmental interference. The state court response has been mixed, with the largest group of states upholding the statutes or ordinances, noting that they do not simply ban juveniles from being "present" in public after dark. Instead, they allow juveniles to be outdoors for certain legitimate reasons or in the company of a parent. See Ramos v. Town of Vernon, 761 A.2d 705 (Conn. 2000). A few state courts have struck down the juvenile curfew laws. See City of Sumner v. Walsh, 61 P.3d 1111 (Wash. 2003); State v. J.P., 907 So. 2d 1011 (Fla. 2004). To gain a better sense of this debate among state courts and lower federal courts, along with some historical background on the use of juvenile curfews, see the web extension for this chapter at *http://www.crimpro.com/extension/ch01*.

2. *Adult curfews.* There is a long and largely disreputable history of adult curfews in the United States. Before the Civil War, curfew laws in the South designated times when slaves could be on the streets. During the late 1800s, curfew ordinances flourished in places where there were large numbers of immigrants, because of fears that immigrants would not properly supervise their children. In 1941, emergency curfews were imposed on American citizens of Japanese ancestry. A variety of adult curfew, loitering, and vagrancy laws were invalidated in the late 1960s through the early 1980s as violations of the basic right of adult citizens to go where they want, whenever they want. See Papachristou v. City of Jacksonville, 405 U.S. 156 (1972) (striking down a vagrancy ordinance); Kolender v. Lawson, 461 U.S. 352 (1983) (rejecting a California statute requiring citizens who loiter to account for their presence and show "reasonable and reliable" identification when required by a police officer; Lawson was detained about 15 times during two-year period for walking in isolated areas at late hours). The Supreme Court reaffirmed this line of cases by striking down the gang loitering ordinance in Chicago v. Morales, 527 U.S. 41 (1999). In a society searching urgently for ways to control crime, should courts reconsider the validity of adult curfew laws? Is the right to prowl at 3 A.M. essential to a free country?

3. *Police as parents.* As a parent, how would you feel about a local curfew law? Would your decision depend on the sanctions attached to the law? Would it depend on your view of the police purpose when enforcing a curfew? Are police exercising a crime control function or a community caretaker function (or something else entirely) when they enforce a curfew?

D. TRADITIONAL AND COMMUNITY POLICING

The idea of what police do, and how they do it, is far from a static concept. From the introduction of police into municipalities in the mid-nineteenth century until the 1940s, local political leaders controlled police departments through job patronage and through investigating complaints from citizens. Police officers in this period responded to a wide variety of social needs including, but not limited to, crime control. The "reform era" followed, lasting from the 1940s until the 1980s. During this period, according to scholars George Kelling and Mark Moore,

> [reformers] rejected politics as the basis of police legitimacy. . . . Civil service eliminated patronage and ward influences in hiring and firing police officers.
>
> [Police] in the reform era moved to narrow their functioning to crime control and criminal apprehension. Police agencies became *law enforcement* agencies. Their goal was to control crime. Their principal means was the use of criminal law to apprehend and deter offenders. Activities that drew the police into solving other kinds of community problems . . . were identified as "social work," and became the object of derision. . . .
>
> During the era of reform policing, the new model demanded an impartial law enforcer who related to citizens in professionally neutral and distant terms. No better characterization of this model can be found than television's Sergeant Friday, whose response, "Just the facts, ma'am," typified the idea: impersonal and oriented toward crime solving rather than responsive to the emotional crisis of a victim.

Kelling and Moore, From Political to Reform to Community: The Evolving Strategy of Police, in Community Policing: Rhetoric or Reality (Jack Greene and Stephen Mastrofski eds., 1988).

In the past 30 years a new conception of the police function has emerged: "community policing." In its broadest outlines, community policing shifts control over police resources from central police management to the community level. Community policing broadens the goals of policing to include community order beyond crime control, and recognizes that fear of crime is a serious matter in its own right. In these sweeping terms, it is difficult to find many police officers, or many departments, that have not embraced this change.

As these changes in police function become pervasive, the trend toward community policing may shift individual and public perceptions of what the police do. In turn, this change may require us to rethink much of modern criminal procedure, which is firmly anchored to the reform-era conception of policing.

The following materials describe in more detail the shifts in policing models over the last generation. The first piece, written during the heyday of reform-era professionalized policing, sets out a classic dichotomy between the "crime control" and "due process" models of criminal justice — two ways of evaluating the work of law enforcement officers and other criminal justice actors. The second piece, written by a national coalition of police chiefs and other police administrators, lays out the distinctive features of the newer community policing model.

As you read the description below of this changing philosophy of policing, keep in mind its possible effect on procedural rules. If you were a city council member, would you pass an ordinance to give the police greater powers to "problem solve"?

For instance, recall the curfew and "civility" cases from the previous sections. It is possible that departments adopting the community policing philosophy should get greater leeway in enforcing civility or juvenile curfews. With the shift to community policing, are procedural controls on the police *less* important or feasible, or are they *more* important than ever — to prevent the officers from making arbitrary and discriminatory use of their more frequent interactions with the public?

■ HERBERT L. PACKER, TWO MODELS OF THE CRIMINAL PROCESS

113 U. Pa. L. Rev. 1 (1964)

. . . The kind of criminal process we have depends importantly on certain value choices that are reflected, explicitly or implicitly, in its habitual functioning. The kind of model we need is one that permits us to recognize explicitly the value choices that underlie the details of the criminal process. In a word, what we need is a *normative* model, or rather two models, to let us perceive the normative antinomy that runs deep in the life of the criminal law. These models may not be labeled Good and Bad, and I hope they will not be taken in that sense. Rather, they represent an attempt to abstract two separate value systems that compete for attention in the operation of the criminal process. . . . I call these two models the Due Process Model and the Crime Control Model. . . .

Crime Control Values

The value system that underlies the Crime Control Model is based on the proposition that the repression of criminal conduct is by far the most important function to be performed by the criminal process. The failure of law enforcement to bring criminal conduct under tight control is viewed as leading to the breakdown of public order and thence to the disappearance of an important condition of human freedom. . . . The claim ultimately is that the criminal process is a positive guarantor of social freedom. In order to achieve this high purpose, the Crime Control Model requires that primary attention be paid to the efficiency with which the criminal process operates to screen suspects, determine guilt, and secure appropriate dispositions of persons convicted of crime. . . .

The model, in order to operate successfully, must produce a high rate of apprehension and conviction and must do so in a context where the magnitudes being dealt with are very large, and the resources for dealing with them are very limited. There must then be a premium on speed and finality. Speed, in turn, depends on informality and on uniformity; finality depends on minimizing the occasions for challenge. The process must not be cluttered with ceremonious rituals that do not advance the progress of a case. Facts can be established more quickly through interrogation in a police station than through the formal process of examination and cross-examination in a court; it follows that extrajudicial processes should be preferred to judicial processes, informal to formal operations. Informality is not enough; there must also be uniformity. Routine stereotyped procedures are essential if large numbers are being handled. The model that will operate successfully on these presuppositions must be an administrative, almost a managerial, model. The image that comes to mind is an assembly line or a conveyor belt down which moves an endless stream of cases, never stopping, carrying the cases to workers who stand at fixed stations and who perform on each case as it comes by the same small but essential operation that brings it one step closer to being a finished product, or, to exchange the metaphor for the reality, a closed file.

The criminal process, on this model, is seen as a screening process in which each successive stage — prearrest investigation, arrest, post-arrest investigation, preparation for trial, trial or entry of plea, conviction, and disposition — involves a series of routinized operations whose success is gauged primarily by their tendency to pass the case along to a successful conclusion.

What is a successful conclusion? One that throws off at an early stage those cases in which it appears unlikely that the person apprehended is an offender and then secures, as expeditiously as possible, the conviction of the rest with a minimum of occasions for challenge, let alone postaudit. By the application of administrative expertness, primarily that of the police and prosecutors, an early determination of probable innocence or guilt emerges. The probably innocent are screened out. The probably guilty are passed quickly through the remaining stages of the process. The key to the operation of the model as to those who are not screened out is what I shall call a presumption of guilt. . . .

The presumption of guilt allows the Crime Control Model to deal efficiently with large numbers. The supposition is that the screening processes operated by police and prosecutors are reliable indicators of probable guilt. Once a man has been investigated without being found to be probably innocent, or, to put it differently, once a determination has been made that there is enough evidence of guilt so that he should be held for further action rather than released from the process, then all subsequent activity directed toward him is based on the view that he is probably guilty. . . .

It would be a mistake to think of the presumption of guilt as the opposite of the presumption of innocence. [The] two concepts embody different rather than opposite ideas. . . . The presumption of innocence is really a direction to the authorities to ignore the presumption of guilt in their treatment of the suspect. It tells them, in effect, to close their eyes to what will frequently seem to be factual probabilities. . . .

For this model . . . the preliminary screening processes operated by the police and the prosecuting officials contain adequate guarantees of reliable factfinding. Indeed, the position is a stronger one. It is that subsequent processes, particularly of a formal adjudicatory nature, are unlikely to produce as reliable factfinding as the expert administrative process that precedes them. . . . It becomes important, then, to place as few restrictions as possible on the character of the administrative factfinding processes and to limit restrictions to those that enhance reliability, excluding those designed for other purposes. . . .

The complementary proposition is that the subsequent stages are relatively unimportant and should be truncated as much as possible. [There] have to be devices for dealing with the suspect after the preliminary screening process has resulted in a determination of probable guilt. The focal device . . . is the plea of guilty; through its use adjudicative factfinding is reduced to a minimum. It might be said of the Crime Control Model that, reduced to its barest essentials and when operating at its most successful pitch, it consists of two elements: (a) an administrative factfinding process leading to exoneration of the suspect, or to (b) the entry of a plea of guilty.

Due Process Values

If the Crime Control Model resembles an assembly line, the Due Process Model looks very much like an obstacle course. Each of its successive stages is designed to present formidable impediments to carrying the accused any further along in the process. . . .

The Due Process Model [takes] a view of informal, nonadjudicative factfinding that stresses the possibility of error: people are notoriously poor observers of disturbing events — the more emotion-arousing the context, the greater the possibility that recollection will be incorrect; confessions and admissions by persons in police custody may be induced by physical or psychological coercion, so that the police end up hearing what the suspect thinks they want to hear rather than the truth; witnesses may be animated by a bias or interest that no one would trouble to discover except one specially charged with protecting the interests of the accused — which the police are not. Considerations of this kind all lead to the rejection of informal factfinding processes as definitive of factual guilt and to the insistence on formal, adjudicative, adversary factfinding processes in which the factual case against the accused is publicly heard by an impartial tribunal and is evaluated only after the accused has had a full opportunity to discredit the case against him. Even then the distrust of factfinding processes that animates the Due Process Model is not dissipated. The possibilities of human error being what they are, further scrutiny is necessary, or at least must be available, lest in the heat of battle facts have been overlooked or suppressed. . . . The demand for finality is thus very low in the Due Process Model.

[Under the Due Process Model, if] efficiency suggests shortcuts around reliability, those demands must be rejected. The aim of the process is at least as much to protect the factually innocent as it is to convict the factually guilty. It somewhat resembles quality control in industrial technology: tolerable deviation from standard varies with the importance of conformity to standard in the destined use of the product. The Due Process Model resembles a factory that has to devote a substantial part of its input to quality control. This necessarily reduces quantitative output.

[The Due Process Model has evolved] from an original matrix of concern with the maximization of reliability into something quite different and more far-reaching. This complex of values can be symbolized although not adequately described by the concept of the primacy of the individual and the complementary concept of limitation on official power.

The combination of stigma and loss of liberty that is embodied in the end result of the criminal process is viewed as being the heaviest deprivation that government can inflict on the individual. Furthermore, the processes that culminate in these highly afflictive sanctions are in themselves coercive, restricting, and demeaning. Power is always subject to abuse, sometimes subtle, other times, as in the criminal process, open and ugly. Precisely because of its potency in subjecting the individual to the coercive power of the state, the criminal process must, on this model, be subjected to controls and safeguards that prevent it from operating with maximal efficiency. According to this ideology, maximal efficiency means maximal tyranny. . . .

The most modest-seeming but potentially far-reaching mechanism by which the Due Process Model implements these antiauthoritarian values is the doctrine of legal guilt. According to this doctrine, an individual is not to be held guilty of crime merely on a showing that in all probability, based upon reliable evidence, he did factually what he is said to have done. Instead, he is to be held guilty if and only if these factual determinations are made in procedurally regular fashion and by authorities acting within competences duly allocated to them. . . .

Another strand in the complex of attitudes that underlies the Due Process Model is the idea — itself a shorthand statement for a complex of attitudes — of equality. . . . Stated most starkly, the ideal of equality holds that "there can be no equal justice where the kind of trial a man gets depends on the amount of money he has." . . . The demands made by a norm of this kind are likely by its very nature to be quite sweeping. . . .

There is a final strand of thought in the Due Process Model whose presence is often ignored but which needs to be candidly faced if thought on the subject is not to be obscured. That is a mood of skepticism about the morality and the utility of the criminal sanction. [We] are told that the criminal law's notion of just condemnation and punishment is a cruel hypocrisy visited by a smug society on the psychologically and economically crippled; that its premise of a morally autonomous will with at least some measure of choice whether to comply with the values expressed in a penal code is unscientific and outmoded. [Doubts] about the ends for which power is being exercised create pressure to limit the discretion with which that power is exercised. . . .

What assumptions do we make about the sources of authority to shape the real-world operations of the criminal process? . . . Because the Crime Control Model is basically an affirmative model, emphasizing at every turn the existence and exercise of official power, its validating authority is ultimately legislative (although proximately administrative). Because the Due Process Model is basically a negative model, asserting limits on the nature of official power and on the modes of its exercise, its validating authority is judicial and requires an appeal to supra-legislative law, to the law of the Constitution. . . . That is at once the strength and the weakness of the Due Process Model: its strength because in our system the appeal to the Constitution provides the last and the overriding word; its weakness because saying no in specific cases is an exercise in futility unless there is a general willingness on the part of the officials who operate the process to apply negative prescriptions across the board. . . .

COMMUNITY POLICING CONSORTIUM, UNDERSTANDING COMMUNITY POLICING: A FRAMEWORK FOR ACTION

Bureau of Justice Assistance (1994)

. . . Experience and research reveal that community institutions are the first line of defense against disorder and crime. Thus, it is essential that the police work closely with all facets of the community to identify concerns and to find the most effective solutions. This is the essence of community policing.

The Role of the Police: A Historical Perspective

... Researchers have suggested that the reform era in government, which began in the early 1900's, coupled with a nationwide move toward professionalization, resulted in the separation of the police from the community. Police managers assigned officers to rotating shifts and moved them frequently from one geographical location to another to eliminate corruption. Management also instituted a policy of centralized control, designed to ensure compliance with standard operating procedures and to encourage a professional aura of impartiality.

This social distancing was also reinforced by technological developments. The expanding role of automobiles replaced the era of the friendly foot patrol officer. By the 1970's, rapid telephone contact with police through 911 systems allowed them to respond quickly to crimes. Answering the overwhelming number of calls for service, however, left police little time to prevent crimes from occurring. As increasingly sophisticated communications technology made it possible for calls to be transmitted almost instantaneously, officers had to respond to demands for assistance regardless of the urgency of the situation. Answering calls severely limited a broad police interaction with the community. The advent of the computer also contributed to the decrease in police contact with the community. Statistics, rather than the type of service provided or the service recipients, became the focus for officers and managers. As computers generated data on crime patterns and trends, counted the incidence of crimes, increased the efficiency of dispatch, and calculated the rapidity and outcome of police response, rapid response became an end in itself.

Random patrolling also served to further break the link between communities and police. Police were instructed to change routes constantly, in an effort to thwart criminals. However, community members also lost the ability to predict when they might be able to interact with their local police....

The police and the public had become so separated from one another that in some communities an attitude of "us versus them" prevailed between the police and community members. One observer of the urban scene characterized the deteriorating police-community relationship this way: "For the urban poor the police are those who arrest you." ...

Community Partnership: Core Component One

Establishing and maintaining mutual trust is the central goal of the first core component of community policing — community partnership. Police recognize the need for cooperation with the community. In the fight against serious crime, police have encouraged community members to come forth with relevant information. In addition, police have spoken to neighborhood groups, participated in business and civic events, worked with social agencies, and taken part in educational and recreational programs for school children.... So how then do the cooperative efforts of community policing differ from the actions that have taken place previously? The fundamental distinction is that, in community policing, the police become an integral part of the community culture, and the community assists in defining future priorities and in allocating resources. The difference is substantial and encompasses basic goals and commitments.

Community partnership ... recognizes the value of activities that contribute to the orderliness and well-being of a neighborhood. These activities could include:

helping accident or crime victims, providing emergency medical services, helping resolve domestic and neighborhood conflicts (e.g., family violence, landlord-tenant disputes, or racial harassment), working with residents and local businesses to improve neighborhood conditions, controlling automobile and pedestrian traffic, providing emergency social services and referrals to those at risk (e.g., adolescent runaways, the homeless, the intoxicated, and the mentally ill), protecting the exercise of constitutional rights (e.g., guaranteeing a person's right to speak, protecting lawful assemblies from disruption), and providing a model of citizenship (helpfulness, respect for others, honesty, and fairness). . . .

To build this trust for an effective community partnership police must treat people with respect and sensitivity. The use of unnecessary force and arrogance, aloofness, or rudeness at any level of the agency will dampen the willingness of community members to ally themselves with the police.

The effective mobilization of community support requires different approaches in different communities. Establishing trust and obtaining cooperation are often easier in middle-class and affluent communities than in poorer communities, where mistrust of police may have a long history. Building bonds in some neighborhoods may involve supporting basic social institutions (e.g., families, churches, schools) that have been weakened by pervasive crime or disorder. . . .

For the patrol officer, police-community partnership entails talking to local business owners to help identify their problems and concerns, visiting residents in their homes to offer advice on security, and helping to organize and support neighborhood watch groups and regular community meetings. For example, the patrol officer will canvass the neighborhood for information about a string of burglaries and then revisit those residents to inform them when the burglar is caught. . . .

Problem Solving: Core Component Two

. . . The theory behind problem-oriented policing is simple. Underlying conditions create problems. These conditions might include the characteristics of the people involved (offenders, potential victims, and others), the social setting in which these people interact, the physical environments, and the way the public deals with these conditions.

A problem created by these conditions may generate one or more incidents. These incidents, while stemming from a common source, may appear to be different. For example, social and physical conditions in a deteriorated apartment complex may generate burglaries, acts of vandalism, intimidation of pedestrians by rowdy teenagers, and other incidents. These incidents, some of which come to police attention, are symptoms of the problems. The incidents will continue so long as the problem that creates them persists. . . .

Determining the underlying causes of crime depends, to a great extent, on an in-depth knowledge of community. Therefore, community participation in identifying and setting priorities will contribute to effective problem-solving efforts by the community and the police. . . .

Neighborhood groups and the police will not always agree on which specific problems deserve attention first. Police may regard robberies as the biggest problem in a particular community, while residents may find derelicts who sleep in doorways, break bottles on sidewalks, and pick through garbage cans to be the number one problem. Under community policing, the problem with derelicts should also receive early attention from the police. . . .

In community policing, the problem-solving process is dependent on input from both the police and the community. Problem solving can involve:

- Eliminating the problem entirely. This type of solution is usually limited to disorder problems. Examples include eliminating traffic congestion by erecting traffic control signs, and destroying or rehabilitating abandoned buildings that can provide an atmosphere conducive to crime.
- Reducing the number of the occurrences of the problem. Drug-dealing and the accompanying problems of robbery and gang violence will be decreased if the police and community work together to set up drug counseling and rehabilitation centers. Longer-range solutions might include intensifying drug education in schools, churches, and hospitals.
- Reducing the degree of injury per incident. For example, police can teach store clerks how to act during a robbery in order to avoid injury or death and can advise women in the community on ways to minimize the chances of being killed or seriously injured if attacked. . . .

The best solutions are those that satisfy community members, improve safety, diminish anxiety, lead to increased order, strengthen the ties between the community and the police, and minimize coercive actions. The following example describes such a solution: A patrol officer faced with chronic nighttime robberies of convenience stores discovered that a major contributing factor was that cash registers could not be seen from the street, either because of their location within the store or because of posters plastered on front windows. The officer did not identify the "root cause" or ultimate cause of crime, but instead identified an underlying condition that, once addressed, held promise of reducing the number of future convenience store robberies. . . .

To maximize the time that the patrol officer can spend interacting with community members, community policing encourages the use of the 911 system only for true emergencies. Non-emergency calls should be handled through other means, including delays in responding and report handling by the police station or sheriff's office over the telephone or by mail. . . .

Implications for Management and the Organizational Structure

. . . Community policing emphasizes the value of the patrol function and the patrol officer as an individual. Patrol officers have traditionally been accorded low status despite the scope and sensitivity of the tasks they perform. Community policing requires the shifting of initiative, decisionmaking, and responsibility downward within the police organization. . . . Assignment stability of these neighborhood officers is also essential if they are to develop close working relationships within their communities because they are expected to engage in activities other than simply reacting to calls for service. . . .

Systems for evaluating personnel performance should reflect the goals of community policing. Emphasizing quality over quantity represents a major difference between traditional policing and community-oriented policing. Patrol officers could be evaluated on how well they know their beats — a prerequisite for identification of problems — and how effectively they and their supervisors have adopted problem-solving techniques. Other relevant performance measures include the extent to which personnel have formed partnerships with the community and the nature of their contributions to this team effort. Since officers are working as part of a team, they should not be evaluated as if they were operating alone. The occasional mistake made by an officer seeking to solve community issues in a proactive manner would be an inappropriate measure of performance. . . .

The backbone of community policing is the patrol officer, and the status, pay, and working conditions of this position should encourage people to spend an entire career in patrol. In effect, what is needed is a system that rewards advancement through skill levels in the same job as much or more than it rewards advancement through the ranks. . . .

The problem-solving orientation of community policing requires a greater emphasis on analytic skills and expert systems management to obtain the most valuable information support. . . . Strategic analysis will require that information be collected by a number of unconventional methods, e.g., conducting neighborhood victimization surveys, canvassing rehabilitation centers and hospitals, interacting with school officials, and assessing the impact of environmental changes on criminal activity. . . .

Wide dissemination and information sharing are essential components of community policing. Pertinent and appropriate information should be made available to members of the community whenever possible. For example, statistics showing an increase in burglaries or rapes in a specific section of town should be shared with the community to further the problem-solving process. . . .

Effective community collaboration and interaction will require patrol officers to be more accessible to community members. "Storefront" police offices or "mini-stations" within neighborhoods can be established quite inexpensively, particularly with assistance from the community. The duties of staffing storefront facilities can be shared among officers, civilian employees, and community residents. [Police departments may supplement automobile patrols with foot, bicycle, scooter, and horseback patrols.]

Assessing Internal Changes

. . . In the past, police efforts usually have been evaluated on a traditional and narrow set of criteria (e.g., crime statistics, the number of 911 calls, the length of police response, the number of arrests and citations, etc.). These assessments were often taken only at times of serious crime increases. Many of the traditional methods of assessment remain valid, but can measure only the effectiveness of crime-fighting tactics and cannot gauge the effect of crime-prevention efforts. . . .

An important goal of community policing is to provide higher-quality service to neighborhoods; therefore, customer satisfaction becomes an important measure of effectiveness. The perception of progress among community members and ongoing feedback from all elements of the community are essential parts of the assessment process. Randomly and routinely conducted surveys will inform the agency of the public view of police performance, the level of fear and concern, and will make the agency aware of the extent to which community members feel as if they are participants in the community policing effort. . . .

Increased levels of community participation in crime reduction and prevention efforts is another indication of program success. Community members will not act if they are afraid or suspicious. Community members should become more willing to work with the police in a variety of ways, ranging from converting abandoned buildings to community assets to involving police actively in neighborhood watch groups. They might also be more comfortable providing information on criminal activity in the area. In fact, calls to report crime may increase considerably during the early phases of community policing implementation, as community confidence in police capability rises and community trust increases. However, the number of 911 calls will likely decrease over time, which will provide a quantitative measure of the strategy's effect. . . .

Notes

1. *Are your police community police?* Do you recognize the community policing approach in the activities and attitudes of your local police? Are there any dangers in the community policing approach?

Periodic surveys of local police departments show that the rhetoric and practices of community policing have become the norm in the United States. As of 2000, about 95 percent of the larger police departments (and about two-thirds of all local police departments) employed at least some "community police" officers. More than three-fourths of larger police departments trained all new officer recruits in community policing methods. On an operational level, police departments in 2000 reported growing use of foot and bicycle patrol, assignment of officers to fixed geographic beats, outreach to neighborhood associations and other community organizations, surveys of citizens about their satisfaction with police services, and use of computers for crime mapping. Bureau of Justice Statistics, Law Enforcement Management and Administrative Statistics, 2000: Data for Individual State and Local Agencies with 100 or More Officers (April 2004, NCJ 203350). How might each of these activities carry out the community policing philosophy?

2. *Community policing and measures of success.* There are theoretical reasons (such as those discussed by Tracey Meares earlier in this chapter) to believe that community policing actually reduces crime. Experience with this concept also offers some encouragement. Once the community policing model became firmly established in the 1990s, the United States also saw a remarkable drop in crime rates. Perhaps more effective policing can take credit for at least part of this good news.

On the other hand, the success or failure of community policing is terribly difficult to measure — especially when police administrators use the label "community policing" to describe virtually any change in management or department structure. Do the advocates of community policing make claims about its social effects that are measurable and verifiable? How would you measure the success of your local "community" police department?

3. *Potential impact on criminal procedure.* Community policing tends to give more authority to the officer on the beat and to give supervisors less control over daily activities and choices of patrol officers. Does this development make it difficult to enforce procedural requirements? Is the decentralizing of authority inconsistent with the very idea of uniform rules of procedure influencing all police officers? As you read cases on searches and seizures in Chapters 2-7, ask yourself how many of the police officers in these cases were acting in a community policing mode. Would

your view of the cases, or the proper rules, change if the police adopted a different philosophy?

4. *Herbert Packer's models of criminal procedure and the community policing philosophy.* Professor Herbert Packer created a way of thinking about criminal procedure that has remained highly influential to this day. His "Crime Control" and "Due Process" models offer a way to identify some of the values and assumptions associated with different approaches to procedural controversies. You might find it useful to refer to these models as organizing principles from time to time as you think about difficult procedural questions later in this course. How do Packer's two models differ in their description of police work? Do the two models share any assumptions about policing? Would a shift to community policing be more appealing to a Crime Control advocate or to a Due Process advocate? Or does community policing promote forms of policing that Packer's account does not address at all? Consider an alternative method of thinking about the criminal process, proposed by John Griffiths:

> . . . Packer's [model] rests not upon two but upon a single, albeit unarticulated, basic conception of the nature of the criminal process — that it is a battleground of fundamentally hostile forces, where the only relevant variable is the "balance of advantage." [Packer] assumes disharmony, fundamentally irreconcilable interests, a state of war. We can start from an assumption of reconcilable — even mutually supportive — interests, a state of love. [There is] a "real-world" institution which occasionally inflicts punishments on offenders for their offenses but which is nonetheless built upon a fundamental assumption of harmony of interest and love. [I therefore offer] a "Family Model" of the criminal process. [People operating within the Family Model would accept] the idea that criminals are just people who are deemed to have offended — that we are all . . . both actual and potential criminals. . . .
>
> What other implications would follow from a Family Model? For one thing, that ideology would necessarily be accompanied by a basic faith in public officials; everyone would assume, as a general matter, that if a public official has a particular role or duty, he can be expected to carry it out in good faith and using his best judgment. . . . Basic faith in public officials would revolutionize American criminal procedure. We are all used to the proposition that legal procedures — indeed, the organization of government in general — must be designed with the bad man, or the man who will unwittingly misuse his powers, primarily in mind. . . . Our assumption that the state and the individual are in battle compels us to believe that any "discretion" — any active responsibility going beyond the umpiring role of a judge — will necessarily be exercised either on behalf of the individual's interest or on behalf of the state's. We see only Packer's two poles as the possible outcomes of discretion.

Griffiths, Ideology in Criminal Procedure, or a Third "Model" of the Criminal Process, 79 Yale L.J. 359 (1970). Is the "family" model more consistent with the realities of police-community relations in a world dominated by the community policing model?

Does Packer's model suggest anything about different ways in which victims of alleged crimes might become involved in criminal investigations or adjudications? For two efforts to supplement the Packer models, see Kent Roach, Four Models of the Criminal Process, 89 J. Crim. L. & Criminology 671 (1999) (proposing "punitive" and "non-punitive" models of victim involvement); Douglas Beloof, The Third Model of Criminal Process: The Victim Participation Model, 1999 Utah L. Rev. 289.

II

Brief Searches and Stops

Police officers sometimes restrict the movement of individuals ("seize" them) or intrude into their privacy to obtain information ("search" them). But in most of these encounters, the stop or search does not last very long or intrude very deeply. Courts and legislatures have established rules to control these encounters between government agents and the public. Yet the restrictions on this police behavior are not as demanding as the rules that apply when government agents attempt to carry out a full-blown search or seizure. This chapter deals with efforts to regulate these lesser searches and seizures.

One of the most important legal constraints on these brief searches and seizures comes from the Fourth Amendment to the U.S. Constitution, which provides as follows:

> The right of the people to be secure in their persons, houses, papers, and effects, against unreasonable searches and seizures, shall not be violated, and no Warrants shall issue, but upon probable cause, supported by Oath or affirmation, and particularly describing the place to be searched, and the persons or things to be seized.

The Fourth Amendment and its analogs in state constitutions have spawned a huge and complex case law. They have also shaped many state and federal statutes, as well as prosecutorial office guidelines and police department directives and training manuals. To understand the complex law of search and seizure, it is helpful (and probably necessary) to approach the material with some general conceptual framework. Two different frameworks for organizing the extensive modern law of search and seizure suggest themselves in the cases and other legal materials.

The traditional framework for searches and seizures begins with the oft-repeated remark that the Fourth Amendment incorporates a strong preference for search warrants (that is, a judicial determination that a proposed search is justified), that warrantless searches are generally considered unreasonable, and that exceptions to the "warrant requirement" are "jealously and carefully drawn." State and federal courts invoke this theme. This preference for warrants grows out of the apparent emphasis on limited warrants in the constitutional text. Some statutes also implicitly make warrants the standard and unwarranted searches the exceptions. For example, Mont. Code Ann. §46-5-101 provides that

> [a] search of a person, object, or place may be made and evidence, contraband, and persons may be seized . . . when a search is made: (1) by the authority of a search warrant; or (2) in accordance with judicially recognized exceptions to the warrant requirement.

Before the late 1960s, the recognized exceptions to the warrant requirement were indeed fairly few. Most prominent were two umbrella categories, exigent circumstances and consent. Warrants were generally required unless the police could show exigent circumstances or consent to search or seize. Within the category of exigent circumstances, courts developed exceptions to the warrant requirement such as risk of flight, destruction of evidence, or an officer's personal observation of a crime.

In the traditional framework, the justification necessary to proceed with a valid search or seizure, whether carried out with or without a warrant, was probable cause. Once a court was convinced that the government's activity amounted to a "search" or "seizure," the court insisted that the government show probable cause to justify its action. A sensible approach for the study of search and seizure in such a legal system is to start with the foundational elements — the process for warrants and the standard of probable cause — and then to identify and study the exceptions.

Organizing a field according to its foundational rules and exceptions works well if the rules are ordinarily followed and the exceptions are modest. But in the modern law of search and seizure the exceptions have swallowed the traditional rules. In doing so, they have changed the entire framework and the best way to study searches and seizures.

Modern search and seizure law is astoundingly complex and contradictory. A survey of current "exceptions" to the warrant requirement — some of which appear in this chapter, and others in Chapters 3 and 4 — suggests how unwieldy the traditional framework has become. A partial list would include exigent circumstances (such as flight or destruction of evidence), plain view, open fields, community caretaker functions, brief frisks for weapons, inventory searches, protective sweeps, automobile searches, border searches, school searches, prison searches, searches incident to arrest, fire investigations, and administrative searches. See Craig Bradley, Two Models of the Fourth Amendment, 83 Mich. L. Rev. 1468 (1985).

What has caused such complexity in this area of the law? Three changes, marked by three U.S. Supreme Court cases decided in 1967 and 1968, rearranged the doctrinal foundations of search and seizure law. Because these cases appear at different points in this volume, a preview here is useful.

The first key case was Katz v. United States, 389 U.S. 347 (1967). In *Katz,* the U.S. Supreme Court changed the method of deciding whether a person had an interest that the Fourth Amendment would protect. In other words, it redefined the basic *conceptual framework* for deciding whether the government had engaged in a "search" that is subject to constitutional limitations. In doing so, the Court moved away from concepts of protected physical spaces (property) and toward concepts of individual privacy.

Katz was convicted of transmitting gambling information by telephone across state lines; crucial evidence in the case came from a wiretap of a public phone booth. The intermediate appeals court found no Fourth Amendment violation and upheld Katz's conviction because the listening device had been placed on the outside of the telephone booth, and thus there was "no physical entrance into the area occupied" by Katz. This was a straightforward application of the "trespass" theory of unreasonable searches, with historical origins in the tort suits that the targets of unreasonable searches filed against the officers who had improperly invaded their property interests. But the Supreme Court reversed Katz's conviction, finding that the Fourth Amendment protected Katz from the government recording his conversation in a telephone booth. The Court described the key doctrinal shift as follows:

> [The] parties have attached great significance to the characterization of the telephone booth from which the petitioner placed his calls. The petitioner has strenuously argued that the booth was a "constitutionally protected area." The Government has maintained with equal vigor that it was not. But this effort to decide whether or not a given "area," viewed in the abstract, is "constitutionally protected" deflects attention from the problem presented by this case. For the Fourth Amendment protects people, not places. What a person knowingly exposes to the public, even in his own home or office, is not a subject of Fourth Amendment protection. But what he seeks to preserve as private, even in an area accessible to the public, may be constitutionally protected.

What are the implications of deciding that the Fourth Amendment "protects people, not places"? The shift to a privacy analysis has drawn a larger number and variety of governmental actions into Fourth Amendment territory. It is far easier to make a claim about "expectations of privacy" in a host of situations than it would be to make a claim based on property interests. As the courts have applied the Fourth Amendment to new settings, they have generated new law and departed more frequently from the concepts of probable cause and warrants.

The second key case to transform search and seizure doctrine is Terry v. Ohio, 392 U.S. 1 (1968), which we will study in section D of this chapter. *Terry* moved beyond the relative simplicity of having a single *standard* — probable cause — to assess the validity of searches and seizures. *Terry* recognized a major category of limited stops and searches that law enforcement officers could conduct on the basis of reasonable suspicion — a standard less than probable cause. By recognizing that standards other than probable cause would be appropriate for justifying various kinds of searches and seizures, the Court invited more deviations from the traditional doctrinal core of the Fourth Amendment.

The third key case is Camara v. Municipal Court, 387 U.S. 523 (1967), which created a new *method* for determining what justification the government would need for a search and what process it would follow to establish that justification. In *Camara,* the Supreme Court approved the granting of warrants for municipal building code enforcement inspections. These inspections took place on the basis of general administrative needs for inspecting an area, without requiring any individualized suspicion that a property owner was violating the law. The Court in *Camara* declared that the Fourth Amendment applied to both civil and criminal law enforcement efforts. With such a diversity of governmental purposes and activities at issue, the complexity of search and seizure doctrine was bound to increase. Furthermore, the opinion in *Camara* announced that it would "balance" competing interests to determine the level of justification and the type of warrant process the government would need to follow before conducting a search: "[There] can be no ready test for determining reasonableness other than by balancing the need to search against the invasion which the search entails."

These cases have fractured search and seizure doctrine and increased the overall complexity of the law. Whether these changes are good or bad, they have made search and seizure law more difficult to learn and apply.

Perhaps some new principle or calculus offers a more satisfying synthesis of these changes in the law than the traditional framework of warrants and probable cause can offer. As you study the materials in the next few chapters, try to construct a coherent explanation for the cases and laws that govern searches and seizures.

In particular, consider the explanatory value of a calculus that weighs three recurring factors in determining the "reasonableness" of a search or seizure: (1) the privacy interest of the person subject to a search; (2) the government's interest in conducting the search; and (3) the degree of intrusion from the search. The balancing of these three factors may solve such crucial puzzles as the level of justification necessary to support the search (such as probable cause, reasonable suspicion, or no individualized suspicion) and the time when the government must give its justification (before the search to obtain a warrant, or after the fact when the target challenges the search).

You will have the opportunity to test this conceptual framework, along with the more traditional framework that emphasizes probable cause and warrants, and to analyze a wide array of government efforts to collect information. The following materials begin with the briefest and most common government searches and seizures.

A. BRIEF INVESTIGATIVE STOPS OF SUSPECTS

Countless times each day, a police officer or some other government agent stops to talk with a member of the general public. Some citizens take part in these conversations willingly; others are more reluctant but feel obliged to stay and continue the conversation. A few do not cooperate at all. What authority does the officer have to insist that a citizen stop for a few moments during an investigation?

■ DELAWARE CODE TIT. 11, §1902

(a) A peace officer may stop any person abroad, or in a public place, who the officer has reasonable ground to suspect is committing, has committed or is about to commit a crime, and may demand the person's name, address, business abroad and destination.

(b) Any person so questioned who fails to give identification or explain the person's actions to the satisfaction of the officer may be detained and further questioned and investigated.

ALASKA STATUTES §28.35.182(b)

A person commits the offense of failure to stop at the direction of a peace officer . . . if the person, while driving or operating a vehicle or motor vehicle . . . knowingly fails to stop as soon as practical and in a reasonably safe manner under the circumstance when requested or signaled to do so by a peace officer.

Notes

1. *Three types of encounters: conversations, stops, and arrests.* These statutes set out a typical set of requirements for police officers who stop a person in a vehicle or on foot in public. While more than 30 states codify these requirements in statutes or rules of criminal procedure, others announce the requirements in judicial opinions. Most are not recent innovations; for instance, the Delaware statute above was adopted in 1951 and is based on the Uniform Arrest Act of 1940. The Supreme Court ratified the constitutionality of this framework in Terry v. Ohio, 392 U.S. 1 (1968), a case we discuss later in this chapter. If you were a police officer, would you prefer explicit statutory authority to stop suspects, or would you rather see the power established and developed in case law? See George Dix, Nonarrest Investigatory Detentions in Search and Seizure Law, 1985 Duke L.J. 849.

These statutes assume the existence of three different levels of controls on the officer. On the first level, where the police officer does not "stop" a person at all but merely engages in a conversation, the officer does not need to justify the decision to focus attention on one person. On the second level, where the officer "stops" a person for a brief time but not long enough to qualify as an arrest, the officer must have "reasonable suspicion" before making the stop. Reasonable suspicion has also been described as "individualized" or "articulable" suspicion. On the third level, where the officer detains a person for a longer time or in a more coercive way, there is an "arrest." Constitutions, statutes, and rules of procedure all require that the officer show "probable cause" that the arrestee has committed a crime.

Thus, for the brief encounters we are now exploring, there are two questions to resolve: Was the interaction between the police officer and the individual a consensual encounter, a limited "stop," or a full arrest? If the incident was a stop, did the government agent have the "reasonable suspicion" needed to justify the stop?

2. *The prevalence of stops and consensual encounters.* Consensual conversations and stops (particularly traffic stops) are the two most common forms of interaction between the police and the public. According to a 2005 national survey, about 19 percent of all persons age 16 or older had at least one contact with a police officer during the year. Just over 40 percent of those contacts occurred during a motor vehicle stop; another 24 percent of the contacts happened when people reported a crime to the police. Only about 3 percent of the contacts occurred because the officer suspected the person of a crime. Bureau of Justice Statistics, Contacts Between Police and the Public, 2005 (April 2007, NCJ 215243).

3. *Ambiguous statutory language.* Will defense counsel and prosecutors in Delaware agree on what constitutes a "reasonable ground" for a stop under the statute? Will they agree on how long the "further" questioning can last under the statute? How should the trial court resolve their disagreements? What sources will be relevant? Is the court's task here the same as when parties dispute the meaning

of some phrase that has developed through the common law? As you read further in this chapter, take special note of the methods courts use to resolve conflicts about the meaning of ambiguous statutory language.

1. *Consensual Encounters and "Stops"*

Conversations change direction. Sometimes a conversation between a police officer and a member of the public will begin as a "consensual encounter" but will transform into a "stop" without the officer's announcement of this fact in so many words. What marks the difference between consensual encounters and coercive stops?

■ UNITED STATES v. SYLVIA MENDENHALL

446 U.S. 544 (1980)

STEWART, J.*

. . . I.

[Sylvia Mendenhall] arrived at the Detroit Metropolitan Airport on a commercial airline flight from Los Angeles early in the morning on February 10, 1976. As she disembarked from the airplane, she was observed by two agents of the Drug Enforcement Administration (DEA), who were present at the airport for the purpose of detecting unlawful traffic in narcotics. After observing the respondent's conduct, which appeared to the agents to be characteristic of persons unlawfully carrying narcotics,[1] the agents approached her as she was walking through the concourse, identified themselves as federal agents, and asked to see her identification and airline ticket. The respondent produced her driver's license, which was in the name of Sylvia Mendenhall, and, in answer to a question of one of the agents, stated that she resided at the address appearing on the license. The airline ticket was issued in the name of "Annette Ford." When asked why the ticket bore a name different from her own, the respondent stated that she "just felt like using that name." In response to a further question, the respondent indicated that she had been in California only two days. Agent Anderson then specifically identified himself as a federal narcotics agent and, according to his testimony, the respondent "became quite shaken, extremely nervous. She had a hard time speaking."

* [Chief Justice Burger and Justices Blackmun and Powell concurred in part and joined in parts I, IIB, IIC, and III of the opinion; Justice Rehnquist joined the opinion, including part IA. — EDS.]

1. The agent testified that the respondent's behavior fit the so-called "drug courier profile" — an informally compiled abstract of characteristics thought typical of persons carrying illicit drugs. In this case the agents thought it relevant that (1) the respondent was arriving on a flight from Los Angeles, a city believed by the agents to be the place of origin for much of the heroin brought to Detroit; (2) the respondent was the last person to leave the plane, "appeared to be very nervous," and "completely scanned the whole area where [the agents] were standing"; (3) after leaving the plane the respondent proceeded past the baggage area without claiming any luggage; and (4) the respondent changed airlines for her flight out of Detroit.

After returning the airline ticket and driver's license to her, Agent Anderson asked the respondent if she would accompany him to the airport DEA office for further questions. She did so, although the record does not indicate a verbal response to the request. The office, which was located up one flight of stairs about 50 feet from where the respondent had first been approached, consisted of a reception area adjoined by three other rooms. At the office the agent asked the respondent if she would allow a search of her person and handbag and told her that she had the right to decline the search if she desired. She responded: "Go ahead." She then handed Agent Anderson her purse, which contained a receipt for an airline ticket that had been issued to "F. Bush" three days earlier for a flight from Pittsburgh through Chicago to Los Angeles. The agent asked whether this was the ticket that she had used for her flight to California, and the respondent stated that it was.

A female police officer then arrived to conduct the search of the respondent's person. . . . The policewoman explained that the search would require that the respondent remove her clothing. . . . As the respondent removed her clothing, she took from her undergarments two small packages, one of which appeared to contain heroin, and handed both to the policewoman. The agents then arrested the respondent for possessing heroin. It was on the basis of this evidence that the District Court denied the respondent's motion to suppress. . . .

II.

The Fourth Amendment provides that "the right of the people to be secure in their persons, houses, papers, and effects, against unreasonable searches and seizures, shall not be violated. . . ."

A.

The Fourth Amendment's requirement that searches and seizures be founded upon an objective justification, governs all seizures of the person, including seizures that involve only a brief detention short of traditional arrest. Terry v. Ohio, 392 U.S. 1 (1968). Accordingly, if the respondent was "seized" when the DEA agents approached her on the concourse and asked questions of her, the agents' conduct in doing so was constitutional only if they reasonably suspected the respondent of wrongdoing. But "obviously, not all personal intercourse between policemen and citizens involves 'seizures' of persons. Only when the officer, by means of physical force or show of authority, has in some way restrained the liberty of a citizen may we conclude that a 'seizure' has occurred." *Terry,* 392 U.S., at 19, n.16.

The distinction between an intrusion amounting to a "seizure" of the person and an encounter that intrudes upon no constitutionally protected interest is illustrated by the facts of Terry v. Ohio, which the Court recounted as follows: "Officer McFadden approached the three men, identified himself as a police officer and asked for their names. . . . When the men 'mumbled something' in response to his inquiries, Officer McFadden grabbed petitioner Terry, spun him around so that they were facing the other two, with Terry between McFadden and the others, and patted down the outside of his clothing." Obviously the officer "seized" Terry and subjected him to a "search" when he took hold of him, spun him around, and patted down the outer surfaces of his clothing. What was not determined in that case, however, was that a seizure had taken place before the officer physically restrained Terry for purposes of searching his person for weapons. The Court "assume[d] that up to that point no intrusion upon constitutionally protected rights had occurred." The Court's assumption appears entirely correct in view of the fact [that police officers enjoy the liberty possessed by every citizen] to address questions to other persons. . . .

We adhere to the view that a person is "seized" only when, by means of physical force or a show of authority, his freedom of movement is restrained. Only when such restraint is imposed is there any foundation whatever for invoking constitutional safeguards. The purpose of the Fourth Amendment is not to eliminate all contact between the police and the citizenry, but to prevent arbitrary and oppressive interference by enforcement officials with the privacy and personal security of individuals. As long as the person to whom questions are put remains free to disregard the questions and walk away, there has been no intrusion upon that person's liberty or privacy as would under the Constitution require some particularized and objective justification.

Moreover, characterizing every street encounter between a citizen and the police as a "seizure," while not enhancing any interest secured by the Fourth Amendment, would impose wholly unrealistic restrictions upon a wide variety of legitimate law enforcement practices. The Court has on other occasions referred to the acknowledged need for police questioning as a tool in the effective enforcement of the criminal laws. Without such investigation, those who were innocent might be falsely accused, those who were guilty might wholly escape prosecution, and many crimes would go unsolved. In short, the security of all would be diminished.

We conclude that a person has been "seized" within the meaning of the Fourth Amendment only if, in view of all of the circumstances surrounding the incident, a reasonable person would have believed that he was not free to leave.[6] Examples of circumstances that might indicate a seizure, even where the person did not attempt to leave, would be the threatening presence of several officers, the display of a weapon by an officer, some physical touching of the person of the citizen, or the use of language or tone of voice indicating that compliance with the officer's request might be compelled. In the absence of some such evidence, otherwise inoffensive contact between a member of the public and the police cannot, as a matter of law, amount to a seizure of that person.

On the facts of this case, no "seizure" of the respondent occurred. The events took place in the public concourse. The agents wore no uniforms and displayed no weapons. They did not summon the respondent to their presence, but instead approached her and identified themselves as federal agents. They requested, but did not demand to see the respondent's identification and ticket. Such conduct without more, did not amount to an intrusion upon any constitutionally protected interest. The respondent was not seized simply by reason of the fact that the agents approached her, asked her if she would show them her ticket and identification, and posed to her a few questions. Nor was it enough to establish a seizure that the person asking the questions was a law enforcement official. In short, nothing in the record suggests that the respondent had any objective reason to believe that she was not free to end the conversation in the concourse and proceed on her way, and for that reason we conclude that the agents' initial approach to her was not a seizure.

6. We agree with the District Court that the subjective intention of the DEA agent in this case to detain the respondent, had she attempted to leave, is irrelevant except insofar as that may have been conveyed to the respondent.

Our conclusion that no seizure occurred is not affected by the fact that the respondent was not expressly told by the agents that she was free to decline to cooperate with their inquiry, for the voluntariness of her responses does not depend upon her having been so informed. We also reject the argument that the only inference to be drawn from the fact that the respondent acted in a manner so contrary to her self-interest is that she was compelled to answer the agents' questions. It may happen that a person makes statements to law enforcement officials that he later regrets, but the issue in such cases is not whether the statement was self-protective, but rather whether it was made voluntarily. [The court also held that Mendenhall had "voluntarily" proceeded to the DEA office, and consented to the search of her person.]

WESLEY WILSON v. STATE

874 P.2d 215 (Wyo. 1994)

TAYLOR, J.

[Limping] severely, Wesley Wilson . . . walked rapidly eastbound on 12th Street in Casper, Wyoming on the morning of June 21, 1991. At 12:31 A.M., Officer Kamron Ritter . . . of the Casper Police Department watched Wilson's "lunging" steps and pulled his patrol car over to the sidewalk. Officer Ritter, believing that a fight may have taken place, asked if Wilson was okay and what happened to his leg. Wilson responded that he had twisted his ankle at a party. Smelling alcohol on Wilson's breath, Officer Ritter requested identification, which Wilson provided. Officer Ritter radioed for a routine warrants check with the National Crime Information Center (NCIC) and local files. This initial encounter with Wilson lasted about a minute and a half.

The conversation with Wilson was interrupted when Officer Ritter detected smoke coming from 12th Street, west of where he was standing. At the same time, two motorcyclists stopped and reported to Officer Ritter that a fire was burning in a building [one block] up the street. Before leaving to check on the fire, Officer Ritter told Wilson to "stay in the area."

Officer Ritter reported the fire to the police dispatcher. . . . After about eight minutes at the scene of the fire, Officer Ritter returned to check on Wilson. He had limped about 40 feet farther east and was attempting to cross 12th Street. As additional fire trucks approached, Officer Ritter helped Wilson cross the street. Officer Ritter then told Wilson to go to a nearby corner and "wait" while the officer returned to the fire scene.

As Officer Ritter provided traffic control, the police dispatcher radioed, at 12:41 A.M., that Wilson had two outstanding arrest warrants. Officer Ritter and Officer Terry Van Oordt then walked down the block to where Wilson was sitting on a lawn at the corner watching the fire. When the officers approached Wilson, they informed him of the outstanding warrants and asked him to stand. Wilson told the officers it was difficult to stand with his injured ankle. The officers noticed an oily patch on the right shoulder of the shirt Wilson was wearing. Both officers touched the stained area and found an oily substance. Wilson volunteered, "What are you doing? I don't smell like smoke." The officers proceeded to arrest Wilson on the outstanding warrants. The following morning, in custody, Wilson made a voluntary statement implicating himself in starting the fire.

At a suppression hearing, Officer Ritter testified about his concerns for Wilson's safety during their initial encounter and that he had no suspicions of Wilson's involvement in the fire or of arresting him for public intoxication. Officer Ritter stated he followed routine Casper Police Department procedure to get the names of subjects police come in "contact" with "at that time of night" and "always" run a warrants check. Officer Ritter said he wanted Wilson to wait until the results of the warrants check were received. During their second encounter, when Officer Ritter helped Wilson cross the street, the officer testified he still had no suspicion of Wilson's potential involvement in the fire but wanted Wilson to wait for the completion of the warrants check. . . .

Wilson, who did not testify at the hearing, argued that the stop was illegal and the evidence gathered from the stop [including his statements about smoke and his confession] should be suppressed.* [The district court denied the suppression motion, and the jury convicted Wilson of felony property destruction.]

Wilson's statement of the issues presumes his appeal is one based on provisions of both the United States Constitution and the Wyoming Constitution. The language of Wyo. Const, art. 1, §4 differs somewhat from its federal counterpart in providing:

> The right of the people to be secure in their persons, houses, papers and effects against unreasonable searches and seizures shall not be violated, and no warrant shall issue but upon probable cause, supported by affidavit, particularly describing the place to be searched or the person or thing to be seized.

[However,] we are unable to consider the impact of those differences in this situation because Wilson . . . failed to offer any argument supporting an independent state constitutional claim. . . . The Fourth Amendment to the United States Constitution grants

> the right of the people to be secure in their persons, houses, papers, and effects, against unreasonable searches and seizures, shall not be violated, and no Warrants shall issue, but upon probable cause, supported by Oath or affirmation, and particularly describing the place to be searched, and the persons or things to be seized.

[The] decision of the United States Supreme Court in Terry v. Ohio, 392 U.S. 1 (1968) marked the initial recognition by the United States Supreme Court of some lesser standard than probable cause for intrusion upon constitutionally guaranteed rights. In *Terry*, a police officer, observing specific conduct which his training and experience taught him was indicative of criminal behavior, conducted a limited seizure to investigate his reasonable suspicions. In the course of such a seizure, the United States Supreme Court approved a limited search for weapons for the protection of the police officer. . . .

From this genesis, a general recognition of the rich diversity of police-citizen encounters has emerged. [Three] categories or tiers of interaction between police and citizens may be characterized. The most intrusive encounter, an arrest, requires

* [The ordinary remedy for the violation of the defendant's constitutional rights is the exclusion of the evidence obtained as a result of the improper seizure during the prosecution's case at trial. Exclusion is not the only possible remedy. See discussion in Chapter 6. — Eds.]

justification by probable cause to believe that a person has committed or is committing a crime. The investigatory stop represents a seizure which invokes Fourth Amendment safeguards, but, by its less intrusive character, requires only the presence of specific and articulable facts and rational inferences which give rise to a reasonable suspicion that a person has committed or may be committing a crime. The least intrusive police-citizen contact, a consensual encounter, involves no restraint of liberty and elicits the citizen's voluntary cooperation with non-coercive questioning.

The proper test for determining when a police-citizen encounter implicates Fourth Amendment rights as a seizure was initially outlined in United States v. Mendenhall, 446 U.S. 544 (1980). [The Court] found no seizure had occurred where federal drug agents approached a woman walking through an airport and requested her identification. [The *Mendenhall* standard] creates an objective test, which makes the subjective intent of the police officer irrelevant unless it is conveyed to the person being detained, and like all search and seizure cases, the inquiry is very fact oriented. The reasonable person standard also means the subjective perceptions of the suspect are irrelevant to the court's inquiry.

[An] analytical difficulty imposed by [this] standard lies in the determination of whether a reasonable person "would have believed that he was not free to leave" when being questioned by a police officer. We find useful instruction in the Model Code of Pre-Arraignment Procedure, §110.1 commentary at 259-60 (A.L.I. 1975):

> The motives that lead one to cooperate with the police are various. To put an extreme case, the police may in purely precatory language request a person to give information. Even if he is guilty, such a person might accede to the request because he has been trained to submit to the wishes of persons in authority, or because he fears that a refusal will focus suspicion, or because he believes that concealment is no longer possible and a cooperative posture tactically or psychologically preferable. Regardless of the particular motive, the cooperation is clearly a response to the authority of the police.
>
> By specifically authorizing law enforcement officers . . . to seek cooperation, the Code rejects the notion that a damaging response to an inquiry from a policeman can never be "voluntary." . . . The extra pressures to cooperate with what is known to be an official request require no further justification than that the request was made in the performance of law enforcement functions. That there exist such pressures seems to us, far from being regrettable, to be a necessary condition of the police's capacity to operate reasonably effectively within their limited grant of powers.

The critical distinction between the position advanced by Wilson and that argued by the State is which type of encounter occurred in this case. Wilson basically contends that he was seized without reasonable suspicion during the period when his identification was being checked for possible warrants. The State asserts that Wilson was never seized in a manner that would implicate Fourth Amendment rights, until he was validly arrested on the outstanding warrants. . . .

The initial encounter between Officer Ritter and Wilson was prompted by the officer's concerns for the safety of a citizen. The officer conducted himself in a reasonable manner by simply pulling his patrol car to the curb to talk with Wilson. No flashing lights or siren sounds were used to signal Wilson to stop. The community caretaker function . . . permits police to act in a manner that enhances public safety. The police officer's observation of specific and articulable facts, Wilson's lunging walk with a severe limp, reasonably justified a brief inquiry into his condition and the possible cause, such as whether Wilson was a victim of criminal conduct. This portion of the initial encounter between Officer Ritter and Wilson occurred in a consensual atmosphere which implicates no Fourth Amendment interest.

When Officer Ritter requested Wilson's name and identification and Wilson complied, the encounter remained consensual. A request for identification is not, by itself, a seizure. Indeed, a reasonable person in physical distress should feel less intimidated by a police officer's offer to help and a request for identification than someone stopped at random. . . .

After obtaining Wilson's identification, Officer Ritter radioed for the NCIC and local warrants check. Despite the request for the computerized warrants check, the encounter remained consensual. Officer Ritter had not imposed any restriction on Wilson's freedom to leave as the warrants check was instituted. . . .

The initial encounter ended when Officer Ritter detected smoke and the two motorcyclists stopped to report a fire. At that point, Officer Ritter told Wilson to "stay in the area." [No seizure occurred at this point] because, when left unattended, [Wilson] limped away from the immediate area where the questioning had occurred. . . .

When Officer Ritter left the fire scene and returned to check on Wilson for the second time, [he] assisted Wilson across the street by grabbing him at the elbow and supporting his weight. [The] physical touching in this instance did not effect a seizure. A reasonable person would not believe that an officer's assistance in crossing a street would represent a restriction on the person's freedom to leave. The aid Officer Ritter provided ensured Wilson's safety by removing him from the path of emergency vehicles.

After Officer Ritter and Wilson crossed the street, the officer instructed Wilson to go to a specific street corner and wait. We hold a seizure occurred at the point when Wilson complied with the instruction to wait given by Officer Ritter in their second encounter. As Officer Ritter directed traffic, he could see Wilson sitting in front of a retail store at the specific corner the officer had directed. The persistence of Officer Ritter in returning to check on Wilson only supplements the determination that a seizure occurred. The show of authority by Officer Ritter restrained Wilson's liberty. A reasonable person would have believed he or she was not free to leave. With his seizure, Wilson's Fourth Amendment right to be free of unreasonable intrusions was implicated.

The narrow issue remaining is whether a brief detention for the purpose of completing a computerized warrants check is an unreasonable seizure. [It] is Casper Police Department policy to conduct NCIC and local warrants checks of everyone police "contact" late at night. The meaning of a "contact" was never defined. However, a seizure to conduct a computerized identification check without reasonable suspicion is not permitted. We acknowledge that where police have been unable to locate a person suspected of involvement in a past crime, the ability to briefly stop that person, ask questions, or check identification in the absence of probable cause promotes the strong government interest in solving crimes and bringing offenders to justice. However, we do not find in the circumstances of Officer Ritter's encounter with Wilson justification for a seizure . . . for the purpose of investigating past crime. . . . Officer Ritter questioned Wilson and requested his identification solely on the basis of the officer's concern for a citizen's safety. The officer lacked any reasonable suspicion of past criminal conduct. . . . When no observed violation of law is present, the intrusion required to run an NCIC or warrants check requires reasonable suspicion of criminal conduct. . . .

Officer Ritter admitted in his testimony that at no time during the first or second encounters did he possess any articulable facts sufficient to create a reasonable suspicion of past or present criminal conduct. Acting in a community caretaker function, Officer Ritter stopped Wilson to inquire about his condition and ensure his safety. A seizure for the purpose of completing an NCIC and local warrants check was impermissible as a matter of law. . . .

In a society burdened by crime, the protection of individual liberties requires difficult choices. All of us want to be able to freely walk the streets of our cities and towns. While we cannot and should not tolerate crime and lawlessness, we equally cannot tolerate the abrogation of basic liberties. Permitting a seizure, without reasonable suspicion of criminal behavior, to complete a computerized identification check of a police "contact" represents an unreasonable intrusion on basic liberties. . . .

The decision of the district court to deny suppression is reversed and this case is remanded for retrial without the tainted evidence.

THOMAS, J., dissenting.

I must dissent from the majority opinion in this case. . . . The contact between the officer and Wilson never went beyond the elicitation of Wilson's voluntary cooperation so as to become a seizure. [Wilson never asked to leave.] The officer testified he would not have pursued Wilson if he had chosen to leave because he had no reason to detain him if Wilson did not consent. . . . Laying aside the question whether there was any constraint upon Wilson's freedom to leave, an elapsed period of ten minutes, during which the officer's attention was devoted to the fire and traffic direction, is not unreasonable. The record reveals, of the ten minutes, Wilson was in the presence of the officer less than three minutes. . . .

The American bench needs to understand that its invocation of the premise of protecting Constitutional rights in reversing criminal convictions has contributed to the development of a society in which violence stalks our streets and fear permeates our neighborhoods. Every decision that tightens the cuffs with which we shackle our law enforcement officers contributes to such evolution. We must remember this rule applies to serial killers and multiple rapists as well as to inept firebugs who are simply a nuisance to property, until someone dies in the fire. . . .

In my judgment, the real question to be addressed in this case is: What was going on that was wrong? The obvious answer is it was wrong for Wilson to set fire to another citizen's garage-workshop. . . . The conclusion Wilson's conviction should not be upheld because of an academic fascination with the supposed wrongful conduct of the police officer does not serve the interests of the citizens of Wyoming and their property rights, which are not constitutionally subordinated to the rights of their persons. . . . I most vigorously dissent.

Notes

1. *Definition of a "stop": majority position.* Most American jurisdictions define a "stop" along the lines set out in United States v. Mendenhall, 446 U.S. 544 (1980). An encounter between a police officer and a citizen becomes a "stop" when a

reasonable person in that situation would not "feel free to leave" or to refuse to cooperate. Jurisdictions have generally adopted this definition in judicial decisions construing the state constitution rather than settling the question through statutes or rules of procedure. Is this the same "reasonable person" you met in Torts?

2. *Does reality matter?* Empirical inquiries could help us answer the question of whether a reasonable person would "feel free to leave" in a given situation. How would you gather such information for a court to use? See David K. Kessler, Free to Leave? An Empirical Look at the Fourth Amendment's Seizure Standard, 99 J. Crim. L. & Criminology 51 (2009) (survey of Boston residents regarding encounters with police). Did the Wyoming court in *Wilson* show any curiosity about the best method for finding a psychologically realistic answer to the question?

3. *The relevant pool.* The concept of the "reasonable person" is familiar in tort law and substantive criminal law. Courts applying the reasonable person concept are sometimes willing to consider particular features of the victim (age or gender, for instance) in their definition of a reasonable person. In effect, courts will sometimes narrow the relevant "pool" of persons from which the reasonable person is drawn.

Should the reasonable person standard for purposes of defining a "stop" consider the experiences and perceptions of different racial groups in their dealings with the police? Different genders? There is ample sociological and survey evidence that black males perceive the police to be more discriminatory and abusive than do white males. If a court is convinced that black males are more likely than other groups to submit passively to police encounters, should it account for this in the totality of the circumstances that go into the definition of a "stop"? See Devon W. Carbado, (E)Racing the Fourth Amendment, 100 Mich. L. Rev. 946, 974-1003 (2002).

4. *Routine check for warrants.* The court ultimately found that Ritter did not seize Wilson when he first requested a warrant check. Do you agree? Did Ritter "seize" Wilson without reasonable suspicion when he followed police department policy and requested an NCIC and warrant check on the person he "contacted" at night? The court concludes that Ritter later detained Wilson for the purpose of "completing" the warrant check. Did Ritter ever tell Wilson that he intended to complete the warrant check before releasing him? Does the status of a warrant check as a "stop" depend on how often police officers allow the individual to walk away before the check is complete? Or is it more important to know how this particular citizen (or a "reasonable" citizen) *believes* the officer would react? See Golphin v. State, 945 So. 2d 1174 (Fla. 2006) (officer's retention of person's identification card while running computer check for outstanding warrants did not necessarily convert consensual encounter into seizure); Montague v. Commonwealth, 684 S.E.2d 583 (Va. 2009) (no "stop" when officers approached suspect in common area of apartment complex, asked for his identity and whether he lived in apartments, and ran a warrants check without informing suspect of that fact).

5. *Limiting stops to investigations of serious crimes.* Should stops be available to police officers investigating misdemeanors? Most states have granted this power to the police, although there are exceptions. See N.Y. Crim. Proc. Law §140.50 (grants power to stop only when officer suspects commission of felony or the most serious misdemeanors); State v. Duvernoy, 195 S.E.2d 631 (W. Va. 1973) (limiting power to stop to investigate nonviolent offenses). Does your position on this issue depend on how effective a policy of investigative stops can be in preventing specific crimes? See Gordon Whitaker, Charles Phillips, Peter Haas & Robert Worden, Aggressive

Policing and the Deterrence of Crime, 7 Law & Pol'y 395 (1985) (investigative stops have strong negative effects on rate of robberies, auto theft, vandalism; smaller effects on rates of burglaries and thefts of property from autos). Does it depend on the racial makeup of the police force?

6. *Duration of stop and subject matter of questions.* When an officer stops a car based on reasonable suspicion that a traffic violation has occurred, it creates an opportunity to investigate other crimes. But the opportunity is limited. It is clear that the stop can only last as long as it would ordinarily take to complete a routine traffic citation. See State v. Joyce, 986 A.2d 642 (N.H. 2009) (motorist seized when officer called for narcotics-sniffing dog after police had been on scene for 10 to 15 minutes). State and federal courts have wrestled with the question of whether there are any limits on the subjects that an officer can discuss during the limited time available during a traffic stop. A rich case law has developed to trace the boundaries of the police power to stop a person, including the power to stop witnesses rather than suspects. For insights into these debates, see the web extension for this chapter at *http://www.crimpro.com/extension/ch02*.

Problem 2-1. Tickets, Please

At 3:30 A.M. on January 23, Mark Battaglia, an investigator from the Sheriff's Department, boarded a bus just as it arrived in Albany from New York City. Battaglia wore civilian clothing with his police badge displayed on his coat. Two uniformed officers accompanied him. Battaglia announced to the 15 passengers on board that he was conducting a drug interdiction. He said that he would ask everyone to produce bus tickets and identification. Battaglia then walked to the rear of the bus and saw Rawle McIntosh and a female companion sitting in the last row of seats. Battaglia noticed that McIntosh pushed a black jacket between himself and his companion. He asked McIntosh for his identification and bus ticket. Battaglia inspected the driver's license and ticket he provided, and asked him about his travel plans. Battaglia then returned the identification and the ticket to McIntosh, and asked the two passengers to stand. As they stood, the jacket remained on the seat. Noticing a bulge in the pocket of the jacket, Battaglia reached into the pocket and found cocaine.

Did Battaglia "stop" McIntosh? If so, exactly when did the stop happen? Would there be a stop if Battaglia questioned McIntosh about his identity and his travel plans without requesting or holding the ticket and identification document? See People v. McIntosh, 755 N.E.2d 329 (N.Y. 2001).

Now suppose that McIntosh refuses to provide the proof of his identity when Officer Battaglia requests it, and he is prosecuted under a statute punishing any person for refusing to provide proof of identity when a police officer makes such a request. The state legislature passed this statute in the aftermath of the terrorist attacks in New York City on September 11, 2001. Is the statute constitutional?

Notes

1. *Asking for name and identification.* Does a stop occur whenever a police officer asks for a person to produce proof of identity? Does it matter how the officer asks

for the identification card or how quickly she returns the card? How could anyone feel free to leave when an officer is holding his driver's license? More than 20 state legislatures have passed statutes empowering police officers to ask for identification. In other states, the judiciary has permitted the police to make this request without specific statutory authority. If a statute authorizes a request for identification only upon reasonable suspicion (as statutes typically do), does that suggest that any police request for a citizen's identification is a stop? Apart from asking for name and identification, are there certain questions a police officer might ask that should automatically convert a conversation into a stop?

Could a statute explicitly oblige citizens to comply with the request for identification and allow officers to restrain citizens who refuse to do so? Is that what the Delaware statute allows? There is little litigation so far over the question of whether such a statute is constitutional. The questions become more immediate in light of the September 11 terrorist attacks. The law in other countries, such as Germany and France, explicitly empowers police officers to insist that people identify themselves. What would you want to know about the operation of such laws to determine whether they offer useful guidance for legislatures in the United States?

2. *Seizures in close quarters.* In Florida v. Bostick, 501 U.S. 429 (1991), the Court considered an encounter between police officers and a suspected drug courier who consented to a search of his luggage during questioning on a bus. Terrance Bostick was reclining on the back seat of the Greyhound bus bound from Miami to Atlanta when two officers wearing badges and sheriff's department jackets boarded the bus during a rest stop. The officers proceeded to the rear of the bus, stood in the aisle in front of Bostick, and questioned him about his destination. They asked to see his ticket and identification. After returning the documents, the officers stated that they were narcotics agents in search of illegal drugs. Then they asked for Bostick's consent to search his bag, telling him that he did not have to consent. He did consent, and they discovered cocaine in the bag. The Supreme Court decided that the agents did not "stop" Bostick when they questioned him on the bus. Although Bostick was not literally "free to leave" during the questioning because the officers were blocking the aisle of the bus, the Court concluded that a reasonable person in Bostick's position could have felt "free to decline the officers' requests or otherwise terminate the encounter." Compare United States v. Drayton, 536 U.S. 194 (2002) (no "stop" when two officers question passengers on bus while standing behind passenger's seat, one officer remains at front of bus watching passengers). Do the police "stop" the driver of a parked car when they position their patrol cars to block the vehicle from moving? Cases analyzing these and other potential stop scenarios appear on the web extension for this chapter at *http://www.crimpro.com/extension/ch02*.

3. *The reasonable person standard and the guilty suspect.* When trying to determine whether police seized a person during a conversation, courts have often stated that the exchange amounts to a seizure only if a "reasonable person" would conclude that he is not free to go. In Florida v. Bostick, the defendant argued that any person carrying contraband in a piece of luggage would not freely consent to a search of the luggage in his presence. Hence, he argued, his agreement to allow the search of his bag demonstrated that he did not feel free to leave. The court replied that the reasonable person standard "presupposes an innocent person." Does this standard lead to the conclusion that *any* refusal to engage in a conversation with a police officer amounts to reasonable suspicion for a stop?

2. *Grounds for Stops: Articulable, Individualized Reasonable Suspicion*

To justify a "stop," the government agent must be able to articulate a reasonable suspicion that the person has committed or will commit a crime. Exactly how can an officer establish reasonable suspicion? This concept is among the most commonly invoked in criminal procedure. Judges and lawyers applying the concept speak with apparent assurance about its meaning. Yet it is surprisingly difficult to find a precise definition of reasonable suspicion. And even a precise standard will leave enormous difficulties when applied to varied circumstances.

Judicial decisions, statutes, and rules of procedure use somewhat different verbal formulations to describe the justification needed for a low-level stop. Some formulations, especially those of the U.S. Supreme Court, emphasize the difference between reasonable suspicion and probable cause (the level of proof necessary to justify an arrest or a full-blown search):

> The Fourth Amendment requires some minimal level of objective justification for making the stop [that] is considerably less than proof of wrongdoing by a preponderance of the evidence. We have held that probable cause means a fair probability that contraband or evidence of a crime will be found, and the level of suspicion required for [reasonable suspicion] is obviously less demanding than that for probable cause. The concept of reasonable suspicion, like probable cause, is not readily, or even usefully, reduced to a neat set of legal rules. . . . In evaluating the validity of a stop such as this, we must consider the totality of the circumstances — the whole picture. [United States v. Sokolow, 490 U.S. 1 (1989).]

Some formulations emphasize that reasonable suspicion must be more than a guess and that it must be based on objective and articulable facts about an individual:

> [In] justifying the particular intrusion the police officer must be able to point to specific and articulable facts which, taken together with rational inferences from those facts, reasonably warrant that intrusion. . . . And in determining whether the officer acted reasonably in such circumstances, due weight must be given, not to his inchoate and unparticularized suspicion or "hunch," but to the specific reasonable inferences which he is entitled to draw from the facts in light of his experience. [Terry v. Ohio, 392 U.S. 1 (1968).]

Still other formulations insist that the reasonable suspicion standard is fact-sensitive, and the facts necessary to meet the standard will change from one context to another.

> The following are among the factors to be considered in determining if the officer has grounds to "reasonably suspect": (1) The demeanor of the suspect; (2) The gait and manner of the suspect; (3) Any knowledge the officer may have of the suspect's background or character; (4) Whether the suspect is carrying anything, and what he is carrying; (5) The manner in which the suspect is dressed, including bulges in clothing, when considered in light of all of the other factors; (6) The time of the day or night the suspect is observed; (7) Any overheard conversation of the suspect; (8) The particular streets and areas involved; (9) Any information received from third persons, whether they are known or unknown; (10) Whether the suspect is consorting with others whose

conduct is "reasonably suspect"; (11) The suspect's proximity to known criminal conduct; (12) Incidence of crime in the immediate neighborhood; (13) The suspect's apparent effort to conceal an article; (14) Apparent effort of the suspect to avoid identification or confrontation by a law enforcement officer. [Ark. Stat. §16-81-203.]

As used in [the following sections], unless the context requires otherwise: . . . "Reasonably suspects" means that a peace officer holds a belief that is reasonable under the totality of the circumstances existing at the time and place the peace officer acts. [Oregon Rev. Stat. §131.605.]

■ STATE v. THEODORE NELSON

638 A.2d 720 (Me. 1994)

GLASSMAN, J.

Theodore Nelson appeals from the judgment entered . . . on a jury verdict finding him guilty of operating a motor vehicle while under the influence of intoxicating liquor. . . . We agree with Nelson that because the stop of his motor vehicle was unlawful, the District Court erred in not granting Nelson's motion to suppress the evidence secured as a result of the stop and we vacate the judgment. . . .

At the hearing before the District Court on Nelson's motion to suppress, the sole witness presented was Officer Michael Holmes, who testified as follows: On December 24, 1991, at approximately 1:30 A.M., while on patrol . . . , he observed an unoccupied automobile he knew belonged to Bruce Moore, a former neighbor of his, in a well-lit parking lot at a housing complex for the elderly located on North Main Street. Because the police department within the prior two weeks had received several complaints of theft during the nighttime, Officer Holmes took up an observation post in a small parking lot adjacent to the driveway to the complex and approximately 50 to 100 yards from the Moore automobile. He observed a white pickup truck occupied by a driver, later identified as Nelson, and one passenger enter the driveway to the complex. The pickup was backed into a parking space beside the Moore vehicle, the motor was shut off, and the headlights extinguished leaving the parking lights illuminated. With the use of binoculars, Officer Holmes recognized the passenger as Moore. He observed each of the occupants of the pickup starting to drink from a 16-ounce Budweiser can. There was no evidence that Officer Holmes observed anything unusual about the appearance of either occupant. After approximately forty-five to fifty minutes, Moore left the pickup truck and entered his own vehicle. The headlights of the pickup truck were turned on and it was again driven past Officer Holmes onto North Main Street. As the pickup passed his observation site, Officer Holmes immediately "pulled out behind it, and turned on [his] blue lights, [and] made an enforcement stop." Nelson promptly brought the pickup to a stop. At no time did Officer Holmes observe anything unusual about the operation of the pickup. There was no evidence of mechanical defects to the pickup or of excessive speed. He stopped the pickup because he "observed the operator . . . drinking a can of beer [and suspected that] the person may be under the influence of intoxicating liquor." The District Court held "Officer Holmes had reasonable articulable suspicion to stop the Defendant's vehicle," and denied Nelson's motion to suppress evidence secured as a result of the claimed illegal stop. . . .

Every person is protected from unreasonable intrusions by police officers and other governmental agents by the Fourth Amendment to the United States Constitution and article I, section 5 of the Maine Constitution. An investigatory stop is justified if at the time of the stop the officer has an articulable suspicion that criminal conduct has taken place, is occurring, or imminently will occur, and the officer's assessment of the existence of specific and articulable facts sufficient to warrant the stop is objectively reasonable in the totality of the circumstances. . . . It is well established that the suspicion for the stop must be based on information available to the officer at the time of the stop and cannot be bolstered by evidence secured by the stop. . . .

In the instant case, we find a clear deficiency in the evidence supporting the reasonableness of the suspicion. The record reveals that the officer observed nothing to support his suspicion that Nelson was operating under the influence of alcohol other than Nelson's consumption of a single can of beer over the course of nearly one hour. An adult's consumption of liquor in a motor vehicle is neither a crime nor a civil violation. The reasonable suspicion standard requires more than mere speculation. There was no evidence that the officer observed indicia of physical impairment or anything unusual in Nelson's appearance. Officer Holmes testified that the pickup truck was not being operated in an erratic manner. The officer offered no reason for his stop of the motor vehicle other than his suspicion that Nelson was under the influence of alcohol.

Based on the whole picture presented by this case, it cannot be said that it was objectively reasonable to believe that criminal activity was afoot. Accordingly, the court should have granted Nelson's motion to suppress the evidence secured as a result of the illegal stop. Judgment vacated.

COLLINS, J., dissenting.

. . . The stop in this instance was not based on mere speculation that Nelson was driving while under the influence. Rather, the officer had observed Nelson drinking a 16-ounce beer, at 1:30 in the morning on Christmas Eve, while parked in the parking lot of a housing complex for the elderly from which several complaints of theft had been registered. These observed facts, in combination with the recognition of the common practice in American society of having a second beer, gave the officer an articulable suspicion that Nelson was operating his truck while under the influence of alcohol. The officer's suspicion was objectively reasonable given the totality of the circumstances. As such, I believe the stop was justified and I would affirm the trial court.

■ STATE v. DAVID DEAN

645 A.2d 634 (Me. 1994)

RUDMAN, J.

[David Dean entered a conditional plea of guilty to charges of operating a vehicle under the influence of alcohol. He now appeals on the ground that the stop was not justified by reasonable suspicion.] The underlying facts are undisputed. At approximately 11:00 P.M. on Tuesday, April 13, 1993, Officer Dennis Sampson of the South Paris Police Department spotted Dean's car while Sampson was patrolling a new residential development on Cobble Hill Road. The road is a dead end, and the development was uninhabited during weekdays. Sampson was patrolling the area at the request of the development's property owners after a number of complaints of vandalism. No complaint had been made that night, and Dean's driving was unremarkable. Sampson stopped him solely because of his presence at that particular time and place. Sampson "wanted to see what they was up to, see if they were landowners or property owners, get some names in case we did have problems up in that area." The District Court, in a well-reasoned opinion, ruled that Sampson had the necessary "reasonable suspicion" to justify the stop. . . .

Dean's contention is that Officer Sampson did not entertain any suspicion that Dean was engaged in criminal activity. Dean raises the specter of random stops in any high-crime area, justified solely by the fact that the person detained happens to be in that area. The District Court, however, understood Dean's contentions and explicitly made the required findings:

> Now, I'll point out that the facts in this case suggest that this particular defendant was driving along a dead-end road at nighttime. The — the structures in the area were uninhabited, and it had been an area which had been the scene of a variety of criminal behavior which, in fact, brought . . . if not residents then the property owners to the police. They asked for increased surveillance. Ordinarily, the officer could not have stopped this particular vehicle. But under the circumstances, given the fact that this occurred well after dark, that the place was virtually uninhabited, that it was a dead-end street and [an area] in which a substantial amount of crime had been perpetrated in the recent past — I find that the officer acted properly because he reasonably suspected, based on prior reports of criminal activity in the area, that this particular Defendant could be engaged in such behavior. . . .

The only real issue is whether the two articulable facts relied on by the court can yield a reasonable suspicion. Those two facts are: (1) Dean's presence in an area of recent crime reports; and (2) the apparent absence of any reason to be in an uninhabited area at night. It is well-settled that a person's mere presence in a high crime area does not justify an investigatory stop. However, the combination of the recent criminal activity with other articulable facts — in this case, the time of day and the fact that the area was uninhabited — creates a reasonable suspicion. Many cases uphold a finding of a reasonable suspicion on similar facts.

In a recent decision, also involving police surveillance of an area due to several complaints, we held that the District Court erred by failing to grant the defendant's motion to suppress. State v. Nelson (Me. 1994). . . . In the *Nelson* case, however, the defendant was sitting in a truck in the parking lot of an occupied housing complex. Dean, in contrast, was driving through an uninhabited development site on a dead end street at 11:00 at night. His situation is distinguishable from that of the defendant in *Nelson*.

Dean's situation is more analogous to that of the defendant in State v. Fitzgerald, 620 A.2d 874 (Me. 1993). After dark, a police officer spotted Fitzgerald's car entering a private turn-around, known to be the site of frequent illegal trash dumping, and posted with "no trespassing" signs by the owner. When the officer's vehicle drove into the turn-around, the defendant was standing next to his car. The defendant then got into his car and drove away. The officer stopped the defendant's vehicle, saw that the defendant displayed evidence of being under the influence of alcohol, and arrested him for operating under the influence. Although the officer never witnessed any illegality or impropriety (Fitzgerald never violated the no trespassing signs), we affirmed the finding that the officer had a reasonable and articulable suspicion, "based on the previous littering and trespassing," the fact that Fitzgerald was outside his car in the dark when the officer approached, and the fact that Fitzgerald tried to leave when he saw the cruiser. Similarly, Officer Sampson's suspicion of Dean was engendered by prior complaints combined with other facts — the time of night and the absence of any apparent reason to be in an uninhabited housing development.

But for Dean's intoxication, this would have been a brief investigatory stop. An investigatory stop of a motor vehicle is normally a minimal intrusion by the state into a person's affairs. Balancing the facts on which Officer Sampson relied to make the stop against Dean's right to be free from any arbitrary intrusions by the State, we find the District Court's findings that the officer's suspicion was reasonable and the stop was justified are not clearly erroneous.

GLASSMAN, J., dissenting.

I respectfully dissent. We have recently reemphasized that the reasonable articulable suspicion standard requires "more than mere speculation" on the part of the police officer to sustain an investigatory stop. State v. Nelson (Me. 1994). Dean's behavior in driving out of a dead-end street at 11:00 P.M. on a Tuesday was in no sense illegal or even inherently suspicious, and the officer's desire to "see what [Dean] was up to" stems, at best, from a hunch.[1] A mere hunch will not justify a stop, and the officer's reasons for stopping the vehicle must not be a mere pretext or ruse. . . .

As the court notes, it is well settled that a person's mere presence in a high-crime area does not justify an investigatory stop. What the court regards as "other articulable facts" justifying the stop, in reality, are mere speculations entertained by the officer because of Dean's presence on a public way in an area where there had been complaints of vandalism or other damage to property. Each of the cases cited by the court to support its position involves additional facts beyond the defendant's mere presence in a crime area, e.g., police observed unusual behavior by the defendant, intrusion onto private property, the unusual operation of a vehicle, or the vehicle's unusual location. The constitutional right to be free from an illegal stop should not be abridged solely on the basis of the day of the week or time of day a car is being operated on a public way. . . .

Notes

1. *Components of reasonable suspicion: majority position.* Courts typically do not specify the general categories of facts that could support a finding of reasonable suspicion. In virtually all cases, however, the conduct of the suspect said to be the basis

1. The court seeks to distinguish *Nelson* by noting that Nelson was sitting in a pickup truck parked in the parking lot of an occupied housing complex whereas Dean was observed driving a motor vehicle on a public way leading out of a largely uninhabited residential development site. This is inapposite because the surroundings in which the police observed Nelson were not at issue in that case, which turned on whether merely drinking a can of beer in a parked car provided a reasonably articulable suspicion that a crime had taken place. This case turns on the site of the stop.

for reasonable suspicion does not violate the criminal law. The observer must infer from the observed facts that there is some correlation between the legal conduct observed and the suspected criminal acts. The officer may observe something resembling criminal conduct (such as the legal acts necessary to prepare for a crime); she might also observe the suspect taking an action that could be designed to hide a crime or to avoid contact with the police (such as avoiding eye contact with the officer or running away from the scene). See Sibron v. New York, 392 U.S. 40 (1968); but cf. State v. Hall, 115 P.3d 908 (Ore. 2005) (fact that suspect repeatedly turned to look at officer's patrol vehicle and then averted his gaze did not amount to reasonable suspicion). The surroundings of the suspect are another common component of reasonable suspicion: For instance, presence near a crime scene soon after the time of a crime would be significant, especially if the suspect has no other apparent reason to be in that location. See State v. Miller, 207 P.3d 541 (Alaska 2009) (officer observed man and woman in vehicle exiting parking lot of tavern soon after receiving 911 call about couple arguing loudly in parking lot). How strong should the correlation be between this innocent conduct and the suspected criminal conduct to establish reasonable suspicion? Why do courts and other legal institutions scrupulously avoid answering this question in terms of numeric probabilities?

A study of stops in New York City gives us one indication of the level of certainty police officers believe in practice to be enough for reasonable suspicion. During a two-year period, a specialized Street Crimes Unit made 45,000 stops, with about 20 percent of those stops resulting in an arrest or criminal charges. See Jeffrey Goldberg, "The Color of Suspicion," N.Y. Times Magazine, June 20, 1999, at 85. Do these figures indicate that police officers have 20 percent confidence that a crime has been or is about to be committed when they make a stop? If so, is that enough certainty?

2. *Do standards matter?* Are *Nelson* and *Dean* consistent; that is, do they reflect a single standard of reasonable suspicion? If you were representing Nelson and Dean, where would you rather argue the case: under the statutory definition of reasonable suspicion in Oregon or Arkansas, or the judicial definition in Maine? Do different formulations of the reasonable suspicion standard make any difference in the outcomes?

3. *Objective basis.* The basis for reasonable suspicion turns on the facts available to the officer; it does not matter whether the officer holds an actual suspicion. In fact, the officer might wrongly believe that reasonable suspicion exists for one crime, when in fact reasonable suspicion exists for another crime. Does an objective "reasonable suspicion" standard promote more careful evaluation of facts by police officers?

4. *Seriousness of crime.* Would the reasonable suspicion determination in *Dean* have turned out differently if the suspected crime had been murder instead of vandalism of property? Was the police officer in *Nelson* concerned about a different crime from the one he ultimately charged? Should the seriousness of the crime committed or soon to be committed affect the determination of reasonable suspicion? See Commonwealth v. Hawkins, 692 A.2d 1068 (Pa. 1997) (rejects concept of fluctuating reasonable suspicion standard based on seriousness of crime suspected; no "gun exception" to reasonable suspicion requirement).

5. *Codified definitions of reasonable suspicion.* This section began with examples of statutes defining reasonable suspicion. Similar definitions appear in some states' rules of criminal procedure. The statutory examples draw on language familiar in

judicial opinions defining the same concept; that is, they codify the common law. Would the presence of such a statute or rule affect a court's willingness to elaborate on the meaning of reasonable suspicion or to adjust it over time?

6. *Role of appellate courts in defining reasonable suspicion.* Under the "totality of the circumstances" test, the factfinder at the trial level takes a central role in deciding whether reasonable suspicion exists. What contributions might an appellate court make? Could an appeals court bring more predictability to the process by describing the sorts of factors that should receive more or less weight? For instance, should an appellate court declare that conduct "as consistent with innocent activity as with criminal activity" should receive little or no weight? See Irwin v. Superior Court of Los Angeles County, 462 P.2d 12, 14 (Cal. 1969) (adopting innocent conduct limit); State v. O'Meara, 9 P.3d 325 (Ariz. 2000) ("totality of circumstances" test for reasonable suspicion allows court to consider conduct susceptible of an innocent explanation; here, unusual meeting in parking lot with drivers switching among four vehicles established reasonable suspicion for stop).

In Ornelas v. United States, 517 U.S. 690 (1996), the U.S. Supreme Court held that appellate courts would determine for themselves, under a de novo standard, the presence or absence of reasonable suspicion. This standard, the Court said, would allow appellate courts to unify precedent and clarify the legal principles at stake, providing law enforcement officers with the tools to reach correct determinations beforehand. At the same time, the Court declared that a reviewing court must give "due weight" to factual inferences drawn by resident judges. In United States v. Arvizu, 534 U.S. 266 (2002), the Court applied this standard of review to affirm a trial judge's finding of reasonable suspicion. A Border Patrol agent stopped Arvizu while driving on an unpaved road in a remote area of southeastern Arizona, and discovered over 100 pounds of marijuana in the minivan. The officer became suspicious when the driver of the minivan slowed dramatically after the patrol car appeared, and the children in the back seat waved to the officer in an "abnormal" and "mechanical" fashion, off and on for about five minutes. While each of these facts was "susceptible to innocent explanations" when viewed in isolation, the trial judge nevertheless could consider them as part of the "totality of the circumstances" to establish reasonable suspicion. An appellate court should not "casually" reject factors such as these "in light of the District Court's superior access to the evidence and the well-recognized inability of reviewing courts to reconstruct what happened in the courtroom." Is this a de novo standard of review at work?

7. *Anonymous tips as the basis for reasonable suspicion.* Ordinarily, the police obtain reasonable suspicion based on their own observations and investigations. But on occasion, the police receive information from an anonymous informant that might contribute later to a finding of "reasonable suspicion." The U.S. Supreme Court has stated that anonymous tips can contribute to a reasonable suspicion finding only if the police can find independent corroboration of "significant details" of the informant's information. Alabama v. White, 496 U.S. 325 (1990). Those significant details must amount to more than innocent conduct that any person could observe. The anonymous tip, standing alone without corroboration, cannot justify a brief seizure of the suspect. See Florida v. J.L., 529 U.S. 266 (2000) (anonymous tip says that young black male standing at a particular bus stop and wearing a plaid shirt was carrying a gun; not enough for reasonable suspicion). You can get a flavor of the state court decisions regarding anonymous tips and reasonable suspicion on the web extension for this chapter at *http://www.crimpro.com/extension/ch02*.

ILLINOIS v. WILLIAM aka "SAM" WARDLOW
525 U.S. 119 (2000)

REHNQUIST, C.J.*

Respondent Wardlow fled upon seeing police officers patrolling an area known for heavy narcotics trafficking. Two of the officers caught up with him, stopped him and conducted a protective pat-down search for weapons. Discovering a .38-caliber handgun, the officers arrested Wardlow. We hold that the officers' stop did not violate the Fourth Amendment to the United States Constitution.

On September 9, 1995, Officers Nolan and Harvey were working as uniformed officers in the special operations section of the Chicago Police Department. The officers were driving the last car of a four car caravan converging on an area known for heavy narcotics trafficking in order to investigate drug transactions. The officers were traveling together because they expected to find a crowd of people in the area, including lookouts and customers.

As the caravan passed 4035 West Van Buren, Officer Nolan observed respondent Wardlow standing next to the building holding an opaque bag. Respondent looked in the direction of the officers and fled. Nolan and Harvey turned their car southbound, watched him as he ran through the gangway and an alley, and eventually cornered him on the street. Nolan then exited his car and stopped respondent. He immediately conducted a protective pat-down search for weapons because in his experience it was common for there to be weapons in the near vicinity of narcotics transactions. During the frisk, Officer Nolan squeezed the bag respondent was carrying and felt a heavy, hard object similar to the shape of a gun. The officer then opened the bag and discovered a .38-caliber handgun with five live rounds of ammunition. The officers arrested Wardlow. The Illinois trial court denied respondent's motion to suppress, finding the gun was recovered during a lawful stop and frisk. Following a stipulated bench trial, Wardlow was convicted of unlawful use of a weapon by a felon. The [Illinois Supreme Court] reversed Wardlow's conviction, concluding that the gun should have been suppressed because Officer Nolan did not have reasonable suspicion. . . .

This case, involving a brief encounter between a citizen and a police officer on a public street, is governed by the analysis we first applied in Terry v. Ohio, 392 U.S. 1 (1968). In *Terry*, we held that an officer may, consistent with the Fourth Amendment, conduct a brief, investigatory stop when the officer has a reasonable, articulable suspicion that criminal activity is afoot. While "reasonable suspicion" is a less demanding standard than probable cause and requires a showing considerably less than preponderance of the evidence, the Fourth Amendment requires at least a minimal level of objective justification for making the stop. The officer must be able to articulate more than an inchoate and unparticularized suspicion or hunch of criminal activity.

Nolan and Harvey were among eight officers in a four car caravan that was converging on an area known for heavy narcotics trafficking, and the officers anticipated encountering a large number of people in the area, including drug customers and individuals serving as lookouts. It was in this context that Officer Nolan decided to investigate Wardlow after observing him flee. An individual's presence in an area

* [Justices O'Connor, Scalia, Kennedy, and Thomas joined in the opinion. — EDS.]

of expected criminal activity, standing alone, is not enough to support a reasonable, particularized suspicion that the person is committing a crime. Brown v. Texas, 443 U.S. 47 (1979). But officers are not required to ignore the relevant characteristics of a location in determining whether the circumstances are sufficiently suspicious to warrant further investigation. Accordingly, we have previously noted the fact that the stop occurred in a "high crime area" among the relevant contextual considerations in a *Terry* analysis.

In this case, moreover, it was not merely respondent's presence in an area of heavy narcotics trafficking that aroused the officers' suspicion but his unprovoked flight upon noticing the police. Our cases have also recognized that nervous, evasive behavior is a pertinent factor in determining reasonable suspicion. Headlong flight — wherever it occurs — is the consummate act of evasion: it is not necessarily indicative of wrongdoing, but it is certainly suggestive of such. In reviewing the propriety of an officer's conduct, courts do not have available empirical studies dealing with inferences drawn from suspicious behavior, and we cannot reasonably demand scientific certainty from judges or law enforcement officers where none exists. Thus, the determination of reasonable suspicion must be based on commonsense judgments and inferences about human behavior. We conclude Officer Nolan was justified in suspecting that Wardlow was involved in criminal activity, and, therefore, in investigating further.

Such a holding is entirely consistent with our decision in Florida v. Royer, 460 U.S. 491 (1983), where we held that when an officer, without reasonable suspicion or probable cause, approaches an individual, the individual has a right to ignore the police and go about his business. And any refusal to cooperate, without more, does not furnish the minimal level of objective justification needed for a detention or seizure. But unprovoked flight is simply not a mere refusal to cooperate. Flight, by its very nature, is not "going about one's business"; in fact, it is just the opposite. Allowing officers confronted with such flight to stop the fugitive and investigate further is quite consistent with the individual's right to go about his business or to stay put and remain silent in the face of police questioning. . . .

STEVENS, J., concurring in part and dissenting in part.*

The State of Illinois asks this Court to announce a "bright-line rule" authorizing the temporary detention of anyone who flees at the mere sight of a police officer. Respondent counters by asking us to adopt the opposite per se rule — that the fact that a person flees upon seeing the police can never, by itself, be sufficient to justify a temporary investigative stop of the kind authorized by *Terry*. The Court today wisely endorses neither per se rule. . . .

Although I agree with the Court's rejection of the per se rules proffered by the parties, unlike the Court, I am persuaded that in this case the brief testimony of the officer who seized respondent does not justify the conclusion that he had reasonable suspicion to make the stop.

. . . The question in this case concerns "the degree of suspicion that attaches to" a person's flight — or, more precisely, what "commonsense conclusions" can be drawn respecting the motives behind that flight. A pedestrian may break into a run for a variety of reasons — to catch up with a friend a block or two away, to seek

* [Justices Souter, Ginsburg, and Breyer joined in this opinion. — EDS.]

shelter from an impending storm, to arrive at a bus stop before the bus leaves, to get home in time for dinner, to resume jogging after a pause for rest, to avoid contact with a bore or a bully, or simply to answer the call of nature — any of which might coincide with the arrival of an officer in the vicinity. A pedestrian might also run because he or she has just sighted one or more police officers. [There] are unquestionably circumstances in which a person's flight is suspicious, and undeniably instances in which a person runs for entirely innocent reasons.[3]

Given the diversity and frequency of possible motivations for flight, it would be profoundly unwise to endorse either per se rule. The inference we can reasonably draw about the motivation for a person's flight, rather, will depend on a number of different circumstances. Factors such as the time of day, the number of people in the area, the character of the neighborhood, whether the officer was in uniform, the way the runner was dressed, the direction and speed of the flight, and whether the person's behavior was otherwise unusual might be relevant in specific cases. . . .

[A] reasonable person may conclude that an officer's sudden appearance indicates nearby criminal activity. And where there is criminal activity there is also a substantial element of danger — either from the criminal or from a confrontation between the criminal and the police. These considerations can lead to an innocent and understandable desire to quit the vicinity with all speed. Among some citizens, particularly minorities and those residing in high crime areas, there is also the possibility that the fleeing person is entirely innocent, but, with or without justification, believes that contact with the police can itself be dangerous, apart from any criminal activity associated with the officer's sudden presence.[7]

[In this case, the] entire justification for the stop is articulated in the brief testimony of Officer Nolan, [who stated,] "He looked in our direction and began fleeing." No other factors sufficiently support a finding of reasonable suspicion. Though respondent was carrying a white, opaque bag under his arm, there is nothing at all suspicious about that. Certainly the time of day — shortly after noon — does not support Illinois' argument. Nor were the officers responding to any call or report of suspicious activity in the area. . . .

The State, along with the majority of the Court, relies as well on the assumption that this flight occurred in a high crime area. Even if that assumption is accurate, it is insufficient because even in a high crime neighborhood unprovoked flight does not invariably lead to reasonable suspicion. On the contrary, because many factors providing innocent motivations for unprovoked flight are concentrated in high crime areas, the character of the neighborhood arguably makes an inference of guilt less appropriate, rather than more so. . . .

3. Compare, e.g., Proverbs 28:1 ("The wicked flee when no man pursueth: but the righteous are as bold as a lion") with Proverbs 22:3 ("A shrewd man sees trouble coming and lies low; the simple walk into it and pay the penalty"). I have rejected reliance on the former proverb in the past, because its "ivory-towered analysis of the real world" fails to account for the experiences of many citizens of this country, particularly those who are minorities. See California v. Hodari D., 499 U.S. 621, 630, n.4 (1991) (Stevens, J., dissenting). That this pithy expression fails to capture the total reality of our world, however, does not mean it is inaccurate in all instances.

7. See Johnson, Americans' Views on Crime and Law Enforcement: Survey Findings, National Institute of Justice Journal 13 (Sept.1997) (reporting study by the Joint Center for Political and Economic Studies in April 1996, which found that 43% of African-Americans consider "police brutality and harassment of African-Americans a serious problem" in their own community); Casimir, Minority Men: We Are Frisk Targets, N.Y. Daily News, Mar. 26,1999, p. 34 (informal survey of 100 young black and Hispanic men living in New York City; 81 reported having been stopped and frisked by police at least once; none of the 81 stops resulted in arrests).

Notes

1. *"Bad neighborhoods" and reasonable suspicion: majority position.* An officer trying to establish reasonable suspicion will at times rely on the amount of crime occurring recently in the neighborhood. The government typically does not support the assertion with any statistical analysis of reported crimes, but bases the claim on the impressions of the officer about neighborhoods. See State v. Moore, 853 A.2d 903 (N.J. 2004) (nature of crime in area may contribute to reasonable suspicion to stop men engaged in suspicious street-side transaction). If you were a judge evaluating the claim of reasonable suspicion, would the reputation of the neighborhood for crime play any part in your decision? If you were a police officer, how might you strengthen such claims? See Margaret Raymond, Down on the Corner, Out in the Street: Considering the Character of the Neighborhood in Evaluating Reasonable Suspicion, 60 Ohio St. L.J. 99 (1999); cf. Brown v. Texas, 443 U.S. 47 (1979) ("The fact that appellant was in a neighborhood frequented by drug users, standing alone, is not a basis for concluding that appellant himself was engaged in criminal conduct").

2. *Neighborhood as proxy for race?* The neighborhoods described in court as "high crime" areas are often the homes for poor and minority residents. Do the demographics of some neighborhoods make crimes committed or reported there easier to notice or remember? Do more crimes occur in poorer neighborhoods because of subtle signals that disorder is tolerated there — the so-called "broken windows" theory of policing? If this is true, then it would make sense to direct more stop-and-frisk activity in places where police find the greatest physical and social disorder. A study of New York City policing by Jeffrey Pagan and Garth Davies, however, found that neighborhood characteristics such as racial composition and poverty levels are better predictors of stop-and-frisk activity than the presence of physical disorder in the neighborhood. They conclude that policing in New York City "is not about disorderly places . . . but about policing poor people in poor places." Fagan & Davies, Street Stops and Broken Windows: *Terry,* Race and Disorder in New York City, 28 Fordham Urban L.J. 457 (2000). If you were a police chief and a reporter called a similar study about your department to your attention, how would you respond?

3. *Avoiding or fleeing the police as basis for reasonable suspicion.* The officers in *Wardlow* noted that the suspect tried to flee the scene and considered the flight to be one factor contributing to reasonable suspicion. Would a suspect's flight from the police be enough, standing alone, to establish reasonable suspicion of criminal activity? A strong majority of state courts have decided that flight contributes to reasonable suspicion, but few cases arise in which flight alone is the basis for a claim of reasonable suspicion. Compare Bost v. State, 958 A.2d 356 (Md. 2008) (reasonable suspicion present when police approached group drinking on side of city street, man immediately walked away, "clutching" something at waistband, picked up pace as he crossed street, looked back at officers), with State v. Hicks, 488 N.W.2d 359 (Neb. 1992) (flight upon approach of police vehicle not sufficient to justify investigative stop).

4. *Seizure by pursuit.* In California v. Hodari D., 499 U.S. 621 (1991), the Court assumed that a suspect's flight, standing alone, did not create reasonable suspicion. Nevertheless, the Court ruled that the officer needed no individualized suspicion

to pursue Hodari because the pursuit did not amount to a "seizure" under the federal constitution. Two officers wearing police department jackets rounded a corner in their patrol car and saw four or five young men gathered around a small car parked at the curb. When the group saw the officers' car approaching, they began to run away. The officers were suspicious and gave chase. One officer left the patrol car and took a route that placed him in front of one of the fleeing suspects. The suspect, looking behind as he ran, did not turn and see the officer until the two were quite close. At that point, he tossed away what appeared to be a small rock and ran in the opposite direction. A moment later, the officer tackled the suspect, handcuffed him, and radioed for assistance. The rock the suspect had discarded was crack cocaine. The Court held that there was no "stop" until the officer tackled Hodari; the pursuit by the officer was not enough.

Courts in about 30 states, reviewing similar cases under their state constitutions, have reached the same conclusion. See State v. Smith, 39 S.W.3d 739 (Ark. 2001). However, most of the remaining states insist that pursuit might sometimes qualify as a seizure. Seizures occur when the "totality of the circumstances" reasonably indicate that the person is not free to leave. See State v. Garcia, 217 P.3d 1032 (N.M. 2009). How might a court reach the conclusion that a person can feel "free to leave," despite the fact that a police officer is chasing her and shouting "stop"? Is it because the suspect is in fact trying to leave? Would it matter if the suspect paused momentarily before or during flight? See State v. Rogers, 924 P.2d 1027 (Ariz. 1996).

5. *Discretion to stop and the definition of crimes.* There is a powerful relationship between reasonable suspicion and the substantive criminal law. If a legislature creates a crime such as "drug loitering," it empowers the police to stop people based on innocent behavior (such as standing on a corner or making signals) that is often a precursor to more harmful criminal activity, such as drug trafficking. See Mich. Comp. L. §750.167(1)(j) (disorderly conduct where a person knowingly loiters in or about a place where an illegal occupation or business is being conducted); Andrew D. Leipold, Targeted Loitering Laws, 3 U. Pa. J. Const. L. 474 (2001). If you were counsel to a police department, would you ask the city council to pass such an ordinance, or would you rather formulate a profile within the department itself?

3. Pretextual Stops

An officer needs reasonable suspicion that a crime has been or will be committed before stopping a person for an investigation. But when the officer has multiple reasons to stop a person, including reasonable suspicion of one crime and a hunch that the person has committed another crime, must the suspicion and the purpose match? In other words, does the police officer invalidate a stop when the crime that she reasonably suspects is only a "pretext" to justify a stop that she intends to use while investigating some other crime? State courts were split on this subject until the U.S. Supreme Court addressed it in Whren v. United States, 517 U.S. 806 (1996). The case created a new shorthand term in criminal procedure: "*Whren* stops" refer to traffic stops based on reasonable suspicion of a traffic violation, but intended to further the investigation of some other crime. Now virtually all state courts addressing this question respond much like the New York court in the following case.

PEOPLE v. FRANK ROBINSON

767 N.E.2d 638 (N.Y. 2001)

SMITH, J.

The issue [in these consolidated cases] is whether a police officer who has probable cause to believe a driver has committed a traffic infraction violates article I, §12 of the New York State Constitution when the officer, whose primary motivation is to conduct another investigation, stops the vehicle. We conclude that there is no violation, and we adopt Whren v. United States, 517 U.S. 806 (1996), as a matter of state law.

People v. Robinson. On November 22, 1993, New York City police officers in the Street Crime Unit, Mobile Taxi Homicide Task Force were on night patrol in a marked police car in the Bronx. Their main assignment was to follow taxicabs to make sure that no robberies occurred. After observing a car speed through a red light, the police activated their high intensity lights and pulled over what they suspected was a livery cab. After stopping the cab, one officer observed a passenger, the defendant, look back several times. The officers testified that they had no intention of giving the driver a summons but wanted to talk to him about safety tips. The officers approached the vehicle with their flashlights turned on and their guns holstered. One of the officers shined his flashlight into the back of the vehicle, where defendant was seated, and noticed that defendant was wearing a bullet proof vest. After the officer ordered defendant out of the taxicab, he observed a gun on the floor where defendant had been seated. Defendant was arrested and charged with criminal possession of a weapon and unlawfully wearing a bullet proof vest. Defendant moved to suppress the vest and gun, arguing that the officers used a traffic infraction as a pretext to search the occupant of the taxicab. The Court denied the motion, and defendant was convicted of both charges. . . .

People v. Reynolds. On March 6, 1999, shortly after midnight, a police officer, on routine motor patrol in the City of Rochester, saw a man he knew to be a prostitute enter defendant's truck. The officer followed the truck and ran a computer check on the license plate. Upon learning that the vehicle's registration had expired two months earlier, the officer stopped the vehicle. The resulting investigation did not lead to any charges involving prostitution. Nevertheless, because the driver's eyes were bloodshot, his speech slurred and there was a strong odor of alcohol, police performed various field sobriety tests, with defendant failing most. . . . Defendant was charged with driving while intoxicated, an unclassified misdemeanor, and operating an unregistered motor vehicle, a traffic infraction. Defendant's motion to suppress was granted by the Rochester City Court, which dismissed all charges.

People v. Glenn. On November 7, 1997, plainclothes police officers were on street crime patrol in an unmarked car in Manhattan. They observed a livery cab make a right hand turn without signaling. An officer noticed one of three passengers in the back seat lean forward. The police stopped the vehicle to investigate whether or not a robbery was in progress. A police officer subsequently found cocaine on the rear seat and, after he arrested defendant, found additional drugs on his person. Defendant was charged with criminal possession of a controlled substance in the third degree and criminally using drug paraphernalia in the second degree. He contended that the drugs should be suppressed, asserting that the traffic infraction was a pretext to investigate a robbery. After his motion to suppress was denied, he pleaded guilty to one count of criminal possession of a controlled substance. . . .

Discussion. The Supreme Court, in Whren v. United States, 517 U.S. 806 (1996), unanimously held that where a police officer has probable cause to detain a person temporarily for a traffic violation, that seizure does not violate the Fourth Amendment to the United States Constitution even though the underlying reason for the stop might have been to investigate some other matter. In *Whren,* officers patrolling a known drug area of the District of Columbia became suspicious when several young persons seated in a truck with temporary license plates remained at a stop sign for an unusual period of time, and the driver was looking down into the lap of the passenger seated on his right. After the car made a right turn without signaling, the police stopped it, assertedly to warn the driver of traffic violations, and saw two plastic bags of what appeared to be crack cocaine in Whren's hands.

After arresting the occupants, the police found several quantities of drugs in the car. The petitioners were charged with violating federal drug laws. The petitioners moved to suppress the drugs, arguing that the stop was not based upon probable cause or even reasonable suspicion that they were engaged in illegal drug activity and that the police officer's assertion that he approached the car in order to give a warning was pretextual. The District Court denied suppression. . . .

The Supreme Court held that the Fourth Amendment had not been violated because "as a general matter, the decision to stop an automobile is reasonable where the police have probable cause to believe that a traffic violation has occurred." The stop of the truck was based upon probable cause that the petitioners had violated provisions of the District of Columbia traffic code. The Court rejected any effort to tie the legality of the officers' conduct to their primary motivation or purpose in making the stop, deeming irrelevant whether a reasonable traffic police officer would have made the stop. According to the Court, "Subjective intentions play no role in ordinary, probable-cause Fourth Amendment analysis." Thus, the "Fourth Amendment's concern with 'reasonableness' allows certain actions to be taken in certain circumstances, whatever the subjective intent." More than forty states and the District of Columbia have adopted the objective standard approved by *Whren* or cited it with approval.

In each of the cases before us, defendant argues that the stop was pretextual and in violation of New York State Constitution, article I, §12. . . . We hold that where a police officer has probable cause to believe that the driver of an automobile has committed a traffic violation, a stop does not violate article I, §12 of the New York State Constitution. In making that determination of probable cause, neither the primary motivation of the officer nor a determination of what a reasonable traffic officer would have done under the circumstances is relevant. . . .

The real concern of those opposing pretextual stops is that police officers will use their authority to stop persons on a selective and arbitrary basis. *Whren* recognized that the answer to such action is the Equal Protection Clause of the Constitution. We are not unmindful of studies . . . which show that certain racial and ethnic groups are disproportionately stopped by police officers, and that those stops do not end in the discovery of a higher proportion of contraband than in the cars of other groups. The fact that such disparities exist is cause for both vigilance and concern about the protections given by the New York State Constitution. Discriminatory law enforcement has no place in our law. . . .

The alternatives to upholding a stop based solely upon reasonable cause to believe a traffic infraction has been committed put unacceptable restraints on law enforcement. This is so whether those restrictions are based upon the primary motivation of an officer or upon what a reasonable traffic police officer would have done under the circumstances. Rather than restrain the police in these instances, the police should be permitted to do what they are sworn to do — uphold the law. . . .

To be sure, the story does not end when the police stop a vehicle for a traffic infraction. Our holding in this case addresses only the initial police action upon which the vehicular stop was predicated. The scope, duration and intensity of the seizure, as well as any search made by the police subsequent to that stop, remain subject to the strictures of article I, §12, and judicial review. . . .

The dissenters concede that . . . an individualized determination of probable cause will generally provide an objective evidentiary floor circumscribing police conduct and thereby prevent the arbitrary exercise of search and seizure power. However, [the] dissenters assert that because motor vehicle travel is so much a part of our lives and is minutely regulated, total compliance with the law is impossible. We see no basis for this differentiation. While New Yorkers may ubiquitously disobey parts of the Vehicle and Traffic Law, that does not render its commands unenforceable. As noted by the unanimous United States Supreme Court, "we are aware of no principle that would allow us to decide at what point a code of law becomes so expansive and so commonly violated that infraction itself can no longer be the ordinary measure of the lawfulness of enforcement." *Whren*, 517 U.S. at 818.

Because the Vehicle and Traffic Law provides an objective grid upon which to measure probable cause, a stop based on that standard is not arbitrary in the context of constitutional search and seizure jurisprudence. Contrary to the dissent's view, probable cause stops are not based on the discretion of police officers. They are based on violations of law. An officer may choose to stop someone for a "minor" violation after considering a number of factors, including traffic and weather conditions, but the officer's authority to stop a vehicle is circumscribed by the requirement of a violation of a duly enacted law. In other words, it is the violation of a statute that both triggers the officer's authority to make the stop and limits the officer's discretion. . . .

The dissent also raises the spectre of "repeatedly documented" racial profiling in the search and seizure context. There is no claim in any of the three cases before us that the police officers engaged in racial profiling. But, if racial profiling is the analytical pivot of our colleagues' dissent, their remedy misses the mark. The dissenters' "reasonable police officer" standard does little to combat or reduce the likelihood of racially motivated traffic stops, since, in their view, an officer's primary motivation is irrelevant.

We conclude, for a number of reasons, that the "reasonable police officer" test should not be followed. The dissenters maintain that under the "reasonable police officer" test, prosecution of a traffic violation would be appropriate even if the stop were pretextual and the other evidence suppressed. . . . We do not see how, in the context before us, a court may separate the fruits of a stop (often a gun or drugs) from the supposed illegality of the stop itself. It would seem that if the stop is arbitrary and, therefore, unlawful, it must be so for all purposes. In the name of protecting the rights of New Yorkers, the dissenters' result would be all too ironic: A police officer could "arbitrarily" stop someone for speeding and the stop would be valid, but a gun seen in plain view in the car during the stop would be suppressed as unlawfully seized.

The invention of the automobile has changed the fabric of American life. While the vast majority of New Yorkers own or drive vehicles, the frequency of their time on the road cannot recast the functional parameters of the Fourth Amendment or article 1, §12. We agree with *Whren* that the reasonable officer standard would result in inappropriate selective enforcement of traffic laws. How is a court to know which laws to enforce? . . . We are simply not free to pick and choose which laws deserve our adherence. If a statute improperly impairs our constitutional liberties, whatever the source, there is a remedy.

We are not confounded by the proposition that police officers must exercise their discretion on a daily basis. Nor are we surprised at the assertion that many New Yorkers often violate some provision of the Vehicle and Traffic Law. But we cannot equate the combination of police officer discretion and numerous traffic violations as arbitrary police conduct. . . . In the cases before us, [we have] a standard that constrains police conduct — probable cause under the Vehicle and Traffic Law and its related regulations that govern the safe use of our highways. . . .

LEVINE, J., dissenting.

[In] the context of pretextual traffic stops — traffic infraction stops that would not have been made but for the aim of the police to accomplish an otherwise unlawful investigative seizure or search — the existence of probable cause that the infraction was committed is manifestly insufficient to protect against arbitrary police conduct. That is so for two reasons. First, motor vehicle travel is one of the most ubiquitous activities in which Americans engage outside the home. Second, it is, by an overwhelming margin, the most pervasively regulated activity engaged in by Americans. . . .

The confluence of the foregoing factors — the dependency of the vast majority of Americans upon private automobile transportation and the virtual impossibility of sustained total compliance with the traffic laws — gives the police wide discretion to engage in investigative seizures, only superficially checked by the probable cause requirement for the traffic infraction that is the ostensible predicate for the stop. . . . Sadly, the pretext stop decisions in lower State and Federal courts confirm that the traffic infraction probable cause standard has left the police with the ability to stop vehicles at will for illegitimate investigative purposes. Typically, the stops are conducted as part of a drug interdiction program by a law enforcement agency. The vehicle and occupants appear to fit within a "drug courier" profile and the driver or occupants may have engaged in some other innocuous behavior which arouses a surmise of criminal conduct. The officer then follows the vehicle until some traffic code violation is observed. At that point, or even later, the vehicle is pulled over and the officer proceeds with the investigation. All occupants may be directed to exit the vehicle; the driver also may be interrogated and asked to consent to a search of the vehicle. . . .

Moreover, as has been repeatedly documented, . . . drug courier interdiction through traffic infraction stops has a dramatically disproportionate impact on young African-American males. Yet both the majority and the *Whren* Court dismiss the relevance of such disparate treatment in the constitutional search and seizure context. They instead suggest that the remedy lies in invoking the Federal Constitution's Equal Protection Clause. The same studies that recognize the existence of a disparate racial impact, however, also demonstrate the inadequacy of the Equal Protection Clause as a remedy for those abuses. A racial profiling claim under the Equal Protection Clause is difficult, if not impossible, to prove. The Equal Protection Clause prohibits race-based selective enforcement of the law only when such enforcement "had a discriminatory effect and . . . was motivated by a discriminatory purpose." United States v Armstrong, 517 U.S. 456 (1996). . . . Moreover, the problems of proof in establishing an equal protection claim may be all but insurmountable. Putting aside the unquestionably expensive and time-consuming process of assembling statistical evidence, it is debatable whether the requisite data would even be available. Supreme Court precedent also suggests that minority motorists alleging that a pretextual traffic stop constituted a denial of equal protection must show that similarly situated white motorists could have been stopped, but were not.

[The petitioners in *Whren*] urged the adoption of an objective standard by which to judge police exploitation of arbitrary traffic code enforcement to conduct investigative stops: whether a reasonable police officer, under the circumstances, would have made the stop for the reasons given. Despite the objective nature of that test, the Supreme Court's primary reason for rejecting it was that it was "driven by subjective considerations" — that is, the improper motivation of the seizing officer to conduct an otherwise unjustified investigative stop. . . . This criticism, in our view, misses the mark. The petitioners in *Whren* claimed that the officers' seizure was unreasonable because it was arbitrary, not because it was either unjustified or improperly motivated. . . .

The *Whren* Court offered only two other reasons for rejecting the test suggested by the petitioners. The first was that "police enforcement practices, even if they could be practicably assessed by a judge, vary from place to place and from time to time. We cannot accept that the search and seizure protections of the Fourth Amendment are so variable . . . and can be made to turn upon such trivialities." Under well-established Federal and State search and seizure doctrine, however, the . . . the basic determination of reasonable suspicion or even probable cause to support a search or seizure will almost always vary from place to place and time to time, depending on the particular circumstances confronting an officer.

[The opinion in *Whren*] also claimed in substance that accepting petitioners' position would place Judges in the role of deciding what traffic code provisions are to be enforced at all. . . . Adoption of the [reasonable officer standard] would do nothing of the sort. It does nothing more than set an objective standard, the violation of which would deprive law enforcement officers only of the use of evidence of crimes unrelated to the traffic infraction obtained in investigative stops effected through arbitrary enforcement of the traffic laws. As to the infraction itself, . . . prosecution of the underlying traffic infraction is not based upon evidence obtained through exploitation of the initial stop, but upon observations made before the stop. . . .

Next to be addressed on these appeals is the standard we would adopt to determine whether the stops in these cases were pretextual. . . . Defendants urge that we adopt a subjective test, whether the "primary motivation" for the stop was to investigate criminal activity rather than to prosecute the traffic offense ostensibly justifying the seizure. We would reject that test [because] courts and commentators have noted the difficulty, if not futility, of basing the constitutional validity of searches or seizures on judicial determinations of the subjective motivation of police officers. . . . Thus, we prefer an objective [standard:] would a reasonable officer assigned to Vehicle and Traffic Law enforcement in the seizing officer's department have made the stop under the circumstances presented, absent a purpose to investigate serious criminal activity of the vehicle's occupants[?] Whether the stop was carried out in accordance with standard procedures of the officer's department would be a highly relevant inquiry in that regard. . . .

Problem 2-2. Asset Management

Under state and federal asset forfeiture laws, the police can seize any "proceeds" or "instrumentalities" of a crime. After a streamlined process to confirm that the assets are indeed connected to a crime, the assets typically are sold; if the asset is cash, it is converted to government use. Under most of these forfeiture laws, the proceeds from the sale go directly into the coffers of the law enforcement agency that seized the asset, not into general revenue to support all governmental operations. This arrangement allows some law enforcement agencies to purchase equipment and support programs without drawing on tax dollars.

In Barbour County, Alabama, Chief Deputy Eddie Ingram specializes in traffic stops that lead to asset forfeiture. He estimates that he and the officers he supervises have discovered more than $11 million in drug assets over the past 15 years. The sheriff's department has used asset forfeiture money to buy bulletproof vests, gun belts, guns, and 9 out of the 14 cars in the department's fleet.

When Ingram is deciding which cars to stop on the U.S. highway that serves as the main north-south thoroughfare through the county, he looks for "things that just are different, and there's no one way to explain it, there's no one indicator. I just look for people that try to fit in that make themselves stand out." For instance, he says, if the speed limit is 65 mph, most people will drive 75 mph. But someone who is committing a crime will travel at 65 mph or less, and avoid eye contact with a deputy who pulls up alongside. Ingram calls these "stress-induced indicators."

Other departments in the region noticed the high levels of asset forfeiture in Barbour County and became interested in Ingram's techniques. He formed his own training academy, which has allowed him to train thousands of officers, some of whom now run their own seminars. After the classroom portion of the training, the students in Ingram's academy go out on the highway to practice the techniques. If they make a stop and find hidden currency, the Barbour County Sheriff's Office keeps 40 percent of the cash.

Several years ago, when Ingram worked on the highway interdiction team at the Villa Rica Police Department in Georgia, the police received complaints of racial profiling. The U.S. Department of Justice investigated and found problems.

Suppose you are a trial judge in Barbour County and you periodically hear claims from defendants about the alleged lack of reasonable suspicion to support a traffic stop that produced evidence of a drug crime. Would the larger pattern of reliance on asset forfeiture by the sheriff's department have any effect on your evaluation of reasonable suspicion in the case at hand? What other forum might be available for motorists to challenge the adequacy of reasonable suspicion to support a stop?

Notes

1. *Pretextual stops: majority position.* Under the federal constitution, courts refuse to question the legitimacy of allegedly pretextual stops, so long as the officer "could have" properly stopped the vehicle based on evidence of a traffic offense. According to the Supreme Court in Whren v. United States, 517 U.S. 806 (1996), any effort to determine whether a reasonable officer "would have" stopped a vehicle for traffic violations alone would be too uncertain: "While police manuals and standard procedures may sometimes provide objective assistance, ordinarily one would be reduced to speculating about the hypothetical reaction of a hypothetical constable — an exercise that might be called virtual subjectivity." The *Whren* decision convinced most states that at one time employed the "would have" doctrine to change approaches for purposes of the state constitution. At this point, over 40 states follow the *Whren* decision. See Mitchell v. State, 745 N.E.2d 775 (Ind. 2001); State v. Pagotto, 762 A.2d 97 (Md. 2000).

One of the few remaining exceptions is the state of Washington. In State v. Ladson, 979 P.2d 833 (Wash. 1999), officers on proactive gang patrol noticed a driver who was rumored to be involved in gang and drug activity. They followed the car and stopped the driver after noticing that the license plate tabs had expired. Their primary reason for the stop was to investigate drug activity, and they found drugs in the passenger's possession. The Washington Supreme Court called pretextual stops "a triumph of form over substance" and worried that approving such searches would mean that "nearly every citizen would be subject to a *Terry* stop simply because he or she is in his or her car." As for how to determine whether a given stop is pretextual, the court adopted a "totality of the circumstances" approach. Trial courts may inquire both about the subjective intent of the officer as well as the objective reasonableness of the officer's behavior to determine whether a stop was pretextual or not. If you wanted to learn whether judicial controls of pretextual stops are workable in practice, what aspect of the Washington system would you study most closely?

2. *State constitutions and the federal constitution.* In *Robinson,* the New York court pointed out that both the state and federal constitutions contain provisions to limit police searches and seizures and to protect privacy. State courts must interpret both constitutional provisions when a litigant presents the issue. The state courts must adhere to the decisions of the U.S. Supreme Court as to the meaning of the federal constitution. State law enforcement officers must comply with certain provisions of the federal constitution — those applicable to the states because the due process clause of the Fourteenth Amendment "incorporates" them. Today, most of the specific Bill of Rights protections for criminal defendants and for citizens generally have been "incorporated" to apply against the states and their agents. See Akhil Reed Amar, The Bill of Rights: Creation and Reconstruction (1998) and Michael Kent Curtis, No State Shall Abridge: The Fourteenth Amendment and the Bill of Rights (1986).

However, a state's supreme court has the ultimate judicial authority over the meaning of its own state constitution. It might interpret the state constitution (or some other provision of state law, such as a statute) to place restrictions on law enforcement officers different from what the federal constitution might require. The federal courts, including the U.S. Supreme Court, must allow a state supreme court's decision in a criminal case to stand so long as the decision does not flatly conflict with binding federal law and rests on "independent and adequate" state law grounds. Periodically, we will consider cases about procedural issues in which state law gives different answers from federal law or asks different procedural questions altogether. This variety in criminal procedure in different jurisdictions makes it possible for lawyers to argue for procedural innovations that might not be apparent from studying federal law alone.

3. *Reading minds.* Do judicial controls on pretextual stops require the judge to read the officer's mind? Is it truly possible to declare that a stop was pretextual based on "objective" evidence (such as the prevalence of traffic stops in that situation, or the officer's compliance with a police department's internal rules about traffic stops)? Or is some finding about subjective intent implicit in any pretext case? Perhaps a court's position on the pretext doctrine reflects an underlying assumption about the trustworthiness of police officers. If a court is unwilling to attempt to control pretextual stops, is it implicitly deciding that the police ordinarily make good faith decisions that ought to be encouraged? Is it making any implicit claims about the truthfulness of police testimony in the ordinary case? See Angela Davis, Race, Cops, and Traffic Stops, 51 U. Miami L. Rev. 425 (1997). Consider how defense attorneys and prosecutors might explain the relevance of a particular officer's habits in making traffic stops. See "State Highway Patrol Trooper Barry Washington Is on the Prowl for Drugs," San Antonio Express-News, July 25, 1996 (trooper seizes more than 1,000 pounds of marijuana and 20,000 grams of cocaine each year; stops up to 40 drivers daily, spending about four minutes with each; sends average of two drug suspects per week into court system).

4. *Highways as a special arena.* The pretext issue takes on special urgency on the highways. Over half of all contacts between adults and police officers take place during traffic stops. In a given year, the police stop about 9 percent of all drivers. See Bureau of Justice Statistics, Characteristics of Drivers Stopped by Police, 2002 (June 2006, NCJ 211471). The vehicle's equipment and the driver's conduct are also regulated in minute detail, allowing a wide variety of stops. The potential grounds for stops cover everything from bumper height, to tire tread, to a burned-out license tag light, or the ever-popular "changing lanes without signaling." In 2005, speeding was the stated reason given to 53 percent of the stopped drivers; 10 percent were stopped for a burned-out light or other vehicle defect; 6 percent were stopped for an improper turn or lane change. Bureau of Justice Statistics, Contacts Between Police and the Public, 2005 (April 2007, NCJ 215243).

Does a healthy legal system depend on lax enforcement of certain laws? In this imperfect world, how many cars and drivers can go for long without some minor violation, such as tag lights or lane violations? If police officers can develop reasonable suspicion against any driver if they persist in the effort, does the *Whren* decision effectively repeal the reasonable suspicion limit for police power on the highways? How does the majority opinion in the New York case answer this question?

5. *Arbitrary enforcement.* Is the pretext doctrine necessary to prevent arbitrary enforcement decisions by the police (including possible harassment of racial minorities), or are other legal doctrines available to prevent arbitrary policing? See Jones v. Sterling, 110 P.3d 1271 (Ariz. 2005) (criminal defendants can assert racial profiling as defense to charges and not rely solely on civil rights claims); David Harris, "Driving While Black" and All Other Traffic Offenses: The Supreme Court and Pretextual Traffic Stops, 87 J. Crim. L. & Criminology 544 (1997) (describing

disproportionate stops of African Americans and Hispanics in Colorado, Florida, Illinois, and Maryland; large-scale study in Florida showed almost 70 percent of drivers stopped were African American or Hispanic, although they constitute about 5 percent of drivers on that highway). Would a challenge based on the equal protection clause of the Constitution be available (or sufficient) to respond to any police use of race as a basis for selecting drivers to stop? See Tracy Maclin, Race and the Fourth Amendment, 51 Vand. L. Rev. 333 (1998).

Would the pretext doctrine give a court a basis to respond to a claim that police officers stop cars on an equal basis, but then treat drivers differently during the stop on the basis of race? See Jeffrey Fagan and Amanda Geller, Profiling and Consent: Stops, Searches and Seizures after *Soto*, available at *http://www.ssrn.com/abstract=1641326* (based on New Jersey data, black and Hispanic drivers when stopped are more than twice as likely as white drivers to be searched).

6. *Police responses to pretext claims.* If you were legal counsel to a police department in a jurisdiction adopting the reasonable officer "would" test for pretext (such as Washington state), what advice would you give the department? For instance, what charges should the arresting officer file — the original offense justifying the stop or the more serious offense or both? What sorts of reasons should an officer give to justify an initial stop? Will the officer fare better if he identifies some grounds for stopping a car other than a traffic violation? See Scott v. State, 877 P.2d 503 (Nev. 1994) (officer stopped car because vehicle might have been stolen). Can the officer overcome the claim of pretext by arguing that he routinely stops several vehicles per month based on similar traffic violations? State v. Wilson, 867 P.2d 1175 (N.M. 1994) (officer testifies that he stops six to eight cars every month for failure to use seat belts; stop upheld).

7. *Department-level pretexts.* Some individual police officers use traffic stops as a means to enforce drug laws. Are pretext claims by defendants stronger or weaker when the use of pretext (such as traffic stops to look for drugs) is a department policy instead of just an individual officer's decision? Other departments (for example, the Kansas City Police Department) use reasonable suspicion stops of cars and persons as a general policy with the goal of finding weapons and enforcing firearms laws. A study of the Kansas City program, which began in 1991, concluded that gun seizures in the 80-by-10-block target area increased by 65 percent, while seizures in a comparable beat went down slightly. Gun crimes in the target beat decreased by 49 percent and increased slightly in the comparison beat. See Lawrence Sherman, James Shaw & Dennis Rogan, The Kansas City Gun Experiment, National Institute of Justice, Research in Brief (Jan. 1995 NCJ 150855). Would a challenge to this Kansas City practice be more difficult than the challenges to the various individual stops in *Robinson*?

4. *Criminal Profiles and Race*

The police officer in the field is not left entirely to her own devices when deciding whether apparently innocent facts are actually indicators of criminal activity. Both police departments and legislative bodies offer guidance on the types of conduct that might create grounds for a stop. Police departments periodically create "criminal profiles," which are lists of personal characteristics and behaviors said to be associated with particular types of crime (most commonly drug trafficking).

Sometimes these profiles are quite specific, while at other times they are relatively short and general. An officer hoping to explain after the fact why she stopped a person might describe the features of the profile that the suspect matched.

The criminal profiles developed in police departments often remain informal and unwritten. Do these "profiles" — collective judgments about suspicious activity — add any weight to the individual police officer's expert judgment in the field as the officer tries to establish reasonable suspicion? Does your response to a criminal profile change if it places some weight on the racial or ethnic identification of the suspect?

■ SAMIR QUARLES v. STATE

696 A.2d 1334 (Del. 1997)

WALSH, J.

In this appeal from the Superior Court, the appellant, Samir Quarles, seeks a reversal of a ruling that denied his motion to suppress evidence of illegal drugs seized from his person during a street encounter with police. . . . We conclude that under a totality of circumstances test the conduct of the appellant, measured from the perspective of experienced police officers, provided a specific and articulable basis for a limited investigative stop. . . .

At approximately 10:00 P.M. on the date in question, Officers Looney and Solge went to the terminal to meet a bus arriving from New York City. Based on their past experience, the officers were aware that the bus in question was often used by persons acting as drug couriers. It was their intention to conduct surveillance of persons departing the bus with the hope of intercepting the flow of drugs into the city. As they watched, fifteen to twenty passengers disembarked from the bus with two individuals, later identified as Quarles and Thomas, exiting last.

Although Quarles and Thomas were conversing as they left the bus, their conversation "came to an abrupt halt" as soon as they observed two uniformed officers standing nearby. The conversation was not reinitiated once the pair passed the officers. The pair then stood motionless on the sidewalk for a few moments before turning to walk north toward Second Street in the opposite direction of the police. The police observed as Quarles began walking at a faster pace ahead of Thomas, who eventually caught up with Quarles after some distance. As Quarles and Thomas proceeded quickly toward Second Street, Quarles looked back on three different occasions to determine the location of the police officers. When Quarles and Thomas reached the intersection of Second and French Streets they turned west on Second Street. After they turned the corner, Quarles observed a third officer, Officer Cunningham, sitting in his patrol car in a parking lot a short distance ahead on Second Street. Upon observing Cunningham's vehicle, Quarles backtracked to the corner and looked around to determine where the two officers on foot were located. According to the officers, Quarles and Thomas seemed "kind of surprised" and in a quandary as to what direction to proceed. At that point Officers Looney and Solge approached the pair and Officer Solge asked if he could speak to them. Quarles and Thomas agreed to speak with the officers.

In the meantime, Officer Cunningham, who had been in radio contact with the other two officers, proceeded the wrong way on Second Street, against traffic, and parked his vehicle partially on the sidewalk prior to joining the group gathered at the corner. The defendants gave inconsistent statements as to their destination and appeared nervous in answering questions about their origin and destination. They were advised that the police were checking for drugs and/or weapons couriers and were asked if they had any drugs or contraband on their persons. The police requested permission to conduct a search of their persons as well as of a bag carried by Quarles. . . . The police proceeded to search both Quarles' bag and his person, uncovering a large quantity of cocaine in Quarles' boot. . . .

Under the Fourth Amendment, a police seizure can be justified only when, based upon specific and articulable facts which, taken together with rational inferences from those facts, reasonably warrant the belief that a crime is being or has been committed. Under this standard, the courts must look for a minimal level of objective "justification" for making the stop. United States v. Sokolow, 490 U.S. 1 (1989). This burden of proof is "considerably less" than proof by a preponderance of the evidence and less demanding than probable cause. When conducting its analysis, the court must consider the totality of the circumstances, the "whole picture," as viewed through the eyes of a police officer who is experienced in discerning the ostensibly innocuous behavior that is indicative of narcotics trafficking.

The United States Supreme Court has stated that the circumstances must be evaluated under an objective/subjective standard as opposed to a purely objective standard. This reflects the reality that:

> [much] of the drug traffic is highly organized and conducted by sophisticated criminal syndicates. The profits are enormous. And many drugs . . . may be easily concealed. As a result, the obstacles to detection of illegal conduct may be unmatched in any other area of law enforcement.

It logically follows that a pattern of behavior interpreted by an untrained observer as innocent could justify an investigatory stop when viewed by experienced law enforcement agents who are cognizant of current drug trafficking operations. United States v. Cortez, 449 U.S. 411 (1981). In *Cortez,* the United States Supreme Court cautioned that terms like "articulable reasons" and "founded suspicion" are not self-defining. But the Court noted that any assessment of police conduct must be two-pronged, based upon: (1) "all the circumstances," including objective observations and "consideration of the modes or patterns of operation of certain kinds of lawbreakers"; and (2) the inferences and deductions that a trained officer could make which "might well elude an untrained person." We believe that standard is an appropriate one for use by courts reviewing the conduct of detaining officers, and we adopt it here.

In our case, the officers relied upon specific factors together with a "drug courier profile" to justify their articulable suspicion. Although the use of "profiling" is vigorously debated in academic circles, it has been accepted by the United States Supreme Court. The Court has stated that a "profile," alone, will not justify a seizure, but when considered in conjunction with police observations, a seizure could be warranted even though the "non-profile" observations by themselves would not justify an investigatory stop. Moreover, the fact that the articulated factors "may be set forth in a 'profile' does not somehow detract from their evidentiary significance as seen by a trained agent." *Sokolow,* 490 U.S. at 9-10.

Here the "profile" characteristics were: (1) the defendants came into Wilmington via bus from New York (a known drug source city); (2) they carried no luggage;

(3) they came in at night, typically when law enforcement activity is at a minimum; and (4) they traveled as a pair. This profile was compiled relying upon police experience, based on past arrests of individuals bringing drugs into the City of Wilmington. The "non-profile" factors relied upon by police were: (1) the defendants' startled reaction to uniformed police officers upon exiting the bus (ceasing their conversation); (2) quickly leaving the bus terminal in a direction away from the officers; (3) . . . repeated glances over their shoulders to see if the officers were following them both before and after turning the corner; (4) rapid stride; and (5) abrupt about face upon seeing a marked police car.

When assessing the relevance of these factors the focus is not on whether the particular conduct is "innocent" or "guilty" but the degree of suspicion that attaches to particular types of conduct. Courts have recognized that wholly lawful and innocent conduct descriptive of a large segment of the population can justify the suspicion that criminal activity is afoot.

When Quarles exited the New York bus in Wilmington, he and his companion satisfied a number of well-known "drug courier profile" characteristics. While this fact alone would not justify a seizure, when combined with the other specific instances of suspicious and odd behavior, police were justified in effectuating a seizure. This Court notes that the conclusions reached by the officers as to Quarles' behavior were based in large part upon their personal experiences in conducting drug courier surveillance at the bus station. Combined, the officers conducted surveillance at the bus station over 90 times, approximately two to three times a month, with, over the past year, Officer Looney personally arresting 12 people for carrying drugs through the station.

The two arresting officers, drawing on their experience of observing hundreds of people move through the bus station, were able to conclude that Quarles' behavior was abnormal and suspicious when compared to other passengers.[5] Quarles' suspicious behavior and the "drug profile," when taken as a whole from the perspective of one who is trained in narcotics detection, produces a reasonable articulable suspicion that a crime was afoot. We therefore conclude that the police officers had a sufficient basis upon which to support an initial stop to question Quarles.

The safeguarding of a citizen's rights against unreasonable stops and seizures by police officers is a cherished protection under the Fourth Amendment and this Court's obligation to advance those rights is clear. But this Court should not turn a blind eye to the realities of society's war against drugs and the experience of the police in combating that problem. We are entitled to test the actions of the police by the exacting standards of the Fourth Amendment jurisprudence, but we should be reluctant to substitute an academic analysis for the on the spot judgment of trained law enforcement officers. . . .

VEASEY, C.J., dissenting.

. . . I submit, respectfully, that the majority opinion rests on a novel rationale — unprecedented deference to subjective police observations based solely

5. With over 90 surveillance operations at the bus station, if each night only one bus carrying twenty passengers came into the station, the two arresting officers would have witnessed the behavior of over 1800 passengers. This vast experience gave the officers an adequate frame of reference for detecting abnormal or suspicious behavior.

upon law enforcement experience. The majority correctly states that . . . "any curtailment of a person's liberty by the police must be supported at least by a reasonable and articulable suspicion that the person seized is engaged in criminal activity." The key words here are "reasonable" and "articulable." These are objective tests. . . . Hunches and subjective impressions of experienced police officers will not suffice. . . .

In this case police did not rely on intelligence reports that drugs were being carried on the bus or that defendant, or anyone fitting his description, was transporting drugs to Wilmington. . . . There were no suspicious hand signals or papers passed secretly. [The] data available to Officers Cunningham, Looney, and Solge at the time they seized Quarles completely lacked specificity and could not have raised a justifiable suspicion that Quarles was engaged in wrongdoing. . . .

Moreover, I question whether the four benign facts cited by the majority establish a profile. . . . These four facts taken as a whole might well describe a number of innocent people. New York City is only 120 miles from Wilmington. Nighttime travel with a companion and without luggage is hardly remarkable. As for New York City being a "known drug source city," what city is not infested with drugs and drug suppliers? Even the trial judge here concluded, "The mere fact that they exited a bus coming from New York City would not give rise to a reasonable suspicion." . . .

At bottom, the majority opinion attaches a novel, and outcome-determinative, deference to experienced police eyes without any expert or empirical evidence. . . . If the precedent embodied in the majority opinion is taken to its logical extreme, police experience alone, and without articulable expert analysis or meticulous police work . . . , will almost always support the seizure. . . .

This case is about constitutional protections that the judicial branch of government is obliged to enforce for the protection of innocent citizens, as well as reprehensible drug traffickers who poison our citizens. With the utmost deference, I must state my concern that the rationale and the unprecedented reach of the majority opinion is dangerous and could lead to a pernicious erosion of our liberty.

Notes

1. *Criminal profiles in the courts: majority position.* The strong majority of courts presented with stops based on facts listed in a criminal profile will not allow the match with the profile, standing alone, to constitute reasonable suspicion. However, courts also often say that the appearance of an observed fact in a profile gives that fact added weight in the reasonable suspicion calculus. See State v. Staten, 469 N.W. 2d 112 (Neb. 1991) (airline passengers fitting drug courier profile may be detained up to one hour). A significant minority of states have rejected or criticized any reliance on the use of profiles to add any weight to facts observed in the field. Commonwealth v. Lewis, 636 A.2d 619 (Pa. 1994). The federal law on profiles seems agnostic, placing no independent weight — positive or negative — on the existence of a profile. See United States v. Sokolow, 490 U.S. 1 (1989); Florida v. Royer, 460 U.S. 491 (1983) (reasonable suspicion established). Some state courts reject particular components of a profile without rejecting the reliance on profiles generally. See State v. Gonzalez-Gutierrez, 927 P.2d 776 (Ariz. 1996) (characteristic of being Mexican did not add weight to reasonable suspicion analysis); Derricott v. State, 611 A.2d 592 (Md. 1992) (criticizing profile that apparently included race of suspect);

Crockett v. State, 803 S.W.2d 308 (Tex. Crim. App. 1991) (no evidence that drug dealers purchase train tickets with cash more frequently than other people).

2. *Dueling profiles and discretion.* Courts seem especially skeptical about profiles phrased broadly enough to "describe a very large category of presumably innocent travelers, who would be subject to virtually random seizures" if a mere match to such a profile were enough to justify a search or seizure. Reid v. Georgia, 448 U.S. 438 (1980). Drug courier profiles sometimes are written broadly enough to attach suspicion both to a particular characteristic (such as exiting a plane first or making eye contact with another passenger) and to its opposite (exiting a plane last or avoiding eye contact with another passenger). What exactly is the problem with a declaration that a particular behavior and its opposite are both suspicious? Judicial opinions dealing with challenges to the use of a criminal profile almost never list the complete provisions of the profile. What does this mean to the attorney hoping to challenge the reliability of the profile as a method of establishing reasonable suspicion?

3. *Officer expertise and subjective standards.* Should the particular expertise of the investigating officer have any bearing on a finding of reasonable suspicion? Or should the court accept only those inferences that any "reasonable person" (that is, a citizen) would draw from the observed facts? If you are willing to account for the special experience of a particular police officer in establishing reasonable suspicion, is this consistent with your views on the "reasonable person" standard we encountered earlier, dealing with the definition of a "stop"? See United States v. Cortez, 449 U.S. 411 (1981) ("when used by trained law enforcement officers, objective facts, meaningless to the untrained, can be combined with permissible deductions from such facts to form a legitimate basis for suspicion of a particular person"); Harris v. State, 806 A.2d 119 (Del. 2002) (to establish reasonable suspicion for stop on basis of drug courier profile, state and federal constitutions require officer to explain how training makes apparently innocent conduct suspicious).

4. *Collective judgments and expertise.* Stops based on criminal profiles differ from other reasonable suspicion stops because they attempt to give the officer on the street the benefit of the collective experience of other officers or the collective judgments of political authorities. The officer makes the stop not only based on his own expertise in law enforcement but also because the "profile" places significance on certain facts. Which is a stronger basis for believing that certain apparently innocent facts are actually indications of criminal activity: the individual training and experience of the officer making the stop, or the statistical and collective experience of police in the department? As the attorney for a person stopped, which of the two bases would you prefer to test on cross-examination? See Wayne LaFave, Controlling Discretion by Administrative Regulations: The Use, Misuse, and Nonuse of Police Rules and Policies in Fourth Amendment Adjudication, 89 Mich. L. Rev. 442 (1990).

5. *Package profiles.* Recall that courts distinguish between "consensual" encounters that do not involve a seizure at all (and therefore require no justification) and stops that do require reasonable suspicion. If the seizure amounts to a full arrest, the government must show probable cause. The same framework applies to property. When the government takes possession (temporary or permanent) of property and the owner later challenges that control as an unconstitutional seizure, courts ask whether the governmental control amounted to a "stop" of the property that required reasonable suspicion.

The U.S. Supreme Court has held that postal authorities must have reasonable suspicion to detain a mail package for a short time and probable cause to seize it outright. United States v. Van Leeuwen, 397 U.S. 249 (1970). The postal service has developed profiles for identifying packages carrying illegal narcotics: packages meeting the profile are delayed for further inspection (often by drug-sniffing dogs) and for controlled delivery to the addressee. One such profile lists the following characteristics: (1) size and shape of the package; (2) package taped to close or seal all openings; (3) handwritten or printed labels; (4) unusual return name and address; (5) unusual odors coming from the package; (6) fictitious return address; and (7) destination of the package. See State v. Cooper, 652 A.2d 995 (Vt. 1994).

Often the challenges to detentions of property involve delays in delivering luggage to airline passengers waiting in baggage claims areas. A brief detention of the luggage also effectively detains the person. Should this make a difference in a court's evaluation of the government's handling of the property?

6. *Efficiency in proof?* Is the problem with criminal profiles that the government has not written specific profiles and has not shown rigorously how the profile features are common to a great number of criminal defendants? Consider a profile constructed as follows. A group of more than 40 representatives from law enforcement agencies in the Phoenix area developed a profile for stopping suspected automobile thieves transporting stolen vehicles to Mexico. The profile was based on an analysis of 10,000 auto thefts in the area over a 17-month period. The profile indicated which vehicles were targeted most often by the thieves: sedans and pickup trucks manufactured by Ford and Chevrolet within the last three years. In addition, the records indicated that the driver of a stolen car would probably be a male between 17 and 27 years of age; he would usually be alone; he would have no apparent luggage; if there was a passenger, there would be no children; and the car's license plate would show a registration to either Pima or Maricopa County. This profile fit only a small percentage of those people driving between Tucson and Nogales. See State v. Ochoa, 544 P.2d 1097 (Ariz. 1976). Could profiles, when carefully constructed and meticulously proven in early cases, prevent duplicative presentation of evidence in later cases?

Problem 2-3. Race and Witness Descriptions

On February 21, at approximately 4:15 A.M., Nancy Henderson approached an automatic teller machine on Main Street. While she was operating the teller machine, but before completing her transaction, someone grabbed her from behind and said, "this is a stick-up" and "I want your money." During a brief struggle, the man pressed a hard, blunt object into her back. He forced Henderson from the front of the bank to a parking lot in back of the building. She gave her money to the man. The man then declared that he planned to rape Henderson. He forced her to walk to the front of the bank and ordered her to get into the driver's seat of her car, threatening to "blow her brains out" if she did not comply. The man positioned himself next to Henderson in the front passenger seat, and directed her where to drive the car.

As Henderson drove, she noticed a pizza shop that appeared to be open. She accelerated the car in that direction and jumped the curb. Then she got out of the car and ran screaming for help. Several people emerged from the shop. During the confusion, the assailant walked away. The police were called, and arrived at the pizza shop within minutes. Henderson described her assailant as "a black male, 5'11" to 6'2", wearing a ski cap, had a mustache, was wearing a light-colored coat, dark pants, white tennis shoes and had medium to dark skin." The police dispatcher sent this description to all officers on patrol.

At 5:25 A.M., another officer on patrol stopped Daniel Coleman in the parking lot of a restaurant located approximately one-half of a mile from the pizza shop. Coleman fit the general description of the assailant, except that he had a goatee as well as a mustache and was not wearing a coat or a cap. The officer questioned Coleman briefly about his identity and destination. Coleman stated that he was coming from his girlfriend's home and that he was on his way to work. During this discussion, another officer drove by with Henderson in the car. She was unable to identify Coleman as her assailant. The officer detained Coleman for a total of about 10 minutes, then released him.

Later that morning, the police viewed a videotape taken by a camera installed near the automatic teller machine. Both of the police officers who had seen Coleman earlier that morning during his brief detention viewed the videotape and identified the assailant on the videotape as Coleman. Coleman was arrested at his place of employment and charged with robbery and attempted rape. When the officers first stopped Coleman, did they have reasonable suspicion? If they ignored information about the race of the suspect, would they have reasonable suspicion? See Coleman v. State, 562 A.2d 1171 (Del. 1989).

Notes

1. *Race and witness descriptions: majority position.* Most courts allow the police to rely on race as one among many components of reasonable suspicion, particularly if the police use the racial element of a description received from a victim or witness of the crime. Note, Developments in the Law — Race and the Criminal Process, 101 Harv. L. Rev. 1473 (1988). Can you imagine a jurisdiction that would bar any use of race in establishing reasonable suspicion, thus requiring the police to point to other factors? For witness identifications, could the police rely on descriptions of clothing or facial hair, while being barred from using information about skin color?

On the other hand, police officers will at times rely on a suspect's race in cases where no witness has described the perpetrator, or even where there is no report of a crime at all. This most often occurs when a person appears to be "out of place": for instance, a black person in a predominantly white neighborhood. Courts have divided on whether such a fact can be the primary component of reasonable suspicion. See, e.g., State v. Dean, 543 P.2d 425 (Ariz. 1975) (Mexican male in dented car in predominantly white neighborhood, reasonable suspicion); State v. Mallory, 337 N.W.2d 391 (Minn. 1983) (black male stopped in white neighborhood where burglary by a black male had occurred recently, reasonable suspicion); State v. Barber, 823 P.2d 1068 (Wash. 1992) (presence of black person in white neighborhood can never amount to reasonable suspicion standing alone).

Officers also sometimes rely on the race of the suspect when it is difficult to articulate other specific grounds for suspicion; courts now tend to invalidate stops in such cases. See United States v. Bellamy, 619 A.2d 515 (D.C. 1993) (no reasonable suspicion where officer stops four black youths in car who teased him about violence against police); Commonwealth v. Phillips, 595 N.E.2d 310 (Mass. 1992) (no reasonable suspicion where Boston police implement policy to "search on sight" young black males suspected of membership in gangs). If most American jurisdictions allow race as one "factor" that contributes to a finding of reasonable suspicion, won't there necessarily be cases where race provides the extra marginal evidence to obtain reasonable suspicion? Would this be objectionable discrimination, or a plausible reaction to probabilities familiar to the police? See Sheri Lynn Johnson, Race and the Decision to Detain a Suspect, 93 Yale L.J. 214 (1983).

2. *Patterns of discrimination in stops.* When the Supreme Court first considered the validity of stops based on reasonable suspicion, in Terry v. Ohio, 392 U.S. 1 (1968), advocates and commentators objected to the police practice, pointing to evidence that police used stops in a discriminatory manner to harass African Americans. More recent observers of police practices argue that officers still choose to stop a disproportionate number of black males. Michael Brown, Working the Street: Police Discretion and the Dilemmas of Reform 166 (1981) ("Race, the field observations [of police] reveal, is one of the most salient criteria to patrolmen in deciding whether or not to stop someone"). An analysis of data concerning traffic stops between 1995 and 2000 concluded that the Maryland State Police "stopped and searched cars with black and Hispanic drivers much more often than cars with white drivers; it is hard to see how they could have produced these results without taking race into account in deciding who to stop and who to search." Although this practice "seems to increase the probability of finding large hauls of drugs," the large hauls are rare, and about "two-thirds of all drivers searched were not carrying any illegal drugs." Most of the drivers who had any drugs in the car were found with trace amounts; among black and Hispanic drivers, "a larger minority of the searches uncovered substantial quantities of illegal drugs." See Samuel R. Gross & Katherine Y. Barnes, Road Work: Racial Profiling and Drug Interdiction on the Highway, 101 Mich. L. Rev. 651 (2002). How might the attorney for an individual who is stopped go about establishing this sort of claim?

Defendants have only rarely convinced courts to outlaw the use of pretextual stops or criminal profiles, but a related claim has achieved more success outside the courts. The related claim is that police stop motorists based at least partly on their race. Such claims are often described in public debates as the creation of a crime called "driving while black" or "DWB."

Claims of DWB are difficult for a criminal defendant to litigate, but state and federal governments now regularly investigate patterns of traffic and drug stops on highways. The New Jersey Attorney General conducted one such investigation. Law enforcement officials prepared the report excerpted below in the aftermath of a tragic shooting incident in 1998 on the New Jersey Turnpike. Troopers were accused of firing 11 shots into a van containing four young men on their way to a basketball tryout. The shots wounded two black men and a Hispanic man. The officers said that they initially stopped the van because it was speeding, and opened fire when the van backed up to hit them. The shooting triggered protests and an internal investigation of claims that officers used racial profiling during stops and investigations on the highway.

■ PETER VERNIERO, ATTORNEY GENERAL INTERIM REPORT OF THE STATE POLICE REVIEW TEAM REGARDING ALLEGATIONS OF RACIAL PROFILING

(April 20, 1999)

. . . This Interim Report specifically focuses on the activities of state troopers assigned to patrol the New Jersey Turnpike. [The] Turnpike is widely believed to be a major drug corridor, thereby providing the State Police with both the impetus and the opportunity to engage in drug interdiction tactics that appear to be inextricably linked to the "racial profiling" controversy. [Based] upon the information that we reviewed, minority motorists have been treated differently than nonminority motorists during the course of traffic stops on the New Jersey Turnpike. For the reasons set out fully in this Report, we conclude that the problem of disparate treatment is real — not imagined. This problem . . . is more complex and subtle than has generally been reported.

[We] define "racial profiling" broadly to encompass any action taken by a state trooper during a traffic stop that is based upon racial or ethnic stereotypes and that has the effect of treating minority motorists differently than nonminority motorists. . . .

Our review has revealed two interrelated problems that may be influenced by the goal of interdicting illicit drugs: (1) willful misconduct by a small number of State Police members, and (2) more common instances of possible de facto discrimination by officers who may be influenced by stereotypes and may thus tend to treat minority motorists differently during the course of routine traffic stops. . . .

Our review has shown that over the years, conflicting messages have been sent regarding the official policy to prohibit any form of race-based profiling. This situation should be rectified by developing a clear and consistent message. We propose that as a matter of policy for the New Jersey State Police, race, ethnicity, and national origin should not be used at all by troopers in selecting vehicles to be stopped or in exercising discretion during the course of a stop (other than in determining whether a person matches the general description of one or more known suspects). In making this recommendation, we propose going beyond the minimum requirements of federal precedent because, simply, it is the right thing to do and because the Executive Branch, no less than its judicial counterpart, has an independent duty to ensure that our laws are enforced in a constitutional, efficient, and even-handed fashion. . . .

Stops. We have received and compiled information regarding stops by troopers assigned to the Moorestown and Cranbury stations from the monthly stop data. . . . Four of every ten stops (40.6 percent) made during the period for which data are available involved black, Hispanic, Asian or other nonwhite people. . . .

Searches. It is obvious from the data provided that very few stops result in the search of a motor vehicle. For example, in those instances for which we have data permitting comparisons between stops and searches, only 627 (0.7 percent) of 87,489 stops involved a search. [The] available data indicate that the overwhelming majority of searches (77.2 percent) involved black or Hispanic persons. Specifically, of the 1,193 searches for which data are available, 21.4 percent involved a white person, more than half (53.1 percent) involved a black person, and almost one of every four (24.1 percent) involved a Hispanic person.

. . . Not surprisingly, most consent searches do not result in a "positive" finding. . . . Specifically, 19.2 percent of the searches we considered resulted in an arrest or seizure of contraband. Accounting for race and ethnicity, 10.5 percent of the searches that involved white motorists resulted in an arrest or seizure of contraband, 13.5 percent of the searches that involved black motorists resulted in an arrest or seizure, and 38.1 percent of the searches of Hispanic motorists resulted in an arrest or seizure.

Arrests. [During the years 1996 through 1998], there were a total of 2,871 arrests [for crimes other than drunk driving]. Of these, 932 (32.5 percent) involved white persons, 1,772 (61.7 percent) involved black persons, and 167 (5.8 percent) involved persons of other races.

Interpretations of the Data and Areas of Special Concern

. . . Information and analysis compiled by the Public Defender's Office . . . suggests that troopers who enjoyed a wider ambit of discretion, by virtue of the nature of their duty assignment, stopped and ticketed minority motorists more often. Specifically, the Public Defender's statistical expert compared the tickets issued on 35 randomly selected days by three different State Police units: (1) the Radar Unit, which uses radar-equipped vans and chase cars and exercises comparatively little discretion; (2) the Tactical Patrol Unit, which focuses on motor vehicle enforcement in particular areas and exercises somewhat greater discretion; and (3) the Patrol Unit, which is responsible for general law enforcement and exercises the most discretion. [The] Radar Unit was found to have issued 18% of its tickets to African-Americans, the Tactical Patrol Unit issued 23.8% of its tickets to African-Americans, and the Patrol Unit issued 34.2% of its tickets to African-Americans. . . . We are concerned by what may be a pattern that when state troopers are permitted more discretion by virtue of their duty assignment, they tended during the time periods examined to ticket African-Americans more often. . . .

The potential for the disparate treatment of minorities during routine traffic stops may be the product of an accumulation of circumstances that can contribute to the use of race- or ethnicity-based criteria by creating the unintended message that the best way to catch drug traffickers is to focus on minorities. To some extent, the State Police as an organization may have been caught up in the martial rhetoric of the "war on drugs," responding to the call to arms urged by the public, the Legislature, and the Attorney General's Statewide Narcotics Action Plans of 1987 and 1993.

[The] officially stated policy has always been to condemn reliance upon constitutionally impermissible factors. . . . The State Police official policy prohibiting racial profiling was announced in a 1990 Standard Operating Procedure. Ironically, the problem of the reliance upon stereotypes may have unwittingly been exacerbated by the issuance of this [1990 Procedure. It] included a discussion of the "sufficiency of objective facts to establish reasonable suspicion or probable cause," explaining that . . . personal characteristics such as race, age, sex, length of hair, style of dress, type of vehicle, and number of occupants of a vehicle "may not be utilized as facts relevant to establish reasonable suspicion or probable cause *unless the [State Police] member can identify and describe the manner in which a characteristic is directly and specifically related to particular criminal activity*." (Emphasis added.) [This] portion of the Standard Operating Procedure, read literally, suggests that a person's race *may* be relied upon by a State Police member if he or she is able to identify and describe the manner in which race is directly and specifically related to a particular criminal activity. This exception has the very real capacity to swallow the rule, and opens the door (or at least fails to shut the door) to the use of stereotypes, especially those that have been "validated" by tautological and self-serving intelligence reports and profiles. . . .

With respect to training programs, . . . inadequate attention may have been paid to the possibility that subtle messages in these lectures and videos would reinforce preexisting stereotypes by, for example, focusing mostly on criminal groups that happen to be comprised of minority citizens or foreign nationals. These kinds of messages may have been further reinforced by statistics compiled by State Police and disseminated to troopers in seminars and bulletins. The very fact that information concerning the racial characteristics of drug traffickers was provided to troopers assigned to patrol duties could have suggested that such characteristics are a legitimate, relevant factor to be taken into account or "kept in mind" in exercising police discretion during a traffic stop.

The State Police reward system, meanwhile, gave practical impetus to the use of these inappropriate stereotypes about drug dealers. [Evidence] has surfaced that minority troopers may also have been caught up in a system that rewards officers based on the quantity of drugs that they have discovered during routine traffic stops. (An internal audit of State Police motor vehicle stops recorded on the Moorestown Station radio logs between May 1, 1996 and July 31, 1996 shows that 34.3% of the 3,524 stops that were conducted by nonminority troopers involved minority motorists. An essentially identical proportion (33.3%) of the 1,751 total stops that were conducted by minority troopers involved minority motorists.) . . . The typical trooper is an intelligent, rational, ambitious, and career-oriented professional who responds to the prospect of rewards and promotions as much as to the threat of discipline and punishment. The system of organizational rewards, by definition and design, exerts a powerful influence on officer performance and enforcement priorities. . . .

The Critical Distinction Between Legitimate Crime Trend Analysis and Impermissible Racial Profiling

[We] start with a discussion of the legitimate use of law enforcement's "collective knowledge and experience." Sophisticated crime analysis is sorely needed if police agencies are to remain responsive to emerging new threats and enforcement opportunities. The law is thus well-settled that in appropriate factual circumstances, police may piece together a series of acts, which by themselves seem innocent, but to a trained officer would reasonably indicate that criminal activity is afoot. State v. Patterson, 270 N.J. Super. 550, 557 (Law Div. 1993). As the court in *Patterson* correctly noted, "it is appropriate and legitimate police work to develop a so-called 'profile' based upon observations made in investigating the distribution or transportation of illicit drugs." Using these and other means, the police can develop a pattern of criminal wrongdoing that justifies their suspicions when they observe features that are in accord with the principal aspects of that pattern. . . . This regularized police experience reflects the collection of historical and intelligence information, careful crime trend analysis, and an examination of the methods of operations, the so-called "modus operandi," of drug traffickers and others engaged in various types of criminal activity. . . .

While police agencies are permitted, indeed are expected, to conduct crime trend analysis and to train officers as to those facts and circumstances that, while innocent on their face, provide a reasonable basis for suspecting criminal activity, the law also provides that certain factors may not be considered by law enforcement. In State v. Kuhn, 213 N.J. Super. 275 (App. Div. 1986), the court held that police are not permitted to draw any inferences of criminal activity from a suspect's race. The court in State v. Patterson expounded on this point, noting that "[certainly] the police cannot conclude that all young, male African-Americans are suspected of involvement in the illicit drug trade." . . .

One need not be a constitutional scholar to understand that race, ethnicity, or national origin cannot be the sole basis for initiating a motor vehicle stop. On this point, everyone seems to agree. The law is far less clear, and opinions within and outside the criminal justice system become far more diverse, with respect to the question whether there are any circumstances when police may legitimately consider these kinds of personal traits and characteristics in drawing rational inferences about criminal activity. No one disputes, of course, that police can take a person's race into account in deciding whether the person is the individual who is described in a "wanted" bulletin; in this instance, race or ethnicity is used only as an "identifier." The issue, rather, and one that has not yet been definitely or at least uniformly resolved by the courts, is whether race, ethnicity, or national origin may be considered as one among an array of factors to infer that a particular individual is more likely than others to be engaged in criminal activity.

We believe that when finally confronted with this issue, the New Jersey Supreme Court would likely . . . hold, based upon independent state constitutional grounds if necessary, that race may play no part in an officer's determination of whether a particular person is reasonably likely to be engaged in criminal activity. In any event, . . . we need not wait for the courts to reach this conclusion before we propose a clear rule to be followed by state troopers assigned to patrol duties. . . .

THE IMPORTANCE OF PERCEPTIONS

[Law] enforcement policy cannot be divorced from public opinion and public perceptions. The New Jersey State Police, no less than any other law enforcement agency, [must] remain responsive to public needs and expectations if it is to achieve its ultimate mission to protect and to serve.

[A] *Star Ledger/Eagleton* poll that was conducted in early May 1998 . . . showed that while the overall job performance rating of the State Police is quite positive in New Jersey, there is a major racial divide among Garden State residents. Black and white New Jerseyans have markedly different views of troopers' fairness in the enforcement of the laws, even-handed treatment of all drivers, judgment in deciding whom to pull over, and courteousness in dealing with stopped motorists. The poll revealed that the vast majority of African-Americans in New Jersey feel that State Police members treat minorities worse than others, and that troopers target cars to pull over based on the race and age of the people in the cars. In stark contrast, the majority of white New Jerseyans feel that troopers treat all motorists the same and seem highly satisfied with all aspects of their job performance. . . .

The Circular Illogic of Race-Based Profiles

. . . We turn now to the specific assumption that is at the heart of the racial profiling controversy: the notion that a disproportionate percentage of drug traffickers and couriers are black or Hispanic, so that race, ethnicity, or national origin can serve as a reliable, accurate predictor of criminal activity. The proponents of this view point to empirical evidence, usually in the form of arrest and conviction statistics, that would appear at first blush to demonstrate quite conclusively that minorities are disproportionately represented among the universe of drug dealers.

The evidence for this conclusion is, in reality, tautological and reflects as much as anything the initial stereotypes of those who rely upon these statistics. . . .

Arrest statistics, by definition, do not show the number of persons who were detained or investigated who, as it turned out, were not found to be trafficking drugs or carrying weapons. Consistent with our human nature, we in law enforcement proudly display seized drug shipments or "hits" as a kind of trophy, but pay scant attention to our far more frequent "misses," that is, those instances where stops and searches failed to discover contraband. . . .

Remedial Steps

[The] State Police has already undertaken a series of initiatives to address these issues, beginning in 1990 with a comprehensive Standard Operating Procedure governing the conduct of motor vehicle stops. That SOP included a number of important and innovative safeguards, including a requirement that state troopers have a reasonable, articulable suspicion to believe that evidence of a crime would be found before asking for permission to conduct a consent search, and a requirement that all consents to search be reduced to writing.

The State Police have also issued policies and procedures that require troopers to advise the dispatcher as to the racial characteristics of motorists who are stopped, that require troopers to record this information on patrol logs, and that prohibit the practice of "spotlighting" vehicles to ascertain the racial characteristics of the occupants of vehicles that have not yet been ordered to pull over. . . . Most recently, pursuant to the Governor's and Attorney General's initiative, State Police vehicles were equipped with video cameras that can be used to provide conclusive evidence of the conduct of motor vehicle stops. . . .

[A] trooper who is bent on finding drugs will . . . engage in comparatively protracted patrol stops, since his or her objective would not be simply to issue a summons or warning, but rather to undertake a full-blown criminal investigation. For this reason, we propose the establishment of a system that would allow supervisors and the State Police hierarchy to monitor the duration of road stops. If, for example, the median length of patrol stops by a given officer is shown to be correlated to the race, ethnicity, or national origin of motorists, that circumstance would trigger the "early warning system" and require appropriate follow-up investigation and explanation. . . .

The Department of Law and Public Safety should prepare and make public on a quarterly basis aggregate statistics compiled pursuant to the databases created in accordance with the recommendations of this Interim Report, detailing by State Police station the proportion of minority and nonminority citizens who were subject to various actions taken by State Police members during the course of traffic stops.

The Superintendent should [establish] a protocol for the use of an "early warning system" to detect and deter the disparate treatment of minority citizens by State Police members assigned to patrol duties. . . . The protocol for use of the "early warning system" should provide for the routine supervisory review of videotapes, patrol officer logs, Traffic Stop Report forms, Search Incident forms, and any other patrol work product. The protocol should also provide for regularly conducted audits of enforcement patterns including traffic stops, the issuance of motor vehicle summons, and search and arrest activity. . . .

The Superintendent should within 90 days of this Report issue a single, comprehensive Standard Operating Procedure [regarding traffic stops]. In preparing the Standard Operating Procedure, the following should be considered:

1. Before exiting his or her police vehicle, a State Police member will inform the dispatcher of the exact reason for the stop (e.g., speeding, 70 mph), a description of the vehicle and, when possible, a description of its occupants (i.e., the number of occupants and the apparent race and gender).
2. A system should be established to monitor the exact duration of all stops.
3. When the patrol vehicle is equipped with a video camera, the State Police person will ensure that the camera is activated before exiting the patrol vehicle and will not turn the camera off until the detained vehicle has been released and departs the scene.
4. In the case of routine stops, the State Police member will at the outset of the stop, introduce him or herself by name, and inform the driver as to the reason for the stop. . . .
5. At the conclusion of the vehicle stop, the State Police person will inform the dispatcher as to the stop outcome (e.g., warning, summons, etc.). . . .
6. All State Police members conducting a motor vehicle traffic stop must utilize a Traffic Stop Report form, which shall record all officer action information necessary for immediate supervisory review or to supplement information recorded by the Computer Aided Dispatch System. . . .
7. All Traffic Stop Report forms are to be reviewed by supervisory personnel at the conclusion of all duty shifts. The information contained in the reports should be entered into the "early warning system" database. . . .

Although the racial profiling issue has gained state and national attention recently, the underlying conditions that foster disparate treatment of minorities have existed for decades in New Jersey and throughout the nation, and will not be changed overnight. Even so, we firmly believe that this Interim Report represents a major step, indeed a watershed event, signaling significant change. We thus hope that this Report, once fully implemented through the issuance of new and comprehensive Standard Operating Procedures, a monitoring system, training, and other reforms, will ensure that New Jersey is a national leader in addressing the issue of racial profiling.

U.S. DEPARTMENT OF JUSTICE, RACIAL PROFILING FACT SHEET

(June 17, 2003)

. . . Racial profiling sends the dehumanizing message to our citizens that they are judged by the color of their skin and harms the criminal justice system by eviscerating the trust that is necessary if law enforcement is to effectively protect our communities.

America has a moral obligation to prohibit racial profiling. Race-based assumptions in law enforcement perpetuate negative racial stereotypes that are harmful to our diverse democracy, and materially impair our efforts to maintain a fair and just society. As Attorney General John Ashcroft said, racial profiling creates a "lose-lose" situation because it destroys the potential for underlying trust that "should support the administration of justice as a societal objective." . . .

The guidance in many cases imposes *more* restrictions on the use of race and ethnicity in federal law enforcement than the Constitution requires. This guidance prohibits racial profiling in federal law enforcement practices without hindering the important work of our nation's public safety officials, particularly the intensified anti-terrorism efforts precipitated by the attacks of September 11, 2001.

Prohibiting Racial Profiling in Routine or Spontaneous Activities in Domestic Law Enforcement: In making routine or spontaneous law enforcement decisions, such as ordinary traffic stops, federal law enforcement officers may *not* use race or ethnicity to any degree, except that officers may rely on race and ethnicity if a specific suspect description exists. This prohibition applies even where the use of race or ethnicity might otherwise be lawful.

Routine Patrol Duties Must Be Carried Out Without Consideration of Race. Federal law enforcement agencies and officers sometimes engage in law enforcement activities, such as traffic and foot patrols, that generally do not involve either the ongoing investigation of specific criminal activities or the prevention of catastrophic events or harm to the national security. Rather, their activities are typified by spontaneous action in response to the activities of individuals whom they happen to encounter in the course of their patrols and about whom they have no information other than their observations. These general enforcement responsibilities should be carried out without *any* consideration of race or ethnicity.

Example: While parked by the side of the highway, a federal officer notices that nearly all vehicles on the road are exceeding the posted speed limit. Although each such vehicle is committing an infraction that would legally justify a stop, the officer may not use race or ethnicity as a factor in deciding which motorists to pull over. Likewise, the officer may not use race or ethnicity in deciding which detained motorists to ask to consent to a search of their vehicles.

Stereotyping Certain Races as Having a Greater Propensity to Commit Crimes Is Absolutely Prohibited. Some have argued that overall discrepancies in crime rates among racial groups could justify using race as a factor in general traffic enforcement activities and would produce a greater number of arrests for non-traffic offenses (*e.g.*, narcotics trafficking). We emphatically reject this view. It is patently unacceptable and thus prohibited under this guidance for federal law enforcement officers to engage in racial profiling.

Acting on Specific Suspect Identification Does Not Constitute Impermissible Stereotyping. The situation is different when a federal officer acts on the personal identifying characteristics of potential suspects, including age, sex, ethnicity or race. Common sense dictates that when a victim or witness describes the assailant as being of a particular race, authorities may properly limit their search for suspects to persons of that race. In such circumstances, the federal officer is not acting based on a generalized assumption about persons of different races; rather, the officer is helping locate a specific individual previously identified as involved in crime.

Example: While parked by the side of the highway, a federal officer receives an "All Points Bulletin" to be on the look-out for a fleeing bank robbery suspect, a man of a particular race and particular hair color in his 30s driving a blue automobile. The officer may use this description, including the race of the particular suspect, in deciding which speeding motorists to pull over.

Prohibiting Racial Profiling in Federal Law Enforcement Activities Related to Specific Investigations: In conducting activities in connection with a specific investigation, federal law enforcement officers may consider race and ethnicity only to the extent that there is trustworthy information, relevant to the locality or time frame, that links persons of a particular race or ethnicity to an identified criminal incident, scheme, or organization. This standard applies even where the use of race or ethnicity might otherwise be lawful. . . .

Example: In connection with a new initiative to increase drug arrests, federal authorities begin aggressively enforcing speeding, traffic, and other public area laws in a neighborhood predominantly occupied by people of a single race. The choice of neighborhood was not based on the number of 911 calls, number of arrests, or other pertinent reporting data specific to that area, but only on the general assumption that more drug-related crime occurs in that neighborhood because of its racial composition. This effort would be *improper* because it is based on generalized stereotypes. . . .

Reliance Upon Generalized Stereotypes Continues to Be Absolutely Forbidden. Use of race or ethnicity is permitted only when the federal officer is pursuing a specific lead concerning the identifying characteristics of persons involved in an *identified* criminal activity. The rationale underlying this concept carefully limits its reach. In order to qualify as a legitimate investigative lead, the following must be true:

- The information must be relevant to the locality or time frame of the criminal activity;
- The information must be trustworthy; and,
- The information concerning identifying characteristics must be tied to a particular criminal incident, a particular criminal scheme, or a particular criminal organization.

Example: The FBI is investigating the murder of a known gang member and has information that the shooter is a member of a rival gang. The FBI knows that the members of the rival gang are exclusively members of a certain ethnicity. This information, however, is not suspect-specific because there is no description of the particular assailant. But because authorities have reliable, locally relevant information linking a rival group with a distinctive ethnic character to the murder, federal law enforcement officers could properly consider ethnicity in conjunction with other appropriate factors in the course of conducting their investigation. Agents could properly decide to focus on persons dressed in a manner consistent with gang activity, but ignore persons dressed in that manner who do not appear to be members of that particular ethnicity.

Example: While investigating a car theft ring that dismantles cars and ships the parts for sale in other states, the FBI is informed by local authorities that it is common knowledge locally that most car thefts in that area are committed by individuals of a particular race. In this example, although the source (local police) is trustworthy, and the information potentially verifiable with reference to arrest statistics, there is no particular incident- or scheme-specific information linking individuals of that race to the particular interstate ring the FBI is investigating. Thus, agents could not use ethnicity as a factor in making law enforcement decisions in this investigation. . . .

Federal Law Enforcement Will Continue Terrorist Identification. Since the terrorist attacks on September 11, 2001, the President has emphasized that federal law enforcement personnel must use every legitimate tool to prevent future attacks, protect our nation's borders, and deter those who would cause devastating harm to our country and its people through the use of biological or chemical weapons, other weapons of mass destruction, suicide hijackings, or any other means.

Therefore, the racial profiling guidance recognizes that race and ethnicity may be used in terrorist identification, but only to the extent permitted by the nation's laws and the Constitution. The policy guidance emphasizes that, even in the national security context, the constitutional restriction on use of generalized stereotypes remains. . . .

Given the incalculably high stakes involved in such investigations, federal law enforcement officers who are protecting national security or preventing catastrophic events (as well as airport security screeners) may consider race, ethnicity, alienage, and other relevant factors. Constitutional provisions limiting government action on the basis of race are wide-ranging and provide substantial protections at every step of the investigative and judicial process. Accordingly, this policy will honor the rule of law and promote vigorous protection of our national security. . . .

Example: U.S. intelligence sources report that Middle Eastern terrorists are planning to use commercial jetliners as weapons by hijacking them at an airport in California during the next week. Before allowing men appearing to be of Middle Eastern origin to board commercial airplanes in California airports during the next week, Transportation Security Administration personnel, and other federal and state authorities, may subject them to heightened scrutiny. . . .

Problem 2-4. Borderline State

In 2010 the Arizona legislature enacted the highly controversial state immigration law known as SB 1070. One aspect of the law that attracts the most public commentary is whether it allows, mandates, invites, or forbids the use of race in police decisions whether to stop a suspect, or whether to investigate their immigration status. The leadership of the Tucson Police Department has hired you to advise them on the relationship between SB 1070 and racial profiling.

Your client asks you to address separately two distinct conceptions of racial profiling: (1) when police officers use race as one element in a decision whether to stop or search, and (2) when race is an unconstitutional or otherwise illegal element in a decision whether to stop or search. With these two definitions in mind, consider the text of A.R.S. §11-1051(B):

> For any lawful stop, detention or arrest made by a law enforcement official or a law enforcement agency of this state or a law enforcement official or a law enforcement agency of a county, city, town or other political subdivision of this state in the enforcement of any other law or ordinance of country, city or town or this state where reasonable suspicion exists that the person is an alien and is unlawfully present in the United States, a reasonable attempt shall be made, when practicable, to determine the immigration status of the person, except if the determination may hinder or obstruct an investigation. Any person who is arrested shall have the person's immigration status determined before the person is released. The person's immigration status shall be verified with the federal government. . . . A law enforcement official or agency of this state or a county, city, town or other political subdivision of this state may not consider race, color or national origin in implementing the requirements of this subsection except to the extent permitted by the United States or Arizona Constitution.

SB 1070 also prohibits government agencies from restricting enforcement of immigration law "to less than the full extent permitted by federal law." A.R.S. §1151(A). The statute creates a citizen suit provision, allowing a judicial challenge of any policy that interferes with the full enforcement of federal law. A.R.S. §11-1051(H).

Arizona Governor Jan Brewer stated that it is "crystal clear and undeniable that racial profiling is illegal, and will not be tolerated in Arizona." The primary author of SB 1070, Arizona State Senator Russell Pearce, wrote that SB 1070 "explicitly prohibits racial profiling." The Arizona Police Office Standards and Training Board, AZPOST, which issues training materials but has no enforcement power, issued training materials and videos stating that race and ethnicity cannot be used in police decisions about whether to investigate immigration status. See *http://www.azpost.state.az.us/SB1070infocenter.htm*.

In United States v. Brignoni-Ponce, 422 U.S. 873, 886-887 (1975), the Supreme Court of the United States held that the U.S. Constitution allows race to be considered in immigration enforcement: "The likelihood that any given person of Mexican ancestry is an alien is high enough to make Mexican appearance a relevant factor." The Arizona Supreme Court has agreed that "enforcement of immigration laws often involves a relevant consideration of ethnic factors." State v. Graciano, 653 P.2d 683, 687 n.7 (Ariz. 1982). In 1996, the Arizona Supreme Court reaffirmed the relevance of race in determinations of reasonable suspicion:

> Mexican ancestry alone, that is, Hispanic appearance, is not enough to establish reasonable cause, but if the occupants' dress or hair style are associated with people currently living in Mexico, such characteristics may be sufficient. The driver's behavior may be considered if the driving is erratic or the driver exhibits an "obvious attempt to evade officers." The type or load of the vehicle may also create a reasonable suspicion.

State v. Gonzalez-Gutierrez, 927 P.2d 776 (Ariz. 1996). See also United States v. Soto-Cervantes, 138 F.3d 1319, 1325 (10th Cir. 1998) (affirming trial court finding of reasonable suspicion of immigration violations based on factors including "the defendant's presence in an area known to be frequented by illegal aliens from

Mexico"); but cf. United States v. Montero-Camargo, 208 F.3d 1122, 1131 (9th Cir. 2000) (en banc) (in a case arising in El Centro, 50 miles north of the Mexican border, "The likelihood that in an area in which the majority — or even a substantial part — of the population is Hispanic, any given person of Hispanic ancestry is in fact an alien, let alone an illegal alien, is not high enough to make Hispanic appearance a relevant factor in the reasonable suspicion calculus"). Notably, modern cases on the question of the explicit relevance of race to stops or searches arise in immigration cases and overwhelmingly involve persons of apparent Hispanic or Mexican origin.

Your counsel to the Tucson Police Department will likely expose the city to lawsuits, regardless of what you say. The Police Department plans to share your advice with other police departments and sheriff's offices throughout Arizona. What is your advice?

Notes

1. *DWB claims.* Claims that police officers stop drivers because of their race and not their behavior are not new, but have become much more prominent over the past several years after a series of prominent law review articles, and some litigation in New Jersey and Maryland. These civil lawsuits, along with defenses raised in criminal proceedings, have produced only modest success. Based on cases such as Whren v. United States, 517 U.S. 806 (1996), described above, most courts have found no constitutional violation. See Tracey Maclin, The Fourth Amendment on the Freeway, 3 Rutgers Race & L. Rev. 117, 117-28 (2001).

2. *DWB legislation.* With DWB making little or no headway as a constitutional claim, state legislatures have taken the lead in efforts to monitor, limit, and sanction racially biased traffic stops. See David A. Harris, Addressing Racial Profiling in the States: A Case Study of the "New Federalism" in Constitutional Criminal Procedure, 3 Pa. J. Const. L. 367 (2001). The statutes pursue different strategies. An Oklahoma statute, 22 Okla. Stat. §34.3, directly forbids the use of race as the "sole" basis for stopping or detaining a person, and makes racial profiling a misdemeanor. The statute also calls for law enforcement agencies to adopt and publicize "a detailed written policy that clearly defines the elements constituting racial profiling." A California statute, Penal Code §13519.4, requires training of officers in topics related to cultural diversity. A Missouri statute, Mo. Stat. §590.650, provides for mandatory collection of data about the race of motorists whom the police stop and search. Which of these strategies is most likely to reduce the amount of racial profiling?

Apart from legislation on the subject, many police departments have now adopted internal guidelines calling on officers to record the age, gender, and race or ethnicity of every person they stop in traffic. See Bureau of Justice Statistics, Traffic Stop Data Collection Policies for State Police, 2004 (2005, NCJ 209156) (22 of 49 state police agencies require officers to record race or ethnicity of motorist in all traffic stops). What (or who) might convince a police department to adopt such a policy?

3. *Race and prevention of terrorism.* Note that the Department of Justice policy on racial profiling creates a special set of rules for terrorism investigations. What justification does the statement offer for creating an exception in this area? Does the legitimacy of such a policy depend on the actual number of terrorist acts committed by Muslim noncitizens, as compared to the number of terrorist acts committed by

tizens (such as the Oklahoma City bombing of 1995)? For a sample of Ch s in this fast-changing area, see the web extension for this chapter at th crimpro.com/extension/ch02.

e in immigration enforcement. For enforcement of general criminal laws, rug crimes, race plays a shadowy, often implicit role as a factor in reason- picion or probable cause determinations. For immigration enforcement, eral law (as in *Brignoni-Ponce*) and state law (as illustrated by the Arizona ed in Problem 2-4) allow *explicit* reliance on race or ethnicity. But only one ethnicity) has been at issue in these cases — being Hispanic. Explicit reli- n race for immigration enforcement has become more awkward, as suggested battles over the text and effect of Arizona Senate Bill 1070. Professor Gabriel Chin and Dean Kevin Johnson, in a July 13, 2010, *Washington Post* op-ed, sug- sted that

> [we] suspect that *Brignoni-Ponce* and its incorporation into S.B. 1070 have escaped the notice of many Americans because of the ways in which racial sensibilities have evolved since the 1954 ruling in *Brown v. Board of Education.* Modern American values and most of modern constitutional law are simply inconsistent with the equation of race and suspicion authorized and encouraged by *Brignoni-Ponce*. Today, being subject to questioning by law enforcement for no other reason than that others of your race, religion or national origin are supposed to commit more of a particular type of crime is nothing short of un-American.

Has *Brignoni-Ponce* been overruled by social norms? Has the United States Supreme Court simply not taken an opportunity to bring doctrine into a more modern line?

5. *Executive branch policies on race*. Arizona Senate Bill 1070 provoked a national controversy, copycat statutes, and federal litigation. On July 28, 2010, a day before the law was to take effect, a federal judge in Phoenix enjoined the most controversial provisions of the law, including §11-1051(B). If race or ethnicity — appearing to be Hispanic or Mexican — are no longer legitimate factors in immigration enforcement, then federal and state executive branch agencies (including police and prosecutors) could choose not to rely on race without waiting for a court order on the issue. Federal authorities and authorities in other states could forbid reliance on race in criminal or immigration enforcement, even without new constitutional rulings. This option might not be available in Arizona under SB 1070, which included provisions requiring state agents to "fully enforce federal law" and made state agencies subject to lawsuits by citizens who could challenge any state or local policy that failed to do so. The federal government, however, has not forbidden reliance on race or ethnicity. To the contrary, the Obama Administration Department of Justice regularly relies on apparent race and ethnicity in federal immigration enforcement. See United States v. Bautista-Silva, 567 F.3d 1266, 1270 (11th Cir. 2009) (reasonable suspicion existed based on seven factors, including that "the driver and all five passengers were Hispanic adult males"), and federal courts regularly accept them. See United States' Response in Opposition to Defendant's Motion to Suppress and Memorandum of Law, in United States v. Gustavo Telles-Montenegro, 2009 WL 6478237, 7 (M.D. Fl. Dec. 21 2009) (reasonable suspicion supported by "the apparent Mexican ancestry of the occupants of the vehicle"), defendant's motion denied, United States v. Telles-Montenegro, 2010 WL 737640, *7 (M.D. Fl. Feb. 4, 2010) ("Agent Fiorita testified that, in his experience, Hispanic

males are typically the drivers of alien smuggling vehicles. Therefore, this relevant consideration.").

B. BRIEF ADMINISTRATIVE STOPS

Among the brief stops and searches that government agents carry out, some are subject to less restrictive rules because of their routine administrative nature. These brief stops are carried out on large numbers of people and further government interests apart from criminal law enforcement. The U.S. Supreme Court determined, in Camara v. Municipal Court, 387 U.S. 523 (1967), that the Fourth Amendment could place limits on government activities even when they are not directed at enforcement of the criminal laws. These "administrative" stops and searches sometimes take place even when the government agents have no reasonable suspicion to believe that a law has been violated. We begin with non-individualized stops of drivers.

■ CITY OF INDIANAPOLIS v. JAMES EDMOND

531 U.S. 32 (2000)

O'CONNOR, J.*

. . . I.

. . . In August 1998, the city of Indianapolis began to operate vehicle checkpoints on Indianapolis roads in an effort to interdict unlawful drugs. The city conducted six such roadblocks between August and November that year, stopping 1,161 vehicles and arresting 104 motorists. Fifty-five arrests were for drug-related crimes, while 49 were for offenses unrelated to drugs. The overall "hit rate" of the program was thus approximately nine percent.

The parties stipulated to the facts concerning the operation of the checkpoints by the Indianapolis Police Department (IPD) for purposes of the preliminary injunction proceedings instituted below. At each checkpoint location, the police stop a predetermined number of vehicles. Approximately 30 officers are stationed at the checkpoint. Pursuant to written directives issued by the chief of police, at least one officer approaches the vehicle, advises the driver that he or she is being stopped briefly at a drug checkpoint, and asks the driver to produce a license and registration. The officer also looks for signs of impairment and conducts an open-view examination of the vehicle from the outside. A narcotics-detection dog walks around the outside of each stopped vehicle.

The directives instruct the officers that they may conduct a search only by consent or based on the appropriate quantum of particularized suspicion. The officers must conduct each stop in the same manner until particularized suspicion develops,

* [Justices Stevens, Kennedy, Souter, Ginsburg, and Breyer joined in this opinion. — EDS.]

and the officers have no discretion to stop any vehicle out of sequence.... According to Sergeant [Marshall] DePew, checkpoint locations are selected weeks in advance based on such considerations as area crime statistics and traffic flow. The checkpoints are generally operated during daylight hours and are identified with lighted signs reading, "NARCOTICS CHECKPOINT ______ MILE AHEAD, NARCOTICS K-9 IN USE, BE PREPARED TO STOP." Once a group of cars has been stopped, other traffic proceeds without interruption until all the stopped cars have been processed or diverted for further processing. Sergeant DePew also stated that the average stop for a vehicle not subject to further processing lasts two to three minutes or less.

Respondents James Edmond and Joell Palmer were each stopped at a narcotics checkpoint in late September 1998. Respondents then filed a lawsuit on behalf of themselves and the class of all motorists who had been stopped or were subject to being stopped in the future at the Indianapolis drug checkpoints. Respondents claimed that the roadblocks violated the Fourth Amendment of the United States Constitution and the search and seizure provision of the Indiana Constitution. Respondents requested declaratory and injunctive relief for the class, as well as damages and attorney's fees for themselves....

II.

The Fourth Amendment requires that searches and seizures be reasonable. A search or seizure is ordinarily unreasonable in the absence of individualized suspicion of wrongdoing. While such suspicion is not an irreducible component of reasonableness, we have recognized only limited circumstances in which the usual rule does not apply. For example, we have upheld certain regimes of suspicionless searches where the program was designed to serve "special needs, beyond the normal need for law enforcement." See, e.g., Vernonia School Dist. 47J v. Acton, 515 U.S. 646 (1995) (random drug testing of student-athletes); Treasury Employees v. Von Raab, 489 U.S. 656 (1989) (drug tests for United States Customs Service employees seeking transfer or promotion to certain positions). We have also allowed searches for certain administrative purposes without particularized suspicion of misconduct, provided that those searches are appropriately limited. See, e.g., New York v. Burger, 482 U.S. 691 (1987) (warrantless administrative inspection of premises of "closely regulated" business).

We have also upheld brief, suspicionless seizures of motorists at a fixed Border Patrol checkpoint designed to intercept illegal aliens, United States v. Martinez-Fuerte, 428 U.S. 543 (1976), and at a sobriety checkpoint aimed at removing drunk drivers from the road, Michigan Dept. of State Police v. Sitz, 496 U.S. 444 (1990). In addition, in Delaware v. Prouse, 440 U.S. 648 (1979), we suggested that a similar type of roadblock with the purpose of verifying drivers' licenses and vehicle registrations would be permissible. In none of these cases, however, did we indicate approval of a checkpoint program whose primary purpose was to detect evidence of ordinary criminal wrongdoing....

In *Sitz,* we evaluated the constitutionality of a Michigan highway sobriety checkpoint program. The *Sitz* checkpoint involved brief suspicionless stops of motorists so that police officers could detect signs of intoxication and remove impaired drivers from the road. Motorists who exhibited signs of intoxication were diverted for a license and registration check and, if warranted, further sobriety tests. This checkpoint program was clearly aimed at reducing the immediate hazard posed by the presence of drunk drivers on the highways, and there was an obvious connection between the imperative of highway safety and the law enforcement practice at issue. The gravity of the drunk driving problem and the magnitude of the State's interest in getting drunk drivers off the road weighed heavily in our determination that the program was constitutional.

In *Prouse,* we invalidated a discretionary, suspicionless stop for a spot check of a motorist's driver's license and vehicle registration. The officer's conduct in that case was unconstitutional primarily on account of his exercise of "standardless and unconstrained discretion." We nonetheless acknowledged the States' "vital interest in ensuring that only those qualified to do so are permitted to operate motor vehicles, that these vehicles are fit for safe operation, and hence that licensing, registration, and vehicle inspection requirements are being observed." Accordingly, we suggested that "questioning of all oncoming traffic at roadblock-type stops" would be a lawful means of serving this interest in highway safety.

We further indicated in *Prouse* that we considered the purposes of such a hypothetical roadblock to be distinct from a general purpose of investigating crime. [We considered the State's primary interest in this setting to be roadway safety.] Not only does the common thread of highway safety thus run through *Sitz* and *Prouse,* but *Prouse* itself reveals a difference in the Fourth Amendment significance of highway safety interests and the general interest in crime control.

III.

It is well established that a vehicle stop at a highway checkpoint effectuates a seizure within the meaning of the Fourth Amendment. The fact that officers walk a narcotics-detection dog around the exterior of each car at the Indianapolis checkpoints does not transform the seizure into a search. See United States v. Place, 462 U.S. 696 (1983). Just as in *Place,* an exterior sniff of an automobile does not require entry into the car and is not designed to disclose any information other than the presence or absence of narcotics. . . . Rather, what principally distinguishes these checkpoints from those we have previously approved is their primary purpose.

As petitioners concede, the Indianapolis checkpoint program unquestionably has the primary purpose of interdicting illegal narcotics. In their stipulation of facts, the parties repeatedly refer to the checkpoints as "drug checkpoints" and describe them as "being operated by the City of Indianapolis in an effort to interdict unlawful drugs in Indianapolis." In addition, the [operating] directives instruct officers to "advise the citizen that they are being stopped briefly at a drug checkpoint." . . . Because the primary purpose of the Indianapolis narcotics checkpoint program is to uncover evidence of ordinary criminal wrongdoing, the program contravenes the Fourth Amendment.

Petitioners propose several ways in which the narcotics-detection purpose of the instant checkpoint program may instead resemble the primary purposes of the checkpoints in *Sitz* and *Martinez-Fuerte*. Petitioners state that the checkpoints in those cases had the same ultimate purpose of arresting those suspected of committing crimes. Securing the border and apprehending drunk drivers are, of course, law enforcement activities, and law enforcement officers employ arrests and criminal prosecutions in pursuit of these goals. If we were to rest the case at this high level of generality, there would be little check on the ability of the authorities to construct roadblocks for almost any conceivable law enforcement purpose. Without drawing the line at roadblocks designed primarily to serve the general interest in crime control, the Fourth Amendment would do little to prevent such intrusions from becoming a routine part of American life. . . .

Nor can the narcotics-interdiction purpose of the checkpoints be rationalized in terms of a highway safety concern similar to that present in *Sitz*. The detection and punishment of almost any criminal offense serves broadly the safety of the community, and our streets would no doubt be safer but for the scourge of illegal drugs. Only with respect to a smaller class of offenses, however, is society confronted with the type of immediate, vehicle-bound threat to life and limb that the sobriety checkpoint in *Sitz* was designed to eliminate. . . .

Of course, there are circumstances that may justify a law enforcement checkpoint where the primary purpose would otherwise, but for some emergency, relate to ordinary crime control. For example, . . . the Fourth Amendment would almost certainly permit an appropriately tailored roadblock set up to thwart an imminent terrorist attack or to catch a dangerous criminal who is likely to flee by way of a particular route. The exigencies created by these scenarios are far removed from the circumstances under which authorities might simply stop cars as a matter of course to see if there just happens to be a felon leaving the jurisdiction. . . .

Petitioners argue that our prior cases preclude an inquiry into the purposes of the checkpoint program. For example, they cite Whren v. United States, 517 U.S. 806 (1996) . . . to support the proposition that "where the government articulates and pursues a legitimate interest for a suspicionless stop, courts should not look behind that interest to determine whether the government's 'primary purpose' is valid." These cases, however, do not control the instant situation.

In *Whren*, we held that an individual officer's subjective intentions are irrelevant to the Fourth Amendment validity of a traffic stop that is justified objectively by probable cause to believe that a traffic violation has occurred. . . . In so holding, we expressly distinguished cases where we had addressed the validity of searches conducted in the absence of probable cause. [While] subjective intentions play no role in ordinary, probable-cause Fourth Amendment analysis, programmatic purposes may be relevant to the validity of Fourth Amendment intrusions undertaken pursuant to a general scheme without individualized suspicion. . . .

Petitioners argue that the Indianapolis checkpoint program is justified by its lawful secondary purposes of keeping impaired motorists off the road and verifying licenses and registrations. If this were the case, however, law enforcement authorities would be able to establish checkpoints for virtually any purpose so long as they also included a license or sobriety check. For this reason, we examine the available evidence to determine the primary purpose of the checkpoint program. While we recognize the challenges inherent in a purpose inquiry, courts routinely engage in this enterprise in many areas of constitutional jurisprudence as a means of sifting abusive governmental conduct from that which is lawful. . . .

Because the primary purpose of the Indianapolis checkpoint program is ultimately indistinguishable from the general interest in crime control, the checkpoints violate the Fourth Amendment. . . .

REHNQUIST, C.J., dissenting.*

The State's use of a drug-sniffing dog, according to the Court's holding, annuls what is otherwise plainly constitutional under our Fourth Amendment jurisprudence: brief, standardized, discretionless, roadblock seizures of automobiles, seizures which effectively serve a weighty state interest with only minimal intrusion on the privacy of their occupants. Because these seizures serve the State's accepted and significant interests of preventing drunken driving and checking for driver's licenses and vehicle registrations, and because there is nothing in the record to indicate that the addition of the dog sniff lengthens these otherwise legitimate seizures, I dissent.

I.

. . . Petitioners acknowledge that the "primary purpose" of these roadblocks is to interdict illegal drugs, but this fact should not be controlling. [The] question whether a law enforcement purpose could support a roadblock seizure is not presented in this case. The District Court found that another "purpose of the checkpoints is to check driver's licenses and vehicle registrations," and the written directives state that the police officers are to "look for signs of impairment." . . . That the roadblocks serve these legitimate state interests cannot be seriously disputed, as the 49 people arrested for offenses unrelated to drugs can attest. . . .

Because of the valid reasons for conducting these roadblock seizures, it is constitutionally irrelevant that petitioners also hoped to interdict drugs. In Whren v. United States, we held that an officer's subjective intent would not invalidate an otherwise objectively justifiable stop of an automobile. The reasonableness of an officer's discretionary decision to stop an automobile, at issue in *Whren,* turns on whether there is probable cause to believe that a traffic violation has occurred. The reasonableness of highway checkpoints, at issue here, turns on whether they effectively serve a significant state interest with minimal intrusion on motorists. . . . Once the constitutional requirements for a particular seizure are satisfied, the subjective expectations of those responsible for it, be it police officers or members of a city council, are irrelevant. It is the objective effect of the State's actions on the privacy of the individual that animates the Fourth Amendment. Because the objective intrusion of a valid seizure does not turn upon anyone's subjective thoughts, neither should our constitutional analysis. . . .

[The] checkpoints' success rate — 49 arrests for offenses unrelated to drugs [or 4.2 percent of the motorists stopped] — only confirms the State's legitimate interests in preventing drunken driving and ensuring the proper licensing of drivers and registration of their vehicles. These stops effectively serve the State's legitimate interests; they are executed in a regularized and neutral manner; and they only minimally intrude upon the privacy of the motorists. They should therefore be constitutional.

* [Justice Thomas joined this opinion; Justice Scalia joined in Part I. — EDS.]

II.

[Expectations] of privacy in an automobile and of freedom in its operation are significantly different from the traditional expectation of privacy and freedom in one's residence. This is because automobiles, unlike homes, are subjected to pervasive and continuing governmental regulation and controls. The lowered expectation of privacy in one's automobile is coupled with the limited nature of the intrusion: a brief, standardized, nonintrusive seizure. . . .

Because of these extrinsic limitations upon roadblock seizures, the Court's newfound non-law-enforcement primary purpose test is both unnecessary to secure Fourth Amendment rights and bound to produce wide-ranging litigation over the "purpose" of any given seizure. Police designing highway roadblocks can never be sure of their validity, since a jury might later determine that a forbidden purpose exists. . . .

IOWA CODE §321K.1

1. The law enforcement agencies of this state may conduct emergency vehicle roadblocks in response to immediate threats to the health, safety, and welfare of the public; and otherwise may conduct routine vehicle roadblocks only as provided in this section. Routine vehicle roadblocks may be conducted to enforce compliance with the law regarding any of the following:

a. The licensing of operators of motor vehicles.

b. The registration of motor vehicles.

c. The safety equipment required on motor vehicles.

d. The provisions of chapters 481A and 483A [dealing with fish and game conservation].

2. Any routine vehicle roadblock conducted under this section shall meet the following requirements:

a. The location of the roadblock, the time during which the roadblock will be conducted, and the procedure to be used while conducting the roadblock, shall be determined by policymaking administrative officers of the law enforcement agency.

b. The roadblock location shall be selected for its safety and visibility to oncoming motorists, and adequate advance warning signs, illuminated at night or under conditions of poor visibility, shall be erected to provide timely information to approaching motorists of the roadblock and its nature.

c. There shall be uniformed officers and marked official vehicles of the law enforcement agency or agencies involved, in sufficient quantity and visibility to demonstrate the official nature of the roadblock.

d. The selection of motor vehicles to be stopped shall not be arbitrary.

e. The roadblock shall be conducted to assure the safety of and to minimize the inconvenience of the motorists involved.

Notes

1. *Automobile checkpoints: majority position.* As the opinion in *Edmond* makes clear, the federal constitution imposes different requirements on sobriety checkpoints and drug enforcement checkpoints. In Michigan Department of Police v. Sitz, 496 U.S. 444 (1990), the Court upheld a sobriety checkpoint where officers stopped vehicles without reasonable suspicion. The opinion emphasized the importance of neutral guidelines for carrying out the roadblock, formulated by supervisors or others besides the officers in the field. Those guidelines reduced both the "objective" intrusion (the duration of the stop and the intensity of the questioning) and the "subjective" intrusion of the stop (the anxiety of law-abiding drivers who are unaware of the purpose of the stop). On the other hand, after the ruling in *Edmond,* governments may not conduct suspicionless stops at drug enforcement checkpoints.

State courts are split on whether suspicionless sobriety checkpoints violate their state constitutions, with a strong majority (nearly 40 states) mirroring the federal position. See State v. Mikolinski, 775 A.2d 274 (Conn. 2001). A minority (about 10) require individualized suspicion before a vehicle stop may occur at a sobriety checkpoint. This group includes Michigan, the state whose appeals court decision was reversed in *Sitz,* which in turn rejected the U.S. Supreme Court's *Sitz* opinion on state constitutional grounds. Sitz v. Department of Police, 506 N.W.2d 209 (Mich. 1993).

2. *Driver's license and other safety reasons for checkpoints.* Police in many jurisdictions stop vehicles without individualized suspicion at a checkpoint to verify the validity of the operators' licenses, following much the same procedures for license checkpoints as they do for sobriety checkpoints. The Iowa statute above approves of roadblocks for purposes of enforcing safety equipment laws but not for purposes of enforcing drunk driving laws. Does this distinction make sense?

The U.S. Supreme Court has approved of license checkpoints so long as they are carried out in a way that does not leave officers in the field with discretion to select the vehicles to stop. Delaware v. Prouse, 440 U.S. 648 (1979). Some states have rejected license checkpoints under their state constitutions. State v. Sanchez, 856 S.W.2d 166 (Tex. Crim. App. 1993) (license and insurance checkpoint set up by four officers); State v. Hicks, 55 S.W.3d 515 (Tenn. 2001) (license checkpoint).

Government agents enforcing health and safety laws other than traffic laws also find it useful to stop and question motorists and persons outside their cars. See People v. McHugh, 630 So. 2d 1259 (La. 1994) (upholding statute authorizing suspicionless stops of hunters who are leaving state wilderness area to inspect hunting license and to request permission to inspect game); but see State v. Medley, 898 P.2d 1093 (Idaho 1995) (disallowing, in an opinion by Justice Trout, a game management checkpoint because of officer discretion in stopping vehicles and presence of criminal law enforcement officials). What set of safety and health concerns convinced the Iowa legislature to pass Section 321K.1?

3. *Which programmatic purpose?* Justice O'Connor, in her majority opinion in *Edmond,* says that "programmatic purposes may be relevant" even though an officer's subjective intentions normally do not matter in evaluating the reasonableness of a seizure. We encountered this issue earlier, in discussing "pretextual" stops. Is it any easier for courts to determine the purpose of a program than to determine the

intentions of a particular officer? What sources of evidence are available to the court making this factual finding? See Crowell v. State, 994 P.2d 788 (Okla. Crim. App. 2000) (use of narcotics detection dog to sniff cars not enough to show that safety roadblock was a pretext for drug enforcement); State v. Sigler, 687 S.E.2d 391 (W. Va. 2009) (police conducting equipment safety checks must follow the same guidelines as they do for sobriety checkpoints; different rules for checkpoints carrying different labels would invite "pretextual" checkpoints).

4. *Warrant clause and reasonableness clause.* A court ruling on the constitutionality of a suspicionless checkpoint stop confronts a question of legal text that we will encounter time and again in search and seizure issues. Recall that the text of the Fourth Amendment provides as follows: "The right of the people to be secure . . . against unreasonable searches and seizures, shall not be violated, and no Warrants shall issue, but upon probable cause. . . . " The first phrase (up to the word "violated") is known as the "reasonableness clause"; the second, the "warrant clause." What is the proper relationship between these clauses? Is the warrant clause a modifier to the reasonableness clause, defining the quintessential "reasonable" search and seizure, or do the clauses have independent meaning? If we are free to define reasonableness apart from the presence of a warrant and probable cause, then courts will need to determine in many different settings the proper measure of reasonableness. But if reasonableness is defined only in light of the warrant and probable cause requirements, then reasonableness in most settings becomes only a matter of determining how feasible it is to require police to show probable cause and obtain warrants.

Sobriety checkpoints take place in the absence of any probable cause or reasonable suspicion to believe that a driver being stopped is violating the law. The Supreme Court in *Sitz* and the other courts that have upheld sobriety checkpoints have used a "balancing" methodology to determine that individualized suspicion is not necessary. These courts balance the needs of law enforcement against the intrusiveness of the search and the individual's interest in privacy. Did the majority opinion in *Edmond* also balance interests? Should courts engage in balancing at all when it comes to constitutionally protected privacy interests? Or should they conclude that the Fourth Amendment and its equivalents have already struck a balance for all cases, requiring individualized suspicion for any "seizure" or "search"?

5. *Effectiveness of checkpoints.* Is it relevant in weighing the government's interest to determine the effectiveness of a particular set of roadblock guidelines in catching drunk drivers or meeting the other objectives of the checkpoint? Would a roadblock that produces one arrest for every 100 cars stopped be more constitutionally suspect than a roadblock that produces one arrest for every 20 cars stopped? How might police supervisors change guidelines to increase the number of arrests? Perhaps courts, police, and legislatures could consider some measure of effectiveness besides the number of arrests. Would courts be more likely to validate sobriety checkpoints if the government shows decreases in alcohol-related fatal crashes?

Consider the type of evidence that supports a decision to establish a random checkpoint and the evidence that supports "individualized" suspicion. Don't both sorts of judgments depend on assessments of similar groups or situations from the past to predict a "hit rate" for future stops? See Christopher Slobogin, Government Dragnets, 73 Law and Contemporary Problems 107 (2010); Bernard E. Harcourt and Tracey L. Meares, Randomization and the Fourth Amendment, 78 Univ. Chi. L. Rev. (forthcoming 2011), available at *http://www.ssrn.com/abstract=1665562*.

6. *Advance notice and neutral plans.* The guidelines for conducting roadblocks often provide for two types of notice. First, there are markers at the scene of the roadblock, announcing to oncoming drivers the purpose of the stop. Second, some guidelines require advance notice in the local media that roadblocks will be taking place in the area on particular days, without announcing the exact locations of the roadblocks. This advance notice is designed to increase the deterrent effect of the roadblocks by influencing the choices of all potential drivers who hear about the stops and to decrease the anxiety of drivers who encounter a roadblock. Such notice was part of the Michigan guidelines considered by the Supreme Court in *Sitz.*

If you were writing roadblock guidelines for a police department, would you include provisions for advance notice? Some courts have concluded that advance notice is not constitutionally required. See People v. Banks, 863 P.2d 769 (Cal. 1993). A few states modify the typical procedures by allowing random stops and giving officers more discretion. See State v. Mitchell, 592 S.E.2d 543 (N.C. 2004) (approves checkpoints based on standing permission from supervisor to operate under unwritten guidelines). Who is in a position to know if the police adequately follow the plan for stopping and questioning drivers? Should the plan be written? If the state's legislature has passed a statute similar to the Iowa statute above, is any further written plan necessary?

The necessary conditions for valid automobile checkpoints have attracted the attention of many state and federal courts. For a sample of these debates, see the web extension for this chapter at *http://www.crimpro.com/extension/ch02*.

7. *Roadblocks to find particular criminal suspects.* Police will occasionally receive information about the location of a suspect for a serious crime and will search all vehicles leaving the area. At least 10 states give police explicit statutory authority to set up roadblocks to find criminal suspects. See Idaho Code §19-621. Courts evaluating these roadblocks tend to approve them more readily if the crime is serious and the officers administer the roadblock in an evenhanded way that minimizes the delay and other intrusions.

What if a car approaching a roadblock makes a U-turn or exits the highway in an apparent attempt to avoid the roadblock? Does that give the police reasonable suspicion to pursue and stop the vehicle? See Commonwealth v. Scavello, 734 A.2d 386 (Pa. 1999) (properly executed turn to avoid passing through roadblock not a basis for stop).

The Supreme Court created a specialized version of the checkpoint rules to apply when the roadblock is designed to obtain information about people other than the motorist stopped. In Illinois v. Lidster, 540 U.S. 419 (2004), a police department seeking information about a fatal hit-and-run accident stopped motorists passing by the scene of the accident several days later. Although one of the stopped motorists was discovered to be driving while intoxicated, the Court ruled that the suspicionless stop was reasonable because the checkpoint sought information rather than arrests of intoxicated drivers.

After this decision, is it still fair to characterize suspicionless searches as "exceptional" techniques that will be approved only under "special" circumstances? Or has the law now evolved (or devolved) to the point that suspicionless searches are regulated and approved on the same basis as more traditional searches?

8. *Fixed and roving stops for immigration enforcement.* Customs and immigration officials routinely stop vehicles crossing the border into the country, and vehicles passing fixed checkpoints near the border. There are criminal sanctions for certain

violations of the immigration laws; indeed, immigration crimes have become some of the most common charges encountered in the federal courts (along with drug and fraud cases).

While the Supreme Court has disapproved of "roving" suspicionless stops of vehicles, it has upheld suspicionless stops of cars for brief questioning at fixed checkpoints at or near the border. See United States v. Martinez-Fuerte, 428 U.S. 543 (1976) (approves fixed checkpoint stops for brief questioning); United States v. Brignoni-Ponce, 422 U.S. 873 (1975) (disapproves roving stops in interior for questioning about immigration status); United States v. Ortiz, 422 U.S. 891 (1975) (disapproves roving immigration stops away from border to search interior of car); cf. United States v. Villamonte-Marquez, 462 U.S. 579 (1983) (approves suspicionless boarding of vessels at sea to inspect documentation). The Court has required reasonable suspicion for unusually long detentions of persons at the border. See United States v. Montoya de Hernandez, 473 U.S. 531 (1985); but cf. United States v. Flores-Montano, 541 U.S. 149 (2004) (Customs officials do not need individualized suspicion before removing, dismantling, and searching fuel tank of vehicle crossing the border, despite the fact that such searches were not routine).

9. *Legislative intent in statutory construction.* Does the Iowa statute reprinted above require each of the listed conditions for a roadblock to be valid? Courts faced with questions about the meaning of a statute will often look beyond the actual language of the statute and will read the language in light of the "legislative intent." Sometimes this legislative intent will be expressed in the "legislative history," a set of documents such as committee reports that discuss the statute before its passage or statements of legislators during floor debates on the bill. Such materials occupy a prominent place in federal statutory construction, although Justice Scalia and several other federal judges have argued for less reliance on legislative history. See INS v. Cardoza-Fonseca, 480 U.S. 421, 452 (1987) (Scalia, J., concurring).

Legislative history is generally less influential in most states. Many state courts do not consider legislative history at all because the state does not even maintain or publish such materials. Other state courts have legislative history available but discount it because it is difficult to know when statements of a single committee or a single legislator reflect the collective views of all those voting for a bill. Nevertheless, even those state courts that ignore or discount legislative history will inquire into the "purpose" of the statute. They might surmise this purpose from the language and structure of the statute (perhaps contained in the title of the statute or in a preamble explicitly stating the statute's purpose) or from a familiarity with the general history of the perceived problem and the statutory solution.

This effort to identify a statutory "purpose" gives courts the opportunity to read different statutes, perhaps passed and amended at different times, as a coherent and rational whole, furthering social purposes of the current day. In an influential text from 1958, Henry Hart and Albert Sacks expressed the interpreting judge's obligation this way: A judge interpreting a statute with ambiguous language "must resolve the uncertainty . . . in a way which is consistent with other established applications of [the statute.] And he must do so in the way which best serves the principles and policies it expresses. If the policy of the [statute] is open to doubt, the official should interpret it in the way which best harmonizes with more basic principles and policies of law." The Legal Process: Basic Problems in the Making and Application of Law 147 (William Eskridge and Phillip Frickey eds., 1994) (1958).

What was the intent of the Iowa legislature in passing its roadblock statute? What would a court need to know to answer this question? If a court determines the general "purpose" of the statute and applies the statute in a way that furthers that purpose, whose "intent" is it furthering?

Problem 2-5. Airport Checkpoints After September 11

You are an associate in a firm representing Los Angeles International Airport (LAX). Airport authorities have decided to install the Secure 2000 scanner. The Secure 2000 is a back-scatter X-ray system for detecting weapons and contraband hidden under a person's clothing. The Secure 2000 covertly scans persons for hidden weapons and explosives as they walk down a hallway. Almost immediately, an image of the person and any concealed objects appears on the monitor. Metal guns and knifes can be detected, as well as nonmetallic objects such as drugs and explosives. The image allows a view under clothes and, indeed, under the skin's surface.

Airport officials ask whether they can implement the Secure 2000 in all of the hallways leading to the terminals. If so, do they need to post a notice, and what does any notice need to say? They ask what authorities should do if the scanner reveals drugs, but not weapons.

Notes

1. *Airport and mass transit security checks.* Passengers who fly on commercial airlines must submit to unusually thorough inspections of their persons and belongings before they may approach the gate for boarding the airplane. What theory best explains this commonly accepted practice? Is it that the inspections do not amount to a "search" for Fourth Amendment purposes? That all passengers "consent" to the search when they purchase their tickets (including all the fine print buried on the back of the ticket or in the recesses of the airline websites)? See United States v. Hartwell, 296 F. Supp. 2d. 596, 602 (E.D. Pa. 2003) ("no consensus has been reached as to the grounds justifying" an airport search). As we saw earlier, drivers do not consent to random searches for any and all of their travels on the road; some special justification is required for searches of cars that are not based on individualized suspicion. Would the rationale for airport searches apply equally well to searches of subway trains and other forms of mass transit? Does the choice of method of travel reflect different levels of privacy expectations?

2. *Changing airport security, changing reasonableness*. The security practices at airports change constantly, in response to the latest efforts by terrorists and criminals to bring weapons and explosives on board flights. If the consent of the people, at least in some broad sense, is necessary to make a search "reasonable," how might the government get feedback from the public about the reasonableness of its ever-changing intrusions into traveler privacy in airports? See Andrew E. Taslitz, Fortune-Telling and the Fourth Amendment: Of Terrorism, Slippery Slopes, and Predicting the Future, 58 Rutgers L. Rev. 195 (2005).

C. GATHERING INFORMATION WITHOUT SEARCHING

Thus far, we have focused on various stops (that is, brief seizures) of persons and their property. We now turn to brief searches, the least intrusive efforts by government agents to collect private information from individuals.

Just as there are some encounters with police that do not count as a "seizure," there are some government efforts to gather information from individuals that do not amount to a "search" at all. Where there is no search, there is no constitutional requirement for the government to justify its efforts to gather information. Under the Fourth Amendment and most of its state equivalents, there is no search within the meaning of the Constitution when the government intrudes into some place or interest where the person has no "reasonable expectation of privacy." The definition contains both a subjective and an objective component. The target of the search must actually expect privacy, and that expectation must be one that society is prepared to recognize as reasonable.

This definition of a "search," now prominent in the case law of every state, derives from Katz v. United States, 389 U.S. 347 (1967). Before *Katz,* searches were defined in terms of property rights. A government agent performed a "search" within the meaning of the constitution when he or she "trespassed" on a protected area. Now under the *Katz* "reasonable expectation of privacy" test, a search might occur even if there is no trespass into a protected place. In the materials that follow, ask yourself what factors might make an expectation of privacy "reasonable."

One of the least intrusive forms of information-gathering occurs when the police simply notice what is in open view of others. Under the Fourth Amendment and its equivalents, there is no reasonable expectation of privacy in matters left within open view. Hence, no "search" has occurred to be evaluated under federal or state law. But when is an item in "open" or "plain" view?

■ STATE v. MIHAI BOBIC

996 P.2d 610 (Wash. 2000)

TALMADGE, J.

We are asked in this case to determine whether an officer's warrantless search of a commercial storage unit was constitutional when the search was made through a small, preexisting hole in an adjoining storage unit. . . . Under the circumstances of this case, we agree the evidence the officers obtained from the storage unit was in open view. . . .

Mihai Bobic and Igor Stepchuk were charged with numerous crimes arising from a sophisticated auto theft conspiracy. Bobic, Stepchuk, or their confederates stole vehicles and stripped them of their contents and key parts. They stored the stolen car parts and other stolen goods in various commercial storage facilities. Insurance carriers subsequently sold the hulks of the cars left by the thieves at auto auctions. Bobic, Stepchuk, or their confederates then purchased the hulks at those auto auctions, giving them clear tide to the vehicles. They then reassembled the vehicles with the stolen car parts and sold them.

Detective Kelly Quirin became suspicious about certain auto thefts and his investigation uncovered a possible connection between auto thefts and storage facilities. On March 1, 1994, Quirin obtained and executed a search warrant to examine certain units at a Shurgard Storage facility. After searching the units in accordance with the warrant, the facility's manager told Quirin that one of the units at his facility, unit E-71, might be connected with stolen vehicles.... On March 8, Quirin went to the storage facility with another officer and asked to look at unit E-71, which was locked. The manager let the officers into an unrented, unlocked storage unit next door to unit E-71. Upon entering the unit, the officers saw a pre-existing hole, "maybe big enough to stick your pinky finger in or a little bigger," about four feet off the ground. (The walls of the units go up to the ceiling.) Quirin looked through the hole, and without aid of a flashlight was able to see items in unit E-71. Based on this information, Quirin obtained a search warrant for unit E-71 and recovered stolen goods.

[Stepchuk and Bobic were charged with theft, trafficking in stolen property, and conspiracy.] Prior to trial, Bobic moved to suppress the evidence recovered during the search of unit E-71. During his pretrial suppression hearing, Bobic testified [that a friend rented unit E-71, but he and the friend shared the unit. Bobic placed a lock on the door of the unit. The rental agreement] permitted the manager to open a unit at any time to uncover illegal activities.[1] ... After a lengthy trial in King County Superior Court, Bobic and Stepchuk were convicted [and Bobic] appealed the lower court's denial of both his motion to suppress evidence seized from unit E-71....

Washington's constitution provides that "[no] person shall be disturbed in his private affairs, ... without authority of law." Const. Art I, §7. A violation of this right turns on whether the State has unreasonably intruded into a person's private affairs. In contrast, a search occurs under the Fourth Amendment if the government intrudes upon a reasonable expectation of privacy. Thus, Washington's "private affairs inquiry" is broader than the Fourth Amendment's "reasonable expectation of privacy inquiry."

Detective Quirin's observations do not constitute a search because the objects under observation were in "open view." Under the open view doctrine, when a law enforcement officer is able to detect something by utilization of one or more of his senses while lawfully present at the vantage point where those senses are used, that detection does not constitute a search. Here, the detective was lawfully inside the adjoining unit because the manager had given him permission to enter. Furthermore, it appears from the record that the detective's observations were made without extraordinary or invasive means and could be seen by anyone renting the unit. [Detective Quirin was able to "look into the hole with one eye"; not utilizing a flashlight because the hole "wasn't big enough to be able to look at to have the flashlight and your eye next to it to see in."]

Bobic contends the search here must nonetheless fail because it invaded a protected privacy interest and was more intrusive than the search in *State v. Rose,* 909 P.2d 280 (1996). In *Rose,* the officer's search was likely *more* intrusive because he

1. The rental agreement states, in pertinent part: "... The Storage Unit may not be used for any unlawful purpose ... nor will Tenant keep in the Storage Unit any ... substances whose storage or use is regulated or prohibited by local, state or federal law or regulation.... Tenant shall give the Landlord permission to enter the Storage Unit at any time for the purpose of removing and disposing of any property in the Storage Unit in violation of this provision.... Tenant represents to Landlord that all personal property to be stored by Tenant in the Storage Unit will belong to Tenant only, and not to any third parties...."

looked with the aid of a flashlight through a window into the defendant's residence during the evening. Here, the detective did not peer through a curtained window; he did not wait until something incriminating came into sight or hearing; and he did not attempt to create a better vantage point.

Moreover, a commercial storage unit is not the kind of location entitled to special privacy protection. For example, a person's home is entitled to heightened constitutional protection relative to other locations. We decline to determine that a commercial storage unit has any special protected status. . . .

In this case, notwithstanding the troubling image of a police officer peering through a peephole in a storage unit, the trial court did not err in denying Bobic's motion to suppress because there was no "search"; the contents of the unit were in open view as that doctrine is understood in our law where the officer was legally at the vantage point, the vantage point was not artificially improved, and the officer perceived what he did with his unaided vision. . . .

STEVEN DEWAYNE BOND v. UNITED STATES

529 U.S. 334 (2000)

REHNQUIST, C.J.*

This case presents the question whether a law enforcement officer's physical manipulation of a bus passenger's carry-on luggage violated the Fourth Amendment's proscription against unreasonable searches. We hold that it did.

Petitioner Steven Dewayne Bond was a passenger on a Greyhound bus that left California bound for Little Rock, Arkansas. The bus stopped, as it was required to do, at the permanent Border Patrol checkpoint in Sierra Blanca, Texas. Border Patrol Agent Cesar Cantu boarded the bus to check the immigration status of its passengers. After reaching the back of the bus, having satisfied himself that the passengers were lawfully in the United States, Agent Cantu began walking toward the front. Along the way, he squeezed the soft luggage which passengers had placed in the overhead storage space above the seats.

Petitioner was seated four or five rows from the back of the bus. As Agent Cantu inspected the luggage in the compartment above petitioner's seat, he squeezed a green canvas bag and noticed that it contained a "brick-like" object. Petitioner admitted that the bag was his and agreed to allow Agent Cantu to open it. Upon opening the bag, Agent Cantu discovered a "brick" of methamphetamine. The brick had been wrapped in duct tape until it was oval-shaped and then rolled in a pair of pants.

Petitioner was indicted for conspiracy to possess, and possession with intent to distribute, methamphetamine. . . . He moved to suppress the drugs, arguing that Agent Cantu conducted an illegal search of his bag. Petitioner's motion was denied, and the District Court found him guilty on both counts and sentenced him to 57 months in prison.

* [Justices Stevens, O'Connor, Kennedy, Souter, Thomas, and Ginsburg joined in this opinion. — EDS.]

[It] is undisputed here that petitioner possessed a privacy interest in his bag. But the Government asserts that by exposing his bag to the public, petitioner lost a reasonable expectation that his bag would not be physically manipulated. The Government relies on our decisions in California v. Ciraolo, 476 U.S. 207 (1986), and Florida v. Riley, 488 U.S. 445 (1989), for the proposition that matters open to public observation are not protected by the Fourth Amendment. In *Ciraolo,* we held that police observation of a backyard from a plane flying at an altitude of 1,000 feet did not violate a reasonable expectation of privacy. Similarly, in *Riley,* we relied on *Ciraolo* to hold that police observation of a greenhouse in a home's curtilage from a helicopter passing at an altitude of 400 feet did not violate the Fourth Amendment. We reasoned that the property was "not necessarily protected from inspection that involves no physical invasion," and determined that because any member of the public could have lawfully observed the defendants' property by flying overhead, the defendants' expectation of privacy was "not reasonable and not one that society is prepared to honor."

But *Ciraolo* and *Riley* are different from this case because they involved only visual, as opposed to tactile, observation. Physically invasive inspection is simply more intrusive than purely visual inspection. For example, in Terry v. Ohio, 392 U.S. 1 (1968), we stated that a "careful [tactile] exploration of the outer surfaces of a person's clothing all over his or her body" is a "serious intrusion upon the sanctity of the person, which may inflict great indignity and arouse strong resentment, and is not to be undertaken lightly." Although Agent Cantu did not "frisk" petitioner's person, he did conduct a probing tactile examination of petitioner's carry-on luggage. Obviously, petitioner's bag was not part of his person. But travelers are particularly concerned about their carry-on luggage; they generally use it to transport personal items that, for whatever reason, they prefer to keep close at hand.

Here, petitioner concedes that, by placing his bag in the overhead compartment, he could expect that it would be exposed to certain kinds of touching and handling. But petitioner argues that Agent Cantu's physical manipulation of his luggage "far exceeded the casual contact [petitioner] could have expected from other passengers." The Government counters that it did not.

Our Fourth Amendment analysis embraces two questions. First, we ask whether the individual, by his conduct, has exhibited an actual expectation of privacy; that is, whether he has shown that he sought to preserve something as private. Here, petitioner sought to preserve privacy by using an opaque bag and placing that bag directly above his seat. Second, we inquire whether the individual's expectation of privacy is "one that society is prepared to recognize as reasonable."[2] When a bus passenger places a bag in an overhead bin, he expects that other passengers or bus employees may move it for one reason or another. Thus, a bus passenger clearly expects that his bag may be handled. He does not expect that other passengers or bus employees will, as a matter of course, feel the bag in an exploratory manner. But this is exactly what the agent did here. We therefore hold that the agent's physical manipulation of petitioner's bag violated the Fourth Amendment.

2. The parties properly agree that the subjective intent of the law enforcement officer is irrelevant in determining whether that officer's actions violate the Fourth Amendment. See Whren v. United States, 517 U.S. 806 (1996) (stating that "we have been unwilling to entertain Fourth Amendment challenges based on the actual motivations of individual officers"). This principle applies to the agent's acts in this case as well; the issue is not his state of mind, but the objective effect of his actions.

BREYER, J., dissenting.*

Does a traveler who places a soft-sided bag in the shared overhead storage compartment of a bus have a "reasonable expectation" that strangers will not push, pull, prod, squeeze, or otherwise manipulate his luggage? Unlike the majority, I believe that he does not.

Petitioner argues . . . that even if bags in overhead bins are subject to general "touching" and "handling," this case is special because Agent Cantu's physical manipulation of petitioner's luggage far exceeded the casual contact he could have expected from other passengers. But the record shows the contrary. . . . On the occasion at issue here, Agent Cantu "felt a green bag" which had "a brick-like object in it." He explained that he felt "the edges of the brick in the bag," and that . . . "when squeezed, you could feel an outline of something of a different mass inside of it." Although the agent acknowledged that his practice was to "squeeze [bags] very hard," he testified that his touch ordinarily was not "[hard] enough to break something inside that might be fragile." Petitioner also testified that Agent Cantu "reached for my bag, and he shook it a little, and squeezed it."

How does the "squeezing" just described differ from the treatment that overhead luggage is likely to receive from strangers in a world of travel that is somewhat less gentle than it used to be? I think not at all. Eagan, Familiar Anger Takes Flight with Airline Tussles, Boston Herald, Aug. 15, 1999, p.8 ("It's dog-eat-dog trying to cram half your home into overhead compartments"). The trial court . . . viewed the agent's activity as "minimally intrusive touching." . . .

Privacy itself implies the exclusion of uninvited strangers, not just strangers who work for the Government. Hence, an individual cannot reasonably expect privacy in respect to objects or activities that he knowingly exposes to the public. . . . Of course, the agent's purpose here — searching for drugs — differs dramatically from the intention of a driver or fellow passenger who squeezes a bag in the process of making more room for another parcel. But in determining whether an expectation of privacy is reasonable, it is the effect, not the purpose, that matters. Few individuals with something to hide wish to expose that something to the police, however careless or indifferent they may be in respect to discovery by other members of the public. Hence, a Fourth Amendment rule that turns on purpose could prevent police alone from intruding where other strangers freely tread. . . .

Nor can I accept the majority's effort to distinguish "tactile" from "visual" interventions, even assuming that distinction matters here. Whether tactile manipulation (say, of the exterior of luggage) is more intrusive or less intrusive than visual observation (say, through a lighted window) necessarily depends on the particular circumstances.

If we are to depart from established legal principles, we should not begin here. At best, this decision will lead to a constitutional jurisprudence of "squeezes," thereby complicating further already complex Fourth Amendment law, increasing the difficulty of deciding ordinary criminal matters, and hindering the administrative guidance (with its potential for control of unreasonable police practices) that a less complicated jurisprudence might provide. At worst, this case will deter law enforcement officers searching for drugs near borders from using even the most non-intrusive touch to help investigate publicly exposed bags. At the same time, the

* [Justice Scalia joined in this opinion. — EDS.]

ubiquity of nongovernmental pushes, prods, and squeezes (delivered by driver, attendant, passenger, or some other stranger) means that this decision cannot do much to protect true privacy. Rather, the traveler who wants to place a bag in a shared overhead bin and yet safeguard its contents from public touch should plan to pack those contents in a suitcase with hard sides, irrespective of the Court's decision today. For these reasons, I dissent.

Notes

1. *Items in plain view: majority position.* If an officer sees an item in plain view, no search has occurred under state or federal law. To qualify for plain view treatment, the police officer must view the item from a place where she has a right to be. The officer might have legal access to the place because it is open to the general public — some state courts, such as those in Florida and Hawaii, call this situation "open view" rather than "plain view." An officer might also have reason to view some item from a vantage point not open to the general public. For instance, the officer might be executing an arrest warrant or might be present in a "community caretaker" capacity. If the officer has a proper reason to be in that non-public location, the discovery of new information from that vantage point is not considered a search. In either setting, plain view or open view, the courts conclude that the target of the investigation has no reasonable expectation of privacy in the item within view of the officer.

What matters other than the location of the officer making the observation? As the Washington court indicates in *Bobic,* the amount of police effort involved in reaching the location might matter. The use of technological enhancements such as flashlights might matter. The nature of the location (a home versus a commercial storage facility) could matter. The U.S. Supreme Court has indicated in several cases that any physical movement of an item makes it much more difficult to claim that the item observed was in plain view. See Arizona v. Hicks, 480 U.S. 321 (1987) (stereo receiver moved inches to observe serial number was not in plain view). Does the opinion in Bond v. United States offer any guidance on the relevance of the *purpose* of the person observing or touching an item? Do you think that Bobic or Bond makes the stronger case that the government conducted a search?

2. *Location of the item; seizing versus viewing.* After an officer has seen some contraband or evidence of a crime in plain view, he may want to seize the item. Even when there has been no "search" of an item in plain view, there are some additional requirements the officer must meet before seizing the item. His ability to complete the seizure will depend primarily on where the item is located. If it is located in an unprotected area (such as the open bed of a pickup truck or an apartment where the officer already has obtained legal access) the officer may seize the item so long as there is probable cause to believe that it is contraband or evidence of a crime or otherwise subject to seizure. If the item is located in a protected area (such as the interior of a building that the officer observes from a point outside), most courts require the officer to obtain a search warrant or to explain why an exception to the warrant requirement is necessary. See Coolidge v. New Hampshire, 403 U.S. 443 (1971) (warrantless seizure of item in plain view is acceptable if officer observes item from lawful location, the discovery is inadvertent, its incriminating nature is immediately apparent, and officer has lawful right of access to the object).

3. *Incriminating nature of the item in plain view.* State and federal courts also require that the incriminating nature of the item in plain view be "immediately apparent" before the officer can seize an item in plain view. When the item in plain view is an illicit drug or other contraband, the incriminating nature of the item is easy to see. In other cases, the incriminating nature of the item might not be apparent to the average observer, but the police officer conducting the search will often know enough about the ongoing investigation to link the items she sees to the crime she is investigating. See State v. Chrisman, 514 N.W.2d 57 (Iowa 1994) (tennis shoes incriminating in light of footprints at crime scene). The incriminating nature of the item is "immediately apparent" if there is probable cause to believe that it is evidence of a crime.

4. *Police "inadvertence" in obtaining the plain view.* Under federal law and the law of most states, the police may observe and seize an item in plain view, even if the officer intended to find it. See Horton v. California, 496 U.S. 128 (1990):

> Evenhanded law enforcement is best achieved by the application of objective standards of conduct, rather than standards that depend upon the subjective state of mind of the officer. The fact that an officer is interested in an item of evidence and fully expects to find it in the course of a search should not invalidate its seizure if the search is confined in area and duration by the terms of a warrant or a valid exception to the warrant requirement.

Roughly 20 states take up a suggestion in older U.S. Supreme Court cases and insist that the police officer "inadvertently" discover the item in plain view before the officer can seize it. If the officer had reason to expect the discovery, he cannot seize the item. See Commonwealth v. Balicki, 762 N.E.2d 290 (Mass. 2002). Why don't most courts care about the motives of the police officer in obtaining the plain view? See State v. Nieves, 999 A.2d 389 (N.H. 2010). What police purpose might be objectionable? Is this debate over "inadvertence" the same as the disagreement reviewed above over "pretextual" stops, or are different interests at stake here?

5. *Plain smell and plain hearing.* If it is possible for an officer to notice an object in "plain view" without conducting a search, is it possible for the officer to notice a "plain smell" without conducting a search? There are cases in which the officer, standing in a proper location, smells something that creates some suspicion or evidence of a crime. State v. Rodriguez, 945 A.2d 676 (N.H. 2008) (officers who smell burning marijuana from exterior of residence need no warrant before entering; reviews divided case law on issue). The same can be said of an investigation based on something an officer hears when standing in a legally sanctioned location (plain hearing): There is no "search" here in the constitutional sense. We will consider the "plain feel" doctrine in section D of this chapter.

Problem 2-6. Plain View from a Ladder

Special Agent Forsythe became aware that football gambling forms were circulating in the town of Farrell. After receiving a tip about the source of the gambling forms, Forsythe began to keep watch at a local print shop. During one October evening, Forsythe noticed that the presses inside the shop were operating, but due to the location and size of the windows, he was unable to observe what was being printed from his position off the premises. The sills of the windows were 7 feet off the ground, so they prevented any view into the shop by someone standing on the ground outside the building. To remedy this problem, Forsythe mounted a 4-foot ladder that he placed on the railroad tracks abutting the print shop property. From a distance of 15 to 20 feet, he observed through a side window some "Las Vegas" football parlay sheets being run off the press. Did Agent Forsythe conduct a "search" within the meaning of state or federal constitutions? Compare Commonwealth v. Hernley, 263 A.2d 904 (Pa. Super. Ct. 1970).

Problem 2-7. The Friendly Skies

Officer Greg Bohlen, an undercover narcotics investigator, received an anonymous telephone call informing him that Bernard Henderson was cultivating and selling marijuana from his home. Bohlen watched the residence carefully for several days but did not observe any illegal activity. Several months later, another officer received a second anonymous call implicating Henderson in marijuana trafficking. Bohlen was unable to obtain a law enforcement helicopter to fly over the property, so he arranged for the use of a helicopter operated by a television station, KUSA. KUSA agreed to provide a helicopter to Officer Bohlen in exchange for the right to report on the drug investigation. On the morning of the scheduled flyover, Bohlen received another anonymous telephone call about Henderson, indicating that Henderson was growing five-foot-tall marijuana plants in a shed behind his house. Officer Bohlen, the helicopter pilot, and a photographer for KUSA made four or five passes over Henderson's residence during a period of approximately five minutes. Officer Bohlen observed a shed, located about 100 yards away from the house. The shed had a plastic roof with "green plant material" (as Bohlen later described it in a warrant application) growing underneath the plastic. Bohlen stated that the helicopter stayed between 500 and 700 feet in altitude. He based his altitude estimate on his experience flying in helicopters. Although he could not describe the plants in detail, based on his special education in drug identification and on his law enforcement experience, Officer Bohlen concluded that the plants were marijuana. A later warranted search of the property and the house produced marijuana plants, along with guns, scales, and other drug paraphernalia. The defendant has filed a motion to suppress the evidence. Will the judge grant it? Compare Henderson v. People, 879 P.2d 383 (Colo. 1994).

Notes

1. *Flyovers and reasonable expectations of privacy: majority position.* Recall that under the Fourth Amendment and its state equivalents, the government has not engaged in a search if it has invaded no "reasonable expectation of privacy." One difficult question about the definition of a search arises when government agents place themselves in unusual — but not necessarily illegal — positions for observing wrongdoing. A situation of this sort that appears frequently in appellate cases is the "flyover" of property by police officers searching for evidence of a crime.

In Florida v. Riley, 488 U.S. 445 (1988), the Supreme Court determined that police observing the defendant's backyard from a helicopter flying in legal airspace did not conduct a search for Fourth Amendment purposes. The defendant lived in a mobile home located on five acres of property. A greenhouse near the residence was obscured from view by a fence, trees, and shrubs. As the result of an anonymous tip, a police helicopter made two passes over the property at an altitude of 400 feet. The observing officer viewed what he thought was marijuana growing in the greenhouse, because two roof panels were missing. One of the primary factors in determining whether the defendant's expectation of privacy was unreasonable was that the helicopter was flying in navigable airspace within the Federal Aviation Administration guidelines. Thus, the Court relied on the fact that the observation itself was legal. The Court also considered the minimal intrusiveness of the observations: the helicopter never "interfered with respondent's normal use of the greenhouse or other parts of the curtilage." Furthermore, "no intimate details connected with the use of the home or curtilage were observed, and there was no undue noise, and no wind, dust, or threat of injury." See also California v. Ciraolo, 476 U.S. 207 (1986) (no search when police officer observes property from fixed-wing aircraft 1,000 feet above property in legal airspace). Do you believe the Supreme Court should have ruled in *Ciraolo* and *Riley* that the government conducted a search? Should the answer depend on whether the police have routine access to helicopters and planes?

Virtually all state courts have agreed with the U.S. Supreme Court's view that a flyover is not a "search" so long as the police aircraft stays within airspace where private aircraft could travel and does not create too much noise, dust, or threat of injury. But see State v. Bryant, 2008 VT 39 (Vt. 2008) (police needed to obtain warrant before helicopter flyover of residential property in search of marijuana, based on reading of state constitution). How might a defendant dispute the government's factual claim about the flight pattern of the aircraft?

2. *Subjective expectations of privacy.* Many courts asking whether government agents have engaged in a search employ a two-part analysis taken from the concurring opinion of Justice Harlan in Katz v. United States, 389 U.S. 347 (1967). A litigant hoping to establish a "search" under the Fourth Amendment must meet "a twofold requirement, first that a person [has] exhibited an actual (subjective) expectation of privacy and, second, that the expectation be one that society is prepared to recognize as 'reasonable.'" Later opinions of the U.S. Supreme Court and of state courts repeat this formulation, but they also suggest that the objective component alone might be enough: a subjective expectation of privacy will not always be a precondition to a conclusion that a search has occurred. See United States v. White, 401 U.S. 745 (1971). Could you imagine courts holding otherwise, that is, insisting on a subjective expectation of privacy before finding that a search took place?

3. *Legal entitlement versus likelihood of observation.* Suppose a litigant could show that flyovers at 500 feet above the property in question are very rare. In what way would this be relevant to the definition of a search? Would such a defendant need to argue that there is a legitimate expectation of lax enforcement of the narcotics laws? Could there be some moral (but extralegal) objection to the police conduct that makes more reasonable an expectation of avoiding such scrutiny?

4. *Police observation versus public observation.* Let us assume that reasonable and law-abiding people leave some things visible to a few members of the public that they would rather not expose to the sustained scrutiny of the police. Can police officers make observations from any place open to the public, or should they be expected to remain outside some areas open to some members of the public? Does the defendant's argument on the "search" issue get stronger when police officers

flying over a property must apply their expertise to interpret what they see below (such as an assertion that a building is "typical" of those used to grow marijuana)?

5. *Other sense enhancements.* So long as the government agent remains in a position properly available to her, many state courts allow the agent to use various devices to get a clearer or closer look at the items in plain view. The clearest cases involve commonly used devices such as flashlights. See State v. Brooks, 446 S.E.2d 579 (N.C. 1994) (officer walking up to car and shining light inside is not a search). A few state and federal courts have been willing to go farther, allowing government agents to use vision-enhancing devices not readily available to most viewers. See Dow Chemical Co. v. United States, 476 U.S. 227 (1986) (no search when agents in airplane over chemical plant use precision aerial-mapping camera). See Chapter 7.

6. *Garbage and abandoned property.* Reasonable expectations of privacy do not attach to property or activities in "plain view" or "open view." Thus, efforts to see such property are not searches in the constitutional sense. The same can be said for property that a person has abandoned, even though it does not lie within plain view of the public or government agents.

The U.S. Supreme Court in California v. Greenwood, 486 U.S. 35 (1988), held that there is no reasonable expectation of privacy in trash put out for collection; thus, there is no constitutionally relevant search if government agents inspect the trash. Over half the states have adopted this same view. See State v. Sampson, 765 A.2d 629 (Md. 2001) (officer collected trash left at curb by suspected drug dealer for six days; not a search). A smaller group (fewer than a dozen) have held in various contexts that there is a reasonable expectation of privacy in garbage, while a good number of high state courts still have not confronted the issue. See Beltz v. State, 221 P.3d 328 (Alaska 2009) (expectation of privacy in garbage placed by curb is reasonable under state constitution).

Privacy interests in a home or building also extend to the area under the eaves and immediately surrounding the building, an area known as the "curtilage." Thus, it could matter where the trash is placed. If the police inspect garbage kept in containers beside a home prior to the day appointed for collection, have they conducted a "search"? For a survey of various state court holdings regarding garbage searches, see the web extension for this chapter at *http://www.crimpro.com/extension/ch02*.

Some have pointed out that the government, under the reasoning of *Greenwood*, can defeat a widely shared expectation of privacy simply by announcing that it plans to conduct a particular form of investigation, thus defeating any expectation of privacy. See Anthony G. Amsterdam, Perspectives on the Fourth Amendment, 58 Minn. L. Rev. 349, 384 (1974). If most Americans today still have an expectation of privacy in their curbside garbage bags, isn't there a reasonable expectation of privacy regardless of what the Supreme Court held in *Greenwood*? See Christopher Slobogin & Joseph Schumacher, Reasonable Expectations of Privacy and Autonomy in Fourth Amendment Cases: An Empirical Look at "Understandings Recognized and Permitted by Society," 42 Duke L.J. 727 (1993) (public survey measuring perceived intrusiveness of various investigative techniques). Should the courts announce decisions about reasonable expectations of privacy on a tentative basis, and overrule themselves if most people don't take the decision to heart?

7. *Computer "trash" cans.* Most electronic message systems allow the computer user to delete messages, but the deleted messages are recoverable until further events take place (e.g., the user turns off the system, or some manager of the

computer system empties the electronic "trash can"). Similarly, it is possible under some circumstances to recover copies of electronic documents or files that a user has attempted to delete. If the government discovers evidence of a crime in these deleted but recoverable messages or files, was there a search at all? If there was a search, was it justified by implied consent?

D. BRIEF SEARCHES OF INDIVIDUALS

The police conduct a great variety of searches, ranging from brief and less intrusive searches of persons or property, up to extensive and very invasive searches. The number of legal standards — constitutional and otherwise — available to limit these searches is not nearly so large. As you read in this section about brief searches of individuals, consider whether the fit between police practices and available legal standards is sufficiently tight and whether different legal standards are likely to change actual behavior.

1. *Frisks for Weapons*

Police encounter people every day who carry hidden handguns. One time-honored police response to this threat is the "frisk," a brief search of a suspect's body. The frisk was a reality long before American courts resolved the question of whether or how the law would regulate the practice. The following case lays out the constitutional controls over frisks, controls at work in every U.S. jurisdiction.

■ JOHN TERRY v. OHIO
392 U.S. 1 (1968)

WARREN, C.J.*

This case presents serious questions concerning the role of the Fourth Amendment in the confrontation on the street between the citizen and the policeman investigating suspicious circumstances.

Petitioner Terry was convicted of carrying a concealed weapon. [The] prosecution introduced in evidence two revolvers and a number of bullets seized from Terry and a codefendant, Richard Chilton, by Cleveland Police Detective Martin McFadden. At the hearing on the motion to suppress this evidence, Officer McFadden testified that while he was patrolling in plain clothes in downtown Cleveland at approximately 2:30 in the afternoon, [he noticed two men, Chilton and Terry, who "didn't look right."] His interest aroused, Officer McFadden took up a post of observation in the entrance to a store 300 to 400 feet away from the two men. "I get more purpose to watch them when I seen their movements," he testified. [One of the men walked away from the corner and past some stores, paused for a moment

* [Justices Black, Brennan, Stewart, Fortas, and Marshall joined in this opinion. Justices Harlan and White concurred in the result. — EDS.]

and looked in a store window, then walked on a short distance, turned around and walked back toward the corner, pausing once again to look in the same store window. Then the second man went through the same series of motions. Each of the two men repeated this ritual five or six times. A third man, Katz, approached them and engaged them briefly in conversation, then walked away. Chilton and Terry resumed their earlier routine. After this had gone on for 10 to 12 minutes, the two men walked off together, following the route taken earlier by Katz.]

By this time Officer McFadden had become thoroughly suspicious. He testified that . . . he suspected the two men of "casing a job, a stick-up," and that he considered it his duty as a police officer to investigate further. He added that he feared "they may have a gun." Thus, Officer McFadden followed Chilton and Terry and saw them stop in front of Zucker's store to talk to [Katz]. Deciding that the situation was ripe for direct action, Officer McFadden approached the three men, identified himself as a police officer and asked for their names. . . . When the men "mumbled something" in response to his inquiries, Officer McFadden grabbed petitioner Terry, spun him around so that they were facing the other two, with Terry between McFadden and the others, and patted down the outside of his clothing. In the left breast pocket of Terry's overcoat Officer McFadden felt a pistol. He reached inside the overcoat pocket, but was unable to remove the gun. At this point, keeping Terry between himself and the others, the officer ordered all three men to enter Zucker's store. As they went in, he removed Terry's overcoat completely, removed a .38-caliber revolver from the pocket and ordered all three men to face the wall with their hands raised. Officer McFadden proceeded to pat down the outer clothing of Chilton and [Katz]. He discovered another revolver in the outer pocket of Chilton's overcoat, but no weapons were found on Katz. The officer testified that he only patted the men down to see whether they had weapons, and that he did not put his hands beneath the outer garments of either Terry or Chilton until he felt their guns. . . . Chilton and Terry were formally charged with carrying concealed weapons.

[The trial court concluded that McFadden did not have probable cause to search or arrest the men, but nonetheless upheld the validity of the search.] The court distinguished between an investigatory "stop" and an arrest, and between a "frisk" of the outer clothing for weapons and a full-blown search for evidence of crime. The frisk, it held, was essential to the proper performance of the officer's investigatory duties, for without it "the answer to the police officer may be a bullet, and a loaded pistol discovered during the frisk is admissible." [The court found Terry and Chilton guilty in a bench trial.]

I.

The Fourth Amendment provides that "the right of the people to be secure in their persons, houses, papers, and effects, against unreasonable searches and seizures, shall not be violated. . . ." This inestimable right of personal security belongs as much to the citizen on the streets of our cities as to the homeowner closeted in his study to dispose of his secret affairs. [However,] what the Constitution forbids is not all searches and seizures, but unreasonable searches and seizures. Unquestionably petitioner was entitled to the protection of the Fourth Amendment as he walked down the street in Cleveland. The question is whether in all the circumstances of this on-the-street encounter, his right to personal security was violated by an unreasonable search and seizure.

[It] is frequently argued that in dealing with the rapidly unfolding and often dangerous situations on city streets the police are in need of an escalating set of flexible responses, graduated in relation to the amount of information they possess. For this purpose it is urged that distinctions should be made between a "stop" and an "arrest" (or a "seizure" of a person), and between a "frisk" and a "search." Thus, it is argued, the police should be allowed to "stop" a person and detain him briefly for questioning upon suspicion that he may be connected with criminal activity. Upon suspicion that the person may be armed, the police should have the power to "frisk" him for weapons. If the "stop" and the "frisk" give rise to probable cause to believe that the suspect has committed a crime, then the police should be empowered to make a formal "arrest," and a full incident "search" of the person. This scheme is justified in part upon the notion that a "stop" and a "frisk" amount to a mere minor inconvenience and petty indignity, which can properly be imposed upon the citizen in the interest of effective law enforcement on the basis of a police officer's suspicion.

On the other side the argument is made that the authority of the police must be strictly circumscribed by the law of arrest and search as it has developed to date in the traditional jurisprudence of the Fourth Amendment. It is contended with some force that there is not — and cannot be — a variety of police activity which does not depend solely upon the voluntary cooperation of the citizen and yet which stops short of an arrest based upon probable cause to make such an arrest. The heart of the Fourth Amendment, the argument runs, is a severe requirement of specific justification for any intrusion upon protected personal security, coupled with a highly developed system of judicial controls to enforce upon the agents of the State the commands of the Constitution. Acquiescence by the courts in the compulsion inherent in the field interrogation practices at issue here, it is urged, would constitute an abdication of judicial control over, and indeed an encouragement of, substantial interference with liberty and personal security by police officers whose judgment is necessarily colored by their primary involvement in the often competitive enterprise of ferreting out crime. This, it is argued, can only serve to exacerbate police-community tensions in the crowded centers of our Nation's cities.

In this context we approach the issues in this case mindful of the limitations of the judicial function in controlling the myriad daily situations in which policemen and citizens confront each other on the street. . . . Street encounters between citizens and police officers are incredibly rich in diversity. They range from wholly friendly exchanges of pleasantries or mutually useful information to hostile confrontations of armed men involving arrests, or injuries, or loss of life. Moreover, hostile confrontations are not all of a piece. Some of them begin in a friendly enough manner, only to take a different turn upon the injection of some unexpected element into the conversation. Encounters are initiated by the police for a wide variety of purposes, some of which are wholly unrelated to a desire to prosecute for crime. . . .

II.

Our first task is to establish at what point in this encounter the Fourth Amendment becomes relevant. That is, we must decide whether and when Officer McFadden "seized" Terry and whether and when he conducted a "search." There is some suggestion in the use of such terms as "stop" and "frisk" that such police conduct is outside the purview of the Fourth Amendment because neither action rises to the level of a "search" or "seizure" within the meaning of the Constitution. We emphatically reject this notion. It is . . . nothing less than sheer torture of the English language to suggest that a careful exploration of the outer surfaces of a person's clothing all over his or her body in an attempt to find weapons is not a "search." . . . It is a serious intrusion upon the sanctity of the person, which may inflict great indignity and arouse strong resentment, and it is not to be undertaken lightly.

The danger in the logic which proceeds upon distinctions between a . . . "frisk" and a "search" is twofold. It seeks to isolate from constitutional scrutiny the initial stages of the contact between the policeman and the citizen. And by suggesting a rigid all-or-nothing model of justification and regulation under the Amendment, it obscures the utility of limitations upon the scope, as well as the initiation, of police action as a means of constitutional regulation. [A] search which is reasonable at its inception may violate the Fourth Amendment by virtue of its intolerable intensity and scope. The scope of the search must be strictly tied to and justified by the circumstances which rendered its initiation permissible. . . .

In this case there can be no question, then, that Officer McFadden "seized" petitioner and subjected him to a "search" when he took hold of him and patted down the outer surfaces of his clothing. We must decide whether at that point it was reasonable for Officer McFadden to have interfered with petitioner's personal security as he did. And in determining whether the seizure and search were "unreasonable" our inquiry is a dual one — whether the officer's action was justified at its inception, and whether it was reasonably related in scope to the circumstances which justified the interference in the first place.

III.

If this case involved police conduct subject to the Warrant Clause of the Fourth Amendment, we would have to ascertain whether "probable cause" existed to justify the search and seizure which took place. However, that is not the case. We do not retreat from our holdings that the police must, whenever practicable, obtain advance judicial approval of searches and seizures through the warrant procedure, or that in most instances failure to comply with the warrant requirement can only be excused by exigent circumstances. But we deal here with an entire rubric of police conduct — necessarily swift action predicated upon the on-the-spot observations of the officer on the beat — which historically has not been, and as a practical matter could not be, subjected to the warrant procedure. Instead, the conduct involved in this case must be tested by the Fourth Amendment's general proscription against unreasonable searches and seizures.

Nonetheless, the notions which underlie both the warrant procedure and the requirement of probable cause remain fully relevant in this context. In order to assess the reasonableness of Officer McFadden's conduct as a general proposition, it is necessary first to focus upon the governmental interest which allegedly justifies official intrusion upon the constitutionally protected interests of the private citizen, for there is no ready test for determining reasonableness other than by balancing the need to search [or seize] against the invasion which the search or seizure entails. And in justifying the particular intrusion the police officer must be able to point to specific and articulable facts which, taken together with rational inferences from those facts, reasonably warrant that intrusion. [When a judge assesses the reasonableness of a search or seizure,] it is imperative that the facts be judged against an objective standard: would the facts available to the officer at the moment of the seizure or the search warrant a man of reasonable caution in the belief that the action taken was appropriate? Anything less would invite intrusions upon constitutionally guaranteed rights based on nothing more substantial than inarticulate hunches, a result this Court has consistently refused to sanction. And simple good faith on the part of the arresting officer is not enough. If subjective good faith alone were the test, the protections of the Fourth Amendment would evaporate, and the people would be secure in their persons, houses, papers, and effects, only in the discretion of the police.

Applying these principles to this case, we consider first the nature and extent of the governmental interests involved. One general interest is of course that of effective crime prevention and detection; it is this interest which underlies the recognition that a police officer may in appropriate circumstances and in an appropriate manner approach a person for purposes of investigating possibly criminal behavior even though there is no probable cause to make an arrest. [In this case, it] would have been poor police work indeed for an officer of 30 years' experience in the detection of thievery from stores in this same neighborhood to have failed to investigate this behavior further.

The crux of this case, however, is not the propriety of Officer McFadden's taking steps to investigate petitioner's suspicious behavior, but rather, whether there was justification for McFadden's invasion of Terry's personal security by searching him for weapons in the course of that investigation. We are now concerned with more than the governmental interest in investigating crime; in addition, there is the more immediate interest of the police officer in taking steps to assure himself that the person with whom he is dealing is not armed with a weapon that could unexpectedly and fatally be used against him. Certainly it would be unreasonable to require that police officers take unnecessary risks in the performance of their duties. American criminals have a long tradition of armed violence, and every year in this country many law enforcement officers are killed in the line of duty, and thousands more are wounded. Virtually all of these deaths and a substantial portion of the injuries are inflicted with guns and knives.

In view of these facts, we cannot blind ourselves to the need for law enforcement officers to protect themselves and other prospective victims of violence in situations where they may lack probable cause for an arrest. When an officer is justified in believing that the individual whose suspicious behavior he is investigating at close range is armed and presently dangerous to the officer or to others, it would appear to be clearly unreasonable to deny the officer the power to take necessary measures to determine whether the person is in fact carrying a weapon and to neutralize the threat of physical harm.

We must still consider, however, the nature and quality of the intrusion on individual rights which must be accepted if police officers are to be conceded the right to search for weapons in situations where probable cause to arrest for crime is lacking. Even a limited search of the outer clothing for weapons constitutes a severe, though brief, intrusion upon cherished personal security, and it must surely be an annoying, frightening, and perhaps humiliating experience. . . .

Petitioner does not argue that a police officer should refrain from making any investigation of suspicious circumstances until such time as he has probable cause to make an arrest; nor does he deny that police officers in properly discharging their investigative function may find themselves confronting persons who might well be armed and dangerous. Moreover, he does not say that an officer is always unjustified in searching a suspect to discover weapons. Rather, he says it is unreasonable for the policeman to take that step until such time as the situation evolves to a point where there is probable cause to make an arrest. When that point has been reached, petitioner would concede the officer's right to conduct a search of the suspect for weapons, fruits or instrumentalities of the crime, or "mere" evidence, incident to the arrest.

[The problem with this line of reasoning, however, is that] it fails to take account of traditional limitations upon the scope of searches, and thus recognizes no distinction in purpose, character, and extent between a search incident to an arrest and a limited search for weapons. The former, although justified in part by the acknowledged necessity to protect the arresting officer from assault with a concealed weapon, is also justified on other grounds, and can therefore involve a relatively extensive exploration of the person. A search for weapons in the absence of probable cause to arrest, however, must, like any other search, be strictly circumscribed by the exigencies which justify its initiation. Thus it must be limited to that which is necessary for the discovery of weapons which might be used to harm the officer or others nearby, and may realistically be characterized as something less than a "full" search, even though it remains a serious intrusion. . . .

Our evaluation of the proper balance that has to be struck in this type of case leads us to conclude that there must be a narrowly drawn authority to permit a reasonable search for weapons for the protection of the police officer, where he has reason to believe that he is dealing with an armed and dangerous individual, regardless of whether he has probable cause to arrest the individual for a crime. The officer need not be absolutely certain that the individual is armed; the issue is whether a reasonably prudent man in the circumstances would be warranted in the belief that his safety or that of others was in danger. And in determining whether the officer acted reasonably in such circumstances, due weight must be given, not to his inchoate and unparticularized suspicion or "hunch," but to the specific reasonable inferences which he is entitled to draw from the facts in light of his experience.

IV.

We must now examine the conduct of Officer McFadden in this case to determine whether his search and seizure of petitioner were reasonable, both at their inception and as conducted. He had observed Terry, together with Chilton and another man, acting in a manner he took to be preface to a "stick-up." We think on the facts and circumstances Officer McFadden detailed before the trial judge a reasonably prudent man would have been warranted in believing petitioner was armed and thus presented a threat to the officer's safety while he was investigating his suspicious behavior. The actions of Terry and Chilton were consistent with McFadden's hypothesis that these men were contemplating a daylight robbery — which, it is reasonable to assume, would be likely to involve the use of weapons. . . . We cannot say his decision at that point to seize Terry and pat his clothing for weapons was the product of a volatile or inventive imagination, or was undertaken simply as an act of harassment; the record evidences the tempered act of a policeman who in the course of an investigation had to make a quick decision as to how to protect himself and others from possible danger, and took limited steps to do so.

The manner in which the seizure and search were conducted is, of course, as vital a part of the inquiry as whether they were warranted at all. The Fourth Amendment proceeds as much by limitations upon the scope of governmental action as by imposing preconditions upon its initiation. . . . We need not develop at length in this case, however, the limitations which the Fourth Amendment places upon a protective seizure and search for weapons. These limitations will have to be developed in the concrete factual circumstances of individual cases. Suffice it to note that such a search, unlike a search without a warrant incident to a lawful arrest, is not justified by any need to prevent the disappearance or destruction of evidence of crime. The sole justification of the search in the present situation is the protection of the police officer and others nearby, and it must therefore be confined in scope to an intrusion reasonably designed to discover guns, knives, clubs, or other hidden instruments for the assault of the police officer.

The scope of the search in this case presents no serious problem in light of these standards. Officer McFadden patted down the outer clothing of petitioner and his two companions. He did not place his hands in their pockets or under the outer surface of their garments until he had felt weapons, and then he merely reached for and removed the guns. He never did invade Katz' person beyond the outer surfaces of his clothes, since he discovered nothing in his pat-down which might have been a weapon. Officer McFadden confined his search strictly to what was minimally necessary to learn whether the men were armed and to disarm them once he discovered the weapons. He did not conduct a general exploratory search for whatever evidence of criminal activity he might find.

V.

We conclude that the revolver seized from Terry was properly admitted in evidence against him. . . . Each case of this sort will, of course, have to be decided on its own facts. We merely hold today that where a police officer observes unusual conduct which leads him reasonably to conclude in light of his experience that criminal activity may be afoot and that the persons with whom he is dealing may be armed and presently dangerous, where in the course of investigating this behavior he identifies himself as a policeman and makes reasonable inquiries, and where nothing in the initial stages of the encounter serves to dispel his reasonable fear for his own or others' safety, he is entitled for the protection of himself and others in the area to conduct a carefully limited search of the outer clothing of such persons in an attempt to discover weapons which might be used to assault him. Such a search is a reasonable search under the Fourth Amendment, and any weapons seized may properly be introduced in evidence against the person from whom they were taken. Affirmed.

HARLAN, J., concurring.

[If] the frisk is justified in order to protect the officer during an encounter with a citizen, the officer must first have constitutional grounds to insist on an encounter, to make a forcible stop. . . . Where such a stop is reasonable, however, the right to frisk must be immediate and automatic if the reason for the stop is, as here, an articulable suspicion of a crime of violence. Just as a full search incident to a lawful arrest requires no additional justification, a limited frisk incident to a lawful stop must often be rapid and routine. There is no reason why an officer, rightfully but forcibly confronting a person suspected of a serious crime, should have to ask one question and take the risk that the answer might be a bullet. . . . Upon the foregoing premises, I join the opinion of the Court.

DOUGLAS, J., dissenting.

[Frisking] petitioner and his companions for guns was a "search." But it is a mystery how that "search" . . . can be constitutional by Fourth Amendment standards, unless there was "probable cause" to believe that (1) a crime had been committed or (2) a crime was in the process of being committed or (3) a crime was about to be committed.

The opinion of the Court disclaims the existence of "probable cause." If loitering were in issue and that was the offense charged, there would be "probable cause" shown. But the crime here is carrying concealed weapons; and there is no basis for concluding that the officer had "probable cause" for believing that that crime was being committed. Had a warrant been sought, a magistrate would, therefore, have been unauthorized to issue one, for he can act only if there is a showing of "probable cause." We hold today that the police have greater authority to make a "seizure" and conduct a "search" than a judge has to authorize such action. We have said precisely the opposite over and over again.

In other words, police officers up to today have been permitted to effect arrests or searches without warrants only when the facts within their personal knowledge would satisfy the constitutional standard of probable cause. At the time of their "seizure" without a warrant they must possess facts concerning the person arrested that would have satisfied a magistrate that "probable cause" was indeed present. The term "probable cause" rings a bell of certainty that is not sounded by phrases such as "reasonable suspicion." Moreover, the meaning of "probable cause" is deeply imbedded in our constitutional history. . . .

The infringement on personal liberty of any "seizure" of a person can only be "reasonable" under the Fourth Amendment if we require the police to possess "probable cause" before they seize him. Only that line draws a meaningful distinction between an officer's mere inkling and the presence of facts within the officer's personal knowledge which would convince a reasonable man that the person seized has committed, is committing, or is about to commit a particular crime. . . .

To give the police greater power than a magistrate is to take a long step down the totalitarian path. Perhaps such a step is desirable to cope with modern forms of lawlessness. But if it is taken, it should be the deliberate choice of the people through a constitutional amendment. Until the Fourth Amendment . . . is rewritten, the person and the effects of the individual are beyond the reach of all government agencies until there are reasonable grounds to believe (probable cause) that a criminal venture has been launched or is about to be launched.

There have been powerful hydraulic pressures throughout our history that bear heavily on the Court to water down constitutional guarantees and give the police the upper hand. That hydraulic pressure has probably never been greater than it is today. Yet if the individual is no longer to be sovereign, if the police can pick him up whenever they do not like the cut of his jib, if they can "seize" and "search" him in their discretion, we enter a new regime. The decision to enter it should be made only after a full debate by the people of this country.

Notes

1. *Frisks for weapons: majority position.* The *Terry* opinion addressed both stops and frisks, and approved a framework already in place in some states at that point. It allowed the police to seize a person for a short time based on reasonable suspicion. We explored this question in section A of this chapter. But the Court considered the brief search — the frisk — to be the "crux" of this case. On the question of frisks, *Terry* has been very influential in the state systems; all the states now approve of frisks for weapons based on some justification less than probable cause. The majority take this position by statute, while others authorize such frisks through judicial rulings. An elaborate body of law in the state courts defines the boundaries of where an officer may search during a frisk, and what techniques he or she may use to identify what they feel inside the clothing. An exploration of these topics appears on the web extension for this chapter at *http://www.crimpro.com/extension/ch02*.

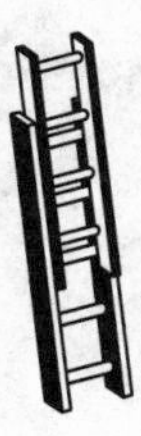

2. *Grounds for a* Terry *search.* Exactly what justification must an officer have before she performs a pat-down search? Why do both Chief Justice Warren and Justice Harlan distinguish between the justification needed for the initial stop and the justification needed for the brief search? Was Justice Douglas right to be concerned that government agents could manipulate too easily any standard less than probable cause?

Some state courts have declared that the police automatically have reasonable suspicion to frisk a person suspected of involvement in drug crimes and burglary. See State v. Evans, 618 N.E.2d 162, 169 (Ohio 1993); State v. Scott, 405 N.W.2d 829, 832 (Iowa 1987). Does the *Terry* opinion leave room for courts to make categorical judgments about reasonable suspicion to frisk, or does it require individualized findings in each case?

3. *Prevalence of frisks.* How often do frisks happen? According to a nationwide survey in 2005, police officers searched 4.8 percent of the drivers they stopped. Bureau of Justice Statistics, Contacts Between Police and the Public, 2005 (April 2007). Police officers in the New York City Police Department conducted 575,304 stops during 2009. The number was up from 97,296 in 2002, more than a fivefold increase in stops during a period when crime rates remained flat. Almost 490,000 of the people stopped were black or Latino, numbers disproportionate to the racial composition of the city population. See *http://www.nyc.gov/html/nypd/html/analysis_and_planning/stop_question_and_frisk_report.shtml.* A spokesperson for the NYPD explained that the stops increased because of a deliberate increased emphasis on enforcement of weapons laws. See Al Baker, Minorities Frisked More But Arrested at Same Rate, N.Y. Times, May 10, 2010. How would you go about determining how often your local police department conducts frisks?

4. Terry *searches before* Terry. Do you believe that police officers frisked suspects based on something less than probable cause before Detective McFadden decided to do so in Cleveland in 1963? Police officers in some states had statutes or department rules explicitly authorizing them to search for weapons without probable cause to arrest. The Uniform Arrest Act of 1942 provided that a "peace officer may search for a dangerous weapon any person whom he has stopped or detained to question . . . whenever he has reasonable ground to believe that he is in danger if the person possesses a dangerous weapon." Rule 470 of the Chicago Police Department

in 1933 also recognized a brief search for weapons without having probable cause: "[When] stopping and questioning a suspicious character [the police officer] shall be on guard against the use of any concealed or deadly weapon by such person. He shall be justified at such times in passing his hands over the clothing for the purpose of finding any deadly weapons." Many other police departments allowed frisks based on grounds less than probable cause but never openly acknowledged the practice.

Only a handful of state courts before 1968 ever explicitly addressed whether police could perform these brief searches without probable cause, with a slight majority of courts approving of the practice. Why did the issue not arise in the Supreme Court until 1968? See Wayne LaFave, "Street Encounters" and the Constitution: *Terry, Sibron, Peters,* and Beyond, 67 Mich. L. Rev. 40 (1968).

5. *The law and self-preservation.* Did the Supreme Court have any choice other than to approve of brief searches for weapons? If police officers felt that their lives were in jeopardy, would they not carry out the search regardless of the legal consequences? If Justice Douglas had written the opinion for the Court, what would have been the impact of the decision on police behavior and on the law of criminal procedure?

6. *Frisks in foreign systems.* In Great Britain, the Police and Criminal Evidence Act of 1984 provides that a constable can stop and search a person in a "public place" based on "reasonable grounds for suspecting" a search will reveal stolen or contraband articles. This level of justification is the same for a full-blown arrest, but it seems to correspond more closely to the American "reasonable suspicion" standard than to the "probable cause" standard. According to the government-issued Code of Practice for the Exercise by Police Officers of the Statutory Powers of Stop and Search, §3.5, a "search" occurring in a "public place" must be limited to a search of the outer garments, while a more thorough search can occur at the police station. In what ways do these legal provisions differ from the law of frisks in the United States? Do you believe that police practices in Great Britain reflect these differences in law? The law in France authorizes the police to conduct an identity check procedure that resembles the American stop and frisk, but the French procedure does not require individualized suspicion and may last up to four hours. See Richard S. Frase, Comparative Criminal Justice as a Guide to American Law Reform: How Do the French Do It, How Can We Find Out, and Why Should We Care? 78 Cal. L. Rev. 542, 576 (1990).

2. *The Scope of a Terry Search*

The frisk for weapons in *Terry* proceeds on a reduced level of justification (reasonable suspicion) because of the especially urgent nature of the government's objective in that setting (the safety of the officer and others in the area) and the limited nature of the search. Could a search based on reasonable suspicion also serve other, non-safety purposes, such as collecting evidence of a crime? What if the search is a bit more intrusive than a weapons frisk? In short, how far do *Terry* searches extend?

■ COMMONWEALTH v. ROOSEVELT WILSON

805 N.E.2d 968 (Mass. 2004)

COWIN, J.

. . . On the night of October 24, 2000, the Brockton police received a telephone call from a person who stated, "This is Stella's Pizza." The caller reported that a person was being beaten with a hammer or being stabbed in a group of ten people huddled across the street from the small commercial area where the pizza parlor was located. A police radio dispatch was broadcast containing this information, and State Trooper Francis Walls, alone in his unmarked vehicle and dressed in plain clothes, was the first officer to arrive at the scene. Walls stopped a short distance from the commercial area, saw a group of nine or ten men standing in a circle, but detected no suspicious activity. He was familiar with the area as one where he had made numerous arrests for drug and weapon violations and fights.

When he saw a backup vehicle close by, Walls pulled up to the group of men. As he got out of his vehicle, Walls made eye contact with the defendant. On making eye contact, the defendant turned, started walking away from Walls, and put his hand "to his waist area." The defendant's back was toward Walls, who, at this point, was concerned that the defendant possessed a gun. Walls grabbed the defendant by the back of his shirt and simultaneously placed his hand on "the area of the defendant's waist" where the defendant's hand had been. As soon as Walls put his hand on the defendant's waist, he felt a bundle of smaller packages, which he recognized by feel as "dime" bags of marijuana. Walls immediately asked the defendant, "You did that for weed? I thought you were putting a gun in your pants." The defendant responded that he did not "mess with guns." Walls retrieved the bag from the defendant's waist and handcuffed him.

Two backup officers, also in an unmarked vehicle and in plain clothes, were getting out of their vehicle as Walls stopped and frisked the defendant. No evidence was found of the assault or beating that had been the subject of the radio dispatch. The defendant was arrested, and an inventory search revealed that in addition to the seized "dime" bags of marijuana, a pager, a cellular telephone, and $476 in cash were in his possession. . . .

The defendant claims that the police lacked the requisite reasonable suspicion to stop him and to initiate a patfrisk. In "stop and frisk" cases our inquiry is two-fold: first, whether the initiation of the investigation by the police was permissible in the circumstances, and, second, whether the scope of the search was justified by the circumstances. In both aspects, the inquiry is whether the police conduct was reasonable under the Fourth Amendment.

In regard to the stop, a police officer may make an investigatory stop where suspicious conduct gives the officer reasonable ground to suspect that a person is committing, has committed, or is about to commit a crime. Concerning the second part of the analysis, a *Terry*-type patfrisk incident to the investigatory stop is permissible where the police officer reasonably believes that the individual is armed and dangerous. Terry v. Ohio, 392 U.S. 1 (1968). The officer's action in both the stop and the frisk must be based on specific and articulable facts and reasonable inferences therefrom, in light of the officer's experience.

Applying these principles to the facts in this case, we first consider the stop. The defendant was seized (or stopped) when Walls grabbed the back of his shirt. At that time, specific and articulable facts supported Walls's belief that the defendant had committed a crime. Walls was responding to a radio dispatch that described ten people involved in a stabbing or beating with a weapon outside Stella's Pizza. On arriving at the location, an area of Brockton where Walls had made numerous arrests for fights and weapon violations, Walls's observations confirmed a group of men huddled on the sidewalk, just as the caller had described. As he left his vehicle, Walls made eye contact with the defendant, who immediately turned away from him, walked away from the group, and simultaneously moved his hand into his "waist area." [Walls testified at the motion hearing that "As soon as he looked at me, he turned around and took his right hand and placed it into his pant line . . . ."] The totality of these facts supports a reasonable belief that the defendant had been involved in a fight with a weapon, and therefore, the stop was proper. The same facts justify the patfrisk, as they establish a reasonable belief that the defendant was armed and dangerous and presented a threat to the officer or others. . . .

The defendant next argues that Walls exceeded the scope of the patfrisk by "exploring" and seizing the package of marijuana he discovered in the defendant's waistband after he had determined it contained no weapon. The scope of a *Terry* search cannot be general; rather it is strictly tied to the circumstances that render its initiation permissible. The Fourth Amendment permits a police officer to conduct a patfrisk for concealed weapons, provided that such a search is confined to what is minimally necessary to learn whether the suspect is armed and to disarm him should weapons be discovered. Terry v. Ohio, 392 U.S. 1, 29-30 (1968).

In Minnesota v. Dickerson, 508 U.S. 366 (1993), the Supreme Court concluded that a police officer may also seize nonthreatening contraband discovered during a *Terry*-type frisk if the "police officer lawfully pats down a suspect's outer clothing and feels an object whose contour or mass makes its identity [as contraband] immediately apparent." If the officer must manipulate or otherwise further physically explore the concealed object in order to discern its identity, then an unconstitutional search has occurred.

The scope of a *Terry* search is not exceeded if, during a lawful patfrisk, it is immediately apparent to the police officer, in light of the officer's training and experience, that a concealed item is contraband. The "plain feel" doctrine is grounded on the same premise that authorizes an officer to frisk the suspect for concealed weapons, i.e., that the weapon will be immediately detected through touch during the patfrisk. As long as the object's contraband identity is immediately apparent to the officer, there is no further "invasion of the suspect's privacy beyond that already authorized by the officer's search for weapons." The "plain feel" doctrine is limited; it does not permit an officer to conduct a general exploratory search for whatever evidence of criminal activity he might find. The contraband nature of the item must be immediately apparent on touch. For these reasons, we conclude that the "plain feel" doctrine is consistent with art. 14, as well as with the Fourth Amendment.

[Several States have adopted the "plain feel" doctrine. See, e.g., People v. Mitchell, 650 N.E.2d 1014 (Ill. 1995); People v. Champion, 549 N.W.2d 849 (Mich. 1996); Commonwealth v. Zhahir, 751 A.2d 1153 (Pa. 2000). Although the Court of Appeals of New York rejected the doctrine, that court did so prior to the Supreme Court's decision in Minnesota v. Dickerson. See People v. Diaz, 612 N.E.2d 298 (N.Y. 1993).]

We consider "plain feel" as analogous to "plain view." As long as the initial search is lawful, the seizure of an item whose identity is already known occasions no further invasion of privacy. The only difference between the two doctrines is the sensory perception used to identify the contraband nature of the object. The "plain feel" doctrine merely recognizes that if contraband is immediately apparent by sense of touch, rather than sight, the police are authorized to seize it.

The "plain feel" doctrine is no more susceptible to fabrication than the "plain view" doctrine. The initial requirement, that the officer be conducting a valid pat-frisk of the suspect, ensures that the officer is lawfully in the position immediately to identify the contraband. Once an otherwise lawful search is in progress, the police may inadvertently discover contraband. Requiring an officer who recognizes contraband by "plain feel" to ignore this fact and walk away from the suspect without seizing the object flies in the face of logic. . . .

When we apply these principles to the facts here, Walls did not exceed the scope of the search because the judge found that it was immediately apparent to Walls when he touched the defendant's waist area that the object in the defendant's waistband was bundles of marijuana, and no manipulation was necessary to determine that fact. Contrast Minnesota v. Dickerson, 508 U.S. at 378-379 (scope of search unconstitutional where officer manipulated contents of defendant's pocket before discerning lump was contraband).

The defendant also contests the judge's finding that Walls knew the item in the defendant's waistband was drugs as soon as he touched it and did not manipulate it. The judge's finding is supported by record evidence. Walls repeatedly stated, despite thorough examination by the defense attorney, that he knew the identity of the object as soon as he touched it, without any manipulation ("The second I hit it, that's what I felt" . . .). Other testimony by Walls supports this finding: his seven years of experience as a State trooper, and his inquiry to the defendant made immediately on touching the object, "You did that for weed?"

Contrary to the defendant's argument that there was no evidence concerning Walls's training and experience in tactile detection of marijuana or its packaging, Walls stated that he has made numerous arrests for drug violations, has seized drugs, and was serving in the "gang unit." From all of this evidence, the judge could reasonably infer that Walls had sufficient personal experience in narcotics packaging and detection to identify immediately the object in the defendant's waistband. . . .

■ ARKANSAS RULE OF CRIMINAL PROCEDURE 3.4

If a law enforcement officer who has detained a person under Rule 3.1 reasonably suspects that the person is armed and presently dangerous to the officer or others, the officer or someone designated by him may search the outer clothing of such person and the immediate surroundings for, and seize, any weapon or other dangerous thing which may be used against the officer or others. In no event shall this search be more extensive than is reasonably necessary to ensure the safety of the officer or others.

■ MONTANA CODE §46-5-401(2)

A peace officer who has lawfully stopped a person [may] frisk the person and take other reasonably necessary steps for protection if the officer has reasonable cause to suspect that the person is armed and presently dangerous to the officer or another person present. The officer may take possession of any object that is discovered during the course of the frisk if the officer has probable cause to believe that the object is a deadly weapon until the completion of the stop, at which time the officer shall either immediately return the object, if legally possessed, or arrest the person.

Notes

1. *"Plain feel": majority position.* Under the "plain feel" or "plain touch" doctrine, if an officer conducts a properly circumscribed *Terry* search for weapons and feels an object that is not a weapon, the officer can seize the item if it is "immediately apparent" that the item is contraband or evidence of a crime. Minnesota v. Dickerson, 508 U.S. 366 (1993). Most state courts to consider the question also have adopted a "plain feel" doctrine under their state constitutions. See People v. Champion, 549 N.W.2d 849 (Mich. 1996). While accepting the basic contours of the doctrine, courts in about half the states apply it strictly. Courts have declared that commonplace items touched during a frisk cannot be seized, because it cannot be "immediately apparent" that the item is contraband or evidence. Murphy v. Commonwealth, 570 S.E.2d 836 (Va. 2002) ("plain feel" doctrine does not permit seizure of baggie containing marijuana felt during pat of outside surface of pants pocket); but cf. State v. Rushing, 935 S.W.2d 30 (Mo. 1996) (applying doctrine more leniently; confiscation of roll of breath mints felt during pat-down was justified because officer's training and experience revealed that breath mint rolls were common cocaine containers).

The high court in New York rejected the "plain touch" doctrine entirely under its state constitution. The court in People v. Diaz, 612 N.E.2d 298 (N.Y. 1993) explained its position as follows:

> The identity and criminal nature of a concealed object are not likely to be discernible upon a mere touch or pat within the scope of the intrusion authorized by *Terry.* While in most instances seeing an object will instantly reveal its identity and nature, touching is inherently less reliable and cannot conclusively establish an object's identity or criminal nature. Moreover, knowledge concerning an object merely from feeling it through an exterior covering is necessarily based on the police officer's expert opinion. . . .
>
> Finally, an opinion of a police officer that the object touched is evidence of criminality will predictably, at least in some circumstances, require a degree of pinching, squeezing or probing beyond the limited intrusion allowed under *Terry.* The proposed "plain touch" exception could thus invite a blurring of the limits to *Terry* searches and the sanctioning of warrantless searches on information obtained from an initial intrusion which, itself, amounts to an unauthorized warrantless search.

What kind of training — formal and informal — would you expect to occur within police departments in jurisdictions that adopt a "plain feel" rule? Should courts evaluate plain feel cases based on what a reasonable officer would know or on what the officer in question knew?

2. *Reasonable suspicion for non-weapons frisks?* The Supreme Court has insisted that a frisk of a person designed to obtain evidence of a crime cannot be based on reasonable suspicion; the officer must have probable cause that the evidence will be on the person, even if the brief search is no more intrusive than a weapons frisk. See Ybarra v. Illinois, 444 U.S. 85 (1979) (frisk of customer in bar where search warrant was being executed). How exactly will the courts make the distinction between permissible weapons frisks and impermissible evidence frisks?

3. *Frisk statutes.* Would the court in *Wilson* have decided the case any differently if a statute identical to the Arkansas statute had been in effect in Massachusetts? What outcome under the Montana statute? Are the police in a better position, generally speaking, in states with a frisk statute or in those where the authority to frisk is based entirely on judicial opinions?

4. *Are courts the agents of legislators or independent interpreters?* Suppose a court is convinced that a state statute regarding the scope of frisks is badly flawed because it does not authorize a frisk beyond the "outer clothing." Should the court feel free to "fix" the problem created by the legislature? Are there canons of construction that would allow a court to read this statute to allow more intrusive (and effective) frisks?

As we have seen earlier, courts look to several different sources of guidance in interpreting the meaning of ambiguous statutory language. They sometimes resort to canons of construction to determine the "plain meaning" of the statutory text. They also often consult the legislative history to determine the legislature's intent in passing the statute. Alternatively, they may refer to the statute's title or language to ascertain the legislative purpose. These different sources may point in different directions in a particular case. What weight will a court give to the various sources of guidance?

The answer to such a question depends on the court's objective: Does the court view itself as an agent of the legislature, or is the court to exercise its own best judgment about how to give meaning to the language? Courts have not agreed on this question. On the one hand, most probably adhere to the view that they interpret statutes as agents of the legislature, to put into effect what the legislators intended in a specific setting (or what they *would have* intended for the setting if they had thought of it). As Justice Oliver Wendell Holmes once stated, "If my fellow citizens want to go to Hell I will help them. It's my job." 1 Holmes-Laski Letters 249 (Mark DeWolfe Howe ed., 1953).

On the other hand, many courts *act* as if they have an independent responsibility to make sense of statutory language. Professor Ernst Freund captured this independent view of courts as interpreters of statutes with the following advice in 1917: "In cases of genuine ambiguity courts should use the power of interpretation consciously and deliberately to promote sound law and sound principles of legislation." Ernst Freund, Interpretation of Statutes, 65 U. Pa. L. Rev. 207 (1917). What objective of statutory interpretation would a court be endorsing if it were to interpret the Arkansas frisk statute to allow frisks of the person beyond the outer clothing?

5. *Purses, briefcases, and bags.* Police also commonly extend protective *Terry* searches to purses, briefcases, and other items a suspect might be holding at the time of a stop. Although the officer might reduce the danger of any weapons in a purse or bag by placing it well out of reach of the suspect, courts and police department rules have not uniformly required the police to do so. Cf. State v. Peterson, 110

P.3d 699 (Utah 2005) (officers could not pat down a jacket before giving it to detained person, who did not request jacket before going outdoors). The search must start with a "frisk" of the exterior of a cloth bag, and the officer may not open the bag to search its contents if the initial frisk confirms that there is no weapon inside.

Problem 2-8. Frisking Car and Driver

Around 12:30 A.M., police officers Josephine Copland and Jess Segundo were patrolling West Oliwood, investigating narcotics sales in that area. As they waited at an intersection for a traffic signal to change, they saw a red Lexus drive through the intersection with a taillight burned out. Officers Copland and Segundo immediately stopped the Lexus, although they typically would not stop a car based only on a problem with the taillight.

When the driver, Steven Worth, pulled over and stopped, he started to move about the inside the vehicle, back and forth in the front seat, and ducked down below the seat. When Officers Copland and Segundo exited their cruiser and approached on foot, they ordered Worth to step out of his vehicle.

Officer Copland ordered Worth to move away from his vehicle, and began examining the interior of the Lexus. She looked around and under the seats and found nothing suspicious. Officer Copland then opened the glove compartment and found what looked to her like a hand-rolled cigarette. Upon picking up and examining the cigarette, she discovered it was filled with tobacco. Officer Copland reached over and lifted the lever next to the driver's seat to disengage the trunk latch. Moving outside to the back of the car, she looked inside the trunk and found an expensive-looking set of golf clubs inside a golf bag. Officer Copland noticed a number of bulges within the golf bag, and she began to unzip the bag's various pockets. In the largest pocket, which ran the length of the bag, Copland discovered a sawed-off shotgun.

Meanwhile, Officer Segundo was examining Worth. She performed a pat-down search of Worth's outer clothing. As part of this frisk, Officer Segundo patted down the knit stocking cap Worth wore, which was rolled over on the edges. Officer Segundo felt a hard object on the right side of Worth's hat. Officer Segundo was not sure what this hard object was, and she reached inside the hat. Grabbing the hard object with her fingers, she felt what she believed (based upon her previous experience) to be crack cocaine. Officer Segundo then removed two pieces of suspected crack cocaine from the hat and arrested Worth for possession of that illegal substance.

Steven Worth was charged with possession of crack cocaine and with possession of an illegal firearm. He filed a motion prior to trial asking the court to suppress the gun recovered from the golf bag and the drugs recovered from his stocking cap. How would you argue in support of the motion?

Problem 2-9. Duty to Cooperate?

The sheriff's department in Humboldt County, Nevada, received an afternoon telephone call reporting an assault. The caller reported seeing a man assault a woman in a red and silver GMC truck on Grass Valley Road. Deputy Sheriff Lee

Dove was dispatched to investigate. When Dove arrived at the scene, he found the truck parked on the side of the road. A man was standing by the truck, and a young woman was sitting inside it. Dove observed skid marks in the gravel behind the vehicle, leading him to believe it had come to a sudden stop.

The officer approached the man, Larry Dudley Hiibel, and explained that he was investigating a report of a fight. Hiibel appeared to be intoxicated. The officer asked him if he had "any identification." Hiibel refused to provide any identification and asked why the officer wanted to see it. Dove responded that he was conducting an investigation (but did not specify the alleged crime he was investigating) and needed to see some identification. Hiibel became agitated and insisted he had done nothing wrong. The officer insisted that he needed to find out who Hiibel was and what he was doing there. After repeated refusals to give the officer any identification, Hiibel became more belligerent, placing his hands behind his back and telling the officer to arrest him and take him to jail, because he would not provide any identification. This routine kept up for several minutes: the officer asked for identification 11 times and was refused each time. During this time, two other officers arrived on the scene. After warning Hiibel that he would be arrested if he continued to refuse to comply, Dove placed Hiibel under arrest.

When Hiibel's daughter shouted her protests over the arrest of her father, three officers removed her from the pickup, pushed her to the ground, handcuffed her, and placed her under arrest as well.

The state charged Hiibel with "willfully resisting, delaying, or obstructing a public officer in discharging or attempting to discharge any legal duty of his office" in violation of Nev. Rev. Stat. (NRS) §199.280. In the trial court, Deputy Dove explained his thinking this way:

> During my conversation with Mr. Hiibel, there was a point where he became somewhat aggressive. I felt based on me not being able to find out who he was, to identify him, I didn't know if he was wanted or what his situation was, I wasn't able to determine what was going on crimewise in the vehicle, based on that I felt he was intoxicated, and how he was becoming aggressive and moody, I went ahead and put him in handcuffs so I could secure him for my safety, and put him in my patrol vehicle.

The government reasoned that Hiibel had obstructed Deputy Dove in carrying out his duties under §171.123:

> 1. Any peace officer may detain any person whom the officer encounters under circumstances which reasonably indicate that the person has committed, is committing or is about to commit a crime. . . .
>
> 3. The officer may detain the person pursuant to this section only to ascertain his identity and the suspicious circumstances surrounding his presence abroad. Any person so detained shall identify himself, but may not be compelled to answer any other inquiry of any peace officer.

Roughly 20 states have enacted similar "stop and identify" statutes. They permit an officer to ask or require a suspect to disclose his identity. A few states model their statutes on the Uniform Arrest Act, a model code that permits an officer to stop a person reasonably suspected of committing a crime and "demand of him his name, address, business abroad and whither he is going."

Hiibel was convicted and fined $250. Does the constitutional bar on "unreasonable searches and seizures" prevent this prosecution of Hiibel? Cf. Hiibel v. Sixth Judicial District Court, 542 U.S. 177 (2004).

Notes

1. Terry *searches of stopped cars*. Although a pat-down search of a person should expose any guns or other large weapons hidden in the clothing, a person stopped while riding in a car might hide a weapon somewhere in the vehicle. How can an officer protect herself from a suspect who keeps a weapon somewhere nearby, but not on his person? The U.S. Supreme Court, in Michigan v. Long, 463 U.S. 1032 (1983), stated that police officers who stop a vehicle and frisk the driver standing outside the car may conduct a further "protective" search of the passenger compartment and any containers inside it that might contain a large weapon such as a gun. Under the federal constitution, the police must have a reasonable suspicion that there may be weapons in the vehicle before the protective search takes place. Most state courts (all but about a half dozen) allow police to conduct protective searches of stopped cars, on terms identical to federal law. They allow the officers to conduct a protective search of the interior and any containers inside (but only those large enough to contain a weapon) if the officers reasonably suspect that there are dangerous weapons in the vehicle. These courts reason that the search of a vehicle is just as important to the officer's safety as a frisk of the person under *Terry*. See State v. Wilkins, 692 A.2d 1233 (Conn. 1997). However, the high court in New York decided in People v. Torres, 543 N.E.2d 61 (N.Y 1989), that police officers could not search the interior of a stopped vehicle for weapons based only on reasonable suspicion. The *Torres* court suggested that the officer stopping the vehicle can reduce any risk by separating the suspect from the vehicle. How might the majority of courts respond to this argument? Would you draw a distinction between a pat-down search of the driver and placing the driver into the patrol car during the stop? See Wilson v. State, 745 N.E.2d 789 (Ind. 2001) (pat-down search of motorist prior to placing him in police car during routine traffic stop violated Fourth Amendment; pat-down search was not supported by particularized reasonable suspicion that motorist was armed).

2. *Orders to exit a vehicle*. When an officer stops a vehicle, he will sometimes but not always ask the driver to get out of the vehicle, out of concern for his own safety. The U.S. Supreme Court has concluded that this intrusion on the driver is minimal and that the officer needs no justification (other than the reasonable suspicion necessary to stop the car) for ordering the driver to get out of the car. Pennsylvania v. Mimms, 434 U.S. 106 (1977); but see State v. Sprague, 824 A.2d 539 (Vt. 2003) (under state constitution, officer conducting routine traffic stop may not automatically order driver to exit vehicle). In Maryland v. Wilson, 519 U.S. 408 (1997), the court extended *Mimms* to hold that officers may order a *passenger* in the car to get out, without any grounds to believe that the passenger is dangerous. Some states previously had rejected that position. See State v. Smith, 637 A.2d 158 (N.J. 1994) (order to passenger to get out of car stopped for minor traffic infraction must be based on articulable suspicion that passenger poses danger). The great majority of

state courts follow both *Mimms* and *Wilson*. Cf. People v. Jackson, 45 P.3d 1237 (Colo. 2002) (police may request identification of passenger in stopped vehicle without individualized suspicion); but see State v. Mendez, 970 P.2d 722 (Wash. 1999). Should the police treat the driver and the passenger differently? Is one any more or less dangerous than the other? Is the intrusion on drivers and passengers the same?

Arizona v. Johnson, 129 S. Ct. 781 (2009), confirms that passengers in a stopped vehicle are also subject to frisk if officer has reasonable suspicion to believe a passenger is armed and dangerous, even if there is no reasonable suspicion that a passenger is involved in crime. In that case, an officer frisked a passenger suspected of membership in a gang whose members frequently carried weapons.

3. Terry *stops and requests for identification.* The Supreme Court in Hiibel v. Sixth Judicial District Court, 542 U.S. 177 (2004), upheld a suspect's conviction for failure to provide his name to an officer during an otherwise valid investigative stop:

> The request for identity has an immediate relation to the purpose, rationale, and practical demands of a *Terry* stop. The threat of criminal sanction helps ensure that the request for identity does not become a legal nullity. On the other hand, the Nevada statute does not alter the nature of the stop itself: it does not change its duration or its location. A state law requiring a suspect to disclose his name in the course of a valid *Terry* stop is consistent with Fourth Amendment prohibitions against unreasonable searches and seizures.

Before *Hiibel*, there was surprisingly little precedent (in either state or federal courts) on the question of whether the state could punish a citizen's refusal to answer an officer's questions during an investigatory stop. Does an effort to investigate and prevent acts of terrorism — an objective of criminal law enforcement that gained new urgency after September 11, 2001 — make this sort of questioning more common and more valuable?

Many states have enacted statutes that compel some level of cooperation with police officers during crime investigations. For a detailed discussion of these statutes, see Margaret Raymond, The Right to Refuse and the Obligation to Comply: Challenging the Gamesmanship Model of Criminal Procedure, 54 Buffalo L. R. 1483 (2007). Related questions involve the subjects a police officer may discuss with occupants of a vehicle after making a stop. An exploration of these topics appears on the web extension for this chapter at *http://www.crimpro.com/extension/ch02*.

The controversial Arizona immigration law enacted in 2010, SB 1070 (codified at A.R.S. §11-1051), creates a presumption of legal residency for people who carry specific identification. The text describes the presumption in these terms:

> A person is presumed to not be an alien who is unlawfully present in the United States if the person provides to the law enforcement officer or agency any of the following:
>
> 1. A valid Arizona driver license.
> 2. A valid Arizona non-operating identification license.
> 3. A valid tribal enrollment card or other form of tribal identification.
> 4. If the entity requires proof of legal presence in the United States before issuance, any valid United States federal, state or local government issued identification.

Arizona legislators declared that they did not intend for SB 1070 to enact a state version of the "Real ID" law, a 2005 federal law that set forth requirements for state driver's licenses and identification cards to be accepted by the federal government for "official purposes," as defined by the Secretary of Homeland Security. Is the new Arizona law in effect a statute requiring people to carry identification? Would it be a good idea for the law to require this of all people?

III

Full Searches of People and Places: Basic Concepts

We now move from brief searches and stops to more extended and complete searches. This chapter describes the origins of the Fourth Amendment and the language of analogous provisions in state constitutions. Then it introduces the three concepts that dominate the case law governing full searches: probable cause, warrants, and consent. Probable cause is the usual justification required to validate a full search. The judicial warrant is the procedure meant to ensure careful and early assessment of probable cause. To obtain a warrant, a government agent must demonstrate to a judge or magistrate, before the search happens, that the plan is justified. The last of the basic concepts, consent, may be the most important of all because police obtain consent from private parties for a large proportion of the searches they conduct. Following this chapter's survey of the most important tools for analyzing full searches, Chapter 4 applies these concepts in several contexts that recur time and again in judicial decisions and in the field.

A. ORIGINS OF THE FOURTH AMENDMENT AND ITS ANALOGS

The police force is a nineteenth-century invention; the repressive government officers that most infuriated the colonists were tax and customs inspectors. These officials often carried out their work by using general warrants, which were broad grants of authority from the king of England or his representatives to search homes and businesses. One goal of this section is to identify the characteristics of government searches that constitutional drafters found most objectionable. Many historians and judges say that Americans were especially concerned with "general warrants." Why were general warrants troubling to colonial lawyers? Did any other characteristics of government searches, apart from their reliance on general warrants, also draw colonial criticism?

1. General Search Warrants

In the 1760s, a series of English cases addressed the validity of general search warrants. The cases were civil tort actions against the individuals who issued and executed the warrants. The plaintiff in the following case, John Entick, published a series of pamphlets critical of the government. A minister of the government, Lord Halifax, considered the pamphlets libelous. He issued to his subordinates a "warrant" authorizing them to search for Entick (without specifying a place where they could look) and to seize him and his papers (without specifying which ones). Halifax's subordinates (or "messengers") executed the warrant and seized a great many of Entick's papers. Entick later brought a tort suit against Carrington, one of the messengers who had executed the warrant. The issue on appeal was whether the warrant was authorized by law (giving the searcher a legal defense) or was beyond the scope of the law, perhaps exposing those who created and executed the warrant to liability for the improper search.

■ JOHN ENTICK v. NATHAN CARRINGTON

95 Eng. Rep. 807 (K.B. 1765)

In trespass; the plaintiff declares that the defendants . . . broke and entered the dwelling-house of the plaintiff . . . and continued there four hours without his consent and against his will, and all that time disturbed him in the peaceable possession thereof, and . . . searched and examined all the rooms, &c. in his dwelling-house, and all the boxes &c. so broke open, and read over, pryed into, and examined all the private papers, books, &c. of the plaintiff there found, whereby the secret affairs, &c. of the plaintiff became wrongfully discovered and made public; and took and carried away . . . printed pamphlets, &c. &c. of the plaintiff there found. [The defendants say] the plaintiff ought not to have his action against them, because they say, that before the supposed trespass . . . the Earl of Halifax was, and yet is, one of the Lords of the King's Privy Council, and one of his principal Secretaries of State, and that the earl . . . made his warrant under his hand and seal directed to the defendants, by which the earl did in the King's name authorize and require the defendants, taking a constable to their assistance, to make strict and diligent search for the plaintiff, mentioned in the said warrant to be the author . . . of several weekly very seditious papers . . . containing gross and scandalous reflections and invectives upon His Majesty's Government, and upon both Houses of Parliament, and him the plaintiff having found, to seize and apprehend and bring together with his books and papers in safe custody, before the Earl of Halifax to be examined. [The defendants argued that such warrants have frequently been granted by Secretaries of State since the Glorious Revolution of 1688 and have never been controverted. The jury found that the agents of Lord Halifax had committed the acts described by the plaintiff and was willing to award damages of 3,000 pounds if the court concluded that these facts constituted a trespass.]

[We] shall now consider the special justification, whether [the defense to a tort claim for trespass] can be supported in law, and this depends upon the jurisdiction of the Secretary of State; for if he has no jurisdiction to grant a warrant to break open doors, locks, boxes, and to seize a man and all his books, &c. in the first instance upon an information of his being guilty of publishing a libel, the warrant will not justify the defendants: it was resolved . . . in the case of Shergold v. Holloway, that a justice's warrant expressly to arrest the party will not justify the officer, there being no jurisdiction. The warrant in our case was an execution in the first instance, without any previous summons, examination, hearing the plaintiff, or proof that he was the author of the supposed libels; a power claimed by no other magistrate whatever . . . ; it was left to the discretion of these defendants to execute the warrant in the absence or presence of the plaintiff, when he might have no witness present to see what they did; for they were to seize all papers, bank bills, or any other valuable papers they might take away if they were so disposed; there might be nobody to detect them.

[In the case of Wilkes v. Wood (1763), involving a member of the House of Commons who had published an attack on the King and his ministers], all his books and papers were seized and taken away; we were told by one of these messengers that he was obliged by his oath to sweep away all papers whatsoever; if this is law it would be found in our books, but no such law ever existed in this country; our law holds the property of every man so sacred, that no man can set his foot upon his neighbour's close without his leave; if he does he is a trespasser, though he does no damage at all; if he will tread upon his neighbour's ground, he must justify it by law. [We] can safely say there is no law in this country to justify the defendants in what they have done; if there was, it would destroy all the comforts of society; for papers are often the dearest property a man can have. This case was compared to that of stolen goods; . . . but in that case the justice and the informer must proceed with great caution; there must be an oath that the party has had his goods stolen, and his strong reason to believe they are concealed in such a place; but if the goods are not found there, he is a trespasser; the officer in that case is a witness; there are none in this case, no inventory taken; if it had been legal many guards of property would have attended it. We shall now consider the usage of these warrants since the [Glorious] Revolution [of 1688]; if it began then, it is too modern to be law; the common law did not begin with the Revolution; the ancient constitution which had been almost overthrown and destroyed, was then repaired and revived; the Revolution added a new buttress to the ancient venerable edifice. [This] is the first instance of an attempt to prove a modern practice of a private office to make and execute warrants to enter a man's house, search for and take away all his books and papers in the first instance, to be law, which is not to be found in our books. It must have been the guilt or poverty of those upon whom such warrants have been executed, that deterred or hindered them from contending against the power of a Secretary of State and the Solicitor of the Treasury, or such warrants could never have passed for lawful till this time. We are . . . all of opinion that it cannot be justified by law. [If] a man is punishable for having a libel in his private custody, as many cases say he is, half the kingdom would be guilty in the case of a favourable libel, if libels may be searched for and seized by whomsoever and wheresoever the Secretary of State thinks fit. . . . Our law is wise and merciful, and supposes every man accused to be innocent before he is tried by his peers: upon the whole, we are all of opinion that this warrant is wholly illegal and void. One word more for ourselves; we are no advocates for libels, all

Governments must set their faces against them, and whenever they come before us and a jury we shall set our faces against them; and if juries do not prevent them they may prove fatal to liberty, destroy Government and introduce anarchy; but tyranny is better than anarchy, and the worst Government better than none at all. Judgment for the plaintiff.

The English controversy in the 1760s over general warrants was familiar to American colonists. A similar practice was creating a popular uproar in the colonies at about this time. Customs agents of the English government, who enforced the highly unpopular and widely flouted tax laws for imports and exports, had all the powers of their English counterparts as they searched for taxable goods. Their power to search for goods sometimes took the form of "writs of assistance." Like a general warrant, the writ of assistance authorized the agent to search private premises, without specifying the place to search or the things to seize. These writs contained no real time limitation, for they expired only upon the death of the king. The writs also obligated all government officials and all subjects of the Crown to assist the customs agent in the search. A reporter of proceedings in the court in the Massachusetts Bay colony offers the following example of a 1755 application for a writ of assistance.

■ THE WRITS OF ASSISTANCE

Quincy's Rep. (Mass.) App., 1:402-04, 453

To the Honourable his Majestys Justices of his Superiour Court for said Province to be held at York in and for the County of York on the third Tuesday of June 1755.

HUMBLY SHEWS Charles Paxton Esqr: That he is lawfully authorized to Execute the Office of Surveyor of all Rates Duties and Impositions arising and growing due to his Majesty at Boston in this Province & cannot fully Exercise said Office in such Manner as his Majestys Service and the Laws in such Cases Require Unless Your Honours who are vested with the Power of a Court of Exchequer for this Province will please to Grant him a Writ of Assistants, he therefore prays he & his Deputys may be Aided in the Execution of said office within his District by a Writ of Assistants under the Seal of this Superiour Court in Legal form & according to Usage in his Majestys Court of Exchequer & in Great Britain, & your Petitioner &Ca:

CHAS PAXTON

[The court issued the writ in the following form:]

GEORGE the Second by the Grace of God of Great Britain, France and Ireland King, Defender of the Faith &c — To all and singular Justices of the Peace, Sheriffs and Constables, and to all other our officers and Subjects within said Prov. & to each of you Greeting —

WHEREAS the Commissioners of our Customs have by their Deputation dated the 8th day of Jany 1752, assignd Charles Paxton Esqr Surveyor of all Rates, Duties, and Impositions arising and growing due within the Port of Boston in said Province as by said Deputation at large appears, WE THEREFORE command you and each of you that you permit ye said C.P. and his Deputies and Servants from Time to time at his or their Will as well in the day as in the Night to enter and go on board any Ship, Boat or other Vessell riding lying or being within or coming to the said Port or any Places or Creeks appertaining to said Port, such Ship, Boat or Vessell then & there found to View & Search & strictly to examine in the same, touching the Customs and Subsidies to us due, And also in the day Time together with a Constable or other public officer inhabiting near unto the Place to enter and go into any Vaults, Cellars, Warehouses, Shops or other Places to search and see whether any Goods, Wares or Merchandises, in ye same Ships, Boats or Vessells, Vaults, Cellars, Warehouses, Shops or other Places are or shall be there hid or concealed, having been imported, ship't or laden in order to be exported from or out of the said Port or any Creeks or Places appertain'g to the same Port; and to open any Trunks, Chests, Boxes, fardells [packages] or Packs made up or in Bulk, whatever in which any Goods, Wares, or Merchandises are suspected to be packed or concealed and further to do all Things which of Rt and according to Law and the Statutes in such Cases provided, is in this Part to be done: And We strictly command you and every of you that you, from Time to Time be aiding and assisting to the said C.P. his Deputies and Servants and every of them in the Execution of the Premises in all Things as becometh: Fail not at your Peril.

Notes

1. *The battle over general warrants and writs of assistance.* The English legal system was rejecting general warrants at the same time colonial officials in America were relying on such warrants more heavily. Lord Camden's decision in Entick v. Carrington is one of several decisions to declare that there was no statutory or other legal authority for general warrants in England. An equally famous decision, Wilkes v. Wood, 19 Howell's State Trials 1153 (C.P. 1763), involved a member of Parliament (John Wilkes) who wrote a series of pamphlets critical of the government and, like John Entick, became the target of government agents executing a general warrant. Did the *Entick* court simply want to encourage Parliament to enact clearer legislation authorizing such warrants? Does the opinion reveal any deeper concerns about their use?

Writs of assistance issued in the American colonies in the 1760s provoked arguments and protests similar to those found in the *Entick* decision. In a now famous (but at the time losing) argument against the validity of writs of assistance, James Otis criticized the writs in these terms:

> Now one of the most essential branches of English liberty, is the freedom of one's house. A man's house is his castle; and while he is quiet, he is as well guarded as a prince in his castle. This writ, if it should be declared legal, would totally annihilate this privilege. Custom house officers may enter our houses when they please — we are commanded to permit their entry — their menial servants may enter — may break locks, bars and every thing in their way — and whether they break through malice or revenge, no man, no court can inquire — bare suspicion without oath is sufficient.

2 Legal Papers of John Adams 113, 142 (L. Wroth and H. Zobel eds., 1965); see generally M. H. Smith, The Writs of Assistance Case (1978).

2. *Fourth Amendment history in the Supreme Court.* The concerns of the Constitution's framers figure into current interpretations of the Fourth Amendment. While the role of history rises and falls in different eras of the Supreme Court's search and seizure jurisprudence, history appears to be on the upswing lately. Consider this assertion by Justice Scalia in Wyoming v. Houghton, 526 U.S. 295, 299-300 (1999): "In determining whether a particular governmental action violates [the Fourth Amendment] provision, we inquire first whether the action was regarded as an unlawful search or seizure under the common law when the Amendment was framed. Where that inquiry yields no answer, we must evaluate the search or seizure under traditional standards of reasonableness. . . ." See David A. Sklansky, The Fourth Amendment and Common Law, 100 Colum. L. Rev. 1739, 1745-70 (2000) (Justices in earlier periods focused on general warrants and writs of assistance and generalized from those controversies to the underlying evils; current justices read the Constitution in light of eighteenth-century common law practices).

3. *What were the offensive characteristics of searches?* In its condemnation of general warrants, did the *Entick* court express concern about the lack of an explanation for a proposed search before it began? Was it concerned with the fact that a government official issued the warrant to his own subordinates? Why does it matter that the general warrants and writs of assistance name no particular target or place for a search? Notice also that the *Entick* court seemed troubled by the fact that the searches under these warrants took place with no witnesses present. What evils would witnesses help prevent? How did the *Entick* court describe a search for "stolen goods"? Was that sort of search more palatable than a search under a general warrant? Try to identify, from these materials, a definition of general warrants that will enable you to spot their possible reemergence in modern doctrine and practice.

4. *Warranted searches and reasonable searches.* The incidents discussed most during constitutional debates involved *warranted* searches rather than warrantless searches. See Thomas Y. Davies, Recovering the Original Fourth Amendment, 98 Mich. L. Rev. 547, 551 (1999) ("the Framers understood 'unreasonable searches and seizures' simply as a pejorative label for the inherent illegality of any searches or seizures that might be made under general warrants"). Warrants issued from an authority with proper jurisdiction became a legal defense for the government officer in any tort suit against him for trespass during the search or seizure. As William Blackstone put it in his influential treatise on the common law of the period, "a lawful warrant will at all events indemnify the officer, who executes the same ministerially." 4 William Blackstone, Commentaries on the Laws of England *286. A messenger executing a warrant could defend against a tort suit by proving that the search was successful. Thus, warrants diminished the power of the jury in a tort suit to control government officers. See Akhil Amar, Fourth Amendment First Principles, 107 Harv. L. Rev. 757 (1994); compare Ronald J. Alien & Ross M. Rosenberg, The Fourth Amendment and the Limits of Theory: Local Versus General Theoretical Knowledge, 72 St. John's L. Rev. 1149, 1169 (1998) (arguing that juries were not granted general power to determine reasonableness of searches).

The various uses of history in the interpretation of the Fourth Amendment will be a recurring theme over the next few chapters of this book. For additional resources in answering these questions, see the web extension for this chapter at *http://www.crimpro.com/extension/ch03*.

5. *Recent appearance of police departments.* The creators of the Fourth Amendment and the earliest analogs in state constitutions did not anticipate possible abuses by

professional police officers, because police departments did not exist at the time. Most law enforcement was carried out by amateurs: citizens who volunteered (or who grudgingly took their turn) as constable or night watchman. There were local sheriffs, but they had no professional staff. Police departments as we think of them did not appear, even in the largest American cities, until late in the nineteenth century. See Lawrence M. Friedman, Crime and Punishment in American History 27-30 (1993); Carol Steiker, Second Thoughts About First Principles, 107 Harv. L. Rev. 820, 830-38 (1994). Does this major change in circumstance make history less relevant for interpreting the Fourth Amendment than it is for other constitutional language? See Anthony Amsterdam, Perspectives on the Fourth Amendment, 58 Minn. L. Rev. 349 (1974) (treating history as unhelpful).

2. American Limits on General Warrants and Other Searches

In June 1776, just before the American colonies declared their independence, Virginia adopted a Declaration of Rights that included this provision:

> That general warrants, whereby any officer or messenger may be commanded to search suspected places without evidence of a fact committed, or to seize any person or persons not named, or whose offense is not particularly described and supported by evidence, are grievous and oppressive, and ought not to be granted.

The Maryland constitution expanded the concern from general warrants to "all warrants." The Pennsylvania Declaration of Rights in the Constitution of 1776 explained the connection between the limits on searches and warrants, and the basic rights of the people:

> That the people have a right to hold themselves, their houses, papers, and possessions free from search and seizure, and therefore warrants without oaths or affirmations first made, affording a sufficient foundation for them, and whereby "any officer or messenger may be commanded or required to search suspected places, or to seize any person [or his] property, not particularly described, are contrary to that right, and ought not to be granted.

When the debate shifted from state constitutions to the new proposed federal constitution, many of the ratifying conventions in the states stipulated that they were approving the proposed federal constitution under the assumption that individual rights were implicit within the document and that an express Bill of Rights would soon be added. The First Congress elected under the new constitution immediately took up the task of drafting constitutional amendments dealing with basic liberties. James Madison presented to the House of Representatives a package of amendments, including one that addressed the problem of improper warrants:

> The rights of the people to be secured in their persons, their houses, their papers, and their other property, from all unreasonable searches and seizures, shall not be violated by warrants issued without probable cause, supported by oath or affirmation, or not particularly describing the places to be searched, or the persons or things to be seized.

After a House committee made some slight changes in language, the amendment came to the full House for a vote. At this point, some remarkable things happened. Rep. Egbert Benson of New York suggested that the provision was "good as far as it went" but was not sufficient. He proposed inserting the phrase "and no warrant shall issue" after the word "violated," so as to create two clauses, one addressing unreasonable searches and seizures generally and the other focused on warrants. Voting records of the convention showed that the House voted down Benson's proposed change "by a considerable majority." After the vote, the House appointed a committee to collect and summarize the various amendments it had approved over several days of debate. This so-called Committee of Three (which included Benson) placed on its list the search and seizure provision — as Benson had proposed amending it! The Senate and House both approved the language in this form, and the state conventions also ratified the text as follows:

> The right of the people to be secure in their persons, houses, papers, and effects, against unreasonable searches and seizures, shall not be violated, and no Warrants shall issue, but upon probable cause, supported by oath or affirmation, and particularly describing the place to be searched, and the persons or things to be seized.

See Nelson Lasson, The History and Development of the Fourth Amendment to the United States Constitution 100-03 (1937); Edward Dumbauld, The Bill of Rights and What It Means Today 35-42 (1957).

3. *The Language of the Fourth Amendment and Its Analogs*

Courts did not treat the Fourth Amendment as a limit on the power of *state* governments (where most crimes are prosecuted) until Wolf v. Colorado, 338 U.S. 25 (1949). Although the federal Bill of Rights originally applied only to the federal government, the Fourteenth Amendment (passed after the Civil War) declared that "no state shall deprive any person of . . . liberty without due process of law." During the 1940s and 1950s, the Supreme Court decided a series of cases, declaring that many of the rights guaranteed in the federal Bill of Rights were such a fundamental part of "due process" that they should apply to the states. The due process clause selectively "incorporated" these rights against state governments. See George C. Thomas, III, When Constitutional Worlds Collide: Resurrecting the Framers' Bill of Rights and Criminal Procedure, 100 Mich. L. Rev. 145 (2001). Before and after *Wolf,* however, states had their own constitutional limitations on state government action, parallel to the Fourth Amendment.

Today all states have a constitutional provision limiting the power of the government to conduct searches and seizures. About half of the states have a provision that tracks the language of the Fourth Amendment, some with only minor modifications. Other states have variations on the Fourth Amendment language that include additional procedural requirements. A typical requirement appears in article II, section 7 of the Colorado constitution, which says that affidavits must be in writing and that the person or thing to be seized must be described "as near as may be." A few states take aim at the specific problem of general warrants. For example, article I, section 7 of the Tennessee constitution states that "general warrants, whereby an officer may be commanded to search suspected places, without evidence of the fact committed, or to seize any person or persons not named, whose offenses are not particularly described and supported by evidence, are dangerous to liberty and ought not to be granted."

Other states emphasize the range of protected privacy rights of individuals. Article I, section 5 of the Louisiana constitution guarantees that the "person, property, communications, houses, papers, and effects" of every person shall be secure against "invasions of privacy." Arizona and Washington State frame the protection even more generally: "No person shall be disturbed in his private affairs, or his home invaded, without authority of law." The constitutions of about ten states contain express protections for individual "privacy" rights. A number of these state constitutional provisions grew out of recent constitutional conventions, some as recent as the 1990s. See Robert Williams, Are State Constitutional Conventions a Thing of the Past? The Increasing Role of the Constitutional Commission in State Constitutional Change, 1 Hofstra L. & Pol'y Symp. 1 (1996).

The varying language of these Fourth Amendment analogs creates room for differing interpretations of the scope of the rights they protect. But variation in language is not determinative: Some states with provisions identical to the Fourth Amendment have interpreted their language differently from one another and differently from federal law; other states with substantially different language in their constitutions have interpreted it in the same way that the U.S. Supreme Court interprets the Fourth Amendment.

In light of the Fourth Amendment and these state provisions, consider three basic issues that underlie many difficult questions regarding the law of search and seizure:

- *The interaction between probable cause and reasonableness.* Do the Fourth Amendment and its state constitutional analogs provide one standard to determine the validity of government searches and seizures? Is that standard probable cause or reasonableness? Are searches without probable cause presumptively (or conclusively) unreasonable? If reasonableness is not defined by reference to probable cause, how should it be defined?
- *The preference for warrants.* Do you think the Fourth Amendment or its state analogs were meant to require that all (or most) searches and seizures take place only after the issuance of a warrant? Or are warrants merely a mechanism for obtaining prior review of the "reasonableness" of searches and seizures, but otherwise not preferred? In other words, how strong is the presumption for warrants?
- *The nature of warrants.* For searches based on warrants, what limits should be placed on the issuance, content, or effect of warrants? Can warrants be issued for more than one person or place? Do warrants need to specify the crime suspected or the nature of the evidence to be sought? Should time limits be placed on the execution of warrants?

What information, principles, or logic should interpreters use to answer these questions? Should the intent of the framers of each provision matter? Can definitions change over time or in different contexts? The remainder of this chapter explores these questions.

B. PROBABLE CAUSE

The two most important standards in modern criminal procedure for justifying stops, searches, and seizures are reasonable suspicion (examined in Chapter 2) and probable cause. Probable cause is the central standard of traditional search and seizure law, and it continues to govern a large portion of full-fledged searches and seizures, including those based on warrants.

1. Defining Probable Cause

Probable cause is constantly applied but only rarely defined. Perhaps this is because the assessment of probable cause is an inherently fact-laden, case-specific sort of judgment. While some situations arise frequently enough for standards to develop (for example, how information from an unnamed informant should be assessed to determine probable cause), general principles are difficult to deduce.

A close analysis of case law and a handful of statutes suggest that general definitions of probable cause do exist and that there is some interesting variation among those definitions. The most common definition emerges from language used by the Supreme Court in Brinegar v. United States, 338 U.S. 160, 175-76 (1949), reprinted below. Four elements, not all of which are present in every definition, tend to capture the variation in definitions of probable cause.

Reasonable to whom. Most jurisdictions focus on the assessment that a "reasonably prudent" or "cautious" person would make in deciding whether probable cause exists. Some jurisdictions, however, focus on the information that a *police officer* knows. Would officers make the same connections and assessment as a citizen without law enforcement experience or training? Kentucky requires the assessment of probable cause to be reasonable to the magistrate. Would experienced magistrates make the same assessments as police?

Strength of inference. Several formulations define the required strength of the link between the facts offered and the conclusion that criminal activity has occurred. One common formulation says the magistrate must determine whether the facts suggest a "probability of criminal activity." Another says the magistrate must determine whether the facts are sufficient "to believe an offense has been committed." Yet another standard requires that the investigator "believe or consciously entertain a strong suspicion that the person is guilty." A few jurisdictions require merely that there be a "substantial basis for concluding that the articles mentioned are probably present" at the place to be searched.

Can these formulations be translated into probabilities of criminal activity? For example, do some of them mean less than 50 percent, while others mean a 50-50 chance, and still others mean more likely than not? Alone among the states, Oregon answers this question by statute. Oregon Rev. Stat. §131.005(11) states that probable cause "means that there is a substantial objective basis for believing that more likely than not an offense has been committed and a person to be arrested has committed it."

Comparison to other standards. Some jurisdictions not only define the probable cause standard but also suggest its limits through comparison with other procedural standards. For example, several states say that probable cause is "more than mere suspicion or possibility but less than certainty." Some states note that the determination of probable cause requires less confidence that a crime has occurred than is required for guilt (that is, proof beyond a reasonable doubt). As we saw in Chapter 2, the "reasonable suspicion" demands less of a showing by police than probable cause.

Quality of information. Some jurisdictions enhance their general definition of probable cause by requiring that the assessment be based on evidence that is reliable, trustworthy, or credible. The following chart excerpts typical language from the case law, constitutional provisions, and statutes in selected states.

State	*Information to Be Considered*	*Quality of Information*	*Perspective*	*Nature of Belief*	*Degree of Certainty*
Arizona	Facts and circumstances,	based on trustworthy information [such that a]	person of reasonable caution [would believe that]	items are related to criminal activity and likely to be found at the place described.	The showing is one of criminal activity, not the rigorous standard required for admissibility of evidence at trial.
California	A particularized suspicion or facts [sufficient]	to entertain a strong suspicion [such that a]	person of ordinary caution [would find that the]	object of the search is in the particular place to be searched.	The government need not demonstrate certainty.
Colorado	Sufficient facts [that a]		person of reasonable caution [would conclude that]	contraband or evidence of criminal activity is located at the place to be searched.	This judgment is one of reasonableness, not pure mathematical probability.
Connecticut	All information set forth in affidavit [such that the]	totality of the circumstances [could lead a]	magistrate [to conclude that]	contraband or evidence will be found in a particular place [with a]	fair probability.
South Dakota	The existence of facts and circumstances within the knowledge of the magistrate [such that a]		reasonable prudent man [would conclude that]	an offense has been or is being committed and the property exists at the place designated [to a]	probability.

Problem 3-1. Applying Different Probable Cause Standards

Consider the following two searches in light of the California and Connecticut standards.

Case 1: One afternoon, Captain Lee and Sergeant Hurter were on patrol in what they described as a "high crime area." Lee, Hurter, and four other officers in two other patrol cars stopped at 1225 6th Alley East, where five or six persons were gathered in front of a shot house (a private residence where illegal whiskey is sold by the shot). Officers had executed a search warrant at this residence two to three weeks earlier. As a result of that search, the owner of the residence had been arrested and charged with the illegal sale of alcohol. Officers during that earlier search found a small quantity of illegal drugs on the front porch, presumably left by people sitting there who dispersed when the police arrived at the house.

The house was located in a mostly African American neighborhood, and the people gathered in front of the house were African American men. Between the porch of the house and the roadway there was a small yard, and there was no sidewalk. Some of the men, including Eddie Tucker, were standing in the yard abutting the roadway, and some were in the roadway leaning on a parked car. There had been no calls or complaints to the police that day concerning any illegal activity at the house or pertaining to any of the people gathered in front of the house. Neither Lee nor Hurter knew Tucker at that point.

The officers testified that they were not aware of anything illegal occurring among the men, but as Lee exited the car, he noticed that Tucker (who was about three feet away from him) had a large bulge in one of his front pants pockets. For safety reasons, Lee asked Tucker what was in his pocket and told him to take whatever it was out so that it could be seen. Tucker took from his pocket a black 35mm film canister with its lid closed. Both officers knew at this point that the object was a film canister and was not a weapon.

Lee then directed his attention to another of the persons present, and Hurter asked Tucker what was in the canister. In response, Tucker put the canister behind his back. Sergeant Hurter then asked to see the canister. Tucker handed the canister to Hurter, who opened it and found five $10 bags of marijuana packaged in cellophane. Did Officer Hurter have probable cause to search the canister? Compare Ex parte Tucker, 667 So. 2d 1339 (Ala. 1995).

Case 2: At 3:20 A.M. on June 10, the Dothan Police Department received a call saying that shots had been fired at the Johnson Homes apartment complex. Officer Jerry Watkins responded to the call. As Watkins arrived, he saw four people standing outside behind the apartments, arguing. The people yelled for Officer Watkins to stop, but when he did, one of the people standing in the group started running. A second man in the group told Watkins that the person who ran away was Kenneth Moffitt, and that Moffitt "had a gun." Watkins followed Moffitt because he believed that he "would probably be pretty dangerous if he was out there shooting." Moffitt ran into the back door of an apartment, and Watkins followed a few seconds later. Watkins searched the kitchen and the living room, and noticed some cocaine on a television, but Moffitt was not in either of those rooms. Officer Watkins then went into the bedroom across the hall, where a small child was sitting on a bed pointing under the bed. Watkins found Moffitt on the floor under the bed. Did Officer

Watkins have probable cause to enter the apartment? Compare Ex parte Moffitt, 844 So. 2d 531 (Ala. 2002).

VIRGIL BRINEGAR v. UNITED STATES

338 U.S. 160 (1949)

RUTLEDGE, J.*

. . . At about six o'clock on the evening of March 3, 1947, Malsed, an investigator of the Alcohol Tax Unit, and Creehan, a special investigator, were parked in a car beside a highway near the Quapaw Bridge in northeastern Oklahoma. The point was about five miles west of the Missouri-Oklahoma line. Brinegar drove past headed west in his Ford coupe. Malsed had arrested him about five months earlier for illegally transporting liquor; had seen him loading liquor into a car or truck in Joplin, Missouri, on at least two occasions during the preceding six months; and knew him to have a reputation for hauling liquor. As Brinegar passed, Malsed recognized both him and the Ford. He told Creehan, who was driving the officers' car, that Brinegar was the driver of the passing car. Both agents later testified that the car, but not especially its rear end, appeared to be "heavily loaded" and "weighted down with something." Brinegar increased his speed as he passed the officers. They gave chase. After pursuing him for about a mile at top speed, they gained on him as his car skidded on a curve, sounded their siren, overtook him, and crowded his car to the side of the road by pulling across in front of it. The highway was one leading from Joplin, Missouri, toward Vinita, Oklahoma, Brinegar's home. [The officers searched the car and found 13 cases of liquor. Brinegar was charged with importing intoxicating liquor into Oklahoma from Missouri in violation of the federal statute that forbids such importation contrary to the laws of any state. The trial judge denied the motion to suppress. Even though the facts described above did not constitute probable cause, the judge believed that certain statements Brinegar made after he was stopped gave the officers probable cause to search].

The crucial question is whether there was probable cause for Brinegar's arrest, in the light of prior adjudications on this problem, more particularly Carroll v. United States, 267 U.S. 132 (1925), which on its face most closely approximates the situation presented here. The *Carroll* [court ruled] that the facts presented amounted to probable cause for the search of the automobile there involved.

In the *Carroll* case three federal prohibition agents and a state officer stopped and searched the defendants' car on a highway leading from Detroit to Grand Rapids, Michigan, and seized a quantity of liquor discovered in the search. About three months before the search, the two defendants and another man called on two of the agents at an apartment in Grand Rapids and, unaware that they were dealing with federal agents, agreed to sell one of the agents three cases of liquor. Both agents noticed the Oldsmobile roadster in which the three men came to the apartment and its license number. Presumably because the official capacity of the proposed purchaser was suspected by the defendants, the liquor was never delivered.

* [Chief Justice Vinson and Justices Black, Reed, Douglas, Burton, and Minton joined in this opinion. Justices Jackson, Frankfurter, and Murphy dissented. — EDS.]

About a week later the same two agents, while patrolling the road between Grand Rapids and Detroit on the lookout for violations of the National Prohibition Act, were passed by the defendants, who were proceeding in a direction from Grand Rapids toward Detroit in the same Oldsmobile roadster. The agents followed the defendants for some distance but lost track of them. Still later, on the occasion of the search, while the officers were patrolling the same highway, they met and passed the defendants, who were in the same roadster, going in a direction from Detroit toward Grand Rapids. Recognizing the defendants, the agents turned around, pursued them, stopped them about sixteen miles outside Grand Rapids, searched their car and seized the liquor it carried.

This Court ruled that the information held by the agents, together with the judicially noticed fact that Detroit was "one of the most active centers for introducing illegally into this country spirituous liquors for distribution into the interior," constituted probable cause for the search.

I.

Obviously the basic facts held to constitute probable cause in the *Carroll* case were very similar to the basic facts here. . . . In each instance the officers were patrolling the highway in the discharge of their duty. And in each before stopping the car or starting to pursue it they recognized both the driver and the car, from recent personal contact and observation, as having been lately engaged in illicit liquor dealings. Finally, each driver was proceeding in his identified car in a direction from a known source of liquor supply toward a probable illegal market, under circumstances indicating no other probable purpose than to carry on his illegal adventure.

[There were also variations in details of the proof in the two cases.] In *Carroll* the agent's knowledge of the primary and ultimate fact that the accused were engaged in liquor running was derived from the defendants' offer to sell liquor to the agents some three months prior to the search, while here that knowledge was derived largely from Malsed's personal observation, reinforced by hearsay; . . . and in *Carroll* the Court took judicial notice that Detroit was on the international boundary and an active center for illegal importation of spirituous liquors for distribution into the interior, while in this case the facts that Joplin, Missouri, was a ready source of supply for liquor and Oklahoma a place of likely illegal market were known to the agent Malsed from his personal observation and experience as well as from facts of common knowledge. . . .

There were of course some legal as well as some factual differences in the two situations. Under the statute in review in *Carroll* the whole nation was legally dry. Not only the manufacture, but the importation, transportation and sale of intoxicating liquors were prohibited throughout the country. Under the statute now in question only the importation of such liquors contrary to the law of the state into which they are brought and in which they were seized is forbidden. . . .

[The probable place of market for Brinegar may have been] the State of Oklahoma as a whole or its populous northeastern region. From the facts of record we know, as the agents knew, that Oklahoma was a "dry" state. At the time of the search, its law forbade the importation of intoxicating liquors from other states. . . . This fact, taken in connection with the known "wet" status of Missouri and the location of Joplin close to the Oklahoma line, affords a very natural situation for persons inclined to violate the Oklahoma and federal statutes to ply their trade. The proof therefore concerning the source of supply, the place of probable destination and illegal market, and hence the probability that Brinegar was using the highway for the forbidden transportation, was certainly no less strong than the showing in these respects in the *Carroll* case.

Finally, as for the most important potential distinction, namely, that concerning the primary and ultimate fact that the petitioner was engaging in liquor running, Malsed's personal observation of Brinegar's recent activities established that he was so engaged quite as effectively as did the agent's prior bargaining with the defendants in the *Carroll* case. He saw Brinegar loading liquor, in larger quantities than would be normal for personal consumption, into a car or a truck in Joplin on other occasions during the six months prior to the search. He saw the car Brinegar was using in this case in use by him at least once in Joplin within that period and followed it. And several months prior to the search he had arrested Brinegar for unlawful transportation of liquor and this arrest had resulted in an indictment which was pending at the time of this trial. . . .

II.

Guilt in a criminal case must be proved beyond a reasonable doubt and by evidence confined to that which long experience in the common-law tradition, to some extent embodied in the Constitution, has crystallized into rules of evidence consistent with that standard. These rules are historically grounded rights of our system, developed to safeguard men from dubious and unjust convictions, with resulting forfeitures of life, liberty and property. . . .

In dealing with probable cause, however, as the very name implies, we deal with probabilities. These are not technical; they are the factual and practical considerations of everyday life on which reasonable and prudent men, not legal technicians, act. The standard of proof is accordingly correlative to what must be proved.

The substance of all the definitions of probable cause is a reasonable ground for belief of guilt. And this means less than evidence which would justify condemnation or conviction. [It] has come to mean more than bare suspicion: Probable cause exists where the facts and circumstances within [the officers'] knowledge and of which they had reasonably trustworthy information [are] sufficient in themselves to warrant a man of reasonable caution in the belief that an offense has been or is being committed.

These long-prevailing standards seek to safeguard citizens from rash and unreasonable interferences with privacy and from unfounded charges of crime. They also seek to give fair leeway for enforcing the law in the community's protection. Because many situations which confront officers in the course of executing their duties are more or less ambiguous, room must be allowed for some mistakes on their part. But the mistakes must be those of reasonable men, acting on facts leading sensibly to their conclusions of probability. The rule of probable cause is a practical, nontechnical conception affording the best compromise that has been found for accommodating these often opposing interests. Requiring more would unduly hamper law enforcement. To allow less would be to leave law-abiding citizens at the mercy of the officers' whim or caprice.

The troublesome line posed by the facts in the *Carroll* case and this case is one between mere suspicion and probable cause. That line necessarily must be drawn by an act of judgment formed in the light of the particular situation and with account taken of all the circumstances. No problem of searching the home or any other place of privacy was presented either in *Carroll* or here. Both cases involve freedom to use public highways in swiftly moving vehicles for dealing in contraband, and to be unmolested by investigation and search in those movements. In such a case the citizen who has given no good cause for believing he is engaged in that sort of activity is entitled to proceed on his way without interference. But one who recently and repeatedly has given substantial ground for believing that he is engaging in the forbidden transportation in the area of his usual operations has no such immunity, if the officer who intercepts him in that region knows that fact at the time he makes the interception and the circumstances under which it is made are not such as to indicate the suspect going about legitimate affairs.

This does not mean, as seems to be assumed, that every traveler along the public highways may be stopped and searched at the officers' whim, caprice or mere suspicion. The question presented in the *Carroll* case lay on the border between suspicion and probable cause. But the Court carefully considered that problem and resolved it by concluding that the facts within the officers' knowledge when they intercepted the *Carroll* defendants amounted to more than mere suspicion and constituted probable cause for their action. We cannot say this conclusion was wrong, or was so lacking in reason and consistency with the Fourth Amendment's purposes that it should now be overridden. Nor, as we have said, can we find in the present facts any substantial basis for distinguishing this case from the *Carroll* case. Accordingly the judgment is affirmed.

Notes

1. *Applying different standards?* Which of the cases described in Problem 3-1 offers a stronger basis — in other words, a stronger argument for probable cause — for a search? Does the relative strength of the cases depend on the standard applied to them, or are all the standards stronger for one of the cases? Consider the Connecticut standard. Can you add (or subtract) a fact that would make a weaker case for probable cause? Would you change different facts to make the case for finding probable cause stronger or weaker under the California standard?

2. *Probable cause and probabilities.* Does probable cause translate into a level of certainty the same as the preponderance of the evidence standard at trial? Courts in all jurisdictions have long insisted that probable cause is something less than "beyond a reasonable doubt" and something more than "mere suspicion," but they have shied away from equating it with the preponderance standard. See Illinois v. Gates, 462 U.S. 213 (1983) (probable cause requires "only the probability, and not a prima facie showing of criminal activity"). In a survey of more than 150 federal judges, about one-third believed that "probable cause" required 50 percent certainty, with the next largest groups of judges calling for 40 percent and 30 percent certainty. See C. M. A. McCauliff, Burdens of Proof: Degrees of Belief, Quanta of Evidence, or Constitutional Guarantees? 35 Vand. L. Rev. 1293 (1982). Does this mean that the judges would not sustain the validity of a search of a house when the police know that one of three possible locations contains evidence of a serious crime? Cf. Maryland v. Pringle, 540 U.S. 366 (2003) (officer who found $763 in glove compartment and cocaine behind armrest in back seat had probable cause to

arrest driver, front seat passenger, and rear passengers when all occupants of car denied knowledge of drugs).

3. *Police expertise in assessing probable cause.* Courts often recognize that officers rely on their training and experience in assessing probable cause. See Ornelas v. United States, 517 U.S. 690 (1996) (reviewing court should give due weight to inferences drawn from historical facts by resident judges and local law enforcement officers; officer may draw inferences "based on his own experience"; the loose panel below the backseat armrest in the automobile in this case may suggest to a layman "only wear and tear, but to Officer Luedke, who had searched roughly 2,000 cars for narcotics, it suggested that drugs may be secreted inside the panel"). As a trial judge in a suppression hearing, would you attribute the same level of expertise to all officers or to those within a particular unit of the police department (such as the narcotics squad)? Or would you insist on some particularized showing of experience from each police officer trying to establish probable cause? See Max Minzer, Putting Probability Back into Probable Cause, 87 Tex. L. Rev. 913 (2009) (proposal for the use of empirical evidence of the success of a given investigating officer or investigative technique in assessing the existence of probable cause to search or seize); Commonwealth v. Thompson, 985 A.2d 928 (Pa. 2009) (officer observed defendant standing on street while exchanging small object for cash from driver; in such a setting, characterization of neighborhood as "high crime" and abstract assertion of police expertise would not suffice for probable cause, but officer here made the requisite connection between his experience and facts in case through testimony that he had observed hundreds of similar transactions that turned out to involve illegal narcotics).

4. *Actual knowledge of officer.* Does one assess probable cause based on what the officer(s) on the scene actually relied on to justify the search or on facts that were available to the officer, whether or not she relied on them? Courts have not entirely agreed on this question, but the existence of probable cause usually depends on the facts available to the officer in the field, not just on facts the officer actually relied on to justify a search or seizure.

Most jurisdictions test probable cause based on the collective information the police have, even if the arresting or searching officer does not hold all of that information. See Prince v. United States, 825 A.2d 928 (D.C. 2003). Does this "collective knowledge" doctrine draw the wrong lessons from the institutional reality of police work? Should search and seizure doctrine generally try to account for the way that organizations (police departments) typically shape the actions of individuals (police officers)? For a comparison of the "collective knowledge" rule and the related "fellow officer" doctrine, see the web extension for this chapter at *http://www.crimpro.com/extension/ch03*.

Recall the discussion in Chapter 2 of "pretextual" stops, and the choice discussed there between objective and subjective standards in criminal procedure. It is possible that the collective knowledge doctrine gives the police too much opportunity for *post hoc* rationalization of the individual officer's decision to conduct a search. What, if anything, is wrong with justifying a search after the fact, based on events that truly did occur?

2. *Sources of Information to Support Probable Cause*

The information needed to show probable cause comes from sources as varied as victims, other witnesses, anonymous sources, confidential informants, and police officers themselves. In the abstract, which of these sources would you expect to be most reliable? Can we judge reliability in the abstract? Jurisdictions have reached different conclusions, and have used different standards, in answering these questions. This section considers how courts assess information from different sources, with particular attention to confidential informants and anonymous sources.

a. Confidential Informants

Much as the law of evidence shows a mistrust of hearsay, so the law of probable cause shows a mistrust of informants, who provide information to the police but are often not available to be questioned further when the time comes to assess probable cause. The U.S. Supreme Court has developed a specialized set of rules for judging the reliability of information from informants. The following two cases trace the impact of a major change in the Supreme Court's approach to such questions.

■ STATE v. TIMOTHY BARTON

594 A.2d 917 (Conn. 1991)

PETERS, J.

The sole issue in this appeal is whether . . . article first, §7, of the Connecticut constitution permits a court to determine the existence of probable cause on the basis of the "totality of the circumstances" when it reviews a search warrant application based on information provided to the police by a confidential informant. The state charged the defendant, Timothy Barton, with possession of over a kilogram of marihuana with intent to sell and with possession of marihuana . . . after police, acting under the authority of a warrant, had searched his home and had seized more than fifty pounds of marihuana there. The defendant moved to suppress the seized evidence, and the trial court granted the defendant's motion on the ground that the affidavit accompanying the search warrant application failed to state the informant's "basis of knowledge." The charges were subsequently dismissed with prejudice. [We] reverse.

[Officers] of the Winsted police department, acting on the authority of a search and seizure warrant obtained that day on the basis of information provided by a confidential informant, searched the defendant's apartment. . . . In the course of their search, the police found some fifty-two pounds of marihuana wrapped in clear plastic bags and kept in larger garbage bags in a bedroom. When the defendant returned home after midnight, the police arrested him.

[At the hearing on the defendant's motion to suppress this evidence, the trial court] applied the two-pronged analysis mandated by this court's decision in State v. Kimbro, 496 A.2d 498 (Conn. 1985), which requires a magistrate, in determining whether probable cause exists for a search or seizure, to evaluate both the "basis of knowledge" and the "veracity" or "reliability" of an informant upon whose information the police have relied. Spinelli v. United States, 393 U.S. 410 (1969); Aguilar v. Texas, 378 U.S. 108 (1964). In the circumstances of this case, [the trial court] concluded that the affidavit in support of the search warrant did not adequately set forth the unnamed informant's basis of knowledge and therefore failed to establish probable cause. . . .

In the present appeal, the state urges us to overrule our holding in *Kimbro*, and to adopt the "totality of the circumstances" standard for determining probable cause used in the federal courts pursuant to the decision of the United States Supreme Court in Illinois v. Gates, 462 U.S. 213 (1983). . . . We agree with the state that application of the standards mandated by *Kimbro* has resulted at times in unduly technical readings of warrant affidavits, and we reject such an inappropriate methodology. . . .

In Illinois v. Gates, the United States Supreme Court rejected the "complex superstructure of evidentiary and analytical rules" that had evolved from its earlier decisions in Aguilar v. Texas and Spinelli v. United States. [The] "two-pronged" *Aguilar-Spinelli* test provides a method for evaluating the existence of probable cause consistent with the requirements of the fourth amendment when a search warrant affidavit is based upon information supplied to the police by a confidential informant. The issuing judge must be informed of (1) some of the underlying circumstances relied on by the informant in concluding that the facts are as he claims they are, and (2) some of the underlying circumstances from which the officer seeking the warrant concluded (a) that the informant, whose identity need not be disclosed, was credible, or (b) that the information was reliable. When the information supplied by the informant fails to satisfy the *Aguilar-Spinelli* test, probable cause may still be found if the warrant application affidavit sets forth other circumstances — typically independent police corroboration of certain details provided by the informant — that bolster the deficiencies.

The *Gates* court identified two principal flaws in the *Aguilar-Spinelli* test. First, because courts and commentators had generally regarded the two prongs of the test to be entirely independent of each other, courts had struggled to formulate rules regarding what types of information and what types of corroboration might satisfy each of the prongs. Specifically, some courts had concluded that independent police investigation might corroborate the "reliability" of the information, but could never satisfy the "basis of knowledge" prong of the test, while ample "self-verifying details" might establish that the informant had personal knowledge of the alleged activity and thus could satisfy the "basis of knowledge" prong, but could never compensate for a deficiency in the "veracity" or "reliability" prong. The "elaborate set of legal rules" that had resulted from this emphasis on the independent character of the two prongs had led courts, in many cases, to dissect warrant applications in an excessively technical manner, "with undue attention being focused on isolated issues that [could not] sensibly be divorced from the other facts presented to the magistrate." Such a result was inconsistent with the nature of a probable cause determination, which, as the *Gates* court noted, involves a "practical, nontechnical conception."

The second principal flaw in the application of the *Aguilar-Spinelli* test, according to the *Gates* court, was that the test had caused reviewing courts, both at suppression hearings and at appellate levels, to test the sufficiency of warrant affidavits by de novo review. Such de novo review, in the view of the *Gates* majority, was inconsistent with the constitution's "strong preference for searches conducted pursuant to a warrant." A reviewing court should rather determine whether the magistrate issuing the warrant had a "substantial basis" for concluding that a search would uncover evidence of criminal activity.

In rejecting the complex structure of rules that had evolved from *Aguilar* and *Spinelli,* however, the *Gates* court did not reject out of hand the underlying concerns that had originally been expressed in *Aguilar.* In that case, the United States Supreme Court invalidated a search warrant supported by an affidavit that stated only that the affiants "have received reliable information from a credible person," without stating any of the underlying circumstances that would support a finding of probable cause. The *Aguilar* court ruled that such a conclusory affidavit failed to state a factual basis on which a neutral and detached magistrate could determine the existence of probable cause. In *Gates,* the court reaffirmed that the "veracity" or "reliability" and the "basis of knowledge" inquiries formulated in *Aguilar* remain "highly relevant" in the determination of probable cause and should be regarded as "closely intertwined issues that may usefully illuminate the commonsense, practical question" of the existence of probable cause to believe that contraband or evidence is located in a particular place. The *Gates* court abandoned only a "rigid compartmentalization" of the inquiries and denied that the court had ever intended them to be understood as "entirely separate and independent requirements to be rigidly exacted in every case."

In the place of the "compartmentalized" *Aguilar-Spinelli* test, the *Gates* court directed lower courts to apply a "totality of the circumstances" analysis more consistent with traditional assessments of probable cause. While still employing the analytical frame of reference established in *Aguilar,* a "totality of the circumstances" analysis permits a judge issuing a warrant greater freedom to assess "the relative weights of all the various indicia of reliability (and unreliability) attending an informant's tip." . . . The task of a subsequent court reviewing the magistrate's decision to issue a warrant is to determine whether the magistrate had a "substantial basis" for concluding that probable cause existed. The court's decision in *Gates* emphasized the necessity of a case-by-case analysis of probable cause based on all of the facts presented to the judge issuing the warrant, not merely on those capable of categorization as indicating the "veracity" or "basis of knowledge" of a particular informant.

[We turn now to a reconsideration of our 1985 decision in State v. Kimbro.] *Kimbro* did not rely upon historical analysis to determine the standard by which probable cause should be measured. We relied, rather, upon our determination that the *Aguilar-Spinelli* test, "with its two prongs of 'veracity' or 'reliability' and 'basis of knowledge,' offers a practical and independent test under our constitution that predictably guides the conduct of all concerned, including magistrates and law enforcement officials, in the determination of probable cause." We regarded the *Gates* "totality of the circumstances" analysis as an "amorphous standard" that inadequately safeguarded the rights of individuals to be free from unjustified intrusions. Upon careful review of that determination, we agree with the conclusion of the United States Supreme Court in *Gates* that the two prongs of the *Aguilar-Spinelli* test are highly relevant evidentiary questions that a magistrate issuing the warrant must consider in deciding whether probable cause for a search or seizure exists, but that they are not wholly independent and dispositive constitutional tests for which de novo review exists at a suppression hearing.

In reaching our present conclusion we return to first principles. Article first, §7, of our constitution . . . safeguards the privacy, the personal security, and the property of the individual against unjustified intrusions by agents of the government. One of the principal means by which the warrant requirement protects the privacy and property of the individual is by the interposition of a neutral and detached magistrate who must judge independently the sufficiency of an affidavit supporting an application for a search warrant. Whether applying the fourth amendment or article first, §7, of our own constitution, we have frequently recognized that a magistrate issuing a warrant cannot form an independent opinion as to the existence of probable cause unless the affidavit supporting the warrant application sets forth some of the facts upon which the police have relied in concluding that a search is justified. . . .

When a police officer seeking a search warrant relies on hearsay information supplied by confidential informants rather than on personal knowledge and observations, certain additional facts are necessary to ensure that the magistrate's decision to issue the warrant is informed and independent. [The *Aguilar* decision began with the commonsensical premise] that confidential informants are themselves often "criminals, drug addicts, or even pathological liars" whose motives for providing information to the police may range from offers of immunity or sentence reduction, promises of money payments, or "such perverse motives as revenge or the hope of eliminating criminal competition." Because such an informant's reliance on rumors circulating on the street is not unlikely and the veracity of such an informant is questionable, a magistrate reviewing a search warrant application based on such an informant's word can best assess the probable reliability of the information if she or he is informed of some of the predicate facts that indicate how the informant gained his information and why the police officer believes that the information is reliable in order to decide, independently, whether the police officer's inferences from the informant's statements are reasonable.

In *Kimbro,* we expressed concern that the "fluid" totality of the circumstances analysis approved in the fourth amendment context of Illinois v. Gates would inadequately inform magistrates and law enforcement officials of their obligation to scrutinize the information gathered from confidential police informants with appropriate caution. In construing article first, §7, of our constitution to require continued application of the *Aguilar-Spinelli* test, we sought to make clear certain benchmarks to guide the discretion of our judges in reviewing ex parte applications for search and seizure warrants based on confidential informants' tips.

Nonetheless, over time, the case law applying the *Aguilar-Spinelli* test has come to be encrusted with an overlay of analytical rigidity that is inconsistent with the underlying proposition that it is the constitutional function of the magistrate issuing the warrant to exercise discretion in the determination of probable cause. That discretion must be controlled by constitutional principles and guided by the evidentiary standards developed in our prior cases, but it should not be so shackled by rigid analytical standards that it deprives the magistrate of the ability to draw reasonable inferences from the facts presented. To the extent that *Kimbro* stands for the proposition that the exercise of discretion by a magistrate is reviewable only according to fixed analytical standards, it is overruled.

Our adoption of a "totality of the circumstances" analysis does not mean, however, that a magistrate considering a search warrant application should automatically defer to the conclusion of the police that probable cause exists. Such deference would be an abdication of the magistrate's constitutional responsibility to exercise an independent and detached judgment to protect the rights of privacy and personal security of the people of Connecticut.

In essence, our adoption of a "totality of the circumstances" analysis of the probable cause requirement of article first, §7, of our constitution means simply this: When a search warrant affidavit is based on information provided to the police by confidential informants, the magistrate should examine the affidavit to determine whether it adequately describes both the factual basis of the informant's knowledge and the basis on which the police have determined that the information is reliable. If the warrant affidavit fails to state in specific terms how the informant gained his knowledge or why the police believe the information to be trustworthy, however, the magistrate can also consider all the circumstances set forth in the affidavit to determine whether, despite these deficiencies, other objective indicia of reliability reasonably establish that probable cause to search exists. In making this determination, the magistrate is entitled to draw reasonable inferences from the facts presented. When a magistrate has determined that the warrant affidavit presents sufficient objective indicia of reliability to justify a search and has issued a warrant, a court reviewing that warrant at a subsequent suppression hearing should defer to the reasonable inferences drawn by the magistrate. . . .

In adopting the *Gates* "totality of the circumstances" analysis, as we have here construed it, as the standard of analysis applicable to article first, §7, of our constitution, we do not intend to dilute the constitutional safeguards of the warrant requirement. This court has both the constitutional duty to construe article first, §7, in a way that adequately protects the rights of individuals in Connecticut and also the supervisory responsibility, as the overseer of the judiciary in Connecticut, to ensure that the standards adopted here require law enforcement officers to provide magistrates with adequate information on which to base their decisions in an ex parte context. . . .

We now consider the affidavit presented in this case in light of the proper constitutional standards. [The critical paragraph of the affidavit] provides: "That the affiants state on Sunday, August 7, 1988 Sgt. Gerald O. Peters received information from a confidential informant at police headquarters pertaining to Tim Barton who resides at 232 Perch Rock Trail, Winsted, Connecticut, first floor that Barton has in his apartment a large quantity of marijuana in plastic garbage bags, which are kept in a closet. That the informant also provided Sergeant Peters of [*sic*] a sample of the marijuana that is in the bags. A field test of the marijuana substance that was provided to Sgt. Peters was field tested and the test results was [*sic*] positive for cannibas [*sic*] substance. The informant further stated that Tim Barton operates a Texas registered vehicle and after being away for approximately one week Barton returned home on Saturday, August 6, 1988 and unloaded several large plastic bags in the evening hours. The informant further stated that shortly after that four to five people arrived at the Barton apartment and stayed a short while and then left with plastic garbage bags." . . .

Reviewing the allegations set forth in the third paragraph of the affidavit in this case, the Appellate Court concluded that the affidavit failed to establish probable cause because it was defective under the "basis of knowledge" prong of the *Aguilar-Spinelli* test mandated by *Kimbro*. The Appellate Court cited the following deficiencies: (1) the affidavit did not expressly indicate that the informant had ever been inside the defendant's apartment; (2) the details regarding the truck and the carrying in and out of garbage bags were "innocuous"; (3) the affidavit did not indicate that the informant had said that he had purchased the marihuana from the defendant, or that he had observed the defendant "constantly in possession" of marihuana in the apartment; and (4) the informant did not give a detailed description of the apartment but merely alleged that the garbage bags were in a closet. We agree that the affidavit does not expressly state that the informant had personal knowledge of the facts described. Legitimate law enforcement efforts, however, should not be unduly frustrated because a police officer, in the haste of a criminal investigation, fails to recite his information in particular formulaic phrases. Probable cause does not depend upon the incantation of certain magic words. Having reviewed the circumstances described by the informant, we conclude that the affidavit provided a substantial basis for the magistrate's inference that the informant was reporting events that he had personally observed.

[Details from the affidavit] support an inference that the informant was sufficiently acquainted with the defendant to have known of a week-long absence and to have been present to observe the defendant's activities upon his return. When considered together with the detail that the garbage bags were kept in a closet and with the fact that the informant provided the police with a marihuana sample purportedly from the same bags, these details support a reasonable, commonsense inference that the informant had personally observed the events he reported and had secured the marihuana sample directly from the defendant at his apartment. . . . Although the magistrate could have properly exercised his discretion to reject the warrant application or to require the affiants to supplement it or corroborate some of its details we conclude that the inference drawn by the magistrate that the informant had firsthand knowledge of the defendant's activities was not unreasonable.

[We also conclude] that the affidavit provided a substantial basis for the magistrate's inference that the informant's information was reliable. The first circumstance supporting an inference of "veracity" or "reliability" is the fact that the informant was not anonymous. . . . Because his identity was known to the police, the informant could expect adverse consequences if the information that he provided was erroneous. Those consequences might range from a loss of confidence or indulgence by the police to prosecution for the class A misdemeanor of falsely reporting an incident . . . had the information supplied proved to be a fabrication.

More significantly, however, the informant supplied the police with a sample of a substance that the police tested and confirmed to be marihuana. By entering the police station with the marihuana in his possession and by exhibiting the marihuana to the police, the informant rendered himself liable to arrest, conviction, and imprisonment. . . . Although the warrant application would have unquestionably been stronger if the affiants had bolstered the reliability of the informant by independently corroborating some of the details he reported we conclude that the affidavit sufficiently set forth some of the underlying circumstances from which the police could have concluded that the informant was credible or that his information was reliable.

As our discussion of this affidavit demonstrates, the determination of an informant's "veracity" or "reliability" and "basis of knowledge" remains highly relevant under the constitutional standard announced in this decision. . . . This is a marginal case; the magistrate could reasonably have demanded more information. We will not invalidate a warrant, however, merely because we might, in the first instance, have reasonably declined to draw the inferences that were necessary here. Having reviewed all the circumstances presented to the magistrate in this affidavit, we conclude that the affidavit provided a substantial basis for concluding that probable cause existed. We accordingly reverse the judgment of the Appellate Court [and] remand the case to the trial court for further proceedings.

GLASS, J., concurring in part, dissenting in part.

I concur in the result reached by the majority in this case because, unlike the majority, I conclude that the disputed warrant meets the established requirements of the time honored *Aguilar-Spinelli* test. Because I disagree with the majority's decision to scrap the *Aguilar-Spinelli* test by overruling State v. Kimbro . . . I write separately in dissent. . . .

Dressed today in Connecticut constitutional finery, the *Gates* approach relegates the principles pertinent to the "veracity" and "basis of knowledge" prongs of the *Aguilar-Spinelli* test to the status of "relevant considerations" among the amorphous "totality of the circumstances." The purported relevance of these "considerations," however, is belied by the majority's suggestion that despite "deficiencies" under both prongs of the *Aguilar-Spinelli* test, a warrant may yet derive sufficient sustenance from the "totality of the circumstances" to satisfy the mandates of our constitution. The majority thus appears to have strayed even further beyond the strictures of *Aguilar-Spinelli* than the *Gates* majority, which proposed that "a deficiency in one [of the prongs of the *Aguilar-Spinelli* test] may be compensated for . . . by a strong showing as to the other, or by some other indicia of reliability." Under the majority's evident reading of *Gates*, a warrant deficient under both prongs of the *Aguilar-Spinelli* test, nevertheless, complies with Connecticut constitutional requirements where the "totality of the circumstances" permit. [Magistrates and police officers,] unfettered by meaningful standards by which to discharge their respective functions in the warrant process, are now granted the unbridled play to accord weight to their subjective preferences in determining the "circumstances" whose "totality" permissibly adds up to probable cause. . . .

The *Aguilar-Spinelli* test, in my opinion, allows ample room for the application of common sense and the evaluation of the unique facts presented by particular cases. I do not, therefore, share the majority's desire to strip probable cause determinations of the "fixed, analytical standards" of *Aguilar-Spinelli* that have served to protect the free men and women of Connecticut from unreasonable government intrusion in a way that the standardless *Gates* approach, I submit, will never do. . . . In my view, the Connecticut constitution is not a document so fragile that a swift stroke of the federal pen suffices, as is allowed today, to erode the substantive protections found not six years ago to be afforded thereunder to the citizens of this state.

■ STATE v. RANDALL UTTERBACK

485 N.W.2d 760 (Neb. 1992)

PER CURIAM

[A] search warrant, to be valid, must be supported by an affidavit establishing probable cause [founded on articulable facts.] When a search warrant is obtained on the strength of an informant's information, the affidavit in support of the issuance of the search warrant must (1) set forth facts demonstrating the basis of the informant's knowledge of criminal activity and (2) establish the informant's credibility, or the informant's credibility must be established in the affidavit through a police officer's independent investigation. The affidavit must affirmatively set forth the circumstances from which the status of the informant can reasonably be inferred.

To determine the sufficiency of an affidavit used to obtain a search warrant, this jurisdiction has adopted the "totality of the circumstances" test set forth by the U.S. Supreme Court in Illinois v. Gates, 462 U.S. 213 (1983). The issuing magistrate must make a practical, commonsense decision whether, given the totality of the circumstances set forth in the affidavit before him, including the veracity and basis of knowledge of the persons supplying hearsay information, there is a fair probability that contraband or evidence of a crime will be found in a particular place. . . .

At approximately 7 A.M. on March 1, 1990, a Fremont police detective and six or seven fellow law enforcement officers executed a no-knock search warrant at Utterback's home. Utterback shared his home with his wife and infant child. In various containers discovered at various locales in the Utterback house, police found 25 separate plastic bags which contained a total of 570 grams of marijuana. . . .

The warrant which the officers executed authorized a search for automatic weapons, drug paraphernalia, and various controlled substances. The police detective obtained the warrant on the previous day from a Dodge County judge. The sworn affidavit executed by the police detective to obtain the search warrant states in pertinent part:

> On February 28, 1990, your affiant was advised by an *individual who is neither a paid nor habitual informant* that a second individual named "Randy" was engaged in the distribution and sale of controlled substances at the residence [at 321 North K Street]. The informant advised that "Randy" lived at the above described residence with his wife. The informant gave a physical description of "Randy" which matches the physical description of Randy Utterback contained in Fremont Police Dept. files. *The informant advised your affiant that in the past six months (the informant) had purchased marijuana from "Randy" at the residence described above,* and had observed other sales of illegal drugs at said residence. The informant further advised your affiant that (the informant) had been inside said residence within the last five days, and had seen a large quantity of marijuana, and lesser quantities of hashish, cocaine, LSD, and PCP. The informant indicated to your affiant that (the informant) was very familiar with illegal drugs, and the information furnished to your affiant indicated such knowledge.
>
> The informant further indicated to your affiant that (the informant) had observed what (the informant) believed to be an AK 47 assault rifle and an Uzi submachine gun in said residence, together with other weapons. The informant advised your affiant that (the informant) had personally inspected these weapons, and that they were loaded with ammunition. The informant gave a description of these weapons to your affiant, and that description is consistent with an AK 47 assault rifle and an Uzi submachine gun.
>
> Your affiant personally drove by the above described residence and observed an older model blue station wagon parked in the driveway of said residence bearing Nebraska license plate No. 5-B8618. According to records of the Dodge County Treasurer said vehicle is registered to Randy and/or Maria Utterback. Your affiant personally checked the records of the Fremont Department of Utilities and determined that the utilities were registered to Maria Utterback. . . .

Utterback argues that the search warrant was invalid in that the affidavit failed to establish the veracity of the confidential informant. To credit a confidential source's information in making a probable cause determination, the affidavit should support an inference that the source was trustworthy and that the source's accusation of criminal activity was made on the basis of information obtained in a reliable way.

Among the ways in which the reliability of an informant may be established are by showing in the affidavit to obtain a search warrant that (1) the informant has given reliable information to police officers in the past, see State v. Hoxworth, 358 N.W.2d 208 (Neb. 1984); (2) the informant is a citizen informant, see State v. Duff, 412 N.W.2d 843 (Neb. 1987); (3) the informant has made a statement that is against his or her penal interest, see State v. Sneed, 436 N.W.2d 211 (Neb. 1989); and (4) a police officer's independent investigation establishes the informant's reliability or the reliability of the information the informant has given, see United States v. Stanert, 762 F.2d 775 (9th Cir. 1985).

Nowhere in the detective's affidavit to obtain the search warrant in this case is there an averment that the detective's informant had given reliable information in the past, nor is there an averment that the informant was a "citizen informant."[Our prior cases have defined a citizen informant as]

> a citizen who purports to be the victim of or to have been the witness of a crime who is motivated by good citizenship and acts openly in aid of law enforcement. [E]xperienced stool pigeons or persons criminally involved or disposed are not regarded as "citizen-informants" because they are generally motivated by something other than good citizenship. . . .

The status of a citizen informant cannot attach unless the affidavit used to obtain a search warrant affirmatively sets forth the circumstances from which the existence of the status can reasonably be inferred. Here, there is nothing in the detective's affidavit used to obtain a search warrant even hinting that the informant was "motivated by good citizenship."

The State argues that the assertion in the detective's affidavit that "[t]he informant advised your affiant that in the past six months (the informant) had purchased marijuana from 'Randy' at the residence described above" was a statement against the penal interest of the informant. An admission by an informant that he or she participated in the crime about which the informant is informing carries its own indicia of reliability, since people do not lightly admit a crime and place critical evidence of that crime in the hands of police.

The act of purchasing marijuana is not a statutorily proscribed act in Nebraska. [Statutes] prohibit the possession of marijuana and . . . being under its influence, but nowhere in the statutes of the State of Nebraska is the purchase of marijuana expressly prohibited. There is nothing in the affidavit used to obtain the search warrant in this case that would establish, unequivocally, that the informant could be prosecuted for the crimes of possession or being under the influence of marijuana. [When] the informant in this case admitted to purchasing marijuana he did not make a statement against his penal interest.

The fourth method of determining the veracity of a confidential informant is through corroboration. Here, the affidavit reveals only that the police corroborated that Utterback lived at the described address, that the car in the driveway was registered to him, that the utilities at the house were registered to Utterback's wife, and that Utterback's physical description matched that given by the informant. If the police had chosen to corroborate the information regarding any criminal activities of Utterback's rather than merely corroborating these innocent details of his life, or had the affidavit contained other corroborative sources of information about the same alleged criminal activity of Utterback's, the veracity of the informant might have been established in the affidavit. However, no such corroboration is reflected in the detective's affidavit used to obtain the search warrant in this case.

We conclude that the affidavit in support of obtaining the search warrant herein fails to establish the veracity and reliability of the confidential informant and that the county judge was clearly wrong in determining that it supported a finding of probable cause to issue a search warrant. . . .

Notes

1. Gates *versus* Aguilar-Spinelli: *majority position.* In Illinois v. Gates, 462 U.S. 213 (1983), the Supreme Court upheld a trial court's finding of probable cause on the following facts. The police received an anonymous letter on May 3 alleging that a husband and wife were engaged in selling drugs; that the wife would drive their car to Florida on May 3 to be loaded with drugs, and the husband would fly down in a few days to drive the car back; that the car's trunk would be loaded with drugs; and that the suspects were storing over $100,000 worth of drugs in their basement. A police officer determined the address of the couple and learned that the husband made a reservation on a May 5 flight to Florida. A federal drug enforcement agent confirmed that the husband took the flight, stayed overnight in a motel room registered in the wife's name, and left the following morning with a woman in a car bearing an Illinois license plate issued to the husband, heading north on an interstate highway. These facts were sufficient under the "totality of the circumstances" test. Could they also support probable cause under the *Aguilar-Spinelli* test?

More than 40 states have adopted the *Gates* "totality of the circumstances" standard, though a handful of states such as Massachusetts, New York, and Tennessee (fewer than 10) have retained the *Aguilar-Spinelli* analysis, relying on state constitutions or statutes. See, e.g., People v. Serrano, 710 N.E.2d 655 (N.Y. 1999). Why have these states rejected the *Gates* standard? A few jurisdictions have adopted a "totality of the circumstances" test but have emphasized the continuing relevance of the *Aguilar-Spinelli* analysis. Is this a preferable compromise position?

The *Barton* court in Connecticut switched from its earlier choice of *Aguilar-Spinelli* to the *Gates* standard, saying the *Aguilar-Spinelli* analysis had become "encrusted with an overlay of analytical rigidity." What evidence did the court offer to support this conclusion? If the claim about "encrustation" is hyperbole, what other reasons might have moved the court to the *Gates* standard?

2. *Fact-based probable cause analysis.* Both *Barton* and *Utterback* adopt the "totality of the circumstances" standard of *Gates.* Which set of facts provided stronger support for a finding of probable cause? Which confidential informant provided

greater detail? Which description could a police officer verify more easily? Do you agree with the court in *Utterback* that an admitted purchase of marijuana is not an admission against penal interest because purchasing is not a crime? The web extension for this chapter, at *http://www.crimpro.com/extension/ch03*, offers photographs of Utterback's home.

The "totality" standard, as the court said in *Barton*, is designed to place more responsibility for the probable cause finding in the hands of the factfinder on the scene: the magistrate reviewing the application for a warrant. Should other institutions allow magistrates to make probable cause determinations by their own lights or should they attempt to standardize the probable cause determination? Do you imagine that magistrates see similar fact patterns repeatedly, ones amenable to legal rules? Or do the warrant applications present such different fact patterns that they cannot usefully be compared?

3. *Legal standards and legal cultures.* How different are the alternative legal standards at issue in these cases? If you were concerned about limiting police powers at a time of rising fear about crime, would you rather be in a state with the *Aguilar-Spinelli* standard or in a state with a legal culture suspicious of government abuses where the courts use the *Gates* standard? Attorneys and others who train police officers very often emphasize the facts central to the *Aguilar-Spinelli* standard, even in jurisdictions that have adopted the *Gates* standard under the state constitution. See Corey Fleming Hirokawa, Making the "Law of the Land" the Law on the Street: How Police Academies Teach Evolving Fourth Amendment Law, 49 Emory L. J. 295 (2000). Why do they make such a choice?

4. *Prevalence of confidential informants.* While officers rely heavily on their own observations in unwarranted searches, cases involving search warrants more often turn on evidence obtained from confidential informants. A survey of warrants issued in drug cases in San Diego in 1998 found that 64 percent of the warrant applications included information from confidential informants, and a quarter of the applications offered information from anonymous tips. Most of the applications gave little information about the informant's reliability or track record; the information offered appeared in standard boilerplate language. However, in almost all cases depending on information from confidential informants (95 percent of them), the police corroborated the tip by conducting a "controlled buy" of narcotics. See Laurence A. Benner and Charles T. Samarkos, Searching for Narcotics in San Diego: Preliminary Findings from the San Diego Search Warrant Project, 36 Cal. W. L. Rev. 221, 238-43 (2000).

5. *The presumption in favor of "citizen informants."* As suggested in dicta in *Utterback*, most courts presume information provided by victims and witnesses to be sufficiently reliable to serve as a basis for finding probable cause without additional proof that the source is credible or the information reliable. See Bryant v. State, 901 So. 2d 810 (Fla. 2005). Why? Does a person lose the status of "citizen informant" if she receives a reward for the information? What if the police pay the citizen small amounts of cash for meals or transportation? See People v. Cantre, 95 A.D.2d 522 (N.Y App. Div. 1983). Can victims or witnesses be liable to suspects for the torts of malicious prosecution or false arrest if they file a complaint with an intent other than the investigation or prosecution of the suspect?

6. *Informer's privilege.* Should suspects be able to challenge information provided by a confidential informant, even at the stage of establishing probable cause? Courts and legislatures have long recognized an "informer's privilege" that allows the government to withhold the name of a confidential informant. Drawing on well-established common law roots in the law of evidence, the Supreme Court in McCray v. Illinois, 386 U.S. 300 (1967), explained the privilege in these terms: "Whether an informer is motivated by good citizenship, promise of leniency or prospect of pecuniary award, he will usually condition his cooperation on an assurance of anonymity — to protect himself and his family from harm, to preclude adverse social reactions." . . .

Typically, the law allows a magistrate or judge (but not the suspect) to learn the informer's identity and to examine the informer in camera if there is some reason to disbelieve the informer's statements. Should the informer's privilege apply when *all* the information supporting a search warrant is withheld from the defendant as confidential? Justice Mosk of the California Supreme Court, in a dissenting opinion in People v. Hobbs, 873 P.2d 1246 (Cal. 1994) characterized this problem as follows:

> A search warrant containing no information other than the address of a home to be searched. Not a word as to what the government seeks to discover and seize. A government informer, his — or, indeed, her — identity kept secret from the suspect, the suspect's counsel, and the public. Both the suspect and counsel barred from a closed proceeding before a magistrate. No record of the proceeding given to the suspect or counsel. Based entirely on the foregoing, a court order approving an unrestricted search of the suspect's home. Did this scenario occur in a communist dictatorship? Under a military junta? Or perhaps in a Kafka novel? No, this is grim reality in California in the final decade of the 20th century.

What if another court — say, the Idaho Supreme Court — reads Justice Mosk's observation, then re-reads Kafka and decides to eliminate the informer's privilege? Could a legal system function if it took the position that no deprivation of liberty, including a search or seizure, could take place without full disclosure to the suspect after the search or arrest?

b. Anonymous Sources

Should courts treat anonymous sources like citizen informants, with presumptions of reliability, or like confidential informants, with a requirement that police show the informant is trustworthy or the information is accurate? Consider the following "wanted" poster, soliciting anonymous and confidential informants, along with the case on the next page.

WANTED: Information

Do you want to help keep Anaconda-Deer Lodge County
DRUG FREE . . . ?
HERE'S YOUR CHANCE!
If you know or suspect that someone is dealing in drugs . . .
TURN THEM IN
Fill out the information below, clip it out, and mail to:

Jim Connors, Police Chief
Anaconda, MT

or phone 555-5242
All information will be kept strictly confidential

....

Who? (name) ______________________ Age ______
Where? (address) ______________________
City, State ______________________
What? Coke __________ Crank __________ Grass __________
Any other info ______________________

■ STATE v. KELLI JOY RAVEYDTS
691 N.W.2d 290 (S.D. 2004)

KONENKAMP, J.

In this appeal, we confront the question of what amount of independent police corroboration is sufficient, when combined with information received from anonymous informants, to establish probable cause for the issuance of a search warrant. . . .

On the morning of July 6, 2003, Deputy Sheriff James Biesheuvel of the Custer County Sheriff's Department received two anonymous telephone calls. The first caller reported that he believed illegal drug activity was taking place in an apartment located in the upstairs portion of his apartment building. Throughout the first caller's explanation of what he thought was suspicious, he stated that he believed the occupant's name was "Kelli," that the address to the apartment building was 886 Montgomery Street, that Kelli had a lot of traffic coming in and out of the building at all hours of the day and night, and that visitors to the apartment complex would only stay for a short period of time. The first caller also indicated that Kelli would whistle to foot and vehicle traffic from her window to signal the visitors. On one occasion, the caller observed a blonde female visit Kelli's apartment at 3 o'clock in the morning. The caller later watched the female leave Kelli's apartment with something in her hand that was small and plastic. Lastly, the first caller provided the officer with a list of vehicle license plate numbers of persons who had visited Kelli's apartment complex within the last few days. The caller did not give his name to the deputy.

The second caller telephoned the sheriff's deputy two hours after the first caller. Like the first caller, this person never gave a name or other identifying information. The second caller, too, claimed to have observed a lot of foot and vehicle traffic coming to and from "Kelli Joy Raveydts's" apartment throughout the middle part of the week. The caller recognized one of Raveydts's visitors as a former, and possibly current, drug dealer. Additionally, a similar list of license plate numbers was provided to the deputy. Finally, because of the caller's claimed experience with illicit drugs, the second caller told the deputy that a particular smell coming from Raveydts's apartment had the odor of marijuana.

Using public records, Deputy Biesheuvel was able to identify the owners of the license plate numbers supplied by the callers. Three of the identified car owners had a questionable, if not criminal, history. Two of the vehicle owners were involved in prior drug violations. Specifically, the deputy indicated in his affidavit that one of the three known vehicle owners and prior arrestees had been recently identified through drug debriefs and interviews as being involved in large marijuana sales throughout the Custer area.

Based on this information provided in the affidavit, a circuit judge issued a search warrant. The warrant authorized law enforcement officers to search Raveydts's apartment, anyone located in the apartment, the urine of anyone located in the apartment, and any vehicle located at the apartment building during the search belonging to Raveydts or any visitor. The search was conducted at approximately 6:40 P.M. the same day that Deputy Biesheuvel received the anonymous telephone calls. Upon entering the apartment, officers apprehended Defendant Robert James Nicholson and seized a hypodermic syringe from his pocket. When Defendants Raveydts and Santana Jean Hansen arrived at the apartment in the course of the search, they were also arrested. Numerous items relating to illegal drugs were found and seized in the apartment, including baggies with residue, documents, prescription tablets, a marijuana pipe, snort tubes, a bindle of opium, plastic bongs, and a small tool with residue. Defendants were all charged with drug-related offenses based on the result of the search and interviews conducted after their arrests. Defendants moved to suppress the evidence obtained, alleging that the warrant and supporting affidavit were deficient for lack of probable cause. The circuit court granted defendants' motion to suppress. . . .

We review the sufficiency of a search warrant by looking at the totality of the circumstances to decide if there was at least a "substantial basis" for the issuing judge's finding of probable cause. State v. Jackson, 616 N.W.2d 412 (S.D. 2000). In Illinois v. Gates, 462 U.S. 213 (1983), a pivotal decision in search and seizure law, the United States Supreme Court abandoned formal application of the two-pronged test enunciated in Aguilar v. Texas, 378 U.S. 108 (1964), and Spinelli v. United States, 393 U.S. 410 (1969). Now the inquiry is whether the information provided to the judge was sufficient for a "common sense" decision that there was a "fair probability" the evidence would be found on the person or at the place to be searched. . . .

Reviewing courts are not empowered to conduct an after-the-fact de novo probable cause determination; on the contrary, the issuing judge's legal basis for granting the warrant is examined with great deference. A deferential standard of review is appropriate to further the Fourth Amendment's strong preference for searches conducted pursuant to a warrant. Under this Court's implementation of the *Gates* standard, we view an anonymous caller's reliability, veracity, and basis of knowledge as relevant considerations in finding probable cause; these considerations, however, are not independent, essential elements. . . .

Two elements are often crucial in deciding whether an anonymous informant's tip provides a "substantial basis" for the issuing court's finding of probable cause. First, an explicit and detailed description of alleged wrongdoing, along with a statement that the event was observed firsthand, entitles the informant's tip to greater weight than might otherwise be the case. Here, the informants provided considerable detail about the activities they personally observed at Raveydts's apartment.

Second, the extent to which the tip is corroborated by the officer's own investigation is important. . . . Deputy Biesheuvel checked the motor vehicle licensing records to identify the individuals who allegedly visited Raveydts's apartment. But he performed no personal surveillance or observation of unusual civilian or vehicular traffic at the address to substantiate either caller's account of presumed illegal conduct. An anonymous tip is insufficient in itself to support a finding of probable cause. See Florida v. J.L., 529 U.S. 266 (2000). The question is whether the checking of the license plate numbers was sufficient independent corroboration.

The case of People v. Titus, 880 P.2d 148, 151-52 (Colo. 1994), provides a helpful counterpoint to our case. Similarly, the issue in *Titus* was law enforcement corroboration of an anonymous informant's list of motor vehicle license plates of alleged drug buyers who frequented a suspect's home. There, the police corroborated that the license plate numbers of the vehicles on the list provided by the anonymous informant matched the description of the vehicles that the informant gave. But this list was innocuous: "There was nothing in the affidavit to suggest . . . that any of these vehicles belonged to known drug offenders. . . ." Thus, the court explained: "The matching of vehicle license plate numbers with vehicle descriptions was not the kind of police corroboration that would serve to establish probable cause in this case. Absent any additional corroboration — for example, that the owners of the vehicles were involved in illegal activity — it was insufficient to support a finding of probable cause."

Here, on the other hand, Deputy Biesheuvel verified that some of the license plate numbers belonged to persons known to have been involved in illegal drug activity. This tended to corroborate the information the two anonymous informants had given. . . . And the two separate anonymous tipsters also tended to corroborate each other. Under the facts of this case, allowing deference to the issuing judge's probable cause determination, we think the corroboration here was sufficient. . . .

MEIERHENRY, J., dissenting.

I respectfully dissent. The majority cites extensively to *Gates*. While *Gates* did abandon the formal application of the two-prong test for anonymous tips in favor of a totality of the circumstances analysis, it still requires "a conscientious assessment of the basis for crediting [anonymous] tips." The Court in *Gates* goes on to state, "Our decisions applying the totality of circumstances analysis outlined above have consistently recognized the value of corroboration of details of an informant's tip by independent police work." . . .

The American Heritage Dictionary defines "corroborate" as follows: "To support or confirm by new evidence; attest the truth or accuracy of." In this case, the officer did nothing to verify that the anonymous caller's information was truthful or accurate. He did not even go to the scene of the alleged criminal activity. It is true that there were two anonymous calls made in this case, but the State acknowledges the calls may have been made by the same person, since they were, after all, anonymous. And while the officer did check the license plate numbers given to him, he never verified that the vehicles had actually been at the apartment. If the "corroboration" that occurred in this case is all we require, an unaccountable, anonymous caller can cause a completely innocent person's home to be raided by simply making up a provocative and entirely untruthful story.

The majority cites to *Titus*. In *Titus* the Colorado Supreme Court found that no probable cause existed where the license plate numbers given by an anonymous tipster were innocuous, and the majority distinguishes it on this basis. However, the majority fails to mention that in *Titus*, the police also sent a police informant to the suspect's home to attempt to purchase drugs, at which time the suspect made a number of suspicious statements, the police performed surveillance of the home, and the officer determined the employment status of the suspect (self-employed). All of this was included in the officer's affidavit. Despite all of this comparatively substantial corroborating evidence, the Colorado court did not believe that probable cause was established.

[In this case, there was no] firsthand observation of the wrongdoing by the tipster or anyone else. Here, the tipster(s) did not claim to have witnessed drug possession, consumption, sales, or purchases. By adopting the majority opinion, we have nearly absolved an officer of the duty to investigate crimes personally, and now allow an officer to rely almost exclusively on unknown, unnamed, and unaccountable tipsters. . . . Simply put, this decision stretches the limits and reduces the requirements for probable cause to a point that puts even the most innocent and law-abiding citizens at risk of a humiliating and demeaning intrusion of their homes.

Problem 3-2. Holding Something Back

During his investigation of a robbery, Detective Sergeant Steven Gibbs received an anonymous phone call telling him that Danny Bradley had committed the crime. He investigated further, then obtained a search warrant based on the following affidavit:

> Det/Sgt Steven T Gibbs of the Marion CSD swears or affirms that he believes and has good cause to believe . . . that certain property hereinafter described is concealed in the following described residence, to wit: a two story yellow frame house with white trim and an enclosed brick porch with the numbers 2021 in the window and located at 2021 N Bellefontaine, Indpls, Marion County, Indiana.
>
> The property is described as follows: A light colored small automatic pistol; a grey sweatshirt with wide red stripes down the sleeves; two diamond rings, a diamond cross necklace, two maroon suitcases, a ladies Gucci watch, a black ladies purse; a maroon John Romaine purse and credit cards and identification in the names of Mary Lou Leonard and Janet M McLaughlin; which constitutes unlawfully obtained property and evidence of an offense.

> In support of your affiant's assertion of probable cause, your affiant would show the court that he has received the following facts from a reliable informant which facts the informant stated to be within the informant's personal knowledge, to wit: On 11-6-89 the informant made a phone call to Det/Sgt Steve Gibbs. The informant stated that he knew an armed robbery had occurred at a motel room near Shadeland Ave the previous Friday or Saturday. The informant said that two older white women had a black male force his way into their motel room and display a weapon. The informant stated that luggage, jewelry, cash and credit cards were taken and that one lady had been injured. The informant stated that this robbery had been done by a Denny Bradley who resides at 2021 Bellefontaine, and that Bradley has a prior history of robbery arrests.
>
> Your affiant believes and has probable cause to believe that the informant's information is reliable, based upon the following facts within your affiant's personal knowledge, to wit: On 11-4-89 (the previous Saturday) at about 2:41 A.M. Det/Sgt Gibbs was sent to 7101 E 21st St, the Knights Inn Motel, room 309 (a block east of Shadeland) to investigate an armed robbery. There I found Mary Lou Leonard wf55 and Janet McLaughlin wf56. They stated that a black male forced his way into their motel room and robbed them at gunpoint. They described all the property mentioned above by the informant as being taken with the exception of the credit cards. Mrs. Leonard had her left finger broken by the robber as he took her wedding band. On 11-6-89 Det/Sgt Gibbs phoned both Leonard and McLaughlin and they stated that their credit cards had also been taken. To your affiant's knowledge, there has been no publicity of this incident prior to receiving the informant's phone call. Checking criminal histories Det/Sgt Gibbs found a Danny Bradley living at 2021 N Bellefontaine with prior robbery arrests. Therefore, your affiant respectfully requests the court to issue a search warrant directing the search for and seizure of the above-described property.

The trial court denied the motion to suppress, but the appellate court reversed, because the affidavit did not establish the credibility of the source and the factual basis for the information. Further, in the court's view, the affidavit did not contain information to show that the totality of the circumstances corroborated the hearsay.

Assuming that this case was decided in a *Gates* jurisdiction, can this outcome be reconciled with the court's holding and reasoning in *Raveydts*? Cf. Bradley v. State, 609 N.E.2d 420 (Ind. 1993).

Notes

1. *Anonymous tips and probable cause: majority position.* Courts do not adopt a special framework for assessing probable cause based on information from an anonymous tip. They usually apply the same basic framework — whether it be *Gates* or *Aguilar-Spinelli* — used to assess the reliability of named and confidential informants. A number of the classic cases on the sources of probable cause, including Illinois v. Gates, 462 U.S. 213 (1983), involved tips from anonymous sources. Of course, the police in such cases face the major difficulty of establishing the reliability of the source without knowing the identity of the source. While a track record for the source might not be available, and an "admission against penal interest" cannot bolster the credibility of an anonymous source, it is still possible that the police will be able to corroborate some details of the tip. See State v. Griggs, 34 P.3d 101 (Mont.

2001) (corroborated facts in anonymous tip must be suspicious and associated with criminal activity to establish probable cause).

In a jurisdiction following the *Aguilar-Spinelli* approach to probable cause, how often will information from an anonymous informant satisfy both prongs? In a *Gates* jurisdiction, would you expect the showing for "basis of knowledge" to be much higher than usual in an anonymous informant case? In assessing the reliability of an anonymous source, does it matter to you whether the anonymous tipster uses a telephone call (as in *Bradley*) or submits a written tip (as requested in the "wanted" poster)? Governments, corporations, and "watchdog" organizations often maintain "whistle blower" sites on the internet, to encourage employees and others who know about wrongdoing to share the information. Should those sites allow for anonymous submissions?

2. *Anonymous tips and reasonable suspicion to stop vehicles.* In Chapter 2, we considered the "reasonable suspicion" necessary to justify a police stop of a person or vehicle. Sometimes anonymous tips give the police a reason to stop a person. Typically, courts require the officer to confirm some of the details that the anonymous tipster related before reasonable suspicion is present. In one common fact pattern, an anonymous tip identifies a driver who might be driving while intoxicated. If the officer stops the vehicle on the basis of the anonymous tip without first developing some independent basis for reasonable suspicion, courts will frequently overturn the stop.

The U.S. Supreme Court has addressed the use of anonymous tips to establish reasonable suspicion to stop a driver suspected of drug activity. In Alabama v. White, 496 U.S. 325, 332 (1990), an anonymous caller gave police specific information about the future travel plans of an alleged drug dealer. The Court agreed that the tip, together with police efforts to corroborate the tip by following the vehicle for a time, amounted to reasonable suspicion, despite the anonymity of the source: "[If] a tip has a relatively low degree of reliability, more information will be required to establish the requisite quantum of suspicion than would be required if the tip were more reliable." The fact that the tip predicted future behavior, which the police were able to verify, gave it extra weight. For a glimpse of the rich case law in the state courts on this question, see the web extension for this chapter at *http://www.crimpro.com/extension/ch03*.

3. *Can a Statute or Rule Clarify the Assessment of Probable Cause?*

If a jurisdiction were committed to consistent determinations of probable cause, would it help if a statute or criminal procedure rule specified the factors for assessing probable cause? Do the following statutes adopt the *Aguilar-Spinelli* or the *Gates* standard? Apply the following statutes to the facts in *Barton* and *Utterback*. Would you reach a different outcome in either of those cases?

ARKANSAS RULE OF CRIMINAL PROCEDURE 13.1

(b) [If] an affidavit or testimony is based in whole or in part on hearsay, the affiant or witness shall set forth particular facts bearing on the informant's reliability and shall disclose, as far as practicable, the means by which the information was obtained. An affidavit or testimony is sufficient if it describes circumstances establishing reasonable cause to believe that things subject to seizure will be found in a particular place. Failure of the affidavit or testimony to establish the veracity and bases of knowledge of persons providing information to the affiant shall not require that the application be denied, if the affidavit or testimony viewed as a whole, provides a substantial basis for a finding of reasonable cause to believe that things subject to seizure will be found in a particular place.

■ IOWA CODE §808.3

[The] magistrate shall endorse on the application the name and address of all persons upon whose sworn testimony the magistrate relied to issue the warrant together with the abstract of each witness' testimony, or the witness' affidavit. However, if the grounds for issuance are supplied by an informant, the magistrate shall identify only the peace officer to whom the information was given. The application or sworn testimony supplied in support of the application must establish the credibility of the informant or the credibility of the information given by the informant. The magistrate may in the magistrate's discretion require that a witness upon whom the applicant relies for information appear personally and be examined concerning the information.

■ IOWA RULE OF CRIMINAL PROCEDURE 2.36, FORM 2

An application for a search warrant shall be in substantially the following form: . . . Being duly sworn, I, the undersigned, say that at the place (and on the person (s) and in the vehicle (s)) described as follows:

in ______ County, there is now certain property, namely:
which is:
______ Property that has been obtained in violation of law.
______ Property, the possession of which is illegal.
______ Property used or possessed with the intent to be used as the means of committing a public offense or concealed to prevent an offense from being discovered.
______ Property relevant and material as evidence in a criminal prosecution.

The facts establishing the foregoing ground(s) for issuance of a search warrant are as set forth in the attachment(s) made part of this application.

ATTACHMENT
Applicant's name: ______________________________
Occupation: ____________________ No. of years: ____________________
Assignment: ____________________ No. of years: ____________________
Your applicant conducted an investigation and received information from other officers and other sources as follows:
(______ See attached investigative and police reports.) . . .

INFORMANT'S ATTACHMENT (Note: Prepare separate attachment for each informant.)
Peace officer ______________ received information from an informant whose name is: ____________
_____ Confidential because disclosure of informant's identity would:
_____ Endanger informant's safety;
_____ Impair informant's future usefulness to law enforcement.

The informant is reliable for the following reason(s):

_____ The informant is a concerned citizen who has been known by the above peace officer for years and who:

_____ Is a mature individual.

_____ Is regularly employed.

_____ Is a student in good standing.

_____ Is a well-respected family or business person.

_____ Is a person of truthful reputation.

_____ Has no motivation to falsify the information.

_____ Has no known association with known criminals.

_____ Has no known criminal record.

_____ Has otherwise demonstrated truthfulness. (State in the narrative the facts that led to this conclusion.)

_____ Other:
_____ The informant has supplied information in the past _____ times.
_____ The informant's past information has helped supply the basis for _____ search warrants.
_____ The informant's past information has led to the making of _____ arrests.
_____ Past information from the informant has led to the filing of the following charges: ______________________________
_____ Past information from the informant has led to the discovery and seizure of stolen property, drugs, or other contraband.
_____ The informant has not given false information in the past.
_____ The information supplied by the informant in this investigation has been corroborated by law enforcement personnel. (Indicate in the narrative the corroborated information and how it was corroborated.)
_____ Other: ______________________________
The informant has provided the following information: ________________

IOWA RULE OF CRIMINAL PROCEDURE 2.36, FORM 3

An endorsement on a search warrant shall be in substantially the following form: . . .

1. In issuing the search warrant, the undersigned relied upon the sworn testimony of the following person(s) together with the statements and information

contained in the application and any attachments thereto. The court relied upon the following witnesses:

Name	Address
____________________	____________________
____________________	____________________
____________________	____________________

2. Abstract of Testimony. (As set forth in the application and the attachments thereto, plus the following information.)

3. The undersigned has relied, at least in part, on information supplied by a confidential informant (who need not be named) to the peace officer(s) shown on Attachment(s) ______.

4. The information appears credible because (select):

______ A. Sworn testimony indicates this informant has given reliable information on previous occasions; or,

______ B. Sworn testimony indicates that either the informant appears credible or the information appears credible for the following reasons (if credibility is based on this ground, the magistrate MUST set out reasons here):

____

5. The information (is/is not) found to justify probable cause.

6. I therefore (do/do not) issue the warrant.

Notes

1. *Statutes and probable cause determinations: majority position.* Only one state (Oregon) offers a general statutory definition of probable cause. However, most states do have statutes or rules of procedure instructing magistrates how to determine whether probable cause exists before issuing a warrant. The statutes often specify the types of sources a magistrate may consider and the inquiries a magistrate must make when assessing "hearsay" information or other questionable sources.

Iowa courts have concluded that the state legislature, in passing section 808.3, was repudiating the decision of the Supreme Court in Illinois v. Gates, 462 U.S. 213 (1983). See State v. Swaim, 412 N.W.2d 568 (Iowa 1987) (interpreting language in statute, "shall include a determination that the information appears credible," as a rejection of *Gates*). What purposes might the other two provisions reprinted above serve?

2. *Rules as requirements and rules as nonbinding guidance.* What should be the effect of a failure to check any boxes on the Iowa form to show why an informant was reliable, in a case where a reviewing court believes that the information provided to the magistrate was enough for probable cause? See State v. District Court of Black Hawk County, 472 N.W.2d 621 (Iowa 1991) (invalidating search warrant based on form application with no checks indicating informant's basis of knowledge). Such checklists are also developed as part of police and prosecutorial manuals. The lists often take the form of computer software, used to prompt an officer to answer specific questions while constructing an application for a search warrant. Should failure to

follow a written executive branch guideline have the same effect on review of probable cause as failure to follow an identical rule of criminal procedure? Should the question simply be whether probable cause exists, with the forms or checklists, whatever their origins, merely serving as evidence for the court assessing or reviewing the probable cause determination?

C. WARRANTS

The U.S. Supreme Court and state supreme courts say it often: Searches and seizures ordinarily must be carried out under warrants obtained from neutral magistrates. See, e.g., Trupiano v. United States, 334 U.S. 699, 705 (1948) ("It is a cardinal rule that, in seizing goods and articles, law enforcement agents must secure and use search warrants wherever reasonably practicable"). Look back at the language of the Fourth Amendment and its equivalents. How would you respond to an argument that searches can be conducted only pursuant to warrants?

Even if an absolute warrant requirement is not plausible, the constitutional language and the oft-stated judicial "preference" for warrants might lead to the expectation that *most* searches are conducted pursuant to a warrant, with exceptions to the warrant requirement being just that — exceptions, and therefore uncommon. Does a judicial preference for warrants mean that warrants are common in practice? It is difficult to determine what proportion of searches are carried out based on warrants, but the current appellate case law suggests a great majority of searches in most contexts are conducted without first obtaining a warrant.

What advantage might warranted searches offer over searches supported by probable cause but no warrant? The special contributions of the warrant involve the timing of the decision and the identity of the decision maker. For warranted searches, the determination of probable cause must occur before the search begins. By settling the issue early, a warrant prevents the use of hindsight. If the probable cause issue waits until after the search produces evidence, judges may feel pressure to accept a search that was based on nothing more than a lucky guess. Some police officers might also feel tempted to lie about the original basis for their search. And for warranted searches, a judicial officer decides whether probable cause is present, rather than the law enforcement officers who are in the thick of the chase. See William Stuntz, Warrants and Fourth Amendment Remedies, 77 Va. L. Rev. 881 (1991).

1. The Warrant Requirement and Exigent Circumstances

Perhaps the largest "exception" to the preference for warrants is the presence of exigent circumstances. When exigent circumstances appear, there is no need for police to obtain a warrant before conducting a search. Exigent circumstances include situations in which an immediate search or seizure is needed to protect the safety of an officer or the public, or when the suspect might escape or destroy evidence. In what proportion of all searches and seizures would you imagine that there is some risk that one of these events might occur? How much risk must the government accept before the circumstances become "exigent"? Can the government take any actions to decrease (or increase) these risks?

■ JOHNNY MANN v. STATE

161 S.W.3d 826 (Ark. 2004)

CORBIN, J.

The record reflects that on or about May 20, 2001, Mitchell Webb, a United States postal inspector in Little Rock, received information from a postal inspector in California of a suspicious package addressed to Clark Nuss, 424 Ashley 81 West, Hamburg, Arkansas. The package had a return address of Crescent City, California. Webb instructed the California office to forward the package to him, via sealed mail. Once Webb received the package, he ran a drug-detection canine by the package, and the dog alerted on it. Another postal inspector then obtained a federal search warrant for the package, which was then opened and discovered to contain approximately eighteen grams of methamphetamine. Webb contacted officers of the Arkansas State Police to see if they were interested in investigating the matter. They indicated that they were, so Webb re-wrapped the package and transported it to Hamburg the following day.

Officers from the state police discovered that Appellant lived at 424 Ashley 81 West in Hamburg. They also ran criminal histories on Appellant and Clark Nuss and discovered that both men had previously lived in Crescent City, California. Officers then decided to make a controlled delivery of the package, with Inspector Webb posing as a rural route carrier in Hamburg. Prior to the actual delivery, Appellant approached his regular mail carrier and asked if there were any packages for him. The mail carrier told Appellant that the mail route for that day was being split up and that another carrier may possibly have his mail.

At the time of the controlled delivery, officers conducted surveillance of the residence at 424 Ashley 81 West, Hamburg. They watched it from the ground, as well as from the air in a state police helicopter. The residence was a mobile home with a screened-in porch area on the front. There was some construction going on at the front of the residence, in an apparent attempt to convert the mobile home into a permanent structure. There was a screen door on the porch and a metal door on the trailer itself.

On the date of the controlled delivery, May 21, 2001, Inspector Webb drove his postal vehicle into Appellant's driveway and honked his horn. Appellant came out and approached Webb. Webb told him that he had two packages that were too big to fit into the mailbox. Webb then asked Appellant if the packages belonged there, and Appellant said that they did. The police officers remained in their surveillance positions for five to six minutes, to give Appellant time to open up the packages. They then approached the residence, entered the screened-in porch, and announced their presence. The metal door to the trailer was open. At some point, either while they were inside the porch area or in the doorway of the trailer, one of the officers heard someone running down the hallway, and he alerted the others. At least two of the officers pursued the runner toward the bathroom, where they discovered Appellant, who was fully clothed, sitting on the commode, which had just been flushed. Appellant was then taken into custody, and officers subsequently obtained his consent to search the residence. The officers then recovered the methamphetamine from the drain of the commode. . . .

Appellant filed a motion to suppress the evidence found during the search of his residence, on the ground that the warrantless entry violated his Fourth Amendment rights. Following a hearing, the trial court denied the motion to suppress, finding that there were exigent circumstances to justify the warrantless entry. Particularly, the trial court found that when the police entered the screened-in porch and announced that they were police, they heard someone running in the residence. According to the trial court: "That led to the reasonable conclusion that Mr. Mann, who they knew was in possession of these drugs at this time, was trying to do something to dispossess himself of them or destroy them." . . .

We begin our analysis by acknowledging the boilerplate principle that a warrantless entry into a private residence is presumptively unreasonable under the Fourth Amendment. See Welsh v. Wisconsin, 466 U.S. 740 (1984). An exception to the warrant requirement is where, at the time of entry, there exists probable cause and exigent circumstances. Exigent circumstances are those requiring immediate aid or action, and, while there is no definite list of what constitutes exigent circumstances, several established examples include the risk of removal or destruction of evidence, danger to the lives of police officers or others, and the hot pursuit of a suspect. The burden is on the State to prove that the warrantless activity was reasonable. . . .

The testimony of the officers during the suppression hearing was inconclusive as to when the exigent circumstances arose. The record reflects that six officers testified at the suppression hearing; however, only two officers, Dennis Roberts, of the Arkansas State Police, and Deputy Jim Culp, of the Ashley County Sheriff's Department, testified that they entered Appellant's residence before he was taken into custody. Roberts initially testified that he was inside the residence when he heard someone running down the hallway. He explained: "We went into the house, and I was one of the first into the house. I heard running down the wooden floor. I announced, 'State Police.' Continued to hear the running. We pursued the running down the hallway and found Mr. Mann inside of the bathroom." Roberts also stated: "Upon entry of the house, just as I was standing, or just as I was hearing the running down the hallway, I saw our package that had been torn open sitting on a kitchen bar right as you walked into the doorway." On cross-examination, Roberts candidly admitted that he could not be certain where he was when he heard someone running down the hallway. He explained: "Immediately, immediately after I heard the running, and I can't tell you where I was, whether I was in the screened-in area or the doorway where I could see the package, I, when I heard the running, I stated, 'state police.' " . . .

During the suppression hearing, the State maintained that the officers' warrantless entry into Appellant's home was based on the exigent circumstance that they feared that evidence was about to be destroyed. This fear was based on the sound of someone running down the hallway. The record reveals that Roberts was apparently the only officer to actually have heard this noise. His testimony, however, is admittedly uncertain as to when he heard the running, i.e., before or after he had entered the home. Our case law requires us to examine only those exigent circumstances that existed at the time of the entry. Obviously, a warrantless entry that occurs before the exigent circumstance exists violates the Fourth Amendment. It was the State's burden to present evidence proving that the warrantless entry was reasonable under the Fourth Amendment. Based on the record before us, we conclude that the State failed to meet its burden and that the trial court erred in concluding that the warrantless entry was reasonable.

Furthermore, regardless of when the exigent circumstance arose, . . . this particular exigent circumstance was effectively created by the police's chosen strategy in this case. At a minimum, the officers reasonably could have foreseen that their decision to approach Appellant's residence without a warrant immediately after completing a controlled delivery of methamphetamine would likely result in an attempt to destroy the evidence. . . .

Here, there is no doubt that the officers had the opportunity to seek and secure a warrant to search Appellant's residence. The officers had probable cause to believe that Appellant was committing the crime of possession of a controlled substance. They had already determined that the package contained a controlled substance, namely methamphetamine, and they had witnessed Appellant accept the package after telling Postal Inspector Webb that the package belonged at his residence. Moreover, they knew that Appellant and the addressee, Clark Nuss, were previously residents of Crescent City, California, where the package originated. The police had two viable options in this case. First, they could have continued their surveillance of Appellant's residence while one or more of them attempted to secure a search warrant. If Appellant would have left the residence with the package during the time that the police were attempting to secure the warrant, they would have had probable cause to stop Appellant and arrest him at that time.

The second option available to police was to obtain an anticipatory search warrant prior to the time that the controlled delivery was executed. An anticipatory warrant is one that is issued before the item to be seized has arrived at the place to be searched. . . . In the present case, the police could have obtained an anticipatory search warrant conditioned upon the delivery of the controlled substance to Appellant's residence. They knew that the package contained a controlled substance and that the package identified a real person at an accurate address.

[The] situations of urgency protected by this exception cannot be created by police officers. This general holding will not dispose of this case or, in fact, of many cases. For in some sense the police always create the exigent circumstances that justify warrantless entries and arrests. Their discovery of the criminal causes him to flee; their discovery of the contraband causes the criminal's attempt to destroy or divert the evidence. For the claim of exigent circumstances to be adequately evaluated, the better question to ask is: how did those urgent circumstances come about? This antecedent inquiry — into the reasonableness and propriety of the investigative tactics that generated the exigency — seems to be what courts have in fact been doing in these kinds of cases. . . . There is no question that the deliberate creation of urgent circumstances is unacceptable. But bad faith is not required to run afoul of the standard. . . .

[The] test for determining whether the exigent circumstances are of the police's own creation [is whether], regardless of good faith, it was reasonably foreseeable that the investigative tactics employed by the police would create the exigent circumstances relied upon to justify a warrantless entry. Applying that test to the facts of this case, we conclude that it was reasonably foreseeable that the police's chosen strategy of approaching Appellant's residence and announcing their presence, only minutes after a controlled delivery had occurred, would create a situation in which Appellant would attempt to destroy the evidence.

[If we] were to uphold the police's actions even though the exigent circumstances were foreseeable, this type of situation may reoccur repeatedly and might lend itself to too easy a by-pass of the constitutional requirement that probable cause should generally be assessed by a neutral and detached magistrate before the citizen's privacy is invaded. [We] conclude that the trial court erred in denying Appellant's motion to suppress. . . . Accordingly, the warrantless entry was unreasonable under the Fourth Amendment, and all evidence gained as a result of the intrusion must be suppressed. . . .

GLAZE, J., dissenting.

[Based on the testimony] before the trial judge at the suppression hearing, the judge quite properly made the following findings and ruling:

> THE COURT: . . . They entered a porch, which was opened, the door was open and the porch as well and the contents of that front porch were visible to anyone on the outside. And at the time they were on this porch, they announced that they were police. They then heard someone running in the trailer. That led to the reasonable conclusion that Mr. Mann, who they knew was in possession of these drugs at this time, was trying to do something to dispossess himself of them or destroy them. [Thus,] there were exigent circumstances concerning their entry that a warrant was not required. . . .

[In] reviewing a ruling denying a defendant's motion to suppress, this court makes an independent determination based on the totality of the circumstances and views the evidence in the light most favorable to the State; we reverse only if the trial court's ruling is clearly against the preponderance of the evidence. Here, the trial court found that, as the officers approached the open door of the porch, Officer Culp heard footsteps inside the trailer home, announced "there's someone running," and then the officers entered the open door of the trailer. When the officers heard someone running in the trailer, they reasonably concluded Mann was trying to destroy the evidence. The majority court simply ignores the trial judge's reasonable analysis of the evidence that supports his ruling to deny Mann's motion to suppress. . . .

[The majority] contends that the officers had the opportunity to secure a warrant to search Mann's trailer; it opines that the officers had probable cause to believe Mann was committing the crime of possession of a controlled substance, since the package he was handed was accepted by him. . . . [Only when the Arkansas officers made a controlled delivery of the package could they] be certain they had probable cause. The majority court here attempts to challenge the officers' failing to obtain a warrant immediately after Mann approached his regular mail carrier and asked if there were any packages for Mann, and his carrier said another carrier may possibly have his mail. Of course, even if the officers suspected at this point that Mann was referring to the Nuss package, they could not be sure until he accepted the package. . . .

In conclusion, it is my strongly held view (and that of the trial judge, I might add) that the officers had not created the exigency in this case. Instead, Mann himself caused the officers to enter the trailer when he started running and the toilet was flushed after the officers identified themselves as they approached the porch leading to the open door of the trailer. . . . The trial judge was correct in denying Mann's motion to suppress, and I would affirm the judge.

Notes

1. *Exigent circumstances: majority position.* Two of the most common grounds for arguing that the police need not obtain a judicial warrant are the potential destruction of evidence and the potential escape of suspects. Williams v. State, 813 A.2d 231 (Md. 2002). Are there exigent circumstances in all cases dealing with evidence (such as narcotics) that is easy to destroy or remove? In all cases where private parties will have access to the area while the police seek a warrant?

Exigent circumstances might also be based on possible danger to the investigating officers or to citizens in the area where the search is to take place. The danger might involve the use of a weapon on the premises, an item creating a risk of fire or explosion, or the possible presence of persons needing medical care, among other things. See People v. Higbee, 802 P.2d 1085 (Colo. 1990) (search for bomb); Holder v. State, 847 N.E.2d 930 (Ind. 2006) (presence of child and adults in home used as methamphetamine lab, combined with health risk to neighbors when smell of ether was present throughout area). See also Michigan v. Fisher, 130 S. Ct. 546 (2009) (exigent circumstances allowed warrantless entry into home when occupant appeared to be injured and was screaming and throwing objects). For a sample of the rich detail of the cases on this question, see the web extension for this chapter at *http://www.crimpro.com/extension/ch03*.

Exigent circumstances can vary with the seriousness of the crime; the showing becomes more difficult as the crime under investigation becomes less serious. See Welsh v. Wisconsin, 466 U.S. 740 (1984) ("application of the exigent-circumstances exception in the context of a home entry should rarely be sanctioned when there is probable cause to believe that only a minor offense [such as driving while intoxicated] has been committed").

When do inconvenient circumstances become "exigent"? That is, how much extra risk must the police accept before they may conclude that obtaining a warrant would be too difficult? Was it feasible in *Mann* for the police to wait to enter the house only after obtaining a warrant? Could they detain any person leaving the premises until officers returned with a warrant?

Exigent circumstances are not the only cases in which courts will allow a warrantless search. As we saw in Chapter 2, many less intrusive searches may be conducted without a warrant. It is useful to make a list of the variety of justifications for warrantless searches.

2. *Maintaining the status quo while seeking a warrant.* May the police enter or remain on the premises long enough to prevent the destruction of evidence or other harms that could occur while they seek a warrant? See Illinois v. McArthur, 531 U.S. 326 (2001) (police obtain probable cause of presence of illegal narcotics in home; occupant required to remain outside home two hours with police officer present while other officers seek search warrant); Segura v. United States, 468 U.S. 796 (1984) (search valid where police officers remained in apartment 19 hours until warrant was obtained); Posey v. Commonwealth, 185 S.W.3d 170 (Ky. 2006) (officers speaking to occupant of home outside front door noticed through open door some marijuana inside the home, and stepped inside to secure evidence until warrant

could be obtained for more thorough search). If it requires too many police officers too long to maintain the status quo, do the police then have exigent circumstances?

3. *The special status of homes.* Courts strike down warrantless searches most often in the context of searches of homes. Many of the exceptions to the warrant requirement applicable outside the home do not apply in the same way within a home, and courts tend to demand greater justifications for warrantless searches of a house. Some courts extend the special protection provided homes to other areas. Indiana, for example, has found a similar preference for warrants when the police search parked and impounded cars. Brown v. State, 653 N.E.2d 77 (Ind. 1995):

> With respect to automobiles generally, it may safely be said that Hoosiers regard their automobiles as private and cannot easily abide their uninvited intrusion. . . . Americans in general love their cars. It is, however, particularly important, in the state which hosts the Indy 500 automobile race, to recognize that cars are sources of pride, status, and identity that transcend their objective attributes. We are extremely hesitant to countenance their casual violation, even by law enforcement officers who are attempting to solve serious crimes.

2. *Requirements for Obtaining Warrants*

Procedures for obtaining warrants typically appear in state statutes, local code provisions, and local rules of court. These rules specify such things as who can issue warrants, the form and content of warrant applications, and the allowable scope of warrants. Several procedural requirements appear on the face of the Fourth Amendment and its analogs. Most constitutions require the applicant to specify the targeted place and the items or person sought. Some also require that the warrant application be in writing or under oath.

a. Neutral and Detached Magistrate

While there are occasional cases litigating the constitutional requirement of a "neutral and detached magistrate," issues of judicial neutrality are more often litigated under judicial ethics rules. Indeed, ethics rules have become a standard avenue for the regulation of lawyers and judges throughout the criminal process, as influential today in practical terms as constitutional provisions.

STATE EX REL. EUSTACE BROWN v. JERRY DIETRICK

444 S.E.2d 47 (W. Va. 1994)

MILLER, J.

[We] consider whether the Circuit Court of Jefferson County was correct in holding that a search warrant issued by a magistrate was void because the magistrate was married to the chief of police and one of his officers had procured the warrant. The lower court determined that because the magistrate was married to the chief of police there was a violation of Canon 3C(1) and 3C(1)(d) of the Judicial Code of Ethics. The former provision requires the recusal of a judge if his impartiality might reasonably be questioned; the latter requires disqualification where the judge's spouse has an interest in the proceeding.[3] We have not had occasion to consider this particular question.

Initially, we note that independent of the Judicial Code of Ethics, the United States Supreme Court has interpreted the Fourth Amendment to the United States Constitution to require that a search warrant be issued by a "neutral and detached magistrate." In Shadwick v. City of Tampa, 407 U.S. 345 (1972), the Supreme Court held that the office of magistrate, in order to satisfy the neutral and detached standard "requires severance and disengagement from activities of law enforcement." By way of illustration, the Supreme Court in *Shadwick* pointed to its earlier case of Coolidge v. New Hampshire, 403 U.S. 443 (1971), where it voided a search warrant issued by the state's attorney general because he "was actively in charge of the investigation and later was to be chief prosecutor at trial." Similarly, in Lo-Ji Sales, Inc. v. New York, 442 U.S. 319 (1979), the magistrate was found not to be neutral and detached when he "allowed himself to become a member, if not the leader, of the search party which was essentially a police operation." In Connally v. Georgia, 429 U.S. 245 (1977), the Supreme Court determined that a magistrate who was compensated based on a fee for the warrants issued could not be considered neutral and detached. It relied on its earlier case of Tumey v. Ohio, 273 U.S. 510 (1927), which invalidated on due process principles the payment of the village mayor, when he acted as a judge, from costs collected in criminal cases brought before him in which there was a conviction.

We afforded the same protection for a neutral and detached magistrate under our search and seizure constitutional provision in . . . State v. Dudick, 213 S.E.2d 458 (W.Va. 1975):

> The constitutional guarantee under W. Va. Const., Article III, §6 that no search warrant will issue except on probable cause goes to substance and not to form; therefore, where it is conclusively proved that a magistrate acted as a mere agent of the prosecutorial process and failed to make an independent evaluation of the circumstances surrounding a request for a warrant, the warrant will be held invalid and the search will be held illegal.

As the foregoing law indicates, where there is a lack of neutrality and detachment in the issuance of the search warrant, it is void. Aside from the constitutional requirements for a neutral and detached magistrate as to warrants, similar standards are imposed by Canon 3C of the Judicial Code of Ethics relating to the disqualification of a judge. The Code defines those situations when a judge may be precluded from presiding over a case. The underlying rationale for requiring disqualification is based on principles of due process. . . .

3. The applicable provisions in 1992 of the Judicial Code of Ethics . . . were in Canon 3C(1) and 3C(1)(d):

A judge should disqualify himself in a proceeding in which his impartiality might reasonably be questioned, including but not limited to instances where: . . .

(d) he or his spouse, or a person within the third degree of relationship to either of them, or the spouse of such a person:

(i) is a party to the proceeding, or an officer, director, or trustee of a party; . . .

(iii) is known by the judge to have an interest that could be substantially affected by the outcome of the proceeding;

(iv) is to the judge's knowledge likely to be a material witness in the proceeding. . . .

Canon 3C(1) contains an initial general admonition that a "judge should disqualify himself in a proceeding in which his impartiality might reasonably be questioned." This admonition is followed by a number of specific instances when disqualification is required. . . . In this case, in addition to the general disqualification standard, it is claimed that the more specific disqualification test contained in Canon 3C(1)(d)(iii) applies. This provision requires disqualification if the judge's spouse has "an interest that could be substantially affected by the outcome of the proceeding." This disqualification is claimed to apply if Chief Boober appeared before his wife to seek a warrant. . . . We have no case law on this point, but we agree with cases from other jurisdictions that support the disqualification.

For example, the Louisiana court in State v. LaCour, 493 So. 2d 756 (La. Ct. App. 1986), set aside a criminal conviction because it found that the judge should have disqualified himself because his son was prosecuting the defendant on another criminal charge in a different county. . . . In Smith v. Beckman, 683 P.2d 1214 (Colo. Ct. App. 1984), the judge's wife was an assistant prosecutor. The record showed that the prosecutor's office had screened her from cases that were before her husband. The court concluded that his disqualification in all criminal cases was warranted because of the appearance of impropriety. . . . The critical point in the court's view was the perception of the closeness created by the marital relationship:

> A husband and wife generally conduct their personal and financial affairs as a partnership. In addition to living together, a husband and wife are also perceived to share confidences regarding their personal lives and employment situations. Generally, the public views married people as "a couple," as "a partnership," and as participants in a relationship more intimate than any other kind of relationship between individuals. In our view the existence of a marriage relationship between a judge and a deputy district attorney in the same county is sufficient to establish grounds for disqualification, even though no other facts call into question the judge's impartiality. . . .

We believe that the foregoing cases and the language in Canon 3C(1) and 3C(1)(d)(i) of the Judicial Code of Ethics relating to the disqualification of a judicial official when his or her impartiality might reasonably be questioned if the official's spouse is a party to the proceeding would foreclose a magistrate from issuing a warrant sought by his or her spouse who is a police officer. However, this situation did not occur here.

The search warrant was issued at the request of Sergeant R. R. Roberts of the Ranson police force. At the hearing below, Magistrate Boober testified that she was the on-call magistrate for emergency matters that might occur after 4:00 P.M. and before 8:00 A.M. the next morning when the magistrate office would be open for normal business.

Magistrate Boober also stated that she was not related to Sergeant Roberts and had no contact with him except through the magistrate system. She also stated that she made an independent review of the affidavit for the search warrant. Her husband's name did not appear on the affidavit nor was there any discussion about her husband with Sergeant Roberts.

There was no evidence to show any actual bias or partiality on the part of Magistrate Boober. The entire argument centered on an implied partiality because of the magistrate's relationship to Chief Boober. We indicated earlier that any criminal matters which the magistrate's husband is involved with cannot be brought before her because of their spousal relationship. We decline to extend such a per se rule with regard to the other members of the Ranson police force. The fact that a magistrate's spouse is the chief of police of a small police force does not automatically disqualify the magistrate, who is otherwise neutral and detached, from issuing a warrant sought by another member of such police force. However, a small police force[14] coupled with the chief's active role in a given case may create an appearance of impropriety that would warrant a right to challenge the validity of a search warrant. Certainly, prudence dictates that Magistrate Boober's involvement with warrants from the Ranson police force should be severely curtailed. . . .

Finally, we are asked to extend the rule of necessity to allow Magistrate Boober to handle warrants when she is the on-call magistrate. The rule of necessity is an exception to the disqualification of a judge. It allows a judge who is otherwise disqualified to handle the case to preside if there is no provision that allows another judge to hear the matter. . . .

The rule of necessity is an exception to the general rule precluding a disqualified judge from hearing a matter. Therefore, it is strictly construed and applied only when there is no other person having jurisdiction to handle the matter that can be brought in to hear it. . . . We would not sanction the use of the rule were it to be offered if Chief Boober appeared seeking the search warrant. In the case of the other police officers from Ranson, we decline to utilize the rule simply because we do not find that Magistrate Boober is automatically barred from issuing warrants at their request. There may be circumstances that can be shown that would cast a shadow over the magistrate's impartiality. In that event, a motion to suppress the evidence obtained under the warrant may be made, and the issue will be resolved at a hearing. . . . The matter is remanded for a further hearing with regard to the warrant if the relators below desire to challenge it on the basis that there are additional facts, other than her marriage to Chief Boober, that demonstrate Magistrate Boober was not neutral and detached. . . .

Notes

1. *Who issues warrants? Majority view.* Most states (more than 30) allow only judges and magistrates to issue warrants. Some state statutes require that magistrates be lawyers, while others list no special statutory qualifications. Judges generally appoint magistrates. They are thus subject to removal by judges or city officials and lack some of the usual privileges accorded to judicial officers. A smaller group of states allow functionaries — who go by titles such as "clerk magistrates," "ministerial recorders," clerks of court, or court commissioners — to issue search warrants. In West Virginia, mayors have the power to issue search warrants pursuant to violations of city ordinances. W. Va. Code §8-10-1.

As noted in *Dietrick,* the Supreme Court, in Connally v. Georgia, 429 U.S. 245 (1977), found unconstitutional a system that compensated magistrates for each warrant they issued. What if, to encourage protection of individual rights, magistrates were paid for warrants they refused to issue?

14. The 1993 West Virginia Blue Book gives the population of the City of Ranson at 2,890. According to the [briefs], there are six other police officers in addition to the Chief of Police.

2. *Neutrality in outcomes.* What if a defendant can show that a particular magistrate has never refused a warrant or approves warrants 98 percent of the time? A major empirical study of the search warrant process in seven jurisdictions made the following observations about the number of warrant applications denied by magistrates:

> It is unfortunate, though not surprising, that documents are not routinely collected that reveal the number of applications that are denied by magistrates. Normally a rejected application is destroyed or revised by the applicant. According to our observations and interviews, the rate of outright rejection is extremely low. Most of the police officers interviewed could not remember having a search warrant application turned down. The estimates by the judges interviewed varied on the number of rejections from almost never to about half. Of the 84 warrant proceedings observed, 7 resulted in denial of the application (8 percent).

Richard van Duizend, Paul Sutton & Charlotte Carter, The Search Warrant Process: Preconceptions, Perceptions, Practices 26-27 (1985). A more recent study of warrant practices in one jurisdiction noted that some judges handled far more than their share of warrant applications. Of the 24 judges available for duty, six judges issued almost three-fourths of the search warrants. Laurence A. Benner and Charles T. Samarkos, Searching for Narcotics in San Diego: Preliminary Findings from the San Diego Search Warrant Project, 36 Cal. W. L. Rev. 221, 226 (2000). Could a defendant strengthen her challenge to the neutrality of a magistrate by demonstrating that the police apply to the particular magistrate in question for search warrants far more often than to other available magistrates?

b. Particularity in Warrants

Remember that the Fourth Amendment, in language echoed in many state provisions, says that "no Warrants shall issue, but upon probable cause, supported by Oath or affirmation, and particularly describing the place to be searched, and the persons or things to be seized." The following classic state cases explore the requirement that warrants be supported by "Oath or affirmation" and that they "particularly" describe the place to be searched and the persons or things to be seized. This "particularity" requirement captures an essential part of the distinction between valid warrants and invalid general warrants.

■ BELL v. CLAPP

10 Johns. 263 (N.Y. 1813)

PER CURIAM

The matter set forth in the plea is a justification of the trespass. The search warrant was founded on oath, and the information stated that one hundred barrels of flour had been stolen from the wharf, in the first ward, by Richard and Isaac Jaques, and that the same, or a part thereof, was concealed in a cellar of Gideon Jaques. The plea then states that the warrant, being under the hand and seal of the magistrate . . . , and being directed to the constables and marshals, authorized and required them to enter the said cellar, in the day-time, and search for the flour, and to bring it, together with the said Gideon, or the person in whose custody it might be found, before the justice; that in pursuance of the warrant, the defendants, the one being a constable and the other a marshal, did go to the cellar, which was part and parcel of the dwelling-house of the plaintiff, and, after being refused entrance, did open the door by force, and seize the flour in as peaceable a manner as possible. This, then, was a valid warrant duly executed by these officers. The warrant had all the essential qualities of a legal warrant. It was founded on oath, and was specific as to place and object, and the stolen goods were taken, and taken in as peaceable a manner as the nature of the case admitted.

In Entick v. Carrington . . . Lord Camden admitted a search warrant, so well guarded, to be a lawful authority. The warrant did not state in whom the property of the flour resided, nor was this essential to its validity: a person may even be indicted and convicted of stealing the goods of a person unknown. Nor did it affect the legality of the warrant that it directed the officer to bring Jaques, to whom the cellar belonged, or the person in whose custody the flour might be found. It was impossible for any warrant to be more explicit and particular; and it would, probably, have been the duty of the officer to have arrested any person in possession of the stolen goods at the place designated, without any directions in the warrant, and to have carried him before the justice for examination.

Sir Mathew Hale, in one part of his treatise, denies to the officer the right of breaking open the door, on a warrant to search for stolen goods. But he, afterwards, admits this power in the officer, if the door be shut, and if upon demand it is refused to be opened. This past opinion is founded on the better reason, for search warrants are often indispensable to the detection of crimes; and they would be of little or no efficacy without this power attached to them. All the checks which the English law, and which even the constitution of the United States, have imposed upon the operation of these search warrants, and with the manifestation of a strong jealousy of the abuses incident to them, would scarcely have been thought of, or have been deemed necessary, if the warrant did not communicate the power of opening the outer door of a house. . . .

The defendants are, accordingly, entitled to judgment upon the demurrers. Judgment for the defendants.

Notes

1. *Particular description of place to be searched: majority position.* The nineteenth-century opinion in *Bell* reflects some very modern concerns. Both state and federal constitutions require that the warrant name with "particularity" the place to be searched and the things to be seized. When a warrant lists property in an urban setting, the street address (including the apartment number, where relevant) is usually particular enough to allow the searching officer "with reasonable effort [to] ascertain and identify the place intended." Steele v. United States, 267 U.S. 498 (1925). Property in a rural setting might be described without an address.

Another famous case from the early nineteenth century offers a useful comparison to *Bell*. In Grummon v. Raymond, 1 Conn. 40 (1814), the court disapproved of a search warrant authorizing government agents to search for stolen goods; the warrant directed the officials to search for the stolen bags "at Aaron Hyatt's, or some other place" among the houses, stores, shops, and barns of the town of Wilton. The officer also was directed to search suspected persons, and arrest them. The court described the proper contents of a warrant as follows: "There must be an oath by the applicant that he has had his goods stolen, and strongly suspects that they are concealed in such a place; and the warrant cannot give a direction to search any other place than the particular place pointed out." What was the difference between the alternative phrasing in the warrants in *Bell* and *Grummon*? Would a warrant listing more than one place to search ever be valid? Does it matter if different people own or occupy the properties? Compare State v. Mehner, 480 N.W.2d 872 (Iowa 1992) (validating warrant listing two house trailers with different occupants) with State v. Marshall, 974 A.2d 1038 (N.J. 2009) (warrant that listed address of house containing duplex units, leaving officers uncertain which unit to search, violated particularity requirement).

Warrants tend to be more specific about the place to be searched than about any persons to be searched. Why is that? If you were a magistrate, what sort of evidence would convince you to issue a warrant authorizing the search of a specific bar and "all persons" found on those premises? See State v. Thomas, 540 N.W.2d 658 (Iowa 1995) (invalidating warrant; application noted numerous prior arrests and controlled purchases of crack cocaine, and observations by undercover officers that most persons present in bar possessed narcotics or weapons).

2. *Particular description of things to be seized: majority position.* Warrants authorize searches for particular objects. The types of objects that may be seized vary somewhat from state to state, although the general categories are fruits, instrumentalities, and evidence of crime. See Ill. Stat. ch. 725, §5/108-3(a) ("any judge may issue a search warrant for the seizure of [any] instruments, articles or things designed or intended for use or which are or have been used in the commission of, or which may constitute evidence of, the offense in connection with which the warrant is issued; or contraband, the fruits of crime, or things otherwise criminally possessed"). The Fourth Amendment requirement of particularity "makes general searches . . . impossible and prevents the seizure of one thing under a warrant describing another. As to what is taken, nothing is left to the discretion of the officer executing the warrant." Marron v. United States, 275 U.S. 192 (1927). What sort of description in the warrant would leave "nothing" to the discretion of the officer? See People v. Brown, 749 N.E.2d 170 (N.Y. 2001) (warrant naming four particular items plus authorizing search for "any other property the possession of which would be considered contraband" was overbroad); State v. Browne, 970 A.2d 81 (Conn. 2009) (supporting affidavit incorporated by reference in search warrant can cure lack of sufficient particularity in description of items to be seized, even if affidavit does not accompany warrant at scene of search; most important protections of warrant occur before search, not at scene of search).

The consequences are severe when the warrant fails to describe particularly the items to be seized. In Groh v. Ramirez, 540 U.S. 551 (2004), the Supreme Court held that a search warrant failing to describe the items to be seized from a home could not be cured by the agent's inclusion of a list of the items in an unincorporated warrant application, or by his oral description to the homeowners of the items to be seized.

Like the federal constitution, most state constitutions and statutes also require a description of the items (or persons) being sought and an explanation for why the applicant believes that the items (or persons) are at the location sought. See Ohio

Rev. Code §2933.24(A) (search warrant shall "particularly name or describe the property to be searched for and seized, the place to be searched, and the person to be searched").

3. *Warrants "in writing" and telephonic warrants.* A majority of states have statutes requiring that warrants be in writing. A number of state constitutions also expressly provide for written warrants. See Neb. Rev. Stat. §29-830; R.I. Const. Art. 1, §6. Requiring warrants to be in writing does not preclude their electronic transmission. See Mich. Comp. Laws §780.651.

Despite the prevalence of constitutional provisions and statutes calling for warrants obtained by testimony made under oath and "in writing," a growing number of states have statutes authorizing the police to obtain warrants over the telephone. Consider, for example, Kan. Stat. Ann. §22-2502(a):

> A search warrant shall be issued only upon the oral or written statement, including those conveyed or received by telefacsimile communication, of any person under oath or affirmation which states facts sufficient to show probable cause that a crime has been or is being committed and which particularly describes a person, place or means of conveyance to be searched and things to be seized. Any statement which is made orally shall be either taken down by a certified shorthand reporter, sworn to under oath and made part of the application for a search warrant, or recorded before the magistrate from whom the search warrant is requested and sworn to under oath. Any statement orally made shall be reduced to writing as soon thereafter as possible. If the magistrate is satisfied that grounds for the application exist or that there is probable cause to believe that they exist, the magistrate may issue a search warrant.

Why does Kansas insist that the person seeking the warrant swear to the statement under oath? Why does the state go to the trouble and expense of reducing the statements to writing? Does the availability of telephonic warrants mean that police can claim exigent circumstances in far fewer cases? One survey of warrant practices discovered that officers rarely used the available procedures for telephonic and electronic search warrants. Laurence A. Benner & Charles T. Samarkos, Searching for Narcotics in San Diego: Preliminary Findings from the San Diego Search Warrant Project, 36 Cal. W. L. Rev. 221, 223 (2000). Why might police officers decline to use such procedures when they are available?

4. *Plain view seizures.* You may recall, from Chapter 2, the "plain view" doctrine, which declares that the police may seize evidence, contraband, or the fruits or instrumentalities of crime that come within the "plain view" of police officers during proper execution of a valid warrant. See Horton v. California, 496 U.S. 128 (1990) (item in plain view is seizable if its incriminating character is immediately apparent to police). Does this authorization to seize items not named in the warrant effectively eliminate any requirement that the warrant "particularly name" the property to be seized?

5. *The advantage for police of warrants listing small items.* The nature of the items sought will determine the permissible scope of the search. If police are looking for an elephant, the search will be limited to places an elephant might hide. If police are looking for a field mouse, the scope of the search would be much broader. See, e.g., State v. Apelt, 861 P.2d 634 (Ariz. 1993) (because warrant included receipts, police could conduct a very detailed search and had a higher possibility of additional "plain view" discovery of evidence than in a more narrowly circumscribed

search). Would it be ethical to advise police to include small items such as receipts in all warrant applications?

6. *The "four corners" rule.* If a defendant challenges the sufficiency of a warrant during a suppression hearing, statutes and court rules in most jurisdictions (and constitutional rulings in a few others) prevent the government from supplementing the warrant application itself with information that the officers knew at the time but failed to present to the magistrate. Some also prevent the government from relying on any information supplementing the application, even if it was actually presented to the magistrate. Greenstreet v. State, 898 A.2d 961 (Md. 2006). The government's defense of the warrant, in other words, must come from within the "four corners" of the application. Some states allow courts to supplement the "four corners" of the affidavit with information that could be "reasonably inferred" from the document, while others (about 10 states) go further and say that the court is free to use outside information at its discretion. See Moore v. Commonwealth, 159 S.W.3d 325, 328 (Ky. 2005). Various applications of the four corners rule can be found on the web extension for this chapter at *http://www.crimpro.com/extension/ch03*.

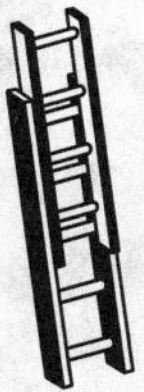

7. *Challenges to facially sufficient warrants.* Defendants sometimes will concede that the facts set forth in the affidavit amount to probable cause but contend that the factual basis for the warrant is untrue. The Supreme Court has held (and state courts have largely agreed) that if a defendant makes a preliminary showing of false statements in the warrant application, the trial court must grant a hearing on the question. Under Franks v. Delaware, 438 U.S. 154 (1978), the defendant's preliminary showing must demonstrate that the government "knowingly and intentionally, or with reckless disregard for the truth," included a false statement in the warrant affidavit. The attack must be "more than conclusory," and must point out "specifically with supporting reasons" the portion of the warrant affidavit that is claimed to be false. It also must be accompanied by affidavits or reliable statements of witnesses, or a satisfactory explanation of their absence. If the unreliable evidence was necessary to the government's showing of probable cause, the defendant gets a hearing and must establish his or her claims by a preponderance of the evidence before the fruits of the search or seizure are excluded from evidence. See State v. Chenoweth, 158 P.3d 595 (Wash. 2007) (state constitution, like federal law, requires suppression of evidence only if officer seeking a search warrant makes an omission or misrepresentation through reckless or intentional disregard for the truth; negligence by affiant does not require suppression).

Problem 3-3. Errors in a Facially Valid Warrant

Officer Holden observed a confidential informant make two illegal purchases of weapons at 916 Varney Street. Both times, the informant entered the building, returned with the weapons, and told Holden that he made the purchases in the "last apartment, of two, on the left" in a hallway down a flight of stairs. With this information, Holden applied for and obtained a warrant to search the apartment. The affidavit accompanying the application described the premises as follows:

> First-floor corner apartment, 916 Varney Street, described as a four-story red-brick structure with a green-colored solid door, with the number 916 affixed to the outside of the main entryway. The corner apartment is described as down one flight of stairs

> where three apartment doors are situated with two on the left side and one on the right side, the door is tan in color and is the second door on the left side in the main hallway at the end of the hall.

Prior to executing the warrant, Holden sent the informant into the building for a third time. After returning outside, he told Holden that the apartment subject to the warrant had a rug in front of the door. When Holden entered the hallway of the building, he realized that the informant was mistaken: There were two doors on the right side of the hallway and only one on the left. Holden decided to search the sole apartment on the left because there was a rug outside the door. He discovered evidence of weapons violations.

In a suppression hearing, will the court treat the evidence as the product of a valid warranted search? Compare Buckner v. United States, 615 A.2d 1154 (D.C. 1992).

Notes

1. *Awareness of the error.* In this problem, the officer was aware of the inaccuracy in the warrant before executing it. Does it make a difference if the officer remains unaware of the inaccuracy until she has begun the search? See Maryland v. Garrison, 480 U.S. 79 (1987) (warrant listing third floor as single apartment, when it was actually divided into separate apartments, could be executed because officers were reasonable in not discovering the inadvertent error in the warrant). What should police officers do when they obtain new information about the person or place named in the warrant before they execute the warrant? Return to the magistrate for an updated finding of probable cause? See State v. Maddox, 98 P.3d 1199 (Wash. 2004) (officers must return to magistrate for updated ruling only if new facts negate probable cause).

2. *The wrong jurisdiction.* Is an otherwise valid warrant still valid if it is executed by police accidentally acting outside of their jurisdiction? See People v. Martinez, 898 P.2d 28 (Colo. 1995) (error in jurisdiction, despite violating statute, not fatal).

3. *Execution of Warrants*

Once the police have obtained a valid warrant, they must "execute" it. That is, the police carry out a search within the limits described in the warrant, and "return" it to the magistrate who issued the warrant. The return serves as a report about the search. Recall that the court in Entick v. Carrington expressed some concern about the lack of any return for a general warrant, and thus the enforcement officer who conducted the search would not be accountable for completing the job properly. Does a return actually prevent abuses by searchers?

Specific procedure rules and statutes address the details of executing warrants. For instance, rules determine the total time that can elapse between issuance and execution of a search warrant. All but three states prescribe a deadline for serving a warrant, at which time the warrant expires. This period ranges from two days (North Carolina and Pennsylvania) to 60 days (Arkansas). The typical time span is 10 days (the period employed in more than 30 states plus the federal system). As one might expect, searches are far more likely to produce the expected evidence if they are executed promptly. See Laurence A. Benner & Charles T. Samarkos, Searching for Narcotics in San Diego: Preliminary Findings from the San Diego Search Warrant Project, 36 Cal. W. L. Rev. 221, 223 (2000).

STATE v. TANYA MARIE ANYAN

104 P.3d 511 (Mont. 2004)

NELSON, J.

. . . ¶3 In late May 2000, Officer Christopher Nichols of the Thompson Falls Police Department was assigned to investigate suspected illegal drug activity occurring at a rented house in Thompson Falls. During the course of the investigation, Officer Nichols determined that the occupants of the house were involved in operating a clandestine methamphetamine lab. Hence, on July 11, 2000, Officer Nichols requested the assistance of Sergeant Allen Bardwell, an officer with the Kalispell Police Department and team leader of the Kalispell SWAT team, in serving a search warrant. After meeting with Officer Nichols and learning that the house to be searched was a large structure consisting of three levels with numerous rooms and that it might be occupied by as many as fifteen individuals, Sergeant Bardwell contacted the Flathead County Sheriff Department's SWAT team for assistance. The commander of the Flathead County SWAT team, Undersheriff Chuck Curry, agreed to assist in the service of the warrant.

¶4 On July 24, 2000, Officer Nichols obtained a warrant to search the residence. In his application for the search warrant, Officer Nichols related that "out of the ordinary traffic" was seen coming [to] and going from the residence and that a great number of the vehicles were from Washington state. Officer Nichols also stated that he checked the license plates on three of the vehicles that he had seen at the residence. One of them was registered to [Troy Klein]. Officer Nichols then checked with Spokane County and discovered that Klein had been charged in the past with committing drug offenses. According to Officer Nichols, Klein also had three active felony warrants.

¶5 Officer Nichols also related in his search warrant application that several other individuals that had been seen near the residence had been charged with drug offenses. In addition, one of the vehicles seen at the residence was registered to an individual who had felony convictions for burglary and child rape. Officer Nichols also related that during his investigation, he discovered that there was a surveillance camera located in the second story east window of the residence and that it appeared to be pointed at the driveway.

¶6 Officer Nichols had discovered during the course of his investigation that an individual matching Klein's description had purchased ammunition from a local hardware store. While he did not include this information in the application for the search warrant, Officer Nichols did share this information with Sergeant Bardwell and Undersheriff Curry. However, the two-and-a-half month investigation, which included surveillance of the home, had yielded no observation or reports of weapons sighted in the home or in the possession of any of the individuals in the home. Officer Nichols also discovered that Klein had a warrant for his arrest in connection with a nonviolent felony parole violation.

¶7 On the night of July 25, 2000, the two SWAT teams, totaling fifteen men, and officers from several other law enforcement agencies converged on Thompson Falls at approximately 1:45 A.M. . . . Officer Nichols ordered two officers to conduct surveillance on the residence from an upstairs bedroom of the house across the street. Officer Shawna Reinschmidt was watching the activities in the front of the house at 2:20 A.M. when a car, which had left the house about five minutes earlier, returned, and the male driver got out of the car and yelled at everyone to get inside and turn off the lights. Officer Reinschmidt reported her observations to the SWAT team assembled at the police department. . . . Officer Reinschmidt continued to observe the house and although she saw some movement in the kitchen, she later testified that her observations were entirely consistent with the occupants preparing to retire for the night.

¶9 Law enforcement officers executed their no-knock raid at 3:00 A.M. As the officers approached the house they observed that it was quiet and most of the lights were off. None of the officers detected any activity or heard anything consistent with attempts to escape or resist arrest. . . .

¶10 The officers approached the home from the west and the north, outside of the range of the surveillance camera located on the east side of the house. The Kalispell SWAT team was assigned to enter the house at the upper level from an outside stairway and the Flathead County SWAT team was assigned to enter the house from the ground floor. At least six officers from the Kalispell SWAT team entered the top floor by using a steel ram to break the doorjamb. They confronted four of the occupants of the house who were in various stages of sleep and preparation for sleep. Another seven or eight officers from the Flathead County SWAT team entered the house through the downstairs kitchen door confronting the two occupants residing in that portion of the house. Another five to ten officers surrounded the house. The officers did not knock and announce their presence prior to entering the house. . . .

¶12 [Several occupants of the house were charged] with conspiracy to manufacture dangerous drugs; criminal production or manufacture of dangerous drugs; criminal possession of dangerous drugs; and possession of dangerous drugs with intent to sell. [They] each filed motions to suppress the evidence seized during the search of the residence, based in part on the officers' failure to knock and announce their presence prior to entering the house to execute the search warrant. The District Court denied the motions. . . .

¶20 This is an issue of first impression in Montana. Montana has no statutory provisions or case law addressing the knock-and-announce rule. Consequently, we look to the relevant federal law and the laws of our sister states to decide this issue. We also look to the greater protections afforded to Montanans in search and seizure matters under Article II, Sections 10 and 11 of the Montana Constitution. . . .

¶22 Underlying the knock-and-announce rule are concerns for the protection of privacy, reduction in the potential for violence, and the prevention of the destruction of property of private citizens. There is nothing more terrifying to the occupants than to be suddenly confronted in the privacy of their home by a police officer decorated with guns and the insignia of his office. This is why the law protects its entrance so rigidly.

> The fear of a smashing in of doors by government agents is based upon much more than a concern that our privacy will be disturbed. It is based upon concern for our safety

> and the safety of our families. Indeed, the minions of dictators do not kick in doors for the mere purpose of satisfying some voyeuristic desire to peer around and then go about their business. Something much more malevolent and dangerous is afoot when they take those actions. . . .

United States v. Lockett, 919 F.2d 585, 592 (9th Cir. 1990). [As] a matter of policy, no-knock warrants are disfavored because of their staggering potential for violence to both the occupants of the residence and the police. "Unannounced breaking and entering into a home could quite easily lead an individual to believe that his safety was in peril and cause him to take defensive measures which he otherwise would not have taken had he known that a warrant had been issued to search his home." State v. Bamber, 630 So. 2d 1048, 1052 (Fla. 1994). . . .

¶25 Because the Fourth Amendment protects property as well as privacy, another purpose of the knock-and-announce rule is to prevent the needless destruction of property. . . .

¶27 [The United States Supreme Court addressed the knock-and-announce principle in Wilson v. Arkansas, 514 U.S. 927 (1995).] After Sharlene Wilson made several narcotics sales to an informant, law enforcement officers with the Arkansas State Police obtained warrants to arrest her and search her home. The affidavit in support of the warrants stated that Wilson's housemate, Bryson Jacobs, had previously been convicted of arson and firebombing. On the afternoon of the search, the officers found the main door to Wilson's home open. As the officers opened an unlocked screen door and entered the residence, they identified themselves as police officers and stated that they had a warrant. They found Wilson in the bathroom flushing marijuana down the toilet. [The Supreme Court held that] the common-law knock-and-announce principle forms a part of the Fourth Amendment reasonableness inquiry. . . .

¶29 In making this determination, the Supreme Court examined in *Wilson* the history of the common-law knock-and-announce rule, noting that although common law generally protected a man's house as "his castle of defense and asylum," common-law courts long held that the sheriff, acting on behalf of the King, could enter a man's house to arrest him "or to do other execution of the King's process," but only after signifying the cause of his coming and requesting that the doors be opened. See 3 W. Blackstone, Commentaries; Semayne's Case, 77 Eng. Rep. 194 (K.B. 1603). . . . In addition, most of the states that ratified the Fourth Amendment enacted constitutional provisions or statutes generally incorporating English common law and a few states enacted statutes specifically embracing the common-law view that the breaking of the door of a dwelling was permitted once admittance was refused. . . . Hence, the Court held that the common-law knock-and-announce principle does form a part of the Fourth Amendment reasonableness inquiry.

¶32 The Court further held, however, that not every entry must be preceded by an announcement. [The] presumption in favor of announcement necessarily would give way to countervailing law enforcement interests. Those interests included circumstances presenting a threat of physical harm to officers, the fact that an officer is pursuing a recently escaped arrestee, and where officers have reason to believe that evidence would likely be destroyed if advance notice were given. . . .

Exigent Circumstances

¶34 Exigent circumstances [are] those circumstances that would cause a reasonable person to believe that entry (or other relevant prompt action) was necessary to prevent physical harm to the officers or other persons, the destruction of relevant evidence, the escape of a suspect, or some other consequence improperly frustrating legitimate law enforcement efforts. . . .

¶35 There are two types of exigencies, those that are foreknown and those unexpected that arise on the scene. . . . In the case before us on appeal, all of the factors that officers actually deemed exigent were actually known well in advance of applying for the search warrant. The SWAT teams became involved in this investigation almost two weeks prior to applying for a search warrant. It was at that point that the decision was made that there would be a no-knock forcible entry into the house. The court issuing the search warrant was never apprised of that decision, nor were any exigent circumstances laid out to the court when the search warrant was applied for.

¶36 Moreover, while peril to officers or the possibility of destruction of evidence or escape may well demonstrate an exigency, mere unspecific fears about those possibilities will not. Were they enough, the knock-and-announce [principle would be inapplicable to virtually all narcotics-based cases. The Supreme Court, however, has] held that the Fourth Amendment does not permit a blanket exception to the knock-and-announce requirement in felony drug investigations. Richards v. Wisconsin, 520 U.S. 385 (1997).

¶37 In *Richards*, law enforcement officers obtained a warrant to search Richards' motel room for drugs and related paraphernalia. One officer, dressed as a maintenance man, knocked on the door and stated that he was with maintenance. With the chain still on the door, Richards cracked it open, but slammed it closed again when he saw a uniformed officer standing behind the "maintenance man." After waiting two or three seconds, the officers kicked in the door. They claimed at trial that they identified themselves as police as they were kicking in the door. The officers caught Richards trying to escape through a window. They found cash and cocaine hidden in plastic bags in the bathroom ceiling.

¶38 Richards sought to have the evidence from his motel room suppressed on the ground that the officers failed to knock and announce their presence prior to forcing entry into the room. The trial court denied the motion. . . . The Wisconsin Supreme Court affirmed, concluding that it was reasonable to assume that all felony drug crimes would involve "an extremely high risk of serious if not deadly injury to the police as well as the potential for the disposal of drugs by the occupants prior to entry by the police." Thus, the Wisconsin Supreme Court concluded that exigent circumstances justifying a no-knock entry are always present in felony drug cases; hence, police officers are never required to knock and announce their presence when executing a search warrant in a felony drug investigation.

¶39 The United States Supreme Court disagreed and determined that the Fourth Amendment does not permit a blanket exception to the knock-and-announce requirement for felony drug investigations. Rather, the Supreme Court held that to justify a no-knock entry, police must have a reasonable suspicion that knocking and announcing their presence, under the particular circumstances, would be dangerous or futile, or that it would inhibit effective investigation of the crime by, for example, allowing the destruction of evidence.

¶40 [The use of blanket exceptions] presented two serious concerns: (1) the exception contains considerable overgeneralization as not every drug investigation poses substantial risks to the officers' safety and the preservation of evidence; and (2) the reasons for creating an exception in one category can, relatively easily, be applied to others and thereby render meaningless the knock-and-announce element of the Fourth Amendment's reasonableness requirement.

¶41 Although the Supreme Court rejected the Wisconsin court's blanket exception to the knock-and-announce requirement in *Richards*, the Supreme Court agreed with the trial court that on the facts of that case, it was reasonable for the officers to believe that Richards knew, after he opened the door, that the men seeking entry to his room were the police and that once the officers reasonably believed that Richards knew who they were, it was reasonable for them to force entry immediately given the disposable nature of the drugs. . . .

Safety Concerns

¶43 Exigent circumstances cannot be predicated upon general fears of the officers executing a search warrant in a narcotics investigation. While peril to officers may well demonstrate an exigency, mere unspecific fears about that possibility will not. [Officers] are concerned about an armed response when they execute any narcotics search warrant. Clearly, though, to expand the exigent circumstances exception to that extent would completely swallow the rule.

¶44 Hence, [evidence] that firearms are within the residence or that a particular defendant is armed is not by itself sufficient to create an exigency. There must be specific information to lead the officers to a reasonable conclusion that the presence of firearms raises concerns for the officers' safety. [Threats] to an officer's safety, a criminal record reflecting violent tendencies, or a verified reputation of a suspect's violent nature can be enough to provide law enforcement officers with justification to forgo the necessity of knocking and announcing their presence.

¶45 In the case sub judice, the officers had no information that any of the occupants of the house possessed weapons. Officer Nichols had information that a person matching Klein's description had purchased ammunition. However, even after months of surveillance, Officer Nichols had no information of weapons being in the residence and no report of anyone seeing any of the occupants of the house, including Klein, with weapons. There was no testimony indicating that any of the occupants of the house were prone to violence or the use of weapons or had ever made threats against law enforcement officers.

¶46 Prior to initiating the raid, Sergeant Bardwell completed a risk analysis report intended to assess the risk associated with specific individuals who the officers anticipate might be present during a raid. Sergeant Bardwell testified that Klein was the only person considered in conjunction with the risk analysis assessment and the only person about whom Sergeant Bardwell had any information prior to the raid. Sergeant Bardwell agreed that the only criterion that applied to Klein from the risk analysis checklist was that he was on probation or parole for a nonviolent offense. . . .

¶48 The State claims that another factor in determining exigency under the safety exception is the inherent danger in methamphetamine labs. In this case, although Officer Nichols expressed concerns regarding the safety of neighborhood residents, he made no attempt to evacuate any residences. . . .

FUTILITY

¶51 The futility exception to the knock-and-announce rule excuses the knock-and-announce requirement where police officers have a reasonable suspicion that the occupants know of the presence and purpose of the police prior to their entry into the residence. . . .

¶55 In the present case, the State conceded in oral argument that the futility exception was not applicable in this case. [The] SWAT teams approached the house from the north and west, thereby effectively remaining outside of the range of the surveillance camera. Additionally, the raid was conducted at night and the officers had no information that the camera was operational, especially in the dark. . . .

DESTRUCTION OF EVIDENCE

¶58 We also conclude that in this case the possibility of destruction of evidence did not create an exigent circumstance justifying the no-knock entry into Appellants' house. [The] government must prove they had a reasonable belief that the loss or destruction of evidence was imminent. The mere possibility or suspicion that a party is likely to dispose of evidence when faced with the execution of a search warrant is not sufficient to create an exigency. . . . The larger the amount of drugs and the more complex the operation, the less likelihood there is that evidence will be destroyed during the period between the knock and announce and the subsequent entry.

¶60 In this case, both Sergeant Bardwell and Undersheriff Curry testified that the mere fact that the residence contained a meth lab would not justify a no-knock entry. Moreover, Sergeant Bardwell testified that the potential for the destruction of the meth lab was not a concern in deciding to take on the assignment. Both Sergeant Bardwell and Undersheriff Curry agreed that a meth lab cannot be destroyed in a matter of five to ten seconds.

CONCLUSION

. . . ¶63 [The] decision to make a no-knock entry should ordinarily be made by a neutral and detached magistrate as part of the application for search warrant. An investigating officer may, however, make this decision based on unexpected exigent circumstances that arise on the scene. When law enforcement officers contemplate a no-knock entry in executing a search warrant, that intention must be included in the application for the search warrant along with any foreknown exigent circumstances justifying the no-knock entry. . . .

¶65 In conclusion, we hold that the law enforcement officers' no-knock entry into Appellants' house to execute the search warrant violated Appellants' federal and state constitutional rights to be free from unreasonable searches and seizures. Consequently, the trial court erred in failing to suppress the evidence resulting from that search. . . .

¶72 [The dissent] objects to our analysis, complaining that we have taken the "totality" out of "totality of the circumstances." Contrary to the dissent's contention, in order to examine the "totality" of the circumstances, each circumstance must first be considered on its own strength. [We] cannot agree that just because there are a number of circumstances, not one of which standing alone would create an exigency, the sheer volume of circumstances without something more is sufficient to create exigent circumstances. [Simply] put, zero plus zero can never equal one. . . .

RICE, J., dissenting.

. . . ¶78 [The Supreme Court in] *Richards* held that, although police should be required to make the necessary showing whenever the reasonableness of a no-knock entry is challenged, the showing itself is "not high." Further, it is not necessary to establish a level of proof satisfying the probable cause standard.

¶79 Indeed, the *Richards* "reasonable suspicion" standard is the same standard applied for the reasonableness of an investigative stop. . . .

¶80 Whether particularized suspicion supports an investigative stop is a question of fact that is analyzed in the context of the totality of the circumstances. In order for the State to prove the existence of particularized suspicion, the State must show: (1) objective data from which an experienced officer can make certain inferences; and (2) a resulting suspicion that the occupant of a certain vehicle is or has been engaged in wrongdoing or was a witness to criminal activity. . . .

¶81 . . . Citing to *Richards*' holding that there can be no "blanket exceptions" to the knock-and-announce rule for felony drug investigations, the Court simply dismisses the nature of the crime here as irrelevant to the inquiry. This is an incorrect application of *Richards*, which also concluded that it is "indisputable that felony drug investigations may frequently involve both" the threat of physical violence and the likelihood of destruction of evidence. [Contrary] to this Court's analysis, the nature of the crime being investigated is nonetheless a key factor which must be considered by police. The law has uniformly recognized that substantial dealers in narcotics possess firearms and that entrance into a situs of drug trafficking activity carries all too real dangers to law enforcement officers. . . .

¶82 [The Court also] dismisses the significance of the kind of drugs involved here — a methamphetamine laboratory. The Court should well know by now that "meth labs" are inherently unstable and dangerous, presenting this additional danger to officers. Nonetheless, the Court concludes this factor is not relevant to the inquiry because police made no attempt to evacuate any residences. Unfortunately, the dismissal of this concern by the Court does not accurately reflect the evidence in the record. To the contrary, Officer Bardwell testified that the situation here — "a meth lab with multiple suspects and they had warrants" — weighed significantly in his mind. . . .

¶83 . . . Klein's ammunition purchase may by itself have been insufficient to establish an exigency, but that did not render this evidence irrelevant to the inquiry. The Court reasons as if the evidence did not exist or was completely inconsequential. To the contrary, Officer Bardwell testified that evidence of the ammunition purchase by Klein, a fugitive felon, was significant to his analysis, and the District Court found this fact to be significant.

¶84 The Court . . . repeatedly focuses on the evidence which the police did not have. . . . Here, because the police had "no information" about whether the occupants were armed and "no information" about weapons being in the house, the Court concludes that the ammunition purchase by Klein is simply immaterial. This is a faulty inquiry. The proper focus in determining reasonable suspicion is what police did observe, and whether an experienced police officer can make certain inferences therefrom. Thus, I disagree with the Court's conclusion about this evidence. Purchase of ammunition by a fugitive felon who is associating with a group operating a meth lab is not a "mere unspecific fear." . . .

¶85 [The] Court illogically reasons that because the surveillance camera would be rendered ineffective by the speed of the no-knock entry, the camera was therefore not a factor to be considered in justifying the no-knock entry. Obviously, the camera would not have been rendered ineffective but for the no-knock entry. In addition to this error in logic, the Court again critically misapprehends Officer Bardwell's testimony. Officer Bardwell offered testimony to the precisely opposite conclusion about the significance of the surveillance camera: . . .

Defense: How did [the presence of a surveillance camera] matter in terms of planning your raid?
Bardwell: That if they have an operation that they deem the expense and trouble to put up counter-surveillance, it's probably a pretty substantial operation that they have. . . .

¶88 Additional factors could be analyzed, but this is enough. Clearly, there were specifically identifiable, objective factors which indicated to police that the situation required a no-knock entry. However, the Court, engaging in a "divide and conquer" analysis, systematically eliminates the effect of each factor. [The Court's analysis] separates and pigeonholes the factors which the police here considered, thereby eliminating all of them. In effect, it has taken the "totality" out of "totality of the circumstances."

¶90 Police here were faced with executing a felony drug warrant in a large structure in which numerous suspects with violent criminal backgrounds were staying. One suspect was known to have purchased ammunition. The suspects had mounted a surveillance camera. A meth lab was housed in the structure, and the size of the structure would inhibit the ability of police to locate and secure the lab. The numbers of suspects known to be inside could present safety and escape concerns. Shortly before the raid, one suspect yelled suspiciously. From a consideration of the totality of these circumstances, I would conclude that police had objective data from which they could reasonably infer, and from which a reasonable suspicion would arise, that a no-knock entry was necessary.

Notes

1. *Use of force in executing warrants and "knock and announce."* Most states have statutes requiring a police officer executing a search warrant to "knock and announce" — that is, to knock on the door before entering, to identify himself as a police officer, and to explain the purpose for seeking entry. See 18 U.S.C. §3109. Those with no statute on point have recognized the doctrine through judicial opinions. Only after entrance has been refused may the officer use force to enter. The knock-and-announce requirement derives from the common law. See Semayne's Case, 77 Eng. Rep. 194 (K.B. 1603). It also has constitutional dimensions: A failure to knock and announce can have some bearing on the constitutional "reasonableness" of a search or seizure. See Wilson v. Arkansas, 514 U.S. 927 (1995).

Once the officers have knocked on the door and announced their identity and purpose for wanting to enter, they may then enter by force after waiting a reasonable time for the occupants to respond to their knock. The amount of delay required in a given case depends on the nature of the evidence involved, the size of the dwelling, the time of day, and many other factors. In United States v. Banks, 540 U.S. 31 (2003), the Court approved of forceful entry by officers after they knocked, announced, and waited for 15 to 20 seconds. The evidence involved (cocaine) was easily disposable, and the apartment was small.

2. *No-knock entry.* There are important exceptions to the knock-and-announce requirement. Typically, the police may enter without notice if they have enough reason to believe that notice would endanger themselves or some other party, or would allow for the destruction of evidence or the escape of a suspect. What common household sounds might justify a forcible no-knock entry to execute a search? See also United States v. Ramirez, 523 U.S. 65 (1998) ("no knock" searches that cause property damage subject to same reasonableness standard as those causing no damage). A number of courts allow police officers to enter without announcing their true intentions if they can gain entry through a ruse such as pretending to be the "pizza man." Adcock v. Commonwealth, 967 S.W.2d 6 (Ky. 1998); State v. Elerieki, 993 P.2d 1191 (Haw. 2000). Is entry through a ruse consistent with the rationale of the knock-and-announce principle?

According to the opinion in Richards v. Wisconsin, 520 U.S. 385 (1997), the exceptions to the knock-and-announce requirement cannot be phrased too broadly. A blanket exception for "drug cases" will not stand; the police must show case-specific facts to demonstrate the need for a no-knock warrant. However, on the specific facts of that case, the officers' decision to enter the location unannounced might be constitutionally reasonable. An exploration of the cases that evaluate no-knock entry by the police appears on the web extension for this chapter at *http://www.crimpro.com/extension/ch03*.

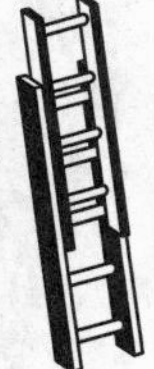

3. *Limits on nighttime searches.* Another common subject for statutes and codes of criminal procedure is the time of day or night an officer may execute a search warrant. More than a dozen states have rules or statutes explicitly authorizing the execution of a search warrant at night, without any special showing or procedures. See Ind. Code §35-33-5-7(c); Va. Code Ann. §19.2-56. However, more than 30 states have statutes or procedural rules imposing some legal limit on the execution of search warrants at night beyond the usual requirements for daytime warrants. These states often require the government agents to make some special showing to the magistrate before conducting a search at night. See Minn. Stat. §626.14 (search warrant may be served only between 7 A.M. and 8 P.M. unless court "determines on the basis of facts stated in the affidavits that a nighttime search outside those hours is necessary to prevent the loss, destruction, or removal of the objects of the search or to protect the searchers or the public"); State v. Jackson, 742 N.W.2d 163 (Minn. 2007) (Fourth Amendment incorporates common law requirement that law enforcement officers have some justification for executing a search warrant at night). Where detailed statutes or procedure rules loom larger than any constitutional requirements, does that tend to make procedure clearer?

4. *Witnesses and returns.* The law in Germany and France requires searches of a home to be witnessed by a resident or someone else not working for the police. See Richard S. Frase & Thomas Weigend, German Criminal Justice as a Guide to American Law Reform: Similar Problems, Better Solutions?, 18 B.C. Int'l & Comp. L. Rev. 317 (1995). In the United States, officers executing a search warrant must fill out the "return," describing to the issuing judge the results of the search. Do these two requirements provide comparable protections to the owner of property that is searched?

5. *Burden of proof.* Most jurisdictions encourage greater police use of search warrants by shifting the burden of proof at a suppression hearing. While the government bears the burden of proof for warrantless searches that are challenged at a suppression hearing, the defendant must carry the burden of proof for warranted searches. Ford v. State, 158 S.W.3d 488 (Tex. Crim. App. 2005) (defendant bears burden of production in motions to suppress, but burden of proof shifts to state if defendant shows that search was warrantless); People v. Syrie, 101 P.3d 219 (Colo. 2004). There is, however, a sizable group of states placing the burden of coming forward and the burden of persuasion on the prosecution for all motions to suppress. See Kan. Stat. Ann. §22-3216 ("the burden of proving that the search and seizure were lawful shall be on the prosecution").

6. *Physical detentions during execution of warrant.* Can the police insist that those present at the location of a warranted search remain there while the search goes forward? Can they use force to prevent those present from moving about? See Muehler v. Mena, 544 U.S. 93 (2005) (execution of search warrant was not unreasonable where officers entered home at 7 A.M., detained occupants of home in handcuffs during hours-long search of home for weapons and gang member, and questioned occupants about their immigration status); Michigan v. Summers, 452 U.S. 692 (1981); Cotton v. State, 872 A.2d 87 (Md. 2005) (officers executing search warrant at residence used to sell drugs may detain person found standing outside the home).

7. *Warrants for computer searches.* Some magistrates place specialized conditions on how computer warrants are executed. The conditions address the on-site seizure of computers, the timing of a later off-site search, the method of the off-site search, and the return of the seized computers after searches are complete. Does the nature of the storage medium for information justify a specialized set of practices for executing a warrant? See Orin S. Kerr, Ex Ante Regulation of Computer Search and Seizure, 96 Va. L. Rev. 1241 (2010).

4. *So You Like Warrants?*

There is surprisingly little empirical literature on how often warrants are actually used across different jurisdictions and for different kinds of searches (for example, for different suspected crimes). The general perception, supported by the limited evidence now available, is that the police conduct most searches, across most crime categories, in most jurisdictions, without obtaining warrants. Consider the following introduction from the van Duizend et al. study of the warrant process:

> [Warrants] do not serve as a primary safeguard of privacy because they are sought in relatively few cases. . . . The most detailed study of warrants prior to this one — the American Bar Foundation's survey of the Administration of Criminal Justice conducted in the late 1950s — found 29 search warrants issued in Detroit, 30 in Milwaukee, and 17 in Wichita during 1956. Following the application of the "exclusionary rule" to state court decisions, there was a substantial increase in the use of search warrants, although the number remains a small proportion of all criminal cases. In Boston, for example, the number of search warrants issued annually averaged 693 between 1961 and 1976. Moreover, the types of cases in which warrants were used appear to be quite limited, according to the literature. . . . Krantz, Gilman, Benda and

> Hallstrom (1979), in their study of Boston police practices, found that 83 percent of the warrants issued during 1976 in the city's three busiest district courts "were to investigate suspected violations of the narcotic drug laws or vice laws." Such offenses accounted for less than 12 percent of all arrests nationally for that year.

What could courts or legislatures or police departments do to encourage police officers to use warrants more often and to make warrants a more significant form of protection against improper searches and seizures? One possibility is to make the warrant requirement a true requirement, subject only to an exception for necessity. In other words, if a warrant can be obtained, it must be obtained or the search will be held invalid. Another approach would be to judge warrantless searches under a different, tougher standard than searches conducted pursuant to a warrant. A third possibility would be to encourage the use of telephonic or electronic warrants. For example, a jurisdiction might allow oral statements to support warrant requests, put cellular phones in police cars, and arrange to have a magistrate available "on call." Consider as well the two approaches we explore in this section, both of which might encourage the use of search warrants.

a. Anticipatory Warrants

The prototypical application for a search warrant describes events that have already occurred and infers from those facts the probable cause to believe that a crime has been committed and that the items sought will be found at the named location. But this creates a timing problem. The officer completes the application after gathering the relevant facts establishing probable cause and before the search takes place. The minutes or hours necessary to obtain a warrant may not be available after the confirmation of probable cause but before the search must happen. To relieve this problem, can the application anticipate future events?

■ MICHAEL DODSON v. STATE

150 P.3d 1054 (Okla. Crim. App. 2006)

C. JOHNSON, J.

. . . ¶3 On September 29, 2003, a Tulsa police drug interdiction officer noticed a suspicious package at the Federal Express facility in Tulsa, Oklahoma. After the officer's drug dog "hit" on the package, the officer obtained a search warrant to open the package. Upon opening the package, the officer found the package contained a manila envelop with Mike Dodson's name on it. Inside the manila envelope was some rolled up tissue paper. Inside the rolled up tissue paper was a baggie. Inside the baggie was approximately one ounce of white crystal substance which field-tested positive for methamphetamine.

¶4 The officer prepared an affidavit for an anticipatory search warrant requesting to search Mike Dodson's residence upon delivery of the package and presented it to a Tulsa County magistrate. After the officer obtained a search warrant, he dressed as a Federal Express driver and delivered the package to Michael Dodson's address. Dodson answered the door, signed for the package and took it inside his residence.

¶5 Tulsa police officers served the search warrant about fifteen minutes later. During the search, they located the baggie containing the white crystal substance and a small quantity of marijuana in the house. No tax stamps were found on either the marijuana or the methamphetamine. . . .

¶6 . . . Mr. Dodson contends the Oklahoma Constitution prohibits the issuance of a warrant based upon future contingent events, making the "house warrant" illegal, and the fruits of its execution inadmissible at trial. This Court has not previously addressed the constitutionality of anticipatory search warrants under our state constitution, but recently the United States Supreme Court, in United States v. Grubbs, 547 U.S. 90 (2006) upheld the constitutionality of anticipatory search warrants under the Fourth Amendment to the United States Constitution.

¶7 Art.2, §30 of the Oklahoma Constitution provides:

> The right of the people to be secure in their persons, houses, papers, and effects against unreasonable searches or seizures shall not be violated; and no warrant shall issue but upon probable cause supported by oath or affirmation, describing as particularly as may be the place to be searched and the person or thing to be seized.

The language of Article II, Section 30 is almost an exact copy of the fourth amendment of the Constitution of the United States and while the language is not in all respects the same in the two provisions, the substance is identical.

¶8 Nothing in the text of Article II, Section 30 requires a showing that the evidence must be in the place to be searched at the time the warrant issues. On the contrary, the provision does not say anything about whether a finding of probable cause can or cannot be based upon the anticipation of some future event. Nothing in the plain language of Article II, Section 30 prohibits the issuance of an anticipatory search warrant and they do not run afoul of plain language of Oklahoma's constitution.

¶9 While anticipatory search warrants may not run afoul of the United States Constitution or the Oklahoma Constitution, we find merit to Mr. Dodson's second proposition that Oklahoma statutes prohibit the issuance of a warrant based upon future contingent events. Sections 1221-1238 of Title 22 outline the requisites for the issuance of a search warrant. Absent specific statutory authority for a separate procedure prior to the filing of a complaint in a criminal case, the State's ability to search for and seize evidence of a crime is limited to the procedure set forth in [the statutes listing] the requisites of a search warrant.

¶10 . . . The plain language of Title 22, Section 1222 requires that the object of the search be currently in the possession of the person or at the location to be searched. It provides that a search warrant may be issued and property seized upon any of the following grounds:

> First: When the property was stolen or embezzled, in which case it may be taken on the warrant, from any house or other place in which it is concealed, or from the possession of the person by whom it was stolen or embezzled, or of any other person in whose possession it may be.
>
> Second: When it was used as the means of committing a felony, in which case it may be taken on the warrant from any house or other place in which it is concealed, or from the possession of the person by whom it was used in the commission of the offense, or of any other person in whose possession it may be.

> Third: When it **is in the possession of any person,** with the intent to use it as the means of committing a public offense, or in the possession of another to whom he may have delivered it for the purpose of concealing it or preventing its being discovered, in which case it may be taken on the warrant from such person, or from a house or other place occupied by him, or under his control, or from the possession of the person to whom he may have so delivered it.
>
> Fourth: When the property constitutes evidence that an offense was committed or that a particular person participated in the commission of an offense.

¶11 The language used in "First," "Second," and "Fourth" subsections clearly presuppose a crime has already been committed which is shown by the use of the past tense in those subsections — *i.e.* "when the property *was stolen or embezzled.*" . . . The language in the "Third" subsection is plain and clear, and is in the present tense — a warrant may be issued when the property "is in the possession of" — which specifically requires the property to currently be in the possession of the person.

¶12 The wording of the "Third" subsection of Section 1222 is applicable to this case. The anticipatory search warrant was issued based upon an affidavit which claimed the defendant "has placed the following described property for concealment, *does now* unlawfully, illegally, knowingly and willfully *keep,* and *does* unlawfully *have in his possession* and under his control certain dangerous substances." Although the affiant expected that certain events (Dodson's possession of illegal substances) would occur *after* the issuance of the warrant, it is that future event which created all of the probable cause for the issuance of the warrant. . . .

¶14 While we recognize that a majority of states have found anticipatory search warrants to be constitutional, several have held they are invalid upon statutory grounds. [The court cited cases from Maryland, Colorado, and Iowa.] Other states which have found the anticipatory search warrants were constitutional but were not permitted by statute subsequently amended their statutes to specifically provide for such warrants. [The court cited cases from Illinois, Alabama, and Hawaii.]

¶15 . . . The utility of anticipatory search warrants in drug investigations, especially when dealing with the activities of persons who traffic in narcotics cannot be ignored. However, it is incumbent upon our legislature to amend §1222 of Title 22 to provide a legal statutory basis for such anticipatory warrants to be issued. . . .

¶21 [Because] the evidence of drug trafficking, possession of marijuana, and failure to affix tax stamp was obtained pursuant to a statutorily invalid warrant, the trial court should have granted the Motion to Suppress. There being no evidence remaining upon which to sustain Mr. Dodson's convictions, his convictions must be reversed and remanded with instructions to dismiss. . . .

LUMPKIN, V.P.J., dissenting.

¶1 I see absolutely no reason — legal, moral, practical, or otherwise — to apply the exclusionary rule's harsh sanction to the facts of this case, for there is no overreaching police conduct to deter. Therefore, I dissent to the Court's opinion and its narrow reading of 22 O.S.2001, §1222.

¶2 Time after time, this Court has instructed police officers who are actively investigating crimes and seeking to conduct a search in that regard to first "obtain your warrants." The policy reason, of course, is that warrantless searches are to be the exception not the rule. Our statutes strongly encourage the participation of a neutral magistrate, detached from the underlying investigation and applying an objective eye to the facts and law involved. This protects all parties involved.

¶3 On this occasion, however, the authorities followed our advice and obtained not one warrant, but two. Through the use of good police work, drugs that were in the process of being illegally distributed from one person to another through a private mail delivery service were intercepted while in transit. After a drug dog hit on a suspicious package, authorities obtained a warrant to open the package. And there they found exactly what they had suspected: methamphetamine, located inside an envelope with Appellant's name written on it.

¶4 At this point, officers had probable cause to search the place where these illegal drugs were scheduled to be delivered, i.e., Appellant's residence. Exercising extreme caution, they obtained another warrant and prepared to serve the warrant at a time when they knew beyond a shadow of a doubt that drugs would be located on the premises. This was extraordinary.

¶5 So now we will punish those same officers for their good work by dismissing the case and allowing another drug trafficker back on the street. And we do this by taking an unconvincing position on the law, a position that is both ill-advised and not required under the statutory language. In other words, the Court is, for some inexplicable reason, straining a gnat's hair to reverse this case.

¶6 Under paragraph two of section 1222, a search warrant may issue and property seized when that property "was used as the means of committing a felony, in which case it may be taken on the warrant from any house or other place in which it is concealed, or from the possession of the person by whom it was used in the commission of the offense, or of any other person in whose possession it may be." It takes no legal gymnastics to find this section may be used to support the warrants issued here. Likewise, the fourth paragraph may be used as the "property" here, the mailed package of drugs, "constitutes evidence that an offense was committed or that a particular person participated in the commission of an offense."

¶7 . . . Officers could have had the magistrate ready to issue the warrant once the drugs were on the property and then executed it minutes later. However, the problem with that scenario is that drugs are too often easily destroyed, i.e. flushing down the toilet, and time, as well as stealth, is of the essence. That is why this case is evidence of nothing more than good, professional police work and that type of professionalism should be commended, not condemned. . . .

Problem 3-4. A New Look

On July 1, an anonymous informant telephoned Detective Wygnanski of the Washoe County Consolidated Narcotics Unit. The informant told Wygnanski that Craig Parent would arrive at the Reno Airport on a Continental Airlines flight from New Orleans on July 3. The informant stated that Parent would be with two women named "Jody" and "Stephanie" and he would have cocaine concealed inside a baby powder bottle in his baggage. The informant also provided Wygnanski with a physical description of Parent, saying that he was 6'1″ tall, with brown "wavy" hair, green eyes, and a moustache. The caller knew Parent's social security number, his FBI number, and his date of birth, and said that he had an extensive criminal record. Wygnanski confirmed the fact that Parent was scheduled to fly on Continental Airlines to Reno on July 3 and determined that he had several criminal convictions on his record. On July 2, Wygnanski obtained a search warrant. Execution of the warrant was conditioned upon the arrival of Continental Airlines flight number 781 from New Orleans on July 3.

On July 3, Parent and two women arrived at the Reno Airport. Police officers observed the threesome as they exited the airplane, and heard Parent call one of the two women "Karen." They noted that his hair was shortly trimmed rather than wavy, and he had no moustache, but Parent otherwise met the description that the informant had provided. The police officers arrested Parent shortly after he retrieved his luggage. A police officer found 3.7 grams of cocaine in a baby powder bottle located inside one of Parent's bags.

The state charged Parent with narcotics crimes, and Parent moved to suppress the evidence. He argues that the justice of the peace improperly issued the search warrant because the Nevada constitution prohibits anticipatory warrants under the circumstances presented in this case. As defense counsel, how would you distinguish the facts in this case from the controlled delivery situation in the *Dodson* case from Oklahoma? Cf. State v. Parent, 867 P.2d 1143 (Nev. 1994).

Notes

1. *Anticipatory warrants: majority position.* The courts in over half of the states upheld the use of anticipatory search warrants, even before the Supreme Court addressed the question in United States v. Grubbs, 547 U.S. 90 (2006). The majority opinion in *Grubbs* drew the following comparison between anticipatory warrants and traditional search warrants:

> An anticipatory warrant is a warrant based upon an affidavit showing probable cause that at some future time (but not presently) certain evidence of crime will be located at a specified place. Most anticipatory warrants subject their execution to some condition precedent other than the mere passage of time — a so-called "triggering condition." . . .
>
> In the typical case where the police seek permission to search a house for an item they believe is already located there, the magistrate's determination that there is probable cause for the search amounts to a prediction that the item will still be there when the warrant is executed. . . . Anticipatory warrants are, therefore, no different in principle from ordinary warrants. They require the magistrate to determine (1) that it is now probable that (2) contraband, evidence of a crime, or a fugitive will be on the described premises (3) when the warrant is executed. It should be noted, however, that where the anticipatory warrant places a condition (other than the mere passage of time) upon its execution, the first of these determinations goes not merely to what will probably be found if the condition is met. . . . Rather, the probability determination for a conditioned anticipatory warrant looks also to the likelihood that the condition will occur, and thus that a proper object of seizure will be on the described premises. In other words, for a conditioned anticipatory warrant to comply with the Fourth Amendment's requirement of probable cause, two prerequisites of probability must be satisfied. It must be true not only that if the triggering condition occurs there is a fair probability that contraband or evidence of a crime will be found in a particular place, but also that there is probable cause to believe the triggering condition will occur. The supporting affidavit must provide the magistrate with sufficient information to evaluate both aspects of the probable-cause determination.

As the *Dodson* court mentioned, a number of state courts (about a half dozen) decided over the years that anticipatory warrants violated state *statutes* defining the use of search warrants. In some jurisdictions, the legislature responded right away with new statutory language authorizing the use of anticipatory warrants. See Ex parte Turner, 792 So. 2d 1141, 1151 (Ala. 2000). Would you expect the federal constitutional ruling in *Grubbs* to influence the way that state courts interpret these state statutes?

2. *Predicting the future.* Are anticipatory warrants likely to involve magistrates in reviewing a larger number of searches? Do they remove the magistrate from effective review, or do they involve the magistrate even more closely than usual in examining warrant applications? Suppose that investigators plan to send a paid informant into two specific locations to purchase illegal drugs. They are confident that the informant will be able to purchase the drugs at one of the two locations, but they are uncertain which location is correct. Could they obtain an anticipatory search warrant for the two locations, conditioned on a positive field test showing that the substance purchased was indeed cocaine? See State v. Gillespie, 530 N.W.2d 446 (Iowa 1995). Would the names of the targets contribute to the showing of probable cause? The dates or the addresses? Does this application amount to a request for the magistrate to pre-approve a standard police operating procedure?

Suppose you serve as counsel to the judicial conference of a state. What guidelines might you set for magistrates to avoid abuse of anticipatory warrants? Would you insist that the magistrate include as a condition in the warrant every detail that the police relate in the application? Over what time span might an anticipatory warrant be valid?

3. *Anticipatory warrants and exigent circumstances.* If anticipatory warrants are both allowed and encouraged in a particular state, what might that do to the state's doctrines regarding exigent circumstances? Should courts require police to obtain anticipatory search warrants and anticipate exigent circumstances that might arise? See Commonwealth v. Killackey, 572 N.E.2d 560 (Mass. 1991) (rejecting requirement that police obtain anticipatory warrant if they can). Will anticipatory warrants reinvigorate the warrant requirement?

b. Administrative Warrants

Anticipatory warrants, considered in the preceding section, encourage the *use* of warrants. Another way to encourage the use of warrants is to allow a standard lower than probable cause (or a different kind of probable cause) for searches when the investigators obtain prior review and approval by magistrates, leaving the ordinary probable cause standard for warrantless searches.

The following case is pivotal in Fourth Amendment jurisprudence. Not only did it open up the possibility of a reduced standard of probable cause in certain settings, but it also established the importance of "balancing" the competing interests in different categories of Fourth Amendment cases. The balancing methodology enables a court to decide what level of justification the government must present to support a valid search in different contexts.

ROLAND CAMARA v. MUNICIPAL COURT OF SAN FRANCISCO

387 U.S. 523 (1967)

WHITE, J.*

. . . On November 6, 1963, an inspector of the Division of Housing Inspection of the San Francisco Department of Public Health entered an apartment building to make a routine annual inspection for possible violations of the city's Housing Code. The building's manager informed the inspector that appellant, lessee of the ground floor, was using the rear of his leasehold as a personal residence. Claiming that the building's occupancy permit did not allow residential use of the ground floor, the inspector confronted appellant and demanded that he permit an inspection of the premises. Appellant refused to allow the inspection because the inspector lacked a search warrant.

[The inspector returned on several later occasions without a search warrant. When Camara refused to allow him to enter, he was charged with refusing to permit a lawful inspection, a misdemeanor. Camara argued that the charges against him were unconstitutional, because they derived from illegitimate power of government agents to search without probable cause or a warrant.]

[In this Court's cases interpreting the Fourth Amendment,] one governing principle, justified by history and by current experience, has consistently been followed: except in certain carefully denned classes of cases, a search of private property without proper consent is "unreasonable" unless it has been authorized by a valid search warrant. . . .

In Frank v. Maryland, 359 U.S. 360 (1959), this Court upheld the conviction of one who refused to permit a warrantless inspection of private premises for the purposes of locating and abating a suspected public nuisance. . . . We proceed to a re-examination of the factors which persuaded the *Frank* majority to adopt this construction of the Fourth Amendment's prohibition against unreasonable searches.

To the *Frank* majority, municipal fire, health, and housing inspection programs "touch at most upon the periphery of the important interests safeguarded by the Fourteenth Amendment's protection against official intrusion," because the inspections are merely to determine whether physical conditions exist which do not comply with minimum [regulatory standards]. We may agree that a routine inspection of the physical condition of private property is a less hostile intrusion than the typical policeman's search for the fruits and instrumentalities of crime. . . . But we cannot agree that the Fourth Amendment interests at stake in these inspection cases are merely "peripheral." It is surely anomalous to say that the individual and his private property are fully protected by the Fourth Amendment only when the individual is suspected of criminal behavior. For instance, even the most law-abiding citizen has a very tangible interest in limiting the circumstances under which the sanctity of his home may be broken by official authority, for the possibility of criminal entry under the guise of official sanction is a serious threat to personal and family security. . . . Like most regulatory laws, fire, health, and housing codes are enforced by criminal processes. . . .

* [Chief Justice Warren and Justices Black, Douglas, Brennan, and Fortas joined this opinion. — EDS.]

The *Frank* majority suggested, and appellee reasserts, two other justifications for permitting administrative health and safely inspections without a warrant. First, it is argued that these inspections are "designed to make the least possible demand on the individual occupant." The ordinances authorizing inspections are hedged with safeguards, and at any rate the inspector's particular decision to enter must comply with the constitutional standard of reasonableness even if he may enter without a warrant. [For instance, the San Francisco Code requires that the inspector display proper credentials, that he inspect "at reasonable times," and that he not obtain entry by force except in emergencies.] In addition, the argument proceeds, the warrant process could not function effectively in this field. The decision to inspect an entire municipal area is based upon legislative or administrative assessment of broad factors such as the area's age and condition. Unless the magistrate is to review such policy matters, he must issue a "rubber stamp" warrant which provides no protection at all to the property owner.

In our opinion, these arguments unduly discount the purposes behind the warrant machinery contemplated by the Fourth Amendment. Under the present system, when the inspector demands entry, the occupant has no way of knowing whether enforcement of the municipal code involved requires inspection of his premises, no way of knowing the lawful limits of the inspector's power to search, and no way of knowing whether the inspector himself is acting under proper authorization. These are questions which may be reviewed by a neutral magistrate without any reassessment of the basic agency decision to canvass an area. . . . The practical effect of [the current] system is to leave the occupant subject to the discretion of the official in the field. This is precisely the discretion to invade private property which we have consistently circumscribed by a requirement that a disinterested party warrant the need to search. We simply cannot say that the protections provided by the warrant procedure are not needed in this context; broad statutory safeguards are no substitute for individualized review, particularly when those safeguards may only be invoked at the risk of a criminal penalty. . . .

In summary, we hold that administrative searches of the kind at issue here are significant intrusions upon the interests protected by the Fourth Amendment, [and] that such searches when authorized and conducted without a warrant procedure lack the traditional safeguards which the Fourth Amendment guarantees to the individual. . . . Because of the nature of the municipal programs under consideration, however, these conclusions must be the beginning, not the end, of our inquiry. . . .

The Fourth Amendment provides that, "no Warrants shall issue, but upon probable cause." Borrowing from more typical Fourth Amendment cases, appellant argues not only that code enforcement inspection programs must be circumscribed by a warrant procedure, but also that warrants should issue only when the inspector possesses probable cause to believe that a particular dwelling contains violations of the minimum standards prescribed by the code being enforced. We disagree.

In cases in which the Fourth Amendment requires that a warrant to search be obtained, "probable cause" is the standard by which a particular decision to search is tested against the constitutional mandate of reasonableness. To apply this standard, it is obviously necessary first to focus upon the governmental interest which allegedly justifies official intrusion upon the constitutionally protected interests of the private citizen. . . .

Unlike the search pursuant to a criminal investigation, the inspection programs at issue here are aimed at securing city-wide compliance with minimum physical standards for private property. The primary governmental interest at stake is to prevent even the unintentional development of conditions which are hazardous to public health and safety. Because fires and epidemics may ravage large urban areas, because unsightly conditions adversely affect the economic values of neighboring structures, numerous courts have upheld the police power of municipalities to impose and enforce such minimum standards even upon existing structures. . . . There is unanimous agreement among those most familiar with this field that the only effective way to seek universal compliance with the minimum standards required by municipal codes is through routine periodic inspections of all structures.

[Camara contends, first], that his probable cause standard would not jeopardize area inspection programs because only a minute portion of the population will refuse to consent to such inspections, and second, that individual privacy in any event should be given preference to the public interest in conducting such inspections. The first argument, even if true, is irrelevant to the question whether the area inspection is reasonable within the meaning of the Fourth Amendment. The second argument is in effect an assertion that the area inspection is an unreasonable search. Unfortunately, there can be no ready test for determining reasonableness other than by balancing the need to search against the invasion which the search entails. But we think that a number of persuasive factors combine to support the reasonableness of area code-enforcement inspections. First, such programs have a long history of judicial and public acceptance. Second, the public interest demands that all dangerous conditions be prevented or abated, yet it is doubtful that any other canvassing technique would achieve acceptable results. Many such conditions — faulty wiring is an obvious example — are not observable from outside the building and indeed may not be apparent to the inexpert occupant himself. Finally, because the inspections are neither personal in nature nor aimed at the discovery of evidence of crime, they involve a relatively limited invasion of the urban citizen's privacy. . . .

Having concluded that the area inspection is a "reasonable" search of private property within the meaning of the Fourth Amendment, it is obvious that "probable cause" to issue a warrant to inspect must exist if reasonable legislative or administrative standards for conducting an area inspection are satisfied with respect to a particular dwelling. Such standards, which will vary with the municipal program being enforced, may be based upon the passage of time, the nature of the building (e.g., a multi-family apartment house), or the condition of the entire area, but they will not necessarily depend upon specific knowledge of the condition of the particular dwelling. It has been suggested that so to vary the probable cause test from the standard applied in criminal cases would be to authorize a "synthetic search warrant" and thereby to lessen the overall protections of the Fourth Amendment. But we do not agree. The warrant procedure is designed to guarantee that a decision to search private property is justified by a reasonable governmental interest. But reasonableness is still the ultimate standard. If a valid public interest justifies the intrusion contemplated, then there is probable cause to issue a suitably restricted search warrant. Such an approach [recognizes] the competing public and private interests here at stake and, in so doing, best fulfills the historic purpose behind the constitutional right to be free from unreasonable government invasions of privacy.

[Most] citizens allow inspections of their property without a warrant. Thus, as a practical matter and in light of the Fourth Amendment's requirement that a warrant specify the property to be searched, it seems likely that warrants should normally be sought only after entry is refused unless there has been a citizen complaint or there is other satisfactory reason for securing immediate entry. . . .

In this case, [there was no emergency demanding immediate access, yet] no warrant was obtained and thus appellant was unable to verify either the need for or the appropriate limits of the inspection. [We] conclude that appellant had a constitutional right to insist that the inspectors obtain a warrant to search and that appellant may not constitutionally be convicted for refusing to consent to the inspection. . . .

CLARK, J., dissenting.*

Today the Court renders . . . municipal experience, which dates back to Colonial days, for naught by . . . striking down hundreds of city ordinances throughout the country and jeopardizing thereby the health, welfare, and safety of literally millions of people. But this is not all. It prostitutes the command of the Fourth Amendment that "no Warrants shall issue, but upon probable cause" and sets up in the health and safety codes area inspection a newfangled "warrant" system that is entirely foreign to Fourth Amendment standards. . . .

There is nothing here that suggests that the inspection was unauthorized, unreasonable, for any improper purpose, or designed as a basis for a criminal prosecution; nor is there any indication of any discriminatory, arbitrary, or capricious action affecting the appellant. . . . The majority say, however, that under the present system the occupant has no way of knowing the necessity for the inspection, the limits of the inspector's power, or whether the inspector is himself authorized to perform the search. [All] of these doubts raised by the Court could be resolved very quickly. Indeed, the inspectors all have identification cards which they show the occupant and the latter could easily resolve the remaining questions by a call to the inspector's superior or, upon demand, receive a written answer thereto. . . .

The Court then addresses itself to the propriety of warrantless area inspections. [These] boxcar warrants will be identical as to every dwelling in the area, save the street number itself. I daresay they will be printed up in pads of a thousand or more — with space for the street number to be inserted — and issued by magistrates in broadcast fashion as a matter of course. I ask: Why go through such an exercise, such a pretense? As the same essentials are being followed under the present procedures, I ask: Why the ceremony, the delay, the expense, the abuse of the search warrant? In my view this will not only destroy its integrity but will degrade the magistrate issuing them and soon bring disrepute not only upon the practice but upon the judicial process. It will be very costly to the city in paperwork incident to the issuance of the paper warrants, in loss of time of inspectors and waste of the time of magistrates and will result in more annoyance to the public. . . .

* [Justices Harlan and Stewart joined this opinion. — EDS.]

Notes

1. *Do administrative warrants honor the Fourth Amendment or undermine it?* Does the majority or dissent in *Camara* do greater honor to the Fourth Amendment? Would the Court have been truer to the Fourth Amendment if it had allowed unwarranted administrative searches on the basis of their reasonableness, modest intrusion, and general applicability, subject to careful guidelines, rather than craft a new kind of warrant? Would the Court have been truer still to the Fourth Amendment if it had barred administrative searches absent consent or individualized suspicion of a civil or criminal violation?

Have you seen administrative warrants before, in another context? Review now the eighteenth-century writ of assistance reprinted in section A of this chapter. Are there significant differences between that writ and the administrative warrants described in the *Camara* decision?

2. *Statutory guidance.* The authority for such warrants is often in statutes. Does a legislative imprimatur help to validate the idea of administrative warrants? Does the legislative approval of the practice answer concerns about the discretion or priorities of police supervisors or field officers? Consider the following language from Mich. Stat. §333.7504(2):

> A magistrate . . . upon proper oath or affirmation showing probable cause, may issue a warrant for the purpose of conducting an administrative inspection authorized by this article or the rules promulgated under this article and seizures of property appropriate to the inspection. Probable cause exists upon showing a valid public interest in the effective enforcement of this article or the rules promulgated under this article sufficient to justify administrative inspection of the area, premises, building, or conveyance in the circumstances specified in the application for the warrant. . . .

3. *Sliding scales.* One of the justifications for allowing administrative search warrants appears to be the modestly invasive nature of the searches they justify. The Supreme Court has declared that the balancing method of determining the reasonableness of a search is available whenever there is a "special need" beyond the normal need for law enforcement. New York v. Burger, 482 U.S. 691 (1987).

Should this "lesser invasion/lesser justification" idea be limited to the context of administrative searches, or should the principle be taken more broadly to require a rough correlation between the intrusiveness of any search (warranted or warrantless) and the justification the government must offer? Is a sliding scale of searches a workable concept? Can it be reconciled with the traditional limits of a warrant requirement and probable cause?

4. *Administrative warrants in highly regulated industries.* There is an important exception to the requirement that the government obtain an administrative warrant. If the target of the search is engaged in a "highly regulated industry," the Supreme Court and an overwhelming number of state courts have concluded that an administrative warrant is not necessary. Instead, the government must show that the warrantless search is necessary, that there is an adequate substitute for the warrant to limit the discretion of the field agent, and that the inspection is limited in time, place, and scope. Donovan v. Dewey, 452 U.S. 594 (1981) (statute authorizing warrantless safety inspections of coal mines). The regulation in question must apply to a focused group of people or enterprises; regulations covering all or most employers, however

intrusive, do not eliminate the need for an administrative warrant. Marshall v. Barlow's, Inc., 436 U.S. 307 (1978) (inspection to enforce OSHA workplace safety rules invalid). Is this exception available because of the consent of the targets? That is, does a liquor or firearms retailer understand when going into the business that warrantless searches will occur? See State v. Larsen, 650 N.W.2d 144 (Minn. 2002) (conservation officer needed warrants to search recreational "ice fishing houses" on frozen lakes; court rejected analogy to closely regulated industries); Scott E. Sundby, Protecting the Citizen "Whilst He Is Quiet": Suspicionless Searches, "Special Needs" and General Warrants, 74 Miss. L. J. 501-52 (2004).

D. CONSENSUAL SEARCHES

The police can conduct a full search *without a warrant and without probable cause* if the target of the search consents. In most jurisdictions, the police conduct far more consensual searches than those justified by probable cause or a search warrant. Indeed, one might ask whether a consensual search is a "search" (within the meaning of the constitution) at all. As you read these materials, compare consensual searches with intrusions, covered in Chapter 2, that are not considered "searches" at all.

1. Components of a Voluntary Choice

Any valid consent to search must be "voluntary," yet this choice rarely takes place in a setting ideally suited to rational deliberation of all available options. What are the minimum elements of voluntariness necessary to make a consensual search legally acceptable?

■ MERLE SCHNECKLOTH v. ROBERT BUSTAMONTE

412 U.S. 218 (1973)

STEWART, J.*

. . . I.

[While on routine patrol in Sunnyvale, California, at approximately 2:40 A.M., Police Officer James Rand stopped an automobile when he observed that one headlight and its license plate light were burned out. Six men were in the vehicle. When the driver, Joe Gonzalez, could not produce a driver's license, Rand asked the others for identification. Only Joe Alcala produced a license,] and he explained that the car was his brother's. After the six occupants had stepped out of the car at the officer's request and after two additional policemen had arrived, Officer Rand asked Alcala if he could search the car. Alcala replied, "Sure, go ahead." Prior to the search

* [Chief Justice Burger and Justices White, Blackmun, Powell, and Rehnquist joined in this opinion. — EDS.]

no one was threatened with arrest and, according to Officer Rand's uncontradicted testimony, it "was all very congenial at this time." [The police officer asked Alcala, "Does the trunk open?" Alcala said, "Yes," and opened up the trunk.] Wadded up under the left rear seat, the police officers found three checks that had previously been stolen from a car wash.

[Bustamonte was brought to trial in a California court on a charge of possessing a check with intent to defraud. The trial judge denied the motion to suppress the checks, and on the basis of the checks and other evidence he was convicted. After his failure to obtain relief on appellate review in state court, Bustamonte challenged his conviction in federal habeas corpus proceedings.]

II.

[The] State concedes that when a prosecutor seeks to rely upon consent to justify the lawfulness of a search, he has the burden of proving that the consent was, in fact, freely and voluntarily given. The precise question in this case, then, is what must the prosecution prove to demonstrate that a consent was "voluntarily" given. . . .

B.

[The] question whether a consent to a search was in fact "voluntary" or was the product of duress or coercion, express or implied, is a question of fact to be determined from the totality of all the circumstances. While knowledge of the right to refuse consent is one factor to be taken into account, the government need not establish such knowledge as the sine qua non of an effective consent. As with police questioning, two competing concerns must be accommodated in determining the meaning of a "voluntary" consent — the legitimate need for such searches and the equally important requirement of assuring the absence of coercion.

In situations where the police have some evidence of illicit activity, but lack probable cause to arrest or search, a search authorized by a valid consent may be the only means of obtaining important and reliable evidence. . . . And in those cases where there is probable cause to arrest or search, but where the police lack a warrant, a consent search may still be valuable. If the search is conducted and proves fruitless, that in itself may convince the police that an arrest with its possible stigma and embarrassment is unnecessary, or that a far more extensive search pursuant to a warrant is not justified. In short, a search pursuant to consent may result in considerably less inconvenience for the subject of the search, and, properly conducted, is a constitutionally permissible and wholly legitimate aspect of effective police activity.

But the Fourth and Fourteenth Amendments require that a consent not be coerced, by explicit or implicit means, by implied threat or covert force. For, no matter how subtly the coercion was applied, the resulting "consent" would be no more than a pretext for the unjustified police intrusion against which the Fourth Amendment is directed. . . .

The problem of reconciling the recognized legitimacy of consent searches with the requirement that they be free from any aspect of official coercion cannot be resolved by any infallible touchstone. To approve such searches without the most careful scrutiny would sanction the possibility of official coercion; to place artificial restrictions upon such searches would jeopardize their basic validity. . . . In examining all the surrounding circumstances to determine if in fact the consent to search was coerced, account must be taken of subtly coercive police questions, as well as the possibly vulnerable subjective state of the person who consents. Those searches that are the product of police coercion can thus be filtered out without undermining the continuing validity of consent searches. In sum, there is no reason for us to depart in the area of consent searches, from the traditional definition of "voluntariness."

The approach of [those courts ruling] that the State must affirmatively prove that the subject of the search knew that he had a right to refuse consent, would, in practice, create serious doubt whether consent searches could continue to be conducted. There might be rare cases where it could be proved from the record that a person in fact affirmatively knew of his right to refuse — such as a case where he announced to the police that if he didn't sign the consent form, "[you] are going to get a search warrant;" or a case where by prior experience and training a person had clearly and convincingly demonstrated such knowledge. But more commonly where there was no evidence of any coercion, explicit or implicit, the prosecution would nevertheless be unable to demonstrate that the subject of the search in fact had known of his right to refuse consent. . . .

One alternative that would go far toward proving that the subject of a search did know he had a right to refuse consent would be to advise him of that right before eliciting his consent. That, however, is a suggestion that has been almost universally repudiated by both federal and state courts, and, we think, rightly so. For it would be thoroughly impractical to impose on the normal consent search the detailed requirements of an effective warning. Consent searches are part of the standard investigatory techniques of law enforcement agencies. They normally occur on the highway, or in a person's home or office, and under informal and unstructured conditions. The circumstances that prompt the initial request to search may develop quickly or be a logical extension of investigative police questioning. . . . These situations are a far cry from the structured atmosphere of a trial where, assisted by counsel if he chooses, a defendant is informed of his trial rights. And, while surely a closer question, these situations are still immeasurably far removed from "custodial interrogation" where, in Miranda v. Arizona, 384 U.S. 436 (1966), we found that the Constitution required certain now familiar warnings as a prerequisite to police interrogation. . . .

C.

It is said, however, that a "consent" is a "waiver" of a person's rights under the Fourth and Fourteenth Amendments. The argument is that by allowing the police to conduct a search, a person "waives" whatever right he had to prevent the police from searching. It is argued that under the doctrine of Johnson v. Zerbst, 304 U.S. 458 (1938) to establish such a "waiver" the State must demonstrate "an intentional relinquishment or abandonment of a known right or privilege." But these standards were enunciated in *Johnson* in the context of the safeguards of a fair criminal trial [such as waiver of counsel at trial or] the right to confrontation, to a jury trial, and to a speedy trial, and the right to be free from twice being placed in jeopardy. . . .

The protections of the Fourth Amendment are of a wholly different order, and have nothing whatever to do with promoting the fair ascertainment of truth at a criminal trial. [The] Fourth Amendment protects the security of one's privacy against arbitrary intrusion by the police. . . . It is no part of the policy underlying the Fourth and Fourteenth Amendments to discourage citizens from aiding to the utmost of their ability in the apprehension of criminals. Rather, the community has a real interest in encouraging consent, for the resulting search may yield necessary evidence for the solution and prosecution of crime, evidence that may insure that a wholly innocent person is not wrongly charged with a criminal offense. [It] would be unrealistic to expect that in the informal, unstructured context of a consent search, a policeman, upon pain of tainting the evidence obtained, could make the detailed type of examination demanded by *Johnson*. . . .

D.

It is . . . argued that the failure to require the Government to establish knowledge as a prerequisite to a valid consent, will relegate the Fourth Amendment to the special province of "the sophisticated, the knowledgeable and the privileged." We cannot agree. The traditional definition of voluntariness we accept today has always taken into account evidence of minimal schooling, low intelligence, and the lack of any effective warnings to a person of his rights; and the voluntariness of any statement taken under those conditions has been carefully scrutinized to determine whether it was in fact voluntarily given.

E.

Our decision today is a narrow one. We hold only that when the subject of a search is not in custody and the State attempts to justify a search on the basis of his consent, the Fourth and Fourteenth Amendments require that it demonstrate that the consent was in fact voluntarily given, and not the result of duress or coercion, express or implied. Voluntariness is a question of fact to be determined from all the circumstances, and while the subject's knowledge of a right to refuse is a factor to be taken into account, the prosecution is not required to demonstrate such knowledge as a prerequisite to establishing a voluntary consent. . . .

MARSHALL, J., dissenting.

[I would] have thought that the capacity to choose necessarily depends upon knowledge that there is a choice to be made. But today the Court reaches the curious result that one can choose to relinquish a constitutional right — the right to be free of unreasonable searches — without knowing that he has the alternative of refusing to accede to a police request to search. I cannot agree, and therefore dissent.

I.

[The Court] imports into the law of search and seizure standards developed to decide entirely different questions about coerced confessions. . . . The inquiry in a case where a confession is challenged as having been elicited in an unconstitutional manner is . . . whether the behavior of the police amounted to compulsion of the defendant. [No] sane person would knowingly relinquish a right to be free of compulsion. Thus, the questions of compulsion and of violation of the right itself are inextricably intertwined. The cases involving coerced confessions, therefore, pass over the question of knowledge of that right as irrelevant, and turn directly to the question of compulsion.

[When] a search is justified solely by consent . . . , the needs of law enforcement are significantly more attenuated, for probable cause to search may be lacking but a search permitted if the subject's consent has been obtained. Thus, consent searches are permitted, not because such an exception to the requirements of probable cause and warrant is essential to proper law enforcement, but because we permit our citizens to choose whether or not they wish to exercise their constitutional rights. . . .

II.

If consent to search means that a person has chosen to forgo his right to exclude the police from the place they seek to search, it follows that his consent cannot be considered a meaningful choice unless he knew that he could in fact exclude the police. . . . I can think of no other situation in which we would say that a person agreed to some course of action if he convinced us that he did not know that there was some other course he might have pursued. . . .

If one accepts this view, the question then is a simple one: must the Government show that the subject knew of his rights, or must the subject show that he lacked such knowledge? I think that any fair allocation of the burden would require that it be placed on the prosecution. . . . If the burden is placed on the defendant, all the subject can do is to testify that he did not know of his rights. And I doubt that many trial judges will find for the defendant simply on the basis of that testimony. [The government, however, might demonstrate the subject's knowledge of his rights by showing his responses at the time of the search.] Denials of knowledge may be disproved by establishing that the subject had, in the recent past, demonstrated his knowledge of his rights, for example, by refusing entry when it was requested by the police. The prior experience or training of the subject might in some cases support an inference that he knew of his right to exclude the police.

The burden on the prosecutor would disappear, of course, if the police, at the time they requested consent to search, also told the subject that he had a right to refuse consent and that his decision to refuse would be respected. . . . The Court contends that if an officer paused to inform the subject of his rights, the informality of the exchange would be destroyed. I doubt that a simple statement by an officer of an individual's right to refuse consent would do much to alter the informality of the exchange, except to alert the subject to a fact that he surely is entitled to know. It is not without significance that for many years the agents of the Federal Bureau of Investigation have routinely informed subjects of their right to refuse consent, when they request consent to search. . . .

I must conclude, with some reluctance, that when the Court speaks of practicality, what it really is talking of is the continued ability of the police to capitalize on the ignorance of citizens so as to accomplish by subterfuge what they could not achieve by relying only on the knowing relinquishment of constitutional rights. Of course it would be "practical" for the police to ignore the commands of the Fourth Amendment, if by practicality we mean that more criminals will be apprehended, even though the constitutional rights of innocent people also go by the board. But such a practical advantage is achieved only at the cost of permitting the police to disregard the limitations that the Constitution places on their behavior, a cost that a constitutional democracy cannot long absorb. . . .

■ PITTSFIELD, MAINE, POLICE DEPARTMENT CONSENT-TO-SEARCH FORM

I, ______, have been informed by ______ and ______ who made proper identification as (an) authorized law enforcement officers of the Pittsfield PD . . . of my CONSTITUTIONAL RIGHT not to have a search made of the premises and property owned by me and/or under my care, custody and control, without a search warrant. Knowing of my lawful right to refuse to consent to such a search, I willingly give my permission to the above named officers to conduct a complete search of the premises and property, including all buildings and vehicles, both inside and outside of the property located at ______.

The above said officers further have my permission to take from my premises and property, any letters, papers, materials or any other property or things which they desire as evidence for criminal prosecution in the case or cases under investigation. This written permission to search without a search warrant is given by me to the above officers voluntarily and without any threats or promises of any kind, at ______ A.M./P.M. on this ______ day of ______, at ______ (place).

PHILADELPHIA POLICE DEPARTMENT DIRECTIVE 7, APPENDIX A

[Officers] will ensure they provide the consenting party with the following warnings:

1. that the consenting party has the right to require the police to obtain a search warrant, and
2. that he/she has the right to refuse to consent to a search. . . .

If the person is in police custody, three additional warnings must be provided:

1. that any items found can and will be confiscated and may be used against them in court;
2. they have the right to consult with an attorney before making a decision to consent; and
3. that they have the right to withdraw their consent at any time.

Problem 3-5. Consent After a Traffic Stop

Robert Robinette was driving his car at 69 miles per hour in a 45-mile-per-hour construction zone on the Interstate. Deputy Roger Newsome, who was on drug interdiction patrol at the time, stopped Robinette for a speeding violation. Before Newsome approached Robinette's vehicle, he decided to issue Robinette only a verbal warning, which was his routine practice regarding speeders in that construction zone. Newsome approached Robinette's vehicle and requested his driver's license. Robinette handed over his license, and Newsome returned to his vehicle to check it. Finding no violations, Newsome returned to Robinette's vehicle. Newsome then asked Robinette to get out of his car and step to the rear of the vehicle. Robinette complied with Newsome's request and stood between his car and the deputy's cruiser. Newsome returned to his vehicle to activate the cruiser's video camera so that he could videotape his interaction with Robinette. Newsome then issued a verbal warning regarding Robinette's speed and returned Robinette's driver's license.

After returning the license, Newsome said to Robinette, "One question before you go: Are you carrying any illegal contraband in your car? Any weapons of any kind, drugs, anything like that?" When Robinette said that he did not have any contraband in the car, Newsome asked if he could search the vehicle. Robinette hesitated briefly, then answered "yes." Upon his search of Robinette's vehicle, Newsome found a small amount of marijuana. Newsome then put Robinette and his passenger in the back seat of the cruiser and continued the search. As a result of this extended search, Newsome found a pill inside a film container; the pill was later determined to be an illegal narcotic. Newsome always asked permission to search the cars he stopped for speeding violations. He had followed this procedure more than 800 times during the previous 12 months. Was Robinette's consent valid? Compare State v. Robinette, 653 N.E.2d 695 (Ohio 1995); Ohio v. Robinette, 519 U.S. 33 (1996).

Notes

1. *Voluntariness of consent: majority position.* Almost all state courts agree with *Bustamonte* that a "totality of the circumstances" determines whether a person consented to a search, and that it is not necessary to inform the person of the right to refuse consent. See Commonwealth v. Cleckley, 738 A.2d 427 (Pa. 1999); but see State v. Johnson, 346 A.2d 66 (N.J. 1975) (party consenting to search must understand right to refuse consent). Whose perceptions of the totality of the circumstances will determine whether the choice was voluntary? Should a court adopt the viewpoint of the person being searched, the officer, or an objective "reasonable person"? Both subjective and objective perspectives operate here. Courts ask about the subjective features of the target of the search, focusing specifically on the consenting person's age, education, and intelligence. Then they consider any objective evidence of coercion, deception, threats, or other undue influence by the police. In light of the police conduct and the defendant's particular subjective circumstances, the court ultimately decides whether the police conduct could have appeared to be coercive to a reasonable person in the defendant's circumstances. See Krause v. Commonwealth, 206 S.W.3d 922 (Ky. 2006) (consent to search was coerced when officer knocked at 4:00 A.M. and requested permission to enter apartment as part of an investigation of a roommate not present at the time, accused of rape of young girl; no sexual assault had occurred, officer's intent was to look for drugs in plain view, but knew that college-educated suspects would refuse consent to search for drugs). Should a person with more education and worldliness have more difficulty arguing that her consent to a search was involuntary? Indeed, after taking this course, would you be able to claim your consent to a search was involuntary on any grounds short of torture?

2. *Why consent?* Why would a "reasonable" person who knows that evidence of a crime is present on the premises ever consent to a search? There is considerable evidence in psychological studies that people unreflectively defer to the wishes of authority figures, including police officers. Is this a sufficient explanation? For a review of the empirical basis for consent doctrine, see Steven L. Chanenson, Get the Facts, Jack! Empirical Research and the Changing Constitutional Landscape of Consent Searches, 71 Tenn. L. Rev. 399 (2004).

3. *Proof of knowledge.* As a prosecutor, how would you try to prove that a person who consented to a search knew that she had the power to refuse? As police counsel, would you recommend that your officers use a consent form in all cases when they

wish to search on the basis of consent? Would it increase the chance that the courts would validate consent searches? Would this practice result in a loss of too many searches? Should the form contain explicit notice that the person can refuse to consent? Note that Directive 7 from the Philadelphia Police Manual provides for some warnings not required as a matter of federal constitutional law. The manual also calls for consent searches only when there is no probable cause and no chance to get a warrant. Why would a police manual contain such provisions?

4. *Consent based on inevitability of a search.* Is consent voluntary when the police claim to have the authority to search immediately, or as soon as they obtain a warrant? In Bumper v. North Carolina, 391 U.S. 543 (1968), the police officer said to a homeowner, "I have a warrant," but the prosecution later justified the search as a consensual search rather than relying on a warrant. The court held that the homeowner's consent to the search was not voluntary because it was induced by a "show of authority" by the police. Was the consent involuntary because of some knowledge the homeowner did not have, such as the invalidity of the warrant? Or was it because the police affirmatively misrepresented the range of options open to her?

Suppose the officer had said, "I can get a warrant if you don't consent." Would your answer change if she had said, "I will seek a warrant"? See State v. Brown, 783 P.2d 1278 (Kan. 1989). Would consent be voluntary if the police ask to search a home while saying that if the owner insists that they obtain a warrant, they plan to return with their "blue lights and sirens blazing" for the benefit of the neighbors?

5. *"Knock and talk" practices.* Police departments encourage their officers to obtain consent to search in many settings. The practice provokes some serious challenges in the setting of searches in a home. When police officers approach a home with no probable cause to search, and plan to request consent to search, this "knock and talk" practice raises difficult factual issues about whether the resident's consent is truly voluntary. Given the special sensitivity of searches in a home, a few jurisdictions declare that officers who approach a home for the sole purpose of obtaining consent to search the home must inform the resident that he or she does not have to consent. State v. Brown, 156 S.W.3d 722 (Ark. 2004) (state constitution requires police officers conducting "knock and talk" to inform home dweller that consent may be refused). Most jurisdictions, however, leave the voluntariness of such consensual searches to the factfinding of the trial judge in the individual case. State v. Smith, 488 S.E.2d 210 (N.C. 1997) ("knock and talk" policy of police department does not violate constitution per se).

6. *Consent while in custody.* Does the driver of a vehicle stopped for a traffic violation voluntarily consent to a search of the car if told that the alternative is to be arrested and taken to jail (and the officer has lawful authority to do just that for traffic violators)? Can a suspect already in custody consent to a search? In United States v. Watson, 423 U.S. 411 (1976), the court approved of a consensual search of a car owned by a person who had been taken into custody in a restaurant and was being held on a public street. As in *Bustamonte,* the Court held that the lack of notice about the right to refuse consent did not make the choice involuntary in this setting. See United States v. Drayton, 536 U.S. 194 (2002) (when armed and uniformed officers of drug interdiction team boarded bus and worked down the aisle questioning passengers, suspect agreed to allow pat-down search of his baggage and person; consent was valid); People v. Anthony, 761 N.E.2d 1188 (Ill. 2001) (suspect wordlessly assuming frisk position after officer's request to search his person is too ambiguous to establish consent; actions might indicate acquiescence to authority).

7. *Consent after a traffic stop.* The Supreme Court held, in Ohio v. Robinette, 519 U.S. 33 (1996), that a police officer asking for consent to search the car at the conclusion of a valid traffic stop need not inform the motorist that he is free to leave and may refuse to consent to the search. However, the Ohio Supreme Court on remand held that the officer's failure to inform the motorist that the stop was over still amounted to one important factor showing lack of consent in the case. State v. Robinette, 685 N.E.2d 762 (Ohio 1997). Roughly 15 states follow Ohio's lead and list a lack of warning as one important component of the voluntariness issue. See Harris v. Commonwealth, 581 S.E.2d 286 (Va. 2003). Courts in other jurisdictions state that consent obtained at the end of any traffic stop deserves heightened review to ensure the voluntariness of the consent. Ferris v. State, 735 A.2d 491 (Md. 1999). In fact, a small group of states (fewer than a half dozen) insist that police may not request consent to search a car stopped for traffic violations unless they have reasonable suspicion of some criminal activity other than the traffic matter. See State v. Smith, 184 P.3d 890 (Kan. 2008). Are these decisions consistent with Schneckloth v. Bustamonte? Is knowledge about the power to refuse consent more important for stopped automobile drivers than for others who are asked to consent to a search? A sampling of consent-to-search cases in the automobile context appears on the web extension of this chapter at *http://www.crimpro.com/extension/ch03*.

Problem 3-6. Scope of Consent

Just past midnight, Sergeant William Planeta and his partner, Officer Joseph Agresta, spotted a 10-year-old black Honda with tinted windows. A computer check on the car failed to turn up any negative information. After following the car for about 20 blocks, the officers pulled it over for excessively tinted windows — a violation of the state motor vehicle code. While his partner spoke with the driver (Gomez), Planeta approached the vehicle, looked through the passenger window, and then inspected the undercarriage of the car for evidence of a hidden compartment. In Planeta's experience, the undercarriage of a vehicle can offer telltale signs of secret compartments used in narcotics trafficking.

Planeta noticed fresh undercoating around the gas tank. Meanwhile, the driver handed Agresta a registration card for the vehicle that showed signs of tampering. The word "Company" had been removed from the name on the card so that it read "Anna Teodora Fermin" rather than "Anna Teodora Fermin Company." The darkly tinted windows, fresh undercoating near the gas tank, and altered registration led Planeta to suspect that the vehicle was being used to transport drugs. Planeta then asked the driver whether he had any guns, knives, cocaine, heroin, or marijuana, and the driver responded, "No." Planeta then asked, "May I search your car, sir?" and the driver said, "Yeah."

Planeta instructed Gomez to stand at the rear of the car, where Officer Agresta patted him down; he then told him to sit on the rear bumper and wait. Planeta unlocked the rear seat and pulled it back. He observed gray "non-factory" carpet in the location above the area where he had spotted the fresh undercoating. He then pulled up the glued carpeting and discovered a cut in the floorboard. Planeta used his pocket knife to pry up the sheet metal. After struggling to reach what he thought was a plastic bag, Planeta returned to his cruiser and retrieved a crowbar, which he brought back to the Honda. Gomez remained silent as Sergeant Planeta began his search again. The crowbar finally enabled him to open part of the gas tank, where he discovered seven bags of cocaine weighing over 1.5 pounds in a hidden compartment.

Gomez has moved to suppress the drugs. He does not contest the voluntariness of his consent to search the vehicle but claims that Planeta's search went beyond the scope of his consent. Will the trial judge grant to motion? Cf. People v. Gomez, 838 N.E.2d 1271 (N.Y. 2005).

Notes

1. *Scope of consent: majority position.* A consent search is valid only if the government agent conducting the search remains within the bounds of the consent granted. The Supreme Court has held that "[t]he standard for measuring the scope of a suspect's consent under the Fourth Amendment is that of 'objective' reasonableness — what would the typical reasonable person have understood by the exchange between the officer and the suspect?" Florida v. Jimeno, 500 U.S. 248 (1991). Virtually all state courts deciding this question have reached the same conclusion.

A court will determine the exact coverage of the agreement by reviewing the language that the officer and the target of the search used, much as a court would examine the language used by contractual parties to determine the meaning of their agreement. Would the use of written consent forms tend to help or hurt police departments in this inquiry? If a person consents generally to a search of his "person" or his "vehicle," does that general statement include consent to search all areas within those bounds? A court will typically find it significant if the government agent tells the search target what he is looking for. If the officer is seeking illegal narcotics, the search might be more thorough and intrusive while still remaining within the bounds of the consent. But a number of courts have insisted that an officer obtain specific consent before searching the crotch area. See Davis v. State, 594 So. 2d 264 (Fla. 1992).

2. *Withdrawal of consent.* A person who has consented to a search can withdraw that consent (or restrict its scope) at any time before the completion of the search. However, the person must make an unequivocal withdrawal, through words or actions or both. An action withdrawing consent must be clearly inconsistent with the prior consent, such as a refusal to open a door or a container. See State v. Smith, 782 N.W.2d 913 (Neb. 2010) (person entering a nightclub requiring all patrons to submit to frisk withdrew that consent when officer tried to reach into his pocket and he grabbed officer's wrist and knocked his hand away).

3. *Duration of consent.* While it is clear that a person must withdraw consent through clear language or action, does that mean that a consent to search remains effective indefinitely, allowing a search several days after the grant of consent? Most courts conclude that an open-ended consent to search contains an implied time limitation: The search must be conducted as soon as it is reasonably possible to do so. But do some circumstances suggest a consent with longer duration? In Caldwell v. State, 393 S.E.2d 436 (Ga. 1990), the defendant called the police at 3:00 P.M. to report the stabbing of her children, invited the police into her apartment, and asked them to search for evidence that would lead to the arrest of the murderer. She then left the premises to spend the night with relatives. The search

continued until 10:00 P.M. the day of the murder, and for several hours the next day. The court concluded that the consent remained valid for the entire period of the search.

2. *Third-Party Consent*

The police can obtain the consent to search property either from the target of the search herself or from some third party. Of course, the third party's consent must be voluntary, just as with the target of the search. In addition, the third party must have the authority (or at least the apparent authority) to consent to the search. The third party's authority to consent to a search of property "does not rest upon the law of property, with its attendant historical and legal refinements, but rests rather on mutual use of the property by persons generally having joint access or control for most purposes." In such a setting, the target of the search has "assumed the risk" that another person with access to the property will consent to a search. United States v. Matlock, 415 U.S. 164 (1974). How might this standard apply in the following problems? Would any recurring fact make a difference to a reviewing court?

Problem 3-7. Co-tenant Consenting for Co-tenant

Gina owned a house, which she rented to her son Dale and another man, Thomas. At about 2:00 A.M. on August 30, several acquaintances of Dale and Thomas were at the house. Two of the guests left for about 30 minutes and returned with more than a half pound of marijuana. Thomas was upset that there was marijuana in the house and complained to Dale, but Dale seemed unconcerned.

Thomas went to the police, where he signed a consent to search the house for the marijuana. Several officers went to the house, drew their weapons, and entered the house without knocking or announcing their purpose or authority. They found marijuana in baggies in a black leather jacket in the kitchen and arrested the guest who owned the jacket. In plain view in the living room was a "sawed off" or "short barreled" shotgun belonging to Dale. Was this a valid consensual search? Compare In re Welfare of D.A.G., 474 N.W.2d 419 (Minn. 1991).

Problem 3-8. Parent Consenting for Child

During a murder investigation, police officers went to a suspect's house and asked his mother for consent to search his room. The suspect, who was 23 years old, slept and stored his clothes and other property in a bedroom upstairs in the house and sporadically paid his mother rent for the room. His mother had regular access to the room for purposes of collecting his laundry. She also stored her sewing machine in the room. Although the room was usually unlocked, on this day it was locked. The suspect's mother opened the door with a key and allowed the police to search his room. They found in the closet a jacket with blood stains matching the blood of the murder victim. Was this a valid consensual search?

Problem 3-9. Child Consenting for Parent

Deputy Sheriff Joe Brown and Officer Chris Nichols planned to arrest Jonathan Lowe. Nichols learned that Lowe was staying at the home of Karen Schwarz, so the two officers drove to Schwarz's home on a Friday night to carry out the arrest. Brittany Glazier, Schwarz's 13-year-old daughter, who had just arrived home from the movies with two girlfriends, answered the door. The three friends had been watching a video while waiting for one girl's ride home; the other friend had permission to spend the night at Brittany's house. Brittany had met Officer Brown at a Girl Scout event. Officer Brown explained to Brittany, who he believed to be either 13 or 14 years old, that he was looking for Lowe. The officers asked for permission to come into the home and "look around" while they waited for Lowe. Brittany agreed.

During the search, Officer Nichols discovered a marijuana pipe and a small plastic container containing a white substance, later determined to be methamphetamine. At some point, Schwarz, who was out bowling, called home and learned of the officers' presence. She immediately drove home. When Schwarz arrived, Officer Nichols told her that he had discovered drugs. Schwarz admitted to owning the pipe and methamphetamine and provided written consent to another search of the entire house. Was this a valid consensual search? Cf. State v. Schwarz, 136 P.3d 989 (Mont. 2006).

■ ARKANSAS RULE OF CRIMINAL PROCEDURE 11.2

The consent justifying a search and seizure can only be given, in the case of: (a) search of an individual's person, by the individual in question or, if the person is under 14 years of age, by both the individual and his parent, guardian, or a person in loco parentis; (b) search of a vehicle, by the person registered as its owner or in apparent control of its operation or contents at the time consent is given; and (c) search of premises, by a person who, by ownership or otherwise, is apparently entitled to give or withhold consent.

Notes

1. *Presence or absence of target and consenting party.* In Problem 3-7, the target of the search was present during the search and did not consent. This situation arises frequently during investigations of alleged domestic abuse. In Georgia v. Randolph, 547 U.S. 103 (2006), Janet Randolph complained to the police that her husband, Scott, had taken their son away after a domestic dispute. She went with an officer to the home she shared with Scott to reclaim the child. When they arrived, Scott said that he had removed the child to a neighbor's house out of concern that Janet might take the boy out of the country. Janet mentioned that her husband used cocaine and left evidence of his use in the bedroom. She gave her consent for the police to search the home, but when an officer asked Scott for permission to search the house, he

unequivocally refused. The Supreme Court held that "a physically present co-occupant's stated refusal to permit entry prevails" over the consent of the other occupant.

Would the analysis change if the target of a search leaves explicit instructions to others with joint control over the property that she does not wish for them to authorize any searches? Or if the consenting party is not at the scene of the search? The court in United States v. Matlock, 415 U.S. 164 (1974), addressed these questions obliquely when it spoke of valid third-party consent against an "absent, nonconsenting" person with an interest in the property. State and federal courts have almost always upheld third-party consents when they contradicted the explicit instructions of the absent search target.

2. *Unequal interests in property.* Parties with different legal interests in a location, such as landlords and tenants, will typically have powers to consent to a search only when contractual terms and other reasonable expectations allow such consent. See State v. Licari, 659 N.W.2d 243 (Minn. 2003) (landlord's contractual right to inspect rented storage unit did not provide actual or apparent authority to consent to police search); Stoner v. California, 376 U.S. 483 (1964) (unwarranted search of hotel room without consent of defendant was unlawful even though police obtained consent of hotel clerk). What happens if the consenting party has a clearly lesser interest in the property than the target of the search? Suppose the target of the search pays rent on an apartment, while the consenting third party is a frequent long-term guest. Should the third party in that setting be able to override the objections of the party with the stronger claim on the property? A few courts require a third party to have at least an equal interest with other owners before allowing that person to consent to a search of the property, at least when the superior interest holder is present and objecting to the search. See Silva v. State, 344 So. 2d 559 (Fla. 1977). Is the principle here that the third party's interests derive from the first party's and therefore cannot override the first party's privacy?

3. *Family member consent.* Family members frequently consent to a search of the shared family home during an investigation of some other occupant of the home, particularly when they are victims of the alleged crime. State v. Ellis, 210 P.3d 144 (Mont. 2009) (police obtained consent from 13-year-old to search her bedroom for evidence of sexual assault by father; state constitutional rule limiting third-party consent for search to those 16 and older provides for no exception for child's own bedroom).

Many third-party consent cases involve spouses or others in a similar relationship. Sometimes one spouse will consent to a search in an effort to injure a partner during a time of conflict. Is it reasonable for the police to rely on consent if it is clear that one party intends only to harm the target of the search? For a perusal of third-party consent cases from the family context, consult the web extension of this chapter at *http://www.crimpro.com/extension/ch03*.

4. *Consent forms and policies.* Would you advise a police department to adopt a special version of its consent-to-search forms for third-party consent searches? Would you advise the police to adopt any rules regarding the proper procedure for obtaining third-party consent?

COMMONWEALTH v. PORTER P.

923 N.E.2d 36 (Mass. 2010)

GANTS, J.

The Commonwealth was granted leave to appeal from an order entered in the Juvenile Court suppressing a gun seized by the police during a search of a room in a transitional family shelter occupied by the juvenile and a statement that he made after his arrest. Having been notified by the shelter's director that the juvenile allegedly possessed a gun, the police officers determined that the director had the authority to consent to their entry and conducted a warrantless search of the juvenile's room with her consent. After the police found the gun, the . . . juvenile was charged with delinquency by reason of the unlawful possession of a firearm and ammunition. [The trial] judge ordered suppression of the gun and the statement to the police. . . . We affirm the allowance of the motion to suppress.

Background. . . . The juvenile and his mother moved into a room at the Roxbury Multi-Service Center, Inc., Family House Shelter in March, 2006. The shelter [contracts with the Commonwealth to provide] temporary housing for otherwise homeless families. . . . Families may remain at the shelter until they find a permanent living situation, unless they commit a violation of the shelter's rules and regulations. The typical stay is between four and eight months. Apart from a key deposit fee of thirty dollars, the families do not pay to live at the shelter.

Each new resident of the shelter, including the juvenile and his mother, as part of the intake procedure, is given a manual setting forth the shelter's rules and regulations. According to the manual, residents . . . are not permitted to enter another resident's room at any time for any purpose. Because residents must commit to being actively engaged at least twenty hours per week in employment, education, or job training, or looking for employment or housing, the residents are required to be out of the shelter from 9 A.M. to 3 P.M. every weekday. . . . Each resident and his or her family is provided a furnished room and given a key to his or her room. The director, however, has a master key that opens every door in the shelter, and the staff members have a master key that opens every resident's room. Members of the shelter's staff have the right to enter any room "for professional business purposes (maintenance, room inspections, etc.)," but only with the knowledge of the director. If a "business professional," such as a repair person or exterminator, requires entry to a resident's room, he or she must be escorted by a staff member, with the director's approval. The shelter staff may conduct "room checks" at any time without warning to monitor compliance with the shelter's "Good Housekeeping Standard" and other rules and regulations, including those affecting health and safety. The manual has a "zero tolerance policy in regards to violent acts committed by residents" and the possession of any weapon; "any resident in possession of a weapon will be terminated immediately." The shelter "reserves the right to contact the Police should the situation warrant," but the manual does not state that the shelter director or a staff member may consent to a police search of a resident's room.

On October 25, 2006, the shelter's director, Cynthia M. Brown, after having heard rumors that the juvenile had a gun, . . . contacted the Boston police department and arranged a meeting for the following morning "to figure out how to proceed." On October 26, 2006, at approximately 10:30 A.M., Detective Frank McLaughlin and four other police officers met with Brown at the shelter. . . . Brown told the officers that the resident's manual authorized her to enter residents' rooms to conduct room checks and that she had inspected residents' rooms several days earlier after reports of suspected drug use. The officers reviewed the portions of the manual authorizing staff to make controlled room entries. Detective McLaughlin confirmed with Brown that her authority to search residents' rooms included the ability to search closets, drawers, bureaus, and other places not in plain view. The detective testified at the evidentiary hearing that he "absolutely" believed that Brown had the authority to consent to a police search of the juvenile's room. He based this belief on the shelter's rules and regulations in the resident's manual, as well as Brown's possession of a master key to the residents' rooms.

Brown and the officers . . . proceeded upstairs to the room, where Brown knocked on the door and announced that she was conducting a room check. When no one answered, she used her master key to open the door. The juvenile was in the room, and it appeared that he had been lying in bed moments before. Brown explained that she was there to conduct a room check and had the police with her because of allegations that the juvenile had a gun in his possession. Detective McLaughlin asked the juvenile to step out of the room into the hallway, and the juvenile complied. Two or three officers began to search the room while the detective and Brown attempted to speak with the juvenile, who denied having a gun. When Brown asked why he was not in school, he stated that he was home sick that day. During their search of the room, the officers found a Glock .40 caliber firearm containing hollow point bullets in the clip underneath a duffel bag in the closet. The juvenile was then handcuffed and placed under arrest. . . .

Discussion. The juvenile argues that the warrantless search of his room at the shelter and the seizure of his firearm violated the Fourth Amendment to the United States Constitution; art. 14 of the Massachusetts Declaration of Rights; and G.L. c. 276, §1. . . .

2. . . . A third party has actual authority to consent to a warrantless search of a home by the police when the third party shares common authority over the home. See Georgia v. Randolph, 547 U.S. 103, 106 (2006); United States v. Matlock, 415 U.S. 164, 171 (1974). The authority which justifies the third-party consent does not rest upon the law of property but rests rather on "mutual use of the property by persons generally having joint access or control for most purposes," so that it is reasonable to recognize that any of the co-inhabitants has the right to permit the inspection in his own right and that the others have assumed the risk that one of their number might permit the common area to be searched.

The reasonableness of a consent search is in significant part a function of commonly held understanding about the authority that co-inhabitants may exercise in ways that affect each other's interests. [Common] authority does not mean simply the right to enter the premises that the police wish to search. Landlords often contractually retain that right, and hotels routinely do, but that does not allow the landlord or hotel manager to consent to a police search of a defendant's apartment or hotel room. United States v. Jeffers, 342 U.S. 48 (1951) (hotel patron gives "implied or express permission [to enter] to such persons as maids, janitors or repairmen in the performance of their duties" but not to police). We have held that, when a college student executes a residence hall contract that permits college officials to enter the student's dormitory room "to inspect for hazards to health or personal safety," the college officials' authority to enter the room to conduct a health and safety inspection does not entitle those officials to consent to a police search for evidence of a crime. Commonwealth v. Neilson, 666 N.E.2d 984 (1996). Here, the shelter's manual allowed shelter staff to enter the room for "professional business purposes," such as to make repairs, exterminate insects and rodents, and monitor compliance with the shelter's "Good Housekeeping Standard," and to escort "business professionals" into the room to accomplish these purposes, but it did not permit shelter staff to allow the police to enter to search for and seize contraband or evidence. . . .

We understand that the police need clear guidance as to who has common authority over a residence and therefore who is entitled to give actual consent, because, as here, they rely on such consent in deciding to conduct a warrantless search, as opposed to securing the residence and applying for a search warrant. Therefore, we declare under art. 14 that a person may have actual authority to consent to a warrantless search of a home by the police only if (1) the person is a co-inhabitant with a shared right of access to the home, that is, the person lives in the home, either as a member of the family, a roommate, or a houseguest whose stay is of substantial duration and who is given full access to the home; or (2) the person, generally a landlord, shows the police a written contract entitling that person to allow the police to enter the home to search for and seize contraband or evidence. No such entitlement may reasonably be presumed by custom or oral agreement.

Co-inhabitancy need not be defined by any legal relationship, such as that of spouses or cotenants on a lease. Rather, it should be defined by the person's demonstrated intent to make a residence his or her home for some substantial period of time. Therefore, an overnight houseguest would lack the authority to consent, unless his or her stay is substantial in its duration, and he or she is given "the run of the house."

Under this standard, Brown did not have actual authority to consent to the police entry into the room to search for a firearm. She was not a co-inhabitant of the room, and the shelter manual did not permit her to allow the police to enter the room to search for contraband or evidence. . . .

3. Having concluded that Brown did not have actual authority to consent to the search of the room by the police, we turn to whether she had the apparent authority to consent.

In Illinois v. Rodriguez, 497 U.S. 177, 179 (1990), the United States Supreme Court held that the Fourth Amendment's proscription of "unreasonable searches and seizures" is not violated when a warrantless entry of a home is based on the consent of a third party who the police, at the time of entry, reasonably, but mistakenly, believed had common authority over the premises. The Court reasoned, "to satisfy the reasonableness requirement of the Fourth Amendment, what is generally demanded of the many factual determinations that must regularly be made by agents of the government — whether the magistrate issuing a warrant, the police officer executing a warrant, or the police officer conducting a search or seizure under one of the exceptions to the warrant requirement — is not that they always be correct, but that they always be reasonable." The Court concluded that "the Constitution is no more violated when officers enter without a warrant because they reasonably (though erroneously) believe that the person who has consented to their entry is a resident of the premises, than it is violated when they enter without a warrant because they reasonably (though erroneously) believe they are in pursuit of a violent felon who is about to escape." Apparent authority is judged against an objective standard: "would the facts available to the officer at the moment . . . warrant a man of reasonable caution in the belief that the consenting party had authority over the premises?"

Federal courts have universally limited apparent authority to reasonable mistakes of fact, not mistakes of law. The *Rodriguez* decision thus applies to situations in which an officer would have had valid consent to search if the facts were as he reasonably believed them to be. An officer's mistaken belief as to the law, even if reasonable, cannot establish apparent authority.

The police officers' mistake in this case was one of law, not of fact. Detective McLaughlin and the other officers took considerable care to ascertain whether Brown had the authority to consent to a search of the room. Prior to entering the room, Detective McLaughlin conferred with Brown and reviewed the portions of the manual pertaining to staff searches of the rooms. They accurately understood the relevant facts regarding Brown's authority to consent to the search. They erred not in their understanding of the facts or in the diligence of their inquiry into Brown's authority to consent to the search, but in their understanding of the law; they believed that these facts gave them valid consent to search the room when, as a matter of law, they did not. Because Brown did not have actual or apparent authority to consent to the search, the warrantless search of the room was not reasonable under the Fourth Amendment or art. 14.

4. [Although the Court concluded that the officers' search of the room was unconstitutional, the Justices went on to decide under art. 14 whether a warrantless search of a home may ever be justified by apparent authority.]

We evaluate the reasonableness of a police officer's conduct based on the information available to him at the time, not on what we later learn to be true. If probable cause in a search warrant affidavit is based on information from a reliable source with personal knowledge, we do not conclude that there has been a violation of art. 14 if the information turns out to be inaccurate, provided the affiant did not know the information to be false or show reckless disregard for its truthfulness. . . . By this same reasoning, we do not believe that art. 14 is violated if a warrantless search of a home occurs after a police officer obtains the voluntary consent of a person he reasonably believes, after diligent inquiry, has common authority over the home, but it turns out that the person lacked common authority. See Illinois v. Rodriguez, 497 U.S. 177, 186 (1990). Apparent authority in the context of consent to search is a police officer's finding of actual authority based on a reasonable mistake of fact.

While we conclude that a search of a home does not violate art. 14 if the police officer has the voluntary consent of an individual with the apparent authority to give such consent, we do so only if the reasonable mistake of fact occurs despite diligent inquiry by the police as to the consenting individual's common authority over the home. To conduct a diligent inquiry, a police officer must take two basic steps. First, the police officer must base his conclusion of actual authority on facts, not assumptions or impressions. He must continue his inquiry until he has reliable information on which to base a finding of actual authority to consent. . . .

Second, even when the consenting individual explicitly asserts that he lives there, if the surrounding circumstances could conceivably be such that a reasonable person would doubt its truth, the police officer must make further inquiry to resolve the ambiguity. The police officer owes a duty to explore, rather than ignore, contrary facts tending to suggest that the person consenting to the search lacks actual authority. Police must not only thoroughly question the individual consenting to the search with respect to his or her actual authority, but also pay close attention to whether the surrounding circumstances indicate that the consenting individual is truthful and accurate in asserting common authority over the premises. . . .

5. Having concluded that the warrantless search was justified by neither Brown's actual authority to consent to the search nor her apparent authority to do so, the firearm seized by the police during the search must be suppressed as fruit of the poisonous tree. . . .

COWIN, J., dissenting.

[Shelter rules regulate the] residents' use of their rooms. Residents "are not allowed access or permitted to enter another resident's room at any time," and they may meet with outside visitors only during stated times at designated locations in the building. The shelter's rules even forbid residents from rearranging the furniture in their rooms, limit the number of suitcases present in the room to "two . . . per family member," and prohibit residents from placing items "on the windowsills." Alcohol and firearms are strictly forbidden in the facility, as are sexual activities (except between residents "coupled" together). [The] shelter requires residents to perform weekly chores and clean their rooms according to enumerated housekeeping standards.

The manual reveals a special concern for eliminating the presence of weapons in the shelter. The shelter forbids possession of "weapons of any kind." The manual defines a weapon as "any item that can be used to threaten or cause physical damage or harm." . . .

[The] shelter director possessed sufficient common authority over the premises to consent to a police search. The staff's plenary authority in the circumstances, including the right to conduct unannounced inspections, meaningfully differentiates the shelter from hotels, apartments, and university dormitories.

The court does not dispute that the conditions of the manual grant shelter staff the authority to enter residents' rooms to search for contraband, but it holds that this power does not extend to granting consent to the police to do the same. This is an entirely unwarranted and impractical distinction, requiring that the shelter staff resort to self-help in order to obtain prompt enforcement of the prohibition on firearms. Shelter staff are not trained in dealing with guns or people armed with guns, and they cannot arrest those in possession of weapons. A commonsense reading of the provisions of the manual regarding weapons plainly communicates that shelter staff, at its choosing, may seek police assistance in undertaking their reserved right to control the premises. In sum, there was no objective basis in these circumstances for any expectation that the juvenile may have had that his room would be immune from the kind of entry that occurred.

Problem 3-10. Divide and Conquer

New Jersey State Troopers Frank Trifari and Thomas Colella were patrolling the southbound lane of Interstate 95 when they observed a 1988 Oldsmobile with out-of-state license plates driving in the left-hand lane for approximately one-half mile. The troopers stopped the car for failing to keep right. . . . The troopers approached the car and asked the driver, Gerald Green, for his license and registration. Both Green and the passenger, Reinaldo Maristany, appeared nervous as they searched for the papers. When Green failed to produce credentials, Trifari asked him to step out of the car and walk to the rear of the vehicle. The officers ordered Maristany to get out of the passenger seat and to sit on the front hood, facing forward.

Trifari and Colella questioned Green and Maristany separately. Green explained that he was returning from a visit with his sick aunt in New York. While Colella remained with Green at the rear of the car, Trifari walked to the front of the car to question Maristany, who claimed that he and Green had been visiting Maristany's children in New York. Because of the inconsistent responses and apparent nervousness, Trifari exchanged places with Colella and requested Green's consent to search the car and trunk. When asked if the trunk contained any luggage, Green indicated that a blue canvas bag and brown suitcase were inside. . . .

After Trifari advised Green of his right to refuse consent, Green agreed to the search and signed a consent-to-search form that authorized Trifari to "conduct a complete search of trunk portion of vehicle including blue canvas bag, brown suitcase, also includes interior portion of vehicle." Maristany, still at the front of the car, did not hear Green consent to a search.

Trifari found no contraband in the car's interior. Green removed the keys from the ignition and opened the trunk for the trooper's inspection. In the blue canvas gym bag, Trifari found three kilograms of cocaine. The bag did not have any identification tags and was empty except for the cocaine. A search of the brown suitcase, likewise showing no identification tag, revealed no contraband. . . . A further search of the car uncovered a rental agreement, indicating that the car had been rented to a Bernadette Harvey. After his arrest, Green claimed that the blue bag belonged to Maristany and that he had no knowledge of its contents.

At the suppression hearing, relying on Green's statement at headquarters, defense counsel argued that Green did not own the blue gym bag, and therefore his consent to search was invalid. According to the State, nothing had indicated that Maristany owned the gym bag, and the trooper saw only a driver who showed apparent ownership and control of the car and who consented to its search. How would you rule on the motion to suppress? Cf. State v. Maristany, 627 A.2d 1066 (N.J. 1993).

Notes

1. *Apparent authority: majority position.* In a number of third-party consent cases, the third party does not actually have authority to consent to the search. Several state courts over the years concluded that these searches were still constitutional so long as the officer had a reasonable belief that the third party had authority to consent. The Supreme Court endorsed this "apparent authority" rule in Illinois v. Rodriguez, 497 U.S. 177 (1990). In that case, the police searched an apartment based on the consent of a former lover of the tenant, who did not have actual authority to consent to a search of the apartment; the Court held that the police were reasonable to search based on her apparent authority. The majority of states addressing this question both before and after *Rodriguez* have reached the same conclusion, approving of searches based on apparent rather than actual authority to consent. See State v. McCaughey, 904 P.2d 939 (Idaho 1995). A few states, however, have disagreed. See State v. McLees, 994 P.2d 683 (Mont. 2000).

The Massachusetts court in *Porter P.* was more explicit than most courts in specifying what the police must do when encountering a claim of authority to consent by a third party; most other courts simply say that the policy must act reasonably under the totality of the circumstances. Can you formulate an alternative description of the police officer's duty to investigate?

2. *Are consent searches reasonable?* One might view consent as a method of making any search a reasonable one. Alternatively, one might say that consent makes reasonableness irrelevant because the party consenting to the search decides not to insist on the probable cause or valid warrant or other circumstances that would make a search reasonable. The latter view might lead a court to reject the apparent authority doctrine: If the search is unreasonable, then actual consent is necessary to salvage it. If, on the other hand, police act reasonably when they conduct a consensual search, then consent that is invalid for reasons not apparent to the police does not make their actions any less reasonable. Is there a principled basis for deciding between these two views?

3. *Voluntariness revisited.* While following *Bustamonte,* courts have stated that consent must still be voluntary, even if the consenting party lacks full knowledge of the nature of his rights. By allowing police to proceed on the apparent authority rather than the actual authority of third parties, have the majority of courts effectively eliminated the voluntariness requirement for a sizable group of cases? Are police training policies and practices likely to increase the number of consent searches based on the apparent authority of third parties?

Problem 3-11. Consent Through Lease Provisions

In response to long-standing problems with drug trafficking and handgun violence in public housing developments in the city, organized groups of tenants urge the housing authority to require all public housing residents to sign leases consenting to police searches of their apartments for drugs or weapons at any time during the lease period. The housing authority tentatively agrees to the plan. In any public housing development where a majority of tenants vote to adopt the plan, the housing authority will include in every lease a provision consenting to searches of the apartment during the lease period.

As legal counsel for the housing authority, what advice would you offer about this plan? Would you amend it?

Notes

1. *Prospective consent and conditioning of government benefits.* Courts limit the extent to which a landlord may waive a tenant's privacy rights and consent to police searches. They enforce lease terms allowing the landlord access only for inspections or emergencies. But suppose the lease includes an explicit clause giving prospective consent for weapons or drug searches. Would you allow tenants prospectively to give consent to searches? If so, should the consent be limited to searches of an individual's home or might it extend to searches of the person?

In Wyman v. James, 400 U.S. 309 (1971), the Supreme Court held that governments could condition the provision of social services (in this instance, Aid to Families with Dependent Children) on agreements to allow home access by aid workers on the grounds that home visits were not searches. To the extent the visits had the appearance of searches, they were reasonable. Finally, relying on *Camara,* the Court noted that the penalty for refusing caseworkers access was termination of benefits, not criminal sanctions.

What arguments would you make for and against applying Wyman v. James to a public housing lease condition allowing prospective searches? The general issue raised here — known as the doctrine of "unconstitutional conditions" — is whether the conditions that the government places on receipt of government support are unconstitutional. The question arises in a variety of contexts, including, for example, the ability of a state university to condition participation on an athletic team on a student's willingness to agree to random or periodic drug tests. See Lynn Baker, The Prices of Rights: Toward a Positive Theory of Unconstitutional Conditions, 75 Cornell L. Rev. 1185 (1990).

2. *Group consent.* Can a majority of a defined group consent for all members of the group? In the public housing situation, if a majority of residents sign leases allowing random searches, do the police have to check a list of who has agreed to the searches or can they treat the situation as one of "group consent"? Could a majority of residents agree to install a metal detector at the entrance to the complex? What percentage of residents would be needed to consent to searches in the common areas of the building?

If collective consent is not allowed as a basis to waive the rights of an entire group, could collective behavior, such as a series of gunshots in a project or a group fight, serve as an exigency that justifies multiple apartment searches? See Pratt v. Chicago Housing Authority, 848 F. Supp. 792 (N.D. Ill. 1994) (rejecting broad-scale searches and sweeps of multiple apartment units, including searches of "closets, drawers, refrigerators, cabinets and personal effects," days after multiple, random gunfire was heard throughout a complex, and despite consent from many tenants).

IV

Searches in Recurring Contexts

Chapters 2 and 3 introduced the basic elements of search and seizure analysis. This chapter explores the recurring situations in which courts, legislatures, and executive branch agencies have applied those elements. Most of these situations actually happen quite often; others appear often in court opinions and statutes but happen less frequently in actual practice.

Review of these commonly encountered problems will offer some worthwhile practice in using concepts introduced in the previous two chapters. Will the government practice be considered a "search" within the meaning of the federal or state constitution? What showing does the government need to make to justify the search: reasonable suspicion, probable cause, or something else? Is a warrant necessary? Is the search acceptable because the target (or someone else with authority) consented to the search, either explicitly or implicitly?

This chapter is divided into categories identified in the text of the Fourth Amendment and many of its analogs. Remember that the Fourth Amendment secures the right of the people to be secure "in their persons, houses, papers, and effects, against unreasonable searches and seizures." Section A considers searches of "persons," along with searches of places or objects based on their proximity to persons. Section B considers issues raised during searches of "houses" and then expands the inquiry to cover other searches where the location of the search matters in creating the relevant legal rules. Section C considers a historic debate (with modern statutory echoes) about the proper treatment of private "papers," a debate that goes to the heart of the types of limits our legal system now places (and refuses to place) on government searches. Section D considers searches of personal property (or "effects"), including searches of cars and containers, which are among the most common recurring situations in law enforcement.

A. "PERSONS"

Searches of the human body intrude into privacy more clearly than most other searches. Do the legal rules about searches of the person reflect the special intrusiveness of these searches? Consider what distinctions in principle or policy explain the various search rules adopted.

1. *Searches Incident to Arrest*

When government agents arrest a person, it has long been clear that they may search the person "incident" to the arrest, without any probable cause or reasonable suspicion to believe that the search will produce any weapon or anything else connected to the crime. This automatic "search incident to arrest" was established in English common law and became part of the law of the American colonies from the very earliest times.

The "search incident to arrest" also extends beyond the body of the arrestee to include areas nearby. But just how near? As a matter of both common law and constitutional law, the answer to this question has fluctuated over time. As Judge Learned Hand once wrote, with typical understatement, "When a man is arrested, the extent to which the premises under his direct control may be searched has proved a troublesome question." United States v. Poller, 43 F.2d 911 (2d Cir. 1930).

■ ARKANSAS RULE OF CRIMINAL PROCEDURE 12.2

An officer making an arrest and the authorized officials at the police station or other place of detention to which the accused is brought may conduct a search of the accused's garments and personal effects ready to hand, the surface of his body, and the area within his immediate control.

■ ANNOTATED LAWS OF MASSACHUSETTS CH. 276, §1

A search conducted incident to an arrest may be made only for the purposes of seizing fruits, instrumentalities, contraband and other evidence of the crime for which the arrest has been made, in order to prevent its destruction or concealment; and removing any weapons that the arrestee might use to resist arrest or effect his escape. Property seized as a result of a search in violation of the provisions of this paragraph shall not be admissible in evidence in criminal proceedings.

■ STATE v. MARC HUFNAGEL

745 P.2d 242 (Colo. 1987)

MULLARKEY, J.

. . . On October 21, 1986, Hufnagel was indicted by the grand jury on charges of selling cocaine and a warrant for his arrest was issued. In the afternoon of the same day, Sheriff Masters, Undersheriff Walters, and Sergeant Berg went to Hufnagel's condominium for the purpose of executing the arrest warrant. The officers did not have a search warrant. When the officers arrived at the defendant's condominium, the door to his unit was open and Undersheriff Walters called out the defendant's name. The defendant, who had been asleep on a sofa in the living area downstairs, responded by calling out "Hello" or "Yo." The officers entered the unit at the top of the stairs leading down to the living area. They saw an eighteen-inch billy club in the entry way and a hatchet downstairs near a fireplace. The officers went downstairs, asked Hufnagel to stand up, and told him that he was under arrest for selling cocaine. He did not overtly resist the arrest, but he was slow to follow their instructions. The officers were in plain clothes and, although armed, did not display their weapons.

Within approximately five minutes after the officers first made verbal contact with the defendant, he was arrested, handcuffed, and led out of the condominium unit. The exact sequence of events within the five minutes is not entirely clear from the record or from the trial court's findings. It is apparent that Hufnagel was patted down for weapons shortly after he stood up and, at that time, he was standing near the sofa and an adjacent, octagonal end table about eighteen inches high. One or two of the officers turned Hufnagel around and handcuffed him with his hands behind his back while Sheriff Masters felt around the edge of the sofa for weapons. As the defendant was being handcuffed, Sheriff Masters saw him look at the end table. Concerned by the defendant's glance, the sheriff flipped open a door in the end table and, inside, he saw a white box. Since the box had no lid, he saw that it contained several baggies, each of which held a white substance which he believed was cocaine. He picked up the box and examined its contents without removing them. He then put the box back into the end table and closed the door.

At approximately the same time that Sheriff Masters searched the sofa and end table, Sergeant Berg made a cursory search of the rest of the condominium to make sure no one else was present. Two of the officers then took the defendant to the sheriff's office; the third remained behind to guard the premises. Later on the same day, Sheriff Masters executed an affidavit for a search warrant, based in part on his observation of the cocaine in the defendant's end table. The warrant was executed, and additional evidence was found and seized.

The defendant moved to suppress the evidence found during the warrantless search incident to his arrest. He conceded that the arrest had been valid, but argued that because he could not have reached into the end table, the search had not been limited to the area within his immediate control. After a hearing, the trial court found as matters of fact that the defendant had been handcuffed before Sheriff Masters searched the sofa and end table and that the door to the end table had been completely closed prior to the search. Based on his finding that the defendant was handcuffed with his hands behind his back, the judge reasoned that the defendant would not have been able to reach into the end table to remove a weapon or to destroy evidence. Therefore, he concluded that the search violated the fourth amendment's prohibition on unreasonable searches and granted the defendant's first motion to suppress. [Because the search warrant was issued on the basis of information obtained in the search incident to the arrest, the trial court concluded that all evidence obtained in the warranted search should also be suppressed.]

As the defendant notes, a warrantless search is generally presumed to be unreasonable and in violation of the fourth amendment. The prosecution has the burden of showing that such a search falls within an exception to the warrant requirement.

In this case, the People rely on the well-settled rule that, when making a lawful arrest, law enforcement officers may search the arrestee's person and the area within the arrestee's immediate control. See Chimel v. California, 395 U.S. 752 (1969). In *Chimel*, the Supreme Court explained that:

> It is entirely reasonable for the arresting officer to search for and seize any evidence on the arrestee's person in order to prevent its concealment or destruction. And the area into which an arrestee might reach in order to grab a weapon or evidentiary items must, of course, be governed by a like rule. A gun on a table or in a drawer in front of one who is arrested can be as dangerous to the arresting officer as one concealed in the clothing of the person arrested. There is ample justification, therefore, for a search of the arrestee's person and the area "within his immediate control" — construing that phrase to mean the area from within which he might gain possession of a weapon or destructible evidence.

The trial court found that the end table door was within "lunging" distance of the defendant and its finding is supported by the record. The end table was directly adjacent to the sofa on which the defendant had been sleeping. When he sat up, he was approximately one to two feet from the end table. He stood up when the officers came downstairs, but did not leave "a very narrow confinement of [the] vicinity" of the end table, according to Sheriff Masters' testimony, and moved only "a few feet," according to his own testimony. This evidence indicates that, prior to being handcuffed, the defendant could have reached the end table and grabbed a weapon or destructible evidence from inside it.

In spite of this, the trial court found that the search was unreasonable because the defendant was handcuffed. We disagree. The search was reasonable in scope and time and was confined to items within the defendant's immediate control. First, it is clear that the police did not engage in a general search of the defendant's home. The search was limited to two items, the sofa and the adjacent end table, which were brought to the officers' attention by the defendant's conduct. As discussed above, Hufnagel had been sleeping on the sofa when the police arrived and he stared at the end table while he was being arrested. Second, the events occurred within a very short time span; the officers spent a total of only about five minutes in the condominium unit. The defendant was not secured when he looked at the end table but he was secured by the time Sheriff Masters flipped open the door. As these findings demonstrate, whether the handcuffs clicked shut before or after the end table search is a matter of split-second timing. We think it would be unwise and highly artificial to make the validity of a search incident to an arrest turn on such a fine point of timing.[2]

Third, the sofa and end table were within the defendant's immediate control. It is well established that, when a search of the arrestee and the area immediately around him or her is incident to a valid, custodial arrest, no additional justification is required for the search. The United States Supreme Court has stated that "the

2. This position has been persuasively explained by Professor LaFave: . . . "A highly sophisticated set of rules, qualified by all sorts of ifs, ands, and buts and requiring the drawing of subtle nuances and hairline distinctions, may be the sort of heady stuff upon which the facile minds of lawyers and judges eagerly feed, but [such rules] may be 'literally impossible of application by the officer in the field.'" LaFave, "Case-by-Case Adjudication" Versus "Standardized Procedures": The *Robinson* Dilemma, 1974 Sup. Ct. Rev. 127.

potential dangers lurking in all custodial arrests make warrantless searches of items within the 'immediate control' area reasonable without requiring the arresting officer to calculate the probability that weapons or destructible evidence may be involved." United States v. Chadwick, 433 U.S. 1 (1977); see also United States v. Robinson, 414 U.S. 218 (1973). This court also has stated that such a search requires no independent justification. Therefore, we have declined to make a separate determination in each case as to whether the arresting officers had reason to believe that the arrestee would grab a weapon or evidence from the surrounding area. As explained below, the danger inherent in any custodial arrest also leads us to hold that a search incident to arrest is constitutional even if the arrestee is handcuffed prior to the search.

Chimel did not decide the exact boundaries of the search incident to arrest exception to the warrant requirement. Therefore, courts have interpreted the exception in a variety of ways. Many courts have considered the fact that the arrestee was handcuffed as one factor in determining the reasonableness of the search. To determine the legal effect of handcuffing an arrestee, courts using this approach have considered the practical effects handcuffs have on the arrestee's "lunging" distance. For example, handcuffs do not completely eliminate an arrestee's ability to reach and grab items. Further, since handcuffs can fail, it is reasonable for the arresting officer to search the area the arrestee could reach after breaking free from them.

Other courts have adopted a rule that a search of the area immediately around the arrestee, made contemporaneously with or immediately following the arrest, is constitutional even if the arrestee is physically unable to reach the area searched at the time of the search.

We believe the second approach, permitting officers to make a reasonable search incident to arrest regardless of whether the arrestee is handcuffed, is the most realistic approach and serves the purposes behind *Chimel.* Arrests are necessarily tense, risky events when many things are happening at once. The difficulty of imposing an orderly chronology after the fact is apparent in this case. Police officers, who must act quickly, cannot reasonably be expected to pay attention to the exact time at which the arrestee is handcuffed and then to make an accurate guess as to how much a reviewing court will think the handcuffs restrict that particular arrestee's "lunging" distance under all the circumstances. . . .

A case-by-case analysis considering all the circumstances of such a search would be impracticable. Further, a case-by-case analysis is not required by *Chimel.* In *Chimel,* the United States Supreme Court rejected the prosecution's argument that an unlimited, warrantless search of an arrestee's house was justified whenever an individual was arrested at home, explaining that "under such an unconfined analysis, Fourth Amendment protection in this area would approach the evaporation point." Instead, the Court concluded that, while legitimate needs of arresting officers to protect themselves and to preserve evidence made warrantless searches "of the person arrested and the area within his reach" reasonable, those needs did not justify "more extensive searches." The Court's goal was to develop a rule that would allow police officers to protect themselves and to preserve evidence without eviscerating arrestees' fourth amendment rights. This goal can be met by limiting searches incident to arrests to the area immediately around the arrestee and the time contemporaneous with or immediately following the arrest.

Therefore, we hold that the People need not show that the arrestee was physically able to reach the exact place searched at the exact second it was searched in order to justify a search incident to arrest. Instead, the prosecution can meet its burden of showing that a warrantless search was reasonable by showing, as it did here, that it was contemporaneous with or immediately following the defendant's arrest and was limited to the area immediately around him. Because we conclude that Sheriff Masters' observation of the contents of the end table was made during a valid search incident to a lawful arrest, we reverse the trial court's order suppressing the evidence found in both searches. . . .

Problem 4-1. Sweeping the Upstairs

The sheriff's office of Shelby County, Tennessee, notified the Stamford Police Department that it had intercepted a Federal Express parcel containing 27 pounds of marijuana, and that the parcel was addressed to a "Sylvia Sloan" at 16 Lipton Place in Stamford. On the basis of this information, the Stamford police went to the address, which appeared to be a multifamily house. Further investigation showed that the house contained three apartments and was owned by an elderly woman who occupied the first-floor apartment. There were also apartments on the second and third floors. Department records revealed that two months earlier officers had responded to a call at that address concerning a domestic disturbance involving Michael Spencer and his wife.

The following morning, the police took possession of the parcel from the Stamford Federal Express office, and a field test revealed that its contents were, in fact, marijuana. They then replaced approximately 5 pounds of the marijuana in the box and resealed it for delivery. Later that morning, working with the statewide narcotics task force, the police conducted a "controlled delivery" of the parcel to 16 Lipton Place. Police officers watched the residence from vantage points 50 to 60 feet away while a task force member, Detective Frederick Caruso, delivered the parcel. Caruso, dressed in a Federal Express coat and carrying the parcel and a pad of delivery invoices, rang the doorbell for the first-floor apartment and knocked on the front door. A man opened the door; in response to Caruso's questions, he verified the address and he told Caruso that his name was Michael Spencer and that he lived on the second floor. When Caruso told him that the delivery was for "Sylvia Sloan," the defendant repeated the name to himself and then told Caruso that he would accept the package. Spencer signed the delivery invoice, took the parcel under his arm and went inside, closing the front door behind him. As Caruso walked away, Spencer came back outside, without the parcel, and looked up and down the street.

At this point, Police Sergeant Eugene Dohmann and three other officers approached the residence and encountered Spencer in the front doorway. They identified themselves as police officers and brought Spencer into the first-floor common hallway, where they saw the Federal Express parcel on a shelf. The officers then read the defendant his *Miranda* rights and placed him under arrest. Spencer denied knowledge of the contents of the parcel or of anybody named Sylvia Sloan, and he claimed that he had accepted the package innocently.

From the bottom of a flight of approximately 12 to 14 steps leading up to the second floor, the officers could see that the door to the defendant's apartment was ajar. Dohmann asked Spencer if anybody else was inside the apartment, but received no response. Two officers then climbed the stairs and entered the second-floor apartment. In Spencer's bedroom in the rear of the apartment, they saw on the bed a homemade "crack" pipe and a dinner plate containing crack cocaine residue, as well as a rolled-up $1 bill containing crack cocaine.

The government charged Spencer with possession of one kilogram or more of a cannabis-type substance with intent to sell and possession of crack cocaine. At trial, the defendant filed a motion to suppress the evidence of crack cocaine seized from his apartment on the ground that the evidence had been obtained illegally as the result of an unconstitutional warrantless search.

The trial court conducted a full evidentiary hearing on the motion to suppress. Sergeant Dohmann testified that the defendant was "kind of reluctant" to tell the officers whether anybody else was in his apartment. According to Dohmann, the defendant "was a bit nervous," and the officers feared that he may have been "hiding something" from them. Therefore, the officers decided to enter the apartment "to make sure no further evidence was being destroyed or possibly other people involved that may be escaping." Dohmann also testified that the officers were concerned for their safety, because weapons often are involved in the narcotics trade:

> It's not unusual for narcotics and weapons to be found in the same building and we wanted to make sure there were no weapons and more importantly nobody up there to use those weapons. I didn't think it was just a coincidence that this package was being delivered there. So, it was our belief that there was somebody in that apartment and we didn't really expect the package to come back to the name on the package because it's not typically done that way for obvious reasons. So, we expected somebody was in that apartment that was expecting a large amount of marijuana and with that we're feeling there's a drug dealer in that apartment. And, if there's a drug dealer in that apartment, we don't know who he is and he could very well be armed.

The sergeant testified that during the search of the apartment the officers did not look in any drawers, and their search was limited to places "where you might find people, human beings."

On cross-examination, Dohmann acknowledged that the investigation prior to the controlled delivery had not revealed that anybody named Sloan was living at 16 Lipton Place. He also acknowledged that his investigation had not indicated that any individual living at that address might be armed or involved in the drug trade. He admitted that there was no other noise in the house: "Nobody came out of their doors to see what was going on or anything else." Finally, defense counsel questioned Dohmann concerning the officers' decision to enter the defendant's apartment:

> *Q.* There came a time when you went up the stairs to go into [the defendant's] home —
>
> *A.* Uh-huh.
>
> *Q.* You had a suspicion that there could be somebody armed upstairs?
>
> *A.* A suspicion? I wouldn't say a suspicion but we had to know.
>
> *Q.* A hunch?
>
> *A.* Not a hunch. You don't even think about it. You just have to eliminate — we have to eliminate the possibility so we went up there with the possibility of that being there and we didn't want to be surprised.

As a trial judge, precisely what factual findings would you need to make to support a valid ruling that the search of the apartment was reasonable? Does it matter that the initial arrest happened outside the house? Compare State v. Spencer, 848 A.2d 1183 (Conn. 2004).

Notes

1. *Search incident to arrest: majority position.* Under the long-standing doctrine of "search incident to arrest," the police may search the person of an arrestee, along with some area near the arrestee, without any independent probable cause or warrant to support the search. As for the amount of area the police may search "incident" to the arrest, the federal standard appears in Chimel v. California, 395 U.S. 752 (1969). The search may extend to the area within the "immediate control" of the arrestee, that is, the area in which the arrestee could reach a weapon or destroy evidence. State courts have by and large adopted this same standard under their state constitutions and statutes. See State v. Lamay, 103 P.3d 448 (Idaho 2004) (backpack that was 10 inches from defendant's hand at start of detention was not within area of immediate control of arrestee). However, as the *Hufnagel* case from Colorado makes clear, there are real disagreements over how to apply this standard. *Hufnagel* represents a strong minority position on the question of handcuffs: A larger group of state courts will consider the fact that an arrestee was handcuffed at the time of a search when determining the area within the "immediate control" of an arrestee. For further exploration of the variety of state court applications of this standard, see the web extension for this chapter at *http://www.crimpro.com/extension/ch04*.

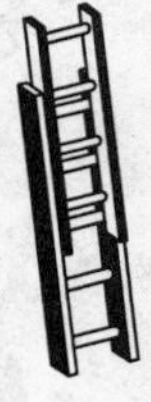

Whether a suspect is handcuffed at the time of a search incident to arrest is only one of a host of facts that courts have used to assess the validity of searches in particular cases. Other factors include: (a) whether there are multiple defendants; (b) whether there are confederates of the suspect nearby who might destroy evidence; (c) whether the officers are between the suspect and the area or object to be searched; (d) whether the officers have control over the area or object to be searched; and (e) any postarrest movement by the arrestee (for example, to get dressed). Which of these factors is subject to the control of the officer? Doesn't assessment of these factors depend on the justification underlying searches incident to arrest?

In the *Hufnagel* case from Colorado, what were the critical factors justifying the search of the end table as a search incident to arrest? How far away from Hufnagel was the end table when the officers entered the apartment? When Hufnagel gave the fatal glance?

2. Chimel *and its predecessors.* The law defining the permissible scope of searches incident to arrest has gone through many changes over the past 70 years. Flexible as *Chimel* may seem, it narrowed the prior rule of Harris v. United States, 331 U.S. 145 (1947), and United States v. Rabinowitz, 339 U.S. 56 (1950), which allowed searches of multiple-room dwellings as searches incident to arrest. An earlier strand of Supreme Court cases — notably Go-Bart Importing Co. v. United States, 282 U.S. 344 (1931), and Trupiano v. United States, 334 U.S. 699 (1948) (rejected by *Rabinowitz)* — suggested that where a search warrant could be obtained before the arrest, it should be.

The court in *Hufnagel,* echoing the U.S. Supreme Court in *Chimel,* justified searches incident to arrest based on the need to find relevant evidence before it is destroyed and the need to protect officers from harm by discovering possible weapons. Which of the two basic justifications supports a more expansive view of searches incident to arrest? What additional theories might justify expansion or contraction of searches incident to arrest? Do the justifications for searches incident to arrest apply most strongly before, during, or after arrest?

3. *Automatic authorization to search.* The distinctive feature of the search incident to arrest is its automatic quality: The police need no justification for the search beyond the justification for the arrest. See United States v. Robinson, 414 U.S. 218 (1973). There is no need to suspect that the person himself is holding a weapon or evidence of a crime; there is no need to suspect that the area within the arrestee's immediate control holds weapons, contraband, or evidence. Is this another example of the courts adopting a "bright line" rule to make the police officer's job more manageable? See Ronald Dworkin, Fact Style Adjudication and the Fourth Amendment, 48 Ind. L.J. 329 (1973).

Statutes in England allow different searches incident to arrest than does American law. Under section 18 of the Police and Criminal Evidence Act of 1984, the constable may search the *premises* of any arrested person (regardless of where the arrest takes place) if there are "reasonable grounds" to believe that the premises contain evidence of the offense that is the basis of the arrest or some similar offense. Section 32 of the Act allows the constable to search a *person,* if the person to be searched has been arrested at a place other than a police station, and if "the constable has reasonable grounds for believing that the arrested person may present a danger to himself or others." The constable may also search the arrested person for evidence of a crime, or for anything he or she might use to escape custody, but only if the constable has "reasonable grounds for believing" that such items will be found in the search. Finally, section 32 also allows the constable "to enter and search any premises in which [the arrested person] was when arrested . . . for evidence relating to the offence for which he has been arrested," but once again, only if the constable has "reasonable grounds for believing that there is evidence . . . on the premises." If an American jurisdiction were to adopt this statute, would it change the practices of the police during arrests in a significant way? Would the police be in greater danger?

4. *Comparison to* Terry *searches.* Courts allow searches of the person incident to arrest to be more intensive than *Terry* searches. See United States v. Robinson, 414 U.S. at 224-229. Why? How long can a search incident to arrest take? Is there any kind of search, either of the person or of a place, that would not be allowed within the justification of a search incident to arrest?

5. *A "life cycle" for procedure issues?* For some time after *Chimel,* state supreme courts actively explored the scope of the area of "immediate control" of the arrestee, considering issues such as the impact of handcuffing the suspect. In recent years the number of cases involving searches incident to arrest in the U.S. and state supreme courts has decreased, and the validity of such searches has been left to trial courts to decide on the facts of each case, with only occasional appeals to lower appellate courts. What characteristics of a criminal procedure issue will make it appear on the docket of a state supreme court? Is there a "life cycle" for criminal procedure issues, in which they become prominent in different institutions in predictable patterns?

6. *Protective sweeps.* Although *Chimel* rejected searches of entire rooms or multiple rooms as part of a search incident to arrest, such searches may still be allowed at the time of arrest on other grounds. One justification for a full-house search is to discover persons who may pose a threat to officers conducting the arrest. In

Maryland v. Buie, 494 U.S. 325 (1990), the Supreme Court upheld two sorts of "protective sweeps" outside the area within the "immediate control" of the arrestee. First, the arresting officers may look in closets and other places immediately adjoining the place of the arrest from which another person might launch an attack on the officers. This search needs no justification beyond the simple fact of the arrest. Second, the officers may search other areas in the house for any persons who might pose a danger to them, but only if they have a reasonable suspicion that the "sweep" will reveal the presence of such a person. In either case, the search is limited to places where a person may be found.

Almost all state courts addressing this subject also allow police to make "protective sweeps" of the premises where an arrest takes place, under the same two-tier analysis that the *Buie* court used. See Commonwealth v. Robertson, 659 S.E.2d 321 (Va. 2008); cf. State v. Davila, 999 A.2d 1116 (N.J. 2010) (protective sweep also available in nonarrest situation if officers are lawfully on premises). Should multiple-room searches for potential accomplices be allowed even when there are no reasonable grounds to believe such accomplices pose a danger to officers but when there is a reasonable suspicion that parties to a multiparty offense are likely to be present or that persons in the house may destroy evidence?

Problem 4-2. Search Incident to (but After) Arrest

An officer looking through binoculars saw a man with a plaid shirt and a blue backpack leaving a field of marijuana plants in a remote, unpopulated canyon. The officer and his partner followed the man in the plaid shirt, whose name turned out to be Howard Boff, and arrested him on a deserted dirt road after he sat down and placed the backpack on the ground about five feet from his body.

The officers drove Boff and his backpack to the sheriff's office, about 45 minutes away in Dove Creek. Three hours after placing Boff in custody, the police officers opened the backpack without a search warrant and found marijuana. Was the search valid as a search incident to arrest? Compare People v. Boff, 766 P.2d 646 (Colo. 1988).

Notes

1. *Subsequent searches: how much time?* Until 1974 the Supreme Court required that searches incident to arrest be "substantially contemporaneous with the arrest." See, e.g., Vale v. Louisiana, 399 U.S. 30 (1970). In 1974 the Court decided United States v. Edwards, 415 U.S. 800, in which it upheld a search of defendant's clothing for paint chips 10 hours after he was arrested. State courts have generally allowed searches at the police station, well after the time of arrest, of objects "immediately associated with the person" that could have been searched at the time of arrest, including clothing, wallets, and purses. See Commonwealth v. Stallworth, 781 A.2d 110 (Pa. 2001); but see State v. Lamay, 103 P.3d 448 (Idaho 2004) (suspect first encountered in hotel room lying on bed next to backpack on floor, then ordered to step into hallway outside hotel room, where he was arrested; later search of backpack not justified as incident to arrest). Professor Myron Moskovitz, based on telephone interviews with police officers and written training materials from various

police departments, concluded that police officers typically handcuff a suspect before searching the vicinity, but they usually obtain a warrant to search an area if they have already removed the arrestee from the scene. Moskovitz, A Rule in Search of a Reason: An Empirical Re-examination of *Chimel* and *Belton,* 2002 Wis. L. Rev. 657, 666-67. This practice, he concludes, is based on police views about the reasonableness of searches rather than their reading of what the courts might allow.

2. *Searches prior to arrest.* The rationale for a search incident to arrest may be strongest immediately prior to arrest, when officers are searching for the person to be arrested or have reasonable grounds to believe that weapons may be present or that evidence might be destroyed. Courts typically allow pre-arrest searches, on the basis of "exigent circumstances," to find a suspect when police are otherwise lawfully within the premises. Courts may also allow pre-arrest searches of areas too small to conceal the offender but large enough to conceal weapons, at least during a "hot pursuit" of the defendant. See Warden v. Hayden, 387 U.S. 294 (1967) (during search for suspect, officer looks in washing machine and discovers evidence). Should such searches generally be allowed as part of arrests within homes? Should officers be able to conduct a "search incident to arrest" beyond the scope of a *Terry* search if they find a person they believe to be the suspect but are not certain?

2. *Intrusive Body Searches*

Strip searches and body cavity examinations are among the most intrusive searches that government agents perform. The police sometimes conduct these searches in the field, either before an arrest or incident to arrest. Sometimes they conduct these searches with the suspect's consent. At other times, officers carry out strip searches at the police station or in a jail or other detention facility, either as part of standard booking procedures or in response to police concerns about an individual.

In recent years, legislatures rather than courts have created the legal limits for these searches. Most states now have statutes placing some limits on the use of strip searches and body cavity searches, and courts have in turn largely ceased their efforts to regulate such searches. Reprinted below are a few examples of these statutes. They highlight how legislatures develop legal rules different from those that courts develop.

Consider the differences between the legislative and judicial rules governing pre-arrest and postarrest searches. Should the extremely intrusive nature of the search technique require some showing beyond probable cause and a judicial warrant in any setting? Or should the regulation of strip searches be more substantial in the field (because of possible abuse), or in the station house (because of the more controlled setting)? Strip search statutes generally require that any allowable strip or body cavity search take place in clean, private surroundings and that the police officers conducting the search must be of the same sex as the person being examined.

As you examine the following three statutes, consider (1) the different levels of justification required for such searches, (2) any special procedures or additional actors who must approve the search, and (3) the use of alternatives to body cavity and strip searches. Then, based on these elements, rank the following statutes in terms of their potential to minimize the number of strip and body cavity searches. What information would you collect to test your assumptions about the impact of different procedures in actual practice?

■ ARKANSAS RULE OF CRIMINAL PROCEDURE 12.3

(a) Search of an accused's blood stream, body cavities, and subcutaneous tissues conducted incidental to an arrest may be made only:

(i) if there is a strong probability that it will disclose things subject to seizure and related to the offense for which the individual was arrested; and

(ii) if it reasonably appears that the delay consequent upon procurement of a search warrant would probably result in the disappearance or destruction of the objects of the search; and

(iii) if it reasonably appears that the search is otherwise reasonable under the circumstances of the case, including the seriousness of the offense and the nature of the invasion of the individual's person.

■ TENNESSEE CODE §40-7-121

(b) No person shall be subjected to a body cavity search by a law enforcement officer or by another person acting under the direction, supervision or authority of a law enforcement officer unless such search is conducted pursuant to a search warrant. . . .

(c) The issue of whether a person subjected to a body cavity search consented to such search is irrelevant and shall not be considered in determining whether the search was a valid one under the provisions of this section, unless the consent is in writing on a preprinted form and contains the following language:

Waiver of Warrant Requirement and Consent to Search Body Cavities

I knowingly and voluntarily consent to have my body cavities searched immediately by law enforcement personnel in the manner provided by the laws of Tennessee. By signing this consent form, I knowingly and voluntarily waive my right to require that a warrant be obtained from an appropriate judge or magistrate before my body cavities are searched. I understand that a body cavity search may involve both visual and physical probing into my genitals and anus. I understand that I would not be prejudiced or penalized by declining to give my consent to be searched in this manner.

■ REVISED CODE OF WASHINGTON §§10.79.080, 10.79.130, 10.79.140

§10.79.080

(1) No person may be subjected to a body cavity search by or at the direction of a law enforcement agency unless a search warrant is issued. . . .

(2) No law enforcement officer may seek a warrant for a body cavity search without first obtaining specific authorization for the body cavity search from the ranking shift supervisor of the law enforcement authority. Authorization for the body cavity search may be obtained electronically: PROVIDED, That such electronic authorization shall be reduced to writing by the law enforcement officer seeking the authorization and signed by the ranking supervisor as soon as possible thereafter.

(3) Before any body cavity search is authorized or conducted, a thorough patdown search, a thorough electronic metal-detector search, and a thorough clothing search, where appropriate, must be used to search for and seize any evidence of a crime, contraband, fruits of crime, things otherwise criminally possessed, weapons, or other things by means of which a crime has been committed or reasonably appears about to be committed. No body cavity search shall be authorized or conducted unless these other methods do not satisfy the safety, security, or evidentiary concerns of the law enforcement agency.

(4) A law enforcement officer requesting a body cavity search shall prepare and sign a report regarding the body cavity search. . . .

§10.79.130

(1) No person [in custody at a holding, detention, or local correctional facility, regardless of whether an arrest warrant or other court order was issued before the person was arrested, may] be strip searched without a warrant unless:

(a) There is a reasonable suspicion to believe that a strip search is necessary to discover weapons, criminal evidence, contraband, or other thing concealed on the body of the person to be searched, that constitutes a threat to the security of a holding, detention, or local correctional facility;

(b) There is probable cause to believe that a strip search is necessary to discover other criminal evidence concealed on the body of the person to be searched, but not constituting a threat to facility security; or

(c) There is a reasonable suspicion to believe that a strip search is necessary to discover a health condition requiring immediate medical attention.

(2) For the purposes of subsection (1) of this section, a reasonable suspicion is deemed to be present when the person to be searched has been arrested for:

(a) A violent offense . . . ;

(b) An offense involving escape, burglary, or the use of a deadly weapon; or

(c) An offense involving possession of a drug or controlled substance . . .

§10.79.140

(1) A person [in custody at a holding, detention, or local correctional facility, regardless of whether an arrest warrant or other court order was issued before the person was arrested or otherwise taken into custody] who has not been arrested for an offense within one of the categories specified in RCW 10.79.130(2) may nevertheless be strip searched, but only upon an individualized determination of reasonable suspicion or probable cause as provided in this section.

(2) With the exception of those situations in which reasonable suspicion is deemed to be present under RCW 10.79.130(2), no strip search may be conducted

without the specific prior written approval of the jail unit supervisor on duty. Before any strip search is conducted, reasonable efforts must be made to use other less-intrusive means, such as pat-down, electronic metal detector, or clothing searches, to determine whether a weapon, criminal evidence, contraband, or other thing is concealed on the body, or whether a health condition requiring immediate medical attention is present. The determination of whether reasonable suspicion or probable cause exists to conduct a strip search shall be made only after such less-intrusive means have been used and shall be based on a consideration of all information and circumstances known to the officer authorizing the strip search, including but not limited to the following factors:

(a) The nature of the offense for which the person to be searched was arrested;

(b) The prior criminal record of the person to be searched; and

(c) Physically violent behavior of the person to be searched, during or after the arrest.

Notes

1. *Strip search statutes: majority position.* In most places, state statutes and police department policies place special limits on strip searches and body cavity searches. More states have statutes or rules addressing this sort of search than virtually any other specific search technique (with the exception of electronic eavesdropping, which we consider in Chapter 7). Is it possible to bar all strip searches? Why does the Washington legislature provide so much more guidance for searches conducted once a person is in custody? Apart from responding to abuses in specific cases, what else might explain the willingness of so many legislatures to address this topic? If legislatures were to leave this question to courts, what standards would courts apply?

2. *Strip searches for misdemeanors and infractions.* Public attention is often drawn to strip searches conducted on people suspected only of minor offenses. See Edwards v. State, 759 N.E.2d 626 (Ind. 2001) (warrantless and suspicionless strip search of misdemeanor arrestees violates federal and state constitutions). Legislatures often claim to sharply limit strip searches for minor offenses. Consider the following illustration from California Penal Code §4030 (f):

> No person arrested and held in custody on a misdemeanor or infraction offense, except those involving weapons, controlled substances or violence . . . shall be subjected to a strip search or visual body cavity search prior to placement in the general jail population, unless a peace officer has determined there is reasonable suspicion based on specific and articulable facts to believe such person is concealing a weapon or contraband, and a strip search will result in the discovery of the weapon or contraband. No strip search or visual body cavity search or both may be conducted without the prior written authorization of the supervising officer on duty. The authorization shall include the specific and articulable facts and circumstances upon which the reasonable suspicion determination was made by the supervisor. . . .

How much protection for citizens suspected of minor offenses does this statute provide? Why do some legislatures create different presumptions for drug and violent offenders? In these states, how important for the ultimate impact of these rules is the definition of a drug or violent offender?

Other state legislatures have passed such statutes in response to notorious and newsworthy cases involving strip searches. See Mary Beth G. v. City of Chicago, 723 F.2d 1263 (7th Cir. 1983) (civil suit brought by women arrested for outstanding parking tickets, challenging city policy requiring a strip search and body cavity search of all women arrested and detained in city lockups, regardless of charges; Illinois legislature amended arrest statute to prohibit strip searches of persons arrested for traffic, regulatory, or misdemeanor offenses absent a reasonable belief that the arrestee is concealing weapons or controlled substances on her person). Often the motivation for these statutes is not the facts of a particular case but the judgment in a lawsuit. Hundreds of lawsuits based on strip suits have been filed over the years.

3. *The relative virtues of process and substantive standards.* Among the statutes addressing strip searches and body cavity searches, there are two distinct limiting techniques at work. Some of the statutory provisions contain substantive "standards," describing a subclass of cases not eligible for this type of search (such as those accused of particular offenses or cases where the police do not have adequate reason to believe that the search will succeed). Others focus on the process of authorizing such a search (by requiring a judicial warrant or supervisor approval or a written record of any decision to conduct such a search). Which regulatory technique offers greater protection to citizens: more intricate process requirements or higher substantive standards?

4. *The mouth exception.* Most of the body cavity statutes do not cover searches of the mouth. Would you expect statutes to have separate mouth search statutes? Why or why not? See State v. Peterson, 515 N.W.2d 23 (Iowa 1994) (upholding forced search of mouth as search incident to arrest).

5. *Consent to strip searches.* Some statutes bar consent to strip searches, others allow consent, still others require special procedures for obtaining consent, and several say nothing about consent. In a jurisdiction whose statute says nothing about consent, what arguments would you make to a court that it should enforce special consent rules for strip and body cavity searches?

Probable cause, a term captured in the text of the Fourth Amendment and many of its analogs, is the core standard for determining when the government may search a place or person. But it is not the only standard. The investigatory searches and stops described in Chapter 2 are governed by the "reasonable suspicion" standard, considered to be less demanding than probable cause. A few other searches — often bodily searches of a highly intrusive nature — are allowed only when the government makes a showing that is even more demanding than probable cause.

The strip search statutes suggest that legislatures will sometimes step in to define sharper limits or higher standards for intrusive body searches. Consider, for example, how the Arkansas, Tennessee, and Washington strip search statutes would apply to the following case. Where legislatures have not acted to limit highly intrusive searches, courts have stepped in to fill that gap.

■ PEOPLE v. ERIC MORE

764 N.E.2d 967 (N.Y. 2002)

LEVINE, J.

Defendant was convicted of criminal possession of a controlled substance in the third degree, criminal possession of a controlled substance in the fifth degree, resisting arrest and false personation. The drug possession counts related to 2.37 grams of crack cocaine which the police extracted from defendant's rectum during a strip search incident to his arrest. . . .

Prior to trial, defendant moved to suppress the drugs seized from his person. At the suppression hearing, a detective in the Troy Police Department Special Operations Unit testified that he and several other officers entered an apartment after obtaining the tenant's permission to do so. The tenant told the police that individuals in the apartment were "cutting up cocaine" for sale and that one of the subjects was wanted on an arrest warrant for assaulting a police officer. Upon entering the apartment, the detective saw defendant sitting on a couch with a woman on his lap. He also saw a "crack pipe and small piece of white rocklike substance" on a nearby table. Based upon his training and experience, the detective believed the substance was crack cocaine. The police arrested defendant and the woman, ordered them onto the floor, handcuffed them and conducted a "quick pat-down" search for weapons. No weapons were found.

The police then separated defendant and the female in order to strip search them. Defendant initially cooperated by taking off most of his clothes, but at some point he protested and scuffled with the officers. During the search, which took place in a bedroom, the police removed a plastic bag, an outer portion of which they saw protruding from defendant's rectum. The bag contained several individually wrapped pieces of a white rock-like substance, which later tested positive for cocaine. Drugs were also recovered from defendant's female companion.

In his motion to suppress the drugs seized from his person, defendant focused his challenge on the legality of his arrest and the strip search incident thereto. He claimed that the arrest was effected without probable cause, presumably as a pretext to justify the search of his person. In addition, he specifically averred that the body cavity search was "illegal and effected in the absence of probable cause, in the absence of a warrant and in the absence of any exigency." County Court denied the motion to suppress in all respects. . . .

The Supreme Court of the United States addressed the constitutionality of a seizure involving an intrusion into the human body in Schmerber v. California, 384 U.S. 757 (1966). Recognizing that it was "writing on a clean slate," the Court held that the police were justified in requiring a person arrested for driving while under the influence of alcohol to submit to a blood test to determine blood alcohol level. The Court framed the relevant issues as "whether the police were justified in requiring petitioner to submit to the blood test, and whether the means and procedures employed in taking his blood respected relevant Fourth Amendment standards of reasonableness."

After concluding that the police had probable cause to arrest the petitioner for driving while under the influence of alcohol, the Supreme Court determined that seizures involving intrusions beyond the body's surface cannot be justified simply because they are made incident to a lawful arrest. The Court reasoned that although a "full search" of a person is allowed incident to a lawful arrest in order to disarm the suspect or preserve evidence, the considerations permitting such a search "have little applicability with respect to searches involving intrusions beyond the body's surface." The Fourth Amendment "forbids any such intrusions on the mere chance that desired evidence might be obtained." Rather, there must exist a "clear indication" that desired evidence will be found. In the absence of such an indication, the Fourth Amendment mandates that the police "suffer the risk that such evidence may disappear unless there is an immediate search."

Moreover, even where there is a "clear indication" that incriminating evidence will be retrieved if the bodily intrusion is permitted, search warrants are "ordinarily required for searches of dwellings, and *absent an emergency,* no less could be required where intrusions into the human body are concerned." Indeed, as the Court stressed, the "importance of informed, detached and deliberate determinations of the issue whether or not to invade another's body in search of evidence of guilt is indisputable and great." The police were not required to obtain a search warrant in *Schmerber* only because of the existence of exigent circumstances — the officer there "might reasonably have believed that he was confronted with an emergency, in which the delay necessary to obtain a warrant, under the circumstances, threatened 'the destruction of evidence.'"

Finally, the *Schmerber* Court concluded that the procedure used to extract the blood from the petitioner was itself reasonable and conducted in a reasonable manner. In upholding the seizure, the Court noted that its decision to allow the intrusion into the petitioner's body "under stringently limited conditions" did not indicate that the Fourth Amendment "permits more substantial intrusions, or intrusions under other conditions."

Undoubtedly, body cavity searches incident to an arrest are at least as intrusive as blood test procedures. This Court has referred to them as "invasive" and "degrading," People v. Luna, 535 N.E.2d 1305 (N.Y. 1989), and other courts have similarly described them. [The court cited federal cases from the First and Seventh Circuits.]

On the suppression record before us, we conclude that the body cavity search of defendant incident to his arrest was unreasonable and invalid. Even assuming that the extraction of the drugs satisfied all of *Schmerber*'s other requirements, the People failed to offer any evidence of exigent circumstances to justify dispensing with the warrant requirement — that a neutral, detached magistrate determine that the search is justified and will be conducted in a reasonable manner. This record is devoid of any evidence from which an officer "might reasonably have believed that he was confronted with an emergency, in which the delay necessary to obtain a warrant" posed a threat to the officer's personal safety or of the destruction of the evidence. Notably, no police officer testified that, despite the available means of incapacitating defendant and keeping him under full surveillance, an immediate body cavity search was necessary to prevent his access to a weapon or prevent his disposing of the drugs. Nor was there any evidence the police were concerned that the drugs — which were wrapped in plastic — could have been absorbed into defendant's body. The absence of exigent circumstances dictates the conclusion that the body cavity search here was unreasonable. . . .

Problem 4-3. Blood Test Consent

Melissa Helton drove her two children, along with her friend, Lori Lathrop, and Lathrop's two children, to a local creek to swim. Helton and Lathrop drank alcohol while the children swam and played. That evening, they all got into the van to drive home. Helton drove the van off the road and struck some trees and shrubs. Lathrop and three of the children were killed in the accident.

Helton was admitted to the university hospital. Two deputy sheriffs asked the medical staff to draw a blood sample from Helton for their investigation, in addition to the blood tests the medical staff was performing to prepare Helton for surgery. Helton was unconscious during the visit of the deputies and the drawing of her blood. The deputies did not have a warrant to support their request for a blood test. The sample showed that Helton had a blood alcohol content of 0.16 percent.

Helton was indicted for four counts of wanton murder and one count of first-offense driving under the influence. She moved to suppress the evidence of her blood alcohol level, arguing that the sample was taken in violation of state statutes and the state and federal constitutions. Section 189A.103 of the state code provides as follows:

> The following provisions shall apply to any person who operates a motor vehicle in this State:
>
> (1) He or she has given his or her consent to one or more tests of his or her blood, breath, and urine, for the purpose of determining alcohol concentration or presence of a substance which may impair one's driving ability, if an officer has reasonable grounds to believe that a violation of the impaired driving laws has occurred;
>
> (2) Any person who is dead, unconscious, or otherwise in a condition rendering him or her incapable of refusal is deemed not to have withdrawn the consent provided in subsection (1) of this section, and the test may be given.

Another statute in the same chapter of the code, Section 189A.105, provides as follows:

> (1) A person's refusal to submit to tests under Section 189A.103 shall result in revocation of his driving privilege as provided in this chapter.
>
> (2) (a) At the time a breath, blood, or urine test is requested, the person shall be informed:
>
> first, that if the person refuses to submit to such tests, the fact of this refusal may be used against him in court as evidence and will result in revocation of his driver's license; and second, that if a test is taken, the results of the test may be used against him in court as evidence of violating the impaired driving laws.
>
> (b) Nothing in this subsection shall be construed to prohibit a judge of a court of competent jurisdiction from issuing a search warrant or other court order requiring a blood or urine test of a defendant charged with a violation of the impaired driving laws when a person is killed or suffers physical injury as a result of the incident in which the defendant has been charged. However, if the incident involves a motor vehicle accident

in which there was a fatality, the investigating peace officer shall seek such a search warrant for blood, breath, or urine testing unless the testing has already been done by consent.

What will the prosecution have to prove to demonstrate compliance with all the relevant statutes and constitutional requirements? Will the judge suppress the evidence? Cf. Helton v. Commonwealth, 299 S.W.3d 555 (Ky. 2009).

Notes

1. *Probable cause "plus": majority position.* Some courts require the government to justify the use of an especially intrusive bodily search with something more than probable cause. Does the New York court in *More* require some "plus," in addition to probable cause? When the government uses invasive medical techniques to carry out a bodily search, the relevant standard under the federal constitution appears in Schmerber v. California, 384 U.S. 757 (1966). There the Court approved the use of evidence derived from a blood sample that a physician had taken from a suspect. The Court found the search reasonable because (1) there was a "clear indication" that the blood sample would produce evidence of a crime; (2) the test was "commonplace" and involved almost no risk or trauma; and (3) the test was conducted in a "reasonable manner," carried out by a physician in a hospital environment. See also Rochin v. California, 342 U.S. 165 (1952) (forced administration of emetic solution to induce vomiting in suspect who had swallowed capsules; barred by due process). Some state courts interpret *Schmerber* to require only probable cause, but most take this language to mean that the government must show exigent circumstances or evidence stronger than probable cause to justify the taking of blood. For further exploration of the variety of state court applications of this standard, see the web extension for this chapter at *http://www.crimpro.com/extension/ch04*.

What role will police expertise play in jurisdictions where officers are left with some discretion to conduct highly intrusive searches in the field? For example, in *More,* how could the police determine before the search whether or not any secreted drugs were in a form that might be destroyed or disappear with further delay? Would the plastic bag and its contents "inevitably" be discovered when a strip search was conducted at the station as part of standard processing before placing the suspect in a jail cell?

2. *Orders for nonintrusive identification evidence.* Should nonintrusive nontestimonial requests — for example, for handwriting, voice, saliva, and hair samples — and other evidence involving the physical state of the suspect be governed by a reasonable suspicion standard, since such information does not require intrusive body searches? See Iowa Code §§810.1-.6 (governing collection of nontestimonial identification evidence including "fingerprints, palm prints, footprints, measurements, hair strands, handwriting samples, voice samples, photographs, blood and saliva samples, ultraviolet or black-light examinations, paraffin tests, and lineups"). Under Iowa Code §810.6, nontestimonial identification orders require the government to establish each of the following:

1. That there is probable cause to believe that a felony described in the application has been committed.

2. That there are reasonable grounds to suspect that the person named or described in the application committed the felony and it is reasonable in view of the seriousness of the offense to subject that person to the requested nontestimonial identification procedures.
3. That the results of the requested nontestimonial identification procedures will be of material aid in determining whether the person named or described in the application committed the felony.
4. That such evidence cannot practicably be obtained from other sources.

In Bousman v. District Court, 630 N.W.2d 789 (Iowa 2001), the Iowa Supreme Court held that this statute and the federal and Iowa constitutions required only reasonable suspicion in support of an order to obtain saliva for a DNA test. The court also held that reasonable suspicion was all that is required to support a brief investigatory detention to gather this information. Is the compelled presence of a suspect at the police station for a physical sample an arrest? If so, why don't the federal and state constitutions require probable cause for the suspect's detention or forced presence, even if they do not require probable cause to compel the nontestimonial evidence?

3. *Noninvasive medical search techniques.* The pumping of a stomach is one medical technique that typically requires the probable cause "plus" showing. Would you require the probable cause "plus" only for physically invasive techniques? How about the use of an X-ray, followed by administration of a laxative? See People v. Thompson, 820 P.2d 1160 (Colo. Ct. App. 1991) (higher justification required for laxative but not for X-ray). Would most people rather be subject to an unwanted X-ray or an unwanted laxative? Which of these procedures can go forward without the assistance of a doctor? A number of cases have approved the taking of a blood sample based only on a showing of probable cause. Would a justification higher than probable cause be necessary if the police officer uses a "stun gun" (a weapon that produces 0.00006 of an amp of electricity to cause muscle contractions and a resulting loss of balance) to disable a resisting suspect long enough to draw the blood sample? See McCann v. State, 588 A.2d 1100 (Del. 1991).

B. "HOUSES" AND OTHER PLACES

We move now to searches of "houses" and other common searches in which the location of the search plays a major part in the legal analysis. Recall from Chapter 2 that the Fourth Amendment and most analogous state provisions protect only a "reasonable expectation of privacy." In Katz v. United States, 389 U.S. 347 (1967), the Supreme Court declared that the Fourth Amendment "protects people, not places." Nevertheless, the location of a search still matters a great deal. We consider in this section searches and seizures that take place in several important recurring locations: in or near homes, workplaces, and institutions such as schools and prisons.

1. *The Outer Boundaries of Houses*

Searches of homes have always presented some of the easiest cases for limiting the power of the government to search. Recall that the most infamous searches of the late eighteenth century — which most influenced the framers of the Fourth Amendment — were searches of homes. But it is not always so easy to tell where a home leaves off and where the rest of the world begins. The area immediately surrounding the home, known as the "curtilage," receives the same protection as the home itself. Areas beyond the curtilage, known as "open fields," traditionally received no Fourth Amendment protection at all. The two cases reprinted in this section explore these two concepts.

CONSTITUTION OF MICHIGAN ART. I, §11

The person, houses, papers and possessions of every person shall be secure from unreasonable searches and seizures. No warrant to search any place or to seize any person or things shall issue without describing them, nor without probable cause, supported by oath or affirmation. The provisions of this section shall not be construed to bar from evidence in any criminal proceeding any narcotic drug, firearm, bomb, explosive or any other dangerous weapon, seized by a peace officer outside the curtilage of any dwelling house in this state.

STATE v. GREGORY FISHER

154 P.3d 455 (Kan. 2007)

NUSS, J.

Gregory C. Fisher was convicted of unlawful manufacture of methamphetamine, possession of ephedrine with the intent to manufacture methamphetamine, possession of anhydrous ammonia in an unapproved container for the production of methamphetamine, possession of methamphetamine, and possession of paraphernalia for use in the manufacture of methamphetamine. [The issue on appeal is as] follows: Did the district court err in failing to suppress evidence obtained pursuant to a search warrant partially based upon the contents of a trash bag seized from Fisher's property? . . .

FACTS

On August 20, 2001, Detective Shane Jager of the Pottawatomie County Sheriff's Department received information from fellow deputy Paul Hoyt concerning suspicious activity at 12420 Highway 63, Emmett, in Pottawatomie County. The property is located in a rural area approximately 4 miles north of the town of Emmett, on the west side of Highway 63. There are no other houses in the general vicinity on the west side of the highway. On the east side of the highway, the closest neighbor's house is approximately a quarter of a mile away.

The property is bounded on the east by Highway 63 and by barbed wire fencing on the north, south, and west which separates the property from surrounding pasture. Photographs reveal the house is approximately 25 yards west of the highway and sits on the northeast part of the property. Its front porch and door face south. A large shed (barn) is located 50 to 60 yards straight west of the house's western exterior near the barbed wire fence. A second, smaller shed sits equidistant between the house and the barn, but somewhat north, actually forming part of the north fence.

From Highway 63, a driveway runs from east to west on the south of the house, curving to the north and ending in a turn-around near the center of the area bounded by the three buildings. The only apparent walkway or sidewalk leads directly south from the house's front door to the driveway. According to photographs in the record, several large trees surround the house inside of the driveway.

According to Jager's suppression hearing testimony, Deputy Hoyt told him that a concerned citizen noticed a strong or peculiar odor emanating from trash being burned on the property and also observed numerous cars stopping there for short intervals of time. Hoyt further relayed to Jager that on August 28, 2001, he received information from another concerned citizen that a white female driving a van — that had been seen coming and going from the residence — drove to a shed located on the property, emptied boxes, placed more boxes in the van, and then left.

At approximately 1 A.M. on the day after Hoyt relayed the information about the delivery of boxes, Jager, Sergeant Chris Schmidt, and Deputy Shane Van Meter went to the area to determine if they could observe anything. While standing in a grass field to the west of the property, and approximately 30 yards west of the barn, Jager noticed a strong odor of ether. Based on his special training, coupled with the prior information of cars stopping at the residence, Jager suspected that methamphetamine was being manufactured and sold there.

Later that morning, Jager returned to the area twice more, once with the county attorney. From his parked position near Highway 63 about 50 yards south of Fisher's driveway, and once again off of Fisher's property, Detective Jager saw a burn barrel and a white translucent plastic trash bag near the barn. He then used binoculars to observe that the bag contained yellow containers. Based upon his training and experience, he associated the yellow bottles with the manufacture of methamphetamine, i.e., Heet bottles. Jager then walked to the field north of the property, where he again smelled ether. Jager testified that at that point he asked the county attorney how he felt about the trash bag. "He said . . . it was not on curtilage, that I could obtain the trash bag, and I advised him that I would like to try . . . to talk to the residents, see what we could obtain from them, and that's when I went to the door of the residence."

Jager testified that after this discussion with the county attorney he got back in his vehicle and

> I pulled my patrol vehicle in the driveway, went to the front door, knocked on the door several times. [After no answer,] I got back in my vehicle and there's a circle driveway that goes around the back side of the residence there, got in, drove by. When I was driving by the white trash bag I noticed Actifed blister packs, several Heet bottles, [and pseudoephedrine and] that's when I collected that white trash bag. . . .

Jager brought the bag to the sheriff's department for examination. In addition to the Heet bottles and 8 to 10 packs of ephedrine, the bag contained plastic gloves, coffee filters with a pinkish powder residue, and miscellaneous trash, including documents identifying Greg Fisher and Betty Harper.

Based upon the tips and Jager's information observed and obtained at the scene, including the contents of the bag, he [obtained and executed a search warrant for the house, outbuildings, and vehicles. The search produced evidence of the manufacture of methamphetamine].

ANALYSIS

. . . Fisher has consistently maintained that the State unlawfully seized the white trash bag from his property because it was within his curtilage. Because the warrant was issued based in part upon facts gleaned from this alleged unconstitutional seizure, he claims the evidence seized pursuant to the improper warrant was fruit of the poisonous tree and should have been suppressed. At oral arguments, the State responded that the bag was outside the curtilage and, if not, it was seized while in Jager's plain view.

When reviewing a motion to suppress evidence, this court reviews the factual underpinnings of a district court's decision by a substantial competent evidence standard and the ultimate legal conclusion drawn from those facts by a de novo standard. This court will not reweigh the evidence. The ultimate determination of the suppression of evidence is a legal question requiring independent review.

In rejecting Fisher's challenge, the district court examined the totality of the circumstances to justify the issuance of the magistrate's search warrant. During this examination, the court found that the bag was seized from outside the curtilage. . . . The district court stated:

> [The] officers went to the house to inquire. They had a right to be there. They have a right to go to the house and knock and talk to the occupants when they have that kind of information. They weren't trespassing. [This] wasn't curtilage as I see it and under these facts. The Heet bottle that [then] became readily apparent, as did [blister packs of pseudoephedrine, after the attempted knock and talk] which are a known precursor for the manufacturing of methamphetamine. They had a right to take the trash . . . .

While Fisher objects to the seizure of the bag, he does not dispute the propriety of the methods or locations, on and off the premises, used for obtaining information, i.e., ether odor and apparent yellow containers in the bag, up to and including Jager's knock and talk. He essentially argues that lawfully made observations do not equate to the right to seize. While the characterization of an observation as a non-search plain view situation settles the lawfulness of the observation itself, it does not determine whether a *seizure* of the observed object would likewise be lawful.

At the scene, however, and now on appeal, the county attorney concluded the bag lawfully observed by Jager could be seized from Fisher's property because (1) it was trash and (2) it was outside the curtilage. Curtilage is the area surrounding the residence, to which historically the Fourth Amendment protection against unreasonable searches and seizures has been extended.

California v. Greenwood, 486 U.S. 35 (1988), is of guidance on the seizure issue. There, the Supreme Court addressed a situation where (1) the trash bag (2) was admittedly outside the curtilage; it determined seizure was proper. Despite the seizure of the bag from outside the curtilage, the Court nevertheless engaged in a reasonable expectation of privacy analysis. Since *Greenwood,* lower courts have struggled with exactly how the concept of curtilage fits into the analysis of trash seizures. In trash cases, this court has not only analyzed whether curtilage exists but also whether the owner has a reasonable expectation of privacy in the trash. . . . To analyze the parties' positions in the instant case, we will therefore examine both curtilage and reasonable expectation of privacy in trash.

CURTILAGE

[The] question of curtilage is a mixed question of fact and law. Accordingly, we review the district court's factual findings for substantial competent evidence and review de novo the district court's legal conclusion whether a particular seizure occurred within the curtilage.

Without elaboration, the district court in the instant case simply concluded that the trash bag was not within the cartilage. [United States v. Dunn, 480 U.S. 294 (1987) holds a central place in the curtilage analysis. The] extent of the curtilage is determined by factors that bear upon whether an individual reasonably may expect that the area in question should be treated as the home itself. [The] central component of this inquiry [is] whether the area harbors the "intimate activity associated with the sanctity of a man's home and the privacies of life." The *Dunn* Court held that curtilage questions should be resolved with particular reference to four factors:

> [1] The proximity of the area claimed to be curtilage to the home, [2] whether the area is included within an enclosure surrounding the home, [3] the nature of the uses to which the area is put, and [4] the steps taken by the resident to protect the area from observation by people passing by.

The *Dunn* Court was also quick to point out, however:

> We do not suggest that combining these factors produces a finely tuned formula that, when mechanically applied, yields a "correct" answer to all extent-of-curtilage questions. Rather, these factors are useful analytical tools only to the degree that, in any given case, they bear upon the centrally relevant consideration — whether the area in question is so intimately tied to the home itself that is should be placed under the home's "umbrella" of Fourth Amendment protection. . . .

The Fisher property is bounded on the east by the highway and on the west, north and south by a barbed wire fence. Outside the fence is farm ground in three directions. According to the photographs, inside the fence is short grass which appears to be mowed and maintained throughout. [Several] large trees surround the house inside of the driveway. Photographs show that vehicles are parked in the area formed by the three buildings. A garden apparently is between the barn and shed in the northwest corner of the property. A power pole with a readable electricity meter is near the curve (from west to north) in the driveway. A "Notice, No Trespassing" sign is on another pole near the entrance to the driveway from the highway. The bag was found between the house and the barn, i.e., within the area bounded by the three buildings.

We begin our determination by observing this is rural property, four miles from the nearest town. There are no other houses in the general vicinity of the house on the west side of the highway. On the east side of the highway, a neighbor's house sits approximately a quarter of a mile away. We next apply the *Dunn* factors.

(1) Proximity of the area claimed to be curtilage to the home: [There] is not any fixed distance at which curtilage ends. Here, although the barn is 50-60 yards west of the house's western edge, the exact distance of the trash bag from any feature is unknown, but it was found between the barn and house, albeit nearer the barn. Several courts have noted that in the context of a rural setting, the area extending to outbuildings may be in the curtilage.

(2) Whether the area is included within an enclosure surrounding the home: There is barbed wire fencing on three sides and highway on another. Moreover, the area within the barbed wire fence appears to be mowed and maintained.

(3) The nature of the uses to which the area is put: the bag was found between the barn and the driveway which splits the area between the house and the barn. Photographs show vehicles are parked on the driveway, between the driveway and the house, and between the driveway and the small shed. Additionally, the barbed wire fence-enclosed area also apparently includes a garden between the barn and shed.

(4) The steps taken by the resident to protect the area from observation by people passing by: The bag was found nearly 100 hundred yards from the highway, *i.e.*, behind the large two-story house whose eastern edge is 25 yards west of the highway and near the barn which, because of the size of the house, is more than 50-60 yards further west of the highway. According to the photographs, from the highway the house would have blocked a direct view of the bag, and the bag would have been observable only from obliques to the house, concomitantly from further distances. Outside of that distance, the house's placement, the remoteness of the house from other rural homes in the area, and a "No Trespassing" sign, however, there is nothing to suggest the residents took any particular precautions to prevent observation. [The] barbed wire fences do not prevent observation. Ether was smelled from outside the property. Yellow containers in the translucent bag were discovered through a detective's use of binoculars while parked near the highway and oblique to the house.

Based upon these facts, particularly this rural environment, we independently conclude the trash bag was found within the curtilage. We hold that in rural Kansas, Fisher's area harbors the "intimate activity associated with the sanctity of a person's home and the privacies of life."

REASONABLE EXPECTATION OF PRIVACY

Even though we have concluded that the trash bag was seized from within the curtilage, we still need to examine whether Fisher maintained a reasonable expectation of privacy in the bag. . . .

An important inquiry in applying the *Greenwood* analysis to garbage within the curtilage is whether the garbage was so readily accessible to the public that its contents were exposed to the public for Fourth Amendment purposes. [In this case, the] trash bag was placed almost 100 yards from the public highway, blocked from the direct east view from the highway by the house, obscured from the direct north view by the small shed, and blocked from the direct west view by the barn; . . . the bag's yellow containers were visible only with use of binoculars. The bag was not exposed for the public to see; indeed, it was not left out for commercial trash collection. Rather, it was placed on the ground near a barrel for eventual disposition by Fisher. . . .

Under these circumstances, we conclude rural residents in Kansas would be quite surprised to learn that highway travelers, children, scavengers, snoops and other members of the public would be fully justified in pawing through the contents of a resident's trash bag placed approximately 100 yards from the highway and behind a rural home. In short, we conclude that Fisher maintained a reasonable expectation of privacy in his trash bag at its specific location — a subjective expectation that was objectively reasonable. Accordingly, the bag's warrantless seizure was per se unreasonable unless permissible under some recognized exception to the warrant requirement.

PLAIN VIEW

The State [argues that] even if the seizure occurred within the curtilage, as we have determined, that the plain view doctrine still justified the seizure. Under the facts of this case, we disagree for several reasons. . . .

It is first important to keep clear the distinctions between the different types of "plain view." As the Supreme Court has stated: "It is important to distinguish 'plain view' as used in Coolidge v. New Hampshire, 403 U.S. 443 (1971) to justify *seizure* of an object, from an officer's mere observation of an item left in plain view. Whereas the latter generally involves no Fourth Amendment search, . . . the former generally does implicate the Amendment's limitations upon seizures of personal property." Horton v. California, 496 U.S. 128, 133 n.5 (1990).

A number of courts have therefore used the term "open view doctrine" to refer to the rule that no Fourth Amendment search occurs where a law enforcement officer observes incriminating evidence or unlawful activity from a nonintrusive vantage point. Thus, the "open view" terminology distinguishes the analysis applicable to warrantless observations from the legally distinct "plain view" doctrine applicable to seizures. It is unclear, however, which of the doctrines the State applies to which events on the day of the seizure.

As for any State contention that the open view of the bag from the highway justified the seizure, we repeat that lawful observation does not equate to lawful seizure. [Absent] a justifiable intrusion onto Fisher's curtilage, the mere observation of the bag from the highway does not itself allow the bag's seizure.

As for any State contention that its justified intrusion was Jager's knock and talk and that the "plain view" of the bag obtained directly thereafter justified the seizure, we hold that the open observation of the bag from the highway — which led to the knock and talk — cannot also serve as a "plain view" of the bag from within the curtilage authorizing the seizure. . . . We specifically disapprove of any State attempt to "piggyback," i.e., to observe an object in open view from off the premises, to use knock and — in these cases, unsuccessful — talk for justified entry onto the premises, and then assert plain view while on the premises as a legal basis to seize the identical object that had been observed earlier. Such piggybacking under these facts would smear the careful distinctions drawn by the *Horton* Court between the right to merely observe an object (here, from off the premises) and the right to seize that object (on the premises). From a practical standpoint, this piggyback practice would grant law enforcement the right to seize virtually any object initially observed from a distance and subsequently located within plain view of a residential doorway by an officer purposely looking for that identical object.

An additional reason for us to reject the State's request to apply the plain view doctrine for justification of the seizure is that Jager's premises search and seizure of the bag exceeded the scope of his justified intrusion. . . . We acknowledge that the knock and talk allows officers to come within the curtilage to ask questions. We also acknowledge that if no one answers the knock, as here, the officers can be justified in knocking on more doors. We also acknowledge that, as here, while driving to and from the parking spot on the driveway, while walking to and from the front door, and while at the front door, the officer may make lawful observations. However, Jager did not have the run of the entire Fisher property. . . . An officer is permitted the same license to intrude as a reasonably respectful citizen. However, a substantial and unreasonable departure from such an area, or a particularly intrusive method of viewing, will exceed the scope of the implied invitation and intrude upon a constitutionally protected expectation of privacy. Accordingly, any observations Jager made while exceeding the scope of his lawful intrusion into the curtilage are unlawful. As a result, any seizure made while Jager was exceeding the scope of his lawful intrusion into the curtilage was also unlawful.

There is little evidence in the record indicating that at the time Jager observed the bag while on the premises he was performing any legitimate functions, i.e., observing while moving around the house exterior to look for another door or observing while on his way back to his vehicle after no one answered the knock. Admittedly, he testified at one point that he was "circling around to leave the property" when he observed the bag's contents. On this record, however, we find the evidence insufficient for the State to meet its burden that Jager did not exceed his lawful intrusion, i.e., the knock and talk.

[Once] Jager's knock and talk was complete, instead of driving away from the house to the highway, he simply drove deeper into the property on the driveway — according to the photographs, perhaps as much as 50 yards — directly to the previously observed bag. Once there, from his vehicle he noticed that it contained Actifed blister packs and, in confirmation of his earlier opinion, Heet bottles. He got out of the vehicle and seized the bag. . . .

REVIEW OF THE EXCISED AFFIDAVIT

Our analysis of the suppression issue does not end here, however. We now examine the validity of the search warrant's issuance based upon the remaining — and lawfully obtained — evidence. [After reviewing the totality of these circumstances presented to the magistrate, the court held] that he had a substantial basis for concluding that a crime had been or was being committed, and there was a fair probability that contraband or evidence of a crime would be found in the places to be searched. Therefore, even absent evidence of the contents of the trash bag, the search warrant was valid. The district court was correct in denying the motion to suppress, albeit for a somewhat different reason.

DAVIS, J., concurring.

I concur in the result of the majority decision affirming the validity of the search warrant. [But] I respectfully disagree with the conclusion that seizure of the trash bag violated the defendant's rights under the Fourth Amendment and would conclude that Officer Jager, in what amounted to an excellent investigation of a clandestine methamphetamine lab, had the right under the "plain view doctrine" to seize the trash bag in question, thereby providing probable cause for a search and seizure of evidence on the defendant's premises. . . .

Officer Jager was lawfully on the defendant's property for a knock and talk. As he was leaving the property by the way offered by the resident, the circle drive, he observed in plain view the contents of the trash bag, which were immediately known by the officer to contain evidence of a crime. This observation provided probable cause to seize the bag.

Notwithstanding the advice of the county attorney, Officer Jager did not seize the bag immediately and did not engage in an exploratory search of the premises (such as the shed from where the ether smell emanated) but observed from his patrol vehicle incriminating evidence in the translucent bag as he was leaving the premises. I would therefore [hold] that the officer's seizure of the bag from defendant's premises was justified by the plain view doctrine, thereby validating the search warrant based upon the contents of the trash bag lawfully seized and other evidence contained in the affidavit. . . .

■ STATE v. THERESA DIXSON

766 P.2d 1015 (Or. 1988)

GILLETTE, J.

The issue in these criminal cases, combined for purposes of appeal, is whether the search and seizure provision in the Oregon Constitution protects land outside the "curtilage" of a residence. . . .

Sheriff's deputies received an informant's tip that marijuana was growing on heavily forested land owned by the Rogge Lumber Company. . . . The officers requested and received the company's permission to search the property for marijuana. [They] drove onto the property by way of a public road until they reached a dirt logging road the informant had described as leading to the marijuana. Unknown to the officers, this road extended onto property [where Lorin and Theresa Dixson lived]. The dirt road had fallen into disuse and no longer was passable by car. The trunk of a large tree lay across the road and, a little further on, a wire cable with a "No Hunting" sign on it stretched across the road. The officers left their car and walked past the fallen tree and wire cable. Just past the cable was another dirt road running along a fence line. This road also had a wire cable and "No Hunting" sign stretched across it. The officers continued walking down this second road. At a bend in the road, they encountered another "No Hunting" sign. The area was rural and covered with thick brush. The officers were able to see marijuana plants only after pushing aside the brush. The plants, which were on the Dixsons' property, were not visible at ground level except from that property. [The officers returned the next day and arrested the defendants near the plants. After charges were filed, the defendants filed a motion to suppress the evidence, based on both the state and federal constitutions.]

The state argues that this court should adopt an "open fields" exception to Article I, section 9, for the reasons expressed in the majority opinion in Oliver v. United States, 466 U.S. 170 (1984). In *Oliver,* the police, without first obtaining a warrant, went to Oliver's farm to investigate reports that he was raising marijuana there. They drove past Oliver's house to a locked gate with a "No Trespassing" sign on it. On foot, they followed a path around the gate and along the road for several hundred yards. As they passed a barn and a parked camper, they heard someone standing by the camper shout, "No hunting is allowed, come back up here." The officers identified themselves and approached the camper, but found no one. They continued walking until they found a field of marijuana over a mile from Oliver's house. . . .

The *Oliver* majority relied on the following rationale for holding that the Fourth Amendment does not protect land outside the curtilage of a dwelling: First, the language of the amendment expressly protects from unreasonable search and seizure only "persons, houses, papers, and effects." The majority concluded that the framers of the Fourth Amendment "would have understood the term 'effects' to be limited to personal, rather than real, property." Second, at common law, a distinction was drawn between the curtilage of a home and other land surrounding the home. In the majority's view, this distinction bolstered its conclusion that the framers of the Fourth Amendment did not intend to extend its protection to land outside the curtilage; it also demonstrated that society historically has had a reduced expectation of privacy in such land.

Third, land outside the curtilage of a dwelling "do[es] not provide the setting for those intimate activities that the Amendment is intended to shelter from government interference or surveillance"; thus, those who perform the activities typically conducted in such areas do not require or expect a great deal of privacy. Finally, the desirability of a uniform rule and the problems inherent in fashioning and enforcing a case-by-case approach outweigh any privacy interests that may exist in land outside the curtilage of a dwelling.

The state [argues] that the above reasons wholly justify an interpretation of Article I, section 9, that parallels the federal rule. Although in interpreting Article I, section 9, we are not bound either by the Supreme Court's holding in *Oliver* or by its method of tackling the problem, we will examine its underlying rationale, to the extent that they are pertinent to an Article I, section 9, inquiry.

At the outset, [a caveat is] in order. [The term "open fields"] encompasses lands that are neither fields nor, in any fair sense of the word, open; the open fields doctrine denies Fourth Amendment protection to all undeveloped and unoccupied land outside the curtilage of a residence. We therefore frame the question presented by this case in what we believe to be more realistic terms — not whether the requirements of Article I, section 9, are subject to an exception for "open fields," but whether that provision prohibits unreasonable searches and seizures conducted on land that falls outside the curtilage of a dwelling.

The Textual Argument

The state argues that, because Article I, section 9, like the Fourth Amendment, expressly protects "persons, houses, papers, and effects," the state provision should be interpreted the same way that the United States Supreme Court has interpreted the Fourth Amendment. That argument has some obvious validity, because the language of a constitutional provision must have some meaning if it is to be interpreted in any principled manner. On the other hand, Article I, section 9, has acquired a meaning over the years that is hard to reconcile with the literal interpretation advocated by the state.

Our prior decisions establish that Article I, section 9, does not protect property alone; in a broader sense, it also protects an individual's "privacy interest," which we have defined as an interest in freedom from certain forms of governmental scrutiny. [A] literal interpretation of Article I, section 9, would afford no protection from such things as the police interception of a private telephone conversation from a public telephone booth. . . .

There is a second problem with the literal interpretation proposed by the state. If we were to rely on the language of Article I, section 9, to limit its protection to "persons, papers, houses, and effects [i.e., personal property]," that interpretation necessarily would exclude all kinds of real property except houses. There would be no principled way to distinguish, based on the language itself, office buildings, churches, schools, commercial establishments, and the like, from other kinds of real property. The drafters of Article I, section 9, are unlikely to have intended to exclude from its protections all real property except houses, i.e., structures where people customarily reside. The scope of the section is broader than a literal reading of its terms.

We conclude that we cannot rely on a literal reading of Article I, section 9. To hold that the provision applies only to those items specifically enumerated therein would undermine the rationale that we have identified as the touchstone of Article I, section 9 — the right to be free from intrusive forms of government scrutiny — and would open up prior decisions of this court . . . to serious question. We decline to take that step. Article I, section 9, protects the privacy of the individual from certain kinds of governmental scrutiny. If the individual has a privacy interest in land outside the curtilage of his dwelling, that privacy interest will not go unprotected simply because of its location. . . .

The Argument Based on the Uses to Which Land Outside the Curtilage of a Dwelling Is Put

[Under Article I, section 9,] the question is whether governmental intrusions into privately owned land would significantly impair an individual's interest in freedom from scrutiny, i.e., his privacy. The answer is: That depends.

Areas such as "the vast expanse of some western ranches or . . . the undeveloped woods of the Northwest" described by the *Oliver* majority may involve little or no privacy interest. Some areas of this state contain large unmarked tracts of land in which it is difficult to tell where one piece of property ends and another begins. The public may be in the habit of using these areas to hike, fish, hunt or camp. However lonely a person usually may be in such places, he or she has no true privacy in them.

On the other hand, owners of even large tracts may, at some expense, take steps to keep out intruders. In this society, signs, such as "No Trespassing" signs, the erection of high, sturdy fences and other, similar measures are all indications that the possessor wishes to have his privacy respected. Allowing the police to intrude into private land, regardless of the steps taken by its occupant to keep it private, would be a significant limitation on the occupant's freedom from governmental scrutiny. Article I, section 9, does not permit such freewheeling official conduct. The remaining question is whether it is possible to fashion a workable test to enable the police to determine whether a particular intrusion constitutes a search under the state constitution. It is.

Case-by-Case Analysis

The rule we announce today is simple and objective. An individual's privacy interest in land he or she has left unimproved and unbounded is not sufficient to trigger the protections of Article I, section 9. Thus, it is not sufficient that the property in question is privately owned, or that it is shielded from view by vegetation or topographical barriers, because those features do not necessarily indicate the owner's intention that the property be kept private. A person who wishes to preserve a constitutionally protected privacy interest in land outside the curtilage must manifest an intention to exclude the public by erecting barriers to entry, such as fences, or by posting signs. This rule will not unduly hamper law enforcement officers in their attempts to curtail the manufacture of and trafficking in illegal drugs, because it does not require investigating officers to draw any deduction other than that required of the general public: if land is fenced, posted or otherwise closed off, one does not enter it without permission or, in the officers' situation, permission or a warrant.

In the present case, the defendants (or someone) had blocked access to their property with cables and posted "No Hunting" signs. However, on this record there was no objective reason for the officers to believe that, in addition to the restriction on hunting, other uses such as hiking were forbidden. In this state, with its expanses of rough and open country, hiking, camping and the like commonly occur on land that is owned by large companies and individuals. See generally, ORS §105.655-.680, dealing with public recreational use of private lands. Unless they intended to hunt, neither the officers nor anyone else would have understood the posted signs to be intended to exclude them from the property entirely. The state carried its burden of showing that there was no violation of the Oregon Constitution in the officer's actions. . . .

Notes

1. *Open fields: majority position.* Under the federal constitution, there is no "search" when officers discover something in "open fields," land beyond the boundaries of a home and its curtilage. The decision in Oliver v. United States, 466 U.S. 170 (1984), affirming the traditional "open fields" doctrine, came as a surprise. After the Supreme Court declared in Katz v. United States, 389 U.S. 347 (1967), that the Fourth Amendment protected expectations of privacy rather than property interests, most lower courts assumed that the old per se rule allowing warrantless and suspicionless searches of open fields was no longer tenable. The *Oliver* decision, however, reaffirmed the traditional "open fields" doctrine (based on Hester v. United States, 265 U.S. 57 (1924)). See Stephen Saltzburg, Another Victim of Illegal Narcotics: The Fourth Amendment (as Illustrated by the Open Fields Doctrine), 48 U. Pitt. L. Rev. 1 (1986).

State courts considering the "open fields" question since 1984 are divided. A majority of state courts have followed the Supreme Court in *Oliver:* For items discovered on property outside the curtilage, no search takes place and no case-by-case consideration of "expectations of privacy" is necessary. See Commonwealth v. Russo, 934 A.2d 1199 (Pa. 2007) (seizure of bear stomach from ground 150 yards from cabin to obtain proof that hunting camp was baited). Roughly 10 states, including New York, Oregon, Vermont, and Washington, have parted company with the federal rule. These courts have ruled that, under state statutes or constitutions, police must have a warrant to enter private property if the owner has taken enough measures to prevent entry onto the land by the public. The adequacy of the property owner's efforts to maintain privacy on the land might be measured case by case or with a relatively clear rule.

2. *Curtilage.* Many cases, both state and federal, have declared that the constitutional protection of privacy is at its highest in the home and the area immediately surrounding it, known as the "curtilage." Does the Michigan constitution make this distinction between the home and all other places explicit?

As the *Fisher* court indicated, United States v. Dunn, 480 U.S. 294 (1987), announced several factors that are now widely used to determine whether property is curtilage. In that case, federal agents suspected that the defendant was operating a drug laboratory in a barn on a ranch. The barn sat 60 yards from a house; a waist-high wooden fence with locked gates enclosed the front of the barn. A fence surrounded the perimeter of the property, and several barbed-wire fences crossed the interior of the property (including a fence surrounding the ranch house and running between the barn and the house). The agents crossed the perimeter fence, several of the barbed-wire fences, and the wooden fence in front of the barn. The court held that the barn was not within the curtilage of the ranch house. The web extension for this chapter, at *http://www.crimpro.com/extension/ch04*, offers diagrams of the properties in *Oliver*, *Fisher*, and *Dunn*.

The *Dunn* case and many others deal with searches of alleged "curtilage" areas in a rural or wooded setting. Are these definitions based on assumptions about land use and habits that do not apply in urban and suburban areas? For instance, would you conclude that a "search" of an item in the curtilage had occurred if police officers walked onto the front porch of a home, rang the doorbell, and then picked up a pair of boots, covered with plaster dust, sitting on a box on the porch (attempting to match the tread of the boots to white footprints found on the carpet at a burglary scene)? See State v. Portrey, 896 P.2d 7 (Or. Ct. App. 1995). Is a home best characterized as a place of activity and industry?

3. *Impermanent homes.* How long must a person occupy a temporary shelter before it can receive all the protections afforded to "houses" under the constitution? See State v. Pruss, 181 P.3d 1231 (Idaho 2008) (privacy expectation in "hooch," wooden frame enclosing a tent, on public land); State v. Mooney, 588 A.2d 145 (Conn. 1991) (privacy expectation in cardboard box hidden under bridge abutment containing effects of homeless man). Does it matter whether the occupant of the temporary shelter is otherwise homeless? For an argument that protections for traditional housing structures reach farther than necessary to protect genuine privacy interests, see Stephanie Stern, The Inviolate Home: Housing Exceptionalism in the Fourth Amendment, 95 Cornell L. Rev. 905 (2010).

4. *Categories covered by constitutional texts.* The Oregon court in *Dixson* was willing to conclude that real property was included within the "persons, houses, papers, and effects" that are protected from unreasonable searches and seizures. Does it matter what the constitutional framers considered to be the meaning of "effects" or "houses"? Where would a lawyer discover the framers' views on this question? Would it matter if the final category were called "possessions" instead of "effects"? See Falkner v. State, 98 So. 691 (Miss. 1924) (term "possessions" embraces "all of the property of the citizen"); State v. Finder, 514 A.2d 1241 (N.H. 1986) (term "possessions" does not include real property beyond curtilage).

5. *Crime scene searches.* Police often search crime scenes. Do they need to obtain warrants at any point? Officers can secure a crime scene without a warrant. Officers can also conduct an initial search in response to emergency situations such as

assisting a victim, searching for other victims, or searching for an offender. Police may also seize evidence in plain view during their emergency search and while securing the crime scene. However, in Mincey v. Arizona, 437 U.S. 385 (1978), the U.S. Supreme Court rejected a "crime scene exception" to the Fourth Amendment, and said that police should have obtained a warrant before they conducted a detailed four-day search of an apartment following the murder of an undercover officer. In Flippo v. West Virginia, 528 U.S. 11 (1999), the U.S. Supreme Court reaffirmed *Mincey* and rejected the warrantless search of a briefcase found (closed) during a murder scene investigation of a vacation cabin in a state park. The briefcase belonged to the husband of the victim, who had called the police to investigate; it contained pictures that established his motive for the murder. How do defendants and their lawyers know what police do at crime scenes, and when they do it?

6. *The "new judicial federalism."* On many constitutional questions arising in the criminal process, the Oregon Supreme Court and others have taken positions different from the federal view under their own state constitutions. One of the recurring questions — on which state courts have reached a wide range of positions — is how much deference state courts should give to U.S. Supreme Court decisions when the state courts are interpreting state law that is analogous to federal provisions. The degree of deference has shifted in response to highly publicized calls, led by Supreme Court Justice William Brennan, for independent state constitutional decision-making. See William Brennan, Jr., State Constitutions and the Protection of Individual Rights, 90 Harv. L. Rev. 489 (1977); James Gardner, The Failed Discourse of State Constitutionalism, 90 Mich. L. Rev. 761 (1992); Barry Latzer, The New Judicial Federalism and Criminal Justice: Two Problems and a Response, 22 Rutgers L. J. 863 (1991).

7. *Independent and adequate state grounds.* The U.S. Supreme Court reviews questions of federal law but cannot question a state court's interpretation of state law. When a state court discusses both state and federal law in its decision (and you have now seen how commonly that occurs), how does the U.S. Supreme Court decide whether it can review the decision? Under Michigan v. Long, 463 U.S. 1032 (1983), the Court requires a "plain statement" sufficient to show that "the federal cases are being used only for the purpose of guidance, and do not themselves compel the result that the court has reached." An assertion by the state court that it has relied independently on state law will not suffice. If the discussion of state law is "interwoven with the federal law, and . . . the adequacy and independence of any possible state law ground is not clear from the face of the opinion," the Supreme Court will treat the decision as one resting on federal law. Is this an appropriate test for judging the intentions of a state court? Does a state court risk reversal if it cites any U.S. Supreme Court cases at all? See Pennsylvania v. Labron, 518 U.S. 938 (1996) (taking jurisdiction and reversing in case where state court cited two federal decisions along with multiple state decisions); Commonwealth v. Labron, 690 A.2d 228 (Pa. 1997) (on remand, reinstating earlier decision and "explicitly noting that it was, in fact, decided upon independent state grounds").

2. Workplaces

Although the Fourth Amendment and its state analogs extend to "homes," all courts have extended the protection against unreasonable searches and seizures to other locations. The nature of the place can profoundly influence the reasonableness of the search. Given the amount of time many people spend in the workplace, it should come as no surprise that police searches of the workplace generate plenty of disputes. In addition to the location of the search, these cases also sometimes raise questions about the relationship between the government and a private employer who participates to some degree in a search.

■ PEOPLE v. CARLOS CHRISTOPHER GALVADON

103 P.3d 923 (Colo. 2005)

MARTINEZ, J.

. . . Galvadon worked as the night manager of a liquor store owned by his mother-in-law. Galvadon and his mother-in-law were the only employees of the store.

The store is located in a strip shopping center and occupies a narrow rectangular retail space. The front two-thirds of the retail space make up the publicly accessible portion of the store. The back of the store, however, is separated from the front of the store by a large refrigerator to create a separate room . . . used for inventory storage, an office and a bathroom. The only access to the back room from the front of the store is through a narrow corridor between the wall of the store and the refrigerator.

The front of the store consists of large glass windows and a glass-paned door with a checkout counter in front. The store has four surveillance video cameras. One is located in the back room and three others are located throughout the front of the store. The video recorder and monitor are also located in the back room.

As night manager, Galvadon was left by himself to take care of the store. His responsibilities included ordering liquor, making bank deposits, writing checks for the store, and restocking shelves. Galvadon used the back room to conduct all of these activities. According to Galvadon, the only people who had unrestricted access to the back room were himself and the owner. Delivery persons were regularly permitted in the back room, but only if supervised or otherwise granted access.

On November 20, 2003, Galvadon was working at the liquor store as night manager. Two other people, Jeffery Hogan and David Flores, were at the store with him for about an hour. Although the record is not clear as to what exactly transpired, the parties recite the same sequence of events: Shortly before midnight, Flores and Hogan were outside of the store standing in the parking lot. Galvadon stood in the open doorway at the front of the store. Flores was sprayed in the face with pepper spray.

At the same time, or immediately thereafter, Sergeant Juhl of the Colorado Springs Police Department drove by the store. Sergeant Juhl became suspicious when he saw Flores drop to the ground. He called for backup officers, turned around and pulled into the parking lot.

When Sergeant Juhl arrived, Galvadon was inside the store, but Hogan and Flores were still in the parking lot. Hogan explained that he and Flores had been "assaulted" by someone around the corner and that Flores was sprayed with pepper spray. Hogan explained that he wanted to take Flores to get his face washed off and then began to escort Flores into the store. Sergeant Juhl followed them.

Once in the store, Hogan asked if he and Flores could use the bathroom. Galvadon stated that no one was allowed in the back. Hogan urged Galvadon that Flores was in pain and needed to use the bathroom to wash off his face. Galvadon again insisted, several times, that no one was allowed in the back room. Hogan, however, ignored Galvadon and escorted Flores to the back room. Sergeant Juhl followed them. Galvadon followed all three of them into the back room.

While Flores was washing his face, backup officers arrived and went to the back room. Galvadon again told everyone in the back room that no one was allowed in back. Galvadon then returned to the front of the store. The officers stayed in the back room with Flores and Hogan while Sergeant Juhl went to the front of the store to speak with Galvadon. While in the back room, one of the officers discovered a "brick" of marihuana sitting in the bottom of an open cardboard box. Shortly thereafter, another brick was discovered sitting in a bag on the floor of the bathroom. Later, the owner of the store arrived and consented to a search of the store. During the search a third brick of marihuana was discovered in the back room.

After Flores, Hogan and the officers cleared out of the back room, Galvadon went into the back room by himself. Sergeant Juhl followed him. When Sergeant Juhl reached Galvadon, he discovered him attempting to hide a surveillance video tape in his pants. Galvadon explained that he had been drinking in the store earlier that night and was hiding the tape because he did not want the owner to find out. The video was later viewed by the investigating officers and showed Galvadon placing what the officers believed to be the bricks of marihuana in the back room.

Galvadon was subsequently charged with possession of marihuana, possession with intent to distribute marihuana and assault in the third degree. Prior to trial, Galvadon sought to suppress the evidence seized from the liquor store as the fruit of an illegal search. In response, the prosecution . . . claimed that because Galvadon was only an employee he could have no reasonable expectation of privacy. In addition, the prosecution asserted that because others had access to the back room and Galvadon was aware he was being videotaped by the in-store surveillance system while in the back room, . . . Galvadon could not have a reasonable expectation of privacy. The trial court disagreed and found that Galvadon had [a] reasonable expectation of privacy in the back room [and that] the warrantless intrusion into the back room could not be justified by any of the exceptions at law argued by the prosecution. Specifically, the court found there were no exigent circumstances, the intrusion was not based on emergency aid and Galvadon did not give consent. . . .

ANALYSIS

. . . Prior to Katz v. United States, 389 U.S. 347 (1967), the Court struggled with a method of determining when a person is afforded Fourth Amendment protection. Protection at the time was generally based on traditional notions of property law, where one must have a property interest in the place or thing searched. Such an inquiry focused on the place or thing searched, rather than the person asserting protection. The Court in *Katz* rejected this idea because it lost sight of what the Fourth Amendment actually protected. The Court held that the Fourth Amendment protects people and their privacy from government intrusion, not simply places based upon a person's property interests or their right to be in that place. . . .

Based upon privacy expectations set forth in *Katz*, the U.S. Supreme Court found that protection afforded by the Fourth Amendment is not limited to a literal reading of "houses," but instead extends beyond the home and may be asserted in the workplace. . . . In Mancusi v. DeForte, 392 U.S. 364 (1968), the defendant was a union official charged with misusing his office for coercion, extortion and conspiracy. The defendant shared an office with several other union officials. When the defendant refused to comply with a subpoena to produce union records, the state officials that served the subpoena searched the office and seized various records without a warrant. The defendant was present for the search and objected to it. The papers seized did not belong to the defendant. The Court applied the expectation of privacy analysis established in *Katz* to hold in *Mancusi* that the defendant could object to the search on Fourth Amendment grounds. . . . The Court found that despite sharing the office with several others, the defendant maintained a reasonable expectation of privacy from government intrusion in the office. . . .

Where the government search at issue takes place in a highly regulated industry such as the liquor business, under certain circumstances proprietors of such businesses might have a diminished expectation of privacy because of long-standing government oversight and consequently have less Fourth Amendment protection. The expectation of privacy in the liquor industry, however, is only diminished to the extent that searches are specifically authorized pursuant to constitutional administrative inspection regulations and conducted pursuant to the purpose of the regulatory scheme. Where, as here, the search of the liquor store was investigatory in nature and not an administrative search conducted pursuant to any regulation or statute, the defendant maintains his otherwise reasonable expectation of privacy. . . .

In examining the circumstances of a particular case [to determine if the defendant maintained a reasonable expectation of privacy in the place searched], courts have chosen to focus on different factors. Some courts look to the "nexus" between the area searched and the work space of the defendant. Other courts have looked to a defendant's right to exclude others from accessing the area for which the defendant asserts privacy. Regardless of the factors considered, an employee's expectation of privacy must be assessed in the context of the employment relation. O'Connor v. Ortega, 480 U.S. 709 (1987).

We look to several factors to determine whether Galvadon's expectation of privacy against government intrusion would exist absent the in-store surveillance system. . . . First, the back room of the liquor store is an exclusive area reserved for use by the owner and Galvadon. Its physical separation from the rest of the store indicates that public access is restricted in this area. The testimony of Sergeant Juhl indicates that even he assumed upon his first entry to the store that the public was not allowed in the back room. The room was specifically set apart as a private place for the owner and Galvadon to conduct the business affairs for the store shielded from the view and access of the public.

Second, Galvadon had the power to exclude access to the back room. As the night manager, and at the time of the police intrusion in this case, Galvadon was in charge and the only person in the store that controlled access to the back room. Because this incident occurred near midnight and Galvadon was left alone by the owner to manage the store, Galvadon could reasonably expect that only persons to whom he granted permission would be given access to the back room. Furthermore, Galvadon attempted several times to keep out Sergeant Juhl, Flores and Hogan, as well as the emergency medical technicians and other officers that arrived at the liquor store. This is a clear manifestation of Galvadon's belief that he could control access to the back room and maintain an expectation of privacy from intrusion of others into that area.

Despite the prosecution's argument to the contrary, the fact that the back room was accessible by a limited number of people does not eliminate Galvadon's expectation of privacy. Galvadon testified that there was a store policy that no one other than himself and the owner were permitted in the back room. Exceptions were made for delivery persons; however, Galvadon's expectation of privacy was not diminished simply because the space was occasionally accessed by someone else. . . . Access could only be granted at the instance of Galvadon or the owner, whoever was present. With respect to delivery persons, such access was only granted for the limited purpose of delivering beer and liquor, a circumstance necessary for the continued operation of the liquor store. Because Galvadon, as night manager and sole person operating the store, could control the access of delivery persons, such access has no effect on Galvadon's reasonable expectation of privacy from government intrusion. . . .

Having found that Galvadon could maintain an expectation of privacy in absence of the in-store surveillance system, we now turn to the question of whether his expectation of privacy from government intrusion was diminished by the presence of the surveillance system. The surveillance system consists of four video cameras; one was located in the back room. The video monitor and tape machine were also located in the back room. The prosecution generally asserts that because Galvadon was aware that the back room was under in-store surveillance, any activities that occurred in the back room were "knowingly exposed" to the store owner and the public. . . . This general assertion, however, ignores the fundamental inquiry supporting Fourth Amendment standing — whether the defendant has a reasonable expectation of privacy from government intrusion. . . .

Galvadon's activities were not exposed to the public through the surveillance system. [There] is no indication that any monitors were viewable from the publicly accessible portions of the store or that the public had access to the video recordings under the normal operation of the store. The owner and Galvadon were the only store employees, the only persons with access to the back room, and thus the only persons with access to the video recording and video monitor located there. The public, under these circumstances, did not have access to view the surveillance monitor or the video recording. As such, we find no support for the proposition that the in-store surveillance system "exposed" Galvadon to the public. . . .

The parties do not dispute that the surveillance system exposed Galvadon's activities in the back room to the owner of the store. As such, we proceed with the analysis to determine if such exposure to the store owner eliminated Galvadon's reasonable expectation of privacy from government intrusion. The U.S. Supreme Court has found that defendant-employees may have little or no expectation of privacy from their employer, but may still maintain a reasonable expectation of privacy from government intrusion. In *Mancusi*, the defendant shared his office with several others. The Court found that this factor alone was insufficient to extinguish the defendant's expectation of privacy from government intrusion. . . . Similarly, we can assume here that because of the surveillance system, Galvadon had a diminished expectation of privacy from the owner of the store. Although the record is void of any reference to how often, if at all, the owner reviewed the surveillance tapes, such evidence would only demonstrate Galvadon's diminished expectation of privacy from the store owner. This, however, does not indicate that he had no reasonable expectation of privacy from government intrusion. . . .

We conclude under the totality of circumstances that the sole person in control of the store, the night manager, maintained a reasonable expectation of privacy from government intrusion in the back room of the store, an area without public access, such that he may assert protection of the Fourth Amendment. The use of a surveillance system reviewable only by the night manager and the owner of the store did not diminish his reasonable expectation of privacy from government intrusion. . . .

MULLARKEY, C.J., dissenting.

The majority concludes that the defendant, Carlos Galvadon, had a reasonable expectation of privacy in the back room of a retail liquor store based on his exclusive control over the back room of the store. I respectfully dissent. I would find that Galvadon, as an employee of a retail liquor store, had no reasonable expectation in the store's back room because it was a liquor storage place subject to inspection at any time when the liquor store did business. . . .

Determination of this question requires examining the law regulating searches of business premises in highly regulated industries and the law defining an employee's reasonable expectation of privacy in his workplace. With respect to highly regulated industries, the Supreme Court has recognized that searches may be conducted without warrants. The liquor business is perhaps the prime example of a highly regulated industry. In Colorado, a retail liquor store may operate only if it complies with the Liquor Code and its implementing regulations. The relevant regulations require a licensed retail liquor store to be open to warrantless inspection by administrative authorities and by peace officers during normal business hours and at all times when activity is occurring on the premises. 1 C.C.R. 203-2, §47-700 (2001). . . .

The Supreme Court has recognized that not all workplaces have identical levels of Fourth Amendment protection. Indeed, the Colorado regulation is consistent with Supreme Court case law that recognizes an explicit exception to the warrant requirement for inspections of business premises within highly regulated industries in Colonnade Catering Corp. v. United States, 397 U.S. 72 (1970) (warrant exception for inspections of the liquor industry); United States v. Biswell, 406 U.S. 311 (1972) (warrant exception applies to firearms industry); and Donovan v. Dewey, 452 U.S. 594 (1981) (extending exception to inspections conducted pursuant to the Federal Mine Safety and Health Act of 1977). Of course, the constitutional rights at issue in these cases protect persons, not places, and the warrant exception at issue applies to the owners or proprietors of businesses within highly regulated industries. In summarizing the effect of these cases, the Supreme Court flatly stated that owners of businesses in highly regulated industries have no reasonable expectation of privacy in the premises. Marshall v. Barlow's Inc., 436 U.S. 307 (1978) (The liquor industry has "such a history of government oversight that no reasonable expectation of privacy . . . could exist for a proprietor over the stock of such an enterprise."). . . .

An employee of a licensed liquor establishment like Galvadon has even more limited rights. In general, an employee's expectation of privacy in the workplace is subordinate to the employer's interests. See O'Connor v. Ortega, 480 U.S. 709, 717 (1987) ("The operational realities of the workplace, however, may make some employees' expectations of privacy unreasonable when an intrusion is by a supervisor rather than a law enforcement official."). Furthermore, when an employee knows, as Galvadon did, that he or she is being watched by an employer, the affected workers are on clear notice from the outset that any movements they might make and any objects they might display within the work area would be exposed to the employer's sight. In light of employees' reduced expectation of privacy vis-à-vis employers, an employee can never be said to have a greater expectation of privacy than an employer. This lower expectation of privacy vis-à-vis the employer is particularly acute where, as here, the employee takes the risk that the employer will find evidence of wrongdoing by means of the video surveillance system in place and turn over such evidence to law enforcement. . . .

The fact that the police officers in this case were not in the back room of the store to conduct an inspection pursuant to the liquor code may be important in cases where there is evidence of bad faith by the police officers. However, there is no allegation of bad faith in this case, and the Supreme Court has made it clear that such bad faith does not affect the analysis of whether the individuals involved had any reasonable expectation of privacy. . . .

Notes

1. *Privacy interests in the workplace: majority position.* American courts have overwhelmingly decided that workers can hold some reasonable expectation of privacy in items kept at their workplace and in their activities at the workplace. The crucial question, as identified in the *Galvadon* opinion from Colorado, is whether the workers have some control over access to the area. Yet the Fourth Amendment and its state analogs speak only about government searches of "persons, houses, papers, and effects." Is a workplace a "house"? What is the justification for treating the workplace as a protected area? What would a society be like that did not limit searches in workplaces?

The government has plenty of reasons to collect information in the workplace. What begins as routine regulatory enforcement might end in a criminal prosecution. For instance, immigration agents may question employees in their workplace about their immigration status. Because of the limited intrusion involved, the questioning does not amount to a "seizure," even if workplace rules require the employees to remain on the site when the government agents arrive. INS v. Delgado, 466 U.S. 210 (1984). Does the access of regulators to the workplace strengthen or weaken the privacy interest of workers in their place of employment?

2. *Private searches.* The federal and state constitutions reach only searches conducted by government agents. A private employer can conduct any sort of search she chooses without engaging in an "unreasonable" search or seizure within the meaning of the federal constitution. See Burdeau v. McDowell, 256 U.S. 465 (1921); but cf. Texas Code Crim. Proc. Article 38.23 ("No evidence obtained by an officer *or other person* in violation of any provisions of the Constitution or laws of the State of Texas, or of the Constitution or laws of the United States of America, shall be admitted in evidence against the accused on the trial of any criminal case."). Statutes and common law rules (or contracts) may limit the private employer's searching power. However, if a private employer acts at the government's behest, a search can become "state action."

Does the power of private employers to gather information about their employees affect the reasonable expectations of privacy that an employee might have in the workplace? Employers may monitor telephone conversations or read computer files at the workplace. Private parties routinely collect and use information about their customers. Credit card companies can track where and what a consumer buys and can sell that information to merchants. As the editors of The Economist magazine put it, as we lose control over our privacy, the "chief culprit is not so much Big Brother as lots of little brothers, all gossiping with each other over computer networks." The Economist, February 10, 1996, at 27. Are statutory protections for privacy in the workplace likely to be enacted? Would they be effective?

The private security industry employs more personnel than federal, state, and local governments combined. As Professor David Sklansky points out, the growing number of private security forces might entail a shift in some of the most basic tenets of criminal procedure. He suggests that this trend will create a body of criminal procedure law that is deconstitutionalized, defederalized, tort-based, and heavily reliant both on legislatures and on juries. See Sklansky, The Private Police, 46 UCLA L. Rev. 1165 (1999); Elizabeth Joh, Conceptualizing the Private Police, 2005 Utah L. Rev. 573.

3. *Government as employer.* If a government agent wishes to search a workplace in the private sector, she usually needs probable cause and a warrant, or consent. But if the government agent represents a government employer conducting a search of a *government* workplace, different constitutional rules apply. Neither a warrant nor probable cause is necessary when the government employer is conducting (1) a non-investigatory work-related search (such as retrieving a file) or (2) an investigation of work-related misconduct. The Supreme Court in O'Connor v. Ortega, 480 U.S. 709 (1987), concluded that the reasonable suspicion standard was the best method of accommodating the employee's privacy interests with the public employer's interests apart from law enforcement. See also City of Ontario, Cal. v. Quon, 130 S. Ct. 2619 (2010) (police chief ordered review of text messages sent by officers on alphanumeric pagers the department recently purchased to determine source of billing overruns, which revealed that officer used pager during work hours for personal messages; review was reasonable because it was motivated by legitimate work-related purpose, and not excessive in scope). Workplace searches that are based on some neutral criteria, but not on individualized suspicion, may also be acceptable. See State v. Ziegler, 637 So. 2d 109 (La. 1994).

3. *Schools and Prisons*

When searches take place in institutions such as schools and prisons, courts tend to evaluate them much more generously than searches of homes or workplaces. These searches fall into a category sometimes known as "administrative" searches, where the government has purposes for its search other than enforcement of the criminal law. In such settings, warrants are often unnecessary, and the level of justification required does not rise to the level of probable cause. As you read the following materials, try to identify the elements of these searches that lead courts to place fewer controls on them than they do for searches in other settings. Could the arguments used to explain the looser supervision of searches in these contexts apply more broadly to others?

IN THE MATTER OF GREGORY M.

627 N.E.2d 500 (N.Y. 1993)

LEVINE, J.

. . . On November 29, 1990 appellant, then 15 years old, arrived at the high school he attended in The Bronx without a proper student identification card. He was directed by a school security officer to report to the office of the Dean to obtain a new card. In accordance with school policy, he was required to leave his cloth book bag with the security officer until he had obtained the proper identification. When appellant tossed the book bag on a metal shelf before proceeding beyond the school lobby to the Dean's office, the security officer heard a metallic "thud" which he characterized as "unusual." He ran his fingers over the outer surface of the bottom of the bag and felt the outline of a gun. The security officer then summoned the Dean who also discerned the shape of a gun upon feeling the outside of appellant's book bag. The bag was brought to the Dean's office and opened by the head of school security, revealing a small hand gun later identified as a .38 Titan Tiger Special. A juvenile delinquency petition was filed in Family Court accusing appellant of [weapons violations]. Family Court denied appellant's motion to suppress the gun. . . .

We affirm [the denial of the appellant's motion to suppress]. Although minimally intrusive, the purposeful investigative touching of the outside of appellant's book bag by the school security officer (i.e., to acquire knowledge about the bag's contents) falls marginally within a search for constitutional purposes. Also, appellant is quite correct in contending that the metallic thud heard by the security officer when appellant put the book bag down was by itself insufficient to furnish a reasonable suspicion that the bag contained a weapon. We conclude, however, that a less rigorous premonition concerning the contents of the bag was sufficient to justify the investigative touching of the outside of the bag. When that touching disclosed the presence of a gun-like object in the bag, there was reasonable suspicion to justify the search of the inside of the bag.

In People v. Scott D., 315 N.E.2d 466 (1974), this Court held that students attending public schools are protected by the constitutional ban against unreasonable searches and seizures. *Scott D.* involved a school search of a student for illegal drugs. We further held in *Scott D.* that inherent in determining whether a school search was reasonable is a "balancing of basic personal rights against urgent social necessities" and that, given the "special responsibility of school teachers in the control of the school precincts and the grave threat, even lethal threat, of drug abuse among school children, the basis for finding sufficient cause for a school search will be less than that required outside the school precincts."

Employing an analysis similar to that of People v. Scott D., the United States Supreme Court in New Jersey v. T.L.O., 469 U.S. 325 (1985), also concluded that the Fourth Amendment of the United States Constitution applies to searches of students by school authorities, but held that less cause is required to justify such a search than is required of law enforcement authorities searching persons or their effects outside school premises. Thus, the Supreme Court held that a determination of the appropriate standard of reasonableness to govern a certain class of searches requires a balancing: "On one side of the balance are arrayed the individual's legitimate expectations of privacy and personal security; on the other, the government's need for effective methods to deal with breaches of public order." The Court in New Jersey v. T.L.O. held that, ordinarily, searches by school authorities of the persons or belongings of students may be made upon "reasonable grounds for suspecting that the search will turn up evidence that the student has violated or is violating either the law or the rules of the school." The Court applied the reasonable suspicion standard in validating a teacher's full search of the inside of a student's purse for cigarettes, during which evidence of her involvement in drug dealing was revealed.

We agree that for searches by school authorities of the persons and belongings of students, such as that conducted in New Jersey v. T.L.O., the reasonable suspicion standard adopted in that case for Fourth Amendment purposes is also appropriate under our State Constitution (N.Y. Const., art. I, §12). In the instant case, however, the investigative touching of the outer surface of appellant's book bag falls within a class of searches far less intrusive than those which, under New Jersey v. T.L.O., require application of the reasonable suspicion standard. Applying the balancing process required under People v. Scott D. and New Jersey v. T. L. O., it is undeniable that appellant had only a minimal expectation of privacy regarding the outer touching of his school bag by school security personnel, even for purposes of learning something regarding its contents, when he left the bag with the security officer pursuant to the school policy requiring this until he obtained a valid identification card. On the other hand, it seems equally undeniable that, in the balancing process, prevention of the introduction of hand guns and other lethal weapons into New York City schools such as this high school is a governmental interest of the highest urgency. The extreme exigency of barring the introduction of weapons into the schools by students is no longer a matter of debate.

Thus, the balancing process ordained by People v. Scott D. and New Jersey v. T.L.O. leads to the conclusion that a less strict justification applies to the limited search here than the reasonable suspicion standard applicable for more intrusive school searches. In this regard, we find it noteworthy that the Supreme Court in New Jersey v. T.L.O. specifically disclaimed that its decision made some quantum of individualized suspicion an essential element of every school search.* The Supreme Court has elsewhere made it clear that, at least outside the context of criminal investigations by law enforcement officers, individualized suspicion is not a constitutional floor below which any search must be deemed unreasonable. There may be circumstances in which, because the privacy interests involved in the case are minimal and are overborne by the governmental interests in jeopardy if a higher standard were enforced, a search may be reasonable despite the absence of such suspicion. See Skinner v. Railway Labor Executives' Assn., 489 U.S. 602 (1989) [approving of drug testing of railway employees involved in train accidents or safety incidents]; United States v. Martinez-Fuerte, 428 U.S. 543 (1976) [brief suspicionless stops of vehicles for questioning at immigration checkpoint at fixed location]. We need not apply these precedents, however, to sustain the actions of the school authorities in the instant case.

* [Footnote 8 of the *T.L.O.* opinion reads as follows: "We do not decide whether individualized suspicion is an essential element of the reasonableness standard we adopt for searches by school authorities. In other contexts, however, we have held that although some quantum of individualized suspicion is usually a prerequisite to a constitutional search or seizure, . . . the Fourth Amendment imposes no irreducible requirement of such suspicion." — EDS.]

Because appellant's diminished expectation of privacy was so clearly outweighed by the governmental interest in interdicting the infusion of weapons in the schools, we think the "unusual" metallic thud heard when the book bag was flung down — quite evidently suggesting to the school security officer the possibility that it might contain a weapon — was sufficient justification for the investigative touching of the outside of the bag, thus rendering that limited intrusion reasonable (and not based on mere whim or caprice) for constitutional purposes. Our application in the instant case of a graduated standard of reasonableness is, of course, sanctioned by and premised on the minimal nature of the search, and that it was conducted by school officials for the special needs of school security and not for a criminal investigative purpose. Once the touching of the outer surface of the bag revealed the presence of a gun-like object inside, school authorities had a reasonable suspicion of a violation of law justifying the search of the contents of the bag.

[Despite] vague professions to the contrary, the dissent is contending that reasonable suspicion is a constitutional floor for purposes of all types of searches, however limited, in a school setting or elsewhere, and irrespective of who conducts the search. [The dissent] supports this position by reliance on Terry v. Ohio, 392 U.S. 1 (1968), and [related New York cases]. The Supreme Court in *Terry* described the intrusion in that case as "a careful exploration of the outer surfaces of a person's clothing all over his or her body in an attempt to find weapons" and characterized it as "a serious intrusion upon the sanctity of the person, which may inflict great indignity."[The Court called the frisk a "limited search" only because] it must be limited to that which is necessary for the discovery of weapons which might be used to harm the officer or others nearby.

People v. Diaz, 612 N.E.2d 298 (N.Y. 1993), declined to extend the *Terry* warrantless search exception to a frisk disclosing other forms of contraband. "Once an officer has concluded that no weapon is present, the search is over and there is no authority for further intrusion." *Diaz* and *Terry* simply do not apply to a less intrusive touching of the outside of a book bag by school personnel, after possession of the bag had been lawfully relinquished.... Thus, Family Court's denial of appellant's motion to suppress should be upheld....

TITONE, J., dissenting.

Acknowledging that there was not even a "reasonable suspicion" of criminality, the Court nevertheless holds that the school security guard was entitled to conduct a search of appellant's book bag. In so ruling, the Court has reduced the privacy protections of the Fourth Amendment and of article I, §12 of the State Constitution below all previously recognized minimum thresholds. While I too am horrified by the recent escalation of deadly weapons in the public schools, I cannot agree that the problem should be remedied by a contraction of even the minimal privacy rights that the Supreme Court has accorded to school children, particularly when there exist other, less intrusive remedies....

The teaching of New Jersey v. T.L.O., on which the majority places heavy reliance, is that search warrants are not constitutionally required for school searches and that such searches may be justified by a lesser showing of reasonable suspicion. Nothing in *T.L.O.,* however, suggests that the serious intrusion of a search may be upheld on even less than reasonable suspicion, much less on the gossamer thread of what the Court has labeled an "unusual" metallic thud....

The majority begins its analysis with the premise that the "investigative touching" of the outside of appellant's book bag was somehow "far less intrusive" than other types of searches. [But] an investigative touching of a closed container requires a degree of pinching, squeezing or probing beyond the limited intrusion allowed under Terry v. Ohio. . . .

The majority also attempts to justify its decision on the theory that appellant had only a "minimal" expectation of privacy "regarding the outer touching of his school bag" when he left it with a security officer pursuant to a school policy. This sweeping conclusion, however, remains unexplained. Significantly, the Supreme Court [in *T.L.O.*] has specifically rejected the contention that a child has a drastically diminished expectation of privacy in articles of personal property that are carried into school. . . .

A further reason offered by the majority for reducing the quantum of information necessary to conduct a school search such as this one is the unquestionably compelling need to prevent the introduction of hand guns and other lethal weapons into the schools. I find this aspect of the majority's rationale unconvincing for several reasons. First, the reduction of students' privacy rights that the majority sanctions is not narrowly tailored to address weapon-related criminal activities. While the search in this case happened to disclose a weapon, the sequence of events that led to that disclosure here could just as easily lead in another case to the discovery of some other illegality or rule infraction such as the possession of drugs or cigarettes. Second, there exist other, more effective means of interdicting weapons in public schools, namely, the installation of metal detectors at the front door. . . .

Third, and most importantly, the constitutional privacy guarantees in our Federal and State Constitutions exist precisely to protect citizens from governmental overreaching in the name of the exigencies of law enforcement. [The majority's rationale is] dangerous, since the same rationale may be trotted out to justify virtually any governmental excess that is aimed at a currently troublesome or rampant form of crime. [T]he need for judicial intervention to bolster the privacy protections would concomitantly increase, rather than diminish, with an increase in the public pressure on law enforcement authorities to take all necessary steps to obliterate a new crime threat. . . .

Finally, even if it is assumed that some lesser showing than the reasonable suspicion approved by the Supreme Court is permissible in these circumstances, the majority has not given any indication of the nature of that showing or of what the lower limits of that showing might be. . . . If, as the majority admits, the "thud" was not sufficient to furnish reasonable suspicion that the bag contained a gun, it is difficult to see how that "thud" could have "evidently suggest[ed] to the school security officer the possibility that [the bag] might contain a weapon." The distinction between a "reasonable suspicion" and an "evident suggestion" is not at all clear to me and will probably be even less meaningful to the school authorities who have to implement this new standard. The significance of the majority's reference to a "premonition" that is "less rigorous" than reasonable suspicion is even more opaque.

The closest the majority has come to actually objectifying the standard it has used is its characterization of the "thud" the guard heard as "unusual." However, what made this sound so "unusual" is far from clear. Students' book bags routinely contain such unexceptional items as make-up cases, portable cassette players and other consumer electronic devices, all of which would likely produce a metallic "thud" when dropped on a hard surface such as a counter. Even more importantly, the "unusual" nature of an event or circumstance does not provide a sound basis for a search of an individual's personal effects. Without more, such an amorphous touchstone would permit intrusions on the most arbitrary of predicates, including a student's "unusual" manner of dress, gait or speech.

. . . While we all have a vital interest in preventing weapons from entering our public school classrooms, that interest could have been served in this case without seriously undermining the student's constitutional rights by either asking the student about the contents of his bag upon his return or by insisting that he empty it or leave it with the guard before re-entering the building. In any event, while I do not advocate anything as sweeping as an over-all constitutional floor of "reasonable suspicion" that would be applicable in all situations, I cannot concur in the majority's decision to sustain this search on a showing that falls well below the minimum requirements approved by the Supreme Court for searches conducted on school premises. Accordingly, I dissent. . . .

OKLAHOMA STATUTES TIT. 70, §24-102

The superintendent, principal, teacher, or security personnel of any public school in the State of Oklahoma, upon reasonable suspicion, shall have the authority to detain and search or authorize the search, of any pupil or property in the possession of the pupil when said pupil is on any school premises, or while in transit under the authority of the school, or while attending any function sponsored or authorized by the school, for dangerous weapons, controlled dangerous substances, . . . intoxicating beverages, . . . or for missing or stolen property if said property be reasonably suspected to have been taken from a pupil, a school employee or the school during school activities. The search shall be conducted by a person of the same sex as the person being searched and shall be witnessed by at least one other authorized person, said person to be of the same sex if practicable.

The extent of any search conducted pursuant to this section shall be reasonably related to the objective of the search and not excessively intrusive in light of the age and sex of the student and the nature of the infraction. In no event shall a strip search of a student be allowed. No student's clothing, except cold weather outerwear, shall be removed prior to or during the conduct of any warrantless search. . . .

Pupils shall not have any reasonable expectation of privacy towards school administrators or teachers in the contents of a school locker, desk, or other school property. School personnel shall have access to school lockers, desks, and other school property in order to properly supervise the welfare of pupils. School lockers, desks, and other areas of school facilities may be opened and examined by school officials at any time and no reason shall be necessary for such search. Schools shall inform pupils in the student discipline code that they have no reasonable expectation of privacy rights towards school officials in school lockers, desks, or other school property.

Notes

1. *Lesser protections in school: majority position.* The decision of the U.S. Supreme Court in New Jersey v. T.L.O., 469 U.S. 325 (1985), reached the same conclusion as

had many of the state courts considering earlier challenges to searches by school officials. Because of the special environment of the school, these courts concluded that neither a warrant nor probable cause was necessary to justify a search by school officials, even if the evidence found during the search ultimately led to a criminal or juvenile conviction. Instead, reasonable suspicion was all that was typically necessary to support a valid search. See also Safford Unified School District #1 v. Redding, 129 S. Ct. 2633 (2009) (search of 13-year-old student's underwear for prescription pain killer without probable cause was unreasonable).

State courts and legislatures visiting this question have continued to take the position that warrants and probable cause are unnecessary in this environment; the statutes printed above are typical in this respect. See State v. Best, 987 A.2d 605 (N.J. 2010) (reasonable suspicion can support search of automobile in school lot for drugs); cf. In re Randy G., 28 P.3d 239 (Cal. 2001) (reasonable suspicion not required to justify school security officer's temporary detention of student).

2. *Individualized suspicion, less than reasonable.* The New York court in *Gregory M.* allowed a search to go forward on the basis of information about an individual student (a backpack making a "thud") that did not amount to reasonable suspicion. Do you agree with the court that the "thud" was not enough for reasonable suspicion? Instead of expanding its own definition of reasonable suspicion, the court decided to recognize a lower level of suspicion in the school context, "evident suggestion." What does the court accomplish (if anything) by creating a new category rather than expanding an old one? Should the new standard apply to exterior touching of purses and backpacks outside the school setting?

3. *Searches of school-owned areas.* School authorities grant students access to lockers and other areas for storage of personal property; sometimes school administrators inform students (either by posting signs or by providing individual notice) that they might search the lockers from time to time. See New Jersey v. T.L.O., 469 U.S. at 338 n.5 (reserving question of proper standard for searches of lockers and desks); Md. Educ. Code §7-308 (authorizes searches of school-owned areas); S.C. Stat. §59-63-1120 (search of school property or student's personal belongings). Under such circumstances, is it reasonable for a student to expect any privacy at all in the locker area? What if the school assumes but does not announce its power to search lockers and exercises that power periodically? Would the same analysis apply to searches of dormitory rooms by school officials in state-supported universities?

4. *School officials as criminal law enforcers.* Part of the justification that courts often give for the relaxed requirements for valid searches in schools is the noncriminal purpose of the searches. School administrators can conduct searches based on reasonable suspicion of a violation of "either the law or the rules of the school." *T.L.O.*, 469 U.S. at 341. But what happens if law enforcement officials approach school officials and ask them to conduct the search? What if the law enforcement agent who initiates the search is stationed full time at the school? Most courts have used the probable cause standard for searches carried out by school officials at the request of the police. Courts use the reasonable suspicion standard for searches initiated by a police officer assigned full time or part time as a liaison to the school. See People v. Dilworth, 661 N.E.2d 310 (Ill. 1996). Should it matter whether the searching police officer has a regular relationship with the school? For further exploration of the variety of state court applications of this standard, including the permissible scope of searches in the school context, see the web extension for this chapter at *http://www.crimpro.com/extension/ch04*.

Would your analysis change if school officials have a general duty to cooperate with criminal law enforcement rather than an intent to do so in a particular case? For instance, Tenn. Code Ann. §49-6-4209 imposes on school officials the legal duty to help enforce the criminal law: "It is the duty of a school principal who has reasonable suspicion to believe, either as a result of a search or otherwise, that any student is committing or has committed any violation of [criminal laws against possession of weapons or drugs], upon the school ground . . . to report [the] suspicion to the appropriate law enforcement officer." Searches in the school context have attracted the attention of about 20 state legislatures. A few statutes place limits on who can conduct searches, or the crimes to be investigated. Others require schools to notify parents about any searches, or to develop a standard search "plan."

Problem 4-4. Gun Lockers

One Friday night in November, students at Madison High School reported hearing gunshots as they left the school following a basketball game. School security guards found spent casings on school grounds the next day. By the following Monday morning, the school staff and security personnel were receiving more reports of guns present in the school building and on school buses, and rumors that a shootout would occur at the school that day. Some staff members and students asked to leave the school out of fear for their safety.

The school principal, Jude, ordered school security personnel to begin a random search of student lockers as a preventive measure while he interviewed selected students. The public school handbook indicates that "lockers are the property of the school system and subject to inspection as determined necessary or appropriate." Students are prohibited from putting private locks on their lockers.

Siena, a Madison High School security aide, searched the school lockers. Using a pass key, he opened the lockers and visually inspected the lockers' contents, moving some articles to see more clearly, and patted down coats in the lockers. Siena did not search every student locker. He chose lockers initially on the lower level of the building, where the largest crowds gathered. He also took care to search the lockers of any known "problem" students and any locker where he saw groups of students congregating.

Altogether, Siena conducted between 75 and 100 locker searches before he opened Baker's locker. At the time, Siena did not know who was assigned to the locker. Baker did not have a history of prior weapon violations, nor did the school officials suspect his involvement in the recent gun incidents. Siena removed a coat from the locker and immediately believed it to be unusually heavy. He found a gun in the coat.

Was the search legal? How would you resolve the case under the constitutional standards described in the *Gregory M.* case? Under the Oklahoma statute reprinted above? Would your analysis change if you knew that the FBI estimates that nearly 100,000 students carry guns to school every day? See Isiah B. v. State, 500 N.W.2d 637 (Wis. 1993).

■ BOARD OF EDUCATION OF INDEPENDENT SCHOOL DISTRICT NO. 92 OF POTTAWATOMIE COUNTY v. LINDSAY EARLS

536 U.S. 822 (2002)

THOMAS, J.*

The Student Activities Drug Testing Policy implemented by the Board of Education of Independent School District No. 92 of Pottawatomie County requires all students who participate in competitive extracurricular activities to submit to drug testing. Because this Policy reasonably serves the School District's important interest in detecting and preventing drug use among its students, we hold that it is constitutional.

I.

The city of Tecumseh, Oklahoma, is a rural community located approximately 40 miles southeast of Oklahoma City. . . . In the fall of 1998, the School District adopted the Student Activities Drug Testing Policy (Policy), which requires all middle and high school students to consent to drug testing in order to participate in any extracurricular activity. In practice, the Policy has been applied only to competitive extracurricular activities sanctioned by the Oklahoma Secondary Schools Activities Association, such as the Academic Team, Future Farmers of America, Future Homemakers of America, band, choir, pom pom, cheerleading, and athletics. Under the Policy, students are required to take a drug test before participating in an extracurricular activity, must submit to random drug testing while participating in that activity, and must agree to be tested at any time upon reasonable suspicion. The urinalysis tests are designed to detect only the use of illegal drugs, including amphetamines, marijuana, cocaine, opiates, and barbituates, not medical conditions or the presence of authorized prescription medications. . . .

Respondent Lindsay Earls was a member of the show choir, the marching band, the Academic Team, and the National Honor Society. Respondent Daniel James sought to participate in the Academic Team. Together with their parents, Earls and James brought a 42 U.S.C. §1983 action against the School District, challenging the Policy both on its face and as applied to their participation in extracurricular activities. They alleged that the Policy violates the Fourth Amendment as incorporated by the Fourteenth Amendment and requested injunctive and declarative relief. [The District Court granted summary judgment to the School District, but the Tenth Circuit reversed.]

II. . . .

Searches by public school officials, such as the collection of urine samples, implicate Fourth Amendment interests. We must therefore review the School District's Policy for "reasonableness," which is the touchstone of the constitutionality of a governmental search. In the criminal context, reasonableness usually requires a showing of probable cause. The probable-cause standard, however, is peculiarly

* [Chief Justice Rehnquist and Justices Scalia, Kennedy, and Breyer joined in this opinion. — EDS.]

related to criminal investigations and may be unsuited to determining the reasonableness of administrative searches where the Government seeks to *prevent* the development of hazardous conditions. The Court has also held that a warrant and finding of probable cause are unnecessary in the public school context because such requirements "would unduly interfere with the maintenance of the swift and informal disciplinary procedures [that are] needed." New Jersey v. T.L.O., 469 U.S. 325, 340-41 (1985).

Given that the School District's Policy is not in any way related to the conduct of criminal investigations, respondents do not contend that the School District requires probable cause before testing students for drug use. Respondents instead argue that drug testing must be based at least on some level of individualized suspicion. It is true that we generally determine the reasonableness of a search by balancing the nature of the intrusion on the individual's privacy against the promotion of legitimate governmental interests. But we have long held that the Fourth Amendment imposes no irreducible requirement of individualized suspicion. In certain limited circumstances, the Government's need to discover such latent or hidden conditions, or to prevent their development, is sufficiently compelling to justify the intrusion on privacy entailed by conducting such searches without any measure of individualized suspicion. Treasury Employees v. Von Raab, 489 U.S. 656 (1989) [allowing drug testing of customs employees in drug enforcement positions]; Skinner v. Railway Labor Executives' Assn., 489 U.S. 602 (1989) [allowing drug testing of railway employees after train accidents]. Therefore, in the context of safety and administrative regulations, a search unsupported by probable cause may be reasonable when "special needs, beyond the normal need for law enforcement, make the warrant and probable-cause requirement impracticable." *T.L.O.* at 351.

Significantly, this Court has previously held that "special needs" inhere in the public school context. While schoolchildren do not shed their constitutional rights when they enter the schoolhouse, "Fourth Amendment rights . . . are different in public schools than elsewhere; the 'reasonableness' inquiry cannot disregard the schools' custodial and tutelary responsibility for children." Vernonia School Dist. 47J v. Acton, 515 U.S. 646, 656 (1995). In particular, a finding of individualized suspicion may not be necessary when a school conducts drug testing.

In *Vernonia,* this Court held that the suspicionless drug testing of athletes was constitutional. The Court, however, did not simply authorize all school drug testing, but rather conducted a fact-specific balancing of the intrusion on the children's Fourth Amendment rights against the promotion of legitimate governmental interests. Applying the principles of *Vernonia* to the somewhat different facts of this case, we conclude that Tecumseh's Policy is also constitutional.

A.

We first consider the nature of the privacy interest allegedly compromised by the drug testing. As in *Vernonia,* the context of the public school environment serves as the backdrop for the analysis of the privacy interest at stake and the reasonableness of the drug testing policy in general. A student's privacy interest is limited in a public school environment where the State is responsible for maintaining discipline, health, and safety. Schoolchildren are routinely required to submit to physical examinations and vaccinations against disease. Securing order in the school environment sometimes requires that students be subjected to greater controls than those appropriate for adults.

Respondents argue that because children participating in nonathletic extracurricular activities are not subject to regular physicals and communal undress, they have a stronger expectation of privacy than the athletes tested in *Vernonia.* [However], students who participate in competitive extracurricular activities voluntarily subject themselves to many of the same intrusions on their privacy as do athletes. Some of these clubs and activities require occasional off-campus travel and communal undress. All of them have their own rules and requirements for participating students that do not apply to the student body as a whole. For example, each of the competitive extracurricular activities governed by the Policy must abide by the rules of the Oklahoma Secondary Schools Activities Association, and a faculty sponsor monitors the students for compliance with the various rules dictated by the clubs and activities. . . . We therefore conclude that the students affected by this Policy have a limited expectation of privacy.

B.

Next, we consider the character of the intrusion imposed by the Policy. Urination is an excretory function traditionally shielded by great privacy. But the degree of intrusion on one's privacy caused by collecting a urine sample depends upon the manner in which production of the urine sample is monitored. Under the Policy, a faculty monitor waits outside the closed restroom stall for the student to produce a sample and must "listen for the normal sounds of urination in order to guard against tampered specimens and to insure an accurate chain of custody." . . . This procedure is virtually identical to that reviewed in *Vernonia*. . . .

In addition, the Policy clearly requires that the test results be kept in confidential files separate from a student's other educational records and released to school personnel only on a "need to know" basis. Respondents nonetheless contend that the intrusion on students' privacy is significant because the Policy fails to protect effectively against the disclosure of confidential information and, specifically, that the school "has been careless in protecting that information: for example, the Choir teacher looked at students' prescription drug lists and left them where other students could see them." But the choir teacher is someone with a "need to know," because during off-campus trips she needs to know what medications are taken by her students. . . . This one example of alleged carelessness hardly increases the character of the intrusion.

Moreover, the test results are not turned over to any law enforcement authority. Nor do the test results here lead to the imposition of discipline or have any academic consequences. Rather, the only consequence of a failed drug test is to limit the student's privilege of participating in extracurricular activities. Indeed, a student may test positive for drugs twice and still be allowed to participate in extracurricular activities. . . . Given the minimally intrusive nature of the sample collection and the limited uses to which the test results are put, we conclude that the invasion of students' privacy is not significant.

C.

Finally, this Court must consider the nature and immediacy of the government's concerns and the efficacy of the Policy in meeting them. This Court has already articulated in detail the importance of the governmental concern in preventing drug use by schoolchildren. The drug abuse problem among our Nation's youth has hardly abated since *Vernonia* was decided in 1995. In fact, evidence suggests that it has only grown worse. As in *Vernonia,* "the necessity for the State to act is magnified by the fact that this evil is being visited not just upon individuals at large, but upon children for whom it has undertaken a special responsibility of care and direction." The health and safety risks identified in *Vernonia* apply with equal force to Tecumseh's children. Indeed, the nationwide drug epidemic makes the war against drugs a pressing concern in every school.

Additionally, the School District in this case has presented specific evidence of drug use at Tecumseh schools. Teachers testified that they had seen students who appeared to be under the influence of drugs and that they had heard students speaking openly about using drugs. A drug dog found marijuana cigarettes near the school parking lot. Police officers once found drugs or drug paraphernalia in a car driven by a Future Farmers of America member. And the school board president reported that people in the community were calling the board to discuss the "drug situation." We decline to second-guess the finding of the District Court that "viewing the evidence as a whole, it cannot be reasonably disputed that the School District was faced with a 'drug problem' when it adopted the Policy." . . .

We also reject respondents' argument that drug testing must presumptively be based upon an individualized reasonable suspicion of wrongdoing because such a testing regime would be less intrusive. [We] question whether testing based on individualized suspicion in fact would be less intrusive. Such a regime would place an additional burden on public school teachers who are already tasked with the difficult job of maintaining order and discipline. A program of individualized suspicion might unfairly target members of unpopular groups. The fear of lawsuits resulting from such targeted searches may chill enforcement of the program, rendering it ineffective in combating drug use. In any case, this Court has repeatedly stated that reasonableness under the Fourth Amendment does not require employing the least intrusive means, because the logic of such elaborate less-restrictive-alternative arguments could raise insuperable barriers to the exercise of virtually all search-and-seizure powers. . . .

III.

Within the limits of the Fourth Amendment, local school boards must assess the desirability of drug testing schoolchildren. In upholding the constitutionality of the Policy, we express no opinion as to its wisdom. Rather, we hold only that Tecumseh's Policy is a reasonable means of furthering the School District's important interest in preventing and deterring drug use among its schoolchildren. . . .

BREYER, J., concurring.

. . . When trying to resolve this kind of close question involving the interpretation of constitutional values, I believe it important that the school board provided an opportunity for the airing of these differences at public meetings designed to give the entire community the opportunity to be able to participate in developing the drug policy. The board used this democratic, participatory process to uncover and to resolve differences, giving weight to the fact that the process, in this instance, revealed little, if any, objection to the proposed testing program.

[A] contrary reading of the Constitution, as requiring "individualized suspicion" in this public school context, could well lead schools to push the boundaries of "individualized suspicion" to its outer limits, using subjective criteria that may "unfairly target members of unpopular groups," or leave those whose behavior is slightly abnormal stigmatized in the minds of others. . . .

GINSBURG, J., dissenting.*

Seven years ago, in Vernonia School Dist. 47J v. Acton, 515 U.S. 646 (1995), this Court determined that a school district's policy of randomly testing the urine of its student athletes for illicit drugs did not violate the Fourth Amendment. In so ruling, the Court emphasized that drug use "increased the risk of sports-related injury" and that Vernonia's athletes were the "leaders" of an aggressive local "drug culture" that had reached "epidemic proportions." Today, the Court relies upon *Vernonia* to permit a school district with a drug problem its superintendent repeatedly described as "not major" to test the urine of an academic team member solely by reason of her participation in a nonathletic, competitive extracurricular activity — participation associated with neither special dangers from, nor particular predilections for, drug use. . . . The particular testing program upheld today is not reasonable, it is capricious, even perverse: Petitioners' policy targets for testing a student population least likely to be at risk from illicit drugs and their damaging effects. I therefore dissent.

I.

[The Court points to] the voluntary character of both interscholastic athletics and other competitive extracurricular activities. . . . The comparison is enlightening. While extracurricular activities are "voluntary" in the sense that they are not required for graduation, they are part of the school's educational program; for that reason, the petitioner . . . is justified in expending public resources to make them available. Participation in such activities is a key component of school life, essential in reality for students applying to college, and, for all participants, a significant contributor to the breadth and quality of the educational experience. Students "volunteer" for extracurricular pursuits in the same way they might volunteer for honors classes: They subject themselves to additional requirements, but they do so in order to take full advantage of the education offered them.

Voluntary participation in athletics has a distinctly different dimension: Schools regulate student athletes discretely because competitive school sports by their nature require communal undress and, more important, expose students to physical risks that schools have a duty to mitigate. . . . Competitive extracurricular activities other than athletics, however, serve students of all manner: the modest and shy along with the bold and uninhibited. Activities of the kind plaintiff-respondent Lindsay Earls pursued — choir, show choir, marching band, and academic team — afford opportunities to gain self-assurance. . . .

Finally, the nature and immediacy of the governmental concern faced by the Vernonia School District dwarfed that confronting Tecumseh administrators. Vernonia initiated its drug testing policy in response to an alarming situation: "[A] large segment of the student body, particularly those involved in interscholastic athletics, was in a state of rebellion . . . fueled by alcohol and drug abuse as well as the students' misperceptions about the drug culture." Tecumseh, by contrast, repeatedly

* [Justices Stevens, O'Connor, and Souter joined in this opinion. — EDS.]

reported to the Federal Government during the period leading up to the adoption of the policy that "types of drugs [other than alcohol and tobacco] including controlled dangerous substances, are present [in the schools] but have not identified themselves as major problems at this time." 1998-1999 Tecumseh School's Application for Funds under the Safe and Drug-Free Schools and Communities Program. . . .

Nationwide, students who participate in extracurricular activities are significantly less likely to develop substance abuse problems than are their less-involved peers. See, *e.g.*, N. Zill, C. Nord, & L. Loomis, Adolescent Time Use, Risky Behavior, and Outcomes 52 (1995) (tenth graders "who reported spending no time in school-sponsored activities were . . . 49 percent more likely to have used drugs" than those who spent 1-4 hours per week in such activities). Even if students might be deterred from drug use in order to preserve their extracurricular eligibility, it is at least as likely that other students might forgo their extracurricular involvement in order to avoid detection of their drug use. Tecumseh's policy thus falls short doubly if deterrence is its aim: It invades the privacy of students who need deterrence least, and risks steering students at greatest risk for substance abuse away from extracurricular involvement that potentially may palliate drug problems.

II.

[Schools'] tutelary obligations to their students require them to "teach by example" by avoiding symbolic measures that diminish constitutional protections. "That [schools] are educating the young for citizenship is reason for scrupulous protection of Constitutional freedoms of the individual, if we are not to strangle the free mind at its source and teach youth to discount important principles of our government as mere platitudes." West Virginia Bd. of Ed. v. Barnette, 319 U.S. 624, 637 (1943). . . .

Notes

1. *Drug testing in schools: majority position.* When the Supreme Court first addressed drug testing in schools in Vernonia School District 47J v. Acton, 515 U.S. 646 (1995), the issue had received little attention in courts or legislatures. The existing statutes and cases validated drug testing of students based on reasonable suspicion of illegal drug use without addressing mandatory random testing. See Tenn. Code Ann. §49-6-4213 (reasonable suspicion testing). In the years between *Vernonia* and *Earls,* very few school districts adopted a policy of random drug testing. See Ronald F. Wright, The Abruptness of *Acton,* 36 Crim. L. Bull. 401 (2000). Do you expect the number of districts adopting this policy to increase more quickly after the *Earls* decision?

A study of 76,000 high school students published in 2003 found that drug testing in schools does not deter drug use among students. Thirty-seven percent of twelfth-graders in schools that tested for drugs said they had smoked marijuana in the last year, compared with 36 percent in schools that did not. The study indicated that about 18 percent of the nation's high schools employed some type of drug testing. See Greg Winter, "Study Finds No Sign That Testing Deters Students' Drug Use," N.Y. Times, May 17, 2003. Does this study suggest to you that schools should spend their limited funds on other forms of drug prevention, or that they should invest more and conduct more reliable and credible urinalysis tests?

If you were sitting on a state supreme court addressing a challenge to a random testing program, would your ruling turn on the types of students subject to the program (for example, all athletes, or all students at particular grade levels)? Would it depend on the uses the school makes of the test results (such as counseling, school sanctions, or criminal prosecution)? See York v. Wahkiakum School District No. 200, 178 P.3d 995 (Wash. 2008) (suspicionless drug testing of student athletes violates state constitution).

2. *Drug testing in other contexts: majority position.* Drug testing occurs more frequently in workplaces than in schools. Some employers require a drug test of all job applicants and probationary employees; among current employees, reasonable suspicion testing is more common. If the employer is a private party, the Fourth Amendment and its state analogs do not apply. Only statutes and common law theories are available to limit the employer's choices, and those statutes tend to regulate but not bar use of random drug testing. See Ariz. Rev. Stat. §23-493.04 (allowing testing "for any job-related purposes"); Minn. Stat. §181.951 (allowing reasonable suspicion testing for all employees and random testing for "safety sensitive" employees). For further exploration of the variety of state court applications of this standard, see the web extension for this chapter at *http://www.crimpro.com/extension/ch04*.

As for public employers, courts have upheld testing programs against most challenges. It is clear that when a public employer has reasonable suspicion of drug use by an employee, drug testing is acceptable. Specific incidents (such as an accident involving a train) might give the employer reasonable suspicion, or at least some individualized suspicion, to test for drug use among the employees involved in the incident. See Skinner v. Railway Labor Executives' Assn., 489 U.S. 602 (1989). Courts have even approved random or routine drug testing, at least for job categories in which drug use presents a special concern for the employer. In National Treasury Employees Union v. Von Raab, 489 U.S. 656 (1989), the Court upheld a program requiring a urinalysis from any Customs Service employee seeking a transfer to a position involving drug interdiction or the carrying of a firearm. Does this opinion suggest that a police department could insist on random drug testing for all of its officers? See McCloskey v. Honolulu Police Department, 799 P.2d 953 (Haw. 1990) (upholding such a program); Guiney v. Police Commissioner of Boston, 582 N.E.2d 523 (Mass. 1991) (striking down such a program). For all members of the Narcotics Bureau within the department? See Delaraba v. Police Dept, 632 N.E. 2d 1251 (N.Y. 1994) (upholding such a program). Collective labor agreements will sometimes limit the power of an employer to implement drug testing. See Fraternal Order of Police, Miami Lodge 20 v. City of Miami, 609 So. 2d 31 (Fla. 1992).

Would you argue that some public employees (within the police department or otherwise) should be subject to drug testing only after officials obtain a warrant based on probable cause? See Chandler v. Miller, 520 U.S. 305 (1997) (Georgia's requirement that candidates for state office pass drug test did not fit within "closely guarded category" of constitutionally permissible suspicionless searches, and was not sufficiently related to requirements of public office).

Problem 4-5. Jail Cell Search

McCoy's first two trials on charges of armed robbery and attempted murder of a police officer ended in mistrials. After his third trial, the jury convicted McCoy, but an appellate court reversed the conviction. On the eve of the scheduled date for the fourth trial, the assistant state attorney assigned to the case, Ketchum, and a police officer, Hagerman, went to McCoy's cell at the local pretrial detention facility.

Hagerman, following instructions from Ketchum, first removed McCoy and his cellmate and then searched the cell for anything McCoy may have written that might contain incriminating statements. As Hagerman searched, Ketchum stood in the doorway of the cell. Hagerman found on a table in the cell a number of depositions, transcripts, offense reports, and personal notes. He seized McCoy's copies of depositions of four state witnesses, which consisted of some 70 pages and included McCoy's copious handwritten notes in the margins. Several of the handwritten notes were incriminating.

McCoy presented no particular security problems at the detention facility, and there was no concrete information suggesting that the papers in his cell would contain incriminating information. How will the trial court rule on his motion to suppress the handwritten notes found on the depositions? Compare McCoy v. State, 639 So. 2d 163 (Fla. Dist. Ct. App. 1994).

Notes

1. *Searches of prison cells: majority position.* State and federal appellate courts have traditionally given a lot of latitude to the decisions of the administrators of prisons, jails, and other detention facilities. They point out the exceptional need for order in such a setting. The Supreme Court in Hudson v. Palmer, 468 U.S. 517 (1984), made a particularly strong statement of this view when it held that the Fourth Amendment does not place any limits on a prison guard's search of the prison cell of a convicted offender. The prisoner in that case claimed that a prison guard had searched his cell and destroyed his property solely to harass the prisoner. The Court replied:

> A right of privacy in traditional Fourth Amendment terms is fundamentally incompatible with the close and continual surveillance of inmates and their cells required to ensure institutional security and internal order. We are satisfied that society would insist that the prisoner's expectation of privacy always yield to what must be considered the paramount interest in institutional security.

468 U.S. at 527-528. A concern for the security and order of prisons led the Court to hold that "the Fourth Amendment has no applicability to a prison cell." Virtually all state courts to consider this question have followed the *Hudson* case and concluded that their analogous state constitutional provisions also have no application to searches of prison cells. Should the exemption from the Fourth Amendment apply only when searches are motivated by the need for order and security in the jail or prison? If so, how should a court determine what motivated the search?

2. *Pretrial detainees versus convicted offenders.* Some persons confined in a cell have been convicted of a crime, while others have only been accused of a crime. Should a

pretrial detainee have a "reasonable expectation of privacy" in a cell when a convicted offender would not? The Supreme Court spoke indirectly to this issue in Bell v. Wolfish, 441 U.S. 520 (1979), when it held that the Fourth Amendment protects neither sentenced nor pretrial detainees from a prison policy requiring inmates to undergo strip and body cavity searches after all contact visits with non-inmates. The Court stated that the security concerns at issue for convicted offenders also exist for pretrial detainees. State courts have split on the question whether constitutional privacy protections apply differently to pretrial detainees and convicted offenders. See DeLancie v. Superior Court, 647 P.2d 142 (Cal. 1982) (invalidating sheriff's routine practice of monitoring conversations between pretrial detainees and visitors); State v. Martin, 367 S.E.2d 618 (N.C. 1988) (search of pretrial detainee's cell by jailer not subject to Fourth Amendment reasonableness test).

In Samson v. California, 547 U.S. 843 (2006), the court heard a challenge to a state law that required parolees to submit to warrantless, suspicionless searches at any time. The Court held that the law did not violate the Fourth Amendment, drawing a parallel between parolees and prisoners, and saying that the public's strong interest in supervising parolees outweighs the parolees' diminished expectation of privacy. Does the lack of a reasonable expectation of privacy, as announced in Hudson v. Palmer, derive from the nature of the person's status (convicted of a crime) or from the nature of the place (a prison)?

3. *Places categorically out of reach of the constitution?* Do *Hudson* and the cases following its lead establish "Fourth-Amendment-free zones"? If prison officials are free to act without legal limits, how will this affect the present or future conduct of the prisoners being punished for violating the criminal law? Are there any alternatives? Consider State v. Berard, 576 A.2d 118 (Vt. 1990) (search and seizure provision in state constitution applies to prison searches, but "special needs" of prison environment allow warrantless random searches of cells). Is *Berard* an improvement over *Hudson* from a prisoner's point of view? From society's point of view? Cf. United States v. Knights, 534 U.S. 112 (2001) (constitution allows police with reasonable suspicion of criminal behavior to conduct a warrantless search of home of a probationer who is subject to a probation condition authorizing warrantless searches).

In Ferguson v. City of Charleston, 532 U.S. 67 (2001), the Supreme Court returned to the question of drug testing in special institutional settings. A state hospital instructed its staff to identify pregnant patients at risk for drug abuse, to test those patients for drug abuse, and to report positive tests to the police. Patients who tested positive for cocaine use were arrested and prosecuted for child abuse. The Court held that this testing was an unreasonable search. Given the amount of cooperation between the hospital and criminal prosecutors in this program, the tests served no "special needs" apart from the State's "general law enforcement interest." The central purpose of the program was the use of criminal law enforcement to coerce patients into substance abuse treatment. Drug testing in these circumstances was a search that was not accomplished through consent and not supported by probable cause.

C. "PAPERS"

There are several methods available to the government to inspect "papers" during criminal law enforcement. One method, which we will explore in Chapter 10, is to issue a subpoena from a grand jury or an administrative agency. The government might also rely on statutory requirements for certain types of businesses to maintain records and to allow the government access to those records. On the other hand, if the government attempts to search and seize papers without using a subpoena or a record-keeping requirement, it must comply with traditional Fourth Amendment requirements: showing probable cause to believe that the papers will provide evidence of a crime, and perhaps obtaining a warrant.

Are there some papers, however, that are so intimately personal that the government cannot obtain them, even if it demonstrates probable cause and obtains a warrant? We start with one of the most important early Supreme Court cases on the Fourth Amendment. The answer that the Court gave in 1886 to the question of "private papers" searches is not the same answer that legal institutions, by and large, give today. This classic opinion, however, does offer us a chance to consider an alternative form of privacy protection, in which rules would absolutely bar the government from searching some areas, regardless of the justifications it might have to conduct the search.

■ EDWARD BOYD v. UNITED STATES
116 U.S. 616 (1886)

BRADLEY, J.*

[The government brought this forfeiture action to obtain 35 cases of glass that Boyd and others allegedly imported from England without paying the proper customs duties. At trial, it became important to show the quantity and value of the glass contained in 29 cases previously imported. The trial court ordered Boyd to produce the invoices for the cases. He did so, but objected to the constitutionality of the 1874 statute giving the judge the power to make such an order. Other provisions of the same statute, which were passed in 1863 and 1867, empowered the judge to issue a warrant to a marshal or customs collector to enter private premises and obtain any papers, books, or invoices that might tend to prove the government's allegations in a civil forfeiture suit under the customs laws. The jury in this case heard the evidence relating to the invoices and rendered a verdict for the United States.]

The clauses of the Constitution, to which it is contended that these laws are repugnant, are the fourth and fifth amendments. . . . The fifth article, amongst other things, declares that no person "shall be compelled in any criminal case to be a witness against himself." . . .

Is a search and seizure, or, what is equivalent thereto, a compulsory production of a man's private papers, to be used in evidence against him in a proceeding to forfeit his property for alleged fraud against the revenue laws — is such a proceeding for such a purpose an "unreasonable search and seizure" within the meaning of the

* [Justices Field, Harlan, Woods, Matthews, Gray, and Blatchford joined in this opinion. — EDS.]

fourth amendment of the Constitution? Or, is it a legitimate proceeding? It is contended by the counsel for the government, that it is a legitimate proceeding, sanctioned by long usage, and the authority of judicial decision. No doubt long usage, acquiesced in by the courts, goes a long way to prove that there is some plausible ground or reason for it in the law. . . .

But we do not find any long usage, or any contemporary construction of the Constitution, which would justify any of the acts of Congress now under consideration. [The] act of 1863 was the first act in this country, and, we might say, either in this country or in England, so far as we have been able to ascertain, which authorized the search and seizure of a man's private papers, or the compulsory production of them, for the purpose of using them in evidence against him in a criminal case, or in a proceeding to enforce the forfeiture of his property. Even the act under which the obnoxious writs of assistance were issued did not go as far as this, but only authorized the examination of ships and vessels, and persons found therein, for the purpose of finding goods prohibited to be imported or exported, or on which the duties were not paid, and to enter into and search any suspected vaults, cellars, or warehouses for such goods.

The search for and seizure of stolen or forfeited goods, or goods liable to duties and concealed to avoid the payment thereof, are totally different things from a search for and seizure of a man's private books and papers for the purpose of obtaining information therein contained, or of using them as evidence against him. . . . In the one case, the government is entitled to the possession of the property; in the other it is not. The seizure of stolen goods is authorized by the common law; and the seizure of goods forfeited for a breach of the revenue laws, or concealed to avoid the duties payable on them, has been authorized by English statutes for at least two centuries past; and the like seizures have been authorized by our own revenue acts from the commencement of the government. . . .

But, when examined with care, it is manifest that there is a total unlikeness of these official acts and proceedings to that which is now under consideration. In the case of stolen goods, the owner from whom they were stolen is entitled to their possession; and in the case of excisable or dutiable articles, the government has an interest in them for the payment of the duties thereon, and until such duties are paid has a right to keep them under observation, or to pursue and drag them from concealment; and in the case of goods seized on attachment or execution, the creditor is entitled to their seizure in satisfaction of his debt. . . . Whereas, by the proceeding now under consideration, the court attempts to extort from the party his private books and papers to make him liable for a penalty or to forfeit his property.

In order to ascertain the nature of the proceedings intended by the fourth amendment to the Constitution under the terms "unreasonable searches and seizures," it is only necessary to recall the contemporary or then recent history of the controversies on the subject, both in this country and in England. The practice had obtained in the colonies of issuing writs of assistance to the revenue officers, empowering them, in their discretion, to search suspected places for smuggled goods, which James Otis [in 1761] pronounced "the worst instrument of arbitrary power, the most destructive of English liberty, and the fundamental principles of law, that ever was found in an English law book;" since they placed "the liberty of every man in the hands of every petty officer." . . .

These things, and the events which took place in England immediately following the argument about writs of assistance in Boston, were fresh in the memories of those who achieved our independence and established our form of government. [The opinion of Lord Camden in the 1765 case of Entick v. Carrington] is regarded as one of the permanent monuments of the British Constitution, and is quoted as such by the English authorities on that subject down to the present time. As every American statesmen, during our revolutionary and formative period as a nation, was undoubtedly familiar with this monument of English freedom, and considered it as the true and ultimate expression of constitutional law, it may be confidently asserted that its propositions were in the minds of those who framed the fourth amendment to the Constitution, and were considered as sufficiently explanatory of what was meant by unreasonable searches and seizures. . . .

The principles laid down in [Entick v. Carrington] affect the very essence of constitutional liberty and security. They reach farther than the concrete form of the case then before the court, with its adventitious circumstances; they apply to all invasions on the part of the government and its employees of the sanctity of a man's home and the privacies of life. It is not the breaking of his doors, and the rummaging of his drawers, that constitutes the essence of the offence; but it is the invasion of his indefeasible right of personal security, personal liberty and private property [that violates the constitutional principle]. Breaking into a house and opening boxes and drawers are circumstances of aggravation; but any forcible and compulsory extortion of a man's own testimony or of his private papers to be used as evidence to convict him of crime or to forfeit his goods, is within the condemnation of that judgment. In this regard the fourth and fifth amendments run almost into each other.

Can we doubt that when the fourth and fifth amendments to the Constitution of the United States were penned and adopted, the language of Lord Camden was relied on as expressing the true doctrine on the subject of searches and seizures, and as furnishing the true criteria of the reasonable and "unreasonable" character of such seizures? [Could the men who proposed those amendments have approved of statutes such as those at issue here?] It seems to us that the question cannot admit of a doubt. They never would have approved of them. The struggles against arbitrary power in which they had been engaged for more than 20 years, would have been too deeply engraved in their memories to have allowed them to approve of such insidious disguises of the old grievance which they had so deeply abhorred. . . .

We have already noticed the intimate relation between the two amendments. They throw great light on each other. For the "unreasonable searches and seizures" condemned in the fourth amendment are almost always made for the purpose of compelling a man to give evidence against himself, which in criminal cases is condemned in the fifth amendment; and compelling a man "in a criminal case to be a witness against himself," which is condemned in the fifth amendment, throws light on the question as to what is an "unreasonable search and seizure" within the meaning of the fourth amendment. And we have been unable to perceive that the seizure of a man's private books and papers to be used in evidence against him is substantially different from compelling him to be a witness against himself. We think it is within the clear intent and meaning of those terms. . . .

Though the proceeding in question is divested of many of the aggravating incidents of actual search and seizure, yet, as before said, it contains their substance and essence, and effects their substantial purpose. . . . We think that the notice to produce the invoice in this case, the order by virtue of which it was issued, and the law which authorized the order, were unconstitutional and void, and that the inspection by the district attorney of said invoice, when produced in obedience to said notice, and its admission in evidence by the court, were erroneous and unconstitutional proceedings. . . .

MILLER, J., concurring.*

. . . While the framers of the Constitution had their attention drawn, no doubt, to the abuses of this power of searching private houses and seizing private papers, as practiced in England, it is obvious that they only intended to restrain the abuse, while they did not abolish the power. Hence it is only unreasonable searches and seizures that are forbidden, and the means of securing this protection was by abolishing searches under warrants, which were called general warrants, because they authorized searches in any place, for the thing. This was forbidden, while searches founded on affidavits, and made under warrants which described the thing to be searched for, the person and place to be searched, are still permitted. . . .

Notes

1. *The erosion of* Boyd: *property and privacy.* The *Boyd* court notes that the government could seize contraband or proceeds of a crime but not papers containing evidence of a crime, because only in the former cases does the government have a proprietary interest in the item stronger than that of the private party. The constitution, under this reading, reinforces the protections of property law.

The linkage between property law and unreasonable searches has changed. For one thing, as we have seen, the definition of a "search" now depends on the "reasonable expectations of privacy" of the target of the search, and not on whether the government has trespassed on any property interest of the target. Katz v. United States, 389 U.S. 347 (1967). For another thing, most courts have now abandoned a traditional limitation on the search power known as the "mere evidence" rule. Under that rule, the government could search for and seize contraband, instrumentalities, or fruits of crime but not mere evidence of crime. Again, the reasoning was grounded in property law: The government had a superior claim to contraband and the like (which the private party had no right to own), but the private party had a superior claim to innocent property that provided evidence of a crime. The U.S. Supreme Court abandoned the mere evidence rule in Warden v. Hayden, 387 U.S. 294 (1967). Every state now interprets its own constitution to allow such searches.

Why might searches of papers become more common after the rejection of the mere evidence rule? Does the mere evidence rule offer more protection to some classes of search targets than to others? See Eric Schnapper, Unreasonable Searches and Seizures of Papers, 71 Va. L. Rev. 869 (1985).

2. *The erosion of* Boyd: *self-incrimination and unreasonable searches.* The *Boyd* court also suggested that the Fourth and Fifth Amendments throw light on each other, or provide mutually reinforcing protections. A search of a person's papers is equivalent to a demand that the person make incriminating testimony. This aspect of the *Boyd* case has also fallen by the wayside. In several cases, such as Andresen v. Maryland, 427 U.S. 463 (1976), the Supreme Court has declared that a search of a person's

* [Chief Justice Waite joined in this opinion. — EDS.]

documents does not amount to compelled "testimony" because the person created the documents voluntarily and does not have to participate in the government's later search or seizure of the documents. Again, state courts have followed suit.

3. *The erosion of* Boyd: *private papers.* Federal and state courts have left more room to wonder if there is still an absolute bar to the search or seizure of private papers such as diaries. The Supreme Court has allowed searches and seizures of business records, see Andresen v. Maryland, but has not squarely addressed private papers. See Daniel Solove, The First Amendment as Criminal Procedure, 82 N.Y.U.L. Rev.112 (2007).

By and large, state courts have taken the next step to conclude that there is no absolute bar to the search of private papers. See State v. Andrei, 574 A.2d 295 (Me. 1990). Every so often, a court says or intimates that some private papers (so long as the papers themselves were not used to commit a crime) might be beyond the reach of a government search, even if supported by probable cause and a warrant. See State v. Bisaccia, 213 A.2d 185 (N.J. 1965). Georgia has passed an unusual statute protecting "private papers" from searches:

> [A judicial officer] may issue a search warrant for the seizure of the following: (1) Any instruments, articles, or things, including the private papers of any person, which are designed, intended for use, or which have been used in the commission of the offense in connection with which the warrant is issued; . . . or (5) Any item, substance, object, thing, or matter, other than the private papers of any person, which is tangible evidence of the commission of the crime for which probable cause is shown.

Ga. Code Ann. §17-5-21(a). Cf. King v. State, 577 S.E.2d 764 (Ga. 2003) (declines to extend to search warrants an earlier holding that use of subpoena to obtain medical records offends Georgia constitution's privacy protection). Does this statutory protection from searches re-create the now-abandoned requirements of *Boyd*? Would it prevent a search for an illegal lottery ticket? For a list of telephone numbers of purchasers of illegal narcotics? If you were restricting the scope of this statute, how might you define "private" papers? See Sears v. State, 426 S.E.2d 553 (Ga. 1993) (interpreting section to bar search for documents only when covered by privilege, such as attorney-client or doctor-patient).

4. *Extra particularity in search warrants for private papers.* While it is not often that a legal system will absolutely bar all searches for private papers, it is more common to see judges insist on extra particularity in a warrant authorizing a search for books or papers. See Lo-Ji Sales, Inc. v. New York, 442 U.S. 319 (1979); Tattered Cover, Inc. v. City of Thornton, 44 P.3d 1044 (Colo. 2002); compare In re C.T., 999 A.2d 210 (N.H. 2010) (when law enforcement seeks privileged medical records, providers must comply with search warrant by producing records for in camera review, allowing patient and provider opportunity to object; state must demonstrate "essential need" for record). Will a more specific warrant address the special intrusiveness of a search for papers? Consider this argument by Telford Taylor, from his renowned essay on the Fourth Amendment:

> [Where] personal papers are concerned, specificity of category is no real safeguard against the most grievous intrusions on privacy, as was pointed out over two hundred years ago during the House of Commons debates on general warrants: "Even a particular warrant to seize seditious papers alone, without mentioning the titles of them, may

prove highly detrimental, since in that case, all a man's papers must be indiscriminately examined. . . ." Of course, a search for a tiny object, such as a stolen or smuggled diamond, which can be concealed among papers or in some other small recess, may involve much the same kind of ransacking search. But at least in such a case it is unnecessary to read papers. [Two Studies in Constitutional Interpretation 67-68 (1969).]

5. *Private records held by third parties: banking records.* Many types of sensitive personal documents, such as banking records or medical records, are held by institutions on behalf of their customers. When government agents investigating a crime try to obtain these records, does the legal system allow the institution to deny the request? Under the Fourth Amendment, the Supreme Court in United States v. Miller, 425 U.S. 435 (1976), decided that a bank's customer has no reasonable expectation of privacy in records relating to the customer's account:

> All of the documents obtained, including financial statements and deposit slips, contain only information voluntarily conveyed to the banks and exposed to their employees in the ordinary course of business. . . . The depositor takes the risk, in revealing his affairs to another, that the information will be conveyed by that person to the Government.

Two years earlier, the California Supreme Court in Burrows v. Superior Court, 529 P.2d 590 (Cal. 1974), set out an argument in favor of giving bank customers standing to challenge unreasonable searches of bank records relating to their accounts:

> A bank customer's reasonable expectation is that, absent compulsion by legal process, the matters he reveals to the bank will be utilized by the bank only for internal banking purposes. . . . For all practical purposes, the disclosure by individuals or business firms of their financial affairs to a bank is not entirely volitional, since it is impossible to participate in the economic life of contemporary society without maintaining a bank account. In the course of such dealings, a depositor reveals many aspects of his personal affairs, opinions, habits and associations. . . .

State courts have divided on the constitutional question, with a strong minority following *Burrows.* See State v. Thompson, 810 P.2d 415 (Utah 1991) (following *Burrows*); State v. Schultz, 850 P.2d 818 (Kansas 1993) (following *Miller*). See Stephen E. Henderson, Learning from All Fifty States: How to Apply the Fourth Amendment and Its State Analogs to Protect Third Party Information from Unreasonable Search, 55 Cath. U. L. Rev. 373 (2006).

Several legislatures have also declared that banking customers may challenge the reasonableness of government efforts to search their banking records. Congress adopted the Right to Financial Privacy Act, 12 U.S.C. §§3401 et seq., as a repudiation of the *Miller* decision: "The Court did not acknowledge the sensitive nature of these records." 1978 U.S.C.C.A.N. 9305. The act requires that the bank customer have notice and an opportunity to object before the financial institution complies with a subpoena seeking the records. About one-third of the states have enacted an equivalent of the Right to Financial Privacy Act. See, e.g., Mo. Rev. Stat. §§408.683 et seq. We will explore the subpoena power and the gathering of documents in complex investigations in Chapter 10.

Do these statutes and cases provide enough protection by allowing the customer to insist that any search of records be reasonable? Should they provide instead for a much higher level of justification by the government to support a search of banking records (similar to bank secrecy provisions in some other nations)? Would a reinvigorated *Boyd* present an absolute bar to a search of banking records? Would you take the same position on a proposed statute protecting the records relating to movie rentals?

D. "EFFECTS"

We now turn to the final interest mentioned in the text of the Fourth Amendment, "effects." Given the variety of property that falls within the meaning of this phrase, and the variety of places where a search of effects could take place, it is difficult to find a unifying theme for all these searches. There are a few settings, however, in which courts and others have created special search rules about personal property. We begin with the "inventory" practices of police departments, the routine methods they use to process the property of those who are taken into custody. We then survey the complex rules surrounding that most American form of personal property, the automobile.

1. *Inventory Searches*

When police officers take a person into custody, some of his personal property comes with him. When the government holds a person's property, it must use ordinary care to maintain the property; the department therefore may need to keep records of the property. This process of examining and storing personal property can often produce evidence of a crime.

PEOPLE v. CURTIS GIPSON

786 N.E.2d 540 (Ill. 2003)

THOMAS, J.

At issue are two questions concerning inventory searches: (1) whether a police officer's unrebutted testimony about police policy on inventory searches can be sufficient evidence of such a policy if the State does not introduce a written policy into evidence; and (2) whether a policy requiring the police to inventory items of value is sufficient to allow the opening of closed containers if the policy does not specifically mention closed containers.

BACKGROUND

. . . Defendant moved to quash his arrest and to suppress the evidence that was found during a search of his car. At the hearing on the motion to suppress, defendant testified as follows. At 12:25 A.M. on January 8, 1998, defendant was driving home from work. When defendant reached the intersection of Jackson and Homan in Chicago, a police car began to follow him. The police car followed him for several minutes. The police car's lights went on when defendant crossed Kedzie, and defendant pulled over. The police officer approached defendant's car and told defendant that he was driving on a revoked license. Defendant gave the officer his identification and proof of insurance, following which the officer put defendant into the backseat of his squad car and locked it. The officer put some information into his computer and told defendant that if he did not have any outstanding warrants, he was free to go.

According to defendant, the officer never told him that he was under arrest. The officer then got out of the squad car and looked under the hood of defendant's car. He searched the passenger compartment of the car and then came back to the squad car. The officer started typing on his computer again and then went back to defendant's car, took the keys out of the ignition, and opened the trunk. Defendant testified that he had a yellow plastic Ameritech bag tied closed in the trunk. Inside of the Ameritech bag was a black plastic bag, containing rocks of cocaine, that was also tied closed. According to defendant, he never gave the officer permission to search his car, and the officer never told him that the car would be towed or that the officer was conducting an inventory search. The officer never told defendant he was under arrest before he searched the car.

The State presented the testimony of Sergeant David Byrd of the Illinois State Police. Byrd testified that he initially began following defendant's car because it had a cracked windshield. A "registration response" on defendant's license plate revealed that the owner's name was Curtis Gipson and that Gipson's driver's license had been revoked. Byrd pulled over defendant and informed him that the reason for the stop was that the car had a defective windshield and that the car's owner had a revoked license. When defendant confirmed that he was Curtis Gipson, Byrd placed defendant in the back of his squad car.

Once defendant was in the car, Byrd called a tow truck and conducted an inventory search of defendant's vehicle. Byrd explained that the State Police policy is to tow the vehicle when someone is arrested for driving on a revoked license. When a vehicle is towed following an arrest, the police policy is that a tow inventory search should be conducted. When asked to explain the police policy on tow inventory searches, Byrd responded: "We are required to check the passenger compartment and trunk area for any valuables, or just for our own — we don't want anything to leave us that might be of value without checking it first and putting it down on the tow sheet."

When Byrd opened the trunk, he found a yellow Ameritech bag. He opened the bag and noticed two smaller bags inside. He opened these and observed what appeared to be crack cocaine. Byrd testified that he never told defendant that he would be free to go at some point. Rather, defendant was arrested and taken into custody. Byrd gave defendant a ticket for having a cracked windshield and driving on a revoked license.

Following arguments by the attorneys, the trial judge recalled Sergeant Byrd to the stand. The following colloquy ensued:

The Court: You are still under oath, sergeant. Is there a printed procedure regarding towing by the Illinois State police?
The Witness: Yes, there is, your Honor. It's in our policy manual.
The Court: It's in the policy manual?
The Witness: Right, and we teach it to all our cadets when they come out on the road.
The Court: Is it a manual that you might have handy?
The Witness: No, it's a —
The Court: Big?
The Witness: Six hundred pages.
The Court: But it is printed in the police procedure?
The Witness: It is printed, tow searches and vehicles being towed and if I may, the reason we do that is because even if somebody is revoked and if they just said, okay, okay, you are going to write the ticket —
Mr. Draper [defendant's attorney]: Objection, judge.
The Court: Okay, all right.

Following further arguments from counsel, the trial court decided to reserve ruling on the motion until the parties submitted further case law. Two months later, the court granted defendant's motion to suppress. The trial judge stated that the police had no right to tow the car and that State Police policy could not supersede the law. The State filed a motion to reconsider, [arguing] that a lawful inventory search pursuant to State Police policy had occurred. The trial judge responded that he was not sure what the State Police policy was because he had never seen it and the officer might have just given his own interpretation. The trial judge then stated that the police could not use a minor traffic ticket to create a basis for a search and that defendant had only been stopped for "a little, minor thing like a cracked windshield." . . . The court denied the motion to reconsider. . . .

ANALYSIS

On review of a trial court's ruling on a motion to suppress, we accord great deference to the trial court's factual findings, and we will reverse those findings only if they are against the manifest weight of the evidence. However, we review de novo the ultimate legal question of whether suppression is warranted.

The State first argues . . . that there is no constitutional requirement that the State produce the actual written policy. We agree with the State.

An inventory search of a lawfully impounded vehicle is a judicially created exception to the warrant requirement of the fourth amendment. In South Dakota v. Opperman, 428 U.S. 364 (1976), the Supreme Court identified three objectives that are served by allowing inventory searches: (1) protection of the owner's property; (2) protection of the police against claims of lost or stolen property; and (3) protection of the police from potential danger.

In conducting such a search, the police must be acting pursuant to standard police procedures. Colorado v. Bertine, 479 U.S. 367 (1987). A single familiar standard is essential to guide police officers, who have only limited time and expertise to reflect on and balance the social and individual interests involved in the specific circumstances they confront. However, as Professor LaFave has noted, the courts have generally not read *Bertine* as requiring that these procedures be in writing. 3 W. LaFave, Search & Seizure §7.4(a), at 550 (3d ed. 1996). Rather, a police officer's testimony that he was following standard procedure is generally deemed to be sufficient. See, e.g., United States v. Lage, 183 F.3d 374, 380 (5th Cir. 1999) (officer's unrebutted testimony that he acted in accordance with standard inventory procedures is sufficient); United States v. Lozano, 171 F.3d 1129, 1132 (7th Cir. 1999) (lack of written policy not dispositive; evidence of "well-honed" police department routine may be sufficient). . . .

We agree . . . that there is no requirement that the procedures be in writing. The Supreme Court requires only that, in conducting inventory searches, the police act in accordance with standardized department procedures. Although it may be easier for the State to show that it was acting in accordance with standard procedures if it can produce a written policy, the Supreme Court has not required, as a matter of constitutional law, that such policies be reduced to writing.

The precise issue we face here is somewhat different. Here, the issue is whether, if the police do have a written policy on inventory searches, the policy itself has to be admitted into evidence, or if an officer's testimony describing the standard procedure can be sufficient. The State contends that the appellate court's decision in this case effectively creates a rule that the State must always produce a written policy on inventory searches if one exists. Defendant contends that we do not need to decide the issue as a matter of law. Rather, the question in any case is simply whether the State introduced sufficient evidence of standardized procedures. Defendant argues that Officer Byrd's testimony was insufficient.

[We] disagree with defendant's assertion that the State did not meet its burden in this case. The defendant bears the burden of proof at a hearing on a motion to suppress. A defendant must make a prima facie case that the evidence was obtained by an illegal search or seizure. If a defendant makes a prima facie case, the State has the burden of going forward with evidence to counter the defendant's prima facie case. However, the ultimate burden of proof remains with the defendant.

Here, defendant made his prima facie case by showing that Sergeant Byrd searched the trunk of defendant's car without a warrant. The State, however, met its burden of going forward with the evidence by establishing that Sergeant Byrd searched defendant's trunk as part of a routine tow inventory search. Sergeant Byrd gave clear, unrebutted testimony of the standard procedures for inventory searches that he was following. Sergeant Byrd testified that it was department policy to tow the vehicle whenever a person is arrested for driving on a revoked license. Before the vehicle is towed, the arresting officer is supposed to do an inventory search of the vehicle and to record anything of value on the tow inventory sheet. The officer is supposed to check the passenger compartment and trunk area for valuables.

Defendant never attempted to challenge this testimony. His attorney did not ask a single question of Sergeant Byrd about the policy and presented no rebuttal testimony on the issue. The attorney did absolutely nothing to cast doubt on Sergeant Byrd's testimony. In his arguments to the trial court, the defense attorney's principal contention was that the police had no right to tow the car. The trial court, not the defense attorney, asked further questions about the policy. But the trial court seemed satisfied with Sergeant Byrd's answer. The trial court asked Sergeant Byrd if the procedure was written down, and Byrd responded that it was in the policy manual that was taught to all cadets. When the trial court asked Byrd if he had the manual handy, Byrd began to answer the question by saying, "No, it's a —," following which the trial court finished Byrd's sentence for him by saying, "Big?" When Byrd tried to give more information about the policy, the court cut him off.

The court later ruled that it did not know what the police policy was because it had not seen the policy. This was error. Sergeant Byrd explained the police policy and defendant did not cross-examine him on the issue or offer any rebuttal to the testimony. The State met its burden of going forward with evidence to rebut the defendant's prima facie case. Sergeant Byrd's testimony established that defendant's trunk was searched as part of a routine tow inventory search. The ultimate burden of proof remained with defendant, and defendant offered nothing to show that the inventory search was improper. . . .

Of course, it would be the better practice for the State to produce the written policy. If it does not, the State leaves itself open to the possibility that the defense will be able to cast doubt on the officer's testimony either through cross-examination or rebuttal testimony. Here, defense counsel did not attempt to do so. Defendant had the burden of proof, and he failed to show that he was subjected to an illegal search.

The [defendant also contends] that Sergeant Byrd was not entitled to open the plastic bags because the State failed to produce any evidence that the inventory search policy allowed the opening of closed containers. In Florida v. Wells, 495 U.S. 1 (1990), the United States Supreme Court upheld the suppression of marijuana found in the trunk of a car during an inventory search. The marijuana was in a locked suitcase in the trunk, and the police forced open the suitcase as part of the inventory search. The record contained no evidence of a police policy on the opening of closed containers during inventory searches. The Supreme Court held that it would be permissible for the police policy to mandate the opening of all containers or no containers, or to allow the police the discretion to decide which containers should be opened, based on the nature of the search and the characteristics of the container. However, because there was no evidence of any policy with respect to closed containers in that case, the Supreme Court held that the search was not sufficiently regulated to satisfy the fourth amendment.

In People v. Hundley, 619 N.E.2d 744 (Ill. 1993), this court held that the general order of the State Police was sufficient to allow the opening of closed containers during an inventory search. The policy introduced into evidence in *Hundley* . . . did not use the words "closed containers." Rather, it required the police to inventory the contents of towed vehicles and to look wherever the owner or operator would ordinarily place or stow property. The officer testified in *Hundley* that he opened a cigarette case because, in his experience, women often put their drivers' licenses and money in such cases. This court held that the general order of the State Police was "adequate to the situation."

Hundley is controlling on this issue. Although defendant is correct that Sergeant Byrd did not specifically mention a closed container policy, he did testify that the policy required the police to check the passenger compartment and the trunk for valuables and to list any valuables on the tow inventory sheet. Obviously, such a policy requires the police to open any containers that might contain valuables. The policy that Sergeant Byrd testified to was more specific than the one at issue in *Hundley*. The *Hundley* policy merely referred to an inventory of the contents of the vehicle. Here, Sergeant Byrd specifically testified that he was supposed to search the trunk and passenger area for "valuables" and to inventory anything of value on the tow sheet. We believe this policy was sufficient to allow Sergeant Byrd to open the plastic bags in the trunk of defendant's car. . . .

Notes

1. *Inventory searches: majority position.* Inventory searches serve "administrative caretaking functions" of protecting against property damage claims and protecting police from dangerous items rather than enforcing criminal law. As a result, the Supreme Court has held that the federal constitution allows a routine (and warrantless) inventory search of impounded automobiles or other personal property without probable cause or individualized suspicion. South Dakota v. Opperman, 428 U.S. 364 (1976). The government must satisfy three requirements for a valid warrantless inventory search of a vehicle: (1) the original impoundment of the vehicle must be lawful; (2) the purpose of the inventory search must be to protect the owner's property or to protect the police from claims of lost, stolen, or vandalized property and to guard the police from danger; and (3) the inventory search must be conducted in good faith pursuant to reasonable standardized police procedures and not as a pretext for an investigatory search. The Supreme Court, in cases such as Colorado v. Bertine, 479 U.S. 367 (1987), has insisted that the inventory search occur under the guidance of "standardized" regulations. According to Florida v. Wells, 495 U.S. 1 (1990), the rules must address the proper treatment of containers found in a car, although those rules may leave some discretion to the officer conducting the inventory to open some containers and to leave others unopened. Most state courts also allow the police to conduct inventory searches without any special justification, so long as the inventory proceeds according to standard rules. The recurring issues in litigation deal with the specificity of the inventory rules and the amount of discretion those rules leave to the police officer in deciding whether to impound a vehicle and whether to open containers.

The issue is not as straightforward as it sounds. Consider this policy of the Illinois State Police, mentioned in the *Gipson* case:

> An examination and inventory of the contents of all vehicles/boats towed or held by authority of Division personnel shall be made by the officer who completes the Tow-In Recovery Report. This examination and inventory shall be restricted to those areas where an owner or operator would ordinarily place or store property or equipment in the vehicle/boat; and would normally include front and rear seat areas, glove compartment, map case, sun visors, and trunk and engine compartments.

Different officers, with different levels of experience, might have very different ideas about where owners "ordinarily" place property. What property do owners normally store in the engine compartment? Do police departments need inventory rules at all? Would consensual inventory searches (and routine requests for that consent) address the problems of safeguarding property in vehicles?

2. *The impoundment decision.* Some jurisdictions address the inventory process at the first possible point and impose various limits on the initial decision whether to impound a vehicle or to leave it at the scene. See Fair v. State, 627 N.E.2d 427 (Ind. 1993) (prosecution must demonstrate (1) that the belief that the vehicle posed some threat or harm to the community or was itself imperiled was consistent with objective standards of sound policing, and (2) that the decision to combat that threat by impoundment was in keeping with established departmental routine or regulation); State v. Huisman, 544 N.W.2d 433 (Iowa 1996) (impoundment decision must be made "according to standardized criteria," and "an administrative or care-taking

reason to impound" must exist). Others, such as the Colorado rules reviewed in *Bertine,* leave some discretion to the individual officer to act within guidelines in deciding whether to impound a car in the first place.

3. *Least intrusive means and investigatory intent.* Defendants often argue that their vehicle was impounded, or the contents inventoried, despite less intrusive means to achieve the stated goals of inventory searches, such as leaving the car where it sits, leaving it with another person, or getting the defendant to sign liability waivers (thus removing the interest in protecting officers against a lawsuit for harm to the personal property). Only a handful of jurisdictions (fewer than a half dozen) recognize such claims when it comes to closed containers; however, a larger group (about 15) require police to give an arrestee a reasonable chance to provide for alternative custody of a vehicle before it is impounded. See, e.g., State v. Perham, 814 P.2d 914 (Haw. 1991) (closed containers). Most courts focus only on whether the administrative rules were followed and whether those rules provide adequate guidance. Isn't a "least intrusive means" test one way to guarantee that officers do not use inventory searches to investigate crimes? Are less intrusive methods easier to see in hindsight than at the moment of decision? The Supreme Court has rejected the argument that the "least intrusive means" is a requirement of the federal constitution. Illinois v. Lafayette, 462 U.S. 640 (1983).

In Colorado v. Bertine, the Supreme Court said that inventory searches could be challenged if they were conducted "in bad faith or for the sole purpose of investigation." Is examination of "bad faith" consistent with the general rejection of "pretext" claims? See Chapter 2. Most state courts discussing inventory searches require that the officer conducting the inventory show "good faith" and prohibit use of the inventory as a "pretext" for a search for incriminating evidence. See State v. West, 862 P.2d 192 (Ariz. 1993). How will this "bad faith" come to light? What if an officer admits to "dual" purposes for an inventory search? See State v. Hauseman, 900 P.2d 74 (Colo. 1995).

4. *Inventory searches of personal belongings at the station.* Inventory searches apply to personal items carried by a person who is arrested and placed in detention. What arguments can you make that the justification for inventory searches is stronger for inventory of personal belongings than for cars? What arguments can you make that the privacy interest of the individual is stronger for personal belongings, especially those held in pockets, outside of public view (such as the content of wallets or purses)? Most states impose fewer restrictions on inventory searches of personal belongings than on inventory searches of cars. See Oles v. State 993 S.W.2d 103 (Tex. Crim. App. 1999) (police did not need probable cause or warrant to take a second look at clothing that had been seized from a defendant a week earlier as part of inventory of his belongings after his arrest). Should similar rules apply to the personal property of civil detainees, such as those who are extremely intoxicated or who suffer from mental illness? See State v. Carper, 876 P.2d 582 (Colo. 1994).

5. *Procedures whose validity turns on the adequacy of executive rules.* There are several types of searches, like inventory searches, in which courts have approved of procedures only when there is a regularized process for police to follow. Consider, for example, the legitimacy of sobriety checkpoints, where the U.S. Supreme Court and state courts have approved only of checkpoints governed by detailed rules. See Chapter 2; Wayne LaFave, Controlling Discretion by Administrative Regulations: The Use, Misuse, and Nonuse of Police Rules and Policies in Fourth Amendment Adjudication, 89 Mich. L. Rev. 442 (1990). Who should issue inventory rules?

Should they be determined by statute? If you were the general counsel to a police department, would you have a responsibility to maximize police power to conduct inventory searches? If police officers are concerned about the length and complexity of the inventory forms and process, how might you address that concern?

Problem 4-6. Personal Inventories

Pursuant to a search warrant, officers entered a house where they found four individuals, including Nancy Filkin, who did not reside there. Filkin and the other three individuals were arrested and removed from the premises. The officer who placed her under arrest did not notice whether Filkin was carrying a purse. However, Deputy Richard McKinny, who transported Filkin to the county jail, testified that she had it with her when he transported her to the jail.

Upon arrival at the county jail, McKinny took Filkin to the female booking area, removed her handcuffs, and remained present during the booking process. The standard operating procedure during the booking process at the county jail was to inventory personal items, to assure that the detainee carries no contraband objects into the jail, and to produce an accurate record so that the prisoner gets everything back when she is released. The search is also designed to protect the safety of the officers. The standard operating procedure for a purse is to remove all items to ensure that it contains no money or valuables.

A female corrections officer inventoried Filkin's closed purse under the watchful eye of McKinny. In the process, the officers discovered and opened a black film canister. The canister contained, among other things, a small self-seal bag holding .05 grams of methamphetamine.

Filkin has filed a motion to suppress the drugs found in the black film canister. How would you rule? Compare State v. Filkin, 494 N.W.2d 544 (Neb. 1993).

2. *Cars and Containers*

Of all the forms of personal property protected from unreasonable searches and seizures, cars and the containers inside them have generated the most litigation. There are distinctive constitutional and statutory rules involving car searches. When reading the following cases, be sure to distinguish the various rationales available to the police to search a car and its contents, and note the ways that the analysis changes because the search involves a car.

■ ARIZONA v. RODNEY GANT

129 S. Ct. 1710 (2009)

STEVENS, J.*

After Rodney Gant was arrested for driving with a suspended license, handcuffed, and locked in the back of a patrol car, police officers searched his car and

* [Justices Scalia, Souter, Thomas, and Ginsburg joined in this opinion. — EDS.]

discovered cocaine in the pocket of a jacket on the backseat. Because Gant could not have accessed his car to retrieve weapons or evidence at the time of the search, the Arizona Supreme Court held that the search-incident-to-arrest exception to the Fourth Amendment's warrant requirement, as defined in Chimel v. California, 395 U.S. 752 (1969), and applied to vehicle searches in New York v. Belton, 453 U.S. 454 (1981), did not justify the search in this case. We agree with that conclusion.

Under *Chimel*, police may search incident to arrest only the space within an arrestee's "immediate control," meaning "the area from within which he might gain possession of a weapon or destructible evidence." The safety and evidentiary justifications underlying *Chimel*'s reaching-distance rule determine *Belton*'s scope. Accordingly, we hold that *Belton* does not authorize a vehicle search incident to a recent occupant's arrest after the arrestee has been secured and cannot access the interior of the vehicle. Consistent with the holding in Thornton v. United States, 541 U.S. 615 (2004), . . . we also conclude that circumstances unique to the automobile context justify a search incident to arrest when it is reasonable to believe that evidence of the offense of arrest might be found in the vehicle.

I.

On August 25, 1999, acting on an anonymous tip that the residence at 2524 North Walnut Avenue was being used to sell drugs, Tucson police officers Griffith and Reed knocked on the front door and asked to speak to the owner. Gant answered the door and, after identifying himself, stated that he expected the owner to return later. The officers left the residence and conducted a records check, which revealed that Gant's driver's license had been suspended and there was an outstanding warrant for his arrest for driving with a suspended license.

When the officers returned to the house that evening, they found a man near the back of the house and a woman in a car parked in front of it. After a third officer arrived, they arrested the man for providing a false name and the woman for possessing drug paraphernalia. Both arrestees were handcuffed and secured in separate patrol cars when Gant arrived. The officers recognized his car as it entered the driveway, and Officer Griffith confirmed that Gant was the driver by shining a flashlight into the car as it drove by him. Gant parked at the end of the driveway, got out of his car, and shut the door. Griffith, who was about 30 feet away, called to Gant, and they approached each other, meeting 10-to-12 feet from Gant's car. Griffith immediately arrested Gant and handcuffed him.

Because the other arrestees were secured in the only patrol cars at the scene, Griffith called for backup. When two more officers arrived, they locked Gant in the backseat of their vehicle. After Gant had been handcuffed and placed in the back of a patrol car, two officers searched his car: One of them found a gun, and the other discovered a bag of cocaine in the pocket of a jacket on the backseat.

Gant was charged with two offenses — possession of a narcotic drug for sale and possession of drug paraphernalia (i.e., the plastic bag in which the cocaine was found). He moved to suppress the evidence seized from his car on the ground that the warrantless search violated the Fourth Amendment. Among other things, Gant argued that *Belton* did not authorize the search of his vehicle because he posed no threat to the officers after he was handcuffed in the patrol car and because he was arrested for a traffic offense for which no evidence could be found in his vehicle. When asked at the suppression hearing why the search was conducted, Officer Griffith responded: "Because the law says we can do it."

The trial court rejected the State's contention that the officers had probable cause to search Gant's car for contraband when the search began, but it denied the motion to suppress. Relying on the fact that the police saw Gant commit the crime of driving without a license and apprehended him only shortly after he exited his car, the court held that the search was permissible as a search incident to arrest. A jury found Gant guilty on both drug counts, and he was sentenced to a 3-year term of imprisonment. . . .

II.

. . . Among the exceptions to the warrant requirement is a search incident to a lawful arrest. The exception derives from interests in officer safety and evidence preservation that are typically implicated in arrest situations. In *Chimel*, we held that a search incident to arrest may only include "the arrestee's person and the area within his immediate control — construing that phrase to mean the area from within which he might gain possession of a weapon or destructible evidence." That limitation, which continues to define the boundaries of the exception, ensures that the scope of a search incident to arrest is commensurate with its purposes of protecting arresting officers and safeguarding any evidence of the offense of arrest that an arrestee might conceal or destroy. If there is no possibility that an arrestee could reach into the area that law enforcement officers seek to search, both justifications for the search-incident-to-arrest exception are absent and the rule does not apply.

In *Belton*, we considered *Chimel*'s application to the automobile context. A lone police officer in that case stopped a speeding car in which Belton was one of four occupants. While asking for the driver's license and registration, the officer smelled burnt marijuana and observed an envelope on the car floor marked "Supergold" — a name he associated with marijuana. Thus having probable cause to believe the occupants had committed a drug offense, the officer ordered them out of the vehicle, placed them under arrest, and patted them down. Without handcuffing the arrestees, the officer "split them up into four separate areas of the Thruway . . . so they would not be in physical touching area of each other" and searched the vehicle, including the pocket of a jacket on the backseat, in which he found cocaine.

The New York Court of Appeals found the search unconstitutional, concluding that after the occupants were arrested the vehicle and its contents were "safely within the exclusive custody and control of the police." The State asked this Court to consider whether the exception recognized in *Chimel* permits an officer to search "a jacket found inside an automobile while the automobile's four occupants, all under arrest, are standing unsecured around the vehicle." We granted certiorari because courts had found no workable definition of "the area within the immediate control of the arrestee" when that area arguably includes the interior of an automobile.

[We] held that when an officer lawfully arrests "the occupant of an automobile, he may, as a contemporaneous incident of that arrest, search the passenger compartment of the automobile" and any containers therein. That holding was based in large part on our assumption that articles inside the relatively narrow compass of the passenger compartment of an automobile are in fact generally, even if not inevitably, within "the area into which an arrestee might reach." . . .

III.

[Our opinion in *Belton*] has been widely understood to allow a vehicle search incident to the arrest of a recent occupant even if there is no possibility the arrestee could gain access to the vehicle at the time of the search. [Although] it is improbable that an arrestee could gain access to weapons stored in his vehicle after he has been handcuffed and secured in the backseat of a patrol car, cases allowing a search in this precise factual scenario are legion. Indeed, some courts have upheld searches under *Belton* even when the handcuffed arrestee has already left the scene.

Under this broad reading of *Belton*, a vehicle search would be authorized incident to every arrest of a recent occupant notwithstanding that in most cases the vehicle's passenger compartment will not be within the arrestee's reach at the time of the search. To read *Belton* as authorizing a vehicle search incident to every recent occupant's arrest would thus untether the rule from the justifications underlying the *Chimel* exception — a result clearly incompatible with our statement in *Belton* that it "in no way alters the fundamental principles established in the *Chimel* case regarding the basic scope of searches incident to lawful custodial arrests." Accordingly, we reject this reading of *Belton* and hold that the *Chimel* rationale authorizes police to search a vehicle incident to a recent occupant's arrest only when the arrestee is unsecured and within reaching distance of the passenger compartment at the time of the search.[4]

Although it does not follow from *Chimel*, we also conclude that circumstances unique to the vehicle context justify a search incident to a lawful arrest when it is "reasonable to believe evidence relevant to the crime of arrest might be found in the vehicle." *Thornton*, 541 U.S., at 632 (Scalia, J., concurring). In many cases, as when a recent occupant is arrested for a traffic violation, there will be no reasonable basis to believe the vehicle contains relevant evidence. But in others, including *Belton* and *Thornton*, the offense of arrest will supply a basis for searching the passenger compartment of an arrestee's vehicle and any containers therein.

Neither the possibility of access nor the likelihood of discovering offense-related evidence authorized the search in this case. Unlike in *Belton*, which involved a single officer confronted with four unsecured arrestees, the five officers in this case outnumbered the three arrestees, all of whom had been handcuffed and secured in separate patrol cars before the officers searched Gant's car. Under those circumstances, Gant clearly was not within reaching distance of his car at the time of the search. An evidentiary basis for the search was also lacking in this case. Whereas Belton and Thornton were arrested for drug offenses, Gant was arrested for driving with a suspended license-an offense for which police could not expect to find evidence in the passenger compartment of Gant's car. Because police could not reasonably have believed either that Gant could have accessed his car at the time of the

4. Because officers have many means of ensuring the safe arrest of vehicle occupants, it will be the rare case in which an officer is unable to fully effectuate an arrest so that a real possibility of access to the arrestee's vehicle remains. But in such a case a search incident to arrest is reasonable under the Fourth Amendment.

search or that evidence of the offense for which he was arrested might have been found therein, the search in this case was unreasonable.

IV. . . .

The State argues that *Belton* searches are reasonable regardless of the possibility of access in a given case because that expansive rule correctly balances law enforcement interests, including the interest in a bright-line rule, with an arrestee's limited privacy interest in his vehicle. For several reasons, we reject the State's argument. First, the State seriously undervalues the privacy interests at stake. Although we have recognized that a motorist's privacy interest in his vehicle is less substantial than in his home, the former interest is nevertheless important and deserving of constitutional protection. It is particularly significant that *Belton* searches authorize police officers to search not just the passenger compartment but every purse, briefcase, or other container within that space. A rule that gives police the power to conduct such a search whenever an individual is caught committing a traffic offense, when there is no basis for believing evidence of the offense might be found in the vehicle, creates a serious and recurring threat to the privacy of countless individuals. Indeed, the character of that threat implicates the central concern underlying the Fourth Amendment — the concern about giving police officers unbridled discretion to rummage at will among a person's private effects.

At the same time as it undervalues these privacy concerns, the State exaggerates the clarity that its reading of *Belton* provides. Courts that have read *Belton* expansively are at odds regarding how close in time to the arrest and how proximate to the arrestee's vehicle an officer's first contact with the arrestee must be to bring the encounter within *Belton*'s purview and whether a search is reasonable when it commences or continues after the arrestee has been removed from the scene. The rule has thus generated a great deal of uncertainty, particularly for a rule touted as providing a "bright line."

Contrary to the State's suggestion, a broad reading of *Belton* is also unnecessary to protect law enforcement safety and evidentiary interests. Under our view, *Belton* and *Thornton* permit an officer to conduct a vehicle search when an arrestee is within reaching distance of the vehicle or it is reasonable to believe the vehicle contains evidence of the offense of arrest. Other established exceptions to the warrant requirement authorize a vehicle search under additional circumstances when safety or evidentiary concerns demand. For instance, Michigan v. Long, 463 U.S. 1032 (1983), permits an officer to search a vehicle's passenger compartment when he has reasonable suspicion that an individual, whether or not the arrestee, is "dangerous" and might access the vehicle to "gain immediate control of weapons." If there is probable cause to believe a vehicle contains evidence of criminal activity, United States v. Ross, 456 U.S. 798 (1982), authorizes a search of any area of the vehicle in which the evidence might be found. . . . *Ross* allows searches for evidence relevant to offenses other than the offense of arrest, and the scope of the search authorized is broader. Finally, there may be still other circumstances in which safety or evidentiary interests would justify a search. Cf. Maryland v. Buie, 494 U.S. 325 (1990) (holding that, incident to arrest, an officer may conduct a limited protective sweep of those areas of a house in which he reasonably suspects a dangerous person may be hiding).

These exceptions together ensure that officers may search a vehicle when genuine safety or evidentiary concerns encountered during the arrest of a vehicle's recent occupant justify a search. Construing *Belton* broadly to allow vehicle searches incident to any arrest would serve no purpose except to provide a police entitlement, and it is anathema to the Fourth Amendment to permit a warrantless search on that basis. For these reasons, we are unpersuaded by the State's arguments that a broad reading of *Belton* would meaningfully further law enforcement interests and justify a substantial intrusion on individuals' privacy. [The court noted that at least eight states — Vermont, New Jersey, New Mexico, Nevada, Pennsylvania, New York, Oregon, and Wyoming have declined to follow a broad reading of *Belton* under their state constitutions, and that a Massachusetts statute provides that a search incident to arrest may be made only for the purposes of seizing weapons or evidence of the offense of arrest. See Commonwealth v. Toole, 448 N.E.2d 1264, 1266-1267 (Mass. 1983) (citing Mass. Gen. Laws, ch. 276, §1).]

V.

Our dissenting colleagues argue that the doctrine of stare decisis requires adherence to a broad reading of Belton even though the justifications for searching a vehicle incident to arrest are in most cases absent. The doctrine of stare decisis is of course essential to the respect accorded to the judgments of the Court and to the stability of the law, but it does not compel us to follow a past decision when its rationale no longer withstands careful analysis.

We have never relied on stare decisis to justify the continuance of an unconstitutional police practice. And we would be particularly loath to uphold an unconstitutional result in a case that is so easily distinguished from the decisions that arguably compel it. The safety and evidentiary interests that supported the search in *Belton* simply are not present in this case. Indeed, it is hard to imagine two cases that are factually more distinct, as *Belton* involved one officer confronted by four unsecured arrestees suspected of committing a drug offense and this case involves several officers confronted with a securely detained arrestee apprehended for driving with a suspended license. This case is also distinguishable from *Thornton*, in which the petitioner was arrested for a drug offense. . . .

We do not agree with the contention in Justice Alito's dissent that consideration of police reliance interests requires a different result. Although it appears that the State's reading of *Belton* has been widely taught in police academies and that law enforcement officers have relied on the rule in conducting vehicle searches during the past 28 years,[11] many of these searches were not justified by the reasons underlying the *Chimel* exception. Countless individuals guilty of nothing more serious than a traffic violation have had their constitutional right to the security of their private effects violated as a result. The fact that the law enforcement community may view the State's version of the *Belton* rule as an entitlement does not establish the sort of reliance interest that could outweigh the countervailing interest that all individuals share in having their constitutional rights fully protected. If it is clear that a practice is unlawful, individuals' interest in its discontinuance clearly outweighs any law enforcement "entitlement" to its persistence. . . .

11. Because a broad reading of *Belton* has been widely accepted, the doctrine of qualified immunity will shield officers from liability for searches conducted in reasonable reliance on that understanding.

The dissent also ignores the checkered history of the search-incident-to-arrest exception. Police authority to search the place in which a lawful arrest is made was broadly asserted in Marron v. United States, 275 U.S. 192 (1927), and limited a few years later in Go-Bart Importing Co. v. United States, 282 U.S. 344 (1931), and United States v. Lefkowitz, 285 U.S. 452 (1932). The limiting views expressed in *Go-Bart* and *Lefkowitz* were in turn abandoned in Harris v. United States, 331 U.S. 145 (1947), which upheld a search of a four-room apartment incident to the occupant's arrest. Only a year later the Court in Trupiano v. United States, 334 U.S. 699 (1948), retreated from that holding, noting that the search-incident-to-arrest exception is "a strictly limited" one that must be justified by "something more in the way of necessity than merely a lawful arrest." And just two years after that, in United States v. Rabinowitz, 339 U.S. 56 (1950), the Court again reversed course and upheld the search of an entire apartment. Finally, our opinion in *Chimel* overruled *Rabinowitz* and what remained of *Harris* and established the present boundaries of the search-incident-to-arrest exception. Notably, none of the dissenters in *Chimel* or the cases that preceded it argued that law enforcement reliance interests outweighed the interest in protecting individual constitutional rights so as to warrant fidelity to an unjustifiable rule.

The experience of the 28 years since we decided *Belton* has shown that the generalization underpinning the broad reading of that decision is unfounded. We now know that articles inside the passenger compartment are rarely "within the area into which an arrestee might reach," and blind adherence to *Belton*'s faulty assumption would authorize myriad unconstitutional searches. The doctrine of stare decisis does not require us to approve routine constitutional violations.

VI.

Police may search a vehicle incident to a recent occupant's arrest only if the arrestee is within reaching distance of the passenger compartment at the time of the search or it is reasonable to believe the vehicle contains evidence of the offense of arrest. When these justifications are absent, a search of an arrestee's vehicle will be unreasonable unless police obtain a warrant or show that another exception to the warrant requirement applies. . . .

SCALIA, J., concurring.

To determine what is an "unreasonable" search within the meaning of the Fourth Amendment, we look first to the historical practices the Framers sought to preserve; if those provide inadequate guidance, we apply traditional standards of reasonableness. Since the historical scope of officers' authority to search vehicles incident to arrest is uncertain, traditional standards of reasonableness govern. It is abundantly clear that those standards do not justify what I take to be the rule set forth in *Belton* and *Thornton*: that arresting officers may always search an arrestee's vehicle in order to protect themselves from hidden weapons. When an arrest is made in connection with a roadside stop, police virtually always have a less intrusive and more effective means of ensuring their safety — and a means that is virtually always employed: ordering the arrestee away from the vehicle, patting him down in the open, handcuffing him, and placing him in the squad car.

Law enforcement officers face a risk of being shot whenever they pull a car over. But that risk is at its height at the time of the initial confrontation; and it is not at all reduced by allowing a search of the stopped vehicle after the driver has been arrested and placed in the squad car. I observed in *Thornton* that the government had failed to provide a single instance in which a formerly restrained arrestee escaped to retrieve a weapon from his own vehicle; Arizona and its *amici* have not remedied that significant deficiency in the present case.

It must be borne in mind that we are speaking here only of a rule automatically permitting a search when the driver or an occupant is arrested. Where no arrest is made, we have held that officers may search the car if they reasonably believe "the suspect is dangerous and . . . may gain immediate control of weapons." Michigan v. Long. In the no-arrest case, the possibility of access to weapons in the vehicle always exists, since the driver or passenger will be allowed to return to the vehicle when the interrogation is completed. The rule of Michigan v. Long is not at issue here. . . .

No other Justice . . . shares my view that application of *Chimel* in this context should be entirely abandoned. It seems to me unacceptable for the Court to come forth with a 4-to-1-to-4 opinion that leaves the governing rule uncertain. I am therefore confronted with the choice of either leaving the current understanding of *Belton* and *Thornton* in effect, or acceding to what seems to me the artificial narrowing of those cases adopted by Justice Stevens. The latter, as I have said, does not provide the degree of certainty I think desirable in this field; but the former opens the field to what I think are plainly unconstitutional searches-which is the greater evil. I therefore join the opinion of the Court.

ALITO, J., dissenting.*

Twenty-eight years ago, in New York v. Belton, this Court held that "when a policeman has made a lawful custodial arrest of the occupant of an automobile, he may, as a contemporaneous incident of that arrest, search the passenger compartment of that automobile." Five years ago, in Thornton v. United States — a case involving a situation not materially distinguishable from the situation here — the Court not only reaffirmed but extended the holding of Belton, making it applicable to recent occupants. Today's decision effectively overrules those important decisions. . . .

To take the place of the overruled precedents, the Court adopts a new two-part rule under which a police officer who arrests a vehicle occupant or recent occupant may search the passenger compartment if (1) the arrestee is within reaching distance of the vehicle at the time of the search or (2) the officer has reason to believe that the vehicle contains evidence of the offense of arrest. The first part of this new rule may endanger arresting officers and is truly endorsed by only four Justices; Justice Scalia joins solely for the purpose of avoiding a "4-to-1-to-4 opinion." The second part of the new rule is taken from Justice Scalia's separate opinion in Thornton without any independent explanation of its origin or justification and is virtually certain to confuse law enforcement officers and judges for some time to come. The Court's decision will cause the suppression of evidence gathered in many searches carried out in good-faith reliance on well-settled case law, and although the Court purports to base its analysis on the landmark decision in Chimel, the Court's

* [Chief Justice Roberts and Justice Kennedy joined in this opinion; Justice Breyer joined in the opinion except for Part II E. — EDS.]

reasoning undermines Chimel. I would follow Belton, and I therefore respectfully dissent.

I.

Although the Court refuses to acknowledge that it is overruling *Belton* and *Thornton*, there can be no doubt that it does so. In *Belton*, an officer on the New York Thruway removed the occupants from a car and placed them under arrest but did not handcuff them. The officer then searched a jacket on the car's back seat and found drugs. . . .

Viewing . . . disagreement about the application of the *Chimel* rule as illustrative of a persistent and important problem, the *Belton* Court concluded that a single familiar standard was essential to guide police officers who make roadside arrests. The Court acknowledged that articles in the passenger compartment of a car are not always within an arrestee's reach, but in order to establish the workable rule this category of cases requires, the Court adopted a rule that categorically permits the search of a car's passenger compartment incident to the lawful arrest of an occupant. . . . The Court stated unequivocally: "[W]e hold that when a policeman has made a lawful custodial arrest of the occupant of an automobile, he may, as a contemporaneous incident of that arrest, search the passenger compartment of that automobile."

Despite this explicit statement, the opinion of the Court in the present case curiously suggests that *Belton* may reasonably be read as adopting a holding that . . . an officer arresting a vehicle occupant may search the passenger compartment "when the passenger compartment is within an arrestee's reaching distance." . . .

II.

Because the Court has substantially overruled *Belton* and *Thornton*, the Court must explain why its departure from the usual rule of stare decisis is justified. I recognize that stare decisis is not an inexorable command, and applies less rigidly in constitutional cases. But the Court has said that a constitutional precedent should be followed unless there is a "special justification" for its abandonment. Relevant factors identified in prior cases include whether the precedent has engendered reliance, whether there has been an important change in circumstances in the outside world, whether the precedent has proved to be unworkable, whether the precedent has been undermined by later decisions, and whether the decision was badly reasoned. These factors weigh in favor of retaining the rule established in *Belton*.

A.

Reliance. While reliance is most important in "cases involving property and contract rights," the Court has recognized that reliance by law enforcement officers is also entitled to weight. . . .

B.

Changed circumstances. Abandonment of the *Belton* rule cannot be justified on the ground that the dangers surrounding the arrest of a vehicle occupant are different today than they were 28 years ago. The Court claims that we now know that articles inside the passenger compartment are rarely within "the area into which an arrestee might reach," but surely it was well known in 1981 that a person who is taken from a vehicle, handcuffed, and placed in the back of a patrol car is unlikely to make it back into his own car to retrieve a weapon or destroy evidence.

C.

Workability. The *Belton* rule has not proved to be unworkable. On the contrary, the rule was adopted for the express purpose of providing a test that would be relatively easy for police officers and judges to apply. The Court correctly notes that even the *Belton* rule is not perfectly clear in all situations. Specifically, it is sometimes debatable whether a search is or is not contemporaneous with an arrest, but that problem is small in comparison with the problems that the Court's new two-part rule will produce.

The first part of the Court's new rule — which permits the search of a vehicle's passenger compartment if it is within an arrestee's reach at the time of the search — reintroduces the same sort of case-by-case, fact-specific decisionmaking that the *Belton* rule was adopted to avoid. As the situation in *Belton* illustrated, there are cases in which it is unclear whether an arrestee could retrieve a weapon or evidence in the passenger compartment of a car.

Even more serious problems will also result from the second part of the Court's new rule, which requires officers making roadside arrests to determine whether there is reason to believe that the vehicle contains evidence of the crime of arrest. What this rule permits in a variety of situations is entirely unclear.

D.

Consistency with later cases. The *Belton* bright-line rule has not been undermined by subsequent cases. On the contrary, that rule was reaffirmed and extended just five years ago in *Thornton*.

E.

Bad reasoning. The Court is harshly critical of *Belton*'s reasoning, but the problem that the Court perceives cannot be remedied simply by overruling *Belton*. *Belton* represented only a modest — and quite defensible — extension of *Chimel*, as I understand that decision.

Prior to *Chimel*, the Court's precedents permitted an arresting officer to search the area within an arrestee's "possession" and "control" for the purpose of gathering evidence. Based on this "abstract doctrine," the Court had sustained searches that extended far beyond an arrestee's grabbing area.

The *Chimel* Court, in an opinion written by Justice Stewart, overruled these cases. Concluding that there are only two justifications for a warrantless search incident to arrest — officer safety and the preservation of evidence — the Court stated that such a search must be confined to "the arrestee's person" and "the area from within which he might gain possession of a weapon or destructible evidence."

Unfortunately, *Chimel* did not say whether "the area from within which [an arrestee] might gain possession of a weapon or destructible evidence" is to be measured at the time of the arrest or at the time of the search, but unless the *Chimel* rule was meant to be a specialty rule, applicable to only a few unusual cases, the Court must have intended for this area to be measured at the time of arrest.

This is so because the Court can hardly have failed to appreciate the following two facts. First, in the great majority of cases, an officer making an arrest is able to handcuff the arrestee and remove him to a secure place before conducting a search incident to the arrest. Second, because it is safer for an arresting officer to secure an arrestee before searching, it is likely that this is what arresting officers do in the great majority of cases. (And it appears, not surprisingly, that this is in fact the prevailing practice.) Thus, if the area within an arrestee's reach were assessed, not at the time of arrest, but at the time of the search, the *Chimel* rule would rarely come into play.

Moreover, if the applicability of the *Chimel* rule turned on whether an arresting officer chooses to secure an arrestee prior to conducting a search, rather than searching first and securing the arrestee later, the rule would create a perverse incentive for an arresting officer to prolong the period during which the arrestee is kept in an area where he could pose a danger to the officer. If this is the law . . . the law would truly be, as Mr. Bumble said, "a ass."

I do not think that this is what the *Chimel* Court intended. Handcuffs were in use in 1969. The ability of arresting officers to secure arrestees before conducting a search — and their incentive to do so — are facts that can hardly have escaped the Court's attention. I therefore believe that the *Chimel* Court intended that its new rule apply in cases in which the arrestee is handcuffed before the search is conducted.

The *Belton* Court, in my view, proceeded on the basis of this interpretation of *Chimel*. [If] we are going to reexamine *Belton*, we should also reexamine the reasoning in *Chimel* on which *Belton* rests. . . .

F.

The second part of the Court's new rule . . . raises doctrinal and practical problems that the Court makes no effort to address. Why, for example, is the standard for this type of evidence-gathering search "reason to believe" rather than probable cause? And why is this type of search restricted to evidence of the offense of arrest? It is true that an arrestee's vehicle is probably more likely to contain evidence of the crime of arrest than of some other crime, but if reason-to-believe is the governing standard for an evidence-gathering search incident to arrest, it is not easy to see why an officer should not be able to search when the officer has reason to believe that the vehicle in question possesses evidence of a crime other than the crime of arrest.

Nor is it easy to see why an evidence-gathering search incident to arrest should be restricted to the passenger compartment. The *Belton* rule was limited in this way because the passenger compartment was considered to be the area that vehicle occupants can generally reach, but since the second part of the new rule is not based on officer safety or the preservation of evidence, the ground for this limitation is obscure. . . .

Notes

1. *Search of automobile incident to arrest: majority position*. Before *Gant*, states were divided on whether to apply an expansive view of the search-incident-to-arrest to cars. About 30 states explicitly adopted New York v. Belton, 453 U.S. 454 (1981), and in doing so they overwhelmingly adopted a broad reading of its rule. About half as many states rejected *Belton* and applied a case-by-case analysis of the scope of searches of cars incident to arrest. To a lesser extent, states and federal courts wrestled with the outer boundaries of the *Belton* line, looking at time, distance, and

other factors to determine when a search was no longer "incident" to arrest. See Crawford v. State, 138 P.3d 254 (Alaska 2006) (center console is "immediately associated with the person" and therefore appropriate for search incident to arrest made after defendant was removed from the car and placed in police cruiser in handcuffs). In *Gant* the Supreme Court rejected the majority reading on *Belton* and adopted a test in line with narrower state constitutional provisions.

How much of a practical barrier will this ruling be to law enforcement? What exactly does the government have to show under the "reasonable to believe" standard? Does this amount to probable cause, reasonable suspicion, or something else?

2. *Passengers and searches of cars incident to arrest.* There was some doubt over the years whether a search of a car incident to the arrest of the driver could also reach property that clearly belonged to a passenger who is not arrested. The Supreme Court resolved this question in Wyoming v. Houghton, 526 U.S. 295 (1999). In that case, an officer stopped a vehicle for speeding and noticed a hypodermic syringe in the driver's shirt pocket. When the driver admitted that he used the syringe to take drugs, the officer arrested him and ordered two female passengers out of the car. He searched the passenger compartment of the car for contraband and discovered drugs in a purse on the back seat belonging to one of the passengers. The Court upheld the search, emphasizing once again the need for bright-line rules that are easy for officers to apply in the field. Do you predict that state courts will follow *Houghton* as they interpret their own constitutions? See State v. Ray, 620 N.W.2d 83 (Neb. 2000) (officer may inspect passenger's knapsack found in passenger compartment, although passenger not arrested at the time). Will this pre-*Gant* decision stand?

3. *Let's be honest: deference to precedent.* Is it better for the Court to admit a change of direction, or to claim a strong foundation in precedent when the prior doctrine was at best questionable in support of the current ruling? Which approach gives greater credibility to the idea of the rule of law? Were *Belton* and *Thornton* as much of a "bright line" as Justice Alito suggests in dissent?

4. *Changing search-incident landscape*. The many variations on car searches will doubtlessly lead to a new wave of litigation on these questions in state and federal courts. For instance, will the second prong of the rule apply to searches of hatchback and trunk areas? You can track developments in this fast-changing area of the law by consulting the web extension of this chapter at *http://www.crimpro.com/extension/ch04*.

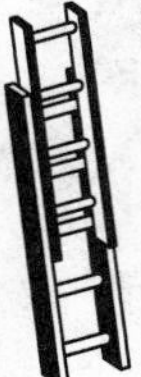

Justice Alito highlights the situation of an officer who arrests some but not all of the occupants of a vehicle. He also points out that persons who were not passengers in the car might attempt to retrieve a weapon or evidence from the car while the officer is still on the scene. How would you counsel a police department to respond to these situations? What are the prospects that *Gant* will influence the search-incident-to-arrest doctrine beyond the vehicle context? See State v. Henning, 209 P.3d 711 (Kan. 2009) (suppressing evidence obtained from search of automobile console after arrest of passenger on outstanding arrest warrant; court overturned statute allowing search incident to arrest for evidence of any crime).

■ CALIFORNIA v. CHARLES ACEVEDO

500 U.S. 565 (1991)

BLACKMUN, J.*

This case requires us once again to consider the so-called "automobile exception" to the warrant requirement of the Fourth Amendment and its application to the search of a closed container in the trunk of a car.

I.

On October 28, 1987, Officer Coleman of the Santa Ana Police Department received a telephone call from a federal drug enforcement agent in Hawaii. The agent informed Coleman that he had seized a package containing marijuana which was to have been delivered to the Federal Express Office in Santa Ana and which was addressed to J. R. Daza at 805 West Stevens Avenue in that city. The agent arranged to send the package to Coleman instead. Coleman then was to take the package to the Federal Express office and arrest the person who arrived to claim it.

Coleman received the package on October 29, verified its contents, and took it to the Senior Operations Manager at the Federal Express office. At about 10:30 A.M. on October 30, a man, who identified himself as Jamie Daza, arrived to claim the package. He accepted it and drove to his apartment on West Stevens. He carried the package into the apartment.

At 11:45 A.M., officers observed Daza leave the apartment and drop the box and paper that had contained the marijuana into a trash bin. Coleman at that point left the scene to get a search warrant. About 12:05 P.M., the officers saw Richard St. George leave the apartment carrying a blue knapsack which appeared to be half full. The officers stopped him as he was driving off, searched the knapsack, and found 11/2 pounds of marijuana.

At 12:30 P.M., respondent Charles Steven Acevedo arrived. He entered Daza's apartment, stayed for about 10 minutes, and reappeared carrying a brown paper bag that looked full. The officers noticed that the bag was the size of one of the wrapped marijuana packages sent from Hawaii. Acevedo walked to a silver Honda in the parking lot. He placed the bag in the trunk of the car and started to drive away. Fearing the loss of evidence, officers in a marked police car stopped him. They opened the trunk and the bag, and found marijuana.

Respondent was charged in state court with possession of marijuana for sale. . . . He moved to suppress the marijuana found in the car. The motion was denied. He then pleaded guilty but appealed the denial of the suppression motion. We granted certiorari to reexamine the law applicable to a closed container in an automobile, a subject that has troubled courts and law enforcement officers since it was first considered in United States v. Chadwick, 433 U.S. 1 (1977). . . .

* [Chief Justice Rehnquist and Justices O'Connor, Kennedy, and Souter joined in this opinion. — EDS.]

II.

. . . In Carroll v. United States, 267 U.S. 132 (1925), this Court established an exception to the warrant requirement for moving vehicles, for it recognized "a necessary difference between a search of a store, dwelling house or other structure in respect of which a proper official warrant readily may be obtained, and a search of a ship, motor boat, wagon or automobile, for contraband goods, where it is not practicable to secure a warrant because the vehicle can be quickly moved out of the locality or jurisdiction in which the warrant must be sought." It therefore held that a warrantless search of an automobile, based upon probable cause to believe that the vehicle contained evidence of crime in the light of an exigency arising out of the likely disappearance of the vehicle, did not contravene the Warrant Clause of the Fourth Amendment. . . .

In United States v. Ross, 456 U.S. 798 (1982), we held that a warrantless search of an automobile under the *Carroll* doctrine could include a search of a container or package found inside the car when such a search was supported by probable cause. The warrantless search of Ross' car occurred after an informant told the police that he had seen Ross complete a drug transaction using drugs stored in the trunk of his car. The police stopped the car, searched it, and discovered in the trunk a brown paper bag containing drugs. We decided that the search of Ross' car was not unreasonable under the Fourth Amendment. [If] probable cause justifies the search of a lawfully stopped vehicle, it justifies the search of every part of the vehicle and its contents that may conceal the object of the search. . . .

Ross distinguished the *Carroll* doctrine from the separate rule that governed the search of closed containers. The Court had announced tins separate rule, unique to luggage and other closed packages, bags, and containers, in United States v. Chadwick, 433 U.S. 1 (1977). In *Chadwick,* federal narcotics agents had probable cause to believe that a 200-pound double-locked footlocker contained marijuana. The agents tracked the locker as the defendants removed it from a train and carried it through the station to a waiting car. As soon as the defendants lifted the locker into the trunk of the car, the agents arrested them, seized the locker, and searched it. In this Court, the United States did not contend that the locker's brief contact with the automobile's trunk sufficed to make the *Carroll* doctrine applicable. Rather, the United States urged that the search of movable luggage could be considered analogous to the search of an automobile. The Court rejected this argument because, it reasoned, a person expects more privacy in his luggage and personal effects than he does in his automobile. Moreover, it concluded that as "may often not be the case when automobiles are seized," secure storage facilities are usually available when the police seize luggage.

In Arkansas v. Sanders, 442 U.S. 753 (1979), the Court extended *Chadwick*'s rule to apply to a suitcase actually being transported in the trunk of a car. In *Sanders,* the police had probable cause to believe a suitcase contained marijuana. They watched as the defendant placed the suitcase in the trunk of a taxi and was driven away. The police pursued the taxi for several blocks, stopped it, found the suitcase in the trunk, and searched it. Although the Court had applied the *Carroll* doctrine to searches of integral parts of the automobile itself (indeed, in *Carroll,* contraband whiskey was in the upholstery of the seats), it did not extend the doctrine to the warrantless search of personal luggage "merely because it was located in an automobile lawfully stopped by the police." Again, the *Sanders* majority stressed the heightened privacy expectation in personal luggage and concluded that the presence of luggage in an automobile did not diminish the owner's expectation of privacy in his personal items.

In *Ross,* the Court endeavored to distinguish between *Carroll,* which governed the *Ross* automobile search, and *Chadwick,* which governed the *Sanders* automobile search. It held that the *Carroll* doctrine covered searches of automobiles when the police had probable cause to search an entire vehicle, but that the *Chadwick* doctrine governed searches of luggage when the officers had probable cause to search only a container within the vehicle. Thus, in a *Ross* situation, the police could conduct a reasonable search under the Fourth Amendment without obtaining a warrant, whereas in a *Sanders* situation, the police had to obtain a warrant before they searched. . . .

III.

The facts in this case closely resemble the facts in *Ross.* In *Ross,* the police had probable cause to believe that drugs were stored in the trunk of a particular car. Here, the [California courts] concluded that the police had probable cause to believe that respondent was carrying marijuana in a bag in his car's trunk. Furthermore, for what it is worth, in *Ross,* as here, the drugs in the trunk were contained in a brown paper bag.

This Court in *Ross* rejected *Chadwick*'s distinction between containers and cars. It concluded that the expectation of privacy in one's vehicle is equal to one's expectation of privacy in the container, and noted that "the privacy interests in a car's trunk or glove compartment may be no less than those in a movable container." [T]he time and expense of the warrant process would be misdirected if the police could search every cubic inch of an automobile until they discovered a paper sack, at which point the Fourth Amendment required them to take the sack to a magistrate for permission to look inside. We now must decide the question deferred in *Ross:* whether the Fourth Amendment requires the police to obtain a warrant to open the sack in a movable vehicle simply because they lack probable cause to search the entire car. We conclude that it does not.

IV.

[A] container found after a general search of the automobile and a container found in a car after a limited search for the container are equally easy for the police to store and for the suspect to hide or destroy. In fact, we see no principled distinction in terms of either the privacy expectation or the exigent circumstances between the paper bag found by the police in *Ross* and the paper bag found by the police here. Furthermore, by attempting to distinguish between a container for which the police are specifically searching and a container which they come across in a car, we have provided only minimal protection for privacy and have impeded effective law enforcement.

The line between probable cause to search a vehicle and probable cause to search a package in that vehicle is not always clear, and separate rules that govern the two objects to be searched may enable the police to broaden their power to make warrantless searches and disserve privacy interests. . . . At the moment when officers stop an automobile, it may be less than clear whether they suspect with a high degree of certainty that the vehicle contains drugs in a bag or simply contains drugs. If the police know that they may open a bag only if they are actually searching the entire car, they may search more extensively than they otherwise would in order to establish the general probable cause required by *Ross*. . . . We cannot see the benefit of a rule that requires law enforcement officers to conduct a more intrusive search in order to justify a less intrusive one.

To the extent that the *Chadwick-Sanders* rule protects privacy, its protection is minimal. Law enforcement officers may seize a container and hold it until they obtain a search warrant. . . . And the police often will be able to search containers without a warrant, despite the *Chadwick-Sanders* rule, as a search incident to a lawful arrest. . . .

Finally, the search of a paper bag intrudes far less on individual privacy than does the incursion sanctioned long ago in *Carroll.* In that case, prohibition agents slashed the upholstery of the automobile. This Court nonetheless found their search to be reasonable under the Fourth Amendment. If destroying the interior of an automobile is not unreasonable, we cannot conclude that looking inside a closed container is. In light of the minimal protection to privacy afforded by the *Chadwick-Sanders* rule, and our serious doubt whether that rule substantially serves privacy interests, we now hold that the Fourth Amendment does not compel separate treatment for an automobile search that extends only to a container within the vehicle.

V.

The *Chadwick-Sanders* rule not only has failed to protect privacy but also has confused courts and police officers and impeded effective law enforcement. The conflict between the *Carroll* doctrine cases and the *Chadwick-Sanders* line has been criticized in academic commentary. One leading authority on the Fourth Amendment, after comparing *Chadwick* and *Sanders* with *Carroll* and its progeny, observed: "These two lines of authority cannot be completely reconciled, and thus how one comes out in the container-in-the-car situation depends upon which line of authority is used as a point of departure." 3 W. LaFave, Search and Seizure 53 (2d ed. 1987).

The discrepancy between the two rules has led to confusion for law enforcement officers. For example, when an officer, who has developed probable cause to believe that a vehicle contains drugs, begins to search the vehicle and immediately discovers a closed container, which rule applies? The defendant will argue that the fact that the officer first chose to search the container indicates that his probable cause extended only to the container and that *Chadwick* and *Sanders* therefore require a warrant. On the other hand, the fact that the officer first chose to search in the most obvious location should not restrict the propriety of the search. The *Chadwick* rule, as applied in *Sanders,* has devolved into an anomaly such that the more likely the police are to discover drugs in a container, the less authority they have to search it. We have noted the virtue of providing clear and unequivocal guidelines to the law enforcement profession. The *Chadwick-Sanders* rule is the antithesis of a "clear and unequivocal" guideline.

[Justice Stevens argues in dissent] that law enforcement has not been impeded because the Court has decided 29 Fourth Amendment cases since *Ross* in favor of the government. . . . In each of these cases, the government appeared as the petitioner. The dissent fails to explain how the loss of 29 cases below, not to mention the many others which this Court did not hear, did not interfere with law enforcement. The fact that the state courts and the Federal Courts of Appeals have been reversed in their Fourth Amendment holdings 29 times since 1982 further demonstrates the extent to which our Fourth Amendment jurisprudence has confused the courts. . . .

VI.

The interpretation of the *Carroll* doctrine set forth in *Ross* now applies to all searches of containers found in an automobile. In other words, the police may search without a warrant if their search is supported by probable cause. [However, probable] cause to believe that a container placed in the trunk of a [vehicle] contains contraband or evidence does not justify a search of the entire [vehicle]. In the case before us, the police had probable cause to believe that the paper bag in the automobile's trunk contained marijuana. That probable cause now allows a warrantless search of the paper bag. The facts in the record reveal that the police did not have probable cause to believe that contraband was hidden in any other part of the automobile and a search of the entire vehicle would have been without probable cause and unreasonable under the Fourth Amendment. . . .

Until today, this Court has drawn a curious line between the search of an automobile that coincidentally turns up a container and the search of a container that coincidentally turns up in an automobile. The protections of the Fourth Amendment must not turn on such coincidences. We therefore interpret *Carroll* as providing one rule to govern all automobile searches. . . .

SCALIA, J., concurring in the judgment.

I agree with the dissent that it is anomalous for a briefcase to be protected by the "general requirement" of a prior warrant when it is being carried along the street, but for that same briefcase to become unprotected as soon as it is carried into an automobile. On the other hand, I agree with the Court that it would be anomalous for a locked compartment in an automobile to be unprotected by the "general requirement" of a prior warrant, but for an unlocked briefcase within the automobile to be protected. I join in the judgment of the Court because I think its holding is more faithful to the text and tradition of the Fourth Amendment, and if these anomalies in our jurisprudence are ever to be eliminated that is the direction in which we should travel.

The Fourth Amendment does not by its terms require a prior warrant for searches and seizures; it merely prohibits searches and seizures that are "unreasonable." What it explicitly states regarding warrants is by way of limitation upon their issuance rather than requirement of their use. For the warrant was a means of insulating officials from personal liability assessed by colonial juries. An officer who searched or seized without a warrant did so at his own risk; he would be liable for trespass, including exemplary damages, unless the jury found that his action was "reasonable." If, however, the officer acted pursuant to a proper warrant, he would be absolutely immune. See Bell v. Clapp, 10 Johns. 263 (N.Y. 1813). By restricting the issuance of warrants, the Framers endeavored to preserve the jury's role in regulating searches and seizures. . . .

Even before today's decision, the "warrant requirement" had become so riddled with exceptions that it was basically unrecognizable. . . . Our intricate body of law regarding "reasonable expectation of privacy" has been developed largely as a means of creating these exceptions, enabling a search to be denominated not a Fourth Amendment "search" and therefore not subject to the general warrant requirement.

Unlike the dissent, therefore, I do not regard today's holding as some momentous departure, but rather as merely the continuation of an inconsistent jurisprudence that has been with us for years. . . . In my view, the path out of this confusion should be sought by returning to the first principle that the "reasonableness" requirement of the Fourth Amendment affords the protection that the common law afforded. I have no difficulty with the proposition that that includes the requirement of a warrant, where the common law required a warrant; and it may even be that changes in the surrounding legal rules (for example, elimination of the common-law rule that reasonable, good-faith belief was no defense to absolute liability for trespass) may make a warrant indispensable to reasonableness where it once was not. But the supposed "general rule" that a warrant is always required does not appear to have any basis in the common law, and confuses rather than facilitates any attempt to develop rules of reasonableness in light of changed legal circumstances. . . .

STEVENS, J., dissenting.*

. . . I.

The Fourth Amendment is a restraint on Executive power. The Amendment constitutes the Framers' direct constitutional response to the unreasonable law enforcement practices employed by agents of the British Crown. Over the years — particularly in the period immediately after World War II and particularly in opinions authored by Justice Jackson after his service as a special prosecutor at the Nuremburg trials — the Court has recognized the importance of this restraint as a bulwark against police practices that prevail in totalitarian regimes. This history is, however, only part of the explanation for the warrant requirement. The requirement also reflects the sound policy judgment that, absent exceptional circumstances, the decision to invade the privacy of an individual's personal effects should be made by a neutral magistrate rather than an agent of the Executive.

[In United States v. Chadwick, we] concluded that neither of the justifications for the automobile exception could support a similar exception for luggage. We first held that the privacy interest in luggage is substantially greater than in an automobile. Unlike automobiles and their contents, we reasoned, luggage contents are not open to public view, except as a condition to a border entry or common carrier travel; nor is luggage subject to regular inspections and official scrutiny on a continuing basis. Indeed, luggage is specifically intended to safeguard the privacy of personal effects, unlike an automobile, whose primary function is transportation. We then held that the mobility of luggage did not justify creating an additional exception to the Warrant Clause. Unlike an automobile, luggage can easily be seized and detained pending judicial approval of a search. . . .

* [Justice Marshall joined this opinion. — EDS.]

II.

In its opinion today, the Court recognizes that the police did not have probable cause to search respondent's vehicle and that a search of anything but the paper bag that respondent had carried from Daza's apartment and placed in the trunk of his car would have been unconstitutional. Moreover, as I read the opinion, the Court assumes that the police could not have made a warrantless inspection of the bag before it was placed in the car. Finally, the Court also does not question the fact that, under our prior cases, it would have been lawful for the police to seize the container and detain it (and respondent) until they obtained a search warrant. Thus, all of the relevant facts that governed our decisions in *Chadwick* and *Sanders* are present here whereas the relevant fact that justified the vehicle search in *Ross* is not present.

The Court does not attempt to identify any exigent circumstances that would justify its refusal to apply the general rule against warrantless searches. Instead, it advances these three arguments: First, the rules identified in the foregoing cases are confusing and anomalous. Second, the rules do not protect any significant interest in privacy. And, third, the rules impede effective law enforcement. None of these arguments withstands scrutiny.

The "Confusion"

. . . In the case the Court decides today, the California Court of Appeal . . . had no difficulty applying the critical distinction. Relying on *Chadwick,* it explained that "the officers had probable cause to believe marijuana would be found only in a brown lunch bag and nowhere else in the car. We are compelled to hold they should have obtained a search warrant before opening it." The decided cases . . . provide no support for the Court's concern about "confusion." The Court instead relies primarily on predictions that were made by Justice Blackmun in his dissenting opinions in *Chadwick* and *Sanders.* The Court, however, cites no evidence that these predictions have in fact materialized. . . .

To the extent there was any "anomaly" in our prior jurisprudence, the Court has "cured" it at the expense of creating a more serious paradox. For surely it is anomalous to prohibit a search of a briefcase while the owner is carrying it exposed on a public street yet to permit a search once the owner has placed the briefcase in the locked trunk of his car. One's privacy interest in one's luggage can certainly not be diminished by one's removing it from a public thoroughfare and placing it — out of sight — in a privately owned vehicle. Nor is the danger that evidence will escape increased if the luggage is in a car rather than on the street. In either location, if the police have probable cause, they are authorized to seize the luggage and to detain it until they obtain judicial approval for a search. Any line demarking an exception to the warrant requirement will appear blurred at the edges, but the Court has certainly erred if it believes that, by erasing one line and drawing another, it has drawn a clearer boundary.

The Privacy Argument

. . . To support its argument that today's holding works only a minimal intrusion on privacy, the Court suggests that "[i]f the police know that they may open a bag only if they are actually searching the entire car, they may search more extensively than they otherwise would in order to establish the general probable cause required by *Ross.*" [T]his fear is unexplained and inexplicable. Neither evidence uncovered in the course of a search nor the scope of the search conducted can be used to provide post hoc justification for a search unsupported by probable cause at its inception.

The Court also justifies its claim that its holding inflicts only minor damage by suggesting that, under New York v. Belton, 453 U.S. 454 (1981), the police could have arrested respondent and searched his bag if respondent had placed the bag in the passenger compartment of the automobile instead of in the trunk. In *Belton,* however, the justification for stopping the car and arresting the driver had nothing to do with the subsequent search, which was based on the potential danger to the arresting officer. The holding in *Belton* was supportable under a straightforward application of the automobile exception. I would not extend *Belton's* holding to this case, in which the container — which was protected from a warrantless search before it was placed in the car — provided the only justification for the arrest. Even accepting *Belton's* application to a case like this one, however, the Court's logic extends its holding to a container placed in the trunk of a vehicle, rather than in the passenger compartment. And the Court makes this extension without any justification whatsoever other than convenience to law enforcement.

The Burden on Law Enforcement

The Court's suggestion that *Chadwick* and *Sanders* have created a significant burden on effective law enforcement is unsupported, inaccurate, and, in any event, an insufficient reason for creating a new exception to the warrant requirement. Despite repeated claims that *Chadwick* and *Sanders* have "impeded effective law enforcement," the Court cites no authority for its contentions. Moreover, all evidence that does exist points to the contrary conclusion. In the years since *Ross* was decided, the Court has heard argument in 30 Fourth Amendment cases involving narcotics. In all but one, the government was the petitioner. All save two involved a search or seizure without a warrant or with a defective warrant. And, in all except three, the Court upheld the constitutionality of the search or seizure.

In the meantime, the flow of narcotics cases through the courts has steadily and dramatically increased. No impartial observer could criticize this Court for hindering the progress of the war on drugs. On the contrary, decisions like the one the Court makes today will support the conclusion that this Court has become a loyal foot soldier in the Executive's fight against crime.

Even if the warrant requirement does inconvenience the police to some extent, that fact does not distinguish this constitutional requirement from any other procedural protection secured by the Bill of Rights. It is merely a part of the price that our society must pay in order to preserve its freedom. . . . I respectfully dissent.

Notes

1. *Searches of containers in cars: majority position.* In California v. Acevedo, the Court resolved the tension between two lines of its earlier cases. It allowed warrantless searches of containers within automobiles so long as the police have probable cause to believe that either the car as a whole or the container itself holds contraband or evidence. Very few state courts have rejected the Court's holding in *Acevedo* as they have interpreted their state constitutions. But see State v. Sawa, 616 A.2d 774 (Vt. 1991). Even in the handful of courts that do require exigent circumstances for

containers in cars, the rule applies only to containers in the trunk or other areas not covered by a search incident to arrest.

The Court made it clear in Wyoming v. Houghton, 526 U.S. 295 (1999), that the *Acevedo* rule also applied to any containers owned by passengers rather than the driver. Police officers with probable cause to search a car may inspect a passengers' belongings inside the car if they are capable of concealing the object of the search. Passengers, just like drivers, possess a reduced expectation of privacy when it comes to property inside cars. Would requiring a warrant in this setting encourage drivers to hide contraband in containers belonging to passengers?

2. *Containers (effects) not in cars.* The decision in the federal courts to apply the automobile exception to containers in cars creates an inconsistency between the status of the containers inside and outside a car. For containers outside of cars, police apparently must find one of the many familiar exigencies to justify a warrantless examination of its contents. In jurisdictions that follow the federal rule, a container becomes subject to warrantless search, so long as the officer has probable cause, as soon as it is placed in a car. Will this wrinkle in the law change a police officer's strategy for the timing of an arrest of a suspect holding a container?

3. *Grounds for searching cars: inventory searches.* As in many areas of search and seizure law, the government may use a number of justifications for a search of an automobile and its contents. A lawyer must assess all the possible theories.

As we saw earlier in this chapter, the justifications for a vehicle search include the need for an inventory of the contents of a vehicle when the vehicle is impounded, or a search of the vehicle when an officer is arresting one of its occupants. See State v. Hundley, 619 N.E.2d 744 (Ill. 1993).

4. *Grounds for searching cars: automobile exception to the warrant requirement.* In Carroll v. United States, 267 U.S. 132 (1925), the Supreme Court upheld a warrantless search by two federal prohibition agents looking for liquor hidden in the upholstery of an automobile. The Court allowed warrantless searches, based on probable cause, of automobiles and other vehicles because "the vehicle can be quickly moved out of the locality or jurisdiction." A second theory justifying reduced Fourth Amendment protection for cars, developed in a series of later cases, is that cars are subject to public view and to pervasive state regulation. Car owners have lower reasonable expectations of privacy than, for example, homeowners.

The power of the police to search cars and other conveyances without a warrant has become known as the "automobile exception." This is an exception to the warrant requirement but not to the probable cause requirement: To exercise this power, police must have probable cause to believe that the car contains evidence or contraband. If police have probable cause, under the automobile exception they may stop the car and conduct a search. A search may be rejected if it exceeds the scope justified by objects which police, based on their finding of probable cause, expect to discover.

The largest group of state courts (about half) have fully embraced the federal view and require no warrant for any search of an automobile. In effect, these courts conclusively presume that exigent circumstances are present for any search of a car, even if the particular car in question was unlikely to move while the officers sought a warrant. A minority of state courts (roughly 15) still explicitly or implicitly require the government to show exigent circumstances to support a warrantless search of a car. The mobility of a car makes this showing quite easy in the ordinary case, but defendants can rebut a presumption of exigency by showing that the car was parked and locked or was otherwise not mobile. See State v. Tibbles, 236 P.3d 885 (Wash. 2010). For a glimpse of the rich case law in the state courts on the automobile exception to the warrant requirement, see the web extension for this chapter at *http://www.crimpro.com/extension/ch04*.

5. *Grounds for searching cars: the application of* Terry. A separate justification for car searches stems from the application of *Terry* searches to cars. As we saw in Chapter 2, the Supreme Court approved such searches in Michigan v. Long. Such searches must satisfy the requirements of *Terry*. In other words, the officer must have a proper basis for stopping the car. Then the officer may automatically order the driver and any passengers out of the car. At that point, if the officer has reasonable suspicion to believe there are weapons in the car, she can search in the passenger compartment, in any areas that could contain an accessible weapon, such as under the seats and inside containers large enough for a weapon. How would this doctrine apply in a case where the driver of a vehicle informs a police officer during a vehicle stop that he is carrying a concealed weapon under the terms of a license allowing him to do so?

6. *Viewing the exterior of cars*. The rules for searching the interior of cars do not apply to examination of the exterior of cars. Following the familiar expectation of privacy analysis of *Katz*, courts have held that no Fourth Amendment issue is raised when police examine the outside of a car or take a picture of it. Courts have also typically refused to apply the Fourth Amendment to examinations of the tread, tire wear, and even the removal of dirt or small samples of paint. See, e.g., Cardwell v. Lewis, 417 U.S. 583 (1974); State v. Skeleton, 795 P.2d 349 (Kan. 1990). Examination of the contents of a car from the outside, including the use of sight, smell, or even a flashlight to enhance the view, usually falls outside the limits of the Fourth Amendment so long as the car is parked in a place that is otherwise accessible to the police.

What about the viewing of the VIN (vehicle identification number)? In cases involving police efforts to obtain the VIN, courts agree that if the VIN is visible through the front windshield (as it is on all modern cars), and the officer simply reads it, there is no search. If the officer must reach into the car, open the door, lift the hood, or look under the vehicle to read the VIN or inspect some other feature of the car, some courts (a minority) still hold that no search has occurred. See, e.g., New York v. Class, 475 U.S. 106 (1986); Wood v. State, 632 S.W.2d 734 (Tex. Crim. App. 1982). About twice as many states, however, conclude that probable cause is required to move items inside a car, open a door, or lift a hood before viewing a VIN. State v. Larocco, 794 P.2d 460 (Utah 1990).

7. *Warrants reconsidered: what is the exception and what is the rule?* After studying the automobile exception, searches of cars incident to arrest, and inventory searches, look again at the following oft-repeated statement, quoted here from United States v. Ross, 456 U.S. 798 (1982), in a manner that emphasizes the statement's pedigree:

> We reaffirm the basic rule of Fourth Amendment jurisprudence stated by Justice Stewart for a unanimous Court in Mincey v. Arizona, 437 U.S. 385, 390: "The Fourth Amendment proscribes all unreasonable searches and seizures, and it is a cardinal principle that 'searches conducted outside the judicial process, without prior approval by judge or magistrate, are per se unreasonable under the Fourth Amendment — subject only to a few specifically established and well-delineated exceptions.' Katz v. United States, 389 U.S. 347, 357."

Consider Justice Scalia's observation in California v. Acevedo, that the warrant requirement has become "so riddled with exceptions" that it is "basically unrecognizable." Is this a problem courts and legislatures should care about, or have they developed an acceptable replacement for a strong warrant requirement? See Joseph Grano, Rethinking the Fourth Amendment Warrant Requirement, 19 Am. Crim. L. Rev. 603 (1982); Tracey Maclin, The Central Meaning of the Fourth Amendment, 35 Wm. & Mary L. Rev. 197 (1993).

Problem 4-7. Mobile . . . Homes

Robert Williams, an agent of the Drug Enforcement Administration, watched Charles Carney approach a youth in downtown San Diego. The youth accompanied Carney to a Dodge Mini Motor Home parked in a nearby lot, a few blocks from the courthouse. Carney and the youth closed the window shades in the motor home. Williams had previously received uncorroborated information that another person who used the same motor home was exchanging marijuana for sex. Williams, with assistance from other agents, watched the motor home for the entire one and one-quarter hours that Carney and the youth remained inside. When the youth left the motor home, the agents followed and stopped him. The youth told the agents that he had received marijuana in return for allowing Carney sexual contacts.

At the agents' request, the youth returned to the motor home and knocked on its door; Carney stepped out. The agents identified themselves as law enforcement officers. Without a warrant or consent, one agent entered the motor home and observed marijuana, plastic bags, and a scale of the kind used in weighing drugs on a table.

Assess the validity of the warrantless search. Compare California v. Carney, 471 U.S. 386 (1985).

V

Arrests

Every year, police in the United States make about 15 million arrests. Arrests are a serious intrusion on liberty, and our legal systems place several types of controls on them. The constraints come from constitutions, statutes, police department rules, the common law of torts, and elsewhere. Despite these multiple limits, police officers in the field still make the most important decisions about arrests.

This chapter surveys the legal rules and institutions that limit the arrest power and studies the operation of that power within (and sometimes outside) those legal boundaries. Section A considers the distinction between arrests and the lesser restraints on liberty known as "stops." Section B identifies the limited situations in which a warrant is necessary to complete a valid arrest. Section C focuses on legal rules dealing with the police officer's decision *not* to make an arrest in certain settings. Section D continues with the theme of police discretion in the arrest decision, looking to the use of the citation power as an alternative to arrests. And finally, Section E introduces the limits on the officer's use of force in carrying out an arrest.

A. STOP OR ARREST?

Police often find it necessary to restrain an individual from moving away from a particular place. They might do so to protect themselves or others from harm. They might do so to investigate a completed crime or to prevent an ongoing or future one. As we saw in Chapter 2, not all of these restraints are equally intrusive, and the different levels of restraint are subject to different legal controls. Some are consensual encounters, some are stops, and some are arrests. How do legal systems distinguish the different types of police efforts to control the movement of citizens?

Answers to this question appear in statutes, in cases, and in the interaction between the two.

■ NEVADA REVISED STATUTES §171.123

1. Any peace officer may detain any person whom the officer encounters under circumstances which reasonably indicate that the person has committed, is committing or is about to commit a crime. . . .

4. A person must not be detained longer than is reasonably necessary to effect the purposes of this section, and in no event longer than 60 minutes. The detention must not extend beyond the place or the immediate vicinity of the place where the detention was first effected, unless the person is arrested.

■ ARKANSAS RULE OF CRIMINAL PROCEDURE 3.1

A law enforcement officer lawfully present in any place may, in the performance of his duties, stop and detain any person who he reasonably suspects is committing, has committed, or is about to commit (1) a felony, or (2) a misdemeanor involving danger of forcible injury to persons or of appropriation of or damage to property, if such action is reasonably necessary either to obtain or verify the identification of the person or to determine the lawfulness of his conduct. An officer acting under this rule may require the person to remain in or near such place in the officer's presence for a period of not more than 15 minutes or for such time as is reasonable under the circumstances. At the end of such period the person detained shall be released without further restraint, or arrested and charged with an offense.

■ ROBERT BAILEY v. STATE

987 A.2d 72 (Md. 2010)

GREENE, J.

In this case, we are asked to determine whether the search and seizure of the petitioner, Robert Bailey, violated the Fourth Amendment to the United States Constitution and the Maryland Declaration of Rights. . . .

I.

On the night of August 16, 2006, Officer Rodney Lewis of the Prince George's County Police Department was patrolling the 6800 block of Hawthorne Street in Landover, Maryland. The area was known for drug activity, though there were no specific complaints on the night in question. At approximately 11:35 P.M., while patrolling on foot, Officer Lewis spotted the petitioner, Robert Bailey, standing alone on the side of 6890 Hawthorne Street. Officer Lewis testified about the encounter at the suppression hearing:

> I observed the defendant standing on the side of a home, . . . just standing in the shadows, at which time I yelled out to him, "Excuse me, sir, do you live there?" I didn't get

> any acknowledgment from the individual, at which time I assumed that he probably didn't hear me. I repeated the same thing, "Excuse me, sir, do you live there," which again I received no acknowledgment from the suspect, at which time myself, along with another officer, walked over to the individual. At that time, I just happened to step out of the shallow [sic] area on the sidewalk where I could visibly see his hands. And from the area at which he was standing at the time, I could smell a strong odor of ether.

When Officer Lewis smelled the odor of ether, he was within a few feet of the petitioner, close enough to "reach out and touch him." The odor was emanating from the petitioner's "body odor." The odor of ether, according to Officer Lewis's testimony, is associated with phencyclidine, more commonly known as PCP. Officer Lewis acknowledged on cross-examination that it is not illegal to possess ether and that ether is a solvent that is used in several household products. Upon smelling the odor of ether, Officer Lewis "reached over and grabbed both of [the petitioner's] hands and . . . had him place them over top of his head." Officer Lewis then conducted a search of the petitioner, which uncovered a glass vial, approximately three to four inches in length and one inch in diameter, half-full of liquid, in the petitioner's right front pants pocket. Field tests confirmed that the liquid contained PCP, and the petitioner was subsequently taken into custody and charged with possession of a controlled dangerous substance. . . .

In addition to observing the odor of ether, Officer Lewis noted that the petitioner had "glossy eyes" and that the petitioner failed to respond to the inquiries about whether he lived in the house. Officer Lewis did not, however, indicate whether he observed the petitioner's glossy eyes before or after he initially seized the petitioner.

The petitioner moved to suppress the physical evidence recovered from the search, asserting that the glass vial was the fruit of an illegal search and seizure under the Fourth Amendment, as well as the Maryland Declaration of Rights. Following a suppression hearing at which Officer Lewis was the sole witness, the trial court found that Officer Lewis had reasonable articulable suspicion to stop and question the petitioner based on the smell of ether, the petitioner's failure to respond to Officer Lewis's questions, and the petitioner's presence in a "high crime drug area with a number of complaints from citizens." The suppression court also determined that Officer Lewis conducted a valid pat-down of the petitioner for "officer safety" and that, based on the totality of the circumstances, the search and seizure were valid.

The petitioner proceeded to trial on an Agreed Statement of Facts. [The] Circuit Court for Prince George's County entered verdicts of guilty to . . . possession of a controlled dangerous substance, and sentenced the petitioner to four years in prison, all but two years suspended, with three years of supervised probation upon release. . . .

III.

. . . This Court analyzed the applicability of the Fourth Amendment to varying levels of police interaction in Swift v. State, 899 A.2d 867 (Md. 2006):

> Many courts have analyzed the applicability of the Fourth Amendment in terms of three tiers of interaction between a citizen and the police. The most intrusive encounter, an arrest, requires probable cause to believe that a person has committed or is committing a crime. The second category, the investigatory stop or detention, known commonly as a *Terry* stop, is less intrusive than a formal custodial arrest and must be supported by reasonable suspicion that a person has committed or is about to commit a crime and permits an officer to stop and briefly detain an individual. . . . The least intrusive police-citizen contact, a consensual encounter, . . . involves no restraint of liberty and elicits an individual's voluntary cooperation with non-coercive police contact. A consensual encounter need not be supported by any suspicion and because an individual is free to leave at any time during such an encounter, the Fourth Amendment is not implicated; thus, an individual is not considered to have been "seized" within the meaning of the Fourth Amendment.

We will consider how the petitioner's encounter with Officer Lewis proceeded from consensual encounter to custodial arrest, in light of settled Fourth Amendment precedent.

IV. Consensual Encounter or Investigatory Stop

. . . Officer Lewis's initial questioning of the petitioner was not an investigative stop, but rather a "consensual encounter" or accosting. [A] consensual encounter does not implicate the Fourth Amendment because the individual with whom the police are interacting is free to leave at any time. . . .

When the police officers asked the petitioner if he lived at the house in whose shadows he was standing, the petitioner could not have reasonably believed that the police were doing anything more than making a routine inquiry. The officers' inquiry was a request for basic information, not an order. Officer Lewis "yelled" the question because of the distance between the officers and the petitioner, and the officers began to walk toward the petitioner only after he did not respond to their questions, presumably to find out why he had not. In sum, the petitioner was not seized by the officers but merely was accosted at the point at which the officers began to approach him. . . .

V. Seizure and Search

An encounter has been described as a fluid situation, and one which begins as a consensual encounter may lose its consensual nature and become an investigatory detention or arrest once a person's liberty has been restrained and the person would not be free to leave. Officer Lewis's testimony indicates that his encounter with the petitioner proceeded quickly from an accosting, in which he shouted questions to the petitioner from the street, to a physical detention, when he grabbed the petitioner's hands.

As the Supreme Court observed in *Terry*, 392 U.S. at 19 n. 16, when the officer, "by means of physical force or a show of authority, has in some way restrained the liberty of a citizen [we may] conclude that a 'seizure' has occurred." In determining whether a person has been seized, the crucial test is whether, taking into account all of the circumstances surrounding the encounter, the police conduct would have communicated to a reasonable person that he was not at liberty to ignore the police presence and go about his business. . . .

In the present case, it is clear that, once Officer Lewis grabbed the petitioner's hands and placed them over his head, a reasonable person in the petitioner's position would have understood that he was physically detained and thus not free to leave or go about his business. Thus, when Officer Lewis grabbed the petitioner's hands, he seized the petitioner for purposes of the Fourth Amendment.

Because the officer seized and searched the petitioner without a warrant, the seizure was presumptively invalid unless it was supported by a reasonable, articulable suspicion of a threat to officer safety or by an exception to the warrant requirement. We must consider whether this seizure of the petitioner was a temporary detention and protective frisk pursuant to *Terry*... or a lawful arrest of the petitioner....

VI. *TERRY* FRISK

We disagree with the Circuit Court's conclusion that the search and seizure of the petitioner was an investigatory stop and protective frisk pursuant to *Terry*.[5] The purpose of a protective *Terry* frisk is not to discover evidence, but rather to protect the police officer and bystanders from harm. Pat-down frisks are proper when the officer has reason to believe that he is dealing with an armed and dangerous individual, regardless of whether he has probable cause to arrest the individual for a crime. The officer has reason to believe that an individual is armed and dangerous if a reasonably prudent person, under the circumstances, would have felt that he was in danger, based on reasonable inferences from particularized facts in light of the officer's experience.

Even if we were to assume that the encounter with the Officer Lewis was a *Terry* stop, the reasonableness of a *Terry* stop is determined by considering whether the officer's action was justified at its inception, and whether it was reasonably related in scope to the circumstances which justified the interference in the first place. Further, assuming *arguendo* that Officer Lewis had reasonable, articulable suspicion to believe that criminal activity was afoot and, accordingly, detain the petitioner, he still lacked the basis for a protective *Terry* frisk. At the suppression hearing, Officer Lewis indicated that he searched the petitioner to "check for weapons," but did not provide any basis for his suspicion that the petitioner was armed and dangerous. Officer Lewis did not testify as to any factors that would lead to a suspicion that the petitioner was carrying a weapon. Further, there are no objective factors in the record that indicate that the petitioner was armed and dangerous. Although the encounter took place at nighttime, the petitioner was alone and the officer "could visibly see his hands," which, presumably because the officer did not indicate otherwise, were empty. There is no indication in the record that the petitioner made

5. This Court need not consider whether Officer Lewis had reasonable articulable suspicion for a *Terry* stop because no investigatory stop took place. Pursuant to Terry v. Ohio, 392 U.S. 1 (1968), and its progeny, a police officer who has reasonable suspicion that a particular person has committed, is committing, or is about to commit a crime may detain that person briefly in order to investigate the circumstances that provoked suspicion. Police conduct a *Terry* investigation by asking the detainee a moderate number of questions to determine his identity and to try to obtain information confirming or dispelling the officer's suspicions. The detainee is not obligated to respond, however, and, unless the detainee's answers provide the officer with probable cause to arrest him, he must be released. In this case, no such questioning took place. Officer Lewis proceeded from an accosting, in which he called out to the petitioner from the street, to a physical detention of the petitioner, when he grabbed the petitioner's hands, without asking any additional questions.

any threatening movements, or any movements at all, nor is there any indication that Officer Lewis suspected that the petitioner was dealing drugs. Thus, we . . . hold that Officer Lewis had no basis to conduct a protective frisk.

Even if Officer Lewis had reasonably believed that the petitioner was armed and dangerous, therefore providing the basis for a proper *Terry* frisk, the search in the present case exceeded the scope of a proper protective frisk. A proper *Terry* frisk is limited to a pat-down of the outer clothing not to discover evidence of a crime, but rather to protect the police officer and bystanders from harm by checking for weapons. . . .

In the present case, Officer Lewis testified that he patted down the petitioner's right front pocket and that he did not manipulate the object contained therein. Officer Lewis testified that he "felt and recognized a glass vial" in the petitioner's pocket. He further testified that generally, in his experience, PCP is "contained in a glass vial." Based on Officer Lewis's testimony, however, the incriminating nature of the object in the defendant's pocket was not immediately apparent upon his initial touch of the object in the pat-down. Rather, Officer Lewis testified that he field-tested the liquid contained in the vial after removing it from the petitioner's pocket, thereby determining that the liquid contained PCP. The removal of the vial from the petitioner's pocket and field test of the liquid contained in the vial constituted a general exploratory search exceeding the permissible scope of a protective *Terry* frisk. Accordingly, we hold that Officer Lewis lacked the proper basis for a *Terry* frisk at the inception of the search, and that the search was a general exploratory search that exceeded the permissible scope of a *Terry* frisk, which serves as a basis to exclude the evidence seized from the petitioner's pocket.

VII. Arrest

We must consider, alternatively, whether Officer Lewis's seizure of the petitioner in the present case constituted a de facto arrest. . . . This Court analyzed what constitutes an arrest in Bouldin v. State, 350 A.2d 130, 133 (Md. 1976).

> It is generally recognized that an arrest is the taking, seizing, or detaining of the person of another . . . by touching or putting hands on him. . . . It is said that four elements must ordinarily coalesce to constitute a legal arrest: (1) an intent to arrest; (2) under a real or pretended authority; (3) accompanied by a seizure or detention of the person; and (4) which is understood by the person arrested.

In Belote v. State, 981 A.2d 1247, 1254 (Md. 2009), this Court further analyzed the factors set forth in *Bouldin:*

> Where a police officer's objective conduct unambiguously reflects an intent to make a custodial arrest, the subjective intent inquiry . . . takes on less significance. In other words, when an arresting officer's objective conduct, which provides significant insight into the officer's subjective intent, is unambiguous, courts need not allocate significant weight to an officer's subjective intent that is revealed partially in the form of his testimony at the suppression hearing; the officer's objective conduct, in effect, will have made his subjective intent clear.

A show of force is objective conduct demonstrating the officer's intent to make an arrest. Generally, a display of force by a police officer, such as putting a person in handcuffs, is considered an arrest. . . . Although the display of force often involves placing the individual who is seized in handcuffs, application of handcuffs is not a necessary element of an arrest. See Grier v. State, 718 A.2d 211, 217 (Md. 1998) ("Once Petitioner was on the ground and in custody and control of the officers, he was certainly under arrest . . . ."); Morton v. State, 397 A.2d 1385, 1388 (Md. 1979) ([arrest occurred] where an officer removed the individual from a recreation center and placed him under guard in a patrol car . . .); Dixon v. State, 758 A.2d 1063, 1073 (Md. App. 2000) (officers exceeded the permissible scope of an investigative *Terry* stop and "arrested appellant at the time they blocked his car, removed him from his vehicle, and handcuffed him").[8]

[Before] the Supreme Court's landmark decision in *Terry,* the Fourth Amendment's guarantee against unreasonable seizures of persons was analyzed in terms of arrest, and probable cause for arrest. *Terry* constituted a limited departure from the requirement of probable cause to support a seizure.[9] If a seizure [amounts to an arrest, it] must be supported by probable cause in order to be lawful.

In this case, Officer Lewis's conduct constituted an unambiguous show of force. He approached the petitioner while in uniform, physically restrained the petitioner, conducted a search of the petitioner's person, and ultimately took the petitioner into physical police custody. [Although] Officer Lewis testified at the suppression hearing that he was checking the petitioner for weapons, this statement is given less weight than his objective conduct on the night in question. . . .

Officer Lewis's conduct on the night in question exceeded the permissible boundaries of an investigative *Terry* stop, both in scope and in duration. A *Terry* stop must be justified both at its inception and be limited in scope, for the specific purpose of searching for weapons to protect the officer's safety, or the safety of bystanders. In the present case, the officer took complete control of the situation in

8. Conversely, even if the officers' physical actions are equivalent to an arrest, the show of force is not considered to be an arrest if the actions were justified by officer safety or permissible to prevent the flight of a suspect. In re David S., 789 A.2d 607, 616 (Md. 2002) (holding that a "hard take down" in which officers forced the individual to the ground and handcuffed him was a limited *Terry* stop, not an arrest, when the "conduct was not unreasonable because the officers reasonably could have suspected that the respondent posed a threat to their safety"). The use of handcuffs in a seizure is not a dispositive factor in determining whether the seizure was a *Terry* stop or an arrest.

9. The Supreme Court of the United States discussed the distinction between an arrest and a *Terry* stop in United States v. Robinson, 414 U.S. 218, 228 (1973):

> An arrest is a wholly different kind of intrusion upon individual freedom from a limited search for weapons, and the interests each is designed to serve are likewise quite different. An arrest is the initial stage of a criminal prosecution. It is intended to vindicate society's interest in having its laws obeyed, and it is inevitably accompanied by future interference with the individual's freedom of movement, whether or not trial or conviction ultimately follows. The protective search for weapons, on the other hand, constitutes a brief, though far from inconsiderable, intrusion upon the sanctity of the person.

The distinction between a *Terry* stop and an arrest is not defined simply by the length of the detention, the investigative activities during the detention, and whether the suspect was removed to a detention or interrogation area. [An] arrest is distinguishable from a *Terry* detention because the *Terry* stop is not only limited in duration, but also has a limited permissible scope. The scope of a *Terry* stop is limited to brief investigatory stops or detentions conducted in furtherance of the goal of protecting the safety of the officer, or the safety of bystanders.

conducting a general exploratory search of the petitioner, removing the vial from his pocket and taking him into custody. . . .

Grabbing the petitioner's wrists when he was not suspected of being armed and dangerous, then conducting a search and removing the vial from his pocket, and, finally, taking him into custody as the initial action leading up to a criminal prosecution, constituted a de facto arrest. Thus, we hold that Officer Lewis's seizure, in which he physically restrained the petitioner and ultimately took him into custody, constituted an arrest.

[The Court went on to conclude that the circumstances present in this case did not create probable cause to support an arrest. Because] Officer Lewis did not make a lawful arrest when he seized the petitioner, the subsequent warrantless search of the petitioner was not within an exception to the warrant requirement and therefore violated the Fourth Amendment. . . .

Notes

1. *Arrest versus stop: majority position.* The difference between an arrest (requiring probable cause) and an investigative detention (requiring reasonable suspicion) turns on several different factors. Courts look to the amount of time the detention lasts, the techniques (such as handcuffs) used to restrain the suspect, the location of the suspect (including the distance covered during any transportation of the suspect), and what the police officers say to the suspect about the purposes of the detention. The judicial opinions often say, using a circular definition, that an arrest takes place when a reasonable person would believe that he or she is under arrest. Medford v. State, 13 S.W.2d 769 (Tex. 2000) (arrest is complete "when a person's liberty of movement is successfully restricted or restrained, whether this is achieved by an officer's physical force or the suspect's submission to the officer's authority [and] only if a reasonable person in the suspect's position would have understood the situation to constitute a restraint on freedom of movement of the degree which the law associates with formal arrest.").

The interaction among all these relevant facts is typically important. In Kaupp v. Texas, 538 U.S. 626 (2003), police officers awakened a 17-year-old boy in his bedroom at 3:00 in the morning, saying, "We need to go and talk." He was taken out in handcuffs, without shoes, dressed only in his underwear in January, driven in a patrol car to the scene of a crime and then to the sheriff's offices, and then taken into an interrogation room and questioned for 10-15 minutes before admitting to participation in a murder. The Court concluded that such police actions were "sufficiently like arrest to invoke the traditional rule that arrests may constitutionally be made only on probable cause."

2. *Time of detention.* The amount of time that the police detain a person is among the most important facts in determining whether a seizure amounted to an arrest or merely a stop. In Florida v. Royer, 460 U.S. 491 (1983), the Supreme Court stated that an investigative detention "must be temporary and last no longer than is necessary to effectuate the purpose of the stop." Most states allow for a flexible determination of the time necessary to convert a stop into an arrest. Why do the Nevada statute and the Arkansas rule choose such different time limits (15 minutes and 60 minutes)? Did the legislators in the two states have different concerns in mind? Courts deciding cases in the absence of a statute also pay close attention to the

amount of time elapsed. While the absolute number of minutes in a detention is important, courts also judge the length of the detention in light of the purposes of the stop and the time reasonably needed to effectuate those purposes, including the diligence of officers in pursuing the investigation. See United States v. Sharpe, 470 U.S. 675 (1985) (approves of 20-minute automobile stop for purpose of investigating potential narcotics violations); People v. Garcia, 11 P.3d 449 (Colo. 2000) (length of valid investigatory stop measured as time required for officers to diligently complete investigation given complexity of situation and protection of personal safety).

Is the amount of time allowed for an investigative stop the kind of factor amenable to bright-line rules? Is it the kind of factor that can be undermined by the use of general standards such as "reasonableness"? If you were to draft a bright-line rule, would you include an "escape" valve for exceptional situations? If you prefer a rule in this situation, would you want that rule to be determined by the legislature or the courts? Do rules as a class tend to favor prosecution or defense?

3. *Conditions of detention.* What can be more typical of arrest than being handcuffed and placed in the back of a police cruiser? If this is true, how can the majority of state courts find that being handcuffed and placed in the back of a cruiser does not, alone, convert an investigative stop into an arrest? See State v. Blackmore, 925 P.2d 1347 (Ariz. 1996) (burglary suspect stopped at gunpoint, handcuffed, placed in back seat of police cruiser; no arrest). Which is more indicative of arrest, the handcuffs or the seat in the police car? Would you support a bright-line rule stating that handcuffs = arrest? For a sampling of the rich case law on this question, consult the web extension for this chapter at *http://www.crimpro.com/extension/ch05*.

4. *Location of detention.* Why do both the Arkansas rule and the Nevada statute require that the detained person remain in the vicinity of the initial stop? Most of the cases on this question allow officers to transport a suspect to some other location nearby to complete an investigation, but longer trips can convert the stop into an arrest. Taking a suspect to the police station is also a key factor in the cases. Can a person be taken to the police station and still not be under arrest? See Dunaway v. New York, 442 U.S. 200 (1979) (recognizing possibility of nonarrest detention based on reasonable suspicion for questioning at police station; however, arrest without probable cause occurred here where defendant was taken to police station for questioning without being told he was under arrest); Collins-Draine v. Knief, 617 N.E.2d 679 (Ill. 2000) (bounds of stop exceeded if officer unnecessarily holds suspect or transports suspect to police station; holding at jail for five hours).

5. *Probable cause to believe what?* Officers need probable cause to justify an arrest. However, an officer might suspect that a person committed one crime although probable cause exists at that time to arrest the person for some other crime. Does it matter which crime the officer has in mind when making the arrest? In Devenpeck v. Alford, 543 U.S. 146 (2004), officers stopped a driver and ultimately arrested him for unlawful audio-taping of a police conversation during the stop, which was later determined not to be a crime. However, the officers on the scene had probable cause to arrest the suspect for impersonating an officer, a sufficient basis to support arrest even though it was not the crime the officers relied upon. Are the arguments in this setting precisely the same as the arguments we encountered in the discussion of "pretextual" stops?

B. ARREST WARRANTS

In Chapter 3, we explored the various ways that the law supposedly encourages the use of a judicial warrant to authorize an officer to conduct a full search. Yet, despite the often-stated "preference" for warrants, most searches take place without a warrant. The same is true for arrests. There are legal rules encouraging or requiring warrants before a police officer can arrest a person in some settings (in particular, arrests made in a home). But in reality, most arrests take place without a warrant. As you read the following materials on the coverage of the warrant requirement for arrests, keep in mind the types of arrests that these rules do not cover.

■ WILLIAM BLACKSTONE, COMMENTARIES ON THE LAWS OF ENGLAND

Vol. 3, p. 288 (1768)

An arrest must be by corporal seising or touching the defendant's body; after which the bailiff may justify breaking open the house in which he is, to take him: otherwise he has no such power; but must watch his opportunity to arrest him. For every man's house is looked upon by the law to be his castle of defence and asylum, wherein he should suffer no violence. Which principle is carried so far in the civil law, that for the most part not so much as a common citation or summons, much less an arrest, can be executed upon a man within his own walls.

■ STATE v. STEVEN THOMAS

124 P.3d 48 (Kan. 2005)

LUCKERT, J.

. . . Just before midnight on March 26, 2002, the Sedgwick County Sheriff's Department received information from a confidential informant that Brandon Prouse was trying to sell the informant 5 or 6 quarts of anhydrous ammonia. Deputies ran a background check on Prouse and discovered that he was wanted on a felony arrest warrant for a probation violation in an aggravated battery case. At around 1:30 A.M. on March 27, 2002, the sheriff's office began surveillance on the house where the informant indicated Prouse might be found. At the time of the surveillance, however, the deputies neither had a search warrant for the house, nor did they know who owned the residence.

At about 2 A.M., Prouse stepped out of the house and walked into the front yard. The uniformed deputies ordered him to stop, but Prouse ran back into the residence through the front door. Four deputies followed Prouse inside. They pursued Prouse through different rooms and then arrested him.

Inside the house, the deputies smelled a strong odor of anhydrous ammonia. As they moved through the residence, the deputies saw in plain view various items that they believed were consistent with a methamphetamine lab. Besides Prouse, the deputies discovered six other individuals inside the house, including Thomas, who owned the residence. A deputy started to open an interior door into the garage to check for more people, but the smell of anhydrous ammonia from the garage was so overwhelming that he immediately shut the door. Because of the strong chemical smell and for safety reasons, the deputies ordered all occupants to go outside onto the front lawn area.

Once the occupants of the house were outside, one of the deputies told his fellow deputies that he would perform a pat-down search of the seven occupants. When the deputy asked Thomas who owned the house, Thomas admitted ownership. During the pat-down search, Thomas said, "You might as well get [my] dope," and indicated that he had methamphetamine in his left front pants pocket. The deputy reached into Thomas' pocket and pulled out a bag containing smaller baggies filled with white rocks. Thomas was then placed under arrest.

At the sheriff's office, [Thomas] admitted ownership of the methamphetamine lab in his house and the drugs found on his person. Thomas told the officers that he learned how to make methamphetamine in prison. He indicated that this was his first attempt at manufacturing methamphetamine and that, sometime before the deputies' arrival at his house, the lab had blown up. . . .

The district court implicitly denied Thomas' motions to suppress, finding Thomas guilty of unlawfully manufacturing a controlled substance, illegal possession of pseudoephedrine, and possession of methamphetamine with intent to sell. . . . The district court found, inter alia, that the deputies intended to wait until Prouse came out of the residence to arrest him. The court also found that the deputies had probable cause to believe that Prouse was the person who came out of the house during the surveillance, that the deputies were in "hot pursuit" of Prouse, and that "exigent circumstances allowed them to enter the house without a warrant." The district court concluded that Thomas' constitutional rights were not violated when the deputies chased Prouse into Thomas' home. . . .

Thomas argues that the arrest warrant upon which the deputies based their chase of Prouse did not authorize their entry without a search warrant into the home of a third party. Further, Thomas contends there were no exigent circumstances to support the entry. . . .

The Fourth Amendment prohibits law enforcement officers from making a warrantless and nonconsensual entry into a home in order to make a routine felony arrest absent exigent circumstances. Payton v. New York, 445 U.S. 573 (1980). The majority in *Payton* noted it was a basic principle of Fourth Amendment law that searches and seizures inside a home without a warrant are "presumptively unreasonable," while "objects . . . found in a public place may be seized by the police without a warrant." The Court concluded that "this distinction has equal force when the seizure of a person is involved" because "an entry to arrest and an entry to search for and to seize property implicate the same interest in preserving the privacy and the sanctity of the home, and justify the same level of constitutional protection." Thus, the Court concluded: "In terms that apply equally to seizures of property and to seizures of persons, the Fourth Amendment has drawn a firm line at the entrance to the house. Absent exigent circumstances, that threshold may not reasonably be crossed without a warrant." . . .

Arrest Warrant Authorizes Entry into Suspect's Home

However, in *Payton* the United States Supreme Court recognized that a search warrant was not constitutionally required if the entry was made into a home where one who was the subject of a felony arrest warrant resided if there was probable cause to believe the subject was present in the home. The Court stated:

> It is true that an arrest warrant requirement may afford less protection than a search warrant requirement, but it will suffice to interpose the magistrate's determination of probable cause between the zealous officer and the citizen. If there is sufficient evidence of a citizen's participation in a felony to persuade a judicial officer that his arrest is justified, it is constitutionally reasonable to require him to open his doors to the officers of the law. Thus, for Fourth Amendment purposes, an arrest warrant founded on probable cause implicitly carries with it the limited authority to enter a dwelling in which the suspect lives when there is reason to believe the suspect is within.

Thus, had the officers followed Prouse into a house in which he resided in order to serve the warrant, the entry would have been constitutional.... In the present case, however, there is nothing in the record to indicate that the officers believed Prouse owned or resided at the house.

THIRD PARTY'S HOUSE

An arrest warrant, standing alone, is not a sufficient basis to enter the home of a third party. The United States Supreme Court reached this holding in Steagald v. United States, 451 U.S. 204 (1981). In *Steagald*, a confidential informant contacted an agent of the Drug Enforcement Administration, suggesting he might be able to locate Ricky Lyons, a federal fugitive wanted on drug charges. Agents found the address where they thought Lyons was located and, 2 days later, drove to the residence. Gary Steagald and Hoyt Gaultney stood outside of the house. After the agents frisked the two men and discovered that neither man was Lyons, they went to the front door. Gaultney's wife answered the door and told the agents she was alone. The agents proceeded, without consent, into the house and searched for Lyons. Although they did not find Lyons, the agents found cocaine. They subsequently obtained a search warrant, and ultimately found 43 pounds of cocaine. Steagald was arrested on federal drug charges.

The Supreme Court stated that the agents had neither consent nor exigent circumstances when they made their initial, warrantless search. The Court phrased its narrow issue for consideration as "whether an arrest warrant — as opposed to a search warrant — is adequate to protect the Fourth Amendment interests of persons not named in the warrant, when their homes are searched without their consent and in the absence of exigent circumstances." The *Steagald* Court recognized that different interests are protected by arrest warrants and search warrants. Arrest warrants protect individuals from unreasonable seizures; search warrants protect against the unjustified intrusion of police into one's home. The Court found that the agents wrongly relied on Lyon's arrest warrant to give them the legal authority to enter into a third person's home. Thus, the third person's privacy interests were left unprotected.

The *Steagald* Court feared that allowing officers, without consent or exigent circumstances, to enter into a third party's residence to search for the subject of an arrest warrant would create a significant potential for abuse and pointed out that officers would then be able to use arrest warrants as a pretext for entering the residences of a suspect's friends and acquaintances or as a pretext for entering residences in which police have mere suspicion, not probable cause, that illegal activity is being committed. The Court held that, under the facts of the case, the warrantless search was unconstitutional.

However, the United States Supreme Court was careful to exempt two circumstances from its holding: consent and exigent circumstances. In this case, the State does not allege there was consent. Rather, the State relies upon exigent circumstances. . . .

EXIGENT CIRCUMSTANCES

The Court of Appeals, in holding that the deputies' conduct was justified by exigent circumstances, found that the present case is similar to United States v. Santana, 427 U.S. 38 (1976). Dominga Santana stood in the doorway of her own house when officers arrived to arrest her. When she saw the police, the defendant went inside the vestibule of the house. The officers followed the defendant inside and arrested her.

Santana filed a motion to suppress the incriminating evidence found during and after her arrest. The federal district court granted Santana's motion, [but the Supreme Court] disagreed with the lower court and determined that Santana's pursuit originated in a public place. Further, "the fact that the pursuit here ended almost as soon as it began did not render it any the less a [hot pursuit] sufficient to justify the warrantless entry into Santana's house." As for the police officers' entry into the defendant's house, the Court concluded: "A suspect may not defeat an arrest which has been set in motion in a public place . . . by the expedient of escaping into a private place."

Santana addressed a situation involving police entry into the suspect's house. The current set of facts involves the warrantless entry of police into a third party's house while trying to apprehend a suspect on an arrest warrant. [The *Steagald* Court discussed] the historical basis for the "hot pursuit doctrine," [and] concluded that English common-law "suggests that forcible entry into a third party's house was permissible only when the person to be arrested was pursued to the house." Later in the decision, the Court dismissed the government's argument that practical problems would arise if law enforcement were required to obtain a search warrant before entering the home of a third party. The Court noted these practical problems were largely ameliorated because "the situations in which a search warrant will be necessary are few." As examples, the Court noted that (1) "an arrest warrant alone will suffice to enter a suspect's own residence"; (2) "if probable cause exists, no warrant is required to apprehend a suspected felon in a public place"; (3) "the subject of an arrest warrant can be readily seized before entering or after leaving the home of a third party"; and (4) under the exigent circumstances doctrine, "a warrantless entry of a home would be justified if the police were in [hot pursuit] of a fugitive." . . .

APPLICATION OF HOT PURSUIT DOCTRINE

Without specific discussion of the hot pursuit exception, Thomas contends there were no exigent circumstances and cites to the list of factors this court has recognized which may be considered in determining if exigent circumstances existed, including: (1) the gravity or violent nature of the offense with which the suspect is to be charged; (2) whether the suspect is reasonably believed to be armed; (3) a clear showing of probable cause; (4) strong reasons to believe that the suspect is in the premises; (5) a likelihood that the suspect will escape if not swiftly apprehended; and (6) the peaceful circumstances of entry. The possible destruction of evidence is also a factor which may be considered. Thomas, as the homeowner, contends that these six or seven factors were not met; therefore, the officers violated his constitutional rights.

Although his argument is unclear, it appears that Thomas seeks a factor-by-factor analysis. Prior cases have not required such a review. [In] Warden v. Hayden, 387 U.S. 294, 299 (1967), the Supreme Court noted the search was "necessary to prevent the dangers that the suspect at large in the house may resist or escape." The United States Supreme Court has recognized that hot pursuit alone justifies a warrantless intrusion into a home. This court has also recognized that hot pursuit is one example of an exigent circumstance. . . .

Here, the deputies had an arrest warrant for Prouse, began surveillance of the house where they reasonably believed he could be found, and then spotted Prouse as he first exited and then reentered the house. The district court found that the deputies initially intended to wait for Prouse and to arrest him outside. There is no evidence, or assertion by Thomas, that the deputies used the arrest warrant as a pretext for entering Thomas' house or for searching it for incriminating evidence.

The district court found the doctrine of hot pursuit applied and also found it was impractical to expect the officers to obtain a warrant once Prouse took refuge in Thomas' house. The district court expressed doubt that a search warrant could have been obtained quickly at 2 o'clock in the morning. Unquestionably, if the officers had sought a search warrant, there was a high possibility that the fugitive named in the arrest warrant would escape apprehension. Indeed, requiring such police conduct would negate the essence of the hot pursuit doctrine. . . .

Furthermore, certain facts in this particular case are important to a conclusion that the officers were justified in making a warrantless entry into a third-party residence. The initial entry and search was limited to the apprehension of Prouse, the suspect named in the arrest warrant. Thomas does not contest the officers' quick protective sweep of the home once they discovered that Prouse was not alone. There is no indication that the deputies dug into drawers or looked into places where the suspect obviously could not hide.

In addition, the evidence pertaining to the methamphetamine lab was in plain view as the deputies pursued Prouse and made a protective sweep of the residence. It is clear that any evidence seized in plain view must be located in places lawfully accessible to officers. The strong smell of anhydrous ammonia was prevalent throughout the house, and various items consistent with the manufacture of methamphetamine sat in plain view in the kitchen area. . . . The Court of Appeals' decision affirming the district court's denial of Thomas' motion to suppress evidence based upon the alleged unauthorized entry into a third-party residence is affirmed.

Problem 5-1. Indoor-Outdoor Arrest

Officer Roy Gows of the Boston Police Department responded to the hospital emergency room to investigate the report of a rape. The victim of the alleged rape told Gows that she had been living in an apartment with Antonio Molina for six weeks. She said that Molina had raped her at knifepoint the previous night in the apartment, using a very large knife drawn from a brown sheath. The witness then gave Officer Gows the address of the apartment. Gows returned to the police station to consult with other officers about the case. Then, along with Detective Martin Nee, Gows proceeded to Molina's apartment to make an arrest.

When they arrived at the apartment, Officer Gows knocked on the front door. People had begun to gather outside the house when Molina opened the door. He fit the physical description provided by the victim and, when asked, identified himself as Molina. Detective Nee and Officer Gows stepped into the living room, which is accessible directly from the front door, and Detective Nee handcuffed Molina while saying that he was under arrest. At that point, a young woman who was also standing in the living room became very angry and began screaming at the officers. Concerned that she might have access to Molina's handgun that was sitting on a table in the living room, Detective Nee moved Molina 10 feet through an adjacent doorway into the kitchen while instructing Officer Gows to deal with the young woman.

Detective Nee informed Molina that the complainant had accused him of rape. While in the kitchen, Nee noticed a two-foot-long knife on the counter. The officers then told Molina that he would be spending the night at the station, and asked if he wanted to retrieve a sweater to wear over his muscle shirt. He agreed, and led the officers to his third-floor bedroom. While in the bedroom, the officers saw a brown knife sheath.

Before his trial for rape, Molina filed a motion to suppress the knife and the sheath as evidence. Will the trial court grant the motion? Cf. Commonwealth v. Molina, 786 N.E.2d 1191 (Mass. 2003).

Notes

1. *Warrants for arrests in a home: majority position.* The federal constitution allows a police officer to make an arrest in a public place without a warrant. When the arrest takes place in a home, however, warrants become more important. As the *Thomas* decision from Kansas explained, the federal constitution requires only an arrest warrant to justify entry into a suspect's home to carry out the arrest, along with some "reason to believe" the suspect is within. Payton v. New York, 445 U.S. 573 (1980); Kirk v. Louisiana, 536 U.S. 635 (2002) (reaffirms *Payton*). This is often the first place a police officer will look when trying to execute an arrest warrant. When an officer enters a third party's home to arrest a suspect, he must have a search warrant, based on probable cause to believe that the suspect (the object of the search) is present in that location. Virtually all state courts have used this same framework under their state constitutions. See State v. Chippero, 987 A.2d 555 (N.J. 2009).

In what ways are arrest warrants different from search warrants? Do separate requirements for search warrants and arrest warrants accomplish anything meaningful for suspects? For nonsuspects?

2. *Warrantless arrests in public places.* The U.S. Constitution does not require warrants for arrests made in a public place, even if the arresting officer could easily have obtained a warrant. In United States v. Watson, 423 U.S. 411 (1976), the Court upheld statutes and regulations granting Postal Service officers the power to make warrantless arrests for felonies. The Court deferred to Congress's judgment about

the meaning of the Fourth Amendment and also relied on "the ancient common-law rule that a peace officer was permitted to arrest without a warrant for a misdemeanor or felony committed in his presence as well as for a felony not committed in his presence if there was reasonable ground for making the arrest," noting that the common law rule had prevailed under state and federal law. See N.D. Cent. Code §29-06-15 (allowing warrantless arrests for misdemeanors only when they are committed in the presence of the arresting officer; exceptions for traffic offenses and domestic violence assaults).

3. *Is crime seriousness a basis for exigency?* In Welsh v. Wisconsin, 466 U.S. 740 (1984), the Supreme Court considered the validity of a night entry of a person's home to arrest him for a nonjailable traffic offense. The Court held that no exigent circumstances could support the arrest in Welsh's home, particularly "when the underlying offense for which there is probable cause to arrest is relatively minor." See also State v. Kiper, 532 N.W.2d 698 (Wis. 1995) (executing arrest warrant for failure to pay fine for allowing minor to drive; no exigent circumstances). Why should exigent circumstances for entering homes vary based on the seriousness of the alleged crime committed? For a sense of the interaction among arrest warrants, search warrants, and the exigent circumstances doctrine, consult the web extension for this chapter at *http://www.crimpro.com/extension/ch05*.

C. POLICE DISCRETION IN THE ARREST DECISION

Police officers remain the critical decisionmakers for arrests. This section considers recent legal reforms that could have contradictory effects on police discretion in arrests. First, statutes have expanded the power of the police to arrest a person without adhering to traditional common law and statutory requirements that the police obtain an arrest warrant in some contexts. In most states, these reforms have eliminated the need for an arrest warrant in most settings. Second, while police officers generally have discretion to decide whether to arrest, statutes and police department rules in special areas now guide the officers in their arrest decisions once there is probable cause to believe that the person has committed a crime. Prominent examples of both of these trends — one expanding the officer's discretion to arrest and the other restricting it — appear in cases involving domestic violence. We begin with the traditional common law rule, which requires a warrant to arrest a person for lesser crimes committed outside the officer's presence.

■ WILLIAM BLACKSTONE, COMMENTARIES ON THE LAWS OF ENGLAND

Vol. 4, p. 287 (1769)

A warrant may be granted . . . ordinarily by justices of the peace. This they may do in any cases where they have a jurisdiction over the offence [and] this extends undoubtedly to all treasons, felonies, and breaches of the peace; and also to all such offences as they have power to punish by statute. [The constable] may, without warrant, arrest any one for a breach of the peace, committed in his view, and carry him before a justice of the peace. And, in case of felony actually committed, or a dangerous wounding whereby felony is likely to ensue, he may upon probable suspicion arrest the felon.

OKLAHOMA STATUTES TIT. 22, §40.3

A. A peace officer shall not discourage a victim of rape, forcible sodomy or domestic abuse from pressing charges against the assailant of the victim.

B. A peace officer may arrest without a warrant a person anywhere, including his place of residence, if the peace officer has probable cause to believe the person within the preceding seventy-two hours has committed an act of domestic abuse . . . although the assault did not take place in the presence of the peace officer. A peace officer may not arrest a person pursuant to this section without first observing a recent physical injury to, or an impairment of the physical condition of, the alleged victim. . . .

CONNECTICUT GENERAL STATUTES §46b-38b

(a) Whenever a peace officer determines upon speedy information that a family violence crime . . . has been committed within his jurisdiction, he shall arrest the person or persons suspected of its commission and charge such person or persons with the appropriate crime. The decision to arrest and charge shall not (1) be dependent on the specific consent of the victim, (2) consider the relationship of the parties or (3) be based solely on a request by the victim.

(b) No peace officer investigating an incident of family violence shall threaten, suggest or otherwise indicate the arrest of all parties for the purpose of discouraging requests for law enforcement intervention by any party. Where complaints are received from two or more opposing parties, the officer shall evaluate each complaint separately to determine whether he should seek a warrant for an arrest.

IOWA CODE §236.12

1. If a peace officer has reason to believe that domestic abuse has occurred, the officer shall use all reasonable means to prevent further abuse including but not limited to the following:

a. If requested, remaining on the scene as long as there is a danger to an abused person's physical safety without the presence of a peace officer, [or] assisting the person in leaving the residence.

b. Assisting an abused person in obtaining medical treatment necessitated by an assault. . . .

c. Providing an abused person with immediate and adequate notice of the person's rights. The notice shall consist of handing the person a copy of the following statement written in English and Spanish, asking the person to read the card and whether the person understands the rights:

> You have the right to ask the court for the following help on a temporary basis:
>
> (1) Keeping your attacker away from you, your home and your place of work.
>
> (2) The right to stay at your home without interference from your attacker.
>
> (3) Getting custody of children and obtaining support for yourself and your minor children if your attacker is legally required to provide such support.
>
> (4) Professional counseling for you, the children who are members of the household, and the defendant.
>
> You have the right to seek help from the court to seek a protective order with or without the assistance of legal representation. . . .
>
> You have the right to file criminal charges for threats, assaults, or other related crimes. You have the right to seek restitution against your attacker for harm to yourself or your property.
>
> If you are in need of medical treatment, you have the right to request that the officer present assist you in obtaining transportation to the nearest hospital or otherwise assist you.
>
> If you believe that police protection is needed for your physical safety, you have the right to request that the officer present remain at the scene until you and other affected parties can leave or until safety is otherwise ensured.

The notice shall also contain the telephone numbers of safe shelters, support groups, or crisis lines operating in the area.

2. a. A peace officer may, with or without a warrant, arrest a person . . . if, upon investigation, . . . the officer has probable cause to believe that a domestic abuse assault has been committed which did not result in any injury to the alleged victim.

b. Except as otherwise provided in subsection 3, a peace officer shall, with or without a warrant, arrest a person [if] the officer has probable cause to believe that a domestic abuse assault has been committed which resulted in the alleged victim's suffering a bodily injury.

c. Except as otherwise provided in subsection 3, a peace officer shall, with or without a warrant, arrest a person [if] the officer has probable cause to believe that a domestic abuse assault has been committed with the intent to inflict a serious injury.

d. Except as otherwise provided in subsection 3, a peace officer shall, with or without a warrant, arrest a person [if] the officer has probable cause to believe that a domestic abuse assault has been committed and that the alleged abuser used or displayed a dangerous weapon in connection with the assault.

3. As described in subsection 2, paragraph "b," "c," or "d," the peace officer shall arrest the person whom the peace officer believes to be the primary physical aggressor. . . . Persons acting with justification . . . are not subject to mandatory arrest. In identifying the primary physical aggressor, a peace officer shall consider the need to protect victims of domestic abuse, the relative degree of injury or fear inflicted on the persons involved, and any history of domestic abuse between the persons involved. A peace officer's identification of the primary physical aggressor shall not be based on the consent of the victim to any subsequent prosecution or on the relationship of the persons involved in the incident, and shall not be based solely upon the absence of visible indications of injury or impairment.

LAWRENCE SHERMAN AND RICHARD BERK, THE MINNEAPOLIS DOMESTIC VIOLENCE EXPERIMENT

(1984)

[The] Minneapolis domestic violence experiment was the first scientifically controlled test of the effects of arrest for any crime. It found that arrest was the most effective of three standard methods police use to reduce domestic violence. The other police methods — attempting to counsel both parties or sending assailants away from home for several hours — were found to be considerably less effective in deterring future violence in the cases examined. [The] preponderance of evidence in the Minneapolis study strongly suggests that the police should use arrest in most domestic violence cases. . . .

POLICING DOMESTIC ASSAULTS

Police have typically been reluctant to make arrests for domestic violence, as well as for a wide range of other kinds of offenses, unless a victim demands an arrest, a suspect insults an officer, or other factors are present. [Two surveys] of battered women who tried to have their domestic assailants arrested report that arrest occurred in only ten percent [and] three percent of the cases. Surveys of police agencies in Illinois and New York found explicit policies against arrest in the majority of the agencies surveyed. Despite the fact that violence is reported to be present in one-third to two-thirds of all domestic disturbances police respond to, police department data show arrests in only five percent of those disturbances in Oakland, . . . and six percent in Los Angeles County. . . .

The apparent preference of many police for separating the parties rather than arresting the offender has been attacked from two directions over the past 15 years. The original critique came from clinical psychologists who agreed that police should rarely make arrests in domestic assault cases and argued that police should mediate the disputes responsible for the violence. A highly publicized demonstration project teaching police special counseling skills for family crisis intervention failed to show a reduction in violence, but was interpreted as a success nonetheless. By 1977, a national survey of police agencies with 100 or more officers found that over 70 percent reported a family crisis intervention training program in operation. Although it is not clear whether these programs reduced separation and increased mediation, a decline in arrests was noted for some. Indeed, many sought explicitly to *reduce* the number of arrests.

By the mid 1970's, police practices were criticized from the opposite direction by feminist groups. Just as psychologists succeeded in having many police agencies respond to domestic violence as "half social work and half police work," feminists began to argue that police put "too much emphasis on the social work aspect and not enough on the criminal." Widely publicized lawsuits in New York and Oakland sought to compel police to make arrests in every case of domestic assault, and state legislatures were lobbied successfully to reduce the evidentiary requirements needed for police to make arrests for misdemeanor domestic assaults. Some legislatures are now considering statutes requiring police to make arrests in these cases.

The feminist critique was bolstered by a study showing that for 85 percent of a sample of spouse killings, police had intervened at least once in the preceding two years. For 54 percent of those homicides, police had intervened five or more times. But it was impossible to determine from the data whether making more or fewer arrests would have reduced the homicide rate.

How the Experiment Was Designed

[To] find which police approach was most effective in deterring future domestic violence, . . . the Minneapolis Police Department agreed to conduct a classic experiment. A classic experiment is a research design that allows scientists to discover the effects of one thing on another by holding constant all other possible causes of those effects. The design of the experiment called for a lottery selection, which ensured that there would be no difference among the three groups of suspects receiving the different police responses. The lottery determined which of the three responses police officers would use on each suspect in a domestic assault case. According to the lottery, a suspect would be arrested, or sent from the scene of the assault for eight hours, or given some form of advice, which could include mediation at an offender's discretion. In the language of the experiment, these responses were called the arrest, send, and advice treatments. The design called for a six-month follow-up period to measure the frequency and seriousness of any future domestic violence in all cases in which the police intervened.

The design applied only to simple (misdemeanor) domestic assaults, where both the suspect and the victim were present when the police arrived. Thus, the experiment included only those cases in which police were empowered, but not required, to make arrests under a recently liberalized Minnesota state law. The police officer must have probable cause to believe that a cohabitant or spouse had assaulted the victim within the past four hours. Police need not have witnessed the assault. Cases of life-threatening or severe injury, usually labeled as a felony (aggravated assault), were excluded from the design.

The design called for each officer to carry a pad of report forms, color coded for the three different police responses. Each time the officers encountered a situation that fit the experiment's criteria, they were to take whatever action was indicated by the report form on the top of the pad. The forms were numbered and arranged for each officer in an order determined by the lottery. . . .

Anticipating something of the background of the victims in the experiment, a predominantly minority, female research staff was employed to contact the victims for a detailed, face-to-face interview, to be followed by telephone follow-up interviews every two weeks for 24 weeks. The interviews were designed primarily to measure the frequency and seriousness of victimizations caused by a suspect after police interventions. The research staff also collected criminal justice reports that mentioned suspects' names during the six-month follow-up period.

Conduct of the Experiment

As is common in field experiments, the actual process in Minneapolis suffered some slippage from the original plan. [The experiment ran from March 17, 1981] until August 1, 1982, and produced 314 case reports. . . . Ninety-nine percent of the suspects targeted for arrest actually were arrested; 78 percent of those scheduled to receive advice did; and 73 percent of those to be sent out of the residence for eight hours actually were sent. One explanation for this pattern . . . is that mediating and sending were more difficult ways for police to control a situation. There was a greater likelihood that an officer might have to resort to arrest as a fallback position. . . .

RESULTS

[Two] measures of repeat violence were used in the experiment. One was a police record of an offender repeating domestic violence during the six-month follow-up period. . . . A second kind of measure came from the interviews in which victims were asked if there had been a repeat incident with the same suspect, broadly defined to include an assault, threatened assault, or property damage. . . .

Figure 1 shows the results taken from the police records on subsequent violence. The arrest treatment is clearly an improvement over sending the suspect away, which produced two and a half times as many repeat incidents as arrest. The advice treatment was statistically not distinguishable from the other two police actions.

Figure 2 shows a somewhat different picture. According to the victims' reports of repeat violence, arrest is still the most effective police action. But the advise category, not sending the suspect away, produced the worst results, with almost twice as much violence as arrest. Sending the suspect away produced results that were not statistically distinguishable from the results of the other two actions. It is not clear why the order of the three levels of repeat violence is different for these two ways of measuring the violence. But it is clear that arrest works best by either measure.

Additional statistical analysis showed that these findings were basically the same for all categories of suspects. Regardless of the race, employment status, educational level, criminal history of the suspect, or how long the suspect was in jail when arrested, arrest still had the strongest violence reduction effect. There was one factor, however, that seemed to govern the effectiveness of arrest: whether the police showed interest in the victim's side of the story.

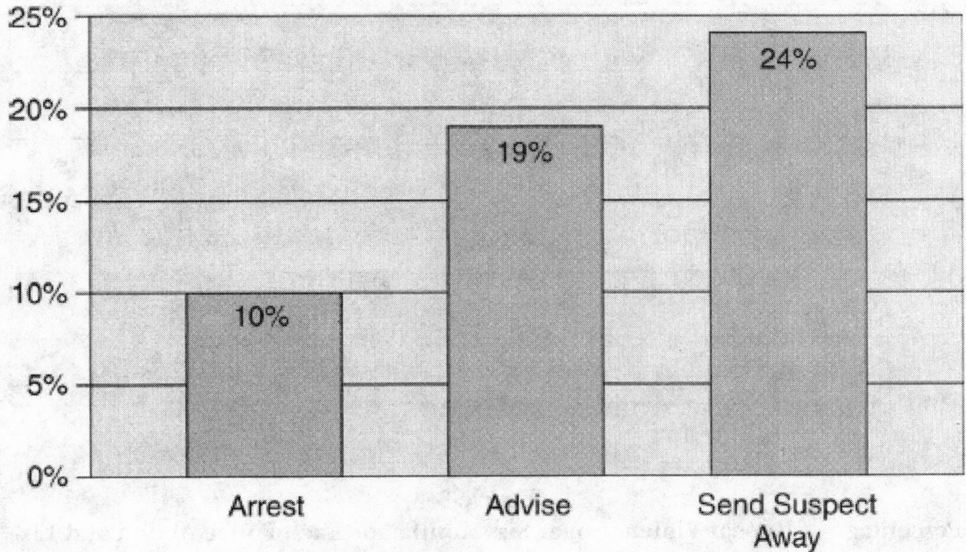

Figure 1
Percentage of Repeat Violence over Six Months for Each Police Action (Office Records N = 314)

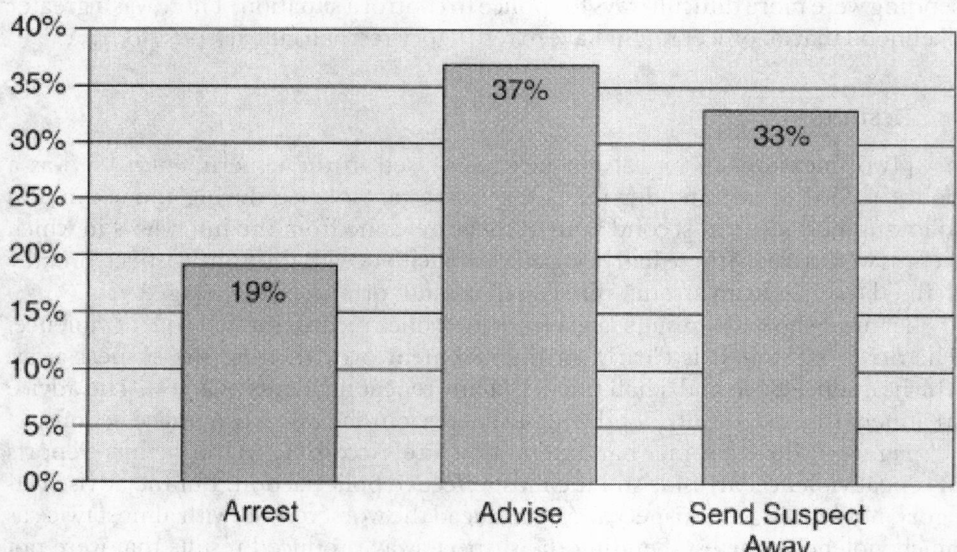

Figure 2
Percentage of Repeat Violence over Six Months for Each Police Action (Victim Interviews N = 161)

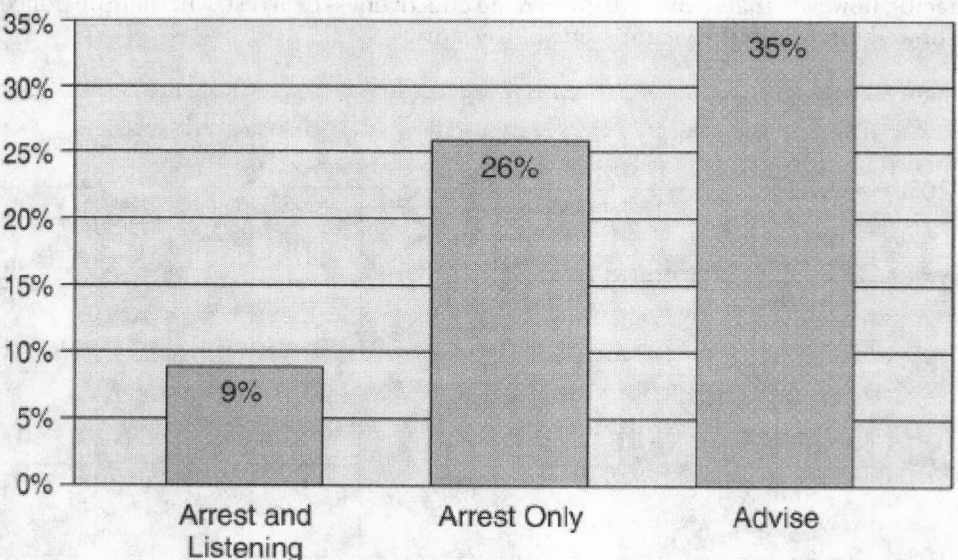

Figure 3
Percentage of Repeat Violence over Six Months for Each Police Action and Listening to Victim (Victim Interviews N = 194)

Figure 3 shows what happens to the effect of arrest on repeat violence incidents when the police do or do not take the time to listen to the victim, at least as the victim perceives it. If police do listen, that reduces the occurrence of repeat violence even more. But if the victims think the police did not take the time to listen, then the level of victim-reported violence is much higher. One interpretation of this finding is that by listening to the victim, the police "empower" her with their strength, letting the suspect know that she can influence their behavior. If police ignore the victim, the suspect may think he was arrested for arbitrary reasons unrelated to the victim and be less deterred from future violence.

Conclusions and Policy Implications

It may be premature to conclude that arrest is always the best way for police to handle domestic violence, or that all suspects in such situations should be arrested. A number of factors suggest a cautious interpretation of the findings, [such as the small sample size, the fact that most arrested suspects in Minneapolis spent the night in jail, and biases in the interview and follow-up process].

But police officers cannot wait for further research to decide how to handle the domestic violence they face each day. They must use the best information available. This experiment provides the only scientifically controlled comparison of different methods of reducing repeat violence. And on the basis of this study alone, police should probably employ arrest in most cases of minor domestic violence. . . .

As a result of the experiment's findings, the Minneapolis Police Department changed its policy on domestic assault in early March of 1984. The policy did not make arrest 100 percent mandatory. But it did require officers to file a written report explaining why they failed to make an arrest when it was legally possible to do so. . . . If the findings are truly generalizeable, the experiment will help ultimately to reduce one of the most common forms of violent crime.

Notes

1. *Common law arrest powers and domestic abuse.* As the passage from Blackstone indicates, officers at common law did not have authority to make a warrantless arrest of a person who committed a misdemeanor out of the presence of the officer, even if the officer had probable cause to believe that the person had committed the crime. This common law limitation often survived in the case law and statutes of states and is still the law in a few locations (fewer than 10 states). This limitation makes it difficult for police officers, without some special statutory authority, to make arrests in the typical domestic abuse call. "Simple assault" is ordinarily classified as a misdemeanor.

2. *The variety of legislative solutions.* Many statutes, like those reprinted above, expand the authority of the officer to arrest an assailant in a domestic abuse setting. Note the different limits that states (for instance, Oklahoma and Connecticut) place on this expanded arrest power. Why do the statutes address the time elapsed between the injury and the arrival of the police? See N.H. Stat. §594:10 (authority to arrest without warrant for misdemeanor domestic abuse occurring within six hours of arrest). Why do some require evidence of a physical injury? See 18 Pa. Cons. Stat. §2711; W. Va. Code §48-27-1002 (listing examples of "credible corroborative

evidence," such as contusions, missing hair, torn clothing, damaged furnishings on premises).

In addition to expanding police authority to arrest in the domestic abuse setting, some of the statutes encourage or require officers to respond in ways other than arresting the assailant. For instance, about a dozen states require the officer on the scene to provide the victim with information about health care and legal protection from further abuse. Why do some statutes call for an automatic warning, such as the one set forth in the Iowa statute? It is also common for statutes to require the officer responding to the call to report the incident to the prosecutor's office, regardless of the arrest decision.

Finally, more than a dozen states have passed statutes encouraging or mandating arrest as the proper police response to evidence of domestic violence. Is the Iowa statute an example of a mandatory statute? While a few statutes only require probable cause that a domestic violence offense has occurred, other statutes impose a number of different preconditions on the mandatory arrest duty of the police. See Utah Code Ann. §77-36-2.2 ("shall arrest" if there is evidence of recent serious injury, or use of dangerous weapon, or probable cause to believe there is potential of continued violence toward victim); Mo. Rev. Stat. §455.085 ("shall" arrest for second incident within 12 hours). Why does Iowa direct a police officer to arrest the person the officer believes to be the "primary physical aggressor," and how does the statute define that term?

The statutes reprinted here do not exhaust the legislative responses to this problem. Other relevant approaches include a Florida statute directing state agencies to collect detailed annual statistics about the enforcement of that state's domestic violence arrest policy and subsequent incidents of violence. See Fla. Stat. §943.1702. Some statutes emphasize training of officers that stresses the criminal nature of domestic abuse rather than the "social work" approach to the problem. Idaho Code §6316.

As the Sherman and Berk study demonstrates, local ordinances or police department policies might adopt a mandatory arrest policy, or a strong preference for arrests, even when state statutes do not. Indeed, almost 90 percent of all police departments have policies dealing with domestic violence. See Bureau of Justice Statistics, Local Police Departments 2003 (June 2006, NCJ 210118).

3. *Arrest statutes for other crimes.* For some other controversial offenses, statutes in many states provide for arrest powers that are broader than common law arrest doctrine would support. One common example is a statute that approves warrantless arrests whenever a driver violates the traffic code or commits related offenses such as driving under the influence. See N.D. Cent. Code §29-06-15(1)(f). These driving violation arrest statutes find additional authority in the quasi-contractual nature of the agreement between the citizen and the state represented by the driver's license: The citizen, it is argued, grants the state additional arrest powers if she exercises the option to drive.

4. *Arrest quotas.* Police department policies *other* than those calling for automatic or presumed arrests in some situations can have a powerful effect on individual officers' arrest decisions. How will officers respond to a departmental policy that evaluates and rewards officers based on the number of arrests they make? See Howie Carr, "Arresting Memo Puts State Cops in a Pinch," Boston Herald, Oct. 21, 1998, at 1 (quoting internal memorandum of Massachusetts State Police, reviewing arrest journal and calling for "corrective action" to "increase the level of activity" because

arrests are a "valid indicator" but not the only indicator of good performance). Is there a plausible legal basis for challenging a system of "arrest quotas" in court? Disputes over these policies more often arise during labor negotiations between police officer unions and department administrators.

5. *History and changes in legal rules.* Lawyers typically face questions about the application or validity of a *current* rule. Because they are not trained as historians and have limited time and resources, it can be difficult for lawyers to trace the evolution of policies and rules. One of the notable aspects of the Sherman and Berk policy paper is its effective use of recent history (the past 20 years) to build an argument for a particular policy position.

The story told by Sherman and Berk offers a telling reminder: Prior policies were passionately supported by smart and principled people, and those policies, too, were bolstered by varying amounts of research. This realization should serve as a warning against assuming that current policies are necessarily an improvement over earlier ones and that the current policy is the best possible policy — the end of the line. About the only thing that can be said with confidence about any policy in effect 10 to 20 years from now is that its proponents will view current policy — the current generation's views — as misguided and ineffective.

6. *The virtues of social science methods.* How persuasive is the bottom line in the analysis of the Minneapolis experiment? If you were the police chief in another city or a legislator in another state, would you change policy on the basis of this publication?

This policy brief, and the movement it captured, is a notable example of the possible influence of social science on criminal procedure. Many states and police departments adopted some version of an "automatic" arrest policy (although most are not truly mandatory arrest policies but strongly encourage such arrests). Despite the warnings about the need for further research, the Minneapolis study was central in promoting these policy changes.

7. *"More research is needed": an important caveat.* A series of replication experiments in six cities only partially confirmed the dramatic findings in Minneapolis. In three cities, the use of arrest actually *increased* later domestic violence. The use of arrest had more of a deterrent effect on suspects who were employed than on those who were unemployed. Arrest also had a positive effect in *neighborhoods* with high rates of employment, and negative effects in neighborhoods with low employment rates. See, e.g., Lawrence W. Sherman, The Police, in James Q. Wilson & Joan Petersilia, Eds., Crime 327, 336-38 (1995) (describing replication studies in Omaha, Charlotte, Milwaukee, Colorado Springs, Bade County). Criminologists remain interested in this topic and continue to generate new data and updated analyses. For references to this sociological literature and a discussion of its ongoing significance, go to the web extension for this chapter at *http://www.crimpro.com/extension/ch05*.

Despite the mixed outcomes of replication studies, policies favoring arrest in domestic assault situations generally have remained in force, and new policies encouraging arrest are still being adopted. Why hasn't the more recent research on domestic assaults and arrest policies produced more targeted policies (for instance, a policy calling for arrest only if the suspect is employed)? Is it easier for police chiefs, mayors, and legislators to apply the gas than the brakes?

Problem 5-2. Arrests and Curfews

The local police department is considering a rule that would require officers to take into custody every juvenile found outdoors after an established curfew hour. The department hopes the new rule will reduce the crime rate by and against juveniles. A recent study found that 40 percent of crimes after curfew are committed against juveniles and that an unknown but significant percentage of all crimes — especially property crimes — are also committed by juveniles.

How would you design a study to test whether the proposed arrest policy would reduce either crimes generally or the percentage of crimes against juveniles? How would you convince the local police department to participate in the study? Would you tell the media about the study?

Problem 5-3. Racial Patterns in Arrests

In the early 1980s, police officers in Georgia arrested more white suspects than black suspects for drug offenses. In a typical year, officers arrested about 10,000 white suspects and 5,000 to 7,000 black suspects. Beginning in the mid-1980s, law enforcement officials decided to increase their emphasis on enforcement of the narcotics laws. As a result, the number of white suspects arrested each year on drug charges increased slightly, while a much steeper increase occurred in arrests of black suspects. Between 1990 and 1995, black suspects accounted for about 119,000 drug arrests; white suspects accounted for about 58,000 arrests, less than a third of the total. The disparity was stronger for cocaine cases than for marijuana cases. About 85 percent of all cocaine arrestees were black, while just over 40 percent of the marijuana arrestees were black.

When these figures are adjusted for the number of blacks and whites in the general population of the state, the arrest rate for African Americans was more than 10,200 arrests (over the five-year period) for every 100,000 black residents of the state. The comparable rate for whites was about 1,600 arrests for every 100,000 white residents. Even for marijuana arrests, where the racial disparities were least pronounced, the adjusted rate of arrest for blacks was about 2,600 per 100,000, while the rate for whites was around 1,200 per 100,000. National surveys at the time suggested that a slightly larger proportion of blacks than whites used illicit drugs. These surveys showed that blacks used drugs at a rate about 20 percent higher than whites.

As a concerned high-ranking police official, how might you react to these developments? Officers in the department tell you that more blacks are arrested for drug trafficking because they tend to make more sales on street corners and other places visible to the public, while white users and sellers tend more often to conduct their operations indoors. Would it address the disparity problem to issue a departmental policy making arrest mandatory whenever a police officer develops probable cause that a narcotics offense has taken place, no matter how small?

Notes

1. *The competing (or complementary) explanations.* For most crimes that generate large numbers of arrests in this country, African Americans are arrested in numbers disproportionate to their percentage of the general population. The disproportion is usually much less dramatic than the numbers described above for drug arrests in Georgia. But the differences are present, nonetheless, for many crimes in many different places (but not for all crimes or places). How might one explain this persistent and discomfiting fact?

Some have postulated racial bias, whether conscious or unconscious, on the part of arresting police officers. See Coramae Richey Mann, Unequal Justice (1993). Consistent with this view, one study of the processing of arrests by prosecutors suggested that blacks were arrested on less stringent legal criteria than whites. John Hepburn, Race and the Decision to Arrest: An Analysis of Warrants Issued, 15 J. Res. Crime & Delinq. 54 (1978). Others conclude that blacks are arrested more often because they more often violate the criminal law. Alfred Blumstein, On the Racial Disproportionality of the United States' Prison Populations, 73 J. Crim. L. & Criminology 1259 (1982). Those who rely on this explanation point to surveys of victims regarding the race of the offenders in their cases (regardless of whether the police were ever involved or whether an arrest was ever made): The information from victims about the race of criminal perpetrators roughly corresponds to the racial makeup of arrestees.

Another line of explanation suggests, based on observations from field studies, that police officers are more likely to arrest suspects who are antagonistic toward them and that black suspects are more likely to meet this description. See Donald Black, The Social Organization of Arrest, 23 Stan. L. Rev. 1087 (1971). Still another group of researchers has argued that police arrest black suspects more frequently because black complainants (who are most often the victims of crimes by black perpetrators) request arrest more often than white complainants. See Richard Lundman, Richard Sykes & John Clark, Police Control of Juveniles: A Replication, 15 J. Res. Crime & Delinq. 74 (1978). Others suggest that blacks are more likely to encounter police officers in poorer neighborhoods and that police officers are more likely to use their discretion to arrest in such neighborhoods. Douglas Smith, Christy Visher & Laura Davidson, Equity and Discretionary Justice: The Influence of Race on Police Arrest Decisions, 75 J. Crim. L. & Criminology 234 (1984). Do these various explanations for racial disparity in arrest rates conflict with one another or are they reconcilable? Further studies of the interaction of race and arrest practices receive attention on the web extension for this chapter at *http://www.crimpro.com/extension/ch05*.

2. *The ethics of police experiments.* Does it trouble you that the Minneapolis police treated similar domestic assault cases differently in the same time period? Do the police have an obligation to apply one, consistent policy at any one time? The recommendation that police officers pursue an arrest policy, in Minneapolis and elsewhere, was not based on a prediction that more arrests would lead to more domestic assault prosecutions. Is there an ethical issue with police using arrest when they know there will not be a prosecution? Does arrest become a form of punishment without trial?

3. *Expungement of arrest records.* Arrests have consequences beyond the initial detention. An arrest record might influence police decisions months or years later about who to investigate, or prosecutorial decisions about whether to charge a person with a new crime. But what if the original arrest was unfounded? Many states provide for "expungement" of arrest records if they do not result in conviction. The state laws vary greatly as to the crimes where they apply (for instance, some make arrests for sex crimes ineligible for expungement). They use different events to judge which arrests were unsubstantiated and therefore subject to expungement: Some use acquittal only, while others include any dismissal without adjudication. Some of them are self-executing, while others depend on a formal request from the arrestee. Should expungement be available automatically (and immediately) whenever a case is dismissed without a prosecution? See Mich. Comp. Laws 28.243 (5); 20 ILCS 2630/5.

D. PAPER ARRESTS: CITATIONS

An arrest is not the only method available to initiate a criminal prosecution or to secure a defendant's presence at judicial proceedings. There are some circumstances when a police officer will issue a "citation" or "appearance ticket" to a person, requiring the person to appear in court regarding a crime the officer believes the person has committed. As in other areas of police officer discretion not to arrest, legal reforms in this field are moving in different directions. On the one hand, the range of offenses where the officer can use citation rather than arrest is expanding. On the other hand, in some limited circumstances the law restricts the officer to using a citation instead of an arrest.

■ NEW YORK CRIMINAL PROCEDURE LAW §§150.10, 150.20, 150.60

§150.10

An appearance ticket is a written notice issued and subscribed by a police officer or other public servant . . . , directing a designated person to appear in a designated local criminal court at a designated future time in connection with his alleged commission of a designated offense. . . .

§150.20

1. Whenever a police officer is authorized . . . to arrest a person without a warrant for an offense other than a class A, B, C or D felony, [the officer may] instead issue to and serve upon such person an appearance ticket.
2. (a) Whenever a police officer has arrested a person without a warrant for an offense other than a class A, B, C or D felony . . . such police officer may, instead of bringing such person before a local criminal court and promptly filing or causing the arresting peace officer or arresting person to file a local

criminal court accusatory instrument therewith, issue to and serve upon such person an appearance ticket. The issuance and service of an appearance ticket under such circumstances may be conditioned upon a deposit of pre-arraignment bail. . . .

§150.60

If after the service of an appearance ticket and the filing of a local criminal court accusatory instrument charging the offense designated therein, the defendant does not appear in the designated local criminal court at the time such appearance ticket is returnable, the court may issue a summons or a warrant of arrest based upon the local criminal court accusatory instrument filed.

Commission Staff Notes on Desk Appearance Ticket Provisions (1970 Comment)*

[An appearance ticket] is issued and served by a police officer or other public servant who has observed the commission of a minor offense, and it requires the offender to appear in a designated court upon a designated return date to answer a charge which the issuer of the ticket will formally file in the court some time after the issuance. In terms of basic function, an appearance ticket is used in some minor cases as a compassionate substitute for an arrest without a warrant, which is also employed to require or compel the court appearance of an offender against whom no formal charges have as yet been lodged.

On a state-wide basis, the use of appearance tickets is at present largely confined to traffic infraction cases. In New York City, however, numerous non-police public officials and employees, such as those of the Sanitation, Fire, Building and Markets Departments, are authorized to issue and serve such tickets in cases involving offenses peculiarly within their ambits. . . .

The theory of the proposed section is that under present law the virtues and advantages of the appearance ticket have not been sufficiently exploited. . . . The results to be expected from the new appearance ticket scheme are (1) an immense saving of police time, (2) elimination of much expense and embarrassment to defendants charged with minor offenses who are excellent risks to appear in court when required, and (3) above all, a significant reduction of that portion of our jail population consisting of unconvicted defendants awaiting trial or other disposition of their cases.

The advantages to the police may be partly appreciated by picturing the predicament of a police officer who observes the commission of a misdemeanor or petty offense by a person whom he either knows to be a resident of the community or whom he finds to have solid roots therein. Absent the appearance ticket device, two very awkward and unsatisfactory courses of action are available to the officer. Normal procedure requires him to arrest the defendant and, dropping his regular duties, take him to the station house to book him, and then to take him to a local criminal court where a formal information must be filed, the defendant arraigned, bail set, and so on. The even less appealing and equally time consuming alternative

* [This is considered the legislative history for these provisions. The following excerpts mix paragraphs from the report for different statutory sections. — Eds.]

entails the officer first going to the court himself, filing an information against the defendant, obtaining a summons or a warrant of arrest and then returning to find the defendant and serve or execute such process; and all this in a case in which the simple issuance of an appearance ticket would almost certainly accomplish the same end result.

■ REVISED STATUTES OF NEBRASKA §§29-435, 29-427

§29-435

Except as provided in section 29-427, for any offense classified as an infraction, a citation shall be issued in lieu of arrest or continued custody. . . .

§29-427

Any peace officer having grounds for making an arrest may take the accused into custody or, already having done so, detain him further when the accused fails to identify himself satisfactorily, or refuses to sign the citation, or when the officer has reasonable grounds to believe that (1) the accused will refuse to respond to the citation, (2) such custody is necessary to protect the accused or others when his continued liberty would constitute a risk of immediate harm, (3) such action is necessary in order to carry out legitimate investigative functions, (4) the accused has no ties to the jurisdiction reasonably sufficient to assure his appearance, or (5) the accused has previously failed to appear in response to a citation.

■ PATRICK KNOWLES v. IOWA

525 U.S. 113 (1998)

REHNQUIST, C.J.*

An Iowa police officer stopped petitioner Knowles for speeding, but issued him a citation rather than arresting him. The question presented is whether such a procedure authorizes the officer, consistently with the Fourth Amendment, to conduct a full search of the car. We answer this question "no."

Knowles was stopped in Newton, Iowa, after having been clocked driving 43 miles per hour on a road where the speed limit was 25 miles per hour. The police officer issued a citation to Knowles, although under Iowa law he might have arrested him. The officer then conducted a full search of the car, and under the driver's seat he found a bag of marijuana and a "pot pipe." Knowles was then arrested and charged with violation of state laws dealing with controlled substances.

Before trial, Knowles moved to suppress the evidence so obtained. He argued that the search could not be sustained under the "search incident to arrest" exception recognized in United States v. Robinson, 414 U.S. 218 (1973), because he had not been placed under arrest. At the hearing on the motion to suppress, the police officer conceded that he had neither Knowles' consent nor probable cause to conduct the search. He relied on Iowa law dealing with such searches.

* [All the Justices joined in this opinion. — EDS.]

Iowa Code Ann. §321.485(1) (a) provides that Iowa peace officers having cause to believe that a person has violated any traffic or motor vehicle equipment law may arrest the person and immediately take the person before a magistrate. Iowa law also authorizes the far more usual practice of issuing a citation in lieu of arrest or in lieu of continued custody after an initial arrest.[1] Section 805.1(4) provides that the issuance of a citation in lieu of an arrest "does not affect the officer's authority to conduct an otherwise lawful search." The Iowa Supreme Court has interpreted this provision as providing authority to officers to conduct a full-blown search of an automobile and driver in those cases where police elect not to make a custodial arrest and instead issue a citation — that is, a search incident to citation. See State v. Meyer, 543 N.W.2d 876, 879 (Iowa 1996). Based on this authority, the trial court denied the motion to suppress and found Knowles guilty. . . .

In *Robinson,* we noted the two historical rationales for the "search incident to arrest" exception: (1) the need to disarm the suspect in order to take him into custody, and (2) the need to preserve evidence for later use at trial. But neither of these underlying rationales for the search incident to arrest exception is sufficient to justify the search in the present case.

We have recognized that the first rationale — officer safety — is both legitimate and weighty. The threat to officer safety from issuing a traffic citation, however, is a good deal less than in the case of a custodial arrest. In *Robinson,* we stated that a custodial arrest involves "danger to an officer" because of "the extended exposure which follows the taking of a suspect into custody and transporting him to the police station." . . . A routine traffic stop, on the other hand, is a relatively brief encounter and is more analogous to a so-called *Terry* stop than to a formal arrest.

This is not to say that the concern for officer safety is absent in the case of a routine traffic stop. It plainly is not. But while the concern for officer safety in this context may justify the "minimal" additional intrusion of ordering a driver and passengers out of the car, it does not by itself justify the often considerably greater intrusion attending a full field-type search. Even without the search authority Iowa urges, officers have other, independent bases to search for weapons and protect themselves from danger. For example, they may order out of a vehicle both the driver, Pennsylvania v. Mimms, 434 U.S. 106, 111 (1977) (per curiam), and any passengers, Maryland v. Wilson, 519 U.S. 408, 414 (1997); perform a "patdown" of a driver and any passengers upon reasonable suspicion that they may be armed and dangerous, Terry v. Ohio, 392 U.S. 1 (1968); conduct a "*Terry* patdown" of the passenger compartment of a vehicle upon reasonable suspicion that an occupant is dangerous and may gain immediate control of a weapon, Michigan v. Long, 463 U.S. 1032 (1983); and even conduct a full search of the passenger compartment, including any containers therein, pursuant to a custodial arrest, New York v. Belton, 453 U.S. 454, 460 (1981).

Nor has Iowa shown the second justification for the authority to search incident to arrest — the need to discover and preserve evidence. Once Knowles was stopped

1. Iowa law permits the issuance of a citation in lieu of arrest for most offenses for which an accused person would be "eligible for bail." See Iowa Code Ann. §805.1(1). In addition to traffic and motor vehicle equipment violations, this would permit the issuance of a citation in lieu of arrest for such serious felonies as second-degree burglary and first-degree theft, both bailable offenses under Iowa law. The practice in Iowa of permitting citation in lieu of arrest is consistent with law reform efforts. See 3 W LaFave, Search and Seizure §5.2(h), p. 99, and n.151 (3d ed. 1996).

for speeding and issued a citation, all the evidence necessary to prosecute that offense had been obtained. No further evidence of excessive speed was going to be found either on the person of the offender or in the passenger compartment of the car.

Iowa nevertheless argues that a "search incident to citation" is justified because a suspect who is subject to a routine traffic stop may attempt to hide or destroy evidence related to his identity (e.g., a driver's license or vehicle registration), or destroy evidence of another, as yet undetected crime. As for the destruction of evidence relating to identity, if a police officer is not satisfied with the identification furnished by the driver, this may be a basis for arresting him rather than merely issuing a citation. As for destroying evidence of other crimes, the possibility that an officer would stumble onto evidence wholly unrelated to the speeding offense seems remote.

In *Robinson*, we held that the authority to conduct a full field search as incident to an arrest was a "bright-line rule," which was based on the concern for officer safety and destruction or loss of evidence, but which did not depend in every case upon the existence of either concern. Here we are asked to extend that "bright-line rule" to a situation where the concern for officer safety is not present to the same extent and the concern for destruction or loss of evidence is not present at all. We decline to do so. . . .

■ GAIL ATWATER v. CITY OF LAGO VISTA

532 U.S. 318 (2001)

SOUTER, J.*

The question is whether the Fourth Amendment forbids a warrantless arrest for a minor criminal offense, such as a misdemeanor seatbelt violation punishable only by a fine. We hold that it does not.

I. . . .

In Texas, if a car is equipped with safety belts, a front-seat passenger must wear one, and the driver must secure any small child riding in front. Violation of either provision is a misdemeanor punishable by a fine not less than $25 or more than $50. Texas law expressly authorizes "any peace officer [to] arrest without warrant a person found committing a violation" of these seatbelt laws, Transp. Code §543.001, although it permits police to issue citations in lieu of arrest.

In March 1997, Petitioner Gail Atwater was driving her pickup truck in Lago Vista, Texas, with her 3-year-old son and 5-year-old daughter in the front seat. None of them was wearing a seatbelt. Respondent Bart Turek, a Lago Vista police officer at the time, observed the seatbelt violations and pulled Atwater over. According to Atwater's complaint (the allegations of which we assume to be true for present purposes), Turek approached the truck and "yelled" something to the effect of "we've

* [Chief Justice Rehnquist and Justices Scalia, Kennedy, and Thomas joined in this opinion. — EDS.]

met before" and "you're going to jail."[1] He then called for backup and asked to see Atwater's driver's license and insurance documentation, which state law required her to carry. When Atwater told Turek that she did not have the papers because her purse had been stolen the day before, Turek said that he had "heard that story two hundred times."

Atwater asked to take her frightened, upset, and crying children to a friend's house nearby, but Turek told her, "you're not going anywhere." As it turned out, Atwater's friend learned what was going on and soon arrived to take charge of the children. Turek then handcuffed Atwater, placed her in his squad car, and drove her to the local police station, where booking officers had her remove her shoes, jewelry, and eyeglasses, and empty her pockets. Officers took Atwater's "mug shot" and placed her, alone, in a jail cell for about one hour, after which she was taken before a magistrate and released on $310 bond.

Atwater was charged with driving without her seatbelt fastened, failing to secure her children in seatbelts, driving without a license, and failing to provide proof of insurance. She ultimately pleaded no contest to the misdemeanor seatbelt offenses and paid a $50 fine; the other charges were dismissed. Atwater and her husband, petitioner Michael Haas, filed suit in a Texas state court under 42 U.S.C. §1983, [alleging that the City] had violated Atwater's Fourth Amendment "right to be free from unreasonable seizure," and sought compensatory and punitive damages.

II.

[An] examination of the common-law understanding of an officer's authority to arrest sheds light on the obviously relevant, if not entirely dispositive, consideration of what the Framers of the Amendment might have thought to be reasonable. . . . Atwater's specific contention is that "founding-era common-law rules" forbade peace officers to make warrantless misdemeanor arrests except in cases of "breach of the peace," a category she claims was then understood narrowly as covering only those nonfelony offenses "involving or tending toward violence." Although her historical argument is by no means insubstantial, it ultimately fails.

A.

We [find that] the common-law commentators (as well as the sparsely reported cases) reached divergent conclusions with respect to officers' warrantless misdemeanor arrest power. . . .

On one side of the divide there are certainly eminent authorities supporting Atwater's position. . . . James Fitzjames Stephen and Glanville Williams both seemed to indicate that the common law confined warrantless misdemeanor arrests to actual breaches of the peace. See 1 J. Stephen, A History of the Criminal Law of England 193 (1883) ("The common law did not authorise the arrest of persons guilty or suspected of misdemeanours, except in cases of an actual breach of the peace either by an affray or by violence to an individual"); G. Williams, Arrest for Breach of the Peace, 1954 Crim. L. Rev. 578, 578 ("Apart from arrest for felony . . . , the only power of arrest at common law is in respect of breach of the peace"). . . .

1. Turek had previously stopped Atwater for what he had thought was a seatbelt violation, but had realized that Atwater's son, although seated on the vehicle's armrest, was in fact belted in. Atwater acknowledged that her son's seating position was unsafe, and Turek issued a verbal warning.

The great commentators were not unanimous, however, and there is also considerable evidence of a broader conception of common-law misdemeanor arrest authority unlimited by any breach-of-the-peace condition. Sir Matthew Hale, Chief Justice of King's Bench from 1671 to 1676, wrote in his History of the Pleas of the Crown that, by his "original and inherent power," a constable could arrest without a warrant "for breach of the peace and some misdemeanors, less than felony." 2 M. Hale, The History of the Pleas of the Crown 88 (1736)....

A second, and equally serious, problem for Atwater's historical argument is posed by the "divers Statutes," M. Dalton, Country Justice ch. 170, §4, p. 582 (1727), enacted by Parliament well before this Republic's founding that authorized warrantless misdemeanor arrests without reference to violence or turmoil. [T]he legal background of any conception of reasonableness the Fourth Amendment's Framers might have entertained would have included English statutes, some centuries old, authorizing peace officers (and even private persons) to make warrantless arrests for all sorts of relatively minor offenses unaccompanied by violence. The so-called "nightwalker" statutes are perhaps the most notable examples. From the enactment of the Statute of Winchester in 1285, through its various readoptions and until its repeal in 1827, night watchmen were authorized and charged "as . . . in Times past" to "watch the Town continually all Night, from the Sun-setting unto the Sun-rising" and were directed that "if any Stranger do pass by them, he shall be arrested until Morning. . . ."

B.

An examination of specifically American evidence is to the same effect. Neither the history of the framing era nor subsequent legal development indicates that the Fourth Amendment was originally understood, or has traditionally been read, to embrace Atwater's position.... During the period leading up to and surrounding the framing of the Bill of Rights, colonial and state legislatures, like Parliament before them, regularly authorized local peace officers to make warrantless misdemeanor arrests without conditioning statutory authority on breach of the peace. See, e.g., First Laws of the State of Connecticut 214-215 (authorizing warrantless arrests of "all Persons unnecessarily travelling on the Sabbath or Lord's Day")....

Nor does Atwater's argument from tradition pick up any steam from the historical record as it has unfolded since the framing, there being no indication that her claimed rule has ever become woven into the fabric of American law. The story, on the contrary, is of two centuries of uninterrupted (and largely unchallenged) state and federal practice permitting warrantless arrests for misdemeanors not amounting to or involving breach of the peace.

[There are] numerous early- and mid-19th-century decisions expressly sustaining (often against constitutional challenge) state and local laws authorizing peace officers to make warrantless arrests for misdemeanors not involving any breach of the peace. See, e.g., Mayo v. Wilson, 1 N.H. 53 (1817) (upholding statute authorizing warrantless arrests of those unnecessarily traveling on Sunday against challenge based on state due process and search-and-seizure provisions).... Small wonder, then, that today statutes in all 50 States and the District of Columbia permit warrantless misdemeanor arrests by at least some (if not all) peace officers without requiring any breach of the peace, as do a host of congressional enactments....

III.

[But] Atwater does not wager all on history. Instead, she asks us to mint a new rule of constitutional law on the understanding that when historical practice fails to speak conclusively to a claim grounded on the Fourth Amendment, courts are left to strike a current balance between individual and societal interests by subjecting particular contemporary circumstances to traditional standards of reasonableness. . . .

If we were to derive a rule exclusively to address the uncontested facts of this case, Atwater might well prevail. She was a known and established resident of Lago Vista with no place to hide and no incentive to flee, and common sense says she would almost certainly have buckled up as a condition of driving off with a citation. In her case, the physical incidents of arrest were merely gratuitous humiliations imposed by a police officer who was (at best) exercising extremely poor judgment. Atwater's claim to live free of pointless indignity and confinement clearly outweighs anything the City can raise against it specific to her case.

But we have traditionally recognized that a responsible Fourth Amendment balance is not well served by standards requiring sensitive, case-by-case determinations of government need, lest every discretionary judgment in the field be converted into an occasion for constitutional review. Often enough, the Fourth Amendment has to be applied on the spur (and in the heat) of the moment, and the object in implementing its command of reasonableness is to draw standards sufficiently clear and simple to be applied with a fair prospect of surviving judicial second-guessing months and years after an arrest or search is made. . . .

At first glance, Atwater's argument may seem to respect the values of clarity and simplicity, so far as she claims that the Fourth Amendment generally forbids warrantless arrests for minor crimes not accompanied by violence or some demonstrable threat of it (whether "minor crime" be defined as a fine-only traffic offense, a fine-only offense more generally, or a misdemeanor). But the claim is not ultimately so simple, nor could it be, for complications arise the moment we begin to think about the possible applications of the several criteria Atwater proposes for drawing a line between minor crimes with limited arrest authority and others not so restricted.

One line, she suggests, might be between "jailable" and "fine-only" offenses, between those for which conviction could result in commitment and those for which it could not. The trouble with this distinction, of course, is that an officer on the street might not be able to tell. It is not merely that we cannot expect every police officer to know the details of frequently complex penalty schemes, but that penalties for ostensibly identical conduct can vary on account of facts difficult (if not impossible) to know at the scene of an arrest. Is this the first offense or is the suspect a repeat offender? Is the weight of the marijuana a gram above or a gram below the fine-only line? Where conduct could implicate more than one criminal prohibition, which one will the district attorney ultimately decide to charge? And so on.

But Atwater's refinements would not end there. She represents that if the line were drawn at nonjailable traffic offenses, her proposed limitation should be qualified by a proviso authorizing warrantless arrests where "necessary for enforcement of the traffic laws or when [an] offense would otherwise continue and pose a danger to others on the road." . . . The proviso only compounds the difficulties.

Would, for instance, either exception apply to speeding? [Is] it not fair to expect that the chronic speeder will speed again despite a citation in his pocket, and should that not qualify as showing that the "offense would . . . continue" under Atwater's rule? . . . Atwater's rule therefore would not only place police in an almost impossible spot but would guarantee increased litigation over many of the arrests that would occur. . . .

An officer not quite sure that the drugs weighed enough to warrant jail time or not quite certain about a suspect's risk of flight would not arrest, even though it could perfectly well turn out that, in fact, the offense called for incarceration and the defendant was long gone on the day of trial. Multiplied many times over, the costs to society of such underenforcement could easily outweigh the costs to defendants of being needlessly arrested and booked. . . .

Just how easily the costs could outweigh the benefits may be shown by asking, as one Member of this Court did at oral argument, "how bad the problem is out there." The very fact that the law has never jelled the way Atwater would have it leads one to wonder whether warrantless misdemeanor arrests need constitutional attention, and there is cause to think the answer is no. [Anyone] arrested for a crime without formal process, whether for felony or misdemeanor, is entitled to a magistrate's review of probable cause within 48 hours. . . . Many jurisdictions, moreover, have chosen to impose more restrictive safeguards through statutes limiting warrantless arrests for minor offenses. [The Court cited statutes from eight states.] It is of course easier to devise a minor-offense limitation by statute than to derive one through the Constitution, simply because the statute can let the arrest power turn on any sort of practical consideration without having to subsume it under a broader principle. It is, in fact, only natural that States should resort to this sort of legislative regulation, for, as Atwater's own *amici* emphasize, it is in the interest of the police to limit petty-offense arrests, which carry costs that are simply too great to incur without good reason.

. . . The upshot of all these influences, combined with the good sense (and, failing that, the political accountability) of most local lawmakers and law-enforcement officials, is a dearth of horribles demanding redress. [The] country is not confronting anything like an epidemic of unnecessary minor-offense arrests. . . . Accordingly, we confirm today [that if] an officer has probable cause to believe that an individual has committed even a very minor criminal offense in his presence, he may, without violating the Fourth Amendment, arrest the offender.

O'CONNOR, J., dissenting.*

. . . I.

[History] is just one of the tools we use in conducting the reasonableness inquiry. And when history is inconclusive, as the majority amply demonstrates it is in this case, we will evaluate the search or seizure under traditional standards of reasonableness by assessing, on the one hand, the degree to which it intrudes upon an individual's privacy and, on the other, the degree to which it is needed for the promotion of legitimate governmental interests. In other words, in determining reasonableness, each case is to be decided on its own facts and circumstances. . . .

* [Justices Stevens, Ginsburg, and Breyer joined in this opinion. — EDS.]

A custodial arrest exacts an obvious toll on an individual's liberty and privacy, even when the period of custody is relatively brief. The arrestee is subject to a full search of her person and confiscation of her possessions. If the arrestee is the occupant of a car, the entire passenger compartment of the car, including packages therein, is subject to search as well. The arrestee may be detained for up to 48 hours without having a magistrate determine whether there in fact was probable cause for the arrest. Because people arrested for all types of violent and nonviolent offenses may be housed together awaiting such review, this detention period is potentially dangerous. And once the period of custody is over, the fact of the arrest is a permanent part of the public record. . . .

Because a full custodial arrest is such a severe intrusion on an individual's liberty, its reasonableness hinges on the degree to which it is needed for the promotion of legitimate governmental interests. In light of the availability of citations to promote a State's interests when a fine-only offense has been committed, I cannot concur in a rule which deems a full custodial arrest to be reasonable in every circumstance. . . . Instead, I would require that when there is probable cause to believe that a fine-only offense has been committed, the police officer should issue a citation unless the officer is able to point to specific and articulable facts which, taken together with rational inferences from those facts, reasonably warrant the additional intrusion of a full custodial arrest. . . .

At bottom, the majority offers two related reasons why a bright-line rule is necessary: the fear that officers who arrest for fine-only offenses will be subject to personal 42 U.S.C. §1983 liability for the misapplication of a constitutional standard, and the resulting systematic disincentive to arrest where arresting would serve an important societal interest. These concerns are certainly valid, but they are more than adequately resolved by the doctrine of qualified immunity.

If, for example, an officer reasonably thinks that a suspect poses a flight risk or might be a danger to the community if released, he may arrest without fear of the legal consequences. Similarly, if an officer reasonably concludes that a suspect may possess more than four ounces of marijuana and thus might be guilty of a felony, the officer will be insulated from liability for arresting the suspect even if the initial assessment turns out to be factually incorrect. . . .

II.

The record in this case makes it abundantly clear that Ms. Atwater's arrest was constitutionally unreasonable. . . . The Court's error, however, does not merely affect the disposition of this case. The per se rule that the Court creates has potentially serious consequences for the everyday lives of Americans. A broad range of conduct falls into the category of fine-only misdemeanors. In Texas alone, for example, disobeying any sort of traffic warning sign is a misdemeanor punishable only by fine, as is failing to pay a highway toll, and driving with expired license plates. Nor are fine-only crimes limited to the traffic context. In several States, for example, littering is a criminal offense punishable only by fine.

[Unbounded] discretion carries with it grave potential for abuse. The majority takes comfort in the lack of evidence of "an epidemic of unnecessary minor-offense arrests." But the relatively small number of published cases dealing with such arrests proves little and should provide little solace. Indeed, as the recent debate over racial profiling demonstrates all too clearly, a relatively minor traffic infraction may often serve as an excuse for stopping and harassing an individual. After today, the arsenal available to any officer extends to a full arrest and the searches permissible concomitant to that arrest. An officer's subjective motivations for making a traffic stop are not relevant considerations in determining the reasonableness of the stop. But it is precisely because these motivations are beyond our purview that we must vigilantly ensure that officers' poststop actions — which are properly within our reach — comport with the Fourth Amendment's guarantee of reasonableness. . . .

Notes

1. *Citations as supplement to arrest: majority position.* Every state gives its law enforcement officers the authority to issue citations (or "appearance tickets") for the violation of some criminal laws. Citations are ordinarily available to address traffic violations, but they are increasingly available for minor nontraffic violations of the criminal law — sometimes all "infractions" or specified misdemeanors. See Cincinnati Police Department Procedure Manual §12.555 (adults charged with misdemeanor offenses are eligible for Notice to Appear, except for specified misdemeanors such as weapons offense, second DUI offense, and three pending summons). The limited evidence on the use of the citation power suggests that officers do not commonly replace arrests with citations outside the traffic enforcement area.

Some foreign jurisdictions make extensive use of devices such as citations to give police officers an alternative to custodial arrest. For instance, in Queensland, Australia, police can issue a "notice to appear" (NTA) for any criminal offense. The NTA can be issued in the field or after taking the person into custody. It is used most frequently for traffic violations, prostitution, drugs, and weapons charges. If police officers in the United States had similarly broad powers to use citations, do you believe they would use it in similar categories of cases? Would citation in the field or at the station prove more popular?

2. *Citations as replacement for arrest.* Almost half of the states now have statutes that attempt to control the choice between citations and arrests for certain traffic offenses. Some simply state that the officer "shall" use the citation, while others (such as the Nebraska statute reprinted above) require the citation unless the officer can demonstrate one of the designated exceptions. Will a law such as the Nebraska statute effectively limit the use of arrest? On the constitutional level, the *Atwater* decision held that the federal constitution does not limit a police officer's power to arrest for a minor crime. Before *Atwater,* state courts were reluctant to declare that state constitutions required use of a citation rather than an arrest. Relatively few state courts have addressed this question under state law, but about half the courts that took up the question after *Atwater* parted ways with the Supreme Court. See State v. Askerooth, 681 N.W.2d 353 (Minn. 2004); State v. Brown, 792 N.E.2d 175 (Ohio 2003). For a sampling of the rich case law on this question, consult the web extension for this chapter at *http://www.crimpro.com/extension/ch05*.

What concerns, if any, might there be with the extensive use of citations? It might help in answering this question to consider it from a number of different perspectives — police, courts, civil rights groups, minority groups, and various kinds of possible defendants. Another way to think about the policy and justice implications of such a reform is to summarize its effect this way: Citations make arrests easier for the police.

3. *Search incident to citation: majority position.* Prior to the Supreme Court's 1998 ruling in *Knowles,* very few courts addressed the question of whether police could conduct a search incident to citation. Why did state courts develop so little case law on this subject? Was the practice of "search incident to citation" simply too rare to generate much litigation? Or was the practice common but unchallenged because prosecutors used other techniques to avoid appellate rulings on the subject? Here, as with many issues surrounding arrest and detention, police department policies often supplement statutes and judicial doctrine. See Phoenix Police Manual Order No. B-5(5)(D) (prohibiting search incident to issuance of a citation). Does *Knowles* apply outside the traffic stop context? See Lovelace v. Commonwealth, 522 S.E.2d 856 (Va. 1999) (applies to brief detention of pedestrian to issue summons).

4. *Pretextual arrests and limiting factors.* Recall the discussion from Chapter 2 about pretextual stops. Are the arguments any stronger or weaker to place controls on pretextual arrests — arrests motivated by some factor other than a desire to enforce some law that the officer has probable cause to believe the suspect has violated? Courts have given comparable treatment to claims about pretextual stops and arrests. See Arkansas v. Sullivan, 532 U.S. 769 (2001) (arrest based on probable cause does not violate Fourth Amendment even if arrest was motivated by desire to conduct search incident to arrest); State v. Hofmann, 537 N.W.2d 767 (Iowa 1995); but see State v. Sullivan, 74 S.W.2d 215 (Ark. 2002) (state constitution bars pretextual arrests for misdemeanor punishable by 90 days in jail).

The court in *Atwater* mentioned several practical limits on the willingness of police officers to arrest for minor crimes, including the amount of time and effort it takes to process an arrest. Does the arrest actually have to happen before the search incident? Could the officer announce an arrest, conduct the search, and then convert the arrest to a citation? See Wayne A. Logan, An Exception Swallows a Rule: Police Authority to Search Incident to Arrest, 19 Yale L. & Pol'y Rev. 381, 406-14 (2001) (distinguishes custodial and noncustodial arrests; argues that search incident should only happen if the officer actually does carry out a custodial arrest).

The *Atwater* court also mentioned the prospect that legislatures would pass statutes to limit any abuses of the arrest power. Under what political circumstances would a state legislature take action to limit the arrest authority of the police? See People v. McKay, 41 P.3d 59 (Cal. 2002) (state statute allows arrest for improper bicycle riding; even if it did not, arrest in violation of statute would not amount to Fourth Amendment violation).

5. *Arrests for minor crimes and race.* Does the officer's discretion to choose between arrest and citation for minor crimes create more risk of racial discrimination in enforcement? If you were advising a police department about a proposed campaign to stop and ticket more drivers who fail to use seat belts, and you knew that Latino and African American drivers use seat belts less frequently than other drivers, what advice would you give about carrying out this program? In the context of drug crimes, could you exercise arrest discretion in a way that equalizes the impact of enforcement on suburban and urban neighborhoods?

E. USE OF FORCE IN MAKING ARRESTS

The prior sections of this chapter have focused on *whether* an officer should make an arrest. In addition, the legal system pays attention to *how* a police officer makes an arrest. Legal controls are most vigorous when a suspect resists the officer's effort to make the arrest and the officer must use force — either deadly or nondeadly — to complete the arrest.

■ WILLIAM BLACKSTONE, COMMENTARIES ON THE LAWS OF ENGLAND

Vol. 4, p. 289 (1769)

[In] case of felony actually committed, or a dangerous wounding whereby felony is likely to ensue, [the constable] may upon probable suspicion arrest the felon; and for that purpose is authorized (as upon a justice's warrant) to break open doors, and even to kill the felon if he cannot otherwise be taken.

■ TENNESSEE v. EDWARD GARNER

471 U.S. 1 (1985)

WHITE, J.*

This case requires us to determine the constitutionality of the use of deadly force to prevent the escape of an apparently unarmed suspected felon. We conclude that such force may not be used unless it is necessary to prevent the escape and the officer has probable cause to believe that the suspect poses a significant threat of death or serious physical injury to the officer or others.

I.

At about 10:45 P.M. on October 3, 1974, Memphis Police Officers Elton Hymon and Leslie Wright were dispatched to answer a "prowler inside call." Upon arriving at the scene they saw a woman standing on her porch and gesturing toward the adjacent house. She told them she had heard glass breaking and that "they" or "someone" was breaking in next door. While Wright radioed the dispatcher to say that they were on the scene, Hymon went behind the house. He heard a door slam and saw someone run across the backyard. The fleeing suspect, who was [Edward Garner], stopped at a 6-feet-high chain link fence at the edge of the yard. With the aid of a flashlight, Hymon was able to see Garner's face and hands. He saw no sign of a weapon, and, though not certain, was "reasonably sure" and "figured" that Garner was unarmed. He thought Garner was 17 or 18 years old and about 5'5" or 5'7" tall.[2] While Garner was crouched at the base of the fence, Hymon called out "police, halt"

* [Justices Brennan, Marshall, Blackmun, Powell, and Stevens joined in this opinion. — EDS.]

2. In fact, Garner, an eighth-grader, was 15. He was 5'4" tall and weighed somewhere around 100 or 110 pounds.

and took a few steps toward him. Garner then began to climb over the fence. Convinced that if Garner made it over the fence he would elude capture,[3] Hymon shot him. The bullet hit Garner in the back of the head. Garner was taken by ambulance to a hospital, where he died on the operating table. Ten dollars and a purse taken from the house were found on his body.

In using deadly force to prevent the escape, Hymon was acting under the authority of a Tennessee statute and pursuant to Police Department policy. The statute provides that "[if], after notice of the intention to arrest the defendant, he either flee or forcibly resist, the officer may use all the necessary means to effect the arrest." Tenn. Code §40-7-108. The Department policy was slightly more restrictive than the statute, but still allowed the use of deadly force in cases of burglary. The incident was reviewed by the Memphis Police Firearm's Review Board and presented to a grand jury. Neither took any action.

Garner's father then brought this action, [seeking damages for asserted violations of Garner's constitutional rights.] After a 3-day bench trial, the District Court entered judgment for all defendants. [The trial court concluded that] Hymon had employed the only reasonable and practicable means of preventing Garner's escape. Garner had "recklessly and heedlessly attempted to vault over the fence to escape, thereby assuming the risk of being fired upon." . . .

II.

Whenever an officer restrains the freedom of a person to walk away, he has seized that person. While it is not always clear just when minimal police interference becomes a seizure there can be no question that apprehension by the use of deadly force is a seizure subject to the reasonableness requirement of the Fourth Amendment.

A police officer may arrest a person if he has probable cause to believe that person committed a crime. [The state argues] that if this requirement is satisfied the Fourth Amendment has nothing to say about how that seizure is made. This submission ignores the many cases in which this Court, by balancing the extent of the intrusion against the need for it, has examined the reasonableness of the manner in which a search or seizure is conducted. To determine the constitutionality of a seizure "[we] must balance the nature and quality of the intrusion on the individual's Fourth Amendment interests against the importance of the governmental interests alleged to justify the intrusion." We have described "the balancing of competing interests" as "the key principle of the Fourth Amendment." Because one of the factors is the extent of the intrusion, it is plain that reasonableness depends on not only when a seizure is made, but also how it is carried out.

[The balancing process] demonstrates that, notwithstanding probable cause to seize a suspect, an officer may not always do so by killing him. The intrusiveness of a seizure by means of deadly force is unmatched. The suspect's fundamental interest in his own life need not be elaborated upon. The use of deadly force also frustrates the interest of the individual, and of society, in judicial determination of guilt

3. When asked at trial why he fired, Hymon stated . . . that the area beyond the fence was dark, that he could not have gotten over the fence easily because he was carrying a lot of equipment and wearing heavy boots, and that Garner, being younger and more energetic, could have outrun him.

and punishment. Against these interests are ranged governmental interests in effective law enforcement. It is argued that overall violence will be reduced by encouraging the peaceful submission of suspects who know that they may be shot if they flee. Effectiveness in making arrests requires the resort to deadly force, or at least the meaningful threat thereof. "Being able to arrest such individuals is a condition precedent to the state's entire system of law enforcement."

Without in any way disparaging the importance of these goals, we are not convinced that the use of deadly force is a sufficiently productive means of accomplishing them to justify the killing of nonviolent suspects. The use of deadly force is a self-defeating way of apprehending a suspect and so setting the criminal justice mechanism in motion. If successful, it guarantees that that mechanism will not be set in motion. And while the meaningful threat of deadly force might be thought to lead to the arrest of more live suspects by discouraging escape attempts, the presently available evidence does not support this thesis. The fact is that a majority of police departments in this country have forbidden the use of deadly force against nonviolent suspects. If those charged with the enforcement of the criminal law have abjured the use of deadly force in arresting nondangerous felons, there is a substantial basis for doubting that the use of such force is an essential attribute of the arrest power in all felony cases. Petitioners and appellant have not persuaded us that shooting nondangerous fleeing suspects is so vital as to outweigh the suspect's interest in his own life.

The use of deadly force to prevent the escape of all felony suspects, whatever the circumstances, is constitutionally unreasonable. It is not better that all felony suspects die than that they escape. Where the suspect poses no immediate threat to the officer and no threat to others, the harm resulting from failing to apprehend him does not justify the use of deadly force to do so. It is no doubt unfortunate when a suspect who is in sight escapes, but the fact that the police arrive a little late or are a little slower afoot does not always justify killing the suspect. A police officer may not seize an unarmed, nondangerous suspect by shooting him dead. The Tennessee statute is unconstitutional insofar as it authorizes the use of deadly force against such fleeing suspects.

It is not, however, unconstitutional on its face. Where the officer has probable cause to believe that the suspect poses a threat of serious physical harm, either to the officer or to others, it is not constitutionally unreasonable to prevent escape by using deadly force. Thus, if the suspect threatens the officer with a weapon or there is probable cause to believe that he has committed a crime involving the infliction or threatened infliction of serious physical harm, deadly force may be used if necessary to prevent escape, and if, where feasible, some warning has been given. As applied in such circumstances, the Tennessee statute would pass constitutional muster.

III.

It is insisted that the Fourth Amendment must be construed in light of the common-law rule, which allowed the use of whatever force was necessary to effect the arrest of a fleeing felon, though not a misdemeanant. As stated in Hale's posthumously published Pleas of the Crown:

> [If] persons that are pursued by these officers for felony or the just suspicion thereof . . . shall not yield themselves to these officers, but shall either resist or fly before they are apprehended or being apprehended shall rescue themselves and resist or fly, so that they cannot be otherwise apprehended, and are upon necessity slain therein, because they cannot be otherwise taken, it is no felony.

2 M. Hale, Historia Placitoram Coronae 85 (1736). See also 4 W. Blackstone, Commentaries *289. Most American jurisdictions also imposed a flat prohibition against the use of deadly force to stop a fleeing misdemeanant, coupled with a general privilege to use such force to stop a fleeing felon.

The State and city argue that because this was the prevailing rule at the time of the adoption of the Fourth Amendment and for some time thereafter, and is still in force in some States, use of deadly force against a fleeing felon must be "reasonable." It is true that this Court has often looked to the common law in evaluating the reasonableness, for Fourth Amendment purposes, of police activity. On the other hand, it "has not simply frozen into constitutional law those law enforcement practices that existed at the time of the Fourth Amendment's passage." Because of sweeping change in the legal and technological context, reliance on the common-law rule in this case would be a mistaken literalism that ignores the purposes of a historical inquiry.

It has been pointed out many times that the common-law rule is best understood in light of the fact that it arose at a time when virtually all felonies were punishable by death. Though effected without the protections and formalities of an orderly trial and conviction, the killing of a resisting or fleeing felon resulted in no greater consequences than those authorized for punishment of the felony of which the individual was charged or suspected. Courts have also justified the common-law rule by emphasizing the relative dangerousness of felons.

Neither of these justifications makes sense today. Almost all crimes formerly punishable by death no longer are or can be. And while in earlier times the gulf between the felonies and the minor offences was broad and deep, today the distinction is minor and often arbitrary. Many crimes classified as misdemeanors, or nonexistent, at common law are now felonies. These changes have undermined the concept, which was questionable to begin with, that use of deadly force against a fleeing felon is merely a speedier execution of someone who has already forfeited his life. They have also made the assumption that a "felon" is more dangerous than a misdemeanant untenable. Indeed, numerous misdemeanors involve conduct more dangerous than many felonies.

There is an additional reason why the common-law rule cannot be directly translated to the present day. The common-law rule developed at a time when weapons were rudimentary. Deadly force could be inflicted almost solely in a hand-to-hand struggle during which, necessarily, the safety of the arresting officer was at risk. Handguns were not carried by police officers until the latter half of the last century. Only then did it become possible to use deadly force from a distance as a means of apprehension. As a practical matter, the use of deadly force under the standard articulation of the common-law rule has an altogether different meaning — and harsher consequences — now than in past centuries. . . .

In evaluating the reasonableness of police procedures under the Fourth Amendment, we have also looked to prevailing rules in individual jurisdictions. The rules in the States are varied. Some 19 States have codified the common-law rule, though in two of these the courts have significantly limited the statute. Four States, though without a relevant statute, apparently retain the common-law rule. Two States have adopted the Model Penal Code's provision verbatim.* Eighteen others allow, in slightly varying language, the use of deadly force only if the suspect has committed a felony involving the use or threat of physical or deadly force, or is escaping with a deadly weapon, or is likely to endanger life or inflict serious physical injury if not arrested. . . .

It cannot be said that there is a constant or overwhelming trend away from the common-law rule. In recent years, some States have reviewed their laws and expressly rejected abandonment of the common-law rule. Nonetheless, the long-term movement has been away from the rule that deadly force may be used against any fleeing felon, and that remains the rule in less than half the States.

This trend is more evident and impressive when viewed in light of the policies adopted by the police departments themselves. Overwhelmingly, these are more restrictive than the common-law rule. The Federal Bureau of Investigation and the New York City Police Department, for example, both forbid the use of firearms except when necessary to prevent death or grievous bodily harm. For accreditation by the Commission on Accreditation for Law Enforcement Agencies, a department must restrict the use of deadly force to situations where "the officer reasonably believes that the action is in defense of human life . . . or in defense of any person in immediate danger of serious physical injury." A 1974 study reported that the police department regulations in a majority of the large cities of the United States allowed the firing of a weapon only when a felon presented a threat of death or serious bodily harm. Overall, only 7.5 percent of departmental and municipal policies explicitly permit the use of deadly force against any felon; 86.8 percent explicitly do not. In light of the rules adopted by those who must actually administer them, the older and fading common-law view is a dubious indicium of the constitutionality of the Tennessee statute now before us.

Actual departmental policies are important for an additional reason. We would hesitate to declare a police practice of long standing "unreasonable" if doing so would severely hamper effective law enforcement. But the indications are to the contrary. There has been no suggestion that crime has worsened in any way in jurisdictions that have adopted, by legislation or departmental policy, rules similar to that announced today. . . .

Nor do we agree with [the state] that the rule we have adopted requires the police to make impossible, split-second evaluations of unknowable facts. We do not deny the practical difficulties of attempting to assess the suspect's dangerousness.

* [Section 3.07(2) (b) of the Model Penal Code provides:

> The use of deadly force is not justifiable . . . unless (i) the arrest is for a felony; and (ii) the person effecting the arrest is authorized to act as a peace officer or is assisting a person whom he believes to be authorized to act as a peace officer; and (iii) the actor believes that the force employed creates no substantial risk of injury to innocent persons; and (iv) the actor believes that (1) the crime for which the arrest is made involved conduct including the use or threatened use of deadly force; or (2) there is a substantial risk that the person to be arrested will cause death or serious bodily harm if his apprehension is delayed.

— Eds.]

However, similarly difficult judgments must be made by the police in equally uncertain circumstances. See, e.g., Terry v. Ohio, 392 U.S. 1 (1968). Nor is there any indication that in States that allow the use of deadly force only against dangerous suspects, the standard has been difficult to apply or has led to a rash of litigation involving inappropriate second-guessing of police officers' split-second decisions. Moreover, the highly technical felony/misdemeanor distinction is equally, if not more, difficult to apply in the field. An officer is in no position to know, for example, the precise value of property stolen, or whether the crime was a first or second offense. . . .

IV.

The [district court did not determine whether Garner presented a danger of physical harm to Officer Hymon or others.] The court did find, however, that Garner appeared to be unarmed, though Hymon could not be certain that was the case. Restated in Fourth Amendment terms, this means Hymon had no articulable basis to think Garner was armed.

[These facts do not justify the use of deadly force.] Officer Hymon could not reasonably have believed that Garner — young, slight, and unarmed — posed any threat. Indeed, Hymon never attempted to justify his actions on any basis other than the need to prevent an escape. [T]he fact that Garner was a suspected burglar could not, without regard to the other circumstances, automatically justify the use of deadly force. Hymon did not have probable cause to believe that Garner, whom he correctly believed to be unarmed, posed any physical danger to himself or others.

The dissent argues that the shooting was justified by the fact that Officer Hymon had probable cause to believe that Garner had committed a nighttime burglary. While we agree that burglary is a serious crime, we cannot agree that it is so dangerous as automatically to justify the use of deadly force. The FBI classifies burglary as a "property" rather than a "violent" crime. Although the armed burglar would present a different situation, the fact that an unarmed suspect has broken into a dwelling at night does not automatically mean he is physically dangerous. This case demonstrates as much. In fact, the available statistics demonstrate that burglaries only rarely involve physical violence. During the 10-year period from 1973-1982, only 3.8 percent of all burglaries involved violent crime.[23] . . .

V.

[We] hold that the statute is invalid insofar as it purported to give Hymon the authority to act as he did. [The] case is remanded for further proceedings consistent with this opinion. So ordered.

23. The dissent points out that three-fifths of all rapes in the home, three-fifths of all home robberies, and about a third of home assaults are committed by burglars. These figures mean only that if one knows that a suspect committed a rape in the home, there is a good chance that the suspect is also a burglar. That has nothing to do with the question here, which is whether the fact that someone has committed a burglary indicates that he has committed, or might commit, a violent crime. The dissent also points out that this 3.8% adds up to 2.8 million violent crimes over a 10-year period, as if to imply that today's holding will let loose 2.8 million violent burglars. The relevant universe is, of course, far smaller. At issue is only that tiny fraction of cases where violence has taken place and an officer who has no other means of apprehending the suspect is unaware of its occurrence.

O'CONNOR, J., dissenting.*

[Although] the circumstances of this case are unquestionably tragic and unfortunate, our constitutional holdings must be sensitive both to the history of the Fourth Amendment and to the general implications of the Court's reasoning. By disregarding the serious and dangerous nature of residential burglaries and the longstanding practice of many States, the Court effectively creates a Fourth Amendment right allowing a burglary suspect to flee unimpeded from a police officer who has probable cause to arrest, who has ordered the suspect to halt, and who has no means short of firing his weapon to prevent escape. I do not believe that the Fourth Amendment supports such a right, and I accordingly dissent.

I.

The facts below warrant brief review because they highlight the difficult, split-second decisions police officers must make in these circumstances. . . . As Officer Hymon walked behind the house, he heard a door slam. He saw Edward Eugene Garner run away from the house through the dark and cluttered backyard. Garner crouched next to a 6-foot-high fence. Officer Hymon thought Garner was an adult and was unsure whether Garner was armed because Hymon "had no idea what was in the hand [that he could not see] or what he might have had on his person." In fact, Garner was 15 years old and unarmed. Hymon also did not know whether accomplices remained inside the house. . . .

The precise issue before the Court deserves emphasis. . . . The issue is not the constitutional validity of the Tennessee statute on its face or as applied to some hypothetical set of facts. Instead, the issue is whether the use of deadly force by Officer Hymon under the circumstances of this case violated Garner's constitutional rights. Thus, the majority's assertion that a police officer who has probable cause to seize a suspect "may not always do so by killing him," is unexceptionable but also of little relevance to the question presented here. . . . The question we must address is whether the Constitution allows the use of such force to apprehend a suspect who resists arrest by attempting to flee the scene of a nighttime burglary of a residence.

II.

[We must balance] the important public interest in crime prevention and detection and the nature and quality of the intrusion upon legitimate interests of the individual. In striking this balance here, it is crucial to acknowledge that police use of deadly force to apprehend a fleeing criminal suspect falls within the "rubric of police conduct . . . necessarily [involving] swift action predicated upon the on-the-spot observations of the officer on the beat." Terry v. Ohio, 392 U.S. 1 (1968). The clarity of hindsight cannot provide the standard for judging the reasonableness of police decisions made in uncertain and often dangerous circumstances. . . .

The public interest involved in the use of deadly force as a last resort to apprehend a fleeing burglary suspect relates primarily to the serious nature of the crime. Household burglaries not only represent the illegal entry into a person's home, but

* [Chief Justice Burger and Justice Rehnquist joined in this opinion. — EDS.]

also "[pose] real risk of serious harm to others." According to recent Department of Justice statistics, "[three-fifths] of all rapes in the home, three-fifths of all home robberies, and about a third of home aggravated and simple assaults are committed by burglars." During the period 1973-1982, 2.8 million such violent crimes were committed in the course of burglaries. Victims of a forcible intrusion into their home by a nighttime prowler will find little consolation in the majority's confident assertion that "burglaries only rarely involve physical violence." Moreover, even if a particular burglary, when viewed in retrospect, does not involve physical harm to others, the "harsh potentialities for violence" inherent in the forced entry into a home preclude characterization of the crime as [innocuous or nonviolent.]

Because burglary is a serious and dangerous felony, the public interest in the prevention and detection of the crime is of compelling importance. Where a police officer has probable cause to arrest a suspected burglar, the use of deadly force as a last resort might well be the only means of apprehending the suspect. With respect to a particular burglary, subsequent investigation simply cannot represent a substitute for immediate apprehension of the criminal suspect at the scene. Indeed, the Captain of the Memphis Police Department testified that in his city, if apprehension is not immediate, it is likely that the suspect will not be caught. Although some law enforcement agencies may choose to assume the risk that a criminal will remain at large, the Tennessee statute reflects a legislative determination that the [provision will] assist the police in apprehending suspected perpetrators of serious crimes and provide notice that a lawful police order to stop and submit to arrest may not be ignored with impunity. . . .

Against the strong public interests justifying the conduct at issue here must be weighed the individual interests implicated in the use of deadly force by police officers. The majority declares that "[the] suspect's fundamental interest in his own life need not be elaborated upon." This blithe assertion hardly provides an adequate substitute for the majority's failure to acknowledge the distinctive manner in which the suspect's interest in his life is even exposed to risk. [The] officer's use of force resulted because the suspected burglar refused to heed [his command to halt] and the officer reasonably believed that there was no means short of firing his weapon to apprehend the suspect. Without questioning the importance of a person's interest in his life, I do not think this interest encompasses a right to flee unimpeded from the scene of a burglary. The legitimate interests of the suspect in these circumstances are adequately accommodated by the Tennessee statute: to avoid the use of deadly force and the consequent risk to his life, the suspect need merely obey the valid order to halt.

A proper balancing of the interests involved suggests that use of deadly force as a last resort to apprehend a criminal suspect fleeing from the scene of a nighttime burglary is not unreasonable within the meaning of the Fourth Amendment. Admittedly, the events giving rise to this case are in retrospect deeply regrettable. No one can view the death of an unarmed and apparently nonviolent 15-year-old without sorrow, much less disapproval. Nonetheless, the reasonableness of Officer Hymon's conduct for purposes of the Fourth Amendment cannot be evaluated by what later appears to have been a preferable course of police action. [Instead], the question is whether it is constitutionally impermissible for police officers, as a last resort, to shoot a burglary suspect fleeing the scene of the crime. . . .

IV.

I cannot accept the majority's creation of a constitutional right to flight for burglary suspects seeking to avoid capture at the scene of the crime. Whatever the constitutional limits on police use of deadly force in order to apprehend a fleeing felon, I do not believe they are exceeded in a case in which a police officer has probable cause to arrest a suspect at the scene of a residential burglary, orders the suspect to halt, and then fires his weapon as a last resort to prevent the suspect's escape into the night. I respectfully dissent.

Problem 5-4. Ruby Ridge

When Randy Weaver failed to appear in court on federal weapons charges, federal marshals decided to arrest him at his home in Ruby Ridge, Idaho. While several agents were walking around the property before approaching the house, a gun battle erupted between the marshals and Weaver's 14-year-old son, who was out walking and carrying a rifle when he encountered the agents. Weaver's son and one of the marshals died in the firefight.

The federal government was aware that other adults and children were on the Weaver property and that Weaver and his family owned and used a large number of firearms. As a result, the FBI sent several SWAT teams and a hostage rescue team to support the marshals in their effort to apprehend Weaver.

The FBI has general policies regarding the use of deadly force by its agents. The standard FBI rules at that time stated that an agent could use deadly force if the agent or some third party is threatened with "grievous" bodily injury. However, when FBI tactical teams are deployed, specialized "rules of engagement" can supplement the general policy. Rules of engagement are instructions that clearly indicate what action agents should take when confronted, threatened, or fired upon by someone. The on-scene commander formulates the rules of engagement. The special rules of engagement in effect at Ruby Ridge stated:

> If any adult in the compound is observed with a weapon after the surrender announcement is made, deadly force can and should be employed to neutralize this individual. If any adult male is observed with a weapon prior to the announcement, deadly force can and should be employed, if the shot can be taken without endangering any children.

The on-scene commander discussed these rules of engagement with supervisors within the FBI but not with legal counsel for the agency.

There were many interpretations of the rules of engagement among the FBI SWAT teams deployed to the Ruby Ridge site. One SWAT team leader recalled the rules as "if you see Weaver or Harris outside with a weapon, you've got the green light." Another member of a SWAT team remembered the rules as, "if you see 'em, shoot 'em."

During the ensuing siege, a member of the FBI's hostage rescue team shot and killed Weaver's wife while she was standing behind a door, holding her 10-month-old baby. Kevin Harris, a member of the Weaver household, was also shot. After the siege ended, Weaver was acquitted of criminal charges. He brought a civil suit against the government and settled the case for $3.1 million. Kevin Harris also filed a civil action against the government and its agents. See Harris v. Roderick, 126 F.3d 1189 (9th Cir. 1997). During Senate hearings on the matter, the FBI announced a new policy on deadly force. The new policy read as follows:

> *Use of Deadly Force Policy*
>
> a. Deadly Force. Officers may use deadly force only when necessary, that is, when the officer has a reasonable belief that the subject of such force poses an imminent danger of death or serious physical injury to the officer or to another person.
>
> b. Fleeing Felons. Deadly force may be used to prevent the escape of a fleeing subject if there is probable cause to believe:
>
> (1) the subject has committed a felony involving the infliction or threatened infliction of serious physical injury or death; and
>
> (2) the escape of the subject would pose an imminent danger of death or serious physical injury to the officer or to another person.
>
> *Use of Nondeadly Force*
>
> If force other than deadly force reasonably appears to be sufficient to accomplish an arrest or otherwise accomplish the law enforcement purpose, deadly force is not necessary.
>
> *Verbal Warnings*
>
> If feasible and if to do so would not increase the danger to the officer or others, a verbal warning to submit to the authority of the officer shall be given prior to the use of deadly force.

See 60 Fed. Reg. 54,569 (October 24, 1995). The policy applies to all federal law enforcement agents. Is each component of the new federal deadly force policy required by Garner? Were the Ruby Ridge rules of engagement consistent with *Garner*? Would you recommend the same deadly force policy for the police officers in Memphis responding to calls about crimes in progress?

Notes

1. *Deadly force: majority position.* In the wake of *Garner,* most states now have statutes either meeting or surpassing the constitutional minimum described in that decision. More than 30 states follow the Model Penal Code provisions on the use of force; more than a dozen of these states adopted (or reaffirmed) this position after the decision in *Garner.* Other states enforce the constitutional requirements through judicial decisions. Police departments now routinely adopt written policies regarding the use of deadly force, even departments that ordinarily do not maintain written operational guidelines. In fact, 100 percent of the police departments serving jurisdictions with populations greater than 10,000 have adopted written deadly force policies. About 90 percent of all police departments have written policies on nondeadly force. Bureau of Justice Statistics, Local Police Departments 2003 (June 2006, NCJ 210118).

Are the situations in which police can use deadly force after *Garner* sufficiently clear to allow police to anticipate and train for those situations? Does *Garner* create an incentive for perjury by officers being sued for their use of force?

2. *Excessive nondeadly force.* The police need not use deadly force to provoke a claim that they used force improperly to carry out an arrest. Many civil damage claims are founded on incidents involving nondeadly force used during arrests. See, e.g., Samaniego v. City of Kodiak, 2 P.3d 78 (Alaska 2000). The use of nondeadly force raises potential claims under the Fourth Amendment that an unreasonable seizure occurred. But in much of the litigation over nondeadly force, traditional doctrines of tort law govern. Claims are made under state tort law, federal civil rights laws, or both. The question in such cases is often whether the officer reasonably believed such force to be necessary to accomplish a legitimate police purpose. Are civil juries less capable of evaluating claims of negligence or gross negligence by the police than they are in other types of tort cases?

3. *Changing times.* What societal changes since 1985 might be the basis for arguing that the Supreme Court should reverse *Garner*? What about the emergence of methamphetamine or the presence of Uzis and Mac 10s? The increase in the number of homicides among youth? What if researchers found an increase in the number of killings committed by burglars?

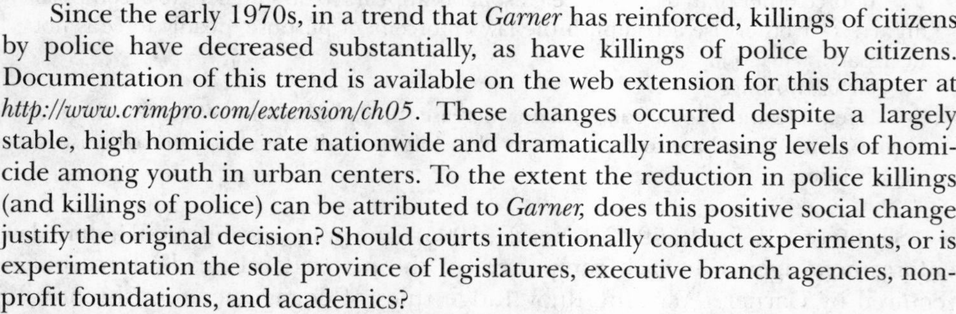

Since the early 1970s, in a trend that *Garner* has reinforced, killings of citizens by police have decreased substantially, as have killings of police by citizens. Documentation of this trend is available on the web extension for this chapter at *http://www.crimpro.com/extension/ch05*. These changes occurred despite a largely stable, high homicide rate nationwide and dramatically increasing levels of homicide among youth in urban centers. To the extent the reduction in police killings (and killings of police) can be attributed to *Garner*, does this positive social change justify the original decision? Should courts intentionally conduct experiments, or is experimentation the sole province of legislatures, executive branch agencies, nonprofit foundations, and academics?

4. *Racial patterns in the use of excessive force.* Criminologists have extensively studied police use of deadly force; one researcher summarized the thrust of the studies as follows: "The literature on police use of deadly force has produced two major findings. First, researchers report extreme variation in rates of police shooting among American jurisdictions. Second, regardless of its geographic scope, the research invariably reports that the percentage of police shootings involving black victims far exceeds the percentage of blacks in the population." James Fyfe, Blind Justice: Police Shootings in Memphis, 73 J. Crim. L. & Criminology 707 (1982); see also Jerome Skolnick & James Fyfe, Above the Law: Police and the Excessive Use of Force (1993). In some places, this pattern might be explained by the disproportionate number of black suspects involved in the most serious violent crimes. In other places, such as Memphis (the location of the shooting in *Garner*) between 1969 and 1976, African Americans were more likely to be injured or killed, even after controlling for seriousness of the suspected crime. Should the *Garner* court have mentioned this sort of evidence as support for its decision?

Police departments have devoted much attention to their policies for the use of force, both deadly and nondeadly. Their efforts go far beyond the constitutional requirements set out in *Garner* or in state constitutional decisions. The following materials suggest, both directly and more obliquely, the forces that compel police departments to develop these rules.

DAVID FRISBY, FLORIDA'S POLICE CONTINUUM OF FORCE

12 Trial Advoc. Q. 37 (1993)

[The] Florida Department of Law Enforcement Bureau of Criminal Justice Standards and Training (FDLE/CJST) in the early 1980's recognized a civil vulnerability of Florida police agencies. [FDLE/CJST created the Use of Force Subcommittee to develop state standards and curricula on use of force]. This committee met formally for the first time in 1986. It completed its initial charge in 1990.

Its product consisted of a use of force matrix and a list of approved police arrest techniques. The arrest techniques had been medically reviewed by a committee of medical doctors and legally reviewed by a committee of attorneys. Both pronounced the techniques appropriate in the context of the use of force matrix. . . . The standard of care established by the police use of force matrix became Florida's official standard of care. . . .

CONTINUUM OF FORCE/LEVELS OF RESISTANCE MATRIX

The matrix defines the relationship between the proper use of force by a police officer and the resistance offered by the offender. The levels of resistance to lawful police authority are broken down into six categories.

RESISTANCE LEVELS

Presence is the first level of resistance. This level of resistance occurs when a person breaks the law by the nature of his very presence in a place, as in a trespass.

The second level of resistance is verbal resistance. A person can violate the law and subject himself to arrest by his speech. Disorderly conduct and variations of "Fire" shouted in a movie theater are typical examples. Verbal resistance, however, is usually a response to a police officer's direction or command.

The third level of resistance is passive physical resistance. Passive physical resistance involves more than mere presence or speech. It occurs when a law breaker, by action or inaction, physically resists the action or direction of a lawful authority. A shoplifter who sits and must be carried away from the store is exhibiting passive resistance.

The fourth level of resistance is active physical resistance. This level includes such behavior as pulling away or fleeing arrest.

The fifth level is aggressive physical resistance. When a person turns his active resistance against the police officer or against another person he achieves this level. Aggressive physical resistance need not necessarily be effective, just threatening.

Florida Use of Force / Levels of Resistance Matrix

Resistance Levels	Arrival	Interview Stance	Touch (consoling)	Verbal Direction	Dialogue	Restraint Devices	Transporters	Take Downs	Pain Compliance	Counter Moves	Intermediate Weapons	Incapacitation	Deadly Force
6 Aggravated Physical	†	†	†	†	†	†	†	†	†	†	†	†	†
5 Aggressive Physical	†	†	†	†	†	†	†	†	†	†	†	†	
4 Active Physical	†	†	†	†	†	†	†	†	†	†	†		
3 Passive Physical	†	†	†	†	†	†	†	†	†				
2 Verbal	†	†	†	†	†	†							
1 Presence	†	†	†	†									
Response Levels	Official Presence 1		Verbal Control 2			Physical Control 3					Intermediate Weapons 4	Incapacitating Conduct 5	Deadly Force 6

Areas with crosses represent suggested, acceptable, beginning response levels. Any response in an area without a cross requires explanation.

Resistance Levels ↑

Response Levels →

The sixth level is aggravated physical resistance. An officer is faced with aggravated physical resistance when a resistor makes overt, hostile, attacking movements, with or without a weapon, with the apparent intent and ability to cause death or great bodily harm.

RESPONSE LEVELS

As the name suggests, the police continuum of force theory defines a spectrum of police response starting at a low level of police response and moving to a high level. It gives rules for escalating and de-escalating the use of force. The police continuum of force sets a standard and makes it clear when a particular example of force is within guidelines or outside acceptable practice. As with the law-breaker's resistance, the police continuum of force defines six levels of police response or police force.

The first and lowest level of police force is presence. Before an officer can even give a lawful command he must establish presence by establishing his identity and authority. He can do this by presenting himself in uniform or by presenting a badge, credentials, and announcing his authority. Presence is often enough force to convince a lawbreaker to stop his unlawful activity.

The second level of force is verbal direction. A police officer uses this force when he requests or commands, verbally or with body language. The third level of force is physical control. Physical control is the most complex level and will be discussed in greater detail later. The fourth level is alternate weapons. This level of force includes the use of police batons, chemical irritants, and stun guns. It is the level automatically in effect whenever the various police specialty weapons are used to obtain compliance. The fifth level of force is incapacitating force. As the name suggests, this level of force is intended to incapacitate a lawbreaker temporarily. Incapacitation techniques include some strikes and blows.

Level six is deadly force. This level of force is reached whenever firearms are used. It is force which is likely to cause serious bodily harm or even death. The deadly force category also includes baton strikes to the head, the use of police vehicles against other occupied vehicles and any other techniques defined as deadly by the local police administration.

The police continuum of force matrix relates these levels of police response to the levels of resistance. It gives a police officer guidance about where to enter the continuum matrix based on the particular bad behavior from the lawbreaker. . . .

Police response in level three is divided into subcategories. Transporters are techniques which are designed to move an arrested person from one place to another. Pain compliance techniques are designed to cause pain but not injury. Such a technique might be appropriate to separate a determined trespasser from a fence when he insists on holding tight. The techniques called takedowns, designed to place an arrestee on the ground for handcuffing, compose another subcategory. The very use of handcuffs, leg irons and other restraint devices is also a level three subcategory. Finally blocks, strikes and reactive techniques designed to control but not incapacitate are classified as level three countermoves. Striking a lawbreaker's hand which is bringing up a weapon is an example of a countermove.

General Rules

There are some general rules for the use of the continuum of force. Usually an officer will escalate up the continuum step by step until the law enforcement goal is achieved. He must then de-escalate as much as possible, consistent with maintaining control. An officer may by-pass steps in the continuum if he can explain why the lesser force would not be effective. An officer who exceeds the recommended level of force must document acceptable justification. For example, an officer might easily justify bypassing intermediate steps and initiating a level four or five response to recapture a desperate escaped murderer. . . .

Local police administrators routinely exercise their legitimate power to set force guidelines different from those of the state. Some department administrators move particular techniques to different places in the continuum because of sensitivity to community feelings. Sometimes they forbid certain types of force. For example, a few police departments in Florida have banned the use of the police baton. This type of practice might lead to increased civil liability if an officer found it necessary to use greater police force because his baton (a level four tool) was not available. Sensitive administrators weigh the benefits of varying from state standards carefully. . . .

Problem 5-5. Bicycle Kicks

Shonna Hobson was the mother of a five-year-old boy, James. Officer Nathan Shoate went to a home in Hobson's neighborhood to interview a child suspected in a bike theft. A child in the neighborhood, Matt, reported to Officer Shoate that he had seen James Hobson riding a bicycle stolen from Matt's sister. When Officer Shoate reached the Hobson home, he saw James near a bicycle. When Shoate got out of his car, James ran into the house.

Officer Shoate met Ms. Hobson at the front door of her home. He told her that her son was seen on a stolen bike and that he would need to talk to James about where he got the bike. Hobson told her son, who was now standing at the front door, to go back into the house. She then told Officer Shoate that James was not on a stolen bicycle, and that he had his own bike. Hobson became a bit irritated and refused to allow Officer Shoate to speak with James. The officer then told Hobson that he would have to take her son to the police station to interview him about the stolen bicycle, and gave her the opportunity to go along to the station. She replied that the officer was not taking her son anywhere.

At that point in the conversation, Officer Shoate called for backup police officers to assist him. When three other officers arrived a few minutes later, Hobson was standing with her son on the front steps of her residence yelling and saying "bullshit" in a loud voice. Officer Shoate then repeated to Hobson that they had to take her son to the police station, to which she again replied, "You aren't taking my son anywhere." Officer Shoate then advised Hobson that she was under arrest for obstructing an officer.

Two officers attempted to handcuff Hobson. When Officer Shoate tried to take hold of Hobson's arm, she pushed him away, saying, "Let me go!" Hobson punched another officer in the face, then was taken to the ground by the three other officers. Once she was on the ground, Hobson continued to flail her arms and legs in an attempt to get away. The officers took her to the police station.

Later investigation determined that the bicycle seen outside the Hobson home did in fact belong to James. Hobson was charged with obstructing an officer, disorderly conduct, and resisting an officer. In an amended complaint filed a few weeks later, the prosecutor added a fourth count: the felony of causing intentional bodily harm (battery) to a peace officer.

Hobson filed a motion to dismiss all the charges because there was no probable cause to support the obstruction or disorderly conduct counts, and her forceful efforts to resist the arrest were legitimate because the arrest was baseless and unlawful. How would you rule? Cf. State v. Hobson, 577 N.W.2d 825 (Wis. 1998).

Notes

1. *Detailed guidance.* Almost all major metropolitan police departments have adopted policies dealing with the use of force, and most of them describe a "continuum" of force similar to the one used in Florida. They vary, however, in the amount of detail they offer to guide police officers in the field. For a point of comparison with the Florida grid reprinted above, you should consult the "Discipline Matrix" of the Tucson Police Department, available on the web extension for this chapter at *http://www.crimpro.com/extension/ch05*.

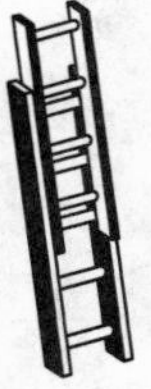

How do you suppose the law enforcement community received the Florida guidelines on the use of force? If you were one of the attorneys asked to review the guidelines during the drafting process, would you have suggested more or fewer categories? Would you change any of the boxes to add or eliminate a particular response level to a particular resistance level? If you were chief of police in Jacksonville, would you issue cards with this chart for every member of the force? Would you publish this chart in the local newspaper?

2. *Extent of the use of force.* The prescribed responses in the lower and middle range of the grid prove just as important as the higher levels of force and resistance because police officers use the lower levels of force much more frequently. The Department of Justice collects statistics regarding use of "excessive force by law enforcement officers," as required by §210402 of the Violent Crime Control and Law Enforcement Act of 1994. In 2005, an estimated 43.5 million persons had a face-to-face contact with a police officer. The police used or threatened to use force against an estimated 700,000 persons, or about 1.6 percent of the total contacts. In 43 percent of those instances, the police pushed or grabbed the suspect; in 9 percent, the officer hit the suspect; and in 15 percent, the officer pointed a gun. The police sprayed chemical or pepper spray in 3 percent of the cases. See Bureau of Justice Statistics, Contacts between Police and the Public, 2005 at Table 12 (April 2007, NCJ 215243).

3. *High-speed chases.* Sometimes police officers must pursue suspects in automobiles, and those pursuits at high speed sometimes result in injuries to the police officers, the suspect, and third parties. Public scrutiny of police departments often centers on the use of force, particularly the damage that officers cause to third parties during high-speed chases. Newspapers routinely publish articles about high-visibility cases, especially those resulting in the payment of tort damages by the city.

More than 90 percent of law enforcement agencies have policies restricting the use of high-speed chases. Most of those policies appeared in the 1970s; about half of the policies have been updated since then to place tighter controls on the occasions for engaging in a high-speed chase. These policies allow high-speed chases more readily to chase suspects involved in more dangerous crimes. Geoffrey Alpert, Police Pursuit: Policies and Training (1997, NCJ 164831); Cal. Pen. Code §13519.8 (mandating creation of department policies). States must waive their sovereign immunity before they can be held liable in tort for injuries resulting from high-speed chases. In what types of cases would you imagine that states have waived their immunity?

Federal law is not hospitable to constitutional tort claims based on high-speed chases. In Sacramento County, California v. Lewis, 523 U.S. 833 (1998), the court affirmed the lower court's dismissal of a suit brought by the estate of a passenger on a motorcycle who was killed after the police and the driver of the motorcycle engaged in a high-speed chase. The court held that the high-speed police chase there did not amount to a Fourth Amendment "seizure" because the chase did not terminate the passenger's "freedom of movement through means intentionally applied." A plaintiff must show that the officers have an "intent to harm suspects physically."

4. *Resisting unlawful arrest*. Although the common law recognized a privilege for citizens to use reasonable force to resist an unlawful arrest, most states now require citizens to submit to unlawful arrests by police officers — about a dozen through judicial opinions and roughly another 20 states through statutes. See State v. Crawley, 901 A.2d 924 (N.J. 2006) (resisting an unlawful arrest or an unsupported stop by a known officer is a violation of state law); Haw. Rev. Stat. §703-304(4)(a) (use of force not justifiable to "resist an arrest which the actor knows is being made by a law enforcement officer, although the arrest is unlawful"). Courts typically address this criminal procedure topic when interpreting the outer boundaries of the substantive criminal law, such as a statute or ordinance making it a crime to "obstruct a police officer lawfully performing an official function by means of flight." What is the case for allowing citizens to use reasonable efforts to resist an unlawful arrest by a police officer?

VI

Remedies for Unreasonable Searches and Seizures

We have seen how the Fourth Amendment and its analogs, along with many statutes, rules, and internal police policies, condemn certain searches and seizures as unreasonable. We now consider the various methods available to remedy the government's violations of law.

A. ORIGINS OF THE EXCLUSIONARY RULE

The texts of the Fourth Amendment and its state constitutional analogs do not usually specify the remedy for the victim of an illegal search or seizure. Up until the twentieth century, courts remedied these violations of the law by allowing the victims to sue the offending government agents in tort (typically for trespass). But when criminal defendants also asked the courts during criminal proceedings to exclude the wrongfully obtained evidence, state and federal courts rejected the suggestion unanimously. As Justice Joseph Story once put it:

> If it is competent or pertinent evidence, and not in its own nature objectionable, as having been created by constraint, or oppression, such as confessions extorted by threats or fraud, the evidence is admissible on charges for the highest crimes, even though it may have been obtained by a trespass upon the person, or by any other forcible and illegal means. The law deliberates not on the mode, by which it has come to the possession of the party, but on its value in establishing itself as satisfactory proof.

United States v. La Jeune, 26 F. Cas. 832 (C.C.D. Mass. 1822). The Supreme Court suggested for the first time in Boyd v. United States, 116 U.S. 616 (1886), that exclusion of evidence might be the proper remedy for evidence obtained through a violation of both the Fourth and Fifth Amendments. A later case, Adams v. New York, 192 U.S. 585 (1904), curtly dismissed the exclusion remedy for a Fourth Amendment violation alone. The following case was the Court's next word on the subject of remedies for illegal searches and seizures.

■ FREMONT WEEKS v. UNITED STATES

232 U.S. 383 (1914)

DAY, J.*

[The defendant was convicted of using the mails for the purpose of transporting lottery tickets, in violation of §213 of the Criminal Code. At the time of his arrest at the Union Station in Kansas City, Missouri, police officers went to the defendant's house to search it. A neighbor told them where to find the key, and they entered the house and took various papers from his room. Later in the same day police officers returned with the United States Marshal, who thought he might find additional evidence,] and, being admitted by someone in the house, probably a boarder, in response to a rap, the Marshal searched the defendant's room and carried away certain letters and envelopes found in the drawer of a chiffonier. Neither the marshal nor the police officers had a search warrant.

The defendant filed in the cause before the time for trial a "Petition to Return Private Papers, Books and Other Property" [claiming that officers of the government had seized his books and papers] "in violation of Sections 11 and 23 of the Constitution of Missouri and of the 4th and 5th Amendments to the Constitution of the United States." [He further argued that the District Attorney's plans to use the papers and property as evidence in the case against him would violate his constitutional rights. The trial court denied the petition.] Among the papers retained and put in evidence were a number of lottery tickets and statements with reference to the lottery, taken at the first visit of the police to the defendant's room, and a number of letters written to the defendant in respect to the lottery, taken by the Marshal upon his search of defendant's room. . . .

The effect of the Fourth Amendment is to put the courts of the United States and Federal officials, in the exercise of their power and authority, under limitations and restraints as to the exercise of such power and authority, and to forever secure the people, their persons, houses, papers and effects against all unreasonable searches and seizures under the guise of law. This protection reaches all alike, whether accused of crime or not, and the duty of giving to it force and effect is obligatory upon all entrusted under our Federal system with the enforcement of the laws. The tendency of those who execute the criminal laws of the country to obtain conviction by means of unlawful seizures and enforced confessions, the latter often obtained after subjecting accused persons to unwarranted practices destructive of rights secured by the Federal Constitution, should find no sanction in the judgments of the courts which are charged at all times with the support of the Constitution and to which people of all conditions have a right to appeal for the maintenance of such fundamental rights.

* [All the Justices joined in this opinion. — EDS.]

[This case] involves the right of the court in a criminal prosecution to retain for the purposes of evidence the letters and correspondence of the accused, seized in his house in his absence and without his authority, by a United States Marshal holding no warrant for his arrest and none for the search of his premises. . . . If letters and private documents can thus be seized and held and used in evidence against a citizen accused of an offense, the protection of the Fourth Amendment declaring his right to be secure against such searches and seizures is of no value, and, so far as those thus placed are concerned, might as well be stricken from the Constitution. The efforts of the courts and their officials to bring the guilty to punishment, praiseworthy as they are, are not to be aided by the sacrifice of those great principles established by years of endeavor and suffering which have resulted in their embodiment in the fundamental law of the land. The United States Marshal . . . acted without sanction of law, doubtless prompted by the desire to bring further proof to the aid of the Government, and under color of his office undertook to make a seizure of private papers in direct violation of the constitutional prohibition against such action. . . . To sanction such proceedings would be to affirm by judicial decision a manifest neglect if not an open defiance of the prohibitions of the Constitution, intended for the protection of the people against such unauthorized action.

The [Government contends that the correct rule of law is] that the letters having come into the control of the court, it would not inquire into the manner in which they were obtained, but if competent would keep them and permit their use in evidence. Such proposition, the Government asserts, is conclusively established by certain decisions of this court. [This doctrine,] that a court will not in trying a criminal cause permit a collateral issue to be raised as to the source of competent testimony, has the sanction of so many state cases that it would be impracticable to cite or refer to them in detail. [The editor of one legal publication has explained the rule as follows:] "Such an investigation is not involved necessarily in the litigation in chief, and to pursue it would be to halt in the orderly progress of a cause, and consider incidentally a question which has happened to cross the path of such litigation, and which is wholly independent thereof."

It is therefore evident that [our prior cases] afford no authority for the action of the court in this case, when applied to in due season for the return of papers seized in violation of the Constitutional Amendment. [Prior cases were distinguishable, however, because they involved] application of the doctrine that a collateral issue will not be raised to ascertain the source from which testimony, competent in a criminal case, comes. . . . The right of the court to deal with papers and documents in the possession of the District Attorney and other officers of the court and subject to its authority [is clearly established.] That papers wrongfully seized should be turned over to the accused has been frequently recognized in the early as well as later decisions of the courts.

We therefore reach the conclusion that the letters in question were taken from the house of the accused by an official of the United States acting under color of his office in direct violation of the constitutional rights of the defendant; that having made a seasonable application for their return, which was heard and passed upon by the court, there was involved in the order refusing the application a denial of the constitutional rights of the accused, and that the court should have restored these letters to the accused. In holding them and permitting their use upon the trial, we think prejudicial error was committed. . . .

Notes

1. *Evidentiary fruits of illegal searches.* Would the exclusionary rule described in the *Weeks* case prevent the government from introducing evidence *derived* from illegally obtained papers rather than the papers themselves? In Silverthorne Lumber Co. v. United States, 251 U.S. 385 (1920), the government had illegally seized corporate papers, returned them before trial, and then issued a subpoena duces tecum to obtain the documents through proper means. The Court declared that the exclusionary rule prevented such a method of curing the effects of an illegal seizure: Exclusion means "that not merely evidence [illegally] acquired shall not be used before the Court but that it shall not be used at all."

2. *The states and the exclusionary rule after 1949.* Because the *Weeks* opinion was based on the federal Bill of Rights, which did not at that time apply to the states, state courts and legislatures were free to adopt or reject the exclusionary remedy. Only a handful of states adopted an exclusionary rule prior to the *Weeks* opinion. See State v. Sheridan, 96 N.W. 730 (Iowa 1903). The *Weeks* opinion did not change this trend in the state courts. Most took the view of Judge Benjamin Cardozo in People v. Defore, 150 N.E. 585 (N.Y. 1926), in which he tartly summarized the exclusionary rule as follows: "There is no blinking the consequences. The criminal is to go free because the constable has blundered. . . . The pettiest peace officer would have it in his power through overzeal or indiscretion to confer immunity upon an offender for crimes the most flagitious."

Thus, for the first half of this century the exclusionary remedy applied only in the federal system and a handful of states. As of 1926, fewer than 15 states had adopted the exclusionary rule and more than 30 had rejected it. Even after the Supreme Court decided to apply the Fourth Amendment to state law enforcement officers in Wolf v. Colorado, 338 U.S. 25 (1949), it did not insist that state courts exclude improperly seized evidence. They were still free to adopt remedies other than the exclusionary rule. About half of the states continued to rely on civil remedies for victims of illegal searches and on criminal charges against police officers who violated the law. But by the 1950s, judges and commentators started having doubts about the success of alternatives to the exclusionary rule — at that time, not just alternatives but the only remedies available in many states.

■ PEOPLE v. CHARLES CAHAN

282 P.2d 905 (Cal. 1955)

TRAYNOR, J.

Defendant and 15 other persons were charged with conspiring to engage in horse-race bookmaking and related offenses. [After a trial without a jury, the court found one defendant not guilty, and all the other defendants, including Cahan, guilty.]

Most of the incriminatory evidence introduced at the trial was obtained by officers of the Los Angeles Police Department in flagrant violation of the United States Constitution (4th and 14th Amendments), the California Constitution (art. I, §19), and state and federal statutes. Gerald Wooters, an officer attached to the intelligence unit of that department testified that after securing the permission of the chief of police to make microphone installations* at two places occupied by defendants, he, Sergeant Keeler, and Officer Phillips one night at about 8:45 entered one "house through the side window of the first floor," and that he "directed the officers to place a listening device under a chest of drawers." Another officer made recordings and transcriptions of the conversations that came over wires from the listening device to receiving equipment installed in a nearby garage. . . . Section 653h of the Penal Code does not and could not authorize violations of the Constitution. . . .

The evidence obtained from the microphones was not the only unconstitutionally obtained evidence introduced at the trial over defendants' objection. In addition there was a mass of evidence obtained by numerous forcible entries and seizures without search warrants. [The officers testified that they obtained evidence by kicking open a door in one location, and by breaking a window at another.]

Thus, without fear of criminal punishment or other discipline, law enforcement officers, sworn to support the Constitution of the United States and the Constitution of California, frankly admit their deliberate, flagrant acts in violation of both Constitutions and the laws enacted thereunder. It is clearly apparent from their testimony that they casually regard such acts as nothing more than the performance of their ordinary duties for which the city employs and pays them.

[Both] the United States Constitution and the California Constitution make it emphatically clear that important as efficient law enforcement may be, it is more important that the right of privacy guaranteed by these constitutional provisions be respected. [The] contention that unreasonable searches and seizures are justified by the necessity of bringing criminals to justice cannot be accepted. It was rejected when the constitutional provisions were adopted and the choice was made that all the people, guilty and innocent alike, should be secure from unreasonable police intrusions, even though some criminals should escape. Moreover, the constitutional provisions make no distinction between the guilty and the innocent, and it would be manifestly impossible to protect the rights of the innocent if the police were permitted to justify unreasonable searches and seizures on the ground that they assumed their victims were criminals. Thus, when consideration is directed to the question of the admissibility of evidence obtained in violation of the constitutional provisions, it bears emphasis that the court is not concerned solely with the rights of the defendant before it, however guilty he may appear, but with the constitutional right of all of the people to be secure in their homes, persons, and effects.

The constitutional provisions themselves do not expressly answer the question whether evidence obtained in violation thereof is admissible in criminal actions. Neither Congress nor the Legislature has given an answer, and the courts of the country are divided on the question. The federal courts and those of some of the states exclude such evidence. In accord with the traditional common-law rule, the courts of a majority of the states admit it, and heretofore the courts of this state have admitted it.

* [Section 653h of the Penal Code provided: "Any person who, without consent of the owner, lessee, or occupant, installs or attempts to install or use a dictograph in any house . . . is guilty of a misdemeanor; provided, that nothing herein shall prevent the use and installation of dictographs by a regular salaried police officer expressly authorized thereto by the head of his office . . . when such use and installation are necessary in the performance of their duties in detecting crime and in the apprehension of criminals." — Eds.]

The decision of the United States Supreme Court in Wolf v. Colorado, 338 U.S. 25 (1949), that the guarantee of the Fourth Amendment applies to the states through the Fourteenth [Amendment,] does not require states like California that have heretofore admitted illegally seized evidence to exclude it now. The exclusionary rule is not "an essential ingredient" of the right of privacy guaranteed by the Fourth Amendment, but simply a means of enforcing that right, which the states can accept or reject. . . .

The rule admitting the evidence has been strongly supported by both scholars and judges. Their arguments may be briefly summarized as follows:

The rules of evidence are designed to enable courts to reach the truth and, in criminal cases, to secure a fair trial to those accused of crime. Evidence obtained by an illegal search and seizure is ordinarily just as true and reliable as evidence lawfully obtained. The court needs all reliable evidence material to the issue before it, the guilt or innocence of the accused, and how such evidence is obtained is immaterial to that issue. It should not be excluded unless strong considerations of public policy demand it. . . .

Exclusion of the evidence cannot be justified as affording protection or recompense to the defendant or punishment to the officers for the illegal search and seizure. It does not protect the defendant from the search and seizure, since that illegal act has already occurred. If he is innocent or if there is ample evidence to convict him without the illegally obtained evidence, exclusion of the evidence gives him no remedy at all. Thus the only defendants who benefit by the exclusionary rule are those criminals who could not be convicted without the illegally obtained evidence. Allowing such criminals to escape punishment is not appropriate recompense for the invasion of their constitutional rights; it does not punish the officers who violated the constitutional provisions; and it fails to protect society from known criminals who should not be left at large. For his crime the defendant should be punished. For his violation of the constitutional provisions the offending officer should be punished. As the exclusionary rule operates, however, the defendant's crime and the officer's flouting of constitutional guarantees both go unpunished. . . .

Opponents of the exclusionary rule also point out that it is inconsistent with the rule allowing private litigants to use illegally obtained evidence, and that as applied in the federal courts, it is capricious in its operation, either going too far or not far enough. So many exceptions to the exclusionary rule have been granted the judicial blessing as largely to destroy any value it might otherwise have had. . . .

Finally it has been pointed out that there is no convincing evidence that the exclusionary rule actually tends to prevent unreasonable searches and seizures and that the disciplinary or educational effect of the court's releasing the defendant for police misbehavior is so indirect as to be no more than a mild deterrent at best.

Despite the persuasive force of the foregoing arguments, we have concluded that evidence obtained in violation of the constitutional guarantees is inadmissible. We have been compelled to reach that conclusion because other remedies have completely failed to secure compliance with the constitutional provisions on the part of police officers with the attendant result that the courts under the old rule have been constantly required to participate in, and in effect condone, the lawless activities of law enforcement officers.

When, as in the present case, the very purpose of an illegal search and seizure is to get evidence to introduce at a trial, the success of the lawless venture depends entirely on the court's lending its aid by allowing the evidence to be introduced. . . .

Out of regard for its own dignity as an agency of justice and custodian of liberty the court should not have a hand in such dirty business.

Courts refuse their aid in civil cases to prevent the consummation of illegal schemes of private litigants; a fortiori, they should not extend that aid and thereby permit the consummation of illegal schemes of the state itself. It is morally incongruous for the state to flout constitutional rights and at the same time demand that its citizens observe the law. The end that the state seeks may be a laudable one, but it no more justifies unlawful acts than a laudable end justifies unlawful action by any member of the public. Moreover, any process of law that sanctions the imposition of penalties upon an individual through the use of the fruits of official lawlessness tends to the destruction of the whole system of restraints on the exercise of the public force that are inherent in the concept of ordered liberty. . . . "Our Government is the potent, the omnipresent teacher. For good or for ill, it teaches the whole people by its example. Crime is contagious. If the Government becomes a lawbreaker, it breeds contempt for law, it invites everyman to become a law unto himself; it invites anarchy." Olmstead v. United States, 277 U.S. 438 (1928) (Brandeis, J., dissenting).

[If the constitutional guarantees against unreasonable searches and seizures] were being effectively enforced by other means than excluding evidence obtained by their violation, a different problem would be presented. If such were the case there would be more force to the argument that a particular criminal should not be redressed for a past violation of his rights by excluding the evidence against him. Experience has demonstrated, however, that neither administrative, criminal nor civil remedies are effective in suppressing lawless searches and seizures. The innocent suffer with the guilty, and we cannot close our eyes to the effect the rule we adopt will have on the rights of those not before the court. "The difficulty with [other remedies] is in part due to the failure of interested parties to inform of the offense. No matter what an illegal raid turns up, police are unlikely to inform on themselves or each other. If it turns up nothing incriminating, the innocent victim usually does not care to take steps which will air the fact that he has been under suspicion." Irvine v. California, 347 U.S. 128 (1954). Moreover, even when it becomes generally known that the police conduct illegal searches and seizures, public opinion is not aroused as it is in the case of other violations of constitutional rights. Illegal searches and seizures lack the obvious brutality of coerced confessions and the third degree and do not so clearly strike at the very basis of our civil liberties as do unfair trials or the lynching of even an admitted murderer. . . . There is thus all the more necessity for courts to be vigilant in protecting these constitutional rights if they are to be protected at all. People v. Mayen, 205 P. 435 (Cal. 1922) [rejecting the exclusionary rule in California] was decided over 30 years ago. Since then case after case has appeared in our appellate reports describing unlawful searches and seizures against the defendant on trial, and those cases undoubtedly reflect only a small fraction of the violations of the constitutional provisions that have actually occurred. On the other hand, reported cases involving civil actions against police officers are rare, and those involving successful criminal prosecutions against officers are nonexistent. In short, the constitutional provisions are not being enforced.

Granted that the adoption of the exclusionary rule will not prevent all illegal searches and seizures, it will discourage them. Police officers and prosecuting officials are primarily interested in convicting criminals. Given the exclusionary rule and a choice between securing evidence by legal rather than illegal means, officers will be impelled to obey the law themselves since not to do so will jeopardize their objectives. [If] courts respect the constitutional provisions by refusing to sanction their violation, they will not only command the respect of law-abiding citizens for themselves adhering to the law, they will also arouse public opinion as a deterrent to lawless enforcement of the law by bringing just criticism to bear on law enforcement officers who allow criminals to escape by pursuing them in lawless ways.

It is contended, however, that the police do not always have a choice of securing evidence by legal means and that in many cases the criminal will escape if illegally obtained evidence cannot be used against him. This contention is not properly directed at the exclusionary rule, but at the constitutional provisions themselves. It was rejected when those provisions were adopted. In such cases had the Constitution been obeyed, the criminal could in no event be convicted. He does not go free because the constable blundered, but because the Constitutions prohibit securing the evidence against him. . . .

In developing a rule of evidence applicable in the state courts, this court is not bound by the decisions that have applied the federal rule, and if it appears that those decisions have developed needless refinements and distinctions, this court need not follow them. . . . Under these circumstances the adoption of the exclusionary rule need not introduce confusion into the law of criminal procedure. Instead it opens the door to the development of workable rules governing searches and seizures and the issuance of warrants that will protect both the rights guaranteed by the constitutional provisions and the interest of society in the suppression of crime. . . .

SPENCE, J., dissenting.

I dissent. The guilt of the appellant is clearly demonstrated by the record before us. . . . In adopting and adhering to the nonexclusionary rule, the law of the State of California has thereby been kept in harmony with the law of the great majority of the other states and of all the British commonwealths; as well as in line with the considered views of the majority of the most eminent legal scholars. Only the federal courts and the courts of a relatively few states have adopted the judicially created exclusionary rule. . . .

The experience of the federal courts in attempting to apply the exclusionary rule does not appear to commend its adoption elsewhere. The spectacle of an obviously guilty defendant obtaining a favorable ruling by a court upon a motion to suppress evidence or upon an objection to evidence, and thereby, in effect, obtaining immunity from any successful prosecution of the charge against him, is a picture which has been too often seen in the federal practice. . . . Furthermore, under the present federal practice, the trial of the accused is interrupted to try the question of whether the evidence was in fact illegally obtained. This question is often a delicate one, and the main trial is at least delayed while the question of whether some other person has committed a wrong in obtaining the evidence has been judicially determined. . . .

[I cannot] ascertain from the majority opinion in the present case the nature of the rule which is being adopted to supplant the well established nonexclusionary rule in California. Is it the exclusionary rule as interpreted in the federal courts with all its technical distinctions, exceptions, and qualifications . . . ? [Neither] the federal courts nor the courts of any of the few states which adopted the exclusionary rule have apparently found a satisfactory solution to [the] problem of developing "workable rules," and it seems impossible to contemplate the possibility that this court can develop a satisfactory solution. At best, this court would have to work out such rules in piecemeal fashion as each case might come before it. In the meantime, what rules are to guide our trial courts in the handling of their problems? If the nonexclusionary rule can be said to have one unquestioned advantage, it is the advantage of certainty. . . .

If, however, reasons may be said to exist for a change in the established policy of this state, I believe that the Legislature, rather than the courts, should make such change. This is particularly true in a situation such as the present one, when the change of policy should be accompanied by "workable rules" to implement such change. . . . In this connection, it is worthy of note that bills have frequently been introduced in the Legislature to accomplish precisely that which is accomplished by the majority opinion, to wit: the supplanting of the nonexclusionary rule by the so-called exclusionary rule, without prescribing any "workable rules" for the latter's application. In the recent legislative sessions of 1951 and of 1953, such bills have been introduced but none has ever been brought to a vote in either house. Under the circumstances, it would be far better for this court to allow the Legislature to deal with this question of policy. . . .

Returning to the precise situation presented by the record before us, it may be conceded that the illegality in obtaining the evidence was both clear and flagrant. It may be further conceded that the crimes which defendants conspired to commit were not in the class of the more serious public offenses. The fact remains, however, that the exclusionary rule, as adopted by the majority, is a rule for all cases and that it deprives society of its remedy against the most desperate gangster charged with the most heinous crime merely because of some degree of illegality in obtaining the evidence against him. . . .

In my opinion, the cost of the adoption of the exclusionary rule is manifestly too great. It would be far better for this state to adhere to the nonexclusionary rule, and to reexamine its laws concerning the sanctions to be placed upon illegal searches and seizures. If the present laws are deemed inadequate to discourage illegal practices by enforcement officers, the Legislature might well consider the imposition of civil liability for such conduct upon the governmental unit employing the offending officer, in addition to the liability now imposed upon the officer himself. It might also consider fixing a minimum amount to be recovered as damages in the same manner that a minimum has been fixed for the invasion of other civil rights. These methods would be far more effective in discouraging illegal activities on the part of enforcement officers and such methods would not be subject to the objection, inherent in the adoption of the exclusionary rule, that "It deprives society of its remedy against one lawbreaker because he has been pursued by another." Irvine v. California, 347 U.S. 128 (1954). . . .

DOLLREE MAPP v. OHIO

367 U.S. 643 (1961)

CLARK, J.*

On May 23, 1957, three Cleveland police officers arrived at appellant's residence in that city pursuant to information that "a person [was] hiding out in the

* [Chief Justice Warren and Justices Black, Douglas, and Brennan joined in this opinion. — EDS.]

home, who was wanted for questioning in connection with a recent bombing, and that there was a large amount of policy paraphernalia being hidden in the home." Miss Mapp and her daughter by a former marriage lived on the top floor of the two-family dwelling. Upon their arrival at that house, the officers knocked on the door and demanded entrance but appellant, after telephoning her attorney, refused to admit them without a search warrant. They advised their headquarters of the situation and undertook a surveillance of the house.

The officers again sought entrance some three hours later when four or more additional officers arrived on the scene. When Miss Mapp did not come to the door immediately, at least one of the several doors to the house was forcibly opened[2] and the policemen gained admittance. Meanwhile Miss Mapp's attorney arrived, but the officers, having secured their own entry, and continuing in their defiance of the law, would permit him neither to see Miss Mapp nor to enter the house. It appears that Miss Mapp was halfway down the stairs from the upper floor to the front door when the officers, in this highhanded manner, broke into the hall. She demanded to see the search warrant. A paper, claimed to be a warrant, was held up by one of the officers. She grabbed the "warrant" and placed it in her bosom. A struggle ensued in which the officers recovered the piece of paper and as a result of which they handcuffed appellant because she had been "belligerent" in resisting their official rescue of the "warrant" from her person. Running roughshod over appellant, a policeman "grabbed" her, "twisted [her] hand," and she "yelled [and] pleaded with him" because "it was hurting." Appellant, in handcuffs, was then forcibly taken upstairs to her bedroom where the officers searched a dresser, a chest of drawers, a closet and some suitcases. They also looked into a photo album and through personal papers belonging to the appellant. The search spread to the rest of the second floor including the child's bedroom, the living room, the kitchen and a dinette. The basement of the building and a trunk found therein were also searched. The obscene [books and pictures] for possession of which she was ultimately convicted were discovered in the course of that widespread search.

At the trial no search warrant was produced by the prosecution, nor was the failure to produce one explained or accounted for. [The Ohio Supreme Court affirmed the conviction because] the evidence had not been taken "from defendant's person by the use of brutal or offensive physical force against defendant." The State says that even if the search were made without authority, or otherwise unreasonably, it is not prevented from using the unconstitutionally seized evidence at trial. . . .

I.

[In] the year 1914, in the *Weeks* case, this Court for the first time held that in a federal prosecution the Fourth Amendment barred the use of evidence secured through an illegal search and seizure. This Court has ever since required of federal law officers a strict adherence to that command which this Court has held to be a clear, specific, and constitutionally required — even if judicially implied — deterrent safeguard without insistence upon which the Fourth Amendment would have been reduced to a form of words. . . .

2. A police officer testified that "we did pry the screen door to gain entrance"; the attorney on the scene testified that a policeman "tried . . . to kick in the door" and then "broke the glass in the door and somebody reached in and opened the door and let them in. . . ."

II.

[Thirty-five years later, in Wolf v. Colorado, 338 U.S. 25 (1949)], the Court decided that the *Weeks* exclusionary rule would not then be imposed upon the States as "an essential ingredient of the right." The Court's reasons for not considering essential to the right to privacy, as a curb imposed upon the States by the Due Process Clause, that which decades before had been posited as part and parcel of the Fourth Amendment's limitation upon federal encroachment of individual privacy, were bottomed on factual considerations.

While they are not basically relevant to a decision that the exclusionary rule is an essential ingredient of the Fourth Amendment as the right it embodies is vouchsafed against the States by the Due Process Clause, we will consider the current validity of the factual grounds upon which *Wolf* was based.

The Court in *Wolf* first stated that "the contrariety of views of the States" on the adoption of the exclusionary rule of *Weeks* was "particularly impressive"; and, in this connection, that it could not "brush aside the experience of States which deem the incidence of such conduct by the police too slight to call for a deterrent remedy by overriding the States' relevant rules of evidence." While in 1949, prior to the *Wolf* case, almost two-thirds of the States were opposed to the use of the exclusionary rule, now, despite the *Wolf* case, more than half of those since passing upon it, [including California], by their own legislative or judicial decision, have wholly or partly adopted or adhered to the *Weeks* rule.

[The] second basis elaborated in *Wolf* in support of its failure to enforce the exclusionary doctrine against the States was that "other means of protection" have been afforded the right to privacy.[7] The experience of California [described in People v. Cahan] that such other remedies have been worthless and futile is buttressed by the experience of other States. . . . It, therefore, plainly appears that the factual considerations supporting the failure of the *Wolf* Court to include the *Weeks* exclusionary rule when it recognized the enforceability of the right to privacy against the States in 1949, while not basically relevant to the constitutional consideration, could not, in any analysis, now be deemed controlling. . . .

III.

. . . Today we once again examine *Wolf*'s constitutional documentation of the right to privacy free from unreasonable state intrusion, and, after its dozen years on our books, are led by it to close the only courtroom door remaining open to evidence secured by official lawlessness in flagrant abuse of that basic right, reserved to all persons as a specific guarantee against that very same unlawful conduct. We hold that all evidence obtained by searches and seizures in violation of the Constitution is, by that same authority, inadmissible in a state court.

7. Less than half [23] of the States have any criminal provisions relating directly to unreasonable searches and seizures. . . .

IV.

Since the Fourth Amendment's right of privacy has been declared enforceable against the States through the Due Process Clause of the Fourteenth, it is enforceable against them by the same sanction of exclusion as is used against the Federal Government. Were it otherwise, then just as without the *Weeks* rule the assurance against unreasonable federal searches and seizures would be "a form of words," valueless and undeserving of mention in a perpetual charter of inestimable human liberties, so too, without that rule the freedom from state invasions of privacy would be so ephemeral and so neatly severed from its conceptual nexus with the freedom from all brutish means of coercing evidence as not to merit this Court's high regard as a freedom "implicit in the concept of ordered liberty." . . . Therefore, in extending the substantive protections of due process to all constitutionally unreasonable searches — state or federal — it was logically and constitutionally necessary that the exclusion doctrine — an essential part of the right to privacy — be also insisted upon as an essential ingredient of the right newly recognized by the *Wolf* case. . . . To hold otherwise is to grant the right but in reality to withhold its privilege and enjoyment. . . .

This Court has not hesitated to enforce as strictly against the States as it does against the Federal Government the rights of free speech and of a free press, the rights to notice and to a fair, public trial, including, as it does, the right not to be convicted by use of a coerced confession, however logically relevant it be, and without regard to its reliability. And nothing could be more certain than that when a coerced confession is involved, "the relevant rules of evidence" are overridden. . . . Why should not the same rule apply to what is tantamount to coerced testimony by way of unconstitutional seizure of goods, papers, effects, documents, etc.? . . .

V.

Moreover, our holding that the exclusionary rule is an essential part of both the Fourth and Fourteenth Amendments is not only the logical dictate of prior cases, but it also makes very good sense. There is no war between the Constitution and common sense. Presently, a federal prosecutor may make no use of evidence illegally seized, but a State's attorney across the street may, although he supposedly is operating under the enforceable prohibitions of the same Amendment. Thus the State, by admitting evidence unlawfully seized, serves to encourage disobedience to the Federal Constitution which it is bound to uphold. Moreover, . . . the very essence of a healthy federalism depends upon the avoidance of needless conflict between state and federal courts. . . . Federal-state cooperation in the solution of crime under constitutional standards will be promoted, if only by recognition of their now mutual obligation to respect the same fundamental criteria in their approaches. . . .

There are those who say, as did Justice (then Judge) Cardozo, that under our constitutional exclusionary doctrine "the criminal is to go free because the constable has blundered." In some cases this will undoubtedly be the result. But . . . there is another consideration — the imperative of judicial integrity. The criminal goes free, if he must, but it is the law that sets him free. Nothing can destroy a government more quickly than its failure to observe its own laws, or worse, its disregard of the charter of its own existence. . . .

The ignoble shortcut to conviction left open to the State tends to destroy the entire system of constitutional restraints on which the liberties of the people rest. Having once recognized that the right to privacy embodied in the Fourth Amendment is enforceable against the States, and that the right to be secure against rude invasions of privacy by state officers is, therefore, constitutional in origin, we can no longer permit that right to remain an empty promise. Because it is enforceable in the same manner and to like effect as other basic rights secured by the Due Process Clause, we can no longer permit it to be revocable at the whim of any police officer who, in the name of law enforcement itself, chooses to suspend its enjoyment. Our decision, founded on reason and truth, gives to the individual no more than that which the Constitution guarantees him, to the police officer no less than that to which honest law enforcement is entitled, and, to the courts, that judicial integrity so necessary in the true administration of justice. . . .

HARLAN, J., dissenting.*

. . . II.

[It] cannot be too much emphasized that what was recognized in *Wolf* was not that the Fourth Amendment as such is enforceable against the States as a facet of due process, . . . but the principle of privacy "which is at the core of the Fourth Amendment." It would not be proper to expect or impose any precise equivalence, either as regards the scope of the right or the means of its implementation, between the requirements of the Fourth and Fourteenth Amendments. [Unlike the Fourteenth, which states a general principle only, the Fourth] is a particular command, having its setting in a pre-existing legal context on which both interpreting decisions and enabling statutes must at least build. . . .

I would not impose upon the States this federal exclusionary remedy. . . . Our concern here, as it was in *Wolf*, is not with the desirability of that rule but only with the question whether the States are Constitutionally free to follow it or not as they may themselves determine, and the relevance of the disparity of views among the States on this point lies simply in the fact that the judgment involved is a debatable one. . . .

The preservation of a proper balance between state and federal responsibility in the administration of criminal justice demands patience on the part of those who might like to see things move faster among the States in this respect. Problems of criminal law enforcement vary widely from State to State. One State, in considering the totality of its legal picture, may conclude that the need for embracing the *Weeks* rule is pressing because other remedies are unavailable or inadequate to secure compliance with the substantive Constitutional principle involved. Another, though equally solicitous of Constitutional rights, may choose to pursue one purpose at a time, allowing all evidence relevant to guilt to be brought into a criminal trial, and dealing with Constitutional infractions by other means. Still another may consider the exclusionary rule too rough-and-ready a remedy, in that it reaches only unconstitutional intrusions which eventuate in criminal prosecution of the victims. Further, a State after experimenting with the *Weeks* rule for a time may, because of

* [Justices Frankfurter and Whittaker joined in this opinion. — EDS.]

unsatisfactory experience with it, decide to revert to a non-exclusionary rule. And so on. . . . For us the question remains, as it has always been, one of state power, not one of passing judgment on the wisdom of one state course or another. . . .

I regret that I find so unwise in principle and so inexpedient in policy a decision motivated by the high purpose of increasing respect for Constitutional rights. But in the last analysis I think this Court can increase respect for the Constitution only if it rigidly respects the limitations which the Constitution places upon it, and respects as well the principles inherent in its own processes. In the present case I think we exceed both, and that our voice becomes only a voice of power, not of reason.

Notes

1. *Power and reason.* Was *Mapp* an appropriate interpretation of the due process clause? Do you believe that conditions had changed significantly between 1949 (the date of the *Wolf* decision) and 1961 (the date of *Mapp*)? Mapp's attorney did not ask the court to overturn the *Wolf* decision, but the American Civil Liberties Union, appearing as *amicus curiae,* raised the issue.

2. *Empirical evidence on the benefits of the exclusionary rule.* The *Cahan* court stated that "there is no convincing evidence that the exclusionary rule actually tends to prevent unreasonable searches and seizures" and that it was "a mild deterrent at best." It is quite difficult to estimate the real impact of the exclusionary rule on police and magistrate practices because the effect of the rule (if any) would be to produce a nonevent. That is, the exclusionary rule would, in theory, prevent improper searches and seizures from occurring. Some have attempted to measure the effects of the exclusionary rule by tracking either the number of search and arrest warrants sought or the number of arrests completed in the same location before and after the exclusionary rule took effect. In some locations, the number of warrants sought went up and the number of arrests went down after *Mapp,* but in other locations there was little or no change.

Others have estimated the deterrent effect of the exclusionary rule by asking police officers themselves how the prospect of losing evidence in a case would affect their decisions in the field. A 1997 survey of law enforcement officers in Ventura County, California, offered equivocal evidence about the deterrent effects of the exclusionary rule. About 20 percent of the officers responding to the survey said that the risk of exclusion of evidence was their primary concern in deciding whether to conduct a search or seizure, while nearly 60 percent considered suppression to be an "important" concern. Officers who had "lost" evidence because of improper searches or seizures in past cases were no more likely than other officers to give correct answers to hypothetical search and seizure questions. See Timothy Perrin, et al., If It's Broken, Fix It: Moving Beyond the Exclusionary Rule — A New and Extensive Empirical Study of the Exclusionary Rule and a Call for a Civil Administrative Remedy to Partially Replace the Rule, 83 Iowa L. Rev. 669 (1998).

3. *Empirical evidence on the costs of the exclusionary rule.* More effort has gone into measuring the "costs" of the exclusionary rule. A number of studies have estimated the number of convictions that the government loses because of concerns about exclusion of evidence obtained from an improper search or seizure. The estimates of arrests lost range from 0.6 percent to 2.35 percent of all felony arrests, with a

higher proportion (in the range of 3 to 5 percent) of arrests on drug and weapons charges. Thomas Davies, A Hard Look at What We Know (and Still Need to Learn) about the "Costs" of the Exclusionary Rule: The NIJ Study and Other Studies of "Lost" Arrests, 1983 Am. B. Found. Res. J. 611. For an attempt to measure the effects of the exclusionary rule on crime rates (as opposed to conviction rates), see Raymond A. Atkins & Paul H. Rubin, Effects of Criminal Procedure on Crime Rates: Mapping Out the Consequences of the Exclusionary Rule, 46 J. L. & Econ. 157 (2003).

Assuming we knew with some confidence how many cases are lost because of improper searches or seizures, how many would be too many? Perhaps the answer depends on whether the exclusionary rule should function as a "sanction" to signal that conduct is wrong and completely intolerable, or as a "price" that tolerates some of the behavior so long as it produces more good than harm overall. See Sharon Davies, The Penalty of Exclusion — A Price or Sanction? 73 S. Cal. L. Rev. 1275 (2000).

4. *The imperative of judicial integrity.* The courts in *Mapp* and *Cahan* each mentioned that the exclusionary rule would serve multiple purposes. In addition to deterring violations of the Constitution, it would also protect judicial integrity. Today, however, the Supreme Court describes the purpose of the exclusionary rule solely in terms of deterrence. See United States v. Janis, 428 U.S. 433, 458 (1976) ("considerations of judicial integrity do not require exclusion of the evidence"). Is the exclusionary rule necessary to protect the integrity of courts? Do courts undermine their integrity when they accept evidence in *civil* cases that was obtained contrary to law? Is the "truth seeking" function of the criminal process the best guarantee of judicial integrity, and does the exclusionary rule harm the truth-seeking function?

5. *Exclusion for violation of state constitutions, statutes, and procedure rules.* When a state court concludes that a search or seizure violated the state constitution rather than the federal constitution, exclusion is almost always the remedy the court adopts. Although exclusion is not required by federal law in such a case, state courts will typically choose exclusion as the proper remedy under state law.

When a search or seizure violates the provisions of a statute (state or federal) rather than a constitution, courts try to determine which remedy the legislature intended. Sometimes an explicit provision in a statute makes this relatively easy. See Ill. Stat. Ann. ch. 720, §5/14-5 (exclusion of any evidence obtained in violation of eavesdropping statute). . . . In other cases, the statutory language does not address remedies, and the legislative history is unhelpful. In such cases, courts tend to use the exclusion remedy for statutory violations when the search or seizure infringed in a "significant" way on "substantial" rights of the defendant. Compare People v. McKinstry, 843 P.2d 18 (Colo. 1993) (no exclusion for failure to include affiant's name in warrant application, as required by statute) with People v. Taylor, 541 N.E.2d 386 (N.Y. 1989) (exclusion required for violation of statutory requirement of contemporaneous recording of evidence supporting warrant application). What remedy would you expect state courts to select when police officers violate departmental policies as they gather evidence?

6. *Silver platters.* It is clear that a federal court cannot receive evidence that state officers obtain in violation of federal law. That is, the state officers may not present the evidence to their federal counterparts on a "silver platter." See Elkins v. United States, 364 U.S. 206 (1960). The same rule prevents federal officers from presenting

evidence to a state court if they obtained it in violation of the federal constitution. But the "silver platter doctrine" does not operate in all possible combinations. Officers from some other jurisdiction (federal or state) may obtain evidence in violation of state law (constitutional or statutory) and present that evidence in the federal courts or in the courts of another state. Local rules about search and seizure do not export to the courts of other jurisdictions. As the reach of federal criminal law grows and the overlap between state and federal criminal justice increases, does the argument get stronger for applying local search and seizure rules in the courts of other jurisdictions? How would traditional conflicts of laws doctrine resolve this issue?

7. *International adoption of exclusionary rule.* Although judges in the United States sometimes claim that no other country in the world uses an exclusionary rule, the claim is not true. For instance, in Germany, judges must consider whether admission of evidence obtained illegally would violate the constitutionally protected privacy interests of the defendant. German judges balance in each case the defendant's interests in privacy against the importance of the evidence and the seriousness of the offense charged. In practice, however, German judges rarely exclude evidence obtained through improper searches.

In Canada, exclusion happens more frequently. The constitutionally based Charter of Rights and Freedoms gives the accused a basis for excluding evidence that was obtained improperly. Evidence is excluded only if a breach of a Charter right or freedom is demonstrated and if the admission of the evidence in the trial would tend to bring the administration of justice "into disrepute." More serious violations are more likely to result in exclusion. Craig Bradley, *Mapp* Goes Abroad, 52 Case Western Res. L. Rev. 375 (2001). In general, judges in other countries distinguish between "real" evidence and interrogation evidence, and are more likely to exclude interrogation evidence. Why would courts make this distinction? The web extension for this chapter, at *http://www.crimpro.com/extension/ch06,* offers further examples of the use of the exclusionary remedy in other countries.

The basis for the exclusionary rule in these and other countries focuses more on judicial integrity than deterrence of police misconduct. If courts in the United States were to emphasize once again the "imperative of judicial integrity," would that open the way to an exclusionary rule that is applied less consistently than it is today?

B. LIMITATIONS ON THE EXCLUSIONARY RULE

We have traced the history of the adoption of the exclusionary rule as a remedy for illegal searches and seizures. The exclusionary rule was a highly controversial choice of remedies at the time of *Weeks, Cahan,* and *Mapp,* and it remains so today. Reservations about the exclusionary rule have not yet led any U.S. legal system to abandon the remedy, but they have led to some serious limitations on its applicability and effects.

1. *Evidence Obtained in "Good Faith"*

COMMONWEALTH v. LOUIS EDMUNDS
586 A.2d 887 (Penn. 1991)

CAPPY, J.

The issue presented to this court is whether Pennsylvania should adopt the "good faith" exception to the exclusionary rule as articulated by the United States Supreme Court in the case of United States v. Leon, 468 U.S. 897 (1984). We conclude that a "good faith" exception to the exclusionary rule would frustrate the guarantees embodied in Article I, Section 8, of the Pennsylvania Constitution. Accordingly, the decision of the Superior Court is reversed. . . .

The pertinent facts can be briefly summarized as follows. On August 5, 1985 State Police Trooper Michael Deise obtained a warrant from a district magistrate to search a white corrugated building and curtilage on the property of the defendant. [The information in the warrant affidavit came from confidential informants and from a later helicopter flyover of the property. When Trooper Deise and three other troopers went to Edmunds's property to execute the warrant, they discovered 17 growing marijuana plants inside the building, rather than outside the building as the informants had alleged. Prior to trial on drug charges, Edmunds moved to suppress the marijuana seized from the building] on the ground that the warrant was constitutionally defective, and probable cause was lacking, because the warrant failed to set forth a time frame in which the informants had observed the marijuana.

Recognizing that the affidavit of probable cause was deficient on its face, the trial court granted the request of the district attorney to convene a supplemental suppression hearing. . . . The express purpose of this hearing was to allow the district attorney to provide oral supplementation of the facts set forth in the written affidavit and warrant, in order to establish a "good faith" exception to the exclusionary rule under the auspices of *Leon.* [District Justice Tlumac] testified that Trooper Deise appeared in her office . . . and related his conversation with the two anonymous informants. She stated that Trooper Deise thereafter dictated the affidavit, which she typed verbatim. She then prepared and issued the search warrant. [She was under the impression that the informants had seen the marijuana the day before Trooper Deise had sought the warrant.]

Upon the close of the supplemental suppression hearing, the trial court found that . . . this warrant would be incapable of establishing probable cause to justify the search of defendant's property. The warrant failed to set forth a time frame from which a neutral and detached magistrate could reasonably infer that the criminal conduct observed was recent and would most likely still be in progress at the time the warrant was requested. [The trial court nevertheless admitted the evidence, because the trooper acted in "good faith" in executing the defective warrant.]

Our starting point must be the decision of the United States Supreme Court in *Leon.* In *Leon,* the Supreme Court in 1984 departed from a long history of exclusionary rule jurisprudence dating back to Weeks v. United States (1914) and Mapp v. Ohio (1961). The Court in *Leon* concluded that the Fourth Amendment does not mandate suppression of illegally seized evidence obtained pursuant to a constitutionally defective warrant, so long as the police officer acted in good faith reliance upon the warrant issued by a neutral and detached magistrate.

In *Leon,* police officers in Burbank, California, had initiated a drug investigation after receiving a tip from a confidential informant that large quantities of cocaine and methaqualone were being sold from a residence. The informant had indicated that he witnessed a sale of methaqualone approximately five months earlier. The Burbank police set up a surveillance of three residences, [and used their observations there to seek a search warrant. A magistrate mistakenly issued the warrant even though the officers had not established probable cause. The search uncovered large quantities of cocaine and methaqualone.]

Justice White, writing for the majority in *Leon,* first indicated that the exclusionary rule was not a "necessary corollary of the Fourth Amendment." Although . . . Mapp v. Ohio had suggested that the exclusion of illegally seized evidence was part-and-parcel of the Fourth Amendment's guaranty, the *Leon* Court took the position that the exclusionary rule operates as "a judicially created remedy designed to safeguard Fourth Amendment rights generally through its deterrent effect, rather than a personal constitutional right of the party aggrieved."

Justice White went on to conclude that the issue of whether the exclusionary rule should be imposed in a particular case "must be resolved by weighing the costs and benefits" of precluding such evidence from the prosecution's case. On the costs side of the analysis, Justice White declared that the exclusionary rule incurs "substantial social costs" in terms of "impeding unacceptably the truthfinding functions of judge and jury." As a result, Justice White noted that "some guilty defendants may go free or receive reduced sentences as a result of favorable plea bargains."

On the benefits side of the analysis, Justice White indicated that the sole purpose of the exclusionary rule under the Fourth Amendment was to "deter police misconduct rather than to punish the errors of judges and magistrates." Given this goal, Justice White concluded that there was no reason to presume that judges or magistrates would be more inclined to "ignore or subvert" the Fourth Amendment if evidence seized pursuant to a defective warrant were admissible. The majority wrote: "Although there are assertions that some magistrates become rubber stamps for the police and others may be unable effectively to screen police conduct . . . we are not convinced that this is a problem of major proportions."

The Court in *Leon* found that the argument that the exclusionary rule "deters future inadequate presentations" by police officers or prevents "magistrate shopping" was "speculative." . . . The *Leon* majority therefore concluded that, where a police officer is acting in objective good faith, based upon a search warrant duly issued by a neutral magistrate or judge, the Fourth Amendment does not require exclusion of such evidence, even where it is later determined that probable cause was lacking for the warrant. Unless the police officer acted "knowingly" or "recklessly" in providing false information to the magistrate, or the affidavit of probable cause is "so lacking in indicia of probable cause as to render official belief in its existence unreasonable," the evidence is admissible. . . .

This Court has long emphasized that, in interpreting a provision of the Pennsylvania Constitution, we are not bound by the decisions of the United States Supreme Court which interpret similar (yet distinct) federal constitutional provisions. [Independent analysis of state constitutions] is a positive expression of the jurisprudence which has existed in the United States since the founding of the nation.

[In Pennsylvania, a court considering differences between state and federal constitutional provisions will analyze] at least the following four factors: 1) text of the

Pennsylvania constitutional provision; 2) history of the provision, including Pennsylvania case-law; 3) related case-law from other states; 4) policy considerations, including unique issues of state and local concern, and applicability within modern Pennsylvania jurisprudence. . . . Depending upon the particular issue presented, an examination of related federal precedent may be useful as part of the state constitutional analysis, not as binding authority, but as one form of guidance. . . .

The text of Article I, Section 8 of the Pennsylvania Constitution [provides:] "The people shall be secure in their persons, houses, papers and possessions from unreasonable searches and seizures, and no warrant to search any place or to seize any person or things shall issue without describing them as nearly as may be, nor without probable cause, supported by oath or affirmation subscribed to by the affiant." Although the wording of the Pennsylvania Constitution is similar in language to the Fourth Amendment of the United States Constitution, we are not bound to interpret the two provisions as if they were mirror images, even where the text is similar or identical.

[Pennsylvania's] Constitution was adopted on September 28, 1776, a full ten years prior to the ratification of the U.S. Constitution. [It] was drafted in the midst of the American Revolution, as the first overt expression of independence from the British Crown. The Pennsylvania Constitution was therefore meant to reduce to writing a deep history of unwritten legal and moral codes which had guided the colonists from the beginning of William Penn's charter in 1681. . . . Thus, contrary to the popular misconception that state constitutions are somehow patterned after the United States Constitution, the reverse is true. The federal Bill of Rights borrowed heavily from the Declarations of Rights contained in the constitutions of Pennsylvania and other colonies. . . .

With respect to Article I, Section 8 of the present Pennsylvania Constitution, which relates to freedom from unreasonable searches and seizures, that provision had its origin prior to the Fourth Amendment, in [the original Commonwealth] Constitution of 1776, drafted by the first convention of delegates chaired by Benjamin Franklin. The primary purpose of the warrant requirement was to abolish "general warrants," which had been used by the British to conduct sweeping searches of residences and businesses, based upon generalized suspicions. Therefore, . . . the issue of searches and seizures unsupported by probable cause was of utmost concern to the constitutional draftsmen. Moreover, as this Court has stated repeatedly in interpreting Article I, Section 8, that provision is meant to embody a strong notion of privacy, carefully safeguarded in this Commonwealth for the past two centuries.

The history of Article I, Section 8, thus indicates that the purpose underlying the exclusionary rule in this Commonwealth is quite distinct from the purpose underlying the exclusionary rule under the Fourth Amendment, as articulated by the majority in *Leon*. The United States Supreme Court in *Leon* made clear that, in its view, the sole purpose for the exclusionary rule under the Fourth Amendment was to deter police misconduct. . . . This reinterpretation differs from the way the exclusionary rule has evolved in Pennsylvania. . . .

Like many of its sister states, Pennsylvania did not adopt an exclusionary rule until the United States Supreme Court's decision in *Mapp* required it to do so. However, at the time the exclusionary rule was embraced in Pennsylvania, we clearly viewed it as a constitutional mandate. . . . During the first decade after *Mapp*, our decisions in Pennsylvania tended to parallel the cases interpreting the Fourth

Amendment. However, beginning in 1973, our case-law began to reflect a clear divergence from federal precedent. The United States Supreme Court at this time began moving towards a metamorphosed view, suggesting that the purpose of the exclusionary rule is not to redress the injury to the privacy of the search victim but, rather, to deter future unlawful police conduct. At the same time this Court began to forge its own path under Article I, Section 8 of the Pennsylvania Constitution, declaring with increasing frequency that Article I, Section 8 of the Pennsylvania Constitution embodied a strong notion of privacy, notwithstanding federal cases to the contrary. . . . Thus, the exclusionary rule in Pennsylvania has consistently served to bolster the twin aims of Article I, Section 8; to-wit, the safeguarding of privacy and the fundamental requirement that warrants shall only be issued upon probable cause. . . .

Citizens in this Commonwealth possess such rights, even where a police officer in "good faith" carrying out his or her duties inadvertently invades the privacy or circumvents the strictures of probable cause. To adopt a "good faith" exception to the exclusionary rule, we believe, would virtually emasculate those clear safeguards which have been carefully developed under the Pennsylvania Constitution over the past 200 years.

A number of states other than Pennsylvania have confronted the issue of whether to apply a "good faith" exception to the exclusionary rule, under their own constitutions, in the wake of *Leon*. [The court reviewed the decisions of eight states approving of *Leon* and 11 rejecting *Leon* on constitutional or statutory grounds.]

We similarly conclude that [allowing] the judicial branch to participate, directly or indirectly, in the use of the fruits of illegal searches would only serve to undermine the integrity of the judiciary in this Commonwealth. From the perspective of the citizen whose rights are at stake, an invasion of privacy, in good faith or bad, is equally as intrusive. This is true whether it occurs through the actions of the legislative, executive or the judicial branch of government.

We recognize that, in analyzing any state constitutional provision, it is necessary to go beyond the bare text and history of that provision as it was drafted 200 years ago, and consider its application within the modern scheme of Pennsylvania jurisprudence. An assessment of various policy considerations, however, only supports our conclusion that the good faith exception to the exclusionary rule would be inconsistent with the jurisprudence surrounding Article I, Section 8.

First, such a rule would effectively negate the judicially created mandate reflected in the Pennsylvania Rules of Criminal Procedure, in [Rule 2003, which] relates to the requirements for the issuance of a warrant, and provides in relevant part:

> (a) No search warrant shall issue but upon probable cause supported by one or more affidavits sworn to before the issuing authority. The issuing authority, in determining whether probable cause has been established, may not consider any evidence outside the affidavits.
>
> (b) At any hearing on a motion for the return or suppression of evidence, or for suppression of the fruits of evidence, obtained pursuant to a search warrant, no evidence shall be admissible to establish probable cause other than the affidavits provided for in paragraph (a).

Rule 2003 thus adopts a "four corners" requirement, and provides that only evidence contained within the four corners of the affidavit may be considered to establish probable cause. . . . Although Rule 2003 is not constitutionally mandated by Article I, Section 8, . . . it reflects yet another expression of this Court's unwavering insistence that probable cause exist before a warrant is issued, and only those facts memorialized in the written affidavit may be considered in establishing probable cause, in order to eliminate any chance of incomplete or reconstructed hindsight. [We] have chosen to adopt that Rule as an administrative matter, and that Rule has now stood in Pennsylvania for 17 years.

In the instant case, probable cause — as defined under Pennsylvania law — is lacking. Two lower courts have so held; we concur. Applying the federal *Leon* test would not only frustrate the procedural safeguards embodied in Rule 2003, but would permit the admission of illegally seized evidence in a variety of contexts where probable cause is lacking, so long as the police officer acted in "good faith." In *Leon* itself probable cause was absent entirely, yet illegally seized evidence was admitted into evidence. We cannot countenance such a wide departure from the text and history of Article I, Section 8, nor can we permit the use of a "good faith" exception to effectively nullify Pa. R. Crim. P. 2003. . . .

A second policy consideration which bolsters our conclusion is that the underlying premise of *Leon* is still open to serious debate. Although it is clear that the exclusionary rule presents some cost to society, in allowing some guilty defendants to go free, the extent of the costs are far from clear. A number of recent studies have indicated that the exclusion of illegally seized evidence has had a marginal effect in allowing guilty criminals to avoid successful prosecution. Nardulli, The Societal Costs of the Exclusionary Rule: An Empirical Assessment, 1983 A. B. Found. Research J. 585. . . . Equally as important, the alternative to the exclusionary rule most commonly advanced — i.e., allowing victims of improper searches to sue police officers directly — has raised serious concern among police officers. Note, The Exclusionary Rule and Deterrence: An Empirical Study of Chicago Narcotics Officers, 54 U. Chi. L. Rev. 1016, 1053 (1987).

A third policy consideration which compels our decisions is that, given the recent decision of the United States Supreme Court in Illinois v. Gates, 462 U.S. 213 (1983), adopting a "totality of the circumstances test" in assessing probable cause, there is far less reason to adopt a "good faith" exception to the exclusionary rule. We have adopted *Gates* as a matter of Pennsylvania law. . . . As a number of jurists have pointed out, the flexible *Gates* standard now eliminates much of the prior concern which existed with respect to an overly rigid application of the exclusionary rule.

Finally, the dangers of allowing magistrates to serve as "rubber stamps" and of fostering "magistrate-shopping," are evident under *Leon*. As the instant case illustrates, police officers and magistrates have historically worked closely together in this Commonwealth. Trooper Deise and District Justice Tlumac prepared the warrant and affidavit with Trooper Deise dictating the affidavit while the magistrate typed it verbatim.

There is no suggestion here that Trooper Deise and District Justice Tlumac acted other than in utmost "good faith" when preparing the warrant. Nevertheless, we are mindful of the fact that both state and federal interpretations of the Fourth Amendment require a warrant to be issued by a "neutral and detached magistrate," because . . . there is a requirement of an independent determination of probable cause. . . .

It must be remembered that a District Justice is not a member of the executive branch — the police — but a member of the judiciary. By falling within the judicial branch of government, the District Justice is thus charged with the responsibility of being the disinterested arbiter of disputes and is charged further with acting as the bulwark between the police and the rights of citizens. Unless and until a magistrate independently determines there is probable cause, no warrant shall issue.

This is not to say that we distrust our police or district justices; far from it. We, in fact, have no doubt that police officers and district justices in Pennsylvania are intelligent, committed and independent enough to carry out their duties under the scheme which has evolved over the past 30 years, in order to safeguard the rights of our citizens. However, requiring "neutral and detached magistrates" furthers the twin aims of safeguarding privacy and assuring that no warrant shall issue but upon probable cause. As such, we see no reason to eliminate this requirement, for if we did, we would eviscerate the purpose of requiring warrants prior to searches. "If it ain't broke, don't fix it."

Thirty years ago, when the exclusionary rule was first introduced, police officers were perhaps plagued with ill-defined, unarticulated rules governing their conduct. However, the past 30 years have seen a gradual sharpening of the process, with police officers adapting well to the exclusionary rule. . . . Although the exclusionary rule may place a duty of thoroughness and care upon police officers and district justices in this Commonwealth, in order to safeguard the rights of citizens under Article I, Section 8, that is a small price to pay, we believe, for a democracy.

PAPADAKOS, J., concurring.

I am compelled to concur in the result because Rule 2003(a) of the Pennsylvania Rules of Criminal Procedure is absolute in requiring that the affidavit of probable cause supporting the issuance of a search warrant must be complete on its face in every essential detail, and that no testimony is permitted after its execution to fill in the blanks. . . .

In view of the clear, unequivocal command of Rule 2003(a), I see no reason for the majority to reinvent the wheel and re-express the rationale underpinning the judicially created rule of procedure. It's all been said before. . . . Were the rule not so absolute on its face, I would gladly join [Justice McDermott] in dissent, for my sympathies and reason lie in his expression of outrage in the result of cases such as this.

McDERMOTT, J., dissenting.

Today we have abandoned the 27 year history of this Court's restrictive use of the exclusionary rule to only those instances where its application would deter misconduct by law enforcement authorities. Now that we have ignored that history and have decided to employ it even in cases where police officers have fulfilled their every obligation to protect the individual constitutional rights of citizens, I dissent.

Until this day we have dutifully followed the canons of the Fourth Amendment prescribed by the Supreme Court of the United States through hundreds of cases. We . . . were obliged to ignore a mountain of illegal contraband that otherwise was palpable indicia of guilt. There is no doubt that the social cost has been more than criminals freed to try again. It has generated a disbelief and a growing disrespect in the efficacy of law that stands mute in the presence of incontrovertible evidence of fire and lets the house burn down because the fireman arrived before he was properly called.[2] United States v. Leon, 468 U.S. 897 (1984), does not open the gates to unauthorized search, it does not dissolve the need for probable cause. It simply and properly shifts the responsibility for determining probable cause to a neutral magistrate and frees the police of his or her mistakes. . . .

The instant case is a classic illustration. The defect in the affidavit of probable cause was that the time of the offense was not specified. What was told the magistrate was that the contraband was "growing," a clear indication of present tense. The informants told the police that they saw it growing and the magistrate was told that it was growing and she issued a search warrant on that premise. When the police arrived it was still growing. All concerned acted in good faith. To suppress the evidence because a date was not specified with exactitude under those circumstances dwindles into practiced absurdity.

The United States Supreme Court has made it abundantly clear that suppression of evidence seized without probable cause is not a constitutional right. This Court has made that clear as well. See Commonwealth v. Miller, 518 A.2d 1187 (Pa. 1986). The United States Supreme Court has made it equally clear that suppression of evidence seized without probable cause is mandated to contain police action. Likewise, we have approved the suppression of evidence only where it will have the benefit of deterring similar police misconduct in the future.

In interpreting our Constitution we are, as are our sister states, always free to give more than that allowed under Federal Constitutional interpretation. I would choose to accept the rationale of the Supreme Court and recognize the "good faith exception" of *Leon* to the exclusionary rule as have 18 of our sister states. . . . Like the United States Supreme Court, I find no evidence that the judiciary has run beyond its responsibilities, or that if they do we cannot correct them. The Supreme Court of the United States is a world landmark for the protection of constitutional rights. What they require we enforce; what they allow we ought not deter except upon clear evidence of positive need. The United States Supreme Court has recognized a positive need to allow, under the canons of *Leon,* a good faith exception. To do otherwise is to provide a sanctuary for the lawless elements seeking profit, particularly in the growing human misery of addiction. . . .

Notes

1. *Good faith exception: majority position.* About 15 states have decided, like Pennsylvania, not to adopt a good faith exception to exclusionary rules under their state constitutions. A majority of states have explicitly adopted *Leon* under state constitutions. See State v. Eason, 629 N.W.2d 625 (Wis. 2001). For a richer account of the courts that accept or reject *Leon,* consult the web extension for this chapter at *http://www.crimpro.com/extension/ch06.* Do you agree with the Pennsylvania court that a state rejecting the good faith exception will maintain stronger privacy protections

2. One rationale, other than deterrence, that has been offered for the use of the exclusionary rule is "the imperative of judicial integrity." However, this rationale has been criticized because [the] layman finds the judicial integrity rationale difficult to grasp, [and] many lawyers think the highest integrity of the adjudicative aspect of the criminal process lies in the separation of the guilty from the innocent on the basis of all the relevant evidence available.

and stronger control over the quality of warranted searches? If you were directing a police training program in a state that had adopted *Leon,* would that decision affect your training priorities or your recommendations to police officers?

2. *Objective good faith and perjury.* As the *Edmunds* court mentions, the officer's good faith reliance on the warrant under *Leon* must be "objectively reasonable." There is no objective good faith when (1) the officer gives to the magistrate information that the officer knew or should have known was false; (2) the magistrate "wholly abandon[s]" the judicial role; (3) the affidavit is "so lacking in indicia of probable cause" that it would be "entirely unreasonable" for a well-trained officer to believe probable cause existed; or (4) the warrant is so facially deficient that the officer could not reasonably believe it is valid. *Leon,* 468 U.S. at 923. See People v. Miller, 75 P.3d 1108 (Colo. 2003) (well-trained officer could not rely on month-old tip with no mention of ongoing activity as basis for probable cause in warrant; no good faith exception). How would a criminal defendant prove that an officer gave false information to the magistrate?

The "four corners" rule, mentioned in the *Edmunds* case from Pennsylvania, is one traditional technique to prevent perjury or other inaccurate police testimony. Is it possible to adopt the good faith exception while continuing to insist that any facts related to the reasonableness of the search appear within the warrant application and supporting affidavits? See State v. Davidson, 618 N.W.2d 418 (Neb. 2000) (inquiry into officers' good faith is not limited to four corners of warrant affidavit).

3. *What counts as a cost?* Are criminal convictions lost because the exclusionary rule is the chosen remedy or are the lost convictions simply the cost of having the Fourth Amendment and its analogs? Since the exclusionary rule arguably returns the parties to their relative positions before the constitutional violation took place, one might consider it a backward-looking "tort" remedy. On the other hand, if one is convinced that the value of the remedy to the defendant (avoiding a criminal conviction) far exceeds the value of any lost privacy, then the difference in value between the loss to the defendant and the loss to the government might be considered a "cost" of the exclusionary rule rather than a cost of the constitutional provision. One might prefer a remedy that more closely matches the defendant's actual loss. Which is the most appropriate measure?

4. *Good faith reliance on legislatures and appellate courts.* Rules or statutes can also work in favor of a good faith exception. In Illinois v. Krull, 480 U.S. 340 (1987), the court extended the good faith exception of *Leon* to include searches by officers who relied in good faith during a search or seizure on a statute later declared to be unconstitutional. See State v. De La Cruz, 969 A.2d 413 (N.H. 2009) (adopting *Krull* while rejecting *Leon*). Does the exclusionary rule help to "deter" the legislature from passing unconstitutional legislation regarding searches and seizures? Do the arguments for the good faith exception change when the police rely on established interpretations of the Fourth Amendment by appellate courts that are later overturned? State v. Dearborn, 786 N.W.2d 97 (Wis. 2010) (applying good faith exception to police action in reliance on established but mistaken appellate interpretations of search incident to arrest law).

5. *Good faith reliance on negligent police action.* The *Leon* decision allows police officers to rely on determinations by a magistrate. In Arizona v. Evans, 514 U.S. 1 (1995), the Court allowed a good faith exception to the exclusionary rule when an officer relied on an inaccurate record showing an outstanding arrest warrant for a person he had stopped. The record was inaccurate because an employee of the clerk

of the court had failed to update a computer database. In Herring v. United States, 129 S. Ct. 695 (2009), in a 5-4 decision authored by Chief Justice Roberts, the Court extended this decision and held that the exclusionary rule does not apply when an illegal search is based on "isolated [police] negligence attenuated from the search." In *Herring*, police relied on a faulty police report of an outstanding arrest warrant for failure to appear on a felony change. This false report led to an arrest, a search incident to arrest, and the discovery of methamphetamine in Herring's pocket and an illegal pistol in his car. The Court held:

> To trigger the exclusionary rule, police conduct must be sufficiently deliberate that exclusion can meaningfully deter it, and sufficiently culpable that such deterrence is worth the price paid by the justice system. As laid out in our cases, the exclusionary rule serves to deter deliberate, reckless, or grossly negligent conduct, or in some circumstances recurring or systemic negligence. The error in this case does not rise to that level.

Is *Herring* a logical extension of *Leon* and *Evans*? Or is it another example of death (to exclusion) by a thousand small (doctrinal) cuts? Thomas K. Clancy, The Irrelevancy of the Fourth Amendment in the Roberts Court, 85 Chicago-Kent L.J. 191 (2010) (attributing decline in the number of cases addressing Fourth Amendment questions in part to *Herring*).

Problem 6-1. Objective Good Faith

The Drug Squad of the Boulder Police Department received an anonymous letter, postmarked from Kansas City, which read as follows:

> This letter is to inform you that the person described below is an active drug dealer and warrants investigation. This is based on firsthand knowledge and eyewitness accounts by me and others. Below are some facts that may help you.
>
> Name: Jeff; Age: 35-40; Height: 5'9"; Weight: 170 lbs.; Race: white; Features: Bald on the top of his head. Crooked front teeth. Address: Lives in Boulder, Colorado, and is a student at the university.
>
> Vehicle: Two-door van with a large window on the driver's side. The passenger side has a sliding door. Color is steel blue. License plate number is MXS 518 or MSX 518, Colorado.
>
> Drugs are collected at a music store located in Kansas City just north of the intersection of 39th and Main on the east side of the street. The collection times may coincide with the vacation times of the university in Colorado. The drugs are then taken to Boulder for resale.
>
> We hope that this information will help you and are sorry that we must remain anonymous as other innocent people may get involved.
>
> Your friends in Kansas City.

Detective Kurt Weiler began an investigation, and confirmed that the vehicle described was registered to Jeffrey Leftwich, that Leftwich was 37 years old, and that his appearance matched the description in the letter. A call to the Kansas City Police Department confirmed that the music store described in the letter was in a "high drug" area.

During spring break at the university, officers noted that no vehicles were parked outside Leftwich's trailer residence. The day after spring break ended, an officer observed a car parked in the driveway of the residence. The parked car belonged to a person who had been convicted two years earlier of possessing cocaine. The next day, officers noted that Leftwich's Ford van was parked in the driveway. Further inquiries confirmed that Leftwich had traveled to Kansas City during spring break.

Detective Weiler then prepared an affidavit for a search warrant for Leftwich's home. The chief deputy district attorney reviewed the affidavit and advised Detective Weiler that the affidavit presented a close case and that a judge might not sign it. Weiler nonetheless filed the application and a district court judge issued a warrant. During the search of Leftwich's home, Weiler found a triple-beam balance and some marijuana.

Assuming that a reviewing court would conclude that the warrant was not supported by probable cause, would the good faith exception apply? Recall that the officer's good faith must be "objectively" reasonable. If this officer did not qualify for the good faith exception, how often will the exception apply in those states adopting it? Compare People v. Leftwich, 869 P.2d 1260 (Colo. 1994).

■ TEXAS CODE OF CRIMINAL PROCEDURE ART. 38.23

(a) No evidence obtained by an officer or other person in violation of any provisions of the Constitution or laws of the State of Texas, or of the Constitution or laws of the United States of America, shall be admitted in evidence against the accused on the trial of any criminal case. . . .

(b) It is an exception to the provisions of subsection (a) of this Article that the evidence was obtained by a law enforcement officer acting in objective good faith reliance upon a warrant issued by a neutral magistrate based on probable cause.

■ COLORADO REVISED STATUTES §16-3-308

(1) Evidence which is otherwise admissible in a criminal proceeding shall not be suppressed by the trial court if the court determines that the evidence was seized by a peace officer . . . as a result of a good faith mistake or of a technical violation.

(2) As used in subsection (1) of this section:

(a) "Good faith mistake" means a reasonable judgmental error concerning the existence of facts or law which if true would be sufficient to constitute probable cause.

(b) "Technical violation" means a reasonable good faith reliance upon a statute which is later ruled unconstitutional, a warrant which is later invalidated due to a good faith mistake, or a court precedent which is later overruled. . . .

(4) (a) It is hereby declared to be the public policy of the state of Colorado that, when evidence is sought to be excluded from the trier of fact in a criminal proceeding because of the conduct of a peace officer leading to its discovery, it will be open to the proponent of the evidence to urge that the conduct in question was taken in

a reasonable, good faith belief that it was proper, and in such instances the evidence so discovered should not be kept from the trier of fact if otherwise admissible. . . .

(b) It shall be prima facie evidence that the conduct of the peace officer was performed in the reasonable good faith belief that it was proper if there is a showing that the evidence was obtained pursuant to and within the scope of a warrant, unless the warrant was obtained through intentional and material misrepresentation.

Problem 6-2. Unwarranted Good Faith

Three undercover police officers went to the Brook Hollow Inn to set up a surveillance of possible illegal activities in one of the rooms. The manager checked the officers into a room that she believed to be vacant. However, when the officers entered the room they noticed that clothing and luggage had been left in the room. One officer called the registration desk to confirm that they were in the right room. Another officer opened the doors of the television cabinet and found cocaine there. After the officers had left the room, Charles Farmer arrived at the room and let himself in with his key. He called the manager from the phone in the room and told her that he had paid for another day and still occupied the room. The manager told Farmer that a terrible mistake had been made.

Would a court in Colorado exclude from evidence the cocaine found in the room? What about a court in Texas? Would this evidence be admissible under *Leon?* Compare Fanner v. State, 759 P.2d 1031 (Okla. Crim. App. 1988).

Notes

1. *Statutory exclusion.* A number of states have passed statutes calling in general terms for the exclusion of evidence obtained through illegal searches or seizures. Would this sort of statute make it more difficult for a court to justify the creation of good faith exceptions or other limitations on the state's exclusionary rule? On the other hand, several jurisdictions have passed statutes allowing admission of evidence obtained illegally, so long as the officer acted in good faith. See Zarychta v. State, 44 S.W.3d 155 (Tex. App. 2001) (narrow interpretation of coverage for Texas good faith statute). Would the passage of such a statute affect your analysis in Problem 6-2? Further examples of statutory exclusionary rules and statutory limits to the remedy appear on the web extension for this chapter at *http://www.crimpro.com/extension/ch06*.

2. *Evidence excluded in which proceedings?* The statutes printed above all address admission of evidence in criminal proceedings. Federal and state constitutions require the exclusion of evidence from the government's case-in-chief at a criminal trial. However, the exclusionary rule usually does not operate in other proceedings. For instance, the government can use such evidence in grand jury proceedings and in most administrative proceedings. See INS v. Lopez-Mendoza, 468 U.S. 1032 (1984) (exclusion does not apply in civil deportation proceedings).

Courts deciding whether to follow the exclusionary rule in various types of proceedings have often relied on the reasoning of the Supreme Court in United States v. Calandra, 414 U.S. 338 (1974). The Court there decided that the exclusionary rule would not apply to grand jury proceedings because the rule would have little additional deterrent value on police, given that the evidence was already excludable from any criminal trial. Would this reasoning apply to investigators for the Immigration and Naturalization Service, or others like them, whose principal task is to enforce civil laws? The exclusionary rule is generally applied to "quasi-criminal" proceedings before judges or administrative agencies such as proceedings to forfeit property (because of its connection with criminal activity). See, e.g., Commonwealth v. One 1985 Ford Thunderbird Automobile, 624 N.E.2d 547 (Mass. 1993). But see Pennsylvania Board of Probation and Parole v. Scott, 524 U.S. 357 (1998) (parole boards are not required by federal law to exclude evidence obtained in violation of Fourth Amendment). Is the deterrent value of the exclusionary rule in quasi-criminal proceedings any greater than in other civil proceedings? A number of state statutes and court rules clarify whether illegally obtained evidence may be admitted in various types of proceedings. See, e.g., La. Code Evid. art. 1101.

3. *Impeachment.* The government can also use improperly obtained evidence as the basis for impeaching a defendant if she testifies at a criminal trial. The Court in United States v. Havens, 446 U.S. 620 (1980), reasoned that exclusion in such cases would not deter police because the usefulness of evidence for impeachment purposes is so difficult to predict. At the same time, allowing the evidence to form the basis of impeachment questions would discourage defendants from committing perjury. See also James v. Illinois, 493 U.S. 307 (1990) (illegally obtained evidence may *not* be used to impeach defense witnesses other than defendant; such impeachment not necessary to discourage perjury of witnesses other than defendant).

2. *Causation Limits: Inevitable Discovery and Independent Source*

Long before *Wolf* and *Mapp*, it was clear that the exclusionary rule applied not only to evidence obtained during an improper search or seizure but also to any "fruits," that is, evidence the government later developed on the basis of leads obtained during an improper search or seizure. A common phrase presents a powerful image: The exclusionary rule, it is said, applies to the "fruit of the poisonous tree." But there must be some end to the consequences of error; a government error early in an investigation cannot bar all subsequent investigation. Courts have wrestled over how far to extend the impact of government errors — what harms can be said to be "caused" by, or fairly attributed to, the initial violation?

Federal and state courts have placed several causal limitations on the fruit-of-the-poisonous-tree doctrine. Two widely acknowledged limitations are known as the "independent source" and "inevitable discovery" rules. Though these are often described as "exceptions" to the exclusionary rule, each amounts to a conclusion that the government would have obtained the evidence in question even without the illegal enforcement activity; thus, the violation did not "cause" the government to hold the evidence. Application of the "inevitable discovery" and "independent source" rules raise a host of questions, many spurred by the fundamental problem of asking judges to decide what could or would have happened in a case, rather than what did in fact happen.

STATE v. CHARLES RABON

930 A.2d 268 (Me. 2007)

LEVY, J.

. . . During the summer of 2004, the Rumford Police Department received information indicating that the Rabons were involved in transporting cocaine from Florida for sale in Maine. . . . The information concerning the Rabons' activities came from a confidential informant who was the subject of a pending criminal charge or charges. . . . The confidential informant claimed that Charles Rabon drives to Florida several times during the year to pick up large amounts of cocaine, brings the cocaine back to the apartment that he shares with his wife Sharon in Rumford, and then distributes most of his cocaine to local dealers for sale at local bars where Charles operates a karaoke business.

[On] August 13, five police officers were sent to the Rabons' apartment to secure the scene in anticipation of the issuance of a search warrant that was to be sought by other officers. The officers arrived at the Rabons' apartment at 11:58 A.M. An officer in plain clothes, but wearing a vest that clearly identified him as a police officer, knocked on the closed front door of the apartment. One of the other officers observed a woman peek through the blinds of a window near the door. One of the officers heard the woman say "Oh shit," and observed her run toward the back of the apartment. The officers immediately opened the door and entered the apartment without consent and located both Rabons. Charles was found sitting at a desk on which there was a container of white powder and a digital scale. The officers handcuffed the Rabons, conducted a brief safety search of the house for firearms or other inhabitants, took photographs of the inside of the apartment, and made a list of the telephone numbers listed in the Rabons' telephone's caller ID. The officers then sat with the Rabons to await the issuance of a search warrant.

The Maine Drug Enforcement Agency (MDEA) agent who participated in the preparation of the warrant request included in paragraphs ten and eleven of his affidavit information concerning the other officers' warrantless entry into the Rabons' apartment. The District Court issued a search warrant at 4:31 P.M. The resulting search of the apartment led to the seizure of cocaine and money.

[The warrant affidavit detailed] the initial information provided by the informant in June of 2004, and on August 11 and 13, 2004, and . . . the extent to which the police were able to corroborate the same. The affidavit reports that the police corroborated that the Rabons' blue van was not at their apartment on August 11 and 12, and that it returned on August 13, a period corresponding to the informant's claim that the Rabons were returning from a drug run to Florida. In addition, the affidavit reports police corroboration of the Rabons' names, telephone number, address, car, color of their apartment building, the fact that Charles Rabon had received a summons for excessive noise and had not been subject to a search, and that two bars in the Rumford and Mexico area, named by the informant as locations where Charles Rabon trafficked in drugs, were known to the police as places where drugs are trafficked. . . .

Following their arrest, the Rabons were each charged with aggravated trafficking of scheduled drugs and a count seeking criminal forfeiture. The Rabons filed a joint motion to suppress all of the evidence obtained from their apartment. . . . The

Superior Court denied the motion to suppress [and] approved the Rabons' conditional guilty pleas. . . . The Rabons' central contention is that because the officers lacked probable cause to search the apartment prior to the warrantless entry, no evidence gathered from the initial warrantless entry into the apartment or from the subsequent search of the apartment pursuant to the warrant can be admitted against them. The State contends that the contested evidence was lawfully seized because the officers' initial warrantless entry into the apartment was justified by the exigent circumstances exception to the warrant requirement; was nonetheless justified as a reasonable, temporary seizure in order to secure the premises and preserve any evidence within it pending the issuance of a search warrant; or because . . . the inevitable discovery exception permits the admission of the evidence seized from the Rabons. . . .

Exigent Circumstances. The exigent circumstances justification for warrantless searches applies when there is a compelling need to conduct a search and insufficient time in which to secure a warrant. However, probable cause is a prerequisite for the exigent circumstances justification to apply. Accordingly, the exigent circumstances exception to the warrant requirement authorizes the warrantless entry in this case only if the officers had probable cause to search the Rabons' apartment at the time they made the decision to enter the Rabons' apartment.

Temporary Seizure of the Premises to Secure the Scene. The temporary seizure of a residence for the purpose of preserving evidence pending the issuance of a warrant is another recognized exception to the warrant requirement. Such a seizure is constitutionally sound under certain circumstances, but only if the officers have probable cause to search at the time they entered the residence. As applied here, if the officers did not have probable cause to search the premises at the time they entered the residence, then this exception is inapplicable and cannot support the denial of the motion to suppress.

The Independent Source Exception. The independent source exception to the exclusionary rule permits the use of evidence that has been obtained in violation of the Fourth Amendment to the United States Constitution and article I, section 5 of the Maine Constitution when that evidence "was gained through an independent source as well as the tainted source." State v. Storer, 583 A.2d 1016 (Me. 1990). An independent source exception analysis is appropriate in circumstances where a search warrant was issued, but some of the information used to establish probable cause is determined to have been illegally obtained. If the magistrate would still have had probable cause to issue the warrant without the allegedly unlawfully obtained information, the independent source exception allows the admission of the evidence, and suppression is not justified.

In the present case, most of the evidence sought to be suppressed was discovered during the search of the Rabons' apartment following the issuance of a search warrant. . . . To determine whether the independent source exception will permit admission of the evidence obtained pursuant to the warrant in this case, we: (1) excise from the affidavit used to obtain the warrant all the information believed to have been illegally obtained, and then (2) determine whether the judge or magistrate would have had probable cause to issue the warrant relying solely on the remaining information. . . .

The Inevitable Discovery Exception. The inevitable discovery exception is an additional analytical framework for considering the suppression of the evidence if we conclude that the initial warrantless entry into the Rabons' apartment prior to the issuance of the search warrant was unlawful because there was no probable cause. The inevitable discovery exception to the exclusionary rule permits the use of evidence that has been obtained in violation of the Fourth Amendment to the United States Constitution and article I, section 5 of the Maine Constitution when that evidence "inevitably would have been discovered by lawful means." *Storer*, 583 A.2d at 1020 (quoting Nix v. Williams, 467 U.S. 431 (1984)). The specific question presented here is whether the evidence discovered by the police when they initially entered the Rabons' apartment with the intent of securing it would have been inevitably discovered through lawful means.

If a warrant would not have issued without the information resulting from the initial warrantless entry reported in paragraphs ten and eleven of the affidavit, there would not be a lawful means to enter the apartment, and it would not be inevitable that the police would have lawfully discovered the evidence they discovered during their initial warrantless entry. Accordingly, for the inevitable discovery exception to apply in this case, it requires that the police had probable cause at the time they entered the Rabons' apartment.

All of the above exceptions to the warrant requirement and the exclusionary rule require the existence of probable cause at the time of the initial warrantless entry into the Rabons' apartment.... To determine probable cause, a magistrate must apply the "totality-of-the-circumstances approach" articulated in Illinois v. Gates, 462 U.S. 213 (1983)....

The warrant affidavit signed by the MDEA agent is based largely on information provided to him by the confidential informant. In viewing the affidavit, as redacted, in its most positive light, we assess the information in the affidavit regarding the informant's: (a) reliability and basis of knowledge; (b) claims regarding the Rabons' criminal activities; and (c) reports of other information concerning the Rabons. We conclude the analysis by applying the totality of the circumstances test.

Informant's Reliability and Basis of Knowledge. The warrant affidavit reveals very little about the informant's background. It reports that the confidential informant contacted the police wishing to share information about drug trafficking occurring in Rumford in order to receive "prosecutorial consideration if any information provided is helpful in a drug trafficking case." The informant is described as not being on probation, but as being on bail for non-drug related offenses; as not receiving any remuneration in exchange for information; and as having provided additional information on other drug trafficking in the area. The affidavit does not provide any details regarding this additional information, or whether it had been found to be accurate.

The affidavit fails to explain the basis for the informant's knowledge that the Rabons were engaged in drug trafficking. The affidavit does not assert that the informant had actually seen firsthand any contraband or criminal activity. The affidavit also does not contain any statement to the effect that the informant has been found or is otherwise believed by the MDEA agent or other law enforcement officials to be a reliable reporter of information....

An affidavit that supplies no information about an informant's reliability or basis of knowledge fails to provide information that is highly relevant to the probable cause determination. The absence of such information does not preclude a finding of probable cause, but... absent that information, "something more" is required.

Corroboration of Informant's Claims of Suspicious or Criminal Activity. Our decisions establish that "something more" is frequently supplied by police corroboration of the informant's reports regarding suspicious or criminal activities by the person suspected of wrongdoing. . . . The affidavit in this case reveals that the police corroborated, to a limited degree, the informant's report that Charles and Sharon Rabon had recently left Florida and were en route back to Rumford in their van in possession of cocaine. . . . The absence of the Rabons' van on August 11 and 12, and its return on August 13 was not, however, contextually suspicious.

Corroboration of Other Information Concerning the Rabons. The MDEA agent's affidavit also corroborates other information provided by the informant, such as the Rabons' names, telephone number, address, car, the color of their apartment building, and the fact that Charles Rabon had received a summons for excessive noise and had not been subject to a search. The corroboration of this readily available information reveals that the informant, or the persons providing information to the informant, were familiar with the Rabons. The informant's identification of two bars in the area known to the police as sites where drugs are trafficked establishes that either the informant, or the persons providing information to the informant, were generally familiar with drug activity in the area. The affidavit contains no corroboration of the informant's claim that Charles Rabon has a karaoke business, nor does it contain information that corroborates whether Charles Rabon was ever present at the two bars where the informant alleges the drugs were sold.

None of the preceding information qualifies as "inside information" that would be uniquely available to an informant with direct knowledge of otherwise uncorroborated criminal activity. An informant's accurate description of readily available information establishes reliability in the limited sense that it will help the police correctly identify the person whom the tipster means to accuse, but it does not show that the tipster has knowledge of concealed criminal activity. . . .

Totality of the Circumstances Analysis. When the police saw the Rabons' van return on August 13, they were in the middle of a promising investigation. Considered in its totality, however, the warrant affidavit, as redacted, does not contain information that establishes the informant's reliability or basis of knowledge, or corroborate in any significant way the informant's claim that the Rabons purchased cocaine in Florida for resale in Maine. . . .

Because probable cause did not exist to search the apartment without the information gained from the warrantless entry into the apartment, none of the above discussed exceptions to the warrant requirement or the exclusionary rule apply, and the evidence seized from the Rabons' apartment during the initial warrantless entry and the subsequent search pursuant to the warrant should have been ordered suppressed.

ALEXANDER, J., concurring.

. . . I write separately because I do not concur in the Court's opinion that probable cause to search was not sufficiently established because the information obtained through the confidential informant was not sufficiently corroborated. . . . Although probable cause to search was sufficiently established without reliance on evidence obtained in the illegal entry, I would vacate because the State failed to meet its burden to establish that discovery of the illegally seized evidence was inevitable. See Nix v. Williams, 467 U.S. 431 (1984) (noting that the prosecution has the burden to prove inevitable discovery by a preponderance of the evidence). . . .

The protections of article I, section 5, and the concurrent protections of the Fourth Amendment of the United States Constitution, cannot be easily circumvented by illegally seizing evidence then asserting that its discovery, by legal means, was "inevitable." Our constitutional protections for person and home can be avoided only for special, narrowly construed purposes, and then, only when justified by a high quality of evidence. [The] inevitable discovery doctrine is available only where there is a high level of confidence that each of the contingencies required for the discovery of the disputed evidence would in fact have occurred. . . .

The First Circuit, in a case originating in Lewiston, outlined a three-step analytical framework for examination of inevitable discovery claims, with the prosecution bearing the burden of proof on each point:

> In evaluating inevitable discovery claims, we ask three questions: first, whether the legal means by which the evidence would have been discovered was truly independent; second, whether the use of the legal means would have inevitably led to the discovery of the evidence; and third, whether applying the inevitable discovery rule would either provide an incentive for police misconduct or significantly weaken constitutional protections.

United States v. Almeida, 434 F.3d 25, 28 (1st Cir. 2006).

We have indicated that evidence may be admitted pursuant to the inevitable discovery doctrine if the prosecution proves two criteria: first, the information in the application for the search warrant that is independent of illegally obtained information must be sufficient to provide probable cause to support the issuance of the warrant, and, second, the independent information would have inevitably led to discovery of the evidence through lawful means.

Whether we apply the First Circuit's three-step analysis or our two-step analysis, the first two steps of either analysis are similar and hold the keys to this case. The third step of the First Circuit's analysis is an important reminder of the significance of the constitutional protections at issue and the caution with which the inevitable discovery doctrine must be applied.

I concur with the Chief Justice that . . . independent of the information derived from the warrantless entry, [the record] demonstrates sufficient probable cause to justify issuing a warrant. . . . There is insufficient evidence, however, to support the second element that use of the legal means would have inevitably led to the discovery of the evidence. Pursuant to *Nix*, the prosecution must prove the elements of the inevitable discovery doctrine by a preponderance of the evidence. Applying the preponderance of the evidence standard to inevitable discovery cases, however, requires a higher standard of quality of evidence. This derives from the conceptual difficulty of proving inevitability to a probability. Thus, . . . the government cannot prevail under the inevitable discovery doctrine merely by establishing that it is more probable than not that the disputed evidence would have been obtained without the constitutional violation. [The] First Circuit requires that inevitability must be demonstrated "to a high degree of probability." . . .

The quality of evidence supporting inevitability of legal discovery of the evidence at the Rabons' home [does not satisfy] the First Circuit's "high degree of probability" test. Instead, the State's evidence presents a logical inconsistency. If it was essential to send five officers to prevent disappearance of the Rabons or the contraband before a warrant could be obtained, then it cannot be inevitable that the

Rabons and the contraband would have been at the apartment five hours later when the warrant was obtained. . . .

The trial court found that, shortly before noon, five Rumford officers, some in uniform and at least one wearing a protective vest, appeared "at the [Rabons'] residence" in order to "secure the premises pending the issuance of a warrant." It is quite a stretch to speculate that this heavy police presence would not have been observed at some time over the next five hours, and that the Rabons, observing the police presence, might not have taken some steps to separate themselves from the contraband or from the premises. Even without the observed police presence, it is also a stretch, inconsistent with the "high degree of probability" standard of evidence, to speculate that the Rabons and the contraband, having arrived at the apartment sometime after 7:30 A.M., would "inevitably" have remained there until sometime after 5:00 P.M. . . .

The court's conclusion of inevitability of the legal discovery of this evidence is speculation, unsupported by any evidence in the record. Basically, the court is bootstrapping the fact that the contraband was discovered upon the illegal entry at noon to infer that, but for the illegal entry, the contraband would have remained in the apartment, inevitably, after 5:00 P.M. The strictures imposed by our Constitution to protect persons and their homes from illegal searches cannot be so easily avoided. The contraband in this case was obtained in a search based on a created exigency that the trial court found was an illegal search. The State failed to meet its burden to prove inevitability of discovery by legal means.

SAUFLEY, C.J., dissenting.

. . . A magistrate reviewing the affidavit would have information demonstrating that the authorities were able to independently confirm much of what was given to them by the confidential informant. This information regarded the Rabons' identities and activities, including their real names, their residence, their vehicle, their travels, and when they were and were not present. The information also related to places where cocaine trafficking was known to be occurring on a regular basis. This information was sufficient to establish the confidential informant's bona fides. The extent, detail, and corroborated nature of the information provided by [the confidential informant] would lead a reasonable person to conclude that there was a "fair probability" that cocaine would be found in the Rabons' home on the date of the search. . . .

The inevitable discovery exception has developed as a logical counterpart to the "fruit of the poisonous tree" doctrine, which reaches out to suppress any evidence obtained as a result of earlier illegal action on the part of law enforcement. Because one of the primary purposes of the judicially-created exclusionary rule, and its extension through the suppression of evidence gained as the "fruit" of other illegally obtained evidence, has been to deter police misconduct, exceptions to the application of the exclusionary rule have been recognized in instances where separate, legitimate investigatory tools would inevitably have turned up the evidence at issue. . . .

We recently applied the inevitable discovery doctrine in a situation where a victim's body was recovered as a result of a custodial interrogation that we presumed to be illegal for purposes of the inevitable discovery analysis. See State v. St. Yves, 751 A.2d 1018 (Me. 2000). There, the police had lawfully and independently gathered the following information prior to any alleged misconduct: (1) the defendant's wife had recently given birth to an infant; (2) the defendant had attempted to obtain food stamps for himself, the infant, and his other daughter, but the infant was nowhere to be seen, and the defendant appeared confused and unkempt; (3) the elder daughter appeared uncared for when the police lawfully entered the defendant's trailer to arrest the defendant's wife; (4) a caseworker had attempted to contact the parents on a number of occasions at their trailer and had heard a child inside, though no adult answered the door; (5) when the police arrived to arrest the defendant's wife, the trailer was cold and filled with refuse, dog feces, and urine; and (6) the defendant and his wife provided conflicting explanations to the police as to the whereabouts of the infant and refused to tell them where the infant could be located.

Taking this information into account, we held that the victim's body would inevitably have been discovered because, if the police had not discovered the victim's body as a result of the interrogation, they would have checked the defendant's wife's story and found that the victim was not with her grandparents. We therefore concluded that, even without the information obtained by interrogating the defendant, the police would have been able to establish probable cause for a warrant to search the defendant's trailer and, after seeking and obtaining a warrant, inevitably would have discovered the victim's body. We concluded, "fairness can be assured by placing the State and the accused in the same positions they would have been in had the impermissible conduct not taken place, and, therefore, the court did not err in determining that the inevitable discovery doctrine saved the evidence from suppression."

In contrast to the search conducted in *St. Yves*, here the challenged evidence was not obtained through an illegal interrogation, and the State did obtain a warrant to search the premises. The warrant, however, was tainted by the inclusion of evidence gained through the initial presumed-illegal entry into the Rabons' residence. Thus, the analysis is similar to that used in *St. Yves*, but turns on whether the warrant would have issued without the offending paragraphs. . . .

I would conclude that the warrant would properly have issued even if the officers had not gone first to the Rabons' home, and even if the paragraphs in the affidavit cataloguing the evidence found in that initial entry had not been added to the affidavit. Thus, the remaining question presented is whether the evidence would inevitably have been discovered when the warrant was issued, several hours after the Rabons' home was secured. [The] warrant was issued and executed approximately four-and-one-half hours after the officers' initial entry. Had the police not secured the Rabons' home prior to seeking the warrant, it is very likely that, based on the urgency of the situation, both the police and the court would have acted upon the warrant request much more quickly. . . .

Problem 6-3. The Search Party

Pamela Powers, a 10-year-old child, disappeared from a YMCA building in Des Moines, Iowa, where she had accompanied her parents to watch an athletic contest. Shortly after she disappeared, Robert Williams was seen leaving the YMCA carrying a large bundle wrapped in a blanket; a 14-year-old boy who had helped Williams open his car door reported that he had seen "two legs in it and they were skinny and white."

Williams' car was found the next day 160 miles east of Des Moines in Davenport, Iowa. Later several items of clothing belonging to the child, some of Williams' clothing, and an army blanket like the one used to wrap the bundle that Williams carried out of the YMCA were found at a rest stop on Interstate 80 near Grinnell, between Des Moines and Davenport. A warrant was issued for Williams' arrest.

Police surmised that Williams had left Pamela Powers or her body somewhere between Des Moines and the Grinnell rest stop, where some of the girl's clothing had been found. On December 26, the Iowa Bureau of Criminal Investigation initiated a large-scale search. Two hundred volunteers divided into teams began the search 21 miles east of Grinnell, covering an area several miles to the north and south of Interstate 80. A snowstorm threatened as the volunteers moved westward from Poweshiek County, in which Grinnell was located, into Jasper County. Searchers were instructed to check all roads, abandoned farm buildings, ditches, culverts, and any other place in which the body of a small child could be hidden.

Suppose that police officers learned the location of the body through an illegal search of Williams' home. The officers found the child's body next to a culvert in a ditch beside a gravel road in Polk County, about two miles south of Interstate 80. At that time, one search team near the Jasper-Polk county line was only two and one-half miles from the location of the body. Will the trial court exclude from trial the evidence obtained from the body? Cf. Nix v. Williams, 467 U.S. 431 (1984).

Problem 6-4. Illegal Stop vs. Outstanding Warrant

A Florida officer observed a person make a left turn without signaling, and then saw a white light emanating from a crack in the plastic lens covering the tail light of the left rear of the defendant's vehicle. On these two grounds, the officer stopped the vehicle, checked the driver's identification, and learned that there was an outstanding warrant for his arrest for failure to appear in another proceeding. As a result of the outstanding warrant, the officer arrested the driver. A search incident to the arrest revealed a firearm, which formed the basis for criminal charges against the driver.

The initial traffic stop was unlawful under Florida law. State v. Riley, 638 So.2d 507 (Fla.1994) (failure to use turn signal without driver's conduct creating reasonable safety concern does not constitute violation of statute), and Doctor v. State, 596 So.2d 442 (Fla.1992) (cracked taillight was not violation of law). The arrest warrant also turned out to be erroneous: A later investigation determined that the arrest warrant was issued due to another person's failure to appear.

Imagine that the defendant moves to suppress the seizure of the firearm, contending (1) that the traffic stop preceding the arrest was unlawful and (2) that the warrant that provided the basis for his arrest was wrongfully issued, and therefore that the government should not be allowed to use the fruits of the search incident to arrest. You are the trial judge. How would you rule? See State v. Frierson, 926 S.2d 1139 (Fla. 2006).

Notes

1. *Inevitable discovery: majority position.* Along with the federal system, Nix v. Williams, 467 U.S. 431 (1984), every state except Texas and Washington recognizes an "inevitable discovery" exception to exclusion. See State v. Winterstein, 220 P.3d 1226 (Wash. 2009). Under this doctrine, a court may use evidence obtained as the fruit of an illegal search or seizure if the government would have learned about the evidence through proper techniques or channels without the illegal search or seizure ever taking place. The inevitable discovery exception is a potentially huge limit on exclusion, particularly if one is willing to presume that the police (or interested citizens) are often capable of solving important crimes. The government must argue more than "if we hadn't done it wrong, we would have done it right." State v. Topanotes, 76 P.3d 1159 (Utah 2003). The level of certainty required in predicting the "inevitability" of the discovery is a key issue.

Under federal law, the government must prove by a preponderance of the evidence the underlying facts necessary to conclude that the discovery was inevitable, and most states have embraced the federal position and use a preponderance standard. A few states require the government to show that discovery was inevitable by "clear and convincing" evidence. See Smith v. State, 948 P.2d 473 (Alaska 1997). But as highlighted in the *Rabon* case, especially by the concurring opinion, many states distinguish between the standard of proof necessary to establish the underlying facts and the level of certainty necessary to reach the conclusion that discovery was "inevitable." See Compare State v. Sugar, 527 A.2d 1377 (N.J. 1987) (body buried in shallow ground would have inevitably been discovered because defendant was attempting to sell the property and prospective buyers would have smelled decomposing body; meets clear and convincing evidence requirement of state law) with Commonwealth v. O'Connor, 546 N.E.2d 336, 340 (Mass. 1989) (question is whether specific facts demonstrate that discovery by lawful means was "certain as a practical matter").

In the typical pretrial motion to suppress (for claims other than inevitable discovery), the standard of proof is a preponderance of the evidence. The defendant carries the burden of proof for warranted searches; the government carries the burden for warrantless searches. Do the factual and legal questions surrounding inevitable discovery justify changes in the ordinary rules about standard of proof and burden of proof?

2. *Potential limits on inevitable discovery doctrine.* A number of state courts endorsing the inevitable discovery exception to the exclusionary rule take great pains to say that they do not consider it a "blanket" exception and that it might be used in some circumstances but not in others. See, e.g., State v. Ault, 724 P.2d 545 (Ariz. 1986) (inevitable discovery doctrine does not apply to illegal search or seizure of items in a home); People v. Stith, 506 N.E.2d 911 (N.Y. 1987) (inevitable discovery exception does not apply to "primary evidence" obtained at time of illegal search; applies only to indirect fruits of illegal search). The web extension for this chapter, at *http://www.crimpro.com/extension/ch06*, offers a richer view of the state cases marking limits on the use of inevitable discovery.

3. *Can inevitable discovery cure intentional illegal searches?* What if the police deliberately conduct an illegal search, knowing that discovery of any evidence is inevitable (say, during a later inventory search)? Should courts apply the inevitable

discovery exception only when the police act in "good faith"? How regularized must the investigative process be to count as "inevitable"? Consider State v. Notti, 71 P.3d 1233 (Mont. 2003) (inevitable discovery of identification of suspect who was in state DNA database and who left DNA on cigarette at murder scene, either through a DNA database computer check or when a Crime Lab employee compared profiles in the "forensic unknown" database with the State's DNA Identification Index).

4. *Inevitable discovery and statutory remedies*. Despite the importance of the issue, and the variety of positions a state might take on this exception to the exclusionary rule, very few states have a statute addressing "inevitable discovery." Why have the legislatures remained silent? If the legislature has adopted a statutory form of the exclusionary rule without providing for an inevitable discovery exception, should a court nevertheless be willing to create the exception?

5. *Independent source: majority position*. All but a few states have declared that the exclusionary rule does not apply to evidence obtained after an improper search or seizure if the government also learned of the evidence through an "independent source." The independent source claim is closely related to inevitable discovery, but it is sometimes distinguishable because it is based on an untainted source that actually did lead the police to the evidence in question, rather than a source or process that hypothetically might have done so. A case like *Rabon* sits on the line, but it would be construed as independent source if officers had later in fact obtained a warrant based on information in their possession before they entered the building. The basis for the proper warranted search was "independent" of anything the police learned during the improper search. See Murray v. United States, 487 U.S. 533 (1988); Segura v. United States, 468 U.S. 796 (1984); compare People v. Weiss, 978 P.2d 1257 (Cal. 1999) (prosecution does not have to show that particular magistrate would have issued warrant if affidavit had not contained illegally obtained information; independent source applies if police would have sought warrant even without tainted information, and redacted affidavit was sufficient for probable cause). In light of the independent source doctrine, do police have anything to lose by routinely conducting a "preliminary" search before seeking a search warrant? See William Stuntz, Warrants and Fourth Amendment Remedies, 77 Va. L. Rev. 881 (1991); State v. Krukowski, 100 P.3d 1222 (Utah 2004) (officer's failure to disclose in search warrant application that he had already conducted an illegal entry of premises cannot be basis for refusing to apply independent source doctrine).

6. *Attenuation*. Even when there is a causal linkage between an improper search or seizure and some evidence obtained later, the evidence can still be admitted if the link is sufficiently "attenuated." An analogy from the law of torts might be the concept of "proximate cause." For instance, in United States v. Ceccolini, 435 U.S. 268 (1978), a police officer during a conversation with a friend at her workplace wrongfully peered into an envelope in the room and discovered gambling paraphernalia, which belonged to the friend's boss. The friend agreed months later to testify against her boss in criminal proceedings. Even though the improper search of the package was a "but for" cause of the government's access to this testimony, it was not excluded because the witness's willingness to testify was more important than the improper search. In this type of case, courts will not exclude the evidence because, they say, police are unlikely to anticipate the chain of events linking their illegal search to some later source of evidence and therefore will not be deterred by the threat of exclusion. Could the officer in *Ceccolini* have anticipated that an unlawful search of the envelope might create an opportunity for his friend to provide

evidence in a criminal trial? See also State v. Guillen, 223 P.3d 658 (Ariz. 2010) (possibly improper dog sniff of garage cured by later consent of homeowner unaware of dog sniff; consent was sufficiently attenuated from tainted conduct).

In Hudson v. Michigan, 547 U.S. 586 (2006), the Supreme Court held that violation of the "knock-and-announce" rule does not require suppression. Justice Scalia, writing for the majority, found the connection between the constitutional violation (knocking, but not waiting long enough before entering) and the harm too attenuated to suppress the evidence.

> [Exclusion] may not be premised on the mere fact that a constitutional violation was a "but-for" cause of obtaining evidence. Our cases show that but-for causality is only a necessary, not a sufficient, condition for suppression. In this case, of course, the constitutional violation of an illegal manner of entry was not a but-for cause of obtaining the evidence. Whether that preliminary misstep had occurred or not, the police would have executed the warrant they had obtained, and would have discovered the gun and drugs inside the house. But even if the illegal entry here could be characterized as a but-for cause of discovering what was inside, we have never held that evidence is "fruit of the poisonous tree" simply because it would not have come to light but for the illegal actions of the police. Rather, but-for cause, or causation in the logical sense alone, can be too attenuated to justify exclusion. . . .
>
> Attenuation can occur, of course, when the causal connection is remote. Attenuation also occurs when, even given a direct causal connection, the interest protected by the constitutional guarantee that has been violated would not be served by suppression of the evidence obtained. . . .

7. *Improper stops and arrests that produce additional information.* If an arrest is improper, the defendant might argue that his very presence in the courtroom is the result of illegal government action, and a conviction would be barred. Both state and federal courts have uniformly rejected this argument because the use of properly obtained evidence to obtain a conviction in criminal proceedings cures any error in the arrest. United States v. Crews, 445 U.S. 463 (1980) (illegal arrest does not taint otherwise valid eyewitness identification of arrestee); Frisbie v. Collins, 342 U.S. 519 (1952) (illegal arrest is no bar to prosecution); People v. Jones, 810 N.E.2d 415 (N.Y. 2004) (police improperly arrested defendant in his home without arrest warrant; identification during lineup conducted while in custody was admissible).

Like the inevitable discovery and independent source rules, the *Frisbie* rule is based on the idea that the illegal government action was not a legally sufficient "cause" of any harm to the defendant. States are divided on whether an outstanding arrest warrant can cure an illegal stop. Consistent with the *Frisbie* doctrine, the majority of states hold that discovery of an outstanding warrant and subsequent arrest and search are attenuated from the initial illegal stop that led to the identification and warrant check, and that this holds true even though the warrant check or search would not have occurred but for that stop. See e.g., Myers v. State, 909 A.2d 1049 (Md. 2006); compare State v. Maland, 103 P.3d 430 (Idaho 2004).

3. Standing to Challenge Illegal Searches and Seizures

One other major limitation on the exclusionary rule restricts the number of people who can challenge an allegedly illegal search or seizure. In some jurisdictions, this is known as the "standing" doctrine. This limitation applies when the government improperly intrudes on a reasonable privacy expectation of one person and finds evidence implicating a second person in a crime. Can the second person challenge the unreasonable intrusion?

■ LOUISIANA CONSTITUTION ART. I, §5

Any person adversely affected by a search or seizure conducted in violation of this Section shall have standing to raise its illegality in the appropriate court.

■ STATE v. JOHN BRUNS
796 A.2d 226 (N.J. 2002)

STEIN, J.

. . . In the early morning hours of July 27, 1997, Officer John Seidler stopped a vehicle for speeding in Lakewood Township. After effectuating the stop, Seidler [determined that the driver, Barbara Edwards, was operating the car with a suspended license. He also discovered two outstanding arrest warrants for Edwards.] Based on the outstanding warrants, Seidler placed Edwards under arrest, handcuffed her, searched her, and seated her in his patrol car.

Seidler next asked the sole passenger in the vehicle, Walter Evans, to step out of the car. Officer Regan, who had been called to the scene as backup, placed Evans in his patrol car. Seidler conducted a search of the passenger compartment after Evans exited the vehicle. He found a handgun and a large knife under the front passenger seat. The object that appeared to be a handgun was later determined to be a toy handgun. [Those two items later became relevant evidence in the investigation of an armed robbery that Evans and John Bruns allegedly committed seven days before the search of Edwards' car.]

In his subsequent trial for armed robbery defendant made a motion to suppress the evidence seized during the search of Edwards' car, alleging that Seidler's search of the vehicle and seizure of the toy handgun and knife were unlawful. The motion judge concluded that the search was incident to Edwards' lawful arrest and that "the steps that the officers took were necessary given the particular circumstances." . . .

The State argues that defendant did not have a proprietary, possessory, or participatory interest in the vehicle searched or the evidence retrieved from it. Therefore, it asserts that defendant did not have standing to move to suppress the evidence. . . .

II.

In order to contest at trial the admission of evidence obtained by a search or seizure, a defendant must first demonstrate that he has standing. Generally speaking, that requires a court to inquire whether defendant has interests that are substantial enough to qualify him as a person aggrieved by the allegedly unlawful search and seizure.

In Rakas v. Illinois, 439 U.S. 128 (1978), the United States Supreme Court held that a defendant must have a legitimate expectation of privacy in the place searched or items seized to establish Fourth Amendment standing. In State v. Alston, 440 A.2d 1311 (N.J. 1981), this Court established a broader standard to determine when a defendant has the right to challenge an illegal search or seizure, rejecting the line of United States Supreme Court cases culminating with Rakas v. Illinois that effectively resolved standing issues only on the basis of a defendant's expectations of privacy. Instead, before reaching the substantive question whether a defendant has a reasonable expectation of privacy, our courts first determine whether that defendant has a proprietary, possessory or participatory interest in the place searched or items seized.

For the twenty years preceding the United States Supreme Court's adoption of the "legitimate expectation of privacy" standard the leading Fourth Amendment standing case was Jones v. United States, 362 U.S. 257 (1960). In *Jones*, the defendant was arrested for the possession and sale of narcotics after federal officers executed a search warrant for narcotics in an apartment in which the defendant was present. The Court rejected the Government's contention that the defendant lacked standing because he did not claim either ownership of the seized narcotics or a property interest in the apartment, but rather was simply a guest in the apartment. Recognizing the predicament a defendant faces when attempting to establish Fourth Amendment standing by demonstrating that he owned or possessed the seized property while at the same time defending against a charge in which an essential element is possession, the Court adopted the so-called "automatic standing rule." The Court . . . concluded that the allegations of possession that led eventually to defendant's conviction afforded him sufficient standing to challenge the search. In addition, acknowledging that the interests of law enforcement would not "be hampered by recognizing that anyone legitimately on premises where a search occurs may challenge its legality by way of a motion to suppress, when its fruits are proposed to be used against him," the Court concluded that his friend's consent to his presence also gave defendant sufficient standing to challenge the search under the Fourth Amendment. That portion of the *Jones* holding became known as the "legitimately on the premises test."

In Rakas v. Illinois, . . . the defendants argued that any person who was a "target" of a search should have standing to object to the search. Reaffirming the principle that Fourth Amendment rights cannot be vicariously asserted, the Court rejected the defendants' argument and [endorsed the "better analysis" that] forthrightly focuses on the extent of a particular defendant's rights under the Fourth Amendment, rather than any theoretically separate, but invariably intertwined concept of standing. The Court in *Rakas* also considered the appropriate scope of the interest protected by the Fourth Amendment. It determined that the "legitimately on the premises" standard applied in *Jones* was too broad, and instead adopted the standard established in Katz v. United States, 389 U.S. 347 (1967), stating that a defendant must have a "legitimate expectation of privacy in the invaded place." Based on that standard the Court held that the defendants had failed to demonstrate that they had a legitimate expectation of privacy in the glove compartment or the area under the front seat of the car in which they were passengers.

In United States v. Salvucci, 448 U.S. 83 (1980), shortly after its decision in *Rakas*, the Court also abolished the "automatic standing" rule of *Jones* and held that defendants who are charged with crimes that have an element of possession can invoke the exclusionary rule only if their own Fourth Amendment rights have in fact been violated. The defendants in *Salvucci* were charged with unlawful possession of stolen mail, and relied solely on the *Jones* automatic standing rule without asserting that they had a legitimate expectation of privacy in the place where the stolen mail was seized. In assessing the trial court's decision to suppress the evidence the Court concluded: "We are convinced that the automatic standing rule of *Jones* has outlived its usefulness in the Court's Fourth Amendment jurisprudence. The doctrine now serves only to afford a windfall to defendants whose Fourth Amendment rights have not been violated. . . ."

In Rawlings v. Kentucky, 448 U.S. 98 (1980), the companion case to *Salvucci*, the Court addressed an argument by the defendant that his ownership of drugs seized by the police entitled him to invoke his Fourth Amendment rights although he claimed no expectation of privacy in the area from which the drugs were seized. The Court rejected defendant's argument, relying on the Court's observation in *Rakas* that "arcane" concepts of property law should not control the analysis of Fourth Amendment standing. [The Court] explained that prior to *Rakas* the defendant "might have been given 'standing' in such a case to challenge a 'search' that netted those drugs but probably would have lost his claim on the merits. After *Rakas*, the two inquiries merge into one: whether governmental officials violated any legitimate expectation of privacy."

Concluding that the United States Supreme Court's decisions such as *Rakas*, *Salvucci*, and *Rawlings* insufficiently guarded against unreasonable searches and seizures, this Court's decision in State v. Alston, 440 A.2d 1311 (N.J. 1981), applied Article I, paragraph 7 of the New Jersey State Constitution to the standing issue in order to afford our citizens greater protection. . . . The more protective approach adopted by this Court was based on the belief that "adherence to the vague 'legitimate expectation of privacy' standard, subject as it is to the potential for inconsistent and capricious application, will in many instances produce results contrary to commonly held and accepted expectations of privacy. . . ."

In *Alston* four defendants charged with the unlawful carrying and possession of weapons moved to suppress the weapons seized as the result of the warrantless search of the vehicle in which they were the driver and passengers. The State argued that the passengers had no standing to challenge the search because they had no ownership interest in the vehicle, and that the driver legitimately possessed the car but lacked a reasonable expectation of privacy in the areas of the vehicle that were searched. The Court rejected the State's arguments, finding that the privacy interests protected by the federal constitution and our State Constitution "flow from some connection with or relation to the place or property searched" and that "it serves the purposes of clarity to emphasize an accused's relationship to property rather than to attempt a definition of expectations in terms of the person." Accordingly, we reiterated our traditional standing rule that requires a defendant to show that "he has a proprietary, possessory, or participatory interest in either the place searched or the property seized," and found that the automatic standing rule conferred standing on all four defendants.

In State v. Mollica, 554 A.2d 1315 (N.J. 1989), we elaborated on the participatory interest portion of our standing rule. Defendants Mollica and Ferrone were charged with various gambling offenses after the state police discovered bookmaking paraphernalia in their hotel rooms. The warrants to search the rooms were based in part on the telephone records for Ferrone's hotel room that the Federal Bureau of Investigation had previously obtained without a warrant as part of its own bookmaking investigation. The State argued that Mollica had no standing to object to the seizure of Ferrone's telephone records even though those records provided the basis for a search warrant that included his hotel room. The Court acknowledged that our standing rule does not automatically provide a defendant charged with a possessory crime "standing to object to prior or antecedent state action that was directed against another person," and observed that Mollica's standing to object to the search and seizure of evidence found in his hotel room did not necessarily give him standing to object to the seizure of Ferrone's telephone records. Nonetheless, the Court considered whether Mollica had a participatory interest in the seized telephone records, noting that a participatory interest "stresses the relationship of the evidence to the underlying criminal activity and defendant's own criminal role in the generation and use of such evidence," and confers standing on a person who "had some culpable role, whether as a principal, conspirator, or accomplice, in a criminal activity that itself generated the evidence." Based on the State's allegation that Mollica participated in illegal bookmaking that included the use of Ferrone's hotel room telephone and resulted in the generation of the telephone records in question, the Court concluded that [there was a] "sufficient connection between the telephone toll records and the underlying criminal gambling for which this defendant is charged, and a sufficient relationship between the defendant and the gambling enterprise, to establish a participatory interest on the part of defendant in this evidence. . . ."

III.

We see no reason to depart from the broad standing rule that entitles a criminal defendant to challenge an unreasonable search and seizure under Article I, paragraph 7 of the New Jersey Constitution if he or she can demonstrate a proprietary, possessory, or participatory interest in the place searched or items seized. Nonetheless, applying that standard to the facts of this case we find that defendant has failed to demonstrate an interest sufficient to give him standing. In reaching that conclusion, we need not specifically delineate the contours of the interest in evidence seized that will justify standing. Defendant's alleged connection to the place searched and items seized simply is far too attenuated to support a constitutional right to object to the search and seizure.

To begin with, based on the record before us defendant cannot claim a proprietary or possessory interest in the vehicle that was searched. During the suppression hearing defense counsel made a vague claim that Edwards had at one point indicated that the vehicle belonged to Bruns. However, the claim was never substantiated and the record confirms that the vehicle was registered in Edwards' name at the time of the search.

Moreover, defendant has failed to demonstrate either an ownership or possessory interest in the weapons seized. We note defense counsel's assertion that there is no reason to believe defendant divested himself of any possessory interest in the weapons, and his hypothetical statement that "for all we know, Mr. Bruns placed the toy gun under the seat ten minutes before the car was stopped and asked those in the car to keep a close watch on it." However, the record contains no evidence whatsoever to support the contention that defendant retained any interest in the weapons at the time of the search.

With no proprietary or possessory interest established, defendant nevertheless asserts that he had a participatory interest in the weapons seized because they were used to commit the robbery for which he was charged. We note first that the toy handgun and knife seized from Edwards' vehicle implicated defendant and Evans in a robbery that took place seven days before the contested search. The evidence was seized as a result of the search incident to Edwards' arrest that occurred after she was pulled over for speeding and a police officer discovered that there were two outstanding warrants for her arrest. Moreover, defendant was not a passenger in the vehicle and he was not in the vicinity of the vehicle at the time it was searched. In *Mollica*, the only case in which we have had occasion to consider whether a defendant's participatory interest was sufficient to confer standing, the Court emphasized the relationship between the evidence seized and the underlying criminal activity with which the defendant was charged, as well as the extent to which a co-defendant played a role in generating and using that evidence.

Defendant points to the relationship between the weapons seized from Edwards' car and the crime with which he was charged. Accepting that generalized connection, however, we are unpersuaded that that connection is adequate to confer standing based on a participatory interest. That evidence implicates a defendant in a crime is not, in and of itself, sufficient to confer standing. There also must be at a minimum some contemporary connection between the defendant and the place searched or the items seized. [Suppression] of the product of a Fourth Amendment violation can be successfully urged only by those whose rights were violated by the search itself, not by those who are aggrieved solely by the introduction of damaging evidence. . . .

Likewise, the weapons seized in this matter did not relate to any ongoing criminal activity between Edwards and defendant, or between Evans and defendant, at the time the allegedly illegal search occurred. The robbery for which defendant was charged occurred seven days before the items were found in Edwards' vehicle. . . .

Although we recognize that in most cases in which the police seize evidence implicating a defendant in a crime that defendant will be able to establish an interest in the property seized or place searched, our broad standing rule necessarily has limits. If substantial time passes between the crime and the seizure of the evidence, and a proprietary connection between defendant and the evidence no longer exists, the defendant's basis for being aggrieved by the search will have diminished. In addition to the temporal aspects of a specific search or seizure, a showing that the search was not directed at the defendant or at someone who is connected to the crime for which he has been charged also will diminish a defendant's interest in the property searched or seized. . . .

Problem 6-5. Place of Business

A citizen in Eagen, Minnesota, was walking by a ground-floor apartment and saw through the window several people putting white powder into bags. He called the police, and Officer James Thielen went to Apartment 103 to investigate. Thielen looked in the same window through a gap in the closed blinds and observed

Wayne Carter, Melvin Johns, and Kimberly Thompson putting the powder into bags for several minutes. While other officers began to prepare affidavits for a search warrant, Thielen remained at the apartment building to keep watch. He then saw Carter and Johns leave the building and drive away. Police stopped the car, and noticed in the passenger compartment some drug paraphernalia and a handgun. They arrested Carter and Johns, and an inventory search of the vehicle uncovered 47 grams of cocaine in plastic sandwich bags.

After seizing the car, the police returned to Apartment 103 and arrested Thompson. A warranted search of the apartment revealed cocaine residue on the kitchen table and plastic bags similar to those found in the car. Thompson was the lessee of the apartment. Carter and Johns lived in Chicago and had come to the apartment for the sole purpose of packaging the cocaine. They had never been to the apartment before and were in the apartment for less than three hours. In return for the use of the apartment, Carter and Johns had given Thompson one-eighth of an ounce of the cocaine.

Carter and Johns were charged with narcotics crimes, and they moved to suppress all evidence obtained from the apartment and the car. Do they have a sufficient privacy interest in the apartment to challenge any illegal search that may have happened there? Compare Minnesota v. Carter, 525 U.S. 83 (1998).

Notes

1. *Standing: majority position.* A majority of states follow the federal "legitimate expectation of privacy" approach when they determine who may invoke the exclusionary rule to remedy an illegal search or seizure. Others, like the New Jersey court in *Bruns*, use some form of the older "legitimately on the premises" test for standing. Often, these courts say that a defendant challenging an illegal search or seizure must demonstrate a "proprietary, possessory, or participatory interest" in the premises searched or the property seized. Try to imagine situations in which the federal test and the "legitimately on the premises" test produce different results.

The Supreme Court attempted, in Rakas v. Illinois, 439 U.S. 128 (1978), to eliminate any distinction between a person's "standing" to challenge an illegal search and the "extent of a particular defendant's rights" under the Fourth Amendment. Rights against unreasonable searches and seizures, said the Court, are personal rights and third parties may not assert them. See Brendlin v. California, 551 U.S. 249 (2007) (when police officer makes traffic stop, passenger in car is seized and may challenge constitutionality of stop). What would be the consequences of allowing a criminal defendant to challenge an allegedly improper search of a third party's property? Consider the Louisiana constitutional provision reprinted above. Why require standing *at all* for a litigant who hopes to challenge governmental misconduct, particularly if deterrence of government wrongdoing is the central purpose of the exclusionary rule?

2. *Standing for searches of residences and business premises.* Even though a defendant, under the federal (and majority) rule, must show a "legitimate" expectation of privacy in the premises searched or the property seized, this does not preclude challenges by those who do not own or lease property. The easier cases to decide involve the search of a residence, where the defendant lives full time even though another person owns or leases the residence. Courts in that setting have no trouble in

concluding that the person living in the house may challenge a search of any common area in the house or any area within the special control of the defendant. How might these residential cases apply to business premises?

More difficult cases involve guests and others who are present in a residence for shorter periods. In Minnesota v. Olson, 495 U.S. 91 (1990), the Court recognized standing for an overnight guest at an apartment: staying overnight in another's home "is a longstanding social custom that serves functions recognized as valuable by society." On the other hand, the Court in Minnesota v. Carter, 525 U.S. 83 (1998), concluded that defendants present in an apartment only for a few hours did not have a "legitimate expectation of privacy" in the premises. What could be said in favor of allowing dinner guests to challenge the admission of evidence obtained when the police make a warrantless entry of a home to arrest the guest or search her possessions? What if the police illegally search the purse of one person and find inside some contraband belonging to another person? See Rawlings v. Kentucky, 448 U.S. 98 (1980) (denying standing in such a setting). What if the nature of the social arrangement between the resident and a guest is unclear at the time of the search? See State v. Hess, 680 N.W.2d 314 (S.D. 2004) (tenant of apartment testified that she had an intimate relationship with owner of drugs found during search, and he had spent the night at her apartment on previous nights, but on this night her plans were unclear and it was "possible" he would spend night); State v. Filion, 966 A.2d 405 (Me. 2009) (long-time friend of lessee of apartment who was frequent social visitor does not have reasonable privacy expectation; key inquiry is defendant's relationship to property, not to the tenant; defendant had never spent the night at apartment, held no key to dwelling, and never visited apartment when friend was absent).

3. *"Automatic" standing for possessory crimes.* Special rules sometimes apply to defendants charged with possessory offenses, such as possession of stolen property or narcotics. The defendant in such a case faces a dilemma. For purposes of standing, she often must establish some ownership interest in the premises that were illegally searched, but for purposes of defending against the charges, she would prefer to deny any connection with the contraband or the premises searched. At one time, most American courts responded to this difficulty by granting "automatic" standing to any defendant who chose to challenge a search or seizure in a possessory crime case. See Jones v. United States, 362 U.S. 257 (1960). Later, the Supreme Court took a different approach to the problem. It held, in Simmons v. United States, 390 U.S. 377 (1968), that the government could not use at trial the defendant's testimony at a suppression hearing, if it was given for the purpose of establishing standing. Because of this "immunity" for the defendant's testimony, the Court decided that "automatic" standing was no longer necessary to protect a defendant. In addition, a defendant might establish a "legitimate" expectation of privacy in some premises searched without necessarily admitting ownership of contraband. See United States v. Salvucci, 448 U.S. 83 (1980). A sizable minority of states have retained the "automatic" standing rule for possessory offenses. See State v. Carvajal, 996 A.2d 1029 (N.J. 2010) (bus passenger who denied ownership of checked luggage abandoned that property and could not later invoke state's automatic standing rule). Some have explained that the "immunity" for the defendant's testimony at a suppression hearing is not adequate because the testimony still might be used to impeach the defendant's trial testimony. Can you think of any other reasons to retain the "automatic" standing rule?

4. *"Target" standing.* Should a court give any special treatment to a claim that the police *intentionally* conducted an illegal search against one party for the purpose of obtaining evidence against another party? In United States v. Payner, 447 U.S. 727 (1980), the Supreme Court applied its usual rules of standing in such a case. A few other courts, however, have responded to purposefully illegal searches of this sort by granting standing to the "target" of the search, even if the target had no legitimate expectation of privacy (or any other interest) in the premises that were searched. See Waring v. State, 670 P.2d 357 (Alaska 1983). What difficulties might a court encounter in applying the "target" standing rule? How often will the doctrine be relevant?

C. ADDITIONS AND ALTERNATIVES TO THE EXCLUSIONARY RULE

As we have seen, the exclusionary rule is not available in many cases to enforce rights against unreasonable searches and seizures. Are there any credible alternatives to the exclusionary rule? Would you embrace any (or all) of these remedies as replacements to the exclusionary rule, or would you adopt them as *additional* remedies and wait for proof of their viability?

1. Administrative Remedies

Police officers are sworn to uphold the law, and supervisors within a police department must ensure that the rank-and-file officers obey the law during criminal investigations. Many police departments hire legal counsel to train and advise investigating officers. What other steps might a police department or a local government adopt to discourage illegal searches and seizures?

Events in Los Angeles in the late 1990s offer a fascinating window into a police department's efforts to punish and prevent misbehavior by individual officers. In 1998, eight pounds of cocaine was found missing from a police evidence locker in the Los Angeles Police Department's Rampart division. Investigations led to officer Raphael Perez, a member of Rampart's elite anti-gang unit known as CRASH, for Community Resources Against Street Hoodlums. Like criminals everywhere, Officer Perez told prosecutors that he had information about other officers that he would trade for a reduced sentence of five years. The information from Officer Perez (much of it later confirmed from independent sources) revealed one of the largest patterns of police misconduct in U.S. history.

Perez told investigators a wild tale of police conspiring to frame innocent suspects, beating suspects, and covering up unjustified shootings. Hundreds of felony cases were tainted by alleged police misconduct. Dozens of officers were fired, relieved of duty, suspended, or quit. The city faced possible civil damages of hundreds of millions of dollars.

Almost every governmental institution that might respond to police abuse did so, including the police department, the Los Angeles District Attorney, the mayor, the city council, and federal civil rights enforcers. The Los Angeles Police assembled a Board of Inquiry to study the corruption scandal. A 362-page Board of Inquiry report blamed the calamity on poor hiring, the isolation of the special CRASH unit, and "rogue cops." L.A. Police Chief Bernard C. Parks explained:

> [The] Board of Inquiry report . . . points out in graphic detail [that] people with troubling backgrounds have been hired as police officers. We need to tighten up that hiring process. Individuals with criminal records or with histories of violent behavior or narcotics involvement have no place in this department. We need to make sure that field officers are supervised closely and that supervisors have the courage to take corrective action when necessary. I recognize there is a fine line between smothering officers under a stifling bureaucratic blanket and beefing up supervision. The Board of Inquiry report tells us how to walk that fine line and how to do it effectively. . . .
>
> [We] do not need to reinvent the wheel. . . . What we do need to do is emphasize a scrupulous adherence to existing policies and standards. We must enhance our ability to detect any individual or collective pattern of performance that falters. We must have the courage to deal with those who are responsible for failures. If we do not do all those things, another Rampart will surely occur.

Chief Parks issued an 18-page order detailing his response to the Rampart scandal, including abolition of the CRASH name in favor of generic "gang details," a limited three-year tour of duty with the new special anti-gang units, and new requirements for members and supervisors of the units.

Chief Parks fired Brian Hewitt (one of the officers that Perez had specifically accused) for the alleged beating of Ismael Jimenez, a gang member. In doing so, Parks followed the recommendation of the Board of Rights, a panel of officers who hear disciplinary cases. Evidence compiled by LAPD detectives against Hewitt included samples of blood splattered on the walls of the Rampart Station, which were matched to the victim's DNA; testimony from an emergency room doctor detailing the victim's injuries; testimony from several citizens and law enforcement personnel; and a piece of carpet from the Rampart Station that was soaked with the victim's bloody vomit.

But county prosecutors, citing a lack of evidence, twice declined to file charges against Hewitt. The prosecutors concluded that there was insufficient evidence to prove in court that Hewitt assaulted Jimenez. The office argued there were no witnesses, except possibly another gang member, and no photographs of his injuries.

Eventually, the federal government entered the scene with an extensive civil rights investigation of the LAPD. Federal officials wanted to know whether Los Angeles ever implemented the recommendations of the 1991 Christopher Commission report, issued following the Rodney King beating and the trials of the officers who beat him. Los Angeles received federal funds to implement those prior recommendations.

ERWIN CHEMERINSKY, WITH PAUL HOFFMAN, LAURIE LEVENSON, R. SAMUEL PAZ, CONNIE RICE, AND CAROL SOBEL, AN INDEPENDENT ANALYSIS OF THE LOS ANGELES POLICE DEPARTMENT'S BOARD OF INQUIRY REPORT ON THE RAMPART SCANDAL

(September 11, 2000)

On March 1, 2000, The Police Department's Board of Inquiry released its report on the "Rampart Area Corruption Incident." This report, [prepared at the request of the Police Protective League], analyzes the Board of Inquiry report and its recommendations. My overall conclusion is that the Board of Inquiry report unjustifiably minimized the magnitude of the scandal and failed to recommend the major changes necessary to reform the Los Angeles Police Department. The Board of Inquiry report is the management account of the Rampart scandal. . . .

1. The Board of Inquiry Report Fails to Identify the Extent of the Problem and, Indeed, Minimizes Its Scope and Nature

[The] Board of Inquiry minimizes the problem, calling it the "Rampart Incident," saying that the problem was a result of a "few" officers, and declaring that corruption is not a problem throughout the Department. These conclusions are at odds with everything that we learned in preparing this report and with the Justice Department's investigation which concluded that abuses occur "on a regular basis."

To ensure that there is a complete and adequate investigation to determine the full extent of the problem, I recommend [that the City of Los Angeles create an independent commission] with the mandate of thoroughly investigating the Los Angeles Police Department, including assessing the extent and nature of police corruption and lawlessness. . . . The Commission should be external to the Police Department and report to the Mayor, the City Council, the City Attorney, the Police Commission, and the people of Los Angeles. Officers with knowledge of wrongdoing in connection with the Rampart scandal should be encouraged to reveal what they know by granting them immunity from discipline for their failure to reveal wrong-doing previously. . . .

2. The Board of Inquiry Report Fails to Recognize That the Central Problem Is the Culture of the Los Angeles Police Department, Which Gave Rise to and Tolerated What Occurred in the Rampart Division and Elsewhere

The culture within the Los Angeles Police Department gave rise to the Rampart scandal and allowed it to remain undetected for so long. Every police department has a culture — the unwritten rules, mores, customs, codes, values, and outlooks — that creates the policing environment and style. . . . The culture of the Los Angeles Police Department emphasizes control and the exclusion of scrutiny by outsiders, including the Police Commission and its Inspector General, as well as courts and prosecutors. The culture of the Los Angeles Police Department exercises control over the rank and file officers through a highly stratified, elaborate discipline system that enforces voluminous rules and regulations, some of them very petty. The result is a startling degree of alienation and hostility to the management of the Department. The culture of the Los Angeles Police Department, as documented by the Christopher Commission, emphasizes overly aggressive policing, resulting in the use of excessive force.

Most importantly, a code of silence is deeply embedded in the Los Angeles Police Department. . . . The code of silence is reinforced in many ways, as the Department punishes whistleblowers and those who expose the wrongdoing of others. Changing the culture of the Police Department and reforming its practices will require many dramatic changes, including a shift from overly aggressive police tactics and a mentality that excludes outside oversight, to one that emphasizes community policing and seeks to end the code of silence. This change will not happen voluntarily. [There] must be judicial enforcement of reforms, either through a consent decree or a court order as part of a judgment.

3. The Board of Inquiry Report Fails to Consider the Need for Structural Reforms in the Department, Including Reforming the Police Commission, Strengthening the Independence and Powers of the Inspector General, and Creating Permanent Oversight Mechanisms for the Department

The Board of Inquiry report identifies no problems with the structure of the Police Department and apparently does not see this as in any way responsible for the Rampart scandal. . . . One essential change is to create a full-time, paid Police Commission and to change the manner of selecting and removing Commissioners to ensure greater independence. Under the Los Angeles City Charter, the Police Commission is the manager for all aspects of the Department, except for police discipline which is the responsibility of the Chief of Police. The Police Commission does not exist only for oversight or policy-making; it is the Department's manager. This task cannot be effectively done by a part-time, unpaid Commission.

Under the Charter, all Commissioners are appointed by, and are removable by, the Mayor. The problem is that Commissioners then are much more likely to reflect one philosophy and, at times, refrain from expressing a difference of opinion because of the risk of being removed by the Mayor or not reappointed. . . . The appointment authority should be dispersed (such as by having the Mayor appoint two police commissioners and having one each by the President of the City Council, the City Attorney, and the City Controller). Removal of a commissioner should require approval of the City Council. . . .

There must be a substantial strengthening of the independence of the Inspector General. . . . The first Inspector General saw her role and powers gutted as she was instructed that she could not report to the Police Commission and could not have access to case files. . . . The Inspector General needs more protection from removal and clearer authority to investigate any matter, unimpeded by the Police Commission.

Finally, there must be an external oversight mechanism for the worst abuses by LAPD officers. A permanent special prosecutor should be created, ideally in the Attorney General's office, to conduct criminal investigations and prosecutions of illegal activity by officers.

4. The Board of Inquiry Report Unduly Minimizes the Problems in the Police Department's Disciplinary System

. . . The Board of Inquiry recommends strengthening the disciplinary system, especially by increasing the powers of the Internal Affairs division and the authority of the Chief of Police. These recommendations fail to deal with the serious distrust in the system among officers or with any of the underlying problems in the disciplinary system. . . .

Assignments to Internal Affairs are for limited time periods, usually no more than two or three years for most individuals, some for far shorter time periods. This turnover in personnel in Internal Affairs often results in significant turnover in handling a single case. More insidiously, it means that officers from Internal Affairs soon will be returning to work with the same officers that they were disciplining. . . .

The Charter provides that disciplinary charges against police officers are adjudicated by a Board of Rights comprised of two command officers and one civilian. . . . [One possible reform] . . . would be to reconstitute the Board of Rights to include one command officer, one officer of the rank of Sergeant II or higher, and one civilian. Another would be binding arbitration. Another, likely the most promising, would be a citizen review board. . . .

Conclusion

. . . Reform is not an event, but a process that will take many years to complete. The hope is that this crisis provides a unique opportunity for reform. This opportunity must not be squandered. . . .

■ ST. PAUL, MINNESOTA, ORDINANCES §§102.01-102.03

Section 102.01

. . . (b) The [police-civilian internal affairs review commission] shall review all complaint investigations concerning members of the police department . . . completed by the internal affairs unit of the police department and subsequent investigations thereof related to alleged acts of excessive force, inappropriate use of firearms, discrimination, . . . poor public relations and such other complaints as may be referred to it by the mayor and/or the chief of police. The commission shall also collect and review summary data on complaints received and report to the mayor and council any patterns which may merit further examination.

Section 102.02

(a) There is hereby created a police-civilian internal affairs review commission consisting of seven voting members to be appointed by the mayor and approved by the council. . . . Five members shall be citizen members and two shall be members of the Saint Paul Police Federation as shall be recommended by the police chief to the mayor for appointment. Members shall, to the extent possible, be representative of the city's diversity of neighborhoods, races and cultures, abilities, incomes and sexual orientations. . . .

SECTION 102.03

. . . (b) Each member of the commission shall, prior to assuming official duties, participate in a training program which shall include topics related to police work, investigation, relevant law, cultural diversity, gender, sexual orientation, disability and the emotional impact of abuse. They shall also participate in ride-alongs with an officer on actual patrol duties. . . .

(d) The investigatory materials prepared by the internal affairs unit of the police department or independent investigators under contract to the city are considered data collected in furtherance of an active investigation and will be reviewed by the commission. The meetings of the commission on such matters will be closed . . . excepting to members of the commission and such other participants as approved by the chair of the commission and the police chief and that will facilitate the review process of the commission.

(e) The commission may request [that] individuals appear before it to state facts to supplement files. The commission may also request internal affairs staff to gather such additional information as may be needed for a determination by the commission. The commission may . . . hire a private investigator as approved by the mayor or chief of police. The commission shall have the power to subpoena witnesses to compel their appearance before it. . . .

(g) The commission, after review and deliberation of an investigation, shall, by majority vote, make its recommendation on the case. Such recommendation by the commission shall be upon a finding that the complaint be sustained; or the complaint not be sustained; or that the officer be exonerated; or the complaint is unfounded; or that the matter does not involve guilt or a lack thereof, but rather a failure of a departmental policy to address the situation. The commission shall also, by majority vote, make a recommendation as to any action to be taken concerning an involved officer. . . .

(j) In the event the chief of police disagrees with the action recommended by the commission, the chief shall notify the commission, in writing, of the action he or she intends to impose. The commission chair and chief of police shall have five working days to discuss any concerns they may have before any action is finalized. This provision does not prohibit the chief of police from taking immediate action in any case. . . .

Notes

1. *Police review boards.* Most police departments of any size have a section (often called "Internal Affairs" or "IAD") that reviews police officer conduct. Sometimes cities establish review boards to help internal affairs divisions or to reconsider the IAD findings. Sometimes special boards are set up to investigate particular allegations of police abuse. More controversial and less common are review boards entirely outside the police department. What are the advantages of an official review board? Who should be its members? What powers should the board have? Review boards have now operated in some jurisdictions for decades, and policy experts have evaluated their work across several dimensions. You can find a sample of those evaluations on the web extension for this chapter at *http://www.crimpro.com/extension/ch06*.

2. *Internal versus external review.* Are internal and external review bodies likely to reach the same results? Two separate reports assessing allegations of "testilying" and other illegal practices by Philadelphia police in the early 1990s reached widely differing conclusions: The internal report identified rogue officers; the external review found fundamental problems with the training and policies of the department. What are the advantages and disadvantages of an "independent" review board? How can internal review efforts be tied to salary raises and promotion decisions?

3. *Review by the media.* Sometimes newspapers or local TV stations will examine allegations of police misconduct. As with unofficial citizen review boards, the formal power of reporters to obtain information is limited, but of course reporters can disclose to the public any refusals to share information. An additional limit on the use of the media to shape officer and department behavior is the risk of libel suits brought by officers against reporters and newspapers. See, e.g., Costello v. Ocean County Observer, 643 A.2d 1012 (N.J. 1994).

4. *Early warning systems.* Police chiefs have a slogan: Ten percent of the officers cause ninety percent of the problems. How can police managers identify the officers who need special training or removal from the field? Some departments (just over a fourth of all departments nationwide) use "early warning" systems (also known as "early intervention" systems) to select officers who might benefit from training or other intervention. See Samuel Walker, Geoffrey P. Alpert & Dennis J. Kenney, Early Warning Systems: Responding to the Problem Police Officer (July 2001, NCJ 188565). Data collection systems flag officers for special attention if they are involved in some requisite number of citizen complaints, firearm discharges, use-of-force reports, civil litigation, high-speed pursuits, or vehicular damage. The supervisor of an officer so identified reviews the incident and counsels the officer; sometimes the department sends the officer to special training classes. Assuming that plaintiffs in civil lawsuits could subpoena this data about individual officers, does it help or hurt the department during the litigation? Do early warning systems encourage inactive policing?

5. *Renegade cops or renegade police culture?* No one defends the brutality of the individual Rampart officers. But is the problem explained by bad cops and weak supervision, or is there a wider problem with the culture of policing? The LAPD has an especially rich history of abuses and breakdowns in supervision, as dramatized in the 1997 movie *L.A. Confidential*. What different responses are called for by the two kinds of problems?

6. *Revocation of officer's license.* State and local police departments hire only individuals who are certified by state licensing authorities to serve as law enforcement officers. Administrative bodies in many states review allegations of police misconduct and sometimes revoke the license of an officer based on that misconduct; the licensing body in Florida is among the most active. The revocation of a license prevents other police forces in the same state from hiring an officer after he or she is fired for misconduct. One database, tracking the work of licensing authorities in 11 states going back to 1973, shows over 5,600 revocations during that time. See Roger L. Goldman, State Revocation of Law Enforcement Officers' Licenses and Federal Criminal Prosecution: An Opportunity for Cooperative Federalism, 22 St. Louis U. Pub. L. Rev. 121 (2003).

2. *Tort Actions and Criminal Prosecutions*

The most common private remedy for illegal searches prior to the use of the exclusionary rule was a tort action against the officer who violated the law during the search. Any victim of a wrongful search (not just those who later face criminal charges) can, in theory, bring a lawsuit against the officer conducting the search, or against the police department or other governmental units, requesting damages or other relief. The search victim might sue in state court based on state common law torts such as false imprisonment or trespass; she might also look to a state statute granting a civil cause of action for wrongful searches or seizures. Some victims also rely on a federal statute, 42 U.S.C. §1983, which creates a cause of action in federal court against any "person" who acts "under color of" state law to deprive another person of federal constitutional or statutory rights.

These lawsuits have not become a common method of dealing with improper searches or seizures. The plaintiffs in such cases face several substantial legal obstacles: The most important are the doctrines of "sovereign immunity" protecting the state or local government from suit, and "qualified immunity," which protects individual police officers who act with "good faith."

The theory behind the tort suit as a remedy for illegal searches and seizures is that civil damages can more precisely measure the violation and the harm. In terms of deterrence, the remedy imposes costs on the officer, the police department, or both; unlike suppression, a tort remedy remains a separate question from whether the suspect committed a criminal offense.

Whether financial costs imposed as result of successful tort claims in fact deter police officers or police departments from unconstitutional actions may turn in part on whether the individual officer (who will often be judgment-proof) or the department (or the county or state government) will pay the damages. One related issue is whether the state is obligated through contract or state law to indemnify the police officer for the costs of defense and any judgment against the officer.

Private enforcement is not the only possibility. In 1994, Congress passed legislation (now codified at 42 U.S.C. §14141) that prohibits state and local governments from engaging in "a pattern or practice of conduct by law enforcement officials" that deprives persons of "rights, privileges, or immunities secured or protected by the Constitution or laws of the United States." The statute authorizes the U.S. Department of Justice to sue in federal court for injunctive and declaratory relief to eliminate the pattern or practice. The Civil Rights Division of the Justice Department filed such a suit against the Los Angeles Police Department in the wake of the Rampart scandal described above; the consent decree resolving that suit is excerpted below. What are the relative merits of public and private civil enforcement?

■ MARK MAIMARON v. COMMONWEALTH

865 N.E.2d 1098 (Mass. 2007)

GREANEY, J.

On November 2, 1998, the plaintiff Mark Maimaron brought an action in the Superior Court under the Massachusetts Tort Claims Act, G.L. c. 258, against State

Trooper David Oxner, several other State troopers, and the Commonwealth, seeking to recover damages for injuries he sustained as the result of an alleged illegal seizure and arrest. The incident involved an altercation in 1995, when Oxner was not on duty. Maimaron asserted that Oxner had violated his civil rights as protected by Federal and State constitutional law and statutes, 42 U.S.C. §1983, and G.L. c. 12, §11I [civil action for violation of constitutional rights], and had committed the intentional torts of assault and battery, malicious prosecution, false arrest, and abuse of process, in making the seizure and arrest. In 2001, the Commonwealth settled Maimaron's claims against it and the State police officers other than Oxner. Thereafter, Maimaron and Oxner agreed to participate in binding arbitration, which resulted in an award and judgment, including attorney's fees, in Maimaron's favor. Unable to satisfy the judgment against him, Oxner entered a settlement agreement and assignment of rights with Maimaron in which Oxner assigned his right to Maimaron to indemnification (of the judgment in the underlying action) by the Commonwealth pursuant to G.L. c. 258, §9A. [The statute] provides, in relevant part:*

> If, in the event a suit is commenced against a member of the state police . . . by reason of a claim for damages resulting from an alleged intentional tort or by reason of an alleged act or failure to act which constitutes a violation of the civil rights of any person under federal or state law, the commonwealth, at the request of the affected police officer, shall provide for the legal representation of said police officer.
>
> The commonwealth shall indemnify members of the state police . . . from all personal financial loss and expenses, including but not limited to legal fees and costs, if any, in an amount not to exceed one million dollars arising out of any claim, action, award, compromise, settlement or judgment resulting from any alleged intentional tort or by reason of an alleged act or failure to act which constitutes a violation of the civil rights of any person under federal or state law; provided, however, that this section shall apply only where such alleged intentional tort or alleged act or failure to act occurred within the scope of the official duties of such police officer.
>
> No member of the state police . . . shall be indemnified for any violation of federal or state law if such member or employee acted in a wilful, wanton, or malicious manner.

Oxner and Maimaron commenced separate actions against the Commonwealth that have been consolidated. In his complaint, Oxner had sought to recover attorney's fees and costs that he incurred defending the underlying action, alleging that the Commonwealth had violated its duty under G.L. c. 258, §9A, in failing to defend him in that action. Maimaron . . . sought to collect the amount of the judgment entered against Oxner in the underlying action, as well as interest, and attorney's fees and costs. . . . A Superior Court judge granted summary judgment in favor of Oxner and Maimaron, and the Commonwealth appealed. . . .

On the evening of November 22, 1995, Oxner and his friend Stephen Roche went to a lounge in Quincy. They were later joined by Oxner's wife and her female friend. Oxner, who was not on duty that evening, had several drinks at the bar.

That same evening, Maimaron, an ironworker, was a patron at the lounge, and had consumed approximately ten beers. Maimaron met Oxner, whom Maimaron believed was actually a coworker from his work site, although Oxner told Maimaron

* [This material was moved from a footnote to text. — Eds.]

that he was a State trooper. Maimaron repeatedly confronted Oxner with this inaccurate belief, despite Oxner's repeated denials.

After midnight, Maimaron and Oxner encountered each other in the parking lot outside the lounge. A heated exchange ensued and Oxner demanded to see Maimaron's identification. Maimaron declined, and was turning to leave, when Oxner hit him on the side of his head and grabbed his shoulder. Fearing for his safety, Maimaron sprayed mace (which he was licensed to carry) into Oxner's face, and then ran down the street.

Oxner pursued Maimaron on foot, holding out his badge, identifying himself as a police officer, whistling, and telling Maimaron to stop because he was under arrest. Roche joined in the pursuit and caught up with Maimaron. Roche struck Maimaron from behind, knocking him to the ground. Maimaron raised his head and tried to get up, at which point Oxner slammed Maimaron down, hitting his face into the pavement.

Oxner and a bystander contacted the Quincy police department. Oxner identified himself as an off-duty officer and requested an ambulance for Maimaron, who was bleeding profusely. Roche disappeared into the crowd of spectators. When Quincy police officers arrived, Oxner told them that he had been assaulted by Maimaron with mace and that an "unknown white male" helped subdue Maimaron by tackling him.

Maimaron suffered extensive injuries, including multiple facial fractures, broken teeth and a detached palate. His jaws were wired shut for six weeks, and he underwent extensive rehabilitation and the implantation of titanium plates in his face. Maimaron sustained long-lasting injuries, including permanent change in his appearance, persistent vertigo and headaches, as well as emotional and psychological distress.

Oxner subsequently filed charges against Maimaron for assault and battery by means of a deadly weapon, as well as for assault and battery on a police officer. The United States Attorney's office conducted an investigation into the altercation. . . . Oxner pleaded guilty to assault and battery of Maimaron and to filing a false written report by a public officer, for which he was sentenced to unsupervised probation for one year.

In January 1997, a trial board of the State police determined that Oxner had violated several State police administrative rules and regulations. The board suspended him without pay for four months, and required that he complete ethics training. On January 3, 1997, the Norfolk County district attorney's office entered a nolle prosequi on the criminal complaint Oxner had filed against Maimaron.

In response to Maimaron's underlying action, Oxner sought defense and indemnification from the Commonwealth during the course of litigation, but the Commonwealth repeatedly declined his requests. After the Commonwealth had settled with Maimaron, Maimaron and Oxner voluntarily entered into binding arbitration. The Commonwealth was notified in writing by Oxner's attorney that the arbitration proceedings were about to begin, and Oxner again demanded that the Commonwealth assume his defense. The Commonwealth responded in writing that it "[declined] to provide . . . indemnification and/or defense of . . . Oxner [and did not] foresee . . . changing its stance on the issue." The Commonwealth did not participate in the arbitration.

In his award, the arbitrator concluded that Oxner had violated Maimaron's civil rights by committing the torts of assault and battery and false arrest. The arbitrator determined that Maimaron was entitled to damages from Oxner in the amount of $363,682. In addition, the arbitrator found the following: at all times during, and after, his confrontation with Maimaron, Oxner was acting within the scope of his employment as a State police officer; Oxner was acting under color of State law throughout the altercation and arrest because, under State police rules and regulations, a State police officer is subject to recall twenty-four hours a day and is instructed to take immediate enforcement action for violations of law observed, and Oxner was following State police regulations in attempting to arrest Maimaron for perceived criminal actions; Oxner violated Maimaron's rights under the Fourth Amendment to the United States Constitution during the assault and battery and subsequent false arrest; Oxner never intended to injure Maimaron during the arrest; and Oxner did not act in a "malicious or wanton" manner. On July 9, 2002, a Superior Court judge entered judgment for Maimaron in the amount of $363,682, and included an award for attorney's fees and costs in the amount of $69,243.52.

In connection with the instant action, the Superior Court judge who ruled on the parties' cross motions for summary judgment . . . concluded that, because the Commonwealth had violated its mandatory duty to defend Oxner against Maimaron's claim in the underlying action, the Commonwealth was bound by the arbitrator's findings and was precluded from arguing that Oxner was not acting within the scope of his official duties or that his conduct was wilful, wanton, or malicious. Judgment entered awarding damages to Maimaron in the amount of $363,682, due to the acts of Oxner; attorney's fees (for litigating the underlying action) to Maimaron in the amount of $69,243.52; attorney's fees (for litigating the instant action) to Maimaron in the amount of $29,951.88; and attorney's fees (for litigating the underlying and instant actions) to Oxner in the amount of $84,879. . . .

1. *Duty to defend.* The judge correctly concluded that the Commonwealth had a mandatory obligation to provide legal representation (the duty to defend) to Oxner under G.L. c. 258, §9A. . . . A review of the plain language of §9A, interpreted in a way to effectuate its purpose, mandates this result.

The first paragraph of G.L. c. 258, §9A, pertains solely to the duty to defend. Its language, "shall provide for the legal representation of said police officer," imposes a mandatory obligation. That obligation arises when (1) a request for legal representation is made by the affected police officer; and (2) a lawsuit is brought against the officer alleging an intentional tort or a violation of civil rights. These requirements were present here.

Relying on language in the second paragraph of G.L. c. 258, §9A, that provides, "this *section* shall apply only where such alleged intentional tort or alleged act or failure to act occurred within the scope of the official duties of such police officer," the Commonwealth maintains that its duty to defend is conditioned on whether the police officer had been acting within the scope of his official duties (emphasis added). We disagree. This language, together with the language also appearing in that paragraph that the indemnification obligation includes "personal financial loss and expenses, including but not limited to legal fees and costs," permits the Commonwealth, if it is *later* determined that the police officer acted outside the scope of his official duties or acted in a wilful, wanton, or malicious manner, to seek reimbursement of legal expenses.[8] To conclude otherwise would undermine the statute's purpose which recognizes that the requirement of mandatory indemnification evidences the Legislature's determination that intentional torts and civil rights violations arise frequently in the scope of police work, and that indemnification of officers against such claims encourages police service. The same applies equally to the duty to defend provision. . . .

2. *Duty to indemnify Maimaron (as assignee).* Under G.L. c. 258, §9A, the Commonwealth is required to indemnify a member of the State police "from all personal financial loss and expenses . . . arising out of any claim, action, award, compromise, settlement or judgment resulting from any alleged intentional tort or by reason of an alleged act or failure to act which constitutes a violation of the civil rights of any person under federal or state law." There are two exclusions: (1) where the alleged act did not occur "within the scope of the official duties of such police officer"; and (2) where the police officer "acted in a wilful, wanton, or malicious manner."

The Commonwealth argues that the judge erred in granting summary judgment on the indemnification issue, maintaining that it should have been permitted to litigate the two exclusions. The judge rejected the Commonwealth's argument on the basis of the rule, applied frequently in insurance cases, that an insurer who has wrongfully refused to defend its insured cannot relitigate coverage issues and, thus, becomes liable to indemnify the damages assessed in the third-party action. . . .

We first address the scope of employment issue as it relates to the color of State law issue that was the concern of the arbitrator in Maimaron's §1983 claim. [The decision in] Pinshaw v. Metropolitan Dist. Comm'n, 524 N.E.2d 1351 (Mass. 1988), established that "the scope of . . . official duties" exclusion in §9A calls for the application of common-law respondeat superior principles. It went on to set forth those principles as follows: . . .

> In determining the scope of employment, the finder of fact must consider whether the conduct complained of is of the kind the employee is hired to perform, whether it occurs within authorized time and space limits, and whether "it is motivated, at least in part, by a purpose to serve the employer." See Restatement (Second) of Agency §228 (1958). . . .
>
> If an employee acts from purely personal motives . . . in no way connected with the employer's interests, he is considered in the ordinary case to have departed from his employment, and the master is not liable. . . . If the act complained of was within the scope of the servant's authority, the master will be liable, although it constituted an abuse or excess of the authority conferred. The master . . . is justly held responsible when the servant, through lack of judgment or discretion, or from infirmity of temper, or under the influence of passion aroused by the circumstances and the occasion, goes beyond the strict line of his duty or authority and inflicts an unjustifiable injury on a third person. . . .

8. The Commonwealth's reasons for refusing its duty to defend, such as the fact that Oxner had pleaded guilty to two criminal charges and was found to be in violation of various State police administrative rules and regulations, do not bear on the Commonwealth's duty to provide a defense. Rather, if such reasons later are found to take Oxner's conduct outside the scope of his official duties or to amount to wilful, wanton, or malicious behavior, the Commonwealth would be entitled to seek reimbursement of the legal fees incurred in his defense.

The determination whether a defendant acted under color of State law is one of two essential requirements for an action under 42 U.S.C. §1983. Generally speaking, there are three basic principles that define the scope of "acting under the color of State law" requirement. First, "a public employee acts under color of State law while acting in his official capacity or while exercising his responsibilities pursuant to State law." That is the basic proposition. Second, a public official . . . acts under color of State law if he acts under "pretense" of law, but not when he is acting as a private individual pursuing his own goals.

Third, and of importance to this case, when a public official "misuses" or "abuses" the authority given him by the State (i.e., if he acts outside the scope of his employment) he nevertheless acts under color of State law where he is "clothed with the authority of State law." Monroe v. Pape, 365 U.S. 167, 184 (1961), overruled in part by Monell v. Department of Social Servs. of the City of N.Y., 436 U.S. 658, 663 (1978) (overruling *Monroe* case "insofar as it holds that local governments are wholly immune from suit under §1983"). Under the third principle, a police officer may be acting under color of State law, but *not* acting within the scope of his employment, because he may have "misused" or "abused," in the Supreme Court's language, the authority given to him by the State. [The] two concepts — acting within the scope of employment and acting under color of State law — do not involve precisely parallel considerations (although there may, in a given case, be some overlap). The scope of employment issue bespeaks a narrower inquiry and, in certain cases, would allow a fact finder to conclude that an officer who is acting under color of State law for purposes of §1983 liability is not acting within the scope of his employment for purposes of G.L. c. 258, §9A, indemnification. . . .

In this case, the arbitrator provided no explanation to support his conclusion that Oxner was acting within the scope of employment, and he did not refer to, much less discuss, the standards governing the scope of official duties exception set forth in the *Pinshaw* decision. . . . The facts found by the arbitrator establish that Oxner was subject to recall twenty-four hours a day; that he eventually displayed his police badge to Maimaron thereby officially identifying himself as a police officer; and that he issued an official command to stop, seeking to arrest Maimaron for some undetermined violation of law. These facts do not, however, compel a conclusion that Oxner was acting within the scope of his employment. Rather, because Oxner could be found to have acted unlawfully and with excessive force in subduing Maimaron (after an encounter in the lounge where Maimaron had done nothing unlawful), a fact finder could conclude that Oxner "abused" his authority, namely, that he was acting outside the scope of his employment, even though he was acting under color of State law. . . .

It was also not necessary for the arbitrator to find in connection with the claims before him that Oxner was not acting wilfully, wantonly, or maliciously. There must be a trial on this exclusion as well. The standard for assessing Oxner's conduct under this exclusion was described in *Pinshaw* in these terms:

> For purposes of §9A, in a civil rights context "wilful, wanton, or malicious" conduct means egregious conduct which would warrant imposition of punitive damages in the underlying action. In Federal civil rights actions, which are among the actions for which §9A provides indemnity, the United States Supreme Court has interpreted the terms "malice," "wanton," and "willful" to constitute a standard for punitive damages "when the defendant's conduct is shown to be motivated by evil motive or intent, or when it

> involves reckless or callous indifference to the federally protected rights of others." Linking the exclusion from indemnification to the standard for punitive damages achieves the Legislature's clear intent; it indemnifies officers for intentional torts and civil rights violations occurring within the scope of their official duties, yet excludes indemnification in egregious cases. It also provides a bright line test for precluding indemnification where punitive damages are awarded in the underlying action.

The arbitrator's conclusion that Oxner had not acted wilfully, wantonly, or maliciously does not, on this record, preclude a finding that Oxner took himself outside the coverage of §9A, when he confronted, and viciously attacked, Maimaron outside the lounge. Oxner's conduct could be found by a trier of fact to be "egregious" (and therefore punitive) in the sense described by the *Pinshaw* case.

Finally, we note that *both* exclusions involve the need for a fact finder to ascertain Oxner's state of mind. Summary judgment, when an actor's state of mind is relevant, is strongly disfavored. . . .

This case, particularly with reference to Oxner's defense by the Commonwealth, has not been handled well. The Commonwealth, to satisfy its defense obligations under §9A, should have defended Oxner under a reservation of rights (and litigated the indemnification issue later). . . . The Commonwealth also could have sought a declaratory judgment in advance of the arbitration to determine whether it was obligated under §9A to defend Oxner. This procedure is utilized in insurance cases to determine an insurer's obligation when there is a legitimate question about provision of a defense, and we discern no reason why the procedure would not have utility in this type of case.

The judgment for the plaintiffs is vacated. The case is remanded to the Superior Court for the entry of a new and partial judgment stating that the Commonwealth breached its duty to defend Oxner under G.L. c. 258, §9A . . . . With respect to the Commonwealth's liability for indemnification to Maimaron (as assignee), the case is remanded for further proceedings consistent with this opinion.

■ OFFICE OF THE ATTORNEY GENERAL, STATE OF ARKANSAS, OPINION NO. 2004-188

(September 8, 2004)

The Honorable Larry Jegley
Prosecuting Attorney, Sixth Judicial District
Little Rock, Arkansas

Dear Mr. Jegley:

You have requested my opinion on certain issues related to chemical testing for the purpose of determining alcohol and drug levels in a suspect's body. You indicate that your questions are related to situations in which police officers arrive at the scene of a motor vehicle accident and find a dead or dying victim of a suspected drunk driver. The suspected drunk driver refuses to submit to chemical testing pursuant to A.C.A. §5-65-208. . . .

Your questions are: . . .

(2) [What] action should police take to enforce the provisions of Section 208? (Should they seek a court order or warrant if a driver refuses consent to testing

(although dissipating drugs or alcohol create a time crunch, often late at night)?) May officers use reasonable force, if needed to obtain the sample, either with or without court order or warrant?

(3) If force is permitted either with or without a warrant, are there any civil liability issues for police agencies enforcing the requirements of A.C.A. §5-65-208, assuming it is mandatory? . . .

Response

[Question 2: What] action should police take to enforce the provisions of Section 208? (Should they seek a court order or warrant if a driver refuses consent to testing (although dissipating drugs or alcohol create a time crunch, often late at night)?) May officers use reasonable force, if needed to obtain the sample, either with or without court order or warrant? . . .

The Arkansas Supreme Court recently stated: "The law is settled that the taking of blood by a law enforcement officer amounts to a Fourth Amendment search and seizure." Haynes v. State, 127 S.W.3d 456, 461 (Ark. 2003), citing Schmerber v. California, 384 U.S. 757 (1966). Accordingly, a warrant is required unless an exception to the warrant requirement can be established. For example, a warrant is not necessary if the suspect gives his consent to the test. Another example of a situation in which a warrant may not be necessary is a situation involving certain exigent circumstances, such as those in which the opportunity to administer the test will exist only for a short time. . . .

Question 3: If force is permitted either with or without a warrant, are there any civil liability issues for police agencies enforcing the requirements of A.C.A. §5-65-208 . . . ?

The answer to this question will depend upon the type of liability to which you are referring. Law enforcement officers, as employees of the state or of political subdivisions of the state, are entitled to certain limited immunity from suit for some types of acts that are performed in the course of their official duties. Law enforcement officers who are employees of the State fall within the provisions of A.C.A. §19-10-305(a), which states: "Officers and employees of the State of Arkansas are immune from liability and from suit, except to the extent that they may be covered by liability insurance, for damages for acts or omissions, other than malicious acts or omissions, occurring within the course and scope of their employment."

It should be noted that the above-quoted grant of immunity applies generally to nonmalicious acts, but that it contains an exception to the extent of liability insurance coverage. Therefore, while law enforcement officers generally cannot be held liable for nonmalicious acts, they can be held liable for such acts to the extent that such acts are covered by liability insurance. They can also, of course, be held liable for malicious acts.

Law enforcement officers who are employees of cities and counties fall within the provisions of A.C.A. §21-9-301, which states:

> It is declared to be the public policy of the State of Arkansas that all counties, municipal corporations, school districts, special improvement districts, and all other political subdivisions of the state shall be immune from liability and from suit for damages, except to the extent that they may be covered by liability insurance. No tort action shall

> lie against any such political subdivision because of the acts of its agents and employees.

Although A.C.A. §21-9-301 speaks only in terms of the immunity of the political subdivision itself, the Arkansas Supreme Court has interpreted the statute as extending immunity to officers and employees of the political subdivisions as well when they negligently commit acts or omissions in their official capacities. Accordingly, a claimant may be able to sue city or county law enforcement officers personally for intentional or malicious acts, or for negligent acts not committed in their official capacities. However, the claimant cannot sue the city or county officer for negligence that was committed in the officer's official capacity (except to the extent that such acts are covered by liability insurance).

In addition to these two types of statutory immunity, law enforcement officers may be entitled to "qualified immunity." Under the doctrine of qualified immunity, an individual is immune from suit if the actions complained of were taken in good faith in the performance of one's duties, and the acts do not violate any clearly established constitutional right. Harlow v. Fitzgerald, 457 U.S. 800 (1982). The test for the applicability of qualified immunity turns upon the "objective legal reasonableness of the action," assessed in light of legal rules that were "clearly established" at the time the action was taken. See Anderson v. Creighton, 483 U.S. 635 (1987). The immunity is "qualified" because it does not obtain where the activity is in violation of clearly established law that a reasonable person would have known.

The question of whether a law enforcement officer is entitled to any type of immunity from a claim arising out of the execution of the testing requirements of A.C.A. §5-65-208 will depend largely upon the facts of each case, including the particular damage claimed, whether that damage resulted from an act committed by the officer in his official capacity, and whether the officer acted negligently or maliciously. . . .

Assistant Attorney General Suzanne Antley prepared the foregoing opinion, which I hereby approve.

Sincerely,
Mike Beebe, Attorney General

■ CONSENT DECREE, UNITED STATES v. CITY OF LOS ANGELES

Civil No. 00-11769 GAF, June 15, 2001

1. The United States and the City of Los Angeles, a chartered municipal corporation in the State of California, share a mutual interest in promoting effective and respectful policing. They join together in entering this settlement in order to promote police integrity and prevent conduct that deprives persons of rights, privileges, or immunities secured or protected by the Constitution or laws of the United States.

2. In its Complaint, plaintiff United States alleges that the City of Los Angeles, the Los Angeles Board of Police Commissioners, and the Los Angeles Police Department (collectively, "the City defendants") are violating 42 U.S.C. §14141 by engaging in a pattern or practice of unconstitutional or otherwise unlawful conduct that

has been made possible by the failure of the City defendants to adopt and implement proper management practices and procedures. In making these allegations, the United States recognizes that the majority of Los Angeles police officers perform their difficult jobs in a lawful manner. . . .

MANAGEMENT AND SUPERVISORY MEASURES TO PROMOTE CIVIL RIGHTS INTEGRITY

39. The City has taken steps to develop, and shall establish a database containing relevant information about its officers, supervisors, and managers to promote professionalism and best policing practices and to identify and modify at-risk behavior (also known as an early warning system). This system shall be a successor to, and not simply a modification of, the existing computerized information processing system known as the Training Evaluation and Management System ("TEAMS"). The new system shall be known as "TEAMS II". . . .

41. TEAMS II shall contain information on the following matters:

a. all non-lethal uses of force that are required to be reported in LAPD "use of force" reports or otherwise are the subject of an administrative investigation by the Department; . . .

c. all officer-involved shootings and firearms discharges, both on-duty and off-duty; . . .

d. all other lethal uses of force;

e. all other injuries and deaths that are reviewed by the LAPD Use of Force Review Board; . . .

f. all vehicle pursuits and traffic collisions; . . .

i. all written compliments received by the LAPD about officer performance;

j. all commendations and awards;

k. all criminal arrests and investigations known to LAPD of, and all charges against, LAPD employees;

l. all civil or administrative claims filed with and all lawsuits served upon the City or its officers . . . resulting from LAPD operations and known by the City, the Department, or the City Attorney's Office; . . .

p. training history and any failure of an officer to meet weapons qualification requirements; and

q. all management and supervisory actions taken pursuant to a review of TEAMS II information, including non-disciplinary actions. . . .

47. The protocol for using TEAMS II shall include the following provisions and elements:

a. The protocol shall require that, on a regular basis, supervisors review and analyze all relevant information in TEAMS II about officers under their supervision to detect any pattern or series of incidents that indicate that an officer, group of officers, or an LAPD unit under his or her supervision may be engaging in at-risk behavior. . . .

c. The protocol shall require that LAPD managers on a regular basis review and analyze relevant information in TEAMS II about subordinate managers and supervisors in their command regarding the subordinate's ability to manage adherence to policy and to address at-risk behavior. . . .

g. The protocol shall require that all relevant and appropriate information in TEAMS II be taken into account when [deciding matters of] pay grade advancement, promotion, assignment as . . . a Field Training Officer, or when preparing annual personnel performance evaluations. . . .

Incidents, Procedures, Documentation, Investigation, and Review

78. The Department shall continue to require officers to report to the LAPD without delay: any conduct by other officers that reasonably appears to constitute (a) an excessive use of force or improper threat of force; (b) a false arrest or filing of false charges; (c) an unlawful search or seizure; (d) invidious discrimination; (e) an intentional failure to complete forms required by LAPD policies and in accordance with procedures; (f) an act of retaliation for complying with any LAPD policy or procedure; or (g) an intentional provision of false information in an administrative investigation or in any official report, log, or electronic transmittal of information. . . . Failure to voluntarily report as described in this paragraph shall be an offense subject to discipline if sustained. . . .

97. [The] City shall develop and initiate a plan for organizing and executing regular, targeted, and random integrity audit checks, or "sting" operations . . . to identify and investigate officers engaging in at-risk behavior, including: unlawful stops, searches, seizures (including false arrests), [or] uses of excessive force. . . . These operations shall also seek to identify officers who discourage the filing of a complaint or fail to report misconduct or complaints. . . . The Department shall use the relevant TEAMS II data, and other relevant information, in selecting targets for these sting audits. . . .

103. LAPD officers may not use race, color, ethnicity, or national origin (to any extent or degree) in conducting stops or detentions, or activities following stops or detentions, except when . . . officers are seeking one or more specific persons who have been identified or described in part by their race, color, ethnicity, or national origin. . . .

104. [The] Department shall require LAPD officers to complete a written or electronic report each time an officer conducts a motor vehicle stop. . . . The report shall include the following: (i) the officer's serial number; (ii) date and approximate time of the stop; (iii) reporting district where the stop occurred; (iv) driver's apparent race, ethnicity, or national origin; (v) driver's gender and apparent age; (vi) reason for the stop . . . ; (vii) whether the driver was required to exit the vehicle; (viii) whether a pat-down/frisk was conducted; (ix) action taken, to include check boxes for warning, citation, arrest, completion of a field interview card, with appropriate identification number for the citation or arrest report; and (x) whether the driver was asked to submit to a consensual search of person, vehicle, or belongings, and whether permission was granted or denied. . . .

105. [The] Department shall require LAPD officers to complete a written or electronic report each time an officer conducts a pedestrian stop. . . .

Community Outreach and Public Information

155. For the term of this Agreement, the Department shall conduct a Community Outreach and Public Information program for each LAPD geographic area. The program shall require . . . at least one open meeting per quarter in each of the 18 geographic Areas for the first year of the Agreement, and one meeting in each

Area annually thereafter, to inform the public about the provisions of this Agreement, and the various methods of filing a complaint against an officer. . . .

156. The LAPD shall prepare and publish on its website semiannual public reports. . . . Such reports shall include aggregate statistics broken down by each LAPD geographic area and for the Operations Headquarters Bureau, and broken down by the race/ethnicity/national origin of the citizens involved, for arrests, information required to be maintained pursuant to paragraphs 104 and 105, and uses of force. Such reports shall include a brief description of [audits completed] and any significant actions taken as a result of such audits or reports, (ii) a summary of all discipline imposed during the period reported by type of misconduct, broken down by type of discipline, bureau and rank, and (iii) any new policies or changes in policies made by the Department to address the requirements of this Agreement. . . .

Notes

1. *The availability of tort remedies for police misconduct.* All states and the federal system offer some kind of tort (or tort-like) remedies for some kinds of police misconduct. In the federal system, private claims can arise under 42 U.S.C. §1983 (civil rights), the Federal Tort Claims Act, or directly under the Constitution in suits known as *Bivens* actions, after Bivens v. Six Unknown Named Agents of Federal Bureau of Narcotics, 403 U.S. 388 (1971). Remedies in federal court may include money damages, injunctive relief, or consent decrees entered between parties in lieu of further litigation. In many states recovery is allowed under statutes providing generally for tort claims against the government and its agents, subject to limitations for sovereign immunity (for governments) and official immunity (for individual officers). Claims may also be made under specialized tort statutes. Surprisingly, very few states have promulgated statutes specifically addressing actions by citizens against the police.

2. *The invisibility of tort claims.* Despite the long history of tort actions to remedy unconstitutional and excessive police action, it is extremely difficult to find any reported cases involving successful claims. Indeed, there are more law review articles discussing tort actions than reported decisions about successful recoveries. See, e.g., John C. Jeffries, Jr., Disaggregating Constitutional Torts, 110 Yale L. J. 259 (2000); Susan Bandes, Patterns of Injustice: Police Brutality in the Courts, 47 Buff. L. Rev. 1275-341 (1999).

The almost complete absence of reported decisions might suggest that tort remedies are entirely illusory, and that the legal barriers to recovery are too high (at least too high to make tort suits a plausible remedy, either for the purposes of the claimant or as a behavior-shaping device). But some plaintiffs who sue the government for improper police conduct do recover damages, despite immunities and other obstacles. Newspapers regularly carry stories of settlements or jury verdicts in civil suits dealing with officer misconduct. The most frequent basis for these claims is excessive use of force.

Cities tend to settle most of these suits for relatively small amounts, with a few high-visibility cases receiving larger settlements or jury verdicts after trial. The unadorned numbers show some large total payments in some cities and much smaller total payments elsewhere. For example, Detroit spent more than 8 percent of its 1993 operating budget, or $27.5 million, on police misconduct damages.

San Francisco paid less than $2 million between 1990 and 1994 to alleged victims of police brutality. Of 31 cases contested in court, city attorneys won all but two, and the city paid $234,600 to the two successful plaintiffs. The city settled 25 cases out of court for $1.54 million, usually in amounts of $10,000 to $20,000. See Dennis Opatrny, Little Danger of Sudden Wealth in Suing the SFPD, City Fights Claims for Misconduct Hard, Rarely Pays Much, San Francisco Examiner, June 11, 1995. Would you devote a major portion of your private practice to representing such clients? What would you need to know before concluding that such a practice would be financially viable?

The news accounts of settlements raise the classic tort question whether civil suits have any impact on police practices. In Pittsburgh, annual civil judgments and settlements exceeding $1 million between 1990 and 1996 convinced the city council to create a citizen police-review board. Many of the settlements, however, include a provision keeping the settlement terms secret. The settlements are often paid from the city's general budget rather than the police department budget, and the officer whose conduct led to the lawsuit is not routinely disciplined as a result of the city's financial loss. Despite these limits, does the amount of money that cities pay to tort plaintiffs each year suggest that civil liability is working reasonably well? Joanna C. Schwartz, Myths and Mechanics of Deterrence: The Role of Lawsuits in Law Enforcement Decisionmaking, 57 UCLA L. Rev. 1023 (2010) (finding that officials rarely have probative information about suits alleging misconduct by their officers). The web extension for this chapter, at *http://www.crimpro.com/extension/ch06*, surveys evidence from a variety of sources about the prevalence and effects of tort suits against police officers.

3. *Qualified good faith immunity for individuals.* The legal barriers to tort claims are very high. State and federal courts have created protections known as a "qualified good faith immunity" or "official immunity" for police officers sued in tort for the illegal acts they commit during the course of their employment. The immunity is "qualified" because an officer loses it when she subjectively knows that she is violating the rights of the victim, or when she objectively should know that she is violating those rights. Does the doctrine of qualified immunity mean that damages will be unavailable in all cases where *Leon* would create a good faith exception to the exclusionary rule? Does it leave plaintiffs without a remedy? See Malley v. Briggs, 475 U.S. 335 (1986) (officer's good faith immunity from tort liability for improper warranted search is same scope as *Leon* good faith exception to exclusionary rule); Hope v. Pelzer, 536 U.S. 730 (2002) (new factual situations calling for new application earlier legal principles could nonetheless violate "clearly established" rights); Pearson v. Callahan, 129 S. Ct. 808 (2009) (judges considering qualified immunity do not face an inflexible requirement to start with question of whether violation occurred, but may begin by asking whether alleged right was clearly established at the time). Practice problems that allow you to apply qualified immunity doctrine in various contexts appear on the web extension of this chapter.

From the standpoint of the plaintiff Maimaron, how sensible are barriers to claims such as qualified immunity? How understandable is the distinction between "acting under color of state law," and acting "outside of" the police officer's authority?

4. *Sovereign immunity and waiver.* Often the victim of an improper search or seizure will prefer to sue the state or local government rather than the judgment-proof individual officer who violated the law. Under traditional common law

principles, such a suit is not possible under state law because of the doctrine of "sovereign immunity," which insulates the government from any monetary claims. Most states have passed statutes that partially waive their sovereign immunity, so they will pay for some wrongdoing committed by state employees (on a respondeat superior basis). Under these tort claims acts, the lawsuit against the state or local government usually becomes the only cause of action for the wrongdoing; the plaintiff can no longer sue the individual employee. However, almost all of these statutes contain exceptions. For instance, most provide that the state or local government will not be liable for "discretionary" actions of officials. Some also exempt any action by officials engaged in the "enforcement" of any law or judicial order. See S.C. Code §15-78-60. Section 1983 does not create respondeat superior liability for state or local government. A plaintiff can sue a local government based on the actions of its police officers only if the officer was acting pursuant to a "policy" or "practice" endorsed by the government.

Beyond the perspective of individual claimants, a more general issue for remedies other than suppression is whether the substantive and procedural barriers to relief make tort claims a plausible and functional alternative. The materials in this chapter only hint at the complexity of Section 1983 and state civil rights and tort claims. That legal complexity is analogous to the complexity involving claims for post-conviction judicial relief, such as claims in habeas corpus. Entire books and law school courses — and entire legal practices — can be built around specialization in these areas. See, e.g., Joseph Cook & John Sobieski, Civil Rights Actions (seven-volume treatise); Sheldon Nahmod, Civil Rights and Civil Liberties Litigation: The Law of Section 1983 (three-volume treatise).

5. *Costs and indemnity for judgments.* Almost all states have statutes that allow the state or local government to pay for the police officer's legal representation so long as the officer was acting within the scope of authority. Many states go further, allowing the state or local government to indemnify the officer for the amount of any judgment paid to the plaintiff. Many states do have statutes authorizing indemnification. See, e.g., Ky. Code §16.185. Do such statutes compromise the power of tort suits to deter officers from making improper searches and seizures? Some states also have statutes authorizing the trial court to order a losing plaintiff to pay the attorney's fees and costs of the defendants if the suit was not substantially justified. See, e.g., Md. State Govt. Code §12-309. In light of the holding of the Massachusetts court in *Maimaron*, would you recommend any amendments to the state laws on indemnity for officers?

6. *Limitations on equitable relief.* Sometimes plaintiffs want injunctive relief rather than, or in addition to, money damages. Although injunctions are now considered a legitimate response to some search and seizure violations, they are still not as widely used as exclusion or damages. When relief is sought in federal court for actions of state actors, federal courts may be reluctant to order or affirm injunctive relief on federalism grounds. Another limitation on the availability of injunctions is the standing doctrine. Who has standing to challenge a police policy or practice? When a plaintiff seeks injunctive relief rather than damages, the Supreme Court has held that the plaintiff must show a likelihood of future harm. In City of Los Angeles v. Lyons, 461 U.S. 95 (1983), a plaintiff who was challenging the use of "chokeholds" by the police department had no standing to obtain injunctive or declaratory relief (as opposed to damages). Although the police had used the chokehold on Adolph Lyons in a situation where the officers faced no threat of injury,

Lyons could not demonstrate a "substantial likelihood" that he personally would be choked again in the future. Is this standing limitation applicable mostly to use of force policies?

State courts may not be constrained by similarly strict standing doctrines, and the federalism concerns will not be present. Is an injunction inherently more intrusive than damage awards or exclusion of evidence in criminal proceedings? Should it be reserved for certain types of violations by law enforcement officials? Keep in mind that an injunction gives a court continuing jurisdiction over the controversy; the court can impose contempt sanctions on any defendant violating the terms of an injunction.

7. *Who benefits from a damages remedy?* Unlike the exclusion remedy, a tort suit can benefit victims of illegal searches and seizures who commit no crime or who are not charged with a crime. This feature of tort suits could make them a better remedy for those injured in the past; does it affect the relative ability of these remedies to prevent future violations? Think about the connection between remedies and rights. If tort suits were the primary method for enforcing the Fourth Amendment, would courts see different types of parties raising these claims? Would the scope of privacy rights change if the remedy were to change?

8. *Federal involvement in police review.* Over the past several years, the U.S. Department of Justice (DOJ) has entered into a series of consent decrees with local and state police departments around the country, focusing on issues such as racial bias in stops, use of deadly force, and mistreatment of citizens. Under 42 U.S.C. §14141, known as the "Police Misconduct Provision," the Department can sue in federal court to prohibit state and local governments from engaging in "a pattern or practice of conduct by law enforcement officials" that deprives persons of "rights, privileges, or immunities secured or protected by the Constitution or laws of the United States." Since 1994, DOJ has investigated dozens of matters under the authority of 14141, and entered several settlements, including the consent decree in Los Angeles. Other consent decrees or "memoranda of understanding" resolved federal lawsuits against Pittsburgh, Cincinnati, the state of New Jersey, Montgomery County (Maryland), and the District of Columbia (see *http://www.usdoj.gov/crt/split/*). Does the Los Angeles consent decree suggest the promise of this new avenue for structural reform? The Los Angeles Consent Decree requires a lot of data, recordkeeping, and monitoring. Can you access this information?

9. *Criminal charges.* It is possible for a prosecutor to file criminal charges against an officer who conducts an illegal search or seizure, either under general criminal statutes (such as false imprisonment or trespass) or under statutes expressly covering police violations of civil rights. See 18 U.S.C. §§241, 242. U.S. Attorneys have to get central DOJ clearance to bring criminal charges against a police officer. Does the potential for criminal charges help prevent illegal searches and seizures? Would these criminal statutes become more effective if they were amended to compel prosecutors to file charges whenever there is probable cause? Local prosecutors are charged with the duty of prosecuting crimes, whether they are committed by citizens or officers. But do prosecutors aggressively prosecute police officers, with whom they work on a daily basis?

Problem 6-6. Legislative Remedies

You work as an adviser to a state senator who wants to limit or abolish the exclusionary rule and to replace it with a genuinely effective, alternative set of tort remedies. Draft a statute creating, to the extent possible, effective remedies for illegal searches and seizures. The remedies can include tort damages, injunctions, and police department training requirements and promotion rules, among other options. The senator has always valued your candid opinion. When you submit this proposal to her, will you recommend that the array of new remedies replace the exclusionary rule?

VII

Technology and Privacy

There was of course no way of knowing whether you were being watched at any given moment. . . . It was even conceivable that they watched everybody all the time. . . . You had to live — did live, from habit that became instinct — in the assumption that every sound you made was overheard, and . . . every moment scrutinized.

George Orwell, *1984*

The cases, statutes, and executive branch policies we have examined thus far have revealed social forces at work, shaping the basic rules constraining searches and seizures. At times and in places where protection of privacy or individual liberty are paramount or where the police are perceived skeptically, the rules of criminal procedure tend to be more restrictive. Where crime control takes the upper hand or where the police are perceived as largely benign, police are given greater power and discretion.

The collective attitudes that influence criminal procedures are constantly shifting. One force that can change attitudes is technology, which alters the ability both to conceal and to detect information. In this chapter, we consider how typical rules governing searches and seizures change when the government uses various technologies to enhance its powers to collect information that no human sense could otherwise detect.

A. ENHANCEMENT OF THE SENSES

New technologies allow searches of vast databases or observation of daily activities such as how people drive and what they say on the phone or online. These technologies raise new questions about the limits on state power and the right to privacy. You should consider not only whether the limits on today's devices (such as wiretaps and infrared) have been resolved wisely but also whether there is a solid foundation of principle and practice that can resolve questions about the flood of new observation and search technologies on the horizon.

Under the widely adopted test in Katz v. United States, 389 U.S. 347 (1967), a "search" subject to constitutional limitations takes place when the government intrudes into a person's "reasonable expectation of privacy." Applying this test, when a government agent sees something in plain view, there is no "search" that is subject to constitutional limits. See Chapter 2, section C. But can the same be said of an item that an officer sees (or smells or hears) with the aid of some device that offers a clearer or closer view or a louder sound or a stronger smell? Since the *Katz* standard first appeared in 1967, federal and state courts have wrestled with a variety of investigative technologies, often on a technology-by-technology basis. Consider whether either of the following two cases provides a useful framework for assessing high technology searches in other contexts.

■ CHARLES KATZ v. UNITED STATES
389 U.S. 347 (1967)

STEWART, J.*

The petitioner was convicted [of] transmitting wagering information by telephone from Los Angeles to Miami and Boston, in violation of a federal statute. At trial the Government was permitted, over the petitioner's objection, to introduce evidence of the petitioner's end of telephone conversations, overheard by FBI agents who had attached an electronic listening and recording device to the outside of the public telephone booth from which he had placed his calls. In affirming his conviction, the Court of Appeals rejected the contention that the recordings had been obtained in violation of the Fourth Amendment, because "there was no physical entrance into the area occupied by [the petitioner]."

[The] parties have attached great significance to the characterization of the telephone booth from which the petitioner placed his calls. The petitioner has strenuously argued that the booth was a "constitutionally protected area." The Government has maintained with equal vigor that it was not. But this effort to decide whether or not a given "area," viewed in the abstract, is "constitutionally protected" deflects attention from the problem presented by this case. For the Fourth Amendment protects people, not places. What a person knowingly exposes to the public, even in his own home or office, is not a subject of Fourth Amendment protection. But what he seeks to preserve as private, even in an area accessible to the public, may be constitutionally protected. . . .

No less than an individual in a business office, in a friend's apartment, or in a taxicab, a person in a telephone booth may rely upon the protection of the Fourth Amendment. One who occupies it, shuts the door behind him, and pays the toll that permits him to place a call is surely entitled to assume that the words he utters into

* [Chief Justice Warren and Justices Brennan, Douglas, Fortas, Harlan, and White joined in this opinion. — EDS.]

the mouthpiece will not be broadcast to the world. To read the Constitution more narrowly is to ignore the vital role that the public telephone has come to play in private communication.

The Government contends, however, that the activities of its agents in this case should not be tested by Fourth Amendment requirements, for the surveillance technique they employed involved no physical penetration of the telephone booth from which the petitioner placed his calls. It is true that the absence of such penetration was at one time thought to foreclose further Fourth Amendment inquiry, Olmstead v. United States, 277 U.S. 438 (1928), for that Amendment was thought to limit only searches and seizures of tangible property. But the premise that property interests control the right of the Government to search and seize has been discredited. Thus, although a closely divided Court supposed in *Olmstead* that surveillance without any trespass and without the seizure of any material object fell outside the ambit of the Constitution, we have since departed from the narrow view on which that decision rested. Indeed, we have expressly held that the Fourth Amendment governs not only the seizure of tangible items, but extends as well to the recording of oral statements, overheard without any technical trespass under local property law. Silverman v. United States, 365 U.S. 505 (1961). Once this much is acknowledged, and once it is recognized that the Fourth Amendment protects people — and not simply "areas" — against unreasonable searches and seizures, it becomes clear that the reach of that Amendment cannot turn upon the presence or absence of a physical intrusion into any given enclosure.

[The] Government's position is that its agents acted in an entirely defensible manner: They did not begin their electronic surveillance until investigation of the petitioner's activities had established a strong probability that he was using the telephone in question to transmit gambling information to persons in other States, in violation of federal law. Moreover, the surveillance was limited, both in scope and in duration, to the specific purpose of establishing the contents of the petitioner's unlawful telephonic communications. The agents confined their surveillance to the brief periods during which he used the telephone booth,[14] and they took great care to overhear only the conversations of the petitioner himself. . . .

The Government urges that, because its agents . . . did no more here than they might properly have done with prior judicial sanction, we should retroactively validate their conduct. That we cannot do. It is apparent that the agents in this case acted with restraint. Yet the inescapable fact is that this restraint was imposed by the agents themselves, not by a judicial officer. . . . Over and again this Court has emphasized that the mandate of the Fourth Amendment requires adherence to judicial processes, and that searches conducted outside the judicial process, without prior approval by judge or magistrate, are per se unreasonable under the Fourth Amendment — subject only to a few specifically established and well-delineated exceptions. . . . These considerations do not vanish when the search in question is

14. Based upon their previous visual observations of the petitioner, the agents correctly predicted that he would use the telephone booth for several minutes at approximately the same time each morning. The petitioner was subjected to electronic surveillance only during this predetermined period. Six recordings, averaging some three minutes each, were obtained and admitted in evidence. They preserved the petitioner's end of conversations concerning the placing of bets and the receipt of wagering information.

transferred from the setting of a home, an office, or a hotel room to that of a telephone booth. Wherever a man may be, he is entitled to know that he will remain free from unreasonable searches and seizures. . . . It is so ordered.

HARLAN, J., concurring.

[As] the Court's opinion states, "the Fourth Amendment protects people, not places." The question, however, is what protection it affords to those people. Generally, as here, the answer to that question requires reference to a "place." My understanding of the rule that has emerged from prior decisions is that there is a twofold requirement, first that a person have exhibited an actual (subjective) expectation of privacy and, second, that the expectation be one that society is prepared to recognize as "reasonable." Thus a man's home is, for most purposes, a place where he expects privacy, but objects, activities, or statements that he exposes to the "plain view" of outsiders are not "protected" because no intention to keep them to himself has been exhibited. On the other hand, conversations in the open would not be protected against being overheard, for the expectation of privacy under the circumstances would be unreasonable. . . .

BLACK, J., dissenting.

[The Fourth Amendment's] first clause protects "persons, houses, papers, and effects, against unreasonable searches and seizures. . . ." These words connote the idea of tangible things with size, form, and weight, things capable of being searched, seized, or both. The second clause of the Amendment still further establishes its Framers' purpose to limit its protection to tangible things by providing that no warrants shall issue but those "particularly describing the place to be searched, and the persons or things to be seized." A conversation overheard by eavesdropping, whether by plain snooping or wiretapping, is not tangible and, under the normally accepted meanings of the words, can neither be searched nor seized. . . . Yet the Court's interpretation would have the Amendment apply to overhearing future conversations which by their very nature are nonexistent until they take place. . . .

Tapping telephone wires, of course, was an unknown possibility at the time the Fourth Amendment was adopted. But eavesdropping (and wiretapping is nothing more than eavesdropping by telephone) was . . . an ancient practice which at common law was condemned as a nuisance. In those days the eavesdropper listened by naked ear under the eaves of houses or their windows, or beyond their walls seeking out private discourse. There can be no doubt that the Framers were aware of this practice, and if they had desired to outlaw or restrict the use of evidence obtained by eavesdropping, I believe that they would have used the appropriate language to do so in the Fourth Amendment. They certainly would not have left such a task to the ingenuity of language-stretching judges. . . .

Since I see no way in which the words of the Fourth Amendment can be construed to apply to eavesdropping, that closes the matter for me. In interpreting the Bill of Rights, I willingly go as far as a liberal construction of the language takes me, but I simply cannot in good conscience give a meaning to words which they have never before been thought to have and which they certainly do not have in common ordinary usage. I will not distort the words of the Amendment in order to "keep the Constitution up to date" or "to bring it into harmony with the times." . . .

With this decision the Court has completed, I hope, its rewriting of the Fourth Amendment, which started only recently when the Court began referring incessantly to the Fourth Amendment not so much as a law against unreasonable searches and seizures as one to protect an individual's privacy. . . . Few things happen to an individual that do not affect his privacy in one way or another. . . .

■ DANNY LEE KYLLO v. UNITED STATES
533 U.S. 27 (2001)

SCALIA, J.*

This case presents the question whether the use of a thermal-imaging device aimed at a private home from a public street to detect relative amounts of heat within the home constitutes a "search" within the meaning of the Fourth Amendment.

I.

In 1991 Agent William Elliott of the United States Department of the Interior came to suspect that marijuana was being grown in the home belonging to petitioner Danny Kyllo, part of a triplex on Rhododendron Drive in Florence, Oregon. Indoor marijuana growth typically requires high-intensity lamps. In order to determine whether an amount of heat was emanating from petitioner's home consistent with the use of such lamps, at 3:20 A.M. on January 16, 1992, Agent Elliott and Dan Haas used an Agema Thermovision 210 thermal imager to scan the triplex. Thermal imagers detect infrared radiation, which virtually all objects emit but which is not visible to the naked eye. The imager converts radiation into images based on relative warmth — black is cool, white is hot, shades of gray connote relative differences; in that respect, it operates somewhat like a video camera showing heat images. The scan of Kyllo's home took only a few minutes and was performed from the passenger seat of Agent Elliott's vehicle across the street from the front of the house and also from the street in back of the house. The scan showed that the roof over the garage and a side wall of petitioner's home were relatively hot compared to the rest of the home and substantially warmer than neighboring homes in the triplex. Agent Elliott concluded that petitioner was using halide lights to grow marijuana in his house, which indeed he was. Based on tips from informants, utility bills, and the thermal imaging, a Federal Magistrate Judge issued a warrant authorizing a search of petitioner's home, and the agents found an indoor growing operation involving more than 100 plants. Petitioner was indicted on one count of manufacturing marijuana. . . . He unsuccessfully moved to suppress the evidence seized from his home and then entered a conditional guilty plea.

[The] District Court found that the Agema 210 "is a non-intrusive device which emits no rays or beams and shows a crude visual image of the heat being radiated from the outside of the house"; it "did not show any people or activity within the walls of the structure"; "the device used cannot penetrate walls or windows to reveal conversations or human activities"; and "no intimate details of the home were observed." Based on these findings, the District Court upheld the validity of the warrant that relied in part upon the thermal imaging. . . .

* [Justices Souter, Thomas, Ginsburg, and Breyer joined in this opinion. — EDS.]

II.

. . . At the very core of the Fourth Amendment stands the right of a man to retreat into his own home and there be free from unreasonable governmental intrusion. With few exceptions, the question whether a warrantless search of a home is reasonable and hence constitutional must be answered no.

On the other hand, the antecedent question of whether or not a Fourth Amendment "search" has occurred is not so simple under our precedent. The permissibility of ordinary visual surveillance of a home used to be clear because, well into the 20th century, our Fourth Amendment jurisprudence was tied to common-law trespass. See, e.g., Olmstead v. United States, 277 U.S. 438 (1928). Visual surveillance was unquestionably lawful because "the eye cannot by the laws of England be guilty of a trespass." Boyd v. United States, 116 U.S. 616 (1886) (quoting Entick v. Carrington, (K.B. 1765)). We have since decoupled violation of a person's Fourth Amendment rights from trespassory violation of his property, but the lawfulness of warrantless visual surveillance of a home has still been preserved. As we observed in California v. Ciraolo, 476 U.S. 207 (1986), "the Fourth Amendment protection of the home has never been extended to require law enforcement officers to shield their eyes when passing by a home on public thoroughfares."

One might think that the . . . validating rationale would be that examining the portion of a house that is in plain public view, while it is a "search" despite the absence of trespass, is not an "unreasonable" one under the Fourth Amendment. But in fact we have held that visual observation is no "search" at all — perhaps in order to preserve somewhat more intact our doctrine that warrantless searches are presumptively unconstitutional. In assessing when a search is not a search, we have applied somewhat in reverse the principle first enunciated in Katz v. United States, 389 U.S. 347 (1967). [Under *Katz,*] a Fourth Amendment search occurs when the government violates a subjective expectation of privacy that society recognizes as reasonable. We have subsequently applied this principle to hold that a Fourth Amendment search does *not* occur — even when the explicitly protected location of a *house* is concerned — unless the individual manifested a subjective expectation of privacy in the object of the challenged search, and society is willing to recognize that expectation as reasonable. . . .

The present case involves officers on a public street engaged in more than naked-eye surveillance of a home. We have previously reserved judgment as to how much technological enhancement of ordinary perception from such a vantage point, if any, is too much. While we upheld enhanced aerial photography of an industrial complex in Dow Chemical v. United States, 476 U.S. 227 (1986), we noted that we found "it important that this is *not* an area immediately adjacent to a private home, where privacy expectations are most heightened."

III.

It would be foolish to contend that the degree of privacy secured to citizens by the Fourth Amendment has been entirely unaffected by the advance of technology. For example . . . the technology enabling human flight has exposed to public view (and hence, we have said, to official observation) uncovered portions of the house and its curtilage that once were private. The question we confront today is what limits there are upon this power of technology to shrink the realm of guaranteed privacy.

The *Katz* test — whether the individual has an expectation of privacy that society is prepared to recognize as reasonable — has often been criticized as circular, and hence subjective and unpredictable. See Posner, The Uncertain Protection of Privacy by the Supreme Court, 1979 S. Ct. Rev. 173. While it may be difficult to refine *Katz* when the search of areas such as telephone booths, automobiles, or even the curtilage and uncovered portions of residences are at issue, in the case of the search of the interior of homes — the prototypical and hence most commonly litigated area of protected privacy — there is a ready criterion, with roots deep in the common law, of the minimal expectation of privacy that *exists*, and that is acknowledged to be *reasonable*. To withdraw protection of this minimum expectation would be to permit police technology to erode the privacy guaranteed by the Fourth Amendment. We think that obtaining by sense-enhancing technology any information regarding the interior of the home that could not otherwise have been obtained without physical intrusion into a constitutionally protected area, constitutes a search — at least where (as here) the technology in question is not in general public use. This assures preservation of that degree of privacy against government that existed when the Fourth Amendment was adopted. On the basis of this criterion, the information obtained by the thermal imager in this case was the product of a search.

The Government maintains, however, that the thermal imaging must be upheld because it detected "only heat radiating from the external surface of the house." The dissent makes this its leading point, contending that there is a fundamental difference between what it calls "off-the-wall" observations and "through-the-wall surveillance." But just as a thermal imager captures only heat emanating from a house, so also a powerful directional microphone picks up only sound emanating from a house — and a satellite capable of scanning from many miles away would pick up only visible light emanating from a house. We rejected such a mechanical interpretation of the Fourth Amendment in *Katz*, where the eavesdropping device picked up only sound waves that reached the exterior of the phone booth. Reversing that approach would leave the homeowner at the mercy of advancing technology — including imaging technology that could discern all human activity in the home. While the technology used in the present case was relatively crude, the rule we adopt must take account of more sophisticated systems that are already in use or in development.[3] . . .

The Government also contends that the thermal imaging was constitutional because it did not "detect private activities occurring in private areas." . . . In the home, [however], *all* details are intimate details, because the entire area is held safe from prying government eyes. . . . Limiting the prohibition of thermal imaging to "intimate details" would not only be wrong in principle; it would be impractical in

3. The ability to "see" through walls and other opaque barriers is a clear, and scientifically feasible, goal of law enforcement research and development. The National Law Enforcement and Corrections Technology Center, a program within the United States Department of Justice, features on its Internet Website projects that include a "Radar-Based Through-the-Wall Surveillance System," "Handheld Ultrasound Through the Wall Surveillance," and a "Radar Flashlight" that "will enable law officers to detect individuals through interior building walls." Some devices may emit low levels of radiation that travel "through-the-wall," but others, such as more sophisticated thermal imaging devices, are entirely passive, or "off-the-wall" as the dissent puts it.

application, failing to provide a workable accommodation between the needs of law enforcement and the interests protected by the Fourth Amendment. To begin with, there is no necessary connection between the sophistication of the surveillance equipment and the "intimacy" of the details that it observes — which means that one cannot say (and the police cannot be assured) that use of the relatively crude equipment at issue here will always be lawful. The Agema Thermovision 210 might disclose, for example, at what hour each night the lady of the house takes her daily sauna and bath — a detail that many would consider "intimate"; and a much more sophisticated system might detect nothing more intimate than the fact that someone left a closet light on. We . . . would have to develop a jurisprudence specifying which home activities are "intimate" and which are not. And even when (if ever) that jurisprudence were fully developed, no police officer would be able to know *in advance* whether his through-the-wall surveillance picks up "intimate" details — and thus would be unable to know in advance whether it is constitutional. . . .

We have said that the Fourth Amendment draws "a firm line at the entrance to the house." That line, we think, must be not only firm but also bright — which requires clear specification of those methods of surveillance that require a warrant. While it is certainly possible to conclude from the videotape of the thermal imaging that occurred in this case that no "significant" compromise of the homeowner's privacy has occurred, we must take the long view, from the original meaning of the Fourth Amendment forward. . . . Where, as here, the Government uses a device that is not in general public use, to explore details of the home that would previously have been unknowable without physical intrusion, the surveillance is a "search" and is presumptively unreasonable without a warrant. Since we hold the Thermovision imaging to have been an unlawful search, it will remain for the District Court to determine whether, without the evidence it provided, the search warrant issued in this case was supported by probable cause — and if not, whether there is any other basis for supporting admission of the evidence that the search pursuant to the warrant produced. . . .

STEVENS, J., dissenting.*

There is, in my judgment, a distinction of constitutional magnitude between "through-the-wall surveillance" that gives the observer or listener direct access to information in a private area, on the one hand, and the thought processes used to draw inferences from information in the public domain, on the other hand. The Court has crafted a rule that purports to deal with direct observations of the inside of the home, but the case before us merely involves indirect deductions from "off-the-wall" surveillance, that is, observations of the exterior of the home. Those observations were made with a fairly primitive thermal imager that gathered data exposed on the outside of petitioner's home but did not invade any constitutionally protected interest in privacy. . . .

* [Chief Justice Rehnquist and Justices O'Connor and Kennedy joined in this opinion. — EDS.]

I.

. . . What a person knowingly exposes to the public, even in his own home or office, is not a subject of Fourth Amendment protection. That is the principle implicated here.

[The] ordinary use of the senses might enable a neighbor or passerby to notice the heat emanating from a building, particularly if it is vented, as was the case here. Additionally, any member of the public might notice that one part of a house is warmer than another part or a nearby building if, for example, rainwater evaporates or snow melts at different rates across its surfaces. Such use of the senses would not convert into an unreasonable search if, instead, an adjoining neighbor allowed an officer onto her property to verify her perceptions with a sensitive thermometer. Nor, in my view, does such observation become an unreasonable search if made from a distance with the aid of a device that merely discloses that the exterior of one house, or one area of the house, is much warmer than another. Nothing more occurred in this case.

Thus, the notion that heat emissions from the outside of a dwelling is a private matter [covered under] the Fourth Amendment (the text of which guarantees the right of people "to be secure *in* their . . . houses" against unreasonable searches and seizures) is not only unprecedented but also quite difficult to take seriously. Heat waves, like aromas that are generated in a kitchen, or in a laboratory or opium den, enter the public domain if and when they leave a building. A subjective expectation that they would remain private is not only implausible but also surely not one that society is prepared to recognize as reasonable. [Based] on what the thermal imager showed regarding the outside of petitioner's home, the officers concluded that petitioner was engaging in illegal activity inside the home. It would be quite absurd to characterize their thought processes as "searches." . . . For the first time in its history, the Court assumes that an inference can amount to a Fourth Amendment violation.

[Public] officials should not have to avert their senses or their equipment from detecting emissions in the public domain such as excessive heat, traces of smoke, suspicious odors, odorless gases, airborne particulates, or radioactive emissions, any of which could identify hazards to the community. In my judgment, monitoring such emissions with sense-enhancing technology, and drawing useful conclusions from such monitoring, is an entirely reasonable public service. On the other hand, the countervailing privacy interest is at best trivial. [Society will not] suffer from a rule requiring the rare homeowner who both intends to engage in uncommon activities that produce extraordinary amounts of heat, and wishes to conceal that production from outsiders, to make sure that the surrounding area is well insulated.

II.

[The contours of the] new rule are uncertain because its protection apparently dissipates as soon as the relevant technology is "in general public use." Yet how much use is general public use is not even hinted at by the Court's opinion, which makes the somewhat doubtful assumption that the thermal imager used in this case does not satisfy that criterion.[5] In any event, putting aside its lack of clarity, this criterion is somewhat perverse because it seems likely that the threat to privacy will grow, rather than recede, as the use of intrusive equipment becomes more readily available. . . .

Although the Court is properly and commendably concerned about the threats to privacy that may flow from advances in the technology available to the law enforcement profession, it has unfortunately failed to heed the tried and true counsel of judicial restraint. Instead of concentrating on the rather mundane issue that is actually presented by the case before it, the Court has endeavored to craft an all-encompassing rule for the future. It would be far wiser to give legislators an unimpeded opportunity to grapple with these emerging issues rather than to shackle them with prematurely devised constitutional constraints.

Problem 7-1. Beepers

James Karo ordered 50 gallons of ether from a government informant, Carl Muehlenweg of Graphic Photo Design. Muehlenweg told Agent Rottinger of the Drug Enforcement Administration (DEA) that Karo planned to use the ether to extract cocaine from clothing he had imported into the United States. DEA agents obtained a court order authorizing the installation and monitoring of a beeper in one of the cans of ether. With Muehlenweg's consent, agents substituted their own can containing a beeper for one of the cans in the shipment and then painted all 10 cans to give them a uniform appearance.

On September 20, agents saw Karo pick up the ether from Muehlenweg. They followed Karo to his house, using visual and beeper surveillance. At one point later that day, agents determined by using the beeper that the ether was still inside the house, but they later determined that it had been moved undetected to the house of a person named Richard Horton, where they located it by using the beeper. The next day, the beeper was no longer transmitting from Horton's house, and agents traced the beeper to a self-storage facility.

Agents detected the smell of ether coming from locker 15 and learned from the manager that Horton had rented that locker using an alias. The agents obtained consent from the manager of the facility to install a closed-circuit video camera in a locker that had a view of locker 15. On February 6, agents monitoring the video camera saw a man and a woman removing the cans from the locker and loading them onto the rear bed of Horton's pickup truck.

At about 6 P.M. on February 6, the pickup left the driveway and traveled along public highways to Taos. During the trip, the agents kept the pickup under both physical and electronic surveillance. When the truck arrived at a house in Taos rented by Horton, the agents decided not to maintain tight surveillance for fear of detection. When the truck left the Taos residence, agents determined, using the monitor, that the beeper can was still inside the house. Again on February 7, the beeper revealed that the ether can was still on the premises. At one point, agents

5. The record describes a device that numbers close to a thousand manufactured units; that has a predecessor numbering in the neighborhood of 4,000 to 5,000 units; that competes with a similar product numbering from 5,000 to 6,000 units; and that is "readily available to the public" for commercial, personal, or law enforcement purposes. . . .

noticed that the windows of the house were wide open on a cold, windy day, leading them to suspect that the ether was being used. On February 8, the agents obtained a warrant to search the Taos residence based in part on information derived through use of the beeper. DEA agents executed the warrant on February 10, and they seized cocaine and laboratory equipment.

Karo was indicted for conspiracy to possess cocaine with intent to distribute it. The trial court granted Karo's pretrial motion to suppress the evidence seized from the Taos residence on the grounds that the initial warrant to install the beeper in the ether container was invalid as an unauthorized "seizure" and that the continued tracking of the beeper as it moved among and inside various homes and the storage locker constituted an unauthorized "search." How would you rule on appeal?

Problem 7-2. Eye in the Sky

Advances in technology are making it easier for police to use video cameras for surveillance of pedestrian areas and busy street intersections. Earlier technologies used analog videotape and were wired to monitoring locations through fiber-optic cable. New cameras use digital images that can be stored and manipulated more easily. The new cameras can be operated by radio commands and can transmit images wirelessly, saving the cost of installing cable.

Police in many jurisdictions are experimenting with video cameras posted in public places. Over two million cameras have been deployed in Great Britain, at busy intersections and in public gathering areas. Many cities in the United States have installed cameras at intersections to record the license plates of drivers who disobey traffic signals; private firms operate the cameras in exchange for a large portion of the revenues from traffic tickets issued.

In Washington, D.C., the police department now has dozens of cameras mounted in downtown areas, monitoring such sites as the White House, the National Mall, and Union Station, as well as cameras attached to police helicopters. Eventually, the system could include more than 200 cameras in stations of the Washington Metro system, another 200 cameras in public schools, and 100 more to be installed by the city traffic department at busy intersections. The first neighborhood to add camera surveillance will probably be Georgetown, a shopping district popular with tourists and college students.

The signals from the cameras all feed into a control room in police headquarters, called the Joint Operations Command Center. The center has 40 video stations angled around a wall of floor-to-ceiling screens. The cameras are programmed to scan public areas automatically, and officers can assume manual control if they see something they want to examine more closely. Eventually, the system could include "biometric" software that will permit an automated match between a face in the crowd and a computerized photo of a suspect. Compare Jess Bravin, "D.C. Cops Build Surveillance Network; New System Will Link Hundreds of Public Cameras," Wall St. Journal, Feb. 13, 2002.

If you were asked to testify before a state legislature about the legal implications of camera surveillance, what would you say? Does the sheer number of existing cameras make it easier or harder to justify further additions to the surveillance area? Would it change your argument if you could demonstrate to the legislature that cameras at traffic intersections cause as many auto collisions as they prevent, because more drivers stop abruptly when a light turns yellow, resulting in more collisions from behind? It has become clear that traffic cameras generate large revenues, both for the local government installing the cameras and the private contractor operating the cameras. Would a profit motive routinely affect the placement or use of the cameras?

Notes

1. *Thermal imaging: majority position.* State and federal law enforcement authorities started using thermal imaging — also commonly referred to as forward-looking infrared radar or "FLIR" — in the late 1980s. Federal circuit courts mostly upheld the constitutionality of thermal imaging without a warrant, analogizing the examination of the heat emitted from the house to examination of garbage left at the curb, and to the molecules sniffed by a dog during the warrantless external examination of a bag, approved by the Supreme Court in United States v. Place, 462 U.S. 696 (1983). In contrast, three of the four state supreme courts that addressed the constitutionality of thermal imaging deemed it unconstitutional. See Commonwealth v. Gindlesperger, 743 A.2d 898 (Pa. 1999); State v. Young, 867 P.2d 593 (Wash. 1994) (based on state constitution). In *Kyllo,* decided 10 years after the first of the thermal imaging cases appeared in federal courts, the Supreme Court held that thermal imaging of a home is a search under the Fourth Amendment. The decision surprised many observers, who saw many doctrinal avenues in the court's existing doctrine for the court to find that thermal imaging was a not a search at all.

2. *New doctrine for new technology?* Both the majority and dissent in *Kyllo* recognize that the *Katz* test, based on individual and societal expectations of privacy, created an inherent tension with new technologies for observation and investigation. First, as a technology becomes widespread it might become unreasonable for an individual to hold a subjective expectation of privacy. If humans develop Superman's X-ray vision, we will all subjectively need to recognize that our walls (and perhaps our clothes) no longer create a barrier to observation. Second, as technology becomes more widespread, members of society might be less and less willing to recognize individual subjective preferences as reasonable. Is either element of the *Katz* test modified by *Kyllo*, or does the court simply apply *Katz* to find that thermal imaging is a search? Does *Kyllo* provide a doctrinal framework that will help courts, legislatures, and executive agencies to resolve questions about the use of other search technologies in the future?

3. *Technology in general use*. The majority in *Kyllo* limited its holding to devices that are "not in general public use." Will this limitation pose the same kind of continual erosion as the original "expectation" doctrine of *Katz*, since technology often becomes cheaper and more widespread over time? Consider, for example, satellite imaging. Commercial satellite cameras supplement the government's spy satellite cameras, and they monitor domestic as well as foreign sites. Given enough commercial and spy satellites, intelligence and law enforcement agencies could realistically achieve constant surveillance of the entire planet. Combine this network of satellite cameras with the street-level cameras discussed in Problem 7-2, and it becomes possible to record much of daily living — particularly urban living — on

camera. Do you expect the law that governs satellites to change as the presence of the cameras becomes more ubiquitous and access to the images grows? For a flavor of the active news media coverage of surveillance cameras for law enforcement, see the web extension for this chapter at *http://www.crimpro.com/extension/ch07*.

4. *Home sweet home.* The majority in *Kyllo* finds thermal imaging inappropriate for the home, which it calls the "prototypical" area of protected privacy. Does the holding apply only to technological searches of the home? The majority also qualifies its holding by observing that the image here provided information "that would previously have been unknowable without physical intrusion." Will *Kyllo* be limited only to devices that provide information that would have required "physical intrusion"?

5. *Beepers: federal position.* In United States v. Knotts, 460 U.S. 276 (1983), the Court held that no search took place when police attached a beeper to a drum of chloroform (a chemical used for making drugs) and then followed the movements of the car using the beeper when they lost visual contact. The Court held that a person "traveling in an automobile on public thoroughfares has no reasonable expectation of privacy in his movements from one place to another." In United States v. Karo, 468 U.S. 705 (1984), the Court held that no seizure took place when the BEA planted a beeper in a drum of ether (another precursor chemical), finding that there was no "meaningful interference with an individual's possessory interests in that property." The *Karo* Court also held that there was no "search" when the drum was transferred to the defendant. However, the Court found that a search occurred when agents used the beeper to track movements within a house.

> In this case, had a DEA agent thought it useful to enter the Taos residence to verify that the ether was actually in the house and had he done so surreptitiously and without a warrant, there is little doubt that he would have engaged in an unreasonable search within the meaning of the Fourth Amendment. For purposes of the Amendment, the result is the same where, without a warrant, the Government surreptitiously employs an electronic device to obtain information that it could not have obtained by observation from outside the curtilage of the house. . . .

There have been relatively few decisions about beepers by state supreme courts since *Knotts* and *Karo*, suggesting that the use of beepers is limited. Most of the state supreme court decisions have held — contrary to the decisions in *Karo* and *Knotts* — that placing a beeper in a car or commercial object is a search. See People v. Oates, 698 P.2d 811 (Colo. 1985).

In the "beeper" cases, courts often point out that a beeper simply reveals the target's location on public highways, something the police could monitor without the special device (and without violating the Fourth Amendment) if they had enough time and resources to follow in another vehicle. Could the same argument apply to other devices now in use, such as police surveillance cameras mounted at stop signs? Does the analysis change if the observation technologies become pervasive?

A technological variation on beepers is the use of GPS to track vehicle movement and record that movement. Would the precision and detail of GPS information lead to a different analysis than for radio beepers? See State v. Jackson 76 P.3d 217 (Wash. 2003) (requiring warrant under state constitution). The vigorous state court activity on the topic of GPS technology used to track vehicle

movement receives further attention on the web extension for this chapter at *http://www.crimpro.com/extension/ch07*.

6. *Beeper statutes.* Mobile tracking devices receive more attention in statutes than in constitutional decisions. The statutes generally treat the use of beepers as a search that must be supported by reasonable suspicion, and some statutes require judicial authorization. For example, a Pennsylvania statute, 18 Pa. Cons. Stat. §5761, authorizes the use of "mobile tracking devices" only after the application for a judicial order and the demonstration of reasonable suspicion. The judicial order authorizes the use of the device only for 90 days. The statute also bars the use of a mobile tracking device to track movement within "an area protected by a reasonable expectation of privacy" unless "exigent circumstances" are present or the government has obtained a judicial order "supported by probable cause."

What explains the prevalence of statutes as opposed to case law on this question? Are statutes of this sort a basis for concluding that legislative procedure tends to create higher barriers than judicial decisions to police action? Has legislation regarding beepers created such onerous conditions that authorities now rarely use the device?

7. *An area ripe for statutory precision?* Do questions about the use of technological enhancement of the senses require answers too precise for judges to give? Can statutes, with their greater possible detail, better limit the misuse of technology? Should police be limited, for example, to use of binoculars of a certain magnification? Statutes have become the most common method of regulating some technological search devices. These include wiretapping and pen registers, which are topics covered later in this chapter.

■ MATTHEW FITZGERALD v. STATE

864 A.2d 1006 (Md. 2004)

RAKER, J.

This case raises the issue of whether a canine sniff of an apartment door is a search under the Fourth Amendment of the United States Constitution. The United States Supreme Court and this Court have held that canine sniffs are non-searches for Fourth Amendment purposes. As the canine sniff doctrine does not depend upon the sniff's location, we shall hold that a sniff of an apartment door from a common area is a permissible non-search under the Fourth Amendment.

I.

In February 2002, an anonymous source informed Detective Leeza Grim of the Howard County Police Department Criminal Investigation Bureau, Vice and Narcotics Division, that Petitioner Fitzgerald and his girlfriend Allison Mancini lived together in an apartment at 3131 Normandy Woods Drive in Ellicott City, Howard County. The source also stated that Fitzgerald and Mancini drove a white pick-up truck and regularly sold a high quality grade marijuana called "Kind Bud." Grim's subsequent investigation confirmed that the couple lived in the building and that the car was registered to Alicia Joy Mancini, apparently Allison Mancini's relative. Grim also learned that Fitzgerald had a juvenile record of separate 1998 arrests for distribution of marijuana near a school and for three first degree burglaries.

Based on these events, Grim met with Officer Larry Brian of the Howard County Police Department's K-9 unit on March 19, 2002. Brian then visited Fitzgerald and Mancini's apartment building accompanied by Alex, Brian's certified drug detecting dog. Alex's olfactory acumen previously had precipitated numerous arrests. Brian and Alex entered the building through unlocked glass doors leading to a vestibule with a stairwell and mailboxes. Brian led Alex to scan apartment doors A, B, C, and D. Alex "alerted" at apartment A, indicating the presence of narcotics. Apartment A was Fitzgerald and Mancini's apartment. Sniffs of the other three apartments did not result in alerts. Alex repeated the sniffs with the identical outcome. Finally, on March 20, the anonymous source contacted Grim again and asserted that Fitzgerald and Mancini continued to sell "Kind Bud" marijuana.

The next day, District Court Judge JoAnn Ellinghaus-Jones issued a search and seizure warrant for Fitzgerald and Mancini's apartment based on Grim's affidavit. The warrant was executed on April 2, 2002. Grim seized substantial amounts of marijuana and other evidence of marijuana use and distribution. Fitzgerald and Mancini were arrested and charged with possession of marijuana with intent to distribute and related offenses. [The trial judge denied Fitzgerald's motion to suppress the evidence, and Fitzgerald was convicted.]

II.

We review first Fitzgerald's contention that a canine sniff of an apartment's exterior is a search under the Fourth Amendment. . . . The United States Supreme Court determined the constitutionality of a warrantless canine sniff in United States v. Place, 462 U.S. 696 (1983). In *Place*, an airline passenger raised the suspicions of law enforcement officers before takeoff. The police officers contacted Drug Enforcement Administration agents in the arrival city. As part of their investigation, the agents had a trained narcotic detection dog sniff the passenger's two pieces of luggage. The Supreme Court held that a canine sniff is not a search under the Fourth Amendment. The Court noted the limited nature of a canine sniff:

> A "canine sniff" by a well-trained narcotics detection dog, however, does not require opening the luggage. It does not expose noncontraband items that otherwise would remain hidden from public view, as does, for example, an officer's rummaging through the contents of the luggage. Thus, the manner in which information is obtained through this investigative technique is much less intrusive than a typical search. Moreover, the sniff discloses only the presence or absence of narcotics, a contraband item. [T]he information obtained is limited [and] ensures that the owner of the property is not subjected to the embarrassment and inconvenience entailed in less discriminate and more intrusive investigative methods. . . . We are aware of no other investigative procedure that is so limited both in the manner in which the information is obtained and in the content of the information revealed by the procedure. . . .

[The Maryland court cited decisions from 28 state courts holding that a canine sniff is not a Fourth Amendment search.]

In United States v. Jacobsen, 466 U.S. 109 (1984), the Supreme Court affirmed the Court's *Place* dog sniff holding. After concluding that federal agents' seizure of a white powdery substance discovered by private freight carrier employees was not unreasonable, the Court held that a chemical test to determine whether the powder was cocaine was not a search. The *Jacobsen* Court . . . based its decision on the test's narrow scope of determining whether or not the powder was cocaine; "It could tell him nothing more, not even whether the substance was sugar or talcum powder." . . .

A review of *Place* and *Jacobsen* indicates that a crucial component of the Supreme Court's holdings is the focus on the scope and nature of the sniff or test, rather than on the object sniffed, in determining whether a legitimate privacy interest exists. . . . The focus . . . is not the object sniffed, the exterior of the luggage in *Place* . . . but rather the narrow yes/no scope of the sniff. The only relevant locational determination is whether the dog was permitted outside the object sniffed.

We applied the binding precedent of *Place* and its progeny in Wilkes v. State, 774 A.2d 420 (Md. 2001). We held, based on *Place* and *Jacobsen*, that a canine scan of a car is not a search under the Fourth Amendment. . . .

Fitzgerald proposes that we differentiate sniffs of the exterior of homes from all other sniffs. . . . To support his argument, he points to United States v. Karo, 468 U.S. 705 (1984) and Kyllo v. United States, 533 U.S. 27 (2001). . . .

In *Karo*, a federal agent learned that Karo and others had ordered 50 gallons of ether from an informant and planned to use the ether to extract cocaine from imported clothing. Pursuant to a court order and the seller's consent, government agents installed a beeper in one can of ether. The agents monitored the beeper through its many travels, including sojourns in private residences. The Court held that monitoring a beeper in a private residence constitutes a Fourth Amendment search.

Fitzgerald is correct that *Karo* emphasized the expectation of privacy in private residences. . . . The Court, though, based its holding on the scope of information a beeper reveals. Comparing the beeper to the obviously impermissible case of an officer entering a private residence to verify the ether's presence, the Court noted:

> For purposes of the [Fourth] Amendment, the result is the same where, without a warrant, the Government surreptitiously employs an electronic device to obtain information that it could not have obtained by observation from outside the curtilage of the house. The beeper tells the agent that a particular article is actually located at a particular time in the private residence and is in the possession of the person or persons whose residence is being watched. . . .

The beeper's broader revelation about the interior of the house is a significant one. In *Karo*, the agents failed to notice that the ether had been moved from one residence to another. Only through using the beeper did they determine that the ether was no longer in the first house and then that the ether was in a second house.

Karo is inapposite to the case sub judice for a number of reasons. First, *Karo*'s rationale does not contradict *Place*'s rationale; the two complement each other. *Place* held that a dog sniff is unique in that it can determine only the presence or absence of contraband, while *Karo* held that a beeper's utility is too broad, because it indicates both the arrival of the ether and its continued presence. Crucial in this respect is *Karo*'s emphasis of the difference between what the government can observe outside the residence and what the beeper tells the government from its presence inside the residence. The dog, Alex in our case, occupied the same position as the government agent; he observed from the public space outside the residence. Were Alex to have entered the residence himself without a warrant, he would have conducted an unconstitutional search.

Second, the object detected in *Karo* was a can of ether. The ether itself was not contraband; it was a potential tool for extracting contraband. In *Place*, the object was contraband itself. A pivotal premise of *Place* was that the sniff "does not expose noncontraband items." . . .

Fitzgerald next cites *Kyllo* for his argument that *Place* and its progeny should not apply to the exterior of residences. In *Kyllo*, the Supreme Court . . . elaborated a "general public use" standard: "We think that obtaining by sense-enhancing technology any information regarding the interior of the home that could not otherwise have been obtained without physical intrusion into a constitutionally protected area constitutes a search — at least where (as here) the technology in question is not in general public use." Fitzgerald argues that this standard includes dog sniffs, which he classifies as "sense-enhancing technology" that is "not in general public use."

Even a perfunctory reading of *Kyllo* reveals that its standard does not apply to dog sniffs. *Kyllo* is an opinion about the need to limit "advancing technology." The *Kyllo* Court sought to draw a line to prevent the police from utilizing continuously advancing technologies to "see" more and more inside the home. . . . The Court viewed the thermal imager as particularly nefarious, even in its crude form, because of its broad potential uses. The imager's utility was not limited to ascertaining whether contraband was present. Instead, the imager could reveal "intimate" details such as "at what hour each night the lady of the house takes her daily sauna and bath."

With this review of *Kyllo*, it is clear that *Kyllo* has no bearing on dog sniffs. First, a dog is not technology — he or she is a dog. A dog is known commonly as "man's best friend." Across America, people consider dogs as members of their family. The same cannot be said of cars, blenders, or thermal imagers. . . .

Second, dogs are not "advancing technology." Even taking into account potential gains from evolution, breeding, and improved nutrition, the limits to dogs' future ability to smell are not far from the current limits. Not so with technology. Technology is constantly advancing; few who have witnessed the computer revolution doubt that technology can advance in the future beyond our wildest dreams today.

Finally, *Kyllo*'s concern with thermal imagers' scope and potential revelation of intimate private details fits neatly with *Place*'s rationale that dog sniffs are unique in their narrow yes/no determination of the presence of narcotic. A person does not have a legitimate expectation of privacy in contraband, but does in bath water. A dog that can determine contraband's existence and nothing else is not a search, even when sniffing the exterior of a home. . . .

In sum, we conclude that binding and persuasive authority compel our holding that a dog sniff of the exterior of a residence is not a search under the Fourth Amendment. To be sure, the dog and police must lawfully be present at the site of the sniff. In the present case, Brian and Alex lawfully were present, as the apartment building's common area and hallways were accessible to the public through an entrance of unlocked glass doors.

Next, we consider Fitzgerald's argument that Alex's sniff was a search because Alex was trained to alert to diazepam tablets, i.e., Valium. . . . Fitzgerald did not raise the diazepam detection issue in either the Circuit Court or the Court of Special Appeals. Consequently, under Maryland Rules of Procedure 8-131(a) and (b), the Court should not review this issue. . . .

III.

Fitzgerald argues that even if Alex's sniff is not a search under the Fourth Amendment, it is a search under Article 26 of the Maryland Declaration of Rights. . . . Fitzgerald argues that his case should be one in which Article 26 holds an action to be a violation (as an illegal search), while the Fourth Amendment permits the action (as a non-search). To support this claim, Fitzgerald argues that Article 26 was designed to protect the sanctity of the home, thus, creating stronger protection than the Fourth Amendment for sniffs outside a residence. . . .

There is no need to determine whether this is a case in which Article 26 mandates our finding an illegal search, . . . because even were we to adopt Fitzgerald's position, we would uphold the sniff's validity. [The] majority of state courts holding a dog sniff to be a search under their constitutions apply a reasonable suspicion standard. There was reasonable suspicion to support a sniff of Fitzgerald's apartment door. . . .

In Terry v. Ohio, 392 U.S. 1 (1968), the Court held that a police officer suspecting criminal activity could conduct a minimally intrusive search for weapons if the officer had a reasonable suspicion that the person was armed and dangerous. In *Place*, Justice Blackmun concurred [and] argued that there were alternative approaches the majority could have taken on dog sniffs. He wrote, . . . "a dog sniff may be a search, but a minimally intrusive one that could be justified in this situation under *Terry* upon mere reasonable suspicion."

Professor LaFave explains the advantage of Justice Blackmun's approach. He notes that narcotics detecting dogs are more likely to alert erroneously when used to sniff "wholesale," such as when a dog sniffs a large group of students in a school. Wayne R. LaFave, Search and Seizure §2.2(f) (3d ed. 1996). Justice Blackmun's reasonable suspicion approach would reduce the likelihood of errors. . . .

Of the states finding a dog sniff to be a search under their state constitutions, almost all have [applied] a reasonable suspicion standard. [The Court cited cases from Alaska, Colorado, Connecticut, Illinois, Minnesota, Montana, New Hampshire, New York, and Pennsylvania.]

The police had reasonable suspicion to conduct a canine sniff of Fitzgerald's door. An anonymous source told Detective Grim Fitzgerald and Mancini's names, their address, and a description of Mancini's truck. The source specified the exact grade of marijuana the source alleged Fitzgerald and Mancini sold on a regular basis. Detective Grim confirmed all the information except the marijuana sales themselves. Further, Detective Grim discovered that Fitzgerald had a juvenile record, including an arrest for distribution of marijuana near a school. These facts confirm that Detective Grim had reasonable suspicion to seek a canine sniff.

Accordingly, we . . . decline to determine whether the Maryland Declaration of Rights deems a dog sniff a search, because even if it did, it would require only reasonable suspicion, which was present in this case.

GREENE, J., dissenting.

. . . One implication of [the Court's] holding is that a canine sniff can never constitute a search provided that the handler and the dog are situated in a place they have a right to be. . . . A far reaching consequence of today's holding is that those who reside in apartment buildings with gated or secured entrances will be afforded greater protections under the law than those who reside in apartment buildings that are left unsecured or open to the public. Moreover, this decision may indeed constitute a logical extension of the rationale of *Place* and *Jacobsen*, resulting, however, in random canine searches in targeted neighborhoods. Because of these and other concerns, I respectfully dissent. . . .

When police intentionally use an investigative technique, in this case a dog, to detect the presence of drugs by directing the dog to a residence or person, that action constitutes a search. I cannot ignore the fact that the police went to that location to detect evidence of criminal activity. . . . For me, the Fourth Amendment draws the line at the entrance to the residence. Absent exigent circumstances, the police may not reasonably cross the threshold without a warrant. The canine sniff at the door of Fitzgerald's apartment was not a detection of something in the hallway, but rather was a detection of something inside Fitzgerald's apartment — a private dwelling.

[The] rationale of *Place* assumes that the dog sniff is accurate and that the privacy interests of those involved will not be compromised. [But mistakes made by the dog and handler sometimes result in a false positive identification of drugs.] One . . . reason dogs may alert falsely is because of the high percentage of cash that contains sufficient quantities of cocaine to trigger a response in a dog. . . . In the present case it was raised on appeal, but not developed at trial, that the dog in this case was trained also to alert on Valium.

[If] the canine sniff is a search, the Fourth Amendment applies requiring a warrant based on probable cause. If is it not a search, the Fourth Amendment is inapplicable. The proper standard, absent exigent circumstances, is a warrant supported by probable cause. . . .

Notes

1. *Are dog sniffs searches? Majority position.* As the court in *Fitzgerald* notes, in United States v. Place, 462 U.S. 696 (1983), the Supreme Court held that dog sniffs are not searches and therefore are not subject to the constraints of the Fourth Amendment. In Illinois v. Caballes, 543 U.S. 405 (2005), the Court confirmed this position, holding that a dog sniff performed on the exterior of a vehicle during a valid traffic stop requires no justification because the dog reveals only the presence or absence of contraband and does not intrude on a reasonable expectation of privacy.

The largest group of state courts read their state constitutions and statutes in a similar fashion to conclude that the use of canines to sniff items in public places does not qualify as a "search." See, e.g., State v. Morrow, 625 P.2d 898 (Ariz. 1981).

A strong minority, however, treat a canine sniff as a "search" under the state constitution. These holdings tend to appear in cases in which the dog is brought into a residence or to the front door of a home. These courts typically require the police to demonstrate reasonable suspicion — not probable cause — to carry out the canine sniff search. See People v. Devone, 931 N.E.2d 70 (N.Y. 2010) (dog sniff of automobile classified as "search" under state constitution, but the government needs only "founded suspicion," less demanding standard than reasonable suspicion, to justify dog sniff). You can sample the state court variety in dealing with canine sniffs on the web extension for this chapter at *http://www.crimpro.com/extension/ch07*.

2. *Plain view and sense enhancements: majority position.* Remember that it is no search for an officer to view objects within "plain" view when the officer is justified in being in a particular place — whether in a home during execution of a warrant or in an area based on consent or some exception to the warrant requirement. See Chapter 2, section C. Most courts draw an analogy between "plain view" and the use of familiar tools that enhance human senses of sight or hearing to provide light, or to change or magnify a view. They often ask whether the officer (or a group of officers) could have made the observation by using normal senses from a permissible location. If the answer to this question is "yes," courts often conclude that the evidence collection is not a search at all; if not, they are more inclined to consider it a search and then evaluate whether the search was reasonable.

More often than not, a court reviewing a police officer's use of sense-enhancing devices will conclude that the officer did not conduct a "search." See Dow Chemical Co. v. United States, 476 U.S. 227 (1986) (no search when government uses $22,000 aerial mapping camera during overflight of industrial plant suspected of environmental crimes). As with other aspects of search and seizure doctrine, the shift in *Katz* from a property-based conception to a privacy-based conception of the Fourth Amendment makes it more difficult for courts to reach categorical conclusions about the use of any particular technological sense-enhancement. The amount of effort a government agent expends in obtaining a "plain" view, the nature of the location observed, the place from which the observation is made, and the public familiarity with a device may all be relevant. For a sample of state court rulings on the use of sense enhancing devices such as high-powered binoculars, flashlights, starscopes, and others, consult the web extension for this chapter at *http://www.crimpro.com/extension/ch07*. Remember that even when use of a sense-enhancing device constitutes a search, a court must address further questions: It must determine what level of justification the government must have to support the search, and then it must evaluate whether the search was reasonable given those particular facts.

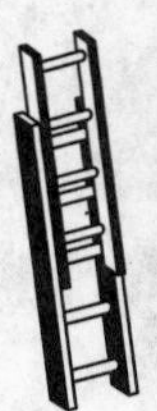

3. *Distinguishing beepers from dogs.* Beepers reveal some information that, at least in theory, would be available to an officer observing a suspect from a legal vantage point. In this sense, beepers differ from dog sniffs because the dog accomplishes what even the most diligent or discerning officer could not. But as the Supreme Court recognized in *Karo*, a beeper can also reveal information (such as the presence or movement of objects within a building) that would not be available to an observing officer at the scene. Do you agree that these different sorts of information deserve different protection under the law?

B. WIRETAPPING

Wiretapping is just one of many technologies that provide the capacity to observe or hear more than would be possible with human senses. This section considers the evolution of the procedures governing wiretapping, from judicial doctrine to statute. The first subsection looks at Olmstead v. United States, one of the earliest wiretapping cases. This case, along with Katz v. United States, invited Congress and state legislatures to occupy the wiretapping field, largely unrestricted by precedent and other limits on judicial authority. The remainder of this section highlights the recurring features of these wiretapping statutes, and reviews some difficult choices about how to extend this regulation to some specialized settings.

1. *Judicial Limits on Wiretaps*

■ ROY OLMSTEAD v. UNITED STATES

277 U.S. 438 (1928)

TAFT, C.J.*

The petitioners were convicted... of a conspiracy to violate the National Prohibition Act by unlawfully possessing, transporting and importing intoxicating liquors and maintaining nuisances, and by selling intoxicating liquors. Seventy-two others in addition to the petitioners were indicted. Some were not apprehended, some were acquitted and others pleaded guilty.

The evidence in the records discloses a conspiracy of amazing magnitude to import, possess and sell liquor unlawfully. . . . Olmstead was the leading conspirator and the general manager of the business. . . . Of the several offices in Seattle the chief one was in a large office building. In this there were three telephones on three different lines. There were telephones in an office of the manager in his own home, at the homes of his associates, and at other places in the city. . . .

The information which led to the discovery of the conspiracy and its nature and extent was largely obtained by intercepting messages on the telephones of the conspirators by four federal prohibition officers. Small wires were inserted along the ordinary telephone wires from the residences of four of the petitioners and those leading from the chief office. The insertions were made without trespass upon any property of the defendants. They were made in the basement of the large office building. The taps from house lines were made in the streets near the houses. The gathering of evidence continued for many months. . . .

The [Fourth] Amendment itself shows that the search is to be of material things — the person, the house, his papers or his effects. The description of the warrant necessary to make the proceeding lawful, is that it must specify the place to be searched and the person or things to be seized. . . . It is plainly within the words of the Amendment to say that the unlawful rifling by a government agent of a sealed letter is a search and seizure of the sender's papers or effects. The letter is a paper, an effect, and in the custody of a Government that forbids carriage except under its

* [Justices McReynolds, Sanford, Sutherland, and Van Devanter joined in this opinion. — EDS.]

protection. The United States takes no such care of telegraph or telephone messages as of mailed sealed letters. The Amendment does not forbid what was done here. There was no searching. There was no seizure. The evidence was secured by the use of the sense of hearing and that only. There was no entry of the houses or offices of the defendants.

By the invention of the telephone, 50 years ago, and its application for the purpose of extending communications, one can talk with another at a far distant place. The language of the Amendment cannot be extended and expanded to include telephone wires reaching to the whole world from the defendant's house or office. The intervening wires are not part of his house or office any more than are the highways along which they are stretched. . . .

Congress may of course protect the secrecy of telephone messages by making them, when intercepted, inadmissible in evidence in federal criminal trials, by direct legislation, and thus depart from the common law of evidence. But the courts may not adopt such a policy by attributing an enlarged and unusual meaning to the Fourth Amendment. . . .

BRANDEIS, J., dissenting.

[At least six] prohibition agents listened over the tapped wires and reported the messages taken. Their operations extended over a period of nearly five months. The typewritten record of the notes of conversations overheard occupies 775 typewritten pages. [The Government concedes] that if wire-tapping can be deemed a search and seizure within the Fourth Amendment, such wire-tapping as was practiced in the case at bar was an unreasonable search and seizure, and that the evidence thus obtained was inadmissible. . . .

When the Fourth and Fifth Amendments were adopted, [force] and violence were then the only means known to man by which a Government could directly effect self-incrimination. It could compel the individual to testify — a compulsion effected, if need be, by torture. It could secure possession of his papers and other articles incident to his private life — a seizure effected, if need be, by breaking and entry. Protection against such invasion of the sanctities of a man's home and the privacies of life was provided in the Fourth and Fifth Amendments by specific language. . . . Subtler and more far-reaching means of invading privacy have become available to the Government. Discovery and invention have made it possible for the Government, by means far more effective than stretching upon the rack, to obtain disclosure in court of what is whispered in the closet.

Moreover, in the application of a constitution, our contemplation cannot be only of what has been but of what may be. The progress of science in furnishing the Government with means of espionage is not likely to stop with wire-tapping. Ways may some day be developed by which the Government, without removing papers from secret drawers, can reproduce them in court, and by which it will be enabled to expose to a jury the most intimate occurrences of the home. Advances in the psychic and related sciences may bring means of exploring unexpressed beliefs, thoughts and emotions. . . . Can it be that the Constitution affords no protection against such invasions of individual security?

[The] tapping of one man's telephone line involves the tapping of the telephone of every other person whom he may call, or who may call him. As a means of espionage, writs of assistance and general warrants are but puny instruments of tyranny and oppression when compared with wire-tapping.

The makers of our Constitution undertook to secure conditions favorable to the pursuit of happiness. They recognized the significance of man's spiritual nature, of his feelings and of his intellect. . . . They conferred, as against the Government, the right to be let alone — the most comprehensive of rights and the right most valued by civilized men. To protect that right, every unjustifiable intrusion by the Government upon the privacy of the individual, whatever the means employed, must be deemed a violation of the Fourth Amendment. . . .

Notes

1. *Constitutional interpretation.* Recall that the Supreme Court overruled *Olmstead* in Katz v. United States, 389 U.S. 347 (1967). Despite their great difference in doctrine and bottom line, *Olmstead* and *Katz* are both splendid examples of constitutional decision making. They each raise some of the foundational issues in any difficult constitutional context: What do the words of the various provisions mean? Should interpretation be limited to the words? If not, what principles limit the power of the court from acting as a superlegislature by interpreting words? On the question of the role a court plays when interpreting the meaning of constitutional terms such as "persons," "houses," or "effects" — much less concepts such as "privacy" and "reasonableness" — consider the following exchange:

> "There's glory for you!"
>
> "I don't know what you mean by 'glory,'" Alice said.
>
> Humpty Dumpty smiled contemptuously. "Of course you don't — till I tell you. I meant there's a nice knock-down argument for you."
>
> "But 'glory' doesn't mean 'a nice knock-down argument,'" Alice objected.
>
> "When I use a word," Humpty Dumpty said in rather a scornful tone, "it means just what I choose it to mean — neither more nor less."
>
> "The question is," said Alice, "whether you can make words mean so many different things."
>
> "The question is," said Humpty Dumpty, "which is to be the master — that's all."

Lewis Carroll, Through the Looking-Glass and What Alice Found There 269 (Martin Gardner ed., 1960).

2. *Wiretap cases between* Olmstead *and* Katz. Even before *Katz*, the Supreme Court had begun to place limits on electronic eavesdropping. In Silverman v. United States, 365 U.S. 505 (1961), the Court found that the government violated the Fourth Amendment when it inserted a "spike mike" into a heating duct. Although the Court concluded that the government had committed a trespass, it emphasized that its decision did "not turn upon the technicality of a trespass upon a party wall as a matter of local law. It is based upon the reality of an actual intrusion into a constitutionally protected area."

3. *Computer searches*. During investigations of certain crimes (think, for instance, of fraud or pornography cases), investigators need to learn about the contents of personal computers. The computer search context calls for some adjustments to traditional search and seizure doctrine. Just as courts in the wiretap context eventually placed less emphasis on whether investigators carried out a physical intrusion

of a protected place, courts that regulate computer searches have placed less weight over time on the physical location where the information is stored.

When the police want access to a personal computer, they typically obtain a warrant. Should the warrant describe the nature of the storage device, or the files or data to be accessed during a later analysis of the storage device? When the government copies data, does that constitute a "search," or does the search occur only when a human being views or analyzes the data? Does the opening or analysis of the data have to occur within a reasonable time from the issuance of the warrant, or is timing relevant only to the physical seizure of the storage device? Thus far, the federal case law is decidedly more developed than the appellate decisions in the state courts. Professor Orin Kerr has explored these topics in a series of law review articles. See Kerr, Searches and Seizures in a Digital World, 119 Harv. L. Rev. 531 (2005). For a glimpse at the evolving answers that courts offer to these questions, see the web extension for this chapter at *http://www.crimpro.com/extension/ch07*.

2. *Statutory Wiretapping Procedures*

Congress took up the Supreme Court's invitation in the *Olmstead* opinion to regulate wiretapping by statute. Indeed, Congress followed the specific recommendation in Chief Justice William Howard Taft's opinion that wiretap evidence be made inadmissible in federal court. Section 605 of the Federal Communications Act of 1934 stated that no person "shall intercept any communication *and* divulge or publish" that communication to any other person, unless the sender authorizes the interception. This ban on divulging wiretap information barred the use in federal court of most intercepted telephone conversations of criminal defendants. Because Congress focused on the admissibility of the evidence and not on its collection, federal agents continued to use wiretaps in investigations. Where the evidence could be used in state prosecutions, federal agents would provide it to the state under what was known as the "silver platter" doctrine (because the federal agents could offer the tainted evidence to the state prosecutors "on a silver platter").

The 1934 statutory limits on federal law enforcement changed when the United States Congress enacted Title III of the Omnibus Crime Control and Safe Streets Act of 1968, which established procedures for authorized wiretapping. The provisions in Title III reflected not only the new constitutional emphasis on privacy in *Katz*, but the specific concerns that led the United States Supreme Court in 1967 — the same year as *Katz* — to reject New York's wiretap statute in Berger v. New York, 388 U.S. 41 (1967). The key provision in the New York statute, authorizing ex parte wiretapping orders, provided as follows:

> An ex parte order for eavesdropping . . . may be issued by any justice of the supreme court or judge of a county court . . . upon oath or affirmation of a district attorney, or of the attorney-general or of an officer above the rank of sergeant of any police department . . . , that there is reasonable ground to believe that evidence of crime may be thus obtained, and particularly describing the person or persons whose communications . . . are to be overheard or recorded and the purpose thereof, and, in the case of a telegraphic or telephonic communication, identifying the particular telephone number or telegraph line involved. . . . Any such order shall be effective for the time specified therein but not for a period of more than two months unless

> extended or renewed by the justice or judge who signed and issued the original order upon satisfying himself that such extension or renewal is in the public interest. . . .

The Court concluded that the statute violated the Fourth Amendment, 388 U.S. at 58-60:

> We believe the statute here is [unconstitutional]. First, . . . eavesdropping is authorized without requiring belief that any particular offense has been or is being committed; nor that the "property" sought, the conversations, be particularly described. The purpose of the probable-cause requirement of the Fourth Amendment . . . is thereby wholly aborted. Likewise the statute's failure to describe with particularity the conversations sought gives the officer a roving commission to "seize" any and all conversations. It is true that the statute requires the naming of "the person or persons whose communications, conversations or discussions are to be overheard or recorded. . . ." But this does no more than identify the person whose constitutionally protected area is to be invaded rather than "particularly describing" the communications, conversations, or discussions to be seized. As with general warrants this leaves too much to the discretion of the officer executing the order.
>
> Secondly, authorization of eavesdropping for a two-month period is the equivalent of a series of intrusions, searches, and seizures pursuant to a single showing of probable cause. Prompt execution is also avoided. During such a long and continuous (24 hours a day) period the conversations of any and all persons coming into the area covered by the device will be seized indiscriminately and without regard to their connection with the crime under investigation. Moreover, the statute permits, and there were authorized here, extensions of the original two-month period — presumably for two months each — on a mere showing that such extension is "in the public interest." . . .This we believe insufficient without a showing of present probable cause for the continuance of the eavesdrop. . . .
>
> Finally, the statute's procedure, necessarily because its success depends on secrecy, has no requirement for notice as do conventional warrants, nor does it overcome this defect by requiring some showing of special facts. On the contrary, it permits unconsented entry without any showing of exigent circumstances. Such a showing of exigency, in order to avoid notice, would appear more important in eavesdropping, with its inherent dangers, than that required when conventional procedures of search and seizure are utilized. Nor does the statute provide for a return on the warrant thereby leaving full discretion in the officer as to the use of seized conversations of innocent as well as guilty parties. In short, the statute's blanket grant of permission to eavesdrop is without adequate judicial supervision or protective procedures.

Before the enactment of Title III in 1968, many states (like the federal government, under the Federal Communications Act of 1934) prohibited wiretapping. After Title III, most states amended their own wiretap laws, authorizing the government to conduct wiretaps under judicial supervision. Wiretapping throughout the United States and in most other countries is now controlled by procedures specified in statutes.

Portions of Title III and selected provisions from several state statutes follow. Title III served as the model for most states. The provisions in state statutes selected for this section highlight only two sets of questions: (1) the basic coverage of the protections for electronic communications and (2) judicial administration of wiretap requests. The statutory schemes governing wiretaps are quite complex and raise many additional issues, a few of which are covered in notes.

Wiretap statutes treat government searches through electronic surveillance differently from other searches. First, the wiretap statutes decide for all cases the question debated as a matter of Fourth Amendment interpretation in *Olmstead* and *Katz:* They declare that wiretaps are searches. Second, Congress and the state legislatures have left little room for the many varieties of exigent circumstances that government agents rely on every day to conduct warrantless searches: If agents want to use wiretaps, they must seek a warrant.

The federal and state statutes do not cover every "intercepted communication." First, most statutes exclude from the wiretap warrant process conversations that are recorded with the consent of one of the parties. Second, the statutes do not apply to all kinds of communications, though the coverage of wiretap statutes has expanded well beyond traditional taps such as those seen in *Olmstead* and *Katz*. The federal wiretap statute originally applied to communications transmitted over a wire, but now it protects wire, oral, and electronic communications, as do most of the state statutes. A wire communication includes any transfer of the human voice by means of a wire, cable, or other connection between the sender and the recipient. See 18 U.S.C. §§2510(4), (18). Electronic communications include those not carried by sound waves, such as electronic mail, video teleconferences, and other data transfers. 18 U.S.C. §2510 (12). Under the federal statute, an "interception" of one of these types of communications occurs when a person uses "any electronic, mechanical, or other device" to make an "aural acquisition" of the "contents" of the communication. How well do these statutory definitions account for future technological changes in communications?

Third, the statutes may not apply to recording of conversations outside the governing jurisdiction or in another country. This question often arises when prosecutors wish to introduce conversations between a party in a different jurisdiction and a second party in the prosecutors' jurisdiction. Should a state statute control law enforcement efforts to intercept calls placed to or from another state? Between two other states? In a federal system, with many different governments intercepting communications (and regulating those interceptions), how will courts resolve conflicts among the different statutory schemes? Will law enforcement agencies convince states to engage in a "race to the bottom" in the regulation of wiretapping? The following two statutes illustrate common features of wiretap statutes.

■ 18 U.S.C. §2511

(1) Except as otherwise specifically provided in this chapter any person who —

(a) intentionally intercepts, endeavors to intercept, or procures any other person to intercept or endeavor to intercept, any wire, oral, or electronic communication; . . .

(c) intentionally discloses, or endeavors to disclose, to any other person the contents of any wire, oral, or electronic communication, knowing or having reason to know that the information was obtained through the interception of a wire, oral, or electronic communication in violation of this subsection;

(d) intentionally uses, or endeavors to use, the contents of any wire, oral, or electronic communication, knowing or having reason to know that the information was obtained through the interception of a wire, oral, or electronic communication in violation of this subsection; . . . shall be punished as provided [elsewhere in this statute] or shall be subject to suit. . . .

(2)(c) It shall not be unlawful under this chapter for a person acting under color of law to intercept a wire, oral, or electronic communication, where such person is a party to the communication or one of the parties to the communication has given prior consent to such interception.

(d) It shall not be unlawful under this chapter for a person not acting under color of law to intercept a wire, oral, or electronic communication where such person is a party to the communication or where one of the parties to the communication has given prior consent to such interception unless such communication is intercepted for the purpose of committing any criminal or tortious act in violation of the Constitution or laws of the United States or of any State.

NEW JERSEY STATUTES §2A:156A-4

It shall not be unlawful under this act for: . . .

b. Any investigative or law enforcement officer to intercept a wire, electronic or oral communication, where such officer is a party to the communication or where another officer who is a party to the communication requests or requires him to make such interception;

c. Any person acting at the direction of an investigative or law enforcement officer to intercept a wire, electronic or oral communication, where such person is a party to the communication or one of the parties to the communication has given prior consent to such interception; provided, however, that no such interception shall be made without the prior approval of the Attorney General or his designee or a county prosecutor or his designee. . . .

STATE v. ALEXANDER FOWLER

139 P.3d 342 (Wash. 2006)

MADSEN, J.

¶1 Petitioner Alexander L. Fowler was convicted by a jury of two counts of incest in the first degree, two counts of incest in the second degree, and one count of rape in the second degree, all stemming from sexual misconduct with his stepdaughter. Fowler asserts that the trial court erred by admitting into evidence recordings of two telephone conversations he had with the victim. The conversations were recorded in Oregon with the consent of and by the victim acting at the request of the Oregon police when they investigated Fowler's possible sexual misconduct. Fowler was in Washington when he spoke on the phone to the victim, and he did not consent to the recordings; the victim was in Oregon at her family home. . . .

Facts

¶3 . . . On September 16, 2002, the alleged victim, M.P., made a telephone call from Oregon to the defendant while the defendant was at a location within Washington State. The alleged victim intentionally and voluntarily recorded the conversation that took place during this phone call without informing the defendant that the recording was being made. On September 26, 2002, the alleged victim made a second call from Oregon to the defendant while the defendant was at a location within Washington State. The alleged victim again intentionally and voluntarily recorded the conversation that occurred during this phone call without informing the defendant that the recording was being made.

¶4 Both telephone calls and the recording of those calls were made by the alleged victim at the request of Detective Mike Wilson of the Oregon State Police for purposes of Detective Wilson's investigation of an alleged sexual offense by the defendant against the victim, which was alleged to have occurred within the state of Oregon. The record does not reflect why Oregon prosecutors did not bring charges against Fowler.

¶5 No Washington State law enforcement officer or other Washington State official requested or in any way encouraged the making of these calls or the recording of these calls. At the time these calls were recorded, there was no investigation ongoing in Washington concerning any alleged offense by the defendant against the alleged victim. In requesting the alleged victim to record these calls, Detective Wilson was following Oregon law, which provided that such a recording is lawful as long as one of the parties gives his or her consent to the recording.

¶6 Based on its findings of fact, the trial court made the following . . . conclusions of law. First, the trial court concluded that RCW 9.73.030 makes it unlawful to record a telephone conversation without the knowledge and consent of both parties to that conversation. Had the alleged victim's recording of her two calls to the defendant been made within the state of Washington, the trial court concluded, such recordings would have been illegal. Second, the trial court held that because the alleged victim consented to the recordings of these two calls and made the recordings while in Oregon, these recordings were lawfully made under Oregon law pursuant to Oregon Revised Statutes §165.540(1)(a). Third, . . . the trial court concluded that because the recordings by the alleged victim were made in Oregon, at the instigation of an Oregon law enforcement officer conducting a criminal investigation within Oregon concerning an offense alleged to have been committed in Oregon, and were made in full conformity with Oregon law, and because there was no request, instigation or involvement by a Washington law enforcement agency or other Washington official with regard to these recordings, the recordings are not rendered inadmissible at the trial of Fowler by the provisions of RCW 9.73.030, and would not be suppressed on that basis.

¶7 At trial, three people testified: M.P., M.P.'s mother, and Detective Wilson of the Oregon police. Fowler did not testify. The State also presented tapes of the two telephone conversations. The jury found Fowler guilty of all charges.

¶8 Fowler appealed, claiming that the trial court erred in denying his motion to suppress the two tape-recorded conversations between him and M.P. . . .

Analysis

¶10 Fowler asserts that taped telephone conversations are unlawful under RCW 9.73.030 and hence inadmissible under RCW 9.73.050. First, Fowler points to RCW 9.73.030(1)(a), which provides that it shall be unlawful for any individual (among others) to intercept or record any "private communication transmitted by telephone, telegraph, radio, or other device between two or more individuals between points within or without the state" by any device designed to record the communication without first obtaining the consent of "all the participants" in the communication. Fowler . . . argues that the fact that the conversations were recorded in Oregon (and were legally recorded in Oregon under Oregon law) is irrelevant because RCW 9.73.030(1)(a) covers telephone calls between two or more persons "within or without the state." Thus, according to Fowler, the recordings are "unlawful" under RCW 9.73.030. . . .

¶12 [The] State argues that Fowler misinterprets the phrase "between points within or without the state" contained in RCW 9.73.030(1)(a). The State claims that that phrase does not refer to the act of intercepting or recording. Rather, the phrase refers to what communications are the concern of RCW 9.73.030. The phrase establishes that "private communications transmitted by telephone, telegraph, radio, or other device" are the concern of RCW 9.73.030 whether those communications are "between points within or without the state." However, according to the State, the phrase "says nothing about what recording location" will bring the recording of communications under the criminal jurisdiction of Washington pursuant to this statute.

¶13 The State points to Kadoranian v. Bellingham Police Department, 829 P.2d 1061 (Wash. 1992), for the proposition that this court has already answered the question as to the relevance of the place of the recordings. In *Kadoranian*, a Canadian citizen sought civil damages in a Washington state court, claiming a violation of RCW 9.73.030. In that case, the Bellingham police recorded the plaintiff's telephone conversation. The call was placed from Washington to Canada, and was tape recorded in Washington with the consent of only one party, the Washington resident. The Canadian citizen first made the argument that the exceptions in the privacy act allowing police to lawfully record conversations with the consent of only one party did not apply to the Bellingham police because the call was received in Canada, not within Washington. This court disagreed, holding that the privacy act does not limit the territory in which telephone calls may be intercepted, as long as the interception occurs in Washington. "Interceptions and recordings occur where made." The court continued and held that "whether the interception of Ms. Kadoranian's conversation was lawful is thus determined according to the laws of the State of Washington, the place where the conversation was intercepted and recorded, not according to the laws of Canada [where the call was received]."

¶14 In reaching this conclusion, the court cited a number of cases which support the view that courts generally determine the validity of a telephone interception by looking to the law of the jurisdiction in which the interception — or the recording — is made. See State v. Fleming, 755 P.2d 725 (Ore. 1988) (Oregon statute requiring 1-party consent controlled the legality of the recording made in Oregon of a call to the defendant in this state from an informant located in Oregon; while the recording was not in accordance with RCW 9.73.030, it was lawful under Oregon law and was thus admissible in Oregon). . . .

¶16 . . . In this case, the two telephone calls were recorded in Oregon with the consent of one of the parties to the call. . . . While Fowler undoubtedly has an expectation of privacy as a Washington resident, he does not have an expectation of privacy related to his behavior in Oregon and the resulting criminal investigation by the Oregon police regarding his sexual misconduct with M.P. while in Oregon.

¶17 Of course, RCW 9.73.030 may be violated by a recording made outside of this state if the recording was made for use of the evidence in Washington by an agent of a Washington official or other person. RCW 9.73.030 makes it clear that it is unlawful for "any individual, partnership, corporation, association, or the state of Washington, its agencies, and political subdivisions" to intercept or record certain recordings. Moreover, RCW 9.73.060 provides that any person "who, directly or by means of a detective agency or any other agent," violates the provisions of this chapter shall be subject to legal action for damages. Thus, when read together, it is clear that these provisions encompass persons acting as "agents" on behalf of someone in Washington.

¶18 In this case, however, the . . . trial court found that no Washington State law enforcement officer or other Washington State official requested or in any way encouraged the making of these calls or the recording of these calls. Thus, because the telephone calls were lawfully recorded in Oregon and were not done at the request of, with the involvement of, or as agents of Washington law enforcement officials otherwise with the intent to use the recordings in Washington, the recordings were not unlawful under RCW 9.73.030 and accordingly are not barred by RCW 9.73.050. See also State v. Brown, 940 P.2d 546 (Wash. 1997) (recording of appellant's statements to California police while appellant was in California did not violate RCW 9.73.030 or .090(1)(b)(i) and were properly admitted in Washington state courts, statements were lawfully recorded under California law, and the California police were not acting as agents of the King County police department). . . .

Notes

1. *Consensual intercepts: majority view.* Most state wiretap statutes follow the federal lead and do not protect interceptions of communications if at least one of the parties to the communication consents to the interception. About a dozen states require the consent of both parties before a conversation maybe recorded (absent judicial authorization). See, e.g., 18 Pa. Cons. Stat. §5704(4) ("It shall not be unlawful under this chapter for [a] person to intercept a wire, electronic or oral communication, where all parties to the communication have given prior consent to such interception"). The New Jersey statute reprinted above takes the unusual position of allowing consensual interceptions only when a government agent provides the consent or directs the interception. Why did the New Jersey legislature require only executive branch review of these interceptions? Will the state attorney general or county prosecutor ever rebuff a police request to seek third-party consent to record a conversation?

2. *Statutes and federalism.* The language of the federal wiretap statute in Title III applies both to federal and state law enforcement officers. The supremacy clause in Article VI of the U.S. Constitution declares that federal legislation is "the supreme Law of the Land." Thus, federal legislation can create binding legal obligations on state law enforcement officials. But is the converse true? Can state statutes (for

instance, those regulating wiretaps more stringently than federal law) create binding obligations on federal law enforcement officers operating within the state? Does it matter whether the evidence that the federal agents collect is presented in a state or federal prosecution? See 18 U.S.C. §2516(2).

3. *Statutes and extraterritorial behavior.* The far-reaching issue in the *Fowler* case was the extraterritorial effect of the state wiretap statute. How important would a state wiretap statute be if it applied only to monitoring of calls between two people located within the state where the crime was committed? Are you satisfied that the Washington court interpreted this statute properly on this issue? Is there any constitutional limitation on the authority of a state legislature to prohibit monitoring activity occurring outside state boundaries? Would you answer questions about extraterritoriality differently if law enforcement agents of another *country* monitored a telephone call between one person in the state and another person in the foreign country and presented the evidence of a criminal violation to state officials? Consider also whether a state court might allow law enforcement agents to follow the law of a foreign jurisdiction, but insist that prosecutors within the state follow domestic law regarding wiretap evidence, such as an obligation to provide defendants with copies of the wiretap warrant. See State v. Capolongo, 647 N.E.2d 1286 (N.Y. 1995). Would the outcome change if both callers were located in the foreign country during the telephone call and discussed a crime that had occurred in the state?

4. *The statutory exclusion remedy.* If a government wiretap violates a constitutional provision, then the constitutional remedy (exclusion of the evidence) will take hold. But what if the government violates statutory limits on wiretapping that are not mandated by the constitution? The state and federal wiretap statutes almost uniformly contain their own exclusionary remedy for at least some statutory violations. See 18 U.S.C. §2515 (designating exclusion as the remedy for unlawful interceptions of wire and oral communications but not electronic communications). In United States v. Giordano, 416 U.S. 505 (1974), the Supreme Court interpreted the federal remedial statute to apply only to violations of provisions that play "a central role in the statutory scheme." How does a court determine which statutory provisions are "central" if the statute itself does not say so? Does it depend on the number of cases in which the government is likely to violate the provision? Is the intent of the investigating officer relevant? Note that the federal statute reprinted above and most state statutes also provide for civil and criminal sanctions against individuals who intentionally violate those statutes.

5. *Statutory procedure.* Congress and state legislatures have taken an active hand in criminal procedure questions. Hardly a legislative session goes by without the passage of some new statute affecting the investigation and prosecution of crime. Wiretap statutes were one of the earliest and most prominent examples of "statutory procedure": an area in which legislatures take the leading role in setting the legal limits on practices in the field.

Legislatures have considerably greater flexibility than courts to fashion procedural rules. Legislatures can, for example, create new institutions or allocate funds to support new procedures. But if legislatures have such flexibility, and are free to adopt or ignore any nonconstitutional precedents on the topic, what principles might legislatures rely on in crafting wise rules?

Are there characteristics of new technologies that make them especially strong candidates for legislative procedure? You can follow an active academic debate on this topic on the web extension for this chapter at *http://www.crimpro.com/extension/ch07*. See Orin Kerr, The Fourth Amendment and New Technologies: Constitutional Myths and the Case for Caution, 102 Mich. L. Rev. 801 (2004).

6. *Statutory interpretation in a constitutional area.* Are the principles of statutory interpretation the same for statutes with constitutional dimensions? The statutory text itself is the starting point, of course, and certain interpretive conventions, called "canons of construction," may enable the interpreter to place the language in context or resolve ambiguous language. In American courts, judges also try to apply statutory language in a manner most consistent with the perceived "purpose" of the legislation. In some jurisdictions (especially under federal law), the judge will settle on a statutory purpose by looking to the intent of the legislators who passed the statute, as embodied in specific sources such as committee reports and floor debates. Do any of these interpretive techniques change when a statute deals with a subject that has been the subject of constitutional litigation, such as the law of searches and seizures? Will courts interpreting a wiretap statute tend to be guided more by their own judicial view of prudent legal controls on government investigations, and consider themselves less obliged to carry out the expressed views of legislators who voted for the bill? In other words, does a constitutional aura around a statute increase the judiciary's interpretive powers?

7. *Cell phones and phone-like technologies.* Starting in the 1970s state and federal courts battled over whether wiretap statutes covered conversations made on cordless or cellular phones. The majority of jurisdictions refused to extend the existing statutes governing "wire" communications to wireless exchanges. Federal law now directly addresses these communications. In the Electronic Communications Privacy Act of 1986, 18 U.S.C. §2510(1), Congress protected conversations over cellular phones, and in the Communications Assistance for Law Enforcement Act, 47 U.S.C. §1001, enacted in 1994, Congress extended this protection to conversations on cordless phones. If the problem of unprotected wireless communications first appeared regularly in appellate decisions in the 1970s, and did not lead to specific statutory coverage until 1994, what does this say about the adaptability of the legal system? Do you conclude from this story that statutes are not capable of responding to changing conditions, because they are too rigid and too difficult to amend? Should legislatures address new technologies quickly, or should courts extend laws to cover them unless and until legislatures say otherwise? For example, what privacy should be recognized in voice or data communications conveyed through satellites? Does it matter whether the user knows that the communication bounces off a satellite?

Problem 7-3. Minimization

The Harford County Narcotics Task Force and Baltimore County authorities jointly investigated Carl Briscoe for suspected cocaine distribution. Along the way, the investigators began to suspect that Roland Mazzone, who lived in Baltimore County, was involved in the distribution ring. On June 19, the State's Attorney for Baltimore County filed ex parte applications with the Circuit Court to intercept and record conversations on two telephones (one at Mazzone's home, the other at his business, the Valley View Inn) from June 20 to July 20. A circuit court judge approved the applications and, on June 19, signed orders authorizing the interceptions. The orders authorized the wiretaps, and placed certain conditions on the operation of the wiretap, including a statement in the orders that the interceptions be conducted "in such a way as to minimize the interception of communications not otherwise subject to interception under Title III or the Maryland wiretap provisions."

At the time the orders were signed, the court also approved written "minimization guidelines," formulated by the State's Attorney. The guidelines included a section on privileged communications:

> Under Maryland Law, we will be concerned with privileged communications involving lawyer-client, husband-wife, priest-penitent, accountant-client and psychologist-patient relationship. Contact the above listed Assistant State's Attorneys for Baltimore County for instructions if you anticipate that you are about to monitor such a conversation and cannot affirmatively decide to minimize it completely. If it appears that the communication does discuss the commission of a designated crime itself, the privilege is breached and the whole conversation is to be monitored. If it appears that the communication might discuss the commission of a designated crime then spot monitoring shall be employed. If the communication does not involve the commission of a crime then the privilege applies absolutely and must be completely minimized as soon as the speakers identify themselves. All husband and wife communications are privileged; but discussions which involve the commission of the designated crime may be intercepted. All other communications must be minimized and spot monitoring must be employed carefully.

On July 12, after the State's Attorney filed further ex parte applications, the court issued new orders to continue the interceptions for an additional 30 days. The court approved a new set of written minimization guidelines, prepared by the State's Attorney, which stated that the minimization guidelines approved on June 19 "will also apply to the operational procedures" authorized on July 12, except for the following changes:

> Information garnered from the wiretaps conducted over Roland Mazzone's residence telephone as well as the business telephone of the Valley View Inn has identified Mazzone's wife, Elizabeth Ann, as being involved in this illegal controlled dangerous substance operation. Thus the privilege that is afforded to them under Maryland Law as husband and wife is breached during the interception of conversations that pertain to Mazzone's illegal drug activity.

During the investigation, the investigating officers learned that David Vita was Mazzone's supplier. Specifically, the officers collected evidence that on June 30, Mazzone paid Vita $14,000 and received from Vita a kilo of cocaine. Agents recorded dozens of phone calls between Roland and Elizabeth. Two provided incriminating evidence. In the first conversation, Roland called Elizabeth and she told him that he should not "come home empty-handed," meaning that he should bring some cocaine home with him. In the second conversation, Elizabeth called Roland at his business to inform him that Vita had arrived at their house.

Before trial, Mazzone moved to suppress all communications intercepted pursuant to the wiretap orders. He argued that the wiretap orders were illegal because the minimization guidelines misstated Maryland law on the marital communication privilege and therefore illegally authorized interception of privileged communications. The marital communications privilege is codified at §9-105. It provides that "one spouse is not competent to disclose any confidential communication between the spouses occurring during their marriage." As Mazzone suggests, Maryland courts have indeed interpreted the marital communications privilege to apply even when the communication furthers a crime.

As the trial judge in this case, you must rule on Mazzone's motion to suppress. Section 10-408(i) of the state wiretap law permits suppression of "any intercepted wire, oral, or electronic communication, or evidence derived therefrom" when "the interception was not made in conformity with the order of authorization."

When evaluating the validity of a wiretap order, Maryland courts distinguish between "preconditions" and "post conditions." Preconditions include the actions that investigators must take before a judge may issue an ex parte wiretap order and the inclusion of certain provisions required to be in the wiretap order. One such precondition is the requirement in §10-408(e)(3) that "every order and extension thereof shall contain a provision that the authorization to intercept . . . shall be conducted in such a way as to minimize the interception of communications not otherwise subject to interception under this subtitle." Maryland courts say that failure of a precondition requires suppression of all the evidence obtained under the wiretap.

Post conditions are the actions that must be taken after the judge issues a valid wiretap order, including compliance with the minimization mandate in the order. Imperfect compliance with a post condition does not require suppression of the evidence obtained under the wiretap order, so long as the level of compliance is "reasonable under the circumstances." Maryland case law designates the following ten factors to be considered in determining the reasonableness of minimization:

> (1) the nature and scope of the crime being investigated; (2) the sophistication of those under suspicion and their efforts to avoid surveillance through such devices as coded conversations; (3) the location and the operation of the subject telephone; (4) government expectation of the contents of the call; (5) the extent of judicial supervision; (6) the duration of the wiretap; (7) the purpose of the wiretap; (8) the length of the calls monitored; (9) the existence of a pattern of pertinent calls, which the monitoring agents could discern so as to eliminate the interception of non-pertinent calls; (10) the absence of monitoring of privileged conversations.

As the trial judge, how would you rule? Would you suppress all the wiretap evidence? Only the recorded calls between husband and wife? None of the statements? Compare State v. Mazzone, 648 A.2d 978 (Md. 1994).

Notes

1. *Minimization: majority view.* Wiretap statutes require the government to "minimize" the number of conversations "intercepted." This limitation prevents the government from listening to all conversations at a given telephone. Instead, agents must stop listening to a call if it does not fall within the coverage of the wiretap order. Reviewing courts, however, rarely invalidate a wiretap on the basis of improper minimization. In Scott v. United States, 436 U.S. 128 (1978), the Supreme Court

held that the monitoring and recording of the entirety of virtually all calls received on a tapped phone over a 30-day period was reasonable under the Fourth Amendment and was not a violation of the statute. The Court noted that the extent of the criminal activity under investigation, the extent to which the phone was used for illegal purposes, and the frequent use of ambiguous language in the conversations justified the full monitoring of every call. Admittedly, the officers knew about the "minimization" requirement contained in the statute and in the judge's order and took no steps to reduce the number of conversations they intercepted. Nevertheless, the Supreme Court decided that the relevant question was not the good faith of the officers (or the lack thereof) but the "objective" reasonableness of the scope of the interceptions. If a target suspects the government is listening to her communications, how could she take advantage of a minimization requirement in jurisdictions where it is enforced more strictly?

2. *Special showing of probable cause.* The court issuing a wiretap order under the typical statute must be convinced that probable cause exists as to several facts: (a) an individual has committed, is committing, or is about to commit a crime designated in the statute; (b) communications about that offense will be obtained through an interception; and (c) the particular facility to be monitored will be used in connection with the offense. See 18 U.S.C. §2518(3); Or. Rev. Stat. §133.724(3). How does this compare to the probable cause finding to support an ordinary search warrant?

Wiretap orders are available only to investigate crimes designated in the statute. While the federal statute includes an extensive list of federal and state crimes, some state statutes are far more selective. Most state statutes extend to violent crimes and narcotics offenses. Compare Utah Code §77-23a-8 (extensive list of crimes punishable by more than one year in prison) with Okla. Stat. tit. 13, §176.7 (murder and drug investigations). The applicant has an incentive to list as many crimes as possible to increase the scope of the permissible interceptions that may take place.

3. *Specifying the targeted person and facility.* Wiretap statutes typically require that applications specify the identity of the person whose communications are to be intercepted, "if known." See, e.g., 18 U.S.C. §2518(1)(b)(iv). Do statutory provisions such as these mean that a person specified in the application must take part in every intercepted conversation, or can the government intercept conversations at the specified facility between two people who were not specified in the application? See United States v. Kahn, 415 U.S. 143 (1974) (approving of interception of conversation between two persons not named in application, where application mentioned "others unknown").

Wiretap statutes also require the application to describe the "nature and location" of the facility from which the communication is to be intercepted. In 1986, Congress amended the federal wiretap statute to allow applications for "roving wiretaps" and "roving oral intercepts." See 18 U.S.C. §2518(11). The USA PATRIOT Act, passed soon after the terrorist attacks of September 11, 2001, expanded the authority for roving wiretaps. More than a dozen states followed suit. See, e.g., Fla. Stat. Ann. §§934.09(10), (11). Under these provisions, the government may intercept any communication of a designated individual about a suspected crime, wherever the communication takes place. The application for a roving wiretap must specify, to a greater extent than an ordinary wiretap application, the targeted individuals. It must also set out facts demonstrating that a wiretap at a specific facility would be ineffective because the target has a purpose to thwart interception by changing facilities. Is the "roving wiretap" the equivalent of a search warrant that fails to "particularly describe" the place to be searched? In 2009, no federal wiretaps were designated as roving, while only 16 state wiretaps were authorized as roving. What might explain numbers this low?

4. *Necessity requirement.* Some items included in the wiretap application are analogous to the kinds of information government agents present in typical applications for search warrants. But some of the information required for wiretaps is entirely new. One important example is the requirement in 18 U.S.C. §2518(c) that government agents describe any "other investigative procedures" that have been tried and an explanation of why those procedures failed or why they "reasonably appear" unlikely to succeed or are "likely" to be too dangerous. The provisions are designed to encourage the government to try measures other than wiretapping as the initial steps in an investigation. As the Court stated in United States v. Kahn, 415 U.S. 143 (1974), interceptions should not be permitted if "traditional investigative techniques would suffice to expose the crime." Courts often note that the "other procedures" provisions do not require the government to show that no other means would work, or that all other means have been tried and failed, but only that some reasonable effort has been made. You can find examples of state courts working in the investigative trenches of the wiretapping laws on the web extension for this chapter at *http://www.crimpro.com/extension/ch07*.

5. *Authority to apply for wiretaps.* Although any police officer can typically apply for an ordinary search warrant, a more limited group of law enforcement officials may apply for an interception order. The federal wiretap statute requires a senior Justice Department official or a United States Attorney (or a designee) to approve any application. See 18 U.S.C. §2516. The Oregon statute is typical in requiring the elected district attorney to apply for the interception order. Or. Rev. Stat. §133.724(1). Other statutes allow state-level officials (such as the attorney general) to apply for an order or to comment on the applications of others. Do these provisions successfully promote political accountability for law enforcement decisions? Does a statute create more or less protection for liberty and privacy by centralizing enforcement choices in the hands of politically accountable officials?

6. *Duration of wiretaps.* All wiretap statutes limit the total length of surveillance allowed. For example, 18 U.S.C. §2518(5) provides that wiretap orders should not authorize interceptions "for any period longer than is necessary to achieve the objective of the authorization, nor in any event longer than thirty days." The judge can grant extensions of a wiretap order if the government renews the application, again for no longer than 30 days. Some state statutes authorize shorter periods of time for surveillance. The average duration of a wiretap in 2009 was 42 days.

7. *The dilemma of placing details in the application.* The application will, in most cases, find its way to the target of the wiretap after the interceptions are complete. 18 U.S.C. §2518(8)(d). Thus, details about the investigation and its goals that are included in the application will likely be available to defense counsel at trial. Does this suggest that the applicant should include as few details as possible? On the other hand, wouldn't a wide range of specified individuals, crimes, and conversations lead to a wiretap order with a broader scope?

8. *Wiretap reports.* State and federal wiretap statutes require various types of reports from the prosecutors executing the order. First, they routinely empower the judge issuing the order to require periodic reports from the officers about the progress of the investigation. Some also require the administrative office of the judiciary or the chief prosecutor to assemble periodic statistics on the overall number of

wiretaps and to describe the characteristics of those investigations. The report goes to the legislature. See 18 U.S.C. §2519; Conn. Gen. Stat. §54-41o. If you were a legislator, which features of these investigations would you want to hear about? At the termination of the interception order, the officers must seal the tapes and records and "return" or file them immediately with the court to prevent tampering. Under certain circumstances, particularly if the target of a wiretap later faces criminal charges based on the wiretap evidence, the target must receive notice that the wiretap took place and must be told about its methods and results. If you were a defense attorney, what would you want to know about the wiretap?

9. *The frequency of wiretaps.* The Administrative Office of the U.S. Courts reports the annual number of wiretap orders issued at the request of both federal and state law enforcement officials. A single court order can involve many telephones. The annual number of wiretap orders remained fairly constant during the 1980s, but has increased since the 1990s.

1985: 784	1997: 1,186	2005: 1,773
1989: 763	2001: 1,491	2007: 2,208
1993: 976	2003: 1,442	2009: 2,376

The number of wiretap orders issued each year appears to be remarkably low, at least by comparison to the number of searches (both warranted and warrantless) that take place each year. The federal courts issue the largest number of wiretap orders, followed closely by courts in California, New York, and New Jersey. In 2009, the average cost per wiretap amounted to $52,200. The Administrative Office reported that "no [wiretap] applications were denied" in 2009. Do the multiple statutory requirements for obtaining a court order, one piled on the other, make the overall process so burdensome that government agents rarely find wiretaps worth the effort?

Looking at the number of wiretaps makes wiretapping seem like a fairly modest practical concern. Another perspective, however, is to consider the number of conversations reached by court-ordered wiretaps. According to the Department of Justice, each wiretap request approved in 2005 reached an average of 107 persons and 2,835 conversations. On average, wiretaps produced evidence of a crime in 22 percent of the conversations intercepted. Links to government reports on wiretap practices appear on the web extension for this chapter at *http://www.crimpro.com/extension/ch07*.

Connecticut requires a special showing from any applicant after the courts issue the first 35 interception orders in a given year. The applicant must show the court why any subsequent requests are based on an emergency situation that "may result in imminent peril to the public health, safety and welfare." See Conn. Gen. Stat.§54-41c(12). How do you suppose the legislature settled on the number 35? Would it be possible for judges, in the absence of a statute, to scrutinize government wiretap requests differently if the number of requests gets too large?

3. Bugs on Agents

Katz firmly established that a search occurs when a government agent plants an electronic bug in a flower vase and leaves the vase in a person's home. But what if a government agent attaches the bug to a flower, places the flower in his lapel, and then converses with a suspect? Which should be the determinative fact — that a conversation is taking place between two people (one of whom could be an agent or could choose to recount that conversation to authorities) or that electronic devices are recording the conversation?

■ STATE v. MICHAEL THADDEUS GOETZ

191 P.3d 489 (Mont. 2008)

GRAY, C.J.:

. . . ¶5 On May 19, 2004, Matt Collar, a detective with the Missouri River Drug Task Force, made contact with Suzanne Trusler, who previously had agreed to act as a confidential informant for the Task Force. Trusler informed Collar she had arranged to purchase a gram of methamphetamine from Goetz. Trusler then met with Collar and Detective Travis Swandal and allowed them to outfit her with a body wire receiving device. The detectives did not seek or obtain a search warrant authorizing use of the body wire. Collar gave Trusler $200 with which to purchase the drug. Trusler then went to Goetz's residence and purchased methamphetamine from him. The conversation between Goetz and Trusler during the drug transaction was monitored and recorded by the detectives via Trusler's body wire. Goetz was unaware of, and did not consent to, the electronic monitoring and recording of his conversation with Trusler.

¶6 The State of Montana subsequently charged Goetz by information with the offense of felony criminal distribution of dangerous drugs. . . . Goetz moved the District Court to suppress the evidence derived from the electronic monitoring and recording of the conversation on the basis that it violated his rights to privacy and to be free from unreasonable searches and seizures as guaranteed by Article II, Sections 10 and 11 of the Montana Constitution. The District Court held a hearing and subsequently denied the motion to suppress. . . .

¶7 On August 4, 2004, Collar made contact with Chrystal White, who previously had agreed to act as a confidential informant with the Task Force. White informed Collar that she had arranged to purchase 1/8 ounce of marijuana for $50 from Hamper. White met with Collar and Swandal and allowed the detectives to outfit her with a body wire receiving device. . . . White met Hamper in a parking lot and purchased marijuana from him. The drug transaction took place in White's vehicle and the conversation between White and Hamper was monitored and recorded by the detectives via White's body wire. The following day, White again contacted Collar and informed him she had arranged to purchase another 1/8 ounce of marijuana from Hamper for $50. . . . White then went to Hamper's residence and purchased marijuana from him. Again, the conversation between White and Hamper regarding the drug transaction was electronically monitored and recorded by the detectives via White's body wire. . . .

¶8 The State subsequently charged Hamper by information with two counts of felony criminal distribution of dangerous drugs. [The District Court denied Hamper's motion to suppress.]

¶10 Were the Defendants' rights under Article II, Sections 10 and 11 of the Montana Constitution violated by the warrantless electronic monitoring and recording of their one-on-one conversations with confidential informants, notwithstanding the confidential informants' consent to the monitoring? . . .

¶13 . . . The Defendants do not dispute that, pursuant to United States Supreme Court jurisprudence, warrantless electronic monitoring of face-to-face conversations, with the consent of one party to the conversation, does not constitute a search and, therefore, does not violate the Fourth Amendment. See e.g. United States v. White, 401 U.S. 745 (1971). They assert, however, that Article II, Sections 10 and 11 of the Montana Constitution afford citizens a greater right to privacy which, in turn, provides broader protection than the Fourth Amendment in situations involving searches and seizures occurring in private settings.

¶14 Article II, Section 10 of the Montana Constitution provides that the "right of individual privacy is essential to the well-being of a free society and shall not be infringed without the showing of a compelling state interest." Article II, Section 11 of the Montana Constitution provides that

> [the] people shall be secure in their persons, papers, homes and effects from unreasonable searches and seizures. No warrant to search any place, or seize any person or thing shall issue without describing the place to be searched or the person or thing to be seized, or without probable cause, supported by oath or affirmation reduced to writing.

[In] light of the constitutional right to privacy to which Montanans are entitled, we have held that the range of warrantless searches which may be lawfully conducted under the Montana Constitution is narrower than the corresponding range of searches that may be lawfully conducted pursuant to the federal Fourth Amendment. . . .

II. Analysis Under Current Montana Constitutional Search and Seizure and Right to Privacy Jurisprudence . . .

¶27 We determine whether a state action constitutes an "unreasonable" or "unlawful" search or seizure in violation of the Montana Constitution by analyzing three factors: 1) whether the person challenging the state's action has an actual subjective expectation of privacy; 2) whether society is willing to recognize that subjective expectation as objectively reasonable; and 3) the nature of the state's intrusion. The first two factors are considered in determining whether a search or seizure occurred, thus triggering the protections of Article II, Sections 10 and 11. . . . Under the third factor, we determine whether the state action complained of violated the Article II, Section 10 and 11 protections because it was not justified by a compelling state interest or was undertaken without procedural safeguards such as a properly issued search warrant or other special circumstances. . . .

A. Did the Defendants Have an Actual Subjective Expectation of Privacy? . . .

¶29 . . . What a person knowingly exposes to the public is not protected, but what an individual seeks to preserve as private, even in an area accessible to the public, may be constitutionally protected. Indeed, in Montana, . . .

> when a person takes precautions to place items behind or underneath seats, in trunks or glove boxes, or uses other methods of ensuring that those items may not be accessed

> and viewed without permission, there is no obvious reason to believe that any privacy interest with regard to those items has been surrendered simply because those items happen to be in an automobile.

State v. Elison, 14 P.3d 456 (Mont. 2000). While *Elison* involved physical items stowed within a vehicle, the same rationale applies to a conversation with another person in a vehicle which cannot be overheard by the public outside the vehicle. Thus, where a person has gone to considerable trouble to keep activities and property away from prying eyes, the person evinces a subjective expectation of privacy in those activities and that property. . . .

¶30 Here, the face-to-face conversations between the Defendants and one other individual were within the Defendants' private homes and, in Hamper's case, in the confines of a vehicle. The Defendants did not conduct their conversations where other individuals were present or physically within range to overhear the conversations. . . . We conclude the Defendants exhibited actual subjective expectations of privacy in the face-to-face conversations they held in private settings.

B. IS SOCIETY WILLING TO RECOGNIZE THE DEFENDANTS' EXPECTATIONS OF PRIVACY AS REASONABLE?

¶31 We next address whether society is willing to recognize an individual's subjective expectation that a one-on-one conversation conducted in a private setting is not being surreptitiously electronically monitored and recorded. Stated differently, does society perceive it is reasonable to expect privacy in a personal conversation held in a private setting? . . .

¶33 We have on prior occasions quoted extensively from — and discussed the debates of — the delegates to the constitutional convention with regard to the inclusion of the right to privacy in the 1972 Montana Constitution. Delegate Campbell stated that the Bill of Rights committee "felt very strongly that the people of Montana should be protected as much as possible against eavesdropping, electronic surveillance, and such type of activities. [We] found that the citizens of Montana were very suspicious of such type of activity." Delegate Dahood reported even more strongly: "It is inconceivable to any of us that there would ever exist a situation in the State of Montana where electronic surveillance could be justified. [Within] the area of the State of Montana, we cannot conceive of a situation where we could ever permit electronic surveillance." Thus, the Constitutional Convention delegates were aware of the great value Montana citizens place on the right to privacy and the clear risk to that privacy engendered by the existence and advancement of electronic technology as used by law enforcement. . . .

¶35 The express statements of the delegates to the 1972 Montana Constitutional Convention regarding the government's use of electronic surveillance against Montana's citizens provide direct support for a conclusion that society is willing to recognize as reasonable the expectation that conversations held in a private setting are not surreptitiously being electronically monitored and recorded by government agents. We are convinced that Montanans continue to cherish the privacy guaranteed them by Montana's Constitution. Thus, while we recognize that Montanans are willing to risk that a person with whom they are conversing in their home or other private setting may repeat that conversation to a third person, we are firmly persuaded that they are unwilling to accept as reasonable that the same conversation is being electronically monitored and recorded by government agents without their knowledge.

¶36 Nor should the underlying purpose or content of the conversations at issue reflect upon society's willingness to accept a subjective expectation of privacy in those conversations as reasonable. [All] of us discuss topics and use expressions with one person that we would not undertake with another and that we would never broadcast to a crowd. Few of us would ever speak freely if we knew that all our words were being captured by machines for later release before an unknown and potentially hostile audience. No one talks to a recorder as he talks to a person. . . .
It is, of course, easy to say that one engaged in an illegal activity has no right to complain if his conversations are broadcast or recorded. If, however, law enforcement officials may lawfully cause participants secretly to record and transcribe private conversations, nothing prevents monitoring of those persons not engaged in illegal activity, who have incurred displeasure, have not conformed or have espoused unpopular causes.

¶37 Based on the foregoing, we conclude each Defendant's expectation of privacy in the conversations at issue here is one society is willing to accept as reasonable. . . . Thus, we further conclude that the electronic monitoring and recording of the Defendants' in-person conversations constituted searches within the contemplation of the Article II, Sections 10 and 11 rights to privacy and to be free from unreasonable searches.

C. NATURE OF THE STATE'S INTRUSION . . .

¶39 [The] Article II, Section 10 right to privacy is not absolute, but may be infringed upon a showing of a compelling state interest to do so. Even upon the showing of a compelling state interest, however, state action which infringes upon an individual's privacy right must be closely tailored to effectuate that compelling interest. Thus, the State may not invade an individual's privacy unless the procedural safeguards attached to the right to be free from unreasonable searches and seizures are met.

¶40 . . . Where, as here, a warrantless search has been conducted, the State bears the burden of establishing that an exception to the warrant requirement justifies the search. The State advances alternative arguments in this regard and we address them in turn.

1. Consent

¶41 The State first argues that the warrantless searches at issue here were authorized by the confidential informants' consent to the monitoring and recording of the conversations. . . . The State asserts that, because the confidential informants in these cases arranged with law enforcement to wear the body wires and clearly consented to the electronic monitoring and recording of the conversations, their consents justified the warrantless searches.

¶42 . . . While we interpret Montana's Constitution to provide greater protections for individuals in the context of search and seizure issues than does the Fourth Amendment to the United States Constitution, we use some federal Fourth Amendment analysis in addressing issues under the Montana Constitution. In that regard, we observe that the Supreme Court recently refined the third-party consent exception in Georgia v. Randolph, 547 U.S. 103 (2006).

¶43 In *Randolph,* the defendant's wife contacted law enforcement regarding a domestic dispute she had with Randolph. The wife informed the officers upon their arrival that Randolph was a drug user and items of drug use were located in the house. Randolph, who was present in the house at the time, denied his wife's allegations and unequivocally refused the officers' request for his consent to search the house. The officers then obtained the wife's consent to search. During the search, the officers observed and seized evidence of drug use. Upon being charged with possession of cocaine, Randolph moved to suppress the evidence on the basis that his wife's consent, given over his express refusal to consent, rendered the searches unlawful. . . .

¶44 The United States Supreme Court . . . held that "a warrantless search of a shared dwelling for evidence over the express refusal of consent by a physically present resident cannot be justified as reasonable as to him on the basis of consent given to the police by another resident."

¶45 . . . Here, the search of conversations by means of electronic monitoring and recording, rather than the search of premises, is at issue. Each party to each conversation was physically present at the time of the search and had an interest — that is, an interest in the nature of a co-tenant in physical premises — in the conversation. Under the *Randolph* rationale . . . the confidential informants' consent to the electronic monitoring and recording of the conversations could not override any objection expressed by the Defendants. Furthermore, because both parties to the conversations were present at the time the searches were conducted, both parties must have the opportunity to object to the search. As the Supreme Court observed, law enforcement may not avoid a refusal of consent by removing a potentially objecting individual from the premises prior to requesting consent. . . .

¶46 Similarly, here, the State cannot justify a search under the consent exception as a result of the simple expedient of failing to inform the potential — and physically present — objecting party that the search is being conducted. We conclude that the warrantless searches of the conversations at issue here cannot be justified by the consent exception to the warrant requirement.

2. Particularized Suspicion Standard

¶47 Alternatively, the State contends that, if we conclude the electronic monitoring and recording of a face-to-face conversation constitutes a search, it should be subject to a particularized suspicion standard rather than the Article II, Section 11 probable cause requirement for the issuance of a search warrant. In essence, the argument is that the State's intrusion into the Defendants' privacy expectations by the electronic monitoring and recording of their conversations was minimal and, therefore, did not rise to a level of requiring probable cause.

¶48 [Throughout] this country, but especially in Montana, . . . a person's residence and his homestead are secure from unwarranted government intrusion, be it by physical or technological means. In two of the searches at issue here, the State intruded into the sanctity of the Defendants' homes for the purpose of performing those searches by technological means. We will not countenance such an intrusion under a lesser standard than probable cause.

¶49 We turn, then, to the State's argument that the particularized suspicion standard should apply to the search of the conversation between Hamper and the confidential informant which took place in the confidential informant's vehicle. . . .

¶52 [We have held that] the dog sniff of the exterior of a vehicle constituted a search, but that such a search may be justified by particularized suspicion of wrongdoing, rather than probable cause sufficient for issuance of a search warrant. State v. Tackitt, 67 P.3d 295 (Mont. 2003). Here, the State asserts that, because the electronic monitoring and recording of a conversation is even less intrusive than a dog sniff, particularized suspicion is a sufficient standard here. We disagree.

¶53 In *Tackitt,* law enforcement officers used a drug-detecting canine to sniff the exterior of the defendant's vehicle parked outside his residence and the canine alerted on the trunk of the vehicle, indicating the presence of drugs. [We] determined that, although warrantless searches generally are *per se* unreasonable, the purpose and minimally intrusive nature of such a canine sniff warranted an exception to the warrant requirement, but would "still require particularized suspicion when the area or object subject to the canine sniff is already exposed to the public." Here, however, the private face-to-face conversation in the vehicle was not exposed to the public. Consequently, we decline to adopt a particularized suspicion standard to justify the warrantless electronic monitoring and recording of a one-on-one conversation occurring in a vehicle. . . .

¶54 For the above-stated reasons, we hold that the electronic monitoring and recording of the Defendants' conversations with the confidential informants, notwithstanding the consent of the confidential informants, constituted searches subject to the warrant requirement of Article II, Section 11 of the Montana Constitution. The electronic monitoring and recording of those conversations without a warrant or the existence of an established exception to the warrant requirement violated the Defendants' rights under Article II, Sections 10 and 11. . . .

LEAPHART, J., specially concurring.

¶56 I specially concur in the court's conclusion that evidence obtained through warrantless, consensual participant recording of a conversation in a home or automobile is not admissible in court. Although the court ties its rationale to the private settings (home and automobile) involved in these cases, I would not limit a Montana citizen's reasonable expectation of conversational privacy to "private settings."

¶57 In my view, Montanans do not have to anticipate that a conversation, no matter what the setting, is being secretly recorded by agents of the state acting without benefit of a search warrant. As Justice Harlan noted in his dissent in United States v. White, 401 U.S. 745, 777 (1971), "it is one thing to subject the average citizen to the risk that participants in a conversation with him will subsequently divulge its contents to another, but quite a different matter to foist upon him the risk that unknown third parties may be simultaneously listening in." . . .

¶58 Article II, Section 11, like the Fourth Amendment, protects people not places. . . . Although an individual's expectation of privacy may be more compelling in one setting (e.g., a home) than another, that is not to say that an individual conversing in a more public setting has no expectation of privacy and must reasonably anticipate the risk of warrantless consensual monitoring. As Justice Harlan observed in *White,* warrantless consensual monitoring undermines "that confidence and sense of security in dealing with one another that is characteristic of individual relationships between citizens in a free society." A "free society" is precisely what

Article 10, Section 10, was designed to foster. This constitutional guarantee ensures that our citizens may continue to engage in private discourse, free to speak with the uninhibited spontaneity that is characteristic of our democratic society. . . .

¶61 . . . There is a theme throughout the dissent that someone who chooses to engage in discourse about criminal endeavors, has no expectation of privacy. The examples and rationales cited are all circuitous in that they assume the "risky" or illegal "nature" of the conversation in question. An officer does not know that a call is obscene or that the conversation relates to a drug sale until after the officer listens in or hears the tape of the conversation. If the officer does have prior reason to believe that an individual has already engaged in obscene calling or drug sales, then the officer has probable cause to obtain a warrant. . . .

RICE, J., dissenting. . . .

¶79 . . . The Court's error springs from an incorrect analytical approach to the issue, resulting in an unnecessarily broad and sweeping decision not predicated on the specific facts of this case. . . .

¶88 The facts of this case do not involve the exercise of "complete discretion" by police to wire someone "just to snoop" or to gather information that might be used or not used at all. The facts here do not involve situations where police did not have particularized suspicion and probable cause. Even before wiring the informants, police had probable cause to believe that both defendants had already committed the crime of criminal distribution of dangerous drugs. Authority to wire aside, the police could have *arrested* the defendants because they had already committed a crime. . . .

¶90 [The] Court issues the sweeping proposition that there is an expectation of privacy in "face-to-face conversations" held in "private settings." This conclusion, disconnected from the facts, *will even prohibit a participant in the conversation from testifying* about what the Defendant said or did, unless a warrant is first obtained. . . .

¶91 This was a commercial transaction. In each of the two cases before us, the seller, for the purpose of making a financial profit, offered and then sold a product to a buyer. But for the seller's financial motive, and the buyer's assurance of payment, these parties would not have met at all. . . .

¶92 As in the typical commercial transaction, the sellers here offered their product to members of the public — they intentionally exposed and sold their product to customers who were non-confidants. The length of each transaction is reflective of its impersonal and commercial nature as each lasted only moments — similar to other retail purchases. These meetings were not social occasions between friends or family. The exchange of product and cash was made and the parties immediately went their own way, because the only purpose of their meeting — the sale — was completed. Thus, in these transactions, the defendants first "knowingly exposed" their business by offering to sell and then exposed their product during the actual exchange to someone who was not a confidant to them.

¶93 The place of the transaction is also a relevant fact, though not necessarily determinative. Goetz invited Trusler, described by the District Court as a "mere visitor," into his home on Main Street and there conducted the brief sales transaction. Hamper met Ms. White first in a parking lot on Main Street, where he got into *her* car for the brief conversation and sale. . . .

¶94 [The] Court only considers whether there exists a reasonable expectation of privacy in "a personal conversation held in a private setting." This statement, and others in the opinion, is so broad that it would apply as readily to governmental recording of a conversation among friends or relatives socially gathered around the living room, as to the facts of this case. Indeed, who would disagree that society reasonably expects the government to not record "conversations held in a private setting" such as the confines of one's home during a family Thanksgiving dinner? I certainly would not disagree — but those are not the facts here. The expectation of privacy in a personal family dinner setting is far different than the expectation of privacy in a commercial transaction where a product is sold to a non-confidant in a brief encounter. . . .

¶96 The public and commercial nature of the criminal enterprise at issue here — the sale of illegal drugs to strangers — separates this case from other kinds of crimes, even drug-related, and further illustrates the necessity of a close factual analysis. For instance, a person joining others at a friend's house to smoke pot, though an illegal act, would have a different privacy expectation than a person who undertakes the risk of meeting with a member of the public to consummate a drug transaction. . . .

¶97 Consistent with its approach of over-generalizing, the Court attempts to summarize the statements of the delegates to the 1972 Montana Constitutional Convention in a manner which appears to provide support for its holding. . . . However, the Court considers only some of the delegates' words, and ignores other specifically applicable words altogether, thereby covering up the reality that the delegates' primary concern was over electronic surveillance and eavesdropping undertaken by the government *without the consent of any party*. [The delegates addressed the factual scenario at issue here. As Delegate Campbell put it:]

> I feel that with "oral communications" you are not excluding the legitimate law enforcement people, who, with the consent of one party, the person who is being threatened by phone calls and things like this, to act on behalf of the victim. The privacy of that individual certainly could be waived with his or her consent, and there's certainly no privacy toward the obscene caller. . . .

¶99 [The] Court appears to distinguish between the risk that a conversation will be repeated and the risk that the same conversation will be consensually electronically monitored by government agents. However, if this is the Court's distinction, it is without a constitutional difference because society would not consider a privacy interest in a non-private commercial drug transaction to be reasonable. Indeed, our constitutional convention delegates did not, and neither did some of the greatest legal minds of our time. . . . Accordingly, I would join them and conclude that no "search" took place.

¶100 However, even assuming *arguendo* that a search did occur, the Court's analysis of the "nature of the State's intrusion" again further ignores the facts of the present case and mischaracterizes the role of consent in our search and seizure jurisprudence. . . .

¶101 . . . The *Randolph* situation cannot fairly be likened to the instant case. [A] conversation, unlike a home, is not a shared space. Once the conversation commences, it becomes the individual property of each participant. Neither participant can prevent the other (absent privilege) from sharing or repeating the conversation because each has full control over it. A conversation is not the same as a dwelling space and, accordingly, consent of both conversationalists is not required in order to monitor the conversation. . . .

¶105 [There are other pertinent details about the nature of the state's intrusion here.] First and foremost, the recording did not produce any evidence beyond what the informant herself could have relayed. . . . The facts clearly distinguish the monitoring here from the "sense enhancing" technologies [that] could be used to surreptitiously monitor the heat signatures generated by activities conducted within the confines of Montanans' private homes and enclosed structures for the purpose of drawing inferences about the legality of such activities.

¶106 It could be argued that consensual monitoring enhances the senses of police because officers can hear a conversation which they otherwise could not. However, this distinction is not one of constitutional dimension, because it relates only to the *mode* by which the information is received, not the *content* of that information. Whether the informant testifies, or the officer testifies with the tape, the evidentiary potential is the same. Thus, it is clear that defendants' constitutional privacy claim really boils down to trial strategy: they do not want the daunting task of fighting against the pesky truthfulness of their very own, recorded words. . . .

¶108 [What is the likely impact of this intrusion] on the individual's sense of security? . . . As Goetz stated while selling drugs to Trusler: "[The] real deal is with this sh__, they are all over. The Feds are f___ing everywhere in this town. The DTF, the FBI, there's reason to be superultra-f___ing-freaked!"

¶109 [The] impact of consensual monitoring upon the "sense of security" of people commercially marketing illegal drugs to the public in an environment of active law enforcement is, respectfully, *very* minimal. This activity is a highly risky venture, and, indeed, one engaging in it truly has good reason to be "freaked" because, consistent with Goetz's knowledge of the risk, law enforcement is engaged. . . .

¶111 Truly, it is a different world today, not only in terms of technological advances, but also in the expectation of the use of technology. I would submit . . . that our citizens, especially young people in today's society who have been raised in the age of *Law and Order* and *CSI,* would think it unusual that a drug dealer would have a *reasonable* expectation that his conversations during a drug sale to a non-confidant were not being consensually monitored. . . .

¶112 Moreover, monitoring provides protection for the informant, who risks physical harm to work with police, and provides for accurate recording and preservation of the evidence of the transaction. Thus, . . . the utility of this technology is very high in the furtherance of the state's compelling state interest in enforcing its criminal laws for the benefit and protection of the citizens. . . .

¶114 . . . Our right of privacy has been hijacked by those engaging in activities which the right was clearly not meant to protect, and has thus been devalued — becoming the new refuge of meth dealers selling to the public by means they well knew risked law enforcement involvement. The delegates to the Constitutional Convention did not countenance such a distortion of the right they found "essential to the well-being of a free society."

¶115 And I would not, either. I dissent. . . .

COTTER, J., concurring . . . .

¶125 While the Dissent complains that the Court's decision is unnecessarily broad and sweeping, so too is its own reach. If the Dissent's rationale is intended to apply equally to the criminal and the law-abiding alike — which I submit, it must — then it stands for the proposition that virtually any commercial transaction may be surreptitiously recorded without a warrant and with only one party's consent, with the resulting recording being admissible in evidence against the speaker. It would, in essence, gut any expectation of privacy one might reasonably have in his commercial conversation, regardless of the lawfulness of the transaction. If, on the other hand, the analysis is intended to apply to only those transactions that are criminal in nature . . . then it runs afoul of our duty to treat all persons the same before the law, without distinction for criminal/non-criminal behavior. Respectfully, either result is unacceptable. . . .

Notes

1. *Bugs on government agents: majority position.* A substantial majority of the states take the federal position as stated in United States v. White, 401 U.S. 745 (1971). Under this reasoning, a conversation between a government agent and a suspect does not become a "search," subject to constitutional limitations, when the agent uses a device to transmit or record the conversation. State courts that reject *White* often rely on distinctive language in a state constitution or a distinctive state constitutional history. State v. Geraw, 795 A.2d 1219 (Vt. 2002); State v. Mullens, 650 S.E. 2d 169 (W.Va. 2007).

A number of state courts that originally rejected *White* have reconsidered their decision (sometimes many years later) and have embraced the federal position. See People v. Collins, 475 N.W.2d 684 (Mich. 1991) (overruling 1975 decision that had rejected *White*); Melanie Black Dubis, The Consensual Electronic Surveillance Experiment: State Courts React to *United States v. White*, 47 Vand. L. Rev. 857 (1994). If a state court has rejected the federal view on a constitutional question, does that decision remain a questionable authority for its entire life span? Is there something special about the issue of consensual electronic surveillance that made these courts willing to reconsider their earlier independent stances?

2. *Confusing bugs and people.* Is the tape recording or transmission of a conversation with a government agent a consensual search, or is it no search at all? When a recording device is on an agent, doesn't the microphone simply serve as a more accurate way to capture and re-create statements? Should the rules be different when the technological enhancement changes the listener's capacity for recollection, but not the capacity to hear the evidence in the first place?

4. *Wiretaps to Fight Terrorism and Crime*

Just as wiretaps are useful for criminal investigations, they can also be useful for espionage. During the Cold War, the FBI and the CIA investigated possible agents of foreign governments operating within the United States. Congressional hearings during the 1970s, however, brought to light some abuses of domestic intelligence, including wiretaps and other surveillance of leaders of the civil rights movement and critics of the Vietnam War. In 1978, Congress passed the Foreign Intelligence Surveillance Act (FISA), creating new legal limits on domestic surveillance of suspected foreign agents.

The provisions of FISA require agents of the government to obtain judicial approval for their wiretaps. The order comes from a specialized federal court, known as the FISA court. While FISA does require probable cause to believe that the target is acting as an agent of a foreign power, the application for a surveillance order under FISA does not require the same detailed showing that is necessary for an ordinary criminal wiretap order under Title III. To prevent criminal investigators from using FISA wiretaps to avoid the more burdensome aspects of Title III, federal courts interpreted the statutes to require a clear separation between criminal and foreign intelligence investigations.

After the terrorist attacks of September 11, 2001, Congress passed the USA PATRIOT Act. One set of provisions in the Act made it easier for different groups of investigators to share information obtained from a FISA wiretap order. As you read the following problem, consider whether the new regime for wiretap orders under FISA will become more commonplace in a wide range of criminal investigations.

Problem 7-4. Crack in the Wall?

You are a judge on the Foreign Intelligence Surveillance Court of Review — a special federal appellate court created by Congress in FISA in 1978 to handle appeals from the FISA court. The Foreign Intelligence Surveillance Court of Review did not hear a single case in its first 25 years of statutory existence. After September 11 and the passage of the USA PATRIOT Act, the first appeal arrives, and the government has filed it. The high-stakes questions for the court are these:

1. Is the order of the FISA court setting limits on the government in this case valid?
2. Is the new rule of the FISA court (calling for the government to disclose connections between any FISA application and any ongoing criminal investigations) required by or allowed by the statute?
3. Is the amendment of FISA by the USA PATRIOT Act constitutional?

As part of its investigation into suspected terrorist groups after the September 11 attacks, the government applied to the FISA court for an order authorizing electronic surveillance. The government's application included some detailed information to support its contention that the target, a United States citizen, was conspiring with others in international terrorism. The FISA court granted the order, but it also placed some limits on the government. The order said that

> law enforcement officials shall not make recommendations to intelligence officials concerning the initiation, operation, continuation or expansion of FISA searches or surveillances. Additionally, the FBI and the Criminal Division of the Department of Justice shall ensure that law enforcement officials do not direct or control the use of the FISA procedures to enhance criminal prosecution, and that advice intended to preserve the option of a criminal prosecution does not inadvertently result in the Criminal Division's directing or controlling the investigation using FISA searches and surveillances toward law enforcement objectives.

To ensure the Justice Department followed these strictures, the court also fashioned a "chaperone requirement." A unit of the Justice Department, the Office of Intelligence Policy and Review (OIPR), composed of 31 lawyers and 25 support staff, must be invited to all meetings between the FBI and the Criminal Division to coordinate their efforts "to investigate or protect against foreign attack, international terrorism, or clandestine intelligence activities by foreign powers." If representatives of OIPR are unable to attend such meetings, "OIPR shall be apprized of the substance of the meetings in writing so that the Court may be notified at the earliest opportunity." Finally, the FISA court issued a new procedural rule, Rule 11, stating that "all FISA applications shall include informative descriptions of any ongoing criminal investigations of FISA targets, as well as the substance of any consultations between the FBI and criminal prosecutors at the Department of Justice."

The FISA court's restrictions were designed to build a "wall" between intelligence officials and law enforcement officers in the Executive branch. Drawing on many other judicial interpretations of FISA, the court meant to approve applications only when the "government's objective is not primarily directed toward criminal prosecution of the foreign agents for their foreign intelligence activity."

Under FISA, the court can approve of electronic surveillance to "obtain foreign intelligence information" if the government shows probable cause to believe that the target is "an agent of a foreign power" and that the communication facility to be monitored "is being used, or is about to be used" by the agent. 50 U.S.C. §1805(a)(3). The statute defines "foreign intelligence information" as

> information that relates to, and if concerning a United States person is necessary to, the ability of the United States to protect against — A) actual or potential attack or other grave hostile acts of a foreign power or an agent of a foreign power; B) sabotage or international terrorism by a foreign power or an agent of a foreign power; or C) clandestine intelligence activities by an intelligence service or network of a foreign power or by an agent of a foreign power.

50 U.S.C. §1801(e)(1). It defines an agent of a foreign power to include any person who "knowingly engages in clandestine intelligence gathering activities . . . which activities involve or may involve a violation of the criminal statutes of the United States" or those involving international terrorist acts, defined as "violent acts or acts dangerous to human life that are a violation of the criminal laws of the United States or of any State."

Section 1804 of FISA requires a national security official to certify in the application that "the purpose" of the surveillance is to obtain foreign intelligence information. That same certification must include a statement of "the basis of the certification that (i) the information sought is the type of foreign intelligence information designated." FISA includes "minimization procedures" designed to prevent the acquisition or sharing within the government of material gathered in an electronic surveillance that is unnecessary to the government's need for foreign intelligence information. 50 U.S.C. §1801(h).

Before 2001, the Department of Justice followed some internal procedures that limited contacts between the FBI and the Criminal Division in cases where FISA surveillance or searches were being conducted by the FBI for foreign intelligence purposes. The 1995 version of those internal procedures states that "the FBI and Criminal Division should ensure that advice intended to preserve the option of a criminal prosecution does not inadvertently result in either the fact or the appearance of the Criminal Division's directing or controlling the foreign intelligence investigation toward law enforcement purposes." Under these procedures, OIPR became a "wall" to prevent the FBI intelligence officials from communicating directly with the Criminal Division about their investigations.

The USA PATRIOT Act made some important changes to this statutory structure. It changed the certification requirement of Section 1804 to declare that "a significant purpose" of the surveillance is to obtain foreign intelligence information (as opposed to "the purpose" under FISA). The statute also explicitly authorized federal officers who conduct foreign intelligence surveillance to "consult with Federal law enforcement officers to coordinate efforts to investigate or protect against" attack, sabotage, international terrorism, or clandestine intelligence activities by foreign agents. 50 U.S.C. §1806(k)(1).

In 2002, the Attorney General modified the 1995 internal procedures. The new procedures eliminated the "directing or controlling" language and allowed the exchange of advice among the FBI, OIPR, and the Criminal Division regarding "the initiation, operation, continuation, or expansion of FISA searches or surveillance."

The government has appealed the order of the FISA court in this case, and also challenges the validity of the court's new Rule 11. Is the FISA court's order in this case consistent with the statute, as amended? Is the order compelled by the constitution? Compare In re Sealed Case, 310 F.3d 717 (Foreign Intelligence Surveillance Court of Review 2002).

Notes

1. *Wiretaps outside FISA.* In December 2005, the public learned that in 2001 the president authorized the National Security Agency to intercept and monitor telephone conversations between some callers in the United States and callers outside the country. Although the details of the program were a mystery, it seemed clear that the intercepts happened without any warrant from the FISA court and thus violated the procedures established in that statute. The Bush administration defended the program on two grounds. First, officials argued that the president has "inherent authority" as "commander in chief" of the armed forces under Article II of the Constitution to order wiretaps, outside the statutory framework of FISA, for electronic surveillance related to the prosecution of a war. Second, they argued that Congress had implicitly created an exception to the FISA procedures on September 14, 2001, when it authorized the president to use "all necessary and appropriate military force" against those responsible for the attacks. Without going into details about the program, officials also asserted that the FISA warrant process was impractical because it generated warrants too slowly and prevented the sort of categorical monitoring that the program required. See Eric Lichtau & Adam Liptak, "Bush Aides Press On in Legal Defense for Wiretapping Program," N.Y. Times, Jan. 28, 2006.

During the public debate about this program, several background facts about espionage wiretaps became clear. First, the NSA's scope was quite extensive, reaching the calls of thousands of Americans. Second, the FISA court granted virtually all government requests for espionage wiretaps. Between 1979 and 2003, the government applied for 16,974 surveillance orders from the FISA court, and the court denied the request in only 4 cases.

Does the existence of this NSA surveillance program affect your views about the validity of Rule 11, as described in Problem 7-4?

C. RECORDS IN THE HANDS OF THIRD PARTIES

Just as technology enables government investigators to monitor a suspect's conversations, it can also enable the government to make the most of available information by assembling small bits of scattered information into larger patterns. When electronic documents are in private hands, courts must confront the question whether an individual maintains any expectation of privacy in those documents. Government access to such records may allow collection of a huge range of information because of the sheer quantity of data that business databases contain, together with the ability to computerize a search of that information.

As we have seen, wiretap statutes tightly regulate the government's electronic eavesdropping on telephone conversations, face-to-face conversations, or electronic communications. Wiretaps can occur only after the government invests extraordinary effort in a detailed application to a judge, and the judge approves the application. Both federal and state law place lesser protections on records of communications held in third party storage, including telephone records, e-mail, and voice mail. The statutes in this area, such as 18 U.S.C. §§2701-2709, give law enforcement officers access, ordinarily pursuant to a warrant or court order or under a subpoena in some cases. The warrant or subpoena used in this setting does not include the exceptionally detailed information necessary for a wiretap order.

A less demanding set of restrictions apply to a third form of communications evidence: the government's use of trap and trace devices and "pen registers," which identify the source and destination of calls made to and from a particular telephone. Devices such as pen registers inspired the passage of many statutes that both obligate the telephone company to cooperate in the use of pen registers and limit the cases in which government may seek a pen register.

■ 18 U.S.C. §3121

(a) [N]o person may install or use a pen register or a trap and trace device without first obtaining a court order. . . .

(c) A government agency authorized to install and use a pen register or trap and trace device under this chapter or under State law shall use technology reasonably available to it that restricts the recording or decoding of electronic or other impulses to the dialing, routing, addressing, and signaling information utilized in the processing and transmitting of wire or electronic communications so as not to include the contents of any wire or electronic communications.

18 U.S.C. §3123

(a) . . . Upon an application made under [this statute], the court shall enter an ex parte order authorizing the installation and use of a pen register or trap and trace device . . . if the court finds that the attorney for the Government [or the State law enforcement or investigative officer] has certified to the court that the information likely to be obtained by such installation and use is relevant to an ongoing criminal investigation. [The law enforcement] agency shall ensure that a record will be maintained which will identify —

(i) any officer or officers who installed the device and any officer or officers who accessed the device to obtain information from the network;

(ii) the date and time the device was installed, the date and time the device was uninstalled, and the date, time, and duration of each time the device is accessed to obtain information;

(iii) the configuration of the device at the time of its installation and any subsequent modification thereof; and

(iv) any information which has been collected by the device.

(b) An order issued under this section —

(1) shall specify —

(A) the identity, if known, of the person to whom is leased or in whose name is listed the telephone line to which the pen register or trap and trace device is to be attached;

(B) the identity, if known, of the person who is the subject of the criminal investigation;

(C) the attributes of the communications to which the order applies, including the number or other identifier and, if known, the location of the telephone line or other facility to which the pen register or trap and trace device is to be attached or applied, and, in the case of an order authorizing installation and use of a trap and trace device [requested by state law enforcement officials], the geographic limits of the order; and

(D) a statement of the offense to which the information likely to be obtained by the pen register or trap and trace device relates. . . .

(c) An order issued under this section shall authorize the installation and use of a pen register or a trap and trace device for a period not to exceed sixty days. . . . Extensions of such an order may be granted, but only upon an application for an order under [this statute] and upon the judicial finding required by subsection (a) of this section. The period of extension shall be for a period not to exceed sixty days.

DAMON RICHARDSON v. STATE

865 S.W.2d 944 (Tex. Crim. App. 1993) (en banc)

CLINTON, J.

Appellant was convicted of the offense of engaging in organized criminal activity . . . and the jury assessed punishment at life confinement in the penitentiary and a $10,000 fine. On appeal he contended . . . that the trial court erred in overruling his motion to suppress evidence obtained by use of a pen register because the use of the pen register was a search in contemplation of Article I, §9 of the Texas Constitution; therefore, Article 18.21 [of the Texas Code of Criminal Procedure] is unconstitutional insofar as it authorizes a search without requiring a showing of probable cause.[1] . . .

In March of 1988, officers of the Texas Department of Public Safety were involved in an extensive investigation of a suspected drug ring operating in Lubbock County. The investigation centered around appellant, who was in the Lubbock County Jail awaiting trial for capital murder, and several other individuals residing at the Seven Acres Lodge, a motel in Lubbock. Despite appellant's incarceration, officers believed that he was controlling a cocaine and crack distribution organization using the telephones located in the county jail, by placing calls to a private telephone located at the Seven Acres Lodge. Due to the difficulty in investigating this case through customary investigative techniques, the officers sought court orders authorizing electronic surveillance to assist in their identification of co-conspirators and the modus operandi of the alleged trafficking organization.

On March 30, 1988, in accordance with the provisions of Article 18.21, the officers applied for and received a court order authorizing the installation of a pen register to catalogue the telephone numbers dialed from (806) 555-4729, a telephone at the Seven Acres Lodge. The officers then combined this information with other information outlined in a 56-page affidavit signed by Officer J. A. Randall, and on April 13, 1988, applied for and received a court order authorizing the wiretapping and recording of communications on the same telephone line. The wiretap intercepted numerous incriminating telephone conversations involving appellant and other targeted suspects. [A second pen register was ordered on April 14, and was installed to record numbers dialed from a limited use telephone in the Lubbock County Jail. Prior to trial, Richardson moved to suppress the evidentiary fruit of the pen registers, arguing that the use of a pen register was a search under Article I, §9 of the Texas Constitution.]

Ultimately, in the context of both the Fourth Amendment and Article I, §9, whether the government's installation and use of a pen register constitutes a search necessarily depends upon whether appellant has a "legitimate expectation of privacy" in the numbers he dialed on the telephone. . . . For purposes of the Fourth Amendment, a 5-3 majority of the Supreme Court has held that the installation and use of a pen register is not a search. This is so, the Court observed, because an individual "in all probability" entertains no actual expectation of privacy in the phone numbers he dials, and, even if he did, such an expectation is not "legitimate." Smith v. Maryland, 442 U.S. 735 (1979). The majority reasoned that telephone users "typically know that they must convey numerical information to the phone company; that the phone company has facilities for recording this information; and

1. Article 18.21 authorizes Texas law enforcement's use of pen registers as a means of electronic surveillance. A pen register is a mechanical or electronic device that attaches to a telephone line and is capable of recording outgoing numbers dialed from that line but is not capable of recording the origin of an incoming communication to that line or the content of a communication carried between that line and another line. Although Article 18.21 does establish a number of prerequisites to the issuance of a court order authorizing the use of a pen register, the statute does not require that an applicant show probable cause. The statute merely requires that the application state the installation and utilization of the pen register will be material to the investigation of a criminal offense. . . .

that the phone company does in fact record this information for a variety of legitimate business purposes." Telephone users, therefore, cannot have an actual expectation that the numbers they dial will remain private.

The *Smith* majority further reasoned that even if an individual did have an actual expectation that the numbers he dials would remain secret, such an expectation is not one that society would recognize as reasonable. To the majority, the disclosure of the telephone numbers was similar to other cases in which the Court held that a person has no legitimate expectation of privacy in information he voluntarily turns over to third parties. In particular, the Court noted United States v. Miller, 425 U.S. 435 (1976), which held that the government could access a bank depositor's financial records, including the depositor's monthly statement, checks and deposit slips, without probable cause. The *Miller* Court noted "that the Fourth Amendment does not prohibit the obtaining of information revealed to a third party and conveyed by him to government authorities, even if the information is revealed on the assumption that it will be used only for a limited purpose and the confidence placed in the third party will not be betrayed." Thus, the bank depositor who has voluntarily disclosed certain financial information to the bank and, necessarily, its employees, takes the risk that the information will be conveyed by the bank or its employees to the government. Having assumed this risk, the bank depositor has no legitimate expectation of privacy.

Similarly, the caller who has voluntarily disclosed the telephone number to the telephone company has assumed the risk that the telephone company would reveal these numbers to the police. For this reason the telephone caller has no legitimate expectation of privacy in the telephone numbers dialed. The installation and use of a pen register to record these numbers is therefore not a search under the Fourth Amendment, and no warrant is required.

The Supreme Court's holding in *Smith* has not gone without criticism. Quite the contrary, a number of legal commentators have rejected the Court's holding as making "a mockery of the Fourth Amendment." 1 W. LaFave, Search and Seizure: A Treatise on the Fourth Amendment §2.7(b), at 507 (2d ed. 1987).... LaFave agreed with Justice Marshall's dissent that the mere fact that a telephone user may know the telephone company can monitor his calls for internal reasons does not necessarily mean that he expects "this information to be made available to the public in general or the government in particular." [It] makes no sense to say that the telephone subscriber... is fair game for unrestrained police scrutiny merely because he has surrendered some degree of his privacy for a limited purpose to those with whom he is doing business....

In addition to the commentators, numerous state courts have criticized the Supreme Court's holding in *Smith*. At least seven States have rejected the reasoning of *Smith*, holding that their state constitutions provide an individual with a protected privacy interest in the telephone numbers dialed from a telephone. [The court cited cases from New Jersey, California, Pennsylvania, Colorado, Washington, Idaho, and Hawaii.] All but one of these cases involve construction of a state constitutional provision that is substantially similar to our Article I, §9....

We agree [with these decisions]. The mere fact that a telephone caller has disclosed the number called to the telephone company for the limited purpose of obtaining the services does not invariably lead to the conclusion that the caller has relinquished his expectation of privacy such that the telephone company is free to turn the information over to anyone, especially the police, absent legal process.

Certainly it is true that a general or indiscriminate disclosure of what otherwise may seem private information by its very nature evinces the lack even of a subjective expectation of privacy. Thus, the drug vendor . . . hawking his wares on the street, does not even demonstrate a subjective belief that his activities will remain private. Even if he did, the open nature of the disclosure obviates any possibility that the public would share his belief, and thus he cannot claim an objectively reasonable expectation of privacy. . . .

But whether an individual "assumes the risk" that a more limited disclosure will open the door to public disclosure depends, we think, upon the reasonableness of his subjective belief (if any) that the disclosure will in fact go no further. A selective disclosure may evidence a subjective expectation of privacy; the circumstances in which information is related to a third party may show a unilateral or even a mutual understanding that the information will remain confidential. This is not an understanding that society is invariably willing to recognize as legitimate, however, for society may have no particular stake in the matter. Thus, a subjective expectation of privacy despite a limited disclosure is not always a "reasonable" one.

There are some subjective expectations of privacy, however, that society does sanction as legitimate in spite of limited, confidential disclosure. We would not want to say, for example, that society does not recognize the confidentiality of information imparted to a physician behind the closed doors of an examination room. That certain facts may be revealed in the necessarily candid process of diagnosis and treatment does not mean we no longer have a collective interest in insulating them from public scrutiny. On the contrary, society accepts — indeed, positively insists — that such information, although of necessity partly exposed, should nevertheless retain its essentially private character. In view of this societal imperative, it is hardly fair to reason that the patient "assumed the risk" of public disclosure because of the forthrightness with which he spoke to his doctor.

Although the argument is not quite as compelling, we believe it would be likewise unfair to hold that the customer "assumes the risk" of public disclosure of a number he dials on the telephone. Other than for billing purposes, the telephone company itself has no interest in memorializing that information. Moreover, the telephone company is fiercely protective of what it considers the privacy interest of its customers even in the information it does record in the ordinary course of business — as any private citizen will discover if he attempts to obtain the telephone bill of another customer without that other's express permission.[8] It goes without saying that telecommunications are pervasive in our society. The telephone company's vigilance in protecting from public disclosure the uses to which its customers put their telephones reflects a value that is equally pervasive. As with information imparted to a doctor, we share a common understanding that the numbers we call remain our own affair, and will go no further. Thus, society recognizes as objectively reasonable the expectation of the telephone customer that the numbers he dials as

8. On page 37 of the prefatory pages of the 1992-1993 Greater Austin Telephone Directory printed by Southwestern Bell we find the heading, "Your Rights As a Customer." Under the subheading, "Telecommunications Privacy," we find the following assurance: "We fully safeguard every individual's right to privacy as an essential aspect of our service. We carefully strive to protect communications services from unlawful wiretapping or other illegal interception. Customer service records, credit information and related confidential personal account information are fully protected."

a necessary incident of his use of the telephone will not be published to the rest of the world.

It follows that the use of a pen register may well constitute a "search" under Article I, §9 of the Texas Constitution. The question remaining is whether such a search would be "unreasonable" in the absence of probable cause. If so, then to the extent it authorizes a court ordered pen register without a showing of probable cause, Article 18.21 violates Article I, §9. Because the court of appeals did not decide the question of reasonableness . . . we remand the cause for further disposition.

CAMPBELL, J., dissenting.

The majority perceives the question presented to be the abstract one of whether the State's use of a pen register may constitute a "search" under Article I, §9, of the Texas Constitution. Clearly, however, that is not the question presented. The true question presented is whether appellant has shown that he, as a pretrial detainee in a county jail, had a reasonable expectation of privacy in the telephone numbers he dialed on the jail telephone. [The dissent argued that the appellant had no reasonable expectation of privacy in calls made from jail, and that in any case society would be unwilling to accept such an expectation of privacy.]

Notes

1. *Pen registers as "searches": majority position.* Most state supreme courts ruling on the constitutional question have concluded (unlike the Supreme Court in Smith v. Maryland, 442 U.S. 735 (1979)), that use of a pen register is a "search" within the meaning of the constitution. The cases also conclude that it is a search for the government to compel a telephone company to provide access to *existing* records, as opposed to the creation of new records, which takes place with a pen register. But see Saldana v. State, 846 P.2d 604 (Wyo. 1993) (no violation of state constitution to subpoena toll records for unlisted number).

The federal statute reprinted above has analogs in almost 40 states. The statutes often authorize the use of a pen register after obtaining a court order, based on a showing that the pen register is "likely" to produce information that is "material" or "relevant" to a criminal investigation. See Fla. Stat. §934.33. Are statutes such as these consistent with the conclusion of many state courts that using a pen register is a constitutionally regulated "search"? These statutes also compel the telephone company to cooperate with the government in placing an authorized pen-register device on a telephone. Would telephone companies oppose the passage of a pen-register statute? For discussion of bank secrecy statutes, see Chapter 4, section C.

2. *Electronic Communications Privacy Act.* The Electronic Communications Privacy Act of 1986, 18 U.S.C. §2703, prohibits any "provider of electronic communications" services to the public from disclosing the contents of electronic communications it stores during the transmission process. The statute does not apply to the internal computer networks of computers operated by many employers; it covers instead any provider of electronic communications or computing services to the public, if the transmission occurs on a system that affects interstate or foreign commerce. Despite the statute's general protection from disclosure of electronic message contents, it creates an exception for disclosure to the government. The statute requires the government to obtain a warrant (based on probable cause)

before it can obtain an electronic communication that has been in "electronic storage" for less than 180 days. For communications stored for more than 180 days, the government can obtain them without probable cause if it notifies the owner of the communication and obtains a subpoena or a court order based on "specific and articulable facts showing that there are reasonable grounds to believe that the contents of a wire or electronic communication . . . are relevant and material to an ongoing criminal investigation." Why the different treatment for messages stored longer than 180 days?

Are Internet service providers (ISPs) required to provide the government with records of usage by its users? If the records being requested by the government involve e-mail and communications, they might be covered by the Electronic Communications Privacy Act. But what if the materials sought by the government are not communications, but stored files and documents? Is the delivery of such information by the service provider a matter covered solely by the contractual relationship between the user and the provider?

Problem 7-5. Prescription Privacy

Marcus Brown, a DEA agent, suspected that Nicholas Russo was abusing prescription medicines. Rumor suggested that Santo Buccheri, a Hartford physician, overprescribed pain killers to Russo and failed to maintain proper records. Brown therefore went to pharmacies located near Buccheri's office and Russo's home. Although Brown had no search warrant or probable cause to believe a crime had occurred, he asked each of the pharmacies to provide him with Russo's prescription records. The records contained information about prescriptions that each pharmacy had filled for Russo, including the name of the prescribing physician, the date Russo submitted the prescription to the pharmacy, the type and quantity of drug prescribed, and the price of the drug. The pharmacies complied with Brown's requests. Those records indicated that Russo had obtained a large amount of Tylenol 3, about 8,000 tablets. Brown therefore returned to each pharmacy and requested copies of the actual prescription forms that Russo presented to the pharmacies. Again, the pharmacists cooperated with Brown's request.

The state filed an information charging Russo with 32 counts of obtaining Tylenol with Codeine No. 3 (the active ingredient in Tylenol 3), a controlled substance, by forging a prescription. Russo moved to suppress the records of his prescriptions that the state obtained from the pharmacies without a warrant and without his consent. Russo contended that he had a reasonable expectation of privacy in his prescription records and, therefore, that the state obtained those records in violation of his rights under the federal and state constitutions. A state statute declares that "prescriptions shall be open for inspection only to federal, state, county and municipal officers, whose duty it is to enforce the laws of this state or of the United States relating to controlled substances." How would you rule on the motion to suppress? See State v. Russo, 790 A.2d 1132 (Conn. 2002).

Problem 7-6. Total Information Awareness

After the terrorist attacks on the World Trade Center and the Pentagon in September 2001, the Department of Defense began developing a data system to identify and stop terrorists. The system collected in one database all the publicly available information about an individual's purchases and other electronic transactions. Sophisticated computer programs could then "mine" this data to uncover patterns of behavior by people who make purchases or transactions that raise suspicions of terrorism. For instance, investigators might use the database to identify people who take commercial flying or scuba diving lessons, or people who purchase large amounts of fertilizer.

A government website describes the sorts of "transactional data" for individuals that would be deposited in the Total Information Awareness database: "financial, educational, travel, medical, veterinary, country entry, place/event entry, transportation, housing, critical resources, government, communications." The individual identifiers would be removed from these transactions until the "data mining" process identified persons who called for further investigation.

The columnist William Safire expressed the concerns of civil libertarians and advocates of limited government about this program:

> Every purchase you make with a credit card, every magazine subscription you buy and medical prescription you fill, every Web site you visit and e-mail you send or receive, every academic grade you receive, every bank deposit you make, every trip you book and every event you attend — all these transactions and communications will go into what the Defense Department describes as "a virtual, centralized grand database." To this computerized dossier on your private life from commercial sources, add every piece of information that government has about you — passport application, driver's license and bridge toll records, judicial and divorce records, complaints from nosy neighbors to the F.B.I., your lifetime paper trail plus the latest hidden camera surveillance — and you have the supersnoop's dream: a "Total Information Awareness" about every U.S. citizen.

Safire, "You Are a Suspect," N.Y. Times, Nov. 14, 2002, at 35. He argued that "the government's infinite knowledge about you is its power over you."

Michael Scardaville of the Heritage Foundation, however, supported the program: "Only those already identified as terrorists have anything to fear." He described as follows the safeguards on privacy the system would use:

> Even if they wanted to, TIA employees simply won't have time to monitor who plays football pools, who has asthma, who surfs what websites, or even who deals cocaine or steals cars. They'll begin with intelligence reports about people already suspected of terrorism. . . . Those already identified as terrorists or potential terrorists by the intelligence community then could be monitored through existing public and private databases to build an in-depth portfolio, including contacts and frequent activities. . . . These portfolios should enable authorities to determine whom to watch and where to find them when they suspect a terror strike is imminent.

Scardaville proposed limiting database access to the FBI, the CIA, and the Department of Homeland Security. The TIA program could develop "limited spinoffs" for use by state and local law enforcement and for those working for aviation security or monitoring for epidemics and biological warfare. Scardaville, Targeting Terrorists, National Review, Nov. 25, 2002.

As a member of Congress, would you vote to fund the further development of this program? In 2003 the Department of Defense announced a name change for the program, which was henceforth to be called the "Terrorism Information Awareness" program because the old name "created in some minds the impression that TIA was a system to be used for developing dossiers on U.S. citizens." Despite the change in names, the description of the program remained mostly the same. Congress ultimately cut off most of the funding for the program.

Problem 7-7. Working Texts

Sergeant Jeff Quon works for the Police Department. The Department acquired several alphanumeric pagers capable of sending and receiving text messages. Under the Department's service contract with Arch Wireless, each pager was allotted a limited number of characters sent or received each month. Text messages that exceeded the contract limits would result in additional fees. The Department issued a pager to Quon, which enabled him to communicate more quickly with his fellow employees.

Months before it distributed the new pagers, the Department announced a "Computer Usage, Internet and E-Mail Policy" that applied to all employees. The policy said that the Department "reserves the right to monitor and log all network activity including e-mail and Internet use, with or without notice. Users should have no expectation of privacy or confidentiality when using these resources." Immediately after the release of the Computer Policy, Quon signed a statement acknowledging that he had read and understood the policy.

The Computer Policy did not apply, on its face, to text messaging. Text messages differ from e-mails in an important way. An e-mail sent on a Department computer is transmitted through the Department's own data servers, but a text message sent on one of the Department's pagers is transmitted using wireless radio frequencies from an individual pager to a receiving station owned by Arch Wireless. The text message is routed through Arch Wireless's computer network, where it remains until the recipient's pager or cellular telephone is ready to receive the message, at which point Arch Wireless transmits the message from the station nearest to the recipient. After delivery, Arch Wireless retains a copy on its computer servers. The message does not pass through computers owned by the Department.

Although the Computer Policy did not cover text messages by its explicit terms, the Department made clear to its employees that it would treat text messages the same way as it treated e-mails. At a staff meeting at which Quon was present, Lieutenant Steven Duke, the administrator responsible for the City's contract with Arch Wireless, told officers that messages sent on the pagers "are considered e-mail messages. This means that text messages would be eligible for auditing."

Within the first or second billing cycle after the pagers were distributed, Quon exceeded his monthly text message character allotment. Duke suggested that Quon could reimburse the Department for the overage fee rather than have Duke audit the messages, so Quon wrote a check to the Department for the overage.

Over the next few months, Quon exceeded his character limit three or four times, and reimbursed the Department each time. At this point, Duke declared that he had become "tired of being a bill collector." He decided to determine whether the existing character limit was too low — that is, whether officers such as Quon were having to pay fees for sending work-related messages — or if the overages were for personal messages.

An administrative assistant for the Department requested the transcripts from Arch Wireless for August and September, and the company sent them after verifying that the Department was the subscriber on the accounts. Duke reviewed the transcripts and discovered that many of the messages sent and received on Quon's pager were not work related, and some were sexually explicit. Quon sent or received 456 messages during work hours in the month of August, of which no more than 57 were work related; he sent as many as 80 messages during a single day at work; and on an average workday, Quon sent or received 28 messages, of which only 3 were related to police business. The Department disciplined Quon for misuse of the equipment.

Quon sued the Department, along with several people who had exchanged texts with him, including his ex-wife, a Department employee who was romantically involved with Quon, and a Department employee who worked on a task force with Quon. The plaintiffs raised privacy claims under the Fourth Amendment, 18 U.S.C. §2701 (popularly known as the Stored Communications Act), and state tort laws. The Stored Communications Act amended the federal wiretap laws to prohibit any "person or entity" providing either "an electronic communication service" or a "remote computing service" to the public from "knowingly" divulging to any person or entity "the contents of a communication while in electronic storage by that service," or divulging a "record or other information pertaining to a subscriber or customer of such service." 18 U.S.C. §2702(a).

You are the district court judge. Did Quon have a reasonable expectation of privacy in the content of his text messages? Does the reasonableness of Duke's audit depend on his intent? For instance, would it matter if the purpose of the audit was to determine if Quon was using his pager to play games and waste time, or if the purpose instead was to determine the efficacy of the existing character limits to ensure that officers were not paying hidden work-related costs? Would you ask the parties to explore alternatives to the audit, such as warning Quon at the beginning of the month that his future messages would be audited, or asking Quon himself to redact the transcript of his messages? Finally, consider whether your analysis would change if the Department were a private security firm instead of an entity of municipal government. See City of Ontario, California v. Quon, 130 S. Ct. 2619 (2010).

Notes

1. *Access to transaction records and encryption.* The government can obtain access to transactional information in the hands of third parties (such as retailers) by warrant or subpoena. More frequently, however, the third party consents to provide the information. When it comes to stored communications, however, none of these techniques will give the government access to information that has been "encrypted" to make it unreadable to anyone other than the intended recipient, who holds the encryption "key." From time to time, the federal government asks the creators of encryption software to give the government a "key" to unlock the encryption, a key that the government would be able to use only after demonstrating

probable cause to search. During 1996 congressional hearings on this question, FBI Director Louis Freeh made the case for government access to encrypted messages:

> [Conventional] encryption not only can prevent electronic surveillance efforts, which in terms of numbers are conducted sparingly, but it also can prevent police officers on a daily basis from conducting basic searches and seizures of computers and files. Without an ability to promptly decrypt encrypted criminal or terrorist communications and computer files, we in the law enforcement community will not be able to effectively investigate or prosecute society's most dangerous felons or, importantly, save lives in kidnappings and in numerous other life and death cases. . . .
>
> In a very fundamental way, conventional encryption has the effect of upsetting the delicate legal balance of the Fourth Amendment, since when a judge issues a search warrant it will be of no practical value when this type of encryption is encountered. Constitutionally-effective search and seizure law assumes, and the American public fully expects, that with warrant in hand law enforcement officers will be able to quickly act upon seized materials to solve and prevent crimes, and that prosecutors will be able to put understandable evidence before a jury. Conventional encryption virtually destroys this centuries old legal principle.

What did Director Freeh fear if unbreakable communications were allowed?

2. *Financial, medical, and other personal information held by third parties.* Pharmaceutical records offer just one important instance of a large range of personal information held by third parties. Major categories of information include banking records and other financial records, and health and medical records. The United States Supreme Court has been unwilling to find constitutional privacy limits on government access to such information. See United States v. Miller, 425 U.S. 435 (1976) (no reasonable expectation of privacy in bank records). State courts have divided on the question of constitutional privacy rights in banking records and pharmaceutical records. See State v. Skinner, 10 So.3d 1212 (La. 2009); State v. McAllister, 875 A.2d 866 (N.J. 2005); Stephen E. Henderson, Learning from All Fifty States: How to Apply the Fourth Amendment and Its State Analogs to Protect Third Party Information from Unreasonable Search, 55 Cath. U. L. Rev. 373 (2006).

Both Congress and state legislatures have often stepped in where courts have hesitated to act. To explore some examples, consult the web extension for this chapter at *http://www.crimpro.com/extension/ch07*.

3. *Combinations of government-held information.* Once the government gains access to information, is any search or seizure issue involved in how the government uses the information? The U.S. Department of the Treasury runs an investigative program, known as "FinCEN," designed to make the most of the information scattered in various government files. The records that FinCEN reviews are based on reports that banks and other institutions and individuals must submit to comply with federal statutes and regulations. By using computers to combine and analyze the information held legitimately in various government files, law enforcers can obtain a more complete picture of an individual's activities or can note trends among certain groups of people that could justify closer scrutiny. This particular program focuses on financial crimes, such as tax evasion or money laundering. Does this technique hold promise for other sorts of investigations? How might one construct an argument that the assembling of many existing bits of data about an individual, contained in different records, creates new information that should be deemed a "search" regulated by the constitution?

Most search and seizure law relates to the government's initial access to information. The FinCEN program offers an example of government *use* of information to which it has undeniable access. Is the use of information relevant to the constitutional requirement of "reasonableness"? See Harold Krent, Of Diaries and Data Banks: Use Restrictions Under the Fourth Amendment, 74 Tex. L. Rev. 49 (1995). If a legislature, or some executive policymaker, decided to place some limit on the government's use of legitimately obtained information, what sort of limit would be feasible? Should the statute or policy impose a time limit on the use of the information? Should it force the government to use the information only in the enforcement of specified laws?

4. *DNA databases.* One especially powerful class of information that the government holds is genetic information, revealed through chemical patterns in an individual's DNA. Most states have now firmly established the validity, as an evidentiary matter, of some types of DNA evidence. Beyond the evidentiary and technical aspects of DNA evidence, its use can be quite dramatic. DNA evidence has proven the innocence of some people wrongly convicted.

But individual use of DNA to establish whether a known individual was (or was not) the likely offender is very different from having a broad database that allows the government to match any genetic material to a particular person. A database containing genetic information about many individuals, and perhaps an entire population, might allow investigators who find hairs, blood, semen, or mucus to identify quickly the most likely suspects.

Every state in the country has passed legislation authorizing a DNA database made up of samples from various categories of citizens, most often groups of criminal offenders or suspects. The military obtains genetic information from every member of the armed services. Some states collect identifying information, such as fingerprints, as part of providing basic services, such as a driver's license. It may not be long until the basic elements of citizenship and commerce obligate individuals to provide a sample of their DNA.

The development of genetic databases raises a huge range of issues. Those issues focus on how the information is obtained, how it may be used, and who will have access to it. Take Massachusetts as an example. The statute authorizes collection and analysis of DNA samples from defendants convicted of any of the 33 enumerated felonies, and it applies retroactively to those currently incarcerated, on probation, or on parole as a result of such a conviction. If a conviction is later dismissed, relevant DNA records may be expunged by court order. Law enforcement officers and correction personnel are authorized to use "reasonable force" to collect the DNA samples. Once samples are collected, the state crime laboratory performs "DNA typing tests" to generate numerical identification information. This numerical identifier becomes part of the state DNA database, and is also forwarded to the Federal Bureau of Investigation for storage and maintenance in a national index system.

The crime lab forwards a DNA record to local police departments, to the Department of Correction, to a sheriff's department, to the parole board, or to prosecuting officers on written or electronic request. The crime lab also must disclose DNA records to "local, state and federal criminal justice and law enforcement agencies, including forensic laboratories serving such agencies, for identification purposes in order to further official criminal investigations or prosecutions." Defendants who are charged with crimes as a result of a DNA database search are provided with a copy of their own DNA record. The director of the crime lab also has discretion to release DNA records for identifying victims of mass disasters or for "advancing other humanitarian purposes."

If you, as an attorney in Massachusetts, hoped to challenge the constitutionality of this law, who would be your ideal client? What constitutional texts and doctrines would you invoke? Landry v. Attorney General, 709 N.E.2d 1085 (Mass. 1999). If you were the director of the state crime laboratory, what regulations would you issue to address any potential constitutional or political difficulties? How would you respond to a legislative proposal to expand the DNA database to all arrestees in the state?

5. *Nongovernmental infringement of privacy (or "private privacy").* Criminal procedure and its constitutional superstructure speak to the relationship between citizens' privacy and their government's power to invade that privacy. On the other hand, infringement of privacy rights by nongovernmental actors has historically been left to private law. Tort claims for trespass, conversion, assault, battery, libel, slander, and invasion of privacy allow private parties to recover damages, and a handful of criminal charges reinforce those privacy interests.

There are various private actors who might collect information about criminal suspects, including family members, friends, employers, teachers, or roommates. Private security firms employ a growing number of people to prevent and ferret out crime. Since traditional constitutional limits on searches and seizures do not apply to "private" searches, police and prosecutors might simply encourage private actors to conduct searches and interrogations, and then turn over their evidence to the authorities. However, courts hold private searchers to public standards when the private action is conducted "at the behest of" or "in partnership with" government authorities.

Courts uniformly assess whether there is a sufficiently close link between a private search and government agents in deciding whether evidence found or obtained from a private search should be admitted. Courts look to a variety of factors, including prior agreements between private actors and government agents that a private agent will conduct a search. The application of this loose standard, however, leads to varying outcomes, both across and within jurisdictions. For an exploration of the wide range of issues involving "private privacy," see the web extension for this chapter at *http://www.crimpro.com/extension/ch07*.

6. *Searches by private security.* Private security agents outnumber sworn law enforcement officers. David Sklansky summarizes the figures as of 1990:

> [There] were 393,000 "proprietary," or in-house, security guards throughout the United States (i.e., guards employed directly by the owner of the property they protect), and 520,000 employees of "contract" guard companies (i.e., companies that hire out guards). [Guards] constitute all but 2-5% of those employed by contract guard companies. The more conservative figure of 5% yields 484,000 contract guards and 877,000 guards overall. There were roughly 600,000 sworn law enforcement officers throughout the country in 1990.

Private Police, 46 UCLA L. Rev. 1165 at n.27 (1999). If the government abolished its police force and a jurisdiction relied entirely on private security, would constitutional limits on search and seizure apply? Should private security agents stay within the same restrictions as other private actors?

7. *Privacy torts in partnership with criminal procedure.* Every state except Rhode Island provides a cause of action for "intentional intrusion upon the solitude or seclusion of another." Some states allow the action as part of common law tort doctrine; in others a cause of action for invasion of privacy appears in state statutes. For instance, Nebraska Statute §20-203 provides that any "person, firm, or corporation that trespasses or intrudes upon any natural person in his or her place of solitude or seclusion, if the intrusion would be highly offensive to a reasonable person, shall be liable for invasion of privacy." Whether based in common law or statutory causes of actions, the law of intentional intrusion on seclusion is relatively unformed. Is this an area of social interaction generally in need of greater legal regulation? If not, are there avenues other than civil tort claims to bolster a sense (and perhaps the reality) of individual privacy, and to limit invasions of privacy by private actors? Are there some actors in particular, such as firms that gather and sell information about individuals, that merit particular regulation?

More familiar than claims for physical invasion of privacy are claims that someone, often a media outlet, has published information that invades the claimant's privacy. It is important to distinguish such claims from claims that another person has reported false information or portrayed the claimant in a false light, which includes causes of action for defamation, libel, and slander.

8. *Web privacy.* Few users of the World Wide Web — a technology whose full name is already an anachronism — know how much information is conveyed when they access a website. Companies and individuals, both legitimate and shady, use the Web to gain information about consumers as a group, and as individuals. The range of issues is substantial. See Daniel J. Solove, Marc Rotenberg & Paul Schwartz, Information Privacy Law (Aspen 2006); The Privacy Law Sourcebook (Marc Rotenberg ed., EPIC 2004). It is helpful to think in terms of the interests and claims that different actors might make in asserting a right to gather information, or the uses of that information, or a right to withhold information. Many websites have privacy policies; when did you last read one?

The technology and its uses shift far more rapidly than existing legal structures. This creates a special challenge for users, lawyers, and courts deciding the limits of existing statutory law and exploring the boundaries of common law claims developed in different times and places. See, e.g., Matthew A. Goldberg, The Googling of Online Privacy: Gmail, Search-Engine Histories and the New Frontier of Protecting Private Information on the Web, 9 Lewis & Clark L. Rev. 249 (2005).

9. *E-mail privacy.* If your employer opens mail that you send from work, the employer may be subject to criminal prosecution under 18 U.S.C. §1702 ("Whoever takes any letter, postal card, or package out of any post office or any authorized depository for mail matter . . . before it has been delivered to the person to whom it was directed, with the design to obstruct the correspondence, or to pry into the business or secrets of another, or opens, secretes, embezzles, or destroys the same, shall be fined under this title or imprisoned not more than five years, or both."). The employer may also be subject to a statutory or common law civil suit for privacy infringement. Add an "e-" to the word "mail," however, and the employer can — and, in the case of many, especially larger employers, probably does — read and review it. See City of Ontario, Cal. v. Quon, 130 S. Ct. 2619 (2010) (review of text messages sent by police officers on departmental pagers to determine source of billing overruns revealed that officer used pager during work hours for personal messages; review was reasonable because it was motivated by legitimate work-related

purpose, and not excessive in scope). The only significant limits on the authority of employers to read employee e-mail come in the contractual relationships between the employee and employer. Of course, employers are not the only potential uninvited readers of a person's e-mail.

The analogy of e-mail to "snail mail" has some vitality with respect to third parties — including the government — seeking to read e-mail without the permission of employers or Internet service providers. However, the analogy has fared poorly with regard to employers or Internet service providers, where the privacy of an individual's communication depends largely on the contract. See Meir S. Hornung, Think Before You Type: A Look at Email Privacy in the Workplace, 11 Fordham J. Corp. & Fin. Law (2005). Should individuals have enforceable privacy interests against nongovernmental parties with respect to e-mail that resides on third-party or corporate computers? Should the answer depend on social norms or laws beyond the scope of any contract between the person and her employer? Limits on employer review of employee e-mail or Web usage may come from quasi-contractual relationships defining professional association, such as the relationship of faculty and students to a university under the principles of academic freedom.

VIII

Interrogations

Some crimes go unsolved unless the perpetrator confesses. Confessions are especially important in some violent crimes, such as murder and robbery; they are less important in possession crimes or transactional crimes (such as drug offenses or fraud), where a greater range of testimonial and physical evidence is often available. Beyond these general observations, however, it is hard to determine the exact number and types of cases in which police interrogation is necessary to solve the crime.

Many police officers are convinced that interrogations and confessions are indispensable in a broad range of cases. Field studies have certainly confirmed that the police interrogate the great majority of all suspects in custody — roughly 80 to 90 percent of them. See Paul Cassell and Bret Hayman, Police Interrogation in the 1990s: An Empirical Study of the Effects of *Miranda,* 43 UCLA L. Rev. 839 (1996); Project, Interrogations in New Haven: The Impact of *Miranda,* 76 Yale L.J. 1519 (1967).

If a suspect does provide the police with incriminating information, this has a considerable effect on the later processing of her case. People who confess to the police are more likely to be charged with a crime, less likely to have the charges against them dismissed, more likely to plead guilty, more likely to be convicted, and more likely to receive a more serious punishment. See Richard Leo, Inside the Interrogation Room, 86 J. Crim. L. & Criminology 266 (1996). Jurors consider evidence of a confession by the defendant to be among the most important types of information that a prosecutor can present. See Saul Kassin & Katherine Neumann, On the Power of Confession Evidence: An Experimental Test of the Fundamental Difference Hypothesis, 21 Law & Hum. Behav. 469 (1997).

In short, the confession of a criminal suspect can be a pivotal moment in the investigation and processing of a criminal case. What are the legal obligations of the police and other government agents who interrogate suspects in the hope of obtaining an outright confession or some admission leading to incriminating evidence?

A. VOLUNTARINESS OF CONFESSIONS

Courts have long declared that an involuntary confession cannot be a valid source of prosecution evidence. However, the precise reasons why involuntary confessions are considered objectionable, and the factors that can demonstrate the involuntariness of the confession, have shifted over the years. The following materials consider the impact of physical abuse, promises, threats, and lies on those courts considering whether a confession is voluntary.

1. *Physical Abuse and Deprivations*

Not so long ago, police in the United States used physical violence widely when they interrogated suspects. In 1931, the National Commission on Law Observance and Enforcement (known as the Wickersham Commission) collected evidence from current and former police officers and from many observers of police interrogation practices. The Commission concluded as follows:

> The third degree — the inflicting of pain, physical or mental, to extract confessions or statements — is widespread throughout the country. Physical brutality is extensively practiced. The methods are various. They range from beating to harsher forms of torture. The commoner forms are beating with the fists or with some implement, especially the rubber hose, that inflicts pain but is not likely to leave permanent visible scars.
>
> The method most commonly employed is protracted questioning. By this we mean questioning — at times by relays of questioners — so protracted that the prisoner's energies are spent and his powers of resistance overcome. . . . Methods of intimidation adjusted to the age or mentality of the victim are frequently used alone or in combination with other practices. The threats are usually of bodily injury. They have gone to the extreme of procuring a confession at the point of a pistol or through fear of a mob. . . .
>
> In considerably over half of the States, instances of the third degree practice have occurred in the last 10 years. . . . Fifteen representative cities were visited during the last 12 months by our field investigators. In 10 of them there was no doubt as to the existence of third-degree practices at that time.

Some police officers argued that third-degree tactics were justified, for a number of reasons (again, as summarized by the Wickersham Commission):

- [The] third degree is used only against the guilty.
- [Obstacles] in the way of the police make it almost impossible to obtain convictions except by third-degree methods. [Through] intimidation, bribery, and all kinds of political connections criminals are often set free. . . . Consequently they hope to build up such a solid case on the basis of a confession that the prisoner will, in spite of all obstacles, be convicted.
- [Police] brutality is an inevitable and therefore an excusable reaction to the brutality of criminals.
- [Restrictions] on the third degree may impair the morale of the police.

- [The] existence of organized gangs in large cities renders traditional legal limitations outworn.

How might you reply to each of these arguments? Could these same arguments be relevant in discussing other interrogation techniques that do not involve physical violence or intimidation?

Five years after the Wickersham Commission report appeared, the Supreme Court issued a major ruling on the question of coerced confessions. As early as 1897, the Court had considered the validity of confessions obtained by federal law enforcement officers, concluding in Bram v. United States, 168 U.S. 532 (1897), that the Fifth Amendment's self-incrimination clause limited coercive police interrogations. However, the Fifth Amendment did not apply to the states at that point, and it was unclear whether federal law placed any limits on the use of an involuntary confession in state court.

ED BROWN v. MISSISSIPPI

297 U.S. 278 (1936)

HUGHES, C.J.*

The question in this case is whether convictions, which rest solely upon confessions shown to have been extorted by officers of the State by brutality and violence, are consistent with the due process of law required by the Fourteenth Amendment of the Constitution of the United States.

[Ed Brown, Henry Shields, and Yank Ellington] were indicted for the murder of one Raymond Stewart, whose death occurred on March 30, 1934. They were indicted on April 4, 1934, and were then arraigned and pleaded not guilty. Counsel were appointed by the court to defend them. Trial was begun the next morning and was concluded on the following day, when they were found guilty and sentenced to death.

Aside from the confessions, there was no evidence sufficient to warrant the submission of the case to the jury. [Defendants testified] that the confessions were false and had been procured by physical torture. The case went to the jury with instructions, upon the request of defendants' counsel, that if the jury had reasonable doubt as to the confessions having resulted from coercion, and that they were not true, they were not to be considered as evidence.

[The state supreme court refused to overturn the convictions on appeal.] The grounds of the decision were (1) that immunity from self-incrimination is not essential to due process of law, and (2) that the failure of the trial court to exclude the confessions after the introduction of evidence showing their incompetency, in the absence of a request for such exclusion, did not deprive the defendants of life or liberty without due process of law. . . .

That the evidence established that [the confessions] were procured by coercion was not questioned. . . . There is no dispute as to the facts upon this point and as they

* [Justices Van Devanter, McReynolds, Brandeis, Sutherland, Butler, Stone, Roberts, and Cardozo joined in this opinion. — EDS.]

are clearly and adequately stated in the dissenting opinion of Judge Griffith . . . — showing both the extreme brutality of the measures to extort the confessions and the participation of the state authorities — we quote this part of his opinion in full, as follows:

> The crime with which these defendants, all ignorant negroes, are charged, was discovered about one o'clock P.M. on Friday, March 30, 1934. On that night one Dial, a deputy sheriff, accompanied by others, came to the home of Ellington, one of the defendants, and requested him to accompany them to the house of the deceased, and there a number of white men were gathered, who began to accuse the defendant of the crime. Upon his denial they seized him, and with the participation of the deputy they hanged him by a rope to the limb of a tree, and having let him down, they hung him again, and when he was let down the second time, and he still protested his innocence, he was tied to a tree and whipped, and still declining to accede to the demands that he confess, he was finally released and he returned with some difficulty to his home, suffering intense pain and agony. The record of the testimony shows that the signs of the rope on his neck were plainly visible during the so-called trial. A day or two thereafter the said deputy, accompanied by another, returned to the home of the said defendant and arrested him, and departed with the prisoner towards the jail in an adjoining county, but went by a route which led into the State of Alabama; and while on the way, in that State, the deputy stopped and again severely whipped the defendant, declaring that he would continue the whipping until he confessed, and the defendant then agreed to confess to such a statement as the deputy would dictate, and he did so, after which he was delivered to jail.
>
> The other two defendants, Ed Brown and Henry Shields, were also arrested and taken to the same jail. On Sunday night, April 1, 1934, the same deputy, accompanied by a number of white men, one of whom was also an officer, and by the jailer, came to the jail, and the two last named defendants were made to strip and they were laid over chairs and their backs were cut to pieces with a leather strap with buckles on it, and they were likewise made by the said deputy definitely to understand that the whipping would be continued unless and until they confessed, and not only confessed, but confessed in every matter of detail as demanded by those present; and in this manner the defendants confessed the crime, and as the whippings progressed and were repeated, they changed or adjusted their confession in all particulars of detail so as to conform to the demands of their torturers. When the confessions had been obtained in the exact form and contents as desired by the mob, they left with the parting admonition and warning that, if the defendants changed their story at any time in any respect from that last stated, the perpetrators of the outrage would administer the same or equally effective treatment. . . .
>
> The evidence upon which the conviction was obtained was the so-called confessions. Without this evidence a peremptory instruction to find for the defendants would have been inescapable. The defendants were put on the stand, and by their testimony the facts and the details thereof as to the manner by which the confessions were extorted from them were fully developed, and it is further disclosed by the record that the same deputy. Dial, under whose guiding hand and active participation the tortures to coerce the confessions were administered, was actively in the performance of the supposed duties of a court deputy in the courthouse and in the presence of *the* prisoners during what is denominated, in complimentary terms, the trial of these defendants. This deputy was put on the stand by the state in rebuttal, and admitted the whippings. It is interesting to note that in his testimony with reference to the whipping of the defendant Ellington, and in response to the inquiry as to how severely he was whipped, the deputy stated, "Not too much for a negro; not as much as I would have done if it were

left to me." Two others who had participated in these whippings were introduced and admitted it — not a single witness was introduced who denied it. . . .

I.

The State stresses the statement in Twining v. New Jersey, 211 U.S. 78 (1908), that "exemption from compulsory self-incrimination in the courts of the States is not secured by any part of the Federal Constitution." . . . But the question of the right of the State to withdraw the privilege against self-incrimination is not here involved. The compulsion to which the quoted statements refer is that of the processes of justice by which the accused may be called as a witness and required to testify. Compulsion by torture to extort a confession is a different matter.

The State is free to regulate the procedure of its courts in accordance with its own conceptions of policy, unless in so doing it "offends some principle of justice so rooted in the traditions and conscience of our people as to be ranked as fundamental." The State may abolish trial by jury. It may dispense with indictment by a grand jury and substitute complaint or information. But the freedom of the State in establishing its policy is the freedom of constitutional government and is limited by the requirement of due process of law. Because a State may dispense with a jury trial, it does not follow that it may substitute trial by ordeal. The rack and torture chamber may not be substituted for the witness stand. The State may not permit an accused to be hurried to conviction under mob domination — where the whole proceeding is but a mask — without supplying corrective process. The State may not deny to the accused the aid of counsel. Nor may a State, through the action of its officers, contrive a conviction through the pretense of a trial which in truth is "but used as a means of depriving a defendant of liberty through a deliberate deception of court and jury by the presentation of testimony known to be perjured." Mooney v. Holohan, 294 U.S. 103 (1935). And the trial equally is a mere pretense where the state authorities have contrived a conviction resting solely upon confessions obtained by violence. . . . It would be difficult to conceive of methods more revolting to the sense of justice than those taken to procure the confessions of these petitioners, and the use of the confessions thus obtained as the basis for conviction and sentence was a clear denial of due process. . . .

II.

. . . In the instant case, the trial court was fully advised by the undisputed evidence of the way in which the confessions had been procured. The trial court knew that there was no other evidence upon which conviction and sentence could be based. Yet it proceeded to permit conviction and to pronounce sentence. The conviction and sentence were void for want of the essential elements of due process. . . .

Notes

1. *Disappearance of the third degree.* Thirty-six years after the appearance of the Wickersham Commission report, another national commission reported the virtual disappearance of physical coercion as an interrogation technique: "today the third

degree is almost non-existent." President's Commission on Criminal Justice and the Administration of Justice, The Challenge of Crime in a Free Society (1967). Physical brutality and intimidation disappeared in part because of political pressure from the public, outraged by the findings of the Wickersham Commission and countless similar news accounts. Would these practices have disappeared, even without the Supreme Court's ruling in *Brown*? During the 30 years following *Brown*, due process claims of involuntary confessions became a staple of the Supreme Court docket. The Court ultimately decided more than 30 such cases. Over time, the nature of the police conduct in question shifted away from physical violence or threats of violence to more subtle physical deprivations and psychological coercion. However, the move away from physical deprivation happened slower in some places than others. In particular, physical abuse of black defendants in Southern states continued through the 1940s. See Michael Klarman, Is the Supreme Court Sometimes Irrelevant? Race and the Southern Criminal Justice System in the World War II Era, 89 J. Am. Hist. 119 (2002). The allegations also still arise in rare cases from the present day. See People v. Richardson, 917 N.E.2d 501 (Ill. 2009) (confession from teenage suspect was voluntary, even though it was obtained a few hours after he was punched by an officer in the jail; interrogating officers worked with separate subdivision of department and in different part of the building from the jail).

2. *Physical deprivations: modern limits.* Although physical abuse such as striking a suspect has largely disappeared from interrogations in this country, one can still find examples of physical deprivations, such as depriving a suspect of food or sleep for some period of time. Courts say that some deprivations are tolerable while others are not. Up to a point, interrogators can limit the sleep or food available to the suspect. See Payne v. Arkansas, 356 U.S. 560 (1958) (confession coerced when defendant given two sandwiches during 40-hour detention and interrogations). What if the interrogator fails to provide the suspect with cigarettes?

After the physical coercion in police interrogations withered away, the legal system still faced questions about psychological manipulation during interrogations. If the *Brown* court prohibited the use of "coerced" or "involuntary" confessions, what types of psychological pressures might qualify under that standard? One recurring source of psychological pressure that has been influential with courts has been the extended isolation of the defendant from family, friends, legal counsel, and other support. See Fikes v. Alabama, 352 U.S. 191 (1957) (isolation for more than a week, confession involuntary).

3. *Length of interrogation.* Interrogators find greater success with suspects after lengthier interrogation sessions. In one survey, 631 police investigators estimated that the mean length of interrogations of suspects is 1.6 hours. See Saul M. Kassin, et al., Police Interviewing and Interrogation: A Self-Report Survey of Police Practices and Beliefs, 31 Law and Human Behavior 381-400 (2007). Criminologist Richard Leo, who observed about 180 police interrogations, conducted a statistical study concluding that the length of an interrogation is one of the strongest determinants of its success. Richard Leo, Inside the Interrogation Room, 86 J. Crim. L. & Criminology 266 (1996). At the same time, lengthy interrogations create a risk that a court will later find any confession to be involuntary. Ashcraft v. Tennessee, 322 U.S. 143 (1944) (continuous 36-hour interrogation, confession involuntary); cf. State v. Harris, 105 P.3d 1258 (Kan. 2005) (detention of a suspect by shackling him to floor of interrogation room for seven hours did not render his subsequent confession involuntary; suspect was questioned for two and a half hours and denied

access to telephone, but allowed to take bathroom breaks). There is no clear time limit that will create an involuntary confession under the "totality of the circumstances," but many interrogators believe that the risk goes up once the session extends past three or four hours.

4. *Delay in presenting a suspect to a judicial officer.* The rules of criminal procedure in most jurisdictions require the police to arrange for the suspect's prompt appearance before a judicial officer. The rules in some states specify a time period. See Ariz. R. Crim. Proc. 4.1 ("A person arrested shall be taken before a magistrate without unnecessary delay. If the person is not brought before a magistrate within 24 hours after arrest, he or she shall immediately be released"); Cal. Penal Code §825 (defendant shall "be taken before the magistrate without unnecessary delay, and, in any event, within 48 hours after his or her arrest, excluding Sundays and holidays").

The Supreme Court has declared that any violation of the time rules contained in the Federal Rules of Criminal Procedure will require suppression of confessions obtained as a result of that delay. This requirement (declared under the Court's so-called supervisory power over federal law enforcement) is known as the *McNabb-Mallory* rule, after McNabb v. United States, 318 U.S. 332 (1943), and Mallory v. United States, 354 U.S. 449 (1957). See also Corley v. United States, 129 S. Ct. 1558 (2009) (federal statute addressing voluntariness of confessions used in federal court did not supplant Federal Rule of Criminal Procedure 5(a), which embodies the "prompt presentment" requirement of *McNabb-Mallory*; statute makes *McNabb-Mallory* inapplicable to voluntary statements obtained within six hours of arrest, but leaves the rule otherwise intact).

Although most states have a time-limit provision in their rules of procedure, most state courts have rejected the *McNabb-Mallory* rule and have declared instead that a violation of the timeliness requirement will not lead to automatic suppression but will be one part of the "totality of the circumstances" that could indicate an involuntary confession. Fewer than 10 states follow the per se federal rule. See Commonwealth v. Perez, 845 A.2d 779 (Pa. 2004) (disavowed state's bright-line rule with a "totality of the circumstances" test for determining the admissibility of statements made during delays in arraignment). Some states have special rules (embodied in statutes, court rules, or constitutional due process rulings) requiring prompt presentation of *juveniles* to a judicial officer. See W. Va. Code, §49-5-8(d); In re Steven William T., 499 S.E.2d 876 (W. Va. 1997).

5. *Vulnerability of suspect.* The Court in *Brown* mentioned the "ignorance" of the suspects. Many other cases assessing the voluntariness of a confession for due process purposes have also considered the vulnerability of the suspect. A suspect who is especially young or who is suffering from illness or injury will be more likely to succeed in claiming that a confession was involuntary. See Beecher v. Alabama, 408 U.S. 234 (1972) (suspect confesses while under influence of morphine and in pain from gunshot wound, confession involuntary); Haley v. Ohio, 332 U.S. 596 (1948) (15-year-old interrogated with no advice from family or friends, confession involuntary). Conversely, a suspect who is mature and well educated will find it more difficult to sustain a claim of involuntariness.

6. *Torture, truth, and need.* Exactly what is objectionable about relying on confessions obtained through torture? If the problem is unreliable information, could that be cured by an evidentiary rule requiring independent corroboration of anything learned through physical abuse of a suspect? If the objection is abuse of police powers, could that risk be addressed through procedures specifying when physical

coercion would be allowed, and the types of physical techniques the police could use? Are there situations in criminal law enforcement that could justify torture? What if the life of a hostage is at stake, or there is a possibility of great loss of life from an act of terror? See John Langbein, Torture and the Law of Proof (1977).

These questions are not merely academic. In the aftermath of the terrorist attacks in New York City and Washington on September 11, 2001, lawyers and government officials started to anticipate settings where torture might be appropriate. During military operations in Afghanistan in 2001 and 2002, U.S. armed forces captured enemy combatants. Agents of the Central Intelligence Agency interrogated the detainees at locations near the fighting, and for months after their capture at the military detention facility at Guantanamo Bay in Cuba. The interrogators used "stress and duress" and "waterboarding" techniques. For instance, detainees who refused to cooperate were kept standing or kneeling for hours while wearing black hoods or spray-painted goggles. Some were allegedly held in awkward and painful positions, or were subjected to 24-hour lighting to disrupt their sleep. In some cases, the United States turned captured combatants over to foreign governments known to use torture during interrogations. News developments related to this topic appear on the web extension for this chapter at *http://www.crimpro.com/extension/ch08*. Do the techniques described above make any confessions of the detainees involuntary? Are such techniques acceptable so long as the government pursues no criminal charges against the detainee? So long as the interrogation takes place outside the territory of the United States?

2. *Promises and Threats*

Only rarely does a suspect volunteer a confession without any effort by the police to convince the suspect that a confession would be worthwhile. When an interrogator tries to convince a suspect of the value of a confession, is it proper to make promises or threats of any type? Are these techniques objectionable for the same reasons that one might object to physical torture during interrogations?

■ STATE v. JAMI DEL SWANIGAN

106 P.3d 39 (Kan. 2005)

NUSS, J.

. . . Shortly before 4 A.M. on October 26, 2000, the Kwik Shop on West Cloud Street in Salina was robbed. According to clerk Krystal Keefer, she saw a black man put his hand up to the glass of the front window and look inside. He then rushed in the front door with a gun. Several times the robber told her to hurry and at one point told her that he would shoot her or kill her if she did not go faster. She opened the cash drawer, grabbed the bills, and handed them to the robber. As she began to grab the change, the robber turned and ran out the front door to the east. The robber stole $100 to $102. . . .

Surveillance cameras at the Kwik Shop captured video images of the robber. The man was wearing a blue bandana over his nose and mouth, blue denim shorts, a long-sleeved black or blue shirt, tennis shoes, and white socks. A photograph of the robber taken from the video was posted at the police station, and Lieutenant Christopher Trocheck believed the person shown to be Jami Swanigan.

Five days after the robbery, Shari Lanham, the lead investigator, [went to Swanigan's home and asked] if he would come to the police department to answer questions about this robbery and other recent convenience store robberies in Salina. He agreed and rode in a patrol car to the station. Upon his arrival, he was placed in a locked waiting room for 30 to 45 minutes before the interrogation began.

The interrogation lasted from 5:03 P.M. until 6:20 P.M., with all but the first few minutes recorded on audiotape. . . . Swanigan first denied knowing anything about the robberies, but eventually said he had heard Marcus Brown was involved. Lanham falsely told Swanigan that his fingerprints had been found at the scene. She also informed him that he had been caught on the surveillance camera. Swanigan had no explanation for either fact, except that he had possibly been at the store before.

After Swanigan took a bathroom break, Lieutenant Mike Sweeney, who was in charge of criminal investigations and who supervised Lanham, joined the interrogation. Swanigan gave Sweeney and Lanham several different stories, but each version contained facts that were contrary to what the officers knew from the eyewitnesses. When confronted with the discrepancies, Swanigan then denied any involvement in the robbery.

Investigator James Feldman then joined the interrogation. Right after Feldman's comments, Swanigan confessed to the robbery. When a discrepancy arose over the clothes the robber had worn, Feldman showed Swanigan a photo from the surveillance video. Swanigan immediately denied the photo was of him and denied that he had any involvement in the robbery. Based primarily upon his interrogation — since latent fingerprints taken from the store, including the front window, were found not to be his — he was arrested and charged with aggravated robbery. . . .

In Swanigan's motion to suppress, he alleged that his statements were not voluntary, knowing, or intelligent under the totality of the circumstances. Specifically, Swanigan alleged that the police used coercive and deceptive tactics, including providing him false information that his fingerprints matched those found at the crime scene and promising that his cooperation in the investigation would help him. [The court denied his motion to suppress the confession.]

In reviewing a district court's decision regarding suppression, this court reviews the factual underpinnings of the decision by a substantial competent evidence standard and the ultimate legal conclusion by a de novo standard with independent judgment. This court does not reweigh evidence, pass on the credibility of witnesses, or resolve conflicts in the evidence. We stated additional considerations specifically concerning confessions in State v. Sanders, 33 P.3d 596 (Kan. 2001):

> In determining whether a confession is voluntary, a court is to look at the totality of the circumstances. The burden of proving that a confession or admission is admissible is on the prosecution, and the required proof is by a preponderance of the evidence. Factors bearing on the voluntariness of a statement by an accused include the duration and manner of the interrogation; the ability of the accused on request to communicate with the outside world; the accused's age, intellect, and background; and the fairness of the officers in conducting the interrogation. The essential inquiry in determining the

> voluntariness of a statement is whether the statement was the product of the free and independent will of the accused.

[The court heard] evidence at the suppression hearing concerning the officers' alleged promises, threats, or both. Regarding promises, the trial court found that "Swanigan was told several times that if he cooperated that that would be conveyed to anybody who might pursue the case." The court further found that although "there was . . . an allegation made that you were promised leniency," that "no specific promises of leniency were made," and that several times "Lieutenant Sweeney indicated that there couldn't be any promises made by those in authority." . . .

Regarding threats, the trial court found: "At no time were any threats uttered." We agree no express threats were uttered, but find that evidence of implied threats exists on the audiotape. The implicit threats are occasionally intertwined with the officers' urgings that Swanigan cooperate. Examples from both categories of interrogation techniques are italicized below:

> [Lanham:] So you need to come clean. You know what's gonna happen after I get done talking with you Jami. I've gotta do a report. Right? You know that. That's all we do here is reports. *And I need to go and put in my report that Jami cooperated. I need to be able to tell Parrish that you, that you cooperated with me and that you came clean and that you got it straight. And that you weren't involved in all of them because you know what Jami? I don't think you're involved in all of them. I think you had a small part in one of them, and that's what I want from you. That's what we need to know from you so that you don't go down for all these robberies. We just want to know your involvement in yours. That's all we want to know from you, so that you don't get charged with all of them.* . . .

Later in the interview Lanham said: "I just need you to tell me how you was involved. Jami, you know it's the right thing to do. *It's gonna help you in the long run and you know it. 'Cause I guarantee there's a lot of difference between going to jail for five robberies than there is for one.*"

[When] Investigator Feldman entered the room, he told Swanigan:

> *You're going to jail. It's guaranteed. You are going to jail. You got one of two options. You can sit there and B.S. and act like we're, we're idiots and tell these lame stories and we'll write every word you say down and send it over to the county attorney and you'll have every lawyer reading that going, "Jesus Christ, this is bullshit!" And you know what they're [county attorney] gonna say? Well, when your lawyer comes up and goes, "Hey, can we get a deal?" You know what they're gonna say? "Read the report. He, he played games the whole time. He doesn't deserve a break. He hasn't learned from any of the mistakes he made."* . . .
>
> *You can show that you made a mistake and you want to take responsibility for your actions and you apologize for it. Or you sit there and play stupid. And then you're gonna fry. Because when the county attorney comes to Sweeney or Lanham and goes, "What do you think? Here's the deal [plea bargain] that I'm being offered." You know what we're gonna say if you're playing games? "Screw ya."*

Lanham then told Swanigan, "And if you don't think they [county attorney] ask our opinion you're crazy cause they do."

Immediately after these comments by officers Feldman and Lanham, the following exchange occurred:

> [*Swanigan:*] Everything happened so fast. I was standing up at the window. I looked in, put my hand up on the window and looked in. I walked inside the store with a gun in my hand. And I pointed it at the um, clerk and asked, and tell him give me all your money. . . . "Give me your money or I'll kill you." So he finally gave me the money. . . .
>
> *F:* What were you wearing?
>
> *S:* I was wearing, I was wearing tan pants and, um, tan shirt that's over at Jessica's house. . . .
>
> *L:* So that outfit that you have on, the other one. There's another outfit there just like this one you have on, right? That what you were wearing?
>
> *S:* Yeah. . . .

In an apparent attempt to wrap up Swanigan's confession, Feldman produced a photograph of the robber from the surveillance video and asked, "That you?" Swanigan vehemently denied it: "Hell no! I can tell you that's not me. I can tell you that's not me." Among other things, Swanigan pointed out that the figure in the photograph was not wearing tan pants and a tan shirt, contrary to what he had just confessed.

From that point until the interrogation ended, Swanigan denied that he was involved in the robbery. When Lanham asked Swanigan how he would therefore know exactly how the robbery happened, he replied, "Because you guys done gave me tips behind how it done happened." When Lanham asked why he would make up the story that he committed the robbery when he actually had not, Swanigan responded, "Because you guys are forcing me to do this." When she denied forcing him into saying anything, he said, "When I try to tell you the truth you guys say it's me."

[The court also heard evidence at the suppression hearing concerning Swanigan's intellect and psychological state.] Dr. Schulman's report on Swanigan was reviewed by the trial court, and in a section titled "examination findings" it states:

> *Estimated intellectual functioning is in the borderline range of intellectual abilities with an estimated IQ of 76.* He says that he missed a lot of school, that he was in regular classes and did not enjoy going to high school. The clinical examination is essentially within normal limits. *He shows some mild depression. He also shows difficulty in dealing with anxiety and is susceptible to being overcome by anxiety but in this setting he shows good control.* There are no indications of any underlying associative thought disturbance. . . .

Swanigan argues the police used [unfair tactics] to overbear his will [by] repeatedly telling him that he would be helping or hurting himself by what he told them. According to him, they urged him to confess to the crime so that they could report that he had cooperated. He claims that when he told them he did not commit the crime, they threatened to report that he was not cooperating, occasionally suggesting that he would be charged with more robberies if he did not confess. At the time, Swanigan was on probation.

Investigator Lanham mentioned the other robberies and the need for Swanigan's cooperation, adding she "needed" to put in her report that he cooperated. . . . Sweeney repeated the need for police to show that Swanigan had cooperated and indicated what would happen if Swanigan did not. "We can write the report where it shows that you're willing to get this straightened out" and, if not,

"Jami, we're going to charge you with aggravated robbery. We're gonna show [the county attorney] that you're not cooperating with us." . . .

Like Lanham and Sweeney, Feldman suggested positive consequences for Swanigan admitting his mistake, i.e., confessing to the robbery, but suggested negative consequences if he did not so "cooperate." He specifically mentioned the influence the interrogators have with the county attorney's office, including what they write in their report. . . .

This court has held that, without more, a law enforcement officer's offer to convey a suspect's cooperation to the prosecutor is insufficient to make a confession involuntary. State v. Banks, 927 P.2d 456 (Kan. 1996) ("it will be noted by the authorities that you did cooperate"). Likewise, we have declined to find a confession involuntary when the police encourage the accused to tell the truth. Kansas appellate courts, however, have not addressed the other side of the same coin, law enforcement conveying a suspect's lack of cooperation to the prosecutor. A growing number of courts have disapproved this tactic. Those not finding that it is coercive per se regard it as another circumstance to be considered in determining the voluntariness of the confession.

[We] fail to see how law enforcement can be . . . allowed to warn [Swanigan] of punishment for his "noncooperation" when [the Fifth Amendment gives him a privilege against self-incrimination]. On the other hand, we do not regard this tactic as one which makes the confession involuntary per se, but rather as one factor to be considered in the totality of circumstances.

Turning now to the assertion that detectives told Swanigan he would be charged for five convenience store robberies instead of just one unless he confessed, we first examine general statements of Kansas law. K.S.A. 60-460(f) provides in relevant part:

> Evidence of a statement which is made other than by a witness while testifying at the hearing, offered to prove the truth of the matter stated, is hearsay evidence and inadmissible except: . . .
>
> (f) *Confessions.* In a criminal proceeding as against the accused, a previous statement by the accused relative to the offense charged, but only if the judge finds that the accused . . . (2) was not induced to make the statement . . . (B) *by threats or promises concerning action to be taken by a public official with reference to the crime, likely to cause the accused to make such a statement falsely, and made by a person whom the accused reasonably believed to have the power or authority to execute the same.*

No Kansas cases have addressed this specific issue. However, Aguilar v. State, 751 P.2d 178 (N.M. 1988), is directly on point. Among other things, during Aguilar's interrogation the police chief implied that if Aguilar did not confess to the burglary, he would be charged in connection with unrelated incidents of vandalism in town. Aguilar then confessed. In examining interrogation techniques quite similar to those in the instant case, the New Mexico Supreme Court held:

> Chief Barela's interrogation alternated between threatening the defendant with charges in connection with unrelated incidents of vandalism in Dexter and assuring the defendant that a confession to the burglary would be looked upon favorably by all concerned. In the totality of the circumstances, this interrogation technique is preponderant. In comparison with all evidence to the contrary, these implied threats

and promises, especially when knowingly made to a defendant with diminished mental capacity, rendered the confession involuntary as a matter of law.

[The] trial court did not specifically assess Swanigan's IQ of 76 as a factor in the voluntariness determination. Nor did the court consider his psychological state during the interrogation, finding only that it was insufficient to make the police interrogation improper at all. Our review of the record, including the audiotape of the October 31 interrogation, discloses that Swanigan's relatively low IQ and his susceptibility to being overcome by anxiety played a part in his alternating denials and confessions (which themselves varied considerably). His confession began to unravel for the last time when the robber in the photo was wearing the wrong clothes. . . .

Although any one of these factors which Swanigan asserts — his low intellect and susceptibility to being overcome by anxiety, the officers' repeated use of false information, and their threats and promises — may not be sufficient to show coercion, the combination of all of them in this case leads us to conclude as a matter of law that Swanigan's October 31 statement was not the result of his free will, but was involuntary. . . .

We acknowledge that there must be a link between the coercive conduct of the State and the confession. A thorough review of the record, as partly evidenced by the facts set forth in this opinion, clearly shows that Swanigan's numerous changes in story, whether in denial or in confession, usually occurred shortly after the officers lied to or threatened him. As such, his October 31 statement should have been excluded as evidence at trial. . . .

Notes

1. *Police promises: majority position.* Most jurisdictions have not taken literally the Supreme Court's prohibition on the use of confessions obtained through "any sort of threats or . . . any direct or implied promises, however slight." Bram v. United States, 168 U.S. 532 (1897). Some promises or threats, standing alone, are indeed enough to render a confession "involuntary." These would include promises to reduce (or decline to file) charges, threats to file more serious charges, or promises to seek more or less serious punishment for the crime. See Lynumn v. Illinois, 372 U.S. 528 (1963) (suspect told that cooperation could lead to lesser charges; failure to cooperate would mean loss of custody of children, confession involuntary); State v. Rezk, 840 A.2d 758 (N.H. 2004) (interrogator said that if defendant confessed, the officer "wouldn't charge him with all the felonies"; confession was involuntary because defendant and police engaged in "station house plea-bargaining" without benefit of defense counsel for the suspect). Improper statements could also include threats to refuse to protect the suspect from mob violence or from a dangerous co-conspirator.

Interrogators can, however, make many other promises or threats without invalidating a confession. They can promise to inform the prosecutor about the defendant's cooperation in making a statement, to ask the prosecutor to discuss lesser charges, or to arrange for treatment programs or similar activities. What distinguishes the acceptable from the unacceptable promises? See People v. Holloway,

91 P.3d 164 (Cal. 2004) (detectives' mention of a possible death penalty and suggestions that defendant would benefit from giving a truthful, mitigated version of the crimes was not an improper promise or threat; court compared these facts to improper interrogations where detectives falsely suggested that suspect would be subject to death penalty, or that statements could not be used in court).

When the police make promises or threats to a *juvenile* suspect, the government has a somewhat more difficult burden to meet in showing that the confession was voluntary. See State v. Presha, 748 A.2d 1108 (N.J. 2000) (courts should consider parent's absence during interview as a highly significant factor in judging voluntariness of juvenile's statement); In re G.O., 727 N.E.2d 1003 (Ill. 2000) (juvenile's confession should not be suppressed simply because he was denied the opportunity to confer with a parent during interrogation, but that factor may be relevant in determining voluntariness).

2. *Proving causation.* The government carries the burden of proving that a confession was voluntary, and the standard of proof is preponderance of the evidence. State v. Agnello 593 N.W.2d 427 (Wis. 1999) (voluntariness of confession need be shown only by a preponderance, not beyond reasonable doubt). As the Kansas court in *Swanigan* indicated, even after a defendant demonstrates that the police made an improper promise or threat, his statement still might be admissible if the promise or threat did not "induce" or "cause" the confession. How would a prosecutor typically prove this causal link?

3. *Do innocent people confess?* Do innocent people really confess to crimes they did not commit? A number of psychologists have investigated the circumstances that lead people to make false confessions. A Royal Commission in Great Britain summarized the findings as follows:

> [There] is now a substantial body of research which shows that there are four distinct categories of false confession:
>
> (i) people may make confessions entirely voluntarily as a result of a morbid desire for publicity or notoriety; or to relieve feelings of guilt about a real or imagined previous transgression; or because they cannot distinguish between reality and fantasy;
>
> (ii) a suspect may confess from a desire to protect someone else from interrogation and prosecution;
>
> (iii) people may see a prospect of immediate advantage from confessing (e.g., an end to questioning or release from the police station), even though the long-term consequences are far worse (the resulting confessions are termed "coerced-compliant" confessions); and
>
> (iv) people may be persuaded temporarily by the interrogators that they really have done the act in question (the resulting confessions are termed "coerced-internalized" confessions).

Report of the Royal Commission on Criminal Justice 57 (1993) (Runciman Commission); see also Saul M. Kassin, Inside Interrogation: Why Innocent People Confess, 32 Am. J. Trial Advoc. 525 (2009).

Two developments over the last generation cast a new light on the question of false confessions. First, the availability of video recordings of many interrogations has created a rich field for psychological and sociological research. Richard Ofshe and Richard Leo have used these materials to develop a model of true and false confessions that emphasizes the misuse of standard interrogation techniques as a major cause of false confessions. They pay particular attention to the "post-admission" portion of an interrogation, when a suspect provides the details that can corroborate or repudiate the suspect's admission of guilt. See Ofshe & Leo, The Decision to Confess Falsely: Rational Choice and Irrational Action, 74 Denv. U. L. Rev. 979 (1997).

Second, the use of DNA evidence to identify clear cases of wrongful convictions allows careful assessments of confessions in cases that go wrong. The research of Brandon Garrett indicates that false confessions account for a substantial number of wrongful conviction cases, and those confessions include many convincing details about the crime that were likely suggested to the suspect by the questioners. See Garrett, The Substance of False Confessions, 62 Stan. L. Rev. 1051 (2010). For a review of the sources, effects, and frequency of false confessions, consult the web extension for this chapter at *http://www.crimpro.com/extension/ch08*.

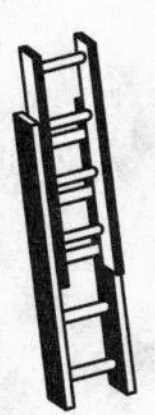

3. *Police Lies*

Police often know facts that suspects do not know and can use those facts to expose a suspect's false story or to encourage a silent suspect to talk. Sometimes police only pretend to know something: They make assertions that are untrue or unsupported, such as stating that a co-defendant has confessed or that a victim has died. Other times police create props, in the form of physical evidence, to increase the chance of obtaining a confession. Are all police lies in the interrogation room a fair and legal part of the "often competitive enterprise of ferreting out crime"? If not, where should courts or police agencies draw the line?

■ RONALD BRISBON v. UNITED STATES
957 A.2d 931 (D.C. App. 2008)

RUIZ, Associate Judge

Appellants Ronald Brisbon and Michael Wonson appeal their convictions for first-degree murder, assault with intent to kill and related offenses. Brisbon challenges the admission of his videotaped confession claiming it was involuntary. . . . Although we consider that the deceptive tactic used by the officers in interrogating Brisbon make the question of voluntariness a close question, we conclude that admission of his videotaped confession was harmless in light of the government's otherwise overwhelming evidence against him.

[Dana Route was "Ronnie T" Brisbon's ex-girlfriend; they remained friends and worked together in Fort Washington, Maryland. On the evening of May 17, she saw Brisbon cleaning two rifles with WD-40 while his friend "Pretty B" Wonson stood nearby. Brisbon and Wonson left the house with the firearms, then returned in under twenty-five minutes, guns still in hand. After they came into the house, Brisbon said to Wonson, "I can't believe that your gun jammed."]

The following day, Thursday, May 18, 2000, Ms. Route was watching the news on TV while at work when she saw a report "that two people were killed on East Capitol Street." . . . Ms. Route put two and two together and confronted Brisbon, [who] told her that "Pretty B was looking for somebody," and when he and Brisbon spotted the target, "Pretty B had got out of the truck and fired [bullets] into a crowd." . . .

Brisbon was arrested at 11:30 A.M. on May 24 at his place of work (C & T Auto Shop) by the Prince George's County, Maryland police. . . . Once they arrived at the D.C. police station, Detective Irving took Brisbon to an interrogation room and told him that he was under arrest for two murders on May 17, and had been "identified as being a shooter that night." [Detectives Credle and Irving began interrogating him. During] the first fifteen minutes, Brisbon denied everything. Detective Irving told him that they had searched the house where Brisbon lived with his mother and grandmother and "that the police recovered drugs and a shotgun out of his grandmother's house," — which was true — and "that his grandmother had got upset and was rushed to the hospital and that his mother was placed under arrest" — which was false. According to the detectives, Brisbon dropped his head and was quiet for a few seconds, then admitted that he "did it," saying that he did not "want anyone else to get in trouble." Detectives Irving and Credle insisted that Brisbon give them all of the details of the crime, because a blanket confession would not convince them that he had told the truth. The detectives denied promising Brisbon that confessing would aid his mother or grandmother. The interrogation continued for two hours, until, at around 9:30 P.M., Brisbon consented to a videotaped confession. . . .

Brisbon moved to suppress the admission of his confession into evidence, claiming that it was an involuntary statement elicited in violation of the Fifth Amendment. . . . Brisbon then took the stand and testified about how he felt pressured to confess when the police had lied to him about the fate of his mother and grandmother. [The] trial judge stated that "even taking into account Mr. Brisbon's testimony, I would find that [the confessed] statements were wholly voluntary."

Once a motion has been made to suppress a confession as involuntary, the burden is on the government to prove that the statements of the accused were voluntarily given without police coercion. Generally, the factors for consideration in determining voluntariness include (1) the circumstances surrounding the questioning, (2) the accused's age, education, and prior experiences with the law, (3) his physical and mental condition at the time the statement was made, (4) other factors showing coercion or trickery, and (5) the delay between the suspect's arrest and the confession. The government must prove voluntariness by a preponderance of the evidence.

[We are] troubled by the deception used by the police officers and its coercive potential. . . . In early Supreme Court jurisprudence, involuntary confessions were held inadmissible, stressing their inherent untrustworthiness.[13] See Brown v. Mississippi, 297 U.S. 278 (1936). In Rogers v. Richmond, 365 U.S. 534 (1961), the Court explained that the reliability of a confession — although obviously important to the truth-seeking purpose of a criminal trial — is not the touchstone of the inquiry:

13. In this case, the record corroborates that Brisbon's confession was truthful because it both contained details that only a participant would be reasonably expected to know and matched up with the eyewitness evidence presented at trial. At the time Brisbon confessed, for example, the detectives were unaware there had been a second shooter.

> [Convictions] following the admission into evidence of confessions which are involuntary, *i.e.*, the product of coercion, either physical or psychological, cannot stand. This is so not because such confessions are unlikely to be true but because the methods used to extract them offend an underlying principle in the enforcement of our criminal law: that ours is an accusatorial and not an inquisitorial system — a system in which the State must establish guilt by evidence independently and freely secured and may not by coercion prove its charge against an accused out of his own mouth. . . .

The Court . . . has never abandoned this due process jurisprudence and its focus on . . . "whether a defendant's will was overborne" by the circumstances surrounding the giving of a confession. To implement these principles, and recognizing the inherent difficulty in ascertaining whether a suspect has been coerced into confessing, we have said that confessions generally are not vitiated when they are obtained by deception or trickery, as long as the means employed are not *calculated* to produce an untrue statement. This short-form guideline reflects the dual due process concerns that a confession may not be obtained by means that are offensive to due process (inquisitorial methods that overbear the suspect's will) and that such undue coercion is likely to lead to a false confession. Thus, we have affirmed a conviction based on a confession obtained after the police used a technique where the police ran a fake lie-detector test on the defendant. Contee v. United States, 667 A.2d 103 (D.C.1995). As we explained, the suspect in a *Contee*-type situation retains ultimate control over his statements because he privately knows whether they are in fact lies. Similarly, in Davis v. United States, 724 A.2d 1163 (D.C.1998), we concluded that the trickery (falsely telling the suspect that his co-perpetrator had said that Davis was carrying a particular weapon) did not require suppression of a confession in part "because it was inconsistent with Davis's own first-hand knowledge," and, therefore, as the defendant himself testified, he was not fooled.

Here, on the other hand, Brisbon was subjected to a very different kind of psychological pressure, unrelated to the evidence the police purport to have that a suspect is guilty of the charged crime. After being told by the officers that his mother and grandmother had been arrested[15] as a result of the discovery of drugs and a shotgun during a search of their house, Brisbon testified, he felt coerced to tell the police "what they wanted to hear," so that his mother and grandmother would be released. The truth of the premise underlying the officers' deception — the existence of contraband of which Brisbon would have known — gave force to the officers' deception. We have not previously been presented with the question whether the technique used here — which could be taken by a suspect in custody as an implicit threat or a promise involving family members — was calculated to exert so much pressure on a suspect as to lead to a confession, whether true or false. Unlike the suspects in *Contee* and *Davis,* . . . Brisbon was confronted with a lie unrelated to the government's evidence of his guilt that had consequences to others, not solely to his own fate. See Holland v. McGinnis, 963 F.2d 1044, 1052 (7th Cir. 1992) (noting that the police tactic used in Lynumn v. Illinois, 372 U.S. 528 (1963), where the suspect was threatened with loss of her children and federal benefits "also distorted

15. While, according to the police, the detectives told Brisbon that his mother was arrested and his grandmother was taken to the hospital, Brisbon testified that he was told that his grandmother also was arrested and had to be taken to the hospital.

the suspect's rational choice . . . by introducing a completely extrinsic consideration: an empty but plausible threat to take away something to which she and her children would otherwise be entitled"). A defendant who is completely innocent might well confess in the latter circumstances for fear of the extraneous adverse consequences; by contrast, an innocent defendant in the former circumstances would have little incentive to render a false confession. This is at least in part because a suspect who is "in the dark" about what he is told is more susceptible to the coercive pressure of trickery, as he is dependent on what the police tell him, than one who can, as in *Contee* and *Davis,* use his own resources to test what he knows against what the police tell him, which would help him withstand the psychological manipulation. Extrinsic pressure not only impairs free choice, but also casts doubt upon the reliability of the resulting confession.

The detectives in this case candidly testified that they lied to Brisbon in order to get him "to admit his involvement in the case" and to "lure the truth" from him. When the officers who question a suspect by using trickery demonstrate an "undeviating intent . . . to extract a confession . . . the confession obtained must be examined with the most careful scrutiny." Spano v. New York, 360 U.S. 315, 324 (1959). We apply that close scrutiny here.

We begin by cautioning that the kind of deception employed here, involving supposed harm to vulnerable family members, could well cross the line beyond the type of tactics *vel non* that a court will tolerate because they are so offensive to a civilized system of justice that they must be condemned under the Due Process Clause. This is especially true if such tactics are used on a suspect particularly susceptible to police pressure. We have already expressed doubt about the police's use of deceptive tactics to "persuade" a suspect that a confession is in his best interest, in light of the evidence already amassed by the government when, in fact, there is no such evidence. See Beasley v. United States, 512 A.2d 1007, 1016 (D.C. 1986) ("We do not condone certain of the tactics used by the police in this case [promise of leniency and deception concerning strength of the government's evidence], and such tactics have made this a close case"). But the use of deception to exert psychological pressure that exploits vulnerabilities extraneous to the offense charged, such as the threat of adverse consequences to family members if the suspect does not confess or cooperate with the investigation, is in a different category that has been singled out for condemnation. See *Rogers,* 365 U.S. at 549 (expressing view that "issue of voluntariness might fairly have gone either way in the whole of the testimony" where detained suspect who initially denied involvement in shooting confessed after being told that his wife would be brought into custody for questioning); *Spano,* 360 U.S. at 324 (confession involuntary where the police used the suspect's "childhood friend," who falsely stated that the suspect's "telephone call [to him] had gotten him into trouble, that his job was in jeopardy, and that loss of his job would be disastrous to his three children, his wife and his unborn child").[17]

Here, the trial court denied Brisbon's motion to suppress without taking note of the questionable mode of psychological pressure employed in this case, and found that his statements were "wholly voluntary," without detailing the factors that

17. Some courts draw a distinction between deceptive and truthful pressure tactics involving family members. See Armstead v. Mississippi, 978 So.2d 642, 648 (Miss. 2008) (finding that "threats to arrest a defendant's family member(s) do not render a confession involuntary so long as probable cause exists to arrest such persons").

led to that determination. We know from the record that the court had just heard the testimony of the officers, who admitted that they lied to Brisbon about his mother's arrest and grandmother's hospitalization in order to get him to confess, but said that they did not promise Brisbon that his confession would result in the exoneration of his mother or Brisbon's ability to see his grandmother. Brisbon, on the other hand, testified that he felt pressured to confess by the officers' deception which included that even his frail elderly grandmother had not only been hospitalized, but also arrested along with his mother. The effect that the officers' tactics reasonably had on Brisbon is a critical element of the voluntariness inquiry. . . . The trial judge's determination, made after hearing the testimony of Brisbon and the officers and seeing the videotape of the confession, where Brisbon denied any coercion,[19] apparently was that the officers' calculated play on his emotional attachment to his mother and grandmother did not equate to unconstitutional coercion. It is of course possible that the unwelcome "news" about his mother's arrest and grandmother's hospitalization, rather than being something that overcame his will and coerced him to confess, could have instead shocked Brisbon into taking responsibility for his actions. In other words, the *truthful* information Brisbon had received about the seizure of drugs and a shotgun from their house might have induced him to want to spare them the "trouble" of being linked to his criminal activities. Brisbon testified that his mother had been arrested the year before on his account; and his mother confirmed in her testimony that she had been arrested, jailed and released, after which Brisbon became very protective of her and his ill grandmother.[20] This previous experience — and whether the officers who interrogated him were aware of it — would be relevant both to an evaluation of the officers' tactics and Brisbon's foreseeable reaction to the officers' deception involving yet another arrest of his mother for which he was to blame. The issue, however, was not explored on the record. Moreover, the officers' exchange with Brisbon about his mother and grandmother preceded the videotaped confession, so the trial judge was not able to evaluate from the tape itself Brisbon's reaction and his statements to the officers when he first confessed.

From our own review of the record, we note other factors that arguably would weigh in favor of a finding of voluntariness. First, although this was the first time Brisbon had been charged and prosecuted, he had a previous arrest, a fact indicating that he had some familiarity with the criminal justice system. But we do not know anything else about the circumstances of Brisbon's prior arrest, or whether he was subject to interrogation at that time. Second, . . . there is no indication based on the record that due to Brisbon's age (twenty-two), educational background, or physical or mental condition, he was particularly susceptible to psychological pressure, save for the obvious emotional "hot buttons" — his concern for his mother and grandmother — that the police sought to manipulate. . . . Finally, Brisbon confessed not only to the murder and assault of two innocent persons in a hail of bullets

19. According to the transcript of the confession, Brisbon denied being coerced by the police: . . .

[Detective]: Has anyone forced you, coerced you, tricked you or did anything in order for you to give this statement?
[Brisbon]: No, sir. . . .

20. Brisbon testified that he was very close to his mother and felt "disturbed" about her situation and that of his grandmother, who was then eighty-two years old and has Alzheimer's disease. Brisbon testified he would be "willing to sacrifice [his] life" for them.

fired into a group at Eastern High, but also went on to confess to other, unrelated crimes — going well beyond what even he testified the officers told him they "wanted to hear." In light of these indications that Brisbon may well have been able to resist the officers' deceptive pressure tactics, we are inclined to conclude that Brisbon did not in fact succumb to them, and that his videotaped confession was therefore voluntary and admissible.

We recognize that the question of voluntariness in this case is a close one, however, and do not decide it, because we can conclude beyond a reasonable doubt that even if the confession should have been suppressed, its admission was harmless. See Arizona v. Fulminante, 499 U.S. 279 (1991) (admission of involuntary confession is "trial error" subject to harmless error analysis). We recognize that a defendant's confession is uniquely powerful evidence and that its erroneous admission will be deemed harmless only rarely, by an overwhelming government case. For the following reasons, we think that even if we assume that Brisbon's confession was involuntary, and its admission unconstitutional, it was nevertheless harmless beyond a reasonable doubt.

This is a case where the government's evidence was not merely sufficient, or even strong, but presented overwhelming evidence of guilt. Apart from the challenged confession, the evidence arrayed against Brisbon consisted of the testimony of several witnesses and other confessions the admissibility of which is not challenged. An eyewitness to the shooting, Jameice Phillips identified Brisbon, who she knew as "Ronnie T," as the shooter. She testified that she had known him through "friends and family," for five years. . . . Nor was Brisbon's videotaped confession to the officers his only admission of guilt. Dana Route testified that Brisbon had also confessed to her, shortly after the shooting. . . .

Even after Brisbon's videotaped confession to the officers was admitted, the issue of its voluntariness and credibility remained for the jury. The jurors were instructed to weigh the credibility of Brisbon's confession in light of his testimony that it had been coerced. . . . Accordingly, we affirm Brisbon's convictions. . . .

Notes

1. *Police lies: majority position.* Most jurisdictions take the view that some police lies will produce a per se "coerced" confession, while others will ordinarily not be enough standing alone to make the confession inadmissible under the "totality of the circumstances." See Frazier v. Cupp, 394 U.S. 731 (1969) (confession voluntary even though police lied to defendant in telling him that another suspect had already confessed and implicated him). Do you agree with the court in *Brisbon* that police lies are especially likely to produce false confessions if they are "unrelated to the government's evidence of his guilt" and relate instead to "extrinsic" considerations? See State v. Kelekolio, 849 P.2d 58 (Haw. 1993) (treating "extrinsic" lies as per se violations of due process and leaving more latitude for police to tell lies regarding matters "intrinsic" to their investigation). If intrinsic lies are more tolerable, why did the *Brisbon* court express doubt about the validity of police efforts to persuade a suspect to confess "in light of the evidence already amassed by the government when, in fact, there is no such evidence"?

Some courts are especially troubled about police lies that relate to the purpose of the interrogation. See State v. McConkie, 755 A.2d 1075 (Me. 2000) (involuntary statement when officer said during police station interview that suspect's statement would "stay confidential"; officers may not affirmatively mislead suspects about the uses to which their statements may be put). Are police falsehoods of this sort more likely to coerce a confession? More detailed treatment of the categories of deception that produce a skeptical judicial response appears on the web extension for this chapter at *http://www.crimpro.com/extension/ch08*. What would be the impact of a legal rule barring the use of a confession obtained because of police lies of *any* sort? See Deborah Young, Unnecessary Evil: Police Lying in Interrogations, 28 Conn. L. Rev. 425 (1996).

2. *False physical evidence and false friends.* Is there any relevant difference between verbal lies about evidence against a defendant and the creation of false physical evidence against a suspect (for instance, forging a report from the forensics laboratory)? Courts seem especially concerned about the latter form of deception. See Commonwealth v. DiGiambattista, 813 N.E.2d 516 (Mass. 2004) (confession coerced by use of fake videotape and forged documentary evidence); Wilson v. State, 311 S.W.3d 452 (Tex. Crim. App. 2010) (use of fictional fingerprint report requires suppression of confession under statutory bar).

Another type of lie that especially troubles courts is the use of "false friends," when the questioner asks the suspect to confess out of friendship or sympathy. In Spano v. New York, 360 U.S. 315 (1959), the questioner was a friend of the suspect and stated (falsely) that if he did not obtain a statement, he would lose his job and his source of support for his family. The resulting confession was held to be involuntary.

3. *Bad confessions or bad police?* Over time the Supreme Court has shifted its views on the role of blameworthy police conduct in evaluating an "involuntary" confession. In Bram v. United States, 168 U.S. 532 (1897), the Court concluded that a coerced confession was a violation of the Fifth Amendment's self-incrimination clause. Hence, the emphasis was on the state of mind of the suspect — the question was whether the statement was "compelled." By 1936, in Brown v. Mississippi, the Court shifted its emphasis to the due process clause as the relevant limitation on the use of coerced confessions. But the Court still seemed most concerned with interrogation practices, such as physical torture in *Brown,* that made the confession, as a matter of fact, "involuntary" and therefore quite possibly false. Later decisions indicated that the state of mind of the defendant, and the consequent risk of false confessions, was not the only concern of courts evaluating the "voluntariness" of a confession. In cases such as Rogers v. Richmond, 365 U.S. 534 (1961), the Court barred use of confessions that were obtained through trickery (a false order to arrest the suspect's ill wife). Even if police conduct does not create a risk of false confession from the defendant, some morally objectionable interrogation tactics might still lead a court to conclude that the confession was "involuntary" based on the totality of the circumstances. The Supreme Court has suggested that wrongful police coercion is "a necessary predicate to the finding that a confession is not Voluntary" under federal law. Colorado v. Connelly, 479 U.S. 157 (1986). If the interrogators have not acted wrongfully (for instance, in failing to appreciate a suspect's unusually limited mental capacity), then the fact that the suspect was coerced is not sufficient.

4. *How common is police lying?* One criminologist who observed more than 180 police interrogations noted that police officers lied to the suspect in about 30 percent of all the interrogations he observed. This technique, he concluded, was among

the most effective methods of obtaining a confession or admission but it was less effective than appeals to the suspect's conscience, identifying contradictions in the story the suspect was telling, or offering excuses for the suspect's alleged conduct. Richard Leo, Inside the Interrogation Room, 86 J. Crim. L. & Criminology 266, 278 (1996). What obstacles might prevent one from learning how often police lie during interrogations? See Laurie Magid, Deceptive Police Interrogation Practices: How Far Is Too Far?, 99 Mich. L. Rev. 1168 (2001) (arguing that deception should be permitted unless it creates an unreasonable risk that an innocent person would falsely confess; until statistically sound research on random sample of confession cases demonstrates the size of this problem, no drastic limit on deceptive techniques is justified).

5. *Training police to lie.* A widely used training manual for police interrogators advises readers to accuse the suspect of committing the crime and if necessary to lie about the evidence available to the police or about other matters: Such "trickery and deceit" is necessary to successful interrogations in the majority of cases. Fred Inbau, et al., Criminal Interrogation and Confessions 484 (4th ed. 2004). Is there a difference between this line of argument and the arguments used to justify the "third degree"? What ethical boundaries should limit police lies or unenforceable (but legally valid) promises? Consider the ethics implicit in the observation of Justice Hugo Black dissenting in a case involving the enforcement of treaties with Native Americans: "Great nations, like great men, should keep their word," FPC v. Tuscarora Indian Nation, 362 U.S. 99 (1960) (Black, J., dissenting).

B. *MIRANDA* WARNINGS

It can be very difficult for a court to determine after the fact whether a confession was "voluntary." In a series of cases between 1936 and 1964, the Supreme Court attempted to highlight the various facts that might, in the "totality of the circumstances," deprive the suspect of the "power of resistance." Fikes v. Alabama, 352 U.S. 191 (1957). As the cases proliferated, it became clear that a great many facts could be relevant to the question of voluntariness. The Supreme Court, perhaps out of frustration with the repeated and difficult application of the "voluntariness" test it had created under the due process clause, began a search in the late 1950s for a more effective and easily administered method of stopping interrogation abuses.

The Court turned first to the possibility of requiring defense lawyers to be present during at least some interrogations. In a series of opinions, several members of the Court indicated that due process required that any suspect in custody should be able to obtain an attorney from the moment of arrest. See Spano v. New York, 360 U.S. 315 (1959). These tentative suggestions soon led to a holding, under the Sixth Amendment right to counsel (rather than the due process clause), that defendants in at least some interrogations had the right to have an attorney present. In Massiah v. United States, 377 U.S. 201 (1964), the defendant had already been indicted for violating narcotics laws and had retained defense counsel when the government recruited his friend to collect more evidence against him. The government placed a radio transmitter in his friend's car. Then the friend struck up a conversation with Massiah in the car about the crimes.

The Court invalidated the use of the confession that Massiah made in the car. The use of the confession at trial, the Court said, violated Massiah's Sixth Amendment right to counsel in all "criminal proceedings." Although these circumstances did not amount to physical or psychological coercion under the customary due process analysis, the Court said that an effective right to counsel "must apply to indirect and surreptitious interrogations as well as those conducted in the jailhouse." The *Massiah* decision created a method for courts to invalidate confessions on the basis of a clear rule, one that could apply regardless of the conditions during the interrogation. But if the rule were applied only to suspects who have already been indicted or to those who are tricked into a confession outside the police station, its impact would be small.

The right to counsel during custodial interrogations occurring *before* indictment received its clearest declaration in Escobedo v. Illinois, 378 U.S. 478 (1964), decided just weeks after *Massiah.* The investigators in that murder case obtained a confession from Escobedo by preventing him from consulting with his retained attorney (who was present at the police station) during the interrogation. The investigators kept Escobedo handcuffed and standing during the interrogation, and they arranged a confrontation with a second suspect, who accused Escobedo of the killing.

Some of the language in the opinion referred broadly to the importance of the presence of counsel at interrogation, which the Court now called a "critical stage" in the criminal process and which was thus covered by the Sixth Amendment right to counsel during a "prosecution." The opinion suggested that all interrogations of persons in custody would have to take place in the presence of counsel:

> The right to counsel would indeed be hollow if it began at a period when few confessions were obtained. There is necessarily a direct relationship between the importance of a stage to the police in their quest for a confession and the criticalness of that stage to the accused in his need for legal advice. [No] system worth preserving should have to fear that if an accused is permitted to consult with a lawyer, he will become aware of, and exercise, these rights. [378 U.S. at 488.]

However, the opinion also lent itself to a narrower reading by emphasizing some of the distinctive facts of the case in its holding:

> We hold, therefore, that where, as here, the investigation is no longer a general inquiry into an unsolved crime but has begun to focus on a particular suspect, the suspect has been taken into police custody, the police carry out a process of interrogations that lends itself to eliciting incriminating statements, the suspect has requested and been denied an opportunity to consult with his lawyer, and the police have not effectively warned him of his absolute constitutional right to remain silent, the accused has been denied "the Assistance of Counsel" in violation of the Sixth Amendment to the Constitution . . . and that no statement elicited by the police during the interrogation may be used against him at a criminal trial. [378 U.S. at 490-91.]

Escobedo suggested the possibility that the Sixth Amendment might require the government to provide suspects with counsel before any interrogation, and the decision sparked a national debate among state courts. Most states restricted the holding to situations in which a defendant had requested counsel, but some states tried to forecast the direction of the Supreme Court and required the government to provide counsel when an interrogation reached the "accusatory" or "critical" stage. See People v. Dorado, 394 P.2d 952 (Cal. 1964) ("The defendant who does not realize his rights under the law and who therefore does not request counsel is the very defendant who most needs counsel"); Neuenfeldt v. State, 138 N.W.2d 252 (Wis. 1965). A few states went in a different direction, requiring police to advise suspects about their right to assistance of counsel and their right to remain silent. See State v. Mendes, 210 A.2d 50 (R.I. 1965). In 1966, two years after *Escobedo,* the Supreme Court decided Miranda v. Arizona.

1. *The* Miranda *Revolution*

■ ERNESTO MIRANDA v. ARIZONA

384 U.S. 436 (1966)

WARREN, C.J.*

The cases before us raise questions which go to the roots of our concepts of American criminal jurisprudence: the restraints society must observe consistent with the Federal Constitution in prosecuting individuals for crime. More specifically, we deal with the admissibility of statements obtained from an individual who is subjected to custodial police interrogation and the necessity for procedures which assure that the individual is accorded his privilege under the Fifth Amendment to the Constitution not to be compelled to incriminate himself.

We dealt with certain phases of this problem recently in Escobedo v. Illinois, 378 U.S. 478 (1964). We granted certiorari in these cases [to explore some facets of the problems] of applying the privilege against self-incrimination to in-custody interrogation, and to give concrete constitutional guidelines for law enforcement agencies and courts to follow. . . .

We start here, as we did in *Escobedo,* with the premise that our holding is not an innovation in our jurisprudence, but is an application of principles long recognized and applied in other settings. . . . Our holding will be spelled out with some specificity in the pages which follow but briefly stated it is this: the prosecution may not use statements, whether exculpatory or inculpatory, stemming from custodial interrogation of the defendant unless it demonstrates the use of procedural safeguards effective to secure the privilege against self-incrimination. By custodial interrogation, we mean questioning initiated by law enforcement officers after a person has been taken into custody or otherwise deprived of his freedom of action in any significant way. As for the procedural safeguards to be employed, unless other fully effective means are devised to inform accused persons of their right of silence and to assure a continuous opportunity to exercise it, the following measures are required. Prior to any questioning, the person must be warned that he has a right to remain silent, that any statement he does make may be used as evidence against him, and that he has a right to the presence of an attorney, either retained or appointed. The defendant may waive effectuation of these rights, provided the waiver is made voluntarily, knowingly and intelligently. If, however, he indicates in

* [Justices Black, Douglas, Brennan, and Fortas joined in this opinion. — EDS.]

any manner and at any stage of the process that he wishes to consult with an attorney before speaking there can be no questioning. Likewise, if the individual is alone and indicates in any manner that he does not wish to be interrogated, the police may not question him. The mere fact that he may have answered some questions or volunteered some statements on his own does not deprive him of the right to refrain from answering any further inquiries until he has consulted with an attorney and thereafter consents to be questioned.

I.

The constitutional issue we decide in each of these cases is the admissibility of statements obtained from a defendant questioned while in custody or otherwise deprived of his freedom of action in any significant way. In each, the defendant was questioned by police officers, detectives, or a prosecuting attorney in a room in which he was cut off from the outside world. In none of these cases was the defendant given a full and effective warning of his rights at the outset of the interrogation process. In all the cases, the questioning elicited oral admissions, and in three of them, signed statements as well which were admitted at their trials. They all thus share salient features — incommunicado interrogation of individuals in a police-dominated atmosphere, resulting in self-incriminating statements without full warnings of constitutional rights.

An understanding of the nature and setting of this in-custody interrogation is essential to our decisions today. . . . From extensive factual studies undertaken in the early 1930's . . . it is clear that police violence and the "third degree" flourished at that time. [These practices] are undoubtedly the exception now, but they are sufficiently widespread to be the object of concern. Unless a proper limitation upon custodial interrogation is achieved — such as these decisions will advance — there can be no assurance that practices of this nature will be eradicated in the foreseeable future. [Furthermore, this] Court has recognized that coercion can be mental as well as physical, and that the blood of the accused is not the only hallmark of an unconstitutional inquisition.

Interrogation still takes place in privacy. Privacy results in secrecy and this in turn results in a gap in our knowledge as to what in fact goes on in the interrogation rooms. A valuable source of information about present police practices, however, may be found in various police manuals and texts which document procedures employed with success in the past, and which recommend various other effective tactics. These texts are used by law enforcement agencies themselves as guides. . . .

The officers are told by the manuals that the "principal psychological factor contributing to a successful interrogation is privacy — being alone with the person under interrogation." The efficacy of this tactic has been explained as follows:

> [The subject] is more keenly aware of his rights and more reluctant to tell of his indiscretions or criminal behavior within the walls of his home. Moreover his family and other friends are nearby, their presence lending moral support. In his own office, the investigator possesses all the advantages. The atmosphere suggests the invincibility of the forces of the law.

To highlight the isolation and unfamiliar surroundings, the manuals instruct the police to display an air of confidence in the suspect's guilt and from outward appearance to maintain only an interest in confirming certain details. The guilt of the subject is to be posited as a fact. The interrogator should direct his comments toward the reasons why the subject committed the act, rather than court failure by asking the subject whether he did it. Like other men, perhaps the subject has had a bad family life, had an unhappy childhood, had too much to drink, had an unrequited desire for women. The officers are instructed to minimize the moral seriousness of the offense, to cast blame on the victim or on society. These tactics are designed to put the subject in a psychological state where his story is but an elaboration of what the police purport to know already — that he is guilty. Explanations to the contrary are dismissed and discouraged. . . .

When the techniques described above prove unavailing, the texts recommend they be alternated with a show of some hostility. One ploy often used has been termed the "friendly-unfriendly" or the "Mutt and Jeff" act:

> In this technique, two agents are employed. Mutt, the relentless investigator, who knows the subject is guilty and is not going to waste any time. . . . Jeff, on the other hand, is obviously a kindhearted man. He has a family himself. He has a brother who was involved in a little scrape like this. He disapproves of Mutt and his tactics and will arrange to get him off the case if the subject will cooperate. He can't hold Mutt off for very long. The subject would be wise to make a quick decision. . . .

The manuals also contain instructions for police on how to handle the individual who refuses to discuss the matter entirely, or who asks for an attorney or relatives. The examiner is to concede him the right to remain silent. "This usually has a very undermining effect. [A] concession of this right to remain silent impresses the subject with the apparent fairness of his interrogator." After this psychological conditioning, however, the officer is told to point out the incriminating significance of the suspect's refusal to talk:

> Joe, you have a right to remain silent. That's your privilege and I'm the last person in the world who'll try to take it away from you. . . . But let me ask you this. Suppose you were in my shoes and I were in yours and you called me in to ask me about this and I told you, "I don't want to answer any of your questions." You'd think I had something to hide, and you'd probably be right in thinking that. That's exactly what I'll have to think about you, and so will everybody else. So let's sit here and talk this whole thing over. . . .

In the event that the subject wishes to speak to a relative or an attorney, the following advice is tendered:

> The interrogator should respond by suggesting that the subject first tell the truth to the interrogator himself rather than get anyone else involved in the matter. If the request is for an attorney, the interrogator may suggest that the subject save himself or his family the expense of any such professional service, particularly if he is innocent of the offense under investigation. The interrogator may also add, "Joe, I'm only looking for the truth, and if you're telling the truth, that's it. You can handle this by yourself."

From these representative samples of interrogation techniques, the setting prescribed by the manuals and observed in practice becomes clear. . . . Even without employing brutality, the "third degree" or the specific stratagems described above, the very fact of custodial interrogation exacts a heavy toll on individual liberty and trades on the weakness of individuals. . . .

In these cases, we might not find the defendants' statements to have been involuntary in traditional terms. Our concern for adequate safeguards to protect precious Fifth Amendment rights is, of course, not lessened in the slightest. In each of the cases, the defendant was thrust into an unfamiliar atmosphere and run through menacing police interrogation procedures. The potentiality for compulsion is forcefully apparent, for example, in State v. Miranda, 401 P.2d 721 (Ariz. 1965), where the indigent Mexican defendant was a seriously disturbed individual with pronounced sexual fantasies, and in People v. Stewart, 400 P.2d 97 (Cal. 1965), in which the defendant was an indigent Los Angeles Negro who had dropped out of school in the sixth grade. [In] none of these cases did the officers undertake to afford appropriate safeguards at the outset of the interrogation to insure that the statements were truly the product of free choice. . . .

The current practice of incommunicado interrogation is at odds with one of our Nation's most cherished principles — that the individual may not be compelled to incriminate himself. Unless adequate protective devices are employed to dispel the compulsion inherent in custodial surroundings, no statement obtained from the defendant can truly be the product of his free choice. From the foregoing, we can readily perceive an intimate connection between the privilege against self-incrimination and police custodial questioning. . . .

II.

[The] constitutional foundation underlying the privilege is the respect a government — state or federal — must accord to the dignity and integrity of its citizens. To maintain a fair state-individual balance, to require the government to shoulder the entire load, to respect the inviolability of the human personality, our accusatory system of criminal justice demands that the government seeking to punish an individual produce the evidence against him by its own independent labors, rather than by the cruel, simple expedient of compelling it from his own mouth. In sum, the privilege is fulfilled only when the person is guaranteed the right to remain silent unless he chooses to speak in the unfettered exercise of his own will.

The question in these cases is whether the privilege is fully applicable during a period of custodial interrogation. . . . An individual swept from familiar surroundings into police custody, surrounded by antagonistic forces, and subjected to the techniques of persuasion described above cannot be otherwise than under compulsion to speak. As a practical matter, the compulsion to speak in the isolated setting of the police station may well be greater than in courts or other official investigations, where there are often impartial observers to guard against intimidation or trickery. . . .

Our holding [in *Escobedo*] stressed the fact that the police had not advised the defendant of his constitutional privilege to remain silent at the outset of the interrogation. . . . A different phase of the *Escobedo* decision was significant in its attention to the absence of counsel during the questioning, [And] *Escobedo* explicated another facet of the pre-trial privilege, noted in many of the Court's prior decisions: the protection of rights at trial. That counsel is present when statements are taken from an individual during interrogation obviously enhances the integrity of the fact-finding processes in court. . . . Without the protections flowing from adequate warnings and the rights of counsel, all the careful safeguards erected around the giving of testimony, whether by an accused or any other witness, would become empty formalities in a procedure where the most compelling possible evidence of guilt, a confession, would have already been obtained at the unsupervised pleasure of the police. . . .

III.

It is impossible for us to foresee the potential alternatives for protecting the privilege which might be devised by Congress or the States in the exercise of their creative rule-making capacities. Therefore we cannot say that the Constitution necessarily requires adherence to any particular solution for the inherent compulsions of the interrogation process as it is presently conducted. Our decision in no way creates a constitutional straitjacket which will handicap sound efforts at reform, nor is it intended to have this effect. . . . However, unless we are shown other procedures which are at least as effective in apprising accused persons of their right of silence and in assuring a continuous opportunity to exercise it, the following safeguards must be observed.

At the outset, if a person in custody is to be subjected to interrogation, he must first be informed in clear and unequivocal terms that he has the right to remain silent. For those unaware of the privilege, the warning is needed simply to make them aware of it — the threshold requirement for an intelligent decision as to its exercise. More important, such a warning is an absolute prerequisite in overcoming the inherent pressures of the interrogation atmosphere. It is not just the subnormal or woefully ignorant who succumb to an interrogator's imprecations, whether implied or expressly stated, that the interrogation will continue until a confession is obtained or that silence in the face of accusation is itself damning and will bode ill when presented to a jury. . . . The Fifth Amendment privilege is so fundamental to our system of constitutional rule and the expedient of giving an adequate warning as to the availability of the privilege so simple, we will not pause to inquire in individual cases whether the defendant was aware of his rights without a warning being given. . . .

The warning of the right to remain silent must be accompanied by the explanation that anything said can and will be used against the individual in court. This warning is needed in order to make him aware not only of the privilege, but also of the consequences of forgoing it. It is only through an awareness of these consequences that there can be any assurance of real understanding and intelligent exercise of the privilege. Moreover, this warning may serve to make the individual more acutely aware that . . . he is not in the presence of persons acting solely in his interest.

The circumstances surrounding in-custody interrogation can operate very quickly to overbear the will of one merely made aware of his privilege by his interrogators. Therefore, the right to have counsel present at the interrogation is indispensable to the protection of the Fifth Amendment privilege under the system we delineate today. Our aim is to assure that the individual's right to choose between silence and speech remains unfettered throughout the interrogation process. A once-stated warning, delivered by those who will conduct the interrogation, cannot itself suffice to that end among those who most require knowledge of their rights. . . . Even preliminary advice given to the accused by his own attorney can be swiftly overcome by the secret interrogation process. Thus, the need for counsel to protect the Fifth Amendment privilege comprehends not merely a right to consult with counsel prior to questioning, but also to have counsel present during any questioning if the defendant so desires.

The presence of counsel at the interrogation may serve several significant subsidiary functions as well. If the accused decides to talk to his interrogators, the assistance of counsel can mitigate the dangers of untrustworthiness. With a lawyer present the likelihood that the police will practice coercion is reduced, and if coercion is nevertheless exercised the lawyer can testify to it in court. The presence of a lawyer can also help to guarantee that the accused gives a fully accurate statement to the police and that the statement is rightly reported by the prosecution at trial.

[An individual's] failure to ask for a lawyer does not constitute a waiver. No effective waiver of the right to counsel during interrogation can be recognized unless specifically made after the warnings we here delineate have been given. The accused who does not know his rights and therefore does not make a request may be the person who most needs counsel. . . .

Accordingly we hold that an individual held for interrogation must be clearly informed that he has the right to consult with a lawyer and to have the lawyer with him during interrogation under the system for protecting the privilege we delineate today. As with the warnings of the right to remain silent and that anything stated can be used in evidence against him, this warning is an absolute prerequisite to interrogation. . . .

If an individual indicates that he wishes the assistance of counsel before any interrogation occurs, the authorities cannot rationally ignore or deny his request on the basis that the individual does not have or cannot afford a retained attorney. The financial ability of the individual has no relationship to the scope of the rights involved here. The privilege against self-incrimination secured by the Constitution applies to all individuals. . . . In fact, were we to limit these constitutional rights to those who can retain an attorney, our decisions today would be of little significance. The cases before us as well as the vast majority of confession cases with which we have dealt in the past involve those unable to retain counsel. . . .

In order fully to apprise a person interrogated of the extent of his rights under this system then, it is necessary to warn him not only that he has the right to consult with an attorney, but also that if he is indigent a lawyer will be appointed to represent him. Without this additional warning, the admonition of the right to consult with counsel would often be understood as meaning only that he can consult with a lawyer if he has one or has the funds to obtain one. . . .

Once warnings have been given, the subsequent procedure is clear. If the individual indicates in any manner, at any time prior to or during questioning, that he wishes to remain silent, the interrogation must cease. At this point he has shown that he intends to exercise his Fifth Amendment privilege; any statement taken after the person invokes his privilege cannot be other than the product of compulsion, subtle or otherwise. Without the right to cut off questioning, the setting of in-custody interrogation operates on the individual to overcome free choice in producing a statement after the privilege has been once invoked. If the individual states that he wants an attorney, the interrogation must cease until an attorney is present. At that time, the individual must have an opportunity to confer with the attorney and to have him present during any subsequent questioning. If the individual cannot obtain an attorney and he indicates that he wants one before speaking to police, they must respect his decision to remain silent.

This does not mean, as some have suggested, that each police station must have a "station house lawyer" present at all times to advise prisoners. It does mean, however, that if police propose to interrogate a person they must make known to him that he is entitled to a lawyer and that if he cannot afford one, a lawyer will be provided for him prior to any interrogation. . . . If the interrogation continues without the presence of an attorney and a statement is taken, a heavy burden rests on the government to demonstrate that the defendant knowingly and intelligently waived his privilege against self-incrimination and his right to retained or appointed counsel. . . .

An express statement that the individual is willing to make a statement and does not want an attorney followed closely by a statement could constitute a waiver. But a valid waiver will not be presumed simply from the silence of the accused after warnings are given or simply from the fact that a confession was in fact eventually obtained. . . . Moreover, where in-custody interrogation is involved, there is no room for the contention that the privilege is waived if the individual answers some questions or gives some information on his own prior to invoking his right to remain silent when interrogated.

Whatever the testimony of the authorities as to waiver of rights by an accused, the fact of lengthy interrogation or incommunicado incarceration before a statement is made is strong evidence that the accused did not validly waive his rights. . . . Moreover, any evidence that the accused was threatened, tricked, or cajoled into a waiver will, of course, show that the defendant did not voluntarily waive his privilege. The requirement of warnings and waiver of rights is a fundamental with respect to the Fifth Amendment privilege and not simply a preliminary ritual to existing methods of interrogation. . . .

The principles announced today deal with the protection which must be given to the privilege against self-incrimination when the individual is first subjected to police interrogation while in custody at the station or otherwise deprived of his freedom of action in any significant way. It is at this point that our adversary system of criminal proceedings commences, distinguishing itself at the outset from the inquisitorial system recognized in some countries. . . .

Our decision is not intended to hamper the traditional function of police officers in investigating crime. When an individual is in custody on probable cause, the police may, of course, seek out evidence in the field to be used at trial against him. Such investigation may include inquiry of persons not under restraint. General on-the-scene questioning as to facts surrounding a crime or other general questioning of citizens in the fact-finding process is not affected by our holding. . . .

In dealing with statements obtained through interrogation, we do not purport to find all confessions inadmissible. Confessions remain a proper element in law enforcement. Any statement given freely and voluntarily without any compelling influences is, of course, admissible in evidence. . . .

IV.

In announcing these principles, we are not unmindful of the burdens which law enforcement officials must bear, often under trying circumstances. [Our] decision does not in any way preclude police from carrying out their traditional investigatory functions. Although confessions may play an important role in some convictions, the cases before us present graphic examples of the overstatement of the "need" for confessions. In each case authorities conducted interrogations ranging up to five days in duration despite the presence, through standard investigating practices, of considerable evidence against each defendant. . . .

Over the years the Federal Bureau of Investigation has compiled an exemplary record of effective law enforcement while advising any suspect or arrested person, at the outset of an interview, that he is not required to make a statement, that any statement may be used against him in court, that the individual may obtain the services of an attorney of his own choice and, more recently, that he has a right to free counsel if he is unable to pay. . . .

The experience in some other countries also suggests that the danger to law enforcement in curbs on interrogation is overplayed. The English procedure since 1912 under the Judges' Rules is significant. As recently strengthened, the Rules require that a cautionary warning be given an accused by a police officer as soon as he has evidence that affords reasonable grounds for suspicion; they also require that any statement made be given by the accused without questioning by police. The right of the individual to consult with an attorney during this period is expressly recognized. . . .

It is also urged upon us that we withhold decision on this issue until state legislative bodies and advisory groups have had an opportunity to deal with these problems by rule making. We have already pointed out that the Constitution does not require any specific code of procedures for protecting the privilege against self-incrimination during custodial interrogation. Congress and the States are free to develop their own safeguards for the privilege, so long as they are fully as effective as those described above in informing accused persons of their right of silence and in affording a continuous opportunity to exercise it. In any event, however, the issues presented are of constitutional dimensions and must be determined by the courts. . . .

V.

Because of the nature of the problem and because of its recurrent significance in numerous cases, we have to this point discussed the relationship of the Fifth Amendment privilege to police interrogation without specific concentration on the facts of the cases before us. We turn now to these facts to consider the application to these cases of the constitutional principles discussed above. . . .

On March 13, 1963, petitioner, Ernesto Miranda, was arrested at his home and taken in custody to a Phoenix police station. He was there identified by the complaining witness. The police then took him to Interrogation Room No. 2 of the detective bureau. There he was questioned by two police officers. The officers admitted at trial that Miranda was not advised that he had a right to have an attorney present. Two hours later, the officers emerged from the interrogation room with a written confession signed by Miranda. At the top of the statement was a typed paragraph stating that the confession was made voluntarily, without threats or promises of immunity and "with full knowledge of my legal rights, understanding any statement I make may be used against me." [One of the officers testified that he read this paragraph to Miranda. Apparently, however, he did not do so until after Miranda had confessed orally.]

At his trial before a jury, the written confession was admitted into evidence over the objection of defense counsel, and the officers testified to the prior oral confession made by Miranda during the interrogation. Miranda was found guilty of kidnapping and rape. He was sentenced to 20 to 30 years' imprisonment on each count, the sentences to run concurrently. On appeal, the Supreme Court of Arizona held that Miranda's constitutional rights were not violated in obtaining the confession and affirmed the conviction. In reaching its decision, the court emphasized heavily the fact that Miranda did not specifically request counsel.

We reverse. From the testimony of the officers and by the admission of respondent, it is clear that Miranda was not in any way apprised of his right to consult with an attorney and to have one present during the interrogation, nor was his right not to be compelled to incriminate himself effectively protected in any other manner. Without these warnings the statements were inadmissible. The mere fact that he signed a statement which contained a typed-in clause stating that he had "full knowledge" of his "legal rights" does not approach the knowing and intelligent waiver required to relinquish constitutional rights. . . .

HARLAN, J., dissenting.*

[The] new rules are not designed to guard against police brutality or other unmistakably banned forms of coercion. Those who use third-degree tactics and deny them in court are equally able and destined to lie as skillfully about warnings and waivers. Rather, the thrust of the new rules is to negate all pressures, to reinforce the nervous or ignorant suspect, and ultimately to discourage any confession at all. The aim in short is toward "voluntariness" in a Utopian sense, or to view it from a different angle, voluntariness with a vengeance. To incorporate this notion into the Constitution requires a strained reading of history and precedent and a disregard of the very pragmatic concerns that alone may on occasion justify such strains. . . .

It is most fitting to begin an inquiry into the constitutional precedents by surveying the limits on confessions the Court has evolved under the Due Process Clause of the Fourteenth Amendment. This is so because these cases show that there exists a workable and effective means of dealing with confessions in a judicial manner. . . .

The earliest confession cases in this Court emerged from federal prosecutions and were settled on a nonconstitutional basis, the Court adopting the common-law rule that the absence of inducements, promises, and threats made a confession voluntary and admissible. [A] new line of decisions, testing admissibility by the Due Process Clause, began in 1936 with Brown v. Mississippi, and must now embrace somewhat more than 30 full opinions of the Court. While the voluntariness rubric was repeated in many instances, the Court never pinned it down to a single meaning but on the contrary infused it with a number of different values. To travel quickly over the main themes, there was an initial emphasis on reliability, supplemented by concern over the legality and fairness of the police practices, in an "accusatorial" system of law enforcement, and eventually by close attention to the individual's state of mind and capacity for effective choice. The outcome was a continuing re-evaluation on the facts of each case of how much pressure on the suspect was permissible.

Among the criteria often taken into account were threats or imminent danger, physical deprivations such as lack of sleep or food, repeated or extended interrogation, limits on access to counsel or friends, length and illegality of detention

* [Justices Stewart and White joined in this opinion. — EDS.]

under state law, and individual weakness or incapacities. Apart from direct physical coercion, however, no single default or fixed combination of defaults guaranteed exclusion, and synopses of the cases would serve little use because the overall gauge has been steadily changing, usually in the direction of restricting admissibility. . . .

There are several relevant lessons to be drawn from this constitutional history. The first is that with over 25 years of precedent the Court has developed an elaborate, sophisticated, and sensitive approach to admissibility of confessions. It is "judicial" in its treatment of one case at a time, flexible in its ability to respond to the endless mutations of fact presented, and ever more familiar to the lower courts . . . . The second point is that in practice and from time to time in principle, the Court has given ample recognition to society's interest in suspect questioning as an instrument of law enforcement . . . .

I turn now to the Court's asserted reliance on the Fifth Amendment, an approach which I frankly regard as a *trompe l'oeil.* The Court's opinion in my view reveals no adequate basis for extending the Fifth Amendment's privilege against self-incrimination to the police station. Far more important, it fails to show that the Court's new rules are well supported, let alone compelled, by Fifth Amendment precedents. . . .

Examined as an expression of public policy, the Court's new regime proves so dubious that there can be no due compensation for its weakness in constitutional law. . . . Without at all subscribing to the generally black picture of police conduct painted by the Court, I think it must be frankly recognized at the outset that police questioning allowable under due process precedents may inherently entail some pressure on the suspect and may seek advantage in his ignorance or weaknesses. . . . The Court's new rules aim to offset these minor pressures and disadvantages intrinsic to any kind of police interrogation. . . .

What the Court largely ignores is that its rules impair, if they will not eventually serve wholly to frustrate, an instrument of law enforcement that has long and quite reasonably been thought worth the price paid for it. There can be little doubt that the Court's new code would markedly decrease the number of confessions. To warn the suspect that he may remain silent and remind him that his confession may be used in court are minor obstructions. To require also an express waiver by the suspect and an end to questioning whenever he demurs must heavily handicap questioning. And to suggest or provide counsel for the suspect simply invites the end of the interrogation. . . .

While passing over the costs and risks of its experiment, the Court portrays the evils of normal police questioning in terms which I think are exaggerated. Albeit stringently confined by the due process standards interrogation is no doubt often inconvenient and unpleasant for the suspect. However, it is no less so for a man to be arrested and jailed, to have his house searched, or to stand trial in court, yet all this may properly happen to the most innocent given probable cause, a warrant, or an indictment. Society has always paid a stiff price for law and order, and peaceful interrogation is not one of the dark moments of the law. . . .

It is also instructive to compare the attitude in this case of those responsible for law enforcement with the official views that existed when the Court undertook . . . major revisions of prosecutorial practice prior to this case. . . . In Mapp v. Ohio, 367 U.S. 643 (1961), which imposed the exclusionary rule on the States for Fourth Amendment violations, more than half of the States had themselves already adopted some such rule. In Gideon v. Wainwright, 372 U.S. 335 (1963), . . . an amicus brief was filed by 22 States and Commonwealths urging that [the Court extend the right to counsel to indigents in state court]; only two States besides that of the respondent came forward to protest. By contrast, in this case new restrictions on police questioning have been opposed by the United States and in an amicus brief signed by 27 States and Commonwealths, not including the three other States which are parties. No State in the country has urged this Court to impose the newly announced rules, nor has any State chosen to go nearly so far on its own. [The] FBI falls sensibly short of the Court's formalistic rules. For example, there is no indication that FBI agents must obtain an affirmative "waiver" before they pursue their questioning. . . .

In closing this [discussion] of policy considerations attending the new confession rules, some reference must be made to their ironic untimeliness. There is now in progress in this country a massive re-examination of criminal law enforcement procedures on a scale never before witnessed. [Legislative] reform is rarely speedy or unanimous, though this Court has been more patient in the past. But the legislative reforms when they come would have the vast advantage of empirical data and comprehensive study, they would allow experimentation and use of solutions not open to the courts, and they would restore the initiative in criminal law reform to those forums where it truly belongs. . . .

WHITE, J., dissenting.*

Decisions like these cannot rest alone on syllogism, metaphysics or some ill-defined notions of natural justice, although each will perhaps play its part. . . . First, we may inquire what are the textual and factual bases of this new fundamental rule. [The] Court concedes that it cannot truly know what occurs during custodial questioning, because of the innate secrecy of such proceedings. It extrapolates a picture of what it conceives to be the norm from police investigatorial manuals. . . . Judged by any of the standards for empirical investigation utilized in the social sciences the factual basis for the Court's premise is patently inadequate. . . .

Even if one were to postulate that the Court's concern is not that all confessions induced by police interrogation are coerced but rather that some such confessions are coerced and present judicial procedures are believed to be inadequate to identify the confessions that are coerced and those that are not, it would still not be essential to impose the rule that the Court has now fashioned. Transcripts or observers could be required, specific time limits, tailored to fit the cause, could be imposed, or other devices could be utilized to reduce the chances that otherwise indiscernible coercion will produce an inadmissible confession.

On the other hand, even if one assumed that there was an adequate factual basis for the conclusion that all confessions obtained during in-custody interrogation are the product of compulsion, the rule propounded by the Court would still be irrational, for, apparently, it is only if the accused is also warned of his right to counsel and waives both that right and the right against self-incrimination that the inherent compulsiveness of interrogation disappears. But if the defendant may not answer without a warning a question such as "Where were you last night?" without having his answer be a compelled one, how can the Court ever accept his negative answer

* [Justices Harlan and Stewart joined in this opinion. — EDS.]

to the question of whether he wants to consult his retained counsel or counsel whom the court will appoint? . . .

The obvious underpinning of the Court's decision is a deep-seated distrust of all confessions. As the Court declares that the accused may not be interrogated without counsel present, absent a waiver of the right to counsel, and as the Court all but admonishes the lawyer to advise the accused to remain silent, the result adds up to a judicial judgment that evidence from the accused should not be used against him in any way, whether compelled or not. . . . I see nothing wrong or immoral, and certainly nothing unconstitutional, in the police's asking a suspect whom they have reasonable cause to arrest whether or not he killed his wife or in confronting him with the evidence on which the arrest was based, at least where he has been plainly advised that he may remain completely silent. . . . Particularly when corroborated, as where the police have confirmed the accused's disclosure of the hiding place of implements or fruits of the crime, such confessions have the highest reliability and significantly contribute to the certitude with which we may believe the accused is guilty. . . .

Much of the trouble with the Court's new rule is that it will operate indiscriminately in all criminal cases, regardless of the severity of the crime or the circumstances involved. It applies to every defendant, whether the professional criminal or one committing a crime of momentary passion. [If] further restrictions on police interrogation are desirable at this time, a more flexible approach makes much more sense than the Court's constitutional straitjacket which forecloses more discriminating treatment by legislative or rule-making pronouncements. . . .

■ LOUISIANA CONSTITUTION ART. 1, §13

When any person has been arrested or detained in connection with the investigation or commission of any offense, he shall be advised fully of the reasons for his arrest or detention, his right to remain silent, his right against self incrimination, his right to the assistance of counsel and, if indigent, his right to court appointed counsel.

■ MASSACHUSETTS GENERAL LAWS, CH. 276, §33A

The police official in charge of the station or other place of detention having a telephone wherein a person is held in custody, shall permit the use of the telephone, at the expense of the arrested person, for the purpose of allowing the arrested person to communicate with his family or friends, or to arrange for release on bail, or to engage the services of an attorney. Any such person shall be informed forthwith upon his arrival at such station or place of detention, of his right to so use the telephone, and such use shall be permitted within one hour thereafter.

Notes

1. *The constitutional basis for* Miranda. What is the legal basis of the *Miranda* decision? The Court indicated that the warnings and the right to counsel it was

announcing were requirements of the Fifth Amendment's self-incrimination clause. Later, the Court refined this position and stated that the *Miranda* rights were "prophylactic" rules that were not, strictly speaking, required by the Fifth Amendment but were necessary to prevent violations of the self-incrimination privilege. See Michigan v. Tucker, 417 U.S. 433 (1974). Why do you suppose the Court based its ruling on the Fifth Amendment rather than the Sixth Amendment's right to counsel? If the *Miranda* warnings are a prophylactic rule rather than a constitutional requirement, did the Court have the authority to impose this requirement on state as well as federal law enforcement officers?

The opinion in *Miranda* creates a relatively detailed set of obligations. Some states and law enforcement agencies, prior to 1966, used warnings to increase the likelihood that a confession would be found voluntary. Would the Court have been wiser to announce more general principles and hope for legislation or police rules to appear before providing any needed specification? See Mark A. Godsey, Rethinking the Involuntary Confession Rule: Toward a Workable Test for Identifying Compelled Self-Incrimination, 93 Cal. L. Rev. 465 (2005) (argues for replacing voluntariness with self-incrimination as basic criterion for admission of confessions; proposes asking whether confession was obtained by using an objective penalty on the suspect to punish silence or provoke speech).

2. *State adoption and modification of* Miranda. The *Miranda* requirements apply to law enforcement officials in all the states. What would occur if the Supreme Court were to modify the *Miranda* decision? A few states, such as Louisiana and Massachusetts, have independently adopted under their state constitutions or statutes a set of required warnings similar to those in *Miranda.* See Traylor v. State, 596 So. 2d 957 (Fla. 1992). Others declare that *Miranda* has no basis in the state constitution. See State v. Bleyl, 435 A.2d 1349 (Me. 1981). Does the Louisiana provision reprinted above impose any requirements different from what the Court required in *Miranda*?

3. *The coercive environment and the "infinite regress" problem.* The *Miranda* opinion is premised on the view that interrogation of a suspect in a police station is inherently coercive. Do you agree with this premise? If so, what makes the interrogation coercive? Is there any legal or practical consequence if a suspect refuses to speak? Consider again the words of the Fifth Amendment: Are you convinced that interrogation in a police station "compels" a person to be a "witness" against himself? As you answer these questions, keep in mind the physical environment of a typical custodial interrogation. The interrogation rooms are designed to isolate suspects, for instance, by locating the rooms in the rear of the building, often with no windows for viewing persons outside the room. The room will contain only a table and a few chairs. Consider also the subject matter of the conversation, and the assertions a questioner will often make. If interrogation is inherently coercive, isn't the decision to waive the right to counsel also made in the same setting? Could the Court respond to this problem by requiring a more specific warning about waiver? A warning about the warning?

4. *Liberal or conservative?* Was *Miranda* a liberal or conservative ruling? Did it legitimize police interrogation through the use of a routine and inconsequential warning? Did it foreclose more intrusive and less predictable judicial supervision of interrogation techniques? See also Charles D. Weisselberg, Mourning *Miranda*, 96 Calif. L. Rev. 1519 (2008) (safeguards of *Miranda* have become ineffective because police training now instructs officers in how to take advantage of court rulings that have weakened the case; *Miranda*'s hollow ritual often forecloses a searching inquiry

into the voluntariness of a statement). Early opinions among police officers about the wisdom of *Miranda* were mixed. Some officers believed that it was a damaging and unnecessary impediment to effective interrogations; others believed that the required warnings were appropriate and would further the professionalism of police work. See Otis Stephens, Robert Flanders & Lewis Cannon, Law Enforcement and the Supreme Court: Police Perceptions of the *Miranda* Requirements, 39 Tenn. L. Rev. 407 (1972). Over the years, police opinion about the decision has become markedly more positive. Various empirical studies of the reception of *Miranda* among law enforcement officers and other groups are discussed on the web extension for this chapter at *http://www.crimpro.com/extension/ch08*.

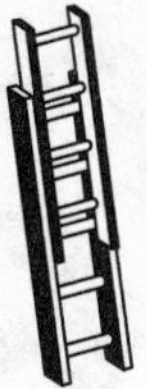

5. *Constitutional foundations of* Miranda, *revisited.* Soon after the *Miranda* decision, Congress enacted 18 U.S.C. §3501, stating that the admissibility of statements made by federal defendants while in police custody should turn only on whether or not they were voluntarily made. While the statute instructed the judge to consider any warnings given to the suspect about the right to silence or to consult an attorney, the "presence or absence" of any such warnings "need not be conclusive on the issue of voluntariness of the confession." For many years and through many administrations, federal prosecutors appear to have made only modest use of §3501. See Paul Cassell, The Statute That Time Forgot: 18 U.S.C. §3501 and the Overhauling of *Miranda,* 85 Iowa L. Rev. 175, 197-225 (1999). The most likely explanation is that §3501 was such a stark rejection of the Supreme Court's decision that most federal prosecutors felt they should not, and perhaps could not, rely upon it, since they are sworn to uphold the constitution.

The Supreme Court finally spoke to the issue in Dickerson v. United States, 530 U.S. 428 (2000). The defendant in the case gave incriminating evidence against himself in an interview that proceeded without proper *Miranda* warnings (although the interrogation was not otherwise coercive). The key question was whether *Miranda* announced a constitutional rule or was merely a regulation of evidence used in federal court.

The Court held that *Miranda,* "being a constitutional decision of this Court, may not be in effect overruled by an Act of Congress, and we decline to overrule *Miranda* ourselves." Over the years, the Court made conflicting statements about the constitutional basis for *Miranda.* Many later decisions referred to *Miranda* as a "prophylactic" rule rather than a constitutional requirement in its own right. See New York v. Quarles, 467 U.S. 649 (1984) (warnings not required when questions were necessitated by an immediate threat to public safety). But in the end, the fact that *Miranda* applied to proceedings in state court demonstrated that the rule was constitutionally required.

6. *Real* Miranda *reforms.* Again and again courts and commentators have noted that the *Miranda* court left open "potential alternatives for protecting the privilege which might be devised by Congress or the States," and allowed legislative solutions different from *Miranda* warnings, so long as the alternatives were "at least as effective in apprising accused persons of their right of silence and in assuring a continuous opportunity to exercise it." If *Miranda* warnings are problematic for law enforcement, why hasn't Congress or a state legislature enacted alternatives more substantial than §3501? What form might this legislation take?

2. *"Triggering"* Miranda *Warnings*

Miranda warnings do not need to be given before *every* conversation between police and citizens. There are two conditions that trigger a need for warnings: First, the suspect must be in custody, and second, the officers must be conducting an interrogation. Even though judges, police, and commentators often join the concepts in the phrase "custodial interrogation," it is important to evaluate custody and interrogation separately.

a. "Custody"

The police are required to give *Miranda* warnings only to suspects who are interrogated while in custody. One study of police work in Salt Lake City found that 30 percent of all interviews occurred in noncustodial settings, including examinations at the crime scene, during field investigations, and during arranged interviews. See Paul Cassell & Bret Hayman, Police Interrogation in the 1990s: An Empirical Study of the Effects of *Miranda,* 43 UCLA L. Rev. 839 (1996). The 30 percent figure relates to full-blown interrogations: It substantially understates the total amount of questions, inquiries, comments, and exchanges that police conduct outside of custodial settings.

■ STATE v. KEVIN FRANKLIN ELMARR

181 P.3d 1157 (Colo. 2008)

RICE, J.

In this interlocutory appeal . . . we review an order from the Boulder County District Court suppressing statements the defendant made in response to police interrogation. We find that the trial court properly suppressed the defendant's statements because the defendant was in custody while interrogated, and it is conceded that he did not receive proper *Miranda* warnings before that custodial interrogation. We therefore affirm the trial court's suppression order and remand for further proceedings.

I. FACTS AND PROCEDURAL HISTORY

On Sunday, May 24, 1987, Detectives Ferguson and Haugse of the Boulder Sheriff's Department and Officer Stiles of the Longmont Police Department visited Defendant Kevin Franklin Elmarr at his home to inform him that his ex-wife, Carol Murphy, was found dead the day before. According to the testimony before the trial court, the detectives were not in uniform, and their weapons were holstered. Officer Stiles was in uniform, but was present more as a friend of Elmarr's family to aid in the notification of death. Two other police officers — Captain Epp and Lieutenant Hopper — later arrived at Elmarr's home in another unmarked police car and were seen there by Elmarr, but they stayed outside.

Detectives Ferguson and Haugse spoke with Elmarr at his home and Elmarr disclosed that he had visited with his ex-wife the day before she was found dead, and had taken her for a ride on his motorcycle. Shortly after this disclosure, Detective Ferguson said the police had more questions for him, and asked him if he would mind accompanying them to the Sheriff's Department at the Boulder Justice Center for further questioning; Elmarr agreed. The detectives drove Elmarr to the Sheriff's Department in their unmarked police car, with Elmarr in the back seat. The detectives did not provide Elmarr the option of driving himself to the station. Elmarr was not handcuffed.

During the drive to the Sheriff's Department, Elmarr volunteered that he had not been entirely truthful in his earlier conversation with the detectives, and provided further information regarding his meeting with his ex-wife the day before she was found dead. The detectives did not say anything while in the car.

The detectives arrived at the Sheriff's Department through the garage in the basement, which is a secure area not open to the public. They escorted Elmarr into an elevator that led to the Sheriff's Department Detective Bureau, which is also not open to the public. Witnesses were unable to recall whether Elmarr was searched before entering the building, but Captain Epp testified that it was standard procedure for persons to be patted down before being transported. Based on this testimony, the trial court found that Elmarr was subjected to a pat-down search upon arrival at the Sheriff's Department. The trial court also found that Elmarr was then placed in a closed interview room measuring seven by ten feet, and told to stay there until officers returned. Captain Epp and Lieutenant Hopper subsequently interrogated Elmarr in that interview room. During the interrogation, Elmarr was seated against the wall, while Captain Epp and Lieutenant Hopper were seated in front of the door. The officers were dressed casually, but the trial court found that they were carrying their weapons. . . . Though the interview room door had a lock on it, no one could recall if it was locked while Elmarr was in the room.

Witnesses testified that Elmarr was never handcuffed or otherwise directly physically restrained, but no one ever told Elmarr that he was free to leave or that he was not under arrest. The interrogation was audio- and video-taped, and the recording shows that Captain Epp began his interrogation by advising Elmarr that he did not have to talk to the police, that he had a right to remain silent, that anything he said that incriminated him would be taken down, and that he had a right to an attorney. Captain Epp then asked if Elmarr wanted to talk to them then. Elmarr answered "sure," and then began speaking about the last time he saw his ex-wife.

Captain Epp then questioned Elmarr about the details of that last meeting with his ex-wife. Though Captain Epp spoke rather slowly and softly, he soon began expressing his doubts about Elmarr's story. For instance, early in the interview Captain Epp told Elmarr, "I hope you're telling me the truth." Later he inspected what he thought were scratches on Elmarr's arms.

Approximately halfway into the interview, Lieutenant Hopper took over much of the questioning, and his tone was more aggressive. He asked Elmarr if he ever thought of hurting his ex-wife; why witnesses would say they saw his ex-wife on a motorcycle matching Elmarr's near the place where her body was found; and whether his ex-wife was "all right" the last time he saw her. Lieutenant Hopper again asked Elmarr why he initially lied when interviewed at his house. [Elmarr said] that he felt he was being accused of murder, and Lieutenant Hopper answered, "You've lied to us already. . . . Put yourself in our place. What would you, what would you think if you were us?"

The recording also shows that near the end of the interrogation, which lasted almost an hour, Captain Epp resumed his questioning, telling Elmarr, "I just get the feeling that you are holding something back." When Elmarr wondered aloud whether he should get a lawyer[2] and protested that he was telling the truth, Captain Epp responded, "Well, I'm not sure. I've got reason to believe that something, that some points here that you're not." Shortly thereafter Lieutenant Hopper explicitly asked Elmarr whether he killed his ex-wife, and Elmarr denied it. Elmarr then said, "I think I would like to talk to a lawyer." At this point the officers stated the interview was over, opened the door, and left the room. They testified that the entire interrogation lasted approximately fifty minutes.

However, Elmarr remained in the Sheriff's Department. The recording shows that he was kept in the interview room for a period of time, after which one of the officers returned and asked him if he would like to take a polygraph test. Elmarr demurred and again stated he wanted to talk to an attorney. The officer left. After a further wait, yet another officer entered the interview room, stated that he wanted to take some photographs of Elmarr, and asked if Elmarr would mind removing his clothes for those pictures, adding, "You really don't have a choice right now." Elmarr complied, after which he asked, "When do I get to go home?" The officer responded, "Shortly here, I hope." Elmarr then asked to make some calls to his family and the officer left, returning later to escort Elmarr out of the interview room to make his calls. Afterwards, Elmarr was escorted back into the interview room, and in the videotape one can hear the door close again. Elmarr again asked how long he would be there, and was told, "At least until your lawyer calls." After a further wait, Elmarr's attorney entered the interview room and the videotape ended, almost an hour after Captain Epp and Lieutenant Hopper had terminated their formal interrogation. . . .

Elmarr was not charged with a crime until almost twenty years later, when in January 2007 he was arrested and charged with first degree murder for the murder of his ex-wife Carol Murphy. [The trial court] suppressed all of the statements Elmarr made at the Sheriff's Department, finding that they were all the product of custodial interrogation.

Because there was no dispute that Elmarr was interrogated, the trial court focused on whether Elmarr was in custody while at the Sheriff's Department. In concluding that Elmarr was indeed in custody, the trial court made the following findings: (1) Elmarr was subjected to a pat-down search upon arrival at the Sheriff's Department; (2) Elmarr was provided with (albeit deficient) *Miranda*-type warnings typically given when a suspect is in custody; (3) Elmarr was placed in a seven-by-ten-foot interview room and told to stay there until the officers returned; (4) Elmarr was interrogated for at least fifty minutes by officers carrying weapons; (5) Captain Epp likely suspected that Elmarr was involved in Carol Murphy's murder and was attempting to elicit incriminating statements from him; (6) Captain Epp and Lieutenant Hopper used a "good-cop-bad-cop" technique upon Elmarr; (6) Elmarr was never handcuffed or overtly restrained, but was never told he was free to leave. . . .

2. The People conceded that this was a sufficient invocation of the right to counsel, and that interrogation should have ceased at this point.

II. Analysis

In their interlocutory appeal, the People . . . argue that Elmarr was not in custody when he was interrogated at the Sheriff's Department, and that the trial court made erroneous factual findings and considered irrelevant evidence in reaching its conclusion. We find that the trial court erroneously considered the police officers' subjective intent in determining whether Elmarr was in custody, but that the court's other factual findings are supported by the record. We hold that those findings, coupled with the undisputed evidence in the record, establish that Elmarr was in custody when he was interrogated at the Sheriff's Department. . . .

For purposes of determining whether *Miranda* warnings are required, a suspect is in custody when his or her "freedom of action is curtailed to a degree associated with formal arrest." People v. Polander, 41 P.3d 698, 705 (Colo.2001) (quoting Berkemer v. McCarty, 468 U.S. 420, (1984)). In assessing the question of custody, we consider such factors as the time, place, and purpose of the interrogation; the persons present during the interrogation; the words the officers spoke to the suspect; the officers' tone of voice and general demeanor; the length and mood of the interrogation; whether any restraint or limitation was placed on the suspect's movement during interrogation; the officers' response to any of the suspect's questions; whether directions were given to the suspect during interrogation; and the suspect's verbal or nonverbal responses to such directions. None of these factors is determinative, and the question of custody is determined in light of the totality of the circumstances.

However, because the test of custody is an objective one, unarticulated thoughts or views of the officers and suspects are irrelevant. See Stansbury v. California, 511 U.S. 318 (1994) (The "initial determination of custody depends on the objective circumstances of the interrogation, not on the subjective views harbored by either the interrogating officers or the person being questioned."). Thus, the People are correct in their argument that the trial court erred when, in determining whether Elmarr was in custody, it relied (in part) upon the finding that Captain Epp likely suspected that Elmarr was involved in Carol Murphy's murder and attempted to elicit incriminating statements from him. That finding has no relevance to the custody question. We therefore review de novo whether the trial court's other factual findings, and the undisputed evidence in the record, establish that Elmarr was in custody.

Our analysis is guided by precedent considering somewhat analogous facts. For instance, in California v. Beheler, 463 U.S. 1121 (1983), officers asked the suspect to accompany them to the police station, transported him there, informed him he was not under arrest, and questioned him for less than thirty minutes before he voluntarily left the police station. The court found that these facts established that the suspect was not in custody. Similarly, in Oregon v. Mathiason, 429 U.S. 492 (1977), the officers asked the suspect to come to the police station to be interviewed. The suspect drove himself to the station, was immediately told he was not under arrest, was told that he was a suspect in a crime, and interviewed for approximately thirty minutes behind closed doors in an interview room before he left the station voluntarily. Again, the court found the suspect was not in custody. We came to the same conclusion in People v. Matheny, 46 P.3d 453 (Colo. 2002), where the suspect was asked to come to the police station to be interviewed, drove himself and the police officers to the station, was escorted to an interview room, was told he was free to leave and not under arrest, and then was interviewed for approximately an hour and a half.

In People v. Trujillo, 784 P.2d 788 (Colo. 1990), however, we found that a suspect was in custody where he was asked to come to the police station for an interview and drove himself to the station; upon arrival, he was never told he was free to leave or not under arrest, was asked accusatory questions for over an hour and a half, was asked to submit to a mug shot and a polygraph test, and was asked to produce certain evidence to the police. Similarly, in People v. Dracon, 884 P.2d 712 (Colo. 1994), we found the suspect was in custody where she agreed to accompany officers to the police station, riding in the front seat of the police car, and was taken through a non-public area to an office and questioned for almost three hours; she was never told she was free to leave or not under arrest, and was made to wait for another three hours in the police station before being interviewed yet again. Finally, we found that a suspect was in custody in People v. Minjarez, 81 P.3d 348 (Colo. 2003), where police officers came to the hospital where the suspect's child was being treated, asked nurses to bring him to a hospital interview room the officers had procured, directed the suspect to sit in a chair away from the closed door, and told the suspect he was free to go but then subjected him to aggressive interrogation — consisting of leading questions and accusations of guilt — for twenty of the forty-five minutes of the interview.

Precedent does not provide a neat formula for deciding the case at hand, and indeed there can be no such formula as each case will present novel factual patterns not previously addressed. We have provided some general rules, however. On the one hand, we have heeded the warning that one is not in custody simply because the questioning takes place in the station house. On the other hand, an officer's statement that a suspect is "free to leave" is not sufficient to establish that an interview is non-custodial, when all the external circumstances appear to the contrary.

Though the case at hand presents a close question, we find that Elmarr was in custody while interrogated by officers in the Sheriff's Department in 1987. No one fact leads us to this conclusion, but rather the totality of the circumstances combine to create a custodial atmosphere. Though Elmarr was asked to accompany police officers to the station for questioning, such a question does not necessarily make the event voluntary, as one could interpret the question to be one where "no" is not an available answer — especially in the circumstances present here. It is significant that Elmarr was transported in the back of a police car to the non-public area of the Sheriff's Department, where he was directed to wait and then interrogated in a small, closed-door interview room. Importantly, he was never told he was not under arrest, or that he was free to leave. In fact, the trial court found that Elmarr was instructed to wait for officers in a closed room, and was thereafter interrogated at length in that room.

Furthermore, it is significant that Elmarr was subjected to aggressive interrogation, where the interrogators expressed doubts regarding his truthfulness, discounted his denials, confronted him with potential evidence of his guilt, and accused him of committing murder. Such interrogation by multiple officers in a small room isolated from others helped create a sense of custody. The custodial atmosphere continued after Elmarr requested an attorney — even then, he was kept in the closed-door interview room and was asked about his willingness to submit to a polygraph test, and then was directed to disrobe for photographs, about which he was told, "You really don't have a choice." All of these factors combined to prompt Elmarr to ask the reasonable question, "When do I get to go home?" All of these facts lead to the conclusion that Elmarr's freedom of action was curtailed to a degree associated with formal arrest, and a reasonable person under those circumstances would feel that he was in custody.[5]

We conclude that all of Elmarr's statements to the police at the Boulder Sheriff's Department in 1987 were the product of custodial interrogation. Because it is conceded that Elmarr did not receive a proper *Miranda* warning, all of those statements must be suppressed. Accordingly, we affirm the trial court's suppression order, and remand for further proceedings consistent with this opinion.

COATS, J., dissenting.

Almost a quarter-century ago, the United States Supreme Court made clear that a suspect is not placed in custody for purposes of the *Miranda* requirements merely by being seized and subjected to an investigatory stop. Berkemer v. McCarty, 468 U.S. 420 (1984). Rather, the prophylactic *Miranda* warnings are triggered only when a suspect's liberty has been infringed upon to an extent commensurate with a formal arrest. And interrogation at a police station, as long as it is consensual, does not constitute a seizure of any kind, much less a seizure tantamount to an arrest.

This jurisdiction was late in acknowledging the distinction between a seizure of the defendant's person and custody for purposes of *Miranda,* and when finally forced to acknowledge the Supreme Court's holdings in *Berkemer* . . . and *Beheler*, we dismissed them as merely reflecting a "fact-specific approach" to the question of custody. Despite grudgingly conceding that *Miranda* is triggered only by a show of force traditionally associated with an arrest, characterized by actions like drawing and pointing weapons, handcuffing, and conducting searches that exceed the limits of a weapons pat-down, and eventually even coming to mouth the words of the Supreme Court's standard, we seem never (as evidenced by today's holding) to have fully embraced the concept.

Once again the majority fails to distinguish objective indications that a suspect has effectively been arrested from indications of a potential suspect's interest in avoiding that eventuality. In the former case, any statements made without an effective waiver of *Miranda* warnings are presumptively the product of police coercion. In the latter, whether motivated more by a desire to assist the investigation or to avoid attracting further suspicion, no such presumption arises. Comparing voluntary witness statements and real evidence is not only a legitimate but in fact a highly desirable and effective technique for solving crimes.

In the absence of actual indicia of an arrest, the majority marshals a laundry list of circumstances or factors, indicative of little more than an interview at the police station. The fact that interview rooms are typically neither large nor public, that two officers are present for an interview, or that they close the door for privacy indicate virtually nothing about the voluntariness of an interviewee's presence. As the

5. The People argue that if the interrogation of Elmarr was custodial, it only became so toward the end of the interview, so that only statements after that point could be suppressed. However, there is no discrete point at which one could say that a non-custodial interview suddenly became custodial. It is the totality of the circumstances, from the time Elmarr was put in a police car until the time he was finally released hours later, that makes the encounter custodial.

Supreme Court has expressly noted, the fact that questioners carry holstered side-arms indicates only that they are police officers, which is understood by the interviewee when he consents to a stationhouse interview. And rather than being an indication of arrest, riding in a police car, only after giving consent and without having been patted-down or handcuffed, would suggest to any reasonable person precisely the opposite.

In the absence of an objectively manifested change in circumstances, the fact that a defendant who is present by agreement is not expressly told that he is free to leave has little meaning; and it seems more than a little disingenuous to suggest it as a worthy practice in light of the trial court's adverse reaction to the police reminder that the defendant was free not to speak with them. To the extent that circumstances actually did change at some point as a result of the defendant's responses, he clearly felt free to, and did, terminate the interview, and only his earlier statements are at issue here. In fact, the majority's substantial reliance on events following termination of the interview is a further indication of its failure to grasp, or at least its failure to apply, the objective standard dictated by the Supreme Court. In the absence of any indication that they already intended, and had already communicated their intent, to arrest him, the subsequent actions of the officers could have no bearing whatsoever on the defendant's perception of his status at the time of his statements.

With its mechanical counting of virtually meaningless factors and its comparisons with fact patterns considered by this court long before the Supreme Court's modern custody jurisprudence became clear to us, I can only assume the majority either fails to appreciate the import of that jurisprudence or despite it, continues to harbor reservations about the use of a defendant's own words to establish his guilt. In either case, I believe the majority's holding today conflicts with the Supreme Court's interpretation of the United States Constitution; can serve only to dissuade law enforcement officers from seeking and preserving a record of voluntary witness interviews; and needlessly hinders the search for truth in the criminal process. I therefore respectfully dissent.

EID, J., dissenting.

. . . In my view, the trial court made two significant and fundamental errors in this case. First, the court found that the incomplete *Miranda* warnings given by the officers created custody: "Defendant was advised of *Miranda* at the very beginning of the questioning, which would indicate to someone familiar with the criminal process that he was being deprived of his freedom." In so holding, the court got it exactly backwards. *Miranda* warnings do not create custody. Instead, custody triggers *Miranda.* [It] would be bizarre to penalize police officers for attempting to give *Miranda* warnings in situations that were later determined by a court to be noncustodial.

The second fundamental error committed by the trial court is the fact that it relied on the officers' subjective intentions in its analysis of whether Elmarr was in custody, concluding that "Captain Epp likely suspected that Defendant was involved in the murder and intended to attempt to elicit incriminating statements from Defendant." As the majority recognizes, and Elmarr acknowledges, the subjective intentions of the officers in questioning the defendant have no role in determining whether the defendant was in custody.

These two errors tainted the entirety of the trial court's analysis and render its fact-finding, upon which the majority relies, suspect. In my view, we should correct the trial court's errors and remand the case for further proceedings. For this reason, I respectfully dissent from the majority's opinion.

Problem 8-1. (Non)Custody: Police Assistance

Shortly after midnight, Police Officer Gene Sheldon was dispatched to the residence of Marvin and Linda Dyer on an emergency call. Ms. Dyer was reportedly suffering from a pleurisy attack. Officer Sheldon arrived at the same time as an ambulance. He followed the ambulance crew into the house and found Ms. Dyer seated on the floor of the bathroom. Emergency medical technicians convinced her to leave the house to seek medical attention. After the rescue unit had left to take Ms. Dyer to the clinic, Officer Sheldon asked Mr. Dyer what had happened, and Mr. Dyer admitted that he had hit his wife. While Sheldon spoke with Mr. Dyer in one room, a volunteer firefighter stayed with the six children in the next room. After a few moments of conversation, Mr. Dyer said that he wanted to go to bed and "if anybody comes back to the bedroom, all they are going to hear is a loud bang." Sheldon stopped Mr. Dyer from leaving the room by standing in the hallway. He convinced Mr. Dyer to sit down. About two hours after Officer Sheldon had arrived at the house, Ms. Dyer returned in the ambulance. Mr. Dyer went outside and Officer Sheldon placed him under arrest. Did Mr. Dyer make his statements while in custody? See State v. Dyer, 513 N.W.2d 316 (Neb. 1994).

Problem 8-2. Blunt Questions

Joseph Turmel and one passenger were traveling northbound on Interstate 89 in New Hampshire. At approximately 5:00 P.M., Trooper James Mayers approached Turmel's car in an unmarked State Police pickup truck. Mayers had five years of experience with undercover narcotics investigations. As Mayers passed Turmel's car at about 70 mph, he noticed that Turmel was holding an unusual cigar in an unusual manner. Based on his training as a drug recognition expert, Mayers believed that the cigar was a "blunt," having part of its tobacco replaced by marijuana. Turmel held the cigar between his thumb and index finger, and "cupped" it inside his hand. Mayers then saw Turmel put the cigar to his mouth, inhale, and pass the cigar to his passenger, who also put the cigar to his mouth and inhaled.

Mayers radioed for a marked police cruiser to assist him. He pulled ahead of Turmel's car and monitored it for three miles until Sgt. Scott Sweet caught up to pursue. Sweet then followed Turmel for six miles, at which point two other marked police cruisers joined the pursuit. Neither Mayers nor Sweet saw Turmel drive erratically or violate any traffic laws. The three police cruisers and Mayers' unmarked truck then pulled the car over to investigate.

Sweet approached on the driver's side and asked Turmel to step out of the car. Sweet and Mayers then took him to the back of the car. Two other officers took the passenger to the front of the car. Mayers smelled marijuana coming from the interior of the car. Mayers introduced himself to Turmel as an officer with the Narcotics Investigation Unit of the State Police, and explained that he had watched him smoking marijuana in the car. Mayers told Turmel that he wanted him to cooperate and asked him if he had been smoking marijuana. Turmel replied, "Yes." Mayers told him that he was not under arrest and asked him whether there were any weapons or drugs in the car. Turmel said there were none, and then Mayers asked for consent to search the vehicle, saying that if no weapons or drugs were found in the car, Turmel and his passenger would "probably" be free to leave. Mayers told Turmel that he did not have to consent to the search, but if he did not consent, Mayers would pursue "other avenues" to search the car. Turmel consented to the search.

Mayers' initial search did not produce any contraband. Following the discovery of a large amount of cash in the trunk, however, a trooper with a drug-sniffing dog were summoned and arrived at the scene 10 minutes later, and the butt of a marijuana cigarette was eventually found in the car's ashtray. Neither Sweet nor Mayers read a *Miranda* warning to Turmel before the questioning or before his consent to search the car. Will the trial court grant a motion to suppress the cash and the marijuana cigarette butt? Does the legal analysis here differ at all from the "stop versus arrest" question explored in Chapter 5? Cf. State v. Turmel, 838 A.2d 1279 (N.H. 2003).

Notes

1. *Subjective versus objective test for custody: majority position.* Federal and state courts determine whether a suspect is in "custody" for purposes of *Miranda* by using an objective test: Would a reasonable person in the suspect's position believe that she has been constrained in a manner akin to an arrest? See Berkemer v. McCarty, 468 U.S. 420 (1984). The particular officer's intentions about the suspect's freedom to leave, and the suspect's actual views about whether she was free to leave, are not controlling under this approach. Many circumstances — the location of the interrogation, the suspect's reason for coming there, the number of officers present, the defendant's conduct after the interrogation — can have a bearing on this objective test. An interrogation does not have to occur in a police station to be custodial. See Orozco v. Texas, 394 U.S. 324 (1969) (custodial interrogation when four police officers wake suspect in bedroom at 4 A.M. and question him). By the same token, an interrogation does not become custodial whenever it occurs within a police station. See California v. Beheler, 463 U.S. 1121 (1983) (suspect arrives at station voluntarily, is told he is not under arrest, and leaves after brief interrogation). When a suspect is "asked" to come to the station, is it a voluntary appearance? If a police officer asks a suspect "to have a seat" in the patrol car, is the suspect in custody? See People v. Taylor, 41 P.3d 681 (Colo. 2002) (roadside stop of driver became custodial for *Miranda* purposes after passenger was arrested on outstanding warrant, officers searched car without consent, and one officer kept driver standing in one place outside car). The dizzying level of detail that seems relevant in answering the custody question gets further attention in the web extension for this chapter at *http://www.crimpro.com/extension/ch08*.

The labels "objective" and "subjective" may not be a reliable guide to which facts will figure in the outcome. See Yarborough v. Alvarado, 541 U.S. 652 (2004) (defendant's age or experience with law enforcement do not qualify as "objective circumstances of the interrogation" in determining the question of custody); Rigterink v. State, 2 So.3d 221 (Fla. 2009) (if reasonable person in suspect's position would understand that the police have probable cause to arrest the suspect for a serious crime, that circumstance militates strongly toward the conclusion that the suspect is in custody).

While the Colorado Supreme Court seems to apply a relatively broad definition of "custody," it is equally easy to find high state courts more skeptical of custody determinations. See State v. Smith, 546 N.W. 2d 916) (Iowa 1996) (no custody where four juveniles under probation in Missouri were brought to a juvenile center by their mothers, interviewed by Iowa officers about a murder because while the interviews took place over many hours, the interview center was "family-centered" and "warm" and had a fish tank, food and drinks were provided, and the questioning was "non-coercive"). Indeed, both high state and lower federal courts sometimes work hard to distinguish United States Supreme Court precedent on the question of custody. See, e.g., Herrera v. State, 241 S.W.3d 520 (Tex. Crim. App. 2007) (no custody for purposes of *Miranda* where suspect already in jail on unrelated charges); cf. Mathis v. United States, 391 U.S. 1 (1968) (custody for purposes of *Miranda* when Internal Revenue Service agents questions suspect in prison serving sentencing for another offense).

2. *"Stop" versus "custody."* Recall that, for purposes of the Fourth Amendment, a "stop" occurs when a reasonable person would not "feel free to leave" (see Chapter 2). If an officer questions a person during such an investigative stop, has a custodial interrogation occurred for purposes of *Miranda*? In Berkemer v. McCarty, 468 U.S. 420 (1984), the Supreme Court decided that a traffic stop does not amount to "custody" under *Miranda.* State courts both before and after *Berkemer* reached the same conclusion. How is an investigative stop different from interrogation in the police station? How are they similar?

3. *Compelled appearances in legal proceedings.* Is a person in "custody" when a court orders her to appear in legal proceedings to answer questions? Under the U.S. Constitution, the courts have concluded that compulsory process is not "custody" for purposes of *Miranda.* See United States v. Mandujano, 425 U.S. 564 (1976) (no *Miranda* warnings required for witnesses compelled to appear before grand jury); State v. Monteiro, 632 A.2d 340 (R.I. 1993) (same); Minnesota v. Murphy, 465 U.S. 420 (1984) (no warnings necessary during required interview with probation officer); but see Estelle v. Smith, 451 U.S. 454 (1981) (suspect is in custody when compelled to attend interview with state-paid psychologist who will testify at sentencing). Given that a refusal to comply with an order to appear can lead to a jail term for contempt, how is this situation different from custodial interrogation in a police station?

b. "Interrogation"

A suspect's conversations while in custody might not rise to the level of interrogations and therefore might not require *Miranda* warnings. Of the many conversations taking place between police officers and suspects, which qualify as "interrogations" that trigger *Miranda* warnings in custodial settings? Again, have the courts drawn the line wisely?

RHODE ISLAND v. THOMAS INNIS

446 U.S. 291 (1980)

STEWART, J.*

In Miranda v. Arizona, 384 U.S. 436 (1966), the Court held that, once a defendant in custody asks to speak with a lawyer, all interrogation must cease until a lawyer is present. The issue in this case is whether the respondent was "interrogated" in violation of the standards promulgated in the *Miranda* opinion.

I.

[Shortly] after midnight, the Providence police received a telephone call from Gerald Aubin, . . . a taxicab driver, who reported that he had just been robbed by a man wielding a sawed-off shotgun [near Mount Pleasant]. While at the Providence police station waiting to give a statement, Aubin noticed a picture of his assailant on a bulletin board [on a poster relating to the murder of a taxicab driver five days earlier. That picture was of Innis].

At approximately 4:30 A.M. on the same date, Patrolman Lovell, while cruising the streets of Mount Pleasant in a patrol car, spotted [Innis, arrested him, and advised him of his *Miranda* rights. Within minutes, Sergeant Sears and Captain Leyden arrived at the scene, and each of them also gave Innis *Miranda* warnings.] The respondent stated that he understood those rights and wanted to speak with a lawyer. Captain Leyden then directed that the respondent be placed in a "caged wagon," a four-door police car with a wire screen mesh between the front and rear seats, and be driven to the central police station. Three officers, Patrolmen Gleckman, Williams, and McKenna, were assigned to accompany the respondent to the central station. They placed the respondent in the vehicle and shut the doors. Captain Leyden then instructed the officers not to question the respondent or intimidate or coerce him in any way. The three officers then entered the vehicle, and it departed.

While en route to the central station, Patrolman Gleckman initiated a conversation with Patrolman McKenna concerning the missing shotgun. As Patrolman Gleckman later testified:

> At this point, I was talking back and forth with Patrolman McKenna stating that I frequent this area while on patrol and [that because a school for handicapped children is located nearby,] there's a lot of handicapped children running around in this area, and God forbid one of them might find a weapon with shells and they might hurt themselves.

Patrolman McKenna apparently shared his fellow officer's concern: "I more or less concurred with him [Gleckman] that it was a safety factor and that we should, you know, continue to search for the weapon and try to find it." While Patrolman Williams said nothing, he overheard the conversation between the two officers: "He [Gleckman] said it would be too bad if the little — I believe he said a girl — would

* [Justices White, Blackmun, Powell, and Rehnquist joined in this opinion. — EDS.]

pick up the gun, maybe kill herself." The respondent then interrupted the conversation, stating that the officers should turn the car around so he could show them where the gun was located. . . . At the time the respondent indicated that the officers should turn back, they had traveled no more than a mile, a trip encompassing only a few minutes. The police vehicle then returned to the scene of the arrest where a search for the shotgun was in progress. There, Captain Leyden again advised the respondent of his *Miranda* rights. The respondent replied that he understood those rights but that he "wanted to get the gun out of the way because of the kids in the area in the school." The respondent then led the police to a nearby field, where he pointed out the shotgun under some rocks by the side of the road.

[The trial court denied Innis's motion to suppress the evidence regarding the gun, concluding that Innis had waived his *Miranda* rights. The jury returned a verdict of guilty on all counts.] We granted certiorari to address for the first time the meaning of "interrogation" under Miranda v. Arizona. . . .

II.

. . . The starting point for defining "interrogation" in this context is, of course, the Court's *Miranda* opinion. There the Court observed that "[by] custodial interrogation, we mean questioning initiated by law enforcement officers after a person has been taken into custody or otherwise deprived of his freedom of action in any significant way." This passage and other references throughout the opinion to "questioning" might suggest that the *Miranda* rules were to apply only to those police interrogation practices that involve express questioning of a defendant while in custody.

We do not, however, construe the *Miranda* opinion so narrowly. The concern of the Court in *Miranda* was that the "interrogation environment" created by the interplay of interrogation and custody would "subjugate the individual to the will of his examiner" and thereby undermine the privilege against compulsory self-incrimination. The police practices that evoked this concern included several that did not involve express questioning. For example, [the Court mentioned] the use of psychological ploys, such as to posit "the guilt of the subject," to "minimize the moral seriousness of the offense," and "to cast blame on the victim or on society." It is clear that these techniques of persuasion, no less than express questioning, were thought, in a custodial setting, to amount to interrogation.

This is not to say, however, that all statements obtained by the police after a person has been taken into custody are to be considered the product of interrogation. [It is clear] that the special procedural safeguards outlined in *Miranda* are required not where a suspect is simply taken into custody, but rather where a suspect in custody is subjected to interrogation. "Interrogation," as conceptualized in the *Miranda* opinion, must reflect a measure of compulsion above and beyond that inherent in custody itself.

We conclude that the *Miranda* safeguards come into play whenever a person in custody is subjected to either express questioning or its functional equivalent. That is to say, the term "interrogation" under *Miranda* refers not only to express questioning, but also to any words or actions on the part of the police (other than those normally attendant to arrest and custody) that the police should know are reasonably likely to elicit an incriminating response from the suspect. The latter portion of this definition focuses primarily upon the perceptions of the suspect, rather than the intent of the police. This focus reflects the fact that the *Miranda* safeguards were designed to vest a suspect in custody with an added measure of protection against coercive police practices, without regard to objective proof of the underlying intent of the police. A practice that the police should know is reasonably likely to evoke an incriminating response from a suspect thus amounts to interrogation.[7] But, since the police surely cannot be held accountable for the unforeseeable results of their words or actions, the definition of interrogation can extend only to words or actions on the part of police officers that they should have known were reasonably likely to elicit an incriminating response.[8]

Turning to the facts of the present case, we conclude that the respondent was not "interrogated" within the meaning of *Miranda.* It is undisputed that the first prong of the definition of "interrogation" was not satisfied, for the conversation between Patrolmen Gleckman and McKenna included no express questioning of the respondent. Rather, that conversation was, at least in form, nothing more than a dialogue between the two officers to which no response from the respondent was invited.

Moreover, it cannot be fairly concluded that the respondent was subjected to the "functional equivalent" of questioning. It cannot be said, in short, that Patrolmen Gleckman and McKenna should have known that their conversation was reasonably likely to elicit an incriminating response from the respondent. There is nothing in the record to suggest that the officers were aware that the respondent was peculiarly susceptible to an appeal to his conscience concerning the safety of handicapped children. Nor is there anything in the record to suggest that the police knew that the respondent was unusually disoriented or upset at the time of his arrest.

The case thus boils down to whether, in the context of a brief conversation, the officers should have known that the respondent would suddenly be moved to make a self-incriminating response. Given the fact that the entire conversation appears to have consisted of no more than a few offhand remarks, we cannot say that the officers should have known that it was reasonably likely that Innis would so respond. This is not a case where the police carried on a lengthy harangue in the presence of the suspect. Nor does the record support the respondent's contention that, under the circumstances, the officers' comments were particularly "evocative." It is our view, therefore, that the respondent was not subjected by the police to words or actions that the police should have known were reasonably likely to elicit an incriminating response from him. . . .

MARSHALL, J., dissenting.*

I am substantially in agreement with the Court's definition of "interrogation" within the meaning of Miranda v. Arizona, 384 U.S. 436 (1966). In my view, the

7. This is not to say that the intent of the police is irrelevant, for it may well have a bearing on whether the police should have known that their words or actions were reasonably likely to evoke an incriminating response. In particular, where a police practice is designed to elicit an incriminating response from the accused, it is unlikely that the practice will not also be one which the police should have known was reasonably likely to have that effect.

8. Any knowledge the police may have had concerning the unusual susceptibility of a defendant to a particular form of persuasion might be an important factor in determining whether the police should have known that their words or actions were reasonably likely to elicit an incriminating response from the suspect.

* [Justice Brennan joined in this opinion. — EDS.]

Miranda safeguards apply whenever police conduct is intended or likely to produce a response from a suspect in custody. [The] Court requires an objective inquiry into the likely effect of police conduct on a typical individual, taking into account any special susceptibility of the suspect to certain kinds of pressure of which the police know or have reason to know.

I am utterly at a loss, however, to understand how this objective standard as applied to the facts before us can rationally lead to the conclusion that there was no interrogation. . . . Since the car traveled no more than a mile before Innis agreed to point out the location of the murder weapon, Officer Gleckman must have begun almost immediately to talk about the search for the shotgun. . . . One can scarcely imagine a stronger appeal to the conscience of a suspect — any suspect — than the assertion that if the weapon is not found an innocent person will be hurt or killed. And not just any innocent person, but an innocent child — a little girl — a helpless, handicapped little girl on her way to school. The notion that such an appeal could not be expected to have any effect unless the suspect were known to have some special interest in handicapped children verges on the ludicrous. . . . I firmly believe that this case is simply an aberration, and that in future cases the Court will apply the standard adopted today in accordance with its plain meaning.

STEVENS, J., dissenting.

. . . I.

[In] my view any statement that would normally be understood by the average listener as calling for a response is the functional equivalent of a direct question, whether or not it is punctuated by a question mark. The Court, however, takes a much narrower view. It holds that police conduct is not the "functional equivalent" of direct questioning unless the police should have known that what they were saying or doing was likely to elicit an incriminating response from the suspect. This holding represents a plain departure from the principles set forth in *Miranda.*

[Once a suspect cuts off questioning,] the police are prohibited from making deliberate attempts to elicit statements from the suspect. Yet the Court is unwilling to characterize all such attempts as "interrogation," noting only that "where a police practice is designed to elicit an incriminating response from the accused, it is unlikely that the practice will not also be one which the police should have known was reasonably likely to have that effect."[8]

[In] order to give full protection to a suspect's right to be free from any interrogation at all, the definition of "interrogation" must include any police statement or conduct that has the same purpose or effect as a direct question. Statements that appear to call for a response from the suspect, as well as those that are designed to do so, should be considered interrogation. By prohibiting only those relatively few statements or actions that a police officer should know are likely to elicit an incriminating response, the Court today accords a suspect considerably less protection. Indeed, since I suppose most suspects are unlikely to incriminate themselves even when questioned directly, this new definition will almost certainly exclude every

8. This factual assumption is extremely dubious. I would assume that police often interrogate suspects without any reason to believe that their efforts are likely to be successful in the hope that a statement will nevertheless be forthcoming.

statement that is not punctuated with a question mark from the concept of "interrogation."

The difference between the approach required by a faithful adherence to *Miranda* and the stinted test applied by the Court today can be illustrated by comparing three different ways in which Officer Gleckman could have communicated his fears about the possible dangers posed by the shotgun to handicapped children. He could have:

1. directly asked Innis: "Will you please tell me where the shotgun is so we can protect handicapped schoolchildren from danger?"
2. announced to the other officers in the wagon: "If the man sitting in the back seat with me should decide to tell us where the gun is, we can protect handicapped children from danger," or
3. stated to the other officers: "It would be too bad if a little handicapped girl would pick up the gun that this man left in the area and maybe kill herself."

In my opinion, all three of these statements should be considered interrogation because all three appear to be designed to elicit a response from anyone who in fact knew where the gun was located. Under the Court's test, on the other hand, the form of the statements would be critical. The third statement would not be interrogation because in the Court's view there was no reason for Officer Gleckman to believe that Innis was susceptible to this type of an implied appeal; therefore, the statement would not be reasonably likely to elicit an incriminating response. Assuming that this is true, then it seems to me that the first two statements, which would be just as unlikely to elicit such a response, should also not be considered interrogation. But, because the first statement is clearly an express question, it would be considered interrogation under the Court's test. The second statement, although just as clearly a deliberate appeal to Innis to reveal the location of the gun, would presumably not be interrogation because (a) it was not in form a direct question and (b) it does not fit within the "reasonably likely to elicit an incriminating response" category that applies to indirect interrogation.

As this example illustrates, the Court's test creates an incentive for police to ignore a suspect's invocation of his rights in order to make continued attempts to extract information from him. If a suspect does not appear to be susceptible to a particular type of psychological pressure, the police are apparently free to exert that pressure on him despite his request for counsel, so long as they are careful not to punctuate their statements with question marks. And if, contrary to all reasonable expectations, the suspect makes an incriminating statement, that statement can be used against him at trial. The Court thus turns *Miranda*'s unequivocal rule against any interrogation at all into a trap in which unwary suspects may be caught by police deception. . . .

II.

. . . In any event, I think the Court is clearly wrong in holding, as a matter of law, that Officer Gleckman should not have realized that his statement was likely to elicit an incriminating response. The Court implicitly assumes that, at least in the absence of a lengthy harangue, a criminal suspect will not be likely to respond to indirect appeals to his humanitarian impulses. [This assumption] is directly contrary to the teachings of police interrogation manuals, which recommend appealing to a suspect's sense of morality as a standard and often successful interrogation technique. . . .

Moreover, there is evidence in the record to support the view that Officer Gleckman's statement was intended to elicit a response from Innis. Officer Gleckman, who was not regularly assigned to the caged wagon, was directed by a police captain to ride with respondent to the police station. . . . The record does not explain why, notwithstanding the fact that respondent was handcuffed, unarmed, and had offered no resistance when arrested by an officer acting alone, the captain ordered Officer Gleckman to ride with respondent. It is not inconceivable that two professionally trained police officers concluded that a few well-chosen remarks might induce respondent to disclose the whereabouts of the shotgun. This conclusion becomes even more plausible in light of the emotionally charged words chosen by Officer Gleckman. . . .

Problem 8-3. Blurting

A suspect in a shooting was taken into custody. The suspect asked to talk with the detectives investigating the case, but they told him that he could do so only after his fingerprints were taken and after he had executed a written waiver of his *Miranda* rights. While a different detective was taking the prints, the suspect blurted out, "This is really going to fuck me up." The detective immediately asked why, and the suspect said that he had handled the gun in question on the previous day but that it had jammed. The detective stopped the defendant from saying anything further. Later tests of the gun yielded no identifiable fingerprints. Was the suspect "interrogated"? Compare Commonwealth v. Diaz, 661 N.E.2d 1326 (Mass. 1996).

Problem 8-4. Public Safety Motivation

At approximately 12:30 A.M., a young woman approached Police Officers Frank Kraft and Sal Scarring and told them that she had just been raped by a black male, approximately six feet tall, who was wearing a black jacket with the name "Big Ben" printed in yellow letters on the back. She told the officers that the man, who was carrying a gun, had just entered a nearby supermarket.

The officers drove the woman to the supermarket, and Officer Kraft entered the store while Officer Scarring radioed for assistance. Officer Kraft quickly spotted Benjamin Quarles, who matched the description given by the woman, approaching a checkout counter. When Quarles saw Kraft, he turned and ran toward the rear of the store, and Kraft pursued him with a drawn gun. Kraft lost sight of him for several seconds but spotted him again and ordered him to stop and put his hands over his head.

Although more than three other officers had arrived on the scene by that time, Officer Kraft was the first to reach Quarles. He frisked him and discovered an empty shoulder holster. After handcuffing him, Officer Kraft asked him where the gun was. Quarles nodded in the direction of some empty cartons and responded, "The gun is over there." Officer Kraft then retrieved a loaded. 38-caliber revolver from one of the cartons, formally placed Quarles under arrest, and read him his *Miranda* rights from a printed card. Quarles indicated that he would be willing to answer questions without an attorney present. Officer Kraft then asked him if he owned the gun and where he had purchased it. Quarles answered that he did own it and that he had purchased it in Miami.

If you were a judge convinced that all of Quarles's statements should be admitted into evidence, how might you draft an opinion to explain this position? Compare New York v. Quarles, 467 U.S. 649 (1984).

Notes

1. *Interrogation by known government agents: majority position.* Virtually all jurisdictions follow the *Innis* definition of "interrogation": words or actions that the police "should know are reasonably likely to elicit an incriminating response from the suspect." See State v. Grant, 944 A.2d 947 (Conn. 2008) (statement to defendant that defendant's blood had been found at murder scene did not constitute interrogation; conduct here was of the sort "normally attendant to arrest" and "a per se rule that confronting a suspect with incriminating evidence constitutes interrogation is not required under *Innis*"). Did the Court apply this test appropriately on the facts of *Innis*? If not, what definition of "interrogation" could better account for the outcome of the case? This definition applies not only in those cases when the police initiate a conversation; it also reaches some cases in which the suspect asks a question or makes a statement, and the officer responds in a way that leads the suspect to make an incriminating reply.

2. *Booking questions.* The definition of an "interrogation" sometimes becomes an issue when a police officer who processes the routine paperwork and fingerprints as part of the suspect's detention makes some comment that elicits an incriminating response from the suspect. In Pennsylvania v. Muniz, 496 U.S. 582 (1990), the Supreme Court determined that some, but not all, of the questions asked of a defendant during a routine booking on DWI charges were "interrogations" that required *Miranda* warnings. Routine questions asking for the suspect's name, address, height, weight, eye color, date of birth, and current age were not considered interrogations. When, however, the booking officer asked the suspect the date of his sixth birthday and the suspect was unable to calculate it, the officer's question qualified as an interrogation. What is it about most of the booking questions that takes them outside the coverage of *Miranda*? Is it the routine nature of booking questions? Consider again the facts of Problem 8-3. See also State v. Goseland, 887 P.2d 1109 (Kan. 1994) (during booking paperwork, officer remarks to suspect in narcotics case, "You need to find something else to do with your life" and suspect replies "No, I'll not stop selling dope, because then you all would not have anything to do"; no interrogation, because officer always makes this remark to suspects being booked).

3. *Interrogation by unknown government agents: majority position.* In all the interrogations we have considered so far, the suspect was aware that the person asking questions was a police officer. But is there an "interrogation" when a suspect in custody is talking with a person that he does not believe to be an agent of the police? The Supreme Court and state high courts say no. In Illinois v. Perkins, 496 U.S. 292 (1990), the Supreme Court held that no *Miranda* warnings were necessary when police placed an undercover agent in same cellblock with a murder suspect detained on other charges, and during discussion of possible escape, the agent asked if the

suspect had ever "done" anybody. The Court held that conversations between suspects and undercover agents "do not implicate the concerns underlying *Miranda.*" But weren't the undercover agent's words "reasonably likely to elicit an incriminating response"? If so, what explains the inapplicability of *Miranda* when undercover agents ask the questions?

4. *"Public safety" exception to* Miranda: *majority position.* In New York v. Quarles, the Court concluded that even though the officer had conducted a custodial interrogation without giving *Miranda* warnings, the suspect's confession was not obtained contrary to the Constitution. The officer's questions about the gun were necessary not only to solve a completed crime but to prevent future crimes or accidents involving the missing gun. The need for "answers to questions in a situation posing a threat to the public safety outweighs the need for the prophylactic rule protecting the Fifth Amendment's privilege against self-incrimination." 467 U.S. at 657. Even if the officer did not ask the questions with the actual purpose of preventing a future mishap with the weapon, a court could later infer a public safety purpose for the questions from the surrounding circumstances. More than half the states allow a "public safety" or related "rescue" exception to *Miranda*. See People v. Davis, 208 P.3d 78 (Cal. 2009) (state's "rescue doctrine" still applies after more than two months elapsed between abduction of young girl and interrogation of suspect, because defendant told others he was "only doing this for the money," raising possibility that victim might still be alive).

Although *Quarles* was partly justified by the idea that warnings about the right to silence are a "prophylactic" rule rather than an actual requirement, the Court has now rejected that reasoning in Dickerson v. United States, 530 U.S. 428 (2000). The uncertain doctrinal footing of Quarles, together with the embrace of the concept in the state courts, deserves further attention. Materials on these questions appear on the web extension for this chapter at *http://www.crimpro.com/extension/ch08*.

3. Form of Warnings

The *Miranda* decision designated four topics that warnings would need to cover before a custodial interrogation could take place. However, the Court did not specify the precise language that the police must use to convey these warnings. How much variation in the language of the warnings is tolerable? When is variation necessary?

In California v. Prysock, 453 U.S. 355 (1981), the Supreme Court confirmed that a "verbatim recital" of the words in the *Miranda* opinion is not necessary to give an adequate warning to a suspect before an interrogation. The warning in that case told the suspect of his right to have an attorney present prior to and during questioning, and of his "right to have a lawyer appointed at no cost if he could not afford one." This was sufficient, even though it might have left the suspect with the impression that an appointed lawyer would become available only after questioning. In Duckworth v. Eagan, 492 U.S. 195 (1989), the Supreme Court considered the constitutionality of an Indiana *Miranda* warning that said, among other things, "we have no way of giving you a lawyer, but one will be appointed for you, if you wish, if and when you go to court." The Court held the warning complied with *Miranda,* noting that "*Miranda* does not require that attorneys be producible on call, but only that the suspect be informed, as here, that he has the right to an attorney before and during questioning, and that an attorney would be appointed for him if he could not afford one."

State courts have also determined that their constitutions allow for some variety (and some ambiguity) in the way the warnings are phrased. A few state statutes provide for additional warnings to some suspects (especially juveniles) before interrogation, but state courts have hesitated to conclude that statutes dealing with warnings for suspects require a particular verbal formula. See, e.g., State v. Bittick, 806 S.W.2d 652 (Mo. 1991) (interpreting warnings listed in Mo. Rev. Stat. §600.048.1). Why haven't more state courts insisted on a uniform and unambiguous method of conveying the *Miranda* warnings? Wouldn't an "inflexible" rule be both realistic and easy to administer because police officers could simply read the warnings from a pocket-sized card?

Some situations might call for additional warnings. A suspect may waive the right to counsel because the prospect of waiting in custody may be unappealing, or because no specific attorney has been identified, or because the suspect doubts that the attorney ultimately assigned to the case will be capable. But what if counsel retained for a specific suspect is available at the police station? Do the interrogating officers have to tell the suspect of the presence of a particular attorney when the additional warning could affect the waiver decision?

■ STATE v. JOHN REED

627 A.2d 630 (N.J. 1993)

HANDLER, J.

In this case, the jury convicted defendant, John Reed, of knowing murder and aggravated criminal sexual contact. Defendant had confessed to those crimes and that confession constituted critically important evidence. The admissibility of defendant's confession presents the sole issue on this appeal. The police refused, before and during defendant's interrogation, to inform defendant that an attorney, who had been brought to police headquarters by a friend of defendant, was present and sought to confer with him. The issue is whether that refusal by the police violated defendant's constitutional rights, including the privilege against self-incrimination, and therefore rendered defendant's confession inadmissible.

[Fran Varga called the police Monday at 8:00 A.M. to inform them that her roommate and boyfriend, John Reed, had found the dead body of Susan Green, one of Reed's coworkers. He found Green's body on the floor of her own apartment, with 53 stab wounds. When detectives Shedden and Importico arrived at the scene, they asked Reed some questions, but had difficulty understanding his answers because Reed suffered from a speech impediment and tended to stutter severely when nervous. He told them that the victim had called him the previous Friday night, afraid because a stranger had been trying to enter her apartment. The stranger had disappeared by the time Reed had arrived to help. He found the body, he said, when he stopped by her apartment on his way to work on Monday morning.

The detectives asked Reed to go to the prosecutor's office to give a statement and provide "elimination" fingerprints. Varga drove him to the prosecutor's office, where they arrived just before 11:00 A.M. The detectives isolated Reed in an interrogation room, and asked Varga to remain in the waiting room. Varga called an attorney, and told him that she and Reed were at the prosecutor's office, that the police were about to question Reed, and that she and Reed needed an attorney. The attorney, William Aitken, agreed to come to the station immediately. Varga informed a police officer that Aitken was on the way.

Meanwhile, Chief Richard Thornburg instructed detectives Shedden and Importico to move Reed to the Major Crimes Building, located a few blocks away. Instead of taking Reed past the area where Varga was waiting and down the elevator, the officers led him down four flights of stairs near the interrogation room and out the back door of the building. Reed signed a *Miranda* waiver form, then gave a different account of the events than he had given earlier.

At approximately 11:25 A.M., Aitken arrived at the prosecutor's office and consulted with Varga. He approached the prosecutor who would eventually present the case against Reed and told him that he was there to represent both Varga and Reed. The prosecutor informed Aitken that Reed was a witness and not a suspect, and stated that, in any event, Aitken had "no right to walk into an investigation." Aitken gave the prosecutor a business card, and the prosecutor assured Aitken that the police would call him if and when Reed requested an attorney. No one informed Reed that a lawyer retained by Varga was waiting to see him.

After a second waiver of *Miranda* rights around noon, Reed spoke with another interrogator, Lt. Mazzei, and told a story markedly different from the second account he had provided. In Reed's third version of the story, he had actually witnessed Green being murdered when, looking through Green's front window, he had seen a "black man" repeatedly stabbing her. After detectives confronted him with the inconsistency, and after further questioning, Reed admitted that he had killed Green. After waiving his *Miranda* rights for a third time, Reed confessed on tape. He explained that he had killed Green in self-defense during a heated argument. The confession was taped at 3:52 P.M.]

Prior to trial, defense counsel moved to suppress defendant's confession on the ground that defendant had not knowingly, voluntarily, and intelligently waived his *Miranda* rights. [The trial court denied the motion because] the police had no duty to inform defendant of the attorney's presence.

[In] Moran v. Burbine, 475 U.S. 412 (1986), [the U.S. Supreme Court] held, as a matter of federal constitutional law, that the police had no obligation to advise a defendant that a third party had summoned an attorney to advise him and that, in the absence of a request by the defendant himself, an attorney's presence at the police station does not affect the right of the police to interrogate him.

In *Moran,* the defendant was in police custody for a burglary. While the defendant was in custody, the police received information connecting the defendant with a murder. The police proceeded to interrogate the defendant about the murder, even though they were aware that a public defender, retained by the defendant's sister in connection with the burglary charge, had called to say that she would act as the defendant's attorney if the police placed him in a lineup or interrogated him. Although the police assured the public defender that they had no plans to question the defendant that evening, nevertheless, shortly after the phone call, the police began interrogating the defendant about the murder. Before each interrogation session, the police informed the defendant of his *Miranda* rights and had him sign waiver forms, but they never informed him that his sister had retained a public defender to assist him or that the public defender was trying to reach him.

Writing for the majority, Justice O'Connor held that the actions of the police did not violate the defendant's fifth, sixth, or fourteenth amendment rights. After noting that the voluntariness of the waiver was not at issue, the Court found that there was no question concerning the defendant's understanding of the *Miranda* warnings and of the consequences of waiving them. In the Court's view, the failure of the police to inform the defendant that an attorney was available to assist him was irrelevant to the question whether he had knowingly waived his rights. . . .

The majority decision in *Moran* signaled a marked departure from the fifth amendment jurisprudence that state and federal courts had established prior to *Moran.* At the time *Moran* was decided, many courts had held that when the police fail to inform a suspect that an attorney is actually available and seeking to render assistance, any subsequent waiver of the suspect's *Miranda* rights was invalid. [The court cited cases from Colorado, Delaware, Florida, Illinois, Louisiana, Massachusetts, North Carolina, Ohio, Oklahoma, Oregon, Pennsylvania, and West Virginia. Since 1986], several state courts have had occasion to consider or reconsider the issue presented in *Moran.* Some of those courts . . . have expressly rejected *Moran* on the grounds that its holding offends state-constitutional provisions protecting the privilege against self-incrimination and due process rights. [The court cited cases from California, Connecticut, Delaware, Florida, Oregon, and Texas. The California case was subsequently overruled by a constitutional amendment.]

In New Jersey, the right against self-incrimination is founded on a common-law and statutory — rather than a constitutional — basis. . . . The common-law right against self-incrimination was first codified in New Jersey in 1855. Subsequently, the Legislature incorporated the right against self-incrimination in its enactment of the Rules of Evidence. Thus, although lacking a constitutional provision expressly establishing the right, the privilege against self-incrimination has been an integral thread in the fabric of New Jersey common law. . . .

The right to counsel has been the object of special judicial solicitude [in New Jersey]. The significance of the right to counsel as an adjunct of the privilege against self-incrimination is evidenced by the special requirements that are affixed to that right. It is not sufficient to advise a suspect subjected to custodial interrogation only that he or she has a generalized right to an attorney. It is essential to inform the suspect that, if the suspect cannot afford one, an attorney will be provided at State expense. It is also essential that the suspect be clearly informed that he or she may ask for counsel at any time during custodial interrogation, and, additionally, that interrogation will be stopped any time the defendant desires counsel. Further, a suspect need not be articulate, clear, or explicit in requesting counsel; any indication of a desire for counsel, however ambiguous, will trigger entitlement to counsel. State v. Bey, 548 A.2d 887 (N.J. 1988).

Our decisional law on the state right against self-incrimination is based on the understanding that the privilege is defined by the ancillary rights, like the right to counsel during custodial interrogation. Moreover, the protections afforded by those ancillary rights provide a metric by which to measure the strength of the privilege. The history of our case law reflects a strong commitment to enhance those ancillary rights to forestall the possible use of coerced confessions. . . .

Many state courts, as already noted, have interpreted their respective state constitutions to require that a suspect exposed to custodial interrogation be apprised of the presence of an attorney seeking to render assistance. Courts have offered different rationales for imposing that duty. Some have based the duty on the fundamental constraints that govern the waiver of the right against self-incrimination. Those constraints are invariably expressed in terms of whether the waiver is "knowing, intelligent, and voluntary."[2] . . . Other courts have derived the duty from notions of due process that insist on reasonable police conduct. . . .

However, we need not engage in an extended debate over the different approaches to dealing with the standards governing the validity of a waiver in this context. For while courts may differ on the rationale for imposing the duty to inform a suspect that an attorney is waiting to confer, they agree on one supervening principle: the atmosphere of custodial interrogation is inherently coercive and protecting the right against self-incrimination entails counteracting that coercion. . . .

The lesson to be drawn from this debate is that a waiver of the right against self-incrimination which, by all subjective indicia, appears knowing, intelligent, and voluntary, may still be deemed invalid when elicited in an atmosphere of coercion. That is because the determination of the subjective mental state that leads to a waiver is often so problematic. [A warning is a clear-cut fact.] Accordingly, the most practical means to overcome coercion will be through normative rules that apply reasonable, specific, and objective standards. . . .

[Our] decision today should be governed by a two-fold purpose: to enhance the reliability of confessions by reducing the inherent coercion of custodial interrogation and diminish the likelihood of unreasonable police conduct in those situations where police, knowing that an attorney has been retained for the suspect and is asking for contact with his or her client, are desperate to acquire a confession before the suspect speaks with the attorney.

The State nevertheless contends that the police had no duty to inform defendant about Aitken's presence because Aitken could not be considered defendant's attorney. The State stresses that defendant never requested an attorney and that Aitken had no legal authority to invoke defendant's rights, and could not exercise, for defendant, the right to counsel. The State thus claims that because no attorney-client relationship existed between defendant and Aitken, law-enforcement authorities could not possibly have interfered in that relationship and defendant's right to counsel. . . .

We are satisfied that an attorney-client relationship should be deemed to exist under such circumstances between the suspect and an attorney when the suspect's family or friends have retained the attorney or where the attorney has represented or is representing the suspect on another matter. When, to the knowledge of the police, such an attorney is present or available, and the attorney has communicated a desire to confer with the suspect, the police must make that information known to the suspect before custodial interrogation can proceed or continue. Further, we hold that the failure of the police to give the suspect that information renders the suspect's subsequent waiver of the privilege against self-incrimination invalid per se.

Our holding is essential to give effect to the right to counsel that, in turn, effectuates the privilege against self-incrimination. Moreover, our holding is supported

2. At least one commentator has argued that in order for a suspect's confession to be valid, the suspect should be provided with "as complete an understanding of his tactical position as possible." See George Dix, Mistake, Ignorance, Expectation of Benefit and the Modern Law of Confessions, 1975 Wash. U. L.Q. 275, 330-331. On this view, deprivation of "crucial information" can convert what otherwise would be a noncoercive situation into a coercive situation. . . . The difficulty with this position is that it is unacceptably overinclusive: it would encompass information such as the death of a critical witness, the successful escape of an accomplice, and the destruction of crucial evidence. Certainly, each of these bits of information would play an important part in the suspect's understanding of his or her "tactical position" and, accordingly, in the suspect's decision to confess.

in large measure by the special and essential role lawyers play in realizing the purpose of the right against self-incrimination. . . . Our holding is also consistent with the Rules of Professional Conduct of the American legal profession. The American Bar Association's Standards for Criminal Justice are unequivocally clear about the need for the earliest possible provision of counsel for an accused in custody. Standards 5-5.1; 5-7.1. . . .

Although we have, today, undoubtedly made explicit an additional responsibility of the State in its conduct toward criminal defendants, we do not believe that burden to be a heavy one. The duty to inform, that we place upon the State, is narrow and specific. It arises only where counsel has made known that he or she has been retained to represent the person held in custody, is present or readily available, and makes a request to consult with the suspect in a reasonably diligent, timely and pertinent fashion.

We do not make incumbent upon the attorney the duty to communicate directly with the interrogating officers. That communication will not, most times, be possible. Rather, whenever the attorney has communicated his presence and desire to confer with the suspect to an agent of the State in a position to contact the interrogating officers, we will impute to those officers knowledge of the attorney's presence and desire to confer with the suspect. . . .

We are satisfied that our holding will fully serve considerations of public policy and not undermine the proper and effective administration of criminal justice. . . . Prior to *Moran,* a majority of states followed a rule similar to the one we enunciate today, without any apparent diminishment in the effectiveness of their law-enforcement agencies. In the states, since 1986, that have rejected *Moran,* no evidence exists that the police have been seriously hindered in their efforts to uphold the law.

[We reject] the dissent's contention that the rule we enunciate today is unfairly biased against the "indigent defendant with no previous experience with law enforcement who is arrested while alone." It is probably true that such a person will be less likely to have a lawyer contacted to see him or her. In an ideal world, every defendant would have the family, friends, financial means, time, energy, and personal resources to mount the best defense. But we do not live in an ideal world.

Regrettably, reality compels us to tolerate significant differences in the empirical operation of the constitutional rules we enunciate. Would anyone dispute, after all, that the Sixth Amendment right to counsel is experienced differently by a well educated defendant with access to any trial lawyer in the country and unlimited financial resources to present a defense, than by an illiterate and indigent defendant, without family or friends, who must rely on a highly competent and committed, but overworked, public defender? Yet we have never taken a disparity in the actual ability of differently-situated defendants to make use of a right as an argument against affording that right.

[The] police conduct in this case illustrates the close correlation between police conduct that can increase the inherently coercive atmosphere of custodial interrogation and conduct that is excessive, shocking, and fundamentally unfair and therefore violative of due process. We are presented with a prosecutor misstating to an attorney retained to represent a client that the client was a witness not a suspect, and refusing to allow that attorney access to the client, thus violating the rules of his profession. In turn, the police hurried defendant down a back stairway to prevent defendant from seeing his girlfriend or the attorney retained to represent him.

This, in turn, prompted the police to aver that taking four flights of stairs to exit a building was "more convenient" than using the elevator next to which defendant's girlfriend was coincidentally sitting. We think that in this case the law-enforcement officers were under great pressure to secure a confession. To prevent defendant from speaking with his attorney, the police engaged in conduct that, if not egregious, exemplifies the ways in which the inherently coercive atmosphere of custodial interrogation can be materially increased in the efforts to obtain a confession.

[Police] and prosecutorial behavior, in denying defendant access to counsel, did not well serve the investigative function. Such conduct does not promote public esteem for the law, and it substantially increases the possibility that a suspect's confession will be involuntary. At a minimum, such conduct must not be encouraged by the courts. . . .

CLIFFORD, J., dissenting.

The importance of the right to counsel in protecting suspects against compelled self-incrimination can hardly be overstated. This Court has traditionally been most solicitous of that right. We have determined that any indication of a suspect's desire for counsel — even if not articulate, clear, or explicit — triggers the right. But today the Court extends that treasured right even farther, concluding that the right to counsel can attach even if a suspect expressly and voluntarily waives that right. That goes too far. . . .

Reed, a quality-control inspector whose work required the reading of complex manuals and engineering drawings, understood that he had the right to an attorney. He understood that an attorney would be provided if he could not afford one. He understood that he could ask for counsel at any time during the investigation and that the interrogation would cease at that point. Fully understanding all of the foregoing, defendant waived those rights — three times. Therefore, the failure to inform defendant of attorney Aitken's desire to communicate cannot be viewed as a violation of defendant's *Miranda* rights. And it should not be viewed as contrary to New Jersey's equivalent common-law protections. . . .

Philosophical as well as practical concerns lead me to disagree with my colleagues' conclusion. First, [a] mentally-competent person's constitutional rights may be asserted only by that person. Therefore, I part company with the Court in its conclusion that a third party — in this case, the attorney in waiting — can assert a suspect's right against self-incrimination.

Moreover, the Court's rule creates an illogical or unfair advantage for some suspects. Those suspects who are taken into custody in the presence of others, or who have previously obtained a private attorney, or who have previously required the services of a public defender — and therefore are more likely to be the beneficiaries of someone's call to an attorney on their behalf — will be found to have been coerced if not alerted should an attorney arrive at the station house. On the other hand, the indigent defendant with no previous experience with law enforcement who is arrested while alone — and hence "out of the loop" as far as legal assistance is concerned — although subjected to identical interrogation techniques will have knowingly and voluntarily waived the right to counsel. The rule therefore results in two classes of suspects and favors those who are more likely to have access to counsel. Such intolerable incongruities result when the emphasis shifts to events entirely unrelated to the suspect's knowledge rather than focusing on the sole person who matters in evaluating the validity of a suspect's waiver — the suspect.

Furthermore, the rule the Court fashions today risks increasing the likelihood of police coercion. Police officers of flexible rectitude who know that the right to question a suspect may terminate once an attorney makes known his or her availability to assist a suspect may be tempted to "turn up the heat" to secure a confession in what the officers may perceive as a limited window of opportunity. . . .

I need hardly add that my resolution of this case in no way constitutes an endorsement of the deplorable bumbling of the law-enforcement personnel who lied to Ms. Varga and Aitken and who scurried through the basement to hide defendant from the attorney who sought to confer with him. I join the majority in its denouncement of such foolishness. However, [the purpose of the majority's decision — to enhance the reliability of confessions by reducing the inherent coercion of custodial interrogation — is] adequately served by careful administering of the *Miranda* warnings, fully complied with in this case, and punctilious observance of the procedures laid out in our case law. . . .

Notes

1. *Informing a suspect about an available retained attorney: majority position.* The Supreme Court decided in Moran v. Burbine, 475 U.S. 412 (1986), that the police had no obligation to tell a suspect about an available attorney if the suspect has already waived the *Miranda* rights. Supreme courts in more than half the states have now faced this issue; a clear majority have disagreed with the Supreme Court and taken the same position as the *Reed* court. Compare Commonwealth v. Mavredakis, 725 N.E.2d 169 (Mass. 2000) (rejecting *Moran*) with Ajabu v. State, 693 N.E.2d 921 (Ind. 1998) (following *Moran* and collecting cases). If an elected prosecutor lived in a jurisdiction following the approach of the Supreme Court in *Moran,* how might she explain this position to a civic organization — say, the Elks Club or the high school's Honor Society? How might an elected prosecutor explain a decision such as the one in *Reed*? Do these questions help to explain why so many states have rejected *Moran*?

2. *Weighting decisions.* If most state courts reject a position taken by the U.S. Supreme Court, what weight should a later state court place on the Supreme Court opinion when interpreting its own state constitution? Should it carry less weight than recent opinions from the highest courts of sister states? Equivalent weight? On what theory of inter-court relations might such a Supreme Court opinion carry greater weight than later decisions from other state courts?

3. *Other variations in the warning.* Some police officers tell suspects that anything they say during an interrogation can be used "for or against" the suspect. Why do you suppose they phrase the warning this way? Is it an acceptable variation on the *Miranda* warnings? See State v. Stanley, 613 A.2d 788 (Conn. 1992) (approving of "for or against" statement on printed waiver form when it is accompanied by other "against" statements); Dunn v. State, 721 S.W.2d 325 (Tex. Crim. App. 1986) (error to give "for or against" warning).

The *Miranda* opinion, after describing the four warnings now known as the *Miranda* warnings, added the following: If the suspect "indicates in any manner that he does not wish to be interrogated, the police may not question him." 384 U.S. at 445. The opinion also refers to "the right to refrain from answering any further inquiries." Should the police be expected to warn suspects about this "fifth right" to cut off questioning? Courts considering this question have almost uniformly said no. See, e.g., State v. Mitchell, 482 N.W.2d 364 (Wis. 1992). If the suspect does indeed have the right to cut off questioning, why should the police be obliged to tell suspects about some of their rights but not this one? Would warnings about this right have any greater effect than the four existing warnings? Cf. United States v. Lombera-Camorlinga, 206 F.3d 882 (9th Cir. 2000) (failure to inform arrested non-citizen of Vienna Convention right to contact consul does not require suppression of statement).

In Florida v. Powell, 130 S. Ct. 1195 (2010), the police informed a suspect before a custodial interrogation that "You have the right to talk to a lawyer before answering any of our questions" and "You have the right to use any of these rights at any time you want during this interview." The suspect waived *Miranda* rights and admitted ownership of a firearm. Although the warning informed a suspect about access to an attorney *before* questioning rather than *during* an interrogation, the Supreme Court held that this combination of warnings satisfied the requirements of *Miranda*. The Court reiterated its view that no particular formulation of words is necessary to convey the essential information about rights of a suspect during custodial interrogation. The two statements that police used in this case, taken together, address the *Miranda* Court's concern that the "circumstances surrounding in-custody interrogation can operate very quickly to overbear the will of one merely made aware of his privilege [to remain silent] by his interrogators."

For an exploration of other variations in the precise wording of the *Miranda* warnings, see the web extension for this chapter at *http://www.crimpro.com/extension/ch08*.

4. *Translation of* Miranda *warnings.* A suspect who has difficulty understanding English must receive the warnings in her own language. For this reason, some police departments maintain a standardized translation of the *Miranda* warnings in languages commonly spoken in the area. See State v. Santiago, 556 N.W.2d 687 (Wis. 1996).

C. INVOCATION AND WAIVER OF *MIRANDA* RIGHTS

After the police give a *Miranda* warning, a suspect may invoke the right to counsel or to silence, or waive these rights and submit to the interrogation. Most suspects waive the right to counsel and the right to silence after receiving *Miranda* warnings. Waiver occurs in at least three-quarters of all custodial interrogations (and probably more). Thus, the legal rules dealing with waiver and invocation of interrogation rights affect more cases than any other aspect of the vast legal doctrine surrounding *Miranda.* In this section, we review how courts determine whether a suspect has invoked or waived *Miranda* rights.

Suspects typically use language that leaves some doubt about their invocation or waiver of the right to counsel or silence. The rules for handling ambiguous words or actions suggesting invocation or waiver can have a huge practical impact: If only crystal clear invocation is valid, there will be more waivers, while if courts insist that government agents treat a range of ambiguous statements or actions as assertions of *Miranda* rights, assertion will be more common. When the suspect makes an ambiguous statement or takes action that might be a waiver of *Miranda* rights, when must the police clarify the waiver before proceeding with the interrogation?

VERMONT STATUTES TIT. 13, §§5234, 5237

§5234

(a) If a person who is being detained by a law enforcement officer . . . is not represented by an attorney under conditions in which a person having his own counsel would be entitled to be so represented, the law enforcement officer, magistrate, or court concerned shall:

(1) Clearly inform him of the right of a person to be represented by an attorney and of a needy person to be represented at public expense; and

(2) If the person detained or charged does not have an attorney and does not knowingly, voluntarily and intelligently waive his right to have an attorney when detained or charged, notify the appropriate public defender that he is not so represented. . . .

(d) Information . . . given to a person by a law enforcement officer under this section gives rise to a rebuttable presumption that the information was effectively communicated if:

(1) It is in writing or otherwise recorded;

(2) The recipient records his acknowledgment of receipt and time of receipt of the information; and

(3) The material so recorded under paragraphs (1) and (2) of this subsection is filed with the court next concerned.

§5237

A person who has been appropriately informed under section 5234 of this title may waive in writing, or by other record, any right provided by this chapter, if the court, at the time of or after waiver, finds of record that he has acted with full awareness of his rights and of the consequences of a waiver and if the waiver is otherwise according to law. The court shall consider such factors as the person's age, education, and familiarity with the English language, and the complexity of the crime involved.

MARY BERGHUIS v. VAN CHESTER THOMPKINS

130 S. Ct. 2250 (2010)

KENNEDY, J.*

. . . I.

On January 10, 2000, a shooting occurred outside a mall in Southfield, Michigan. Among the victims was Samuel Morris, who died from multiple gunshot wounds. . . . Thompkins, who was a suspect, fled. About one year later he was found in Ohio and arrested there.

* [Justices Alito, Scalia, and Thomas and Chief Justice Roberts joined in this opinion. — EDS.]

Two Southfield police officers traveled to Ohio to interrogate Thompkins, then awaiting transfer to Michigan. The interrogation began around 1:30 P.M. and lasted about three hours. The interrogation was conducted in a room that was 8 by 10 feet, and Thompkins sat in a chair that resembled a school desk (it had an arm on it that swings around to provide a surface to write on). At the beginning of the interrogation, one of the officers, Detective Helgert, presented Thompkins with a form derived from the *Miranda* rule. It stated:

> 1. . . . You have the right to remain silent.
> 2. Anything you say can and will be used against you in a court of law.
> 3. You have a right to talk to a lawyer before answering any questions and you have the right to have a lawyer present with you while you are answering any questions.
> 4. If you cannot afford to hire a lawyer, one will be appointed to represent you before any questioning, if you wish one.
> 5. You have the right to decide at any time before or during questioning to use your right to remain silent and your right to talk with a lawyer while you are being questioned.

Helgert asked Thompkins to read the fifth warning out loud. Thompkins complied. Helgert later said this was to ensure that Thompkins could read, and Helgert concluded that Thompkins understood English. Helgert then read the other four *Miranda* warnings out loud and asked Thompkins to sign the form to demonstrate that he understood his rights. Thompkins declined to sign the form. The record contains conflicting evidence about whether Thompkins then verbally confirmed that he understood the rights listed on the form. . . . Compare [Record on Appeal] at 9a (at a suppression hearing, Helgert testified that Thompkins verbally confirmed that he understood his rights), with *id.*, at 148a (at trial, Helgert stated, "I don't know that I orally asked him" whether Thompkins understood his rights).

Officers began an interrogation. At no point during the interrogation did Thompkins say that he wanted to remain silent, that he did not want to talk with the police, or that he wanted an attorney. Thompkins was largely silent during the interrogation, which lasted about three hours. He did give a few limited verbal responses, however, such as "yeah," "no," or "I don't know." And on occasion he communicated by nodding his head. Thompkins also said that he "didn't want a peppermint" that was offered to him by the police and that the chair he was "sitting in was hard."

About 2 hours and 45 minutes into the interrogation, Helgert asked Thompkins, "Do you believe in God?" Thompkins made eye contact with Helgert and said "Yes," as his eyes welled up with tears. Helgert asked, "Do you pray to God?" Thompkins said "Yes." Helgert asked, "Do you pray to God to forgive you for shooting that boy down?" Thompkins answered "Yes" and looked away. Thompkins refused to make a written confession, and the interrogation ended about 15 minutes later.

Thompkins was charged with first-degree murder, assault with intent to commit murder, and certain firearms-related offenses. He moved to suppress the statements made during the interrogation. He argued that he had invoked his Fifth Amendment right to remain silent, requiring police to end the interrogation at once, see

Michigan v. Mosley, 423 U.S. 96, 103 (1975), that he had not waived his right to remain silent, and that his inculpatory statements were involuntary. The trial court denied the motion. . . . The jury found Thompkins guilty on all counts. He was sentenced to life in prison without parole. . . .

III.

A.

Thompkins makes various arguments that his answers to questions from the detectives were inadmissible. He first contends that he invoked his privilege to remain silent by not saying anything for a sufficient period of time, so the interrogation should have ceased before he made his inculpatory statements.

This argument is unpersuasive. In the context of invoking the *Miranda* right to counsel, the Court in Davis v. United States, 512 U.S. 452, 459 (1994), held that a suspect must do so "unambiguously." If an accused makes a statement concerning the right to counsel "that is ambiguous or equivocal" or makes no statement, the police are not required to end the interrogation or ask questions to clarify whether the accused wants to invoke his or her *Miranda* rights. . . .

The Court has not yet stated whether an invocation of the right to remain silent can be ambiguous or equivocal, but there is no principled reason to adopt different standards for determining when an accused has invoked the *Miranda* right to remain silent and the *Miranda* right to counsel at issue in *Davis*. Both protect the privilege against compulsory self-incrimination by requiring an interrogation to cease when either right is invoked.

There is good reason to require an accused who wants to invoke his or her right to remain silent to do so unambiguously. A requirement of an unambiguous invocation of *Miranda* rights results in an objective inquiry that avoids difficulties of proof and provides guidance to officers on how to proceed in the face of ambiguity. If an ambiguous act, omission, or statement could require police to end the interrogation, police would be required to make difficult decisions about an accused's unclear intent and face the consequence of suppression if they guess wrong. Suppression of a voluntary confession in these circumstances would place a significant burden on society's interest in prosecuting criminal activity. Treating an ambiguous or equivocal act, omission, or statement as an invocation of *Miranda* rights might add marginally to *Miranda*'s goal of dispelling the compulsion inherent in custodial interrogation. But as *Miranda* holds, full comprehension of the rights to remain silent and request an attorney are sufficient to dispel whatever coercion is inherent in the interrogation process.

Thompkins did not say that he wanted to remain silent or that he did not want to talk with the police. Had he made either of these simple, unambiguous statements, he would have invoked his "right to cut off questioning." Here he did neither, so he did not invoke his right to remain silent.

B.

We next consider whether Thompkins waived his right to remain silent. Even absent the accused's invocation of the right to remain silent, the accused's statement during a custodial interrogation is inadmissible at trial unless the prosecution can establish that the accused in fact knowingly and voluntarily waived

Miranda rights when making the statement. The waiver inquiry has two distinct dimensions: waiver must be voluntary in the sense that it was the product of a free and deliberate choice rather than intimidation, coercion, or deception, and made with a full awareness of both the nature of the right being abandoned and the consequences of the decision to abandon it.

Some language in *Miranda* could be read to indicate that waivers are difficult to establish absent an explicit written waiver or a formal, express oral statement. *Miranda* said "a valid waiver will not be presumed simply from the silence of the accused after warnings are given or simply from the fact that a confession was in fact eventually obtained." . . . In addition, the *Miranda* Court stated that "a heavy burden rests on the government to demonstrate that the defendant knowingly and intelligently waived his privilege against self-incrimination and his right to retained or appointed counsel."

The course of decisions since *Miranda,* informed by the application of *Miranda* warnings in the whole course of law enforcement, demonstrates that waivers can be established even absent formal or express statements of waiver that would be expected in, say, a judicial hearing to determine if a guilty plea has been properly entered. . . .

One of the first cases to decide the meaning and import of *Miranda* with respect to the question of waiver was North Carolina v. Butler, 441 U.S. 369 (1979). . . . *Butler* interpreted the *Miranda* language concerning the "heavy burden" to show waiver in accord with usual principles of determining waiver, which can include waiver implied from all the circumstances. . . .

The prosecution therefore does not need to show that a waiver of *Miranda* rights was express. An implicit waiver of the right to remain silent is sufficient to admit a suspect's statement into evidence. *Butler* made clear that a waiver of *Miranda* rights may be implied through the defendant's silence, coupled with an understanding of his rights and a course of conduct indicating waiver. . . .

If the State establishes that a *Miranda* warning was given and the accused made an uncoerced statement, this showing, standing alone, is insufficient to demonstrate "a valid waiver" of *Miranda* rights. The prosecution must make the additional showing that the accused understood these rights. Where the prosecution shows that a *Miranda* warning was given and that it was understood by the accused, an accused's uncoerced statement establishes an implied waiver of the right to remain silent.

Although *Miranda* imposes on the police a rule that is both formalistic and practical when it prevents them from interrogating suspects without first providing them with a *Miranda* warning, it does not impose a formalistic waiver procedure that a suspect must follow to relinquish those rights. As a general proposition, the law can presume that an individual who, with a full understanding of his or her rights, acts in a manner inconsistent with their exercise has made a deliberate choice to relinquish the protection those rights afford. . . . *Miranda* rights can therefore be waived through means less formal than a typical waiver on the record in a courtroom, given the practical constraints and necessities of interrogation and the fact that *Miranda*'s main protection lies in advising defendants of their rights.

The record in this case shows that Thompkins waived his right to remain silent. There is no basis in this case to conclude that he did not understand his rights; and on these facts it follows that he chose not to invoke or rely on those rights when he did speak. [First, there] was more than enough evidence in the record to conclude that Thompkins understood his *Miranda* rights. Thompkins received a written copy of the *Miranda* warnings; Detective Helgert determined that Thompkins could read and understand English; and Thompkins was given time to read the warnings. Thompkins, furthermore, read aloud the fifth warning, which stated that "you have the right to decide at any time before or during questioning to use your right to remain silent and your right to talk with a lawyer while you are being questioned." He was thus aware that his right to remain silent would not dissipate after a certain amount of time and that police would have to honor his right to be silent and his right to counsel during the whole course of interrogation. . . . Helgert, moreover, read the warnings aloud.

Second, Thompkins's answer to Detective Helgert's question about whether Thompkins prayed to God for forgiveness for shooting the victim is a course of conduct indicating waiver of the right to remain silent. If Thompkins wanted to remain silent, he could have said nothing in response to Helgert's questions, or he could have unambiguously invoked his *Miranda* rights and ended the interrogation. [His] course of conduct indicating waiver . . . is confirmed by the fact that before then Thompkins had given sporadic answers to questions throughout the interrogation.

Third, there is no evidence that Thompkins's statement was coerced. Thompkins does not claim that police threatened or injured him during the interrogation or that he was in any way fearful. The interrogation was conducted in a standard-sized room in the middle of the afternoon. It is true that apparently he was in a straight-backed chair for three hours, but there is no authority for the proposition that an interrogation of this length is inherently coercive. Indeed, even where interrogations of greater duration were held to be improper, they were accompanied, as this one was not, by other facts indicating coercion, such as an incapacitated and sedated suspect, sleep and food deprivation, and threats. The fact that Helgert's question referred to Thompkins's religious beliefs also did not render Thompkins's statement involuntary. The Fifth Amendment privilege is not concerned with moral and psychological pressures to confess emanating from sources other than official coercion. In these circumstances, Thompkins knowingly and voluntarily made a statement to police, so he waived his right to remain silent.

C.

Thompkins next argues that, even if his answer to Detective Helgert could constitute a waiver of his right to remain silent, the police were not allowed to question him until they obtained a waiver first. *Butler* forecloses this argument. The *Butler* Court held that courts can infer a waiver of *Miranda* rights "from the actions and words of the person interrogated." This principle would be inconsistent with a rule that requires a waiver at the outset. . . . Any waiver, express or implied, may be contradicted by an invocation at any time. . . .

Interrogation provides the suspect with additional information that can put his or her decision to waive, or not to invoke, into perspective. As questioning commences and then continues, the suspect has the opportunity to consider the choices he or she faces and to make a more informed decision, either to insist on silence or to cooperate. When the suspect knows that *Miranda* rights can be invoked at any time, he or she has the opportunity to reassess his or her immediate and long-term interests. Cooperation with the police may result in more favorable treatment for the suspect; the apprehension of accomplices; the prevention of continuing injury and fear; beginning steps towards relief or solace for the victims; and the beginning of the suspect's own return to the law and the social order it seeks to protect. . . .

SOTOMAYOR, J., dissenting.*

The Court concludes today that a criminal suspect waives his right to remain silent if, after sitting tacit and uncommunicative through nearly three hours of police interrogation, he utters a few one-word responses. The Court also concludes that a suspect who wishes to guard his right to remain silent against such a finding of "waiver" must, counterintuitively, speak — and must do so with sufficient precision to satisfy a clear-statement rule that construes ambiguity in favor of the police. Both propositions mark a substantial retreat from the protection against compelled self-incrimination that Miranda v. Arizona, 384 U.S. 436 (1966), has long provided during custodial interrogation. . . .

I.

. . . The strength of Thompkins' *Miranda* claims depends in large part on the circumstances of the 3-hour interrogation, at the end of which he made inculpatory statements later introduced at trial. The Court's opinion downplays record evidence that Thompkins remained almost completely silent and unresponsive throughout that session. One of the interrogating officers, Detective Helgert, testified that although Thompkins was administered *Miranda* warnings, the last of which he read aloud, Thompkins expressly declined to sign a written acknowledgment that he had been advised of and understood his rights. There is conflicting evidence in the record about whether Thompkins ever verbally confirmed understanding his rights. The record contains no indication that the officers sought or obtained an express waiver.

As to the interrogation itself, Helgert candidly characterized it as "very, very one-sided" and "nearly a monologue." Thompkins was "peculiar," "sullen," and "generally quiet." Helgert and his partner "did most of the talking," as Thompkins was "not verbally communicative" and "largely" remained silent. To the extent Thompkins gave any response, his answers consisted of "a word or two. A 'yeah,' or a 'no,' or 'I don't know.' And sometimes he simply sat down with his head in his hands looking down. Sometimes he would look up and make eye-contact would be the only response." After proceeding in this fashion for approximately 2 hours and 45 minutes, Helgert asked Thompkins three questions relating to his faith in God. The prosecution relied at trial on Thompkins' one-word answers of "yes."

Thompkins' nonresponsiveness is particularly striking in the context of the officers' interview strategy, later explained as conveying to Thompkins that "this was his opportunity to explain his side" of the story because everybody else, including his co-defendants, "had given their version," and asking him "who is going to speak up for you if you don't speak up for yourself?" Yet, Helgert confirmed that the "*only* thing" Thompkins said relative to his involvement in the shooting occurred near the end of the interview — *i.e.*, in response to the questions about God. The only other responses Helgert could remember Thompkins giving were that he "didn't want a peppermint" and "the chair that he was sitting in was hard." Nevertheless, the Michigan court concluded on this record that Thompkins had not invoked his right to remain silent because "he continued to talk with the officer, albeit sporadically," and that he voluntarily waived that right. . . .

* [Justices Breyer, Ginsburg, and Stevens joined this opinion. — EDS.]

Miranda and our subsequent cases . . . require police to respect the accused's decision to exercise the rights outlined in the warnings. If an individual indicates in any manner, at any time prior to or during questioning, that he wishes to remain silent or if he states that he wants an attorney, the interrogation "must cease." . . . A heavy burden rests on the government to demonstrate that the defendant knowingly and intelligently waived his privilege against self-incrimination and his right to retained or appointed counsel. . . .

The question whether a suspect has validly waived his right is entirely distinct as a matter of law from whether he invoked that right. The questions are related, however, in terms of the practical effect on the exercise of a suspect's rights. A suspect may at any time revoke his prior waiver of rights — or, closer to the facts of this case, guard against the possibility of a future finding that he implicitly waived his rights — by invoking the rights and thereby requiring the police to cease questioning.

II.

. . . Even in concluding that *Miranda* does not invariably require an express waiver of the right to silence or the right to counsel, this Court in North Carolina v. Butler, 441 U.S. 369 (1979), made clear that the prosecution bears a substantial burden in establishing an implied waiver. The Federal Bureau of Investigation had obtained statements after advising Butler of his rights and confirming that he understood them. When presented with a written waiver-of-rights form, Butler told the agents, "I will talk to you but I am not signing any form." He then made inculpatory statements, which he later sought to suppress on the ground that he had not expressly waived his right to counsel.

[The] question is whether the defendant in fact knowingly and voluntarily waived the rights delineated in the *Miranda* case. *Miranda,* we observed, "unequivocally said . . . mere silence is not enough." While we stopped short in *Butler* of announcing a *per se* rule that the defendant's silence, coupled with an understanding of his rights and a course of conduct indicating waiver, may never support a conclusion that a defendant has waived his rights, we reiterated that courts must presume that a defendant did not waive his rights; the prosecution's burden is "great." . . .

Together, *Miranda* and *Butler* establish that a court must presume that a defendant did not waive his rights; the prosecution bears a "heavy burden" in attempting to demonstrate waiver; the fact of a "lengthy interrogation" prior to obtaining statements is "strong evidence" against a finding of valid waiver; "mere silence" in response to questioning is not enough; and waiver may not be presumed "simply from the fact that a confession was in fact eventually obtained."

It is undisputed here that Thompkins never expressly waived his right to remain silent. His refusal to sign even an acknowledgment that he understood his *Miranda* rights evinces, if anything, an intent not to waive those rights. That Thompkins did not make the inculpatory statements at issue until after approximately 2 hours and 45 minutes of interrogation serves as strong evidence against waiver. *Miranda* and *Butler* expressly preclude the possibility that the inculpatory statements themselves are sufficient to establish waiver.

In these circumstances, Thompkins' actions and words preceding the inculpatory statements simply do not evidence a "course of conduct indicating waiver" sufficient to carry the prosecution's burden. . . . Unlike in *Butler,* Thompkins made no initial declaration akin to "I will talk to you." . . .

Today's decision thus ignores the important interests *Miranda* safeguards. The underlying constitutional guarantee against self-incrimination reflects many of our fundamental values and most noble aspirations, our society's preference for an accusatorial rather than an inquisitorial system of criminal justice; a fear that self-incriminating statements will be elicited by inhumane treatment and abuses and a resulting distrust of self-deprecatory statements; and a realization that while the privilege is sometimes a shelter to the guilty, it is often a protection to the innocent. For these reasons . . . a criminal law system which comes to depend on the confession will, in the long run, be less reliable and more subject to abuses than a system relying on independent investigation. By bracing against the possibility of unreliable statements in every instance of in-custody interrogation, *Miranda*'s prophylactic rules serve to protect the fairness of the trial itself. Today's decision bodes poorly for the fundamental principles that *Miranda* protects.

III.

Thompkins separately argues that his conduct during the interrogation invoked his right to remain silent, requiring police to terminate questioning. . . . I cannot agree with the Court's much broader ruling that a suspect must clearly invoke his right to silence by speaking. Taken together with the Court's reformulation of the prosecution's burden of proof as to waiver, today's novel clear-statement rule for invocation invites police to question a suspect at length — notwithstanding his persistent refusal to answer questions — in the hope of eventually obtaining a single inculpatory response which will suffice to prove waiver of rights. . . .

In Michigan v. Mosley, 423 U.S. 96 (1975), the Court said that a critical safeguard of the right to remain silent is a suspect's "right to cut off questioning." . . . Thompkins contends that in refusing to respond to questions he effectively invoked his right to remain silent, such that police were required to terminate the interrogation prior to his inculpatory statements. . . .

The Court [extends] *Davis* to hold that police may continue questioning a suspect until he unambiguously invokes his right to remain silent. Because Thompkins neither said "he wanted to remain silent" nor said "he did not want to talk with the police," the Court concludes, he did not clearly invoke his right to silence.

I disagree with this novel application of *Davis*. Neither the rationale nor holding of that case compels today's result. *Davis* involved the right to counsel, not the right to silence. [A request to have counsel present and a request to remain silent each trigger different procedural safeguards. The police may reapproach a suspect who invokes the right to remain silent under certain circumstances; the same does not hold true for a suspect who invokes the right to counsel.] The different effects of invoking the rights are consistent with distinct standards for invocation. . . .

In addition, the suspect's equivocal reference to a lawyer in *Davis* occurred only *after* he had given express oral and written waivers of his rights. . . . The Court ignores this aspect of *Davis,* as well as the decisions of numerous federal and state courts declining to apply a clear-statement rule when a suspect has not previously given an express waiver of rights. . . .

The suspect's right to cut off questioning must be "scrupulously honored." Such a standard is necessarily precautionary and fact specific. The rule would acknowledge that some statements or conduct are so equivocal that police may scrupulously honor a suspect's rights without terminating questioning — for instance, if a suspect's actions are reasonably understood to indicate a willingness to listen before deciding whether to respond. But other statements or actions — in particular, when a suspect sits silent throughout prolonged interrogation, long past the point when he could be deciding whether to respond — cannot reasonably be understood other than as an invocation of the right to remain silent. Under such circumstances, "scrupulous" respect for the suspect's rights will require police to terminate questioning.[8] . . .

Davis' clear-statement rule is also a poor fit for the right to silence. Advising a suspect that he has a "right to remain silent" is unlikely to convey that he must speak (and must do so in some particular fashion) to ensure the right will be protected. By contrast, telling a suspect he has the right to the presence of an attorney, and that if he cannot afford an attorney one will be appointed for him prior to any questioning if he so desires, implies the need for speech to exercise that right. . . .

Conversely, the Court's concern that police will face difficult decisions about an accused's unclear intent and suffer the consequences of "guessing wrong," is misplaced. If a suspect makes an ambiguous statement or engages in conduct that creates uncertainty about his intent to invoke his right, police can simply ask for clarification. It is hardly an unreasonable burden for police to ask a suspect, for instance, "Do you want to talk to us?" . . . Police may well prefer not to seek clarification of an ambiguous statement out of fear that a suspect will invoke his rights. But our system of justice is not founded on a fear that a suspect will exercise his rights. If the exercise of constitutional rights will thwart the effectiveness of a system of law enforcement, then there is something very wrong with that system.

The Court asserts in passing that treating ambiguous statements or acts as an invocation of the right to silence will only "marginally" serve *Miranda*'s goals. Experience suggests the contrary. In the 16 years since *Davis* was decided, ample evidence has accrued that criminal suspects often use equivocal or colloquial language in attempting to invoke their right to silence. A number of lower courts that have (erroneously, in my view) imposed a clear-statement requirement for invocation of the right to silence have rejected as ambiguous an array of statements whose meaning might otherwise be thought plain. At a minimum, these decisions suggest that differentiating "clear" from "ambiguous" statements is often a subjective inquiry. [When] a suspect "understands his (expressed) wishes to have been ignored in contravention of the rights just read to him by his interrogator, he may well see further objection as futile and confession (true or not) as the only way to end his interrogation. . . .

Today's decision turns *Miranda* upside down. Criminal suspects must now unambiguously invoke their right to remain silent — which, counterintuitively, requires them to speak. At the same time, suspects will be legally presumed to have waived their rights even if they have given no clear expression of their intent to do so. Those results, in my view, find no basis in *Miranda* or our subsequent cases and

8. Indeed, this rule appears to reflect widespread contemporary police practice. Thompkins' *amici* collect a range of training materials that instruct police not to engage in prolonged interrogation after a suspect has failed to respond to initial questioning. One widely used police manual, for example, teaches that a suspect who indicates, "even by silence itself," his unwillingness to answer questions "has obviously exercised his constitutional privilege against self-incrimination."

are inconsistent with the fair-trial principles on which those precedents are grounded. . . .

Problem 8-5. Ambiguous Assertion?

The police were investigating the murder of a woman and her two young children. The killer had used a knife and a shotgun, and had stolen several items from the home, including an automobile. The police identified the stolen car on the road at 10:15 P.M., several hours after the murders. They arrested the driver, 16-year-old Jason Williams, and took him to the police station.

At 5:20 A.M., the police took Williams from his detention cell to an interview room located across the hall. Detectives Bozovsky and Christensen were waiting in the interview room when Williams arrived. They introduced themselves and sat at opposite ends of the table, while Williams sat between them with his back to the door. Williams was not wearing handcuffs. After Williams sat down, Detective Bozovsky recited a full *Miranda* warning and asked Williams if he understood the rights. Williams said yes. Bozovsky then asked Williams if he was willing to talk with them, and Williams replied "Yes, I'll talk with you." He signed a waiver of his *Miranda* rights.

Williams had not yet been informed about the homicide investigation. Instead, he was questioned about being in a stolen car. Williams initially maintained that he had stolen the car from a man who had left the keys in its ignition while parked outside of a liquor store. Approximately 45 minutes into the interview, Detective Bozovsky informed Williams that the car had been stolen from the home of people who had been murdered. Bozovsky noticed an injury to Williams' hand, and said that he suspected Williams had injured his hand during the murders. Williams denied any involvement in the homicides. Detective Christensen then explained that the homicide scene would be processed for fingerprints and blood analysis, and hypothesized that if the adult female victim had been sexually assaulted, physical evidence, such as semen, could be traced back to the assailant. Williams emphatically denied his involvement in anything like that, and Christensen accused him of lying. Williams then lost his composure, stood up from his chair, turned toward Christensen and said, "I don't have to take any more of your bullshit." Then Williams walked out of the interrogation room, into the hall, and back to his detention cell, where he was placed by the detention officer. This episode occurred approximately one hour into the interview.

Detectives Christensen and Bozovsky allowed Williams about five minutes to cool down. They would like to continue the interrogation with Williams. You are an attorney working for the police department, and you approach the detectives in the police station at this point. Bozovsky and Chritensen want to know what they should do next. Has Williams now invoked his right to silence? What advice will you give the detectives? Cf. State v. Williams, 535 N.W.2d 277 (Minn. 1995).

Suppose instead that Williams had said, "That's the end of this conversation, I'm done!" as he left the room. Would your advice change? Cf. State v. Schroeder, 777 N.W.2d 793 (Neb. 2010).

Notes

1. *Unambiguous assertion of* Miranda *rights: majority position.* The judicial opinions on assertions of *Miranda* rights divide into three groups. A small group holds that any statements that might be interpreted as an assertion of rights puts an end to the interrogation. A second group says that when a suspect makes an ambiguous statement that could be an assertion of rights, the interrogator must stop the questioning about the crime and obtain a clarification about the meaning of the statement. The largest group, represented by Davis v. United States, 512 U.S. 452 (1994), declares that a suspect must make a clear and unequivocal statement to invoke the *Miranda* right to counsel.

The *Thompkins* case expanded *Davis* to cover both the right to silence and the right to counsel. State courts and lower federal courts are wrestling with the question of which words or actions of a suspect amount to an "unambiguous" invocation of the right to silence. Will the courts encounter greater ambiguity in the invocation of the right to silence than they find in the invocation of the right to counsel? You can track current developments on this question on the web extension for this chapter at *http://www.crimpro.com/extension/ch08*.

2. *Interaction among supreme courts.* In Davis v. United States, 512 U.S. 452 (1994), the Supreme Court addressed an issue that many state courts had already answered, and it adopted a position taken by a minority of state courts until that time. Should the positions of state courts on a question of federal constitutional law have any significance when the U.S. Supreme Court considers the question? If so, is their significance any different from that of lower federal courts? After *Davis,* the state courts moved decisively toward the "unambiguous assertion" position. See State v. Eastlack, 883 P.2d 999 (Ariz. 1994) (follows *Davis,* although officer asked clarifying questions). A few courts, however, reaffirmed their earlier allegiance to some other approach. See State v. Hoey, 881 P.2d 504 (Haw. 1994). How would you explain the apparent, but incomplete, influence of the U.S. Supreme Court on state supreme courts deciding this question, one that arises often in every jurisdiction?

3. *Timing of invocation.* Even if the suspect uses unambiguous words, she must use them at the right time. Courts have not allowed suspects to make "anticipatory assertions" of rights, before interrogation begins. See, e.g., Sapp v. State, 690 So. 2d 581 (Fla. 1997); People v. Villalobos, 737 N.E.2d 639 (Ill. 2000). Although a questioner may continue questioning after an ambiguous statement from a suspect, courts sometimes require them to respond to clear questions from the suspect that do not invoke *Miranda* rights. See Almeida v. State, 737 So. 2d 520 (Fla. 1999) (suspect asks "Well, what good is a lawyer going to do?"; questioner must reply that decision belongs to suspect).

Some courts apply different tests for invocation, depending on whether the invocation happens at the start of the interrogation or in mid-stream, after an initial waiver of *Miranda* rights. See State v. Turner, 305 S.W.3d 508 (Tenn. 2010) (the *Davis* rule requiring unambiguous assertion of right to counsel applies only after a suspect initially waived *Miranda* rights). Does the nature of the interaction between the suspect and questioner change during an interview in ways that justifies a change in the standard for invoking *Miranda* rights?

4. *Ambiguous waiver: majority position.* There are many instances in which a defendant says or does something that might be interpreted to constitute a waiver (rather

than an assertion) of *Miranda* rights. This could be something as simple as refusing to answer any questions about waiver but discussing the crime with the interrogating officer. In North Carolina v. Butler, 441 U.S. 369 (1979), the Court said that "an explicit statement of waiver is not invariably necessary to support a finding that the defendant waived the right to remain silent or the right to counsel guaranteed by the *Miranda* case." Virtually all state courts have agreed that a suspect can implicitly waive *Miranda* rights through conduct or ambiguous statements. Garvey v. State, 873 A.2d 291 (Del. 2005) (suspect who responded to *Miranda* advisory by saying, "Depends on what you ask me," effectively waived interrogation rights, indicating intent to selectively waive rights and an understanding of those rights).

Does the *Thompkins* case mean that any suspect responses to questions during an interrogation will now amount to a waiver of the right to silence? Do you predict any serious changes in interrogation techniques based on this opinion?

Consider how legislation on the topic of waiver might look different from constitutional rulings on the subject. Does the Vermont statute reprinted above prevent the use of a confession obtained after a suspect orally waives his rights but refuses to sign any waiver form? See State v. Caron, 586 A.2d 1127 (Vt. 1990). The Vermont statute is taken in large part from the Model Public Defender Act, adopted in 1970 by the National Conference of Commissioners on Uniform State Laws.

5. *Standard of proof for waiver.* In Lego v. Twomey, 404 U.S. 477 (1972), the Court ruled that the constitution requires the government to show that a confession was voluntary by a preponderance of the evidence. The same standard of proof applies when the government must prove the knowing and intelligent waiver of *Miranda* rights. Colorado v. Connelly, 479 U.S. 157 (1986). In both cases, the Court emphasized the distinction between proving the essential elements of a crime (which bears directly on the reliability of the jury's verdict) and establishing the voluntariness of a confession (which bears on the admissibility of evidence). Most state courts have also adopted the preponderance standard. See, e.g., People v. Clark, 857 P.2d 1099 (Cal. 1993); but see State v. Gerald, 549 A.2d 792 (N.J. 1988) (beyond reasonable doubt). Do doubts about the validity of a waiver of *Miranda* rights translate into doubts about the accuracy of the prosecution's evidence?

6. *Why do suspects waive their rights?* Can a suspect gain anything by talking to the police? Perhaps suspects believe they can convince the officers to look elsewhere for the culprit or to drop the investigation. Observers of interrogations say that it is standard practice for police interrogators at the beginning of an interrogation to encourage the suspect to speak with the officer as a way of telling "his side" of the story and to learn more about the evidence the police have collected. The officer will be careful to engage in small talk, to cover routine booking questions, and to talk about the advantages of waiver before allowing the suspect to answer any questions about *Miranda* rights. At that point, the questioner will often speak of the *Miranda* waiver as a formality that is surely very familiar to the suspect. If the suspect announces a decision about waiver too early, the officer has no opportunity to persuade the suspect to waive, and the relevant legal rules make it difficult to follow up after an invocation of rights. David Simon, Homicide: A Year on the Killing Streets (1991). Suspects with a prior felony record are far less likely than other suspects to waive their *Miranda* rights. The web extension for this chapter, at *http://www.crimpro.com/extension/ch08*, reviews the legal and criminological studies of interrogation practices. In hindsight, if the Warren Court was concerned about the

coercive nature of the interrogation environment in the police station, was it a mistake to allow a suspect to waive the right to silence without an attorney present?

Problem 8-6. Capacity to Waive

Donald Cleary forced his way into a home, struggled with the occupant, held her at gunpoint, and fled. About an hour later, an investigator from the state's attorney's office and a sergeant from the sheriff's department stopped defendant as he was driving his truck because he fit the general description of the assailant. The sergeant read Cleary his *Miranda* rights twice, and Cleary signed a statement purporting to waive those rights. He then confessed, admitting that he had entered the victim's house and accosted her, and that he had intended to rape her.

At the hearing on the defense motion to suppress this statement, Cleary relied on expert testimony from a psychiatrist, Dr. Robert Linder. Linder had evaluated Cleary in connection with several prior criminal charges. He estimated that Cleary had an IQ of 65, which translated into a mental age between ten and twelve, and only a limited ability to read and write. Cleary was 26 years old at the time of the hearing. Dr. Linder testified that Cleary had difficulty thinking abstractly and anticipating future events, which would limit his ability to comprehend the language of the *Miranda* warnings. He conceded, however, that Cleary could understand that he did not have to talk to the police, that he could speak with an attorney if he wished, and that he could stop answering questions whenever he chose. However, he believed that Cleary might have difficulty understanding the future legal impact of waiving his rights. Dr. Linder believed that Cleary would not be able to look beyond his immediate concerns to a future court proceeding in which comments he had made earlier would be used against him. Instead, Cleary would speak to police to take the shortest route to his immediate needs — to please the officers, to make himself feel better, and to go home.

Under cross-examination, Dr. Linder conceded that defendant had undergone a learning process through his prior contacts with the police and court system. Cleary had been questioned in previous arson and sexual assault investigations, and now understood that the prosecutor sought to put him in jail. Those previous charges had all been dismissed. He was declared incompetent to stand trial for one of the charges.

Cleary's former mental health services counselor also testified, and estimated his mental capacity to be that of a seven- or eight-year-old child and his emotional level to be that of a four- or five-year-old child. Cleary himself testified at the hearing that he spoke to the officers because he thought they would help him and because he could not leave until he spoke to them.

According to the U.S. Supreme Court in Fare v. Michael C., 442 U.S. 707, 725 (1979), an analysis of a defendant's capacity to waive *Miranda* rights requires a "totality-of-the-circumstances approach," that mandates an evaluation of the defendant's "age, experience, education, background, and intelligence," and an inquiry into "whether he has the capacity to understand the warnings given him, the nature of his Fifth Amendment rights, and the consequences of waiving those rights." Courts typically say that a suspect's mental impairment is a highly significant circumstance to be considered among all the others in deciding the voluntariness question.

The trial judge found that Cleary had attended special education classes in school through the eleventh grade and had limited ability to read, write, and do mathematics. He read at a second-grade level. He had also participated in programs for mentally retarded adults and continued to work actively with two counselors. She stated that Cleary, "in spite of his intellectual limitations, has the ability to learn and puts his learning to practical use." For example, Cleary operated his own logging business for seven years. He purchased and maintained equipment for the business and negotiated bank loans, timber contracts, and truck transportation for his timber. Cleary had a driver's license, maintained a vehicle, was knowledgeable about how it worked, and purchased parts for it.

Assume that the trial court rules that Cleary voluntarily waived his *Miranda* rights. Recall that the government carries the burden of proof on questions of the voluntariness of a waiver. As an appellate judge, would you conclude that this ruling was an abuse of discretion? Cf. State v. Cleary, 641 A.2d 102 (Vt. 1994).

Notes

1. *Capacity to waive under* Miranda: *majority position.* Analysis of the capacity of suspects to waive their *Miranda* rights is highly case-specific. Courts assess a variety of factors to resolve these frequently litigated claims of incapacity, such as the defendant's prior experience with the criminal justice system, the defendant's intelligence and education, mental illness, vocabulary and literacy, state of intoxication, and emotional state. Courts also look at the conduct of the police in eliciting a confession. For example, the U.S. Supreme Court in Colorado v. Connelly, 479 U.S. 157 (1986), considered a case involving the confession of a suspect who suffered from a psychosis. Because the police could not reasonably have known about the condition and did not engage in any "overreaching" conduct during the interrogation, the Court held that the waiver of *Miranda* rights was knowing and voluntary. See also State v. Chapman, 605 A.2d 1055 (N.H. 1992). How are the police interrogators to determine whether and to what degree a suspect is mentally disabled?

Note that a suspect's capacity to waive *Miranda* rights is distinct from the voluntariness of the confession. The mental illness of a suspect might interfere with that person's ability to understand *Miranda* rights even if the police do nothing blameworthy to affect the voluntariness of the confession. Capacity questions are also connected to the accuracy of confessions. The availability of DNA evidence has uncovered a number of wrongful convictions over the years, some based substantially on false confessions. It is quite common in these false-confession cases to find that the defendant had some form of mental impairment that raised questions about the capacity to waive *Miranda* rights.

Appellate courts defer to trial court judgments of capacity; the appellate case law is full of decisions affirming a trial court's finding of waiver, even on fairly dramatic facts. Is a per se rule or rebuttable presumption of incapacity appropriate for some defendants? See Morgan Cloud, George B. Shepherd, Alison Nodvin Barkoff & Justin V. Shur, Words Without Meaning: The Constitution, Confessions, and Mentally Retarded Suspects, 69 U. Chi. L. Rev. 495 (2002) (authors tested sample of mentally impaired individuals to determine if they could understand *Miranda* warnings; mentally impaired suspects do not understand legal consequences of confessing or meaning of sentences comprising warnings).

2. *Intoxication and capacity to waive.* Suspects under the influence of alcohol or drugs very rarely convince a court that they did not have the capacity to waive their *Miranda* rights. In State v. Keith, 628 A.2d 1247 (Vt. 1993), for example, the court affirmed a finding of valid waiver where defendant had a blood-alcohol level of .203 at the time he was interrogated and gave several inconsistent stories of his whereabouts at the time of a suspicious fire. James Keith had refused to sign the waiver form, saying, "every time I sign something I get in trouble," but he was willing to talk to Sergeant Bombardier of the arson squad, who later expressed his belief that the defendant was just "playing head games." Courts in these cases often point out that the defendant voluntarily got himself into the intoxicated condition. Does the blameworthiness of the defendant have any bearing on her capacity to waive rights? Is a claim that intoxication negates the capacity to waive *Miranda* rights different from the claim that the influence of alcohol or drugs eliminates criminal responsibility for purposes of substantive criminal law?

3. *Juveniles and* Miranda *waivers.* The youth of a suspect in custody can be an important factor for courts determining whether the suspect has the capacity to make a knowing and voluntary waiver. Most states follow the totality-of-the-circumstances rule of Fare v. Michael C., 442 U.S. 707 (1979). See Commonwealth v. Williams, 475 A.2d 1283 (Pa. 1984). A few states, however, require that a juvenile consult with an "interested adult" before she can waive *Miranda* rights. See In re K.W.B., 500 S.W.2d 275 (Mo. 1973); Conn. Gen. Stat. Ann. §46b-137(a). Is a per se consultation rule appropriate for juveniles as a group? Perhaps your answer to this question will depend on how many juveniles you believe will misunderstand the rights explained to them. One empirical study, which sought to determine the capacity of juveniles to comprehend the meaning and significance of their *Miranda* rights, concluded that juveniles younger than 15 years old typically did not adequately comprehend their *Miranda* rights and that one-third to one-half of 15-year-olds showed an inadequate understanding of the *Miranda* warnings. The study further found that 55.3 percent of the children demonstrated an inadequate understanding of at least one of the four warnings, and that 63.3 percent of the juveniles misunderstood at least one of the crucial words used in the standard *Miranda* warnings. Adequate understanding of the warnings was achieved by only 20.9 percent of the juveniles. See Thomas Grisso, Juveniles' Capacities to Waive *Miranda* Rights: An Empirical Analysis, 68 Cal. L. Rev. 1134 (1980).

4. *Language barriers.* Courts have also treated language barriers as one circumstance that might contribute to a finding of incapacity. See People v. Jiminez, 863 P.2d 981 (Colo. 1993) (suspect spoke no English and little Spanish, mostly Kickapoo; no valid waiver when warnings were delivered in Spanish). How might you argue for resolving language-barrier cases with a more clear-cut rule than the approach taken for alcohol, mental disability, or youthfulness claims?

D. EFFECT OF ASSERTING *MIRANDA* RIGHTS

The *Miranda* opinion appeared to bar police efforts to change a suspect's decision after he or she invoked *Miranda* rights during an interrogation: "If the individual indicates in any manner, at any time prior to or during questioning, that he wishes to remain silent, the interrogation must cease. At this point, he has shown that he intends to exercise his Fifth Amendment privilege; any statement taken after the person invokes his privilege cannot be other than the product of compulsion, subtle or otherwise." It later became clear, however, that a suspect could waive *Miranda* rights even after initially invoking them. Indeed, the police in some circumstances can take actions to encourage this later waiver.

The U.S. Supreme Court distinguished between the effects of invoking the *right to silence* and the *right to counsel.* In Michigan v. Mosley, 423 U.S. 96 (1975), the Court upheld the use of a confession despite the fact that the suspect earlier invoked his right to silence. Under the circumstances of that case, the Court concluded that the police "scrupulously honored" Mosley's initial invocation of the privilege, even though they had initiated a later conversation about the criminal investigation that led to his waiver and confession. In Edwards v. Arizona, 451 U.S. 477 (1981), however, the Court insisted on a different rule for those who invoke the right to counsel: Such a person "is not subject to further interrogation, by the authorities until counsel has been made available to him, unless the accused himself initiates further communication, exchanges or conversations with the police." 451 U.S. at 484. Consider the following judicial efforts to apply these rules regarding waiver after an initial invocation.

■ CHARLES GLOBE v. STATE

877 So.2d 663 (Fla. 2004)

PER CURIAM.

. . . Globe was convicted of the July 3, 2000, first-degree murder of Elton Ard. Ard was a fellow inmate at the Columbia Correctional Institution (CCI). Globe and his codefendant and fellow inmate, Andrew D. Busby, had been planning to murder an inmate or correctional officer for two weeks before Ard's murder. Ard was Busby's cellmate and was one of seven potential victims targeted by Globe and Busby because he was harassing Busby. Globe and Busby talked for days about killing Ard and devised a plan to do so. Using part of a linen sheet and broken ballpoint pens, Globe made two garrotes approximately two weeks prior to the murder. Globe intended to use these garrotes to strangle his victim.

On the morning of July 3, 2000, at approximately 7 A.M., Globe slipped into the prison cell shared by Ard and Busby. After locking the cell door and covering the window, Globe grabbed Ard around the neck and they began to struggle. Globe placed one of the garrotes around Ard's neck, but it broke as he and Busby were strangling Ard. Ard pled for his life, offering to give Globe all of his money, a total of forty-five dollars. Globe told Ard that he didn't want his money "but his fucking life." Globe then struck Ard in the face, causing him to bleed. Globe flushed the broken garrote down the toilet and after discovering that Ard was still alive tied the second garrote around Ard's neck. Globe then lit a cigarette and watched Ard gasp for air six times before he finally died. After Ard died, Globe took the garrote from Ard's neck and tied it around Ard's wrist. He put a cigarette in Ard's mouth and placed a lighter in his hand. . . .

Evidence recovered from the murder scene included photographs of writing on the prison wall, photographs of bloody fingerprints, the cigarette lighter found in Ard's hand, the cigarette from Ard's mouth, the magic marker used to write on the wall, and the wingtip piece from a pair of glasses. The phrases "Call FDLE" and

"Remember Andy and K.D., 7/3/2000," were written in magic marker on the cell door. "Don't forget to look on the door" was written in magic marker on the cell wall. Karen Smith, a crime laboratory analyst and forensic document examiner with FDLE, testified that Globe had written "Call FDLE" and "Remember Andy and K.D., 7/3/2000." . . .

Several hours after the murder, FDLE agent Bill Gootee met with Globe, advised him of his *Miranda* rights, and asked Globe if he wanted to make a statement. Globe replied, "Not at this time," but did not request an attorney. Gootee terminated the interview and passed this information on to FDLE Agent Don Ugliano. Approximately seven hours later, Ugliano was standing in a hallway and heard Globe say something to the effect of "that guy doesn't need to be here." Globe had just finished being photographed and Busby was a short distance away inside the inspector's office talking to his father on the phone. Ugliano asked Globe "why," and Globe said, "The whole place is just screwed up. It is all messed up." Ugliano then asked Globe if he was willing to make a statement. Globe answered that he would, if he could be with Busby. After Globe and Busby were advised of their *Miranda* rights, they gave a tape recorded statement in which they admitted to killing Ard. After the statement was taken, Globe was moved to Florida State Prison and placed under a higher level of security than was available at CCI.

Inspector Jack Schenck, a senior inspector with the Florida Department of Corrections, Office of the Inspector General, interviewed Globe on July 7, 2000, at Florida State Prison. Schenck was present for Globe's July 3, 2000, statement. After being advised of his *Miranda* rights, Globe discussed how he had been planning to murder an inmate and how he had actually murdered Ard. Counsel was appointed for Globe, and he was arraigned on September 7, 2000. While sitting outside the judge's chambers that day, Globe said to Ugliano, "It's stupid to have to go through all this bullshit. I know I am going to get the needle for killing him." Ugliano told Globe that he was not allowed to speak to him anymore because Globe was represented by an attorney. Globe replied, "Shit. We have already confessed to killing the dude. What's it matter?" . . .

The jury convicted Globe of first-degree murder on September 11, 2001, and on September 14, 2001, recommended death by a vote of nine to three. The trial court followed the jury's recommendation and imposed a death sentence, finding and weighing four aggravating factors, no statutory mitigating factors, and eleven nonstatutory mitigating factors. . . .

Globe argues that the trial court erred by denying his motion to suppress the July 3 and July 7 statements. The court denied Globe's motion to suppress his statements "upon a finding that the statements were made freely, voluntarily, and knowingly after full and complete advisal and waiver of *Miranda* rights." . . .

The State must establish, by a preponderance of the evidence, that the waiver of *Miranda* rights is knowing, intelligent, and voluntary. Whether *Miranda* rights were validly waived must be ascertained from two separate inquiries. . . . First, the relinquishment of the right must have been voluntary in the sense that it was the product of free and deliberate choice rather than intimidation, coercion, or deception. Second, the waiver must have been made with a full awareness of both the nature of the right being abandoned and the consequences of the decision to abandon it. Only if the "totality of the circumstances surrounding the interrogation" reveal both an uncoerced choice and the requisite level of comprehension may a court properly conclude that the *Miranda* rights have been waived. . . .

[Police-initiated] questioning of a person in custody is not absolutely foreclosed if he or she invokes the right to remain silent but not the right to counsel. We implicitly recognized the distinction between assertion of the two rights in Traylor v. State, 596 So. 2d 957, 966 (Fla. 1992):

> If the suspect indicates in any manner that he or she does not want to be interrogated, interrogation must not begin or, if it has already begun, must immediately stop. If the suspect indicates in any manner that he or she wants the help of a lawyer, interrogation must not begin until a lawyer has been appointed and is present or, if it has already begun, must immediately stop until a lawyer is present. Once a suspect has requested the help of a lawyer, no state agent can reinitiate interrogation on any offense throughout the period of custody unless the lawyer is present, although the suspect is free to volunteer a statement to police on his or her own initiative at any time on any subject in the absence of counsel.

In Michigan v. Mosley, 423 U.S. 96 (1975), the United States Supreme Court held that resolution of the question of the admissibility of statements obtained after a person in custody has invoked his or her right to remain silent depends upon whether the person's decision to assert his or her "right to cut off questioning" was "scrupulously honored." In holding that no *Miranda* violation occurred in *Mosley*, the Court stated:

> This is not a case, therefore, where the police failed to honor a decision of a person in custody to cut off questioning, either by refusing to discontinue the interrogation upon request or by persisting in repeated efforts to wear down his resistance and make him change his mind. In contrast to such practices, the police here immediately ceased the interrogation, resumed questioning only after the passage of a significant period of time and the provision of a fresh set of warnings, and restricted the second interrogation to a crime that had not been a subject of the earlier interrogation.

We applied *Mosley* in Henry v. State, 574 So. 2d 66, 69 (Fla. 1991), when analyzing the resumption of questioning on the same offense after invocation of the right to silence. We recognized that in *Mosley* the Supreme Court neither set out "precise guidelines" for what constitutes scrupulous adherence to *Miranda* nor stated that "any factor standing by itself would be dispositive of the issue." However, we recognized five factors the Court in *Mosley* found to be relevant:

> First, Mosley was informed of his rights both times before questioning began. Second, the officer immediately ceased questioning when Mosley unequivocally said he did not want to talk about the burglaries. Third, there was a significant lapse of time between the questioning on the burglary and the questioning on the homicide. Fourth, the second episode of questioning took place in a different location. Fifth, the second episode involved a different crime.

In *Henry*, we determined that variance as to one or more of the five factors was not dispositive, and therefore applied a totality of the circumstances approach. We apply the same analysis in this case.

Globe argues that his right to remain silent was not "scrupulously honored" because of Agent Ugliano's request for a statement approximately seven hours after he declined to give a statement to Agent Gootee. The trial court's factual findings are supported by competent, substantial evidence and are entitled to a presumption of correctness. Applying the five factors set out in *Mosley* and *Henry* to the facts in this case, it is evident that four of the five factors are present: (1) *Miranda* warnings were given several times, including right before each request for a statement; (2) interrogations ceased immediately when Globe expressed his desire to remain silent; (3) there was a significant time lapse between the questioning in that the second request for a statement was made seven and a half hours after the first request; and (4) the second questioning took place at a different location. We conclude that it is not dispositive that the second questioning involved the same crime. We consider not only that four of the five factors weigh in favor of admissibility but also that when Globe initially invoked his right to silence he said only that he did not want to make a statement "at this time," leaving open the prospect of future questioning on the crime. We hold that Globe's right to remain silent was scrupulously honored. Accordingly, the trial court did not err when it denied Globe's motion to suppress the July 3, 2000, statement.

The July 7 statement was taken at Florida State Prison, where Globe had been moved for security reasons. Globe alleges that the July 7 statement was the fruit of the illegally obtained July 3 statement; that it was not made voluntarily, intelligently, or knowingly; and that it was taken in violation of Florida Rule of Criminal Procedure 3.130.

Globe's first argument fails because the July 3 statement was not illegally obtained, as discussed above. Globe's second argument also is without merit. Before making his July 7 statement, Globe was advised of his *Miranda* rights by Agent Ugliano. [The] proper inquiry is whether the "totality of the circumstances surrounding the interrogation" reveal both an uncoerced choice and the requisite level of comprehension. In this case, Globe was read his rights. He was asked if he understood his rights and responded, "Sure." He was then asked, "With your rights in mind, would you like to answer questions and make a statement at this time?" Although Globe's response was inaudible on the tape recording, he proceeded to make a statement. All of this occurred after Globe had been read his rights twice before on July 3. The trial court's factual findings are supported by competent, substantial evidence and are entitled to a presumption of correctness. The totality of the circumstances in this case demonstrate that Globe voluntarily waived his rights and was fully aware of the consequences of his decision. Globe's right to remain silent was scrupulously honored.

Globe also argues that the July 7 statement is inadmissible because he was in custody on July 3 and should have been brought before a judge within twenty-four hours pursuant to Florida Rule of Criminal Procedure 3.130. Florida Rule of Criminal Procedure 3.130 states that "every arrested person shall be taken before a judicial officer . . . within 24 hours of arrest." Globe asserts that although he was not formally arrested, he was de facto arrested when he was removed from the open population at Columbia Correctional and was taken to Florida State Prison. The State argues that Globe was in custody pursuant to a lawful conviction unrelated to the murder for which he was under investigation.

[We] noted in Chavez v. State, 832 So. 2d 730 (Fla. 2002), that where a defendant has been sufficiently advised of his rights, a confession that would otherwise be admissible is not subject to suppression merely because the defendant was deprived of a prompt first appearance. "When a defendant has been advised of his rights and makes an otherwise voluntary statement, the delay in following the strictures of

[Rule 3.130] must be shown to have induced the confession." A first appearance "serves as a venue for informing the defendant of certain rights, and provides for a determination of the conditions for the defendant's release."

In this case, Globe was repeatedly advised of his *Miranda* rights, would not have been subject to release because of his prior convictions, and did not invoke his right to counsel. Additionally, Globe made his most incriminating statement, the July 3 statement, less than twenty-four hours after he alleges he was de facto arrested. There is no showing that the delay in following the strictures of rule 3.130 induced the confession. Therefore, under the narrow circumstances in this case, we hold that the trial court did not err in denying the motion to suppress. However, we remind the State of its obligation under rule 3.130 to take every arrested person, including those already in custody on other grounds, before a magistrate within twenty-four hours of arrest. . . .

MARYLAND v. MICHAEL BLAINE SHATZER

130 S. Ct. 1213 (2010)

SCALIA, J.*

We consider whether a break in custody ends the presumption of involuntariness established in Edwards v. Arizona, 451 U.S. 477 (1981).

I.

In August 2003, a social worker assigned to the Child Advocacy Center in the Criminal Investigation Division of the Hagerstown Police Department referred to the department allegations that respondent Michael Shatzer, Sr., had sexually abused his 3-year-old son. At that time, Shatzer was incarcerated at the Maryland Correctional Institution-Hagerstown, serving a sentence for an unrelated child-sexual-abuse offense. Detective Shane Blankenship was assigned to the investigation and interviewed Shatzer at the correctional institution on August 7, 2003. Before asking any questions, Blankenship reviewed Shatzer's *Miranda* rights with him, and obtained a written waiver of those rights. When Blankenship explained that he was there to question Shatzer about sexually abusing his son, Shatzer expressed confusion — he had thought Blankenship was an attorney there to discuss the prior crime for which he was incarcerated. Blankenship clarified the purpose of his visit, and Shatzer declined to speak without an attorney. Accordingly, Blankenship ended the interview, and Shatzer was released back into the general prison population. Shortly thereafter, Blankenship closed the investigation.

Two years and six months later, the same social worker referred more specific allegations to the department about the same incident involving Shatzer. Detective Paul Hoover, from the same division, was assigned to the investigation. He and the social worker interviewed the victim, then eight years old, who described the incident in more detail. With this new information in hand, on March 2, 2006, they went to the Roxbury Correctional Institute, to which Shatzer had since been transferred,

* [Chief Justice Roberts and Justices Kennedy, Ginsburg, Breyer, Alito, and Sotomayor joined in this opinion; Justice Thomas joined in part III. — EDS.]

and interviewed Shatzer in a maintenance room outfitted with a desk and three chairs. Hoover explained that he wanted to ask Shatzer about the alleged incident involving Shatzer's son. Shatzer was surprised because he thought that the investigation had been closed, but Hoover explained they had opened a new file. Hoover then read Shatzer his *Miranda* rights and obtained a written waiver on a standard department form.

Hoover interrogated Shatzer about the incident for approximately 30 minutes. Shatzer denied ordering his son to perform fellatio on him, but admitted to masturbating in front of his son from a distance of less than three feet. Before the interview ended, Shatzer agreed to Hoover's request that he submit to a polygraph examination. At no point during the interrogation did Shatzer request to speak with an attorney or refer to his prior refusal to answer questions without one.

Five days later, on March 7, 2006, Hoover and another detective met with Shatzer at the correctional facility to administer the polygraph examination. After reading Shatzer his *Miranda* rights and obtaining a written waiver, the other detective administered the test and concluded that Shatzer had failed. When the detectives then questioned Shatzer, he became upset, started to cry, and incriminated himself by saying, "I didn't force him. I didn't force him." After making this inculpatory statement, Shatzer requested an attorney, and Hoover promptly ended the interrogation.

The State's Attorney for Washington County charged Shatzer with second-degree sexual offense, sexual child abuse, second-degree assault, and contributing to conditions rendering a child in need of assistance. Shatzer moved to suppress his March 2006 statements pursuant to *Edwards*. The trial court held a suppression hearing and later denied Shatzer's motion. The *Edwards* protections did not apply, it reasoned, because Shatzer had experienced a break in custody for *Miranda* purposes between the 2003 and 2006 interrogations. . . . Based on the proffered testimony of the victim and the "admission of the defendant as to the act of masturbation," the trial court found Shatzer guilty of sexual child abuse of his son. . . .

II.

. . . In Miranda v. Arizona, 384 U.S. 436 (1966), the Court adopted a set of prophylactic measures to protect a suspect's Fifth Amendment right from the "inherently compelling pressures" of custodial interrogation. . . . Critically, however, a suspect can waive [*Miranda*] rights. To establish a valid waiver, the State must show that the waiver was knowing, intelligent, and voluntary under the high standard of proof for the waiver of constitutional rights set forth in Johnson v. Zerbst, 304 U.S. 458 (1938). In *Edwards,* the Court determined that *Zerbst*'s traditional standard for waiver was not sufficient to protect a suspect's right to have counsel present at a subsequent interrogation if he had previously requested counsel; "additional safeguards" were necessary. The Court therefore superimposed a second layer of prophylaxis. *Edwards* held:

> [When] an accused has invoked his right to have counsel present during custodial interrogation, a valid waiver of that right cannot be established by showing only that he responded to further police-initiated custodial interrogation even if he has been advised of his rights. [He] is not subject to further interrogation by the authorities until

> counsel has been made available to him, unless the accused himself initiates further communication, exchanges, or conversations with the police.

The rationale of *Edwards* is that once a suspect indicates that he is not capable of undergoing custodial questioning without advice of counsel, any subsequent waiver that has come at the authorities' behest, and not at the suspect's own instigation, is itself the product of the "inherently compelling pressures" and not the purely voluntary choice of the suspect. Arizona v. Roberson, 486 U.S. 675, 681 (1988). Under this rule, a voluntary *Miranda* waiver is sufficient at the time of an initial attempted interrogation to protect a suspect's right to have counsel present, but it is not sufficient at the time of subsequent attempts if the suspect initially requested the presence of counsel. The implicit assumption, of course, is that the subsequent requests for interrogation pose a significantly greater risk of coercion. That increased risk results not only from the police's persistence in trying to get the suspect to talk, but also from the continued pressure that begins when the individual is taken into custody as a suspect and sought to be interrogated — pressure likely to "increase as custody is prolonged," Minnick v. Mississippi, 498 U.S. 146 (1990). The *Edwards* presumption of involuntariness ensures that police will not take advantage of the mounting coercive pressures of prolonged police custody by repeatedly attempting to question a suspect who previously requested counsel until the suspect is badgered into submission.

We have frequently emphasized that the *Edwards* rule is not a constitutional mandate, but judicially prescribed prophylaxis. Because *Edwards* is our rule, not a constitutional command, it is our obligation to justify its expansion. Lower courts have uniformly held that a break in custody ends the *Edwards* presumption. . . .

A judicially crafted rule is justified only by reference to its prophylactic purpose, and applies only where its benefits outweigh its costs. We begin with the benefits. *Edwards*' presumption of involuntariness has the incidental effect of conserving judicial resources which would otherwise be expended in making difficult determinations of voluntariness. Its fundamental purpose, however, is to preserve the integrity of an accused's choice to communicate with police only through counsel, by preventing police from badgering a defendant into waiving his previously asserted *Miranda* rights. Thus, the benefits of the rule are measured by the number of coerced confessions it suppresses that otherwise would have been admitted.

It is easy to believe that a suspect may be coerced or badgered into abandoning his earlier refusal to be questioned without counsel in the paradigm *Edwards* case. That is a case in which the suspect has been arrested for a particular crime and is held in uninterrupted pretrial custody while that crime is being actively investigated. After the initial interrogation, and up to and including the second one, he remains cut off from his normal life and companions, thrust into and isolated in an unfamiliar, police-dominated atmosphere, where his captors appear to control his fate. That was the situation confronted by the suspects in *Edwards, Roberson,* and *Minnick,* the three cases in which we have held the *Edwards* rule applicable. Edwards was arrested pursuant to a warrant and taken to a police station, where he was interrogated until he requested counsel. The officer ended the interrogation and took him to the county jail, but at 9:15 the next morning, two of the officer's colleagues reinterrogated Edwards at the jail. Roberson was arrested at the scene of a just-completed burglary and interrogated there until he requested a lawyer. A different officer interrogated him three days later while he was still in custody pursuant to the arrest. Minnick was arrested by local police and taken to the San Diego jail, where two FBI agents interrogated him the next morning until he requested counsel. Two days later a Mississippi Deputy Sheriff reinterrogated him at the jail. None of these suspects regained a sense of control or normalcy after they were initially taken into custody for the crime under investigation.

When, unlike what happened in these three cases, a suspect has been released from his pretrial custody and has returned to his normal life for some time before the later attempted interrogation, there is little reason to think that his change of heart regarding interrogation without counsel has been coerced. He has no longer been isolated. He has likely been able to seek advice from an attorney, family members, and friends. And he knows from his earlier experience that he need only demand counsel to bring the interrogation to a halt; and that investigative custody does not last indefinitely. In these circumstances, it is far fetched to think that a police officer's asking the suspect whether he would like to waive his *Miranda* rights will any more wear down the accused than did the first such request at the original attempted interrogation — which is of course not deemed coercive. His change of heart is less likely attributable to "badgering" than it is to the fact that further deliberation in familiar surroundings has caused him to believe (rightly or wrongly) that cooperating with the investigation is in his interest. Uncritical extension of *Edwards* to this situation would not significantly increase the number of genuinely coerced confessions excluded. . . .

At the same time that extending the *Edwards* rule yields diminished benefits, extending the rule also increases its costs: the in-fact voluntary confessions it excludes from trial, and the voluntary confessions it deters law enforcement officers from even trying to obtain. Voluntary confessions are not merely a proper element in law enforcement, they are an unmitigated good, essential to society's compelling interest in finding, convicting, and punishing those who violate the law.

The only logical endpoint of *Edwards'* disability is termination of *Miranda* custody and any of its lingering effects. Without that limitation — and barring some purely arbitrary time-limit — every *Edwards* prohibition of custodial interrogation of a particular suspect would be eternal. The prohibition applies, of course, when the subsequent interrogation pertains to a different crime, *Roberson,* when it is conducted by a different law enforcement authority, *Minnick,* and even when the suspect has met with an attorney after the first interrogation, *ibid.* And it not only prevents questioning *ex ante*; it would render invalid *ex post,* confessions invited and obtained from suspects who (unbeknownst to the interrogators) have acquired *Edwards* immunity previously in connection with any offense in any jurisdiction. In a country that harbors a large number of repeat offenders, this consequence is disastrous.

We conclude that such an extension of *Edwards* is not justified; we have opened its protective umbrella far enough. The protections offered by *Miranda,* which we have deemed sufficient to ensure that the police respect the suspect's desire to have an attorney present the first time police interrogate him, adequately ensure that result when a suspect who initially requested counsel is reinterrogated after a break in custody that is of sufficient duration to dissipate its coercive effects.

If Shatzer's return to the general prison population qualified as a break in custody (a question we address in Part III), there is no doubt that it lasted long enough (2 1/2 years) to meet that durational requirement. But what about a break that has lasted only one year? Or only one week? It is impractical to leave the answer to that question for clarification in future case-by-case adjudication; law enforcement officers need to know, with certainty and beforehand, when renewed interrogation is lawful. . . .

We think it appropriate to specify a period of time to avoid the consequence that continuation of the *Edwards* presumption will not reach the correct result most of the time. It seems to us that period is 14 days. That provides plenty of time for the suspect to get reacclimated to his normal life, to consult with friends and counsel, and to shake off any residual coercive effects of his prior custody.

The 14-day limitation meets Shatzer's concern that a break-in-custody rule lends itself to police abuse. He envisions that once a suspect invokes his *Miranda* right to counsel, the police will release the suspect briefly (to end the *Edwards* presumption) and then promptly bring him back into custody for reinterrogation. But once the suspect has been out of custody long enough (14 days) to eliminate its coercive effect, there will be nothing to gain by such gamesmanship — nothing, that is, except the entirely appropriate gain of being able to interrogate a suspect who has made a valid waiver of his *Miranda* rights.[7] . . .

III.

The facts of this case present an additional issue. . . . After the 2003 interview, Shatzer was released back into the general prison population where he was serving an unrelated sentence. The issue is whether that constitutes a break in *Miranda* custody.

We have never decided whether incarceration constitutes custody for *Miranda* purposes. . . . Whether it does depends upon whether it exerts the coercive pressure that *Miranda* was designed to guard against — the danger of coercion that results from the *interaction* of custody and official interrogation. . . . Without minimizing the harsh realities of incarceration, we think lawful imprisonment imposed upon conviction of a crime does not create the coercive pressures identified in *Miranda*.

Interrogated suspects who have previously been convicted of crime live in prison. When they are released back into the general prison population, they return to their accustomed surroundings and daily routine — they regain the degree of control they had over their lives prior to the interrogation. Sentenced prisoners, in contrast to the *Miranda* paradigm, are not isolated with their accusers. They live among other inmates, guards, and workers, and often can receive visitors and communicate with people on the outside by mail or telephone.

Their detention, moreover, is relatively disconnected from their prior unwillingness to cooperate in an investigation. The former interrogator has no power to increase the duration of incarceration, which was determined at sentencing. And even where the possibility of parole exists, the former interrogator has no apparent power to decrease the time served. . . .

7. A defendant who experiences a 14-day break in custody after invoking the *Miranda* right to counsel is not left without protection. *Edwards* establishes a *presumption* that a suspect's waiver of *Miranda* rights is involuntary. Even without this second layer of prophylaxis, a defendant is still free to claim the prophylactic protection of *Miranda* — arguing that his waiver of *Miranda* rights was in fact involuntary under Johnson v. Zerbst.

Shatzer's experience illustrates the vast differences between *Miranda* custody and incarceration pursuant to conviction. At the time of the 2003 attempted interrogation, Shatzer was already serving a sentence for a prior conviction [in a medium-security correctional facility]. Inmates in these facilities generally can visit the library each week, have regular exercise and recreation periods, can participate in basic adult education and occupational training, are able to send and receive mail, and are allowed to receive visitors twice a week. His continued detention after the 2003 interrogation did not depend on what he said (or did not say) to Detective Blankenship, and he has not alleged that he was placed in a higher level of security or faced any continuing restraints as a result of the 2003 interrogation. The "inherently compelling pressures" of custodial interrogation ended when he returned to his normal life.

IV.

A few words in response to Justice Stevens' concurrence. [We] are not talking about "reinterrogating" the suspect; we are talking about *asking his permission* to be interrogated. An officer has in no sense lied to a suspect when, after advising, as *Miranda* requires, "You have the right to remain silent, and if you choose to speak you have the right to the presence of an attorney," he promptly ends the attempted interrogation because the suspect declines to speak without counsel present, and then, two weeks later, reapproaches the suspect and asks, "Are you now willing to speak without a lawyer present?" . . .

The concurrence also accuses the Court of ignoring that when a suspect asks for counsel, until his request is answered, there are still the same "inherently compelling" pressures of custodial interrogation on which the *Miranda* line of cases is based. We do not ignore these pressures; nor do we suggest that they disappear when custody is recommenced after a break. But if those pressures are merely "the same" as before, then *Miranda* provides sufficient protection — as it did before. The *Edwards* presumption of involuntariness is justified only in circumstances where the coercive pressures have increased so much that suspects' waivers of *Miranda* rights are likely to be involuntary most of the time. . . .

THOMAS, J., concurring in part and concurring in the judgment.

I join Part III of the Court's opinion, which holds that release into the general prison population constitutes a break in custody. I do not join the Court's decision to extend the presumption of involuntariness established in *Edwards* for 14 days after custody ends.

It is not apparent to me that the presumption of involuntariness the Court recognized in *Edwards* is justifiable even in the custodial setting to which *Edwards* applies it. Accordingly, I would not extend the *Edwards* rule beyond the circumstances present in *Edwards* itself. But even if one believes that the Court is obliged to apply *Edwards* to any case involving continuing custody, the Court's opinion today goes well beyond that. It extends the presumption of involuntariness *Edwards* applies in custodial settings to interrogations that occur after custody ends. . . .

Our precedents insist that judicially created prophylactic rules like those in *Edwards* and *Miranda*, maintain the closest possible fit between the rule and the Fifth Amendment interests they seek to protect. The Court's 14-day rule does not satisfy this test. The Court relates its 14-day rule to the Fifth Amendment simply by asserting that 14 days between release and recapture should provide "plenty of time for the suspect . . . to shake off any residual coercive effects of his prior custody."

This *ipse dixit* does not explain why extending the *Edwards* presumption for 14 days following a break in custody — as opposed to 0, 10, or 100 days — provides the closest possible fit with the Self-Incrimination Clause. Nor does it explain how the benefits of a prophylactic 14-day rule (either on its own terms or compared with other possible rules) outweigh its costs (which would include the loss of law enforcement information as well as the exclusion of confessions that are in fact voluntary). . . .

STEVENS, J., concurring in the judgment.

While I agree that the presumption from *Edwards* is not eternal, and does not mandate suppression of Shatzer's statement made after a 2 1/2-year break in custody, I do not agree with the Court's newly announced rule: that *Edwards always* ceases to apply when there is a 14-day break in custody. . . .

I.

The most troubling aspect of the Court's time-based rule is that it disregards the compulsion caused by a second (or third, or fourth) interrogation of an indigent suspect who was told that if he requests a lawyer, one will be provided for him. When police tell an indigent suspect that he has the right to an attorney, that he is not required to speak without an attorney present, and that an attorney will be provided to him at no cost before questioning, the police have made a significant promise. If they cease questioning and then reinterrogate the suspect 14 days later without providing him with a lawyer, the suspect is likely to feel that the police lied to him and that he really does not have any right to a lawyer.[2] [The detainee] may well see further objection as futile and confession (true or not) as the only way to end his interrogation. . . .

II.

The Court never explains why its rule cannot depend on, in addition to a break in custody and passage of time, a concrete event or state of affairs, such as the police having honored their commitment to provide counsel. Instead, the Court simply decides to create a time-based rule, and in so doing, disregards much of the analysis upon which *Edwards* and subsequent decisions were based. . . . The Court, moreover, ignores that when a suspect asks for counsel, until his request is answered, there are still the same "inherently compelling" pressures of custodial interrogation on which the *Miranda* line of cases is based, and that the concern about compulsion is especially serious for a detainee who has requested a lawyer, an act that signals his inability to cope with the pressures of custodial interrogation.

2. The Court states that this argument rests on a fallacy because "we are not talking about 'reinterrogating' the suspect; we are talking about asking his permission to be interrogated." Because, however, a suspect always has the right to remain silent, this is a distinction without a difference: Any time that the police interrogate or reinterrogate, and read a suspect his *Miranda* rights, the suspect may decline to speak. . . .

Instead of deferring to these well-settled understandings of the *Edwards* rule, the Court engages in its own speculation that a 14-day break in custody eliminates the compulsion that animated *Edwards*. But [he has asked for a lawyer, he does not have one, he is in custody, and] police are still questioning him. A 14-day break in custody does not change the fact that custodial interrogation is inherently compelling. It is unlikely to change the fact that a detainee considers himself unable to deal with the pressures of custodial interrogation without legal assistance. . . .

The Court [speculates] that once a suspect has been out of *Miranda* custody for 14 days, "he has likely been able to seek advice from an attorney, family members, and friends." . . . As a factual matter, we do not know whether the defendant has been able to seek advice: First of all, suspects are told that if they cannot afford a lawyer, one will be provided for them. Yet under the majority's rule, an indigent suspect who took the police at their word when he asked for a lawyer will nonetheless be assumed to have been able to seek advice from an attorney. Second, even suspects who are not indigent cannot necessarily access legal advice (or social advice as the Court presumes) within 14 days. Third, suspects may not realize that they *need* to seek advice from an attorney. Unless police warn suspects that the interrogation will resume in 14 days, why contact a lawyer? . . .

The many problems with the Court's new rule are exacerbated in the very situation in this case: a suspect who is in prison. Even if, as the Court assumes, a trip to one's home significantly changes the *Edwards* calculus, a trip to one's prison cell is not the same. A prisoner's freedom is severely limited, and his entire life remains subject to government control. Such an environment is not conducive to "shaking off any residual coercive effects of his prior custody." Nor can a prisoner easily seek advice from an attorney, family members, and friends, especially not within 14 days; prisoners are frequently subject to restrictions on communications. [For] a person whose every move is controlled by the State, it is likely that his sense of dependence on, and trust in, counsel as the guardian of his interests in dealing with government officials intensified. . . .

III.

Because, at the very least, we do not know whether Shatzer could obtain a lawyer, and thus would have felt that police had lied about providing one, I cannot join the Court's opinion. I concur in today's judgment, however, on another ground: Even if Shatzer could not consult a lawyer and the police never provided him one, the 2 1/2-year break in custody is a basis for treating the second interrogation as no more coercive than the first. Neither a break in custody nor the passage of time has an inherent, curative power. But certain things change over time. An indigent suspect who took police at their word that they would provide an attorney probably will feel that he has been denied the counsel he has clearly requested, when police begin to question him, without a lawyer, only 14 days later. But, when a suspect has been left alone for a significant period of time, he is not as likely to draw such conclusions when the police interrogate him again. . . .

Notes

1. *Effect of invoking right to counsel: majority position.* The Supreme Court now applies the two-part test elaborated in Oregon v. Bradshaw, 462 U.S. 1039 (1983), to determine whether a suspect's statement is admissible when made after an earlier invocation of the right to counsel. First, the court asks who "initiated" any post-invocation conversation about the crime. If the police initiate the conversation (by word or deed), then they violate Edwards v. Arizona, 451 U.S. 477 (1981), and the confession must be suppressed. If the suspect initiates "a generalized discussion about the investigation," a court will proceed to the second step and ask whether the defendant waived the right to counsel knowingly and intelligently, despite the earlier invocation of the right. In *Bradshaw,* the defendant "initiated" the conversation by asking, "Well, what is going to happen to me now?" This basic approach has also met with approval in most state courts. See, e.g., Ex parte Williams, 31 So. 3d 670 (Ala. 2010). However, it is not always easy to determine who "initiates" a "generalized" conversation about the investigation. For instance, what should a police officer do if a suspect who has invoked the right to counsel asks, after a lineup procedure, "What happened?"

The Supreme Court has been unwilling to recognize many alternative methods of reopening an interrogation of the suspect who has asked for an attorney. See also Arizona v. Roberson, 486 U.S. 675 (1988) (*Edwards* rule applies even when the second interrogation deals with unrelated crime). Does the *Edwards* rule sufficiently protect the suspect's privilege against self-incrimination? New York provides that a suspect who has invoked the right to counsel should never be allowed to initiate a conversation with the police about the crime unless counsel is present. See People v. Cunningham, 400 N.E.2d 360 (N.Y 1980) (barring any interrogation after invocation of right to counsel unless waiver made with attorney present). This position has attracted virtually no following among the other states. State v. Piorkowski, 700 A.2d 1146 (Conn. 1997) (rejects New York rule on waiver, defendant may make post-arraignment waiver of counsel in counsel's absence). Why do you suppose so many jurisdictions decline to take this approach?

2. *Effect of invoking right to silence: majority position.* As the *Globe* case from Florida indicates, it is easier for the police to initiate a new interrogation after a suspect has invoked the right to silence, as opposed to the right to counsel. Most state courts have read their state constitutions to reach results consistent with the holding in Michigan v. Mosley, 423 U.S. 96 (1975). As the *Globe* case suggests, it is still not entirely clear which of the various facts in *Mosley* were essential to the holding there. See Wilson v. State, 562 S.E.2d 164 (Ga. 2002) (reinterrogation under *Mosley* not available for same crime after 17-hour interval; later interrogation must address different crime). A sampling of the complex state court rulings on this topic appear on the web extension for this chapter at *http://www.crimpro.com/extension/ch08*.

Is it appropriate to place different obligations on the police, depending on which right the defendant invokes? What practical differences are there, if any, between the invocation of the right to counsel and the right to silence? Consider People v. Pettingill, 578 P.2d 108 (Cal. 1978) (rejecting the *Mosley* rule and disallowing any government initiation of interrogation after invocation of right to silence).

3. *Effect of invoking rights: foreign practice.* Under the government-issued Code of Practice in Great Britain, authorities may continue to question a suspect even after

he has asserted a right to silence, so long as the continued questioning is not oppressive. They may question suspects who request a solicitor only under "exigent circumstances" and a few other exceptional cases. Code of Practice for the Detention, Treatment, and Questioning of Persons by the Police, para. 6.6. See also Craig Bradley, The Emerging International Consensus as to Criminal Procedure Rules, 14 Mich. J. Int'l L. 171 (1993).

E. SIXTH AMENDMENT RIGHT TO COUNSEL DURING INVESTIGATIONS

The Fifth Amendment to the U.S. Constitution, as interpreted in *Miranda,* is not the only source of a right to counsel during the investigative stage of the criminal process. Indeed, the Sixth Amendment provides an explicit right to counsel: "In all criminal prosecutions, the accused shall enjoy the right to . . . have the Assistance of Counsel for his defence." Recall that shortly before it decided *Miranda,* the U.S. Supreme Court suggested, in Escobedo v. Illinois, 378 U.S. 478 (1964), that the Sixth Amendment right to counsel might apply before the start of any formal criminal process. But it eventually became clear that the Sixth Amendment right to counsel attaches only after the initiation of formal proceedings, which typically means some form of charging (initial arraignment, indictment or information). State courts have given the same meaning to state constitutions.

The Sixth Amendment thus provides an alternative — and indeed a clear, textually-based alternative — right to counsel after charging. This separate source of a right to counsel for some defendants raises the fundamental question whether the scope and impact of the Fifth and Sixth Amendment rights to counsel are the same. For example, must defendants be informed of the Sixth Amendment right to counsel, or is the notice regarding the Fifth Amendment right to counsel — through *Miranda* — sufficient? Must a defendant assert the Sixth Amendment right, or does it automatically attach after charging? Will the detailed rules that govern notice, assertion and waiver of the right to counsel under *Miranda* also apply after indictment?

Part D examined the effect of assertion of the Fifth Amendment right to counsel under *Miranda.* The following case and problem examine the effect of asserting a Sixth Amendment right to counsel after charges are filed. Notice any differences between the standards applied under the two constitutional clauses. The specific legal question is whether a government agent can ask subsequent questions to the defendant after the Sixth Amendment counsel right attaches.

■ STATE v. BENJAMIN APPLEBY

221 P.3d 525 (Kan. 2009)

LUCKERT, J.

Benjamin A. Appleby was convicted of the attempted rape and capital murder of A.K., a 19-year-old college student, in Johnson County, Kansas.

Factual and Procedural Background

On June 18, 2002, A.K. was murdered while working alone as an attendant at a swimming pool near her family's home. Her [father] found A.K. in the pool's pump room, lying face down under a pool cover. . . .

Soon after this tragic discovery, police arrived and secured the pool area. In doing so, an officer recorded the name of everyone present at the scene, including a "Teddy Hoover" who was later identified as Appleby. The police also secured evidence, some of which was tested for DNA. This testing revealed DNA that did not match A.K.'s. Few other leads developed from the initial investigation. . . .

Several months after A.K.'s death, Sergeant Scott Hansen of the Leawood Police Department went to Appleby's home in Kansas City, Kansas. At that point in time, the police knew Appleby by his alias of Teddy Hoover. Appleby agreed to speak with Sergeant Hansen and indicated that he was a self-employed pool maintenance contractor. Hansen requested a DNA elimination sample from Appleby, who said he would talk to his attorney about providing a sample. When Hansen tried to follow up later, he discovered that Appleby had left town.

Subsequent leads caused police to seek more information from Appleby, who they still knew as Teddy Hoover. In November 2004, the investigation led Kansas detectives to Connecticut, where Appleby was living. Connecticut State Police discovered an outstanding arrest warrant for Appleby from 1998 and agreed to execute the warrant when Kansas detectives could be present. The purpose of this arrest was to give Kansas detectives an opportunity to question Appleby. . . .

Connecticut police arrested Appleby at his home and executed the residential search warrant. While the search warrant was being executed, Appleby was transported to a nearby Connecticut police station by Connecticut Detective Daniel Jewiss. On the way, Appleby volunteered that after some "trouble" in his past, he had taken on the name of his childhood friend, Teddy Hoover, who had died in an accident.

At the police station, [detectives processed Appleby on the Connecticut arrest warrant and executed a search warrant that allowed swabbing Appleby's inner mouth for purposes of DNA testing. Detective Jewiss then] told Appleby that other detectives wanted to speak to him about "an unrelated matter" and asked if Appleby was willing to talk to them. Appleby agreed and was taken upstairs to an interrogation room where the Kansas detectives waited. The detectives asked Appleby if he would answer some questions about A.K.'s murder. Up to this point, Appleby had not been told that Kansas detectives were involved or that some of the warrants were related to the A.K. murder investigation.

Appleby told the Kansas detectives he wanted to speak with them and straighten out some details from the time Sergeant Hansen interviewed him at his home in Kansas City. [The] detectives repeatedly asked Appleby if he had been at the pool where A.K. died, but Appleby told them he had never been there. After approximately one hour, the detectives moved him to an adjoining interview room. The second room contained items from the police investigation, such as a time line of the investigation, A.K.'s photograph and obituary, an aerial photograph of the pool, a videotape, a notebook labeled with the name Teddy Hoover, and two additional notebooks labeled as crime scene and autopsy photographs. The detectives then confronted Appleby with the fact that an officer at the pool on the day of the murder had logged the presence of a man who gave the name Teddy Hoover and a telephone number. At that point, Appleby acknowledged he had been at the pool that day.

About 15 or 20 minutes later, Appleby admitted he had killed A.K. Appleby told the detectives A.K. was in the pump room when he arrived at the pool. Finding A.K. attractive, Appleby tried to "hit on her," but A.K. rejected his advances and tried to leave the pump room. Appleby stood in her way and tried to grab her breasts and her waist. A.K. pushed Appleby and then punched him. This angered Appleby, who "lost it" and, in his own words, "just beat the shit out of her." [He attempted to have sex with her after she lost consciousness, but could not obtain an erection.]

DNA testing performed by two crime labs matched Appleby's DNA to the DNA found mixed with A.K.'s. . . . The State charged Appleby with capital murder for the death of A.K. . . . and attempted rape. The jury found Appleby guilty of both charges. The trial court imposed a hard 50 life imprisonment sentence for the murder conviction and a consecutive sentence of 228 months' imprisonment for the attempted rape conviction. Appleby now appeals. . . .

Suppression of Confession

. . . Appleby contends the trial court erred by admitting into evidence the incriminating statements he made to Kansas detectives. Appleby argues the statements must be suppressed because he asked about an attorney while he was being booked on the Connecticut arrest warrant. . . .

This argument differs from the typical issue arising from the application of Miranda v. Arizona, 384 U.S. 436 (1966), in that Appleby was arrested in another state on unrelated charges, and the arresting officer, Detective Jewiss, had no intention of interrogating Appleby; typically a *Miranda* issue arises when there is custodial interrogation related to the crime on which the arrest was based. Under the circumstances of this case, the State argues Appleby's questions about whether he would be allowed to talk to an attorney were, at most, an invocation of Sixth Amendment rights related to the Connecticut charges. Appleby argues that he was asserting his Fifth Amendment rights and the assertion applied to both cases. To understand these arguments, a more detailed discussion of the interaction is necessary.

When Appleby was arrested in Connecticut, he was arrested on the Connecticut charges only, even though the arrest was timed to occur when Kansas detectives were in Connecticut and the arrest may not have occurred if Kansas law enforcement had not contacted the Connecticut State Police Department to request assistance in investigating Appleby. But this involvement was behind the scene; the Kansas detectives did not directly participate when Detective Jewiss took Appleby into custody at his home, and Appleby was not aware of their presence until after he had asked the Connecticut detectives the four questions about whether he could talk to an attorney. Appleby did ask Detective Jewiss why there were so many officers at his house, and the detective explained a search warrant was being executed and the officers were going to search the home. Appleby questioned what the search was about, and Jewiss replied that he "wasn't going to talk to him any further about the case; that somebody else would talk to him." . . .

When Detective Jewiss and Appleby arrived at the station, Detective Jewiss began the routine book-in process on the Connecticut arrest warrant. At this point, before Appleby had been *Mirandized,* Appleby asked "if he was going to have the opportunity to talk to an attorney." Detective Jewiss replied "absolutely." Detective Jewiss testified he understood this to be a question regarding procedure, not an invocation of the right. While testifying at the suppression hearing, Detective Jewiss was asked if he was questioning Appleby at this point in time. He answered: "Not at all. I even informed him that I wouldn't be questioning him, and that I wouldn't talk to him about either of these cases."

After Appleby asked about an attorney, he was read a notice of rights form that listed the three Connecticut charges — risk of injury to a minor, disorderly conduct, and public indecency. The form also advised of *Miranda* rights and stated in part: "You may consult with an attorney before being questioned; you may have an attorney present during questioning, and you cannot be questioned without your consent." Appleby signed the notice of rights form, which was an acknowledgment, not a waiver of rights.

Soon after that exchange, another Connecticut detective advised Appleby of the search warrant that authorized the officer to swab the inside of Appleby's mouth in order to obtain a DNA sample. Detective Jewiss testified that Appleby asked if he had the right to say "no" and then asked if he could speak to an attorney about his right to refuse the testing. According to Detective Jewiss, the detectives advised Appleby he could not talk to an attorney at that point regarding a search that had been authorized by a judge.

Following the DNA swabbing, Detective Jewiss continued with the book-in process on the Connecticut charges. Appleby was fingerprinted and photographed, the property on his person was inventoried, and a personal information data sheet was completed. During that process, Appleby asked two more times whether he would have an opportunity to talk to an attorney.

At the suppression hearing, Detective Jewiss repeatedly testified that he understood Appleby to be "asking about our procedure as in . . . will he have the opportunity to talk to an attorney." According to Detective Jewiss, the question was never in the context of, "I don't want to talk to you" or "I don't want to talk to anybody without an attorney here."

Detective Jewiss testified that during the book-in process he asked Appleby his name, date and place of birth, residence, and similar book-in questions. The only other question he asked came about 30 minutes after they arrived at the police station when Detective Jewiss asked Appleby if he wanted to talk to some people about an unrelated matter. Appleby said he would. Detective Jewiss was asked if Appleby brought up the word "attorney" at that time, and he replied, "No, he didn't."

Detective Jewiss was also asked why he did not give Appleby the opportunity to speak to an attorney before sending him upstairs to be interrogated by the Kansas detectives. Detective Jewiss, who had repeatedly stated that he had understood Appleby to be asking about procedure and had explained that a defendant would typically be allowed to contact an attorney only after the book-in process was complete, testified that "there was still some processing that I had to continue with."

When Detective Jewiss transferred Appleby to the Kansas detectives, he reported that Appleby had not invoked his right to counsel, "but he has asked something about an attorney when the [DNA] search warrant was being conducted." Detective Jewiss did not tell the Kansas detectives about the other instances when Appleby asked whether he would be able to talk to an attorney.

After Detective Jewiss left, the two Kansas detectives asked Appleby if he wanted to answer some questions about the murder of A.K. He said he wanted to talk to them, and the detectives then told him he would be read his *Miranda* rights again since he was being interviewed "on a different charge from what he was arrested." After being read his rights, Appleby said he understood them and was willing to answer some questions. He was questioned for approximately 2 and 1/2 hours, the final 20 minutes on videotape. At no point during the questioning by the Kansas detectives did Appleby indicate he wished to speak to or have the assistance of an attorney. . . .

Appleby filed three pretrial motions to suppress the statements he made to the Kansas detectives. . . . The trial court recognized there are two questions to ask in the determination of whether a suspect has invoked his or her Fifth Amendment right to counsel: (1) whether the suspect articulated a desire to have an attorney present sufficiently clearly that a reasonable officer in the circumstances would understand the statement to be a request for an attorney and (2) whether an attorney is being requested for purposes of interrogation rather than in regard to later hearings or proceedings. See State v. Walker, 80 P.3d 1132 (Kan. 2003). The trial court concluded Appleby clearly requested an attorney, but he did not make it clear he wanted the attorney to assist with questioning rather than to have assistance with his case. . . .

Appleby argues his requests for an attorney were clear and sufficient to require the Kansas detectives to refrain from questioning him until his requests were honored or until he had initiated contact with them. Appleby . . . argues the trial court's reasoning imposes too exacting a standard, essentially requiring the suspect to use the specific words of "I want an attorney to assist me with your purposed custodial interrogation," and that his statements to Detective Jewiss were sufficiently clear to invoke his Fifth Amendment right to counsel.

In making these arguments, Appleby groups together all of the instances where he referred to an attorney during the book-in process. Nevertheless, as we analyze his arguments, we recognize that one of the instances was of a different character than the others; that was the one made in response to the execution of the search warrant for purposes of obtaining DNA swabs. In that instance, Appleby clearly asked if he could talk to his attorney about whether he could refuse to allow the swabbing. In the three other instances, his questions were more general, as he asked whether he would have the opportunity to talk to an attorney.

[The] State contends that Appleby's requests for an attorney are more akin to a Sixth Amendment invocation of the right to counsel than a Fifth Amendment invocation of the right to counsel. It argues Appleby's requests could not reasonably be construed to be requests for assistance with custodial interrogation because he was not being interrogated at the time he made those requests. In addition, the State asserts that the *Miranda* right to counsel may not be anticipatorily invoked.

The State's arguments bring into issue the interrelationship of Fifth and Sixth Amendment rights, which was discussed by the United States Supreme Court in McNeil v. Wisconsin, 501 U.S. 171 (1991), under circumstances similar to those in this case — *i.e.,* where an arrest is made in one case and an interrogation relates to another. In *McNeil,* the defendant was arrested in Omaha, Nebraska, pursuant to a Wisconsin warrant based on charges of an armed robbery outside Milwaukee. Milwaukee detectives went to Omaha to retrieve McNeil. The detectives advised McNeil of his *Miranda* rights and began to ask questions. McNeil refused to answer any questions, the interview ended, and he was taken to Wisconsin where an attorney was appointed to represent him.

Later that day, McNeil was visited by officers from a different Wisconsin county. The county detectives advised McNeil of his *Miranda* rights, and McNeil signed a form waiving those rights. The county detectives then asked McNeil about charges of murder, attempted murder, and armed robbery. McNeil denied any involvement in the crimes. Two days later the county detectives returned and again advised McNeil of his *Miranda* rights. McNeil again waived his rights and this time confessed.

McNeil sought suppression of his statement to the county detectives asserting a Sixth Amendment right to counsel, but the Supreme Court determined his confession was admissible. The ruling was based on the distinction between McNeil's Fifth and Sixth Amendment rights. The Supreme Court explained that the Sixth Amendment right to counsel had attached in the Milwaukee case [because the] Sixth Amendment right to counsel attaches on filing of formal charges, indictment, [information or] arraignment. . . . But that right, the Court explained, is offense specific and cannot be invoked once for all future prosecutions. As a result, "incriminating statements pertaining to other crimes, as to which the Sixth Amendment right has not yet attached, are, of course, admissible at the trial of those offenses."

A similar dividing line is not drawn, however, when the Fifth Amendment right to counsel — which is protected by Miranda v. Arizona, 384 U.S. 436 (1966) — is invoked (which McNeil did not do in arguing his appeal). In other words, Fifth Amendment rights are not offense specific. Thus, the *McNeil* Court noted that "once a suspect invokes the *Miranda* right to counsel for interrogation regarding one offense, he may not be reapproached regarding *any* offense unless counsel is present." Further, Edwards v. Arizona, 451 U.S. 477 (1981), established a second layer of prophylaxis for the *Miranda* right to counsel: Once a suspect asserts the right, not only must the current interrogation cease, but he may not be approached for further interrogation until counsel has been made available to him — which means . . . that counsel must be present, Minnick v. Mississippi, 498 U.S. 146 (1990). If the police do subsequently initiate an encounter in the absence of counsel (assuming there has been no break in custody), the suspect's statements are presumed involuntary and therefore inadmissible as substantive evidence at trial, even where the suspect executes a waiver and his statements would be considered voluntary under traditional standards. This is designed to prevent police from badgering a defendant into waiving his previously asserted *Miranda* rights.

Recently, in Montejo v. Louisiana, 129 S. Ct. 2079 (2009), the Supreme Court reaffirmed this Fifth Amendment jurisprudence, concluding the three layers of protection — *Miranda, Edwards,* and *Minnick* — are sufficient. However, the *Montejo* Court modified some aspects of its Sixth Amendment jurisprudence. Specifically, it overruled Michigan v. Jackson, 475 U.S. 625 (1986), because of that decision's "wholesale importation of the *Edwards* rule into the Sixth Amendment."

However, . . . the *Montejo* Court did not modify *McNeil's* dividing lines between Fifth and Sixth Amendment analysis. . . . In particular, the *Montejo* Court did not alter the *McNeil* requirement that, even if Sixth Amendment rights have been invoked, a defendant must affirmatively assert Fifth Amendment rights if subjected to a custodial interrogation in another case. As a result, if Appleby asserted Sixth Amendment rights, as the State suggests, the assertion was effective only in the Connecticut case. . . .

Because the accused's purpose in requesting an attorney must be determined in order to sort the interplay of these rights, the *McNeil* Court concluded that an effective invocation of the Fifth Amendment right to counsel applies only when the suspect has expressed his wish for the particular sort of lawyerly assistance that is the subject of *Miranda.* It requires, at a minimum, "some statement that can reasonably be construed to be an expression of a desire for the assistance of an attorney *in dealing with custodial interrogation by the police.*" *McNeil,* 501 U.S. at 178.

[Some] courts have been very restrictive in defining "imminent," allowing no intervening activity between the invocation of the right and the planned initiation of questioning. . . . This restrictive view is supported by the statements in *Montejo* that the Court had "in fact never held that a person can invoke his *Miranda* rights anticipatorily, *in a context other than custodial interrogation.*" . . .

Yet the Court did not clearly explain what was meant by the context of a custodial interrogation or a context other than a custodial interrogation, and the facts of *Montejo* are very different from those in this case and therefore do not help to explain the meaning as it would be applied in this case. As in *McNeil,* the focus in *Montejo* was whether there had been an assertion of Sixth Amendment rights that prevented further interrogation. In fact, upon his arrest, Montejo waived his *Miranda* rights and gave police various versions of events related to the crime. A few days later at a preliminary hearing, known in Louisiana as a "72-hour hearing," counsel was appointed for Montejo even though he had not requested the appointment and had stood mute when asked if he wanted the assistance of an attorney. Later that same day, police approached Montejo, *Mirandized* him again, and asked him to accompany them to locate the murder weapon. During the drive, Montejo wrote an inculpatory letter of apology to the victim's widow. After the drive, Montejo met his attorney for the first time. At trial, he objected to the admission of the letter, basing his objection on *Jackson.* The Supreme Court held that the letter need not be suppressed based on an objection under *Jackson,* which it overruled. The Court concluded Montejo had not asserted his Sixth Amendment right to counsel. Yet, the Court concluded the case should be remanded to allow Montejo to assert an objection under *Edwards,* in other words, a Fifth Amendment objection. . . .

Here, Appleby does not assert that a Sixth Amendment right to counsel requires the suppression of his confession. Nor did the trial court suppress on that basis. The trial court merely pointed to the possibility of a Sixth Amendment assertion in another case — or perhaps even the Kansas case — as a circumstance that caused Appleby's assertion to be ambiguous. He relies on a Fifth Amendment right to counsel and suggests his questions during the book-in process asserted that right. This argument brings us to the State's position that the right was not effectively asserted because Appleby was not in the interrogation room. . . .

This approach is similar to that followed by the trial court in this case and in past decisions of this court where the context of a statement regarding an attorney has been analyzed to view whether an objective law enforcement officer would understand there had been an invocation of Fifth Amendment rights. For example, in State v. Gant, 201 P.3d 673 (Kan. 2009), . . . this court recently held a defendant did not assert his Fifth Amendment rights when he yelled to his companions while being arrested that they should call a lawyer. Although we did not consider the question of whether interrogation must be imminent, we did conclude the factual context revealed the defendant was directing his comments toward his companions, not police, and was not clearly and unambiguously asserting his right to counsel.

Now, we explicitly recognize what was implicit in many of our prior decisions: The timing as well as the content and context of a reference to counsel may help determine whether there has been an unambiguous assertion of the right to have the assistance of an attorney in dealing with a custodial interrogation by law enforcement officers.

This is the approach adopted by the trial court. In reaching the conclusion that the context in this case created ambiguity, the trial court made several findings that are supported by substantial competent evidence. Specifically, the trial court found that Appleby was aware he was being arrested by Connecticut authorities and was being charged for crimes committed in Connecticut. Further, Appleby had not been subjected to interrogation at that point in time about anything, in either the Connecticut or the Kansas case, and no one had indicated to him that his arrest was in any way connected the murder of A.K. Moreover, Detective Jewiss had informed Appleby that he would not be questioning him and that someone else would be talking to him about "the case." At that point in time, Appleby only knew of the Connecticut case. Hence, when Appleby asked whether he would have a chance to talk to an attorney, he knew he was not going to be questioned by Detective Jewiss. At that point in time, interrogation was clearly not imminent or impending.

It was not until minutes before the custodial interrogation with the Kansas detectives that Appleby was asked by Detective Jewiss if he would talk to some people about an unrelated matter. The trial court concluded that at that time: "Appleby undoubtedly believed that matter to be the [A.K.] murder investigation." Yet Appleby agreed without hesitation to speak to the detectives. Then Appleby was given his *Miranda* rights, which he clearly waived. He never asked about an attorney again. Thus, when questioning was imminent — when Appleby was approached for interrogation — he clearly waived his right to counsel.

We agree with the conclusion reached by the trial court that Appleby's references to an attorney during the book-in process on the Connecticut charges did not constitute a clear and unambiguous assertion of his Fifth Amendment right as protected by *Miranda.* The trial court did not err in denying Appleby's motion to suppress his custodial statements made to the Kansas detectives. . . .

JOHNSON, J., concurring in part and dissenting in part:

. . . I would not require a detainee to possess the knowledge of a constitutional scholar well-versed in Fifth and Sixth Amendment jurisprudence. Rather, I would view the circumstances from the perspective of an objectively reasonable layperson interacting with an objectively reasonable law enforcement officer. In that context, even though only the officer knew that the arrest was pretextual, both could not have questioned that Appleby was actually in custody on the 6-year-old Connecticut charges, so as to trigger the protections applicable to custodial interrogations.

In that setting, Appleby asked Detective Jewiss about consulting with an attorney not once, but four times. The trial court found that Appleby had asserted his right to an attorney, albeit perhaps only for Sixth Amendment purposes. The majority questions, but does not decide, whether the wording of Appleby's requests was sufficient to support the trial court's finding. Without belaboring the point, I would simply submit that one might expect a detainee, who has been confronted in his home by a multitude of armed officers, arrested, and taken to jail, to propound a request for an attorney in a most polite and nonconfrontational manner. Moreover, Appleby's persistence in making a number of requests in a short period of time belies any equivocation as to his desire to have an attorney present or as to Detective Jewiss' understanding of that desire.

[A] detainee would need to possess excellent clairvoyance — or astute constitutional acumen — to ascertain that, if there is any way in which the detainee's request for an attorney might be construed as being for Sixth Amendment purposes, then the right would not actually accrue or the request become effective until some undisclosed later time, after the detainee has been subjected to a custodial interrogation. . . .

Problem 8-7. Christian Burial Speech

On the afternoon of December 24, 1968, 10-year-old Pamela Powers went with her family to the YMCA in Des Moines, Iowa, to watch a wrestling tournament in which her brother was participating. When she failed to return from a trip to the washroom, a search for her began; it was unsuccessful.

Robert Williams, who had recently escaped from a mental hospital, was a resident of the YMCA. Soon after the girl's disappearance Williams was seen in the YMCA lobby carrying some clothing and a large bundle wrapped in a blanket. As Williams placed the bundle into his car, a witness noticed a body under the blanket. Williams immediately drove away. His abandoned car was found the following day in Davenport, Iowa, roughly 160 miles east of Des Moines. A warrant was then issued in Des Moines for his arrest on a charge of abduction.

On the morning of December 26, a Des Moines lawyer named Henry McKnight went to the Des Moines police station and informed the officers present that he had just received a long-distance call from Williams and that he had advised Williams to turn himself in to the Davenport police. Williams did surrender that morning to the police in Davenport, and they booked him on the charge specified in the arrest warrant and gave him the warnings required by Miranda v. Arizona. The Davenport police then telephoned their counterparts in Des Moines to inform them that Williams had surrendered. McKnight, the lawyer, was still at the Des Moines police headquarters, and Williams spoke with McKnight on the telephone. McKnight advised Williams that Des Moines police officers would be driving to Davenport to pick him up, that the officers would not interrogate him or mistreat him, and that Williams was not to talk to the officers about Pamela Powers until after consulting with McKnight upon his return to Des Moines. As a result of these conversations, McKnight and the Des Moines police officials agreed that Detective Cleatus Learning and a fellow officer would drive to Davenport to pick up Williams, that they would bring him directly back to Des Moines, and that they would not question him during the trip.

In the meantime Williams was arraigned before a judge in Davenport on the outstanding arrest warrant. The judge advised him of his *Miranda* rights and committed him to jail. Before leaving the courtroom, Williams conferred with a lawyer named Thomas Kelly, who advised him not to make any statements until consulting with McKnight back in Des Moines.

Soon after Detective Learning and his fellow officer arrived in Davenport, they met with Williams and Kelly. Detective Learning repeated the *Miranda* warnings, and told Williams: "We both know that you're being represented here by Mr. Kelly and you're being represented by Mr. McKnight in Des Moines, and I want you to remember this because we'll be visiting between here and Des Moines." Kelly reiterated to Detective Learning that Williams was not to be questioned about the disappearance of Pamela Powers until after he had consulted with McKnight back in Des Moines. When Learning expressed some reservations, Kelly firmly stated that the agreement with McKnight was to be carried out — that there was to be no interrogation of Williams during the journey to Des Moines. Kelly was denied permission to ride in the police car back to Des Moines with Williams and the two officers. The two detectives, with Williams in their charge, then set out on the 160-mile drive. Williams said several times during the trip that "when I get to Des Moines and see Mr. McKnight, I am going to tell you the whole story."

Detective Learning knew that Williams was a former mental patient, and knew also that he was deeply religious. Learning and Williams soon embarked on a conversation covering a variety of topics, including the subject of religion. Learning addressed Williams as "Reverend." He then made this speech:

> I want to give you something to think about while we're traveling down the road. Number one, I want you to observe the weather conditions, it's raining, it's sleeting, it's freezing, driving is very treacherous, visibility is poor, it's going to be dark early this evening. They are predicting several inches of snow for tonight, and I feel that you yourself are the only person that knows where this little girl's body is, that you yourself have only been there once, and if you get a snow on top of it you yourself may be unable to find it. And, since we will be going right past the area on the way into Des Moines, I feel that we could stop and locate the body, that the parents of this little girl should be entitled to a Christian burial for the little girl who was snatched away from them on Christmas Eve and murdered. And I feel we should stop and locate it on the way in rather than waiting until morning and trying to come back out after a snow storm and possibly not being able to find it at all.

Williams asked Detective Learning why he thought their route to Des Moines would be taking them past the girl's body, and Learning responded that he knew the body was in the area of Mitchellville — a town they would be passing on the way to Des Moines. (In fact, Learning did not know where the body was.) Learning then added, "I do not want you to answer me. I don't want to discuss it any further. Just think about it as we're riding down the road."

As the car approached Grinnell, a town approximately 100 miles west of Davenport, Williams asked whether the police had found the victim's shoes. When Detective Learning replied that he was unsure, Williams directed the officers to a service station where he said he had left the shoes; a search for them proved unsuccessful. As they continued toward Des Moines, Williams asked whether the police had found the blanket, and directed the officers to a rest area where he said he had disposed of the blanket. Nothing was found. The car continued toward Des Moines, and as it approached Mitchellville, Williams said that he would show the officers where the body was. He then directed the police to the body of Pamela Powers.

Williams was indicted for first-degree murder. Because a warrant had been issued for Williams' arrest, and because he had been arraigned and confined to jail, Williams' Sixth Amendment right to counsel attached. Before trial, his counsel moved to suppress all evidence resulting from any statements Williams had made during the automobile ride from Davenport to Des Moines. Should the judge grant the motion? Compare Brewer v. Williams, 430 U.S. 387 (1977); Yale Kamisar, Brewer v. Williams — A Hard Look at a Discomfiting Record, 66 Geo. L.J. 209 (1977).

Notes

1. *The Sixth Amendment right to counsel and "deliberately eliciting" a confession.* The Sixth Amendment to the U.S. Constitution provides for a right to counsel "in all criminal prosecutions." The U.S. Supreme Court, along with most states applying analogous state constitutional provisions, has held that Sixth Amendment counsel rights attach after the initiation of formal proceedings, whether by way of indictment, information, or initial arraignment.

In Brewer v. Williams, 430 U.S. 387 (1977), the case on which Problem 8-7 is based, the Court held that Detective Learning violated that right by "deliberately eliciting" information from Williams while his counsel was absent, and that Williams had not waived his right to counsel: "It is true that Williams had been informed of and appeared to understand his right to counsel. But waiver requires not merely comprehension but relinquishment, and Williams's consistent reliance upon the advice of counsel in dealing with the authorities refutes any suggestion that he waived that right." How do the facts compare in the *Innis* case, reprinted in Part B, where the Court held that no interrogation occurred, and in *Williams,* where the Court concluded that the police deliberately elicited information? Are the Fifth and Sixth Amendment definitions of "interrogation" comparable? Compare Fellers v. United States, 540 U.S. 519 (2004) (officer who went to home of indicted defendant to arrest him violated right to counsel by discussing charge in absence of attorney; contact need not amount to an "interrogation" to violate Sixth Amendment).

2. *Waiver and invocation of Sixth Amendment rights.* In Michigan v. Jackson, 475 U.S. 625 (1986), the Court explained that Sixth Amendment rights deserve at least as much protection as Fifth Amendment rights, and applied Edwards v. Arizona, 451 U.S. 477 (1981), to hold that government agents could not initiate a conversation with a defendant after the Sixth Amendment right to counsel had attached. As with *Edwards,* the Court did not preclude a later confession where the defendant initiated a later conversation. In Montejo v. Louisiana, 129 S. Ct. 2079 (2009), however, the Court overruled *Jackson*. After defendant Montejo had been assigned counsel, two police detectives visited him at the prison and asked him to help them locate the murder weapon. During the search for the weapon, Montejo wrote an inculpatory letter of apology to the victim's widow. The Court held that a defendant may waive the Sixth Amendment right to counsel — so long as relinquishment of the right is voluntary, knowing, and intelligent — even if the government initiates the conversation after the assignment of counsel to the defendant. The majority considered the *Edwards* rule to be sufficient to prevent police from badgering a defendant into waiving his previously asserted *Miranda* rights; the Court did not consider it necessary to create any separate protection for Sixth Amendment interests.

3. *Sixth Amendment right to counsel and cellmate confessions.* In Kuhlmann v. Wilson, 477 U.S. 436 (1986), the U.S. Supreme Court deferred to the factual findings of the

trial court that prisoner Benny Lee was not acting as a government interrogator when the government planted Lee in Wilson's cell. *Kuhlmann* addresses the recurring question of whether government agents "deliberately elicit" a confession from a defendant whose Sixth Amendment rights have attached. In this fact-sensitive area, one can find enormous variety in the decisions of state and lower federal courts; a review of some representative holdings appear on the web extension for this chapter at *http://www.crimpro.com/extension/ch08*. Why is there a different standard for assessing when government agents have violated defendants' Fifth Amendment and Sixth Amendment rights to counsel?

4. *Scope of the Sixth Amendment right to counsel for "other" offenses.* Can government agents interrogate a defendant about a crime other than an offense for which the government has initiated formal proceedings? In McNeil v. Wisconsin, 501 U.S. 171 (1991), the Court explained that "The Sixth Amendment right [to counsel] is offense specific. It cannot be invoked once for all future prosecutions, for it does not attach until a prosecution is commenced, that is, at or after the initiation of adversary judicial criminal proceedings — whether by way of formal charge, preliminary hearing, indictment, information, or arraignment." In Texas v. Cobb, 532 U.S. 162 (2001), the Court addressed the issue of what constituted the "same offense." Some state court and lower federal court decisions treated "factually related" crimes as the "same offense." The Supreme Court, however, held that the determination of whether a second offense was the "same offense" under the Sixth Amendment should be determined under the narrow standards applied under federal law to determine whether double jeopardy barred the filing of two separate charges for the "same offence." See Blockburger v. United States, 284 U.S. 299 (1932), discussed in Chapter 14. Thus, a second offense would not be considered the "same offense" and would allow subsequent interrogation when each of two statutory provisions "requires proof of a fact which the other does not."

F. *MIRANDA* CURES, IMPACTS, AND ALTERNATIVES

The decades-long debate over the wisdom of *Miranda* turns in part on how much of an impact it has on criminal investigations and prosecutions. The first part of this section considers whether a *Miranda* error can be fixed, thus lessening any harm to the prosecution from failure to give proper warnings. The second part considers evidence about the impact of *Miranda* on the criminal justice system. The final part considers whether there are alternatives to giving *Miranda* warnings that would encourage voluntary confessions.

1. *Cures and Remedies for* Miranda *Violations*

In the ordinary case, a *Miranda* violation will mean that the confession obtained as a result of the tainted interrogation will be inadmissible as evidence. But what about physical evidence or testimony of witnesses obtained as a result of the improper interrogation? Will this derivative evidence — the "fruit of the poisonous tree" — be admissible? There are a number of circumstances under which courts will admit evidence obtained after a *Miranda* violation, even if the improper interrogation was the "but for" cause of the police obtaining the evidence. As you read the following materials, try to sort out the various arguments in favor of ignoring the original violation of law.

■ MISSOURI v. PATRICE SEIBERT

542 U.S. 600 (2004)

SOUTER, J.*

This case tests a police protocol for custodial interrogation that calls for giving no warnings of the rights to silence and counsel until interrogation has produced a confession. Although such a statement is generally inadmissible, since taken in violation of Miranda v. Arizona, 384 U.S. 436 (1966), the interrogating officer follows it with *Miranda* warnings and then leads the suspect to cover the same ground a second time. The question here is the admissibility of the repeated statement. Because this midstream recitation of warnings after interrogation and unwarned confession could not effectively comply with *Miranda*'s constitutional requirement, we hold that a statement repeated after a warning in such circumstances is inadmissible.

Respondent Patrice Seibert's 12-year-old son Jonathan had cerebral palsy, and when he died in his sleep she feared charges of neglect because of bedsores on his body. In her presence, two of her teenage sons and two of their friends devised a plan to conceal the facts surrounding Jonathan's death by incinerating his body in the course of burning the family's mobile home, in which they planned to leave Donald Rector, a mentally ill teenager living with the family, to avoid any appearance that Jonathan had been unattended. Seibert's son Darian and a friend set the fire, and Donald died.

Five days later, the police awakened Seibert at 3 A.M. at a hospital where Darian was being treated for burns. In arresting her, Officer Kevin Clinton followed instructions from Rolla, Missouri, officer Richard Hanrahan that he refrain from giving *Miranda* warnings. After Seibert had been taken to the police station and left alone in an interview room for 15 to 20 minutes, Hanrahan questioned her without *Miranda* warnings for 30 to 40 minutes, squeezing her arm and repeating "Donald was also to die in his sleep." After Seibert finally admitted she knew Donald was meant to die in the fire, she was given a 20-minute coffee and cigarette break. Officer Hanrahan then turned on a tape recorder, gave Seibert the *Miranda* warnings, and obtained a signed waiver of rights from her. He resumed the questioning with "Ok, 'trice, we've been talking for a little while about what happened on Wednesday the twelfth, haven't we?," and confronted her with her prewarning statements:

> *Hanrahan:* Now, in discussion you told us, you told us that there was an understanding about Donald.
> *Seibert:* Yes. . . .
> *Hanrahan:* And what was the understanding about Donald?
> *Seibert:* If they could get him out of the trailer, to take him out of the trailer. . . .
> *Hanrahan:* 'Trice, didn't you tell me that he was supposed to die in his sleep?

* [Justices Stevens, Ginsburg, and Breyer joined in this opinion; Justice Kennedy concurred in the judgment. — EDS.]

Seibert: If that would happen, 'cause he was on that new medicine, you know. . . .
Hanrahan: The Prozac? And it makes him sleepy. So he was supposed to die in his sleep?
Seibert: Yes.

After being charged with first-degree murder for her role in Donald's death, Seibert sought to exclude both her prewarning and postwarning statements. At the suppression hearing, Officer Hanrahan testified that he made a "conscious decision" to withhold *Miranda* warnings, thus resorting to an interrogation technique he had been taught: question first, then give the warnings, and then repeat the question "until I get the answer that she's already provided once." He acknowledged that Seibert's ultimate statement was "largely a repeat of information . . . obtained" prior to the warning.

The trial court suppressed the prewarning statement but admitted the responses given after the *Miranda* recitation. A jury convicted Seibert of second-degree murder. . . .

[Giving *Miranda*] warnings and getting a waiver has generally produced a virtual ticket of admissibility; maintaining that a statement is involuntary even though given after warnings and voluntary waiver of rights requires unusual stamina, and litigation over voluntariness tends to end with the finding of a valid waiver. To point out the obvious, this common consequence would not be common at all were it not that *Miranda* warnings are customarily given under circumstances allowing for a real choice between talking and remaining silent.

The technique of interrogating in successive, unwarned and warned phases raises a new challenge to *Miranda.* Although we have no statistics on the frequency of this practice, it is not confined to Rolla, Missouri. [The] Police Law Institute, for example, instructs that "officers may conduct a two-stage interrogation. . . . At any point during the pre-*Miranda* interrogation, usually after arrestees have confessed, officers may then read the *Miranda* warnings and ask for a waiver. If the arrestees waive their *Miranda* rights, officers will be able to repeat any *subsequent* incriminating statements later in court." Police Law Institute, Illinois Police Law Manual 83 (Jan. 2001-Dec. 2003) (hereinafter Police Law Manual). . . .

The inquiry is simply whether the warnings reasonably convey to a suspect his rights as required by *Miranda.* The threshold issue when interrogators question first and warn later is thus whether it would be reasonable to find that in these circumstances the warnings could function "effectively" as *Miranda* requires. Could the warnings effectively advise the suspect that he had a real choice about giving an admissible statement at that juncture? Could they reasonably convey that he could choose to stop talking even if he had talked earlier? For unless the warnings could place a suspect who has just been interrogated in a position to make such an informed choice, there is no practical justification for accepting the formal warnings as compliance with *Miranda,* or for treating the second stage of interrogation as distinct from the first, unwarned and inadmissible segment. . . .

By any objective measure, applied to circumstances exemplified here, it is likely that if the interrogators employ the technique of withholding warnings until after interrogation succeeds in eliciting a confession, the warnings will be ineffective in preparing the suspect for successive interrogation, close in time and similar in content. After all, the reason that question-first is catching on is as obvious as its manifest purpose, which is to get a confession the suspect would not make if he understood his rights at the outset; the sensible underlying assumption is that with one confession in hand before the warnings, the interrogator can count on getting its duplicate, with trifling additional trouble. . . . What is worse, telling a suspect that "anything you say can and will be used against you," without expressly excepting the statement just given, could lead to an entirely reasonable inference that what he has just said will be used, with subsequent silence being of no avail. Thus, when *Miranda* warnings are inserted in the midst of coordinated and continuing interrogation, they are likely to mislead and deprive a defendant of knowledge essential to his ability to understand the nature of his rights and the consequences of abandoning them. . . .

Missouri argues that a confession repeated at the end of an interrogation sequence envisioned in a question-first strategy is admissible on the authority of Oregon v. Elstad, 470 U.S. 298 (1985), but the argument disfigures that case. In *Elstad,* the police went to the young suspect's house to take him into custody on a charge of burglary. Before the arrest, one officer spoke with the suspect's mother, while the other one joined the suspect in a "brief stop in the living room," where the officer said he "felt" the young man was involved in a burglary. The suspect acknowledged he had been at the scene. This Court noted that the pause in the living room "was not to interrogate the suspect but to notify his mother of the reason for his arrest," and described the incident as having "none of the earmarks of coercion." The Court, indeed, took care to mention that the officer's initial failure to warn was an "oversight" that "may have been the result of confusion as to whether the brief exchange qualified as 'custodial interrogation' or . . . may simply have reflected . . . reluctance to initiate an alarming police procedure before [an officer] had spoken with respondent's mother." At the outset of a later and systematic station house interrogation going well beyond the scope of the laconic prior admission, the suspect was given *Miranda* warnings and made a full confession. In holding the second statement admissible and voluntary, *Elstad* rejected the "cat out of the bag" theory that any short, earlier admission, obtained in arguably innocent neglect of *Miranda,* determined the character of the later, warned confession; on the facts of that case, the Court thought any causal connection between the first and second responses to the police was "speculative and attenuated." Although the *Elstad* Court expressed no explicit conclusion about either officer's state of mind, it is fair to read *Elstad* as treating the living room conversation as a good-faith *Miranda* mistake, not only open to correction by careful warnings before systematic questioning in that particular case, but posing no threat to warn-first practice generally.

The contrast between *Elstad* and this case reveals a series of relevant facts that bear on whether *Miranda* warnings delivered midstream could be effective enough to accomplish their object: the completeness and detail of the questions and answers in the first round of interrogation, the overlapping content of the two statements, the timing and setting of the first and the second, the continuity of police personnel, and the degree to which the interrogator's questions treated the second round as continuous with the first. In *Elstad,* it was not unreasonable to see the occasion for questioning at the station house as presenting a markedly different experience from the short conversation at home; since a reasonable person in the suspect's shoes could have seen the station house questioning as a new and distinct experience, the *Miranda* warnings could have made sense as presenting a genuine choice whether to follow up on the earlier admission.

At the opposite extreme are the facts here, which by any objective measure reveal a police strategy adapted to undermine the *Miranda* warnings.[6] The unwarned interrogation was conducted in the station house, and the questioning was systematic, exhaustive, and managed with psychological skill. When the police were finished there was little, if anything, of incriminating potential left unsaid. The warned phase of questioning proceeded after a pause of only 15 to 20 minutes, in the same place as the unwarned segment. [The] police did not advise that her prior statement could not be used. Nothing was said or done to dispel the oddity of warning about legal rights to silence and counsel right after the police had led her through a systematic interrogation. . . . The impression that the further questioning was a mere continuation of the earlier questions and responses was fostered by references back to the confession already given. It would have been reasonable to regard the two sessions as parts of a continuum, in which it would have been unnatural to refuse to repeat at the second stage what had been said before. . . .

Because the question-first tactic effectively threatens to thwart *Miranda*'s purpose of reducing the risk that a coerced confession would be admitted, and because the facts here do not reasonably support a conclusion that the warnings given could have served their purpose, Seibert's postwarning statements are inadmissible. . . .

BREYER, J., concurring.

In my view, the following simple rule should apply to the two-stage interrogation technique: Courts should exclude the "fruits" of the initial unwarned questioning unless the failure to warn was in good faith. I believe this is a sound and workable approach to the problem this case presents. Prosecutors and judges have long understood how to apply the "fruits" approach, which they use in other areas of law. And in the workaday world of criminal law enforcement the administrative simplicity of the familiar has significant advantages over a more complex exclusionary rule.

I believe the plurality's approach in practice will function as a "fruits" test. The truly "effective" *Miranda* warnings on which the plurality insists will occur only when certain circumstances — a lapse in time, a change in location or interrogating officer, or a shift in the focus of the questioning — intervene between the unwarned questioning and any postwarning statement. . . .

KENNEDY, J., concurring in the judgment.

. . . The *Miranda* rule has become an important and accepted element of the criminal justice system. At the same time, not every violation of the rule requires suppression of the evidence obtained. Evidence is admissible when the central concerns of *Miranda* are not likely to be implicated and when other objectives of the criminal justice system are best served by its introduction. . . .

Oregon v. Elstad, 470 U.S. 298 (1985), reflects this approach. . . . In my view, *Elstad* was correct in its reasoning and its result. . . . An officer may not realize that a suspect is in custody and warnings are required. The officer may not plan to question the suspect or may be waiting for a more appropriate time. Skilled investigators often interview suspects multiple times, and good police work may involve referring to prior statements to test their veracity or to refresh recollection. In light

6. Because the intent of the officer will rarely be as candidly admitted as it was here (even as it is likely to determine the conduct of the interrogation), the focus is on facts apart from intent that show the question-first tactic at work.

of these realities it would be extravagant to treat the presence of one statement that cannot be admitted under *Miranda* as sufficient reason to prohibit subsequent statements preceded by a proper warning. That approach would serve "neither the general goal of deterring improper police conduct nor the Fifth Amendment goal of assuring trustworthy evidence." . . .

This case presents different considerations. The police used a two-step questioning technique based on a deliberate violation of *Miranda*. The *Miranda* warning was withheld to obscure both the practical and legal significance of the admonition when finally given. . . . The technique used in this case distorts the meaning of *Miranda* and furthers no legitimate countervailing interest. . . .

The plurality concludes that whenever a two-stage interview occurs, admissibility of the postwarning statement should depend on "whether the *Miranda* warnings delivered midstream could have been effective enough to accomplish their object" given the specific facts of the case. This test envisions an objective inquiry from the perspective of the suspect, and applies in the case of both intentional and unintentional two-stage interrogations. In my view, this test cuts too broadly. *Miranda*'s clarity is one of its strengths, and a multifactor test that applies to every two-stage interrogation may serve to undermine that clarity. I would apply a narrower test applicable only in the infrequent case, such as we have here, in which the two-step interrogation technique was used in a calculated way to undermine the *Miranda* warning. . . .

O'CONNOR, J., dissenting.*

The plurality devours Oregon v. Elstad, 470 U.S. 298 (1985), even as it accuses petitioner's argument of "disfiguring" that decision. I believe that we are bound by *Elstad* to reach a different result, and I would vacate the judgment of the Supreme Court of Missouri. . . . I would analyze the two-step interrogation procedure under the voluntariness standards central to the Fifth Amendment and reiterated in *Elstad*. . . .

Problem 8-8. Hot Load

Officers Mike Hannan and Terry Thomas of the Tennessee Highway Patrol stopped a speeding vehicle driven by Kellie Alisha Jones. When Jones was unable to find the vehicle's registration, Officer Hannan asked her to accompany him to his squad car while he wrote out a traffic citation. While Jones went to the squad car, the passenger, Hosie Smith, looked in the glove compartment for the vehicle's registration. Officer Thomas, who was on the passenger's side of the car, asked Smith questions regarding ownership of the car and the couple's destination. After this brief conversation with Smith, Thomas returned to the squad car and sat in the back seat. While waiting for radio verification of Jones's license and the vehicle's registration, both officers continued to question Jones about the ownership of the car and her destination. When asked who her passenger was, Jones stated that it was her boyfriend, but she could only give the name "Pumpkin" when asked about his name. Because Smith and Jones appeared to be extremely nervous, and had given

* [Chief Justice Rehnquist and Justices Scalia and Thomas joined in this opinion. — EDS.]

inconsistent answers to the questions about their destination and the ownership of the car, the officers became suspicious and asked Jones if she was carrying any illegal items, weapons, or contraband. Jones denied knowledge of such cargo, and consented to a search of the car.

Officer Thomas re-approached the station wagon on the passenger side and asked Smith if there were any illegal items in the car. Smith denied knowledge of any such contraband. Thomas then told Smith that he had permission to look through the vehicle, and asked again about any illegal items in the car. Smith said, "Yes, it was probably a hot load." Thomas then asked, "By a hot load, do you mean cash, marijuana, or cocaine, one of the three?" Smith responded, "Probably." Thomas searched the car and found 22 pounds of pure cocaine in the locked glove compartment. At 6:25 P.M., the officers placed both Smith and Jones under arrest, read them their *Miranda* rights, and transported them to Highway Patrol Headquarters.

At 9:45 P.M., Smith was questioned by Officer Lonnie Hood. Before he was questioned, Smith was read his *Miranda* rights again and signed a written waiver of those rights. During the course of the interrogation, Smith gave Officer Hood an incriminating account of his employment to drive the station wagon with Jones from Oklahoma City, Oklahoma, to Fayetteville, North Carolina. This statement was reduced to writing by Officer Hood and signed by Smith.

Smith filed a motion to suppress the cocaine found in the car, his statements to Thomas beside the road, and those to Hood at Highway Patrol Headquarters.

Instead of following *Elstad* under state law, the court (like about 15 other state courts) embraced the earlier "cat out of the bag" theory of United States v. Bayer, 331 U.S. 532 (1947). In *Bayer,* the Court recognized:

> Of course, after an accused has once let the cat out of the bag by confessing, no matter what the inducement, he is never thereafter free of the psychological and practical disadvantages of having confessed. He can never get the cat back in the bag. The secret is out for good. In such a sense, a later confession always may be looked upon as fruit of the first.

The Tennessee court rejected the idea that all subsequent warnings could cure prior invalid confessions, but it also rejected the idea that all invalid confessions tainted all later confessions. State v. Smith, 834 S.W.2d 915 (Tenn. 1992). The Tennessee court held that unwarned confessions raised a "rebuttable presumption" that a subsequent confession is tainted by the initial illegality." The prosecution can overcome that presumption by establishing that "the taint is so attenuated as to justify admission of the subsequent confession."

Under the state constitution, the "crucial inquiry" for the courts is "whether the events and circumstances surrounding and following the initial, illegal conduct of the law enforcement officers prevented the accused from subsequently (1) making a free and informed choice to waive the State constitutional right not to provide evidence against one's self, and (2) voluntarily confessing his involvement in the crime." In addressing these questions, Tennessee courts examine the following factors:

1. The use of coercive tactics to obtain the initial, illegal confession and the causal connection between the illegal conduct and the challenged, subsequent confession;
2. The temporal proximity of the prior and subsequent confessions;
3. The reading and explanation of *Miranda* rights to the defendant before the subsequent confession;
4. The circumstances occurring after the arrest and continuing up until the making of the subsequent confession including, but not limited to, the length of the detention and the deprivation of food, rest, and bathroom facilities;
5. The coerciveness of the atmosphere in which any questioning took place including, but not limited to, the place where the questioning occurred, the identity of the interrogators, the form of the questions, and the repeated or prolonged nature of the questioning;
6. The presence of intervening factors including, but not limited to, consultations with counsel or family members, or the opportunity to consult with counsel, if desired;
7. The psychological effect of having already confessed, and whether the defendant was advised that the prior confession may not be admissible at trial;
8. Whether the defendant initiated the conversation that led to the subsequent confession; and
9. The defendant's sobriety, education, intelligence level, and experience with the law, as such factors relate to the defendant's ability to understand the administered *Miranda* rights.

If you were arguing this motion for Smith, how would you try to persuade the trial court that the state constitutional standard is more protective of *Miranda* rights than the more recent *Seibert* case? What would be the outcome of the *Smith* facts under *Seibert*? Will states like Tennessee now revert to the new federal position?

Notes

1. *Out-of-court statements obtained after earlier* Miranda *violations: majority position.* Unlike illegal searches and seizures, an unwarned interrogation will not necessarily require a later court to exclude all the evidence derived from the tainted statement. Although any statement made during an unwarned interrogation must not come into evidence, later statements of the suspect might still be admissible — even though the statements appear to be the "fruit of the poisonous tree."

In Oregon v. Elstad, 470 U.S. 298 (1985), the Supreme Court held that the state could use as evidence a subsequent confession. According to the Court, when the initial unwarned statement was given voluntarily,

> a careful and thorough administration of *Miranda* warnings serves to cure the condition that rendered the unwarned statement inadmissible. The warning conveys the relevant information and thereafter the suspect's choice whether to exercise his privilege to remain silent should ordinarily be viewed as an act of free will.

470 U.S. at 310. Before *Seibert* was decided, a significant minority of states (around 15) rejected the *Elstad* decision, placing a burden on the government to overcome a presumption of compulsion for subsequent confessions. See, e.g., Commonwealth v. Smith, 593 N.E.2d 1288 (Mass. 1992). Do you expect those states to revise their state constitutional doctrine in light of *Seibert*? For a glimpse of the vigorous state court rulings on the question of "cures" for improper *Miranda* warnings, see the web extension for this chapter at *http://www.crimpro.com/extension/ch08*.

2. *Use of statements for impeachment at trial.* Although state and federal courts exclude *Miranda*-tainted statements from the prosecution's case in chief, they allow the prosecution to use such statements (and the evidentiary fruit of those statements) to impeach a defendant's testimony at trial. See Oregon v. Hass, 420 U.S. 714 (1975); Harris v. New York, 401 U.S. 222 (1971). Again, not all states agree. See Commonwealth v. Triplett, 462 Pa. 244, 341 A.2d 62 (1975) (under Pennsylvania Constitution, statement obtained in violation of an accused's *Miranda* rights cannot be used to impeach his trial testimony).

The Supreme Court authorized a new use of defendant statements for impeachment purposes in Kansas v. Ventris, 129 S. Ct. 1841 (2009). Prior to the murder trial of Ventris, the government planted an informant in his cell; the informant heard him admit to shooting and robbing the victim. When Ventris testified at trial that his co-defendant committed the crimes, the government asked the informant to testify about his alleged confession. The Supreme Court held that such impeachment use of the statement was constitutionally acceptable, even though the statement was obtained in violation of the defendant's Sixth Amendment rights as interpreted in *Massiah*. Justice Scalia's opinion for the Court distinguished between "core" or "substantive" protections and "prophylactic" protections. For the latter category, impeachment uses of illegally obtained evidence are allowed. He argued that violations of the *pretrial* right to counsel belong to the former category, because the violation occurs when the statement is obtained, not when the government attempts to introduce the evidence at trial.

In light of these rulings, will police officers routinely violate *Miranda* after a suspect invokes the right to silence or to an attorney, simply to provide the prosecutor with potential impeachment evidence? See Richard Leo, The Impact of *Miranda* Revisited, 86 J. Crim. L. & Criminology 621 (1996) (in study of more than 180 interrogations, observing only one instance of interrogator pursuing questions in known violation of *Miranda*); Charles Weisselberg, Saving *Miranda*, 84 Cornell L. Rev. 109 (1998) (collecting evidence of training that encourages interrogations outside *Miranda*).

3. *Harmless error.* There are some constitutional errors in a trial that an appellate court will consider "harmless" because the verdict likely would have remained the same even if the errors had not occurred. There are other errors that courts say can never be harmless. For a number of years after the *Miranda* decision, courts said that the introduction into evidence of a coerced confession qualified as one such error. This type of error was said to involve a right so basic to a fair trial that courts would not bother with a harmless-error inquiry. In Arizona v. Fulminante, 499 U.S. 279 (1991), however, the Supreme Court decided that the introduction of coerced confessions could be treated as a harmless error after all. We discuss this issue further in Chapter 20, dealing with appeals.

4. *Section 1983 and coercive questioning*. The remedy for improper efforts to obtain confessions has been exclusion of the confession. If the confession was

coerced (as opposed to a technical violation of the *Miranda* requirements), any evidentiary fruits of the confession are also inadmissible. Is some alternative remedy possible? Are damage suits, injunctions, or administrative sanctions workable alternatives?

Both federal and state law allow criminal suspects to sue police officers for the use of illegal interrogation techniques. Although there are some important barriers to recovery in both state and federal courts (as we saw in Chapter 6), plaintiffs sometimes can recover damages after they have been subjected to illegal interrogations, including *Miranda* violations and the use of physical deprivations.

Problem 8-9. Inevitable Discovery

Elizabeth Reed, an attendant at a county landfill, died from a shotgun wound fired at close range as she was preparing to leave work. The killer left Reed's body hidden in some brush beside a dirt road, approximately 95 feet from the landfill office. The police soon began to focus their investigation on Kenneth DeShields, who had been seen that day driving Reed's car. They arrested him the morning after the murder.

Before any questioning began, DeShields requested an attorney and said that he did not wish to speak about the incident. However, the investigating officers persisted in their questions, and DeShields ultimately gave a series of statements. Although DeShields initially denied any knowledge of the murder, he eventually told the police that he had been with a man named "Blair" when Blair had killed Reed during an attempt to rob her. DeShields also said that after he and Blair had left the landfill, Blair had thrown a rake into a ditch and driven down a dirt road in the nearby woods to discard several items from the robbery. Detective Hudson then searched the dirt road that DeShields had described. He found an expended shotgun shell casing and the victim's wallet approximately 15 feet east of the dirt road and approximately 1,000 feet from the dump site.

At trial, the state did not introduce any of DeShields's postarrest statements into evidence. However, the shell casing and wallet were admitted into evidence, and an expert testified that the shell casing had been fired from DeShields's shotgun. The shell casing was the only direct evidence linking the killing to his shotgun. Two police officers testified that it was routine police practice to search the general area extensively in a homicide case and that this practice was followed in this case. By the time Hudson found the evidence, the police had already searched the landfill compound and several county roads that crisscrossed the area.

Did the trial court rule correctly in admitting the shell casing and wallet into evidence? Compare DeShields v. State, 534 A.2d 630 (Del. 1987).

Note

1. *Tainted leads to witnesses and physical evidence.* An improper interrogation might give the authorities information that can lead them to other witnesses or to physical evidence. In Michigan v. Tucker, 417 U.S. 433 (1974), the Supreme Court allowed the use of prosecution witnesses whose names had been obtained during an interrogation where proper *Miranda* warnings had not been given. While recognizing

that a truly involuntary confession, obtained in violation of the due process clause, could be remedied only by complete exclusion of all evidentiary "fruits" of the confession, this was not such a case. The failure to give proper *Miranda* warnings was merely a violation of a "prophylactic" rule rather than a constitutional violation as such. For *Miranda* violations that do not create an involuntary (and thus unconstitutional) confession, the Court believed that exclusion of evidence would be too costly. See also United States v. Patane, 542 U.S. 630 (2004) (physical evidence produced through unwarned but voluntary statements was admissible, even though police deliberately violated *Miranda*).

State courts have not often rejected this analysis explicitly, but many seem to assume that any evidentiary "fruit" from a confession obtained in violation of *Miranda* must be excluded unless one of the traditional exceptions to the "fruits" rule is present. A deliberate violation of *Miranda* by interrogators also has led some state courts to limit the use of evidentiary fruit. See Commonwealth v. Martin, 827 N.E.2d 198 (Mass. 2005) (rejects *Patane*; state constitution requires suppression of physical evidence derived from unwarned statements); State v. Peterson, 923 A.2d 585 (Vt. 2007) (state constitution requires suppression of tangible fruits of *Miranda* violation).

2. *Systemwide Impacts*

Miranda has been criticized on both doctrinal and practical grounds. The practical critiques take many forms, but they boil down to the question of how many convictions are "lost" because *Miranda* warnings were given. Before reading the following study, it is worth thinking in the abstract about the challenge of measuring the impact of *Miranda*. The article illustrates recent efforts, 30 years after the decision, to study its continuing impact. Is it possible to reach a conclusion about the impact of *Miranda*, either 30 years ago or today? Can the benefits of *Miranda* be quantified?

■ PAUL CASSELL AND BRET HAYMAN, POLICE INTERROGATION IN THE 1990S: AN EMPIRICAL STUDY OF THE EFFECTS OF *MIRANDA*

43 UCLA L. Rev. 839 (1996)

[We] undertook an empirical survey of confessions and their importance [in Salt Lake City, Utah]. We collected the basic data for the study by attending "screening" sessions held at the Salt Lake County District Attorney's office during a six-week period in the summer of 1994. Prosecutors in the District Attorney's Office screen all felony cases for prosecutive merit. . . . The screening session is a forty-five-minute interview by the prosecutor of the police officer concerning the evidence supporting the filing of charges. . . . There were 219 suspects in our sample. . . .

A. The Frequency of Questioning, Waivers, and Confessions

One important issue that has not been the subject of much empirical study is the frequency with which suspects are questioned. Not every person who is arrested will be questioned. In our sample, police questioned 79.0% of the suspects. This means that a surprisingly large percentage (21.0%) were not questioned.

[We also] collected information on why police failed to interrogate suspects (as reported by the officer at screening). [In] two cases (4.9% of the nonquestioning cases), the reason for not questioning was a belief that the suspect would invoke *Miranda*. In two other cases (4.9% of the nonquestioning cases), the police cited the fact that a suspect had an attorney as the obstacle to questioning, a reason that has a possible connection with *Miranda*. . . . The most often-given reason for nonquestioning [accounting for 34.1% of the nonquestioning cases] was that a suspect's whereabouts was unknown at the time police screened the case. The second most common reason [26.8%] for failure to question was the officer's belief that the case against the suspect was overwhelming. . . .

One of the most important questions about the *Miranda* regime is how often suspects invoke their *Miranda* rights, preventing any police questioning. A suspect can claim *Miranda* rights in two ways. First, he can refuse at the start of an interview to waive his rights (including the right to remain silent and the right to counsel), thus precluding any interview. Second, even if he initially waives his rights, he can assert them at any point in the interview. If a suspect asserts *Miranda* rights, police questioning must stop. . . . Surprisingly very little information is available on such a fundamental subject. The previously published evidence . . . suggests that about 20% of all suspects invoke their *Miranda* rights.

We gathered data on how often and in what ways suspects asserted their *Miranda* rights. [Of] suspects given their *Miranda* rights, 83.7% waived them. Reflecting the practices of the local law enforcement agencies, virtually all of these waivers were verbal rather than written. At the same time, 16.3% invoked their rights. Of the twenty-one suspects who invoked their rights, nine invoked their right to an attorney (two even before *Miranda* warnings could be read), six invoked their right not to make a statement, and six either refused to execute a waiver or otherwise invoked their rights.

[Five] suspects who initially waived their rights [3.9% of the total] changed their minds later and invoked their rights during the interview. Of these five suspects, three asked for an attorney during the interview (two after giving incriminating statements, one after giving a denial with an explanation), and two asserted their right to remain silent during the interview (one after giving a flat denial, one after giving a denial with an explanation). . . . If these three are added to suspects who invoked their rights initially, then a total of 18.6% of the suspects in our sample who were given *Miranda* rights invoked them before police succeeded in obtaining incriminating information. . . .

Perhaps the critical issue in the debate over *Miranda* is how often today suspects confess or otherwise make incriminating statements. Surprisingly little information is available on this subject, despite frequent definitive pronouncements that many suspects still confess.

[We] divided the outcomes into "successful" and "unsuccessful" categories — looking at the results from law enforcement's point of view. The result of questioning was "successful" when the police: (1) obtained a written confession;

(2) obtained a verbal confession; (3) obtained an incriminating statement; or (4) locked a suspect into a false alibi.

A written or verbal "confession" was "any substantial acknowledgment by the suspect that he or she committed the crime." Simply put, the suspect had to say in essence "I did it." . . . A "confession" could include statements in mitigation. . . .

Our next category was for "incriminating statements." Because this category is somewhat subjective and because its scope makes a critical difference in determining the scope of police success statistics, it is worth explaining in detail. An "incriminating statement" was "any statement that tends to establish guilt of the accused or from which with other facts guilt may be inferred or which tends to disprove some anticipated defense."

We found that such statements generally occurred in one of three situations. First, a suspect might give a statement that linked him to the crime or crime scene without admitting his guilt. For example, in an attempted homicide case the police asked the suspect if a certain car, known to have been involved in the crime, was his. He responded that it was, but denied any involvement in the crime. . . . A second kind of incriminating statement was a partial admission of guilt. For example, in one case involving a burglary, a suspect admitted being in the house unlawfully, but said he was there because of something the victim had done to his girlfriend, not to steal anything. . . .

Table 4 — Results
(N = 219 overall; 173 for those questioned)

	No.	*Questioned Only* %	*Overall* %
Invoked rights	21	12.1	9.5
Successful	73	42.2	33.3 . . .
Unsuccessful	79	45.7	36.1 . . .
Not questioned	46	—	21.0
Total	219	100	100

Third, a suspect might make statements to the police that tended to call into question his truthfulness or make him appear suspicious. For example, in one case an officer suspected a car was stolen and pulled over the suspect. The officer asked the suspect certain questions concerning his license, registration, and his relationship to the car. The suspect was visibly shaken by the questions and gave stammering and sometimes contradictory answers. We classified these statements as "incriminating."

After confessions and incriminating statements, the final category of "successful" outcomes was for a suspect who was "locked into a false alibi." . . .

The number of incriminating statements and denials we found are shown in Table 4. Overall, 9.5% of the suspects invoked their rights, 33.3% were successfully questioned, 36.1% were questioned unsuccessfully, and 21.0% were not questioned. Because some might argue that only suspects who were in fact questioned should be included in determining a confession rate, we also report percentages for only those suspects who were questioned. As can also be seen in Table 4, of all police interviews, 12.1% produced an immediate invocation of *Miranda* rights, 42.2% were successful, and 45.7% were unsuccessful. It should also be noted that, however measured, our "success" rate is artificially inflated because of the point at which our sample was drawn. We sampled cases from screening sessions where police officers believed they had gathered sufficient evidence for prosecution. As a consequence, our sample excludes a significant number of cases that police thought were too weak to warrant prosecution — including cases that were too weak because of an unsuccessful outcome of police questioning. . . .

[We] also examined whether suspects for particular types of crimes were more likely to confess. The limited previous research on this issue, from studies conducted in the 1960s, suggests that suspects are less likely to confess to violent crimes than to property crimes. Our data trend in this direction; . . . police were less successful in interrogating suspects for crimes of violence than for property crimes, although the result is not statistically significant at the conventional . . . confidence level. . . .

Although our success rate is inflated, it is lower than success rates found in this country before *Miranda,* suggesting that *Miranda* has hampered law enforcement efforts to obtain incriminating statements. [The] available pre- and post-*Miranda* information on confession rates in this country . . . suggests that interrogations were successful, very roughly speaking, in about 55% to 60% of interrogations conducted before the *Miranda* decision. For example, the earliest academic study in this country reported confession rates of 88.1% and 58.1% in two cities in California in 1960.[149] Similarly, a 1961 survey in Detroit reported a 60.8% confession rate, which fell slightly to 58.0% in 1965. [These figures] avoid the problem of anticipatory implementation of *Miranda* in various jurisdictions. In particular, confession rates after June 1964 might be dampened by the Supreme Court's *Escobedo* decision, which led some police to adopt *Miranda*-style warnings even before the decision. Our 33.3% overall success rate (and even our 42.2% questioning success rate) is well below the 55%-60% estimated pre-*Miranda* rate and, therefore, is consistent with the hypothesis that *Miranda* has harmed the confession rate.

B. Questioning Inside and Outside the *Miranda* Regime

One question that has not been the subject of any substantial empirical research is the extent to which police questioning falls inside or outside the *Miranda* regime and whether this makes any difference to ultimate outcomes. . . .

The *Miranda* rules cover only "custodial" interrogation. Evidence suggests that police have adjusted to *Miranda* by shifting to noncustodial "interviews" to skirt *Miranda*'s requirements. In talking to police officers, the researchers found some anecdotal evidence supporting this view. In a few screenings, officers (mostly from one large department) referred to giving suspects a "*Beheler*" warning, as in "I gave him *Beheler*." This is a reference to the Supreme Court's decision in California v. Beheler, 463 U.S. 1121 (1983), which held that a suspect was not in custody when he "voluntarily agreed to accompany police to the station house [and] the police specifically told [him] that he was not under arrest." . . . On the other hand, in a few cases in our sample it appeared that officers Mirandized when not required to do so. . . .

149. Edward Barren, Jr., Police Practices and the Law — from Arrest to Release or Charge, 50 Cal. L. Rev. 11 (1962).

To date, no one has quantified how often police interview in noncustodial settings. In our sample, 69.9% of the interviews were custodial while 30.1% were noncustodial. Of the noncustodial interviews, 40.3% were at the scene, 26.9% were field investigations, and 32.7% were arranged interviews (that is, interviews where police officers had previously contacted the suspects to set up an interview time).

Even if police are able to avoid *Miranda*'s requirements by conducting various noncustodial interviews, the question would remain whether such interviews are less effective in obtaining incriminating information. We found that police were less successful in noncustodial interviews [with a 30% success rate, compared to 56.9% in custodial interrogations].

Notes

1. *Number of attempted interrogations.* Would the *Miranda* decision be likely to affect the number of cases in which the police at least attempt an interrogation? Should a study of the impact of *Miranda* include cases in which the suspect was not available for questioning? The Salt Lake City study did so. One prominent *Miranda*-era study — of the pseudonymous "Seaside City," California — concluded that officers failed to interrogate only 2 percent of the suspects "actually arrested and incarcerated." James Witt, Non-Coercive Interrogation and the Administration of Criminal Justice: The Impact of *Miranda* on Police Effectuality, 64 J. Crim. L. & Criminology 320 (1973).

2. *Number of waivers.* The most current studies have concluded that roughly 80 percent of all suspects waive their *Miranda* rights and make statements without counsel present. Some studies have found waiver rates in excess of 90 percent. See Paul Cassell, *Miranda*'s Social Costs: An Empirical Reassessment, 90 Nw. U. L. Rev. 387 (1996) (collecting studies of waiver rate). A study in Great Britain suggested that about 68 percent of suspects in 1991 requested legal advice, after receiving warnings similar to those in *Miranda.* David Brown, Tom Ellis & Karen Larcombe, Changing the Code: Police Detention Under the Revised PACE Codes of Practice, Home Office Research and Planning Unit, London HMSO (1992). The tendency to waive the right to counsel or the right to silence is especially strong among suspects with no prior criminal convictions. Richard Leo, Inside the Interrogation Room, 86 J. Crim. L. & Criminology 266 (1996). Would the repeat offenders who tend more often to invoke their rights be more or less likely than the average offender to provide an incriminating statement in the absence of a warning? If so many suspects waive their rights, is that an indication of *Miranda*'s failure or success? See George Thomas, Is *Miranda* a Real-World Failure? A Plea for More (and Better) Empirical Evidence, 43 UCLA L. Rev. 821 (1996).

3. *Number of confessions or admissions.* The major concern of *Miranda*'s critics is that the warnings change the dynamic between the questioner and the suspect and reduce the number of successful interrogations, even when the suspect agrees to talk to the police. A number of empirical studies attempt to measure the "success rate" for interrogations immediately before and after the *Miranda* decision. A Pittsburgh study concluded that 48.5 percent of suspects confessed before *Miranda* while 32.3 percent confessed after *Miranda.* Richard Seeburger & Stanton Wettick, *Miranda* in Pittsburgh — A Statistical Analysis, 29 U. Pitt. L. Rev. 1 (1967). The "Seaside City"

(California) study noted above pointed to a pre-*Miranda* confession rate of 68.9 percent and a post-*Miranda* rate of 66.9 percent. This study included only suspects who were arrested and incarcerated; it excluded cases in which suspects were detained for questioning but never incarcerated. The Salt Lake City study, based on cases investigated in 1994, found a success rate of 33.3 percent overall and 42.2 percent of cases where questioning actually occurred. In contrast, a study of interrogations in three California cities in 1992-1993 concluded that 64 percent of all the observed interrogations produced a confession or incriminating admission. Richard Leo, Inside the Interrogation Room, 86 J. Crim. L. & Criminology 266 (1996).

One difficulty in studying this issue is defining what constitutes a "successful" interrogation. The studies all include outright confessions, in which the suspect tells the police that he committed the crime. Many also include some partially successful interrogations leading to "admissions": statements that police and prosecutors can use to prove one or more elements of the crime. Do you agree with the way Cassell and Hayman resolved this issue in the Salt Lake City study? A second difficulty in this debate comes from the (possibly) changing effects of *Miranda* over the 30-plus years since the decision appeared. Is it plausible to think that the confession rate "rebounded" after an initial drop, once police officers adjusted their practices to the new requirements and found the best ways to prevent lost confessions? A reporter who spent one year with homicide detectives in Baltimore (research that later formed the basis for the television series *The Wire*) concluded that the police are able to use the *Miranda* warnings to create an atmosphere of cooperation with at least some suspects. He observed cases in which the suspect's act of acknowledging an understanding of the rights, followed by a waiver of those rights, created some momentum for cooperation during the interrogation. David Simon, Homicide: A Year on the Killing Streets (1991). At the same time, early studies may have *understated* the current effects of *Miranda* because over the years the nature of *Miranda* rights have become more broadly known and understood.

Another difficulty in measuring the effects of *Miranda* on the confession rate is that the warnings and a request for waiving the rights might simultaneously discourage and encourage confessions. Some suspects will refuse to talk once they hear the warnings, while the process of explaining the *Miranda* rights and obtaining a waiver may create a more cooperative atmosphere and lead to more (or more damaging) admissions. George Thomas reviewed the available empirical studies and concluded that they are inconclusive, but still consistent with the view that *Miranda* helps as much as it hurts. Thomas, Plain Talk About the *Miranda* Empirical Debate: A "Steady-State" Theory of Confessions, 43 UCLA L. Rev. 933 (1996).

4. *Number of convictions.* Another measurement of *Miranda*'s effects might come from estimating its impact on the conviction rate. There are two methods of arriving at this number. First, one might compare the percentage of all suspects convicted of crimes in the same location immediately before and after the Court's decision, and presume that some or all of the change in conviction rates was attributable to *Miranda.* Using this method, the Pittsburgh study concluded that the conviction rate was unchanged after the *Miranda* decision. The Seaside City study found a 9 percent decline in the conviction rate (from 92 percent to 83 percent). Is there any problem with this method of estimating the decision's impact on convictions? Second, one might start with an estimate of the number of confessions lost and combine it with some estimate of the proportion of cases in which a confession is essential to obtain a conviction. Multiplying the lost confessions by the number of

cases in which confessions are necessary results in a final estimate. A researcher might estimate the number of cases in which a confession is important by asking for the opinion of prosecutors and others involved in the case. She might also review the case files herself to imagine which cases might have ended differently if a confession were or were not available. Using these methods (or a combination of them), most studies have estimated that confessions are essential in 13 percent to 28 percent of all cases. See Paul Cassell, *Miranda*'s Social Costs, 90 Nw. U. L. Rev. 387 (1996) (summarizing studies and reaching average of 23.8 percent). In choosing which studies of this question are most reliable, what would you want to know?

5. *Number of reversals on appeal.* Yet another measure of *Miranda*'s effects is the number of convictions overturned on appeal because of *Miranda* violations. All the evidence suggests that a trivial number of cases are lost on appeal because of *Miranda.* Peter Nardulli, The Societal Costs of the Exclusionary Rule Revisited, 1987 U. Ill. L. Rev. 223 (confessions suppressed in 0.04 percent of all cases). Why might this be the case when other measures show evidence of a larger *Miranda* impact?

6. *Clearance rates.* An ideal measurement of *Miranda*'s costs over time (such as a reliable account of confession rates before *Miranda* and during the years since) is not available. One indirect measurement of the effects is the "clearance rate," that is, the percentage of reported crimes that the police declare "solved." Those rates, which have been collected and reported since at least 1950, declined just after the *Miranda* decision and have remained at the lower levels since that time. Paul Cassell and Richard Fowles analyzed this data. After attempting to control for other possible explanations for the lower clearance rates, they conclude that "without *Miranda,* the number of crimes cleared would be substantially higher — by as much as 6.6-29.7% for robbery, 6.2-28.9% for burglary, 0.4-11.9% for larceny, and 12.8-45.4% for vehicle theft." Cassell & Fowles, Handcuffing the Cops? A Thirty-Year Perspective on *Miranda*'s Harmful Effects on Law Enforcement, 50 Stan. L. Rev. 1055, 1126 (1998). For what crimes would you expect *Miranda* to have the greatest effect? Would you expect clearance rates to show more or less of an impact than confession rates? See Floyd Feeney, Police Clearances: A Poor Way to Measure the Impact of *Miranda* on the Police, 32 Rutgers L.J. 1 (2000).

7. *Acceptable costs and benefits.* After resolving all the factual disputes about the actual effects of the *Miranda* decision, one is left with a different type of question: How much of the undesirable effect is too much? If the effects of *Miranda* described thus far could be considered the "costs" of the decision, are there any corresponding benefits? What are those benefits and how might one measure them and compare them to the costs?

3. Alternatives to **Miranda**

Miranda continues to be the subject of criticism, though law enforcement officers in particular have become more supportive of *Miranda* as they have made it part of their routine. Remember that the Court in *Miranda* expressly invited legislatures to find alternative methods for protecting the privilege against self-incrimination.

> It is impossible for us to foresee the potential alternatives for protecting the privilege which might be devised by Congress or the States in the exercise of their creative

> rule-making capacities. Therefore we cannot say that the Constitution necessarily requires adherence to any particular solution for the inherent compulsions of the interrogation process as it is presently conducted. Our decision in no way creates a constitutional straitjacket which will handicap sound efforts at reform, nor is it intended to have this effect. . . . Congress and the States are free to develop their own safeguards for the privilege, so long as they are fully as effective as those described above in informing accused persons of their right of silence and in affording a continuous opportunity to exercise it.

What are the alternatives to *Miranda*? The Court in Dickerson v. United States, 530 U.S. 428 (2000), struck down one such effort, a federal statute instructing judges to judge the admissibility of confessions only by the traditional standards of voluntariness. What sort of alternatives might succeed where the 1968 federal statute failed?

Perhaps a legislature could revise the *Miranda* warning to remove aspects most often criticized as obstacles to proper crime-solving techniques. Perhaps interrogations should occur before a judicial officer. Or perhaps a trial jury might later be told of any refusal to make a statement to the magistrate, or the refusal to make a statement to the judicial officer might be punishable as contempt of court. See Akhil Amar & Renee Lettow, Fifth Amendment First Principles: The Self-Incrimination Clause, 93 Mich. L. Rev. 857 (1995); Donald Dripps, Foreword: Against Police Interrogation — And the Privilege Against Self-Incrimination, 78 J. Crim. L. & Criminology 699 (1988). Consider the following approach to interrogations, made possible by technological advances.

■ TEXAS CODE OF CRIMINAL PROCEDURE ART. 38.22

Sec. 2. No written statement made by an accused as a result of custodial interrogation is admissible as evidence against him in any criminal proceeding unless it is shown on the face of the statement that:

(a) the accused, prior to making the statement, . . . received from the person to whom the statement is made a warning that:

(1) he has the right to remain silent and not make any statement at all and that any statement he makes may be used against him at his trial; (2) any statement he makes may be used as evidence against him in court; (3) he has the right to have a lawyer present to advise him prior to and during any questioning; (4) if he is unable to employ a lawyer, he has the right to have a lawyer appointed to advise him prior to and during any questioning; and (5) he has the right to terminate the interview at any time; and

(b) the accused, prior to and during the making of the statement, knowingly, intelligently, and voluntarily waived the rights set out in the warning prescribed by Subsection (a) of this section.

Sec. 3. (a) No oral or sign language statement of an accused made as a result of custodial interrogation shall be admissible against the accused in a criminal proceeding unless:

(1) an electronic recording, which may include motion picture, video tape, or other visual recording, is made of the statement; (2) prior to the statement

but during the recording the accused is given the warning in Subsection (a) of Section 2 above and the accused knowingly, intelligently, and voluntarily waives any rights set out in the warning; (3) the recording device was capable of making an accurate recording, the operator was competent, and the recording is accurate and has not been altered; (4) all voices on the recording are identified; and (5) not later than the 20th day before the date of the proceeding, the attorney representing the defendant is provided with a true, complete, and accurate copy of all recordings of the defendant made under this article. . . .

(c) Subsection (a) of this section shall not apply to any statement which contains assertions of facts or circumstances that are found to be true and which conduce to establish the guilt of the accused, such as the finding of secreted or stolen property or the instrument with which he states the offense was committed. . . . (e) The courts of this state shall strictly construe Subsection (a) of this section and may not interpret Subsection (a) as making admissible a statement unless all requirements of the subsection have been satisfied by the state, except that: (1) only voices that are material are identified; and (2) the accused was given the warning in Subsection (a) of Section 2 above or its fully effective equivalent.

Sec. 4. When any statement, the admissibility of which is covered by this article, is sought to be used in connection with an official proceeding, any person who swears falsely to facts and circumstances which, if true, would render the statement admissible under this article is presumed to have acted with intent to deceive and with knowledge of the statement's meaning for the purpose of prosecution for aggravated perjury. . . . No person prosecuted under this subsection shall be eligible for probation.

Sec. 5. Nothing in this article precludes the admission of a statement made by the accused in open court at his trial, before a grand jury, or at an examining trial . . . , or of a statement that does not stem from custodial interrogation, or of a voluntary statement, whether or not the result of custodial interrogation, that has a bearing upon the credibility of the accused as a witness, or of any other statement that may be admissible under law.

DONALD STEPHAN v. STATE

711 P.2d 1156 (Alaska 1985)

BURKE, J.

More than five years ago, in Mallott v. State, 608 P.2d 737 (Alaska 1980), we informed Alaska law enforcement officials that "it is incumbent upon them to tape record, where feasible, any questioning [of criminal suspects,] and particularly that which occurs in a place of detention." This requirement (hereinafter the *Mallott* rule) was again noted in S.B. v. State, 614 P.2d 786 (Alaska 1980), with the observation that an electronic record of such interviews "will be a great aid" when courts are called upon to determine "the circumstances of a confession or other waiver of [a suspect's] *Miranda* rights." In a third case, McMahan v. State, 617 P.2d 494 (Alaska 1980), the recording requirement was repeated, with the further statement that "if *Miranda* rights are read to the defendant, this too should be recorded." Today, we hold that an unexcused failure to electronically record a custodial interrogation conducted in a place of detention violates a suspect's right to due process, under the Alaska Constitution, and that any statement thus obtained is generally inadmissible.[2]

The relevant facts in the two cases now before us are similar. Malcolm Scott Harris and Donald Stephan, petitioners, were arrested on unrelated criminal charges, taken to police stations and questioned by police officers. Harris was interrogated on two separate occasions; Stephan was interrogated only once. Both men made inculpatory statements. In each instance, a working audio or video recorder was in the room and was used during part, but not all, of the interrogation. The officers, in each case, offered no satisfactory excuse for their clear disregard of the *Mallott* rule.[3]

Prior to their respective trials, Harris and Stephan both moved to suppress confessions made during their interrogations. At the suppression hearings there was conflicting testimony about what occurred during the unrecorded portions of the interviews. Harris claimed that, in his first interrogation, he was not informed of his *Miranda* rights at the beginning of the session, that the questioning continued after he asserted his right to remain silent, and that the officer made threats and promises during the untaped portions. Stephan claimed that his ultimate confession was induced by promises of leniency and was obtained in the absence of an attorney, after he requested one. In both cases, the officers' testimony was to the contrary. Without a full recording to resolve the conflict, the superior court was required to evaluate the credibility of the witnesses and choose which version of the unrecorded events to believe. In each case, the court chose the police officers' recollections and determined that the confession was voluntary and, thus, admissible at trial. Harris and Stephan were ultimately found guilty and filed notices of appeal. . . .

In its decision, the court of appeals acknowledged: "The supreme court has clearly stated in three separate cases that the police are under a duty to record statements which suspects make where recording is feasible. That admonition cannot be ignored." The court, nevertheless, refused to adopt a general exclusionary rule, stating:

> We believe that the issue of what sanction is appropriate is best approached on a case by case basis. . . . Exactly what sanction, if any, to apply for the failure to record a defendant's statement in a given case is a decision which is best left to the sound discretion of the trial court. . . .

The court of appeals' refusal to adopt an exclusionary rule in these circumstances is perhaps due to failure on our part to adequately explain the full significance of our prior decisions. Electronic recording of suspect interrogations was

2. We are not alone in recognizing the importance of recording custodial interrogations. See Hendricks v. Swenson, 456 F.2d 503 (8th Cir. 1972) (suggesting that videotapes of interrogations protect a defendant's rights and are a step forward in the search for truth); Ragan v. State, 642 S.W.2d 489 (Tex. Crim. App. 1982) (Tex. Code Crim. Proc. Ann. art. 38.22, §3, requiring that oral statements of the accused during custodial interrogations must be recorded in order to be admissible); Model Code of Pre-Arraignment Procedure §130.4 (Proposed Official Draft 1975) (requiring sound recordings of custodial interviews). . . .

3. One officer stated that it was "normal practice" to get the suspect's statement "laid out in the desired manner," and only then record the full, formal confession. Another officer explained that a suspect is more at ease and likely to talk without a tape recorder running.

described in those cases, rather ambiguously, as "part of a law enforcement agency's duty to preserve evidence." Today, we resolve that ambiguity. Such recording is a requirement of state due process when the interrogation occurs in a place of detention and recording is feasible. We reach this conclusion because we are convinced that recording, in such circumstances, is now a reasonable and necessary safeguard, essential to the adequate protection of the accused's right to counsel, his right against self incrimination and, ultimately, his right to a fair trial. . . . Thus, as we have done on previous occasions, we construe Alaska's constitutional provision, in this instance, as affording rights beyond those guaranteed by the United States Constitution. . . .

The contents of an interrogation are obviously material in determining the voluntariness of a confession. The state usually attempts to show voluntariness through the interrogating officer's testimony that the defendant's constitutional rights were protected. The defendant, on the other hand, often testifies to the contrary. The result, then, is a swearing match between the law enforcement official and the defendant, which the courts must resolve.

> The difficulty in depicting what transpires at such interrogations stems from the fact that in this country they have largely taken place incommunicado. . . . Interrogation still takes place in privacy. Privacy results in secrecy and this in turn results in a gap in our knowledge as to what in fact goes on in the interrogation rooms. [Miranda v. Arizona, 384 U.S. at 445, 448.]

Thus, we believe a recording requirement is justified, because a tape recording provides an objective means for evaluating what occurred during interrogation. . . .

In the absence of an accurate record, the accused may suffer an infringement upon his right to remain silent and to have counsel present during the interrogation. Also, his right to a fair trial may be violated, if an illegally obtained, and possibly false, confession is subsequently admitted. An electronic recording, thus, protects the defendant's constitutional rights, by providing an objective means for him to corroborate his testimony concerning the circumstances of the confession.

The recording of custodial interrogations is not, however, a measure intended to protect only the accused; a recording also protects the public's interest in honest and effective law enforcement, and the individual interests of those police officers wrongfully accused of improper tactics. A recording, in many cases, will aid law enforcement efforts, by confirming the content and the voluntariness of a confession, when a defendant changes his testimony or claims falsely that his constitutional rights were violated. In any case, a recording will help trial and appellate courts to ascertain the truth.

The concept of due process is not static; among other things, it must change to keep pace with new technological developments. For example, the gathering and preservation of breath samples was previously impractical. Now that this procedure is technologically feasible, many states require it, either as a matter of due process or by resort to reasoning akin to a due process analysis. The use of audio and video tapes is even more commonplace in today's society. The police already make use of recording devices in circumstances when it is to their advantage to do so. Examples would be the routine video recording of suspect behavior in drunk driving cases and, as was done in these cases, the recording of formal confessions. Furthermore, media reports indicate that many Alaska police officers have purchased their own recorders, carry them while on duty and regularly record conversations with suspects or witnesses, in order to protect themselves against false accusations. When a portable recorder has not been available, some officers have even used their patrol car radio to record conversations through the police dispatch center.

In both of the cases before us, the police were engaged in custodial interrogations of suspects in a place of detention. A working recording device was readily available, but was used to record only part of the questioning. Compliance with the recording rule is not unduly burdensome under these circumstances. Turning the recorder on a few minutes earlier entails minimal cost and effort. In return, less time, money and resources would have been consumed in resolving the disputes that arose over the events that occurred during the interrogations.

The only real reason advanced by police for their frequent failure to electronically record an entire interrogation is their claim that recordings tend to have a "chilling effect" on a suspect's willingness to talk. Given the fact that an accused has a constitutional right to remain silent, under both the state and federal constitutions, and that he must be clearly warned of that right prior to any custodial interrogation, this argument is not persuasive.

In summary, the rule that we adopt today requires that custodial interrogations in a place of detention, including the giving of the accused's *Miranda* rights, must be electronically recorded. To satisfy this due process requirement, the recording must clearly indicate that it recounts the entire interview. Thus, explanations should be given at the beginning, the end and before and after any interruptions in the recording, so that courts are not left to speculate about what took place.

Since its announcement, the *Mallott* rule has always included a proviso, "when feasible." The failure to electronically record an entire custodial interrogation will, therefore, be considered a violation of the rule, and subject to exclusion, only if the failure is unexcused. Acceptable excuses might include an unavoidable power or equipment failure, or a situation where the suspect refuses to answer any questions if the conversation is being recorded. We need not anticipate all such possible excuses here, for courts must carefully scrutinize each situation on a case-by-case basis. Any time a full recording is not made, however, the state must persuade the trial court, by a preponderance of the evidence, that recording was not feasible under the circumstances, and in such cases the failure to record should be viewed with distrust.

[We] adopt a general rule of exclusion. While other remedies may each have their merits, we believe an exclusionary rule will best protect the suspects' constitutional rights, provide clear direction to law enforcement agencies and lower courts, and preserve the integrity of our justice system.

[Law] enforcement agencies and lower courts have repeatedly failed to give due regard to the protections the *Mallott* rule is intended to provide, even though the rule was first announced over five years ago. We believe that a strong and certain remedy will have a considerable deterrent effect in future cases. Compliance imposes such minimal costs and burdens on law enforcement agencies that they will have little to gain from noncompliance. . . .

The imposition of sanctions against an individual officer will not necessarily solve what appears to be a systemic problem. Agency policy and operations must change, not simply individual behaviors. Once they are fully aware of the consequences of unexcused violations of the *Mallott* rule, we are confident that law enforcement agencies will establish effective procedures to implement the rule and provide adequate training for their personnel. Suppression of statements taken in violation of the rule will, therefore, deter continued disregard of its requirements by officers, agencies and courts.

Another purpose is also served by the rule that we now adopt. The integrity of our judicial system is subject to question whenever a court rules on the admissibility of a questionable confession, based solely upon the court's acceptance of the testimony of an interested party, whether it be the interrogating officer or the defendant. This is especially true when objective evidence of the circumstances surrounding the confession could have been preserved by the mere flip of a switch. Routine and systematic recording of custodial interrogations will provide such evidence, and avoid any suggestion that the court is biased in favor of either party.

Most importantly, an exclusionary rule furthers the protection of individual constitutional rights. Strong protection is needed to insure that a suspect's right to counsel, his privilege against self incrimination, and due process guarantees are protected. A confession is generally such conclusive evidence of guilt that a rule of exclusion is justified, when the state, without excuse, fails to preserve evidence of the interchange leading up to the formal statement. [E]xclusion of the defendant's statement is the only remedy which will correct the wrong that has been done and place the defendant in the same position he or she would have been in had the evidence been preserved and turned over in time for use at trial.

Thus, we conclude that exclusion is the appropriate remedy for an unexcused failure to electronically record an interrogation, when such recording is feasible. A general exclusionary rule is the only remedy that provides crystal clarity to law enforcement agencies, preserves judicial integrity, and adequately protects a suspect's constitutional rights. The necessity for this strong remedy remains, even when we consider society's interests in crime prevention and the apprehension of criminal offenders. Exclusion of reliable, yet unrecorded, statements will not occur frequently when compliance is widespread.[33]

Despite what we have said thus far, we recognize that nearly every rule must have its exceptions, and that exclusion of a defendant's statements in certain instances would be wholly unreasonable. A violation of the *Mallott* rule does not, therefore, require exclusion of the defendant's statements in all cases. Thus, the holding in this case does not bar the admission of statements obtained before a violation of the recording rule occurs. Where recording ceases for some impermissible reason, properly recorded statements made prior to the time recording stops may be admitted, even when the failure to record the balance of the interrogation is unexcused, since such prior statements could not be tainted by anything that occurred thereafter. Also, failure to record part of an interrogation does not bar the introduction of a defendant's recorded statements, if the unrecorded portion of the interrogation is, by all accounts, innocuous. In such cases, there is no reason to

33. Caveat: We recognize that many custodial interrogations must take place in the field, where recording may not be feasible. Because of this, the rule that we announce today has limited application; it applies only to custodial interrogations conducted in a place of detention, such as a police station or jail, where it is reasonable to assume that recording equipment is available, or can be made available with little effort. In a future case, however, we may be persuaded to extend the application of this rule, particularly if it appears that law enforcement officials are engaging in bad faith efforts to circumvent the recording requirement set forth in this opinion.

exclude the defendant's recorded statements, because no claim of material misconduct will be presented. See Alaska R. Crim. P. 47(a) (errors which do not affect substantial rights shall be disregarded). For the same reason, a defendant's unrecorded statement may be admitted if no testimony is presented that the statement is inaccurate or was obtained improperly, apart from violation of the *Mallott* rule. . . .

Notes

1. *Video recording as a constitutional requirement: majority position.* Only the Alaska Supreme Court has required that interrogations be recorded as a constitutional matter. Compare In re Jerrell C.J., 699 N.W.2d 110 (Wis. 2005) (under judicial supervisory power, court requires all station house custodial interrogations of juveniles to be electronically recorded). While the argument has been made in a number of jurisdictions, courts typically have not received it with any sympathy. See, e.g., Brashars v. Commonwealth, 25 S.W.3d 58 (Ky. 2000); State v. Lockhart, 4 A.3d 1176 (Conn. 2010). After *Stephan* was decided the Minnesota Supreme Court, relying on its supervisory authority, mandated recordings of "custodial interrogations" when they occur "at a place of detention." See State v. Scales, 518 N.W.2d 587, 592 (Minn. 1994). Other courts have indicated that recording will weigh strongly in favor of findings of voluntariness.

Was it appropriate for the Alaska Supreme Court to "warn" police and prosecutors about the possibility of a judicially mandated rule unless a recording rule was adopted voluntarily? Would a long history *of Miranda* and voluntariness violations in a particular state provide a justification for a state court to mandate a recording rule? Can constitutional remedies be supported by the failure of all other remedies to end or diminish serious constitutional violations? See People v. Cahan, reprinted in Chapter 6 (arguing that the exclusionary rule was necessary because no other remedy had worked to control police searches and seizures).

2. *Video recording as a statutory requirement.* Texas is one of only a few states in which the legislature has implemented a statutory video recording requirement. See Brandon Garrett, Judging Innocence, 108 Colum. L. Rev. 55, 123 (2008) (documents spreading use of video recorded interrogations in police departments, and legislation in six jurisdictions — the District of Columbia, Illinois, Maine, New Mexico, Texas, and North Carolina — requiring video recording of interrogations for at least some categories of investigations). It may be easy to understand why other states have not been swayed by the Alaska decision in *Stephan* to mandate recording as a constitutional matter, but why have states been reluctant to mandate recording by statute? Why not video record every interrogation and confession? Do police departments think use of video recording will lead to fewer confessions? Do legislatures think that video recording policies should be left to local police and prosecutors to implement? If you drafted a new law requiring that in general interrogations and confessions be video recorded, what requirements, exceptions, and limitations would you include?

3. *Police discretion to video record interrogations and confessions.* A 1990 survey showed that about one-sixth of the 14,000 police and sheriffs' departments, and one-third of the 710 departments serving populations over 50,000, video recorded some interrogations or confessions. William Geller, Videotaping Interrogations and Confessions: NIJ Research in Brief (NCJ 139962, 1993). Given the prevalence of the

technology and prominent recommendations for its use, video recording of interrogations and confessions may now be even more likely to happen. The use of DNA evidence to establish definitively that false confession led to a surprising number of wrongful convictions has added momentum to the voluntary adoption of video recording by police departments. See Jeremy W. Peters, "Wrongful Conviction Prompts Detroit Police to Videotape Certain Interrogations," N.Y. Times, April 11, 2006 (at least 450 police departments in United States record interrogations, in some cases prompted by concerns about false confessions).

Periodic surveys of law enforcement agencies find that they record interrogations most often in homicide and rape investigations and for other serious crimes. The officers in jurisdictions that use video recording believe that it leads to better preparation by detectives and better monitoring of detectives' work by supervisors. They also believe that it produces stronger evidence of guilt and induces more guilty pleas. Most agencies find suspects less willing to talk when video recording takes place. Not surprisingly, surveys find that video recording leads to fewer claims against police that they had coerced or intimidated a suspect or fabricated a confession. Prosecutors are generally more supportive of video recording interrogations than are defense attorneys, who find video recordings harder to attack than written or audio recorded confessions. Detectives tend at first to disapprove of recording, but most jurisdictions find a strong shift among detectives in favor of recording once they had experience with its use. See Thomas P. Sullivan, et al., The Case for Recording Police Interrogations, Litigation, Volume 34, Number 3 (Spring 2008) (telephone survey of more than 600 departments that record interrogations).

4. *Administrative issues in recording.* Most police departments record interrogations openly or ask the subject about recording. Some police departments, however, use surreptitious recording equipment. Such practices reduce the chance that the use of video recording will discourage suspects from confessing (since they will not know they are being recorded). What reasons might there be not to record surreptitiously? See Matthews v. Commonwealth, 168 S.W.3d 14 (Ky. 2005) (police interrogators may lie to suspect about whether they are recording his statements). Must police record the whole interrogation, or is it necessary to record only the defendant's confession and summary after interrogation? Suppose the interrogation takes seven hours but the summary only 30 minutes. Should the cost of the recording medium factor into the decision whether to record the entire confession? What about the cost of making transcripts? Does the emergence of technology that automatically makes a rough transcription of speech ironically make recording interrogations more functional? See State v. Barnett, 789 A.2d 629 (N.H. 2001) (under supervisory power, court requires any video recording of interrogation admitted into evidence to be complete). In some jurisdictions defense counsel are not given immediate access to recorded interrogations and confessions. Some prosecutors show defense counsel recorded confessions but object to making copies. Other jurisdictions do not give defense counsel access to video recordings until after indictment or for a period of time after the interrogation.

5. *Is video recording an "alternative" to* Miranda? What would be the judicial response to fully video recorded but unwarned confessions in a jurisdiction whose legislature took the U.S. Supreme Court's invitation and passed a mandatory recording statute expressly to take the place of *Miranda* warnings in protecting each suspect's Fifth Amendment rights? Is there any reason not to record interrogations and confessions along with providing *Miranda* warnings? Would you expect foreign

jurisdictions, without the constraints or protections of *Miranda,* to be more or less hesitant to adopt recording procedures? The 1991 Code of Practice for Interrogation in England requires that all interviews be recorded, wherever they occur, unless it is impracticable to do so. See M. McConville & P. Morrell, Recording the Interrogation: Have the Police Got It Taped?, 1983 Crim. L. Rev. 159 (noting an increase after appearance of Code of Practice in spontaneous confessions allegedly spoken before the video was running); Paul Marcus & Vicki Waye, Australia and the United States: Two Common Criminal Justice Systems Uncommonly at Odds, 12 Tulane J. Int'l & Comp. L. 27 (2004).

6. *Confessions, lies, and video recording.* Recording interrogations and confessions seems to solve a number of problems, such as reducing or eliminating the frequent claims by suspects that they were threatened or that they did not in fact confess or say what the police say they did. But does recording make all confessions look voluntary even when they have been compelled by forces not visible (or audible) on the recording? Won't recording create a whole new set of factual issues about whether the recording is complete? Is taping of interrogations and confessions a great reform for a past era?

Perhaps it is not the requirement of warnings but the content of the warnings that needs rethinking. Consider the following reform in Great Britain and its implications for the warnings offered suspects during investigations.

■ UNITED KINGDOM, CRIMINAL JUSTICE AND PUBLIC ORDER ACT OF 1994, §34

(1) Where, in any proceedings against a person for an offence, evidence is given that the accused . . . at any time before he was charged with the offence, on being questioned under caution by a constable trying to discover whether or by whom the offence had been committed, failed to mention any fact relied on in his defence in those proceedings . . . being a fact which in the circumstances existing at the time the accused could reasonably have been expected to mention when so questioned, charged or informed, as the case may be, subsection (2) below applies.

(2) Where this subsection applies . . . the court, in determining whether there is a case to answer; [or] the court or jury, in determining whether the accused is guilty of the offence charged, may draw such inferences from the failure as appear proper.

Notes

1. *Warnings in Great Britain and elsewhere in Europe.* Great Britain changed the law relating to the warnings that suspects must receive before interrogation. Under the old law (which goes back to the nineteenth century and was embodied in the Police and Criminal Evidence Act of 1984), suspects were told, "You do not have to say anything unless you wish to do so, but what you say may be given in evidence." The 1984 act (and the related Code of Practice promulgated by the government a year later) also required that the police inform suspects in custody that they have a right to consult an attorney before any interrogation, that the police make available a

"duty solicitor" for suspects who want advice, and that the warnings be given both orally and in writing. How does the 1994 statute, reprinted above, change these practices?

Some form of warnings about the right to silence and the consequences of speaking (or not speaking) are now standard practice in many European nations. For instance, suspects in France are informed of the right to silence and to consult counsel during detention, but they are not entitled to have counsel present during interrogation. In Germany, police must inform suspects of the right to remain silent when they become the focus of an investigation. The warnings also inform suspects of their right to consult a defense attorney *prior* to interrogation, although there is no right to counsel during interrogation. If the suspect chooses to remain silent, police may continue to question the suspect. German courts prohibit the police from making affirmative misrepresentations during interrogations. See Christopher Slobogin, An Empirically Based Comparison of American and European Regulatory Approaches to Police Investigation, 22 Mich. J. Int'l L. 423, 442-45 (2001); Stephen C. Thaman, *Miranda* in Comparative Law, 45 St. Louis U. L.J. 581 (2001).

2. *Warnings about silence*. Would the 1994 English statute be consistent with the Fifth Amendment to the U.S. Constitution? Would it have any effect on the everyday practices of criminal investigators? Should the Fifth Amendment also require a warning to a suspect that "silence cannot be used against you"?

IX

Identifications

Eyewitnesses to crime can provide some of the most convincing evidence to support a conviction. This is especially true when the physical evidence linking the defendant to the crime is thin, or when the offender is a stranger to others at the scene (as in many robbery cases). All too often, however, this important evidence turns out to be unreliable. How do legal institutions respond to the special value and risks of eyewitness identifications?

This chapter explores this question. Section A reviews some of the psychological literature detailing the risks of eyewitness identifications. Section B surveys the conditions that lead courts to exclude evidence coming from in-person identifications (both in the field and at the police station) and from identifications of photographs. Section C considers the remedies other than exclusion of evidence that are available to a defendant who believes that an identification procedure was unreliable.

A. RISKS OF MISTAKEN IDENTIFICATION

Eyewitnesses are wrong in a disturbing number of cases. One famous example involves the case of Ronald Cotton. One night in 1984, a man broke into the apartment of Jennifer Thompson, who was then a 22-year-old college student in Burlington, North Carolina. The intruder raped Thompson. When police received an anonymous tip in the case, they showed Thompson several photographs of potential suspects, and she picked the photograph of Ronald Cotton. Cotton was a plausible suspect, who had been convicted in 1980 of attempted rape and had recently been released from prison. Although there was no physical evidence linking

Cotton to the crime, the jury convicted based on Thompson's confident identification of Cotton during the trial as the man who had raped her. The judge sentenced him to 50 years in prison. Eleven years later, lawyers for Cotton arranged for DNA tests on some of the physical evidence in the case. The tests conclusively established that Cotton was the wrong man. The evidence pointed instead to Bobby Poole — already convicted and serving a prison term for another sexual assault — and Poole later confessed to the rape of Thompson. Jennifer Thompson-Cannino, Ronald Cotton, & Erin Torneo, Picking Cotton: Our Memoir of Injustice and Redemption (2009).

One famous example, of course, does not tell us how often the problem arises in criminal justice systems that produce millions of criminal convictions each year. How often does a mistaken identification lead to an erroneous conviction? Nobody really knows since we have no convincing way to identify all the wrongful convictions.

It is possible, however, to estimate the importance of mistaken identifications *relative to other causes* of the wrongful convictions we have learned about over the years. Over the last few years, the widespread availability of DNA testing has confirmed many examples of wrongful convictions. Far and away the most common cause of these errors is mistaken identifications by eyewitnesses. See Brandon L. Garrett, Convicting the Innocent: Where Criminal Prosecutions Go Wrong (2011).

Psychologists have studied witness memory in great detail over the years. The following summary of psychological research may suggest some of the reasons why eyewitness identifications sometimes lead to erroneous convictions. Given the commonplace nature of these identification errors, what are the implications for legal systems? What changes in the pertinent rules might address these predictable failures of witnesses?

■ RALPH NORMAN HABER AND LYN HABER, EXPERIENCING, REMEMBERING AND REPORTING EVENTS

6 Psychol. Pub. Pol'y & L. 1057-91 (2000)

[Consider] the following description of a bank robbery, drawn from actual cases. Several men entered a bank, tied up the only guard in the lobby, told the customers to lie down on the floor, and demanded that the tellers hand over all their money. The robbers then left. There were five tellers, two officers, one guard, and five customers in the bank at the time. When the police took their statements over the next hour, there was little consensus among the thirteen witnesses as to the number of robbers, what they looked like, what they did, the presence of weapons, or the duration of the robbery.

Video cameras in the bank recorded the robbery. Comparing these recordings to the descriptions provided by the witnesses, it was found that no single witness gave an accurate report of the sequence of events, nor did any single witness provide a consistently accurate description of any of the robbers. Further, in subsequent photo identification line-ups, half of the witnesses made serious errors: Four of the thirteen witnesses erroneously selected as a perpetrator one of the other people who had been in the bank at the time of the robbery (a teller or a customer), and three of the thirteen erroneously selected a photograph of someone who had not been there at all at the time. All seven of these witnesses asserted that they were sure they had correctly identified one of the robbers and that they were willing to so testify. . . .

The purpose of this article is to summarize the scientific evidence on the accuracy of eyewitness testimony, with specific attention to the factors that enhance or impair the likelihood of accuracy. . . .

Observing and Encoding Events into Memory

In this first section, we consider the factors that might lead witnesses to make and remember differing observations of the same event. . . .

Observational point of view. In the bank robbery described earlier, the customers forced to lie down on the floor had less opportunity to view from the front those robbers who approached the teller booths, whereas some of the tellers had frontal views. Therefore, those tellers should be able to give more detailed descriptions of the appearance of those robbers, and in the absence of other factors, those descriptions are more likely to be accurate. It is critical in evaluating a witness's statements about an event to be sure that the witness had a sufficient opportunity to view the event from a position consistent with the statements being given. . . . In addition to distance, lighting conditions, especially back lighting, reflections, and shadows impact the ability to see fine details. . . .

Allocation of Attention. Attention is memory's gatekeeper. At any moment your five senses are bombarded with vast amounts of external stimulation. [For] encoding to occur, you must attend to [stimulation] during the time it impinges on your senses. [The] deployment of attention has two consequences: it allows you to encode and retain memory of some aspects of what happens to you, and it allows the remainder to slip away and be lost forever.

[You] can switch attention quickly. Any change in stimulation, such as a loud noise, or a movement off to the side, will cause you to orient your attention to it. That re-orientation allows you to encode sudden changes in what is happening, though at the expense of what you had been attending to just previously, which then stops being accessible for encoding into memory. When driving comfortably, it is possible to divide your attention so you can control the car while conversing with a passenger. However, a sudden squeal of brakes refocuses your attention exclusively on the emergency, and you cannot remember what your passenger said during that interval.

This focusing is not simply like moving your eyes. [What] you as an observer will encode about an event depends on where and how your attention is focused, not just where you happen to be looking. Most important, it is possible for events to occur directly in front of you, well within your range of seeing and hearing, and yet make no impact on your memory if you were attending to something else at the time. . . .

Bias in Attentional Focus. [Frequently] some aspect of an event causes an involuntary narrowing of attention to some particular detail, so much so that other parts of the event are not attended to at all, and therefore not encoded into memory. One area of great legal importance concerns the narrowing of attention that occurs for most witnesses when they detect the presence of a weapon. People focus their attention on the weapon so much that almost everything else that's happening goes unnoticed and therefore unremembered. . . . Specifically, scientific research on "weapon focus" has shown that, when a weapon is present, witnesses are far less able to remember distinctive features of the people present, including those of the person holding the weapon. Hence, a witness's chances of making a correct identification of a person are reduced if that person held a weapon.

It is equally likely that a narrowing of attention will occur, with its concomitant loss in encoding, whenever any component of the event is highly dramatic, frightening, violent, or distasteful to the witness. It should always be assumed that violence in any form narrows attention, and that which is outside the resultant narrowed attention is encoded less completely, if at all. . . .

Knowledge, Familiarity, and Expertise with the Content of the Event. In the course of everyday life, you are highly familiar with aspects of your work, both inside your home and at your jobsite. If you work as a supermarket clerk, you are likely to be far more knowledgeable than most people about a wide range of edible products; if you are a car salesman, you know a lot about the makes of cars. Within your own sphere, you are an expert. Bystander-witnesses are often required to testify about details of what they observed, such as the characteristics of a vehicle or a weapon. If the eyewitness has little knowledge of that class of objects, the witness's reports about the object are often incomplete or simply wrong. . . .

Similarly, lack of familiarity has been demonstrated in scientific experiments to lead to inaccurate identification of people. The adage that "all Asians look alike (to non-Asians)" is in fact mostly true. In experiments on cross-racial identification, in which the race of the criminal is different from that of the witness and the witness has few close interactions with people of that race, the witness cannot provide as many identifying features of the criminal he observed, thereby making it less likely that subsequent identifications will be accurate. . . .

Witness Expectations and Interpretation of the Event. Research has shown that the beliefs of the witness produce fundamental changes in the reports of what was observed. For example, one study [from 1947] concerned with racial prejudice asked subjects/witnesses to view a scene depicting two men in which one man held a knife: The witnesses were to describe the scene to other people who had not seen it. The two critical contents of the scene that were varied were whether both men were the same race and which one held the knife. When both men were of the same race, nearly all witnesses correctly described the critical element of who held the knife, as well as most of the details of dress and the position of the two men. However, if one man was Black and one White, most witnesses (Black and White alike) reported that the Black man held the knife even when it was held by the White man. Some witnesses who correctly described who held the knife incorrectly added that the White man was defending himself (there was nothing in either man's posture or position to suggest this conclusion). All of the witnesses stated that they believed that crimes were more likely to be committed by Blacks than by Whites. The results suggest that eyewitnesses sometimes encode and remember the event so as to be consistent with their beliefs rather than the way it actually happened. . . .

Remembering Events

Experts on memory research refer to a witness's first report of an observed event, when it is given after the event, as an independent memory. . . . A witness's independent memory report of an event is normally the most accurate description the witness will ever be able to produce. . . .

In normal life, your own independent memories often undergo influences that, in psychological parlance, "taint" them: You dress your stories up for your listeners who did not observe the events, and you discuss the events with other people who also observed them and you incorporate what they say as part of your memory. A tainted memory is not necessarily a false or inaccurate memory, but it is no longer your own, original, independent encoding of the event. It is a compendium of information and detail, some of which you yourself did not see or remember. In this respect, it is analogous to hearsay. . . .

The Inevitably Wrong Focus of Autobiographical Memory. . . . Typically, as an event unfolds, you as an observer are not thinking about describing the other people and their actions: you see the event in terms of how it affects you. The event has all of the properties of a story, with a beginning, middle, and end, and a sequence of actions with one or more actors. The most important actor — the protagonist in your story — is you. . . . As an example of how an eyewitness describes events from a personal point of view, consider one of the eyewitness accounts from a woman who was in the bank described above:

> I stopped at the bank to cash a check. I was putting the money in my purse when armed men ran into the bank, waved their guns at everyone and ordered me to lie down on the floor. One gigantic man, who looked like a football player, stepped over me and I was afraid he would take all of the money I just got I was so scared he would hurt me. He went to the same teller who had just helped me, threatened her with his pistol, and stuffed what she handed him into his bag. After what seemed like hours of terror, all the robbers ran out. They didn't take my money.

This report has little helpful content for the policeman who wants to identify the robbers. The policeman asked her: How many robbers were there? Which ones had guns? What did each of the robbers look like? What were they wearing? What did each of the other robbers do? Every investigator and every interrogator forces the witness to switch from "What happened to you?" to "What happened in the bank?" Hence, almost immediately, the eyewitness is required to change from an autobiographical and psychological focus to an objective focus. This translation usually produces changes in the report, changes that may introduce inaccuracies about the physical reality. . . . In trying to answer the interrogator's questions, the witness often adds content and details that "must have happened" — details not present in independent memory. . . .

Systematic Changes in the Content of Memory with Each Repetition. Unlike a video recording, which remains the same each time it is played, memory undergoes changes with rehearsal. [Each] further repetition of the report produces predictable changes in the report. These predictable changes are, first, that many of the details drop out of the subsequent reports altogether and are never reported again and, second, that other details are altered or additions are made to fit more consistently with the overall description provided by the observer. . . . Further, not surprisingly, observers also are shown to alter their descriptions depending on the audience to whom they are speaking. . . .

These facts about alterations of memory produced by rehearsal are particularly relevant to testimony made by witnesses in court. By the time the witness reaches the stand and is questioned by counsel, she has told her story dozens of times. Often, the first time the story is told is to other observers or to the first new arrivals at the scene. That description, the closest one available from the independent memory of the observer, is usually unrecorded. The first recorded description, taken down by one of the officers at the scene, may already have undergone many changes after several prior rehearsals, each with its smoothings, rearrangements of facts, and attempts to be congruent with what has been learned from other witnesses. This is only the beginning of the rehearsals required of the witness. More than one policeman will demand a repetition; then come the investigators and the lawyers. . . .

Post-Event Information Can Create New (and Potentially) False Memories. The single most dramatic finding in recent memory research concerns changes in reports made by witnesses when other people give them information. Two insidious facts have emerged: First, witnesses are unaware that they have acquired new information from somebody else — the information is treated as if it were part of what they themselves originally observed; and second, witnesses usually are unaware that they have changed their report based on that new information. . . .

Consider some findings from recent research: (a) Embedding a false presupposition into a question (asking "Did the red car stop or run the light just before the crash?" when the car's color has not been previously specified) will often change the witness's subsequent testimony as to the color of the car; (b) varying the intensity of verbs in a question (asking "Did the car hit . . . , Did the car collide . . . , Did the car smash . . . , Did the car demolish . . . ?") will often change the witness's subsequent testimony about the speed of the car; (c) showing a witness line-up pictures of people not involved in the observed event will often result in the witness subsequently choosing one of those innocent people as the criminal, even when the real criminal is present in the later line-up; (d) allowing the witness to overhear a new or different description about the event or about the persons involved will often lead the witness to include the divergent information in subsequent testimony. . . .

Why is it so easy for post-event information to become incorporated into memory? Research has shown that the main reason is that human beings do not have a particularly good memory for the sources of their knowledge about events. When you acquire information about an event from several sources, regardless of how accurate you are in remembering the information itself, you are less accurate about remembering from which source you acquired it. . . .

Encoding, Remembering, and Identifying Strangers

In the preceding sections, we have discussed memory processes without differentiating between memory of events and memory of people. An eyewitness is frequently required to identify an unfamiliar person who might have perpetrated a crime. Such identifications often comprise the only evidence against the defendant. In this section, we focus specifically on what is known about the accuracy of a witness's identification of unfamiliar people from memory. . . .

In a large number of controlled experiments, witnesses have been asked to observe a realistic enactment of a crime committed by a stranger and then to give descriptions of the criminal. Then, after differing periods of time, these witnesses have been asked to attempt to identify whether the perpetrator they observed is present in a line-up. The observation factors studied have included the type of event being observed, length of time of observation, distance and viewing conditions, amount of activity by the stranger, presence of a weapon, presence of frightening events, number of different strangers, amount of stress felt by the eyewitness, and post-event exposure to other people who had been present at the event or who talk to the eyewitness about the event.

[Consider] identification accuracy for research line-ups that are constructed with the known perpetrator present. The first kind of accuracy of concern is whether the witness can discriminate between the true perpetrator and the remaining foils who are innocent of the crime. Based on a large number of experiments, about 75% of the time the perpetrator is correctly selected (true positive); the remaining 25% of the time the witness identifies someone who either was not present at the crime scene, or was a bystander at the scene, but not the criminal (false positive). If no weapon is present, no violence, no bystanders, no post-event contamination, and little delay, true-positive rates can approach 90% (with false-positive rates dropping to a low of about 10%). Conversely, if a weapon is present, the scene is violent, bystanders are present, post-event information is available, the witness feels great stress, and there is a long time delay between observation and identification, the true-positive rate for correct identification of the perpetrator drops well below 50%, with the false-positive rate exceeding 50%. These percentages just quoted are rough consensual estimates, based on the results of perhaps 100 experiments with line-ups. . . .

The fallibility of the eyewitness becomes even more evident when results of lineup research are considered in which the perpetrator is known not to be in the lineup. Now the correct response for the eyewitness is to say "no," none of the people in the line-up is the perpetrator. The results show that, on average, under normal observation conditions, eyewitnesses still say "yes" (that someone present is the perpetrator) about 60% of the time when the perpetrator is known to be absent! All of these "yes" responses are false positives: The eyewitness has identified an innocent person. Only under the most favorable observation conditions (as described in the previous section) is there some reduction in the false-positive rates (with the perpetrator absent). Even more seriously, "yes" responses are found to increase to a high of 90% (a 90% false-positive rate of identifying an innocent person incorrectly as the perpetrator who committed the crime) when the observation conditions are poor, and the eyewitness is led to believe that the perpetrator is present. . . .

We have presented an array of scientific research evidence showing that, by the time an eyewitness testifies in court, the identification and testimony offered may not accurately reflect either what actually happened, or what was originally observed. . . . The recent examples of DNA evidence being used to reverse convictions that had been originally based on only eyewitness identifications suggest that there are in fact many innocent people who have been wrongly convicted on the basis of erroneous eyewitness testimony. . . .

Notes

1. *Relative importance of different memory problems.* The psychological studies described above identify problems at the encoding, storage, and retrieval phases of memory that might affect the accuracy of an eyewitness identification. Which of the various problems a witness might encounter will have the largest impact on the memory? In one effort to answer this question, researchers performed a statistical analysis (known as a "meta-analysis") on the results of more than 190 studies of eyewitness performance. The analysis measured the relative effects of many different obstacles and aids to accurate memory. The authors concluded that "context

reinstatement" was among the most important contributing factors to an accurate identification: For instance, if the target was placed in the same pose at the initial exposure and at the later time of recognition (or asked to wear a distinctive piece of clothing or speak words that the witness recalled from the original incident), the accuracy of the witness identifications increased. The other factors having the largest effect on witness accuracy include the distinctiveness of the target, exposure time, age of the witness, cross-racial identification, and amount of time elapsed between the original event and the recognition exercise. See Peter Shapiro & Steven Penrod, Meta-Analysis of Facial Identification Studies, 100 Psychol. Bull. 139 (1986). For a sampling of the rich psychological literature on eyewitness observation and memory, consult the web extension for this chapter at *http://www.crimpro.com/extension/ch09*.

The psychological experiments described above test human memory, but they often take place in a setting different from what an actual crime victim might face. What might those differences be? Would they make a crime witness more or less likely than an experimental "subject" to give an accurate identification?

2. *Cross-racial identifications*. Unfortunately, there is some truth to the distasteful phrase, "They [people of another race] all look alike." Research studies for over thirty years have found an empirical basis for saying that people of one race find it more difficult to identify people of another race. A witness's difficulty in making such identifications seems to be tied to unfamiliarity: People who have more regular contact with those of another race have less difficulty making such identifications. The so-called "own-race bias" accounts for about 15 percent of the variation in the ability of witnesses to identify another person. See Christian A. Meissner & John C. Brigham, Eyewitness Identification: Thirty Years of Investigating the Own-Race Bias in Memory for Faces: A Meta-Analytic Review, 7 Psychol. Pub. Pol'y & L. 3 (2001).

3. *Individual recognition skills and witness certainty*. It is important to remember that these difficulties with memory address only trends and averages: Any individual witness might be affected less (or more) by such problems. Unfortunately, it is difficult to determine whether a particular witness is above average or below average in her ability to identify a crime suspect. The age of a witness is one of the few consistently helpful indicators: Children tend to make less accurate identifications, mostly because they are substantially more suggestible than adults. See M. Bruck & S. J. Ceci, The Description of Children's Suggestibility, in Memory for Everyday and Emotional Events (Stein, Ornstein, Tversky & Brainerd eds., 1997). Witnesses over 70 are less accurate when describing events that are especially unfamiliar, or those that unfold quickly with many distractions present. See Daniel Yarmey, The Elderly Witness, in Psychological Issues in Eyewitness Identification (Sporer, Malpass & Koehnken eds., 1996).

One might be tempted to rely on the witness's level of certainty to identify the most "able" witnesses, i.e., the witness who says, "I'm absolutely sure it was him." But witness certainty, it turns out, is not a good measure of accuracy. As one summary of the psychological literature put it, "[The] eyewitness accuracy-confidence relationship is weak under good laboratory conditions and functionally useless in forensically representative settings." Gary Wells & Donna Murray, Eyewitness Confidence, in Eyewitness Testimony: Psychological Perspectives 155 (Gary Wells & Elizabeth Loftus eds., 1984).

4. *Police officers as witnesses.* Sometimes the witness to a crime is a police officer, who may have special training in facial recognition techniques. Does the special training and experience of police officers increase their accuracy as eyewitnesses? The evidence on this question is equivocal. On the one hand, police officers (as well as untrained witnesses) tend to have more complete and accurate memories if they are able to anticipate an event and know that they will later need to recall it accurately. A police officer may be in a good position to anticipate the need for later recall. On the other hand, a number of studies have concluded that police officers and others with special training fare no better than other witnesses under realistic eyewitness conditions.

5. *Early forgetting.* Some of the earliest research in memory showed that more forgetting happens early. We forget very rapidly immediately after an event — usually within a few hours — but forgetting becomes more and more gradual as time passes. See Elizabeth Loftus, Eyewitness Testimony 21-83 (1979). What are the implications of this research for police work?

6. *Words and memory.* Some memory problems arise simply from the fact that investigators ask the witness to express the memory in words. Laboratory studies found that memories for a mock criminal's face were much poorer among eyewitnesses who had described what the perpetrator looked like shortly after seeing him compared with those who had not formulated a description in words. The problem is known as "verbal overshadowing of visual memories." Bruce Bower, Words Get in the Way: Talk Is Cheap, but It Can Tax Your Memory, Science News, April 19, 2003.

B. EXCLUSION OF IDENTIFICATION EVIDENCE

Witnesses identify potential suspects in several settings. The most formal identification procedures — and the easiest to subject to legal controls — occur in the police station. The "lineup" places a small group of persons before the witness; the witness is asked if any person in the lineup is the person who committed the crime. In another identification technique that often takes place in a police station, the witness reviews photographs of different persons to identify a suspect. Finally, there are "confrontations" or "showups," in which the police ask the witness to view the suspect alone. This sort of identification occurs most frequently in the field, near the crime scene, but it can also occur at the station.

Until the mid-1960s, the legal system relied on adversarial testing of evidence to control these identification procedures. If a "showup" produced unreliable evidence, defense counsel was expected to point this out. But in recent decades, federal and state constitutions (and to a lesser extent, statutes and court rules) have required the exclusion of some evidence obtained during identification procedures. The constitutional controls derive from (1) the right to counsel clauses and (2) the due process clauses of the federal and state constitutions. Courts have declared a select group of identification procedures invalid unless they take place with counsel for the defendant present. For a larger group of identification procedures, defendants make claims based on the due process clause, arguing that the identifications were too unreliable to be admitted as evidence. The following materials explore the right-to-counsel and due process limitations in several common settings.

1. *Exclusion on Right to Counsel Grounds*

The Sixth Amendment to the U.S. Constitution provides that "In all criminal prosecutions, the accused shall . . . have the Assistance of Counsel for his defence." Every state constitution except one (Virginia's) also provides explicitly for legal counsel in criminal cases. A number describe the point at which the right to counsel attaches by using phrases such as "appear" or "defend," as in New York's article I, section 6: "In any trial in any court whatever the party accused shall be allowed to appear and defend in person and with counsel. . . ." Others speak in terms of a right to be "heard" through counsel, as in New Hampshire's article 15: "Every subject shall have a right . . . to be fully heard in his defense, by himself, and counsel." In what way are these constitutional provisions relevant to police efforts to obtain eyewitness identifications of suspects?

■ UNITED STATES v. BILLY JOE WADE

388 U.S. 218 (1967)

BRENNAN, J.*

The question here is whether courtroom identifications of an accused at trial are to be excluded from evidence because the accused was exhibited to the witnesses before trial at a post-indictment lineup conducted for identification purposes without notice to and in the absence of the accused's appointed counsel.

The federally insured bank in Eustace, Texas, was robbed on September 21, 1964. A man with a small strip of tape on each side of his face entered the bank, pointed a pistol at the female cashier and the vice president, the only persons in the bank at the time, and forced them to fill a pillowcase with the bank's money. [Wade was indicted for the robbery on March 23, 1965, and arrested on April 2. Counsel was appointed to represent him on April 26.] Fifteen days later an FBI agent, without notice to Wade's lawyer, arranged to have the two bank employees observe a lineup made up of Wade and five or six other prisoners and conducted in a courtroom of the local county courthouse. Each person in the line wore strips of tape such as allegedly worn by the robber and upon direction each said something like "put the money in the bag," the words allegedly uttered by the robber. Both bank employees identified Wade in the lineup as the bank robber.

At trial, the two employees, when asked on direct examination if the robber was in the courtroom, pointed to Wade. The prior lineup identification was then elicited from both employees on cross-examination. At the close of testimony, Wade's counsel moved for a judgment of acquittal or, alternatively, to strike the bank officials' courtroom identifications on the ground that conduct of the lineup, without notice to and in the absence of his appointed counsel, violated his . . . Sixth Amendment right to the assistance of counsel. The motion was denied, and Wade was convicted. . . .

* [Justice Clark joined in this opinion. Chief Justice Warren and Justices Douglas and Fortas joined in this opinion except for part I, which is not reprinted here. Justice Black joined in parts II through IV of this opinion. Justices White, Harlan, and Stewart joined in parts I and III of this opinion. — EDS.]

II.

. . . The Framers of the Bill of Rights envisaged a broader role for counsel than under the practice then prevailing in England of merely advising his client in "matters of law," and eschewing any responsibility for "matters of fact." The constitutions in at least 11 of the 13 States expressly or impliedly abolished this distinction. . . .

When the Bill of Rights was adopted, there were no organized police forces as we know them today. The accused confronted the prosecutor and the witnesses against him, and the evidence was marshalled, largely at the trial itself. In contrast, today's law enforcement machinery involves critical confrontations of the accused by the prosecution at pretrial proceedings where the results might well settle the accused's fate and reduce the trial itself to a mere formality. In recognition of these realities of modern criminal prosecution, our cases have construed the Sixth Amendment guarantee to apply to "critical" stages of the proceedings. The guarantee reads: "In all criminal prosecutions, the accused shall enjoy the right . . . to have the Assistance of Counsel for his defence." The plain wording of this guarantee thus encompasses counsel's assistance whenever necessary to assure a meaningful "defence." . . . The presence of counsel at such critical confrontations, as at the trial itself, operates to assure that the accused's interests will be protected consistently with our adversary theory of criminal prosecution. . . .

III.

The Government characterizes the lineup as a mere preparatory step in the gathering of the prosecution's evidence, not different — for Sixth Amendment purposes — from various other preparatory steps, such as systematized or scientific analyzing of the accused's fingerprints, blood sample, clothing, hair, and the like. We think there are differences which preclude such stages being characterized as critical stages at which the accused has the right to the presence of his counsel. Knowledge of the techniques of science and technology is sufficiently available, and the variables in techniques few enough, that the accused has the opportunity for a meaningful confrontation of the Government's case at trial through the ordinary processes of cross-examination of the Government's expert witnesses and the presentation of the evidence of his own experts. . . .

IV.

But the confrontation compelled by the State between the accused and the victim or witnesses to a crime to elicit identification evidence is peculiarly riddled with innumerable dangers and variable factors which might seriously, even crucially, derogate from a fair trial. The vagaries of eyewitness identification are well-known; the annals of criminal law are rife with instances of mistaken identification. . . . A major factor contributing to the high incidence of miscarriage of justice from mistaken identification has been the degree of suggestion inherent in the manner in which the prosecution presents the suspect to witnesses for pretrial identification. [It] is a matter of common experience that, once a witness has picked out the accused at the lineup, he is not likely to go back on his word later on, so that in practice the issue of identity may (in the absence of other relevant evidence) for all practical purposes be determined there and then, before the trial.

[As] is the case with secret interrogations, there is serious difficulty in depicting what transpires at lineups and other forms of identification confrontations. [The] defense can seldom reconstruct the manner and mode of lineup identification for judge or jury at trial. Those participating in a lineup with the accused may often be police officers; in any event, the participants' names are rarely recorded or divulged at trial. The impediments to an objective observation are increased when the victim is the witness. Lineups are prevalent in rape and robbery prosecutions and present a particular hazard that a victim's understandable outrage may excite vengeful or spiteful motives. In any event, neither witnesses nor lineup participants are apt to be alert for conditions prejudicial to the suspect. . . . Improper influences may go undetected by a suspect, guilty or not, who experiences the emotional tension which we might expect in one being confronted with potential accusers. Even when he does observe abuse, if he has a criminal record he may be reluctant to take the stand and open up the admission of prior convictions. Moreover, any protestations by the suspect of the fairness of the lineup made at trial are likely to be in vain; the jury's choice is between the accused's unsupported version and that of the police officers present. In short, the accused's inability effectively to reconstruct at trial any unfairness that occurred at the lineup may deprive him of his only opportunity meaningfully to attack the credibility of the witness' courtroom identification. . . .

The potential for improper influence is illustrated by the circumstances, insofar as they appear, surrounding the prior identifications in the three cases we decide today. [The companion cases were Gilbert v. California, 388 U.S. 263 (1967), and Stovall v. Denno, 388 U.S. 293 (1967).] In the present case, the testimony of the identifying witnesses elicited on cross-examination revealed that those witnesses were taken to the courthouse and seated in the courtroom to await assembly of the lineup. The courtroom faced on a hallway observable to the witnesses through an open door. The cashier testified that she saw Wade "standing in the hall" within sight of an FBI agent. . . . The lineup in *Gilbert* was conducted in an auditorium in which some 100 witnesses to several alleged state and federal robberies charged to Gilbert made wholesale identifications of Gilbert as the robber in each other's presence, a procedure said to be fraught with dangers of suggestion. And the vice of suggestion created by the identification in *Stovall,* was the presentation to the witness of the suspect alone handcuffed to police officers. It is hard to imagine a situation more clearly conveying the suggestion to the witness that the one presented is believed guilty by the police. . . .

Insofar as the accused's conviction may rest on a courtroom identification in fact the fruit of a suspect pretrial identification which the accused is helpless to subject to effective scrutiny at trial, the accused is deprived of that right of cross-examination which is an essential safeguard to his right to confront the witnesses against him. . . . The trial which might determine the accused's fate may well not be that in the courtroom but that at the pretrial confrontation, with the State aligned against the accused, the witness the sole jury, and the accused unprotected against the overreaching, intentional or unintentional, and with little or no effective appeal from the judgment there rendered by the witness — "that's the man." . . .

No substantial countervailing policy considerations have been advanced against the requirement of the presence of counsel. Concern is expressed that the requirement will forestall prompt identifications and result in obstruction of the confrontations. As for the first, we note that in the two cases in which the right to counsel is today held to apply, counsel had already been appointed and no argument is made in either case that notice to counsel would have prejudicially delayed the confrontations. [Law] enforcement may be assisted by preventing the infiltration of taint in the prosecution's identification evidence. That result cannot help the guilty avoid conviction but can only help assure that the right man has been brought to justice.[29] Legislative or other regulations, such as those of local police departments, which eliminate the risks of abuse and unintentional suggestion at lineup proceedings and the impediments to meaningful confrontation at trial may also remove the basis for regarding the stage as "critical." But neither Congress nor the federal authorities have seen fit to provide a solution. What we hold today in no way creates a constitutional straitjacket which will handicap sound efforts at reform, nor is it intended to have this effect.

V.

We come now to the question whether the denial of Wade's motion to strike the courtroom identification by the bank witnesses at trial because of the absence of his counsel at the lineup required . . . the grant of a new trial at which such evidence is to be excluded. We do not think this disposition can be justified without first giving the Government the opportunity to establish by clear and convincing evidence that the in-court identifications were based upon observations of the suspect other than the lineup identification. [T]he appropriate procedure to be followed is to vacate the conviction pending a hearing to determine whether the in-court identifications had an independent source, or whether, in any event, the introduction of the evidence was harmless error, and for the District Court to reinstate the conviction or order a new trial, as may be proper. . . .

WHITE, J., dissenting in part and concurring in part.*

The Court has again propounded a broad constitutional rule barring use of a wide spectrum of relevant and probative evidence, solely because a step in its ascertainment or discovery occurs outside the presence of defense counsel. This was the approach of the Court in Miranda v. Arizona, 384 U.S. 436 (1966). I objected then to what I thought was an uncritical and doctrinaire approach without satisfactory factual foundation. I have much the same view of the present ruling and therefore dissent. . . .

The Court's opinion is far-reaching. . . . It matters not how well the witness knows the suspect, whether the witness is the suspect's mother, brother, or long-time associate, and no matter how long or well the witness observed the perpetrator at the scene of the crime. . . .

To find the lineup a "critical" stage of the proceeding and to exclude identifications made in the absence of counsel, the Court must [assume] that there is now no adequate source from which defense counsel can learn about the circumstances

29. Many other nations surround the lineup with safeguards against prejudice to the suspect. In England the suspect must be allowed the presence of his solicitor or a friend; Germany requires the presence of retained counsel; France forbids the confrontation of the suspect in the absence of his counsel; Spain, Mexico, and Italy provide detailed procedures prescribing the conditions under which confrontation must occur under the supervision of a judicial officer who sees to it that the proceedings are officially recorded to assure adequate scrutiny at trial.

* [Justices Harlan and Stewart joined in this opinion. — EDS.]

of the pretrial identification in order to place before the jury all of the considerations which should enter into an appraisal of courtroom identification evidence. But [I am not willing to assume] that the police and the witnesses will forget or prevaricate, that defense counsel will be unable to bring out the truth and that neither jury, judge, nor appellate court is a sufficient safeguard against unacceptable police conduct occurring at a pretrial identification procedure. I am unable to share the Court's view of the willingness of the police and the ordinary citizen-witness to dissemble. . . .

Identifications frequently take place after arrest but before an indictment is returned or an information is filed. The police may have arrested a suspect on probable cause but may still have the wrong man. Both the suspect and the State have every interest in a prompt identification at that stage, the suspect in order to secure his immediate release and the State because prompt and early identification enhances accurate identification and because it must know whether it is on the right investigative track. Unavoidably, however, the absolute rule requiring the presence of counsel will cause significant delay and it may very well result in no pretrial identification at all. . . . Nor do I think the witnesses themselves can be ignored. They will now be required to be present at the convenience of counsel rather than their own. Many may be much less willing to participate if the identification stage is transformed into an adversary proceeding not under the control of a judge. . . .

Finally, I think the Court's new rule is vulnerable in terms of its own unimpeachable purpose of increasing the reliability of identification testimony. Law enforcement officers have the obligation to convict the guilty and to make sure they do not convict the innocent. . . . To this extent, our so-called adversary system is not adversary at all; nor should it be. But defense counsel has no comparable obligation to ascertain or present the truth. Our system assigns him a different mission. [As] part of our modified adversary system and as part of the duty imposed on the most honorable defense counsel, we countenance or require conduct which in many instances has little, if any, relation to the search for truth. [Defense counsel] will not only observe what occurs and develop possibilities for later cross-examination but will hover over witnesses and begin their cross-examination then, menacing truthful factfinding as thoroughly as the Court fears the police now do. . . . In my view, the State is entitled to investigate and develop its case outside the presence of defense counsel. . . .

■ PEOPLE v. JONATHAN HICKMAN

684 N.W.2d 267 (Mich. 2004)

CORRIGAN, C.J.

In this case, we must determine when the right to counsel attaches to corporeal identifications. We adopt the analysis of Moore v. Illinois, 434 U.S. 220 (1977), and hold that the right to counsel attaches only to corporeal identifications conducted at or after the initiation of adversarial judicial criminal proceedings. To the extent that People v. Anderson, 205 N.W.2d 461 (Mich. 1973), goes beyond the constitutional text and extends the right to counsel to a time before the initiation of adversarial criminal proceedings, it is overruled. . . .

Factual History and Procedural Posture

Defendant was convicted of possession of a firearm during the commission or attempted commission of a felony, conspiracy, and armed robbery, for robbing the complainant of $26 and two two-way radios. The complainant testified that two men approached him from behind and robbed him. He testified that one of the men, later identified as defendant, pointed a gun at his face while the other person took the radios and money. The complainant then called the police and gave a description of the two men, as well as a description of the gun.

An officer soon saw a man fitting the description of the man with the gun. The man, later identified as defendant, was caught after a foot chase. During the chase, the police saw defendant throw something and they later recovered a chrome handgun that matched the complainant's description of the gun. Defendant was carrying one of the two-way radios.

Approximately ten minutes later, an officer took the complainant to a police car in which defendant was being held. The officer asked the complainant if the person sitting in the police car was involved in the robbery. The complainant immediately responded that defendant was the man who had the gun.

Defendant's motion to suppress an on-the-scene identification by the victim on the ground that defendant was not represented by counsel at the time of the identification was denied, and defendant was convicted. The Court of Appeals affirmed defendant's conviction. The Court held that the prompt on-the-scene identification did not offend the requirements set forth in *Anderson* and rejected defendants due process claim, holding that the identification was not unduly suggestive. Defendant appealed, and this Court granted leave, limited to the issue whether counsel is required before an on-the-scene identification can be admitted at trial. . . .

People v. Anderson

In *Anderson,* the right to counsel was extended to all pretrial corporeal identifications, including those occurring before the initiation of adversarial proceedings. This extension of United States v. Wade, 388 U.S. 218 (1967), to all pretrial identification procedures was based on "psychological principles," and "social science." Notably absent was any grounding in our federal constitution or state constitution. In People v. Jackson, 217 N.W.2d 22 (Mich. 1974), this Court acknowledged that the *Anderson* rules were not [mandated under the federal constitution]. The *Jackson* Court affirmed the *Anderson* rules, however, as an exercise of the Court's "constitutional power to establish rules of evidence applicable to judicial proceedings in Michigan courts and to preserve best evidence eyewitness testimony from unnecessary alteration by unfair identification procedures." Finally, in People v. Cheatham, 551 N.W.2d 355 (Mich. 1996), this Court noted in obiter dictum that the right to counsel under Const. 1963, art. 1, §20 "attaches only at or after the initiation of adversary judicial proceedings by way of formal charge, preliminary hearing, indictment, information, or arraignment." Thus, the *Anderson* rules lack a foundation in any constitutional provision, whether state or federal. Instead, the rules reflect the policy preferences of the *Anderson* Court. . . .

MOORE V. ILLINOIS

In *Moore,* the United States Supreme Court adopted the plurality opinion in Kirby v. Illinois, 406 U.S. 682 (1972), holding:

> [The] right to counsel announced in *Wade* and Gilbert v. California, 388 U.S. 263 (1967), attaches only to corporeal identifications conducted at or after the initiation of adversary judicial criminal proceedings — whether by way of formal charge, preliminary hearing, indictment, information, or arraignment . . . because the initiation of such proceedings marks the commencement of the criminal prosecutions to which alone the explicit guarantees of the Sixth Amendment are applicable.

The Court further noted that identifications conducted before the initiation of adversarial judicial criminal proceedings could still be challenged: "In such cases, however, *due process* protects the accused against the introduction of evidence of, or tainted by, unreliable pretrial identifications obtained through unnecessarily suggestive procedures." Therefore, it is now beyond question that, for federal Sixth Amendment purposes, the right to counsel attaches only at or after the initiation of adversarial judicial proceedings.

This conclusion is also consistent with our state constitutional provision, Const. 1963, art. 1, §20, which provides: "*In every criminal prosecution,* the accused shall have the right . . . to have the assistance of counsel for his or her defense. . . ." This Court has already noted . . . that a defendant's right to counsel under art. 1, §20 attaches only at or after the initiation of adversarial judicial proceedings. This Court also held in People v. Reichenbach, 587 N.W.2d 1 (Mich. 1998) [that] no peculiar state or local interests exist in Michigan to warrant a different level of protection with regard to the right to counsel in the instant case. Both the federal and the state provisions originated from the same concerns and to protect the same rights.

Because the *Moore* analysis is consistent with both U.S. Const., Am. VI and Const. 1963, art. 1, §20, which expressly apply only to criminal prosecutions, we adopt that analysis and hold that the right to counsel attaches only to corporeal identifications conducted at or after the initiation of adversarial judicial criminal proceedings.

[The] *Anderson* decision generated considerable confusion regarding its proper application. [There is no] simple, practical standard regarding on-the-scene corporeal identifications. In People v. Dixon, 271 N.W.2d 196 (Mich. App. 1978), the Court held that if the police have "more than a mere suspicion" that the suspect is wanted for the crime, there can be no on-the-scene corporeal identification; rather, the suspect must be taken to the police station and participate in a lineup with counsel present. In People v. Turner, 328 N.W.2d 5 (Mich. App. 1982), however, the Court found the *Dixon* rule too difficult and, instead, held that police may conduct on-the-scene identifications without counsel unless the police have "very strong evidence" that the person stopped is the perpetrator. "Very strong evidence" was defined as "where the suspect has himself decreased any exculpatory motive, *i.e.,* where he has confessed or presented the police with either highly distinctive evidence of the crime or a highly distinctive personal appearance."

[The] *Turner* "strong evidence" rule is hardly more workable than *Dixon's* "more than a mere suspicion" rule. Rather than perpetuate the confusion in this area, we take this opportunity to adopt the *Moore* analysis and clarify that the right to counsel attaches only to corporeal identifications conducted at or after the initiation of adversarial judicial criminal proceedings. This eliminates any unwarranted confusion and allows the focus to be on whether the identification procedure used violates due process. . . .

The on-the-scene identification in this case was made before the initiation of any adversarial judicial criminal proceedings; thus, counsel was not required. . . .

The *Anderson* rule, extending the right to counsel to all pretrial identifications, is without constitutional basis. Consistently with both the United States Constitution and the Michigan Constitution, we adopt the straightforward analysis of Moore v. Illinois and hold that the right to counsel attaches only to corporeal identifications conducted at or after the initiation of adversarial judicial criminal proceedings. . . .

KELLY, J., dissenting.

To the casual reader, the rationale for today's majority decision may be elusive. After all, as the majority correctly notes, the case deals with law that has been relatively well-settled for close to thirty years: a potential criminal defendant does not have a Sixth Amendment right to counsel during identifications that occur before the initiation of adversarial judicial proceedings, such as a formal charge or preliminary hearing. Moore v. Illinois, 434 U.S. 220, 226-227 (1977); People v. Jackson, 217 N.W.2d 22 (Mich. 1974).

Nor has this Court held that the protective rules enumerated by People v. Anderson and its progeny apply to on-the-scene identification procedures and require counsel during those procedures. In fact, the opposite is true.

Yet the majority undertakes today ostensibly to resolve these issues. Its purpose is to take away the potential defendant's entitlement to counsel during all preindictment proceedings by overruling *Anderson* and its progeny. Hereafter, a defendant, in custody but not yet indicted, will no longer have the practical ability to challenge photographic or corporeal identification procedures. The police will be able to conduct such procedures without allowing a defendant's attorney to be present. Moreover, even after the initiation of adversarial judicial procedures, a criminal defendant will no longer have the right to counsel during a photographic showup. Because I do not see any good reason to depart from longstanding precedent, I must respectfully dissent.

The majority is not correct in its assertion that, under *Anderson*, "the right to counsel was extended to all pretrial corporeal identifications, including those occurring before the initiation of adversarial proceedings." *Anderson*, which itself dealt with the right to counsel for pretrial custodial photographic showup procedures, set forth "justified" exceptions, albeit arguably in dicta, for the absence of counsel at eyewitness identification procedures. Notably included as exceptions were emergency situations requiring immediate identification and "prompt, on-the-scene corporeal identifications within minutes of the crime. . . ." We have since specifically affirmed the *Anderson* exception for prompt on-the-scene identifications. City of Troy v. Ohlinger, 475 N.W.2d 54 (Mich. 1991).

The majority could reaffirm the *Anderson* exception for prompt on-the-scene identifications, or perhaps enlarge the explanation of the exception to provide a workable framework for the lower courts. Instead, it unnecessarily chooses to remove the *Anderson* protections from all preindictment identification procedures.

It is an ill-conceived decision that ignores principles of stare decisis. It also fails to consider the adverse effect on defendants' rights to be assured that pretrial identifications are not obtained through mistake or unnecessarily suggestive procedures. . . .

Apparently the majority's own "policy preferences" outweigh those of the members of the *Anderson* Court and the *Jackson* Court, as well as other members of this Court. Unlike the majority, I believe *Anderson* was decided with due deference to the practical problems of ensuring accurate identifications. I am concerned that the majority's policy decision gives insufficient thought to the underlying rationale for our long-existing decision to grant counsel to defendants where practicable.

Anderson discussed at length the scope of the problem of misidentifications, particularly in the use of photographic identification procedures. These concerns have certainly not diminished with time. [The] past century has seen the accumulation of literally thousands of studies on the weakness of eyewitness testimony.

[After] DNA identification techniques became more common, the United States Justice Department conducted a study of exonerated defendants and prepared a research report. Connors, *Convicted by juries, exonerated by science: Case studies in the use of DNA evidence to establish innocence after trial* (1996). The study was commissioned by the National Institute of Justice. It reviewed twenty-eight cases where the defendants had been exonerated through the use of DNA identification techniques.

Among the conclusions reached was that, in the majority of cases, "eyewitness testimony was the most compelling evidence. Clearly, however, those eyewitness identifications were wrong." Notably, one of the significant factors of misidentification listed in the Justice Department report involves an issue directly raised in the instant case and the majority's decision to overrule *Anderson:* the potential susceptibility of eyewitnesses to suggestions from the police, whether intentional or unintentional.

One of the major underpinnings of the *Anderson* decision, and the later affirmation in *Jackson,* was the recognition of difficulties with obtaining reliable identification evidence. Courts and scholars have recognized the continued validity of these concerns. Nonetheless, this Court refuses to recognize that *Anderson's* rules were, in fact, grounded on more than a transient notion of what the Sixth Amendment requires.

The majority does so with barely a nod to the principle of stare decisis. . . . Even if this Court has found that an error occurred, before it overrules a decision deliberately made, it should be convinced not merely that the case was wrongly decided, but also that less injury will result from overruling than from following it. . . .

In the instant case, the injury done by unnecessarily overruling *Anderson* is grave. Conversely, the continued use of its precedent would harm no one but those who fail in their duty to ensure that identifications are made under circumstances that render them reliable. The use of counsel during preindictment procedures has become part of the accepted practice in Michigan courts. I see nothing even approaching a special justification to depart from precedent here. . . .

The fact that the majority has seen fit to unnecessarily overturn *Anderson* creates a Catch-22 for defendants during other preindictment identification procedures. Until today, a defendant who was not "formally" charged but in custody was entitled to an attorney during any identification procedure. Now, the only required persons in the room will be the investigating officer and the witness. Where the defendant is presented to a potential witness during an on-the-scene identification, the defendant himself is present to observe the actions and words of the officer. Arguably, a defendant who has been subjected to an unnecessarily suggestive on-the-scene identification procedure has the opportunity to present a coherent rationale for his arguments.

In contrast, a defendant who seeks to challenge a corporeal identification procedure will be effectively unable to do so. He must stand before the one-way glass and trust the competence and conscience of the investigating officer. I doubt that J.R.R. Tolkien's image of Wormtongue whispering quietly into the ear of Theoden, King of Rohan will be one that is frequently repeated in practice. However, even an inadvertent suggestion will be imperceptible to a defendant who remains precluded from witnessing it. The majority is essentially creating a black box into which the defendant will not be allowed to peer. It then requires him to refute the premise that what occurred inside did not violate his right to due process. . . .

I agree wholeheartedly with Justice Brennan's dissenting statement in Kirby v. Illinois, 406 U.S. 682, 699 n.8 (1972): . . . "the establishment of the date of formal accusation as the time wherein the right to counsel at lineup attaches could only lead to a situation wherein substantially all lineups would be conducted prior to indictment or information." Until today, Michigan has not known this to occur. However, I seriously doubt that it will long be the case after the majority's ruling. . . .

In conclusion, . . . the decision to overrule *Anderson* is misguided. It has been made without due deference to the principles of stare decisis and without a comprehension of the practical realities of frequent eyewitness misidentifications.

U.S. DEPARTMENT OF JUSTICE, TECHNICAL WORKING GROUP FOR EYEWITNESS EVIDENCE

Eyewitness Evidence: A Guide for Law Enforcement (1999)

PROCEDURES FOR EYEWITNESS IDENTIFICATION OF SUSPECTS

A. COMPOSING LINEUPS . . .

Procedure [for Live Lineups]:

In composing a live lineup, the investigator should:

1. Include only one suspect in each identification procedure.
2. Select fillers who generally fit the witness' description of the perpetrator. When there is a limited/inadequate description of the perpetrator provided by the witness, or when the description of the perpetrator differs significantly from the appearance of the suspect, fillers should resemble the suspect in significant features.
3. Consider placing suspects in different positions in each lineup, both across cases and with multiple witnesses in the same case. Position the suspect randomly unless, where local practice allows, the suspect or the suspect's attorney requests a particular position.
4. Include a *minimum* of four fillers (nonsuspects) per identification procedure.
5. When showing a new suspect, avoid reusing fillers in lineups shown to the same witness.

6. Consider that complete uniformity of features is not required. Avoid using fillers who so closely resemble the suspect that a person familiar with the suspect might find it difficult to distinguish the suspect from the fillers.
7. Create a consistent appearance between the suspect and fillers with respect to any unique or unusual feature (e.g., scars, tattoos) used to describe the perpetrator by artificially adding or concealing that feature. . . .

B. INSTRUCTING THE WITNESS PRIOR TO VIEWING A LINEUP . . .

Procedure [for Live Lineup]:

Prior to presenting a live lineup, the investigator should:

1. Instruct the witness that he/she will be asked to view a group of individuals.
2. Instruct the witness that it is just as important to clear innocent persons from suspicion as to identify guilty parties.
3. Instruct the witness that individuals present in the lineup may not appear exactly as they did on the date of the incident because features such as head and facial hair are subject to change.
4. Instruct the witness that the person who committed the crime may or may not be present in the group of individuals.
5. Assure the witness that regardless of whether an identification is made, the police will continue to investigate the incident.
6. Instruct the witness that the procedure requires the investigator to ask the witness to state, in his/her own words, how certain he/she is of any identification. . . .

C. CONDUCTING THE IDENTIFICATION PROCEDURE . . .

Procedure: [Simultaneous Live Lineup]

When presenting a simultaneous live lineup, the investigator/lineup administrator should: . . .

2. Instruct all those present at the lineup not to suggest in any way the position or identity of the suspect in the lineup.
3. Ensure that any identification actions (e.g., speaking, moving) are performed by all members of the lineup.
4. Avoid saying anything to the witness that may influence the witness' selection.
5. If an identification is made, avoid reporting to the witness any information regarding the individual he/she has selected prior to obtaining the witness' statement of certainty. . . .
7. Document the lineup in writing, including [identification] information of lineup participants, [names] of all persons present at the lineup, [and date] and time the identification procedure was conducted.
8. Document the lineup by photo or video. This documentation should be of a quality that represents the lineup clearly and fairly.
9. Instruct the witness not to discuss the identification procedure or its results with other witnesses involved in the case and discourage contact with the media.

Sequential Live Lineup:

When presenting a sequential live lineup, the lineup administrator/investigator should: . . .

2. Provide the following additional viewing instructions to the witness:
   a. Individuals will be viewed one at a time.
   b. The individuals will be presented in random order.
   c. Take as much time as needed in making a decision about each individual before moving to the next one.
   d. If the person who committed the crime is present, identify him/her.
   e. All individuals will be presented, even if an identification is made; or the procedure will be stopped at the point of an identification (consistent with jurisdictional/departmental procedures).
3. Begin with all lineup participants out of the view of the witness.
4. Instruct all those present at the lineup not to suggest in any way the position or identity of the suspect in the lineup.
5. Present each individual to the witness separately, in a previously determined order, removing those previously shown.
6. Ensure that any identification actions (e.g., speaking, moving) are performed by all members of the lineup.
7. Avoid saying anything to the witness that may influence the witness' selection.
8. If an identification is made, avoid reporting to the witness any information regarding the individual he/she has selected prior to obtaining the witness' statement of certainty. . . .

D. RECORDING IDENTIFICATION RESULTS . . .

Procedure:

When conducting an identification procedure, the investigator should:

1. Record both identification and nonidentification results in writing, including the witness' own words regarding how sure he/she is.
2. Ensure results are signed and dated by the witness.
3. Ensure that no materials indicating previous identification results are visible to the witness.
4. Ensure that the witness does not write on or mark any materials that will be used in other identification procedures.

Summary:

Preparing a complete and accurate record of the outcome of the identification procedure improves the strength and credibility of the identification or nonidentification results obtained from the witness. This record can be a critical document in the investigation and any subsequent court proceedings.

Notes

1. *Availability of counsel during in-person identifications: majority position.* The decisions in *Wade* and Gilbert v. California, 388 U.S. 263 (1967), gave a dramatic debut to the constitutional right to counsel for identification procedures. The Supreme Court spoke broadly of the unreliability of this type of evidence and of the need for defense counsel to help counter this problem. But five years later, in Kirby v. Illinois, 406 U.S. 682 (1972), the Court sharply limited the type of lineup procedures in which counsel would be required under the Constitution: The *Wade-Gilbert* rule applied only to lineups occurring "at or after the initiation of adversary judicial criminal proceedings." For purposes of the federal constitution, that point arrives as early as the pre-indictment "preliminary hearing" in which a magistrate determines if there is probable cause to bind the defendant over to the grand jury. Moore v. Illinois, 434 U.S. 220 (1977).

Most states have adopted the *Kirby* rule to determine which identification procedures fall within the reach of the constitutional right to counsel. Fewer than a half dozen states extend the right to counsel to lineups occurring earlier in the process. In these states, counsel must be present at any postarrest in-person identification. See State v. Mitchell, 593 S.W.2d 280 (Tenn. 1980) (applies to all warranted arrests).

No state has applied the right to counsel to field confrontations or showups, in which the police bring the crime victim together with a single suspect near the time and place where the crime occurred. To require counsel in such a setting would amount to a constitutional ban on the use of evidence from a field confrontation. How much does the refusal of the legal system to require counsel at field interrogations diminish the counsel requirement of *Wade*?

2. *How much does counsel see?* If you were a lawyer, would you want to know where the witness had been in the station prior to the lineup? Whom she had seen? What route your client took to get to the station? In light of the importance of what the witness has to say immediately after the lineup, can a defense attorney be excluded from the interview? Is this consistent with the reasoning of *Wade*? Cases that address this question generally uphold police efforts to exclude defense counsel from these conversations.

3. *The role of counsel in creating a record.* What should an attorney do at a lineup? Silently observe any suggestive police practices, or object to them? If the attorney takes an observer role, does he have to terminate representation of the defendant later in order to become a witness in the case? If the primary function of the defense counsel is to create a record for possible challenges to the use of the identification evidence at trial, could a state conduct a lineup without counsel present, so long as it is recorded? See Utah Code §77-8-4: "The entire lineup procedure shall be recorded, including all conversations between the witnesses and the conducting peace officers. The suspect shall have access to and may make copies of the record and any photographs taken of him or any other persons in connection with the lineup." In addition, Utah Code §77-8-2 provides suspects with a right to counsel during post-indictment lineups.

4. *Police rules as substitute for counsel? Wade* addressed the possibility of statutes or police regulations as a substitute for a right to counsel: "Legislative or other regulations, such as those of local police departments, which eliminate the risks of abuse

and unintentional suggestion at lineup proceedings and the impediments to meaningful confrontation at trial may also remove the basis for regarding the stage as 'critical.' " Could a police department adopting regulations along the lines of the Department of Justice recommendations reprinted above make an argument that the lineup is no longer a "critical" stage and therefore that the right to counsel does not apply? Are there any reasons to believe that police will not follow the procedures that the department's legal counsel drafts?

5. *Best practices during lineups.* The extensive academic research on the subject of eyewitness testimony produces a long list of possible improvements to current police practices. The U.S. Department of Justice sponsored a Technical Working Group that published the recommended practices reprinted above. Under the guidelines, witnesses should be told that the perpetrator may or may not be present in the lineup. Research indicates that this latter instruction greatly decreases the number of false positives. See Gary L. Wells, Police Lineups: Data, Theory, and Policy, 7 Psychol. Pub. Pol'y & L. 791 (2001).

However, the Department of Justice recommendations stop short of imposing two further requirements that find strong support in the academic research. It is clear that "blind presentations" of the lineup (that is, the officer conducting the lineup procedure does not know which participant is the suspect) improve the accuracy of witness identification. Officers who know the identity of the suspect can signal to the witness, either through words or subtle body language, which is the "correct" choice. A second technique involves "sequential" lineups, where the officer presents to the witness one person at a time, asking each time whether he or she is the perpetrator. Sequential lineups encourage witnesses to compare each person to their memory of the events, rather than asking which lineup participant (relatively speaking) most closely resembles the original description. Dawn McQuiston-Surrett, Roy S. Malpass, & Colin G. Tredoux, Sequential vs. Simultaneous Lineups: A Review of Methods, Data, and Theory, 12 Psychol. Pub. Pol'y & L. 137 (2006).

What might prevent the Department of Justice from recommending these two techniques that so clearly contribute to more accurate identifications? See Kate Zernike, "Study Fuels a Growing Debate Over Police Lineups," N.Y. Times, April 19, 2006 (describing experiment by Chicago Police Department to use sequential lineups and blind presentations for some eyewitness identifications; sequential lineups made witnesses less likely to choose any suspect, and when they did pick, they were more likely to select an innocent person). The debates among local actors about the best identification procedures are lively and have not thus far led to a consensus about best practices. For examples of such debates, see the web extension for this chapter at *http://www.crimpro.com/extension/ch09*.

6. *Right to counsel for photographic identifications: majority position.* Rather than arranging an acceptable in-person encounter, it is often easier for police investigators to show pictures of potential suspects to a witness. Furthermore, pictures can be matched on more features. Are concerns about the reliability of the witness's identification different when investigators use photographs or other recorded images of a suspect? Do different types of legal regulation then become more or less feasible?

In United States v. Ash, 413 U.S. 300 (1973), the Court held that the federal Constitution does not require the presence of counsel at *any* photographic identification, whether it is conducted before or after the start of adversarial criminal proceedings. It reasoned that a photographic display, unlike an in-person lineup, does not involve a "trial-like confrontation" between the defendant and the witness.

Thus, the presence of a lawyer is less important to a defendant whose picture is used in a photo array. Is this distinction convincing?

Most state courts have followed *Ash* and concluded that there is no right to counsel for photographic identifications. See Barone v. State, 866 P.2d 291 (Nev. 1993) (reversing a 1969 decision that had granted right to counsel for photo identification). A handful do require the presence of defense counsel for at least some photo identifications.

7. *The exclusion remedy.* If police fail to allow counsel to be present during identification when such presence is constitutionally required, then the judge must exclude at trial any evidence of the pretrial identification. In addition, any identification of the defendant by the witness *at trial is* excludable unless the prosecution can demonstrate that the witness's ability to recognize the defendant at trial has an "independent basis" apart from the tainted pretrial identification. Justice White's dissent in *Wade* predicted that trial identifications would rarely meet this standard, but one limited survey of case law in the years immediately after *Wade* found that courts still routinely allowed at-trial identifications, Joseph Quinn, In the Wake of *Wade:* The Dimensions of the Eyewitness Identification Cases, 42 U. Colo. L. Rev. 135 (1970) (citing six cases as illustrations of larger trend).

8. *Counsel at identification procedures in foreign practice.* Several legal systems outside the United States rely on counsel at formal identification procedures more heavily than the U.S. system does. For instance, in England and Wales, Code D of the Police and Criminal Evidence Act of 1984 provides for defense counsel at any formal "identification parade." Case law in Israel provides that a suspect must be informed of the right to counsel during a lineup. See Eliahu Harnon and Alex Stein, Israel, in Criminal Procedure: A Worldwide Study (Craig Bradley, 2d ed. 2007). In civil law systems (said to be less "adversarial" than common law systems), would you expect defense counsel to take part in lineups?

2. *Exclusion on Due Process Grounds*

As we saw in the preceding subsection, federal and state constitutions generally require the presence of counsel only for lineups taking place after the initiation of adversary criminal proceedings (typically post-indictment lineups). This accounts for a small number of the identification procedures that take place. Are there any limitations — constitutional or otherwise — on the larger number of lineups and "field confrontations" that occur earlier in the investigative process?

For more than a generation, courts have insisted that due process will prevent the use of the least reliable identification procedures, regardless of the presence or absence of counsel. In Stovall v. Denno, 388 U.S. 293 (1967), decided the same day as United States v. Wade, the Supreme Court refused to exclude evidence of a pretrial identification under the due process clause because the identification was unduly "suggestive." While investigating a stabbing case, the police entered the victim's hospital room with the suspect handcuffed to an officer and asked the victim if the suspect was the person who had committed the crime. Because the police had no viable alternative to the procedure used here, it was not "unnecessarily suggestive."

The Supreme Court appeared to shift its emphasis in two later cases, Neil v. Biggers, 409 U.S. 188 (1972), and Manson v. Brathwaite, 432 U.S. 98 (1977). While the Court had focused in *Stovall* on the suggestiveness of the identification procedures used, that was not enough to show a due process violation in *Biggers* or *Brathwaite*. Even though the police had used suggestive "showups" to identify suspects in those cases, the Court reasoned that a witness with an adequate memory of the original crime could reliably identify the criminal despite the suggestive procedure followed at the time of the identification. The Court went on to describe the factors it would consider, as part of the "totality of the circumstances," that could outweigh a suggestive identification procedure. Thus, the Court rejected a "per se" rule that would exclude all evidence obtained through unduly suggestive identification procedures, in favor of a "reliability test" that would allow some identification evidence to stand because other factors supported its accuracy. The following case describes this "totality" approach to identification evidence obtained at the police station and offers an alternative version of the legal standard.

■ STATE v. TYRONE DUBOSE

699 N.W.2d 582 (Wis. 2005)

N. PATRICK CROOKS, J.

¶1 Petitioner Tyrone Dubose [argues that] the circuit court erred in denying Dubose's motion to suppress the victim's out-of-court identifications of him. . . .

¶2 We agree with Dubose that the circuit court erred in denying his motion to suppress the out-of-court identification evidence. However, we decline to adopt his proposed per se exclusionary rule regarding such evidence. Instead, we adopt standards for the admissibility of out-of-court identification evidence similar to those set forth in the United States Supreme Court's decision in Stovall v. Denno, 388 U.S. 293 (1967). . . .

I.

¶3 Timothy Hiltsley and Ryan Boyd left the Camelot Bar in Green Bay, Wisconsin, at approximately 1:00 A.M. on January 9, 2002. Hiltsley had been drinking at the bar and admitted to being "buzzed" when he left. In the parking lot, Hiltsley and Boyd encountered a group of men, some of whom Hiltsley recognized as regular customers of a liquor store where he worked. Dubose, an African-American, was one of the men he allegedly recognized. After a brief conversation, Hiltsley invited two of the men, along with Boyd, to his residence to smoke marijuana.

¶4 When they arrived at Hiltsley's apartment, Hiltsley sat down on the couch to pack a bowl of marijuana. At that time, Dubose allegedly held a gun to Hiltsley's right temple and demanded money. After Hiltsley emptied his wallet and gave the men his money, the two men, both African-Americans, left his apartment.

¶5 Within minutes after the incident, at approximately 1:21 A.M., one of Hiltsley's neighbors called the police to report a possible burglary. She described two African-American men fleeing from the area, one of whom was wearing a large hooded flannel shirt. At the same time, Hiltsley and Boyd attempted to chase the men. . . . During his search, Hiltsley flagged down a police officer that was responding to the burglary call. Hiltsley told the officer that he had just been robbed at gunpoint. He described the suspects as African-American, one standing about 5-feet 6-inches, and the other man standing a little taller.

¶6 Another police officer also responded to the burglary call. As he neared the scene, he observed two men walking about one-half block from Hiltsley's apartment. This officer, Jeffrey Engelbrecht, was unable to determine the race of the individuals, but noted that one of the men was wearing a large hooded flannel shirt. When the officer turned his squad car around to face the men, they ran east between two houses. The police quickly set up a one-block perimeter in order to contain the suspects.

¶7 The officer subsequently requested headquarters to dispatch a canine unit to help search for the men. While he waited at the perimeter for the canine unit, police headquarters reported another call in regard to an armed robbery at Hiltsley's apartment. The report indicated that the two suspects were African-American males, that one was possibly armed, and that the two calls were probably related. Upon their arrival, the canine unit officer and his dog began tracking the suspects within the perimeter. The dog began barking near a wooden backyard fence, and the officer demanded that the person behind the fence come out and show his hands. A male voice responded that he was going to surrender and asked why the police were chasing him. The male who came out from behind the fence was Dubose, who was subsequently arrested.

¶8 Dubose, who was not wearing a flannel shirt, told the police that he had been in an argument with his girlfriend and that he had just left her house. He thought she might have called the police on him, which is why he ran when he saw the squad car. After his arrest, he was searched. The search did not uncover any weapons, money, or contraband. Dubose was then placed in the back of a squad car and driven to an area near Hiltsley's residence.

¶9 At this location, the officers conducted a showup procedure, giving Hiltsley the opportunity to identify one of the alleged suspects. The officers placed Hiltsley in the backseat of a second squad car, which was parked so that its rear window was three feet apart from the rear window of the squad car containing Dubose. The dome light was turned on in the car containing Dubose. The officers told Hiltsley that Dubose was possibly one of the men who had robbed him at gunpoint, and asked Hiltsley if he could identify the man in the other squad car. Hiltsley told the police that he was 98 percent certain that Dubose, who sat alone in the back seat of the other squad car, was the man who held him at gunpoint. Hiltsley also told the police that he recognized him due to his small, slender build and hairstyle.

¶10 The squad cars separated and took both Hiltsley and Dubose to the police station. Approximately 10 to 15 minutes after the first showup, the police conducted a second showup. There, Hiltsley identified Dubose, alone in a room, through a two-way mirror. Hiltsley told police that Dubose was the same man he observed at the previous showup, and that he believed Dubose was the man who robbed him. A short time after the second showup, the police showed Hiltsley a mug shot of Dubose, and he identified him for a third time.

¶11 The State of Wisconsin charged Dubose with armed robbery. Dubose filed a motion to suppress all identifications of him in connection with the case. . . . The [trial judge] denied Dubose's motion and scheduled a jury trial. At trial, Hiltsley testified about the events and subsequent showups that occurred on January 9, 2002. He also identified Dubose in the courtroom as the man who held him at gunpoint on the night in question. The jury convicted Dubose of armed robbery on September 5, 2002. . . .

III.

¶17 Our analysis begins with a summary of the law relating to the right to due process in out-of-court identification procedures. In Stovall v. Denno, 388 U.S. 293 (1967), the United States Supreme Court considered for the first time whether, and under what circumstances, out-of-court identification procedures could implicate a defendant's right to due process. The defendant in that case, an African-American male, was arrested for murder. Without time to consult with or retain counsel, the defendant was taken to the hospital room of the only surviving witness to the alleged crime. The witness had been stabbed multiple times and was awaiting surgery. The defendant was handcuffed to one of five police officers who, along with two prosecutors, brought him into the hospital room. He was the only African-American in the room. The witness subsequently identified the defendant from her hospital bed after a police officer asked her if he "was the man," and the defendant uttered a few words for the purpose of voice identification. The witness later recovered, and testified at the defendant's trial as to the events that occurred in her hospital room. At that time, she also made an in-court identification of the defendant.

¶18 The United States Supreme Court considered whether the confrontation in the hospital room was "so unnecessarily suggestive and conducive to irreparable mistaken identification that he was denied due process of law." . . . The Court determined that necessity is a key factor in reviewing whether a showup violates due process. Although the identification was suggestive, the Court determined that it did not violate the defendant's right to due process because the procedure was necessary. It held:

> Here was the only person in the world who could possibly exonerate Stovall. Her words, and only her words, "He is not the man" could have resulted in freedom for Stovall. The hospital was not far distant from the courthouse and jail. No one knew how long Mrs. Behrendt might live. Faced with the responsibility of identifying the attacker, with the need for immediate action and with the knowledge that Mrs. Behrendt could not visit the jail, the police followed the only feasible procedure and took Stovall to the hospital room. Under these circumstances, the usual police station line-up, which Stovall now argues he should have had, was out of the question.

Thus, while the out-of-court identification was not suppressed in that case, *Stovall* established a due process right of criminal suspects to be free from confrontations that, under all circumstances, are unnecessarily suggestive. The right was enforceable by exclusion at trial of evidence of the constitutionally invalid identification. . . .

¶20 [The] United States Supreme Court next considered the identification issue in Simmons v. United States, 390 U.S. 377 (1968). In that case, the defendant was convicted of armed robbery based on in-court identification. However, the in-court identification witnesses had been shown photographs of the defendant prior to trial. The defendant argued that the in-court identifications were tainted, because the out-of-court photo identification was suggestive.

¶21 The Court, attempting to follow the "totality test" developed in *Stovall*, determined that the in-court identification was not tainted. [The Court held] "that convictions based on eyewitness identification at trial following a pretrial identification by photograph will be set aside . . . only if the photographic identification procedure was so impermissibly suggestive as to give rise to a very substantial likelihood of irreparable misidentification." In so holding, however, the Supreme Court [replaced] "conducive to irreparable mistaken identification" with "a very substantial likelihood of irreparable misidentification" [and thus required] a much higher level of proof on the part of the defendant. . . .

¶23 In Neil v. Biggers, 409 U.S. 188 (1972), the United States Supreme Court shifted away from its reliance on the "necessity" of the out-of-court identification as set forth in *Stovall* and, instead, emphasized the standard of reliability established in *Simmons*. In *Biggers*, the police conducted a showup that consisted of two detectives walking the defendant past the victim at the police station. At the victim's request, the police directed the respondent to say "shut up or I'll kill you." The victim identified the defendant after the showup and then later at trial. The defendant objected to the admissibility of the out-of-court identification.

¶24 The Supreme Court determined that . . . evidence from a suggestive identification would be admissible if a court can find it reliable under the totality of the circumstances. In order to determine if an identification is reliable under the totality of the circumstances, the Court developed a five-part test: (1) the opportunity of the witness to view the defendant at the time of the crime; (2) the witness' degree of attention; (3) the accuracy of the witness' prior description of the defendant; (4) the level of certainty demonstrated by the witness at the confrontation; and (5) the length of time between the crime and the confrontation.

¶25 The United States Supreme Court's next significant eyewitness identification case was Manson v. Brathwaite, 432 U.S. 98 (1977). In that case, a police officer made a positive out-of-court photo identification of the defendant two days after he conducted an undercover purchase of drugs from the defendant. Both parties agreed that the identification was improperly suggestive. The Supreme Court held that, under the totality of the circumstances, the identification was reliable even though the confrontation procedure was suggestive. The Court reaffirmed *Biggers* and held that "reliability is the linchpin in determining the admissibility of identification testimony. . . ."

¶26 With guidance from the United States Supreme Court, this court has adopted the test set forth in *Biggers* and *Brathwaite* in an attempt to minimize the misidentification of defendants in Wisconsin. See State v. Wolverton, 533 N.W.2d 167 (Wis. 1995); Fells v. State, 223 N.W.2d 507 (Wis. 1974) (in a case involving lineup and photo identifications, the proper procedure is to first determine if the identification was "unnecessarily suggestive," and, if so, decide whether, under the totality of circumstances, the identification was nevertheless reliable). In *Wolverton*, this court decided a case that presented similar factual circumstances to the case presently before us. There, the police conducted showups in driveways of different witnesses to different incidents. The suspect was positively identified while sitting alone in the back of a squad car. The identifications took place shortly after the alleged incidents, and the witnesses later identified the suspect at trial.

¶27 In relying on *Biggers* and *Brathwaite*, we held that if the criminal defendant demonstrates that the showup was impermissibly suggestive, the burden shifts to the state to demonstrate that under the totality of the circumstances the identification was reliable. Accordingly, we upheld the admissibility of the out-of-court identifications, not under standards involving due process and necessity as set forth in *Stovall*, but because under the totality of the circumstances, such identifications were determined to be reliable.

IV.

¶28 . . . Dubose asks us to abandon [our reliability test] and apply a per se exclusionary rule in cases where out-of-court identifications were impermissibly suggestive.

¶29 We begin our assessment by recognizing that much new information has been assembled since we last reviewed the showup procedure in *Wolverton*. Over the last decade, there have been extensive studies on the issue of identification evidence, research that is now impossible for us to ignore. See Nancy Steblay, et al., Eyewitness Accuracy Rates in Police Showup and Lineup Presentations: A Meta-Analytic Comparison, 27 Law & Hum. Behav. 523 (2003); U.S. Department of Justice, Eyewitness Evidence: A Guide for Law Enforcement (1999), available at *http://www.ncjrs.org/pdffiles1/nij/178240.pdf*.

¶30 These studies confirm that eyewitness testimony is often hopelessly unreliable. The research strongly supports the conclusion that eyewitness misidentification is now the single greatest source of wrongful convictions in the United States, and responsible for more wrongful convictions than all other causes combined. In a study conducted by . . . the Innocence Project at the Benjamin Cardozo School of Law, mistaken identifications played a major part in the wrongful conviction of over two-thirds of the first 138 postconviction DNA exonerations. . . .

¶31 In light of such evidence, we recognize that our current approach to eyewitness identification has significant flaws. [It] is extremely difficult, if not impossible, for courts to distinguish between identifications that were reliable and identifications that were unreliable. . . . Because a witness can be influenced by the suggestive procedure itself, a court cannot know exactly how reliable the identification would have been without the suggestiveness. . . .

¶33 With *Stovall* as our guide, we now adopt a different test in Wisconsin regarding the admissibility of showup identifications. We conclude that evidence obtained from an out-of-court showup is inherently suggestive and will not be admissible unless, based on the totality of the circumstances, the procedure was necessary. A showup will not be necessary, however, unless the police lacked probable cause to make an arrest or, as a result of other exigent circumstances, could not have conducted a lineup or photo array. A lineup or photo array is generally fairer than a showup, because it distributes the probability of identification among the number of persons arrayed, thus reducing the risk of a misidentification. . . .

¶34 We emphasize that our approach . . . is not a per se exclusionary rule like Dubose requests. Showups have been a useful instrument in investigating and prosecuting criminal cases, and there will continue to be circumstances in which such a procedure is necessary and appropriate.

¶35 If and when the police determine that a showup is necessary, special care must be taken to minimize potential suggestiveness. We recommend procedures similar to those proposed by the Wisconsin Innocence Project to help make showup identifications as non-suggestive as possible. For example, it is important that showups are not conducted in locations, or in a manner, that implicitly conveys to the witness that the suspect is guilty. Showups conducted in police stations, squad cars, or with the suspect in handcuffs that are visible to any witness, all carry with them inferences of guilt, and thus should be considered suggestive. Next, officers investigating the matter at issue should proceed with caution in instructing the witness. [An] eyewitness should be told that the real suspect may or may not be present, and that the investigation will continue regardless of the result of the impending identification procedure. Finally, it is important that a suspect be shown to the witness only once. If a suspect is identified, the police have no reason to conduct further identification procedures. Conversely, if the suspect is not identified by the witness, he or she should not be presented to that witness in any subsequent showups. While this list is far from complete, a showup conducted in accord with these standards will do much to alleviate the inherent suggestiveness of the procedure.

¶36 Applying this approach to the facts before us, it is clear that the showups conducted were unnecessarily suggestive, and that the admission of identification evidence denied Dubose a right to due process under Article I, Section 8 of the Wisconsin Constitution. First, there existed sufficient facts at the time of Dubose's arrest to establish probable cause for his arrest. It was not necessary for the police to conduct the showups, since they had sufficient evidence against Dubose to arrest him without such showups. Next, the officers handcuffed Dubose and placed him in the back seat of a squad car. . . . Third, the police officers told the witness, Hiltsley, that they may have caught "one of the guys" who had robbed him. . . .

¶37 Finally, after the first showup was conducted and Dubose was positively identified, the police still conducted two more identification procedures, another showup and a photo of Dubose, at the police station shortly after Dubose's arrival. These subsequent identification procedures were unnecessarily suggestive. . . .

¶38 On remand, we recognize that the exclusion of evidence of the out-of-court identifications does not deprive the prosecutor of reliable evidence of guilt. The witness would still be permitted to identify the defendant in court if that identification is based on an independent source. And properly conducted pretrial viewings can still be proven at trial and would be encouraged by the rule prohibiting use of suggestive ones. . . . The in-court identification is admissible if the State carries the burden of showing by clear and convincing evidence that the in-court identifications were based upon observations of the suspect other than the out-of-court identification. . . .

¶42 We gain support for our reliance on the Wisconsin Constitution by noting that the federal standard in out-of-court eyewitness identifications has also not been accepted, on state constitutional grounds, in two prominent states — New York and Massachusetts. See Commonwealth v. Johnson, 650 N.E.2d 1257 (Mass. 1995); People v. Adams, 423 N.E.2d 379 (N.Y. 1981). Although these states have adopted a per se exclusionary rule under their respective state constitutions, and thus provide a different approach than this court, we recognize nevertheless that Wisconsin does not stand alone on out-of-court identification issues.

¶43 We also recognize that this case is not the first to result in a change in principles based on extensive new studies completed after a court decision that was premised on constitutional interpretation and application. For example, in Brown v. Board of Education, 347 U.S. 483 (1954), the United States Supreme Court relied on comprehensive studies to support its legal conclusion that the doctrine of separate but equal was violative of the United States Constitution and, thus, that Plessy v. Ferguson, 163 U.S. 537 (1896) should be overruled. For support of this much-needed shift in constitutional law, the United States Supreme Court based its decision on several modern studies and on the effects of segregation in public education. . . .

LOUIS B. BUTLER, JR., J., concurring.

. . . ¶47 I agree with Justice Roggensack that with respect to identification testimony in criminal trials, reliability should be the key to admissibility. . . . However, I part ways with the dissent precisely because showup identifications have been shown to be unreliable, thereby undercutting the legal fiction that we have operated under with respect to eyewitness testimony.

¶48 Some of the very research relied upon by the dissent to illustrate the disagreements about the unreliability of showups sets forth an overall accuracy rate of 69 percent for showups, compared to 51 percent for lineups. Nancy Steblay, et al., Eyewitness Accuracy Rates in Police Showup and Lineup Presentations: A Meta-Analytic Comparison, 27 Law and Human Behavior 523, 535 (2003). Although not mentioned by the dissent, that research further indicates that when the target is in the display, a correct identification occurs only 47 percent of the time in showups, compared to 45 percent of the time in lineups. Moreover, when the target is not in the display, a false identification of an innocent suspect . . . occurs 23 percent of the time in showups, as opposed to 17 percent of the time in lineups.

¶49 This is not "disputed social science theory." This is data relied upon by the dissent. What we are dealing with is a serious failure rate with respect to eyewitness identifications. Whether we are looking at the dissent's failure rate for showups of 53 percent, 31 percent, 23 percent, or 16 percent, that rate is simply unacceptable. The dissent cannot seriously argue that any of these statistical misidentification rates lead to the conclusion that eyewitness identifications are inherently reliable. What we have here is a legal fiction that is simply not borne out by the facts. Unless, and until, we improve eyewitness identification procedures so that the likelihood of irreparable misidentification is significantly reduced, we can no longer proceed as though all is good in the Land of Oz. . . .

¶51 The reasons supporting our approach should be readily apparent. If the wrong person is incorrectly identified, an innocent person faces potential prosecution, incarceration, and conviction. More important, however, is the fact that the guilty perpetrator remains at large, able to wreak havoc upon an unsuspecting populace. No one wants that. I therefore join the majority opinion in this matter. . . .

JON P. WILCOX, J., dissenting.

¶61 Today the majority [abandons a] long line of well-established precedent, contending that the Due Process Clause of the Wisconsin Constitution now affords greater protections than its federal counterpart. In doing so, the majority provides no legal justification for its decision other than its raw power to do so. The majority . . . fails to articulate a rationale for how identical language in the two documents can mean the same thing for a number of years and now suddenly mean something different. . . .

¶65 Furthermore, I, too, am troubled by the majority's reliance on recent social science "studies," presented by advocacy groups, to justify its departure from stare decisis. Not only is such data disputed, . . . but, more importantly, it is not a valid basis to determine the meaning of our constitution. The majority fails to adequately explain how the meaning of the text of the constitution can change every time a new series of social science "studies" is presented to the court. If the text is so fluid, then our constitution is no constitution at all, merely a device to be invoked whenever four members of this court wish to change the law.

¶66 It is not the function of this court to create what it considers to be good social policy based on data from social science "studies." That is the province of the legislature. Our task is to render decisions based on legal principles and constitutional authority.

DAVID T. PROSSER, J., dissenting.

¶69 As in any case, the facts are critical. After committing an armed robbery against Timothy Hiltsley, two men fled from Hiltsley's residence in Green Bay. A few minutes later, at about 1:21 A.M., a neighbor called the police to report the two men fleeing the scene. Police officers arrived immediately, and one of the responding officers observed two men walking near the apartment. When the officer turned his vehicle around to investigate, the men fled between two houses, into the middle of a residential block.

¶70 The police immediately set up a perimeter around the block. By all accounts, this took less than 90 seconds. Upon searching the area, the police quickly discovered Dubose. The officers placed Dubose in the back of a squad car and drove him to Hiltsley's location, where they conducted a showup. Hiltsley immediately identified Dubose as the man who robbed him at gunpoint, mentioning that he recognized Dubose due to his build and hairstyle. . . . All of this occurred within minutes after the robbery.

¶72 Shortly thereafter, other officers located a semi-automatic pistol within the perimeter, near the houses where the two unidentified men ran after being pursued by the police. . . .

¶74 The facts in this case are not sufficient to justify the majority's conclusion that this defendant's due process rights were violated. Nothing in these facts is so inherently unfair or suggestive that it justifies this court-ordered sea change in the law. . . .

¶76 By sheer volume of cases, the Supreme Court has developed substantial experience interpreting constitutional provisions. Matters reaching the Supreme Court are of such import that they are also likely to be better briefed and argued than issues in the state court system. When state courts adopt myriad different interpretations of state constitutions, the level of uncertainty rises exponentially. A suspect's constitutional rights may change dramatically depending on which side of a state line he robs an acquaintance. . . .

PATIENCE DRAKE ROGGENSACK, J., dissenting.

¶79 [The] majority requires the suppression of identifications of defendants charged with crimes, no matter how reliable the identification. This holding substitutes a search for the truth, which should form the foundation for every criminal prosecution, with one social science theory that showup identifications are "unnecessarily suggestive." . . . I dissent because reliability, and not a disputed social science theory, must be the key to admissibility of all identification testimony in criminal trials and because I conclude that the totality of circumstances bearing on the identification in this case resulted in a reliable identification of Dubose as the perpetrator of the armed robbery of which he was convicted. . . .

¶80 The term "due process of law" comes from the Magna Charta's promise of a trial directed by the "law of the land" as established by the legislative body of government. One of the four paintings in the Wisconsin Supreme Court hearing room depicts the signing of the Magna Charta. . . . I note this because constitutional principles are not to change depending on what social science theory is in fashion. . . .

¶83 There are many factors that bear on whether an identification is reliable. Showup identifications that are done soon after the commission of the crime, while the appearance of the perpetrator is fresh in a witness's mind, have more reliability than identifications done after the passage of considerable time. Additionally, showup identifications are done in-person, and corporeal identifications are generally held more reliable than photo identifications. *Simmons*, 390 U.S. at 386 n.6 (citing P. Wall, Eye-Witness Identification in Criminal Cases 83 (1965); Williams, Identification Parades, [1955] Crim. L. Rev. 525, 531).

¶87 The rule of law announced today is not based on constitutional principle. This is demonstrated in part by the majority opinion's decision that if officers lack probable cause to arrest, then a showup is permissible. [This places] a defendant in the unusual position of arguing that law enforcement had probable cause to arrest, so the showup identification was unnecessary and accordingly should be suppressed. This is an odd position in which to place a defendant whose defense is, "It wasn't me." . . .

¶90 The research cited by the majority does not represent the only social science theory on the subject of identifications. Hard data that social scientists have analyzed have resulted in disagreements about the unreliability of showups. One social science study reports that "overall, the results present surprising commonality in outcome between [showups and lineups] and . . . an apparent contradiction of the ambient knowledge that showups are more dangerous for innocent suspects than are lineups." Nancy Steblay, et al., Eyewitness Accuracy Rates in Police Showup and Lineup Presentations: A Meta-Analytic Comparison, 27 Law and Human Behavior 523, 535 (2003). Steblay reported that

> when overall identification decisions are tabulated, showups produce an accuracy advantage over lineups (69% vs. 51%). This initial result is qualified by subsequent analyses. As anticipated, a consideration of specific subject choices provides a more complete picture. Correct identification (hit) rate within the context of a target-present condition is nearly identical for the two types of procedures: Approximately 46% of witnesses shown either a lineup or a showup correctly identified the perpetrator when he or she was present. False suspect identification rates in a target-absent display are also approximately equal between showups and lineups, at about 16%. . . .

¶94 No one wants the wrong person identified as the perpetrator of a crime. However, where I part company with the majority opinion and the concurrence is that I am not willing to throw out identifications like the one now before us that are reliable, as the means of addressing those identifications that are not reliable. . . .

¶95 All identification procedures, from showups to lineups to photo arrays, can be improved by crafting better techniques for these methods to reduce suggestiveness and increase reliability. Proposed improvements include videotaping eyewitness identifications and making standard the need for officers to inform eyewitnesses that the suspect in the showup may not be the perpetrator or that the perpetrator may not be included in the lineup or array. See Gary L. Wells & Elizabeth A. Olson, Eyewitness Testimony, 54 Ann. Rev. Psychol. 277, 286 (2003).... Other proposed enhancements include allowing expert testimony on the reliability of eyewitness identifications or jury instructions on eyewitness identification. None of these well-respected sources advocate the ban of showup identifications as the majority opinion has done. Instead, they advocate for law enforcement education on how to better conduct eyewitness identifications and for a more complete presentation of the problems with eyewitness identification at trial.

¶96 In sum, because reliability, and not a disputed social science theory, must be the key to admissibility of all identification testimony in criminal trials and because I conclude that the totality of circumstances bearing on the identification in this case resulted in a reliable identification of Dubose as the perpetrator of the armed robbery of which he was convicted, I would affirm the court of appeals....

Problem 9-1. The Pizza Hut Robbery

Shortly before 1:00 A.M., Kathy Davis was preparing to leave the Pizza Hut where she worked as manager. Her husband, John Davis, and her brother, Gerald Wilson, had come to visit her and accompany her home. As they left the building, they were accosted by a man wearing a white scarf across his face and carrying a metal pipe ("the pipe man"). He demanded that they give him the bank bag with the day's receipts. Wilson attempted to grapple with the robber. The robber hit Wilson with the pipe and then told a second robber ("the gunman") that if Wilson moved again, the gunman should kill him.

This was the first indication that a second robber was present. The gunman was crouched near the corner of the building, about 25 feet away from the victims, holding a gun. The man, who wore a hat and covered the lower part of his face with a scarf, held the gun on Wilson while Kathy and John went back into the building. They brought the bank bag out to the robbers, who then fled. The victims reported the robbery to the police, who responded within a few minutes.

Wilson described the gunman as a male Mexican, five feet nine inches to six feet tall, wearing a blue sweater and jeans, with a white scarf around the lower part of his face. He described the pipe man in more detail: male Mexican, 21 to 22 years old, five feet seven inches to five feet eight inches tall, 155 to 160 pounds, shaggy brown hair, brown eyes, wearing a blue sweater and Levi's and a white scarf over the lower part of his face, one front tooth missing, and a bald spot on the side of his head.

A short time after the robbery, police officers apprehended Livio Ramirez, who had been walking with another man, who fled at the sight of a police car. Ramirez was wearing jeans, a blue sweatshirt with paint spattered on the front, and a brown baseball cap. Ramirez also had readily visible tattoos on his arms. They searched Ramirez and handcuffed him to the fence by placing a second set of handcuffs through the fence and attaching them to the handcuffs Ramirez was wearing.

Roughly 45 minutes after the end of the robbery, the police drove Kathy Davis, John Davis, and Gerald Wilson to the location where Ramirez was handcuffed to the fence to determine whether they could identify him as one of the robbers. The police told them they had found someone who matched the description of one of the robbers.

Ramirez, a dark-complexioned Apache Indian with long hair, was the only suspect present and was surrounded by police officers. The police turned the headlights and spotlights from the police cars on Ramirez to provide adequate light. The witnesses viewed Ramirez by looking at him from the back seat of a police car. Of the three witnesses, only Wilson identified Ramirez as the masked man with the gun; the other two witnesses were unable to identify him as one of the robbers. Following the identification, Ramirez was placed under arrest and was charged with the robbery.

Assume that the state Supreme Court has interpreted the state constitution to diverge from the federal test of Neil v. Biggers when it comes to the reliability of suggestive identification procedures. Under the modified state rule, trial courts considering a motion to suppress identification evidence should not consider the level of certainty expressed by the witness, and should consider whether the identification remained consistent over time. Wilson mentioned tattoos and a hat in his description of the gunman for the first time during the suppression hearing. If the trial court admitted this evidence into the trial, could an appellate court fairly apply this modified test to affirm? Compare State v. Ramirez, 817 P.2d 774 (Utah 1991).

Suppose now that Kathy Davis, John Davis, and Gerald Wilson had their first opportunity to identify a suspect during a lineup at the police station two days after the Pizza Hut robbery. Would the due process clause (federal or state) bar the introduction at trial of any evidence of the pretrial identification or an at-trial identification under the following circumstances?

(a) Before the lineup takes place, a police officer mentions to the witnesses that "we have arrested someone for this crime and have included that person in this lineup."
(b) During the lineup, John says (in the presence of Kathy and Gerald), "It's definitely the third guy — I can tell by his eyes." Kathy and Gerald agree that the third lineup participant was the gunman in the robbery.
(c) After the three witnesses have identified a lineup participant as the gunman, a detective says, "You picked out the guy we had arrested for the crime."

■ NEW YORK CITY POLICE DEPARTMENT, LEGAL BUREAU, EYEWITNESS IDENTIFICATION PROCEDURES: SHOWUPS

A. The one-on-one display of a suspect to a victim is *generally prohibited* as being unnecessarily suggestive, *except:*

1. where it is conducted promptly on-the-scene; or,

2. where there is an emergency hospital situation (witness critically injured and likely to die). . . .

C. Showup Procedures — A police officer should consider the following factors when determining if a prompt on-the-scene showup is permissible:

1. The time elapsed since crime [was] committed. There is no set time limit. However, if more than a few hours have elapsed since the commission of the crime, a showup should *not* be employed. Usually, the apprehension of a suspect and return to the scene for viewing will be within minutes, not hours, of the crime. . . .

4. Showups should not be conducted at a stationhouse.

5. Manner in which suspect is displayed.

a. Never tell the witness that the perpetrator has been "caught," and that the witness must view him for identification purposes.

b. If a witness becomes aware that a "suspect" is in custody, emphasize before the viewing that it is *only a suspect,* and that the witness must not assume it is the perpetrator before even viewing the suspect. . . .

D. Group Identifications

1. Occasions will arise where an officer will ask a witness if he can pick out the suspect from a group of persons not in police custody. [For example, an officer may ask the witness to] observe suspect among a group of individuals (unarranged confrontation). [An officer also might accompany] a witness to an area where suspect is likely to be with other persons, i.e., let witness watch person coming and going from suspect's place of employment, at a park, playground, etc. Procedures:

a. Allow witness to view area, with instructions to look carefully at people on street, in doorways or in stores, etc.

b. If police officer sees a possible suspect, he may draw witness' attention in that direction.

c. Avoid pointing out a single individual, or if necessary, do so in a non-suggestive manner. Don't say, "That looks like him, doesn't it?"

E. There is no right to counsel at any showup procedure.

Notes

1. *Due process limits on suggestive identifications: majority position.* Virtually all jurisdictions have followed the federal position set out in the *Biggers* case and in Manson v. Brathwaite, 432 U.S. 98 (1977). When applying state constitutions to suggestive identifications, courts look to the totality of the circumstances, emphasizing the five factors listed in *Biggers* to determine the "reliability" of an identification despite suggestiveness in the identification procedure. A growing number of state courts, however, now de-emphasize the importance of witness certainty. Courts applying this test refuse to overturn convictions in the overwhelming majority of due process challenges to "suggestive" identifications, although there are exceptions.

Massachusetts employs a per se rule and excludes from evidence *any* identification produced by an unduly suggestive process. See Commonwealth v. Johnson, 650 N.E.2d 1257 (Mass. 1995). The *Johnson* court explained its decision as follows:

> [Mistaken] identification is believed widely to be the primary cause of erroneous convictions. Compounding this problem is the tendency of juries to be unduly receptive to eyewitness evidence. We have stated that "the law has not taken the position that a jury can be relied on to discount the value of an identification by a proper appraisal of the unsatisfactory circumstances in which it may have been made." . . . The "reliability test" is unacceptable because it provides little or no protection from unnecessarily suggestive identification procedures, from mistaken identifications and, ultimately, from wrongful convictions.

Do you agree? Does the per se rule make a defendant better off than she would have been in the absence of any suggestive identification procedure at all?

2. *Unreliable measures of reliability.* Some state courts have criticized the federal "reliability" factors from Neil v. Biggers, 409 U.S. 188 (1972), because they are inconsistent with "empirical" findings of psychologists studying eyewitness memory. One "reliability" factor said to be overrated is the level of certainty a witness displays: Many studies have suggested a very weak correlation, at best, between witness certainty and witness accuracy. A second questionable "reliability" factor is the amount of time a witness originally has to view the suspect. Although the amount of initial exposure is indeed related to the accuracy of memory, most people tend to overestimate the amount of time that elapsed during events that they witness. Did the Wisconsin court in *Dubose* respond adequately to these alleged problems with the federal "reliability" test? Is the court's modified test more empirically grounded? Will it lead to different results?

3. *Showups and lineups.* All other factors being equal, showups are thought to be more suggestive than lineups. Does the due process limitation on the use of identification evidence give police enough reason to avoid showups in favor of lineups whenever possible? Note that the New York City police policy allows showups in the field, but only those occurring within a "reasonable time" (ordinarily within a few hours) of the crime. What proportion of total identification procedures would you imagine occur in this setting? In light of the rapid deterioration of human memory, does the short time lapse between the crime and the identification make the showup, on balance, as reliable as a lineup occurring several hours, days, or weeks later? See Nancy Steblay, Jennifer Dysart, Solomon Fulero & R. C. L. Lindsay, Eyewitness Accuracy Rates in Police Showup and Lineup Presentations: A Meta-Analytic Comparison, 27 Law & Hum. Behav. 523 (2003) (in target-present conditions, showups and lineups yield approximately equal hit rates, whereas in target-absent conditions, showups produce a higher level of correct rejections; false identifications are more numerous for showups when innocent suspect resembles perpetrator).

The recommended procedures for eyewitness evidence issued by the U.S. Department of Justice allow police officers to conduct a showup. Because of the "inherent suggestiveness" of the showup, the witness should be cautioned that the person may not be the perpetrator. According to the guidelines, if one witness identifies a suspect during a showup, the police should use other identification procedures for other witnesses.

4. *Statutory limits on lineups.* For many years, few jurisdictions passed statutes or court rules addressing the use of identification procedures by police. Exonerations based on DNA evidence, however, pointed to identification procedures as a major source of errors in criminal justice and convinced many state legislatures to address

the question. See, e.g., North Carolina General Statutes §15A-284.52 (specifying "warning" statements to be given to witnesses before making identification, and requiring extensive documentation of identification procedures used during investigation). For recent legislative developments in this field, see the web extension for this chapter at *http://www.crimpro.com/extension/ch09*. How do legislatures compare to state appellate courts as the institution to take the lead in changing identification procedures? See Sandra Guerra Thompson, Eyewitness Identifications and State Courts as Guardians Against Wrongful Conviction, 7 Ohio St. J. Criminal Law 603 (2010).

5. *Detention for identification.* Do the police have the power to compel a person who is not currently in custody to participate in a lineup? Many states do address this question by statute and court-issued rules of procedure. See Model Code of Pre-Arraignment Criminal Procedure, art. 170. Nebraska Revised Statutes §29-3303 is typical. It authorizes a judge to order a person to submit to a lineup or some other identification procedure (such as fingerprinting). The order may issue upon a showing that (1) there is probable cause to believe that an offense has been committed; (2) identification procedures may contribute to the identification of the individual who committed the offense; and (3) the identified or described individual has refused, or will refuse, to participate voluntarily.

Such a court order is not necessary if a suspect is already in police custody. A few state rules and statutes allow the detention of persons for the purpose of participating in lineups or other identification procedures, even in the absence of probable cause to believe the detained person committed the crime. See State v. Rodriguez, 921 P.2d 643 (Ariz. 1996). Courts have approved of this practice even in the absence of a statute or rule authorizing it. See State v. Hall, 461 A.2d 1155 (N.J. 1983) (court can compel participation in lineup without probable cause). Are identification procedures sufficiently similar to fingerprinting to allow a judicial order of detention based on less than probable cause? Note that detention for fingerprinting at the station house, based on less than probable cause, would likely be an unconstitutional "seizure" if it took place without a judicial order. See Davis v. Mississippi, 394 U.S. 721 (1969). In a state allowing the police to detain a suspect for identification purposes, should a defendant have a comparable power to obtain a court order forcing *another* suspect to attend a lineup? Should citizens generally have an obligation to take part in a lineup along with a suspect who physically resembles them? Would you willingly take part in a lineup? For modest compensation, say, $100?

■ JOHN J. FARMER, ATTORNEY GENERAL GUIDELINES FOR PREPARING AND CONDUCTING PHOTO AND LIVE LINEUP IDENTIFICATION PROCEDURES

Attorney General of New Jersey, April 18, 2001

I. Composing the Photo or Live Lineup

The following procedures will result in the composition of a photo or live lineup in which a suspect does not unduly stand out. An identification obtained through a lineup composed in this manner should minimize any risk of misidentification and have stronger evidentiary value than one obtained without these procedures.

A. In order to ensure that inadvertent verbal cues or body language do not impact on a witness, whenever practical, considering the time of day, day of the week, and other personnel conditions within the agency or department, the person conducting the photo or live lineup identification procedure should be someone other than the primary investigator assigned to the case. The Attorney General recognizes that in many departments, depending upon the size and other assignments of personnel, this may be impossible in a given case. In those cases where the primary investigating officer conducts the photo or live lineup identification procedure, he or she should be careful to avoid inadvertent signaling to the witness of the "correct" response.

B. The witness should be instructed prior to the photo or live lineup identification procedure that the perpetrator may not be among those in the photo array or live lineup and, therefore, they should not feel compelled to make an identification.

C. When possible, photo or live lineup identification procedures should be conducted sequentially, i.e., showing one photo or person at a time to the witness, rather than simultaneously.

D. In composing a photo or live lineup, the person administering the identification procedure should ensure that the lineup is comprised in such a manner that the suspect does not unduly stand out. However, complete uniformity of features is not required.

E. *Photo Lineup.* In composing a photo lineup, the lineup administrator or investigator should:

1. Include only one suspect in each identification procedure.
2. Select fillers (non-suspects) who generally fit the witness' description of the perpetrator. When there is a limited or inadequate description of the perpetrator provided by the witness, or when the description of the perpetrator differs significantly from the appearance of the suspect, fillers should resemble the suspect in significant features.
3. Select a photo that resembles the suspect's description or appearance at the time of the incident if multiple photos of the suspect are reasonably available to the investigator.
4. Include a minimum of five fillers (nonsuspects) per identification procedure.
5. Consider placing the suspect in different positions in each lineup when conducting more than one lineup for a case due to multiple witnesses.
6. Avoid reusing fillers in lineups shown to the same witness when showing a new suspect. . . .

9. Preserve the presentation order of the photo lineup. In addition, the photos themselves should be preserved in their original condition. . . .

II. Conducting the Identification Procedure . . .

B. *Sequential Photo Lineup.* When presenting a sequential photo lineup, the lineup administrator or investigator should:

1. Provide viewing instructions to the witness as outlined in subsection I B, above.

2. Provide the following additional viewing instructions to the witness:

a. Individual photographs will be viewed one at a time.

b. The photos are in random order.

c. Take as much time as needed in making a decision about each photo before moving to the next one.

d. All photos will be shown, even if an identification is made prior to viewing all photos; or the procedure will be stopped at the point of an identification (consistent with jurisdiction/departmental procedures).

3. Confirm that the witness understands the nature of the sequential procedure.

4. Present each photo to the witness separately, in a previously determined order, removing those previously shown.

5. Avoid saying anything to the witness that may influence the witness' selection.

6. If an identification is made, avoid reporting to the witness any information regarding the individual he or she has selected prior to obtaining the witness' statement of certainty.

7. Record any identification results and witness' statement of certainty. . . .

9. Instruct the witness not to discuss the identification procedure or its results with other witnesses involved in the case and discourage contact with the media.

Problem 9-2. Photo Lineups

On August 8, a man robbed the Fort Gratiot branch of the People's Bank in Port Huron, Michigan, of more than $22,000 (including approximately $600 in Canadian currency). Three bank tellers, the branch manager, and a customer witnessed the robbery and gave descriptions of the robber and his car to investigators. Bank teller Mary Kamendat described the robber as approximately 45 or 46 years old, almost six feet tall, weighing about 210 pounds, with dust or some other substance on his face. She also described him as needing a haircut. Another bank teller, Cindy Dortman, noticed that the robber was wearing a light-colored shirt, a baseball cap, dark sunglasses, and had longer hair than normal for a man of his age. She also described him as wearing flared jeans, with a chain hanging out of his pocket and his shirt pulled over his pants. She said that the robber had a "long, very distinguished" nose.

The bank's surveillance camera took photographs of the robber. After the local newspaper published two of the surveillance photographs a few days after the crime, the St. Glair County Sheriff's Department received several phone calls regarding the robbery. One caller identified Albin Kurylczyk as the man in the photographs. This information prompted a detective and an FBI agent to visit Kurylczyk at his home on August 17. At their request, Kurylczyk permitted the officers to search his house and his car, which was similar to the getaway car the eyewitnesses had described. He also agreed to accompany the investigators to the local police station for further interviews. Once there, he consented to be photographed. At that time, he was not represented by counsel, nor did he request an attorney.

On the same day, other deputies responded to a call from the bank. The bank tellers Dortman and Kamendat believed the robber had returned when a customer dressed like the robber entered the bank and attempted to exchange some

Canadian currency. The tellers detained him by delaying his transaction until the deputies arrived. However, after an investigation, the law enforcement authorities were satisfied that this customer was not the bank robber. He was not included in any of the identification procedures used later in the investigation.

Two days later, on August 19, a detective assembled an array of six photographs, including the photograph he had taken of Kurylczyk and one of another suspect. Kurylczyk was the only man in the photographic array dressed in clothing that matched the description of the eyewitnesses. In particular, his photo showed him wearing a chain attached to his belt and extending to a wallet in the rear pocket of his jeans. None of the others in the photographic lineup wore such a trucker's wallet. This same type of wallet was visible in the bank's surveillance photographs, as published in the local paper. In addition, Kurylczyk's photograph was taken from a closer distance, so that his image appeared larger than the others. Three of the men in the array had mustaches; Kurylczyk did not have a mustache, and none of the witnesses described the robber as having a mustache.

The detective showed the photo array to Kamendat and Dortman, and both identified Kurylczyk as the bank robber. As a result, the government charged him with the crime. Before trial, Kurylczyk moved to exclude the identification testimony of the eyewitnesses. First, he contended that he was entitled to the assistance of counsel during the photographic lineup. Second, he argued that the photographic lineup was impermissibly suggestive in violation of his Fourteenth Amendment right of due process. How should the trial court rule? Compare People v. Kurylczyk, 505 N.W.2d 528 (Mich. 1993).

Problem 9-3. Videorecorded Lineups

At 2:20 A.M., a man entered a gas station and asked Roy Beals, the attendant, for permission to use the telephone. He was followed by a second man, holding what appeared to be a .45-caliber automatic pistol, and by a third man, whom Beals was unable to see. The three men robbed the gas station. Beals told police after the robbery that the gunman was approximately 5"6' or 5"7' tall, and wore a knee-length brown vinyl coat, with a fleecy lining and collar. From the loose fit of the coat, Beals assumed the man was thin. The man wore what appeared to be uniform pants and a security guard's cap, with a badge, and had a second badge pinned on his collar. The fleecy coat collar was turned up around the man's face, and the bill of his cap came down to his eyebrows. Beals was therefore able to observe only a portion of the man's face. From his observation, Beals could tell that the gunman was a black man and that he was not wearing glasses, but could not describe him further. He could not describe the man's hair or estimate his age.

The gunman told Beals to turn around, go into a back room, and lie face down on the floor. Following Beals into the backroom, the gunman then asked where "the money" was. Beals answered that the money was in a locked box on a post outside. The man demanded a key, but Beals did not have one. At one point, the gunman struck him with the weapon he was carrying. The robbers were in the station for about five minutes, and Beals spent most of this time face down on the floor.

Later that same day, the police stopped a car containing four young black men, including Oscar McMillian. The four occupants of the car were taken into custody. At some point, the police staged a lineup, consisting of these four men, in connection with the investigation of an unrelated crime, a purse-snatching. The lineup was recorded on videotape with an audio recording of the men speaking. No attorney was present at this lineup.

Several days later, McMillian was charged with armed robbery. Soon thereafter, the police showed the videotaped lineup to Beals. McMillian was given no notice that Beals was to view the recorded lineup, and defense counsel was not present at the viewing. Based on the defendant's height, build, and voice, Beals identified McMillian as the gunman in the gas station robbery. Was it error to allow Beals to view the videotape without McMillian's attorney being present? Will the trial court allow Beals to identify McMillian at trial? Compare McMillian v. State, 265 N.W.2d 553 (Wis. 1978).

Notes

1. *Due process limits on photo identifications.* As with in-person identifications, the due process clause creates a second constitutional restraint on photographic identifications. If the photo array is unduly suggestive, *and* if the totality of the circumstances suggests that the improper identification procedure created an undue risk of misidentification, the court will exclude at trial any evidence based on that tainted identification. See Commonwealth v. Silva-Santiago, 906 N.E.2d 299 (Mass. 2009) (court described the preferred procedures for presenting photographic arrays to eyewitnesses, and declared that it expected law enforcement agencies to follow these protocols in future; double-blind procedure is best practice but not required in every case; no suppression of identification in this case).

Many of the claims of unduly "suggestive" photo arrays derive from the showing of multiple photo arrays to the witness when the suspect's picture appears in each of the arrays. Courts virtually always reject challenges based on these claims. See, e.g., State v. Rezk, 609 A.2d 391 (N.H. 1992) (approves an identification in second photo lineup when defendant was the only subject pictured also in first photo lineup and was the only person pictured in prison overalls).

2. *Departmental policies and photospreads.* The New Jersey Attorney General policy on photo identifications reprinted above is based in part on recommendations from the U.S. Department of Justice. What would motivate a law enforcement official to recommend procedures that are more specific than what the courts have required in constitutional litigation? The New Jersey policy differs from the DOJ policy in stating a preference for sequential lineups and "blind" presentations. What are the arguments against these two requirements?

3. *Whose pictures?* When the police have no suspect, they will sometimes ask the witness to review a large number of photos in the hope that the perpetrator's picture will appear. Which pictures can the police show to a witness? Can the photos include only those who have been convicted of a crime similar to the one now at issue? Any arrested person? Any person at all? Suppose the police collect pictures of persons from one ethnic group, awaiting those occasions when a crime victim is attempting to identify, say, an Asian perpetrator? See San Jose Recorder, Jan. 31, 1996 (lawsuit settlement by the town of San Jose, California, paying $150,000 in damages to person who spent three months in jail after being identified by witness to armed robbery; witness selected photograph from mug book containing pictures

only of Asians, many of whom — like plaintiff — had never been arrested or convicted). More recently, computer programs have enabled the police to create a digitized image based on the description by a witness, and to match that digitized image to photographs in existing databases such as arrest files or drivers' license pictures. For a survey of the typical features of this software, see the web extension of this chapter at *http://www.crimpro.com/extension/ch09*.

C. OTHER REMEDIES FOR IMPROPER IDENTIFICATION PROCEDURES

As we have seen, one remedy for improper pretrial identification procedures is the exclusion at trial of any evidence of the pretrial identification, along with the possible exclusion of any at-trial identification based on the earlier procedure. But the exclusion remedy is extreme. Recall that identifications tend to be important to the prosecution in cases charging very serious crimes such as rape and robbery. Perhaps for this reason, courts invoke the remedy in only a small number of cases. Whatever problems might be present with the identification procedure, courts have concluded most of the time that the improper identification method was a "harmless error" of sorts — that it did not cause the witness to make an improper identification.

In sum, the exclusion remedy is available to very few defendants who have legitimate complaints about improper identification procedures. Is there some way other than exclusion for these defendants to reduce the chances of an erroneous conviction?

The following case considers the need for a jury instruction that highlights the difficulties of cross-racial identifications. Do you believe that the arguments in favor of such an instruction are basically the same as those supporting instructions about identifications more generally, or is there something distinctively difficult about cross-racial identifications? Will jury instructions of the sort described in this opinion actually change juror conduct?

■ STATE v. McKINLEY CROMEDY

727 A.2d 457 (N.J. 1999)

COLEMAN, J.

This appeal involves a rape and robbery in which a cross-racial identification was made of defendant as the perpetrator seven months after the offenses occurred. The identification of the perpetrator was the critical issue throughout the trial. The trial court denied defendant's request to have the jury instructed concerning the cross-racial nature of the identification. . . . The novel issue presented is whether a cross-racial identification jury instruction should be required in certain cases before it is established that there is substantial agreement in the scientific community that cross-racial recognition impairment of eyewitnesses is significant enough to warrant a special jury instruction. Our study of the recommendations of a Court-appointed Task Force, judicial literature, and decisional law from other jurisdictions persuades us that there exists a reliable basis for a cross-racial identification charge. We hold that the trial court's failure to submit to the jury an instruction similar to the one requested by defendant requires a reversal of defendant's convictions.

On the night of August 28, 1992, D.S., a white female student then enrolled at Rutgers University in New Brunswick, was watching television in her basement apartment. While she was relaxing on the couch, an African-American male entered the brightly lit apartment and demanded money from D.S., claiming that he was wanted for murder and that he needed funds to get to New York. After D.S. told the intruder that she had no money, he spotted her purse, rifled through it, and removed money and credit cards.

The intruder then [demanded that she remain quiet and led her by the arm into the brightly lit kitchen. He sexually assaulted her.] Throughout the sexual assault, D.S. was facing the kitchen door with her eyes closed and hand over her mouth to avoid crying loudly. Once the assault was over, D.S. faced her attacker who, after threatening her again, turned around and left the apartment. At the time of the second threat, D.S. was standing approximately two feet away from her assailant. The attacker made no attempt to conceal his face at any time. D.S. immediately called the New Brunswick Police Department after the intruder left the apartment. . . .

D.S. described her assailant as an African-American male in his late 20s to early 30s, full-faced, about five feet five inches tall, with a medium build, mustache, and unkempt hair. She stated that the intruder was wearing a dirty gray button-down short-sleeved shirt, blue warm-up pants with white and red stripes, and a Giants logo on the left leg. . . . Three days later, a composite sketch was drawn by an artist with her assistance. The following day at police headquarters, D.S. was shown many slides and photographs, including a photograph of defendant, in an unsuccessful attempt to identify her assailant.

On April 7, 1993, almost eight months after the crimes were committed, D.S. saw an African-American male across the street from her who she thought was her attacker. She spotted the man while she was standing on the corner of a street in New Brunswick waiting for the light to change. As the two passed on the street, D.S. studied the individual's face and gait. Believing that the man was her attacker, D.S. ran home and telephoned the police, giving them a description of the man she had just seen. Defendant was picked up by the New Brunswick police and taken to headquarters almost immediately. Within fifteen minutes after seeing defendant on the street, D.S. viewed defendant in a "show-up" from behind a one-way mirror and immediately identified him as the man she had just seen on the street and as her attacker. Defendant was then arrested and, with his consent, saliva and blood samples were taken for scientific analysis. [The State Police Laboratory was unable to determine whether those samples matched the samples obtained from D.S. at the time of the crime.]

Because of the nature of the crimes, the races of the victim and defendant, and the inability of the victim to identify defendant from his photograph, and because defendant was not positively identified until almost eight months after the date of the offenses, defense counsel sought a cross-racial identification jury charge. The following language was proposed:

> [Y]ou know that the identifying witness is of a different race than the defendant. When a witness who is a member of one race identifies a member who is of another race we say there has been a cross-racial identification. You may consider, if you think it is

> appropriate to do so, whether the cross-racial nature of the identification has affected the accuracy of the witness's original perception and/or accuracy of a subsequent identification.

In support of that request, defendant cited the June 1992 New Jersey Supreme Court Task Force on Minority Concerns Final Report, 131 N.J. L.J. 1145 (1992) (Task Force Report).

The trial court denied the request because this Court had not yet adopted the Task Force Report and because there had been no expert testimony with respect to the issue of cross-racial identification. The trial court instead provided the jury with the Model Jury Charge on Identification. The jury convicted defendant of first-degree aggravated sexual assault. . . .

For more than forty years, empirical studies concerning the psychological factors affecting eyewitness cross-racial or cross-ethnic identifications have appeared with increasing frequency in professional literature of the behavioral and social sciences. People v. McDonald, 690 P.2d 709, 717-18 (Cal. 1984). [Studies] have concluded that eyewitnesses are superior at identifying persons of their own race and have difficulty identifying members of another race. See generally Gary Wells & Elizabeth Loftus, Eyewitness Testimony: Psychological Perspectives 1 (1984); Elizabeth Loftus, Eyewitness Testimony (1979). This phenomenon has been dubbed the "own-race" effect or "own-race" bias. Its corollary is that eyewitnesses experience a "cross-racial impairment" when identifying members of another race. Studies have consistently shown that the "own-race effect" is strongest when white witnesses attempt to recognize black subjects.

Although researchers generally agree that some eyewitnesses exhibit an own-race bias, they disagree about the degree to which own-race bias affects identification. In one study, African-American and white "customers" browsed in a convenience store for a few minutes and then went to the register to pay. Researchers asked the convenience store clerks to identify the "customers" from a photo array. The white clerks were able to identify 53.2% of the white customers but only 40.4% of the African-American subjects. Stephanie Platz & Harmon Hosch, Cross-Racial/Ethnic Eyewitness Identification: A Field Study, 18 J. Applied Soc. Psychol. 972, 977-78 (1988). . . .

Many studies on cross-racial impairment involve subjects observing photographs for a few seconds. Because the subjects remembered the white faces more often than they recalled the African-American faces, researchers concluded that they were biased towards their own race. See Paul Barkowitz & John C. Brigham, Recognition of Faces: Own-Race Bias, Incentive, and Time Delay, 12 J. Applied Soc. Psychol. 255 (1982). Yet, there is disagreement over whether the results of some of the tests can be generalized to real-world situations in which a victim or witness confronts an assailant face-to-face and experiences the full range of emotions that accompany such a traumatic event.

The debate among researchers did not prevent the Supreme Court of the United States, in the famous school desegregation case of Brown v. Board of Education of Topeka, 347 U.S. 483, 494 n.11 (1954), from using behavioral and social sciences to support legal conclusions without requiring that the methodology employed by those scientists have general acceptance in the scientific community. . . . Thus, Brown v. Board of Education is the prototypical example of an appellate court using modern social and behavioral sciences as legislative evidence to support its choice of a rule of law.

In United States v. Telfaire, 469 F.2d 552 (D.C. Cir. 1972), Chief Judge Bazelon urged in his concurring opinion that juries be charged on the pitfalls of cross-racial identification. He believed that the cross-racial nature of an identification could affect accuracy in the same way as proximity to the perpetrator and poor lighting conditions. He felt that a meaningful jury instruction would have to apprise jurors of that fact. . . . Judge Bazelon rejected the notion that instructions on interracial identifications "appeal to racial prejudice." Rather, he believed that an explicit jury instruction would safeguard against improper uses of race by the jury and would delineate the narrow context in which it is appropriate to consider racial differences. . . .

The Supreme Court of the United States has acknowledged that problems exist with eyewitness identifications in general and cross-racial identifications in particular. Manson v. Brathwaite, 432 U.S. 98 (1977). Although there have been no reported decisions in our own State addressing the propriety of requiring a cross-racial identification jury instruction, decisions have been rendered by courts in other jurisdictions. The majority of courts allowing cross-racial identification charges hold that the decision to provide the instruction is a matter within the trial judge's discretion. Omission of such a cautionary instruction has been held to be prejudicial error where identification is the critical or central issue in the case, there is no corroborating evidence, and the circumstances of the case raise doubts concerning the reliability of the identification. See United States v. Thompson, 31 M.J. 125 (C.M.A. 1990) (calling for cross-racial identification instruction when requested by counsel and when cross-racial identification is a "primary issue"); People v. Wright, 755 P.2d 1049 (Cal. 1988). . . .

Courts typically have refused the instruction where the eyewitness or victim had an adequate opportunity to observe the defendant, there was corroborating evidence bolstering the identification, and/or there was no evidence that race affected the identification. See Commonwealth v. Hyatt, 647 N.E.2d 1168 (Mass. 1995) (declining instruction in rape and robbery case where victim was terrorized for fifteen to twenty minutes in broad daylight and could see the attacker's face).

A number of courts have concluded that cross-racial identification simply is not an appropriate topic for jury instruction. See State v. Willis, 731 P.2d 287, 292-93 (Kan. 1987); People v. McDaniel, 630 N.Y.S.2d 112, 113 (N.Y. App. Div. 1995). Those courts have determined that the cross-racial instruction requires expert guidance, and that cross-examination and summation are adequate safeguards to highlight unreliable identifications. Other jurisdictions have denied the instruction, finding that the results of empirical studies on cross-racial identification are questionable. People v. Bias, 475 N.E.2d 253, 257 (Ill. App. Ct. 1985) (rejecting instruction in robbery case where eyewitness failed to describe key distinguishing facial features and gave inconsistent descriptions because empirical studies are not unanimous). One jurisdiction has even rejected cross-racial identification instructions as improper commentary on "the nature and quality" of the evidence. See State v. Hadrick, 523 A.2d 441, 444 (R.I. 1987) (rejecting such instruction in robbery case where victim viewed perpetrator for two to three minutes at close range during robbery and identified him from a line-up). . . .

It is well-established in this State that when identification is a critical issue in the case, the trial court is obligated to give the jury a discrete and specific instruction that provides appropriate guidelines to focus the jury's attention on how to analyze and consider the trustworthiness of eyewitness identification. State v. Green, 430 A.2d 914 (N.J. 1981). *Green* requires that as a part of an identification charge a trial court inform the jury that [it] should consider, among other things, "the capacity or the ability of the witness to make observations or perceptions . . . at the time and under all of the attendant circumstances for seeing that which he says he saw or that which he says he perceived with regard to his identification." What defendant sought through the requested charge in the present case was an instruction that informed the jury that it could consider the fact that the victim made a cross-racial identification as part of the "attendant circumstances" when evaluating the reliability of the eyewitness identification.

The Court-appointed Task Force discussed and debated the issue of the need for a cross-racial and cross-ethnic identification jury instruction for more than five years. That Task Force was comprised of an appellate judge, trial judges, lawyers representing both the prosecution and defense, social scientists, and ordinary citizens. . . . Task Force sessions were conducted in much the same way as legislative committees conduct hearings on proposed legislation. . . . Ultimately, in 1992 the Task Force submitted its final report to the Court in which it recommended, among other things, that the Court develop a special jury charge regarding the unreliability of cross-racial identifications.

The Court referred that recommendation to the Criminal Practice Committee. . . . The Criminal Practice Committee has submitted that proposed charge to the Model Jury Charge Committee for its review. That Committee is withholding further consideration of the proposed charge pending the Court's decision in the present case.

We reject the State's contention that we should not require a cross-racial identification charge before it has been demonstrated that there is substantial agreement in the relevant scientific community that cross-racial recognition impairment is significant enough to support the need for such a charge. This case does not concern the introduction of scientific evidence to attack the reliability of the eyewitness's identification. Defendant's requested jury instruction was not based upon any "scientific, technical, or other specialized knowledge" to assist the jury. N.J.R.E. 702. He relied instead on ordinary human experience and the legislative-type findings of the Task Force because the basis for his request did not involve a matter that was beyond the ken of the average juror.

[I]n a prosecution in which race by definition is a patent factor, race must be taken into account to assure a fair trial. At the same time, we recognize that unrestricted use of cross-racial identification instructions could be counter-productive. Consequently, care must be taken to insulate criminal trials from base appeals to racial prejudice. An appropriate jury instruction should carefully delineate the context in which the jury is permitted to consider racial differences. The simple fact pattern of a white victim of a violent crime at the hands of a black assailant would not automatically give rise to the need for a cross-racial identification charge. More is required.

A cross-racial instruction should be given only when, as in the present case, identification is a critical issue in the case, and an eyewitness's cross-racial identification is not corroborated by other evidence giving it independent reliability. Here, the eyewitness identification was critical; yet it was not corroborated by any forensic evidence or other eyewitness account. The circumstances of the case raise some doubt concerning the reliability of the victim's identification in that no positive identification was made for nearly eight months despite attempts within the first five days following the commission of the offenses. Under those circumstances, turning over to the jury the vital question of the reliability of that identification without acquainting the jury with the potential risks associated with such identifications could have affected the jurors' ability to evaluate the reliability of the identification. We conclude, therefore, that it was reversible error not to have given an instruction that informed the jury about the possible significance of the cross-racial identification factor, a factor the jury can observe in many cases with its own eyes, in determining the critical issue — the accuracy of the identification. . . .

Because of the widely held commonsense view that members of one race have greater difficulty in accurately identifying members of a different race, expert testimony on this issue would not assist a jury, and for that reason would be inadmissible. We request the Criminal Practice Committee and the Model Jury Charge Committee to revise the current charge on identification to include an appropriate statement on cross-racial eyewitness identification that is consistent with this opinion. . . .

Notes

1. *Jury instructions about eyewitness testimony: majority position.* Judicial instructions to the jury can remind jurors about the vagaries of human memory. Such instructions are sometimes called *Telfaire* instructions, after one of the first cases to approve of their use. See United States v. Telfaire, 469 F.2d 552 (D.C. Cir. 1972) (describing a suggested jury instruction). Most states leave it to the trial judge to decide whether to grant a defense request for such an instruction. About 30 states allow (but do not require) the trial judge to grant a request for such jury instructions. Roughly 10 states do require jury instructions, at least when there is some special reason to question the identification. See State v. Ledbetter, 881 A.2d 290 (Conn. 2005) (under supervisory power, court requires jury instructions whenever police fail to tell witness that suspect might not be present in the lineup); Brodes v. State, 614 S.E.2d 766, 769 (Ga. 2005) (jury instructions on factors affecting reliability of eyewitness testimony may not state that witness certainty is an indicator of accuracy).

As the court in *Cromedy* discussed, there may be special reasons to instruct the jury on this issue when the prosecution depends on a cross-racial identification. However, a small but growing number of states prohibit the use of such instructions. See Graham v. Commonwealth, 250 Va. 79 (1995). If jury instructions provide enough specific information about the circumstances that tend to produce less reliable eyewitness testimony, are they an adequate replacement for exclusion? See Edith Greene, Eyewitness Testimony and the Use of Cautionary Instructions, 8 U. Bridgeport L. Rev. 15 (1987) (study of impact of standard jury instructions regarding eyewitness memory, concluding they do not improve juror performance).

2. *Admissibility of expert testimony on eyewitness memory.* Starting in the early 1980s, a few defendants asked courts to allow experts to testify about recurring problems with witness memory. At first, very few courts allowed those experts to testify. Since then, the trend has been toward allowing such testimony. The high state courts addressing this question fall into several different groups. Appellate courts in fewer than 10 states still instruct trial courts that such expert testimony is not admissible

in the ordinary criminal case because it invades the province of the jury. The largest group of appellate courts (over 30 states) now allow the trial court the discretion to admit or exclude the testimony. See Weatherred v. State, 15 S.W.3d 540 (Tex. Crim. App. 2000) (trial court excluded, affirmed on appeal); State v. Clopten, 223 P.3d 1103 (Utah 2009) (expert testimony regarding the reliability of eyewitness identification is admissible under the general standard that governs all expert testimony). There are still very few appellate courts that will overturn a trial court's decision to exclude such testimony as an abuse of discretion. Under what circumstances might a court conclude that such testimony is necessary to a fair trial? See People v. LeGrand, 867 N.E.2d 374 (N.Y. 2007) (it can be an abuse of discretion for the trial court to exclude expert testimony about "weapon focus" if guilt or innocence turns on accuracy of eyewitness identifications and there is little or no corroborating evidence connecting defendant to the crime).

3. *The experts on expert testimony.* Social scientists have concluded that there is a great need for expert testimony about eyewitness identifications. Studies of jurors have indicated (with the usual ambiguity of social science studies) that jurors (1) place great weight on eyewitness testimony as they deliberate and reach their verdicts and (2) often have misconceptions about the reliability of eyewitness testimony and the conditions that pose the greatest risks for misidentification. See Brian Cutler, Steven Penrod, & Hedy Dexter, Juror Sensitivity to Eyewitness Identification Evidence, 14 Law & Hum. Behav. 185 (1990) (study showing jurors remain unaffected by factors that should influence accuracy of witness's memory); but cf. Rogers Elliott, B. Farrington, & H. Manheimer, Eyewitnesses Credible and Discredible, 18 J. Appl. Soc. Psychol. 1411 (1988) (recounts difficulty in replicating early studies showing that jurors rely heavily on eyewitness testimony). Social scientists are split on the question of whether expert testimony can correct juror misconceptions about eyewitness memory without affecting their overall willingness to believe eyewitness testimony. Compare Brian Cutler, Steven Penrod, & Hedy Dexter, The Eyewitness, the Expert Psychologist, and the Jury, 13 Law & Hum. Behav. 311 (1989); with E. B. Ebbesen & V. J. Konecni, Eyewitness Memory Research: Probative v. Prejudicial Value, 5 Expert Evidence 2-28 (1997) (prejudicial outweighs probative value).

4. *Expert testimony as a substitute for exclusion.* In light of the rare use of the exclusion remedy, is expert testimony a more effective method of preventing wrongful convictions? Is due process satisfied whenever the defense can counter any prosecution eyewitness testimony with expert testimony about human memory? Must the government pay for such experts to testify for indigent criminal defendants? See Espinosa v. State, 589 So. 2d 887 (Fla. 1991) (trial court did not abuse discretion in refusing to order state to pay for defense expert on eyewitness memory); State v. Broom, 533 N.E.2d 682 (Ohio 1988) (refusal to appoint eyewitness identification expert to aid in indigent's defense was no due process violation; defendant made no particularized showing of reasonable probability that such an expert would aid in his defense).

5. *Corroboration.* Would it make sense to exclude identification evidence — regardless of any violations of due process or right to counsel — unless there is independent evidence to corroborate the identification evidence? See Regina v. Turnbull, [1977] 1 Q.B. 224 (1976):

> When, in the judgment of the trial judge, the quality of the identifying evidence is poor, as for example when it depends solely on a fleeting glance or on a longer observation

made in difficult conditions, [the] judge should then withdraw the case from the jury and direct an acquittal unless there is other evidence which goes to support the correctness of the identification. [For] example, X sees the accused snatch a woman's handbag; he gets only a fleeting glance of the thief's face as he runs off but he does see him entering a nearby house. [Although this is poor identification evidence, the judge need not withdraw the case from the jury] if there was evidence that the house into which the accused was alleged by X to have run was his father's.

6. *Prosecutors as the cure.* Is the prosecutor's power to decline to file charges against a defendant the ultimate remedy for weak identification evidence? Do prosecutors have adequate incentives and ability to screen out cases with the most questionable eyewitness-identification evidence? When Samuel Gross studied the records available in a large number of misidentification cases, he reached the following conclusions:

> (1) More often than not, a misidentified defendant was originally suspected because of his appearance. (2) A misidentified defendant is more likely to be cleared before his case comes to trial than after. (3) If he is not exonerated before trial, a misidentified defendant will almost certainly go to trial rather than plead guilty, even in return for an attractive plea bargain. (4) A misidentified defendant who is convicted at trial may still be exonerated, but the chances decrease over time.

Gross, Loss of Innocence: Eyewitness Identification and Proof of Guilt, 16 J. Legal Stud. 395 (1987).

X

Complex Investigations

Most crime investigations last for a short time and involve the efforts of only a few law enforcement officers. Different procedural issues crop up when investigations last longer and involve more people. In this chapter, we consider two central issues that arise in complex investigations. In the first section, we consider whether the legal system places any limits on the government's choice and pursuit of targets. In the second section, we consider the power of the grand jury to investigate crimes and the legal and practical limits on that power.

A. SELECTION AND PURSUIT OF TARGETS

1. *Selective Investigations*

The typical crime investigation is reactive: It aims to collect evidence of a known and completed crime. What if an investigation focuses instead on a person when there is no evidence of wrongdoing, or on a specific area where crimes might be committed? Does the government ever have to justify its decision to investigate, so long as it does not conduct a "search" or "seizure"? In this section, we consider whether targets of investigations can object to the criteria that the government uses to select places or persons to investigate.

What criteria *should* government agents use — or not use — to focus attention on settings when there is not yet any evidence that a crime has taken place? The Department of Justice memorandum below represents one internal effort by a law enforcement agency to select the highest priority investigative targets. The following two cases identify the possible grounds for constitutional challenges to investigators' choices. In Chapter 13, we will consider the distinct but related question of "selective prosecution": challenges to the decision of a prosecutor (as opposed to an investigator) to file criminal charges in some but not all similar cases when there is sufficient evidence of a crime.

■ MEMORANDUM FOR SELECTED UNITED STATES ATTORNEYS

FROM: David W. Ogden, Deputy Attorney General
SUBJECT: Investigations and Prosecutions in States Authorizing the Medical Use of Marijuana
DATE: October 19, 2009

This memorandum provides clarification and guidance to federal prosecutors in States that have enacted laws authorizing the medical use of marijuana. These laws vary in their substantive provisions and in the extent of state regulatory oversight, both among the enacting States and among local jurisdictions within those States. Rather than developing different guidelines for every possible variant of state and local law, this memorandum provides uniform guidance to focus federal investigations and prosecutions in these States on core federal enforcement priorities.

The Department of Justice is committed to the enforcement of the Controlled Substances Act in all States. Congress has determined that marijuana is a dangerous drug, and the illegal distribution and sale of marijuana is a serious crime and provides a significant source of revenue to large-scale criminal enterprises, gangs, and cartels. One timely example underscores the importance of our efforts to prosecute significant marijuana traffickers: marijuana distribution in the United States remains the single largest source of revenue for the Mexican cartels.

The Department is also committed to making efficient and rational use of its limited investigative and prosecutorial resources. In general, United States Attorneys are vested with "plenary authority with regard to federal criminal matters" within their districts. USAM 9-2.001. In exercising this authority, United States Attorneys are "invested by statute and delegation from the Attorney General with the broadest discretion in the exercise of such authority." This authority should, of course, be exercised consistent with Department priorities and guidance.

The prosecution of significant traffickers of illegal drugs, including marijuana, and the disruption of illegal drug manufacturing and trafficking networks continues to be a core priority in the Department's efforts against narcotics and dangerous drugs, and the Department's investigative and prosecutorial resources should be directed towards these objectives. As a general matter, pursuit of these priorities should not focus federal resources in your States on individuals whose actions are in clear and unambiguous compliance with existing state laws providing for the medical use of marijuana. For example, prosecution of individuals with cancer or other serious illnesses who use marijuana as part of a recommended treatment regimen consistent with applicable state law, or those caregivers in clear and unambiguous compliance with existing state law who provide such individuals with marijuana, is unlikely to be an efficient use of limited federal resources. On the other hand, prosecution of commercial enterprises that unlawfully market and sell marijuana for profit continues to be an enforcement priority of the Department. To be sure, claims of compliance with state or local law may mask operations inconsistent with the terms, conditions, or purposes of those laws, and federal law enforcement should not be deterred by such assertions when otherwise pursuing the Department's core enforcement priorities.

Typically, when any of the following characteristics is present, the conduct will not be in clear and unambiguous compliance with applicable state law and may indicate illegal drug trafficking activity of potential federal interest:

- Unlawful possession or unlawful use of firearms;
- Violence;
- Sales to minors;
- Financial and marketing activities inconsistent with the terms, conditions, or purposes of state law, including evidence of money laundering activity and/or financial gains or excessive amounts of cash inconsistent with purported compliance with state or local law;
- Amounts of marijuana inconsistent with purported compliance with state or local law;
- Illegal possession or sale of other controlled substances; or
- Ties to other criminal enterprises.

Of course, no State can authorize violations of federal law, and the list of factors above is not intended to describe exhaustively when a federal prosecution may be warranted. . . .

This guidance regarding resource allocation does not "legalize" marijuana or provide a legal defense to a violation of federal law, nor is it intended to create any privileges, benefits, or rights, substantive or procedural, enforceable by any individual, party or witness in any administrative, civil, or criminal matter. Nor does clear and unambiguous compliance with state law or the absence of one or all of the above factors create a legal defense to a violation of the Controlled Substances Act. Rather, this memorandum is intended solely as a guide to the exercise of investigative and prosecutorial discretion.

Finally, nothing herein precludes investigation or prosecution where there is a reasonable basis to believe that compliance with state law is being invoked as a pretext for the production or distribution of marijuana for purposes not authorized by state law. Nor does this guidance preclude investigation or prosecution, even when there is clear and unambiguous compliance with existing state law, in particular circumstances where investigation or prosecution otherwise serves important federal interests.

Your offices should continue to review marijuana cases for prosecution on a case-by-case basis, consistent with the guidance on resource allocation and federal priorities set forth herein, the consideration of requests for federal assistance from state and local law enforcement authorities, and the Principles of Federal Prosecution.

■ AH SIN v. GEORGE WITTMAN

198 U.S. 500 (1905)

MCKENNA, J.*

[Ah Sin filed a petition] alleging that he was a subject of the Emperor of China, and was restrained of his liberty by . . . the chief of police of the city and county of San Francisco, under a judgment of imprisonment rendered in the police court of said city for the violation of one of its ordinances. [Defendant was convicted under a city ordinance making it "unlawful for any person within the limits of the city and county of San Francisco to exhibit or expose to view in . . . any place built or protected in a manner to make it difficult of access or ingress to police officers when three or more persons are present, any cards, dice, dominoes, fan-tan table or layout, or any part of such layout, or any gambling implements whatsoever." The ordinance also made it unlawful to "visit or resort to" such a house or room, and provided for punishment upon conviction by a fine not to exceed five hundred dollars, or by imprisonment in the county jail for not more than six months, or both.]

Plaintiff in error avers "That said ordinance and the provisions thereof are enforced and executed by the said municipality of San Francisco, and said State of California, solely and exclusively against persons of the Chinese race, and not otherwise." The contention is that Chinese persons are thereby denied the equal protection of the law in violation of the Fourteenth Amendment of the Constitution of the United States. Yick Wo v. Hopkins, 118 U.S. 356 (1886), is cited to sustain the contention. . . . That case concerned the use of property for lawful and legitimate purposes. The case at bar is concerned with gambling, to suppress which is recognized as a proper exercise of governmental authority, and one which would have no incentive in race or class prejudice or administration in race or class discrimination. In the *Yick Wo* case there was not a mere allegation that the ordinance attacked was enforced against the Chinese only, but it was shown that not only the petitioner in that case, but two hundred of his countrymen, applied for licenses, and were refused, and that all the petitions of those not Chinese, with one exception, were granted. The averment in the case at bar is that the ordinance is enforced "solely and exclusively against persons of the Chinese race and not otherwise." There is no averment that the conditions and practices to which the ordinance was directed did not exist exclusively among the Chinese, or that there were other offenders against the ordinance than the Chinese as to whom it was not enforced. No latitude of intention should be indulged in a case like this. There should be certainty to every intent.

Plaintiff in error seeks to set aside a criminal law of the State, not on the ground that it is unconstitutional on its face, not that it is discriminatory in tendency and ultimate actual operation as the ordinance was which was passed on in the *Yick Wo* case, but that it was made so by the manner of its administration. This is a matter of proof, and no fact should be omitted to make it out completely, when the power of a Federal court is invoked to interfere with the course of criminal justice of a State. We think, therefore, the judgment of the Superior Court should be and it is hereby affirmed.

* [Chief Justice Fuller and Justices Harlan, Brewer, Brown, White, Holmes, and Day joined in this opinion. — EDS.]

DENNIS BALUYUT v. SUPERIOR COURT

911 P.2d 1 (Cal. 1996)

BAXTER, J.

Petitioners below are defendants charged with violation of Penal Code section 647(a)[1] in the Municipal Court for the Santa Clara County Judicial District. They sought dismissal of the charges on the ground that the Mountain View police who arrested them engaged in a pattern of discriminatory arrest and prosecution of homosexuals under this statute, thereby denying them equal protection of the law. [The trial court denied the motion to dismiss.]

In support of their motion to dismiss, defendants presented ten arrest reports spanning a two-year period. The reports described decoy officers' arrests of men in and outside an adult bookstore in Mountain View for violations of section 647(a). The arrests involved a decoy officer who had engaged a person in small talk. [After] the person eventually made it clear that he was interested in a sexual encounter the officer suggested that the person accompany the officer to the officer's car. Once at the officer's car, the person was arrested for soliciting a lewd act to be performed in a public place. . . . Other evidence was offered that the modus operandi of the decoy officers was typical of a "cruising" pattern of homosexual men and that it invited homosexual men to make contact with the decoy officer.

Mountain View police records for the two years prior to the arrest of defendants were reviewed by the municipal court which also heard testimony about the decoy operation. The court concluded that the operation was focused solely on persons who had a proclivity to engage in homosexual conduct, [and that] it did so without any relationship to the alleged problems at that location for which the citizen complaint had been initially lodged.

Based on these factual conclusions, and applying this court's decision in Murgia v. Municipal Court, 540 P.2d 44 (Cal. 1975), the municipal court ruled that defendants had established there was improper selectivity — discrimination — in prosecution and that the discrimination had an invidious basis. It was unjustifiable, arbitrary, and without a rational relationship to legitimate law enforcement interests. Notwithstanding these conclusions and the court's belief that the complaints should be dismissed, the court felt bound by People v. Smith, 155 Cal. App. 3d 1103 (1984) to deny the motion to dismiss because defendants had not established that the Mountain View police had a specific intent to punish the defendants for their membership in a particular class. . . .

Although referred to for convenience as a "defense," a defendant's claim of discriminatory prosecution goes not to the nature of the charged offense, but to a defect of constitutional dimension in the initiation of the prosecution. The defect lies in the denial of equal protection to persons who are singled out for a prosecution that is "deliberately based upon an unjustifiable standard such as race, religion, or other arbitrary classification." When a defendant establishes the elements of discriminatory prosecution, the action must be dismissed even if a serious crime is charged unless the People establish a compelling reason for the selective enforcement.

1. . . . Section 647: "Every person who commits any of the following acts is guilty of disorderly conduct, a misdemeanor: (a) Who solicits anyone to engage in or who engages in lewd or dissolute conduct in any public place or in any place open to the public or exposed to public view."

Unequal treatment which results simply from laxity of enforcement or which reflects a nonarbitrary basis for selective enforcement of a statute does not deny equal protection and is not constitutionally prohibited discriminatory enforcement. However, the unlawful administration by state officers of a state statute that is fair on its face, which results in unequal application to persons who are entitled to be treated alike, denies equal protection if it is the product of intentional or purposeful discrimination.

In *Murgia* this court explained the showing necessary to establish discriminatory prosecution: "In order to establish a claim of discriminatory enforcement a defendant must demonstrate [1] that he has been deliberately singled out for prosecution on the basis of some invidious criterion, [and (2) that] the prosecution would not have been pursued except for the discriminatory design of the prosecuting authorities." The *Smith* court elaborated on these elements and in so doing appeared to hold that the defendant must show not only that an invidious discriminatory purpose underlies the prosecution, but also that this purpose is to punish the defendant for his membership in a particular class. . . .

Nothing in *Murgia* . . . or the controlling decisions of the United States Supreme Court supports the imposition of this additional burden on a defendant. Showing an intent to punish for membership in a group or class is not necessary to establish a violation of an individual's right to equal protection under the Fourteenth Amendment to the United States Constitution. There must be discrimination and that discrimination must be intentional and unjustified and thus "invidious" because it is unrelated to legitimate law enforcement objectives, but the intent need not be to "punish" the defendant for membership in a protected class or for the defendant's exercise of protected rights. . . .

Murgia arose in the context of a motion for discovery by defendants who claimed that they were being discriminatorily prosecuted under various statutes on the basis of their membership in or support of the United Farm Workers Union (UFW) and sought information relevant to that claim. Discovery had been denied on the ground that the evidence sought was irrelevant as defendants had violated the laws under which they were charged. [We held as follows:] "Neither the federal nor state Constitution countenances the singling out of an invidiously selected class for special prosecutorial treatment, whether that class consists of black or white, Jew or Catholic, Irishman or Japanese, United Farm Worker or Teamster. If an individual can show that he would not have been prosecuted except for such invidious discrimination against him, a basic constitutional principle has been violated, and such prosecution must collapse upon the sands of prejudice."

[*Murgia* recognized that] an equal protection violation does not arise whenever officials prosecute one and not [another] for the same act; instead, the equal protection guarantee simply prohibits prosecuting officials from purposefully and intentionally singling out individuals for disparate treatment on an invidiously discriminatory basis. [But the suggestion] that discriminatory enforcement is not established unless the defendant establishes that the law enforcement officers responsible had a specific intent to punish the defendants for their membership in a particular classification finds no support in [*Murgia*]. Rather, the purpose or intent that must be shown is simply intent to single out the group or a member of the group on the basis of that membership for prosecution that would not otherwise have taken place. When there is no legitimate law enforcement purpose for singling out those persons for prosecution, the prosecution is arbitrary and unjustified and thus results in invidious discrimination. . . .

Subsequent to *Murgia* and the United States Supreme Court decisions on which it relied, the high court again visited the question and reaffirmed the factors which establish a violation of a defendant's right to equal protection, noting that ordinary equal protection principles apply in assessing discriminatory prosecution claims. In Wayte v. United States, 470 U.S. 598 (1985), the court considered a "passive enforcement" policy under which the federal government prosecuted persons who failed to register for the draft. Under that policy the government prosecuted only persons who reported themselves as unwilling to register. Those who reported themselves were known by the government as likely to be persons who for moral or religious reasons were vocal opponents of the registration requirement. At the time the policy existed, the Selective Service system was unable to develop a more active enforcement system.

Wayte . . . was one of the first persons indicted under the passive enforcement policy. He claimed to be a victim of selective or discriminatory enforcement and asserted that the indictment violated his First Amendment rights. The district court dismissed the indictment, ruling that the government had not rebutted Wayte's prima facie case of selective prosecution. [The Supreme Court held, however, that the prosecution could go forward because Wayte had failed to show that the government focused its investigation on him because of his protest activities.]

The court held that even if the government's passive enforcement policy had a discriminatory effect, Wayte had not shown that the government intended that result. Although he had shown that the government was aware that the likely impact of its passive enforcement policy was prosecution of vocal objectors, a showing of "discriminatory purpose" required more. That showing is that the government selected the course of action "at least in part 'because of,' not merely 'in spite of,' its adverse effects upon an identifiable group." . . .

We are not free to adopt a narrower construction of the protection afforded by the equal protection clause of the Fourteenth Amendment than that enunciated by the United States Supreme Court. Requiring a defendant to show that the government had a specific intent to punish a person singled out as a member of a class for criminal prosecution finds no support in the controlling precedent of the United States Supreme Court cases. . . .

Problem 10-1. Selection of Participants

A Brockton police officer arrested Ann O'Connor for two violations of the city ordinance against prostitution. After being charged with these offenses, she filed a motion to dismiss the complaints, arguing that the police had engaged in improper selective enforcement of the prostitution laws. O'Connor claimed that no male was arrested with her on either charge, because it is the police department's policy and practice to arrest only prostitutes and not their clients.

The ordinance in question was amended three years prior to O'Connor's arrest, to apply both to the prostitute and the client:

> Any person who engages, agrees to engage, or offers to engage in sexual conduct with another person in return for a fee, or any person who pays, agrees to pay or offers to

pay another person to engage in sexual conduct, or to agree to engage in sexual conduct with another natural person may be punished by imprisonment in a jail or house of correction for not more than one year, or by a fine of not more than five hundred dollars, or by both such fine and imprisonment.

One Brockton police detective testified at the motion hearing about the department's typical methods of surveillance of female suspects on certain streets in Brockton. The police officer typically would observe (1) females on the street waving at males in cars, (2) a female entering a vehicle and driving off with a male, (3) both returning after an interval, and then (4) a repetition of the process with a different male. The detective testified that, in such circumstances, "ordinarily" the police do not arrest the driver of the vehicle. In cases in which the officer follows the vehicle and discovers two passengers in the vehicle engaged in a sexual act, only the female is arrested.

The detective stated that the basic reason for the policy was that complaints from area citizens related "mainly to the girls," and that the women arrested are known to the police whereas the men are not. The department's arrest records for the previous year show that 36 of the 37 persons arrested for prostitution were female and that 23 of the 25 persons arrested for soliciting prostitution were female.

Will the court grant O'Connor's motion to dismiss? On the basis of a constitutional provision, or on some other basis? Compare Commonwealth v. An Unnamed Defendant, 492 N.E.2d 1184 (Mass. 1986) (constitutional violation for selective enforcement of prostitution laws) with City of Minneapolis v. Buschette, 240 N.W. 2d 500 (Minn. 1976) (no constitutional violation).

Notes

1. *Discriminatory selection of investigative targets: majority position.* Courts in almost all jurisdictions agree about the basic steps to follow in resolving a constitutional challenge to an investigator's selection of a target. Under the equal protection clause of the federal Constitution, "no state shall" make any law denying persons "the equal protection of the laws." When criminal defendants have claimed that the government's "selective enforcement" of a law violates the equal protection clause, courts have asked the defendant to address several issues. First, the defendant must show that others similarly situated were treated differently (that is, the police did not make an arrest or follow up on a viable investigative lead). Second, the defendant must show that differences between the groups receiving different treatment are legally significant (for instance, different treatment of racial or gender groups). Finally (and this is the most difficult showing), a defendant must demonstrate that the government agents intentionally discriminated against the group — that is, they chose the target *because of* the group membership, and not *in spite of* the group membership. See Wayte v. United States, 470 U.S. 598 (1985).

2. *Proving intent.* If the investigator's state of mind is critical to a claim of discriminatory investigation, how would a defendant get evidence of such a state of mind? As we will see in Chapter 13, courts have created a difficult standard for defendants to satisfy before they can obtain discovery on such questions. See United States v. Armstrong, 517 U.S. 456 (1996) (defendant must show that the government declined to prosecute similarly situated suspects of other races). What

showings do the courts in *Ah Sin* and *Baluyut* require of a defendant challenging an alleged discriminatory investigation? Note the California court's use of the doctrine of "specific intent," drawn from substantive criminal law. Although the term is slippery, courts speaking of specific intent usually mean (a) an awareness of some specific circumstance surrounding the crime (e.g., knowledge that property is stolen, to be convicted of receiving stolen property), or (b) an intent to do some future act beyond the act that forms the basis for a crime (e.g., a specific intent to deprive the owner of property permanently, as an element of larceny). See Joshua Dressier, Understanding Criminal Law §10.06 (5th ed. 2009). Exactly what state of mind of the investigator does the California court in *Baluyut* require the defendant to prove?

3. *Public selection of enforcement priorities.* Recall from Chapter 1 the discussion of "community policing" and its emphasis on public input into enforcement priorities. Is it adequate for the police to explain their enforcement policy by saying that they enforce certain laws only in situations when a citizen complains about a possible violation? In *Baluyut,* suppose all the complaints about violations of the public lewdness ordinance dealt with homosexual activity. Is there any danger in a police policy that ensures responsiveness to public concerns? Compare State v. Anonymous, 364 A.2d 244 (Conn. C.P. 1976) (invalidating police policy of enforcing Sunday "blue laws" only upon receiving a citizen complaint) with State v. Russell, 343 N.W.2d 36 (Minn. 1984) (denying challenge to police policy of concentrating enforcement efforts in burglary cases in one predominantly black precinct receiving most reports of burglary).

State and local law enforcement agencies often face a choice of whether to treat federal immigration laws as an enforcement priority. Some police departments routinely refer arrestees to federal immigration authorities when they have reason to believe that they are in violation of the immigration laws. In some states, such as Arizona, state legislators instruct law enforcement agencies throughout the state to pursue this strategy. In other jurisdictions, local law enforcement does not routinely cooperate with federal immigration authorities, and instead cultivates cooperation in immigrant communities in the detection and prevention of other crimes. See Jesse McKinley, "San Francisco Alters When Police Must Report Immigrants", N.Y. Times, October 21, 2009.

4. *Resources as a selection criterion.* Police departments and other criminal investigators, just like everyone else, must economize on a limited budget. Is the resource constraint, in the end, the best constraint on investigative decisions? Will budgetary considerations, like Adam Smith's invisible hand, lead investigators to direct their efforts to solve and prevent the greatest number of crimes that are of greatest concern to the community? Could the rules of legal ethics effectively supplement prosecutorial budgets by requiring prosecutors to advise criminal investigators to go forward only when the investigation is "proportional" to the suspected conduct?

For some special investigators, resource questions essentially do not exist. So-called special prosecutors (formerly known in the federal system as the "independent counsel") are typically appointed to investigate politically sensitive cases in which the public might not trust the judgment of the ordinary prosecutors or investigators. Special prosecutors do not have to apportion a limited investigative budget over a large number of potential criminal cases. If there is no effective limit on the amount of time government agents can spend investigating a single person, do the legal and political systems have any workable way to prevent abuses of the investigative power? See Julie O'Sullivan, The Independent Counsel Statute: Bad Law, Bad Policy, 33 Am. Crim. L. Rev. 463 (1996).

5. *Impact of written guidelines.* Written guidelines to govern the selection of investigative targets are the exception rather than the rule. Typically, the criteria for the selection of investigative targets are informal and unwritten, although federal investigators put these policies in writing more often than state investigators, and they tend to appear in white-collar crime settings. For examples of such policies in the investigation of immigration violations, environmental crimes, and corporate crimes, see the web extension for this chapter at *http://www.crimpro.com/extension/ch10*.

Although written policies are exceptional, law enforcement agencies routinely make decisions about how to allocate their resources. Some of these choices involve "proactive" efforts to uncover crimes that have not yet been committed or reported to the police. Is the guidance provided by the Department of Justice memorandum on case selection better than the ad hoc, oral standards recounted in Problem 10-1? If so, what are the differences between them? Or are these policies all equally futile or misleading because a certain amount of arbitrariness in enforcement is inevitable?

2. *Entrapment Defenses*

Some crimes, such as prostitution, drug trafficking, or price fixing, involve voluntary transactions that are difficult for anyone other than the participants to observe. Sometimes government agents investigate such crimes through "undercover" operations, not revealing to their targets the fact that they are law enforcement officers. The undercover agent might pretend to participate in a crime as it takes place rather than inquiring after a crime has happened. The agent might also create the opportunity for some person to commit a crime under "simulated" conditions. How should judges, legislators, and enforcement officials respond to the dangers — and perhaps the necessity — of these enforcement techniques? When will a defendant escape a conviction because the government "entrapped" him? The case and statutes that follow take up the central question surrounding the entrapment doctrine: whether the defendant's state of mind, the activities of the government, or some combination of the two should be the key concept in resolving entrapment claims.

■ PEOPLE v. JESSIE JOHNSON

647 N.W.2d 480 (Mich. 2002)

YOUNG, J.

This case involves the defense of entrapment. The circuit court found that defendant was entrapped by the police and dismissed two charges of possession with intent to deliver more than 225, but less than 650, grams of cocaine. The Court of Appeals affirmed in a split decision. We conclude that the lower courts clearly erred in finding that defendant was entrapped under Michigan's current entrapment test. . . .

Facts and Proceedings

Defendant was a police officer in the city of Pontiac. He also owned a house in the city of Pontiac that he rented out as a residence.

Defendant became the subject of a criminal investigation after one of defendant's former tenants turned informant and reported to the Pontiac police department that defendant was instrumental in operating his rented house as a drug den. The informant indicated that he sold crack cocaine from defendant's house with defendant's full knowledge and consent. Further, according to the informant, defendant arranged, oversaw, and protected the drug-selling operation. In exchange, defendant received a substantial portion of the profits from the drug sales.

The Pontiac police called in the state police for assistance in their investigation of defendant. An undercover officer from the state police department, Lieutenant Sykes, was introduced by the informant to defendant as a major drug dealer in Detroit and Mount Clemens who wished to expand his operations into Pontiac. Defendant agreed to meet with Sykes, but not pursuant to any police investigation he was conducting himself. Defendant was propositioned by Sykes to serve as protection and security from "rip-offs" and police raids for Sykes' drug operations, as well as to identify potential locations for drug dens in Pontiac. Defendant was to be compensated for his services. Defendant agreed to participate only after he determined that Sykes was not an undercover officer known to defendant's fellow Pontiac officers. Defendant made no attempt to arrest Sykes or report his illegal activities for further investigation.

At Sykes' request, defendant agreed to accompany Sykes to a mall on February 7, 1992, to assist him in purchasing drugs from a supplier. The supplier was in reality another undercover state police officer.

Defendant and Sykes arrived at the mall parking lot in different vehicles. After some preliminary discussions, Sykes drove over to the undercover officer to make the staged drug deal, while defendant walked. Armed with a gun in his pocket, defendant stood one and a half car lengths from the passenger side of the second undercover officer's vehicle. After the transaction began, Sykes directed defendant to come to the driver's side of the undercover officer's vehicle. Sykes then handed defendant the package of drugs received from the supplier in the staged drug deal. Defendant took the package and returned to Sykes' vehicle and waited for Sykes. At that time, defendant expressed some confusion regarding the exact procedures he was to follow, stating that he needed to know what to do "from A to Z." Sykes testified, and audiotapes of the February 7, 1992, drug deal confirm, that Sykes wanted defendant to take the drugs back to his car, check them, ensure that the package was correct, and notify Sykes of any problems. Sykes stated that in order for defendant to fulfill his duty to protect against "rip-offs," defendant would be required to hold and examine the drugs purchased. Sykes explained that he could not watch the supplier and the package at the same time. After this conversation, while defendant and Sykes weighed the cocaine, defendant indicated that as a result of their discussion he had a better understanding of what Sykes wanted him to do. Defendant did not express his unwillingness to perform the duties explained by Sykes. Sykes then paid defendant $1,000 for his assistance.

Sometime after this first drug deal, Sykes asked defendant if he wished to participate in future drug deals and told him that it was okay if he no longer wanted to participate. Defendant indicated that he wanted to be included in future transactions. As a result, a second, similarly staged drug deal occurred on March 4, 1992, immediately after which defendant was arrested.

Defendant was charged with two counts of possession with intent to deliver more than 225, but less than 650, grams of cocaine. [Johnson] moved to dismiss the charges on the basis of an entrapment theory. The trial court granted defendant's motion to dismiss, reasoning that Sykes had changed defendant's duty during the first transaction from one of protection to one of actual drug possession, thus entrapping defendant into the drug possessions.

As indicated, the Court of Appeals affirmed in a split decision. The majority wrote that "because many of the factors indicative of entrapment existed in this case, we hold that defendant has met his burden of proving that the police conduct would have induced an otherwise law-abiding person in similar circumstances as defendant to commit the offenses charged." It also concluded that "Sykes' conduct in this case was so reprehensible as to constitute entrapment." . . .

Analysis

Under the current entrapment test in Michigan, a defendant is considered entrapped if either (1) the police engaged in impermissible conduct that would induce a law-abiding person to commit a crime in similar circumstances or (2) the police engaged in conduct so reprehensible that it cannot be tolerated. People v. Ealy, 564 N.W.2d 168 (Mich. App. 1997). However, where law enforcement officials present nothing more than an opportunity to commit the crime, entrapment does not exist.

Inducing Criminal Conduct

When examining whether governmental activity would impermissibly induce criminal conduct, several factors are considered: (1) whether there existed appeals to the defendant's sympathy as a friend, (2) whether the defendant had been known to commit the crime with which he was charged, (3) whether there were any long time lapses between the investigation and the arrest, (4) whether there existed any inducements that would make the commission of a crime unusually attractive to a hypothetical law-abiding citizen, (5) whether there were offers of excessive consideration or other enticement, (6) whether there was a guarantee that the acts alleged as crimes were not illegal, (7) whether, and to what extent, any government pressure existed, (8) whether there existed sexual favors, (9) whether there were any threats of arrest, (10) whether there existed any government procedures that tended to escalate the criminal culpability of the defendant, (11) whether there was police control over any informant, and (12) whether the investigation was targeted. People v. Juillet, 475 N.W.2d 786 (Mich. 1991).

In holding that defendant was entrapped, the Court of Appeals found that defendant had not previously committed the possession with intent to deliver offenses charged, the procedures employed by the government escalated defendant's conduct to the charged offense, and the offer of consideration was excessive. On the basis of these three factors, it held that "because many of the factors indicative of entrapment existed," the defendant "met his burden of proving that the police conduct would have induced an otherwise law-abiding person in similar circumstances as defendant to commit the offenses charged." We respectfully disagree.

First, while the Court of Appeals noted that defendant had "merely owned" a crack house and that no evidence existed that defendant was a drug dealer or even a drug user, it ignored ample evidence presented that defendant had in fact previously committed the offense of possession with intent to deliver. To be convicted of the charge of possession with intent to deliver, the defendant must have knowingly possessed a controlled substance, intended to deliver that substance to someone else, and the substance possessed must have actually been cocaine and defendant must have known it was cocaine. Actual physical possession is unnecessary for a conviction of possession with intent to deliver; constructive possession will suffice. Constructive possession exists when the totality of the circumstances indicates a sufficient nexus between defendant and the contraband. Possession is attributed not only to those who physically possess the drugs, but also to those who control its disposition. In addition, possession may be either joint or exclusive.

Defendant owned a home that he rented to tenants who operated it as a drug house. Despite being a police officer in the jurisdiction in which the house was located, defendant knew and consented to the house being used for drug sales. Further, defendant provided protection for the operation and received a portion of the profits from the drug sales, specifically $200 for each quarter ounce of drugs sold from the house. . . .

Our conclusion that defendant previously possessed cocaine is one that we make as a matter of law. [We] do not limit our review of whether the lower courts clearly erred to the hearing testimony, but rather review the entire record. While the hearing testimony arguably lends itself to different conclusions, the audio tapes admitted into the record . . . undisputedly establish that defendant played a role in the drug operation:

> *[Informant]:* So I can take the hundred and invest it or what?
> *[Defendant]:* Alright, man, I'm gonna give you one more shot.
> *[Informant]:* Okay, dig, the same arrangement, the two off every quarter?
> *[Defendant]:* Yeah.

As far as corroboration of defendant's past participation in drug activities, this first taped telephone conversation between the informant and defendant is clear evidence that defendant previously received $200 for every quarter ounce of cocaine sold by the informant at the house and that defendant wished and agreed to continue this arrangement.

Under these circumstances, it is clear these alleged previous actions by defendant could serve as the foundation for a conviction for possession with intent to deliver under a constructive possession theory. Defendant had a duty to arrest the informant, yet not only did he permit the informant to sell drugs, he accepted money to provide protection for the operation. Without such protection, drugs would not have been sold from the house. Accordingly, defendant controlled the disposition of drugs at the house he owned and shared in the profits in so doing. For these reasons, we find clear error in the lower court's deduction that there was insufficient evidence to surmise that defendant had not previously committed the offense of possession with intent to deliver cocaine. [The] defendant's prior actions, at the very least, are sufficient to establish the charge of possession with intent to deliver cocaine as an aider and abettor.

Second, contrary to the Court of Appeals majority, we are not convinced that the procedures employed by the police escalated defendant's criminal culpability. The Court of Appeals majority wrote:

> The procedures employed by the police escalated defendant's conduct from merely owning a drug house to possession with intent to deliver cocaine. Sykes initially "hired" defendant to protect against arrest and theft and to inform Sykes of any potential drug raids. At the first staged drug buy, however, Sykes called defendant over and handed defendant the package of cocaine. It was only after the first transaction that defendant was informed that he was expected to handle the drugs, check them, and ensure that the package was "right." This active involvement was not contemplated prior to the buy. Sykes' actions, therefore, served to escalate defendant's passive involvement in the enterprise to active participation beyond the scope of what defendant had agreed to beforehand and pressured defendant into complying with Sykes' requests in order to remain a part of the enterprise. . . .

As discussed above, defendant's previous actions concerning his drug house operation amounted to possession with intent to deliver. Both offenses charged as a result of the undercover operation were possession with intent to deliver. Therefore, no conduct by the state police in the undercover operation could serve to escalate defendant's prior criminal activity. Rather, the government simply provided defendant with an additional opportunity to commit a crime that he had previously committed. . . .

Similarly, defendant's culpability was not escalated at the scene of the first transaction in regard to the role defendant agreed to play in the undercover drug transaction. The touchstone of the Court of Appeals opinion in this regard was that placing the drugs in the hands of defendant at the scene of the first drug deal was a violation of what defendant had agreed to do. However, our review of the record leads us to conclude that touching the drugs should not have come as a surprise to defendant.

Although the taped recording of the first drug transaction suggests that defendant was unsure precisely what he was to do beyond providing "protection," that confusion was not based on defendant's lack of agreement to do more. [Defendant] was hired by Sykes to protect and secure against arrests, police raids, and "rip-offs." While the Court of Appeals construed "rip-off" as narrowly as possible by equating it with "theft," protecting against a "rip-off" would seem to include ensuring that drug packages received at drug deals contain actual drugs in the negotiated quantity and quality, a task that necessarily requires taking possession of the drugs in order to properly inspect them. A recorded audiotape of defendant and Sykes discussing their arrangement before the first staged drug transaction demonstrates that Sykes informed defendant that he would have to handle the drugs on occasion:

> *Sykes:* . . . And probably on occasion, I'm gonna need your expertise to accompany me to pick up a package or two, okay. . . . So if, you know, just run here, run there, pick up some, and we'll be straight, okay. That's, that's basically all that you got to do, I'll run the rest.
>
> *Defendant:* Okay.

In addition, defendant's willingness to participate in the crimes charged is evidenced by his agreement to participate in further transactions after he participated in the first transaction, which included his taking possession of the drugs. We further note that the second drug transaction between defendant and the undercover police officers exposes a consideration that the lower courts appear to have overlooked during their review. Initial entrapment does not immunize a defendant from criminal liability for subsequent transactions that he readily and willingly undertook. . . .

For these reasons, it is apparent that Sykes' handing the drugs to defendant for inspection during the first transaction failed to escalate defendant's criminal culpability. As a result, the Court of Appeals clearly erred in concluding otherwise.

Finally, the Court of Appeals majority clearly erred in holding that the amount of money offered for defendant's services was excessive and unusually attractive. [Given] defendant's understanding that he would receive $1,000 for each transaction, the compensation was neither excessive or unusually attractive. Each transaction involved approximately ten ounces of cocaine, which had an estimated street value of $75,000. A $1,000 fee for a transaction involving almost $75,000, roughly one percent of the street value, is not excessive. This is especially evident given that defendant previously earned a $200 profit, or nearly thirty percent of the street value, for the sale of one quarter ounce of cocaine at his crack house, which the record reflects had a street value of approximately $700. Thus, the Court of Appeals clearly erred in ascertaining that defendant was impermissibly induced because the consideration for his illegal services was excessive or unusually attractive.

In sum, we have concluded that the Court of Appeals clearly erred in regard to each of the three factors that persuaded that Court to conclude that the police engaged in conduct that would induce a law-abiding person to commit a crime in similar circumstances. Therefore, because none of the remaining *Juillet* factors are at issue, we hold that defendant failed to establish by a preponderance of the evidence that the police engaged in conduct that would induce a law-abiding person to commit a crime in similar circumstances.

Reprehensible Conduct

The Court of Appeals alternatively held that the police conduct was so reprehensible that, as a matter of public policy, it could not be tolerated regardless of its relationship to the crime and therefore constituted entrapment. The majority based its reasoning primarily on its escalation analysis. . . .

As we discussed above, defendant was hired to protect against arrests, raids, and "rip-offs." In light of his alleged familiarity with drug operations, defendant should have expected that ensuring against "rip-offs" would include, among other things, examining the drugs for their legitimacy and holding the drugs to prevent a theft at the scene of the drug deal. More importantly, as indicated above, the negotiations between defendant and Sykes before the first transaction support this understanding. [Further, defendant willingly participated in the criminal enterprise and even met with Sykes at the Pontiac police department station before these drug deals in order to determine whether Sykes was an undercover officer who would be recognized by defendant's fellow officers.] Given our conclusion that defendant had previously committed the offense of possession with intent to deliver and that he agreed to provide protection against "rip-offs," which clearly includes handling the drugs in order to inspect them, the police did nothing more than provide defendant with an opportunity to commit a crime. Such conduct was not reprehensible and does not establish entrapment.

For these reasons, we conclude that the Court of Appeals clearly erred in finding that defendant established by a preponderance of the evidence that the police conduct in this case was so reprehensible as to constitute entrapment.

THE ENTRAPMENT TEST IN MICHIGAN

We originally granted leave to appeal in this case to consider whether the current entrapment test in Michigan, a modified objective test, is the most appropriate one. Accordingly, we asked the parties to address whether this Court should adopt the federal subjective test for entrapment. Sorrells v. United States, 287 U.S. 435 (1932). However, because defendant's case fails to meet even the current, more lenient modified objective test, we do not need to reach that question.

Nevertheless, after review of our entrapment defense law, we note that Chief Justice Corrigan has raised serious questions regarding the constitutionality of any judicially created entrapment test in Michigan. People v. Maffett, 633 N.W.2d 339 (Mich. 2001) (Corrigan, C. J., dissenting). Accordingly, we urge the Legislature to consider these questions and determine whether a legislative response is warranted. . . .

CAVANAGH, J., dissenting.

I concur in the majority's holding that the police conduct did not entrap defendant into the second transaction. However, I would conclude that the police conduct did entrap defendant into the first transaction; therefore, I respectfully dissent.

The majority's conclusion that defendant constructively possessed cocaine and, therefore, was not entrapped into committing the possession crimes is based on repeated references to the informant's claim that defendant "arranged, oversaw, and protected" the drug sales at the home defendant owned. [The informant, however,] did not testify at the entrapment hearing. Rather, the information that the informant allegedly relayed to the police came into evidence through the police officer the informant contacted about defendant. This officer testified as follows:

> *Q.* Now did this [informant] tell you how he [defendant] was involved? . . .
> *A.* He said he was running a dope house. [The defendant] owned the house and [the informant] was selling crack out of the house with [defendant's] full knowledge and consent and more or less participation; not in the actual sale, but in setting it up and providing protection and in running the operation. . . .

The most crucial part of the officer's testimony, which sheds light on the Court of Appeals reasoning, is omitted.

> *Q.* Did you ever run across any . . . evidence other than [the informant's] statements that [defendant] had been involved in the — this purported dope house? . . .
> *A.* Yes.
> *Q.* And what was that?

A. I checked records on the house that was pointed out and [defendant] did in fact own that house; to me that was corroboration. . . .

The police officer initially stated that the informant told him defendant set up, ran, and supervised the drug house. However, when asked what information corroborated what the informant allegedly said, the officer pointed to only the fact that defendant owned the home and accepted money to look the other way. The trial court made its credibility determination on this testimony that defendant had no other involvement beyond owning the drug house and bribery. Contrary to the picture the majority paints of defendant's part in the drug sales occurring in the home he owned, the record supports the Court of Appeals conclusion that defendant did nothing more than own a crack house and accept money to keep silent. Thus, the majority's mischaracterization of defendant's involvement directly conflicts with this Court's duty to give deference to credibility determinations in light of direct testimony supporting them.[1] . . .

I cannot join a decision that not only mischaracterizes the facts in favor of a result, but also strips the deference that is due credibility determinations made by lower courts in such a way as the majority does today. Accordingly, I would reverse in part the decision of the Court of Appeals holding defendant was entrapped into the second possession transaction and affirm in part the decision of the Court of Appeals holding defendant was entrapped into the first.

MODEL PENAL CODE §2.13

American Law Institute (1962)

(1) A public law enforcement official or a person acting in cooperation with such an official perpetrates an entrapment if for the purpose of obtaining evidence

1. [The] following is an excerpt from the body recordings of the undercover officer and defendant, which again proves that the majority's heavy reliance upon ambiguous dialog between defendant and the undercover officer before the February 7 audio tape is suspect. Even after the ambiguous discussion, which the majority quoted, defendant clearly stated that he thought his involvement was to protect.

[Undercover Officer]: Ah man, alright, alright look, the reason, the reason I got you there is so that you there not eight places away. If you eight places away, you ain't doing me no good.

[Defendant]: Two cars away.

[Undercover Officer]: That ain't doing me no good. [You] got to be there, that's why I said ride up in the car with me. That way I can, if something happens man, I'm still stuck with the Goddamn package. I want to pitch it. . . . That's, that's what I want.

[Defendant]: Oh, you want me to handle it.

[Undercover Officer]: I don't want, no, no, no, no, I, but if you're in the car, just roll down the window. I can pitch it in there. I ain't got, I ain't holding nothing. That's what I'm talking about, see? But you standing way over there, now I got to hold it and hold it, and hold it, until you get there because I, I, I can't check the package and check him too. Alright. That's my boy, but business is business.

[Defendant]: I thought you wanted protection, that's what I was under the impression that you wanted me for.

This conversation took place after the first transaction, thus revealing that defendant did not know he was to "handle" the drugs, but only thought he was to protect the undercover officer before the first transaction.

of the commission of an offense, he induces or encourages another person to engage in conduct constituting such offense by either:

(a) making knowingly false representations designed to induce the belief that such conduct is not prohibited; or

(b) employing methods of persuasion or inducement that create a substantial risk that such an offense will be committed by persons other than those who are ready to commit it.

(2) Except as provided in Subsection (3) of this Section, a person prosecuted for an offense shall be acquitted if he proves by a preponderance of evidence that his conduct occurred in response to an entrapment. The issue of entrapment shall be tried by the Court in the absence of the jury.

(3) The defense afforded by this Section is unavailable when causing or threatening bodily injury is an element of the offense charged and the prosecution is based on conduct causing or threatening such injury to a person other than the person perpetrating the entrapment.

■ MISSOURI REVISED STATUTES §562.066

1. The commission of acts which would otherwise constitute an offense is not criminal if the actor engaged in the prescribed conduct because he was entrapped by a law enforcement officer or a person acting in cooperation with such an officer.

2. An "entrapment" is perpetuated if a law enforcement officer or a person acting in cooperation with such an officer, for the purpose of obtaining evidence of the commission of an offense, solicits, encourages or otherwise induces another person to engage in conduct when he was not ready and willing to engage in such conduct.

3. The relief afforded by subsection 1 is not available as to any crime which involves causing physical injury to or placing in danger of physical injury a person other than the person perpetrating the entrapment.

4. The defendant shall have the burden of injecting the issue of entrapment.

Notes

1. *Entrapment: majority position.* The Supreme Court first recognized an entrapment defense in Sorrells v. United States, 287 U.S. 435 (1932). In that case, a government agent posed as a tourist and befriended Sorrells. The agent asked Sorrells to get him some illegal liquor. At first, Sorrells declined. Eventually, however, Sorrells obtained a half gallon of whiskey for the agent. The Supreme Court stated that improper entrapment occurs when "the criminal design originates with the officials of the Government, and they implant in the mind of an innocent person the disposition to commit the alleged offense and induce its commission in order that they may prosecute." The concurring opinions focused on the objective conduct of law enforcement personnel rather than on the subjective predisposition of the defendant.

The opinions in *Sorrells* were the origins of the "subjective" and "objective" approaches to entrapment. See also Sherman v. United States, 356 U.S. 369 (1958) (improper entrapment sets a "trap for the unwary innocent [rather than a] trap for the unwary criminal"); United States v. Russell, 411 U.S. 423 (1973) (also recognizing due process defense of "outrageous governmental conduct"). The *Sorrells* and *Sherman* cases were not constitutional rulings. The courts instead based the entrapment defense on the presumed intent of the legislators that had passed the criminal statutes involved. The courts reasoned that Congress did not mean to criminalize acts that were entirely the creations of government action.

More than 30 states follow the "subjective" test developed in the federal courts. Roughly 10 states apply the "objective" approach, exemplified in the Michigan opinion in *Johnson*. See People v. Barraza, 591 P.2d 947 (Cal. 1979). Another group of about a half dozen states use a "hybrid" approach, combining both subjective and objective elements. England v. State, 887 S.W.2d 902 (Tex. Crim. App. 1994); State v. Vallejos, 945 P.2d 957 (N.M. 1997). The subjective component of this mixed test requires evidence that the accused himself was actually induced to commit the charged offense by the persuasiveness of the police conduct. As for the objective component, the issue becomes whether the persuasion was enough to cause an ordinarily law-abiding person nevertheless to commit the offense.

If you were a prosecutor, would you systematically prefer one test over the other or would you guess that each test will be favorable to you in some factual settings and not in others? State courts sometimes adopt the entrapment doctrine (whether subjective or objective) through constitutional rulings or through their supervisory powers, whereas in many states the legislature codifies the defense. Section 2.13 of the Model Penal Code, which opts for the objective approach, has been influential. What might lead a legislature to adopt instead the subjective standard for entrapment? Could it be that those who are entrapped lack the criminal intent that the legislature was targeting when it defined the crime? If one reason to adopt an objective entrapment standard is to protect the integrity of the courts, should the legislatures attempt to address this question or should they leave it to the courts themselves?

2. *The pliability of subjective standards.* Under the "subjective" version of the entrapment defense, a defendant must demonstrate that the government "induced" him to commit the crime and that he was not "predisposed" to commit the crime. In Jacobson v. United States, 503 U.S. 540 (1992), the Supreme Court applied once again its subjective standard of entrapment. The opening words of the opinion tell the reader right away about the Court's view of the case:

> In February 1984, petitioner, a 56-year-old veteran-turned-farmer who supported his elderly father in Nebraska, ordered two magazines and a brochure from a California adult bookstore. The magazines . . . contained photographs of nude preteen and teenage boys. The contents of the magazines startled petitioner, who testified that he had expected to receive photographs of "young men 18 years or older." [Postal] inspectors found petitioner's name on the mailing list of the California bookstore. . . . There followed over the next two and one half years, repeated efforts by two Government agencies, through five fictitious organizations and a bogus pen pal, to explore petitioner's willingness to break the new [child pornography] law by ordering sexually explicit photographs of children through the mail.

The Court explained that the evidence must demonstrate predisposition both prior to and independent of the government's acts. On the evidence presented, the Court found that neither Jacobson's prior behavior nor his response to the agencies' inducements was enough to establish predisposition. Does this mean that the government must have reasonable suspicion of wrongdoing before proceeding with a sting operation against a target? See Foster v. State, 13 P.3d 61 (Nev. 2000) (undercover police need not have grounds for believing that target is predisposed; overrules earlier case requiring reasonable cause).

3. *Physical injury limitation.* Note that the Model Penal Code provision on entrapment makes the defense unavailable when the crime threatens violence to someone other than the government agent making the proposition. Why does the code make this exception? Does the threat of violence have any bearing on the defendant's predisposition? On the acceptability of the government's conduct? This statutory limitation appears in many state codes and is equally common in statutes adopting subjective and objective standards for entrapment. Ky. Rev. Stat. §505.010 (subjective standard); Utah Code Ann. §76-2-303 (objective standard). Would this exception cover drug trafficking cases?

4. *Entrapment and trial strategy.* When a defendant raises the entrapment defense, it has some important consequences at trial. Perhaps most important is the effect on the usual rules of evidence. Once a defendant claims entrapment, the rules barring the introduction of evidence of a defendant's prior criminal conduct are suspended. That evidence becomes relevant to proving predisposition; it also may be relevant to the reasonableness of the government's actions if government agents knew about the conduct. Because of this change in the rules of evidence, many defense lawyers consider entrapment to be a high-risk defense. Raising entrapment also affects the instructions a trial jury could receive about possible defenses, the allocation of authority between judge and jury, and other procedural issues. For an exploration of these trial issues, see the web extension for this chapter at *http://www.crimpro.com/extension/ch10*.

Problem 10-2. Outrageous Government Conduct

During the summer of 1988, defendants Jerome Johnson, a New Jersey state trooper, and Wanda Bonet, Johnson's girlfriend, met a person who became their cocaine supplier. On one occasion, Johnson told his supplier, "I would like to rip off a drug dealer with a lot of cocaine and then I could turn around and sell it and make some money." Some months later, Johnson's supplier was arrested while delivering a large quantity of cocaine to an undercover agent of the Drug Enforcement Administration Task Force. The supplier decided to cooperate with law enforcement authorities by becoming an informant. He told DEA agents that Johnson was willing to "rip off" drugs from a drug dealer and then sell those drugs for money.

The federal agents and the New Jersey State Police jointly developed a plan to give Johnson the opportunity to steal drugs from a drug dealer and to sell those drugs. The plan contemplated that the informant would tell Johnson that he knew of an opportunity for Johnson to steal drugs from a drug courier and make a lot of money; that he, the informant, was acting as a broker for the sale of a kilogram of cocaine; that he had arranged for a "mule," a paid courier, to transport the drugs by car to a meeting place with a prospective buyer; and that the informant and the seller of the cocaine would be in a second car following the mule. According to the plan, Johnson, wearing his state trooper uniform, would pretend to make a traffic stop of the mule's car at a prearranged location and then would seize the cocaine.

The seller of the cocaine, following in the car with the broker-informant, would see the seizure and chalk up the loss of the cocaine as a cost of doing business. Johnson then would meet the broker at Johnson's apartment and sell the cocaine to the mule for $5,000.

When the informant presented and explained the scheme to Johnson, he agreed to participate and added new elements to the plan. He requested $1,000 cash in advance, an unmarked car, and a portable flashing red light to use to make the traffic stop. Johnson also indicated he would change shifts so that he would be off-duty at the time of the stop. On December 22, 1988, the informant and a detective, acting as the mule, met with Johnson and Bonet in their Newark apartment. The parties reviewed and discussed the details of the plan. The next day Johnson stopped the mule as planned and seized one kilogram of cocaine. The informant and a special agent, posing as the seller, drove off. Johnson drove to his apartment, followed by the mule. On his arrival at approximately 12:05 P.M., Johnson was arrested.

Johnson was indicted for drug offenses and for crimes related to the abuse of his office. He moved to dismiss the indictment on two grounds. First, he argued that the sting involved such outrageous government conduct that it violated state due process standards. Second, he claimed that the sting violated the New Jersey statutory entrapment defense, N.J. Stat. Ann. §2C:2-12, which provides as follows:

> A public law enforcement official or a person engaged in cooperation with such an official or one acting as an agent of a public law enforcement official perpetrates an entrapment if for the purpose of obtaining evidence of the commission of an offense, he induces or encourages and, as a direct result, causes another person to engage in conduct constituting such offense by [employing] methods of persuasion or inducement which create a substantial risk that such an offense will be committed by persons other than those who are ready to commit it.

How would you rule? Compare State v. Johnson, 606 A.2d 315 (N.J. 1992).

CINCINNATI POLICE DIVISION, PROCEDURE MANUAL §12.131 CONFIDENTIAL INFORMANT MANAGEMENT AND CONTROL

A. A person must meet three criteria to establish them as a CI: (1) the person is in a unique position to help the Division in a present or future investigation, (2) the person will not compromise Division interests or activities, (3) the person will accept the direction necessary to effectively use their services.

B. Precautions when dealing with CIs:

1. Never provide CIs with knowledge of police facilities, operations, activities, or personnel.

2. Two police officers must be capable of contacting a CI. Two officers will be present at all contact with CIs unless otherwise approved by a supervisor. [When] dealing with CIs of the opposite sex or homosexual CIs, two officers will always be present. [T]wo officers will always be present when paying CIs.

3. Immediately document initial debriefing contacts with CIs on the Confidential Informant Registration and Reliability Report.

4. Document all significant contacts with CIs on the Controlling District/Section/Unit Debriefing Report. Examples of significant contact are: (a) receiving information about criminals or criminal activity including information from phone conversations, (b) any compensation made to CIs, (c) any contact that results in an arrest or the execution of a search warrant. . . .

D. Undesirable CIs are those who (1) commit an act which could endanger the life or safety of a police officer, (2) reveal the identity of a police officer to suspects, or in any other way compromise an official investigation, (3) try to use the Division to further criminal goals, (4) provide false or misleading information to police officers, (5) engage in conduct that brings discredit or embarrassment upon the Division. . . .

L. Controlled Purchases Using Confidential Informants:

(1) Get permission from an immediate supervisor before making controlled purchases.

(2) When possible, use CIs to introduce police officers to make purchases.

(3) Use a concealed body transmitting device and/or recording devices on CIs whenever possible. Never destroy recordings before the conclusion of court proceedings, including appeals.

(4) Search all CIs before and after conducting a controlled purchase of drugs. The Strip Search Law does not apply to the voluntary search of CIs. . . .

(5) Currency used in controlled purchases: (a) photocopy and record serial numbers, (b) two officers will witness buy money given to CIs.

(6) When possible, use two or more officers for surveillance of CIs during controlled purchases.

Notes

1. *Outrageous conduct: majority position.* Most state and federal courts recognize, at least theoretically, a constitutional defense to criminal charges based on the overly aggressive tactics of government investigators. In some jurisdictions, it is called "due process entrapment," while in others (including the federal system) it is known as "outrageous governmental conduct." United States v. Russell, 411 U.S. 423 (1973). However, the defense rarely succeeds. There is no clear consensus among courts on the elements necessary to prove the defense, although many courts consider the four issues raised by the New Jersey Supreme Court in State v. Johnson, 606 A.2d 315 (N.J. 1992), the case on which Problem 10-2 was based.

> Relevant factors are (1) whether the government or the defendant was primarily responsible for creating and planning the crime, (2) whether the government or the defendant primarily controlled and directed the commission of the crime, (3) whether objectively viewed the methods used by the government to involve the defendant in the commission of the crime were unreasonable, and (4) whether the government had a legitimate law enforcement purpose in bringing about the crime. Although courts have used varying formulations of the primary factors governing due process entrapment,

> the factors most invoked center around two major recurrent concerns: the justification for the police in targeting and investigating the defendant as a criminal suspect; and the nature and extent of the government's actual involvement in bringing about the crime.

606 A.2d at 323. The defense commonly appears in drug cases because it would be difficult to prosecute many narcotics violations (which are often consensual transactions leaving behind little evidence and few willing witnesses) without undercover operations.

Most courts and commentators note that there is some overlap between the defenses of subjective entrapment, objective entrapment, and due process "outrageous conduct." See Elizabeth E. Joh, Breaking the Law to Enforce It: Undercover Police Participation in Crime, 62 Stan. L. Rev. 155 (2009). The various tests all allow for some inquiry into both the predisposition of the defendant and the reasonableness of the government's conduct.

Most courts declare that they will assess outrageous misconduct claims by weighing factors on a case-by-case basis. On occasion, a court will declare a particular government tactic, regardless of the other circumstances in the case, to be outrageous conduct per se. One court has declared the use of contingency fees for informants to be outrageous governmental conduct per se. See State v. Glosson, 462 So. 2d 1082 (Fla. 1985); but see State v. Florez, 636 A.2d 1040 (N.J. 1994) (court considers contingency fee for confidential informant a troubling tactic, but not enough standing alone to warrant dismissal of charges). For a sampling of the judicial reaction to government involvement in crimes as part of the investigative enterprise, see the web extension for this chapter at *http://www.crimpro.com/extension/ch10*.

2. *Regulation or ban on undercover operations?* Are undercover operations simply too corrosive to tolerate in an open and democratic society? Consider this description of the use of informants in Communist East Germany: "Of all aspects of the MfS [Ministry for State Security], the generation of an army of individuals, willing to report suspicious information about acquaintances, friends, and family roused the fiercest resentment — and fear. The end result was to turn citizens against one another and to create an atmosphere of debilitating apprehension." Nancy Travis Wolfe, Policing a Socialist Society: The German Democratic Republic 78 (1992).

Police forces in nations other than the United States have been slower to adopt undercover techniques in the enforcement of ordinary criminal laws. For instance, Italian law evaluates the actions of government agents under the ordinary complicity doctrines of criminal law, meaning that an agent must not aid or abet a crime. See Jacqueline E. Ross, Impediments to Transnational Cooperation in Undercover Policing: A Comparative Study of the United States and Italy, 52 Am. J. Comparative Law 569 (2004). What would a society look like if the law prohibited undercover police operations? Conversely, what if the law gave judges no role in regulating undercover operations? See Richard H. McAdams, The Political Economy of Entrapment, 96 J. Crim. L. & Criminology 107 (2005).

3. *Confidential informant guidelines.* The use of a confidential informant raises special difficulty for law enforcement agencies because the government has less control over the actions of its agent. The problem is most pronounced when the informant participates in a crime while being paid by the government, as opposed to simply telling a police officer about past crimes. The Cincinnati police guidelines regarding confidential informants illustrate how executive branch agencies respond

to these special concerns. What dangers were the drafters of the Cincinnati guidelines trying to prevent? See Alexandra Natapoff, Snitching: The Institutional and Communal Consequences, 73 U. Cin. L. Rev. 645 (2004) (use of informants is usually framed as a threat to accuracy, but practice is understood through its connections to plea bargaining, prosecutorial discretion, administrative nature of American criminal justice; all of these realities threaten principles of accountability, consistency, predictability, and other rule of law precepts).

4. *Undercover operations guidelines.* The Federal Bureau of Investigation has guidelines on undercover operations that involve government agents rather than informants. They address the selection of targets for sting operations and the methods used to carry them out. The guidelines require a field agent to obtain prior authorization for certain undercover operations, including those that will last more than six months, target public officials or the news media, or require government agents to engage in a felony. See S. Rep. No. 682, 97th Cong., 2d Sess. 536-52 (1982). A review by the Inspector General for the Department of Justice in 2005 concluded that the FBI complied effectively with the undercover operation guidelines, but deviations from the Department's guidelines on confidential informants were more common. Office of the Inspector General, The Federal Bureau of Investigation's Compliance with the Attorney General's Investigation Guidelines (September 2005). Why might one expect to find more violations of confidential informant guidelines than undercover operation guidelines?

Most large police departments also have policies that address undercover operations, especially for narcotics and vice officers. For instance, the narcotics division of the Dallas Police Department requires written approval for all "long-term undercover operations" (longer than one to two hours). The undercover officer works with a partner whenever possible; when the officer must work undercover alone, a partner is still assigned to maintain daily contact, "cover" the undercover officer during sales, and maintain records and chain of custody for all evidence. The policy also forbids the officer to consume any narcotic unless forced to do so "under threat of immediate bodily injury." If you were drafting police guidelines on the subject of undercover investigations, what criteria would you set out for selecting the targets of undercover investigations? If you were drafting a statute on the subject, as opposed to internal guidelines, would the content of the provisions change?

5. *Supervision by prosecutors.* Prosecutors are often involved in planning and executing undercover operations. Although prosecutors have absolute immunity from any tort suit for their "prosecutorial" decisions, that immunity does not extend to a prosecutor's actions when advising criminal investigators about an undercover operation. See Burns v. Reed, 500 U.S. 478 (1991) (granting qualified "good faith" immunity but not absolute immunity to prosecutors for participation in investigations). What tort claims might arise against a prosecutor who is advising criminal investigators?

Problem 10-3. The Mayor

Federal prosecutors and FBI investigators became convinced in the early 1980s that Mayor Marion Barry of the District of Columbia was involved in various illegal activities. Over an eight-year period, federal law enforcement agencies carried out

10 separate investigations of potential illegal actions by Barry, including bribery, campaign finance fraud, prostitution, and drug use. A grand jury heard accusations from several of Barry's associates (some of them convicted for selling drugs) that the mayor had purchased and used cocaine, but Barry testified before the grand jury that he never used cocaine. None of these investigations resulted in any criminal charges.

In December 1988, district police were notified that Charles Lewis, a friend of Barry, had offered drugs to a maid at a downtown hotel. The detectives were on their way to Lewis's room but left the hotel when they learned that Barry was in the room with Lewis. That incident renewed the government's interest in the mayor's long-rumored drug use.

To create an opportunity for Barry to commit a crime, the government asked for help from a former intimate friend of Barry's, Rasheeda Moore. Moore was willing to cooperate because she was facing criminal charges herself. In January 1990, the government flew Moore to Washington from California and got her a room at the Vista International Hotel. They paid to have her hair styled. On January 18, three days before Barry planned to announce his plans to seek reelection, the agents asked Moore to invite the mayor to her hotel room.

When Barry met Moore in the hotel lobby, he was at first reluctant to go up to her room. She convinced him to accompany her to the room, along with a woman she described as her cousin, Wanda. Wanda was actually an FBI agent. Once in the room, Barry engaged Moore in small talk and drank cognac. Then Barry asked, "Can we make love before you leave, before you leave town?" Moore complained that Barry wasn't sufficiently romantic: "I can't just jump into it." Then she said, "So what are you going to do? Let's do something."

A few minutes later, Barry asked Moore about Wanda, who had left the room a few minutes earlier: "Your friend mess around?" Moore, taking the question as one about drugs, responded, "She has some, yeah, sometimes. . . . She toots [snorts cocaine] more than she'll do anything else." Soon afterward, Barry said, "I don't have anything. What about you?" A short time later, Wanda returned to the room with crack cocaine. Moore presented Barry with a pipe loaded with crack cocaine, and Barry paid for it. Then Barry looked at the pipe and said "How does this work? . . . I never done it before."

Moore replied, "That's what we used to do all the time, what are you talking about?" Barry, however, insisted that he had never "done that before." Moore then said, "Put it in there. . . . Let me give you a lighter." Barry replied "You do it," but Moore said "No, I'm not doing nothing." Each insisted several more times that the other light the pipe. Moore asked, "Are you chicken?"

Eventually Barry lit the crack pipe, put it to his mouth and inhaled twice. Almost immediately, the mayor picked up his jacket and started for the door, as Moore asked if he wanted to smoke more of the crack. "No. You're crazy," Barry responded. Barry then turned for the door, and law enforcement agents burst in from the adjoining room.

A medic told Barry that he had been exposed to a dangerous substance and asked whether the mayor wanted to go to the hospital. Barry said no. "Man, I should have followed my first instincts, I tell you," he said. Then D.C. Police Sergeant James Pawlik said, "I mean, we really didn't want this to happen."

"I didn't want it to happen, either," Barry replied. "I should, if I had followed my instincts tonight, I'd have been all right. I should have stayed downstairs.

Bitch kept insisting coming up here." After complaining about the tightness of the handcuffs, Barry spoke further about Moore: "She was slick, though. I should have known better when she wouldn't do it first. I should have known something was up." He repeatedly muttered, "Damn bitch set me up."

Pawlik asked Barry if he hadn't expected to be caught in a sting sooner or later. "I don't know," Barry said. "I guess you all been checking on me for a long time, huh?" "Obviously," Pawlik responded. "Some day it's got to happen."

"I guess you all figured that I couldn't resist that lady," Barry said. As the agents prepared to lead Barry from the room, Pawlik said, "When it's all over, it'll be better for everybody." Barry responded, "You think so?"

The government brought charges against Barry for perjury (based on his testimony to the grand jury that he had never used cocaine) and for possession of cocaine (a misdemeanor). The FBI's guidelines on undercover operations state that sting operations should be directed toward obtaining evidence of serious crimes by major criminal figures. The same guidelines suggest that officers should ordinarily arrest a suspect immediately after taking possession of cocaine (or making a purchase) and before the suspect smokes or inhales the drug.

Why did the prosecutors decide to give Barry an opportunity to commit only a misdemeanor (possession of a small amount of crack cocaine)? What form of the entrapment defense (if any) would you advise Barry to pursue? What outcome would you predict?

B. THE INVESTIGATIVE GRAND JURY

Efforts by police officers to gather information about criminal suspects have occupied most of our attention thus far. The police are indeed the government agents who gather information in most criminal law enforcement. But in more complex investigations, other institutions such as grand juries and regulatory bodies, often acting under prosecutorial guidance, become important players in the effort to build a file that could lead to criminal charges. These investigations typically pursue suspicions about alleged white-collar crimes such as fraud. Such complex investigations, although making up only a tiny fraction of the criminal cases ultimately filed, require an enormous amount of resources for both the prosecution and defense, and receive much media attention.

The grand jury is the central investigative tool in these complex cases. Unlike police departments, which emerged in this country late in the nineteenth century, the grand jury is an ancient institution. It can trace its heritage at least as far back as twelfth-century England. The grand jury began as a body of citizens that the courts empowered to investigate criminal violations in the vicinity. Initially, the criminal charges that the grand jury issued were based on the personal knowledge of grand jurors. Only later did they acquire the power to call witnesses and to consider evidence that representatives of the Crown placed before them.

The grand jury thrived when first transplanted to England's American colonies. Each state entering the Union prior to the Civil War created grand juries and gave them broad powers to call witnesses and to gather documents. Later in the nineteenth century, voters grew less enthusiastic about the institution (especially in new states, such as Colorado and Nebraska) and passed constitutional provisions allowing the legislature to abolish the grand jury altogether. Although many of the newer states no longer *required* indictments as the method of initiating charges in serious criminal cases, they retained the grand jury as one method of investigating important cases, particularly those involving political corruption, where the independence of the police or prosecutor might be in question. Because of special investigative powers given to grand juries, prosecutors found it convenient to rely on them to gather evidence in cases, such as those involving conspiracies and documentary material, where routine police work could not produce enough evidence.

The grand jury is technically an arm of the court, and a judge supervises some of its activities. For instance, a judge hears any motions to quash a grand jury subpoena and will enforce a subpoena if a witness refuses to comply. The court instructs the grand jurors at the beginning of their term about their general responsibilities. Despite this supervisory power, the judge is generally not present during grand jury proceedings, and state and federal courts have proven reluctant to interfere in the affairs of the grand jury.

In this section, we consider issues relating to the special investigative powers of grand juries and similar governmental bodies to subpoena testimony and evidence. We postpone until Chapter 13 our discussion of the charging functions of the grand jury.

1. *Grand Jury Secrecy*

A witness who receives a subpoena to testify before a grand jury enters an unfamiliar room where the prosecuting attorney asks most of the questions, the grand jurors listen, and the stenographer records everything said. The witness usually knows very little about the grand jury's overall investigation or her place in that investigation. In this setting, most of the information flows in one direction. The grand jury can obtain a lot of information without revealing much of its investigative strategy.

Witnesses, however, often have legal counsel who can make the grand jury less intimidating. In an ordinary criminal case, an attorney enters the scene only after the government already has gathered most of its evidence. But lawyers have the opportunity to become involved earlier in more complex investigations because of the long time period involved: A white-collar crime case will often take months, or even years, to investigate. Lawyers also get involved earlier in the more complex cases because larger amounts of money are often at stake, and the targets of the investigation can afford to hire an attorney. As you read the statutes and notes below, consider the intricate game that occurs when counsel and sophisticated grand jury witnesses face off against prosecutors trying to get the most information from witnesses without revealing too much about the grand jury's investigation.

■ FEDERAL RULE OF CRIMINAL PROCEDURE 6

. . . (d) Who May Be Present.

(1) While the Grand Jury Is in Session. The following persons may be present while the grand jury is in session: attorneys for the government, the witness being

questioned, interpreters when needed, and a court reporter or an operator of a recording device.

(2) During Deliberations and Voting. No person other than the jurors, and any interpreter needed to assist a hearing-impaired or speech-impaired juror, may be present while the grand jury is deliberating or voting.

(e) Recording and Disclosing the Proceedings.

(1) Recording the Proceedings. Except while the grand jury is deliberating or voting, all proceedings must be recorded by a court reporter or by a suitable recording device. But the validity of a prosecution is not affected by the unintentional failure to make a recording. Unless the court orders otherwise, an attorney for the government will retain control of the recording, the reporter's notes, and any transcript prepared from those notes.

(2) Secrecy. . . .

(B) Unless these rules provide otherwise, the following persons must not disclose a matter occurring before the grand jury: (i) a grand juror; (ii) an interpreter; (iii) a court reporter; (iv) an operator of a recording device; (v) a person who transcribes recorded testimony; (vi) an attorney for the government; or (vii) [government personnel who assists the attorney for the government].

■ COLORADO REVISED STATUTES §16-5-204(4)(d)

Any witness subpoenaed to appear and testify before a grand jury or to produce books, papers, documents, or other objects before such grand jury shall be entitled to assistance of counsel during any time that such witness is being questioned in the presence of such grand jury, and counsel may be present in the grand jury room with his client during such questioning. However, counsel for the witness shall be permitted only to counsel with the witness and shall not make objections, arguments, or address the grand jury. Such counsel may be retained by the witness or may, for any person financially unable to obtain adequate assistance, be appointed in the same manner as if that person were eligible for appointed counsel. An attorney present in the grand jury room shall take an oath of secrecy. If the court, at an in camera hearing, determines that counsel was disruptive, then the court may order counsel to remain outside the courtroom when advising his client. No attorney shall be permitted to provide counsel in the grand jury room to more than one witness in the same criminal investigation, except with the permission of the grand jury.

Problem 10-4. Selecting Witnesses

Janet Terreton has contacted the federal government with information about possible corruption in New Jersey's state and local governments. Terreton's former employer, Anderson Hagelman, is the sole proprietor of two companies that do business with various units of local governments in New Jersey. She alleges that Hagelman, along with many others who sell goods and services to state and local governments, have bribed governmental contracting officials to obtain the government contracts. Terreton resigned from her management position in Hagelman's firm two months before she contacted the government, after a dispute over her retirement compensation. Terreton's information ultimately arrives in the office of the U.S. Attorney. As the government attorney assigned to this matter, how would you begin the investigation? Should you, or the agents working with you, attempt to interview any witnesses outside the presence of the grand jury?

Notes

1. *Grand jury secrecy.* The proceedings of grand juries traditionally are secret. The federal rules of criminal procedure, like the rules and statutes of most states, codify the traditional practice: Only the grand jurors, attorneys for the government, the witness, and (sometimes) a court reporter can be present in the room. Each of these parties except for the witness has an obligation not to disclose what happens in the grand jury room. A classic explanation for the secrecy of grand jury proceedings appears in United States v. Amazon Industrial Chemical Corp., 55 F.2d 254, 261 (D. Md. 1931):

> The reasons which lie behind the requirement of secrecy may be summarized as follows: (1) To prevent the escape of those whose indictment may be contemplated; (2) to insure the utmost freedom to the grand jury in its deliberations, and to prevent persons subject to indictment or their friends from importuning the grand jurors; (3) to prevent subornation of perjury or tampering with the witnesses who may testify before the grand jury and later appear at the trial of those indicted by it; (4) to encourage free and untrammeled disclosures by persons who have information with respect to the commission of crimes; (5) to protect the innocent accused who is exonerated from disclosure of the fact that he has been under investigation, and from the expense of standing trial where there was no probability of guilt.

About 20 states have statutes or court rules, like the Colorado statute reprinted above, that allow a grand jury witness to bring an attorney into the grand jury room. See also Fla. Stat. §§905.17(1), (2). Rules of evidence do not apply to grand jury proceedings, and the witness's attorney typically may not object to any questions. What, then, is the attorney's function? Will the presence of an attorney in the grand jury room influence the type of questions asked or the witnesses selected to testify?

2. *Makeup and selection of the grand jury.* At common law, a grand jury had anywhere between 12 and 23 members. Federal grand juries have 16 to 23 members, and most state grand juries stay within the common-law size limits. See Alaska Stat. §12.40.020 (12 to 18 jurors). Some jurisdictions have grand juries that sit routinely, and the court impanels such a grand jury on its own initiative; elsewhere, the prosecutor requests the court to impanel a grand jury for some special purpose. The clerk of the court summons the potential grand jurors, typically (as in the federal system) from the list of registered voters. The judge may excuse some potential jurors if service would be particularly burdensome to them. See Sara Sun Beale, et al., Grand Jury Law and Practice §§3:04, 3:05, 4:8 (2d ed. 1997). What sorts of document requests will an investigative body of this type tend to make? How might the grand jury's requests for testimony and documents change if the court assigned staff members or experts to advise the grand jurors?

3. *Witness debriefing.* Although attorneys for grand jury witnesses are not allowed in the grand jury room in a majority of American jurisdictions, they still obtain

information about the grand jury's questions and the witness's answers by debriefing their clients immediately after the testimony. Many attorneys also encourage their clients to step outside the grand jury room periodically (perhaps after each question) for a consultation. See Sara Sun Beale, et al., Grand Jury Law and Practice §6:28 (2d ed. 1997) (surveying statutory and common law protections for witnesses' ability to consult counsel outside grand jury room). Some attorneys attempt to debrief witnesses who are not their clients. Statutes and rules of criminal procedure typically impose an obligation of secrecy on the grand jurors and the government attorneys but not on grand jury witnesses. See Fed. R. Crim. P. 6(e)(2); Ill. Code Crim. Proc. §112-6. About a dozen states have statutes or rules that prevent a grand jury witness from discussing her testimony with anyone other than her attorney. See N.C. Gen. Stat. §§15A-623(e), (g). What would be the likely attitude of government attorneys about witness debriefing? Is there anything government attorneys can or should do about it? See In re Grand Jury Proceedings, 558 F. Supp. 532 (W.D. Va. 1983) (defense lawyers may debrief all witnesses, but government attorneys may request grand jury witnesses not to discuss their testimony with others).

4. *Warnings to grand jury witnesses: constitutional requirements.* The witness who receives a subpoena to testify before the grand jury can be held in contempt of court for failing to appear, even if the witness plans only to invoke the Fifth Amendment privilege. Despite this element of coercion, the Supreme Court has decided (along with the great majority of state courts) that prosecutors need not give *Miranda* warnings to grand jury witnesses. United States v. Mandujano, 425 U.S. 564 (1976); State v. Driscoll, 360 A.2d 857 (R.I. 1976). Would you require a warning only for those witnesses who become "targets" of a grand jury investigation? Again, most jurisdictions have not required such warnings as a constitutional matter. See United States v. Washington, 431 U.S. 181 (1977) (no warning of "target" status is required by federal Constitution); People v. J.H., 554 N.E.2d 961 (Ill. 1990) (same for Illinois constitution); but see People ex rel. Gallagher v. District Court, 601 P.2d 1380 (Colo. 1979) (Colorado constitution requires warnings).

5. *Nonconstitutional requirements of warnings.* Despite a lack of success on the constitutional front, witnesses still often receive various warnings before appearing in front of the grand jury. In the federal system, the U.S. Attorney's Manual requires prosecutors to inform witnesses of their right to silence, the fact that statements to the grand jury can be used against the witness, and the fact that those who have retained attorneys may consult with their attorneys outside the grand jury room. See §9-11.151. The manual also requires prosecutors to inform grand jury witnesses (and some nonwitnesses) of their status as "targets" of the investigation. See §§9-11.151 to 155. What would be the remedy for a violation of this written prosecutorial policy? In a strong minority of states, statutes require the prosecutor to inform grand jury witnesses of their right to silence, especially when the witness is a target of the investigation. Ill. Rev. Stat. ch. 38, para. 112-4(b); Tex. Code Crim. Proc. art. 20.17. Some state statutes also require the state to notify subpoena recipients if they are targets of the investigation. See Ind. Code Ann. §35-34-2-5. Why would a potential witness want to know if he is a target of the investigation? Some state statutes provide certain advantages (such as the right to consult with counsel in the grand jury room) only to targets and not to other witnesses.

6. *Grand jury witnesses versus police interrogation.* The question of warnings for grand jury witnesses calls for a comparison between interrogation during grand jury proceedings and custodial interrogation in a police station. There are certain

similarities in the two experiences: In both cases, the witness is confined against her will, and the questioning takes place in isolation and in an unfamiliar setting. The two forms of questioning are also different: A person in police custody can end all questioning by invoking the right to silence, while a grand jury witness has no general right to silence and can be imprisoned for contempt of court for refusing to answer questions (unless the answers would be self-incriminating). Can you think of other parallels and differences between the two forms of questioning? Who goes to the grand jury and who goes to the police station?

7. *The legal ethics of contacting represented persons.* There may be times when a prosecutor would prefer to speak to witnesses outside the grand jury room. Such an interview can save the witness the trouble of appearing at a specific time and place to testify, and it allows the prosecutor to screen out all but the most relevant inculpatory evidence from the grand jury. But if the witness is represented by counsel, can the prosecutor accomplish these purposes? Can the prosecutor (or an investigator working with the prosecuting attorney) interview the witness without the witness's attorney present? The Model Rule of Professional Conduct 4.2 has some bearing on this question: "In representing a client, a lawyer shall not communicate about the subject of the representation with a person the lawyer knows to be represented by another lawyer in the matter, unless the lawyer has the consent of the other lawyer or is authorized by law to do so."

In light of this ethical rule, will criminal suspects be able to protect themselves from interrogation by placing a lawyer on retainer and notifying the government of that fact? There is a lively debate about whether state bar authorities can appropriately enforce this rule against federal prosecutors. For a sample of the arguments, see the web extension for this chapter at *http://www.crimpro.com/extension/ch10*.

2. *Immunity for Witnesses*

Although the grand jury can ask for a very broad range of testimony and documents, there is still some evidence beyond its reach. For instance, a grand jury cannot obtain information protected by common law privileges, such as the attorney-client privilege. There is also an important constitutional limit on the statements that a grand jury may obtain from a witness. The Fifth Amendment to the U.S. Constitution, and analogous provisions in almost every state constitution (all but two), create a privilege against self-incrimination:

> No person . . . shall be compelled in any criminal case to be a witness against himself. . . . [U.S. Const., amend. 5]
> No subject shall be . . . compelled to accuse or furnish evidence against himself. [N.H. Const., pt. I, art 15]

A witness who receives a subpoena to appear and testify before a grand jury (or before a magistrate, administrative agency, or congressional committee, as the case may be) can invoke this constitutional privilege and refuse to answer questions when the answers would incriminate the witness. But this does not end the matter. Once the witness has invoked the privilege against self-incrimination, the prosecutor has another option. She can ask a court to order the witness to testify despite the risk of self-incrimination; in exchange, the prosecutor promises that no government agent will use the "compelled" testimony to further a later criminal prosecution against the witness. This promise is known as "immunity."

The question of immunity offers a useful vantage point for studying the privilege against self-incrimination. Just as the nature of a contract can be understood by exploring remedies for breach of contract, so the nature of the privilege against self-incrimination becomes clear when one explores the nature of the immunity necessary to overcome that privilege. The following case explores exactly what sort of promises a prosecutor must make to an immunized witness. Although the case deals with witnesses at trial, the same constitutional reasoning would apply to the immunity offered to grand jury witnesses.

■ COMMONWEALTH v. PATRICIA SWINEHART

664 A.2d 957 (Pa. 1995)

CAPPY, J.

This case presents the question of whether the use and derivative use immunity provided in 42 Pa. C.S. §5947,[1] is consistent with the Pennsylvania constitutional privilege at Article I, Section 9, against compelled self-incrimination. For the reasons that follow we find that use and derivative use immunity is consistent with the protection provided under our state constitution.

[After the murder of David Swinehart, authorities charged his nephew, Thomas DeBlase, with the crime. Preliminary rulings and interlocutory appeals delayed his trial for several years. In the meantime,] Patricia Swinehart, the wife of the decedent, was arrested and charged with the murder of her husband, and with being a co-conspirator of DeBlase. DeBlase was subpoenaed as a witness in the Patricia Swinehart trial and offered a grant of immunity pursuant to 42 Pa. C.S. §5947. DeBlase moved to quash the subpoena and objected to the grant of immunity. . . . The trial court refused to quash the subpoena, approved the grant of immunity to DeBlase, and then when DeBlase still refused to answer, found him to be in both civil and criminal contempt. [Without DeBlase's testimony, the trial of Patricia Swinehart resulted in an acquittal. This is DeBlase's appeal of his contempt conviction.]

DeBlase asserts that the Act, which grants an immunized witness use and derivative use immunity, offers insufficient safeguards in exchange for the considerable protection guaranteed under Article I, Section 9 of the Pennsylvania Constitution which the immunized witness is forced to forsake. DeBlase acknowledges that the United States Supreme Court has upheld use and derivative use immunity as sufficient protection under the Fifth Amendment to the United States Constitution in

1. The pertinent portions of the immunity statute that are at issue provide: . . .

(c) Whenever a witness refuses, on the basis of his privilege against self-incrimination, to testify or provide other information in a [judicial proceeding, and the judge] communicates to the witness an immunity order, that witness may not refuse to testify based on his privilege against self-incrimination.

(d) No testimony or other information compelled under an immunity order, or any information directly or indirectly derived from such testimony or other information, may be used against a witness in any criminal case, except that such information may be used . . . in a prosecution [for perjury or false swearing.]

Kastigar v. United States, 406 U.S. 441 (1972). He argues, however, that the Pennsylvania Constitutional protection is broader and can only be satisfied by a grant of transactional immunity.[5]

[We] will begin our analysis with a review of the text of the constitutional provision at issue, the history of that provision as related through legislative enactments and prior decisions of this Court, related case law from our sister states, and finally, policy considerations which include matters unique to our Commonwealth.

Article I, Section 9 [says that] "In all criminal prosecutions the accused . . . cannot be compelled to give evidence against himself. . . . A comparison of the actual language in Article I, Section 9 and the Fifth Amendment does not reveal any major differences in the description of the privilege against self-incrimination within the two Constitutions. As the words themselves are not persuasive of either interpretation on the issue at bar, we turn to the prior decisions of this Court which interpreted the right against self-incrimination as contained within the Pennsylvania Constitution.

[It] was not until after the United States Supreme Court decision in Counselman v. Hitchcock, 142 U.S. 547 (1892), that this Court addressed the question of immunity in relation to the privilege against self-incrimination. In *Counselman,* the United States Supreme Court rejected a federal statute which conferred only use immunity as being an insufficient substitute for the privilege guaranteed under the Fifth Amendment. . . . The Court then went on to conclude that a statutory grant of immunity, in order to be valid as against the Fifth Amendment, "must afford absolute immunity against future prosecution for the offense to which the question relates." In the wake of *Counselman,* only those legislative grants of immunity which compelled testimony from a witness in exchange for transactional immunity were found to be valid.

Thus, from 1892 until 1978, Pennsylvania recognized only transactional immunity as a sufficient exchange for compelling a witness to forsake the privilege against self-incrimination. The courts in Pennsylvania followed the lead of the United States Supreme Court on this issue.

The Pennsylvania Legislature also adhered to the dictates of the United States Supreme Court when drafting legislation on the issue of immunity grants for witnesses. Prior to the 1978 revisions, which are at issue in this case, the immunity conferred under the Act was transactional immunity. This shift in the type of immunity authorized by the Act can easily be traced to the United States Supreme Court decision in Kastigar v. United States, 406 U.S. 441 (1972).

In *Kastigar,* the United States Supreme Court found use and derivative use immunity to adequately protect the privilege against compulsory self-incrimination contained within the Fifth Amendment. The Court reconsidered its opinion in

5. Generally three types of immunity are recognized, although some scholars treat "use" and "use and derivative use" immunity as one and the same. "Use" immunity provides immunity only for the testimony actually given pursuant to the order compelling said testimony. "Use and derivative use" immunity enlarges the scope of the grant to cover any information or leads that were derived from the actual testimony given under compulsion. Thus, under either "use" or "use and derivative use" immunity a prosecution against the witness is not foreclosed; any prosecution must, however, arise from evidence unrelated to the information which is derived from the witness's own mouth. "Transactional" immunity is the most expansive, as it in essence provides complete amnesty to the witness for any transactions which are revealed in the course of the compelled testimony.

Counselman and determined that although use immunity offers insufficient protection under the Fifth Amendment, transactional immunity offers greater protection than is necessary and thus concluded that use and derivative use immunity would thereafter be sufficient.

> [The] privilege has never been construed to mean that one who invokes it cannot subsequently be prosecuted. Its sole concern is to afford protection against being forced to give testimony leading to the infliction of penalties affixed to criminal acts. Immunity from the use of compelled testimony, as well as evidence derived directly and indirectly therefrom, affords this protection. It prohibits the prosecutorial authorities from using the compelled testimony in any respect, and it therefore insures that the testimony cannot lead to the infliction of criminal penalties on the witness.

This shift by the United States Supreme Court away from transactional immunity in favor of use and derivative use immunity was commented upon by this Court in [1975. Following the *Kastigar* decision and our 1975 decision commenting favorably on *Kastigar*,] the immunity statute was revised to its present form wherein transactional immunity was replaced with use and derivative use immunity. [It] is clear that Pennsylvania, for the most part, followed the lead of the United States Supreme Court. . . .

Turning to our sister states, we find that they are evenly split on the issue of whether their state constitutions afford protection against compulsory self-incrimination greater than the Fifth Amendment in the wake of *Kastigar*. The six states that have rejected *Kastigar* and found their constitutions to require transactional immunity are [Alaska, Hawaii, Massachusetts, Mississippi, Oregon, and South Carolina].[13]

In each of [these six states], the state courts, relying upon their constitutional self-incrimination clauses, rejected legislation that had been developed post-*Kastigar* replacing transactional immunity with use/derivative use immunity. South Carolina and Alaska found the protection of use/derivative use immunity to be too cumbersome to enforce, citing the practical problems in determining whether or not later prosecutions stemmed from the immunized testimony. Mississippi had the same practical reasons for rejecting *Kastigar* as South Carolina and Alaska. Mississippi more bluntly phrased the problem as being one of having to rely upon the good faith of the prosecutor in use/derivative use situations. . . . Oregon found the rationale of *Kastigar* unpersuasive and chose to remain consistent with their case law which had always followed the reasoning of *Counselman*. . . .

The six states which have found use and derivative use immunity consistent with the self-incrimination clauses in their state constitutions are [Arizona, Indiana, Maryland, New Jersey, New York, and Texas].[14] [These courts] accepted use and derivative use immunity grants as consistent with their state constitutions [because

13. Eleven jurisdictions provide for transactional immunity through legislation. [These include California, Idaho, Illinois, Maine, Michigan, Nevada, New Hampshire, Rhode Island, Utah, Washington, and West Virginia.]

14. Eighteen jurisdictions have provided for use/derivative use immunity through legislation passed after *Kastigar*. [These include Arkansas, Colorado, Connecticut, Delaware, Florida, Georgia, Iowa, Kansas, Louisiana, Minnesota, Montana, Nebraska, New Mexico, North Carolina, North Dakota, South Dakota, Vermont, and Wisconsin.]

they] found the state constitutional privilege at issue to be coextensive with the Fifth Amendment.

In reviewing the relevant opinions and legislation from our sister states we find no clear preference among the jurisdictions. "What appears most striking among the courts which reject use/derivative use immunity is the concern for the practical effect of separating out the information garnered from the compelled testimony when later prosecuting the individual. It is this fear that the individual will be condemned by his/her own words, even inadvertently, which caused South Carolina, Alaska, Mississippi, and to some extent, Oregon, to reject use/derivative use immunity as inconsistent with the protection from self-incrimination found within their state constitutions. . . . To complete our analysis of this issue we now turn to a consideration of policy concerns which would affect our conclusion.

This case involves the juxtaposition of the privilege against self-incrimination and the need to compel testimony. The inherent conflict between these two important concepts is the heart of this case. Each of these concepts [carries] historical baggage of considerable proportion. Our system of jurisprudence abhors the ancient star chamber inquisitions which forced a witness into "the cruel trilemma of self-accusation, perjury or contempt." On the other hand, of equal importance to our system of justice is the ancient adage that "the public has a right to every man's evidence." The concept of compelling a witness to testify has been recognized in Anglo-American jurisprudence since the Statute of Elizabeth, 5 Eliz. 1, c.9, §12 (1562). Immunizing a witness has always been a feature of Pennsylvania jurisprudence. The dilemma in balancing these competing concerns centers on the type of immunity which can best provide the public with the information to which it is entitled in order to ferret out criminal activity and at the same time protect the rights of the witness being forced to testify under compulsion.

In urging this Court to declare the present immunity statute unconstitutional, DeBlase places great emphasis on the fact that Pennsylvania has historically required transactional immunity as the only adequate safeguard for compelling a witness's testimony in violation of the right against self-incrimination. As with most critics of use/derivative use immunity, DeBlase asserts that only transactional immunity can truly protect a witness from later being condemned by his own words. The strongest argument for rejecting use/derivative use immunity is what has been commonly referred to as the "web effect." . . .

In fact in the instant case DeBlase argues that if forced to testify against his co-conspirator he will forever be caught within the web and his ability to receive a fair trial forever tainted. Specifically, the untraceable effects of his immunized testimony will impact upon the selection of his jury, the presentation of a defense, the ability to utilize character witnesses and infringe upon his decision to testify in his own behalf. The practical consequences of rejecting transactional immunity and leaving a witness clothed in only the protection of use/derivative use immunity constitutes the most salient argument against the constitutionality of 42 Pa. C.S. §5947.

On the other hand, there is no dispute that immunization of a witness is a necessary, effective and ancient tool in law enforcement. As the United States Supreme Court stated in *Kastigar,* "many offenses are of such a character that the only persons capable of giving useful testimony are those implicated in the crime." The very nature of criminal conspiracies is what forces the Commonwealth into the Hobson's choice of having to grant one of the parties implicated in the criminal scheme immunity in order to uncover the entire criminal enterprise. Thus, in order to serve justice an accommodation must be made; however, that arrangement should not place the "witness" in a better position as to possible criminal prosecution than he had previously enjoyed. A grant of immunity should protect the witness from prosecution through his own words, yet it should not be so broad that the witness is forever free from suffering the just consequences of his actions, if his actions can be proven by means other than his own words.

Clearly, there are compelling "pros" and "cons" on the question of the right against self-incrimination versus the need to immunize the witness. However, to elevate the right against self-incrimination above the right of the public to every person's evidence would not achieve a proper balance of these competing interests. Transactional immunity offers complete amnesty to the witness, a measure of protection clearly greater than the privilege against self-incrimination. The practical consequences, otherwise known as the "web effect," created by immunizing a witness should not tip the balance so far in favor of the witness that the Commonwealth is only left with the option of granting complete amnesty to a witness in order to fully investigate criminal enterprises and serve the public need for justice. Use/derivative use immunity strikes a better balance between the need for law enforcement to ferret out criminality and the right of the witness to be free of self-incrimination.

In this case we find that Article I, Section 9 is, in fact, more expansive than the Fifth Amendment; it is not, however, so expansive that the privilege against self-incrimination would require greater protection than that provided within the Act. . . . Recognizing the serious practical concerns which almost always accompany a later prosecution of the immunized witness, we hold that in the later prosecution, the evidence offered by the Commonwealth shall be reviewed with the most careful scrutiny. That is, the Commonwealth must prove, of record, by the heightened standard of clear and convincing evidence, that the evidence upon which a subsequent prosecution is brought arose wholly from independent sources. Accordingly, . . . the decision of the Superior Court is affirmed and this matter is remanded to the trial court for further proceedings consistent with this opinion. . . .

Notes

1. *Transactional and use immunity: majority position.* As the *Swinehart* court indicates, "use/derivative use" immunity is sufficient to satisfy the federal constitution, while states are divided over the type of immunity that prosecutors must offer to witnesses before a court will compel the witness to give self-incriminating testimony. Roughly 20 states require use immunity, while a slightly smaller group requires transactional immunity. In other states, the type of immunity needed varies, depending on factors such as the seriousness of the offense being investigated. Note that more states resolve this question by statute than by a constitutional court ruling. Immunity orders do not occur in a large number of cases. For instance, in 2007, prosecutors in the federal system requested immunity for 1,134 witnesses. U.S. Dept. of Justice, Sourcebook of Criminal Justice Statistics, table 5.1.2007, available at *http://www.albany.edu/sourcebook/pdf/t512007.pdf*

2. *Simple use immunity.* The Supreme Court's *Kastigar* decision approved of "use/derivative use" immunity: Later prosecution of an immunized witness is possible, but only if the prosecution's case is not based on the witness's statements or on any

investigative leads obtained from that testimony. But was the Court correct to insist on this form of immunity, instead of "simple" use immunity? Simple use immunity would prevent use of immunized testimony in a later prosecution, but it would leave the prosecution free to use evidence obtained from investigative leads created by the witness's compelled testimony. For instance, the judicially compelled testimony of a murder suspect could not be introduced at the suspect's trial, but the murder weapon found through leads obtained during compelled testimony might come into evidence. Simple use immunity was an acceptable form of overcoming the self-incrimination privilege in most states during the nineteenth century. See State ex rel. Hackley v. Kelly, 24 N.Y. 74 (1861). Courts in England today do not exclude the fruits of testimony compelled under an immunity order. Does this approach, which bars only the use of a witness's actual statements, make the most sense of the Fifth Amendment's language: "No person . . . shall be compelled . . . to be a *witness* against himself"? Would your attitude about simple use immunity be different if you were interpreting a state provision such as the one in Texas, "[The] accused . . . shall not be compelled to give evidence against himself"? Tex. Const, art. I, §10. For a constitutional defense of simple use immunity, see Akhil Amar & Renee Lettow, Fifth Amendment First Principles: The Self-Incrimination Clause, 93 Mich. L. Rev. 857 (1995).

3. *The history of the privilege against self-incrimination.* What exactly does the privilege against self-incrimination — in a federal or state constitution — protect? Because an immunity order must substitute for the privilege against self-incrimination, it creates an occasion for addressing this question. What are the relevant sources for an answer? The precise words of the constitutional provision surely should have some role. What is the relevance of the *history* of the self-incrimination concept? See generally Richard Helmholtz et al., The Privilege Against Self-Incrimination: Its Origins and Development (1997).

The Latin maxim *nemo tenetur seipsum prodere* ("no one is obliged to accuse himself") originated in the medieval law of the Roman Catholic Church: It confirmed that even though a believer had a duty to confess sins to a priest, that obligation did not extend to criminal proceedings. The concept first became prominent in England in the ecclesiastical courts which were investigating and prosecuting those who resisted Anglican religious practice and belief. Puritans and other nonconformists invoked the concept to prevent their investigation and prosecution by ecclesiastical courts. See Michael Macnair, The Early Development of the Privilege Against Self-Incrimination, 10 Oxford J. Legal Stud. 66 (1990). One of the most famous of these crusaders for religious toleration and civil liberties was John Lilburn (a leader in a movement known as the "Levellers"), who invoked the privilege against self-incrimination as a natural right in various pamphlets and at his trial for treason. Lilburn also gave a pragmatic defense of the privilege: The privilege was necessary because "most men once entrusted with authority . . . pervert the same to their own domination and to the prejudice of our Peace and Liberties." Lilburn, An Agreement of the Free People of England (1649).

Despite these early uses in ecclesiastical courts, an evidentiary privilege against the use of self-incriminating statements did not operate in the English common law criminal courts until late in the eighteenth century, when defense counsel first became widely available and it was possible for a defendant to offer a defense without testifying himself. See John Langbein, The Historical Origins of the Privilege Against Self-Incrimination at Common Law, 92 Mich. L. Rev. 1047 (1994).

The American drafters of constitutions in the late eighteenth century all included a privilege against self-incrimination as part of a cluster of rights designed to reinforce the importance of the jury in a criminal trial as the central guarantee against oppressive government. But as Eben Moglen argues, the new constitutional provision was not meant to alter existing practices, and those practices included widespread techniques to encourage an accused to testify. See Eben Moglen, Taking the Fifth: Reconsidering the Origins of the Constitutional Privilege Against Self-Incrimination, 92 Mich. L. Rev. 1086 (1994); cf. Katharine B. Hazlett, The Nineteenth Century Origins of the Fifth Amendment Privilege Against Self-Incrimination, 42 Am. J. Legal Hist. 235 (1998). Defendants in custody had to appear before a magistrate who would routinely question the defendant about his involvement in the alleged crime. If the defendant confessed, the confession could form the basis for a summary conviction before the magistrate (for lesser offenses) or could be introduced at a later trial. If the defendant refused to answer a magistrate's questions, that fact could be revealed at trial. Does this history point in the direction of transactional immunity, use/derivative use immunity, or simple use immunity? Does it point in any direction at all?

4. *The purpose of the privilege.* If the text and history leave some doubt about the proper scope of the privilege, should legislators (who draft immunity statutes) and judges (who apply them) engage in some form of moral or political philosophy to flesh out the meaning of the privilege that is most attractive, or one most in keeping with our governmental structure and traditions? David Dolinko summarized the philosophical support for the privilege as follows:

> The rationales for the privilege fall, very roughly, into two categories. Systemic rationales are policies their proponents believe to be crucial to our particular kind of criminal justice system. Individual rationales are principles claimed to be entailed by a proper understanding of human rights or by a proper respect for human dignity and individuality. Among systemic rationales are the suggestions that the privilege encourages third-party witnesses to appear and testify by removing the fear that they might be compelled to incriminate themselves and removes the temptation to employ short cuts to conviction that demean official integrity. Individual rationales include the arguments that compelled self-incrimination works an unacceptable cruelty or invasion of privacy, as well as the notion of respect for the inviolability of the human personality, and the belief that punishing an individual for silence or perjury when he has been placed in a position in which his natural instincts and personal interests dictate that he should lie is an intolerable invasion of his personal dignity.

Dolinko, Is There a Rationale for the Privilege Against Self-Incrimination? 33 UCLA L. Rev. 1063 (1986). The philosopher Jeremy Bentham criticized some of the leading arguments in favor of the privilege. He listed them as follows:

> 2. The old woman's reason. The essence of this reason is contained in the word *hard:* 'tis hard upon a man to be obliged to criminate himself. Hard it is upon a man, it must be confessed, to be obliged to do any thing that he does not like. That he should not much like to do what is meant by his criminating himself, is natural enough; for what it leads to, is, his being punished. [But] did it ever yet occur to a man to propose a general abolition of all punishment, with this hardship for a reason for it? . . .
>
> You know of such or such a paper; tell us where it may be found. A request thus simple, your tenderness shudders at the thoughts of putting to a man: his

answer might lead to the execution of that justice, which you are looking out for pretences to defeat. This request, you abhor the thought of putting to him: but what you scruple not to do (and why should you scruple to do it?) is, to dispatch your emissaries in the dead of night to his house, to that house which you call his castle, to break it open, and seize the documents by force. . . .

3. The fox-hunter's reason. This consists in introducing upon the carpet of legal procedure the idea of *fairness,* in the sense in which the word is used by sportsmen. The fox is to have a fair chance for his life: he must have . . . leave to run a certain length of way, for the express purpose of giving him a chance for escape. . . . In the sporting code, these laws are rational, being obviously conducive to the professed end. Amusement is that end. [The] use of a fox is to be hunted; the use of a criminal is to be tried. . . .
4. Confounding interrogation with torture: with the application of physical suffering, till some act is done; in the present instance, till testimony is given to a particular effect required. [The] act of putting a question to a person whose station is that of defendant in a cause, is no more an act of torture than the putting the same question to him would be, if, instead of being a defendant, he were an extraneous witness. [If] any thing he says should be mendacious, he is liable to be punished for it. . . .
5. Reference to unpopular institutions. Whatever Titius did was wrong: but this is among the things that Titius did; therefore this is wrong: such is the logic from which this sophism is deduced. In the apartment in which the court called the Court of Star-chamber sat, the roof had stars in it for ornaments. [The] judges of this court conducted themselves very badly: therefore judges should not sit in a room that has had stars in the roof. [Using this reasoning, lawyers claim that the Star Chamber was a bad court because of its] abominable practice of asking questions, by the abominable attempt to penetrate to the bottom of a cause.

5 Bentham, Rationale of Judicial Evidence 230-43 (1827). Which of the possible rationales can best explain limitations on the applicability of the concept (i.e., its use to protect a person from criminal but not civil consequences of wrongdoing, or its application only to "testimony" and not other forms of compelled cooperation with a prosecution, such as participation in a lineup)? Which of the "principled" rationales described above might support transactional immunity? For an assessment of the effect of the self-incrimination privilege in modern practice, where most cases do not go to trial, see Stephanos Bibas, The Right to Remain Silent Helps Only the Guilty, 88 Iowa L. Rev. 421 (2003).

5. *Prosecution based on independent sources.* As the *Swinehart* court indicates, the government might successfully prosecute an immunized witness for the crime that is the subject of the testimony, but only under limited circumstances. The prosecutors must show that the evidence upon which a subsequent prosecution is brought "arose wholly from independent sources" and that they did not use the compelled testimony "in any respect." If you were a prosecutor in such a case, how would you attempt to prove that your evidence was based on "independent" sources? Consider this policy from the U.S. Department of Justice Criminal Resource Manual, §9-706:

> [Prosecutors] should take the following precautions in the case of a witness who may possibly be prosecuted for an offense about which the witness may be questioned

during his/her compelled testimony: (1) Before the witness testifies, prepare for the file a signed and dated memorandum summarizing the existing evidence against the witness and the date(s) and source(s) of such evidence; (2) ensure that the witness's immunized testimony is recorded verbatim and thereafter maintained in a secure location to which access is documented; and (3) maintain a record of the date(s) and source(s) of any evidence relating to the witness obtained after the witness has testified pursuant to the immunity order.

How often will these procedures be feasible? How often will they suffice when the defendant raises a constitutional challenge to the prosecution?

6. *Effect of immunity in other jurisdictions.* If a state prosecutor immunizes a grand jury witness and compels self-incriminating testimony, what assurance does the witness have that federal prosecutors will not use the testimony as a basis for federal criminal charges? The Supreme Court has declared that the Fifth Amendment requires federal prosecutors to respect the immunity grants of state governments. Murphy v. Waterfront Commission, 378 U.S. 52 (1964). Does this ruling create a potential source of conflict between state and federal authorities? If so, how might the various actors respond to the conflict?

7. *Invoking the privilege based on potential future prosecutions.* Although the Fifth Amendment speaks of a privilege "in any criminal case," a person need not testify in a criminal courtroom to invoke the privilege. In fact, it is extraordinarily easy to invoke Fifth Amendment protections, because they apply to any legally compelled statements that *could* lead to the discovery of incriminating evidence, even though the statements themselves are not incriminating and are not introduced into evidence. Such statements would include grand jury testimony or testimony in a civil trial. For further discussion of the invocation and effects of the privilege in grand jury investigations, see the web extension for this chapter at *http://www.crimpro.com/extension/ch10*.

3. Document Subpoenas

Documents are the stock in trade of an investigative grand jury. The grand jury obtains documents by issuing subpoenas to document holders, compelling them to appear before the grand jury with the documents in hand. In reality, the prosecutor who advises the grand jury draws up the subpoena duces tecum describing the documents the grand jury demands. The terms of the subpoena are often very broad, and courts and legislatures have placed few if any bounds on the document requests. There is no requirement for the grand jury to show probable cause or reasonable suspicion that the documents they request will contain evidence of a crime. Historically, the documents needed only to be relevant to some legitimate grand jury inquiry. In the following case, consider whether the Supreme Court places any limits on the documents a grand jury may request.

UNITED STATES v. R. ENTERPRISES, INC.

498 U.S. 292 (1991)

O'CONNOR, J.*

This case requires the Court to decide what standards apply when a party seeks to avoid compliance with a subpoena duces tecum issued in connection with a grand jury investigation.

I.

Since 1986, a federal grand jury sitting in the Eastern District of Virginia has been investigating allegations of interstate transportation of obscene materials. In early 1988, the grand jury issued a series of subpoenas to three companies — Model Magazine Distributors, Inc. (Model), R. Enterprises, Inc., and MFR Court Street Books, Inc. (MFR). Model is a New York distributor of sexually oriented paperback books, magazines, and videotapes. R. Enterprises, which distributes adult materials, and MFR, which sells books, magazines, and videotapes, are also based in New York. All three companies are wholly owned by Martin Rothstein. The grand jury subpoenas sought a variety of corporate books and records and, in Model's case, copies of 193 videotapes that Model had shipped to retailers in the Eastern District of Virginia. All three companies moved to quash the subpoenas, arguing that the subpoenas called for production of materials irrelevant to the grand jury's investigation and that the enforcement of the subpoenas would likely infringe their First Amendment rights. [The district court denied the motions.]

II.

The grand jury occupies a unique role in our criminal justice system. It is an investigatory body charged with the responsibility of determining whether or not a crime has been committed. Unlike this Court, whose jurisdiction is predicated on a specific case or controversy, the grand jury can investigate merely on suspicion that the law is being violated, or even just because it wants assurance that it is not. The function of the grand jury is to inquire into all information that might possibly bear on its investigation until it has identified an offense or has satisfied itself that none has occurred. As a necessary consequence of its investigatory function, the grand jury paints with a broad brush. A grand jury investigation is not fully carried out until every available clue has been run down and all witnesses examined in every proper way to find if a crime has been committed. [The] Government cannot be required to justify the issuance of a grand jury subpoena by presenting evidence sufficient to establish probable cause because the very purpose of requesting the information is to ascertain whether probable cause exists.

[Any requirement that the government show probable cause or the relevance of a request in a grand jury subpoena] ignores that grand jury proceedings are subject to strict secrecy requirements. See Fed. R. Crim. P. 6(e). Requiring the Government to explain in too much detail the particular reasons underlying a subpoena

* [The Justices were unanimous in joining parts I and II of this opinion. Chief Justice Rehnquist and Justices White, Kennedy, and Souter joined in parts III and IV; Justice Scalia joined in parts IIIA and IV. — EDS.]

threatens to compromise the indispensable secrecy of grand jury proceedings. Broad disclosure also affords the targets of investigation far more information about the grand jury's internal workings than the Federal Rules of Criminal Procedure appear to contemplate.

III.

A.

The investigatory powers of the grand jury are nevertheless not unlimited. Grand juries are not licensed to engage in arbitrary fishing expeditions, nor may they select targets of investigation out of malice or an intent to harass. In this case, the focus of our inquiry is the limit imposed on a grand jury by Federal Rule of Criminal Procedure 17(c), which governs the issuance of subpoenas duces tecum in federal criminal proceedings. The Rule provides that "[the] court on motion made promptly may quash or modify the subpoena if compliance would be unreasonable or oppressive."

This standard is not self-explanatory. [What] is reasonable depends on the context. . . . In the grand jury context, the decision as to what offense will be charged is routinely not made until after the grand jury has concluded its investigation. One simply cannot know in advance whether information sought during the investigation will be relevant and admissible in a prosecution for a particular offense.

To the extent that Rule 17(c) imposes some reasonableness limitation on grand jury subpoenas, however, our task is to define it. In doing so, we recognize that a party to whom a grand jury subpoena is issued faces a difficult situation. As a rule, grand juries do not announce publicly the subjects of their investigations. A party who desires to challenge a grand jury subpoena thus may have no conception of the Government's purpose in seeking production of the requested information. Indeed, the party will often not know whether he or she is a primary target of the investigation or merely a peripheral witness. Absent even minimal information, the subpoena recipient is likely to find it exceedingly difficult to persuade a court that compliance would be unreasonable. . . .

Our task is to fashion an appropriate standard of reasonableness, one that gives due weight to the difficult position of subpoena recipients but does not impair the strong governmental interests in affording grand juries wide latitude, avoiding minitrials on peripheral matters, and preserving a necessary level of secrecy. We begin by reiterating that the law presumes, absent a strong showing to the contrary, that a grand jury acts within the legitimate scope of its authority. Consequently, a grand jury subpoena issued through normal channels is presumed to be reasonable, and the burden of showing unreasonableness must be on the recipient who seeks to avoid compliance. . . . Drawing on the principles articulated above, we conclude that where, as here, a subpoena is challenged on relevancy grounds, the motion to quash must be denied unless the district court determines that there is no reasonable possibility that the category of materials the Government seeks will produce information relevant to the general subject of the grand jury's investigation. . . .

B.

It seems unlikely, of course, that a challenging party who does not know the general subject matter of the grand jury's investigation, no matter how valid that party's claim, will be able to make the necessary showing that compliance would be unreasonable. After all, a subpoena recipient cannot put his whole life before the court in order to show that there is no crime to be investigated. Consequently, a court may be justified in a case where unreasonableness is alleged in requiring the Government to reveal the general subject of the grand jury's investigation before requiring the challenging party to carry its burden of persuasion. We need not resolve this question in the present case, however, as there is no doubt that respondents knew the subject of the grand jury investigation pursuant to which the business records subpoenas were issued. . . .

IV.

Applying these principles in this case demonstrates that the District Court correctly denied respondents' motions to quash. It is undisputed that all three companies — Model, R. Enterprises, and MFR — are owned by the same person, that all do business in the same area, and that one of the three, Model, has shipped sexually explicit materials into the Eastern District of Virginia. The District Court could have concluded from these facts that there was a reasonable possibility that the business records of R. Enterprises and MFR would produce information relevant to the grand jury's investigation into the interstate transportation of obscene materials. Respondents' blanket denial of any connection to Virginia did not suffice to render the District Court's conclusion invalid. A grand jury need not accept on faith the self-serving assertions of those who may have committed criminal acts. Rather, it is entitled to determine for itself whether a crime has been committed. . . .

STEVENS, J., concurring in part and concurring in the judgment.*

Federal Rule of Criminal Procedure 17(c) authorizes a federal district court to quash or modify a grand jury subpoena duces tecum "if compliance would be unreasonable or oppressive." This Rule requires the district court to balance the burden of compliance, on the one hand, against the governmental interest in obtaining the documents on the other. A more burdensome subpoena should be justified by a somewhat higher degree of probable relevance than a subpoena that imposes a minimal or nonexistent burden. Against the procedural history of this case, the Court has attempted to define the term "reasonable" in the abstract, looking only at the relevance side of the balance. Because I believe that this truncated approach to the Rule will neither provide adequate guidance to the district court nor place any meaningful constraint on the overzealous prosecutor, I add these comments.

The burden of establishing that compliance would be unreasonable or oppressive rests, of course, on the subpoenaed witness. . . . This showing might be made in various ways. Depending on the volume and location of the requested materials, the mere cost in terms of time, money, and effort of responding to a dragnet subpoena could satisfy the initial hurdle. Similarly, if a witness showed that compliance with the subpoena would intrude significantly on his privacy interests, or call for the disclosure of trade secrets or other confidential information, further inquiry would

* [Justices Marshall and Blackmun joined in this opinion. — EDS.]

be required. Or, as in this case, the movant might demonstrate that compliance would have First Amendment implications.

The trial court need inquire into the relevance of subpoenaed materials only after the moving party has made this initial showing. And, as is true in the parallel context of pretrial civil discovery, a matter also committed to the sound discretion of the trial judge, the degree of need sufficient to justify denial of the motion to quash will vary to some extent with the burden of producing the requested information. For the reasons stated by the Court, in the grand jury context the law enforcement interest will almost always prevail, and the documents must be produced. I stress, however, that the Court's opinion should not be read to suggest that the deferential relevance standard the Court has formulated will govern decision in every case, no matter how intrusive or burdensome the request.

■ OHIO REVISED CODE §2939.12

When required by the grand jury, prosecuting attorney, or judge of the court of common pleas, the clerk of the court of common pleas shall issue subpoenas and other process to any county to bring witnesses to testify before such jury.

■ ARKANSAS STATUTES §16-43-212

(a) The prosecuting attorneys and their deputies may issue subpoenas in all criminal matters they are investigating and may administer oaths for the purpose of taking the testimony of witnesses subpoenaed before them. Such oath when administered by the prosecuting attorney or his deputy shall have the same effect as if administered by the foreman of the grand jury. . . .

(b) The subpoena provided for in subsection (a) of this section shall be served in the manner as provided by law and shall be returned, and a record made and kept, as provided by law for grand jury subpoenas. . . .

Notes

1. *Breadth of document subpoena.* As *R. Enterprises* states, a recipient of a grand jury subpoena can challenge both the breadth of the subpoena and the burden of compliance. The Supreme Court stated in Oklahoma Press Publishing Co. v. Walling, 327 U.S. 186 (1946), that an unreasonably indefinite or overbroad subpoena might violate the Fourth Amendment or perhaps due process; in many states, such a subpoena would also violate statutes or rules of procedure. Note that in *R. Enterprises,* Federal Rule of Criminal Procedure 17(c) placed the most pertinent limit on the range of documents requested: Compliance must not be "unreasonable or oppressive." What specific facts might convince a court that a particular subpoena is overbroad or too indefinite? Does the subject matter of the grand jury's investigation matter? How about the cost of collecting relevant documents? The proportion of a business's documents falling within the terms of the subpoena (as opposed to the absolute number of documents)?

2. *The justification needed for a subpoena.* The *R. Enterprises* court followed the majority position in concluding that the prosecution does not need to make any preliminary showing of the relevance of testimony or other evidence sought through a grand jury subpoena. The probable cause necessary to support a search warrant is not a prerequisite for a grand jury subpoena. As the Court reasoned in United States v. Dionisio, 410 U.S. 1 (1973), a subpoena is different from an arrest, or even a more limited "stop," because the subpoena is served like any other legal process and involves no stigma and no force. Although the recipient of a subpoena to testify before a grand jury might challenge it on relevance grounds, it is very difficult to succeed on such a claim, in light of the breadth of the grand jury's duties to investigate any violations of the criminal law. Again, the *R. Enterprises* court is typical in its willingness to allow the grand jury to obtain documents and testimony relevant to a broad range of *potentially* criminal conduct. A few jurisdictions have required a modest grand jury showing of relevance. A grand jury subpoena in these courts is enforceable only if the grand jury (or the prosecutor on behalf of the grand jury) affirms that the testimony or documents it seeks will be relevant to a legitimate subject of inquiry. See In re Grand Jury Proceeding, Schofield I, 486 F.2d 85 (3d Cir. 1973); Robert Hawthorne, Inc. v. County Investigating Grand Jury, 412 A.2d 556 (Pa. 1980). Would this preliminary statement from the grand jury make it any easier for the subpoena recipient to show that the subpoena is not relevant to some possible investigation? Should the level of justification to support a grand jury subpoena turn on the type of document involved? See State v. Nelson, 941 P.2d 441 (Mont. 1997) (state constitution requires state to show probable cause to support investigative subpoena for discovery of medical records).

3. *The prosecutor and grand jury subpoenas.* The subpoenas requiring witnesses to appear before a grand jury are, strictly speaking, issued under the authority of the grand jury itself. In practice, however, the prosecutor coordinating the grand jury's investigation has virtually complete control over the subpoenas that issue. Some statutes, such as the Ohio statute above, give independent authority to the prosecutor to issue grand jury subpoenas. State v. Guido, 698 A.2d 729 (R.I. 1997) (prosecutor used subpoena to obtain document for delivery to State Attorney General, grand jury did not see it, information issued on basis of document; no abuse of grand jury power). Others give the prosecutor the power to subpoena a witness only if the grand jury approves of the request, either before or after the subpoena issues.

The Arkansas statute reprinted above is an unusual one, giving the prosecutor the subpoena power completely separate from the grand jury. See also Mich. Comp. Laws 767A.1 et seq. (empowers prosecutors to issue investigatory subpoenas; judge must find probable cause that felony has been committed and that the person subpoenaed "may have knowledge regarding the commission of the felony," before authorizing investigative subpoena); Oman v. State, 737 N.E.2d 1131 (Ind. 2000) (prosecutor acting without grand jury must get court approval to subpoena documents). In the many states where prosecutors have no such subpoena power, do they miss significant investigative opportunities? Must they conduct all their witness interviews in front of the grand jury? How do prosecutors ever speak in private with hostile witnesses during an investigation? Some states (fewer than a dozen) allow a magistrate to issue a subpoena to witnesses during an investigation, requiring the witness to appear before the magistrate rather than a grand jury. This system is sometimes called the "one-man grand jury." See Idaho Code §19-3004. Would you insist on secrecy in such proceedings, as in grand jury proceedings? Would you allow the witness to have counsel present during the testimony?

Problem 10-5. Subpoena Versus Search Warrant

After a violent clash at Stanford University between student antiwar protesters and local police officers, the district attorney's office opened a grand jury investigation to determine the identity of any students who assaulted the officers. Some of the students had assaulted the officers with sticks and clubs, and both students and officers were seriously injured. A few days after the grand jury started to hear testimony, a special edition of the *Stanford Daily*, a student newspaper, carried articles and photographs about the student protest and the violent events of that day. The photographs were the work of a staff photographer for the *Daily*. The police believed that the staff photographer might have taken additional pictures that would help identify the students who had assaulted the officers.

The day after the pictures were published, the district attorney's office secured a warrant to search the *Daily*'s offices for negatives, film, and pictures showing the events and occurrences at the protest. The warrant affidavit contained no allegation that members of the *Daily* staff were in any way involved in unlawful acts during the protest. Four police officers executed the search warrant later the same day. While staff members at the *Daily* looked on, the officers searched photographic laboratories, filing cabinets, desks, and wastepaper baskets. Some of the files they searched contained notes and correspondence. Some of the materials were confidential, although no staff member informed the officers of that fact. The search revealed only the photographs that had already been published in the *Daily*, and the police removed no materials from the *Daily*'s office.

The *Daily* and various members of its staff brought a civil action in federal court against the police officers who conducted the search, the chief of police, the district attorney and one of his deputies, and the judge who had issued the warrant. The complaint alleged that the search of the *Daily's* office was a violation of the First, Fourth, and Fourteenth Amendments of the U.S. Constitution. Assuming there was probable cause to support the search warrant, how would you argue this case on behalf of the *Daily*? Compare Zurcher v. Stanford Daily, 436 U.S. 547 (1978).

Notes

1. *Subpoenas and search warrants.* A prosecutor advising a grand jury during an investigation may have the choice of obtaining documents through a subpoena or a search warrant. What considerations will help the prosecutor make the choice? As we have seen, a subpoena requires the government to show no reasonable suspicion or probable cause to believe that the subpoena will produce evidence of a crime, and it requires virtually no showing of relevance. A search warrant, of course, must be based on probable cause and must particularly describe the place to be searched and the things to be seized. Does a subpoena give the government a way to bypass all the ordinary restraints on searches and seizures? Is the deference to grand jury requests a relic, or are grand jury investigations truly different from investigations that would

require a search warrant? Which method is likely to produce more evidence? Which will be more intrusive and which will cost the recipient more to comply with? State and federal statutes make it a crime for a person to destroy or alter documents that have been subpoenaed by a grand jury. How might these statutes affect a prosecutor's choice about the timing, scope, and recipients of subpoenas?

2. *Searches and freedom of the press.* In Zurcher v. Stanford Daily, 436 U.S. 547 (1978), the Supreme Court considered the validity of a search warrant authorizing the search of a newspaper's offices for photographs of demonstrators who had injured several police officers. The Court concluded that the Constitution imposed no special requirements for "third party" searches: The probable cause necessary to obtain a warrant was sufficient justification for a search, even if the target of the search was a newspaper not itself involved in wrongdoing. Congress responded to this decision by passing the Privacy Protection Act of 1980, 42 U.S.C. §2000aa. The statute, recognizing the special threats to the constitutional freedom of the press that are involved with searches of newspaper offices, creates a presumption in favor of subpoenas rather than search warrants to obtain documents from publishers. It prevents all criminal law enforcement agents (both state and federal) from searching for or seizing any "work-product materials" possessed by a publisher or broadcaster, unless there is probable cause to believe that the publisher has committed a crime relating to the documents or that immediate seizure is necessary to prevent death or serious bodily injury. Is this statute sufficient to protect the special First Amendment concerns involved in the search of newspaper offices? Cf. Branzburg v. Hayes, 408 U.S. 665 (1972) (enforcing grand jury subpoena for testimony of news reporter despite claim of privilege for news sources). Department of Justice regulations establish a similar presumption in favor of subpoenas rather than search warrants for document searches in the offices of attorneys, physicians, and clergy. 28 C.F.R. §59.4(b). Those regulations (unlike the statute) apply only to searches by federal agents. Why treat these categories of document holders any differently from other third parties who hold possible evidence of a crime?

3. *Attorneys as subpoena and search targets.* Internal guidelines at the Department of Justice require special authorization before seeking a subpoena of an attorney to obtain information about that attorney's representation of a client. Before a federal prosecutor may request such a subpoena, the U.S. Attorneys' Manual §9-13.410 requires certification of the following: (1) information is not privileged, (2) information is reasonably necessary to complete investigation, (3) alternative sources of the information are not available, and (4) need for information outweighs "potential adverse effects" on attorney-client relationship. What sorts of harms might flow from issuing a subpoena to an attorney? One of the ABA Model Rules of Professional Conduct, Rule 3.8(f), at one time required a prosecutor to obtain judicial approval after an adversarial hearing before she could issue a grand jury subpoena to a lawyer. The rule has since been revised to remove the requirement of judicial approval, but ethics rules in a handful of states still retain it. Is the requirement consistent with the guidelines in the U.S. Attorneys' Manual?

Section 9-13.420 of the U.S. Attorney's Manual creates special rules for the use of search warrants to search the offices of attorneys who are suspects, subjects, or targets of a criminal investigation. The application may go forward only if there is a "strong need" for material and if alternatives (such as a subpoena) will not work because of a risk of destroyed documents. The rules call for the creation of a "privilege team" consisting of agents and lawyers not involved in the investigation, who must review seized documents to identify those containing possibly privileged information. The privilege team cannot reveal the contents of privileged documents to the investigating agents and attorneys. Why do the rules for search warrants not require a pre-search certification that it will not reach privileged documents?

4. *Negotiations over terms of compliance.* If your client receives a grand jury subpoena for documents, and you conclude that there is no viable constitutional basis for objecting to the subpoena, is there anything left to do except collect the documents and turn them over? Can you negotiate some less onerous form of compliance? What negotiating leverage do you have, if any?

5. *The contents of incriminating documents.* When a grand jury forces a witness to provide documents, including some that the witness created personally, is it forcing him to "witness" against himself? Should the privilege against self-incrimination apply to the contents of all documents a suspect creates? Under federal law, it is now clear that the contents of preexisting documents are not "testimonial" and therefore the privilege against self-incrimination cannot stop the grand jury from obtaining such documents. See Fisher v. United States, 425 U.S. 391 (1976). All the states addressing this question have followed the federal lead. How much documentary evidence would be beyond the reach of a grand jury if the contents of documents were considered privileged when self-incriminating? If the government can force a person to turn over written statements that incriminate, does a privilege against oral testimony mean much at all?

6. *Act of production doctrine.* There is an exception to the *Fisher* rule regarding the contents of incriminating documents. Compliance with a subpoena is an implicit admission that the records requested in the subpoena exist, that they are in the possession or control of the subpoena recipient, and that they are authentic. The U.S. Supreme Court, along with all the state courts to address the issue, recognizes that the *act* of producing documents under a grand jury subpoena can give the government valuable information that might ultimately help convict the document holder of a crime. The contents of the documents, as opposed to the act of producing the documents, remains a valid source of evidence. Is this "act of production" any more "testimonial" than the contents of the documents? See United States v. Doe, 465 U.S. 605 (1984) (act of producing incriminating business records is itself testimonial self-incrimination); Braswell v. United States, 487 U.S. 99 (1988) (individual representative of legal entity must submit subpoenaed documents to grand jury, but prosecution may not use act of production evidence against individual).

This area of law is nuanced, including complex fields such as the "collective entity" doctrine, the self-incrimination privilege for corporate entities, and the "required records" doctrine. For a review of these interconnected doctrines and practices, see the web extension for this chapter at *http://www.crimpro.com/extension/ch10*.

7. *Other acts compelled by the grand jury.* Is a person serving as a "witness" against herself if the grand jury asks for a blood sample for testing? Handwriting exemplars? Are these actions any different from the act of producing documents? In Schmerber v. California, 384 U.S. 757 (1966), the Court held that there is no compelled self-incrimination when a grand jury orders a witness to provide a blood sample. Some states make an exception to the grand jury's broad subpoena power when it comes to the most intrusive grand jury requests for evidence. For instance, grand juries will sometimes subpoena witnesses and ask for fingerprints, hair

samples, or voice exemplars. Compare Woolverton v. Multi-County Grand Jury, 859 P.2d 1112 (Okla. Crim. App. 1993) (requiring showing of probable cause to support request for blood samples, reasonable suspicion for palm prints) with United States v. Dionisio, 410 U.S. 1 (1973) (upholding subpoena for voice exemplar with no special government justification). Is there an argument for treating voice exemplars differently from palm prints? From blood samples?

PART TWO

EVALUATING CHARGES

XI

Defense Counsel

During the earliest phases of the criminal process, defense lawyers are rarely to be seen. But as the prosecution and police formulate and file charges against some suspects, and as the courts begin to process those charges, defense counsel becomes involved.

In this chapter, we introduce the various sources of law that make it possible for a criminal defendant to get a lawyer. We also consider the practical value of these legal entitlements to the ordinary criminal defendant. Does having an attorney really matter to defendants? What do defense lawyers do? Can you imagine a criminal justice system without them?

A. WHEN WILL COUNSEL BE PROVIDED?

Not every person charged with a crime consults a lawyer. The most common reason for a defendant to face charges alone, without a lawyer, is financial — defendants often cannot afford counsel. But our legal systems have not left matters there. The same government that pays the judge, the prosecutor, and the investigators will also (at least in some cases) pay for the defendant's lawyer.

The question that has persisted over many decades is when the state will pay for defense counsel and when it will not. Some cases involve charges that are not serious enough to require counsel; some proceedings are too early or late in the process to require counsel. This section reviews the law on (1) the types of charges necessary to invoke constitutional and statutory rights to counsel and (2) the types of criminal proceedings that trigger a defendant's right to counsel.

1. *Types of Charges*

Constitutions have much to say about the availability of defense counsel. The Sixth Amendment to the federal constitution states that "In all criminal prosecutions, the accused shall enjoy the right . . . to have the assistance of counsel for his defence." Almost every state constitution has an equivalent provision.

The most important early decision regarding the Sixth Amendment right to counsel was Powell v. Alabama, 287 U.S. 45 (1932). The defendants were nine young black men who were accused of raping two young white women on a train near Scottsboro, Alabama. The case against the defendants attracted much local attention: Soldiers escorted the defendants to and from their proceedings to protect them from hostile mobs. None of the defendants was literate, and none was a resident of Alabama.

The defendants were divided into three groups for trial. The first trial began six days after indictment, and each of the three trials was completed within one day. Until the morning of the first trial, the court named no particular lawyer to represent the defendants. The trial judge instead appointed all the members of the Scottsboro bar "for the limited purpose of arraigning" the defendants. Some members of the bar consulted with the defendants in jail, but did nothing further. A colloquy on the morning of the trial left it unclear which attorney, if any, would represent the defendants at trial. An attorney sent from Tennessee by people concerned about the young men's situation was unprepared to serve as lead counsel, but members of the Scottsboro bar were quick to say they would "assist" the newly arrived lawyer. The juries found all the defendants guilty and imposed the death penalty upon each of them.

The Supreme Court concluded that appointment of a primary defense lawyer, at least under these circumstances, was a requirement of due process. The Court made some general observations about the value of legal counsel:

> The right to be heard would be, in many cases, of little avail if it did not comprehend the right to be heard by counsel. Even the intelligent and educated layman has small and sometimes no skill in the science of law. If charged with crime, he is incapable, generally, of determining for himself whether the indictment is good or bad. He is unfamiliar with the rules of evidence. Left without the aid of counsel he may be put on trial without a proper charge, and convicted upon incompetent evidence, or evidence irrelevant to the issue or otherwise inadmissible. He lacks both the skill and knowledge adequately to prepare his defense, even though he had a perfect one. He requires the guiding hand of counsel at every step in the proceedings against him. Without it, though he be not guilty, he faces the danger of conviction because he does not know how to establish his innocence.

287 U.S. at 68-69. The opinion also stressed some of the more compelling facts in the case:

> In the light [of] the ignorance and illiteracy of the defendants, their youth, the circumstances of public hostility, the imprisonment and the close surveillance of the defendants by the military forces, the fact that their friends and families were all in other states and communication with them [was] necessarily difficult, and above all that they stood in deadly peril of their lives, . . . the necessity of counsel was so vital and imperative that the failure of the trial court to make an effective appointment of counsel

> was . . . a denial of due process within the meaning of the Fourteenth Amendment. Whether this would be so in other criminal prosecutions, or under other circumstances, we need not determine. . . . In a case such as this, whatever may be the rule in other cases, the right to have counsel appointed, when necessary, is a logical corollary from the constitutional right to be heard by counsel.

287 U.S. at 71. The Scottsboro case became an international *cause célèbre.* A crusading New York lawyer, Samuel Leibowitz, participated in the defense during the second trial, which also ended in the conviction of all defendants by an all-white jury. After the later convictions were overturned on appeal in the state system, the government agreed to a plea agreement allowing for the release of four defendants and prison terms for the other five. See James Goodman, Stories of Scottsboro (1994); Michael J. Klarman, *Powell v. Alabama*: The Supreme Court Confronts "Legal Lynchings," in Criminal Procedure Stories (Carol Steiker, ed., 2006).

After a series of later Supreme Court cases considering the right to appointed counsel at trial, Betts v. Brady, 316 U.S. 455 (1942), settled on the "special circumstances" test to govern the appointment of counsel; that is, counsel would be constitutionally required only under "special circumstances," and not in every criminal case. Betts was indicted for robbery. Due to lack of funds, he was unable to employ counsel, and asked the judge to appoint counsel for him. The judge refused because the local practice was to appoint counsel only in prosecutions for murder and rape. Betts then pleaded not guilty and elected to be tried without a jury. Witnesses were summoned on his behalf. He cross-examined the State's witnesses and examined his own alibi witnesses. Betts did not take the witness stand. The judge found him guilty and sentenced him to eight years in prison. The Court concluded that due process did not require the appointment of counsel under these circumstances.

In the following case, the Supreme Court returned to the question of appointed counsel, this time giving a different answer.

■ CLARENCE EARL GIDEON v. LOUIE WAINWRIGHT

372 U.S. 335 (1963)

BLACK, J.*

Petitioner was charged in a Florida state court with having broken and entered a poolroom with intent to commit a misdemeanor. This offense is a felony under Florida law. Appearing in court without funds and without a lawyer, petitioner asked the court to appoint counsel for him. [When the Court denied his request, Gideon objected: "The United States Supreme Court says I am entitled to be represented by Counsel."]

Put to trial before a jury, Gideon conducted his defense about as well as could be expected from a layman. He made an opening statement to the jury, cross-examined the State's witnesses, presented witnesses in his own defense, declined to testify himself, and made a short argument "emphasizing his innocence to the charge contained in the Information filed in this case." The jury returned a verdict of guilty, and petitioner was sentenced to serve five years in the state prison. [The

* [Chief Justice Warren and Justices Douglas, Brennan, Stewart, White, and Goldberg joined in this opinion. — EDS.]

state Supreme Court later denied habeas corpus relief.] Since 1942, when Betts v. Brady, 316 U.S. 455, was decided by a divided Court, the problem of a defendant's federal constitutional right to counsel in a state court has been a continuing source of controversy and litigation in both state and federal courts. To give this problem another review here, we granted certiorari. . . .

I.

The facts upon which Betts claimed that he had been unconstitutionally denied the right to have counsel appointed to assist him are strikingly like the facts upon which Gideon here bases his federal constitutional claim. Betts was indicted for robbery in a Maryland state court. On arraignment, . . . Betts was advised that it was not the practice in that county to appoint counsel for indigent defendants except in murder and rape cases. He then pleaded not guilty, had witnesses summoned, cross-examined the State's witnesses, examined his own, and chose not to testify himself. He was found guilty by the judge, sitting without a jury. [Upon review of the conviction, this Court] held that a refusal to appoint counsel for an indigent defendant charged with a felony did not necessarily violate the Due Process Clause of the Fourteenth Amendment. . . . The Court said: "Asserted denial [of due process] is to be tested by an appraisal of the totality of facts in a given case. That which may, in one setting, constitute a denial of fundamental fairness, shocking to the universal sense of justice, may, in other circumstances . . . fall short of such denial."

Treating due process as "a concept less rigid and more fluid than those envisaged in other specific and particular provisions of the Bill of Rights," the Court held that refusal to appoint counsel under the particular facts and circumstances in the *Betts* case was not so "offensive to the common and fundamental ideas of fairness" as to amount to a denial of due process. Since the facts and circumstances of the two cases are so nearly indistinguishable, we think the Betts v. Brady holding if left standing would require us to reject Gideon's claim that the Constitution guarantees him the assistance of counsel. Upon full reconsideration we conclude that Betts v. Brady should be overruled.

II.

The Sixth Amendment provides, "In all criminal prosecutions, the accused shall enjoy the right . . . to have the Assistance of Counsel for his defence." We have construed this to mean that in federal courts counsel must be provided for defendants unable to employ counsel unless the right is competently and intelligently waived. [In *Betts,* the Court] set out and considered "relevant data on the subject . . . afforded by constitutional and statutory provisions subsisting in the colonies and the States prior to the inclusion of the Bill of Rights in the national Constitution, and in the constitutional, legislative, and judicial history of the States to the present date." On the basis of this historical data the Court concluded that appointment of counsel is not a fundamental right, essential to a fair trial, [and thus was not a due process requirement applicable to the States.]

We accept Betts v. Brady's assumption, based as it was on our prior cases, that a provision of the Bill of Rights which is "fundamental and essential to a fair trial" is made obligatory upon the States by the Fourteenth Amendment. We think the Court in *Betts* was wrong, however, in concluding that the Sixth Amendment's guarantee of counsel is not one of these fundamental rights. Ten years before Betts v. Brady, this Court, after full consideration of all the historical data examined in *Betts,* had unequivocally declared that "the right to the aid of counsel is of this fundamental character." Powell v. Alabama, 287 U.S. 45, 68 (1932). While the Court at the close of its *Powell* opinion did by its language, as this Court frequently does, limit its holding to the particular facts and circumstances of that case, its conclusions about the fundamental nature of the right to counsel are unmistakable. Several years later, in 1936, the Court reemphasized what it had said about the fundamental nature of the right to counsel in this language:

> We concluded that certain fundamental rights, safeguarded by the first eight amendments against federal action, were also safeguarded against state action by the due process of law clause of the Fourteenth Amendment, and among them the fundamental right of the accused to the aid of counsel in a criminal prosecution.

Grosjean v. American Press Co., 297 U.S. 233, 243-44 (1936). [Similar statements appear in several other decisions. In] deciding as it did — that "appointment of counsel is not a fundamental right, essential to a fair trial" — the Court in Betts v. Brady made an abrupt break with its own well-considered precedents. In returning to these old precedents, sounder we believe than the new, we but restore constitutional principles established to achieve a fair system of justice.

Not only these precedents but also reason and reflection require us to recognize that in our adversary system of criminal justice, any person haled into court, who is too poor to hire a lawyer, cannot be assured a fair trial unless counsel is provided for him. This seems to us to be an obvious truth. Governments, both state and federal, quite properly spend vast sums of money to establish machinery to try defendants accused of crime. Lawyers to prosecute are everywhere deemed essential to protect the public's interest in an orderly society. Similarly, there are few defendants charged with crime, few indeed, who fail to hire the best lawyers they can get to prepare and present their defenses. That government hires lawyers to prosecute and defendants who have the money hire lawyers to defend are the strongest indications of the widespread belief that lawyers in criminal courts are necessities, not luxuries. The right of one charged with crime to counsel may not be deemed fundamental and essential to fair trials in some countries, but it is in ours. From the very beginning, our state and national constitutions and laws have laid great emphasis on procedural and substantive safeguards designed to assure fair trials before impartial tribunals in which every defendant stands equal before the law. This noble ideal cannot be realized if the poor man charged with crime has to face his accusers without a lawyer to assist him. . . .

The Court in Betts v. Brady departed from the sound wisdom upon which the Court's holding in Powell v. Alabama rested. Florida, supported by two other States, has asked that Betts v. Brady be left intact. Twenty-two States, as friends of the Court, argue that *Betts* was "an anachronism when handed down" and that it should now be overruled. We agree. . . .

HARLAN, J., concurring.

I agree that Betts v. Brady should be overruled, but consider it entitled to a more respectful burial than has been accorded, at least on the part of those of us who were not on the Court when that case was decided. I cannot subscribe to the view that

Betts v. Brady represented "an abrupt break with its own well-considered precedents." In 1932, in Powell v. Alabama, a capital case, this Court declared that under the particular facts there presented — "the ignorance and illiteracy of the defendants, their youth, the circumstances of public hostility . . . and above all that they stood in deadly peril of their lives" — the state court had a duty to assign counsel for the trial as a necessary requisite of due process of law. It is evident that these limiting facts were not added to the opinion as an afterthought; they were repeatedly emphasized, and were clearly regarded as important to the result.

Thus when this Court, a decade later, decided Betts v. Brady, it did no more than to admit of the possible existence of special circumstances in noncapital as well as capital trials, while at the same time insisting that such circumstances be shown in order to establish a denial of due process. The right to appointed counsel had been recognized as being considerably broader in federal prosecutions, but to have imposed these requirements on the States would indeed have been "an abrupt break" with the almost immediate past. . . .

The principles declared in *Powell* and in *Betts,* however, have had a troubled journey throughout the years that have followed first the one case and then the other. . . . In noncapital cases, the "special circumstances" rule has continued to exist in form while its substance has been substantially and steadily eroded. [Since 1950] there have been not a few cases in which special circumstances were found in little or nothing more than the "complexity" of the legal questions presented, although those questions were often of only routine difficulty. The Court has come to recognize, in other words, that the mere existence of a serious criminal charge constituted in itself special circumstances requiring the services of counsel at trial. In truth the Betts v. Brady rule is no longer a reality. This evolution, however, appears not to have been fully recognized by many state courts, in this instance charged with the front-line responsibility for the enforcement of constitutional rights. To continue a rule which is honored by this Court only with lip service is not a healthy thing and in the long run will do disservice to the federal system.

The special circumstances rule has been formally abandoned in capital cases, and the time has now come when it should be similarly abandoned in noncapital cases, at least as to offenses which, as the one involved here, carry the possibility of a substantial prison sentence. (Whether the rule should extend to all criminal cases need not now be decided.) This indeed does no more than to make explicit something that has long since been foreshadowed in our decisions. . . .

■ In re ADVISORY OPINION TO THE GOVERNOR (APPOINTED COUNSEL)

666 A.2d 813 (R.I. 1995)

WEISBERGER, C.J.

To His Excellency Lincoln Almond, Governor of the State of Rhode Island and Providence Plantations: We have received from Your Excellency a request seeking the advice of the justices of this Court in accordance with article X, section 3, of the Rhode Island Constitution on the following question of law:

> In view of the historical development of the law relating to the right of appointed counsel under the federal and state constitutions, and the more recent developments

> in federal case law, is the State of Rhode Island required by the Rhode Island Constitution to provide free counsel to indigents notwithstanding that the trial justice determines that no incarceration will be imposed?

[The governor submitted this question to the Court in preparation for proposing to the legislature an annual operating budget for the state.] In response, we issued an order inviting briefs from various specified parties and all other interested parties. . . .

The Sixth Amendment to the United States Constitution mandates that "in all criminal prosecutions, the accused shall enjoy the right . . . to have the assistance of counsel for his defense." In 1963, the United States Supreme Court made this requirement applicable to the states via the Fourteenth Amendment in Gideon v. Wainwright, 372 U.S. 335.

The *Gideon* decision, however, did not reveal the contours of the right to counsel inasmuch as that holding was limited to facts that involved a felony conviction. The issue of the right to counsel was revisited in Argersinger v. Hamlin, 407 U.S. 25 (1972), in which the Supreme Court was asked to rule on whether indigent defendants facing misdemeanor charges are entitled to appointed counsel. The *Argersinger* Court concluded that the rationale of the *Gideon* decision "has relevance to any criminal trial, where an accused is deprived of his liberty." *Argersinger* went on to hold that any criminal prosecution resulting in the actual deprivation of an indigent defendant's liberty must be accompanied by the appointment of counsel for that defendant.

Although *Argersinger* did not specifically address the question of whether counsel must be appointed when no imprisonment will result, the Supreme Court did reach this issue seven years later, in Scott v. Illinois, 440 U.S. 367 (1979). Scott, an indigent defendant, was convicted of shoplifting and fined $50 after a trial in which he was not assisted by appointed counsel. In an opinion by Justice Rehnquist, the Court held that the right to appointed counsel under the Sixth and Fourteenth Amendments of the United States Constitution requires "only that no indigent criminal defendant be sentenced to a term of imprisonment unless the State has afforded him the right to assistance of appointed counsel in his defense." . . .

The Rhode Island constitutional analogue to the Sixth Amendment guarantee of the right to counsel is found in article I, section 10, of the Rhode Island Constitution. This section protects a defendant's right to assistance of counsel in terms almost identical to those of its federal counterpart: "In all criminal prosecutions, accused persons shall . . . have the assistance of counsel in their defense." In 1971, prior to the Supreme Court's rulings in *Argersinger* and *Scott,* this provision was interpreted in State v. Holliday, 280 A.2d 333 (R.I. 1971). In *Holliday,* this Court . . . construed article I, section 10, broadly to require appointment of counsel for indigent defendants charged with misdemeanors that carry a potential prison sentence in excess of six months, even if no imprisonment is actually imposed. . . . In *Holliday* this Court had no means of ascertaining the direction that the Supreme Court would take, and it is clear that our prognostication in *Holliday* was inaccurate. . . .

[The] balance achieved by the Supreme Court of the United States is as favorable to the perceived rights of defendants as should rationally be applied in criminal cases. We are unwilling to interpret article I, section [10] of the Rhode Island Constitution in such fashion as further to subordinate societal interests in effective prosecution of the guilty. . . . Moreover, this Court has recognized the validity of considering budgetary limitations in determining the extent of state-funded benefits for indigents. . . .

Certain of the *amici* would have this Court provide heightened constitutional protection to indigent criminal defendants who, although they may face no threat of imprisonment, may suffer such consequences as denial of public housing and loss of professional licenses. It is well settled, however, that the full panoply of due-process protections attaches only when loss of a fundamental liberty results from state action. . . . Although loss of a license or permit and denial of public housing are grave occurrences, they do not rise to the level of deprivation characterized by incarceration. An automobile driver, for instance, is not entitled to confer with counsel when asked to submit to a breathalyzer test, even though submission to or refusal of that test may result in loss of that driver's license, because there is no fundamental constitutional right to operate a motor vehicle. Therefore, we disagree with *amici* that counsel must be provided in a criminal proceeding simply because an indigent defendant may subsequently lose a comparable property right. . . .

We conclude that it is (1) within the authority of the General Assembly to determine that the public interest would be served by increasing appropriations to provide counsel in situations not constitutionally required and (2) not the province of this Court to impose upon the state obligations that have no constitutional or statutory basis. We therefore advise Your Excellency that the United States Supreme Court's interpretation of the Sixth Amendment as a guarantee of a criminal defendant's right to counsel only when imprisonment is actually imposed represents the appropriate standard that should be applied under article I, section 10, of the Rhode Island Constitution. In conclusion, therefore, we respond to Your Excellency's question in the negative.

MURRAY, J., dissenting.

I respectfully dissent. [This] state has a proud history of affording its citizens the right to counsel and has specifically declined to follow the United States Supreme Court in limiting the provision of counsel to indigents. In 1941, long before Gideon v. Wainwright, 372 U.S. 335 (1963), Rhode Island established a public counsel system for accused felons. Thirty years later, before the United States Supreme Court decided Argersinger v. Hamlin, 407 U.S. 25 (1972), this court, in State v. Holliday, 280 A.2d 333 (R.I. 1971), extended the right to counsel for indigent defendants charged with serious misdemeanors which could subject them to an imposition of penalty in excess of six months' imprisonment. In 1987, after the Supreme Court decided Scott v. Illinois, 440 U.S. 367 (1979), we stated in State v. Moretti, 521 A.2d 1003 (R.I. 1987), and in State v. Medeiros, 535 A.2d 766 (R.I. 1987), that the Rhode Island Constitution provides a broader right to counsel than that provided under the Federal Constitution.

Specifically, we found in *Moretti* that "the confluence of the federal and the state guarantees is if an indigent Rhode Island criminal defendant faces a potential sentence of more than six months, Rhode Island constitutional law guarantees to a defendant appointed counsel, even if the trial justice predetermines that no prison sentence will be imposed. If the potential sentence is less than six months, federal constitutional law guarantees the defendant appointed counsel unless the trial justice predetermines that no prison sentence will be imposed." . . .

As a final matter, it should be stressed that we should not attempt to peer into the minds of trial justices. By answering His Excellency's request in the negative, the majority's decision effectively reduces the range of discretion previously afforded to trial justices in misdemeanor cases. The majority would have each trial justice determine whether incarceration may be imposed at the initial stages of an action, regardless of any later developments that may require the trial justice to impose a sanction of imprisonment. . . .

ALABAMA v. LeREED SHELTON

535 U.S. 654 (2002)

GINSBURG, J.*

This case concerns the Sixth Amendment right of an indigent defendant charged with a misdemeanor punishable by imprisonment, fine, or both, to the assistance of court-appointed counsel. Two prior decisions control the Court's judgment. First, in Argersinger v. Hamlin, 407 U.S. 25 (1972), this Court held that defense counsel must be appointed in any criminal prosecution, whether classified as petty, misdemeanor, or felony, "that actually leads to imprisonment even for a brief period." Later, in Scott v. Illinois, 440 U.S. 367 (1979), the Court drew the line at "actual imprisonment," holding that counsel need not be appointed when the defendant is fined for the charged crime, but is not sentenced to a term of imprisonment.

Defendant-respondent LeReed Shelton, convicted of third-degree assault, was sentenced to a jail term of 30 days, which the trial court immediately suspended, placing Shelton on probation for two years. The question presented is whether the Sixth Amendment right to appointed counsel, as delineated in *Argersinger* and *Scott,* applies to a defendant in Shelton's situation. We hold that a suspended sentence that may "end up in the actual deprivation of a person's liberty" may not be imposed unless the defendant was accorded "the guiding hand of counsel" in the prosecution for the crime charged.

I.

After representing himself at a bench trial in the District Court of Etowah County, Alabama, Shelton was convicted of third-degree assault, a class A misdemeanor carrying a maximum punishment of one year imprisonment and a $2000 fine. He invoked his right to a new trial before a jury in Circuit Court where he again appeared without a lawyer and was again convicted. The court repeatedly warned Shelton about the problems self-representation entailed but at no time offered him assistance of counsel at state expense.

The Circuit Court sentenced Shelton to serve 30 days in the county prison. As authorized by Alabama law, however, the court suspended that sentence and placed Shelton on two years' unsupervised probation, conditioned on his payment of court costs, a $500 fine, reparations of $25, and restitution in the amount of $516.69. Shelton appealed his conviction and sentence on Sixth Amendment grounds. . . .

* [Justices Stevens, Souter, O'Connor, and Breyer joined in this opinion. — EDS.]

II.

Three positions are before us in this case. . . . Shelton argues that an indigent defendant may not receive a suspended sentence unless he is offered or waives the assistance of state-appointed counsel. Alabama now concedes that the Sixth Amendment bars *activation* of a suspended sentence for an uncounseled conviction, but maintains that the Constitution does not prohibit *imposition* of such a sentence as a method of effectuating probationary punishment. To assure full airing of the question presented, we invited an *amicus curiae* to argue in support of a third position, one Alabama has abandoned: Failure to appoint counsel to an indigent defendant does not bar the imposition of a suspended or probationary sentence upon conviction of a misdemeanor, even though the defendant might be incarcerated in the event probation is revoked. . . .

B.

Applying the "actual imprisonment" rule to the case before us, we take up first the question we asked *amicus* to address: Where the State provides no counsel to an indigent defendant, does the Sixth Amendment permit activation of a suspended sentence upon the defendant's violation of the terms of probation? We conclude that it does not. A suspended sentence is a prison term imposed for the offense of conviction. Once the prison term is triggered, the defendant is incarcerated not for the probation violation, but for the underlying offense. The uncounseled conviction at that point results in imprisonment; it "ends up in the actual deprivation of a person's liberty." This is precisely what the Sixth Amendment, as interpreted in *Argersinger* and *Scott,* does not allow.

Amicus resists this reasoning primarily on two grounds. First, he attempts to align this case with our decisions in Nichols v. United States, 511 U.S. 738 (1994), and Gagnon v. Scarpelli, 411 U.S. 778 (1973). We conclude that Shelton's case is not properly bracketed with those dispositions.

Nichols presented the question whether the Sixth Amendment barred consideration of a defendant's prior uncounseled misdemeanor conviction in determining his sentence for a subsequent felony offense. Nichols pleaded guilty to federal felony drug charges. Several years earlier, unrepresented by counsel, he was fined but not incarcerated for the state misdemeanor of driving under the influence (DUI). Including the DUI conviction in the federal Sentencing Guidelines calculation allowed the trial court to impose a sentence for the felony drug conviction 25 months longer than if the misdemeanor conviction had not been considered. We upheld this result, concluding that "an uncounseled misdemeanor conviction, valid under *Scott* because no prison term was imposed, is also valid when used to enhance punishment at a subsequent conviction." In *Gagnon,* the question was whether the defendant, who was placed on probation pursuant to a suspended sentence for armed robbery, had a due process right to representation by appointed counsel at a probation revocation hearing. We held that counsel was not invariably required in parole or probation revocation proceedings; we directed, instead, a "case-by-case approach" turning on the character of the issues involved.

Considered together, *amicus* contends, *Nichols* and *Gagnon* establish this principle: Sequential proceedings must be analyzed separately for Sixth Amendment purposes and only those proceedings resulting "in *immediate* actual imprisonment" trigger the right to state-appointed counsel. . . . *Gagnon* and *Nichols* do not stand for the broad proposition *amicus* would extract from them. The dispositive factor in those cases was not whether incarceration occurred immediately or only after some delay. Rather, the critical point was that the defendant had a recognized right to counsel when adjudicated guilty of the felony offense for which he was imprisoned. Unlike this case, in which revocation of probation would trigger a prison term imposed for a misdemeanor of which Shelton was found guilty without the aid of counsel, the sentences imposed in *Nichols* and *Gagnon* were for felony convictions — a federal drug conviction in *Nichols,* and a state armed robbery conviction in *Gagnon* — for which the right to counsel is unquestioned. Thus, neither *Nichols* nor *Gagnon* altered or diminished *Argersinger*'s command that "no person may be imprisoned *for any offense* . . . unless he was represented by counsel at his trial." . . .

Amicus also contends that "practical considerations clearly weigh against" the extension of the Sixth Amendment appointed-counsel right to a defendant in Shelton's situation. He cites figures suggesting that although conditional sentences are commonly imposed, they are rarely activated. . . . *Amicus* does not describe the contours of the hearing that, he suggests, might precede revocation of a term of probation imposed on an uncounseled defendant. In Alabama, [the] proceeding is an "informal" one at which the defendant has no right to counsel, and the court no obligation to observe customary rules of evidence. More significant, the sole issue at the hearing — apart from determinations about the necessity of confinement — is whether the defendant breached the terms of probation. The validity or reliability of the underlying conviction is beyond attack.

We think it plain that a hearing so timed and structured cannot compensate for the absence of trial counsel, for it does not even address the key Sixth Amendment inquiry: whether the adjudication of guilt corresponding to the prison sentence is sufficiently reliable to permit incarceration. Deprived of counsel when tried, convicted, and sentenced, and unable to challenge the original judgment at a subsequent probation revocation hearing, a defendant in Shelton's circumstances faces incarceration on a conviction that has never been subjected to "the crucible of meaningful adversarial testing." The Sixth Amendment does not countenance this result.

In a variation on *amicus'* position, the dissent would limit review in this case to the question whether the *imposition* of Shelton's suspended sentence required appointment of counsel. . . . The dissent imagines a set of safeguards Alabama might provide at the probation revocation stage sufficient to cure its failure to appoint counsel prior to sentencing, including, perhaps, complete retrial of the misdemeanor violation with assistance of counsel. But there is no cause for speculation about Alabama's procedures; they are established by Alabama statute and decisional law, and they bear no resemblance to those the dissent invents in its effort to sanction the prospect of Shelton's imprisonment on an uncounseled conviction. . . .

Nor do we agree with *amicus* or the dissent that our holding will substantially limit the states' ability to impose probation or encumber them with a large, new burden. Most jurisdictions already provide a state-law right to appointed counsel more generous than that afforded by the Federal Constitution. All but 16 States, for example, would provide counsel to a defendant in Shelton's circumstances, either because he received a substantial fine or because state law authorized incarceration for the charged offense or provided for a maximum prison term of one year. There is thus scant reason to believe that a rule conditioning imposition of a suspended sentence on provision of appointed counsel would affect existing practice in the large majority of the States. And given the current commitment of most jurisdictions to affording court-appointed counsel to indigent misdemeanants while simultaneously preserving the option of probationary punishment, we do not share *amicus*' concern that other States may lack the capacity and resources to do the same.

Moreover, even if *amicus* is correct that some courts and jurisdictions at least cannot bear the costs of the rule we confirm today, those States need not abandon probation or equivalent measures as viable forms of punishment. Although they may not attach probation to an imposed and suspended prison sentence, States unable or unwilling routinely to provide appointed counsel to misdemeanants in Shelton's situation are not without recourse to another option capable of yielding a similar result.

That option is pretrial probation, employed in some form by at least 23 States. Under such an arrangement, the prosecutor and defendant agree to the defendant's participation in a pretrial rehabilitation program, which includes conditions typical of post-trial probation. The adjudication of guilt and imposition of sentence for the underlying offense then occur only if and when the defendant breaches those conditions. [Pretrial] probation also respects the constitutional imperative that "no person may be imprisoned for any offense . . . unless he was represented by counsel at his trial." . . .

SCALIA, J., dissenting.*

In Argersinger v. Hamlin we held that "absent a knowing and intelligent waiver, *no person may be imprisoned* for any offense . . . unless he was represented by counsel at his trial." Although, we said, the "run of misdemeanors will not be affected" by this rule, "in those *that end up in the actual deprivation of a person's liberty,* the accused will receive the benefit" of appointed counsel (emphasis added). We affirmed this rule in Scott v. Illinois, drawing a bright line between imprisonment and the mere threat of imprisonment: "The central premise of *Argersinger* — that actual imprisonment is a penalty different in kind from fines *or the mere threat of imprisonment* — is eminently sound and warrants adoption of *actual imprisonment* as the line defining the constitutional right to appointment of counsel" [emphasis added]. We have repeatedly emphasized actual imprisonment as the touchstone of entitlement to appointed counsel.

Today's decision ignores this long and consistent jurisprudence, extending the misdemeanor right to counsel to cases bearing the mere threat of imprisonment. Respondent's 30-day suspended sentence, and the accompanying 2-year term of probation, are invalidated for lack of appointed counsel even though respondent has not suffered, and may never suffer, a deprivation of liberty. The Court holds that the suspended sentence violates respondent's Sixth Amendment right to counsel because it "*may* end up in the actual deprivation of [respondent's] liberty," *if* he someday violates the terms of probation, *if* a court determines that the violation merits revocation of probation, and *if* the court determines that no other punishment will "adequately protect the community from further criminal activity" or

* [Chief Justice Rehnquist and Justices Kennedy and Thomas joined in this opinion. — EDS.]

"avoid depreciating the seriousness of the violation." And to all of these contingencies there must yet be added, before the Court's decision makes sense, an element of rank speculation. Should all these contingencies occur, the Court speculates, the Alabama Supreme Court would mechanically apply its decisional law applicable to routine probation revocation (which establishes procedures that the Court finds inadequate) rather than adopt special procedures for situations that raise constitutional questions in light of *Argersinger* and *Scott*. The Court has miraculously divined how the Alabama justices would resolve a constitutional question. . . .

In the future, *if and when* the State of Alabama seeks to imprison respondent on the previously suspended sentence, we can ask whether the procedural safeguards attending the imposition of that sentence comply with the Constitution. But that question is *not* before us now. . . .

Our prior opinions placed considerable weight on the practical consequences of expanding the right to appointed counsel beyond cases of actual imprisonment. Today, the Court gives this consideration the back of its hand. Its observation that all but 16 States already appoint counsel for defendants like respondent is interesting but quite irrelevant, since today's holding is not confined to *defendants like respondent*. Appointed counsel must henceforth be offered before *any* defendant can be awarded a suspended sentence, no matter how short. Only 24 States have announced a rule of this scope. Thus, the Court's decision imposes a large, new burden on a majority of the States, including some of the poorest (e.g., Alabama, Arkansas, and Mississippi). That burden consists not only of the cost of providing state-paid counsel in cases of such insignificance that even financially prosperous defendants sometimes forgo the expense of hired counsel; but also the cost of enabling courts and prosecutors to respond to the "over-lawyering" of minor cases. Nor should we discount the burden placed on the minority 24 States that currently provide counsel: that they keep their current disposition forever in place, however imprudent experience proves it to be.

Today's imposition upon the States finds justification neither in the text of the Constitution, nor in the settled practices of our people, nor in the prior jurisprudence of this Court. I respectfully dissent.

FLORIDA RULE OF CRIMINAL PROCEDURE 3.111

(a) A person entitled to appointment of counsel as provided herein shall have counsel appointed when the person is formally charged with an offense, or as soon as feasible after custodial restraint, or at the first appearance before a committing judge, whichever occurs earliest.

(b)(1) Counsel shall be provided to indigent persons in all prosecutions for offenses punishable by incarceration including appeals from the conviction thereof. In the discretion of the court, counsel does not have to be provided to an indigent person in a prosecution for a misdemeanor or violation of a municipal ordinance if the judge, at least 15 days prior to trial, files in the cause a written order of no incarceration certifying that the defendant will not be incarcerated in the case pending trial or probation violation hearing, or as part of a sentence after trial, guilty or nolo contendere plea, or probation revocation. This 15-day requirement may be waived by the defendant or defense counsel.

(A) If the court issues an order of no incarceration after counsel has been appointed to represent the defendant, the court may discharge appointed counsel unless the defendant is incarcerated or the defendant would be substantially disadvantaged by the discharge of appointed counsel. . . .

(C) If the court withdraws its order of no incarceration, it shall immediately appoint counsel if the defendant is otherwise eligible for the services of the public defender. The court may not withdraw its order of no incarceration once the defendant has been found guilty or pled nolo contendere.

(2) Counsel may be provided to indigent persons in all proceedings arising from the initiation of a criminal action against a defendant, including postconviction proceedings and appeals therefrom, extradition proceedings, mental competency proceedings, and other proceedings that are adversary in nature, regardless of the designation of the court in which they occur or the classification of the proceedings as civil or criminal.

(3) Counsel may be provided to a partially indigent person on request, provided that the person shall defray that portion of the cost of representation and the reasonable costs of investigation as he or she is able without substantial hardship to the person or the person's family, as directed by the court.

(4) "Indigent" shall mean a person who is unable to pay for the services of an attorney, including costs of investigation, without substantial hardship to the person or the person's family; "partially indigent" shall mean a person unable to pay more than a portion of the fee charged by an attorney, including costs of investigation, without substantial hardship to the person or the person's family.

■ VERMONT STATUTES TIT. 13, §§5231, 5201

§5231

A needy person who is being detained by a law enforcement officer without charge or judicial process, or who is charged with having committed or is being detained under a conviction of a serious crime, is entitled:

(1) To be represented by an attorney to the same extent as a person having his own counsel; and

(2) To be provided with the necessary services and facilities of representation. Any such necessary services and facilities of representation that exceed $1,500 per item must receive prior approval from the court after a hearing involving the parties. . . . This obligation and requirement to obtain prior court approval shall also be imposed in like manner upon the Attorney General or a State's Attorney prosecuting a violation of the law. . . .

§5201

In this chapter, the term . . . "Serious crime" includes: (A) A felony; (B) A misdemeanor the maximum penalty for which is a fine of more than $1,000 or any period of imprisonment unless the judge, at the arraignment but before the entry of a plea, determines and states on the record that he will not sentence the defendant to a fine of more than $1,000 or period of imprisonment if the defendant is convicted of the misdemeanor. . . .

Notes

1. *Constitutional right to appointed defense counsel in minor cases: majority position.* The Rhode Island advisory opinion reflects the overwhelming majority view in this country: Provision of counsel is constitutionally required for any defendant charged with a felony and for any defendant charged with a misdemeanor that results in actual imprisonment, even if less than six months. The decision in Scott v. Illinois, 440 U.S. 367 (1979), declared that only misdemeanors resulting in "actual imprisonment" would require appointed counsel. Prior to the *Scott* decision, more than 20 states provided counsel (by statute or under the federal or state constitution) for a broader range of misdemeanors, and not just those involving actual imprisonment. Today, fewer states go beyond the "actual imprisonment" rule as a matter of state constitutional law. See Commonwealth v. Thomas, 507 A.2d 57 (Pa. 1986) (adopting actual imprisonment rule).

What explains this shift in constitutional rules over the years? Is it an example of the leading role the U.S. Supreme Court can play in constitutional interpretation? Does it exemplify what can happen when legal rules created in a system dealing with a relatively small number of cases are used in a system processing much larger numbers of cases? Is it significant that Rhode Island's governor requested an advisory opinion on the extent of the right to counsel when formulating the state budget?

What do the courts in *Gideon* and in the Rhode Island advisory opinion believe that lawyers do? Are attorneys indispensable to criminal justice, or an impediment to criminal justice, or both? Consider, in this connection, what happened to Clarence Gideon. After the Supreme Court reversed Gideon's conviction, an attorney defended Gideon at his retrial on the charges. He was acquitted. See Anthony Lewis, Gideon's Trumpet 223-38 (1964).

2. *Statutory right to appointed counsel in minor cases.* There is more variation among state statutes providing counsel than among state constitutional interpretations. Some states have statutes or rules that track the federal and state constitutional requirements. States such as Vermont, however, add to the list of crimes for which the state must provide counsel for indigent defendants. As the opinions in *Shelton* indicated, a number of state statutes provided counsel for defendants who receive a suspended sentence even before it became clear that the constitution requires defense lawyers in such cases. Some states also provide counsel for some cases involving large criminal fines.

Perhaps the most important statutory provisions and rules on this subject are the ones (like the Florida rule above) giving a trial judge the *discretion* to appoint counsel in any criminal proceedings, regardless of the crime involved. The critical decisions here are funding decisions, which are often made at the local rather than state level. See Bureau of Justice Statistics, Indigent Defense Services in Large Counties, 1999 at 3 (Nov. 2000, NCJ 184932) (in largest 100 counties, 69 percent of funds for indigent defense comes from county or city government, 25 percent from state). Will a city provide enough money to fund attorneys for all those accused of violating its criminal ordinances? As a trial judge, can you identify any class of cases where you would not routinely appoint counsel even if the funds were available?

Funding for indigent criminal defense takes place against a complex political background, which receives fuller attention on the web extension for this chapter at *http://www.crimpro.com/extension/ch11*.

3. *Determination of indigence.* The trial court typically determines, in a hearing soon after charges are filed, whether or not the defendant qualifies as an indigent to receive state-provided counsel. The trial judge must consult factors listed in appellate opinions, statutes, or procedure rules, but those factors tend to be general enough to leave the trial judge with much discretion in deciding which defendants qualify. The judge often must consider such factors as the seriousness of the crime, the amount of bail bond required, the defendant's assets and debts, and the defendant's employment status. See Tenn. Code §40-14-202(c). The state might provide counsel and later attempt to collect the attorneys' fees from defendants who have more resources than they originally appeared to have. In the end, the great majority of felony defendants are indigents who receive public defenders or appointed counsel. By some estimates, more than three-quarters of all defendants charged with eligible crimes are provided with counsel. Bureau of Justice Statistics, Defense Counsel in Criminal Cases (Nov. 2000, NCJ 179023) (82 percent of felony defendants in state court represented by publicly financed counsel).

Why bother to distinguish between indigent and non-indigent defendants? Would the criminal justice system improve if the state offered to pay for an attorney (at state-determined rates) for any criminal defendant charged with an eligible crime — no questions asked about the defendant's ability to pay? Would this make the provision of defense counsel more like Social Security benefits, an entitlement with broad political support because it benefits a broad group?

4. *Recoupment of fees.* State statutes typically allow the state to recoup some fees for the services of the defense attorney if the defendant is convicted and the court later finds that the defendant has the funds for at least a partial payment of the attorney's fees. See State v. Dudley, 766 N.W.2d 606 (Iowa 2009) (statute requiring acquitted indigent defendants to reimburse cost of defense, if applied without means test, violates right to counsel). In most jurisdictions, judges tell the defendant about these recoupment laws when asking whether the defendant wants to waive counsel. Exactly how would you word this notice to defendants if you were a trial judge?

5. *Constitutional sources of the right to counsel.* Keep in mind the different constitutional sources for the right to counsel. In some settings (a "criminal prosecution"), the Sixth Amendment requires counsel to be available. When it comes to police station interrogations, as we have seen in Chapter 8, the Fifth Amendment requires that a defendant be told about the right to have counsel present. In others (such as some postconviction proceedings), the due process clause requires counsel. In still other settings, the equal protection clause requires the state to provide counsel to all if it allows counsel for some. Recall also that most states have analogues to these federal constitutional provisions. What constitutional source was the basis for the *Gideon* decision?

What does the text of the Sixth Amendment suggest about the types of cases in which the state must provide counsel? On the one hand, the amendment does provide for a right to counsel "in *all* criminal prosecutions." Thus it would seem to cover any misdemeanor — even one not resulting in imprisonment. On the other hand, the Sixth Amendment was originally thought to address access to *retained* counsel, not defense counsel provided by the state. The Sixth Amendment right to counsel apparently was drafted as a repudiation of the common law of England, which prevented those accused of most felonies from relying upon retained counsel to conduct their defense at trial.

6. *Incorporation.* Long before *Gideon,* the Supreme Court had declared that the Sixth Amendment required the government to appoint counsel for all criminal defendants in *federal* court. See Johnson v. Zerbst, 304 U.S. 458 (1938). The language of the Sixth Amendment and the rest of the Bill of Rights applied only to the federal government, not to the states. Thus, the *Gideon* Court had to resolve the larger question (given the relative sizes of the federal and state criminal systems) of whether the due process clause of the Fourteenth Amendment — which did apply to the states — "incorporated" the specific guarantees of the Bill of Rights.

The majority in *Gideon* argued that the *Betts* rule was an aberration and a departure from earlier cases dealing with the incorporation of the right to counsel; Justice John Marshall Harlan suggested instead that the *Betts* case was a plausible but impracticable extension of earlier cases. Who was right?

The Supreme Court has decided that due process "selectively" incorporates some Bill of Rights guarantees. *Gideon* was an important development in this broader constitutional trend. While there has been debate over the years about the extent to which the framers and adopters of the Fourteenth Amendment intended to incorporate provisions of the Bill of Rights, the current consensus seems to be that the Court was substantially correct to incorporate most, if not all, of the provisions. See Michael Kent Curtis, No State Shall Abridge: The Fourteenth Amendment and the Bill of Rights (1986); Akhil Amar, The Bill of Rights and the Fourteenth Amendment, 101 Yale L.J. 1193 (1992).

7. *Actual imprisonment for later crimes.* A conviction for a misdemeanor that is not punished with a prison sentence might become relevant at a later time, during sentencing for some different crime. Can a sentencing judge use an earlier uncounseled misdemeanor conviction to lengthen the prison term imposed for the later offense? In Nichols v. United States, 511 U.S. 738 (1994), the Supreme Court decided that a sentencing court may consider a defendant's previous uncounseled misdemeanor conviction in sentencing him for a subsequent offense. The opinion argued that the later sentencing decision does not convert the punishment for the original crime into a prison term, and that sentencing judges often rely on past conduct not proven in a criminal trial as a part of sentencing. Should the state provide counsel for *any* crime if a conviction for that crime will affect a person's liberty, whether now or later? Compare State v. Kelly, 999 So.2d 1029 (Fla. 2008) (state constitution prevents state from using an initial uncounseled DUI conviction to elevate later "wobbler" misdemeanor DUI convictions into felony convictions, unless defendant waived counsel for original conviction; rejects *Nichols*).

Problem 11-1. Lawyers and Experts

Paul Husske was charged with rape. Part of the government's case against him was a DNA analysis of tissue obtained from the rape victim. Several months before trial, the defendant filed a motion asserting his indigence and requesting that the trial court appoint an expert, at the government's expense, to help him challenge the DNA evidence that the prosecution intended to use. Husske asserted that because DNA evidence is "of a highly technical nature," it is "difficult for a lawyer to challenge DNA evidence without expert assistance." He expressed concern about the use of DNA evidence because the state's laboratory in the Division of Forensic Science had a "well-known record" for incompetent or biased testing. He also attached an affidavit from a local attorney who had read extensively on the subject of DNA and who also asserted the need for expert assistance to test the reliability of such evidence. Even though the trial court denied the defendant's motion, the court appointed the local attorney as co-counsel to assist the defendant, because he was "the most knowledgeable member of the local bar in the area of forensic DNA application."

A researcher from the Division of Forensic Science and a faculty member from a nearby state university testified at trial for the government as expert witnesses on the subject of DNA analysis. The experts each testified that the defendant's DNA profile matched the profile of the individual who had attacked the victim. They said that the DNA analysis did not exclude the defendant as a contributor of the genetic material that the assailant left on the victim's body and clothing. They also stated that the statistical probability of randomly selecting a person unrelated to the defendant in the Caucasian population with the same DNA profile was 1 in 700,000. Was the trial judge obliged to appoint an expert to assist defense counsel? Compare Husske v. Commonwealth, 476 S.E.2d 920 (Va. 1996).

Problem 11-2. Universal Appointment

The director of the Indigent Defense Services office for the largest county in the state would like to expand the coverage of the service. Currently about three-quarters of the criminal defendants in the state court are eligible to receive services from IDS. She would like to convince judges in the county to make appointments of counsel available to all criminal defendants, regardless of their income levels, the seriousness of the crimes charged, or the types of punishments they face. If they were to do so, she believes the overall quality of representation for defendants would increase, and public satisfaction with public services would improve. The county might have to increase funding for the office by modest amounts — experience would determine the necessary funding levels over time — but the current rules for recoupment of fees from defendants who are financially capable of paying should keep any budget shortfall within reasonable limits. Defendants would remain free, of course, to hire private defense counsel if they want to reject the appointment of an attorney from IDS. Defendants could also waive counsel if they prefer not to wait for the attorney to prepare for the representation.

What are the prospects for the director's idea? Which arguments might be most persuasive to the local judges? Which other figures in local government, state government, the local bar, and the community might determine the type of reception that the director's proposal receives? The director's favorite analogy when talking about universal appointment of counsel is the Medicare program: The federal program that provides basic medical services to older citizens is broadly popular, and is thought to deliver cost-effective medical care. Will this argument resonate with the relevant actors?

Notes

1. *Appointment of experts*. In Ake v. Oklahoma, 470 U.S. 68 (1985), the Supreme Court held that the due process and equal protection clauses (but not the Sixth Amendment) require a state to provide an indigent defendant with access to a psychiatrist if the defendant makes a preliminary showing that his sanity will be a "significant issue" at trial. Later litigation focused on the question of when an appointed expert is one of the "raw materials integral to building an effective defense." See Caldwell v. Mississippi, 472 U.S. 320 (1985) (trial court properly denied an indigent defendant's requests for the appointment of a criminal investigator, a fingerprint expert, and a ballistics expert). Most courts that have considered the appointment of a non-psychiatric expert have held that state constitutions require the appointment of non-psychiatric experts to indigent defendants where they make a "particularized" showing of the need for the assistance. See Rey v. State, 897 S.W.2d 333 (Tex. Crim. App. 1995) (requiring appointment of pathologist to assist in cross-examination of state pathologist regarding autopsy). Some states determine the "particularized need" by asking the defendant to show prejudice if the expert is not available. See Dowdy v. Commonwealth, 686 S.E.2d 710 (Va. 2009) (defendant failed to show adequate prejudice from failure of state to provide investigator to locate alibi witnesses).

2. *Distribution of offenses*. The decision to provide counsel for different classes of misdemeanants has serious consequences, not the least of them fiscal. If felonies rest at the top of a "pyramid" of criminal charges, the least serious misdemeanors are the charges at the broad bottom of the pyramid: In most systems, they are by far the most numerous charges. See Bureau of Justice Statistics, Prosecutors in State Courts, 2005 at 6 (July 2006, NCJ 213799) (prosecutors' offices close three times more misdemeanor cases than felony cases). As a result, choices about the appointment of counsel for the lowest-level charges will generally have the largest impact on the system for providing counsel. The federal system is atypical on this score, since only about a quarter of all charges filed in a given year are misdemeanors. Many states create special court systems to handle the lowest-level offenses, with names such as "misdemeanor court" or "district court."

2. *Type of Proceedings*

For typical crimes, it would probably be unworkable to provide counsel (or even to give notice of the right to counsel) as soon as a person becomes a suspect or interacts with the police. Consider, in this regard, the great variety of interactions between citizens and police. The right to counsel more plausibly could attach whenever a person is arrested, though no jurisdiction has found a right to counsel based simply on the fact of arrest. Perhaps no right to counsel should attach until a person appears in court and is asked to plead guilty or not guilty, or at some other point in the standard criminal process.

Courts trying to determine when the right to counsel attaches have concluded that different constitutional provisions create obligations arising at different points in the process. There are at least two distinct counsel rights — one based on the

Sixth Amendment and its state analogues, the other based on the Fifth Amendment privilege against self-incrimination.

The Fifth Amendment right to counsel — a right derived from the inherently compulsory nature of custodial interrogation and from the need to protect against compulsory self-incrimination — was recognized in Miranda v. Arizona, 384 U.S. 436 (1966) (see Chapter 8). The Fifth Amendment right to counsel arises whenever the police conduct a custodial interrogation. Because interrogations usually occur before charging (since they are used to gather evidence), the Fifth Amendment right to counsel will often arise before any Sixth Amendment right to counsel.

The Sixth Amendment provides that in "all criminal prosecutions, the accused shall . . . have the assistance of counsel for his defense." The language raises the question: What is a "criminal prosecution"? The legal test is phrased in these general terms: The analysis of whether a Sixth Amendment right to counsel attaches turns on whether the procedure is considered (1) a "critical stage" of the criminal process, (2) taking place after the "initiation" of the adversarial judicial proceedings. We saw one application of the right to counsel in Chapter 9 — the U.S. Supreme Court considers post-indictment lineups to be a "critical stage" of the criminal process. What is it that makes a police technique or judicial hearing a "critical stage" after the initiation of adversarial proceedings?

■ ALABAMA RULE OF CRIMINAL PROCEDURE 6.1(a)

A defendant shall be entitled to be represented by counsel in any criminal proceedings held pursuant to these rules and, if indigent, shall be entitled to have an attorney appointed to represent the defendant in all criminal proceedings in which representation by counsel is constitutionally required. The right to be represented shall include the right to consult in private with an attorney or the attorney's agent, as soon as feasible after a defendant is taken into custody, at reasonable times thereafter, and sufficiently in advance of a proceeding to allow adequate preparation therefor.

■ MISSOURI SUPREME COURT RULES 31.01, 31.02

31.01

Every person arrested and held in custody by any peace officer in any jail, police station or any other place, upon or without a warrant or other process for the alleged commission of a criminal offense, or upon suspicion thereof, shall promptly, upon request, be permitted to consult with counsel or other persons in his behalf, and, for such purpose, to use a telephone.

31.02

(a) In all criminal cases the defendant shall have the right to appear and defend in person and by counsel. If any person charged with an offense, the conviction of which would probably result in confinement, shall be without counsel upon his first appearance before a judge, it shall be the duty of the court to advise him of his right to counsel, and of the willingness of the court to appoint counsel to represent him if he is unable to employ counsel. Upon a showing of indigency, it shall be the duty of the court to appoint counsel to represent him. If after being informed as to his rights, the defendant requests to proceed without the benefit of counsel, and the court finds that he has intelligently waived his right to have counsel, the court shall have no duty to appoint counsel. . . .

WALTER ROTHGERY v. GILLESPIE COUNTY, TEXAS

554 U.S. 191 (2008)

SOUTER, J.*

This Court has held that the right to counsel guaranteed by the Sixth Amendment applies at the first appearance before a judicial officer at which a defendant is told of the formal accusation against him and restrictions are imposed on his liberty. See Brewer v. Williams, 430 U.S. 387, 398-399 (1977). The question here is whether attachment of the right also requires that a public prosecutor (as distinct from a police officer) be aware of that initial proceeding or involved in its conduct. We hold that it does not.

I.

Although petitioner Walter Rothgery has never been convicted of a felony, a criminal background check disclosed an erroneous record that he had been, and on July 15, 2002, Texas police officers relied on this record to arrest him as a felon in possession of a firearm. The officers lacked a warrant, and so promptly brought Rothgery before a magistrate judge, as required by Tex. Crim. Proc. Code Ann., Art. 14.06(a). Texas law has no formal label for this initial appearance before a magistrate, which is sometimes called the "article 15.17 hearing"; it combines the Fourth Amendment's required probable-cause determination with the setting of bail, and is the point at which the arrestee is formally apprised of the accusation against him.

Rothgery's article 15.17 hearing followed routine. The arresting officer submitted a sworn "Affidavit of Probable Cause" that described the facts supporting the arrest and charged that Rothgery committed the offense of unlawful possession of a firearm by a felon. . . . After reviewing the affidavit, the magistrate judge determined that probable cause existed for the arrest. The magistrate judge informed Rothgery of the accusation, set his bail at $5,000, and committed him to jail, from which he was released after posting a surety bond. . . . The release was conditioned on the defendant's personal appearance in trial court "for any and all subsequent proceedings that may be had relative to the said charge in the course of the criminal action based on said charge."

Rothgery had no money for a lawyer and made several oral and written requests for appointed counsel, which went unheeded. [Rothgery also requested counsel at the article 15.17 hearing itself, but the magistrate judge informed him that the appointment of counsel would delay setting bail, so Rothgery waived the right to

* [Chief Justice Roberts and Justices Stevens, Scalia, Kennedy, Ginsberg, Breyer, and Alito joined in this opinion. — EDS.]

have appointed counsel present at the hearing.] The following January, he was indicted by a Texas grand jury for unlawful possession of a firearm by a felon, resulting in rearrest the next day, and an order increasing bail to $15,000. When he could not post it, he was put in jail and remained there for three weeks.

On January 23, 2003, six months after the article 15.17 hearing, Rothgery was finally assigned a lawyer, who promptly obtained a bail reduction (so Rothgery could get out of jail), and assembled the paperwork confirming that Rothgery had never been convicted of a felony. Counsel relayed this information to the district attorney, who in turn filed a motion to dismiss the indictment, which was granted.

Rothgery then brought this 42 U.S.C. §1983 action against respondent Gillespie County, claiming that if the County had provided a lawyer within a reasonable time after the article 15.17 hearing, he would not have been indicted, rearrested, or jailed for three weeks. The County's failure is said to be owing to its unwritten policy of denying appointed counsel to indigent defendants out on bond until at least the entry of an information or indictment. Rothgery sees this policy as violating his Sixth Amendment right to counsel. [Such a policy, if proven, arguably would also be in violation of Texas state law, which appears to require appointment of counsel for indigent defendants released from custody, at the latest, when the "first court appearance" is made. See Tex. Crim. Proc. Code Ann., Art. 1.051(j).]

The District Court granted summary judgment to the County, and the Court of Appeals affirmed. The Court of Appeals [held] that the Sixth Amendment right to counsel did not attach at the article 15.17 hearing, because "the relevant prosecutors were not aware of or involved in Rothgery's arrest or appearance before the magistrate on July 16, 2002," and there is also "no indication that the officer who filed the probable cause affidavit at Rothgery's appearance had any power to commit the state to prosecute without the knowledge or involvement of a prosecutor." We granted certiorari, and now vacate and remand.

II.

A.

The Sixth Amendment right of the "accused" to assistance of counsel in "all criminal prosecutions" is limited by its terms: it does not attach until a prosecution is commenced. We have, for purposes of the right to counsel, pegged commencement to the initiation of adversary judicial criminal proceedings — whether by way of formal charge, preliminary hearing, indictment, information, or arraignment. Kirby v. Illinois, 406 U.S. 682, 689 (1972) (plurality opinion). The rule is not mere formalism, but a recognition of the point at which "the government has committed itself to prosecute, the adverse positions of government and defendant have solidified, and the accused finds himself faced with the prosecutorial forces of organized society, and immersed in the intricacies of substantive and procedural criminal law. The issue is whether Texas's article 15.17 hearing marks that point, with the consequent state obligation to appoint counsel within a reasonable time once a request for assistance is made.

[We have held] that the right to counsel attaches at the initial appearance before a judicial officer. See Brewer v. Williams, 430 U.S. 387 (1977); Michigan v. Jackson, 475 U.S. 625 (1986). This first time before a court, also known as the "preliminary arraignment" or "arraignment on the complaint," is generally the hearing at which the magistrate informs the defendant of the charge in the complaint, and of various rights in further proceedings, and determines the conditions for pretrial release. Texas's article 15.17 hearing is an initial appearance: Rothgery was taken before a magistrate judge, informed of the formal accusation against him, and sent to jail until he posted bail.

The *Brewer* defendant surrendered to the police after a warrant was out for his arrest on a charge of abduction. He was then arraigned before a judge on the outstanding arrest warrant, and at the arraignment, the judge advised him of his *Miranda* rights and committed him to jail. After this preliminary arraignment, and before an indictment on the abduction charge had been handed up, police elicited incriminating admissions that ultimately led to an indictment for first-degree murder. Because neither of the defendant's lawyers had been present when the statements were obtained, the Court found it "clear" that the defendant was deprived of the right to the assistance of counsel. [The] defendant's right had clearly attached for the reason that a warrant had been issued for his arrest, he had been arraigned on that warrant before a judge in a courtroom, and he had been committed by the court to confinement in jail.

[By] the time a defendant is brought before a judicial officer, is informed of a formally lodged accusation, and has restrictions imposed on his liberty in aid of the prosecution, the State's relationship with the defendant has become solidly adversarial. And that is just as true when the proceeding comes before the indictment (in the case of the initial arraignment on a formal complaint) as when it comes after it (at an arraignment on an indictment).

[The] overwhelming consensus practice conforms to the rule that the first formal proceeding is the point of attachment. We are advised without contradiction that not only the Federal Government, including the District of Columbia, but 43 States take the first step toward appointing counsel before, at, or just after initial appearance. . . .

C.

The Court of Appeals thought *Brewer* and *Jackson* could be distinguished on the ground that neither case addressed the issue of prosecutorial involvement, and the cases were thus "neutral on the point." [Under the Circuit Court's] standard of prosecutorial awareness, attachment depends not on whether a first appearance has begun adversary judicial proceedings, but on whether the prosecutor had a hand in starting it. That standard is wrong.

[An] attachment rule that turned on determining the moment of a prosecutor's first involvement would be wholly unworkable and impossible to administer, guaranteed to bog the courts down in prying enquiries into the communication between police (who are routinely present at defendants' first appearances) and the State's attorneys (who are not). And it would have the practical effect of resting attachment on such absurd distinctions as the day of the month an arrest is made, [since] jails may be required to report their arrestees to county prosecutor offices on particular days; or the sophistication, or lack thereof, of a jurisdiction's computer intake system, [since] some Texas counties have computer systems that provide arrest and detention information simultaneously to prosecutors, law enforcement officers, jail personnel, and clerks. . . .

It is not that the Court of Appeals believed that any such regime would be desirable, but it thought originally that its rule was implied by this Court's statement that the right attaches when the government has "committed itself to prosecute." *Kirby*, 406 U.S., at 689. . . . But what counts as a commitment to prosecute is an issue of federal law unaffected by allocations of power among state officials under a State's law, and under the federal standard, an accusation filed with a judicial officer is sufficiently formal, and the government's commitment to prosecute it sufficiently concrete, when the accusation prompts arraignment and restrictions on the accused's liberty to facilitate the prosecution. From that point on, the defendant is "faced with the prosecutorial forces of organized society, and immersed in the intricacies of substantive and procedural criminal law" that define his capacity and control his actual ability to defend himself against a formal accusation that he is a criminal. *Kirby*, 406 U.S. at 689. By that point, it is too late to wonder whether he is "accused" within the meaning of the Sixth Amendment, and it makes no practical sense to deny it. All of this is equally true whether the machinery of prosecution was turned on by the local police or the state attorney general. In this case, for example, Rothgery alleges that after the initial appearance, he was "unable to find any employment for wages" because "all of the potential employers he contacted knew or learned of the criminal charge pending against him." One may assume that those potential employers would still have declined to make job offers if advised that the county prosecutor had not filed the complaint.

[The County] tries to downplay the significance of the initial appearance by saying that an attachment rule unqualified by prosecutorial involvement would lead to the conclusion "that the State has statutorily committed to prosecute every suspect arrested by the police," given that state law requires an article 15.17 hearing for every arrestee. The answer, though, is that the State has done just that, subject to the option to change its official mind later. The State may rethink its commitment at any point: it may choose not to seek indictment in a felony case, say, or the prosecutor may enter nolle prosequi after the case gets to the jury room. But without a change of position, a defendant subject to accusation after initial appearance is headed for trial and needs to get a lawyer working, whether to attempt to avoid that trial or to be ready with a defense when the trial date arrives. . . .

The County stipulates that "the properly formulated test is not . . . merely whether prosecutors have had any involvement in the case whatsoever, but instead whether the State has objectively committed itself to prosecute." It then informs us that prosecutorial involvement "is merely one form of evidence of such commitment." Other sufficient evidentiary indications are variously described: first (expansively) as "the filing of formal charges . . . by information, indictment or formal complaint, or the holding of an adversarial preliminary hearing to determine probable cause to file such charges"; then (restrictively) as a court appearance following "arrest . . . on an indictment or information." Either version, in any event, runs up against *Brewer* and *Jackson*: an initial appearance following a charge signifies a sufficient commitment to prosecute regardless of a prosecutor's participation, indictment, information, or what the County calls a "formal" complaint.

[According] to the County, our cases (*Brewer* and *Jackson* aside) actually establish a "general rule that the right to counsel attaches at the point that [what the County calls] formal charges are filed," with exceptions allowed only in the case of "a very limited set of specific preindictment situations." The County suggests that the latter category should be limited to those appearances at which the aid of counsel is urgent and the dangers to the accused of proceeding without counsel are great. Texas's article 15.17 hearing should not count as one of those situations, the County says, because it is not of critical significance, since it "allows no presentation of witness testimony and provides no opportunity to expose weaknesses in the government's evidence, create a basis for later impeachment, or even engage in basic discovery."

[The] Court in *Brewer* and *Jackson* . . . found the attachment issue an easy one. [If the County] had simply taken the cases at face value, it would have avoided the mistake of merging the attachment question (whether formal judicial proceedings have begun) with the distinct "critical stage" question (whether counsel must be present at a postattachment proceeding unless the right to assistance is validly waived). Attachment occurs when the government has used the judicial machinery to signal a commitment to prosecute as spelled out in *Brewer* and *Jackson*. Once attachment occurs, the accused at least is entitled to the presence of appointed counsel during any "critical stage" of the postattachment proceedings; what makes a stage critical is what shows the need for counsel's presence. Thus, counsel must be appointed within a reasonable time after attachment to allow for adequate representation at any critical stage before trial, as well as at trial itself.

The County thus makes an analytical mistake in its assumption that attachment necessarily requires the occurrence or imminence of a critical stage. On the contrary, it is irrelevant to attachment that the presence of counsel at an article 15.17 hearing, say, may not be critical, just as it is irrelevant that counsel's presence may not be critical when a prosecutor walks over to the trial court to file an information. . . .

III.

Our holding is narrow. We do not decide whether the 6-month delay in appointment of counsel resulted in prejudice to Rothgery's Sixth Amendment rights, and have no occasion to consider what standards should apply in deciding this. We merely reaffirm what we have held before and what an overwhelming majority of American jurisdictions understand in practice: a criminal defendant's initial appearance before a judicial officer, where he learns the charge against him and his liberty is subject to restriction, marks the start of adversary judicial proceedings that trigger attachment of the Sixth Amendment right to counsel. . . .

ALITO, J., concurring.*

I join the Court's opinion because I do not understand it to hold that a defendant is entitled to the assistance of appointed counsel as soon as his Sixth Amendment right attaches. As I interpret our precedents, the term "attachment" signifies nothing more than the beginning of the defendant's prosecution. It does not mark the beginning of a substantive entitlement to the assistance of counsel. . . .

The Sixth Amendment . . . defines the scope of the right to counsel in three ways: It provides who may assert the right ("the accused"); when the right may be asserted (in "all criminal prosecutions"); and what the right guarantees (the right "to have the Assistance of Counsel for his defence").

It is in the context of interpreting the Amendment's answer to the second of these questions — when the right may be asserted — that we have spoken of the

* [Chief Justice Roberts and Justice Scalia joined in this opinion. — EDS.]

right "attaching." . . . Because pretrial criminal procedures vary substantially from jurisdiction to jurisdiction, there is room for disagreement about when a "prosecution" begins for Sixth Amendment purposes. As the Court, notes, however, we have previously held that "arraignments" that were functionally indistinguishable from the Texas magistration marked the point at which the Sixth Amendment right to counsel "attached."

It does not follow, however, and I do not understand the Court to hold, that the county had an obligation to appoint an attorney to represent petitioner within some specified period after his magistration. . . . To recall the framework laid out earlier, we have been asked to address only the when question, not the what question. . . . Whereas the temporal scope of the right is defined by the words "[in] all criminal prosecutions," the right's substantive guarantee flows from a different textual font: the words "Assistance of Counsel for his defence."

In interpreting this latter phrase, we have held that "defence" means defense at trial, not defense in relation to other objectives that may be important to the accused. We have thus rejected the argument that the Sixth Amendment entitles the criminal defendant to the assistance of appointed counsel at a probable cause hearing. See Gerstein v. Pugh, 420 U.S. 103, 122-123 (1975) (observing that the Fourth Amendment hearing "is addressed only to pretrial custody" and has an insubstantial effect on the defendant's trial rights). More generally, we have rejected the notion that the right to counsel entitles the defendant to a "preindictment private investigator." United States v. Gouveia, 467 U.S. 180 (1984).

At the same time, we have recognized that certain pretrial events may so prejudice the outcome of the defendant's prosecution that, as a practical matter, the defendant must be represented at those events in order to enjoy genuinely effective assistance at trial. Thus, we have held that an indigent defendant is entitled to the assistance of appointed counsel at a preliminary hearing if "substantial prejudice . . . inheres in the . . . confrontation" and "counsel [may] help avoid that prejudice." Coleman v. Alabama, 399 U.S. 1, 9 (1970) (plurality opinion). We have also held that the assistance of counsel is guaranteed at a pretrial lineup, since "the confrontation compelled by the State between the accused and the victim or witnesses to a crime to elicit identification evidence is peculiarly riddled with innumerable dangers and variable factors which might seriously, even crucially, derogate from a fair trial." See United States v. Wade, 388 U.S. 218, 228 (1967). Other "critical stages" of the prosecution include pretrial interrogation, a pretrial psychiatric exam, and certain kinds of arraignments.

Weaving together these strands of authority, I interpret the Sixth Amendment to require the appointment of counsel only after the defendant's prosecution has begun, and then only as necessary to guarantee the defendant effective assistance at trial. It follows that defendants in Texas will not necessarily be entitled to the assistance of counsel within some specified period after their magistrations. Texas counties need only appoint counsel as far in advance of trial, and as far in advance of any pretrial "critical stage," as necessary to guarantee effective assistance at trial. . . .

THOMAS, J., dissenting.

. . . Given the Court's repeated insistence that the right to counsel is textually limited to "criminal prosecutions," . . . I think it appropriate to examine what a "criminal prosecution" would have been understood to entail by those who adopted the Sixth Amendment.

There is no better place to begin than with Blackstone, whose works constituted the preeminent authority on English law for the founding generation. . . . Blackstone organized the various stages of a criminal proceeding "under twelve general heads, following each other in a progressive order." The first six relate to pretrial events: "1. Arrest; 2. Commitment and bail; 3. Prosecution; 4. Process; 5. Arraignment, and it's incidents; 6. Plea, and issue." Thus, the first significant fact is that Blackstone did not describe the entire criminal process as a "prosecution," but rather listed prosecution as the third step in a list of successive stages. For a more complete understanding of what Blackstone meant by "prosecution," however, we must turn to chapter 23, entitled "Of the Several Modes of Prosecution." There, Blackstone explained that — after arrest and examination by a justice of the peace to determine whether a suspect should be discharged, committed to prison, or admitted to bail — the "next step towards the punishment of offenders is their prosecution, or the manner of their formal accusation."

Blackstone thus provides a definition of "prosecution": the manner of an offender's "formal accusation." The modifier "formal" is significant because it distinguishes "prosecution" from earlier stages of the process involving a different kind of accusation: the allegation of criminal conduct necessary to justify arrest and detention. Blackstone's discussion of arrest, commitment, and bail makes clear that a person could not be arrested and detained without a "charge" or "accusation," i.e., an allegation, supported by probable cause, that the person had committed a crime. But the accusation justifying arrest and detention was clearly preliminary to the "formal accusation" that Blackstone identified with "prosecution." . . .

"Prosecution," as Blackstone used the term, referred to "instituting a criminal suit," by filing a formal charging document — an indictment, presentment, or information — upon which the defendant was to be tried in a court with power to punish the alleged offense. . . .

With Blackstone as our guide, it is significant that the Framers used the words "criminal prosecutions" in the Sixth Amendment rather than some other formulation such as "criminal proceedings" or "criminal cases." Indeed, elsewhere in the Bill of Rights we find just such an alternative formulation: In contrast to the Sixth Amendment, the Fifth Amendment refers to "criminal case[s]."

[On] this understanding of the Sixth Amendment, it is clear that petitioner's initial appearance before the magistrate did not commence a "criminal prosecution." No formal charges had been filed. The only document submitted to the magistrate was the arresting officer's affidavit of probable cause. . . . The magistrate certified that he had examined the affidavit and "determined that probable cause existed for the arrest of the individual accused therein." Later that day, petitioner was released on bail, and did not hear from the State again until he was indicted six months later. . . .

[Our] reasoned precedents provide no support for the conclusion that the right to counsel attaches at an initial appearance before a magistrate. Kirby v. Illinois, 406 U.S. 682 (1972) (plurality opinion), explained why the right attaches "after the initiation of adversary judicial criminal proceedings":

> The initiation of judicial criminal proceedings is . . . the starting point of our whole system of adversary criminal justice. For it is only then that the government has committed itself to prosecute, and only then that the adverse positions of government and defendant have solidified. It is then that a defendant finds himself faced with the

> prosecutorial forces of organized society, and immersed in the intricacies of substantive and procedural criminal law. . . .

None of these defining characteristics of a "criminal prosecution" applies to petitioner's initial appearance before the magistrate. The initial appearance was not an "adversary" proceeding, and petitioner was not "faced with the prosecutorial forces of organized society." Instead, he stood in front of a "little glass window," filled out various forms, and was read his *Miranda* rights. The State had not committed itself to prosecute — only a prosecutor may file felony charges in Texas, and there is no evidence that any prosecutor was even aware of petitioner's arrest or appearance. The adverse positions of government and defendant had not yet solidified — the State's prosecutorial officers had not yet decided whether to press charges and, if so, which charges to press. And petitioner was not immersed in the intricacies of substantive and procedural criminal law — shortly after the proceeding he was free on bail, and no further proceedings occurred until six months later when he was indicted. . . .

Neither petitioner nor the Court identifies any way in which petitioner's ability to receive a fair trial was undermined by the absence of counsel during the period between his initial appearance and his indictment. Nothing during that period exposed petitioner to the risk that he would be convicted as the result of ignorance of his rights. [The] Sixth Amendment protects against the risk of erroneous conviction, not the risk of unwarranted prosecution. . . .

Problem 11-3. Lawyers in Psychiatric Examinations

Raymond Larsen was charged with murder in Illinois. He admitted that he killed the victim but relied on the affirmative defense of insanity at the time of the slaying. The state filed a written pretrial motion to require Larsen to submit to examination by a state-designated psychiatrist as provided by statute. The court appointed Dr. Robert Reifman, assistant director of the Psychiatric Institute of the Circuit Court of Cook County, to conduct an examination "on August 23, or on any date subsequent, necessary to complete such examination." The defendant's counsel did not receive notice of the location and time, or of the name of the psychiatrist, prior to the examination, which was conducted on August 24.

Based on the court-ordered psychiatric examination, Dr. Reifman testified for the state on rebuttal at trial. He opined that the defendant had an antisocial personality but did not suffer from a mental defect or disease and had substantial capacity to conform his conduct to the requirement of the law and to appreciate the criminality of his conduct. On appeal the defendant argues that the psychiatric examination was a "critical stage" of the proceedings and that he had the right to notice and presence of counsel. How would you rule? See People v. Larsen, 385 N.E. 2d 679 (Ill. 1979).

Notes

1. *Initiation of adversarial proceedings: majority position.* The federal constitutional right to counsel applies only when two preconditions are met. First, the right attaches only after the initiation of an "adversarial proceeding." Second, even after the initiation of adversarial proceedings, the government must allow a defense attorney to participate only during a "critical stage" of those proceedings. Most state courts adopt this same two-part test to determine when the right to counsel under the state constitution applies. The precise methods for filing criminal charges and the exact functions of early judicial hearings differ from state to state; as the *Rothgery* case indicates, the "initiation" prong of the test does not depend on the involvement of the prosecutor or the potential contributions of defense counsel at the proceeding. The federal constitutional right to counsel does not begin with arrest, or even with a postarrest probable cause hearing required by Gerstein v. Pugh, 420 U.S. 103 (1975).

Some high state courts have read their state constitutions to provide for a right to counsel earlier than in the federal system. See Page v. State, 495 So. 2d 436 (Miss. 1986) (right to counsel attaches before arraignment, when proceedings reach "accusatory" stage); cf. McCarter v. State, 770 A.2d 195 (Md. 2001) (statute gives defendant right to counsel at initial appearance; not necessary to decide if initial appearance is "critical stage" for constitutional counsel right). You may also recall from Chapter 9 that a minority of states have concluded that a postarrest identification lineup or photo identification can qualify as a "critical stage" that triggers the right to counsel. See, e.g., Commonwealth v. Richman, 320 A.2d 351 (Pa. 1974) (lineup). Some states also conclude that it is a violation of the right to counsel to fail to inform a suspect during interrogation that his attorney is trying to make contact. See Haliburton v. State, 514 So. 2d 1088 (Fla. 1987). See Chapter 8.

2. *Critical stages before trial: majority position.* The second prong of the test depends on the value that defense counsel might contribute during a particular proceeding, with the ultimate objective of ensuring a fair trial. The right to counsel extends to preliminary hearings in which the government must demonstrate a prima facie case against the defendant, Coleman v. Alabama, 399 U.S. 1 (1970), because defense counsel at such a hearing can obtain discovery of the state's evidence, make a record for later impeachment of state witnesses at trial, and preserve defense witness testimony. See also Cooks v. State, 240 S.W.3d 906 (Tex. Crim. App. 2007) (period of 30 days for filing of motion for new trial is a "critical stage").

State constitutions are almost always interpreted to cover the same pretrial proceedings as the federal constitution. Typically, a state's rules of criminal procedure will track these constitutional boundaries and will provide for the appointment of legal counsel at the defendant's initial appearance before a magistrate, when the defendant is informed of the charges. The Missouri rule reprinted above is typical.

3. *Defense counsel for initial bail determination.* Defense attorneys are usually not available when the judge makes the first determination of bail or pretrial detention at the initial appearance. See, e.g., Fenner v. State, 846 A.2d 1020 (Md. 2004). Roughly 20 states provide no counsel at the time of bail. About half the states, however, do provide counsel at the time of bail in urban centers, even though defense lawyers are not available elsewhere in the state. A study of the Baltimore courts compared defendants who were all charged with similar nonviolent offenses, some

represented by counsel and others not. The presence of counsel made an enormous difference in outcomes: two and a half times as many represented defendants were released on recognizance as unrepresented defendants. More than twice as many represented defendants had their bail reduced to affordable amounts. See Douglas L. Colbert, Ray Paternoster & Shawn D. Bushway, Do Attorneys Really Matter? The Empirical and Legal Case for the Right of Counsel at Bail, 23 Cardozo L. Rev. 1719 (2002).

4. *Defense counsel for DWI examinations: majority position.* In most states, there is no constitutional or statutory right to counsel for DWI examinations if they precede formal charging. Roughly a dozen high state courts have granted a person arrested on DWI charges the right to consult with retained counsel before performing sobriety tests. See State v. Spencer, 750 P.2d 147 (Or. 1988). Does this position create a special rule for DWI defendants not applicable to most criminal defendants? Are DWI defendants as a class different from other criminal defendants? Will the lawyer be able to persuade a problem drinker to seek treatment?

For a review of the state court and legislative variety on the right to counsel during the production of blood samples or handwriting exemplars, see the web extension for this chapter at *http://www.crimpro.com/extension/ch11*.

5. *Are psychiatric examinations a "critical stage"?* Should there be a rule governing whether all psychiatric examinations are a critical stage in the proceedings, or should it depend on the use of the information gained by the examination? Courts in about a dozen states have concluded that there is a right to counsel during at least some psychiatric exams, and these opinions typically state that the examination might be a "critical stage" in some cases but not in others. More than 20 states have declared that there is no constitutional right to counsel during any psychiatric exams. Should competency examinations be treated differently from examinations used to undermine potential defenses? Those used at sentencing? Those used to establish aggravating factors for a capital sentence? In Estelle v. Smith, 451 U.S. 454 (1981), the Supreme Court held that use of a psychiatrist's testimony at a capital sentencing proceeding based on a pretrial psychiatric examination at which defendant had not been represented by counsel violated defendant's Fifth Amendment rights against compulsory self-incrimination. What would a lawyer do at a psychiatric examination? Would a lawyer have a right to review a psychiatrist's questions before the examination?

6. *Right to counsel at sentencing.* The Sixth Amendment and its state constitutional analogues apply to sentencing hearings; the government must provide the defendant with an attorney at these hearings. Mempa v. Rhay, 389 U.S. 128 (1967); State v. Alspach, 554 N.W.2d 882 (Iowa 1996) (right to counsel at postconviction hearing to challenge amount of restitution). However, counsel is not required if the trial court sentences a defendant to probation and the state later attempts to convince the judge to revoke the defendant's probation (and send the defendant to prison) because she has violated the conditions of probation. Gagnon v. Scarpelli, 411 U.S. 778 (1973). If the end result is the same for the offender (a prison term), what is the constitutional distinction between sentencing hearings and probation revocation hearings?

7. *Right to counsel on appeal.* The criminal prosecution ends with a conviction and sentence. If the defendant appeals the case, the government is defending the

judgment rather than "prosecuting" the case. As a result, courts say, the Sixth Amendment right to counsel does not apply to criminal appeals. The federal constitutional right to counsel on the first appeal as of right is based instead on both due process and equal protection principles. See Douglas v. California, 372 U.S. 353 (1963). The federal constitutional right does not extend to discretionary appeals. Ross v. Moffitt, 417 U.S. 600 (1974). The government also has no federal constitutional obligation to supply counsel for postconviction proceedings such as habeas corpus. See Murray v. Giarratano, 492 U.S. 1 (1989). Once again, state courts have by and large followed the federal lead when interpreting their own constitutional provisions. Nevertheless, many states do appoint counsel for at least some defendants during these postconviction proceedings. See, e.g., Mont. Code Ann. §§46-8-103, 46-8-104 ("Any court of record may assign counsel to defend any defendant, petitioner, or appellant in any postconviction criminal action or proceeding if he desires counsel and is unable to employ counsel").

B. SELECTION AND REJECTION OF COUNSEL

Although the government may have an obligation to offer an attorney to most criminal defendants, not all defendants accept the offer. Some will insist on representing themselves, while others will be unhappy with the assigned lawyer and will ask for some other attorney. Which legal institutions must respond to these sorts of requests?

The U.S. Supreme Court, for one, has declared a general principle that the Sixth Amendment right to counsel includes a right to self-representation. In Faretta v. California, 422 U.S. 806 (1975), the Court pointed to historical practices giving the defendant power to waive counsel. The Sixth Amendment made the assistance of counsel "an aid to a willing defendant — not an organ of the State interposed between an unwilling defendant and his right to defend himself personally."

The right to self-representation, however, is far different from what most defendants might prefer: the right to select the attorney who will be appointed to represent them. Most defendants who choose to represent themselves do so after a frustrating experience with an attorney assigned to their case (or an attorney assigned to some earlier case). But it is clear that poor defendants do not have the legal right to select which attorney will represent them. Courts do not grant indigent defendants such a power, nor do most managers of public defender organizations. The decision about self-representation, then, is part of a broader negotiation between the defendant, the judge, the former attorney, and a prospective new attorney about who will represent the defendant. What interests will each of these parties bring to the negotiation?

■ STATE v. JOSEPH SPENCER

519 N.W.2d 357 (Iowa 1994)

McGIVERIN, C.J.

The question presented here is whether a criminal defendant suffered a violation of his sixth amendment right to self-representation when the district court appointed counsel for him over his objection. . . . On July 18, 1990, Monona County Sheriff Dennis Smith went to Joseph Spencer's rural home to investigate complaints that Spencer was discharging firearms on his property. Sheriff Smith [observed marijuana growing in Spencer's garden, obtained a search warrant, and seized marijuana plants, cocaine, and firearms from the house]. On August 20, trial informations were filed charging Spencer with possession of marijuana with intent to manufacture, unauthorized possession of firearms, possession of cocaine, and possession of marijuana. . . .

Defendant Spencer retained a private attorney, Richard Mock of Onawa, to represent him and pleaded not guilty. Attorney Mock filed a motion to suppress drugs and weapons seized during the execution of the search warrant. After an evidentiary hearing, the district court overruled the motion.

A trial date was set. On May 17, 1991, a few days before trial, attorney Mock moved to withdraw from his representation of defendant Spencer. During the hearing on that motion, the question arose as to who would represent defendant at trial. Defendant Spencer told the court he wished to represent himself but admitted he did not know legal procedures or how to object to improper evidence. After a lengthy colloquy, the district court stated, "As far as I'm concerned, although he indicates he wants to do it himself, I don't see that he's competent and qualified to do it himself." The district court then appointed attorney Richard McCoy of Sioux City to represent Spencer. The case was continued and went to trial about one year later. Attorney McCoy fully represented defendant prior to and during the trial. Spencer was found guilty by a jury and was sentenced on the four charges. Spencer appealed, contending through new counsel that the district court denied his right to self-representation. [He] contends that the district court forced counsel upon him, contrary to his rights under the sixth amendment of the federal constitution. . . .

The sixth amendment provides that an accused "shall enjoy the right . . . to have the assistance of counsel for his defence." The fourteenth amendment of the federal constitution extends this right to state prosecutions. In Faretta v. California, 422 U.S. 806 (1975), the Supreme Court held that the right to self-representation to make one's own defense is necessarily implied by the structure of the Sixth Amendment. However, the Supreme Court also recognized an important limitation on that right: Although the defendant may elect to represent himself (usually to his detriment), the trial court "may — even over objection by the accused — appoint a 'standby counsel' to aid the accused if and when the accused requests help, and to be available to represent the accused in the event that termination of the defendant's self-representation is necessary." Such an appointment serves "to relieve the judge of the need to explain and enforce basic rules of courtroom protocol or to assist the defendant in overcoming routine obstacles that stand in the way of the defendant's achievement of his own clearly indicated goals." McKaskle v. Wiggins, 465 U.S. 168 (1984). . . .

Moreover, a defendant waives his right to self-representation unless he asserts that right by "knowingly and intelligently forgoing his right to counsel." This waiver may occur despite the defendant's statement that he wishes to represent himself if he makes that statement merely out of brief frustration with the trial court's decision regarding counsel and not as a clear and unequivocal assertion of his constitutional rights. In addition, a waiver [of the right to self-representation] may be found if it reasonably appears to the court that defendant has abandoned his initial request to represent himself.

We believe that the trial court did not err in appointing an attorney for Spencer. The intent behind the appointment, from the comments of both the court and Mock, defendant's withdrawing attorney, was to provide Spencer with "standby counsel" as envisioned in *Faretta* and *McKaskle*. The following comments were made at the hearing on attorney Mock's application to withdraw:

> *The Court:* Well, I don't think that you're [the defendant] in the position of being able to defend yourself. And the least I would do is have somebody appointed to sit and be available as your counsel. But, frankly, I'm not going to put the court in the position whereby you defend yourself and then it's reversed if there is a conviction, just because there was no attorney present. It's as simple as that. Now, do you have any other person in mind?
>
> *The Defendant:* No, sir . . .
>
> *The Court:* Well, what familiarity do you have with the legal system?
>
> *The Defendant:* I don't have any, Your Honor. . . .
>
> *The Court:* An ordinary citizen can defend himself, but frankly an ordinary citizen is going to have a little difficulty following the procedures, making the proper objections and defending his own interests, unless he's familiar with the procedure in court. That's the problem I have. If you think you can do that, that's one thing; otherwise, what will happen is, if there is a conviction, it will be appealed and they will say you should have had somebody here to protect your rights.

The court thus properly appointed attorney McCoy over defendant's objection. If defendant had wished to treat this appointed attorney as standby counsel, he could have done so. The record here, however, evinces Spencer's initial desire to be represented by counsel (in employing attorney Mock), leading us to conclude that even if he wished to proceed pro se at the time of the withdrawal hearing, he waived and abandoned that right by acquiescing to attorney McCoy's full representation of his case for the following year leading up to and during the jury trial. . . .

Spencer's request for self-representation came out of frustration rather than a distinct and unequivocal request for that constitutional right. When Spencer was first charged in August 1990, he hired a private attorney (Richard Mock). Spencer worked with him until his motion to suppress evidence was overruled. Then, in May 1991, Mock moved to withdraw. Defendant was exasperated and did not want to pay for another attorney. Yet he willingly accepted attorney McCoy's name and address from the court and clearly relied on McCoy's representation during the following year and throughout trial. Spencer never attempted to try the jury case himself with McCoy as standby counsel. He never again raised the self-representation issue in the trial court. . . . Finally, defendant Spencer has pointed to nothing that he would have done differently had he represented himself at trial, nor has he demonstrated any way in which attorney McCoy denied him "a fair chance to present his case in his own way." *McKaskle*, 465 U.S. at 177. . . .

We believe that the trial court's appointment of attorney McCoy to be available as standby counsel satisfied Spencer's request to represent himself but ensured that Spencer's other rights were protected as well. By his later acts Spencer waived and abandoned any right to self-representation that he may have had. . . .

LAVORATO, J., dissenting.

In a state criminal trial, a defendant has a Sixth and Fourteenth Amendment right under the federal Constitution to self-representation. Faretta v. California, 422 U.S. 806 (1975). Before the right attaches, the defendant must voluntarily elect to proceed without counsel by "knowingly and intelligently" waiving his Sixth Amendment right to counsel. In addition, the defendant's request to proceed without counsel must be "clear and unequivocal." Before a trial court accepts the request, the court must make the defendant aware of the dangers and disadvantages of self-representation, so that the record will establish that "he knows what he is doing and his choice is made with eyes open." *Faretta,* 422 U.S. at 835. A trial court may not bar a defendant from proceeding without counsel even though the defendant is not technically competent in the law. The defendant must only be competent to make the choice to proceed without counsel. . . .

I easily infer from the record that Spencer is above average in intelligence. He has college training in electronics and math. His work experience included several years in the Air Force. He also worked as an electronics technician at General Dynamics. . . .

Unlike the majority, I believe the following colloquy between the court and Spencer shows that (1) Spencer made a clear and unequivocal request — not once, but several times — to proceed without counsel, (2) his request was knowingly and intelligently made, and (3) the trial court understood Spencer was making a clear and unequivocal request to proceed without counsel: . . .

> *The Court:* . . . Do you want to get another attorney or do you want to go to trial tomorrow with him?
>
> *The Defendant:* I feel I would be better off defending myself, Your Honor. He doesn't want to listen to what I'm telling him. . . . I'll have to go pro — I'll have to defend myself.
>
> *The Court:* Before I would let you do that, I would appoint somebody. If your status is as it appears to be, that you have property, those will be assessed — the fees of whoever is appointed will be assessed against that.
>
> *The Defendant:* I don't see how you can force me to do that, Your Honor.
>
> *The Court:* Well, I don't think that you're in the position of being able to defend yourself. And the least I would do is have somebody appointed to sit and be available as your counsel. But, frankly, I'm not going to put the court in the position whereby you defend yourself and then it's reversed if there is a conviction, just because there was no attorney present. It's as simple as that. [What] familiarity do you have with the legal system?
>
> *The Defendant:* I don't have any, Your Honor. Shouldn't make the legal system that way where I can't defend myself. I'm the one that's familiar with the case. I'm the one that's arrested. I know what my best interest is.
>
> *The Court:* Well, if I understand your complaint, [Mr. Mock] wanted to plead it and you wanted to fight it. Now, the question is, how are you going to fight it in the courtroom? My problem with it is that I don't want you to sit in the courtroom not being prepared for the procedures and end up with a verdict against you because you weren't familiar with the procedures. Do you understand what I'm saying?
>
> *The Defendant:* I understand what you're saying, but I don't understand why you make them that way.
>
> *The Court:* Why do we make what that way?
>
> *The Defendant:* Court procedures that way. Ordinary citizen can't come in and defend himself. . . .

The Court: Okay. During the interim, the court has attempted to contact an attorney to represent the defendant in this case. I have contacted Richard McCoy in Sioux City. He practices in criminal court and he's . . . tried a lot of cases and I feel that he's a good attorney. He's indicated that he would be willing to take your case. . . . Does that meet with your approval?

The Defendant: Doesn't meet with my approval, Your Honor, but if you're going to force it on me, I'm going to have to take it. . . .

The Prosecutor: The appointment of Mr. McCoy is pursuant to [section] 815.10(2) then?

The Court: That's right. And I can appreciate that it says, "if a person desires legal assistance and is not indigent." As far as I'm concerned, although he indicates he wants to do it himself, I don't see that he's competent and qualified to do it himself. There should be somebody there. And on that basis, [the] court interprets that section to apply. . . .

Spencer captured the essence of *Faretta* when he insisted that we "shouldn't make the legal system that way where I can't defend myself. I'm the one that's familiar with the case. I'm the one that's arrested. I know what my best interest is." On this point, *Faretta* eloquently says:

> . . . To force a lawyer on a defendant can only lead him to believe that the law contrives against him. Moreover, it is not inconceivable that in some rare instances, the defendant might in fact present his case more effectively by conducting his own defense. Personal liberties are not rooted in the law of averages. The right to defend is personal. [Although the defendant] may conduct his own defense ultimately to his own detriment, his choice must be honored out of "that respect for the individual which is the lifeblood of the law."

The majority . . . attempts to finesse the trial court's denial of Spencer's request to defend himself by simply characterizing the court's actions as appointment of standby counsel. [However, the] role of standby counsel is limited to assisting a pro se defendant when such defendant wants assistance. A pro se defendant has the right to control the case the defendant chooses to present to the jury. That means a trial court must permit the pro se defendant to control the organization and content of the defense, to make motions, to argue points of law, to participate in voir dire, to question witnesses, and to address the court and jury at appropriate points in the trial. . . . If the trial court permits standby counsel to participate in the defense over the defendant's objections, such participation effectively allows counsel to make or substantially interfere with any significant tactical decisions, or to control questioning of witnesses, or to speak instead of the defendant on any matter of importance. Such interference is a denial of the pro se defendant's right to self-representation. . . .

These stringent limitations were recently spelled out in McKaskle v. Wiggins, 465 U.S. 168 (1984), the first case in which the Supreme Court has described the role of standby counsel. Because the role of standby counsel is severely restricted, trial courts contemplating appointment of standby counsel should — at a minimum — explain the limitations I have sketched out above from *McKaskle.* The reason is obvious: if the right to self-representation is to mean anything, a defendant who is appointed standby counsel should know how far the defendant can go in defending himself or herself without interference.

Here the trial court should have granted Spencer's request to defend himself. If the court was still concerned, the court should have then explicitly told Spencer he was appointing standby counsel and should have explained the limitations on standby counsel's role. Although above average in intelligence, Spencer is still a layperson untrained in the intricacies of criminal law. . . . After the colloquy between the court and himself, Spencer could only have had one thought: appointed counsel was being forced upon him and he was not going to be allowed to defend himself. . . .

At English common law the insistence upon a right of self-representation was the rule, rather than the exception. It is ironic that in the long history of British criminal jurisprudence there was only one tribunal that ever adopted the practice of forcing counsel upon an unwilling criminal defendant. That tribunal was the Star Chamber, a tribunal that for centuries symbolized the disregard of basic human rights. And the insistence upon a right to self-representation was, if anything, more fervent in the American colonies than at English common law. As *Faretta* points out, [the] "value of state-appointed counsel was not unappreciated by the Founders, yet the notion of compulsory counsel was utterly foreign to them. And whatever else may be said of those who wrote the Bill of Rights, surely there can be no doubt that they understood the inestimable worth of free choice." In sum, I would hold that the trial court denied Spencer the right to represent himself. I would therefore reverse and remand for a new trial.

Problem 11-4. Competence to Stand Trial, Competence to Waive Counsel

Ahmad Edwards tried to steal a pair of shoes from an Indiana department store. After he was discovered, he drew a gun, fired at a store security officer, and wounded a bystander. He was arrested and charged with attempted murder, battery with a deadly weapon, criminal recklessness, and theft. His mental condition became the subject of a series of competency proceedings and self-representation requests.

Several months after Edwards' arrest, his court-appointed counsel asked for a psychiatric evaluation of the defendant's competence to stand trial. During this hearing, Edwards' counsel presented psychiatric and neuropsychological evidence showing that Edwards was suffering from serious thinking difficulties and delusions. A testifying psychiatrist reported that Edwards could understand the charges against him, but he was "unable to cooperate with his attorney in his defense because of his schizophrenic illness"; his "delusions and his marked difficulties in thinking" made it "impossible for him to cooperate with his attorney." The court concluded that Edwards was not then competent to stand trial and ordered his recommitment to the state hospital.

About eight months after his commitment, the hospital reported that Edwards' condition had again improved to the point that he had again become competent to stand trial. Almost one year after that report, Edwards' trial began. Just before trial, Edwards asked to represent himself. He also asked for a continuance, which he said he needed to prepare for pro se representation. The judge refused the continuance; Edwards then proceeded to trial represented by counsel. The jury convicted him of criminal recklessness and theft but failed to reach a verdict on the charges of attempted murder and battery.

The State decided to retry Edwards on the attempted murder and battery charges. Just before the retrial in December 2005, Edwards again asked the court to permit him to represent himself. Referring to the lengthy record of psychiatric reports, the judge noted that Edwards still suffered from schizophrenia and concluded that "he's competent to stand trial but I'm not going to find he's competent to defend himself." The court denied Edwards' self-representation request. Edwards was represented by appointed counsel at his retrial. The jury convicted Edwards on both of the remaining counts.

Edwards appeals from this conviction, and argues that the trial court's refusal to permit him to represent himself at his retrial deprived him of his constitutional right of self-representation. Consider two legal standards relevant to Edwards' claim. First, according to Drope v. Missouri, 420 U. S. 162 (1975), the Constitution does not permit trial of an individual who lacks "mental competency." The trial judge must determine (1) whether the defendant has "a rational as well as factual understanding of the proceedings against him" and (2) whether the defendant "has sufficient present ability to consult with his lawyer with a reasonable degree of rational understanding." A person who lacks the capacity to understand the nature and object of the proceedings against him, to consult with counsel, and to assist in preparing his defense may not be subjected to a trial.

Second, in Godinez v. Moran, 509 U.S. 389 (1993), the Court declared that a defendant who was marginally competent to stand trial could also plead guilty after waiving his rights to counsel and trial. According to the Court, the decision to plead guilty "is no more complicated than the sum total of decisions that a [represented] defendant may be called upon to make during the course of a trial." As a result, "there is no reason to believe that the decision to waive counsel requires an appreciably higher level of mental functioning than the decision to waive other constitutional rights." The competence that is required of a defendant seeking to waive his right to counsel is the competence to waive the right, not the competence to represent himself: "the defendant's technical legal knowledge is not relevant to the determination." Thus, due process does not require a state to set the standard for competence to waive the right to trial or the right to counsel at a level higher than the standard for competence to stand trial.

Given these legal principles, how could you argue on behalf of the state that the trial court's denial of Edwards' motion to represent himself was correct? Cf. Indiana v. Evans, 554 U.S. 164 (2008).

Notes

1. *Knowing and voluntary waiver of counsel: majority position.* Once the right to counsel has attached, the defendant can waive that right, but only if the choice is "knowing and voluntary." Johnson v. Zerbst, 304 U.S. 458 (1938). In Faretta v. California, 422 U.S. 806 (1975), the Supreme Court declared that the right to "assistance" of counsel logically implied a defendant's right to represent herself at trial without counsel. How does this square with the Court's observation in *Gideon* that a lawyer is a "necessity, not a luxury"?

As *Spencer* indicates, there is no simple answer to the question of how a trial court will determine that the defendant's request is a knowing and voluntary waiver of the right to counsel. Typically, courts say that the defendant can waive counsel and invoke the *Faretta* right to self-representation only if (1) the trial court informs the defendant about the dangers of such a strategy, or (2) it otherwise appears from the record that the defendant understood the dangers. See People v. Adkins, 551 N.W.2d 108 (Mich. 1996) (waiver of counsel requires an unequivocal request by defendant, offer by trial court to appoint counsel, explanation of dangers of self-representation and the punishment for the crime charged, and a finding that self-representation will not disrupt trial). Courts often say that a waiver hearing expressly addressing the disadvantages of a pro se defense is much preferred but not absolutely necessary. The ultimate test, they say, is not the trial court's express advice but the defendant's understanding.

Defendants who represent themselves sometimes claim after conviction that the trial judge did not adequately warn them about the perils of acting as their own counsel. What warnings should judges give? State v. Cornell, 878 P.2d 1352 (Ariz. 1994) (no reversible error where court did not warn defendant that self-representation would undermine his planned insanity defense). Should courts, legislatures, or drafters of procedural rules design the standard *Faretta* warnings? See People v. Arguello, 772 P.2d 87 (Colo. 1989) (model inquiry); Michigan Court Rules 6.005(D) and (E) (court must advise the defendant of the charge, the maximum possible prison sentence for the offense, any mandatory minimum sentence required by law, and the risk involved in self-representation).

2. *Timeliness and manner of request*. Trial judges commonly explain their denial of a defendant's motion for self-representation on timeliness grounds. If the request arrives too close to the start of trial, a continuance might become necessary to allow the defendant to prepare for trial. People v. Lynch, 237 P.3d 416 (Cal. 2010) (timeliness of defendant's request to represent himself is not merely a matter of calendar days remaining before trial; trial judge may consider age of alleged victims, complexity of case, and any factor that makes it more or less feasible to delay trial). Under what circumstances do you imagine that trial judges would grant a self-representation motion filed after the start of the trial? Commonwealth v. El, 977 A2d 1158 (Pa. 2009) (request for self-representation was not timely when submitted after motion for bench trial and motion to bar admission of evidence).

Defendants sometimes take actions that amount to a request for self-representation, including physical attacks against the appointed attorney. State v. Holmes, 302 S.W.3d 831 (Tenn. 2010) (trial judge compelled defendant to stand trial with only standby counsel after he attacked his attorney by knocking his glasses askew; while defendant's actions were serious, they fell short of "extremely serious misconduct" that would justify sanction of total forfeiture of Sixth Amendment right to counsel; court suggested appointment of new counsel and warning to defendant regarding consequences of further misconduct).

3. *Reasons for waiver of counsel*. The old bromide says that "the man who represents himself has a fool for a client." Is the decision to waive an attorney indeed a foolish choice in most cases? See State v. Jones, 228 P.3d 394 (Kan. 2010) (pretrial denial of *Faretta* rights can never amount to harmless error because exercise of the right normally increases likelihood of outcome unfavorable to defendant). It is difficult to answer such a question at the system level. A study of federal pro se defendants determined that very few of them showed signs of mental illness, and

the outcomes in their cases compared favorably with the outcomes for defendants represented by counsel. See Erica Hashimoto, Defending the Right of Self Representation: An Empirical Look at the Felony Pro Se Defendant, 85 N.C. L. Rev. 423 (2007). Is it possible to conclude from this observation that defendants waive counsel in cases where the evidence is especially strong or especially weak? Or that defendants who waive have realistic concerns about the quality of the effort that busy defense lawyers can offer?

Another study, based on state court data, noted that defendants waive counsel far more often in misdemeanor cases (even those misdemeanors where the law requires the government to provide counsel upon request) than in felony cases. The study found no evidence to confirm the hypothesis that concerns about money — either an up-front "application fee" or later recoupment of a portion of the attorney's fees — influenced the waiver decision. Ronald F. Wright & Wayne A. Logan, The Political Economy of Application Fees for Indigent Criminal Defense, 47 Wm. & Mary L. Rev. 2045 (2006). How might an observer learn whether costs influence some defendants who waive counsel?

4. *Standby counsel.* Often a judge will respond to a request for self-representation by appointing "standby counsel." Even if the standby counsel gives the defendant unwelcome advice and direction, a conviction can be upheld. See McKaskle v. Wiggins, 465 U.S. 168 (1984) (appointment of standby counsel does not violate self-representation right unless counsel interferes with substantial tactical decisions of defendant); Partin v. Commonwealth, 168 S.W.3d 23 (Ky. 2005) (rights to self-representation and confrontation satisfied even though trial court prohibited defendant from personally cross-examining his wife during trial on domestic violence charges; cross-examination conducted by standby counsel). Is the obligation of the trial judge to warn the defendant about the dangers of self-representation lower when the defendant's lawyer accepts "standby counsel" status at the time defendant asks to represent herself? See State v. Layton, 432 S.E.2d 740 (W. Va. 1993) (allowing less extensive warning about self-representation when standby counsel played relatively active role at trial); Anne Bowen Poulin, The Role of Standby Counsel in Criminal Cases: In the Twilight Zone of the Criminal Justice System, 75 N.Y.U. L. Rev. 676 (2000).

The law in some states allows a defendant to partially waive the right to counsel; the defendant may rely on an appointed lawyer for some purposes, but also serve as co-counsel and examine some witnesses himself or herself. See Hill v. Commonwealth, 125 S.W.3d 221 (Ky. 2004) (judge must hold *Faretta* hearing before granting defendant's request to waive a portion of right to counsel and serve as co-counsel at trial).

5. *The constituency for* Faretta *rights.* In *Spencer,* what could the defendant have said to the trial judge to convince the appellate court that he had tried to exercise his right to represent himself? If trial judges can appoint counsel over requests like Spencer's, how vibrant is the right to self-representation? Which constituency, if any, keeps *Faretta* rights alive? If you were a prosecutor, would you argue on behalf of defendants who want to represent themselves?

If lawyers are essential to justice, shouldn't *Faretta* be reversed? In Martinez v. Court of Appeal of California, 528 U.S. 152 (2000), the Supreme Court refused to extend the *Faretta* right of self-representation to a direct appeal. The appellate courts may properly appoint counsel for the appellant, even if the appellant objects. Are trial judges better able than appellate judges to manage the difficulties presented by defendants who represent themselves? Are a defendant's interests in self-representation stronger at trial than during an appeal? See State v. Rafay, 222 P.3d 86 (Wash. 2009) (state constitution guarantees right to represent oneself on appeal; rejects *Martinez*).

6. *Competence to stand trial and to waive the right to counsel.* Some defendants are not competent to make a "knowing and voluntary waiver" of the right to counsel. In Godinez v. Moran, 509 U.S. 389 (1993), the Supreme Court held that the due process clause does not require a higher standard to assess whether a defendant is competent to waive counsel or plead guilty than is used to assess competency to stand trial. In Indiana v. Edwards, 554 U.S. 164 (2008), however, the Court ruled that a state can declare a defendant incompetent to conduct his or her own defense at trial, even if the state also concluded that the defendant was competent to stand trial. As the Court explained:

> Mental illness itself is not a unitary concept. It varies in degree. It can vary over time. It interferes with an individual's functioning at different times in different ways. . . . In certain instances an individual may well be able to satisfy [the trial] competence standard, for he will be able to work with counsel at trial, yet at the same time he may be unable to carry out the basic tasks needed to present his own defense without the help of counsel.

Is there a convincing way to reconcile *Edwards* and *Godinez*? For a more thorough treatment of competence hearings, see the web extension for this chapter at *http://www.crimpro.com/extension/ch11*

7. *Performance standards for pro se counsel.* In practice, trial courts appear to give some leeway to lay lawyers, but appellate cases consistently hold that the ordinary standards of practice and evidence are to be applied to defendants who appear pro se. See Commonwealth v. Jackson, 647 N.E.2d 401 (Mass. 1995). Should judges assist pro se litigants in questioning witnesses? Should judges give pro se litigants miniature "lessons" in trial procedure and the rules of evidence? See Sharon Finegan, Pro Se Criminal Trials and the Merging of Inquisitorial and Adversarial Systems of Justice, 58 Cath. U. L. Rev. 445 (2009) (procedures followed during pro se criminal trials have evolved to look less like classic adversarial trial and more like inquisitorial model of justice with more active role for judge).

8. *Selection of appointed counsel.* Defendants who retain their own lawyers may retain any lawyer they can afford who will agree to take the case (assuming the lawyer has no conflict of interest). This ability of the client to choose a particular lawyer helps to create a cooperative relationship. The lawyer is urged to "establish a relationship of trust and confidence with the accused." ABA Standards for Criminal Justice 4-3.1 (1980). An indigent defendant, however, may not choose his appointed counsel. In the homely phrase of the Nebraska trial judge in State v. Green, 471 N.W.2d 402 (Neb. 1991), "beggars can't be choosey." This is a fair, if blunt, assessment of the law in almost every jurisdiction. See Morris v. Slappy, 461 U.S. 1 (1983) (upholds trial court's refusal to grant continuance necessary to allow original counsel to represent defendant; trial proceeded with new appointed counsel). Does this rule suggest we are committed to providing counsel only in the most minimal sense to indigent defendants? If you were a supervisor in a public defender's office, would you institute a rule that allowed clients to take part in the choice of their lawyers?

Should a judge appointing defense counsel place any weight on a defendant's request to work with an attorney with specific qualities? Consider this possible conversation between a lawyer and client:

> "I want a Black lawyer to represent me." These are the first words you hear after you introduce yourself to your new client. . . . You are white. He is Black. You answer that you are an experienced criminal lawyer and will represent him to the best of your ability, regardless of his or your race. He responds that he too is experienced with the criminal justice system — a system that targets Black men, like himself, for prosecution far more than whites, that sentences Black men to prison more frequently and for a longer duration than whites, and that fails to acknowledge or address the role that race and racism play in the development, enforcement, and execution of the criminal laws established by "the system." . . . He explains that an African-American lawyer will be better able to understand and appreciate the circumstances that resulted in the bringing of these charges and that he, the client, can trust a Black lawyer more than a white one.

Kenneth P. Troccoli, "I Want a Black Lawyer to Represent Me": Addressing a Black Defendant's Concerns with Being Assigned a White Court-Appointed Lawyer, 20 Law and Inequality: A Journal of Theory and Practice 1 (Winter 2002). See also Marcus T. Boccaccini & Stanley L. Brodsky, Characteristics of the Ideal Criminal Defense Attorney from the Client's Perspective: Empirical Findings and Implications for Legal Practice, 25 Law & Psychol. Rev. 81, 116 (2001) (client survey lists the following, in descending order, as most desired attorney characteristics: advocates for client's interest, works hard, keeps client informed, cares about the client, honest, gets favorable outcome, "would not do whatever prosecution says," listens to client, spends time with client before court date).

9. *Law students as counsel.* Almost every state allows some law students to participate in the defense of criminal cases. Statutes and court rules typically allow law students to represent indigent criminal defendants, so long as the defendant is informed that the representative is a law student and consents to the representation, and a licensed attorney supervises the student's efforts. See Rules Regulating the Florida Bar 11-1.2(b); Miss. Code Ann. §73-3-207. What would you say to a defendant to convince her to allow a law student to "practice" on her case?

C. ADEQUACY OF COUNSEL

Constitutions and other laws not only govern the availability of a lawyer; they also address the quality of the legal representation that the attorney must give the client. So long as lawyers make mistakes, courts and other legal institutions must decide whether the client will be the one who pays. The next case lays down a legal standard now followed almost uniformly by courts trying to determine whether an attorney has provided a client with the "effective assistance of counsel" necessary for a constitutionally acceptable criminal conviction.

■ CHARLES STRICKLAND v. DAVID WASHINGTON

466 U.S. 668 (1984)

O'CONNOR, J.*

This case requires us to consider the proper standards for judging a criminal defendant's contention that the Constitution requires a conviction or death sentence to be set aside because counsel's assistance at the trial or sentencing was ineffective.

I.

A.

During a 10-day period in September 1976, respondent planned and committed three groups of crimes, which included three brutal stabbing murders, torture, kidnapping, severe assaults, attempted murders, attempted extortion, and theft. After his two accomplices were arrested, respondent surrendered to police and voluntarily gave a lengthy statement confessing to the third of the criminal episodes. The State of Florida indicted respondent for kidnapping and murder and appointed an experienced criminal lawyer to represent him.

Counsel actively pursued pretrial motions and discovery. He cut his efforts short, however, and he experienced a sense of hopelessness about the case, when he learned that, against his specific advice, respondent had also confessed to the first two murders. [Respondent also acted against counsel's advice in pleading guilty to all charges, and waiving the right to an advisory jury at his capital sentencing hearing.]

In preparing for the sentencing hearing, counsel spoke with respondent about his background. He also spoke on the telephone with respondent's wife and mother, though he did not follow up on the one unsuccessful effort to meet with them. He did not otherwise seek out character witnesses for respondent. Nor did he request a psychiatric examination, since his conversations with his client gave no indication that respondent had psychological problems. [To establish his claim of "emotional stress" as a "mitigating factor" against a death sentence, counsel decided to rely on the defendant's statements at the guilty plea colloquy about his emotional state, and not to introduce further evidence on the question. By foregoing the opportunity to present new evidence on these subjects, counsel prevented the State from cross-examining respondent on his claim and from putting on psychiatric evidence of its own.]

Counsel also excluded from the sentencing hearing other evidence he thought was potentially damaging. He successfully moved to exclude respondent's "rap sheet." Because he judged that a presentence report might prove more detrimental than helpful, as it would have included respondent's criminal history and thereby would have undermined the claim of no significant history of criminal activity, he did not request that one be prepared.

* [Chief Justice Burger and Justices White, Blackmun, Powell, Rehnquist, and Stevens joined in this opinion. — EDS.]

[Because the sentencing judge had a reputation as a person who thought important for a convicted defendant to own up to his crime, counsel argued at sen tencing that Washington's remorse and acceptance of responsibility justified spar ing him from the death penalty. Counsel also argued that respondent had no history of criminal activity and that respondent committed the crimes under extreme mental or emotional disturbance, thus coming within the statutory list of mitigating circumstances. The trial judge found numerous aggravating circumstances and no significant mitigating circumstances, and sentenced respondent to death on each of the three counts of murder.]

B.

Respondent subsequently sought collateral relief in state court on numerous grounds, among them that counsel had rendered ineffective assistance at the sentencing proceeding. Respondent challenged counsel's assistance in six respects. He asserted that counsel was ineffective because he failed to move for a continuance to prepare for sentencing, to request a psychiatric report, to investigate and present character witnesses, to seek a presentence investigation report, to present meaningful arguments to the sentencing judge, and to investigate the medical examiner's reports [about the condition of the victims' bodies] or cross-examine the medical experts. [The state trial court, the state appellate courts, and the federal district court all refused to find ineffective assistance of counsel, and therefore refused to grant postconviction relief. The federal appeals court announced a new legal standard for claims of ineffective assistance of counsel and remanded the case for further fact-finding under the new standards. This appeal followed.]

II.

In a long line of cases that includes Powell v. Alabama, 287 U.S. 45 (1932) . . . and Gideon v. Wainwright, 372 U.S. 335 (1963), this Court has recognized that the Sixth Amendment right to counsel exists, and is needed, in order to protect the fundamental right to a fair trial [in the adversary system. It has also] recognized that the right to counsel is the right to the effective assistance of counsel. . . .

The Court has not elaborated on the meaning of the constitutional requirement of effective assistance in [cases] presenting claims of "actual ineffectiveness." In giving meaning to the requirement, however, we must take its purpose — to ensure a fair trial — as the guide. The benchmark for judging any claim of ineffectiveness must be whether counsel's conduct so undermined the proper functioning of the adversarial process that the trial cannot be relied on as having produced a just result. . . .

III.

A convicted defendant's claim that counsel's assistance was so defective as to require reversal of a conviction or death sentence has two components. First, the defendant must show that counsel's performance was deficient. This requires showing that counsel made errors so serious that counsel was not functioning as the "counsel" guaranteed the defendant by the Sixth Amendment. Second, the defendant must show that the deficient performance prejudiced the defense. This requires showing that counsel's errors were so serious as to deprive the defendant of a fair trial, a trial whose result is reliable. Unless a defendant makes both showings, it cannot be said that the conviction or death sentence resulted from a breakdown in the adversary process that renders the result unreliable. . . .

A.

. . . When a convicted defendant complains of the ineffectiveness of counsel's assistance, the defendant must show that counsel's representation fell below an objective standard of reasonableness. More specific guidelines are not appropriate. The Sixth Amendment refers simply to "counsel," not specifying particular requirements of effective assistance. It relies instead on the legal profession's maintenance of standards sufficient to justify the law's presumption that counsel will fulfill the role in the adversary process that the Amendment envisions. The proper measure of attorney performance remains simply reasonableness under prevailing professional norms.

Representation of a criminal defendant entails certain basic duties. Counsel's function is to assist the defendant, and hence counsel owes the client a duty of loyalty, a duty to avoid conflicts of interest. Cuyler v. Sullivan, 446 U.S. 335 (1980). From counsel's function as assistant to the defendant derive the overarching duty to advocate the defendant's cause and the more particular duties to consult with the defendant on important decisions and to keep the defendant informed of important developments in the course of the prosecution. Counsel also has a duty to bring to bear such skill and knowledge as will render the trial a reliable adversarial testing process.

These basic duties neither exhaustively define the obligations of counsel nor form a checklist for judicial evaluation of attorney performance. In any case presenting an ineffectiveness claim, the performance inquiry must be whether counsel's assistance was reasonable considering all the circumstances. Prevailing norms of practice as reflected in American Bar Association standards and the like, e.g., ABA Standards for Criminal Justice 4-1.1 to 4-8.6 (2d ed. 1980), are guides to determining what is reasonable, but they are only guides. No particular set of detailed rules for counsel's conduct can satisfactorily take account of the variety of circumstances faced by defense counsel or the range of legitimate decisions regarding how best to represent a criminal defendant. Any such set of rules would interfere with the constitutionally protected independence of counsel and restrict the wide latitude counsel must have in making tactical decisions. Indeed, the existence of detailed guidelines for representation could distract counsel from the overriding mission of vigorous advocacy of the defendant's cause. Moreover, the purpose of the effective assistance guarantee of the Sixth Amendment is not to improve the quality of legal representation, although that is a goal of considerable importance to the legal system. The purpose is simply to ensure that criminal defendants receive a fair trial.

Judicial scrutiny of counsel's performance must be highly deferential. It is all too tempting for a defendant to second-guess counsel's assistance after conviction or adverse sentence, and it is all too easy for a court, examining counsel's defense after it has proved unsuccessful, to conclude that a particular act or omission of counsel was unreasonable. A fair assessment of attorney performance requires that every effort be made to eliminate the distorting effects of hindsight, to reconstruct the circumstances of counsel's challenged conduct, and to evaluate the conduct from counsel's perspective at the time. Because of the difficulties inherent in making the evaluation, a court must indulge a strong presumption that counsel's conduct falls within the wide range of reasonable professional assistance; that is, the defendant must overcome the presumption that, under the circumstances, the challenged action might be considered sound trial strategy. There are countless ways to provide effective assistance in any given case. Even the best criminal defense attorneys would not defend a particular client in the same way.

The availability of intrusive post-trial inquiry into attorney performance or of detailed guidelines for its evaluation would encourage the proliferation of ineffectiveness challenges. Criminal trials resolved unfavorably to the defendant would increasingly come to be followed by a second trial, this one of counsel's unsuccessful defense. Counsel's performance and even willingness to serve could be adversely affected. . . .

B.

An error by counsel, even if professionally unreasonable, does not warrant setting aside the judgment of a criminal proceeding if the error had no effect on the judgment. The purpose of the Sixth Amendment guarantee of counsel is to ensure that a defendant has the assistance necessary to justify reliance on the outcome of the proceeding. Accordingly, any deficiencies in counsel's performance must be prejudicial to the defense in order to constitute ineffective assistance under the Constitution.

In certain Sixth Amendment contexts, prejudice is presumed. Actual or constructive denial of the assistance of counsel altogether is legally presumed to result in prejudice. So are various kinds of state interference with counsel's assistance. Prejudice in these circumstances is so likely that case-by-case inquiry into prejudice is not worth the cost. Moreover, such circumstances involve impairments of the Sixth Amendment right that are easy to identify and, for that reason and because the prosecution is directly responsible, easy for the government to prevent.

One type of actual ineffectiveness claim warrants a similar, though more limited, presumption of prejudice. In Cuyler v. Sullivan, 446 U.S. 335 (1980), the Court held that prejudice is presumed when counsel is burdened by an actual conflict of interest. In those circumstances, counsel breaches the duty of loyalty, perhaps the most basic of counsel's duties. Moreover, it is difficult to measure the precise effect on the defense of representation corrupted by conflicting interests. Given the obligation of counsel to avoid conflicts of interest and the ability of trial courts to make early inquiry in certain situations likely to give rise to conflicts, it is reasonable for the criminal justice system to maintain a fairly rigid rule of presumed prejudice for conflicts of interest. . . .

Conflict of interest claims aside, actual ineffectiveness claims alleging a deficiency in attorney performance are subject to a general requirement that the defendant affirmatively prove prejudice. . . . It is not enough for the defendant to show that the errors had some conceivable effect on the outcome of the proceeding. Virtually every act or omission of counsel would meet that test, and not every error that conceivably could have influenced the outcome undermines the reliability of the result of the proceeding. . . .

On the other hand, we believe that a defendant need not show that counsel's deficient conduct more likely than not altered the outcome in the case. [The "more likely than not altered the outcome" test, which is used to decide whether to grant a new trial based on new evidence,] is not an apt source from which to draw a prejudice standard for ineffectiveness claims. The high standard for newly discovered evidence claims presupposes that all the essential elements of a presumptively accurate and fair proceeding were present in the proceeding whose result is challenged. An ineffective assistance claim asserts the absence of one of the crucial assurances that the result of the proceeding is reliable, so finality concerns are somewhat weaker and the appropriate standard of prejudice should be somewhat lower. The result of a proceeding can be rendered unreliable, and hence the proceeding itself unfair, even if the errors of counsel cannot be shown by a preponderance of the evidence to have determined the outcome.

Accordingly, the appropriate test for prejudice finds its roots in the test for materiality of exculpatory information not disclosed to the defense by the prosecution, and in the test for materiality of testimony made unavailable to the defense by Government deportation of a witness. The defendant must show that there is a reasonable probability that, but for counsel's unprofessional errors, the result of the proceeding would have been different. A reasonable probability is a probability sufficient to undermine confidence in the outcome. . . .

IV.

Although we have discussed the performance component of an ineffectiveness claim prior to the prejudice component, there is no reason for a court deciding an ineffective assistance claim to approach the inquiry in the same order or even to address both components of the inquiry if the defendant makes an insufficient showing on one. In particular, a court need not determine whether counsel's performance was deficient before examining the prejudice suffered by the defendant as a result of the alleged deficiencies. The object of an ineffectiveness claim is not to grade counsel's performance. If it is easier to dispose of an ineffectiveness claim on the ground of lack of sufficient prejudice, which we expect will often be so, that course should be followed. . . .

V.

Having articulated general standards for judging ineffectiveness claims, we think it useful to apply those standards to the facts of this case in order to illustrate the meaning of the general principles. . . . With respect to the performance component, the record shows that respondent's counsel made a strategic choice to argue for the extreme emotional distress mitigating circumstance and to rely as fully as possible on respondent's acceptance of responsibility for his crimes. . . . The trial judge's views on the importance of owning up to one's crimes were well known to counsel. The aggravating circumstances were utterly overwhelming. Trial counsel could reasonably surmise from his conversations with respondent that character and psychological evidence would be of little help. Respondent had already been able to mention at the plea colloquy the substance of what there was to know about his financial and emotional troubles. Restricting testimony on respondent's character to what had come in at the plea colloquy ensured that contrary character and psychological evidence and respondent's criminal history, which counsel had successfully moved to exclude, would not come in. On these facts, there can be little question, even without application of the presumption of adequate performance, that trial counsel's defense, though unsuccessful, was the result of reasonable professional judgment.

With respect to the prejudice component, the lack of merit of respondent's claim is even more stark. The evidence that respondent says his trial counsel should have offered at the sentencing hearing would barely have altered the sentencing profile presented to the sentencing judge. [At] most this evidence shows that numerous people who knew respondent thought he was generally a good person and that a psychiatrist and a psychologist believed he was under considerable emotional stress that did not rise to the level of extreme disturbance. Given the overwhelming aggravating factors, there is no reasonable probability that the omitted evidence would have changed the conclusion that the aggravating circumstances outweighed the mitigating circumstances and, hence, the sentence imposed. Indeed, admission of the evidence respondent now offers might even have been harmful to his case: his "rap sheet" would probably have been admitted into evidence, and the psychological reports would have directly contradicted respondent's claim that the mitigating circumstance of extreme emotional disturbance applied to his case.

[Respondent] has made no showing that the justice of his sentence was rendered unreliable by a breakdown in the adversary process caused by deficiencies in counsel's assistance. . . .

MARSHALL, J., dissenting.

[State] and lower federal courts have developed standards for distinguishing effective from inadequate assistance. Today, for the first time, this Court attempts to synthesize and clarify those standards. For the most part, the majority's efforts are unhelpful. . . .

I.

A.

My objection to the performance standard adopted by the Court is that it is so malleable that, in practice, it will either have no grip at all or will yield excessive variation in the manner in which the Sixth Amendment is interpreted and applied by different courts. To tell lawyers and the lower courts that counsel for a criminal defendant must behave "reasonably" . . . is to tell them almost nothing. In essence, the majority has instructed judges called upon to assess claims of ineffective assistance of counsel to advert to their own intuitions regarding what constitutes "professional" representation, and has discouraged them from trying to develop more detailed standards governing the performance of defense counsel. In my view, the Court has thereby not only abdicated its own responsibility to interpret the Constitution, but also impaired the ability of the lower courts to exercise theirs.

The debilitating ambiguity of an "objective standard of reasonableness" in this context is illustrated by the majority's failure to address important issues concerning the quality of representation mandated by the Constitution. . . . Is a "reasonably competent attorney" a reasonably competent adequately paid retained lawyer or a reasonably competent appointed attorney? It is also a fact that the quality of representation available to ordinary defendants in different parts of the country varies significantly. Should the standard of performance mandated by the Sixth Amendment vary by locale? The majority offers no clues as to the proper responses to these questions. . . .

I agree that counsel must be afforded wide latitude when making tactical decisions regarding trial strategy, but many aspects of the job of a criminal defense attorney are more amenable to judicial oversight. For example, much of the work involved in preparing for a trial, applying for bail, conferring with one's client, making timely objections to significant, arguably erroneous rulings of the trial judge, and filing a notice of appeal if there are colorable grounds therefor could profitably be made the subject of uniform standards.

B.

I object to the prejudice standard adopted by the Court for two independent reasons. First, it is often very difficult to tell whether a defendant convicted after a trial in which he was ineffectively represented would have fared better if his lawyer had been competent. Seemingly impregnable cases can sometimes be dismantled by good defense counsel. On the basis of a cold record, it may be impossible for a reviewing court confidently to ascertain how the government's evidence and arguments would have stood up against rebuttal and cross-examination by a shrewd, well-prepared lawyer. The difficulties of estimating prejudice after the fact are exacerbated by the possibility that evidence of injury to the defendant may be missing from the record precisely because of the incompetence of defense counsel. . . .

Second and more fundamentally, the assumption on which the Court's holding rests is that the only purpose of the constitutional guarantee of effective assistance of counsel is to reduce the chance that innocent persons will be convicted. In my view, the guarantee also functions to ensure that convictions are obtained only through fundamentally fair procedures. The majority contends that the Sixth Amendment is not violated when a manifestly guilty defendant is convicted after a trial in which he was represented by a manifestly ineffective attorney. I cannot agree. Every defendant is entitled to a trial in which his interests are vigorously and conscientiously advocated by an able lawyer. [I would hold] that a showing that the performance of a defendant's lawyer departed from constitutionally prescribed standards requires a new trial regardless of whether the defendant suffered demonstrable prejudice thereby. . . .

IV.

[I must also] dissent from the majority's disposition of the case before us. It is undisputed that respondent's trial counsel made virtually no investigation of the possibility of obtaining testimony from respondent's relatives, friends, or former employers pertaining to respondent's character or background. Had counsel done so, he would have found several persons willing and able to testify that, in their experience, respondent was a responsible, nonviolent man, devoted to his family, and active in the affairs of his church. . . . Had this evidence been admitted, respondent argues, his chances of obtaining a life sentence would have been significantly better. . . .

The State makes a colorable — though in my view not compelling — argument that defense counsel in this case might have made a reasonable "strategic" decision not to present such evidence at the sentencing hearing on the assumption that an unadorned acknowledgment of respondent's responsibility for his crimes would be more likely to appeal to the trial judge, who was reputed to respect persons who accepted responsibility for their actions. But however justifiable such a choice might have been after counsel had fairly assessed the potential strength of the mitigating evidence available to him, counsel's failure to make any significant effort to find out what evidence might be garnered from respondent's relatives and acquaintances surely cannot be described as "reasonable." . . . If counsel had investigated [and presented the available mitigating evidence], there is a significant chance that respondent would have been given a life sentence. . . .

MICHAEL BRUNO v. STATE

807 So. 2d 55 (Fla. 2001)

PER CURIAM

Michael J. Bruno, under sentence of death, appeals the denial of relief following an evidentiary hearing on his first motion filed pursuant to Florida Rule of Criminal Procedure 3.850, [the statute providing for collateral review of convictions]. For the reasons expressed below, we affirm the denial of relief. . . .

On August 8, 1986, appellant Michael Bruno and his fifteen-year-old son, Michael Jr., were in the apartment of a friend, Lionel Merlano, when Bruno beat Merlano with a crowbar. Bruno then sent Michael Jr. elsewhere in the apartment to fetch a handgun and, when the boy returned with a gun, Bruno shot Merlano twice in the head. Bruno was arrested several days later and gave a taped statement wherein he at first denied any knowledge of the murder but then later admitted committing the crime, claiming it was self-defense. Michael Jr. also gave a full statement to police. Prior to being arrested, Bruno made numerous inculpatory statements to friends concerning both his plan to commit the murder and the commission of the crime itself. Police found the gun in a canal where a friend, Jody Spalding, saw Bruno throw it.

Bruno was charged with first-degree murder and robbery (he stole a stereo from the apartment after the murder) and his strategy at trial was to raise a reasonable doubt in jurors' minds by claiming that Jody Spalding was the killer. He was convicted as charged, and the judge followed the jury's eight-to-four vote and imposed a sentence of death based on three aggravating circumstances and no mitigating circumstances. This Court affirmed. Bruno filed the present rule 3.850 motion and the trial court conducted an evidentiary hearing at which Bruno presented six witnesses and the State presented one witness. The trial court denied the motion. Bruno appeals. . . .

Bruno argues that the trial court erred in denying his postconviction claims concerning alleged ineffective assistance of counsel. The test to be applied by the trial court when evaluating an ineffectiveness claim is two-pronged: The defendant must show both that trial counsel's performance was deficient and that the defendant was prejudiced by the deficiency. The standard of review for a trial court's ruling on an ineffectiveness claim also is two-pronged: The appellate court must defer to the trial court's findings on factual issues but must review the court's ultimate conclusions on the deficiency and prejudice prongs de novo.

In his brief before this Court, Bruno asserts several instances of ineffectiveness. . . . In subclaim two, Bruno contends that defense counsel was ineffective during the trial due to alcohol and drug impairments. Bruno points to the previous hospitalization of trial counsel for drug and alcohol use. Private counsel was retained in August 1986 to represent Bruno. Over the next few months, counsel developed a drinking problem and, when he was drinking, would occasionally use cocaine. He enrolled in Alcoholics Anonymous on October 15, 1986, and remained alcohol and drug free from then until March 1987, when he began drinking again but not using cocaine. He admitted himself into a hospital on March 15, 1987, for his drinking problem, remained hospitalized for twenty-eight days, and subsequently remained alcohol- and drug-free. After being released, counsel apprised both Bruno and the court of his problem and offered to withdraw, but Bruno asked him to continue as counsel. The trial, which originally had been set for March 30, 1987, was rescheduled for August 5, 1987, and began on that date. Counsel testified at the evidentiary hearing below that he never was under the influence of alcohol or drugs while working on this case. The trial court concluded that Bruno "failed to meet his burden of demonstrating how [counsel's] drug and alcohol usage prior to trial rendered ineffective his legal representation to the Defendant and how such conduct prejudiced the Defendant." We agree.

In subclaim three, . . . Bruno argues that defense counsel repeatedly divulged confidential and damaging information to the trial court. [One] example of the alleged conflict of interest relates to comments made by defense counsel during the penalty phase. The comments were made in response to Dr. Stillman's testimony that Bruno was insane at the time of the offense. Shortly after Dr. Stillman's testimony, defense counsel requested a side-bar conference and told the trial court that he was surprised by the testimony, as Dr. Stillman had previously informed defense counsel that Bruno was sane at the time of the offense. At the evidentiary hearing below, defense counsel explained that he conveyed his surprise to the court in order to justify his subsequent motion for an additional psychological examination. [The trial court found that the defense attorney's] "statements to the Trial Judge were made as a justification for his seeking leave of court to file a belated notice of intent to rely on an insanity defense. . . . The Defendant has failed to show that he was prejudiced by [defense counsel]'s statements to the trial judge." . . .

In subclaim four, Bruno argues that counsel was ineffective because he failed to present a defense of voluntary intoxication. At the evidentiary hearing below, defense counsel testified that Bruno adamantly refused the presentation of a voluntary intoxication defense. In rejecting this claim, the trial court stated that the "decision not to present the affirmative defense of 'voluntary intoxication' was based on a strategy decision which was motivated by the Defendant's conscious decision, rather than a result of [counsel's] legal incompetency." We agree with the trial court that Bruno has failed to satisfy the first prong of the *Strickland* test.

In subclaim five, Bruno asserts that counsel negligently failed to move to suppress Bruno's initial statement to the police. . . . Bruno was first interrogated by the police on August 12, 1986. Bruno alleges that he was not given *Miranda* warnings at this time. During the interrogation, Bruno told the police that he knew the victim and had previously consumed a few beers with the victim at the victim's apartment, which was located in the Candlewood apartment complex. Bruno told the police that, the weekend the crime was committed, he was working on Jody Spalding's car, with the exception of going to the Candlewood apartment complex to obtain a receipt for a refrigerator. . . . Bruno claims that this statement provided the police with additional evidence, as it contradicted the later statement in which Bruno claimed that he killed the victim in self-defense, it contradicted other testimony about his whereabouts in the days following the killing, and shows guilty knowledge. . . . The trial court concluded that Bruno failed to meet the second prong of the *Strickland* test. We agree. . . .

In subclaim ten, Bruno argues that counsel was ineffective in failing to investigate and present available mitigation. The trial court rejected this claim as follows:

> The testimony and exhibits presented at the evidentiary hearing reflect that the Defendant's mis-information to, and his failure to fully cooperate with [counsel] in the preparation of his defense, prevented [counsel] from initially obtaining information relating to the Defendant's previous hospitalization at Pilgrim State Hospital. . . . Dr. Stillman's trial testimony . . . acquainted the jury with the Defendant's extensive emotional and drug history, and drug use at the time of the murder. The Defendant's parents testified that Mr. Bruno had tried to commit suicide, and was briefly hospitalized until his sister had him released. The fact that there could have been a more detailed presentation of these circumstances does not establish that defense counsel's performance was deficient. Defense counsel cannot be faulted for failing to investigate background information, which he had no reason to suspect existed.

We agree. The trial court noted that Bruno's failure to cooperate with counsel prevented counsel from initially obtaining relevant information pertaining to the penalty phase. Despite this obstacle, counsel still presented evidence concerning several potential mitigating circumstances: Bruno's extensive emotional and drug history, Bruno's drug use at the time of the murder, Dr. Stillman's testimony that Bruno had organic brain damage as a result of his drug use, and testimony that Bruno had attempted suicide and was briefly hospitalized. . . . Counsel's performance in this case may not have been perfect, but it did not fall below the required standard. [Even] assuming that counsel's performance was deficient, we agree with the trial court that Bruno has failed to satisfy the second prong of the *Strickland* test. . . .

Bruno claims that counsel was ineffective in failing to provide Dr. Stillman with sufficient background information. Bruno argues that counsel's neglect prevented Dr. Stillman from sufficiently assessing Bruno's competence to stand trial and potential mitigating circumstances.

Prior to trial, Dr. Stillman was appointed to evaluate whether Bruno was insane at the time of the offense or incompetent to stand trial. The record reveals that Dr. Stillman informed defense counsel on two separate occasions that he did not believe that Bruno was either insane at the time of the offense or incompetent to stand trial. Subsequently, Dr. Stillman was called as a defense witness during the penalty phase. In preparing for this testimony, Dr. Stillman interviewed, for the first time, members of Bruno's family and a jail nurse who had contact with Bruno. These meetings occurred within two days of Dr. Stillman's testimony. During the State's cross-examination, Dr. Stillman opined that he believed that Bruno was insane at the time of the offense. Dr. Stillman testified that despite his previous determinations that Bruno was not insane, he still had a suspicion, and that this suspicion was confirmed upon meeting with members of Bruno's family and the nurse. . . . The trial court below rejected this claim as follows:

> Since Dr. Stillman is dead, there is no way for the court to ascertain what factors he considered, or did not consider, in the way of background material on the Defendant. . . . Dr. Stillman interviewed the defendant twice for a total of two and a half hours. He . . . spoke with the defendant's sister and parents, [and] was aware of the Defendant's

> extensive drug usage, and his stay at Pilgrim State hospital. . . . The fact that the defendant and his family withheld information from [counsel] does not render [counsel's] performance deficient.

We agree. As far as Dr. Stillman's penalty phase testimony, it is clear from the record that Dr. Stillman had been provided with all necessary information at the time of his testimony. In regards to whether Bruno was competent to stand trial or insane at the time of the offense, we find no negligence on the part of defense counsel. Defense counsel asked Dr. Stillman to evaluate Bruno prior to trial. Dr. Stillman rendered an opinion, on two separate occasions, that Bruno was neither incompetent to stand trial nor insane at the time of the offense. Bruno has not established that Dr. Stillman told defense counsel that he needed more information in order to form this opinion. [We] find no merit to this claim. . . .

Based on the foregoing, we affirm the trial court's denial of Bruno's motion for postconviction relief. . . .

ANSTEAD, J., concurring in part and dissenting in part.

. . . While I agree with the majority's analysis and rejection of claims of error as to eight of [the ineffective assistance] claims, it appears that two of Bruno's claims present valid instances of ineffectiveness. They include: (1) the improper and prejudicial disclosure of confidential information by counsel; and (2) counsel's critical failure to investigate and present mitigating evidence on behalf of the defendant to the sentencing jury and judge.

Bruno argues that his trial counsel substantially prejudiced the outcome of his penalty phase proceedings when trial counsel divulged confidential and damaging information to the trial court by informing the court during the penalty phase that he was completely surprised by Dr. Stillman's testimony that Bruno was "insane" at the time of the offense. After Stillman made the surprise disclosure that he believed Bruno was insane at the time of the crime, defense counsel approached both the court and the prosecutor and told them that Stillman had personally assured him many times just the opposite — that Bruno was "totally competent." Critically, the prosecutor later used this assurance during closing argument to completely impeach Stillman's testimony, and the sentencing court subsequently rejected Stillman's penalty phase testimony *in toto*. Bruno claims that his lawyer was ineffective because counsel's disclosures completely discredited Bruno's most important mitigation witness and his only expert witness, thereby conceding away virtually his entire case for mitigation. . . .

During direct examination, Stillman actually testified to the existence of some mitigation. According to Stillman, Bruno suffered from a passive-aggressive personality, and he also exhibited signs of a schizophrenic-type disorder when he was under the influence of drugs. . . . Stillman testified that Bruno started using L.S.D. and marijuana when he was married and that his drug abuse progressively worsened over the years. When his wife left him, he tried to kill himself by taking Quaaludes and by attempting to drown himself in the ocean. Further, Stillman testified that Bruno had been using an ounce of cocaine every day for weeks prior to the offense.

However, during cross-examination, Stillman proclaimed for the first time that he believed Bruno was insane at the time of the murder. He claimed that at the prior times he had evaluated the defendant, he suspected that Bruno may have been insane at the time of the offense but the lack of corroborating evidence prevented him from reaching such a conclusion. Stillman testified that he received the corroborating evidence just a few days before trial, when he discussed Bruno with his parents and sister . . . and a nurse who worked with Bruno at the jail. . . .

In an apparent panic, trial counsel reacted to Stillman's revelation by immediately disclosing to the court two confidential letters to trial counsel in which Stillman had opined that Bruno was competent to stand trial and was not insane. Trial counsel told the court that he thought he was duty bound to bring this patent inconsistency in Stillman's evaluations to the trial court's attention.

At the evidentiary hearing in the 3.850 proceeding, trial counsel sought to justify his breach of confidence by claiming that he acted in order to justify his subsequent motion for an additional psychological examination. However, the record directly refutes this assertion. In the actual motion for psychiatric evaluation, which was filed after the jury's recommendation for death but prior to the trial court's sentencing, trial counsel made absolutely no reference to the fact that Stillman had changed his opinion concerning Bruno's sanity. Rather, the motion . . . alleges that trial counsel and Stillman were unaware of Bruno's psychological history until trial counsel talked with Bruno's sister and learned about Bruno's history of drug use, attempted suicide, and hospitalization for mental problems.

Thus, trial counsel's stated tactical reason for disclosing this obviously damaging and confidential information to the court is not supported by the record. Rather, trial counsel's reason for disclosing this confidential information appears to have been prompted more by counsel's interest in maintaining his own credibility with the court and demonstrating that he had not been negligent in failing to present an insanity defense during the guilt phase, than by an interest in securing a future psychiatric examination for his client. . . .

The only other witnesses trial counsel presented were Bruno's parents, who provided marginal evidence of mitigation. At the close of all the evidence, the jury recommended death by a vote of eight to four and the court imposed death, *finding no mitigating circumstances.* Because the trial court in this case ultimately rejected Stillman's testimony and found no mitigating evidence, counsel's error in revealing damaging, confidential information to the trial court against his most important witness clearly affected the jury's and the trial court's evaluation of the evidence and the outcome of the case.

Bruno further claims that counsel was manifestly ineffective in his more or less complete failure to investigate and present evidence of the abundant mitigating evidence that actually existed of Bruno's troubled history of mental problems and drug abuse. [The] trial court allowed no break between the finding of guilt by the jury and the penalty phase of the trial; indeed, the penalty phase began the very next morning. Trial counsel acceded to this procedure.

[The defense attorney did call] Bruno's parents to testify. Bruno's mother described Bruno as he was as a young man, claiming that he was "good boy." However, she testified that after he left home and got married, he changed drastically. He started wearing his hair long (in a mohawk), tattooed his body, and started hanging around with a motorcycle group and bands. She testified that after his marriage ended he went "berserk," lost the desire to live and attempted to commit suicide by drowning himself and overdosing on drugs. . . .

Critically, however, at the end of her testimony, when trial counsel asked her whether she had anything to say to the jury about the possible punishment her son should receive, Bruno's mother declared: "All I can say is that I don't have much time, neither does my husband. But if that's your wish [i.e., the imposition of the punishment of death] and you think you are doing right, God bless you. But other than that I don't know what to say. I just feel sorry for my husband, but if a child does something wrong, he should be punished. That is my belief." [Unlike] Bruno's mother, Bruno's father testified that he did not believe that Bruno deserved the death penalty. . . .

On direct examination during the penalty phase, counsel did not elicit a single affirmative opinion from Stillman concerning the applicability of mitigators to this crime. Counsel was apparently unaware of his obligation to do so. Importantly, the record reflects that Dr. Stillman was appointed by the court *only* to assess Bruno's sanity and competency for guilt phase purposes, and not to evaluate Bruno and his background to determine the existence of mitigation for penalty phase purposes. . . . Counsel never sought a mental health evaluation of his client for mitigation purposes, an evaluation that is fundamental in defending against the death penalty.

Further, the record reflects that although trial counsel presented Bruno's parents and Dr. Stillman as witnesses at the penalty phase, counsel did nothing to prepare these witnesses for testifying and, most tellingly, was unaware of the content of their testimony beforehand, especially regarding the opinion of Bruno's mother that he must accept his punishment. . . . At the time of the penalty phase, counsel did not even know who comprised the members of Bruno's immediate family — he did not know of the existence of Bruno's younger sister, who held key mental health information concerning him. . . .

The postconviction record reveals that copious mitigation actually existed in this case. . . . Bruno has a life-long and extensive record of drug abuse beginning with sniffing glue and lacquer thinner at ages eleven to thirteen. At the postconviction evidentiary hearing, Bruno called . . . Dr. Dee, a neuropsychologist. . . . Dr. Dee testified that Bruno suffers from organic brain syndrome as a result of his continuous, heavy, chronic drug use, which included cocaine, LSD, and marijuana. The most significant injury to his brain is manifested by impaired memory, increased impulsivity, difficulty in impulse control, deteriorated work performance, and inability to hold a job. According to Dr. Dee, at the time of the murder, Bruno was under the influence of extreme mental or emotional disturbance due to cerebral damage and drug usage.

Dr. Dee testified that according to Bruno's son Michael, on the day of the murder, Bruno free-based cocaine mid-day and used it continuously throughout the day until he and his son left for the victim's apartment. Bruno had also taken three purple micro-dots of LSD and eight or nine Quaaludes. Dr. Dee also testified that Bruno's ability to appreciate the criminality of his conduct or conform his conduct to the requirements of the law was substantially impaired, also due to his cerebral impairment and intoxication. As for nonstatutory mitigation, Dr. Dee testified that Bruno and his siblings were physically beaten and abused by their mother as young children. This finding, based on accounts from Bruno's family members, differ significantly from Bruno's mother's testimony during the penalty phase proceedings that Bruno grew up in a happy home. . . .

Bruno has clearly demonstrated deficient performance by his counsel which prejudiced the outcome of the penalty phase of the proceedings. [The] jury recommended death by a vote of eight to four, four votes for life even without the substantial mitigation we now know existed all the time. In the words of the United States Supreme Court in *Strickland,* it is apparent that confidence in the outcome of Bruno's penalty phase proceeding has been substantially undermined by counsel's neglect and lack of preparation.

Problem 11-5. *Cronic* Errors

Joe Elton Nixon was convicted of first-degree murder, kidnapping, robbery, and arson; the court sentenced him to death. Nixon's trial counsel made the following remarks during his opening statement in the guilt phase:

> In this case, there will be no question that Jeannie [sic] Bickner died a horrible, horrible death. In fact, that horrible tragedy will be proved to your satisfaction beyond any reasonable doubt. In this case, there won't be any question, none whatsoever, that my client, Joe Elton Nixon, caused Jeannie [sic] Bickner's death. This case is about the death of Joe Elton Nixon and whether it should occur within the next few years by electrocution or maybe its natural expiration after a lifetime of confinement.

During his closing argument, Nixon's counsel said:

> Ladies and gentlemen of the jury, I wish I could stand before you and argue that what happened wasn't caused by Mr. Nixon, but we all know better. I know what you will decide will be unanimous. You will decide that the State of Florida, through Mr. Hankinson and Mr. Guarisco, has proved beyond a reasonable doubt each and every element of the crimes charged, first-degree premeditated murder, kidnapping, robbery, and arson.

Nixon filed a motion for collateral review, claiming that his trial counsel was ineffective during the guilt phase of the trial. Nixon argues that these comments were the equivalent of a guilty plea by his attorney. He claims that he did not give his attorney consent to enter a guilty plea or to admit guilt as part of a trial strategy.

Nixon argues that his counsel's conduct in this case amounted to per se ineffective assistance of counsel and that the proper test for assessing counsel arises under United States v. Cronic, 466 U.S. 648 (1984), rather than Strickland v. Washington. In *Cronic,* decided the same day as *Strickland,* the Supreme Court created an exception to the *Strickland* standard for ineffective assistance of counsel and acknowledged that certain circumstances are so egregiously prejudicial that ineffective assistance of counsel will be presumed. In *Cronic,* the Supreme Court stated:

> [There are] circumstances that are so likely to prejudice the accused that the cost of litigating their effect in a particular case is unjustified. Most obvious, of course, is the complete denial of counsel. [A] trial is unfair if the accused is denied counsel at a critical stage of his trial. Similarly, if counsel entirely fails to subject the prosecution's case to meaningful adversarial testing, then there has been a denial of Sixth Amendment rights that makes the adversary process itself presumptively unreliable.

How would you rule on Nixon's motion? Compare Nixon v. Singletary, 758 So. 2d 618 (Fla. 2000); Florida v. Nixon, 543 U.S. 175 (2004).

Notes

1. *The test for ineffective assistance of counsel: majority position.* The *Strickland* opinion was the Supreme Court's first substantial effort to define the quality of representation required by the Sixth Amendment. In *Strickland,* the court announced its two-part standard: (1) counsel's performance must be "reasonably effective" and cannot fall below an "objective standard" of reasonableness, and (2) the defendant must show a "reasonable probability" that the outcome in the proceedings changed because of the attorney's deficient performance. The *Strickland* opinion has been enormously influential, with states overwhelmingly adopting its framework under state constitutions. Why did it take until 1984 (almost 200 years) to get a square decision from the U.S. Supreme Court on standards of attorney competence? Note that the Court did not explicitly require access to counsel as an element of due process in state criminal trials until Powell v. Alabama, 287 U.S. 45 (1932), and it was not until Gideon v. Wainwright, 372 U.S. 335 (1963), that state-provided attorneys became the rule rather than the exception. See David Cole, *Gideon v. Wainwright* and *Strickland v. Washington*: Broken Promises, in Criminal Procedure Stories (Carol Steiker ed., 2006).

In *Strickland,* Justice O'Connor describes the effectiveness standard as an "objective" standard. What makes a standard "objective" or "subjective"? Why does the court create a "strong presumption" of sound lawyering? Is that an objective standard?

2. *Measuring prejudice.* The prejudice standard under *Strickland,* requiring a "reasonable probability" of a different outcome absent attorney error, calls for a counterfactual inquiry into what the outcome would have been in a hypothetical trial without attorney error. Is the prejudice standard too restrictive or too liberal? How can courts best account for the effects of what counsel *failed* to do? In Sears v. Upton, 130 S. Ct. 3259 (2010), defense counsel selected one theory of mitigation in a capital trial but failed to investigate others. Although the chosen mitigation theory was a reasonable one, the Supreme Court held that prejudice still might flow from the failure to investigate alternatives: Sears might be prejudiced by his counsel's failures, whether his haphazard choice was reasonable or not.

Should a court insist on reaching the difficult and counterfactual prejudice issue only after finding substandard attorney performance? The bulk of the appellate cases on ineffective assistance (and it is indeed a bulky body of cases) turn on prejudice rather than ineffectiveness. You can find a sampling of these cases from the state courts on the web extension of this chapter at *http://www.crimpro.com/extension/ch11*.

How should the standard for prejudice change when the defendant pleads guilty rather than going to trial? The majority of courts declare that a defendant can be prejudiced by an attorney's failure to explain a potential defense during consultations about a guilty plea, even if the defense would not have succeeded. See Grosvenor v. State, 874 So. 2d 1176 (Fla. 2004).

3. *Measuring performance.* The defendant has the burden of proving unreasonable performance, by a preponderance of the evidence. The most straightforward cases of substandard performance involve an attorney's failure to consult a client (or failure to follow client instructions) over the basic direction of the litigation, such as

a decision whether to file a notice of appeal, or a decision to concede guilt and concentrate on the sentencing phase of a capital case. See Roe v. Flores-Ortega, 528 U.S. 470 (2000) (ineffectiveness often present but not presumed when counsel fails to consult client about appeal and misses deadline for filing); Padilla v. Kentucky, 130 S. Ct. 1473 (2010) (when immigration consequences of criminal conviction are clear, competent counsel must inform defendant about those consequences prior to entry of guilty plea).

The more common and more difficult claims about attorney performance involve questionable choices about trial preparation and presentation of evidence. The U.S. Supreme Court has applied the *Strickland* standard lately to emphasize the reasonableness of the investigation that *precedes* an attorney's trial choices, rather than focusing on the reasonableness of the trial decision itself. See Rompilla v. Beard, 545 U.S. 374 (2005) (unreasonable performance during pretrial investigation of prior related conviction that prosecution would emphasize as aggravating fact in capital case); Porter v. McCollum, 130 S. Ct. 447 (2009) (state court was unreasonable to conclude that defense counsel in capital case was not deficient; attorney failed to uncover and present during penalty phase any mitigating evidence regarding client's mental health, family background, or military service). Does the legal standard in *Strickland* prevent a finding of unreasonable performance in any case where the attorney (or an appellate court) can construct a *post hoc* justification for the choice? When a defendant complains about a large collection of attorney decisions, does the standard require a court to consider them one at a time, or can the court consider the collective impact of many borderline attorney choices?

With sad regularity, attorneys are accused of sleeping, being drunk or drugged, or otherwise being physically unable to present an effective defense. Courts sometimes hold that such impairments do not deny defendants effective counsel without specific proof about faulty legal decisions caused by the impairment. See, e.g., McFarland v. Texas, 928 S.W.2d 482 (Tex. Crim. App. 1996) (72-year-old lawyer who said he "customarily" takes a "short nap in the afternoon" held not to be ineffective assistance where napping might have been a "strategic" move to generate jury sympathy and where co-counsel remained awake). Are attorneys impaired if they do not know the most basic law governing the case? Should courts give experienced attorneys a stronger presumption of reasonable performance than newer attorneys?

4. *Structural ineffectiveness and presumed prejudice*. In a few settings, the trial might occur in a setting so likely to produce error that prejudice can be presumed; no attorney is likely to provide adequate defense in these settings. Examples of "structural" ineffectiveness appear in conflict of interest cases, in which an attorney represents multiple clients and runs the risk of harming one client while furthering the interests of the other. If defense counsel raises at trial the issue of potential conflict of interest, and the trial court fails to appoint new counsel or to hold a hearing to determine the risk of a conflict, prejudice is presumed. See People v. Hernandez, 896 N.E.2d 297 (Ill. 2008) (defendant whose attorney had been retained by victim of alleged offense, in a crime allegedly committed against the current defendant years earlier, could now rely on presumption of prejudice, and would not have to show that attorney was "actively" representing the victim). If the defendant raises the issue after trial, she must prove that there was an "actual conflict of interest" that "adversely affected" her lawyer's performance, but there is no need to prove that the adverse effects on lawyer performance changed the outcome at trial. See Cuyler v. Sullivan, 446 U.S. 335 (1980); but see Mickens v. Taylor, 535 U.S. 162 (2002)

(defendant must show prejudice where defense lawyer had *potential* conflict of interest based on former representation of murder victim in juvenile proceedings).

Structural ineffectiveness (and the presumption of prejudice) is more difficult to establish in other settings. In United States v. Cronic, 466 U.S. 648 (1984), a companion case to *Strickland,* the Court rejected a presumption of ineffectiveness when an inexperienced lawyer was appointed shortly before a complex case. However, the court noted that such a presumption could be found "if the accused is denied counsel at a critical stage of his trial," or "if counsel entirely fails to subject the prosecution's case to meaningful adversarial testing." See, e.g., Florida v. Nixon, 543 U.S. 175 (2004) (attorney predicted that prosecution's evidence of guilt in murder trial would be virtually impossible to refute, and proposed to defendant a strategy of conceding guilt to focus on urging leniency at penalty phase, but defendant did not respond; no presumption of prejudice under *Cronic* for conceding guilt under these circumstances).

5. *Public and private incompetence.* Should the judicial standards for ineffective assistance of counsel be the same for public defenders and private attorneys practicing criminal defense? There was a time when courts in some jurisdictions used different standards for publicly provided and privately retained defense counsel, applying a less demanding standard when reviewing the work of privately retained counsel because the work of such an attorney was not considered "state action." See People v. Stevens, 53 P.2d 133 (Cal. 1935). However, in Cuyler v. Sullivan, 446 U.S. 335, 344-45 (1980), the Supreme Court rejected the idea that private attorneys are to be judged by some lesser standard of constitutional scrutiny: "Since the State's conduct of a criminal trial itself implicates the State in the defendant's conviction, we see no basis for drawing a distinction between retained and appointed counsel that would deny equal justice to defendants who must choose their own lawyers."

Although it is clear that retained attorneys cannot be scrutinized less carefully than appointed counsel, could they be scrutinized *more* carefully? On average, which type of attorney do you suppose would be more effective? Does your answer change for different types of criminal cases? See Bureau of Justice Statistics, Defense Counsel in Criminal Cases (Nov. 2000, NCJ 179023) (in both federal and state courts, conviction rates were the same for defendants represented by publicly and privately financed counsel; pretrial release less common for state court defendants with public counsel; state defendants with public counsel sentenced more often to prison or jail but for shorter terms than those with private lawyers).

6. *Does quality of counsel matter?* By focusing on the effectiveness of lawyers, do we lose sight of more important questions about the *contents* of procedural rules that the lawyers must use? If you are convinced that the law of criminal procedure is designed first and foremost to produce convictions efficiently, would you conclude that lawyers (regardless of their effectiveness) will rarely have any procedural claims available that could prevent a conviction from happening? Conversely, if you are convinced that the law of criminal procedure focuses more on police shortcomings than on a defendant's guilt or innocence, would you conclude that judges will find a way to review police conduct, whether or not a lawyer raises the claim in a timely and effective manner?

AMERICAN BAR ASSOCIATION, DEFENSE FUNCTION STANDARDS (3d ed. 1993)

STANDARD 4-1.3 . . . WORKLOAD

(e) Defense counsel should not carry a workload that, by reason of its excessive size, interferes with the rendering of quality representation, endangers the client's interest in the speedy disposition of charges, or may lead to the breach of professional obligations. Defense counsel should not accept employment for the purpose of delaying trial.

STANDARD 4-3.6 PROMPT ACTION TO PROTECT THE ACCUSED

Many important rights of the accused can be protected and preserved only by prompt legal action. Defense counsel should inform the accused of his or her rights at the earliest opportunity and take all necessary action to vindicate those rights. Defense counsel should consider all procedural steps which in good faith may be taken, including, for example, motions seeking pretrial release of the accused, obtaining psychiatric examination of the accused when a need appears, moving for change of venue or continuance, moving to suppress illegally obtained evidence, moving for severance from jointly charged defendants, and seeking dismissal of charges.

STANDARD 4-4.1 DUTY TO INVESTIGATE

(a) Defense counsel should conduct a prompt investigation of the circumstances of the case and explore all avenues leading to facts relevant to the merits of the case and the penalty in the event of conviction. The investigation should include efforts to secure information in the possession of the prosecution and law enforcement authorities. The duty to investigate exists regardless of the accused's admissions or statements to defense counsel of facts constituting guilt or the accused's stated desire to plead guilty. . . .

STANDARD 4-6.1 DUTY TO EXPLORE DISPOSITION WITHOUT TRIAL

(a) Whenever the law, nature, and circumstances of the case permit, defense counsel should explore the possibility of an early diversion from the criminal process through the use of other community agencies.

(b) Defense counsel may engage in plea discussions with the prosecutor. Under no circumstances should defense counsel recommend to a defendant acceptance of a plea unless appropriate investigation and study of the case has been completed, including an analysis of controlling law and the evidence likely to be introduced at trial.

RULE 33, COURT OF COMMON PLEAS, CUYAHOGA COUNTY, OHIO

No attorney will be assigned to defend any indigent person in a criminal case unless his or her name appears on the applicable list of approved trial counsel. . . . The approved trial counsel list shall remain in effect for a period of two years. . . . Counsel whose name appears on the approved trial counsel list shall file an application for renewal to serve as appointed counsel in order to remain on the approved trial counsel list. . . . The following experience qualifications shall be a prima facie basis for the inclusion of a lawyer on the lists designated below:

(A) Assigned counsel for murder cases (including charges of murder, aggravated murder and aggravated murder with specifications).

(1) Trial counsel in a prior murder trial; or

(2) Trial counsel in four first degree felony jury trials; or

(3) Trial counsel in any ten felony or civil jury trials;

(4) No lawyer may appear on the list for murder cases unless he is also listed as counsel for major felony cases described below.

(B) Assigned counsel for major felony cases (first, second and third degree felonies).

(1) Trial counsel in two previous major felony jury trials (first, second or third degree felonies); or

(2) Trial counsel in any four previous criminal jury trials; or

(3) Trial counsel in any previous six criminal or civil jury trials; or

(4) Trial counsel in any two criminal jury trials plus assistant trial counsel in any two criminal jury trials.

(C) Assigned counsel for fourth degree felony cases.

(1) Trial counsel in any previous criminal or civil jury trial; or

(2) Assistant counsel in any two civil or criminal jury trials. . . .

To assist attorneys in obtaining trial experience in criminal cases, and for the purposes of obtaining experience necessary for inclusion on one of the above lists, this Court will cooperate with programs organized by local bar associations in which interested attorneys may be assigned as assistant trial counsel on a non-fee basis in cooperation with regularly retained or assigned counsel in criminal case trials in this county, under the supervision of the trial judge. . . .

The office of the Cuyahoga County Public Defender shall be assigned no less than 35 percent defendants in each category of cases described above for which counsel are selected for indigent defendants. The assigned Public Defender, before being assigned to represent an indigent defendant, shall also meet the established criteria. . . .

Problem 11-6. More Objective Competence Standards

Assume that you are chief counsel to the senate rules committee in a state where the legislature promulgates rules of criminal procedure. The chair of the committee, with the support of the chief justice of the state supreme court, has asked you to draft specific competence standards for the pretrial process. In particular, you are directed to research and draft standards providing guidance on the following three questions:

- How soon must attorneys see a new client?
- How much time must attorneys have, at a minimum, to prepare for plea negotiations?
- What obligations, if any, should counsel have with respect to researching alibi or character witnesses?

How specific can such rules be without interfering with effective defense in some cases? Do nonbinding guidelines accomplish anything? Would you recommend ultimate adoption of these types of rules, or would you encourage the committee and the courts to rely on the *Strickland* standards without additional guidance?

Notes

1. *Rules and standards.* The majority in *Strickland* said that "specific guidelines are not appropriate." Was Justice O'Connor correct in concluding that courts should not specify what is adequate representation of a criminal defendant? What is the significance of the fact that a few states had begun to announce specific expectations for defense counsel to meet? Is any institution other than the judiciary more capable of specifying the standards for effective assistance of counsel, or is lawyering an activity that simply cannot be reduced to enforceable standards? Cf. Bobby v. Van Hook, 130 S. Ct. 13 (2009) (reversing a grant of habeas corpus relief for ineffective assistance that was based heavily on defense counsel's failure to satisfy 2003 ABA standards for uncovering and presenting mitigating evidence during preparation for a trial years earlier).

2. *Performance standards versus experience standards.* The Cuyahoga County rules take a fairly typical approach to the problem of attorney competence: Like the court rules in many other local jurisdictions, these rules focus on the prior experience of attorneys rather than specifying the tasks a competent attorney should perform. Are the approaches embodied in the ABA Standards and the Cuyahoga County standards compatible? Were both standards drafted based on the same goals or assumptions? Do prospective standards for appointment prevent incompetent representation better than retrospective claims by disgruntled clients? For further examples of performance standards adopted by the ABA and other professional organizations to promote effective representation in criminal cases, go to the web extension for this chapter at *http://www.crimpro.com/extension/ch11*.

3. *Caseload limits as a competence strategy*. The seeming numerical gold standard for indigent defense caseloads was established in 1973 by the National Advisory Council of the Federal Law Enforcement Assistance Administration. The council's Standard 13.12 provides that the caseload of a public defender attorney "should not exceed" 150 felonies per year, 400 misdemeanors, 200 juvenile cases, 200 mental commitment cases, or 25 appeals. Those numbers have been cited and adopted as a rough measure of appropriate caseloads by the American Bar Association and by many state-level professional organizations. It is common to find evaluations of

criminal defense services that point out the excessive caseload of defense attorneys, using these numbers as benchmark.

What enforcement mechanisms are available to prevent violations of these caseload targets? According to ABA Formal Opinion 06-441 (2006), lawyers who represent indigent criminal defendants have an ethical obligation to refuse new cases if their workloads are so excessive that they cannot competently represent their clients. The opinion states that many factors determine when a caseload becomes excessive, including these numerical standards as well as the complexity of cases, availability of support services, the experience and ability of individual lawyers and the lawyer's duties other than representing clients.

4. *Malpractice liability for defense attorneys.* If substandard work by criminal defense counsel injures a client, can the client sue for malpractice? While malpractice suits in criminal cases are possible, they face more obstacles than civil malpractice claims. For suits against publicly financed attorneys, sovereign immunity and various official immunities block the suit unless state law waives those defenses. Often state law allows criminal defendants to bring malpractice suits only if they can prove they were actually innocent; it is not enough to claim that the attorney caused an overly severe sentence. See Meredith J. Duncan, Criminal Malpractice: A Lawyer's Holiday, 37 Ga. L. Rev. 1251 (2003); Schreiber v. Rowe, 814 So. 2d 396 (Fla. 2002) (public defenders cannot assert judicial immunity in malpractice cases, but former defendant must prove actual innocence to maintain suit); cf. Hilario v. Reardon, 960 A.2d 337 (N.H. 2008) (civil plaintiff who claims that malpractice of criminal defense attorney occurred after the plea and sentencing, and prevented him from enjoying some benefits of plea bargain, does not have to make the normally required showing that that he was factually innocent of the underlying charges).

Compare malpractice suits to an alternative form of accountability for attorneys, embodied in Rule 13 of the Rules of the Supreme Court of the State of Hawaii. Under Rule 13, after a conviction has been overturned because of ineffective assistance of counsel, the Supreme Court appoints a special master who can recommend "corrective action" against the attorney such as remedial education, suspension of the attorney's license to practice law, and referral to the state legal ethics authorities.

D. SYSTEMS FOR PROVIDING COUNSEL

We have surveyed the legal standards designed to ensure that individual defense counsel will provide effective assistance of counsel. The methods the government uses to fund and deliver legal services to the indigent also have a powerful effect on the performance of the defense counsel in individual cases. What institutions and sources of law shape entire systems for providing counsel?

The first method of providing defense counsel to indigent defendants in this country was the appointment of a private attorney to the case. The attorney might have handled the case as an unpaid volunteer or might have received some small compensation from the government. Early in the twentieth century, however, organizations of full-time defense attorneys began to spring up in major urban areas.The first appeared in Los Angeles in 1914. Supporters of these "defender organizations" (public agencies and private charitable groups) hoped that they would provide criminal defense at less expense to the public and would avoid the distracting and needlessly confrontational style of the "shyster" lawyers who often accepted court appointments. As one prominent defense attorney put it, the publicly accountable defense attorney could join forces with the prosecutor to see that "no innocent man may suffer or guilty man escape." Mayer Goldman, The Need for a Public Defender, 8 J. Crim. L. & Criminology 273 (1917-1918).

Today, most places still use more than one method of providing defense counsel, but the "organizational" defenders have become the most important piece of the puzzle. Those who create and fund the defender organizations hope to control the costs of providing adequate criminal defense and to do so without compromising either the fairness or the efficiency of the criminal justice system. As you read the following materials, think about how to determine the proper goals of a system for delivering criminal defense services. Do the different systems provide defense counsel with different incentives to handle criminal cases in particular ways, such as choosing between plea bargains and trials?

DONALD J. FAROLE AND LYNN LANGTON COUNTY-BASED AND LOCAL PUBLIC DEFENDER OFFICES, 2007

Bureau of Justice Statistics, September 2010 (NCJ 231175)

In 2007, 49 states and the District of Columbia had public defender offices to provide legal representation for some or all indigent defendants. In 27 states and the District of Columbia, counties or local jurisdictions funded and administered public defender offices. In the remaining 22 states, one office oversaw indigent defense operations throughout the state. . . . County-based public defender offices employed 71% of the nation's 15,026 public defenders in 2007. . . .

In 1963 the United States Supreme Court ruled in Gideon v. Wainwright that state courts are required to ensure that the provisions of the right to counsel under the Sixth and Fourteenth Amendments apply to indigent defendants. Since the *Gideon* ruling, states, counties, and jurisdictions have established varying means of providing public representation for defendants unable to afford a private attorney. Indigent defense systems typically provide representation through some combination of three methods:

1. A public defender office.
2. An assigned counsel system in which the court schedules cases for participating private attorneys.
3. A contract system in which private attorneys contractually agree to take on a specified number of indigent defendants or indigent defense cases. . . .

The 27 states and the District of Columbia with county-based public defender offices operated a total of 530 offices. . . . In 2007, 83% of county-based public defender offices reported using formal criteria to determine if a defendant qualified as indigent and was eligible for public representation. . . . Judges (52%) and public defenders (47%) were the most common entities responsible for screening potential clients for indigency in jurisdictions served by county-based public defender offices. . . .

Public defender offices had various procedures to handle cases in which there was a conflict of interest, such as a co-defendant already handled by the defender office. The majority (52%) of county-based public defender offices reported handling conflict cases through a court administered assigned counsel program; about a quarter (23%) of offices handled conflict cases through previously established contracts with private attorneys. Less than 1 in 10 (7%) county-based public defender offices used an ethical screen, whereby an office would take a case regardless of the conflict but preclude an attorney with conflicting connections from involvement in the case. . . .

Vertical representation refers to the practice of one attorney representing a client from arraignment through the duration of the case. It is distinguished from horizontal representation in which a different attorney represents the same client at various stages of the case. Sixty percent of county-based public defender offices had a written policy requiring vertical representation of indigent cases. About 7 in 10 (71%) offices reported providing primarily vertical representation in felony, non-capital cases (these offices may or may not have had written policies requiring vertical representation). . . . The majority of county-based public defender offices had formal policies that required the most experienced attorneys to handle the most complex cases (58%) and about a quarter (28%) required that an attorney be appointed to the case within 24 hours of client detention. . . .

Eighty-two percent of county-based public defender offices allowed for some form of cost recoupment for public defender services in 2007. Among the offices that permitted cost recoupment, the most widely available fee was a charge based on the cost for the defender's services (69% of offices). . . . More than 2 in 5 (44%) offices charged an up-front application or administrative fee, which typically ranged from $10 to $200 depending on the state and the type of case. . . .

In 2007, 15% of county-based public defender offices had formal caseload limits, and 36% had the authority to refuse appointments due to excessive caseloads. About 6 in 10 (59%) offices reported having neither caseload limits nor the authority to refuse cases. About half (49%) of offices that received more than 5,000 cases reported having the authority to refuse appointments due to excess caseload, compared to 28% of offices that received fewer than 1,000 cases in 2007. . . .

County-based public defender offices received a median of 853 felony non-capital cases and 1,000 misdemeanor cases, and employed a median of 7 full-time equivalent (FTE) litigating public defenders per office in 2007. . . . The National Advisory Commission (NAC) guidelines recommend a caseload for each public defender's office, not necessarily each attorney in the office. They state that "the caseload of a public defender office should not exceed the following: felonies per attorney per year: not more than 150; misdemeanors (excluding traffic) per attorney per year: not more than 400; juvenile court cases per attorney per year: not more than 200; Mental Health Act cases per attorney per year: not more than 200; and appeals per attorney per year: not more than 25." . . . One way to examine the numeric caseload guideline is to assess the number of cases received per FTE litigating attorney. . . . Using this estimation method, a public defender office would meet the guideline for cases received in 2007 if the FTE litigating attorneys received no more than 75 felony non-capital and 200 misdemeanor cases.

This conservative measure also assumes that attorneys did not have any cases pending from previous years and did not handle any other type of case. Still, 36% of county-based public defender offices met the guideline for felony non-capital cases per attorney, and 66% met the guideline for the number of misdemeanor cases per attorney. Offices with larger overall caseloads were more likely than those with smaller caseloads to exceed the maximum recommended limit for both felony and misdemeanor cases. About 4 in 5 offices that received more than 2,500 cases in 2007 failed to meet the national guideline of felony non-capital cases per attorney.

Another way to examine caseloads is to calculate the number of defenders needed to meet the nationally accepted caseload guideline. . . . To meet this guideline in 2007, the median office would have needed 11 attorneys who only handled the median number of felony, misdemeanor, juvenile-related, or appellate cases reported. . . . The median office reported employing 7 FTE litigating attorneys, approximately 64% of the estimated number needed. Twenty-seven percent of county-based public defender offices reported sufficient numbers of litigating attorneys to handle the cases received in those offices in 2007. About a quarter (23%) of all offices reported less than half of the number of litigating attorneys required to meet the professional guidelines for the number of cases received in 2007.

[Professional guidelines recommend 1 managerial attorney for every 10 staff attorneys.] The 273 county-based offices with 5 or more litigating attorneys reported a median of 1.7 managerial attorneys for every 10 assistant public defenders. [Professional guidelines recommend 1 investigator per 3 litigating attorneys.] County-based public defender offices employed about 1,500 investigators and 800 paralegals. . . . In 2007, 7% of the 469 county-based public defender offices with at least 1.5 FTE litigating attorneys met the accepted professional guideline for the ratio of investigators to attorneys. . . . Forty percent of all county-based offices employed no investigators. Among offices receiving less than 1,000 cases in 2007, nearly 9 in 10 (87%) had no investigators on staff. . . .

The median salary for entry-level assistant public defenders ranged from $42,000 to $45,000. With 6 years or more experience, assistant public defenders earned a median salary in the range of $54,000 to $68,000. Assistant public defenders in higher caseload offices received higher salaries in general. . . .

STATE v. LEONARD PEART

621 So. 2d 780 (La. 1993)

CALOGERO, C.J.

In this case we assess a multifaceted ruling made by the trial judge in Section E of Orleans Parish Criminal District Court. . . . Because we find that the provision of indigent defense services in Section E is in many respects so lacking that defendants who must depend on it are not likely to receive the reasonably effective assistance of counsel the constitution guarantees, we remand this case to the trial court and instruct the judge of Section E of Criminal District Court, when hearing Leonard Peart's case and others in which similar claims are asserted by indigent defendants pre-trial, to hold individual hearings for each defendant and apply a rebuttable presumption that indigents are not receiving assistance of counsel sufficiently effective to meet constitutionally required standards. . . .

The legislature has [established] Louisiana's indigent defender system. LSA-R.S. 15:144 creates Indigent Defender Boards to oversee indigent defense operations in each judicial district. . . . LSA-R.S. 15:146 sets up a mechanism for local funding of individual districts' indigent defender systems. LSA-R.S. 15:304 is a general statute which requires all parishes and the city of New Orleans to pay "all expenses . . . whatever attending criminal proceedings. . . ."[2]

Facts

Leonard Peart was charged with armed robbery, aggravated rape, aggravated burglary, attempted armed robbery, and first degree murder. He is indigent.

In New Orleans, the Indigent Defender Board ("IDB") has created the Orleans Indigent Defender Program ("OIDP"). OIDP operates under a public defender model. The trial court appointed Rick Teissier, one of the two OIDP attorneys assigned to Section E, to defend Peart against all the above charges except first degree murder.

. . . At the time of his appointment, Teissier was handling 70 active felony cases. His clients are routinely incarcerated 30 to 70 days before he meets with them. In the period between January 1 and August 1, 1991, Teissier represented 418 defendants. Of these, he entered 130 guilty pleas at arraignment. He had at least one serious case set for trial for every trial date during that period. OIDP has only enough funds to hire three investigators. They are responsible for rendering assistance in more than 7,000 cases per year in the ten sections of Criminal District Court, plus cases in Juvenile Court, Traffic Court, and Magistrates' Court. In a routine case Teissier receives no investigative support at all. There are no funds for expert witnesses. OIDP's library is inadequate.

The court found that Teissier was not able to provide his clients with reasonably effective assistance of counsel because of the conditions affecting his work, primarily the large number of cases assigned to him. The court further ruled that "the system of securing and compensating qualified counsel for indigents" in LSA-R.S. 15:145, 15:146 and 15:304 was "unconstitutional as applied in the City of New Orleans" because it does not provide adequate funding for indigent defense and because it places the burden of funding indigent defense on the city of New Orleans. The trial judge ordered short and long term relief. In the short term, he ordered Teissier's caseload reduced; ordered the legislature to provide funding for an improved library and for an investigator for Teissier; and announced his intention to appoint members of the bar to represent indigents in his court. For the long term, he ordered that the legislature provide funds to OIDP to pay additional attorneys, secretaries, paralegals, law clerks, investigators, and expert witnesses.

2. [Indigent Defender Boards] choose between public defender, contract attorney, and assigned counsel models, or may use a combination of these models. LSA-R.S. 15:146 sets up a mechanism for local funding of individual districts' indigent defender systems. This provision, unique in the United States, creates a system whereby almost all of the funds for indigent defense come from criminal violation assessments [in] an amount ranging from $17.50 to $25.00 for each violation. Parking violations are excepted. . . .

[While the State's appeal of this ruling was pending, Peart was tried and acquitted of armed robbery.] In a second trial, in which he was represented by other counsel, he was acquitted on the murder charge. He is awaiting trial on the aggravated rape charge. Teissier again represents him.[5] . . .

LAW

. . . We begin with the proposition that because there is no precise definition of reasonably effective assistance of counsel, any inquiry into the effectiveness of counsel must necessarily be individualized and fact-driven. In different contexts, Louisiana courts have found a wide variety of attorneys' failings to constitute ineffective assistance. These courts [have determined] whether an individual defendant has been provided with reasonably effective assistance, and no general finding by the trial court regarding a given lawyer's handling of other cases, or workload generally, can answer that very specific question as to an individual defendant and the defense being furnished him.

[The] language of La. Const. art. 1 sec. 13 is unequivocal: "At each stage of the proceedings, every person is entitled to the assistance of counsel . . . appointed by the court if he is indigent and charged with a crime punishable by imprisonment." That assistance must be reasonably effective. Article 1 sec. 13 also provides that "the legislature shall provide for a uniform system for securing and compensating qualified counsel for indigents." As noted above, the legislature has enacted statutes responsive to these constitutional requirements.

However, we cannot say that the system these statutes have put in place invariably — or, in Section E, even regularly — affords indigent defendants reasonably effective assistance of counsel. We take reasonably effective assistance of counsel to mean that the lawyer not only possesses adequate skill and knowledge, but also that he has the time and resources to apply his skill and knowledge to the task of defending each of his individual clients.

[This] system has resulted in wide variations in levels of funding, both between different IDB's and within the same IDB over time. The general pattern has been one of chronic underfunding of indigent defense programs in most areas of the state. The system is so underfunded that [one recent study committee, appointed by the state judiciary, concluded that] there is a "desperate need to double the budget for indigent defense in Louisiana in the next two years." The unique system which funds indigent defense through criminal violation assessments, mostly traffic tickets, is an unstable and unpredictable approach.[10] . . .

The conditions in Section E should be contrasted with the American Bar Association Standards for Criminal Justice (1991). These conditions routinely

5. Ironically, the trial court judgment indicates that at the time of the judgment Peart himself was receiving the effective assistance of counsel guaranteed him by the constitution. As the trial judge wrote, "each of Mr. Teissier's clients is entitled to the same kind of defense Leonard Peart is receiving." That Peart himself could receive effective assistance, while Teissier's other clients do not, reflects the fact that indigent defenders must select certain clients to whom they give more attention than they give to others. . . . We therefore anticipate, although we do not decide, that the State may well be able to rebut the presumption of ineffectiveness in the pending rape case against Peart.

10. Examples of the approach's unpredictability abound. One particularly stark example: when the City of East Baton Rouge ran out of pre-printed traffic tickets in the first half of 1990, the indigent defender program's sole source of income was suspended while more tickets were being printed.

violate the standards on workload (Std. 4-1.3(e)) ("defense counsel should not carry a workload that, by reason of its excessive size, interferes with the rendering of quality representation"); initial provision of counsel (Std. 5-6.1) ("counsel should be provided to the accused . . . at appearance before a committing magistrate, or when criminal charges are filed, whichever occurs earliest"); investigation (Std. 4-4.1) ("defense counsel should conduct a prompt investigation of the circumstances of the case and explore all avenues leading to facts relevant to the merits of the case"); and others. We know from experience that no attorney can prepare for one felony trial per day, especially if he has little or no investigative, paralegal, or clerical assistance. As the trial judge put it, "not even a lawyer with an S on his chest could effectively handle this docket." We agree. Many indigent defendants in Section E are provided with counsel who can perform only pro forma, especially at early stages of the proceedings. . . . In light of the unchallenged evidence in the record, we find that because of the excessive caseloads and the insufficient support with which their attorneys must work, indigent defendants in Section E are generally not provided with the effective assistance of counsel the constitution requires.

Remedies

Having found that indigent defendants in Section E cannot all be receiving effective assistance of counsel, we must decide what remedy this Court should impose. Louisiana is not the only state to have faced a crisis in its indigent defense system. Over the last decade, numerous states have addressed problems like those Louisiana faces. In some states, legislatures have on their own initiative improved provision of indigent defense services. For example, in 1989 alone the legislatures of New Mexico, Missouri and Kentucky provided for large increases in the budgets of their statewide public defender offices; the Tennessee and Georgia legislatures established new statewide public defender offices. In other states, litigation challenging the adequacy of defense services has resulted in systemic changes. [The court cited cases from Arkansas, Florida, Kansas, New Hampshire, and Oklahoma.]

By virtue of this Court's constitutional position as the final arbiter of the meaning of the state constitution and laws, we have a duty to interpret and apply the constitution. In addition, the constitution endows this Court with general supervisory jurisdiction over all other courts. . . . Acting pursuant to the established sources of authority noted above, . . . we find that a rebuttable presumption arises that indigents in Section E are receiving assistance of counsel not sufficiently effective to meet constitutionally required standards. See State v. Smith, 681 P.2d 1374 (Ariz. 1984). This presumption is to apply prospectively only; it is to apply to those defendants who were represented by attorney Teissier when he filed the original "Motion for Relief" who have not yet gone to trial; and it will be applicable to all indigent defendants in Section E who have OIDP attorneys appointed to represent them hereafter, so long as there are no changes in the workload and other conditions under which OIDP assigned defense counsel provide legal services in Section E. If legislative action is not forthcoming and indigent defense reform does not take place, this Court, in the exercise of its constitutional and inherent power and supervisory jurisdiction, may find it necessary to employ the more intrusive and specific measures it has thus far avoided to ensure that indigent defendants receive reasonably effective assistance of counsel. We decline at this time to undertake these more intrusive and specific measures because this Court should not lightly tread in the affairs of other branches of government and because the legislature ought to assess such measures in the first instance. . . .

We instruct the judge of Section E, when trying Leonard Peart's motion and any others which may be filed, to hold individual hearings for each such moving defendant and, in the absence of significant improvement in the provision of indigent defense services to defendants in Section E, to apply a rebuttable presumption that such indigents are not receiving assistance of counsel effective enough to meet constitutionally required standards. If the court, applying this presumption and weighing all evidence presented, finds that Leonard Peart or any other defendant in Section E is not receiving the reasonably effective assistance of counsel the constitution requires, and the court finds itself unable to order any other relief which would remedy the situation, then the court shall not permit the prosecution to go forward until the defendant is provided with reasonably effective assistance of counsel. . . . Reversed and remanded.

DENNIS, J., dissenting.

[The] conditions that affect indigent services in Orleans Parish obviously are not limited to Section E. To deny this is as whimsical as saying that a person in early term is "only a little bit pregnant." On the other hand, the majority, without articulating constitutional principles or legal assistance guidelines, sweepingly creates a presumption that indigent defense services in Section E are ineffective and invites the trial judge to halt trials until the presumption has been overcome by the state. Evidently, my colleagues intend to offer up Section E as a lamb for burnt offering, hoping that an all-knowing, benevolent deity will miraculously cure the ills of the indigent defense system in that section and perhaps elsewhere. I respectfully decline to join the majority's decision because it does not realistically and thoroughly address or attempt to remedy the systemic constitutional deficiencies affecting the provision of indigent defense services in Orleans and perhaps other parishes. . . .

The Legislature and the Executive branch of Louisiana have a duty to correct the constitutional deficiencies in the system. However, without a clear explanation by this court of the controlling constitutional principles and standards, the legislature cannot know exactly what is required to bring the indigent defender system into constitutional alignment; and it is unlikely that the legislature will be inspired or impelled to take satisfactory action without adequate guidance from this court. . . .

This court should establish standards by setting limits on the number of cases handled by indigent defense attorneys, by requiring a minimum number of investigators to be assigned to each defender, and by requiring specified support resources for each attorney. If a defendant demonstrates future error due to funding and resource deficiencies, the courts should be instructed to view the harm as state-imposed error, which would require reversal of the conviction unless the state demonstrates that the error was harmless.

In State v. Smith, 681 P.2d 1374 (Ariz. 1984), the Arizona Supreme Court found that a county's bid system [produced inadequate representation, so] the court required the county to follow a series of guidelines in order to maintain a contract defense system. The county's failure to comply would result in the automatic reversal of any conviction obtained under the system and appealed by the defendant, unless the state could demonstrate that the error was harmless. The decision prompted the county to begin paying appointed counsel on an hourly basis, increasing the county's expenditure on defense services and improving the quality of representation.

The majority has created a *Smith*-type presumption but has failed to set forth any standards to give the legislative and executive branches guidance in bringing the system into constitutional compliance. Furthermore, the majority has adopted a per se rule that would allow the trial court to prevent criminal trials in Section E until the defense counsel system is in compliance with the constitution. In my opinion, the per se rule may be too drastic at this time. Utilizing the *Smith*-type harmless error standard alone would be appropriate and would ensure that the criminal justice system continues to operate while the state attempts to comply with the constitutional requirements. . . .

■ KIMBERLY HURRELL-HARRING v. STATE

930 N.E.2d 217 (N.Y. 2010)

LIPPMAN, C.J.

. . . Gideon v. Wainwright, 372 U.S. 335 (1963), is not now controversial either as an expression of what the Constitution requires or as an exercise in elemental fair play. Serious questions have, however, arisen in this and other jurisdictions as to whether *Gideon's* mandate is being met in practice.

In New York, the Legislature has left the performance of the State's obligation under *Gideon* to the counties, where it is discharged, for the most part, with county resources and according to local rules and practices. Plaintiffs in this action, defendants in various criminal prosecutions ongoing at the time of the action's commencement in Washington, Onondaga, Ontario, Schuyler and Suffolk counties, contend that this arrangement, involving what is in essence a costly, largely unfunded and politically unpopular mandate upon local government, has functioned to deprive them and other similarly situated indigent defendants in the aforementioned counties of constitutionally and statutorily guaranteed representational rights. They seek a declaration that their rights and those of the class they seek to represent are being violated and an injunction to avert further abridgment of their right to counsel; they do not seek relief within the criminal cases out of which their claims arise.

This appeal results from dispositions of defendants' motion pursuant to CPLR 3211 to dismiss the action as nonjusticiable. Supreme Court denied the motion, but [the Appellate Division granted it]. We now reinstate the action, albeit with some substantial qualifications upon its scope.

[Defendants claim that the action is not justiciable, because there is no cognizable claim for ineffective assistance of counsel apart from one seeking relief from a conviction. They argue that the case law conditions] relief for constitutionally ineffective assistance upon findings that attorney performance, when viewed in its total, case specific aspect, has both fallen below the standard of objective reasonableness, see Strickland v. Washington, 466 U.S. 668, 687-688 (1984), and resulted in prejudice, either with respect to the outcome of the proceeding or, under this Court's somewhat less outcome oriented standard of "meaningful assistance," to the defendant's right to a fair trial. People v. Benevento, 697 N.E.2d 584 (N.Y. 1998). Defendants reason that the prescribed, deferential and highly context sensitive inquiry into the adequacy and particular effect of counsel's performance cannot occur until a prosecution has concluded in a conviction, and that, once there is a conviction, the appropriate avenues of relief are direct appeals and the various other established means of challenging a conviction. . . .

These arguments possess a measure of merit. A fair reading of *Strickland* and our relevant state precedents supports defendants' contention that effective assistance is a judicial construct designed to do no more than protect an individual defendant's right to a fair adjudication; it is not a concept capable of expansive application to remediate systemic deficiencies. The cases in which the concept has been explicated are in this connection notable for their intentional omission of any broadly applicable defining performance standards. . . .

Having said this, however, we would add the very important caveat that *Strickland's* approach is expressly premised on the supposition that the fundamental underlying right to representation under *Gideon* has been enabled by the State in a manner that would justify the presumption that the standard of objective reasonableness will ordinarily be satisfied. The questions properly raised in this Sixth Amendment-grounded action, we think, go not to whether ineffectiveness has assumed systemic dimensions, but rather to whether the State has met its foundational obligation under *Gideon* to provide legal representation. . . .

According to the complaint, 10 of the 20 plaintiffs — two from Washington, two from Onondaga, two from Ontario and four from Schuyler County — were altogether without representation at the arraignments held in their underlying criminal proceedings. Eight of these unrepresented plaintiffs were jailed after bail had been set in amounts they could not afford. It is alleged that the experience of these plaintiffs is illustrative of what is a fairly common practice in the aforementioned counties of arraigning defendants without counsel and leaving them, particularly when accused of relatively low level offenses, unrepresented in subsequent proceedings where pleas are taken and other critically important legal transactions take place. . . .

In addition to the foregoing allegations of outright nonrepresentation, the complaint contains allegations to the effect that although lawyers were eventually nominally appointed for plaintiffs, they were unavailable to their clients — that they conferred with them little, if at all, were often completely unresponsive to their urgent inquiries and requests from jail, sometimes for months on end, waived important rights without consulting them, and ultimately appeared to do little more on their behalf than act as conduits for plea offers, some of which purportedly were highly unfavorable. It is repeatedly alleged that counsel missed court appearances, and that when they did appear they were not prepared to proceed, often because they were entirely new to the case, the matters having previously been handled by other similarly unprepared counsel. . . .

The allegations of the complaint must at this stage of the litigation be deemed true and construed in plaintiffs' favor, affording them the benefit of every reasonable inference, the very limited object being to ascertain whether any cognizable claim for relief is made out. . . . The above summarized allegations, in our view, state cognizable Sixth Amendment claims.

[The right to counsel] attaches at arraignment and entails the presence of counsel at each subsequent "critical" stage of the proceedings. As is here relevant, arraignment itself must under the circumstances alleged be deemed a critical stage since . . . it is clear from the complaint that plaintiffs' pretrial liberty interests were on that occasion regularly adjudicated with most serious consequences, both direct and collateral, including the loss of employment and housing, and inability to support and care for particularly needy dependents. There is no question that a bail hearing is a critical stage of the State's criminal process.

Recognizing the crucial importance of arraignment and the extent to which a defendant's basic liberty and due process interests may then be affected, CPL 180.10(3) expressly provides for the "right to the aid of counsel at the arraignment and at every subsequent stage of the action" and forbids a court from going forward with the proceeding without counsel for the defendant, unless the defendant has knowingly agreed to proceed in counsel's absence. Contrary to defendants' suggestion and that of the dissent, nothing in the statute may be read to justify the conclusion that the presence of defense counsel at arraignment is ever dispensable, except at a defendant's informed option. . . . Nor is there merit to defendants' suggestion that the Sixth Amendment right to counsel is not yet fully implicated. See Rothgery v. Gillespie County, Texas, 554 U.S. 191 (2008). . . .

These allegations state a claim, not for ineffective assistance under *Strickland*, but for basic denial of the right to counsel under *Gideon*. . . . While it may turn out after further factual development that what is really at issue is whether the representation afforded was effective — a subject not properly litigated in this civil action — at this juncture . . . the complaint states a claim for constructive denial of the right to counsel by reason of insufficient compliance with the constitutional mandate of *Gideon*. See United States v. Cronic, 466 U.S. 648 (1984). The dissent's conclusion that these allegations assert only performance based claims, and not claims for nonrepresentation, seems to us premature. . . .

Strickland itself, of course, recognizes the critical distinction between a claim for ineffective assistance and one alleging simply that the right to the assistance of counsel has been denied and specifically acknowledges that the latter kind of claim may be disposed of without inquiring as to prejudice:

> In certain Sixth Amendment contexts, prejudice is presumed. Actual or constructive denial of the assistance of counsel altogether is legally presumed to result in prejudice. So are various kinds of state interference with counsel's assistance. Prejudice in these circumstances is so likely that case-by-case inquiry into prejudice is not worth the cost. Moreover, such circumstances involve impairments of the Sixth Amendment right that are easy to identify and, for that reason and because the prosecution is directly responsible, easy for the government to prevent.

The allegations before us state claims falling precisely within this described category. It is true, as the dissent points out, that claims, even within this category, have been most frequently litigated postconviction, but it does not follow from this circumstance that they are not cognizable apart from the postconviction context. Given the simplicity and autonomy of a claim for nonrepresentation, as opposed to one truly involving the adequacy of an attorney's performance, there is no reason . . . why such a claim cannot or should not be brought without the context of a completed prosecution.

[We] perceive no real danger that allowing these claims to proceed would impede the orderly progress of plaintiffs' underlying criminal actions. Those actions have, for the most part, been concluded, and we have, in any event, removed from the action the issue of ineffective assistance, thus eliminating any possibility that the collateral adjudication of generalized claims of ineffective assistance might be used to obtain relief from individual judgments of conviction. Here we emphasize that our recognition that plaintiffs may have claims for constructive denial of counsel should not be viewed as a back door for what would be nonjusticiable assertions of ineffective assistance seeking remedies specifically addressed to attorney performance, such as uniform hiring, training and practice standards. To the extent that a cognizable Sixth Amendment claim is stated in this collateral civil action, it is to the effect that in one or more of the five counties at issue the basic constitutional mandate for the provision of counsel to indigent defendants at all critical stages is at risk of being left unmet because of systemic conditions, not by reason of the personal failings and poor professional decisions of individual attorneys. . . .

It is, of course, possible that a remedy in this action would necessitate the appropriation of funds and perhaps, particularly in a time of scarcity, some reordering of legislative priorities. But this does not amount to an argument upon which a court might be relieved of its essential obligation to provide a remedy for violation of a fundamental constitutional right. See Marbury v. Madison, 5 U.S. 137 (1803) ("every right, when withheld, must have a remedy, and every injury its proper redress"). We have consistently held that enforcement of a clear constitutional or statutory mandate is the proper work of the courts, and it would be odd if we made an exception in the case of a mandate as well-established and as essential to our institutional integrity as the one requiring the State to provide legal representation to indigent criminal defendants at all critical stages of the proceedings against them. . . . Accordingly, the order of the Appellate Division should be modified . . . by reinstating the complaint in accordance with this opinion. . . .

PIGOTT, J., dissenting.

. . . The allegations in the complaint can be broken down into two categories: (1) the deprivation of "meaningful and effective assistance of counsel," and (2) the deprivation of the right to counsel at a "critical stage" of the proceedings, i.e., the arraignment. The claims under the former category are many: lack of a sufficient opportunity to discuss the charges with their attorney or participate in their defense; lack of preparation by counsel; denial of investigative services; lack of "vertical representation;" refusal of assigned counsel to return phone calls or accept collect calls; inability to leave messages on assigned counsel's answering machine due to a full voicemail box, etc.

[The majority] reads the complaint as stating a claim for "constructive denial" of the right to counsel, i.e., that upon having counsel appointed, plaintiffs received only nominal representation, such that there is a question as to whether the counties were in compliance with the constitutional mandate of *Gideon*. In support of this rationale, the majority relies on United States v. Cronic, 466 U.S. 648 (1984), which recognizes a "narrow exception" to *Strickland's* requirement that a defendant asserting an ineffective assistance of counsel claim must demonstrate a deficient performance and prejudice. . . .

Cronic's "narrow exception" applies to individual cases where: (1) there has been a "complete denial of counsel"; i.e., the defendant is denied counsel at a critical stage of the trial; (2) "counsel entirely fails to subject the prosecution's case to meaningful adversarial testing"; or (3) "the likelihood that any lawyer, even a fully competent one, could provide effective assistance is so small that a presumption of prejudice is appropriate without inquiry into the actual conduct of the trial." *Cronic's* holding is instructive, if only to point out that the Supreme Court was reaching the obvious conclusion that, in *individual cases,* the absence or inadequacy of counsel must generally fall within one of those three narrow exceptions. Constructive denial of counsel is a branch from the *Strickland* tree, with *Cronic* applying only when the appointed attorney's representation is so egregious that it's as if defendant had no attorney at all. Therefore, whether a defendant received ineffective assistance of counsel under *Strickland* or is entitled to a presumption of prejudice under *Cronic* is a determination that can only be made *after* the criminal proceeding has ended. . . .

That is not to say that a claim of constructive denial could never apply to a class where the State effectively deprives indigent defendants of their right to counsel, only that the various claims asserted by plaintiffs here do not rise to that level. Here, plaintiffs' complaint raises basic ineffective assistance of counsel claims in the nature of *Strickland* (i.e., counsel was unresponsive, waived important rights, failed to appear at hearings, and was unprepared at court proceedings) and not the egregious type of conduct found in *Cronic*. Plaintiffs' mere lumping together of 20 generic ineffective assistance of counsel claims into one civil pleading does not ipso facto transform it into one alleging a systemic denial of the right to counsel.

[The] majority posits that plaintiffs have stated a cognizable claim because 10 of them were arraigned without counsel, and eight of those remained in custody because they could not meet the bail that was set. The framework of CPL article 180 . . . presupposes that a criminal defendant, upon arraignment, may not have yet retained counsel or, due to indigency, requires the appointment of one. CPL 180.10 mandates that, in addition to apprising him of, and furnishing him with, a copy of the charges against him, the court must also inform an unrepresented defendant that he is entitled to, among other things, "an adjournment for the purpose of obtaining counsel" and the appointment of counsel by the court if "he is financially unable to obtain the same." . . .

Giving plaintiffs the benefit of every favorable inference, the complaint nevertheless fails to state a cause of action for the deprivation of the right to counsel at arraignment. One reason is that there is no allegation that the failure to have counsel at one's first court appearance had an adverse effect on the criminal proceedings. . . . There is nothing in New York law which in any way prevents counsel's later taking advantage of every opportunity or defense which was originally available to a defendant upon his initial arraignment. . . . As pleaded, none of the 10 plaintiffs arraigned without counsel entered guilty pleas and, indeed, in compliance with the strictures of CPL 180.10, all met with counsel shortly after the arraignment. . . .

While the perfect system of justice is beyond human attainment, plaintiffs' frustration with the deficiencies in the present indigent defense system is understandable. Legal services for the indigent have routinely been underfunded, and appointed counsel are all too often overworked and confronted with excessive caseloads, which affects the amount of time counsel may spend with any given client. [The Legislature is] the proper forum for weighing proposals to enhance indigent defense services in New York. This complaint is, at heart, an attempt to convert what are properly policy questions for the Legislature into constitutional claims for the courts. . . .

Notes

1. *Local variety in indigent defense systems.* As the materials above indicate, jurisdictions have created several different systems for providing defense counsel to indigent criminal defendants. Although public defender services are the exclusive method of providing defense counsel in less than a third of all jurisdictions, they tend to be used in the largest jurisdictions, meaning that the majority of criminal defendants in this country receive their attorney through a public defender's office. Bureau of Justice Statistics, Indigent Defense Services in Large Counties, 1999 at Table 7 (Nov. 2000, NCJ 184932) (82 percent of cases in 100 largest counties handled through public defender programs). The federal system continues to rely on different systems from district to district. This local variation in the federal system is the legacy of one of the great justice reform reports in U.S. history, the Report of the Attorney General's Committee on Poverty and the Administration of Federal Criminal Justice (1963), known after its chair as the "Allen Report." The Allen Report led to the federal Criminal Justice Act of 1964, which provided a framework for funding indigent defense in the federal system.

In most states, local governments choose and finance systems of indigent defense. A growing group of states — currently over 20 of them — fund and operate statewide indigent defender services with full authority to provide legal services. See Mary Sue Backus & Paul Marcus, The Right to Counsel in Criminal Cases: A National Crisis, 57 Hastings L.J. 1031, 1046-53 (2006) (summarizing the work of the National Committee on the Right to Counsel). Other states create a statewide commission to provide uniform policies and training for public defenders but leave the choice and funding of systems to the local government. There is more statewide uniformity for police practices and trial procedures (through state statutes, constitutional rulings, and procedural rules) than for the provision of defense counsel. Why have the local governments rather than the state governments become the focal point for choices about defense counsel?

2. *Caseloads and legal challenges to public defender systems.* On a regular basis, criminal defendants or civil plaintiffs litigate claims of systemic failure of the public defender system. As the Louisiana and New York opinions indicate above, the doctrinal challenge for these claims is to demonstrate how they are different from individual claims of ineffective assistance of counsel. The litigation tends to be filed in jurisdictions during acute funding crises. For surveys of some recent litigation to challenge system conditions for public defender offices, go to the web extension for this chapter at *http://www.crimpro.com/extension/ch11*. In particular, the web extension offers a case study of the turmoil in the Georgia system in recent years.

On those relatively rare occasions when defendants challenge the overall effectiveness of a public defender program, the caseload of the attorneys is always a key variable. See In re Order on Prosecution of Criminal Appeals by the Tenth Judicial Circuit Public Defender, 561 So. 2d 1130 (Fla. 1990) (backlog of appellate cases assigned to public defenders supports habeas corpus relief for indigent appellants unless new funds appropriated within 60 days); Cara H. Drinan, The Third Generation of Indigent Defense Litigation, 33 N.Y.U. Rev. L. & Social Change 427 (2009) (first-generation suits were reactive and sought limited relief from the courts for extraordinary workloads; second-generation suits were marked by their empirical grounding, extensive alliances of support, and requests for sweeping reform).

The ABA standards recommend annual caseloads of no more than 150 non-capital felonies per attorney, 400 misdemeanors, 200 juvenile cases, or 25 appeals. ABA Standards for Criminal Justice, Providing Defense Services §5-5.3 cmt. (3d ed. 1992). How do these standards compare with the workload of Rick Teissier, the defense attorney in *Peart*? Several states have statutes directing public defenders not to accept additional cases if the heavier caseload would prevent them from providing effective representation. A handful of states have statutes adopting specific annual caseload caps for public defender programs. See N.H. Rev. Stat. §604-B:6; Wash. Rev. Code §10.101.030; Wis. Stat. §977.08(5)(bn).

3. *Volunteer lawyers and conscripted lawyers.* Almost all jurisdictions rely on volunteer attorneys to represent some indigent defendants. Sometimes these attorneys take cases when the public defender organization has a conflict of interest; in other places, the court appoints attorneys for all cases from a list of volunteers. The amount of compensation varies. A volunteer attorney can ordinarily expect some compensation for "overhead" expenses and some reduced compensation for her time. But payment in some systems is discretionary, and the lawyers on the list do not have complete freedom to accept or refuse appointments from the court, depending on schedule and income needs. In a companion case to *Peart,* the Louisiana court in State v. Clark, 624 So. 2d 422 (La. 1993), upheld a contempt finding against an attorney who had refused to accept an appointment to represent a criminal defendant. The attorney, who had placed himself on the volunteer list, had been appointed to five felony cases over a four-month period; he refused to represent the fifth defendant because his private practice was suffering from neglect. The Louisiana court said that attorneys must represent indigents unless a court decides that the appointment is "unreasonable and oppressive," and that these circumstances were not enough to meet the standard. See also State ex rel. Missouri Public Defender Comm'n v. Pratte, 298 S.W.3d 870 (Mo. 2009) (reaffirms traditional power of court to appoint any lawyer in the state to represent indigent criminal defendants, with exception of public defenders, who are prohibited by statute from private practice and therefore cannot be appointed to cases that defender office cannot accept through ordinary means).

Broad-based challenges to appointment systems do not occur routinely. A few systemic lawsuits have produced more funding and better organization for appointed counsel systems, including litigation in New York City. See New York County Lawyer's Ass'n v. State, 763 N.Y.S.2d 397, 400 (N.Y. Sup. 2003). More often, however, courts conclude that the level of compensation at issue, while perhaps in need of an increase, does not create a constitutional problem. See Lewis v. Iowa District Court for Des Moines County, 555 N.W.2d 216 (Iowa 1996). Why are systemic judicial challenges to public defender systems more common than systemic challenges to appointed systems? Do lawyers simply decline to participate in the appointment system (when the choice is theirs) rather than litigate over the adequacy of the compensation?

4. *Judicial and legislative remedies.* The most vexing question in much of the litigation challenging systems for providing defense counsel is the question of remedy. If an attorney is placed in a situation in which effective assistance is difficult or impossible for her to provide, what should the court do? Overturn individual convictions of those who challenge the effectiveness of their attorneys? Order the legislature to provide additional funding? Mandate a minimally acceptable caseload or fee schedule? After *Peart* was decided, the Louisiana legislature created

the Louisiana Indigent Defender Board and gave it a $10 million budget to use for studying problems with indigent defense in the state and for granting operating funds in trouble areas, such as appointment of defense experts in particular cases. It also transferred fiscal responsibility for indigent defense from the parishes to the state. The legislature later cut the budget to $5 million, and it soon became clear that funding from the state would not improve the workload situation for most public defenders. In State v. Citizen, 898 So. 2d 325 (2005), the court reviewed the anemic state funding and ruled that an appointed attorney could file a motion to determine the availability of funds for payment of fees. If the revenue is not available, the judge must order the state to cease its prosecution. Does this aftermath of the *Peart* litigation tell you anything about the remedies a court should impose? Do judicial interventions in indigent defense systems have to occur regularly, say, every 10 years?

5. *Self-help for public defenders*. Sometimes the remedy for inadequate funding of a defense system occurs without any judicial order, when the leaders of a public defense organization refuse to accept additional cases until the caseload on its attorneys becomes lighter. Indeed, ABA guidelines adopted in 2009 call for public defense providers to "file motions asking a court to stop the assignment of new cases and to withdraw from current cases, as may be appropriate, when workloads are excessive and other adequate alternative are unavailable." American Bar Association, Eight Guidelines of Public Defense Related to Excessive Workloads, Guideline 6 (2009). The guidelines also suggest strategies such as arranging for some cases to be assigned to private lawyers, urging prosecutors not to initiate criminal prosecutions when civil remedies are adequate, or negotiating informal arrangements with courts regarding case assignments.

6. *Incentives for aggressive representation*. Which system — public defender organizations, appointed counsel, or contract attorneys — provides an acceptable defense for the least amount of money? The best defense for an acceptable amount of money? There is no single answer to these questions. As the Bureau of Justice Statistics indicates, the funding, staffing, and caseloads for public defender offices vary quite a lot. One often hears the assertion that defender organizations are funded at a level that compels the attorneys to urge their clients to plead guilty in most cases. Is it inevitable that defense attorneys who regularly accept money from the government will, in the long run, moderate their demands on prosecutors, police, and judges?

Some believe that "organizational" defenders are more cost-efficient because they represent many defendants at once and work in criminal justice full time. Thus, legislatures tend to create public defender programs because of potential cost savings. Are public defenders more efficient than appointed counsel, or do they choose certain cases and issues to pursue aggressively while allowing the other cases and clients to suffer from neglect? Would an appointed attorney be better able to represent each client more thoroughly, without trading off one client's needs against those of another? Are attorneys who spend all their time representing criminal defendants in the best position to bring systemwide challenges to the practices of police, prosecutors, or judges?

7. *Funding parity*. If popular support for prosecution of crimes is higher than the support for funding criminal defense, is the answer to require parity of funding between prosecution and defense? How would you accomplish this most effectively — through a constitutional ruling, a statute, or a local ordinance?

There is little doubt that the total resources available for the investigation and prosecution of crime are greater than those available for defending against criminal charges. See David Luban, Are Criminal Defenders Different? 91 Mich. L. Rev. 1729 (1993) (resources for prosecution versus public and private defense counsel may be at roughly comparable levels, but only when ignoring prosecutorial access to police and forensic expert support). If it is true that prosecutors and police combined receive more resources than defense counsel, is that a problem? Perhaps one might respond that prosecutors have more funding because they perform a wider range of functions than defense counsel. For instance, they make screening decisions on cases that are never charged. Alternatively, one might ask whether the increased demands on defense counsel really translate into worse outcomes for clients.

Apart from the question of funding for entire offices, is there any justification for paying individual prosecutors a higher salary than individual defense attorneys? See Ariz. Stat. §11-582 (public defender salary to be at least 70 percent of prosecutor salary); Tenn. Code §16-2-518 ("any increase in local funding for positions or office expense for the district attorney general shall be accompanied by an increase in funding of 75 percent of the increase in funding to the office of the public defender in such district"). For an effort to contrast the "ex post" evaluation of a lawyer's performance under *Strickland* with an "ex ante" evaluation of the resources available to prosecution and defense, see Donald Dripps, Ineffective Assistance of Counsel: The Case for an Ex Ante Parity Standard, 88 J. Crim. L. & Criminology 242-308 (1997); cf. Ronald F. Wright, Parity of Resources for Defense Counsel and the Reach of Public Choice Theory, 90 Iowa L. Rev. 219 (2004).

■ STATE v. DELBERT LYNCH

796 P.2d 1150 (Okla. 1990)

KAUGER, J.

In these cases of first impression, we are asked to decide whether the trial court erred in declaring 21 O.S. Supp. 1985 §701.14 unconstitutional because court appointed counsel were forced to represent indigent defendants without the assurance of receiving adequate, speedy, and certain compensation for such representation. We find that: 1) Although the statute is not facially unconstitutional, it is unconstitutional in application; 2) The present system presses lawyers into service without affording a post-appointment opportunity to show cause why they should not be forced to accept the appointment; and 3) The statute provides an arbitrary and unreasonable rate of compensation for lawyers which may result in an unconstitutional taking of private property depending on the facts of each case. While we recognize the responsibility of members of the Oklahoma bar to assist in the provision of legal representation to indigent defendants, we find that in some instances the arbitrary and unreasonable statutory scheme contravenes the due process clause of the Okla. Const. art. 2, §7. . . .

Two Seminole County lawyers, Jack Mattingly and Rob Pyron, were appointed by the district court to represent Delbert Lynch, an indigent who had been charged with first degree murder. Although the State had sought the death penalty, after a complicated trial, which began on August 21, 1989, and ended on August 31, 1989, the jury rendered a guilty verdict and gave Lynch a life sentence. Following Lynch's sentencing on September 6, 1989, the lawyers petitioned the court for fees and expenses.

At the hearing on counsel fees, Mattingly testified that he had spent 169 hours on the case, and incurred $173.03 in out of pocket expenses, requesting a $17,073.03 fee. Pyron's testimony was that he had expended 109.55 hours on Lynch's behalf, and he sought a $10,995.00 fee. Mattingly submitted a statement documenting his hourly overhead rate for 1986, 1987, 1988, which ranged from $45.80 to $53.53 — averaging $50.88. Pyron submitted his overhead figures for 1988, reflecting an average hourly rate of $48.00. Had the two lawyers split the maximum statutory fee of $3,200, Mattingly would have received $9.47 per hour, with Pyron receiving $14.61 per hour. Based on these computations, Mattingly would lose $41.41 and Pyron would lose $33.39 in overhead expenses for every hour that they worked on the defense. These figures do not reflect any compensation for the attorneys' services. The trial court approved the requested fees, finding that the $3,200 restriction on attorney fees was unconstitutional. . . .

The parties do not dispute that Oklahoma is required to provide attorneys for indigent defendants who are charged in Oklahoma courts with felonies, certain misdemeanors, competency to stand trial, contempt proceedings, and guardianship matters, or that the State of Oklahoma has attempted to provide such representation. The basic concern is not with the constitutional requirements of the Okla. Const. art. 2, §20, or the public policy which requires representation of indigent defendants; but, rather, with the practical application of the public policy and its impairment of constitutionally guaranteed private property rights. The State asserts that compensation should only exceed the statutory limit when extraordinary circumstances are shown as established in Bias v. State, 568 P.2d 1269 (Okla. 1977), and that an unconstitutional taking does not occur when a court-appointed attorney is required to represent indigent defendants.

The Okla. Const. art. 2, §7 provides that "No person shall be deprived of life, liberty, or property without due process of law." The lawyers contend that under this constitutional provision mandatory representation without just compensation is unconstitutional. The Oklahoma Constitution . . . also requires that competent counsel be provided for indigent defendants. [A] criminal defendant has a fundamental right to the reasonably effective assistance of counsel, regardless of whether counsel is appointed or retained. This means a lawyer must render the same obligations of loyalty, confidentiality, and competence to a court-appointed client as a retained client would receive. Oklahoma has fulfilled the constitutional requirement of competent counsel by utilizing public defenders' offices, voluntary pools, and court appointments. In order for the system to work, a balance must be maintained between the lawyer's [professional obligations], an indigent's fundamental right to counsel, and the avoidance of state action tantamount to confiscation of a lawyer's practice.

To achieve an appropriate balance of constitutional interests the rights of both the indigent defendant and the lawyer must be protected. Here, the constitutional right of the indigent to counsel is not at issue — the due process rights of appointed counsel for indigent defendants are. Although it is obvious that while Oklahoma's statutorily mandated cap may not be facially defective, and that in some instances payment of the statutory fee might even be an excessive rate of compensation, there is a substantial probability that it will be defective in application. Here, it is apparent that the maximum statutory fee is inadequate to compensate the lawyers who represented Lynch.[13]

In Bias v. State, a lawyer had been compelled both to subsidize indigent representation and to forsake his regular law practice during the representation of the indigent defendant. The *Bias* Court recognized that such circumstances may constitute a taking of private property without compensation. In order to harmonize conflicting interests, the Court authorized payment in excess of the statutorily prescribed norms for extraordinary expenditures of time and expense. . . .

Clearly, there is a substantial risk of the erroneous deprivation of property rights under the current appointment system. A lawyer's skills and services are his/her only means of livelihood. The taking thereof, without adequate compensation, is analogous to taking the goods of merchants or requiring free services of architects, engineers, accountants, physicians, nurses or of one of the 34 other occupations or professions in this state which require a person to be licensed before practicing the occupation or profession. None of the licensing statutes require that the members of those professions donate their skills and services to the public. We know that many of these professionals do so. We also know that it would be unusual for the various licensing boards to force their licensees to proffer their services to indigents or to offer cut-rate prices on haircuts, perms, embalming, dentures, or surgeries. . . .

Nevertheless, we also recognize that a lawyer's calling is different from that of other licensed professions. We are a government of laws and not of men and women. At the foundation of this republic is the respect for enforcement of the law in a neutral way. The services of competent counsel are necessary to insure that our system of justice functions smoothly, that justice is dispensed even handedly, and that the rights and interests of indigent defendants are safeguarded in a truly adversarial forum. A lawyer is weighted with responsibility which is uncommon to the ordinary professional, and as a member of the integrated bar, an Oklahoma lawyer has a duty to the oath of office, to the Courts, to his/her clients, and to the public at large to be more than a tradesperson.

Procedural due process of law requires adequate notice, a realistic opportunity to appear at a hearing, and the right to participate in a meaningful manner before one's rights are irretrievably altered. We find that in order to provide safeguards which will bring the system into compliance with due process, trial courts must proffer a post-appointment opportunity for the lawyer to appear and to show cause without penalty, why he/she should not be appointed to represent an indigent defendant. [This is] in accord with the Model Rules of Professional Conduct, 5 O.S. Supp. 1988 Ch.1, App. 3-A, Rule 6.2 and the committee comments thereto, which provide that a lawyer may refuse an appointment for the representation of an indigent upon a showing of good cause.

13. The maximum statutory fee set by the legislature is: 1) in capital cases, $200 for services rendered before the preliminary hearing, $500 for services rendered during the preliminary hearing, $2,500 for services rendered from the time the defendant is bound over until final disposition in the trial court; 2) in other criminal cases, the fee is not to exceed $500; 3) in juvenile and guardianship cases, the fee is not to exceed $100 in a preliminary hearing, $500 if the cause goes to trial and $100 for post-disposition hearings. . . .

We find that good cause consists of, but is not limited to the following factors: 1) the lawyer is not qualified to provide competent representation; 2) the representation will result in a conflict of interest; and 3) the case is so repugnant to the lawyer that it would impair either the attorney-client relationship or the lawyer's ability to represent the client. Title 5 O.S. Supp. 1988 Ch. 1, App. 3-A, Rule 6.2. We also find that Rule 1.16 of the Model Rules of Professional Conduct, 5 O.S. Supp. 1988 Ch. 1, App. 3-A, is applicable to all client representation, and that it should be construed with the "good cause" factors. This rule provides that a lawyer may refuse to represent a client if: 1) the representation would violate the Rules of Professional Conduct or other law; 2) the lawyer's physical or mental condition materially impairs the lawyer's representation of the client; 3) the client persists in conduct involving the lawyer's service which the lawyer believes is criminal or fraudulent; 4) the client has used the lawyer's services to perpetrate a crime or fraud; or 5) the client discharges the lawyer. . . .

For all practical purposes [Oklahoma statutes] exempt attorneys in counties which have public defenders' offices from representing indigent defendants in state courts. Lawyers in these counties are subject to appointment only when a conflict of interest arises in the public defender's office. Currently, these attorneys are neither faced with impending financial disaster nor forced to ignore their practice in order to provide effective counsel for an indigent. Except in rare circumstances, these attorneys have been granted an "immunity" by the legislature. . . . Because lawyers who practice in certain counties are immunized from the representation of indigent defendants, not all Oklahoma lawyers are treated equally. [D]iscrimination between attorneys who may be forced to represent indigent defendants based solely on the population of the county in which they practice law is unconstitutional under any level of scrutiny. . . .

We applaud individual attorneys or associations of attorneys who volunteer to provide either pro bono legal representation or representation of indigent defendants at rates which may be drastically under the market value of the lawyers' skills and services. It reflects pride in the practice of law, and it exemplifies the best of many virtues found in the practicing bar. The provision of legal services to indigents is one of the responsibilities assumed by the legal profession, and personal involvement in the problems of the disadvantaged can be one of the most rewarding experiences in the life of a lawyer.

Every lawyer, regardless of professional prominence or professional workload, should find time to participate in or otherwise support the provision of legal services to the disadvantaged. We strongly urge the continuation of these services. We believe that attorneys would voluntarily donate their skills and services were they not unduly burdened with compulsory appointments. We also believe that Oklahoma lawyers will form local, county, district, and intrastate voluntary pools to assume this responsibility and to relieve lawyers who practice in counties with few lawyers from an unfair court-imposed case load. We also recognize that at this time voluntary services are insufficient to accommodate the right of indigent citizens to the effective assistance of counsel where that right is implicated.

[The State] has an obligation to pay appointed lawyers sums which will fairly compensate the lawyer, not at the top rate which a lawyer might charge, but at a rate which is not confiscatory, after considering overhead and expenses. The basis of the amount to be paid for services must not vary with each judge; rather there must be a statewide basis or scale for ascertaining a reasonable hourly rate in order to avoid the enactment of a proscribed special law.

Although we invite legislative attention to this problem, in the interim, we must establish guides which will apply uniformly without either violating due process rights or granting constitutional immunities. *Bias* provided some relief to Oklahoma lawyers; however, it did not address the constitutional infirmities which are squarely presented here. Therefore, in order to correct the defects which render the present statutory scheme unconstitutional, we must build on the foundation which was laid in *Bias.* We find that the most even handed approach in setting fees is to tie the hourly rate of the counsel appointed for the indigent defendant to the hourly rate of the prosecutor/district attorney and the public defenders.

[A]ll district attorneys receive the same salary — $56,180 per year or $29.26 per hour. We find that the trial court may award the attorney from $14.63 to $29.26 based on the attorney's qualifications. This range is tied to the salary range paid to assistant district attorneys and the district attorneys. (As a matter of course, when the district attorneys' and public defenders' salaries are raised by the Legislature so, too, would the hourly rate of compensation for defense counsel.) The overhead and the litigation expense of the district attorney are furnished by the state. In order to place the counsel for the defense on an equal footing with counsel for the prosecution, provision must be made for compensation of defense counsel's reasonable overhead and out of pocket expenses.

However, before the lawyer can be compensated for overhead, the percentage of reasonable hourly overhead rate directly attributable to the case in controversy, and the amount of out-of-pocket expenses incurred, must be presented to the trial court. . . . To receive payment for the reasonable overhead, attorney fees, and out of pocket expenses charged to the case, the lawyer must present accurate itemizations of overhead expenditures, time sheets, and invoices to support the number of hours reasonably spent on the defense.

Mattingly and Pyron have complied with the guidelines we are establishing. Were this not so, we would remand for further proceedings. We find that they are seasoned lawyers who should be paid an hourly rate of $29.26 per hour; that the average overhead rate and out of pocket expenses presented are reasonable; and that the lawyers spent the time alleged in the pursuit of Lynch's defense.

[T]he provision of counsel for indigent defendants, and the compensation of such counsel also lie within the Legislative sphere, and its consideration of the myriad problems presented is invited. This is an important area, which the Legislature should act to address. Nevertheless, until such time as the Legislature considers these matters . . . these guidelines shall become effective [immediately] in all cases in which the State of Oklahoma is required to provide assistance of counsel, insofar as the appointment of counsel and the implementation of post-appointment show cause hearings are concerned. [R]ecovery of attorney fees under the new guidelines will not be effective in non-capital cases until August 24, 1992, to allow the Legislature to address the problem, and to enact corrective legislation.

DOOLIN, J., dissenting.

The present traditional method of compensation and appointment of competent counsel to represent indigent defendants has worked well and existed in the

British Colonial system when John Adams represented the British Troops who perpetrated the Boston Massacre, not to mention the example of Abe Fortas when he sounded *Gideon*'s trumpet in "Modern Times." I dissent.

SIMMS, J., dissenting.

Under our system of criminal jurisprudence, a licensed attorney finds himself in a very unique position. That lawyer is an officer of the court. And as such, is bound to render service when required by his or her appointment to represent an indigent defendant. However, he is not [an] "officer" within the ordinary meaning of that term. An attorney is not in the same category as marshals, bailiffs, court clerks or judges. A lawyer is engaged in a private profession, important though it be to our system of justice. [B]ecause of this unique relationship a lawyer enjoys with our system of criminal justice, fulfilling his legally recognized duty to render services when required by an appointment to represent an indigent defendant, cannot to me, be described in most instances in terms of a taking of his "property" without due process of law. . . .

We should direct the Legislature's attention to the Criminal Justice Act which the Congress of the United States enacted, titled "Adequate Representation of Defendants." . . . The federal act further provides for a uniform hourly rate for time expended in court or before a magistrate and a uniform hourly rate for time expended out of court. I would submit that enactment of a state statute closely paralleling [the federal act] might be a simple and direct answer to the problems raised by the majority opinion in this case. We should emphasize that the solutions to these problems are within the expertise and proper power of the Legislature and not this Court.

HODGES, J., concurring specially.

. . . I write separately to state that today's decision is merely a stopgap measure to remedy constitutional infirmities in the present system. The legislature is free to adopt any solution that is consistent with the Oklahoma and United States Constitutions. . . .

Dramatic changes have impaired the traditional method of compensation and appointment of counsel to represent indigent defendants. Recent years have witnessed increased complexity, specialization, and costs in criminal defense work. Added to this, the "War on Drugs" is fueling a dramatic increase in the number of criminal cases heaped upon an already heavily burdened system. These exacerbating factors have led to the emerging view that the responsibility to provide the Sixth Amendment right to counsel is a public responsibility that is not to be borne entirely by the private bar. . . . It is up to the Legislature to fulfill that obligation.

OPALA, V.C.J., concurring in part and dissenting in part.

. . . I join in concluding that the regime of assigning lawyers for criminal defense work in counties which are without public defender services is tainted by a constitutional infirmity. I recede from the court's interim institutional design that is to govern until the legislature overhauls the system. In my view, the whole scheme is affected by a fatal and incurable flaw. It saddles the judiciary with the responsibility of operating defense services in 75 counties — a function properly to be performed by the executive department. Until the legislature establishes a professionally independent statewide public defender system within the executive department, I would, merely as a stopgap measure, (1) develop guidelines that would equalize, on a statewide basis, the Bar's burden for providing defense services in those 75 counties and (2) call upon the Oklahoma Bar Association [hereafter called the Bar] to manage a statewide service pool of qualified lawyers for deployment in criminal as well as other mandated public-service work. . . .

The law must insulate from anyone's interference — judicial, legislative or executive — all aspects of a public defender's attorney/client relationship. The litigation-related strategy choices, as well as any other facet of professional decision-making in the conduct of a person's defense, must be beyond the pale of outsiders' meddling. Nevertheless, the essence of the service to be provided is correctly characterized as extraneous to the judicial or legislative function and akin to that of the executive. It is the executive's responsibility to seek reversal-proof convictions in judicial tribunals properly constituted to administer that standard of adjudicative process which conforms to the dictates of our fundamental law. In short, in the aftermath of *Gideon* and its progeny, defense, as much as prosecution, is an essential component of government service for the enforcement of criminal laws. . . .

■ AMERICAN BAR ASSOCIATION, MODEL RULE OF PROFESSIONAL CONDUCT 1.5(d)

A lawyer shall not enter into an arrangement for, charge, or collect . . . a contingent fee for representing a defendant in a criminal case.

Problem 11-7. Flat Fees for Service

From 1967 to 1988, the Detroit Recorder's Court used an "event based" fee system to compensate counsel assigned to represent indigent criminal defendants. Under this system, a separate fee was paid for pre-preliminary examination jail visits, preliminary examinations, two post-preliminary examination jail visits, investigation and trial preparation, written motions filed and heard, calendar conferences, arraignments on the information, final conferences, evidentiary hearings, pleas, and forensic hearings. The system also provided compensation for each day of trial necessary to dispose of any particular case, and for counsel appearances in court for sentencing of the defendant.

In an effort to reduce jail overcrowding, a jail oversight committee studied the Recorder's Court and found a direct correlation between jail bed demand and the length of the criminal docket. The committee concluded that a substantial savings in jail bed demand could be recognized by reducing the time between a defendant's arrest and the ultimate disposition of the case. The committee was concerned that the event-based system gave assigned counsel an incentive to prolong final disposition of cases to earn a larger fee.

The committee asked the clerk of the Detroit Recorder's Court to devise a compensation system that would promote docket efficiency without reducing the overall level of compensation paid to assigned counsel. A statistical analysis revealed that attorneys tended to perform more "events" for clients who faced charges punishable by longer prison terms. The clerk grouped all assigned cases for the previous two years by potential maximum sentence and averaged the fees paid in each group of cases. The clerk then proposed a fee system that would pay attorneys a flat fee for representing a defendant, regardless of the number of "events" the attorney performed. Assigned counsel would be entitled to the full fee, regardless of whether the case is dismissed at the preliminary examination, the defendant pleads guilty at the arraignment on the information, or the case is ultimately disposed of after a jury trial. The flat fee would vary for different types of offenses and would reflect the average fees paid for defending such cases under the old system. The fixed rates would range from $475 for a 24-month maximum crime to $1,400 for a first-degree murder case.

The local court adopted the fixed fee system, and it succeeded in speeding up the docket. By shortening the time between arrest and disposition, the system alleviated some of the pressure for more jail space. A lawyer could earn $100 an hour for a guilty plea, typically three to four hours of work. If she went to trial the earnings could be $15 an hour or less. Prosecutors also noted a decrease in the number of "frivolous" defense motions and increased pressure from the defense bar for the prosecutor to dismiss weak cases at an earlier stage.

The fee system permits assigned counsel to petition the chief judge of the Recorder's Court for payment of extraordinary fees in cases requiring above-average effort. However, undercompensated attorneys have hesitated to petition for extraordinary fees, believing that such requests would either prove futile or perhaps even adversely affect their prospects of receiving future assignments. While more than 3,000 indigent criminal defense assignments were made in the Court during 1989, only 29 petitions were filed for extraordinary fees, of which 23 were granted, totaling $11,175. This is approximately 1.6 percent of the total indigent attorney fees paid for that year.

In Michigan, assigned counsel have a statutory right to compensation for providing criminal defense services to the indigent. The controlling statute provides that the chief judge "shall appoint" an attorney "to conduct the accused's examination and to conduct the accused's defense." The attorney appointed "shall be entitled to receive from the county treasurer, on the certificate of the chief judge that the services have been rendered, the amount which the chief judge considers to be reasonable compensation for the services performed." Mich. Comp. Laws §775.16. Does the fixed fee system provide assigned counsel "reasonable compensation for the services performed"? Does it violate indigent defendants' right to effective assistance of counsel? Compare Recorder's Court Bar Ass'n. v. Wayne Circuit Court, 503 N.W.2d 885 (Mich. 1993).

Problem 11-8. The Neighborhood Defender

The Neighborhood Defender Service (NDS) of Harlem created a new method of organizing public defense resources. The differences between NDS and the more typical public defender's office were manifest in the outreach efforts of the office, the range of legal services offered to clients, and the assignment of staff to clients.

Rather than placing its offices in one location near the courthouse, NDS placed several offices around the community to make the organization more visible and available to its clients. The service also placed posters, business cards, and other outreach devices in the community so that people in the neighborhood would be familiar with the service before they or their family members needed legal representation in a criminal matter. NDS hoped that this would help attorneys establish a relationship with their clients earlier in the criminal process and would give clients more reason to trust and cooperate with their attorneys.

NDS also shifted its focus from trial to the early stages of cases (sometimes even before arrest), emphasizing investigation and early resolution of charges. Through mediation, attorneys in NDS could sometimes resolve conflicts between victims and defendants, leading the victim to ask the prosecutor to drop charges. The service also continued to advise clients after conviction, to avoid problems during probation or parole. On occasion, NDS would represent clients or their family members in civil matters closely connected to a criminal charge (for instance, possible eviction from public housing based on drug trafficking charges).

As for assignment of staff to the clients, NDS moved away from the typical arrangement of placing one attorney alone in charge of a proportional share of cases the office receives. Each NDS client is represented by a team, consisting of a lead attorney, secondary attorneys, community workers, an investigator, and an administrative assistant. Each NDS attorney is assigned to more total cases than he would handle alone under the traditional arrangement, but the attorneys share the workload on each of the cases. If a client ever has a second case, the same team handles the client's case again. The strategy is to assign more tasks to nonlawyers and to ensure continuity of representation over time and more widespread responsibility for making early progress on the cases.

Is this organizational model for public defender services likely to work in many different communities? If not, what are the conditions necessary for a neighborhood defender service to succeed? See National Inst. of Justice, Public Defenders in the Neighborhood: A Harlem Law Office Stresses Teamwork, Early Investigation (1997, NCJ 163061).

Notes

1. *Legal challenges to adequacy of payments to appointed lawyers*. Lawyers raising constitutional challenges to the adequacy of payments for their work as appointed or contract counsel in individual criminal cases have found modest but consistent success. Courts do sometimes recognize that lawyers can be asked to perform enough services for so little compensation that a due process or takings clause violation occurs. See State v. Young, 172 P.3d 138 (N.M. 2007) (fees in complex capital case amounted to less than $73 per hour; court ruled the compensation inadequate and presumed ineffectiveness without inquiry into actual performance). The challenge could also be based on a violation of the client's constitutional right to counsel or on violations of the ethical obligations of attorneys. See People v. Doolin, 198 P.3d 11 (Calif. 2009) (rejecting capital defendant's claim that county's compensation system for appointed counsel violated state constitutional right to conflict-free counsel by allowing attorney to keep any funds from flat fee not spent on defense).

2. *Contingent fees*. Would private defense attorneys be more willing to represent criminal defendants if they could make contingent fee arrangements with their clients, calling for different levels of compensation depending on the outcome of the proceedings? The ABA standard reprinted above, barring the use of contingent fees in criminal cases, reflects the law of all the states. Why are contingent fees prohibited in criminal cases when they have been such an effective method (some might

say too effective) for providing counsel to civil litigants? For further reading, see Pamela Karlan, Contingent Fees and Criminal Cases, 93 Colum. L. Rev. 595 (1993).

3. *Challenges to contract attorney systems: majority position.* In contract attorney programs, the government (typically at the county level) agrees with a private law firm, bar association, or nonprofit organization to provide indigent defense. The contract may cover all criminal cases or specific classes of cases (such as all juvenile cases or adult cases in which the public defender's office has a conflict of interest). These contracts become especially attractive in jurisdictions where the costs of appointed attorneys have increased. For instance, Oklahoma turned to lowest-bidder contract providers after the *Lynch* case was decided.

The method of pricing the services is the difficult issue. Some jurisdictions use a fixed price contract, in which the provider agrees to perform defense services at the stated price, regardless of the number of cases that actually arise. Although this method of setting the contract amount is relatively common, it has only rarely been challenged on constitutional grounds. In State v. Smith, 681 P.2d 1374 (Ariz. 1984), a defendant convicted of burglary argued that he was denied effective assistance of counsel because of his attorney's "shocking, staggering and unworkable" caseload, which was the product of a fixed price contract. The county had granted the contract to the lowest bidder, but the contract did not allow for support costs such as investigators, paralegals, and secretaries and did not consider the experience or competence of the attorney. Smith's attorney handled a "part time" caseload of 149 felonies, 160 misdemeanors, 21 juvenile cases, and 33 other cases in the year Smith was convicted, in addition to a private civil practice. The court therefore found that the bid system violated the rights of defendants to due process and the right to counsel. Would a government avoid these problems by entering a contract that pays a fixed fee per case?

The American Bar Association's Criminal Justice Standards discourage local governments from awarding an indigent-services contract based on a fixed price for a time period. The standards recommend that contracts include detailed information about minimum attorney qualifications, attorney workloads, use of support services, and so forth. ABA Standards for Criminal Justice, Providing Defense Services §5-3.3(b) (3d ed. 1992). Will a contracting government be able to follow these standards and still obtain the predictability of legal expenses so necessary to government budgeting and administration?

E. THE ETHICS OF DEFENDING CRIMINALS

If you are a defense lawyer, you may often hear the question, "how can you defend those people?" Should all lawyers be required to defend criminals, regardless of the crime of which the defendant is accused or the lawyer's view of the defendant's guilt? The following selections represent a range of time-honored answers to this question. As you read them, try to come up with a short phrase to describe the position suggested in each passage. Which of the positions reflects the current mainstream of thought among American lawyers? Among law students? What are the institutional and ethical implications of each position?

■ SPEECHES OF LORD ERSKINE
(James High ed., 1876)

In every place where business or pleasure collects the public together, day after day, my name and character have been the topics of injurious reflection.* And for what? Only for not having shrunk from the discharge of a duty which no personal advantage recommended, but which a thousand difficulties repelled. Little indeed did they know me, who thought that such calumnies would influence my conduct. I will forever, at all hazards assert the dignity, independence and integrity of the English Bar, without which impartial justice, the most valuable part of the English Constitution, can have no existence. From the moment that any advocate can be permitted to say that he will or will not stand between the Crown and the subject arraigned in the court where he daily sits to practice, from that moment the liberties of England are at an end. If the advocate refuses to defend, from what he may think of the charge or of the defense, he assumes the character of the judge; nay he assumes it before the hour of judgment; and in proportion to his rank and reputation puts the heavy influence of perhaps a mistaken opinion into the scale against the accused in whose favor the benevolent principles of English law makes all presumptions. . . .

■ JOHN DOS PASSOS, THE AMERICAN LAWYER
158 (1907)

I do not place the right of the lawyer to defend a client when he believes him to be guilty upon the ground that he cannot know that his client is guilty until his guilt has been officially and finally declared by a court and jury, because he often does know, in the sense that he has a moral conviction of the guilt of his client which he has derived through the ordinary channels of information. I place the right of the lawyer upon the ground that he is an officer of the law, and that it is his *duty* to see that the forms of law are carried out, quite irrespective of individual knowledge.

AMERICAN BAR ASSOCIATION AND ASSOCIATION OF AMERICAN LAW SCHOOLS, PROFESSIONAL RESPONSIBILITY: REPORT OF THE JOINT CONFERENCE (1958)

The Joint Conference on Professional Responsibility* was established in 1952 by the American Bar Association and the Association of American Law Schools. [T]hose who had attempted to teach ethical principles to law students found that the students were uneasy about the adversary system, some thinking of it as an unwholesome compromise with the combativeness of human nature, others vaguely approving of it but disturbed by their inability to articulate its proper limits. . . . Confronted by the layman's charge that he is nothing but a hired brain and voice, the lawyer often finds it difficult to convey an insight into the value of the adversary system. . . .

* [Lord Erskine was defense counsel for Thomas Paine, the influential pamphleteer. — Eds.]
* [The conference was chaired by Lon Fuller and John Randall. — Eds.]

Accordingly, it was decided that the first need was for a reasoned statement of the lawyer's responsibilities, set in the context of the adversary system. . . .

THE LAWYER'S ROLE AS ADVOCATE IN OPEN COURT

The lawyer appearing as an advocate before a tribunal presents, as persuasively as he can, the facts and the law of the case as seen from the standpoint of his client's interest. . . . In a very real sense it may be said that the integrity of the adjudicative process itself depends upon the participation of the advocate. This becomes apparent when we contemplate the nature of the task assumed by any arbiter who attempts to decide a dispute without the aid of partisan advocacy.

Such an arbiter must undertake, not only the role of judge, but that of representative for both of the litigants. Each of these roles must be played to the full without being muted by qualifications derived from the others. When he is developing for each side the most effective statement of its case, the arbiter must put aside his neutrality and permit himself to be moved by a sympathetic identification. . . . When he resumes his neutral position, he must be able to view with distrust the fruits of this identification and be ready to reject the products of his own best mental efforts. The difficulties of this undertaking are obvious. If it is true that a man in his time must play many parts, it is scarcely given to him to play them all at once.

It is small wonder, then, that failure generally attends the attempt to dispense with the distinct roles traditionally implied in adjudication. What generally occurs in practice is that at some early point a familiar pattern will seem to emerge from the evidence; an accustomed label is waiting for the case and, without further proofs, this label is promptly assigned to it. [W]hat starts as a preliminary diagnosis designed to direct the inquiry tends, quickly and imperceptibly, to become a fixed conclusion, as all that confirms the diagnosis makes a strong imprint on the mind, while all that runs counter to it is received with diverted attention.

An adversary presentation seems the only effective means for combating this natural human tendency to judge too swiftly in terms of the familiar that which is not yet fully known. The arguments of counsel hold the case, as it were, in suspension between two opposing interpretations of it. While the proper classification of the case is thus kept unresolved, there is time to explore all of its peculiarities and nuances. . . .

Viewed in this light, the role of the lawyer as a partisan advocate appears not as a regrettable necessity, but as an indispensable part of a larger ordering of affairs. The institution of advocacy is not a concession to the frailties of human nature, but an expression of human insight in the design of a social framework within which man's capacity for impartial judgment can attain its fullest realization. . . .

THE REPRESENTATION OF UNPOPULAR CAUSES

One of the highest services the lawyer can render to society is to appear in court on behalf of clients whose causes are in disfavor with the general public. . . . Where a cause is in disfavor because of a misunderstanding by the public, the service of the lawyer representing it is obvious, since he helps to remove an obloquy unjustly attaching to his client's position. But the lawyer renders an equally important, though less readily understood, service where the unfavorable public opinion of the client's cause is in fact justified. It is essential for a sound and wholesome development of public opinion that the disfavored cause have its full day in court, which includes, of necessity, representation by competent counsel. Where this does not occur, a fear arises that perhaps more might have been said for the losing side and suspicion is cast on the decision reached. Thus, confidence in the fundamental processes of government is diminished.

The extent to which the individual lawyer should feel himself bound to undertake the representation of unpopular causes must remain a matter for individual conscience. The legal profession as a whole, however, has a clear moral obligation with respect to this problem. . . . No member of the Bar should indulge in public criticism of another lawyer because he has undertaken the representation of causes in general disfavor. Every member of the profession should, on the contrary, do what he can to promote a public understanding of the service rendered by the advocate in such situations. . . .

These are problems each lawyer must solve in his own way. But in solving them he will remember, with Whitehead, that moral education cannot be complete without the habitual vision of greatness. And he will recall the concluding words of a famous essay by Holmes:

> Happiness, I am sure from having known many successful men, cannot be won simply by being counsel for great corporations and having an income of fifty thousand dollars. An intellect great enough to win the prize needs other food besides success. The remoter and more general aspects of the law are those which give it universal interest. It is through them that you not only become a great master in your calling, but connect your subject with the universe and catch an echo of the infinite, a glimpse of its unfathomable process, a hint of the universal law.

■ JOHN KAPLAN, DEFENDING GUILTY PEOPLE

7 U. Bridgeport L. Rev. 223 (1986)

I would like to address an often asked, many times answered, but still extremely complex question: Why would lawyers want to defend guilty people? I will try to do so by examining first a somewhat different issue: Why should society as a whole want guilty people to be represented by lawyers? . . . The first means of approach is to ask two related questions: "Why do we want lawyers to represent criminal defendants at all?" and, second, "How does this rationale change in the case when we know that the defendant is guilty?" . . .

The first of the questions seems simple, but there are three quite different reasons why we wish those accused of crimes to be defended by lawyers. The most obvious reason is that defense lawyers improve the accuracy of the fact-finding process in which they are engaged. Many people may dispute this, since over the years the adversary system has played, at best, to mixed reviews. . . . Often it was said that a system where each of the two sides was trying to put something over on the decision maker was a crazy method of deciding important questions. . . .

The second major reason why we want defendants in criminal cases to be defended by counsel is much more complex. [The] basic idea is that one major characteristic of the due process model of criminal litigation is the use of the criminal process to check and regulate its own institutions. Thus, in a particular case, the defendant's lawyer will litigate much more than whether the defendant has violated a particular law with the appropriate state of mind. The lawyer also will be making sure that the arms of the state have complied with the many legal rules which bind them. . . .

The third major reason for providing an attorney for those accused of crimes involves the symbolic statement that it makes about us and our society; it is a multifaceted statement. It says that we are a compassionate people and that in our society even the worst off (and it is hard to think of any who, as a class, are worse off than those accused of crimes) are entitled to have one person in their corner to help them. It underlines the value we place upon equality, because though lawyers vary considerably in their ability to manipulate our complex system of jury trials, their variation is far less than that among criminal defendants. [Our] trial system makes the statement that in our society the individual has rights against the state which can actually be enforced through the legal system. . . .

Next we move to the second question — which of these three reasons for having the defendant represented by an attorney no longer applies when we know that the defendant is guilty. [It] seems that only the first reason, improving the accuracy of the fact-finding process, loses its force. Of course, when the defendant is by hypothesis guilty, we need not worry about the accuracy of the process by which this is determined.

With respect to the second reason, checking the operation of the institutions of the criminal law, most of the checks are expected to apply where the accused is guilty of the crimes charged. . . . There is a thin line between arguing that a defendant is innocent — a matter that goes to fact-finding — and arguing that the police and prosecutors improperly brought the case on insufficient evidence — a matter involving the checking function.

The closeness of these two functions at this point is also seen when we adopt a dynamic, rather than a static, view of the criminal process. We must remember that when prosecutors and police do their jobs well, they do so in part because of the discipline imposed upon them by the fact that they will have to prove their case against a defendant represented by a lawyer. If that should cease, it may be impossible to guarantee that the police and prosecutors will continue at the same level of competence, energy, and integrity. The perhaps apocryphal example of a mountain village may be instructive: it is said that the town fathers took down the "dangerous curve ahead" sign because no one had gone off the road there. They had therefore concluded that the curve was no longer dangerous.

The fact that innocent defendants may benefit from some applications of the checking function, such as those related to the strength of the prosecution's case, might lead to the argument that at least as to these applications, the checking function should not be applied where the defendant is guilty. So far as the checking function is concerned, a defense lawyer is unnecessary in those cases where we know that the defendant is guilty. If enough innocent defendants went to trial so that we could perform the checking function adequately in their cases, why should a lawyer do so on behalf of one who is guilty? The problem . . . is that our criminal justice system is so heavily structured to produce guilty pleas that there may not be enough innocent defendants going to trial to raise the inadequacies of the police and prosecutorial screening in their cases. . . .

Similarly, the third major reason for having attorneys represent criminal defendants is not affected by whether the defendant is guilty. Indeed, the symbolic value of having an attorney represent a defendant may even be increased when we know the accused is guilty. The statement, then, becomes that much louder that the rights of those defendants whose guilt has not been officially and fairly determined are so fixed and important that, even if we knew they were guilty, these rights would remain. . . .

The last question we need to ask is, "Why would anyone want to make a living this way?" The answer to that question involves a very different kind of discourse, but my answer is simple. The question should not be asked. It is important to remember that, for one reason or another, criminal lawyers want to defend criminal defendants. Their taste may be as baffling to us as is the proctologist's, but we need both and should not try to dissuade either from pursuing his or her profession. Instead, we ought to encourage both because, whether they realize it or not — or even care — they are doing exactly what we want them to do.

■ AARON CUTLER, IS A LAWYER BOUND TO SUPPORT AN UNJUST CAUSE? A PROBLEM OF ETHICS

300-302 (1952)

The layman's question which has most tormented the lawyer over the years is: "How can you honestly stand up and defend a man you know to be guilty?" [Advocates] enjoy reciting the following colloquy attributed to Samuel Johnson by his famous biographer, James Boswell:

> *Boswell:* But what do you think of supporting a cause which you know to be bad?
>
> *Johnson:* Sir, you do not know it to be good or bad till the Judge determines it. You are to state facts clearly; so that your thinking, or what you call knowing, a cause to be bad must be from reasoning, must be from supposing your arguments to be weak and inconclusive. But Sir, that is not enough. An argument which does not convince yourself may convince the judge to whom you urge it; and if it does convince him, why then, sir, you are wrong and he is right. . . .
>
> *Boswell:* But, Sir, does not affecting a warmth when you have no warmth, and appearing to be clearly of one opinion when you are in reality of another opinion, does not such dissimulation impair one's honesty? Is there not some danger that a lawyer may put on the same mask in common life in the intercourse with his friends?
>
> *Johnson:* Why, no, Sir. Everybody knows you are paid for affecting warmth for your client, and it is therefore properly no dissimulation: the moment you come from the Bar you resume your usual behaviour. Sir, a man will no more carry the artifice of the Bar into the common intercourse of society, than a man who is paid for tumbling upon his hands will continue to tumble on his hands when he should walk upon his feet. . . .

Such an attitude we submit entirely overlooks the bifurcated roles of a lawyer. The duty is not simply one which he owes his client. Just as important is the duty which the lawyer owes the court and society. Great as is his loyalty to the client, even greater is his sacred obligation as an officer of the court. He cannot ethically, and should not by preference, present to the court assertions he knows to be false. . . .

It is only when a lawyer really believes his client is innocent that he should undertake to defend him. All our democratic safeguards are thrown about a person accused of a crime so that no innocent man may suffer. Guilty defendants, though they are entitled to be defended sincerely and hopefully, should not be entitled to the presentation of false testimony and insincere statements by counsel.

It is too glibly said a lawyer should not judge his own client and that the court's province would thus be invaded. In more than 90 percent of all criminal cases a lawyer knows when his client is guilty or not guilty. The facts usually stand out with glaring and startling simplicity.

If a lawyer knows his client to be guilty, it is his duty in such case to set out the extenuating facts and plead for mercy in which the lawyer sincerely believes. In the infrequent number of cases where there is doubt of the client's guilt and the lawyer sincerely believes his client is innocent, he of course should plead his client's cause to the best of his ability.

In civil cases, the area of doubt is undoubtedly considerably greater. At a guess, only one-third [of] the cases presented to a lawyer are pure black or pure white. In only one-third of the cases does the lawyer indubitably know his client is wrong or right. In the other two-thirds gray is the predominant color. It is the duty of the advocate to appraise the client's cause in his favor, after giving due consideration to the facts on the other side. In such a case, it is of course the duty of the advocate to present his client's case to the best of his ability. . . .

A lawyer should worship truth and fact. He should unhesitatingly cast out the evil spirits of specious reasoning, of doubtful claims, of incredible or improbable premises. Truly, the best persuader is one who has first really persuaded himself after a careful analysis of the facts that he is on the right side. Some assert that lawyers must be actors. That is only partially true. An actor can portray abysmal grief or ecstatic happiness without having any such corresponding feeling in his own heart. A young actor can well portray the tragedy of King Lear, though his face is unwrinkled and unmarred after his make-up is removed. [But the] true lawyer can only be persuasive when he honestly believes he is right. . . .

Whatever the situation was in Johnson's day, there should be no artifice at the Bar. Nor should a man "resume his usual behaviour" the moment he comes from the Bar. The lawyer's usual behavior both in his office, and at the Bar and in Society, should be that of a man of probity, integrity and absolute dependability.

The argument that a lawyer should be a mouthpiece for his client, indelicate as that connotation may be, is specious and only logical to a limited extent. A lawyer should not be merely a mechanical apparatus reproducing the words and thoughts and alibis of his client, no matter how insincere or dishonest. Rather the lawyer should refuse to speak those words as a mouthpiece, unless the utterances of his client are filtered and purified by truth and sincerity. . . .

■ LETTER FROM WILLIAM TOWNSEND

4 N.Y. L. Rev. 173 (1926)

To William H. Townsend, of the Lexington, Kentucky, bar, writing for the February American Bar Association Journal, we are indebted for some interesting light upon Abraham Lincoln's views. . . . Mr. Townsend writes:

> Lincoln was regarded as a really formidable antagonist only when he was thoroughly convinced of the justice of his cause. He seemed utterly incapable of that professional partisanship that enlisted the best efforts of his colleagues at the bar, regardless of the

side they were on. He would never argue a case before a jury when he believed he was wrong. His associate, Henry C. Whitney, says of him in this respect: "No man was stronger than he when on the right side, and no man weaker than he when on the opposite. A knowledge of this fact gave him additional strength before a court or a jury."

Leonard Swett (one of Lincoln's closest friends) and Lincoln were once defending a man charged with murder, and, after all the evidence was in, Lincoln believed their man was guilty. "You speak to the jury," he said to Swett, "if I say a word they will see from my face that the man is guilty and convict him."

In another murder case, the circumstantial evidence of guilt seemed almost conclusive and, when Lincoln, who had never wavered in his masterly defense, arose to address the jury, he frankly conceded that the testimony for the State was exceedingly strong. He said, in his slow, drawling way, that he had thought a great deal about the case and that the guilt of his client seemed probable. "But I am not sure," he said as his honest gray eyes looked the jury squarely in the face, "are you?" It was an application of the rule of reasonable doubt which secured an acquittal.

From the foregoing it would seem that Lincoln had no scruple against effort to acquit a guilty client, only that he preferred that associate counsel should do the summing up. In the other example Lincoln invoked the rule of reasonable doubt artfully and dramatically and the client whose guilt Lincoln conceded to be probable, was cleared of the crime.

Notes

1. *The line between obligation and excuse.* In England the question appears to be not whether lawyers should choose to represent those who are guilty but whether any advocate can or should ever refuse to represent a defendant. A barrister cannot refuse to take a case, whether to act as an advocate or to advise, "unless the barrister is professionally committed already, has not been offered a proper fee, is professionally embarrassed by a prior conflict of interest or lacks sufficient experience or competence to handle the matter." Anthony Thornton, Responsibility and Ethics of the English Bar, in Legal Ethics and Professional Responsibility 68 (Ross Cranston ed., 1995). In the United States, lawyers can choose whether to take a case and then are asked to defend this choice. Is the English practice the best way, in the end, to reduce public criticism of criminal defense work?

The ethics of defending criminals is a topic that commands the attention of attorneys in criminal practice, and not just legal ethicists. See Lisa J. McIntyre, The Public Defender: The Practice of Law in the Shadows of Repute 139-70 (1987) (based on interviews with public defenders in Cook County, Illinois). For some attorneys who represent criminal defendants, no line of argument about the defense lawyer's specialized role can counter the emotional costs of defending people accused of terrible crimes. See Susan A. Bandes, Repression and Denial in Criminal Lawyering, 9 Buff. Crim. L. Rev. 339 (2006). For others, a more heroic conception of the defense attorney supplements the traditional need to test factual and legal claims through an adversarial system. See Margareth Etienne, The Ethics of Cause Lawyering: An Empirical Examination of Criminal Defense Lawyers as Cause Lawyers, 95 J. Crim. L. & Criminology 101 (2005) (based on data from interviews with 40 criminal defense attorneys, concludes that many criminal defense attorneys consider themselves to be "cause lawyers" who are committed to individual clients but also to the cause of legal reform in criminal law).

2. *Asking the question.* Some of the justifications for representing potentially guilty defendants depend on the possibility (however slim) that a client could be innocent of the charges. If a defense lawyer learns that a particular client did indeed commit the crime as charged, what justifications remain for going forward with the case? Should a defense lawyer ever ask a client, "Are you guilty?" Experienced lawyers give different answers to this question. Some insist on asking their clients, because they believe they cannot prepare a good defense unless they know "the whole truth." Others do not ask, because they believe the answer would be irrelevant to the defense.

3. *Ethical deliberation for lawyers.* Even if a theory supporting the strong defense of criminal defendants, including those clients a lawyer believes to be guilty, provides general justification for an individual lawyer to defend criminals, these theories hardly answer the difficult questions that arise in actually defending clients. There are more than a few difficult questions of application. What ought a defense attorney to do if she believes her client is lying? Is it appropriate for a defense attorney to use procedural tactics or create scheduling conflicts to increase the chance that the state's case will weaken and that the memory of witnesses will fade? Some of these questions will receive further attention in later chapters. Each deserves considered reflection by a lawyer before the moment of decision. As Monroe Freedman explains: "In making a series of ethical decisions, we create a kind of moral profile of ourselves. You should be conscious, therefore, of how your own decisions on issues of lawyers' ethics establish your moral priorities and thereby define your own moral profile. In understanding lawyers' ethics, you may come to better understand your moral values, and yourself." Freedman, Understanding Lawyers' Ethics (1990); cf. Freedman, An Ethical Manifesto for Public Defenders, 39 Val. U. L. Rev. 911 (2005).

XII

Pretrial Release and Detention

Not long after the police arrest a suspect, the government must decide what charges (if any) to file against the suspect. More or less contemporaneously with the preliminary charging decision, the court must decide whether to release the suspect from custody. Questions about charging and release arise, sometimes repeatedly, in a group of preliminary proceedings that differ in title and in detail from jurisdiction to jurisdiction. This chapter explores the decision whether to release or detain a suspect, and Chapter 13 considers the related decision of what charges to file.

As we saw in Chapter 5, a police officer will sometimes issue a citation instead of arresting a suspect. For many other suspects, the release decision is resolved at the police station, without any appearance before a judicial officer. Most jurisdictions allow "station-house bail" for minor crimes: An administrative official within the law enforcement agency (or perhaps an administrative employee of the courts) releases the suspect by following routine requirements. For instance, the suspect might make a written promise to appear at later proceedings or might pay a modest amount of money "bail" that would be forfeited upon a failure to appear.

Release decisions may also occur a few hours later, when the suspect appears before a judge or magistrate. This "initial appearance" before a judicial officer combines several functions: (1) a determination of whether the government had probable cause to support an arrest of the suspect, (2) an inquiry into whether the court must assign defense counsel to the defendant, and (3) the decision whether to release the suspect. The release decision might be the first determination of a bail amount (or other conditions of release), or it might involve an adjustment of a bail amount set earlier.

Finally, the release decision can occur at a later proceeding, when a judge reconsiders the bail amount or other conditions of release. The later proceeding might be a "preliminary hearing," when a judge also determines whether there is enough evidence to hold the defendant for trial; the later proceeding might also be a "bail hearing," devoted exclusively to the question of release or detention. Defense counsel could be involved at the earliest judicial determination of bail amounts, but usually counsel has little opportunity to become familiar with the defendant's circumstances and to make an effective argument at that point. Only when the court revisits the release decision (often several days after the arrest) can defense counsel develop and present relevant facts.

A great deal is at stake in pretrial release decisions. Most obviously, the liberty of a person who is presumed innocent is weighed against the risk of flight or the possibility that the suspect will commit further crimes after being released. The costs of pretrial detention are also relevant here. The jail facilities required to house pretrial detainees are expensive to build and operate; there were over 400,000 pretrial detainees in jails at mid-year 2009, more than 60 percent of the total jail detainees. Any laws or practices that might change those numbers will drive major budget choices, especially at the local government level.

The release decision has changed dramatically over the past few generations, and it is still in flux. Section A below highlights the reform movement, begun more than 50 years ago and still a vibrant part of federal and state law, to make it easier for defendants to gain release from custody before trial. The section also describes the factors that influence the release decision and the institutions most responsible for making that choice. Section B then traces a more recent movement — in part a reaction to the first reform — to expand the state's power to detain some defendants until the time of trial in an effort to protect the public from further crimes the defendant might commit. Section C tracks the use of detentions without criminal trial in the related arena of terrorism investigations and prevention.

A. PRETRIAL RELEASE

Bail procedures have been the subject of extensive social science research. The researchers' interest in bail stems from the pervasiveness of bail determinations, the relative ease of quantifying bail determinations, and the moral problems raised by detaining those who have not yet been tried (and are, therefore, presumptively innocent) and releasing those who threaten additional harm. A classic illustration of the use of social science as an engine of reform is the Manhattan Bail Project conducted by the Vera Institute of Justice. In reading the following account of the bail experiment, consider the project's origin, implementation (including the essential role of law students), and effects.

■ VERA INSTITUTE OF JUSTICE, FAIR TREATMENT FOR THE INDIGENT: THE MANHATTAN BAIL PROJECT

Ten-Year Report, 1961-1971 (May 1972)

There are many penalties imposed upon an accused person who is detained in jail because he is too poor to post bail. [The] detainee is more apt to be convicted than if he were free on bail; and, if convicted, he is more apt to receive a tougher sentence. [Detainees] lose income while they are away from their jobs, and suffer dislocation and sometimes even permanent rupture in their family lives. They frequently suffer social stigmatization and loss of self respect because of their confinement — even though they have not been convicted of anything and must be presumed innocent, and may eventually be acquitted. . . .

In a large city like New York, these people can also expect to be detained in jails where conditions are comparable to maximum security prisons. . . . Meanwhile, detained persons' defense preparations suffer as it is difficult or impossible for them to consult with attorneys, communicate with family or friends, locate witnesses, or gather evidence.

The Origins and Evolution of Bail

The concept of bail has a long history and deep roots in English and American law. In medieval England, the custom grew out of the need to free untried prisoners from disease-ridden jails while they were waiting for the delayed trials conducted by traveling justices. Prisoners were bailed, or delivered, to reputable third parties of their own choosing who accepted responsibility for assuring their appearance at trial. If the accused did not appear, the bailor would stand in his place.

Eventually it became the practice for property owners who accepted responsibility for accused persons to forfeit money when their charges failed to appear for trial. From this grew the modern practice of posting a money bond through a commercial bondsman who receives a cash premium for his service, and usually demands some collateral as well. In the event of non-appearance the bond is forfeited, after a grace period of a number of days during which the bondsman may produce the accused in court.

The Constitution of the United States did not specifically grant the right to bail, although the Eighth Amendment stipulated that "excessive bail shall not be required." The Judiciary Act of 1789 and subsequent statutes in all but seven of the states did require admission to bail, however, in all non-capital cases. . . .

The emergence of the bondsman as a commercial adjunct to the processes of American criminal justice brought with it certain advantages — he was added to the agencies seeking to enforce court appearance, for example — but it also brought serious drawbacks. Abuses tended to creep into the system, such as collusive ties some bondsmen developed with police, lawyers, court officials and also with organized crime. But more important, the central determinant in whether an accused person would go free on bail pending trial became the decision of a businessman who was interested not in the evenhanded application of justice, but in profit. . . .

Vera Takes Action

[Vera instigators] felt that the best course might be to establish a bail fund, limited perhaps to helping youthful defendants between the ages of 16 and 21. It was thought that such a fund might pay the premiums on bail bonds for these young persons, and at the same time carry out research that would help identify who the good risks might be, and why; how a defendant behaves while his trial is pending; and how the cases were concluded. The fund might later be broadened to include older defendants.

[During discussions with city officials and legal experts, however,] the concept of a fund began to show serious defects. Successful operation of a bail fund would not change bail-setting procedures, and would promote the idea that an unfair system could somehow be made to function equitably with the help of private philanthropic support. It seemed clear that the whole system needed reform and should not be encouraged to rely upon private philanthropy. . . .

Real reform was indeed possible. . . . This was the idea of encouraging judges to release far more accused persons on their honor pending trial, and providing the judges with verified information about the accused on which such releases could be based. It was an obvious, but . . . daring idea: find out who can be trusted, and trust them to appear for trial.

What was needed was a carefully designed project that would . . . develop information about defendants which would enable the courts to grant release to good risks. . . . A project based on these concepts quickly took form:

1. Indigent defendants awaiting arraignment in Manhattan's criminal courts would be questioned by Vera staff interviewers to determine how deep their community roots were and thus whether they could be relied upon to return to court for trial if they were released without bail.
2. The test of indigency would be representation by a Legal Aid lawyer.
3. Questioners would develop information about the defendant's length of residence in the city, his family ties, and his employment situation.
4. Responses of the defendant would be verified immediately in personal or telephone interviews with family, friends, and employers.
5. When verified information indicated that an individual was trustworthy and could be depended on to return for trial, the Vera staff member would appear at arraignment and recommend to the judge that the accused be released on his own recognizance (R.O.R. or pretrial parole) pending trial.

A Demonstration Project Is Set Up

It was anticipated that such a simple but radical change in generally accepted procedures would meet opposition from those accustomed to the old ways or fearful of the new, and so the entire project was devised as a demonstration — an experiment to see whether people would return for trial if released without bail and, in general, how their cases compared with the cases of those not granted release as well as those released on bail. . . .

The experiment was scheduled to begin in the fall of 1961 in the arraignment part of the Manhattan Magistrate's Felony Court. [Students] from the School of Law at New York University were recruited as Vera staff interviewers and received a period of training during which they learned how the arraignment court functioned. The Law School agreed to give the students credit for their Vera work in conjunction with a University seminar on legal problems of the indigent. The entire experience was thought to be an important introduction to the criminal justice process for the aspiring young lawyer. . . .

On October 16, 1961 after months of detailed planning, the Manhattan Bail Project began operations. Specifics attending the launching were carefully arranged:

1. No publicity was given the inauguration of the venture, on grounds that it would be most effective as a demonstration to the community if the results could later speak for themselves. . . .
2. The answers sought through the project were limited and precise: (a) Would judges release more defendants on their own recognizance if they were given verified information about the defendants than they would without such information? (b) Would released defendants return for trial at the same rate as those released on bail? (c) How would the cases of released defendants compare with a control group not recommended for release, both in convictions and in sentencing? . . .
4. All magistrates who would be sitting in court during the project were visited personally by Vera staff members prior to its initiation so that they would understand fully what was happening and why.
5. Since a primary function of the project was to demonstrate to the public and to those within the criminal justice system that pretrial parole was a device that could serve the public's interest as well as the defendant's, some offenders were excluded at the outset from the experiment. These were homicide, forcible rape, sodomy involving a minor, corrupting the morals of a child, and carnal abuse — crimes that were all thought to be too sensitive and controversial to be associated with a release program; narcotics offenses, because of special medical problems and . . . a greater risk of flight; and assault on a police officer, where intervention by Vera might, it was feared, arouse police hostility.
6. Comprehensive follow-up procedures were devised to be sure that released defendants knew when they were expected in court for further appearances in connection with their trials. These procedures included mailed reminders, telephone calls, visits at home or work, and special notifications in the defendant's language, if he did not speak English.

[The] law students began their interviews in the detention pens in the arraignment court. At first, they were asked to make subjective evaluations of the defendant's eligibility for pretrial parole after they had verified their community ties. It was discovered, however, that pressures were developing that caused some interviewers to withhold recommendations for release in cases where it was probably justified. To relieve the individual of these pressures and of the personal responsibility that, in part, created them, a weighted system of points was developed and the sole determinant as to whether or not a defendant would be recommended for release without bail was his achieving a point score of five or above. This development of a set of objective criteria on which to base release recommendations proved to be an important innovation. . . .

POINT SCORING SYSTEM: MANHATTAN BAIL PROJECT

To be recommended, defendant needs [a] New York area address where he can be reached and [a] total of five points from the following categories:

Prior Record

1 No convictions.

0 One misdemeanor conviction.
−1 Two misdemeanor or one felony conviction.
−2 Three or more misdemeanors or two or more felony convictions.

Family Ties (in New York Area)

3 Lives in established family home AND visits other family members (immediate family only).
2 Lives in established family home (immediate family).
1 Visits others of immediate family.

Employment or School

3 Present job one year or more, steadily.
2 Present job 4 months. . . .
1 Has present job which is still available,
or Unemployed 3 months or less and 9 months or more steady prior job,
or Unemployment Compensation,
or Welfare.
3 Presently in school, attending regularly.
2 Out of school less than 6 months but employed or in training.
1 Out of school 3 months or less, unemployed and not in training.

Residence (in New York Area steadily)

3 One year at present residence.
2 One year at present [and] last prior residence or 6 months at present residence.
1 Six months at present and last prior residence or in New York City 5 years or more.

Discretion

1 Positive, over 65, attending hospital, appeared on some previous case.
0 Negative — intoxicated — intention to leave jurisdiction.

Comparing the Experimental and the Control Groups

. . . Vera was especially anxious to compare the experiences of those who had been recommended for release with the experiences of the control group, a statistically identical group for which recommendations had not been made to the judges. It found that 59 percent of its pretrial parole recommendations were followed by the court and that only 16 percent of the control group was released without bail by the judges acting on their own. Judges were clearly basing their actions on the availability of reliable information about the defendants. More significantly, *60 percent of those released pending trial during the first year eventually were acquitted or had their case dismissed, compared with only 23 percent of the control group. And only 16 percent of the released defendants who were convicted were sentenced to prison, where 96 percent of those convicted in the control group received prison sentences.* Unquestionably, detention was resulting in a higher rate of convictions and in far more punitive dispositions. At the end of the second year, the control group was dropped. . . .

Modifications in Project Procedures

Further innovations came in the third year of the project. An important one was that the number of offenses that had been excluded for political reasons was sharply reduced to include only homicide and certain narcotics offenses. Also, the indigency requirement was dropped. It was felt that bail costs should not be imposed on a defendant merely because he had funds; the test for those with money, as well as for those without, should be the same: will the accused return to court for trial? . . .

Meanwhile, in 1963, two developments suggested that a large potential existed for applying new concepts of bail reform outside of New York City. One of these was the strong interest expressed by the United States Department of Justice in helping to sponsor a national conference on bail. The other was the speed with which civic leaders in Des Moines, Iowa, learned from the news media of the Vera experiment, decided to investigate the possibility of a bail project in Des Moines, then designed and adopted such a project.

[The] Bail Reform Act of 1966 [was] signed into law by President Lyndon B. Johnson on June 22, 1966 — the first change in federal bail law since the Judiciary Act of 1789. [The] Act seemed a fitting climax to the effort begun just five years earlier. The Act stipulated that persons should not be detained needlessly in the federal courts to face trial, to testify, or to await an appeal; that release should be granted in non-capital cases where there is reasonable assurance the individual will reappear when required; that the courts should make use of a variety of release options, depending on the circumstances (for example, release in custody of a third party, or with cash deposit, or bail, or with restricted movements); and that information should be developed about the individual on which intelligent selection of alternatives could be based. The Act guaranteed the right to judicial review of release conditions, and also the right to appeal.

[In] the fall of 1964, the New York City Office of Probation took over the administration of the Vera project. . . . During the three years [of the Bail Project] 3,505 defendants had been released on their own recognizance following the recommendations of Vera staff members, out of a total of some 10,000 defendants who had been interviewed. *Only 56 of these parolees, or 1.6 percent of the total, willfully failed to appear in court for trial. During the same period, 3 percent of those released on bail failed to appear, or nearly twice as many as had been released without bail.* The figures strongly suggested that bail was not as effective a guarantee of court appearance as was release on verified information.

Over the thirty-five months, a little less than half — 48 percent — of those released through the Vera project were acquitted or had their cases dismissed, while the remaining 52 percent were found guilty. Of those found guilty, 70 percent received suspended sentences, 10 percent were given jail terms, and 20 percent were given the alternative of a fine or jail sentence.

During the Vera operation, staff recommendations became increasingly liberal as experience established that more and more persons could be released safely on their assurances that they would return for trial. Also judicial acceptance of the recommendations rose sharply. At the outset, Vera urged release for 28 percent of the defendants interviewed, while two and a half years later the figure was 65 percent. Judges were following Vera's advice 55 percent of the time in 1961, and 70 percent of the time in 1964. . . .

■ ALABAMA RULES OF CRIMINAL PROCEDURE 7.2, 7.3

RULE 7.2

(a) Before conviction. Any defendant charged with an offense bailable as a matter of right may be released pending or during trial on his or her personal recognizance or on an appearance bond unless the court or magistrate determines that such a release will not reasonably assure the defendant's appearance as required, or that the defendant's being at large will pose a real and present danger to others or to the public at large. If such a determination is made, the court may impose the least onerous condition or conditions contained in Rule 7.3(b) that will reasonably assure the defendant's appearance or that will eliminate or minimize the risk of harm to others or to the public at large. In making such a determination, the court may take into account the following:

(1) The age, background and family ties, relationships and circumstances of the defendant.

(2) The defendant's reputation, character, and health.

(3) The defendant's prior criminal record, including prior releases on recognizance or on secured appearance bonds, and other pending cases.

(4) The identity of responsible members of the community who will vouch for the defendant's reliability.

(5) Violence or lack of violence in the alleged commission of the offense.

(6) The nature of the offense charged, the apparent probability of conviction, and the likely sentence, insofar as these factors are relevant to the risk of nonappearance. . . .

(11) Residence of the defendant, including consideration of real property ownership, and length of residence in his or her place of domicile.

(12) In cases where the defendant is charged with a drug offense, evidence of selling or pusher activity should indicate a substantial increase in the amount of bond.

(13) Consideration of the defendant's employment status and history, the location of defendant's employment, e.g., whether employed in the county where the alleged offense occurred, and the defendant's financial condition. . . .

RULE 7.3

(a) Mandatory conditions. Every order of release under this rule shall contain the conditions that the defendant:

(1) Appear to answer and to submit to the orders and process of the court having jurisdiction of the case;

(2) Refrain from committing any criminal offense;

(3) Not depart from the state without leave of court; and

(4) Promptly notify the court of any change of address.

(b) Additional conditions. An order of release may include any one or more of the following conditions reasonably necessary to secure a defendant's appearance:

(1) Execution of an appearance bond in an amount specified by the court, either with or without requiring that the defendant deposit with the clerk security in an amount as required by the court;

(2) Execution of a secured appearance bond;

(3) Placing the defendant in the custody of a designated person or organization agreeing to supervise the defendant;

(4) Restrictions on the defendant's travel, associations, or place of abode during the period of release;

(5) Return to custody after specified hours; or

(6) Any other conditions which the court deems reasonably necessary.

THOMAS H. COHEN AND BRIAN A. REAVES, PRETRIAL RELEASE OF FELONY DEFENDANTS IN STATE COURTS

Bureau of Justice Statistics (November 2007, NCJ 214994)

. . . From 1990 to 2004, an estimated 62% of State court felony defendants in the 75 largest counties were released prior to the disposition of their case (table 1). Defendants were about as likely to be released on financial conditions requiring the posting of bail (30%) as to be granted a non-financial release (32%). Among the 38% of defendants detained until case disposition, about 5 in 6 had a bail amount set but did not post the financial bond required for release.

Table 1. Type of pretrial release or detention for State court felony defendants in the 75 largest counties, 1990-2004

Detention-release outcome	*Number [of defendants]*	*Percent*
. . . **Released before case disposition**	264,604	62
Financial conditions	125,650	30
Surety bond	86,107	20
Deposit bond	23,168	6
Full cash bond	12,348	3
Property bond	4,027	1
Non-financial conditions	136,153	32
Personal recognizance	85,330	20
Conditional release	32,882	8
Unsecured bond	17,941	4
Emergency release	2,801	1
Detained until case disposition	159,647	38
Held on bail	132,572	32
Denied bail	27,075	6

[A pronounced trend] was observed in the type of release used. From 1990 to 1998, the percentage of released defendants under financial conditions rose from 24% to 36%, while non-financial releases dropped from 40% to 28%. From 1990 to 2004, surety bond (33%) and release on recognizance (32%) each accounted for about a third of all releases. . . . The trend away from non-financial releases to financial releases was accompanied by an increase in the use of surety bonds and a decrease in the use of release on recognizance (ROR). From 1990 through 1994, ROR accounted for 41% of releases, compared to 24% for surety bond. In 2002 and 2004, surety bonds were used for 42% of releases, compared to 23% for ROR. . . .

Commercial Bail and Pretrial Release

An estimated 14,000 commercial bail agents nationwide secure the release of more than 2 million defendants annually. . . . Bond forfeiture regulations and procedures vary by jurisdiction, but most States regulate commercial bail and license bail agents through their departments of insurance. Four States do not allow commercial bail: Illinois, Kentucky, Oregon, and Wisconsin. Also, the District of Columbia, Maine, and Nebraska have little commercial bail activity.

Bail agents generally operate as independent contractors using credentials of a surety company when posting appearance bond for their client. For a fee, the surety company allows the bail agent to use its financial standing and credit as security on bonds. In turn, the bail agent charges the defendant a fee (usually 10% of the bail amount) for services. In addition, the bail agent often requires collateral from the defendant.

A bail agent usually has an opportunity to recover a defendant if they fail to appear. If the defendant is not returned, the agent is liable to the court for the full bail amount. Most jurisdictions permit revocation of the bond, which allows the agent to return the defendant to custody before the court date, freeing the agent from liability. The agent may be required to refund the defendant's fee in such cases. Courts can also set aside forfeiture judgments if good cause is shown as to why a defendant did not appear.

Many Factors Influence the Pretrial Release Decision

[Courts typically use an offense-based schedule when setting bail. After assessing the likelihood that a defendant, if released, will not appear in court and assessing any danger the defendant may present to the community, the court may adjust the bail higher or lower. In the most serious cases, the court may deny bail altogether. The use of a high bail amount or the denial of bail was most evident in cases involving serious violent offenses.]

Murder defendants (19%) had the lowest probability of being released, followed by those charged with robbery (44%), burglary (49%), motor vehicle theft (49%), or rape (53%). Defendants charged with fraud (82%) were the most likely to be released.

Female defendants (74%) were more likely than males (60%) to be released pretrial. By race and Hispanic origin, non-Hispanic whites (68%) had a higher probability of release than Hispanics (55%). Pretrial detention rates for Hispanics may have been influenced by the use of immigration holds to detain those illegally in the U.S.

Defendants on parole (26%) or probation (43%) at the time of their arrest for the current offense were less likely to be released than those without an active criminal justice status (70%). Defendants who had a prior arrest, whether they had previously failed to appear in court (50%) or not (59%), had a lower probability of release than those without a prior arrest (79%).

Defendants with a prior conviction (51% . . .) had a lower probability of being released than those without a conviction (77%). This was true even if the prior convictions were for misdemeanors only (63%). . . .

A Third of Released Defendants Were Charged with Pretrial Misconduct Within 1 Year After Release

From 1990 through 2004, 33% of defendants were charged with committing one or more types of misconduct after being released but prior to the disposition of their case. A bench warrant for failure to appear in court was issued for 23% of released defendants. An estimated 17% were arrested for a new offense, including 11% for a felony. Overall misconduct rates varied only slightly from 1990 through 2004, ranging from a high of 35% to a low of 31%for surety bond releases (19%). . . .

By type of release, the percent of the defendants who were fugitives after 1 year ranged from 10% for unsecured bond releases to 3% of those released on surety bond. Overall, 28% of the defendants who failed to appear in court and had a bench warrant issued for their arrest were still fugitives at the end of a 1-year study period. This was 6% of all defendants released pretrial. . . . Compared to the overall average, the percentage of absconded defendants who remained a fugitive was lower for surety bond releases (19%). . . .

Defendants who had an active criminal justice status at the time of arrest — such as pretrial release (48%), parole (47%), or probation (44%) — had a higher misconduct rate than those who were not on a criminal justice status (27%). This difference was observed for both failure to appear and rearrest.

Defendants with a prior failure to appear (49%) had a higher misconduct rate than defendants who had previously made all court appearances (30%) or had never been arrested (23%). Defendants with a prior failure to appear (35%) were about twice as likely to have a bench warrant issued for failing to appear during the current case than other defendants (18%).

Defendants with at least one prior felony conviction (43%) had a higher rate of pretrial misconduct than defendants with misdemeanor convictions only (34%) or no prior convictions (27%).

Notes

1. *Statutory fruits of 1960s bail reform: majority view.* The thrust of efforts to change the bail system in the 1950s and 1960s was to increase the use of nonfinancial techniques such as release on recognizance and to standardize the criteria used for release decisions as a way of preventing the wealth of defendants from dominating the release decision. See Daniel Freed & Patricia Wald, Bail in the United States (1964). The efforts bore fruit in the 1966 Federal Bail Reform Act, 18 U.S.C. §3146(b). Unlike the federal statute at work until that time, which gave essentially no guidance to the judge on release and bail decisions, the 1966 statute required

courts to consider standard criteria in reaching their decisions. The statutory factors included "(1) the nature of the offense charged; (2) the weight of the evidence against the accused; (3) the accused's family ties; (4) employment; (5) financial resources; (6) character; (7) mental health; (8) the length of residence in the community; (9) a record of convictions; and (10) a record of failure to appear at court appearances or of flight to avoid prosecution." The ABA Standards on Criminal Justice, Pretrial Release (1968), also embodied many of the aspirations of critics of the money bail system. Both the 1966 Bail Reform Act and the ABA standards influenced state legislatures to revise their criteria for making release decisions, and most states have a similar (though not identical) list of factors. See, e.g., Cal. Penal Code §1275. Around 10 jurisdictions have statutes without lists of factors and leave the determination to the discretion of the judge or magistrate. See, e.g., Mass. Gen. L. ch. 276, §57. A similar number of states include only a very short list of factors. See, e.g., Fla. Stat. §903.03. State rules based on the ABA standards or the 1966 federal statute explicitly make ROR the presumptive outcome for defendants.

This era of federal and state legislation, together with changes in local practices, resulted in higher numbers of defendants being released before trial or guilty plea. While it was common earlier in the century for a state to release fewer than one-third of all defendants, it is now more common to release close to two-thirds of defendants. Would this change in practice have occurred without changes in the federal and state statutes?

2. *Rates of failure to appear.* Of course, some of the defendants released before trial or the entry of a guilty plea fail to appear at their later court proceedings. How many? Statistics compiled every two years between 1990 and 2006 in large urban jurisdictions show consistent results: between 18 and 24 percent of the felony defendants who were released before case disposition failed to appear. Bureau of Justice Statistics, Felony Defendants in Large Urban Counties, 2006, Table 9 (2010, NCJ 228944). These statistics, however, include "technical defaults" where defendants miss the initial court date but come voluntarily at a later time for rescheduled hearings or trials. The FTA rate typically improves when a jurisdiction establishes a system of notification and supervision of those who are released before trial. Who should notify the defendant of the upcoming proceeding, and what form should the notice take?

3. *Bond dealers and bounty hunters.* In jurisdictions requiring payment of the full amount of money bail prior to release (known as full cash bond) or the posting of a surety bond, many defendants rely on the services of bail bond dealers. Surety bonds remain the most common form of financial release, and the trend over the last two decades has been toward greater use of surety bonds. The bond dealer makes the required payment to the court in the form of a bond obligating the dealer to pay the amount of the bail if the defendant does not appear for court proceedings. The dealer charges the defendant a nonrefundable fee, often around 10 percent of the total bond amount, although it varies with the dealer's assessment of the risk that a particular defendant will flee. See Smith v. Leis, 835 N.E.2d 5 (Ohio 2005) (state constitution requires availability of bond rather than "cash bail" requiring defendant to deposit entire bail amount in cash).

About half of the states grant express authority to the dealer and their agents — often called "bounty hunters" — to arrest a defendant who tries to flee. See Ala. Code §15-13-117. Nineteenth-century authority confirms the substantial powers of bond dealers and bounty hunters, which in some respects exceeds that of government agents trying to recapture a fugitive. Reese v. United States, 76 U.S. 13 (1869); Taylor v. Taintor, 83 U.S. 366 (1872). This authority creates a potential for rough practices — and for adventures that have occasionally become the subject of front-page stories and the plot lines for movies, classic and otherwise. For photos, graphics, and other multimedia materials related to the bail bond industry, see the web extension for this chapter at *http://www.crimpro.com/extension/ch12*.

4. *Abolition of surety bonds.* Critics of the surety bond system argue that it fosters violence and leaves defendants with no financial incentive to appear in court after their release. Jurisdictions have taken a number of steps to reduce the importance of bond dealers. A handful of states have directly outlawed the offering of surety bonds. See Wis. Stat. §969.12. Around 20 states have made the surety bond less attractive to defendants by using "deposit" bonds, allowing defendants themselves to deposit a portion of their bail — usually 10 percent — comparable to the rates charged by sureties. See, e.g., Cal. Penal Code §1295; Ohio R. Crim. P. 46. Because the cash deposit to the state is refundable and the fee to the bond dealer is not, defendants have little reason to call on the dealer. The state can also profit from the use of cash bail because courts often do not collect bonds from sureties when the defendant fails to appear. Given all these advantages of cash bail, why does the surety bond system remain the most common form of financial release?

Consider this alternative to bond dealers. Jails can now install an interactive kiosk allowing detainees to use a credit card to make bail. For relatively minor crimes with bails under $5,000, the necessary amount falls with the limit that many people carry on their credit cards. If the defendants do appear for their hearings, the county refunds the bail amount to the defendant's credit card account; the fees for the transaction are far lower than the 10 percent typically charged by bond dealers.

5. *Nonfinancial release conditions.* A defendant's pretrial release might be conditioned not on payment of bail but on performance of certain nonfinancial conditions. The most common nonfinancial release condition is a requirement that the defendant maintain regular contact with a pretrial program. It is also common for the judge to insist that the defendant avoid any contact with the victim of the alleged crime. An increasingly common condition of release is regular drug monitoring or treatment. See Kan. Stat. §22-2802 (drug testing limited to those charged with felonies). Testing positive for some drugs (particularly cocaine) is a predictor, according to some studies, of a higher rate of nonappearance and arrests for crimes committed after release. Peggy Tobolowsky & James Quinn, Drug-Related Behavior as a Predictor of Defendant Pretrial Misconduct, 25 Tex. Tech L. Rev. 1019 (1994). If positive drug tests do not predict a failure to appear, should the tests still be administered? What is the rationale for requiring drug treatment? Another increasingly common nonfinancial condition of release is the use of electronic monitoring. An electronic device attached to the defendant's person (often a wrist or an ankle bracelet) allows the government to monitor his proximity to home or to some other location. Should electronic monitoring be used primarily for those who receive ROR or for those who would otherwise remain in jail?

6. *Racial and gender bias in release and bail decisions.* Evidence periodically surfaces to suggest that black and Hispanic defendants receive less favorable bail and release decisions than white defendants. One study of bail practices in Connecticut by Professors Ian Ayres and Joel Waldfogel revealed that bond dealers charged lower bond rates to black and Hispanic defendants than to white defendants, suggesting that judges set the bail amounts for black and Hispanic defendants higher than the real

risk of flight. The "competitive market" — in the form of the bond dealers — thus was able to discount the rate for minority defendants and still make a profit. Ian Ayres, Pervasive Prejudice? Unconventional Evidence of Race and Gender Discrimination (2001). Studies have also consistently indicated that female defendants are more likely than male defendants to obtain pretrial release and to receive nonfinancial conditions of release. Why might a judge make more "lenient" release decisions for female defendants? See Ellen Steury & Nancy Frank, Gender Bias and Pretrial Release: More Pieces of the Puzzle, 18 J. Crim. Justice 417 (1990) (finding most of differential treatment for women explained by seriousness of offense and prior record).

7. *Effects of pretrial release on acquittal rates.* Bail researchers have long believed that a defendant's odds of acquittal at trial go down if the defendant fails to obtain pretrial release. They reason that a defendant who remains in jail is less able to locate witnesses and otherwise prepare a defense. Caleb Foote's study of bail practices in Philadelphia in the 1950s observed that 67 percent of the defendants charged with violent crimes were acquitted if they were released before trial, while only 25 percent of jailed defendants were acquitted. Foote, Compelling Appearance in Court: Administration of Bail in Philadelphia, 102 U. Pa. L. Rev. 1031 (1954). A number of later studies found a causal relationship (and not just a statistical association) between pretrial release and acquittal rates. However, the trend (not uniform) among more recent studies is to conclude that pretrial release is correlated with — but does not necessarily cause — high acquittal rates. For instance, the seriousness of a charge is a factor both in making release less likely and in making conviction more likely because (among other reasons) prosecution witnesses are more likely to show up. See Gerald Wheeler & Carol Wheeler, Bail Reform in the 1980s: A Response to the Critics, 18 Crim. L. Bull. 228 (1982).

8. *Effects of pretrial release on sentences.* There is stronger evidence of a causal linkage between the pretrial release decision and the choice of punishment after a conviction. The best evidence indicates that defendants not released before their conviction are more likely to receive prison sentences than those who are released. For instance, one analysis of the New York City data produced in the Vera Institute study found that 64 percent of persons detained received prison sentences, compared to only 17 percent of those released before disposition of the charges. See Anne Rankin, The Effect of Pretrial Detention, 39 N.Y.U. L. Rev. 641 (1964).

Problem 12-1. Who Sets Bail?

The trial judges in the state courts of Spokane County meet periodically to discuss issues related to the administration of the state courts in the county. During the most recent meeting of the judges, the Chief Judge for the District Courts in Spokane, Christine Cary, proposed to the other judges that they issue a General Order regarding bail for domestic violence offenses. A draft of her proposed order, entitled "Domestic Violence Offense — Mandatory Court Appearance — No Bail," provides as follows:

> Any person arrested for a crime classified under Section 10.99 of the Revised Code of Washington as Domestic Violence shall be held in jail without bail pending their first

> appearance. This order shall apply to all offenses listed under Section 10.99, irrespective of their classification as a Felony, Gross Misdemeanor, or Misdemeanor.

The proposed General Order also states that a trial judge will always be "on call" to set bail prior to the defendant's preliminary appearance in appropriate cases.

Chief Judge Cary argued to her colleagues that her proposed General Order would exercise authority granted to the trial judges under Rule 3.2(a) of the Criminal Rules for Courts of Limited Jurisdiction: "A court of limited jurisdiction may adopt a bail schedule for persons who have been arrested on probable cause but have not yet made a preliminary appearance before a judicial officer. With the exception of [certain traffic offenses], the adoption of such a schedule or whether to adopt a schedule, is in the discretion of each court of limited jurisdiction."

Under current practices in Spokane County, jail personnel determine bail according to a preset bail schedule and grant release to some defendants prior to any preliminary court appearance. In some cases, the government might not file formal charges against the defendant until after the preliminary appearance. The preliminary appearance occurs within 24 hours of arrest, while the charges might be delayed by as much as 72 hours after arrest (not including Saturdays, Sundays, or holidays). The practical effect of the new General Order, therefore, would be to delay the release of most persons arrested for domestic violence crimes until the arrestee's first appearance before a judge or magistrate, typically on the day after the arrest, because the majority of domestic violence arrests occur in the evening.

Chief Judge Cary's proposed General Order does not specify the length of detention. Rule 3.2.1(d)(1) requires that an accused "detained in jail must be brought before a court of limited jurisdiction as soon as practicable after the detention is commenced, but in any event before the close of business on the next court day."

Another District Court judge in Spokane County, Salvatore Cozza, noted at the meeting that the proposed General Order might conflict with other provisions of state law. In particular, he noted that Washington's constitution has a specific provision creating a right to bail. Article 1, section 20 of the Washington Constitution provides that "all persons charged with crime shall be bailable by sufficient sureties, except for capital offenses when the proof is evident, or the presumption great." The issue, Judge Cozza said, is the point at which the right to bail attaches. Perhaps the right attaches immediately following arrest; maybe it attaches within a reasonable time following the incidents of arrest. Or perhaps the right does not attach until a judicial determination can be made.

After the judges' meeting ended, word of Chief Judge Cary's proposal spread to other government officials and community figures. Within two days, the District Attorney for Spokane County, Donald Brockett, wrote a letter to all of the District Court judges, urging them not to adopt the proposed General Order. He believes that the order would violate the state constitutional right to bail and would expose the county to tort liability. The Spokane County public defender's office also wrote a letter in opposition to the order. The Sheriff, who is responsible for operating the county jail, wrote to the judges (with a copy to all the county commissioners who set the budget for the jail), noting his concern that the new General Order would increase operating expenses at the jail, given the large number of domestic violence arrestees. Officials from the Young Women's Christian Association (YWCA), an organization that operates a shelter for battered women, sent a letter to the judges in favor of the General Order, arguing that a forced overnight separation of a couple during a domestic violence event can prevent additional violence against the victim.

You are one of the District Court judges in Spokane County, and you must decide how you plan to vote on Chief Judge Cary's proposed General Order at the next meeting of the judges. Will you propose instead to retain current practices? To delay the bail decision until after charges are filed?

Give particular consideration to the constitutional arguments about this order. What do you make of the "charged with crime" language in the state constitution? Does that language trigger the point at which the right attaches, or does it modify only the word "persons"? Your own research on the legal history of the state constitutional right to bail reveals that the drafters of section 20 in 1889 changed the proposed language from "all prisoners" to the current language of "all persons charged with crime." The records do not articulate a reason for the substituted language. At the time the constitution was adopted, the Code of 1881 provided that bail could be granted only by judges and the amount set on a case-by-case basis. Section 778 of the Code of 1881 is similar to the adopted version of Const. art. 1, §20 and reads:

> Every person charged with an offense except that of murder in the first degree, where the proof is evident or the presumption great, may be bailed by sufficient sureties . . . : Provided, That all persons accused of crime in any court of this Territory, whether by indictment or otherwise, shall be admitted to bail by the court, where the same is pending, . . . and the bail bond in such cases shall be reasonable and at the sound discretion of the court.

You should also consider any possible due process issues connected with this proposal. A government action affecting an individual's liberty interest is constitutional only if it furthers compelling state interests and is narrowly drawn to serve those interests. The government has compelling interests in preventing crime and ensuring that those accused of crimes are available for trial and to serve their sentences if convicted. For instance, County of Riverside v. McLaughlin, 500 U.S. 44 (1991), recognizes that a police officer may detain an individual without a warrant if the officer has probable cause to believe that the arrestee committed an offense, so long as a judge makes a fair and reliable determination of probable cause within 48 hours of the arrest.

What will you say and how will you vote at the next judges' meeting? Cf. Westerman v. Cary, 892 P.2d 1067 (Wash. 1994).

Notes

1. *Bail schedules*. The earliest available point of release, "station-house bail," often occurs when officers use a "bail schedule," a listing of the presumptive amount of bail to require from various types of offenders. Most often, the presumptive bail is linked to the criminal charge a defendant is facing. For example, a recent Los Angeles County bail schedule made $60,000 the presumptive bail amount for voluntary manslaughter; for kidnapping for ransom, $500,000; and for bookmaking, $2,500. For additional examples of bail schedules and a discussion of how they operate in practice, see the web extension for this chapter at *http://www.crimpro.com/extension/ch12*.

2. *Rules and discretion in bail: majority view.* Most systems leave substantial discretion in the hands of judges in setting bail amounts. Many jurisdictions rely on bail schedules set at local levels. See, e.g., Mont. Code §46-9-302 ("A judge may establish and post a schedule of bail for offenses over which the judge has original jurisdiction"). Tennessee allows magistrates substantial discretion but imposes statewide caps on bail amounts based on the nature of the offense. See Tenn. Code §40-11-105. A few states such as Alabama, Kentucky, and Utah have more specific statewide bail schedules.

What is likely to be the posture of trial judges toward the use of bail schedules? Which crimes (in addition to the domestic violence crimes at issue in Problem 12-1) are likely to create the most pressure on the judges and other actors with power to release arrestees before trial? Are specific bail guidelines useful? Who should develop guidelines?

Would evidence of discriminatory bail practices support use of bail schedules? Recall that the 1994 study by Professors Ayres and Waldfogel offered evidence of such discrimination. Would factors in bail schedules need to be tested to make sure they did not incorporate a racial bias? If wealth is a significant predictor of likelihood of appearance, then which principle should govern: using accurate appearance rules or avoiding wealth-based discrimination?

3. *Appellate court controls on bail.* There are constitutional limits on the amount of bail a trial court can set. According to Stack v. Boyle, 342 U.S. 1 (1951), the "excessive bail" clause of the Eighth Amendment prevents a trial court from setting bail "higher than an amount reasonably calculated to fulfill the purpose" of ensuring the accused's presence at trial. A slight majority of states have an even stronger constitutional provision guaranteeing a right to bail. Do these constitutional provisions suggest that the appellate courts are the institution with the ultimate authority in setting bail? Should appellate courts actively review bail determinations? What impact would bail guidelines have on appellate review of individual cases?

4. *Consultation with victims.* All 50 states have passed statutes offering protections to victims during the criminal justice process, and about 30 have given some of these protections constitutional status. These provisions all require authorities to provide information to victims, such as explaining the possibility of pretrial release, notifying victims after a suspect is arrested, and notifying victims about the time and place of release hearings. See, e.g., Cal. Penal Code §4024.4 (granting power to local governments to contract for victim notification). About half of the states require that victims be notified of a suspect's release, and the terms of release, including the amount of any bail, though many states require the victim to make a written request for such information. A few "victims' rights" provisions indicate that the judge should consider the concerns of the victim of the alleged crime when determining the conditions to place upon the defendant during pretrial release. See Texas Code Crim. Proc. art. 56.02 ("A victim, guardian of a victim, or close relative of a deceased victim [has] the right to have the magistrate take the safety of the victim or his family into consideration as an element in fixing the amount of bail for the accused"). A few states allow the victim to have some input prior to the bail decision. See, e.g., Mo. Const. art. I, §32 (crime victims have the right "to be informed of and heard at . . . bail hearings, . . . unless in the determination of the court the interests of justice require otherwise"). Are such provisions likely to change the release decisions that judges make? Are they consistent with the practice of station-house bail?

5. *Prosecutors and bail.* Statutes and rules tell judges what they should consider in their bail and pretrial release decisions. What factors actually influence judges the most? Judges are less likely to release a defendant already on parole or probation at the time of the current charges; the same is true for defendants with prior arrests or convictions, and those currently charged with violent offenses. In particular, less than ten percent of murder defendants are released before trial.

Some observers of bail practices contend that the recommendation of the prosecutor is the single most influential variable as judges make bail and release decisions. A classic study of San Diego judges reached this conclusion. When researchers presented the judges with several hypothetical case files and asked them to set bail, the local ties of the defendant was the most important variable. However, when observers watched judges decide actual cases, the recommendation of the prosecutor became the most important variable in setting bail amounts — more important than severity of the crime, prior record, defense attorney recommendation, or local ties. The prosecutors, for their part, were most heavily influenced by the severity of the crime and (to a lesser extent) the defendant's local ties. See Ebbe Ebbeson & Vladimir Konecni, Decision Making and Information Integration in the Courts: The Setting of Bail, 32 J. Personality & Soc. Psychol. 805 (1975). Why did the researchers observe judges in the courtroom in addition to asking them about simulated case files?

B. PRETRIAL DETENTION

Until the 1980s, a substantial majority of state constitutions guaranteed a right to bail except in capital cases. Earlier in our history, the capital case exception applied to a large number of defendants because a wide range of crimes (from murder to burglary) were punishable by death. Once capital punishment became available only for a subset of murders, however, the state constitutional right to bail extended to a much larger group — indeed, to most criminal defendants.

These constitutional provisions never meant that all defendants were to be released before trial. A judge could, consistent with these constitutional provisions, deny bail altogether or set bail in prohibitively high amounts when necessary to ensure a defendant's appearance at trial or to prevent the defendant from threatening witnesses or otherwise undermining the integrity of the judicial process. These hard-to-identify practices blunted the practical impact of the constitutional provisions and statutes declaring in broad terms the "right to bail."

However, the success of the bail reform movement of the 1960s and 1970s in decreasing the use of money bail and increasing the number of defendants released before trial gave new visibility and urgency to an old question: What are the purposes of pretrial release and detention? Should systems refuse to release a defendant before trial only when necessary to preserve the integrity of the judicial process? Or could a judge deny bail altogether if necessary to serve different purposes, such as protecting the public from further wrongdoing by the defendant before trial?

In 1970, only four years after the 1966 Bail Reform Act, Congress passed a controversial pretrial detention law for the District of Columbia that allowed detention on the basis of the threat of additional criminal acts by the defendant before trial.

In 1984 Congress declared, in a new Bail Reform Act, that prevention of future wrongdoing was indeed a proper basis for detaining a defendant in custody before trial. That declaration gave momentum to a movement that has now become the law in over half the states.

The federal statute, reprinted below, creates a rebuttable presumption of detention under subsection (e)(2), which is based on the defendant's criminal history and prior performance while on pretrial release. That presumption can be established only after the judge holds a hearing under subsection (f)(1). Federal prosecutors can request these hearings only for defendants who are charged with certain crimes, or who present a serious risk of flight or jury tampering. An alternative form of the rebuttable presumption, described under subsection (e)(3), requires no such hearing. Once a judge concludes that there is probable cause to believe that the defendant committed one of the enumerated charges, the judge need not hold a hearing or make any criminal history determinations to detain the defendant without bail. Note that for both sections, relevant charges include drug trafficking with penalties of 10 years or more, which includes most drug charges prosecuted in federal court.

U.S. CONSTITUTION AMENDMENT VIII

Excessive bail shall not be required, nor excessive fines imposed, nor cruel and unusual punishments inflicted.

TENNESSEE CONSTITUTION ART. I, §§15, 16

15. That all prisoners shall be bailable by sufficient sureties, unless for capital offences, when the proof is evident or the presumption great. And the privilege of the writ of habeas corpus shall not be suspended, unless when in case of rebellion or invasion, the General Assembly shall declare the public safety requires it.

16. That excessive bail shall not be required, nor excessive fines imposed, nor cruel and unusual punishments inflicted.

18 U.S.C. §3142(e), (f)

(e) (1) If, after a hearing pursuant to the provisions of subsection (f) of this section, the judicial officer finds that no condition or combination of conditions will reasonably assure the appearance of the person as required and the safety of any other person and the community, such judicial officer shall order the detention of the person before trial.

(2) In a case described in subsection (f)(1) of this section, a rebuttable presumption arises that no condition or combination of conditions will reasonably assure the safety of any other person and the community if such judicial officer finds that —

(A) the person has been convicted of a Federal offense that is described in subsection (f)(1) of this section, or [a similar] State or local offense . . . ;

(B) the offense described in paragraph (1) of this subsection was committed while the person was on release pending trial for a Federal, State, or local offense; and

(C) a period of not more than five years has elapsed since the date of conviction, or the release of the person from imprisonment, for the offense described in paragraph (1) of this subsection, whichever is later.

(3) Subject to rebuttal by the person, it shall be presumed that no condition or combination of conditions will reasonably assure the appearance of the person as required and the safety of the community if the judicial officer finds that there is probable cause to believe that the person committed . . . an offense for which a maximum term of imprisonment of ten years or more is prescribed in the [federal laws proscribing drug trafficking, crimes of violence, and certain crimes with victims less than 18 years old].

(f) The judicial officer shall hold a hearing to determine whether any condition or combination of conditions . . . will reasonably assure the appearance of such person as required and the safety of any other person and the community —

(1) upon motion of the attorney for the Government, in a case that involves — (A) a crime of violence [or an offense involving specified forms of terrorism, for which a maximum term of imprisonment of 10 years or more is prescribed]; (B) an offense for which the maximum sentence is life imprisonment or death; (C) an offense for which a maximum term of imprisonment of ten years or more is prescribed in the [federal drug trafficking laws]; (D) any felony if such person has been convicted of two or more offenses described in subparagraphs (A) through (C) of this paragraph, or two or more [similar] State or local offenses . . . , or a combination of such offenses; or (E) any felony that is not otherwise a crime of violence that involves a minor victim or that involves the possession or use of a firearm or destructive device . . . or any other dangerous weapon, or involves a failure to register [as a sex offender]; or

(2) Upon motion of the attorney for the Government or upon the judicial officer's own motion, in a case that involves — (A) a serious risk that the person will flee; or (B) a serious risk that the person will obstruct or attempt to obstruct justice, or threaten, injure, or intimidate, or attempt to threaten, injure, or intimidate, a prospective witness or juror. . . .

The facts the judicial officer uses to support a finding pursuant to subsection (e) that no condition or combination of conditions will reasonably assure the safety of any other person and the community shall be supported by clear and convincing evidence. . . .

■ UNITED STATES v. ANTHONY SALERNO

481 U.S. 739 (1987)

REHNQUIST, C.J.*

The Bail Reform Act of 1984 allows a federal court to detain an arrestee pending trial if the Government demonstrates by clear and convincing evidence after an adversary hearing that no release conditions "will reasonably assure . . . the safety of

* [Justices White, Blackmun, Powell, O'Connor, and Scalia joined this opinion. — EDS.]

any other person and the community."... We hold that, as against the facial attack mounted by these respondents, the Act fully comports with constitutional requirements....

I.

Responding to "the alarming problem of crimes committed by persons on release," S. Rep. No. 98-225, p.3 (1983), Congress formulated the Bail Reform Act of 1984, 18 U.S.C. §3141 et seq., as the solution to a bail crisis in the federal courts. The Act represents the National Legislature's considered response to numerous perceived deficiencies in the federal bail process. By providing for sweeping changes in both the way federal courts consider bail applications and the circumstances under which bail is granted, Congress hoped to give the courts adequate authority to make release decisions that give appropriate recognition to the danger a person may pose to others if released.

To this end, §3141(a) of the Act requires a judicial officer to determine whether an arrestee shall be detained. Section 3142(e) provides that "if, after a hearing pursuant to the provisions of subsection (f), the judicial officer finds that no condition or combination of conditions will reasonably assure the appearance of the person as required and the safety of any other person and the community, he shall order the detention of the person prior to trial." ... If the judicial officer finds that no conditions of pretrial release can reasonably assure the safety of other persons and the community, he must state his findings of fact in writing, §3142(i), and support his conclusion with "clear and convincing evidence,"§3142(f).

The judicial officer is not given unbridled discretion in making the detention determination. Congress has specified the considerations relevant to that decision. These factors include the nature and seriousness of the charges, the substantiality of the Government's evidence against the arrestee, the arrestee's background and characteristics, and the nature and seriousness of the danger posed by the suspect's release. §3142(g). Should a judicial officer order detention, the detainee is entitled to expedited appellate review of the detention order. §§3145(b), (c).

Respondents Anthony Salerno and Vincent Cafaro were arrested on March 21, 1986, after being charged in a 29-count indictment alleging various Racketeer Influenced and Corrupt Organizations Act (RICO) violations, mail and wire fraud offenses, extortion, and various criminal gambling violations. The RICO counts alleged 35 acts of racketeering activity, including fraud, extortion, gambling, and conspiracy to commit murder. At respondents' arraignment, the Government moved to have Salerno and Cafaro detained pursuant to §3142(e), on the ground that no condition of release would assure the safety of the community or any person. The District Court held a hearing at which the Government made a detailed proffer of evidence. The Government's case showed that Salerno was the "boss" of the Genovese crime family of La Cosa Nostra and that Cafaro was a "captain" in the Genovese family. According to the Government's proffer, based in large part on conversations intercepted by a court-ordered wiretap, the two respondents had participated in wide-ranging conspiracies to aid their illegitimate enterprises through violent means. The Government also offered the testimony of two of its trial witnesses, who would assert that Salerno personally participated in two murder conspiracies. Salerno opposed the motion for detention, challenging the credibility of the Government's witnesses. He offered the testimony of several character witnesses as well as a letter from his doctor stating that he was suffering from a serious medical condition. Cafaro presented no evidence at the hearing, but instead characterized the wiretap conversations as merely "tough talk."

The District Court granted the Government's detention motion, concluding that the Government had established by clear and convincing evidence that no condition or combination of conditions of release would ensure the safety of the community or any person. . . . Respondents appealed, contending that to the extent that the Bail Reform Act permits pretrial detention on the ground that the arrestee is likely to commit future crimes, it is unconstitutional on its face. . . .

II.

A facial challenge to a legislative Act is, of course, the most difficult challenge to mount successfully, since the challenger must establish that no set of circumstances exists under which the Act would be valid. . . . We think respondents have failed to shoulder their heavy burden to demonstrate that the Act is "facially" unconstitutional.

Respondents present two grounds for invalidating the Bail Reform Act's provisions permitting pretrial detention on the basis of future dangerousness. First, they [argue] that the Act exceeds the limitations placed upon the Federal Government by the Due Process Clause of the Fifth Amendment. Second, they contend that the Act contravenes the Eighth Amendment's proscription against excessive bail. We treat these contentions in turn.

A.

The Due Process Clause of the Fifth Amendment provides that "No person shall . . . be deprived of life, liberty, or property, without due process of law. . . ." Respondents first argue that the Act violates substantive due process because the pretrial detention it authorizes constitutes impermissible punishment before trial. The Government, however, has never argued that pretrial detention could be upheld if it were "punishment." The Court of Appeals assumed that pretrial detention under the Bail Reform Act is regulatory, not penal, and we agree that it is. . . .

To determine whether a restriction on liberty constitutes impermissible punishment or permissible regulation, we first look to legislative intent. Unless Congress expressly intended to impose punitive restrictions, the punitive/regulatory distinction turns on whether an alternative purpose to which the restriction may rationally be connected is assignable for it, and whether it appears excessive in relation to the alternative purpose assigned to it.

We conclude that the detention imposed by the Act falls on the regulatory side of the dichotomy. The legislative history of the Bail Reform Act clearly indicates that Congress did not formulate the pretrial detention provisions as punishment for dangerous individuals. Congress instead perceived pretrial detention as a potential solution to a pressing societal problem. There is no doubt that preventing danger to the community is a legitimate regulatory goal.

Nor are the incidents of pretrial detention excessive in relation to the regulatory goal Congress sought to achieve. The Bail Reform Act carefully limits the circumstances under which detention may be sought to the most serious of crimes. See 18 U.S.C. §3142(f) (detention hearings available if case involves crimes of violence, offenses for which the sentence is life imprisonment or death, serious drug offenses, or certain repeat offenders). The arrestee is entitled to a prompt detention hearing, and the maximum length of pretrial detention is limited by the stringent time limitations of the Speedy Trial Act. Moreover, . . . the conditions of confinement envisioned by the Act appear to reflect the regulatory purposes relied upon by the Government. [The] statute at issue here requires that detainees be housed in a facility "separate, to the extent practicable, from persons awaiting or serving sentences or being held in custody pending appeal." 18 U.S.C. §3142(i)(2). We conclude, therefore, that the pretrial detention contemplated by the Bail Reform Act is regulatory in nature, and does not constitute punishment before trial in violation of the Due Process Clause.

[The] Government's regulatory interest in community safety can, in appropriate circumstances, outweigh an individual's liberty interest. For example, in times of war or insurrection, when society's interest is at its peak, the Government may detain individuals whom the Government believes to be dangerous. See Ludecke v. Watkins, 335 U.S. 160 (1948) (approving unreviewable executive power to detain enemy aliens in time of war); Moyer v. Peabody, 212 U.S. 78 (1909) (rejecting due process claim of individual jailed without probable cause by Governor in time of insurrection). Even outside the exigencies of war, we have found that sufficiently compelling governmental interests can justify detention of dangerous persons. Thus, we have found no absolute constitutional barrier to detention of potentially dangerous resident aliens pending deportation proceedings. Carlson v. Landon, 342 U.S. 524 (1952). We have also held that the government may detain mentally unstable individuals who present a danger to the public, Addington v. Texas, 441 U.S. 418 (1979), and dangerous defendants who become incompetent to stand trial, Jackson v. Indiana, 406 U.S. 715 (1972). We have approved of postarrest regulatory detention of juveniles when they present a continuing danger to the community. Schall v. Martin, 467 U.S. 253 (1984). Even competent adults may face substantial liberty restrictions as a result of the operation of our criminal justice system. If the police suspect an individual of a crime, they may arrest and hold him until a neutral magistrate determines whether probable cause exists. Gerstein v. Pugh, 420 U.S. 103 (1975). Finally, . . . an arrestee may be incarcerated until trial if he presents a risk of flight . . . or a danger to witnesses.

Respondents characterize all of these cases as exceptions to the "general rule" of substantive due process that the government may not detain a person prior to a judgment of guilt in a criminal trial. Such a "general rule" may freely be conceded, but we think that these cases show a sufficient number of exceptions to the rule that the congressional action challenged here can hardly be characterized as totally novel. Given the well-established authority of the government, in special circumstances, to restrain individuals' liberty prior to or even without criminal trial and conviction, we think that the present statute providing for pretrial detention on the basis of dangerousness must be evaluated in precisely the same manner that we evaluated the laws in the cases discussed above.

The government's interest in preventing crime by arrestees is both legitimate and compelling. In *Schall*, we recognized the strength of the State's interest in preventing juvenile crime. This general concern with crime prevention is no less compelling when the suspects are adults. . . . The Bail Reform Act of 1984 responds to an even more particularized governmental interest than the interest we sustained in *Schall*. The statute we upheld in *Schall* permitted pretrial detention of any juvenile arrested on any charge after a showing that the individual might commit some undefined further crimes. The Bail Reform Act, in contrast . . . operates only on individuals who have been arrested for a specific category of extremely serious offenses. Congress specifically found that these individuals are far more likely to be responsible for dangerous acts in the community after arrest. Nor is the Act by any means a scattershot attempt to incapacitate those who are merely suspected of these serious crimes. The Government must first of all demonstrate probable cause to believe that the charged crime has been committed by the arrestee, but that is not enough. In a full-blown adversary hearing, the Government must convince a neutral decisionmaker by clear and convincing evidence that no conditions of release can reasonably assure the safety of the community or any person. While the Government's general interest in preventing crime is compelling, even this interest is heightened when the Government musters convincing proof that the arrestee, already indicted or held to answer for a serious crime, presents a demonstrable danger to the community. Under these narrow circumstances, society's interest in crime prevention is at its greatest.

On the other side of the scale, of course, is the individual's strong interest in liberty. We do not minimize the importance and fundamental nature of this right. But, as our cases hold, this right may, in circumstances where the Government's interest is sufficiently weighty, be subordinated to the greater needs of society. We think that Congress' careful delineation of the circumstances under which detention will be permitted satisfies this standard. When the Government proves by clear and convincing evidence that an arrestee presents an identified and articulable threat to an individual or the community, we believe that, consistent with the Due Process Clause, a court may disable the arrestee from executing that threat. . . .

B.

Respondents also contend that the Bail Reform Act violates the Excessive Bail Clause of the Eighth Amendment. . . . The Eighth Amendment addresses pretrial release by providing merely that "excessive bail shall not be required." This Clause, of course, says nothing about whether bail shall be available at all. Respondents nevertheless contend that this Clause grants them a right to bail calculated solely upon considerations of flight. They rely on Stack v. Boyle, 342 U.S. 1, 5 (1951), in which the Court stated that "bail set at a figure higher than an amount reasonably calculated [to ensure the defendant's presence at trial] is 'excessive' under the Eighth Amendment." In respondents' view, since the Bail Reform Act allows a court essentially to set bail at an infinite amount for reasons not related to the risk of flight, it violates the Excessive Bail Clause. Respondents concede that the right to bail they have discovered in the Eighth Amendment is not absolute. A court may, for example, refuse bail in capital cases. [A] court may [also] refuse bail when the defendant presents a threat to the judicial process by intimidating witnesses. Respondents characterize these exceptions as consistent with what they claim to be the sole purpose of bail — to ensure the integrity of the judicial process.

While we agree that a primary function of bail is to safeguard the courts' role in adjudicating the guilt or innocence of defendants, we reject the proposition that the Eighth Amendment categorically prohibits the government from pursuing other admittedly compelling interests through regulation of pretrial release. The above-quoted dictum in Stack v. Boyle is far too slender a reed on which to rest this argument. [T]he statute before the Court in that case in fact allowed the defendants to be bailed. Thus, the Court had to determine only whether bail, admittedly available in that case, was excessive if set at a sum greater than that necessary to ensure the arrestees' presence at trial.

The holding of *Stack* is illuminated by the Court's holding just four months later in Carlson v. Landon, 342 U.S. 524 (1952). In that case, remarkably similar to the present action, the detainees had been arrested and held without bail pending a determination of deportability. The Attorney General refused to release the individuals, "on the ground that there was reasonable cause to believe that [their] release would be prejudicial to the public interest and would endanger the welfare and safety of the United States." The detainees brought the same challenge that respondents bring to us today: the Eighth Amendment required them to be admitted to bail. The Court squarely rejected this proposition:

> The bail clause was lifted with slight changes from the English Bill of Rights Act. In England that clause has never been thought to accord a right to bail in all cases, but merely to provide that bail shall not be excessive in those cases where it is proper to grant bail. When this clause was carried over into our Bill of Rights, nothing was said that indicated any different concept. [342 U.S. at 545.]

Nothing in the text of the Bail Clause limits permissible Government considerations solely to questions of flight. The only arguable substantive limitation of the Bail Clause is that the Government's proposed conditions of release or detention not be "excessive" in light of the perceived evil. Of course, to determine whether the Government's response is excessive, we must compare that response against the interest the Government seeks to protect by means of that response. Thus, when the Government has admitted that its only interest is in preventing flight, bail must be set by a court at a sum designed to ensure that goal, and no more. We believe that when Congress has mandated detention on the basis of a compelling interest other than prevention of flight, as it has here, the Eighth Amendment does not require release on bail.

III.

In our society liberty is the norm, and detention prior to trial or without trial is the carefully limited exception. We hold that the provisions for pretrial detention in the Bail Reform Act of 1984 fall within that carefully limited exception. The Act authorizes the detention prior to trial of arrestees charged with serious felonies who are found after an adversary hearing to pose a threat to the safety of individuals or to the community which no condition of release can dispel. The numerous procedural safeguards detailed above must attend this adversary hearing. We are unwilling to say that this congressional determination, based as it is upon that primary concern of every government — a concern for the safety and indeed the lives of its citizens — on its face violates either the Due Process Clause of the Fifth Amendment or the Excessive Bail Clause of the Eighth Amendment. The judgment of the Court of Appeals is therefore reversed.

MARSHALL, J., dissenting.*

This case brings before the Court for the first time a statute in which Congress declares that a person innocent of any crime may be jailed indefinitely, pending the trial of allegations which are legally presumed to be untrue, if the Government shows to the satisfaction of a judge that the accused is likely to commit crimes, unrelated to the pending charges, at any time in the future. Such statutes, consistent with the usages of tyranny and the excesses of what bitter experience teaches us to call the police state, have long been thought incompatible with the fundamental human rights protected by our Constitution. . . .

II.

[In connection with the Due Process challenge,] the majority concludes that the Act is a regulatory rather than a punitive measure. The ease with which the conclusion is reached suggests the worthlessness of the achievement. . . . Let us apply the majority's reasoning to a similar, hypothetical case. After investigation, Congress determines (not unrealistically) that a large proportion of violent crime is perpetrated by persons who are unemployed. It also determines, equally reasonably, that much violent crime is committed at night. From amongst the panoply of "potential solutions," Congress chooses a statute which permits, after judicial proceedings, the imposition of a dusk-to-dawn curfew on anyone who is unemployed. Since this is not a measure enacted for the purpose of punishing the unemployed, and since the majority finds that preventing danger to the community is a legitimate regulatory goal, the curfew statute would, according to the majority's analysis, be a mere "regulatory" detention statute, entirely compatible with the substantive components of the Due Process Clause.

The absurdity of this conclusion arises, of course, from the majority's cramped concept of substantive due process. The majority proceeds as though the only substantive right protected by the Due Process Clause is a right to be free from punishment before conviction. The majority's technique for infringing this right is simple: merely redefine any measure which is claimed to be punishment as "regulation," and, magically, the Constitution no longer prohibits its imposition. Because . . . the Due Process Clause protects other substantive rights which are infringed by this legislation, the majority's argument is merely an exercise in obfuscation.

The logic of the majority's Eighth Amendment analysis is equally unsatisfactory. [The majority] declares, as if it were undeniable, that: "this Clause, of course, says nothing about whether bail shall be available at all." If excessive bail is imposed the defendant stays in jail. The same result is achieved if bail is denied altogether. Whether the magistrate sets bail at $1 billion or refuses to set bail at all, the consequences are indistinguishable. It would be mere sophistry to suggest that the Eighth Amendment protects against the former decision, and not the latter. Indeed, such a result would lead to the conclusion that there was no need for Congress to pass a preventive detention measure of any kind; every federal magistrate and district judge could simply refuse, despite the absence of any evidence of risk of flight or danger to the community, to set bail. . . .

* [Justice Brennan joined this opinion. — EDS.]

III.

The essence of this case may be found, ironically enough, in a provision of the Act to which the majority does not refer. Title 18 U.S.C. §3142(j) provides that "nothing in this section shall be construed as modifying or limiting the presumption of innocence." But the very pith and purpose of this statute is an abhorrent limitation of the presumption of innocence. . . .

The statute does not authorize the Government to imprison anyone it has evidence is dangerous; indictment is necessary. But let us suppose that a defendant is indicted and the Government shows by clear and convincing evidence that he is dangerous and should be detained pending a trial, at which trial the defendant is acquitted. May the Government continue to hold the defendant in detention based upon its showing that he is dangerous? The answer cannot be yes, for that would allow the Government to imprison someone for uncommitted crimes based upon "proof" not beyond a reasonable doubt. The result must therefore be that once the indictment has failed, detention cannot continue. But our fundamental principles of justice declare that the defendant is as innocent on the day before his trial as he is on the morning after his acquittal. Under this statute an untried indictment somehow acts to permit a detention, based on other charges, which after an acquittal would be unconstitutional. The conclusion is inescapable that the indictment has been turned into evidence, if not that the defendant is guilty of the crime charged, then that left to his own devices he will soon be guilty of something else. . . .

The finding of probable cause conveys power to try, and the power to try imports of necessity the power to assure that the processes of justice will not be evaded or obstructed. [Detention under] this statute bears no relation to the Government's power to try charges supported by a finding of probable cause, and thus the interests it serves are outside the scope of interests which may be considered in weighing the excessiveness of bail under the Eighth Amendment. . . .

IV.

Throughout the world today there are men, women, and children interned indefinitely, awaiting trials which may never come or which may be a mockery of the word, because their governments believe them to be "dangerous." Our Constitution, whose construction began two centuries ago, can shelter us forever from the evils of such unchecked power. Over 200 years it has slowly, through our efforts, grown more durable, more expansive, and more just. But it cannot protect us if we lack the courage, and the self-restraint, to protect ourselves. Today a majority of the Court applies itself to an ominous exercise in demolition. Theirs is truly a decision which will go forth without authority, and come back without respect. I dissent.

STEVENS, J., dissenting.

There may be times when the Government's interest in protecting the safety of the community will justify the brief detention of a person who has not committed any crime. [It] is indeed difficult to accept the proposition that the Government is without power to detain a person when it is a virtual certainty that he or she would otherwise kill a group of innocent people in the immediate future. Similarly, I am unwilling to decide today that the police may never impose a limited curfew during a time of crisis. These questions are obviously not presented in this case, but they lurk in the background and preclude me from answering the question that is presented in as broad a manner as Justice Marshall has. Nonetheless, I firmly agree with Justice Marshall that the provision of the Bail Reform Act allowing pretrial detention on the basis of future dangerousness is unconstitutional. Whatever the answers are to the questions I have mentioned, it is clear to me that a pending indictment may not be given any weight in evaluating an individual's risk to the community or the need for immediate detention.

If the evidence of imminent danger is strong enough to warrant emergency detention, it should support that preventive measure regardless of whether the person has been charged, convicted, or acquitted of some other offense. In this case, for example, it is unrealistic to assume that the danger to the community that was present when respondents were at large did not justify their detention before they were indicted, but did require that measure the moment that the grand jury found probable cause to believe they had committed crimes in the past. It is equally unrealistic to assume that the danger will vanish if a jury happens to acquit them. . . .

■ NEW MEXICO CONSTITUTION ART. II, §13

All persons shall before conviction be bailable by sufficient sureties, except for capital offenses when the proof is evident or the presumption great and in situations in which bail is specifically prohibited by this section. Excessive bail shall not be required, nor excessive fines imposed, nor cruel and unusual punishment inflicted.

Bail may be denied by the district court for a period of sixty days after the incarceration of the defendant by an order entered within seven days after the incarceration, in the following instances:

A. the defendant is accused of a felony and has previously been convicted of two or more felonies, within the state, which felonies did not arise from the same transaction or a common transaction with the case at bar;

B. the defendant is accused of a felony involving the use of a deadly weapon and has a prior felony conviction, within the state.

The period for incarceration without bail may be extended by any period of time by which trial is delayed by a motion for a continuance made by or on behalf of the defendant. . . .

■ VIRGINIA CODE §19.2-120

. . . A. A person who is held in custody pending trial or hearing for an offense, civil or criminal contempt, or otherwise shall be admitted to bail by a judicial officer, unless there is probable cause to believe that:

1. He will not appear for trial or hearing or at such other time and place as may be directed, or

2. His liberty will constitute an unreasonable danger to himself or the public.

B. The judicial officer shall presume, subject to rebuttal, that no condition or combination of conditions will reasonably assure the appearance of the person or the safety of the public if the person is currently charged with:

1. An act of violence as defined in [this code];

2. An offense for which the maximum sentence is life imprisonment or death;

3. A violation . . . involving a Schedule I or II controlled substance if (i) the maximum term of imprisonment is ten years or more and the person was previously convicted of a like offense or (ii) the person was previously convicted as a "drug kingpin" as defined in [this code];

4. A violation . . . which relates to a firearm and provides for a mandatory minimum sentence;

5. Any felony, if the person has been convicted of two or more offenses described in subdivision 1 or 2 . . . ;

6. Any felony committed while the person is on release pending trial for a prior felony under federal or state law or on release pending imposition or execution of sentence or appeal of sentence or conviction;

7. [Felony sexual assault] and the person had previously been convicted of [felony sexual assault] and the judicial officer finds probable cause to believe that the person who is currently charged with one of these offenses committed the offense charged;

8. A violation of [the statutes prohibiting the activities of criminal street gangs, acts of terrorism, or acts of bioterrorism against agricultural crops or animals]; or

9. A violation [involving driving while intoxicated] and the person has, within the past five years of the instant offense, been convicted three times on different dates of a violation of any combination of these Code sections, or any [similar ordinance or statute], and has been at liberty between each conviction. . . .

C. The judicial officer shall presume, subject to rebuttal, that no condition or combination of conditions will reasonably assure the appearance of the person or the safety of the public if the person is being arrested pursuant to [the enforcement of federal immigration laws].

D. The court shall consider the following factors and such others as it deems appropriate in determining, for the purpose of rebuttal of the presumption against bail described in subsection B, whether there are conditions of release that will reasonably assure the appearance of the person as required and the safety of the public:

1. The nature and circumstances of the offense charged;

2. The history and characteristics of the person, including his character, physical and mental condition, family ties, employment, financial resources, length of residence in the community, community ties, past conduct, history relating to drug or alcohol abuse, criminal history, membership in a street gang . . . , and record concerning appearance at court proceedings; and

3. The nature and seriousness of the danger to any person or the community that would be posed by the person's release.

Problem 12-2. The Next Danger

Yaser Mohammed Jawad was charged in Virginia with first-degree murder and the use of a firearm in the commission of first-degree murder. At the bail hearing, Antwoin Boyd, an eyewitness to the shooting, testified for the prosecution. Boyd worked at a barbershop that was located in the shopping center that Jawad owned.

The barbershop was also two doors down from Jawad's convenience store. Boyd testified that, as he was leaving the barbershop, he saw two men "tussling" and "wrestling" in front of the door to Jawad's store. They banged into the door of Jawad's store twice and were causing a "big commotion." Nobody was entering or leaving the store because of the fighting.

From approximately 50 feet away, Boyd saw Jawad come out of the store and attempt to pull the two men apart. Jawad was yelling and cursing at the men. One of the men involved in the fighting, Benjamin Jones, told Jawad that they were cousins and were not fighting. Jones then stopped fighting with his cousin and started "fussing with Jawad face to face." Jawad spat in Jones's face. Jones, who was very upset and angry, spat in Jawad's face and attempted to attack him, but his "cousin" held him back. Jawad went back into his store and Jones started to walk to his car.

At that point, according to Boyd, Jawad came back outside holding a handgun. He shot the gun once in the air. Jawad and Jones continued to "fuss" with each other while standing twenty feet apart. Jawad then ran up and pinned Jones against the car. After Jones dared him three times to shoot, Jawad stepped back and shot Jones in the face. Boyd also testified that, eight or nine months before the shooting of Jones, he had seen Jawad chase a suspected shoplifter down the sidewalk with a gun.

Jones had a lengthy felony record, including two weapons convictions. Two security guards who knew Jones testified that he was a violent person. Jawad's attorney told the trial court that there would be a factual question at trial about "whether or not the defendant was the aggressor or whether the alleged victim engaged in conduct that brought about his own demise."

Jawad testified on his own behalf at the bail hearing. According to his testimony, he has never "failed to appear for anything in court" and intends "to appear for all court appearances" in this case. He is married to an American citizen and lives with his wife, 14-month-old son, father, mother, and brother in a home in Chesapeake owned by his parents and brother. He has lived in the United States consistently for eight years and in Chesapeake for three years. He has no immediate family still living in Pakistan. Nearly 32 years of age, he is in good physical health, has never been treated for any mental conditions, and has never abused drugs or alcohol. He has no prior criminal record.

Jawad and other members of his family own the shopping center where the shooting occurred. An electrical engineer by education, Jawad managed the convenience store in the shopping center, but discontinued working there after the shooting. He says that he will look for "a separate line of work" upon his release on bail. Outside of his interest in the shopping center, his financial resources are minimal. He testified that has no money or property in Pakistan.

A citizen of Pakistan, Jawad surrendered his expired Pakistani passport to the trial court. Robert Lindemann, the family's business attorney who had been practicing law for 23 years, testified to Jawad's reputation for honesty and fair dealing. He testified that, in all his dealings with him, Jawad "always kept his word on anything he said he was going to do." Jawad, Lindemann said, was a hard worker who, together with his family, transformed the shopping center from a facility in disrepair to a financially successful operation. Lindemann also testified to Jawad's reputation in the community for peacefulness. He opined that Jawad would not flee and would comply with all terms of bond.

Several members of Jawad's family, his wife's family, his employees, customers of his store, and others in the community who knew him, including his accountant, were present at the hearing and identified to the court as appearing on his behalf. They did not testify.

Imagine that you are the trial judge in this case, and you must decide whether to set bail under the terms of Virginia Code §19.2-120, reprinted above. Subsection (b) of the statute creates a presumption against the granting of bail. How would that presumption figure into your ruling on Jawad's release? Jawad's attorney has argued that a "presumption" against bail based simply on the seriousness of the charge he faces is inconsistent with the due process protections discussed in United States v. Salerno, 481 U.S. 739 (1987). Is this argument consistent with your reading of *Salerno*?

If you decide to release Jawad, what factual findings will best insulate that ruling from reversal on appeal? What financial and nonfinancial conditions would you place on his release? For a comparison point of typical bail amounts, see *http://bjs.ojp.usdoj.gov/content/pub/pdf/fdluc06.pdf*, at Table 6. Cf. Commonwealth v. Jawad, 2002 WL 31655285 (Va. App. 2002).

Notes

1. *Preventive detention: majority position.* Like the federal system, about half the states authorize courts to detain defendants before trial for the purpose of preventing the commission of new crimes ("preventive detention"). See, e.g., Mass. Gen. L. ch. 276, §58A. On the other hand, about 25 states have constitutional provisions that, like Tennessee, guarantee the right to bail except in capital cases. See People v. Purcell, 778 N.E.2d 695 (Ill. 2002) (strikes down law requiring defendant to show that guilt is not evident, because allocation of burden to accused is inconsistent with state constitution's presumption of bail); Ariana Lindermayer, What the Right Hand Gives: Prohibitive Interpretations of the State Constitutional Right to Bail, 78 Fordham L. Rev. 267 (2009). Detention based on risk of future crime is often distinguished from detention based on fear of flight or threat to witnesses. Do the categories of fear of flight or threat to witnesses overlap with risk of future crime?

Among states that authorize detention, the details of their statutes and constitutions vary substantially. Some states limit preventive detention to "serious crimes"; others limit detention to offenders with specific combinations of prior record and sufficiently serious current charges. A handful of states have enacted limits on the maximum time a defendant may be detained to prevent crimes. See, e.g., Mass. Gen. L. ch. 276, §58A (90 days); Wis. Stat. §969.035 (60 days). For a taxonomy of the state statutes that authorize pretrial detention and an analysis of trends, see the web extension for this chapter at *http://www.crimpro.com/extension/ch12*.

Why have so many states continued to reject preventive detention laws over the more than 15 years since passage of the federal Bail Reform Act and the decision of the Supreme Court in *Salerno*? Are other states likely, over time, to make the statutory and constitutional changes necessary to allow preventive detention? Some state constitutional provisions that seemed to bar the use of preventive detention have either been amended by the voters (e.g., Ohio Const. art. I, §9 was amended in 1997) or read restrictively to avoid any inconsistency with a new preventive detention statute. See State v. Ayala, 610 A.2d 1162 (Conn. 1992); Mo. Rev. Stat. §544.457 (allowing preventive detention "notwithstanding" constitutional guarantee of bail).

2. *Presumption of innocence.* The justices in *Salerno* disagreed about the meaning of the presumption of innocence. See Daniel Richman, *United States v. Salerno*: The Constitutionality of Regulatory Detention, in Criminal Procedure Stories (Carol Steiker, ed., 2006). A critic of the majority opinion might draw a comparison to the following passage from Lewis Carroll's *Through the Looking Glass,* where the Queen and Alice discuss the consequences of having a memory that works both ways:

> "I'm sure mine only works one way," Alice remarked. "I can't remember things before they happen."
>
> "It's a poor sort of memory that only works backward," the Queen remarked.
>
> "What sort of things do you remember best?" Alice ventured to ask.
>
> "Oh, things that happened the week after next," the Queen replied in a careless tone.
>
> "For instance, now," she went on, sticking a large piece of plaster on her finger as she spoke, "there's the King's Messenger. He's in prison now, being punished: and the trial doesn't even begin till next Wednesday: and of course the crime comes last of all."
>
> "Suppose he never commits the crime?" said Alice.
>
> "That would be all the better, wouldn't it?" the Queen said, as she bound the plaster round her finger with a bit of ribbon.
>
> Alice felt there was no denying that. "Of course it would be all the better," she said: "but it wouldn't be all the better his being punished."
>
> "You're wrong there, at any rate," said the Queen: "Were you ever punished?"
>
> "Only for faults," said Alice.
>
> "And you were all the better for it, I know!" the Queen said triumphantly.
>
> "Yes, but then I had done the things I was punished for," said Alice: "that makes all the difference."
>
> "But if you hadn't done them," the Queen said, "that would have been better still; better, and better, and better!" . . .
>
> Alice was just beginning to say, "There's a mistake somewhere — ," when the Queen began screaming, so loud that she had to leave the sentence unfinished. "Oh, oh, oh!" shouted the Queen, shaking her hand about as if she wanted to shake it off. "My finger's bleeding! Oh, oh, oh, oh!" . . .
>
> "What is the matter?" she said, as soon as there was a chance of making herself heard.
>
> "Have you pricked your finger?"
>
> "I haven't pricked it yet," the Queen said, "but I soon shall — oh, oh, oh!"

Is this the message of the *Salerno* opinion? If not, in what sense can we say that *Salerno* respects the presumption of innocence?

3. *Limitation to serious felonies and repeat offenders.* Most of the states passing new statutory or constitutional provisions to allow preventive detention have limited its use to criminal defendants who are accused of committing a select group of serious or violent felonies. See Mendonza v. Commonwealth, 673 N.E.2d 22 (Mass. 1996) (upholding revised statute under federal and state constitutions because it applies to felonies involving the use, or threatened use, of violence or abuse, or the violation of protective orders). Some, like the New Mexico constitutional provision above, apply only to those accused of a felony who have also been convicted of one or more felonies in the past. See also Colo. Const. art. II, §19 (new bail denied to those accused of committing violent crime while on prior bail, parole, or probation for previous charges of violent crime). Do both the "serious crime" and "repeat

offender" limitations serve the same purpose? Another variety of selective detention statutes applies only to defendants accused of a particularly high-priority crime, such as stalking or domestic violence. See Ill. Rev. Stat. ch. 725, para. 5/110-4. Do these provisions raise any concerns different from a provision focusing on all serious felonies?

4. *How many defendants are detained?* The number of defendants detained in the federal system is creeping upward. Among federal defendants in 1983 (the year before the passage of the Bail Reform Act), 24 percent remained in custody until their prosecutions were completed. In 1985 the figure rose to 29 percent (including those who failed to make bail and those who were ordered detained). In 2007 over 63 percent of federal defendants were not released before disposition of their cases. Bureau of Justice Statistics, Federal Justice Statistics, 2007 — Statistical Tables, at Table 3.1 (August 2010, NCJ 230889). As for the state systems, in large counties in 2006, 42 percent of defendants were detained until case disposition. See *http://bjs.ojp.usdoj.gov/content/pub/pdf/fdluc06.pdf*, at Table 6. These national average statistics obscure some real differences among jurisdictions.

What is the proper practical balance between the 1960s reform encouraging presumptive release and the 1980s reform encouraging open detention for those who threaten harm? Does detention until trial of almost one-third of those charged with felonies in the federal system seem too high? Does the federal system reflect the victory of candor? Is open preventive detention preferable to continued sub-rosa detention through unrealistically high bail requirements in states where there is no legal authority to detain defendants for the purpose of protecting the public from the commission of additional crimes?

5. *Compensation for wrongful detention.* Should the government compensate people who are detained under the Bail Reform Act or analogous state statutes and are later found at trial to be not guilty? See Masson v. Netherlands, 22 EHRR 491 (1996) (European Court of Human Rights reviewing domestic law that allows civil court, after a failure to convict a suspect in criminal proceedings, to grant compensation at expense of the state for damage suffered as a result of wrongful pretrial detention).

6. *Civil detention after completion of sentence.* States are now using post-sentence detention to extend their control over some persons convicted of sex offenses. Statutes passed since the mid-1990s authorize the government to request continued detention of convicted sex offenders after they have completed their sentences. These statutes typically require the government to demonstrate, on a year-to-year basis, that the offender remains "dangerous." The Supreme Court has upheld statutes against challenges based on the due process, ex post facto, and double jeopardy clause of the federal constitution. Kansas v. Hendricks, 521 U.S. 346 (1997). Employing the same distinction that it used in *Salerno,* the court said that this detention was "regulatory" rather than "punitive." See also Kansas v. Crane, 534 U.S. 407 (2002) (Constitution does not require judicial finding of total or complete lack of control to support regulatory detention of sexual offender, but Constitution does require a showing that person does lack some control over his or her behavior); United States v. Comstock, 130 S. Ct. 1949 (2010) (Necessary and Proper clause gives Congress authority to enact civil commitment statute that authorizes detention of sexually dangerous, mentally ill federal prisoners).

7. *The revenge of social science.* Social science studies were the driving force behind legal changes to make pretrial release easier and less dependent on money bail.

Similarly, social science figured prominently in the movement to expand the power of judges to detain defendants before trial. These studies focused on the number of defendants released before trial who were soon rearrested for committing additional crimes. In 2006, for example, 18 percent of released defendants were rearrested for a new offense allegedly committed within one year of release.

Over the past generation, we have reduced the number of people who are detained and have changed the acceptable reasons for detaining persons, allowing the detention of some defendants who at one time would have been released on bail. Do we now have it just about right? Are we now detaining the right people? Does this trend reflect a shift in the fundamental basis for the criminal law, punishing criminal propensities rather than criminal acts?

C. DETENTION OF EXCLUDABLE ALIENS AND ENEMY COMBATANTS

After the terrorist attacks of September 11, 2001, the federal government detained several groups of people as part of the effort to investigate the previous attacks and to prevent future terrorist crimes. First, the government detained a large number of noncitizens from Arab nations, present within the United States, on the basis of potential immigration violations such as expired student visas. Under the immigration laws, the government incarcerated these noncitizens for several months with limited access to counsel, while government agents investigated their potential immigration violations, along with their potential involvement in terrorist activities. The government did not release the precise number and identity of these detainees; estimates range from 1,200 to 2,000 persons. Many of these detainees were ultimately deported for their immigration violations, and a few were charged with crimes (although none were charged with crimes directly connected to terrorism). The government also declared that the immigration proceedings related to these people were closed to the public, and no individualized showing was needed to establish that secrecy was necessary in each particular case.

Second, the government detained dozens of people in the United States as "material witnesses" who might have information relating to the attacks. The traditional use of the federal material witness statute was to hold reluctant or fearful witnesses for a short time (typically a few days) to obtain their grand jury testimony. During this investigation, FBI agents obtained judicial approval for warrants allowing them to detain material witnesses, and then held them for several months; only about half the witnesses ever testified before a grand jury.

Third, the United States military captured men during the fighting in Afghanistan and transported several hundred of them to a military detention facility in Cuba. These men were held for questioning without criminal charges and without access to counsel. Problem 12-3 deals with the third category.

Problem 12-3. Traditions in Trying Times

During combat in Afghanistan in late 2001 and early 2002, U.S. military forces captured several hundred people on the battlefield. The military transported those captives to Guantanamo Bay in Cuba. The U.S. government designated those people as "enemy combatants" and detained them under the executive authority entrusted to the president as commander in chief of the armed forces.

The president issued a military order in November 2001 setting out procedures for the detention, treatment, and trial of "certain non-citizens in the war against terrorism." The order stipulated that it applied to any individual who was not a citizen of the United States, after the president determined in writing that there was reason to believe (1) that such individual was a member of al-Qaeda or (2) that he was engaged in international terrorism, or (3) that it was in the interests of the United States that he should be subject to the order. The order provided that any such individual would be detained at an appropriate location and treated humanely. It stated that any individual "when tried" would be tried by a military tribunal, and it contained extensive provisions relating to such a trial. It further declared:

> With respect to any individual subject to this order . . . the individual shall not be privileged to seek any remedy or maintain any proceeding, directly or indirectly, or to have any such remedy or proceeding sought on the individual's behalf, in (i) any court of the United States, or any State thereof, (ii) any court of any foreign nation, or (iii) any international tribunal.

One of these enemy combatants, Feroz Ali Abbasi, was a British national. His family filed a lawsuit in the British courts, asking the judge to order the Foreign Office to "make representations" on behalf of Abbasi to the United States government. The British court refused to grant this relief to Abbasi's family. The judge, however, also observed that subjecting a person to indefinite detention without giving the person any opportunity to challenge the detention before a court or tribunal appeared to violate basic principles of Anglo-American justice:

> The United States executive is detaining Mr. Abbasi . . . in circumstances where Mr. Abbasi can make no challenge to his detention before any court or tribunal. How long this state of affairs continues is within the sole control of the United States executive. . . .
>
> The United Kingdom and the United States share a great legal tradition, founded in the English common law. One of the cornerstones of that tradition is the ancient writ of habeas corpus, recognised at least by the time of Edward I, and developed by the 17th Century into "the most efficient protection yet developed for the liberty of the subject". . . .
>
> The underlying principle, fundamental in English law, is that every imprisonment is prima facie unlawful, and that no member of the executive can interfere with the liberty . . . of a British subject except on the condition that he can support the legality of his action before a court of justice. This principle applies to every person, British citizen or not, who finds himself within the jurisdiction of the court. . . . It applies in war as in peace; in Lord Atkin's words (written in one of the darkest periods of the last war): "In this country, amid the clash of arms, the laws are not silent. They may be changed, but they speak the same language in war as in peace." . . . As one would expect, endorsement of this common tradition is no less strong in the United States. . . . The

> recognition of this basic protection in both English and American law long pre-dates the adoption of the same principle as a fundamental part of international human rights law. . . .

Imagine that you work as an attorney at the U.S. Department of State. The Senate has begun to consider various legislative proposals to regulate the detention of "enemy combatants" such as Abbasi. The Senate Judiciary Committee, with jurisdiction over these bills, wants you to testify and to evaluate in general terms the regulation of detainees suspected of being terrorists or enemy combatants. In particular, the senators hope that your testimony will focus on the potential impact of detention practices on the nation's international relationships. Can the United States reassure other nations that specialized rules for detention of suspected terrorists will be used only in that specialized context?

Is it possible to maintain a distinction between detention for criminal purposes and detention for military purposes? As you think about this question, imagine that some additional terrorist atrocity is committed, perhaps by a group based in China. If investigators detained a large number of suspects of Chinese origin, what limits would apply to that detention? Cf. Feroz Abbasi v. Secretary of State, 2002 EWCA Civ. 1598 (Court of Appeal, Civil Division, 2002).

Notes

1. *Detention of excludable aliens.* In Zadvydas v. Davis, 533 U.S. 678 (2001), the Supreme Court interpreted a statute that, according to the government, allowed an alien who is subject to a final order of removal to be detained beyond a 90-day statutory "removal period" at the discretion of the attorney general. The Court construed the statute narrowly to avoid constitutional problems, and observed that as a matter of due process aliens could not be detained indefinitely following a final order of removal and that the attorney general had to justify continued detention. Two years later, however, the Court in Demore v. Kim, 538 U.S. 510 (2003), upheld a statute requiring mandatory detention for deportable criminal aliens, as applied to a lawful permanent resident who entered the United States at age six and was convicted of burglary and "petty theft with priors." Is it significant that *Zadvydas* was decided shortly before September 11 and *Demore* a year and a half after September 11?

2. *Migration of anti-terrorism practices to anti-crime efforts*. The ongoing efforts to resolve the questions surrounding detainees at Guantanamo Bay, together with the lively debate about the legitimacy of the government's use of the material witness statute as a detention device, receive fuller treatment on the web extension to this chapter at ***http://www.crimpro.com/extension/ch12***.

To what extent do government practices that develop in response to threats from terrorists ultimately spread to more ordinary anti-crime contexts? Scholars sometimes try to answer this question historically, by studying government responses to various emergencies around the world over the years. For instance, some criminologists characterize the government response to violence in Northern Ireland as a "contagion." According to this thesis, Northern Ireland served as a testing ground for repressive police practices that would later spread elsewhere to extend the authority of the state. See Aogàn Mulcahy, The "Other" Lessons from

Ireland? Policing, Political Violence and Policy Transfer, 2 Eur. J. Criminology 185 (2005) (based on qualitative interview data about impact of Northern Ireland conflict, assessing both the contagion thesis and more positive lessons other jurisdictions learned from the conflict); Oren Gross, Chaos and Rules: Should Responses to Violent Crises Always Be Constitutional? 112 Yale L.J. 1011 (2003) (collecting studies of impact of conflict in Northern Ireland and other prolonged "emergency" settings).

XIII

Charging

Soon after arrest, suspects learn why they have been detained. Most often, this occurs when the arresting officer files a form (sometimes called a complaint, sometimes an investigation report) indicating the charges to be filed against the arrestee. Those charges are subject to change at many points later in the process. A prosecutor ordinarily decides whether to accept the police officer's proposed charge and files that charge or another at an initial appearance before a judicial officer, a hearing that is given various names in different jurisdictions. This hearing takes place within a short period (typically 48 hours, or some other time defined by rule or statute). The charges can also change at an arraignment, when the defendant indicates how he will plead, or at a later hearing to test the adequacy of the evidence for trial, sometimes known as a preliminary examination. Charges can also be dismissed later in the process.

You might think of the charging process as a set of screens following investigation: Various government institutions help decide which persons in custody will become criminal defendants and which charges they will face. The arresting police officer and the officer's supervisor have some input into the charging decision. Prosecuting attorneys usually have the most important voice in determining whether to charge and what charges to select; criminal codes commonly give the prosecutor more than one legally viable option in a particular case. The prosecutor might follow personal criteria, policies and principles established for the office, or (less frequently) statutes dictating the charging decision. Courts are usually less involved in the charging decision than in most other procedural choices. Much of the time, courts review charging decisions only to confirm that there is a minimal amount of evidence supporting the charge, enough to justify "binding over" the case for trial. Grand juries are another special institution designed in part to determine whether there is probable cause to charge defendants, especially in more serious cases.

Because the prosecutor's choices dominate the charging phase, we concentrate in this chapter on sources of law other than appellate opinions, statutes, and rules. As you survey the charging process, ask whether the various executive branch guidelines and practices at work here are comparable in any way — in origins, function, evolution, and so on — to the way legislatures and courts craft rules.

A. POLICE SCREENING

Should police officers make an independent judgment about whether to file charges for every crime that might be charged? Should police departments set up internal mechanisms to review arrests before submitting a file or report to prosecutors? On what grounds might a police supervisor reject a charge when the facts appear to satisfy the elements of the crime?

Police screening of charges is largely hidden in the modern, big-city criminal process. Hints about the extent of police screening can be seen in occasional studies of "clearance rates" and case "attrition." Clearance rates refer to the percentage of complaints made to police that are solved in some fashion. Attrition is the term describing how initial complaints drop out of the criminal process and why only a relatively small percentage of complaints end with convictions.

The amount of case attrition in a system depends on the interaction between police and prosecutors. Where the police and prosecutors have different ideas about which cases are worthwhile, many cases that the police assemble will fall out of the system, some sooner and some later. Police screening represents an effort to anticipate how the prosecutor will evaluate the case.

In the following rules from two different police departments, what differences do you see in the working relationships between police and prosecutors as they decide on charges? The correspondence reprinted below reveals the tensions between prosecution and police departments that can arise when the prosecutor and law enforcement do not agree on charging priorities. The county in question is a rural jurisdiction that faces significant crime concerns in connection with illegal immigration.

■ PHILADELPHIA POLICE DEPARTMENT, DIRECTIVE 50, SUBJECT: INVESTIGATION AND CHARGING PROCEDURE

I. Policy

A. All adults arrested for a felony or misdemeanor offense will be investigated, processed and charged in accordance with the procedures outlined in this directive. . . .

C. The Complaint Fact Sheet (CFS) will serve as the police report for the District Attorney's Charging Unit (DACU). Prior to slating a defendant, the DACU should receive the CFS from the investigating unit to clarify certain facts or to supply needed information. . . .

E. The Criminal Complaint will be prepared and delivered to the Arraignment Court by the DACU.

II. Investigating Unit Procedure

A. The assigned investigator will prepare the following forms:

1. Arrest Report
2. Hearing Sheet
3. Investigator's Aid to Interview
4. Complaint Fact Sheet. . . .
5. Investigation Report

B. The assigned investigator will ensure that:

1. When charging a suspect with a misdemeanor or felony offense, appropriate summary offenses are included in the Arrest Reports and Complaint Fact Sheet. Substantiated facts and testimony will be included in these reports to support all charges listed. . . .

3. The CFS is promptly submitted to the unit supervisor for review. . . .

4. In division/units electronically equipped with a facsimile transceiver, the CFS will be transmitted to the DACU immediately after review and approval by the supervisor. . . .

C. The investigating unit supervisor will ensure that:

1. The Complaint Fact Sheet is properly prepared and the charges are appropriate for the facts and testimony as listed on the CFS.

2. Review and approve CFS.

3. The CFS is promptly transmitted to the DACU if electronically equipped to do so. . . .

6. When any charges are modified or disapproved by the DACU, attach the Record of Declination form (when received) to the CFS . . . , and submit to the commanding officer for review. . . .

D. Commanding Director of the Investigating Unit will [review] all modified and disapproved CFS and compare with submitted [CFS] for consistency [and forward] a memorandum through the chain of command describing any case where modification or disapproval appears to be totally unjustified or inconsistent with previous DACU decisions and policies.

HOUSTON POLICE DEPARTMENT GENERAL ORDER 500-7

Effective law enforcement requires cooperation between police officers and members of the district attorney's office. It is the purpose of this General Order to establish procedural guidelines for officers to use when consulting with the district attorney's office regarding the filing of charges.

1. Consultation With an Assistant District Attorney

Before using the computer terminal to file any charges with the district attorney's office, the officer filing the charges must speak with an assistant district attorney to ensure that the charges will be accepted. During the consultation, the officer shall provide the elements of the offense, sufficient details to show that probable cause existed to arrest the person and evidence that the person being charged did in fact commit the offense. These probable cause details should be included in the charges filed via the [computer]. It is important that an adequate probable-cause statement be contained in the warrant because this is sometimes the only information available to the assistant district attorney when the defendant is arraigned before a magistrate during a probable-cause hearing.

An assistant district attorney also will be consulted before the simultaneous filing of both county *and* municipal charges against *one* suspect if these charges are based on the same set of circumstances or the same criminal action. This consultation eliminates the possibility of a case being dismissed because of noncompliance with the Speedy Trial Act or because of violations of legal restraints against placing a defendant in double jeopardy.

Whenever an officer is unsure of the elements of a particular case, he shall discuss the matter with his immediate supervisor or contact the district attorney's office. Under no circumstances will a lesser charge be filed merely as a matter of convenience. For example, a charge of public intoxication will not be filed if the actual offense was driving while intoxicated. Appropriate charges shall be filed according to the elements of the offense.

2. Rejection of Charges by Assistant District Attorneys

If an officer tries to file charges through the district attorney's intake office and these charges are rejected, he will include the following information in his original or supplemental offense report: a) Time and date the officer spoke with the assistant district attorney about filing charges in the case; b) Name of the assistant district attorney who rejected the charges; [and] c) Reasons given by the assistant district attorney for rejecting the charges.

If the charges are rejected because of alleged mishandling by an officer, the officer will refer the case to his supervisor for review. If the supervisor does find mishandling on the part of the officer, he shall instruct the officer on policy and proper procedures, to avert recurrences. . . .

■ CORRESPONDENCE IN COCHISE COUNTY, ARIZONA

Dear Chief Nichols:

In the past, I have spoken a couple of times about Cochise County being the only county in the state where police officers file their own felony criminal complaints without the complaints first being reviewed by a prosecutor. Indeed, since taking office last year, I have learned that most counties discontinued this practice years ago.

As you know, when an arrest is made for a felony offense, a felony complaint must be filed within 48 hours of the arrest, or the charge must be dismissed and the subject must be released from custody. If the felony complaint is filed within 48 hours and the subject is in custody, the County Attorney's Office must indict within 10 days of the initial appearance, or the subject must be released from custody. . . .

We all know that a high number of cases forwarded to the County Attorney's Office each week end up being dismissed, without prejudice, because, either they cannot be fit into the grand jury's schedule for that week, or the case, in the opinion of the reviewing prosecutor, requires further investigation and/or additional evidence. Another reason why cases are dismissed is that evidence is at the lab awaiting analysis and, sometimes, it is not until the evidence is analyzed that we can be sure a crime has been committed, or what crime to charge. . . . I would estimate that of the cases which are submitted to this office after a felony complaint has been filed, virtually half are dismissed without prejudice for one or more of the reasons cited above.

When a suspect is arrested and a felony complaint is filed, legal wheels start turning and resources are expended, primarily in the form of Justice Court time and costs of incarceration in the county jail. When that same felony complaint is dismissed by this office, more costs are incurred in reversing the arrest, initial appearance and incarceration processes. What's more, all of these costs are incurred by the taxpayers of Cochise County with absolutely no benefit to the taxpayers. On top of that, I believe that many people, not the least of which are those who are arrested and charged, misunderstand what has happened and mistakenly believe that once the charge(s) has been dismissed, the case is over and the suspect has gotten away with a crime. I think that the creation of this misperception does a disservice to the citizens of Cochise County.

Even though I have spoken in the past about moving toward a system where all cases are reviewed by a prosecutor before a felony complaint is filed, I have hesitated to do so for several reasons. First and foremost, I don't want anyone in the field of law enforcement to perceive the change as being, in any way, a criticism of law enforcement procedures. Police officers are not lawyers. They cannot be expected to . . . anticipate the chances of successful prosecution by way of either a plea agreement, or a jury trial. In having police officers file felony complaints, it puts them in a position of having to arrive at conclusions that they are, simply, not trained, or experienced enough to draw. They should not have to handle this burden.

Secondly, it will require some amount of reorganization in the County Attorney's Office. Since we have 48 hours in which to file a felony complaint after an arrest is made, there's no need for an officer to consult with a prosecutor immediately after an arrest. . . . When reports are ready, they can be faxed to the County Attorney's Office and then the reviewing prosecutor can speak directly to the case officer. We will, of course, have to organize our office so that a prosecutor will be available. The only times an officer will have to contact the prosecutor off hours is when an arrest is made, for instance, on a Friday night and the felony complaint must be filed by Sunday evening, or when there is a long weekend. . . .

I have enclosed a new checklist form which, I believe, will further streamline the interaction between prosecutors and officers by eliminating, as much as possible, repeated contacts between prosecutors and officers to communicate what evidence exists and what additional evidence may be needed. Additionally, we continue to have significant disclosure problems which have had an impact on admissible evidence at trial. . . . By using the checklist, both officers and prosecutors will be on the same page, when discussing the case, and whether to file a felony complaint. [The checklist] should virtually eliminate the problem of the case officer claiming that a report was sent and our office claiming it was never received. . . .

I suspect that some officers may perceive that the checklist will increase the amount of work they have to do, but I think it merely "front loads" the process. In other words, all of the things on the checklist are things which have to be provided sooner or later; this just rearranges the sequence so that these things are provided at the beginning of the prosecution. . . .

Let me emphasize, however, that when an arrest is made of a dangerous person, or someone who *absolutely has to be kept in custody,* we will definitely not sacrifice the safety of the public in favor of following these procedures. Under those circumstances, the highest priority must be public safety and we will make sure that that remains our highest priority.

I am proposing that we look at implementing these procedures 60 days after the date of this letter. I would also propose that I come to each department and meet with as many officers as possible to discuss the implementation of these procedures. I will be available seven days a week, day or night, to do this. [I am also] more than willing to meet with the Chiefs and Sheriff as a group, or individually.

Thank you for the support you all have given me over the past year, and I look forward to working with you to better serve our respective communities and Cochise County as a whole.

Sincerely,
Edward G. Rheinheimer, Cochise County Attorney

Mr. Rheinheimer:

The Chiefs of Police, whose signatures appear on this letter, have reviewed and discussed your recent letter with the attached felony submission checklist. We would like to share the following comments with you regarding your proposal. . . .

We certainly understand the timeliness requirements surrounding felony complaints, but your letter does not give sufficient information on the problems encountered by your office that would encourage us to support your proposals. The truth is, you have not provided information on how many cases are presented, how many go to Grand Jury, and how many are dismissed. Certainly the newspaper, which received a copy of your letter, is unaware of these facts. Additionally, you provide a number of justifications for case dismissals in your letter. These justifications may delay a case for trial, but certainly not for grand jury.

We are extremely concerned with the dismissal of cases and your inability to take them to a grand jury. It also appears that you are asking for unrealistic burdens beyond the evidentiary requirement of probable cause for grand jury presentations. Does the prosecutor, who enjoys absolute immunity, shift a civil burden to the officer, who only enjoys qualified immunity, when a decision is made by your office that insufficient evidence exists to take a case to grand jury? . . . If your estimates are correct and half of the felony cases filed in your office are dismissed for evidentiary requirements beyond those to establish probable cause, we submit this whole exercise is truly a red herring.

We would all hope that your intent in the [fifth paragraph of your letter] is to not inflame an already rocky relationship with law enforcement officials, but your statements are hasty generalizations. Certainly some officers have more experience than some prosecutors and vice versa. Police officers are not lawyers and thank goodness for that! If lawyers had to make decisions in the split seconds our police officers have, people would be needlessly injured! There is a strong argument that the police officers need to know the law better than the lawyers, because of the need to apply it in immediate situations. . . .

It is of great comfort that you agree in cases where someone *absolutely* has to be kept in custody, your office will not sacrifice the safety of the public. We could be mistaken, but that decision should be made by courts in the bond process and not by the prosecutor in a decision on whether to proceed to grand jury. We are already releasing arrestees on citations when possible, but [an unjustified release] does a disservice to the victims that have called the police and expect that the suspect will be arrested. . . . We already receive complaints when the officers fail to make arrests and quite frankly the public doesn't care about the burdens placed on the criminal justice system when they are victimized. They pay taxes for the police to make arrests, the prosecutors to take the cases to trial, and when found guilty, the public expects the perpetrator to receive some sort of punishment through the courts.

In reviewing the proposed checklist, we can only expect that this system is doomed for failure. We already know that case reports are lost, so unless your office has another filing system in mind, multiple cases and checklists will still be confused and lost. If we are still talking about grand jury requirements, too many of the questions on the checklist will go unanswered. There are a multitude of duplicated information requests on the form as well as questions that the case officer will not be able to answer or provide immediately after an arrest. There are requests for tapes, photos, diagrams, lab analysis and other documents that will be impossible to provide within 48 hours. This process will still require multiple submissions, a goal that this checklist is trying to defeat. . . .

In summary, we would certainly support a working group to investigate these issues. . . . It may even help to hire an outside consultant to review these problems and make recommendations to a governing body like the County Board of Supervisors. There are obvious problems that even the layperson would be able to identify. [It] is clear that one day of grand jury per week is not sufficient for a county with our current population and crime rates. It won't matter what system we use for the approval of felony complaints, unless we ignore the crime taking place, these cases will either be presented to the Grand Jury, reduced to misdemeanors, or be dismissed for some other reason and perhaps never prosecuted.

Our police officers are risking their lives to protect the community they serve. We don't believe they will sit back and listen to someone who insults their intelligence and minimizes the importance of their duty. The officers are frustrated with the criminal justice system, as it currently exists in Cochise County. . . . Shifting burdens or pointing fingers will not fix the criminal justice system. There needs to be a concerted effort on all of our parts to participate in a solution, but one that truly identifies the problem and is not based upon unsupported conclusions.

Respectfully,
Glenn Nichols; Chief of Police; Benson, Arizona
James Elkins; Chief of Police; Bisbee, Arizona
Charles Austin; Chief of Police; Douglas, Arizona
Dennis Grey; Chief of Police; Huachuca City, Arizona
David Santor; Chief of Police; Sierra Vista, Arizona
Jake Weaver; Chief of Police; Willcox, Arizona

Notes

1. *Police screening.* Police departments have many different approaches to screening cases. Many departments do not openly acknowledge that officers screen cases *after* arrest, even though almost all police officials recognize the substantial discretion of police officers in making arrest decisions. See Chapter 5. Some departments train officers to select certain kinds of charges from among different possible charges. Other departments institute a formal screening process, either at the scene of an arrest or as part of the booking process at jail. This screening can take the form of review by a supervisor or by an officer trained to examine the facts of cases and the charges filed. Many departments establish methods of pretransfer review by prosecutors. Under the Philadelphia and Houston police department policies reprinted above, how early do prosecutors review the charges? Which system gives the police greater control over the selection of initial charges?

2. *Police-prosecutor cooperation in the charging decision.* In some jurisdictions, the police and the prosecutors pursue conflicting visions of the best charging practices. As the letters from Cochise County indicate, the police might evaluate cases in light of the probable cause standard necessary to support an indictment or information, while the prosecutor might evaluate the case in light of the standard of proof at trial. At a deeper level, police officers and prosecutors might differ about the value of testing the evidence assembled against a defendant through an adversarial process. How would you advise Mr. Rheinheimer to respond to the letter from the police chiefs? Following up on the suggestion in the police chiefs' letter, Cochise County did rely on independent consultants, who recommended that the county implement felony complaint filing by the Cochise County Attorney's Office and discontinue the practice of law enforcement agencies filing felony complaints. The consultants also interviewed prosecutors and police officers in the county, and made a series of observations about the communications necessary to bridge the gap in perceptions between the police and prosecutors. A copy of the consultants' report appears on the web extension for this chapter at *http://www.crimpro.com/extension/ch13*.

In Houston, the general order reprinted above represents a long-term effort to avoid wasting resources when police and prosecutors do not coordinate their charging decisions. Trial lawyers staff the charging unit to answer inquiries from the police 24 hours a day. Police call from crime scenes and roadside stops for advice. Typically, the officers will not arrest or charge a suspect if the consulting prosecutor will not agree to accept charges. From the prosecutors' vantage point, this process serves the purpose of educating police officers about the proof required for conviction of various crimes; it also strengthens cases when the prosecutor advises the officer to take pictures, record statements, or pursue other investigative leads. Because the line prosecutors who receive the calls from the police must sign the charges they accept, they have some professional stake in the viability of the charges. They sometimes must persuade officers who are frustrated with belligerent suspects not to file charges based on that short-term frustration.

3. *Police cautions in England.* Because the police in England make the initial decision whether to prosecute a criminal case, a practice has grown up (without a statutory basis) known as a "police caution." The caution is a warning to an arrested person, delivered by a senior police officer. If the person accepts the caution, the police agree not to refer the case to the Crown Prosecution Service. The caution

becomes part of the offender's prior record. The Home Secretary has issued "National Standards for Cautioning" to guide police decisions in this area. See Home Office Circular 18/1994, The Cautioning of Offenders; Andrew Ashworth, The Criminal Process (2d ed. 1998). Does the consent of the suspect (when he accepts a caution) make the caution fundamentally different from a conviction in police court?

4. *Screening and "the tank."* Police departments exercising a screening function may release a person under arrest before the time for an initial appearance. In the meantime, arrestees can spend one or two nights in the local jail or holding facility before release. What circumstances might properly lead a police department to arrest and then release a person without filing formal charges? Are the police effectively given the power to punish citizens for short periods of time without prosecutorial or judicial supervision? Should prosecutors review all arrests, even when the police department does not believe charges should be pursued?

B. PROSECUTORIAL SCREENING

Prosecutors (who go by various names, such as "district attorneys," "county attorneys," "state's attorneys," or simply "prosecuting attorneys") have the most to say about whether to file charges against a suspect and which charges to select. Granted, they react to an initial charge proposed by the police, and they may have to convince a judge or a grand jury that there is enough evidence to justify going forward with a prosecution. But in the end, the prosecutor can overrule police charging decisions without interference, and judges and grand juries only rarely refuse to go forward with the prosecutor's charging decisions.

The prosecutor's broad charging discretion has a long history in the common law. Judges today explain their reluctance to become involved in charging decisions on three grounds: (1) under the separation of powers doctrine, the executive branch has the responsibility to enforce the criminal law; (2) judges are poorly situated to make judgments about allocation of limited prosecutorial resources; and (3) overbroad provisions in criminal codes require selection from among the possible charges that could be filed.

The charging decision is subject to some limits. The constraining rules come primarily from prosecutorial office policies, but they also appear at times in statutes and in a few judicial decisions. Even when charging decisions are not subject to such limits, external influences make them somewhat patterned and predictable. What considerations — both legal and otherwise — direct this prosecutorial decision?

1. *Encouraging or Mandating Criminal Charges*

Should prosecutors pursue every crime brought to them? Could they? Are there instances in which the substantial discretion of prosecutors should be limited or removed?

Many jurisdictions have restricted the power of prosecutors to decline or divert domestic assault cases, because these cases present distinctive challenges for prosecutors. "No-drop" prosecutorial policies combine with other system-wide policy initiatives regarding domestic assaults, including mandatory arrest policies (considered in Chapter 5), detention policies (considered in Chapter 12), and sentencing policies.

The scope of the domestic violence problem is daunting. Domestic violence is found at all socio-economic levels, among all races and age groups, and among people with all levels of education. More than one million American women are battered each year by their husbands or partners. Patricia Tjaden & Nancy Thoennes, U.S. Dept. of Justice, NCJ 183781, Full Report of the Prevalence, Incidence, and Consequences of Intimate Partner Violence Against Women: Findings from the National Violence Against Women Survey, at iv (2000), available at *http://www.ojp.usdoj.gov/nij/pubs-sum/183781.htm*.

Victims of abuse are often reluctant to testify in criminal cases against their partners, preferring that prosecutors drop the charges. Immediately following an assault, an abusive spouse is typically apologetic and attentive, promising to change. Later, tension builds and the abusive spouse becomes unpredictable and threatening again, often leading to another episode of battering. Victim advocates report that an abused woman will return to her partner an average of six times before she leaves permanently. A battered spouse is often isolated, having few friends or sources of support. She also might find the criminal process to be daunting and frustrating, particularly if the prosecutor fails to file serious charges in the case or delays its progress.

A prosecutor's office can address some of these problems by adopting a "no-drop" policy, mandating prosecution for all domestic violence cases filed. Such a policy takes the victim "off the hook" and insulates her from pressure to drop the case coming from her partner, family, and friends. These policies also emphasize that society at large has an interest in deterring domestic violence. Domestic violence can lead to murder or to injuries that require medical treatment. Children growing up in violent families are more likely to suffer from alcohol or drug abuse, and are more likely to commit violent crimes themselves later in life.

The materials that follow offer several different responses to the special problems of domestic violence. The provisions from Italy, Germany, and West Virginia that close this unit place the issue of mandatory prosecution in a more general context.

■ FLORIDA STATUTES §741.2901

(1) Each state attorney shall develop special units or assign prosecutors to specialize in the prosecution of domestic violence cases, but such specialization need not be an exclusive area of duty assignment. These prosecutors, specializing in domestic violence cases, and their support staff shall receive training in domestic violence issues.

(2) It is the intent of the Legislature that domestic violence be treated as a criminal act rather than a private matter. . . . The state attorney in each circuit shall adopt a pro-prosecution policy for acts of domestic violence. . . . The filing, nonfiling, or diversion of criminal charges, and the prosecution of violations of injunctions for protection against domestic violence by the state attorney, shall be determined by these specialized prosecutors over the objection of the victim, if necessary. . . .

WISCONSIN STATUTES §968.075

(7) Each district attorney's office shall develop, adopt and implement written policies encouraging the prosecution of domestic abuse offenses. The policies shall include, but not be limited to, the following:

(a) A policy indicating that a prosecutor's decision not to prosecute a domestic abuse incident should not be based:

1. Solely upon the absence of visible indications of injury or impairment;

2. Upon the victim's consent to any subsequent prosecution of the other person involved in the incident; or

3. Upon the relationship of the persons involved in the incident.

(b) A policy indicating that when any domestic abuse incident is reported to the district attorney's office, including a report [which police officers are required by law to submit after responding to a domestic abuse incident], a charging decision by the district attorney should, absent extraordinary circumstances, be made not later than two weeks after the district attorney has received notice of the incident. . . .

(9) Each district attorney shall submit an annual report to the department of justice listing [the] number of arrests for domestic abuse incidents in his or her county as compiled and furnished by the law enforcement agencies within the county [and the] number of subsequent prosecutions and convictions of the persons arrested for domestic abuse incidents. . . .

PROSECUTION GUIDELINES FOR DULUTH, MINNESOTA

The prosecution guidelines of the Duluth City Attorney's Office were first conceived in 1982. The current guidelines are a result of revisions made in 1989. The guidelines were developed through extensive meetings and discussions between prosecutors in the criminal division of the City Attorney's Office and staff persons of the Domestic Abuse Intervention Project (DAIP). The guidelines are used consistently by prosecutors in Duluth in the prosecution of domestic abuse cases.

These guidelines provide a framework upon which to base decisions. They do not make up a specific set of absolute procedures to fit the myriad possibilities these cases present. The prosecution goals stated below sometimes come into conflict and need to be balanced, based on the circumstances of each case. Because of the complex nature of victims' reluctance to testify against abusers, the prosecutor should not be motivated by a desire to punish the victim in effectuating the goals of this policy.

The goals of prosecution in domestic abuse cases are: 1) to protect the victim from additional acts of violence committed by the defendant, 2) to deter the defendant from committing continued acts of violence against others in the community, [and] 3) to create a general deterrence to battering in the community. In the prosecution of cases, the prosecutor will assist in maximizing the ability of the court to place controls on the abuser and in deterring continued use of violence by following these guidelines:

1) The prosecutor will seek to obtain convictions as an optimum result and will avoid entering into conditional deferrals, except where supported by statute, ordinance, case law, the Minnesota Rules of Criminal Procedure, and rules of conduct for prosecutors.
2) The prosecutor will attempt to proceed with these cases with as few continuances as possible to increase the likelihood of a conviction and to decrease the abuser's opportunity to pressure the victim and to continue to commit violent acts against her/him.
3) Whenever possible, the prosecutor and law enforcement officials will sign the complaint.
4) The prosecutor will subpoena the victim to shield her/him from pressure from the abuser or other parties who do not want the victim to participate in the case as a witness.
5) The prosecutor will approach plea agreements with the intent of expediting the goals of the prosecution, especially that of protecting the victim. Plea agreements will not be used to reduce the prosecutor's case load or the court's calendar. . . .
6) To ensure that victims have access to advocacy, the prosecutor will make a reasonable effort to provide information to the shelter . . . regarding cases charged in which no arrest procedure occurred. . . .
7) The prosecutor will review police investigation reports submitted by the police department in cases which did not result in an arrest but in which police officers believe that prosecution is warranted. . . .
8) The prosecutor shall make available to the shelter and the DAIP information regarding the disposition of all cases and actions taken on police investigation reports. . . .

■ ITALIAN CONSTITUTION ART. 112

The public prosecutor has the duty to exercise criminal proceedings.

■ GERMAN CODE OF CRIMINAL PROCEDURE 152(2)

[The public prosecutor] is required . . . to take action against all judicially punishable . . . acts, to the extent that there is a sufficient factual basis. [Translator: John Langbein]

■ WEST VIRGINIA CODE §7-4-1

It shall be the duty of the prosecuting attorney to attend to the criminal business of the State in the county in which he is elected and qualified, and when he has information of the violation of any penal law committed within such county, he shall institute and prosecute all necessary and proper proceedings against the offender, and may in such case issue or cause to be issued a summons for any witness he may deem material. . . .

Notes

1. *Discretion in filing charges: majority position.* At common law, each local prosecutor had complete discretion to refuse to file charges or to dismiss charges after they had been filed. See Wilson v. Renfroe, 91 So. 2d 857 (Fla. 1956). This remains the dominant position for most crimes in almost all jurisdictions, but there are three limited exceptions to this general rule. First, for some crimes (including domestic assault and weapons charges) some jurisdictions have implemented mandatory prosecution policies. See Daniel C. Richman, "Project Exile" and the Allocation of Federal Law Enforcement Authority, 43 Ariz. L. Rev. 369 (2001) (weapons offenses). Second, a few jurisdictions have statutes suggesting that prosecutors have an obligation to prosecute crimes for which they believe probable cause exists. See, e.g., Ala. Code §12-17-184. Third, some jurisdictions provide the state attorney general with varying degrees of supervisory power over all local prosecutors. See Conn. Gen. Stat. §§51-275 to 51-277; Del. Code Ann. tit. 29, §2502.

2. *No-drop policies for domestic abuse cases.* Several states, including Florida and Wisconsin, have enacted laws encouraging or requiring the development of plans and policies to increase prosecutions and convictions in domestic abuse cases. Many jurisdictions, however, have implemented written or unwritten guidelines within the prosecutor's office about domestic abuse cases in the absence of specific legislative guidance. A growing group of state attorneys general (for instance, in New Jersey and North Carolina) have adopted statewide policies discouraging local prosecutors from dropping domestic violence charges. Policies like the one set out in the Florida statute, encouraging the prosecutor to proceed over the victim's objections, are known as "hard no-drop" policies; the more common policies, focusing on victim support and encouragement, are known as "soft no-drop" policies. Other approaches require the prosecutor to consult with the victim or with other individuals or agencies before dismissing a prosecution. Should the decision be left to the police, or should it depend on the victim's willingness to make an initial complaint?

Academic researchers and policy innovators devote considerable attention to the effects of no-drop policies. Advocates of no-drop policies for domestic violence cases start with the observation that the rate of prosecution for domestic violence complaints remains lower than the rate of prosecution for other types of complaints. They devise various methods of measuring whether these prosecutorial policies change the prosecution rate. They also inquire about the effects of no-drop policies on later stages of the criminal process, and of course, the effects of the policy on the actual levels of domestic violence. For some selections from the ever-growing body of research on this question, go to the web extension for this chapter at *http://www.crimpro.com/extension/ch13*.

3. *Case "attrition."* The phenomenon of cases "falling out" of the criminal justice process is commonly referred to as case "attrition." One possible reaction to the level of case attrition is to claim that police and prosecutors are failing in their obligation to protect the public. What are other possible implications of case attrition? A famous study conducted in the 1970s closely examined case attrition for felony cases in New York City. Vera Institute of Justice, Felony Arrests: Their Prosecution and Disposition in New York City's Courts (Malcolm Feeley ed., rev. ed. 1980). It found an unexpectedly high level of prior relationships throughout felony crime

categories, and it attributed the bulk of case attrition to the relationships between the parties involved.

> [Criminal] conduct is often the explosive spillover from ruptured personal relations among neighbors, friends and former spouses. Cases in which the victim and defendant were known to each other constituted 83 percent of rape arrests, 69 percent of assault arrests, 36 percent of robbery arrests, and 39 percent of burglary arrests. The reluctance of the complainants in these cases to pursue prosecution (often because they were reconciled with the defendants or in some cases because they feared the defendants) accounted for a larger portion of the high dismissal rate than any other factor.

Does this study suggest that the problems with domestic abuse victims as reliable complainants are also commonplace for other crimes? Does this study suggest reasons to hesitate in implementing a no-drop policy for domestic abuse cases, or does it offer a reason to consider no-drop policies for some other crimes? From another perspective, is there a proper ratio of convictions to complaints (or arrests) for most types of crimes?

4. *Specialized units in prosecutors' offices.* Although the criminal code might give prosecutors huge amounts of discretion over whether to file criminal charges, the legislature or the chief prosecutor might structure the prosecutor's office in ways that will encourage the filing of some criminal charges and discourage the filing of others. For instance, the office might have specialized units whose work is easy to monitor. Line items in budgets offer strong incentives to pursue certain charges. Some investigative techniques or charging decisions require special authorization from those high in the prosecutorial hierarchy. These office structures establish predictable limits on the reach of substantive criminal laws, even when those criminal laws are drafted very broadly and delegate nominally large powers to the prosecutor.

5. *Charging discretion in foreign legal systems.* The civil law tradition that prevails in most legal systems of the world nominally denies the prosecutor discretion in charging. The "legality" principle requires the prosecutor to file charges whenever they have evidence to support the charges. Studies of such systems — especially the Italian, German, and French systems, which have received relatively close examination — suggest that prosecutors, in fact, exercise a substantial degree of discretion in charging. See, e.g., Marco Fabri, Theory Versus Practice of Italian Criminal Justice Reform, 77 Judicature 211 (Jan.-Feb. 1994). As the volume increases in criminal justice systems, the prosecutors divert more cases from full adjudication. Some civil law systems now recognize a principle of "expediency" that ratifies this prosecutorial power to set priorities among cases. See Jorg-Martin Jehle & Marianne Wade, Coping with Overloaded Criminal Justice Systems: The Rise of Prosecutorial Power Across Europe (2006).

Meanwhile, even in common law jurisdictions such as England, judges hold more influence over charging decisions than they do in the United States. Judges can review the reasonableness of a prosecutor's decision not to prosecute, a decision to prosecute, or a police decision to issue a formal "caution" instead of forwarding the case to the prosecutorial service. See R. v. Chief Constable of Kent ex rel. L, (1991) 93 Cr. App. R. 416 (review of juvenile case based on prosecutors' own Code for Crown Prosecutors policy); R. v. DPP ex rel. Kebilene, [2000] 2 AC 326 (review of decision to prosecute adults in a select set of offenses).

6. *Mandatory charging statutes in the United States.* The West Virginia Code creates what seems to be a nondiscretionary charging obligation, in sync with the provisions from Italy and Germany. However, prosecutors retain substantial discretion in West Virginia despite the mandatory language of the statute. See State ex rel. Bailey v. Facemire, 413 S.E.2d 183 (W. Va. 1991). The Colorado Criminal Code permits a person to challenge the district attorney's decision not to charge, but the Colorado Supreme Court has warned that the statute does not permit a judge to substitute her judgment for that of the prosecutor. Colo. Rev. Stat. §16-5-209. The court must find that the "district attorney's decision was arbitrary or capricious and without reasonable excuse" before it will step in. Landis v. Farish, 674 P.2d 957, 958 (Colo. 1984). Are there universal realities of justice systems that make mandatory charging provisions unlikely to succeed?

2. *Declination and Diversion*

The initial question that a prosecutor faces is whether to file criminal charges at all. Many times when the police believe a person has committed a crime, the prosecutor "declines" to file charges. Prosecutors can also "divert" charges from the criminal process by suspending any decision about filing criminal charges while the potential defendant completes some agreed-upon rehabilitative or restitution program. If the person carries out the agreement, the prosecutor declines to file charges (or drops existing charges). If the defendant does not meet the conditions, the prosecutor goes forward with the charges. Are the legal and practical controls on declination and diversion decisions likely to be the same?

a. Declination Policies

Declinations are typically based on a prosecutor's ad hoc discretionary decision that the pursuit of criminal charges is not a good use of the limited resources of the office or is not a proper use of the criminal sanction. Sometimes, however, these discretionary decisions will develop into a pattern that may become formalized in internal office policies or rules. Chief prosecutors will at times create declination policies to control the decisions of the attorneys in the office. On rare occasions, statutes or judicial rulings require the creation of general policies to govern declinations.

The Justice Department produced the first two documents reprinted below in response to two critical reports from the General Accounting Office, a research arm of Congress. The most controversial of those reports was titled "U.S. Attorneys Do Not Prosecute Many Suspected Violators of Federal Law" (February 27, 1978). The third document contains federal guidelines for charging corporate defendants.

■ U.S. DEPARTMENT OF JUSTICE, UNITED STATES ATTORNEYS' WRITTEN GUIDELINES FOR THE DECLINATION OF ALLEGED VIOLATIONS OF FEDERAL CRIMINAL LAWS

A Report to the United States Congress (November 1979)

This report examines the written guidelines issued by various United States Attorneys concerning the types of alleged violations of federal criminal laws they will normally decline to prosecute. . . . They are promulgated by United States Attorneys, with the Department's knowledge and encouragement, as a means of formalizing and crystallizing prosecutorial priorities, thereby increasing the effectiveness of limited prosecutorial and investigative resources. Written guidelines represent United States Attorneys' attempts to respond to local demands and circumstances within the context of national law enforcement priorities. They are typically formulated after consideration of Department policies and consultation with federal investigative agencies. . . .

Although written declination guidelines are sometimes referred to as "blanket" declinations, they are, either explicitly or implicitly, made subject to the caveat that unusual or aggravating circumstances should always be considered before any complaint is declined. Decisions to decline cases pursuant to written guidelines are also typically subject to reconsideration, for example, if matters are referred to state and local prosecutors and declined or not pursued by them. In addition, alleged offenses that would otherwise be subject to the guidelines may be prosecuted in clusters at a later date if enough similar offenses accumulate and prosecution would have a significant deterrent impact.

Written declination guidelines are applied with varying degrees of frequency to different categories of federal criminal offenses. [They] are usually expressed in terms of the amount of money or value of property involved, whether the offense appears to be connected with other criminal activity, or other similar factors. The ranges and distributions of declination "cut-off points" vary across districts. For some offenses, the declination cut-off points of the various districts congregate around similar values and factors, while for others, the declination guidelines show considerable variation among districts. . . . Of the 94 United States Attorneys' offices, 83 reported written declination guidelines in some form. The remaining 11 offices reported that they did not have written guidelines, but instead made all declination decisions on a case-by-case basis.

[Declination] policies are a crucial part of the investigative and prosecutorial system. Investigators and prosecutors alike rely upon such policies to help channel limited law enforcement resources toward their most productive uses. Indeed, since law enforcement resources are limited, it is clearly impossible to investigate and prosecute every alleged criminal violation. Some priorities are required to reduce wastage and to increase the effective deployment of scarce investigative and prosecutorial time and effort. . . .

WRITTEN DECLINATION GUIDELINES CURRENTLY IN USE BY UNITED STATES ATTORNEYS

The specific written declination guidelines supplied by U.S. Attorneys were applicable to 42 categories of criminal offenses. [For] a number of categories of offenses, only a few districts have written declination guidelines. For other types of offenses, written guidelines are very frequently in force. The following 11 categories of offenses are the ones most frequently made subject to written guidelines by U.S. Attorneys:

CATEGORIES OF CRIMINAL OFFENSES MOST FREQUENTLY SUBJECT TO WRITTEN DECLINATION GUIDELINES

Written	*Category of Offense Number of Districts with Declination Policies*
1. Theft from Interstate Shipment	61
2. Interstate Transportation of Stolen Property	51
3. Bank Fraud and Embezzlement	51
4. Forgery of U.S. Treasury Checks	51
5. Theft of Government Property	48
6. Dyer Act: Interstate Transportation of a Stolen Vehicle	45
7. Crimes on Government Reservations	36
8. Bank Robbery and Related Offenses	33
9. Fraud Against the Government	28
10. Drug Offenses	24
11. Immigration and Naturalization — Illegal Aliens	24

A review of the written declination policies for various offenses indicates a number of general characteristics:

- Written guidelines are typically categorized by the type of criminal offense or the statutory provisions involved. . . .
- Written guidelines are more prevalent for non-violent criminal offenses, though some exist for violent crimes.
- Written guidelines are usually expressed in terms of the gravity of the alleged offense, the history and circumstances of the defendant involved, and the connection of the alleged offense to a pattern of illegal activity.
- Other frequently mentioned declination determining factors include the sufficiency and strength of the Government's evidence and the availability of alternatives to federal prosecution.

The most frequently used measurement of the gravity of the offense is the value of property or loss involved. Using Theft from Interstate Shipment as an example, the value of property involved is used by 52 of 61 districts as a declination-determining factor. . . . Written declination guidelines [use varying] ranges and distributions of declination cut-off points (e.g., monetary value, quantity of drugs) from district to district and from offense to offense. The variation among districts is illustrated again by the policies with respect to Theft from Interstate Shipment. [T]he range of declination cut-off points goes from $100 to $5,000 in property value, with many districts clustered around $500 (15 districts), $1,000 (11 districts), and $5,000 (10 districts). The declination cut-off points for other offenses are differently distributed across ranges of differing size. . . .

■ STATEMENT OF ASSISTANT ATTORNEY GENERAL PHILIP HEYMANN

Before the Committee on the Judiciary of the United States Senate (April 23, 1980)

Winning convictions is only half of a prosecutor's job. Equally vital is to sort out which cases to prosecute and which to decline.

Declinations are the rule, not the exception. Of 171,000 criminal matters referred to federal prosecutors in Fiscal Year 1976, 108,000 were declined — a declination rate of 63 percent. Many other uncounted declinations are made by the investigative agencies, in accord with guidelines agreed on with federal prosecutors.

Cases are declined for a variety of reasons. The first is scarcity of resources; the federal system cannot handle every allegation of a federal criminal violation generated in a country of 200 million people. We try to make our resources have the most effect by selecting areas where deterrence is especially important, where the federal interest is the greatest, cases of the greatest culpability and cases where we have a good chance of winning. To conserve resources, we will often defer to state and local prosecution, or in appropriate cases of lesser culpability, to administrative discipline by a suspect's employer or professional association.

The more important reason for declining is lack of merit in the prosecution. Often, upon investigation, we discover that there simply is no evidence supporting the initial allegation. In other cases the available evidence turns out to be weak; there is a vast difference between making an allegation and mustering sufficient proof to convince 12 jurors beyond a reasonable doubt. Declining a weak case is part of the prosecutor's duty of fairness, for the burdens of indictment and trial were never intended to be a form of curbstone punishment to be used without a reasonable chance of securing a conviction. Declining weak cases is also important because too many losses at trial would seriously weaken the credibility of the Department's future prosecutions. . . .

Judging what is a weak case is partly a technical evaluation of the evidence — what witnesses are likely to be available, what they will testify to and with what credibility. It is also a matter of gauging whether the jury is likely to be impressed by the wrongfulness of the defendant's conduct. The phenomenon of jury nullification is not unknown in the federal system and elements of a crime such as "corrupt intent" provide another way for jurors to act on their assessment of the wrongfulness of conduct. . . .

It is important to have public support and understanding of this part of the job of prosecutors and investigators. . . . Without public understanding of the declination function, the temptation always will be to prolong investigations that deserve to be closed, to reveal information that should be kept a confidential part of the investigative process, even to charge and prosecute where no indictment deserves to be brought.

[There] are a number of common reasons why the declination function may have been misunderstood. First, that declinations are so common an occurrence in law enforcement is a fact frankly unfamiliar to many citizens, legislators and writers. For instance, when GAO published a study two years ago describing the 63 percent declination rate common to federal prosecutors, several Committees in the House and Senate issued a request for a study of "recommendations for improving the percentage of such [criminal] complaints which are prosecuted by the Department."

Second, it can be hard to keep in clear view the difference between scandalous behavior and criminal behavior, and the difference between suspecting criminal behavior and proving it — particularly when a matter is being discussed in the non-technical confines of a journal or newspaper. When we pursue an investigation, often we find that the suspect behaved badly, may even have acted like a scoundrel, and yet has not committed a federal criminal violation. . . . Sometimes we end up at the conclusion of an investigation strongly suspecting that a person is guilty of a criminal offense, but unable to assemble adequate admissible evidence. Keeping these distinctions in mind is essential in understanding that a declination does not amount to approval or condoning of the examined behavior.

Another cause of potential misunderstanding is that we can't talk very much about our declinations. Investigative information is generally to be presented in court or not at all. By law we can't make grand jury information public, and by ethical practice, to protect privacy, we generally refrain from disclosing other investigative information except in the confines of an indictment and trial or in response to oversight requests from the Congress on closed cases. Certainly, as an agency following the rule of law, we have no business broadcasting our "suspicions" or "hunches" about guilt. So the public is often not given any detailed information on the reason for a declination; they simply learn that an investigation of an obvious scoundrel has been closed. This may contribute to suspicion that the real reason for the declination is political. . . .

I do not make light of the public's responsibility for scrutinizing the actions of law enforcement and prosecutorial agencies. That is a very strong long-term safeguard against abuse. But at the same time, we must avoid creating a system in which the only incentive is to prosecute, no matter how weak or nonexistent the case. . . . When we decline to prosecute unmeritorious cases, it is as much a part of a system of justice as when we prosecute the guilty.

■ FEDERAL PROSECUTION OF BUSINESS ORGANIZATIONS

United States Attorney Manual, Chapter 9-28.000 et seq. (2008)

9-28.100 Duties of Federal Prosecutors and Duties of Corporate Leaders

The prosecution of corporate crime is a high priority for the Department of Justice. By investigating allegations of wrongdoing and by bringing charges where appropriate for criminal misconduct, the Department promotes critical public interests. These interests include, to take just a few examples: (1) protecting the integrity of our free economic and capital markets; (2) protecting consumers, investors, and business entities that compete only through lawful means; and (3) protecting the American people from misconduct that would violate criminal laws safeguarding the environment. . . .

In carrying out this mission with the diligence and resolve necessary to vindicate the important public interests discussed above, prosecutors should be mindful of the common cause we share with responsible corporate leaders. Prosecutors should also be mindful that confidence in the Department is affected both by the results we achieve and by the real and perceived ways in which we achieve them. [Professionalism] and civility play an important part in the Department's discharge of its responsibilities in all areas, including the area of corporate investigations and prosecutions. . . .

9-28.300 Factors to Be Considered

A. *General Principle:* Generally, prosecutors apply the same factors in determining whether to charge a corporation as they do with respect to individuals. See USAM §9-27.220, et seq. Thus, the prosecutor must weigh all of the factors normally considered in the sound exercise of prosecutorial judgment: the sufficiency of the evidence; the likelihood of success at trial; the probable deterrent, rehabilitative, and other consequences of conviction; and the adequacy of noncriminal approaches. However, due to the nature of the corporate "person," some additional factors are present. In conducting an investigation, determining whether to bring charges, and negotiating plea or other agreements, prosecutors should consider the following factors in reaching a decision as to the proper treatment of a corporate target:

1. the nature and seriousness of the offense, including the risk of harm to the public, and applicable policies and priorities, if any, governing the prosecution of corporations for particular categories of crime;
2. the pervasiveness of wrongdoing within the corporation, including the complicity in, or the condoning of, the wrongdoing by corporate management;
3. the corporation's history of similar misconduct, including prior criminal, civil, and regulatory enforcement actions against it;
4. the corporation's timely and voluntary disclosure of wrongdoing and its willingness to cooperate in the investigation of its agents;
5. the existence and effectiveness of the corporation's pre-existing compliance program;

6. the corporation's remedial actions, including any efforts to implement an effective corporate compliance program or to improve an existing one, to replace responsible management, to discipline or terminate wrongdoers, to pay restitution, and to cooperate with the relevant government agencies;
7. collateral consequences, including whether there is disproportionate harm to shareholders, pension holders, employees, and others not proven personally culpable, as well as impact on the public arising from the prosecution;
8. the adequacy of the prosecution of individuals responsible for the corporation's malfeasance; and
9. the adequacy of remedies such as civil or regulatory enforcement actions.

B. *Comment:* The factors listed in this section are intended to be illustrative of those that should be evaluated and are not an exhaustive list of potentially relevant considerations. Some of these factors may not apply to specific cases, and in some cases one factor may override all others. For example, the nature and seriousness of the offense may be such as to warrant prosecution regardless of the other factors. In most cases, however, no single factor will be dispositive. In addition, national law enforcement policies in various enforcement areas may require that more or less weight be given to certain of these factors than to others. . . .

9-28.700 The Value of Cooperation

A. *General Principle:* In determining whether to charge a corporation and how to resolve corporate criminal cases, the corporation's timely and voluntary disclosure of wrongdoing and its cooperation with the government's investigation may be relevant factors. In gauging the extent of the corporation's cooperation, the prosecutor may consider, among other things, whether the corporation made a voluntary and timely disclosure, and the corporation's willingness to provide relevant information and evidence and identify relevant actors within and outside the corporation, including senior executives.

Cooperation is a potential mitigating factor, by which a corporation — just like any other subject of a criminal investigation — can gain credit in a case that otherwise is appropriate for indictment and prosecution. Of course, the decision not to cooperate by a corporation (or individual) is not itself evidence of misconduct, at least where the lack of cooperation does not involve criminal misconduct or demonstrate consciousness of guilt (e.g., suborning perjury or false statements, or refusing to comply with lawful discovery requests). Thus, failure to cooperate, in and of itself, does not support or require the filing of charges with respect to a corporation any more than with respect to an individual.

B. *Comment:* In investigating wrongdoing by or within a corporation, a prosecutor is likely to encounter several obstacles resulting from the nature of the corporation itself. It will often be difficult to determine which individual took which action on behalf of the corporation. Lines of authority and responsibility may be shared among operating divisions or departments, and records and personnel may be spread throughout the United States or even among several countries. . . . Accordingly, a corporation's cooperation may be critical in identifying potentially relevant actors and locating relevant evidence, among other things, and in doing so expeditiously. . . .

Cooperation benefits the government — and ultimately shareholders, employees, and other often blameless victims — by allowing prosecutors and federal agents, for example, to avoid protracted delays, which compromise their ability to quickly uncover and address the full extent of widespread corporate crimes. With cooperation by the corporation, the government may be able to reduce tangible losses, limit damage to reputation, and preserve assets for restitution. At the same time, cooperation may benefit the corporation by enabling the government to focus its investigative resources in a manner that will not unduly disrupt the corporation's legitimate business operations. . . .

9-28.710 Attorney-Client and Work Product Protections

The attorney-client privilege and the attorney work product protection serve an extremely important function in the American legal system. The attorney-client privilege is one of the oldest and most sacrosanct privileges under the law.

[Waiving] the attorney-client and work product protections has never been a prerequisite under the Department's prosecution guidelines for a corporation to be viewed as cooperative. Nonetheless, [everyone] agrees that a corporation may freely waive its own privileges if it chooses to do so; indeed, such waivers occur routinely when corporations are victimized by their employees or others, conduct an internal investigation, and then disclose the details of the investigation to law enforcement officials in an effort to seek prosecution of the offenders. . . .

What the government seeks and needs to advance its legitimate (indeed, essential) law enforcement mission is not waiver of those protections, but rather the facts known to the corporation about the putative criminal misconduct under review. In addition, while a corporation remains free to convey non-factual or "core" attorney-client communications or work product — if and only if the corporation voluntarily chooses to do so — prosecutors should not ask for such waivers and are directed not to do so. [The] analysis parallels that for a non-corporate defendant, where cooperation typically requires disclosure of relevant factual knowledge and not of discussions between an individual and his attorneys.

[A] corporation's failure to provide relevant information does not mean the corporation will be indicted. It simply means that the corporation will not be entitled to mitigating credit for that cooperation. Whether the corporation faces charges will turn, as it does in any case, on the sufficiency of the evidence, the likelihood of success at trial, and all of the other factors [identified above]. The converse is also true: The government may charge even the most cooperative corporation pursuant to these Principles if, in weighing and balancing the factors described herein, the prosecutor determines that a charge is required in the interests of justice.

9-28.900 Restitution and Remediation

A. *General Principle:* Although neither a corporation nor an individual target may avoid prosecution merely by paying a sum of money, a prosecutor may consider the corporation's willingness to make restitution and steps already taken to do so. A prosecutor may also consider other remedial actions, such as improving an existing compliance program or disciplining wrongdoers, in determining whether to charge the corporation and how to resolve corporate criminal cases.

B. *Comment:* . . . A corporation's response to misconduct says much about its willingness to ensure that such misconduct does not recur. Thus, corporations that fully recognize the seriousness of their misconduct and accept responsibility for it should be taking steps to implement the personnel, operational, and organizational changes necessary to establish an awareness among employees that criminal conduct will not be tolerated. Among the factors prosecutors should consider and weigh are whether the corporation appropriately disciplined wrongdoers, once those employees are identified by the corporation as culpable for the misconduct. . . .

In addition to employee discipline, two other factors used in evaluating a corporation's remedial efforts are restitution and reform. As with natural persons, the decision whether or not to prosecute should not depend upon the target's ability to pay restitution. A corporation's efforts to pay restitution even in advance of any court order is, however, evidence of its acceptance of responsibility and . . . may be considered in determining whether to bring criminal charges. Similarly, although the inadequacy of a corporate compliance program is a factor to consider when deciding whether to charge a corporation, that corporation's quick recognition of the flaws in the program and its efforts to improve the program are also factors to consider as to appropriate disposition of a case.

9-28.1200 Selecting Charges

A. *General Principle:* Once a prosecutor has decided to charge a corporation, the prosecutor at least presumptively should charge, or should recommend that the grand jury charge, the most serious offense that is consistent with the nature of the defendant's misconduct and that is likely to result in a sustainable conviction.

B. *Comment:* Once the decision to charge is made, the same rules as govern charging natural persons apply. These rules require a faithful and honest application of the Sentencing Guidelines and an individualized assessment of the extent to which particular charges fit the specific circumstances of the case, are consistent with the purposes of the Federal criminal code, and maximize the impact of Federal resources on crime. . . .

REVISED CODE OF WASHINGTON §9.94A.411(1)

Standard

A prosecuting attorney may decline to prosecute, even though technically sufficient evidence to prosecute exists, in situations where prosecution would serve no public purpose, would defeat the underlying purpose of the law in question or would result in decreased respect for the law.

Guideline/Commentary

. . . The following are examples of reasons not to prosecute which could satisfy the standard.

(a) Contrary to Legislative Intent — It may be proper to decline to charge where the application of criminal sanctions would be clearly contrary to the intent of the legislature in enacting the particular statute.

(b) Antiquated Statute — It may be proper to decline to charge where the statute in question is antiquated in that: (i) it has not been enforced for many years; and (ii) most members of society act as if it were no longer in existence; and (iii) it serves no deterrent or protective purpose in today's society; and (iv) the statute has not been recently reconsidered by the legislature. This reason is not to be construed as the basis for declining cases because the law in question is unpopular or because it is difficult to enforce.

(c) De Minimus Violation — It may be proper to decline to charge where the violation of law is only technical or insubstantial and where no public interest or deterrent purpose would be served by prosecution.

(d) Confinement on Other Charges — It may be proper to decline to charge because the accused has been sentenced on another charge to a lengthy period of confinement; and (i) conviction of the new offense would not merit any additional direct or collateral punishment; (ii) the new offense is either a misdemeanor or a felony which is not particularly aggravated; and (iii) conviction of the new offense would not serve any significant deterrent purpose.

(e) Pending Conviction on Another Charge — It may be proper to decline to charge because the accused is facing a pending prosecution in the same or another county; and (i) conviction of the new offense would not merit any additional direct or collateral punishment; (ii) conviction in the pending prosecution is imminent; (iii) the new offense is either a misdemeanor or a felony which is not particularly aggravated; and (iv) conviction of the new offense would not serve any significant deterrent purpose.

(f) High Disproportionate Cost of Prosecution — It may be proper to decline to charge where the cost of locating or transporting, or the burden on, prosecution witnesses is highly disproportionate to the importance of prosecuting the offense in question. This reason should be limited to minor cases and should not be relied upon in serious cases.

(g) Improper Motives of Complainant — It may be proper to decline charges because the motives of the complainant are improper and prosecution would serve no public purpose, would defeat the underlying purpose of the law in question or would result in decreased respect for the law.

(h) Immunity — It may be proper to decline to charge where immunity is to be given to an accused in order to prosecute another where the accused's information or testimony will reasonably lead to the conviction of others who are responsible for more serious criminal conduct or who represent a greater danger to the public interest.

(i) Victim Request — It may be proper to decline to charge because the victim requests that no criminal charges be filed and the case involves the following crimes or situations: (i) assault cases where the victim has suffered little or no injury; (ii) crimes against property, not involving violence, where no major loss was suffered; (iii) where doing so would not jeopardize the safety of society. Care should be taken to insure that the victim's request is freely made and is not the product of threats or pressure by the accused. . . . The prosecutor is encouraged to notify the victim, when practical, and the law enforcement personnel, of the decision not to prosecute.

Notes

1. *Number of declinations.* The precise number of criminal matters that are declined for prosecution each year is hard to pin down. In the federal system, where the best data are available, U.S. Attorneys' offices decline to prosecute a large proportion of criminal matters they receive. In 2009, federal prosecutors filed charges in district court in 48 percent of the "criminal matters" referred to them for investigation or prosecution. They declined to prosecute 15 percent of the matters and referred 37 percent of the suspects to federal magistrates (who handle misdemeanors and charges that are ultimately dismissed and prosecuted instead in state court).

The number of declinations in the typical state system also makes up a significant proportion of the criminal matters that a prosecutor's office handles. Among felony defendants in large urban counties in 2006, charges were dismissed for 23 percent of all defendants initially charged with a felony. Bureau of Justice Statistics, Felony Defendants in Large Urban Counties, 2006, table 11 (May 2010, NCJ 228944). Of course, the dismissal rate does not capture the total number of *arrests* declined for prosecution. Earlier studies have estimated that more than 40 percent of all felony arrests are declined for prosecution, while a similarly large group of felony arrestees are ultimately charged with misdemeanors. See Vera Institute of Justice, Felony Arrests: Their Prosecution and Disposition in New York City's Courts (Malcolm Feeley ed., rev. ed. 1980).

2. *Reasons for declinations.* The reasons individual prosecutors decline to file charges are even more elusive than the number of declinations they make. Over the years, several scholars, commissions, and associations have described some common reasons for individual prosecutors to choose not to file criminal charges in a particular case. Frank Miller offered one such typology of reasons prosecutors decline charges, listing attitude of the victim, cost to the system, undue harm to the suspect, adequacy of alternative procedures, and willingness of the suspect to cooperate in achieving other enforcement goals. See Miller, Prosecution: The Decision to Charge a Suspect with a Crime (1969). The National District Attorneys Association, in its National Prosecution Standards, §42.3 (2d ed. 1991), lists several possible grounds for a prosecutor to decline a criminal case, including "doubt as to the accused's guilt," "possible improper motives of a victim or witness," "undue hardship caused to the accused," "the expressed desire of an accused to release potential civil claims against victims, witnesses, law enforcement agencies and their personnel, and the prosecutor and his personnel," and "any mitigating circumstances." How do these reasons compare to those in the Washington statute reprinted above?

How often do prosecutors actually rely on these plausible reasons for declination? In 2003, federal prosecutors gave the following reasons for their declinations: no crime committed (22 percent of the declinations), matter handled in other prosecutions (21 percent), pretrial diversion (1.6 percent), weak evidence (22 percent), minimal federal interest (3.6 percent), U.S. Attorney policy (2.7 percent), lack of resources (5.7 percent), and several others. What trends would you expect to find over time in the mix of reasons that federal prosecutors give for their declinations? See Michael Edmund O'Neill, Understanding Federal Prosecutorial Declinations: An Empirical Analysis of Predicative Factors, 41 Am. Crim. L. Rev. 1439 (2004).

Once again, data for state systems are sketchier. According to one study of prosecution data from New Orleans during the 1990s, prosecutors explained that

38 percent of the charges they declined to prosecute were not necessary because they were "prosecuting on other charges." Various evidentiary flaws in the charges accounted for 26% of the declinations, while concerns about the victim of the crime explained 18% of the charges declined. Marc L. Miller and Ronald F. Wright, The Black Box, 94 Iowa L. Rev. 125 (2008).

3. *Written reasons, public reasons.* Most larger prosecutors' offices require a prosecutor who declines to file charges to give reasons in some written form in the case file. What purposes might the requirement of written reasons serve? If, as chief prosecutor, you supervised an office that required line prosecutors to record their reasons, would you reveal to the public the prosecutor's reasoning in each case? Would you release aggregate statistics that reveal the reasons used in multiple cases? A few states (although a growing number) have statutes requiring a prosecutor to explain in writing each refusal to prosecute a case. See Mich. Stat. §767.41; Neb. Rev. Stat. §29-1606.

4. *Declination policies versus ad hoc judgments.* Although most declination decisions fall within the discretion of the individual prosecutor, many offices develop written policies to govern the declination decision for at least some types of cases. We have already seen one type of declination policy earlier in this chapter: "no-drop" policies for domestic violence crimes. It is quite common to find such articulated (often written) office policies that declare certain crimes to be a high priority for the office.

Just as important, many offices articulate general policies that declare certain crimes to hold a low priority for the office. For example, the prosecutor's office in Kitsap County, Washington, issues "standards and guidelines" stating explicitly that the office will devote relatively fewer resources to crimes and activities, such as "economic crime" and "confiscation of the fruits of drug crime" that appear toward the bottom of the declared priority list. The charging standards also explicitly state a more demanding standard for charging crimes against property (evidence that "would justify conviction") than for charging crimes against persons (evidence that makes conviction "probable"). This detailed and substantive charging policy is posted, along with other office charging policies, on the web extension for this chapter at *http://www.crimpro.com/extension/ch13*.

Declination policies also address categories of criminal suspects. For instance, many offices adopt specialized charging rules for juvenile suspects and for repeat felony offenders. As we saw above, the U.S. Department of Justice has created written guidelines to govern the charging of corporate entities in particular.

5. *Declination policies that require internal consultation.* A declination policy is only one method of discouraging the use of criminal charges for specific types of cases. Prosecutors' offices will sometimes adopt policies requiring the "line" prosecutors to consult with supervisors or others in the office with special expertise before filing criminal charges under certain statutes. See U.S. Attorneys' Manual §9-2.400 (requiring line prosecutor to consult with supervisors before filing charges against member of news media or for desecration of flag, draft evasion, obscenity, RICO, and other offenses). Is it possible to predict which offenses are most likely to be singled out for a prior consultation requirement?

6. *Prosecutorial policy and office size.* The size and structure of the prosecutor's office determines to some extent whether explicit declination policies will be in place and what topics the policies will address. As of 2005, the chief prosecutors in 46 of the 50 states were elected locally, most for four-year terms. Full-time

prosecutors' offices in jurisdictions with large populations (one million persons or more) had a median of 141 assistant prosecutors; offices in jurisdictions serving populations between 250,000 and one million residents employed a median of 34 assistant prosecutors; smaller offices employed a median of three assistant prosecutors. Bureau of Justice Statistics, Prosecutors in State Courts, 2005 (July 2006, NCJ 213799). There are 2,344 separate prosecutor offices that try felony cases in the state courts. What effects does a decentralized structure have on the declination policies to be adopted or followed in prosecutors' offices?

7. *Judicial review of declinations and decisions to file charges.* Judges might overturn a prosecutor's decision to file charges or not to file charges, but only in rare circumstances. See State v. Foss, 556 N.W.2d 540 (Minn. 1996) (acknowledging power of trial court to stay adjudication of guilt over prosecutor's objection in "special circumstances"; such circumstances existed in an earlier case involving consensual sex with 14-year-old when victim and her mother did not desire criminal prosecution, but no special circumstances exist in typical misdemeanor assault case).

If an individual prosecutor appears to be violating a known office policy by filing criminal charges when the policy calls for declination, can the defendant convince a court to enforce the policy? See United States v. Caceres, 440 U.S. 741 (1979) (defendant may not enforce internal rules of law enforcement agency, such as IRS rule requiring internal approval before eavesdropping). Would the result depend on whether the policy includes an explicit disclaimer that it does not create any enforceable rights? On whether it is written? Are written policies a meaningful limit on prosecutorial choices if defendants cannot enforce them? See Kenneth Culp Davis, Discretionary Justice (1969); Gerard E. Lynch, Our Administrative System of Criminal Justice, 66 Fordham L. Rev. 2117 (1998).

8. *Dismissals after charges are filed.* At English common law, the power of the prosecutor to dismiss a charge — to enter a plea of *nolle prosequi* — was every bit as broad as the discretion to file charges initially. An illustration of this power appears in the following conversation between an advocate, Lacy, and Chief Justice John Holt in seventeenth-century England. Lacy asked the chief justice to dismiss seditious libel charges against other members of his religious sect:

> *Lacy:* I come to you, a prophet from the Lord God, who has sent me to thee, and would have thee grant a nolle prosequi for John Atkins, His servant, whom thou hast cast into prison.
>
> *Chief Justice Holt:* Thou art a false prophet, and a lying knave. If the Lord God had sent thee, it would have been to the attorney general, for He knows that it belongeth not to the Chief Justice to grant a nolle prosequi; but I, as Chief Justice, can grant a warrant to commit thee to bear him company.

See 2 Francis Wharton, A Treatise on Criminal Procedure §1310 (10th ed. 1918). This common-law rule on dismissals took hold in the United States and was especially useful in systems that allowed private prosecutors to file charges without consulting the public prosecutor. Today, however, a strong majority of jurisdictions (more than 30) give prosecutors less control over dismissals than over the initial decision whether to charge. They require the prosecutor to state reasons and obtain the leave of the court before dismissing charges. See Mich. Comp. Laws §767.29; Fed. R. Crim. P. 48(a) (indictment, information or complaint can be dismissed "with leave of court"). For reasons you can well imagine, judges rarely deny a prosecutor's motion to dismiss charges.

9. *Declinations and the community prosecution model.* Ideally, the cases that a prosecutor's office accepts or declines for prosecution reflect some coherent set of priorities for the office. Cases that reinforce the highest priorities for the office would, of course, be the least likely to be declined. To what extent do you imagine you could reconstruct the priorities of an office by analyzing the pattern of declinations?

Some prosecutors talk about a shift in philosophy, moving to a "community prosecution" model that parallels the "community policing" model that is now at least one generation old. According to this approach, prosecutors place less emphasis on obtaining convictions in the courtroom or through plea agreements. Instead, the prosecutor mobilizes legal resources and leads other government agencies to address community problems to prevent crime rather than respond to crime. They use their legal authority to motivate slumlords to comply with housing codes, prevent liquor law violators from obtaining new liquor licenses, and place high priorities on crimes committed in public parks and other areas where the public is highly aware of crime. See Walter J. Dickey & Peggy A. McGarry, The Search for Justice and Safety Through Community Engagement: Community Justice and Community Prosecution, 42 Idaho L. Rev. 313 (2006). If a new chief prosecutor were to embrace a community prosecution approach, what specific changes in declination patterns would you expect to see?

10. *Corporations and declinations.* In August 2008, the U.S. Department of Justice revised for the third time its instructions for line prosecutors around the country regarding the decision of whether to charge a corporate entity with a crime. The first version of the policy, created by then-Deputy Attorney General Eric Holder, appeared in 1999. The Department revised the charging policies in 2003 (the "Thompson memo"), following the Enron and WorldCom accounting scandals, and again in 2006 (the "McNulty memo"). The 2008 version appeared after federal legislators, business groups, bar associations, and civil liberties advocates objected to the guidelines. The earlier versions, these advocates complained, placed such heavy weight on the "cooperation" of a corporation under investigation that the policy unfairly forced a corporation to waive its attorney-client and work-product privileges.

Deputy Attorney General Mark Filip announced the revised charging guidelines for corporations during a press conference at the New York Stock Exchange. Can you think of any comparable examples of the targets of criminal investigations successfully pressuring the prosecutor to clarify the limits on its charging authority? Do the relevant factors discussed in the DOJ policy on corporations differ from the factors relevant to deciding whether to charge an individual? Are guidelines in the federal system more likely to be revised on a regular basis than guidelines of local prosecutors in the state courts?

b. Diversion of Defendants

Prosecutors file charges in some cases and decline to charge in others, but they have other options as well. The prosecutor may, for example, "divert" the suspect from the criminal justice system into an alternative program for rehabilitation and restitution. Diversion occurs in some states before charges are ever filed: The prosecutor agrees to withhold any criminal charges, provided the suspect successfully completes the designated program or other conditions that the prosecutor specifies. Diversion can also take place after charges are filed, in which case the prosecution is suspended while the defendant completes the diversion program. If the defendant succeeds, the prosecutor dismisses the criminal charges. The archetypal "diversion" case involves a first-time offender who has committed a nonviolent crime. Some diversion programs explicitly focus on classes of offenders, such as nonviolent drug offenders.

As you read the following materials, consider whether the prosecutor is properly situated to identify "good" cases for diversion and to set the proper conditions for a successful diversion program. Will a prosecutor systematically place requirements on a defendant that a judge at sentencing would not? Will defendants respond differently to diversion programs than they would to requirements imposed at sentencing after a conviction?

MONTANA CODE §46-16-130

(1)(a) Prior to the filing of a charge, the prosecutor and a defendant who has counsel or who has voluntarily waived counsel may agree to the deferral of a prosecution for a specified period of time based on one or more of the following conditions:

(i) that the defendant may not commit any offense;

(ii) that the defendant may not engage in specified activities, conduct, and associations bearing a relationship to the conduct upon which the charge against the defendant is based;

(iii) that the defendant shall participate in a supervised rehabilitation program, which may include treatment, counseling, training, or education;

(iv) that the defendant shall make restitution in a specified manner for harm or loss caused by the offense; or

(v) any other reasonable conditions. . . .

(d) The agreement must be terminated and the prosecution automatically dismissed with prejudice upon expiration and compliance with the terms of the agreement. . . .

(3) After a charge has been filed, a deferral of prosecution may be entered into only with the approval of the court.

(4) A prosecution for a violation of [laws that prohibit driving while impaired] may not be deferred.

MONTANA COMMISSION ON CRIMINAL PROCEDURE: COMMENTS

A provision regulating pretrial diversion, sometimes called deferred prosecution, is new to Montana, although the practice has been statutorily recognized since at least 1979. The Commission believed a pretrial diversion provision was necessary because prosecutors have long employed diversion on an informal, individual basis by deferring prosecution if, for example, the accused agreed to undergo rehabilitative treatment. Since the President's Commission on Law Enforcement and Administration of Justice recommended such programs in its 1967 report, many states have formalized diversion by statute or court rule. Pretrial diversionary programs are premised on the belief that it is not always necessary and, in fact, may often be detrimental to pursue formal courtroom prosecution for every criminal violation. In most situations, the criminal prosecution is suspended subject to the defendant's consent to treatment, rehabilitation, restitution, or other noncriminal or nonpunitive alternatives.

The statute contemplates that the decision to divert lies with the prosecutor in an exercise of his powers and is not ordinarily subject to judicial review. This conforms with existing practice in that several Montana County Attorneys conduct formal diversion programs, yet no Montana case has been found that discusses the practice. However, some litigation has occurred in other jurisdictions. . . .

■ STATE v. WALLACE BAYNES

690 A.2d 594 (N.J. 1997)

GARIBALDI, J.

The Court again addresses whether a trial court correctly reversed a prosecutor's rejection of a defendant's admission into a Pretrial Intervention (PTI) Program. In particular, we must determine whether the Monmouth County prosecutor's decision, based on his stated policy of denying admission into PTI to any defendant charged with possession of a controlled dangerous substance within 1,000 feet of a school zone, constitutes a "patent and gross abuse of discretion."

The facts of this case are undisputed. On September 28, 1994, at approximately 5:30 P.M., defendant, Wallace Baynes, purchased .44 grams of heroin from Jose Morales. The purchase was made outside of the Rainbow Liquor Store, [which was under police surveillance at the time.] The location of the purchase occurred approximately 900 feet from the Garfield Primary School. Baynes was arrested and subsequently indicted [for possession of heroin within 1,000 feet of a school zone]. Drug possession is a third-degree crime.

Defendant claims that he purchased the heroin because he was having difficulty dealing with the serious illness of his mother, who has since passed away. At the time of his application for admission into the Monmouth County Pretrial Intervention Program, defendant was a 43-year-old gainfully employed father of one, residing with and supporting his elderly mother and his 17-year-old son. He had completed two years of college. According to defendant, he had been employed by the same employer for the previous nine years. . . .

The Director of the PTI program accepted Baynes's application for admission. Further, the head of the narcotics team that arrested Baynes did not object to Baynes's diversion. The prosecutor, however, advised Baynes in an April 27, 1995, memorandum that his PTI application was rejected because of that prosecutor's acknowledged policy to deny PTI admission to defendants charged with "school zone offenses," including those involving possession of controlled dangerous substances (CDS) for personal use.

On June 23, 1995, a hearing was held before the trial court for reconsideration of the prosecutor's decision. In reversing the prosecutor's decision and referring the matter back to the prosecutor for reconsideration, the court observed that "the prosecutor [had failed] to consider all the relevant factors" in this case. The decision to refer the matter back to the prosecutor follows our past decisions, finding remand to the prosecutor useful where "the prosecutorial decision was based upon a consideration of inappropriate factors or not premised upon a consideration of all relevant factors. . . ." State v. Bender, 402 A.2d 217 (N.J. 1979).

In a letter to the trial court, the prosecutor advised the court that he had reviewed all the information again and continued to oppose defendant's diversion into PTI. After a second hearing appealing that decision, the trial court ordered Baynes's admission into the PTI program over the prosecutor's objection, stating that [the prosecutor's decision was]"so clearly unreasonable that it shocks the judicial conscience, subverts the goals of PTI, and constitutes a clear error of judgment because it could not have reasonably been made upon a fair weighing of all relevant factors." . . .

PTI is a diversionary program through which certain offenders are able to avoid criminal prosecution by receiving early rehabilitative services expected to deter future criminal behavior. [The Supreme Court initially established PTI by Rule 3:28 in 1970, creating] the vocational-service pretrial intervention program operated by the Newark Defendants Employment Project. By October 1976, the Court had approved programs for 12 counties. In 1979, the Legislature authorized a statewide PTI program as part of the Criminal Code of Justice. The Code provisions generally mirrored the procedures and guidelines previously established under Rule 3:28.

Admission into PTI is based on a recommendation by the criminal division manager, as Director of the PTI Program, with the consent of the prosecutor. The Court has provided criteria for making PTI decisions in its Guidelines for Operation of Pretrial Intervention. Guidelines 1, 2, 3, and 8 are particularly relevant to this case. Guideline 1 sets forth the purposes of PTI:

> (1) to enable defendants to avoid ordinary prosecution by receiving early rehabilitative services expected to deter future criminal behavior; (2) to provide defendants who might be harmed by the imposition of criminal sanctions with an alternative to prosecution expected to deter criminal conduct; (3) to avoid burdensome prosecutions for "victimless" offenses; (4) to relieve overburdened criminal calendars so that resources can be expended on more serious criminal matters; and (5) to deter future criminal behavior of PTI participants.

Guideline 2 provides that any defendant "accused of crime shall be eligible for admission into a PTI program." Thus, . . . PTI decisions are primarily individualistic in nature and a prosecutor must consider an individual defendant's features that bear on his or her amenability to rehabilitation.

Guideline 3 refers to and supplements N.J.S.A. 2C:43-12(e), which presents 17 criteria that prosecutors and criminal division managers are to consider in formulating their PTI recommendation. Guideline 3(i) clarifies how "the nature of the offense" is to be used in assessing a defendant's PTI eligibility. That guideline explains that although all defendants are eligible for enrollment in a PTI program, the nature of the crime is only one factor to be considered. Moreover, Guideline 3(i) states that there is a presumption against acceptance into a program when "the crime was (1) part of organized criminal activity; or (2) part of a continuing criminal business or enterprise; or (3) deliberately committed with violence or threat of violence against another person; or (4) a breach of the public trust." A presumption against acceptance into a PTI program also exists when the defendant is "charged with a first or second degree offense or sale or dispensing of Schedule I or II narcotic drugs [and is] not drug dependent." Finally, Guideline 8 requires a judge, prosecutor, or criminal division manager, making a PTI decision, to provide the defendant with a statement of reasons justifying the decision, as well as demonstrating that all of the facts have been considered. That statement may not simply parrot the language of relevant statutes, rules, and guidelines. Additionally, the statement cannot be vague; it must be sufficiently specific to provide the defendant with an opportunity to demonstrate that the reasons are unfounded.

The decision to divert a defendant from criminal prosecution implicates both judicial and prosecutorial functions. . . . Judicial review of the prosecutor's PTI decision is strictly limited, but necessary because "PTI involves far more than merely an exercise of the charging function." State v. Leonardis, 375 A.2d 607 (N.J. 1977). "It is one thing not to charge and let the accused go totally free, but it may be quite another to withhold a charge, and hence not to invoke the jurisdiction of the court system, on condition that an uncharged, untried, unconvicted person submit to a correctional program."

[Our expectation is] that a prosecutor's decision to reject a PTI applicant will rarely be overturned. A prosecutor's decision is to be afforded great deference. In fact, the level of deference which is required is so high that it has been categorized as "enhanced deference" or "extra deference." Absent evidence to the contrary, a reviewing court must assume that all relevant factors were considered by the prosecutor's office. That presumption makes it difficult to reverse a prosecutor's decision. A reviewing court may order a defendant into PTI over the prosecutor's objection, only if the defendant can clearly and convincingly establish that the prosecutor's refusal to sanction admission into the program was based on a patent and gross abuse of discretion. In State v. Bender, 402 A.2d 217, 222 (N.J. 1979), the Court defined the "patent and gross abuse of discretion" standard:

> Ordinarily, an abuse of discretion will be manifest if defendant can show that a prosecutorial veto (a) was not premised upon a consideration of all relevant factors, (b) was based upon a consideration of irrelevant or inappropriate factors, or (c) amounted to a clear error in judgment. In order for such an abuse of discretion to rise to the level of "patent and gross," it must further be shown that the prosecutorial error complained of will clearly subvert the goals underlying Pretrial Intervention. . . .

In this case, the prosecutor's rejection of Baynes's PTI application falls under categories (a) and (c), as set forth in *Bender.* First, the prosecutor's rejection in this case was not based on all of the relevant factors. After the initial remand for reconsideration by the trial court, the prosecutor claimed to have considered all of the relevant factors. We do not doubt his veracity, in the sense that he re-read the application and the police report. He could not, however, have considered all relevant factors, because the per se rule under which he made his decision had effectively denied Baynes's application from the moment Baynes was charged with possession of CDS in a school zone.

By their nature, per se rules require prosecutors to disregard relevant factors, contrary to the guidelines, and when a defendant demonstrates that a prosecutor has relied on such a rule, the presumption that the prosecutor has considered all relevant facts is overcome. As a result, the June 23, 1995, memorandum denying Baynes's application was merely an impermissible "parrot-like" recitation of the language of relevant statutes, rules, and guidelines.

The State correctly points out that prosecutors may rely on the nature of the offense, in "appropriate circumstances," as the sole basis for making PTI decisions. Although caselaw supports the proposition that certain offensive conduct can outweigh all other factors considered, no court has indicated that possession of CDS for personal use is an "appropriate circumstance" that alone can justify denying PTI.

Where courts have found a prosecutor's reliance on the nature of the offense charged to be an appropriate basis for a PTI decision, the crime was of a more serious nature than possession of CDS for personal use. In State v. Wallace, 684 A.2d 1355 (N.J. 1996), for example, . . . Wallace had entered his former girlfriend's house with a loaded gun and threatened to kill her. He was charged with second-degree possession of a firearm for an unlawful purpose and third-degree making of terroristic threats. In supporting her decision, . . . the prosecutor primarily relied on a prosecutorial guideline that discourages PTI for those defendants charged with either first- or second-degree offenses [or criminal acts committed with violence].

Under the caselaw of this jurisdiction, it is, therefore, appropriate for prosecutors to base their rejections solely on the nature of an offense for which the Guidelines express a presumption against admission. . . . Our prior opinions indicate that possession of CDS for personal consumption does not fall into [this category].

In addition to satisfying the first category of abuse of discretion set forth in *Bender,* the prosecutor's veto also fulfills the third, i.e., it was a "clear error in judgment." A prosecutor will be found to have made a "clear error in judgment," when the decision was premised on appropriate factors and rationally explained but is contrary to the predominate views of others responsible for the administration of justice. Although a reviewing court cannot substitute its own judgment for that of the prosecutor, others responsible for the administration of justice in New Jersey hold contrary views of how first-time offenders charged with possession of drugs for personal use should, as a class, be treated.

The 1987 Comprehensive Drug Reform Act simply does not indicate the intent prescribed to it by the Monmouth County prosecutor. [The] Legislature created a new crime, covering possession with intent to distribute or actual distribution of drugs in a school zone. Under that section, proof that the offensive conduct occurred within a school zone is an element of the offense, and if the defendant is found guilty a jail term must be imposed as well as a minimum term. The penalty structure for this type of offense is similar to that for second-degree offenses for which admission to PTI is presumptively unavailable.

Possession of CDS in a school zone, on the other hand, is not a separate crime. Rather, it is a sentencing factor that requires the court to impose 100 hours of community service as a condition of probation if the defendant is not given a prison term. . . .

The Monmouth County Prosecutor's Office is the only prosecutor's office in the State to have adopted the policy that a simple possession offense makes a defendant ineligible for admission into PTI. Nor has the Attorney General adopted such a policy. [A 1997 Directive from the Attorney General] prohibits a prosecutor from consenting to PTI for a person charged with simple possession of drugs within 1,000 feet of school property unless, as a condition of PTI, the defendant serves not less than 100 hours of community service and pays a Drug Enforcement and Demand Reduction penalty. . . . Clearly, that policy is inconsistent with the Monmouth County prosecutor's policy of excluding from PTI all defendants charged with simple possession of drugs in a school zone. In fact, early diversion programs were begun in many jurisdictions in order to cope with both the non-addict first offender and the drug-dependent defendant.

As a first-time offender charged with a non-violent, third-degree offense, Baynes is eligible for diversion into the PTI program. By abandoning his discretion in favor of a per se rule, the prosecutor made a decision unsupported by the legislative purpose behind both the PTI Statute and the Comprehensive Drug Reform Act, by the Guidelines, and by caselaw. Thus, the rejection of Baynes's PTI application was an abuse of discretion under two of the three categories of the *Bender* test. . . .

■ KITSAP COUNTY PROSECUTING ATTORNEY MISSION STATEMENT AND STANDARDS AND GUIDELINES

(2007)

. . . In this office we utilize three kinds of diversion programs. In dealing with juvenile offenders, the legislature has obligated us to divert all youth the first time they commit a minor offense. In the District and Municipal Courts, we use pre-trial diversion agreements (PDAs) to relieve court congestion by diverting first-time offenders and defendants in problematic cases. Our adult felony diversion program offers an opportunity to avoid felony conviction to certain low risk property offenders and to select drug offenders.

Juvenile Diversions: "Diversion — A first time misdemeanor offender will be sent to the Juvenile Department Diversion Unit. A second misdemeanor offense may be sent to diversion if the circumstances warrant. Factors the charging deputy shall consider in determining whether to divert the second offense include: length, seriousness, and recency of the alleged offender's criminal history and the circumstances surrounding the commission of the alleged offense." RCW 13.40.050. Following the law, we cooperate with the Superior Court Juvenile Department by determining which offenders qualify under the statute.

Pre-Trial Diversion Agreements (PDAs), District and Municipal Courts: The decision when to PDA a case is less-than-scientific. Generally, most non-DV or non-DUI/Physical Control cases will be PDA'd if no aggravating factors are present. PDAs may also be offered the morning of trial due to court congestion and/or speedy trial problems. However, when faced with the need to choose among a number of cases all set for trial on the same day, priority should be given to the most aggravated Domestic Violence and DUI cases. . . .

DUI cases may be offered a PDA if a first offense, no aggravating factors are present, and a BAC of 0.12 or less. DUI PDA cases will not be dismissed, however. The typical DUI PDA will be to amend the charge to first degree negligent driving upon successful PDA compliance.

DV cases can and do become more problematic over time so evidence problems often result in a PDA being offered even with the presence of aggravating factors. The DPA, if possible, should speak with a Division Chief or a Senior DPA if significant aggravating factors are present, however, prior to offering a PDA in a DV case based upon proof problems.

If aggravating factors are present but a case is problematic (i.e. conviction by jury is unlikely), less-than-one-year DPAs are expected to speak with a Division Chief or a Senior DPA prior to offering a PDA if possible. Of course, if in a time crunch in court, the DPA should always make his or her best call and thereafter speak with the Division Chief to discuss the DPA's decision. Continuing cases for a DPA to speak with a Division Chief or Senior DPA (or to permit the defense attorney to speak with a Division Chief or a Senior DPA) is discouraged due to court congestion problems.

Felony Diversions: Many minor non-violent felony offenses are committed by first time offenders as a result of substance abuse and/or unusually bad judgment. If an offender is addicted to controlled substances, criminal behavior is likely to continue unless the offender receives treatment. In other minor felony cases involving first time offenders, less expensive alternatives to costly incarceration exist, and those alternatives may succeed at lessening the risk of further criminal behavior. In addition, the conditions of diversion will allow more supervision than currently available for a minor felony conviction.

One alternative is Drug Court. We screen the referrals of felony possession of controlled substances for prior sex offenses or violent crimes, including burglary and eluding a police vehicle. If there are none, in most cases we will offer the offender the opportunity to take judicially supervised treatment instead of going to jail. If the offender completes the program, the charge is dismissed. If they fail, having already confessed to the crime, they are convicted of the underlying offense and sentenced. . . .

Felony Diversion Screening Factors: To identify offenders who will be offered diversion either through Drug Court or some other option, we will use the following criteria.

1. The Seriousness of the Current Offense. No sex crimes or violent crime, including eluding a police vehicle, will be considered for diversion. First Degree Burglary (a violent offense) and Residential Burglary are excluded from consideration. Second Degree Burglary generally will not be considered for diversion. However, it may be considered if approved by the Chief of Case Management or the Prosecutor. If a case of second degree burglary is considered, particular attention will be paid to the likelihood that the offender would have encountered another person in the course of the crime.

2. Criminal History. Generally a history of sex or violent offenses, including eluding a police vehicle, will disqualify an offender.A history of Residential Burglary will also generally disqualify an offender unless the offense was disposed of in Juvenile Court. Exceptions must be approved by the Chief Deputy supervising the program or by the Prosecutor.

3. Strength of the Case. In considering Drug Court, the strength of the State's case should generally not be a factor. However, in diversion other than Drug Court, if, in the opinion of the Chief of Case Management or the Prosecutor, there would be value in exerting some control over the offender through a diversion program, a problematic case may be considered.

4. Ability to Pay Associated Costs. No person shall be denied diversion solely on present inability to pay the associated costs. However, the willingness to commit to pay future costs or to perform alternative community service is a factor that may be used in determining eligibility for a diversion program.

Notes

1. *Prevalence of diversion.* Diversion of arrestees is not as common as the outright rejection of criminal charges or the filing of felony charges. Prosecutors are most likely to offer diversion to suspects who face misdemeanor charges. About 8 percent of all felony arrestees in the largest urban counties in 2006 took part in diversion or "deferred adjudication" programs. Bureau of Justice Statistics, Felony Defendants in Large Urban Counties, 2006 (May 2010, NCJ 228944). Federal diversion programs are small: About 1,100 suspects were handled through pretrial diversion in 2003 (compared with more than 80,000 defendants prosecuted and 33,000 defendants whose cases were declined).

2. *Authority for diversion.* Prosecutors do not always have clear legal authority to take part in diversion programs. In some states, programs have statewide statutory authority (illustrated by the Montana statute reprinted above). Elsewhere, judges establish and supervise diversion programs (as in the New Jersey program described in *Baynes*). In a few jurisdictions, prosecutors send offenders into diversion programs without any explicit statutory authority to do so. Combinations of these situations are also possible: A statute might authorize diversion of offenders only after the filing of charges, yet the prosecutor may decide unilaterally to send some offenders into diversion programs before filing charges. For a sample of these state statutes, rules, and judicial decisions, go to the web extension for this chapter at *http://www.crimpro.com/extension/ch13*. Did the origins of the New Jersey program in the judicial branch influence the outcome or analysis in *Baynes*? Would the source of authority affect the level of funding for the program or the prosecutor's control over the conditions that program participants must meet?

3. *Who decides who enters the program?* State statutes dealing with pretrial diversion programs most often empower judges to approve of prosecutorial recommendations of individual offenders. Yet, as the New Jersey court in *Baynes* recognized, in practice prosecutors decide which defendants or suspects will enter a pretrial diversion program, and a court will give great deference to the prosecutor's decision. Indeed, in many states courts refuse to review the prosecutor's decision on whether to offer diversion to a suspect unless the prosecutor relies on unconstitutional grounds such as race. Flynt v. Commonwealth, 105 S.W.3d 415 (Ky. 2003) (court must have prosecutor's approval to admit defendant into diversion program; separation-of-powers doctrine requires this reading of statute). Statutes in about a dozen states give prosecutors complete control over who may enter pretrial diversion programs. Prosecutors' offices sometimes create policies to govern eligibility for diversion, at least for some types of cases.

Legislatures also create some preconditions for defendants or suspects to participate in pretrial diversion programs. See, e.g., Ind. Code §33-39-1-8 (prosecutor "may" withhold prosecution against a person charged with a misdemeanor if person agrees to listed conditions of pretrial diversion program). If the prosecutor and the suspect disagree about the proper interpretation of the statute defining eligibility requirements, can a court review the prosecutor's decision based on its independent interpretation of the statute? Or must it defer to the prosecutor's reading of the statute?

4. *Who decides whether the defendant has completed the program?* Suppose a defendant believes she has fulfilled all the conditions of the diversion program but the prosecutor disagrees and files criminal charges. Will a court review the prosecutor's conclusion that the defendant failed to complete the program? Is there any reason to treat this question differently from the question of who will enter a diversion program? Among states with statutes addressing this question, most require court approval for a decision to remove an offender from a diversion program, but some (fewer than 10) have statutes granting this decision exclusively to the prosecutor. See Fla. Stat. §948.08. What circumstances might enable a court to make an independent judgment about the defendant's success or failure in the program?

5. *Statement of reasons.* A few diversion programs require the prosecutor to provide an applicant to the program with written notice of rejection, along with the reasons for the rejection. The statement of reasons facilitates judicial review of the prosecutor's decision and is thought to help the courts identify arbitrary and abusive denials by the prosecutor. However, fewer than 10 states have a statewide legal requirement that the prosecutor give written reasons. Why do most states refuse to require a statement of reasons from the prosecutor? Have they concluded that such statements are pointless?

Problem 13-1. Youth Court

There are approximately 500 "youth courts" in the United States. These courts are intended to provide prosecutors, police, and schools with an alternative to juvenile courts. Often the "judges" in youth courts are not lawyers; sometimes they are not even adults, but rather the offender's peers. Does the creation of diversion courts (as opposed to diversion programs) exacerbate, undermine, or sidestep concerns about prosecutorial power and discretion? Consider the Utah statutes reprinted below, which provide for the creation and operation of youth courts; youth courts had been created on an ad hoc basis prior to the statute's enactment. Youth court jurisdiction in Utah extends to "status offenses" (offenses that would not be a crime if committed by an adult), lesser misdemeanors, infractions, and violations of municipal and county ordinances. Youth court jurisdiction in Utah does not extend to felonies, class A misdemeanors, possession of controlled substances, offenses committed as part of gang activity, or any offense where a dangerous weapon is used. Youth courts can be established by nonprofit entities.

If you were a district attorney, would you encourage the development and use of youth courts in your state? What other kinds of offenders or offenses might be handled with similar group diversion models?

■ UTAH CODE ANN. §78A-6-1203

(1) Youth Court is a diversion program which provides an alternative disposition for cases involving juvenile offenders in which youth participants, under the

supervision of an adult coordinator, may serve in various capacities within the courtroom, acting in the role of jurors, lawyers, bailiffs, clerks, and judges.

(a) Youth who appear before youth courts have been identified by law enforcement personnel, school officials, a prosecuting attorney, or the juvenile court as having committed acts which indicate a need for intervention to prevent further development toward juvenile delinquency, but which appear to be acts that can be appropriately addressed outside the juvenile court process.

(b) Youth Courts may only hear cases as provided for in this chapter.

(c) Youth Court is a diversion program and not a court established under the Utah Constitution. . . .

(2) Any person may refer youth to a Youth Court for minor offenses. Once a referral is made, the case shall be screened by an adult coordinator to determine whether it qualifies as a Youth Court case.

(3) Youth Courts have authority over youth:

(a) referred for a minor offense or offenses, or who are granted permission for referral under this chapter;

(b) who, along with a parent, guardian, or legal custodian, voluntarily and in writing, request Youth Court involvement;

(c) who admit having committed the referred offense;

(d) who, along with a parent, guardian, or legal custodian, waive any privilege against self-incrimination and right to a speedy trial; and

(e) who, along with their parent, guardian, or legal custodian, agree to follow the Youth Court disposition of the case. . . .

(5) Youth Courts may exercise authority over youth described in Subsection (4), and over any other offense with the permission of the juvenile court and the prosecuting attorney in the county or district that would have jurisdiction if the matter were referred to juvenile court. . . .

(7) Youth Courts may decline to accept a youth for Youth Court disposition for any reason and may terminate a youth from Youth Court participation at any time.

(8) A youth or the youth's parent, guardian, or custodian may withdraw from the Youth Court process at any time. The Youth Court shall immediately notify the referring source of the withdrawal.

(9) The Youth Court may transfer a case back to the referring source for alternative handling at any time.

(10) Referral of a case of Youth Court may not prohibit the subsequent referral of the case to any court.

■ UTAH CODE ANN. §78A-6-1205

(1) Youth Court dispositional options include:

(a) community service;

(b) participation in law-related educational classes, appropriate counseling, treatment, or other educational programs;

(c) providing periodic reports to the Youth Court;

(d) participating in mentoring programs;

(e) participation by the youth as a member of a Youth Court;

(f) letters of apology;

(g) essays; and

(h) any other disposition considered appropriate by the Youth Court and adult coordinator.

(2) Youth Courts may not impose a term of imprisonment or detention and may not impose fines.

(3) Youth Court dispositions shall be completed within 180 days from the date of referral.

(4) Youth Court dispositions shall be reduced to writing and signed by the youth and a parent, guardian, or legal custodian indicating their acceptance of the disposition terms.

(5) Youth Court shall notify the referring source if a participant fails to successfully complete the Youth Court disposition. The referring source may then take any action it considers appropriate.

3. *Private Prosecution*

If prosecutors won't prosecute, perhaps an aggrieved citizen will. Indeed, there is a long tradition of private rather than public prosecution. Public prosecutors — like many of the institutions of criminal justice, including police and public defense counsel — are a modern invention. Throughout much of the eighteenth and nineteenth centuries, it was common for private citizens to bring complaints to a grand jury or a magistrate, *and* to hire private attorneys to assist the public prosecutor or to prosecute the criminal case alone. Only at the turn of the twentieth century did the public prosecutor become the primary method for initiating criminal charges.

Remnants of true private prosecution exist still in United States law. The "victim's rights" concept has strengthened the accountability of public prosecutors to victims of crime. Prosecutors also reflect the political priorities of the voters or the Executive who appoints them, and the Legislature that funds them.

As traditional and well recognized as interest group politics may be, the link between private preferences and public prosecution is not widely recognized. Consider the legal and policy dimensions of the modern forms of private prosecution described in the following statute, case, and problem.

■ WISCONSIN STATUTES §968.02

(1) Except as otherwise provided in this section, a complaint charging a person with an offense shall be issued only by a district attorney of the county where the crime is alleged to have been committed. A complaint is issued when it is approved for filing for the district attorney. . . .

(3) If a district attorney refuses or is unavailable to issue a complaint, a circuit judge may permit the filing of a complaint, if the judge finds there is probable cause to believe that the person to be charged has committed an offense after conducting a hearing. If the district attorney has refused to issue a complaint, he or she shall be informed of the hearing and may attend. The hearing shall be ex parte without the right of cross-examination.

■ STATE v. DONALD CULBREATH

30 S.W.3d 309 (Tenn. 2000)

ANDERSON, C.J.

. . . In December of 1995, Larry Parrish, an attorney in Memphis, Tennessee, was approached by the executive director of an organization known as the Citizens for Community Values, Inc., ("CCV"), who asked him to meet with two Shelby County assistant district attorneys, Amy Weirich and Jennifer Nichols, regarding the prosecution of obscenity cases. Parrish, a former Assistant United States Attorney, was experienced in the prosecution of obscenity cases.

Parrish met with Weirich and Nichols for three hours. When they asked for his help, Parrish replied, "I haven't been asked." On the following day, then-Shelby County District Attorney John Pierotti contacted Parrish and requested his assistance. Pierotti told Parrish that his office could not pay for Parrish's services but could reimburse expenses. When Parrish asked if he could be compensated by outside sources, Pierotti agreed. . . .

Thereafter, Parrish conducted an extensive investigation into sexually-oriented businesses in Shelby County, Tennessee, with the assistance of two assistant district attorneys, an investigator from the District Attorney General's office, and investigators from the Tennessee Bureau of Investigation and the Department of Revenue. Parrish met with these employees in his law firm office on a daily basis for several months. Beginning in January of 1996, the group's investigation consisted of conducting surveillance of sexually-oriented establishments and taking statements from a large number of witnesses. Although Parrish testified that it was "understood" that General Pierotti had the ultimate decision-making authority, there were no procedures or guidelines establishing Parrish's specific duties or Pierotti's oversight.

The initial agreement called for the District Attorney General's office to pay for expenses incurred during the investigation, but Parrish began to pay expenses from contributions by CCV and numerous members of the community. Parrish testified that CCV received a monthly statement itemizing his time and expenses, just as any other client. Parrish's expenses included the use of court reporters to take statements, a TV/VCR, copying and courier expenses, video monitors, special telephone lines, and various office supplies and equipment. The expenses were paid from CCV contributions. . . .

On July 11, 1996, Parrish was "appointed" as a "Special Assistant District Attorney" by General Pierotti and was administered an oath of office for the first time. On the same day, a civil nuisance suit seeking injunctive relief against several sexually-oriented businesses was filed in Shelby County Chancery Court. . . . At Pierotti's request, Parrish was appointed as additional counsel in matters relating to the civil cases in chancery court by Governor Don Sundquist on August 30, 1996. The letter of appointment noted that Parrish would not be compensated by the State, that Parrish would disclose the amount and source of any compensation received, that such information was a matter of public record, and that Parrish was under the direct supervision of General Pierotti.

When Pierotti resigned, effective November 1, 1996, his successor, William Gibbons, continued to work with Parrish in the investigation and prosecution of sexually-oriented businesses. In addition to the civil nuisance suit already filed in chancery court, Gibbons sought criminal indictments from the grand jury. In December of 1996, the grand jury returned an 18-count indictment against the defendant, Donald L. Culbreath, [including ten counts of promoting prostitution, six counts of prostitution, and two counts of public indecency].

The trial court found that over a 19-month period, Parrish received $410,931.87 for his services from CCV and other private contributors between December of 1995 and July of 1997. Of this amount, Parrish's expenses exceeded $100,000. The trial court found that Parrish's substantial involvement in the prosecution of these cases and his "enormous" compensation from a private, special interest group created a conflict of interest that required Parrish's disqualification. . . .

In determining whether to disqualify a prosecutor in a criminal case, the trial court must determine whether there is an actual conflict of interest, which includes any circumstances in which an attorney cannot exercise his or her independent professional judgment free of "compromising interests and loyalties." See Tenn. R. Sup. Ct. 8, EC 5-1. If there is no actual conflict of interest, the court must nonetheless consider whether conduct has created an appearance of impropriety. See Tenn. R. Sup. Ct. 8, EC 9-1, 9-6. If disqualification is required under either theory, the trial court must also determine whether the conflict of interest or appearance of impropriety requires disqualification of the entire District Attorney General's office. . . .

A District Attorney General is an elected constitutional officer whose function is to prosecute criminal offenses in his or her circuit or district. Tenn. Const. art. VI, §5. The District Attorney General "[shall] prosecute in the courts of the district all violations of the state criminal statutes and perform all prosecutorial functions attendant thereto. . . ." Tenn. Code Ann. §8-7-103(1). . . .

The proper role of the prosecutor in our criminal justice system has been addressed on numerous occasions by various courts and ethical rules. . . . The United States Supreme Court has said that a prosecutor:

> is the representative not of an ordinary party to a controversy, but of a sovereignty whose obligation to govern impartially is as compelling as its obligation to govern at all; and whose interest, therefore, in a criminal prosecution is not that it shall win a case, but that justice shall be done. As such, he is in a peculiar and very definite sense the servant of the law the twofold aim of which is that guilt shall not escape or innocence suffer. He may prosecute with earnestness and vigor — indeed, he should do so. But, while he may strike hard blows, he is not at liberty to strike foul ones.

Berger v. United States, 295 U.S. 78 (1935).

These principles are likewise embodied within the ethical considerations of the Model Code of Professional Responsibility governing the conduct of prosecutors:

> The responsibility of a public prosecutor differs from that of the usual advocate; his duty is to seek justice, not merely to convict. This special duty exists because: (1) the prosecutor represents the sovereign and therefore should use restraint in the discretionary exercise of governmental powers, such as in the selection of cases to prosecute; (2) during trial the prosecutor is not only an advocate but also may make decisions normally made by an individual client, and those affecting the public interest should be fair to all; and (3) in our system of criminal justice the accused is to be given the benefit of all reasonable doubts.

Tenn. R. Sup. Ct. 8, EC 7-13; see ABA Standards for Criminal Justice, Standard 3-1.1(c) (1979) ("[The] duty of the prosecutor is to seek justice, not merely to convict"). The Model Code also discusses the differences in the role of the prosecutor from that of the private attorney:

> With respect to evidence and witnesses, the prosecutor has responsibilities different from those of a lawyer in private practice; the prosecutor should make timely disclosure to the defense of available evidence, known to the prosecutor, that tends to negate the guilt of the accused, mitigate the degree of the offense, or reduce the punishment. Further, a prosecutor should not intentionally avoid pursuit of evidence merely because the prosecutor believes it will damage the prosecutor's case or aid the accused. [Tenn. R. Sup. Ct. 8, EC 7-13.]

In short, public prosecutors hold a unique office in our criminal justice system. [Prosecutors] are expected to be impartial in the sense that they must seek the truth and not merely obtain convictions. They are also to be impartial in the sense that charging decisions should be based upon the evidence, without discrimination or bias for or against any groups or individuals. Yet, at the same time, they are expected to prosecute criminal offenses with zeal and vigor within the bounds of the law and professional conduct.

Under English common law, the criminal justice system required the victim of a criminal offense, or the victim's family, to initiate and pursue criminal proceedings. Although the development and role of the public prosecutor in the United States over the past several centuries has largely supplanted the English common law in this regard, many jurisdictions still allow a private attorney to be retained or appointed to assist in the prosecution of a criminal case.

Numerous courts and commentators have recognized, however, that the use of a private attorney in the prosecution of a criminal case may present ethical dilemmas, including conflicts of interest. The private attorney must comply with the standards and ethical responsibilities for a public prosecutor — to not merely seek convictions but also to pursue justice. At the same time, however, the private attorney's ethical duty "both to client and to the legal system, is to represent the client zealously within the bounds of the law, which include Disciplinary Rules and enforceable professional regulations." Tenn. R. Sup. Ct. 8, EC 7-1.

In Tennessee, [a statute] provides for the employment of additional counsel [to prosecute an alleged crime]:

> [Where] the interest of the state requires . . . additional counsel to the attorney general and reporter or district attorney general, the governor shall employ such counsel, who shall be paid such compensation for services as the governor, secretary of state, and attorney general and reporter may deem just, the same to be paid out of any money in the treasury not otherwise appropriated. [Tenn. Code Ann. §8-6-106.]

Although the statutory provisions in Tennessee, similar to the laws in other jurisdictions, purport to address the potential conflicts by requiring that the private attorney work under the supervision of the District Attorney or be compensated by the state, they do not foreclose the risk that a conflict of interest, or appearance of such a conflict, may exist under the circumstances of a particular case. For example, there is a conflict of interest whenever an attorney is retained to assist the prosecution and acquires a direct financial interest in the proceeding. . . . Accordingly, a court must review the facts and circumstances of each case with these standards in mind.

In this case, Parrish's involvement began without any formal appointment by the Governor and no oath of office, and it continued in this manner for eight months from December of 1995 to July 1996. Parrish was compensated for his services by a private, special interest group that he billed each month. During this time, Parrish spearheaded a comprehensive investigation with a "staff" that included two assistant district attorneys and three investigators. There was no specific agreement or arrangement as to Parrish's role, the extent of his participation, or the extent of District Attorney General Pierotti's supervision — for all practical purposes, there appeared to be little supervision or control by Pierotti. . . .

Although General Pierotti purportedly appointed Parrish as a special prosecutor on the same day the [civil nuisance] suit was filed, there was (and is) no constitutional or statutory authority for such an appointment to be made. Moreover, although Parrish was later appointed as additional counsel by the Governor, there was (and is) no legal authority allowing Parrish to be compensated on an hourly basis by a private, special interest group. . . .

Parrish had an actual conflict of interest under the circumstances of this case. He was privately compensated by a special interest group and thus owed a duty of loyalty to that group; at the same time, he was serving in the role of public prosecutor and owed the duty of loyalty attendant to that office. Moreover, because Parrish was compensated on an hourly basis, the reality is that he acquired a direct financial interest in the duration and scope of the ongoing prosecution. . . .

The State contends that there was no conflict of interest because Parrish and the prosecution had the same interest — eradicating sexually-oriented businesses. The prosecutor's discretion about whom to prosecute and to what extent they should be prosecuted, however, is vast and to a large degree, not subject to meaningful review. Moreover, as the United States Supreme Court has recognized, the prosecutor's discretion goes beyond initial charging decisions [to include matters such as] "what information will be sought as evidence, which persons should be charged with what offenses, which persons should be utilized as witnesses, whether to enter into plea bargains and the terms on which they will be established, and whether any individuals should be granted immunity. . . ." Young v. United States ex rel. Vuitton et Fils S.A., 481 U.S. 787, 807 (1987). [The] foundation for the exercise of the vast prosecutorial discretion is freedom from conflict of interest and fidelity to the public interest.

Finally, we agree that the trial court did not abuse its discretion in disqualifying the District Attorney General's staff based on the appearance of impropriety created by Parrish's conflict of interest. . . . Despite Parrish's extensive contact with the office of the District Attorney General, including daily working involvement with two assistant district attorneys and several investigators, there were no guidelines as to Parrish's duties and no efforts to screen Parrish from other members of the District Attorney General's office. . . . Moreover, the trial court found that on one occasion, Pierotti, Gibbons, and Parrish attended a fund-raiser which "stressed the necessity to continue on with the prosecution of criminal activity in topless clubs and the need for continued donations to pursue these goals." . . .

Here, the private attorney's conflict of interest tainted the entire prosecution of the case well before the charges were presented to the grand jury. Accordingly, we conclude that the proceedings were inherently improper and that dismissal of the indictments is the appropriate remedy to redress the constitutional error. . . .

Problem 13-2. Private Money, Public Prosecutions

The Massachusetts legislature created the Insurance Fraud Bureau (IFB) to investigate charges of fraudulent insurance transactions and to refer any violation of law regarding insurance fraud to the appropriate prosecutor. The IFB is governed by a board of fifteen members, five each from the governing committees of two insurance rating bureaus (one for auto insurance and the other for workers' compensation insurance) and five public officials, including the Commissioner of Insurance and the Commissioner of the Department of Industrial Accidents.

According to the statute, every insurer "having reason to believe that an insurance transaction may be fraudulent" must report its suspicions to the IFB. The IFB must review each report and may investigate further. Whenever the IFB's executive director is satisfied that a material fraud or intentional misrepresentation has been committed in an insurance transaction, he must "refer the matter to the attorney general, the appropriate district attorney or the United States attorney, and to appropriate licensing agencies." A person convicted of any law concerning insurance fraud, following an IFB referral for prosecution, "shall be ordered to make restitution to the insurer for any financial loss sustained as a result of such violation."

The IFB receives reports of suspected insurance fraud from a variety of sources. During the IFB's first seven years, slightly more than half of these reports came from insurance companies. Other reports came from government agencies, professional organizations, and the public. Of the more than 12,800 reports received in those seven years, more than 5,000 were accepted for investigation, 64 percent of which were from insurance companies.

The Commissioner of Insurance must cover the IFB's investigation costs through annual assessments against the two insurance rating bureaus, which are themselves funded by insurance companies operating in the state. For fiscal year 1999, the appropriation from the general fund for the investigation and prosecution of automobile insurance fraud was $270,871, and the assessment against the auto insurance rating bureau was $250,000. In that same year, the legislative appropriation for the investigation and prosecution of workers' compensation fraud was $463,159 and the assessment against workers' compensation rating board was $250,000.

The commissioner must also collect from the rating bureaus enough money to cover funds spent for fringe benefits "attributable to personnel costs of the attorney general's office related to the purposes" of the program. Under this law, the Attorney General uses the assessments to hire 13 assistant attorneys general, six for automobile insurance fraud matters and seven for workers' compensation insurance fraud matters.

James Ellis and Nicholas Ellis were partners in a law firm that represented plaintiffs in workers' compensation and personal injury cases. Along with other associates, employees and clients, they were charged with insurance fraud and related offenses. Both defendants moved to dismiss the indictments based on the partiality of the attorneys prosecuting the cases. They challenged the constitutionality of the statutorily funding scheme.

The state argued in reply that routine cooperation from a victim of a crime is often necessary and should be encouraged. Victims of commercial or corporate crimes may assist the prosecution by collecting and organizing necessary information and may properly hire private investigators for external investigation of suspected crimes. In addition, the state noted that assessments are made industry-wide, rather than on one particular victim corporation, and are spent on investigation and prosecution of automobile and workers' compensation insurance fraud generally, rather than for the particular benefit of any one victim. How would you rule on the motion to dismiss? Compare Commonwealth v. Ellis, 708 N.E. 2d 644 (Mass. 1999).

Notes

1. *Private filing of complaints.* Most states give the public prosecutor exclusive authority to file criminal complaints. See Cal. Govt. Code §26500 ("The public prosecutor shall attend the courts, and within his or her discretion shall initiate and conduct on behalf of the people all prosecutions"). The same is true in the federal system. The court in Harman v. Frye, 425 S.E.2d 566 (W. Va. 1992), considered criminal complaints for battery that two participants in a fight filed against each other. The opinion summarized the reasons why most states have required the public prosecutor to approve of the filing of any criminal charges:

> [Citizens] can misuse the right to file a criminal complaint before a magistrate by exaggerating the facts or omitting relevant facts they disclose to the magistrate so as to transform a noncriminal dispute into a crime. The magistrate, who must remain neutral, is not in the same position as the prosecuting attorney or law enforcement officers to ascertain whether all of the relevant facts have been disclosed accurately. . . . When citizens file criminal complaints before the magistrate which later prove to be frivolous, retaliatory or unfounded, the prosecuting attorney is required to take the time to investigate the complaint before moving a nolle pros to dismiss. . . . Moreover, additional time and expense are also incurred when either the public defender or an attorney-at-law must be appointed to represent indigent persons against whom frivolous, retaliatory or unfounded charges have been filed. . . . Finally, private citizens have not undergone the same professional training as prosecuting attorneys or law enforcement officers nor are they subject to the same rules of professional conduct and discipline which are imposed on prosecuting attorneys and law enforcement officers.

In a few states, statutes authorize citizens to file criminal complaints even when the prosecutor has declined to do so. Most of these statutes (like the Wisconsin statute reprinted above) allow the private complaint to occur only after the public prosecutor has affirmatively decided not to file charges, and they require the citizen to obtain approval for the charges from a judge or grand jury. A few of the statutes apply only to particular crimes, such as domestic violence or issuance of a worthless check. See W. Va. Code §§48-27-902, 61-3-39a. Can the public prosecutor prevent any abuses of private complaints simply by dismissing charges once they are filed? If the prosecutor retains the power to dismiss charges filed by a private citizen, has the mechanism accomplished anything other than creating paperwork?

2. *Historical roots of victim rights during prosecution.* By the turn of the twentieth century the public prosecutor became the primary method for initiating criminal charges. Private prosecutions became the exception rather than the rule as public prosecutors became more professionalized and independent of the courts, professional police departments became more common in metropolitan areas, and acquittal rates rose for privately initiated complaints.

Traces of the older private prosecution system remain visible today, and are gaining renewed attention as a method of empowering the victims of crime. More than half the states still have statutes or constitutional provisions that allow private counsel, retained by a crime victim, to participate in criminal proceedings. In most jurisdictions, the private prosecutor may only assist the prosecutor, while in a few the private prosecutor has more authority to direct the criminal proceedings. See, e.g., Pa. Stat. tit. 16, §1409 (the court may "direct any private counsel employed by [a complainant] to conduct the entire proceeding").

Most states, however, do not give the victim any right to "consult" with the prosecutor about the charges to be filed. They simply instruct the prosecutor to inform the victim about the charges to be filed or about the decision not to file charges. See Ariz. Stat. §13-4408 (prosecutor to give victim notice of the charge against defendant and concise statement of procedural steps in criminal prosecution, and to inform victim of decision to decline prosecution, with reasons for declination). Are these "notice" statutes an inevitable response to the abandonment of private prosecutions? To get a sense of the range of these efforts to allow victim representation in the criminal process, go to the web extension for this chapter at *http://www.crimpro.com/extension/ch13*.

Are private prosecutions of crime an effective way to supplement the limited resources of a public prosecutor, much as we rely on "private attorneys general" to help enforce some civil statutes? See Roger A. Fairfax, Jr. Delegation of the criminal prosecution function to private actors. 43 UC Davis L. Rev. 411 (2009).

3. *Private financial aid to public prosecution.* What is wrong with private parties funding public prosecutions so long as the public prosecutor makes the decisions? In Commonwealth v. Ellis, 708 N.E. 2d 644 (Mass. 1999), which provides the basis for Problem 13-2, the Massachusetts Supreme Court upheld the statutory industry funding scheme for insurance and fraud prosecutions, finding no appearance of conflict. The court observed: "where the question is whether the appearance of an arrangement may support a determination of unconstitutionality, the fact that the Legislature has endorsed the plan, has supervisory authority over it, and appropriates funds for it substantially changes appearances."

Can you distinguish the outcomes in *Culbreath* and *Ellis?* See also Hambarian v. Superior Court, 44 P.3d 102 (Cal. 2002) (prosecutor's office need not be removed despite use of accountant paid by victim). A prosecutor who is paid by a private interest but is working under the direction of a public prosecutor can be said to serve two (or more) clients. Who are the clients, and do their interests conflict?

4. *Special prosecutors.* Almost all states have statutes empowering a judge (or a prosecuting attorney) to appoint a "special prosecutor" to file and prosecute criminal charges. The court appoints the special prosecutor when the district attorney "refuses to act" or "neglects" to perform a duty. See Ala. Code §12-17-186; Tenn. Const. art. 6, §5 ("In all cases where the Attorney for any district fails or refuses to attend and prosecute according to law, the Court shall have power to appoint an Attorney pro tempore"). Courts will also order the use of a special prosecutor when

the prosecuting attorney has a conflict of interest regarding a suspect, a complainant, or some other person involved in a potential criminal case. If an independent official who decides whether to file criminal charges does not operate within a limited budget and does not compare the current case to all other potential criminal cases that an office might prosecute, will the quality of the prosecutorial decision improve? Are budget constraints a necessary evil, or are they the essence of prosecutorial accountability?

4. *Selection of Charges and System*

Up to this point, we have focused on prosecutorial choices that would place a suspect either "in" or "out" of the criminal justice system. But prosecutors also make important choices about each criminal defendant who will be charged. For one thing, the prosecutor selects among a range of criminal charges that could apply to the case. For another, prosecutors might select which judicial system (state or federal, juvenile or adult) will adjudicate the charges.

a. Selection Among Charges

U.S. DEPARTMENT OF JUSTICE, PRINCIPLES OF FEDERAL PROSECUTION

(1980)

SELECTING CHARGES

1. Except as hereafter provided, the attorney for the government should charge, or should recommend that the grand jury charge, the most serious offense that is consistent with the nature of the defendant's conduct, and that is likely to result in a sustainable conviction.

2. Except as hereafter provided, the attorney for the government should also charge, or recommend that the grand jury charge, other offenses only when, in his judgment, additional charges:

(a) are necessary to ensure that the information or indictment: (i) adequately reflects the nature and extent of the criminal conduct involved; and (ii) provides the basis for an appropriate sentence under all the circumstances of the case; or

(b) will significantly enhance the strength of the government's case against the defendant or a codefendant.

3. The attorney for the government may file or recommend a charge or charges without regard to the provisions of paragraphs 1 and 2, if such charge or charges are the subject of a pre-charge plea agreement. . . .

MINNESOTA STATUTES §388.051

(1) The county attorney shall [prosecute] felonies, including the drawing of indictments found by the grand jury, and, to the extent prescribed by law, gross

misdemeanors, misdemeanors, petty misdemeanors, and violations of municipal ordinances, charter provisions and rules or regulations. . . .

(3) [Each] county attorney shall adopt written guidelines governing the county attorney's charging . . . policies and practices. The guidelines shall address, but need not be limited to, the . . . factors that are considered in making charging decisions. . . .

■ PEOPLE v. JALEH WILKINSON

94 P.3d 551 (Cal. 2004)

GEORGE, C.J.

[In] the early morning hours of February 27, 1999, a motorist observed defendant driving erratically on a street in the City of Santa Monica. Defendant's vehicle crossed over the center divider, struck a parked car, and continued down the street, swerving between lanes. Defendant eventually stopped her car at a curb and placed her head on the front passenger seat. [Officers] tapped on the window of defendant's parked car, whereupon defendant looked at one of the officers and drove off. The police gave chase for three blocks before defendant stopped. Defendant, who smelled strongly of alcohol and exhibited slurred speech, indicated she had consumed some drinks but not many. She could not complete a field sobriety test and did not respond when told she was required to submit to a blood or breath test for alcohol.

Officers transported defendant to the police station. She was belligerent during booking and resisted a patsearch. At one point, defendant grabbed a custodial officer's arm with both hands, causing a visible welt. When taken to a holding cell, defendant charged at an officer and yelled, kicked, and banged at the door. After the police reminded defendant that she would have to submit to a blood or breath test, defendant covered her ears, stated "I can't hear you," and began running around inside the cell. An officer testified defendant appeared to be under the influence of alcohol but not of drugs.

Defendant testified in her own defense as follows. On the night in question, defendant, a bank vice-president, went to a bar, where she met a man who offered to buy her a drink. She accepted and eventually consumed two glasses of wine. The man invited defendant to dinner, and they agreed to meet at a Santa Monica restaurant. At the restaurant, defendant consumed three alcoholic beverages over the course of three hours while she waited for the man, but he never arrived. She left her drink several times to use the restroom and to smoke a cigarette outside. She eventually left the restaurant, driving away without feeling any signs of intoxication. The next thing she remembered was waking up in jail, with no recollection of her encounter with the officers. After her release from custody, defendant filed a police complaint alleging she had been drugged.

A toxicologist, testifying on behalf of the defense, expressed the opinion that on the night in question defendant was under the influence of alcohol and gamma hydroxy butyrate (hereafter GHB), commonly known as a "date rape" drug, basing his opinion on a review of the police report and a videotape of defendant's conduct in the holding cell. GHB depresses the nervous system, exaggerates the effects of alcohol, and may cause drowsiness and memory loss. Depending upon a person's personality, the drug may make a person more emotional and combative. . . .

The jury convicted defendant as charged, and the trial court placed defendant on formal probation for three years. . . . Defendant was convicted of violating Penal Code section 243.1, which states in full: "When a battery is committed against the person of a custodial officer as defined in Section 831 of the Penal Code, and the person committing the offense knows or reasonably should know that the victim is a custodial officer engaged in the performance of his or her duties, and the custodial officer is engaged in the performance of his or her duties, the offense shall be punished by imprisonment in the state prison." Section 831, subdivision (a), in turn, defines a "custodial officer" as "a public officer, not a peace officer, employed by a law enforcement agency of a city or county who has the authority and responsibility for maintaining custody of prisoners and performs tasks related to the operation of a local detention facility used for the detention of persons usually pending arraignment or upon court order either for their own safekeeping or for the specific purpose of serving a sentence therein." Because section 243.1 provides for a punishment of imprisonment in state prison, but does not otherwise specify the term of imprisonment, under section 18 the offense is punishable "by imprisonment in any of the state prisons for 16 months, or two or three years. . . ."

At the time section 243.1 was enacted in 1976, section 243 prescribed the punishment (1) for simple battery (which section 243 made punishable as a misdemeanor), (2) for battery against a person who the defendant knew or should have known was a "peace officer or fireman engaged in the performance of his duties" (which section 243 made punishable as either a felony or a misdemeanor, commonly known as a "wobbler"), and (3) for battery resulting in the infliction of "serious bodily injury" (which section 243 also made punishable as a wobbler, prescribing a punishment of two, three, or four years' imprisonment for a felony violation).

In 1981, the Legislature divided section 243 into subdivisions, with subdivision (a) covering simple battery (punishable as a misdemeanor with a maximum jail sentence of six months), subdivision (b) covering battery on a person who the defendant knows or should know is a peace officer, firefighter, etc. (punishable as a misdemeanor with a maximum jail sentence of one year), subdivision (c) covering battery on a peace officer, firefighter, etc., that results in the infliction of injury (a wobbler with a possible state prison term of 16 months, two years, or three years), and subdivision (d) covering battery that results in serious bodily injury (a wobbler with a possible prison term of two, three, or four years). The following year, in 1982, the Legislature added a reference to custodial officers to subdivisions (b) and (c) of section 243, defining custodial officers by reference to section 831. . . .

On appeal, defendant [contends] that the current statutory scheme pertaining to battery on a custodial officer is "irrational" and violates the federal and state guarantees of equal protection because one who commits the "lesser" offense of battery on a custodial officer without injury can receive felony punishment under section 243.1 while a person committing the "greater" offense of battery on a custodial officer with injury can be convicted of a wobbler offense under section 243, subdivision (c)(1) and can receive a misdemeanor sentence. . . .

We begin our discussion with an overview of relevant case authority. . . . In People v. Chenze, 97 Cal. App. 4th 521 (Cal. App. 2002), the defendant contended that he was improperly charged and convicted under section 243.1 because that provision had been "impliedly repealed" when the Legislature amended section 243 to include references to custodial officers. . . . The Court of Appeal in *Chenze* disagreed that the two statutes were in irreconcilable conflict and thus rejected the claim of implied repeal. The court cited an enrolled bill report . . . which explained the need for an amendment to section 243 to include references to custodial officers notwithstanding the existence of section 243.1: "According to the bill's sponsors, simple battery charges against custodial officers are rarely pursued by local prosecutors because the present law only provides for felony charges with imprisonment in a state prison. Thus, these violators are rarely, if ever, punished. By providing for the option of county jail and/or fine for such violations, proponents hope that simple battery charges will be prosecuted more vigorously. Felony battery charges can still be pursued for the more serious cases." . . . But the Legislature also apparently envisioned that there might be circumstances under which no or only slight injury was inflicted, but felony charges would nonetheless still be appropriate. . . .

The United States Supreme Court's decision in United States v. Batchelder, 442 U.S. 114 (1979), . . . concluded that the defendant properly could be sentenced under one federal firearms statute, although an almost identical statute prescribed a lesser punishment. In *Batchelder*, the court took note of legislative history indicating that Congress "intended to enact two independent gun control statutes, each fully enforceable on its own terms." The court in *Batchelder* then stated that . . . "when an act violates more than one criminal statute, the Government may prosecute under either so long as it does not discriminate against any class of defendants." The high court concluded that the statutory scheme at issue fell under this rule: "There is no appreciable difference between the discretion a prosecutor exercises when deciding whether to charge under one of two statutes with different elements and the discretion he exercises when choosing one of two statutes with identical elements. In the former situation, once he determines that the proof will support conviction under either statute, his decision is indistinguishable from the one he faces in the latter context. The prosecutor may be influenced by the penalties available upon conviction, but this fact, standing alone, does not give rise to a violation of the Equal Protection or Due Process Clause." . . .

Batchelder instructs us that neither the existence of two identical criminal statutes prescribing different levels of punishments, nor the exercise of a prosecutor's discretion in charging under one such statute and not the other, violates equal protection principles. Thus, defendant may not complain that she was charged with a felony violation under section 243.1 even though section 243, subdivision (b) is an identical statute prescribing a lesser punishment. [Numerous] factors properly may enter into a prosecutor's decision to charge under one statute and not another, such as a defendant's background and the severity of the crime, and so long as there is no showing that a defendant has been singled out deliberately for prosecution on the basis of some invidious criterion [such as race or religion], that is, one that is arbitrary and thus unjustified because it bears no rational relationship to legitimate law enforcement interests, the defendant cannot make out an equal protection violation. Defendant does not allege that her prosecution was motivated by improper considerations.

[Defendant's argument] is based upon the questionable premise that battery on a custodial officer without injury always is a less serious offense than battery with injury, so as to warrant inevitably a lesser punishment. [Consider, however,] whether a hypothetical defendant who, in the course of grabbing the arm of a correctional officer, inflicts a puncture wound with her fingernail that requires medical attention would be more culpable than a defendant who repeatedly hits and kicks the correctional officer, intending to cause serious injury but does not do so through no lack of effort. [The Legislature amended section 243] to allow misdemeanor prosecutions of batteries committed on custodial officers, and the Legislature did not repeal section 243.1 to allow felony prosecutions for more serious cases, even if no injury was inflicted. . . .

The only difference between sections 243.1 and 243, subdivision (b) on the one hand, and section 243, subdivision (c)(1) on the other, is that, because section 243, subdivision (c)(1) is a wobbler, a trial court has discretion at sentencing either to impose misdemeanor punishment or grant probation and later, upon the defendant's successful completion of probation, declare the offense to be a misdemeanor. . . .

The circumstance that the Legislature did not grant to the trial court the same discretion in prosecutions under section 243.1 to reduce the charge to a misdemeanor as it did for prosecutions under section 243, subdivision (c) does not render the statutory scheme unconstitutional. A rational basis for these statutes exists; the Legislature reasonably could have concluded that reduction of the section 243.1 offense is not appropriate in cases of a battery on a custodial officer that is deemed serious enough by the prosecutor to warrant felony prosecution under the latter statute. . . . Because a rational basis exists for the statutory scheme pertaining to battery on a custodial officer, these statutes are not vulnerable to challenge under the equal protection clause. . . .

KENNARD, J., dissenting.

[The] statutory scheme lacks any rational basis, in my view, and thereby violates the constitutional guarantee of equal protection of the laws. . . . The first prerequisite to a meritorious claim under the equal protection clause is a showing that the state has adopted a classification that affects two or more similarly situated groups in an unequal manner. In this case, persons who commit the same illegal act — a battery on a custodial officer causing injury — are in that respect similarly situated, but they are treated differently depending on whether they are charged under section 243.1, which does not require proof of injury, or under section 243(c), which does. . . .

[The] current scheme encourages arbitrary, irrational charging. In the case of a battery on a custodial officer that causes injury, there would be no incentive for the prosecutor to charge the defendant under section 243(c). [Under section 243.1], the prosecutor is spared the burden of proving the injury and the trial court is precluded from treating the offense as a misdemeanor, an option that would be available to the court if the defendant had been charged with, and convicted of a violation of section 243(c). . . .

Other consequences of the statutory scheme are even more perplexing, as illustrated by the problems involved in instructing a jury in the trial of a defendant charged with a violation of section 243(c). A trial court must instruct the jury on a lesser included offense when the evidence raises a question whether all of the elements of the charged crime are present, and the evidence would support a conviction of the lesser offense. [When] a defendant is charged with a battery on a custodial officer with injury or serious bodily injury, and there is a question whether the injury occurred, the trial court must instruct on the necessarily included offense of battery in violation of section 243.1 (battery on a custodial officer without injury). If the jury then found the defendant guilty as charged of a battery on a custodial officer causing injury (§243(c)), the court would have discretion to impose a misdemeanor sentence. But if the jury, because it entertained a reasonable doubt that the battery had caused an injury to the custodial officer, found the defendant guilty only of the necessarily included offense of battery on a custodial officer (§243.1), the trial court would be required to sentence the defendant as a felon.

I can perceive no rational basis for this rather startling statutory scheme. The majority does, however. The majority first questions whether the offense defined in section 243.1 (battery on a custodial officer without injury) is actually less serious than the offense defined in section 243(c) (battery on a custodial officer with injury). It observes that if we compare two different batteries, it is possible that a particular battery without injury could be more heinous than another battery that did cause an injury. By the same reasoning, however, a particular petty theft could, depending on the circumstances, be more serious than a particular grand theft, and a particular grand theft could be more serious than a particular robbery, and so forth. Under this reasoning, the legal classification of crimes as inherently "greater" or "lesser" becomes meaningless and a rational ordering of crimes and punishment in the penal law becomes impossible. In deciding which of two crimes is the greater, the only meaningful comparison is between the elements of each crime, . . . not the particular circumstances of their commission. . . .

The majority holds that section 243.1 (battery on a custodial officer without injury) does not violate the principle of equal protection of the laws because the Legislature could have rationally concluded that reduction of this offense to a misdemeanor is not appropriate whenever the prosecutor deems the offense serious enough for felony prosecution. This reasoning misses the point. Equal protection analysis requires comparing two statutes. . . . The majority offers no rational basis for the distinction between them.[4] . . . Could the Legislature rationally believe that some batteries without injury are so serious that the prosecutor must be given unfettered, unreviewable power to ensure that they are prosecuted as felonies, but that this is not the case for batteries causing injury? Conversely, could the Legislature rationally believe that the courts could be trusted to determine when batteries causing injury should be treated as felonies rather than misdemeanors, but could not be trusted to make the same determination as to batteries that did not cause injury? The answer is inescapable: the statutory distinction has no rational basis, thus denying defendant the equal protection of the laws. . . .

Here, after charging defendant with a felony battery under section 243.1, the prosecutor offered to dismiss the felony charge if defendant would plead guilty to a misdemeanor battery, which would be further reduced to an infraction if she successfully completed probation. Defense counsel refused the offer. The prosecutor then offered to dismiss the battery charge if defendant would plead guilty to the misdemeanor of driving under the influence of alcohol or drugs. Defense counsel rejected this offer as well. The case was then prosecuted as a felony. The trial court

4. The majority mistakenly relies on United States v. Batchelder, 442 U.S. 114 (1979), a case involving a federal statutory scheme that defined two crimes with essentially the same elements but different penalties. . . . The court was not faced with a statutory scheme like the one at issue here, which defines two closely related crimes and permits lesser punishment for the crime that differs only in requiring one additional aggravating element. . . . I note, moreover, that the Colorado Supreme Court found the reasoning in *Batchelder* unpersuasive and declined to follow it in construing the equal protection clause of its own state constitution. People v. Estrada, 601 P.2d 619 (Colo. 1979).

expressed dismay that the case had not been settled, and, after the jury found defendant guilty as charged, the court placed defendant on probation instead of sending her to prison for the felony conviction.

[These] facts show that the prosecutor did not consider defendant's conduct so egregious as to require felony punishment. A prosecutor taking that view would not have been so eager to induce defendant to plead guilty to crimes punishable only as misdemeanors. But because defendant was charged under section 243.1, a mandatory felony, the trial court was prevented from exercising the discretion the Legislature gave it to treat the more serious crime of battery on a custodial officer with injury (§243(c)) as a misdemeanor. This kind of injustice is the predictable result of the current irrational statutory scheme. . . .

In 1988, the Florida legislature revised the state's "habitual offender" statute. Under the new statute, a prosecutor's decision to charge an eligible defendant as a habitual offender translated into longer prison sentences. Within a few years, defendants and others began to complain that prosecutors were using their new charging power in an arbitrary and discriminatory manner. Legislative committees asked for a study of the use of the habitual offender statute. The study, completed in 1992, concluded as follows:

> [First, in] most circuits, and certainly on a statewide basis, the statute has not been limited to use against the very worst offenders but has been applied more frequently to the less serious offenders. . . . Second, the circuit in which an offender is prosecuted is of enormous importance to the risk of habitualization. This means that for the roughly one third of all guilty adjudications who are eligible for habitualization, Florida does not have a single statewide system of reasonably uniform sentencing. For this group of offenders . . . there are effectively 20 separate sentencing systems that vary widely in their treatment of offenders eligible for habitualization.
>
> Third, in all but two circuits [those encompassing Miami and Sarasota], the habitual offender sanctions are much more likely to be used against black offenders than non-black offenders, even after adjusting for prior record, the nature of the current offense and a variety of other factors that might have a bearing on the decision to habitualize. It was also found that, on a statewide basis, prosecutors were much more likely to use the statute against male offenders than similarly situated female offenders. . . .

After receiving this report, several state legislators called for revisions to the statute that would restrict or remove the prosecutor's power to decide when to charge an offender as a habitual felon. Consider the following statement that a group of prosecutors in the state made in this volatile context.

FLORIDA PROSECUTING ATTORNEYS' ASSOCIATION, STATEMENT CONCERNING IMPLEMENTING OF HABITUAL OFFENDER LAWS

(1993)

The Florida Prosecuting Attorneys' Association desires to provide continuing effective protection to the public from habitual offenders by discouraging the legislature from the total elimination of habitual offender laws and minimum mandatory sentence laws through the voluntary adoption by the State Attorneys of implementation criteria for use of habitual offender laws.

To fulfill this desire, the State Attorneys of the State of Florida adopt the criteria set forth below for the implementation of the habitual offender laws of Florida in their respective circuits to be utilized whenever such utilization would not result in the interference with the proper and fair administration of the duties of a State Attorney, as shall be determined by the respective State Attorney. Recognizing that there will be cases which would justify habitual offender treatment which will not meet these criteria, such cases shall have the reasons set forth in writing and signed by the designated Assistant State Attorney(s), and the State Attorneys filing such cases shall notify this Organization's President of such filings.

I. Habitual Violent Felony Offenders

A. Charged offense must be a second degree felony or higher . . . , AND
B. Charged offense must be an enumerated violent felony, AND
C. Defendant must have at least one prior conviction for an enumerated violent felony, AND
D. The felony for which the defendant is to be sentenced was committed within five years of the date of the conviction for the last enumerated violent felony or within five years of the defendant's release, on parole or otherwise, from a prison sentence or other commitment imposed as a result of the prior enumerated felony conviction.

II. Habitual Felony Offenders

A. *Violent Offenses:* Defendants charged with a second degree or higher enumerated violent felony . . . must have at least two prior felony convictions of any type.
B. *Second Degree Felonies (Excluding Sale or Purchase of or Trafficking in Controlled Substances and Burglary Cases):* Defendants charged with a non-violent, second degree or higher offense (excluding Sale or Purchase of or Trafficking in a Controlled Substance and Burglary) must have at least three prior felony convictions of any type, or two prior enumerated violent felony convictions.
C. *Second Degree Burglary:* Defendants charged with a second degree or higher Burglary must have at least two prior felony convictions of any type.
D. *Sale of or Trafficking in Controlled Substances:* Defendants charged with a second degree or higher sale of or trafficking in a Controlled Substance (including attempts and conspiracies of a second degree or higher) must have at least two prior felony convictions for sale of or trafficking in Controlled Substances (including attempts or conspiracies but not including Counterfeit Drugs); OR two prior enumerated violent felony convictions; OR one sale or trafficking in a Controlled Substance (including attempts and conspiracies but not including Counterfeit Drugs) conviction and one enumerated violent felony conviction.

E. *Third Degree Felonies:* Defendants charged with third degree felonies shall receive habitual offender sanctions only if they meet one of the following criteria:

1. The defendant is charged with: Aggravated Assault, OR Aggravated Stalking, OR Attempted Sexual Battery (victim 12 or older, no physical force), OR Battery on a Law Enforcement Officer, OR Child Abuse, OR Felony DUI, OR Resisting Arrest with Violence, OR . . . Vehicular Homicide, AND the defendant has at least four prior felony convictions of any type, or two prior enumerated violent convictions; OR
2. The defendant is charged with Burglary of a Structure AND the defendant has at least two prior felony convictions, one of which is a Burglary of a Dwelling or Structure; OR
3. The defendant is charged with Grand Theft of a Motor Vehicle AND the defendant has at least four prior felony convictions, three of which must be for Grand Theft of a Motor Vehicle. . . .

Problem 13-3. Available Charges

On the evening of January 9, Ida County deputy sheriff Randy Brown was on patrol in Ida Grove. He observed three snowmobiles traveling on a downtown sidewalk and then on the streets in a careless and reckless manner. Once Brown began pursuit, the trio split up. With the aid of another deputy, Brown eventually stopped and arrested Mitch Peters.

At the time of arrest, Peters had a strong odor of alcohol on his breath. The deputies took him to the Ida County sheriff's office, where they administered sobriety tests. Peters failed the horizontal gaze nystagmus test and the preliminary breath test, registering above .10. Peters was charged with operating a motor vehicle while intoxicated, second offense, under Iowa Code §321J.2, which provides as follows:

> A person commits the offense of operating while intoxicated if the person operates a motor vehicle in this state [while] under the influence of an alcoholic beverage or other drug or a combination of such substances, [or while] having an alcohol concentration . . . of .10 or more.

Peters objects to the charge, claiming that he could be prosecuted only under section 321G.13(3), which provides as follows: "A person shall not drive or operate an all-terrain vehicle or snowmobile [while] under the influence of intoxicating liquor or narcotics or habit-forming drugs." This statute carries a lesser punishment than §321J.2. The trial court rejected Peters's claim. After conviction Peters appealed, claiming that §321J.2 did not apply to his conduct. How would you rule? Compare State v. Peters, 525 N.W.2d 854 (Iowa 1994); People v. Rogers, 475 N.W.2d 717 (Mich. 1991).

Notes

1. *Selection among charges: majority view.* According to judges in the United States, prosecutors may select among all applicable statutes in deciding what charges to bring, with no outside interference. The occasional claim by defendants that one crime better fits the offense and offender than another virtually always fails. In United States v. Batchelder, 442 U.S. 114 (1979), the Supreme Court considered two overlapping criminal statutes. Although both statutes prohibited convicted felons from possessing firearms, one provision imposed only a two-year maximum penalty while the second imposed a maximum penalty of five years. The Court held that Batchelder's conviction and sentence to the maximum term under the five-year statute did not violate the due process, equal protection, or separation of powers doctrine. While some courts reach this result as a matter of constitutional doctrine, others rely on statutory interpretation. These courts apply a technique of statutory interpretation or "rule of construction" referred to by its Latin name, *in pari materia,* which leads courts to presume that all related statutes make up a single, coherent statutory scheme, regardless of when they were enacted.

Such a hands-off judicial attitude is easiest to explain when the two statutes involve a greater offense and a lesser-included offense. It is more difficult to justify, however, when two statutes with different penalties require the prosecutor to prove precisely the same elements. A few courts create rules of statutory interpretation that apply the lesser penalty in a situation where two identical statutes impose different penalties, assuming that the legislature made an error. See State v. McAdam, 83 P.3d 161 (Kan. 2004).

2. *Structuring the charging discretion.* Does the absence of judicial regulation of charge selection create the need for detailed charging guidelines? What institutions could develop charging policies? Should legislatures draft policies or should they follow the Minnesota legislature's approach, simply directing that each chief prosecutor draft charging policies?

Consider again the Justice Department's Principles of Federal Prosecution. Do they give any surprising or meaningful direction to a prosecutor making a charging decision? The National District Attorneys Association lists the following among the appropriate factors for a prosecutor to consider in selecting charges: "the probability of conviction," "the willingness of the offender to cooperate with law enforcement," "possible improper motives of a victim or witness," "excessive cost of prosecution in relation to the seriousness of the offense," "recommendations of the involved law enforcement agency," and "any mitigating circumstances." National Prosecution Standards §43.6 (2d ed. 1991). Does this list differ in emphasis or in particulars from the federal standards?

Habitual felon laws, such as the one discussed in the Florida guidelines, typically leave prosecutors with charging discretion that can make exceptionally large differences in the sentence. Compare the Florida policy with the office policy of the Los Angeles District Attorney regarding the application of California's Three Strikes law. Special Directive 00-02, available at *http://da.co.la.ca.us/3strikes.htm,* declares that if a defendant has two or more qualifying prior felony convictions, charges under a relevant statute are presumed to justify a "Third Strike" filing, which warrants a minimum 25-years-to-life sentence. This presumption may be rebutted "if the current offense does not involve the use or possession of a firearm or deadly weapon, injury to a victim, [or] violence or the threat of violence." For such cases, the Head Deputy can authorize dismissal of a strike after consideration of the "remoteness of the strikes," whether "the strikes arose from one incident or transaction," and "any other mitigating or aggravating factors enumerated in the California Rules of Court, Rules 421 and 423." How does the Los Angeles Special Directive compare to the Florida guidelines? For additional examples and discussion of prosecutorial office policies that govern the selection among charges, go to the web extension for this chapter at *http://www.crimpro.com/extension/ch13*.

3. *Charges of overcharging.* Defense attorneys and many observers of the criminal justice system claim that prosecutors routinely "overcharge" cases in anticipation of plea bargain negotiations. Standard 3-3.9 of the ABA Standards for Criminal Justice (3d ed. 1993) advises prosecutors against bringing charges greater than necessary "to reflect the gravity of the offense" or charges where there is not "sufficient admissible evidence to support a conviction." How can we know when prosecutors are "overcharging" for strategic reasons? If it is difficult to prove that an abuse is taking place at all, is there any hope of reducing the amount of any abuse?

4. *Statutory limits on multiple convictions.* About a half-dozen states have statutes that approach the question of charge selection at the "back end" of convictions rather than the "front end" of charges. These statutes limit the number of convictions that can result from overlapping charges. Consider Mo. Ann. Stat. §556.041:

> When the same conduct of a person may establish the commission of more than one offense he may be prosecuted for each such offense. He may not, however, be convicted of more than one offense if [the] offenses differ only in that one is defined to prohibit a designated kind of conduct generally and the other to prohibit a specific instance of such conduct. . . .

But cf. Ill. Ann. Stat. ch. 720, para. 5/3-3 ("When the same conduct of a defendant may establish the commission of more than one offense, the defendant may be prosecuted for each such offense"). Is a statute directed to the trial judge who enters final judgment more likely to produce consistent punishment for similar conduct than any effort to influence the charging decision more directly?

5. *Criminal code reform.* Would a well-drafted criminal code reduce concerns about consistent and fair charging? See Paul Robinson, Are Criminal Codes Irrelevant? 68 S. Cal. L. Rev. 159 (1994). Are there fewer overlaps and conflicts between statutes in states with a uniform criminal code? The majority of states revised their criminal codes in the decades following the promulgation of the path-breaking Model Penal Code by the American Law Institute in 1962. Criminal codes before reform often include hundreds or, in some cases, thousands of separate crimes. Going forward, imagine the practices or institutions that might produce well-drafted criminal codes. Whenever there is an apparent conflict between two statutory provisions, should the courts (or the lawyers) notify the appropriate legislative committees? Consider again the overlapping statutes in the *Wilkinson* case from California and the two statutes described in Problem 13-3. Why do you suppose the state legislatures passed these overlapping statutes? Was it an oversight that could be rationalized through criminal code reform?

b. Selection of System

Most of the crimes committed by defendants under 18 years old are handled in specialized juvenile courts as "delinquency" cases. Juvenile courts (which go by various names, such as "Family Court") operate differently from the adult criminal justice system. Their informal processes, which are considered civil rather than criminal proceedings, are designed to emphasize rehabilitation and avoid the stigma associated with adult criminal punishment. The juvenile justice system loses its authority over offenders when they reach age 18 or 21.

While most juvenile offenders have their cases adjudicated in the juvenile system, some are transferred to the adult criminal justice system. Less than 5 percent of all adjudicated juvenile cases transfer into the adult system. States have created a variety of mechanisms and presumptions to direct juvenile offenders into one system or the other. As with other charging decisions, the prosecutor is the key decisionmaker over this transfer decision, while the legislature also sets some important parameters. Do the limitations on the prosecutor's choice between systems differ from the limits on other prosecutorial charging decisions?

■ HOWARD N. SNYDER, MELISSA SICKMUND, AND EILEEN POE-YAMAGATA, JUVENILE TRANSFERS TO CRIMINAL COURT IN THE 1990'S: LESSONS LEARNED FROM FOUR STUDIES

National Center for Juvenile Justice (August 2000)

Juveniles may be prosecuted in criminal court under certain circumstances, and State law determines the conditions under which youth charged with a criminal law violation can be processed in the criminal, rather than the juvenile, justice system. The legal mechanisms for "transferring" juveniles from the juvenile to the criminal justice system differ from State to State. . . . These mechanisms, while having different labels across the States, fall into three general categories, according to who makes the transfer decision. The three mechanisms are judicial waiver, statutory exclusion, and concurrent jurisdiction; the decisionmakers are, respectively, the juvenile court judge, the legislature, and the prosecutor.

Judicial waiver (the juvenile court judge). In judicial waivers, a hearing is held in juvenile court, typically in response to the prosecutor's request that the juvenile court judge "waive" the juvenile court's jurisdiction over the matter and transfer the juvenile to criminal court for trial in the "adult" system. Most State statutes limit judicial waiver by age and offense criteria and by "lack of amenability to treatment" criteria. States often limit waiver to older youth or to youth who have committed certain serious offenses. Amenability determinations are typically based on a juvenile's offense history and previous dispositional outcomes but may also include psychological assessments. Under many State statutes, a court making an amenability determination must also consider the availability of dispositional alternatives for treating the juvenile, the time available for sanctions (for older juveniles), public safety, and the best interests of the child. Judicial waiver provisions vary in the degree of flexibility they allow the court in decisionmaking. Some provisions make the waiver decision entirely discretionary. Others establish a presumption in favor of waiver or specify circumstances under which waiver is mandatory.

Regardless of the degree of flexibility accorded to the court, the waiver process must adhere to certain constitutional principles of fairness. The U.S. Supreme Court, in Kent v. United States (1966), held that juvenile courts must provide "the essentials of due process" when transferring juveniles to criminal court. In 1996, approximately 10,000 cases — or 1.6 percent of all formally processed delinquency cases disposed in juvenile courts that year — were judicially waived to criminal court.

Statutory exclusion (the legislature). In a growing number of States, legislatures have statutorily excluded certain young offenders from juvenile court jurisdiction based on age and/or offense criteria. Perhaps the broadest such exclusion occurs in States that have defined the upper age of juvenile court jurisdiction as 15 or 16 and thus excluded large numbers of youth under age 18 from the juvenile justice system. . . .

Many States also exclude certain individuals charged with serious offenses from juvenile court jurisdiction. Such exclusions are typically limited to older youth. The offenses most often targeted for exclusion are capital and other murders and violent offenses; however, an increasing number of States are excluding additional felony offenses. . . .

Concurrent jurisdiction (the prosecutor). Under this transfer option, State statutes give prosecutors the discretion to file certain cases in either juvenile or criminal court because original jurisdiction is shared by both courts. State concurrent jurisdiction provisions, like other transfer provisions, typically are limited by age and offense criteria.

Prosecutorial transfer, unlike judicial waiver, is not subject to judicial review and is not required to meet the due process requirements established in *Kent.* According to some State appellate courts, prosecutorial transfer is an "executive function" equivalent to routine charging decisions. Some States, however, have developed guidelines for prosecutors to follow in "direct filing" cases. . . .

State legislation delineates the conditions under which individuals charged with a violation of the law (and whose age places them under the original jurisdiction of the juvenile court) may or must be processed in the adult criminal system. Historically, the majority of States have relied on judicial waiver as the mechanism for transferring juveniles to criminal court. . . . Statutory exclusion and concurrent jurisdiction provisions have been relatively less common, but the number of States in which these options exist is growing. Between the 1992 and 1997 legislative sessions, 45 States expanded their statutory provisions governing the transfer of juveniles to criminal court. Generally, States have done so by adding statutory exclusion provisions, lowering minimum ages, adding eligible offenses, or making judicial waiver presumptive. As of the end of 1997, legislatures in 28 States had statutorily excluded from juvenile court jurisdiction cases involving certain offenses and certain age youth, and, in 15 States, prosecutors had the discretion to file certain cases in criminal court.

Nearly all States rely on a combination of transfer provisions to move juveniles to the criminal system. As of the end of 1997, the most common combination (18 States) was judicial waiver together with statutory exclusion. Relying on judicial waiver alone was the second most common transfer arrangement (16 States). . . .

What Criteria Are Used in the Transfer Decision?

Although there is a general sense that transfer should be reserved for the most serious juvenile cases, numerous studies have shown that a significant proportion of transfers seem to fall outside that category, calling into question the decisionmaking of the juvenile court judges and/or prosecutors who control transfer decisions. Other than the general seriousness of an offense, what characteristics make a case more likely to result in transfer? For example, does the likelihood of transfer vary with the seriousness of a victim's injury, the use of weapons (especially firearms), the presence of gang motivation in the underlying incident, or a juvenile's history of substance abuse or prior offending? Are there interactions between these characteristics?

[Recent studies of juvenile justice in South Carolina, Utah, and Pennsylvania offer insight into the factors that influence the assignment of cases to the juvenile or criminal system.] Judges concurred with most waiver requests made by prosecutors (solicitors) in South Carolina and Utah. Two factors distinguished cases that were waived from those that were not: the extent of a juvenile's court history and the seriousness of his or her offense. . . . In South Carolina, offense seriousness was . . . a key determinant in the waiver decision. Regardless of a youth's court history, cases involving serious person offenses were more likely to be approved for waiver than other types of cases. Although the seriousness of the offense category alone was not as key in Utah as it was in South Carolina, [characteristics] of the crime incident were important in decisions to waive in Utah. Waiver was most likely to be granted in cases involving serious person offenders who used weapons and seriously injured someone, regardless of the offenders' court history. Even first-time offenders in Utah were waived if they seriously injured their victim. For other types of cases, the court looked to a youth's court history to decide whether to waive the matter to criminal court. In these cases, youth with long histories were more likely to be waived than those with shorter histories. . . .

What Was the Impact of New Legislation That Excludes Additional Offenders from Juvenile Court Jurisdiction?

Of those States that have passed laws that make it easier to try juveniles in criminal court, the most common change was the enactment or expansion of statutory exclusion provisions. Legislatures responded to public outcry regarding "failures" of the juvenile justice system and proposed exclusion as at least a partial solution. The phrase "Do the adult crime, do the adult time" became a cliché. The efficacy of exclusion provisions, however, was not well established. Were more or different juveniles tried in the criminal system in jurisdictions that had enacted new statutory exclusion provisions? Did excluded juveniles receive harsher sanctions under new exclusion provisions than they would have received under prior judicial waiver provisions?

[Under Pennsylvania's 1996 exclusion law], when a case is not dismissed at the preliminary hearing, the criminal court judge's decision to keep the case in criminal court or to decertify it to juvenile court must be based on the same factors that a juvenile court judge uses to decide whether a youth should be waived to criminal court: the youth's age, prior referrals to juvenile court, and amenability to treatment.

The juvenile courts in the three Pennsylvania study counties judicially waived 277 youth in 1995. In the transition year of 1996, when the State's exclusion law took effect, the number of waivers dropped to 157 — a decrease of 120 youth. Of the 473 youth excluded from juvenile court jurisdiction in these counties in 1996, a total of 109 were convicted in criminal court. Assuming that cases still open in criminal court at the end of the study period resulted in the same proportion of convictions and dismissals, approximately 135 of the 473 excluded youth eventually would have been convicted in criminal court. The drop in the number of waived youth between 1995 and 1996 — 120 — is close to the number of excluded youth convicted in criminal court when all cases are closed — 135. These numbers suggest that the ultimate impact of Pennsylvania's 1996 exclusion legislation was to retain in criminal court those cases that the juvenile court would have judicially waived had it been given the opportunity. Consequently, regardless of the transfer path in Pennsylvania — judicial waiver or legislative exclusion — about the same number of youth were sentenced to an adult correctional facility.

Therefore, considering only case outcomes, the impact of Pennsylvania's new exclusion statute was negligible. The statute, however, increased the processing time for cases eventually handled within the juvenile justice system and placed an additional burden on local jails and the criminal courts. . . .

Findings from the project's four transfer studies can be summarized as follows:

Juvenile court judges largely concur with prosecutors as to which juveniles should be transferred to criminal court. These studies show that the juvenile court supports the prosecutor's request for transfer in approximately four out of five cases — indicating that these two key decisionmakers generally agree about who should be waived and who should not. Anecdotal evidence from the Utah study, in fact, indicates that in many cases in which a waiver petition was denied, the denial was based on a prosecutor's recommendation to withdraw the petition (following a plea bargaining agreement). It may be that the high proportion of judicial approval of waiver requests indicates that prosecutors are able to gauge which cases juvenile court judges will agree to waive and request waivers in only those cases. However, the study of exclusions in Pennsylvania implies that criminal court judges agree with juvenile court judges as to which youth should receive criminal court sanctions. . . .

The system adapts to large changes in structure. The structure of transfer decisions has changed in response to the public's concern over the increase in juvenile violence. Data in these studies confirm that the decisionmaking process will adapt to changing legal conditions and social pressure. For example, the study of the implementation of Pennsylvania's exclusion law found that even though the justice system adopted the State's new set of rules and followed new paths, case processing resulted in the same outcomes that would have occurred if the rules had not changed. There had been an expectation that the changed statutory exclusion provision would result in many, many more juveniles being tried in criminal court and in many of these youth ending up incarcerated in adult correctional facilities. However, Pennsylvania's exclusion legislation has had little overall impact on either the number of juveniles handled in criminal court or the proportion incarcerated in adult correctional facilities.

There was also an underlying assumption that transfer decisionmaking by juvenile court judges in Pennsylvania tended to favor juveniles and that decisionmaking by criminal court judges under the new provisions would be different. However, this study found that, in Pennsylvania, the decisionmaking process followed by criminal court judges regarding decertification was much the same as that followed by juvenile court judges regarding waiver. . . .

■ KRISTY MADDOX v. STATE

931 S.W.2d 438 (Ark. 1996)

BROWN, J.

This is a juvenile-transfer case. On October 16, 1995, an information was filed charging appellant Kristy Maddox with criminal mischief in the first degree, a Class C felony. She was accused of intentionally throwing a Mountain Dew bottle from a moving vehicle and striking the victim's automobile, causing damage in excess of $500. Maddox, who was 17 years old at the time of the alleged incident, and who turned 18 on February 4, 1996, moved to have the charge transferred to juvenile court. Her motion was denied. She now appeals that denial.

Only two witnesses testified at the juvenile-transfer hearing. Pamela Maddox, the appellant's mother, related to the court that at the time of the hearing, Maddox was living with her and assisting around the house by doing chores and taking care of her younger siblings. She testified that Maddox was not currently in high school, but that she was working on her G.E.D. and planned to attend college in the Fall. She stated that she had a good relationship with her daughter, but that she did have to call the police on one occasion for an undisclosed "family disturbance." She and the prosecutor agreed that Maddox had no prior criminal history.

Sherry Lynn Kinnamon, the victim, was called as a witness by the prosecution. She testified that on April 20, 1995, she was driving her grandparents from Huntsville to the VA Hospital in Fayetteville when she noticed a red pick-up truck following very closely behind her. She stated that she tapped her brakes a few times to get the driver's attention and slowed so that the truck could pass, but that the driver would not do so. Even when given a straight stretch of road with no cars approaching, the driver of the truck would not pass her. She explained that the driver instead pulled alongside her car several times, and that the driver and two passengers would simply look at her, then drop back behind her car, where they made obscene gestures. She stated that she slowed her car to two miles an hour so that the truck would pass, but that it again would not. Finally, she accelerated, and the truck pulled alongside her car. Maddox hung out of the window on the passenger's side of the truck, held by her belt loops. She was holding a full glass bottle of Mountain Dew, and she and the other occupants of the truck were yelling obscenities at Kinnamon. Kinnamon testified that Maddox then intentionally threw the glass bottle at her car. It dented the front of the hood and cracked the windshield. Kinnamon said that after she regained her composure, she pursued the truck and got its license plate number. No one was injured, but she estimated that the damage to her car was about $800.

The trial court denied the motion to transfer after determining that Maddox's intentional throwing of the Mountain Dew bottle at Kinnamon's car was not only a serious act but a violent one. The court emphasized the harassing nature of the episode and referred to an incident in Oklahoma where a person was killed because an object had been thrown at his vehicle. The court noted that Maddox had no prior criminal record and mentioned that there had been no evidence introduced, one way or the other, with regard to her prospects for rehabilitation.

Maddox claims in her appeal that the trial court clearly erred in retaining jurisdiction of this matter. The Arkansas Juvenile Code provides that the circuit court shall consider the following factors in determining whether to retain jurisdiction or transfer a case to juvenile court: 1) The seriousness of the offense, and whether violence was employed by the juvenile in the commission of the offense; 2) Whether the offense is part of a repetitive pattern of adjudicated offenses which would lead to the determination that the juvenile is beyond rehabilitation under existing rehabilitation programs, as evidenced by past efforts to treat and rehabilitate the juvenile and the response to such efforts; and 3) The prior history, character traits, mental maturity, and any other factor which reflects upon the juvenile's prospects for rehabilitation. Ark. Code §9-27-318(e). The decision to retain jurisdiction must be supported by clear and convincing evidence. Ark. Code §9-27-318(f). In making its decision, the trial court need not give equal weight to each of the statutory factors. Furthermore, the trial court's denial of a motion to transfer will be reversed only if its ruling was clearly erroneous.

Maddox asserts a twofold challenge to the denial of her motion to transfer. She first urges that the trial court did not recognize the relevance of her mother's testimony and emphasizes that her mother presented sufficient evidence of her character traits to support a positive finding on the issue of her prospects for rehabilitation. She further argues that the charge of criminal mischief is a crime against property which the trial court improperly characterized as "violent" in order to keep the matter in circuit court.

The State responds that criminal mischief is a Class C felony that satisfies the seriousness criterion for purposes of section 9-27-318(e) and that violence was employed in the commission of this offense. The State also questions whether the mother's testimony was really relevant to the criterion of rehabilitation, when there was no showing that Maddox was remorseful or willing to accept responsibility for her actions. Finally, the State contends that the fact Maddox was 18 at the time of her hearing is sufficient, standing alone, to affirm the trial court's ruling.

In recent years, this court has fashioned the following rule in juvenile-transfer cases: The use of violence in the commission of a serious offense is a factor sufficient in and of itself for a circuit court to retain jurisdiction of a juvenile's case, but the commission of a serious offense without the use of violence is not sufficient grounds to deny the transfer. Sebastian v. State, 885 S.W.2d 882 (Ark. 1994). In Green v. State, 916 S.W.2d 756 (Ark. 1996), this court noted that manslaughter, a Class C felony, was a serious offense: "No doubt the offense charged is serious. Manslaughter is a Class C felony. If [the appellant] were convicted he would be sentenced to imprisonment for not less than three nor more than ten years." Criminal mischief in the first degree is also a Class C felony, and it satisfies the seriousness requirement.

The question we next address is whether the trial court was correct in its finding that Maddox committed a violent act. We agree with the trial court that she did. This is not a case where a juvenile merely committed a crime against property such as we had in Pennington v. State, 807 S.W.2d 660 (1991). In *Pennington,* two 17-year-olds broke about 30 tombstones in a cemetery and were charged with criminal mischief. The circuit court refused to transfer the cases to juvenile court, and we reversed on the basis that the trial court gave too much deference to the prosecutor, after the court acknowledged that violence was not embraced in the young men's actions.

In the instant case, the trial court noted that these facts would likely support an aggravated assault charge as well as a charge of criminal mischief. This court has observed that the crime of aggravated assault is not only serious, but that no violence beyond that necessary to commit aggravated assault is necessary to meet the requirement under Ark. Code §9-27-318(e)(1). We conclude that a violent act lies at the core of the alleged crime in the instant case — the willful throwing of a glass bottle at a moving vehicle containing three passengers, as testified to by Kinnamon. These facts are sufficient to sustain a refusal to transfer in our judgment.

There is, too, the fact that Maddox has now turned 18. Young people over age 18 can no longer be committed to the Division of Youth Services for rehabilitation unless they are already committed at the time they turn 18. The fact that Maddox cannot now be committed to the Division of Youth Services is highly relevant to her prospects for rehabilitation as a juvenile and is a factor that this court considers important in reviewing a trial court's denial of a motion to transfer. This circumstance lends additional support to an affirmance.

ROAF, A.J., dissenting.*

In 1989, the Arkansas General Assembly enacted . . . the Arkansas Juvenile Code of 1989. A declaration of purpose for this legislation is found at Ark. Code §9-27-302. It is important in the context of this appeal and warrants our reconsideration:

> This subchapter shall be liberally construed to the end that its purposes may be carried out:
>
> (1) To assure that all juveniles brought to the attention of the courts receive the guidance, care and control, preferably in each juvenile's own home, which will best serve the emotional, mental, and physical welfare of the juvenile and the best interests of the state;
>
> (2) To preserve and strengthen the juvenile's family ties whenever possible, removing him from the custody of his parents only when his welfare or the safety and protection of the public cannot adequately be safeguarded without such removal; . . .
>
> (3) To protect society more effectively by substituting for retributive punishment, whenever possible, methods of offender rehabilitation and rehabilitative restitution, recognizing that the application of sanctions which are consistent with the seriousness of the offense is appropriate in all cases;
>
> (4) To provide means through which the provisions of this subchapter are executed and enforced and in which the parties are assured a fair hearing and their constitutional and other legal rights recognized and enforced.

Since 1991, this court has been called upon numerous times to interpret the provisions of the juvenile code dealing with how we treat youth who are charged with criminal offenses. The General Assembly has in turn had the opportunity on several occasions to react to our holdings. I submit that this court and the General Assembly have so woefully failed to consider a significant portion of the stated purposes underpinning the juvenile code that this language has become meaningless.

* [Associate Justice Roaf incorporated by reference here the dissenting opinion from another case, Butler v. State, 922 S.W.2d 685 (Ark. 1996). — EDS.]

We have neither liberally construed the statute to the benefit of the emotional, mental, and physical welfare of the juveniles, nor even for the best interests of the state. We have failed to insure that methods of rehabilitation and restitution are substituted wherever possible, for retributive punishment, and we have surely failed to provide that juveniles are assured fair hearings and that their constitutional and other rights provided by this statute are uniformly recognized and enforced. We share this responsibility equally with our elected state representatives.

Today, we once again affirm a trial court's refusal to transfer a criminal case involving a juvenile to juvenile court. The trial court's ruling, and our affirmance, were foregone conclusions because of the prior holdings of this court, because of the weight of stare decisis, and because of the legislature's failure to revisit this legislation in light of our holdings. Children between the ages of 14 and 17 years are paying the price for our failures. We cannot even take comfort in the notion that the best interests of the state are being served, for many of these juveniles will return to our midst as adults, and the opportunity to use our best efforts to rehabilitate, guide and care for them will have been lost.

The landmark case which has led us down this path is, of course, Walker v. State, 803 S.W.2d 502 (Ark. 1991). In *Walker,* by a 4 to 3 decision, this court reached several significant holdings which have been repeatedly reavowed and reaffirmed since *Walker* — that a juvenile movant has the burden of proof when seeking to transfer a case from circuit court to juvenile court — that the trial court need not give equal weight to the three factors that the statute directs it to consider in determining whether to transfer a case — that the prosecutor is not even required to introduce proof on each of the three factors that the trial court is directed to consider — that the criminal information alone can provide a sufficient basis for the denial of a transfer to juvenile court — that a trial court does not have to make findings of fact or provide a rationale for its decision in a juvenile transfer proceeding. We have also held that juveniles "ultimately" charged and tried in circuit court are subject to the procedures prescribed for adults, and are not afforded the protections provided by the juvenile code, such as the requirement of parental consent to a waiver of right to counsel.

I am not unmindful of the fact that since 1991, the general assembly has twice amended Ark. Code §9-27-318, which deals with waiver and transfer to circuit court, each time to the detriment of juvenile defendants. However, they have not seen fit to amend the stated purposes for the juvenile code. I suggest that they do so at the next opportunity. Until then, our decisions and their inaction are in direct conflict with these purposes. I dissent.

Notes

1. *Choice of system for juvenile offenders: majority position.* The choice between the adult and juvenile systems is cluttered with various starting presumptions, shifting burdens of proof or persuasion, and opportunities to reconsider the choice of systems. In the end, the statutes in almost every state (along with the federal juvenile system) initially assign the great majority of juveniles to the juvenile court, and then allow a judge in the juvenile court to "waive" jurisdiction after an investigation, a hearing, and a statement of reasons by the court. See Kent v. United States, 383 U.S. 541 (1966). See Dia N. Brannen, et al., Transfer to Adult Court: A National

Study of How Juvenile Court Judges Weigh Pertinent *Kent* Criteria, 12 Psychol. Pub. Pol'y & L. 332 (2006).

About 15 states give prosecutors the power in some cases to select between the adult and juvenile systems when there is "concurrent" jurisdiction (ordinarily for the most serious offenses and the oldest juveniles). Most states initially place into the adult system the oldest juveniles who commit the most serious crimes, and place into the juvenile system (at least initially) the youngest juveniles and those who commit the least serious crimes. Various studies of juvenile justice suggest that major changes in the laws dealing with the assignment of juveniles to the adult criminal justice system have made little difference in the numbers of juvenile cases actually resolved in the adult system. In 2002, two-thirds of the juveniles transferred to criminal court were charged with a violent offense. The proportion of delinquency cases that were waived into the adult system was 1.4 percent in 1985; the proportion reached 1.5 percent in 1991 and then dropped to 0.8 percent by 2002. Howard N. Snyder & Melissa Sickmund, Juvenile Offenders and Victims: 2006 National Report 187 (2006).

Where the law gives the prosecutor the initial choice of systems, that decision is usually subject to judicial review, and the burden of proof usually falls on the party seeking to transfer the case (that is, the juvenile attempting to move into the juvenile court). In Arkansas, as we saw in the *Maddox* case, the trial court in the adult system may retain jurisdiction if there is "clear and convincing evidence" that the juvenile should be tried as an adult. In many other states, such as North Dakota, the trial court in the adult system retains jurisdiction if there are "reasonable grounds" (in essence, probable cause) to believe that the juvenile committed the crime as charged and would not be "amenable to rehabilitation" in the juvenile system. See In the Interest of A.E., 559 N.W.2d 215 (N.D. 1997). Does *Maddox* convince you that the statutory requirement of judicial review makes little difference in transfer cases?

2. *Constitutional challenges to charging of juveniles.* Juveniles in several states have challenged the constitutionality of statutes that mandate the choice of the adult system for some cases or that give prosecutors the discretion to file charges in the adult system. These challenges are based on many different clauses in state constitutions, most frequently due process and equal protection clauses. See In re William M., 196 P.3d 456 (Nev. 2008) (statute that creates rebuttable presumption that certain juveniles are certifiable for trial in adult court offends the constitutional privilege against self-incrimination). More often than not, however, the challenges have failed. See Manduley v. Superior Court, 41 P.3d 3 (Cal. 2002) (upholds constitutionality of system allowing prosecutor to choose juvenile versus adult system for certain defendants).

Juveniles have also found very limited success in challenging the procedures used at a judicial hearing to determine whether to transfer a case from one system to another, and in challenging the complete absence of such a judicial hearing. See In re Boot, 925 P.2d 964 (Wash. 1996) (statute giving exclusive original jurisdiction over juveniles charged with specified crimes to adult criminal court does not permit hearing on juvenile court jurisdiction; assignment to adult court without declination hearing does not violate procedural or substantive due process or equal protection).

3. *Right to counsel in juvenile delinquency proceedings.* The right to retained counsel in delinquency proceedings was made a federal constitutional requirement in In re Gault, 387 U.S. 1 (1967). Because counsel is not appointed or is often waived, less

than half of all juveniles are represented by legal counsel in their delinquency proceedings. Barry Feld, Criminalizing the American Juvenile Court 222 (1993). Statutes in many states have created systems for appointing counsel for at least some juvenile proceedings. Roughly 10 states have mandatory appointment statutes; about half the states make appointment of counsel discretionary. See Tory Caeti, Craig Hemmens & Velmer Burton, Jr., Juvenile Right to Counsel: A National Comparison of State Legal Codes, 23 Am. J. would be required for comparable charges in the adult system. But see In re L.M., 186 P.3d 164 (Kan. 2008) (because the goals and processes of the revised juvenile justice code are now patterned on the adult criminal system, with a reduced emphasis on rehabilitation and the State's parental role in providing guidance and discipline, procedural protections in juvenile proceedings must now include a jury trial, not just bench trial). In situations where transfer into the adult criminal courts means that the state will appoint an attorney and provide a jury, will a juvenile welcome the transfer?

4. *Abolition of juvenile court?* The first juvenile court was created in Chicago after the Illinois legislature passed the Illinois Juvenile Court Act of 1899. By 1925, 46 states, 3 territories, and the District of Columbia had separate juvenile courts. See Robert E. Shepherd, The Juvenile Court at 100 Years: A Look Back, Juv. Just. Dec. 1999 at 13. About 20 states have created "family courts" with broader jurisdiction to handle the full range of criminal and civil issues involving children. Now, 100 years after their creation, the basic premises that support the creation of juvenile courts are in doubt. Are children who commit crimes better served by having a separate system for adjudicating their crimes and imposing sentences? Or would they be better off in a single criminal justice system, perhaps with special allowances made for their age?

5. *Disparate racial impact in juvenile justice.* The juvenile justice system entrusts prosecutors and judges with even larger zones of discretion than they utilize in the adult criminal justice system. As a result, a great deal of research has taken place in the juvenile justice system. One topic of continuing concern is the presence of any racial disparities in the outcomes of the juvenile system. On the whole, the research has found racial disparities that are larger than disparities found in some studies of the adult criminal justice system. As a legislator, how would you respond to research findings of this sort study? Would you argue to transfer fewer juveniles into the adult system (even though the racial disparities in the adult system might be smaller overall)? To make the juvenile system less discretionary? For a sample of the voluminous research about the operation of the juvenile justice systems in various states, go to the web extension for this chapter at *http://www.crimpro.com/extension/ch13*.

Another critical choice of system for many serious cases is between state and federal court, or between different state courts. For large classes of drug and firearm cases, for example, there is overlapping state and federal jurisdiction. Consider the following problem.

Problem 13-4. Federal Day

In Manhattan, federal prosecutors have developed a program known as "Federal Day." One day each week chosen at random, all drug arrests obtained by state and local police agencies are processed in federal court, where sentences for drug crimes are much higher than they are in the state courts. Prosecutors say that the program is designed to help the overwhelmed state courts and to deter criminal activity by imposing the stiffer sentences. Since 2007 there have been between 100 and 200 federal indictments per year in cases that the local police have developed. For instance, 231 cases went to federal district court under the Federal Day program between January 2008 and May 2010. During that same period, New York police made 5,837 felony narcotics arrests. Of the 5,606 cases sent to the state prosecutor in Manhattan, 1,172 resulted in state felony indictments. A total of 1,043 other cases were reduced to state misdemeanors.

A U.S. senator has heard about the Federal Day program and plans to introduce legislation requiring all U.S. Attorneys' offices to institute such programs. Would you advise the U.S. Attorney for Manhattan to continue the program? Under what conditions? Do you believe that those who support the Manhattan policy will also support the proposed legislation, and vice versa? What are the prospects for its passage? Compare Katherine Bishop, "Mandatory Sentences in Drug Cases: Is the Law Defeating Its Purpose?" N.Y. Times, June 8, 1990, at B16.

Notes

1. *The federalization trend.* It is often said that criminal justice remains primarily a state and local function, and in terms of volume that remains true. The federal courts still produce less than 10 percent of the felony convictions in this country each year, and virtually all misdemeanor convictions come out of the state courts. But the areas of potential overlap between the federal and state criminal justice systems have been growing. The federal government has been exerting more authority and money on criminal matters during the last few decades than at any previous point in the nation's history. In particular, the federal presence in narcotics enforcement has grown enormously over the years. See Michael M. O'Hear, Federalism and Drug Control, 57 Vand. L. Rev. 783 (2004).

The 1999 report of the American Bar Association's Task Force on Federalization of Criminal Law documents various aspects of this growth. Federal crime legislation has become more common: "more than forty percent of the federal criminal provisions enacted since the Civil War have been enacted since 1970." The number of federal investigators and prosecutors has expanded along with the number of available federal crimes. The report lists some negative consequences of federalization: "diminution of the stature of the state courts in the perception of citizens" and "disparate results for the same conduct." What would be a legitimate basis for extending federal law to criminalize additional conduct? Would the same arguments support a new emphasis in enforcing existing federal laws? See Michael A. Simons, Prosecutorial Discretion and Prosecution Guidelines: A Case Study in Controlling Federalization, 75 N.Y.U. L. Rev. 893 (2000).

2. *Sorting institutions for federal and state criminal systems.* Informal discussions between federal and state prosecutors normally determine whether a case will be routed through the federal or the state system. The federal system can normally devote more resources to a case, and a federal conviction normally produces a more

severe sentence than would result from a state conviction. For these reasons, combined with the overwhelming volume of cases in the state system, the federal prosecutor normally can take her choice of cases that violate the criminal laws of both jurisdictions.

Informal working groups of state and federal investigators and prosecutors, known as "inter-agency task forces" or some comparable label, might develop over time some predictable criteria for assignment of prosecutions to the state or federal systems. For further exploration of the devices used to coordinate federal and state law enforcement (along with the related questions of coordination among different states), go to the web extension for this chapter at *http://www.crimpro.com/extension/ch13*.

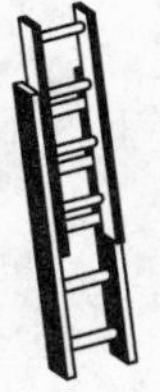

3. *Potential limits on the federalization of crime*. Some restraint on the growth of federal criminal law might come from various constitutional provisions, such as the commerce clause, that were designed to limit the authority of the federal government and to preserve essential areas of state authority. Those constitutional limits, however, have produced very few rulings that in fact limit congressional authority to create federal crimes. In United States v. Lopez, 514 U.S. 549 (1995), the Supreme Court held that possession of a gun near a school is not an economic activity that has a "substantial effect" on interstate commerce; thus, Congress went beyond its constitutional authority in passing a federal crime to cover this activity. More typical of recent cases, however, is Sabri v. United States, 541 U.S. 600 (2004), where the Court held that Congress had constitutional authority to make it a federal crime to bribe officials of a local organization or government that receives federal program funds, even when the bribe has nothing to do with the federal funds. Even a remote connection to federal funds makes such a law a valid exercise of Congress's authority under the Constitution's spending clause.

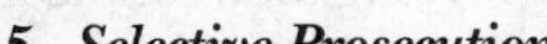

5. *Selective Prosecution*

For each of the prosecutorial charging decisions considered in this chapter, judges mostly refuse to second-guess the exercise of charging discretion. A prosecutor might make very different charging decisions in two similar cases and will not have to explain those choices. In all of these cases, however, judges asked to review the prosecutor's decision point out that if a prosecutor bases the charging decision on some constitutionally suspect grounds — such as the defendant's race or gender — the court stands willing to step in. Similarly, the prosecutor cannot file a charge as a way of punishing a defendant for taking constitutionally protected action, such as exercising free speech or insisting on a jury trial. Thus, a prosecutor can have many different reasons for a charging decision, but she cannot rely on a limited set of constitutionally improper reasons. How is a defendant to know the prosecutor's reason for a particular charging decision?

UNITED STATES v. CHRISTOPHER ARMSTRONG

517 U.S. 456 (1996)

REHNQUIST, C.J.*

In this case, we consider the showing necessary for a defendant to be entitled to discovery on a claim that the prosecuting attorney singled him out for prosecution on the basis of his race. We conclude that respondents failed to satisfy the threshold showing: They failed to show that the Government declined to prosecute similarly situated suspects of other races.

In April 1992, respondents were indicted in the United States District Court for the Central District of California on charges of conspiring to possess with intent to distribute more than 50 grams of cocaine base (crack) and conspiring to distribute the same, [and federal firearms offenses]. In response to the indictment, respondents filed a motion for discovery or for dismissal of the indictment, alleging that they were selected for federal prosecution because they are black. In support of their motion, they offered only an affidavit by a "Paralegal Specialist," employed by the Office of the Federal Public Defender representing one of the respondents. The only allegation in the affidavit was that, in every one of the 24 [narcotics] cases closed by the office during 1991, the defendant was black. Accompanying the affidavit was a "study" listing the 24 defendants, their race, whether they were prosecuted for dealing cocaine as well as crack, and the status of each case.

The Government opposed the discovery motion, arguing, among other things, that there was no evidence or allegation "that the Government has acted unfairly or has prosecuted non-black defendants or failed to prosecute them." The District Court granted the motion. It ordered the Government (1) to provide a list of all cases from the last three years in which the Government charged both cocaine and firearms offenses, (2) to identify the race of the defendants in those cases, (3) to identify what levels of law enforcement were involved in the investigations of those cases, and (4) to explain its criteria for deciding to prosecute those defendants for federal cocaine offenses.

The Government moved for reconsideration of the District Court's discovery order. With this motion it submitted affidavits and other evidence to explain why it had chosen to prosecute respondents and why respondents' study did not support the inference that the Government was singling out blacks for cocaine prosecution. The federal and local agents participating in the case alleged in affidavits that race played no role in their investigation. An Assistant United States Attorney explained in an affidavit that the decision to prosecute met the general criteria for prosecution, because

> there was over 100 grams of cocaine base involved, over twice the threshold necessary for a ten year mandatory minimum sentence; there were multiple sales involving multiple defendants, thereby indicating a fairly substantial crack cocaine ring; . . . there were multiple federal firearms violations intertwined with the narcotics trafficking; the overall evidence in the case was extremely strong, including audio and videotapes of defendants; . . . and several of the defendants had criminal histories including narcotics and firearms violations.

* [Justices O'Connor, Scalia, Kennedy, Souter, Thomas, and Ginsburg joined this opinion. Justice Breyer concurred in part and concurred in the judgment. — EDS].

The Government also submitted sections of a published 1989 Drug Enforcement Administration report which concluded that large-scale, interstate trafficking networks "controlled by Jamaicans, Haitians and Black street gangs dominate the manufacture and distribution of crack." In response, one of respondents' attorneys submitted an affidavit alleging that an intake coordinator at a drug treatment center had told her that there are "an equal number of caucasian users and dealers to minority users and dealers." Respondents also submitted an affidavit from a criminal defense attorney alleging that in his experience many nonblacks are prosecuted in state court for crack offenses. . . . The District Court denied the motion for reconsideration. When the Government indicated it would not comply with the court's discovery order, the court dismissed the case. [The Court of Appeals affirmed the order.]

A selective-prosecution claim is not a defense on the merits to the criminal charge itself, but an independent assertion that the prosecutor has brought the charge for reasons forbidden by the Constitution. Our cases delineating the necessary elements to prove a claim of selective prosecution have taken great pains to explain that the standard is a demanding one. These cases afford a "background presumption" that the showing necessary to obtain discovery should itself be a significant barrier to the litigation of insubstantial claims.

A selective-prosecution claim asks a court to exercise judicial power over a "special province" of the Executive. The Attorney General and United States Attorneys retain "broad discretion" to enforce the Nation's criminal laws. Wayte v. United States, 470 U.S. 598 (1985). They have this latitude because they are designated by statute as the President's delegates to help him discharge his constitutional responsibility to "take Care that the Laws be faithfully executed." U.S. Const., Art. II, §3. . . .

Of course, a prosecutor's discretion is subject to constitutional constraints. One of these constraints, imposed by the equal protection component of the Due Process Clause of the Fifth Amendment, is that the decision whether to prosecute may not be based on "an unjustifiable standard such as race, religion, or other arbitrary classification," Oyler v. Boles, 368 U.S. 448, 456 (1962). A defendant may demonstrate that the administration of a criminal law is "directed so exclusively against a particular class of persons . . . with a mind so unequal and oppressive" that the system of prosecution amounts to "a practical denial" of equal protection of the law. Yick Wo v. Hopkins, 118 U.S. 356, 373 (1886).

In order to dispel the presumption that a prosecutor has not violated equal protection, a criminal defendant must present clear evidence to the contrary. We explained in *Wayte* why courts are "properly hesitant to examine the decision whether to prosecute." Judicial deference to the decisions of these executive officers rests in part on an assessment of the relative competence of prosecutors and courts. "Such factors as the strength of the case, the prosecution's general deterrence value, the Government's enforcement priorities, and the case's relationship to the Government's overall enforcement plan are not readily susceptible to the kind of analysis the courts are competent to undertake." It also stems from a concern not to unnecessarily impair the performance of a core executive constitutional function. "Examining the basis of a prosecution delays the criminal proceeding, threatens to chill law enforcement by subjecting the prosecutor's motives and decisionmaking to outside inquiry, and may undermine prosecutorial effectiveness by revealing the Government's enforcement policy."

The requirements for a selective-prosecution claim draw on ordinary equal protection standards. The claimant must demonstrate that the federal prosecutorial policy had a discriminatory effect and that it was motivated by a discriminatory purpose. To establish a discriminatory effect in a race case, the claimant must show that similarly situated individuals of a different race were not prosecuted. This requirement has been established in our case law since Ah Sin v. Wittman, 198 U.S. 500 (1905). Ah Sin, a subject of China, petitioned a California state court for a writ of habeas corpus, seeking discharge from imprisonment under a San Francisco county ordinance prohibiting persons from setting up gambling tables in rooms barricaded to stop police from entering. He alleged in his habeas petition "that the ordinance is enforced solely and exclusively against persons of the Chinese race and not otherwise." We rejected his contention that this averment made out a claim under the Equal Protection Clause, because it did not allege "that the conditions and practices to which the ordinance was directed did not exist exclusively among the Chinese, or that there were other offenders against the ordinance than the Chinese as to whom it was not enforced."

The similarly situated requirement does not make a selective-prosecution claim impossible to prove. Twenty years before *Ah Sin,* we invalidated an ordinance, also adopted by San Francisco, that prohibited the operation of laundries in wooden buildings. *Yick Wo,* 118 U.S. at 374. The plaintiff in error successfully demonstrated that the ordinance was applied against Chinese nationals but not against other laundry-shop operators. The authorities had denied the applications of 200 Chinese subjects for permits to operate shops in wooden buildings, but granted the applications of 80 individuals who were not Chinese subjects to operate laundries in wooden buildings "under similar conditions." . . .

Having reviewed the requirements to prove a selective-prosecution claim, we turn to the showing necessary to obtain discovery in support of such a claim. If discovery is ordered, the Government must assemble from its own files documents which might corroborate or refute the defendant's claim. Discovery thus imposes many of the costs present when the Government must respond to a prima facie case of selective prosecution. It will divert prosecutors' resources and may disclose the Government's prosecutorial strategy. The justifications for a rigorous standard for the elements of a selective-prosecution claim thus require a correspondingly rigorous standard for discovery in aid of such a claim.

The parties [describe] the requisite showing to establish entitlement to discovery . . . with a variety of phrases, like "colorable basis," "substantial threshold showing," "substantial and concrete basis," or "reasonable likelihood." However, the many labels for this showing conceal the degree of consensus about the evidence necessary to meet it. The Courts of Appeals require some evidence tending to show the existence of the essential elements of the defense, discriminatory effect and discriminatory intent.

In this case we consider what evidence constitutes "some evidence tending to show the existence" of the discriminatory effect element. . . . The vast majority of the Courts of Appeals require the defendant to produce some evidence that similarly situated defendants of other races could have been prosecuted, but were not, and this requirement is consistent with our equal protection case law.

The Court of Appeals [in this case] reached its decision in part because it started "with the presumption that people of all races commit all types of crimes — not with the premise that any type of crime is the exclusive province of any particular racial or ethnic group." It cited no authority for this proposition, which seems contradicted by the most recent statistics of the United States Sentencing Commission. Those statistics show that: More than 90 percent of the persons sentenced in 1994 for crack cocaine trafficking were black, 93.4 percent of convicted LSD dealers were white, and 91 percent of those convicted for pornography or prostitution were white. Presumptions at war with presumably reliable statistics have no proper place in the analysis of this issue.

The Court of Appeals also expressed concern about the "evidentiary obstacles defendants face." But . . . if the claim of selective prosecution were well founded, it should not have been an insuperable task to prove that persons of other races were being treated differently than respondents. For instance, respondents could have investigated whether similarly situated persons of other races were prosecuted by the State of California, were known to federal law enforcement officers, but were not prosecuted in federal court. We think the required threshold — a credible showing of different treatment of similarly situated persons — adequately balances the Government's interest in vigorous prosecution and the defendant's interest in avoiding selective prosecution.

In the case before us, respondents' "study" did not constitute some evidence tending to show the existence of the essential elements of a selective-prosecution claim. The study failed to identify individuals who were not black, could have been prosecuted for the offenses for which respondents were charged, but were not so prosecuted. This omission was not remedied by respondents' evidence in opposition to the Government's motion for reconsideration. . . . Respondents' affidavits, which recounted one attorney's conversation with a drug treatment center employee and the experience of another attorney defending drug prosecutions in state court, recounted hearsay and reported personal conclusions based on anecdotal evidence. The judgment of the Court of Appeals is therefore reversed, and the case is remanded for proceedings consistent with this opinion. It is so ordered.

STEVENS, J., dissenting.

Federal prosecutors are respected members of a respected profession. Despite an occasional misstep, the excellence of their work abundantly justifies the presumption that they have properly discharged their official duties. Nevertheless, the possibility that political or racial animosity may infect a decision to institute criminal proceedings cannot be ignored. For that reason, it has long been settled that the prosecutor's broad discretion to determine when criminal charges should be filed is not completely unbridled. . . .

The Court correctly concludes that in this case the facts presented to the District Court in support of respondents' claim that they had been singled out for prosecution because of their race were not sufficient to prove that defense. Moreover, I agree with the Court that their showing was not strong enough to give them a right to discovery, either under Rule 16 or under the District Court's inherent power to order discovery in appropriate circumstances. [However], I am persuaded that the District Judge did not abuse her discretion when she concluded that the factual showing was sufficiently disturbing to require some response from the United States Attorney's Office. Perhaps the discovery order was broader than necessary, but I cannot agree with the Court's apparent conclusion that no inquiry was permissible.

The District Judge's order should be evaluated in light of three circumstances that underscore the need for judicial vigilance over certain types of drug prosecutions. First, the Anti-Drug Abuse Act of 1986 and subsequent legislation established a regime of extremely high penalties for the possession and distribution of so-called "crack" cocaine. Those provisions treat one gram of crack as the equivalent of 100 grams of powder cocaine. The distribution of 50 grams of crack is thus punishable by the same mandatory minimum sentence of 10 years in prison that applies to the distribution of 5,000 grams of powder cocaine. . . . Second, the disparity between the treatment of crack cocaine and powder cocaine is matched by the disparity between the severity of the punishment imposed by federal law and that imposed by state law for the same conduct. For a variety of reasons, often including the absence of mandatory minimums, the existence of parole, and lower baseline penalties, terms of imprisonment for drug offenses tend to be substantially lower in state systems than in the federal system. The difference is especially marked in the case of crack offenses. . . . Finally, it is undisputed that the brunt of the elevated federal penalties falls heavily on blacks. While 65 percent of the persons who have used crack are white, in 1993 they represented only 4 percent of the federal offenders convicted of trafficking in crack. Eighty-eight percent of such defendants were black. . . . Those figures represent a major threat to the integrity of federal sentencing reform, whose main purpose was the elimination of disparity (especially racial) in sentencing. . . .

The extraordinary severity of the imposed penalties and the troubling racial patterns of enforcement give rise to a special concern about the fairness of charging practices for crack offenses. Evidence tending to prove that black defendants charged with distribution of crack in the Central District of California are prosecuted in federal court, whereas members of other races charged with similar offenses are prosecuted in state court, warrants close scrutiny by the federal judges in that District. In my view, the District Judge, who has sat on both the federal and the state benches in Los Angeles, acted well within her discretion to call for the development of facts that would demonstrate what standards, if any, governed the choice of forum where similarly situated offenders are prosecuted. . . .

The majority discounts the probative value of the [defendant's] affidavits, claiming that they recounted "hearsay" and reported "personal conclusions based on anecdotal evidence." But [it] was certainly within the District Court's discretion to credit the affidavits of two members of the bar of that Court, at least one of whom had presumably acquired a reputation by his frequent appearances there, and both of whose statements were made on pains of perjury. The criticism that the affidavits were based on "anecdotal evidence" is also unpersuasive. I thought it was agreed that defendants do not need to prepare sophisticated statistical studies in order to receive mere discovery in cases like this one. . . .

Even if respondents failed to carry their burden of showing that there were individuals who were not black but who could have been prosecuted in federal court for the same offenses, it does not follow that the District Court abused its discretion in ordering discovery. There can be no doubt that such individuals exist, and indeed the Government has never denied the same. In those circumstances, I fail to see why the District Court was unable to take judicial notice of this obvious fact and demand information from the Government's files to support or refute respondents' evidence. The presumption that some whites are prosecuted in state court is not "contradicted" by the statistics the majority cites, which show only that high percentages of blacks are convicted of certain federal crimes, while high percentages of whites are convicted of other federal crimes. Those figures are entirely consistent with the allegation of selective prosecution. The relevant comparison, rather, would be with the percentages of blacks and whites who commit those crimes. But, as discussed above, in the case of crack far greater numbers of whites are believed guilty of using the substance. The District Court, therefore, was entitled to find the evidence before her significant and to require some explanation from the Government.[6] I therefore respectfully dissent. . . .

Notes

1. *Selective prosecution: majority position.* The U.S. Supreme Court makes it clear from time to time that it is possible, at least in theory, for a court to overturn a prosecutor's charging decision when it is based on a constitutionally impermissible ground such as race, religion, or sex. A defendant who makes such a claim must establish that (a) the prosecutor made different charging decisions for similarly situated suspects (a discriminatory effect), and (b) the prosecutor intentionally made the decision on the basis of an "arbitrary" classification (a discriminatory intent). Arbitrary classifications would include "suspect classes" under equal protection doctrine and those exercising their constitutional liberties such as freedom of speech or religion. See Oyler v. Boles, 368 U.S. 448 (1962); Wayte v. United States, 470 U.S. 598 (1985).

Although a selective prosecution claim remains theoretically available, the claim is very difficult for a defendant to win. The *Wayte* decision made it clear that the government must choose the defendant for prosecution "because of" and not "despite" the protected conduct or status of the defendant. In that case, the government had prosecuted for draft evasion a person who had publicly criticized the military draft. The government had chosen to prosecute the case under a "passive enforcement" policy, in which the government filed charges only when told about a person's refusal to register for the draft and only when the person refused to comply with the law after a specific request. The government carried out this policy in Wayte's case, despite (and not because of) his speech criticizing the draft. This basic federal framework for analyzing constitutional challenges to discriminatory charging policies has also been very influential in state courts. See, e.g., Salaiscooper v. Eighth Judicial District Court ex rel. County of Clark, 34 P.3d 509 (Nev. 2001) (disparate treatment of prostitutes and customers is not discrimination on basis of sex).

2. *Discovery to support selective prosecution claims.* According to the opinion in *Armstrong,* a court hearing a claim of selective prosecution may grant discovery to the defendant if there is "some evidence" to support each of the elements of the claim. Do you agree with the court that the defendants in *Armstrong* failed to produce "some evidence"? See also United States v. Bass, 536 U.S. 862 (2002) (overturns trial court order for discovery concerning capital charging practices; defendant failed to show disparate treatment of similarly situated persons).

What sort of evidence is likely to be available to support a selective prosecution claim? To show disparate treatment, a defendant must prove that he is "similarly

6. Also telling was the Government's response to respondents' evidentiary showing. It submitted a list of more than 3,500 defendants who had been charged with federal narcotics violations over the previous 3 years. It also offered the names of 11 nonblack defendants whom it had prosecuted for crack offenses. All 11, however, were members of other racial or ethnic minorities. . . .

situated" to a pool of other suspects who were not prosecuted. Those who are similarly situated would have committed basically the same act as the defendant. Further, there could be no significant difference in the harm caused by these similar acts, and prosecution of one case could not be significantly less costly or difficult than the others. Where can a defendant get information about this pool of unprosecuted suspects?

Will it ever be possible to prove disparate impact in those prosecutorial offices (the overwhelming majority) in which the prosecuting attorneys keep no records of the cases they decline to charge or of the reasons for the declination? Cf. Commonwealth v. Washington W., 928 N.E.2d 908 (Mass. 2010) (juvenile charged with homosexual statutory rape was entitled to discovery of prosecutor office statistics on charges brought in other juvenile cases; juvenile records, unlike those in adult courts, are closed to public and would prevent investigation of potential claim of selective prosecution). Very few courts have reversed convictions on selective prosecution grounds, and no Supreme Court opinions have done so on racial grounds except for Yick Wo v. Hopkins, 118 U.S. 356 (1886). Does this pattern prove anything? What did the claimants in *Yick Wo* do that claimants today might emulate?

3. *Racial patterns in charging.* It is clear that racial minorities are charged with crimes at a rate disproportionate to their numbers. But is the rate higher after accounting for different levels of participation in crime? Criminologists addressing this question have studied records of large numbers of cases using statistical techniques (especially "regression" analysis) to compare similar cases and sort out racial and nonracial influences over charging decisions. For instance, one study by Richard Berk analyzed the correlation between race and crack cocaine charging practices in Los Angeles between 1990 and 1992. The study indicates that the U.S. Attorney prosecuted black offenders at a higher rate than comparable white offenders. Richard Berk & Alec Campbell, Preliminary Data on Race and Crack Charging Practices in Los Angeles, 6 Fed. Sentencing Rep. 36 (1993). Does any of this analysis support the conclusion that selective prosecution doctrine fails to control biased prosecution? If racial discrimination in charging is indeed widespread, is it unrealistic to ask a defendant to make a prediscovery showing?

For an exploration of other studies of racial disparities in charging decisions, go to the web extension for this chapter at *http://www.crimpro.com/extension/ch13*. The methodological issues involved in designing a credible study in this field are serious, and receive some attention on the web extension.

4. *Prosecutorial vindictiveness.* If all criminal defendants were to insist on exercising all of their constitutional and statutory procedural rights, they could make life difficult for a prosecutor. Can a prosecutor charge defendants more severely if they insist on a jury trial, an appeal, or some other procedural right? In Blackledge v. Perry, 417 U.S. 21 (1974), a defendant was initially charged in state district court with misdemeanor assault. After conviction, he requested a trial de novo on the charges in state superior court, and the prosecutor changed the charges to felony assault. The Supreme Court concluded that a prosecutor in such a situation would have an incentive to "retaliate" against the defendant for taking an action that the prosecutor finds inconvenient. Thus, the prosecutor would have to demonstrate on the record that the change in charges was based on some factor other than the defendant's exercise of procedural rights. The limit on "prosecutorial vindictiveness" set out in Blackledge v. Perry does not apply, however, to a prosecutor's *pretrial* decision to add or reduce charges based on a defendant's willingness to waive

procedural rights. See United States v. Goodwin, 457 U.S. 368 (1982) (no presumption of vindictiveness where prosecutor changes misdemeanor charges to felony after defendant requests jury trial); State v. Knowles, 239 P.3d 129 (Mont. 2010) (during plea negotiations following hung jury in first trial, increase of charges from 5-year maximum statute to 20-year maximum statute because of defendant's rejection of prosecutor's plea offer constituted vindictive prosecution; no new factual information was uncovered after first trial). Is this distinction a meaningful one?

5. *Prosecution in the sunshine.* Would prosecutors benefit or lose more from the collection and publication of data on the race of every defendant and victim for every criminal matter the office encounters? If a chief prosecutor were to carry out this policy (either voluntarily or pursuant to a statute), would she want to show the data broken down by type of crime and by the action the office chose to pursue? If you believe prosecutors would resist the collection and publication of such data, what arguments might they raise against this proposal? What if the legislature were willing to provide funds for any extra personnel needed to collect and analyze the data? See Angela J. Davis, Prosecution and Race: The Power and Privilege of Discretion, 67 Fordham L. Rev. 13 (1998) (proposing a requirement that prosecutors publish "racial impact studies").

C. GRAND JURY AND JUDICIAL SCREENING

The grand jury would indict a hamburger.

—Traditional courthouse wisdom

Pretrial judicial hearings that go by names such as "initial appearance" and "preliminary examination" serve multiple functions. At the initial appearance, the magistrate informs the defendant about the nature of the charges, the right to remain silent, the right to appointed counsel, and other features of the criminal process. An initial appearance also gives the magistrate an occasion to assign counsel to indigent defendants (or at least to ascertain whether a defendant is eligible for appointed counsel) and to set bail or other conditions of pretrial release.

For our present purposes, we focus on the ability of judges in these pretrial hearings to screen out charges without enough factual support. The prosecutor (in consultation with the police, as we have seen) can file charges through a charging instrument known as the "complaint" or "information." Then the charges are tested in judicial proceedings. If the prosecutor, in the adversarial "preliminary examination," is not able to produce evidence showing probable cause to believe that the defendant committed the crime as charged, then the charges are dismissed and the defendant released. If probable cause is present, the magistrate will "bind over" the defendant for arraignment and trial in a court with jurisdiction to try the offense.

There are alternatives to the use of the preliminary judicial hearing as the initial filter in the accusatory process. In just under half of the states, a defendant can insist that the prosecutor seek the permission of a grand jury before filing felony charges. If the grand jury agrees with the prosecutor's request to charge an individual, the charges appear in a grand jury "indictment." In Chapter 10 we studied the role of the grand jury in investigating crimes — the grand jury as a "sword."

Now we consider the grand jury's function as a "shield" against unfounded prosecutions, and the interaction between the grand jury and the judicial "preliminary examination" as screening devices.

The traditional image of the grand jury as a shield might be misleading. By all accounts, grand juries indict in virtually all cases when a prosecutor requests the indictment. There are several possible reasons for this, all built into the structure of the grand jury. See Andrew Leipold, Why Grand Juries Do Not (and Cannot) Protect the Accused, 80 Cornell L. Rev. 260 (1995). First, the grand jury's review standard is quite low: It must determine only whether there is probable cause to believe that the accused has committed the crime that the prosecutor has specified. Second, the grand jury proceedings are not adversarial. Only the prosecutor presents evidence to the grand jury, and he has no obligation (in most states) to present any exculpatory evidence. In most jurisdictions, no representatives of the grand jury witnesses or targets are even present in the grand jury room during testimony or deliberations.

■ NEW YORK CONSTITUTION ART. I, §6

No person shall be held to answer for a capital or otherwise infamous crime . . . unless on indictment of a grand jury, except that a person held for the action of a grand jury upon a charge for such an offense, other than one punishable by death or life imprisonment, with the consent of the district attorney, may waive indictment by a grand jury and consent to be prosecuted on an information filed by the district attorney; such waiver shall be evidenced by written instrument signed by the defendant in open court in the presence of his or her counsel. . . .

The power of grand juries to inquire into the wilful misconduct in office of public officers, and to find indictments or to direct the filing of informations in connection with such inquiries, shall never be suspended or impaired by law. . . .

■ ILLINOIS ANNOTATED STATUTES CH. 725, PARA. 5/111-2

(a) All prosecutions of felonies shall be by information or by indictment. No prosecution may be pursued by information unless a preliminary hearing has been held or waived . . . and at that hearing probable cause to believe the defendant committed an offense was found. . . .

(b) All other prosecutions may be by indictment, information or complaint. . . .

(f) Where the prosecution of a felony is by information or complaint after preliminary hearing, or after a waiver of preliminary hearing in accordance with paragraph (a) of this Section, such prosecution may be for all offenses, arising from the same transaction or conduct of a defendant even though the complaint or complaints filed at the preliminary hearing charged only one or some of the offenses arising from that transaction or conduct.

COMMONWEALTH v. KHARI WILCOX

767 N.E.2d 1061 (Mass. 2002)

GREANEY, J.

After hearing six days of evidence during a three-month period, a Suffolk County grand jury indicted the defendant on charges of armed robbery and home invasion. The defendant moved for discovery of the grand jury attendance records to ascertain whether at least twelve of the grand jurors who voted to indict him had heard "all of the evidence" presented against him. (Of particular concern to the defendant was whether fewer than the required minimum of twelve grand jurors voting to indict him had heard certain exculpatory evidence, including evidence suggesting that he had been erroneously identified.) A judge in the Superior Court allowed the defendant's motion, but stayed discovery to give the Commonwealth an opportunity to seek interlocutory review of her order. . . .

The grand jury as known to the common law always has been regarded as a bulwark of individual liberty and a fundamental protection against despotism and persecution. It is an institution preserved by our State Constitution, which asserts the "great principle . . . that no man shall be put to answer a criminal charge [for a capital or otherwise infamous offense] until the criminating evidence has been laid before a grand jury," Commonwealth v. Holley, 69 Mass. 458 (1855). See Mass. R. Crim. P. 3(b)(1), 378 Mass. 847 (1979) ("A defendant charged with an offense punishable by imprisonment in state prison shall have the right to be proceeded against by indictment except when the offense charged is within the concurrent jurisdiction of the District and Superior Courts and the District Court retains jurisdiction"). For an indictment to stand, the grand jury must hear sufficient evidence to establish the identity of the accused and probable cause to arrest him.

The defendant's discovery motion is predicated on the argument that the requirement in Mass. R. Crim. P. 5(e), 378 Mass. 850 (1979), of a "concurrence" of at least twelve grand jurors to return an indictment, mandates that a core of at least twelve grand jurors heard all of the evidence and voted to indict. He asserts that the word "concurrence" presumes that a grand juror has been present to hear all of the evidence presented before joining in a decision to indict, and that such an obligation is necessitated by the grand jurors' oath. The defendant urges us to follow the "better-reasoned decisions from other jurisdictions" that "recognize that an informed grand jury that truly concurs to indict, based on hearing all of the evidence, ensures the integrity of the grand jury process." We decline to add such a requirement to rule 5.

Rule 5(e) has its origins in the common law. By the common law, a grand jury "may consist of not less than thirteen, nor more than twenty-three persons," Crimm v. Commonwealth, 119 Mass. 326 (1876), and a concurrence of at least twelve was required to return an indictment. Both the maximum number of grand jurors and the minimum number required to indict prescribed by the common law [were] kept intact by statute and rule. See G.L. c. 277, §§1, 2A-2G (twenty-three grand jurors shall be selected to serve); Mass. R. Crim. P. 5(a), 378 Mass. 850 (1979) ("the court shall select not more than twenty-three grand jurors to serve"); Mass. R. Crim. P. 5(e) ("An indictment may be found only upon the concurrence of twelve or more jurors"). The common law quorum requirement of thirteen remains in place, unaltered by statute or rule.

Rule 5 is modeled in large part on its Federal counterpart, Fed. R. Crim. P. 6. The Federal rule requires that every grand jury session be attended by "not less than 16 nor more than 23 members," Fed. R. Crim. P. 6(a)(1), and, for an indictment to be found, requires "the concurrence of 12 or more jurors," Fed. R. Crim. P. 6(f). Federal courts have nearly uniformly rejected the argument raised by the defendant that the grand jurors voting to indict be required to hear all of the evidence presented. See United States v. Byron, 994 F.2d 747, 748 (10th Cir. 1993); but see United States v. Provenzano, 688 F.2d 194, 202-203 (3d Cir. 1982) (expressing uneasiness with approach followed by other Federal courts and providing procedure whereby replacement and absentee grand jurors are given transcript of missed proceedings as well as an opportunity to recall witnesses for questioning). Often quoted and relied on in these Federal decisions is the reasoning stated by Judge Learned Hand, writing for the court in United States ex rel. McCann v. Thompson, 144 F.2d 604, 607 (2d Cir. 1944):

> Since all the evidence adduced before a grand jury — certainly when the accused does not appear — is aimed at proving guilt, the absence of some jurors during some part of the hearings will ordinarily merely weaken the prosecution's case. If what the absentees actually hear is enough to satisfy them, there would seem to be no reason why they should not vote. Against this we can think of nothing except the possibility that some of the evidence adduced by the prosecution might conceivably turn out to be favorable to the accused; and that, if the absentees had heard it, they might have refused to vote a true bill. No one can be entirely sure that this can never occur; but it appears to us so remote a chance that it should be left to those instances in which it can be made to appear that the evidence not heard was of that character, in spite of the extreme difficulty of ever proving what was the evidence before a grand jury. Indeed, the possibility that not all who vote will hear all the evidence, is a reasonable inference from the fact that sixteen is a quorum. Were the law as the relator argues, it would practically mean that all jurors present at the beginning of any case, must remain to the end, for it will always be impossible to tell in advance whether twelve will eventually vote a true bill, and if they do, who those twelve will be. The result of such a doctrine would therefore be that in a long case, or in a case where there are intervals in the taking of evidence, the privilege of absence would not exist. That would certainly be an innovation, for the contrary practice has, so far as we are aware, been universal; and it would be an onerous and unnecessary innovation.

We reject the defendant's contention that the reasoning stated in the *Thompson* case is "unpersuasive." In most instances, grand jurors hear only inculpatory evidence. Commonwealth v. O'Dell, 466 N.E.2d 828 (Mass. 1984) (stating that prosecutors are not required "to bring exculpatory evidence to the attention of grand juries"). It is only when the prosecutor possesses exculpatory evidence that would greatly undermine either the credibility of an important witness or evidence likely to affect the grand jury's decision, or withholds exculpatory evidence causing the presentation to be "so seriously tainted," that the prosecutor must present such evidence to the grand jury. See Commonwealth v. Vinnie, 698 N.E.2d 896 (Mass. 1998). On the occasion when a grand juror "misses" inculpatory evidence, such a circumstance, as stated by Judge Hand, may work in the accused's favor if that grand juror has not otherwise heard sufficient evidence to establish the probable cause standard. On the other hand, the "missed" evidence may have been cumulative of other evidence presented.

In the *Thompson* case, the existence of the quorum requirement served as a reasonable basis for inferring that not all of the grand jurors voting on an indictment will necessarily have heard all of the evidence. This same inference may be drawn from the common-law quorum requirement existing in the Commonwealth, as well as from the fact that grand jurors may be replaced pursuant to statute. Provisions governing grand jurors, which we decline to change, take into account the lengthy terms for which many grand juries sit, usually a number of months. The provisions also, as acknowledged by the defendant, insure that the grand jury can continue functioning despite absent members. See 1 S.S. Beale, Grand Jury Law and Practice §4:8, at 4-35 (2d ed. 2001) ("It is not unusual for individual grand jurors to miss a number of the sessions, yet to participate in the ultimate decision whether to indict or not. In this respect, the grand jury process differs radically from the trial process, where it would be unthinkable for a juror to miss several days of evidence, yet be permitted to deliberate and vote on the defendant's guilt"). Adoption of the rule the defendant proposes may cause the prosecution to seek to indict an accused on the basis of whatever evidence it can present in one day. In such circumstances, the prosecution may not be able to present the direct testimony of several witnesses, relying instead on the hearsay statements of one witness. While proceedings conducted in this manner would not be impermissible, see Commonwealth v. O'Dell, 466 N.E.2d 828 (Mass. 1984) ("an indictment may be based solely on hearsay"), they would run contrary to our "preference for the use of direct testimony before grand juries," Commonwealth v. St. Pierre, 387 N.E.2d 1135 (Mass. 1979), which inures to the accused's benefit. The defendant's rule would also be disruptive of witnesses, police and their schedules, court sessions, and the daily encumbered lives of grand jurors and their families.

Although the defendant correctly identifies that other States, either by statute, rule, or decision, have adopted the requirement that the grand jurors voting to indict have heard all the evidence presented, see, e.g., Ariz. Rev. Stat. Ann. §21-406(B); Me. R. Crim. P. 6(j); N.D. Cent. Code §29-10.1-20; Or. Rev. Stat. §132.360; Commonwealth v. Levinson, 389 A.2d 1062 (Pa. 1978) (explaining when "a substantial percentage of the total membership of the jury is absent from a significant portion of the presentation of evidence, it can no longer be said with confidence that the deliberations were not affected"), some State courts have followed the Federal approach. See, e.g., People v. Martin-Trigona, 444 N.E.2d 527 (Ill. App. 1982); State v. Blyth, 226 N.W.2d 250 (Iowa 1975); Johnston v. State, 822 P.2d 1118 (Nev. 1991). We join this latter group of courts. We add that it is precisely the unique and limited function of the grand jury that permits their proceedings, including those rules pertaining to grand jurors, to vary from the rules governing trials and petit jurors. That these rules vary does not vitiate the defendant's constitutional right to be indicted by a grand jury, of which at least twelve grand jurors agree that probable cause exists to indict. As has been explained, the grand jury are expected to follow their oath faithfully, as they may not return an indictment unless they have heard sufficient evidence to establish the identity of the accused and probable cause to arrest him.

The case is remanded to the county court for entry of an order vacating the order of the Superior Court judge allowing the defendant's motion for discovery of the grand jury attendance records, and directing the entry of an order denying the motion. . . .

Notes

1. *Which crimes require an indictment?* In almost half the states, a grand jury indictment rather than a prosecutor's information is necessary for at least some charges. In some of these jurisdictions, such as New York, the constitution requires a grand jury indictment; in other "indictment" states, the state constitution allows the legislature to decide which if any crimes must be charged through grand jury indictment. For the most part, the "indictment" states have retained the traditional requirement embodied in the Fifth Amendment to the federal constitution: Indictment must occur in all capital and "infamous" crimes — that is, felonies. A few require indictments only for crimes punishable by death or life imprisonment. The grand jury requirement is one of the few provisions of the federal Bill of Rights that has not yet been "incorporated" against the states through the due process clause of the Fourteenth Amendment. Hurtado v. California, 110 U.S. 516 (1884).

In most states and for most charges, the grand jury is optional. Prosecutors can decide whether to proceed under an information or a grand jury indictment (as in Illinois, under the statute reprinted above). Indictments have become one weapon in the prosecutor's arsenal of ways to investigate and charge crimes. Prosecutors often use grand juries to charge politically sensitive crimes (to share responsibility for the charging decision) or to charge crimes that come to light as the result of grand jury investigations.

2. *Grand jury versus preliminary examinations.* In cases where the prosecutor files an information rather than seeking an indictment from the grand jury, the factual and legal basis for the prosecutor's charge is usually tested before trial in a judicial proceeding, usually called a "preliminary examination" or "preliminary hearing." Some defendants might actually prefer a preliminary examination over a grand jury indictment, because the judge might evaluate the evidence more skeptically than the grand jury, given that the grand jurors only hear the prosecution's side of the case. Defendants also may attend the preliminary examination, giving them discovery opportunities that are not generally available from the grand jury. Although the use of a preliminary examination might give such practical advantages to the defendant, the government holds the power to choose between the grand jury and preliminary examination options. The majority view is that there is no constitutional right to a preliminary hearing once a prosecutor has decided to seek an indictment. See People v. Glass, 627 N.W.2d 261 (Mich. 2001) (overruling earlier case granting right to preliminary examination to all defendants, including indictees).

Further, there is no federal constitutional requirement that either a judge or a grand jury determine whether probable cause supports the criminal charges filed against a defendant. Lem Woon v. Oregon, 229 U.S. 586 (1913) (upholding statute providing for no preliminary examination after information). All states have statutes offering at least some defendants a determination of probable cause underlying the charges, whether the determination comes from a judge in a preliminary hearing or from a grand jury indictment. A few states provide, as an alternative charging method, for "direct filing" of charges by the prosecutor without testing in a preliminary hearing or indictment. These states usually allow the defendant to file a motion to dismiss the charges after discovery is complete.

3. *Waiver of indictment.* In the jurisdictions requiring indictment for some crimes, defendants often waive their right to indictment and proceed without any grand

jury or judicial screening of the charges. Are there times when the legal system might prevent defendants from waiving the right to indictment? See N.Y. Crim. Proc. Law §195.20(a) (waiver must be written, executed in open court in presence of counsel); N.C. Gen. Stat. §15A-642(b) (waiver allowed except for offenses punishable by death or cases in which defendant waives counsel).

4. *Nonadversarial proceedings.* Time and again, judicial opinions point out that grand jury proceedings are not adversarial and are not a "mini-trial." Truer words have never been spoken. To begin with, the grand jury's task is far different from that of a trial jury: The grand jury need only decide whether the prosecutor has demonstrated probable cause to believe that the defendant committed the crime charged. In most jurisdictions, only the prosecutor presents testimony and documents to the grand jury, and none of it is subject to cross-examination or the rules of evidence. Costello v. United States, 350 U.S. 359 (1956). In a strong minority of states, attorneys for some grand jury witnesses may observe the testimony of their clients, but the attorneys may not question the witness or make any statements to the grand jury. See, e.g., Ill. Ann. Stat. ch. 725, para. 5/112-4.1.

In most systems, the prosecutor has no obligation to present exculpatory evidence, United States v. Williams, 504 U.S. 36 (1992), although support for this traditional position is eroding. More than a dozen states have statutes or judicial rulings that require the prosecutor to present exculpatory evidence under some circumstances. See Schuster v. Eighth Judicial District Court, 160 P.3d 873 (Nev. 2007) (state statute requires district attorney to subject to grand jury any evidence that will "explain away the charge," but statute does not impose duty on district attorney to explain to jurors the importance of the evidence); People v. Lancaster, 503 N.E.2d 990 (N.Y. 1986). Prosecutorial policies also sometimes recognize the obligation of a prosecutor to present exculpatory evidence that would lead the grand jury to refuse to indict. See U.S. Attorneys' Manual §9-11.233; see also ABA Standards for Criminal Justice, Prosecution Function Standard 3-3.6(b) ("No prosecutor should knowingly fail to disclose to the grand jury evidence which tends to negate guilt or mitigate the offense"). Sometimes the target of a grand jury investigation must have notice and an opportunity to testify before the grand jury can indict. See Sheriff of Humboldt County v. Marcum, 783 P.2d 1389 (Nev. 1989).

5. *Judicial review of indictments.* As you might imagine based on the other materials in this chapter, judicial dismissal of charges contained in an indictment is a rare event. Only about 10 states even authorize courts to inquire into the sufficiency of the evidence to support an indictment. See, e.g., Colo. Rev. Stat. §16-5-204(4)(k). Challenges based on prosecutorial misconduct are only slightly more successful as a basis for dismissal of an indictment.

Assuming that a court is willing to review an indictment, will there be a record of the proceedings sufficient to allow judicial review? Statutes and rules of procedure in the federal system and in a majority of the states require recording of at least the testimony that a grand jury hears, and a strong minority also require recording of other statements made to the grand jury, such as the commentary of the prosecutor. Virtually nowhere are the deliberations and votes of the grand jury recorded.

6. *Timing of initial appearance and preliminary hearing.* The federal constitution requires that the initial determination of probable cause to support an *arrest* (but not to support the charges) occur within 48 hours of the arrest. County of Riverside v. McLaughlin, 500 U.S. 44 (1991) (delay longer than 48 hours presumptively unreasonable). Some states have rules calling for such a hearing in even less time,

but most simply require a hearing within a "reasonable" time. As for the determination of whether there is probable cause to support the crimes charged, the hearing usually takes place within 10 to 20 days of the initial appearance if the defendant does not waive the hearing or if the grand jury does not return an indictment in the meantime.

7. *Attendance of the defendant.* Statutes and rules (not to mention due process principles) generally grant defendants the right to attend the initial appearance and the preliminary examination. This presents a logistical challenge in some jurisdictions, requiring the authorities to shuttle many detained defendants from the jail to the courthouse and back again. One response to this administrative burden has been the use of videoconference technology linking the courtroom with a designated hearing room in the jail. If you were representing a defendant, would you be more effective during a preliminary examination by remaining with your client at the jail, or by being present in the courtroom with the judge? See Anne Bowen Poulin, Criminal Justice and Videoconferencing Technology: The Remote Defendant, 78 Tulane L. Rev. 1089 (2004).

8. *Staff for grand jury.* The grand jury depends on the prosecutor for legal advice and most of the logistics of its operation. Would grand juries assert more independence in the evaluation of criminal charges if they could employ their own legal counsel and other experts and staff? Fewer than 10 states have statutes authorizing support staff for grand juries, such as legal counsel, accountants, or detectives. See Kan. Stat. §22-3006. More frequently, statutes authorize the prosecutor to attend the sessions of the grand jury (except during deliberations and voting), to examine witnesses, and to provide legal advice to the grand jury. Fla. Stat. §905.19. The supervising judge for the grand jury is also available to provide legal advice, although the grand jury rarely requests advice from the judge. But other sources of staff support for the grand jury have not developed in most places.

Consider this lack of support staff against the background of a growing bureaucracy attached to virtually every other governmental institution early in the twentieth century. Grand jurors were no longer personally aware of crimes committed or conditions to investigate, as they once were. They were without the increasingly specialized auditing and management skills necessary to investigate crimes or to monitor government. Given the complexity of governance, what institution of government could survive without support staff? Could Congress or the president perform their duties without the benefit of their own counsel? For an exploration of the idea of grand jury staff and other innovations to revitalize this ancient institution, go to the web extension for this chapter at *http://www.crimpro.com/extension/ch13*.

XIV

Jeopardy and Joinder

Chapter 13 addressed the legal forces at work when a prosecutor chooses whether to charge a suspect and which charges to select. We concentrate now on those cases in which the prosecutor could file multiple charges. When several related criminal incidents happen, a prosecutor might file a single count or multiple counts in a single prosecution against one or more defendants, or she might instead file separate criminal cases.

Several sources of law shape the prosecutor's grouping of multiple charges. First, the constitutional bar against "double jeopardy," embodied in the Fifth Amendment of the U.S. Constitution and in most state constitutions, puts some pressure on the prosecutor to include more charges and more conduct within a single initial prosecution, because double jeopardy might bar any later attempt to pursue the related charges. Section A considers these double jeopardy issues.

Prosecutors must also consider statutes and procedural rules on the conceptually related concepts of "joinder" and "severance" of charges and defendants. These rules define both the maximum and minimum range of charges that a prosecutor can join together into a single proceeding. Under the joinder and severance rules, both the prosecutor and the trial court decide whether to include or exclude charges or defendants in a single proceeding. Section B explores these rules.

A. DOUBLE JEOPARDY

A prosecutor must plan for the future when filing charges. If she chooses not to combine related charges in an initial set of proceedings and instead files some of the charges later, there is a risk that the court will bar the later charges. As mentioned above, the legal basis for this decision is the double jeopardy clause of the federal constitution and of most state constitutions. The Fifth Amendment to the federal constitution provides: "No person shall . . . be subject for the same offence to be twice put in jeopardy of life or limb. . . ."

Double jeopardy, it is often said, protects criminal defendants from (1) a second prosecution after acquittal, (2) a second prosecution after conviction, and (3) multiple punishments for the same offense within the same proceeding. The materials in this part touch on some prominent double jeopardy issues that flow from the charging decision. First, we consider a controversial and revealing limitation on the operation of the double jeopardy principle — the "dual sovereign" exception. Second, we consider which charges in a later proceeding amount to the "same offence" that was charged in a prior proceeding.

1. Multiple Sovereigns

Federal and state governments have overlapping responsibilities for enforcing criminal laws. Many economic and other activities cross state lines, and the criminal codes of most states and the federal government now reach much of the same conduct. Often a person who engages in criminal behavior could face charges in two states, or in both state and federal systems.

The overlap between the federal and state criminal laws is a recurring issue for double jeopardy purposes. In United States v. Lanza, 260 U.S. 377 (1922), several defendants were convicted under state law in Washington for manufacturing, transporting, and possessing liquor and were fined $750 each. When the federal government also brought criminal charges under the National Prohibition Act, Lanza raised a double jeopardy objection to the federal prosecution. He noted that the Eighteenth Amendment, prohibiting the manufacture, sale, or transportation of intoxicating liquors, gave both Congress and the states "concurrent power to enforce" the prohibition. According to Lanza, the state and the federal criminal statutes were punishing the "same offense" because they each derived from the same constitutional authority.

The Court rejected this argument and embraced instead the doctrine known as the "dual sovereign" exception to double jeopardy:

> We have here two sovereignties, deriving power from different sources, capable of dealing with the same subject-matter within the same territory. Each may, without interference by the other, enact laws to secure prohibition. . . . Each government in determining what shall be an offense against its peace and dignity is exercising its own sovereignty, not that of the other.

260 U.S. at 382.

The following materials trace the continuing vitality of the "dual sovereign" doctrine during a time when the overlap between federal and state criminal laws has grown larger.

ALFONSE BARTKUS v. ILLINOIS

359 U.S. 121 (1959)

FRANKFURTER, J.*

Petitioner was tried in the Federal District Court for the Northern District of Illinois on December 18, 1953, for robbery of a federally insured savings and loan association, the General Savings and Loan Association of Cicero, Illinois, in violation of 18 U.S.C. §2113. The case was tried to a jury and resulted in an acquittal. On January 8, 1954, an Illinois grand jury indicted Bartkus. The facts recited in the Illinois indictment were substantially identical to those contained in the prior federal indictment. The Illinois indictment charged that these facts constituted a violation of [the Illinois robbery statute. Bartkus entered a plea of autrefois acquit, which the trial court rejected. Bartkus was tried, convicted, and sentenced to life imprisonment.]

The state and federal prosecutions were separately conducted. It is true that the agent of the Federal Bureau of Investigation who had conducted the investigation on behalf of the Federal Government turned over to the Illinois prosecuting officials all the evidence he had gathered against the petitioner. Concededly, some of that evidence had been gathered after acquittal in the federal court. The only other connection between the two trials is to be found in a suggestion that the federal sentencing of the accomplices who testified against petitioner in both trials was purposely continued by the federal court until after they testified in the state trial. The record establishes that the prosecution was undertaken by state prosecuting officials within their discretionary responsibility. . . . It establishes also that federal officials acted in cooperation with state authorities, as is the conventional practice between the two sets of prosecutors throughout the country. It does not support the claim that the State of Illinois in bringing its prosecution was merely a tool of the federal authorities, who thereby avoided the prohibition of the Fifth Amendment against a retrial of a federal prosecution after an acquittal. It does not sustain a conclusion that the state prosecution was a sham and a cover for a federal prosecution. . . . Since the new prosecution was by Illinois, and not by the Federal Government, the claim of unconstitutionality must rest upon the Due Process Clause of the Fourteenth Amendment. . . .

Time and again this Court has attempted by general phrases not to define but to indicate the purport of due process and to adumbrate the continuing adjudicatory process in its application. The statement by Mr. Justice Cardozo in Palko v. Connecticut, 302 U.S. 319, 324-325 (1937), has especially commended itself and been frequently cited in later opinions. Referring to specific situations, he wrote:

> In these and other situations immunities that are valid as against the federal government by force of the specific pledges of particular amendments have been found to be implicit in the concept of ordered liberty, and thus, through the Fourteenth Amendment, become valid as against the states.

[He suggested that due process] prohibited to the States only those practices "repugnant to the conscience of mankind." In applying these phrases in *Palko*, the

* [Justices Clark, Harlan, Whittaker, and Stewart joined this opinion. — EDS.]

Court ruled that, while at some point the cruelty of harassment by multiple prosecutions by a State would offend due process, the specific limitation imposed on the Federal Government by the Double Jeopardy Clause of the Fifth Amendment did not bind the States. [*Palko* sustained a first-degree murder conviction returned in a second trial after an appeal by the State from an acquittal of first-degree murder.]

The Fifth Amendment's proscription of double jeopardy has been invoked and rejected in over twenty cases of real or hypothetical successive state and federal prosecution cases before this Court. While United States v. Lanza, 260 U.S. 377 (1922), was the first case in which we squarely held valid a federal prosecution arising out of the same facts which had been the basis of a state conviction, the validity of such a prosecution by the Federal Government has not been questioned by this Court since the opinion in Fox v. Ohio, 46 U.S. 410 (1847), more than one hundred years ago.

In Fox v. Ohio, argument was made to the Supreme Court that an Ohio conviction for uttering counterfeit money was invalid. This assertion of invalidity was based in large part upon the argument that since Congress had imposed federal sanctions for the counterfeiting of money, a failure to find that the Supremacy Clause precluded the States from punishing related conduct would expose an individual to double punishment. Mr. Justice Daniel, writing for the Court [recognized] a possibility of double punishment, but denied that from this flowed a finding of pre-emption, concluding instead that both the Federal and State Governments retained the power to impose criminal sanctions, the United States because of its interest in protecting the purity of its currency, the States because of their interest in protecting their citizens against fraud. . . .

The experience of state courts in dealing with successive prosecutions by different governments is obviously also relevant in considering whether or not the Illinois prosecution of Bartkus violated due process of law. Of the twenty-eight States which have considered the validity of successive state and federal prosecutions as against a challenge of violation of either a state constitutional double-jeopardy provision or a common-law evidentiary rule of autrefois acquit and autrefois convict, twenty-seven have refused to rule that the second prosecution was or would be barred. These States were not bound to follow this Court and its interpretation of the Fifth Amendment. The rules, constitutional, statutory, or common law which bound them, drew upon the same experience as did the Fifth Amendment, but were and are of separate and independent authority. . . .

With this body of precedent as irrefutable evidence that state and federal courts have for years refused to bar a second trial even though there had been a prior trial by another government for a similar offense, it would be disregard of a long, unbroken, unquestioned course of impressive adjudication for the Court now to rule that due process compels such a bar. A practical justification for rejecting such a reading of due process also commends itself in aid of this interpretation of the Fourteenth Amendment. In Screws v. United States, 325 U.S. 91 (1945), defendants were tried and convicted in a federal court under federal statutes with maximum sentences of a year and two years respectively. But the state crime there involved was a capital offense. Were the federal prosecution of a comparatively minor offense to prevent state prosecution of so grave an infraction of state law, the result would be a shocking and untoward deprivation of the historic right and obligation of the States to maintain peace and order within their confines. It would be in derogation of our federal system to displace the reserved power of States over state offenses by reason of prosecution of minor federal offenses by federal authorities beyond the control of the States.[25] . . .

The entire history of litigation and contention over the question of the imposition of a bar to a second prosecution by a government other than the one first prosecuting is a manifestation of the evolutionary unfolding of law. Today a number of States have statutes which bar a second prosecution if the defendant has been once tried by another government for a similar offense. A study of the cases under the New York statute, which is typical of these laws, demonstrates that the task of determining when the federal and state statutes are so much alike that a prosecution under the former bars a prosecution under the latter is a difficult one. [Experience] such as that of New York may give aid to Congress in its consideration of adoption of similar provisions in individual federal criminal statutes or in the federal criminal code.

Precedent, experience, and reason alike support the conclusion that Alfonse Bartkus has not been deprived of due process of law by the State of Illinois. Affirmed.

BLACK, J., dissenting.*

. . . Fear and abhorrence of governmental power to try people twice for the same conduct is one of the oldest ideas found in western civilization. Its roots run deep into Greek and Roman times. Even in the Dark Ages, when so many other principles of justice were lost, the idea that one trial and one punishment were enough remained alive through the canon law and the teachings of the early Christian writers. By the thirteenth century it seems to have been firmly established in England, where it came to be considered as a "universal maxim of the common law." [Some] writers have explained the opposition to double prosecutions by emphasizing the injustice inherent in two punishments for the same act, and others have stressed the dangers to the innocent from allowing the full power of the state to be brought against them in two trials. . . .

The Court apparently takes the position that a second trial for the same act is somehow less offensive if one of the trials is conducted by the Federal Government and the other by a State. Looked at from the standpoint of the individual who is being prosecuted, this notion is too subtle for me to grasp. If double punishment is what is feared, it hurts no less for two "Sovereigns" to inflict it than for one. If danger to the innocent is emphasized, that danger is surely no less when the power of State and Federal Governments is brought to bear on one man in two trials, than when one of these "Sovereigns" proceeds alone. In each case, inescapably, a man is forced to face danger twice for the same conduct.

The Court, without denying the almost universal abhorrence of such double prosecutions, nevertheless justifies the practice here in the name of "federalism." This, it seems to me, is a misuse and desecration of the concept. Our Federal Union was conceived and created "to establish Justice" and to "secure the Blessings of Liberty," not to destroy any of the bulwarks on which both freedom and justice depend. We should, therefore, be suspicious of any supposed "requirements" of "federalism"

25. Illinois had on additional and unique interest in Bartkus beyond the commission of this particular crime. If Bartkus was guilty of the crime charged he would be an habitual offender in Illinois and subject to life imprisonment. The Illinois court sentenced Bartkus to life imprisonment on this ground.

* [Chief Justice Warren and Justice Douglas joined this opinion. — EDS.]

which result in obliterating ancient safeguards. I have been shown nothing in the history of our Union, in the writings of its Founders, or elsewhere, to indicate that individual rights deemed essential by both State and Nation were to be lost through the combined operations of the two governments. . . .

The Court's argument also ignores the fact that our Constitution allocates power between local and federal governments in such a way that the basic rights of each can be protected without double trials. The Federal Government is given power to act in limited areas only, but in matters properly within its scope it is supreme. It can retain exclusive control of such matters, or grant the States concurrent power on its own terms.

[This] practice, which for some 150 years was considered so undesirable that the Court must strain to find examples, is now likely to become a commonplace. For, after today, who will be able to blame a conscientious prosecutor for failing to accept a jury verdict of acquittal when he believes a defendant guilty and knows that a second try is available in another jurisdiction and that such a second try is approved by the Highest Court in the Land? Inevitably, the victims of such double prosecutions will most often be the poor and the weak in our society, individuals without friends in high places who can influence prosecutors not to try them again. The power to try a second time will be used, as have all similar procedures, to make scapegoats of helpless, political, religious, or racial minorities and those who differ, who do not conform and who resist tyranny.

There are some countries that allow the dangerous practice of trying people twice. [Such practices] are not hard to find in lands torn by revolution or crushed by dictatorship. I had thought that our constitutional protections embodied in the Double Jeopardy and Due Process Clauses would have barred any such things happening here. Unfortunately, [today's decision causes] me to fear that in an important number of cases it can happen here. I would reverse.

BRENNAN, J., dissenting.*

Bartkus was tried and acquitted in a Federal District Court of robbing a federally insured savings and loan association in Cicero, Illinois. He was indicted for the same robbery by the State of Illinois less than three weeks later, and subsequently convicted and sentenced to life imprisonment. The single issue in dispute at both trials was whether Bartkus was the third participant in the robbery along with two self-confessed perpetrators of the crime.

The Government's case against Bartkus on the federal trial rested primarily upon the testimony of two of the robbers, Joseph Cosentino and James Brindis, who confessed their part in the crime and testified that Bartkus was their confederate. The defense was that Bartkus was getting a haircut in a barber shop several miles away at the time the robbery was committed. The owner of the barber shop, his son and other witnesses placed Bartkus in the shop at the time. The federal jury in acquitting Bartkus apparently believed the alibi witnesses and not Cosentino and Brindis.

The federal authorities were highly displeased with the jury's resolution of the conflicting testimony, and the trial judge sharply upbraided the jury for its verdict.

* [Chief Justice Warren and Justice Douglas joined this opinion. — EDS.]

The federal authorities obviously decided immediately after the trial to make a second try at convicting Bartkus, and since the federal courthouse was barred to them by the Fifth Amendment, they turned to a state prosecution for that purpose. It is clear that federal officers solicited the state indictment, arranged to assure the attendance of key witnesses, unearthed additional evidence to discredit Bartkus and one of his alibi witnesses, and in general prepared and guided the state prosecution. . . .

I think that the record before us shows that the extent of participation of the federal authorities here [made this state prosecution into] a second federal prosecution of Bartkus. The federal jury acquitted Bartkus late in December 1953. Early in January 1954 the Assistant United States Attorney who prosecuted the federal case summoned Cosentino to his office. Present also were the FBI agent who had investigated the robbery and the Assistant State's Attorney for Cook County who later prosecuted the state case. The Assistant State's Attorney said to Cosentino, "Look, we are going to get an indictment in the state court against Bartkus, will you testify against him?" Cosentino agreed that he would. Later Brindis also agreed to testify. Although they pleaded guilty to the federal robbery charge in August 1953, the Federal District Court postponed their sentencing until after they testified against Bartkus at the state trial, which was not held until April 1954. . . . Both Cosentino and Brindis were also released on bail pending the state trial, Brindis on his own recognizance.

In January, also, an FBI agent who had been active in the federal prosecution purposefully set about strengthening the proofs which had not sufficed to convict Bartkus on the federal trial. . . . He uncovered a new witness against Bartkus, one Grant Pursel. . . . The first time that Pursel had any contact whatsoever with a state official connected with the case was the morning that he testified. . . .

Given the fact that there must always be state officials involved in a state prosecution, I cannot see how there can be more complete federal participation in a state prosecution than there was in this case. I see no escape from the conclusion that this particular state trial was in actuality a second federal prosecution — a second federal try at Bartkus in the guise of a state prosecution. If this state conviction is not overturned, then, as a practical matter, there will be no restraints on the use of state machinery by federal officers to bring what is in effect a second federal prosecution. . . .

Of course, cooperation between federal and state authorities in criminal law enforcement is to be desired and encouraged, for cooperative federalism in this field can indeed profit the Nation and the States in improving methods for carrying out the endless fight against crime. But the normal and healthy situation consists of state and federal officers cooperating to apprehend lawbreakers and present the strongest case against them at a single trial, be it state or federal. . . .

U.S. ATTORNEYS' MANUAL §9-2.031, DUAL PROSECUTION AND SUCCESSIVE PROSECUTION POLICY (*PETITE POLICY*)

A. Statement of Policy: This policy establishes guidelines for the exercise of discretion by appropriate officers of the Department of Justice in determining whether to bring a federal prosecution based on substantially the same act(s) or transactions involved in a prior state or federal proceeding. See Rinaldi v. United States, 434 U.S. 22, 27 (1977); Petite v. United States, 361 U.S. 529 (1960). Although there is no general statutory bar to a federal prosecution where the defendant's conduct already has formed the basis for a state prosecution, Congress expressly has provided that, as to certain offenses, a state judgment of conviction or acquittal on the merits shall be a bar to any subsequent federal prosecution for the same act or acts. See 18 U.S.C. §§659 [interstate or foreign shipments by carrier], 660 [embezzling carrier's funds derived from commerce], 2101 [travel in interstate commerce to incite a riot].

The purpose of this policy is to vindicate substantial federal interests through appropriate federal prosecutions, to protect persons charged with criminal conduct from the burdens associated with multiple prosecutions and punishments for substantially the same act(s) or transaction(s), to promote efficient utilization of Department resources, and to promote coordination and cooperation between federal and state prosecutors.

This policy precludes the initiation or continuation of a federal prosecution, following a prior state or federal prosecution based on substantially the same act(s) or transaction(s) unless three substantive prerequisites are satisfied: first, the matter must involve a substantial federal interest; second, the prior prosecution must have left that interest demonstrably unvindicated; and third, applying the same test that is applicable to all federal prosecutions, the government must believe that the defendant's conduct constitutes a federal offense, and that the admissible evidence probably will be sufficient to obtain and sustain a conviction by an unbiased trier of fact. In addition, there is a procedural prerequisite to be satisfied, that is, the prosecution must be approved by the appropriate Assistant Attorney General. . . .

In order to insure the most efficient use of law enforcement resources, whenever a matter involves overlapping federal and state jurisdiction, federal prosecutors should, as soon as possible, consult with their state counterparts to determine the most appropriate single forum in which to proceed to satisfy the substantial federal and state interests involved, and, if possible, to resolve all criminal liability for the acts in question.

B. Types of Prosecution to Which This Policy Applies: [This] policy applies whenever the contemplated federal prosecution is based on substantially the same act(s) or transaction(s) involved in a prior state or federal prosecution. This policy constitutes an exercise of the Department's prosecutorial discretion, and applies even where a prior state prosecution would not legally bar a subsequent federal prosecution under the Double Jeopardy Clause because of the doctrine of dual sovereignty (see Abbate v. United States, 359 U.S. 187 (1959)), or a prior prosecution would not legally bar a subsequent state or federal prosecution under the Double Jeopardy Clause because each offense requires proof of an element not contained in the other. See United States v. Dixon, 509 U.S. 688 (1993); Blockburger v. United States, 284 U.S. 299 (1932).

This policy does not apply, and thus prior approval is not required, where the prior prosecution involved only a minor part of the contemplated federal charges. For example, a federal conspiracy or RICO prosecution may allege overt acts or predicate offenses previously prosecuted as long as those acts or offenses do not represent substantially the whole of the contemplated federal charge, and, in a RICO prosecution, as long as there are a sufficient number of predicate offenses to sustain the RICO charge if the previously prosecuted offenses were excluded. . . .

D. Substantive Prerequisites for Approval of a Prosecution Governed by This Policy: As previously stated there are three substantive prerequisites that must be met before approval will be granted for the initiation or a continuation of a prosecution governed by this policy.

The first substantive prerequisite is that the matter must involve a substantial federal interest. This determination will be made on a case-by-case basis, applying the considerations applicable to all federal prosecutions. See Principles of Federal Prosecution, USAM 9-27.230. Matters that come within the national investigative or prosecutorial priorities established by the Department are more likely than others to satisfy this requirement.

The second substantive prerequisite is that the prior prosecution must have left that substantial federal interest demonstrably unvindicated. In general, the Department will presume that a prior prosecution, regardless of result, has vindicated the relevant federal interest. That presumption, however, may be overcome when there are factors suggesting an unvindicated federal interest.

The presumption may be overcome when a conviction was not achieved because of the following sorts of factors: first, incompetence, corruption, intimidation, or undue influence; second, court or jury nullification in clear disregard of the evidence or the law; third, the unavailability of significant evidence, either because it was not timely discovered or known by the prosecution, or because it was kept from the trier of fact's consideration because of an erroneous interpretation of the law; fourth, the failure in a prior state prosecution to prove an element of a state offense that is not an element of the contemplated federal offense; and fifth, the exclusion of charges in a prior federal prosecution out of concern for fairness to other defendants, or for significant resource considerations that favored separate federal prosecutions.

The presumption may be overcome even when a conviction was achieved in the prior prosecution in the following circumstances: first, if the prior sentence was manifestly inadequate in light of the federal interest involved and a substantially enhanced sentence — including forfeiture and restitution as well as imprisonment and fines — is available through the contemplated federal prosecution, or second, if the choice of charges, or the determination of guilt, or the severity of sentence in the prior prosecution was affected by the sorts of factors listed in the previous paragraph. An example might be a case in which the charges in the initial prosecution trivialized the seriousness of the contemplated federal offense, for example, a state prosecution for assault and battery in a case involving the murder of a federal official.

The presumption also may be overcome, irrespective of the result in a prior state prosecution, in those rare cases where the following three conditions are met: first, the alleged violation involves a compelling federal interest, particularly one implicating an enduring national priority; second, the alleged violation involves egregious conduct, including that which threatens or causes loss of life, severe economic or physical harm, or the impairment of the functioning of an agency of the federal government or the due administration of justice; and third, the result in the prior prosecution was manifestly inadequate in light of the federal interest involved.

The third substantive prerequisite is that the government must believe that the defendant's conduct constitutes a federal offense, and that the admissible evidence probably will be sufficient to obtain and sustain a conviction by an unbiased trier of fact. This is the same test applied to all federal prosecutions. See Principles of Federal Prosecution, USAM 9-27.200 et seq. . . .

E. Procedural Prerequisite for Bringing a Prosecution Governed by This Policy: Whenever a substantial question arises as to whether this policy applies to a prosecution, the matter should be submitted to the appropriate Assistant Attorney General for resolution. Prior approval from the appropriate Assistant Attorney General must be obtained before bringing a prosecution governed by this policy. The United States will move to dismiss any prosecution governed by this policy in which prior approval was not obtained, unless the Assistant Attorney General retroactively approves it on the following grounds: first, that there are unusual or overriding circumstances justifying retroactive approval, and second, that the prosecution would have been approved had approval been sought in a timely fashion. Appropriate administrative action may be initiated against prosecutors who violate this policy.

F. . . . No Substantive or Procedural Rights Created: This policy has been promulgated solely for the purpose of internal Department of Justice guidance. It is not intended to, does not, and may not be relied upon to create any rights, substantive or procedural, that are enforceable at law by any party in any matter, civil or criminal, nor does it place any limitations on otherwise lawful litigative prerogatives of the Department of Justice.

■ NEW JERSEY STATUTES §2C:1-11

When conduct constitutes an offense within the concurrent jurisdiction of this State and of the United States, a prosecution in the District Court of the United States is a bar to a subsequent prosecution in this State under the following circumstances:

a. The first prosecution resulted in an acquittal or in a conviction, or in an improper termination . . . and the subsequent prosecution is based on the same conduct, unless (1) the offense of which the defendant was formerly convicted or acquitted and the offense for which he is subsequently prosecuted each requires proof of a fact not required by the other and the law defining each of such offenses is intended to prevent a substantially different harm or evil or (2) the offense for which the defendant is subsequently prosecuted is intended to prevent a substantially more serious harm or evil than the offense of which he was formerly convicted or acquitted or (3) the second offense was not consummated when the former trial began; or

b. The former prosecution was terminated, after the information was filed or the indictment found, by an acquittal or by a final order or judgment for the defendant which has not been set aside, reversed or vacated and which acquittal, final order or judgment necessarily required a determination inconsistent with a fact which must be established for conviction of the offense of which the defendant is subsequently prosecuted.

OHIO REVISED CODE §2925.50

If a violation of this chapter is a violation of the federal drug abuse control laws . . . a conviction or acquittal under the federal drug abuse control laws for the same act is a bar to prosecution in this state.

Problem 14-1. Rodney King's Attackers

Rodney King was driving while intoxicated on a major freeway in Los Angeles. California Highway Patrol officers spotted King driving more than 80 miles per hour and decided to follow him with red lights and sirens activated. They ordered him by loudspeaker to pull over, but he continued to drive. Los Angeles Police Department officers joined in the pursuit, including Officer Laurence Powell. King left the freeway and eventually stopped at an entrance to a recreation area. LAPD Sergeant Stacey Koon arrived at the scene and took charge.

The officers ordered King and his two passengers to exit the car and to lie face down on the pavement with legs spread and arms behind their backs. King's two friends complied. King got out of the car but put his hands on the hood of the car rather than lying down. The officers again ordered King to assume a prone position. King got on his hands and knees but did not lie down. Several officers tried to force King down and to handcuff him, but King resisted, so the officers retreated. Koon then fired taser darts (designed to stun a combative suspect) into King.

King rose from the ground and stepped toward Officer Powell. Powell used his baton to strike King on the side of his head. King fell to the ground. King attempted to rise, but Powell and another officer each struck him with their batons to prevent him from doing so. For about one minute after this point, several officers struck King more than 50 times with their batons and kicked or stepped on him. King remained on the ground. He was eventually hospitalized for facial fractures, a broken leg, and other injuries.

A bystander captured most of the events on videotape, and it was broadcast right away on the local and national media. Within one week of the beating, Los Angeles District Attorney Ira Reiner sought charges against the officers for excessive use of force. The Los Angeles County grand jury returned an indictment.

When the trial judge in Los Angeles County refused to grant the defendants' motion to change venue, they appealed and the ruling was overturned. The case was then reassigned to a different court, in suburban Ventura County. The district attorney's office did not appeal the intermediate appellate court's decision to transfer venue, nor did it challenge the selection of Ventura County as the new venue site. Trial commenced in Simi Valley before a predominantly white jury, containing no African American jurors; King was an African American. The prosecution's case at trial relied heavily on the videotape. The prosecution did not call an expert on the use of force by police until the rebuttal phase of the trial. The prosecutors also did not present any civilian witnesses to the beating. Rodney King did not testify in the case because of his prior criminal background and his inconsistent prior statements about the beating.

The state court jury acquitted all the officers of the excessive force and assault charges. Following the verdict, riots erupted in Los Angeles; at least 45 people were killed and more than 5,000 buildings were destroyed. Political and community leaders in Los Angeles asked for a federal prosecution of the officers. The President announced on television that he was surprised by the verdict and that the federal authorities would renew their investigation of the matter.

Federal prosecutors could charge the officers under 18 U.S.C. §242 with willfully violating the civil rights of Rodney King. Section 242 provides in pertinent part:

> Whoever, under color of any law . . . willfully subjects any inhabitant of any State . . . to the deprivation of any rights, privileges, or immunities secured or protected by the Constitution or laws of the United States [shall] if bodily injury results . . . be fined under this title or imprisoned not more than ten years, or both. . . .

A provision of the California constitution and a California statute both prohibit a state prosecution if the federal government has already prosecuted the defendant for the "same offense." Cal. Const. art I, §15; Cal. Penal Code §§656, 793-794. As U.S. Attorney for the Central District of California, would you file charges against the officers? What legal considerations would be relevant to your choice? What other considerations? Compare Laurie Levenson, The Future of State and Federal Civil Rights Prosecutions: The Lessons of the Rodney King Trial, 41 UCLA L. Rev. 509 (1994); Powell v. Superior Court, 283 Cal. Rptr. 777 (Ct. App. 1991) (venue); United States v. Powell, 34 F.3d 1416 (9th Cir. 1994); Koon v. United States, 518 U.S. 81 (1996) (sentencing).

Notes

1. *Double jeopardy and dual sovereigns: majority position.* The Supreme Court ultimately decided, in Benton v Maryland, 395 U.S. 784 (1969), that the due process clause of the Fourteenth Amendment incorporates double jeopardy requirements against state governments. The Supreme Court, however, never repudiated its 1959 decision in *Bartkus*, despite all the changes in state-federal relations that it wrought through its incorporation decisions from that same era. See United States v. Lara, 541 U.S. 193 (2004) (dual sovereign doctrine permits federal government to prosecute Native Americans for offenses after they have already been convicted of similar offenses in tribal courts). See Anthony J. Colangelo, Double Jeopardy and Multiple Sovereigns: A Jurisdictional Theory, 86 Wash. U. L. Rev. 769 (2009).

A substantial majority of states follow the U.S. Supreme Court and hold, under state constitutional provisions, that the double jeopardy bar does not prohibit a second prosecution by a different sovereign, even for an offense defined by identical elements that would be considered the "same offence" within one jurisdiction. See State v. Franklin, 735 P.2d 34 (Utah 1987) (avowed racist killed two black men who were jogging in park with two white women; federal conviction for civil rights crime does not bar state murder trial under state statute or constitution). A few states have extended their constitutional double jeopardy provisions to bar a second prosecution for the same offense — or sometimes a similar offense — if it has been prosecuted in another jurisdiction.

2. *Dual sovereign statutes.* In contrast to the narrow constitutional rulings, more than a dozen states reject the dual sovereignty doctrine by statute. See, e.g., Cal. Penal Code §656 ("Whenever on the trial of an accused person it appears that

upon a criminal prosecution under the laws of another State, Government, or country, founded upon the act or omission in respect to which he is on trial, he has been acquitted or convicted, it is a sufficient defense"). Most statutory limits on second prosecutions are limited to particular categories of offenses, such as the Ohio statute relating to drug offenses. Typically, these statutes are based on either the Uniform Narcotic Drug Act or the Uniform Controlled Substances Act. Unif. Narcotic Drug Act 21, 9B U.L.A. 284 (1958); Unif. Controlled Substances Act 418, 9 U.L.A. 596 (1990). See State v. Hansen, 627 N.W.2d 195 (Wis. 2001) (state statute applicable to controlled substance offenses bars prosecution of defendant by state officials for offenses arising out of the same conduct for which the defendant has been federally prosecuted). Why might legislatures restrict statutory double jeopardy provisions to specified types of crimes? The statutes are intended to prevent the unfairness of multiple prosecutions and to avoid the unnecessary use of state resources to prosecute cases already adequately prosecuted in federal courts. They often provide for exceptions when a reprosecution serves a different purpose or addresses a different evil from the earlier prosecution. See Ga. Code Ann. §16-1-8(c) (barring reprosecution except to prevent a "substantially more serious" or different harm or evil). For an exploration of the variety of state statutes on dual prosecutions, see the web extension for this chapter at *http://www.crimpro.com/extension/ch14*.

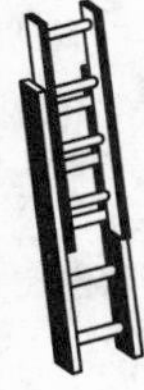

3. *Silver platters and dual sovereigns.* When more than one system can prosecute a criminal case, choice of law questions will crop up. For instance, which system's rules will be used to evaluate the work of the government agents who collected the evidence? Will the agents of one sovereign, acting in violation of the rules of their own government, be able to offer any evidence they obtain on a "silver platter" to prosecutors in another jurisdiction? When the federal constitution creates the obligations for the government agents, the answer is clear: No court (state or federal) may rely on evidence obtained by any state or federal agents in violation of the federal constitution. But what happens when the states have different rules from the federal government? If a state has its own rules (constitutional or statutory) to control government agents, and its agents violate those rules and offer the tainted evidence to federal prosecutors, the federal courts will admit the evidence. See United States v. Wright, 16 F.3d 1429 (6th Cir. 1994). State courts also accept evidence from government agents in another jurisdiction that violate the rules of that other jurisdiction. See Burge v. State, 443 S.W.2d 720 (Tex. Crim. App. 1969). Should a prosecutorial office policy dealing with prosecutions by multiple jurisdictions also address the use of evidence obtained in violation of law in another jurisdiction?

4. *Creation of the federal* Petite *policy.* Some jurisdictions that do not have constitutional or statutory limitations on filing cases already prosecuted in another jurisdiction nonetheless have *internal* prosecutorial rules or guidelines limiting successive prosecutions. The best-known illustration is the federal *Petite* policy. One week after the decision in *Bartkus,* which made it clear that the "dual sovereign" exception to the constitutional doctrine of double jeopardy would allow both state and federal prosecutions of the same crime, the Department of Justice issued a policy limiting federal prosecution after a state prosecution. The policy allows a federal prosecution following a state prosecution only when necessary to advance compelling interests of federal law enforcement. The policy later took its name from Petite v. United States, 361 U.S. 529 (1960), in which the Court noted with approval the existence of the policy. It was designed to limit successive prosecutions for the

same offense to situations involving distinct federal and state interests. In announcing the policy, Attorney General William Rogers stated:

> We should continue to make every effort to cooperate with state and local authorities to the end that the trial occur in the jurisdiction, whether it be state or federal, where the public interest is best served. If this be determined accurately, and is followed by efficient and intelligent cooperation of state and federal law enforcement authorities, then consideration of a second prosecution very seldom should arise.

Dept. of Justice Press Release, Apr. 6, 1959, at 3. The policy creates internal guidance only and does not create any rights that a defendant can enforce in court. See United States v. Snell, 592 F.2d 1083 (9th Cir. 1979). Are such policies properly considered "law"?

5. *Double jeopardy and international extradition.* The law in some other nations clearly rejects any dual sovereignty exception. As global legal regimes emerge, should double jeopardy principles bar multiple prosecutions by different countries? Is the principle barring double jeopardy an essential element of human rights? A partial answer to this question may be worked out on a bilateral basis as part of extradition treaties, for if a country cannot obtain control over the defendant, it is difficult to conduct a trial or to punish a person.

The European Union (EU) Convention implementing the Schengen Agreement of 1985 states in Article 54 that "[a] person who has been finally judged by a Contracting Party may not be prosecuted by another Contracting Party for the same offences provided that, where he is sentenced, the sentence has been served or is currently being served or can no longer be carried out under the sentencing laws of the Contracting Party." In two consolidated cases, the European Court of Justice held in 2003 that under this provision a person cannot be prosecuted in another member state even if (1) his case was discontinued by the prosecution after payment of a certain amount of money (based on a procedure of discontinuation) or (2) the case was settled out of court through a monetary payment (also based on national procedure). C-187/01 *Hyüseyin Gözütok* and C-385/01 *Klaus Brügge* (Feb. 11, 2003). Article 54 sweeps far more broadly than internal United States double jeopardy barriers. The decision is noteworthy because it equates the discontinuation of procedures through a decision by the public prosecutor with a trial (or other judicial action).

6. *Double jeopardy and the Interstate Agreement on Detainers.* Even in the domestic U.S. context, one state's refusal to extradite a suspect could limit the capacity of another state to try that person regardless of the double jeopardy law in either jurisdiction. The possibility of such conflicts, however, has been reduced through the Interstate Agreement on Detainers, which provides a regular method of processing criminal charges filed by more than one state. The IAD is an interstate compact that most state legislatures have adopted. See Calif. Penal Code §1389. It allows prosecutors to notify officials holding a criminal defendant in an out-of-state facility that the state wishes to pursue criminal charges against the defendant; such notice is called a "detainer." The IAD also allows the defendant to request that the state issuing the detainer dispose of the charges promptly.

2. *"Same Offence"*

The limitations on double jeopardy apply only when a person is placed twice in jeopardy for the "same offence." Determining whether a second offense is the "same" offense as the first one raises difficult challenges. First, many criminal codes include hundreds or even thousands of crimes with overlapping elements, aimed at punishing similar harms. The federal code, for example, includes more than 3,000 separate offenses. Because of the intricacy of most criminal codes (to put it kindly), courts have conceded that charges need not be brought twice under precisely the same statute before concluding that the prosecutions are for the same offense. How to determine whether charges under different code provisions should be considered the same offense is the topic of this subsection.

The Supreme Court has tried several approaches to the problem. In Blockburger v. United States, 284 U.S. 299 (1932), the defendant was convicted of three counts of violating the Harrison Narcotics Act based on the sale of small amounts of morphine hydrochloride. One of the counts of conviction charged a sale of eight grains of the drug not from the original stamped package; another count alleged that the same sale was not made according to a written order of the purchaser, as required by the statute. The court sentenced Blockburger to five years in prison and imposed a fine of $2,000 upon each count, the terms of imprisonment to run consecutively. Blockburger asserted that these two counts constituted one offense for which only a single penalty could be imposed. The Court disagreed, holding that "where the same act or transaction constitutes a violation of two distinct statutory provisions, the test to be applied to determine whether there are two offenses or only one is whether each provision requires proof of an additional fact which the other does not." 284 U.S. at 304.

The *Blockburger* test was criticized because the government could so easily obtain multiple convictions based on the same conduct, but it remained the applicable standard in federal courts and in most state courts until 1990, when the Court decided Grady v. Corbin, 495 U.S. 508 (1990). Thomas Corbin drove his car across the center line while intoxicated, killing Brenda Dirago and injuring her husband, Daniel. Corbin was charged with two misdemeanors, driving while intoxicated and failing to keep right of the median. He pleaded guilty and was punished with a $350 fine, a $10 surcharge, and a six-month license revocation. Two months later a grand jury indicted Corbin for reckless manslaughter, second-degree vehicular manslaughter, and criminally negligent homicide for causing the death of Brenda Dirago, third-degree reckless assault for causing physical injury to Daniel Dirago, and driving while intoxicated. The bill of particulars supporting the indictment alleged that Corbin operated a motor vehicle on a public highway in an intoxicated condition, failed to keep right of the median, and drove approximately 45 to 50 miles per hour in heavy rain, "a speed too fast for the weather and road conditions then pending." Corbin challenged the indictment as a violation of double jeopardy. The Court agreed, and added a "same conduct" test on top of the *Blockburger* "same elements" test for those cases when the government pursues successive prosecutions:

> If *Blockburger* constituted the entire double jeopardy inquiry in the context of successive prosecutions, the State could try Corbin in four consecutive trials: for failure to keep right of the median, for driving while intoxicated, for assault, and for homicide.

> The State could improve its presentation of proof with each trial, assessing which witnesses gave the most persuasive testimony, which documents had the greatest impact, and which opening and closing arguments most persuaded the jurors. Corbin would be forced either to contest each of these trials or to plead guilty to avoid the harassment and expense.
>
> Thus, a subsequent prosecution must do more than merely survive the *Blockburger* test. [The] Double Jeopardy Clause bars any subsequent prosecution in which the government, to establish an essential element of an offense charged in that prosecution, will prove conduct that constitutes an offense for which the defendant has already been prosecuted. This is not an "actual evidence" or "same evidence" test. The critical inquiry is what conduct the State will prove, not the evidence the State will use to prove that conduct. [The] presentation of specific evidence in one trial does not forever prevent the government from introducing that same evidence in a subsequent proceeding. [495 U.S. at 520-521.]

Applying the new standard, the Court held that the double jeopardy clause barred the second prosecution because "the State has admitted that it will prove the entirety of the conduct for which Corbin was convicted — driving while intoxicated and failing to keep right of the median — to establish essential elements of the homicide and assault offenses."

Three years later, the Court overruled *Grady* and reinstated the "same elements" test as the basic way to identify double jeopardy violations in United States v. Dixon, 509 U.S. 688 (1993). The complex facts in *Dixon* concerned two cases in which contempt judgments — in one case for violation of a condition of release, and in the other for violation of civil protection orders — were entered before each defendant was prosecuted for the offenses underlying the contempt violation.

> *Grady* must be overruled. Unlike *Blockburger* analysis, whose definition of what prevents two crimes from being the "same offence," has deep historical roots and has been accepted in numerous precedents of this Court, *Grady* lacks constitutional roots. The "same-conduct" rule it announced is wholly inconsistent with earlier Supreme Court precedent and with the clear common-law understanding of double jeopardy. . . . *Grady* was not only wrong in principle; it has already proved unstable in application. [We] think it time to acknowledge what is now, three years after *Grady*, compellingly clear: the case was a mistake.

509 U.S. at 704, 709, 711. The first of the following two cases shows the *Blockburger* test at work. The second case discusses the choices among different tests for the "same offense" and illustrates the response of state courts to the leadership of the U.S. Supreme Court in this difficult area.

■ ROBERT TAYLOR v. COMMONWEALTH

995 S.W.2d 355 (Ky. 1999)

COOPER, J.

. . . On the afternoon of October 9, 1996, Appellant, then seventeen years of age, his girlfriend, Lucy Cotton, and Cotton's infant son had attended the Daniel Boone Festival and were traveling through rural Knox County in a 1985 Buick owned by Cotton's mother. They had with them a .22 rifle, a .38 Derringer handgun, and two shotguns. When the vehicle stalled, Appellant sought assistance from Herman McCreary, who lived nearby. McCreary agreed to help and drove his 1984 Ford pickup truck to the location of the stalled vehicle. Upon arrival, he observed Cotton sitting in the passenger seat of the Buick holding a child in her lap. Several attempts to jump-start the Buick failed. According to Cotton, Appellant told her, "If it don't start this time, I'm gonna take his truck," and armed himself with the .22 rifle and the .38 handgun. According to Appellant, Cotton pointed the .38 handgun at him and threatened to shoot him if he did not steal McCreary's truck.

When a final attempt to jump-start the Buick was unsuccessful, Appellant got out of the vehicle, pointed the .22 rifle at McCreary, and ordered him to lie on the ground. When McCreary complied, Appellant fired a round from the rifle into the ground near McCreary's head. According to Cotton, Appellant then struck McCreary in the head with the stock of the rifle. McCreary temporarily lost consciousness. Upon regaining consciousness, McCreary experienced dizziness and noticed blood coming from the left side of his head. Appellant then told McCreary to get into the ditch beside the road or he would "blow his head off." McCreary again complied, whereupon Appellant, Cotton and the child departed the scene in McCreary's truck. McCreary walked to a neighbor's house and called the police. [Taylor and Cotton were later apprehended and Taylor was convicted of assault in second degree, robbery in first degree, and possession of handgun by a minor. He was sentenced to two ten-year prison terms, to be served consecutively, for the assault and robbery charges, along with a twelve-month term for the weapons charge, to be served concurrently. Taylor] asserts that his convictions violated the constitutional proscription against double jeopardy. U.S. Const. amend. V; Ky. Const. §13.

In Commonwealth v. Burge, 947 S.W.2d 805, 809-11 (1997), we reinstated the "*Blockburger* rule," Blockburger v. United States, 284 U.S. 299 (1932), as incorporated in KRS §505.020, as the sole basis for determining whether multiple convictions arising out of a single course of conduct constitutes double jeopardy. The test in this case is not whether all three convictions were premised upon the use or possession of a firearm, or whether both the assault and the robbery occurred in the course of a single transaction. Where the "same act or transaction constitutes a violation of two distinct statutory provisions, the test to be applied to determine whether there are two offenses or only one is whether each provision requires proof of an additional fact which the other does not." Blockburger v. United States, 284 U.S. 299, 304 (1932).

KRS §515.020(1) defines robbery in the first degree as follows:

> A person is guilty of robbery in the first degree when, in the course of committing a theft, he uses or threatens the immediate use of physical force upon another person with intent to accomplish the theft and when he:
>
> (a) Causes physical injury to any person who is not a participant in the crime; or
>
> (b) Is armed with a deadly weapon; or
>
> (c) Uses or threatens the use of a dangerous instrument upon any person who is not a participant in the crime.

The first paragraph of the statute sets forth three elements which must be proven in any robbery case, viz: (1) In the course of committing a theft, (2) the defendant used or threatened the immediate use of physical force upon another person (3) with the intent to accomplish the theft. Subsections (a), (b), and (c) of the statute then describe three separate and distinct factual situations, any one of which could constitute the fourth element of the offense. The indictment of Appellant for robbery in the first degree in this case charged that he committed the offense "by being armed with a deadly weapon." The jury was instructed that it could convict Appellant of robbery in the first degree only if it believed beyond a reasonable doubt that "when he did so, he was armed with a .22 rifle." Thus, both the indictment and the instruction were predicated upon a violation of KRS 515.020(1)(b). Neither the indictment nor the instruction required Appellant to have caused a physical injury to McCreary or to have used or threatened the use of a dangerous instrument upon McCreary.

KRS 508.020(1) defines assault in the second degree as follows:

> A person is guilty of assault in the second degree when:
> (a) He intentionally causes serious physical injury to another person; or
> (b) He intentionally causes physical injury to another person by means of a deadly weapon or a dangerous instrument; or
> (c) He wantonly causes serious physical injury to another person by means of a deadly weapon or a dangerous instrument.

The statute sets forth three alternative factual situations by which the offense can be committed. Although the indictment charged Appellant with having committed the offense "by striking Herman McCreary with a pistol," the jury instruction conformed to the testimony of Lucy Cotton, who provided the only evidence with respect to this offense:

> You will find the defendant guilty under this instruction if, and only if, you believe from the evidence beyond a reasonable doubt all of the following: (a) that in this county on or about October 9, 1996 and before the finding of the indictment herein, he inflicted an injury upon Herman McCreary by striking him with a .22 rifle, a deadly weapon; AND (b) that in so doing, the defendant intentionally caused physical injury to Herman McCreary.[1]

Thus, conviction of either the assault or the robbery of McCreary required proof of an element not required to prove the other. The conviction of robbery required proof of a theft, which was not required to convict of assault. The conviction of assault required proof of a physical injury to McCreary, whereas the conviction of robbery required proof only that Appellant used or threatened the use of physical force upon McCreary while armed with a .22 rifle. . . .

STUMBO, J., dissenting.

Respectfully, I must dissent. I believe Appellant's convictions for both assault and robbery violated the prohibition against double jeopardy. . . . As written, the

1. Appellant did not object to the variance of this instruction from the language of the indictment. The indictment described the weapon used to inflict the injury as a pistol, whereas the instruction described the weapon as a .22 rifle. Generally, instructions should be based on the evidence introduced at trial, and any variance between the language of the indictment and the language of the instruction is not deemed prejudicial unless the defendant was misled.

indictment did not violate the double jeopardy prohibition. The indictment charged Appellant with "Assault in the Second Degree by striking Herman McCreary with a pistol" and "Robbery in the First Degree by being armed with a deadly weapon while in the course of committing a theft of Herman McCreary." Clearly, these offenses arise from two distinct statutes. As charged, each would have required proof of a fact which the other did not. For the assault, the prosecution would have had to prove that Appellant struck McCreary with the .38 pistol causing a physical injury. For the robbery, the prosecution would have had to prove Appellant used or threatened to use physical force on McCreary while armed with a deadly weapon (presumably the .22 rifle) during the course of the theft of his truck.

In the end, however, the prosecution was unable to maintain this logically sound but practically impossible distinction. By the time the jury was instructed, the assault had merged into the robbery so that one was clearly included within the other. This is so because the jury instruction on second-degree assault required the jury to find the offense was accomplished "by striking him with a .22 rifle, a deadly weapon." The jury instruction on first-degree robbery required the jury to find Appellant "used or threatened the immediate use of physical force upon Herman McCreary; AND (c) that when he did so, he was armed with a .22 rifle." This melding of the charges allowed the jury to consider any assault with the .22 rifle during the incident as an element of the robbery and thus made the assault charge a lesser included offense of the robbery charge. . . .

PEOPLE v. MELISSA NUTT

677 N.W.2d 1 (Mich. 2004)

YOUNG, J.

. . . On December 10, 1998, Darrold Smith's home in Lapeer County was burglarized. Four firearms and a bow and arrows were stolen from the home. Lapeer County police officers and those of adjacent Oakland County conducted a joint investigation concerning three Lapeer County burglaries, including the burglary of Smith's home. The officers obtained a search warrant for a cabin in Oakland County that was occupied by defendant and John Crosley. During the execution of the warrant on December 14, 1998, three of Smith's stolen firearms were found hidden underneath a mattress inside the cabin. Smith's bow and arrows and property stolen from another residence were also seized during the search.

Defendant confessed to a Lapeer County detective that she participated as a getaway driver during three burglaries that occurred the week of December 10, 1998, including the burglary of the Smith residence. Defendant admitted that three of the guns stolen from Smith were concealed underneath a mattress in the Oakland County cabin.

In January 1999, defendant was charged in Lapeer County with three counts of second-degree home invasion and three counts of larceny in a building. Meanwhile, on February 16, 1999, an arrest warrant was issued in Oakland County alleging that defendant had committed one offense of receiving and concealing a stolen firearm.

On February 22, 1999, defendant pleaded guilty in Lapeer County of one charge of second-degree home invasion in connection with the burglary of the Smith residence and the theft of the firearms. The remaining five charges [from

Lapeer County] were dismissed pursuant to a plea agreement. Defendant was sentenced to probation.

In July 1999, defendant was bound over for trial in Oakland County on the charge of receiving and concealing a stolen firearm. Defendant moved to dismiss the charge, contending that it constituted an improper successive prosecution in violation of the double jeopardy clauses of the federal and state constitutions. Defendant argued that pursuant to People v. White, 212 N.W.2d 222 (Mich. 1973), the state was required to join at one trial all charges arising from a continuous time sequence that demonstrated a single intent and goal. Thus, defendant maintained, she could not be tried in Oakland County for possession of the same firearms that she was alleged to have stolen during the home invasion for which she was convicted in Lapeer County. The trial court granted defendant's motion to dismiss. . . .

The United States and Michigan Constitutions protect a person from being twice placed in jeopardy for the same offense. The prohibition against double jeopardy provides three related protections: (1) it protects against a second prosecution for the same offense after acquittal; (2) it protects against a second prosecution for the same offense after conviction; and (3) it protects against multiple punishments for the same offense. The first two of these three protections concern the "successive prosecutions" strand of the Double Jeopardy Clause, which is implicated in the case before us. In particular, because our Double Jeopardy Clause is essentially identical to its federal counterpart, we must determine whether the term "same offense" in our Constitution was, in *White*, properly accorded a meaning that is different from the construction of that term in the federal Constitution. . . .

Federal Successive Prosecutions Protection and the Same-Elements Test

Application of the same-elements test, commonly known as the "*Blockburger* test," is the well-established method of defining the Fifth Amendment term "same offence." The test, which has deep historical roots, focuses on the statutory elements of the offense. If each requires proof of a fact that the other does not, the *Blockburger* test is satisfied, notwithstanding a substantial overlap in the proof offered to establish the crimes.

[The Double Jeopardy Clause] was designed to embody the protection of the English common-law pleas of former jeopardy, "auterfoits acquit" (formerly acquitted) and "auterfoits convict" (formerly convicted), which applied only to prosecutions for the identical act and crime. An examination of the historical record reveals that the English practice, as understood in 1791, did not recognize auterfoits acquit and auterfoits convict as good pleas against successive prosecutions for crimes whose elements were distinct, even though based on the same act. . . .

Although Justice William Brennan was a persistent advocate of the same transaction test, see Werneth v. Idaho, 449 U.S. 1129 (1981) (Brennan, J., dissenting), the idea that crimes arising from the same criminal episode constitute the same offenses for double jeopardy purposes has been consistently rejected by the United States Supreme Court. Instead, the . . . *Blockburger* same-elements analysis was consistently applied by the Court . . . until the Court in Grady v. Corbin, 495 U.S. 508 (1990), adopted a "same-conduct" rule — a somewhat compromised version of Justice Brennan's "same transaction" test — as an additional step to be performed in addressing successive prosecutions claims. In an opinion authored by Justice William Brennan, the Court held that "the Double Jeopardy Clause bars a subsequent prosecution if, to establish an essential element of an offense charged in that prosecution, the government will prove conduct that constitutes an offense for which the defendant has already been prosecuted."

Justice Scalia dissented, noting that the majority's holding was wholly without historical foundation and that it created a procedural mandatory joinder rule: "In practice, [the majority's holding] will require prosecutors to observe a rule we have explicitly rejected in principle: that all charges arising out of a single occurrence must be joined in a single indictment." Looking to the text of the Double Jeopardy Clause and its origins in the common law, Justice Scalia opined that the *Blockburger* rule best gave effect to the plain language of the Clause, "which protects individuals from being twice put in jeopardy 'for the same offense,' not for the same conduct or actions."

The *Grady* same-conduct test was short-lived. In United States v. Dixon, 509 U.S. 688 (1993), the Court overruled *Grady* as wrongly decided for the reasons expressed in Justice Scalia's *Grady* dissent and returned to the *Blockburger* formulation of the test for both successive prosecutions and multiple punishments. . . .

Meaning of "Same Offense" in Michigan's Double Jeopardy Provision

. . . In accordance with the principle that our double jeopardy provision was intended to embody English common-law tenets of former jeopardy, this Court more than one hundred years ago rejected the "same transaction" approach and instead embraced the federal same-elements test as supplying the functional definition of "same offense" under our Constitution's Double Jeopardy Clause. In People v. Parrow, 45 N.W. 514 (Mich. 1890), this Court held that Const. 1850, art. 6, §29 did not preclude the defendant's prosecution for larceny of money stolen during an alleged burglary where the defendant had previously been acquitted of burglary. . . .

However, in People v. White, 212 N.W.2d 222 (Mich. 1973), the majority . . . adopted the same transaction test advocated unsuccessfully by Justice William Brennan — one even more expansive than the defunct compromise *Grady* test. The defendant in *White* followed the victim to her home in Inkster, forced her to get into his car, drove her to Detroit, and, while in Detroit, raped her. The defendant was first tried and convicted in Wayne Circuit Court on a kidnapping charge. Subsequently, the defendant was tried and convicted in Detroit Recorder's Court on charges of rape and felonious assault.

[The Court] held that the rape and felonious assault convictions were violative of art. 1, §15. We noted that several other states had adopted the same transaction test, either under their own constitutions or under statutes requiring mandatory joinder, and that . . . the same transaction test was necessary to effectuate the intent of the framers that the state not be allowed to make repeated attempts to convict a defendant. Without reference to our Constitution, its text, or its ratification process, the *White* Court opined that the same transaction test fostered sound policy:

> In a time of overcrowded criminal dockets, prosecutors and judges should attempt to bring to trial a defendant as expeditiously and economically as possible. A far more

> basic reason for adopting the same transaction test is to prevent harassment of a defendant. The joining of all charges arising out of the same criminal episode at one trial . . . will enable a defendant to consider the matter closed and save the costs of redundant litigation. It will also help . . . to equalize the adversary capabilities of grossly unequal litigants and prevent prosecutorial sentence shopping.

The *White* Court also noted that the equivalent of the same transaction test had long been the standard applied to civil actions by the court rule governing joinder and by the doctrines of collateral estoppel and res judicata. Finally, the Court concluded that the three crimes committed by the defendant were all part of a single criminal transaction because they "were committed in a continuous time sequence and displayed a single intent and goal — sexual intercourse with the complainant.". . .

In Crampton v. 54-A Dist. Judge, 245 N.W.2d 28 (Mich. 1976), this Court, recognizing the difficulty of applying the same transaction test, introduced a different inflection on the *White* "single intent and goal" factor where some of the offenses at issue did not involve criminal intent: . . . "where one or more of the offenses does not involve criminal intent, the criterion is whether the offenses are part of the same criminal episode, and whether the offenses involve laws intended to prevent the same or similar harm or evil, not a substantially different, or a very different kind of, harm or evil." . . .

In our 1963 Constitution the narrower language of the 1850 and 1908 double jeopardy provisions was replaced with language similar to that of the original Constitution of 1835 and the Fifth Amendment: "No person shall be subject for the same offense to be twice put in jeopardy." Art. 1, §15.

It is immediately striking that the plain language of the provision provides no support for the conclusion that the term "same offense" should be interpreted by reference to whether a crime arises out of the "same transaction" as another. Rather, we believe that the plain and obvious meaning of the term "offense" is "crime" or "transgression.". . .

The ultimate inquiry, of course, is the meaning ascribed to the phrase "same offense" by the ratifiers of our 1963 Constitution. Examination of the record of the Constitutional Convention of 1961 provides the historical context and persuasive support for our decision to return to the original meaning given to the Fifth Amendment–based double jeopardy language in art. 1, §15.

Constitutional Convention Committee Proposal Number 15 recommended that Const. 1908, art. 2, §14 be revised to mirror the language of the Fifth Amendment, with the deletion of the "archaic" words "of life and limb." Delegate Stevens explained that the "Supreme Court of Michigan . . . has virtually held that [Const. 1908, art. 2, §14] means the same thing as the provision in the federal constitution, and that is what we have put in. . . ." It was reported that the change was not substantive and that the judiciary committee wished simply to bring the text of the double jeopardy provision "in line with the law as it now stands in the state of Michigan" and "in line with the federal constitution."

Of even greater significance to our analysis is the Address to the People[26] accompanying Const. 1963, art. 1, §15:

> . . . The new language of the first sentence involves the substitution of the double jeopardy provision from the U.S. Constitution in place of the present provision which merely prohibits "acquittal on the merits." This is more consistent with the actual practice of the courts in Michigan. Thus, the ratifiers were advised that (1) the double jeopardy protection conferred by our 1963 Constitution would parallel that of the federal constitution, and (2) . . . the proposal was meant to bring our double jeopardy provision into conformity with what this Court had already determined it to mean. . . .

In 1973, this Court disregarded decades of precedent and, without consideration of the will of the people of this state in ratifying the Double Jeopardy Clause in our 1963 Constitution, adopted Justice William Brennan's long-rejected "same transaction" test. . . . In the absence of any evidence that the term "offense" was understood by the people to comprise all criminal acts arising out of a single criminal episode, we are compelled to overrule *White*. [The] same-elements test best gives effect to the intent of the ratifiers of the 1963 Constitution.[28]

Application

Defendant's Oakland County prosecution for possession of stolen firearms, following her conviction for second-degree home invasion in Lapeer County, withstands constitutional scrutiny under the same-elements test. Defendant was convicted of home invasion pursuant to MCL 750.110a(3), which provided: "A person who breaks and enters a dwelling with intent to commit a felony or a larceny in the dwelling or a person who enters a dwelling without permission with intent to commit a felony or a larceny in the dwelling is guilty of home invasion in the second degree." Required for a conviction of this offense was proof that defendant (1) entered a dwelling, either by a breaking or without permission, (2) with the intent to commit a felony or a larceny in the dwelling.

Defendant now stands charged with receiving and concealing a stolen firearm in violation of MCL 750.535b(2), which provides: "A person who receives, conceals, stores, barters, sells, disposes of, pledges, or accepts as security for a loan a stolen firearm or stolen ammunition, knowing that the firearm or ammunition was stolen, is guilty of a felony. . . ." Thus, the Oakland County Prosecutor is required to prove that defendant (1) received, concealed, stored, bartered, sold, disposed of, pledged, or accepted as security for a loan (2) a stolen firearm or stolen ammunition (3) knowing that the firearm or ammunition was stolen.

Clearly, there is no identity of elements between these two offenses. Each offense requires proof of elements that the other does not. Because the two offenses

26. The Address to the People, widely distributed to the public prior to the ratification vote in order to explain the import of the sundry proposals, is a valuable tool in determining whether a possible "common understanding" diverges from the plain meaning of the actual words of our Constitution.

28. [Principles] of collateral estoppel and properly adopted procedural joinder rules might well compel the dismissal of charges in certain circumstances. Nevertheless, collateral estoppel and joinder are discrete, nonconstitutional concepts that should not be conflated with the constitutional double jeopardy protection. [We] will be requesting the Committee on the Rules of Criminal Procedure to consider whether our permissive joinder rule, MCR 6.120(A), should be amended to impose mandatory joinder of all the charges against a defendant arising out of the same transaction. . . .

are nowise the same offense under either the Fifth Amendment or art. 1, §15, we . . . hold that defendant is not entitled to the dismissal of the Oakland County charge.

RESPONSE TO THE DISSENT

[The dissent] asserts that we have given short shrift to the purpose of the double jeopardy provision's successive prosecutions strand, which is to prevent the state from making repeated attempts to obtain a conviction for an alleged offense. However, the instant case in fact illustrates that this venerable purpose is in no way served by the ill-conceived rule set forth in *White*. Defendant was not subjected to repeated attempts to convict her of "an alleged offense." Rather, she was subjected to prosecution for two independent offenses in two separate jurisdictions. Application of the *White* rule, rather than ensuring that the state would not get more than "one bite at the apple," would preclude the state from ever trying defendant for one of the charges against her. This is not at all consistent with the purpose of the double jeopardy protection. . . .

CAVANAGH, J., dissenting.

. . . This Court's decision to overrule *White* is grounded in the improper belief that the same elements test is the sole test used by the United States Supreme Court to protect citizens' constitutional rights under the United States Constitution. However, the same elements test, also referred to as the *Blockburger* test, is not as entrenched in federal jurisprudence as the majority claims. . . .

In numerous cases, the United States Supreme Court has used other tests because it recognized that the same elements test is not an adequate safeguard to protect a citizen's constitutional right against double jeopardy. In Ashe v. Swenson, 397 U.S. 436 (1970), the United States Supreme Court held that the double jeopardy clause includes a collateral estoppel guarantee. . . . As stated in Albernaz v. United States, 450 U.S. 333, 340 (1981), "The *Blockburger* test is a rule of statutory construction, and because it serves as a means of discerning congressional purpose the rule should not be controlling where, for example, there is a clear indication of contrary legislative intent." Further, in In re Nielsen, 131 U.S. 176 (1889), a conviction for unlawful cohabitation precluded a subsequent charge of adultery because the incident occurred during the same two and a half year period as that for unlawful cohabitation. In Harris v. Oklahoma, 433 U.S. 682 (1977), the defendant was convicted of felony murder after a store clerk was killed during a robbery. After the defendant's conviction for felony murder, the defendant was tried and convicted of robbery with firearms. The United States Supreme Court held that when "conviction of a greater crime . . . cannot be had without conviction of the lesser crime, the Double Jeopardy Clause bars prosecution for the lesser crime after conviction of the greater one." And in Brown v. Ohio, 432 U.S. 161 (1977), double jeopardy barred a subsequent prosecution for a greater offense even though the greater offense required proof of an additional element. . . .

Our Double Jeopardy Clause is meant to protect our citizens from government zeal and overreaching; yet, the same elements test permits multiple prosecutions stemming from a single incident. "The same-elements test is an inadequate safeguard, for it leaves the constitutional guarantee at the mercy of a legislature's decision to modify statutory definitions." United States v. Dixon, 509 U.S. 688, 735 (1993) (White, J., dissenting). Notably, a technical comparison of the elements is neither constitutionally sound nor easy to apply. While the same elements test appears at first glance to be easy to apply, this Court's recent struggle with whether materiality is an element of perjury in People v. Lively, 664 N.W.2d 223 (Mich. 2003), provides proof to the contrary. . . . If our courts struggle with the basics of determining what elements constitute a crime, it is inevitable that these struggles will continue when courts attempt to determine whether two crimes contain the same elements.

In contrast to the same elements test, the same transaction test requires the government to join at one trial all the charges against a defendant arising out of a continuous time sequence, when the offenses shared a single intent and goal. Although a single transaction can give rise to distinct offenses, the charges must be joined at one trial. However, the same transaction test also offers flexibility for certain circumstances, such as when facts necessary to sustain a charge have not yet occurred or have not been discovered despite due diligence. . . .

In this case, defendant pleaded guilty of second-degree home invasion, MCL 750.110a(3). She was subsequently charged with receiving and concealing stolen firearms, MCL 750.535b. Notably, defendant was the driver in the home invasion during which the guns were stolen. She also admitted that the guns concealed were the ones stolen during the home invasion. Defendant's actions represent a single intent and goal, as well as the events being part of a continuous time sequence. Almost universally, inherent in stealing an item is receiving it and concealing it, if only for a brief time. Defendant's intent when she participated in the home invasion was to successfully steal the guns. Defendant's intent when she participated in the concealing of the guns was to successfully steal the guns. The subsequent prosecution for receiving and concealing stolen firearms violated defendant's double jeopardy rights. . . .

Without double jeopardy protections, our citizens are at risk of facing multiple prosecutions by the government, regardless of a prior acquittal. Further, because the state can devote its resources to improving the presentation of its case, the probability of a conviction may increase with each retrial. Accordingly, [after] pleading guilty of second-degree home invasion, defendant's subsequent prosecution for receiving and concealing stolen firearms violated her double jeopardy rights.

NEW YORK CRIMINAL PROCEDURE LAW §40.20

1. A person may not be twice prosecuted for the same offense.

2. A person may not be separately prosecuted for two offenses based upon the same act or criminal transaction unless:

(a) The offenses as defined have substantially different elements and the acts establishing one offense are in the main clearly distinguishable from those establishing the other; or

(b) Each of the offenses as defined contains an element which is not an element of the other, and the statutory provisions defining such offenses are designed to prevent very different kinds of harm or evil; or

(c) One of such offenses consists of criminal possession of contraband matter and the other offense is one involving the use of such contraband matter, other than a sale thereof; or

(d) One of the offenses is assault or some other offense resulting in physical injury to a person, and the other offense is one of homicide based upon the death of such person from the same physical injury, and such death occurs after a prosecution for the assault or other non-homicide offense; or

(e) Each offense involves death, injury, loss or other consequence to a different victim; or

(f) One of the offenses consists of a violation of a statutory provision of another jurisdiction, which offense has been prosecuted in such other jurisdiction and has there been terminated by a court order expressly founded upon insufficiency of evidence to establish some element of such offense which is not an element of the other offense, defined by the laws of this state; or

(g) The present prosecution is for a consummated result offense . . . which occurred in this state and the offense was the result of a conspiracy, facilitation or solicitation prosecuted in another state. . . .

Notes

1. *Determining whether two charges are for the "same offence": majority position.* The Supreme Court's decision in United States v. Dixon, 509 U.S. 688 (1993), reestablished the "same elements" test of Blockburger v. United States, 284 U.S. 299 (1932). Under this test, if the two offenses *each* have at least one distinct "element," they are not treated as the same offense. Hence, multiple trials or multiple punishments based on these offenses do not violate the protection against double jeopardy.

About 30 state courts follow *Dixon* and have adopted (or readopted) the *Blockburger* "same elements" test under state law. See, e.g., State v. Alvarez, 778 A.2d 938 (Conn. 2001). About 10 jurisdictions have interpreted their state constitutions to employ the *Grady* "same conduct" test (or the closely related "same evidence" test) in addition to the *Blockburger* analysis as a limit on multiple prosecutions. See State v. Lessary, 865 P.2d 150 (Haw. 1994). A smaller group of states (about a half dozen) apply a test that places even stronger limits on government attempts to bring multiple prosecutions: the "same transaction" test (also called the "same episode" or "same incident" test) suggested by Justice Brennan in his concurring opinion in Ashe v. Swenson, 397 U.S. 436 (1970). See, e.g., State v. Farley, 725 P.2d 359 (Or.1986). Around 15 states have adopted statutory tests for whether a second charge is for the "same offense"; some statutes mirror the *Blockburger* test, Fla. Stat. §775.021(4)(a), while others add a "same facts" or "same conduct" test.

Trial judges pay close attention to their jury instructions relating to the "same elements" test; as a result, these instructions offer some of the clearest available descriptions of the doctrine. Samples of such instructions appear on the web extension for this chapter at *http://www.crimpro.com/extension/ch14*. The extension also explores some of the many suggestions in the academic literature for reworking this doctrine from the ground up.

2. *Punishment for greater and lesser included offenses.* A lesser included offense is one that is necessarily included within the statutory elements of another offense. Thus, if Crime 1 has elements A and B, it is a lesser included offense for Crime 2, with elements A, B, and C. In a straightforward application of the *Blockburger* test, a prosecution for either Crime 1 or Crime 2 would prevent a later prosecution or punishment for the second crime. An exception to this bar would allow a prosecution

for Crime 2 after a prosecution for Crime 1, if the additional element C had not yet occurred at the time of the Crime 1 prosecution (for instance, if an assault victim dies after the trial for assault goes forward). See Brown v. Ohio, 432 U.S. 161, 169 n.7 (1977).

But the courts have gone beyond this literal understanding of lesser included offenses. Both federal and state courts declare that double jeopardy limits for the "same offense" also apply to "a species of lesser included offense." In Harris v. Oklahoma, 433 U.S. 682 (1977), the court held that a conviction for felony murder barred a later trial of the defendant for the underlying robbery. Strictly speaking, the robbery and felony murder statutes pass the *Blockburger* test: Felony murder requires proof of a killing (robbery does not), and robbery requires proof of forcible taking of property (which felony murder does not necessarily require). But the court was willing to treat robbery and felony murder as the "same offense" because in the *case at hand*, the prosecution was relying on forcible taking of property to establish the predicate felony for felony murder. See also United States v. Dixon, 509 U.S. 688, 697-700 (1993) (criminal contempt of court for violation of judicial order not to commit "any criminal offense" and possession of cocaine with intent to distribute are the same offense); State v. Quick, 206 P.3d 985 (N.M. 2009) (double jeopardy prevents use of single act of drug possession to form basis for possession and possession with intent to distribute convictions; government may not divide stash of drugs into subgroups to support both convictions). On the other hand, the same logic does not seem to apply to conspiracy or "continuing criminal enterprise" crimes. See United States v. Felix, 503 U.S. 378, 387-92 (1992) (conspiracy to manufacture narcotics is not same offense as manufacturing narcotics); Garrett v. United States, 471 U.S. 773, 777-86 (1985) (distribution of marijuana is not same offense as conducting a continuing criminal enterprise to distribute marijuana).

3. *The "multiple punishment" prong of double jeopardy.* Unlike the relatively clear rule against multiple *prosecutions* for the same offense, there are looser limits when the prosecutor files multiple charges in a *single proceeding*, and the defendant claims that the charges are actually an attempt to impose multiple punishments for what is really a single offense. In this setting, the legislature sets the constraints on the prosecutor. In Missouri v. Hunter, 459 U.S. 359 (1983), the Supreme Court held that "the Double Jeopardy Clause does no more than prevent the sentencing court from prescribing greater punishment than the legislature intended." The defendant in *Hunter* was convicted after a single trial for robbery and armed criminal action. The armed criminal action statute explicitly provided that any penalty imposed for the crime "shall be in addition to any punishment provided by law" for any other crime committed with the weapon in question. The Court upheld the convictions and sentences even though the two crimes would be considered the "same offence" for *Blockburger* purposes.

Most states follow Missouri v. Hunter and hold that in the context of a single prosecution, the *Blockburger* test (or an alternative test) only helps determine whether the legislature intended to allow separate convictions and punishments for a single criminal episode or event. See, e.g., State v. Adel, 965 P.2d 1072 (Wash. 1998). The courts reason that the legislature can select from a wide range of punishments for any particular offense. Other states have rejected the majority rule and have applied state law to limit cumulative punishments regardless of the legislature's intent. In one especially difficult area, states are split on whether punishment is acceptable for both felony murder and the underlying felony when they are tried together. See, e.g., Todd v. State, 917 P.2d 674 (Alaska 1996) (allowing multiple punishment); cf. Boulies v. People, 770 P.2d 1274 (Colo. 1989) (state merger rule barring multiple punishment).

What reasons might justify the different treatment of "multiple proceedings" on the one hand, and "multiple punishment" for the same conduct in a single proceeding on the other hand? Does this distinction make sense? See Nancy King, Portioning Punishment: Constitutional Limits on Successive and Excessive Penalties, 144 U. Pa. L. Rev. 101 (1995) (points to illogic of cases allowing multiple punishments in a single trial but not in successive trials; argues for limiting Eighth Amendment to a remedy for excessive punishments imposed in multiple proceedings).

4. *When do double jeopardy claims arise?* Double jeopardy claims can arise at a variety of points in the criminal justice process. A defendant can raise double jeopardy claims as soon as she is charged with multiple counts in a single proceeding. A defendant might challenge even a single count, claiming that jeopardy already attached at an earlier proceeding. Jeopardy "attaches" at an initial trial when the jury is sworn in (for jury trials) or when the first witness is sworn in (for a bench trial) or when the court accepts a guilty plea. The defendant might raise a double jeopardy challenge at the time of sentencing, claiming that the state has requested multiple punishments for the same offense. Double jeopardy challenges might also arise when the state attempts to impose some civil penalties before or after adjudicating the criminal charges.

It is important to recognize that double jeopardy influences the work of all three branches of government. Double jeopardy rules have a substantial impact on what kinds of charges the prosecution chooses to file. Principles of prior jeopardy may also shape the actions of judges at sentencing, when the judge can group together charges to produce a single sentence lower than what technically could be imposed for each separate conviction. Finally, legislators will have a powerful effect on the grouping of crimes when they define the elements of different crimes. Ultimately, are double jeopardy principles anything more than instructions to legislatures to draft cleanly?

5. *Double jeopardy after mistrial.* Most mistrials do not bar a retrial, even though jeopardy has attached; retrial is possible so long as the earlier declaration of mistrial was a "manifest necessity." Mistrials declared after a jury deadlocks typically fall into this category. See Renico v. Lett, 130 S. Ct. 1855 (2010) (trial court declaration of mistrial after jury deadlocked was based on manifest necessity). Errors that happen during the trial itself are more difficult to classify. If *every* declaration of mistrial could bar subsequent prosecution, defense attorneys could manipulate the outcome. Whenever a trial starts to go badly, their own misconduct in the later stages of a trial could gain the attorneys a second chance in a new trial. As a result, most declarations of mistrial based on defense errors are considered to be manifest necessities. The same risk of manipulation would hold true for prosecutors if *no* mistrial ever barred subsequent prosecution. Thus, mistrials declared after prosecutorial misconduct at trial or other errors within the control of the prosecutor are less likely to be classified as "manifest necessities."

6. *Consistency and respect.* What principles of decision making underlie the Supreme Court's boomerang from *Grady* (1990) to *Dixon* (1993)? It is arguable that *Grady* and *Dixon* both reveal substantial departures from established rules (*Grady* from *Blockburger*, and *Dixon* from *Grady*). All courts offer words of respect

for stare decisis. Should courts have a different stare decisis rule with respect to constitutional and nonconstitutional decisions? Should all constitutional decisions have a natural life span? Should readers discount all constitutional decisions by the age of the justices and the number of justices who decided the case who are still active — a kind of actuarial jurisprudence?

Problem 14-2. Multiplicity

On December 11, Ronald Gardner, Cato Peterson, Amir Wilson, and Aaron Banks were traveling in a white Cougar automobile from Detroit to Muskegon. Muskegon County Sheriff Deputy Al VanHemert received a tip from a confidential informant that Aaron Banks and several other persons would be transporting crack cocaine to a Muskegon Heights neighborhood that afternoon. Two deputies executed a legal stop and search of the vehicle. They seized 222 grams of crack cocaine and arrested the occupants of the car.

Ronald Gardner, Cato Peterson, and Amir Wilson each made statements to the officers. Gardner said that Ricky Franklin paid him two hundred dollars to drive Peterson, Wilson, and Banks to the Muskegon Heights area. He admitted that he had previously transported sellers and drugs to that area. Gardner also stated he had picked up money at the home of "Miss Louise" in Muskegon and transported the cash back to Detroit. He stated that cocaine was sometimes transported in the spare tire in the trunk. Gardner called Franklin the head of the organization, while Banks was the boss of the Muskegon portion of the operation.

Peterson stated to the officers that he was traveling to Muskegon to sell crack cocaine, that this was his second trip to Muskegon, and that Franklin was the head of the organization.

Wilson also made a statement to the Muskegon authorities after his arrest. He stated that he sold crack cocaine for Ricky Franklin and that he had sold drugs on three previous trips to Muskegon. He stated that Banks would stay at Miss Louise's house and dispense the crack baggies to the sellers there. The cocaine was transported in the spare tire in the trunk. Robert Johnson was also involved in the sale of cocaine.

On June 6, a Muskegon County jury convicted Amir Wilson of possession with intent to deliver and conspiracy to deliver between 50 and 225 grams of cocaine. On July 3, Wilson was sentenced to two concurrent prison terms of eight to twenty years.

On July 5, police arrested Gerald Hill in Southfield (in Oakland County, near Muskegon County) for possession with intent to deliver between 225 and 649 grams of cocaine. Southfield police made the arrest after a routine traffic stop of the vehicle in which Hill and Ricky Franklin were passengers. The police allowed Hill to go into a store across the street from where the vehicle was stopped. After Hill left the area, store employees alerted police officers that they had found cocaine in a jacket behind the store. The Muskegon and Oakland County Sheriff Departments joined efforts to investigate the "Franklin organization."

In November, an Oakland County grand jury indicted Wilson, Banks, Hill, Johnson, and another individual, Terrence Moore, on charges of conspiring over a 26-month period to possess with intent to deliver over 650 grams of cocaine. Wilson moved to set aside the indictment on the basis of a violation of double jeopardy.

Should the trial judge in Oakland County grant the motion? Compare People v. Wilson, 563 N.W.2d 44 (Mich. 1997).

Notes

1. *Multiplicity: majority view.* At what point does the commission of one offense end and the commission of a second offense begin? This can be a very difficult question with criminal acts that occur in several locations (such as drug sales), through multiple events (such as conspiracies based on a series of conversations), or over extended periods of time. All jurisdictions must face claims that multiple, identical charges are applied to what is only a single event. See State v. Leyda, 138 P.3d 610 (Wash. 2006) (when defendant obtained victim's credit card and used it to make four purchases, the "unit of prosecution" for crime of identity theft was the act of obtaining identification of another person with criminal intent, rather than each discrete use).

In fact, in *Blockburger* itself the defendant claimed that two drug sales on successive days constituted one offense. Shortly after delivery of the drug that was the subject of the first sale, the purchaser paid for an additional quantity to be delivered the next day. The defendant argued that these two sales to the same purchaser, with no substantial interval of time between the delivery of the drug in the first transaction and the payment for the second quantity sold, constituted a single continuing offense. 284 U.S. at 301. The Court rejected the claim: "The Narcotic Act does not create the offense of engaging in the business of selling the forbidden drugs, but penalizes any sale made. . . . Each of several successive sales constitutes a distinct offense, however closely they may follow each other." 284 U.S. at 302.

Some courts refer to the issue of dividing one offender's behavior into distinct offenses as the problem of "multiplicity." Though not all jurisdictions use the term, the question of multiplicity is common to all jurisdictions. See Vincent v. Commonwealth, 281 S.W.3d 785 (Ky. 2009) (defendant not prejudiced when prosecutor alleged 294 counts of sexual offenses; prosecutor did not intentionally stack indictment to prejudice defendant, because victims of alleged crimes were uncertain of number of incidents and locus of some alleged offenses was uncertain). To what extent does application of the *Blockburger* test answer the question of how many different crimes can be charged? Beyond the scope of *Blockburger,* what principles should govern?

2. *The special problem of conspiracies.* The puzzle of determining how many separate charges are possible is especially difficult in the context of conspiracies — especially drug conspiracies — which tend to take place over time and space and to involve multiple participants. To determine whether criminal conduct amounted to one conspiracy or two, courts consult the "totality of the circumstances," with special emphasis on (1) the time of the conduct, (2) the persons acting as co-conspirators, (3) the overlap among the statutory offenses charged in the indictments, (4) the overt acts charged by the government or any other description of the offenses charged that indicate the nature and scope of the activity that the government sought to punish in each case, and (5) places where the events alleged as part of the conspiracy took place. The procedural difficulties regarding the parsing of conspiracies reflect the substantive battles over the scope of conspiracy law.

3. *Collateral Estoppel*

The common-law doctrine of collateral estoppel raises a question related to double jeopardy: When has an issue or a fact been resolved in one proceeding in a way that will bind the parties in later disputes? The prototypical case illustrating this doctrine is Ashe v. Swenson, 397 U.S. 436 (1970). During a late-night poker game in a basement, three or four masked men entered with weapons and robbed the six men playing cards. In Ashe's trial for robbing one of the card players, defense counsel cross-examined the prosecution witnesses on the identification of Ashe as one of the robbers and offered no other defense to the charges. The jury found him not guilty. When the government brought Ashe to trial again six weeks later for the robbery of the second card player, the defendant moved to dismiss the charge, based on his previous acquittal. The Supreme Court later agreed that the jury's verdict in the first trial prevented a second robbery trial.

■ EX PARTE PHILIP TAYLOR

101 S.W.3d 434 (Tex. Crim. App. 2002)

COCHRAN, J.

Appellant lost control of his car on a rural road and collided with an oncoming car. Appellant's two passengers died in the accident. A jury acquitted appellant of intoxication manslaughter in causing the death of one passenger. The State had alleged that appellant was intoxicated by alcohol. The State now seeks to prosecute appellant for intoxication manslaughter in causing the death of his second passenger. This time, however, the State alleges that appellant was intoxicated by either alcohol and marijuana or by marijuana alone. We must determine whether the appellant's acquittal in the first trial, of intoxication manslaughter, prevents the State from attempting to prove, in another criminal proceeding, an alternate theory of intoxication for causing the death of his second passenger. . . .

I.

. . . The evidence showed that appellant was driving his Ford Thunderbird on a rural road in Brazos County late one afternoon. His fiancee, Kyla Blaisdell, sat in the front passenger seat and her best friend, Michelle James, sat in the back seat. It was not disputed that appellant was speeding, but witnesses' estimates of his actual speed varied widely. As appellant came out of a curve, the Thunderbird's right front wheel left the paved surface and veered onto a grassy, gravely area. According to the defense expert, appellant overcorrected as he attempted to bring his front wheel back onto the pavement. Consequently, he lost control of the car, which veered into the left lane and collided with [Patricia] Varner's oncoming Suburban. According to the State's expert, appellant lost control of the car as he entered the curve at a high speed. Because of his speeding through the curve, the car headed into a ditch on the right hand side, and appellant pulled the steering wheel too much to the left, sending the car into the left lane. Regardless of where appellant lost control of the car, Kyla Blaisdell and Michelle James died in the collision. Ms. Varner and appellant were both seriously injured.

At the hospital, medical technicians drew a sample of appellant's blood to determine its blood alcohol concentration ("BAC"). Their analysis resulted in a .137 BAC reading. The DPS twice reanalyzed this blood sample, using more sensitive equipment. Its analysis returned BAC readings of .124 and .119. DPS took another blood sample from appellant more than three hours after the first sample. This second sample indicated a BAC of .06. Appellant's blood also tested positive for the presence of marijuana, but there was no evidence that he had smoked marijuana on that particular day. The prosecutor, agreeing that traces of marijuana may linger in the body for days after its actual use, did not oppose appellant's motion in limine barring any mention of marijuana during the trial. Kyla Blaisdell tested negative for both alcohol and drugs; Michelle James tested negative for drugs, but .04 for alcohol; and Ms. Varner tested negative for both drugs and alcohol. Appellant's toxicology expert testified that, according to his calculations, appellant's BAC at the time of the accident must have been between .07 and .09.

Kelsey Blaisdell, Kyla's brother, testified that the trio spent most of the afternoon at his parent's home. He said that they came over to do laundry and to "hang out." They had some wine with them and were drinking from about 2:30 until 6:00 P.M. Kelsey testified that appellant did not seem drunk or otherwise intoxicated: appellant did not slur his speech or have poor balance. . . .

At the conclusion of all evidence, the trial judge charged the jury that, if it believed from the evidence, beyond a reasonable doubt, that appellant [operated a motor vehicle] while intoxicated, "either by not having the normal use of his mental or physical faculties by reason of the introduction of alcohol into his body or by having an alcohol concentration of .10 or more, and by reason of that intoxication, if any, by accident or mistake, caused the death of Michelle James, you will find [appellant] guilty of intoxication manslaughter." The jury was also instructed, as an alternate basis for a finding of guilt, that if it believed from the evidence, beyond a reasonable doubt, that appellant [recklessly caused the death of Michelle James] by "operating a motor vehicle at an excessive speed and by driving into a motor vehicle occupied by Patricia Varner, you will find [appellant] guilty of manslaughter." . . .

The jury acquitted appellant of all counts of intoxication manslaughter and reckless manslaughter of Michelle James. The State subsequently dismissed appellant's indictment for causing Kyla Blaisdell's death. But later the State learned that appellant, sometime after the trial, allegedly told Kyla Blaisdell's mother that he and the girls had been smoking marijuana cigarettes on the afternoon of the accident. Based upon this newly discovered evidence, the State re-indicted appellant for intoxication manslaughter in causing the death of Kyla Blaisdell, alleging that he had lost the normal use of his mental and physical faculties by reason of the introduction of alcohol, marijuana, or a combination of alcohol and marijuana.

Appellant filed an application for a pretrial writ of habeas corpus, contending that the doctrine of collateral estoppel barred any further State efforts to prosecute him for causing this accident based upon his alleged intoxication. The trial court largely denied appellant relief, concluding that only the issue of intoxication by reason of alcohol had been litigated in the first trial, but not the distinct factual question of whether marijuana, either alone or in combination with alcohol, had rendered him intoxicated. Appellant then filed a pretrial appeal [to the intermediate appellate court, which disagreed with the trial court and concluded that the ultimate issue of fact decided by the jury was that appellant was not intoxicated;

therefore, the issue of intoxication could not be relitigated in any further criminal proceeding. The government appealed this ruling.]

II.

At issue in this appeal is the scope of the factual finding that the jury made when it acquitted appellant. The State assumes that the first jury concluded that appellant was not intoxicated because of alcohol. It contends that this finding does not preclude the State from prosecuting appellant for the death of a second accident victim, when the State alleged intoxication by alcohol and marijuana or by marijuana alone. . . .

The first prosecution was for killing Michelle James; the second, for killing Kyla Blaisdell. For double jeopardy purposes, the unlawful killing of each victim is a separate offense. In its seminal case on collateral estoppel, Ashe v. Swenson, 397 U.S. 436 (1970), the Supreme Court noted that the defendant's reprosecution was not barred by double jeopardy under the usual *Blockburger* test because the second prosecution was for a different offense, namely the robbery of a different victim attending the same poker party. Thus, the Supreme Court had to turn to the related doctrine of collateral estoppel, which prevents a party who lost a fact issue in the trial of one cause of action from relitigating the same fact issue in another cause of action against the same party. The situation is the same in this case. If the State had prosecuted appellant for the same offense (causing the death of Michelle James) on a different theory, we would not have to resort to collateral estoppel. Reprosecution would be barred by autrefois acquit under *Blockburger*.

In Ashe v. Swenson, the Supreme Court stated that collateral estoppel "means simply that when an issue of ultimate fact has once been determined by a valid and final judgment, that issue cannot again be litigated between the same parties in any future lawsuit." To determine whether collateral estoppel bars a subsequent prosecution (or permits prosecution but bars relitigation of certain specific facts) courts employ a two-step analysis. Courts must determine: (1) exactly what facts were "necessarily decided" in the first proceeding; and (2) whether those "necessarily decided" facts constitute essential elements of the offense in the second trial.

In each case, courts must review the entire trial record to determine — "with realism and rationality" — precisely what fact or combination of facts the jury necessarily decided and which will then bar their relitigation in a second criminal trial. In Ashe v. Swenson, the Supreme Court emphasized that:

> the rule of collateral estoppel is not to be applied with the hypertechnical and archaic approach of a 19th century pleading book, but with realism and rationality. . . . Any test more technically restrictive would, of course, simply amount to a rejection of the rule of collateral estoppel in criminal proceedings, at least in every case where the first judgment was based upon a general verdict of acquittal.

Although Texas courts have rarely discussed the scope of a fact barred by collateral estoppel, cases from other jurisdictions have held that collateral estoppel operates only if the "very fact or point now in issue" was determined in the prior proceeding. It must be precisely the same issue in both cases. Thus, issue preclusion is limited to cases where the legal and factual situations are identical. . . . On the other hand, issue preclusion cannot be defeated simply by advancing new or different evidence to support the same issue already litigated. Thus, a party who neglects to submit the evidence that would support a legal theory that the party withheld in a first proceeding, cannot later point to its own omission as justification for pursuing a second proceeding.

In sum, there are no hard and fast rules concerning which factual issues are legally identical and thus barred from relitigation in a second criminal proceeding. . . . In each case, the entire record — including the evidence, pleadings, charge, jury arguments, and any other pertinent material — must be examined to determine precisely the scope of the jury's factual findings. In one case, for example, a jury's acquittal might rest upon the proposition that the defendant was "not intoxicated," while in another, that same verdict might rest upon the narrower proposition that the defendant was "not intoxicated" by a particular substance, but he might well have been intoxicated by a different substance. Generally, then, the scope of the facts that were actually litigated determines the scope of the factual finding covered by collateral estoppel.

Given the pleadings, the jury charge, the disputed issues, and the evidence presented by both the State and the defense at the trial, the jury in this particular case necessarily concluded that, at the time of the accident: 1) Appellant had not lost the normal use of his mental or physical faculties by reason of the introduction of alcohol; 2) Appellant did not have an alcohol concentration of .10 or more; and 3) Appellant did not recklessly drive at an excessive speed into another vehicle.

Thus, these three facts have been established, and they cannot be relitigated in any future criminal proceeding against appellant. But do these discrete factual findings leave open the possibility that appellant was intoxicated, but by some substance other than alcohol?

Not here. The only witness who testified to appellant's possible loss of normal use of mental or physical faculties was Kelsey Blaisdell, the brother of one of the victims. He stated that appellant and the two girls had some wine that afternoon. . . . Because the trial court granted appellant's unopposed motion in limine, there was no mention at trial of any other possible source of intoxication and no other evidence that appellant had lost the normal use of his mental or physical faculties.

The source of appellant's intoxication was not a disputed issue in the first trial. It was only the more general issue of intoxication — was he or wasn't he — that was disputed, and upon this issue, the appellant prevailed. Had appellant's defense been one of conceding the fact of intoxication, but contesting the manner in which he became intoxicated, the situation would, of course, be different. Thus, considering the question in a practical, common-sense manner, it is evident that there is no reasonable possibility that the jury in the first trial could have decided, based upon this evidence, that appellant was intoxicated but not because of alcohol. . . .[29]

The State argues that it now possesses more and different evidence — namely that appellant admitted to Mrs. Blaisdell, after his acquittal, that both he and the

29. The dissent argues that the jury could have decided that appellant was, in fact, intoxicated but that "his intoxication was not a contributing factor to the accident." This is, of course, a possibility, but that factual finding would not prevent the application of collateral estoppel. Quite the reverse. . . . If that were the fact that the jury necessarily decided, then collateral estoppel would apply to causation, rather than intoxication. [If an acquittal could have been based on either fact A or fact B, and the government is required to prove both fact A and fact B in a subsequent trial, collateral estoppel bars relitigation of either fact.]

girls had smoked marijuana that day. But here, as in Harris v. Washington, 404 U.S. 55 (1971), when an ultimate issue has been decided, the constitutional guarantee of collateral estoppel applies "irrespective of whether the jury considered all relevant evidence, and irrespective of the good faith of the State in bringing successive prosecutions." [In Harris v. Washington, a jury acquitted the defendant of murder, finding that the defendant had not mailed the bomb which killed the victim and his infant son and seriously injured the victim's wife. The Supreme Court found that the State could not reprosecute the defendant for killing the infant based upon additional evidence, namely a threatening letter that the defendant had allegedly sent to the victim's family.]

The State also argues that, because it was required [under State v. Carter, 810 S.W.2d 197 (Tex. Crim. App. 1991) to allege in the charging instrument] which type of intoxicant appellant consumed, collateral estoppel applies only to that specific intoxicant. Accordingly, the State contends, resolving whether collateral estoppel applies depends entirely upon the precise indictment allegations, regardless of the actual evidence or the facts "necessarily" found by the jury. But application of collateral estoppel depends not merely upon the pleadings, but also upon the evidence, charge, jury argument, and any other relevant material. The State fails to point to any evidence, argument, or other material in this record which would support its theory that this jury could have concluded appellant was intoxicated, but not by alcohol.... Therefore, we affirm the court of appeals.

HERVEY, J., dissenting.

...After examining relevant portions of the record from the first criminal prosecution, I cannot conclude that the jury in that case necessarily found that appellant was not intoxicated by alcohol. The offenses submitted to the jury in that prosecution were intoxication manslaughter and manslaughter. The jury was instructed to find appellant guilty of intoxication manslaughter if it found that appellant's intoxication, if any, caused the victim's death.... The charge instructed the jury to convict appellant of intoxication manslaughter if it believed beyond a reasonable doubt that appellant [operated] a motor vehicle in a public place "while intoxicated, either by not having the normal use of his mental or physical faculties by reason of the introduction of alcohol into his body or by having an alcohol concentration of .10 or more, and by reason of that intoxication, if any, by accident or mistake, caused the death of [the victim]." ...

The State's theory was that appellant's alcohol intoxication caused him to drive recklessly at an excessive rate of speed which caused the accident resulting in the victim's death. Appellant's theory was that he was not intoxicated by any of the two manner and means submitted to the jury but that, if he was, his intoxication was not a contributing factor to the accident.... Appellant's accident reconstructionist supported these assertions at trial [and] contradicted other aspects of the prosecution's theory of how the accident occurred such as when appellant began to lose control of his vehicle (before the curve at a lower speed limit or after the curve at a higher speed limit).

It was undisputed that appellant had been drinking wine before the fatal accident. Responding to the prosecution's evidence that appellant's BAC at the time of the accident was above .10, the best appellant's toxicology expert could do was to admit that appellant's BAC at the time of the accident was between .07 and

.09. . . . Significantly, appellant's toxicology expert also admitted that a BAC of .07 to .09 would cause most people to lose "some of the normal use of their abilities." . . .

During closing jury arguments, the defense argued that . . . the prosecution failed to prove that appellant's intoxication, if any, caused the fatal accident. The last thing the defense told the jury was that it should still acquit appellant even if the jury found that he was intoxicated.

> They haven't proved that he had an alcohol content of above .10 at the time he was driving, and they haven't proved that [appellant] had an accident because . . . he was intoxicated. [What] could have caused this accident? . . . Could be that the Varner vehicle was towards the middle of the road. It could be inattentiveness. It could be an animal ran out. . . . We will never know what caused that accident. . . . This is a tragedy. A verdict of not guilty does not mean that it isn't tragic. A verdict of not guilty means the government has not proved these allegations . . . beyond a reasonable doubt. Even if you find he was intoxicated, if you don't find that intoxication beyond a reasonable doubt caused this accident, you must return a verdict of not guilty. . . .

These portions of the record demonstrate that the jury could have acquitted appellant . . . because it did not believe that this intoxication was a contributing factor to the accident which the record reflects was one of the theories appellant urged at the first trial. . . .

The Court's opinion concedes that it is "a possibility" that the jury did not necessarily find that appellant was not intoxicated by alcohol. This should be fatal to appellant's collateral estoppel claim. But, the Court still concludes that this prosecution is jeopardy-barred because, even if the jury found that appellant was intoxicated, it nevertheless could have found that the "intoxication itself was not a contributing factor to the accident" in which case "collateral estoppel would apply to causation, rather than intoxication."

But, in analyzing the collateral estoppel issue this way, the Court concludes that this prosecution is jeopardy-barred even though it is unable to decide what the jury necessarily found in the first trial. In other words, the Court apparently bases its decision on what the jury could have found without deciding what the jury necessarily found. My understanding of collateral estoppel law, however, is that for the collateral estoppel bar to apply, the Court must be able to decide what the jury necessarily found in the first trial, not what it could have found.

The Court's analysis involving what the jury could have found in appellant's first trial also fails to take into account that it is entirely possible that the jury did not speak with one voice in acquitting appellant. For example, it is possible that some of the jurors believed that appellant was not intoxicated, some of the jurors believed that he was intoxicated but his intoxication was not a contributing factor to the accident, and some of the jurors believed that appellant should have been acquitted for other reasons. Cf. Schad v. Arizona, 501 U.S. 624 (1991) (Scalia, J., concurring) (stating the general rule that "when a single crime can be committed in various ways, jurors need not agree upon the mode of commission"). Under these circumstances, it cannot be said that the jury necessarily found anything in the first trial except possibly that it had a reasonable doubt of appellant's guilt. . . .

Apparently the Court decides that federal constitutional collateral estoppel principles prevent the prosecution from litigating these two issues of intoxication in this proceeding because it was the more general issue of intoxication — was he or wasn't he — that was disputed in the first trial and because the prosecution could have but did not litigate these other two theories of intoxication in the first trial. But federal constitutional collateral estoppel principles only prohibit a party from relitigating an issue that was necessarily decided in the first trial, and it is clear that the only issue litigated (and that could possibly have been decided) in the first trial was whether appellant was intoxicated by alcohol.

In deciding that the prosecution cannot litigate the other two theories of intoxication (marijuana and combination of marijuana and alcohol) in this proceeding because the prosecution could have litigated them in the first trial, the Court adds a new element to the federal constitutional collateral estoppel doctrine that *Ashe* and other United States Supreme Court cases do not require. The Court's decision expands *Ashe* to preclude litigating in a second trial issues of ultimate fact that could have been decided in the first trial. But the federal constitutional collateral estoppel doctrine applies only to issues of ultimate fact that were actually decided in the first trial. I respectfully dissent.

Notes

1. *Collateral estoppel: majority position.* The U.S. Supreme Court declared in Ashe v. Swenson, 397 U.S. 436 (1970), that the federal guarantee against double jeopardy includes the concept of collateral estoppel: "when an issue of ultimate fact has once been determined by a valid and final judgment, that issue cannot again be litigated between the same parties in any future lawsuit." There are several limitations, however, that prevent collateral estoppel from having an impact in a wide range of cases. First, the doctrine typically does not apply to matters resolved by guilty plea. Federal and state courts agree that collateral estoppel applies only after an "adjudication on the merits after full trial." Ohio v. Johnson, 467 U.S. 493, 500 (1984).

Second, as *Ex parte Taylor* illustrates, it is often difficult, based on a jury's general verdict, to determine exactly what factual findings were the basis for a jury's acquittal. This problem is commonplace because defendants are prone to give the jury more than one possible theory for an acquittal. See Yeager v. United States, 129 S. Ct. 2360 (2009) (in original trial, jury acquitted Yeager of securities fraud counts, and was unable to reach verdict on additional counts; collateral estoppel bars retrial because acquittal necessarily reflected finding by jury that Yeager did not possess relevant information, and courts should treat the deadlock on other counts as a nonevent). Would the use of special interrogatories to the jury (to be completed only after the jury has delivered its general verdict) make the collateral estoppel doctrine a more meaningful limitation on multiple criminal trials?

2. *Parties and proceedings covered.* Although collateral estoppel binds the government, most courts say that the doctrine is asymmetrical; that is, it does not bind defendants. If a factfinder determines some fact against a defendant in one criminal proceeding, the defendant may still ask a factfinder in some later criminal case to find that same fact in his favor. On the other hand, in most jurisdictions the collateral estoppel doctrine benefits the defendant only at the first trial, and does not extend to any co-defendants. A jury's finding concerning a factual issue at the trial of one co-defendant does not preclude the prosecution from relitigating the same issue at a subsequent trial of another co-defendant.

Can a finding of fact made in an administrative or civil proceeding be the basis for collateral estoppel in a later criminal proceeding? Typically, the courts do not apply the doctrine to bar such prosecutions. For instance, if a defendant in license revocation proceedings convinces the factfinder that some critical factual element of drunken driving charges is missing, that finding generally does not bar a later criminal prosecution for driving while impaired. Courts point out that the two proceedings operate under two different standards of proof: preponderance of the evidence in the administrative proceedings, and beyond a reasonable doubt in the criminal proceedings.

These arguments about the reach of collateral estoppel to parties and proceedings beyond the prototypical setting of two criminal trials involving a single criminal defendant generate a complex case law. You can work through some of the implications of this doctrine on the web extension for this chapter at *http://www.crimpro.com/extension/ch14*.

3. *Collateral estoppel and dual sovereigns.* It is common to find the collateral estoppel principle embodied in state statutes barring or limiting multiple prosecutions. Around 10 states have statutes recognizing collateral estoppel based on adverse factual findings made in criminal proceedings in another jurisdiction. See Colo. Rev. Stat. §18-1-303(1)(b). Recall that the common-law doctrine of collateral estoppel required "mutuality of parties" — that is, the same two parties had to be involved in both the original proceedings and the later relitigation of the same factual issue. Is there any reason to insist on "mutuality of parties" when it comes to dual sovereigns prosecuting the same person for crimes based on the same factual premise? In other words, should one government's loss in a criminal trial prevent another government from relitigating the same factual issue?

B. JOINDER

Constitutional and statutory double jeopardy rules require prosecutors to choose carefully when grouping together the potential charges to be brought against a defendant. We now look at some doctrinal cousins to double jeopardy: the statutory and court rules that govern "joinder" and "severance" of potentially related charges. As you read the following materials, consider to what extent the joinder and severance rules further interests different from the constitutional or statutory bar on double jeopardy.

The most common joinder rules (exemplified by Rule 8 of the Federal Rules of Criminal Procedure) are known as "permissive" joinder rules. They define the outer boundaries of the prosecutor's power to join charges together for a single trial, that is, the *maximum* range of charges that can be grouped together. These rules address both the joinder of separate offenses filed against a single defendant and joinder of multiple defendants in a single trial. Some states also have "compulsory" or "mandatory" joinder rules. These rules identify the *minimum* range of charges that the prosecutor must group together for a single trial. Like the doctrines of double jeopardy and collateral estoppel, these compulsory joinder rules require dismissal of charges if they should have been tried in an earlier proceeding dealing with related charges. Rules on "severance" address the power of the court to override a prosecutor's joinder decisions and order separate trials for charges that were otherwise properly joined. This is sometimes necessary to prevent an undue prejudicial effect on the defense.

The joinder rules may on first inspection seem dry and technical. But joinder and severance rules are enormously important to defendants and prosecutors because they define the possible strategies at trial and very often determine the outcome of the case. The issues appeal to lawyers who enjoy puzzles.

1. Discretionary Joinder and Severance of Offenses

When a prosecutor files multiple charges against a defendant, the charges usually fall within the minimum and maximum range of charges that a prosecutor has the power to group together in a single case. If the prosecutor fails to join the charges and the defendant wishes to resolve them in one trial, the court has the discretion to join the charges even though the prosecutor did not file them together. The parties can also urge the trial court to sever the joined charges as a discretionary matter to avoid prejudice. Review the federal rules and Vermont rules reprinted below, then read the following case. Would the outcome of the case change under the Vermont rules?

■ FEDERAL RULE OF CRIMINAL PROCEDURE 8(a)

The indictment or information may charge a defendant in separate counts with two or more offenses if the offenses charged — whether felonies or misdemeanors or both — are of the same or similar character, or are based on the same act or transaction, or are connected with or constitute parts of a common scheme or plan.

■ FEDERAL RULE OF CRIMINAL PROCEDURE 13

The court may order that separate cases be tried together as though brought in a single indictment or information if all offenses . . . could have been joined in a single indictment or information.

■ FEDERAL RULE OF CRIMINAL PROCEDURE 14

(a) Relief. If the joinder of offenses or defendants in an indictment, an information, or a consolidation for trial appears to prejudice a defendant or the government, the court may order separate trials of counts, sever the defendants' trials, or provide any other relief that justice requires.

(b) Defendant's Statements. Before ruling on a defendant's motion to sever, the court may order an attorney for the government to deliver to the court for in camera inspection any defendant's statement that the government intends to use as evidence.

VERMONT RULE OF CRIMINAL PROCEDURE 8(a)

Two or more offenses may be joined in one information or indictment, with each offense stated in a separate count, when the offenses, whether felonies or misdemeanors or both,

(1) are of the same or similar character, even if not part of a single scheme or plan; or

(2) are based on the same conduct or on a series of acts connected together or constituting parts of a single scheme or plan.

VERMONT RULE OF CRIMINAL PROCEDURE 14

(a) The court may order a severance of offenses or defendants before trial if a severance could be obtained on motion of a defendant or the prosecution under subdivision (b) of this rule.

(b)(1) Severance of Offenses.

(A) Whenever two or more offenses have been joined for trial solely on the ground that they are of the same or similar character, the defendant shall have a right to a severance of the offenses.

(B) The court, on application of the prosecuting attorney, or on application of the defendant other than under subparagraph (A), shall grant a severance of offenses whenever,

(i) if before trial, it is deemed appropriate to promote a fair determination of the defendant's guilt or innocence of each offense; or

(ii) if during trial upon consent of the defendant, or upon a finding of manifest necessity, it is deemed necessary to achieve a fair determination of the defendant's guilt or innocence of each offense.

VERMONT REPORTER'S NOTES — 1995 AMENDMENT

[Rule 8] is taken from ABA Minimum Standards (Joinder and Severance) §§1.1, 1.2, and is similar to Federal Rule 8. Rule 8(a) permits joinder of offenses either because they are of similar character though factually unrelated or because they are factually related. Note that each offense must be pleaded in a separate count. . . . Under the federal rule the phrase "same character" adopted for Rule 8(a)(1) has been ordinarily held to mean the same crime committed against distinct objects upon distinct occasions. Although joinder of similar offenses has been criticized as tending to prejudice the defendant through its cumulative effect, the ABA recommends the provision, because it may actually work to the defendant's advantage in preventing multiple trials and facilitating concurrent sentencing. Prejudice will be avoided because under Rule 14(b)(1)(A) defendant has an absolute right to severance of such offenses for trial. ABA Minimum Standards §1.1(a), Commentary. . . .

Rule 8(a)(2) is, of course, a rule of permissive joinder. As a practical matter, if the same facts are centrally involved in two offenses, joinder is virtually compelled. Otherwise, acquittal of the defendant upon one offense will bar prosecution for the second offense by virtue of the Fifth Amendment's Double Jeopardy Clause, which includes the principles of collateral estoppel. Ashe v. Swenson, 397 U.S. 436 (1970).

[Rule 14] is based on ABA Minimum Standards (Joinder and Severance) §§2.1-2.4, 3.1, with variations reflecting Vermont practice. It is similar in effect to the more complicated provisions of Federal Rule 14. Note that Rule 14 is a grant of discretion to sever a joinder otherwise proper under Rule 8 in the interests of fairness or to avoid prejudice. If a joinder is improper under Rule 8, a severance must be granted or it is reversible error. Rule 14(a) is based on ABA Minimum Standards §3.1(b). A power in the court to sever on its own motion, like the comparable power to join under Rule 13(a), is necessary to allow the court to carry out its responsibilities for the orderly conduct of the trial. The federal courts have recognized a power in the court to act on its own motion under Federal Rule 14. . . . Rule 14(b)(1), dealing with severance of offenses, is taken from ABA Minimum Standards §2.2. Subparagraph (A), conferring an absolute right of severance where offenses have been joined solely by virtue of Rule 8(a)(1) because they are of the same or similar character, is a necessary protection for defendants against what would otherwise be potential prejudice in such joinders. That prejudice may consist in the defendant's fear of testifying in his own behalf on one count because of the effect of such testimony on the other count, or in the danger that proof of one count will have prejudicial effect on the other count as inadmissible evidence of another crime. In requiring severance in these circumstances the rule is stricter than Federal Rule 14, although individual decisions under the latter rule have allowed severance for similar purposes. The rule is stricter than prior Vermont practice, which gave the court discretion as to severance even where unrelated offenses were involved. See State v. Dopp, 255 A.2d 186 (Vt. 1969). Severance of offenses joined under Rule 8(a)(2) as arising from the same or connected conduct or a single scheme is available to either party under Rule 14(b)(1)(A) when necessary in the interests of fair trial. . . .

DAMIAN LONG v. UNITED STATES

687 A.2d 1331 (D.C. 1996)

FERREN, J.

A jury found appellant, Damian Long, guilty of assault with intent to rob three victims while armed on September 8, 1992, at about 10:30 P.M., at 12th and Orren Streets, N.E. He also was found guilty of attempted robbery while armed and felony murder while armed of another victim several minutes later on Trinidad Avenue, N.E., a block away from the first crime. Long contends . . . the trial court erroneously joined the Orren Street and Trinidad Avenue offenses for trial and then abused its discretion in denying the defense motion for severance. . . . We affirm in part, reverse in part, and remand for reconsideration of Long's severance motion.

[Around 5:30 to 6:00 P.M. on September 8], appellant Long left the apartment of Scholethia Monk, located at Holbrook Terrace, N.E., where he had been spending time with Ms. Monk, her brother (David), and Kimberly Bridgeford. Long was dressed in a black suede jacket with fringe, a black shirt, black jeans, black boots, and a black silk-stocking skull cap. The Holbrook Terrace apartment was only a few blocks from the area where the Orren Street and Trinidad Avenue incidents at issue here took place.

Several hours later, at about 10:30 P.M., a man dressed in a black fringed jacket, black pants, and black shoes — later identified as Damian Long — approached the three Orren Street victims, Sabrina Fox, Carla Davis, and Guy Foster, who were standing in the street on the driver's side of the car that was parked against the curb in front of Fox's home. They were attempting to open the door and window of the car with a coat hanger because they had inadvertently locked the keys inside. Long crossed over to them from the opposite side of the street, pointed a revolver at them, and said something to the two women that sounded like "get the fuck out of here." He then pressed the pistol against Foster's head and demanded his money. When Foster protested that he had none, Long put his hand in Foster's pants pockets and satisfied himself that this was true. Long then ordered Foster to crawl under the car, and Long walked away in the direction of Trinidad Avenue.

Fox and Davis had fled in the same direction. They feared that their assailant was following them, so they hid in an alleyway a few blocks away from where the car was parked. Fox and Davis then heard gunshots and unsuccessfully tried to flag down a passing police cruiser. They hailed a taxi and went to a nearby police precinct where they told their story and gave a description of the perpetrator.

In the meantime, Fox's mother, Penelope Boyd-Fox, who had witnessed the assault on the three from the porch of her home on Orren Street, had immediately telephoned "911" for help. While she was still on the phone to the police department emergency number, she heard gunshots nearby. At about the same time, Foster came out from under the car and fled to his home on Orren Street. He telephoned the police to report the crime. While on the phone with the police, he heard gunshots and reported that as well.

Deborah Alford . . . was sitting on her front porch [on Trinidad Avenue] with several family members at approximately 10:30 P.M. the same night. A few minutes earlier, she had seen [her neighbor Louis Johnson] park his Suzuki sports vehicle on the street and enter his home several doors away. Apparently returning home from work, Johnson had been wearing his Army uniform. Shortly thereafter, Alford saw Johnson walking from his home, dressed in his bathrobe, and returning to his Suzuki. At this moment, Alford saw a man dressed in a black jacket ("I didn't know it had suede fringes on it"), black pants, and a black skull cap walking in Trinidad Street alongside the parked cars. Alford saw the man in black, after he had passed by Johnson, take out a pistol from his jacket and turn back toward Johnson as Johnson put the keys into the car's doorlock. Alford next saw the man in black and her neighbor "tussling." Frightened by the sight of the pistol, she and the others fled into their home. A few seconds later, Alford heard a series of gunshots. Johnson was later pronounced dead of gunshot wounds.

Kimberly Bridgeford testified that at around 5:00 P.M. on September 8, 1992, she and her boyfriend, David Monk, had gone with Damian Long to David's sister's, Scholethia Monk's, apartment on Holbrook Terrace. After awhile, Long left the apartment and, shortly thereafter, Bridgeford and David Monk left to go to the store. On the way to the store, Bridgeford heard gunshots, saw an ambulance, and walked by the Trinidad Avenue murder scene where she saw Johnson lying on the street with blood all over him. Bridgeford and David Monk then returned to the Holbrook Terrace apartment and found Long on the front porch. Long told Bridgeford that he had "shot a man on Trinidad Avenue because the man tried to rob him with a knife."

Scholethia Monk testified that Long returned later to her Holbrook Terrace apartment on September 8, 1992, "panicking and sweating." Long had told Monk that "two dudes" had tried to rob him on Trinidad Avenue and that he had just shot one of them. There was blood on Long's face, he no longer wore a skull cap, and he was carrying a pistol. Long put the gun under a couch. Monk told Long to get his pistol out of her apartment. He then wrapped it in a plastic bag and took it outside. Ten days later, the police recovered a gun from under the seat of the car where Long's close friend, Monk's brother, had been sitting just before they found the gun. A ballistics expert was "positive" that a bullet recovered from the scene of the murder on Trinidad Avenue had been fired by that pistol.

Homicide detective Willie Toland investigated the Trinidad Avenue case. When he arrived at the scene, he noticed a black skull cap seven feet from the place where Johnson had been shot, and Johnson's keys were still in the Suzuki's passenger door lock. As Toland investigated the crime scene, Foster arrived and informed Toland of what had happened earlier on Orren Street. Toland spoke with Davis and Fox later the same night and a few days later conducted a video lineup in which they identified Long as their attacker. . . .

Long's argument, raised before trial and renewed at the end of the government's case, [is] that the Orren Street and Trinidad Avenue charges had been improperly joined for trial. Specifically, Long protested joinder because the offenses were "not similar offenses, [nor] offenses committed in a single act or transaction, nor a series of offenses that [were] sufficiently connected to each other."

Super. Ct. Crim. R. 8(a) provides for joinder of offenses when the offenses charged "are of the same or similar character or are based on the same act or transaction or on two or more acts or transactions connected together or constituting parts of a common scheme or plan." We review the trial court's joinder decision de novo.

The government urges that joinder was proper because the Orren Street offenses had been "connected together" with the Trinidad Avenue offenses in the sense that proof of the Orren Street offenses "constitut[ed] a substantial portion of the proof" of the Trinidad Avenue offenses. The facts, however, do not support the government's argument. None of the witnesses to the Orren Street incident saw the Trinidad Avenue incident, and neither crime depended on the other for its furtherance or success.

The government also argues that the Orren Street and Trinidad Avenue offenses had been properly joined as part of a "common scheme or plan," because Long had been "walking the neighborhood in search of people to rob." We have previously rejected such an argument when considering joinder of defendants under Super. Ct. Crim. R. 8(b), and we reject the argument in this context as well. See Jackson v. United States, 623 A.2d 571 (D.C. 1993) ("The goal of obtaining property from others, here money and guns, was too general for joinder of offenses under Rule 8(b).").

The government contends, finally, that the Orren Street offenses were similar in character to the Trinidad Avenue offenses, and we agree. The "similarity of offenses [under Rule 8(a)] is determined by the content of the indictment"; it is not dependent on whether evidence of one crime would be admissible in the trial of the other. In this case . . . the two crimes, as charged, "both involved armed robberies which were closely related in time and place." Accordingly, it cannot plausibly be maintained that they are insufficiently similar to one another to warrant initial joinder under Rule 8(a). We must conclude that the two sets of offenses were properly joined.

Long contends the trial court erred nonetheless in denying his severance motion under Super. Ct. Crim. R. 14. He says the Orren Street offenses should have been severed from the Trinidad Avenue charges because the evidence of each would be inadmissible in a separate trial of the other. Long adds he was further prejudiced because he was "precluded from presenting separate defenses" to each group of charges.[4]

We have noted that

> [e]ven when offenses are properly joined, it is within the trial court's discretion to sever counts and order separate trials if the defendant would be prejudiced by joinder. Our standard of review of such rulings is abuse of discretion, and appellant must make a showing of compelling prejudice to show such error. Of course, there is a potential for prejudice whenever similar, but unrelated offenses are charged. However, the requisite prejudicial effect for a severance will not be found where the evidence [1] can be kept separate and distinct at trial or [2] is mutually admissible at separate trials. [Cox v. United States, 498 A.2d 231, 235 (D.C. 1985).]

Because the incidents were not tried separately and distinctly,[5] resolution of the severance issue turns on mutual admissibility: whether the evidence of each joined offense would be admissible at a separate trial of the other. The first sentence of Super. Ct. Crim. R. 14 provides:

> [If] it appears that a defendant or the government is prejudiced by a joinder of offenses or of defendants in an indictment or information or by such joinder for trial together, the Court may order an election or separate trials of counts, grant a severance of defendants or provide whatever other relief justice requires.

In response to Long's contention, the government argues that the severance motion was properly denied because evidence of each group of offenses would have been admissible in a separate trial of the other "to explain the immediate circumstances surrounding the offense charged." Technically speaking, such evidence "is not other crimes evidence because it is too intimately entangled with the charged criminal conduct."[6] Alternatively, the government argues that the evidence of each

4. Long apparently wanted to present a misidentification defense as to Orren Street and to claim self-defense at Trinidad Avenue, but realistically separate defenses appeared to be possible only if the offenses were tried separately. . . .

5. The evidence as to each offense was not "kept separate and distinct such that it would not be amalgamated in the jury's mind into a single inculpatory mass." Although the prosecutor attempted to structure the trial to separate the incidents, calling first the Orren Street witnesses and then the Trinidad Avenue witnesses, the evidence of the two crimes was closely tied together by some of the witnesses whose testimony pertained to both crimes, e.g., Scholethia Monk, Kimberly Bridgeford, and the homicide investigator, Willie Toland. Moreover, the government's closing argument also brought together evidence of the two crimes. Finally, the strong identification evidence and intent-to-rob evidence from the Orren Street incident served to supply identification and motive evidence for the Trinidad Avenue incident, so there was a substantial likelihood that the jury would cumulate the evidence. Accordingly, we cannot uphold the denial of severance based on the "separate and distinct" — sometimes known as the "simple and distinct" — theory.

6. The trial court accepted the government's . . . theory in denying Long's renewed motion to sever: "[T]his matter is so inextricably intertwined each with each other that there is no way the Government can separate it all and make sense of the whole matter. They absolutely need for identification purposes, if for nothing else, they absolutely have to have these cases tried together, they should be tried together temporally. And by temporally, I mean both time and place they are as connected as can be." Recently our en banc court discerned three subcategories of evidence embraced by [the]" immediate circumstances" rationale: such evidence (1) is direct and substantial proof of the charged crime, (2) is

incident would be admissible in a trial of the other as "other crimes" evidence tending to prove "identity."[7]

Commonly, the question is whether uncharged criminal conduct shall be admitted in a trial of the charged crime, but in this case the question is the admissibility of a charged crime in the trial of another charged crime. If each would be admissible in the other, then there would be no reason why the two should not be tried together; but, if one or both would not meet the test for admissibility in the other, then severance is required. . . .

In this case, Long presented a misidentification defense at trial. Thus, identity was a contested issue. . . . We therefore believe it appropriate to scrutinize the evidence of each incident, as it bears on proving identity of the assailant in the other. . . . The Orren Street evidence informed the jury that, at about 10:30 P.M., on September 8, 1992, a man identified as Damian Long, dressed entirely in black (including a fringe jacket and skull cap) and carrying a gun, had . . . attempted a robbery at gunpoint. After the assault, the witnesses saw Long headed toward nearby Trinidad Avenue. They heard gunshots soon thereafter.

As for Trinidad Avenue, earlier on the same day at about 5:30 to 6:00 P.M., Scholethia Monk and Kimberly Bridgeford saw Long, dressed entirely in black (including a fringe jacket and skull cap), leave Monk's apartment. Bridgeford saw Long depart in the direction of Trinidad Avenue. Later that evening shortly after 10:30 P.M., Deborah Alford, from her front porch on Trinidad Avenue, saw a man dressed in a black jacket (she did not notice fringe on it), black pants, and a black skull cap walk past her neighbor, Louis Johnson, who was standing next to his car. . . . Alford never identified the assailant. Both Monk and Bridgeford, however, witnessed Long's return to Monk's apartment "panicking and sweating," admitting he had "shot a man on Trinidad Avenue because the man tried to rob him with a knife." Long had blood on his face and was carrying a pistol. His skull cap was missing. The police later found a black skull cap seven feet from where Johnson had been shot. Monk's apartment on Holbrook Terrace was but a few blocks away from where the offenses occurred on Orren Street and Trinidad Avenue.

We believe that the testimony of the Orren Street witnesses, Davis and Fox (who identified Long as a would-be robber), that they saw Long heading in the direction of Trinidad Avenue nearby, and then heard gunshots — all around 10:30 P.M., on September 8, 1992 — provided powerful evidence of the Trinidad Avenue assailant's identity. Indeed, this evidence was particularly significant for the Trinidad Avenue prosecution, when coupled with Monk's and Bridgeford's testimony about Long's admission that he had shot a man on Trinidad Avenue, because the only person who saw the assailant approach Johnson, Deborah Alford, was unable to identify Johnson's killer (although Alford provided a description consistent with Fox's, Davis's, Monk's, and Bridgeford's description of Long). The Orren Street evidence also revealed the assailant's possible motive for approaching Johnson on Trinidad Avenue (robbery).

---

closely intertwined with the evidence of the charged crime, or (3) is necessary to place the charged crime in an understandable context.

7. . . . "[O]ther crimes" evidence is admissible only if [it is introduced to show] motive, intent, absence of mistake or accident, common scheme or plan, or identity as reflected in Fed. R. Evid. 404(b).

We also recognize that the Trinidad Avenue evidence was probative of the identity of the Orren Street attacker. Alford's description of an unidentified, black-jacketed, gun-carrying assailant on Trinidad Avenue, combined with the Monk/Bridgeford testimony that Damian Long had come to Monk's apartment with a gun, "panicking and sweating," tended to identify Long as the Orren Street assailant dressed in black seen heading toward Trinidad Avenue just before shots were fired around 10:30 P.M. The fact that Monk testified that Long's skull cap was missing when he returned to her apartment, coupled with the police officer's finding a skull cap on Trinidad Avenue, adds to Long's connection with the Orren Street attack by a man wearing a black skull cap.

Accordingly, without regard to the required probative value/prejudicial impact analysis, we can say that the Orren Street and Trinidad Avenue offenses [would be mutually admissible] in separate trials (and thus would not be joined prejudicially if prosecuted in a joint trial).

We turn to the ruling on probative value/prejudicial impact. The motions judge said, "I don't see prejudice under [Super. Ct. Civ. R.] 14 that would justify severance." The trial judge, in considering the renewed severance motion at trial, referred to the motions judge's ruling and then added his own belief that [a joint trial was permissible] because the cases were "inextricably intertwined."

The trial judge, therefore, said not a word about probative value relative to prejudice. That was unfortunate. At least as to admissibility of Trinidad Avenue evidence in an Orren Street trial, we see a serious question whether probative value outweighs prejudicial impact. Monk and Bridgeford identified the man — Damian Long — whom Alford apparently had seen accosting Johnson: a man fitting the description of the person who had attempted the robbery only blocks away on Orren Street minutes earlier. This identification evidence from Trinidad Avenue, however, was cumulative of — and of far less probative value than — the direct eyewitness testimony from Fox and Davis . . . that Long was the would-be bandit on Orren Street. Furthermore, this weaker identification evidence includes the powerfully prejudicial testimony that Long had committed a murder, not merely an assault, on Trinidad Avenue.

The trial judge, after a pretrial severance motion has been denied, has a continuing obligation to grant a severance if undue prejudice arises as a result of joinder at any time during trial. The trial judge recognized this obligation: "the Court of Appeals seems to indicate that I have to listen [to severance motions] again and again and again and again." Here, however, in denying the renewed severance motion, the trial judge, for his prejudice analysis, merely referred to the ruling of the motions judge, who did not "see prejudice" from a pretrial perspective. . . .

The probative/prejudicial analysis is a discretionary evaluation which an appellate court cannot undertake itself when the trial court fails to do so unless it is clear from the record, as a matter of law, that the trial court had "but one option." In this case, admissibility of the Trinidad Avenue murder evidence in an Orren Street trial appears to be a more difficult discretionary call than admissibility of the Orren Street assault in a Trinidad Avenue trial, but as to either case we find no sound basis on the record for this court to take over the trial court's function by ruling on probative value/prejudicial impact.

We, therefore, must remand the case for the trial judge to make a probative/prejudicial ruling for each case and thus to rule once again on the severance motion — including consideration of Long's contention that he was prejudiced by his inability, in a single trial, to present separate defenses (Orren Street, misidentification; Trinidad Avenue, self-defense). The judge shall order a new trial of the Orren Street prosecution if he concludes that the murder evidence from Trinidad Avenue should have been omitted from the Orren Street trial. Otherwise, the Orren Street convictions . . . shall stand, without prejudice to Long's right to appeal the severance ruling on remand.[17] Similarly, the judge shall make a probative/prejudice ruling on admissibility of Orren Street evidence in the Trinidad Avenue trial, and also shall rule on Long's claim of prejudice from his practical inability to claim self-defense for Trinidad Avenue at a joint trial. The judge shall order a new trial, or not, as indicated. Absent a new trial order, the Trinidad Avenue conviction shall stand, subject to Long's right of appeal of that severance ruling. . . .

Problem 14-3. Compulsory Joinder

Matthew Hensley was involved in a bar fight in Kanawha County, West Virginia on November 16, 1991. Ambulances arrived at the scene took several people from the bar to a local hospital. Hensley and four other people were arrested at the scene and were immediately charged in magistrate court with public intoxication and destruction of property, both misdemeanors. On November 21, one of the victims of the fight, Barbara Lane, provided a statement to a detective with the Sheriff's Department regarding injuries she suffered during the fight. Lane told the detective that Hensley threw a cue ball, hitting her in her left eye, causing bone fractures and resulting in plastic and reconstructive surgery. However, no additional charges were brought against Hensley prior to his trial in magistrate court on March 13, 1992. He was acquitted of both misdemeanors following the trial in magistrate court.

The Sheriff's Department did not tell the prosecutor's office about the nature of Lane's injuries until January 1994, over two years after the bar fight and nearly two years after the acquittal in magistrate court. Soon after learning about the severity of Lane's injuries, the prosecutor charged Hensley with malicious assault, a

17. We have indicated that other crimes evidence on occasion should be tailored to minimize prejudice. Theoretically, it would be possible to sanitize the Trinidad Avenue evidence for a separate Orren Street trial. In such a trial, the Trinidad Avenue identification testimony would have to be trimmed to leave out reference to a murder, and Deborah Alford would be limited to testifying that an unidentifiable man in black had accosted Johnson with a gun at about 10:30 P.M. Scholethia Monk and Kimberly Bridgeford would be limited to saying that Long — dressed in black — had returned to the apartment shortly after 10:30 P.M., admitting he had just assaulted someone on Trinidad Avenue. The police could then testify about finding a black skull cap on Trinidad Avenue nearby.

The trial court will have to decide, as part of the required probative value/prejudicial impact analysis, (1) whether the preferred approach would be admission of sanitized Trinidad Avenue evidence in a separate Orren Street trial, in order to keep prejudicial homicide evidence from that jury, or (2) whether, because (a) the Fox/Davis identification evidence was strong, (b) the Monk/Bridgeford testimony could be limited to identification of Long as the man who returned "panicking and sweating" at about 10:30 P.M., (c) the murder evidence was highly prejudicial, and (d) because sanitizing the evidence would be complicated, the Trinidad Avenue murder evidence should be kept out of the Orren Street trial altogether, or (3) whether sanitizing the Trinidad Avenue evidence would not work, and the probative value of that evidence outweighs prejudice. If either of the first two instances applies, the court should grant the severance motion; in the third, the court should deny it.

felony. Hensley moved to dismiss the indictment under Rule 8(a) of the West Virginia Rules of Criminal Procedure based on the failure of the State to join the felony charge with the misdemeanor charges prior to the trial in magistrate court in March 1992.

Rule 8(a) of West Virginia Rules of Criminal Procedure provides:

> Joinder of Offenses. — Two or more offenses may be charged in the same indictment or information in a separate count for each offense if the offenses charged, whether felonies or misdemeanors or both, are of the same or similar character. All offenses based on the same act or transaction or on two or more acts or transactions connected together or constituting parts of a common scheme or plan shall be charged in the same indictment or information in a separate count for each offense, whether felonies or misdemeanors or both.

West Virginia courts have developed several exceptions to the application of the rule despite the absence of explicit language within the rule. The first exception is that all offenses, even though based on the same act or transaction or constituting parts of a common scheme or plan, must have occurred in the same jurisdiction before there is a compulsion to charge all offenses in the same charging documents. The second exception applies when the prosecuting attorney does not know and has no reason to know about all the offenses. The third exception happens when the prosecuting attorney had no opportunity to attend the proceeding where the first offense is presented. See Cline v. Murensky, 322 S.E.2d 702 (W. Va. 1984) (two people involved in bar fight were charged and pled guilty in magistrate court to misdemeanor offense of brandishing weapon, all within few hours of fight; both were later indicted in Circuit Court for carrying weapon without license, state not precluded because prosecutor did not have opportunity to attend magistrate court's hearing).

If you were the trial judge in Hensley's felony case, what issues would you ask the parties to address during the hearing on the motion to dismiss? How would you expect to rule? Would your ruling change if the felony charges were already pending in Circuit Court at the time of the acquittal in magistrate court? Would the outcome change if West Virginia had adopted a rule identical to Federal Rule of Criminal Procedure 8(a)? Compare State ex rel. Forbes v. Canady, 475 S.E.2d 37 (W.Va. 1996).

Problem 14-4. Protective Order

Aurelio Chenique-Puey and Susan Lane cohabited from 1983 until 1987, and they had a daughter in 1986. After their separation in 1987, Chenique-Puey harassed Lane by banging on the door and windows of her New Jersey home, and by threatening to kill her. Lane obtained a domestic violence restraining order, which prohibited Chenique-Puey from "returning to the scene of the domestic violence" and "from having any contact with the plaintiff or harassing plaintiff or plaintiff's relatives in any way." It also curtailed his child-visitation rights.

Chenique-Puey was convicted and imprisoned on unrelated charges, so Lane did not have any further contact with him until 1991. Five days after his release from prison, Chenique-Puey came to Lane's apartment to see his daughter. At the time,

Lane was watching a football game on television with two of her children and her boyfriend, John Clifford. Lane refused to admit Chenique-Puey and told him to leave. The parties disagree about what happened at that point. According to Lane, Chenique-Puey taunted Clifford through an open rear window. He reached his arm through the window bars and waved a knife at them. After failing to provoke Clifford, Chenique-Puey threatened to return to the apartment with a shotgun and kill the couple.

Chenique-Puey claimed that he went to the open rear window with his companions, Pedro and Marisa Mondo, and looked inside the apartment. Lane told them that she would not let them in and that they should leave. Chenique-Puey then told Lane that he would return on another day and they left. He says that there was no knife and that he made no threats to Lane and Clifford.

When Chenique-Puey and his companions left the premises, Lane called the police and filed a criminal complaint against him. He was indicted on charges of third-degree terroristic threats and fourth-degree contempt of a judicial restraining order. At the start of trial, the defendant moved for a severance of the contempt charge. He argued that joinder of this offense would prejudice him because evidence of the restraining order would convince the jury that he had in fact made the alleged terroristic threats against Lane.

In New Jersey, joinder of offenses is governed by Rule 3:7-6, which provides that two or more offenses may be charged together if they are "of the same or similar character or are based on the same act or transaction or on two or more acts or transactions connected together or constituting parts of a common scheme or plan." Mandatory joinder under Rule 3:15-1(b) is required when multiple criminal offenses charged are "based on the same conduct or arise from the same episode." Rule 3:15-2(b) vests a trial court with discretion to order separate trials if a defendant or the State is "prejudiced" by permissive or mandatory joinder of offenses.

To convict a defendant of the fourth-degree crime of contempt of a domestic violence restraining order, the State must prove that (1) a restraining order was issued under the act, (2) the defendant violated the order, (3) the defendant acted purposely or knowingly, and (4) the conduct that constituted the violation also constituted a crime or disorderly persons offense. The crime of terroristic threats in the third degree occurs if a person "threatens to kill another with purpose to put him in imminent fear of death under circumstances reasonably causing the victim to believe the immediacy of the threat and the likelihood that it will be carried out."

As a trial court judge, would you grant the motion to sever the offenses? Would you grant other relief? As an appellate court judge, would you reverse a trial court that had refused to grant the severance? Compare State v. Chenique-Puey, 678 A.2d 694 (N.J. 1996).

Notes

1. *Permissive joinder of offenses: majority view.* The rules governing joinder and severance work together to define the permissible bounds for single prosecutions and the extent of allowable judicial discretion. A slight majority of states track the federal rule on permissive joinder and allow prosecutors or judges to join offenses for trial, whether they are "related" charges ("based on the same act or transaction or on two or more acts or transactions connected together or constituting parts of a

common scheme or plan") or similar but "unrelated" charges (having the "same or similar character"). A significant minority of states authorize joinder only for "related" offenses utilizing a variety of formulations. See, e.g., Fla. R. Crim. P. 3.150; Ill. Ann. Stat. ch. 725, para. 5/111-4; State v. Ramos, 818 A.2d 1228 (N.H. 2003) (adopts ABA standards for joinder, because former, more permissive approach produced inconsistent results; when two or more unrelated offenses are joined for trial, both prosecution and defense have absolute right to severance). Given that "related" offenses can include two or more acts "connected together or constituting parts of a common scheme or plan," will the results of this rule be much different from the results of a rule allowing joinder of acts with the "same or similar character"?

2. *The effects of joinder.* Joinder may offer some benefits for defendants, since an attorney can charge less money to represent a defendant at a single trial than at multiple trials. Generally speaking, however, the conventional wisdom is that joint trials provide more advantages to the prosecution. What particular advantages might the prosecutor gain by combining related charges into a single trial?

One careful study of joinder in the federal courts compared outcomes at trial for joined offenses and separately tried offenses. After controlling for the seriousness of the charges and other variables, the study concluded that trial defendants who face multiple counts are roughly 10 percent more likely to be convicted of the most serious charge than a defendant who stands trial on a single count. Andrew D. Leipold & Hossein A. Abbasi, The Impact of Joinder and Severance on Federal Criminal Cases: An Empirical Study, 59 Vand. L. Rev. 101 (2006). If you were studying the effects of joinder in a state felony court system, what variables other than the number of counts would you want to investigate?

3. *Severance of offenses: majority view.* A majority of states have rules or statutes that address severance separately from the joinder question. Most states with severance provisions require severance upon a finding of prejudice, or if necessary to promote a "fair determination of innocence or guilt." A few authorize severance in the "interests of justice." A group of about a half dozen states (represented by the Vermont rule reprinted above) follow the recommendations of the ABA Standards for Criminal Justice by giving the defendant the absolute right to sever "unrelated but similar" offenses. This approach bars the joinder of the unrelated but similar offenses unless the defendant consents. See, e.g., Mich. R. Crim. P. 6.121. What reasons might lead a defendant to accept joinder of unrelated but similar offenses?

The *Long* decision from the District of Columbia reviews the most important sources of prejudice to defendants during a trial of properly joined offenses. First, a defendant might want to pursue separate and inconsistent defenses to the different charges. Was Long asking for the opportunity to mislead two different juries? A second common source of prejudice to defendants from a joint trial of separate offenses involves "other crimes" evidence. The rules of evidence limit the prosecutor's ability to introduce evidence of one crime during the trial of another crime, because the jury might infer that a person who committed one crime is more likely to have committed a second crime. Joinder of offenses might allow a prosecutor to overcome this evidentiary rule; thus, severance is often granted when a court determines that the rules of evidence would exclude evidence of one charge in a separate trial of the other charge. Federal Rule of Evidence 404(b) governs such questions in the federal system. Evidence of "other crimes" is admissible to show a defendant's motive, intent, absence of mistake or accident, common scheme or plan, or identity, but not her propensity to commit a crime.

Even when the rules of evidence might exclude evidence of one crime during a separate trial for the other crime, the charges can still be joined if the evidence remains "simple and distinct" at trial. See United States v. Lotsch, 102 F.2d 35 (2d Cir. 1939) (Hand, J.) ("Here we can see no prejudice from the joining of the three charges: The evidence to each was short and simple; there was no reasonable ground for thinking that the jury would not keep separate what was relevant to each"). "Simple and distinct" (or "separate and distinct") refers both to the content of the evidence and to the method the prosecution uses to present it. If witnesses for one crime are presented together, followed by a different set of witnesses for the other crime, the evidence is more likely to be considered "simple and distinct."

4. *Appellate review of joinder and severance decisions.* Appellate courts rarely overturn a trial court's joinder and severance decisions. The standard of review in virtually all jurisdictions is "abuse of discretion." Did the trial court in *Long* abuse its discretion? Given that most joinder and severance decisions are resolved before trial and are based on the charges in the indictment or information rather than testimony of witnesses at trial, are trial courts really better situated to resolve these claims than an appellate court?

5. *Mandatory joinder: majority position.* About 10 states have adopted a "mandatory" or "compulsory" joinder requirement, either by statute, procedural rule, or judicial ruling. See N.Y. Crim. Proc. Law §40.40 ("Where two or more offenses are joinable in a single accusatory instrument against a person by reason of being based upon the same criminal transaction . . . such person may not . . . be separately prosecuted for such offenses"); Va. Code §19.2-294. A larger group of states, following the federal approach embodied in Fed. R. Crim. P. 8(a), maintain a "permissive" joinder rule, which defines the maximum range of charges that the prosecutor can bring together in the same trial but does not speak to any minimum range of charges that the prosecutor must join together. Note that in a permissive joinder jurisdiction, double jeopardy principles and the related doctrine of collateral estoppel still define a minimum range of charges that must be resolved in a single criminal proceeding. Thus, the mandatory joinder jurisdictions have supplemented double jeopardy and collateral estoppel principles.

6. *Misjoinder.* The converse of mandatory joinder is "misjoinder." When a defendant believes that a prosecutor has grouped together more charges than the permissive joinder rules will allow, she can request the trial court to declare misjoinder. The remedy is separate trials, not dismissal of the charges. Misjoinder can occur in any jurisdiction, whether it has a permissive or compulsory joinder rule, because all jurisdictions define the maximum range of charges that may be grouped together. But not all jurisdictions declare the same maximum. Some follow the model of Fed. R. Crim. P. 8(a), allowing joinder of offenses based on (1) acts that are of the same or similar character or (2) the "same act or transaction" or (3) two or more acts or transactions connected together or constituting parts of a common scheme or plan. Another group of states do not include the first ground for joinder, acts of the "same or similar character." Can you imagine a class of cases in which this first ground for joinder would make a difference in the outcome on a motion to declare misjoinder, or do you expect the different formulations to produce essentially the same results?

The relationships among the doctrines of permissive joinder, mandatory joinder, misjoinder, and severance are complex. You can find diagrams to sort out these overlapping spheres on the web extension for this chapter at *http://www.crimpro.com/extension/ch14*.

2. *Joint Trials of Defendants*

The joinder and severance questions we have considered thus far all deal with multiple offenses and an individual defendant. Related questions arise when prosecutors charge two or more defendants with committing essentially the same crime. Under what circumstances will the co-defendants receive separate trials?

The key phrases in procedural rules such as the ones reprinted below are framed generally and require further elaboration by courts presented with recurring factual situations. Cases have generally held that a defendant should obtain severance from a co-defendant when (1) evidence admitted against one defendant is facially incriminating to the other defendant, such as a prior statement of one co-defendant that incriminates the other co-defendant; (2) evidence admitted against one defendant influences the jury so strongly that it has a harmful "rub-off effect" on the other defendant; (3) there is a significant disparity in the amount of evidence introduced against each of the two defendants; or (4) co-defendants present defenses that are so antagonistic that they are mutually exclusive.

Only clear examples of these types of prejudice will convince an appellate court to reverse a trial court's decision to require a joint trial. For instance, to determine if a "rub off" problem exists, the court must ask whether the jury can keep separate the evidence that is relevant to each defendant and render a fair and impartial verdict as to each. Even in some cases where such prejudicial factors are strong enough to warrant a severance, courts sometimes decide that curative jury instructions can remove any risk of prejudice that might result from a joint trial.

■ FEDERAL RULE OF CRIMINAL PROCEDURE 8(b)

The indictment or information may charge two or more defendants if they are alleged to have participated in the same act or transaction, or in the same series of acts or transactions, constituting an offense or offenses. The defendants may be charged in one or more counts together or separately. All defendants need not be charged in each count.

■ VERMONT RULE OF CRIMINAL PROCEDURE 8(b)

Two or more defendants may be joined in the same information or indictment:

(1) when each of the defendants is charged with accountability for each offense included;

(2) when each of the defendants is charged with conspiracy and some of the defendants are also charged with one or more offenses alleged to be in furtherance of the conspiracy; or

(3) when, even if conspiracy is not charged and all of the defendants are not charged in each count, it is alleged that the several offenses charged

(A) were part of a common scheme or plan; or

(B) were so closely connected in respect to time, place, and occasion that it would be difficult to separate proof of one charge from proof of others.

VERMONT RULE OF CRIMINAL PROCEDURE 14(b)(2)

Whenever two or more defendants have been joined together in the same information or indictment,

(A) On motion of the prosecuting attorney or a defendant before trial, the court shall grant severance of one or more defendants if the court finds that they are not joinable under Rule 8(b)(2).

(B) On motion of the prosecuting attorney before trial, other than under subparagraph (A) of this paragraph, the court shall grant severance of one or more defendants if the court finds that there is no reasonable likelihood of prejudice to any defendant. On motion of the prosecuting attorney during trial, the court shall grant severance of one or more defendants only with the consent of the defendant or defendants to be severed or upon a finding of manifest necessity.

(C) On motion of a defendant for severance because an out-of-court statement of a codefendant makes reference to, but is not admissible against, the moving defendant, the court shall determine whether the prosecution intends to offer the statement in evidence as part of its case in chief. If so, the court shall require the prosecuting attorney to elect one of the following courses:

(i) a joint trial at which the statement is not admitted into evidence:

(ii) a joint trial at which the statement is admitted into evidence only after all references to the moving defendant have been deleted, provided that the court finds that the statement, with the references deleted, will not prejudice the moving defendant; or

(iii) severance of the moving defendant.

(D) On motion of a defendant other than under subparagraph (A) or (C) of this paragraph, the court shall grant severance of the moving defendant unless the court finds that there is no reasonable likelihood that that defendant would be prejudiced by a joint trial.

(E) In determining whether there is no reasonable likelihood that a defendant would be prejudiced, the court shall consider among other factors whether, in view of the number of offenses and defendants charged and the complexity of the evidence to be offered, the trier of fact will be able to distinguish the evidence and apply the law intelligently as to each offense and as to each defendant.

(F) The court may, at any time, grant severance of one or more defendants with the consent of the prosecution and the defendant or defendants to be severed.

VERMONT REPORTER'S NOTES — 1995 AMENDMENT

Rule 14(b)(2) is amended to eliminate the absolute right of severance for a defendant in a felony case and to provide guidelines under which a motion for severance of defendants is to be considered. Under the prior rule, in misdemeanor cases severance or whatever other relief justice required was to be granted when either a defendant or the State was prejudiced by joinder. The amended rule applies to both felonies and misdemeanors. The amendment is based on ABA Standard 13-3.2. The purposes of the amendment are to give the court flexibility and to strike a proper balance between avoidance of multiple trials for victims and the right of defendants to a fair trial. . . .

When two or more defendants have been joined, the first issue for determination is whether the joinder is proper under the terms of that rule. Amended Rule 14(b)(2)(A) requires the court to grant a pretrial request by either prosecution or defense for severance on grounds of misjoinder, regardless of whether there is prejudice. If a defect in joinder appears during trial, a severance on that ground is to be considered in accordance with the standards of subparagraphs (B) and (D).

Under Rule 14(b)(2)(B), even if joinder is proper pursuant to Rule 8(b), the prosecutor will be granted a severance on motion before trial if the court finds "no reasonable likelihood" that any defendant would be prejudiced by the severance. . . . On an appropriate motion by a defendant under Rule 14(b)(2)(C), the court must determine whether Bruton v. United States, 391 U.S. 123 (1968), affects the severance decision. Under *Bruton,* the trial court must protect the confrontation rights of a nonconfessing defendant where a codefendant has confessed and that confession is admissible only against the confessing defendant. Rule 14(b)(2)(C)(i)-(iii) set out the options which must be followed for compliance with *Bruton*. . . .

If a defendant moves for severance before trial on grounds other than misjoinder or the potential use of a codefendant's confession, the court under Rule 14(b)(2)(D) is to sever the moving defendant unless it finds that there is no reasonable likelihood of prejudice to that defendant from the joinder. The standard for determining prejudice is set forth in Rule 14(b)(2)(E). That standard departs from the formulation, "fair determination of guilt or innocence," found in ABA Standard 13-3.2(b)(i), (ii). In deciding the question, the court is to consider "prejudice" in terms of the impact of the challenged joinder on each defendant's right to a fair trial where the prosecution makes the motion and on the moving defendant's fair trial right where a defendant makes the motion. [T]here is a reasonable likelihood of prejudice where the jury might consider evidence against one defendant that is properly offered only against a codefendant, either on the merits or as to character or credibility. Where the evidence against both defendants is substantially similar, however, they may be tried jointly in the absence of other factors giving rise to a reasonable likelihood of prejudice. . . .

Problem 14-5. Antagonistic Brothers

Brothers Durid and Kafan Hana were arrested following a controlled narcotics purchase that took place at the Sterling Heights home in which the brothers lived with their parents and siblings. The drug transaction arose out of a conversation between James Hornburger and Raed Alsarih at the Sterling Heights High School where they were students. Hornburger approached Alsarih about obtaining twelve ounces of cocaine for Stephen Putnam, who happened to be an undercover narcotics police officer. Alsarih agreed to the transaction after contacting Kafan. Hornburger, Putnam, and Alsarih drove to Kafan's home. Alsarih went to the door and spoke with Durid, who contacted Kafan by beeper and reported that Kafan would be back in 15 minutes. When the purchasers returned to the house later that evening, they saw Kafan drive up and Alsarih and Kafan went into the house together.

According to Alsarih, testifying pursuant to a plea bargain, he went with Kafan to a back bedroom where Durid was sleeping. Durid awoke when Kafan turned on the light. While Kafan opened a safe, Durid asked Alsarih whether the person outside was a police officer and whether Alsarih had dealt with him before. Kafan removed a plastic bag from the safe, mixed it with the contents from some other bags and gave it to Alsarih. They returned to the front of the house, and Kafan watched while Alsarih went out to Putnam's car. Durid was watching from the living room window. Alsarih then got in the back seat and gave the bag of cocaine to Putnam. Putnam signaled to a surveillance team, which moved in and arrested Hornburger, Alsarih, Kafan, and Durid. A subsequent search of the home, pursuant to a search warrant, disclosed that the safe contained three kilograms of cocaine, miscellaneous jewelry and papers, a telephone recorder, and a telephone beeper. Both Kafan and Durid initially denied knowing the combination to the safe. However, Kafan later supplied the combination, and Durid admitted that the safe was his.

Both Durid and Kafan filed pretrial motions for separate trials. Michigan Court Rule 6.121 provides for permissive joinder and conditional severance:

> (A) Permissive Joinder. An information or indictment may charge two or more defendants with the same offense. [T]wo or more informations or indictments against different defendants may be consolidated for a single trial whenever the defendants could be charged in the same information or indictment under this rule. . . .
>
> (C) Right of Severance; Related Offenses. On a defendant's motion, the court must sever the trial of defendants on related offenses on a showing that severance is necessary to avoid prejudice to substantial rights of the defendants.
>
> (D) Discretionary Severance. On the motion of any party, the court may sever the trial of defendants on the ground that severance is appropriate to promote fairness to the parties and a fair determination of the guilt or innocence of one or more of the defendants. Relevant factors include the timeliness of the motion, the drain on the parties' resources, the potential for confusion or prejudice stemming from either the number of defendants or the complexity or nature of the evidence, the convenience of the witnesses, and the parties' readiness for trial. . . .

In a supporting affidavit, Durid's counsel explained the results of a meeting with Kafan's attorneys:

> At said meeting affiant was advised by both counsel that the defense theory of the above case was that evidence would show that the controlled substances seized from 3105 Metropolitan Parkway were the property of, or possessed by, Durid Bajhat Hana and not by Kafan Hana. Given the fact that Durid Bajhat Hana's theory of the case is that the controlled substances seized from 3105 Metropolitan Parkway were the property of, or possessed by, Kafan Hana, and not by Durid Bajhat Hana, Durid Bajhat Hana will be compelled to act, for all practical purpose, as an assistant prosecutor as to Kafan Hana.

The trial court heard argument on the motions. Durid's attorney argued that "the two defenses could not be more antagonistic. Two people are pointing the finger at each other and the case is clear that severance must be granted." The prosecutor argued that it took more than "a mere allegation of pointing fingers at one another" to warrant separate trials. The trial court denied the motion.

The brothers were tried jointly before a jury. Durid was tried on an aiding and abetting theory. In his opening statement, Kafan's attorney told jurors that their deliberations necessarily pitted brother against brother. During closing argument, Durid's attorney similarly described the defense postures as "brother pitted against brother." In closing arguments, Kafan's attorney disputed the theory that his client had control over the three kilograms of cocaine seized from the safe:

> We know he used the Cadillac, we know he used the house, we know he used the safe, but we know he didn't own the Cadillac and own the house and own the safe. Everybody who has ever shared a locker in school or anybody who's ever shared an apartment, everybody who's ever lived in a rooming house and had to share a bathroom knows that you can share special areas and have absolutely no right to control something that belongs to somebody else.

The prosecutor pointed out the conflict during rebuttal closing argument when she noted: "That's real convenient for these two boys to sit here and say that the drugs belonged to one another." This remark was stricken. The prosecutor later stated:

> The position that Durid Hana and Kafan Hana took in this trial is saying that the drugs did not belong to them, but they were in their bedroom and they were in a safe that they both had access to, and if you believe both Durid Hana and Kafan Hana, the good fairy must have delivered the drugs and locked them in the safe. It's not reasonable to believe that they did not know that they were there. Someone put those drugs in that safe, and if you look at all of the evidence that occurred that night, it is reasonable to believe that both of them knew it. . . .

The prosecutor further explained in closing argument: "As to Durid Hana, it is the People's theory that Durid aided his brother in the delivery of cocaine in the sum of 225 to 649 grams of cocaine, that he provided support, advice and encouragement and took an active role in that delivery. It is further alleged that Durid Hana knew that the cocaine was being stored in that safe and that he had dominion and control over the contents of what was kept in that safe, as did his brother Kafan Hana." Neither Durid nor his brother testified. Durid and Kafan were both convicted of possession of more than 650 grams of cocaine and delivery of more than 225, but less than 650, grams of cocaine.

Durid appeals, alleging that the trial court erred in denying his motion for a separate trial given the antagonistic defenses of the two brothers. He argues that the events at trial support his claim of antagonistic defenses. How would you rule? Compare People v. Hana, 524 N.W.2d 682 (Mich. 1994).

Notes

1. *Joinder of defendants: majority view.* Joint trials account for almost one-third of all federal criminal trials, a rate much higher than in most state systems. As a result, the federal courts have dealt extensively with severance issues. See Richardson v. Marsh, 481 U.S. 200 (1987). In general, the federal courts have shown a strong preference for joint trials. This preference has become even more pronounced in recent years, and severance requests in the federal courts are now routinely denied. Interestingly, one empirical study of the joinder of federal defendants concluded that joining co-defendants in a single trial had virtually no impact on the likelihood of conviction. Andrew D. Leipold & Hossein A. Abbasi, The Impact of Joinder and Severance on Federal Criminal Cases: An Empirical Study, 59 Vand. L. Rev. 101 (2006).

A majority of states leave decisions on the joinder and severance of trials for multiple defendants to the discretion of the trial judge. Defendants in these jurisdictions find courts generally unreceptive when they request separate trials based on the special legal and practical difficulties of defending against conspiracy charges. As the reporter's notes to Vermont Rule 14(b)(2) indicate, Vermont had a mandatory severance rule but amended it in 1995, in line with the dominant view, allowing the trial judge some discretion over whether to order joint trials. See Kan. Stat. §22-3204. A significant minority of states, including Vermont, provide more detailed rules to guide courts in assessing out-of-court statements by co-defendants. See, e.g., Fla. R. Crim. P. 3.152(b).

2. *Remedies short of severance.* Courts take several approaches short of severing trials to deal with conflicts among co-defendants. The most common is simply to issue cautionary instructions to the jury before it retires to consider the case. Sometimes the judge also instructs the jury at the beginning of the trial or when particular evidence is presented. Occasionally courts will bar the use of evidence that would be admissible at a trial of a co-defendant tried separately. A more complex option, which has been tried in a number of states, is the use of "dual" juries to hear the same case. Each jury considers the charges against one defendant. The court will excuse one of the juries when evidence is presented against one defendant that could not be presented against the other. For a general discussion of "mega-trials" in the federal courts, see James Jacobs et al., Busting the Mob: United States v. Cosa Nostra (1994).

PART THREE

RESOLVING GUILT AND INNOCENCE

XV

Discovery and Speedy Trial

The most critical task for the attorney preparing for trial is to gather information about the events in question. Much of the best information is in the hands of the other party. The rules of discovery govern how and when the parties exchange information that may be relevant in resolving the charges, whether through trial or guilty plea. These rules are grounded in constitutions, statutes, court rules, and local policies and practices.

Adequate preparation takes time. But all the while, the defendant must live with the shame of accusation and the inconvenience and expense of preparing for trial. For defendants who are detained, the period before trial can destroy employment and personal relationships. Many defendants, and especially those in detention, want a "speedy" trial. In this chapter, we review the tools for discovering information and the many sources of law that give parties the ability, and the incentive, to speed up or slow down the trial date.

A. DISCOVERY

In all litigation, there are rules about exchanging information among the parties and gathering information from nonparties. What the parties learn during discovery determines in large part the evidence they will have at their disposal at trial. Even more important for most defendants, discovery allows them to estimate their chances of success at trial and to enter plea bargain negotiations with that information in mind.

Two sets of interrelated questions dominate the law of discovery in criminal cases. First, discovery rules must resolve whether shared information or independent information is the norm. The answer to this question reflects the expected relationship among prosecutors, judges, and defense attorneys. Less exchange of information reflects a more adversarial and independent model, where each side develops its own evidence; more exchange reflects a more cooperative model of litigation, with the court taking a stronger role in coordinating a collective search for truth. When describing the criminal discovery process on this score, it may be helpful to draw a comparison to discovery in civil litigation. It is commonplace to hear that criminal discovery is less extensive than civil discovery. Is this claim accurate today? If so, will it remain true in the future? As you read and discuss the materials in this section, try to draw comparisons to civil discovery techniques and to identify trends over time toward more or less extensive criminal discovery.

The second set of questions deals with the symmetry of discovery. Will prosecution and defense have an equal ability to obtain information from the opposing side? In a system with other asymmetries built into it (such as the "beyond a reasonable doubt" standard of proof, the privilege against self-incrimination, and the government's funding of prosecutors and investigators), are asymmetrical discovery rights necessary or desirable?

1. *Prosecution Disclosure of Inculpatory Information*

A defense attorney with enough time, ingenuity, and resources could learn much about the government's evidence in a criminal case. Rules of procedure and statutes in most jurisdictions set out the obligations of the prosecution to disclose some of the incriminating evidence against the accused, but only after the defendant requests it. Local court rules sometimes supplement the statewide rules.

Despite these discovery rules, however, the defense attorney frequently knows much less than the prosecutor about the case at the time of plea bargaining or trial. Some of the functional limits on discovery are built into the rules themselves, and others are a function of the defense attorney's limited time and resources.

The criminal discovery rules show remarkable variety from jurisdiction to jurisdiction. Federal Rule of Criminal Procedure 16 and the South Carolina rule reprinted below are typical of the more restrictive rules, which give the defendant access to only a handful of documents and tangible objects before trial. Most states go beyond these limited categories to allow defense discovery of a wider range of prosecution information. The ABA Standards for Criminal Justice have been an influential model for those states moving in the direction of wider discovery. The New Jersey rule reprinted below illustrates the broader scope of documents and other information that some states consider essential to the preparation of a defense.

Use the following problem as a setting for applying the New Jersey and South Carolina rules. Under each of these approaches to criminal discovery, what information gets exchanged, and what types of evidence go unmentioned? How will a plea negotiation or a trial progress if the defense lawyer does not have access to such information before trial? Can defense counsel develop the same information through different avenues?

Problem 15-1. Exchanging Words

Two groups in a bar were arguing one night. One group, which included Wayne Galvan, left shortly before the bar closed, while the other group, which included Perry Sutton, waited inside a few minutes longer, hoping to avoid any contact outside with the other group. When Sutton and his friends went outside, Galvan and his friends appeared from around the corner and started taunting Sutton's group. Soon the two groups were involved in a heated argument. In the midst of the noise and confusion, Galvan drew a small handgun and fired two shots while standing less than five feet from Sutton. The second shot killed Sutton. Galvan ran away. Several of Sutton's friends knew Galvan by name and identified him to police officers. The officers later arrested Galvan at his cousin's home, where they also found a small handgun.

You have been appointed to represent Galvan. During his initial conversation with you, Galvan claimed that he meant to frighten Sutton and his friends by firing his handgun into the air, but that he did not intend to harm Sutton. Galvan said that he had discussed the incident with two other detainees in the county jail.

You have obtained from your client the names and addresses of some of his friends who were present that evening. During telephone conversations with two of those friends, you learn that one was interviewed within a week of the shooting by a police officer and an attorney from the district attorney's office, both of whom were taking notes. The second was interviewed by a police officer alone, and the officer did not take any notes. You learned from Galvan's friends the name of one of Sutton's friends who was present on the night of the shooting, but that person refuses to talk to you.

Galvan has authorized you to engage in plea negotiations. What sort of discovery will you request before plea negotiations begin? Consider each of the following categories of potentially useful information:

- Any statements that Galvan made to police officers, prosecutors, his friends, or members of the rival group. Does it matter whether the statements have been recorded in a document?
- Any statements that members of the rival group made to police or prosecutors about what they saw or heard that night. Can you insist that the police tell you what they know about the background and reliability of these witnesses?
- Any statements that members of Galvan's group made to the police or prosecutors. Can the prosecutors gain discovery of these statements? Is there anything you can or should do to prepare these potential defense witnesses for an interview with the police or cross-examination at trial by the prosecutor?
- Any ballistics or other scientific tests performed on the gun, along with any medical examinations performed on Sutton.

Anticipate how the prosecutors might respond if the relevant discovery rules are similar to those in South Carolina. Then compare the government's response if the rules look like those in New Jersey. Would any of the evidence you might obtain through requests under these discovery rules dramatically change the course of the plea negotiations?

Think also about the timing of discovery. Suppose you are assigned to the case at the arraignment, less than a month after the charges are filed. The median time it takes to process felony cases in the state is 80 days (roughly the national median time), although a few cases last a good deal longer. About 10 percent of the felony cases require more than a year to resolve.

Finally, consider the investigative resources at your disposal. You work full time as a defense attorney, and you represent about 150 felony defendants per year (the maximum workload prescribed in the ABA Standards on Criminal Justice, but lighter than the load many defense attorneys actually carry). Your office employs a former police detective as an investigator, but seven other criminal defense attorneys in your office share the services of this investigator. In light of these resource constraints and the legal rules described below, what would be your strategy for obtaining the types of information listed above?

■ SOUTH CAROLINA RULE OF CRIMINAL PROCEDURE 5(A)

(1) *Information Subject to Disclosure*.

(A) *Statement of Defendant*. Upon request by a defendant, the prosecution shall permit the defendant to inspect and copy or photograph: any relevant written or recorded statements made by the defendant, or copies thereof, within the possession, custody, or control of the prosecution, the existence of which is known, or by the exercise of due diligence may become known, to the attorney for the prosecution; the substance of any oral statement which the prosecution intends to offer in evidence at the trial made by the defendant whether before or after arrest in response to interrogation by any person then known to the defendant to be a prosecution agent.

(B) *Defendant's Prior Record*. Upon request of the defendant, the prosecution shall furnish to the defendant such copy of his prior criminal record, if any, as is within the possession, custody, or control of the prosecution, the existence of which is known, or by the exercise of due diligence may become known, to the attorney for the prosecution.

(C) *Documents and Tangible Objects*. Upon request of the defendant the prosecution shall permit the defendant to inspect and copy books, papers, documents, photographs, tangible objects, buildings, or places, or copies or portions thereof, which are within the possession, custody, or control of the prosecution, and which are material to the preparation of his defense or are intended for use by the prosecution as evidence in chief at the trial, or were obtained from or belong to the defendant.

(D) *Reports of Examinations and Tests*. Upon request of a defendant the prosecution shall permit the defendant to inspect and copy any results or reports of physical or mental examinations, and of scientific tests or experiments, or copies thereof, which are within the possession, custody, or control of the prosecution, the existence of which is known, or by the exercise of due diligence may become known, to the attorney for the prosecution, and which are material to the preparation of the defense or are intended for use by the prosecution as evidence in chief at the trial.

(2) *Information Not Subject to Disclosure*. Except as provided in paragraphs (A), (B), and (D) of subdivision (a)(1), this rule does not authorize the discovery or inspection of reports, memoranda, or other internal prosecution documents made by the attorney for the prosecution or other prosecution agents in connection with the investigation or prosecution of the case, or of statements made by prosecution witnesses or prospective prosecution witnesses provided that after a prosecution witness has testified on direct examination, the court shall, on motion of the defendant, order the prosecution to produce any statement of the witness in the possession of the prosecution which relates to the subject matter as to which the witness has testified; and provided further that the court may upon a sufficient showing require the production of any statement of any prospective witness prior to the time such witness testifies.

(3) *Time for Disclosure*. The prosecution shall respond to the defendant's request for disclosure no later then thirty days after the request is made, or within such other time as may be ordered by the court.

NEW JERSEY COURT RULE 3:13-3

(a) Where the prosecutor has made a pre-indictment plea offer, the prosecutor shall upon request permit defense counsel to inspect and copy or photograph any relevant material which would be discoverable following an indictment pursuant to section (b) or (c).

(b) A copy of the prosecutor's discovery shall be delivered to the criminal division manager's office, or shall be available at the prosecutor's office, within 14 days of the return or unsealing of the indictment. . . . A defendant who does not seek discovery from the State shall so notify the criminal division manager's office and the prosecutor, and the defendant need not provide discovery to the State [except as] otherwise required by law. . . .

(c) The prosecutor shall permit defendant to inspect and copy or photograph the following relevant material if not given as part of the discovery package under section (b):

(1) books, tangible objects, papers or documents obtained from or belonging to the defendant;

(2) records of statements or confessions, signed or unsigned, by the defendant or copies thereof, and a summary of any admissions or declarations against penal interest made by the defendant that are known to the prosecution but not recorded;

(3) results or reports of physical or mental examinations and of scientific tests or experiments made in connection with the matter or copies thereof, which are within the possession, custody or control of the prosecutor;

(4) reports or records of prior convictions of the defendant;

(5) books, papers, documents, or copies thereof, or tangible objects, buildings or places which are within the possession, custody or control of the prosecutor;

(6) names, addresses, and birthdates of any persons whom the prosecutor knows to have relevant evidence or information including a designation by the prosecutor as to which of those persons may be called as witnesses;

(7) record of statements, signed or unsigned, by such persons or by co-defendants which are within the possession, custody or control of the prosecutor and any relevant record of prior conviction of such persons;

(8) police reports which are within the possession, custody, or control of the prosecutor;

(9) names and addresses of each person whom the prosecutor expects to call to trial as an expert witness, the expert's qualifications, the subject matter on which the expert is expected to testify, a copy of the report, if any, of such expert witness, or if no report is prepared, a statement of the facts and opinions to which the expert is expected to testify and a summary of the grounds for each opinion. . . .

Notes

1. *Defendant and co-defendant statements.* Discovery rules in all jurisdictions allow defense counsel at least some access to the government's evidence regarding statements that the defendant made about the alleged crime. This does not mean, however, that the government must turn over all statements by a defendant. Under Fed. R. Crim. P. 16(a)(1)(A), the defense may obtain "written or recorded" statements of a defendant and written evidence of "oral statements" made by a defendant in response to interrogation by a known government agent. The ABA Standard for Criminal Justice, Discovery 11-2.1(a)(i) (3d ed. 1996) calls for the prosecutor to disclose "all written and oral statements of the defendant or any co-defendant," along with any documents "relating to the acquisition of such statements." See also Fla. R. Crim. P. 3.220(b)(1)(C). What sorts of statements does the ABA standard cover that the Federal Rule does not? Does a defense attorney really need to obtain such statements from the government when he could simply ask his client about any statements he made? How would he use documents "relating to the acquisition" of a defendant's statement?

Note that Rule 16 makes no provision for the discovery of co-defendant's statements. Cf. Fla. R. Crim. P. 3.220(b)(1)(D) (discovery of "any written or recorded statements and the substance of any oral statements made by a codefendant if the trial is to be a joint one"). When might defense counsel use such a statement? Does defense counsel have an alternative method of preparing for any co-defendant statements that might be used at trial?

2. *Prosecution expert witnesses.* Criminal discovery rules, like their civil counterparts, recognize the special challenges of preparing for the trial testimony of expert witnesses. Fed. R. Crim. P. 16(a)(1)(E) calls for disclosure of a "written summary of testimony the government intends to use" from experts in its case in chief, which includes the expert's opinions, the bases and the reasons for the opinions, and the expert's qualifications. Once again, many states give the defense more information, by including disclosure of the reports or statements of any experts (such as the results of tests) made "in connection with" a particular case, whether or not the government plans to call the expert at trial. Fla. R. Crim. P. 3.220(b)(1)(J). The rules typically impose on both parties the same obligations of disclosure about their experts.

3. *Nonexpert witnesses and potential witnesses.* Perhaps the greatest variety in discovery rules involves information about nonexpert witnesses and potential witnesses. Federal Rule of Criminal Procedure 26.2 provides for disclosure *at trial* by both the prosecution and defense of written "statements" of any witnesses other than the defendant. Any disclosure of witness statements before trial (or before entry of a guilty plea) results from negotiations between the parties. What impact would this timing question have on the course of plea negotiations?

What is the rationale for providing such limited discovery of potential witnesses? To some extent, such discovery rules endorse the classic adversarial model of justice. Rules that limit disclosure of prosecution witnesses also reflect worries that defendants will engage in witness tampering, bribery, and intimidation. To the extent that defendants can use broader discovery to fine-tune misleading or perjured defenses, broader discovery could undermine the basic truth-finding function of criminal adjudication.

Discovery rules in other jurisdictions treat information about potential witnesses as a matter that the defense cannot develop alone before trial. The rules commonly require the government to give the defense — before trial — the names and addresses of its witnesses and other persons who have knowledge of the events surrounding the alleged crime. See Fla. R. Crim. P. 3.220(b)(1)(A); National District Attorneys Association, National Prosecution Standards 53.2 (3d ed. 2009) (covering prosecution witnesses but not potential witnesses). The rules also oblige the government to provide the defense with potential impeachment material, such as the prior criminal record of any witnesses or the nature of any cooperation agreement between the government and the witness. The rules also typically extend to any written summaries of witness statements, even if the statements are not "adopted" or "verbatim." See ABA Standard 11-2.1(a)(ii); Fla. R. Crim. P. 3.220(b)(1)(B). Is all of this discovery about witnesses necessary? Once a defense attorney has the name and address of a potential witness, can she obtain statements from the witness on equal terms with the government?

4. *Open file policies.* A few jurisdictions (such as New Jersey, as indicated in the provisions reprinted above) have embraced "open file" discovery — rules that require the prosecutor to keep any written records about the case completely open to the defense attorney. While such a position is unusual to find in statewide statutes or rules, it is commonplace to find individual prosecutors' offices that have committed themselves to open file discovery. Why would prosecutors create discovery rules that go well beyond the requirements of the applicable law? Does it save them the trouble of sorting through documents to comply with discovery requests? Keep in mind that prosecutors adopting an open file policy still must identify material exculpatory evidence for defense attorneys and offer such information to the defense, even if there is no specific request for it. Does an open file policy best achieve the discovery objectives identified by the National District Attorneys Association: "to provide information for informed pleas, expedite trials, minimize surprise, afford the opportunity for effective cross-examination, meet the requirements of due process, and otherwise serve the interests of justice"? National Prosecution Standards 52.1 (2d ed. 1991). Can a prosecutor's office count on the limited time available to a defense attorney in most smaller cases to minimize the impact of an open file policy? Cf. ABA Standard 11-1.2 (discovery "may be more limited" in cases involving minor offenses).

5. *Writings already in existence.* Even with open file policies, the emphasis is on written materials rather than the knowledge of the people who provide or analyze the evidence. Is this why the federal system, with its first-class capacity for developing written evidence and keeping records, has more restrictive discovery rules than most jurisdictions? Note that most of the discovery provisions described above require the prosecution to hand over existing documents, but they do not oblige the prosecutor to create or compile information (which is more common under civil discovery rules). There are a few exceptions to this pattern: Some discovery rules call on the prosecutor to commit to writing any known oral statement of the defendant, and to summarize information about expert witnesses. Given that criminal justice systems rely so heavily on guilty pleas rather than development of the facts during a trial, should the systems move in the direction of forcing the parties to summarize evidence before trial?

6. *Depositions.* Depositions of witnesses and other third parties, the lifeblood of civil discovery, does not hold an important place in criminal discovery. In the federal system and in most states, depositions are available only to preserve the testimony of a witness who is unlikely to be available at trial. A few states, however, have begun to make it easier to obtain depositions and to use them in criminal proceedings. These are sometimes called "discovery" depositions, as opposed to depositions used to preserve testimony. See Fla. R. Crim. P. 3.220(h). Why have criminal discovery innovators focused their attention on the available documents rather than the deposition or written interrogatory?

Despite the rarity of criminal depositions in most jurisdictions, the parties do interview witnesses before trial. Does this voluntary system of gathering evidence give the parties equal access to information? See ABA Standard 11-6.3 (neither prosecutor nor defense should advise persons other than defendant to refrain from speaking with counsel for opposing side).

7. *Remedies.* Discovery rules typically leave courts with a great deal of discretion in selecting a remedy for a violation of the law. The most common remedies are continuances (to allow the party time to develop a response to the evidence) and exclusion of the evidence that the party should have disclosed (particularly where the aggrieved party can show some prejudice flowing from the discovery violation). Trial courts have also dismissed charges for more serious discovery violations by a prosecutor. State ex rel. Rusen v. Hill, 454 S.E.2d 427 (W. Va. 1994). If an appellate court decides that a discovery violation occurred, it can reverse the conviction if the defendant shows prejudice. Contempt citations against the attorney or later disciplinary proceedings by the state bar are also possibilities.

8. *Discovery by any other name.* The rules of pretrial discovery are not the defendant's only method of finding out about the government's evidence. The preliminary hearing, where the government establishes probable cause to support the charges in the case, often gives defense counsel a glimpse of the government's theory of the case. Defendants will also on occasion request a "bill of particulars," a document that supplements the indictment or information when necessary to give proper notice to the defendant of the charges he must defend against.

9. *Other pre-trial motions.* The parties file discovery motions along with motions on many other issues. Which issues can the parties raise before trial, and which *must* they raise before trial? What procedures does the court follow to resolve these motions? The web extension for this chapter, at *http://www.crimpro.com/extension/ch15*, collects materials that explore these interrelated questions surrounding motions practice.

2. *Prosecution Disclosure of Exculpatory Information*

Under the criminal discovery rules, the defense lawyer must ask before receiving material from the government. But the prosecutor's duty sometimes goes beyond responding to valid defense requests for discovery. There are several types of information that the law requires the prosecution to disclose to the defense, even if the defense lawyer never asks for the information.

One disclosure duty that courts place on prosecutors involves perjured testimony of government witnesses. If the prosecutor knows or should know that government witnesses are presenting false testimony or evidence, due process requires the prosecutor to disclose this fact to the defendant and to the court. A conviction must be set aside if there is any reasonable likelihood that the false testimony could have affected the judgment of the jury. See Mooney v. Holohan, 294 U.S. 103 (1935); Napue v. Illinois, 360 U.S. 264 (1959).

A second constitutional duty to disclose derives from Brady v. Maryland, 373 U.S. 83 (1963). In that case, a defense attorney in a murder case asked to review all the extrajudicial statements of a coconspirator, but the prosecutor withheld a statement in which the coconspirator admitted to shooting the victim. The Supreme Court ruled that the constitution's due process clause requires the prosecution to disclose "evidence favorable to an accused" if that evidence is "material either to guilt or to punishment." The Court expanded this disclosure duty in United States v. Agurs, 427 U.S. 97 (1976). The obligation to disclose all *material* evidence favorable to the accused, the Court said, applies even when the defendant makes only a general request for exculpatory information or makes no discovery request at all. Such material evidence includes evidence that the defense might use to impeach prosecution witnesses, along with evidence that more directly points to the defendant's innocence. See United States v. Bagley, 473 U.S. 667 (1985). Failure to disclose *non-material* evidence does not violate *Brady*, regardless of whether defense counsel requested disclosure.

Litigation over *Brady* issues remains quite common. Courts struggle to identify which prosecutorial failures to disclose are important enough to justify overturning a conviction. This difficult question necessarily calls for the court to speculate: What would have happened if the prosecutor had disclosed the material? How certain does the reviewing court have to be?

A third constitutional duty relates to the incentives of the prosecution's witnesses. In Giglio v. United States, 405 U.S. 150 (1972), the Court overturned a conviction based on the prosecutor's failure to disclose a promise made to its key witness that he would not be prosecuted if he testified for the Government. Such "*Giglio* material" is now a routine part of the disclosure obligations of the prosecutor.

In the following case, the Illinois Supreme Court unanimously found that the government had committed a *Brady* violation. How could lower courts reach a different result on these facts? What office practices become necessary for Illinois prosecutors as a result of this case?

■ PEOPLE v. ALAN BEAMAN

890 N.E.2d 500 (Ill. 2008)

KILBRIDE, J.

The petitioner, Alan Beaman, appeals the dismissal of his postconviction petition. His petition stems from a first degree murder conviction, and sentence of 50 years. [Petitioner] asserts several claims, including that the State violated his constitutional right to due process of law by failing to disclose information about a viable alternative suspect in the murder. We conclude that the State violated petitioner's right to due process under Brady v. Maryland, 373 U.S. 83 (1963), by failing to disclose material information about the alternative suspect. . . .

I. BACKGROUND

Jennifer Lockmiller, an Illinois State University student, was found dead in her apartment in Normal, Illinois, on August 28, 1993. A clock radio electrical cord was wrapped around her neck, and she had been stabbed in the chest with scissors. Her shirt and bra were pushed up around her neck, and her shorts and underwear were pulled down. A box fan was lying across her face.

Seven fingerprints were recovered from the clock radio. Two of the fingerprints were from petitioner, four belonged to Jennifer's boyfriend Michael Swaine, and one was unidentified. Based on the crime scene and Jennifer's class schedule, the State argued that the time of death was shortly after 12 P.M. on Wednesday, August 25, 1993. In a bill of particulars, the State asserted the murder occurred between 12 P.M. and 2 P.M. on that date.

Prior to trial, the State filed a motion *in limine* seeking to exclude evidence of Jennifer's relationships with men other than petitioner and Michael Swaine. The State argued that petitioner should not be allowed to offer alternative-suspect evidence unless he could establish it was not remote or speculative. The prosecutor informed the court that the State did not possess nonspeculative evidence of a third-party suspect. The court reserved ruling on the motion.

Before the jury trial, the prosecutor and defense counsel discussed Jennifer's relationship with a person identified as John Doe. The prosecutor informed the court that Doe had "nothing to do with this case." Petitioner conceded that he did not have any specific evidence showing that another person committed the offense. The trial court then granted the motion *in limine*, ruling that petitioner could not present any evidence of an alternative suspect.

At trial, petitioner testified that he began dating Jennifer in July of 1992. During the following year, petitioner and Jennifer ended and then restarted their relationship a number of times. Petitioner was a student at Illinois Wesleyan University in Bloomington during that time. He often used Jennifer's clock radio to wake up for class. In several letters to Jennifer, petitioner expressed his desire to have a monogamous relationship. The letters indicated that petitioner believed Jennifer was involved with other men. . . .

Petitioner testified that one night in the spring of 1993, Jennifer called and told him that she wanted to end their relationship. He went to Jennifer's apartment to get his compact disc player. When he arrived, he saw John Doe's car in the parking lot. Petitioner pounded on the door to Jennifer's apartment, but she refused to let him inside. Petitioner continued pounding and kicking the door until it broke. After he discovered Jennifer and Doe inside, he took his compact disc player from the apartment and left. Petitioner was yelling while inside the apartment, but he did not touch either Jennifer or Doe.

Additionally, Jennifer and petitioner's roommate, Michael Swaine, began a relationship during the summer of 1993. One night in early July, petitioner suspected that Swaine was at Jennifer's apartment. Petitioner pounded and kicked the door until it broke. He entered the apartment, but could not find Swaine. Petitioner did not touch Jennifer, but confronted her verbally and left after 30 to 45 minutes.

On July 25, 1993, petitioner searched Swaine's room and discovered letters that Jennifer had written to Swaine. Petitioner located Swaine and screamed at him about "seeing" Jennifer. Petitioner then went to Jennifer's apartment, pounded on her door, and when she let him inside, he confronted her by reading the letters. Petitioner emptied a bathroom garbage can on the floor looking for used contraceptives. He left after 15 to 20 minutes. At that point, petitioner considered the relationship to be over.

[After a brief trip to Cincinnati], petitioner returned to Normal on August 4, 1993. He stopped at Jennifer's apartment, had a short conversation with her, and drove her to class before saying goodbye. Petitioner then moved back to his parents' home in Rockford, Illinois.

Jennifer called petitioner at his home in Rockford several times, including a call on August 23, 1993. Petitioner testified that Jennifer asked him if they could get back together when the school year began. Petitioner told her "no, we're through," and hung up the telephone. . . .

After Jennifer's body was found in her apartment, police detectives interviewed petitioner several times. Petitioner stated he had not seen Jennifer since August 4. When he was asked to account for his activities between August 23 and August 27, petitioner began with August 25. Petitioner wrote that he went to a church function at 7 P.M., followed by a church music rehearsal, and a party. Petitioner then went to Monday, August 23, and wrote, "Jen called, I hung up, about five minutes." Petitioner then filled out the rest of the week. The date of Jennifer's murder had not been announced publicly at that time. Petitioner denied any involvement in the murder.

Petitioner presented evidence that his car was driven 322 miles between August 24 and August 30. . . . Petitioner also presented testimony that he drove 305.6 miles that week in his daily activities in Rockford to show that he could not have driven approximately 140 miles to Normal on August 25. The parties presented conflicting testimony on whether petitioner's odometer had been subject to tampering.

Petitioner also testified that he worked a night shift at his uncle's grocery store, ending at 9 A.M. on August 25. He went home, picked up some cash and a check, and drove to his bank to make a deposit. A bank security videotape showed petitioner leaving the bank at 10:11 A.M. After returning from the bank, petitioner went to sleep in his room until approximately 5 P.M.

Telephone records showed that calls were made from the Beaman residence to their church at 10:37 A.M. and to Mitchell Olson's residence at 10:39 A.M. Olson was the church's director of music and youth ministries. The evidence showed that only petitioner or his mother, Carol Beaman, could have made those calls. Petitioner testified that he did not remember making the calls, but it was "entirely possible" that he made them.

Olson testified that petitioner occasionally played music during church services and they had scheduled a rehearsal for the evening of August 25. Olson did not recall speaking with anyone in petitioner's family that morning, but remembered speaking with Carol Beaman when he called the residence around 2:30 or 3 P.M.

Carol Beaman testified that she did not make the phone calls from her residence at 10:37 and 10:39 A.M. She left home around 7 o'clock that morning. She drove to Independence Village, her mother's assisted-living facility, and took her mother to a clinic for blood tests. They returned to Independence Village at 10 A.M. Carol spent 15 to 20 minutes taking her mother to her room and helping her get settled. She then went to a Wal-Mart store located directly across the street. She checked out at 11:10 A.M., as shown by her receipt. . . .

After leaving Wal-Mart, she went to other stores. Her final stop was at a grocery store where she checked out at 2:03 P.M. She went directly home because she had perishable items. She subsequently timed the drive from the grocery store to her residence at 9 to 13 minutes. Accordingly, she testified that she arrived home by 2:16 P.M. However, she previously informed police officers that she arrived home around 3 P.M. When she arrived, petitioner's car was in the driveway and his dog was sitting in front of his bedroom door. She woke petitioner for dinner at approximately 6 P.M.

Normal Police Detective Timothy Freesmeyer testified about drive times and distances relevant to defendant's opportunity to commit the murder. Freesmeyer testified that the distance from petitioner's bank to Jennifer's apartment was 126.7 miles. Freesmeyer's drive time test indicated that petitioner could have arrived at Jennifer's apartment just before noon if he left the bank at 10:11 A.M. and drove 10 miles per hour over the speed limit. The distance from petitioner's home to Jennifer's apartment was 139.7 miles. Petitioner could have driven from Jennifer's apartment to his residence in Rockford in just under two hours, driving 10 miles per hour over the speed limit. . . .

In terms of other possible suspects, the State presented evidence that Swaine was working at his former high school's bookstore in Elmhurst, Illinois, on August 25. Jennifer's former long-term boyfriend, Stacey Gates, also known as "Bubba," testified that he was employed as a teacher in Peoria, Illinois, and he worked that day.

In closing argument, the State maintained that the evidence clearly established petitioner's motive and opportunity to commit the offense. According to the State, petitioner drove to Normal after he left the bank at 10:11 A.M., arriving at around noon. When he walked into Jennifer's apartment, he saw Swaine's property. At that point, he "snapped" and committed the murder. Petitioner left the apartment by 12:15 P.M. and drove back to Rockford, arriving home around 2:10 P.M. The State argued that petitioner's guilt was also shown by his immediate focus on August 25 when asked to account for his time that week.

The State further argued that petitioner did not make the telephone calls from the Beaman residence at 10:37 and 10:39 A.M. According to the State, Carol Beaman could have driven home after taking her mother back to Independence Village, placed the calls, and then driven back to Wal-Mart. The State concluded that the circumstantial evidence "weaves around this defendant a web . . . that's so powerful that you can rest assured that you have the right person here."

Defense counsel responded that the evidence against petitioner was almost nonexistent, and the State had improperly focused its investigation on him to the exclusion of other potential suspects. Defense counsel explained that petitioner began with the evening of August 25 in accounting for the week because certain events stood out in his memory that day, including a church event, his music rehearsal, and a party. The rest of the week was, for the most part, routine. Counsel argued that the evidence against Swaine was as strong as the evidence presented against petitioner. . . .

In rebuttal, the prosecutor defended the State's investigation. He argued, "Alibis, we proved up everybody else's, but — we just jumped right in there and cleared all these other people, and we just didn't do the same for him." The prosecutor further argued, "Did we look at Mr. Swaine? You bet we did. Did we look at Bubba? You bet we did. Did we look at a lot of people and interview a lot of witnesses? You bet we did. And guess who sits in the courtroom . . . with the gap in his alibi still unclosed even after all this?" . . .

The jury found petitioner guilty of first degree murder and the trial court sentenced him to 50 years' imprisonment. The appellate court affirmed the trial court's judgment. . . . Petitioner then filed a postconviction petition [alleging that] the State violated his constitutional right to due process of law under *Brady* by failing to disclose material information supporting John Doe's viability as a suspect. . . .

At the evidentiary hearing, retired Normal Police Lieutenant Tony Daniels testified about the John Doe evidence. Doe and Jennifer had previously been involved in a romantic relationship. He lived in Bloomington, approximately 1.5 miles from Jennifer's apartment. Daniels testified that it would take Doe four to six minutes to drive to Jennifer's apartment and back. Doe told police officers that he and Jennifer were about to renew their relationship before her death. Jennifer and Michael Swaine came to his apartment a few days before the murder. Doe stated that he had supplied Jennifer with marijuana and other drugs, and she owed him money.

Daniels interviewed Doe twice in early September 1993 and found him to be "somewhat evasive" and "very nervous." In his first interview, Doe stated that he went out of town on August 24, the day before the murder. In the second interview a few days later, Doe informed Daniels that he did not leave Bloomington until 4 P.M. on August 25. He was in his apartment until 4 P.M. that day. Doe's girlfriend stated that she was with him from just after 1 P.M. until 4 P.M. that day. Doe did not provide any verification of his location before his girlfriend arrived around 1 P.M.

Daniels explained that he asked Doe to take a polygraph examination, but the examiner was unable to start the test because Doe failed to follow his directions. The polygraph examiner testified that the failure to follow the instructions could have been an intentional avoidance tactic. He further testified that Doe was being examined as a suspect in the murder. Daniels asked Doe to try again. Doe initially agreed, but the polygraph examination never occurred due to Doe's lack of cooperation.

Daniels further testified that Doe was charged with domestic battery and possession of marijuana with intent to deliver prior to petitioner's trial. A witness to the domestic battery indicated that Doe had his girlfriend on the floor and was elbowing her in the chest. Doe's girlfriend stated that Doe had physically abused her on numerous previous occasions. Additionally, she stated that Doe was using steroids, causing him to act erratically. Daniels testified that he considered Doe a viable suspect in the murder at the time of petitioner's trial, and he believed that Doe remained a viable suspect. . . .

Following the evidentiary hearing, the circuit court concluded that... petitioner's *Brady* claim failed because the undisclosed information on Doe's polygraph and his domestic battery charge was inadmissible at trial. Additionally, the court found that the evidence pointing to Doe as a viable suspect was remote and speculative. The court found that petitioner had "not provided enough evidence that if presented at the [motion *in limine* hearing], the trial court would have allowed the defense to present John Doe I as a suspect." ...

II. ANALYSIS

... We first address petitioner's claim under Brady v. Maryland that the State violated his right to due process by failing to disclose material information on a viable alternative suspect. Petitioner argues that the State's evidence based on his motive and opportunity to commit the offense was entirely circumstantial. He contends there is a reasonable probability that the jury would have acquitted him had it known there was another suspect with motive and opportunity to commit the murder. The State responds that the withheld evidence was not favorable to petitioner's defense or material to his guilt or punishment. Accordingly, the State argues petitioner's right to due process was not violated by the failure to disclose the evidence....

In *Brady,* the Supreme Court held that the prosecution violates an accused's constitutional right to due process of law by failing to disclose evidence favorable to the accused and material to guilt or punishment. This rule encompasses evidence known to police investigators, but not to the prosecutor. To comply with *Brady,* the prosecutor has a duty to learn of favorable evidence known to other government actors, including the police. The Supreme Court has, therefore, noted "the special role played by the American prosecutor in the search for truth in criminal trials." The prosecutor's interest in a criminal prosecution "is not that it shall win a case, but that justice shall be done."

A *Brady* claim requires a showing that: (1) the undisclosed evidence is favorable to the accused because it is either exculpatory or impeaching; (2) the evidence was suppressed by the State either wilfully or inadvertently; and (3) the accused was prejudiced because the evidence is material to guilt or punishment. Evidence is material if there is a reasonable probability that the result of the proceeding would have been different had the evidence been disclosed. To establish materiality, an accused must show "the favorable evidence could reasonably be taken to put the whole case in such a different light as to undermine confidence in the verdict."

In making the materiality determination, courts must consider the cumulative effect of all the suppressed evidence rather than considering each item of evidence individually. After a reviewing court has found a *Brady* violation, the constitutional error cannot be found harmless.

Here, the undisclosed evidence consists of four points: (1) John Doe failed to complete the polygraph examination; (2) Doe was charged with domestic battery and possession of marijuana with intent to deliver prior to petitioner's trial; (3) Doe had physically abused his girlfriend on numerous prior occasions; and (4) Doe's use of steroids had caused him to act erratically. Petitioner's attorney testified at the evidentiary hearing that he did not receive this evidence. In its brief to this court, the State does not dispute that it knew of the evidence and failed to disclose it. In fact, the State refers to the evidence as being "withheld." Accordingly, petitioner has established that the evidence was suppressed by the State.

The State, however, argues that the evidence was not favorable to petitioner or material to his guilt or punishment. Initially, we note that the circuit court held the State did not violate *Brady* by failing to disclose the polygraph evidence and the domestic battery charge because that evidence would not have been admissible at trial. In addressing whether the undisclosed evidence was favorable to petitioner, however, we need not decide whether each of the individual items of undisclosed evidence would have been admissible at trial. In this case, petitioner's essential claim is that he could have used the undisclosed evidence, along with the disclosed evidence tending to show Doe's possible involvement in the offense, to present Doe as an alternative suspect. Thus, even if some of the undisclosed evidence would have been inadmissible at trial, it still may have been favorable to petitioner in gaining admission of critical alternative suspect evidence. . . .

An accused in a criminal case may offer evidence tending to show that someone else committed the charged offense. Evidence of an alternative suspect should be excluded as irrelevant, however, if it is too remote or speculative. Generally, evidence is relevant if it tends to make the existence of any fact in consequence more or less probable than it would be without the evidence.

The undisclosed evidence is clearly favorable to petitioner in establishing Doe as an alternative suspect. First, the circumstances of the polygraph examination indicate that Doe intentionally avoided the test. He did not comply with the polygraph examiner's instructions during the first attempt and failed to cooperate in scheduling a second attempt. Moreover, the polygraph examiner testified that the police had identified Doe as a suspect in the murder. . . .

The evidence that Doe was charged with domestic battery and had physically abused his girlfriend on many prior occasions also could have been used by petitioner at a pretrial hearing to establish Doe as a viable suspect. That evidence is relevant to Doe's likelihood to commit a violent act against his girlfriend. The evidence that Doe had physically abused his girlfriend on numerous occasions, together with the evidence that he was in the process of renewing his romantic relationship with Jennifer prior to her death, provided additional support of Doe as a viable suspect. Further, the undisclosed evidence of Doe's steroid abuse may have explained his violent outbursts toward his girlfriend and supported an inference of a tendency to act violently toward others.

Finally, the undisclosed evidence that Doe had been charged with possession of marijuana with intent to deliver could have been used by petitioner as part of Doe's motive to commit the murder. That evidence tends to establish Doe as a drug dealer and, with evidence of Jennifer owing Doe money for drugs, it could have been offered to support a motive to commit the murder.

In analyzing whether the undisclosed evidence is favorable to petitioner, we also note that the Supreme Court recently examined the constitutionality of a rule of evidence restricting a criminal defendant from introducing proof of "third-party guilt" in cases where the prosecution offered forensic evidence that, if believed, strongly supported a guilty verdict. Holmes v. South Carolina, 547 U.S. 319 (2006). In finding the rule of evidence unconstitutional, the Court concluded that "by evaluating the strength of only one party's evidence, no logical conclusion can be reached regarding the strength of contrary evidence offered by the other side to rebut or cast doubt." This observation is applicable to whether the undisclosed evidence here is favorable and material. The impact or strength of the undisclosed evidence can only be determined by also viewing the strength of the evidence presented against petitioner.

Here, the State summarizes its evidence against petitioner as resting "on more than mere opportunity: petitioner's fingerprints were on the murder weapon; petitioner demonstrated knowledge of when Jennifer was murdered; and petitioner had every reason to kill Jennifer when he arrived at her apartment and saw, for the first time, definitive proof that Jennifer and Swaine had been sleeping together." In our view, the State's evidence against petitioner was not particularly strong. The State essentially presented evidence of motive, evidence of opportunity that was strongly disputed by petitioner, inferences from petitioner's statements to police officers that he knew the date of the murder, and fingerprints on the clock radio that were explained by petitioner's relationship with Jennifer and made less important by the State's concession that it would not have been necessary to touch the clock radio in committing the murder. This evidence is tenuous and supports admission by petitioner of the similarly probative alternative suspect evidence on Doe. We conclude that the evidence withheld by the State is favorable to petitioner because it supports Doe's viability as an alternative suspect. . . .

Having found that the withheld evidence is favorable to petitioner, we must next determine whether it is material. As noted, evidence is material if there is a reasonable probability that the result would have been different had it been disclosed. An accused must show "the favorable evidence could reasonably be taken to put the whole case in such a different light as to undermine confidence in the verdict." Again, the impact of the alternative-suspect evidence on the verdict cannot be determined without viewing the strength of the evidence presented by petitioner as well as the evidence presented by the State.

The State's evidence against petitioner showed that he had a motive to commit the murder based on his jealousy. Additionally, the State established that petitioner had been violent toward objects, but not people, on several occasions during his involvement with Jennifer. The evidence of petitioner's opportunity to commit the offense was strongly disputed. . . . The State's timeline depended on petitioner driving 10 miles per hour over the speed limit to Normal and back to Rockford. Additionally, the timeline required petitioner to commit the offense and stage the crime scene in an extremely quick and efficient manner. . . .

The State's other evidence against petitioner was based on inferences from his statements to police officers and his fingerprints on the clock radio. That evidence, however, was explained by petitioner. Petitioner explained that he began with August 25 in accounting for his time the week of the murder because he had events that day that stood out in his memory. The rest of the week was routine. . . .

We also note that the State's argument relied upon the assertion that all other potential suspects had been eliminated from consideration. The prosecutor informed the jury that the State had "proved up everybody else's" alibi and petitioner was the one "who sits in the courtroom . . . with the gap in his alibi still unclosed." The prosecution presented testimony to establish the alibis of two named suspects, Swaine and Gates. The prosecution's argument that all other potential suspects had been eliminated from consideration was a key part of the State's case given the tenuous circumstantial evidence of petitioner's guilt. . . .

We conclude that there is a reasonable probability that the result of the trial would have been different if petitioner had presented the evidence establishing Doe as an alternative suspect. We cannot have confidence in the verdict finding petitioner guilty of this crime given the tenuous nature of the circumstantial evidence against him, along with the nondisclosure of critical evidence that would have countered the State's argument that all other potential suspects had been eliminated from consideration. Accordingly, we conclude that the State's suppression of the withheld evidence violated petitioner's constitutional right to due process under *Brady.* Based on this record, the circuit court's dismissal of petitioner's *Brady* claim was manifest error.

A *Brady* violation cannot be found harmless. Petitioner's conviction must, therefore, be reversed and the matter remanded for further proceedings. . . .

HAWAII PENAL PROCEDURE RULE 16

(b) Disclosure by the Prosecution.

(1) Disclosure of Matters Within Prosecution's Possession. The prosecutor shall disclose to the defendant or the defendant's attorney the following material and information within the prosecutor's possession or control: . . . (vii) any material or information which tends to negate the guilt of the defendant as to the offense charged or would tend to reduce the defendant's punishment therefor.

(2) Disclosure of Matters Not Within Prosecution's Possession. Upon written request of defense counsel and specific designation by defense counsel of material or information which would be discoverable if in the possession or control of the prosecutor and which is in the possession or control of other governmental personnel, the prosecutor shall use diligent good faith efforts to cause such material or information to be made available to defense counsel; and if the prosecutor's efforts are unsuccessful the court shall issue suitable subpoenas or orders to cause such material or information to be made available to defense counsel. . . .

(d) Discretionary Disclosure. Upon a showing of materiality and if the request is reasonable, the court in its discretion may require disclosure as provided for in this Rule 16 in cases other than those in which the defendant is charged with a felony, but not in cases involving violations.

(e) Regulation of Discovery.

(1) Performance of Obligations. Except for matters which are to be specifically designated in writing by defense counsel under this rule, the prosecution shall disclose all materials subject to disclosure pursuant to subsection (b)(1) of this rule to the defendant or the defendant's attorney within ten calendar days following arraignment and plea of the defendant. The parties may perform their obligations of disclosure in any manner mutually agreeable to the parties or by notifying the attorney for the other party that material and information, described in general terms, may be inspected, obtained, tested, copied or photographed at specified reasonable times and places.

(2) Continuing Duty of Disclose. If subsequent to compliance with these rules or orders entered pursuant to these rules, a party discovers additional material or information which would have been subject to disclosure pursuant to this Rule 16, that party shall promptly disclose the additional material or information, and if the additional material or information is discovered during trial, the court shall be notified.

UTAH CRIMINAL PROCEDURE RULE 16

(a) Except as otherwise provided, the prosecutor shall disclose to the defense upon request the following material or information of which he has knowledge: . . . (4) evidence known to the prosecutor that tends to negate the guilt of the accused, mitigate the guilt of the defendant, or mitigate the degree of the offense for reduced punishment. . . .

(b) The prosecutor shall make all disclosures as soon as practicable following the filing of charges and before the defendant is required to plead. The prosecutor has a continuing duty to make disclosure.

Problem 15-2. Preserving Evidence

Kanju Osakalumi and several other residents of New York City traveled to the home of Allison Charlton in Bluefield, West Virginia, bringing with them an assortment of drugs and firearms. On the afternoon of June 14, one of the persons from New York City, Chandel Fleetwood, died from a single gunshot wound to the head, fired from his own revolver. Osakalumi and others who were present took the body to a wooded area approximately one mile away. They also disposed of the victim's revolver and a bloodied cushion from the couch where the victim had been sitting. The following day, Osakalumi and his friends returned to New York City.

Officers from the Bluefield Police Department soon began hearing rumors that someone had been shot at the Charlton home. About seven months after Fleetwood's death, two detectives visited the home. Upon observing a stained couch, the detectives took samples from it and from the carpet surrounding it. Approximately two months later, police officers returned to the Charlton home, and inspected the couch again. This time, they discovered a bullet hole in it. Detective Ted Jones inserted a writing pen into the bullet hole to determine the trajectory of the bullet. He extracted a badly deformed bullet as well as some hair and bone fragments. The officers confiscated the couch and stored it at the police department.

The couch gave off an unpleasant odor and was both a fire and health hazard. As a result, the police (with the consent of the prosecutor's office) soon disposed of the couch at the county landfill. The police did not measure either the proportions of the couch, the location of the bullet hole in the couch, or the trajectory of the bullet. Neither did they photograph the couch or the bullet hole.

Two years after Fleetwood's death, a passerby discovered his skeletal remains in the woods. After the Bluefield police completed their investigation, Osakalumi was arrested in New York. He claimed that Fleetwood was under the influence of marijuana when he loaded one round of ammunition into his own revolver, spun the cylinder, put it to his own head and shot himself. Osakalumi said that he and the others in the house panicked and disposed of the body and the revolver in a nearby wooded area.

The only evidence that Fleetwood had been murdered was the trial testimony of Dr. Irvin Sopher, medical examiner for the state of West Virginia. Dr. Sopher testified that approximately 9 months after Fleetwood's death (but approximately 14 months before his body was found), Detective Ted Jones delivered to him the bullet, blood samples, and bone fragments. In addition, Detective Jones drew for

Dr. Sopher a diagram of the couch, along with the location of the bullet hole and the position of the bullet when officers found it.

Although Jones's diagram of the couch was lost, Dr. Sopher drew Detective Jones's couch diagram from memory at trial. Dr. Sopher testified that based upon examination of the skull and the purported right-to-left, straight-line trajectory of the bullet through the couch, the manner of Fleetwood's death was homicide. Dr. Sopher testified that he came to this conclusion when he lined up the trajectory of the bullet through the skull with the right-to-left path of the bullet through the couch, as drawn by Detective Jones. Dr. Sopher determined that Fleetwood was held down on the couch and was shot through the head, with the bullet traveling in a straight line.

The jury convicted Osakalumi of first-degree murder. On appeal he claims that the trial court erred when it allowed Dr. Sopher to testify based on the condition of the couch. As the appellate court judge, how do you rule? Compare State v. Osakalumi, 461 S.E.2d 504 (W. Va. 1995).

Notes

1. *Disclosure of evidence favorable to the accused: majority position.* The Supreme Court decision in Brady v. Maryland, 373 U.S. 83 (1963), remains central to discovery practice in American criminal justice. Because the disclosure duty described in *Brady* is a requirement of federal due process, it applies in every criminal case unless the defendant expressly waives the disclosure. As illustrated by the Hawaii and Utah rules reprinted above, over 40 states have passed rules or statutes codifying the *Brady* disclosure requirement, although many of these rules and statutes (unlike the constitutional requirement) only take effect after a request from the defense. See Ohio R. Crim. P. 16(A) (disclosure upon defendant's request).

Defendants often win *Brady* claims that are appealed in the state courts, at least when those claims are the focus of the appeal (as opposed to one in a laundry list of claims, especially in capital cases). See, e.g., State v. Higgins, 788 So. 2d 238 (Fla. 2001) (prosecutors failed to turn over a statement by a minor witness that a prosecution witness might herself have been seen driving the victim's vehicle). But *Brady* claims appear to be appealed infrequently, so the relative success of defendants in this context says little if anything about discovery practice in the mine run of cases.

2. *Exculpatory evidence in government hands.* The defendant who seeks dismissal of charges because of a *Brady* violation need not show bad faith by the prosecutor. The prosecutor does not even have to know about the evidence that must be disclosed: Evidence in the hands of government agents (such as criminal investigators) who regularly report to the prosecutor can be the basis for a *Brady* violation because the prosecutor has a duty to inquire about such information. See Kyles v. Whitley, 514 U.S. 419 (1995); Banks v. Dretke, 540 U.S. 668 (2004) (reiterating the affirmative duty on prosecutors to disclose *Brady* material and observing that a rule "declaring 'prosecutor may hide, defendant must seek,' is not tenable. . . ."); but see Yearby v. State, 997 A.2d 144 (Md. 2010) (no *Brady* violation if the defendant knew or reasonably should have known about the existence of the prejudicial or material information).

3. *Impeachment as exculpatory evidence.* The *Brady* disclosure duty reaches both exculpatory evidence and evidence that the defense might use to impeach a

prosecution witness. While the potential impeachment evidence might take many forms, much litigation centers on disclosure of any rewards that the prosecution offers to its witnesses. A prosecution witness cannot lie about any lenient treatment the witness expects to receive from the government as a result of cooperating. Attorneys who practice in this arena refer to such evidence as *Giglio* material, named for Giglio v. United States, 405 U.S. 150 (1972). In that case, the Court declared that reversal is required when a witness falsely denies any arrangement for lenient treatment, even though the promise of leniency came from another prosecutor and was unknown to the government attorney at trial. The test for materiality under *Giglio* is whether there is a "reasonable probability" that the false evidence may have affected the judgment of the jury. Even if the prosecution witness does not lie at trial about any promise of leniency, the existence of such deals with witnesses typically qualifies as *Brady* material. See United States v. Bagley, 473 U.S. 667 (1985) (evidence of government agreement to pay money to witnesses commensurate with the information they furnished did qualify as impeachment evidence, but it did not satisfy materiality requirement).

4. *Materiality of exculpatory evidence.* The major limit on the *Brady* disclosure duty is the requirement that the undisclosed evidence be "material" to the defense. Under federal law, all *Brady* violations share a uniform materiality standard: The defendant must show a "reasonable probability" that the verdict would have been different if the prosecution had disclosed the exculpatory evidence. It does not affect the standard one way or the other if the defendant requests the disclosure.

State courts have split over the proper materiality standard. About 30 states have adopted the federal "uniform" standard, but a strong minority grant defendants a more favorable materiality standard in cases where the defense makes specific requests for the information. People v. Vilardi, 555 N.E.2d 915 (N.Y. 1990). Does a specific request for discovery from the defense change the legitimate expectations of both parties? Note also that many state rules of criminal procedure (like the Utah rule reprinted above), include something similar to the *Brady* disclosure duty without including any materiality requirement; most of these rules, however, depend on a request from the defense.

5. Brady *and plea bargaining.* While *Brady* information might affect the outcome at trial, it could also affect the negotiating strength of the defendant during plea bargaining. Given the dominance of guilty pleas and plea bargaining in American criminal justice, it is critical to know whether a defendant can challenge the validity of a guilty plea if she discovers later that the prosecutor failed to disclose *Brady* material. A few states have statutes or rules that explicitly link the prosecutor's disclosure obligation to a defendant's not-guilty plea at arraignment. See N.H. Super. Ct. R. 98 (prosecutor to disclose exculpatory material within 30 days from a not-guilty plea). The U.S. Supreme Court addressed one aspect of this question in United States v. Ruiz, 536 U.S. 622 (2002), stating that "the Constitution does not require the Government to disclose material impeachment evidence prior to entering a plea agreement with a criminal defendant." Ruiz was challenging a provision in a proposed plea agreement that required her to waive certain *Brady* rights as part of the arrangement, but the Court's statement appears broad enough to cover guilty pleas reached without any explicit waiver of *Brady* rights in a plea agreement. Note that the ruling extends to impeachment material but not to exculpatory material.

State courts are split over whether *Brady* violations by the prosecution invalidate a defendant's guilty plea. The web extension for this chapter, at *http://www.crimpro.com/extension/ch15*, explores the range of state court rulings on this critical topic. See State v. Harris, 680 N.W.2d 737, 741 (Wis. 2004) (imposes disclosure at guilty plea stage as matter of state law).

6. *Preservation of evidence.* It is often said that the duty to disclose evidence would be meaningless if the prosecutor were free to destroy evidence. Is this true? The Supreme Court has addressed the government's obligation, under the due process clause, to preserve some types of evidence. In Arizona v. Youngblood, 488 U.S. 51 (1988), the police failed to preserve semen samples from the victim's body and clothing. The defendant, accused of child molestation and sexual assault, argued that he could have performed tests on the samples that might have established his defense of mistaken identity. However, the Supreme Court noted that the state did not attempt to use the materials in its own case in chief, and it limited the government's duty to preserve evidence as follows:

> [Requiring] a defendant to show bad faith on the part of the police both limits the extent of the police's obligation to preserve evidence to reasonable bounds and confines it to that class of cases where the interests of justice most clearly require it, i.e., those cases in which the police themselves by their conduct indicate that the evidence could form a basis for exonerating the defendant. We therefore hold that unless a criminal defendant can show bad faith on the part of the police, failure to preserve potentially useful evidence does not constitute a denial of due process of law.

Years later, Youngblood was found to be innocent on the basis of other DNA evidence, and was released two days before completing his original sentence. See also Illinois v. Fisher, 540 U.S. 544 (2004) (distinguishing between exculpatory information and information that is merely useful to the defense; exculpatory information must be turned over to the defense even without any showing of bad faith).

Once again, there is dissension among state courts on an important aspect of this discovery issue. Most states directly addressing the question have accepted the holding in *Youngblood.* About a dozen states, however, have declared that bad faith is not a necessary part of the defendant's showing because the destruction of evidence often reflects some negligence by the government and because the evidence could sometimes be crucial to the defense. See State v. Tiedemann, 162 P.3d 1106 (Utah 2007) (state due process claim does not require showing of bad faith by government officials when they destroy evidence that is potentially useful to defense); Cynthia E. Jones, The Right Remedy for the Wrongly Convicted: Judicial Sanctions for Destruction of DNA Evidence, 77 Fordham L. Rev. 2893 (2009). Why do state courts seem so willing to part ways with the Supreme Court on constitutional questions involving discovery? Do the state courts take more responsibility for their own litigation management, in light of the state's needs and practices?

The preservation of evidence has made a critical difference in more cases lately as DNA testing procedures become available. These tests make it possible to reevaluate the convictions of some defendants in cases (such as rape and murder cases) where blood or other biological material from the perpetrator is available at the crime scene or from the victim. The incentive to test this material and to match it to the convicted defendant is very strong in capital cases, and a few capital defendants have been released on the basis of DNA test information.

7. *The extent of disclosure violations.* How often do prosecutors and defense attorneys fail to disclose the information that they should to the opposing party? Periodic newspaper reports on "prosecutorial misconduct" focus on discovery violations; they suggest (inconclusively) that discovery violations by prosecutors occur regularly. Recent examples appear on the web extension for this chapter at *http://www.crimpro.com/extension/ch15*, exploring the range of state court rulings on this critical topic. How would you measure in a reliable way whether prosecutors are now committing more discovery violations than in the past? If such a trend were proven, could it be traced to the number of new prosecutors hired in a given time period?

8. *Remedies for prosecutorial disclosure violations.* As we have seen, courts might reverse criminal convictions if the prosecutor fails to disclose material information when required by law. Will the state bar authorities also sanction prosecutors who violate their legal obligations to disclose information, even when the evidence is not material? Examples of disciplinary proceedings against prosecutors for discovery violations do get reported from time to time. For example, disciplinary proceedings in 2007 served as a remedy for multiple violations of the discovery rules during criminal proceedings against several members of the Duke University lacrosse team members. Prosecutor Mike Nifong made inflammatory remarks to the press about the three indicted players and their teammates, withheld key DNA evidence, and lied to the court, all in violation of the North Carolina professional responsibility rules. The state bar revoked Nifong's license to practice law. See North Carolina State Bar v. Nifong, N.C. State Bar Disciplinary Hearing Commission, No. 06 DHC 35, June 16, 2007. However, state bar authorities discipline criminal prosecutors far less often than they discipline private attorneys. One survey of state bar records revealed that criminal attorneys (both prosecutors and defense attorneys) are sanctioned far less often than attorneys in civil practice, and that discipline rarely occurs after a "first offense." See Fred C. Zacharias, The Professional Discipline of Prosecutors, 79 N.C. L. Rev. 721 (2001). What might explain the relatively infrequent disciplinary actions against criminal prosecutors? See also Van De Kamp v. Goldstein, 129 S. Ct. 855 (2009) (prosecutors who fail to properly train and supervise subordinates in complying with discovery and disclosure obligations regarding impeachment material about confidential informers are protected from civil rights actions by absolute immunity).

■ AMERICAN BAR ASSOCIATION, MODEL RULES OF PROFESSIONAL CONDUCT

Rule 3.8, Special Responsibilities of a Prosecutor

The prosecutor in a criminal case shall: . . .

(d) make timely disclosure to the defense of all evidence or information known to the prosecutor that tends to negate the guilt of the accused or mitigates the offense, and, in connection with sentencing, disclose to the defense and to the tribunal all unprivileged mitigating information known to the prosecutor, except when the prosecutor is relieved of this responsibility by a protective order of the tribunal; . . .

(g) When a prosecutor knows of new, credible and material evidence creating a reasonable likelihood that a convicted defendant did not commit an offense of which the defendant was convicted, the prosecutor shall:

(1) promptly disclose that evidence to an appropriate court or authority, and

(2) if the conviction was obtained in the prosecutor's jurisdiction,

(i) promptly disclose that evidence to the defendant unless a court authorizes delay, and

(ii) undertake further investigation, or make reasonable efforts to cause an investigation, to determine whether the defendant was convicted of an offense that the defendant did not commit.

(h) When a prosecutor knows of clear and convincing evidence establishing that a defendant in the prosecutor's jurisdiction was convicted of an offense that the defendant did not commit, the prosecutor shall seek to remedy the conviction.

U.S. DEPARTMENT OF JUSTICE, MEMORANDUM FOR DEPARTMENT PROSECUTORS

January 4, 2010

FROM: David W. Ogden, Deputy Attorney General
SUBJECT: Guidance for Prosecutors Regarding Criminal Discovery

The discovery obligations of federal prosecutors are generally established by Federal Rules of Criminal Procedure 16 and 26.2, 18 U.S.C. §3500 (the Jencks Act), Brady v. Maryland, 373 U.S. 83 (1963), and Giglio v. United States, 405 U.S. 150 (1972). In addition, the United States Attorney's Manual describes the Department's policy for disclosure of exculpatory and impeachment information. *See* USAM §9-5.001. In order to meet discovery obligations in a given case, Federal prosecutors must be familiar with these authorities and with the judicial interpretations and local rules that discuss or address the application of these authorities to particular facts. In addition, it is important for prosecutors to consider thoroughly how to meet their discovery obligations in each case. Toward that end, the Department has adopted the guidance for prosecutors regarding criminal discovery set forth below. The guidance is intended to establish a methodical approach to consideration of discovery obligations that prosecutors should follow in every case to avoid lapses that can result in consequences adverse to the Department's pursuit of justice. [This memorandum] provides prospective guidance only and is not intended to have the force of law or to create or confer any rights, privileges, or benefits. . . .

Step 1: Gathering and Reviewing Discoverable Information

A. Where to look — The Prosecution Team

Department policy states: "It is the obligation of federal prosecutors, in preparing for trial, to seek all exculpatory and impeachment information from all members of the prosecution team. Members of the prosecution team include federal, state, and local law enforcement officers and other government officials participating in the investigation and prosecution of the criminal case against the defendant." USAM §9-5.001. . . .

Many cases arise out of investigations conducted by multi-agency task forces or otherwise involving state law enforcement agencies. In such cases, prosecutors should consider (1) whether state or local agents are working on behalf of the prosecutor or are under the prosecutor's control; (2) the extent to which state and federal governments are part of a team, are participating in a joint investigation, or are sharing resources; and (3) whether the prosecutor has ready access to the evidence. Courts will generally evaluate the role of a state or local law enforcement agency on a case-by-case basis. . . .

Prosecutors are encouraged to err on the side of inclusiveness when identifying the members of the prosecution team for discovery purposes. Carefully considered efforts to locate discoverable information are more likely to avoid future litigation over *Brady* and *Giglio* issues and avoid surprises at trial. . . .

B. What to Review

To ensure that all discovery is disclosed on a timely basis, generally all potentially discoverable material within the custody or control of the prosecution team should be reviewed. The review process should cover the following areas:

1. *The Investigative Agency's Files:* With respect to Department of Justice law enforcement agencies, with limited exceptions, the prosecutor should be granted access to the substantive case file and any other file or document the prosecutor has reason to believe may contain discoverable information related to the matter being prosecuted. Therefore, the prosecutor can personally review the file or documents or may choose to request production of potentially discoverable materials from the case agents. With respect to outside agencies, the prosecutor should request access to files and/or production of all potentially discoverable material. The investigative agency's entire investigative file, including documents such as FBI Electronic Communications (ECs), inserts, emails, etc. should be reviewed for discoverable information. If such information is contained in a document that the agency deems to be an "internal" document such as an email, an insert, an administrative document, or an EC, it may not be necessary to produce the internal document, but it will be necessary to produce all of the discoverable information contained in it. Prosecutors should also discuss with the investigative agency whether files from other investigations or non-investigative files such as confidential source files might contain discoverable information. . . .

2. *Confidential Informant (CI)/Witness (CW)/Human Source (CHS)/Source (CS) Files:* The credibility of cooperating witnesses or informants will always be at issue if they testify during a trial. Therefore, prosecutors are entitled to access to the agency file for each testifying CI, CW, CHS, or CS. Those files should be reviewed for discoverable information and copies made of relevant portions for discovery purposes. The entire informant/source file, not just the portion relating to the current case, including all proffer, immunity and other agreements, validation assessments, payment information, and other potential witness impeachment information should be included within this review. . . .

Prosecutors should take steps to protect the non-discoverable, sensitive information found within a CI, CW, CHS, or CS file. Further, prosecutors should consider whether discovery obligations arising from the review of CI, CW, CHS, and CS files may be fully discharged while better protecting government or witness interests such as security or privacy via a summary letter to defense counsel rather than producing the record in its entirety. . . .

3. *Evidence and Information Gathered During the Investigation:* Generally, all evidence and information gathered during the investigation should be reviewed, including anything obtained during searches or via subpoenas, etc. . . .

4. *Substantive Case-Related Communications*: "Substantive" case-related communications may contain discoverable information. Those communications that contain discoverable information should be maintained in the case file or otherwise preserved in a manner that associates them with the case or investigation. "Substantive" case-related communications are most likely to occur (1) among prosecutors and/or agents, (2) between prosecutors and/or agents and witnesses and/or victims, and (3) between victim-witness coordinators and witnesses and/or victims. Such communications may be memorialized in emails, memoranda, or notes. "Substantive" communications include factual reports about investigative activity, factual discussions of the relative merits of evidence, factual information obtained during interviews or interactions with witnesses/victims, and factual issues relating to credibility. Communications involving case impressions or investigative or prosecutive strategies without more would not ordinarily be considered discoverable, but substantive case-related communications should be reviewed carefully to determine whether all or part of a communication (or the information contained therein) should be disclosed.

Prosecutors should also remember that with few exceptions (*see, e.g.*, Fed. R. Crim. P. 16(a)(1)(B)(ii)), the format of the information does not determine whether it is discoverable. For example, material exculpatory information that the prosecutor receives during a conversation with an agent or a witness is no less discoverable than if that same information were contained in an email. When the discoverable information contained in an email or other communication is fully memorialized elsewhere, such as in a report of interview or other document(s), then the disclosure of the report of interview or other document(s) will ordinarily satisfy the disclosure obligation. . . .

5. *Potential* Giglio *Information Relating to Non-Law Enforcement Witnesses*: . . . All potential *Giglio* information known by or in the possession of the prosecution team relating to non-law enforcement witnesses should be gathered and reviewed. That information includes, but is not limited to:

- Prior inconsistent statements . . .
- Statements or reports reflecting witness statement variations . . .
- Benefits provided to witnesses, including dropped or reduced charges, immunity, expectations of downward departures or motions for reduction of sentence, assistance in a state or local criminal proceeding, . . . stays of deportation or other immigration status considerations, . . . monetary benefits, non-prosecution agreements, letters to other law enforcement officials (*e.g.* state prosecutors, parole boards) setting forth the extent of a witness's assistance or making substantive recommendations on the witness's behalf, relocation assistance, [or] benefits to culpable or at risk third-parties
- Other known conditions that could affect the witness's bias such as . . . animosity toward defendant, animosity toward a group of which the

defendant is a member or with which the defendant is affiliated, relationship with victim, [or] known but uncharged criminal conduct . . .

- Prior convictions under Fed.R.Evid. 609
- Known substance abuse or mental health issues or other issues that could affect the witness's ability to perceive and recall events

6. *Information Obtained in Witness Interviews:* Although not required by law, generally speaking, witness interviews should be memorialized by the agent. Agent and prosecutor notes and original recordings should be preserved, and prosecutors should confirm with agents that substantive interviews should be memorialized. . . . Whenever possible, prosecutors should not conduct an interview without an agent present to avoid the risk of making themselves a witness to a statement and being disqualified from handling the case if the statement becomes an issue. . . .

a. *Witness Statement Variations and the Duty to Disclose:* Some witnesses' statements will vary during the course of an interview or investigation. For example, they may initially deny involvement in criminal activity, and the information they provide may broaden or change considerably over the course of time, especially if there are a series of debriefings that occur over several days or weeks. Material variances in a witness's statements should be memorialized, even if they are within the same interview, and they should be provided to the defense as *Giglio* information.

b. *Trial Preparation Meetings with Witnesses:* Trial preparation meetings with witnesses generally need not be memorialized. However, prosecutors should be particularly attuned to new or inconsistent information disclosed by the witness during a pre-trial witness preparation session. New information that is exculpatory or impeachment information should be disclosed. . . .

c. *Agent Notes:* Agent notes should be reviewed if there is a reason to believe that the notes are materially different from the memorandum, if a written memorandum was not prepared, if the precise words used by the witness are significant, or if the witness disputes the agent's account of the interview. . . .

STEP 2: CONDUCTING THE REVIEW

. . . It would be preferable if prosecutors could review the information themselves in every case, but such review is not always feasible or necessary. The prosecutor is ultimately responsible for compliance with discovery obligations. Accordingly, the prosecutor should develop a process for review of pertinent information to ensure that discoverable information is identified. . . . This process may involve agents, paralegals, agency counsel, and computerized searches. Although prosecutors may delegate the process and set forth criteria for identifying *potentially* discoverable information, prosecutors should not delegate the disclosure determination itself. In cases involving voluminous evidence obtained from third parties, prosecutors should consider providing defense access to the voluminous documents to avoid the possibility that a well-intentioned review process nonetheless fails to identify material discoverable evidence. . . .

STEP 3: MAKING THE DISCLOSURES

[Prosecutors are] encouraged to provide discovery broader and more comprehensive than the discovery obligations. If a prosecutor chooses this course, the defense should be advised that the prosecutor is electing to produce discovery beyond what is required under the circumstances of the case but is not committing to any discovery obligation beyond the discovery obligations. . . .

A. *Considerations Regarding the Scope and Timing of the Disclosures:* Providing broad and early discovery often promotes the truth-seeking mission of the Department and fosters a speedy resolution of many cases. It also provides a margin of error in case the prosecutor's good faith determination of the scope of appropriate discovery is in error. . . . But when considering providing discovery beyond that required by the discovery obligations or providing discovery sooner than required, prosecutors should always consider any appropriate countervailing concerns in the particular case, including, but not limited to: protecting victims and witnesses from harassment or intimidation; protecting the privacy interests of witnesses; protecting privileged information; protecting the integrity of ongoing investigations; protecting the trial from efforts at obstruction; protecting national security interests; investigative agency concerns; enhancing the likelihood of receiving reciprocal discovery by defendants; any applicable legal or evidentiary privileges; and other strategic considerations that enhance the likelihood of achieving a just result in a particular case. . . .

Prosecutors should never describe the discovery being provided as "open file." Even if the prosecutor intends to provide expansive discovery, it is always possible that something will be inadvertently omitted from production and the prosecutor will then have unintentionally misrepresented the scope of materials provided. Furthermore, because the concept of the "file" is imprecise, such a representation exposes the prosecutor to broader disclosure requirements than intended or to sanction for failure to disclose documents, *e.g.* agent notes or internal memos, that the court may deem to have been part of the "file." . . .

B. *Timing*: Exculpatory information, regardless of whether the information is memorialized, must be disclosed to the defendant reasonably promptly after discovery. Impeachment information, which depends on the prosecutor's decision on who is or may be called as a government witness, will typically be disclosed at a reasonable time before trial to allow the trial to proceed efficiently. [Witness] security, national security, or other issues may require that disclosures of impeachment information be made at a time and in a manner consistent with the policy embodied in the Jencks Act. . . .

Discovery obligations are continuing, and prosecutors should always be alert to developments occurring up to and through trial of the case that may impact their discovery obligations and require disclosure of information that was previously not disclosed.

C. *Form of Disclosure:* There may be instances when it is not advisable to turn over discoverable information in its original form, such as when the disclosure would create security concerns or when such information is contained in attorney notes, internal agency documents, confidential source documents, Suspicious Activity Reports, etc. If discoverable information is not provided in its original form and is instead provided in a letter to defense counsel, including particular language, where pertinent, prosecutors should take great care to ensure that the full scope of pertinent information is provided to the defendant.

Step 4: Making a Record

One of the most important steps in the discovery process is keeping good records regarding disclosures. Prosecutors should make a record of when and how information is disclosed or otherwise made available. While discovery matters are often the subject of litigation in criminal cases, keeping a record of the disclosures confines the litigation to substantive matters and avoids time-consuming disputes about what was disclosed. . . .

Conclusion

Compliance with discovery obligations is important for a number of reasons. First and foremost, however, such compliance will facilitate a fair and just result in every case, which is the Department's singular goal in pursuing a criminal prosecution. This guidance does not and could not answer every discovery question because those obligations are often fact specific. However, prosecutors have at their disposal an array of resources intended to assist them in evaluating their discovery obligations including supervisors, discovery coordinators in each office, the Professional Responsibility Advisory Office, and online resources available on the Department's intranet website, not to mention the experienced career prosecutors throughout the Department. And, additional resources are being developed through efforts that will be overseen by a full-time discovery expert who will be detailed to Washington from the field. By evaluating discovery obligations pursuant to the methodical and thoughtful approach set forth in this guidance and taking advantage of available resources, prosecutors are more likely to meet their discovery obligations in every case and in so doing achieve a just and final result in every criminal prosecution. . . .

Notes

1. *Interaction among discovery obligations.* Consider the relationship between jurisdiction-wide and local court rules that define discovery obligations, constitutional obligations under *Brady* and *Giglio*, state ethics rules such as those embodied in Model Rule 3.8, and discovery policies internal to the prosecutor's office. Note, for instance, that the DOJ memorandum reprinted above adopts an expansive view of materiality — indeed, it does not even discuss a materiality limit on disclosure obligations. Meanwhile, Model Rule 3.8 covers more information than *Brady* but requires proof of a knowing violation to prove a violation of the rule. See ABA Formal Ethics Op. 09-454 (2009) ("Rule 3.8(d) is more demanding than the constitutional case law, in that it requires the disclosure of evidence of information favorable to the defense without regard to the anticipated impact of the evidence or information on a trial's outcome. . . . Further, this ethical duty of disclosure is not limited to admissible 'evidence,' . . . it also requires disclosure of favorable 'information.'").

2. *Motivations for office policies.* What might convince a chief prosecutor to adopt formal guidance on discovery, or a supervisory structure that promotes compliance with discovery rules? The DOJ memorandum was issued soon after publicity about disclosure violations in a major prosecution involving corruption charges against

Alaska Senator Ted Stevens. Do you believe that discovery policies are more common in large or small offices?

3. *Internal enforcement practices*. Prosecutors' offices sometimes evaluate the performance of their own attorneys and create systems to sanction wrongdoers and to train less experienced attorneys to avoid discovery violations. One such mechanism is the Office for Professional Responsibility (OPR) within the U.S. Department of Justice.

Suppose you are the senior career attorney in a prosecutor's office, and the chief prosecutor has asked you to take charge of the discovery practices in the office. What training programs would you create? Would you limit those training programs to new attorneys when they first join the office? Would you institute any supervisor review of discovery decisions of line prosecutors as their cases progress? How about any auditing of discovery decisions after the conclusion of a case? Consider the resources and routines that the "discovery coordinators" mentioned in the DOJ memorandum might create for each U.S. Attorney's Office. See New Perspectives on *Brady* and Other Disclosure Obligations: Report of the Working Groups on Best Practices, 31 Cardozo L. Rev. 1961 (2010). Compliance with discovery obligations is a major quality-control topic for managers in prosecutors' offices. For a sampling of materials that supervisors develop and use to promote compliance, consult the web extension for this chapter at *http://www.crimpro.com/extension/ch15*.

3. Defense Disclosures

The trend over the past several decades has been toward broader criminal discovery rights for both the defense and the prosecution. The most potent arguments against expanding discovery at each juncture have pointed to some necessary limits on defense disclosures. There may be constitutional difficulties in forcing a defendant to disclose certain information to the prosecution. Among other things, forced disclosure might be considered self-incrimination in violation of the constitutional privilege. Faced with this sort of barrier, prosecutors have resisted the general expansion of criminal discovery on the basis of litigation fairness. If the defendant does not have to disclose evidence, prosecutors argue, then neither should they.

In the end, the arguments for limiting criminal discovery have lost more often than they have won — in part because the constitutional problems with compelling the defendant to disclose evidence have turned out to be surprisingly small. Where the Constitution has created no barrier, both defense and prosecution disclosures have increased.

If the Constitution will stop only a few types of defense disclosures, what are other possible grounds for evaluating discovery innovations? Are there some types of information that the prosecution will not develop if the defendant does not provide it? What, if anything, do we gain from a truly adversarial system of developing and presenting evidence?

PENNSYLVANIA RULE OF CRIMINAL PROCEDURE 573(C)

(1) In all court cases, if the Commonwealth files a motion for pretrial discovery, upon a showing of materiality to the preparation of the Commonwealth's case and that the request is reasonable, the court may order the defendant, subject to the defendant's rights against compulsory self-incrimination, to allow the attorney for the Commonwealth to inspect and copy or photograph any of the following requested items:

(a) results or reports of physical or mental examinations, and of scientific tests or experiments made in connection with the particular case, or copies thereof, within the possession or control of the defendant, that the defendant intends to introduce as evidence in chief, or were prepared by a witness whom the defendant intends to call at the trial, when results or reports relate to the testimony of that witness, provided the defendant has requested and received discovery under paragraph (B)(1)(e); and

(b) the names and addresses of eyewitnesses whom the defendant intends to call in its case-in-chief, provided that the defendant has previously requested and received discovery under paragraph (B)(2)(a)(i).

(2) If an expert whom the defendant intends to call in any proceeding has not prepared a report of examination or tests, the court, upon motion, may order that the expert prepare and the defendant disclose a report stating the subject matter on which the expert is expected to testify; the substance of the facts to which the expert is expected to testify; and a summary of the expert's opinions and the grounds for each opinion.

PENNSYLVANIA RULE OF CRIMINAL PROCEDURE 567(A)

A defendant who intends to offer the defense of alibi at trial shall file with the clerk of courts not later than the time required for filing the omnibus pretrial motion provided in Rule 579 a notice specifying an intention to offer an alibi defense, and shall serve a copy of the notice and a certificate of service on the attorney for the Commonwealth.

(1) The notice and a certificate of service shall be signed by the attorney for the defendant, or the defendant if unrepresented.

(2) The notice shall contain specific information as to the place or places where the defendant claims to have been at the time of the alleged offense and the names and addresses of the witnesses whom the defendant intends to call in support of the claim.

STATE v. JOHN LUCIOUS

518 S.E.2d 677 (Ga. 1999)

HUNSTEIN, J.

The State is seeking imposition of the death penalty against John R. Lucious for the murder of Mohammad A. Aftab in Clayton County. Lucious was indicted on charges of malice murder, two counts of felony murder, possession of a firearm during the commission of a felony, and misdemeanor possession of marijuana in connection with the alleged 1996 murder and armed robbery. During pretrial proceedings, the State refused to open its file except to the extent mandated by the Georgia and United States Constitutions because Lucious elected not to participate in Georgia's Criminal Procedure Discovery Act, OCGA §17-16-1 et seq. Lucious filed an omnibus motion seeking an order of the trial court declaring the Act unconstitutional. The trial court denied the motion but granted Lucious the unilateral right to discover specific material, including the State's trial witness list, scientific reports, and scientific work product. [The] State filed an application to appeal asserting that Lucious was not entitled to the pretrial discovery information granted by the trial court because of his election not to participate in the Act.

Prior to passage of the Act, there was no comprehensive Georgia statute or rule of law which governed discovery in criminal cases. Enacted in 1994, the Act [provides] for the "comprehensive regulation of discovery and inspection in criminal cases [and repeals] conflicting laws." . . . Ga. L. 1994, pp. 1895-1896. The Act, which applies only to those cases in which the defendant elects by written notice to have it apply, broadens discovery in felony cases by imposing corresponding discovery obligations upon both the defendant and the State. For example, the Act requires the State and the defendant to disclose, inter alia, the identities and addresses of all persons they intend to call as witnesses at trial, relevant written or recorded statements of all witnesses, and scientific reports, physical or mental reports, and other evidence intended for use at trial or evidence obtained from or that belongs to the defendant regardless of whether the State intends to use such evidence at trial. The Act also [provides] for discovery of a custodial statement and [requires] notice of an intent to offer an alibi defense and a list of witnesses to be offered to rebut the defense of alibi. These provisions reveal that the Act provides a comprehensive scheme of reciprocal discovery in criminal felony cases. . . .

Lucious contends the Act's discovery provisions violate his right to due process under the United States and Georgia Constitutions. We disagree. In Wardius v. Oregon, 412 U.S. 470 (1973), the Supreme Court held that under the due process clause a defendant cannot be compelled to disclose to the State evidence or witnesses to be offered in support of an alibi defense absent reciprocal discovery of the State's rebuttal witnesses. The *Wardius* Court reviewed its earlier decision in Williams v. Florida, 399 U.S. 78 (1970), which upheld Florida's notice-of-alibi statute because such statute provided reciprocal discovery, and stated:

> [although] the Due Process Clause has little to say regarding the amount of discovery which the parties must be afforded, it does speak to the balance of forces between the accused and his accuser. The Williams Court was therefore careful to note that "Florida law provides for liberal discovery by the defendant against the State, and [Florida's] notice-of-alibi rule is itself carefully hedged with reciprocal duties requiring state disclosure to the defendant." . . . We do not suggest that the Due Process Clause of its own force requires [a state] to adopt [reciprocal discovery] provisions. But we do hold that in the absence of a strong showing of state interests to the contrary, discovery must be a two-way street. [412 U.S. at 474-475.]

The Court in *Wardius* thus articulated a due process requirement of reciprocity in criminal discovery statutes in the absence of a strong state interest to the contrary. This same requirement has been held to apply under the due process clause of the

Georgia Constitution. See Rower v. State, 443 S.E.2d 839 (Ga. 1994) (to satisfy due process, discovery practices in criminal cases must provide a balance of forces between the defendant and the State). Applying this due process standard to the Act, we find that the Act furthers legitimate State interests by establishing a closely symmetrical scheme of discovery in criminal cases that maximizes the presentation of reliable evidence, minimizes the risk that a judgment will be predicated on incomplete or misleading evidence, and fosters fairness and efficiency in criminal proceedings. Because the Act provides for reciprocal discovery in criminal felony cases with any imbalance favoring the defendant, the Act does not violate the due process clause of the United States or Georgia Constitutions.

Nor do the Act's discovery provisions violate Lucious's right to confrontation. The right to confrontation is a "trial right," guaranteeing a defendant the ability to confront and question adverse witnesses at trial. See Pennsylvania v. Ritchie, 480 U.S. 39, 52-53 (1987). As a trial right, it "does not include the power to require the pretrial disclosure of any and all information that might be useful in contradicting unfavorable testimony," and does not guarantee "cross-examination that is effective in whatever way, and to whatever extent, the defense might wish." Delaware v. Fensterer, 474 U.S. 15, 20 (1985). Because the confrontation clause guarantees only the right to confront and cross-examine those individuals called to testify against a defendant at trial and the pretrial discovery provisions of the Act do not implicate or infringe upon such right, we find no merit to this argument.

[Lucious argues further] that the Act's reciprocal discovery provisions violate his right to effective representation of counsel by denying him the benefit of defense counsel's judgment of whether and when to reveal aspects of his case to the State. The Act simply requires disclosure of witnesses and evidence a defendant intends to introduce at trial as part of a reciprocal discovery process. The United States Supreme Court has affirmed the right of states to experiment with systems of broad discovery designed to aid in the administration of justice and to enhance the fairness of the adversary system. That the Act provides for discovery before trial rather than after a witness has testified is of no constitutional significance. See United States v. Nobles, 422 U.S. 225, 241 (1975) (the Sixth Amendment "does not confer the right to present testimony free from the legitimate demands of the adversarial system").

Because there is no general constitutional right to discovery in a criminal case, the election not to invoke the discovery provisions of the Act necessarily entitles a defendant to only that discovery specifically afforded by the Georgia and United States Constitutions, statutory exceptions to the Act, and non-conflicting rules of court. This panoply of discovery rights exists separately from the Act and provides abundant discovery opportunities for all criminal defendants, including death penalty defendants, who elect not to have the Act apply to their case. We therefore find that the trial court erred in granting Lucious those discovery rights identified below which are not guaranteed under the United States or Georgia Constitutions or otherwise provided for by statute or court rule.

Specifically, the trial court erred by holding that a defendant who chooses not to participate in the Act is entitled to discover all of the State's scientific reports. In a broadly-worded order the trial court directed the State to produce its Georgia Bureau of Investigation "Crime Lab reports and any and all other scientific reports." A defendant's right to discover scientific reports is a procedural right derived from former OCGA §17-7-211, a statute expressly repealed by passage of the Act. Procedural rights which flow from a repealed criminal discovery statute can be eliminated. In order to obtain discovery of scientific reports, therefore, a defendant must elect to proceed under the provisions of the Act.

For the same reasons, we find the trial court erred in holding that a defendant who chooses not to opt into the Act is entitled to discover all of the State's scientific work product. The trial court's order provides that the State must produce "any and all . . . memos, notes, graphs, computer print-outs, photographs, and other data that the State's experts will rely on to support their testimony during direct examination." To the extent such information may be discoverable in felony criminal cases, its production is now governed by the Act and a defendant is entitled to this information only if he invokes the Act. Because the right to subpoena work product was derived from former OCGA §17-7-211 and is not a substantive right apart from the discovery provisions of the Act, [defendants may not] unilaterally obtain evidence of scientific work product.

The trial court also erred in holding that Lucious was entitled to the witness list provided by Uniform Superior Court Rule 30.3. Rule 30.3 provides that upon request of defense counsel, the State shall furnish the addresses and telephone numbers of trial witnesses known to the State. The Legislature intended, in enacting the Act, to amend the criminal discovery procedures and to provide certain criminal defendants the opportunity to discover information well in excess of that mandated by either the United States or Georgia Constitutions, including the opportunity to receive from the State a continuing list of trial witnesses and related information. Under the Act, a defendant is entitled to a trial witness list and information concerning trial witnesses only if he chooses to have the Act apply, thereby agreeing to the reciprocal discovery provisions of the Act. Because Rule 30.3 conflicts with OCGA §§17-16-3 and 17-16-8 in that it requires the State to furnish a trial witness list without imposing reciprocal discovery obligations upon the defendant, we find the Rule to be unenforceable. Rule 30.3 must yield to the substantive law contained in these statutes.

Although Lucious did not choose to have the Act apply to his case and, therefore, is not entitled to a list of trial witnesses pursuant to Rule 30.3, Lucious remains entitled to a list of witnesses who appeared before the grand jury and upon whose testimony the charges against him are founded. See Ga. Const., Art. I, Sec. I, Par. XIV; Evans v. State, 150 S.E.2d 240 (Ga. 1966).

Finally, we find the Act is inapplicable to presentence hearings. Discovery in presentence hearings in both capital or non-capital cases remains governed by OCGA §17-10-2, which was not among the various discovery statutes related to felony cases specifically repealed or amended by the enactment of the Act.

FLETCHER, P.J., concurring in part and dissenting in part.

Because the majority opinion interprets the discovery act as repealing by implication the defendant's right to the state's trial witness lists, scientific reports, and scientific work product, I dissent [from that portion of the opinion].

The majority construes too narrowly the constitutional requirement that the defendant shall be furnished "a list of witnesses on whose testimony such charge is founded." In Sutton v. State, 228 S.E.2d 820 (Ga. 1976), we held that the constitutional right to be furnished a list of witnesses "is the right, on demand, to be furnished by the district attorney's office, prior to arraignment, with the list of witnesses who will testify for the state on the trial."

As a matter of due process and fundamental fairness, I would continue to interpret the constitutional provision as requiring the state to provide a list of its trial witnesses despite the repeal of the statute. The requirement enables the defendant to prepare a defense by interviewing potential trial witnesses; it aids judicial economy by requiring defense counsel to investigate and interview the witnesses before trial, thus avoiding the need for a continuance; and it places no undue burden on the prosecutor, as shown by the attorney general office's practice of furnishing a list of potential trial witnesses in all criminal cases.

Even in the absence of a constitutional right, the better policy and practice is for prosecutors to furnish a list of potential trial witnesses to avoid unfair surprise and make trials more efficient. The discovery act repealed former OCGA §17-7-110, which required disclosure of witness lists and the indictment, but reenacted that provision to apply in misdemeanor cases. Because persons charged with less serious offenses are entitled to the names of trial witnesses, persons charged with felonies should receive the same information from the state.

The due process clause of the United States Constitution guarantees a defendant the right to an independent examination of critical evidence. Depending on the case, this right may include the state's scientific reports and data on which its experts will rely at trial. Despite the majority's unsupported assertion, the repeal of OCGA §17-7-211 cannot eliminate the defendant's due process right to scientific reports and work product when they are critical evidence. Any doubts about the importance of the evidence should weigh in favor of disclosure towards the defendant.

Both the Georgia Attorney General and the Georgia Association of Criminal Defense Lawyers agree that a defendant preparing for trial is entitled to a significant amount of information under the United States Constitution and the Georgia Constitution, statutes, court rules, and court decisions. Specifically, they agree that a defendant is entitled to the following:

1. Exculpatory material as set forth in Brady v. Maryland, 373 U.S. 83 (1963).
2. Evidence of an understanding, agreement, or promise of leniency under Giglio v. United States, 405 U.S. 150 (1972), and Patillo v. State, 368 S.E.2d 493 (Ga. 1988).
3. Evidence in aggravation that the state intends to rely on at presentence hearings and victim impact evidence under OCGA §17-10-1.2 and Livingston v. State, 444 S.E.2d 748 (Ga. 1994).
4. Independent examination of critical evidence under the due process clause of the United States Constitution.
5. Materials used by a witness to refresh memory as set forth in Sterling v. State, 477 S.E.2d 807 (Ga. 1996), and Johnson v. State, 383 S.E.2d 118 (Ga. 1989).
6. Notice of state's intent to introduce evidence of similar transactions that do not involve prior difficulties between the defendant and victim under Uniform Superior Court Rule 31.3 and Wall v. State, 500 S.E.2d 904 (Ga. 1998).
7. Certain information from the Georgia Crime Information Center under OCGA §35-3-34.
8. Notice of the state's intention to rebut evidence of specific acts of violence by the victim against third persons under Chandler v. State, 405 S.E.2d 669 (Ga. 1991), and Uniform Superior Court Rule 31.6.
9. Pre-trial examination of known handwriting samples under OCGA §24-7-7.

10. Disclosure of the name of an informant in certain circumstances under Roviaro v. United States, 353 U.S. 53 (1957), and Wilson v. State, 433 S.E. 2d 703 (Ga. App. 1993).
11. Examination of any report prepared under OCGA §17-4-20.1 about an act of family violence for which the defendant has been arrested.
12. Presentation of evidence at a court proceeding by way of a notice to produce, if the matter would be admissible and the defendant needs it for use as evidence on his own behalf.
13. Access to records under the Open Records Act, OCGA §50-18-70.

These rights remain available despite a defendant's decision not to have the criminal discovery statute apply. . . .

Notes

1. *Reciprocal discovery: majority position.* The trend in American jurisdictions is toward increasingly reciprocal discovery. These statutes usually survive constitutional challenges. See State v. Brown, 940 P.2d 546 (Wash. 1997). However, the full "two-way street" form of discovery is more rare. Some courts have struck down the most ambitious efforts to create reciprocal discovery, particularly those requiring the defendant to reveal information about potential witnesses that she does *not* plan to call at trial. The Georgia decision in *Lucious* is typical in focusing on whether the material that the defense must disclose under the statute would be disclosed later at trial. The most common constitutional objections are based on the self-incrimination privilege, the right to cross-examination, the right to effective assistance of counsel, and due process. For a sampling of the wide-ranging state court decisions on defense disclosures in criminal discovery, consult the web extension for this chapter at *http://www.crimpro.com/extension/ch15*.

Discovery rules in most states regulate specialized defenses such as alibis, self-defense, or insanity. The Supreme Court has upheld the constitutionality of such statutes in Williams v. Florida, 399 U.S. 78 (1970). The defenses must be reciprocal: The Supreme Court has struck down a statute that required the defense to provide notice of an alibi defense without requiring the prosecution to disclose its alibi-rebuttal witnesses. Wardius v. Oregon, 412 U.S. 470 (1973). Why are alibi, self-defense, and insanity the three types of defense evidence that appear most often in the statutes and rules regarding disclosure? At least two of these defenses (alibi and insanity) require the development of evidence unrelated to the events of the alleged crime. But why should the government obtain special notice about self-defense? And once the government knows that a defendant plans to pursue an insanity defense, why should the government have access to defense experts? Can't the prosecution hire its own experts?

2. *Consensual discovery.* Statutes in many states finesse the constitutional questions involved in compelling defendant disclosures by giving the defendant the choice of opting out of extensive discovery. Only if the defendant obtains full discovery rights against the government must she also comply with the disclosure duties. Note that the *Lucious* court mentioned the consent feature of the Georgia statute. Does a defendant "waive" objections to disclosure in the same sense that he

or she can "waive" the right to trial or to an appointed attorney? Does consensual discovery protect a true adversarial option?

3. *Work-product doctrine in criminal cases.* Recall that discovery rules usually include a privilege, developed at common law, for the "work product" of attorneys and their agents. The privilege limits the disclosures of both defense and prosecution. The U.S. Supreme Court recognized the work-product doctrine in Hickman v. Taylor, 329 U.S. 495 (1947), establishing a qualified privilege for certain materials prepared by an attorney in anticipation of litigation. The Court explained the decision as follows:

> Historically, a lawyer is an officer of the court and is bound to work for the advancement of justice while faithfully protecting the rightful interests of his clients. In performing his various duties, however, it is essential that a lawyer work with a certain degree of privacy, free from unnecessary intrusion by opposing parties and their counsel. Proper preparation of a client's case demands that he assemble information, sift what he considers to be the relevant from the irrelevant facts, prepare his legal theories and plan his strategy without undue and needless interference. . . . This work is reflected, of course, in interviews, statements, memoranda, correspondence, briefs, mental impressions, personal beliefs, and countless other tangible and intangible ways — aptly though roughly termed . . . as the [work] product of the lawyer. Were such materials open to opposing counsel on mere demand, much of what is now put down in writing would remain unwritten. An attorney's thoughts, heretofore inviolate, would not be his own. Inefficiency, unfairness and sharp practices would inevitably develop in the giving of legal advice and in the preparation of cases for trial. The effect on the legal profession would be demoralizing. And the interests of the clients and the cause of justice would be poorly served.

329 U.S. at 510-11. There are two levels of "work-product" protections. An "absolute" privilege attaches to any mental impressions, conclusions, opinions or legal theories of an attorney; that is, any document containing such material must be redacted to remove it before disclosure to another party. On the other hand, a "qualified" privilege attaches to other materials created "in anticipation of litigation." An opposing party can obtain this material if there is a strong enough reason for the disclosure. Is a state that has embraced broad defense disclosures likely to weaken the work-product doctrine? Is the work-product privilege based on a view of an independent and adversarial development of information that is incompatible with extensive discovery?

4. *Effective advocacy and reciprocal discovery.* Which of the following sorts of information would an advocate most want to withhold from the other party before trial: information about fact witnesses, expert witnesses, or documents? Do the discovery rules in criminal cases provide the most protection to information that requires the most effort to develop? Or do they protect the information that will have the most impact at trial? Or is the objective instead to require disclosure of information precisely *because* it is likely to have an impact at trial or *because* it is difficult to develop? Discovery rules that restrict independent development of evidence to peripheral issues make a profound statement about the adversary system. For instance, in Germany, the judge and the defense attorney have full access to the prosecution file, but the defense has no corresponding duty to disclose its information to the court or the prosecution. Do our discovery rules now declare that an adversarial development of evidence is more likely to obscure truth than to further it? As you evaluate

the rules of criminal discovery, try to anticipate how lawyers in the adversarial tradition will react to rules that attempt to shift that tradition toward reciprocal discovery.

4. *Discovery Ethics*

During discovery, defense attorneys could face one of the classic puzzles of legal ethics. If a client gives her lawyer incriminating physical evidence, what are the lawyer's obligations? Do the obligations change if the material comes from a third party? If the client or a third party tells the lawyer about the location of such material? Finally, does defense counsel have an affirmative ethical obligation to seek out incriminating evidence?

Problem 15-3. Defense Attorney as Repository

Michael Hitch was indicted for first-degree murder and is currently awaiting trial on that charge. In the course of their investigation, the police interviewed Hitch's girlfriend, Diane Heaton, who told them that the victim was wearing a certain wristwatch shortly before his death. Later, an investigator for the Public Defender's Office contacted Ms. Heaton, and she informed the investigator that she had found a wristwatch in Hitch's suit jacket. She also stated that she did not want to turn the evidence over to the police. The investigator contacted the defendant's attorney, who told him to bring the watch to the attorney's office. The attorney indicated that he did this for two reasons. First, he wanted to examine the watch to determine whether it was the same one that Ms. Heaton had described to the police. Second, he was afraid that she might destroy or conceal the evidence. Shortly thereafter, Hitch informed the police that he had taken a watch from the victim. The police were, however, unaware of the location of that watch.

The defense attorney filed a petition with the Ethics Committee of the State Bar, requesting an opinion concerning his duties with respect to the wristwatch. You are a practicing attorney in the state and serve as a volunteer member of the Ethics Committee. After reviewing the California and North Carolina ethics opinions reprinted below, what guidance would you give to Hitch's attorney? If the attorney ignores the guidance from the committee, does that constitute grounds for discipline against him? Cf. Hitch v. Pima County Superior Court, 708 P.2d 72 (Ariz. 1985).

■ STANDING COMMITTEE ON PROFESSIONAL RESPONSIBILITY AND CONDUCT, STATE BAR OF CALIFORNIA, CALIFORNIA FORMAL ETHICS OPINION 1984-76

Issue: What are the ethical obligations of a criminal defense attorney during the course of a pending criminal matter when the client places upon the attorney's desk or informs the attorney of the location of the instrumentality, fruits, or other physical evidence of the crime? . . .

Fundamental to this discussion is Section 954 of the Evidence Code, which provides that a client "has a privilege to refuse to disclose, and to prevent another from disclosing, a confidential communication between client and lawyer. . . ." Likewise, Business and Professions Code Section 6068, subdivision (e) places upon the attorney the duty "to maintain inviolate the confidence, and at every peril to himself to preserve the secrets, of his client." The rationale behind the evidentiary privilege and the professional obligation of the attorney is to allow the client to make disclosures to the attorney "without fear that his attorney may be forced to reveal the information confided to him." People v. Meredith, 29 Cal.3d 682, 690 (1981).

On the other hand, by the provisions of Section 135 of the Penal Code, it is a violation of the law for one knowingly to conceal or destroy any "instrument in writing or other matter or thing [that] is about to be produced in evidence upon any trial, inquiry or investigation whatever, authorized by law . . . ", and it is clear that the attorney-client privilege does not grant to the client the power permanently to "sequester physical evidence such as a weapon or any other article used in the perpetration of a crime by delivering it to his attorney." People v. Lee, 3 Cal. App. 3d 514, 526 (1970). Likewise, rule 7-107(A) of the California Rules of Professional Conduct states: "A member of the State Bar shall not suppress any evidence that he or his client has a legal obligation to reveal or produce."

The California Supreme Court in People v. Meredith has determined that physical evidence of a crime over which the lawyer has exercised dominion and control, thus taking possession, is not protected by the attorney-client privilege. Other jurisdictions have imposed a clear legal and ethical duty upon the lawyer to turn that evidence over to the prosecution. State v. Olwell, 394 P.2d 681 (Wash. 1964); Anderson v. State 297 So. 2d 871 (Fla. App. 1974). . . .

In considering the attorney's legal obligations to his client under the Sixth Amendment to provide effective counsel, the attorney should advise the client of the attorney's ethical as well as legal obligation with respect to the duty to deliver physical evidence of the crime to the prosecution if the attorney takes possession of such physical evidence. It is at this stage of representation that the impact upon the attorney-client relationship is at its greatest. The client is informed of the duties the attorney may have in the search-for-truth aspect of the adversary system, even to the extent of a legal duty imposed upon the attorney to participate in the very case against his client by delivering material evidence of the crime to the prosecution.

Although the fact of the delivery of the physical evidence of a crime by the client to the attorney is within the protection of the attorney-client privilege, the physical evidence itself is not. As a corollary, however, although it was held in Anderson v. State that the attorney acted properly under the circumstances that confronted him by turning the stolen items over to the police, "in order for the attorney-client privilege to be meaningfully preserved, the state cannot introduce evidence that it received the items from the attorney's office."

It was also held in State v. Olwell [that the] "attorney should not be a depository for criminal evidence. . . . Such evidence given the attorney during legal consultation . . . and used by the attorney in preparing the defense of his client's case . . . could clearly be withheld for a reasonable period of time. It follows that the attorney after a reasonable period, should, as an officer of the court, on his own motion turn the same over to the prosecution." The prosecution, however, must take "extreme precautions" to make certain that the source of the evidence is not disclosed at trial. Thus, in its *Olwell* decision, the court was seeking the proper balance between truth seeking by the prosecution, and the attorney-client privilege of the defense.

[The] criminal defense attorney, after holding for a reasonable time for the purpose of preparing his client's defense, the instrumentality, fruits, or other physical evidence of the crime placed upon his desk by the client, is thereafter both legally and ethically obligated on his own motion to turn such evidence over to the prosecution.

It is apparent, however, that there is a significant difference in the legal and ethical obligations of an attorney when given possession of the physical evidence of a crime, as opposed to merely being told by his client of the location of the physical evidence of the crime.

[In] the situation wherein the client informs the attorney of the location of the physical evidence of the crime, or the attorney merely observes it without taking possession, the attorney need not disclose to the prosecution either its location or his or his agent's physical observations of the same. When, however, the defense attorney removes the physical evidence from its original location or takes possession of it, the evidence must, after reasonable time for investigation, be delivered to the prosecution and the location of its discovery will be subject to disclosure.

A criminal defense attorney should give careful consideration to the consequences of his actions before accepting possession of physical evidence or revealing any oral or observation evidence to the prosecution in light of the client's Sixth Amendment right to effective counsel and Business and Professions Code Section 6068, subdivision (e), requiring confidentiality. [Case law suggests] that all investigation and examination by a criminal defense attorney (with the exception of possession of physical evidence) is within the self-incrimination privilege of the defendant. . . .

This opinion is . . . advisory only. It is not binding upon the courts, The State Bar of California, its Board of Governors, any persons or tribunals charged with regulatory responsibilities, or any member of the State Bar.

NORTH CAROLINA STATE BAR, RECEIPT OF EVIDENCE OF CRIME BY LAWYER FOR DEFENDANT, ETHICS OPINION 221 (1995)

Inquiry #1: Attorney A and Attorney B work for different law firms. They have been appointed to represent Defendant, who is charged with first-degree murder. Defendant's wife, W, was apparently present during the altercation that led to the victim's death. During Attorney A and Attorney B's investigation, Defendant implicated W in the matter and told the attorneys that he had knowledge of relevant physical evidence. The police detectives who investigated the death are in possession of a stick they believe Defendant used to commit the murder, but neither the police detectives nor the prosecutors are aware of the existence of other physical evidence.

Defendant brought the physical evidence to Attorney B's office. Attorney B took possession of the physical evidence for purposes of examination and consultation with Attorney A concerning the extent to which the physical evidence might incriminate or exculpate Defendant.

Attorney A and Attorney B interviewed W, who incriminated herself. The story W told Attorney A and Attorney B is different from the statement that she gave to the police officers during the initial investigation.

Must Attorney A or Attorney B notify the district attorney's office or the investigating law enforcement agency of the existence of the physical evidence?

Opinion #1: No. On the one hand, a lawyer has a duty to preserve the confidences of the client and to zealously represent the client within the bounds of the law. Rule 4 and Canon VII of the Rules of Professional Conduct. On the other hand, a lawyer is an officer of the court and should not engage in conduct that is prejudicial to the administration of justice. Rule 1.2(d). In the absence of a court order or a common law or statutory obligation to disclose the location or deliver an item of inculpatory physical evidence that is not contraband (the possession of which is in and of itself a crime, such as narcotics) to law enforcement authorities, a defense lawyer may take such evidence into his or her possession for the purpose of testing, examination, or inspection. The defense lawyer should return the evidence to the source from whom the lawyer received it. In returning the item to the source, the lawyer must advise the source of the legal consequences pertaining to the possession or destruction of the evidence by that person or others. This advice should include the advice to retain the evidence intact and not engage in conduct that might be a violation of criminal statutes relating to evidence. See generally ABA Standards for Criminal Justice: Prosecution Function and Defense Function (3rd ed.), Standard 4-4.6(a)-(c), "Physical Evidence," and Commentary. If a defense lawyer receives a subpoena for inculpatory physical evidence in his or her possession, the lawyer may take appropriate steps to contest the subpoena in order to protect the interests of the client. However, the lawyer must comply with a court order to produce the evidence.

Similarly, pursuant to N.C.G.S. §15A-905, a defense lawyer must comply with any order entered by the court to produce evidence the defendant intends to introduce at trial.

Inquiry #2: What specific information, if any, is Attorney A or Attorney B allowed to disclose to the district attorney or the law enforcement agency regarding the weapon or how it was obtained?

Opinion #2: See opinion #1 above.

Inquiry #3: W provided information to Attorney A and Attorney B which would assist Defendant in his defense. Since Attorney A and Attorney B might be witnesses for Defendant, do they have to withdraw from the representation of Defendant?

Opinion #3: No. Rule 5.2(b) requires a lawyer to withdraw from the representation of a client if, "after undertaking employment in contemplated or pending litigation, a lawyer learns or it is obvious that he or a lawyer in his firm ought to be called as a witness on behalf of his client." However, he may continue the representation and he or a lawyer in his firm may testify under the circumstances enumerated in Rule 5.2(a). It is not "obvious" that Attorney A or Attorney B "ought" to be called as a witness for their client. Any information gained by Attorney A and Attorney B during the professional relationship with Defendant, including information obtained from third parties such as W, is confidential information. Rule 4(a); see also N.C.G.S. §15A-906. Unless Defendant consents to disclosure of the information gained from W, the lawyers may not testify about what W told them. Even if Defendant consents to the use of this information, W may be called as a witness herself, thus avoiding the need for Attorney A or Attorney B to testify. A problem of this nature can be avoided by having a nonlawyer present at all interviews with prospective trial witnesses.

Inquiry #4: Defendant has consented to the disclosure by Attorney A and Attorney B of the substance of W's statements to them. At trial, W is called as a witness and testifies contrary to her earlier statements to Attorney A and Attorney B. If the testimony of Attorney A or Attorney B is necessary to rebut the testimony of W, must one or both of them withdraw from the representation?

Opinion #4: Withdrawal may not be required. It is possible that by aggressive cross-examination of W, the need for one of the lawyers to testify will be avoided. If Lawyer A or Lawyer B must testify in order to rebut the testimony of W, moreover, the lawyers might conclude that an exception in Rule 5.2(a)(4) applies which would allow the lawyer to testify without withdrawing from the representation. Rule 5.2(b). Rule 5.2(a)(4) allows a lawyer to continue the representation despite acting as a witness in the trial if withdrawal "would work a substantial hardship on the client because of the distinctive value of the lawyer . . . as counsel in the particular case."

If it is necessary for one of the lawyers to testify, the lawyer who testifies may have to withdraw from the representation but the other lawyer may remain in the case. Rule 5.2(b) only requires the lawyer who testifies for his client and the other members of his firm to withdraw from the representation.

Notes

1. *Ethical obligations to turn over physical evidence.* The rules governing a defense lawyer's obligations to disclose physical evidence are largely uniform. If a defense lawyer receives incriminating *testimony* from a client, the attorney-client privilege and the self-incrimination clause combine to prevent the attorney from revealing that information to the government. But if the defense lawyer receives incriminating *physical* evidence, the outcome is different. Discovery rules do not address this question. Instead, Rule 3.4 of the Model Rules of Professional Conduct, adopted as law in many states, provides the starting point for analyzing the attorney's duties:

> A lawyer shall not . . . unlawfully obstruct another party's access to evidence or unlawfully alter, destroy or conceal a document or other material having potential evidentiary value. A lawyer shall not counsel or assist another person to do any such act.

Hence, the key question is whether a lawyer's act is an "unlawful" obstruction of access or tampering with evidence. Most states have statutes that prohibit obstruction of investigations or tampering with evidence. In some places, an investigation must be pending before the destruction or concealment of potential evidence becomes unlawful, while elsewhere the intent to prevent detection of a crime is the critical element, regardless of the timing of the destruction or concealment. The courts addressing these situations have held that the attorney who takes possession of contraband relevant to a criminal investigation against a client must ordinarily give the evidence to the government. The attorney can return the evidence to its original location only if the return of the evidence does not create a risk that the evidence will be concealed or altered. See Rubin v. State, 602 A.2d 677 (Md. 1992). The National Legal Aid and Defender Association recommends that a lawyer deliver physical evidence to the government only if delivery is required by law or court order, or if "the item received is contraband, or if in the lawyer's judgment the lawyer cannot retain the item in a way that does not pose an unreasonable risk of physical harm to anyone."

What would you say to your client or a third party about incriminating physical evidence? If you decided to deliver the physical evidence to the government, exactly how would you proceed? Could you deliver the item to some third party (say, a member of the Ethics Committee of the state bar) and ask that person to deliver the evidence anonymously?

2. *Source and type of evidence.* Does it matter that the watch in Problem 15-3 was not contraband (that is, it was not illegal for anyone to possess the watch)? Does it matter that the attorney learned of the location of the wristwatch from a third party rather than from the client? Can the prosecutor reveal to the jury that defense counsel was the source of the watch when it comes into evidence at trial? See State v. Olwell, 394 P.2d 681 (Wash. 1964) (if client provides defense counsel with evidence that must be given to government, attorney-client privilege prevents prosecutor from informing jury about source of evidence).

3. *Ethics rules and prosecutorial disclosures.* Rules of ethics often recognize a distinctive set of duties for prosecuting attorneys. How might these rules be relevant during the discovery process? Rule 3.8 of the ABA's Model Rules of Professional Conduct, the basis for most state bar ethics rules, is reprinted earlier in this chapter. Consider as well the following passage from Rule 8 of the Supreme Court of Tennessee, EC 7-13:

> The responsibility of a public prosecutor differs from that of the usual advocate; the public prosecutor's duty is to seek justice, not merely to convict. . . . With respect to evidence and witnesses, the prosecutor has responsibilities different from those of a lawyer in private practice; the prosecutor should make timely disclosure to the defense of available evidence, known to the prosecutor, that tends to negate the guilt of the accused, mitigate the degree of the offense, or reduce the punishment. Further, a prosecutor should not intentionally avoid pursuit of evidence merely because the prosecutor believes it will damage the prosecutor's case or aid the accused.

If you were a chief prosecutor in the district, what office policies would you consider to ensure that the trial attorneys in your office follow the requirements of *Brady* and other disclosure and discovery laws? Is it more important to hire good people as line prosecutors, or to establish proper routines, monitoring, and incentives for the people who work in the office? See Model Rule of Professional Conduct 5.1 ("A lawyer having direct supervisory authority over another lawyer shall make reasonable efforts to ensure that the other lawyer conforms to the Rules of Professional Conduct").

B. SPEEDY TRIAL PREPARATION

An old bromide reminds us that "justice delayed is justice denied." This can be true both for the prosecution and the defense in criminal cases. If preparations for trial last too long, the evidence becomes less reliable for both sides. The uncertainty about the criminal charges may harm the defendant's reputation and can make it difficult for the defendants and the victims of the alleged crime to move ahead with their lives. The need for speedy resolution of criminal charges has been mentioned in some of the earliest documents in our legal tradition, including the Magna Carta of 1215, which states, "we will not deny or defer to any man either justice or right."

The right to a speedy trial appears in constitutional provisions, both state and federal. The Sixth Amendment guarantees a "speedy and public trial," and most states have similar provisions. The federal and state due process clauses prevent some extreme forms of delay. Recent constitutional amendments recognizing the rights of victims of crime have declared that victims, too, have a right to a speedy trial. Many state and federal statutes also hurry the criminal process along. These include statutes of limitation (requiring charges to be filed within a limited time from the events in question) and speedy trial acts (requiring the parties and the courts to bring the matter to trial within a specified period from the start of the process).

Despite all this emphasis on speed, another bromide reminds us that "haste makes waste." Both prosecution and defense have some reasons to slow down the process. Some of their reasons may be less than noble. If testimony is going to damage one side or another, a witness's fading memory may make the testimony less convincing and more susceptible to attack. If a defendant remains in custody before trial, a prosecutor may not be so anxious to risk an acquittal that would release the defendant from custody; a defendant not in custody may want to delay the day of reckoning. But other reasons for delay are surely necessary, even praiseworthy, including a desire to complete the discovery processes examined in the previous section.

1. *Pre-accusation Delay*

Once a crime occurs and an investigation begins, the matter typically becomes the basis for criminal charges or is declined for criminal charges within a matter of days. Among the handful of matters that take more time, a small proportion can remain active for many months or years after the events take place. What legal principles and institutions are available to limit the amount of time that can pass between the commission of a crime and the filing of criminal charges? Once a state legislature has passed a statute of limitations, is any further limitation necessary to avoid delays that might create hardship or unreliable outcomes?

■ NEW YORK CRIMINAL PROCEDURE LAW §30.10

1. A criminal action must be commenced within the period of limitation prescribed in the ensuing subdivisions of this section.

2. Except as otherwise provided in subdivision three:

(a) A prosecution for a class A felony or rape in the first degree . . . or aggravated sexual abuse in the first degree . . . or course of sexual conduct against a child in the first degree . . . may be commenced at any time;

(b) A prosecution for any other felony must be commenced within five years after the commission thereof;

(c) A prosecution for a misdemeanor must be commenced within two years after the commission thereof;

(d) A prosecution for a petty offense must be commenced within one year after the commission thereof.

3. Notwithstanding the provisions of subdivision two, the periods of limitation for the commencement of criminal actions are extended as follows in the indicated circumstances:

(a) A prosecution for larceny committed by a person in violation of a fiduciary duty may be commenced within one year after the facts constituting such offense are discovered or, in the exercise of reasonable diligence, should have been discovered by the aggrieved party or by a person under a legal duty to represent him who is not himself implicated in the commission of the offense. . . .

(f) For purposes of a prosecution involving a sexual offense . . . committed against a child less than 18 years of age [other than those delineated in paragraph (a)], the period of limitation shall not begin to run until the child has reached the age of 18 or the offense is reported to a law enforcement agency. . . .

4. In calculating the time limitation applicable to commencement of a criminal action, the following periods shall not be included:

(a) Any period following the commission of the offense during which (i) the defendant was continuously outside this state or (ii) the whereabouts of the defendant were continuously unknown and continuously unascertainable by the exercise of reasonable diligence. However, in no event shall the period of limitation be extended by more than five years beyond the period otherwise applicable under subdivision two.

(b) When a prosecution for an offense is lawfully commenced within the prescribed period of limitation therefor, and when an accusatory instrument upon which such prosecution is based is subsequently dismissed by an authorized court under directions or circumstances permitting the lodging of another charge for the same offense or an offense based on the same conduct, the period extending from the commencement of the thus defeated prosecution to the dismissal of the accusatory instrument does not constitute a part of the period of limitation applicable to commencement of prosecution by a new charge.

■ COMMONWEALTH v. STEPHEN SCHER

803 A.2d 1204 (Pa. 2002)

NEWMAN, J.

. . . Martin Dillon died of a gunshot wound to the chest on June 2, 1976 at the Dillon family recreational property called "Gunsmoke" in Susquehanna County. Scher was the only other individual present when Dillon died. How Dillon died, and whether that death was an accident or an intentional act of murder, is a story that evolved in fits and starts in the intervening two decades, culminating in murder charges being filed against Scher in 1996 and his conviction for first degree murder following a six-week jury trial in 1997. . . .

The Scene

Andrew Russin, a neighbor whose house was approximately two miles from Gunsmoke, testified that, on the day Dillon died, Scher appeared at Russin's house with his hands and mouth covered in blood and asked Russin to call the authorities because Dillon had been shot. [The men drove separately to Gunsmoke, and walked] towards the skeet shooting area, where Russin saw Dillon's body. . . . Russin then watched as Scher picked up the gun that was lying near Dillon's body and smashed it against a tree, breaking the barrel from the stock.

Trooper William Hairston of the Pennsylvania State Police . . . arrived at Gunsmoke with John Conarton, the Susquehanna County Coroner, . . . and walked up the path that led to a clearing where Dillon's body lay on its back. A pair of hunting goggles and shooting "earmuffs" were on the ground nearby. . . .

In his June 2, 1976 statement, Scher told Trooper Hairston: (1) he and Dillon had come to Gunsmoke to skeet shoot; (2) after firing about twenty rounds, they decided to take a break and returned to the trailer for some beer and potato chips; (3) the two sat in the trailer discussing an upcoming murder trial in which Dillon, a lawyer, was representing the defendant; (4) they then went back to the trail towards the clearing where the skeet-shooting trap was set up and fired a few more rounds; (5) Dillon then wanted to go back to the trailer to get cigarettes, so Scher loaded his shotgun, a sixteen-gauge, to be ready for the next round of firing, while Dillon unloaded his twenty-gauge shotgun and placed it on a nearby stump; (6) Scher and Dillon then walked down the trail, and Scher placed his loaded shotgun on a metal gun stand, approximately 120 feet from the skeet-shooting area; (7) as they went further down the trail, Dillon turned around and saw something in the open field that he thought was a porcupine, ran back up the trail and grabbed Scher's gun from the stand; (8) Scher heard Dillon cock the gun and heard it fire, but he could not see Dillon; (9) Scher then walked up the trail and found Dillon lying on the ground, face down; (10) Scher, a physician, ran up to Dillon and turned him over, saw that Dillon was bleeding from the chest and tried to stop the bleeding, but knew that Dillon was dead; (11) Scher took the car keys from Dillon's pocket and drove to Russin's house; (12) Scher and Russin returned to the scene, and Scher noticed that the trigger of the sixteen-gauge shotgun had a twig in it; (13) Scher then smashed the shotgun against the tree, and stated, "I know I shouldn't have done that." This June 2, 1976 statement to Trooper Hairston, as Scher's trial testimony more than twenty years later admitted, was a lie. . . .

On June 4, 1976, at 11:30 A.M., two days after his statement to Trooper Hairston, Scher came to the District Attorney's Office at the Susquehanna County Courthouse in Montrose, at the request of the investigators, and gave a statement. . . .When asked whether he and Dillon had any disagreements, Scher said, "No. We were talking about this rumor. I told him I was thinking of leaving town. It was rough on him. He sat and told me I was just a quitter and chicken — 'don't run away . . . it was just small people talking.'" After giving this answer, Scher became angry, terminated the interview, and left the room.

Edward Little, the District Attorney of Susquehanna County from 1968 to 1980, testified at pretrial hearings on Scher's Motion to Dismiss . . . and explained why no charges were filed during his tenure in office. . . . Dr. James Grace, a general practitioner who conducted an autopsy of Dillon on June 3, 1976, had issued a report that . . . listed the cause of death as "gunshot wound of the chest," but made no determination whether the death was the result of a homicide. Coroner Conarton, who was present when Scher gave his June 2, 1976 statement to Trooper Hairston, had determined that Dillon's death was accidental and had listed this as the manner of death on Dillon's death certificate. . . . Little explained that he . . . was not convinced that Dillon's death was an accident and requested that Coroner Conarton delay issuance of the death certificate in order to allow additional time to conduct the investigation. Little testified, however, that he never brought charges against Scher because he felt that there was insufficient evidence of murder to prosecute the case successfully. . . .

The Reactivated Investigation

Jeffrey Snyder was the District Attorney of Susquehanna County from 1988 until 1996. In 1989 [at the request of Martin Dillon's father, Lawrence Dillon], Snyder agreed to have the facts as developed by the investigation to that point presented to a panel of medical experts who were holding a conference at the University of Pennsylvania. . . . Following this presentation, a significant majority of the conference members opined that a self-inflicted gunshot wound, either accidental or intentional, caused Dillon's death. Snyder viewed this vote as "an overwhelming defeat for the prosecution" and concluded that no successful prosecution could be mounted at that time.

[In 1994], again at the urging of the Dillon family, two Pennsylvania State Police officers who had no previous involvement in the case were brought in to reexamine the evidence, conduct interviews with witnesses, and, in Snyder's words, "winnow out the rumor, the innuendo, that in my opinion riddled much of the material that was already on file." The "rumor" referred to by Snyder was the report that Scher and Dillon's wife, Patricia, had been having an affair before Dillon's death. [Patricia Dillon married Scher in 1978. The officers put in charge of the case in 1994 developed evidence] that Scher and Patricia had been having an extramarital affair prior to Dillon's death. In 1995, the Commonwealth successfully petitioned, in spite of the objection of Patricia Scher, to have Dillon's body exhumed for a second autopsy. Following this second autopsy in April of 1995, the Commonwealth obtained support from its expert forensic pathologist, Dr. Mihalikis, for the position that the physical evidence of Dillon's gunshot wound was not consistent with an accidental discharge of a dropped shotgun. The Commonwealth concluded that it possessed sufficient evidence to prosecute murder charges successfully and charged Scher with first-degree murder in June of 1996.

Scher's Trial Testimony

. . . Confronted with the Commonwealth's case, Scher took the stand and admitted that his previous statements to the investigators in June of 1976 were false. He proceeded to explain what happened that day at Gunsmoke. . . .

> He looked right at me in the eye. He said, I have to know. Are you and Pat having an affair? And I just had — I had to tell him the truth. He was looking me in the eye. I

> could no longer keep it from him. I said, Yes, we're having, not a love affair, but a physical affair. . . .
>
> Then I hear a scream, yell. And I look up and he has the sixteen gauge gun in his hand, reached around and I — I knew — I just knew I had to get that gun away. . . . I didn't know what he was going to do with it. I just knew with his state of mind at that time and my state of mind that it wasn't good to have a hold of a gun and I lunged. In a matter of that much time, I grabbed the gun and pulled away. We struggled and the gun went off.

Scher then explained why he decided to engage in a cover-up . . . and why he had lied to investigators, to the press, and to the public for the next twenty-one years.

> I was thinking, How can I tell anybody this accident happened like this and have anybody believe me in Montrose, what with all the rumors that were going on and me being a relative newcomer to the area and Marty's father is the mayor and I'm the only Jew in town, in the county? And I felt I couldn't tell anybody. . . .
>
> And I decided since it was an accident that I was going to make it into another accident. . . . So I made up that story and took the gun that I dropped right when it discharged and wiped off the barrel with a handkerchief and put it back into my pocket. I took the gun and I put it with the muzzle facing his head where he laid. Then I untied his shoelace to make it look like there was something he tripped over. . . .

The jury convicted Scher of first-degree murder and the trial court sentenced him to life imprisonment on October 22, 1997. On appeal to the Superior Court, Scher [claimed] that the twenty-year delay in filing charges against him violated his right to due process of law as guaranteed by the United States and Pennsylvania Constitutions. The Superior Court reversed the Judgment of Sentence. . . .

THE DUE PROCESS STANDARD

. . . United States v. Marion, 404 U.S. 307 (1971), was the seminal case to address whether a defendant's federal constitutional rights are violated by an extensive delay between the occurrence of a crime and the indictment or arrest of a defendant for the crime. In *Marion*, the defendants were charged with having engaged in a fraudulent business scheme beginning in March of 1965 and ending in January of 1966. The federal prosecutor in *Marion* did not empanel a grand jury to investigate the scheme until September of 1969, and no indictment was returned until March of 1970. [The Supreme Court held that constitutional speedy trial claims do] not apply until "either a formal indictment or information or else the actual restraints imposed by arrest and holding to answer a criminal charge," which was not implicated in defendants' complaints of pre-arrest delay. Concerning the defendants' Fifth Amendment due process claims, the Court noted that the primary guarantee against the bringing of overly stale charges was whatever statute of limitations applied to the crime. The Court went on to note, however, "the statute of limitations does not fully define the appellees' rights with respect to the events occurring prior to indictment." The following passage from *Marion* is significant:

> Thus, the Government concedes that the Due Process Clause of the Fifth Amendment would require dismissal of the indictment if it were shown at trial that the pre-indictment delay in this case caused substantial prejudice to appellees' rights to a fair trial and that the delay was an intentional device to gain tactical advantage over the accused. Cf. Brady v. Maryland, 373 U.S. 83 (1963). However, we need not, and could not now, determine when and in what circumstances actual prejudice resulting from pre-accusation delays requires the dismissal of the prosecution. . . .

Six years after *Marion*, the United States Supreme Court revisited the due process implications of pre-arrest delay in United States v. Lovasco, 431 U.S. 783 (1977). Eugene Lovasco was indicted in March of 1975 for possessing firearms stolen from the mail beginning in July and ending in August of 1973. Lovasco moved to dismiss the indictment, claiming that the prosecutor's delay in bringing the indictment caused him prejudice through the deaths of two favorable witnesses and therefore violated his due process rights. [The Court stated that] the due process inquiry must consider the reasons for the delay as well as the prejudice to the accused. In [its] discussion of the "reasons for the delay," the Court stated, "in our view, investigative delay is unlike delay undertaken by the Government solely to gain a tactical advantage over the accused." . . .

We [read] *Marion* and *Lovasco* [to mean] that delay intentionally undertaken by the prosecution to gain a tactical advantage over the defendant is one case, but not the only case, where pre-arrest delay would violate due process. However, [there is no] obligation on the Commonwealth to conduct all criminal investigations pursuant to a due diligence or negligence standard, measured from the moment when criminal charges are filed and the defendant raises his due process claim. Such a standard would be too onerous, requiring judicial oversight of decisions traditionally entrusted to the prosecutor. Furthermore, a due diligence or negligence standard would require an inquiry into the methods, resources, and techniques of law enforcement in conducting a criminal investigation that would amount to judicial second-guessing of how the Commonwealth must build its case. We are mindful of the Supreme Court's admonition in *Lovasco* against placing too stringent a responsibility on the prosecution to justify the delay in the face of these claims: "The Due Process Clause does not permit courts to abort criminal prosecutions simply because they disagree with a prosecutor's judgment as to when to seek an indictment."

[The] test that we believe is the correct one must take into consideration all of the facts and circumstances surrounding the case, including: the deference that courts must afford to the prosecutor's conclusions that a case is not ripe for prosecution; the limited resources available to law enforcement agencies when conducting a criminal investigation; the prosecutor's motives in delaying indictment; and the degree to which the defendant's own actions contributed to the delay. Therefore, . . . in order to prevail on a due process claim based on pre-arrest delay, the defendant must first show that the delay caused him actual prejudice, that is, substantially impaired his or her ability to defend against the charges. The court must then examine all of the circumstances to determine the validity of the Commonwealth's reasons for the delay. Only in situations where the evidence shows that the delay was the product of intentional, bad faith, or reckless conduct by the prosecution, however, will we find a violation of due process. Negligence in the conduct of a criminal investigation, without more, will not be sufficient to prevail on a due process claim based on pre-arrest delay. With this clarification of the standard in mind, we turn to Scher's case.

Actual Prejudice

. . . In order for a defendant to show actual prejudice, he or she must show that he or she was meaningfully impaired in his or her ability to defend against the state's charges to such an extent that the disposition of the criminal proceedings was likely affected. This kind of prejudice is commonly demonstrated by the loss of documentary evidence or the unavailability of an essential witness. It is not sufficient for a defendant to make speculative or conclusory claims of possible prejudice as a result of the passage of time. Where a defendant claims prejudice through the absence of witnesses, he or she must show in what specific manner missing witnesses would have aided the defense. Furthermore, it is the defendant's burden to show that the lost testimony or information is not available through other means.

Scher claims that he suffered prejudice because certain witnesses died and important evidence was lost by the time of trial that would have aided his defense that the shooting of Dillon was accidental, not intentional. Specifically, he . . . claims prejudice from the decomposition of Dillon's body that occurred during the twenty-year period, and from the Commonwealth's conduct of the second autopsy in 1995, which he claims interfered with his ability to present expert testimony in support of his position that Dillon's death was accidental. Further, Scher argues that the loss or destruction of other evidence, such as . . . the audio recording of the June 1976 autopsy; certain photographs taken of the scene; . . . and any bloodstains on the inside of the shotgun, impaired his ability to show that the shooting was accidental and not a premeditated act of murder.

In order to argue prejudice from the loss or destruction of evidence in these due process claims, the defendant must show that the loss or destruction of evidence related to the delay in filing charges. With respect to some of the items that Scher claims were lost or destroyed, the delay in filing charges clearly had no role in causing these items to be lost or destroyed. First, Scher contends that by the time charges were filed against him, the shotgun had been fired numerous times, thus eliminating any bloodstains that may have been inside the barrel, which would have tended to prove a close range of fire consistent with Scher's story that the shooting was an accident. However, one of Scher's experts, George Fassnacht, a forensic firearms consultant, testified that the repeated firing of the shotgun in 1976 by the police during testing of the weapon would have removed any bloodstains from inside the barrel. Accordingly, the loss of this evidence cannot be attributed to the delay in indicting Scher for murder. . . .

Scher claims prejudice from the [death of the County Coroner, Dr. John Conarton]. Scher notes that Dillon's death certificate, completed by Conarton, lists the cause of Dillon's death as accidental. Scher contends that he was prejudiced when he lost the opportunity to have Conarton explain why he believed Dillon's death was accidental. What Scher ignores, however, is that in the section of the death certificate that asks, "How did injury occur?" Coroner Conarton wrote, "Running with gun, fell, gun went off." As Scher admitted in his trial testimony, this is not how Dillon died, and his stories to Conarton, Collier, and the other investigating officers to this effect were lies. Conarton was present when Scher gave his statement to Trooper Hairston at the scene, which related the false story of how Dillon tripped while running with the shotgun. The record strongly suggests that Conarton formed his opinion as to the cause of Dillon's death based mainly on Scher's false statement and a cursory review of the scene where Dillon's body lay positioned in a manner, with shoelaces untied, that Scher deliberately set to make it appear that Dillon tripped and fell while carrying the shotgun. . . . Consequently, we cannot credit Scher's complaints of prejudice from the absence of Conarton's testimony . . . when it is apparent that Conarton accepted a version of the "accident" that Scher himself admitted was false and upon which he did not base his defense.

The most serious claim of prejudice raised by Scher concerns the death of [Dr. James Grace, who conducted the autopsy,] and the loss of audio recordings from the June 3, 1976 autopsy performed by Dr. Grace, as well as the alteration of Dillon's body during the second autopsy in 1995. The critical issue to Scher's defense was whether the physical evidence was consistent with an accidental discharge of the weapon during a struggle. Evidence of the angle of Dillon's chest wound, . . . the presence or absence of gunpowder around the wound, and the size of the wound were relevant to the determination of whether Dillon was shot from a close range, consistent with a struggle, or a more distant range that could not have been caused by an accidental discharge during a struggle.

In support of his defense theory, Scher presented a number of expert witnesses. John Shane, M.D., a pathologist, reviewed, among other evidentiary items: twenty-seven black and white photographs of the scene; the clothes worn by Dillon, the photographs taken during Dr. Grace's autopsy; photographs taken during the second autopsy in 1995; forty-three microscopic slides of tissue taken from Dillon's body; Dr. Grace's autopsy report; and the shot cup retrieved from Dillon's body. . . . Dr. Shane testified that the presence of gunpowder residue in the wound tract signaled that the range of fire would have been within eighteen inches, due to the limited distance that gunpowder travels from the barrel when a firearm is discharged. [Scher also presented the testimony of two other expert witnesses who reviewed the available autopsy reports, photographs, clothing, and tissue samples; both concluded that the shot was fired from less than one foot from Dillon's body.]

The ability of Scher's experts to support his defense by offering opinions to a reasonable degree of medical certainty based on a review of the evidence available to them demonstrates why Scher's claims of prejudice fail. [There] was sufficient evidence, including photographs and Dr. Grace's report, for Scher's experts to offer specific opinions concerning the presence of gunpowder in the wound tract, the range of fire, and whether the physical evidence was consistent with a struggle. . . .

REASONS FOR THE DELAY

[In] order for there to be a violation of due process, the Commonwealth's behavior must be more than merely negligent in causing the delay. Only where the Commonwealth has intentionally delayed in order to gain a tactical advantage or acted recklessly to such a degree as to shock one's conscience and offend one's sense of justice will we find a deprivation of due process. We do not find the Commonwealth's behavior in this case to be so outrageous as to meet that standard. There has been no allegation that the Commonwealth intentionally delayed indicting Scher in order to gain a tactical advantage over him, and the record contains credible denials from a succession of Susquehanna County District Attorneys that they ever intentionally employed delay tactics. Furthermore, we cannot accept the

Superior Court's conclusion that the Commonwealth's actions were "grossly negligent." Astonishingly, the Superior Court's opinion makes no mention of the watershed moment in this case: when Scher admitted that he had lied to investigators about how Dillon's death occurred and that, for the past twenty years, he lied when he denied having had an affair with Patricia prior to the incident at Gunsmoke. [Scher] staged the scene and fabricated a story that gained some credence with investigators. Perhaps, as Scher argues, those investigators should have been more circumspect in accepting his tale and pursued their suspicions more thoroughly, but we cannot find the Commonwealth's actions towards Scher so egregious when, in a small town, in a rural part of Pennsylvania with a part-time District Attorney, those responsible for enforcing the law would find it difficult to disbelieve the word of a respected physician. Nor can we ignore the benefit that Scher gained by lying to authorities rather than remaining silent: he enjoyed his liberty for twenty years. In these circumstances, we cannot find that the Commonwealth's failure to charge Scher with murder sooner violated his right to due process of law. . . .

CASTILLE, J., concurring.

[The] lead opinion rejects the prevailing view in the federal Circuit Courts. That view would require the defendant to prove that the pre-arrest delay was intentionally undertaken by the government for the purpose of gaining a tactical advantage over the accused in the prosecution. Instead of this bad faith standard, which derives from the explicit language employed by the United States Supreme Court in its decisions in *Marion* and *Lovasco*, the lead opinion would adopt a subjective recklessness/conscience-shocking standard. It is here that I part ways with the lead opinion. [A] proper assessment of the reasons for the delay in initiating prosecution must be confined to the question of the prosecution's bad faith — i.e., whether the delay was intentionally undertaken by the prosecution to gain a tactical advantage over the defendant. . . .

Although the lead opinion recognizes that a negligence standard is unworkable, the recklessness standard it would approve amounts to nothing more than a heightened negligence standard. [A negligence standard would] require judicial oversight of decisions traditionally entrusted to the prosecutor. Consequently, the lead opinion's standard opens the door to the type of hindsight and second-guessing employed here by the Superior Court and eschewed by the Supreme Court. . . .

ZAPPALA, C.J., dissenting.

. . . The Commonwealth's inordinate and unexcused delay in filing charges against Dr. Scher resulted in actual prejudice to Dr. Scher's ability to defend himself against the charges. At trial, the pivotal issue was whether Mr. Dillon's death resulted from an accidental firing of the shotgun as he and Dr. Scher struggled with the shotgun or resulted from the intentional and deliberate firing of the shotgun by Dr. Scher at a distance of several feet away from Dillon. The Commonwealth premised its theory on the testimony of expert witnesses following an autopsy conducted 18 years after Dillon's death. The expert testimony sought to contradict the findings made by Dr. James Grace based upon the autopsy he conducted immediately after Dillon's death. During the trial, the competency of Dr. Grace to conduct the autopsy and the findings themselves were challenged by the Commonwealth.

The Commonwealth went to great lengths to disparage and criticize Dr. Grace's abilities and to undermine specific critical physical findings made by Dr. Grace regarding the condition of the wound. Dr. Grace's findings were contrary to the Commonwealth's theory of the case and undermined the testimony of Commonwealth experts who had not examined the body until it was exhumed eighteen years later. While Dr. Grace's observations of the body and the shotgun wound were of paramount importance in determining whether the shotgun fired accidentally, the Commonwealth's delay in bringing the prosecution resulted in the unavailability of Dr. Grace as a witness. . . .

While Dr. Grace lived for 19 years after the shooting incident, the Commonwealth lost the audio recording made during the 1976 autopsy performed by Dr. Grace and failed to subsequently preserve his recollection of the examination of crucial evidence. . . .

The resulting prejudice to Dr. Scher's defense due to the unavailability of this crucial witness was compounded by the Commonwealth's deliberate tactics at trial to disparage the findings made by Dr. Grace which were contrary to the prosecution's theory. In order to support its theory of the shooting, the Commonwealth attempted to flatly contradict Dr. Grace's observations by suggesting to the jury that as a physician he was incompetent to make even the simplest physical observations and claimed that the observations recorded by Dr. Grace in his autopsy report were not those that Dr. Grace actually intended to make.

[Throughout the twenty years that elapsed after the shooting, the Commonwealth possessed all] of the physical evidence that was collected after the shooting. This evidence included: the clothing worn by Dr. Scher and Mr. Dillon on the date of the shooting; Dr. Scher's 16-gauge shotgun, Mr. Dillon's 20-gauge shotgun, ammunition and shells found at the scene of the shooting, shooting glasses and ear protectors found at the scene, clay birds, bird thrower, and sections of a log. . . . District Attorney Snyder was critical of the investigation that had been done. He testified that the investigation was "not getting done; not properly." [Any of the witnesses interviewed by the troopers in the renewed investigation would have been available to be interviewed in 1976. The facilities and experts who conducted the testing were available to the Commonwealth when the investigation began. Any new tests performed by the Commonwealth and the Federal Bureau of Investigation failed to reveal any new and/or relevant information that could not have been discovered by testing procedures available to them in 1976.]

This record demonstrates that there was no ongoing investigation into the death of Mr. Dillon. The investigation was dormant for most of the 20 years of pre-arrest delay. Indeed, for 8 of those years, the "investigation" was non-existent. . . . There is no basis to conclude that the pre-arrest delay was required for further investigation. The record establishes that the Commonwealth did not have a proper reason for the inordinate delay. . . .

Problem 15-4. Child Victims

Gilbert Vernier is a 69-year-old grandfather. In July 1999, M.E., then 7 years old, supported by her sister, J.V., informed their mother, "Grandpa touched me in a bad way." The Wyoming Department of Family Services and the county sheriff's department investigated the claim. Two interviews of the victim and her sister were recorded on audiotape. A lieutenant in the sheriff's department who was present during the interview transcribed the second tape. No charges were filed at that time.

Ten years later, in 2009, another granddaughter, L.L., reported to the sheriff's department that in 1992 Vernier had molested her when she was 9 years old and was living with her grandparents. Two weeks after L.L. made this report, M.E. again informed the sheriff's department that Vernier had sexually assaulted her in 1999. J.V. corroborated M.E.'s statements, recalling that Vernier routinely took M.E. into a locked bedroom. During the same time frame in 2009, other evidence emerged about sexual abuse perpetrated by Vernier. D.H. and D.P., Vernier's daughters, recounted repeated sexual abuse and rape by their father when D.H. was between the ages of 12 and 16 and D.P. between the ages of 8 and 13.

Following the 2009 investigation, the state charged Vernier with two counts of indecent liberties and one count of second-degree sexual assault based on the alleged incidents in 1999. At his arraignment, Vernier entered a plea of not guilty and filed a motion to dismiss, claiming the state intentionally had delayed filing charges. Although Wyoming has no statute of limitations for prosecuting crimes, Vernier claimed that the delay violated his due process rights. He argued that the 10-year delay impaired his efforts to defend himself against the charges. During that time, the government lost the two 1999 audiotapes of conversations between M.E. and investigators. The transcript of the second tape still exists, however, along with the deputy's notes reflecting her own observations about the interview. Vernier also argued that in 1999 he might have recalled an alibi that would have been helpful.

The district court denied the motion. How would you rule on appeal? How would you respond if Vernier asks your court to create a specific limitations period for crimes in the absence of a statute of limitations, either as a matter of constitutional law or as an exercise of the court's "supervisory" power over the state's criminal justice system? Compare Vernier v. State, 909 P.2d 1344 (Wyo. 1996).

Notes

1. *Pre-accusation delay: majority position.* All state courts have interpreted the due process provisions of their state constitutions to limit a few types of pre-accusation delay, applying the test that the U.S. Supreme Court created in United States v. Lovasco, 431 U.S. 783 (1977). A defendant raising a constitutional objection to a delay between the date of an alleged crime and the time of the indictment or information must show (1) the prejudice that the delay caused for the defense and (2) the reason for the delay. There are two basic approaches in the state courts on the burden of proving these elements. One group requires the defendant to prove both prejudice and an intentional prosecutorial delay to achieve a tactical advantage. See State v. Lacy, 929 P.2d 1288 (Ariz. 1996). A roughly equal number of states give the defendant the initial burden of proving prejudice and then require the government to prove a valid reason for the delay. See also People v. Nelson, 185 49 (Cal. 2008) (pre-indictment delay between 1976 rape and murder and 2001 filing of charges in "cold-hit" DNA case did not cause unconstitutional prejudice; unavailability of defense witnesses and loss of other evidence is outweighed by prerogative of state to allocate investigative resources; record does not demonstrate prosecutorial negligence). In states that have passed statutes of limitations (as almost all states have),

does the *Lovasco* analysis enable the courts to identify correctly the "stale" cases that the statute of limitations does not reach? Or does the constitutional analysis merely make the law less predictable, without systematically improving on the statutory limits? The breakdown among the state courts on this issue receives some attention on the web extension for this chapter at *http://www.crimpro.com/extension/ch15*.

2. *Reasons for delay.* The *Lovasco* Court declared categorically that there can be no due process violation if "good-faith investigative delay" is responsible for the timing of the charges. Courts also say that a delay created solely to gain a "tactical advantage" for the prosecution does create a due process problem. The longer the delay, the more willing courts are to find an improper reason for it.

A central question in the pre-accusation delay cases seems to be the good faith of the prosecutor. Compare this interpretation of the requirements of due process with the more general judicial reluctance to become involved in the prosecutor's charging decision in ordinary cases. See Chapter 13. Will an inquiry into the prosecutor's state of mind regarding a delay lead to more judicial scrutiny of prosecutorial charging decisions than traditional doctrine has allowed? In other words, is the test for pre-accusation delay more intrusive than the test for selective prosecution? Did the prosecutors in *Scher* and in Problem 15-4 delay charges for different reasons, or did they each just change their minds about criminal charges?

Problem 15-4 illustrates one reason for delay: Crime victims in some cases — notably for intrafamily sexual assaults on children — do not make allegations for many years after the incidents. Should special constitutional rules apply to such cases? See State v. Gray, 917 S.W.2d 668 (Tenn. 1996) (dismissal of charges of sexual abuse brought 42 years after incident involving 9-year-old girl). Specialized statutes of limitation in many states address this type of case (as does the New York statute above).

3. *Source of constitutional protections.* Although the federal constitution and most state constitutions provide specifically for a "speedy trial," these provisions do not apply to delays that occur before criminal charges are filed. The U.S. Supreme Court took the lead on this question in United States v. Marion, 404 U.S. 307 (1971). A review of the text and history of the Sixth Amendment's speedy trial clause (which speaks of a speedy trial for the "accused") convinced the Court that only "a formal indictment or information or else the actual restraints imposed by arrest and holding to answer a criminal charge" would trigger the protections of the speedy trial clause. See also United States v. MacDonald, 456 U.S. 1 (1982) (no speedy trial protection for period between dismissal of first charges and second indictment). As you read further materials in this chapter and encounter cases decided under the Sixth Amendment or analogous state constitutional clauses, consider whether the due process cases dealing with pre-accusation delay would be decided differently if they were analyzed under the more specific constitutional language requiring a "speedy trial."

4. *Statutes of limitation.* The Court in United States v. Marion noted that statutes of limitation provide "the primary guarantee against bringing overly stale criminal charges." The New York statute above is typical in several respects. First, it provides longer limitation periods for more serious crimes. Second, it creates special rules for marking the beginning of the limitation period for certain crimes unlikely to be detected or reported immediately. The statute leaves it for judges to answer the difficult question of when a continuing crime, such as conspiracy, is "committed" in the

sense necessary to trigger the statute. Finally, the statute defines certain events that can "toll" (i.e., suspend) the statute after it has begun to run. Should the drafters of the New York statute have included a provision that would allow judges to create additional "tolling" rules "in the interest of justice"?

Should statutes of limitation influence a court ruling on a constitutional challenge to pre-accusation delay? More specifically, if a statute gives extra latitude to a prosecutor in some cases, should that lead a court to give prosecutors extra latitude for delay under the due process clause? Or should the due process protections be strongest when legislatures have provided less statutory protection against delay?

Perhaps the rationale for a statute of limitations is based on something other than deterioration of evidence. Should we keep statutes of limitations because criminals tend to be more short-sighted than the general public, and the deterrent power of criminal charges is lost if the case is not filed relatively quickly? See Yair Listokin, Efficient Time Bars: A New Rationale for the Existence of Statutes of Limitations in Criminal Law, 31 J. Legal Stud. 99 (2002) (because potential criminals tend to discount the future at higher rates than society, punishing crimes long after they are committed will have only a nominal deterrent effect, while they may cost society substantial sums).

2. *Constitutional Protections for Speedy Trial After Accusation*

Once the prosecution obtains an indictment or files an information against a defendant, a wider array of legal provisions become available to move the process along. The Sixth Amendment grants to "the accused" the right to a "speedy and public trial." Analogous state constitutional clauses announce such rights in similarly general terms. The federal Speedy Trial Act creates a more specific obligation for the government to process all criminal trials within 70 days of the indictment or information, although it provides several ways to exclude days from the tally. Most states have statutes limiting the time between an accusation and the start of trial (or entry of a guilty plea). Statutes and judicial orders also allocate judicial resources to keep criminal dockets moving.

The deadlines become relevant in a great number of cases. In large urban jurisdictions in 2006, the median time it took to adjudicate a felony case was 92 days (up from 79 days in 1998). Just under half the cases were adjudicated within three months. Twelve percent of the felony cases were still unresolved after a year had passed since the arrest. See Bureau of Justice Statistics, Felony Defendants in Large Urban Counties, 2006, at table 10 (2010, NCJ 228944).

From its earliest opportunity, the U.S. Supreme Court has insisted that the constitutional guarantee of a "speedy" trial is a "necessarily relative" concept. See Beavers v. Haubert, 198 U.S. 77 (1905). The same length of time between accusation and resolution of criminal charges might be acceptable in one case and unacceptable in another, depending on the prosecutor's reasons, the harm that the defendant suffered, and other circumstances. In Barker v. Wingo, 407 U.S. 514 (1972), the Court settled on four circumstances that every court must consider when resolving a claim that the government has violated a defendant's constitutional right to a speedy trial. As you read the following exercise in applying the four-part *Barker* standard, consider how the four factors interact and ask whether some pertinent questions have now been placed out of view.

■ VERMONT v. MICHAEL BRILLON

129 S. Ct. 1283 (2009)

GINSBURG, J.*

This case concerns the Sixth Amendment guarantee that in "all criminal prosecutions, the accused shall enjoy the right to a speedy . . . trial." Michael Brillon, defendant below, respondent here, was arrested in July 2001 on felony domestic assault and habitual offender charges. Nearly three years later, in June 2004, he was tried by jury, found guilty as charged, and sentenced to 12 to 20 years in prison. The Vermont Supreme Court vacated Brillon's conviction and held that the charges against him must be dismissed because he had been denied his right to a speedy trial. . . . We hold that the Vermont Supreme Court erred. . . .

I.

On July 27, 2001, Michael Brillon was arrested after striking his girlfriend. Three days later he was arraigned in state court in Bennington County, Vermont and charged with felony domestic assault. His alleged status as a habitual offender exposed him to a potential life sentence. The court ordered him held without bail.

Richard Ammons, from the county public defender's office, was assigned on the day of arraignment as Brillon's first counsel. In October, Ammons filed a motion to recuse the trial judge. It was denied the next month and trial was scheduled for February 2002. In mid-January, Ammons moved for a continuance, but the State objected, and the trial court denied the motion.

On February 22, four days before the jury draw, Ammons again moved for a continuance, citing his heavy workload and the need for further investigation. Ammons acknowledged that any delay would not count (presumably against the State) for speedy-trial purposes. The State opposed the motion,[2] and at the conclusion of a hearing, the trial court denied it. Brillon, participating in the proceedings through interactive television, then announced: "You're fired, Rick." Three days later, the trial court — over the State's objection — granted Ammons' motion to withdraw as counsel, citing Brillon's termination of Ammons and Ammons' statement that he could no longer zealously represent Brillon. The trial court warned Brillon that further delay would occur while a new attorney became familiar with the case. The same day, the trial court appointed a second attorney, but he immediately withdrew based on a conflict.

On March 1, 2002, Gerard Altieri was assigned as Brillon's third counsel. On May 20, Brillon filed a motion to dismiss Altieri for, among other reasons, failure to file motions, "virtually no communication whatsoever," and his lack of diligence "because of heavy case load." At a June 11 hearing, Altieri denied several of

* [Chief Justice Roberts and Justices Scalia, Kennedy, Souter, Thomas, and Alito joined this opinion. — EDS.]

2. . . . Under Vermont procedures, the judge presiding over the trial was scheduled to "rotate" out of the county where Brillon's case was pending in March 2002. Thus, a continuance past March would have caused a different judge to preside over Brillon's trial, despite the denial of his motion to recuse the initial judge. Ammons requested a continuance until April.

Brillon's allegations, noted his disagreement with Brillon's trial strategy,[4] and insisted he had plenty of time to prepare. The State opposed Brillon's motion as well. Near the end of the hearing, however, Altieri moved to withdraw on the ground that Brillon had threatened his life during a break in the proceedings. The trial court granted Brillon's motion to dismiss Altieri, but warned Brillon that "this is somewhat of a dubious victory in your case because it simply prolongs the time that you will remain in jail until we can bring this matter to trial."

That same day, the trial court appointed Paul Donaldson as Brillon's fourth counsel. At an August 5 status conference, Donaldson requested additional time to conduct discovery in light of his caseload. A few weeks later, Brillon sent a letter to the court complaining about Donaldson's unresponsiveness and lack of competence. Two months later, Brillon filed a motion to dismiss Donaldson — similar to his motion to dismiss Altieri — for failure to file motions and "virtually no communication whatsoever." At a November 26 hearing, Donaldson reported that his contract with the Defender General's office had expired in June and that he had been in discussions to have Brillon's case reassigned. The trial court released Donaldson from the case without making any findings regarding the adequacy of Donaldson's representation.

Brillon's fifth counsel, David Sleigh, was not assigned until January 15, 2003; Brillon was without counsel during the intervening two months. On February 25, Sleigh sought extensions of various discovery deadlines, noting that he had been in trial out of town. On April 10, however, Sleigh withdrew from the case, based on "modifications to [his] firm's contract with the Defender General."

Brillon was then without counsel for the next four months. On June 20, the Defender General's office notified the court that it had received funding from the legislature and would hire a new special felony unit defender for Brillon. On August 1, Kathleen Moore was appointed as Brillon's sixth counsel. The trial court set November 7 as the deadline for motions, but granted several extensions in accord with the parties' stipulation. On February 23, 2004, Moore filed a motion to dismiss for lack of a speedy trial. The trial court denied the motion on April 19.

The case finally went to trial on June 14, 2004. Brillon was found guilty and sentenced to 12 to 20 years in prison. The trial court denied a post-trial motion to dismiss for want of a speedy trial, concluding that the delay in Brillon's trial was "in large part the result of his own actions" and that Brillon had "failed to demonstrate prejudice as a result of [the] pre-trial delay."

On appeal, the Vermont Supreme Court held 3 to 2 that Brillon's conviction must be vacated and the charges dismissed for violation of his Sixth Amendment right to a speedy trial. Citing the balancing test of Barker v. Wingo, 407 U.S. 514 (1972), the majority concluded that all four of the factors described in *Barker* — length of delay, the reason for the delay, the defendant's assertion of his right, and prejudice to the defendant — weighed against the State.

The court first found that the three-year delay in bringing Brillon to trial was "extreme" and weighed heavily in his favor. In assessing the reasons for that delay, the Vermont Supreme Court separately considered the period of each counsel's

4. Specifically, Altieri appeared reluctant to follow Brillon's tactic that he "bring in a lot of people" at trial, "some of them young kids and relatives . . . in an attempt by Mr. Brillon — this is his theory — I don't want to use the words trash, [to] impeach [the victim]."

representation. It acknowledged that the first year, when Brillon was represented by Ammons and Altieri, should not count against the State. But the court counted much of the remaining two years against the State for delays "caused, for the most part, by the failure of several of defendant's assigned counsel, over an inordinate period of time, to move his case forward." As for the third and fourth factors, the court found that Brillon "repeatedly and adamantly demanded to be tried," and that his "lengthy pretrial incarceration" was prejudicial, despite his insubstantial assertions of evidentiary prejudice. . . .

II.

The Sixth Amendment guarantees that in "all criminal prosecutions, the accused shall enjoy the right to a speedy . . . trial." . . . In *Barker*, the Court refused to quantify the right into a specified number of days or months or to hinge the right on a defendant's explicit request for a speedy trial. Rejecting such "inflexible approaches," *Barker* established a balancing test, in which the conduct of both the prosecution and the defendant are weighed. Some of the factors that courts should weigh include length of delay, the reason for the delay, the defendant's assertion of his right, and prejudice to the defendant.

Primarily at issue here is the reason for the delay in Brillon's trial. *Barker* instructs that "different weights should be assigned to different reasons," and in applying *Barker*, we have asked "whether the government or the criminal defendant is more to blame" for the delay. Doggett v. United States, 505 U.S. 647, 651 (1992). Deliberate delay to hamper the defense weighs heavily against the prosecution. More neutral reasons such as negligence or overcrowded courts weigh less heavily but nevertheless should be considered since the ultimate responsibility for such circumstances must rest with the government rather than with the defendant.

In contrast, delay caused by the defense weighs against the defendant: If delay is attributable to the defendant, then his waiver may be given effect under standard waiver doctrine. That rule accords with the reality that defendants may have incentives to employ delay as a defense tactic: delay may work to the accused's advantage because witnesses may become unavailable or their memories may fade over time.

Because the attorney is the defendant's agent when acting, or failing to act, in furtherance of the litigation, delay caused by the defendant's counsel is also charged against the defendant. Coleman v. Thompson, 501 U.S. 722, 753 (1991).[6] The same principle applies whether counsel is privately retained or publicly assigned, for once a lawyer has undertaken the representation of an accused, the duties and obligations are the same whether the lawyer is privately retained, appointed, or serving in a legal aid or defender program. Except for the source of payment, the relationship between a defendant and the public defender representing him is identical to that existing between any other lawyer and client. Unlike a prosecutor or the court, assigned counsel ordinarily is not considered a state actor.

6. Several States' speedy-trial statutes expressly exclude from computation of the time limit continuances and delays caused by the defendant or defense counsel. [The Court cited statutes or rules of procedure from California, New York, Alaska, Arkansas, and Indiana.]

III.

Barker's formulation necessarily compels courts to approach speedy trial cases on an ad hoc basis, and the balance arrived at in close cases ordinarily would not prompt this Court's review. But the Vermont Supreme Court made a fundamental error in its application of *Barker* that calls for this Court's correction. The Vermont Supreme Court erred in attributing to the State delays caused by "the failure of several assigned counsel . . . to move his case forward," and in failing adequately to take into account the role of Brillon's disruptive behavior in the overall balance.

The Vermont Supreme Court's opinion is driven by the notion that delay caused by assigned counsel's "inaction" or failure "to move the case forward" is chargeable to the State, not the defendant. In this case, that court concluded, a significant portion of the delay in bringing defendant to trial must be attributed to the state, even though most of the delay was caused by the inability or unwillingness of assigned counsel to move the case forward.

We disagree. An assigned counsel's failure "to move the case forward" does not warrant attribution of delay to the State. Contrary to the Vermont Supreme Court's analysis, assigned counsel generally are not state actors for purposes of a speedy-trial claim. While the Vermont Defender General's office is indeed "part of the criminal justice system," the individual counsel here acted only on behalf of Brillon, not the State.

Most of the delay that the Vermont Supreme Court attributed to the State must therefore be attributed to Brillon as delays caused by his counsel. During those periods, Brillon was represented by Donaldson, Sleigh, and Moore, all of whom requested extensions and continuances. Their "inability or unwillingness" to move the case forward may not be attributed to the State simply because they are assigned counsel.

A contrary conclusion could encourage appointed counsel to delay proceedings by seeking unreasonable continuances, hoping thereby to obtain a dismissal of the indictment on speedy-trial grounds. Trial courts might well respond by viewing continuance requests made by appointed counsel with skepticism, concerned that even an apparently genuine need for more time is in reality a delay tactic. Yet the same considerations would not attend a privately retained counsel's requests for time extensions. We see no justification for treating defendants' speedy-trial claims differently based on whether their counsel is privately retained or publicly assigned.

In addition to making assigned counsel's "failure to move the case forward" the touchstone of its speedy-trial inquiry, the Vermont Supreme Court further erred by treating the period of each counsel's representation discretely. [The] Vermont Supreme Court failed appropriately to take into account Brillon's role during the first year of delay. . . .

Brillon sought to dismiss Ammons on the eve of trial. His strident, aggressive behavior with regard to Altieri, whom he threatened, further impeded prompt trial and likely made it more difficult for the Defender General's office to find replacement counsel. Even after the trial court's warning regarding delay, Brillon sought dismissal of yet another attorney, Donaldson. Just as a State's deliberate attempt to delay the trial in order to hamper the defense should be weighted heavily against the State, so too should a defendant's deliberate attempt to disrupt proceedings be weighted heavily against the defendant. Absent Brillon's deliberate efforts to force the withdrawal of Ammons and Altieri, no speedy-trial issue would have arisen. The effect of these earlier events should have been factored into the court's analysis of subsequent delay.

The general rule attributing to the defendant delay caused by assigned counsel is not absolute. Delay resulting from a systemic breakdown in the public defender system could be charged to the State. But the Vermont Supreme Court made no determination, and nothing in the record suggests, that institutional problems caused any part of the delay in Brillon's case.

In sum, delays caused by defense counsel are properly attributed to the defendant, even where counsel is assigned. Any inquiry into a speedy trial claim necessitates a functional analysis of the right in the particular context of the case, and the record in this case does not show that Brillon was denied his constitutional right to a speedy trial. . . .

BREYER, J., dissenting.*

We granted certiorari in this case to decide whether delays caused "solely" by a public defender can be "charged against the State pursuant to the test in Barker v. Wingo. The case, in my view, does not squarely present that question, for the Vermont Supreme Court, when it found Michael Brillon's trial unconstitutionally delayed, did not count such delays against the State. . . . Given these circumstances, I would dismiss the writ of certiorari as improvidently granted.

The relevant time period consists of slightly less than three years, stretching from July 2001, when Brillon was indicted, until mid-June 2004, when he was convicted and sentenced. In light of Brillon's improper behavior, the Vermont Supreme Court did not count months 1 through 12 (mid-July 2001 through mid-June 2002) against the State. Noting the objection that Brillon had sought to "intentionally sabotage the criminal proceedings against him," the Vermont Supreme Court was explicit that this time period "does not count against the State."

The Vermont Supreme Court did count months 13 through 17 (mid-June 2002 through November 2002) against the State. It did so under circumstances where (1) Brillon's counsel, Paul Donaldson, revealed that his contract with the defender general's office had expired in June 2002 — shortly after (perhaps before!) he took over as Brillon's counsel, (2) he stated that this case was "basically the beginning of [his] departure from the contract," and (3) he made no filings, missed several deadlines, did "little or nothing" to "move the case forward," and made only one brief appearance at a status conference in mid-August. I believe it fairer to characterize this period, not as a period in which "assigned counsel" failed to move the case forward, but as a period in which Brillon, in practice, had no assigned counsel. And, given that the State conceded its responsibility for delays caused by another defender who resigned for "contractual reasons," it is hardly unreasonable that the Vermont Supreme Court counted this period of delay against the State.

The Vermont Supreme Court also counted months 18 through 25 (the end of November 2002 through July 2003) against the State. It did so because the State conceded in its brief that this period of delay cannot be attributed to the defendant. This concession is not surprising in light of the fact that during much of this period, Brillon was represented by David Sleigh, a contract attorney, who during the course

* [Justice Stevens joined this opinion. — EDS.]

of his representation filed nothing on Brillon's behalf except a single motion seeking to extend discovery. The record reflects no other actions by Sleigh other than a letter sent to Brillon informing him that as a result of "modifications to our firm's contract with the Defender General, we will not be representing you in your pending case." Brillon was left without counsel for a period of nearly six months. The State explained in conceding its responsibility for this delay that Sleigh had been forced to withdraw "for contractual reasons," and that the defender general's office had been unable to replace him "for funding reasons."

Finally, the Vermont Supreme Court counted against the State the last 11 months — from August 2003 to mid-June 2004. But it is impossible to conclude from the opinion whether it did so because it held the State responsible for the defender's failure to "move the case forward," or for other reasons having nothing to do with counsel, namely the judge's unavailability, or the fact that the case files were incomplete and "additional documents were needed from the State."

[The] Vermont Supreme Court has considerable authority to supervise the appointment of public defenders. See Vt. Stat. Ann., Tit. 13, §§5204, 5272 (1998); see also Vt. Rule Crim. Proc. 44 (2003). It consequently warrants leeway when it decides whether a particular failing is properly attributed to assigned counsel or instead to the failure of the defender general's office properly to assign counsel. I do not believe the Vermont Supreme Court exceeded that leeway here. . . .

Notes

1. *Constitutional speedy trial rights: majority position.* The Supreme Court has incorporated the "speedy trial" clause of the Sixth Amendment as a component of the Fourteenth Amendment's due process clause that applies to the states. Klopfer v. North Carolina, 386 U.S. 213 (1967). In addition, virtually all states have used the four-part test from Barker v. Wingo, 407 U.S. 514 (1972), to determine the speedy trial rights of defendants under their state constitutions. As illustrated in the *Brillon* case, the analysis of constitutional speedy trial claims often requires courts to answer a series of questions, assigning responsibility for each period of delay. The first *Barker* factor (the length of the delay) is a necessary threshold. Only when the delay becomes long enough will the court analyze the other factors. Although the exact length of time necessary is a question for common-law development, a delay of just under one year is usually sufficient to obtain a full review of the four factors. Once the full inquiry takes place, often the most important factor is whether the defendant has been prejudiced.

2. *Ranking reasons for delay.* Courts in most jurisdictions have followed the *Barker* Court's suggestion that a "deliberate attempt to delay the trial in order to hamper the defense" is weighed heavily against the government, while a "valid reason" such as a missing witness would justify some delay. Reasons such as prosecutorial negligence or lack of resources will count against the government, but not heavily. See State v. Spivey, 579 S.E.2d 251 (N.C. 2003) (delay of over four years in starting murder trial acceptable under *Barker*; reasons for delay included numerous homicide cases on docket, courthouse renovations). Does it make sense to make defendants bear the cost of inadequate public defender funding? Does a similar ranking system apply to a defendant's reasons for contributing to the delay? Will the defendant's actions only be weighed "heavily" against her claim if she has made a deliberate

attempt to hamper the prosecution through delay? See State v. Azania, 865 N.E.2d 994 (Ind. 2007) (time elapsed during pursuit of collateral relief after first trial is attributed to defendant, the party with the obligation to go forward in such proceedings, and does not require dismissal of charges before re-trial after grant of habeas relief).

3. *Prejudice.* The *Barker* Court listed three types of prejudice that a speedy trial could avoid: (a) "oppressive pretrial incarceration"; (b) "anxiety and concern of the accused"; and (c) "the possibility that the defense will be impaired." Courts routinely say that the third type of prejudice, which can include disappearance of witnesses or loss of memory, is the most serious. If there is a statistical relationship between pretrial detention and conviction for the charged crime, is it plausible to argue that any prejudice of the first type (pretrial detention) also must count as prejudice of the third type (impairment of defense)? Does it matter what grounds the government has for holding the defendant? Speedy trial rights extend to persons imprisoned for other offenses. See Smith v. Hooey, 393 U.S. 374 (1969). Will incarceration for another offense weigh less heavily in favor of the defendant than incarceration only for the current charges? There are cases in which the other *Barker* factors create such a strong showing for the defendant that the court will presume prejudice. According to Doggett v. United States, 505 U.S. 647 (1992), the presumption of prejudice strengthens over time. The eight-year delay between indictment and arrest in *Doggett* was a product of the defendant's choice to leave the country (unaware that he was under indictment) and the government's negligence in pursuing him. The Court was willing to presume that such a lengthy delay would impair the defense. But see People v. Martinez, 996 P.2d 32 (Cal. 2000) (refuses to adopt federal rule that defendant need not show specific prejudice if delay is sufficiently long; defendant must always show prejudice under state law).

4. *Remedy.* What should a court do if it is convinced that the government has violated a defendant's constitutional speedy trial rights? According to Strunk v. United States, 412 U.S. 434 (1973), dismissal of the charges with prejudice is the only proper remedy for a violation of the Sixth Amendment speedy trial right. State courts by and large have interpreted their own constitutions the same way. Can you imagine any alternative remedies that would effectively prevent delay without losing convictions of guilty persons? How about a reduction of sentence to reflect the amount of improper delay? What about money damages for improper pretrial incarceration or prolonged anxiety? If these alternatives were available to state courts, would they become more willing to find a constitutional violation? Should a court be able to select a nondismissal remedy only for particular kinds of prejudice (such as anxiety or loss of reputation) but not for others (such as impairment of defense)? See Akhil Amar, The Constitution and Criminal Procedure: First Principles 96-116 (1997).

5. *Victim's right to speedy trial.* Over the past generation, state constitutional amendments and statutes have recognized some of the interests and procedural rights of victims of alleged crimes. A majority of states now have statutory or constitutional provisions requiring the trial court to consider the interests of crime victims (especially youthful or elderly victims) when responding to requests for continuances. A few states declare more generally that victims have a right to a speedy trial. Take, for instance, Utah Code §77-38-7:

> (1) In determining a date for any criminal trial or other important criminal or juvenile justice hearing, the court shall consider the interests of the victim of a crime to a speedy resolution of the charges under the same standards that govern a defendant's or minor's right to a speedy trial. . . .
>
> (3)(a) In ruling on any motion by a defendant or minor to continue a previously established trial or other important criminal or juvenile justice hearing, the court shall inquire into the circumstances requiring the delay and consider the interests of the victim of a crime to a speedy disposition of the case. . . .

What assurance does a crime victim have that a trial court will carry out these directives? Is the statute enforceable on appeal?

3. *Statutory Protections for Speedy Trial After Accusation*

Almost all states now have statutes or procedural rules that oblige the government to complete criminal trials promptly. These "speedy trial acts" show some important differences from one another. First, these statutes and rules differ in how specifically they define the time period that may elapse between accusation and the start of trial. Most, like the federal Speedy Trial Act, give the state a specific number of days (70 days in the federal system) to process the case. Within the group of states that specify the time period, many allow more days to bring to trial a defendant who is not in custody than one who is in custody. See Ill. Ann. Stat. ch. 725, para. 5/103-5 (120 days for defendants in custody, 160 days for defendants released pretrial). A smaller group of states do not specify a number of days at all, but simply require the trial to take place within a "reasonable" time. Mich. R. Crim. P. 6.004 (provides that the "defendant and the people are entitled to a speedy trial and to a speedy resolution of all matters before the court," but states no specific time period for trial of charges against defendants not in custody).

Second, the statutes differ from one another in the methods available to extend the number of days the parties may use to prepare for trial. Some, like the federal statute, exhaustively list the events that can add time to the available days; a number of statutes allow the trial court to extend the time period for "good cause" (or on some other generally phrased grounds). Third, the statutes differ from one another in the remedies they provide for violations. The federal statute is typical of one group, giving the trial judge considerable discretion to choose whether to dismiss the charges with or without prejudice. Other statutes make it clear that one form of dismissal or the other is strongly preferred or required.

Can you identify a combination of features described above that is likely to have the most effect on the amount of time available to prepare a case for trial? The least effect? As you reflect on these statutes, keep a close eye on the interaction between rights and remedies. Is there a relationship between the clarity of the speedy trial obligations that the government faces and the stringency of the remedy for violations? Do these statutes "codify" the constitutional analysis or do they pursue different objectives, using different means?

Problem 15-5. The Fierce Urgency of Now

In recent years, the Superior Court of fast-growing Riverside County, California, has been severely overburdened by the substantial number of criminal cases awaiting trial in that county. Section 1382 of the Penal Code, reprinted below, establishes a presumptive time period of 60 days for bringing a felony case to trial. Nonetheless, a 2007 survey revealed that nearly 25 percent of jail inmates had been awaiting trial for more than one year. One hundred seventy-seven inmates had been awaiting trial for more than two years, thirty-two inmates were awaiting trial for more than four years, and in one case the delay was an astonishing eight years.

To address this problem, the Chief Justice of the California Supreme Court assigned numerous retired judges and active judges from outside the county to assist the Riverside Superior Court. Furthermore, the Riverside Superior Court itself devoted virtually all of its resources — superior court judges and courtrooms — ordinarily intended for the trial of civil cases instead to the trial of criminal cases, an effort that, at the time, seriously compromised that court's ability to conduct civil trials.

The case of Terrion Marcus Engram illustrates some of the delay issues in Riverside County. Engram initially was charged with attempted premeditated murder and first-degree burglary. At his first trial, the jury acquitted Engram of the attempted murder charge but found him guilty of burglary. On appeal, the Court of Appeal, concluding that the trial court committed prejudicial instructional error with regard to the burglary charge, reversed the conviction and remanded the matter to the trial court for a new trial on the burglary charge. Engram was released from custody on his own recognizance pending retrial and remained free from custody throughout the later proceedings.

The initial retrial of the burglary charge began on May 20. On May 27, after deliberating, the jury was unable to agree on a verdict and the trial court declared a mistrial. The trial court denied defendant's motion to dismiss the burglary charge, and set a third jury trial on the burglary charges for July 14.

When that trial date arrived, the prosecution moved to postpone the trial until July 28, the last day for trial under the then-governing time waiver executed by defendant. The assigned deputy district attorney gave four reasons to support the request: (1) "I have a last-day case set for today," (2) "I also have two last-day cases on July 21," (3) "I need time to prepare one of these cases as a hand-off for another Deputy District Attorney to try," and (4) "I need time to coordinate witness schedules." The trial court granted the prosecution's motion.

On that date, defendant moved to continue the trial to August 28, based on his counsel's declaration that he was unable to complete discovery and investigation pending receipt of the trial transcripts from the second trial. The court granted the motion without objection by the prosecution and continued the trial to the date requested. At that time, counsel stipulated that the last day for trial under defendant's then-applicable time waiver was September 8.

On August 28, the prosecution moved to continue the trial to September 8. A declaration filed by the deputy district attorney stated: (1) "I will be out of town the week of September 1-5," (2) "I recently finished trial" in another case, (3) "I have another case that has a current last day of September 8, and I need time to prepare this case as a 'hand off' for another Deputy District Attorney," and (4) "I need time to coordinate witness schedules and prepare for trial." The trial court, without a waiver of time by defendant, granted the motion and continued the trial to September 8.

On September 8, the prosecution again moved to continue the trial, this time until September 17. A declaration filed in support of the motion stated that although the deputy district attorney assigned to the case had expected to be available and able to proceed on September 8, that attorney still was out of the state and unavailable, attending to his brother who unexpectedly had contracted a staph infection and had been hospitalized. Without opposition by the defendant, the trial court granted the motion and continued the trial to September 17. At that point, counsel for both parties stipulated that the last day for trial was September 29.

On September 11, the prosecution once again moved to postpone the trial to September 29. The assigned deputy district attorney stated that the prosecution was unable to proceed on September 17 because (1) "I will be out of town the week of September 15-18," (2) "I have two other cases that have a current last day of September 19 and September 22," (3) "I need time to prepare this or the other two cases as a 'hand off' for another Deputy District Attorney," and (4) "I need time to coordinate witness schedules and prepare for trial." When the case was called on September 17, the trial court, without a waiver of time by defendant, granted the prosecution's motion to postpone the trial until September 29.

When the case was called for trial on September 29, defense counsel announced he was ready for trial and that Engram objected to any further delay of trial. The elected district attorney appeared for the prosecution and informed the judge that in addition to the present case involving defendant Engram, there were 17 other "last-day" cases (one other felony case and 16 misdemeanor cases) that were before the court on September 29, each of which presented a statutory speedy-trial issue. In each of the cases, after defense counsel announced ready for trial and stated that the defendant objected to any further delay, the trial court informed counsel for both parties that there were no available courtrooms to which the case could be assigned for trial.

Although none of the ordinary criminal courtrooms were available for the criminal cases at issue, the district attorney urged the court instead to use courtrooms currently devoted to juvenile, probate, and family law matters for these criminal cases. The court replied that all of the regular civil departments of the Superior Court were already temporarily diverted to use for criminal cases, and denied the district attorney's further request to conduct criminal trials in the juvenile, probate, and family law departments. The judge explained her decision as follows:

> In juvenile court, that's a court where neglected and abused children as well as children who are accused of crime get the attention of the court all to the aim of letting them grow up safely in decent surroundings and becoming productive citizens, rather than letting them go into the adult criminal law system. It would be an injustice to those children, to their parents, and to society to close down juvenile court in order to try other cases, important as these cases are. We will not be closing down juvenile court in order to squeeze out one or two more trials. On a practical note, those courtrooms don't have jury boxes.
>
> With respect to probate, this is where we deal with guardianship situations where we decide where children are to live when both parents are in prison or strung out on drugs or dead. Probate also deals with conservatorship, where retarded adults and

> other incompetent adults have their cases come up so they are cared for and they don't live in misery or get exploited. Probate also deals with the administration of estates and money issues, but when you're trying to figure out where the deceased person's money goes, again there are very great human issues there.
>
> As for the family law department, those courtrooms don't have jury boxes. Again, we're dealing with child custody, child support issues of huge human and social importance. The judges in each of these departments are burdened with heavy caseloads. We will not be displacing family law or probate or juvenile.

The district attorney responded with a request for a "good cause" exception to the requirements of the speedy trial preparation statute: "If the Court doesn't have sufficient resources to try these cases and the Court has done everything that the Court can do to find courtrooms for these cases, that should amount to good cause to continue each of these matters at least one day."

Imagine that you are the trial judge in this case. How would you rule on Engram's motion to dismiss under Section 1382? What facts and sources of law would be relevant to you in determining whether there is "good cause" for a further delay? See People v. Johnson, 606 P.2d 738 (Cal. 1980) (ordinary court congestion arising from inadequate resources is not good cause, but congestion arising from extraordinary and nonrecurring circumstances can qualify as good cause). Would your decision be different if the Chief Justice had not already devoted extra judicial resources to the county? Cf. People v. Engram, 240 P.3d 237 (Cal. 2010).

If you grant the motion, what should be the remedy under Section 1387? What would be the outcome if the controlling statute were the federal Speedy Trial Act, reprinted below?

Speedy-trial statutes give priority to criminal matters over civil matters; among criminal matters, they give priority to felonies and cases involving defendants who are detained before trial. See Cal. Penal Code §§1048, 1050. In a world where ordinary civil litigation must wait in line behind criminal cases, does this give every segment of society a concrete interest in speedy trials? Is this what courts mean when they speak of the "public's interest" in speedy trials?

■ CALIFORNIA PENAL CODE §1382

(a) The court, unless good cause to the contrary is shown, shall order the action to be dismissed in the following cases: . . .

(2) In a felony case, when a defendant is not brought to trial within 60 days of the defendant's arraignment on an indictment or information, or reinstatement of criminal proceedings . . . or, in case the cause is to be tried again following a mistrial, an order granting a new trial from which an appeal is not taken, or an appeal from the superior court, within 60 days after the mistrial has been declared. . . . However, an action shall not be dismissed under this paragraph if either of the following circumstances exists:

(A) The defendant enters a general waiver of the 60-day trial requirement. . . .

(B) The defendant requests or consents to the setting of a trial date beyond the 60-day period. . . . Whenever a case is set for trial beyond the 60-day period by request or consent, expressed or implied, of the defendant without a general waiver, the defendant shall be brought to trial on the date set for trial or within 10 days thereafter.

(c) If the defendant is not represented by counsel, the defendant shall not be deemed under this section to have consented to the date for the defendant's trial unless the court has explained to the defendant his or her rights under this section and the effect of his or her consent.

CALIFORNIA PENAL CODE §1387

(a) An order terminating an action pursuant to [section 1382] is a bar to any other prosecution for the same offense if it is a felony or if it is a misdemeanor charged together with a felony and the action has been previously terminated pursuant to [section 1382], or if it is a misdemeanor not charged together with a felony, except in those [cases in which] the judge or magistrate finds any of the following:

(1) That substantial new evidence has been discovered by the prosecution which would not have been known through the exercise of due diligence at, or prior to, the time of termination of the action.

(2) That the termination of the action was the result of the direct intimidation of a material witness, as shown by a preponderance of the evidence. . . .

(b) Notwithstanding subdivision (a), an order terminating an action pursuant to this chapter is not a bar to another prosecution for the same offense if it is . . . an offense based on an act of domestic violence, . . . and the termination of the action was the result of the failure to appear by the complaining witness, who had been personally subpoenaed. This subdivision shall apply only within six months of the original dismissal of the action, and may be invoked only once in each action. . . .

18 U.S.C. §3161

(c)(1) In any case in which a plea of not guilty is entered, the trial of a defendant charged in an information or indictment with the commission of an offense shall commence within 70 days from the filing date (and making public) of the information or indictment, or from the date the defendant has appeared before a judicial officer of the court in which such charge is pending, whichever date last occurs. . . .

(h) The following periods of delay shall be excluded in computing the time within which an information or an indictment must be filed, or in computing the time within which the trial of any such offense must commence:

(1) Any period of delay resulting from other proceedings concerning the defendant. . . .

(2) Any period of delay during which prosecution is deferred by the attorney for the Government pursuant to written agreement with the defendant, with the approval of the court, for the purpose of allowing the defendant to demonstrate his good conduct.

(3) . . . Any period of delay resulting from the absence or unavailability of the defendant or an essential witness. . . .

(5) If the information or indictment is dismissed upon motion of the attorney for the Government and thereafter a charge is filed against the defendant for the same offense, or any offense required to be joined with that offense, any

period of delay from the date the charge was dismissed to the date the time limitation would commence to run as to the subsequent charge had there been no previous charge.

(6) A reasonable period of delay when the defendant is joined for trial with a codefendant as to whom the time for trial has not run and no motion for severance has been granted.

(7)(A) Any period of delay resulting from a continuance granted by any judge on his own motion or at the request of the defendant or his counsel or at the request of the attorney for the Government, if the judge granted such continuance on the basis of [findings on the record] that the ends of justice served by taking such action outweigh the best interest of the public and the defendant in a speedy trial. . . .

(B) The factors, among others, which a judge shall consider in determining whether to grant a continuance under subparagraph (A) of this paragraph in any case are as follows:

(i) Whether the failure to grant such a continuance in the proceeding would be likely to make a continuation of such proceeding impossible, or result in a miscarriage of justice.

(ii) Whether the case is so unusual or so complex, due to the number of defendants, the nature of the prosecution, or the existence of novel questions of fact or law, that it is unreasonable to expect adequate preparation for pretrial proceedings or for the trial itself within the time limits established by this section. . . .

(iv) Whether the failure to grant such a continuance in a case which, taken as a whole, is not so unusual or so complex as to fall within clause (ii), would deny the defendant reasonable time to obtain counsel, would unreasonably deny the defendant or the Government continuity of counsel, or would deny counsel for the defendant or the attorney for the Government the reasonable time necessary for effective preparation, taking into account the exercise of due diligence.

(C) No continuance under subparagraph (A) of this paragraph shall be granted because of general congestion of the court's calendar, or lack of diligent preparation or failure to obtain available witnesses on the part of the attorney for the Government. . . .

■ 18 U.S.C. §3162

(a)(2) If a defendant is not brought to trial within the time limit required by section 3161(c) as extended by section 3161(h), the information or indictment shall be dismissed on motion of the defendant. The defendant shall have the burden of proof of supporting such motion but the Government shall have the burden of going forward with the evidence in connection with any exclusion of time under subparagraph 3161(h)(3). In determining whether to dismiss the case with or without prejudice, the court shall consider, among others, each of the following factors: the seriousness of the offense; the facts and circumstances of the case which led to the dismissal; and the impact of a reprosecution on the administration of this chapter and on the administration of justice. . . .

Notes

1. *Speedy-trial statutes and the federal constitution.* Almost all states have statutes or court rules addressing speedy trial preparation. Some of these statutes are intended to implement the constitutional speedy-trial right, while others serve the additional purpose of clearing court dockets. Do these provisions add a new dimension to the constitutional analysis simply because they are more specific than a general right to a "speedy trial"? In the minority of states where statutes or rules use general language (such as a statutory bar against "unreasonable delay"), does the statute or rule add anything at all to the constitutional inquiry? Why would drafters of rules or statutes bother to pass a provision without specific time limits?

2. *Time allowed for preparation.* Speedy-trial statutes select many different time periods to allow the parties to prepare for trial. The federal statute's 70-day limit is one of the shorter periods; some state statutes allow periods longer than six months. Most have tighter time limits for defendants in custody than for those who have been released before trial. It is also customary for these statutes to provide longer time limits for felonies than for misdemeanors, and some create even finer distinctions between the more serious and less serious offenses. See Ohio Rev. Stat. §2945.71. The statutes list several events that can start the speedy-trial "clock." Under the federal statute, an arrest starts a time period that must end within 30 days in an indictment or information, while the indictment or information starts the 70-day countdown to the trial. Under most of the state statutes, an indictment or information starts the clock for felonies, and the filing of a complaint begins the period for misdemeanors. Trials that end in mistrials or in convictions reversed on appeal have their own specialized timing rules.

If you were drafting a speedy-trial statute, would you anticipate the ways that the parties might try to manipulate the time periods? For instance, would you address the defendant's ability to enter a plea agreement and withdraw it near the arrival of the statutorily designated number of days from the filing of the charge? How would you respond to the prosecutor's power to enter a nolle prosequi as the deadline nears and to refile charges when the case is ready to try?

3. *Speedy-trial rights for crime victims.* Generally speaking, the victims of alleged crimes prefer not to wait for trial to begin. What are the shortest preparation periods that a statute could grant to a defendant without being unconstitutional? Under the federal statute, a trial cannot commence "less than 30 days from the date on which the defendant first appears through counsel" unless the defendant consents to a quicker deadline. 18 U.S.C. §3161(c)(2). A minority of states have statutes setting a minimum time period for trial preparation. This question ordinarily arises as a constitutional challenge (based on due process or the right to counsel) to a trial court's refusal to grant a defense motion for a continuance; appellate courts almost always defer to the trial court's discretion on this question.

4. *Excluded time periods.* One major difference among speedy-trial statutes appears in the method of identifying "excluded" days, those that do not count toward the speedy-trial deadline. Most jurisdictions, represented by the federal statute reprinted above, list the particular events that can be excluded from the speedy-trial countdown. See Bloate v. United States, 130 S. Ct. 1345 (2010) (under federal Speedy Trial Act, days granted to defendant to prepare pretrial motions are not automatically excludable from the 70-day time limit for bringing defendant to trial;

days may be excluded only if trial court makes case-specific findings that the ends of justice served by granting a continuance outweigh the best interest of the public and the defendant in a speedy trial).

A minority of states, represented by the California statute above, do not specify the grounds for excluding days, instead allowing judges to determine in a particular case whether "good cause" exists to allow an exclusion. See Bulgin v. State, 912 So.2d 307 (Fla. 2005) (if state officials do not obtain express waiver of speedy trial rights, days that defendant spent cooperating with investigators must count against statutory limit of 175 days to begin trial). Some statutes say simply that any delay "caused" by the defendant is excluded from the countdown. Consult the federal statute again, giving particular attention to section 3161(h)(8). Does this provision convert the statute's itemized list into a less predictable standard? Is it inevitable that an itemized list of grounds for excluding days will include reasons such as these?

5. *Sanctions for violations of statutes.* Another major difference among speedy-trial statutes is the remedy they require or encourage for statutory violations. As you saw in the federal statute reprinted above, dismissal without prejudice is the preferred remedy under some speedy-trial statutes. Is dismissal without prejudice a toothless remedy? Consult again the New York statute of limitations reprinted at the beginning of this section and consider whether such provisions make the dismissal without prejudice remedy more effective. It is more common to find speedy-trial statutes or rules of procedure that make dismissal with prejudice the preferred remedy. See Neb. Stat. §29-1208. Does the California statute reprinted above make dismissal with prejudice the preferred remedy?

Is the dismissal remedy for speedy-trial violation similar to the exclusionary rule for unconstitutional searches and seizures because it rewards some guilty defendants out of proportion to the wrong that the state has committed? Would monetary damages be a better remedy, at least for defendants who make no showing that the delay impaired their defense? A Massachusetts statute offers compensation to some defendants whose cases are delayed beyond the statutory limits. See Commonwealth v. Bunting, 518 N.E.2d 1159 (Mass. 1988) (in action to recover damages for statutory speedy-trial delays, state can still litigate question of whether defendant consented to delays, even after dismissal of criminal charges on speedy-trial grounds).

XVI

Pleas and Bargains

In criminal courts in this country, guilty pleas before trial occur far more often than verdicts after trial. In large urban counties in 2006, 9 of 10 felony convictions were based on a guilty plea rather than a trial. Only murder charges produced trials in more than 10 percent of the cases; the rate of guilty pleas was even higher than 90 percent for misdemeanor charges. Most of the time, in most places in this country, the overwhelming majority of criminal charges are resolved through guilty pleas.

Why do we see so few criminal trials? Plea bargains are the short — and incomplete — answer. A large proportion of felony defendants enter pleas of guilty only after they have reached an agreement with the prosecutor, obliging the prosecutor to make some concessions. Perhaps the prosecutor will agree to dismiss some pending charges or to reduce the pending charge to something less serious (this is known as a "charge bargain"). Or perhaps the prosecutor will agree to recommend a particular sentence or to refrain from making certain recommendations (a "sentence bargain"). Other agreement terms are possible, such as a promise not to file charges against third parties.

But plea agreements are not the only explanation for guilty pleas. Some defendants plead guilty as charged without extracting any promises at all from the prosecutor (an "open" plea). These defendants (and their attorneys) know that judges tend to impose less severe sentences on offenders who plead guilty, compared to those who go to trial. This "plea discount" is a reality in virtually every court, but it is rare to find formal acknowledgment of the practice in case law, statutes, or procedural rules.

Anyone who wants to understand American criminal justice must study both guilty pleas and plea bargains. The numbers suggest that these topics are more fundamental than criminal trials. Of course, it may be that plea bargaining takes place in the "shadow" of criminal trials, so that the terms of any agreement reflect the parties' predictions about what *would* have happened at a trial. But it is also possible that some types of cases are resolved by guilty pleas so often that the rules of trial have little importance, while the trials that do occur represent some different universe of cases.

The materials in this chapter survey the boundaries that our legal institutions place on the practice of plea bargaining. We begin inside those boundaries, examining some of the typical topics for bargaining and the ordinary motives of parties who enter plea agreements. We then move out to the boundaries, looking at the types of bargains that the negotiating parties are willing to accept but the legal system as a whole rejects. Categorical constraints on plea bargains come from legislatures, the executive branch, and (less frequently) judges. As always, we will consider whether these different institutions create distinctive answers to the puzzle of what makes a fair plea bargain. Running throughout the chapter is a question about the controlling substantive principles: Does the common law of contracts provide the necessary guidance for determining which plea agreements are enforceable and which are not? The chapter closes with a discussion of the largest questions about plea bargaining: Is the practice inevitable, and is it desirable?

A. BARGAIN ABOUT WHAT?

Every defendant who pleads guilty gives up the right to a jury trial, and the concomitant rights to be represented by counsel, compel witnesses to testify, and confront adverse witnesses. Why would a defendant waive these key rights — essentially those guaranteed by the Fifth and Sixth Amendments to the federal Constitution and their state analogs — along with the chance of an acquittal? And why would prosecutors be willing to bargain away the chance of a conviction in court, with the public affirmation of justice and the publicity that go along with it? The materials in this section explore the objectives of the prosecution and defense as they bargain over a possible plea of guilty. This section also pursues a second theme: Are there some terms that are implicit in every plea bargain?

■ FEDERAL RULE OF CRIMINAL PROCEDURE 11(a), (c)

(a)(1) A defendant may plead not guilty, guilty, or (with the court's consent) nolo contendere.

(2) With the consent of the court and the government, a defendant may enter a conditional plea of guilty or nolo contendere, reserving in writing the right to have an appellate court review an adverse determination of a specified pretrial motion. A defendant who prevails on appeal may then withdraw the plea.

(3) Before accepting a plea of nolo contendere, the court must consider the parties' views and the public interest in the effective administration of justice.

(4) If a defendant refuses to enter a plea or if a defendant organization fails to appear, the court must enter a plea of not guilty.

(c)(1) An attorney for the government and the defendant's attorney, or the defendant when proceeding pro se, may discuss and reach a plea agreement. The court must not participate in these discussions. If the defendant pleads guilty or nolo contendere to either a charged offense or a lesser or related offense, the plea agreement may specify that an attorney for the government will:

(A) not bring, or will move to dismiss, other charges;

(B) recommend, or agree not to oppose the defendant's request, that a particular sentence or sentencing range is appropriate or that a particular provision of the Sentencing Guidelines, or policy statement, or sentencing factor does or does not apply (such a recommendation or request does not bind the court); or

(C) agree that a specific sentence or sentencing range is the appropriate disposition of the case, or that a particular provision of the Sentencing Guidelines, or policy statement, or sentencing factor does or does not apply (such a recommendation or request binds the court once the court accepts the plea agreement).

(2) The parties must disclose the plea agreement in open court when the plea is offered, unless the court for good cause allows the parties to disclose the plea agreement in camera.

(3)(A) To the extent the plea agreement is of the type specified in Rule 11(c)(1)(A) or (C), the court may accept the agreement, reject it, or defer a decision until the court has reviewed the presentence report.

(B) To the extent the plea agreement is of the type specified in Rule 11(c)(1)(B), the court must advise the defendant that the defendant has no right to withdraw the plea if the court does not follow the recommendation or request.

PEOPLE v. GREGORY LUMZY

730 N.E.2d 20 (Ill. 2000)

HEIPLE, J.

. . . On June 10, 1997, defendant was charged with the offenses of aggravated battery and robbery. On June 23, 1997, defendant pled guilty to robbery in exchange for the State's dismissal of the aggravated battery charge. The circuit court of Lee County sentenced defendant to seven years in prison.

On August 1, 1997 defendant's attorney filed a motion to reconsider defendant's sentence. Defendant did not move to withdraw his guilty plea. The trial court denied defendant's motion and defendant filed a notice of appeal. . . .

The State argued that defendant's plea was a "negotiated plea" because the State had agreed to drop the aggravated battery charge in exchange for defendant's guilty plea. Accordingly, under the rationale of People v. Evans, 673 N.E.2d 244 (Ill.1996), defendant could not ask the court to reconsider the length of his sentence without having first filed a motion to withdraw his guilty plea. The appellate court, with one justice dissenting, held that defendant could properly challenge the length of his sentence even though he had not filed a motion to withdraw his guilty plea. . . .

In *Evans,* this court held that . . . in a challenge to a sentence entered pursuant to a negotiated plea agreement, the defendant must (1) move to withdraw the guilty plea and vacate the judgment, and (2) show that the granting of the motion is necessary to correct a manifest injustice. While that terminology used in *Evans* was perfectly appropriate and adequate to dispose of the issue before the court in that case, it did not, nor did it purport to, address every conceivable type of plea agreement.

As Justice Freeman correctly observed in his special concurrence in People v. Linder, 708 N.E.2d 1169 (Ill. 1999), "not all 'negotiated' pleas are the same." Indeed, there are at least four distinct plea scenarios which can occur when a defendant decides to enter a plea of guilty. First, a defendant may simply enter a "blind," or "open," plea without any inducement from the State. In such a case, both the defendant and the State may argue for any sentence permitted by law. Likewise, the trial court in such a case exercises its full discretion and selects the defendant's sentence from the range provided by the relevant statute. . . .

At the other extreme, a defendant may enter a fully negotiated plea under which he agrees to plead guilty in exchange for a specific sentencing recommendation by the State. This was the fact pattern addressed in *Evans.* In that case, two defendants had each pled guilty pursuant to plea agreements under which the State agreed to drop other pending charges and to recommend a specific sentence. The trial courts accepted the plea agreements and entered judgment thereon. Subsequently, however, each defendant sought to reduce his respective sentence by filing a motion for sentence reconsideration. After those motions were denied, the defendants filed appeals arguing that their sentences were excessive.

Relying primarily on contract-law principles, this court in *Evans* rejected the defendants' attempts to reduce the sentences to which they had agreed as part of their plea bargains without first moving to withdraw their guilty pleas. This court recognized that a contrary rule would permit defendants to hold the State to its side of the bargain, by eliminating the possibility of convictions on the dropped charges or sentences in excess of the agreed-upon recommendation, while reneging on the agreement by trying to unilaterally reduce the sentences to which they had agreed.

This court considered a slightly different type of plea agreement in People v. Linder, 708 N.E.2d 1169 (Ill. 1999). In that case, we considered the consolidated appeals of two defendants who pled guilty pursuant to agreements under which the State agreed to drop other pending charges and to recommend a sentence not to exceed an agreed-upon cap. Under this third type of plea bargain, the State's ability to argue for the full range of penalties provided for in the Unified Code of Corrections was constrained by the terms of its agreements with the defendants. After the trial judges in *Linder* accepted the defendants' guilty pleas and imposed sentences within the caps, both defendants sought on appeal to challenge the sentences imposed upon them as excessive. Once again relying upon the contract-law principles described in *Evans,* this court held that such appeals were improper where the defendants had not moved to withdraw their guilty pleas. . . . Accordingly, this court held that it would be fundamentally unfair to permit defendants to unilaterally modify their sides of the plea bargains while simultaneously holding the State to its side of the bargain.

The instant case involves a fourth type of guilty plea which is fundamentally different from the pleas this court considered in *Evans* and *Linder.* Here, as in *Evans* and *Linder,* the State agreed to drop certain charges against defendant in exchange for defendant's plea of guilty to another charge. In stark contrast to the facts of *Evans* and *Linder,* however, the plea bargain in the instant case was utterly silent as to the sentence which defendant would receive. In this case, therefore, both the State and the defendant were free to argue for any sentence provided for in the Unified

Code of Corrections. Likewise, the trial court was able to exercise its full discretion in selecting any sentence permitted by law.

Accordingly, where the record is clear that *absolutely no agreement existed* between the parties as to defendant's sentence, defendant manifestly cannot be breaching such a nonexistent agreement by arguing that the sentence which the court imposed was excessive. For the reasons stated above, the judgment of the appellate court . . . is affirmed.

FREEMAN, J., specially concurring.

[The] State argues that, by reducing the charges, the State did make a sentencing concession because the sentence would have been greater had the aggravated battery charge not been dropped. I disagree. [An] agreement by the State to reduce or dismiss charges against a defendant in exchange for the defendant's plea to the reduced or remaining charges, which has the effect of reducing the sentencing range or the number of sentences a defendant could face, does not constitute an implicit agreement as to sentence. By agreeing to drop a charge, the State has made only the concession of forgoing its right to establish defendant's guilt of that charge. To imply a sentencing concession on the part of the State in this circumstance would require this court to presume that defendant was, in fact, guilty of the charge. Such a presumption would, of course, fly in the face of the presumption of innocence that exists in our criminal justice system.

The rule enunciated in *Evans* focused on returning the parties to their status quo. When a defendant pleads guilty solely in return for the dismissal of charges, the State and defendant receive just what they bargained for, *i.e.*, a guilty plea in exchange for dismissing charges. The parties have not agreed as to the length of the sentence, which is left to the circuit court's full discretion. Thus, no part of the bargain would be undermined by allowing defendant to seek reconsideration of the sentence decided by the circuit court alone. [W]e should avoid a bright-line rule that places meaningless procedural obstacles in the path of an appeal. For these reasons and those expressed in the court's opinion, I concur in today's holding.

BILANDIC, J., dissenting.

. . . This court in People v. Evans, 673 N.E.2d 244 (Ill. 1996), interpreted Supreme Court Rule 604(d), which provides that a defendant may not appeal from a judgment entered upon a plea of guilty unless the defendant timely "files in the trial court a motion to reconsider the sentence, if only the sentence is being challenged, or, if the plea is being challenged, a motion to withdraw his plea of guilty and vacate the judgment." This court held that the motion-for-sentence-reconsideration provisions of Rule 604(d) apply only to "open," as opposed to "negotiated," guilty pleas. We defined an open guilty plea as one in which a defendant pleads guilty "without receiving *any* promises from the State in return." (Emphasis added.) Accordingly, we concluded that, following the entry of judgment on a negotiated guilty plea, a defendant must move to withdraw the guilty plea and vacate the judgment, even if the defendant wants to challenge only his sentence.

Evans explained that allowing a defendant to challenge only his sentence following the entry of judgment on a negotiated guilty plea would violate basic contract law principles. In such a circumstance, the defendant is attempting to hold the State to its part of the bargain while unilaterally reneging on or modifying the terms that the defendant had previously agreed to accept. For example, the defendants in

Evans agreed to plead guilty and, in exchange, the State promised to dismiss other charges and recommend a specific sentence. . . .

Subsequently, in People v. Linder, 708 N.E.2d 1169 (Ill. 1999), this court determined that the holding in *Evans* applies to plea agreements in which the defendant agrees to plead guilty in exchange for the State's promises to dismiss other charges and to recommend a cap on the length of the defendant's sentence. We reasoned that, by agreeing to plead guilty in exchange for the sentencing cap, the defendant is effectively agreeing not to challenge a sentence imposed below the cap.

In this case, defendant was charged with robbery, a Class 2 felony, and aggravated battery, a Class 3 felony. At a hearing, the circuit court advised defendant of the charges against him and that he faced possible prison sentences of three to seven years for the robbery, and two to five years for the aggravated battery. The circuit court further advised defendant that he could receive extended prison terms and therefore be sentenced to prison terms of 14 and 10 years, respectively. Defendant and the State ultimately reached a plea agreement. Defendant agreed to plead guilty to robbery in exchange for the State's promise to dismiss the aggravated battery charge against defendant. The parties presented the plea agreement to the circuit court. The circuit court again advised defendant that he could be sentenced to a maximum of 14 years' imprisonment for the robbery. The circuit court accepted the plea agreement and, following defendant's guilty plea to robbery, sentenced defendant to seven years in prison.

Defendant's plea agreement is negotiated within the meaning of *Evans*. Defendant pled guilty in exchange for the State's promise to dismiss the aggravated battery charge against him. Because defendant obtained the State's promise to dismiss this charge, the prison sentence that defendant could have expected to receive was reduced from 12 years to 7 years if extended sentences were not imposed, and from 24 years to 14 years if extended sentences were imposed. The plea agreement that the parties negotiated, therefore, provided defendant the valuable benefit of a less severe sentence than he could have received had he been convicted of both robbery and aggravated battery.

Moreover, by pleading guilty to robbery in exchange for the State's promise to dismiss the aggravated battery charge, defendant, in effect, agreed that a sentence within the statutory range for robbery was appropriate. Defendant was in fact sentenced to seven years in prison for the robbery — a sentence within the statutory range.

Allowing defendant to modify unilaterally this plea agreement while holding the State to the terms of the agreement will discourage prosecutors from entering into plea agreements. . . . I therefore respectfully dissent.

Problem 16-1. Waiving the Right to Appeal a Sentence

The United States Attorney for your district adopted a policy to encourage defendants to waive the right to appeal. The new office policy states that any plea agreements with federal criminal defendants must include the following language:

> The defendant is aware that Title 18, United States Code, Section 3742 affords a defendant the right to appeal the sentence imposed. Acknowledging this, the defendant knowingly waives the right to appeal any sentence within the maximum provided in the

> statute(s) of conviction (or the manner in which that sentence was determined) on the grounds set forth in Title 18, United States Code, Section 3742 or on any ground whatever, in exchange for the concessions made by the United States in this plea agreement. The defendant also waives his right to challenge his sentence or the manner in which it was determined in any collateral attack. . . .

Any proposed plea agreements that do not include this language must receive approval from a supervisory committee, and the committee will grant these "exceptions" only under "extraordinary circumstances." The policy calls on prosecutors to negotiate for the government to retain its right to appeal any legal error in the application of the federal sentencing guidelines.

The policy recognizes that a sentencing appeal waiver provision does not waive all claims on appeal. The federal courts of appeals have held that appellate review of some claims cannot be waived, such as a defendant's claim that he was denied the effective assistance of counsel at sentencing, that he was sentenced on the basis of his race, or that his sentence exceeded the statutory maximum. The memo also warns that prosecutors must not use the appeal waiver provision "to promote circumvention of the sentencing guidelines."

You are the director of the office of the Federal Public Defender in this district. How will you respond to the new bargaining policy of the federal prosecutors? How do you predict this new policy will be received by the courts? Can you predict whether the policy will be difficult for the prosecutors to implement in particular types of cases? Develop some alternative bargaining strategies for the public defenders in your office to pursue. See United States v. Guevara, 941 F.2d 1299 (4th Cir. 1991); Memo from John Keeney, Acting Assistant Attorney General, October 4, 1995.

Notes

1. *Common types of bargains.* Prosecutors and defendants are allowed to bargain over a wide variety of topics. What do prosecutors typically offer during plea negotiations? Under a "charge bargain" (see Federal Rule 11(c)(1)(A) above), the prosecutor agrees to reduce charges or to drop some counts entirely. The prosecutor might also agree not to file charges in the future against the defendant or some third party based on the events in question. Under a "sentence bargain" (see Rule 11(c)(1)(B) above), a prosecutor agrees to ask the sentencing judge for a certain outcome, or to refrain from asking for a certain outcome, or to make no sentencing recommendation at all.

What does a defendant typically offer? The most important and obvious benefit the defendant can offer is to waive the trial and all its accompanying procedural protections, such as the right to confront witnesses. The waiver of a trial saves the government the expense of preparing and conducting a trial, along with the uncertainty about the outcome at trial. See Commonwealth v. Stagner, 3 S.W.3d 738 (Ky. 1999) (allowing defendant to plead guilty while jury is deliberating; some other jurisdictions prevent guilty pleas after the jury receives case because bargain no longer serves public function of clearing docket). A defendant can also offer to cooperate during investigations of other defendants and other crimes.

There are several ways for a defendant to give up some procedural options while preserving others. The "conditional plea" (see Rule 11(a) above) allows the defendant to plead guilty while reserving the right to appeal on a defined pretrial issue, such as the voluntariness of a confession. If the defendant succeeds on appeal, the guilty plea can be withdrawn. Although it is used less often than the conditional plea, the "slow plea" is another way for a defendant to preserve some options while waiving others. Under a slow plea, the defendant and the prosecution stipulate to the existence of some facts, and then go forward with an abbreviated bench trial to resolve the remaining factual and legal issues.

Finally, a defendant might offer a plea of nolo contendere rather than a plea of guilty. A plea of nolo contendere (meaning "I will not contest" the charges) allows the court to impose criminal sanctions, just as a guilty plea would, but the nolo plea cannot be used against the defendant in any later civil litigation as an admission of guilt. The court (and in some jurisdictions, the prosecutor) must agree before a defendant enters a nolo plea rather than a guilty plea.

2. *Why plead guilty? Plea discounts.* Defendants considering a guilty plea surely know the conventional wisdom that those who plead guilty receive less severe sentences than those who are convicted after a trial. The size of the so-called plea discount varies from place to place, and it is difficult to measure because where the plea discount is most effective (not necessarily where it is most generous) it results in very few trials as a point of comparison. One estimate placed the discount in the federal system at about 30 to 40 percent of the typical sentence imposed on those convicted after trial. See U.S. Sentencing Commission, Supplemental Report on the Initial Sentencing Guidelines and Policy Statements 48 (1987); Jeffery Todd Ulmer et al., Trial Penalties in Federal Sentencing: Extra-Guidelines Factors and District Variation, 27 Justice Quarterly 560 (2010). Many consider the fact of a plea bargain to be an illegitimate basis for sentencing some offenders less severely than others. See ABA Standards for Criminal Justice: Prosecution Function 14-1.8 (guilty plea alone is not sufficient grounds for leniency in sentence). For a more detailed examination of the empirical studies of the plea discount, go to the web extension for this chapter at *http://www.crimpro.com/extension/ch16*.

Would a legislature improve the certainty and honesty of criminal justice by specifying the proper size for a plea discount? The Italian criminal code offers an example of such an explicit plea discount. It provides for a one-third reduction in applicable sentence after guilty plea, provided that maximum sentence does not exceed two years; for more serious charges, the code offers an "abbreviated trial" with one-third reduction in applicable sentence upon conviction. See Codice di procedura penale art. 442, 444.

3. *Presumed good faith in bargaining.* Courts in the United States, since at least the middle of the twentieth century, have generally presumed that plea bargaining is both an appropriate and necessary part of the criminal justice system. As the U.S. Supreme Court put it in Santobello v. New York, 404 U.S. 257 (1971), plea bargaining is "not only an essential part of the process but a highly desirable part for many reasons." The courts have also presumed, except in extraordinary cases, that a prosecutor who negotiates a plea bargain does so for proper reasons (such as faster disposition of cases and elimination of uncertainty) and not improper ones (such as obtaining convictions based on questionable evidence, or punishing the defendant's exercise of rights). For instance, the Supreme Court has rejected claims that a prosecutor acted "vindictively" and contrary to due process by increasing

the charges against a defendant who rejected an initial offer of a plea bargain. Bordenkircher v. Hayes, 434 U.S. 357 (1978). What sort of prosecutorial motives for entering plea negotiations might be improper ones? Is it possible for courts to identify such cases?

4. *Waiver of appeal.* Most state and federal courts have concluded that a defendant may explicitly waive the right to appeal a conviction as part of a plea agreement. See People v. Seaberg, 541 N.E.2d 1022 (N.Y. 1989). A few courts maintain that public policy forbids prosecutors from insulating themselves from review by bargaining away a defendant's appeal rights. Cf. State v. Ethington, 592 P.2d 768 (Ariz. 1979) (defendant can appeal conviction, notwithstanding agreement not to appeal). Is it necessary for a defendant to waive the right to appeal explicitly, or does it go without saying that a defendant who pleads guilty will not attack the conviction on appeal? If a defendant wants to appeal some aspect of a conviction based on a guilty plea, should she explicitly condition the guilty plea on the outcome of the planned appeal? For a survey of typical practices in federal court regarding this negotiation term, see Nancy J. King & Michael E. O'Neill, Appeal Waivers and the Future of Sentencing Policy, 55 Duke L.J. 209 (2005).

5. *Waivable and nonwaivable procedural rights.* When defendants attempt to raise challenges in appellate or post-conviction review on issues that they waived in plea agreements, claiming that the agreement is unenforceable, courts typically dismiss the challenge. Courts allow defendants to bargain away rights of all sorts. See United States v. Mezzanatto, 513 U.S. 196 (1995) (allowing defendant to waive protections of Rule 11(e)(6), which prevented later introduction into evidence of statements made during plea negotiations); People v. Stevens, 610 N.W.2d 881 (Mich. 2000) (statements made during plea negotiations are admissible in prosecution's case-in-chief); Cowan v. Superior Court, 926 P.2d 438 (Cal. 1996) (allowing waiver of statute of limitations).

There are a few legal challenges to a conviction that some courts say a defendant may not waive, even if the waiver appears explicitly in a plea agreement. Courts have taken this position on constitutional speedy trial rights, People v. Callahan, 604 N.E.2d 108 (N.Y. 1992). Courts are split on whether the parties can agree to a sentence outside the statutorily authorized range of punishments; often they enforce illegal sentences falling below the authorized range of punishments but not illegal sentences set above the authorized range. Ex parte Johnson, 669 So. 2d 205 (Ala. 1995) (enforces prosecutor's agreement to two-year prison term, even though prosecutor failed to account for sentencing enhancements requiring additional minimum sentences). Is there any pattern that separates the waivable from the nonwaivable rights? Are the waivable rights the least important ones? See Nancy J. King, Priceless Process, 47 UCLA L. Rev. 113 (1999) (nonwaivable rights should focus on constitutional claims with impact on third parties, since legislature can decide whether to protect statutory rights from waiver).

6. *Forfeiture of claims.* In some contexts, a guilty plea will lead a court to conclude that the defendant forfeited a legal challenge, even though the defendant did not knowingly and intelligently relinquish a known right. This "forfeiture" (as opposed to "waiver") of claims occurs most often when a defendant raises a claim in collateral proceedings such as habeas corpus, which take place after the direct appeal. A guilty plea will automatically bar most postconviction collateral challenges to the conviction based on events occurring before the entry of the plea, because those errors could be cured by recharging or trying the case. See United States v. Broce,

488 U.S. 563 (1989) (guilty plea bars later double jeopardy claim when further evidence is necessary to determine whether one conspiracy or two were present); Tollett v. Henderson, 411 U.S. 258 (1973) (forfeiture of claim of racial discrimination in grand jury selection); McMann v. Richardson, 397 U.S. 759 (1970) (forfeiture of claims regarding jury exposure to coerced confessions). For some exceptional claims, however, a defendant can raise the issue on collateral attack. See Blackledge v. Perry, 417 U.S. 21 (1974) (allowing petitioner for habeas corpus to raise claim of vindictive prosecutorial charging decision). The Supreme Court in *Blackledge* explained that these exceptional claims are not forfeited, despite the guilty plea, because they go to "the very power of the State" to charge the defendant. See also Menna v. New York, 423 U.S. 61 (1975) (allowing habeas petitioner to raise double jeopardy claim despite guilty plea).

B. CATEGORICAL RESTRICTIONS ON BARGAINING

As we have seen, both the prosecution and the defense have reasons to make concessions during plea negotiations, and there are few categorical restrictions on topics for bargaining. But the parties do not act alone in reaching or enforcing agreements. Because the parties are negotiating about criminal punishments, many different people and institutions have an interest in the outcome. There are times when government officials will not approve the "deal" that the parties have reached. Officials may sometimes refuse to enforce the deal, or they may take measures to prevent similar deals in the future. In short, various actors remove terms from the bargaining table. In this section, we survey the limits that legislatures, prosecutorial supervisors, and judges have placed on the terms available to the negotiating parties during plea bargaining. In what ways do the unacceptable bargains differ from the acceptable ones? Consider as well the ways that these institutions have developed distinctive approaches to plea bargaining limits.

1. Legislative Limits

Until recently, legislatures did not explicitly limit the power of the prosecution and defense to enter plea agreements. Even now, it is unusual to find a statute that addresses the topic of plea agreements directly, except to authorize the prosecuting attorney in general terms to enter such agreements. It is common to find statutes setting out the procedures necessary to ensure that a defendant enters a guilty plea knowingly and voluntarily, but these procedures apply both to negotiated pleas and non-negotiated (or "open") pleas.

Yet, in many jurisdictions, statutes have profound — even if indirect — effects on plea bargaining. Most states have at least some statutes that specify mandatory minimum penalties for certain crimes. The statutes do not require the prosecutor to charge the crime in question whenever there is sufficient evidence, and they do not stop the prosecutor from reducing or dismissing charges when this crime occurs. Nevertheless, these statutes do influence bargaining, for once the prosecutor obtains a conviction for the designated crime, the prosecutor has limited influence over the sentence and the judge has fewer sentencing options.

In addition to these sentencing statutes, some state legislatures have addressed more directly the prosecutor's power to negotiate over charges and sentences. Three examples follow. In what ways do the statutes represent different strategies for limiting plea bargains? Which strategies are likely to have the most impact on actual charging and negotiating practices?

CALIFORNIA PENAL CODE §1192.7

(a)(1) It is the intent of the Legislature that district attorneys prosecute violent sex crimes under statutes that provide sentencing under a "one strike," "three strikes," or habitual sex offender statute instead of engaging in plea bargaining over those offenses.

(2) Plea bargaining in any case in which the indictment or information charges any serious felony, any felony in which it is alleged that a firearm was personally used by the defendant, or any offense of driving while under the influence of alcohol, drugs, narcotics, or any other intoxicating substance, or any combination thereof, is prohibited, unless there is insufficient evidence to prove the people's case, or testimony of a material witness cannot be obtained, or a reduction or dismissal would not result in a substantial change in sentence.

(3) If the indictment or information charges the defendant with a violent sex crime [such as rape, sexual penetration, sodomy, oral copulation, or continuous sexual abuse of a child], that could be prosecuted under [enhanced penalty provisions such as the "three strikes" habitual felon law], plea bargaining is prohibited unless there is insufficient evidence to prove the people's case, or testimony of a material witness cannot be obtained, or a reduction or dismissal would not result in a substantial change in sentence. At the time of presenting the agreement to the court, the district attorney shall state on the record why a sentence under one of those sections was not sought.

(b) As used in this section "plea bargaining" means any bargaining, negotiation, or discussion between a criminal defendant, or his or her counsel, and a prosecuting attorney or judge, whereby the defendant agrees to plead guilty or nolo contendere, in exchange for any promises, commitments, concessions, assurances, or consideration by the prosecuting attorney or judge relating to any charge against the defendant or to the sentencing of the defendant.

(c) As used in this section, "serious felony" means any of the following: (1) Murder or voluntary manslaughter; (2) mayhem; (3) rape; (4) sodomy by force, violence, duress, menace, threat of great bodily injury, or fear of immediate and unlawful bodily injury on the victim or another person; (5) oral copulation by force, violence, duress, menace, threat of great bodily injury, or fear of immediate and unlawful bodily injury on the victim or another person; (6) lewd or lascivious act on a child under 14 years of age; (7) any felony punishable by death or imprisonment in the state prison for life; (8) any felony in which the defendant personally inflicts great bodily injury on any person, other than an accomplice, or any felony in which the defendant personally uses a firearm; (9) attempted murder; (10) assault with intent to commit rape or robbery; (11) assault with a deadly weapon or instrument on a peace officer; (12) assault by a life prisoner on a non-inmate; (13) assault with a deadly weapon by an inmate; (14) arson; (15) exploding a destructive device or any explosive with intent to injure; (16) exploding a destructive device or any explosive causing bodily injury, great bodily injury, or mayhem; (17) exploding a destructive device or any explosive with intent to murder; (18) any burglary of the first degree; (19) robbery or bank robbery; (20) kidnapping; . . . (23) any felony in which the defendant personally used a dangerous or deadly weapon; (24) selling, furnishing, administering, giving, or offering to sell, furnish, administer, or give to a minor any heroin, cocaine, phencyclidine (PCP), or any methamphetamine-related drug, . . . (26) grand theft involving a firearm; (27) carjacking; . . . (31) assault with a deadly weapon, firearm, machinegun, assault weapon, or semiautomatic firearm or assault on a peace officer or firefighter . . . (32) assault with a deadly weapon against a public transit employee, custodial officer, or school employee . . . (33) discharge of a firearm at an inhabited dwelling, vehicle, or aircraft . . . (37) intimidation of victims or witnesses . . . (38) terrorist threats . . . ; and (41) any conspiracy to commit an offense described in this subdivision.

■ NEW YORK CRIMINAL PROCEDURE LAW §220.10

The only kinds of pleas which may be entered to an indictment are those specified in this section:

1. The defendant may as a matter of right enter a plea of "not guilty" to the indictment.

2. Except as provided in subdivision five, the defendant may as a matter of right enter a plea of "guilty" to the entire indictment.

3. Except as provided in subdivision five, where the indictment charges but one crime, the defendant may, with both the permission of the court and the consent of the people, enter a plea of guilty of a lesser included offense.

4. Except as provided in subdivision five, where the indictment charges two or more offenses in separate counts, the defendant may, with both the permission of the court and the consent of the people, enter a plea of:

(a) Guilty of one or more but not all of the offenses charged; or

(b) Guilty of a lesser included offense with respect to any or all of the offenses charged; or

(c) Guilty of any combination of offenses charged and lesser offenses included within other offenses charged.

5. (a)(i) Where the indictment charges one of the class A felonies . . . or the attempt to commit any such class A felony, then any plea of guilty entered pursuant to subdivision three or four must be or must include at least a plea of guilty of class B felony. . . .

(iii) Where the indictment charges one of the class B felonies . . . then any plea of guilty entered pursuant to subdivision three or four must be or must include at least a plea of guilty of a class D felony.

REVISED CODE OF WASHINGTON §§9.94A.450, 9.94A.460

§9.94A.450

(1) Except as provided in subsection (2) of this section, a defendant will normally be expected to plead guilty to the charge or charges which adequately describe the nature of his or her criminal conduct or go to trial.

(2) In certain circumstances, a plea agreement with a defendant in exchange for a plea of guilty to a charge or charges that may not fully describe the nature of his or her criminal conduct may be necessary and in the public interest. Such situations may include the following:

(a) Evidentiary problems which make conviction on the original charges doubtful;

(b) The defendant's willingness to cooperate in the investigation or prosecution of others whose criminal conduct is more serious or represents a greater public threat;

(c) A request by the victim when it is not the result of pressure from the defendant;

(d) The discovery of facts which mitigate the seriousness of the defendant's conduct;

(e) The correction of errors in the initial charging decision;

(f) The defendant's history with respect to criminal activity;

(g) The nature and seriousness of the offense or offenses charged;

(h) The probable effect on witnesses.

§9.94A.460

The prosecutor may reach an agreement regarding sentence recommendations. The prosecutor shall not agree to withhold relevant information from the court concerning the plea agreement.

Notes

1. *Codifying plea considerations.* The Washington statute lists several considerations that prosecutors traditionally describe as reasons to reduce charges or to recommend a lesser sentence as part of a plea bargain. The National District Attorneys Association lists similar factors for a prosecutor to consider before negotiating a plea agreement, including the following: "the nature of the offense(s)"; "age, background, and criminal history of the defendant"; "sufficiency of admissible evidence to support a verdict"; "undue hardship caused to the defendant"; "possible deterrent value of prosecution"; "age of the case"; "willingness of the defendant to waive (release) his right to pursue potential civil causes of action arising from his arrest"; and "availability and willingness [of witnesses] to testify." National Prosecution Standards 68.1 (2d ed. 1991). A few other states have similar statutes. See also Oregon Code §135.415 (nonexclusive list of criteria the prosecutor may consider in making plea agreements). Would the passage of such a statute alter any practices in a prosecutor's office? What would motivate a legislature to pass such a statute?

2. *Particular charges.* In recent years, it has become more common for legislatures to instruct prosecutors not to dismiss or reduce charges for specific crimes. As you might imagine, the crimes involved are usually those that have become high priorities for the public. See Nev. Rev. Stat. §§483.560, 484.3792 (prosecutor may not dismiss charges for driving with suspended or revoked license, or for drunk driving offenses, unless there is no probable cause to support charge). Cf. Miss. Stat. §43-21-555 (no plea bargaining in youth court).

3. *Size of discount.* The New York statute does not bar plea bargains for any particular crimes. Rather, it defines the maximum reduction in charges and authorized sentences that the prosecutor may offer. A statute specifying the size of the discounts a prosecutor can offer may create a very visible incentive to plead guilty. For instance, in Corbitt v. New Jersey, 439 U.S. 212 (1978), the Supreme Court upheld the constitutionality of a statute that required a mandatory term of life imprisonment for a conviction after trial; the same statute allowed either a life term or a 30-year term for a conviction under the statute based on a guilty or nolo plea. Compare United States v. Jackson, 390 U.S. 570 (1968) (overturning statute as undue burden on right to jury trial where death penalty is authorized only for defendants who go to trial); Shumpert v. Department of Highways, 409 S.E.2d 771 (S.C. 1991) (statute reducing period of driver's license suspension for those pleading guilty of drunk driving offenses is overturned as burden on trial rights).

4. *Exceptions under the California statute.* Section 1192.7 of the California Penal Code became law as a result of a voter referendum in 1982. Other provisions of the "victims' rights" referendum included greater admissibility of evidence of a defendant's prior convictions and increased penalties for repeat felony offenders. The statute has been amended often over the years, sometimes through ordinary legislation and at other times through voter initiatives (for instance, the "serious felonies" numbered higher than 27 were added as part of the 2000 Juvenile Crime Initiative). Subsection (a)(3) of the statute was not included in the original language. What does this portion of the statute change?

The plea bargain limitations for "serious felonies," however, never reduced the number of cases resolved through guilty pleas and plea negotiations in California. One study of California plea bargaining concluded that the statutory ban never reduced the use of guilty pleas because §1192.7 applied only to cases in superior court. Since virtually all serious felonies are charged initially in municipal court and transferred to superior court only after the preliminary examination, the prosecution and defense can negotiate a plea bargain in almost any case during the first few days after the filing of the charge, before any preliminary examination and before much discovery has taken place. See Candace McCoy, Politics and Plea Bargaining: Victims' Rights in California (1993). Even if the bar on plea negotiations were to apply to all court systems, how many dismissals and reductions of charges would it prevent? Consider the exceptions in subsections (a)(2) and (a)(3), allowing plea bargaining when there is "insufficient evidence" or when a material witness is not available, or when no substantial reduction in sentence would result. How many cases would fall within these subsections, and who would determine the breadth of coverage for this statutory language?

2. *Judicial Rules*

Judges are pulled in two directions when it comes to plea bargains. On the one hand, plea bargaining appears to be an extension of the prosecutor's charging decision, and judges are reluctant to become involved in charging decisions. See Chapter 13. On the other hand, plea bargaining is a key determinant in sentencing, and judges have customarily considered sentencing to be a judicial function. As a result, judges usually accept the practice of negotiated guilty pleas and allow prosecutors to dismiss or reduce charges. But they resist more strenuously when plea bargaining takes the form of a sentence bargain.

What form does judicial resistance to sentence bargains take? It is rare to find judges creating rules of criminal procedure or making other general pronouncements that place whole categories of agreements out of bounds. But they do frequently insist on the power, in individual cases, to make an independent judgment about any sentence that the parties might have selected under their agreement. This means that judges have been especially skeptical about agreements that give the judge only one sentencing option (the one that the prosecution and the defense have negotiated) and allow the defendant to withdraw the plea if the judge does not enter the sentence specified in the agreement. See Fed. R. Crim. P. 11(c)(1)(C) (parties may "agree that a specific sentence is the appropriate disposition of the case"). The following case indicates when judges are likely (or unlikely) to limit or scrutinize entire classes of plea bargains. Later in this chapter (in section C), we consider the role of the judge during plea negotiations in individual cases.

RAYMOND ESPINOZA v. HON. GREGORY MARTIN

894 P.2d 688 (Ariz. 1995)

CORCORAN, J.

Petitioner Raymond Espinoza, a criminal defendant in Maricopa County, challenges the policy adopted by a group of Maricopa County Superior Court judges of summarily rejecting all plea agreements containing stipulated sentences. . . .

The criminal divisions of the Maricopa County Superior Court are divided into four groups designated as quadrants A through D. Quadrant B [consists] of 5 judges. [The] quadrant B judges issued a memorandum detailing a new plea agreement policy that was scheduled to take effect on January 25, 1993. The policy stated that quadrant B judges would no longer accept any plea agreements containing stipulated sentences because sentencing "is a judicial function which should not be subjected to limitations which are imposed by the parties, but are not required by law." . . . The relevant section of that policy reads as follows:

> 1. Plea agreements may stipulate to "probation," or "department of corrections" [DOC] for felonies, or "county jail" for misdemeanors. Agreements may not stipulate to any term of years (other than lifetime probation in dangerous crimes against children) or to any non-mandatory terms and conditions of probation . . . , or to sentences running concurrently or consecutively. . . .

The only 2 exceptions to the quadrant B policy are as follows:

> 2. Exceptions will be made for legitimate cooperation agreements. If the state wishes to make stipulated sentencing concessions in exchange for information, testimony or cooperation from a defendant, that fact should be made known to the judge in an appropriate manner prior to the change of plea. . . .
>
> 4. Stipulations in capital murder cases to life imprisonment are viewed by the judges as charging concessions and not true sentencing stipulations. Therefore, such stipulations are unaffected by the policy.

On June 2, 1993, Espinoza was indicted on one count of offering to sell narcotic drugs and one count of misconduct involving weapons. At his arraignment, the case was assigned to respondent, quadrant B Judge Gregory Martin. On August 11, 1993, Espinoza appeared before Judge Martin in chambers to enter a plea of guilty to both counts pursuant to a plea agreement, which stipulated that the sentences would run concurrently with each other and with an unrelated probation revocation. Judge Martin summarily rejected Espinoza's plea agreement because the stipulation to concurrent sentences violated the quadrant B policy. . . .

Rule 17.4, Arizona Rules of Criminal Procedure, governs plea negotiations and agreements. This court has stated that "the rules [of criminal procedure] recognize that properly negotiated plea agreements . . . are an essential part of the criminal process and can enhance judicial economy, protect the resources of the State, and serve the ends of justice for the defendant, the State and the victim." State v. Superior Court, 611 P.2d 928 (Ariz. 1980).

This case turns on the meaning of rule 17.4(a), which reads as follows: "The parties may negotiate concerning, and reach an agreement on, any aspect of the disposition of the case. The court shall not participate in any such negotiation." The plain language of rule 17.4(a) gives the parties the right to negotiate and reach agreement on "any aspect of the disposition of the case." This means that the State and the defendant may bargain both as to the plea of guilty and as to the sentence to be imposed.

Although rule 17.4(a) allows the parties to negotiate plea agreements, including sentences, rule 17.4 also grants trial courts considerable discretion in deciding whether to accept or reject such agreements. Rule 17.4(d) provides in part:

> After making such determinations [of the accuracy of the agreement and the voluntariness and intelligence of the plea] and considering the victim's view, if provided, the court shall either accept or reject the tendered negotiated plea.*

Furthermore, even if a trial court accepts a plea agreement, it is not bound by negotiated provisions regarding the sentence or the terms of probation if a review of the presentence report reveals the inadequacy of those provisions.

In order to ensure that agreements negotiated pursuant to rule 17.4(a) have some meaningful effect, we interpret rule 17.4 as guaranteeing the parties the right

* [Rule 17.4(d) continues as follows: "The court shall not be bound by any provision in the plea agreement regarding the sentence or the term and conditions of probation to be imposed, if, after accepting the agreement and reviewing a presentence report, it rejects the provision as inappropriate." Section (e) states as follows: "If an agreement or any provision thereof is rejected by the court, it shall give the defendant an opportunity to withdraw his or her plea, advising the defendant that if he or she permits the plea to stand, the disposition of the case may be less favorable to him or her than that contemplated by the agreement." — Eds.]

to present their negotiated agreement to a judge, to have the judge consider the merits of that agreement in light of the circumstances of the case, and to have the judge exercise his or her discretion with regard to the agreement. Instead of hampering judicial sentencing discretion, the current version of rule 17.4, taken as a whole, contemplates the exercise of judicial discretion when determining whether to accept or reject each particular plea agreement. In exercising that discretion, the trial court must review the plea agreement to see if the ends of justice and the protection of the public are being served by such agreement. . . .

After giving full consideration to the appropriateness of a plea agreement, the trial court has the discretion to either accept or reject the entire plea agreement, or to accept the agreement and later reject the sentencing provisions if deemed inappropriate after further inquiry. Therefore, there [is no need] to try to further enhance judicial sentencing discretion by approving a policy that limited the parties' right to negotiate. . . .

Espinoza agreed to plead guilty to two charges: attempting to knowingly sell a narcotic drug and knowingly possessing a deadly weapon during the commission of a felony. In exchange, the parties agreed that the sentences imposed on both charges would be served concurrently, and that those sentences would also be concurrent with a probation revocation. . . . Judge Martin did not consider the particular circumstances of the case and made no findings regarding the appropriateness of the negotiated sentence. Instead, the presence of a stipulated sentence in the agreement triggered the quadrant B policy and precluded any individualized exercise of discretion. Absent the quadrant B policy, Judge Martin could have weighed the merits of the plea agreement and accepted it, rejected it entirely, or rejected the sentencing provisions as inappropriate once he had reviewed the presentence report. This is the type of discretion contemplated by rule 17.4, and trial courts are obligated to exercise it.

[Groups] of judges may not implement policies to automatically reject all such plea agreements without considering whether a stipulated sentence is appropriate in light of the circumstances of the case. Our holding applies equally to the actions of individual judges. [A trial judge may not] automatically reject a plea agreement without individualized consideration because it contains a stipulated sentence. . . .

FELDMAN, C.J., specially concurring.

I fully concur in the majority opinion. Two comments in Justice Martone's dissent, however, require a response from the Chief Justice.

Because the dissent departs from the issue before us to castigate the court for failing to adopt the petition to amend Ariz. R. Crim. Proc. 17.4, it is appropriate to explain why we did not adopt that proposal. The dissent makes much of the number of comments favoring the petition, but, as is often the case, the numbers do not paint an accurate picture. Other than judges, only three writers, none of whom is a practicing lawyer, supported the rule change. The dissent fails to mention that, in fact, several judges opposed the change and that the comments of representatives of the lawyers who would have had to practice under the proposed rule were unanimously unfavorable. The prosecutors opposed it on the grounds that it was contrary to the interests of victims and the public, and the defense bar opposed it on the grounds that it would significantly hinder their attempts to obtain fair treatment for their clients under a mandatory sentencing regime. . . .

This debate is, of course, a non-issue in this case. Those readers who desire an in-depth review, however, should peruse the comment to the petition to amend Rule 17.4 filed by Judge Ronald Reinstein, Presiding Criminal Judge of the Maricopa County Superior Court. [I] quote here one paragraph of that comment:

> While some have argued that sentencing stipulations are regularly crafted by inexperienced young attorneys, and judges are best suited to determine in the first instance what an appropriate disposition in a case should be, the fact is that most of the more significant and sensitive cases in the justice system are handled by experienced prosecutors and defense attorneys who have lived and breathed these cases for months. The sentencing judge on the other hand more than likely only reviews the presentence report the night before sentencing. Many of those judges, while perhaps experienced in life and the law, at least in the beginning of their judicial careers or their assignment to the criminal bench, have no experience at all in criminal sentencing. We are not all anointed with mystical and instant wisdom when we don our judicial robes.

Some may believe that we should damn the torpedoes and go forward with a rule opposed by all who would have to practice under it, but I disagree. Although we may empathize with the judges who seek to regain some of the discretion taken from them by mandatory sentencing, we must listen to those who would have had to practice under the changed rule. [I]t would be an abuse of power to impose the rule until it was first tried with a group willing to experiment. . . .

ZLAKET, J., dissenting.

The majority concedes that judges are empowered to reject plea agreements. I am of the additional opinion that they should be permitted to summarily reject those containing stipulated sentences for that reason alone, without having to go through the charade of considering each case individually. My hope is that most judges would not routinely follow such a course of action, at least until we can be sure it causes no damage to the plea-bargaining process that constitutes an integral part of our criminal justice system. Nevertheless, arriving at a general principle applicable to a class of plea agreements, after full consideration of the issue, seems to me more honest, more efficient, and every bit as thoughtful as pondering each agreement individually before rejecting it. . . .

I believe the court's ruling today not only threatens [judicial] candor but also reinforces the purely ministerial role about which [judges have] so vehemently and properly complained. Sentencing is, or at least should be, a judicial function. Regrettably, mandatory sentencing schemes have eliminated a great deal of judicial discretion in such matters. I prefer not to support a rule interpretation that potentially contributes to further erosion of this authority, especially where it is unnecessary to resolve the pending case.

MARTONE, J., dissenting.

I dissent. I would support the efforts of five trial judges to improve our criminal justice system. . . . The quadrant B policy was not in conflict with Rule 17.4. While Rule 17.4(a) allows the parties to agree on the disposition of a case, Rule 17.4(d) allows the court to "either accept or reject the tendered negotiated plea." Even after acceptance, the court may reject sentencing stipulations. Rule 17.4(d). If, after looking at the document, a judge is opposed to any part of the plea, he or she may summarily reject it. And that is precisely what Judge Martin did here. That he and other judges agreed to exercise their rights under Rule 17.4(d) does not make his decision conflict with the rule. Indeed, their agreement is collectively supportive of the rule. No one forced Judge Martin to participate in the policy. He was free to accept or reject it, altogether or in a specific case. He accepted it because he thought it was a good idea. The quadrant B policy was not binding on any judge who did not want to be bound by it.

[The] Superior Court in Maricopa County has petitioned to amend Rule 17.4 to prohibit sentencing stipulations and the majority rejected it. See In re Rule 17.4, Rules of Criminal Procedure, R-94-0007.* We are considering an experiment with the proposed amendment, but the majority rejected Maricopa County's request to participate in it.

I believe that this court should be in the business of rewarding creative efforts that arise elsewhere in the system. We have not been at the forefront of reform in the criminal justice system. . . . The trial judges are trying new ideas as we approach the next millennium. We should support them.

Problem 16-2. Bargaining Ban in a Lower Court

The trial courts in New Jersey include superior courts, which are the courts of general jurisdiction, and municipal courts, which are courts of limited jurisdiction to try lesser criminal offenses. In 1974, the New Jersey Supreme Court passed a rule prohibiting all plea bargaining in municipal courts in the state.

In passing this rule, the court expressed the concern that plea bargaining might be abused in municipal court because of the part-time nature of the personnel in many municipal courts and the informal nature of the proceedings. For instance, municipal courts are not required to maintain stenographic records or audio recordings of proceedings and most municipal courts do not have a prosecutor or a public defender assigned full time to the court. In the view of the Supreme Court, this structure left the municipal courts vulnerable to allegations of improper "back room deals."

For several years, the Supreme Court maintained its rule on plea bargaining and emphasized that the ban was particularly important in drunken-driving offenses. In 1983, Chief Justice Robert Wilentz issued a reminder to judges on assignment in municipal courts that "without in any way affecting the generality of the plea bargaining prohibition, I suggest that you emphasize the particular importance of not allowing plea bargaining in drunken driving cases."

In 1988, the Supreme Court Task Force on the Improvement of Municipal Courts recommended the authorization of plea bargaining in the municipal courts, giving the following reasons:

* [This note is asterisked in the original dissenting opinion.] Of the approximately 60 comments received, over 40 were in favor of prohibiting sentencing agreements. . . . The majority is persuaded by the opposition of institutional bar groups. It is natural enough for lawyers to not want to surrender their sentencing power to judges. But if judges, and not lawyers, ought to possess the power to sentence, the reluctance of lawyers to transfer that power ought not carry the day. . . .

> The existence of a regulated plea agreement process is essential to serve both the ends of justice and the effective response to burgeoning municipal court caseloads. It will foster increases in the productivity and professionalism of the municipal court bench, administrators, clerks and staff. The process provides for the certainty and fairness of punishment to better protect the rights of the defendants, victims and the interests of society.
>
> The municipal courts have a volume of cases in excess of 6 million that must be processed and resolved in an expeditious and summary manner. The Committee has been advised and is of the opinion that unless plea agreements are permitted in the carefully defined fashion being proposed, they will certainly take place in an unregulated fashion. Certainly, in the absence of some form of expeditious disposition, these courts would not be able to cope with their heavy calendars given the part-time nature of the courts and the part-time nature of the judges, most of whom have full-time law practices.

The committee, while acknowledging the feasibility of plea bargaining in general in the municipal courts, determined that drunken-driving offenses posed special problems. It noted the extraordinary emotional and fiscal costs of drunken driving, and "the public's concern that the process of plea bargaining, as applied to alcohol and drug offenses, might undermine the deterrent thrust of New Jersey's tough laws in these areas." Accordingly, the committee's report recommended that while the ban on municipal court plea bargaining should be lifted, the prohibition on plea agreements in drunken-driving offenses should continue.

In 1990, the court instituted a regulated system of plea agreements in municipal courts. It allowed plea bargaining pursuant to New Jersey Court Rule 7:4-8. The guidelines that the court issued with the court rules specified that their purpose was "to allow for flexibility in the definitions and exclusions relating to the plea agreement process as that process evolves and certain offenses come to demand lesser or greater scrutiny." Guideline 4 adopted the recommendation of the committee that plea bargaining not be allowed in drunken-driving cases.

As a member of the New Jersey Supreme Court, how would you respond to the recommendations of the committee? What more would you like to know about the municipal courts and their caseloads before you decide? Compare State v. Hessen, 678 A.2d 1082 (N.J. 1996).

Notes

1. *Reasons for rejection of a plea agreement.* Statutes and rules give judges the opportunity to approve or disapprove plea agreements. The court must decide whether to accept or reject the defendant's plea of guilty; if the plea grows out of an objectionable plea agreement, the court can simply refuse to accept the guilty plea. Further, rules and statutes in more than 30 states require prosecutors to obtain the consent of the court to dismiss a charge. Does the court need any justification, or any particular type of justification, to reject a guilty plea based on a plea agreement or to refuse to dismiss a charge? Almost all appellate courts allow trial courts to reject guilty pleas or dismissals of charges without any serious review of the judge's reasons for refusing. A few cases, however, have held that a trial judge must state reasons for rejecting a guilty plea; the judge may refuse the guilty plea or the dismissal of charges only if the prosecutor has abused his discretion by failing to consider facts

important to the public interest in the case. Sandy v. District Court, 935 P.2d 1148 (Nev. 1997); United States v. Ammidown, 497 F.2d 615 (D.C. Cir. 1973). Limits on the judicial power to reject guilty pleas are based on separation of powers concepts and on judges' limited knowledge both about the relative strengths of individual cases and about the most efficient allocation of prosecutorial resources. Would you expect such limits on judicial power to apply equally to charging agreements and sentencing agreements?

2. *Stipulated sentences.* As described in the *Espinoza* case from Arizona, the state supreme court had considered (and rejected) an amendment to the guilty plea rules dealing with "stipulated sentences," and the trial judges of quadrant B created their own rule about stipulated sentences. What exactly can a trial judge do when the parties present a stipulated or "negotiated" sentence? The details vary from place to place. Most jurisdictions (including the federal courts) allow the parties to choose the type of agreement they will present to the judge: They can agree either to recommend a sentence (leaving the judge free to accept or reject the recommendation) or to offer the judge only a stipulated sentence that the judge must simply accept or reject as a package with the guilty plea. See People v. Johnson, 929 N.E.2d 361 (N.Y. 2010) (judge's decision that stipulated sentence was inadequate invalidated waiver of appeal contained in plea agreement). A few states recognize only the "binding" form of sentencing agreements. See People v. Killebrew, 330 N.W.2d 834 (Mich. 1982) (when judge plans to impose sentence that exceeds sentence recommendation or agreement, defendant may withdraw guilty plea). Other states have statutes or rules to preserve the judge's power, in all cases, to accept a guilty plea but still depart from the sentence the parties recommend. See State v. Strecker, 883 P.2d 841 (Mont. 1994). English law permits plea bargaining but not negotiated sentences. See R. v. Turner (F.R.) [1970] 2 Q.B. 321, 54 Crim. App. 352 (guidelines for plea bargaining). For an overview of the cases on binding sentence bargains, go to the web extension for this chapter at *http://www.crimpro.com/extension/ch16*.

Even though most criminal procedure rules allow the parties to stipulate to a particular sentence, stipulated sentences are far less common in practice than charge bargains or nonbinding sentencing recommendations. Many judges declare that they will not accept "binding" sentence recommendations, even though the relevant rules of procedure authorize such agreements. Why does this pattern emerge in most places? Did the trial judges in Maricopa County need to create a common policy for the jurisdiction?

3. *Disfavored classes of agreements.* What was it about plea negotiations in the municipal courts (described in Problem 16-2) that made such practices a special concern to the New Jersey courts? See State v. Hessen, 678 A.2d 1082 (N.J. 1996). What features of drunken-driving cases created the need for special treatment? Were any of these features present in the types of plea bargains that the trial courts tried to ban in the *Espinoza* case from Arizona? Is there any explanation for the different outcomes in these cases, a ban on a category of plea bargains upheld in one case but not the other? Cf. State v. Hager, 630 N.W.2d 828 (Iowa 2001) (despite trial court rule forbidding plea bargains on day of trial, abuse of discretion not to consider plea entered on day of trial).

One type of agreement that courts have rejected categorically is known as the "consistency" agreement, in which a defendant receives charging concessions in exchange for an agreement to testify against another defendant and to testify consistently with past statements that the defendant has made. See State v. Rivera,

109 P.3d 83 (Ariz. 2005) (prosecutor may enter plea agreement that requires defendant to avow accuracy of prior statements to police and to provide truthful testimony in future, but may not enter agreement that requires defendant to testify in future consistently with prior statements). Why are judges in most jurisdictions willing to ban this type of agreement when they allow the parties to negotiate over so many other potential terms of agreement?

4. *Prosecutor's objection to guilty plea and sentence.* We have considered the situation in which the judge objects to a sentence that the parties have negotiated. Can a judge side with a defendant against a prosecutor and accept a guilty plea (and impose a sentence or dismiss a charge) over the prosecutor's objection? The prosecutor's ability to object to the sentence that the defendant proposes derives from a charge bargain or a binding sentence bargain. The prosecutor has no power to object to the sentence imposed when a defendant pleads to the court, and thus to the whole indictment.

Most courts give the prosecutor the power to block a guilty plea if the judge plans to dismiss charges or impose a sentence below what the plea agreement specifies. See State v. Vasquez-Aerreola, 940 S.W.2d 451 (Ark. 1997) (court may not dismiss charge of gang activity and accept guilty plea on other charges over prosecutor's objection); People v. Siebert, 537 N.W.2d 891 (Mich. 1995) (court may not accept a plea bargain containing a sentence agreement but impose a lower sentence than that agreed to; in such a case, prosecutor must be given opportunity to withdraw from agreement). Nonetheless, a few courts insist, at least for sentence bargains, that the prosecutor cannot prevent the judge from selecting the sentence to impose. See State v. Warren, 558 A.2d 1312 (N.J. 1989) (prohibits use of plea agreements in which prosecutor reserves right to withdraw from plea agreement if court-imposed sentence is more lenient than one agreed to by parties or recommended to court by prosecutor).

3. Prosecutorial Guidelines

Decisions whether to offer or accept plea bargains, like decisions about charging a suspect, are often governed by executive branch policies. These policies vary in their level of detail; in many smaller offices, prosecutors follow consistent plea practices that may reflect unwritten (but articulated) guidelines, or they may simply reflect shared office culture and experience. Sometimes prosecutors develop formal plea review standards, describing substantively the types of bargains that are acceptable. Other times they create procedural review mechanisms, such as supervisory review or committee review of possible plea bargains. These guidelines or procedures might apply only for identified types of cases, such as those involving drugs or those likely to attract publicity.

Federal prosecutors, under the central control of the attorney general, have developed a detailed set of written plea bargaining policies. In addition to the nationwide guidelines set out below, many of the U.S. Attorneys' offices in the 94 federal districts around the country have developed additional guidance to reflect the distinctive caseloads, resources, and other factors in each district.

The federal executive branch plea policies that follow were created against a background of major changes in sentencing law. At the time of the 1980 policy printed below, the federal system (and all but a handful of state systems) still had a highly discretionary sentencing system. Under discretionary sentencing systems the legislature defined most crimes to include a wide range of possible sentences, sometimes covering (for a single crime) everything from nonprison sanctions, such as fines or probation, to long prison terms. In theory, the law left huge discretion to the sentencing judge to set terms within the statutorily authorized range. The actual sentence to be served was often determined through "back-end" review by parole boards once the offender had spent a minimum required portion of the judicially imposed term in prison. In such systems, the charge might have only a modest binding effect. In practice, however, the processing of many cases by the same "working group" of attorneys and judges within the criminal court culture would lead to very firm expectations or "prices" for various crimes. See Milton Heumann, Plea Bargaining: The Experiences of Prosecutors, Judges, and Defense Attorneys (1978).

Remember as you read these policies that the Federal Rules of Criminal Procedure authorize three kinds of pleas: (1) agreements to enter a guilty plea to one or more charges in return for dismissal of other charges (a "charge" bargain under Rule 11(c)(1)(A)); (2) agreements to recommend a sentence in exchange for a guilty plea, subject to the judge's power to select the final sentence after accepting the guilty plea (a "sentence" bargain under Rule 11(c)(1)(B)); and (3) an agreement to a particular sentence in exchange for a guilty plea (a stipulated sentence plea under Rule 11(c)(1)(C)).

U.S. DEPARTMENT OF JUSTICE, PRINCIPLES OF FEDERAL PROSECUTION

(1980)

Entering into Plea Agreements

1. The attorney for the government may, in an appropriate case, enter into an agreement with a defendant that, upon the defendant's plea of guilty or nolo contendere to a charged offense or to a lesser or related offense, he will move for dismissal of other charges, take a certain position with respect to the sentence to be imposed, or take other action.

2. In determining whether it would be appropriate to enter into a plea agreement, the attorney for the government should weigh all relevant considerations, including:

(a) the defendant's willingness to cooperate in the investigation or prosecution of others;

(b) the defendant's history with respect to criminal activity;

(c) the nature and seriousness of the offense or offenses charged;

(d) the defendant's remorse or contrition and his willingness to assume responsibility for his conduct;

(e) the desirability of prompt and certain disposition of the case;

(f) the likelihood of obtaining a conviction at trial;

(g) the probable effect on witnesses;

(h) the probable sentence or other consequences if the defendant is convicted;

(i) the public interest in having the case tried rather than disposed of by a guilty plea;

(j) the expense of trial and appeal; and

(k) the need to avoid delay in the disposition of other pending cases.

Comment: . . . The provision is not intended to suggest the desirability or lack of desirability of a plea agreement in any particular case. . . . A plea disposition in one case may facilitate the prompt disposition of other cases, including cases in which prosecution might otherwise be declined. This may occur simply because prosecutorial, judicial, or defense resources will become available for use in other cases, or because a plea by one of several defendants may have a "domino effect," leading to pleas by other defendants. In weighing the importance of these possible consequences, the attorney for the government should consider the state of the criminal docket and the speedy trial requirements in the district, the desirability of handling a larger volume of criminal cases, and the workloads of prosecutors, judges, and defense attorneys in the district.

3. If a prosecution is to be concluded pursuant to a plea agreement, the defendant should be required to plead to a charge or charges:

(a) that bears a reasonable relationship to the nature and extent of his criminal conduct;

(b) that has an adequate factual basis;

(c) that makes likely the imposition of an appropriate sentence under all the circumstances of the case; and

(d) that does not adversely affect the investigation or prosecution of others.

Comment: [The] considerations that should be taken into account in selecting the charge or charges to which a defendant should be required to plead guilty . . . are essentially the same as those governing the selection of charges to be included in the original indictment or information.

(a) Relationship to criminal conduct — The charge or charges to which a defendant pleads guilty should bear a reasonable relationship to the defendant's criminal conduct, both in nature and in scope. . . . In many cases, this will probably require that the defendant plead to the most serious offense charged. . . . The requirement that a defendant plead to a charge that bears a reasonable relationship to the nature and extent of his criminal conduct is not inflexible. There may be situations involving cooperating defendants in which [lesser charges may be appropriate].

(c) Basis for sentencing — [The] prosecutor should take care to avoid a "charge agreement" that would unduly restrict the court's sentencing authority. [If] restitution is appropriate under the circumstances of the case, a sufficient number of counts should be retained under the agreement to provide a basis for an adequate restitution order. . . .

Notes

1. *The shift away from discretionary sentencing*. Since the early 1980s the federal system and about half of the states have shifted to a more rule-bound sentencing process known as "guideline" or "structured" sentencing. The effect of such laws has been to take away some sentencing discretion from the judge. Sometimes the new laws also created more "determinate" systems that abolished or restricted the use of parole to adjust the sentence to be served. In such a system, the judge announces

the sentence that corresponds closely to the sentence that the offender will actually serve.

2. *Federal sentencing guidelines*. In the Sentencing Reform Act of 1984, Congress designed a radically new sentencing system. In place of the indeterminate sentencing system that allowed judges to choose sentences from a broad range of available outcomes, Congress created a new agency — the United States Sentencing Commission — to draft detailed sentencing guidelines. The U.S. Sentencing Commission, following general statutory guidance, produced a lengthy set of guidelines in 1987. The guidelines direct federal judges in most cases to impose sentences from a much narrower range than before.

Under the sentencing guidelines, the trial judge calculates an "offense level" (ranging on a scale from 1 to 43) to measure the seriousness of the offense, and a "criminal history category" (ranging on a scale from 1 to 6) to account for the offender's prior criminal convictions. To combine these scores, the guidelines create a grid, placing the offense levels on a vertical axis, and the criminal history categories on the horizontal axis. Each combination of the two scores corresponds to one of the 258 boxes in the grid, and each box contains a presumptive sentencing range (expressed as months of imprisonment, such as 51-63 months) for that particular offense level and criminal history score.

The guidelines begin with a "base offense level" for each crime and instruct the judge to adjust that number up or down, in specified amounts, based on specific characteristics of the case. These factors focus mostly on offense information, such as the amount of drugs sold, whether the offender used a gun, or whether the offender played a leading or minor role in a multi-person offense. Because these particular factual findings can have such a clear impact on the sentence, the guidelines have spawned a new kind of bargaining — "fact bargaining" — in which the parties agree to the presence or absence of these relevant sentencing facts in a given case.

The offense levels are based not only on the elements of the offenses charged but also on other activities of the defendant (called "relevant conduct") that are related to the charged offense. Relevant conduct can include uncharged behavior, behavior underlying dismissed charges, and even behavior underlying prior acquittals. For instance, the government might charge a defendant with participating in one sale of a small amount of narcotics, although there is evidence that he participated in larger, related sales. The sentencing judge can consider both the sale that formed the basis for the charge and the uncharged sales in setting the sentence for the crime of conviction. Thus, charge bargains are less likely to have an impact on the ultimate sentence because the sentencing guidelines instruct the judge to consider the underlying conduct regardless of the charges.

Once the judge determines the designated sentencing range under the guidelines, she must also decide whether to "depart" up or down from the narrow range of sentences specified under the guidelines. A sentencing court departing from the guidelines can be overturned on appeal more easily if the ground for departure is not acceptable under the standard of 18 U.S.C. §3553(b) (part of the Sentencing Reform Act). Under that statute, departures may occur only in unusual cases, when "there exists an aggravating or mitigating circumstance of a kind, or to a degree, not adequately taken into consideration by the Sentencing Commission in formulating the guidelines."

The web extension for this chapter, at *http://www.crimpro.com/extension/ch16*, contains worksheets, exercises, and other materials that will familiarize you with basic sentencing guidelines vocabulary and concepts.

3. *Guidance from Main Justice*. The U.S. Department of Justice issued special guidance to prosecutors that appeared simultaneously with the guidelines. Excerpts from the 1987 "Redbook" are reprinted below. Is this internal guidance to prosecutors consistent with the statute and with the policy statements? What changes does it make to the 1980 Principles of Federal Prosecution?

After the first few months of practice under the new sentencing and plea bargaining rules, officials in the Department of Justice believed that federal prosecutors in the field were not adhering closely enough to the department's plea bargaining policies. Consequently, the leadership of the Department (housed in "Main Justice" in Washington, D.C.) revised the 1987 Redbook by issuing the 1989 "Thornburgh Bluesheet," also reprinted below. The revision of the policy was aimed at increasing compliance with the plea practices that the leadership of the department wanted.

4. *Change of administrations*. After the 1992 elections, the incoming Clinton administration appointed new leadership to the Department of Justice. The new Attorney General, Janet Reno, reviewed plea bargaining policies and issued a "Bluesheet" of her own. It is reprinted below. In most districts, this policy was carried out by newly appointed U.S. Attorneys, along with many career attorneys who had also served under the previous administration.

■ U.S. SENTENCING GUIDELINES §§6B1.2, 6B1.4 (POLICY STATEMENTS)

§6B1.2

(a) In the case of a plea agreement that includes the dismissal of any charges or an agreement not to pursue potential charges [under Rule 11(c)(1)(A)], the court may accept the agreement if the court determines, for reasons stated on the record, that the remaining charges adequately reflect the seriousness of the actual offense behavior and that accepting the agreement will not undermine the statutory purposes of sentencing or the sentencing guidelines. Provided, that a plea agreement that includes the dismissal of a charge or a plea agreement not to pursue a potential charge shall not preclude the conduct underlying such charge from being considered under the provisions of §1B1.3 (Relevant Conduct) in connection with the count(s) of which the defendant is convicted.

(b) In the case of a plea agreement that includes a nonbinding recommendation [under Rule 11(c)(1)(B)], the court may accept the recommendation if the court is satisfied either that: (1) the recommended sentence is within the applicable guideline range; or (2) the recommended sentence departs from the applicable guideline range for justifiable reasons.

(c) In the case of a plea agreement that includes a specific sentence [under Rule 11(c)(1)(C)], the court may accept the agreement if the court is satisfied either that: (1) the agreed sentence is within the applicable guideline range; or (2) the agreed sentence departs from the applicable guideline range for justifiable reasons.

§6B1.4

(a) A plea agreement may be accompanied by a written stipulation of facts relevant to sentencing. [Stipulations] shall: (1) set forth the relevant facts and circumstances of the actual offense conduct and offender characteristics; (2) not contain misleading facts; and (3) set forth with meaningful specificity the reasons why the sentencing range resulting from the proposed agreement is appropriate. . . .

(d) The court is not bound by the stipulation, but may with the aid of the presentence report, determine the facts relevant to sentencing.

PROSECUTORS' HANDBOOK ON SENTENCING GUIDELINES ("THE REDBOOK")

William Weld, Assistant Attorney General (1987)

[The] validity and use of the Commission's policy statements by prosecutors should depend upon whether the agreement reflects charge bargaining or sentence bargaining under [Rule 11(c)].

SENTENCE BARGAINING

A significant problem with the Commission's policy statements on plea bargains which include a specific sentence under [Rule 11(c)(1)(B) and (C)], §6B1.2(b) and (c), is that the standard they set forth for acceptance or rejection of a sentence that departs from the guidelines appears to be of doubtful validity under the Sentencing Reform Act (SRA). The standard for departure from the guidelines is set forth in the Act and requires a finding that an aggravating or mitigating circumstance exists that was not adequately taken into consideration by the Commission in formulating the guidelines. Yet the Commission's policy statements relating to sentence bargains authorize departure "for justifiable reasons." We do not believe it is possible to argue that the Commission has not adequately taken into consideration the value of a plea agreement as a mitigating factor so as to support a departure. . . . We recognize, nonetheless, that many judges might be tempted to take a realistic approach; a sentence outside the guidelines in the context of a plea agreement is unlikely to result in an appeal of the sentence. Therefore, if urged to accept a plea agreement that departs from the guidelines, they will follow the policy statements despite their questionable basis.

[Prosecutors] should not recommend or agree to a lower-than-guideline sentence merely on the basis of a plea agreement. They may, however, recommend or agree to a sentence at the low end of an applicable sentencing range [within the guidelines. Departure] from the guidelines may be warranted and may be included in the recommended or agreed-upon sentence if the [statutory standard] is met. That is, a mitigating circumstance must exist (other than the reaching of a plea agreement) that was not adequately taken into consideration by the Commission in formulating the guidelines and that should result in a sentence different from that described. Moreover, a departure from the guidelines may also be reflected in a plea agreement if the defendant provided substantial assistance in the investigation or prosecution of another person who has committed an offense. . . .

The basic reason for rejecting the Commission's policy statements on sentence bargains and treating sentences which are the subject of a sentence bargain in the same manner as sentences which result from conviction after trial is that any other result could seriously thwart the purpose of the SRA to reduce unwarranted disparity in sentencing [among defendants with similar records who have been found guilty of similar criminal conduct].

Charge Bargaining

[It] is our view that moderately greater flexibility legally can and does attach to charge bargains than to sentence bargains. While, as indicated previously, the Commission's quite liberal policy statements on sentence bargaining appear to be inconsistent with the controlling (and stricter) statutory departure standard, the statutory departure standard is not applicable in the charge-bargain context. . . .

Nevertheless, in order to fulfill the objectives of the Sentencing Reform Act prosecutors should conduct charge bargaining in a manner consistent with the direction in the applicable policy statement, §6B1.2(a), i.e., subject to the policy statement's instruction that the "remaining charges [should] adequately reflect the seriousness of the actual offense behavior" and that the agreement not undermine the statutory purposes of sentencing. In our view, this translates into a requirement that readily provable serious charges should not be bargained away. The sole legitimate ground for agreeing not to pursue a charge that is relevant under the guidelines to assure that the sentence will reflect the seriousness of the defendant's "offense behavior" is the existence of real doubt as to the ultimate provability of the charge. Concomitantly, however, the prosecutor is in the best position to assess the strength of the government's case and enjoys broad discretion in making judgments as to which charges are most likely to result in conviction on the basis of the available evidence. . . .

It is appropriate that the sentence for an offender who agrees to plead guilty to relatively few charges should be different from the sentence for an offender convicted of many charges since guilt has not been determined as to the dismissed charges. At the same time, however, sentence bargaining should not result in a vastly different sentence as compared to a sentence following trial. . . . The overriding principle governing the conduct of plea negotiations is that plea agreements should not be used to circumvent the guidelines. . . .

A subsidiary but nonetheless important issue concerns so-called "fact" bargaining or stipulations. [The policy statement §6B1.4] attaches certain conditions to such stipulations. The most important condition, with which the Department concurs, is that stipulations shall "not contain misleading facts." Otherwise, the basic purpose of the SRA to reduce unwarranted sentence disparity will be undermined. Thus, if the defendant can clearly be proved to have used a weapon or committed an assault in the course of the offense, the prosecutor may not stipulate, as part of a plea agreement designed to produce a lower sentence, that no weapon was used or assault committed. If, on the other hand, certain facts surrounding the offense are not clear, e.g., the extent of the loss or injury resulting from the defendant's fraud, the prosecutor is at liberty to stipulate that no loss or injury beyond that clearly provable existed. . . .

■ PLEA POLICY FOR FEDERAL PROSECUTORS ("THORNBURGH BLUESHEET")

Richard Thornburgh, Attorney General (1989)

. . . Department policy requires honesty in sentencing; federal prosecutors are expected to identify for U.S. District Courts departures when they agree to support them. For example, it would be improper for a prosecutor to agree that a departure is in order, but to conceal the agreement in a charge bargain that is presented to a court as a fait accompli so that there is neither a record of nor judicial review of the departure. . . .

The basic policy is that charges are not to be bargained away or dropped, unless the prosecutor has a good faith doubt as to the government's ability readily to prove a charge for legal or evidentiary reasons. It would serve no purpose here to seek to further define "readily provable." The policy is to bring cases that the government should win if there were a trial. There are, however, two exceptions.

First, if the applicable guideline range from which a sentence may be imposed would be unaffected, readily provable charges may be dismissed or dropped as part of a plea bargain. . . . Second, federal prosecutors may drop readily provable charges with the specific approval of the United States Attorney or designated supervisory level official for reasons set forth in the file of the case. This exception recognizes that the aims of the Sentencing Reform Act must be sought without ignoring other, critical aspects of the federal criminal justice system. For example, approval to drop charges in a particular case might be given because the United States Attorney's office is particularly overburdened, the case would be time-consuming to try, and proceeding to trial would significantly reduce the total number of cases disposed of by the office. . . .

The Department's policy is only to stipulate to facts that accurately represent the defendant's conduct. If a prosecutor wishes to support a departure from the guidelines, he or she should candidly do so and not stipulate to facts that are untrue. Stipulations to untrue facts are unethical. If a prosecutor has insufficient facts to contest a defendant's effort to seek a downward departure or to claim an adjustment, the prosecutor can say so. . . .

■ CHARGING AND PLEA DECISIONS ("RENO BLUESHEET")

Janet Reno, Attorney General (1993)

As first stated in the preface to the original 1980 edition of the Principles of Federal Prosecution, "they have been cast in general terms with a view to providing guidance rather than to mandating results. The intent is to assure regularity without regimentation, to prevent unwarranted disparity without sacrificing flexibility."

It should be emphasized that charging decisions and plea agreements should reflect adherence to the Sentencing Guidelines. However, a faithful and honest application of the Sentencing Guidelines is not incompatible with selecting charges or entering into plea agreements on the basis of an individualized assessment of the extent to which particular charges fit the specific circumstances of the case, are consistent with the purposes of the federal criminal code, and maximize the impact of federal resources on crime. Thus, for example, in determining "the most serious offense that is consistent with the nature of the defendant's conduct, that is likely to result in a sustainable conviction," it is appropriate that the attorney for the government consider, inter alia, such factors as the sentencing guideline range yielded by the charge, whether the penalty yielded by such sentencing range (or potential mandatory minimum charge, if applicable) is proportional to the seriousness of the defendant's conduct, and whether the charge achieves such purposes of the criminal law as punishment, protection of the public, specific and general deterrence, and rehabilitation. . . .

To ensure consistency and accountability, charging and plea agreement decisions must be made at an appropriate level of responsibility and documented with an appropriate record of the factors applied.

Notes

1. *The 1992 Terwilliger Bluesheet*. After a few years of experience with the new system, officials in the Department of Justice remained unsatisfied with the plea bargaining practices of its attorneys in the field. In a 1992 revision of the plea bargaining policy, known as the "Terwilliger Bluesheet," the department moved away from an emphasis on describing the types of bargains that are acceptable. Instead, the revised policy strengthened the procedural review process for plea agreements:

> All negotiated plea agreements to felonies or misdemeanors negotiated from felonies shall be in writing and filed with the court. . . . There shall be within each office a formal system for approval of negotiated pleas. The approval authority shall be vested in at least a supervisory criminal Assistant United States Attorney . . . who will have the responsibility of assessing the appropriateness of the plea agreement under the policies of the Department of Justice pertaining to pleas. . . .

The 1992 policy allowed for categorical review of certain plea bargains. Fact situations that "arise with great frequency and are given identical treatment" could be handled through a "written instruction" that "describes with particularity the standard plea procedure to be followed, so long as that procedure is otherwise within Departmental guidelines." The policy listed as an example "a border district which routinely deals with a high volume of illegal alien cases daily." What do you suppose were the effects of these 1992 policy changes? The full texts of the 1987 Redbook, the 1989 Thornburgh Bluesheet, the 1992 Terwilliger Bluesheet, and the 1993 Reno Bluesheet, appear on the web extension for this chapter, at *http://www.crimpro.com/extension/ch16*. The web extension also offers further background on the creation of these policies.

2. *Policies and political accountability*. In response to the Reno Bluesheet, on January 13, 1994, Senator Orrin Hatch (R-Utah), the ranking minority member on the Judiciary Committee, sent Attorney General Janet Reno a letter strongly opposing her directive:

> The Department's new policy now permits prosecutors to make independent decisions about whether a prescribed guideline sentence or mandatory minimum charge is not

"proportional to the seriousness of the defendant's conduct." In other words, this new policy increases the potential for the unwarranted softening of sentences for violent offenders. . . .

I do not support the Department's announcement to drug traffickers and violent criminals that certain illegal conduct may not be charged because a Department employee may find the prescribed punishment too severe. If the Administration believes that existing sentences for drug cases and violent criminals are too severe, then it should seek to change the law or the relevant sentencing guidelines — not ignore them.

Reno responded on March 8, 1994:

[It] remains the directive of the Department of Justice that prosecutors charge the most serious offense that is consistent with the nature of the defendant's conduct, that is likely to result in a sustainable conviction; that prosecutors adhere to the Sentencing Guidelines; and that charging and plea agreements be made at an appropriate level of responsibility with appropriate documentation. In short, contrary to what you suggest, individual prosecutors are not free to follow their own lights or to ignore legislative directives.

3. *Congress reasserts control over federal sentencing*. In 2003 Congress enacted the USA PROTECT Act, Public Law 108-21, 117 Stat. 650. Although the statute dealt primarily with crimes involving child abuse, it also changed several features of federal sentencing law more generally, making downward departures from the sentencing prescribed by the federal guidelines more difficult for judges to invoke. Congress also asked the attorney general to submit a report to the House and Senate Judiciary Committees, detailing the policies the Department would follow to discourage downward departures.

4. *The Ashcroft and Holder memos*. In response to the PROTECT Act, Attorney General John Ashcroft issued policies concerning "sentencing recommendations and sentencing appeals." The policies emphasized "honesty in sentencing, both with respect to the facts and the law." A prosecutor's sentencing recommendations to the court "must honestly reflect the totality and seriousness of the defendant's conduct and must be fully consistent with the Guidelines," regardless of whether the individual prosecutor agrees with the policy embodied in the sentencing guidelines. Two months later, Attorney General Ashcroft issued a second policy statement, this one dealing with selection of charges and plea agreements. The policy is reprinted below.

With the arrival of the Obama administration in 2008, another change in charging and plea bargaining policy issued from Main Justice. Attorney General Eric Holder's statement is also excerpted here. This policy was issued in the context of a series of Supreme Court opinions, such as United States v. Booker, 543 U.S. 220 (2005), and Kimbrough v. United States, 552 U.S. 85 (2007), which loosened the binding effect of the federal sentencing guidelines on the decisions of federal sentencing judges, converting them into "advisory" guidelines.

DEPARTMENT POLICY CONCERNING CHARGING CRIMINAL OFFENSES, DISPOSITION OF CHARGES, AND SENTENCING

John Ashcroft, Attorney General (September 22, 2003)

. . . Just as the sentence a defendant receives should not depend upon which particular judge presides over the case, so too the charges a defendant faces should not depend upon the particular prosecutor assigned to handle the case. . . .

I. Department Policy Concerning Charging and Prosecution of Criminal Offenses

. . . It is the policy of the Department of Justice that, in all federal criminal cases, federal prosecutors must charge and pursue the most serious, readily provable offense or offenses that are supported by the facts of the case, except as authorized by an Assistant Attorney General, United States Attorney, or designated supervisory attorney in the limited circumstances described below. The most serious offense or offenses are those that generate the most substantial sentence under the Sentencing Guidelines, unless a mandatory minimum sentence or count requiring a consecutive sentence would generate a longer sentence. A charge is not "readily provable" if the prosecutor has a good faith doubt, for legal or evidentiary reasons, as to the Government's ability readily to prove a charge at trial. Thus, charges should not be filed simply to exert leverage to induce a plea. . . .

There are, however, certain limited exceptions to this requirement:

1. *Sentence would not be affected.* First, if the applicable guideline range from which a sentence may be imposed would be unaffected, prosecutors may decline to charge or to pursue readily provable charges. [Counts] essential to establish a mandatory minimum sentence must be charged and may not be dismissed, except to the extent provided elsewhere below.

2. *"Fast-track" programs.* [Early disposition or "fast-track" programs allow the Department to handle the high volume of cases (particularly immigration cases) in some districts. As a matter of Department policy, Attorney General authorization is necessary for any fast-track program.] Such programs are intended to be exceptional and will be authorized only when clearly warranted by local conditions within a district. . . .

3. *Post-indictment reassessment.* In cases where post-indictment circumstances cause a prosecutor to determine in good faith that the most serious offense is not readily provable, because of a change in the evidence or some other justifiable reason (*e.g.*, the unavailability of a witness or the need to protect the identity of a witness until he testifies against a more significant defendant), the prosecutor may dismiss the charge(s) with the written or otherwise documented approval of [a supervisory attorney]. . . .

5. *Statutory enhancements.* The use of statutory enhancements is strongly encouraged, and federal prosecutors must therefore take affirmative steps to ensure that the increased penalties resulting from specific statutory enhancements [such as use of a weapon] are sought in all appropriate cases. . . . In many cases, however, the filing of such enhancements will mean that the statutory sentence exceeds the applicable Sentencing Guidelines range, thereby ensuring that the defendant will not

receive any credit for acceptance of responsibility and will have no incentive to plead guilty. [A] supervisory attorney may authorize a prosecutor to forgo the filing of a statutory enhancement, but *only* in the context of a negotiated plea agreement. . . .

6. *Other Exceptional Circumstances.* Prosecutors may decline to pursue or may dismiss readily provable charges in other exceptional circumstances with the [documented approval of a supervisory attorney. Case-specific] approval to dismiss charges in a particular case might be given because the United States Attorney's Office is particularly over-burdened, the duration of the trial would be exceptionally long, and proceeding to trial would significantly reduce the total number of cases disposed of by the office. However, such case-by-case exceptions should be rare; otherwise the goals of fairness and equity will be jeopardized.

II. Department Policy Concerning Plea Agreements

[It] remains Department policy that the sentencing court should be informed if a plea agreement involves a "charge bargain." Accordingly, a negotiated plea that uses any of the options described in Section I(B)(2), . . . (5), or (6) must be made known to the court at the time of the plea hearing and at the time of sentencing, *i.e.*, the court must be informed that a more serious, readily provable offense was not charged or that an applicable statutory enhancement was not filed. . . . Charges may be declined or dismissed pursuant to a plea agreement only to the extent consistent with the principles set forth in Section I of this Memorandum.

[As for sentence bargains], prosecutors may enter into a plea agreement for a sentence that is within the specified guideline range. For example, when the Sentencing Guidelines range is 18-24 months, a prosecutor may agree to recommend a sentence of 18 or 20 months rather than to argue for a sentence at the top of the range. . . .

In passing the PROTECT Act, Congress has made clear its view that there have been too many downward departures from the Sentencing Guidelines. . . . Accordingly, federal prosecutors must not request or accede to a downward departure except in the limited circumstances specified in this memorandum and with authorization from [a supervisory] attorney. . . .

Federal criminal law and procedure apply equally throughout the United States. As the sole federal prosecuting entity, the Department of Justice has a unique obligation to ensure that all federal criminal cases are prosecuted according to the same standards. . . .

DEPARTMENT POLICY ON CHARGING AND SENTENCING

Eric H. Holder, Jr., Attorney General (May 19, 2010)

. . . Decisions about whether to initiate charges, what charges and enhancements to pursue, when to accept a negotiated plea, and how to advocate at sentencing, are among the most fundamental duties of federal prosecutors. For nearly three decades, the Principles of Federal Prosecution, as reflected in Title 9 of the U.S. Attorneys' Manual, Chapter 27, have guided federal prosecutors in the discharge of these duties in particular and in their responsibility to seek justice in the enforcement of the federal criminal laws in general. The purpose of this memorandum is to reaffirm the guidance provided by those Principles.

Persons who commit similar crimes and have similar culpability should, to the extent possible, be treated similarly. Unwarranted disparities may result from disregard for this fundamental principle. They can also result, however, from a failure to analyze carefully and distinguish the specific facts and circumstances of each particular case. Indeed, equal justice depends on individualized justice, and smart law enforcement demands it. Accordingly, decisions regarding charging, plea agreements, and advocacy at sentencing must be made on the merits of each case, taking into account an individualized assessment of the defendant's conduct and criminal history and the circumstances relating to commission of the offense (including the impact of the crime on the victims), the needs of the communities we serve, and federal resources and priorities. Prosecutors must always be mindful of our duty to ensure that these decisions are made without unwarranted consideration of such facts as race, gender, ethnicity, or sexual orientation.

Charging Decisions: Charging decisions should be informed by reason and by the general purposes of criminal law enforcement: punishment, public safety, deterrence, and rehabilitation. These decisions should also reflect the priorities of the Department and of each district. [A] federal prosecutor should ordinarily charge "the most serious offense that is consistent with the nature of the defendant's conduct, and that is likely to result in a sustainable conviction" [USAM 9-27.300]. This determination, however, must always be made in the context of "an individualized assessment of the extent to which particular charges fit the specific circumstances of the case, are consistent with the purpose of the Federal criminal code, and maximize the impact of Federal resources on crime" [USAM 9-27-300]. . . .

All charging decisions must be reviewed by a supervising attorney. All but the most routine indictments should be accompanied by a prosecution memorandum that indentifies the charging options supported by the evidence and the law and explains the charging decision therein. Each office shall promulgate written guidance describing its internal indictment review process.

Plea Agreements: Plea agreements . . . are governed by the same fundamental principle as charging decisions: prosecutors should seek a plea to the most serious offense that is consistent with the nature of the defendant's conduct and likely to result in a sustainable conviction, informed by an individualized assessment of the specific facts and circumstances of each particular case. Charges should not be filed simply to exert leverage to induce a plea. [All plea agreements] must be reviewed by a supervisory attorney. Each office shall promulgate written guidance regarding the standard elements required in its plea agreements, including the waivers of a defendant's rights.

Advocacy at Sentencing: . . . Congress has identified the factors for courts to consider when imposing sentences pursuant to 18 U.S.C. §3553. Consistent with the statute and with the advisory sentencing guidelines as the touchstone, prosecutors should seek sentences that reflect the seriousness of the offense, promote respect for the law, provide just punishment, afford deterrence, protect the public, and offer defendants an opportunity for effect rehabilitation. In the typical case, the appropriate balance among these purposes will continue to be reflected by the applicable guidelines range, and prosecutors should generally continue to advocate for a sentence within that range. [Given] the advisory nature of the guidelines, advocacy at sentencing — like charging decisions and plea agreements — must also follow from an individualized assessment of the facts and circumstances of each particular case. . . .

Notes

1. *Prosecutor plea policies and legislative oversight.* The Ashcroft Memo was intended as a response to Congress's request to reduce the number of downward departures from the federal sentencing guidelines. One distinguishing feature of the memo was the policy decision to equate the criteria for initial selection of charges (Section I of the Memos) and the criteria for evaluating charge bargains (Section II of the Memos). The memo also spotlights the role of supervisor review and documentation of non-guideline sentences. Meanwhile, the Holder Memo attempts to invoke historical precedents within the Department while leaving some room for individualized assessment of charges, plea agreements, and sentencing advocacy. It reflects the shift of the federal guidelines from binding status to advisory status, opening up a range of purposes that charges, plea agreements, and sentencing might serve. The Holder Memo, unlike the Reno Bluesheet, stresses supervisory control and documentation. Like the Ashcroft Memo, it uses consistent criteria in evaluating charges and plea agreements. Further details and evaluation of these Department policies appear on the web extension for this chapter at *http://www.crimpro.com/extension/ch16*.

2. *Written and unwritten guidance.* A striking feature of the plea bargaining policies in the federal system is the fact that they are written. Many other prosecutors' offices in state systems have pursued goals similar to those of the Department of Justice in creating its plea policies. They hope to maintain adequate control over prosecutors in the field and to send appropriate public signals about sentencing and plea bargaining. Nonetheless, within the state systems, such policies are rarely written, even when they are explicit. Why might a supervising prosecutor choose to keep such a critical office policy unwritten?

3. *Uniformity within a jurisdiction.* The federal plea bargaining policies reprinted above apply to U.S. Attorneys' offices throughout the country. While these offices still have a great deal of independence, and vary from one another in their plea bargaining practices, they are still subject to more centralized control than the various prosecutors' offices located throughout a given state. Since prosecutors often create plea bargaining policies for their own offices, shouldn't there be great variety in plea bargaining practices among the different prosecutors within a state? Or are there institutions or incentives that produce similar prosecutorial plea policies throughout a state or even across different states? The following case addresses this topic.

STATE v. CHRISTOPHER BRIMAGE

706 A.2d 1096 (N.J. 1998)

Garibaldi, J.

We are again presented with issues relating to Section 12 of the Comprehensive Drug Reform Act of 1987, N.J.S.A. 2C:35-1 to 36A-1 ("CDRA"). Under N.J.S.A.

2C:35-12 ("Section 12"), a prosecutor may, through a negotiated plea agreement or post-conviction agreement with a defendant, waive the mandatory minimum sentence specified for any offense under the CDRA. To satisfy the constitutional requirements of the separation of powers doctrine, N.J. Const. art. III, ¶1, this Court in State v. Vasquez, 609 A.2d 29 (N.J. 1992), held that prosecutorial discretion under Section 12 must be subject to judicial review for arbitrary and capricious action. To further that review, the Court held that prosecutors must adhere to written guidelines governing plea offers and state on the record their reasons for waiving or not waiving the parole disqualifier in any given case.

In response to that holding, the Attorney General promulgated plea agreement guidelines. . . . Although the Guidelines prescribe statewide minimum plea offers, they also direct each county prosecutor's office to adopt its own written plea agreement policy. . . . We must determine whether the Attorney General's Plea-Bargaining Guidelines are adequate to satisfy the separation of powers doctrine, as enunciated in *Vasquez*, and to meet the statutory goals of uniformity in sentencing.

I.

On May 12, 1995, the Franklin Township Police, armed with a search warrant, conducted a search of the Brimage residence. According to defendant's statements at the plea hearing, during the search defendant turned over to the police eighteen bags of cocaine totaling about six grams. . . . Defendant's residence was within 1000 feet of Franklin Township High School. In September 1995, defendant was indicted under the CDRA for possession of a controlled dangerous substance with intent to distribute . . . ; possession of a controlled dangerous substance with intent to distribute within 1000 feet of school property, contrary to N.J.S.A. 2C:35-7; and possession of a controlled dangerous substance, . . . all third degree offenses. . . .

The Somerset County Prosecutor's Office offered, in exchange for defendant's guilty plea, to recommend the presumptive sentence for a third degree crime — four years incarceration — plus the mandatory three-year period of parole ineligibility specified in N.J.S.A. 2C:35-7 for the school zone offense. The prosecutor proffered the following reasons for not waiving the parole ineligibility term of N.J.S.A. 2C:35-7: the proofs available to sustain a conviction of defendant were very strong, including defendant's taped confession that he intended to sell cocaine for profit; defendant did not offer to cooperate in any other drug-related investigations; and the Somerset County Prosecutor's Office had sufficient resources to litigate this matter, unlike various other counties that were plagued with a lack of resources or with case management problems. . . .

Defendant then accepted the prosecutor's original plea agreement offer and pled guilty to all counts in the indictment, although he reserved the right to challenge the validity of the Guidelines and the applicability of the mandatory three-year parole disqualifier to his case. [At the hearing on his motion for waiver of the mandatory minimum sentence, Brimage] argued that the standard plea offer required by the Attorney General's Guidelines for a school zone offense was . . . probation conditioned on 364 days in county jail . . . and that the prosecutor acted arbitrarily and capriciously by not making that offer to defendant. . . . Finding that nonwaiver of the mandatory parole disqualifier was standard policy in Somerset County for school zone cases and that the Guidelines' lesser plea offer was only applicable when the prosecutor in his discretion decided to waive that disqualifier, the court denied defendant's motion. [The] court sentenced defendant to four years imprisonment with three years of parole ineligibility, in accordance with the prosecutor's recommendation. . . .

II.

. . . N.J.S.A. 2C:35-7 of the CDRA ("Section 7") requires a mandatory minimum custodial sentence between one-third and one-half of the sentence imposed, but no less than three years for those convicted of dispensing or possessing with the intent to distribute drugs within a school zone. [The] Legislature's intention, as stated in its Declaration of Policy and Legislative Findings for the CDRA, [was] to "provide for the strict punishment, deterrence and incapacitation of the most culpable and dangerous drug offenders." N.J.S.A. 2C:35-1.1(c). To foster that policy, the Legislature included in the CDRA mandatory periods of parole ineligibility for various crimes.

Despite the nondiscretionary nature of N.J.S.A. 2C:35-7, that section, like other mandatory parole bar provisions in the CDRA, contemplates exceptions to its rule as provided by N.J.S.A. 2C:35-12 ("Section 12"). Section 12 allows a prosecutor to waive the period of parole ineligibility imposed under Section 7 as part of a plea or post-conviction agreement with a defendant. . . .

The primary purpose of the Section 12 waiver provision is to provide an incentive for defendants, especially lower and middle level drug offenders, to cooperate with law enforcement agencies in the war against drugs. Another goal of N.J.S.A. 2C:35-12, as enunciated in the Department of Law and Public Safety's report on the CDRA, is to encourage plea bargaining so as not to plague the courts with too many defendants who, without any incentive to plead guilty, demand jury trials and thus overburden and backlog the system. . . .

To achieve the Legislature's specific goal of encouraging cooperation and turning State's evidence and to prevent sentencing courts from undermining the effectiveness of prosecutors' strategies, N.J.S.A. 2C:35-12 requires the sentencing court to enforce all agreements reached by the prosecutor and a defendant under that section and prohibits the court from imposing a lesser term of imprisonment than that specified in the agreement. That shift in sentencing power from the judiciary to the prosecutor is uncommon. . . .

As a result of the atypical grant of sentencing power to the prosecutor in N.J.S. A. 2C:35-12, that statute has been the subject of various constitutional challenges on separation of powers grounds. We first considered the interaction of Section 7 and Section 12 in [State v. Vasquez.] In *Vasquez*, . . . we upheld the transfer of sentencing authority under Section 12, but stated that judicial oversight was "mandated to protect against arbitrary and capricious prosecutorial decisions." To enable judicial review, we required prosecutors to state on the record their reasons for waiving or not waiving the parole disqualifier in any given case and to promulgate written guidelines governing their exercise of discretion. [Only] those defendants who showed "clearly and convincingly that the exercise of discretion was arbitrary and capricious would be entitled to relief." . . .

THE GUIDELINES

In response to this Court's ruling in *Vasquez*, on September 15, 1992 the Attorney General promulgated plea agreement guidelines for charges brought under the

Comprehensive Drug Reform Act. . . . Recognizing the various goals of the Legislature in enacting the CDRA as well as the intentions of the Court in *Vasquez,* the Introduction to the 1992 Guidelines states: "In order to satisfy the principal goal of the Legislature to ensure a uniform, consistent and predictable sentence for a given offense, these decisions require that the prosecutorial decision-making process must be guided by uniform standards that channel the exercise of discretion and reduce the danger of uneven application." . . .

The Guidelines continue by asserting that the "specified mandatory term of imprisonment and minimum term of parole ineligibility" should be treated as norms and that prosecutors "should exercise caution and reluctance in deciding whether to waive the minimum sentence or parole ineligibility."§II.1. More specifically, in Section II.3 of those Guidelines, the Attorney General requires that all plea agreements for a CDRA offense impose on defendants a mandatory minimum term of incarceration, except where the agreement is or was necessary to obtain cooperation of "substantial value" to the State. That term must be a state prison term, except in the case of a school zone offense under N.J.S.A. 2C:35-7. The 1992 version of the Guidelines provides that the "minimum term of imprisonment for a school zone offense shall include the imposition of 364 days incarceration in a county jail as a condition of probation". . . . In Section II.9, the Guidelines specify various requirements for cooperation agreements. Finally, in Section II.5, the Guidelines outline criteria for deciding whether to approve or disapprove a plea agreement that incorporates an upward or downward departure from any plea agreement policy.

Despite those specific provisions in the Guidelines, Section II.4 directs each county prosecutor's office to adopt and implement its own written policy governing plea and post-conviction agreements, using the Guidelines as a model, and suggests that the counties may also promulgate their own "standardized plea offers for typical cases and offenders." The Guidelines state that the counties, in formulating those plea offers, may consider certain factors such as the nature and extent of the drug distribution and use problem, the number and type of drug arrests in the jurisdiction, and the backlog of drug and non-drug cases in the courts. They should also consider the seriousness of the offense, the role of the actor in the crime, the amount of time that has passed since the offense was committed, whether the defendant has previously been convicted of an offense, and the amount of resources already expended on the particular case. Finally, Section II.4 specifically states that "nothing contained in these guidelines shall preclude a prosecutor from adopting more stringent policies or standardized plea offers consistent with the needs, resources and enforcement priorities of each county." . . .

Although the Introduction to the Guidelines recognizes the need to "guard against sentencing disparity," the Guidelines actually generated such disparity. The inter-county disparity created by the Guidelines is evidenced in the actual policies that have been adopted throughout the jurisdictions. . . . Although the standard plea offer in Gloucester and Hudson Counties [for a person in Brimage's situation] would have been probation with 364 days in jail, the pre-indictment offer in Mercer and Salem Counties was one year without parole. Meanwhile, the plea in Camden and Cumberland Counties would have been three years flat and three to five years flat, respectively. . . .

THE SUPPLEMENTAL DIRECTIVE

Subsequent to Brimage's plea, the Attorney General issued additional guidelines in its 1997 Supplemental Directive; however, the Supplemental Directive fails to limit the discretion authorized by Section II.4 and thus maintains the resulting inter-county disparity. The Supplemental Directive was developed in response to Governor Christine Todd Whitman's Drug Enforcement, Education and Awareness Program, which required the Attorney General to issue new, revised guidelines concerning prosecutorial charging, case disposition, and plea bargaining policies to ensure that the CDRA is aggressively and uniformly enforced in court. The Supplemental Directive mandates, among other requirements, that each county reduce its plea policies to writing and review the policies at least once a year; that downward departures shall not be permitted except as provided in the Attorney General's Guidelines; that both downward and upward departures and all cooperation agreements shall be memorialized in writing; . . . and that offenders may be sentenced to treatment in lieu of imprisonment only if they meet a long list of explicit conditions. [While] the Directive states that the Guidelines are "intended and shall hereinafter be interpreted to establish drug prosecution policies that must be followed by every county prosecutor's office," the Directive nevertheless permits each county to adopt its own standards pursuant to Section II.4. . . .

III.

By permitting each county to adopt its own standard plea offers and policies, neither the former nor the current Guidelines serve as the universal, equitable prototype that the *Vasquez* line of cases had in mind. Although the guidelines adopted within each county may avoid arbitrariness with respect to decision-making among individual prosecutors, and while we concede that some disparity in sentencing is inevitable in the administration of criminal justice, the formalization of disparity from county to county is clearly impermissible. The inter-county disparity authorized by the Attorney General's Guidelines, both before and after their amendment, violates the goals of uniformity in sentencing and, thus, not only fails on statutory grounds, but also threatens the balance between prosecutorial and judicial discretion that is required under *Vasquez*. The Guidelines fail to appropriately channel prosecutorial discretion, thus leading to arbitrary and unreviewable differences between different localities. . . .

Accordingly, to meet the requirements of the *Vasquez* line of cases, the plea agreement guidelines for N.J.S.A. 2C:35-12 must be consistent throughout the State. [Prosecutors] must be guided by specific, universal standards in their waiver of mandatory minimum sentences under the CDRA.

Although the record does not indicate that the availability of county resources has been a significant factor in causing sentencing disparity between the counties, we recognize . . . the need for some flexibility among the different counties and some accommodation of local concerns and differences. The Declaration of Policy for the CDRA states that one of the goals of the Act is to "ensure the most efficient and effective dedication of limited investigative, prosecutorial, judicial and correctional resources," N.J.S.A. 2C:35-1.1. [Using] the waiver power to advance this legislative goal would not be an abuse of power. Consistent with that authority, we believe that differences in available county resources as well as varying backlog and caseload situations are legitimate factors that prosecutors may consider in deciding whether or not to waive a mandatory minimum sentence under N.J.S.A. 2C:35-12. However, before a prosecutor may take any such factors into account, those factors must be explicitly set forth in . . . the Attorney General's Guidelines, just as the requirements for cooperation agreements are precisely and distinctly enumerated. Although . . . flexibility among the prosecutors of different counties may sometimes be necessary, that does not justify the adoption of different guidelines in every county in contravention of the goals of uniformity and the *Vasquez* line of cases. Any flexibility on the basis of resources or local differences must be provided for and explicitly detailed within uniform, statewide guidelines. . . .

We therefore order the Attorney General to review and promulgate, within ninety days, new plea offer guidelines, which all counties must follow. . . . The new guidelines should specify permissible ranges of plea offers for particular crimes and should be more explicit regarding permissible bases for upward and downward departures. The Attorney General may, if he chooses, provide for differences in treatment among various offenders based on specific factors of flexibility among the counties, such as resources or backlog, in certain circumstances. As in all plea offers, the individual characteristics of the crime and of the defendant, such as whether the defendant is a first or second time offender, must be considered. Finally, to permit effective judicial review, prosecutors must state on the record their reasons for choosing to waive or not to waive the mandatory minimum period of parole ineligibility specified in the statute. Additionally, for proper judicial review, if a prosecutor departs from the guidelines, the reasons for such departure must be clearly stated on the record. . . .

Problem 16-3. Statewide Bargaining Guidelines

Soon after the New Jersey Supreme Court issued its decision in *Brimage*, the state attorney general issued a 64-page set of "*Brimage* Guidelines." The drafters patterned their prosecutor guidelines after judicial sentencing guidelines, including a grid laying out the offense seriousness on a vertical axis and the defendant's criminal history on a horizontal axis. Each box of the grid showed three different plea agreements a prosecutor might offer, with more favorable outcomes going to those defendants accepting offers earlier before the start of trial.

The immediate effect of the guidelines was probably an increase in the seriousness of drug charges that urban defendants faced. The more severe charging practices of the less urban counties became more standard across the state, and the guidelines left urban prosecutors less room to negotiate in the initial filing of charges or in the disposition of cases.

A few years later, a new state attorney general considered potential changes in the *Brimage* Guidelines. After consultations with county prosecutors, defense attorneys, and judges, the attorney general became concerned about the fairness of sentences in cases involving drug sales in school zones. The urban-suburban divide (and thus a racial divide) was stark for these crimes. In most urban areas, virtually all drug sales happened within 1,000 feet of a school; in less densely populated parts of the state, many more drug sales happened outside the 1,000-foot boundary.

The new attorney general is now considering revised guidelines that depend less on the crime of conviction. The plea agreements that prosecutors would be authorized to offer account for more specific offense characteristics (such as the amount of drugs and the presence of a weapon) and offender characteristics (such as gang membership or prior criminal record). The revisions also increase the minimum "authorized plea offers" available in cases involving defendants who carry or use weapons, while making more lenient offers possible for other drug defendants with prior records, or those who sold drugs near a school but presented no particular threat of violence. Prosecutors could also "depart" from the presumptive charge or disposition that is preferred under the guidelines if the evidence in the case is weak or if the defendant offers cooperation in other cases.

Suppose you are advising the attorney general. Who is likely to support or oppose this collection of policy changes? What arguments will they present? See *http://www.state.nj.us/lps/dcj/pdfs/agdir.pdf*.

Problem 16-4. Sharkfest

In one county in Arizona, most of the plea bargaining takes place during what defense attorneys call "Sharkfest." On a designated day each week, the deputy county attorneys, deputy public defenders, and a few private defense attorneys gather in one large room. The location of Sharkfest alternates between the county attorney's office and the public defender's office.

Each defense attorney pulls out an open case file, finds the deputy county attorney assigned to the case, argues over the facts and the legal issues, and inquires about possible plea agreements. As the prosecutor and defense attorney make their arguments to one another, their colleagues might be listening — although they might also be engaged in their own negotiations at that moment — and chime in with their own thoughts. Colleagues might comment on the facts, note a similar case the attorney had in the past and the resolution to that case, or mention applicable case law. The defense attorneys generally rely on the input of their colleagues more often than the prosecutors do. The prosecutors generally operate within office policies about acceptable plea agreements, and must resolve the case within parameters set forth by the "charging department," unless new information about the case comes to light during the negotiation.

After the two attorneys reach a potential plea agreement in a case, but before the defense attorney can take that plea bargain to her client, the prosecutor takes the proposed plea bargain to the chief deputy county attorney for approval. Because there is only one chief deputy county attorney in the office, much of the attorney time spent at Sharkfest involves waiting for him to make his way around the room.

What motivates prosecutors and public defenders to attend Sharkfest every week? Why don't more private defense counsel attend? How might the results of Sharkfest resemble the results one might obtain from a carefully crafted set of written office guidelines for plea bargaining?

Notes

1. *Uniformity in guidelines.* The New Jersey decision in *Brimage* is unusual; courts do not often order prosecutors to create statewide policies on questions of plea bargaining or requests for sentencing enhancements. Prosecutors themselves do

not often create statewide guidelines for such matters, either. Instead, it is more common to find policies about plea bargaining and related matters set at the local office level. See Pamela Utz, Settling the Facts (1978) (comparing practices in California jurisdictions).

How are prosecutors likely to respond to a judicial requirement that they create statewide guidelines? Is there such a thing as too much uniformity from office to office? Within a single office? See State v. Pettitt, 609 P.2d 1364 (Wash. 1980) (striking down prosecutor's office policy mandating the filing of habitual criminal complaints against any defendant who had three or more prior felonies as abuse of discretion where policy resulted in mandatory life sentence for a defendant with three nonviolent property crimes).

2. *Priority crimes.* Prosecutorial office policies on plea bargaining often restrict the power of the individual prosecutor to negotiate terms for a select group of high-priority crimes. While the line prosecutors remain free to reach plea agreements in less serious cases (which are by far the most numerous), the guidelines prohibit dismissal of charges or sentencing concessions in cases involving violent crimes such as murder, rape, or armed robbery. Alternatively, in such cases the guidelines may require special justifications for plea agreements or may limit the acceptable bargaining outcomes. How do supervising prosecutors choose the priority crimes that will be subject to these special bargaining limitations? Do they take their cues from crime legislation and limit bargaining whenever the legislature has emphasized the importance of a crime by enhancing its penalty? See Milton Heumann & Colin Loftin, Mandatory Sentencing and the Abolition of Plea Bargaining: The Michigan Felony Firearm Statute, 13 Law & Soc'y Rev. 393 (1979) (evaluating mandatory-minimum-sentence statute for firearms cases, and contemporaneous county prosecutor's no-plea-bargaining policy for crimes charged under the statute).

3. *Internal review.* One common prosecutorial policy on plea bargaining is procedural rather than substantive. Instead of banning plea bargains for some crimes or limiting the outcomes that a prosecutor can accept in certain cases, these policies simply require the line prosecutor to obtain approval from a supervisor (or some committee of supervisors) before entering a plea agreement. See Richard Kuh, Plea Bargaining: Guidelines for the Manhattan District Attorney's Office, 11 Crim. L. Bull. 48 (1975) (supervisor review for proposed agreements reducing charges to extent greater than ordinarily allowed under office policy). The web extension for this chapter, at *http://www.crimpro.com/extension/ch16*, offers examples of such office policies regarding plea negotiations.

4. *Victim Consultation*

Many prosecutors feel obliged to inform crime victims about their efforts to negotiate a guilty plea. But only recently have legal provisions and institutions reinforced this sense of obligation. Over the past generation, a majority of states have enacted statutes and constitutional provisions requiring prosecutors to inform or consult the victims of alleged crimes about any plea agreements in their case. These laws differ in the type of information the victim and the prosecutor must exchange and in the timing of the exchange. But they share the assumption that the involvement of a crime victim will change the outcomes in at least some plea negotiations. Will the timing of the victim's involvement make a difference in many plea negotiations?

MAINE REVISED STATUTES TIT. 15, §812; TIT. 17-A, §§1172, 1173

TITLE 15, §812

1. The Legislature finds that there is citizen dissatisfaction with plea bargaining which has resulted in some criticism of the criminal justice process. The Legislature further finds that part of the dissatisfaction is caused because victims of crimes and law enforcement officers who respond to those crimes have no subsequent contact with the cases as they proceed through the courts for judicial disposition. Victims and law enforcement officers are many times not informed by prosecutors of plea agreements which are to be submitted to the court for approval or rejection. . . . It is the intent of this section to alleviate these expressions of citizen dissatisfaction and to promote greater understanding by prosecutors of citizens' valid concerns. This is most likely to be accomplished by citizens and law enforcement officers being informed of the results of plea negotiations before they are submitted to the courts. This notification will in no way affect the authority of the judge to accept, reject or modify the terms of the plea agreement.

2. Before submitting a negotiated plea to the court, the attorney for the State shall advise the relevant law enforcement officers of the details of the plea agreement reached in any prosecution where the defendant was originally charged with murder, a Class A, B or C crime or [an assault crime, sex offense, or kidnapping,] and shall advise victims of their rights under Title 17-A, section 1173.

TITLE 17-A, §1172

1. When practicable, the attorney for the State shall make a good faith effort to inform each victim of a crime of the following: A) the details of a plea agreement before it is submitted to the court; B) the right to comment on the plea agreement pursuant to section 1173; C) the time and place of the trial; D) the time and place of sentencing; and E) the right to participate at sentencing. . . .

TITLE 17-A, §1173

When a plea agreement is submitted to the court . . . , the attorney for the State shall disclose to the court any and all attempts made to notify each victim of the plea agreement and any objection to the plea agreement by a victim. A victim who is present in court at the submission of the plea may address the court at that time.

STATE v. PATRICK WILLIAM CASEY

44 P.3d 756 (Utah 2002)

DURRANT, J.

¶1 The central issue presented in this appeal is whether the district court deprived M.R., a victim of sexual abuse, of his constitutional and statutory right to be heard at defendant's change of plea hearing. . . .

¶3 On November 3, 1999, the Tooele County Attorney's Office charged defendant with aggravated sexual abuse of a child, a first degree felony. . . . Following a preliminary hearing in which both the victim, M.R., and his mother testified, the district court bound defendant over for trial.

¶4 A few weeks later the prosecutor handling defendant's case sent M.R.'s mother a letter explaining that defendant had requested a plea bargain. After receiving this letter, M.R.'s mother, according to her affidavit, met with the prosecutor and obtained an assurance that the first degree felony charge would not be reduced due to the strong evidence of guilt compiled against defendant.

¶5 Nevertheless, the prosecutor subsequently offered to reduce the first degree felony charge to lewdness involving a child, a class A misdemeanor, in return for a guilty plea. M.R.'s mother, upon learning of the State's extension of this offer and defendant's acceptance, contacted the prosecutor and expressed a desire to tell the district court how her family, including M.R., felt about the proposed plea. The prosecutor advised her to attend the change of plea hearing scheduled for October 24, 2000.

¶6 M.R. and his mother appeared at this change of plea hearing as directed. At a recess during this proceeding, M.R.'s mother approached the prosecutor, objected to the reduced charge, and reiterated M.R.'s, and her own, desire to make a statement. She later testified that she believed the prosecutor was going to inform the district court of her request. . . .

¶7 Notwithstanding his conversations with M.R.'s mother, the prosecutor did not inform the district court that M.R. and his mother had requested to be heard at the change of plea hearing. M.R. and his mother also failed to bring the issue to the court's attention. The court therefore proceeded with defendant's change of plea hearing unaware of M.R.'s request. Noting the "dramatic" reduction in the charge, the court refused to be limited to the four-month sentence recommended in the stipulated plea agreement. The State and defendant responded to the court's concern by agreeing to delete the stipulated sentence provision. The court then accepted defendant's guilty plea to the class A misdemeanor charge and set the matter for sentencing.

¶8 Subsequently, M.R.'s mother, acting on behalf of M.R., obtained legal assistance and filed two motions with the district court: a motion for a misplea and a motion to reject the plea bargain. In response, the prosecutor and defendant filed separate motions to strike M.R.'s pleadings, claiming that M.R. lacked standing to set aside the plea because he was not a party to the criminal proceeding.

¶9 Without ruling on whether M.R. had standing to challenge defendant's guilty plea, the district court held defendant's sentencing hearing on November 27, 2000. At the start of this hearing, M.R.'s counsel moved the court to set aside the accepted plea. . . .

¶10 M.R. and his mother testified that the court should have rejected the plea bargain. Specifically, M.R. declared, "I don't think it's right that defendant gets that less of a plea agreement because of what he's done. He's done it to me . . . and . . . he's hurt my whole family." M.R.'s mother testified that "the court should reject the plea bargain because a misdemeanor sentence did not truly reflect the seriousness of the offenses committed by defendant the same way that a felony conviction would." . . .

¶11 . . . M.R.'s counsel argued that the Victims' Rights Amendment of the Utah Constitution placed M.R. on equal footing with defendant and envisioned that M.R. could employ an attorney in exercising his legal rights. M.R.'s counsel then argued that (1) M.R. had the right to be heard before the court's acceptance of defendant's plea, (2) M.R.'s right to be heard had been violated, and (3) the court should grant a misplea and hear from M.R. before accepting any subsequent plea between the State and defendant. . . .

¶12 [The] court decided to "informally" reopen the plea hearing in order to accept the testimony that it had just heard from M.R. and his mother. Having accepted this testimony, the court "reaffirmed" defendant's plea at the class A level. The court then denied both of M.R.'s pending motions, sentenced defendant to eight months in jail on the class A misdemeanor charge, and fined him.

¶14 On appeal, M.R., by and through his legal guardian, contends that (1) he had the right to seek appellate review of the district court's adverse rulings on his two motions, (2) he had the right to be heard through counsel with respect to legal issues related to the constitutional and statutory rights afforded him as a victim, (3) he had a constitutional and statutory right to be heard regarding the appropriateness of the plea bargain, (4) he properly invoked his right to be heard at defendant's change of plea hearing by submitting a request to the prosecutor, and (5) the court, through the negligence of the prosecutor, denied him his right to be heard by accepting the plea bargain without hearing from him. . . .

¶18 In 1987, the Utah Legislature enacted the Victims' Rights Act. See Utah Code Ann. §§77-37-1 to -5. This statute included, among other things, a bill of rights for victims, and declared that these rights must be "protected in a manner no less vigorous than protections afforded criminal defendants."§77-37-1. The Utah Legislature then passed the Victims' Rights Amendment, which was ratified by Utah citizens. . . . Utah Const. art. I, §28. This constitutional amendment bestowed specific rights upon crime victims and gave the Utah Legislature the power to "enforce and define [its terms] by statute." Acting pursuant to this authority, the Utah Legislature subsequently enacted the Rights of Crime Victims Act. Utah Code Ann. §§77-38-1 to -14. This act elaborated upon the rights afforded crime victims under the Victims' Rights Amendment and defined several terms included in the amendment. . . .

¶21 Applying the principles outlined above, we first address whether M.R. had the right to appeal the district court's rulings regarding his right to be heard. The Victims' Rights Amendment does not address the question of M.R.'s right to appeal decisions impacting his right to be heard. The Rights of Crime Victims Act is on point, however, and we conclude that M.R. had the right to seek appellate review pursuant to the plain meaning of that statute.

¶22 We resolve this issue under a plain meaning analysis for two reasons. First, subsection 77-38-11(2)(b) explicitly provides that adverse rulings on a motion or request "brought by a victim of a crime . . . may be appealed under the rules governing appellate actions, provided that no appeal shall constitute grounds for delaying any criminal . . . proceeding." Second, subsection 77-38-11(2)(c) of the Utah Code declares that an appellate court "shall review all such properly presented issues, including issues that are capable of repetition but would otherwise evade review." In short, these two provisions demonstrate (1) that crime victims possess the right to appeal rulings on motions related to their rights as a victim and (2) that an appellate court must review appeals of such a nature. Accordingly, M.R.'s appeal is properly before us.

¶23 We next address whether M.R. had the right to be heard at defendant's change of plea hearing. . . . In pertinent part, the Victims' Rights Amendment states as follows: "To preserve and protect victims' rights to justice and due process, victims of crimes have [the right, upon request, to be] heard at important criminal justice hearings related to the victim, either in person or through a lawful representative, once a criminal information or indictment charging a crime has been publicly filed in court." Utah Const. art. I, §28(1)(b). Using comparable language, section 77-38-4 of the Rights of Crime Victims Act similarly declares that the victim of a crime "shall have . . . the right to be heard at . . . important criminal . . . justice hearings."

¶25 [The] question that arises is what constitutes an "important criminal justice hearing" under the Victims' Rights Amendment and the Utah Code. Section 77-38-2 of the Rights of Crime Victims Act answers this question with respect to both the Utah Constitution and the Utah Code; it defines "important criminal justice hearings" involving the disposition of charges in this way: "For the purposes of this chapter and the Utah Constitution, important criminal justice hearings [means] any court proceeding involving the disposition of charges against a defendant [except for] unanticipated proceedings to take an admission or a plea of guilty as charged to all charges previously filed or any plea taken at an initial appearance." . . .

¶26 Here, the change of plea hearing conducted by the district court fell within the definition of an important criminal justice hearing because it disposed of a first degree felony charge filed against defendant in return for a guilty plea on a class A misdemeanor. Further, neither exception applied because the hearing was not an initial appearance and the defendant did not accept responsibility for the first degree felony charge previously filed. . . .

¶27 While it is clear that the Utah Constitution and the Utah Code afforded M.R. the right to be heard upon request at defendant's change of plea hearing, neither the constitution nor the code mandates how M.R.'s request must be submitted. Relying on the Victims' Rights Act and the Rights of Crime Victims Act, M.R. argues that a request to be heard at a plea hearing suffices if it is submitted either to the district court or to the prosecutor. The State contends that the two statutes require a crime victim to petition the court directly. . . .

¶28 We begin our analysis with the Victims' Rights Amendment. This constitutional provision merely notes that the right to be heard is activated "upon request." Utah Const. art. I, §28(b). . . . The Victims' Rights Act states that victims have the "right to be informed and assisted as to their role in the criminal justice process," and all criminal justice agencies have "the duty to provide this information and assistance." Utah Code Ann. §77-37-3(1)(b). Additionally, the Victims' Rights Act declares that victims have a "right to clear explanations regarding relevant legal proceedings," and all "criminal justice agencies have the duty to provide these explanations." Id. §77-37-3(1)(c). Because prosecutors are a component of the criminal justice system and the Victims' Rights Act applies to "all criminal justice agencies," the aforementioned duties necessarily fall upon prosecutors. . . .

¶30 We further conclude that a prosecutor's obligation to provide "assistance" to the victim should mean, at a minimum, that a victim may submit a request to be heard at a plea hearing to a prosecutor and expect that the request will be forwarded to the court. Likewise, a prosecutor's obligation to provide a "clear explanation" of events occurring at a plea hearing should mean that a victim can rely on a prosecutor's statement indicating he or she will convey a request to be heard to the district court. . . .

¶32 In addition to having a duty to convey requests to be heard under the Victims' Rights Act and the Rights of Crime Victims Act, prosecutors also have a duty to convey requests to be heard as officers of the court. Prosecutors must convey such requests because they are obligated to alert the court when they know that the court lacks relevant information. This duty, which is incumbent upon all attorneys, is magnified for prosecutors because, as our case law has repeatedly noted, prosecutors have unique responsibilities. Specifically, a prosecutor is a minister of justice, possessing duties that rise above those of privately employed attorneys. The prosecutor "is the representative not of an ordinary party to a controversy, but of a sovereignty whose obligation to govern impartially is as compelling as its obligation to govern at all; and whose interest . . . in a criminal prosecution is not that it shall win . . . but that justice shall be done." State v. Emmett, 839 P.2d 781, 787 (Utah 1992). . . .

¶38 Based on the prosecutor's failure to relay M.R.'s request to be heard, the district court initially deprived M.R. of his right to speak at the change of plea hearing. At defendant's sentencing hearing, however, the court learned of M.R.'s earlier desire to be heard. The court then permitted M.R. and his mother to take the stand and testify regarding the appropriateness of defendant's plea bargain. The court also permitted extensive argument by M.R.'s counsel. Restricted in no respect by the court, all three individuals claimed that the plea bargain should have been rejected. After hearing this testimony and argument, the court "informally" reopened defendant's change of plea hearing and accepted the testimony that it had just heard from M.R. and his mother. The court then reaffirmed defendant's plea at the Class A level.

¶39 By taking these steps, the district court remedied its initial denial of M.R.'s right to be heard. Our conclusion is based on the following rationale. First, we note that the plea was subject to review up until the time of sentencing. Accordingly, in exercising its power to reopen the plea, the court permitted M.R. to be heard at a time when he could have persuaded the court to reject the proposed plea. Second, the record clearly demonstrates that the court reaffirmed the plea only after having accepted M.R.'s and his mother's testimony, and permitting argument by his counsel.

¶40 Thus, although M.R. was entitled to be heard at defendant's change of plea hearing, we conclude that he has enjoyed the fruits of the right he now claims he was denied. Accordingly, we hold that the district court, to its credit, cured the error initially committed at the change of plea hearing and honored M.R.'s right to be heard as soon as it discovered M.R. wished to be heard.[14] . . .

WILKINS, J., concurring:

. . . ¶44 [When] the trial court was finally informed of M.R.'s desire to be heard, it was clearly insufficient for the trial court to "informally" reopen the change of plea hearing and "consider" M.R.'s concerns before summarily reaffirming the "accepted" plea. Doing so merely compounded the error invited by the prosecution in failing to promptly inform the court of M.R.'s initial request to be heard at the change of plea hearing. [The] defendant's plea had not yet been finally accepted at

14. Because the district court upheld M.R.'s right to be heard in the present case, we decline to address what remedies are available for the hypothetical denial of a victim's right to be heard. We do note, however, that the Utah Legislature established a framework in which only three remedies were provided for the violation of a victim's right: injunctive relief, declaratory relief, and writ of mandamus. Utah Code Ann. §§77-38-11(1)-(2)(i). [Even] if the declaration of a misplea were assumed to be an available remedy, such a declaration would raise constitutional issues regarding the double jeopardy clauses of both the United States Constitution and the Utah Constitution.

the time the trial court became aware of M.R.'s desire to be heard on the matter. The correct course would have been for the trial court to reopen the hearing, after notice to all concerned.

¶46 The constitutional provisions granting M.R. his right to be heard, however, also limit this right. Subsection (2) of the Victims' Rights Amendment, Article I, Section 28 of the Utah Constitution, specifically prohibits construing the rights afforded M.R. in such a way as to provide "relief from any criminal judgment." The defendant's plea, once accepted by the court and sentence imposed, is a criminal judgment. Consequently, once the trial court accepted defendant's plea and entered the judgment of sentence on the plea, M.R.'s rights as a victim could not result in the "misplea" M.R. sought. Only while the plea was still not final, that is, prior to the entry of sentence, could M.R.'s motion for misplea have been granted on the basis of M.R. having been denied his constitutional right to speak at the change of plea hearing.

¶47 A second difficulty is created by the provisions of the Rights of Crime Victims Act, Utah Code Ann. §77-38-11(2)(b), that authorize appellate review of an adverse ruling by the trial court on M.R.'s motions, but specifically provide that no such appeal "shall constitute grounds for delaying any criminal . . . proceeding." When juxtaposed with the rights of the criminal defendant to a speedy trial and the necessity to move forward with the criminal process despite an otherwise valid appeal by a victim, appellate relief for M.R. is a practical impossibility. Moreover, the same statute limits M.R.'s remedies to injunctive relief, declaratory relief, and writ of mandamus. If the criminal action proceeds, and if the victim is denied his or her constitutional right to address the court, the victim has little hope of a meaningful remedy. While the criminal proceeding moves forward, the victim denied rights may seek only an injunction or writ of mandamus that will preserve the right to speak if such an appeal can be filed, perfected, heard, and decided before entry of the criminal judgment. This will often not be the case. . . .

¶48 So, our hands are tied by the same constitutional and statutory provisions that gave M.R. his right to be heard in the first place. We cannot order the plea "undone" once the sentence and judgment have been entered by the trial court. We cannot impose any corrective action on the failure of the prosecutor to inform the court of the request to speak, or the failure of the trial court to fully reconsider the change of plea, with all due formality, thereby according M.R. his constitutional right to actually be heard.

¶49 As it works in practice, the right of a victim to be heard at a change of plea hearing is fragile at best, and may be made illusory by the intentional or unintentional mishandling of the situation by the prosecutor or the trial court, all without meaningful remedy. Perhaps the legislature may find it wise to reconsider the provisions of the statute addressing appellate review of the denial of a victim's request to assert the rights granted by the Victims' Rights Amendment. There may be other circumstances under which those rights may be just as easily and negligently denied as were M.R.'s in this case.

Notes

1. *Informing victims of plea agreements: majority position.* A majority of states now have statutes or constitutional provisions dealing with the rights of crime victims in

the criminal process. Virtually all of these laws address plea bargains. The most common type of provision requires the prosecutor, when feasible, to inform a victim that the prosecutor plans to recommend that a court accept a guilty plea based on a plea agreement. The statutes also typically instruct the prosecutor to inform the victim of the time and place for the plea hearing. See U.S. Dept. of Justice, Victim Input into Plea Agreements (2002) (survey of state laws). Does a law requiring notice about a public document (the plea agreement) and a public hearing (the plea hearing) give crime victims anything of practical value? Would the notice requirement have a different effect if it were to apply before the prosecutor finalizes any plea negotiations? Does a notice requirement remain ineffective until the legislature authorizes funds to hire extra prosecutorial staff members to provide support to victims?

A smaller number of statutes require the prosecution to "consult" with the victim before recommending a plea agreement. See Ind. Code §35-35-3-5; W. Va. Code §61-11A-6(a)(5)(C). A few laws also authorize the victim to make a statement to the court during the plea hearing or require the prosecutor to inform the court about the victim's views on any proposed plea agreement. R.I. Gen. Laws §§12-28-3 (14), 12-28-4.1. What might the victim say to the prosecutor or the judge that would provide new information relevant to the case?

2. *Responsiveness to victims.* Are prosecutors free to give controlling weight to the views of victims? The victims' rights laws described above all assume the validity of a prosecutor's partial reliance on the wishes of crime victims. When defendants raise constitutional and other legal challenges to prosecutorial decisions based partly on the views of victims, courts have upheld the decisions. See Commonwealth v. Latimore, 667 N.E.2d 818 (Mass. 1996) (district attorney's decision not to accept defendant's offer of guilty plea to lesser offense, based in part on victim's family's desire to pursue murder conviction, was not prosecutorial misconduct). Would you predict the same result if a statute explicitly provided the victim with controlling authority — a "veto" power over any proposed plea agreement? What if a prosecutor adopted such a policy in the absence of a statute? Does the legitimacy of the victim's input change if he has filed a civil suit to recover monetary damages from the defendant? See N.D. Cent. Code §§29-01-16 and 29-01-17 (provides for "compromise" of a misdemeanor; victim accepts civil settlement, and there is no criminal conviction).

3. *The impact of victims' rights laws.* All 50 states have some statutory protections for the rights of victims during the criminal process, and about 30 states have amended their constitutions to provide for such rights. But some states have stronger requirements than others. Does the type of law at work in a state influence the way that government officials deal with the victim of an alleged crime? Does a stronger law change the likely reaction of the victim? Scholars from a variety of disciplines have studied the impact of victims' rights laws. For an overview of those empirical surveys, go to the web extension for this chapter at *http://www.crimpro.com/extension/ch16*.

C. VALIDITY OF INDIVIDUAL PLEA BARGAINS

Most of the statutes and judicial opinions on the subject of guilty pleas do not address plea bargaining as an institution. Instead, they focus on the validity of the guilty plea in an individual case. There are three essential ingredients for a valid plea of guilty, whether the plea is "open" or "negotiated": The plea must reflect a knowing waiver of trial rights, the defendant must waive those rights voluntarily, and there must be an adequate "factual basis" to support the charges to which the defendant pleads guilty.

1. Lack of Knowledge

A defendant who pleads guilty must know about the nature of the charges and some of the consequences of waiving the right to trial and accepting a conviction. In essence, the defendant must see two future paths. Down one path, she must visualize the events likely to occur at a trial and after a possible conviction; down another path, she must picture the events likely to occur after a conviction based on a plea of guilty. But predicting the future is no easy task. Courts do not require that a defendant know every single consequence of pleading guilty; the challenge is to select *which* consequences a defendant must understand before entering a valid plea of guilty. Traditional doctrine states that the defendant must understand the "direct" consequences of the conviction but not the "collateral" consequences. A rich case law has developed in an effort to sort out direct from collateral consequences.

The rules of criminal procedure give the trial judge the primary responsibility for ensuring that defendants understand the consequences of waiving trial and pleading guilty. This judicial responsibility is also grounded in the federal constitution. In Boykin v. Alabama, 395 U.S. 238 (1969), the Supreme Court declared that guilty pleas will not be constitutionally valid unless the record affirmatively shows that defendants understand their privilege against self-incrimination, their right to trial by jury, and their right to confront their accusers. During a *Boykin* hearing, the judge asks the defendant a routine set of questions about these rights and other matters before the court will accept a plea of guilty or nolo contendere.

The defense attorney, however, also carries important responsibilities in educating the defendant. A failure to explain to the client the nature of the charges and the relevant consequences of a conviction could amount to ineffective assistance of counsel and affect the validity of the guilty plea. Given the centrality of plea negotiations to modern criminal practice, an ability to explain a guilty plea to a client numbers among the most important skills for a defense lawyer.

■ FEDERAL RULE OF CRIMINAL PROCEDURE 11(b)

(1) Before the court accepts a plea of guilty or nolo contendere, the defendant may be placed under oath, and the court must address the defendant personally in open court. During this address, the court must inform the defendant of, and determine that the defendant understands, the following:

(A) the government's right, in a prosecution for perjury or false statement, to use against the defendant any statement that the defendant gives under oath;

(B) the right to plead not guilty, or having already so pleaded, to persist in that plea;

(C) the right to a jury trial;

(D) the right to be represented by counsel — and if necessary have the court appoint counsel — at trial and at every other stage of the proceeding;

(E) the right at trial to confront and cross-examine adverse witnesses, to be protected from compelled self-incrimination, to testify and present evidence, and to compel the attendance of witnesses;

(F) the defendant's waiver of these trial rights if the court accepts a plea of guilty or nolo contendere;

(G) the nature of each charge to which the defendant is pleading;

(H) any maximum possible penalty, including imprisonment, fine, and term of supervised release;

(I) any mandatory minimum penalty;

(J) any applicable forfeiture;

(K) the court's authority to order restitution;

(L) the court's obligation to impose a special assessment;

(M) the court's obligation to apply the Sentencing Guidelines, and the court's discretion to depart from those guidelines under some circumstances; and

(N) the terms of any plea-agreement provision waiving the right to appeal or to collaterally attack the sentence.

JOSE PADILLA v. KENTUCKY

130 S. Ct. 1473 (2010)

STEVENS, J.*

Petitioner Jose Padilla, a native of Honduras, has been a lawful permanent resident of the United States for more than 40 years. Padilla served this Nation with honor as a member of the U.S. Armed Forces during the Vietnam War. He now faces deportation after pleading guilty to the transportation of a large amount of marijuana in his tractor-trailer in the Commonwealth of Kentucky.

In this postconviction proceeding, Padilla claims that his counsel not only failed to advise him of this consequence prior to his entering the plea, but also told him that he "did not have to worry about immigration status since he had been in the country so long." Padilla relied on his counsel's erroneous advice when he pleaded guilty to the drug charges that made his deportation virtually mandatory. He alleges that he would have insisted on going to trial if he had not received incorrect advice from his attorney.

Assuming the truth of his allegations, the Supreme Court of Kentucky denied Padilla postconviction relief without the benefit of an evidentiary hearing. The court held that the Sixth Amendment's guarantee of effective assistance of counsel does not protect a criminal defendant from erroneous advice about deportation because it is merely a "collateral" consequence of his conviction. . . . We agree with Padilla that constitutionally competent counsel would have advised him that his conviction for drug distribution made him subject to automatic deportation. Whether he is entitled to relief depends on whether he has been prejudiced, a matter that we do not address.

* [Justices Breyer, Ginsburg, Kennedy, and Sotomayor joined this opinion. — EDS.]

I.

The landscape of federal immigration law has changed dramatically over the last 90 years. While once there was only a narrow class of deportable offenses and judges wielded broad discretionary authority to prevent deportation, immigration reforms over time have expanded the class of deportable offenses and limited the authority of judges to alleviate the harsh consequences of deportation. [Deportation] or removal is now virtually inevitable for a vast number of noncitizens convicted of crimes.

[In the Immigration and Nationality Act of 1917, Congress for the first time] made classes of noncitizens deportable based on conduct committed on American soil. Section 19 of the 1917 Act authorized the deportation of "any alien who is hereafter sentenced to imprisonment for a term of one year or more because of conviction in this country of a crime involving moral turpitude, committed within five years after the entry of the alien to the United States."

[The] Act also included a critically important procedural protection to minimize the risk of unjust deportation: At the time of sentencing or within 30 days thereafter, the sentencing judge in both state and federal prosecutions had the power to make a recommendation "that such alien shall not be deported." This procedure, known as a judicial recommendation against deportation, or JRAD, had the effect of binding the Executive to prevent deportation; the statute was consistently interpreted as giving the sentencing judge conclusive authority to decide whether a particular conviction should be disregarded as a basis for deportation. Thus, from 1917 forward, there was no such creature as an automatically deportable offense. Even as the class of deportable offenses expanded, judges retained discretion to ameliorate unjust results on a case-by-case basis. . . .

However, the JRAD procedure is no longer part of our law. Congress first circumscribed the JRAD provision in the 1952 Immigration and Nationality Act (INA), and in 1990 Congress entirely eliminated it. In 1996, Congress also eliminated the Attorney General's authority to grant discretionary relief from deportation, an authority that had been exercised to prevent the deportation of over 10,000 noncitizens during the 5-year period prior to 1996. Under contemporary law, if a noncitizen has committed a removable offense . . . his removal is practically inevitable but for the possible exercise of limited remnants of equitable discretion vested in the Attorney General to cancel removal for noncitizens convicted of particular classes of offenses. Subject to limited exceptions, this discretionary relief is not available for an offense related to trafficking in a controlled substance.

These changes to our immigration law have dramatically raised the stakes of a noncitizen's criminal conviction. The importance of accurate legal advice for noncitizens accused of crimes has never been more important. These changes confirm our view that, as a matter of federal law, deportation is an integral part — indeed, sometimes the most important part — of the penalty that may be imposed on noncitizen defendants who plead guilty to specified crimes.

II.

Before deciding whether to plead guilty, a defendant is entitled to the effective assistance of competent counsel. The Supreme Court of Kentucky rejected Padilla's ineffectiveness claim on the ground that the advice he sought about the risk of deportation concerned only collateral matters, i.e., those matters not within the sentencing authority of the state trial court. . . .

We, however, have never applied a distinction between direct and collateral consequences to define the scope of constitutionally "reasonable professional assistance" required under *Strickland* v. Washington, 466 U.S. 668 (1984). Whether that distinction is appropriate is a question we need not consider in this case because of the unique nature of deportation.

We have long recognized that deportation is a particularly severe "penalty," Fong Yue Ting v. United States, 149 U.S. 698 (1893); but it is not, in a strict sense, a criminal sanction. Although removal proceedings are civil in nature, deportation is nevertheless intimately related to the criminal process. Our law has enmeshed criminal convictions and the penalty of deportation for nearly a century. And, importantly, recent changes in our immigration law have made removal nearly an automatic result for a broad class of noncitizen offenders. Thus, we find it most difficult to divorce the penalty from the conviction in the deportation context. Moreover, we are quite confident that noncitizen defendants facing a risk of deportation for a particular offense find it even more difficult.

Deportation as a consequence of a criminal conviction is, because of its close connection to the criminal process, uniquely difficult to classify as either a direct or a collateral consequence. The collateral versus direct distinction is thus ill-suited to evaluating a *Strickland* claim concerning the specific risk of deportation. We conclude that advice regarding deportation is not categorically removed from the ambit of the Sixth Amendment right to counsel. *Strickland* applies to Padilla's claim.

III.

Under *Strickland*, we first determine whether counsel's representation fell below an objective standard of reasonableness. Then we ask whether there is a reasonable probability that, but for counsel's unprofessional errors, the result of the proceeding would have been different. The first prong — constitutional deficiency — is necessarily linked to the practice and expectations of the legal community: the proper measure of attorney performance remains simply reasonableness under prevailing professional norms. We long have recognized that prevailing norms of practice as reflected in American Bar Association standards and the like are guides to determining what is reasonable. Although they are only guides, and not inexorable commands, these standards may be valuable measures of the prevailing professional norms of effective representation, especially as these standards have been adapted to deal with the intersection of modern criminal prosecutions and immigration law.

The weight of prevailing professional norms supports the view that counsel must advise her client regarding the risk of deportation. National Legal Aid and Defender Assn., Performance Guidelines for Criminal Representation §6.2 (1995); Chin & Holmes, Effective Assistance of Counsel and the Consequences of Guilty Pleas, 87 Cornell L. Rev. 697, 713-718 (2002); ABA Standards for Criminal Justice, Prosecution Function and Defense Function 4-5.1(a), p. 197 (3d ed. 1993). . . .

We too have previously recognized that preserving the client's right to remain in the United States may be more important to the client than any potential jail sentence. INS v. St. Cyr, 533 U.S. 289, 323 (2001). Likewise, we have recognized that preserving the possibility of discretionary relief from deportation under §212(c) of the 1952 INA, repealed by Congress in 1996, would have been one of the principal benefits sought by defendants deciding whether to accept a plea offer or instead to proceed to trial. We expected that counsel who were unaware of the discretionary relief measures would follow the advice of numerous practice guides to advise themselves of the importance of this particular form of discretionary relief.

In the instant case, the terms of the relevant immigration statute are succinct, clear, and explicit in defining the removal consequence for Padilla's conviction. See 8 U.S.C. §1227(a)(2)(B)(i) ("Any alien who at any time after admission has been convicted of a violation of . . . any law or regulation of a State, the United States or a foreign country relating to a controlled substance . . . , other than a single offense involving possession for one's own use of 30 grams or less of marijuana, is deportable"). Padilla's counsel could have easily determined that his plea would make him eligible for deportation simply from reading the text of the statute, which addresses not some broad classification of crimes but specifically commands removal for all controlled substances convictions except for the most trivial of marijuana possession offenses. Instead, Padilla's counsel provided him false assurance that his conviction would not result in his removal from this country. This is not a hard case in which to find deficiency: The consequences of Padilla's plea could easily be determined from reading the removal statute, his deportation was presumptively mandatory, and his counsel's advice was incorrect.

Immigration law can be complex, and it is a legal specialty of its own. Some members of the bar who represent clients facing criminal charges, in either state or federal court or both, may not be well versed in it. There will, therefore, undoubtedly be numerous situations in which the deportation consequences of a particular plea are unclear or uncertain. The duty of the private practitioner in such cases is more limited. When the law is not succinct and straightforward (as it is in many of the scenarios posited by Justice Alito), a criminal defense attorney need do no more than advise a noncitizen client that pending criminal charges may carry a risk of adverse immigration consequences. But when the deportation consequence is truly clear, as it was in this case, the duty to give correct advice is equally clear.

Accepting his allegations as true, Padilla has sufficiently alleged constitutional deficiency to satisfy the first prong of *Strickland*. Whether Padilla is entitled to relief on his claim will depend on whether he can satisfy *Strickland*'s second prong, prejudice, a matter we leave to the Kentucky courts to consider in the first instance.

IV.

The Solicitor General has urged us to conclude that *Strickland* applies to Padilla's claim only to the extent that he has alleged affirmative misadvice. In the United States' view, counsel is not constitutionally required to provide advice on matters that will not be decided in the criminal case, though counsel is required to provide accurate advice if she chooses to discusses these matters. Respondent and Padilla both find the Solicitor General's proposed rule unpersuasive, although it has support among the lower courts. [We believe, however, that] that there is no relevant difference between an act of commission and an act of omission in this context.

A holding limited to affirmative misadvice would invite two absurd results. First, it would give counsel an incentive to remain silent on matters of great importance, even when answers are readily available. Silence under these circumstances would be fundamentally at odds with the critical obligation of counsel to advise the client of "the advantages and disadvantages of a plea agreement." Libretti v. United States, 516 U.S. 29, 50-51 (1995). When attorneys know that their clients face possible exile from this country and separation from their families, they should not be encouraged to say nothing at all. Second, it would deny a class of clients least able to represent themselves the most rudimentary advice on deportation even when it is readily available. It is quintessentially the duty of counsel to provide her client with available advice about an issue like deportation and the failure to do so clearly satisfies the first prong of the *Strickland* analysis. . . .

There is no reason to doubt that lower courts — now quite experienced with applying *Strickland* — can effectively and efficiently use its framework to separate specious claims from those with substantial merit.

It seems unlikely that our decision today will have a significant effect on those convictions already obtained as the result of plea bargains. For at least the past 15 years, professional norms have generally imposed an obligation on counsel to provide advice on the deportation consequences of a client's plea. We should, therefore, presume that counsel satisfied their obligation to render competent advice at the time their clients considered pleading guilty.

Likewise, although we must be especially careful about recognizing new grounds for attacking the validity of guilty pleas, in the 25 years since we first applied *Strickland* to claims of ineffective assistance at the plea stage, practice has shown that pleas are less frequently the subject of collateral challenges than convictions obtained after a trial. Pleas account for nearly 95% of all criminal convictions. But they account for only approximately 30% of the habeas petitions filed. The nature of relief secured by a successful collateral challenge to a guilty plea — an opportunity to withdraw the plea and proceed to trial — imposes its own significant limiting principle: Those who collaterally attack their guilty pleas lose the benefit of the bargain obtained as a result of the plea. Thus, a different calculus informs whether it is wise to challenge a guilty plea in a habeas proceeding because, ultimately, the challenge may result in a less favorable outcome for the defendant, whereas a collateral challenge to a conviction obtained after a jury trial has no similar downside potential.

Finally, informed consideration of possible deportation can only benefit both the State and noncitizen defendants during the plea-bargaining process. By bringing deportation consequences into this process, the defense and prosecution may well be able to reach agreements that better satisfy the interests of both parties. As in this case, a criminal episode may provide the basis for multiple charges, of which only a subset mandate deportation following conviction. Counsel who possess the most rudimentary understanding of the deportation consequences of a particular criminal offense may be able to plea bargain creatively with the prosecutor in order to craft a conviction and sentence that reduce the likelihood of deportation, as by avoiding a conviction for an offense that automatically triggers the removal consequence. At the same time, the threat of deportation may provide the defendant with a powerful incentive to plead guilty to an offense that does not mandate that penalty in exchange for a dismissal of a charge that does.

In sum, we have long recognized that the negotiation of a plea bargain is a critical phase of litigation for purposes of the Sixth Amendment right to effective assistance of counsel. The severity of deportation — the equivalent of banishment or exile — only underscores how critical it is for counsel to inform her noncitizen client that he faces a risk of deportation.[15]

V.

It is our responsibility under the Constitution to ensure that no criminal defendant — whether a citizen or not — is left to the mercies of incompetent counsel. To satisfy this responsibility, we now hold that counsel must inform her client whether his plea carries a risk of deportation. Our longstanding Sixth Amendment precedents, the seriousness of deportation as a consequence of a criminal plea, and the concomitant impact of deportation on families living lawfully in this country demand no less.

Taking as true the basis for his motion for postconviction relief, we have little difficulty concluding that Padilla has sufficiently alleged that his counsel was constitutionally deficient. . . .

ALITO, J., concurring in the judgment.*

I concur in the judgment because a criminal defense attorney fails to provide effective assistance within the meaning of Strickland v. Washington, 466 U.S. 668 (1984), if the attorney misleads a noncitizen client regarding the removal consequences of a conviction. In my view, such an attorney must (1) refrain from unreasonably providing incorrect advice and (2) advise the defendant that a criminal conviction may have adverse immigration consequences and that, if the alien wants advice on this issue, the alien should consult an immigration attorney. I do not agree with the Court that the attorney must attempt to explain what those consequences may be. As the Court concedes, immigration law can be complex; it is a legal specialty of its own; and some members of the bar who represent clients facing criminal charges, in either state or federal court or both, may not be well versed in it. The Court nevertheless holds that a criminal defense attorney must provide advice in this specialized area in those cases in which the law is "succinct and straightforward" — but not, perhaps, in other situations. This vague, halfway test will lead to much confusion and needless litigation.

I.

Under *Strickland*, an attorney provides ineffective assistance if the attorney's representation does not meet reasonable professional standards. Until today, the longstanding and unanimous position of the federal courts was that reasonable defense counsel generally need only advise a client about the direct consequences of a criminal conviction. While the line between "direct" and "collateral" consequences is not always clear, the collateral-consequences rule expresses an important truth: Criminal defense attorneys have expertise regarding the conduct of criminal

15. To this end, we find it significant that the plea form currently used in Kentucky courts provides notice of possible immigration consequences. Further, many States require trial courts to advise defendants of possible immigration consequences. See, e.g., Cal. Penal Code Ann. §1016.5; Fla. Rule Crim. Proc. 3.172(c)(8); N.Y. Crim. Proc. Law Ann. §220.50(7); N. C. Gen. Stat. Ann. §15A-1022; Ohio Rev. Code Ann. §2943.031; Tex. Code. Ann. Crim. Proc., Art. 26.13(a)(4).

* [Chief Justice Roberts joined this opinion. — EDS.]

proceedings. They are not expected to possess — and very often do not possess — expertise in other areas of the law, and it is unrealistic to expect them to provide expert advice on matters that lie outside their area of training and experience.

This case happens to involve removal, but criminal convictions can carry a wide variety of consequences other than conviction and sentencing, including civil commitment, civil forfeiture, the loss of the right to vote, disqualification from public benefits, ineligibility to possess firearms, dishonorable discharge from the Armed Forces, and loss of business or professional licenses. A criminal conviction may also severely damage a defendant's reputation and thus impair the defendant's ability to obtain future employment or business opportunities. All of those consequences are serious, but this Court has never held that a criminal defense attorney's Sixth Amendment duties extend to providing advice about such matters. . . .

Because many criminal defense attorneys have little understanding of immigration law, it should follow that a criminal defense attorney who refrains from providing immigration advice does not violate prevailing professional norms. But the Court's opinion would not just require defense counsel to warn the client of a general risk of removal; it would also require counsel in at least some cases, to specify what the removal consequences of a conviction would be.

The Court's new approach is particularly problematic because providing advice on whether a conviction for a particular offense will make an alien removable is often quite complex. . . . Defense counsel who consults a guidebook on whether a particular crime is an "aggravated felony" will often find that the answer is not easily ascertained. . . .

The Court tries to downplay the severity of the burden it imposes on defense counsel by suggesting that the scope of counsel's duty to offer advice concerning deportation consequences may turn on how hard it is to determine those consequences. . . . This approach is problematic for at least four reasons.

First, it will not always be easy to tell whether a particular statutory provision is "succinct, clear, and explicit." How can an attorney who lacks general immigration law expertise be sure that a seemingly clear statutory provision actually means what it seems to say when read in isolation? What if the application of the provision to a particular case is not clear but a cursory examination of case law or administrative decisions would provide a definitive answer?

Second, if defense counsel must provide advice regarding only one of the many collateral consequences of a criminal conviction, many defendants are likely to be misled. To take just one example, a conviction for a particular offense may render an alien excludable but not removable. If an alien charged with such an offense is advised only that pleading guilty to such an offense will not result in removal, the alien may be induced to enter a guilty plea without realizing that a consequence of the plea is that the alien will be unable to reenter the United States if the alien returns to his or her home country for any reason, such as to visit an elderly parent or to attend a funeral. Incomplete legal advice may be worse than no advice at all because it may mislead and may dissuade the client from seeking advice from a more knowledgeable source.

Third, the Court's rigid constitutional rule could inadvertently head off more promising ways of addressing the underlying problem — such as statutory or administrative reforms requiring trial judges to inform a defendant on the record that a guilty plea may carry adverse immigration consequences. [Twenty-eight] states and the District of Columbia have already adopted rules, plea forms, or statutes requiring courts to advise criminal defendants of the possible immigration consequences of their pleas. A nonconstitutional rule requiring trial judges to inform defendants on the record of the risk of adverse immigration consequences can ensure that a defendant receives needed information without putting a large number of criminal convictions at risk; and because such a warning would be given on the record, courts would not later have to determine whether the defendant was misrepresenting the advice of counsel. . . .

Fourth, the Court's decision marks a major upheaval in Sixth Amendment law. This Court decided *Strickland* in 1984, but the majority does not cite a single case, from this or any other federal court, holding that criminal defense counsel's failure to provide advice concerning the removal consequences of a criminal conviction violates a defendant's Sixth Amendment right to counsel. . . .

II.

While mastery of immigration law is not required by *Strickland*, several considerations support the conclusion that affirmative misadvice regarding the removal consequences of a conviction may constitute ineffective assistance.

First, a rule prohibiting affirmative misadvice regarding a matter as crucial to the defendant's plea decision as deportation appears faithful to the scope and nature of the Sixth Amendment duty this Court has recognized in its past cases. [Thorough] understanding of the intricacies of immigration law is not within the range of competence demanded of attorneys in criminal cases. By contrast, reasonably competent attorneys should know that it is not appropriate or responsible to hold themselves out as authorities on a difficult and complicated subject matter with which they are not familiar. . . .

Second, incompetent advice distorts the defendant's decisionmaking process and seems to call the fairness and integrity of the criminal proceeding itself into question. When a defendant opts to plead guilty without definitive information concerning the likely effects of the plea, the defendant can fairly be said to assume the risk that the conviction may carry indirect consequences of which he or she is not aware. That is not the case when a defendant bases the decision to plead guilty on counsel's express misrepresentation that the defendant will not be removable. . . .

In concluding that affirmative misadvice regarding the removal consequences of a criminal conviction may constitute ineffective assistance, I do not mean to suggest that the Sixth Amendment does no more than require defense counsel to avoid misinformation. When a criminal defense attorney is aware that a client is an alien, the attorney should advise the client that a criminal conviction may have adverse consequences under the immigration laws and that the client should consult an immigration specialist if the client wants advice on that subject. By putting the client on notice of the danger of removal, such advice would significantly reduce the chance that the client would plead guilty under a mistaken premise. . . .

SCALIA, J, dissenting.*

In the best of all possible worlds, criminal defendants contemplating a guilty plea ought to be advised of all serious collateral consequences of conviction, and surely ought not to be misadvised. The Constitution, however, is not an all-purpose tool for judicial construction of a perfect world; and when we ignore its text in order to make it that, we often find ourselves swinging a sledge where a tack hammer is needed.

The Sixth Amendment guarantees the accused a lawyer "for his defense" against a criminal prosecution — not for sound advice about the collateral consequences of conviction. For that reason, and for the practical reasons set forth in Part I of Justice Alito's concurrence, I dissent from the Court's conclusion that the Sixth Amendment requires counsel to provide accurate advice concerning the potential removal consequences of a guilty plea. For the same reasons, but unlike the concurrence, I do not believe that affirmative misadvice about those consequences renders an attorney's assistance in defending against the prosecution constitutionally inadequate; or that the Sixth Amendment requires counsel to warn immigrant defendants that a conviction may render them removable. Statutory provisions can remedy these concerns in a more targeted fashion, and without producing permanent, and legislatively irreparable, overkill. . . .

There is no basis in text or in principle to extend the constitutionally required advice regarding guilty pleas beyond those matters germane to the criminal prosecution at hand — to wit, the sentence that the plea will produce, the higher sentence that conviction after trial might entail, and the chances of such a conviction. Such matters fall within the range of competence demanded of attorneys in criminal cases. We have never held, as the logic of the Court's opinion assumes, that once counsel is appointed all professional responsibilities of counsel — even those extending beyond defense against the prosecution — become constitutional commands. Because the subject of the misadvice here was not the prosecution for which Jose Padilla was entitled to effective assistance of counsel, the Sixth Amendment has no application.

Adding to counsel's duties an obligation to advise about a conviction's collateral consequences has no logical stopping-point. [It] seems to me that the concurrence suffers from the same defect. The same indeterminacy, the same inability to know what areas of advice are relevant, attaches to misadvice. And the concurrence's suggestion that counsel must warn defendants of potential removal consequences — what would come to be known as the "*Padilla* warning" — cannot be limited to those consequences except by judicial caprice. It is difficult to believe that the warning requirement would not be extended, for example, to the risk of heightened sentences in later federal prosecutions pursuant to the Armed Career Criminal Act, 18 U.S.C. §924(e). . . .

The Court's holding prevents legislation that could solve the problems addressed by today's opinions in a more precise and targeted fashion. If the subject had not been constitutionalized, legislation could specify which categories of misadvice about matters ancillary to the prosecution invalidate plea agreements, what collateral consequences counsel must bring to a defendant's attention, and what warnings must be given. Moreover, legislation could provide consequences for the

* [Justice Thomas joined this opinion. — EDS.]

misadvice, nonadvice, or failure to warn, other than nullification of a criminal conviction after the witnesses and evidence needed for retrial have disappeared. Federal immigration law might provide, for example, that the near-automatic removal which follows from certain criminal convictions will not apply where the conviction rested upon a guilty plea induced by counsel's misadvice regarding removal consequences. Or legislation might put the government to a choice in such circumstances: Either retry the defendant or forgo the removal. But all that has been precluded in favor of today's sledge hammer. . . .

Problem 16-5. Direct and Collateral Effects

Donald Ross pleaded guilty to three counts of second-degree child rape committed against his former stepdaughter. Those offenses carried a maximum sentence of 10 years and a $20,000 fine, a minimum sentence of 67 months, and a mandatory 12-month community placement. As part of the plea negotiations, the government agreed to recommend a prison term of 89 months. Ross did not receive an explicit warning of his mandatory one-year community placement term prior to entering his plea.

At the sentencing hearing, the judge imposed an 89-month sentence plus the mandatory one-year community placement. In addition to the standard community placement conditions, the court adopted special conditions recommended by the pre-sentence investigator: no contact with the victim; no contact with females under 16 years old; Department of Corrections approval of residence location and living arrangements; and urinalysis and polygraph at the will of his community corrections officer.

Ross then filed a motion to withdraw his guilty plea as involuntary. The state's rules of criminal procedure say this about knowing and intelligent pleas of guilt:

> The court shall not accept a plea of guilty, without first determining that it is made voluntarily, competently and with an understanding of the nature of the charge and the consequences of the plea. The court shall not enter a judgment upon a plea of guilty unless it is satisfied that there is a factual basis for the plea.

The trial court denied withdrawal, concluding that the omission of the mandatory 12-month community placement represented merely a "collateral" consequence of his plea. His lack of knowledge about this potential consequence, the court said, was not a sufficient basis for withdrawing the guilty plea.

Will an appellate court uphold the denial of the motion to withdraw the guilty plea? Appellate decisions in this state distinguish "direct" from "collateral" consequences by asking whether the component of the sentence represents "a definite, immediate and largely automatic effect on the range of the defendant's punishment." Cf. State v. Ross, 916 P.2d 405 (Wash. 1996).

Notes

1. *Knowledge of nature of charges and procedural rights.* The federal constitution requires a defendant to understand the nature of the charges before pleading guilty

to them. Although defense counsel usually explains the elements of the offense to the client, the judge ordinarily confirms that the defendant understood what he was told. In Henderson v. Morgan, 426 U.S. 637 (1976), a defendant with below-average intelligence pleaded guilty to second-degree murder while insisting that he "meant no harm" to the victim. Because the judge during the plea colloquy did not explain to the defendant that intent was a "critical" element of the crime, the Court overturned the conviction, even though there was overwhelming evidence of the defendant's guilt. The *Henderson* decision, however, does not require the judge to explain every element of every crime to every defendant. The opinion addressed only "critical" elements of the offense. See Bradshaw v. Stumpf, 545 U.S. 175 (2005) (guilty plea is valid when "the record accurately reflects that the nature of the charge and the elements of the crime were explained to the defendant by his own, competent counsel").

Defendants must also understand the nature of trial rights they are waiving, such as confrontation of witnesses, representation by counsel, and jury factfinding. As with the nature of the charges, the judge need not describe every detail of the procedural rights that the defendant is waiving. In Iowa v. Tovar, 541 U.S. 77 (2004), the defendant pled guilty to a DUI charge after waiving the right to counsel. When the sentence for a later conviction was enhanced based on the earlier conviction, Tovar challenged the validity of his waiver of counsel in the initial proceedings because the trial judge had only explained the disadvantages of self-representation in general terms. The Supreme Court held that a trial court must inform the accused of the nature of the charges against him, of his right to be counseled regarding his plea, and of the range of allowable punishments. The judge is not required to advise the defendant more specifically that an attorney might identify a viable defense that a layperson might overlook, or that an attorney can offer an independent opinion on whether it is wise to plead guilty. Compare Hopper v. State, 934 N.E.2d 1086 (Ind. 2010) (under court's supervisory power, it requires trial court to inform defendants who propose to waive right to counsel and enter guilty plea about "the value of counsel's experience in bargaining for a plea and ability to identify chinks in the State's armor to fortify a negotiating position").

2. *Knowledge of direct penal consequences.* A valid plea of guilty does not require the defendant to understand each and every consequence of the sentence that could be imposed: in traditional terminology, the defendant must understand the "direct" consequences of the conviction but not the "collateral" consequences. In general terms, consequences that occur farther in the future and more contingent on later events or the decisions of other governmental actors are more likely to be declared "collateral." Direct consequences include the maximum sentence authorized and some information about the prison term a defendant should expect. See State v. Cozart, 897 N.E.2d 478 (Ind. 2008) (judicial explanation of maximum and minimum limits of sentence range was adequate, even without explanation that court had no discretion to suspend sentence below the minimum term). Most courts also conclude that any substantial restitution payments would be a direct consequence.

On the other hand, eligibility for parole tends to fall into the "collateral" category. The courts are split over requirements that sex offenders register with law enforcement officers near their residence after the completion of any prison term. State v. Bellamy, 835 A.2d 1231 (N.J. 2003) (court must advise a guilty-pleading defendant of possible future civil commitment as a sexually violent predator); but cf.People v. Gravino, 928 N.E.2d 1048 (N.Y. 2010) (judges need not advise defendants pleading guilty of sex crimes involving children about registration obligations or possible probation conditions that would prohibit contact with their own minor children); Ward v. State, 315 S.W.3d 461 (Tenn. 2010) (trial judge must inform defendant at guilty plea colloquy about mandatory lifetime community supervision component of sentence, but not mandatory sex offender registration requirement).

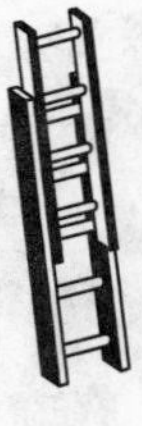

For a sampling of the many state court decisions that distinguish the "collateral" consequences of a conviction from the "direct" consequences, go to the web extension for this chapter at *http://www.crimpro.com/extension/ch16*.

3. *Guilty pleas and incompetent lawyers.* A defendant who pleads guilty must be represented by counsel or must waive the right to counsel. Moore v. Michigan, 355 U.S. 155 (1957). Furthermore, if a lawyer gives constitutionally inadequate representation that causes a defendant to enter a guilty plea, the defendant may later withdraw the plea. But this does not mean that any faulty legal advice will invalidate a plea. In Brady v. United States, 397 U.S. 742 (1970), counsel gave the defendant incorrect but competent advice about the constitutionality of the death penalty statute at issue in the case; the incorrect advice of counsel was not sufficient reason to invalidate the defendant's "knowing" waiver of trial rights. See also Davie v. People, 675 S.E.2d 416 (S.C. 2009) (when counsel fails to communicate plea offer to defendant, court should decide on case-by-case basis whether prejudice is inherent in failure and whether defendant needs to show object evidence of prejudice to establish ineffective assistance and involuntary guilty plea; surveys fractured jurisprudence in other states).

As the Supreme Court noted in *Padilla*, many state courts, state procedural rules, and professional standards address the question of whether the defense lawyer must inform the defendant about the immigration consequences of a guilty plea and conviction. State institutions have also addressed the parallel obligations of the judge to inform the defendant about immigration consequences. The web extension for this chapter collects the pronouncements of these different institutions about the obligations of defense counsel and trial judges regarding immigration consequences of criminal convictions; you can find these materials on the web extension for this chapter at *http://www.crimpro.com/extension/ch16*.

4. *Guilty pleas before discovery.* If defendants must know about the nature of the charges and the direct consequences of a guilty plea, must they also know about the basic facts the prosecutor could present against them at trial? According to United States v. Ruiz, 536 U.S. 622 (2002), federal prosecutors are not constitutionally required, before entering into a binding plea agreement with a criminal defendant, to disclose "impeachment information relating to any informants or other witnesses." The Supreme Court's decision in *Ruiz* is typical in its refusal to declare a per se rule against bargaining away discovery rights. A few courts, however, have concluded that in some cases, accepting a guilty plea based on a plea agreement that prevents the defendant from engaging in discovery violates due process. See State v. Draper, 784 P.2d 259 (Ariz. 1989) (due process and right to counsel sometimes may prohibit plea agreement conditioned on defendant not interviewing victim of alleged crime; remand to determine defendant's access to state's evidence through other witnesses). Can you identify circumstances in which a defendant could make a "knowing" waiver of the right to a jury trial without taking advantage of a discovery right? The *Ruiz* court found it significant that the condition relating to discovery was non-mandatory because the defendant could choose to go forward

with discovery and forgo the plea agreement. Are there any terms that prosecutors simply may not offer because they prevent the defendant from making a knowing waiver?

5. *Professional obligations during plea negotiations.* Several sources of law address the information that attorneys for the prosecution and defense reveal to each other and to the defendant during plea negotiations. First, ethics rules and aspirational standards instruct a defense lawyer to inform the defendant about the terms of any proposed plea agreement because the client must decide what plea to enter. See ABA Model Rule of Professional Conduct 4.1; ABA Standards for Criminal Justice: Defense Function 4-6.2(a), (b); see also People v. Whitfield, 239 N.E.2d 850 (Ill.1968) (overturning conviction after trial because defense counsel failed to communicate plea bargain offer to client). These ethics rules and aspirational standards state that it is unprofessional conduct for an attorney (prosecution or defense) to knowingly make false statements during plea negotiations. ABA Model Rule 4.1 (lawyer shall not knowingly make a false statement of material fact or law to a third person); ABA Standards 3-4.1(c), 4-6.2. To what extent do discovery rules provide for disclosure of information before the entry of a guilty plea? Do professional obligations require greater or earlier disclosures than those required under the rules of discovery? See State v. Gibson, 514 S.E.2d 320 (S.C. 1999) (prosecutor's failure to disclose *Brady* information can undermine voluntariness of guilty plea).

6. *Hearing procedures.* The decision in Boykin v. Alabama, 395 U.S. 238 (1969), gave a constitutional foundation to some of the information a defendant must know before entering a guilty plea. The record must show the defendant's awareness of three major constitutional rights waived through entry of a guilty plea: the privilege against self-incrimination, the right to jury trial, and the right to confront adverse witnesses. In addition to these constitutional requirements, many rules of procedure have added requirements such as knowledge regarding the nature of the charges, the direct consequences of a conviction, and the factual basis for the charge. Trial courts engage in lengthy (and elaborately scripted) "plea colloquies" to create a record establishing that a defendant knows what is necessary before pleading guilty. What happens if the trial court fails to cover one of the necessary questions and thereby violates a rule of procedure? Fed. R. Crim. P. 11(h) allows a federal court to uphold a plea if the violation of the rule's requirements was "harmless error." Compare State v. Hoppe, 765 N.W.2d 794 (Wis. 2009) (guilty plea was not knowing, even though trial court found that defendant read and understood a form that includes a guilty plea questionnaire and waiver of rights; plea colloquy must satisfy ten requirements as described in state case law, and the form that the defendant read here failed to inquire into promises or threats were made in connection with plea or about information regarding potential range of punishments).

2. *Involuntary Pleas*

Time and again, procedural rules and judicial opinions say that a plea of guilty or nolo contendere must be "voluntary." The question of voluntariness raises a familiar theme in criminal procedure: In what sense can we say that a defendant *chooses* to waive procedural advantages such as a right to jury trial? Surely a defendant is choosing among unpleasant options when she decides to plead guilty. Is it possible for the government to restrict the defendant's options in such a way that the defendant's decision to plead guilty is no longer a "choice" in any meaningful sense? In this section, we consider three settings in which defendants have repeatedly claimed that their decision to plead guilty was not truly voluntary.

a. *Alford* Pleas

A defendant who pleads guilty stands ready to accept punishment for the crime as charged. Is this decision coerced if the defendant insists that he did not commit the crime?

■ FEDERAL RULE OF CRIMINAL PROCEDURE 11(b)

(2) Before accepting a plea of guilty or nolo contendere, the court must address the defendant personally in open court and determine that the plea is voluntary and did not result from force, threats, or promises (other than promises in a plea agreement).

(3) Before entering judgment on a guilty plea, the court must determine that there is a factual basis for the plea.

■ NORTH CAROLINA v. HENRY ALFORD

400 U.S. 25 (1970)

WHITE, J.*

On December 2, 1963, Alford was indicted for first-degree murder, a capital offense under North Carolina law. The court appointed an attorney to represent him, and this attorney questioned all but one of the various witnesses who appellee said would substantiate his claim of innocence. The witnesses, however, did not support Alford's story but gave statements that strongly indicated his guilt. Faced with strong evidence of guilt and no substantial evidentiary support for the claim of innocence, Alford's attorney recommended that he plead guilty, but left the ultimate decision to Alford himself. The prosecutor agreed to accept a plea of guilty to a charge of second-degree murder, and on December 10, 1963, Alford pleaded guilty to the reduced charge.

Before the plea was finally accepted by the trial court, the court heard the sworn testimony of a police officer who summarized the State's case. Two other witnesses besides Alford were also heard. Although there was no eyewitness to the crime, the testimony indicated that shortly before the killing Alford took his gun from his house, stated his intention to kill the victim, and returned home with the declaration that he had carried out the killing. After the summary presentation of the State's case, Alford took the stand and testified that he had not committed the murder but that he was pleading guilty because he faced the threat of the death penalty if he did not do so.[2] In response to the questions of his counsel, he acknowledged

* [Chief Justice Burger and Justices Harlan, Stewart, and Blackmun joined this opinion. — EDS.]

2. After giving his version of the events of the night of the murder, Alford stated: "I pleaded guilty on second degree murder because they said there is too much evidence, but I ain't shot no man, but I take the fault for the other man. We never had an argument in our life and I just pleaded guilty because

that his counsel had informed him of the difference between second- and first-degree murder and of his rights in case he chose to go to trial. The trial court then asked appellee if, in light of his denial of guilt, he still desired to plead guilty to second-degree murder and appellee answered, "Yes, sir. I plead guilty on — from the circumstances that he [Alford's attorney] told me." After eliciting information about Alford's prior criminal record, which was a long one, the trial court sentenced him to 30 years' imprisonment, the maximum penalty for second-degree murder. [Alford sought postconviction relief, first in the state court, and later in federal habeas corpus proceedings.]

We held in Brady v. United States, 397 U.S. 742 (1970), that a plea of guilty which would not have been entered except for the defendant's desire to avoid a possible death penalty and to limit the maximum penalty to life imprisonment or a term of years was not for that reason compelled within the meaning of the Fifth Amendment. . . . The standard was and remains whether the plea represents a voluntary and intelligent choice among the alternative courses of action open to the defendant. That he would not have pleaded except for the opportunity to limit the possible penalty does not necessarily demonstrate that the plea of guilty was not the product of a free and rational choice, especially where the defendant was represented by competent counsel whose advice was that the plea would be to the defendant's advantage. . . .

Ordinarily, a judgment of conviction resting on a plea of guilty is justified by the defendant's admission that he committed the crime charged against him and his consent that judgment be entered without a trial of any kind. The plea usually subsumes both elements, and justifiably so, even though there is no separate, express admission by the defendant that he committed the particular acts claimed to constitute the crime charged in the indictment. Here Alford entered his plea but accompanied it with the statement that he had not shot the victim. If Alford's statements were to be credited as sincere assertions of his innocence, there obviously existed a factual and legal dispute between him and the State. Without more, it might be argued that the conviction entered on his guilty plea was invalid, since his assertion of innocence negatived any admission of guilt. . . .

In addition to Alford's statement, however, the court had heard an account of the events on the night of the murder, including information from Alford's acquaintances that he had departed from his home with his gun stating his intention to kill and that he had later declared that he had carried out his intention. Nor had Alford wavered in his desire to have the trial court determine his guilt without a jury trial. Although denying the charge against him, he nevertheless preferred the dispute between him and the State to be settled by the judge in the context of a guilty plea proceeding rather than by a formal trial. Thereupon, with the State's telling evidence and Alford's denial before it, the trial court proceeded to convict and sentence Alford for second-degree murder.

State and lower federal courts are divided upon whether a guilty plea can be accepted when it is accompanied by protestations of innocence and hence contains only a waiver of trial but no admission of guilt. Some courts, giving expression to the principle that "our law only authorizes a conviction where guilt is shown," Harris v.

---

they said if I didn't they would gas me for it, and that is all." [Alford later described his decision as follows:] "I'm still pleading that you all got me to plead guilty. I plead the other way, circumstantial evidence. . . . You told me to plead guilty, right. I don't — I'm not guilty but I plead guilty."

State, 172 S.W. 975 (Tex. 1915), require that trial judges reject such pleas. [The court cited cases from Michigan, New Jersey, New Mexico, and Washington along with lower federal court cases.] But others have concluded that they should not . . . force any defense on a defendant in a criminal case . . . particularly when advancement of the defense might "end in disaster. . . ." Tremblay v. Overholser, 199 F. Supp. 569 (D.D.C. 1961). They have argued that, since [guilt is at times uncertain, an accused who believes in his own innocence] might reasonably conclude a jury would be convinced of his guilt and that he would fare better in the sentence by pleading guilty. [The court cited cases from Idaho, Illinois, Iowa, Minnesota, Pennsylvania, and several lower federal courts.]

This Court has not confronted this precise issue, but prior decisions do yield relevant principles. . . . The issue in Hudson v. United States, 272 U.S. 451 (1926), was whether a federal court has power to impose a prison sentence after accepting a plea of nolo contendere, a plea by which a defendant does not expressly admit his guilt, but nonetheless waives his right to a trial and authorizes the court for purposes of the case to treat him as if he were guilty. The Court held that a trial court does have such power, and . . . the federal courts have uniformly followed this rule, even in cases involving moral turpitude. Implicit in the nolo contendere cases is a recognition that the Constitution does not bar imposition of a prison sentence upon an accused who is unwilling expressly to admit his guilt but who, faced with grim alternatives, is willing to waive his trial and accept the sentence. These cases would be directly in point if Alford had simply insisted on his plea but refused to admit the crime. The fact that his plea was denominated a plea of guilty rather than a plea of nolo contendere is of no constitutional significance with respect to the issue now before us, for the Constitution is concerned with the practical consequences, not the formal categorizations, of state law. . . .

Nor can we perceive any material difference between a plea that refuses to admit commission of the criminal act and a plea containing a protestation of innocence when, as in the instant case, a defendant intelligently concludes that his interests require entry of a guilty plea and the record before the judge contains strong evidence of actual guilt. Here the State had a strong case of first-degree murder against Alford. Whether he realized or disbelieved his guilt, he insisted on his plea because in his view he had absolutely nothing to gain by a trial and much to gain by pleading. . . . In view of the strong factual basis for the plea demonstrated by the State and Alford's clearly expressed desire to enter it despite his professed belief in his innocence, we hold that the trial judge did not commit constitutional error in accepting it.[11] . . .

Alford now argues in effect that the State should not have allowed him this choice but should have insisted on proving him guilty of murder in the first degree. The States in their wisdom may take this course by statute or otherwise and may prohibit the practice of accepting pleas to lesser included offenses under any circumstances. But this is not the mandate of the Fourteenth Amendment and the Bill of Rights. The prohibitions against involuntary or unintelligent pleas should

11. Our holding does not mean that a trial judge must accept every constitutionally valid guilty plea merely because a defendant wishes so to plead. A criminal defendant does not have an absolute right under the Constitution to have his guilty plea accepted by the court, although the States may by statute or otherwise confer such a right. . . .

not be relaxed, but neither should an exercise in arid logic render those constitutional guarantees counterproductive and put in jeopardy the very human values they were meant to preserve. . . .

Notes

1. *Guilty pleas by defendants claiming innocence: majority position.* Although there was once a real dispute among state courts about the constitutionality of accepting guilty pleas from defendants who maintained their innocence, that dispute is now largely resolved. A substantial majority of states follow the lead of the U.S. Supreme Court and allow a defendant to plead guilty, despite claims of innocence, so long as the prosecution establishes a strong factual basis to support the conviction. See People v. Canino, 508 P.2d 1273 (Colo. 1973). Fewer than a half-dozen states prevent trial judges from accepting *Alford* pleas. See Ross v. State, 456 N.E.2d 420 (Ind. 1983).

The live question in connection with *Alford* pleas is whether the trial judge has discretion to *reject* an *Alford* plea. The Supreme Court (in footnote 11) suggested that an individual trial judge, or a state court system as a whole through its rules of procedure, might refuse to accept such guilty pleas. Many individual judges do refuse to accept *Alford* pleas, and the majority of appellate courts uphold their discretion to do so. See Albert Alschuler, The Defense Attorney's Role in Plea Bargaining, 84 Yale L.J. 1179 (1975). If a state system decides not to prohibit *Alford* pleas, should it place controls on the power of the trial judge to refuse to accept such pleas? Would this step ensure the equal treatment of defendants and prevent litigants from shopping for judges? See ABA Standards for Criminal Justice: Pleas of Guilty 14-1.6 (defendant's offer to plead guilty should not be refused "solely" because defendant refuses to admit culpability). What reasons might a judge give to refuse an offer of an *Alford* plea in a specific case, apart from a general ban on such pleas?

2. Alford *pleas and free will.* If a defendant is *not* coerced when she pleads guilty while insisting that she is innocent, who *is* coerced into pleading guilty? Defendants who offer an *Alford* plea have a very limited set of options. We can presume that defendants prefer to have the option of entering an *Alford* plea rather than face the expense or publicity of a trial, along with the risk of a more severe sentence after trial. Are there reasons why the public should deny this option to the bargaining parties?

As you might expect, a defendant who enters any guilty plea must be mentally competent; otherwise, the court cannot consider the plea to be knowing and voluntary. See Godinez v. Moran, 509 U.S. 389 (1993) (same competence standard used for entry of guilty plea and capacity to stand trial); State v. Engelmann, 541 N.W.2d 96 (S.D. 1995) (allows withdrawal of *Alford* plea based on lack of mental competence at arraignment).

3. Alford *pleas and the truth.* If trials always uncovered the truth about the events surrounding alleged crimes, would there be any reason to allow *Alford* pleas? Is a system that accepts such pleas implicitly admitting that trials often fail to uncover the truth and that an innocent defendant might be justifiably concerned about an erroneous conviction after trial? The factual basis for an *Alford* plea must come from sources other than the statements of the defendant. Compare State v. Case, 213 P.3d 429 (Kan. 2009) (defendant's *Alford* plea to aggravated endangering of child and

admission of a factual basis for that charge did not amount to stipulation to prosecutor's characterization of the offense as sexual abuse; sentencing judge not authorized to increase period of supervised release under statute applicable to sexually motivated crimes).

Most courts say that it is not necessary that the factual basis establish guilt beyond a reasonable doubt. The Supreme Court's opinion in *Alford* called the factual basis in that case "strong" and "overwhelming"; state courts have suggested several formulations to describe the necessary level of proof. Clewley v. State, 288 A.2d 468 (Me. 1972) (not unreasonable to conclude guilt); Re Guilty Plea Cases, 235 N.W. 2d 132, 145 (Mich. 1975) (might have been convicted at trial); State v. Hagemann, 326 N.W.2d 861 (N.D. 1982) ("strong" proof of guilt). Would the "beyond a reasonable doubt" standard seriously reduce the number of *Alford* pleas accepted? See Ala. Code §15-15-23 (adopting beyond-reasonable-doubt standard for acceptance of guilty pleas); Richard Uviller, Pleading Guilty: A Critique of Four Models, 41 Law & Contemp. Probs. 102 (1977) (clear and convincing evidence). It is also possible to view an *Alford* plea as the most honest route available in a system in which some defendants want to avoid a trial even though they believe in their own innocence. When a state bans *Alford* pleas, does it invite defendants to lie to their attorneys and to the court?

Problem 16-6. An Offer You Can't Refuse

Joan Capriccioso worked as a waitress at a diner in Staten Island, where she met Philip Fiumefreddo. After a two-month courtship, the two were married; she was then 39 and he was 68. Throughout four years of marriage to Philip, Joan often complained to acquaintances about him, saying that she wished him dead.

Eventually, Joan's father Salvatore Capriccioso withdrew $3,200 from the bank and gave it to Joseph Gurrieri, with the understanding that Gurrieri would arrange for the murder of Philip Fiumefreddo. Gurrieri hired Christopher Munroe to kill Fiumefreddo for $1,000. Munroe went to the Fiumefreddo residence at 6:30 A.M. Joan let him in. After offering to fix breakfast for him, she told Munroe to make the house look burglarized, gave him a pillow, and instructed him to use it to kill her husband, who was still sleeping. She then left for work. Munroe suffocated Philip with the pillow as he slept.

Becoming increasingly distressed about the murder, Gurrieri went to the police and confessed. Joan Fiumefreddo and her father were indicted for second-degree murder, second-degree conspiracy, and second-degree solicitation. On the same day, Munroe and Gurrieri were indicted for various crimes in connection with the killing; these latter two defendants soon pleaded guilty to the charges. On the day jury selection was scheduled to begin, Fiumefreddo and her attorney, John Collins, met for over an hour with the trial judge; her father; his attorney, Joseph Lamattina; and the prosecutor. Immediately following this discussion, Collins told the court: "My client is now prepared to plead with only one promise having been made by me. That promise is with her pleading to this top count that the Court would sentence her to 18 years to life." Lamattina stated that Salvatore Capriccioso was prepared to plead guilty to second-degree conspiracy in exchange for a sentence promise of one to three years.

Nine days after the plea colloquy, defendant made a motion pro se to withdraw her guilty plea. In the accompanying affidavit she stated that

> while I acknowledge that the Court advised me that I had certain rights, I nevertheless did not then, nor do I now realize the full consequences of my plea of guilty. I am not guilty of the offenses to which I pleaded guilty. I pleaded guilty with the promise that I would be sentenced to 18 to life and co-defendant's sentence would be lighter if the defendant pleads guilty to second degree murder.

The judge denied the motion to withdraw her plea, and sentenced her and her father to the agreed-upon terms of imprisonment. Was Fiumefreddo's guilty plea voluntary? Compare People v. Fiumefreddo, 626 N.E.2d 646 (N.Y. 1993).

Notes

1. *"Package" deals.* Can the prosecutor increase the cost of the trial by threatening to prosecute third parties, such as family members of the defendant? Courts have not announced any outright bans of "package deals" or "connected pleas," but they review them with some suspicion. What should a defendant emphasize to convince a court that her particular "package deal" produced an involuntary plea? How will the defendant obtain the evidence necessary to make this showing? Does the fact that a defendant's sentence is near the minimum available sentence help or hurt her claim that the plea was involuntary? See State v. Danh, 516 N.W.2d 539 (Minn. 1994) (requiring contingent terms of package-deal guilty plea to be explained on the record to trial court to allow assessment of voluntariness). Does the difficulty with package deals come from the defendant's reduced capacity to make decisions (because the package deal offers the defendant options that cannot be compared in a rational manner) or from the public's unease about using family or other intimate bonds to gain a litigation advantage?

2. *Coercive overcharging.* A prosecutor can make the decision to go to trial very costly, through a combination of serious charges and an attractive plea agreement. These decisions, however, will usually not provoke a court to rule that the defendant's guilty plea was involuntary. In Brady v. United States, 397 U.S. 742 (1970), the fact that the defendant believed that a decision to go to trial would expose him to a possible death penalty was not enough to invalidate the guilty plea. Nonetheless, some statutes and aspirational standards instruct the prosecutor not to "overcharge." Take, for instance, a North Carolina statute, N.C. Gen. Stat. §15A-1021(b), which forbids state agents from placing "improper pressure" on a defendant to plead guilty. According to the drafters' commentary, the statute (based on the American Law Institute's Model Code of Pre-Arraignment Procedure) was meant to prevent the prosecutor from filing charges not supported by provable facts or charges not ordinarily filed based on the conduct in question. See also ABA Standards for Criminal Justice, Prosecution Function 3-3.9(f) (prosecutor should not bring charges greater than "can reasonably be supported with evidence at trial" or greater than necessary to reflect gravity of offense).

3. *Civil consequences.* Do the prosecutor's proposed bargain terms become coercive when they move beyond matters of criminal charges and sentences to include civil consequences, matters that other legal institutions ordinarily decide? State

courts have not expressed any special concern about such agreements. See Gustine v. State, 480 S.E.2d 444 (S.C. 1997) (prosecutor offers plea agreement on child sex-abuse charges contingent on defendant's giving up parental rights to step-daughter; court does not declare parental rights term coercive as a matter of law but calls for case-by-case inquiry into knowing and voluntary nature of guilty plea). Is it wise to assume that criminal consequences are the most serious problems facing a defendant?

4. *Breaching a contract and breaking a plea bargain*. Coercive negotiation techniques by a prosecutor call into question the authenticity of any "meeting of the minds" between the government and the defendant. Indeed, the law of plea bargains is often described by analogy to the law of contract. In both areas courts must decide when an agreement is made, what terms the agreement includes, whether a breach has occurred, and the appropriate remedies.

The basic federal law for deciding when a bargain is made comes from the U.S. Supreme Court decisions in Santobello v. New York, 404 U.S. 257 (1971), and Mabry v. Johnson, 467 U.S. 504 (1984). In *Santobello,* the Supreme Court stated: "If the guilty plea is part of a plea bargain, the State is obligated to comply with any promises it makes." 404 U.S. 262. In *Mabry,* the Court explained that the enforceability of bargains was guaranteed by the due process clause, but that a plea was not binding until it was entered and accepted by a court: Until that point the plea bargain was a "mere executory agreement" without "constitutional significance." In general, therefore, a prosecutor can withdraw an offer any time before the formal plea is accepted by the court. A majority of state courts have adopted this framework.

Once it becomes clear that the parties have indeed entered a binding plea agreement, courts also must determine whether either of the parties has breached that agreement. Further, they wrestle with the question of proper remedies for breaches of a plea agreement. An extensive discussion of these interrelated questions appears on the web extension for this chapter at *http://www.crimpro.com/extension/ch16*. Along the way, this web material considers in more detail the contractual dimensions of plea bargains.

b. Judicial Overinvolvement

Earlier in this chapter we considered judicial efforts to place limits on the institution of plea bargaining, and the individual judge's responsibility during a plea hearing to confirm and document that the defendant is entering the guilty plea knowingly and voluntarily. But what is the individual judge's role prior to the guilty plea? Rules of procedure paint very different portraits of the judge's involvement in plea negotiations. Some rules, such as Fed. R. Crim. P. 11(c)(1), state that the trial judge "shall not participate in any" plea discussions. Others do not tell the judge what to do during the negotiations. Rules and statutes in a few states authorize the trial judge to take part in negotiations. See N.C. Gen. Stat. §15A-1021(a) ("The trial judge may participate in the discussions"). Do these rules reflect profound differences in practice, or do they reflect an ambiguity about what qualifies as judicial "participation" in the plea negotiations?

STATE v. LANDOUR BOUIE

817 So. 2d 48 (La. 2002)

CALOGERO, C.J.

We granted this writ application to determine whether the district court abused its discretion in not allowing the defendant to withdraw his plea of guilty, given that the trial judge had previously interjected his own opinions into the plea negotiations as to whether the defendant would be acquitted or found guilty. . . .

The state charged the defendant and his co-defendant, Cornelius Johnson, with attempted second degree murder. . . . The charge arose out of the shooting of Eddie Hughes, who had intervened in an attempt by [Bouie] and Johnson to secure the services of a prostitute doing business near Hughes's home. Using a rifle that [Johnson] retrieved from [Bouie's] house, where the two men had driven after the initial dispute with Hughes, Johnson confronted Hughes on the street outside his home and fired a bullet that struck the victim in the throat, severing his spinal column. The victim survived. . . .

From the outset, the defendant indicated that he wanted to go to trial, and throughout the discussions, he consistently indicated that he believed he was innocent of the charge of attempted second degree murder. . . . At the outset of the day set for trial, the defendant, represented by appointed counsel, stated that he understood that he was going to trial, and asserted that he *wanted* to go to trial. Immediately, the trial judge told the defendant that he was being tried for attempted second degree murder and that "if you go to trial, the penalty for that charge is fifty years at hard labor." The trial judge followed up by telling the defendant that, because he had been on probation at the time of the offense, he could be found guilty of being a second felony offender and receive a sentence of up to 100 years. But if he pleaded guilty, . . . and if the state filed a multiple offender bill, the trial judge would give the defendant the minimum twenty-five years at hard labor, or as low as ten years if the state did not file the multiple offender bill.

When the defendant was asked if this information helped him to make up his mind, the defendant responded affirmatively, but he also asserted, "Your Honor — uh — I'm just going you know, I haven't did anything." The trial judge quickly responded with his view on the certainty that the defendant would be convicted if he chose to go to trial: . . .

Court: You may be able to be found not guilty. . . . But I can tell you this, all of the years that I've been either a prosecutor or a judge, I don't think I've ever seen more than one or two people who went to trial found not guilty. The D.A. knows what they're doing when they try somebody, generally, and the jury seems to believe them, generally. And the odds are not in your favor of going to trial and winning a case. Do you understand that? Do you?

Bouie: Yes, sir.

Court: And when I say all the years I've been doing that, that's been since 1981, so how long is that? Sixteen years I've been doing this, either a judge or an assistant district attorney and I think I've found two people found not guilty — uh — seen two people found not guilty in felony trials. Now, if you go to trial, I'm telling you the odds are against you winning. Do you understand that?

Bouie: Yes, sir.

Court: All right, then if you lose, then you're looking at the hundred years. . . . If you plead guilty, you're looking at no more than twenty-five and maybe as low as ten. Do you understand that?
Bouie: Yes, sir.

At this point, the defendant was allowed to confer with his counsel and the matter of his co-defendant was taken up by the trial judge. Johnson, too, expressed indecision and questioned the state's version of the facts, but, after discussions with the trial judge, in which the judge offered the same deal and stated that a hundred-year sentence meant that Johnson would die in prison, Johnson eventually entered a plea of guilty as charged in return for a sentencing commitment by the court of twenty-five years imprisonment at hard labor, the minimum term for a second offender convicted of attempted murder and sentenced as a multiple offender. In its recitation of the case, the state indicated that Johnson had given a video-taped statement in which he stated that the defendant had encouraged him to retrieve the weapon and to shoot the victim. According to the state, Johnson said that, on the way back to the scene, the two men had struck a bargain in which the defendant agreed to drive the getaway car and Johnson vowed to shoot the victim. Johnson, in court, disagreed with the state's recitation, but he conceded that there had been a shooting and that what the state had said had basically happened "in so many ways."

After Johnson's plea was completed, the defendant returned to court. [The] defendant was asked what he thought he was facing and he replied, "Whew, um, I really don't know." Expressing some frustration, "All right, that's why I keep trying to explain it to you," the trial judge reiterated that the defendant was charged with attempted second degree murder, which carries a sentence of up to 50 years at hard labor, that a jury was waiting upstairs and would return a verdict in a few days if he elected to go to trial that day, that the defendant in fact had a prior felony conviction, and that the sentence would be up to 100 years at hard labor as a second felony offender if he went to trial, but only 25 years if he pleaded guilty. After conferring with his attorney, the defendant agreed to plead guilty, and the *Boykin* examination commenced. See Boykin v. Alabama, 395 U.S. 238 (1969).

During the colloquy, the trial judge gave a similar response anytime the defendant vacillated. When the defendant indicated that he thought he had been promised 10 years, the trial judge responded that it was only if the state chose not to file a multiple offender bill would he impose a sentence between 10 and 25 years at hard labor. The trial judge then asked if the defendant wanted to plead guilty. When he received no response, the trial judge stated that if not, "we've got the people waiting upstairs to get the trial started." The defendant responded, "I — whew, um — ." The trial judge again asked if the defendant wanted to finish the guilty plea and if he understood what was happening. The defendant said he did "in a way" and expressed doubt about the evidence against him. The trial judge then explained the law of principals, using the getaway driver of an armed robbery as an example. The trial judge [said that if the jury concluded that Bouie] provided a gun to Johnson, drove him back to the scene, and encouraged him to shoot the victim, then the defendant would be as guilty as if he had shot the victim.

The trial judge then had the state repeat its case against the defendant for the record. Unlike his co-defendant Johnson, the defendant expressed considerable doubt that he was guilty of any crime for transporting Johnson back and forth from the scene of the shooting. In his own statement to the police, the defendant had acknowledged only that he had been on the scene with Johnson to pick up a prostitute, that after the initial confrontation with the victim he had driven Johnson back to his (the defendant's) house where Johnson retrieved a rifle that he (Johnson) had hidden there earlier that evening, and that he (the defendant) had then returned with Johnson to the scene to "turn a trick" with the prostitute. The defendant had denied in his statement that he knew beforehand that Johnson would shoot the victim and he continued to insist in court that the two men had gone back "to see . . . where the trick was. [Johnson] got out the car and the only thing I heard was a shot. . . ." [After Bouie observed that "everything is pointing at me," the trial judge returned to the question of a guilty plea]:

> *Court:* Do you think it's in your best interest at this point to go ahead and accept a guilty plea and get the lesser years that you've been offered rather than running the risk of going to trial and getting the Habitual Act charged against you and getting, maybe, up to a hundred years?
>
> *Bouie:* (no answer)
>
> *Court:* Do you think this guilty plea today, right now, is better than doing that? In other words, this is in your best interest at this point.
>
> *Bouie:* It seems like, Your Honor.

The trial court then accepted the defendant's guilty plea.[2] However, after the state filed a multiple offender bill, but before sentencing, the defendant moved to withdraw his plea, alleging that he had been under "extreme emotional stress" when he entered the plea. At the hearing on the motion, the defendant testified that the court had, in effect, stampeded him into pleading guilty, not simply by the sentencing offer of 25 years imprisonment at hard labor but also by informing him, in effect, that "if I take you to trial, I was not going to win in your courtroom. You was going to give me fifty to a hundred years. So I feel as though I wasn't going to win no matter what." On the basis of that testimony, the attorney representing the defendant asked the court at the close of the hearing, "You saw [two acquittals] in nearly a twenty-year period. . . . How is he going to knowingly and intentionally plead guilty after he hears that, Your Honor?"

The trial judge denied the motion on grounds that it had spent over an hour and a half with the defendant in a painstaking effort to persuade him that a guilty plea was in his best interests "because he probably would have gotten convicted and been sentenced to fifty to a hundred years. [Instead] of doing that, I gave him twenty-five, and, certainly . . . that was in his best interest." The court . . . sentenced him to the promised term of 25 years imprisonment at hard labor. . . .

A trial judge has broad discretion in ruling on a defendant's motion to withdraw his guilty plea before sentencing. La. Code Crim. Proc. art. 559. When circumstances indicate that the plea was constitutionally invalid, the trial judge should allow the defendant to withdraw his plea. . . . However, as a general rule, an otherwise valid plea of guilty is not rendered involuntary merely because it was entered to

2. Notably, the trial judge never explained to the defendant that, to prove him guilty of attempted second degree murder, the state was required to prove that the defendant, even as a principal, had possessed the requisite specific intent to kill the victim. Consequently, whether a jury accepting the defendant's story as true could have rationally found the requisite specific intent proved beyond a reasonable doubt appears less certain than the trial judge advocated.

limit the possible maximum penalty to less than that authorized by law for the crime charged.

[The] defendant contends that the nature and extent of the district court judge's participation in the plea agreement had a coercive effect on his decision to plead guilty. While this court has not directly addressed the issue of a judge's participation in negotiating a plea agreement, in State v. Chalaire, 375 So. 2d 107, fn.2 (La. 1979), albeit in dicta, we stated: "Although not objected to in this appeal, the judge's active participation in the plea negotiations evokes our concern. The ABA Standards recommend that the trial judge should not be involved with plea discussions before the parties have reached an agreement. ABA Standards, The Function of the Trial Judge §4.1 (Approved Draft 1972); accord, Fed. R. Crim. P. [11(c)(1)]." As we noted in *Chalaire,* the reasons for proscribing judicial participation in plea negotiations, according to the ABA Standards Commentary, are:

> (1) judicial participation in the discussions can create the impression in the mind of the defendant that he would not receive a fair trial were he to go to trial before this judge; (2) judicial participation in the discussions makes it difficult for the judge objectively to determine the voluntariness of the plea when it is offered; (3) judicial participation to the extent of promising a certain sentence is inconsistent with the theory behind the use of the presentence investigation report; and (4) the risk of not going along with the disposition apparently desired by the judge may seem so great to the defendant that he will be induced to plead guilty even if innocent. ABA Standards, Pleas of Guilty §3.3(a) Commentary 73 (Approved Draft 1968).

On the other hand, we also pointed out that . . . removal of the judge from the bargaining process usually places the sentencing prerogative in the district attorney's office. [We] concluded that . . . "any judge who directly participates in plea discussions should take extreme care to avoid the dangers described in the ABA commentary."

In our decision today, we do not adopt a rule absolutely prohibiting the participation of Louisiana trial judges in plea negotiations, such as that provided by the Federal Rules of Criminal Procedure [11(c)(1)] ("The court shall not participate in any such discussions"). Instead, we find that the interjection of the trial judge's personal knowledge and opinion in the plea discussions under the circumstances of this case did, or probably did, have a coercive effect on this particular defendant's decision that a guilty plea was in his best interest.

In the present case, the trial judge's explanations of the penalties the defendant faced if he went to trial and if he were convicted by a jury, and of the trial judge's discretion to impose greater penalties after conviction than offered in the course of plea negotiations, were not inherently coercive because the advice concerned information that an accused ought to possess to enter a knowing and intelligent guilty plea. Furthermore, the court's explanation of the law of principals under La. Rev. Stat. 14:24, which would form the basis of any verdict rendered by a jury, also served the same end.

However, when the trial judge coupled those lengthy explanations with his personal view that the result of a jury trial was all but a foregone conclusion, he went beyond simply facilitating the entry of a knowing and voluntary guilty plea. The trial judge's discussion of the chances of an acquittal at a jury trial conveyed the court's personal experience over the years in unrelated cases and its confidence in the soundness of the exercise of the charging discretion of the District Attorney's Office. No matter how benign the judge's intent, and no matter how solicitous of the defendant's interests, the trial judge clearly conveyed his opinion that this particular defendant had no realistic choice other than to plead guilty or face penalties ranging from two to four times as great as the court offered. Aside from the question of its reliability, such a message was inherently coercive because it came from the court, not from the prosecutor. . . . See Standley v. Warden, 990 P.2d 983, 985 (Nev. 1999) ("Appellant had good reason to fear offending the judge if he declined [the plea offer] because the same judge would have presided over the trial and, if the trial resulted in a conviction, the judge would have determined the appropriate sentence"). The defendant here voiced those concerns in his own words at the hearing on his motion to withdraw his guilty plea when he explained to the court that he took the sentencing offer because, "You told me, if I take you to trial, I'm not going to win in your courtroom."

We recognize that a defendant may enter a voluntary guilty plea even while he continues to protest his innocence. North Carolina v. Alford, 400 U.S. 25 (1970). . . . However, *Alford* presupposes that the defendant "must be permitted to judge for himself in this respect." Therefore, whether the offered plea agreement was in fact in the defendant's best interest was not for the court to decide, but for the defendant to determine with the advice of his counsel.

We concede that a fine line may at times separate a trial judge's attempts to insure that the defendant understands that a guilty plea might serve his best interest and the overbearing of a defendant's will to reach a result the court, with the best of intentions, deems appropriate. However, we find that the trial judge in this case, by stating his personal views on the virtual certainty that the defendant would be convicted by a jury, as well as on the prospect of a sentence much greater than that offered, when this judge would be determining the sentence to be imposed following the guilty verdict, overstepped his bounds and acted as more of an advocate than as a neutral arbiter of the criminal prosecution. We conclude that the defendant's guilty plea under these circumstances was not knowingly and voluntarily entered, such that the district court abused its discretion in not granting the defendant's motion to withdraw the guilty plea. . . .

WEIMER, J., dissenting.

. . . I do not believe the statements were sufficient to coerce the defendant or unreasonably persuade him to plead guilty. It has not been alleged that anything the trial court stated was inaccurate. . . . It should be noted that defendant's admitted behavior in the events surrounding the shooting subjected him to a risk of conviction. This risk of conviction was amplified when the statement of his co-defendant, which implicated the defendant, was considered. . . .

Certainly, the trial court can and must inform the defendant of the consequences of his plea. However, in doing so, the court must avoid the impression of coercing or persuading the defendant to plead guilty. Despite the defendant's allegations, I believe the court succeeded in avoiding that impression.

Notes

1. *Legal limits on judicial participation in plea negotiations.* States have addressed the role of the judge during plea negotiations through statutes, rules of criminal procedure, rules of judicial ethics, and in judicial opinions interpreting constitutional provisions. More than half of the states instruct the judge not to "participate" in the plea discussions, the position embodied in the Federal Rules of Criminal Procedure. See People v. Collins, 27 P.3d 726 (Cal. 2001) (judge's promise of "some benefit" for giving up jury trial right rendered guilty plea involuntary); State v. Wakefield, 925 P.2d 183 (Wash. 1996); Colo. Rev. Stat. §16-7-302; Ga. Unif. Super. Ct. R. 33.5(a); Mass. R. Crim. P. 12(b) (reporter's notes). Does this mean that the judges cannot even be present as an observer during such discussions?

Another group of states discourages judges from participating in plea negotiations but does not prohibit it. Judicial opinions in these states suggest that judicial participation in negotiations, while not the best practice, is not a reason to invalidate a conviction on constitutional or other grounds. State v. Niblack, 596 A.2d 407 (Conn. 1991); State v. Ditter, 441 N.W.2d 622 (Neb. 1989). A small but growing number of states (now over a dozen) have rules or statutes that do not discourage judicial participation, and some even authorize judges to take part. See Mont. Code §46-12-211; N.C. Gen. Stat. §15A-1021(a). Some of the laws authorizing judges to participate extend only to limited types of participation. For instance, some states allow judges to take part only when the parties extend an invitation. People v. Cobbs, 505 N.W.2d 208 (Mich. 1993). Others limit the judge to commenting on the acceptability of charges and sentences that the parties themselves propose. See Ill. Sup. Ct. R. 402(d); State v. Warner, 762 So. 2d 507, 514 (Fla. 2000) (once invited by parties, court may actively discuss potential sentences and comment on proposed plea agreements). Do these limits identify the judicial practices with the most potential for making a guilty plea involuntary?

The ABA Standards for Criminal Justice, Pleas of Guilty 14-3.3, have embodied over the years an ambivalence about judicial involvement in plea discussions. The original 1968 version of Standard 14-3.3 completely barred judicial participation in plea negotiations. The 1980 edition of the Standards established a more active role for judges as a participant in plea negotiations. The parties could request to meet with the judge to discuss a plea agreement, and the judge could "serve as a moderator in listening to their respective presentations" and could "indicate what charge or sentence concessions would be acceptable." On the other hand, "the judge should never through word or demeanor, either directly or indirectly, communicate to the defendant or defense counsel that a plea agreement should be accepted or that a guilty plea should be entered." The 1997 edition of the Standards set out a more limited role for the judge: "a judge may be presented with a proposed plea agreement negotiated by the parties and may indicate whether the court would accept the terms as proposed and, if relevant, indicate what sentence would be imposed."

2. *Judicial involvement in practice.* Judges do participate in plea negotiations. As the variety of legal rules on the subject suggests, the practice varies from place to place. One study from the late 1970s concluded that about a third of judges in felony and misdemeanor courts nationwide attended plea negotiations. Most of the judges attending the negotiations "reviewed" recommendations by the parties, while a few

judges made their own recommendations to the parties. These nationwide figures concealed some variety among different jurisdictions. Judges in states with rules clearly barring their participation in plea bargaining were much less likely to attend the negotiations than judges in other states. John Paul Ryan & James Alfini, Trial Judges' Participation in Plea Bargaining: An Empirical Perspective, 13 Law & Soc'y Rev. 479 (1979). See also Allen Anderson, Judicial Participation in the Plea Negotiation Process: Some Frequencies and Disposing Factors, 10 Hamline J. Pub. L. & Pol'y 39 (1990).

3. *Judicial neutrality and plea negotiations.* Critics of judicial participation in plea negotiations have argued that a judge who proposes or ratifies the terms of a plea agreement cannot properly perform judicial duties later in the case. For instance, they say, such a judge cannot properly decide at the plea hearing whether the defendant is entering the guilty plea voluntarily. If the defendant rejects a proposed offer, it may be difficult for the negotiating judge to preside at the trial. The participating judge may also find it difficult at sentencing to give proper consideration to a presentence investigation that recommends some sentence different from the negotiated recommendation. See Richard Klein, Due Process Denied: Judicial Coercion in the Plea Bargaining Process, 32 Hofstra L. Rev. 1349 (2004). Are these concerns realistic? Are there ways to avoid these problems in systems that permit judges to participate in plea discussions? Should rules require different judges for the plea and the trial?

4. *Judicial coercion and plea negotiations.* The most common objection to judicial participation in plea discussions is that the judge will coerce the defendant into accepting a plea agreement. While the prosecutor does not hold ultimate authority to impose a sentence in most cases, the judge can say with certainty what sentence she will impose after trial or after a guilty plea. If the judge indicates that a particular outcome is a "good deal," does the defendant have much hope for a better outcome? One might conclude alternatively that judges who participate in plea discussions merely give the defendant more accurate and complete information about what will occur at sentencing. Their presence might prevent prosecutors from misrepresenting local sentencing practices or from proposing unreasonable outcomes. Albert Alschuler, The Trial Judge's Role in Plea Bargaining (pt. 1), 76 Colum. L. Rev. 1059 (1976). For reasons such as these, a law reform commission in Great Britain has called for a return to the practice of "sentence canvassing," in which a judge can tell a defendant in private the most severe sentence he might expect after a guilty plea. The courts in Great Britain have put a stop to this traditional practice. Report of the Royal Commission on Criminal Justice 112-13 (1993) (Runciman Commission).

How does judicial participation in plea negotiations compare to other sources of coercion to plead guilty? If a defendant can voluntarily plead guilty while claiming innocence, and can voluntarily plead guilty when the prosecutor plans to seek more severe sanctions against the defendant's family members unless they all enter guilty pleas, why object to a judge who tells the defendant the going rate for an offense?

D. THE FUTURE OF BARGAINING

Is plea bargaining bad or good? If courts and executive branch policies actually do "regulate" plea bargaining — as the materials in this chapter suggest — are those regulations effective at limiting the undesirable aspects of plea bargaining? Should we ban plea bargaining altogether?

1. *Legitimacy of Bargaining*

Many scholars, judges, and lawyers believe that plea bargaining is inevitable. They say that the use of other processes (especially trials) to decide guilt or innocence would at best be hugely expensive and at worst cause a meltdown of the justice system. But before we consider whether it is feasible to ban plea bargaining, we need to know whether an attempted ban would be worth the effort. Is plea bargaining legitimate? Would we keep it in an ideal world?

■ ALBERT ALSCHULER, IMPLEMENTING THE CRIMINAL DEFENDANT'S RIGHT TO TRIAL: ALTERNATIVES TO THE PLEA BARGAINING SYSTEM

50 U. Chi. L. Rev. 931 (1983)

. . . Plea bargaining makes a substantial part of an offender's sentence depend, not upon what he did or his personal characteristics, but upon a tactical decision irrelevant to any proper objective of criminal proceedings. In contested cases, it substitutes a regime of split-the-difference for a judicial determination of guilt or innocence and elevates a concept of partial guilt above the requirement that criminal responsibility be established beyond a reasonable doubt. This practice also deprecates the value of human liberty and the purposes of the criminal sanction by treating these things as commodities to be traded for economic savings — savings that, when measured against common social expenditures, usually seem minor.

Plea bargaining leads lawyers to view themselves as judges and administrators rather than as advocates; it subjects them to serious financial and other temptations to disregard their clients' interests; and it diminishes the confidence in attorney-client relationships that can give dignity and purpose to the legal profession and that is essential to the defendant's sense of fair treatment. In addition, this practice makes figureheads of court officials who typically prepare elaborate presentence reports only after the effective determination of sentence through prosecutorial negotiations. Indeed, it tends to make figureheads of judges, whose power over the administration of criminal justice has largely been transferred to people of less experience, who commonly lack the information that judges could secure, whose temperaments have been shaped by their partisan duties, and who have not been charged by the electorate with the important responsibilities that they have assumed. Moreover, plea bargaining perverts both the initial prosecutorial formulation of criminal charges and, as defendants plead guilty to crimes less serious than those that they apparently committed, the final judicial labeling of offenses.

The negotiation process encourages defendants to believe that they have, [in the words of a Chicago defense attorney], "sold a commodity and . . . , in a sense, gotten away with something." It sometimes promotes perceptions of corruption. It has led the Supreme Court to a hypocritical disregard of its usual standards of waiver in judging the most pervasive waiver that our criminal justice system permits. The practice of plea bargaining is inconsistent with the principle that a decent society should want to hear what an accused person might say in his defense — and with constitutional guarantees that embody this principle and other professed ideals for the resolution of criminal disputes. Moreover, plea bargaining has undercut the goals of legal doctrines as diverse as the fourth amendment exclusionary rule, the insanity defense, the right of confrontation, the defendant's right to attend criminal proceedings, and the recently announced right of the press and the public to observe the administration of criminal justice. This easy instrument of accommodation has frustrated both attempts at sentencing reform and some of the most important objectives of the due process revolution.

Plea bargaining provides extraordinary opportunities for lazy lawyers whose primary goal is to cut corners and to get on to the next case; it increases the likelihood of favoritism and personal influence; it conceals other abuses; it maximizes the dangers of representation by inexperienced attorneys who are not fully versed in an essentially secret system of justice; it promotes inequalities; it sometimes results in unwarranted leniency; it merges the tasks of adjudication, sentencing, and administration into a single amorphous judgment to the detriment of all three; it treats almost every legal right as a bargaining chip to be traded for a discount in sentence; and it almost certainly increases the number of innocent defendants who are convicted. In short, an effort to describe comprehensively the evils that plea bargaining has wrought requires an extensive tour of the criminal justice system. . . .

At the end of a long investigation of plea bargaining, I confess to some bafflement concerning the insistence of most lawyers and judges that plea bargaining is inevitable and desirable. Perhaps I am wrong in thinking that a few simple precepts of criminal justice should command the unqualified support of fair-minded people:

- that it is important to hear what someone may be able to say in his defense before convicting him of crime;
- that, when he denies his guilt, it is also important to try to determine on the basis of all the evidence whether he is guilty;
- that it is wrong to punish a person, not for what he did, but for asking that the evidence be heard (and wrong deliberately to turn his sentence in significant part on his strategies rather than on his crime);
- and, finally, that it is wrong to alibi departures from these precepts by saying that we do not have the time and money to listen, that most defendants are guilty anyway, that trials are not perfect, that it is all an inevitable product of organizational interaction among stable courtroom work groups, and that any effort to listen would merely drive our failure to listen underground.

From my viewpoint, it is difficult to understand why these precepts are controversial; what is more, I do not understand why the legal profession, far from according them special reverence, apparently values them less than the public in general does. Daniel Webster thought it a matter of definition that "law" would hear before it condemned, proceed upon inquiry, and render judgment only after trial. Apparently the legal profession has lost sight of Webster's kind of law. . . .

■ FRANK EASTERBROOK, PLEA BARGAINING AS COMPROMISE

101 Yale L.J. 1969 (1992)

Is plea bargaining good or bad? Should we keep it or kick it? . . .

The analogy between plea bargains and contracts is far from perfect. Courts use contract as an analogy when addressing claims for the enforcement of plea bargains, excuses for nonperformance, or remedies for their breach. But plea bargains do not fit comfortably all aspects of either the legal or the economic model. Courts refuse to enforce promises to plead guilty in the future, although the enforcement of executory contracts is a principal mission of contract law.

On the economic side, plea bargains do not represent Pareto improvements. Instead of engaging in trades that make at least one person better off and no one worse off, the parties dicker about how much worse off one side will be. In markets persons can borrow to take advantage of good deals or withdraw from the market, wait for a better offer, and lend their assets for a price in the interim. By contrast, both sides to a plea bargain operate under strict budget constraints, and they cannot bide their time. They bargain as bilateral monopolists (defendants can't shop in competitive markets for prosecutors) in the shadow of legal rules that work suspiciously like price controls. Judges, who do not join the bargaining, set the prices, increasingly by reference to a table of punishments that looks like something the Office of Price Administration would have promulgated. Plea bargaining is to the sentencing guidelines as black markets are to price controls.

Black markets are better than no markets. Plea bargains are preferable to mandatory litigation — not because the analogy to contract is overpowering, but because compromise is better than conflict. Settlements of civil cases make both sides better off; settlements of criminal cases do so too. Defendants have many procedural and substantive rights. By pleading guilty, they sell these rights to the prosecutor, receiving concessions they esteem more highly than the rights surrendered. Rights that may be sold are more valuable than rights that must be consumed, just as money (which may be used to buy housing, clothing, or food) is more valuable to a poor person than an opportunity to live in public housing.

Defendants can use or exchange their rights, whichever makes them better off. So plea bargaining helps defendants. Forcing them to use their rights at trial means compelling them to take the risk of conviction or acquittal; risk-averse persons prefer a certain but small punishment to a chancy but large one. Defendants also get the process over sooner, and solvent ones save the expense of trial. Compromise also benefits prosecutors and society at large. In purchasing procedural entitlements with lower sentences, prosecutors buy that most valuable commodity, Time. With time they can prosecute more criminals. When [eighty] percent of defendants plead guilty, a given prosecutorial staff obtains five times the number of convictions it could achieve if all went to trial. Even so, prosecutors must throw back the small fish. The ratio of prosecutions (and convictions) to crimes would be extremely low if compromises were forbidden. Sentences could not be raised high enough to maintain deterrence, especially not when both economics and principles of desert call for proportionality between crime and punishment.

True, defense lawyers and prosecutors are imperfect agents of their principals. Of what agents is this not true? Real estate agents? Corporate managers? Agency costs are endemic and do not justify abandoning consensual transactions. . . . Monitoring the performance of agents is difficult, and serious monitoring means substantially increasing the time and number of lawyers devoted to each case. Critics of plea bargaining commit the Nirvana Fallacy, comparing an imperfect reality to a perfection achievable only in imaginary systems. . . .

Why should we interfere with compromises of litigation? If the accused is entitled to a trial at which all his rights are honored and the sentence is appropriate to the crime, yet prefers compromise, who are we to disagree? . . . Why is liberty too important to be left to the defendant whose life is at stake? Should we not say instead that liberty is too important to deny effect to the defendant's choice?

Every day people choose where (if at all) to obtain an education, what occupation to pursue, whom to marry, whether to bear children, and how to raise them. Often they choose in ignorance — not simply because they do not know whether Yale offers a better education than the University of Southern Mississippi, but also because they do not know what the future holds. Technological changes or fluctuations in trade with foreign nations will make some educations obsolete and raise the value of others. People may, without the approval of regulators, climb mountains, plummet down slopes at eighty miles per hour on waxed boards, fail to exercise, eat fatty foods, smoke cigarettes, skip physical checkups, anesthetize their minds by watching television rather than reading books, and destroy their hearing by listening to rock music at high volumes. Sometimes courts say that the Constitution protects the right to make these choices, precisely because they are so important. . . .

Courts give effect not only to life-and-death choices actually made but also to elections by inaction. When a defendant's lawyer fails to make an important motion or omits an essential line of argument, we treat the omission as a forfeiture. How bizarre for a legal system that routinely puts persons in jail for twenty years following their agents' oversight to deny them the right to compromise the same dispute, advertently, for half as much loss of liberty. . . .

Curtailing the discount for pleading guilty has been justified in the name of equality. Yet the greatest disparity in sentencing is between those convicted at trial and those not prosecuted. A reduction in the number of convictions attributable to a decline in the number of pleas would dramatically increase the effective disparity in the treatment of persons suspected of crime. . . .

Plea bargains are compromises. Autonomy and efficiency support them. "Imperfections" in bargaining reflect the imperfections of an anticipated trial. To improve plea bargaining, improve the process for deciding cases on the merits. When we deem that process adequate, there will be no reason to prevent the person most affected by the criminal process from improving his situation through compromise.

Notes

1. *Plea bargains: contract or charade?* Some scholars have accepted the essentially contractual nature of plea bargaining, and have suggested that the problem with

plea bargaining law is that it does not take the contracting analogy seriously enough.Robert Scott and William Stuntz, for example, focus on the risk of convicting an innocent defendant, arguing that "by following appropriate contract models, one can devise different rules that reduce the harm to innocent defendants and meanwhile reduce transaction costs and inefficiency for everyone else." Scott & Stuntz, Plea Bargaining as Contract, 101 Yale L.J. 1909 (1992). Critics of plea bargaining, such as Professor Stephen Schulhofer, have rejected the notion that plea bargains are fair simply because the defendant agreed to the terms and because the agreement puts the defendant in a better position than if the defendant went to trial. Schulhofer, Plea Bargaining as Disaster, 101 Yale L.J. 1979 (1992). Schulhofer and other critics focus on the public interest in criminal justice that the contract model obscures. Does plea bargaining undermine public confidence in the criminal justice system? Stanley Cohen & Anthony Doob, Public Attitudes to Plea Bargaining, 32 Crim. L.Q. 85 (1989-1990) (1988 survey found that more than two-thirds of Canadians disapprove of plea bargaining). What is Judge Easterbrook's attitude toward the use of contract law to explain plea bargaining? Does he take account of the public interest arguments? Does Professor Alschuler account for the contractarian argument that plea bargains are the fairest (most preferable) means for the defendant to address criminal charges, except in very limited circumstances? Would the fairness of plea bargaining be cast into doubt if there were no trials at all? See Malcolm Feeley, The Process Is the Punishment (1979) (of 1,640 misdemeanor cases, not one defendant requested jury trial). Is there such a thing as a "natural" rate of trials?

2. *The public interest in trials.* Judge Easterbrook treats plea bargains as the best way to honor the rights of the defendant, including the right to autonomy — to determine one's own destiny. But do not offenders forgo any such right when they commit a crime? Do criminal defendants have a constitutional right to bargain? Why should society care about giving free choice to a person who has acted in a way that denies rights (life, health, autonomy, ownership, and so forth) to others? Might the public have a greater interest in public trials than in more convictions? Might the public have an interest in convictions and sentences as close as possible to conceptions of what "really" happened, whether the conviction and sentence follow a trial or a nonbargained guilty plea?

3. *Bargaining and bribery.* Sometimes the government will enter a plea bargain with a defendant in exchange for the defendant's cooperation in other criminal investigations, including testimony against other criminal defendants. Does this sort of plea bargain amount to bribing a witness? Courts never took such an argument seriously until a panel of the U.S. Court of Appeals for the Tenth Circuit reversed a money laundering conviction on the ground that the government had bribed the cooperating witness. A few months later, the en banc court changed direction and upheld the conviction. The "anti-gratuity statute," 18 U.S.C. §201(c)(2), declares that whoever "directly or indirectly, gives, offers, or promises anything of value to any person, for or because of the testimony under oath or affirmation given or to be given by such person" has committed a crime. The en banc court read the word "whoever" to exclude prosecuting attorneys acting within the normal course of their authority. Any other result, the court said, would be a "a radical departure from the ingrained legal culture of our criminal justice system." United States v. Singleton, 165 F.3d 1297 (10th Cir. 1999) (en banc). What would be the effects if prosecutors stopped promising to enter lenient plea agreements with

cooperative witnesses? Try to formulate alternatives that prosecutors might adopt to obtain cooperation from witnesses who were involved in alleged crimes.

2. *Efforts to Ban Bargaining*

Courts and commentators occasionally refer to plea bargaining as eternal and inevitable. It may be inevitable, though it is surely not eternal. Research suggests that plea bargaining was forbidden (at least formally) in the first two-thirds of the nineteenth century, and emerged in the last third of that century, becoming institutionalized and widespread in the twentieth century. See Lawrence Friedman, Plea Bargaining in Historical Perspective, 13 Law & Soc'y Rev. 247 (1979); Albert Alschuler, Plea Bargaining and Its History, 13 Law & Soc'y Rev. 211 (1979).

Professor George Fisher, through careful study of the origins of plea bargaining in nineteenth-century Massachusetts, revealed how plea bargaining first thrived for crimes that gave judges little choice over sentences (and therefore gave added importance to the prosecutor's choice of charges). Bargaining also became more attractive to prosecutors after the appearance of probation as a sentencing option. Judges became more amenable to plea bargaining after a flood of railroad tort suits created civil docket pressures. Fisher, Plea Bargaining's Triumph, 109 Yale L.J. 857 (2000).

Do the following cases indicate that plea bargaining was banned in fact, or do they instead imply a ban in law but a reality of underground bargains? As a historian, how would you determine which of the two stories — true bans, or de jure bans combined with de facto bargains — was closer to the truth?

■ COMMONWEALTH v. JOHN BATTIS

1 Mass. 95 (1804)

The Court will not direct an immediate entry of the plea of guilty to an indictment for a capital crime, but will give a reasonable time to the prisoner to consider the same, that he may, if he think proper, retract his plea.

The defendant, John Battis, a Negro of about twenty years of age, was indicted for the murder of one Salome Talbot, a white girl of the age of thirteen years, on the twenty-eighth day of June last. The indictment contained three counts. The 1st count charged the killing to have been with a stone, with which he beat and broke her skull, and etc. The 2d stated that the killing was by drowning; and the 3d charged the killing to have been by beating and breaking her skull with a stone, and throwing her body into the water, and suffocating and drowning. There was another indictment against the prisoner for committing a rape on the body of the said Salome, on the same day on which the murder was charged to have been committed.

On the second day of the term, in the forenoon, the prisoner was set to the bar, and had both indictments read to him, and pleaded guilty to each. The Court informed him of the consequence of his plea, and that he was under no legal or moral obligation to plead guilty; but that he had a right to deny the several charges, and put the government to the proof of them. He would not retract his pleas; whereupon the Court told him that they would allow him a reasonable time to consider of what had been said to him: and remanded him to prison. They directed the clerk not to record his pleas, at present.

In the afternoon of the same day, the prisoner was again set to the bar, and the indictment for murder was once more read to him; he again pleaded guilty. Upon which the Court examined, under oath, the sheriff, the jailer, and the justice (before whom the examination of the prisoner was had previous to his commitment) as to the sanity of the prisoner; and whether there had not been tampering with him, either by promises, persuasions, or hopes of pardon, if he would plead guilty. On a very full inquiry, nothing of that kind appearing, the prisoner was again remanded, and the clerk directed to record the plea on both indictments.

On the last day of the term, the prisoner was brought to the bar, and the Attorney-general (Sullivan) moved for sentence; which the chief justice delivered in solemn, affecting, and impressive address to the prisoner. The sentence was entered on the indictment for the rape. He has since been executed.

■ GEORGE EDWARDS v. PEOPLE

39 Mich. 760 (1878)

CAMPBELL, C.J.

Plaintiff in error was informed against on a charge of larceny, in the daytime, from a shop, of a gold watch of the value of twenty-five dollars. The information was sworn to on the 25th of June, averring the offense on the 11th. On the same 25th day of June the prisoner was arraigned, pleaded guilty and was sentenced to the Ionia house of correction for three years. . . . The error relied on to reverse the judgment is that the court did not make the proper investigation before proceeding to sentence the prisoner, to ascertain whether he ought not to have been put on trial.

It has always been customary, and is according to many authorities essential before sentence to inquire of the prisoner whether he has anything to say why sentence should not be pronounced against him; and that it is generally said should appear of record. . . .

The Legislature of 1875, having in some way had their attention called to serious abuses caused by procuring prisoners to plead guilty when a fair trial might show they were not guilty, or might show other facts important to be known, passed a very plain and significant statute designed for the protection of prisoners and of the public. It was thereby enacted as follows:

> That whenever any person shall plead guilty to an information filed against him in any circuit court, it shall be the duty of the judge of such court, before pronouncing judgment or sentence upon such plea, to become satisfied, after such investigation as he may deem necessary for that purpose, respecting the nature of the case, and the circumstances of such plea, that said plea was made freely, with full knowledge of the nature of the accusation, and without undue influence. And whenever said judge shall have reason to doubt the truth of such plea of guilty, it shall be his duty to vacate the same, direct a plea of not guilty to be entered, and order a trial of the issue thus formed. . . .

It is contrary to public policy to have any one imprisoned who is not clearly guilty of the precise crime charged against him, and thus equally contrary to policy and justice to punish any one without some regard to the circumstances of the case. By confining this statute to information and not extending it to indictments, it is easy to see that the Legislature thought there was danger that prosecuting attorneys, either to save themselves trouble, to save money to the county, or to serve some other improper purpose, would procure prisoners to plead guilty by assurances they have not power to make of influence in lowering the sentence, or by bringing some other unjust influence to bear on them. It is to be presumed they had evidence before them of serious abuses under the information system which in their judgment required checking by stringent measures.

Every one familiar with the course of criminal justice knows that those officers exercise very extensive and dangerous powers, that in the hands of an arbitrary or corrupt man are capable of great abuse. And unless the general impression is wrong, great abuses have been practiced by this very device of inveigling prisoners into confessions of guilt which could not be lawfully made out against them, and deceiving them concerning the precise character of the charges which they are led to confess. And it has also happened, as is generally believed, that by receiving a plea of guilty from a person whose offense is not aggravated, worse criminals who have used him for their purposes remain unpunished, because the facts which would convict them have not been brought out.

This statute not only requires the judge to examine carefully into the facts of the case, which can require no less than a search into the depositions if they have been returned or similar evidence if they have not been taken, but also compels him to examine the prisoner himself concerning the circumstances which induced him to plead guilty. It is evident that for this purpose it would be highly improper to take any thing on the statement of the prosecuting attorney, or to allow him to be present at the examination of the prisoner. . . . It could not have been contemplated that this should be done during the routine business of court and in presence of all the officers of justice and the prosecutor.

Without deciding that the absence from the record of a recital of such investigation must in all cases void the validity of a sentence on such plea, we have no hesitation in saying that the record ought to show the fact, and unless it does so, must show at least a reasonable delay between plea and sentence which may justify some presumption that this duty has been performed. . . .

Being of opinion that the record before us furnishes presumptive evidence at least that the statute was disregarded, we feel compelled to reverse the judgment. It is to be hoped that some express provision of law will require the record to note what is done in these cases. The statute is a wholesome one, but in the evident want to care in carrying it out we do not feel warranted in holding that a failure to note the fact on the record is conclusive. It is too important a matter to be left without some more positive direction concerning its appearance on the court journals. Judgment must be reversed, and the prisoner discharged.

Plea bargaining bans are not only part of history. Bans have also appeared from time to time in modern criminal justice. The following article describes several bans on plea bargains, along with other efforts by prosecutors to limit their reliance on plea negotiations. Before reading this article, consider what you would expect to happen when legal systems try to ban plea bargaining. Does the account of New Orleans practices confirm or challenge your expectations?

■ RONALD WRIGHT AND MARC MILLER, THE SCREENING/BARGAINING TRADEOFF

55 Stanford L. Rev. 29 (2002)

When it comes to plea bargaining, we have created a false dilemma. . . . Scholars, judges, prosecutors, defense lawyers, and politicians have offered only two basic responses to the fact that guilt is mostly resolved through negotiated guilty pleas: They take it or they leave it.

Some take the system more or less as it is. They accept negotiated pleas in the ordinary course of events, either because such a system produces good results or because it is inevitable. They might identify some exceptional cases that create an intolerable risk of convicting innocent defendants, or unusual cases where there are special reasons to doubt the knowing and voluntary nature of the defendant's plea. These special cases might call for some regulation. But the mine run of cases, in this view, must be resolved with a heavy dose of plea bargains and a sprinkling of trials.

Then there are those who leave it, arguing that our system's reliance on negotiated guilty pleas is fundamentally mistaken. Some call for a complete ban on negotiated guilty pleas. Others, doubting that an outright ban is feasible, still encourage a clear shift to more short trials to resolve criminal charges. Restoring the criminal trial to its rightful place at the center of criminal justice might require major changes in public spending, and it might take a lifetime, but these critics say the monstrosity of the current system demands such a change.

This dilemma about plea bargaining — take it or leave it — is a false one. It is based on a false dichotomy. It errs in assuming that criminal trials are the only alternative to plea bargains. In this erroneous view, fewer plea bargains lead inexorably to more trials; indeed, the whole point in limiting plea bargains is to produce more trials.

This paper offers a different choice, and points to prosecutorial "screening" as the principal alternative to plea bargains. Of course all prosecutors "screen" when they make any charging decision. By prosecutorial screening we mean a far more structured and reasoned charge selection process than is typical in most prosecutors' offices in this country. The prosecutorial screening system we describe has four interrelated features, all internal to the prosecutor's office: early assessment, reasoned selection, barriers to bargains, and enforcement.

First, the prosecutor's office must make an early and careful assessment of each case, and demand that police and investigators provide sufficient information before the initial charge is filed. Second, the prosecutor's office must file only appropriate charges. Which charges are "appropriate" is determined by several factors. A prosecutor should only file charges that the office would generally want to result in a criminal conviction and sanction. In addition, appropriate charges must reflect reasonably accurately what actually occurred. They are charges that the prosecutor can very likely prove in court. Third, and critically, the office must severely restrict all plea bargaining, and most especially charge bargains. Prosecutors should also recognize explicitly that the screening process is the mechanism that makes such restrictions possible. Fourth, the kind of prosecutorial screening we advocate must include sufficient training, oversight, and other internal enforcement mechanisms to ensure reasonable uniformity in charging and relatively few changes to charges after they have been filed. If prosecutors treat hard screening decisions as the primary alternative to plea bargaining, they can produce changes in current criminal practice that would be fundamental, attractive, and viable. . . .

Traditional Alternatives to Plea Bargaining

. . . For those who wish to establish that plea bargaining is an inevitable and irrepressible force in American criminal justice, Philadelphia is a problem. The city has long operated a system that relies more on short bench trials than on pleas of guilty. A number of scholars conducted case studies in Philadelphia (and a few other cities with high rates of bench trials) and concluded that the trials in those cities were not truly adversarial trials. Instead, they were "slow pleas" of guilt. The brief trials allowed the defendant to present evidence about the circumstances of the case, not to obtain an acquittal, but to influence the judge at sentencing.

Stephen Schulhofer visited the Philadelphia courts and took away a different impression. [He] observed a large number of bench trials in the city and concluded that they were genuinely adversarial proceedings where defendants retained many of the constitutional protections sacrificed during plea bargaining. Schulhofer called for other jurisdictions to follow Philadelphia's lead and to treat short trials as a viable alternative to plea bargaining. . . .

Explicit efforts to shorten trials have not been the preferred technique among American prosecutors who want to limit the reach of negotiated pleas. Instead, the handful of prosecutors who aspire to "ban" plea bargaining — either for targeted crimes or for the entire criminal docket — have issued strong ukases against bargaining, enforced by more rigorous screening and modest staffing increases, as their most workable solution. . . .

Among the most famous American plea bargaining bans occurred in Alaska during the 1970s and 1980s. In 1975, state Attorney General Avrum Gross declared that prosecutors would no longer engage in charge bargaining or sentence bargaining. Attorney General Gross hoped to restore public confidence in the system, increase the number of trials, improve the litigation skills of prosecutors, and return prosecutors to their traditional roles of evaluating evidence and trying cases instead of negotiating.

Major studies in 1978 and 1991 evaluated the impact of the Alaska plea ban. By all accounts, both charge bargaining and sentence bargaining became rare events during the first ten years of the policy. During the late 1980s, charge bargains reappeared, but prosecutors continued to avoid sentence bargains. For a few years, the trial rate increased modestly. Seven percent of charged cases went to trial before the ban, and the rate moved to 10% before returning to 7% by the end of the 1980s.

Since the cases were not ending in negotiated pleas or trials, what was happening to them? The answer was a combination of aggressive screening and open guilty pleas. Before the ban, prosecutors in Fairbanks refused to prosecute about 4% of the felonies referred to them by the police or other investigators. After the ban, the proportion of felonies that prosecutors declined to prosecute increased to about 44%. A large portion of the case load (about 23%) was disposed of through open pleas of guilt. This was part of the Attorney General's thinking when he created the plea ban. More careful selection of cases would make it possible to stick with the initial charges, even in front of a judge or jury.

The Alaska experience received lackluster academic reviews. Some implied that the failure to increase trials proved that unseen bargains were still driving the system, and explained the high number of open guilty pleas. Others pointed to the reappearance of charge bargaining after ten years, and suggested that it is futile to place controls on the quintessential prosecutorial decision of charge selection. Some implied that Alaska was too unusual a jurisdiction to offer any guidance to prosecutors in most major American cities. However, other jurisdictions scattered around the country have duplicated pieces of the Alaska experience over the years. Some prosecutors in other locales have picked out priority crimes like homicide and banned plea bargains for those cases.[53] Some of the bans target particular forms of bargaining rather than particular crimes.[54] The reaction to these experiences, like the reaction to the Alaska plea ban, has been subdued. If these prosecutors were not increasing their trial rates, the critics found the effort unimportant.

These experiences do not mean that any ban on charge reductions will produce small trial increases and large numbers of open guilty pleas. If prosecutors do not change their screening principles to insist on more declinations of cases referred to the office, the dispositions shift in other directions. In El Paso County, Texas during the 1980s, the chief prosecutor announced an end to all plea bargaining in burglary cases. There was no organized effort to change the screening of such cases, and the number of trials increased enough to create a serious backlog of untried cases. Partial bans on plea bargaining appear regularly around the country. Most prosecutors today who plan to restrict plea negotiations focus on priority crimes, such as homicide or sex crimes. Some of the bans are limited to particular courts or phases of litigation, such as the statutory ban on plea bargains for most serious felonies in Superior Court in California, or the ban on plea bargaining in the Supreme Court in the Bronx in the mid-1990s.

When plea bans are limited to a particular court (such as the highest trial court), the effects are usually minimal because the bargainers simply move to a different (typically earlier) point in the process. Plea bans exist today, but we know little about their effects on case dispositions and sentences. The attention of academic observers has strayed to other areas, even as prosecutors keep innovating. . . . Thirty years of scholarship has missed a fundamental perspective on plea bargaining: there are in fact many alternative points of comparison when assessing the wisdom and necessity of plea bargains. . . .

53. In the 1970s, the prosecutor in Maricopa County (Phoenix), Arizona barred plea bargains in cases involving designated crimes such as drug sales, homicide, robbery, burglary, assault with a deadly weapon, and sexual misconduct. The policy did not increase trial rates for these crimes because more defendants pled guilty as charged. Moise Berger, *The Case Against Plea Bargaining*, 62 A.B.A. J. 621 (1976). Similar reports came after prosecutors in Multnomah County, Oregon and Black Hawk County, Iowa banned plea bargaining for selected crimes during the early 1970s. Note, The Elimination of Plea Bargaining in Black Hawk County: A Case Study, 60 Iowa L. Rev. 1053 (1975). . . .

54. In an example of one such effort to discourage some forms of bargaining, the District Attorney for Manhattan in the mid-1970s prohibited his attorneys from recommending sentences and established (and published!) a 1974 memorandum suggesting specific charge discounts to offer in exchange for guilty pleas. Richard H. Kuh, Plea Bargaining: Guidelines for the Manhattan District Attorney's Office, 11 Crim. L. Bull. 48 (1975). Thomas Church documented the efforts of a county in a Midwestern state during the early 1970s to eliminate charge bargaining in drug sale cases. Thomas Church, Jr., Plea Bargains, Concessions and the Courts: Analysis of a Quasi-Experiment, 10 Law & Soc'y Rev. 377 (1976). The prosecutor left sentence bargaining in place, and the proportion of the cases resolved through defendants pleading guilty as charged increased from 17 to 90% between 1972 and 1974. In Church's view, the county's experience demonstrated the inevitability of plea bargaining. But his interviewees believed that the concessions the defendants were promised after the ban were far less reliable and valuable than the concessions they negotiated before the ban.

THE SCREENING/BARGAINING TRADEOFF IN PRACTICE: NODA DATA

A chief prosecutor attempting to change plea practices faces both administrative and political hurdles. Will her proposed policy actually change the use of negotiated guilty pleas? If so, can the office sustain it over the long haul? We do not believe that plea bargaining is inevitable, but plea bargaining surely is pervasive and deeply entrenched. Any effort to limit plea bargaining must confront the habits and relationships of prosecutors and defense attorneys.

Reform efforts emerging voluntarily from within one criminal justice institution may have a greater chance to succeed than reforms imposed externally. A single institution can set up review and reward systems, allowing for more supervision — and, we believe, more consistency — than external constraints can provide. Among the many virtues we see in the screening/bargaining tradeoff described in this paper is the authority of a chief prosecutor, acting alone, to set this change in motion.

What should we expect to happen when a prosecutor decides to shift the screening/bargaining tradeoff in the direction of screening? As for changes in case processing, the most direct effect should be measurable: fewer plea bargains. The kinds of plea bargains that are easiest to track are charge reductions after cases are filed. A jurisdiction with hard screening practices should produce fewer and smaller charge reductions than jurisdictions with weaker screening practices.

[We can] test the plausibility of the screening/bargaining tradeoff using previously unstudied and unreported data about one major urban prosecutor's office: the New Orleans District Attorney's Office, or NODA. This data exists because the District Attorney for Orleans Parish, Harry Connick, has remained committed to principled screening throughout his long term in office. . . .

Harry Connick was elected as the District Attorney for Orleans Parish in 1974. He has remained in that office for the past twenty-eight years. Connick first ran for office in 1969 against incumbent Jim Garrison, the flamboyant District Attorney made famous in the film JFK. His first unsuccessful campaign did not focus on plea bargaining. He promised faster prosecution and better tracking of defendants who failed to appear for trial. His 1973 campaign began with a similar emphasis on swift prosecution. As the campaign wore on, however, Connick's speeches began to feature attacks on plea bargaining. . . .

Connick told voters that widespread plea bargaining was wrong; years later, he explained that victims were right to resent it when cases were bargained away simply because of a "lazy" prosecutor. He promised to eliminate "baseless" plea bargaining and to hire full-time prosecutors who would not use plea bargains just to move cases from the docket.

As in other American cities, the criminal courts in New Orleans deal with enormous volume. In the face of this large urban caseload, Connick needed a strategy to carry out his campaign statements about plea bargaining. During the weeks between his election victory and taking office, he started speaking publicly about a plan with two central components. First, Connick planned to devote expertise and resources to screening. He proposed a screening procedure that "would weed out those cases really not worthy of being on the criminal docket, so more courtroom emphasis can be devoted to the violent offender." Second, he instructed his prosecutors not to engage in plea bargaining — particularly charge bargaining — except under very limited circumstances. . . .

The distinctiveness of the screening process in the NODA office is apparent from a closer examination of the path each new case takes through the system. Police officers develop a case folder after they complete an investigation and file charges with the magistrate. The first stop for the case folder in the NODA office is the Magistrate Section, where the least experienced assistants work. They typically have logged six months or fewer on the job. The ADA from the Magistrate Section appears for the state at the first appearance and bail hearing before the magistrate. A public defender is also present for the first appearance, but the case is reassigned immediately after the hearing and there is typically no further defense presence or participation in the case until after the DA files an information or obtains an indictment.

After any proceedings in the Magistrate Division, the folder moves to the Screening Section of the NODA office. Connick devotes extraordinary resources to this operation. For instance, in the late 1990s, about fifteen of the eighty-five attorneys in the office worked in Screening. . . . All attorneys in the Screening Section served previously (usually a couple of years) in the Trial Section. This level of experience comes at a premium in New Orleans, where the turnover among prosecuting attorneys is quite high. The average tenure of an ADA in the NODA office is around two years.

Within the Screening Section, designated cases such as homicide or rape get assigned to screeners with special expertise. Drug cases and a few other high-volume cases go to a subgroup known as Expedited Screening. Ordinary cases go to the Screening Attorney on duty for that day. The screener reviews the investigation file, speaks to all the key witnesses and the victims (often by telephone, but sometimes in person), and generally gauges the strength of the case. If the police report neglects to mention a factual issue that is likely to arise at trial, the screening attorney will speak directly with the police officer to resolve it. There is a powerful office expectation that the Screening Attorney will make a decision within ten days of receiving the folder.

NODA instituted a variety of measures to ensure reasonable uniformity in screening decisions. Connick committed his screening principles to writing in an office policy manual. The general office policy is to charge the most serious crime the facts will support at trial. The policy does not, on its face, allow individual prosecutors to consider for themselves the equities in the case when selecting the charge. By the same token, however, Connick insists that overcharging is unacceptable, because the charges chosen for the information will stay in place through the trial. If screening prosecutors overcharge cases too often, the Chief of the Trial Section might send the screening attorney back into the courtroom on at least one of those overcharged matters to "get his teeth kicked in."

Supervisors review all refusals to charge. Attorneys say they often compare notes, especially in early morning discussions, and this helps to educate and develop shared charging norms in the office. Office policy discourages refusal for select categories of crimes, notably domestic violence cases. For the most serious crimes, including rape and homicide, the office conducts "charge conferences" with senior prosecutors and police present to discuss the facts and potential charges.

Neither Connick nor any attorneys in his office claim to have abolished plea bargaining entirely from the New Orleans system. Prosecutors in the office acknowledge that sometimes new information appears and changes the value of a case. Witnesses leave town, victims decide not to testify, new witnesses appear, and investigators find new evidence. On occasion, the screening attorney makes a bad judgment and overcharges, and a plea could save the case.

Nevertheless, office policy tries to keep these changes in charges to a minimum. A supervisor must approve any decision to drop or change charges after the information is filed. The attorney requesting the change must complete a special form naming the screening and trial attorneys, and explaining the reason for the decision, drawing from a list of acceptable reasons. The ADAs believe there is a "stigma" involved in reducing charges, however strong the reasons for a reduction might be.

Attorneys from the NODA office believe that they decline to prosecute an exceptional number of cases. They view this as a necessary part of training police officers to investigate more thoroughly. The relatively high rate of declination also created a political challenge for Connick over the years. During each of his reelection campaigns — in 1978, 1984, 1990, and 1996 — Connick's challengers criticized the number of cases that the NODA office declined to prosecute. As his opponent Morris Reed put it in many public debates, "the PD arrests them and the DA turns them loose." Connick had several replies. Poor police work made declinations necessary. Further, he pointed to specific examples of how his office dealt severely with defendants once they were charged. Connick also explicitly linked his screening policies to his plea bargaining policies: Tough screening, he said, made it possible to keep plea bargaining at low levels.

Connick drew on case data to make specific claims about low rates of plea bargaining in the office: He asserted that plea bargaining in Jim Garrison's day reached 60 to 70%, but fell to 7 or 8% of all cases filed under his office policy. He also routinely mentioned the high number of trials in New Orleans compared to other Louisiana jurisdictions. In addition, Connick pointed to his routine use of the habitual felon law to enhance sentences. By the end of each of the four reelection campaigns, Connick convinced the voters that it was possible both to decline many cases and to run a tough prosecutor's office at the same time. . . .

The data mostly support District Attorney Harry Connick's claims to have implemented a screening/bargaining tradeoff over the last thirty years. Several kinds of information bolster that judgment, but the most substantial and useful by far is the data that Connick has kept to assist in his administration of the office. New Orleans shows that the screening/bargaining tradeoff does not necessarily lead to a disabling number of trials. The office also shows that a committed prosecutor can implement the screening/bargaining tradeoff even without the conscious support of other actors in the system. . . . Plea bargaining's triumph, and the cynical products of that triumph, are simply not as absolute as a century of practice and study suggest.

Notes

1. *The isolated popularity of bans.* Though a minor theme in current criminal justice debates, bans on plea bargaining occasionally become a topic of public concern, and they remain a subject of intense scholarly interest. Jurisdictions other than Alaska have experimented with formal plea bans, though none have been statewide; most are implemented by a single prosecutor with a particular vision for improving the criminal justice system. Other modern efforts to abolish plea bargaining include a ban in El Paso, Texas; a Detroit ban on bargaining in felony

firearm cases; another effort in Michigan to abolish charge bargaining in drug trafficking cases; and a judge-imposed ban in Superior Court in New Hampshire. See Amy Fixsen, Plea Bargaining: The New Hampshire "Ban," 9 New Eng. J. on Crim. & Civ. Confinement 387 (1983); Robert Weninger, The Abolition of Plea Bargaining: A Case Study of El Paso County, Texas, 35 UCLA L. Rev. 265 (1987); see generally 13 Law & Soc'y Rev. (1979). A recent effort in the Bronx District Attorney's office banned bargains in felony cases after indictment. See Kenneth Jost, Critics Blast New York Plea Ban, 9 CQ Researcher No. 6, at 124 (Feb. 12, 1999). Which aspect of plea bargaining do these reforms target? Is selective restriction on bargaining preferable to a total ban?

2. *Alternatives to plea bargaining.* If bargains are banned, what takes their place? The Alaska and New Orleans experiences suggest that guilty plea rates may remain quite high even in the absence of bargains. Why might this be so? Professor Schulhofer and others have argued that it is possible to offer meaningful trials in place of bargains, including greater use of bench rather than jury trials. See Stephen Schulhofer, Is Plea Bargaining Inevitable? 97 Harv. L. Rev. 1037 (1984) (discussing use of short trials in Philadelphia). In an article excerpted at the beginning of this section, Professor Alschuler makes a particularly eloquent argument in favor of offering some kind of trial over any kind of bargain: "In providing elaborate trials to a minority of defendants while pressing all others to abandon their right to trial, our nation allocates its existing resources about as sensibly as a nation that attempted to solve its transportation problem by giving Cadillacs to ten percent of the population while requiring everyone else to travel by foot. [Less] would be more. . . . ." Does the New Orleans District Attorney offer defendants, as a group, less procedural protection or less favorable outcomes than they might receive in a jurisdiction that negotiates more routinely for reduced charges?

3. *The inevitability of plea bargaining reconsidered.* The Alaska experience suggests that in some jurisdictions, at least, it is possible to have not only a formal plea ban, but one that causes substantial changes in the behavior of the key actors. But even in Alaska pressures led, over the course of a decade, to decay in the original stark vision of a land without bargains. Are bans likely to be effective only for a short time? Are plea bargains an inevitable answer to pressures within the justice system (whether political, legal, social, or economic)? See generally Milton Heumann, Plea Bargaining: The Experiences of Prosecutors, Judges, and Defense Attorneys (1978). Can individual lawyers or judges "ban" bargaining? For a ban to work, does there need to be a more proportional and modest system of punishments? Is plea bargaining a necessity or virtue in highly punitive times? In other words, does a world with no plea bargaining require penalties that judges and prosecutors are actually comfortable enforcing?

XVII

Decisionmakers at Trial

More than 90 percent of all criminal convictions are obtained through plea bargains and guilty pleas, leaving comparatively few cases for trial. Looking at trials from this vantage point, however, obscures four important points. First, for some kinds of offenses and offenders, the trial rate is considerably higher. For example, in 2006 in large urban counties, about 49 percent of murder convictions were obtained through trial. Generally, trial rates for violent offenses against persons are higher than for property, drug, and weapons offenses.

Second, 10 percent of all convictions may seem small compared with the proportion of charges settled through plea bargains, but there are still a large number of criminal trials in most U.S. jurisdictions. In 2004, for example, there were over 1,075,000 felony convictions in state courts. While 95 percent of the convictions were obtained through guilty pleas, there were still over 53,000 felony trials. A small change in the plea rate can have a major impact on the number of trials and the operation of court systems.

Third, there is not just one kind of trial. Public perception often seems to be shaped by long, high-profile trials. But in fact, most trials are short. In 2009, for example, of the 8,051 federal criminal trials, 63 percent were completed in a single day, 12 percent lasted two days, and 9 percent took three days. Thus, more than four-fifths of federal criminal trials were completed in three days or less. Just under half of state felony trials are handled by judges sitting without a jury. Judges try a much higher percentage of misdemeanor trials, though the rate varies enormously among the states and the proportion of the roughly 12 million misdemeanors each year that go to trial is difficult to determine.

Finally, plea bargaining practices do not develop in a vacuum: They reflect to some degree the availability, benefits, and costs of trials. For example, when sanctions imposed after trials start to resemble sanctions imposed after guilty pleas, more defendants are likely to go to trial since there is always some chance that the government will fail to prove the case or that a jury or judge will find the defendant not guilty for some other reason.

A useful perspective for studying the U.S. trial system is to consider the very different processes used in other countries. For example, the paradigm decisionmaker in U.S. criminal trials — the criminal jury — is virtually unknown in some other lands. Other countries employ institutions not familiar in the United States, such as multi-judge panels in criminal cases. In Germany lone judges try minor offenses, but more serious offenses are tried before panels made up of "professional" and "lay" judges.

The fact that other places conduct trials in other ways serves as a reminder that the U.S. justice system involves choices. One fundamental question about U.S. criminal trials is why they are relatively rare, compared with plea bargains, and whether that is a good or bad thing. If public criminal trials are preferred to private (and regulated) bargains, will different rules produce more trials?

This chapter examines different decisionmakers at trial. The first section examines the choice between jury and judge trials. The second and third sections study the procedures for selecting jurors and guiding juries as they perform their function. The final section considers the role of a decisionmaker in a larger sense — the public — in watching and evaluating criminal trials.

A. JUDGE OR JURY?

Perhaps the most distinctive feature of American criminal trials is the criminal jury. While studying these materials and the law related to juries, you should also sit as a judge, assessing the continuing vitality and relevance of this complicated and expensive institution. Consider whether the original assumptions and justifications for the criminal jury remain true today, or whether some other institution (perhaps judges) or some other form (perhaps smaller juries or juries that can convict on a majority vote) would be more appropriate.

1. Availability of Jury Trial

The Sixth Amendment provides in part: "In all criminal prosecutions, the accused shall enjoy the right to a speedy and public trial, by an impartial jury." The U.S. Supreme Court determined in Duncan v. Louisiana, 391 U.S. 145 (1968), that this fundamental right applies to the states through the due process clause of the Fourteenth Amendment. Despite the absolute language of the amendment ("*all* criminal prosecutions"), the right is not absolute; the constitutional guaranty of a jury trial does not cover "petty offenses." The *Duncan* Court explained that jury trials were not available historically for petty crimes and that non-jury trials are faster and less expensive than jury trials.

The question of which crimes qualify as "petty" crimes has enormous practical consequences because the largest number of cases in American criminal justice systems involve less serious (but not necessarily "petty") crimes. The Court in Baldwin v. New York, 399 U.S. 66 (1970), relied on the history of the Sixth Amendment in concluding that it was meant to protect jury trials only in cases that were triable by a jury at common law. In later cases, it has become clear that a "serious" offense covered by the federal right to jury trial must be punishable by a prison term of more than six months. In Blanton v. City of North Las Vegas, 489 U.S. 538, 541-42 (1989), the Court stated the test as follows:

> In determining whether a particular offense should be categorized as "petty," our early decisions focused on the nature of the offense and on whether it was triable by a jury at common law. In recent years, however, we have sought more objective indications of the seriousness with which society regards the offense. We have found the most relevant such criteria in the severity of the maximum authorized penalty. . . . In using the word "penalty," we do not refer solely to the maximum prison term authorized for a particular offense. A legislature's view of the seriousness of an offense also is reflected in the other penalties that it attaches to the offense. . . . Primary emphasis, however, must be placed on the maximum authorized period of incarceration.

The Court in *Blanton* held that a charge under Nevada's DUI statute, which had a maximum authorized prison term of six months as well as other possible penalties (including fines and wearing distinctive clothing to identify the offender as a convicted drunk driver), was not "constitutionally serious." In United States v. Nachtigal, 507 U.S. 1 (1993), the Court reiterated that "offenses for which the maximum period of incarceration is six months or less are presumptively 'petty.' . . . A defendant can overcome this presumption, and become entitled to a jury trial, only by showing that the additional mix of penalties, viewed together with the maximum prison term, are so severe that the legislature clearly determined that the offense is a 'serious' one." In *Nachtigal,* the Court held that a DUI charge with a maximum penalty of six months' imprisonment, a $5,000 fine, a five-year term of probation, and several other penalties, was not constitutionally serious.

Most state constitutions, like the federal constitution, protect the right to a jury trial. State courts interpreting these provisions have most often determined, like the U.S. Supreme Court, that the right to a jury trial applies only to "serious" offenses. However, most state courts have chosen a different line of demarcation between serious and petty offenses. State legislatures have also passed statutes guaranteeing a jury trial in a wider range of cases than the state or federal constitutions require. The majority and dissenting opinions in the following case offer two very different and archetypal approaches to the question of when a case is serious enough to warrant a jury trial.

■ STATE v. KENT BOWERS

498 N.W.2d 202 (S.D. 1993)

MILLER, C.J.

. . . On April 12, 1990, a large group of people, which included [Kent Bowers and four other appellants], gathered at the Women's Medical Clinic in Sioux Falls, South Dakota, to protest against abortions taking place there and to dissuade patients from entering the clinic to obtain an abortion. Prior to this protest, the organizers had met with police in hopes of keeping their protest peaceful. The protest consisted of praying, singing and reading the bible. The protesters congregated on the parking lot and lawn of the clinic and blocked the south and east doors into the clinic. Although the protesters made no threats and induced no violence, they obstructed at least one person's access to the clinic.

The police were called to the clinic. Anticipating a violent protest, they called in seventy-seven officers, including twenty-one off-duty officers. . . . An officer, using a bull horn to amplify his voice, read a statement to the protesters ordering them to leave the clinic's property. [Protesters] crossed the police barrier to go back onto clinic property and to resume blocking the south and east doors of the clinic. The police then began to arrest protesters. . . . The arrested protesters were charged with one count of unlawful occupancy of property in violation of [a state misdemeanor statute] and one count of disorderly assembly in violation of [a Sioux Falls ordinance].

The protesters requested jury trials. . . . The magistrate judge denied the motions for jury trials, assuring the protesters that he would impose no jail sentences in the event they were found guilty. . . . The protesters were found guilty on both counts. The magistrate judge then imposed fines and jail sentences which included seven to fourteen days jail time which was suspended on the condition of no like offenses for one year. [On appeal, the] circuit judge affirmed the convictions but modified the sentences imposed by deleting the suspended jail time. This appeal followed.

The United States Constitution provides in part: "In all criminal prosecutions, the accused shall enjoy the right to a speedy and public trial, by an impartial jury of the State and district wherein the crime shall have been committed." U.S. Const. Amend. VI. This right, however, does not extend to crimes which carry a possible jail penalty of only six months' imprisonment. Baldwin v. New York, 399 U.S. 66 (1970).

The South Dakota Constitution provides in part: "In all criminal prosecutions the accused shall have the right to . . . a speedy public trial by an impartial jury of the county or district in which the offense is alleged to have been committed." S.D. Const. Art. VI, §7; SDCL 23A-16-3. In State v. Wikle, 291 N.W.2d 792 (S.D. 1980), this court explained that the right to a jury trial extends to a criminal prosecution for which there could be imposed "a direct penalty of incarceration for any period of time." In 1984, this court modified *Wikle* when we held "a court may deny a jury trial request in a criminal prosecution when the court assures the defendant at the time of request that no jail sentence will be imposed. This is, of course, limited to prosecution of offenses with maximum authorized jail sentences of less than six months." State v. Auen, 342 N.W.2d 236 (S.D. 1984). Appellants argue that the magistrate judge erred because the sentences imposed on them are beyond the scope of *Auen*.

Violators of either the state law, a Class 2 misdemeanor, or the municipal ordinance here at issue could, at the time of the alleged offenses, be punished by a maximum of thirty days in a county jail, a $100 fine, or both. When the magistrate judge was presented with the requests for jury trials, he noted that although he has granted jury trials in petty theft cases, he would not grant appellants jury trials. The magistrate judge assured appellants he would impose no jail sentences in the event they were found guilty. Nevertheless, after the trial the magistrate judge imposed suspended jail sentences as well as fines. The magistrate judge then placed appellants on probation for one year. . . .

On appeal, the circuit court noted that as the magistrate court "denied the jury trial upon this assurance [of no jail sentence], a final judgment entered imposing a suspended seven days in the county jail was contrary to the assurance of the court." The circuit court then modified the sentences imposed and deleted the portions of the judgments which imposed jail time. We agree with the circuit court judge that the magistrate judge improperly imposed a one-year probation with suspended jail sentences. . . . The circuit court's subsequent judgment cured the magistrate judge's improper sentencing.

We note further that appellants were not denied their Sixth Amendment right to a jury trial by being placed on probation for one year. No jail sentence remains which can be imposed on appellants even in the event that their suspended sentences are revoked. Of that part of the sentence which remained after the circuit court's judgment, not "one day of the defendant's freedom was involved . . . but only his pocketbook." *Wikle,* 291 N.W.2d at 795 (Henderson, J., concurring specially). Appellants were not improperly denied a jury trial. . . . Affirmed.

HENDERSON, J., concurring in part, dissenting in part.

. . . In the case before us, appellants were charged with disorderly assembly and unlawful occupancy of property. Whereas both offenses carry a maximum jail time of six months, the magistrate trial judge denied the request for a jury trial: "I'm not, first of all, going to open up the Pandora's box of giving trials to every Class 2 offense. I have done that in petty theft cases because no one wants to be a thief, but otherwise I'm not going to open up that box . . . so the request for a jury trial will be denied."

Attempting to follow *Auen,* the magistrate trial court assured the appellants that they would receive no jail sentence. Nevertheless, after the trial, the magistrate court imposed suspended sentences, community service, fines and probation. Although the circuit court eliminated the suspended sentences . . . , the one-year probation remained intact.

Both the magistrate court and circuit court erred in denying appellants a jury trial based upon the crime being a petty offense with no jail time. The first problem is defining "petty." Although the meaning and scope of petty crimes are not statutorily defined, the Court announced a formula in *Wikle* to distinguish the two. Courts must look to the maximum punishment and the nature of the offense, consider the common law background of the offense, determine if society views the offense with sufficient opprobrium, and consider the consequences of conviction.

Furthermore, Baldwin v. New York, 399 U.S. 66 (1970), does not hold that offenses which carry a maximum punishment of six months or less are automatically petty offenses. Rather, when deciding if an offense is "petty," the U.S. Supreme Court seeks out objective criteria reflecting the seriousness with which society regards the offense, and "we have found the most relevant such criteria in the severity of the maximum authorized penalty." Attempting to heed to that holding, this state broadly defines a "petty crime" as an offense that carries a maximum jail time of six months or less. *Auen.* What happened to our "eternal vigilance" here — as commanded by Thomas Jefferson, as being "the price of liberty?"

Under *Baldwin,* we are supposed to be looking at the maximum penalty, not simply jail time. Had appellants been charged with the state law version of disorderly assembly, rather than the city version, they would have violated a Class 1 misdemeanor with a maximum incarceration of one year. Thus, under state law, the court could not deny the appellants their mandatory and constitutionally guaranteed jury trial. Admittedly, these appellants were not charged with the state version.

However, the inequity is obvious: Prosecutors can deftly deny a defendant a jury trial by simply charging him with the city version of a crime.

Granted, police and prosecutors may arrest and charge at their own discretion. But in Sioux Falls, a person can be denied a jury trial if the city officials believe the actions are petty, even though the state categorizes the actions as serious or when the judge decides not to "open up the Pandora's box," or when the prosecutor, as he stated during the motion hearing, does not want the appellants to use "the Court system as a forum by which to politicize their beliefs."

Despite the majority's labeling it as such, this protest was anything but petty. Before the protests began, organizers met with the police in hopes of keeping their assembly peaceful. Anticipating problems, the police, on the other hand, called in 21 off-duty officers, sent 77 officers to the protest, rented buses, brought video cameras, instituted new methods for arresting and identifying arrestees who might not be carrying identification. This was all set up in advance at an expense of nearly $5,000. Police Captain Gerald Kiesacker stated that he had anticipated more violence and more resistance than at previous similar demonstrations. Consider: The press was given its own observation area during the arrests. Petty? Baloney! . . .

Additionally, placing appellants on a one-year probation without benefit of a jury trial also denied them their Sixth Amendment rights. . . . Probation is an alternative to confinement where the defendant is under the control of the trial court in a manner designed to avoid incarceration. Public protection is provided through the ability of the trial court to revoke probation and impose a sentence should the defendant violate the terms of the probation. . . .

Thus, appellants were subject to a one-year punishment, a violation of which could subject them to jail time. Furthermore, though they may not be incarcerated, their actions are still under the disciplinary eye of the trial court. Appellants Dorr and Ellenbecker took jail time in lieu of the fine. . . . Today's holding permits a penalty beyond [the] six-month boundary. Probation, in itself, involves the freedom of a defendant. Even under the logic of *Baldwin* and *Auen,* the defendant escapes the grasp of the State within six months. Is not the purpose of the courts to protect, not chisel away, the rights of the accused? . . .

When the shadows are cast upon my judicial mantel, I am comforted with the conviction that I stood for jury trials and not against them. As Teddy Roosevelt once expressed: "I shall not join those weak and timid souls who know neither victory nor defeat." I have fought the good fight. Under the Statist's muskets, I have again fallen. So what. "Woe unto you, when all men shall speak well of you!" [Luke 6:26]. And so it may be said of these appellants.

■ MARYLAND COURTS AND JUDICIAL PROCEEDINGS CODE §12-401

(d) A defendant who has been found guilty of a municipal infraction . . . or a Code violation . . . may appeal from the final judgment entered in the District Court. . . .

(f) [In any criminal case, including a] case in which sentence has been imposed or suspended following a plea of nolo contendere or guilty, and an appeal in a municipal infraction or Code violation case, an appeal shall be tried de novo [in the trial court of original jurisdiction for felonies, the Circuit Court].

(g) In a criminal appeal that is tried de novo, there is no right to a jury trial unless the offense charged is subject to a penalty of imprisonment or unless there is a constitutional right to a jury trial for that offense.

Notes

1. *Jury trials and petty offenses under state constitutions: majority position.* Virtually all state constitutions guarantee the right to a jury trial, often by stating that the right "shall remain inviolate." Does this language suggest an effort to preserve a right in its limited historical form rather than an effort to declare a more extensive right based in natural law? Most state courts have concluded that the state constitution does not require a jury trial for all offenses, but only for "serious" (as opposed to "petty") offenses. However, most state courts disagree with the federal constitutional definition of a "petty" crime. The federal courts look primarily to the length of imprisonment imposed as an "objective" measure of a crime's seriousness for purposes of a jury trial. A crime whose punishment is more than six months' imprisonment is "presumptively" serious; any crime that is punished by a shorter term of imprisonment is very difficult to establish as "serious" under the Sixth Amendment, even when coupled with substantial fines and other penalties. Some state courts agree with this approach. See, e.g., State v. Smith, 672 P.2d 631 (Nev. 1983) (no jury trial for six-month prison term authorized for drunken-driving offense). A larger group of states adopt the federal methodology (focusing on the length of the prison term) but conclude that some shorter period of potential or actual imprisonment is enough to trigger the right to a jury trial. The majority opinion in *Bowers* offers an example of this approach. Many states declare that any defendant facing the possibility of incarceration is entitled to a jury trial. See Opinion of the Justices (DWI Jury Trials), 608 A.2d 202 (N.H. 1992).

A substantial number of state courts reject the federal methodology for determining the scope of the right to a jury trial. Some of these courts continue to insist that jury trials are available only for the most serious crimes, but they give great weight to factors other than the length of potential or actual incarceration in deciding which crimes are serious. The dissenting opinion in *Bowers* illustrates this approach. See also Fisher v. State, 504 A.2d 626 (Md. 1986) (considers historical treatment of offense, "infamous" nature of offense, maximum authorized sentence, and place of incarceration). Other courts inquire about the "punitive" nature of the fines imposed. A number of courts turn to history to determine whether the offense is analogous to some crime that was tried by jury at the time the federal constitution was adopted. Medlock v. 1985 Ford F-150 Pick Up, 417 S.E.2d 85 (S.C. 1992). State courts in more than 10 states have declared that the state constitution requires jury trials for all "offenses." The only exceptions involve crimes with trivial punishments or other characteristics that make them criminal offenses in name only. See Mitchell v. Superior Court, 783 P.2d 731 (Cal. 1989) (en banc) (jury trial for all misdemeanors and felonies and all infractions punishable by imprisonment). If you were a state legislator hoping to draft a new criminal statute, would you prefer your state courts to use one of these constitutional approaches over the others?

2. *Statutory right to jury trials.* It is common to find state statutes that extend the right to a jury trial to a broader range of cases than the federal or state constitution requires. Some statutes provide a jury trial for a particular offense without declaring

any general rule about the availability of jury trials. Others declare generally the minimum lengths of incarceration or minimum fine amounts that will create a right to a jury. See Ohio Rev. Code §2945.17(B)(2) (jury trial for any offense punishable by a fine exceeding $1000); Ill. Ann. Stat. ch. 725, para. 5/103-6 (jury trial for "[every] person accused of an offense"); see also ABA Standards for Criminal Justice, Trial by Jury 15-1.1(a) (3d ed. 1996) (jury trial should be available in prosecutions in which confinement in jail or prison may be imposed). Another type of statute grants a right to jury trial for less serious cases but places conditions on the exercise of the right, such as the payment of a fee. See Colo. Stat. §16-10-109 (granting jury trial for petty offenses, provided defendant pays $25 fee). A common form of this "conditional" statutory right to a jury trial appears in two-tiered court systems; the Maryland statute offers an example. These laws provide for jury trials in all cases falling within the jurisdiction of a felony-level trial court, and allow any defendant in a case initially charged and tried in the misdemeanor-level trial court to appeal the case for a trial de novo (before a jury) in the felony-level court. This system, in effect, gives even those charged with misdemeanors a statutory right to a jury trial, but only for those who persist in an appeal from the misdemeanor court. See, e.g., Ark. Code §16-17-703. Do such "conditional" systems effectively deny the right to a jury trial to those defendants without the resources or persistence to jump through the proper hoops before receiving a jury? For further analysis of the variety of statutory jury trial rights in the states, go to the web extension for this chapter at *http://www.crimpro.com/extension/ch17*.

3. *Combining petty offenses.* Will a defendant receive a jury trial if she faces several "petty" charges, where convictions on the multiple counts would authorize the judge to impose a sentence longer than six months? In Lewis v. United States, 518 U.S. 322 (1996), the Court held that a defendant who is prosecuted in a single proceeding for multiple petty offenses does not have a Sixth Amendment right to a jury trial. Lewis was charged with two counts of obstructing the mail, each charge carrying a maximum authorized prison sentence of six months. The Court concluded that Congress, by setting the maximum prison term at six months, had categorized the offense as petty. Congress's judgment, and not the punishment imposed in a particular case, determines the seriousness of an offense under the Sixth Amendment. See also People v. Foy, 673 N.E.2d 589 (N.Y. 1996).

4. *Trial at option of prosecutor or judge.* As the *Bowers* case from South Dakota illustrates, judges in most courts can avoid a jury trial for some crimes that authorize prison or jail sentences if they commit before the trial not to incarcerate the defendants after conviction. The trial court in *Bowers* made such a promise but imposed a "suspended" prison term, which the offender does not serve unless he fails to complete the nonprison components of a sentence, such as payment of a fine. Should courts consider suspended sentences as incarceration for purposes of the right to a jury trial? Is it appropriate to allow trial judges to "override" the legislature's decision to make a crime eligible for jury trials?

Prosecutors also have much to say about the availability of a jury trial. The prosecutor can charge a defendant with multiple counts of a petty offense rather than a more serious one, or charge the lesser of two alternative offenses if the more serious offense triggers a jury trial. See City of Casper v. Fletcher, 916 P.2d 473 (Wyo. 1996) (prosecutor in battery case could choose between municipal ordinance, for which jury trial did not attach, and state statute that would qualify for jury trial). Is there any problem with the prosecutor initially filing the more serious charge, and revising the charge to some lesser crime (a non-jury trial offense) only for defendants who insist on a jury trial?

2. *Waiver of Jury Trial*

The seemingly simple question of how many trials are resolved by juries and how many by judges is surprisingly difficult to answer because of the lack of uniform records and lack of interest in low-level cases. In 2006, about 4 percent of all felony convictions in state courts resulted from jury trials, while about 2 percent of the convictions resulted from bench trials. But this overall rate of felony bench trials hides real differences among types of crimes and among jurisdictions. Juries are much more likely to try violent offenses, and judges are more likely to try drug offenses. In the federal system in 2008, about 12 percent of criminal trials (395 of 3,184) were bench trials. Fewer than 10 percent of the felony trials are before the bench in some states (such as Alaska and New Jersey), while more than two-thirds of the trials are before the bench in other states (such as Virginia). See Sean Doran, John Jackson & Michael Seigel, Rethinking Adversariness in Nonjury Criminal Trials, 23 Am. J. Crim. L. 1 (1995). Note that these figures deal only with felony trials. A much smaller proportion of misdemeanor cases are tried before juries.

The number of bench trials taking place each year is not simply a product of the legal rules that entitle some defendants and not others to a jury trial. Many defendants who could insist on a trial by jury instead waive the right and proceed to a bench trial with the judge as the sole factfinder. Sometimes the waiver of a jury trial will be welcome news to the government and to the public since jury trials are expensive and difficult to administer. Judges may even encourage some defendants to waive jury trials, perhaps by discounting the sentence in cases tried to the bench. However, there are times when the prosecutor or the judge will not share the defendant's desire to bypass the jury. In felony cases juries appear to convict at substantially higher rates than judges, though judges have a higher conviction rate for misdemeanors. See Kenneth Klein, Unpacking the Jury Box, 47 Hastings L.J. 1325 (1996). The defendant may believe the judge will better understand a complex defense or will react with more restraint to an abhorrent crime. What interests might lead a judge or a prosecutor to resist a defendant's waiver in such cases? Should defendants have a right to choose between jury and bench trials?

■ STATE v. TYERIC LAMAR LESSLEY

779 N.W.2d 825 (Minn. 2010)

ANDERSON, J.

. . . Early in the morning of March 17, 2008, respondent Tyeric Lamar Lessley, Lessley's cousin, and a friend finished spending the evening at a nightclub on Hennepin Avenue in Minneapolis. When the three men left the nightclub at closing time, the police were responding to an unrelated fight outside the nightclub and the three men were maced. All three men got into a car driven by Lessley's cousin. They began to drive to a service station in order to wash out their eyes. While on their way to the service station, their car collided with a pickup truck near the intersection of Third Street and Park Avenue in Minneapolis.

The pickup truck was occupied by three or four men. The occupants of the truck were coming from a bar on Hiawatha Avenue in Minneapolis. After the collision, the car in which Lessley was a passenger kept going, prompting the occupants of the truck to follow the car. While the car was being followed, Lessley pulled out a revolver. The men in the truck were able to stop the car.

After the car was stopped, Lessley got out and began to walk away from the two vehicles. An occupant of the pickup truck, Darby Claar, got out of the truck and followed Lessley on foot. Claar caught up with Lessley and punched Lessley "once or twice," including once in the jaw. Armed with the revolver — a .44-caliber Smith and Wesson — Lessley shot twice at Claar and hit him once. Lessley then left the scene. Police officers investigating the traffic accident discovered Claar's body about a half-block from the scene of the traffic accident. An autopsy determined that Claar died from a single bullet wound. . . .

There is some dispute as to the distance from which Lessley shot Claar. The criminal complaint quotes Lessley as saying the men were about six feet apart, but the medical examiner testified [at a pre-trial hearing] that the gun was fired from a range of "two centimeters . . . up to three feet." Lessley told the police that he shot Claar in self-defense. Lessley also told the police that he fired twice at Claar after Claar attempted to make him return to the scene of the accident. Lessley said that he left the shooting scene because he had a gun and was scared.

The State charged Lessley with murder in the second degree (intentional). Later, the State added a second count of murder in the second degree (unintentional — during commission of a felony). . . . The State exercised its right under Minn. R. Crim. P. 26.03, subd. 13(4) to remove the judge who was initially assigned to the case. The case was reassigned to a second judge and Lessley exercised his right under Rule 26.03 to remove that judge. The case was then reassigned to a third judge.

Lessley filed several pretrial motions. He moved to dismiss the second-degree murder charge on the basis that there was insufficient probable cause that he had acted with intent to kill. He also moved to dismiss on the ground that the State had failed to meet its burden of disproving beyond a reasonable doubt that he had acted in self-defense. [The judge denied the motions.]

On the scheduled day of trial, Lessley . . . waived his right to a jury trial. Immediately after Lessley testified that he wanted to waive a jury trial, the State said that it would ask the judge to remove himself from the case. . . . The State said that the judge had "indicated to everyone that our case was very weak, that our Second Degree Murder . . . was thin." The State also said the judge had "indicated to us in chambers and on the record that this is more of a manslaughter matter. . . . And I think that unfortunately the Court has shown bias toward the defendant in this case, and I respectfully ask that you recuse yourself." The judge denied the State's motion to remove him from the case. [The State filed an appeal with the Chief Judge of the Fourth Judicial District to remove the trial judge for cause. The Chief Judge denied the State's motion, concluding that the trial judge showed no bias or prejudice in any of the pre-trial proceedings.]

The State then moved to have the trial judge deny Lessley's jury-trial-waiver request. The judge denied the State's motion, stating that it did not appear that the State had a right to a jury trial and that denial of the waiver request would be an abuse of discretion. The judge then accepted Lessley's waiver request and told the parties to proceed. The State waived its right to make an opening argument and said it was prepared to call its first witness.

At this point, the Hennepin County Attorney entered the courtroom and requested a stay of proceedings in order to seek review by the Minnesota Court of Appeals. [The judge denied the request and the State filed a pretrial notice of appeal with the court of appeals. The court of appeals dismissed the State's appeal, and the State sought review in this court.]

The State argues that we should read article I, section 4, of the Minnesota Constitution to require the State's consent before a criminal defendant may waive a jury trial and be tried by a judge of the district court. We first examine language itself and its context, and then explain why our case law, Minnesota statutes and rules, and the history of the constitution support a reading that article I, section 4 confers no such right on the State. . . .

The State's first argument involves the text of the Minnesota Constitution Bill of Rights section that mentions jury-trial waiver. The section entitled "Trial by Jury" reads:

> The right of trial by jury shall remain inviolate, and shall extend to all cases at law without regard to the amount in controversy. *A jury trial may be waived by the parties in all cases in the manner prescribed by law.* The legislature may provide that the agreement of five-sixths of a jury in a civil action or proceeding, after not less than six hours' deliberation, is a sufficient verdict. The legislature may provide for the number of jurors in a civil action or proceeding, provided that a jury have at least six members.

Minn. Const. art. I, §4 (emphasis added). The second sentence of section 4 is known as the jury-waiver clause. . . .

The State argues that article I, section 4, by its plain language, allows a criminal defendant to waive a jury trial only with the State's consent. The State contends that the phrase "by the parties" means that all parties in a case must waive, and that the State is a party in this case. The State additionally argues that the phrase "in all cases" means both criminal and civil cases. . . .

We acknowledge that the second sentence of article I, section 4, by itself, may be read to suggest that the State has a right to object to a criminal defendant's jury-trial-waiver request. Such a reading is based on the rationale that "all cases" includes criminal cases and "by the parties" includes the State as well as the defendant. But we conclude that the jury-waiver clause is properly read as applying specifically to civil cases. This conclusion is based on the context of article I, section 4, which clearly alludes to civil actions. The first sentence of section 4 mentions "cases at law" and "amount in controversy," signaling a reference to civil actions for recovery of money damages. In addition, the third and fourth sentences of section 4 refer explicitly to civil actions. Thus, read as a whole, the language of section 4's strongly suggests that this entire section applies only to civil trials. . . .

It is essential that — to paraphrase John Marshall, the fourth Chief Justice of the United States Supreme Court — we remember that it is a *Bill of Rights* we are expounding. See M'Culloch v. Maryland, 17 U.S. 316 (1819). . . . The Minnesota Constitution is, in essence, a contract between the people and those persons whom the people choose to put in a position of having sovereign power. Our constitution is a limited contract, and the Bill of Rights is the part of that contract that reserves rights to the people and protects them from the improper exercise of government power. [Given] the purpose of Minnesota's Bill of Rights, it would be counterintuitive for us to construe the section 4 jury-trial-waiver provision as granting rights to the State as opposed to reserving rights to the people. [We] conclude that section 4 is reserved limited to civil matters. . . .

To the extent that the jury-waiver clause of article I, section 4, could be considered ambiguous, an abundance of other authority supports our view that this section does not require a defendant to obtain the State's consent in order to waive a jury trial. . . . Here, not only the purpose of our Bill of Rights, but also our case law on article I, section 4, Minnesota's statutes and procedural rules regarding jury-trial waiver, and the history and circumstances of section 4 all support our reading that the jury-waiver clause does not give the State the right to consent or block a criminal defendant's jury-trial waiver. We next elaborate on these sources.

Case Law

The State contends that our case law supports its reading of article I, section 4 that the State's consent is required before a criminal defendant can waive a jury trial. But we have specifically rejected the reading that the State proposes.

In Whallon v. Bancroft, decided in 1860 — just three years after Minnesota's constitution was adopted — a challenger to a county officer's election contended in his court action that he was entitled under article I, section 4 to a jury trial. 4 Minn. 109, 113 (1860). We concluded that article I, section 4 did not entitle the challenger to a jury trial. In *Whallon,* we said that section 4 "has reference only to civil matters, as it authorizes a waiver of the right conferred in *all cases,* which is not true of criminal cases, and also as criminal cases are specially provided for in section 6 of the same article." . . . In subsequent cases, we have not questioned our statement in *Whallon* that article I, section 4 "has reference only to civil matters."

More recently, in Gaulke v. State, 184 N.W.2d 599 (1971), we were dubious about the idea that the State's consent was required for a criminal defendant to waive a jury trial. In *Gaulke,* the district court denied a defendant's request to waive a jury trial and be tried by the court. On appeal, the defendant claimed that he was denied a right guaranteed to him by Minn. Const. article I, section 4, and Minn. Stat. §631.01.[9] We denied Gaulke's claim because we concluded that he needed to bring the claim on direct appeal, rather than by postconviction petition. In dicta, we were skeptical of Gaulke's argument that a criminal defendant has an absolute right under Minn. Const. article I, section 4, and Minn.Stat. §631.01 to waive jury trial. We stated: "Considering the historical antecedents of our constitution, it is doubtful that the legislature intended to grant the accused an absolute right of waiver. Although we perceive no intent that the [defendant's jury trial] waiver be subject to the consent of the prosecution, it has long been considered to be subject to the approval of the trial court."

9. Minnesota Statutes §631.01 reads, in relevant part: "Except where defendant waives a jury trial, every issue of fact shall be tried by a jury of the county in which the indictment was found or information filed. . . . If the defendant shall waive a jury trial, such waiver shall be in writing signed by him in open court after he has been arraigned and has had opportunity to consult with counsel and shall be filed with the clerk. Such waiver may be withdrawn by the defendant at any time before the commencement of the trial."

In *Gaulke,* we contrasted Rule 23(a) of the Federal Rules of Criminal Procedure, which allows a defendant to waive a jury trial only with the approval of the court and the consent of the government, with Minn.Stat. §631.01, Minnesota's counterpart rule at the time. Minnesota Statutes §631.01 did not expressly condition waiver "on the consent of either the prosecutor or the court." Notably, in *Gaulke* we did not question the constitutionality of Minn.Stat. §631.01. . . .

Statutes and Rules

Minnesota statutes and our criminal rules further inform our conclusion. Minnesota has had statutory provisions in place for jury-trial waiver since at least 1935. In 1935, the legislature adopted the [language quoted in footnote 9]. In 1975, the jury-trial-waiver procedures were incorporated into the Minnesota Rules of Criminal Procedure, and section 631.01 was later repealed. Jury-trial waiver is now governed exclusively by the Minnesota Rules of Criminal Procedure, more specifically Rule 26.01, which read at the time of Lessley's jury-trial-waiver request as follows:

> Waiver on the Issue of Guilt. The defendant, with the approval of the court may waive jury trial on the issue of guilt provided the defendant does so personally in writing or orally upon the record in open court, after being advised by the court of the right to trial by jury and after having had an opportunity to consult with counsel.

Nothing in the procedure established by the rule makes the criminal defendant's jury-trial waiver subject to the consent of the State. Our Advisory Committee on the Rules of Criminal Procedure recommended the rule language that we adopted in 1975 after soliciting comments and holding a public hearing. In 1977, the committee recommended amending the rule to allow the State to object to a defendant's jury-trial waiver, but we did not adopt the change. . . .

In Minnesota, the criminal-justice system has operated for more than 75 years under procedures that do not make the criminal defendant's jury-trial waiver subject to the consent of the State. During that time, the legislature could have acted to recognize such a right on the part of the State, but has never done so. Our court has interpreted the jury-waiver clause of article I, section 4 on multiple occasions, yet we have never read the clause to require the State's consent before a defendant can waive a jury trial.

Constitutional Convention Debates

Minnesota's first and only constitutional convention, called to order on July 13, 1857, was "somewhat of a mess." Bickering Democrats and Republicans split into two constitutional conventions, each of which produced its own document. Each of the separate conventions proceeded on the assumption that it was the genuine convention and therefore the only one with the authority to write Minnesota's constitution. Each convention produced a document that was later considered by a compromise committee.

The Democrats produced the following jury-trial language as the fifth item in their Bill of Rights: "The right of Trial by Jury shall be secured to all, and remain inviolate forever; but a Jury Trial *may be waived by the parties in all civil cases,* in the manner to be prescribed by law."

The Republican debate regarding jury-trial waiver was more extensive, although its ultimate meaning is unclear. The Republicans on July 24, 1857, debated the following language that had been reported from committee: "The right of trial by jury shall remain inviolate; and shall extend to all cases at law without regard to the amount in controversy; but a jury trial *may be waived by the parties in all cases* in the manner prescribed by law." David Morgan, a delegate from Hennepin County, moved to amend the section's waiver language by adding the word "civil" before the word "cases." . . . Delegate N.P. Colburn opposed the amendment, seeing no objection to allowing a criminal defendant "to waive his right of trial by jury, if he chooses." [One] delegate, David Secombe, noted that a territorial statute in place "for the last six years" allowed an offender arraigned before a magistrate to waive a jury trial without consultation with the prosecutor. . . . Morgan's amendment failed and [the delegates adopted] a version of the second sentence of article I, section 4 that closely resembled the provision that the Republicans considered in their debates.

The State argues that the debates prove that the Republicans meant to apply section 4 to criminal cases, because the Republicans enacted the "all cases" language of section 4 after rejecting delegate Morgan's proposal to add the word "civil." But the debates also suggest that the delegates wanted to continue allowing criminal defendants, by statute, the right to jury-trial waiver. . . . Thus, we conclude that the debates do not definitively settle the question of what the framers intended and do not direct us to read section 4 in the manner argued by the State. . . .

Policy Arguments

Last, we note that the State and amicus Minnesota County Attorneys Association propound a number of essentially policy-based arguments for why we should read article I, section 4 to make a criminal defendant's jury-trial waiver subject to the consent of the State. The State asserts that 30 states currently require the prosecutor's consent before a defendant may waive a jury trial; notes that an American Bar Association standard advocates such a requirement; and points to the federal system, in which Rule 23(a) of the Federal Rules of Criminal Procedure require a jury-waiving defendant to obtain the government's consent. But we emphasize that the question before us is not whether it might be wise policy for a criminal defendant to need the consent of the State in order to waive a jury trial. Rather, the question is whether the State's consent is required by article I, section 4 of the Minnesota Constitution. In sum, our analysis leads us to the conclusion that article I, section 4 of the Minnesota Constitution does not require the State's consent before a defendant seeks to waive a jury trial. . . .

GILDEA, J., dissenting.

. . . The district court granted Lessley's request for a bench trial because it concluded that (1) the State did not have a constitutional right to a jury trial, and (2) it would be an abuse of discretion to deny Lessley's request. . . . I would resolve this case based on the language of the applicable criminal rule, Minn. R. Crim. P. 26.01, and our precedent, rather than reaching the constitutional question. Under the rule and our precedent, the district court abused its discretion in granting Lessley's request, and I would therefore reverse. . . .

Lessley moved that the district court allow him to plead guilty to the lesser offense of second-degree manslaughter. The court denied that motion, [but observed] that "the State's evidence of intent is limited," and that "[Lessley's] remorse is . . . compelling." A few days later, Lessley, by submitting a request to waive a jury trial, asked this judge to be the finder of fact in his case. Lessley's desired fact-finder had earlier questioned the credibility of the State's witnesses and characterized the case — on the record — as one involving "idiocy" and "a bunch of drunkards." . . .

In ruling on Lessley's request, the court noted that it had "some discretion." But the court viewed its discretion as "limited to those cases where the court thinks that for some reason the defendant's decision to waive the jury is not smart, often pro se people. . . . I suspect it would be an abuse of discretion for me to deny the right to the waiver, although frankly my job would be much easier. That's not one of the choices I get." . . .

The court's ruling constitutes nothing more than a reflexive grant of Lessley's request. But we have repeatedly recognized that the defendant does not have an unconditional right to a bench trial. Rather, we have said that the court must, in the exercise of its sound discretion, decide whether to approve the request. The district court's duty in considering a jury-waiver request is not discharged "as a mere matter of rote, but with sound and advised discretion, with an eye to avoid unreasonable or undue departures" from the jury-trial process. Patton v. United States, 281 U.S. 276, 312-13 (1930). In my view, the district court's automatic and unreasoned approval of Lessley's request runs afoul of this precedent.

[We have] we recognized that the perceived fairness of the process properly [informs] the decision on a jury-waiver request. . . . There might be a case where the objection offered by the State to a defendant's request for a bench trial is done purely for an "ignoble purpose." Singer v. United States, 380 U.S. 24, 36 (1965). In such a situation, the district court would be well within its discretion under Rule 26.01 in refusing to give the State's objection any weight. But that is not this case. . . .

I would hold that it was an abuse of discretion to grant Lessley's request for a bench trial. [To] grant Lessley's request risks undermining the public's trust and confidence in our judicial system. [Given] the judge's comments that I referenced above and the judge's refusal to remove himself from the case, there was a basis for concern as to the appearance of the fairness of the proceeding if that judge acted as the fact-finder in this case. The record does not provide any countervailing factor that would support granting Lessley's request for a bench trial. For example, the record does not reflect any concerns over pretrial publicity. The record likewise does not provide any other basis for me to conclude that the "tribunal which the constitution regards as most likely to produce a fair result," *Singer*, 380 U.S. at 36, has been undermined so as to outweigh the appearance concerns the judge's comments created. I would therefore reverse and remand the matter for a jury trial.

Notes

1. *Waiver of jury trial: majority position.* Almost all jurisdictions allow a defendant to waive the right to a jury trial; more than 30 states, however, condition the defendant's waiver of the jury on the judge's agreement that a bench trial is appropriate.

N.Y. Crim. Proc. Law §320.10; Or. Rev. Stat. §136.001(2). About 10 states give the defendant the unilateral power to select a bench trial over a jury trial. See, e.g., Iowa R. Crim. P. 2.17(1). North Carolina stands alone in forbidding jury waiver through an explicit constitutional text. N.C. Const. art. I, §24 ("No person shall be convicted of any crime but by the unanimous verdict of a jury in open court"). About 30 states and the federal courts also empower the prosecutor to block the defendant's choice of a bench trial. Fed. R. Crim. P. 23(a); Cal. Const. art. I, §16 ("consent of both parties"); Fla. R. Crim. P. 3.260; see also ABA Standards for Criminal Justice: Trial by Jury 15-1.2 (3d ed. 1996) (waiver must be "with the consent of the prosecutor"). For a graphic summary of the state positions on this issue, go to the web extension for this chapter at *http://www.crimpro.com/extension/ch17*.

Until the early twentieth century, very few states gave defendants facing felony charges the option to waive jury trial for bench trial; amendments to the rules allowing waiver of jury trial occurred at the same time that plea bargaining began to dominate criminal practice in the United States. Is there any connection between these developments? See George Fisher, Plea Bargaining's Triumph: A History of Plea Bargaining in America (2003).

Like the U.S. Supreme Court in Singer v. United States, 380 U.S. 24 (1965), most state courts have rejected constitutional challenges to rules and statutes that require the consent of the prosecution and the court before a waiver takes effect. People v. Kirby, 487 N.W.2d 404 (Mich. 1992); but see State v. Baker, 976 P.2d 1132 (Ore. 1999) (statute granting the prosecution right to insist on jury trial despite defendant's waiver violates the waiver provision of Oregon Constitution's jury trial guarantee). In jurisdictions that permit the court to deny a defendant's request for a bench trial, the rules often say that a trial court has discretion to deny such a request, and an appellate court can review that decision for an abuse of discretion. What circumstances might amount to an abuse of discretion? The dissenting justice in *Lessley* discusses the interests of both the accused and the general public in trying a case before a jury. What is relevant in deciding exactly who has a right to a jury trial?

2. *Law-trained judges.* Most state court systems have different levels of trial courts, with "limited jurisdiction" courts to try misdemeanors and other minor offenses in the first instance, and "general jurisdiction" courts to try all felonies and (sometimes) the cases of defendants who appeal a conviction from the limited jurisdiction court. Judges in the general jurisdiction courts virtually always have legal training. However, a number of judges in limited jurisdiction courts do not have legal training. Courts have usually turned aside due process challenges to this arrangement, but the opinions often rely on the fact that cases tried before a nonlawyer judge will ultimately receive meaningful review by a law-trained judge. See North v. Russell, 427 U.S. 328 (1976); Amrein v. State, 836 P.2d 862 (Wyo. 1992); but see Gordon v. Justice Court for Yuba, 525 P.2d 72 (Cal. 1974) (criminal trials before nonlawyer judges violate due process). What differences would you expect in the arguments that lawyers make to nonlawyer judges?

3. *Other decisionmakers.* Many other countries involve citizens on panels resembling juries to decide criminal cases. See Neil Vidmar, World Jury Systems (2000). But the details vary in important ways. Some foreign legal systems utilize decisionmakers other than lone judges or juries. Consider, for example, the use of multimember panels in Germany to try serious offenses. The panels are made up of three "professional" and two "lay" judges. See William Pizzi & Walter Perron, Crime

Victims in German Courtrooms: A Comparative Perspective on American Problems, 32 Stan. J. Int'l L. 37 (1996). Some parties in the United States hire a "private" judge — an arbitrator who mediates a settlement between the defendant and the crime victim, as part of a pretrial "diversion" program. What conditions would allow the use of alternative judges to flourish? History has given us judges and juries, but times and technologies change. What new forms of trial can you imagine?

B. SELECTION OF JURORS

Jury members are selected in two stages. The first stage involves the selection of the "venire" — the pool of potential jurors. Early in American history, only adult white males who owned a certain amount of property were eligible to serve on a jury. Over time, eligibility for service expanded in steps, first covering white males without property and eventually reaching all adults. As legal eligibility for jury service expanded, however, the actual methods for selecting the jury venire did not keep pace. Under the "key man" selection system used in many states, public officials or prominent citizens served as jury commissioners (the "key men") to nominate potential jurors. Not surprisingly, their nominations did not reflect a demographic cross section of the eligible jurors in the community.

The Supreme Court periodically has decided cases requiring the states to change their selection processes to produce venires that better represent the community. In the first case to deal with the question, Strauder v. West Virginia, 100 U.S. 303 (1880), the Court sustained an equal protection challenge to a statute excluding blacks from the jury venire. In Norris v. Alabama, 294 U.S. 587 (1935), the Court quashed an indictment because blacks were excluded *in fact* from serving on grand juries in the jurisdiction, even though they were legally eligible to participate. In later cases, the Court did not require the defendant to show complete exclusion of a racial group from jury service: A substantial disparity between the racial mix of the county's population and the racial mix of the venire, together with an explanation of how the jury selection process had created this outcome, would be enough to establish a prima facie case of discrimination. The government would then have to rebut the presumption of discrimination. See Turner v. Fouche, 396 U.S. 346 (1970) (underrepresentation of African Americans); Castaneda v. Partida, 430 U.S. 482 (1977) (underrepresentation of Mexican Americans).

The Supreme Court has also recognized a defendant's right to challenge the process of creating the venire in the Sixth Amendment's promise of an "impartial jury." In Taylor v. Louisiana, 419 U.S. 522 (1975), the Court held that a Louisiana law placing on the venire only those women who affirmatively requested jury duty violated the Sixth Amendment's requirement that the jury represent a "fair cross section" of the community. Duren v. Missouri, 439 U.S. 357 (1979), summarized the current test followed in both federal and state courts for challenging a venire under the Sixth Amendment and its analogs. The defendant must show that (1) the group allegedly excluded is a "distinctive" group in the community, (2) the representation of this group in venires is not reasonable in relation to the number of such persons in the community, and (3) this underrepresentation is a result of "systematic" exclusion of the group (not necessarily intentional discrimination) in the jury selection process. At that point, the burden of proof shifts to the government to show a "significant state interest" that justifies use of the method that systematically excludes a group. Courts have determined the distinctiveness of groups that are "cognizable" under the Sixth Amendment by looking to the shared attitudes and experiences of the group. By and large, this has meant that racial groups and gender are considered distinctive, while age groups (such as 18- to 24-year-olds) are not. For a sample of the state and federal constitutional cases on the construction of the jury venire, go to the web extension for this chapter at *http://www.crimpro.com/extension/ch17*.

1. *Voir Dire*

A second stage of juror selection takes place for each case. From among a large pool of prospective jurors at the courthouse on a given day, a random group will be called to a particular courtroom for a specific case. An initial group of jurors are seated in the jury box, and then the judge and lawyers determine which individuals will serve on the jury for that case. There are two ways to remove a potential juror from the box. First, there are removals "for cause": The judge removes from the panel any jurors who are not qualified to serve or are not capable of performing their duties. Second, the attorneys may remove a limited number of qualified jurors through "peremptory" challenges.

Each of these methods of removing potential jurors requires the judge and the attorneys to learn something about the attitudes and experiences of the individual jurors. Jurors are questioned in a process known as *voir dire* ("to speak the truth," or, more literally, "to see to say"). In most jurisdictions, statutes and rules of procedure allow both the judge and the attorneys to formulate the questions; often the judge asks questions proposed by counsel, but sometimes the attorneys query potential jurors directly. Fewer than 10 states allow the attorneys to conduct all the questioning. Some questions are directed to the jurors as a group, while follow-up questions with individual jurors are typical in most places. Regardless of the voir dire process described in statutes or procedure rules, the trial judge retains discretion to control the questions that attorneys can ask at voir dire.

The best approach to voir dire is a subject of great interest among trial attorneys. One influential publication on the topic starts with advice about the basic objectives of the questioner: "Lawyers can approach the voir dire process as an interrogation, [as a] job interview, or as a conversation." A conversational style of questioning, carried out with empathy and friendly interest, is most likely to bring out open and candid answers from jurors. Jeffrey T. Fredrick, Mastering Voir Dire and Jury Selection: Gaining an Edge in Questioning and Selecting a Jury 83-87 (2005). Jurors also tend to like lawyers who are similar to them, and offer more complete and revealing answers to such lawyers. The questioner can encourage this process by pointing out experiences that the juror and the lawyers have shared, such as attendance at the same university or growing up in the same neighborhood.

The juror's ability to identify with the defendant is also critical from the point of view of defense counsel. The legendary trial attorney Clarence Darrow, in a 1936 magazine article, argued that an attorney can make informed guesses on this question by noting the religion and ethnicity of the potential jurors.

Every knowing lawyer seeks for a jury of the same sort of men as his client; men who will be able to imagine themselves in the same situation and realize what verdict the client wants. . . . In this undertaking, everything pertaining to the prospective juror needs to be questioned and weighed: his nationality, his business, religion, politics, social standing, family ties, friends, habits of life and thought; the books and newspapers he likes and reads, and many more matters that combine to make a man; all of these qualities and experiences have left their effect on ideas, beliefs and fancies that inhabit his mind. . . .

A skillful lawyer does not tire himself hunting for learning or intelligence in the box; if he knows much about man and his malting, he knows that all beings act from emotions and instincts, and that reason is not a motive factor. If deliberation counts for anything, it is to retard decision. . . .

The most important point to learn is whether the prospective juror is humane. This must be discovered in more or less devious ways. As soon as "the court" sees what you want, he almost always blocks the game. Next to this, in having more or less bearing on the question, is the nationality, politics, and religion of the person examined for the jury. . . .

An Irishman is called into the box for examination. There is no reason for asking about his religion; he is Irish; that is enough. We may not agree with his religion, but it matters not, his feelings go deeper than any religion. You should be aware that he is emotional, kindly and sympathetic. If he is chosen as a juror, his imagination will place him in the dock; really, he is trying himself. You would be guilty of malpractice if you got rid of him, except for the strongest reasons.

An Englishman is not so good as an Irishman, but still, he has come through a long tradition of individual rights, and is not afraid to stand alone; in fact, he is never sure that he is right unless the great majority is against him. The German is not so keen about individual rights except where they concern his own way of life; liberty is not a theory, it is a way of living. Still, he wants to do what is right, and he is not afraid. He has not been among us long, his ways are fixed by his race, his habits are still in the making. We need inquire no further. If he is a Catholic, then he loves music and art; he must be emotional, and will want to help you; give him a chance.

If a Presbyterian enters the jury box and carefully rolls up his umbrella, and calmly and critically sits down, let him go. He is cold as the grave; he knows right from wrong, although he seldom finds anything right. He believes in John Calvin and eternal punishment. Get rid of him with the fewest possible words before he contaminates the others; unless you and your clients are Presbyterians you probably are a bad lot, and even though you may be a Presbyterian, your client most likely is guilty. . . .

Never take a wealthy man on a jury. He will convict, unless the defendant is accused of violating the anti-trust law, selling worthless stocks or bonds, or something of that kind. Next to the Board of Trade, for him, the penitentiary is the most important of all public buildings. . . .

Clarence Darrow, "How to Pick A Jury" (Esquire, May 1936).

■ ANDREW HILL v. STATE

661 A.2d 1164 (Md. 1995)

BELL, J.

This case requires that we revisit the issue of when, and define the circumstances under which, at the request of the defendant, voir dire in a criminal case must include a question regarding racial bias or prejudice. In line with what this

Court consistently has held to be the overarching purpose of the voir dire examination — "to ascertain the existence of cause for disqualification . . ." — we shall hold that under the circumstances of the case sub judice, the trial court should have inquired, as requested, into the venire's racial bias. . . .

The State's only witness at trial was Barron Burch, a Baltimore City police officer. He testified that, while on armed robbery detail, he responded to the 2100 block of Booth Street, in answer to a call for a black male, wearing a black jacket and blue jeans, armed with a gun. When he arrived at that location, Officer Burch stated that he saw Andrew Hill, the petitioner. Observing that he matched the description he had been given, the officer approached the petitioner, placed him against the police cruiser Officer Burch was driving, and conducted a pat down search of the petitioner's clothing. He did not [discover a gun, but he did notice] that the petitioner was holding a box, inscribed with the word, "Dominoes." Despite the petitioner's express confirmation that the box did, indeed, contain Dominoes, Officer Burch took the box from the petitioner, opened it, and recovered 14 vials of cocaine.

The petitioner was charged with cocaine possession offenses. He elected to be tried by a jury. The petitioner being African-American and Officer Burch Caucasian, the petitioner requested the Circuit Court for Baltimore City to propound the following question during the voir dire examination of the venire:

> You have taken note, the defendant is African/American. Both sides to this case, and certainly the court want to make it abundantly clear to you that the racial background of the defendant is not to be considered against him in any way. It is imperative that the defendant be judged only upon the evidence or lack of evidence, without any regard whatever to whether he is African/American or white. If there is in your background any experience, or attitude, or predisposition, or bias, or prejudice, or thought that will make it more difficult for you to render a verdict in favor of this defendant because of his race, then I ask that you raise your hand.

The trial court refused to ask the question. It did ask, however, whether any member of the jury panel "knew of anything that would keep her or him from giving a fair and impartial verdict," and "whether any member knew of any reason why he or she should not serve on the jury." The jury having returned a guilty verdict as to both the possession and possession with intent to distribute cocaine charges, the petitioner, relying on the voir dire issue, among others, filed an appeal.

[In] Maryland, the principles governing jury voir dire are well settled. Of course, the nature and extent of the voir dire procedure, as well as the form of the questions propounded, are matters that lie initially within the discretion of the trial judge. [Informing] the trial court's exercise of discretion regarding the conduct of the voir dire, is a single, primary, and overriding principle or purpose: to ascertain the existence of cause for disqualification. This is consistent with the fundamental tenet underlying the trial by jury that each juror, as far as possible, be impartial and unbiased. Thus, the purpose of the voir dire examination is to exclude from the venire those potential jurors for whom there exists cause for disqualification, so that the jury that remains is capable of deciding the matter before it based solely upon the facts presented, uninfluenced by any extraneous considerations.

[Where] a defendant's proposed voir dire questions concern a specific cause for disqualification, he or she has "a right to have [those] questions propounded to prospective jurors. . . ." That "right" to examine prospective jurors to determine whether any cause exists for disqualification is guaranteed by Article 21 of the Maryland Declaration of Rights, [which guarantees the right to a speedy trial by an "impartial jury"]. And the proper focus of the voir dire examination is the venireperson's state of mind and the existence of bias, prejudice, or preconception, i.e., "a mental state that gives rise to cause for disqualification. . . ."

In Davis v. State, 633 A.2d 867 (Md. 1993), we quite recently identified yet again areas of inquiry which, if reasonably related to the case at hand, are mandatory subjects of the voir dire examination. . . . Among the areas of inquiry is prospective jurors' possible racial bias. . . . Racial prejudice and bias has not been eradicated even as of today. And, as *Davis* recognized, a prospective juror who is prejudiced or biased based on race would be unable objectively to decide a matter in which a person of that race is a party.

In this case, the petitioner is an African-American on trial for a drug possession crime, whose guilt or innocence must be determined by the jury. We hold that he was entitled to have questions propounded to the venire on its voir dire concerning this possible prejudice or racial bias. The trial court's failure to propound such a question was an abuse of discretion.

We are aware, of course, that the Supreme Court of the United States has held that "there is no per se constitutional rule . . . requiring inquiry as to racial prejudice" based solely on an alleged criminal confrontation between an African-American assailant and a white victim. Ristaino v. Ross, 424 U.S. 589 (1976). That Court determined that the constitutional necessity to question prospective jurors concerning their racial or ethnic bias arises only when "special circumstances," of the kind reflected in Ham v. South Carolina, 409 U.S. 524 (1973), are present.

In *Ham,* the African-American civil rights activist, who was charged with a drug offense, defended on the basis that the police framed him in retaliation for his active, and widely known, civil rights activities. Noting that "Ham's reputation as a civil rights activist and the defense he interposed were likely to intensify any prejudice that individual members of the jury might harbor," the *Ristaino* Court concluded that "racial issues . . . were inextricably bound up with the conduct of the trial" and that gave rise to the consequent need for voir dire "questioning specifically directed to racial prejudice" to assure the empanelling of an impartial jury.* In Rosales-Lopez v. United States, 451 U.S. 182, 189 (1981), the Court explained the *Ristaino* holding as follows:

> Only when there are more substantial indications of the likelihood of racial or ethnic prejudice [than an interracial confrontation] affecting the jurors in a particular case does the trial court's denial of a defendant's request to examine the juror's ability to deal impartially with this subject amount to an unconstitutional abuse of discretion.

In [*Rosales-Lopez*], the Supreme Court characterized the racial discrimination issue as one involving a conflict affecting the appearance of justice. Acting pursuant

* [In Ristaino v. Ross, 424 U.S. 589 (1976), James Ross was tried in a Massachusetts court with two other black men for armed robbery and assault. The victim of the alleged crimes was a white man employed as a uniformed security guard. Under a state statute, the court was required during voir dire to inquire generally into prejudice. Ross asked the judge to question the prospective jurors specifically about racial prejudice. The judge refused to ask the more specific question. The Supreme Court held that a specific inquiry was not required in this case, based on the "mere fact that the victim of the crimes alleged was a white man and the defendants were Negroes." — EDS.]

to its supervisory authority over the federal courts, the Court acknowledged, as it previously had done in *Ristaino,* that "it is usually best to allow the defendant to resolve this conflict by making the determination of whether or not he would prefer to have the inquiry into racial or ethnic prejudice pursued." . . .

In Bowie v. State, 595 A.2d 448 (Md. 1991), we held that, where the defendant and the victim are of different races and the case involves the violent victimization of other persons, inquiry into juror racial bias is required. This is the first occasion that we have had to address the situation where voir dire into racial or ethnic bias was requested in a case which did not involve interracial violence. We agree with the Supreme Court that determining an appropriate nonconstitutional standard involves resolution of a conflict concerning the appearance of justice. Also like that Court, we agree that how the conflict is to be resolved ordinarily should be determined by the defendant. Unlike that Court, however, we strike a different balance when the trial court does not defer to the defendant's preferred resolution.

In Aldridge v. United States, 283 U.S. 308, 314-315 (1931), in which an African-American was tried [in federal court] for the murder of a white police officer, the Court explained why it was proper for the venire to be questioned with regard to racial prejudice:

> The argument is advanced on behalf of the government that it would be detrimental to the administration of the law in the courts of the United States to allow questions to jurors as to racial or religious prejudices. We think that it would be far more injurious to permit it to be thought that persons entertaining a disqualifying prejudice were allowed to serve as jurors and that inquiries designed to elicit the fact of disqualification were barred. No surer way could be devised to bring the processes of justice into disrepute. . . .

While we have not heretofore embraced, in total, the *Aldridge* analysis, we do so now. We hold, as a matter of Maryland nonconstitutional criminal law, that the refusal to ask a voir dire question on racial or ethnic bias or prejudice under the circumstances of this case constituted reversible error. . . .

Problem 17-1. "Racially Sensitive Cases" and Voir Dire

Brian Glaspy and Victor Jackson were students enrolled in the Johnstown Campus of the University of Pittsburgh. Both were African Americans. They attended a small party in the dormitory suites of some friends. The events at the party are in dispute.

According to Glaspy and Jackson, a woman at the party engaged in sexual activity with Jackson; Glaspy rubbed up against the woman while she danced and had sexual relations with Jackson. The woman, however, told the police that Glaspy held her while Jackson removed her clothes and performed various sexual acts on her, and that Glaspy also penetrated her anally. The woman was white. Various witnesses noticed the activities of these three; some believed that she consented to the activity, while others believed that she did not.

Jackson and Glaspy were both charged with rape. During the empanelling of the jury, defense counsel asked the trial judge for permission to conduct individual voir dire for all the jurors, to explore any racial prejudices that the jurors may harbor. Pennsylvania Rule of Criminal Procedure 1106(e) provides that, in all non-capital cases, the trial judge "shall select the method" of voir dire — either individual voir dire or, in the alternative, group voir dire.

There are two leading cases in the jurisdiction to guide the trial judge's discretion in ruling on this motion. First, in Commonwealth v. Christian, 389 A.2d 545 (Pa. 1978), a black defendant was charged with the rape and murder of an elderly white woman. The prosecution planned to introduce testimony of a witness who said that the victim refused a sexual advance by the defendant on the same evening as the murder. The defendant asked for permission to pose two questions to each venire member individually: "Do you feel that blacks have sexual drives that differ from whites?" and "Do you believe that there is anything wrong with a black man showing affection to a white woman?" The trial court denied the motion, but the Supreme Court reversed the conviction. Because the alleged crime — the rape and other sexual molestation of an elderly woman — was itself shocking, and the prosecution witness would testify about the defendant's advances toward a white woman, the case was "racially sensitive, and one in which there was need on voir dire for inquiry into the possible racial prejudices of potential jurors."

The second relevant case is Commonwealth v. Richardson, 473 A.2d 1361 (Pa. 1984). The trial court refused to allow a black defendant accused of raping a white victim to question jurors about their potential racial bias. On appeal after the conviction, the Supreme Court refused to order a new trial; by "posing such questions" the trial court "would have risked creating racial issues in a case where such issues would not otherwise have existed."

Can the trial judge, consistent with the *Christian* and *Richardson* cases, grant the motion of Glaspy and Jackson to conduct individual voir dire on the question of potential racial bias? If the *Hill* decision from Maryland were instead a binding precedent in Pennsylvania, could the judge reconcile the three relevant cases?

Suppose that the trial judge denies the motion, but asks a question about potential racial bias during group voir dire of the entire panel. One prospective juror admits that he is racially biased, and would not be able to render a fair verdict because of the race of the defendants. The judge excuses the juror from the case. Now Glaspy and Jackson renew their motion to pursue individual voir dire on this question. Does this pretrial event strengthen or weaken the case for granting the motion? Would the Supreme Court be justified in modifying its past case law to declare that "any case involving allegations of sexual misconduct where the parties are of different races" is per se "racially sensitive"? Cf. Commonwealth v. Glaspy, 616 A.2d 1359 (Pa. 1992).

Problem 17-2. Defendant Bias and Voir Dire

The decomposed body of Delores Jackson, a black female, was found in a wooded area in Riceland County, South Carolina. The pathologist determined that she died from a blow to the head from a blunt instrument. After the media publicized the discovery of the body, several witnesses reported to the authorities that Charles Cason had admitted killing a black woman in October of the previous year. Further investigation led police to other witnesses, who said that Cason had been drinking on the day of the alleged murder. He was angry because his sister-in-law failed to pick him up at work as promised. Jackson jeered at Cason on the bus ride home and during their walk down Decker Boulevard towards their respective homes. Cason's neighbors told police that he had in his possession some of Jackson's personal effects after she disappeared, suggesting a robbery. Two witnesses said that Cason admitted several days later that he killed Jackson, and used appalling language to describe the victim: "I killed a nigger bitch."

Prior to trial, defense counsel requested a specific voir dire to ascertain racial bias on the part of the jury. They requested the specific voir dire because two prosecution witnesses planned to testify at trial about Cason's description of the victim. The prosecutors objected to the voir dire question; they said that they planned to use Cason's pejorative words to show his state of mind and not to show that race was a motive for the crime.

The trial judge refused defense counsel's request for the specific voir dire question about race. Rather, the trial judge asked a general question as to bias or prejudice. The trial judge explained that a specific question related to race is required only when there are "special circumstances creating a constitutionally significant likelihood that, absent questioning about racial prejudice, the jurors would not be indifferent in the matter."

S.C. Code Ann. §14-7-1020 provides in pertinent part as follows:

> The court shall, on motion of either party in the suit, examine on oath any person who is called as a juror therein to know whether he . . . has any interest in the case, has expressed or formed any opinion or is sensible of any bias or prejudice therein. . . . If it appears to the court that the juror is not indifferent in the cause, he shall be placed aside as to the trial of that cause and another shall be called.

The jury convicted, and Cason appealed. How would you rule? Compare State v. Cason, 454 S.E.2d 888 (S.C. 1995).

Notes

1. *Racial bias questions on voir dire: majority position.* As the Maryland opinion in *Hill* indicates, the federal constitution requires the judge to ask specific voir dire questions about racial prejudice only when "special circumstances" in the case create a "reasonable possibility" that the jury will be influenced by racial prejudice. Virtually all state courts now agree on this general principle, saying that some "special circumstances" must be present before a trial court is obliged to ask racial prejudice questions on voir dire. See State v. Taylor, 423 A.2d 1174 (R.I. 1980). What did the *Hill* court hold about the necessary "circumstances"? Older decisions more often declared in general terms a defendant's right to insist on questions about racial prejudice. See Pinder v. State, 8 So. 837 (Fla. 1891) (requiring questions on racial prejudice in murder case because such information is of "most vital import" to defendant).

Most state courts say that special circumstances must amount to more than the fact that the defendant and the victim (or the arresting officer) are of different races. See Commonwealth v. Moffett, 418 N.E.2d 585 (Mass. 1981). But beyond this, there is little agreement about what qualifies as a "special" circumstance. State courts are split over whether charges of a "violent" crime are enough to invoke racial prejudice questions. Some conclude that a violent crime is enough, but others require some more specific showing. People v. Peeples, 616 N.E.2d 294 (Ill. 1993) (murder, no questions required); State v. Hightower, 680 A.2d 649 (N.J. 1996) (murder, questions required). Rape cases present some of the most compelling cases for questions about racial prejudice. In such cases, courts have concluded more often than not that racial prejudice questions were necessary in the case at hand, even if a blanket rule was not necessary.

Why have so few courts adopted a per se rule allowing the parties to insist on specific voir dire questioning about racial prejudice in any criminal case? Do such questions cause any harm? Do the questions create racial tensions or stereotyping where they would not otherwise appear? Do they allow a party to begin arguing a case before the evidence is introduced, by casting a case in racial terms?

2. *Voir dire questions on other matters.* The trial court has substantial discretion over the content of voir dire questions regarding questions other than race. However, if the particular circumstances of a case make it reasonably likely that some potential jurors will not be able to render an impartial verdict, the court will inquire into those subjects if the parties request it. See State v. Thomas, 798 A.2d 566 (Md. 2002) (trial court may not refuse voir dire about attitudes toward crime charged; judge refused to ask venirepersons whether they had any "strong feelings regarding violations of the narcotics laws"). For instance, when a case has received media attention before trial, the judge asks specific questions about the juror's familiarity with the news coverage. Again, however, the trial court has broad discretion to decide how many questions to ask and whether to question jurors individually or as a group. For a sampling of the state court rulings on individual voir dire questions, go to the web extension for this chapter at *http://www.crimpro.com/extension/ch17*.

3. *Follow-up questions.* When a trial court allows specific questioning about juror prejudices — racial or otherwise — but limits it to one or two questions directed to the group of jurors as a whole, appellate courts are especially reluctant to rule that the trial court abused its discretion. See State v. Windsor, 316 N.W.2d 684 (Iowa 1982); but see State v. Tucker, 629 A.2d 1067 (Conn. 1993) (court should allow wide latitude to counsel in inquiring into possible prejudice of jurors whose preliminary responses to voir dire may indicate prejudice). If you were representing a defendant and the judge allowed only a single question about juror prejudice, would you use the question? How much success would counsel have in discovering racial prejudice through sharply limited questioning?

4. *Investigating venire members.* In the few cases in which the parties are able to spend lots of time and resources, they may decide to investigate the background of jury venire members prior to any voir dire questions. The parties also might hire jury consultants to assist in the selection of jurors. Part of the background investigation of the jurors involves a search for any record of prior criminal convictions or arrests. How might you argue as defense counsel that the government must share any information about prior criminal records of panel members? See State v. Bessenecker, 404 N.W.2d 134 (Iowa 1987) (prosecution must obtain court order before using arrest record of prospective juror, and defense counsel must have access to same report); Losavio v. Mayber, 496 P.2d 1032 (Colo. 1972) (granting public defender access to arrest records of prospective jurors when prosecution routinely obtained such information).

2. *Dismissal for Cause*

Recall that there are two methods to remove potential jurors from the panel: dismissal of any unqualified jurors "for cause," and dismissal of a limited number of qualified jurors based on "peremptory challenges" by the parties. We now consider the first of these methods of removal.

A potential juror might be unqualified to serve in any cases at all: For instance, the juror might be unable to understand English or might be a felon ineligible for jury duty. The juror might also be qualified to serve in some cases but not in others, as when a juror is closely related to the defendant or the alleged victim. More generally, the judge must dismiss a juror for cause whenever it appears that the juror cannot keep an open mind about the evidence and apply the relevant law. All these standards are straightforward, but they play out in a complex setting. Many jurors would prefer to avoid lengthy jury duty; the judge would prefer to seat the jury as quickly as possible without excusing many potential jurors; and the parties would prefer to convince the judge to remove unsympathetic jurors from the panel rather than using their limited peremptory challenges. Everyone concerned must predict the jurors' future behavior based on brief answers to questions that are continually being rephrased.

■ TEXAS CODE OF CRIMINAL PROCEDURE ART. 35.16

(a) A challenge for cause is an objection made to a particular juror, alleging some fact which renders the juror incapable or unfit to serve on the jury. A challenge for cause may be made by either the state or the defense for any one of the following reasons:

1. That the juror is not a qualified voter in the state and county under the Constitution and laws of the state; provided, however, the failure to register to vote shall not be a disqualification;
2. That the juror has been convicted of misdemeanor theft or a felony;
3. That the juror is under indictment or other legal accusation for misdemeanor theft or a felony;
4. That the juror is insane;
5. That the juror has such defect in the organs of feeling or hearing, or such bodily or mental defect or disease as to render the juror unfit for jury service . . . ;
6. That the juror is a witness in the case;
7. That the juror served on the grand jury which found the indictment;
8. That the juror served on a petit jury in a former trial of the same case;
9. That the juror has a bias or prejudice in favor of or against the defendant;
10. That from hearsay, or otherwise, there is established in the mind of the juror such a conclusion as to the guilt or innocence of the defendant as would influence the juror in finding a verdict. To ascertain whether this cause of challenge exists, the juror shall first be asked whether, in the juror's opinion, the conclusion so established will influence the juror's verdict. If the juror answers in the affirmative, the juror shall be discharged without further interrogation by either party or the court. If the juror answers in the negative, the juror shall be further examined as to how the juror's conclusion was formed, and the extent to which it will affect the juror's action; and . . . if the juror states that the juror feels

able, notwithstanding such opinion, to render an impartial verdict upon the law and the evidence, the court, if satisfied that the juror is impartial and will render such verdict, may, in its discretion, admit the juror as competent to serve in such case. If the court, in its discretion, is not satisfied that the juror is impartial, the juror shall be discharged;

11. That the juror cannot read or write.

No juror shall be impaneled when it appears that the juror is subject to the second, third or fourth grounds of challenge for cause set forth above, although both parties may consent. All other grounds for challenge may be waived by the party or parties in whose favor such grounds of challenge exist. . . .

(b) A challenge for cause may be made by the State for any of the following reasons:

1. That the juror has conscientious scruples in regard to the infliction of the punishment of death for crime, in a capital case, where the State is seeking the death penalty;

2. That he is related within the third degree of consanguinity or affinity [to the defendant]; and

3. That he has a bias or prejudice against any phase of the law upon which the State is entitled to rely for conviction or punishment.

(c) A challenge for cause may be made by the defense for any of the following reasons:

1. That he is related within the third degree of consanguinity or affinity . . . to the person injured by the commission of the offense, or to any prosecutor in the case; and

2. That he has a bias or prejudice against any of the law applicable to the case upon which the defense is entitled to rely, either as a defense to some phase of the offense for which the defendant is being prosecuted or as a mitigation thereof or of the punishment therefor.

STATE v. RECHE SMITH

607 S.E.2d 607 (N.C. 2005)

WAINWRIGHT, J.

On 8 March 2002, defendant Reche Smith was convicted of first-degree murder and felony larceny. The jury found defendant guilty of first-degree murder on the basis of malice, premeditation, and deliberation and under the felony murder rule. Following a capital sentencing hearing, the jury recommended a sentence of death for the murder. The trial court accordingly imposed a sentence of death for the murder and further imposed a sentence of fifteen to eighteen months imprisonment for the felony larceny.

The evidence at trial showed the following: At 6:00 A.M. on 10 March 2001, the victim, Charles King, was at his home in Plymouth, North Carolina, when defendant knocked on his door. King, wearing a bathrobe and thermal shirt and pants, answered the door, and defendant asked him for a glass of water. King invited defendant into his home and headed toward his kitchen to get the water. However, before King reached the kitchen, defendant grabbed King around his neck and choked him until he became unconscious. Defendant then bound King's wrists with clear packaging tape, went to another room in King's house, found a clock, and used the clock's extension cord first to bind King's wrists and then his ankles. Next defendant covered King's entire face, including his nose and mouth, with clear packaging tape and pushed King under a hospital bed. Defendant left King under the bed to die of asphyxiation while he searched King's house for something to steal. As King lay suffocating under his bed, defendant took $250 from an envelope in King's bedroom, $20 from King's wallet, King's cell phone, bank card, and car keys. After thirty minutes of searching King's house and stealing these items, defendant took King's car, drove to Williamston, North Carolina, rented a room at a motel, and bought crack cocaine. . . .

Defendant first argues the trial court erred by denying his challenge for cause to prospective juror Charles Hassell. During voir dire, Hassell indicated he was strictly against drug use. Defense counsel then asked Hassell the following question: "Your position is such concerning drug use and abuse that in the event evidence came out in this trial that drug use was involved, it would affect or impair — substantially impair your ability to be fair and impartial; is that correct?" Hassell replied "yes" to this question. Defendant then challenged Hassell for cause. In response, the trial court engaged in the following colloquy with Hassell:

> *The Court:* Well let me — Mr. Hassell, let me ask you . . . just a couple of questions if I could. I don't mean to embarrass you. There are no right or wrong answers, and I want to make sure I understand what you're saying, and I'm trying to frame the question in a way that — are you saying to me, sir, that your personal feelings about the use . . . of or possession of drugs is such that it would interfere or prevent you from following the law in this — as I would instruct you as it relates to this case?
>
> *Mr. Hassell:* Well, I could follow the law.
>
> *The Court:* All right. Now — and so I want to make sure what you're saying — you know, many people don't like drugs, don't approve of drugs, and I don't believe that's the question that [the defense attorney] was asking you, and that may have been how — that may have been what you are saying. I don't know one way or the other.
>
> I'm not trying to put words in your mouth, but I — I'm just making sure I understand that's what you were saying or whether what you were saying is you didn't like drugs or are you saying to me that your feeling is such — I'm asking you as to whether or not your personal feelings about particular crimes or particular types of conduct are such that it would overwhelm your reason and common sense and your ability to follow the law as I would instruct you on should we reach some aspect of the case that may relate to the consumption or use or possession of drugs?
>
> *Mr. Hassell:* No. It wouldn't do that.
>
> *The Court:* You would be able and could and would follow the law as I would instruct you on regardless of what your own personal feelings would be as it relates to the use or possession of or consumption of drugs; is that correct?
>
> *Mr. Hassell:* Yes.
>
> *The Court:* Are you sure of that answer, sir?
>
> *Mr. Hassell:* Yeah.
>
> *The Court:* All right. The Challenge for cause is denied.

Defendant properly preserved error by exhausting the peremptory challenges available to him, renewing his challenge to prospective juror Hassell, and having his renewed challenge denied. N.C.G.S. §15A-1214(h). However, in addition to preserving error, defendant must show error by (1) demonstrating that the trial court abused its discretion in denying the challenge, and (2) showing defendant was prejudiced by this abuse of discretion.

Defendant contends the trial court improperly rehabilitated Hassell with leading questions, despite the prohibition against reducing determinations of juror bias "to question-and-answer sessions which obtain results in the manner of a catechism." Wainwright v. Witt, 469 U.S. 412, 424 (1985). However, we conclude that the trial court did not lead Hassell to answer that he would follow the law. Rather, the trial court questioned Hassell in an effort to determine whether, despite Hassell's feelings about drug use, he could follow the law.

We further conclude that the trial court did not abuse its discretion by denying defendant's challenge for cause. As the United States Supreme Court further stated in *Wainwright*:

> What common sense should have realized experience has proved: many veniremen simply cannot be asked enough questions to reach the point where their bias has been made "unmistakably clear"; these veniremen may not know how they will react when faced with imposing the death sentence, or may be unable to articulate, or may wish to hide their true feelings. Despite this lack of clarity in the printed record, however, there will be situations where the trial judge is left with the definite impression that a prospective juror would be unable to faithfully and impartially apply the law. . . . This is why deference must be paid to the trial judge who sees and hears the juror.

Thus, we must give substantial weight to the trial court's determination that Hassell was not biased. We defer to the trial court who could see and hear Hassell, and we conclude that the trial court did not abuse its discretion by denying defendant's challenge for cause. Defendant's assignment of error is overruled.

Next, defendant contends the trial court erred by failing to give him an additional peremptory challenge. Defendant claims he was entitled to an additional peremptory challenge because the trial court removed a seated juror for cause before the end of jury selection and after defendant had used all but one of his remaining peremptory challenges.

After both defendant and the prosecution accepted prospective juror Gloria Cox, Cox brought the trial court a note from her doctor recommending that she be excused from jury duty because serving as a juror would be too stressful for her. The trial court dismissed Cox for cause. Defendant then requested an additional peremptory challenge, stating that he had undergone a substantial portion of jury selection believing that Cox would be a juror. The trial court denied defendant's request.

Defendant contends the trial court erred by failing to use its inherent authority to restore a peremptory challenge to remedy a prejudicial development in jury selection. However, we disagree. Although a trial court must grant a defendant an additional peremptory challenge if, upon reconsideration of the defendant's previously denied challenge for cause, "the judge determines that the juror should have been excused for cause," N.C.G.S. §15A-1214(i), trial courts generally have no authority to grant additional peremptory challenges. In fact, trial courts are "precluded from authorizing any party to exercise more peremptory challenges than specified by statute." State v. Dickens, 484 S.E.2d 553, 561 (N.C. 1997) (holding that the trial court did not err by refusing to grant the defendant an additional peremptory challenge following the reexamination and excusal for cause of a juror). Because the trial court had no authority to provide defendant with additional peremptory challenges, defendant's argument is without merit and we overrule this assignment of error.

Next, defendant contends the trial court failed to comply with the N.C.G.S. §15A-1214(a) requirement for random jury selection when it placed a prospective juror in a specific seat after that juror was randomly called to fill another seat. Prospective juror Jonas Simpson, who had been summoned in the initial group of venire members to be examined for fitness to serve, was not present when the clerk called his name. The trial court called another prospective juror in Simpson's place. The trial court then examined this prospective juror and two other prospective jurors. Following a recess, Simpson arrived at the courtroom. The trial court placed him in panel A, seat twelve, the panel and seat for which he was originally called. After the trial court and the prosecutor questioned Simpson, the trial court allowed the prosecutor's request to challenge Simpson for cause, finding that Simpson was unequivocally opposed to the death penalty.

Defendant contends the trial court violated the §15A-1214(a) requirement for random jury selection when it placed Simpson in a specific seat. However, defendant has waived review of this issue . . . because he failed to follow the N.C.G.S. §15A-1211(c) procedure for challenging the randomness of jury selection. Subsection 15A-1211(c) states that all such challenges must be in writing, must "specify the facts constituting the ground of challenge," and must be "made and decided before any juror is examined." These challenges must be made at the trial court level. Defendant did not object to the trial court's placement of Simpson in a specific seat. Therefore, defendant has failed to preserve this issue for review, and we overrule his assignment of error. . . .

Notes

1. *Dismissals for cause: majority position.* The judge must confirm that each of the potential jurors meets the general requirements for service, such as residency and literacy requirements. At that point, the judge evaluates possible sources of bias against the defendant or against the government. The most common source of potential bias is a personal relationship between the juror and some person connected with the case, such as one of the attorneys. The judge also inquires into the prior experiences of the jurors; for instance, the judge might ask if a juror has been a victim of a crime. This ground leads to disqualification less often than do personal relationships. A juror who has learned before trial about the events that will be disputed at trial will receive special scrutiny. Although prior knowledge of the case alone does not disqualify a juror, a judge will sometimes conclude that the juror who has already learned about the events in question will be unable to keep an open mind and base a verdict only on the evidence presented at trial. Even if the judge allows the juror to remain on the panel, one of the parties will almost always remove the knowledgeable juror with a peremptory challenge. Does this special scrutiny of jurors who are aware of the relevant events systematically remove the most informed and intelligent candidates from the jury? Or is this a concern only in cases receiving unusual pretrial publicity?

2. *Excused for hardship.* The judge will at times "excuse" jurors who are qualified in general and who have no particular reason to favor one party or another. Statutes and procedural rules often specify that the judge may exempt jurors for "undue hardship" or "extreme inconvenience." Jurors themselves frequently raise this issue with the judge by describing the financial hardship of jury duty. See Sudler v. State, 611 A.2d 945 (Del. 1992) (trial court's excusal of five jurors based on their unavailability after holiday weekend violated defendant's right to jury trial). H. L. Mencken, the American satirist and journalist of the early twentieth century, defined a jury with this dynamic in mind: "Jury — A group of twelve men who, having lied to the judge about their hearing, health, and business engagements, have failed to fool him." What behavior might one expect from a juror who faces unusual hardships while serving on a jury? Would the juror predictably favor the prosecution or the defense?

The judge's decision about whether to excuse a juror for hardships interacts with rules about the length of service expected of jurors and the sanctions for citizens who do not appear for jury duty. How do you suppose a judge would react to a juror asking for a hardship excuse in a system requiring 10 days of service from jurors, and where only 5 percent of all citizens who are summoned actually appear for jury duty? Would the judge's response to the hardship request change in a "one day or one trial" system? Under the "one day or one trial" system, prospective jurors serve in a maximum of one trial and complete their service after one day if they are not chosen for a trial. For a survey of court strategies to reduce the inconvenience of jury service, go to the web extension for this chapter at *http://www.crimpro.com/extension/ch17*.

3. *Dismissals for cause in death penalty cases.* Special problems arise during voir dire in cases in which the prosecutor plans to seek the death penalty. Many jurors have pronounced views about the use of capital punishment, and those who strongly favor or oppose its use may still serve on the jury if they remain able to apply the law that dictates the cases eligible for the death penalty. However, if a juror declares that he would always vote to impose the death penalty, or to recommend against the death penalty, then he will be excluded for cause. See Witherspoon v. Illinois, 391 U.S. 510 (1968). If you were a prosecutor and a juror declares that she believes in the biblical injunction "an eye for an eye," what follow-up questions would you ask?

4. *Harmless error in denial of challenge for cause.* If the trial court refuses to excuse a juror for cause but the juror does not serve on the panel because the defendant uses a peremptory challenge to remove the juror, has any reversible error occurred? What if the defendant had peremptory challenges to spare? Cf. United States v. Martinez-Salazar, 528 U.S. 304 (2000) (when judge fails to remove juror for cause, defendant must allow the juror on the panel to challenge the decision on appeal); Busby v. State, 894 So. 2d 88 (Fla. 2004) (defendant can challenge decision on removal for cause even if juror excluded from panel based on peremptory; no actual harm must be shown).

3. Peremptory Challenges

In addition to removal of jurors for cause, all states allow the parties to "strike" additional jurors without any initial requirement of a reason or explanation. Such strikes are called "peremptory challenges." The following Idaho statute sets out the traditional definition: "A peremptory challenge . . . is an objection to a juror for which no reason need be given, but upon which the court must exclude him." Idaho Stat. §19-2015.

States usually allow a specific number of peremptory challenges, ranging from 2 to 20 or more. In some states, the parties have equal numbers of peremptories, while elsewhere the defense may excuse more jurors than the prosecution.

The procedures for exercising peremptory challenges vary enormously. Statutes and court rules describe the order in which peremptories must be exercised, often establishing a back-and-forth pattern between defense and prosecution. Challenges in some jurisdictions are made in the presence of jurors; in some jurisdictions challenges must be made in writing. Generally, to preserve a challenge about jury selection on appeal, a party must exhaust all peremptory challenges. The use of objections for cause and peremptory challenges involves an intense mix of law and trial strategy.

Why allow peremptory challenges? A number of theories have been advanced. Consider the following explanation of the functions of peremptory challenges.

> The peremptory challenge has traditionally served two principal functions. First, the peremptory challenge provides a margin of protection for challenges for cause. [The] difficulties of developing information about bias, together with the risk of error in adjudicating claims of bias, combine to make the peremptory challenge an essential fallback for use when a challenge for cause is rejected. . . . This device has the advantage of saving the time of attorneys, jurors, and the court that would otherwise be spent in probing the true extent, if any, of the bias of potential jurors. . . .
>
> The second principal function of the peremptory challenge is to provide the parties with an opportunity to participate in the construction of the decision-making body, thereby enlisting their confidence in its decision. To fulfill this function, the peremptory challenge gives the parties the power to exclude jurors who are indisputably free of bias, merely because the parties would prefer to be judged by others instead. . . .

Barbara Underwood, Ending Race Discrimination in Jury Selection: Whose Right Is It, Anyway? 92 Colum. L. Rev. 725 (1992).

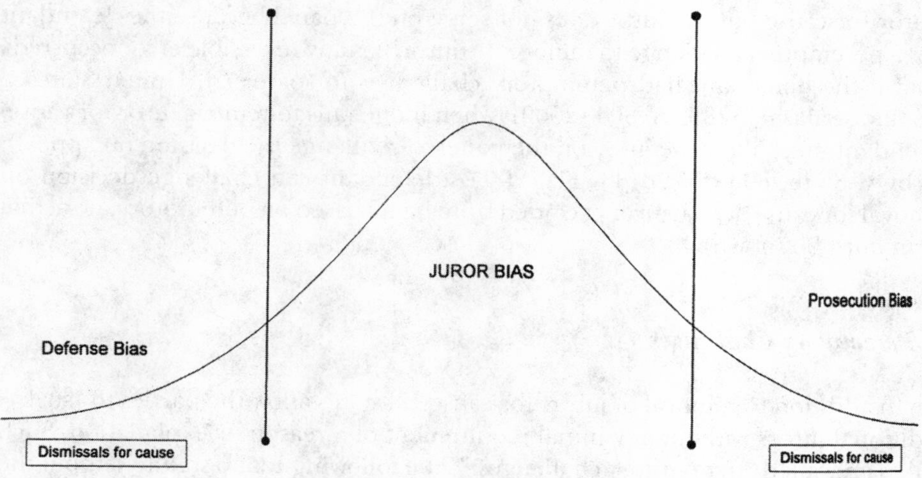

It may be helpful to think about a range of potential jurors, some of whom are biased for the prosecution, and others for the defense; indeed it may be helpful to picture the array of jurors along a bell curve (without making any necessary assumptions about the shape of the curve). Some of those biased jurors (and perhaps some unbiased jurors) will be dismissed by the court for "cause," either on the decision of the court or the motion of counsel. But some jurors in the middle of the bell curve will remain who the lawyers believe are likely to favor one side or the other. In theory, peremptory challenges allow the parties to shape a fair jury for their perspective, which may mean both avoiding antagonistic jurors and finding sympathetic ones.

Should lawyers ever be required to explain why they struck a particular juror? Until fairly recent times, these questions had relatively clear answers: peremptory strikes were just that, with no explanation required. Only if prosecutors engaged in a pattern of peremptory strikes across several cases that revealed racial discrimination would a review of those peremptory decisions be allowed. Strauder v. West Virginia, 100 U.S. 303 (1880); Swain v. Alabama, 380 U.S. 202 (1965). In 1978 California became the first state to prohibit race-based peremptory challenges in individual cases as a matter of state constitutional law, People v. Wheeler, 583 P.2d 748 (Cal. 1978). Massachusetts took a similar position in 1979, Commonwealth v. Soares, 387 N.E.2d 499 (Mass. 1979), as did Florida in 1984, State v. Neil, 457 So. 2d 481 (Fla. 1984). In 1986, the U.S. Supreme Court addressed the claim that the federal constitution prohibited race-based peremptory challenges in Batson v. Kentucky.

JAMES BATSON v. KENTUCKY

476 U.S. 79 (1986)

POWELL, J.*

This case requires us to reexamine that portion of Swain v. Alabama, 380 U.S. 202 (1965), concerning the evidentiary burden placed on a criminal defendant who claims that he has been denied equal protection through the State's use of peremptory challenges to exclude members of his race from the petit jury.

I.

Petitioner, a black man, was indicted in Kentucky on charges of second-degree burglary and receipt of stolen goods. On the first day of trial in Jefferson Circuit Court, the judge conducted voir dire examination of the venire, excused certain jurors for cause, and permitted the parties to exercise peremptory challenges. The prosecutor used his peremptory challenges to strike all four black persons on the venire, and a jury composed only of white persons was selected. Defense counsel moved to discharge the jury before it was sworn on the ground that the prosecutor's removal of the black veniremen violated petitioner's rights under the Sixth and Fourteenth Amendments to a jury drawn from a cross section of the community, and

* [Justices Brennan, White, Marshall, Blackmun, Stevens, and O'Connor joined this opinion. — EDS.]

under the Fourteenth Amendment to equal protection of the laws. Counsel requested a hearing on his motion. Without expressly ruling on the request for a hearing, the trial judge observed that the parties were entitled to use their peremptory challenges to "strike anybody they want to." The judge then denied petitioner's motion, reasoning that the cross-section requirement applies only to selection of the venire and not to selection of the petit jury itself. The jury convicted petitioner on both counts. . . .

II.

In Swain v. Alabama, this Court recognized that a "State's purposeful or deliberate denial to Negroes on account of race of participation as jurors in the administration of justice violates the Equal Protection Clause." This principle has been "consistently and repeatedly" reaffirmed, in numerous decisions of this Court both preceding and following *Swain.* We reaffirm the principle today.

A.

More than a century ago, the Court decided that the State denies a black defendant equal protection of the laws when it puts him on trial before a jury from which members of his race have been purposefully excluded. Strauder v. West Virginia, 100 U.S. 303 (1880). That decision laid the foundation for the Court's unceasing efforts to eradicate racial discrimination in the procedures used to select the venire from which individual jurors are drawn.

[A] defendant has no right to a petit jury composed in whole or in part of persons of his own race. . . . But the defendant does have the right to be tried by a jury whose members are selected pursuant to nondiscriminatory criteria. The Equal Protection Clause guarantees the defendant that the State will not exclude members of his race from the jury venire on account of race, or on the false assumption that members of his race as a group are not qualified to serve as jurors.

Purposeful racial discrimination in selection of the venire violates a defendant's right to equal protection because it denies him the protection that a trial by jury is intended to secure. "The very idea of a jury is a body . . . composed of the peers or equals of the person whose rights it is selected or summoned to determine; that is, of his neighbors, fellows, associates, persons having the same legal status in society as that which he holds." *Strauder*. . . .

The harm from discriminatory jury selection extends beyond that inflicted on the defendant and the excluded juror to touch the entire community. Selection procedures that purposefully exclude black persons from juries undermine public confidence in the fairness of our system of justice. . . .

B.

In *Strauder,* the Court invalidated a state statute that provided that only white men could serve as jurors. We can be confident that no State now has such a law. The Constitution requires, however, that we look beyond the face of the statute defining juror qualifications and also consider challenged selection practices to afford protection against action of the State through its administrative officers in effecting the prohibited discrimination. Thus, the Court has found a denial of equal protection where the procedures implementing a neutral statute operated to exclude persons from the venire on racial grounds, and has made clear that the Constitution prohibits all forms of purposeful racial discrimination in selection of jurors. . . .

Accordingly, the component of the jury selection process at issue here, the State's privilege to strike individual jurors through peremptory challenges, is subject to the commands of the Equal Protection Clause. Although a prosecutor ordinarily is entitled to exercise permitted peremptory challenges for any reason at all, as long as that reason is related to his view concerning the outcome of the case to be tried, the Equal Protection Clause forbids the prosecutor to challenge potential jurors solely on account of their race or on the assumption that black jurors as a group will be unable impartially to consider the State's case against a black defendant.

III.

The principles announced in *Strauder* never have been questioned in any subsequent decision of this Court. Rather, the Court has been called upon repeatedly to review the application of those principles to particular facts. A recurring question in these cases, as in any case alleging a violation of the Equal Protection Clause, was whether the defendant had met his burden of proving purposeful discrimination on the part of the State. That question also was at the heart of the portion of Swain v. Alabama we reexamine today. . . .

A.

. . . The record in *Swain* showed that the prosecutor had used the State's peremptory challenges to strike the six black persons included on the petit jury venire. While rejecting the defendant's claim for failure to prove purposeful discrimination, the Court nonetheless indicated that the Equal Protection Clause placed some limits on the State's exercise of peremptory challenges.

The Court sought to accommodate the prosecutor's historical privilege of peremptory challenge free of judicial control, and the constitutional prohibition on exclusion of persons from jury service on account of race. While the Constitution does not confer a right to peremptory challenges, those challenges traditionally have been viewed as one means of assuring the selection of a qualified and unbiased jury. To preserve the peremptory nature of the prosecutor's challenge, the Court in *Swain* declined to scrutinize his actions in a particular case by relying on a presumption that he properly exercised the State's challenges.

[On the other hand, it] was impermissible for a prosecutor to use his challenges to exclude blacks from the jury "for reasons wholly unrelated to the outcome of the particular case on trial" or to deny to blacks "the same right and opportunity to participate in the administration of justice enjoyed by the white population." [An] inference of purposeful discrimination would be raised on evidence that a prosecutor, "in case after case, whatever the circumstances, whatever the crime and whoever the defendant or the victim may be, is responsible for the removal of Negroes who have been selected as qualified jurors by the jury commissioners and who have survived challenges for cause, with the result that no Negroes ever serve on petit juries." Evidence offered by the defendant in *Swain* did not meet that standard. . . .

A number of lower courts following the teaching of *Swain* reasoned that proof of repeated striking of blacks over a number of cases was necessary to establish a violation of the Equal Protection Clause. Since this interpretation of *Swain* has placed on defendants a crippling burden of proof, prosecutors' peremptory challenges are now largely immune from constitutional scrutiny. For reasons that follow, we reject this evidentiary formulation as inconsistent with standards that have been developed since *Swain* for assessing a prima facie case under the Equal Protection Clause.

B.

Since the decision in *Swain*, we have explained that [circumstantial] evidence of invidious intent may include proof of disproportionate impact. . . . Moreover, since *Swain*, we have recognized that . . . a defendant may make a prima facie showing of purposeful racial discrimination in selection of the venire by relying solely on the facts concerning its selection in his case. . . . A single invidiously discriminatory governmental act is not "immunized by the absence of such discrimination in the making of other comparable decisions." For evidentiary requirements to dictate that several must suffer discrimination before one could object would be inconsistent with the promise of equal protection to all.

C.

[A] defendant may establish a prima facie case of purposeful discrimination in selection of the petit jury solely on evidence concerning the prosecutor's exercise of peremptory challenges at the defendant's trial. To establish such a case, the defendant first must show that he is a member of a cognizable racial group, and that the prosecutor has exercised peremptory challenges to remove from the venire members of the defendant's race. Second, the defendant is entitled to rely on the fact, as to which there can be no dispute, that peremptory challenges constitute a jury selection practice that permits those to discriminate who are of a mind to discriminate. Finally, the defendant must show that these facts and any other relevant circumstances raise an inference that the prosecutor used that practice to exclude the veniremen from the petit jury on account of their race. This combination of factors in the empanelling of the petit jury, as in the selection of the venire, raises the necessary inference of purposeful discrimination.

In deciding whether the defendant has made the requisite showing, the trial court should consider all relevant circumstances. For example, a "pattern" of strikes against black jurors included in the particular venire might give rise to an inference of discrimination. Similarly, the prosecutor's questions and statements during voir dire examination and in exercising his challenges may support or refute an inference of discriminatory purpose. These examples are merely illustrative. We have confidence that trial judges, experienced in supervising voir dire, will be able to decide if the circumstances concerning the prosecutor's use of peremptory challenges creates a prima facie case of discrimination against black jurors.

Once the defendant makes a prima facie showing, the burden shifts to the State to come forward with a neutral explanation for challenging black jurors. Though this requirement imposes a limitation in some cases on the full peremptory character of the historic challenge, we emphasize that the prosecutor's explanation need not rise to the level justifying exercise of a challenge for cause. But the prosecutor may not rebut the defendant's prima facie case of discrimination by stating merely that he challenged jurors of the defendant's race on the assumption — or his intuitive judgment — that they would be partial to the defendant because of their shared race. Just as the Equal Protection Clause forbids the States to exclude black persons from the venire on the assumption that blacks as a group are unqualified to serve as jurors, so it forbids the States to strike black veniremen on the assumption that they will be biased in a particular case simply because the defendant is black. The core guarantee of equal protection, ensuring citizens that their State will not discriminate on account of race, would be meaningless were we to approve the exclusion of jurors on the basis of such assumptions, which arise solely from the jurors' race. Nor may the prosecutor rebut the defendant's case merely by denying that he had a discriminatory motive or affirming his good faith in making individual selections. . . . The prosecutor therefore must articulate a neutral explanation related to the particular case to be tried. The trial court then will have the duty to determine if the defendant has established purposeful discrimination. . . .

IV.

[We] do not agree that our decision today will undermine the contribution the challenge generally makes to the administration of justice. The reality of practice, amply reflected in many state- and federal-court opinions, shows that the challenge may be, and unfortunately at times has been, used to discriminate against black jurors. By requiring trial courts to be sensitive to the racially discriminatory use of peremptory challenges, our decision enforces the mandate of equal protection and furthers the ends of justice. In view of the heterogeneous population of our Nation, public respect for our criminal justice system and the rule of law will be strengthened if we ensure that no citizen is disqualified from jury service because of his race. . . .

MARSHALL, J., concurring.

I join Justice Powell's eloquent opinion for the Court, which takes a historic step toward eliminating the shameful practice of racial discrimination in the selection of juries. . . . I nonetheless write separately to express my views. The decision today will not end the racial discrimination that peremptories inject into the jury-selection process. That goal can be accomplished only by eliminating peremptory challenges entirely. . . .

II.

Merely allowing defendants the opportunity to challenge the racially discriminatory use of peremptory challenges in individual cases will not end the illegitimate use of the peremptory challenge. . . . First, defendants cannot attack the discriminatory use of peremptory challenges at all unless the challenges are so flagrant as to establish a prima facie case. This means . . . that where only one or two black jurors survive the challenges for cause, the prosecutor need have no compunction about striking them from the jury because of their race. See Commonwealth v. Robinson, 415 N.E.2d 805 (Mass. 1981) (no prima facie case of discrimination where defendant is black, prospective jurors include three blacks and one Puerto Rican, and prosecutor excludes one for cause and strikes the remainder peremptorily, producing all-white jury). Prosecutors are left free to discriminate against blacks in jury selection provided that they hold that discrimination to an "acceptable" level.

Second, when a defendant can establish a prima facie case, trial courts face the difficult burden of assessing prosecutors' motives. Any prosecutor can easily assert facially neutral reasons for striking a juror, and trial courts are ill equipped to second-guess those reasons. How is the court to treat a prosecutor's statement that he struck a juror because the juror had a son about the same age as defendant, or seemed uncommunicative, or "never cracked a smile"? . . .

Nor is outright prevarication by prosecutors the only danger here. . . . A prosecutor's own conscious or unconscious racism may lead him easily to the conclusion that a prospective black juror is "sullen," or "distant," a characterization that would not have come to his mind if a white juror had acted identically. A judge's own conscious or unconscious racism may lead him to accept such an explanation as well supported. . . .

III.

Some authors have suggested that the courts should ban prosecutors' peremptories entirely, but should zealously guard the defendant's peremptory as essential to the fairness of trial by jury. . . . I would not find that an acceptable solution. Our criminal justice system "requires not only freedom from any bias against the accused, but also from any prejudice against his prosecution. Between him and the state the scales are to be evenly held." Hayes v. Missouri, 120 U.S. 68 (1887). We can maintain that balance, not by permitting both prosecutor and defendant to engage in racial discrimination in jury selection, but by banning the use of peremptory challenges by prosecutors and by allowing the States to eliminate the defendant's peremptories as well. . . .

BURGER, C.J., dissenting.*

Today the Court sets aside the peremptory challenge, a procedure which has been part of the common law for many centuries and part of our jury system for nearly 200 years. . . . The peremptory challenge has been in use without scrutiny into its basis for nearly as long as juries have existed. "It was in use amongst the Romans in criminal cases, and the Lex Servilia (B.C. 104) enacted that the accuser and the accused should severally propose one hundred judices, and that each might reject fifty from the list of the other, so that one hundred would remain to try the alleged crime." W. Forsyth, History of Trial by Jury 175 (1852). . . .

Permitting unexplained peremptories has long been regarded as a means to strengthen our jury system. . . . One commentator has recognized:

> The peremptory, made without giving any reason, avoids trafficking in the core of truth in most common stereotypes. . . . Common human experience, common sense, psychosociological studies, and public opinion polls tell us that it is likely that certain classes of people statistically have predispositions that would make them inappropriate jurors for particular kinds of cases. But to allow this knowledge to be expressed in the evaluative terms necessary for challenges for cause would undercut our desire for a society in which all people are judged as individuals and in which each is held reasonable and open to compromise. . . . Instead we have evolved in the peremptory challenge a system that allows the covert expression of what we dare not say but know is true more often than not.

* [Justice Rehnquist joined this opinion. — EDS.]

Babcock, Voir Dire: Preserving "Its Wonderful Power," 27 Stan. L. Rev. 545 (1975).... A moment's reflection quickly reveals the vast differences between the racial exclusions involved in *Strauder* and the allegations before us today:

> [Excluding] a particular cognizable group from all venire pools is stigmatizing and discriminatory in several interrelated ways that the peremptory challenge is not. The former singles out the excluded group, while individuals of all groups are equally subject to peremptory challenge on any basis, including their group affiliation. Further, venire-pool exclusion bespeaks a priori across-the-board total unfitness, while peremptory-strike exclusion merely suggests potential partiality in a particular isolated case.... To suggest that a particular race is unfit to judge in any case necessarily is racially insulting. To suggest that each race may have its own special concerns, or even may tend to favor its own, is not.

United States v. Leslie, 783 F.2d 541 (5th Cir. 1986) (en banc). Unwilling to rest solely on jury venire cases such as *Strauder,* the Court also invokes general equal protection principles in support of its holding. [However,] in making peremptory challenges, both the prosecutor and defense attorney necessarily act on only limited information or hunch. The process cannot be indicted on the sole basis that such decisions are made on the basis of assumption or intuitive judgment. As a result, unadulterated equal protection analysis is simply inapplicable to peremptory challenges exercised in any particular case. A clause that requires a minimum "rationality" in government actions has no application to "an arbitrary and capricious right." *Swain.*

[If] conventional equal protection principles apply, then presumably defendants could object to exclusions on the basis of not only race, but also sex, age, religious or political affiliation, mental capacity, number of children, living arrangements, and employment in a particular industry or profession. In short, it is quite probable that every peremptory challenge could be objected to on the basis that, because it excluded a venireman who had some characteristic not shared by the remaining members of the venire, it constituted a "classification" subject to equal protection scrutiny....

Our system permits two types of challenges: challenges for cause and peremptory challenges. Challenges for cause obviously have to be explained; by definition, peremptory challenges do not.... Analytically, there is no middle ground: A challenge either has to be explained or it does not. It is readily apparent, then, that to permit inquiry into the basis for a peremptory challenge would force the peremptory challenge to collapse into the challenge for cause....

A "clear and reasonably specific" explanation of "legitimate reasons" for exercising the challenge will be difficult to distinguish from a challenge for cause. Anything short of a challenge for cause may well be seen as an "arbitrary and capricious" challenge, to use Blackstone's characterization of the peremptory. Apparently the Court envisions permissible challenges short of a challenge for cause that are just a little bit arbitrary — but not too much. While our trial judges are experienced in supervising voir dire, they have no experience in administering rules like this.

[One] painful paradox of the Court's holding is that it is likely to interject racial matters back into the jury selection process, contrary to the general thrust of a long line of Court decisions and the notion of our country as a "melting pot." ... Today we mark the return of racial differentiation as the Court accepts a positive evil for a perceived one. Prosecutors and defense attorneys alike will build records in support of their claims that peremptory challenges have been exercised in a racially discriminatory fashion by asking jurors to state their racial background and national origin for the record, despite the fact that such questions may be offensive to some jurors and thus are not ordinarily asked on voir dire. . . .

REHNQUIST, J., dissenting.*

. . . In my view, there is simply nothing "unequal" about the State's using its peremptory challenges to strike blacks from the jury in cases involving black defendants, so long as such challenges are also used to exclude whites in cases involving white defendants, Hispanics in cases involving Hispanic defendants, Asians in cases involving Asian defendants, and so on. This case-specific use of peremptory challenges by the State does not single out blacks, or members of any other race for that matter, for discriminatory treatment. Such use of peremptories is at best based upon seat-of-the-pants instincts, which are undoubtedly crudely stereotypical and may in many cases be hopelessly mistaken. But as long as they are applied across-the-board to jurors of all races and nationalities, I do not see — and the Court most certainly has not explained — how their use violates the Equal Protection Clause. [Given] the need for reasonable limitations on the time devoted to voir dire, the use of such "proxies" by both the State and the defendant may be extremely useful in eliminating from the jury persons who might be biased in one way or another. . . .

■ RODNEY LINGO v. STATE

437 S.E.2d 463 (Ga. 1993)

HUNT, P.J.

Rodney Dwayne Lingo was convicted of murder, theft by taking of a motor vehicle, and armed robbery. He was indicted for but found not guilty of rape. The state unsuccessfully sought a death sentence. Lingo received a life sentence for murder, a consecutive life sentence for armed robbery, and a consecutive 20-year sentence for theft by taking.

At the time the victim, Tracy Plank, was killed, Lingo was living with a friend or acquaintance of the victim, Teresa Cooper. The evidence showed that on the evening of November 4, 1985, the victim and Lingo left the home of a mutual friend together in the victim's car. Several hours later, Lingo was seen driving the victim's car alone. The next day, Lingo was seen wearing the victim's jacket and trying to sell parts of the victim's car. The victim's body was found in a roadside wooded area about five days later. She had been shot twice in the head with a gun belonging to Lingo. In statements given to the police, Lingo claims that another friend, who was riding around with him and the victim, was the one who actually shot the victim. In subsequent statements, Lingo implicates two other, different people with pulling the trigger. . . .

Lingo, who is black, contests the trial court's ruling that the reasons given by the prosecutor for the exercise of his peremptory strikes were adequate under Batson v. Kentucky, 476 U.S. 79 (1986), and its progeny. We find that notwithstanding the

* [Chief Justice Burger joined this opinion. — EDS.]

prima facie inference of racial discrimination, the record supports the trial court's findings that the prosecutor's reasons for his strikes were racially neutral, and shows that the prosecutor was able to overcome the prima facie case.

The venire was made up of 50 qualified jurors, and the petit jury was selected from the first 47 jurors called. Of those 47 jurors, 34 were white and 13 were black. The state exercised its ten peremptory strikes against the first ten black venire members called. After the state had exhausted its peremptory strikes, two black jurors were added to the petit jury by the defense. The state then used its only peremptory strike for alternate jurors on the first black potential alternate juror to be called. The record does not indicate the race of the three qualified jurors who remained after the jury was empanelled. Therefore, at least 13 and no more than 16 of the 50 qualified jurors were black (26 percent to 32 percent), and 2 of the 12 jurors who served were black (16.7 percent). The prosecutor exercised 100 percent of his peremptory strikes to exclude black jurors and did not accept any of the black jurors called before he exhausted his strikes.

This overwhelming pattern of strikes establishes a prima facie inference of racial discrimination. Ford v. State, 423 S.E.2d 245 (Ga. 1992). To overcome this inference of discrimination, the prosecutor must present concrete, tangible, race-neutral and neutrally-applied reasons for the strikes exercised against black venire members. The greater the disparity between the percentage of black jurors in the venire and the percentage of strikes exercised by the state against black jurors, the more likely it becomes that racial bias underlies the exercise of the peremptory challenges, and the greater the scrutiny the trial court must apply to the prosecutor's proffered explanations. . . .

Thus, we must review the prosecutor's stated reasons for his strikes to determine whether they overcame the defendant's prima facie case of discrimination. In so doing, we must give the trial court's factual findings great deference. We may only disregard those findings if they are clearly erroneous. Of course, we may still disagree with the trial court's conclusions based on those findings and where there is a strong prima facie case, as here, we must carefully scrutinize those conclusions. We review each of the prosecutor's strikes as follows:

(1) The prosecutor gave as his reasons in support of his first strike, which was against a black woman, the fact that the woman was "indecisive" about the death penalty, and preferred a life sentence, and that she had a hearing problem. . . .

(2) The prosecutor's reasons for his second strike, against a black man, were that he was strongly opposed to the death penalty, and had a DUI conviction. . . .

(3) The prosecutor's reasons for his third strike, against a black woman, were that she was hesitant about the death penalty, and initially stated she would not stand up and affirm a verdict of death and the death penalty, and that she was familiar with the case and a witness in the case. . . .

(4) The prosecutor gave as his reasons for his fourth strike, against a black woman, the fact that she was opposed to the death penalty, and knew a witness in the case. . . .

(5) The prosecutor's reason in support of his fifth strike, against a black man, was that the juror made it very clear he did not want to serve, that the prosecutor was concerned the juror would be preoccupied with his

financial problems, and that the prosecutor had difficulty in getting the juror to respond or pay attention to his questions. The trial court found these reasons to be race-neutral, specifically recalling that the juror could not keep still during the voir dire, and, itself, questioning whether "from his demeanor" this juror was "competent to handle this type of situation."

(6) The prosecutor's reasons in support of his sixth strike, also against a black man, were that the juror was opposed to the death penalty, and was familiar with the defendant and with a witness. . . .

(7) The prosecutor's reasons in support of his seventh strike, against a black woman, were that she was very opposed to the death penalty, and that if she served, the prosecutor was concerned she would be preoccupied with a sick child at home. The trial court . . . noted his recollection that the juror clearly did not want to be there, and someone had to be sent to get her for jury duty.

(8) The prosecutor's reasons for his eighth strike, against a black man, were that he was initially hostile in his responses, and this juror and the prosecutor "got off on the wrong foot at the very start." The prosecutor also gave as reasons the fact that the juror's criminal justice degree might affect his objectivity, and that the juror had testified as a character witness on behalf of a defendant in a prior case. The trial court, in accepting the prosecutor's reasons as race-neutral, specifically recalled this juror's responses as belligerent.

(9) The prosecutor's reasons for his ninth strike, against a black woman, were that she knew a witness in the case, could not give her sentence if polled, and that she had a conviction for shoplifting. . . .

(10) The prosecutor gave as his reason for his tenth strike, against a black man, that the juror had a prior conviction, and had indicated on the jury questionnaire that he had a "bad check problem." . . .

(11) Finally, the prosecutor gave as his reasons for striking an alternate juror, a black woman, the fact that she was opposed to the death penalty, as well as the fact that she was a teacher and school was to start the following Monday. . . .

The record supports the trial court's findings that the reasons given by the prosecutor were not racially motivated, and demonstrates that the prosecutor was able to overcome the very strong prima facie inference of racial discrimination.

The dissent correctly cites Strozier v. Clark, 424 S.E.2d 368 (Ga. Ct. App. 1992), a recent Court of Appeals case, for the rule that where racially-neutral and neutrally-applied reasons are given for a strike, the simultaneous existence of any racially motivated explanation results in a *Batson* violation.[4] However, the dissent would

4. . . . *Strozier* stands for the proposition that where it can be determined that the racially-neutral explanation is, in fact, pretextual since there is a racially motivated reason that can be independently determined, the jury selection process is invalid under *Batson*. *Strozier* does not hold that where one racially-neutral reason is given for striking a juror, any additional reason, not also used against a juror of another race, is per se racially motivated. The cases cited by *Strozier* illustrate that there must be some indication that the "additional reason" is, in fact, racially motivated. In Moore v. State, 811 S.W.2d 197 (Tex. Ct. App. 1991), the prosecutor stated that she struck one juror, in part, because that juror was a member of a minority club. Of course, this was not a racially-neutral reason, notwithstanding that the

misapply this rule by creating a presumption that any reason for striking a black juror, not also used against a white juror — regardless of other reasons for striking a black juror — is per se racially motivated. This is not what *Batson* or *Strozier* hold, or even imply. Rather, there is a *Batson* violation only where the prosecutor's explanation is determined to be racially motivated. Where there are multiple reasons for striking a juror, white or black, it cannot be presumed that a reason applied to one juror, of one race, but not applied to another juror, of another race, is racially motivated.

Of course we are required, in a strong prima facie case such as here, to carefully examine the prosecutor's remaining reasons, to determine if there is an underlying racial motive. And, where a reason is given against a black juror, not also used against a white juror, the reason is particularly suspect. However, we are not authorized to create an inference of discrimination where none is apparent, and where none has been found by the trial court, to whose findings we must give great deference. . . . While we are required to carefully review the record in a case involving a *Batson* challenge, especially where a strong prima facie case is made, we are still required to give the trial court's findings "great deference," and we are not authorized to ignore them. Here, the trial court's findings are not clearly erroneous. . . . Judgment affirmed.

SEARS-COLLINS, J., dissenting.

When it comes to grappling with racial issues in the criminal justice system today, often white Americans find one reality while African-Americans see another. This perception gap is evident in the majority's affirmance of Rodney Dwayne Lingo's conviction. As I cannot ignore the race-based innuendo and subtle stereotyping used to exclude people of color from Lingo's jury, I must dissent.

The prosecutor exercised 100 percent of his peremptory strikes to exclude the first ten black jurors called from the venire. He was content with none of the African-American jurors called before he exhausted his strikes. This is an "overwhelming pattern" of strikes, as recognized by the majority, and establishes a powerful prima facie inference of racial discrimination. It is up to the prosecutor to present "concrete, tangible, race-neutral and neutrally-applied" reasons for the strikes exercised against black venire members. Ford v. State. In deciding whether the reasons given by the prosecutor were "neutrally applied," we consider whether the reasons given could apply equally to white jurors who were not struck by the prosecutor. "A prosecutor's failure to explain the apparently disparate treatment of similarly situated white and black jurors . . . diminishes the force of his explanation for striking a black juror." Ford v. State.

Even if racially-neutral and neutrally-applied reasons are given, the simultaneous existence of any racially motivated explanation "vitiates the legitimacy of the entire (jury selection) procedure." Strozier v. Clark, 424 S.E.2d 368 (Ga. Ct. App. 1992). . . .

---

prosecutor also gave, as a reason for striking this juror, that the juror was hesitant to impose a life sentence. In State v. Tomlin, 384 S.E.2d 707 (S.C. 1989) the prosecutor gave the racially-neutral reason for striking a juror as the fact that the juror was unemployed, but also stated that the juror "shucked and jived." In *Strozier* itself, the prosecutor, in addition to stating the apparently neutral reason of the juror's age as his reason for striking her, also gave his completely unsupported opinion that the juror was dishonest in her answer to questions, an opinion he stated was based on an experience the prosecutor had previously, with other jurors, in an unrelated case. Thus, . . . it is apparent that the "additional reasons," in themselves, were racially motivated and, accordingly, rendered the selection process invalid under *Batson*.

The prosecutor explained that one potential black juror was struck because: he was "touchy" about one of the prosecutor's first questions and "hostile from there on"; he had previously testified in a trial as a character witness; and he had taken some criminal justice classes. The voir dire examination of this juror is set forth . . . as follows:

> *Q:* Mr. Cothran, [this] is a potential death penalty case, and because of that I have to begin by asking you this question: Are you so conscientiously opposed to capital punishment that you would not vote for the death penalty under any circumstances?
> *A:* No.
> *Q:* Okay. . . . In a death penalty case, what happens is, and you may already be aware of this — you're a criminal justice major; you've taken some courses in criminal justice; is that right?
> *A:* How was that revealed to you, sir? Was I supposed to answer that?
> *Q:* Well, that's fine, but you put it on your questionnaire.
> *A:* Oh, okay. I have forgot I put it down there, but I have taken some courses.
> *Q:* So you already know this, . . . but in a death penalty case what happens is that trial is divided into two parts. The first part is called a guilt-innocence phase. [If] and only if in phase one they find the defendant guilty of murder, then they move into phase two which we call the sentencing phase. . . . You understand that . . . the Court would authorize you to consider the death penalty as a sentence, but you'd also be obligated to consider life as a sentence? Now, would you be able to consider both of those options?
> *A:* Yes.
> *Q:* Okay . . . if the Court charges you that proof beyond a reasonable doubt is not proof beyond all doubt, but is simply proof to a moral and a reasonable certainty, would you follow that charge?
> *A:* If within myself, with the evidence that I have heard and able to reach an agreement within myself, then I would follow that.
> *Mr. Lukemire:* Thank you.

With respect to this juror, the trial court stated:

> As far as Mr. Cothran was concerned, that one got very close to the line, but I do recall when he did make the response concerning the criminal justice degree that it definitely, just from an oral response, I was not looking at him, it caught my attention that he did seem to be belligerent, and I will be very candid about this, had there been no blacks on this jury, the court would have had real trouble with not possibly finding there might have been some type of pattern, just with [this juror].

Contrary to the trial court's statement, however, the fact that two black jurors were added to the jury after the prosecutor had exhausted his peremptory strikes is irrelevant to the inquiry of whether this juror was struck because of racial bias and does not eliminate the obvious racial discrimination in the prosecutor's strike against this juror. Moreover, the trial court's statement indicates that but for this irrelevancy it would have found racial bias in the striking of this juror. Furthermore, the above portion of the record reveals that other than being initially surprised by the prosecutor's knowledge of information the juror had provided on his juror questionnaire, the juror showed no indication of being "hostile" towards the prosecutor. Even giving great deference to the trial court, I still cannot believe that a white juror who gave exactly the same responses to the voir dire questions that this juror gave would have been labeled "hostile" and "belligerent." The hostility and belligerence found so readily by the prosecutor and the trial judge from this juror's one response evoke stereotypical images of the angry black man, who, at the slightest provocation and at even the faintest appearance of challenging the status quo will be tagged "hostile" or "belligerent."

The prosecutor further explained that he excluded this juror because he had served as a character witness in another proceeding. This reason was not neutrally applied, however, because the prosecutor accepted without complaint a white juror who had previously testified in a trial as a character witness. The prosecutor also explained that he did not want this juror on the panel because he had taken criminal justice classes. While a juror's legal background often justifies a strike, in this case the prosecutor asked the juror not one question as to whether the juror would be influenced by the classes he had taken, and when asked specifically whether he could follow the charge of the court the juror responded that he could do so.

To conclude, even assuming that the fact that the juror had taken some criminal justice classes was a non-racially motivated reason for striking this juror, both the prosecutor's application of the racial stereotype of the "hostile black male" and his failure to neutrally apply his other reason for striking this juror force me to conclude that improper racial motives played a role in the prosecutor's striking the juror.

The prosecutor explained that he struck one prospective juror, who was young, black, unemployed, and lived with his unemployed girlfriend and her three children, because he "made it very clear he did not want to be here" due to his financial problems, and might not be able to concentrate. When asked if he would have problems with service, this juror responded as follows: ". . . It's going to cause me a heap of problems. See, I've got a heap — I've got bills all the way up to my neck to pay. . . . I can't keep running down here and all because my girlfriend ain't working, and it's kind of hard on me. I can't go."

The record reveals that when asked, the juror stated that he would not have a problem focusing his attention on the trial. Moreover, the prosecutor accepted a white juror who was unemployed, and at least three other white jurors with whom the prosecutor was content stated specifically that jury service would be inconvenient or would pose a financial hardship for them. Compare the explanation given by one of the white jurors who expressed a problem with service on financial grounds:

> . . . I work for General Telephone, and if I don't work, I don't get paid, you know. I have no sick leave, no vacation leave, and I support my family, and it's, you know — you know, I know I have a civil duty to be here, but it's hard to make a living on . . . the money we receive.

While the white juror may have been better able to articulate his position, he made it no less clear that he did not want to be there. Yet the prosecutor accepted the white juror.

I would find on the basis of either of the above jurors alone that the prosecutor failed to overcome the powerful prima facie case of racial discrimination. In rebuffing the *Batson* challenge, the majority stresses the *Batson* edict that the trial court is to be afforded "great deference." I do not believe that "great deference" means ignoring blatant discrimination. . . .

With respect to seven of the black jurors struck by the prosecutor (including a prospective alternate juror), the prosecutor explained that the jurors had some aversion to the death penalty. The record reveals that one of the black jurors struck for this reason repeatedly indicated she was willing to impose a death sentence if warranted by the circumstances, and two others were hesitant about the death penalty, but said that they could consider it as a form of punishment after hearing the evidence. However, in ruling in the state's favor on the defendant's *Batson* motion, the trial court stated his recollection that while both black and white jurors expressed hesitancy about the death penalty, the black jurors struck for that reason were more adamant against the death penalty than were the white jurors. Even if we defer to the trial court's decision that this is a race-neutral reason, the fact remains that included among the prosecutor's reasons for striking those jurors were other reasons that were not well-founded in the record or were not neutrally applied among the black and white jurors. For example, the prosecutor reasoned that one potential juror would not be able to state her decision when polled in court. The record reveals, however, that the juror initially misunderstood the prosecutor's question; when it was clarified, she said that she would be able to give her decision when polled. Also, the prosecutor stated that one black prospective juror was struck because the juror had a hearing problem. While the prosecutor said that the juror had a hearing problem, the record indicates that the juror never claimed to have a hearing problem, and the state had no objection to a white juror who told the prosecutor twice during voir dire that he had a hearing problem.

The prosecutor stated that four black jurors were struck, among other reasons, because they knew witnesses. The record reveals that the state accepted six white jurors who also knew witnesses. Two of the four black jurors struck for this reason indicated they knew witnesses by sight but did not have personal relationships with those witnesses. Among the white jurors accepted by the state who knew witnesses, however, one played cards with two witnesses, while another had lived in the same neighborhood and belonged to the same church as a witness. . . .

The majority states that I would apply Strozier v. Clark to "create a presumption that any reason for striking a black juror, not also used against a white juror — regardless of other reasons for striking a black juror — is, per se racially motivated." That is not correct. To the contrary, as the majority itself notes, the inference of discrimination in this case is created by the prima facie case, which the prosecutor carries the burden of overcoming. I would apply to this case the rule established by this court that where there is a strong prima facie case, the prosecutor's reason for his strikes must be neutrally applied. Moreover, contrary to the implication in the majority, I do not say that any one non-neutrally applied reason renders the jury selection invalid, but that when inequity in application so permeates the process, the fact that a race-neutral reason was also given cannot . . . remedy the discrimination. The majority opinion does not refute the *Strozier* rule, but implies that it should not apply in this case because the "bad" reasons in *Strozier* were facially race-based or pretextual, whereas in this case it is necessary to look at all of the reasons given by the prosecutor to discern the overriding racial foundation for the strikes. I believe that this is a dangerous distinction without a difference, as subtle racial discrimination is just as damaging, if not more so, as overt racial discrimination.

We stand at the edge of the 21st century and many people of color in this country are still not free from insidious racial discrimination such as that manifested in this case. The constitutions of the United States and of Georgia demand the total, uncompromising racial neutrality of the jury selection process to ensure every American's right to fully participate, and Rodney Dwayne Lingo did not receive that neutrality. My candor in this dissent may lead some to believe that I am "hostile." I am not. I am, however, fully committed to the promise of the U.S. and Georgia Constitutions to afford their rights and privileges to all citizens.

Notes

1. *Number and theory of peremptory challenges: majority view.* States generally allow the most peremptory challenges in capital cases and the least in misdemeanor cases. In capital cases, most states allow somewhere between 12 and 20 challenges per party. Some of these states grant the defense more challenges than the prosecution. For noncapital felonies, states allow between 3 (Hawaii and New Hampshire for most felonies) and 20 (New Jersey defendants) peremptory challenges, with about a third of states allowing 6 challenges. As with capital cases, a significant minority of states provide the prosecution with fewer possible challenges than the defense. For misdemeanor jury trials, the number of peremptory challenges allowed ranges between 2 (Missouri) and 10 (California and New Jersey), with almost half the states allowing 3 possible challenges. Bureau of Justice Statistics, State Court Organization 2004, at table 41 (August 2006, NCJ 212351). In felony cases the federal system currently allows 10 strikes for the defense but only 6 for the prosecution. Fed. R. Crim. P. 24. Under what theory are far greater numbers of challenges allowed in more serious cases? What differences explain the wide range in the numbers of peremptory challenges allowed in capital and serious felony cases?

2. *Stages of a* Batson *claim.* Many difficult legal and strategic questions arise under *Batson*. However, it is not legal but factual and strategic decisions that dominate day-to-day jury practice. The court in *Batson* sketched the basic procedure for resolving allegations of racial bias in the exercise of peremptory challenges, which largely mirrors federal discrimination claims made under Title VII. First, the defendant must establish a prima facie case of intentional discrimination; second, the prosecutor must offer a neutral explanation for why it struck black jurors; finally, the trial court determines whether or not there has been "purposeful discrimination." In 1995 the Supreme Court, in the case of Purkett v. Elem, 514 U.S. 765 (1995), strengthened the analogy between *Batson* claims and claims made under Title VII when it held that the government's burden at the second stage is merely a burden of production that can be satisfied by virtually any race-neutral explanation (including a "silly" or "superstitious" explanation), and that it is the defendant who carries the burden of persuasion that purposeful discrimination has in fact occurred. See also Johnson v. California, 545 U.S. 162 (2005) (party trying to establish prima facie case under *Batson* need not show by preponderance of evidence that peremptory challenge was based on improper bias).

Trial courts are relatively amenable to hearing *Batson* challenges — in other words, recognizing that a prima facie case has been made — but find purposeful discrimination and grant relief much less often. For a discussion of the empirical

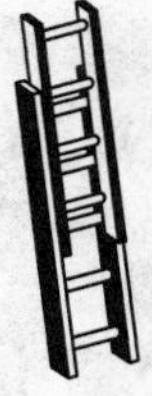

research on the success rates of parties who file *Batson* claims, go to the web extension for this chapter at *http://www.crimpro.com/extension/ch17*.

3. *Pretext and truth.* The *Lingo* case illustrates both the established dynamic for *Batson* claims and the difficulty, for both trial and appellate courts, in assessing whether intentional discrimination has occurred. The key element of a *Batson* battle is the explanation the prosecutor gives for striking one or more jurors. While courts hesitate to find a prima facie case when the defendant identifies only a single juror strike as discriminatory, the decisions of trial and appellate courts often turn on the reasons the prosecutor gives for striking several jurors in a single case, as in *Lingo.* It is relatively easy to offer some race-neutral explanation for every juror: The difficult questions are whether the explanation, if honest, is sufficient and whether the explanation in each case is the "true" reason for a strike or is a pretext for striking a juror on the basis of race.

The *Lingo* case from Georgia provides several illustrations of the reasons that prosecutors offer for strikes, including opposition to the death penalty (especially in death penalty cases), prior criminal record on the part of the juror, relationship or acquaintance with a witness, and involvement in prior court proceedings. Are there particular kinds of explanations that should not be allowed because trial courts cannot easily assess whether they are the real reason? Which of the following reasons given by prosecutors for striking jurors seem most likely to be true, and which seem to be a pretext? Does the difficulty of this judgment reveal the flaws or virtues of the *Batson* approach?

- Appearance, e.g., shoulder-length, curly, unkempt hair, along with a mustache and a goatee-type beard; overweight; "a young, pretty woman" who might be "attracted to defendant or defense counsel"
- Unemployment, e.g., "unemployed people are less likely to be sympathetic to the prosecution"
- Age, e.g., "every juror below the age of 30 because . . . from my experience as a prosecutor and defense lawyer . . . older jurors are generally more likely to be prosecution minded or favorable to the prosecution"
- Place of residence, e.g., "high-crime area"
- Habits, e.g., "excessively verbal"; "loner"; "inattentive"

Most courts reject simple "gut feelings" or "hunches" as a reason to strike a juror, though it is sometimes difficult to distinguish gut feelings from the reasons that are offered. See Commonwealth v. Maldonado, 788 N.E.2d 968 (Mass. 2003) (reasons based on subjective data such as juror's looks or gestures, or attorney's "gut" feeling should "rarely be accepted as adequate because such explanations can easily be used as pretexts for discrimination"). Is it possible to categorize explanations for strikes and to provide different standards of review to different types of explanations? If not, is the whole *Batson* scheme unworkable?

4. *Race-neutral reasons and appellate courts*. The trial court initially evaluates the reasons that a party gives for striking jurors and determines whether the race-neutral reason was a genuine explanation for the strikes. What sort of deference should this finding of the trial judge receive on appellate review? The Supreme Court offered some guidance on the proper role of appellate review in Miller-El v. Dretke, 545 U.S. 231 (2005). The court described several reasons to treat the prosecutor's race-neutral reason as a pretext:

> Out of 20 black members of the 108-person venire panel for Miller-El's trial, only 1 served. Although 9 were excused for cause or by agreement, 10 were peremptorily struck by the prosecution. The prosecutors used their peremptory strikes to exclude 91% of the eligible African-American venire members. Happenstance is unlikely to produce this disparity. More powerful than these bare statistics, however, are side-by-side comparisons of some black venire panelists who were struck and white panelists allowed to serve. If a prosecutor's proffered reason for striking a black panelist applies just as well to an otherwise-similar nonblack who is permitted to serve, that is evidence tending to prove purposeful discrimination. . . .

The opinion also reviewed the history of overt racial discrimination in the selection of jurors by prosecutors in the jurisdiction and noted systematic differences in the questions that prosecutors asked black and white jurors in this case. The Supreme Court then insisted that every judge evaluating a *Batson* claim — at both the trial and appellate levels — concentrate on the reason that the party gave at the time rather than strengthening the rationale later: "A *Batson* challenge does not call for a mere exercise in thinking up any rational basis. If the stated reason does not hold up, its pretextual significance does not fade because a trial judge, or an appeals court, can imagine a reason that might not have been shown up as false."

5. *Race and decision making.* Did the Court in *Batson* assume that jurors of different races will systematically reach different judgments? Is such a belief necessary to justify the decision? Researchers in psychology have conducted a number of experiments in an effort to learn about racial differences among individual juror judgments, the effects of racial composition on the group decision dynamics of juries, and the influence of a defendant's race on individual juror judgments. A review of this literature appears in Samuel R. Sommers & Omoniyi O. Adekanmbi, Race and Juries: An Experimental Psychology Perspective, in Critical Race Realism: Intersections of Psychology, Race, and Law 78 (Gregory S. Parks, Shayne Jones, and Jonathan Cardi, eds. 2008). For further exploration of this research, go to the web extension for this chapter at *http://www.crimpro.com/extension/ch17*.

Problem 17-3. Extending *Batson*

Defendant Edward Lee Davis, an African American man, was charged with aggravated robbery. No jurors were struck for cause during the jury selection. The defense, however, exercised four of its five peremptory strikes, while the state used one of its three. When the state used the one peremptory to strike a black man from the jury panel, defense counsel objected and asked for a race-neutral explanation. The prosecutor, in response, stated for the record that the prospective juror would have been a very good juror for the state and that race had nothing to do with her decision to strike. She explained:

> However, it was highly significant to the State that the man was a Jehovah's Witness. I have a great deal of familiarity with the sect of Jehovah's Witness. I would never, if I had a peremptory challenge left, fail to strike a Jehovah's Witness from my jury. In my experience that faith is very integral to their daily life in many ways. At least three times a week he goes to church for separate meetings. The Jehovah's Witness faith is of a

mind the higher powers will take care of all things necessary. In my experience Jehovah's Witnesses are reluctant to exercise authority over their fellow human beings in this Court House.

The prosecutor concluded her statement by saying she did not feel it appropriate "to pry" into this matter with the juror because there was no need to do so when exercising a peremptory on race-neutral grounds. Defense counsel had nothing further to add, and the trial judge ruled the peremptory strike would stand.

The defendant concedes the state's peremptory was exercised for race-neutral reasons but contends that the race-neutral explanation offered by the state is constitutionally impermissible as religious discrimination. How would you rule on appeal? See State v. Davis, 504 N.W.2d 767 (Minn. 1993).

Notes

1. *Extending* Batson *claims to other groups: majority view.* The U.S. Supreme Court has extended the coverage of *Batson* from jurors who are racial minorities to other groups. A prima facie case of racial discrimination arises when a party uses peremptory strikes to exclude Latinos from the jury. Hernandez v. New York, 500 U.S. 352 (1991). The Court applied the *Batson* framework to claims of gender discrimination in J.E.B. v. Alabama ex rel. T.B., 511 U.S. 127 (1994). State courts continue to wrestle with the application of *Batson* and analogous state decisions to nonracial challenges. For example, states are divided on whether to extend *Batson* to claims based on religious orientation. See Casarez v. State, 913 S.W.2d 468 (Tex. Crim. App. 1994) (allowing peremptory challenges based on religious orientation); State v. Hodge, 726 A.2d 531 (Conn. 1999). The battle over the extension of *Batson* does not extend only to groups subject to heightened standards of review under equal protection analysis. See, e.g., Commonwealth v. Carleton, 641 N.E.2d 1057 (Mass. 1994) (applying *Batson* to prosecutor's effort to strike all jurors with Irish-sounding names).

2. *Extending* Batson *to other proceedings and parties.* The federal and state courts have also extended the *Batson* limits on peremptory challenges to parties other than the prosecutor and to proceedings other than a criminal trial. In Powers v. Ohio, 499 U.S. 400 (1991), the Court held that any litigant, regardless of race, could raise a claim of racially discriminatory peremptory challenges. In Edmonson v. Leesville Concrete Co., Inc., 500 U.S. 614 (1991), the Court extended the prohibition against race-based strikes to civil trials. A year after *Edmonson,* the Court accepted challenges by prosecutors to race-based peremptory strikes by defendants in Georgia v. McCollum, 505 U.S. 42 (1992). While *Batson* claims can be made now in civil or criminal cases, and by defendants or prosecutors, criminal defendants still make the majority of *Batson* claims. See Kenneth Melilli, *Batson* in Practice: What We Have Learned About *Batson* and Peremptory Challenges, 71 Notre Dame L. Rev. 447 (1996).

Does this expansion of the coverage of *Batson* make the peremptory challenge less valuable than ever for litigants? Do these developments point to the eventual abolition of peremptory challenges, the position that Justice Marshall advocated in his concurring opinion in *Batson*?

3. *Remedies for* Batson *violations.* One of the many complicated questions courts have tried to answer in the wake of *Batson* is the question of the proper remedy. Should the judge start with a fresh venire, or reseat the improperly excluded jurors, or reseat all jurors excluded after the first improper peremptory strike? Some jurisdictions require trial courts, as a general rule, to disallow the strike and reseat the improperly stricken juror. A few states require the trial court to conduct jury selection from a newly convened venire. Most courts, however, have allowed the trial judge to choose among available remedies, without designating a preferred or required remedy. See Jefferson v. State, 595 So. 2d 38 (Fla. 1992); People v. Willis, 43 P.3d 130 (Cal. 2002). If the preferred remedy for a *Batson* violation is dismissal of the initial panel and selection of the jury from a fresh venire, would the parties ever have an incentive to create a deliberate *Batson* violation? Which remedy is most consistent with the view that the jury serves important functions for the jurors themselves and for the public at large?

4. *Removal of judges.* Just as jurors can be excluded when they are unable to find the facts impartially, a judge presiding at a trial may be removed from a case if she is not able to preside impartially. A party who questions the judge's impartiality may request that the judge recuse herself from the case. Statutes typically list some specific grounds for mandatory recusal, along with an instruction that the judge recuse herself whenever her "impartiality might reasonably be questioned." See 28 U.S.C. §455 (lists personal knowledge of disputed facts, family relationship with a party or attorney, and financial interest in outcome among the grounds for recusal). These statutory standards give specific content to the constitutional requirement that judges be impartial. See Tumey v. Ohio, 273 U.S. 510 (1927) (due process requires recusal of judge who has direct pecuniary interest in outcome of case).

In addition to challenges for cause and recusal of judges, about 20 states allow defendants to have one automatic strike — a kind of peremptory challenge — to the trial judge. See, e.g., Ill. Rev. Stat. ch. 38, para. 114-5(a). Some statutes that appear to require evidence of bias in fact operate as essentially automatic challenge provisions; others, including several federal statutes, that appear on their face to allow peremptory challenges to judges in fact require some evidence of bias. See, e.g., 28 U.S.C. §144; Liteky v. United States, 510 U.S. 540 (1994) (recusal and removal statutes require "extrajudicial source" of bias; bias allegations cannot be sustained solely on rulings by judge or information judge received during judicial proceedings). Is the presumption that judges are neutral stronger than for jurors?

C. JURY DELIBERATIONS AND VERDICTS

Once the jury is seated, the trial begins. In a few jurisdictions, the judge delivers preliminary instructions regarding the task at hand, along with an outline of the procedures for the jury to follow at trial and during deliberation. More often, the jury hears right away the opening statements of the attorneys, followed by the government's case in chief. Assuming that the judge denies the customary defense motion to dismiss the charges at the close of the prosecution's case, the jury then hears the defense evidence, if indeed the defendant chooses to present a defense. After closing statements from the attorneys, the judge instructs the jury on the law relevant to the case, using a combination of standard jury instructions for criminal cases and a few customized instructions that the parties suggest. The case then rests in the hands of the jury. In this section, we consider the rules governing the jury's deliberations.

1. *Deadlocked Juries*

Although most juries reach a unanimous verdict, many start out with divided views among the panel members about the proper outcome. Divisions among jurors may be easier to resolve when juries are presented with a range of offenses, including lesser included charges, that create room for negotiation. But courts are sometimes faced with deadlocked juries. What devices may the court use to encourage the jurors to reach a common decision?

■ NEW YORK CRIMINAL PROCEDURE LAW §310.30

At any time during its deliberation, the jury may request the court for further instruction or information with respect to the law, with respect to the content or substance of any trial evidence, or with respect to any other matter pertinent to the jury's consideration of the case. Upon such a request, the court must direct that the jury be returned to the courtroom and, after notice to both the people and counsel for the defendant, and in the presence of the defendant, must give such requested information or instruction as the court deems proper. With the consent of the parties and upon the request of the jury for further instruction with respect to a statute, the court may also give to the jury copies of the text of any statute which, in its discretion, the court deems proper.

■ COMMONWEALTH v. BENJAMIN GREER

951 A.2d 346 (Pa. 2008)

CASTILLE, C.J.

. . . On February 5, 2004, Bin Zhang was working at the Golden Dragon Restaurant in Philadelphia when he received a telephone call requesting a food delivery. Zhang recognized the number as one used in a previous robbery, and so he called the police. In response, the Burglary Detail Unit of the Philadelphia Police Department posted officers at the delivery address. Meanwhile, at the instruction of the officers, Zhang took an empty box to that address. When Zhang arrived, he was approached by two men who took his cell phone and then attempted to flee. One man escaped, but the second man, appellee Benjamin Greer, was thwarted by Zhang, who grabbed his clothing. Appellee and Zhang fell to the ground, causing Zhang to break his ankle. The police then apprehended appellee, who was charged with criminal conspiracy, aggravated assault, and robbery.

Appellee was tried by a jury sitting before the Honorable Gary S. Glazer. After two days of testimony, the jury began deliberations late in the afternoon of February 10, 2005, breaking after less than an hour that day. The jury resumed deliberations the following morning. The jury then sent a note to Judge Glazer, asking that certain testimony be read back and seeking clarification regarding the law of criminal conspiracy. The relevant testimony was read back to the jury, Judge Glazer gave a supplemental instruction, and deliberations resumed at approximately 11:00 A.M. That afternoon, the jury sent the first of two additional notes to Judge Glazer. The first note, which was signed by the jury's forewoman and stated that it was written at 12:30 P.M., volunteered that the jurors had reached a verdict of not guilty on the robbery charge, but were unable to reach a verdict on criminal conspiracy and aggravated assault. The note also volunteered that the jurors were divided 10-2 in favor of guilt for conspiracy, with jurors nine and ten favoring a not guilty verdict; and that juror number ten was the sole juror in favor of a not guilty verdict for aggravated assault. The note further volunteered that the holdout jurors "have reasonable doubt about evidence." At no point had Judge Glazer inquired as to the numerical split of the jury or the identity of the jurors in the minority.

At 1:30 P.M., Judge Glazer informed trial counsel that he had received a note from the jury stating that it was having difficulty reaching a verdict on conspiracy and aggravated assault, but he did not reveal that the note also outlined the numerical division of the jury, the identities of the "holdout" jurors, and their concerns. Judge Glazer suggested issuing a jury charge deriving from Commonwealth v. Spencer, 275 A.2d 299 (Pa. 1971), *i.e.*, a non-coercive charge instructing the jurors to be true to their convictions, but to reconsider their original views. Both attorneys agreed, and Judge Glazer issued a supplemental instruction. . . .

Following this charge, the jury again requested that certain testimony be read back and that they be reinstructed on conspiracy. Judge Glazer complied and the jury resumed deliberations at 2:05 P.M. Forty-five minutes later, at approximately 2:50 P.M., the court received a second note signed by the jury forewoman, entitled "Reason for Hung Jury." The note volunteered that: juror number nine was "not convinced" of (1) the police account of how they actually apprehended appellee, and (2) "the discrepancy between" Zhang's testimony and the police testimony; and juror number ten was "not convinced" that the evidence "concluded" that appellee was "the actual perp." Judge Glazer informed counsel of the note, this time also apparently revealing that it identified the holdout jurors. Judge Glazer suggested that he make "one last comment" to the jury and then take a verdict at 4 P.M. As the court and counsel were discussing the options, the jury was brought back into the courtroom. Judge Glazer then addressed the jury with another *Spencer* charge, which consisted of the following:

> I'm just going to ask that you go back for a little bit. What this indicates to me is either someone is not talking or someone is not listening. And, you know, I mean you owe that to the parties here. I mean again, I have a sense of fairness to the people here. That's why you're here. That's why you were picked. You promised us that you would be fair and that you would listen to your fellow jurors, and that you would give us a fair verdict. I mean that's really all that we we're asking for. Parties just want a fair shot which is what everybody is entitled to.
>
> And a jury verdict is . . . a jury of 12 people speaking as one. And, you know, if it were easy, anybody could do it. . . . But it's not easy. This is one of the most serious, difficult citizen participation functions that we have in American government. . . . Parties entrust you to reach a verdict.
>
> Now, you're almost there. You're there on one count. But we need your best efforts. We need you to talk. This is not time for people to stand on ego. There's people's lives that are depending on your verdict and on your participation, if you can fairly do so. If you can.

> And there's always that caveat because, as I said, you know — this is probably the third or fourth time — don't ask people to surrender deeply-held beliefs just to get out of here and reach a verdict because that's not right. On the other hand, each of you has views and just judging by what the note says, you're close, but no cigar. So we need you to go back and try to do and resolve this case.
>
> [We've] been here almost a week. It's a lot of time. It's a lot of your time. I'm here everyday, I work here. But you are serving the system and the community in an effort to reach a verdict, if you can fairly do so. So I'm going to [ask] you to go back. We're not going to keep you here over the weekend. Don't worry about that. We're going to ask you to go back and try because I think you can do it. But just keep an open mind. Listen to each other. Okay? Go on.

The jury resumed deliberations at 3:20 P.M., whereupon appellee objected to the above charge, arguing that it was directed at the two holdout jurors and pressured them to convict. Appellee suggested that the court declare a hung jury on the two deadlocked counts. Judge Glazer rejected the argument. . . . At 3:53 P.M., the jury returned with a unanimous verdict of not guilty on the charge of robbery, and guilty on the charges of criminal conspiracy and aggravated assault.

[Greer requested a retrial because] counsel had not been made aware at the time of trial that the jury forewoman's first signed note had identified the holdout jurors and the nature of their concerns. . . . Citing Brasfield v. United States, 272 U.S. 448 (1926), a case where the judge inquired into the nature of the deadlocked jury's division, appellee forwarded the absolutist claim that "it is a *per se* mistrial when the jury reveals its numerical division." . . . Judge Glazer denied the motion and sentenced appellee to three to six years of incarceration for aggravated assault, to run concurrently with a one-to-two-year sentence for criminal conspiracy. [Greer appealed to Superior Court, and that court vacated the convictions, concluding that the instruction here coerced the jury to reach a verdict.]

This Court granted the Commonwealth's request for discretionary review. We review jury charges, including supplemental jury charges, for an abuse of discretion. Further, the question of the proper duration of jury deliberations is one that rests within the sound discretion of the trial court, whose decision will not be disturbed unless there is a showing that the court abused its discretion or that the jury's verdict was the product of coercion or fatigue. . . .

Proper disposition of this appeal requires appreciation of the origins and subsequent experience of the *Allen* charge, particularly as the charge has been employed in Pennsylvania. Allen v. United States, 164 U.S. 492 (1896), involved a federal capital prosecution. The judge's supplemental charge in *Allen* is not set out verbatim in the opinion; rather, the High Court summarized the substance of the charge as follows:

> [That] in a large proportion of cases absolute certainty could not be expected; that, although the verdict must be the verdict of each individual juror, and not a mere acquiescence in the conclusion of his fellows, yet they should examine the question submitted with candor, and with a proper regard and deference to the opinions of each other; that it was their duty to decide the case if they could conscientiously do so; that they should listen, with a disposition to be convinced, to each other's arguments; that, if much the larger number were for conviction, a dissenting juror should consider whether his doubt was a reasonable one which made no impression upon the minds of so many men, equally honest, equally intelligent with himself. If, upon the other hand,

> the majority were for acquittal, the minority ought to ask themselves whether they might not reasonably doubt the correctness of a judgment which was not concurred in by the majority.

The *Allen* Court found "no error" in this charge.... Nothing in the *Allen* opinion suggested that the rule thus stated was of constitutional dimension.

The *Allen* charge came to be commonly used in both the state and federal courts, but over time, various courts raised concerns respecting that part of the charge encouraging jurors in the minority to reconsider their views in light of the majority vote, with the fear being that such an emphasis might be unduly coercive. Nevertheless, the U.S. Supreme Court has not disavowed the *Allen* charge....

Strict constitutional concerns aside, courts have taken greater control over supplemental charges as a supervisory matter. The U.S. Supreme Court did so in *Brasfield,* where the issue was not the propriety of the *Allen* charge, but the distinct and narrower question of the propriety of the trial judge inquiring into the numerical division of the jury. Other courts have taken on the specifics of the *Allen* charge, motivated by a concern with jury coercion, a concern with constitutional implications. This brings us to *Spencer.*

[The issue in *Spencer*] was whether the *Allen* charge has a prohibited coercive effect. The defendant argued that the portion of the charge which directed jurors in the minority to listen with deference to the majority and re-examine their minority position implied two troublesome points: (1) that jurors in the minority should yield to the majority; and (2) that those without reasonable doubt (the majority) need not re-examine their position despite the existence of reasonable doubt in the mind of a minority juror. *Spencer* noted that "each notion is contrary to the hallowed tradition of trial by jury" secured by both the federal and the Pennsylvania Constitutions [and declared] "that the *Allen* charge should not be employed by trial judges of this Commonwealth after the date of this opinion."...

[The *Spencer* court also] cited with approval to then-recently promulgated guidelines from the American Bar Association governing jury deadlock, noting that such guidelines "may avoid the evils inherent in the *Allen* charge and with proper usage may aid in the alleviation of problems which arise when juries are deadlocked." Those guidelines provided as follows:

> (a) Before the jury retires for deliberation, the court may give an instruction which informs the jury:
>
> (i) that in order to return a verdict, each juror must agree thereto;
>
> (ii) that jurors have a duty to consult with one another and to deliberate with a view to reaching an agreement, if it can be done without violence to individual judgment;
>
> (iii) that each juror must decide the case for himself, but only after an impartial consideration of the evidence with his fellow jurors;
>
> (iv) that in the course of deliberations, a juror should not hesitate to reexamine his own views and change his opinion if convinced it is erroneous; and
>
> (v) that no juror should surrender his honest conviction as to the weight or effect of the evidence solely because of the opinion of his fellow jurors, or for the mere purpose of returning a verdict.
>
> (b) If it appears to the court that the jury has been unable to agree, the court may require the jury to continue their deliberations and may give or repeat an instruction as provided in subsection (a).

With this background in mind, we turn to this appeal. [Preliminarily, we note that] Pennsylvania is not a *Brasfield/Allen* jurisdiction. This Court has imposed no *per se* supervisory rule in Pennsylvania concerning inquiries into jury divisions, much less have we held that such a rule, once imposed, should be extended to prohibit issuing non-coercive *Spencer* charges *anytime* the Court learns the identity of initial holdout jurors.

[In *Spencer,* this Court engaged in a] totality of circumstances analysis precisely because *Allen* charges contain the "potential abuses" of suggesting that minority jurors should yield to the majority, and that the majority need not re-examine their positions in light of the minority jurors' views. [The] relevant question of Pennsylvania law . . . is whether the supplemental charge in this case comported with *Spencer* or was unlawfully coercive. Joining that question squarely now, we see no abuse of discretion by the trial court.

First of all, the supplemental charge did not begin to approach the substance of the supplemental *Allen* charge that this Court found to be potentially coercive in *Spencer*. The trial court here . . . did not purport to separately address the jurors in the minority, nor did it suggest to jurors holding a minority view that they should defer to the majority view. The court did not say anything along the lines of "a dissenting juror should consider whether his doubt is a reasonable one if it made no impression upon the minds of so many other jurors." Nor did the court suggest that jurors in the minority should distrust their own judgment because their views differ from that of the majority. Rather, the trial court addressed the jury as a whole, and while repeatedly advising the jurors that they were not expected to surrender deeply-held views, reminded them of their duty and function, and directed them to continue to deliberate and to try to reach a verdict. In addition, as the Commonwealth has stressed, the court did not pressure the jury to reach a verdict under pain of being inconvenienced over the upcoming weekend; rather, it made clear that the jury would not be kept over the weekend.

Second, we are not persuaded by the argument that the fact that the court knew the nature of the jury's numerical division and the identity of the holdouts (here, via volunteered information from the jury forewoman) can make an otherwise non-coercive *Spencer* charge coercive. While the U.S. Supreme Court held in *Brasfield* that inquiry into the numerical division of a jury is inappropriate as a supervisory matter . . . this Court has never held, for *Spencer* purposes, that the Court's awareness of the jury's division precludes issuing a non-coercive *Spencer* charge. [When the jury voluntarily reveals its numerical split, a number of courts have observed that the judge has a heightened duty to avoid utilizing coercive language in its supplemental charge. The trial court here, however, did not utilize this information in the instructions that followed. Although the court addressed the jury twice, and the charge was extensive], the charge still was addressed to the jury as a whole and did not purport to single out the jurors in the minority. We do not believe that the court's awareness of the division in the jury made the charge coercive.

Turning to the fact that the court was aware of the identity of the holdouts, we likewise do not believe that that fact renders an otherwise proper *Spencer* charge unlawfully coercive. Again, unlike in the *Allen* situation . . . a proper *Spencer* charge does not address jurors in the minority separately, but directs all jurors to be open to reconsideration. More importantly, as a matter of logic, the jurors already are acutely aware of where they stand relative to the private jury vote-whether the specific outcome of that poll is revealed to the trial court or not.

No doubt, jurors in a minority position always feel some form of pressure to bow down to the will of the majority. [Even if the trial court is completely unaware of the nature of the jury's division, a charge to continue deliberating may cause jurors in the minority to feel more pressure to change their views than jurors in the majority.]

By the same token, a charge to continue deliberating theoretically could cause jurors in a majority position to feel pressure to switch views, if only to get the matter over with. Indeed, it is also possible that jurors may want to just throw up their hands at the first sign of disagreement and declare themselves deadlocked in the hope they will be discharged from service. These sorts of ephemeral psychological pressures are both inherent in the jury function and difficult to measure. We . . . should tread carefully before allowing speculation about such effects to control the relevant jurisprudence.

Nothing in the law requires that deliberations be aborted because jurors may feel uncomfortable in being directed to listen to each other and to attempt to hammer out their differences. Indeed, if avoidance of conflict or discomfort were the prime directive, we could do away with deliberation entirely and tally private, individual votes from the jury. As the *Allen* Court noted . . .

> The very object of the jury system is to secure unanimity by a comparison of views, and by arguments among the jurors themselves. It certainly cannot be the law that each juror should not listen with deference to the arguments and with a distrust of his own judgment, if he finds a large majority of the jury taking a different view of the case from what he does himself. It cannot be that each juror should go to the jury room with a blind determination that the verdict shall represent his opinion of the case at that moment; or, that he should close his ears to the arguments of men who are equally honest and intelligent as himself.

Allen, 164 U.S. at 501-02. To this, we would add (and this is what *Spencer* refines *Allen* to accomplish), there is nothing improper in directing all jurors to be open to the arguments of their fellow jurors.

Finally, we turn to the two phrases in the court's second *Spencer* charge which were of particular concern to the [defendant], *i.e.,* the statements that "this is not the time for people to stand on ego," and that "each of you has views and just judging by what the note says, you're close, but no cigar." We fail to see the coercive effect of telling jurors not to "stand on ego." The expression "close but no cigar" is more troublesome, and it would have been better to avoid that language. But, we do not believe the phrase altered the essentially non-coercive charge that was issued. Again, the court was careful to direct its charge to the jury as a whole, and emphasized, yet again, that jurors were not to surrender deeply-held beliefs merely to reach a verdict. Nor did the court suggest that jurors in the minority had a special obligation to reconsider, over and above that of all the jurors. Finally, the general thrust of the charge was rather modest. The court began this portion of the charge by stating, "I'm just going to ask that you go back for a little bit" and ended it by saying: "We're going to ask you to go back and try because I think you can do it. But just keep an open mind. Listen to each other. Okay? Go on." This hardly smacks of coercion. We see no abuse of discretion in the charge. . . .

SAYLOR, J., concurring.

. . . Presently, while the trial judge qualified his language with many of the beneficial aspects of *Spencer,* he also suggested, after learning of the 10-2 split, that "what this indicates to me is that someone is not talking or someone is not listening," "you're almost there," and "you're close but no cigar." I believe that these types of admonitions might be perceived as being directed primarily toward the dissenting jurors, much in the same fashion as an *Allen* charge. The first reference — reflecting the trial judge's belief that "someone is not talking or someone is not listening" — might be taken by jurors as a criticism of their conduct in the deliberations. Particularly given that trial judges have limited information regarding the actual dynamics of jury deliberations as they unfold in the jury room, and jurors must adhere to their "individual judgment" and "honest conviction as to the weight or effect of the evidence," *Spencer,* 275 A.2d at 304 n. 7, I believe these types of comments should be avoided. Likewise, the references to the jurors being "almost there" and "close but no cigar" seem to me to beg the question, "close to what?" In circumstances in which ten jurors favor conviction, such references could reasonably be regarded as being directed toward the minority jurors. . . .

I am ultimately able to join the result reached by the majority because, in my view, any potential coercion by the trial judge was adequately ameliorated by the remaining portions of the charge reflecting *Spencer* principles. Left to my own devices, however, I would accompany the disposition with a caveat to the effect that trial courts should do their best to adhere to the guidelines approved in *Spencer,* and avoid any additional types of collateral remarks that could carry a risk of having coercive effects.

Notes

1. *"Dynamite" charges: majority position.* The dynamite charge (or "hammer" charge) originated in Commonwealth v. Tuey, 62 Mass. 1 (1851), and came to national attention in Allen v. United States, 164 U.S. 492 (1896). The instruction produced verdicts, and its use spread rapidly. More recently, many courts have limited or abandoned the *Allen* instruction. About half the states have disapproved dynamite charges, in whole or in part. See People v. Gainer, 566 P.2d 997 (Cal. 1977); State v. Fool Bull, 766 N.W.2d 159 (S.D. 2009). The case law on the subject is extensive. Some courts have limited the instruction through procedural devices, such as preventing judges from giving the instruction too early during the jury's deliberations or from giving it more than once. Along these lines, some courts say that an *Allen* charge is acceptable only if the judge delivered an identical charge to the jury at the start of its deliberations. Other courts focus on the content of the instructions. Appellate courts pay special attention to the balance between statements about the need for agreement and statements about the duty of individual jurors to stand by their own considered opinions. The alternative presented in the ABA standards (as discussed in *Greer*) influences many courts. Do you believe that the ABA alternative creates a different reaction among jurors than the traditional *Allen* charge? See also Lowenfield v. Phelps, 484 U.S. 231 (1988) (approving charge

that does not instruct minority jurors to reconsider in light of majority views but does tell jurors not to hesitate to "reexamine" their views and to "change" their opinion if they are convinced that they are wrong). The dynamite charge has become the subject of some empirical studies that attempt to measure its impact on jury deliberations. For a survey of the state cases and the empirical work, go to the web extension for this chapter at *http://www.crimpro.com/extension/ch17*.

2. *Numerical breakdowns.* When a jury sends out word that it is divided and cannot reach a consensus, two questions spring to mind: How many jurors are "holding out," and which side does the majority favor? Appellate courts usually express concern if a trial judge inquired about the numerical division of the jury, explaining that such inquiries might create undue pressure on the minority jurors to change their votes. However, courts are divided over whether such inquiries, standing alone, constitute legal error. The larger group, including the federal courts, say that a judge's inquiries about the jury's numerical division are per se error. See Brasfield v. United States, 272 U.S. 448 (1926); People v. Wilson, 213 N.W.2d 193 (Mich. 1973). In the other states, this type of inquiry becomes a ground for reversal when combined with other circumstances, such as the judge's further inquiry about whether the majority favors conviction, acquittal, or some other option. On the other hand, if the jury *volunteers* information about its numerical division, the judge typically must inform the parties. Statutes and court rules typically state that the parties must be informed about any statement that the jury makes during its deliberations, and they must have an opportunity to argue to the judge about what she should say to the panel.

There is some social science evidence that jurors who cling most tenaciously to their views are also those who reach their views most quickly and are most likely to take a more absolutist view of the case. Deanna Kuhn, Michael Weinstock & Robin Flaton, How Well Do Jurors Reason? Competence Dimensions of Individual Variation in a Juror Reasoning Task, 5 Psychol. Sci. 289 (1994). If this description is generally true, should we give judges more opportunities to convince jurors with minority views to rethink their positions?

3. *Lesser-included offenses and jury deliberations.* Experimental data suggest that juries presented with alternatives for verdicts other than acquittal or the most serious available charge produce fewer acquittals and fewer hung juries. See Neil Vidmar, Effects of Decision Alternatives on the Verdicts and Social Perceptions of Simulated Jurors, 22 J. Personality & Soc. Psychol. 211 (1972) (in 54 percent of mock homicide trials, jury acquitted when choice of verdict was guilty of first-degree murder or not guilty; when jury had four options, jurors returned verdicts of first-degree murder in 8 percent of the cases, second-degree murder in 64 percent, manslaughter in 21 percent, and not guilty in 8 percent). Depending on the case, as a strategic matter the prosecution or the defense may favor or oppose the judge instructing the jury about lesser included offenses.

In cases involving lesser-included offenses or multiple charges, the judge may encourage agreement among jurors by providing instructions on the order for them to consider lesser-included offenses. Two instructions are common. Under an "acquittal first" instruction, the judge tells the jury to reach a unanimous decision to acquit on the most serious charge before moving on to consider conviction for a lesser offense. See State v. Tate, 773 A.2d 308 (Conn. 2001) (if jury that has received "acquittal first" instruction asks for clarification about a lesser included offense and then reports itself deadlocked, trial court should first ask jury if it has reached a partial verdict before declaring mistrial). An alternative is the "unable to agree" or "reasonable efforts" instruction, which permits a jury to consider lesser included offenses if, after reasonable efforts, the jury cannot agree on a verdict on the more serious offense. The acquittal-first instruction was the more traditional of the two, but the reasonable efforts instruction is gaining a strong following among state courts. See State v. Thomas, 533 N.E.2d 286 (Ohio 1988). As defense counsel, which of these instructions would you ordinarily prefer? Under what circumstances might you prefer the other instruction?

In some cases, the defendant asks the judge to present the jury with an "all or nothing" choice: they convict the defendant of either the most serious charge, or nothing at all. Because of the jury's traditional freedom to accept or reject evidence selectively, courts usually disfavor such instructions. In other circumstances, the defendant finds the all-or-nothing strategy to be too risky. Where one of the elements of the offense charged remains in doubt, but the defendant is plainly guilty of some offense, the jury might "resolve its doubts in favor of conviction." Keeble v. United States, 412 U.S. 205, 213 (1973). The judge's willingness to discuss lesser-included offenses in the jury instructions depends in part on whether the prosecution filed the lesser offenses in the indictment or information, and whether the defense attorney made the lesser offense central to her theory of the case.

4. *Sequestration of juries.* One powerful practical force working in favor of jury agreement is the fact that jurors are forced to remain together in a single room, at least during working hours, until their task is complete. Indeed, for some cases involving an unusual amount of publicity that could taint the jurors, the court will "sequester" the jury and order them to remain together in a hotel during their meals, evenings, and off-days. See Tex. Code Crim. Proc. art 35.23. At one time, this process was much more explicitly designed to produce a verdict. Consider William Blackstone's description of the environment for jury deliberations: "the jury, . . . in order to avoid intemperance and causeless delay, are to be kept without meat, drink, fire, or candle, unless by permission of the judge, till they are all unanimously agreed." Blackstone, 3 Commentaries on the Laws of England 375 (1768).

5. *Prevalence of hung juries.* In the popular imagination, the "hung jury" is a common occurrence. A study of juries in the 1960s found that hung juries occurred in 5.5 percent of the cases studied. Harry Kalven & Hans Zeisel, The American Jury 57 (1966). The rate of deadlocked juries differs from place to place. For instance, rates of hung juries in Los Angeles are higher than in other jurisdictions: 13 to 16 percent in Los Angeles, compared to 6.2 percent nationwide. In federal criminal trials, the rate of hung juries remains around 2 to 3 percent. See Paula L. Hannaford, Valerie P. Hans & G. Thomas Munsterman, How Much Justice Hangs in the Balance? 83 Judicature 59 (1999). Keep in mind that these rates reflect the number of juries that end their deliberations in deadlock; there are no data on the extent to which juries declare themselves deadlocked and ultimately reach a verdict. What outcomes would you expect during any later retrials of cases that initially produced a hung jury?

2. Changes to Jury Structure

The classic structure for a criminal jury calls for 12 members whose names are known to the parties. The jurors must agree unanimously on a verdict, based on their unaided memory of the testimony and other evidence. What effects might we anticipate from changes to this traditional structure?

GEORGIA CONSTITUTION ART. I, §I, PARA. XI

(a) The right to trial by jury shall remain inviolate. . . . In criminal cases, the defendant shall have a public and speedy trial by an impartial jury; and the jury shall be the judges of the law and the facts.

(b) A trial jury shall consist of 12 persons; but the General Assembly may prescribe any number, not less than six, to constitute a trial jury in courts of limited jurisdiction and in superior courts in misdemeanor cases. . . .

MONTANA CODE §46-16-110

(1) The parties in a felony case have a right to trial by a jury of 12 persons.

(2) The parties may agree in writing at any time before the verdict, with the approval of the court, that the jury shall consist of any number less than that to which they are entitled.

(3) Upon written consent of the parties, a trial by jury may be waived.

STATE v. SHERRIE TUCKER

657 N.W.2d 374 (Wis. 2003)

BABLITCH, J.

We are asked to decide under what circumstances a circuit court may restrict the disclosure of juror information in a criminal trial, and, if juror information is restricted, what precautions must be taken to avoid prejudice to the criminal defendant. . . .

In March 1998, law enforcement officers executed a search warrant at an apartment shared by Tucker and her boyfriend, Damien McCray (McCray). In the apartment, officers found cocaine in a bag marked "Shiree Tucker," a .38 caliber revolver, and bullets. Tucker made a statement to police after a *Miranda* warning was given, in which she admitted that the cocaine belonged to her and that she had been selling cocaine for about a month. Tucker was tried and convicted of possession of cocaine with intent to deliver within 1,000 feet of a school while armed with a dangerous weapon, which resulted in a seven year prison sentence. The circuit court judge stayed the prison sentence and instead ordered seven years of probation for Tucker.

Prior to jury selection for Tucker's trial, the circuit court judge told counsel off the record that "it has been my practice to use numbers and not names in this court. . . . What I'm prohibiting is the names of jurors being stated in the courtroom and for the record when other people may be sitting in the audience and using those names for any other reason." When defense counsel objected, the judge explained that the use of numbers is appropriate because this was a case "involving drugs and an allegation of drug dealing which I think raises the bar to some extent in terms of any danger to jurors." . . . During the trial, the judge corrected defense counsel when he referred to a juror by name, stating "it's my practice to refer to the jurors by number, so please follow the practice." There was no other statement made in front of the jury regarding the use of numbers instead of their names. . . .

Both parties had access to all the juror information, including the jurors' names. Furthermore, the public presumably could have obtained the jurors' names by inquiring at the clerk of courts' office. A jury is typically deemed "anonymous" when juror information is withheld from the public and the parties themselves. Therefore, the jury in this case was not a classic "anonymous" jury. Notwithstanding whether the jury in this case is characterized as an "anonymous" or a "numbers" jury, if restrictions are placed on juror identification or information, due process concerns are raised regarding a defendant's rights to an impartial jury and a presumption of innocence. Accordingly, although this case does not deal with the classic "anonymous" jury, the reasoning in cases involving anonymous juries is beneficial to our analysis.

The empanelling of an anonymous jury is a relatively recent phenomenon that was rarely utilized before the Second Circuit's opinion in United States v. Barnes, 604 F.2d 121 (2d Cir. 1979). The court in *Barnes* addressed juror anonymity with respect to its effect on the practice of voir dire. In *Barnes*, the district court ordered that the jurors' identities, addresses, religious affiliations, and ethnic backgrounds remain anonymous, even from the parties themselves. The court . . . examined each of the restrictions placed on juror information and concluded that the jurors' demeanors and responses to questions regarding their family, education and other matters would provide substantially the same information as the juror information that was restricted. Consequently, the court rejected the argument that the defendant was denied the ability to intelligently exercise peremptory challenges. . . . Although not explicit, the court essentially weighed the need to protect the jury, which was prompted by the defendant's ties to the mafia, against the rights of the defendant to an impartial jury.

A few years later, the Second Circuit addressed a different concern with the use of an anonymous jury in United States v. Thomas, 757 F.2d 1359 (2d Cir. 1985). In *Thomas*, the defendants argued that an anonymous jury is an unconstitutional infringement on a defendant's presumption of innocence because it gives jurors the impression that the defendant is dangerous and a threat to the jurors' safety. The court in *Thomas* acknowledged the fundamental tenet that a defendant is presumed innocent until proven guilty, but nevertheless determined that an anonymous jury might be permissible if jurors are in need of protection. Therefore, the court rejected a per se rule against empanelling an anonymous jury, but concluded that an anonymous jury is warranted only if there is a "strong reason" to believe that the jury needs protection and if the court takes "reasonable precautions" to minimize the impact of anonymity on the jurors' views of the defendant. The court noted that reasonable precautions were taken in that case, in part, because the judge gave the jury an "intelligent, reasonable and believable explanation for his actions that did not cast the defendants in an unfavorable light." In other words, the curative or precautionary instruction served to rebut any notion that the use of an anonymous jury was somehow a negative reflection on the defendant's guilt or character. The Second Circuit's approach in *Thomas* has been widely adopted by both federal and state courts. . . .

[We also find the reasoning in *Thomas* persuasive.] Therefore, before a circuit court restricts any juror information in an individual case, it should determine that the jurors are in need of protection and take reasonable precautions to avoid prejudice to the defendant. In this case, Tucker concedes that her opportunity for voir dire was not impeded since both parties had access to all the juror information. However, Tucker claims that her presumption of innocence was eroded by the circuit court's use of numbers without an individualized determination that the jury needed protection nor a precautionary statement made to the jury regarding the use of numbers instead of names.

Serious concerns regarding a defendant's presumption of innocence are raised when juror information is restricted, as in this case. [The] empanelment of an anonymous jury triggers due process scrutiny because this practice is likely to taint the jurors' opinion of the defendant, thereby burdening the presumption of innocence. Therefore, courts must attempt to ensure that juror anonymity should not cast any adverse reflection upon the defendant.

[Accordingly, we] conclude that if a court withholds any juror information, it must both: (1) find that a jury needs protection; and (2) take reasonable precautions to avoid prejudicing the defendant. We now examine whether the circuit court in this case satisfied this two prong test. [We] hold that the circuit court erroneously exercised its discretion by failing to apply the correct standard of law. . . .

First, the circuit court did not make an individualized determination that the jurors needed protection based on the specific circumstances present in Tucker's case. Rather, the court informed counsel that "it has been my practice to use numbers and not names" in drug cases. The circuit court repeatedly referred to its "practice" of using numbers without specifically noting any particular factors that warranted the use of numbers in Tucker's case.

There are various factors that may be taken into account in making an individualized determination that a jury needs protection. Such factors may include, but are not limited to: (1) the defendant's involvement in organized crime; (2) the defendant's participation in a group with the capacity to harm jurors; (3) the defendant's past attempts to interfere with the judicial process; and (4) extensive publicity that could enhance the possibility that jurors' names would become public and expose them to intimidation or harassment.

Second, the circuit court did not take necessary precautions to minimize any prejudicial effect to Tucker. Although the circuit court explained the use of numbers instead of jurors' names to counsel off the record, the court did not make any statement to the jurors regarding its use of numbers. Rather, the jurors were just referred to by number instead of name. The only statement heard by the jurors regarding the use of numbers was when the circuit court corrected defense counsel by stating, "it's my practice to refer to the jurors by number, so please follow the practice." The circuit court did instruct the jury on Tucker's presumption of innocence and on the State's burden of proving guilt beyond a reasonable doubt. However, we conclude that this instruction, by itself, was insufficient. When jurors' names are withheld, as in this case, the circuit court, at a minimum, must make a precautionary statement to the jury that the use of numbers instead of names should in no way be interpreted as a reflection of the defendant's guilt or innocence. . . .

Any additional precautionary statements that are made to a jury when juror information is restricted should be based on factors and influences that may be present in a case, which could warrant withholding juror information. A precautionary statement must not mislead a jury, but must be based on factors and influences that are relevant in a particular case. . . .

Although the circuit court erred [in its use of numbered jurors in this case], the error in this case was harmless. An error is harmless if it is clear beyond a reasonable doubt that a rational jury would have found the defendant guilty absent the error. . . . In this case, Tucker admitted to police after she was given a *Miranda* warning that the cocaine belonged to her and that she had been selling cocaine for about a month. . . . In addition, the cocaine found in Tucker and McCray's apartment was in a plastic bag marked "Shiree Tucker." . . .

BRADLEY, J., concurring.

. . . If this were an anonymous jury, then I agree with the majority that the circuit court was required to make an individualized determination of the need for such a jury. I part ways with the majority because it fails to draw a distinction between a numbers jury, as here, and an anonymous jury. The result of this failure is that in concluding that harmless error applies in this "numbers only" situation, it incorrectly extends harmless error as a remedy in all truly anonymous jury cases. Such a widespread extension is contrary to precedent. . . .

Ultimately, I concur in the mandate of the majority because I conclude that there was no error. The defendant had access to all juror information, including their names. Given that the only limitation here was how the jurors were addressed and that the judge advised the jury that it was her practice to use numbers rather than names, I do not find that the defendant's rights were violated.

Measures to shield juror information not only implicate the defendant's rights, but also contradict the presumption of openness that defines the American judicial system. The selection of jurors has always presumptively been a public process.

Since the sixteenth century jurors have been selected in public. It is not surprising that trials in colonial America adopted the presumptive openness of the jury selection process that developed in England. This openness enhances both the basic fairness of the criminal trial and the appearance of fairness so essential to public confidence in the system. . . .

A few years ago this court unanimously rejected a petition for an administrative rule governing juror confidentiality. The petition provided that jurors be referred to only by number and that no personal juror identifying information could be elicited during voir dire. It allowed that a party may, after the trial, petition the court for access to personal juror identifying information for purposes of developing a motion for a new trial.

The breadth of such a proposal and its effect on our tradition of public trials were apparent to many who appeared in opposition to the proposal at the public hearing. The State Bar of Wisconsin was one of the groups that appeared in opposition to the petition. It cautioned that an anonymous jury should be used only in "an extremely rare circumstance."

A trial is a public event and a public trial lies at the foundation of our legal tradition. The public trial is rooted in the "principle that justice cannot survive behind walls of silence." Sheppard v. Maxwell, 384 U.S. 333 (1966).

The majority's failure to distinguish between a numbers jury and an anonymous jury serves to dilute the jurisprudence on anonymous juries. It compounds this problem by applying an across the board "no harm, no foul" analysis of the harmless error rule thus serving to make the use of anonymous juries more commonplace. [Instead, the use of an anonymous jury should be] the "last resort" and "a drastic measure." . . .

The most common rationale for an anonymous jury is the protection of the jurors. A jury that sits in fear may not fill the expectation of impartiality. Yet, the use of an anonymous jury is a double edged sword — it can give a sense of security or it can breed and feed fear. When fear is the result, then jury anonymity is a solution that exacerbates the problem it was intended to solve.

SYKES, J., concurring.

. . . The parties and the public had unrestricted access to all juror identifying information. As such, the anonymous jury case law does not apply. The majority opinion nevertheless applies the anonymous jury case law, assumes that the presumption of innocence has been violated, and imposes the procedural requirements prescribed by the inapplicable anonymous jury cases. . . . I cannot agree with this approach.

Voir dire by number does not implicate the presumption of innocence in the same way that the cases have assumed the use of an anonymous jury does. It has not been demonstrated — in this case or in the case law — that mere voir dire by number, without any restriction on access to juror information, has any serious adverse impact on the presumption of innocence. Any suggestion that it does is pure speculation. Indeed, the majority engages in no evaluation of this point at all, but merely extrapolates a presumption of innocence/due process violation from cases that involved true anonymous juries rather than the far more innocuous practice of voir dire by number.

Our courthouses today are equipped with various security precautions — metal detectors at courthouse entrances, security glass in individual courtrooms, armed deputy sheriffs in the courtroom and in the courthouse hallways — all of which suggest at least some level of risk to the people who work and visit there, including the jurors. It cannot seriously be suggested that the presumption of innocence has necessarily been compromised by the use of any of these sorts of generalized protections. Certain special security precautions are sometimes taken in individual cases, such as posting extra deputies in the courtroom, without encumbering the presumption of innocence or requiring particularized due process justifications. Voir dire by number (if a circuit court chooses to use this technique) falls within this category of routine security measures, whether used as a general practice, in a certain class of cases, or case by case.

In my view, voir dire by number, without any other restriction on the scope of voir dire or the parties' or the public's access to juror identifying information, does not rise to the level of an encumbrance on the presumption of innocence so as to implicate the defendant's right to due process. . . .

Problem 17-4. Non-unanimous Verdicts

> A jury too frequently have at least one member, more ready to hang the panel than to hang the traitor.
>
> — Abraham Lincoln to Erastus Corning, June 12, 1863

As in many states, prosecutors and citizens in California have expressed concern that too many trials result in hung juries and that a requirement of unanimity provides radical or irrational jurors with the power to block a just outcome. A Blue Ribbon Commission on Jury System Improvement in California recommended the following jury reform:

> The Legislature should propose a constitutional amendment which provides that, except for good cause when the interests of justice require a unanimous verdict, trial judges shall accept an 11-1 verdict after the jury has deliberated for a reasonable period of time (not less than six hours) in all felonies, except where the punishment may be death or life imprisonment, and in all misdemeanors where the jury consists of twelve persons. . . .

The commission explained that "eliminating the unanimity requirement is intended primarily to address the problem of an 11-1 or 10-2 hung jury where the hold-out jurors are refusing to deliberate, are engaging in nullification, or are simply [being] unreasonable (e.g., ignoring the evidence)." A slight majority of the commission preferred allowing only 11-1 and not 10-2 verdicts because "where two jurors share the same minority position, it seems less likely that the basis for the minority position is irrationality rather than a legitimate disagreement."

The commission's recommendation was a version of the "modified unanimity" approach — adopted in England and used in civil cases in several states — that gives judges the power to allow non-unanimous verdicts after a period of time (two hours in England). Opting for a time delay before allowing non-unanimous verdicts "forces the jury to begin its deliberations listening to all jurors and counting the votes of all jurors."

As a legislator in California, would you support a bill implementing the commission's recommendation? See Clark Kelso, Final Report of the Blue Ribbon Commission on Jury System Improvement, 47 Hastings L.J. 1433 (1996).

Notes

1. *Jury size: majority position.* Starting in 1970, the Supreme Court permitted experimentation with the size of criminal juries. In Williams v. Florida, 399 U.S. 78 (1970), the Court upheld the use of a 6-person jury in a criminal case; however, in Ballew v. Georgia, 435 U.S. 223 (1978), the Court struck down the use of a 5-person jury as a violation of the Sixth Amendment. A handful of states took up this invitation and now allow felonies (other than capital cases) to be tried by juries of either 6 or 8 members, including Arizona (8-member juries except where sentences are 30 years or more), Utah (8-member juries), Connecticut (6-member juries), and Florida (6-member juries). Another small group of states, including Indiana and Massachusetts, allow 6-member juries for felony trials in limited jurisdiction courts but require full 12-member juries in general jurisdiction courts. In contrast, for misdemeanors, more than half of the states mandate that juries consist of 6 members, and another large group of states specify a jury size between 6 and 12 members. State Court Organization 2004 (August 2006, NCJ 212351). Efforts in a few states to reduce the size of the criminal jury have been rejected on state constitutional grounds. See, e.g., Byrd v. State, 879 S.W.2d 435 (Ark. 1994). Perhaps reducing the expense and difficulty of selecting and maintaining juries makes it possible to offer

juries in a broader range of cases. Will a smaller jury function differently? In a predictable direction?

2. *Does jury size matter?* Social science played a role in the U.S. Supreme Court's decision in Ballew v. Georgia, 435 U.S. 223 (1978), which drew a constitutional line at a jury of six. The *Ballew* Court cited 19 studies on jury size conducted since 1970. An extensive discussion of these studies led the Court to conclude as follows:

> First, recent empirical data suggest that progressively smaller juries are less likely to foster effective group deliberation. . . . Second, the data now raise doubts about the accuracy of the results achieved by smaller and smaller panels. . . . Third, the data suggest that the verdicts of jury deliberation in criminal cases will vary as juries become smaller, and that the variance amounts to an imbalance to the detriment of one side, the defense. . . . Fourth, [smaller juries create] problems not only for jury decisionmaking, but also for the representation of minority groups in the community. . . . We readily admit that we do not pretend to discern a clear line between six members and five. But the assembled data raise substantial doubt about the reliability and appropriate representation of panels smaller than six. [435 U.S. at 232-39].

Does study of internal jury dynamics offer the proper test for the optimal jury size?

3. *Non-unanimous verdicts.* In Apodaca v. Oregon, 406 U.S. 404 (1972), the Supreme Court reversed earlier cases and interpreted the Sixth Amendment right to jury trial to allow convictions based on 11-1 and 10-2 votes. A companion case, Johnson v. Louisiana, 406 U.S. 356 (1972), upheld a conviction based on a 9-3 vote. However, in Burch v. Louisiana, 441 U.S. 130 (1979), the Court concluded that a conviction based on a 5-1 vote violated the right to a jury trial. States have not rushed into this constitutional opening. Only Louisiana and Oregon currently allow juries to convict defendants of felonies on a non-unanimous vote, although this reform is suggested fairly often, as the California proposal in Problem 17-4 illustrates. Some states have adopted non-unanimous verdict rules for misdemeanor trials, and a substantial number allow special exceptions to the unanimity requirement for verdicts, including consent of the parties.

The most famous study of non-unanimous juries is Reid Hastie, Steven D. Penrod & Nancy Pennington, Inside the Jury (1983). The study found several differences between behavior on unanimity-rule and majority-rule juries. Majority-rule juries reach a verdict more quickly; they tend to vote early and conduct discussions in a more adversarial manner; holdouts are more likely to remain at the conclusion of deliberations; members of small groups are less likely to speak; and large factions attract members more quickly. Is there a rational explanation for a constitutional doctrine that allows a 9-3 verdict but not a 5-1 verdict? Does democratic theory support any non-unanimous verdict that mimics what a simple majority of society at large would decide in a case?

4. *Different rationales for one verdict.* The unanimity requirement calls for each juror to agree to the group outcome, whether it be conviction or acquittal of each possible charge. Jurors may, however, take different routes to reach the same conclusion. For instance, a statute might list more than one method of committing a crime, and jurors may have differing views about which method the defendant used. In Schad v. Arizona, 501 U.S. 624 (1991), a defendant was indicted for first-degree murder, and the prosecutor argued both premeditated- and felony-murder theories. It was not clear whether the jurors all agreed on one theory when they

returned a guilty verdict. The Court held that there was no due process violation because the state statute treated felony murder and premeditation as alternative *means* of establishing the single criminal element. Thus, the key question is whether the statute makes a particular fact an element of the offense or instead an alternative means of establishing a crime element. State courts have also framed the question in these terms. See State v. Fortune, 909 P.2d 930 (Wash. 1996). However, it has proven difficult to determine which facts are the "means" (over which jurors may disagree) and which are the "elements" (on which jurors must agree). See State v. Boots, 780 P.2d 725 (Or. 1989) (Linde, J.); Richardson v. United States, 526 U.S. 813 (1999) (interpreting the federal Continuing Criminal Enterprise statute to require jury to agree unanimously on the "violations" that make up the "series of continuing violations" that define the enterprise; violations are elements of the offense, not merely the means of committing an element). For a sampling of the varied state court rulings on this question, go to the web extension for this chapter at *http://www.crimpro.com/extension/ch17*.

5. *Special verdicts: majority position.* Special verdicts require the jury to answer specific questions about its subsidiary findings of fact, and they instruct the jury about the sequence for proceeding from preliminary findings to final conclusions. Although a special verdict allows judicial review of improper verdicts, they are not often used in criminal cases, and some courts have struck down convictions based on special verdicts. See State v. Dilliner, 569 S.E.2d 211 (W. Va. 2002) (use of special interrogatories in criminal case in absence of statutory authorization is reversible error). According to the seminal case on this question, United States v. Spock, 416 F.2d 165 (1st Cir. 1969), special verdicts may coerce a jury into reaching a guilty verdict: "There is no easier way to reach, and perhaps force, a verdict of guilty than to approach it step by step. A juror, wishing to acquit, may be formally catechized." Despite this general disinclination to use special verdicts, some state statutes or procedural rules provide for special verdicts in particular types of cases, such as those in which the defendant presents an insanity defense.

6. *Inconsistent verdicts.* When there are multiple defendants in a trial or multiple counts against a single defendant, the jury could reach inconsistent conclusions for the different defendants or charges. Yet because of the preference for general verdicts, there is no explanation available for how the jury reached its incongruent outcomes. Faced with this situation, the federal courts have decided that consistency among verdicts is not necessary when a defendant is convicted on one or more counts but acquitted on others. Dunn v. United States, 284 U.S. 390 (1932) (Holmes, J.). The incompatible results, these courts conclude, could be a product of jury lenity, but that does not invalidate the guilty verdict the jury did return.

State courts have by and large followed the *Dunn* rule for inconsistent verdicts. People v. Caldwell, 681 P.2d 274 (Cal. 1984); Commonwealth v. Campbell, 651 A.2d 1096 (Pa. 1994). A small minority of state courts still hold that inconsistent verdicts require reversal. Many courts, however, recognize an exception for "logically" inconsistent verdicts (as opposed to "factually" inconsistent verdicts). When a jury has returned verdicts convicting a defendant of two or more crimes, and the existence of an element of one of the crimes negates the existence of a necessary element of the other crime, courts generally say that the verdicts should not be sustained. Why do courts hope to avoid inquiries into the reasons for inconsistent verdicts? If the primary objective is to avoid speculation about the basis for verdicts, would a presumption in favor of dismissing all inconsistent verdicts work just as well as the current majority rule?

7. *Jury reform: juror note-taking.* Traditionally jurors in criminal cases have been barred from taking notes during trial. However, the majority of states (around 35) and the federal courts have begun to allow note-taking subject to judicial approval. See, e.g., Wash. Superior Ct. Crim. R. 6.8; Mich. R. Crim. P. 6.414. Another group of states authorize note-taking without leaving the decision to the trial court in ordinary cases. See Minn. R. Crim. P. 26.03; Md. Crim. R. 4-326; see also ABA Standards for Criminal Justice: Trial by Jury 15-3.5 (3d ed. 1996). About five states still prohibit note-taking. See, e.g., Pa. R. Crim. P. 644. In states where statutes and procedural rules do not address the question, courts often authorize note-taking. See, e.g., People v. Hues, 704 N.E.2d 546 (N.Y. 1998) (survey of cases). Research suggests higher juror satisfaction and no change in outcomes when jurors are allowed to take notes. See Larry Heuer & Steven Penrod, Increasing Juror Participation in Trials Through Note Taking and Question Asking, 79 Judicature 256 (1996).

Problem 17-5. Jury Nullification and Social Justice

Defense counsel has asked the trial judge to instruct the jury as follows:

> The Court instructs the Jury that under the Constitution of the United States, the Jury has a paramount right to acquit an accused person for whatever reason and to find him not guilty, even though the evidence may support a conviction, and this is an important part of the jury trial system guaranteed by the Constitution.
>
> The Court further instructs the Jury that this principle of jury nullification is just as important to the constitutional process as any other instruction which the Court has given to this Jury, and that in the final analysis, you, the members of the Jury, are the sole judges of whether or not it is right and fair to convict the Accused or whether under the totality of the circumstances, the Accused should be found not guilty. In arriving at your verdict you are not compelled to answer to anyone or to the State, nor are you required at any time by the Court or any person or party to give a reason or to be brought to accountability for your decision and vote.

Alternatively, counsel has asked the court for permission to make such an argument to the jury in the closing statement. The prosecutor has objected to the proposed instruction and will object if defense counsel makes such an argument in the closing statement.

This issue has arisen in four cases. In State v. Adams, the defendant is charged with destruction of government property and criminal trespass because she scaled a fence at a military installation and spray-painted antinuclear slogans on military equipment used to maintain nuclear weaponry. In State v. Baker, the defendant is charged with criminal trespass for blocking the doorway to an abortion clinic. He was protesting the practices of the clinic and calling for an end to legal abortions.

In State v. Cunningham, the defendant is charged with robbery in the first degree. The prosecution will present evidence that the defendant took two 12-packs of beer at gunpoint from a convenience store. The minimum sentence for this crime is 10 years. The state has also charged the defendant with being a "persistent felony offender" in the second degree because of his prior felony convictions. If the jury finds him guilty on this charge, the judge will impose a 20-year mandatory minimum sentence.

In State v. Derby, the defendant is an African American man who is charged with distribution of crack cocaine. The government will present evidence that the defendant sold two ounces of crack to an undercover agent. Venue for the trial is set in a location where it is likely that a number of the jurors will be African Americans.

As trial judge in each of these cases, would you grant the motions? What particular circumstances that you do not yet know would influence your decision? Would it matter to you if there were a state constitutional provision stating that the "jury shall have the right to determine the law and the facts"? Compare Davis v. State, 520 So. 2d 493 (Miss. 1988); State v. Wentworth, 395 A.2d 858 (N.H. 1978); Medley v. Commonwealth, 704 S.W.2d 190 (Ky. 1985).

Notes

1. *Authority of jury to nullify: majority position.* During its deliberations, the jury resolves factual disputes based on the evidence the parties present. It then applies the facts to the relevant legal principles that the judge provides in her instructions. But does the jury also have the power to interpret the law in light of its own values and priorities? Judicial opinions on this subject widely recognize that the jurors have the "power" to ignore the law or to interpret the law themselves. This power has come to be known as "jury nullification." Nevertheless, judges usually consider jury nullification to be illegitimate. Hence, most courts refuse to instruct a jury that they have the power to "nullify" the law, and most do not allow defense counsel to make such an argument to the jury.

State constitutions and statutes fall into two camps on the issue of the jury's authority to decide questions of law (and thus to decide not to apply the law when an injustice would result). The state constitutions of Georgia (art. I, §1, para. 11, §A), Indiana (art. I, §19), Maryland (art. XXIII), and Oregon (art. I, §16) declare that the jury has authority over both the factual and legal aspects of each case. Other state statutes take an opposite view. Cal. Penal Code §1126 ("In a trial for any offense, questions of law are to be decided by the court, and questions of fact by the jury").

Some states acknowledge the power of the jury to assess law and facts by the rather subtle shift from general jury instructions directing the jury that if it finds the facts to be true it "must" find the defendant guilty to language suggesting to the jury that it "should" or "may" find the defendant guilty. A handful of states allow the judge to instruct the jury more directly about its power. Some even allow attorneys to argue nullification directly to the jury if the trial judge allows it. See State v. Bonacorsi, 648 A.2d 469 (N.H. 1994).

The jury's power to nullify the law presents profound questions about the connection between public opinion and criminal enforcement in a democratic society. Legal scholars have approached these issues from several intriguing angles.For a sample of these essays, go to the web extension for this chapter at *http://www.crimpro.com/extension/ch17*.

2. *Jury information and jury tampering.* Suppose a nullification enthusiast tries to hand out a jurors' rights tract or any other literature at a courthouse to those wearing a juror badge. What can a prosecutor or judge do? The legal lines become quite clear when any person tries to influence an active juror: such conduct is known as

jury tampering, and the right to a free and fair trial overcomes any claim of a right to free speech. The legal lines are less clear, however, when people distribute literature outside the courthouse to all citizens, or only to those who are not specifically identified as jurors. Professor Nancy King has analyzed these tactics and concludes that they are constitutionally acceptable. King, Silencing Nullification Advocacy Inside the Jury Room and Outside the Courtroom 65 U. Chi. L. Rev. 433 (1998).

3. *Juror misbehavior.* Imagine that a juror lies during voir dire with the goal of exercising the "right" to nullify a conviction (or at least the power of a single juror to hang a jury). Or suppose a juror makes remarks during deliberations suggesting a racial motive in decision making (whether in favor of a guilty or not guilty verdict). What happens in these cases? If jurors violate direct instructions from the judge or lie during voir dire, and it comes to light before the jury starts deliberations, the jurors can be removed from the case and alternates put in their place. If their misbehavior comes to light after a verdict has been reached, depending on the nature and severity of the misbehavior, jurors may be prosecuted for jury tampering. Most states and the federal system place sharp limits on the introduction of information from or about jury deliberations in an effort to protect jury secrecy and maintain a focus on issues of guilt and innocence.

California now employs a jury instruction that requires jurors to inform the judge whenever a fellow member of the jury refuses to deliberate based on his or her disagreement with the law. People v. Williams, 21 P.3d 1209 (Cal. 2001) (upholding conviction after trial court replaced juror who was reported by fellow juror; replaced juror disagreed with statutory rape law as applied to 18-year-old male defendant and 16-year-old female victim). Do you expect to see this device spread eventually to many other states?

D. THE PUBLIC AS DECISIONMAKER

1. Public Access to Trials

The Sixth Amendment to the U.S. Constitution provides defendants with a right to a "speedy and public trial," as do analogous state constitutional provisions. A public trial might mean that any person could attend, including reporters. Or the right to a public trial might be a personal right of the defendant, giving the defendant a right *not* to have a public trial — the right to a closed trial — as well.

Courts have recognized both a private and a public interest in open trials. The presumption in favor of an open trial is not absolute, and the courts have wrestled with issues such as when the defense or prosecution has a right to a closed proceeding, and when the media has a right of access to proceedings even against the wishes of both parties. Questions regarding media coverage, particularly with cameras and microphones, have taken a higher profile with the creation of specialized television channels devoted to trials, and the increasing capacity through technology to create much wider access to trials. Consider whether the court in the following case properly balances the prosecutor's request to close the trial during the testimony of one key witness and the defendant's request that the trial remain open.

■ STATE v. BARRY GARCIA

561 N.W.2d 599 (N.D. 1997)

MESCHKE, J.

Barry Caesar Garcia appeals a jury verdict and a criminal judgment finding him guilty of murder and aggravated assault, and sentencing him to life imprisonment without parole. We affirm. . . .

During the evening of November 15, 1995, juveniles Jaime Guerrero, Juan Guerrero, Michael Charbonneau, Ray Martinez, Angel Esparza, and Garcia drove around Fargo-Moorhead in a brown, 1975, Minnesota-licensed, Ford sedan owned by Juan Guerrero's mother. The young men took along 10 to 15 red and green shotgun shells and a sawed-off shotgun owned by the Skyline Piru Bloods, a street gang whose members included Jaime Guerrero, Juan Guerrero and Martinez. While driving in a West Fargo residential area near 10 P.M., Garcia asked the driver to stop. Garcia and Charbonneau, who is much taller than Garcia, left the car. Garcia took the shotgun. Their car continued down the street and came to a stop, and Garcia and Charbonneau began walking around the neighborhood.

In the same neighborhood, Pat and Cherryl Tendeland were dropping off their friend, Connie Guler, who had accompanied them to a prayer service in Hillsboro. In the Tendeland car parked in Guler's driveway, while seated and talking, Guler saw a "taller boy . . . maybe six feet or taller" and a "shorter one . . . five feet or less tall" walking down the sidewalk toward them. Guler thought the shorter boy was carrying a gun, but Pat thought it was an umbrella. After the boys stood near Guler's driveway for awhile, they began walking back toward the brown Ford sedan. From their suspicious behavior, Pat decided to back up and follow the boys "to see where they [were] going."

As the Tendeland car slowly approached the Ford sedan, Guler saw the taller boy walking briskly toward the Ford and the shorter boy with the gun lagging behind. The Ford's lights were on, and it started to pull away. Cherryl read off the car's license number. Guler testified about the next thing she remembered:

> I caught out of the sight of my eye something, and I turned, and this shorter boy was coming down off my berm, and he was so close, he could have opened my car door. And the next — our eyes met, and all I remember was these cold, dark eyes. And that's all I know. I don't have a face. And it just — he just raised it. I said, "My God, he's going to shoot," and it went off. I mean, it wasn't a matter of — it was just (indicating), like a click of the finger. It was so quick. . . .

Cherryl was shot in the forehead and shotgun pellets also struck Pat's face, knocking a lens from his glasses. Guler was not struck by the blast. Pat, who had difficulty seeing with blood running down his face and without the lost lens, decided to drive to a nearby police station. [Cherryl Tendeland died from the shotgun wounds.]

Jaime Guerrero, who had remained in the Ford, testified he did not see the gunshot, but he heard it. Guerrero said Charbonneau and Garcia got back in the car about 20 seconds after he heard the shotgun blast. According to Guerrero, Garcia, who was still carrying the shotgun, said "they got her," and "next time, don't look at me."[Based on descriptions of witnesses, the police located the Ford sedan that night.] Police recovered a sawed-off shotgun with a warm barrel from the backseat of the car along with several red and green shotgun shells. Shortly, the police chasing after Garcia captured him in an athletic field at Moorhead State University. When arrested, Garcia possessed one green and three red shotgun shells. . . .

The spent shotgun shell recovered at the scene had been fired from the sawed-off shotgun found in the brown Ford sedan. Neither Pat nor Guler could positively identify Garcia as the person who shot into the Tendeland car. No usable fingerprints were found on the shotgun. Atomic absorption tests on Garcia, Martinez, and Jaime and Juan Guerrero showed significant levels of antimony and barium on all four individuals, thus evidencing each of them could have recently fired a gun or handled a gun that had been recently fired. The pattern on the sole of Garcia's tennis shoes corresponded with shoeprints found at the scene of the shooting.

The Tendeland shooting brought on much publicity, and the trial court allowed expanded media coverage of Garcia's jury trial. See N.D. Admin. R. 21.* At the trial, the State called Jaime Guerrero as a witness. When asked his name, Guerrero replied, "I am not going to say nothing."

Away from the jury, the trial court learned Guerrero had not been granted immunity to testify, warned Guerrero he may be subject to contempt penalties, and also informed him of his Fifth Amendment rights to remain silent and to speak to a lawyer. Guerrero asked to speak with a lawyer, and the trial court appointed the same lawyer who was representing Guerrero in juvenile court to advise him. The court recessed, and Guerrero consulted his lawyer during the lunch hour.

When the trial court reconvened out of the presence of the jury [the] State's attorney explained to the court:

> Mr. Guerrero has indicated some willingness to proceed and provide testimony to matters which he has already provided us information. I'm concerned — and it's been relayed to me — that there may be some concern about the media coverage, particularly the television camera, and also the number of viewers and spectators in the audience of the courtroom.
>
> It is — it's my request at this time that, for the testimony of Jaime Guerrero, that the Court terminate expanded media coverage, terminate the use of the television camera, terminate the feed to the television and/or radio just for that testimony, and

* N.D. Admin. R. 21 provides in pertinent part as follows:

d. "Expanded media coverage" includes broadcasting, televising, electronic recording, or photographing of a judicial proceeding for the purpose of gathering and disseminating information to the public by media personnel. . . .

Section 4. The court may permit expanded media coverage of a judicial proceeding in the courtroom while the judge is present, and in adjacent areas as the court may direct. Expanded media coverage provided for in this rule may be exercised only by media personnel. . . .

b. The judge may deny expanded media coverage of any proceeding or portion of a proceeding in which the judge determines on the record, or by written findings:

1. Expanded media coverage would materially interfere with a party's right to a fair trial;

2. A witness or party has objected and shown good cause why expanded media coverage should not be permitted; . . .

4. Expanded media coverage would include testimony of a juvenile victim or witness in a proceeding in which illegal sexual activity is an element of the evidence. . . .

c. The judge may limit or end expanded media coverage at any time during a proceeding, if the judge determines on the record, or by written findings:

1. The requirements of this rule or additional guidelines imposed by the judge have been violated; or

2. The substantial rights of an individual participant, or rights to a fair trial will be prejudiced by the expanded media coverage if it is allowed to continue.

> that the Court also order that anybody other than the family of Barry Garcia or the family of Cherryl Tendeland be excused from the courtroom, to present — to present a more friendly environment, if you will, for the testimony of this child, who is only 15 years of age. I think there are good arguments to be made for the termination of the expanded coverage for a person only 15 years of age. There is some reason to believe that he is concerned about other persons' opinions and feelings and actions if he decides to go ahead and testify. . . .

Garcia's attorney resisted the State's request, arguing there was "no compelling reason to shut things down at this point." . . . The State's attorney explained he had promised to dismiss with prejudice the juvenile court charges against Guerrero if he testified truthfully in Garcia's trial. Guerrero's lawyer told the court Guerrero "is a juvenile, and he is intimidated by the audience and media coverage," and elaborated on Guerrero's reluctance to testify:

> I think he's intimidated by the whole spectacle of the trial, that he will be on television, he will be in the newspaper again. And it would put him at ease not to have to experience this. And he is a juvenile and does want his confidentiality preserved, if possible, but I guess that's . . . not really possible. But those are some of the factors that make him not want to testify. This would put him at ease if he didn't have to kind of run the gauntlet. . . .

Garcia's lawyer again objected to any closure of the trial. The State's attorney explained:

> I would like, just for the record, to note that in support of our request and our position, we are aware of another witness, not Mr. Guerrero, but another witness who has indicated a reluctance to provide testimony, who has been subpoenaed, because of actual repercussions that he's already experienced. So we are basing these requests on some real events, not just speculation. At least that's what I have been told. . . .

The court outlined its "initial thoughts," but recessed and deferred ruling until the media had an opportunity to be heard. After hearing argument from a media representative, the trial court ruled:

> [It] is in the interests of justice to suspend the expanded media coverage order for this witness, and to suspend the rule as regards media coverage. Exercising the inherent powers of the Court to control the courtroom, I am going to order that the courtroom be cleared, that the feeds to the radio and the television be terminated, and that all persons, except for counsel, Mr. Garcia, and Detective Warren, and the immediate family of — was it — of Mr. Garcia, and the immediate family of Mrs. Tendeland. . . .
>
> The cautionary instruction I intend to give . . . will read as follows: Ladies and gentlemen of the jury, as you are aware, Mr. Guerrero has indicated an unwillingness to testify. He has expressed a concern about all the media coverage, all of the people — and all the people in the courtroom. Taking into consideration the youth of Mr. Guerrero and his concerns, the Court has determined that in order to facilitate his testimony, the courtroom will be cleared of all persons. You are not to draw any conclusions or inferences from the clearance of the courtroom.

The court also allowed a single pool representative, chosen by the media, to remain in the courtroom. The court gave the jury the cautionary instruction, and Guerrero testified in the partially closed courtroom.

Garcia claims his constitutional rights to a public trial were violated when the trial court temporarily terminated expanded media coverage and excluded the general public from the courtroom for Guerrero's testimony.

The Sixth Amendment to the United States Constitution guarantees a criminal defendant "the right to a speedy and public trial. . . ." See also N.D. Const. Art. I, §12. Although the guarantee of a public trial was created for the benefit of criminal defendants, see In re Oliver, 333 U.S. 257 (1948), the right is also shared with the public; the common concern is to assure fairness. Press-Enterprise Co. v. Superior Court of Cal., 478 U.S. 1 (1986). "In addition to ensuring that judge and prosecutor carry out their duties responsibly, a public trial encourages witnesses to come forward and discourages perjury." Waller v. Georgia, 467 U.S. 39 (1984). The Supreme Court explained in Gannett Co., Inc. v. DePasquale, 443 U.S. 368 (1979): "Openness in court proceedings may improve the quality of testimony, induce unknown witnesses to come forward with relevant testimony, cause all trial participants to perform their duties more conscientiously, and generally give the public an opportunity to observe the judicial system." Precedents demonstrate, however, that the right to a public trial is not absolute and must give way in rare instances to other interests essential to the fair administration of justice.

The contours of a criminal defendant's right to a public trial in the context of total closure of an entire pretrial suppression hearing were confronted by the Supreme Court in *Waller.* The *Waller* Court ruled that defendant's public-trial guarantee had been violated, and explained:

> [The] party seeking to close the hearing must advance an overriding interest that is likely to be prejudiced, the closure must be no broader than necessary to protect that interest, the trial court must consider reasonable alternatives to closing the proceeding, and it must make findings adequate to support the closure. [467 U.S. at 48.]

The *Waller* Court made clear that a trial court's power to exclude the public from a criminal trial should be exercised sparingly and then only for the most unusual of circumstances.

We used the *Waller* standard to measure a trial court's temporary closure of a defendant's criminal trial on charges of gross sexual imposition during the testimony of the child victim, the defendant's adopted son. State v. Klem, 438 N.W.2d 798 (N.D. 1989). Klem's first trial had been entirely open to the public while the child victim testified, and had resulted in a hung jury. At the second trial, when the child witness was first seated to testify, the State's attorney abruptly requested closure of the trial for the child's testimony because the "sensitive nature" of the case "may be very distracting and very embarrassing for him in front of all these people and the people in the Courtroom may inhibit the testimony." After the defendant objected to the proposed closure, the court summarily ruled, "I think I will clear the Courtroom," and did so.

A majority of this Court concluded the trial court, in closing the trial to all but court personnel, parties, attorneys, jurors, and a public media representative during the child's testimony, deprived the accused of his right to a public trial. [The] majority concluded the trial court had failed to satisfactorily comply with the *Waller* requirements: "There was no hearing, no weighing of competing interests, and no findings to support closure." 438 N.W.2d at 801.

Garcia argues the trial court in this case, like the trial court in *Klem,* largely ignored the *Waller* requirements in ordering the partial closure of the courtroom, so that a reversal and a remand for a new trial are necessary. We disagree.

This case differs from *Klem* in several major ways. We pointed out in *Klem* that, ordinarily, a motion to close a trial to the public should be made before trial to avoid unfair surprise and to give the trial court the benefit of research and arguments, but the reasons for closure could not have been reasonably anticipated in this case. The mid-trial motion in *Klem* could have been made before trial, and the reasons for it were given in generalities as the child witness was seated to testify. The witness had in fact testified publicly in the first trial, so there was no apparent reason for either the closure motion or the order.

Here, Guerrero had given a sworn statement in exchange for the State's promise not to attempt to transfer his case from juvenile to adult court. Not until Guerrero was called as a witness for the State, refused to respond to any questions, and consulted with his attorney was the State's attorney or anyone else expecting Guerrero to decline to testify.

This trial court's actions show the careful consideration and weighing of competing interests so sorely lacking in *Klem.* In contrast to the summary ruling in *Klem,* this trial court held an in-chambers hearing, two open court hearings out of the jury's presence, and delayed ruling until the media could also be heard on the request for closure. Although this trial court did not hold a formal evidentiary hearing on the motion, an evidentiary hearing is not necessarily required unless requested.

The *Klem* trial court's exclusion of the general public, except for one media representative, more closely resembled a complete or total closure of the courtroom than what the trial court did here. This court allowed the Tendeland and Garcia family members to remain in the courtroom. This was only a partial closure, one that generally results in the exclusion of certain members of the public while other members of the public are permitted to remain in the courtroom. When a trial court orders a partial, rather than a total, closure of a court proceeding at the request of a party, a "substantial reason," less stringent than the *Waller* "overriding interest" requirement, can justify the closure. We believe this trial court had a substantial reason to partially and temporarily close Garcia's trial during Guerrero's testimony.

This trial court was aware of the widespread publicity generated by this case and the effect of the television camera in the courtroom. Allegations of street-gang activity dramatized this case. The State's attorney told the court about possible "repercussions" experienced by another subpoenaed witness. Guerrero's attorney explained his juvenile client's understandable intimidation from being seen testifying on television and publicized in newspapers that brought about his reluctance to testify. We would have much preferred the trial court to have gotten the explanation for Guerrero's reluctance to testify from Guerrero himself rather than filtered through the State's attorney and Guerrero's lawyer. But extensive interviews with the reluctant witness, while no doubt the better practice, are not constitutionally compelled. . . . Here, Guerrero's intimidation and hesitation to testify were amply demonstrated to the trial court by his opening refusal to even give his name.

A trial court can properly weigh an accused's right to a public trial against the interests of protecting a witness from intimidation to enable the witness to testify with more composure. A trial court may exclude members of the public from a trial if a witness will be inhibited or embarrassed to testify in the presence of an audience from his tender age or the nature of his testimony, from actual threats, or from the possibility of reprisals by others if the witness testifies. In this case, allegations of gang-related activities and possible "repercussions" like those experienced by another potential witness added to the weighing process. . . .

We disagree with Garcia that the trial court's partial closure order went further than necessary. . . . Garcia did not ask the court to allow other relatives or friends to remain in the courtroom during Guerrero's testimony, although he could have. If Garcia wanted others to remain, he should have pointed them out to the trial court and asked they be allowed to stay. The trial court's order for partial closure lasted only during Guerrero's testimony, and then those excluded were readmitted. . . .

A trial court must also consider reasonable alternatives to a partial closure. We recognize that closure of the courtroom to the public "is not the only, nor necessarily the most effective, response to [witness] intimidation." We also recognize, however, that other alternatives sometimes provoke serious confrontation problems. This record is shallow on consideration of reasonable alternatives. The State's attorney, however, identified confrontation problems in possible alternatives in stating: "[We're] not asking that Mr. Garcia in any way be deprived of any of his rights of confrontation, cross-examination, so forth. We're merely here to try and search for the truth through all the evidence that's available to us. . . ." The trial court considered variations for the partial closure order, at one point telling the attorneys:

> . . . My initial thoughts were — was to clear the courtroom of everyone except the immediate family of the Garcias. And my initial thought was to order the media not to publish in any fashion any of the testimony that's offered, but not necessarily exclude them from the courtroom. . . . Then, you know, as far as the jury is concerned, the only people that would be missing would be all the spectators.

Although this case poses a difficult question, we conclude the court properly considered reasonable alternatives, and found the partial closure to be the only adequate solution for the problem confronting the court. While it would have been helpful if the trial court had made more explicit findings about possible alternatives, we see no constitutional error here. . . .

We stress again that trial courts should not lightly close a criminal trial in any manner, and when dealing with a request for closure, a court must take pains to develop a complete record and make detailed findings about all the circumstances. More explicit findings would have facilitated review in this case. But, considering the circumstances with the findings the trial court did make, we conclude Garcia's constitutional rights to a public trial were not violated by the brief, narrowly tailored, and partial closure ordered for Guerrero's testimony. . . .

Notes

1. *"Public trial": majority view.* The defendant, prosecution, reporters, and the public may all have different interests with respect to whether a trial remains open. The public nature of criminal trials derives both from the express guarantee of the

Sixth Amendment and its state analogs and from the First Amendment rights of both the defendant and the press. The presumption of open trials is usually tested when one party wants to close the proceedings and the other does not. A defendant might want to avoid publicity or retribution, exclude people who might provide new evidence, or reduce the risk of a biased jury. The government might want to protect the identity of an informant, undercover police officer, victim, or witness by limiting the number of people who watch the testimony. See, e.g., People v. Jones, 750 N.E. 2d 524 (N.Y. 2001) (undercover officer). Courts are often most sympathetic to victim and witness concerns, especially in cases involving children and in cases of sexual assault and abuse. See generally Vivian Berger, Man's Trial, Woman's Tribulation: Rape Cases in the Courtroom, 77 Colum. L. Rev. 1 (1977). In which North Dakota case was the privacy interest of the witness greater — the child sexual victim in *Klem* or the gang member in *Garcia*? In which case did the state have a greater interest in closing the trial?

2. *Media access to the courtroom: majority view.* Journalists are members of the public and have the same initial rights as any other person to watch trials. In addition to recognizing the right to court access shared by all citizens, the U.S. Supreme Court has enumerated a qualified First Amendment right in the press to attend criminal trials. See Globe Newspaper Co. v. Superior Court for Norfolk County, 457 U.S. 596 (1982); Richmond Newspapers, Inc. v. Virginia, 448 U.S. 555, 572 (1980). But when the defendant or the government makes a strong claim for closure, the Sixth Amendment right to a fair trial and the less specific rights of the government or witnesses conflict with the First Amendment claims of the press. Federal and state law have created a framework governing press access that leaves substantial discretion in the hands of the trial judge, and newspapers and other media regularly sue for access to proceedings or materials. See, e.g., State ex rel. the Missoulian v. Judicial District, 933 P.2d 829 (Mont. 1997).

In addition to general claims for access, reporters often want to bring their cameras and microphones with them. Courts have largely rejected claims that the media have a constitutional right to bring cameras and microphones into the courtroom. However, almost all states currently allow cameras at trials (with various limitations on the placement and use of flash), and over 35 states allow trials to be filmed — a dramatic shift since Florida first allowed cameras into its courtrooms in 1977. See Ruth Strickland & Richter Moore, Cameras in State Courts: A Historical Perspective, 78 Judicature (1994). As in North Dakota, state rules often leave the degree of access to the discretion of the trial judge. In contrast, the federal courts have experimented with but largely rejected the use of cameras in the courtroom. Trial judges seem always to face new questions about communications technologies, such as text messages, Twitter updates, and cameras in telephones. For a window into the changing role of communication technologies in the courtroom, go to the web extension for this chapter at *http://www.crimpro.com/extension/ch17*.

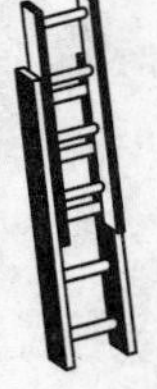

3. *What parts of the trial process must be public?* The general requirement of public trials does not mean that all parts of all trials must be open to the public. The trial proceedings may include bench conferences or discussions between judge and counsel in chambers. Submissions will often be made in writing. Physical evidence may be difficult to view at a distance, or in the form presented in court. Does the defendant have a right to make these proceedings public? Pretrial proceedings often reveal information that, if reported, might influence the judgment of jurors at trial, and courts have been more willing to restrict access at this stage. See, e.g.,

State v. Archuleta, 857 P.2d 234 (Utah 1993); but see State v. Densmore, 624 A.2d 1138 (Vt. 1993) (allowing media access to psychosexual evaluation submitted by defendant for sentencing). Some information provided at pretrial proceedings, including detention and competency hearings, may be irrelevant to questions of guilt and innocence. Other proceedings, such as voir dire hearings, are closely linked to trial, and for these proceedings the rules governing media at trial apply. See Presley v. Georgia, 130 S. Ct. 721 (2010) (trial judges must consider all available methods to preserve public access to jury selection before closing proceedings to public; court should not consider just those alternatives that defendant suggests).

4. *Televising appeals.* Is there a difference between televising trials and televising appellate arguments? Are trials or appellate proceedings likely to be of greater public interest? It is very difficult for most U.S. citizens to attend arguments in the U.S. Supreme Court, but the Court has fiercely resisted all efforts to film its arguments. Why? Should audio recordings of state and U.S. Supreme Court arguments be made more widely available?

5. *Press shield laws.* Reporters not only cover events in the courtroom, but also interview victims, witnesses and others outside the courtroom. Some states have "press shield" statutes that allow reporters to refuse to reveal their sources of information to criminal investigators. See Miller v. Superior Court, 986 P.2d 170 (Cal. 1999) (interpreting statute to protect reporter's interviews with offender; reporter cannot be jailed for refusing to turn over interview non-broadcast material to court under subpoena from prosecutor). Do these laws promote more active public scrutiny of the criminal justice system?

2. *Community Courts*

Must the key decisionmakers in criminal justice — those who choose which citizens to bring before a court and those who adjudicate and sentence people convicted of offenses — be lawyers? If citizens are to have a voice in criminal justice decisions (beyond the role of complainant, victim or witness), does the long tradition of the American jury satisfy that need? Jurors are chosen for their lack of knowledge. Should they be chosen for their knowledge?

Two substantial movements are changing the forms of criminal adjudication in the United States. Both movements have deep historical roots.

One movement involves the creation of "drug courts" and other specialized "therapeutic" courts. There are now more than 2,000 drug courts in the United States in action or in active planning. Drug courts address specific groups of offenders, typically drug offenders whose activities do not include violence. The offenders adjudicated in drug court must plead guilty, and must return to court often as they serve their sentences to update the court on their status. The first modern "drug court" was established in 1989. Drug courts provide a familiar kind of forum (a court) and a familiar decisionmaker (a judge), but with purposes distinct from general criminal courts. Drug courts reflect a rebirth of the goal of rehabilitation as a justification for punishment and social control, and a recognition that a general jurisdiction court handling serious cases of personal violence might have different purposes and priorities than an offense-specific court.

A second and even newer movement appears in the form of "community courts," which have close links to the idea of community policing and the philosophical aim of "restorative justice." The first modern community court opened in New York City in 1993; dozens more have begun operating in other states since that time, suggesting that the idea of community courts is spreading, just as the model of drug courts spread a few years ago.

Unlike drug courts, community courts typically offer a different forum (a conference room) and a different decisionmaker (community members). The goals of community court and the tools to achieve those goals also contrast with traditional criminal courts. Consider the case of four men cited for urinating in public in Manhattan, at different times and in different places. See Center for Court Innovation, "There Are No Victimless Crimes": Community Impact Panels at the Midtown Community Court (BJA 2000). About a month after they were charged, all four were summoned to a meeting with five other people — a "discussion facilitator" and a community panel made up of four people who live or work in the neighborhood: a man and woman in their 60s, a priest, and an out-of-uniform police officer.

The accused citizens are asked to explain what brought them to community court. Two are students from a local university, another is an immigrant cab driver. Each describes the time and place of his infraction. The cab driver explains that "The paper says 'public urination,' [but] it was not in public. It was dark. It was nine o'clock. No people, no vehicles, nothing. [I was] in front of Javits Center, on 38th Street. But there was no single person. Nothing!"

The community members then ask questions, such as "Everyone has to urinate; what do cabbies usually do?" and express their frustrations: "I'm on a community board and I've heard a number of complaints about cabbies who open their door and urinate on the street. It's very offensive, it bothers a lot of people, it's not hygienic. It helps to change the quality of a neighborhood. It's sort of like there's a pact people have in society. You behave in a certain way or you find yourself in a community that's known for breaking the laws."

All participants discuss the reasons for public urination by taxi drivers, students, and others. One of the students says, "I definitely would not want anybody in my doorway using it as a bathroom. But I understand it because I'm on this side. . . . There are a lot of clubs in the area, and a lot of people have the same problem. And it's not a problem that's going to go away by just talking about it; if you have to go and you're drunk, you're going to go."

After two hours of discussion, participants fill out post meeting questionnaires. One of the offenders walks around the table to shake hands with each of the community representatives, who have been asked to remain in the room for a short post-meeting debriefing with the facilitator. Outside in the hallway a few moments later, one of the students reflects on what he just experienced as he waits for the elevator. "It was nice," he says. "Well, not really 'nice,' but we got to experience the other side. We got to meet with the people, and that was good. We got a sense of the community."

Asked if the experience will influence his decision to urinate in public again, he pauses to think before answering. "I went in there knowing I did something wrong. I pissed in the street. Having to face these people made me feel worse. It gets to you more on a personal level than just having to pay a fine."

Consider what the creation of new kinds of courts says about our current criminal justice process. Should traditional courts be more like community courts? What percentage of the work of community courts will reflect "net widening" — the assessment of matters that would not have been handled within the criminal justice system? Should participation in community courts be voluntary?

JOHN FEINBLATT AND GREG BERMAN, RESPONDING TO THE COMMUNITY: PRINCIPLES FOR PLANNING AND CREATING A COMMUNITY COURT

(Feb. 2001, NCJ 185986)

For many years an important element has been missing from the criminal justice system. Although courts, police, and prosecutors have become increasingly modernized in recent years, they still often fail to meet the needs of the justice system's primary consumers: the neighborhoods that experience crime and its consequences every day. This problem was first recognized by advocates of community policing, who argued that police officers could address neighborhood crime and disorder more effectively if they established a close relationship with community residents and neighborhood groups. The idea of community justice has since spread to other branches of the justice system including courts, probation departments, prosecutors, and corrections offices. . . .

New York City's Midtown Community Court, which opened in October 1993, differs dramatically from the way that lower courts have operated in the city for many years. Nevertheless, it reflects a return to an old idea. In 1962, New York City closed a network of neighborhood magistrate's courts that handled intake for the city's court system. These courts arraigned defendants and disposed of low-level offenses that did not need to be forwarded to a higher tribunal. . . . While this change increased efficiency to an extent, its cost was remoteness — the new centralized courts were removed from the communities they served. As caseloads increased, felony cases naturally began to claim more and more attention. Fewer resources were devoted to quality-of-life misdemeanors like shoplifting, prostitution, and subway fare cheating, and judges were under tremendous pressure to dispose of such cases quickly. All too often defendants arrested for low-level offenses were released after being sentenced to either "time served" while awaiting their court appearance, a fine that might or might not be paid, or community service that might or might not be performed.

[The] planners of the Midtown Community Court sought to recreate neighborhood-based intake and arraignment along the lines of the magistrate's courts. . . . With the help of the local community board — the smallest unit of government in New York City — planners found a location for the court near Times Square on the West Side of Manhattan, an area teeming with quality-of-life crimes. The 1896 building, which was once a magistrate's court, was renovated. . . . The court's location, architecture, and technology are part of a larger strategy to honor the idea of community by making justice restorative. Offenders are sentenced to make restitution to the community through work projects in the neighborhood: caring for trees lining the streets, removing graffiti, cleaning subway stations, and sorting cans and bottles for recycling. At the same time, the court uses its legal leverage to link offenders with drug treatment, health care, education, and other social services. . . .

Midtown Community Court's planning team pursued . . . goals they considered to be at the heart of community justice. [The goals included principles for restoring the community:]

- Recognize that communities are victims. Quality-of-life crimes damage communities. If unaddressed, low-level offenses erode communal order, leading to disinvestment and neighborhood decay and creating an atmosphere in which more serious crime can flourish. . . .
- Use punishment to pay back the community. Standard sentences that involve jail, fines, and probation may punish offenders, but they do little to make restitution for the damage caused by crime. A community court requires offenders to compensate neighborhoods through community service.
- Combine punishment with help. By permanently altering the behavior of chronic offenders, social service programs can play an important role in crime control. Encouraging offenders to deal with their problems honors a community's ethical obligation to people who break its laws because they have lost control of their lives.
- Give the community a voice in shaping restorative sanctions. The most effective community courts open a dialog with neighbors, seeking their input in developing appropriate community service projects. A community advisory board can offer residents an institutionalized mechanism for interacting with the judge and court administrators. . . .

[Community courts also embody principles for bridging the gap between communities and courts:]

- Make justice visible. A community court puts offenders to work in places where neighbors can see what they are doing, outfitting them in ways that identify them as offenders performing community service. . . .
- Make justice accessible. A community court welcomes observers and visitors from the community, giving them an opportunity to see justice in action. Calendars and other information about activities in the courtroom are available to the public on computer terminals in the lobby. . . .
- Reach out to victims. A community court can be a safe haven for victims, offering them assistance and a voice in the criminal justice process. Because it is based in the neighborhood where victims live, a community court may be able to provide access to services more quickly and in a less intimidating setting than larger, centralized courts.

[These courts carry out principles for knitting together a fractured criminal justice system, and for helping offenders deal with problems that lead to crime:]

- Use the court's authority to link criminal justice agencies. Too often, criminal justice agencies work in isolation, moving cases from street to court to cell and back again without communicating or taking the time to solve problems. . . .
- Explore crossing jurisdictional lines. The problems citizens face often do not conform to the narrow jurisdictional boundaries imposed by modern

court systems. A criminal defendant also may be involved in a landlord-tenant dispute or a small claims matter. Handling all of a defendant's cases in one place enhances the court's ability to address the defendant's underlying problems. . . .

- Use the court as a gateway to treatment. The trauma of arrest may prompt a defendant to seek help. A court can use its coercive power to reinforce that impulse.
- Remain involved beyond disposition of the immediate case. A judge in a community court can monitor offenders' experiences in treatment, using the court's authority to reward progress or impose new sanctions for failure.

. . . Many quality-of-life problems in a community are not violations of the law and do not come to the attention of the police or the courts. The Midtown Community Court has sought to address these problems in [several] ways. First, the court established a mediation service to resolve neighborhood disputes (for example, the opening of an adult movie house or the operation of a noisy repair shop) before they escalate to legal battles. In addition to helping the community deal with such problems, the service conveys the court's commitment to the community and its quality of life. Second, the court set up a street outreach unit, staffed by police officers and caseworkers from the court, to enroll potential clients in court-based social service programs before they get into trouble with the law. Four mornings a week, outreach teams scour the neighborhood, encouraging likely clients — prostitutes, substance abusers, and homeless people — to come in for help voluntarily. . . .

Police and community groups lose heart in fighting low-level crime when they lack a reliable way to measure progress. To measure its impact on the community, a community court should deploy researchers, compile results, and publicize success. . . . Besides the traditional work of caseload and sentencing outcome analysis, research staff at the Midtown Community Court study problems raised by neighbors. The court's researchers monitor patterns of prostitution and drug dealing as well as street sanitation. To help community groups and police target resources, the researchers have developed neighborhood-specific computer software to map arrests, complaints, and other quality-of-life indicators. When the research confirms success, a community court should be ready to make this success known locally and to other communities that have established community courts. A court can create its own newsletter and Internet Web site and should promote media coverage to ensure feedback on successes to the community.

[To] be effective a community court must address the needs of the court system's most important constituency: the people who live and work in neighborhoods affected by crime. To address these needs, a community court must ask a new set of questions. What can a court do to solve neighborhood problems? What can courts bring to the table beyond their coercive power and symbolic presence? And what roles can community residents, businesses, and service providers play in improving justice? . . .

Notes

1. *Special courts.* The dramatic emergence in the 1990s of special courts to handle drug offenders, the mentally ill, and now low-level community offenders

have their roots in the many police and magistrate courts common throughout the United States until the middle of the twentieth century. Advocates of court unification in the early twentieth century, such as Harvard Law School Dean Roscoe Pound, eliminated many special courts. Special juvenile courts and family courts, however, remained in place in many jurisdictions through the twentieth century, the remnants of special courts.

Special courts have reemerged with a vengeance. Indeed some types, like drug courts, are proliferating at such a high rate that it is hard even to count them. The web extension for this chapter, at *http://www.crimpro.com/extension/ch17*, tracks recent trends in the use of specialized therapeutic and community-based courts.

2. *Do special courts work?* Special courts excite their supporters; whether they work is another question. For one early evaluation, see Denise C. Gottfredson, Stacy S. Najaka & Brook Kearley, Effectiveness of Drug Treatment Courts: Evidence from a Randomized Trial, 2 Criminology & Pub. Pol'y 171 (2003). Many supporters of special courts do not stop to define the measures of success, pointing instead to the failures of traditional criminal courts, the need to do something different, and to anecdotes of apparent success. Advocates of community courts chose the story about public urination to illuminate the idea and virtue of community courts: Is this a story of success?

Perhaps community courts are still too young for complete assessment. What should the measures of success for any special court be? Will it vary by the type of court?

3. *The limits of the criminal law.* Community courts, drug courts, family courts and other special courts appear to address problems related to, but beyond, the traditional core of the criminal justice system. Among their common features are less legal process and fewer lawyers, but also less severe sanctions. What are the virtues and dangers and blurring the lines between criminal and civil justice systems? What are, and what should be, the limits of the criminal justice system to respond to the problems of society?

XVIII

Witnesses and Proof

A complete understanding of felony trials requires a knowledge of substantive criminal law, the law of evidence, trial strategy, and procedural rules. Yet it is possible to boil down this wide-ranging material into a few core principles of procedure that define criminal trials. At a general level, these principles are familiar to lawyers and nonlawyers alike.

The first core principle is the presumption of innocence — the idea that a person is not guilty of a crime until the state proves to a factfinder that the person has committed a criminal act with the requisite mental state. The state must prove its case "beyond a reasonable doubt."

The second principle — the right to confront witnesses — is our central tool for squeezing truth from the evidence. It is not hard to imagine a system (however unpalatable) that does not presume innocence or that allows conviction on some standard lower than beyond a reasonable doubt, but it is difficult to imagine a system that does not allow a defendant the right to challenge and test witnesses and other evidence.

The defendant can confront any government witness, and the government can confront any defense witness. But can the government call any witness to prove a case? The third principle — the privilege against self-incrimination — recognizes the single great exception to the power of the government to call relevant witnesses. The principle recognizes that a defendant cannot be forced to testify, either by threat of prison or by calling the defendant's silence to the attention of the factfinder. This principle may preclude the government from calling the single person who may know most about the alleged offense.

This chapter explores these core principles. The first section examines the meaning and role of the reasonable doubt standard, since this concept sets up the hurdles that the prosecution must clear during its presentation of witnesses and other evidence. The second section considers the law of confrontation, looking primarily at the defendant's power to test the evidence that the government presents. The third section studies the implementation of the privilege against self-incrimination at trial. The fourth section highlights one of the most important ethical dilemmas in an adversary trial system devoted to finding the truth: What should a defense lawyer do if the lawyer believes the client or a witness is lying? What should a prosecutor do if the prosecutor believes a key witness is lying?

A. BURDEN OF PROOF

Some trial court observers are skeptical about the practical consequences of using various standards of proof in civil and criminal cases. Perhaps jurors would reach the same verdicts whether they were told to decide cases on preponderance-of-the-evidence, "clear and convincing" proof, or beyond-a-reasonable doubt standards. But the idea (if not the precise language) of the reasonable doubt standard has ancient roots, and the higher burden on the government to obtain a conviction in criminal cases is the cornerstone for principles and practices that appear throughout the criminal trial.

1. *Reasonable Doubt*

How should we define reasonable doubt? How should juries be instructed to decide when the government has proven its case "beyond" that point? The very phrase "beyond a reasonable doubt" suggests a tension that makes the concept difficult to grasp: Doubt is a negative concept, but to go "beyond" a given amount of evidence is a positive concept. This tension — between a positive and a negative conception of reasonable doubt — is reflected in various definitions and rules that the states have adopted. Is there a single point at which reasonable doubt is passed, or do these positive and negative notions together define a range for juries to apply?

Some courts simply direct jurors to decide whether the government has proven all elements beyond a reasonable doubt, and allow no further explanation of the reasonable doubt concept. See Romano v. State, 909 P.2d 92 (Okla. Crim. App. 1995). A leading nineteenth-century treatise explains this position: "There are no words plainer than reasonable doubt and none so exact to the idea meant." 1 Joel Prentiss Bishop, New Criminal Procedure, §1094 (1895). Most jurisdictions either direct or allow judges to define reasonable doubt more precisely. Should judges be limited to a standard definition? If so, which one?

■ STEVE WINEGEART v. STATE

665 N.E.2d 893 (Ind. 1996)

DICKSON, J.

How to instruct juries regarding reasonable doubt has long been a subject on which courts, individual judges, and lawyers have taken differing approaches. Today we seek not only to resolve conflicting opinions among different panels of the Court of Appeals but also to foster the improved wording of instructions so that we may achieve greater juror understanding and better application of the rudimentary principle of proof beyond a reasonable doubt.

Following a jury trial, defendant-appellant Steve Winegeart was convicted of the crime of burglary. . . . In his appeal from the conviction, the defendant contends that the trial court erred in instructing the jury regarding reasonable doubt. . . . The defendant asserts that the following instruction, which used the words "actual," "fair," and "moral certainty," permitted the jury to find guilt based upon a degree of proof below that required by the Due Process Clause of the Fourteenth Amendment to the United States Constitution. After stating that the burden is upon the State to prove guilt beyond a reasonable doubt, the challenged instruction explained:

> A reasonable doubt is such doubt as you may have in your mind when having fairly considered all of the evidence, you do not feel satisfied to a moral certainty of the guilt of the defendant. A reasonable doubt is a fair, actual and logical doubt that arises in the mind as an impartial consideration of all the evidence and the circumstances in the case. It is not every doubt, however, it is a reasonable one. You are not warranted in considering as reasonable those doubts that may be merely speculative or products of the imagination, and you may not act upon mere whim, guess or surmise or upon the mere possibility of guilt. A reasonable doubt arises, or exists in the mind, naturally, as a result of the evidence or the lack of evidence. There is nothing in this that is mysterious or fanciful. It does not contemplate absolute or mathematical certainty. Despite every precaution that may be taken to prevent it, there may be in all matters depending upon human testimony for proof, a mere possibility of error.
>
> If, after considering all of the evidence, you have reached such a firm belief in the guilt of the defendant that you would feel safe to act upon that belief, without hesitation, in a matter of the highest concern and importance to you, then you have reached that degree of certainty which excludes reasonable doubt and authorizes conviction. . . .

Winegeart contends that the giving of the reasonable-doubt instruction blatantly violated constitutional principles and deprived his jury trial of fairness. He asserts that in the reasonable-doubt instruction used in his jury trial, the words "actual" and "fair" expand the quantum of doubt needed to constitute "reasonable" doubt, and that the instruction refers to "moral certainty" instead of "evidentiary certainty," thus authorizing the jury to find guilt based on a degree of proof below that required by the Due Process Clause.

The Due Process Clause of the Fourteenth Amendment protects an accused "against conviction except upon proof beyond a reasonable doubt of every fact necessary to constitute the crime with which he is charged." In re Winship, 397 U.S. 358 (1970). Because of the transcending interest a criminal defendant has in his liberty, the risk of an erroneous conviction necessitates that a substantial burden of proof be placed upon the prosecution. The standard of proof beyond a reasonable doubt serves to impress upon the fact-finder "the need to reach a subjective state of near certitude of the guilt of the accused." Jackson v. Virginia, 443 U.S. 307 (1979). While the federal constitution requires that juries be instructed "on the necessity that the defendant's guilt be proven beyond a reasonable doubt," it does not require the use of "any particular form of words." Victor v. Nebraska, 511 U.S. 1 (1994). However, the jury instructions, taken as a whole, must correctly express the concept of reasonable doubt to the jury.

In Cage v. Louisiana, 498 U.S. 39 (1990) (per curiam), a reasonable-doubt instruction was determined to be constitutionally defective. In defining reasonable doubt, the instruction included language that equated reasonable doubt with "a grave uncertainty" and "an actual substantial doubt" and stated, "What is required is not an absolute or mathematical certainty, but a moral certainty." The Court found that the words "substantial" and "grave" suggested a "higher degree of doubt than is required for acquittal under the reasonable-doubt standard," and that these statements, together with the reference to "moral certainty," rather than "evidentiary certainty," permitted a finding of guilt based upon a degree of proof below that required by the Due Process Clause.

These principles were discussed and applied by the United States Supreme Court in the recent companion cases of Victor v. Nebraska and Sandoval v. California, 511 U.S. 1 (1994), which approved reasonable-doubt instructions that included phrases such as "to a moral certainty," and "actual and substantial doubt." In both of the instructions approved in *Victor* and *Sandoval,* the moral certainty language appeared in very similar sentences, which stated that reasonable doubt occurs when, after "consideration of all the evidence," the juror does not have "an abiding conviction, to a moral certainty" of the guilt of the accused. In this context, the Supreme Court explained that "the reference to moral certainty, in conjunction with the abiding conviction language," sufficiently emphasized "the need to reach a subjective state of near certitude of the guilt of the accused." The *Victor* court also distinguished its "moral certainty" instructions from the one in *Cage,* noting that "the problem in *Cage* was that the rest of the instruction provided insufficient context to lend meaning to the phrase." The Court noted, "Instructing the jurors that they must have an abiding conviction of the defendant's guilt does much to alleviate any concerns that the phrase moral certainty might be misunderstood in the abstract." Although clearly stating that the Justices "do not condone" and "do not countenance" the inclusion of the phrase moral certainty in a reasonable-doubt instruction, the Court found that in the context of the entire instruction, which explicitly directed the jurors to base their conclusion on the evidence of the case and not to engage in speculation or conjecture, the inclusion of the moral certainty language did not render the instruction unconstitutional. Similarly, while noting that equating reasonable doubt with substantial doubt is "somewhat problematic," the Court found that the context of the instruction, unlike that in *Cage,* contrasted substantial doubt with fanciful conjecture. It concluded that "taken as a whole, the instructions correctly conveyed the concept of reasonable doubt to the jury."

The challenged words and phrases in the reasonable-doubt instruction given to the *Winegeart* jury contain both significant differences from, and substantial similarities to, the instructions approved in *Victor.* The *Winegeart* instruction's reference to "moral certainty" lacks the "abiding conviction" language noted in *Victor.* On the other hand, the "actual and substantial doubt" wording in the Nebraska instruction in *Victor* is similar to the "fair, actual, and logical doubt" phrase used in Winegeart's trial. Moreover, the *Winegeart* jury was directed to base its decision on all the evidence; to disregard whim, guess, surmise, or mere possibility of guilt; and to consider the "hesitate to act" benchmark — all factors that the *Victor* court found significant. . . .

The proper constitutional inquiry "is not whether the instruction 'could have' been applied in an unconstitutional manner, but whether there is a reasonable likelihood that the jury did so apply it." *Victor.* [We] conclude that there is not a reasonable likelihood that the jurors who determined the defendant's guilt applied the instruction in a way that violated the Due Process Clause. . . . However, we disapprove of the continued use of this instruction in the future.

The instruction uses 300 words in 11 sentences to explain reasonable doubt. This is not atypical for reasonable-doubt instructions, which often appear to be a conglomeration of phrases providing supplemental or alternative explication of reasonable doubt. Through the years, appellate decisions have held a wide variety of reasonable-doubt instructions to satisfy the minimal constitutional requirements. After a particular phrase has been thus tolerated by appellate courts, trial courts will often — usually in response to requests by counsel — incorporate such "approved" phrases into reasonable-doubt instructions. As a result, most reasonable-doubt instructions commonly in use in our courts today have not been crafted for the purpose of most effectively explaining the concept of reasonable doubt to jurors but rather are used primarily because the language therein is considered adequate to avoid appellate reversal.

As courts utilize such longer, more intricate explanations of reasonable doubt, juries are likely to draw an overall impression which may transcend the literal meaning of the substance of the words. Such lengthy and conceptually challenging instructions often present a drumbeat repetition, declaring that reasonable doubt is not every doubt, not whim, not guess, not surmise, not mere possibility, not fanciful, etc.; and that to qualify as reasonable doubt, such doubt must be fair, actual, logical, natural, etc. It is not surprising that jurors often have difficulty in synthesizing and comprehending reasonable doubt or that they may perceive that the instructing judge is minimizing the degree of doubt that will preclude a finding of guilt.

Although reluctant to find reversible error in instructions purporting to explain reasonable doubt, the United States Supreme Court has acknowledged: "Attempts to explain the term 'reasonable doubt' do not usually result in making it any clearer to the minds of the jury." Miles v. United States, 103 U.S. 304 (1881). The Seventh Circuit has declared:

> "Reasonable doubt" must speak for itself. Jurors know what is "reasonable" and are quite familiar with the meaning of "doubt." Judges' and lawyers' attempts to inject other amorphous catch-phrases into the "reasonable doubt" standard, such as "matter of the highest importance" only muddy the water. . . . It is, therefore, inappropriate for judges to give an instruction defining "reasonable doubt," and it is equally inappropriate for trial counsel to provide their own definition.

United States v. Glass, 846 F.2d 386, 386 (7th Cir. 1988). This view has found support in several other jurisdictions. [The court cited cases from Illinois, Kansas, Missouri, and the U.S. Court of Appeals for the Fourth Circuit.]

Professor Wigmore, noting that "various efforts have been made to define more in detail this elusive and undefinable state of mind," states: "In practice, these detailed amplifications of the doctrine have usually degenerated into a mere tool for counsel . . . to save a cause for a new trial. . . . The effort to [develop these elaborate unserviceable definitions] should be abandoned." 9 John Henry Wigmore, Evidence in Trials at Common Law §2497, 406-409 (James Chadbourn rev. 1981).

Substantial research by linguists, psychologists, and others suggests that many jurors have difficulty understanding jury instructions but much less difficulty understanding those that have been rewritten in light of psycholinguistic principles. See

Peter Tiersma, Reforming the Language of Jury Instructions, 22 Hofstra L. Rev. 37 (1993). Researchers have provided valuable suggestions on how to write more comprehensible jury instructions, including the [elimination] of jargon and modifying clauses and the use of simpler language. Summarizing the suggestions of psycholinguists, Professor Tanford provides ten guidelines for the improvement of instructions.

1. Eliminate nominalizations (making nouns out of verbs) and substitute verb forms; e.g., changing "an offer of evidence" to "items were offered into evidence."
2. Replace the prepositional phrase "as to" with "about"; e.g., changing "you must not speculate as to what the answer might have been" to "you must not speculate about what the answer might have been."
3. Relocate prepositional phrases so they do not interrupt a sentence; e.g., avoiding sentences such as "proximate cause is a cause which, in a natural and continuous sequence, produces the injury."
4. Replace words that are difficult to understand with simple ones; e.g., changing "agent's negligence is imputed to plaintiff" to "agent's negligence transfers to plaintiff."
5. Avoid multiple negatives in a sentence; e.g., "innocent mis-recollection is not uncommon."
6. Use the active rather than passive voice; e.g., changing "no emphasis is intended by me" to "I do not intend to emphasize."
7. Avoid "whiz" deletions (omitting words "which is"); e.g., by changing "statements of counsel" to "statements which are made by counsel."
8. Reduce long lists of words with similar meanings to only one or two; e.g., shortening "knowledge, skill, experience, training, or education" to "training or experience."
9. Organize instructions into meaningful discourse structures that avoid connecting unrelated ideas in ways that make them seem related.
10. Avoid embedding subordinate clauses in sentences; e.g., "you must not speculate to be true any insinuation suggested by a question asked a witness."

J. Alexander Tanford, The Law and Psychology of Jury Instructions, 69 Neb. L. Rev. 71 (1990).

We agree in principle with the . . . jurisdictions that have concluded that the phrase "reasonable doubt" may suffice without further explication and that many attempts to provide effective additional explanation have fallen short. However, we are not convinced that the task is impossible in light of recent and ongoing research, and we thus prefer to endorse for use in Indiana courts a reasonable-doubt instruction that, to the maximum extent possible, reflects the wisdom of the various available resources.

There is an inherent challenge in devising a comprehensible and succinct instruction explaining to lay jurors the concept of reasonable doubt. They must be informed that their determination of guilt depends upon the absence of reasonable doubt. The existence of reasonable doubt precludes a finding of guilt. Viewed in this way, the reasonable-doubt instruction is necessarily an attempt to define a negative concept. When court instructions proceed to define this concept by stating what it is not, the resulting double negative concept diminishes juror comprehension even further. In addition, we perceive that instructions containing repeated statements narrowing the class of doubts eligible for consideration as reasonable doubt may have a cumulative effect of minimizing the value and importance of this bedrock principle of criminal justice.

Although not utilized by the trial court in the present case, one attempt to suggest an improved reasonable-doubt instruction is found in Indiana Pattern Jury Instruction 1.15:

> A reasonable doubt is a fair, actual and logical doubt that arises in your mind after an impartial consideration of all of the evidence and circumstances in the case. It should be a doubt based upon reason and common sense and not a doubt based upon imagination or speculation.
>
> To prove the defendant's guilt of the elements of the crime charged beyond a reasonable doubt, the evidence must be such that it would convince you of the truth of it, to such a degree of certainty that you would feel safe to act upon such conviction, without hesitation, in a matter of the highest concern and importance to you.

1 Indiana Pattern Jury Instructions — Criminal, instruct. 1.15 (2d ed. 1991). This instruction seeks to explain what reasonable doubt is and is not and then proceeds to equate "beyond a reasonable doubt" with the degree of probability a juror would require to act unhesitatingly "in a manner of highest concern and importance to" himself or herself. Such attempts to quantify the degree of probability have received mixed reviews.

The "hesitate to act" analogy is discussed in *Victor.* The *Victor* majority comments that "the hesitate to act standard gives a common-sense benchmark for just how substantial such a doubt must be."[However, a committee of distinguished federal judges, reporting to the Judicial Conference of the United States, has criticized this "hesitate to act" formulation."] The committee explained:

> [The] analogy it uses seems misplaced. In the decisions people make in the most important of their own affairs, resolution of conflicts about past events does not usually play a major role. Indeed, decisions we make in the most important affairs of our lives — choosing a spouse, a job, a place to live, and the like — generally, involve a very heavy element of uncertainty and risk-taking. They are wholly unlike the decisions jurors ought to make in criminal cases.

Federal Judicial Center, Pattern Criminal Jury Instructions (1987). We find such reasoning persuasive and believe that, while the "hesitate to act" language may bolster an otherwise marginal instruction against constitutional challenge, use of this analogy is neither required nor particularly desirable in explaining the concept of reasonable doubt.

In contrast to the Indiana Pattern Jury Instruction and other common instructions that attempt to define the negative concept of reasonable doubt, a proposal from the Federal Judicial Center focuses upon the positive concept of proof beyond a reasonable doubt. It defines that term, succinctly, as proof "that leaves you firmly convinced," and explains that reasonable doubt is a greater degree of doubt than merely "possible doubt." It explains that a juror's choice between guilty and not guilty should be equated to the distinction between "firmly convinced" of guilt versus "a real possibility" that the defendant is not guilty. The instruction states:

> [The] government has the burden of proving the defendant guilty beyond a reasonable doubt. Some of you may have served as jurors in civil cases, where you were told that it is only necessary to prove that a fact is more likely true than not true. In criminal cases, the government's proof must be more powerful than that. It must be beyond a reasonable doubt.
>
> Proof beyond a reasonable doubt is proof that leaves you firmly convinced of the defendant's guilt. There are very few things in this world that we know with absolute certainty, and in criminal cases the law does not require proof that overcomes every possible doubt. If, based on your consideration of the evidence, you are firmly convinced that the defendant is guilty of the crime charged, you [should] find [him/her] guilty. If on the other hand, you think there is a real possibility that [he/she] is not guilty, you [should] give [him/her] the benefit of the doubt and find [him/her] not guilty. [Federal Judicial Center, Pattern Criminal Jury Instructions (1987).]

In the exercise of our inherent and constitutional supervisory responsibilities, see Ind. Const. Art. VII, §4, we seek to assure that juries in criminal cases are equipped with instructions that will allow them to understand and apply correctly the concept of reasonable doubt. Informed by numerous studies and recommendations from academic and judicial authorities, we acknowledge the shortcomings in Indiana Pattern Jury Instruction 1.15, in the instruction at Winegeart's trial, and in the various other reasonable-doubt explanations commonly in use. A substantial improvement in effective communication may be achieved by utilization of the Federal Judicial Center's proposed instruction. We therefore authorize and recommend (but, acknowledging that two of the five members of this Court find the present Indiana Pattern Jury Instruction preferable, do not mandate) that Indiana trial courts henceforth instruct regarding reasonable doubt by giving the above-quoted Federal Judicial Center instruction, preferably with no supplementation or embellishment. We also request that this instruction be added to the next revision of the Indiana Pattern Jury Instructions — Criminal.

While the challenged instruction in the present case is less effective than we would prefer, it is not so deficient as to be constitutionally defective. We therefore reject the defendant's contention of reversible error regarding the trial court's reasonable-doubt instruction. . . .

DEBRULER, J., concurring in result.

I do not share the majority's perception of deep problems within this area, nor the belief that the Federal Judicial Center, Pattern Criminal Jury Instructions are the appropriate remedy. Specifically, I do not believe that "firmly convinced" equates to "beyond a reasonable doubt." Both objectively and subjectively, "firmly convinced" seems more similar to "clear and convincing" than to "beyond a reasonable doubt." I find the Indiana Pattern Jury Instruction more than adequate.

JOHN P. CRONAN, IS ANY OF THIS MAKING SENSE? REFLECTING ON GUILTY PLEAS TO AID CRIMINAL JUROR COMPREHENSION

39 Am. Crim. L. Rev. 1187 (2002)

... The unfortunate truth is that jury instructions are written with almost no focus on comprehensibility of such instructions. ... A growing mountain of empirical research is concluding, with shocking accord, that jurors retain alarmingly low comprehension of the most fundamental aspects of their roles. In fact, several studies have discovered that subjects who received no instructions comprehended the law better than subjects who received pattern instructions. ... Of greatest concern, scholarly studies and anecdotal evidence suggest that jurors conflate reasonable doubt with the civil standard of preponderance of the evidence. ... Regardless of whether a jury's confusion serves to benefit or to harm a criminal defendant, the consequence is repugnant because it distorts the constitutional accuracy of our criminal verdicts. ...

As early as 1895, the Supreme Court established that a trial judge's role in instructing a jury is to direct the application of the law, stated accurately and correctly. Juries receive instructions at various stages of the trial. After jury selection and before opening statements, judges usually provide the jury with preliminary instructions on the law. Although the extent and detail of preliminary instructions varies considerably, their basic purpose is to orient the jurors to their roles and prepare jurors for what to expect during the trial. ... Throughout the trial, judges deliver evidentiary instructions that explicate proper consideration of particular pieces of evidence. ...

The most significant instructions are the "substantive law instructions" that the judge delivers at the end of the trial, either before or after closing arguments. Substantive law instructions set forth the specific criminal charges, the mens rea necessary for conviction, lesser-included offenses, affirmative defenses, the presumption of innocence, and definitions of other important legal terms that arise in the case. [Judges] are required to provide both parties with the opportunity to file in writing proposed instructions with the judge, copies of which must be furnished to their adversaries. ... The specific procedures for delivering instructions ... vary greatly among jurisdictions and even among judges within the same court.

[The] primary evidence of juror confusion comes from an abundance of empirical research in this area. Scholars began to explore juror confusion in the 1970s, laying the groundwork for a wave of scholarship attempting to pinpoint the extent and source of juror confusion. Although their conclusions differ on the magnitude of the problem, almost all studies concur that a very real problem exists. ...

David U. Strawn and Raymond W. Buchanan conducted the first major study on juror comprehension in 1975 by comparing comprehension of subjects who received Florida's pattern criminal jury instructions to subjects who did not receive the instructions. David U. Strawn & Raymond W. Buchanan, Jury Confusion: A Threat to Justice, 59 Judicature 478 (1976). The study concluded that, although the instructions improved comprehension to some extent, the instructed jurors still missed twenty-seven percent of the test items and failed to show any improved comprehension for four of nine crucial content areas addressed by the instruction. For example, despite the instruction that the defendant must be proved guilty beyond a reasonable doubt, only half of the jurors understood that the defendant did not have to present evidence establishing his innocence. In addition, forty-three percent of the subjects blatantly misunderstood the instruction on circumstantial evidence, erroneously believing that circumstantial evidence held no probative value.

Several other researchers have followed Strawn and Buchanan's groundbreaking work. [Professors Amiram Elwork, Bruce D. Sales and James J. Alfini studied jury comprehension in Michigan criminal trials in their 1982 book, *Making Jury Instructions Understandable*. The authors] reached the shocking conclusion that subjects receiving pattern instructions demonstrated inferior comprehension than subjects receiving no instructions. The authors concluded that prior to deliberating on a defendant's guilt, the average jury understands only about half of the legal instructions presented by the judge. These observations led the authors to the ominous conclusion that many verdicts in criminal trials result from misunderstandings of the law.

Professors Geoffrey P. Kramer and Dorean M. Koenig also concluded that Michigan's pattern instructions for criminal trials inadequately assist juror comprehension of critical criminal law issues. Geoffrey P. Kramer & Dorean M. Koenig, Do Jurors Understand Criminal Jury Instructions? Analyzing the Results of the Michigan Juror Comprehension Project, 23 U. Mich. J.L. Reform 401 (1990). The authors tested likely problematic instructions, based on a 1987 study of Michigan judges, by comparing the responses of subjects who received a particular standard instruction with the responses of subjects who did not receive any instruction. The subjects reflected representative cross-sections of gender, age, and educational level. Kramer and Koenig's findings also were disheartening. The . . . subjects demonstrated poor comprehension of the reasonable doubt standard, with particular confusion concerning the difference between reasonable doubt and any doubt and whether jurors are allowed to draw inferences from the evidence in order to reach a verdict. In fact, these two concepts were better understood by the uninstructed subjects than by the instructed subjects. Moreover, although the study also found relatively high comprehension of witness credibility, comprehension was lower for the group receiving the instruction than for the uninstructed group. . . . From these findings, Kramer and Koenig concluded that "jury instructions are often lost on jurors, and can sometimes even backfire."

A 1989 study by Professor Phoebe C. Ellsworth unearthed flaws in California jury instructions. Phoebe C. Ellsworth, Are Twelve Heads Better Than One?, 52 Law & Contemp. Probs. 205 (1989). Two hundred sixteen subjects viewed a two-and-one-half-hour videotape of a mock trial, covering all phases including the instructions. After watching a mock trial, the subjects were divided into twelve-person juries for deliberations. Ellsworth videotaped these deliberations and, upon their conclusions, distributed questionnaires testing juror comprehension of certain factual and legal aspects. Although the jurors sorted out the factual issues "fairly well," they encountered significant difficulty with the legal questions. Despite using a standard characterized as "lenient" and awarding credit for partial accuracy, Ellsworth concluded that the subjects made correct references to the law only fifty-one percent of the time. The subjects made unclear references to the law twenty-eight percent of the time and definitely incorrect references twenty-one percent of the time. Deliberations failed to abet comprehension. The jurors shifted from a correct view of the law to an incorrect one as frequently as vice versa. The questionnaires yielded similar results. On average, the jurors answered correctly only 11.7 percent of the true-false questions regarding the legal elements from the instructions.

[Professor Bradley Saxton tested actual jurors.] Bradley Saxton, How Well Do Jurors Understand Jury Instructions? A Field Test Using Real Juries and Real Trials in Wyoming, 33 Land & Water L. Rev. 59, 112 (1998). Saxton studied forty-nine civil and criminal trials in Wyoming by questioning jurors, judges, and trial lawyers. These questionnaires focused on the procedures used to instruct the jury and the jurors' comprehension of the instructions. Saxton crafted the jurors' questionnaires to test the understanding of the particular instruction received and distributed the questionnaires immediately after the jurors completed deliberations and reached verdicts. To gather control data, Saxton distributed questionnaires to individuals who never served on a jury and therefore were never exposed to the tested instruction. Saxton found a disconnect between the jurors' confidence that they understood the instructions and their actual comprehension. Despite spending a significant amount of time deliberating and believing that they understood the instructions, many jurors unknowingly misunderstood essential aspects of the instructions. Of greater concern, several areas of confusion, such as the weight given to circumstantial evidence and the burdens of proof in criminal and civil trials, could directly affect and skew the reliability of the verdict. Based on these findings, Saxton proposed detailed recommendations for Wyoming judges to ameliorate juror confusion. . . .

Some researchers concentrate on instructions in particular areas of the law. Shari Seidman Diamond and Judith N. Levi tested juror comprehension of the Illinois Pattern Jury Instructions for capital cases. Shari Seidman Diamond & Judith N. Levi, Improving Decisions on Death by Revising and Testing Jury Instructions, 79 Judicature 224 (1996). The subjects, who were 170 jury-eligible citizens, were divided into groups and listened to an audiotaped description of the evidence from an actual capital case as well as its jury instructions. The subjects heard either the actual Illinois Pattern Instructions used in the case or a revised set of instructions. The rewritten instructions focused on common linguistic problems and topics likely to cause the greatest confusion. One group of six subjects from each session was randomly selected to deliberate, while the remaining subjects individually answered a set of written questions testing their comprehension of the instructions. These questions focused on three areas of comprehension: unenumerated mitigators, non-unanimity on mitigators, and evidentiary weight. After the deliberating subjects concluded or after forty minutes, the subjects individually answered the same set of questions.

Although Diamond and Levi's study revealed great confusion in all three areas, comprehension improved dramatically when the instructions were rewritten with an eye on clarity. Questions about the pattern instruction on [weighing the evidence] resulted in an average of fifty-one percent correct answers and forty-two percent incorrect answers. After receiving the rewritten instructions, correct answers rose to sixty-six percent, and incorrect answers dropped to thirty percent. . . .

Although myriad factors contribute to juror confusion, the problem arises primarily from the insufficient effort many judges make to ensure that the average juror can comprehend the instructions. . . . More specifically, scholars identify the use of legal jargon and arcane legalese as the most serious flaws of contemporary instructions. . . .

Besides the complexity of legal topics, confusion also arises from the syntax and organization. Too often, judges present instructions in disorganized structures that are likened to "a hastily-sewn tapestry of ill-fitting sentences and paragraphs." The Charrow study was the first comprehensive study of the linguistic problems of jury instructions that cause confusion. Robert P. Charrow & Veda R. Charrow, Making Legal Language Understandable: A Psycholinguistic Study of Jury Instructions, 79 Colum. L. Rev. 1306 (1979). The study found that the use of nominalizations, "as to" instructions, misplaced prepositional phrases, obscure legal terms, double and triple negatives, and poor organization hinder juror comprehension. Charrow and Charrow identified, for example, one particularly confusing phrase commonly found in instructions that includes a triple negative and a nominalization: "innocent misrecollection is not uncommon." This complex phrase could be rephrased to the far simpler, "people often forget things." Steele and Thornburg agreed: the jury's efforts to understand the instructions "are seriously undermined because of the badly organized, jargon-filled, convoluted prose" of jury instructions. Walter W. Steele & Elizabeth G. Thornburg, Jury Instructions: A Persistent Failure To Communicate, 67 N.C. L. Rev. 77 (1988). . . .

A related problem is the understandable difficulty jurors encounter in trying to remember verbal instructions. A person's rate of recall of spoken words is lower than of written words. . . .

The first reform, of course, is rewriting instructions in plain language. While this reform will go a long way in improving clarity, other reforms merit consideration as well. In addition, although studies universally agree that writing instructions in plain language improves comprehension, comprehension of rewritten instructions still falls short of ideal. . . .

Problem 18-1. A Doubt with a Reason

At 10:40 P.M. on October 29, Trooper Radford stopped Warren Manning on Highway 34 for a defective headlight. After writing Manning a warning ticket, Radford learned from his dispatcher that Manning was driving with a suspended license. Radford placed Manning under arrest and the two left the scene with Manning in the back seat of the patrol car.

Radford's patrol car was spotted early the next morning half-submerged in Reedy Creek Pond. He had been shot twice through the head with his own revolver and severely pistol-whipped. The prosecutor charged Manning with murder. The State's theory of the case was that Manning used his own .25 caliber pistol to threaten Radford. The prosecutor argued that Manning forced the trooper to drive to Reedy Creek Pond, where Manning murdered him and attempted to submerge the patrol car. Radford's revolver was found in a tobacco barn 75 yards behind Manning's home.

Manning testified on his own behalf that after he and Trooper Radford left in the patrol car, the trooper stopped another car traveling in front of them after a bag was thrown from its window. There were four people in the car. Radford approached the vehicle and while he was talking with the driver, Manning ran away from the patrol car unobserved. He walked to a friend's house and was driven back to his car.

After the close of evidence at trial, the judge gave the following charge on reasonable doubt:

> Beyond a reasonable doubt, in telling you that that is the degree of proof by which the State must prove, that phrase means exactly what it states in the English language, and that is a doubt for which you can give a real reason. That excludes a whimsical doubt, fanciful doubt. You could doubt any proposition if you wanted to. A reasonable doubt is a substantial doubt for which honest people, such as you, when searching for the truth can give a real reason. So it's to that degree of proof that the State is required to establish the elements of a charge.

Later in the charge, the judge added this thought about the meaning of reasonable doubt: "I instruct you to seek some reasonable explanation of the circumstances proven other than the guilt of the Defendant and if such a reasonable explanation can be found you should find the Defendant not guilty." As defense counsel, how would you argue that this charge was invalid? Compare State v. Manning, 409 S.E.2d 372 (S.C. 1991).

Notes

1. *Defining reasonable doubt: majority position.* As the Indiana court in *Winegeart* indicated, the federal constitution requires that the government prove all elements of an offense beyond a reasonable doubt, In re Winship, 397 U.S. 358 (1970), but it does not require that courts define reasonable doubt in a particular way. States have adopted a range of positions specifying both what is required and what is forbidden in defining reasonable doubt.

Several modern definitions trace their wording back to a famous decision by Chief Justice Lemuel Shaw, in Commonwealth v. Webster, 59 Mass. 295, 320 (1850):

> [What] is reasonable doubt? It is a term often used, probably pretty well understood, but not easily defined. It is not mere possible doubt; because every thing related to human affairs, and depending on moral evidence, is open to some possible or imaginary doubt. It is that state of the case, which, after the entire comparison and consideration of all the evidence, leaves the minds of the jurors in that condition that they cannot say they feel an abiding conviction, to a moral certainty, of the truth of the charge.

About 20 states emphasize the negative perspective, defining reasonable doubt as a doubt that would cause a reasonable person to "hesitate to act in their most important affairs." Another group of about 20 states requires the doubt to be "based on reason" or "a valid reason." Roughly 10 states refer to "actual and substantial doubt" or "serious and substantial doubt" or "fair and actual doubt." A handful require that the doubt be articulable, that it be "doubt for which a reason can be given," although some states forbid such formulations because they require jurors to be articulate and place the burden on the defendant to show reasonable doubt. See People v. Antommarchi, 604 N.E.2d 95 (N.Y. 1992). About a dozen states define reasonable doubt in positive terms, focusing on the "moral certainty of guilt" or saying the juror must be "firmly convinced of guilt." (Several states tolerate several different approaches, and thus the preceding categories total more than 50.) See Steve

Sheppard, The Metamorphoses of Reasonable Doubt: How Changes in the Burden of Proof Have Weakened the Presumption of Innocence, 78 Notre Dame L. Rev. 1165 (2003) (tracking twentieth-century shift to interpretation that emphasizes assignment of reasons as operational meaning of reasonableness).

State courts also diverge on the question whether to define reasonable doubt at all. About a dozen states allow the trial judge to avoid the issue by providing no definition to the jury, while two states forbid trial judges from giving definitions. Paulson v. State, 28 S.W.3d 570 (Tex. Crim. App. 2000) (best practice is not to define reasonable doubt for jury). Five states have statutory mandates to define reasonable doubt in all cases; about a dozen states have reached the same position through case law. A few states require a definition only if the defendant requests it, and another handful require a definition to be given only in complex cases. For a graphic showing the distribution of states on this issue, go to the web extension for this chapter at *http://www.crimpro.com/extension/ch18*.

One danger of using a negative definition of "reasonable doubt" is that it seems to place a burden on the defendant to show reasonable doubt instead of placing the burden on the government to dispel reasonable doubt (or to offer proof "beyond" reasonable doubt). The positive formulation of the instruction — found in the Federal Judiciary Center version of the instruction, which requires a juror to be "firmly convinced that the defendant is guilty of the crime charged" — has gained legal momentum with the decision of the Indiana Supreme Court in *Winegeart* and a 1995 decision by the Arizona Supreme Court mandating the use of this instruction. State v. Portillo, 898 P.2d 970 (Ariz. 1995). The U.S. Supreme Court has refused to mandate a particular definition for all federal courts, and the circuits have adopted a range of positions parallel to those taken among the states.

2. *Do definitions help?* States that forbid trial courts from defining reasonable doubt, or those that leave the decision to the trial judge, echo the long-standing skepticism of observers like Joel Bishop and John Henry Wigmore. Definitions, they say, do not help jurors decide cases. But the difficulty of applying the concept suggests that if states or individual judges want to leave jurors to use their own conceptions of reasonable doubt, they may be saying more about their view of the jury's role than about reasonable doubt. Professor Richard Uviller has observed that most people "require considerable explanation, example, and parallel articulation to grasp the basic contours" of the concept of reasonable doubt, and that a reasonable doubt instruction, unadorned by explanation, "is an invitation to clothe it by invention, its flexibility an opportunity to bend it to prefigured purposes." Richard Uviller, Acquitting the Guilty: Two Case Studies on Jury Misgivings and the Misunderstood Standard of Proof, 2 Crim. L.F. 1, 38 (1990). Would the criminal trial be fairer if courts adopted a uniform definition of reasonable doubt? Is such consistency a virtue, or is simply having *some* definition the real virtue? See Peter Tiersma, The Rocky Road to Legal Reform: Improving the Language of Jury Instructions, 66 Brook. L. Rev. 1081 (2001) (trial courts unlikely to improve jury instructions; drafters of standardized jury instructions are more likely mechanism for reform).

Problem 18-2. Words and Numbers

Joseph McCullough was charged with possession of a controlled substance (marijuana) and possession of stolen property (a 1974 Chevrolet "Luv" pickup truck). During the voir dire examination of potential jurors, the district judge attempted to illustrate the concept of reasonable doubt with a numerical scale. On a scale of 0 to 10, the judge placed the preliminary hearing standard of probable cause at about 1 and the burden of persuasion in civil trials at just over 5. She then twice described reasonable doubt as about "seven and a half, if you had to put it on a scale." The judge also provided the jurors with the reasonable doubt standard described in Nev. Rev. Stat. §175.211, which provides as follows:

> A reasonable doubt is one based on reason. It is not mere possible doubt, but is such a doubt as would govern or control a person in the more weighty affairs of life. If the minds of the jurors, after the entire comparison and consideration of all the evidence, are in such a condition that they can say they feel an abiding conviction of the truth of the charge, there is not a reasonable doubt. Doubt to be reasonable must be actual and substantial, not mere possibility or speculation.

After introducing the jurors to the reasonable doubt standard provided by the Nevada statute, the judge again noted, "I have tried to give you that on a zero to ten scale." The jury convicted the defendant of both charges. He appeals, claiming that the judge's attempt to quantify reasonable doubt impermissibly lowered the prosecution's burden of proof and confused the jury rather than clarifying the reasonable doubt concept. How would you rule? See McCullough v. State, 657 P.2d 1157 (Nev. 1983).

Problem 18-3. Presumed Innocent or Not Guilty?

Jose Flores was tried and convicted of first-degree murder. The trial court instructed the jury by using a modified version of Oklahoma Uniform Jury Instruction — Criminal No. 903. The instruction read as follows:

> You are instructed that the defendant is presumed to be not guilty of the crime charged against him in the Information unless his guilt is established by evidence beyond a reasonable doubt and that presumption of being not guilty continues with the defendant unless every material allegation of the Information is proven by evidence beyond a reasonable doubt.

This jury instruction reflected the terms of Okla. Stat. tit. 22, §836, which provides that a defendant in a criminal action "is presumed to be innocent until the contrary is proved, and in case of a reasonable doubt as to whether his guilt is satisfactorily shown, he is entitled to be acquitted."

Flores now argues that the jury instruction diluted the presumption of innocence and diminished the State's burden of proving him guilty beyond a reasonable doubt. He argues the instruction also failed to advise the jury that the presumption of innocence remains in effect until the jury is convinced of guilt. Was the jury instruction erroneous? Is it more accurate to instruct the jury that a defendant is presumed innocent or presumed not guilty? Compare Flores v. State, 896 P.2d 558 (Okla. Crim. App. 1995); State v. Pierce, 927 P.2d 929 (Kan. 1996).

Notes

1. *Quantifying reasonable doubt.* Most state and federal courts discourage or prohibit trial judges from efforts to quantify the reasonable doubt standard. See State v. Cruz, 639 A.2d 534 (Conn. 1994). Can the preponderance standard for civil cases be quantified? Don't the preponderance, clear and convincing, and reasonable doubt standards all express degrees of certainty? Did the Nevada judge in Problem 18-2 just choose the wrong numbers? Some judges have used sports analogies rather than numerical descriptions. What if the judge said that the prosecution had to "take the ball way past the 50-yard line, but you don't have to go a hundred yards for a guilty finding"? See State v. DelVecchio, 464 A.2d 813 (Conn. 1983). Studies conducted in the 1970s found that jurors quantified reasonable doubt at around 86 percent certainty of guilt. See Saul Kassin & Lawrence Wrightsman, On the Requirements of Proof: The Timing of Judicial Instruction and Mock Juror Verdicts, 37 J. Personality & Soc. Psychol. 282 (1979). Another study suggests that jurors take a wide range of positions, associating the concept of "reasonable doubt" with anything from 50 to 100 percent certainty of guilt. See Terry Connolly, Decision Theory, Reasonable Doubt, and the Utility of Erroneous Acquittals, 11 Law & Hum. Behav. 101 (1987). For a review of the empirical studies of juror understanding of the reasonable doubt standard, go to the web extension for this chapter at *http://www.crimpro.com/extension/ch18*.

2. *Presumption of innocence and burden of proof.* Is the presumption of innocence anything more than another way to refer to the prosecution's burden of proof? In other words, when a defendant is said to be "presumed innocent," does that statement have legal ramifications beyond requiring the state to prove all elements of the offense beyond a reasonable doubt? Does it remind the jury not to place any evidentiary weight on the mere fact that the defendant has been charged with a crime? Most states declare that a separate instruction on presumption of innocence is not necessary in every case, while about 15 states do require a separate instruction. See, e.g., Ohio Rev. Stat. §2938.08 ("The presumption of innocence places upon the state (or the municipality) the burden of proving him guilty beyond a reasonable doubt. In charging a jury the trial court shall state the meaning of the presumption of innocence and of reasonable doubt in each case"). Does the presumption of innocence tell the jury anything about how long the government bears its burden of proof? Consider this typical description from Horn v. Territory, 56 P. 846, 848 (Okla. 1899):

> A defendant's friends may forsake him, but the presumption of innocence, never. It is present throughout the entire trial; and, when the jury go to their room to deliberate, the "presumption of innocence" goes in with them, protesting against the defendant's guilt. And it is only after the jury has given all the evidence in the case a full, fair, and impartial consideration, and have been able to find beyond a reasonable doubt that the defendant is guilty as charged, that the presumption of innocence leaves him.

In Taylor v. Kentucky, 436 U.S. 478 (1978), the Supreme Court found a federal due process violation when a Kentucky judge refused to instruct the jury on the presumption of innocence. The Court cited Coffin v. United States, 156 U.S. 432 (1895), to establish that the presumption of innocence in favor of the accused "is the undoubted law, axiomatic and elementary, and its enforcement lies at the foundation of the administration of our criminal law." A year later, however, the Court held that a presumption-of-innocence instruction was not a constitutional requirement in all cases. Kentucky v. Whorton, 441 U.S. 786 (1979). The instruction was necessary in *Taylor* only because of "skeletal" jury instructions and the prosecutor's repeated suggestions that the defendant's status as a person charged with a crime tended to establish his guilt.

3. *Guilty clothing*. The presumption of innocence can have an impact on the operation of the courtroom beyond the jury instructions. For example, courts generally forbid the state from requiring the defendant to appear in prison garb or surrounded by armed guards. However, the defendant must object to the clothing or other circumstances. Estelle v. Williams, 425 U.S. 501 (1976). Federal and state courts allow the conspicuous use of security guards more readily than they will tolerate shackles or distinctive clothing on the defendant. See Holbrook v. Flynn, 475 U.S. 560 (1986) (upholding four uniformed state troopers sitting in the front spectator row during trial as security measure); Sterling v. State, 830 S.W.2d 114 (Tex. Crim. App. 1992) (seven uniformed deputies in courtroom). Cf. John Schwartz, "Extreme Makeover: Criminal Court Edition," N.Y. Times, Dec. 5, 2010 (judge granted defense motion to allow defendant to cover swastika tattooed on his neck with makeup during jury trial).

2. *Presumptions*

Judges instruct juries, and lawyers argue to juries, about evidentiary presumptions — asserting either that the jurors should assume a fact to be true or that if one fact is found then another fact or conclusion is more likely to be true. These presumptions can undermine the requirement that crime elements be proven beyond a reasonable doubt. In Sandstrom v. Montana, 442 U.S. 510 (1979), the U.S. Supreme Court rejected an instruction in a deliberate homicide case where intent was an element of the offense. The instruction said, "the law presumes that a person intends the ordinary consequences of his voluntary acts." The defendant had confessed to the killing, making his mental state the key issue. The Court found that, from the standpoint of the reasonable juror, this instruction shifted the burden of proof from the state to the defendant.

In Francis v. Franklin, 471 U.S. 307 (1985), a Georgia prisoner attempting escape killed a man when he fired a gun through a door at the moment the victim slammed it. Again, the sole defense was lack of intent to kill. The trial court, using an instruction with a long pedigree, instructed the jury that the acts of a "person of sound mind and discretion are presumed to be the product of the person's will, but the presumption may be rebutted. A person of sound mind and discretion is presumed to intend the natural and probable consequences of his acts but the presumption may be rebutted. A person will not be presumed to act with criminal intention but the trier of facts . . . may find criminal intention upon a consideration of the words, conduct, demeanor, motive and all of the circumstances connected with the act for which the accused is prosecuted." The jury was also instructed that the defendant was presumed innocent and that the State was required to prove every element of the offense beyond a reasonable doubt. The Supreme Court again rejected the instruction. Even though the trial court had stated that "the presumption may be rebutted," such qualifying language did not prevent a reasonable juror from believing that the defendant bore the burden of showing he did not intend to kill. The *Franklin* Court distinguished valid and invalid instructions involving evidentiary presumptions as follows:

> The court must determine whether the challenged portion of the instruction creates a mandatory presumption, or merely a permissive inference. A mandatory presumption instructs the jury that it must infer the presumed fact if the State proves certain predicate facts. A permissive inference suggests to the jury a possible conclusion to be drawn if the State proves predicate facts, but does not require the jury to draw that conclusion.

471 U.S. at 313. The following case from South Carolina analyzes jury instructions within this framework of mandatory presumptions and permissive inferences.

■ STATE v. JOHNNY RUFUS BELCHER

685 S.E.2d 802 (S.C. 2009)

KITTREDGE, J.

Appellant Johnny Rufus Belcher was convicted of murder and possession of a firearm during the commission of a violent crime following the shooting of his cousin, Fred Suber. [Suber] was shot and killed during a cookout with family and friends. Those in attendance included Suber's ex-girlfriend and Hansel Brown, whom Suber believed was the father of his ex-girlfriend's child. Suber confronted Brown and an argument ensued. Belcher interceded.

The testimony presented at trial revealed conflicting versions of the event. The State's view tended to show that after Belcher confronted Suber, Belcher retrieved a gun from Brown and, with no justification or excuse, fatally shot Suber. Conversely, Belcher presented evidence that after the confrontation between Suber and Brown was seemingly resolved, Suber without provocation confronted him (Belcher) with a gun. Belcher fled to Brown's truck where he retrieved a gun from Brown and fired it at Suber while he (Suber) was approaching, gun in hand. . . .

The trial court charged the jury, in part, as follows:

> Murder is the unlawful killing of another person with malice aforethought either expressed or inferred. [Malice can] be inferred from facts and circumstances that are proven by the State. Malice may be inferred by the use of a deadly weapon. But these inferences are evidentiary only and may be considered by you along with all the other evidence and given such weight, if any, as you determine that they should receive. . . .

Where a jury is asked to consider a lesser included offense of murder or a defense, Belcher asserts the permissive inference charge violates our common law and our constitutional prohibition against charging juries on the facts. S.C. Const. art. V, §21 ("Judges shall not charge juries in respect to matters of fact, but shall declare the law."). We elect to decide this appeal solely under the common law. Relying on Belcher's common law challenge, we conclude that our modern day usage of this jury charge has strayed from this Court's original jurisprudence. . . .

We begin with State v. Hopkins, 15 S.C. 153 (1881). Hopkins was convicted of murder. He pled accident, and objected to the following "use of a deadly weapon" implied malice instruction: "In every case of intentional homicide the presumption of malice arises, and the fact of killing intentionally by the use of a deadly weapon being shown in any case, the burden of proof is thereby imposed upon the defendant to rebut such presumption, unless the facts and circumstances shown in the testimony in behalf of the State incidentally rebut it."[3] Under the circumstances, the charge was error, and Hopkins was granted a new trial.

Hopkins cited to the rule that there is "no doubt whatever of the isolated proposition that the law presumes malice from the mere fact of homicide, but there are cases as made by the proof to which the rule is inapplicable." The Court explained that, "when all the circumstances of the case are fully proved there is no room for presumption. The question becomes one of fact for the jury, under the general principle that he who affirms must prove, and that every man is presumed innocent until the contrary appears."

[In State v. Levelle, 13 S.E. 319 (S.C. 1891), the Court recognized that "It is true that the inference of malice drawn from the use of a deadly weapon may be rebutted by testimony, but, in the absence of any such testimony, malice may be and is inferred from the use of a deadly weapon causing death.] *Levelle* never expanded upon the "in the absence of any such testimony [rebutting malice]" qualification, perhaps because it was not necessary to the disposition of the appeal. We are persuaded, though, that this qualification relates to homicide prosecutions where the evidence shows the death may have been something less than murder — that is, mitigated, excused or justified.

[We] view the approach to the "use of a deadly weapon" implied malice charge as seemingly settled law from *Hopkins* and the *Levelle* . . . qualification. This Court, however, then began a slow, and at first an almost imperceptible, retreat, as State v. Byrd, 51 S.E. 542 (S.C. 1905), illustrates.

In *Byrd,* this Court, in reviewing the jury instruction stated that: "The use of a deadly weapon presumes malice, *but the presumption may be rebutted.* So, after all, it is left for the jury to say, from all the facts and circumstances, whether the killing was done with malice, or not." (emphasis added). Relying on *Levelle* . . . , the *Byrd* Court found no error associated with the jury charge [and] approved of the charge even with evidence of mitigation.

The Court never expressly confronted the contradiction of inviting a jury to infer malice from the use of a deadly weapon where evidence was presented that would reduce, mitigate, excuse or justify the homicide, which was the core feature of *Hopkins.* [With] this Court's continuing imprimatur, by the 1970s, juries were routinely charged in any murder prosecution involving a deadly weapon that "malice is presumed from the use of a deadly weapon." The critical observation is that the charge was proper even where evidence was presented that would reduce, mitigate, excuse or justify the killing.

The law, of course, today speaks in terms of "permissive inferences," not "presumptions." This transition resulted from the United States Supreme Court's pronouncement that the Due Process Clause of the Fourteenth Amendment is violated when a jury charge creates a mandatory presumption and impermissibly shifts

3. In reviewing this dated precedent, we note that the law then imposed the burden of proving various defenses (self-defense, for example) on the defendant. Under modern jurisprudence, burden shifting is not permitted. For this reason, we analyze this older precedent in light of prevailing law that forbids burden shifting.

the burden of proof to the defendant. See Sandstrom v. Montana, 442 U.S. 510 (1979) (holding that "burden-shifting presumptions" or "conclusive presumptions" deprive a defendant of the "due process of law" and are therefore unconstitutional); Mullaney v. Wilbur, 421 U.S. 684 (1975) (holding that the "Due Process Clause" forbids a state from placing the burden on the accused to prove his actions reduced the crime from "murder to manslaughter").

Following *Sandstrom* and its progeny, this Court followed suit. In State v. Mattison, 277 S.E.2d 598 (S.C. 1981), we stated that an "appropriate instruction on implied malice would deal with the evidentiary nature of the presumption and that the implication does not require the jury to infer malice but only permits it."

Mattison, however, expressed no reluctance with the underlying premise that malice is inferred from the use of a deadly weapon. The jury in *Mattison* was charged: "The law says that if one intentionally kills another with a deadly weapon, the implication of malice arises. In other words, the law implies malice from the use of a deadly weapon." As discussed more fully below, the transparent error in the use of the word "intentional" is that self-defense involves an intentional act.

Two years later, in State v. Elmore, 308 S.E.2d 781 (S.C. 1983), this Court again addressed the challenged jury instruction in light of the burden shifting jurisprudence of the United States Supreme Court. The instruction used in Elmore's trial was held to have been a mandatory presumption, rather than a permissive inference, and therefore unconstitutional. The *Elmore* Court went on to set forth a jury charge it felt comported with the Due Process Clause.

> The law says if one intentionally kills another with a deadly weapon, the implication of malice may arise. If facts . . . are proved beyond a reasonable doubt, sufficient to raise an inference of malice to your satisfaction, this inference would be simply an evidentiary fact to be taken into consideration by you, the jury, along with other evidence in the case, and you may give it such weight as you determine it should receive.

The Court noted that "only slight deviations from this charge will be tolerated." *Elmore* articulated the contemporary jury charge, until today.

In examining the legal proposition in a homicide prosecution that an inference of malice may arise from the use of a deadly weapon, we are unable to harmonize the earlier writings of this Court with our modern jurisprudence.

One appellate court has described this jury charge as a "half-truth." Glenn v. State, 511 A.2d 1110, 1126 (Md. App. 1986). In discussing its meaning behind this observation, *Glenn* notes that malice includes the absence of justification, excuse and mitigation.[5] When malice is viewed in light of these component parts, it becomes clear that inferring malice from the use of a deadly weapon is indeed only a "half-truth." The absence of justification, excuse or mitigation cannot be inferred from the use of a deadly weapon standing alone. Other facts and evidence (or the absence of other facts and evidence) are required for the fulfillment of these component parts. . . .

Under our policy-making role in the common law, we hold that the "use of a deadly weapon" implied malice instruction has no place in a murder (or assault and

5. Under South Carolina law, malice is a legal term implying wickedness and excluding a just cause or excuse. The term malice indicates a formed purpose and design to do a wrongful act under the circumstances that exclude any legal right to do it.

battery with intent to kill) prosecution where evidence is presented that would reduce, mitigate, excuse or justify the killing (or the alleged assault and battery with intent to kill).

The use of the term "intentional" is instructive. Say, for example, a homicide occurs by the use of a deadly weapon under circumstances warranting a self-defense instruction. The killing would be intentional, yet under our currently sanctioned charge, the jury would be permitted to find malice merely because "if one intentionally kills another with a deadly weapon, the implication of malice may arise." That highlights the "half-truth" nature of the charge.

Today's decision does not stand alone.* Other states that have addressed this issue have rejected the charge under similar circumstances. See e.g., Farris v. Commonwealth, 77 Ky. 362 (Ky. 1878) (noting that when "there is evidence before the jury from which they might conclude that the killing was done in necessary self-defense or in the sudden heat of passion, such an instruction may be fatally misleading"); Glenn v. State (Md. App. 1986); Erwin v. State, 29 Ohio St. 186, 191 (Ohio 1876) ("Where the attending circumstances [of the killing] are shown in detail, some of which tend to disprove the presence of malice or purpose to kill, it is misleading and erroneous to charge a jury that in such a case the law raises a presumption of malice and intent to kill from the isolated fact that death was caused by the use of a deadly weapon"); State v. Jenkins, 443 S.E.2d 244 (W.Va. 1994) ("It is erroneous in a first degree murder case to instruct the jury that if the defendant killed the deceased with the use of a deadly weapon, then intent, malice, willfulness, deliberation, and premeditation may be inferred from that fact, where there is evidence that the defendant's actions were based on some legal excuse, justification, or provocation"). For a discussion surrounding the history of this charge, see Bruce A. Antkowiak, The Art of Malice, 60 Rutgers L. Rev. 435 (2008).

We do not reach our decision lightly. The State understandably urges this Court to honor what has been treated as a settled fixture in our criminal law. The able trial judge diligently prepared the charge in faithful adherence to our precedent. Moreover, the trial court charged the jury that the "killing has to be unlawful" and that there has to be "a deliberate and intentional design to use or employ or handle a deadly weapon so as to endanger the life of another without just cause or excuse." Thus, while we acknowledge the State's argument, we are firmly convinced that instructing a jury that "malice may be inferred by the use of a deadly weapon" is confusing and prejudicial where evidence is presented that would reduce, mitigate, excuse or justify the homicide. A jury charge is no place for purposeful ambiguity.

Errors, including erroneous jury instructions, are subject to harmless error analysis. In many murder prosecutions, as Belcher concedes, there will be overwhelming evidence of malice apart from the use of a deadly weapon. [When a defendant walks into the store and shoots and robs the clerk, a charge that the jury may infer malice is not prejudicial to the defendant.] Here, however, the error in charging that malice may be inferred by the use of a deadly weapon cannot be considered harmless. Evidence of self-defense was presented, thereby highlighting the prejudice resulting from the charge. It is entirely conceivable that the only evidence of malice was Belcher's use of a handgun. We need go no further than saying we cannot conclude the error was harmless beyond a reasonable doubt.

* [The material in this paragraph appeared in footnote 7 in the original. — Eds.]

Today we return to the rationale underlying *Hopkins* [and] *Levelle* and hold that where evidence is presented that would reduce, mitigate, excuse or justify a homicide (or assault and battery with intent to kill) caused by the use of a deadly weapon, juries shall not be charged that malice may be inferred from the use of a deadly weapon.[9] The permissive inference charge concerning the use of a deadly weapon remains a correct statement of the law where the only issue presented to the jury is whether the defendant has committed murder (or assault and battery with intent to kill).

Because our decision represents a clear break from our modern precedent, today's ruling is effective in this case and for all cases which are pending on direct review or not yet final where the issue is preserved. Our ruling, however, will not apply to convictions challenged on post-conviction relief. We reverse and remand for a new trial.

Problem 18-4. Presumption in the Fire

James Jubilee, an African American, moved with his family from California to Virginia Beach in April 1998. After a few weeks in the new neighborhood, he asked his new neighbor, Susan Elliott, about shots being fired from behind the Elliott home. Elliott explained to Jubilee that her son shot firearms as a hobby, and used the backyard as a firing range.

A few nights later, Elliott's son Richard drove a truck onto Jubilee's property, planted a cross, and set it on fire. He was trying to "get back" at Jubilee for complaining about the shooting in the backyard. Elliott was not affiliated with the Ku Klux Klan. The next morning, as Jubilee was pulling his car out of the driveway, he noticed the partially burned cross approximately 20 feet from his house. After seeing the cross, Jubilee was very nervous because "a cross burned in your yard tells you that it's just the first round." He worried about the violence that might follow.

A separate cross burning incident took place elsewhere in the state a few months later. One August night, Barry Black led a Ku Klux Klan rally in Carroll County. Twenty-five to 30 people attended this gathering, which occurred on private property with the permission of the owner, who also attended the rally. When the sheriff of the county learned that a Klan rally was occurring in his jurisdiction, he went to observe it from the side of the road. Over the next hour or so, about 40 to 50 cars passed the site, and a few of the drivers stopped to ask the sheriff what was happening on the property.

Eight to 10 houses were located nearby. Rebecca Sechrist, who was related to the owner of the property where the rally took place, sat and watched to see what was going on from the lawn of her in-laws' home. She heard Klan members speak about what they believed in. As she put it, the speakers "talked real bad about the blacks and the Mexicans." One speaker told the assembled gathering that "he would love to take a .30/.30 and just randomly shoot the blacks." The speakers also talked about "President Clinton and Hillary Clinton," and about how their tax money "goes to

9. [We] neither restrict the State from arguing to the jury for a finding of malice from the use of a deadly weapon, nor restrict a defendant from arguing the absence of malice or the presence of reasonable doubt in this regard. It is axiomatic that some matters appropriate for jury argument are not proper for charging. . . .

the black people." This language made Sechrist feel "very scared." At the conclusion of the rally, the crowd circled around a 25- to 30-foot cross, which was placed 325 yards away from the road. As the sheriff and others looked on, the cross went up in flame. The sheriff then went down the driveway, entered the rally, and asked who was responsible for burning the cross. Black responded, "I guess I am because I'm the head of the rally." The sheriff then told Black, "There's a law in the State of Virginia that you cannot burn a cross and I'll have to place you under arrest for this."

Barry Black and Richard Elliott were both charged with of violating Virginia's cross burning statute. Section 18.2-423 provides:

> It shall be unlawful for any person or persons, with the intent of intimidating any person or group of persons, to burn, or cause to be burned, a cross on the property of another, a highway or other public place. . . . Any such burning of a cross shall be prima facie evidence of an intent to intimidate a person or group of persons.

At Black's trial, the judge instructed the jury that "intent to intimidate means the motivation to intentionally put a person or a group of persons in fear of bodily harm. Such fear must arise from the willful conduct of the accused rather than from some mere temperamental timidity of the victim." The trial court also instructed the jury that "the burning of a cross by itself is sufficient evidence from which you may infer the required intent." The jury found Black guilty and fined him $2,500.

At Elliott's trial, the court instructed the jury that the Commonwealth must prove that "the defendant intended to commit cross burning," that he "did a direct act toward the commission of the cross burning," and that he "had the intent of intimidating any person or group of persons." The court did not instruct the jury on the meaning of the word "intimidate" or on the prima facie evidence provision of §18.2-423. The jury found Elliott guilty of attempted cross burning and sentenced him to 90 days in jail and a $2,500 fine.

Did either the statute or the judge's instructions in either of the two trials create an unconstitutional presumption of guilt? Cf. Virginia v. Black, 538 U.S. 343 (2003).

Notes

1. *Presumptions: majority position.* Both federal and state courts have followed the constitutional structure that the U.S. Supreme Court built in *Sandstrom* and *Franklin.* Federal and state courts differ, however, on the particular kinds of language that create an impermissible mandatory presumption. For instance, courts disagree on whether presumptions such as "a person generally intends the consequences of his acts" can be cured by additional language saying that such presumptions are rebuttable. *Sandstrom* claims apply as well to arguments made by the prosecutor in closing arguments.

Despite the best efforts of trial courts instructing juries, *Sandstrom* claims continue to arise. Should legislatures bar the use of all evidentiary presumptions? Doesn't all circumstantial evidence require reliance on presumptions? Don't all findings about mens rea require jurors to rely on presumptions even if they are unstated?

2. *Reasonable doubt about what?* Every defendant benefits from the requirement that the state prove all elements of any criminal offense beyond a reasonable doubt.

But what are "elements" of offenses, and what are "defenses" that the defendant must prove? Can states define crimes any way they want? The U.S. Supreme Court at times has wrestled with the idea that the federal constitution might place some controls on what the state can designate as an element of a crime or a defense to the charges. Current doctrine, however, reinforces the view that states have substantial discretion in defining crimes. In Patterson v. New York, 432 U.S. 197 (1977), the Supreme Court rejected a due process challenge to a New York law that made the defense of extreme emotional disturbance an affirmative defense that the defendant must prove by a preponderance of the evidence. The Court emphasized that "preventing and dealing with crime is much more the business of the States than it is of the Federal Government." The federal constitution limits the capacity of states to define crimes only to the extent that the state law "offends some principle of justice so rooted in the traditions and conscience of our people as to be ranked as fundamental." The court declined to adopt "as a constitutional imperative, operative countrywide, that a State must disprove beyond a reasonable doubt every fact constituting any and all affirmative defenses related to the culpability of an accused."

Thus, states appear to have substantial discretion within federal constitutional boundaries to define crimes and defenses and to allocate the burden of proving or disproving an element to either the prosecution or the defense. Sometimes the argument is not about whether the state *can* place a particular burden on the state or the defendant, but whether it has in fact done so.

3. *The burden on affirmative defenses: majority view.* States divide on the general issue of whether the prosecution carries the burden of proof on affirmative defenses. Roughly 35 states require the defendant to carry the burden of proof on all affirmative defenses, but they usually require only that the defendant prove the defense by a preponderance of the evidence. See, e.g., Ohio Rev. Code §2901.05 (The burden of proof "for all elements of the offense is upon the prosecution. The burden of going forward with the evidence of an affirmative defense, and the burden of proof, by a preponderance of the evidence, for an affirmative defense, is upon the accused"). A handful of states require the state to carry the burden of proof on all affirmative defenses, though usually the defendant has the burden of going forward with facts sufficient to raise the defense. It is most common for states to require the prosecution to carry the burden on self-defense, while about half the states place the burden of proving insanity and related defenses on the defendant.

4. *Elements and facts enhancing punishment.* Are facts that increase punishment — such as a finding that the defendant used a gun during the offense, or the amount of drugs involved — "elements" of the offense that the government must prove beyond a reasonable doubt? In McMillan v. Pennsylvania, 477 U.S. 79 (1986), the Supreme Court held that the reasonable doubt standard applied only to facts that "bear on the defendant's guilt," and upheld a statute enhancing the sentence if the prosecution proved by a preponderance of the evidence that the defendant "visibly possessed a firearm." The majority of states also allow the government to prove sentencing facts, including facts related to the prior criminal history of the defendant, at standards lower than reasonable doubt. See People v. Wims, 895 P.2d 77 (Cal. 1995).

The Supreme Court periodically addresses the question of whether particular facts are "elements" of a crime (to be decided by a trial jury using the beyond a reasonable doubt standard) or are instead "sentencing enhancement" (to be decided after trial using a lower standard of proof). The decisions in Apprendi v. New Jersey, 530 U.S. 466 (2000), and Blakely v. Washington, 542 U.S. 296 (2004), are discussed in Chapter 19.

5. *Statutory definitions of sufficient evidence.* As we have seen, a legislature is free by and large to define the elements of crimes; it is more limited in its power to declare what inferences about crime elements that a jury must draw from the proven facts. However, the legislature may specify the type of evidence that is *not* sufficient to prove the elements. For instance, some statutes specify the minimum number of witnesses the prosecution must present to support a conviction for a particular crime (e.g., the traditional "two witness rule" for perjury convictions).

Issues about the proper burden of proof and crime definitions draw from a mixture of substantive criminal law, constitutional law, criminal procedure, sentencing law, and evidence, and often from a blend of statutes, case law, and other kinds of legal authority. The mixed nature of questions about defining crimes means that a legislature might accomplish a goal with a rule of evidence that might be invalid as a crime definition. See Montana v. Egelhoff, 518 U.S. 37 (1996) (upholding state statute barring evidence of voluntary intoxication in determining the mental element of an offense).

B. CONFRONTATION OF WITNESSES

An adversarial legal system, by its very nature, places great value on the testing of evidence. Cross-examination of witnesses presents the attorneys with their best opportunity to test the reliability of evidence.

State and federal constitutions recognize the importance of this adversarial testing of evidence. Often, however, the constitutional provisions refer to "confrontation" of witnesses rather than to cross-examination. Consider the relevant clause from the Sixth Amendment to the federal constitution: "In all criminal prosecutions, the accused shall enjoy the right . . . to be confronted with the witnesses against him. . . ." In this section, we consider the devices available to test evidence.

1. The Value of Confrontation

Ordinarily the prosecution presents witnesses who testify at trial in the presence of the defendant, and the defense counsel cross-examines the witnesses with the defendant present. But does the presence of the defendant add anything? Is there some value in the "confrontation" of witnesses that goes beyond an effective cross-examination? See Richard D. Friedman, Confrontation: The Search for Basic Principles, 86 Geo. L.J. 1011 (1998).

Problem 18-5 presents a common dilemma in the criminal courtroom: the tradeoff between the values of confrontation and the costs of presenting evidence in a format that allows live testing of the evidence in the courtroom. The Texas case reprinted below deals with an unusual trial setting in which a witness is disguised during testimony. As you read it, reflect on what makes a cross-examination effective and what additional functions confrontation might serve. The second case, an opinion of the European Court of Human Rights, plays a variation on this theme:

efforts by prosecutors in the Netherlands to use witnesses whose names remain unknown to the defendant. As you read the case, try to sort out which of the concepts discussed would be familiar to an American court and which would be unthinkable. What does this European decision tell us about criminal justice in the United States?

A word is in order about the European Court of Human Rights. More than 30 nations have signed a treaty known as the European Convention for the Protection of Human Rights and Fundamental Freedoms. The treaty was signed in 1950, after the revelation of outrageous human rights abuses during World War II and during a time when some European nations felt the need to distinguish their democratic forms of government from Communist legal systems during the Cold War.

Under the European Convention, an individual who is convicted in the criminal courts of a signatory nation can challenge that conviction if it was obtained in violation of the convention. The challenge first goes to the European Commission on Human Rights; either the defendant or the government may appeal the commission's decision to the European Court of Human Rights. The judges of the court are drawn from various signatory nations. They interpret the convention in light of broad principles of international and domestic law. The European Court of Human Rights both reflects and develops a consensus among nations about human rights, including the nature of a fair criminal trial.

Problem 18-5. Child Testimony

Teresa Brady was born in 1997. Her father and mother, Michael Brady and Carla Myers, were married at the time of her birth but were divorced in 1998. Under a court visitation order, Teresa spent a Friday night and a Saturday night in April 2001 with her father at the home of Michael's mother, Rosemary Brady. Michael returned Teresa to Carla's home on Sunday at 6:00 P.M. On Monday morning, one of Teresa's teachers discovered her hiding in the bathroom closet and complaining about genital pain. A physical examination produced evidence of sexual abuse. During the three months following the discovery of the child's injury, she made several statements to investigators that her father had hurt her. The state filed charges against Michael in July 2001.

In January 2002, the State asked the court to order that Teresa's testimony be videotaped for use at trial, using the statutory procedures for recording the testimony of children. In February, the trial court ruled that it was more likely than not that it would be traumatic for Teresa to testify in court and ordered that the videotape testimony be taken. In March, Teresa's videotape testimony was taken and was subsequently admitted at trial over appellant's objection and viewed by the jury. The tape had been taken at home in Teresa's kitchen and bedroom. The judge, prosecutor, defense attorney, investigator, Teresa's mother, and the operator of the video equipment were present during the videotaping. The videotape session lasted approximately two hours. Michael was situated in the garage of the house, and he was able to see and hear Teresa via closed-circuit television as she was questioned. Michael was also able to speak with defense counsel by a microphone hook-up. Teresa was not able to see or hear appellant and was not aware of his presence. All of these arrangements carefully followed the statutory requirements.

Michael Brady maintains that this statute is unconstitutional on its face because it infringes upon his right to confront the witnesses against him as guaranteed by the Sixth Amendment of the United States Constitution and the analogous provision of the state constitution. The statute in question in this case is similar to the Maryland statute that the United States Supreme Court reviewed in Maryland v. Craig, 497 U.S. 836 (1990). The Supreme Court upheld the constitutionality of the Maryland statute as it found that the admission of the child victim's live testimony at the time of trial, transmitted to the courtroom and the trier of fact via one-way closed-circuit television, was consistent with the Confrontation Clause. The Supreme Court found it significant that Maryland's procedure preserves all of the elements of the confrontation right apart from the physical presence of the witness in the courtroom: "the child witness must be competent to testify and must testify under oath; the defendant retains full opportunity for contemporaneous cross-examination; and the judge, jury, and defendant are able to view (albeit by videotape monitor) the demeanor (and body) of the witness as he or she testifies."

The Supreme Court went on to state that in some cases the State's interest in protecting a child witness from serious emotional distress and trauma occasioned by testifying in the courtroom and in the presence of the defendant may outweigh a defendant's right to face his or her accusers in court. In such instances, the Supreme Court concluded that it was not necessary that the child witness be able to view, to hear, or otherwise perceive the presence of the defendant, who is viewing and listening in at the time.

The statute operating in this case resembles in some respects the Maryland statute at issue in *Craig*. The single significant dissimilarity in the two statutes appears to be that the statute here, unlike the Maryland statute, authorizes the use of videotaped pre-trial statements as well as the use of closed-circuit television during trial. How would you rule on Brady's claim? Cf. Brady v. State, 575 N.E.2d 981 (Ind.1991).

ISRAEL ROMERO v. STATE

173 S.W.3d 502 (Tex. 2005)

KELLER, P.J.

The question before us is whether the defendant's Sixth Amendment right to confront witnesses was violated when a witness testified in disguise. Although this is a very close issue, and one undecided by the United States Supreme Court, we answer that question "yes." . . .

Appellant was indicted for aggravated assault. On the morning of trial, Cesar Hiran Vasquez, one of the State's key witnesses, arrived at the courthouse but refused to enter the courtroom to testify. Vasquez, who had been subpoenaed by the State, notified the State that he "would rather go to jail than testify in this case" because of his fear of appellant. [Vasquez spoke little English, and all of his communications were through an interpreter.] The State informed the trial court of Vasquez's fear and his refusal to testify, and the trial court responded by threatening to fine Vasquez $500 for failing to obey the State's subpoena. Vasquez persisted in his refusal to testify, however, stating that, because he was worried for himself and his children, he "would prefer to pay" the fine rather than testify. The trial court then imposed the fine. Shortly thereafter, Vasquez entered the courtroom wearing dark sunglasses, a baseball cap pulled down over his forehead, and a long-sleeved jacket with its collar turned up and fastened so as to obscure Vasquez's mouth, jaw, and the lower half of his nose. The net effect and apparent purpose of Vasquez's "disguise" was to hide almost all of his face from view. The record reflects that, at the time of trial, appellant was aware of Vasquez's name and address.

Appellant objected to the "disguise" on the basis of his "right to confrontation" and, more generally, his right to a fair trial. The trial court overruled these objections.

The State then called Vasquez to the stand, outside the presence of the jury, to testify regarding appellant's motion to suppress Vasquez's in-court identification of appellant. Vasquez testified that he was operating a taxicab on May 10, 2002, at approximately 1:45 A.M., outside the Cosmos nightclub in Houston, when he saw appellant run toward the nightclub and, for no apparent reason, fire several shots in that direction. Given Vasquez's proximity to the nightclub's entrance, appellant's shots came fairly close to him. A security guard at the nightclub returned fire and hit appellant in the back. Appellant then retreated to a pickup truck and sped away, stopping once to fire again in the direction of the nightclub. Vasquez's testimony continued:

Q: [DEFENSE COUNSEL] If the Court were to order you not to wear your sunglasses, your hat, and your jacket with my client present in the courtroom, are you still going to testify. . . .
A: For my safety, I wouldn't do it. . . .
Q: [PROSECUTOR] Why are you afraid to testify against this defendant?
A: Because of the way that it could be seen that he was going to attack the security guard. It can be seen that he's a person who's dangerous on the street. . . .
Q: What are you afraid that he would do?
A: To take revenge. . . .
Q: [DEFENSE COUNSEL] Well, my client's never threatened you, has he?
A: No.
Q: All right. He's given you no reason to be afraid of him, right?
A: Didn't you see the way he's looking at me? . . .
Q: You just don't like the way he's looking at you, right, basically?
A: No.
Q: Then what is it?
A: The way I saw him attack with the gun. . . .

On direct appeal, appellant . . . argued that the trial court's ruling denied him his Sixth Amendment right to confrontation because Vasquez's "ball cap, large opaque sunglasses and mask [sic] prevented a face-to-face confrontation" and hindered the jury's ability to observe Vasquez's demeanor and assess his credibility. [The court of appeals] reversed the judgment of the trial court, and remanded the case to the trial court for further proceedings. . . .

The Sixth Amendment's Confrontation Clause ("In all criminal prosecutions, the accused shall enjoy the right . . . to be confronted with the witnesses against him") reflects a strong preference for face-to-face confrontation at trial. An encroachment upon face-to-face confrontation is permitted only when necessary to further an important public interest and when the reliability of the testimony is otherwise assured.

Reliability

Whether the reliability of the testimony is otherwise assured turns upon the extent to which the proceedings respect the four elements of confrontation: physical presence, oath, cross-examination, and observation of demeanor by the trier of fact. In Maryland v. Craig, 497 U.S. 836 (1990), the Supreme Court found sufficient assurance of reliability in a procedure that denied one of these elements — physical presence — where the remaining three elements were unimpaired. In that case, a child witness testified in front of a one-way closed-circuit monitor that prevented her from seeing the defendant but permitted the judge, jury, and defendant to see the witness. Because the witness was under oath, subject to contemporaneous cross-examination, and her demeanor was on display before the trier of fact, the Supreme Court found that the procedure adequately ensured that the testimony was "both reliable and subject to rigorous adversarial testing in a manner functionally equivalent to that accorded live, in person testimony."

In this case, as with *Craig*, the presence element of confrontation was compromised. Although the physical presence element might appear, on a superficial level, to have been satisfied by Vasquez's taking the witness stand, it is clear that Vasquez believed the disguise would confer a degree of anonymity that would insulate him from the defendant. The physical presence element entails an accountability of the witness to the defendant. The Supreme Court has observed that the presence requirement is motivated by the idea that a witness cannot "hide behind the shadow" but will be compelled to look the defendant "in the eye" while giving accusatory testimony. Coy v. Iowa, 487 U.S. 1012 (1988). In the present case, accountability was compromised because the witness was permitted to hide behind his disguise.

But unlike *Craig*, the present case also involves a failure to respect a second element of confrontation: observation of the witness's demeanor. Although Vasquez's tone of voice was subject to evaluation and some body language might have been observable, the trier of fact was deprived of the ability to observe his eyes and his facial expressions. And while wearing a disguise may itself be an aspect of demeanor that jurors could consider in assessing credibility, that fact cannot by any stretch of the imagination be considered an adequate substitute for the jurors' ability to view a witness's face, the most expressive part of the body and something that is traditionally regarded as one of the most important factors in assessing credibility. To hold otherwise is to remove the "face" from "face-to-face confrontation."

Important Interests

While there may be circumstances sufficient to justify a procedure that overrides not just one but two elements of a defendant's right to confrontation, those circumstances should rise above the "important" interests referred to in *Craig* to interests that are truly compelling. But we do not see an important interest served in the present case, much less a compelling one.

One important, even compelling, interest might be to protect a witness from retaliation, but the disguise in this case did little to further such an interest because Vasquez's name and address, but not his face, were already known to the defendant. Although Vasquez might reasonably fear that the defendant would be able to connect his facial features and appearance to his name and address, this connection could easily be made without any in-court appearance. A defendant seeking retaliation could simply knock on the door at the known address and ask for the named person. Moreover, this is not a case in which the defendant gave the victim or the authorities any concrete reason for suspecting retaliation, nor is this a case in which the defendant was shown to belong to a crime syndicate or a street gang from which retaliation might be anticipated.

At best, the disguise worked to allay the witness's subjective fear of retaliation. But some degree of trauma is to be expected in face-to-face confrontations. *Coy*, 487 U.S. at 1020 ("face-to-face presence may, unfortunately, upset the truthful rape victim or abused child; but by the same token it may confound and undo the false accuser, or reveal the child coached by a malevolent adult. It is a truism that constitutional protections have costs"). Calming an adult witness's fears is quite a different thing from protecting a child victim from serious emotional trauma. Adults are generally considered to be made of sterner stuff and capable of looking after their own psychological well-being. And the difference is especially great when the adult witness is not the victim, but merely a bystander who observed events, and when the basis of the witness's fear is simply that the defendant committed a violent crime and gave the witness a bad look. If those circumstances are sufficient to justify infringing on a defendant's right to face-to-face confrontation, then such infringement can be carried out against anyone accused of a violent crime. That outcome would violate the principle that face-to-face confrontation may be deprived only in exceptional situations. . . . We affirm the judgment of the Court of Appeals.

MEYERS, J., dissenting.

Mr. Israel G. Romero, this is your lucky day. You're going to get a new trial. The trial judge erred by allowing an eye witness to your crime to wear a ball cap, jacket, and sunglasses while testifying. . . .

The majority says that two elements of the confrontation clause were compromised — that being presence and demeanor. While I'm unsure what compromise means here, I'm fairly confident that the witness was there face-to-face to testify, was cross-examined, and that his demeanor showed that he was scared to death of the defendant. In Texas, is an accused entitled to more than this? Apparently so. Since Mr. Vasquez spoke through an interpreter, I really think this whole controversy is probably "lost in translation." . . .

The central concern of the Confrontation Clause is to ensure the reliability of the evidence against a criminal defendant by subjecting it to rigorous testing in the context of an adversary proceeding before the trier of fact. [As the Supreme Court noted in its earliest case interpreting the Confrontation Clause]:

> The primary object of the constitutional provision in question was to prevent depositions or ex parte affidavits, such as were sometimes admitted in civil cases, being used against the prisoner in lieu of a personal examination and cross-examination of the witness in which the accused has an opportunity, not only of testing the recollection and sifting the conscience of the witness, but of compelling him to stand face to face with the jury in order that they may look at him, and judge by his demeanor upon the stand and the manner in which he gives his testimony whether he is worthy of belief. Mattox v. United States, 156 U.S. 237, 242-243 (1895). . . .

But here's the catch, the defense basically neutralized the witness's disguise. Mr. Vasquez was the only one in the courtroom who thought he was The Phantom of the Opera. The only effect that wearing a hat and sunglasses had was to make Mr. Vasquez more comfortable on the stand and to limit the trauma he felt when testifying against someone whom he feared. This is similar to the cases cited by the parties, Coy v. Iowa, 487 U.S. 1012 (1988), and Maryland v. Craig, 497 U.S. 836 (1990), in which measures were used to prevent face-to-face contact between the defendant and the witness in order to prevent trauma to the victims. However, unlike the screen in *Coy* and the closed circuit television in *Craig*, in this case, the outfit worn by Mr. Vasquez did not prevent or encroach upon face-to-face contact between the defendant and the witness.

Attorneys often change the appearance of witnesses appearing in court. Drunks are sobered up, addicts are cleaned up, and the homeless are dressed up; prostitutes even appear in business suits. These modifications are intended to persuade the jury that the witness is reliable. Mr. Vasquez's additions were not intended to fool the jury. Rather it was simply a method to allay his fears about testifying. Nothing was compromised — just slightly camouflaged.

I agree with the trial court's decision to allow the witness to appear as secret agent man. Therefore, I respectfully dissent.

HOLCOMB, J., dissenting.

. . . After considering the record and the arguments of the parties, I conclude that an important state interest is implicated in this case. On this record, the trial court could have reasonably concluded that Vasquez's disguise was necessary to further the important state interest in protecting the physical well-being of witnesses who have a well-founded fear of retaliation on the part of the defendant. Vasquez testified that he witnessed appellant engage in an unprovoked, determined, and lethal attack on a nightclub in Houston. Vasquez also [remarked] about how appellant was looking at him in the courtroom, apparently in a threatening manner. On this record, the trial court could have reasonably concluded that Vasquez reasonably believed appellant was a dangerous person, possibly a sociopath, and that Vasquez had a well-founded fear of retaliation on appellant's part. The fact that the trial court made no such finding on the record is not determinative. Nothing in Maryland v. Craig requires that a trial court make explicit, as opposed to implicit, findings regarding the necessity of a special procedure to protect a witness. . . .

Finally, I conclude that the reliability of Vasquez's testimony was otherwise assured, because (1) both parties were aware of his name and residence address, i.e., he was not an anonymous witness; (2) he testified in the courtroom and under oath, thus impressing him with the seriousness of the matter and the possibility of a penalty for perjury; (3) he was able to see appellant's face in the courtroom, thus reducing the risk that he would wrongfully implicate an innocent person; (4) he was subject to cross-examination; and (5) the jury was able to hear his voice and observe his overall demeanor.

Undoubtedly, the Sixth Amendment does not always require that the jurors have the ability to see the witness's eyes or see his mouth move as he talks. In some situations, for example, a witness may be blind and may wear sunglasses over his sightless eyes; in other situations, a witness may testify in sign language. In my view, the Sixth Amendment was satisfied in this case. . . .

■ DÉSIRÉ DOORSON v. NETHERLANDS

22 Eur. Ct. H.R. 330 (1996)

In August 1987 the prosecuting authorities decided to take action against the nuisance caused by drug trafficking in Amsterdam.* The police compiled photographs of persons suspected of being drug dealers, and showed the photos to about 150 drug addicts to collect statements from them. However, most of the witnesses were only prepared to make statements on condition that their identity was not disclosed to the drug dealers they identified. Witnesses who had testified during a similar enforcement effort in 1986 had received threats.

In September 1987 the police received information from a drug addict that Doorson was engaged in drug trafficking. The police then included a 1985 photograph of Doorson in the collection of photographs they showed to other drug addicts. A number of addicts recognized Doorson from his photograph and told police that he had sold drugs. Six of these drug addicts remained anonymous; they were referred to by the police under the code names Y05, Y06, Y13, Y14, Y15 and Y16. The identity of two others was disclosed, namely R and N.

On 12 April 1988 Doorson was arrested on suspicion of having committed drug offenses. During the preliminary judicial investigation, Doorson's lawyer requested an examination of the witnesses referred to in the police report. The investigating judge ordered the police to bring these witnesses before him on 30 May 1988 between 09.30 and 16.00. Doorson's lawyer was notified and invited to attend the questioning of these witnesses before the investigating judge.

On 30 May 1988 Doorson's lawyer arrived at the investigating judge's chambers at 09.30. However, after an hour and a half had elapsed and none of the witnesses had appeared, he concluded that no questioning would take place. The attorney left for another appointment, after the judge promised him that if the witnesses should turn up later that day, they would not be heard but would be required to appear for questioning at a later date so that he would be able to attend. After the lawyer had left, two of the eight witnesses referred to in the police report turned up and were heard by the investigating judge in the absence of the lawyer, witness Y15 at about 11.15 and witness Y16 at about 15.00. Y15 and Y16 did not keep a promise to return for further questioning on 3 June.

In proceedings before the Regional Court, the named witness N appeared, but R did not. Both the prosecution and the defense were given the opportunity to put questions to N. Asked to identify Doorson, N stated that he did not recognize him. On being shown Doorson's photograph, he said that he recognized it as that of a man who had given him heroin when he was ill. However, towards the end of his examination he stated that he was no longer quite sure of recognizing the man in the photograph; it might be that the man who had given him the heroin only resembled that man. He also claimed that when shown the photographs by the police, he had only identified Doorson's photograph as that of a person from whom he had bought drugs because at the time he had felt very ill and had been afraid that the police might not give him back the drugs which they had found in his possession.

* [Material in this opinion preceding paragraph 53 has been edited without indication. — Eds.]

After the Regional Court convicted Doorson of drug trafficking and sentenced him to 15 months' imprisonment, he appealed to the Amsterdam Court of Appeal. Doorson's lawyer requested the procurator general of the Court of Appeal to summon the anonymous witnesses and the named witnesses N and R for questioning at that Court's hearing. The procurator general replied that he would summon N and R but not the anonymous witnesses, because he wished to preserve their anonymity.

The Court of Appeal decided to verify the necessity of maintaining the anonymity of the witnesses and referred the case back to the investigating judge for this purpose. The Court of Appeal also requested the investigating judge to examine the witnesses — after deciding whether their anonymity should be preserved or not — and to offer Doorson's lawyer the opportunity both to attend this examination and to put questions to the witnesses.

On 14 February 1990 the investigating judge heard the witnesses Y15 and Y16 in the presence of Doorson's lawyer. The lawyer was given the opportunity to put questions to the witnesses but was not informed of their identity. The identity of both witnesses was known to the investigating judge.

Both witnesses expressed the wish to remain anonymous and not to appear in court. Witness Y16 stated that he had in the past suffered injuries at the hands of another drug dealer after he had cooperated with the police, and he feared similar reprisals from Doorson. Witness Y15 stated that he had in the past been threatened by drug dealers if he were to talk. He also said that Doorson was aggressive. The investigating judge concluded that both witnesses had sufficient reason to wish to maintain their anonymity and not to appear in open court.

At its next hearing on the case, the Court of Appeal heard the witness N in Doorson's presence and his lawyer was given the opportunity to question the witness. N said that his statement to the police had been untrue and that he did not in fact know Doorson. The named witness R was initially present at these proceedings. Before he was heard, he asked the Court usher who was guarding him for permission to leave for a minute; he then disappeared and could not be found again.

The Court of Appeal decided to refer the case once again back to the investigating judge, requesting her to record her findings as to the reliability of the witnesses Y15 and Y16. On 19 November 1990 the investigating judge drew up a record of her findings regarding the reliability of the statements made to her by Y15 and Y16 on 14 February 1990. She stated in this document that she could not remember the faces of the two witnesses but, having re-read the records of the interrogations, could recall more or less what had happened. She had the impression that both witnesses knew whom they were talking about and had identified Doorson's photograph without hesitation. As far as she remembered, both witnesses had answered all questions readily and without hesitating, although they had made a "somewhat sleepy impression."

On 6 December 1990, the Court of Appeal found Doorson guilty of the deliberate sale of quantities of heroin and cocaine. As regards Doorson's complaint that the majority of the witnesses had not been heard in the presence of Doorson or his lawyer, the Court stated that it had based its conviction on evidence given by the witnesses N, R, Y15 and Y16. Doorson brought this appeal to the European Court of Human Rights.

53. The applicant alleged that the taking of, hearing of and reliance on evidence from certain witnesses during the criminal proceedings against him

infringed the rights of the defence, in violation of Article 6(1) and (3)(d) of the Convention, which provide as follows:

> 1. In the determination . . . of any criminal charge against him, everyone is entitled to a fair . . . hearing [by an] impartial tribunal. . . .
>
> 3. Everyone charged with a criminal offence has the following minimum rights: . . . (d) to examine or have examined witnesses against him and to obtain the attendance and examination of witnesses on his behalf under the same conditions as witnesses against him. . . .

54. The applicant claimed in the first place that, in obtaining the statements of the anonymous witnesses Y15 and Y16, the rights of the defence had been infringed to such an extent that the reliance on those statements by the Amsterdam Court of Appeal was incompatible with the standards of a "fair" trial. . . .

Although he conceded that in the course of the appeal proceedings Y15 and Y16 had been questioned by [the Investigating Judge] in the presence of his Counsel and had identified him from a photograph taken several years previously, that was not a proper substitute for a confrontation with him in person. Not knowing the identity of the persons concerned, he could not himself cross-examine them to test their credibility. Nor could the possibility of mistakes be ruled out. It would, in his submission, have been possible to examine the witnesses in his presence, protecting them, if need be, by the use of disguise, voice-distorting equipment or a two-way mirror.

In fact, he questioned the need for maintaining the anonymity of Y15 and Y16 at all. Both had stated before the investigating judge that they feared reprisals but there was nothing to suggest that they were ever subjected to, or for that matter threatened with, violence at the hands of the applicant. Moreover, the basis of the investigating judge's assessment of the need for anonymity was not made clear to the defence. . . .

55. In the second place, the applicant complained about the reliance on the evidence of the named witness R. Although R had been brought to the hearing of the Court of Appeal for questioning, he had — in the applicant's submission — been allowed to abscond under circumstances which engaged the Court of Appeal's responsibility. . . . Since he — the applicant — had not been able to cross-examine R, his statement to the police should not have been admitted as evidence. . . .

67. The Court of Appeal had been entitled to consider the reliability of the statements of Y15 and Y16 sufficiently corroborated by the findings of the investigating judge, as officially recorded on 19 November 1990, and by the statement in open court of the [investigating police officer] that the witnesses in the case had been under no constraint. In any case, the Court of Appeal had noted in its judgment that it had made use of the anonymous statements with "the necessary caution and circumspection." . . .

69. As the Court has held on previous occasions, the Convention does not preclude reliance, at the investigation stage, on sources such as anonymous informants. The subsequent use of their statements by the trial court to found a conviction is however capable of raising issues under the Convention. See Kostovski v. Netherlands, 12 Eur. Ct. H.R. 344 (1990).

[Under the *Kostovski* judgment, the use of statements by anonymous witnesses is acceptable when the statement is taken down by a judge who (a) is aware of the identity of the witness, (b) has expressed, in the official record of the hearing of such a witness, his reasoned opinion as to the reliability of the witness and as to the reasons for the witness's wish to remain anonymous, and (c) has provided the defence with some opportunity to put questions or have questions put to the witness. This rule is subject to exceptions; thus, according to the same judgment, the statement of an anonymous witness may be used in evidence despite the absence of the safeguards mentioned above if (a) the defence has not at any stage of the proceedings asked to be allowed to question the witness concerned, and (b) the conviction is based to a significant extent on other evidence not derived from anonymous sources, and (c) the trial court makes it clear that it has made use of the statement of the anonymous witness with caution and circumspection.]

70. It is true that Article 6 does not explicitly require the interests of witnesses in general, and those of victims called upon to testify in particular, to be taken into consideration. However, their life, liberty or security of person may be at stake, as may interests coming generally within the ambit of Article 8 of the Convention.* Such interests of witnesses and victims are in principle protected by other, substantive provisions of the Convention, which imply that Contracting States should organise their criminal proceedings in such a way that those interests are not unjustifiably imperilled. Against this background, principles of fair trial also require that in appropriate cases the interests of the defence are balanced against those of witnesses or victims called upon to testify.

71. As the Amsterdam Court of Appeal made clear, its decision not to disclose the identity of Y15 and Y16 to the defence was inspired by the need, as assessed by it, to obtain evidence from them while at the same time protecting them against the possibility of reprisals by the applicant. . . .

Although, as the applicant has stated, there has been no suggestion that Y15 and Y16 were ever threatened by the applicant himself, the decision to maintain their anonymity cannot be regarded as unreasonable per se. Regard must be had to the fact, as established by the domestic courts and not contested by the applicant, that drug dealers frequently resorted to threats or actual violence against persons who gave evidence against them. Furthermore, the statements made by the witnesses concerned to the investigating judge show that one of them had apparently on a previous occasion suffered violence at the hands of a drug dealer against whom he had testified, while the other had been threatened. In sum, there was sufficient reason for maintaining the anonymity of Y15 and Y16. . . .

73. In the instant case the anonymous witnesses were questioned at the appeals stage in the presence of Counsel by an investigating judge who was aware of their identity, even if the defence was not. . . . In this respect the present case is to be distinguished from that of *Kostovski.* Counsel was not only present, but he was put in a position to ask the witnesses whatever questions he considered to be in the interests of the defence except in so far as they might lead to the disclosure of their identity, and these questions were all answered. . . .

* [Article 8 provides: "Everyone has the right to respect for his private and family life, his home and his correspondence." — EDS.]

74. While it would clearly have been preferable for the applicant to have attended the questioning of the witnesses, the Court considers, on balance, that the Amsterdam Court of Appeal was entitled to consider that the interests of the applicant were in this respect outweighed by the need to ensure the safety of the witnesses. More generally, the Convention does not preclude identification — for the purposes of Article 6(3)(d) — of an accused with his Counsel. . . .

76. Finally, it should be recalled that, even when "counterbalancing" procedures are found to compensate sufficiently the handicaps under which the defence labours, a conviction should not be based either solely or to a decisive extent on anonymous statements. That, however, is not the case here: it is sufficiently clear that the national court did not base its finding of guilt solely or to a decisive extent on the evidence of Y15 and Y16.

Furthermore, evidence obtained from witnesses under conditions in which the rights of the defence cannot be secured to the extent normally required by the Convention should be treated with extreme care. The Court is satisfied that this was done in the criminal proceedings leading to the applicant's conviction, as is reflected in the express declaration by the Court of Appeal that it had treated the statements of Y15 and Y16 "with the necessary caution and circumspection." . . .

83. None of the alleged shortcomings considered on their own lead the Court to conclude that the applicant did not receive a fair trial. Moreover, it cannot find, even if the alleged shortcomings are considered together, that the proceedings as a whole were unfair. In arriving at this conclusion the Court has taken into account the fact that the domestic courts were entitled to consider the various items of evidence before them as corroborative of each other. . . . For these reasons, the Court holds, by seven votes to two, that there has been no violation of Article 6(1) taken together with Article 6(3)(d) of the Convention. . . .

RYSSDAL, J., dissenting.

It is not only in drug cases that problems may arise in relation to the safety of witnesses. It is not permissible to resolve such problems by departing from such a fundamental principle as the one that witness evidence challenged by the accused cannot be admitted against him if he has not had an opportunity to examine or have examined, in his presence, the witness in question.

In the instant case the applicant had this opportunity in respect of witness N, who withdrew his earlier statement. The applicant did not have such an opportunity in relation to witness R, who "disappeared," or witnesses Y15 and Y16, who were heard only in the presence of his lawyer. Moreover, Y15 and Y16 were anonymous witnesses whose identity was only known to the investigating judge but not to the applicant and his lawyer, nor to the Regional Court and the Court of Appeal.

Notes

1. *Anonymous witnesses: majority position.* In the United States, a witness is usually required to divulge both his name and address on cross-examination. This is said to allow the defendant to put the witness in a "proper setting" and to test the witness's credibility. See Smith v. Illinois, 390 U.S. 129 (1968). At the same time, the right to cross-examine prosecution witnesses about their identities or addresses is not considered absolute, and a trial court has discretion to restrict cross-examination on

such topics if there is an adequate showing that the safety of the witness is at risk. Alvarado v. Superior Court, 5 P.3d 203 (Cal. 2000) (prosecution may not permanently withhold identities of key witnesses; although disclosure may be delayed until trial, safety concerns of prisoner-witnesses must be addressed by means less drastic than anonymous testimony if testimony is crucial to prosecution's case); State v. Vandebogart, 652 A.2d 671 (N.H. 1994) (witness allowed not to reveal address; she was victim of prior assault by defendant). Recall also that the government often may shield the identity of "confidential informants" during the investigation stage.

Courts in a number of nations have upheld convictions based on the testimony of "anonymous witnesses." Legislation in some nations (such as New Zealand) allows undercover police officers to testify without revealing their identities. The general trend has been to allow the use of anonymous witnesses only when accompanied by the sort of safeguards described in the *Doorson* opinion from the European Court of Human Rights. As European nations move toward more of a hybrid between common law and civil law processes (and thus a hybrid between adversarial and inquisitorial development of proof), will they become less likely to rely on devices such as anonymous witnesses?

2. *The value of comparative law.* The concept of confronting witnesses is a familiar one even in civil law legal systems, which are based on an "inquisitorial" model of factfinding (in which the judge takes responsibility for developing facts) rather than an "adversarial" model (in which the parties present their own facts and take responsibility for testing the factual claims of their adversaries). But the confrontation rights of defendants in civil law systems do not exactly track the confrontation rights of defendants in U.S. courts. Do the practices and values of European criminal justice systems have any relevance for American lawyers, legislators, or judges? See Diane Marie Amann, Harmonic Convergence? Constitutional Criminal Procedure in an International Context, 75 Ind. L.J. 809 (2000).

3. *Confrontation of child witnesses: majority position.* Under the federal constitution, some witnesses may testify outside the courtroom and outside the presence of the defendant if the defendant is able to monitor the testimony and communicate with the defense attorney conducting the cross-examination. According to Maryland v. Craig, 497 U.S. 836 (1990), the trial court must make a case-specific finding that the witness would suffer from extreme emotional trauma during traditional testimony that would prevent the witness from reasonably communicating. The *Craig* Court distinguished Coy v. Iowa, 487 U.S. 1012 (1988), which struck down a statute protecting child witnesses without an individualized assessment of the potential trauma to the child.

Most high state courts to address this issue (more than 25) follow the federal position and allow prosecuting witnesses to testify outside the courtroom (and outside the defendant's physical presence) so long as the arrangement is "necessary to further an important public policy" and "the reliability of the testimony is otherwise assured." People v. Wrotten, 923 N.E.2d 1099 (N.Y. 2009) (two-way video testimony authorized by statute for child witnesses and within inherent authority of trial judge for other witnesses, based on finding of necessity). The cases often require that the defendant be able to monitor the cross-examination from a remote location or from a hidden or screened location in the room. Another group of high state courts (fewer than 10) have concluded that the defendant must be present (and visible to the witness) during the direct testimony and cross-examination. See People v. Fitzpatrick,

633 N.E.2d 685 (Ill. 1994) (striking down statute that allowed cross-examination on closed-circuit television).

The states departing from the federal position, by and large, are those with specific "face to face" provisions in their state constitutions. Almost 30 state constitutions track the language of the Sixth Amendment to the federal constitution and speak of the right of the accused to be "confronted" with adverse witnesses. About 20 state constitutions mention a defendant's right to meet adverse witnesses "face to face." For a sampling of the state court rulings and statutes on this topic, go to the web extension for this chapter at *http://www.crimpro.com/extension/ch18*.

Which of the various elements of the classic courtroom confrontation create more reliable testimony? Does it matter that the testimony takes place during trial rather than during an earlier deposition? Does it matter whether the testimony takes place in a courtroom? Note that the statute described in Problem 18-5 required a video image of the defendant to be present during the testimony. Would a cardboard cutout image of the defendant suffice?

4. *Reliability of out-of-court statements by child witnesses.* Social science and psychology researchers have explored at great length the factors associated most strongly with reliable and unreliable child testimony. As one might expect, older children are more reliable witnesses than younger children. Young children depend more heavily than older children on "recognition memory" (responding to specific questions about an event rather than volunteering information in response to a general question). Suggestive questioning is more likely to influence younger children, and small differences in age can mean large differences in reliability. The number of times a child is questioned before trial also affects reliability. See Stephen Ceci & Maggie Bruck, Suggestibility of the Child Witness: A Historical Review and Synthesis, 113 Psychol. Bull. 403 (1993). Contrary to expectations, promptness in coming forward with an accusation or consistency in the details of a story is not a good indicator of a reliable child witness.

5. *Defendant's presence at trial.* Both federal and state courts have concluded that defendants have a right, both under confrontation clauses and due process clauses, to be present at "every stage" of the trial. Does a defendant waive the right to be present during the trial by engaging in disruptive behavior? See Illinois v. Allen, 397 U.S. 337 (1970) (no constitutional error to remove defendant from courtroom after repeated outbursts, if defendant is allowed to return to courtroom after promise of better behavior). By escaping from jail before trial? Crosby v. United States, 506 U.S. 255 (1993) (interpreting Fed. R. Crim. P. 43 to prevent trial in absentia of defendant who escapes jail before trial begins, but to allow such trials for defendants who escape after trial has begun). By failing to appear on the day set for trial after being released before trial? See People v. Johnston, 513 N.E.2d 528 (Ill. 1987) (failure to appear at trial, after appearing at pretrial hearing, is waiver of right to be present).

6. *Victims and sequestration of witnesses.* A traditional rule of evidence allows a party to insist that the judge exclude a witness from the courtroom until that witness has testified. This rule of "sequestration of witnesses" makes cross-examination more effective because it prevents the witness from changing her testimony to remain consistent with (or to rebut) the evidence presented up until that time. The judge's power to exclude witnesses existed at common law, and many states now have rules of evidence codifying this discretionary rule. Others, such as Fed. R. Evid. 615, give the parties an absolute right to exclude a witness; the judge has no discretion on the question for most witnesses.

The sequestration rule sometimes conflicts with the notion that the victim of an alleged crime has a special interest in attending a trial. Consider the following typical effort to reconcile these competing principles, contained in Utah R. Evid. 615(1):

> At the request of a party the court shall order witnesses excluded so that they cannot hear the testimony of other witnesses, and it may make the order on its own motion. This rule does not authorize exclusion of . . . a victim in a criminal trial or juvenile delinquency proceeding where the prosecutor agrees with the victim's presence.

Compare Mich. Comp. Laws §780.761(11) ("The victim has the right to be present throughout the entire trial of the defendant, unless the victim is going to be called as a witness. If the victim is going to be called as a witness, the court may, for good cause shown, order the victim to be sequestered until the victim first testifies"). Under these rules and statutes, does the victim now have a right to presence at trial comparable to the defendant's right to be present? Does the presence of the victim in the courtroom influence other witnesses as they testify (creating a sort of "confrontation" right for a crime victim)?

2. *Unavailable Prosecution Witnesses*

How can a defendant confront the person who accuses her if the accuser is not present in the courtroom? There may be many reasons for a witness or victim's absence from the courtroom. For the most part, the law of evidence dictates when statements made by unavailable witnesses will be admitted at trial. There is, however, a constitutional component to these questions as well. The two cases below deal with statements made to the police by a person other than the accused who was not available to testify at trial. Such statements raise the question whether the defendant is able to "confront" her accuser.

MICHAEL CRAWFORD v. WASHINGTON

541 U.S. 36 (2004)

SCALIA, J.*

Petitioner Michael Crawford stabbed a man who allegedly tried to rape his wife, Sylvia. At his trial, the State played for the jury Sylvia's tape-recorded statement to the police describing the stabbing, even though he had no opportunity for cross-examination. The Washington Supreme Court upheld petitioner's conviction after determining that Sylvia's statement was reliable. The question presented is whether this procedure complied with the Sixth Amendment's guarantee that, "[in] all criminal prosecutions, the accused shall enjoy the right . . . to be confronted with the witnesses against him."

* [Justices Stevens, Kennedy, Souter, Thomas, Ginsburg, and Breyer joined this opinion. — EDS.]

I.

On August 5, 1999, Kenneth Lee was stabbed at his apartment. Police arrested petitioner later that night. After giving petitioner and his wife *Miranda* warnings, detectives interrogated each of them twice. Petitioner eventually confessed that he and Sylvia had gone in search of Lee because he was upset over an earlier incident in which Lee had tried to rape her. The two had found Lee at his apartment, and a fight ensued in which Lee was stabbed in the torso and petitioner's hand was cut. Petitioner gave the following account of the fight:

> *Q.* Okay. Did you ever see anything in [Lee's] hands?
> *A.* I think so, but I'm not positive.
> *Q.* Okay, when you think so, what do you mean by that?
> *A.* I coulda swore I seen him goin' for somethin' before, right before everything happened. He was like reachin', fiddlin' around down here and stuff . . . and I just . . . I don't know, I think, this is just a possibility, but I think, I think that he pulled somethin' out and I grabbed for it and that's how I got cut . . . but I'm not positive. . . .

Sylvia generally corroborated petitioner's story about the events leading up to the fight, but her account of the fight itself was arguably different — particularly with respect to whether Lee had drawn a weapon before petitioner assaulted him:

> *Q.* Did Kenny do anything to fight back from this assault?
> *A.* (pausing) I know he reached into his pocket . . . or somethin' . . . I don't know what.
> *Q.* After he was stabbed? . . .
> *A.* Okay, he lifted his hand over his head maybe to strike Michael's hand down or something and then he put his hands in his . . . put his right hand in his right pocket . . . took a step back . . . Michael proceeded to stab him . . . then his hands were like . . . how do you explain this . . . open arms . . . with his hands open and he fell down . . . and we ran (describing subject holding hands open, palms toward assailant).
> *Q.* Okay, when he's standing there with his open hands, you're talking about Kenny, correct?
> *A.* Yeah, after, after the fact, yes.
> *Q.* Did you see anything in his hands at that point?
> *A.* (pausing) um um (no).

The State charged petitioner with assault and attempted murder. At trial, he claimed self-defense. Sylvia did not testify because of the state marital privilege, which generally bars a spouse from testifying without the other spouse's consent. In Washington, this privilege does not extend to a spouse's out-of-court statements admissible under a hearsay exception, so the State sought to introduce Sylvia's tape-recorded statements to the police as evidence that the stabbing was not in self-defense. Noting that Sylvia had admitted she led petitioner to Lee's apartment and thus had facilitated the assault, the State invoked the hearsay exception for statements against penal interest, Wash. Rule Evid. 804(b)(3).

Petitioner countered that, state law notwithstanding, admitting the evidence would violate his federal constitutional right to be "confronted with the witnesses against him." According to our description of that right in Ohio v. Roberts, 448 U.S. 56 (1980), it does not bar admission of an unavailable witness's statement against a criminal defendant if the statement bears "adequate indicia of reliability." To meet that test, evidence must either fall within a "firmly rooted hearsay exception" or bear "particularized guarantees of trustworthiness." The trial court here admitted the statement on the latter ground, offering several reasons why it was trustworthy: Sylvia was not shifting blame but rather corroborating her husband's story that he acted in self-defense or "justified reprisal"; she had direct knowledge as an eyewitness; she was describing recent events; and she was being questioned by a "neutral" law enforcement officer. The prosecution played the tape for the jury and relied on it in closing, arguing that it was "damning evidence" that "completely refutes [petitioner's] claim of self-defense." The jury convicted petitioner of assault.

The Washington Court of Appeals reversed. It applied a nine-factor test to determine whether Sylvia's statement bore particularized guarantees of trustworthiness, and noted several reasons why it did not: The statement contradicted one she had previously given; it was made in response to specific questions; and at one point she admitted she had shut her eyes during the stabbing. . . . The Washington Supreme Court reinstated the conviction [and we] granted certiorari to determine whether the State's use of Sylvia's statement violated the Confrontation Clause.

II.

The Sixth Amendment's Confrontation Clause provides that, "[in] all criminal prosecutions, the accused shall enjoy the right . . . to be confronted with the witnesses against him." . . . Petitioner argues that [the *Roberts*] test strays from the original meaning of the Confrontation Clause and urges us to reconsider it.

The Constitution's text does not alone resolve this case. One could plausibly read "witnesses against" a defendant to mean those who actually testify at trial, those whose statements are offered at trial, or something in-between. We must therefore turn to the historical background of the Clause to understand its meaning.

The right to confront one's accusers is a concept that dates back to Roman times. The founding generation's immediate source of the concept, however, was the common law. English common law has long differed from continental civil law in regard to the manner in which witnesses give testimony in criminal trials. The common-law tradition is one of live testimony in court subject to adversarial testing, while the civil law condones examination in private by judicial officers.

Nonetheless, England at times adopted elements of the civil-law practice. Justices of the peace or other officials examined suspects and witnesses before trial. These examinations were sometimes read in court in lieu of live testimony. . . . The most notorious instances of civil-law examination occurred in the great political trials of the 16th and 17th centuries. One such was the 1603 trial of Sir Walter Raleigh for treason. Lord Cobham, Raleigh's alleged accomplice, had implicated him in an examination before the Privy Council and in a letter. At Raleigh's trial, these were read to the jury. Raleigh argued that Cobham had lied to save himself: "Cobham is absolutely in the King's mercy; to excuse me cannot avail him; by accusing me he may hope for favour." 1 D. Jardine, Criminal Trials 435 (1832). Suspecting that Cobham would recant, Raleigh demanded that the judges call him to appear, arguing that "[the] Proof of the Common Law is by witness and jury: let Cobham be here, let him speak it. Call my accuser before my face. . . ." The judges refused, and, despite Raleigh's protestations that he was being tried "by the Spanish Inquisition," the jury convicted, and Raleigh was sentenced to death. . . .

Through a series of statutory and judicial reforms, English law developed a right of confrontation that limited these abuses. For example, treason statutes required witnesses to confront the accused "face to face" at his arraignment. Courts, meanwhile, developed relatively strict rules of unavailability, admitting examinations only if the witness was demonstrably unable to testify in person. Several authorities also stated that a suspect's confession could be admitted only against himself, and not against others he implicated.

One recurring question was whether the admissibility of an unavailable witness's pretrial examination depended on whether the defendant had had an opportunity to cross-examine him. In 1696, the Court of King's Bench answered this question in the affirmative, in the widely reported misdemeanor libel case of King v. Paine, 87 Eng. Rep. 584. The court ruled that, even though a witness was dead, his examination was not admissible where "the defendant not being present when [it was] taken before the mayor . . . had lost the benefit of a cross-examination." . . .

Controversial examination practices were also used in the Colonies. . . . A decade before the Revolution, England gave jurisdiction over Stamp Act offenses to the admiralty courts, which followed civil-law rather than common-law procedures and thus routinely took testimony by deposition or private judicial examination. Colonial representatives protested that the Act subverted their rights "by extending the jurisdiction of the courts of admiralty beyond its ancient limits." John Adams, defending a merchant in a high-profile admiralty case, argued: "Examinations of witnesses upon Interrogatories, are only by the Civil Law. Interrogatories are unknown at common Law, and Englishmen and common Lawyers have an aversion to them if not an Abhorrence of them."

Many declarations of rights adopted around the time of the Revolution guaranteed a right of confrontation. The proposed Federal Constitution, however, did not. At the Massachusetts ratifying convention, Abraham Holmes objected to this omission precisely on the ground that it would lead to civil-law practices: "The mode of trial is altogether indetermined; . . . whether [the defendant] is to be allowed to confront the witnesses, and have the advantage of cross-examination, we are not yet told. [We] shall find Congress possessed of powers enabling them to institute judicatories little less inauspicious than a certain tribunal in Spain, . . . the *Inquisition.*" 2 Debates on the Federal Constitution 110-111 (J. Elliot 2d ed. 1863). . . . The First Congress responded by including the Confrontation Clause in the proposal that became the Sixth Amendment. Early state decisions shed light upon the original understanding of the common-law right. State v. Webb, 2 N.C. 103 (1794) (per curiam), decided a mere three years after the adoption of the Sixth Amendment, held that depositions could be read against an accused only if they were taken in his presence. . . .

III.

This history supports two inferences about the meaning of the Sixth Amendment. . . . First, the principal evil at which the Confrontation Clause was directed was the civil-law mode of criminal procedure, and particularly its use of *ex parte* examinations as evidence against the accused. It was these practices that the Crown deployed in notorious treason cases like Raleigh's; . . . that English law's assertion of a right to confrontation was meant to prohibit; and that the founding-era rhetoric decried. The Sixth Amendment must be interpreted with this focus in mind.

Accordingly, we once again reject the view that the Confrontation Clause applies of its own force only to in-court testimony, and that its application to out-of-court statements introduced at trial depends upon "the law of Evidence for the time being." Leaving the regulation of out-of-court statements to the law of evidence would render the Confrontation Clause powerless to prevent even the most flagrant inquisitorial practices. Raleigh was, after all, perfectly free to confront those who read Cobham's confession in court.

This focus also suggests that not all hearsay implicates the Sixth Amendment's core concerns. An off-hand, overheard remark might be unreliable evidence and thus a good candidate for exclusion under hearsay rules, but it bears little resemblance to the civil-law abuses the Confrontation Clause targeted. On the other hand, *ex parte* examinations might sometimes be admissible under modern hearsay rules, but the Framers certainly would not have condoned them.

The text of the Confrontation Clause reflects this focus. It applies to "witnesses" against the accused — in other words, those who "bear testimony." 1 N. Webster, An American Dictionary of the English Language (1828). "Testimony," in turn, is typically "[a] solemn declaration or affirmation made for the purpose of establishing or proving some fact." An accuser who makes a formal statement to government officers bears testimony in a sense that a person who makes a casual remark to an acquaintance does not. The constitutional text, like the history underlying the common-law right of confrontation, thus reflects an especially acute concern with a specific type of out-of-court statement. . . .

Regardless of the precise [definition of testimonial statements], some statements qualify under any definition — for example, *ex parte* testimony at a preliminary hearing. Statements taken by police officers in the course of interrogations are also testimonial under even a narrow standard. Police interrogations bear a striking resemblance to examinations by justices of the peace in England. . . . In sum, even if the Sixth Amendment is not solely concerned with testimonial hearsay, that is its primary object, and interrogations by law enforcement officers fall squarely within that class.[4] . . .

The historical record also supports a second proposition: that the Framers would not have allowed admission of testimonial statements of a witness who did not appear at trial unless he was unavailable to testify, and the defendant had had a prior opportunity for cross-examination. The text of the Sixth Amendment does not suggest any open-ended exceptions from the confrontation requirement to be developed by the courts. Rather, the "right . . . to be confronted with the witnesses against him," is most naturally read as a reference to the right of confrontation at common law, admitting only those exceptions established at the time of the founding. As the English authorities above reveal, the common law in 1791 conditioned admissibility of an absent witness's examination on unavailability and a prior

4. We use the term "interrogation" in its colloquial, rather than any technical legal, sense. Cf. Rhode Island v. Innis, 446 U.S. 291 (1980). Just as various definitions of "testimonial" exist, one can imagine various definitions of "interrogation," and we need not select among them in this case. Sylvia's recorded statement, knowingly given in response to structured police questioning, qualifies under any conceivable definition.

opportunity to cross-examine. The Sixth Amendment therefore incorporates those limitations. . . .

This is not to deny . . . that "[there] were always exceptions to the general rule of exclusion" of hearsay evidence. Several had become well established by 1791. But there is scant evidence that exceptions were invoked to admit *testimonial* statements against the accused in a *criminal* case.[6] Most of the hearsay exceptions covered statements that by their nature were not testimonial — for example, business records or statements in furtherance of a conspiracy. . . .

V.

Roberts conditions the admissibility of all hearsay evidence on whether it falls under a "firmly rooted hearsay exception" or bears "particularized guarantees of trustworthiness." This test departs from the historical principles identified above in two respects. First, it is too broad: It applies the same mode of analysis whether or not the hearsay consists of *ex parte* testimony. This often results in close constitutional scrutiny in cases that are far removed from the core concerns of the Clause. At the same time, however, the test is too narrow: It admits statements that *do* consist of *ex parte* testimony upon a mere finding of reliability. This malleable standard often fails to protect against paradigmatic confrontation violations. . . .

Where testimonial statements are involved, we do not think the Framers meant to leave the Sixth Amendment's protection to the vagaries of the rules of evidence, much less to amorphous notions of "reliability." . . . To be sure, the Clause's ultimate goal is to ensure reliability of evidence, but it is a procedural rather than a substantive guarantee. It commands, not that evidence be reliable, but that reliability be assessed in a particular manner: by testing in the crucible of cross-examination. . . .

The Raleigh trial itself involved the very sorts of reliability determinations that *Roberts* authorizes. In the face of Raleigh's repeated demands for confrontation, the prosecution responded with many of the arguments a court applying *Roberts* might invoke today: that Cobham's statements were self-inculpatory, that they were not made in the heat of passion, and that they were not "extracted from [him] upon any hopes or promise of Pardon." It is not plausible that the Framers' only objection to the trial was that Raleigh's judges did not properly weigh these factors before sentencing him to death. Rather, the problem was that the judges refused to allow Raleigh to confront Cobham in court, where he could cross-examine him and try to expose his accusation as a lie.

Dispensing with confrontation because testimony is obviously reliable is akin to dispensing with jury trial because a defendant is obviously guilty. This is not what the Sixth Amendment prescribes. . . .

The legacy of *Roberts* in other courts vindicates the Framers' wisdom in rejecting a general reliability exception. . . . Reliability is an amorphous, if not entirely subjective, concept. There are countless factors bearing on whether a statement is reliable; the nine-factor balancing test applied by the Court of Appeals below is representative. See, e.g., People v. Farrell, 34 P.3d 401 (Colo. 2001) (eight-factor

6. The one deviation we have found involves dying declarations. . . . Although many dying declarations may not be testimonial, there is authority for admitting even those that clearly are. We need not decide in this case whether the Sixth Amendment incorporates an exception for testimonial dying declarations. If this exception must be accepted on historical grounds, it is *sui generis*.

test). Whether a statement is deemed reliable depends heavily on which factors the judge considers and how much weight he accords each of them. Some courts wind up attaching the same significance to opposite facts. . . .

Roberts' failings were on full display in the proceedings below. Sylvia Crawford made her statement while in police custody, herself a potential suspect in the case. Indeed, she had been told that whether she would be released depended on "how the investigation continues." In response to often leading questions from police detectives, she implicated her husband in Lee's stabbing and at least arguably undermined his self-defense claim. Despite all this, the trial court admitted her statement, listing several reasons why it was reliable. In its opinion reversing, the Court of Appeals listed several *other* reasons why the statement was *not* reliable. Finally, the State Supreme Court relied exclusively on the interlocking character of the statement and disregarded every other factor the lower courts had considered. The case is thus a self-contained demonstration of *Roberts'* unpredictable and inconsistent application. . . .

We have no doubt that the courts below were acting in utmost good faith when they found reliability. The Framers, however, would not have been content to indulge this assumption. They knew that judges, like other government officers, could not always be trusted to safeguard the rights of the people. . . . By replacing categorical constitutional guarantees with open-ended balancing tests, we do violence to their design. . . .

Where nontestimonial hearsay is at issue, it is wholly consistent with the Framers' design to afford the States flexibility in their development of hearsay law — as does *Roberts,* and as would an approach that exempted such statements from Confrontation Clause scrutiny altogether. Where testimonial evidence is at issue, however, the Sixth Amendment demands what the common law required: unavailability and a prior opportunity for cross-examination. We leave for another day any effort to spell out a comprehensive definition of "testimonial." Whatever else the term covers, it applies at a minimum to prior testimony at a preliminary hearing, before a grand jury, or at a former trial; and to police interrogations. These are the modern practices with closest kinship to the abuses at which the Confrontation Clause was directed. . . .

REHNQUIST, C.J., concurring in the judgment.*

I dissent from the Court's decision to overrule Ohio v. Roberts, 448 U.S. 56 (1980). I believe that the Court's adoption of a new interpretation of the Confrontation Clause is not backed by sufficiently persuasive reasoning to overrule long-established precedent. . . .

The Court's distinction between testimonial and nontestimonial statements, contrary to its claim, is no better rooted in history than our current doctrine. Under the common law, although the courts were far from consistent, out-of-court statements made by someone other than the accused and not taken under oath, unlike *ex parte* depositions or affidavits, were generally not considered substantive evidence upon which a conviction could be based. Testimonial statements such as accusatory statements to police officers likely would have been disapproved of in the 18th century, not necessarily because they resembled *ex parte* affidavits or depositions as the

* [Justice O'Connor joined this opinion. — EDS.]

Court reasons, but more likely than not because they were not made under oath. Without an oath, one usually did not get to the second step of whether confrontation was required. Thus, while I agree that the Framers were mainly concerned about sworn affidavits and depositions, it does not follow that they were similarly concerned about the Court's broader category of testimonial statements. . . .

With respect to unsworn testimonial statements, there is no indication that once the hearsay rule was developed courts ever excluded these statements if they otherwise fell within a firmly rooted exception. Dying declarations are one example. . . . It is an odd conclusion indeed to think that the Framers created a cut-and-dried rule with respect to the admissibility of testimonial statements when the law during their own time was not fully settled. . . .

Exceptions to confrontation have always been derived from the experience that some out-of-court statements are just as reliable as cross-examined in-court testimony due to the circumstances under which they were made. . . . That a statement might be testimonial does nothing to undermine the wisdom of one of these exceptions. [Cross-examination] is a tool used to flesh out the truth, not an empty procedure. In a given instance cross-examination may be "superfluous." 5 J. Wigmore, Evidence §1420, at 251 (J. Chadbourn rev. 1974).

[The] thousands of federal prosecutors and the tens of thousands of state prosecutors need answers as to what beyond the specific kinds of "testimony" the Court lists is covered by the new rule. They need them now, not months or years from now. Rules of criminal evidence are applied every day in courts throughout the country, and parties should not be left in the dark in this manner. . . .

Notes

1. *Hearsay exceptions and confrontation: majority position.* Rules of evidence in all jurisdictions exclude out-of-court hearsay statements (that is, statements made out of court by someone other than the witness, offered to prove the truth of the matter addressed in the statement) but then make exceptions to allow into evidence some of the more reliable statements. Before the Supreme Court decided *Crawford*, federal and state law allowed the government to use hearsay statements of a person who would not testify at trial so long as the evidence fell within a "firmly rooted" exception to the bar on hearsay. When no such exception was available, the confrontation clause prevented use of the evidence unless the judge found some "particularized guarantees of trustworthiness." Ohio v. Roberts, 448 U.S. 56 (1980).

Does the older "reliability" test or *Crawford*'s "testimonial" test better capture the modern-day meaning of the Sixth Amendment's text, embodying a right for a defendant "to be confronted with the witnesses against him"? In a world that relies so much on guilty pleas and so little on trials to adjudicate criminal cases, is the right to confront witnesses in the courtroom only one means to an end — reliable evidence to support a conviction?

In domestic violence cases, the government traditionally introduced into evidence a recording of the alleged victim's emergency call to the police. This happened even when the victim did not testify at trial. What other crime categories are most affected by the *Crawford* decision's application of confrontation rights to all "testimonial" evidence? For a sampling of the complex and changing case law

in the state courts on this topic, go to the web extension for this chapter at *http://www.crimpro.com/extension/ch18*.

2. *The role of timing and motives*. What sorts of prosecutions depend most heavily on "testimonial" statements and are thus most affected by *Crawford*? The timing of the statement is part of the equation, along with the purposes of the questioner. In Davis v. Washington, 547 U.S. 813 (2006), the Supreme Court evaluated, under *Crawford*, statements made to police officers during an investigation. Statements made in the course of police interrogations are not "testimonial," and hence not subject to the Confrontation Clause, if they were made under circumstances "objectively indicating" that the primary purpose of the interrogation was to enable police assistance to meet an "ongoing emergency." It is fair to assume that the motives of the police for obtaining witness statements, along with the witness's motives for providing the statements, are often mixed: they hope for immediate help to prevent an ongoing harm, and to collect evidence for prosecution of the alleged offender. Does this *Davis* test weaken the *Crawford* holding?

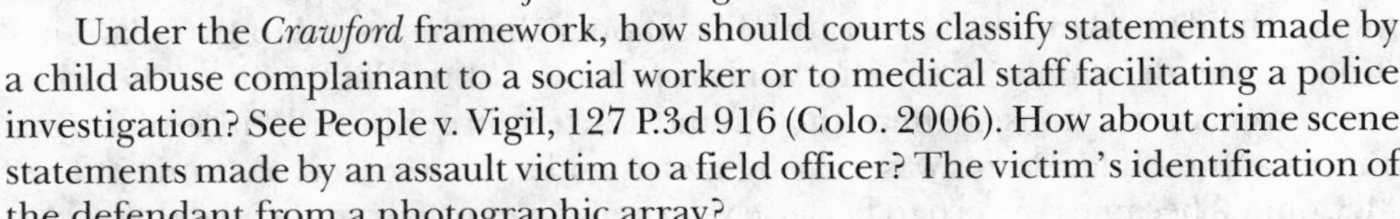

Under the *Crawford* framework, how should courts classify statements made by a child abuse complainant to a social worker or to medical staff facilitating a police investigation? See People v. Vigil, 127 P.3d 916 (Colo. 2006). How about crime scene statements made by an assault victim to a field officer? The victim's identification of the defendant from a photographic array?

3. *Scientific evidence and confrontation*. In Melendez-Diaz v. Massachusetts, 129 S. Ct. 2527 (2009), the Supreme Court decided that sworn reports of analysts for state crime laboratories, describing the results of scientific testing of the state's evidence, are "testimonial." As a result, defendants have a right under the Confrontation Clause to cross-examine the analysts, and the government cannot prove the facts relevant to the lab tests through the introduction of sworn "certificates of analysis." How might this holding influence governmental choices in funding and staffing state crime labs? How would it affect the scheduling of drunk driving cases for trial in the state courts?

4. *Forfeiture by wrongdoing*. If an out-of-court "testimonial" statement becomes unavailable as evidence when the witness is not available to testify at trial, does this give defendants an incentive to prevent prosecution witnesses from appearing at trial? Under the "forfeiture by wrongdoing" doctrine, a defendant who takes action designed to prevent the testimony of a prosecution witness at trial waives the right to confront that witness. See Giles v. California, 554 U.S. 353 (2008) (state must prove intent of defendant to prevent testimony before invoking forfeiture by wrongdoing doctrine); People v. Stechly, 870 N.E.2d 333 (Ill. 2007).

■ COMMONWEALTH v. JOHN BACIGALUPO

918 N.E.2d 51 (Mass. 2009)

COWIN, J.

The defendant and a codefendant, Gary Carter, were convicted by a jury in the Superior Court of murder in the first degree on the theory of deliberate premeditation. Both men were also convicted of two counts of armed assault with intent to murder; two counts of assault and battery by means of a dangerous weapon; one count of unlawful possession of a firearm; and one count of unlawful possession of ammunition. The defendant appeals from the convictions and from the denial of his motions for a new trial. We reverse the defendant's convictions because, in contravention of Bruton v. United States, 391 U.S. 123 (1968), the codefendant's extrajudicial confession implicating the defendant was admitted in evidence. . . .

Facts and Procedural Background

[We] summarize the evidence in the light most favorable to the Commonwealth. Two shootings occurred in the early morning of November 24, 1996: the first at Club Caravan in Revere at shortly after 1 A.M., and the second outside the Comfort Inn in Saugus at about 1:30 A.M. The two locations were only minutes apart by car at that time of night. Each of the victims of the first shooting, confederate drug dealers Charles McConnell and Vincent Portalla, survived. Robert Nogueira, Portalla's "enforcer," died in the second shooting.

Just after midnight on November 24, 1996, McConnell and Portalla were looking for the defendant and Carter to collect money that they owed to Portalla. They drove to the defendant's home in Winthrop but could not locate him. They then drove to Carter's house, where they found Carter sitting outside in a blue Ford Taurus automobile. Carter was wearing gloves and appeared nervous and "jittery." McConnell became concerned because wearing gloves usually indicated that a person is "up to something." Carter told Portalla that he had heard that Portalla was looking for him and asked if Portalla was "out to hurt [him]." Carter then told the two men to follow him, and they did so, as he drove to Club Caravan in Revere.

Outside the club, Carter and Portalla left their respective automobiles and, for approximately ten minutes, engaged in a heated discussion, which McConnell observed. Carter repeated that he had heard that Portalla had been "looking for us" and wanted to "hurt us." Portalla denied this and pulled up his shirt to indicate that he was unarmed. The men then spoke in normal tones. Shortly thereafter, the defendant "came ripping around the corner" in a black Lincoln Town Car automobile. He put on a glove and jumped out, holding a pistol. Portalla and the defendant wrestled over the gun. When the defendant's pistol discharged into the air, Portalla, who was unarmed, ran into the club. The defendant fired approximately five times at him, hitting him in the buttocks. As McConnell fled in Portalla's car, the defendant and Carter simultaneously fired at McConnell, shooting him in the back and arm. Neither McConnell nor Portalla originally identified the shooters to police. In a recorded conversation with a friend the day after the shootings, McConnell identified the defendant and Carter as his assailants. [The conversation was recorded because, unbeknownst to McConnell, his friend was a Federal government informant.]

An employee at Club Caravan ran outside immediately after the shooting. He observed a dark blue or black car going around the rotary. It was a large car, "like a Cadillac or a Continental"; he considered a Lincoln Town Car to be a Continental. When the police responded to Club Caravan, they discovered a blue Ford Taurus rental car in the parking lot. The car had been rented to Carter, and in it was a clip "fully loaded" with nine millimeter ammunition. This ammunition was of the same type as casings found at the scene of the later shooting in Saugus.

As stated, the third victim was Nogueira, Portalla's "enforcer." He "handled" Portalla's "problems," i.e., he collected the money people owed Portalla for drug purchases. Nogueira had a reputation in the community for violence and was "a dangerous guy." On the night of the shooting, Nogueira was at a Comfort Inn on the Revere-Saugus border, where he had been staying for a "good couple of weeks." At about 1 A.M., the night clerk at the Comfort Inn saw Nogueira leave the motel; the clerk heard shots immediately thereafter. Nogueira was shot twenty times.

The ballistics evidence recovered from the body of Nogueira and from the two crime scenes established that two different weapons, one revolver and one semiautomatic firearm, were used in the shootings and that one of the weapons, the semiautomatic, had been used at both locations. State police ballistics evidence indicated that a copper-jacketed bullet found in McConnell's getaway car and a full metal-jacketed bullet recovered from Nogueira's body were fired from the same weapon. Although the ballistics evidence established that a second weapon was used at each scene, no determination could be made whether the second weapon was the same one used at both scenes.

Prior to trial, the defendant moved to sever his trial from Carter's because Carter had earlier recounted to John Patti the roles that he and the defendant played in the shootings. Carter's confession to Patti implicated the defendant, and the Commonwealth planned to call Patti as a witness. The judge denied the motion but stated that, when Carter's confession was introduced, he would exclude any testimony that referred to the defendant. . . .

THE *BRUTON* ISSUE

The defendant claims that the testimony given by the witness, John Patti, recounting Carter's confession to him shortly after the shootings incriminates the defendant and violates the principle of *Bruton.* Patti's testimony on direct examination referred to the defendant solely as Carter's unnamed "friend" (in compliance with the judge's order) and included statements that the "friend" drove up to Club Caravan and got out of his car immediately before the shooting of Portalla and McConnell. In addition, on cross-examination, Patti agreed that Carter said that "Johnny" shot Nogueira at the Comfort Inn. Earlier in his testimony, Patti had referred to the defendant as "Johnny." The judge instructed emphatically that none of Carter's statements could be used against the defendant.

In *Bruton,* the United States Supreme Court reversed the defendant's conviction because the introduction of a nontestifying codefendant's confession implicating the defendant violated the defendant's right to confront the witnesses against him in contravention of the confrontation clause of the Sixth Amendment to the United States Constitution. The confession added "substantial, perhaps even critical, weight to the Government's case in a form not subject to cross-examination since [the codefendant] did not take the stand. [The defendant] was thus denied his constitutional right of confrontation." The Court also doubted that a curative instruction would alleviate the prejudice and concluded that the risk that the jury may not follow such an instruction is too great. "[We] cannot accept limiting instructions as an adequate substitute for [the defendant's] constitutional right of cross-examination. The effect is the same as if there had been no instruction at all."

The *Bruton* rule was limited by Richardson v. Marsh, 481 U.S. 200 (1987). In *Richardson,* the Court held that "the Confrontation Clause is not violated by the admission of a nontestifying codefendant's confession with a proper limiting instruction when . . . the confession is redacted to eliminate not only the defendant's name, but any reference to his or her existence."[11] The Court specifically declined to consider at that time the admissibility of a confession in which the defendant's name "has been replaced with a symbol or neutral pronoun."

The question whether the use of a symbol or neutral pronoun would violate the *Bruton* rule was resolved in Gray v. Maryland, 523 U.S. 185 (1998). In *Gray,* a nontestifying codefendant's confession was redacted by substituting the word "deleted" or "deletion" each time Gray's name appeared. The Supreme Court held that such a redacted confession was within the class of statements protected by *Bruton* and that the nonconfessing defendant's name could not be replaced with an obvious blank space, a word such as "deleted," a symbol, or other similarly conspicuous type of alteration. Because the redacted confession still referred "directly to the existence of the nonconfessing defendant" and incriminated him, the Court held that it fell within the *Bruton* rule.

Patti's reference to Carter's "friend" suggested to the jury that Carter was referring to the defendant. This implication was strengthened by the fact that only two people were on trial for the shootings that Carter said were committed by himself and a "friend." Thus, the jury logically would have inferred that the "friend" was the defendant. In addition, repeated objections by the defendant's counsel, the judge's forceful instructions that Patti's testimony did not concern the defendant, and the judge's repeated admonitions to Patti on how to respond properly to the questions (to testify only to "what . . . Carter did, not what anybody else did") only emphasized to the jury that the "friend" was indeed the defendant.[12] This is particularly so given

11. In *Richardson,* a joint murder trial of two defendants, the confession of one defendant, Williams, was redacted to omit all reference to the other codefendant, Marsh. There was no indication in the confession that anyone other than Williams and a third person took part in the crime. The jury were also instructed not to consider the confession against Marsh. As redacted, the confession indicated that only Williams and the third person had discussed the murder in the front seat of a car while driving to the victim's house. There was no suggestion in the confession that Marsh or any other person was in the back seat of the car at the time.

12. The pertinent portions of Patti's testimony are the following (emphasis added):

Q.: "What did he tell you happened?"
A.: "He said a *friend* of his came flying up in the hot box." . . .
Q.: "What did Mr. Carter tell you he did at that point in time, if anything?"
A.: "*His friend* was exiting the car that he pulled up in, the hot box. And then he tried to wave *his friend* off. He put his arms up and yelled, no, stop." . . .
Q.: "What did Mr. Carter tell you he did?"
A.: "*His friend* started — "
THE JUDGE: "No. What did Carter tell you he did."
ATTORNEY FOR DEFENDANT: "I make the same motion again."
THE JUDGE: "Overruled. Now, would you — hold it for just a minute. Let me get this straight. Do you understand his question?"
A.: "Yes."
THE JUDGE: "He's asking you what did Carter say that he did, he, Carter did, not what anybody else did, what Carter did. Do you understand that question?"
A.: "Yes, I —"
THE JUDGE: "Are you able to answer the question?"
A.: "Yeah."
THE JUDGE: "Directly?"
A.: "Yes."
THE JUDGE: "All right. Well, answer it, then."
A.: "He said he pulled his gun and started firing at Charlie."
Q.: "And do you know who Charlie is?"
A.: "Charlie McConnell."

that McConnell's earlier testimony named Carter and the defendant as the two shooters at Club Caravan. Moreover, when Carter's attorney cross-examined Patti, Patti agreed that "Johnny" shot at Nogueira at the Comfort Inn, and Patti had earlier referred in his testimony to the defendant as "Johnny."[13] Pursuant to *Gray*, nicknames fall under the rule of *Bruton* as much as full names. This reference plainly incriminated the defendant. It was just as "blatant and incriminating" as the word "deleted" in the *Gray* case. The fact that the remark was made during cross-examination by the attorney for the codefendant does not reduce its prejudicial effect on the defendant.

Other courts have similarly determined that there was a *Bruton* error in the admission of a nontestifying codefendant's accusation of a "friend." See, e.g., People v. Fletcher, 917 P.2d 187 (Cal. 1996); People v. Hernandez, 521 N.E.2d 25 (Ill. 1988). Most of these decisions preceded the United States Supreme Court's decision in *Gray*, suggesting the logic of the Supreme Court's holding in *Gray*: even if the defendant is not named, out-of-court statements that clearly refer to the defendant should not be admitted.

Having concluded that a *Bruton* error occurred, we consider the effect of this improperly admitted evidence. A *Bruton* error is one of constitutional dimension. Preserved constitutional errors are reviewed to determine whether they are harmless beyond a reasonable doubt. The essential question is whether the error had, or might have had, an effect on the jury and whether the error contributed to or might have contributed to the verdicts. . . .

McConnell, the witness whose testimony was crucial to the defendant's convictions in regard to the Revere shootings, was a convicted felon testifying pursuant to a proffer agreement with the Commonwealth. He did not name his assailants to the government until, four years after the shootings, he was in jeopardy of being charged with serious offenses. Thus, the introduction of an inadmissible confession by a codefendant, naming a "friend" as participating in the shootings, buttressed the testimony of McConnell (testimony that the jury may otherwise have rejected). Identification of one of the shooters of Nogueira as "Johnny" significantly added to the Commonwealth's case against the defendant for Nogueira's murder. Accordingly, we conclude that the error "had, or might have had," an effect on the jury; the evidence of Carter's statement implicated the defendant in each of the shootings and requires reversal of all his convictions. . . .

Notes

1. *Out-of-court statements by co-defendants: majority position.* A co-defendant who has confessed and implicated the defendant may be unavailable for testimony or

13. On cross-examination, Patti's relevant testimony was as follows:

Q.: "Okay. Sir, you told the grand jury that Johnny put his arm out the window, fired a bunch of shots at Bobby and then put two more in his head; right?"
A.: "Yes."
Q.: "That's what you told the grand jury?"
A.: "That's what he told me."
Q.: "And that's what Gary Carter told you?"
A.: "Exactly."

cross-examination at trial because of the co-defendant's privilege against self-incrimination. In Bruton v. United States, 391 U.S. 123 (1968), the Court prevented the use of the co-defendant's statement in a joint jury trial, even if the judge cautions the jury to consider the confession as evidence only against the co-defendant. When the co-defendant takes the stand at trial (and is therefore available for cross-examination), the co-defendant's confession may come into evidence.

In many trial settings, the law assumes that judicial instructions to a jury will eliminate the ill effects of the jury's exposure to prejudicial evidence. Why do the courts declare that exposure to a co-defendant statement, untested by cross-examination, is an exception to that usual approach?

2. *Redacted statements.* The decision in Gray v. Maryland, 523 U.S. 185 (1998), considered the types of redactions to a co-defendant confession that would make the statement admissible against the co-defendant in a joint trial. Redactions of a co-defendant's out-of-court statement do not comply with *Bruton* if the context makes it obvious that the statement refers to the defendant. See Jefferson v. State, 198 S.W.3d 527 (Ark. 2004) (in a case involving a small cast of characters, replacing defendant's name in co-defendant's confession did not solve *Bruton* problem). Should it matter whether the co-defendant's attorney (as opposed to the prosecutor) links the defendant to the co-defendant's out-of-court statement? For a survey of the fact-sensitive cases on this topic, go to the web extension for this chapter at *http://www.crimpro.com/extension/ch18*.

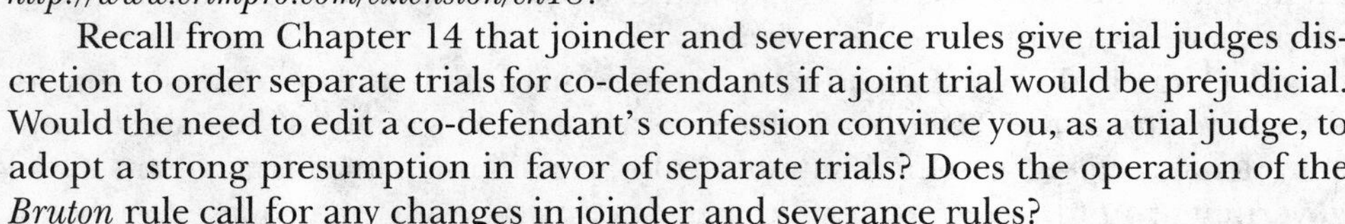

Recall from Chapter 14 that joinder and severance rules give trial judges discretion to order separate trials for co-defendants if a joint trial would be prejudicial. Would the need to edit a co-defendant's confession convince you, as a trial judge, to adopt a strong presumption in favor of separate trials? Does the operation of the *Bruton* rule call for any changes in joinder and severance rules?

3. Bruton *and* Crawford. The decisions in United States v. Bruton and Crawford v. Washington both interpret the confrontation clause. Are they consistent with one another? Suppose, for instance, that two co-defendants in a murder case make statements to friends and relatives, and each statement implicates both the speaker and the co-defendant in the crime. Can the government introduce each statement at a joint trial, without redaction, because the statements are not "testimonial"? See Thomas v. United States, 978 A.2d 1211 (D.C. 2009).

3. Unavailable Topics

Rules of evidence limit the sorts of inquiries a party may pursue at trial. Clearly this has an effect on the defendant's ability to confront and cross-examine prosecution witnesses. Perhaps the most striking of these rules are those that limit the questions the defense may ask about past and current criminal charges against the prosecution's witness. These evidentiary rules are based on the assumption that prior convictions or other wrongdoing could lead the jury to conclude too hastily that the witness is not credible. The following case explores the outer reach of such evidentiary limits on the power to cross-examine.

JOHNNY CARROLL v. STATE

916 S.W.2d 494 (Tex. Crim. App. 1996)

BAIRD, J.

Appellant was convicted of murder and sentenced to 30 years confinement. . . . We granted review to determine whether [a State's witness may] be cross-examined concerning pending criminal charges. We will reverse and remand.

The right of confrontation has ancient roots. Over 2,000 years ago the Roman Governor Porcius Festus reported to King Agrippa: "It is not the manner of the Romans to deliver any man up to die before the accused has met his accusers face to face, and has been given a chance to defend himself against the charges." The right of confrontation was also recognized in English common law. Initially, the right of the accused to confront witnesses was recognized in trials for treason. Arguably, the most notorious treason trial in England was that of the Sir Walter Raleigh, accused of conspiring to overthrow the King of England. Raleigh was charged with treason after a third party, Cobham, confessed under torture, to conspiring with Raleigh. At trial, Raleigh was denied the opportunity to confront Cobham and Cobham's statement was used to convict and ultimately execute Raleigh. . . .

Cross-examination serves three general purposes: cross-examination may serve to identify the witness with his community so that independent testimony may be sought and offered concerning the witness' reputation for veracity in that community; cross-examination allows the jury to assess the credibility of the witness; and, cross-examination allows facts to be brought out tending to discredit the witness by showing that his testimony in chief was untrue or biased. Alford v. United States, 282 U.S. 687 (1931). Cross-examination is by nature exploratory and there is no general requirement that the defendant indicate the purpose of his inquiry. Indeed, the defendant should be granted a wide latitude even though he is unable to state what facts he expects to prove through his cross-examination.

The Constitutional right of confrontation is violated when appropriate cross-examination is limited. The scope of appropriate cross-examination is necessarily broad. A defendant is entitled to pursue all avenues of cross-examination reasonably calculated to expose a motive, bias or interest for the witness to testify. . . . This broad scope necessarily includes cross-examination concerning criminal charges pending against a witness and over which those in need of the witness' testimony might be empowered to exercise control. A witness' pecuniary interest in the outcome of the trial is also an appropriate area of cross-examination.

Nevertheless, there are several areas where cross-examination may be inappropriate and, in those situations the trial judge has the discretion to limit cross-examination. Specifically, a trial judge may limit cross-examination when a subject is exhausted, or when the cross-examination is designed to annoy, harass, or humiliate, or when the cross-examination might endanger the personal safety of the witness. See generally Delaware v. Van Arsdall, 475 U.S. 673 (trial judge may exercise discretion to prevent harassment, prejudice, confusion of the issues, the witness' safety, and repetitive or marginally relevant interrogation.); Tex. R. Crim. Evid. 608, 609, 404 and 405.

In the instant case, the State presented two witnesses who testified they were present at the time of the murder. Charles Fitzgerald testified he and the victim were at a bar when they saw appellant. Appellant showed Fitzgerald a pistol and shortly thereafter got into an argument with the victim. Fitzgerald and the victim moved to a table and appellant followed. Appellant shot the victim with the pistol, and continued shooting as the victim moved toward the back of the bar. Although Fitzgerald testified he only consumed two beers, the officers who interviewed him the night of the murder testified Fitzgerald was intoxicated. Appellant impeached Fitzgerald's testimony with proof of his intoxication at the time of the killing.

Herman Russell testified appellant and the victim argued over a mutual girlfriend. When the victim indicated the girlfriend had moved in with him, appellant pulled a pistol and told the victim he should not talk to the girl. Appellant then put the pistol into his waistband and Russell went to a back room. In less than a minute Russell heard a gunshot and saw the victim running while holding his arm. Russell testified appellant continued to shoot the victim.[7]

Appellant sought to impeach Russell's testimony with evidence that Russell was currently incarcerated and awaiting trial on an aggravated robbery charge and that he had several prior felony convictions. The State asked the trial judge to prohibit appellant from conducting such cross-examination, contending such evidence was not relevant. Appellant contended Russell's testimony had a potential for bias because Russell's testimony in the instant case might favorably affect the outcome in the aggravated robbery case. Appellant further contended Russell's previous convictions could be used to enhance the felony charge, thus increasing the punishment range and creating a greater likelihood for bias. The trial judge agreed with the State and prohibited the testimony. The Court of Appeals affirmed, holding that Tex. R. Crim. Evid. 608(b) specifically prohibited the use of the pending aggravated robbery charge for impeachment.[9]

There exists a long line of federal and state authority holding a pending criminal charge is an appropriate area of cross-examination. Davis v. Alaska, 415 U.S. 308 (1974); Carmona v. State, 698 S.W.2d 100 (Tex. Crim. App. 1985). Indeed, the instant situation differs little from that confronted by the Supreme Court in Alford v. United States, 282 U.S. 687 (1931), where a prosecution witness testified to Alford's actions and incriminating statements. On cross-examination, Alford sought to elicit testimony that the witness was in federal custody "for the purpose of showing whatever bias or prejudice he may have." However, the trial judge refused to allow such evidence because it was not based upon a final conviction.

The Supreme Court reversed, holding cross-examination is a matter of right. Although the extent of cross-examination is subject to the sound discretion of the trial judge, the trial judge abuses that discretion when he prevents appropriate cross-examination. And inquiry into a witness' potential bias arising from incarceration was appropriate. Indeed, the Supreme Court held Alford should have been allowed to cross-examine the witness to demonstrate the "testimony was biased because given under a promise or expectation of immunity, or under the coercive effect of his detention by officers [who were] conducting the present prosecution." . . .

7. [Carroll] testified he did not display his weapon. Instead, he and the victim were discussing the mutual girlfriend when the victim used profanity and reached into his pants as if to retrieve a weapon. Appellant shot the victim because the girlfriend had informed him that the victim "had something that would take care of [him]."

9. Tex. R. Crim. Evid. 608(b) provides: "Specific instances of the conduct of a witness, for the purpose of attacking or supporting his credibility, other than conviction of crime as provided in Rule 609, may not be inquired into on cross-examination of the witness nor proved by extrinsic evidence."

In Harris v. State, 642 S.W.2d 471 (Tex. Crim. App. 1982), the defendant sought to question the State's witness concerning her pending juvenile charges. The trial judge sustained the State's objections to such cross-examination. On appeal the defendant contended he was entitled to cross-examine the witness concerning any probable bias or interest in her testimony. [We] reversed stating the defendant "had an unqualified right to ask . . . the only witness linking him with the offense, whether she too had been 'accused' of the offense on trial, and to receive her answer. . . ." The jury was entitled to the "whole picture" in order to evaluate and judge the witness' credibility.

Alford and *Harris* control our resolution of the instant case. Appellant's cross-examination was clearly an attempt to demonstrate that Russell held a possible motive, bias or interest in testifying for the State. Appellant's inquiry into Russell's incarceration, his pending charge and possible punishment as a habitual criminal, was appropriate to demonstrate Russell's potential motive, bias or interest to testify for the State. A defendant is permitted to elicit any fact from a witness intended to demonstrate that witness' vulnerable relationship with the state.

The State contends appellant's cross-examination was impermissible because no agreement existed between the State and Russell which might affect Russell's motive to testify for the State. However, the existence of such an agreement is not determinative. [It] is possible, even absent an agreement, that Russell believed his testimony in this case would be of later benefit. . . .

Finally, the Court of Appeals' holding that appellant was unable to impeach Russell under Rule 608(b) is erroneous for at least two reasons. First, appellant's cross-examination concerning Russell's incarceration was not an inquiry into a specific instance of conduct. Instead, appellant's cross-examination focused on Russell's possible motive, bias or interest in testifying for the State. To understand this distinction we draw upon . . . Ramirez v. State, 802 S.W.2d 674 (Tex. Crim. App. 1990), which involved the interpretation and application of Rule 608(b). In *Ramirez*, the mother of an eight-year-old victim testified she did not believe appellant sexually assaulted the victim. The State cross-examined the mother regarding her prior use of heroin suggesting that, at the time of the offense, she was under its influence and unaware of what happened to her child. The State offered no evidence to show the mother either previously used heroin, or was under its influence at the time of the incident. Relying on Rule 608(b), we held the State was improperly allowed to question the mother about a specific instance of conduct.

In the instant case the Court of Appeals improperly relied upon Rule 608(b) because appellant . . . did not seek to cross-examine Russell about the underlying facts which gave rise to the aggravated robbery charge. Rather, appellant attempted to inform the jury that Russell had a vulnerable relationship with the State at the time of his testimony. . . . Consequently, the Court of Appeals erred in relying on Rule 608(b) to uphold the trial judge's limitation on appellant's cross-examination of Russell.

Second, although we see no conflict between the right to cross-examine a witness about a pending charge and Rule 608(b), if such a conflict existed, the constitutional right of confrontation would prevail. . . . Accordingly, the judgment of the Court of Appeals is reversed and the case is remanded to that Court. . . .

MEYERS, J., concurring.

In this case the charges pending against the State's witness originated in the same jurisdiction and were brought by the identical authorities as those for which the appellant stands accused. I therefore agree with the decision of our lead opinion to allow the defendant to use these charges for impeachment on cross-examination of this witness. However, in future contexts, should these charges emanate from another jurisdiction or authority, I would hold that release of the information to the jury is subject to a discretionary ruling of the trial court under Rule 403 of the Texas Rules of Criminal Evidence. With these additional comments, I join the opinion of the Court.

MANSFIELD, J., dissenting.

The State presented two witnesses who testified they were in the bar at the time the murder was committed. Charles Fitzgerald testified appellant showed him a pistol and observed him arguing with Robert Brzowski, the victim. Fitzgerald testified further appellant followed him and Mr. Brzowski to another table, shot Mr. Brzowski with the pistol and continued shooting at Mr. Brzowski as he fled toward the back of the bar. Appellant introduced evidence, including the testimony of two police officers who interviewed Fitzgerald after the shooting, that Fitzgerald was intoxicated at the time of the shooting.

The second witness, Herman Russell, the bartender, testified and gave essentially the same version of what occurred as Fitzgerald. Russell testified appellant and Mr. Brzowski argued over a mutual female acquaintance and things went down hill from there, concluding with appellant shooting and killing Mr. Brzowski.

At trial, appellant sought to impeach Russell with evidence of prior felony convictions, i.e., two convictions for cattle theft from 1962 and 1965. Though conceding Texas Rule of Criminal Evidence 609(b)* would ordinarily bar use of the convictions for impeachment as the convictions were too remote (over ten years old), appellant claimed they were relevant as they could be used to enhance punishment if Russell were convicted of his pending charge. Additionally, appellant sought to impeach Russell with evidence of a pending aggravated robbery charge and that he was currently incarcerated awaiting trial on that charge. Appellant alleged Russell was potentially biased because his testimony in the present case might affect the outcome in his pending aggravated robbery case, and he was entitled to show the jury Russell's testimony might be influenced by the charge pending against him.

At the hearing, Russell testified there had been no deals made with the State concerning the pending aggravated robbery charge in relation to his testimony in the present case. He testified he had already given a statement regarding the present case (the killing occurred on April 11, 1992) prior to being arrested on the aggravated robbery charge (the robbery allegedly was committed in 1988). Finally, he testified his testimony in the present case would not be affected by the case pending against him, which was scheduled to be prosecuted in a different court. The trial court denied appellant's motion, and Russell testified without being impeached by evidence of his prior convictions or of the pending aggravated robbery charge. . . .

* [Rule 609 enables the court to admit into evidence the prior conviction of a witness for impeachment purposes, if the crime was a felony or involved moral turpitude and the court determines that the probative value of admitting this evidence outweighs its prejudicial effect. Evidence of a conviction is not admissible if more than 10 years have elapsed since the date of conviction or release from prison, whichever is later. — EDS.]

Texas Criminal Evidence Rule 608(b) does not allow a witness to be impeached, for purposes of attacking his credibility, by proof of specific instances of conduct, other than conviction of crimes as provided by Rule 609, either on cross-examination or by extrinsic evidence. . . . Rule 608(b) is much more restrictive as to impeachment of witnesses by instances of conduct other than convictions than its federal counterpart. . . .

Appellant cites Davis v. Alaska, 415 U.S. 308 (1974), in support of his claim that the Confrontation Clause of the U.S. Constitution requires that he be permitted to show any fact, including a pending charge, which would tend to establish bias or motive of a witness (i.e. Russell) testifying against him. The majority, I respectfully assert, reads *Davis* in a too-broad manner. In *Davis,* counsel for petitioner was denied the opportunity to cross-examine a State's witness as to his status as a probationer, which counsel alleged would tend to show possible motive or bias on the part of the witness. The Supreme Court held "petitioner was thus denied the right of effective cross-examination which would be constitutional error of the first magnitude and no amount of showing or want of prejudice would cure it."

The present case differs markedly from the facts of *Davis.* First, the witness in *Davis* was on probation resulting from a recent adjudication of delinquency in a juvenile court and likely could have been impeached with that adjudication under Rule 609(d) had this been a Texas case. Second, unlike in *Davis,* appellant in the present case had available to him, under Rule 612, for impeachment purposes, Russell's statement taken at the time of the killing and before he was arrested on the aggravated robbery charge. Third, in the present case, a hearing was held at which the witness (Russell) testified that he would testify truthfully, he would not be affected by his pending charge as to his testimony and no "deal" had been made with the State concerning his testimony. No such examination of the witness (Green) for bias or motive took place in *Davis.* Fourth, a juvenile adjudication is a final determination by a court and is analogous to a conviction. In the present case the witness had merely been charged with a crime and had not been even tried, much less been convicted. Given these differences, appellant's right to an effective cross-examination was not denied.

There is little doubt — notwithstanding Rule 608(b) — *Davis* mandates that a criminal defendant be permitted to impeach a State witness on cross-examination with evidence of a pending charge against the witness where a deal concerning the witness' testimony with the State existed or was under discussion. Similarly, *Davis* would be implicated where, unlike in the present case, the defendant had no other reasonable means to impeach the witness (e.g. by a prior statement if inconsistent with his testimony) or had not been afforded a hearing by the court at which he could support his claim of bias or motive of the witness which could be shown only by allowing him to cross-examine the witness — before the jury — as to a pending charge. . . . I respectfully dissent.

KELLER, J., dissenting.

. . . Under the majority's analysis the failure to allow cross-examination regarding a pending charge is always error. I agree that, ordinarily, the mere existence of a pending charge gives rise to an inference that the witness may have been influenced. But in some cases, additional facts in the record may show that such an inference is not warranted. . . . When a witness' testimony corresponds with his statement given prior to the point at which the motive for bias arose, and the defendant does not otherwise show that the pending charge may have influenced the witness' testimony at trial, I believe that it is not an abuse of discretion to disallow cross-examination regarding an unrelated pending criminal charge that is alleged to be the motive for bias. Such are the facts in this case. Accordingly, I dissent.

Problem 18-6. Evidence Off Limits

James Egelhoff spent an evening drinking with two friends. Some time after 9 P.M., Egelhoff and his friends left a party in a station wagon. Egelhoff bought beer at 9:20 P.M. At about midnight, the sheriff's department received reports of a possible drunken driver. The deputies who responded to the call discovered the station wagon stuck in a ditch along a U.S. highway. In the front seat were Egelhoff's two friends, each dead from a single gunshot to the head. Egelhoff lay in the rear of the station wagon, yelling obscenities. His blood-alcohol level measured .36, more than one hour later. On the floor of the car, near the brake pedal, lay Egelhoff's .38 caliber handgun, with four loaded rounds and two empty casings. He had gunshot residue on his hands.

At his trial for deliberate homicide, Egelhoff testified that his intoxication made it impossible for him to commit the crime. Although he remembered "sitting on a hill passing a bottle of Black Velvet back and forth" with his friends, he recalled nothing further because of his extreme intoxication. Because he was physically incapable of carrying out the killing and could not remember the events of the evening, Egelhoff concluded that some fourth party had killed his friends.

Deliberate homicide, under state law, occurs when a person "purposely" or "knowingly" causes the death of another human being. Although the trial court allowed Egelhoff to testify about his intoxication, the judge also instructed the jury, consistent with a state statute, that it could not consider Egelhoff's "intoxicated condition in determining the existence of a mental state which is an element of the offense." The jury found Egelhoff guilty as charged.

The defendant argues on appeal that the state statute violated his due process right to present to the jury all relevant evidence to rebut the state's evidence on all elements of the offense charged. Evidence of his intoxication was relevant to deciding whether he had killed the victims "knowingly" or "purposely." The exclusion of this evidence, he says, lessened the government's burden of proof in establishing the mens rea for the crime. How would you rule on the defendant's appeal? Compare Montana v. Egelhoff, 518 U.S. 37 (1996).

Notes

1. *Cross-examination about pending charges: majority position.* Rules of evidence control the scope of questions that lawyers can ask during cross-examination. For instance, the rules restrict the cross-examining lawyer to questions related to the subjects covered during direct examination. They also limit questions about prior convictions or pending criminal charges against the witness. However, the constitutional right to confrontation sometimes allows a defendant to go beyond these usual restrictions on cross-examination to ask questions that the prosecuting attorney

could not ask. In Delaware v. Van Arsdall, 475 U.S. 673 (1986), the Court held that a defendant's rights secured by the confrontation clause were violated when the trial court prohibited "all inquiry" into the possibility that a witness would be biased after agreeing to testify in exchange for favorable treatment in a different criminal matter. The Court noted that the witness's agreement about the pending charges could show a "prototypical form of bias." The jury "might have received a significantly different impression" of the witness's credibility if defense counsel had been permitted to pursue the proposed line of cross-examination. See also Davis v. Alaska, 415 U.S. 308 (1974) (refusal to allow defendant to cross-examine key prosecution witness to show his probation status for juvenile offense denied defendant his constitutional right to confront witnesses, notwithstanding state policy protecting anonymity of juvenile offenders).

State courts have also concluded that their constitutions allow defendants to pursue lines of cross-examination that the rules of evidence would not allow for other litigants. About 30 states have endorsed the federal position. Like the Supreme Court in *Van Arsdall,* these courts ask if the proposed questions would explore a "prototypical form of bias." They most often conclude that defense counsel may ask questions about criminal charges pending against the witness. See State v. Mizzell, 563 S.E.2d 315 (S.C. 2002) (trial court violated confrontation rights by forbidding defense counsel to elicit from prosecution witness, charged with same crime as defendant "Tootie" Mizzell, the punishment he could receive if convicted). However, state courts will sometimes uphold a trial court that restricts defense cross-examination on this subject, if the witness asserts that she expects no benefit to flow from testifying. See Marshall v. State, 695 A.2d 184 (Md. 1997). Can an appellate court develop sound rules on this question, or is the issue better left to the discretion of the trial court?

2. *Prior criminal record of prosecution witnesses.* On topics of cross-examination other than pending criminal charges against the witness, trial courts tend to have more discretion to limit cross-examination. This is true, for instance, when defense counsel tries to explore the prior criminal record of prosecution witnesses. Although trial judges often allow at least some cross-examination on this subject, appellate courts uphold most efforts to limit questioning on the topic. Many state courts conclude that the prior convictions of a witness do not demonstrate a "prototypical form" of bias against the defendant, but are simply a generalized attack on the witness's credibility that might confuse the jury. Trial judges can impose reasonable limits on cross-examination to guard against harassment, prejudice, confusion of the issues, or waste of time. See State v. Lanz-Terry, 535 N.W.2d 635 (Minn. 1995). Why do courts treat prior convictions differently from pending criminal charges against a prosecution witness?

3. *Ethics of cross-examination.* Sometimes a judge's evidentiary ruling arrives too late. An attorney's leading question on cross-examination might suggest an answer to the jury, even if the witness never has to answer the question. In response to this problem, rules of legal ethics typically instruct attorneys not to ask a question on cross-examination if there is no reasonable factual basis for the question. See ABA Model Rule of Professional Conduct 3.4(e) (lawyer at trial shall not "allude to any matter that the lawyer does not reasonably believe is relevant or that will not be supported by admissible evidence"). If you were a staff attorney working within the disciplinary body of the state bar, how would you expect to enforce this rule?

4. *Legislative limits on defense evidence.* Our discussion has focused on the defendant's power to "confront" adverse witnesses and test the prosecution's case, mostly through cross-examination of witnesses. Defendants will also answer the prosecution's case by presenting their own evidence. As with cross-examination, a range of legal rules can restrict the evidence a defendant might present. Rules of evidence require generally that any evidence be relevant to an issue in controversy and that its probative value outweigh its prejudicial impact. See Fed. R. Evid. 403 ("Although relevant, evidence may be excluded if its probative value is substantially outweighed by the danger of unfair prejudice, confusion of the issues, or misleading the jury, or by considerations of undue delay, waste of time, or needless presentation of cumulative evidence"). States sometimes enact rules or statutes for a particular subject matter that defendants might try to raise at trial. For instance, most jurisdictions have "rape shield" laws, which limit the power of a defendant in a sexual assault case from inquiring into certain aspects of the sexual history of the victim of the alleged crime.

Statutes and rules of evidence in some jurisdictions also limit the defendant's ability to introduce evidence of voluntary intoxication. In Montana v. Egelhoff, 518 U.S. 37 (1996), the basis for Problem 18-6 above, the Court upheld the constitutionality of a statute that precluded the jury from considering evidence of intoxication when it determined whether the defendant had the mens rea to commit the crime. The Court indicated that 10 states had enacted similar statutes or rules; since the *Egelhoff* decision appeared, the number has grown. The statute in *Egelhoff* appears to place a new type of limit on defense efforts to present evidence. The Montana legislature did not justify its rule by arguing that intoxication evidence is unreliable, cumulative, privileged, or irrelevant. The state instead adopted the rule to deter irresponsible behavior, to incapacitate those who cannot control violent impulses while drunk, and to express society's moral judgment that persons who voluntarily become intoxicated should remain responsible for their actions.

After *Egelhoff,* is there any legal or practical limit on the legislature's power to prevent the defendant from presenting evidence that many juries might find convincing? See Holmes v. South Carolina, 547 U.S. 319 (2006) (defendant's federal constitutional rights violated by an evidence rule precluding defense from introducing proof that third party committed the crime charged, even if the prosecution has introduced forensic evidence that strongly supports a guilty verdict against the defendant); Clark v. Arizona, 548 U.S. 735 (2006) (upholding state statute limiting defense uses of evidence of defendant's mental illness; statute required defendant to assert affirmative defense of insanity rather than using evidence of paranoid schizophrenia to deny specific intent to shoot a police officer).

5. *Commentary on evidence.* Although judges constantly evaluate evidence and rule on its admissibility, many states have constitutional or statutory provisions that prohibit the judge from "commenting" on the evidence or the credibility of witnesses. See Wash. Const. art. IV, §16; Ga. Code §17-8-57. There is, however, no per se federal constitutional bar to judicial commentary on evidence, and some states do not impose such a bar. See Quercia v. United States, 289 U.S. 466 (1933) (no error for judge to comment on evidence so long as the comment does not "excite [in the jury] a prejudice which would preclude a fair and dispassionate consideration of the evidence"; court here committed error by saying that witness displayed mannerisms of a person who is lying).

C. SELF-INCRIMINATION PRIVILEGE AT TRIAL

Once the prosecution has presented its case in chief, the defendant may present evidence as well. The central strategic question for the defendant at this point is whether to testify. While the defendant might present testimony from other witnesses, that evidence is not likely to carry the same weight as a defendant's personal denial of the crime and personal explanation of the prosecution's key evidence. At the same time, a defendant might not feel capable of making a convincing denial at trial, because of nervousness, concern about charges of perjury, or for some other reason.

In the United States, as in most Western legal systems, the law allows the defendant alone to choose whether to testify at trial. The privilege against self-incrimination allows the defendant to refuse to cooperate during certain phases of an investigation, but the privilege provides the clearest protections during a criminal trial. Professor John Langbein has traced the origins of the privilege to the emergence in the eighteenth century of adversary criminal procedure and a prominent role for defense counsel who could speak for the defendant and challenge the government's evidence. See John Langbein, The Historical Origins of the Privilege Against Self-Incrimination at Common Law, 92 Mich. L. Rev. 1047 (1994).

Because of the privilege against self-incrimination, a criminal defendant may refuse to cooperate in some investigative efforts and may refuse to testify at trial. Is there any price for such refusals? As a practical matter, some disadvantages do flow from invoking the privilege. A jury or judge might infer from a defendant's silence that she is guilty or at least that she has no answer to the government's evidence. But can the prosecutor urge the factfinder to draw such inferences? Should the judge do or say anything to prevent the jury from drawing such conclusions? The *Griffin* case reprinted below announced the bright-line constitutional rule that all American courts follow on this question; the following *Murray* opinion from the European Court of Human Rights describes a position encountered in other Western legal systems.

■ EDDIE DEAN GRIFFIN v. CALIFORNIA
380 U.S. 609 (1965)

DOUGLAS, J.*

Petitioner was convicted of murder in the first degree after a jury trial in a California court. He did not testify at the trial on the issue of guilt, though he did testify at the separate trial on the issue of penalty. The trial court instructed the jury on the issue of guilt, stating that a defendant has a constitutional right not to testify. But it told the jury:

> As to any evidence or facts against him which the defendant can reasonably be expected to deny or explain because of facts within his knowledge, if he does not testify or if, though he does testify, he fails to deny or explain such evidence, the jury may take that

* [Justices Black, Clark, Brennan, and Goldberg joined this opinion. — EDS.]

> failure into consideration as tending to indicate the truth of such evidence and as indicating that among the inferences that may be reasonably drawn therefrom those unfavorable to the defendant are the more probable.

It added, however, that no such inference could be drawn as to evidence respecting which he had no knowledge. It stated that failure of a defendant to deny or explain the evidence of which he had knowledge does not create a presumption of guilt nor by itself warrant an inference of guilt nor relieve the prosecution of any of its burden of proof.

Petitioner had been seen with the deceased the evening of her death, the evidence placing him with her in the alley where her body was found. The prosecutor made much of the failure of petitioner to testify:

> The defendant certainly knows whether Essie Mae had this beat up appearance at the time he left her apartment and went down the alley with her. . . . He would know that. He would know how she got down the alley. He would know how the blood got on the bottom of the concrete steps. He would know how long he was with her in that box. He would know how her wig got off. He would know whether he beat her or mistreated her. He would know whether he walked away from that place cool as a cucumber when he saw Mr. Villasenor because he was conscious of his own guilt and wanted to get away from that damaged or injured woman. These things he has not seen fit to take the stand and deny or explain. And in the whole world, if anybody would know, this defendant would know. Essie Mae is dead, she can't tell you her side of the story. The defendant won't.

The death penalty was imposed and the California Supreme Court affirmed. The case is here on a writ of certiorari which we granted to consider whether comment on the failure to testify violated the Self-Incrimination Clause of the Fifth Amendment which we made applicable to the States by the Fourteenth in Malloy v. Hogan, 378 U.S. 1 (1964). . . .[3]

If this were a federal trial, reversible error would have been committed. Wilson v. United States, 149 U.S. 60 (1893), so holds. It is said, however, that the *Wilson* decision rested not on the Fifth Amendment, but on an Act of Congress, now 18 U.S.C. §3481.[4] That indeed is the fact. . . . But that is the beginning, not the end, of our inquiry. The question remains whether, statute or not, the comment rule, approved by California, violates the Fifth Amendment.

We think it does. It is in substance a rule of evidence that allows the State the privilege of tendering to the jury for its consideration the failure of the accused to testify. No formal offer of proof is made as in other situations; but the prosecutor's comment and the court's acquiescence are the equivalent of an offer of evidence and its acceptance. The Court in the *Wilson* case stated:

3. [Most states do not allow] comment on the defendant's failure to testify. The legislatures or courts of 44 States have recognized that such comment is, in light of the privilege against self-incrimination, "an unwarrantable line of argument."

4. Section 3481 reads as follows: "In [a federal criminal trial] the person charged shall, at his own request, be a competent witness. His failure to make such request shall not create any presumption against him."

> . . . It is not every one who can safely venture on the witness stand though entirely innocent of the charge against him. Excessive timidity, nervousness when facing others and attempting to explain transactions of a suspicious character, and offences charged against him, will often confuse and embarrass him to such a degree as to increase rather than remove prejudices against him. It is not every one, however honest, who would, therefore, willingly be placed on the witness stand. The statute, in tenderness to the weakness of those who . . . may have been in some degree compromised by their association with others, declares that the failure of the defendant in a criminal action to request to be a witness shall not create any presumption against him.

[Comment] on the refusal to testify is a remnant of the inquisitorial system of criminal justice, which the Fifth Amendment outlaws. It is a penalty imposed by courts for exercising a constitutional privilege. It cuts down on the privilege by making its assertion costly. It is said, however, that the inference of guilt for failure to testify as to facts peculiarly within the accused's knowledge is in any event natural and irresistible, and that comment on the failure does not magnify that inference into a penalty for asserting a constitutional privilege. What the jury may infer, given no help from the court, is one thing. What it may infer when the court solemnizes the silence of the accused into evidence against him is quite another. [We] hold that the Fifth Amendment, in its direct application to the Federal Government, and in its bearing on the States by reason of the Fourteenth Amendment, forbids either comment by the prosecution on the accused's silence or instructions by the court that such silence is evidence of guilt. Reversed.

STEWART, J., dissenting.*

. . . Article I, §13, of the California Constitution establishes a defendant's privilege against self-incrimination and further provides: ". . . whether the defendant testifies or not, his failure to explain or to deny by his testimony any evidence or facts in the case against him may be commented upon by the court and by counsel, and may be considered by the court or the jury." In conformity with this provision, the prosecutor in his argument to the jury emphasized that a person accused of crime in a public forum would ordinarily deny or explain the evidence against him if he truthfully could do so. Also in conformity with this California constitutional provision, the judge instructed the jury [that they could draw a negative inference from the defendant's failure to deny to explain evidence or facts if he had the knowledge to make such an explanation].

We must determine whether the petitioner has been "compelled . . . to be a witness against himself." Compulsion is the focus of the inquiry. Certainly, if any compulsion be detected in the California procedure, it is of a dramatically different and less palpable nature than that involved in the procedures which historically gave rise to the Fifth Amendment guarantee. When a suspect was brought before the Court of High Commission or the Star Chamber, he was commanded to answer whatever was asked of him, and subjected to a far-reaching and deeply probing inquiry in an effort to ferret out some unknown and frequently unsuspected crime. He declined to answer on pain of incarceration, banishment, or mutilation. And if he spoke falsely, he was subject to further punishment. Faced with this formidable array of alternatives, his decision to speak was unquestionably coerced.

* [Justice White joined this opinion. — EDS.]

Those were the lurid realities which lay behind enactment of the Fifth Amendment, a far cry from the subject matter of the case before us. I think that the Court in this case stretches the concept of compulsion beyond all reasonable bounds, and that whatever compulsion may exist derives from the defendant's choice not to testify, not from any comment by court or counsel. . . .

It is not at all apparent to me, on any realistic view of the trial process, that a defendant will be at more of a disadvantage under the California practice than he would be in a court which permitted no comment at all on his failure to take the witness stand. How can it be said that the inferences drawn by a jury will be more detrimental to a defendant under the limiting and carefully controlling language of the instruction here involved than would result if the jury were left to roam at large with only its untutored instincts to guide it, to draw from the defendant's silence broad inferences of guilt? The instructions in this case expressly cautioned the jury that the defendant's failure to testify "does not create a presumption of guilt or by itself warrant an inference of guilt"; it was further admonished that such failure does not "relieve the prosecution of its burden of proving every essential element of the crime." . . .

I think the California comment rule is not a coercive device which impairs the right against self-incrimination, but rather a means of articulating and bringing into the light of rational discussion a fact inescapably impressed on the jury's consciousness. The California procedure is not only designed to protect the defendant against unwarranted inferences which might be drawn by an uninformed jury; it is also an attempt by the State to recognize and articulate what it believes to be the natural probative force of certain facts. . . .

No constitution can prevent the operation of the human mind. Without limiting instructions, the danger exists that the inferences drawn by the jury may be unfairly broad. Some States have permitted this danger to go unchecked, by forbidding any comment at all upon the defendant's failure to take the witness stand. Other States have dealt with this danger in a variety of ways, as the Court's opinion indicates. Some might differ, as a matter of policy, with the way California has chosen to deal with the problem, or even disapprove of the judge's specific instructions in this case. But, so long as the constitutional command is obeyed, such matters of state policy are not for this Court to decide. I would affirm the judgment.

■ KEVIN SEAN MURRAY v. UNITED KINGDOM

22 Eur. Ct. H.R. 29 (1996)

. . . The applicant was arrested by police officers at 17.40 on 7 January 1990. . . . Pursuant to Article 3 of the Criminal Evidence (Northern Ireland) Order 1988, he was cautioned by the police in the following terms:

> You do not have to say anything unless you wish to do so but I must warn you that if you fail to mention any fact which you rely on in your defence in court, your failure to take this opportunity to mention it may be treated in court as supporting any relevant evidence against you. If you do wish to say anything, what you say may be given in evidence.

In response to the police caution the applicant stated that he had nothing to say. . . .

13. At 21.27 on 7 January a police constable cautioned the applicant pursuant to Article 6 of the Order, inter alia, requesting him to account for his presence at the house where he was arrested. He was warned that if he failed or refused to do so, a court, judge or jury might draw such inference from his failure or refusal as appears proper. He was also served with a written copy of Article 6 of the Order. In reply to this caution the applicant stated: "nothing to say." . . .

15. The applicant was interviewed by police detectives at Castlereagh Police Office on 12 occasions during 8 and 9 January. In total he was interviewed for 21 hours and 39 minutes. At the commencement of these interviews he was either cautioned pursuant to Article 3 of the Order or reminded of the terms of the caution.

16. During the first 10 interviews on 8 and 9 January the applicant made no reply to any questions put to him. He was able to see his solicitor for the first time at 18.33 on 9 January. At 19.10 he was interviewed again and reminded of the Article 3 caution. He replied: "I have been advised by my solicitor not to answer any of your questions." A final interview, during which the applicant said nothing, took place between 21.40 and 23.45 on 9 January. His solicitor was not permitted to be present at any of these interviews.

17. In May 1991 the applicant was tried by a single judge, the Lord Chief Justice of Northern Ireland, sitting without a jury, for the offences of conspiracy to murder, the unlawful imprisonment, with seven other people, of a certain Mr. L and of belonging to a proscribed organisation, the Provisional Irish Republican Army (IRA).

18. According to the Crown, Mr. L had been a member of the IRA who had been providing information about their activities to the Royal Ulster Constabulary. On discovering that Mr. L was an informer, the IRA tricked him into visiting a house in Belfast on 5 January 1990. He was falsely imprisoned in one of the rear bedrooms of the house and interrogated by the IRA until the arrival of the police and the army at the house on 7 January 1990. It was also alleged by the Crown that there was a conspiracy to murder Mr. L as punishment for being a police informer.

19. In the course of the trial, evidence was given that when the police entered the house on 7 January the applicant was seen by a police constable coming down a flight of stairs wearing a raincoat over his clothes and was arrested in the hall of the house. Mr. L testified that he was forced under threat of being killed to make a taped confession to his captors that he was an informer. He further said that on the evening of 7 January he had heard scurrying and had been told to take off his blindfold. . . . The applicant had told him that the police were at the door and to go downstairs and watch television. While he was talking to him the applicant was pulling tape out of a cassette. On a search of the house by the police . . . a tangled tape was discovered in the upstairs bedroom. The salvaged portions of the tape revealed a confession by Mr. L that he had agreed to work for the police. . . . At no time, either on his arrest or during the trial proceedings, did the applicant give any explanation for his presence in the house.

20. At the close of the prosecution case the trial judge, acting in accordance with Article 4 of the Order, called upon [Murray to give evidence in his own defense]:

> I am also required by law to tell you that if you refuse to come into the witness box to be sworn or if, after having been sworn, you refuse, without good reason, to answer any question, then the court in deciding whether you are guilty or not guilty may take into

account against you to the extent that it considers proper your refusal to give evidence or to answer any questions.

21. Acting on the advice of his solicitor and counsel, the applicant chose not to give any evidence. No witnesses were called on his behalf. Counsel . . . submitted, inter alia, that the applicant's presence in the house just before the police arrived was recent and innocent.

22. On 8 May 1991 the applicant was found guilty of the offence of aiding and abetting the unlawful imprisonment of Mr. L and sentenced to eight years' imprisonment. He was acquitted of the remaining charges. . . .

25. In concluding that the applicant was guilty of the offence of aiding and abetting false imprisonment, the trial judge drew adverse inferences against the applicant under both Articles 4 and 6 of the Order. The judge stated that in the particular circumstances of the case he did not propose to draw inferences against the applicant under Article 3 of the Order. . . .

27. Criminal Evidence (Northern Ireland) Order 1988 includes the following provisions:

> Article 3: Circumstances in which inferences may be drawn from accused's failure to mention particular facts when questioned, charged, etc.
>
> (1) Where, in any proceedings against a person for an offence, evidence is given that the accused
>
> (a) at any time before he was charged with the offence, on being questioned by a constable trying to discover whether or by whom the offence had been committed, failed to mention any fact relied on in his defence in those proceedings; or
>
> (b) on being charged with the offence or officially informed that he might be prosecuted for it, failed to mention any such fact, being a fact which in the circumstances existing at the time the accused could reasonably have been expected to mention when so questioned, charged or informed, as the case may be, paragraph (2) applies.
>
> (2) [The] court or jury, in determining whether the accused is guilty of the offence charged, may . . . draw such inferences from the failure as appear proper [and] on the basis of such inferences treat the failure as, or as capable of amounting to, corroboration of any evidence given against the accused in relation to which the failure is material. . . .
>
> Article 4: Accused to be called upon to give evidence at trial . . .
>
> (2) Before any evidence is called for the defence, the court . . . shall tell the accused that he will be called upon by the court to give evidence in his own defence, and . . . shall tell him in ordinary language what the effect of this Article will be if . . . when so called upon, he refuses . . . to answer any question. . . .
>
> (3) If the accused . . . refuses to be sworn, . . . paragraph (4) applies.
>
> (4) The court or jury, in determining whether the accused is guilty of the offence charged, may . . . draw such inferences from the refusal as appear proper [and] treat the refusal as, or as capable of amounting to, corroboration of any evidence given against the accused in relation to which the refusal is material. . . .
>
> Article 6: Inferences from failure or refusal to account for presence at a particular place
>
> (1) Where (a) a person arrested by a constable was found by him at a place or about the time the offence for which he was arrested is alleged to have been committed, and (b) the constable reasonably believes that the presence of the person at that place and at that time may be attributable to his participation in the commission of the offence,

and (c) the constable informs the person that he so believes, and requests him to account for that presence, and (d) the person fails or refuses to do so, then if, in any proceedings against the person for the offence, evidence of those matters is given, paragraph (2) applies.

(2) [The] court or jury, in determining whether the accused is guilty of the offence charged, may . . . draw such inferences from the failure or refusal as appear proper [and] treat the failure or refusal as, or as capable of amounting to, corroboration of any evidence given against the accused in relation to which the failure or refusal is material.

(3) Paragraphs (1) and (2) do not apply unless the accused was told in ordinary language by the constable when making the request mentioned in paragraph (1)(c) what the effect of this Article would be if he failed or refused to do so. . . .

40. The applicant alleged that there had been a violation of the right to silence and the right not to incriminate oneself contrary to Article 6(1) and (2) of the Convention. . . . The relevant provisions provide as follows:

1. In the determination of . . . any criminal charge against him, everyone is entitled to a fair and public hearing within a reasonable time by an independent and impartial tribunal. . . .

2. Everyone charged with a criminal offence shall be presumed innocent until proved guilty according to law. . . .

41. In the submission of the applicant, the drawing of incriminating inferences against him under the Criminal Justice (Northern Ireland) Order 1988 violated Article 6(1) and (2) of the Convention. It amounted to an infringement of the right to silence, the right not to incriminate oneself and the principle that the prosecution bear the burden of proving the case without assistance from the accused.

He contended that a first, and most obvious element of the right to silence is the right to remain silent in the face of police questioning and not to have to testify against oneself at trial. In his submission, these have always been essential and fundamental elements of the British criminal justice system. Moreover the Commission in Saunders v. United Kingdom, No. 19187/91, Comm. Rep. 10.5.94 (1994) and the Court in Funke v. France, 1 C.M.L.R. 897 (1993) have accepted that they are an inherent part of the right to a fair hearing under Article 6. In his view these are absolute rights which an accused is entitled to enjoy without restriction.

A second, equally essential element of the right to silence was that the exercise of the right by an accused would not be used as evidence against him in his trial. However, the trial judge drew very strong inferences, under Articles 4 and 6 of the Order, from his decision to remain silent under police questioning and during the trial. Indeed, it was clear from the trial judge's remarks . . . that the inferences were an integral part of his decision to find him guilty.

Accordingly, he was severely and doubly penalised for choosing to remain silent: once for his silence under police interrogation and once for his failure to testify during the trial. To use against him silence under police questioning and his refusal to testify during trial amounted to subverting the presumption of innocence and the onus of proof resulting from that presumption: it is for the prosecution to prove the accused's guilt without any assistance from the latter being required. . . .

43. The Government . . . emphasised that the Order did not detract from the right to remain silent in the face of police questioning and explicitly confirmed the right not to have to testify at trial. They further noted that the Order in no way

changed either the burden or the standard of proof: it remained for the prosecution to prove an accused's guilt beyond reasonable doubt. What the Order did was to confer a discretionary power to draw inferences from the silence of an accused in carefully defined circumstances. [The] Order merely allows the trier of fact to draw such inferences as common sense dictates. The question in each case is whether the evidence adduced by the prosecution is sufficiently strong to call for an answer. . . .

45. Although not specifically mentioned in Article 6 of the Convention, there can be no doubt that the right to remain silent under police questioning and the privilege against self-incrimination are generally recognised international standards which lie at the heart of the notion of a fair procedure under Article 6. By providing the accused with protection against improper compulsion by the authorities these immunities contribute to avoiding miscarriages of justice and to securing the aim of Article 6.

46. The Court does not consider that it is called upon to give an abstract analysis of the scope of these immunities and, in particular, of what constitutes in this context "improper compulsion." What is at stake in the present case is whether these immunities are absolute in the sense that the exercise by an accused of the right to silence cannot under any circumstances be used against him at trial or, alternatively, whether informing him in advance that, under certain conditions, his silence may be used, is always to be regarded as "improper compulsion."

47. On the one hand, it is self-evident that [it] is incompatible with the immunities under consideration to base a conviction solely or mainly on the accused's silence or on a refusal to answer questions or to give evidence himself. On the other hand, the Court deems it equally obvious that these immunities cannot and should not prevent that the accused's silence, in situations which clearly call for an explanation from him, be taken into account in assessing the persuasiveness of the evidence adduced by the prosecution. Wherever the line between these two extremes is to be drawn, it follows from this understanding of "the right to silence" that the question whether the right is absolute must be answered in the negative. . . .

48. As regards the degree of compulsion involved in the present case, it is recalled that the applicant was in fact able to remain silent. Notwithstanding the repeated warnings as to the possibility that inferences might be drawn from his silence, he did not make any statements to the police and did not give evidence during his trial. [His] insistence in maintaining silence throughout the proceedings did not amount to a criminal offence or contempt of court. . . .

50. Admittedly a system which warns the accused — who is possibly without legal assistance (as in the applicant's case) — that adverse inferences may be drawn from a refusal to provide an explanation to the police . . . involves a certain level of indirect compulsion. However, since the applicant could not be compelled to speak or to testify, as indicated above, this factor on its own cannot be decisive. The Court must rather concentrate its attention on the role played by the inferences in the proceedings against the applicant and especially in his conviction.

51. In this context, it is recalled that these were proceedings without a jury, the trier of fact being an experienced judge. Furthermore, the drawing of inferences under the Order is subject to an important series of safeguards designed to respect the rights of the defence and to limit the extent to which reliance can be placed on inferences.

In the first place, before inferences can be drawn under Article 4 and 6 of the Order appropriate warnings must have been given to the accused as to the legal effects of maintaining silence. Moreover, . . . the prosecutor must first establish a prima facie case against the accused, i.e. a case consisting of direct evidence which, if believed and combined with legitimate inferences based upon it, could lead a properly directed jury to be satisfied beyond reasonable doubt that each of the essential elements of the offence is proved.

The question in each particular case is whether the evidence adduced by the prosecution is sufficiently strong to require an answer. The national court cannot conclude that the accused is guilty merely because he chooses to remain silent. It is only if the evidence against the accused "calls" for an explanation which the accused ought to be in a position to give that a failure to give an explanation "may as a matter of common sense allow the drawing of an inference that there is no explanation and that the accused is guilty." Conversely if the case presented by the prosecution had so little evidential value that it called for no answer, a failure to provide one could not justify an inference of guilt. In sum, it is only common sense inferences which the judge considers proper, in the light of the evidence against the accused, that can be drawn under the Order.

In addition, the trial judge has a discretion whether, on the facts of the particular case, an inference should be drawn. [The] judge must explain the reasons for the decision to draw inferences and the weight attached to them. The exercise of discretion in this regard is subject to review by the appellate courts.

52. In the present case, the evidence presented against the applicant by the prosecution was considered by the Court of Appeal to constitute a "formidable" case against him. It is recalled that when the police entered the house some appreciable time after they knocked on the door, they found the applicant coming down the flight of stairs in the house where Mr. L had been held captive by the IRA. [Soon after the police arrived, the] applicant was pulling a tape out of a cassette. The tangled tape and cassette recorder were later found on the premises. Evidence by the applicant's co-accused that he had recently arrived at the house was discounted as not being credible. . . .

54. In the Court's view, having regard to the weight of the evidence against the applicant, as outlined above, the drawing of inferences from his refusal, at arrest, during police questioning and at trial, to provide an explanation for his presence in the house was a matter of common sense and cannot be regarded as unfair or unreasonable in the circumstances. [The] courts in a considerable number of countries where evidence is freely assessed may have regard to all relevant circumstances, including the manner in which the accused has behaved or has conducted his defence, when evaluating the evidence in the case. [What] distinguishes the drawing of inferences under the Order is that, in addition to the existence of the specific safeguards mentioned above, it constitutes, as described by the Commission, "a formalised system which aims at allowing common sense implications to play an open role in the assessment of evidence." . . .

55. The applicant submitted that it was unfair to draw inferences under Article 6 of the Order from his silence at a time when he had not had the benefit of legal advice. . . . In this context he emphasised that under the Order once an accused has remained silent a trap is set from which he cannot escape: if an accused chooses to give evidence or to call witnesses, he is, by reason of his prior silence, exposed to the risk of an Article 3 inference sufficient to bring about a conviction; on the other hand, if he maintains his silence inferences may be drawn against him under other provisions of the Order.

56. The Court [will not] speculate on the question whether inferences would have been drawn under the Order had the applicant, at any moment after his first interrogation, chosen to speak to the police or to give evidence at his trial or call witnesses. Nor should it speculate on the question whether it was the possibility of such inferences being drawn that explains why the applicant was advised by his solicitor to remain silent.

Immediately after arrest the applicant was warned in accordance with the provisions of the Order but chose to remain silent. [There] is no indication that the applicant failed to understand the significance of the warning given to him by the police prior to seeing his solicitor. Under these circumstances the fact that during the first 48 hours of his detention the applicant had been refused access to a lawyer does not detract from the above conclusion that the drawing of inferences was not unfair or unreasonable. . . .

57. [The] Court does not consider that the criminal proceedings were unfair or that there had been an infringement of the presumption of innocence. . . . For these reasons, the Court [holds] by 14 votes to 5 that there has been no violation of Article 6(1) and (2) of the Convention arising out of the drawing of adverse inferences on account of the applicant's silence. . . .

WALSH, partly dissenting.

1. In my opinion there have been violations of Article 6(1) and (2) of the Convention. The applicant was by Article 6(2) guaranteed a presumption of innocence in the criminal trial of which he complains. Prior to the introduction of the Criminal Evidence (Northern Ireland) Order 1988 a judge trying a case without a jury could not lawfully draw an inference of guilt from the fact that an accused person did not proclaim his innocence. Equally in a trial with a jury it would have been contrary to law to instruct the jurymen that they could do so. [The] object and effect of the 1988 Order was to reverse that position. . . .

3. . . . To permit such a procedure is to permit a penalty to be imposed by a criminal court on an accused because he relies upon a procedural right guaranteed by the Convention. I draw attention to the decision of the Supreme Court of the United States in Griffin v. California, 380 U.S. 609 (1965), which dealt with a similar point in relation to the Fifth Amendment of the Constitution by striking down a Californian law which permitted a court to make adverse comment on the accused's decision not to testify. . . .

Problem 18-7. Telling the Jury

Two police officers on patrol learned of an activated security alarm around 2:25 A.M. at Pleasants Hardware Store in the Pinewood Shopping Center. As they approached the plaza, the officers observed a car parked about 100 yards from the shopping center facing away from the hardware store. The store was not lit, and the parking lot was empty. When the officers got out of their car and inspected the premises, they noticed a large hole in the concrete block wall at the rear of the building.

After this initial investigation, the officers drove to the location of the car they had seen earlier to obtain license tag numbers but discovered that it was gone. Within two minutes, they observed the car traveling north on Highway 321 at a high speed with its headlights off. After a brief pursuit, the driver of the car pulled over.

The driver, Joseph Reid, told the officers he had stopped in the area of the shopping center because his car had run out of gas. When the officers asked why the car was running at that time, Reid said it had started unexpectedly. The officers found a sledgehammer near the location where Reid stopped his car.

Reid was tried in superior court on the charge of breaking and entering with intent to commit the felony of larceny. During the prosecution's closing argument to the jury, the following exchange took place:

> *The State:* Now defendant hasn't taken the stand in this case —
> *Defense Counsel:* Objection to his remarks about that, Your Honor.
> *The Court:* Overruled.
> *Defense Counsel:* Exception.
> *The State:* The defendant hasn't taken the stand in this case. He has that right. You're not to hold that against him. But we have to look at the other evidence to look at intent in this case.

The prosecutor's remark that the defendant had not testified mirrored the North Carolina Pattern Jury Instructions regarding a criminal defendant's right not to testify. Did the prosecutor commit reversible error by quoting to the jury from the pattern jury instructions? Compare State v. Reid, 434 S.E.2d 193 (N.C. 1993).

Problem 18-8. Pre-arrest Silence

At 2:30 A.M., Patrick Easter's Isuzu Trooper collided with a yellow taxicab. Easter was returning from a wedding reception to his home near the accident site. The cab was carrying six university students. Easter suffered injuries in the accident, and four of the students were seriously injured. A test administered shortly after the accident showed Easter's blood alcohol content was approximately .11. Several days later, Easter was arrested and charged with four counts of vehicular assault.

Easter did not testify at trial. The state and the defense presented evidence supporting different versions of how the accident happened. Officer Fitzgerald's testimony occupied much of the trial, although he did not observe the accident or take a statement from a witness. He testified that he arrived within minutes of the accident and found Easter in the bathroom of a gas station at the intersection, with torn clothes, a cut forehead, and blood on his elbows and knees. He testified that Easter then "totally ignored" him when he asked what happened. He also testified that when he continued to ask questions, Easter looked down, "once again ignoring me, ignoring my questions."

Fitzgerald said that he "felt the defendant was being smart drunk." The officer explained that when he used the term "smart drunk," he meant to say that Easter "was evasive, wouldn't talk to me, wouldn't look at me, wouldn't get close enough for me to get good observations of his breath and eyes, I felt that he was trying to hide or cloak."

Fitzgerald testified he took Easter back to the intersection and told him he would be placed under arrest or he could submit to a voluntary blood-alcohol test at a hospital. Fitzgerald suspected Easter was intoxicated because of Easter's slightly slurred speech, bloodshot eyes, and the odor of alcohol on his breath, although Easter had no coordination problems, walked without difficulty, and produced his license without fumbling or stumbling. After learning that he would be arrested, Easter's attitude changed. He asked for business papers in the truck and for a friend to be telephoned. Easter answered questions about his driver's license and said his home was a mile north of the accident scene.

In closing, the prosecutor argued that the trial testimony was best summed up with the words "smart drunk." He referred several times to testimony that Easter was a "smart drunk" who had ignored Officer Fitzgerald, except when asking about his papers and friend, and concluded, "Easter is a smart drunk." He closed his final argument with these words: "I urge you to find Mr. Easter, the smart drunk in this case, guilty." Did the prosecutor and the prosecution witness improperly comment on the defendant's invocation of his right to silence? See State v. Easter, 922 P.2d 1285 (Wash. 1996).

Notes

1. *Commenting on silence: majority position.* The Supreme Court's broad holding in *Griffin* that a prosecutor may not comment on a defendant's silence at trial has taken an even broader form over time in the state and federal courts. The *Griffin* rule applies not only to a prosecutor's statements literally pointing out that a defendant has not testified. It also prevents the prosecutor from calling the defendant to the witness stand to allow the jury to see the defendant invoke the privilege. The principle also covers veiled references to a defendant's failure to testify. See State v. McLamb, 69 S.E.2d 537 (N.C. 1952) (argument that defendant was "hiding behind his wife's coattail" was equivalent to comment on defendant's failure to testify on his own behalf). Most state courts say that the constitutional rule bars any comments "manifestly intended" to note a defendant's silence, or statements that are reasonably likely to draw a jury's attention to the fact that the defendant did not testify. See People v. Arman, 545 N.E.2d 658 (Ill. 1989). If a prosecutor makes an improper statement and the defense counsel objects, most states require the trial court to give a curative instruction to the jury immediately.

While the prosecutor may usually comment on a defendant's failure to produce *other* witnesses or exculpatory evidence to contradict the government's evidence, even a statement that the government's proof is "uncontradicted" could run afoul of the *Griffin* rule when it is highly unlikely that anyone other than the defendant could rebut the evidence. See Smith v. State, 787 A.2d 152 (Md. 2001) (prosecutor in closing argument improperly commented that the defendant had given "zero" answer to key piece of incriminating evidence; proper test is whether the prosecutor's comment is "susceptible of the inference" by the jurors that they were to consider silence). On the other hand, the prosecutor has a bit more latitude in comments that respond directly to defense attorney claims about the quality of the government's case. See United States v. Robinson, 485 U.S. 25 (1988) (prosecutor may refer to defendant's failure to testify when defense counsel claims in closing argument that government did not allow defendant to explain defendant's side of story); Tate v. State, 20 So.3d 623 (Miss. 2009) (no error when prosecutor says in closing argument that child sex-abuse cases often amount to "her word against his," responding to defense arguments about daughter's motives to frame her father for the crime). For a sampling of state court cases that carry out the ban on commentary

about a defendant's silence at trial, go to the web extension for this chapter at *http://www.crimpro.com/extension/ch18*.

2. *Jury instructions about silence*. The constitutional right to silence at trial encompasses a right to have the judge instruct the jury not to draw any inferences from the defendant's decision not to testify. As the court said in Carter v. Kentucky, 450 U.S. 288, 303 (1981), "No judge can prevent jurors from speculating about why a defendant stands mute in the face of a criminal accusation, but a judge can, and must, if requested to do so, use the unique power of the jury instruction to reduce that speculation to a minimum." Most jurisdictions rely on pattern jury instructions about a defendant's silence, along these lines: "The defendant has an absolute right not to testify. The fact that the defendant did not testify should not be considered by you in any way in arriving at your verdict." As defense counsel, would you rather have the judge deliver this jury instruction, or would you rather not call attention to the defendant's silence?

3. *Inferences based on silence at trial: other legal systems*. The European Court of Human Rights, as indicated by the *Murray* opinion, reflects a common position in foreign legal systems. Not all systems allow the defendant to remain silent at trial; even among those allowing silence, most empower the judge to draw inferences against the defendant based on this silence. See Criminal Procedure Act of Norway, ch. 9, §93 ("If the person charged refuses to answer, or states that he reserves his answer, the president of the court may inform him that this may be considered to tell against him"). In the United States, the federal and state constitutions as well as some statutes and rules of evidence prevent the factfinder from drawing inferences based on the defendant's silence at trial. See Conn. Gen. Stat. §54-84(b). Is there any value in preventing comments on silence if the factfinder is a judge rather than a jury? Would it be more consistent with truth-seeking if the judge (but not the prosecutor) could tell the jury it may draw inferences from silence?

4. *Incentives to remain silent*. Do juries act differently when none of the attorneys mention the defendant's silence, or is that something a jury will consider regardless of what the attorneys say? Even if a defendant is convinced that the jury looks unfavorably on a decision not to testify, there are some powerful reasons to remain silent at trial. Once a defendant chooses to take the stand at trial, he may not selectively invoke the privilege to avoid answering the most difficult questions. The defendant is subject to the ordinary scope of cross-examination. For many defendants, this means that the prosecutor can introduce evidence of some prior convictions as a method of impeaching the defendant's credibility as a witness. See Theodore Eisenberg & Valerie P. Hans, Taking a Stand on Taking the Stand: The Effect of a Prior Criminal Record on the Decision to Testify and on Trial Outcomes, 94 Cornell L. Rev. 1353 (2009). What remedy is appropriate if a defendant takes the stand but refuses to answer some questions on cross-examination?

5. *Use at trial of pretrial silence*. Although it is clear that a prosecutor cannot make even an indirect reference to the defendant's silence at trial, there is more leeway to comment at trial on some forms of *pretrial* silence by the defendant. The Supreme Court has drawn fine distinctions under the federal constitution. The prosecutor may not comment on any pretrial silence of the defendant *after* arrest and the delivery of *Miranda* warnings. Doyle v. Ohio, 426 U.S. 610 (1976). However, the government can use a defendant's *pre-arrest* silence as a basis for impeachment during the defendant's testimony at trial. The same is true for post-arrest silence when there is no indication that *Miranda* warnings were delivered. Fletcher v. Weir, 455 U.S. 603

(1982) (post-arrest, pre-*Miranda* silence); Jenkins v. Anderson, 447 U.S. 231 (1980) (pre-arrest silence); cf. Anderson v. Charles, 447 U.S. 404 (1980) (defendant made inconsistent factual statements at trial and during interrogation after waiver of *Miranda* rights; prosecution may properly comment on factual inconsistency). Is there any real difference in the evidentiary value of these various forms of silence?

State courts are about evenly divided between those that follow this cluster of federal rulings and those that depart from one or more of the components. It is most common to find state courts ruling that post-arrest unwarned silence cannot be used as impeachment material at trial. These courts base such rulings both on state constitutional provisions and on rules of evidence. See Reynolds v. State, 673 S.E.2d 854 (Ga. 2009) (while federal law allows impeachment use of evidence of pre-arrest, pre-*Miranda* silence, state evidence rules make it improper for prosecutor to comment on defendant's pre-warning silence or failure to come forward); Weitzel v. State, 863 A.2d 999 (Md. 2005) (discussing division of authority on question of whether substantive use of pre-arrest silence violates state constitutional rights); State v. Leach, 807 N.E.2d 335 (Ohio 2004) (allowing use of pre-arrest silence for impeachment, but not as substantive evidence of guilt). Note that the prosecutor in Problem 18-8 above used the defendant's pre-arrest silence not for impeachment purposes but during direct examination of a prosecution witness and during closing arguments. Should the use of such evidence depend on the defendant's choice to take the stand at trial?

In 1994 the British Parliament changed the rule regarding silence before trial. A 1984 statute required the police to inform suspects in custody that they have a right to consult an attorney before any interrogation. Under §34 of the Criminal Justice and Public Order Act of 1994, a court may draw inferences from the fact that a person is questioned and fails to mention a fact that an innocent person could reasonably be expected to mention during questioning, so long as the constable warns the accused of this fact at the time of questioning.

6. *Compulsory process for defense witnesses.* The defendant who hopes to call witnesses and collect evidence to undermine the prosecution's case receives some significant help from the government. Provisions in the federal constitution and in virtually all state constitutions give the defendant the power of "compulsory process," that is, the power to subpoena witnesses who must inform the court of what they know about the events in question. For instance, the Sixth Amendment to the federal constitution grants to the accused the right "to have compulsory process for obtaining witnesses in his favor." Statutes and rules of procedure also confirm the defendant's power to obtain government support in presenting witnesses.

7. *Threats of perjury charges against defense witnesses.* While it is surely true that the law makes it easier for defendants to obtain favorable testimony, there are also some legal obstacles to finding defense witnesses. To begin with, the defense witnesses might invoke the privilege against self-incrimination. Further, the potential witnesses might fear that if they testify, they will create a risk of perjury charges if the prosecutor believes that the testimony is not truthful. To what extent can government agents, such as judges or prosecutors, use these incentives to make it more difficult for the defendant to obtain witnesses?

The due process clause of the federal constitution controls the statements of prosecutors and judges about possible criminal charges to be filed against defense witnesses. In the leading Supreme Court decision, Webb v. Texas, 409 U.S. 95 (1972), a trial judge warned the defendant's only witness against committing perjury and explained the consequences of a perjury conviction. The Court held that the judge's statements violated due process. See also State v. Finley, 998 P.2d 95 (Kan. 2000) (right to present defense infringed when prosecutor suggests state will charge potential defense witness with felony murder based on her testimony).

High state courts have read *Webb* flexibly to mean that the judge or prosecutor can sometimes mention possible criminal charges to a defense witness. Applying federal due process principles rather than state constitutional provisions, the courts often condemn a prosecutor for saying that she "will" bring criminal charges against the defense witness if the witness testifies. See Mills v. State, 733 P.2d 880 (Okla. Crim. App. 1985). However, when a prosecutor tells a defense witness that testimony "could" expose the witness to criminal charges, courts are less likely to find a due process violation. The same distinction applies to a trial judge who informs the witness about possible criminal charges which could result from testifying. See Jones v. State, 655 N.E.2d 49 (Ind. 1995). Should it matter whether the prosecutor speaks directly to the defense witness or instead sends a message by way of the defense attorney or some other third party?

Defendants have much less success when they complain that the government has deported aliens whom the defendant planned to call as defense witnesses. United States v. Valenzuela-Bernal, 458 U.S. 858 (1982) (no due process violation in prosecution for illegal transportation of aliens when government deports all aliens who would have testified for defendant). Can you explain why these claims are more difficult to sustain than those dealing with threats of criminal charges against witnesses?

8. *Defense grants of immunity.* If a prosecution witness invokes her privilege against self-incrimination, the prosecutor has the option of "immunizing" the witness from later prosecution based on the testimony, and the court will compel the witness to testify despite the privilege. (Recall the discussion of this issue in Chapter 10.) However, the defense does not have a comparable power to immunize defense witnesses who invoke the privilege. Defendants sometimes ask the court to order the prosecution to grant immunity to a defense witness, but courts routinely deny the requests. See State v. Roy, 668 A.2d 41 (N.H. 1995). Why have defendants been so unsuccessful in obtaining grants of immunity, even for their most crucial witnesses? When a defendant requests a grant of immunity for a witness and does not receive it, should the judge explain to the jury that the defendant had hoped to call a witness who is now "missing" because of the privilege against self-incrimination?

D. ETHICS AND LIES AT TRIAL

Ethical issues arise at all stages in the prosecution and defense of criminal defendants. Issues before trial include the conduct of interrogations, the grounds for filing charges, and the statements made while negotiating plea bargains. During trial preparation, ethical obligations may require discovery disclosures beyond those required by constitutional doctrine, statutes, or rules of procedure. Throughout the criminal process, ethical dilemmas for defense counsel arise from the tension between the search for truth and the zealous representation of the defendant. For the prosecutor, ethical dilemmas arise from the conflict between the obligation to seek justice on behalf of the public as a whole and the need to consult and defer to the wishes of crime victims.

Some of the most difficult ethical questions in all of legal practice arise when the lawyer believes the client is acting illegally or is lying. Related problems arise when a lawyer believes that a friendly witness is lying. Consider the extent to which the ethical obligations of defense lawyers and prosecutors at trial are — or should be — different. Is this difference on obligations simply an outgrowth of the burden of proof and the beyond-a-reasonable-doubt standard in criminal cases?

■ PEOPLE v. DEREK ANDRADES

828 N.E.2d 599 (N.Y. 2005)

G.B. SMITH, J.

In People v. DePallo, 96 N.Y.2d 437 (N.Y. 2001), we held that defense counsel properly balanced the duties he owed to his client and the duties he owed to the court and to the criminal justice system when, during a jury trial, counsel notified the court that his client had offered perjured testimony and refused to use that testimony in his closing argument to the jury. We left open the question of the propriety of a similar disclosure under circumstances where the court sits as the factfinder. We address that issue in the case now before us and hold that counsel's disclosure to the court, which was open to the inference that his client intended to perjure himself upon taking the stand, did not deprive defendant of a fair hearing or of the effective assistance of counsel.

Defendant became enraged when he heard rumors that Magalie Nieves, a woman with whom he had had a sexual relationship, was infected with the HIV virus. Defendant, with the aid of 14-year-old Ericka Cruz, confronted Nieves and a fight ensued. Subsequently, defendant and Cruz lured Nieves to an isolated area where defendant choked her with a bandana, and he and Cruz stabbed her in the ear and in the breast, killing her. Days later, the police arrested Cruz, who offered a confession of the killing. The next day, defendant was arrested and charged, inter alia, with second degree murder and first degree manslaughter. Upon his arrest, defendant was read his *Miranda* rights and gave both written and videotaped statements in which he admitted to acting in concert with Cruz in killing Nieves.

Defendant moved to suppress his confessions. . . . Prior to the hearing, defendant's attorney asked to be relieved as counsel, stating, "There is an ethical conflict with my continuing to represent [defendant] and I can't go any further than that." The prosecutor opposed the application, citing the age of the case. The court asked defense counsel to state the nature of the ethical dilemma without disclosing privileged information so that the court could make an effective ruling. Counsel stated, however, that he could not elaborate. The court then presumed that counsel's ethical dilemma concerned defendant's right to testify. The court denied counsel's application and told him that if the problem arose, he would have to offer more specific information to the court.

After the People presented their case at the . . . hearing, defense counsel informed the court that defendant intended to testify. Outside defendant's presence, counsel stated:

> As part and parcel of my request to be relieved in this matter, I think I should tell the Court and place on the record that I did tell [defendant] and advise [defendant] that he should not testify at the hearing and as a result of the problem that I'm having, the ethical problem I'm having. What I'm going to do is just basically direct his attention to date, time and location of the statement and let him run with the ball.

The court, recognizing that defense counsel was not permitted to divulge privileged matters to the court, concluded that counsel's conduct complied with his ethical obligations under the disciplinary rules given his anticipation that defendant "could possibly, could commit perjury on the witness stand." The court further concluded that counsel could still afford defendant the effective assistance of counsel. [The court also concluded that it was not necessary for defendant to be present during the conference because it did not constitute a critical stage of his trial.]

Defendant thereafter testified on his own behalf, largely in narrative form, with the court and counsel asking clarifying questions. Defendant testified that at the time he provided his statements to the police, he did not remember the events leading to Nieves's death and specifically did not recall stabbing her. He stated that during his interrogation, the police informed him of Cruz's version of the events, and he believed what she said because he did not think that Cruz would lie about him. Defendant stated that he initially refused to sign the written confession drafted by the police officers because its contents were not true, but that later he signed it only after one of the officers took him into a private room. Defendant further testified that when he gave his videotaped statement, he simply restated Cruz's rendition of the killing as described to him by the officers. Thus, he claimed that this confession was not a recounting of events from his own memory. Finally, defendant stated that by the time he had provided the videotaped confession at approximately 10:00 P.M., he was hungry because he had not eaten all day, and was not permitted food until after he had given that statement.

Defense counsel offered no closing argument, choosing instead to rest on the record and the papers submitted. Following the People's closing statement, the court denied defendant's motion to suppress his confessions. In a subsequent written decision, the court noted that it "did not find the defendant's testimony credible or worthy of belief." The court held that defendant made his written and videotaped statements after voluntarily waiving his constitutional rights. Upon a jury trial, at which defendant largely defended himself, defendant was convicted of second degree murder and sentenced to a prison term of 25 years to life. . . .

In *DePallo*, we recognized that a defense attorney's duty to zealously represent a client must be circumscribed by his or her duty as an officer of the court to serve the truth-seeking function of the justice system. Moreover, as perjury is a criminal offense, defense counsel has a duty to refrain from participating in the client's commission of it. Thus, we stated that while counsel must pursue all reasonable means to reach the objectives of the client, counsel must not in any way assist a client in presenting false evidence to the court. See Nix v. Whiteside, 475 U.S. 157 (1986).

Indeed, New York's Code of Professional Responsibility specifically addresses an attorney's ethical obligations in providing lawful representation. Disciplinary Rule 7-102 expressly states that an attorney may not "knowingly use perjured testimony or false evidence," DR 7-102(a)(4); "knowingly make a false statement of law or fact," DR 7-102(a)(5); "participate in the creation or preservation of evidence when the lawyer knows or it is obvious that the evidence is false," DR 7-102(a)(6);

"counsel or assist the client in conduct that the lawyer knows to be illegal or fraudulent," DR 7-102(a)(7); or "knowingly engage in other illegal conduct," DR 7-102(a)(8).

In light of the ethical obligations of an attorney in this state, and in accordance with United States Supreme Court jurisprudence, an attorney faced with a client who intends to commit perjury has the initial responsibility to attempt to dissuade the client from pursuing the unlawful course of action. Nix v. Whiteside, 475 U.S. at 169-170. Should the client insist on perjuring himself, counsel may seek to withdraw from the case. If counsel's request is denied, defense counsel, bound to honor defendant's right to testify on his own behalf, should refrain from eliciting the testimony in traditional question-and-answer form and permit defendant to present his testimony in narrative form. However, in accordance with DR 7-102(a)(4), counsel may not use the perjured testimony in making argument to the court.

Here, defense counsel properly discharged his ethical obligations under the circumstances presented. Counsel clearly advised defendant against lying on the witness stand; indeed, counsel encouraged defendant not to take the stand at all. Yet defendant insisted on testifying at the hearing, and his attorney believed that the evidence he intended to present was false. Thus, it was entirely proper for counsel to seek to withdraw as defendant's attorney prior to the hearing based on his perceived ethical dilemma.

While defendant does not argue the propriety of his attorney's actions up to that point, he does take issue with his attorney's telling the court that the ethical dilemma he faced concerned defendant's right to testify at the hearing. Defendant argues that such a disclosure signifies defendant's intention to commit perjury to the court which sits as the factfinder for the hearing. He contends that such a disclosure inevitably affected the court's ability to assess his credibility in determining the outcome of the hearing.[3] In that same vein, defendant argues that his attorney should not have told the court of his intent to question defendant in the narrative before having done so. Defendant asserts that his attorney should have said nothing, proceeded to question defendant in the narrative, and if counsel's suspicions about defendant's testimony ripened into a reality, counsel could simply refrain from using the perjured testimony in his closing argument.

We disagree. As an initial matter, we note that at no time did counsel ever disclose to the court that defendant intended to commit perjury or otherwise disclose any client secrets. Rather, the court inferred defendant's perjurious intent based upon the nature of counsel's application. However, counsel could have properly made such a disclosure since a client's intent to commit a crime is not a protected confidence or secret. See Nix v. Whiteside, 475 U.S. at 174; Code of Professional Responsibility DR 4-101(c)(3). Moreover, counsel's ethical obligations do not

3. In support of his position, defendant relies on Lowery v. Cardwell, 575 F.2d 727 (9th Cir. 1978). In that case, defendant testified at her bench trial and perjured herself, to the surprise of her attorney. Counsel requested a recess, at which time he unsuccessfully attempted to withdraw from the case. Counsel then ended the defendant's testimony and made no reference to the defendant's perjured testimony during his closing arguments. The [court] held that counsel's actions denied the defendant a fair trial because counsel's actions gave the judge the impression that counsel believed that the defendant had testified falsely. The court . . . suggested that it would have been the better practice for the attorney to have made a record for his own protection in the event that he was ever questioned about his professional conduct. We expressly reject this approach because it requires an attorney to remain silent while the client commits perjury, which is wholly incompatible with counsel's role as an officer of the court and, more specifically, counsel's obligation to reveal fraud perpetrated by a client upon the court.

change simply because a judge rather than a jury is sitting as the factfinder. Moreover, as a practical matter, defendant's suggestion would solve nothing because counsel would likely find it difficult to allow defendant to testify in the narrative without prior explanation. Like the direct examination of any witness, defendant's examination must be guided by proper questioning. Had counsel attempted to offer defendant's testimony in the narrative, it would have been subject to objection either by the prosecutor or the court. Even if counsel were permitted to present defendant's testimony in narrative form without objection, the very fact of defendant testifying in such a manner would signify to the court that counsel believes that his client is perjuring himself.

We therefore conclude that defense counsel properly balanced his duties to his client with his duties to the court and the criminal justice system and that in doing so, defendant was not denied his right to a fair hearing. Furthermore, absent a breach of any recognized professional duty, defendant's claim that he was denied the effective assistance of counsel must also fail.

Finally, we reject defendant's contention that he was denied his right to be present during a material stage of the trial because he was absent during the colloquy between the court and the attorneys regarding defense counsel's intent to present defendant's testimony in the narrative. [A] colloquy of this nature involves procedural matters at which a defendant can offer no meaningful input. Therefore, defendant had no right to be present. . . .

PEOPLE v. VICTOR REICHMAN

819 P.2d 1035 (Colo. 1991)

PER CURIAM.

This is an attorney discipline case. A hearing panel approved the findings and recommendation of a majority of the hearing board that the respondent receive a public censure for conduct involving dishonesty, fraud, deceit or misrepresentation, and conduct prejudicial to the administration of justice. We accept the recommendation of the hearing panel and publicly censure the respondent and order that he be assessed the costs of these proceedings.

[The] respondent was the duly appointed or elected District Attorney of the Sixth Judicial District, which includes La Plata County. . . . In the spring of 1987, the respondent and other members of law enforcement in the Sixth Judicial District formed a de facto task force, or "LEADS committee," to conduct undercover operations to investigate and prosecute drug trafficking in the district. A police officer from outside the judicial district was retained to conduct the undercover investigations, and the officer chose the fictitious identity of one "Colton Young," an unemployed biker. The respondent served as the head of the task force.

After several months undercover, "Young" had developed a list of names of suspected drug traffickers in the judicial district. In addition, two individuals had told "Young" that an attorney, Robin Auld, accepted drugs in lieu of fees.[2] Then, in September 1987, "Young" called an emergency meeting of the task force to

2. On March 19, 1990, this court suspended Robin Auld from the practice of law for six months for his involvement in the occurrences which form the basis for this proceeding.

announce that he believed his undercover identity may have been compromised. The task force decided to rehabilitate "Young's" identity. With the respondent's approval, "Young" was "arrested" for a traffic violation on the main street of Durango outside of the business establishment of a significant target of the task force. Auld was not this target. A search of "Young" was then conducted in such a way that the fruits of the search could be easily suppressed and the charges dismissed. "Young" was instructed to contact Robin Auld and retain him as defense counsel.[3]

As part of the plan, fictitious charges were lodged against "Young" with the respondent's knowledge and approval. The respondent, either personally or through his agents, filed a false criminal complaint against "Young," charging him with the illegal possession of a firearm and of marihuana in the County Court of La Plata County. Other documents filed by or on behalf of the respondent in the "Young" case included a surety bond and an offense report, falsely stating "Young's" name and address, and falsely stating that "Young" had committed certain criminal offenses. In addition, with the respondent's knowledge and approval, "Young" appeared in county court and made false statements to the county judge, who was unaware of the deception.

A majority of the hearing board concluded that the respondent's conduct in filing the false documents and the fictitious criminal complaint, and otherwise creating and maintaining the deception of the county court, violated DR 1-102(A)(4) (conduct involving dishonesty or misrepresentation), and DR 1-102(A)(5) (conduct prejudicial to the administration of justice).

The respondent argues that his conduct was not unethical and he points to a number of cases in which prosecutors engaged in deception during "sting" operations. . . . United States v. Murphy, 768 F.2d 1518 (7th Cir. 1985), discussed the participation of the FBI and federal prosecutors in Operation Greylord. The defendant in Murphy, a former associate judge of the Circuit Court of Cook County, Illinois, was convicted of accepting bribes to fix the outcomes of hundreds of criminal cases that came before him. As part of Operation Greylord, FBI agents posed as corrupt lawyers, and other agents testified in made-up criminal cases heard by Judge Murphy. Murphy argued that his convictions were invalid because the Operation Greylord "cases" were frauds on the court, and the undercover agents committed perjury. The court of appeals disagreed, finding that while the agents' acts appeared criminal, the acts were not crimes because they were performed without the requisite criminal intent. Further, *Murphy* held, "The FBI and prosecutors behaved honorably in establishing and running Operation Greylord. They assure us that they notified the Presiding Judge of the Circuit Court's Criminal Division, the State's Attorney of Cook County, the Attorney General of Illinois, and the Governor of Illinois." . . .

Prosecutorial deception may not always constitute prosecutorial misconduct for purposes of determining whether a criminal complaint or indictment must be dismissed. It does not necessarily follow, however, that prosecutorial deception of a

3. The actual objective of the "arrest" and the filing of the fictitious charges against "Young" was hotly disputed. The special assistant disciplinary counsel sought to establish that the respondent's intention was to coerce Auld into betraying Auld's client or clients. The hearing board did not find that this was the respondent's design by clear and convincing evidence. For the purpose of this opinion, we assume that the respondent's intention was to rehabilitate "Young's" undercover identity.

type which results in directly misleading a court should be exempted from the proscriptions of the Code of Professional Responsibility simply because the deception is not such as to warrant the dismissal of a criminal case.

In the case of In re Friedman, 392 N.E.2d 1333 (Ill. 1979), the attorney-respondent, Friedman, was a state prosecutor. In two separate investigations involving bribery of two police officers, Friedman instructed the police officers to testify falsely in court hearings. [Defense attorneys had attempted to bribe the officers to testify falsely in favor of their clients, and the prosecutor instructed the officers to do so as part of a bribery investigation directed at the defense attorneys.] Four justices of the Supreme Court of Illinois found that Friedman's conduct violated the Code of Professional Responsibility notwithstanding his motives. Two justices found that Friedman's conduct was unethical but did not merit discipline because he "acted without the guidance of precedent or settled opinion and because there is apparently considerable belief . . . that the respondent acted properly in conducting the investigation. . . ." Two justices concurred in the decision of the court not to impose discipline because they determined that Friedman did not violate the Code of Professional Responsibility. Two justices concluded that Friedman's conduct was unethical and warranted censure.

[The *Friedman* court rejected the argument that the attorney's] conduct was not unethical because he was motivated by . . . his public responsibilities. This argument is the equivalent of the contention that the end justifies the means, and "that pernicious doctrine," Olmstead v. United States, 277 U.S. 438 (1928) (Brandeis, J., dissenting),[5] is unacceptable in the administration of the criminal law.

[We] conclude, as did the hearing panel and the majority of the hearing board, that the respondent's conduct violated DR 1-102(A)(1), and DR 1-102(A)(5). District attorneys in Colorado owe a very high duty to the public because they are governmental officials holding constitutionally created offices. This court has spoken out strongly against misconduct by public officials who are lawyers. The respondent's responsibility to enforce the laws in his judicial district grants him no license to ignore those laws or the Code of Professional Responsibility. While the respondent's motives and the erroneous belief of other public prosecutors that the respondent's conduct was ethical do not excuse these violations of the Code of Professional Responsibility, they are mitigating factors to be taken into account in assessing the appropriate discipline. The respondent has no prior discipline. We find, therefore, that the respondent's misconduct warrants discipline consistent with our duties to protect the public and maintain the integrity of the legal profession.

Accordingly, we accept the recommendation of the hearing panel and publicly censure the respondent Victor Reichman. While the surrounding circumstances may tend to explain and mitigate the misconduct, they do not excuse the deception imposed on the court. We therefore publicly reprimand Reichman and assess him the costs of these proceedings in the amount of $4,851.28. . . .

5. As Justice Brandeis said in dissent in *Olmstead:*

> Crime is contagious. If the Government becomes a lawbreaker, it breeds contempt for law; it invites every man to become a law unto himself; it invites anarchy. To declare that in the administration of the criminal law the end justifies the means — to declare that the Government may commit crimes in order to secure the conviction of a private criminal — would bring terrible retribution. Against that pernicious doctrine this Court should resolutely set its face.

Notes

1. *Lying clients: majority view.* As the U.S. Supreme Court made clear in Nix v. Whiteside, 475 U.S. 157 (1986), the federal constitutional right to effective counsel does not compel an attorney to remain silent when a client plans to commit perjury during testimony. Nor does the Constitution require the attorney to take any other particular action, such as withdrawing from the case or informing the court of the client's plans. The same can be said for state constitutional rulings: They leave the attorney with several acceptable options. The most pertinent legal requirements in this situation come not from constitutions, but from the rules of legal ethics, sometimes embodied in state statutes. The first ethical duty of the defense attorney who learns that a client might commit perjury at trial is to convince the client not to commit perjury. What exactly does an attorney tell a client accused of a crime who apparently plans to lie during testimony?

Before taking any further steps, the attorney must have sufficient reason to believe that her client plans to lie during testimony, despite her best efforts to convince him otherwise. ABA Model Rule of Professional Conduct 3.3(a)(4) phrases it this way: "A lawyer shall not knowingly offer evidence that the lawyer knows to be false." How will an attorney "know" that a client's testimony will be false? State courts sometimes require the attorney to be convinced "beyond a reasonable doubt" that the client plans to commit perjury. Other formulations include "good cause to believe the defendant's proposed testimony would be deliberately untruthful," a "firm factual basis," a "good-faith determination," and "actual knowledge." See Commonwealth v. Mitchell, 781 N.E.2d 1237 (Mass. 2003) (reviewing standards and adopting "firm basis in fact" because standard of beyond reasonable doubt would "eviscerate" attorney's ethical obligation of candor to tribunal).

2. *Defense counsel responses to perjury.* If the attorney knows that a client plans to commit perjury, or has already committed perjury at trial, several options are open to her under the rules of ethics. One possibility is to withdraw from the case. Ethics rules allow (or even require) the attorney in most pretrial situations to make the motion, although courts often will deny the motion. ABA Model Rule of Professional Conduct 1.16(a)(1) (a lawyer "shall withdraw from the representation of a client if . . . the representation will result in violation of the rules of professional conduct or other law"). What should the attorney say in the motion to withdraw? Suppose the case is set for a bench trial. Does withdrawal prevent any harm from befalling the client or the tribunal?

The attorney who does not withdraw must deal with a "trilemma — that is, the lawyer is required to know everything, to keep it in confidence, and to reveal it to the court." Monroe Freedman, Lawyers' Ethics in an Adversary System 28 (1975). Since the appearance of the ABA's Model Rules of Professional Conduct in 1983 (now adopted in over 40 jurisdictions), the states have moved toward rules requiring counsel to reveal the potential perjury to the court. In the words of Rule 3.3(a)(2), a lawyer "shall not knowingly . . . fail to disclose a material fact to a tribunal when disclosure is necessary to avoid assisting a criminal or fraudulent act by the client."

The defense attorney might allow the client to testify but use a "narrative" form of testimony, in which the attorney asks an open-ended question, such as, "tell us what happened," and the defendant relates his story without further questions from defense counsel. See State v. Chambers, 994 A.2d 1248 (Conn. 2010) (no violation of state constitution or ethics rules). Does this response strike the right balance among the defense lawyer's ethical obligations? Is this an appropriate response to perjury by a defense witness other than the defendant?

3. *Lying prosecution witnesses.* The *Reichman* case from Colorado dealt with perjury by prosecution witnesses in the context of a disciplinary proceeding against a prosecutor. The same issue also comes up when defendants challenge the validity of a conviction based on false testimony by prosecution witnesses. A prosecutor who knowingly allows prosecution witnesses to present false testimony about a material fact violates the federal due process clause. This is true even if the government attorney who knows about the false testimony is not the same as the trial attorney. Once the prosecution witness has delivered the false testimony, the prosecutor must inform the court of the falsehood. See Giglio v. United States, 405 U.S. 150 (1972); Mooney v. Holohan, 294 U.S. 103 (1935).

Some courts go a step further, and overturn convictions based on false testimony of prosecuting witnesses even if the prosecutor was unaware of the perjury. These courts require a defendant to demonstrate that the perjury came to his attention after trial (despite his due diligence in preparing for trial), and that the jury probably would have acquitted if it had not heard the perjured testimony. Ex parte Chabot, 300 S.W.3d 768 (Tex. Crim. App. 2009).

What inquiries would you expect prosecutors to make about the truthfulness of the testimony from government witnesses? What if the local police department has developed a reputation for "testilying" (providing false testimony to strengthen the prosecution's case)? For a review of empirical investigations into the extent and effects of testilying, go to the web extension for this chapter at *http://www.crimpro.com/extension/ch18*.

PART FOUR

MEASURING PUNISHMENT AND REASSESSING GUILT

XIX Sentencing

Criminal adjudication points toward sentencing. At sentencing, the system finally announces a "bottom line" outcome for those defendants who have proceeded all the way through the criminal process. Along the way, defense counsel, prosecutors, judges, and police make choices with one eye on the possible sentence. This anticipation of sentencing is perhaps most evident in plea bargaining.

Just as much of criminal procedure looks ahead to sentencing, the sentencing phase offers a chance to look back on the earlier steps in the process. At sentencing, the criminal justice system surveys once again all the major decisions it has reached regarding an offender, from investigation through conviction. It also takes a broader view of the offender's past and future, the victim's past and future, and the community's present attitude toward the crime. After this panoramic survey is complete, the sentencing authority selects a sanction.

One major puzzle for modern sentencing procedures can be summed up in this question: Why go to all the trouble of following intricate procedures for police and prosecutors, before and during trial, if the last step in the system ignores those procedural protections? This question, however, raises another: If the sentencing authority had to be bound by all determinations made prior to conviction, would convicted offenders receive undue protection, as if they were still presumed innocent?

A. WHO SENTENCES?

In most criminal justice systems, several institutions share the decision about the proper sentence to impose: Legislatures and judges always have a say in the sentence, and juries, parole commissions, or sentencing commissions sometimes participate. But the precise division of labor in deciding on sentencing policy and sentences in particular cases varies a great deal from place to place.

1. Indeterminate Sentencing

Until recently, sentencing in the United States was an area characterized more by discretion than procedure. In 1950 every state and the federal system had an "indeterminate" sentencing system. Under this type of system, the legislature prescribed broad potential sentencing ranges, and the trial judge sentenced without meaningful legal guidance and typically without offering any detailed explanation for the sentence. An executive branch agency (usually a parole board) ultimately determined the actual sentence each defendant would serve. There were virtually no judicial opinions explaining or reviewing a sentence, and legal counsel ordinarily made oral arguments at sentencing hearings without any written submissions to the court. The unwritten nature of the arguments and the decisions, together with the unavailability of pre-sentence investigation reports, made it difficult to get a handle on sentencing law and practice in an indeterminate system. Perhaps that reveals the most important point about such a system: Sentencing happened without much law.

The following materials offer a glimpse of indeterminate sentencing systems at work. The U.S. Supreme Court decision in Williams v. New York, which came at the high water mark for indeterminate sentencing, captures not only the huge discretion given to trial judges but also some of the principles underlying that discretion. The next document is a written opinion of a sentencing judge in the Australian territory of Victoria, where it is common for judges to record their thought processes as they exercise sentencing discretion. The opinion illustrates the types of arguments and reasoning that operate in the many cases sentenced in indeterminate sentencing systems in the United States.

■ SAMUEL WILLIAMS v. NEW YORK

337 U.S. 241 (1949)

BLACK, J.*

A jury in a New York state court found appellant guilty of murder in the first degree. The jury recommended life imprisonment, but the trial judge imposed sentence of death. In giving his reasons for imposing the death sentence the judge discussed in open court the evidence upon which the jury had convicted stating that this evidence had been considered in the light of additional information obtained through the "Probation Department, and through other sources." [A New York statute authorized the court to consider "any information that will aid the court in determining the proper treatment of such defendant." Williams claimed that the

* [Chief Justice Vinson and Justices Reed, Frankfurter, Douglas, Jackson, and Burton joined this opinion. — EDS.]

sentence, which was based on information supplied by witnesses, violated due process because the defendant had no chance to confront or cross-examine the witnesses or to rebut the evidence.]

The record shows a carefully conducted trial lasting more than two weeks in which appellant was represented by three appointed lawyers who conducted his defense with fidelity and zeal. The evidence proved a wholly indefensible murder committed by a person engaged in a burglary. . . .

About five weeks after the verdict of guilty with recommendation of life imprisonment, and after a statutory pre-sentence investigation report to the judge, the defendant was brought to court to be sentenced. [The] judge gave reasons why he felt that the death sentence should be imposed. . . . He stated that the pre-sentence investigation revealed many material facts concerning appellant's background which though relevant to the question of punishment could not properly have been brought to the attention of the jury in its consideration of the question of guilt. He referred to the experience appellant "had had on 30 other burglaries in and about the same vicinity" where the murder had been committed. The appellant had not been convicted of these burglaries although the judge had information that he had confessed to some and had been identified as the perpetrator of some of the others. The judge also referred to certain activities of appellant as shown by the probation report that indicated appellant possessed "a morbid sexuality" and classified him as a "menace to society." The accuracy of the statements made by the judge as to appellant's background and past practices were not challenged by appellant or his counsel, nor was the judge asked to disregard any of them or to afford appellant a chance to refute or discredit any of them by cross-examination or otherwise.

The case presents a serious and difficult question. The question relates to the rules of evidence applicable to the manner in which a judge may obtain information to guide him in the imposition of sentence upon an already convicted defendant. . . . To aid a judge in exercising this discretion intelligently the New York procedural policy encourages him to consider information about the convicted person's past life, health, habits, conduct, and mental and moral propensities. The sentencing judge may consider such information even though obtained outside the courtroom from persons whom a defendant has not been permitted to confront or cross-examine. . . .

Tribunals passing on the guilt of a defendant always have been hedged in by strict evidentiary procedural limitations. But both before and since the American colonies became a nation, courts in this country and in England practiced a policy under which a sentencing judge could exercise a wide discretion in the sources and types of evidence used to assist him in determining the kind and the extent of punishment to be imposed within limits fixed by law. Out-of-court affidavits have been used frequently, and of course in the smaller communities sentencing judges naturally have in mind their knowledge of the personalities and backgrounds of convicted offenders. . . .

In addition to the historical basis for different evidentiary rules governing trial and sentencing procedures there are sound practical reasons for the distinction. In a trial before verdict the issue is whether a defendant is guilty of having engaged in certain criminal conduct of which he has been specifically accused. Rules of evidence have been fashioned for criminal trials which narrowly confine the trial contest to evidence that is strictly relevant to the particular offense charged. These rules rest in part on a necessity to prevent a time consuming and confusing trial of collateral issues. They were also designed to prevent tribunals concerned solely with the issue of guilt of a particular offense from being influenced to convict for that offense by evidence that the defendant had habitually engaged in other misconduct. A sentencing judge, however, is not confined to the narrow issue of guilt. His task within fixed statutory or constitutional limits is to determine the type and extent of punishment after the issue of guilt has been determined. Highly relevant — if not essential — to his selection of an appropriate sentence is the possession of the fullest information possible concerning the defendant's life and characteristics. And modern concepts individualizing punishment have made it all the more necessary that a sentencing judge not be denied an opportunity to obtain pertinent information by a requirement of rigid adherence to restrictive rules of evidence properly applicable to the trial.

Undoubtedly the New York statutes emphasize a prevalent modern philosophy of penology that the punishment should fit the offender and not merely the crime. The belief no longer prevails that every offense in a like legal category calls for an identical punishment without regard to the past life and habits of a particular offender. This whole country has traveled far from the period in which the death sentence was an automatic and commonplace result of convictions — even for offenses today deemed trivial. . . . Indeterminate sentences, the ultimate termination of which are sometimes decided by nonjudicial agencies, have to a large extent taken the place of the old rigidly fixed punishments. . . . Retribution is no longer the dominant objective of the criminal law. Reformation and rehabilitation of offenders have become important goals of criminal jurisprudence. . . .

Under the practice of individualizing punishments, investigation techniques have been given an important role. Probation workers making reports of their investigations have not been trained to prosecute but to aid offenders. Their reports have been given a high value by conscientious judges who want to sentence persons on the best available information rather than on guesswork and inadequate information. To deprive sentencing judges of this kind of information would undermine modern penological procedural policies that have been cautiously adopted throughout the nation after careful consideration and experimentation. We must recognize that most of the information now relied upon by judges to guide them in the intelligent imposition of sentences would be unavailable if information were restricted to that given in open court by witnesses subject to cross-examination. And the modern probation report draws on information concerning every aspect of a defendant's life. The type and extent of this information make totally impractical if not impossible open court testimony with cross-examination. Such a procedure could endlessly delay criminal administration in a retrial of collateral issues.

The considerations we have set out admonish us against treating the due-process clause as a uniform command that courts throughout the Nation abandon their age-old practice of seeking information from out-of-court sources to guide their judgment toward a more enlightened and just sentence. . . . So to treat the due-process clause would hinder if not preclude all courts — state and federal — from making progressive efforts to improve the administration of criminal justice. We hold that appellant was not denied due process of law. Affirmed.

MURPHY, J., dissenting.*

[Williams] was convicted of murder by a jury, and sentenced to death by the judge. . . . In our criminal courts the jury sits as the representative of the community; its voice is that of the society against which the crime was committed. A judge even though vested with statutory authority to do so, should hesitate indeed to increase the severity of such a community expression.

He should be willing to increase it, moreover, only with the most scrupulous regard for the rights of the defendant. The [evidence here] would have been inadmissible at the trial. Some, such as allegations of prior crimes, was irrelevant. Much was incompetent as hearsay. All was damaging, and none was subject to scrutiny by the defendant.

Due process of law includes at least the idea that a person accused of crime shall be accorded a fair hearing through all the stages of the proceedings against him. I agree with the Court as to the value and humaneness of liberal use of probation reports as developed by modern penologists, but, in a capital case, against the unanimous recommendation of a jury, where the report would concededly not have been admissible at the trial, and was not subject to examination by the defendant, I am forced to conclude that the high commands of due process were not obeyed.

THE QUEEN v. ROBERT ARNAUTOVIC

[2007] VCC 597 (9 June 2005)
County Court of Victoria, Melbourne Criminal Division

Her Honour, Judge Gaynor:

1. Robert James Arnautovic, you have pleaded guilty before me to seven counts of burglary, seven counts of theft and one count of armed robbery and have admitted prior convictions. The facts underlying the offending which took place between November 1998 and March 2002 are as follows.

2. Counts 1 and 2 relate to an incident which occurred on the afternoon of 13 November 1998 when you entered the rear yard of a house at 56 Stafford Street, Abbotsford, smashing two windows to gain entry. You stole from that house property to the value of approximately $18,300 consisting of electronic equipment, computer equipment, a mobile phone, a watch, cameras, camera equipment, VCRs, CD players, disk players and CDs. . . .

3. [Counts 3-10 relate to similar criminal incidents during 1999 and 2000.]

7. Count 11 refers to an incident on the morning of 4 December 2001 when you forced a side window of a house at 5 York Street, Albion through which you gained entry and then stole a bag which you filled with items of property. While you were in the house the occupier, one Xavier Haveraux and his three year old daughter Kemely returned home entering through the front door. You rushed at Mr. Haveraux striking him to the head three times with a flat instrument similar to a small jemmy bar causing Mr. Haveraux to fall on the floor. Whilst he was on the floor you searched him taking his watch which was valued at $65 and demanding money from him, you ultimately being given $10. Whilst this was occurring you kept

* [Justice Rutledge joined this opinion. — EDS.]

accusing Mr. Haveraux of "ripping you off" to the tune of $50 a couple of weeks earlier and claimed you had followed him home.

8. You then asked Mr. Haveraux to drive you in his car to get more money but Mr. Haveraux talked you out of this and got you to leave. You then left the premises and walked down the street before which you apologised to Mr. Haveraux's three year old daughter who was present during the entire incident. Once you had left Mr. Haveraux grabbed an old cricket bat and followed you to see where you were going and as he followed you down the street you turned back towards him and approached him saying, "Come on."

9. You and Mr. Haveraux then struggled, wrestling to the ground during the course of which Mr. Haveraux managed to hit you over the head with the cricket bat causing you to bleed. Eventually you both stood up and you walked off, Mr. Haveraux going back to his house and calling police. A sample of your bloodstains obtained from the footpath in York Street was subsequently obtained and examined.

10. [Counts 12 through 15 relate to further burglaries and thefts in 2001 and 2002.]

13. You have admitted extensive prior convictions, they being 39 prior convictions for burglary, 57 prior convictions for theft, and you have in the course of your offending previously received eight gaol terms and in that course breaching three suspended sentences imposed upon you.

14. You are now 30 years of age, the youngest of three children born to your parents who separated when you were still a baby. Your mother was a heroin addict who now resides in a nursing home after suffering a stroke as a result of a heroin overdose about five years ago. You have had virtually no contact with your father who remarried, had further children and was himself gaoled for subsequent criminal behaviour.

15. At the age of one you were placed in foster care and remained in departmental care for the next 15 years. Your placements were changed every two to three years. You were rarely visited by your mother who continued with drug problems and was apparently regularly in and out of gaol. . . .

17. At the age of 15 you were placed to live with your mother for six months, she then just having come out of gaol. She introduced you to heroin. You quickly became addicted and this has been the drug that has bedevilled you ever since although there is also some history of earlier amphetamine use.

18. You have a limited employment history, in 1997 working as a furniture removalist for about eight months, then briefly as a truck jockey and then with a garden program. The dominating theme of your life however from the age of 15 until two years ago was your heroin addiction and associated offending in support of that habit. [That offending saw you] in July 1999 placed on a combined custody and treatment order and in August 2000 you were sentenced to a total effective sentence of 14 months. . . .

20. On your release from prison in October 2001, you admitted yourself to a rehabilitation centre to detoxify but stayed only eight weeks before moving to various boarding houses in Footscray. In that time you met Rebecca Gibbons, also a heroin user with whom you commenced a relationship. On 15 October 2002 your daughter Shakira was born. Her birth saw a remarkable transformation by you in terms of your drug addiction and lifestyle.

21. Before turning to this aspect of your life however, the observations and psychological testing upon you by forensic psychologist Dr. Carla Lechner as contained in her report of 27 May 2005 are important. . . .

22. It is Dr. Lechner's view that you demonstrate symptoms [consistent] with a diagnosis of clinical depression and states that you told her you had been depressed for as long as you can remember, your mood at present being further lowered by an intense anxiety over the outcome of this proceeding and your fear of prison and of course the effect of that upon your daughter, Shakira.

23. Dr. Lechner says you impressed as cognitively and emotionally immature, which she attributed to a retardation of your emotional development in the years of your heavy drug use. Formal psychological testing to determine your level of comprehension, reason and judgment skills rated you in the low average borderline range of verbal intelligence with approximately 91 per cent of the adult population performing better than you.

24. I now return to the issue of your daughter. Shakira, as I have stated, was born on 15 October 2002. According to the report of Dr. Juliana Antolovic, a paediatrician in child development and rehabilitation at the Royal Children's Hospital, whose report, dated 20 March 2005, was tendered on your behalf, Shakira was born with a significant medical condition, Pierre Robin Syndrome, which is associated with abnormal development of the jaw, tongue and mouth, and children with this condition often have a cleft palate and can have significant problems with breathing and feeding.

25. Indeed, according to Dr. Antolovic, who appears to have been Shakira's paediatrician since her birth, Shakira had a number of complications related to this condition and since her birth has had multiple admissions to hospital, a number of investigations and surgery to repair her very large cleft palate. For the first 18 months of her life she was dependent upon tube feeding for her growth and nutrition. Dr. Antolovic states: "Shakira's care needs have been extremely high. In addition to two weekly visits to the Child Development and Rehabilitation Centre, Shakira and her family have also regularly attended the Royal Children's Hospital for routine follow up with a dietician and in a cleft palate splint. During the time Shakira was fed by a nasogastric tube (the first 18 months of her life) there were multiple visits to the emergency department for replacement of her neo-gastric tube. These visits sometimes occurred up to three times a week, which is not uncommon in the circumstances."

26. At the age of 17 a daughter was born to you and your then partner, a lady named Narelle. That daughter and her mother were taken in by the maternal grandmother with whom they still live and with whom you continue to have contact. However, you did not play a significant parenting role in that daughter's life, you remaining in the grip of your heroin addiction and continuing to offend in support of it and to be gaoled regularly by the court.

27. However, it is clear that the birth of this second gravely physically compromised daughter has wrought the transformation in you and you have entirely devoted yourself to her care since her birth. You have been her primary caregiver since her birth. Concomitant with this dedication to your daughter and her various needs, you have entirely ceased heroin use and criminal offending.

28. In December 2004 the Department of Human Services became involved because of concerns over verbal domestic violence taking place between yourself

and Rebecca, who had remained a drug user, you perceiving that she was failing to fulfil her role as Shakira's mother.

29. Shakira was removed from your care for one night then returned to you as her sole carer and you remain in that position to this day. You and the child's mother, Rebecca, remained in a relationship until December 2004. . . .

40. Howard Draper, a solicitor who represented you in the Children's Court proceedings relating to Shakira [notes that in] February 2005 the Children's Court made an interim protection order placing the child in your care on certain conditions and that by the return of that order on 16 May 2005 DHS was recommending that there was no need for any further involvement by that department due to the progress made by you. He states: "According to the latest DHS report, 16 May 2005, my client is currently on methadone and is no longer required to provide drug screens to DHS. It appears that DHS is satisfied that my client is not abusing substances." . . .

42. Mr. Draper concludes, "As a legal practitioner I have been practising in the Children's Court for about 21 years and for the past seven to eight years most of my practice has involved Children's Court matters. I have no hesitation in noting that the efforts of Mr. Arnautovic in addressing the protective concerns and providing a safe and secure environment for his daughter, have been exceptional." . . .

52. I am satisfied that since the birth of Shakira you have ceased to use heroin. You did admit, when giving evidence in the pre-sentence before me, to occasionally smoking marijuana at night after Shakira was in bed. I am satisfied that you have ceased offending and have carried out to the fullest extent to which you are capable, care which has proved difficult and demanding, of your disabled child.

53. This is, however, not the only aspect to which the court must have regard. A medical report dated 8 October 2003 from Dr. Denis Yeung of the Sunshine Brimbank Clinic, notes that the victim of the armed robbery, Mr. Haveraux, sustained the following injuries as a result upon your assault upon him — bruising on the left side of his skull, sore fingers on the left hand, abrasions on the right little finger, bruises on the back of the right hand and wrist, and whilst X-ray did not show any fracture, a diagnosis of ligamentous strain was made.

54. In his victim impact statement dated 27 May 2005 Mr. Haveraux stated: "For the next week after the attack I found it difficult to enter the empty house. This was the reason for installing the alarm as it would give me prior warning. I do feel that I have been affected psychologically as I now tend to enter empty rooms as if somebody may be waiting around the corner for me."

55. He further states: "I feel that no mercy should be shown because of the fact that the attack took place in front of my three year old daughter and that he wanted to take a hostage to the bank so we could give him all we had. If this attack had involved a weaker person (that is somebody that hadn't played soccer for 20 years) what damage could he have caused? Put him away before he really hurts somebody."

56. Your counsel informed me that regularly throughout the years of your drug addiction you would turn to the use of prescription drugs when your heroin supply failed and at the time of the armed robbery you had taken Rohypnol to this end. . . . These courts are sadly familiar with the elevation in violent offending that can occur when the offender is under the influence of this prescription drug. This appears to have been the case at the time of the armed robbery, the violence involved not being characteristic of your previous offending. . . .

58. Appallingly, this violent offending, however, took place before the undoubtedly terrified gaze of a three year old child. This offending in particular was abhorrent in the extreme. In the absence of mitigatory material, indeed in the absence of any but the most compelling mitigatory material, the court would, in a case such as this involving the intrusion into a home, a violent attack upon the occupier of the house, the terrifying of a little girl in her own home, watching her father being assaulted, would undoubtedly result in a sentence of imprisonment to be served immediately. Such offending cannot and should not be tolerated. I make it clear to you, Mr. Arnautovic, that I condemn your behaviour and I do so in the strongest possible terms. The fact of your difficult personal history, the fact of your heroin addiction, the fact of your Rohypnol use at the time, are of no moment. This was an appalling and dangerous attack and one cannot wonder at the sentiments expressed by Mr. Haveraux in the victim impact statement. . . .

60. The question is whether your undoubted reformation, together with the needs of your highly dependent little daughter, are such that a sentence of imprisonment to be immediately served should be averted. This is the course that I am urged to take by your counsel on the basis of your reformation and the needs of your daughter. This course is resisted by the prosecution, which contends that a sentence of imprisonment to be immediately served should indeed be visited upon you. It is their contention firstly that the hardship to your daughter, should you be incarcerated, would not be such as to answer the "test" contained in the judgment of Wells, J. in Worth (1976) 14 S.A.S.R. 291 where . . . His Honour stated: "the hardship caused directly or indirectly by a proposed sentence of imprisonment to the family of or to others closely associated with the offender [should] be taken into account by the court in mitigation of that sentence . . . where the circumstances are highly exceptional where it would be, in effect, inhuman to refuse to do so."

61. Insofar as your rehabilitation is concerned the prosecution referred to the case of DPP v. Jovasici, a decision of the Court of Appeal of the Supreme Court of Victoria delivered on March 22, 2001. There, in essence, it was held that notwithstanding the demonstrated rehabilitation of two professional burglars, including drug rehabilitation, the requirement for general and specific deterrence, denunciation and punishment, were such that gaol sentences to be immediately served, which had been received in the first instance, were in fact manifestly inadequate and were, accordingly, increased by the Court of Appeal. There are, however, in my view, important distinguishing factors between those authorities and this case. Dealing first with the case of *Jovasici*, this involves the participation of perpetrators in a highly organised professional ring of burglars which targeted goods of particular value centring around a particular receiver of stolen goods and the activities of which clearly resulted in the theft and on selling of a vast array of valuable items stolen from a myriad of residences. It involved organised and sophisticated offending. Further, it was not accepted by the sentencing judge in that case that either of the perpetrators, neither of whom gave evidence in their hearings, were remorseful, nor was it accepted that the offending occurred solely to support the drug addiction suffered by both men.

62. During the plea before me you did give evidence on oath, saying there were no apologies you could make to Mr. Haveraux that he could accept. You said you did not blame him for his comments relating to you and described what you had done to him as the "lowest act" you had committed in your life. You said you were still dealing with what you had done in that it continued to play on your conscience. You

were concerned that you could have "devastated that little girl" and said that you thought about what you have done all the time. . . .

66. I am satisfied . . . that the hardship which would be faced by Shakira if you were incarcerated would amount to be extreme and exceptional circumstances as demanded by the authority. Shakira is only two and a half years old, a far more vulnerable age than the child in the case of Holland. She has disabilities that require particular care and according to the evidence of Ms. Matthew, this will be ongoing for some four years.

67. Further, and unusually, she has no meaningful relationships with any adult other than yourself, thus she is in familial terms, apart from yourself, an isolated, disabled toddler, and your removal from her life would see her placed either in foster care with strangers or, if the department was willing to consider the few persons named by you when pressed in cross-examination as possibly suitable, with adults who are neither related to her or whom it appears she knows particularly well. Mention has been made in more than one report and by myself earlier in this judgment of your social isolation as a result of your change of lifestyle. . . .

69. [It] is my view that Shakira's case is one in which mercy should be exercised. If I be wrong in that it is my view that Shakira's dependence upon you, coupled with your personal transformation and general remorse, are sufficient that I should sentence you in a way which does not require your immediate incarceration. I should add, Mr. Arnautovic, however, that I have made this decision only after anxiously considering all the competing sentencing demands and emphasise that I am fully alive to the appalling and noxious nature of your offending. It is my view, however, that the long term interests of the community and Shakira are best served by your continuing on your path of reformation and your care of your daughter. It is my view that were you to be incarcerated and separated from Shakira the effects upon her would be grievous, long lasting and possibly irretrievable. The effect upon yourself would likely ignite such anxiety in view of your daughter's position that you could well collapse, and even did you not, the additional problems faced by you on your release insofar as the traumatising effects upon Shakira as a result of your separation, could interfere substantially with, if not destroy, your capacity to continue to care for her and her to respond and thus the exceptional work of the past two years be totally undone.

70. I therefore propose to deal with you by way of a non-custodial disposition which will involve not only suspended sentences but the imposition of a community based order for which you have been assessed as suitable. . . .

71. I am including a community based order in the disposition, both because I think the gravity of your offending requires it and because, in my view, you have ongoing personal difficulties and frailties which require attention and you have indicated through your work with DHS that you are capable of taking advantage of assistance offered to you and, indeed, have been reliant upon it to such an extent that it appears your main social interaction in life is with DHS workers. That support is to be withdrawn in June of this year and it is my view that replacement of it with the supports that can be obtained by a Community Based Order is important in terms of your ongoing reform which is, of course, inextricably linked with Shakira's welfare. . . .

73. I therefore sentence you as follows, and can you stand up, please? On counts 1, 3, 5, 7, 9, 12 and 14 you are sentenced to 12 months' imprisonment. On Count 4 you are sentenced to six months' imprisonment. On counts 6, 8, 10, 13 and 15 you

are sentenced to nine months' imprisonment. On Count 11 you are sentenced to two years and nine months' imprisonment. I order that 12 days of each of the sentences imposed on counts 1, 3, 5, 7, 9, 12 and 14 be served cumulatively to the sentence imposed on Count 11 and to each other, giving a total effective sentence of three years. This sentence is to be wholly suspended for a period of three years. On Count 2 you are placed on a community based order for two years. . . .

75. The order will last for two years. You must attend at the Sunshine Community Corrections Centre at 10 Foundry Road, Sunshine within two clear working days, all right? . . . You must report to and receive visits from a Community Corrections officer. You must notify an officer at the specified Community Corrections Centre of any change of address or employment within two clear working days of that change. You may not leave Victoria without the consent of the specified Community Corrections officer and you must obey all lawful instructions and directions of the Community Corrections officer.

76. I order that you perform 150 hours of unpaid community work over a 24 month period as directed. I order that you be under the supervision of a Community Corrections officer. [An onerous level of unpaid community work may place you under a detrimental amount of pressure and may affect your ability to successfully negotiate both your parenting and order commitments.] I order that you undergo assessment and treatment for alcohol or drug addiction or submit to medical, psychological or psychiatric assessment and treatment as directed by the regional manager. I order that you submit to testing for alcohol or drug use as directed by the regional manager and I further order, as a special condition, that you undergo programs to reduce the risk of re-offending and participate in such programs as directed by the Community Corrections officer. . . .

100. . . . Can you stand up Mr. Arnautovic? Because before you leave I have to explain to you the consequences of breaching the suspended sentence. . . . The legislation makes it very clear that unless there are exceptional circumstances, if a person breaches a suspended sentence the court must make that person serve the whole of the sentence that was suspended. So if you commit an offence — you need to have a look at your marijuana smoking in that respect as well, OK?

102. PRISONER: Yes.

103. HER HONOUR: If you commit an offence you will be looking at three years' imprisonment. I imagine that would ruin your life and it would certainly ruin Shakira's life. Do you understand? All right. I am confident enough in your progress to place you on a disposition which can be very dangerous for persons who have got long offending histories and drug addictions, all right? You just keep going the way you are going and all will be well, but you need to understand that for the next three years you have got to be incredibly careful. All right?

104. PRISONER: Yes.

105. HER HONOUR: Thank you. You can have a seat.

Notes

1. *Informal procedure at sentencing: majority position.* The New York statute discussed in *Williams,* which allowed the sentencing judge to consider evidence inadmissible under the rules of evidence, typifies sentencing practices in most states. See also Tex. Crim. Proc. Code Ann. §37.07(3). The informal presentation of

evidence supposedly supports an effort to obtain the most information possible about the offender and the offense and to make an individualized (perhaps even clinical) decision. Many different actors participate over time in the decision about how best to respond to an individual offender. Thus, the indeterminate sentencing system is one of "multiple discretions." Professor Franklin Zimring describes the system as follows:

> The best single phrase to describe the allocation of sentencing power in state and federal criminal justice is multiple discretion. Putting aside the enormous power of the police to decide whether to arrest, and to select initial charges, there are four separate institutions that have the power to determine criminal sentences — the legislature, the prosecutor, the judge, and the parole board or its equivalent. . . . With all our emphasis on due process in the determination of guilt, our machinery for setting punishment lacks any principle except unguided discretion. Plea bargaining, disparity of treatment and uncertainty are all symptoms of a larger malaise — the absence of rules or even guidelines in determining the distribution of punishments. . . .

Zimring, Making the Punishment Fit the Crime: A Consumer's Guide to Sentencing Reform, 12 Occasional Papers of the University of Chicago Law School (1977). More than half of the states use such an indeterminate sentencing system for large groups of cases, although many of these same states might use more narrowly circumscribed sentencing rules for some crimes.

2. *Williams revisited.* Samuel Titto Williams, a black man, was 18 years old at the time he killed 15-year-old Selma Graff, who surprised him during a burglary. He had no record of prior convictions, but he had been accused of burglary at age 11. The judgment in juvenile court was suspended. The probation report — a report prepared by probation officers prior to sentencing, also called a pre-sentence investigation report — informed the judge that Williams was suspected of (but not charged with) committing 30 burglaries during the two months before the murder. A seven-year-old girl who was present during one of those burglaries told the probation department that Williams had molested her sexually. She identified Williams as the perpetrator two weeks after the incident. The probation report also stated that Williams was living with two women, and had brought different men into the apartment for the purpose of having sexual relations with the women. It alleged that he had once gone to a local school to photograph "private parts of young children." Finally, the sentencing judge relied on injuries inflicted on the murder victim's brother during the burglary. The prosecutor had not brought any charges based on the assault. See Kevin Reitz, Sentencing Facts: Travesties of Real-Offense Sentencing, 45 Stan. L. Rev. 523 (1993). Is the problem in *Williams* the new offender information at sentencing or the defendant's lack of an opportunity to challenge that information?

3. *Capital punishment and informal procedure.* Although the *Williams* Court emphasized that rehabilitative purposes of sentencing required far-reaching information about an offender, the proposed "treatment" for Williams was execution. It brings to mind the statement attributed to the comedian W. C. Fields, who quoted a condemned prisoner on his way to the electric chair, saying, "This will certainly be a lesson to me." *Williams* is still cited with approval in support of informal sentencing procedures generally. However, it has been partially overruled in the context of

capital sentencing. In Gardner v. Florida, 430 U.S. 349 (1977), the trial judge sentenced a defendant to death after consulting confidential and unrebutted information in the pre-sentence investigation report. A plurality of the Supreme Court found that due process required, at least in capital cases, that the defendant have access to information that will influence the sentencing judge and have an opportunity to test its reliability.

4. *Recurring themes in discretionary sentencing.* When judges describe the factors they consider in sentencing under an indeterminate system, they often list the types of considerations that the judge discussed in the *Arnautovic* case. One study of sentences in white-collar crime cases in federal court concluded that judges considered three common principles during sentencing: (1) the harm the offense produced; (2) the blameworthiness of the defendant, judged both from the defendant's criminal intent and from other details of the crime and defendant's earlier life; and (3) the consequences of the punishment, both for deterring future wrongdoing and for the well-being of the defendant's family and community. Despite the presence of these common principles for sentencing, judges selected very different sentences because they did not agree on how to measure each of the principles or the relative weight to place on each. See Stanton Wheeler, Kenneth Mann, & Austin Sarat, Sitting in Judgment: The Sentencing of White-Collar Criminals (1988).

Observers in higher-volume courts, such as state misdemeanor courts, have described a very different reality. During plea bargaining the parties settle quickly on a proper sentence, hinging largely on the charges finally filed and on the parties' interpretation of the facts as reflected in the police reports. These negotiations do not often involve individualized haggling, as in a Middle Eastern bazaar. Rather, they are "more akin to modern supermarkets in which prices for various commodities have been clearly established and labeled." Malcolm Feeley, The Process Is the Punishment: Handling Cases in a Lower Criminal Court 187 (1979).

It is extremely rare for sentencing judges in discretionary systems in the United States to produce written opinions explaining their reasons for selecting a particular punishment. One intriguing exception occurred in the case of Colonel Oliver North, who was prosecuted for crimes connected to his involvement with funding for Nicaraguan military insurgent during the Reagan administration. The attorneys and the sentencing judge in that case produced remarkable documents for those sentencing proceedings, which are available on the web extension for this chapter at *http://www.crimpro.com/extension/ch19*.

5. *Sentencing juries.* In some states, juries not only rule on guilt or innocence but also decide the sentence to impose, even in noncapital cases. In about six of these states, the jury's choice is binding; in a few others, the jury only recommends a sentence to the judge. See Fla. Stat. §921.141 (jury recommends sentence); Tex. Crim. Proc. Code Ann. §37.07 (judge can assess punishment if defendant does not request probation or jury sentence; jury must be instructed about parole and other devices for reducing actual amount of prison time offender must serve). Sentencing juries tend to impose longer prison terms than sentencing judges would impose in comparable cases. See Nancy J. King & Rosevelt L. Noble, Felony Jury Sentencing in Practice: A Three-State Study, 57 Vand. L. Rev. 885 (2004). Even in a system that gives no formal sentencing power to juries, the jury might consider likely punishments as it deliberates on the verdict in the case. The jury might acquit if it believes the sanction is too severe.

Should the sentencing jury be required to vote unanimously for a particular sentence? Should its voting rules be the same as the rules for its vote on guilt and innocence? See Manual for Courts-Martial, Rule 1006(d) (Exec. Order No. 12,473) (members of court martial may propose sentences; panel must consider each proposed sentence from least severe to most severe; unanimous vote needed for death penalty; three-fourths of members must recommend confinement for more than 10 years; two-thirds of members must recommend other sentences).

2. *Legislative Sentencing*

Although indeterminate sentencing has been the norm in this country for most of the twentieth century, new arrangements have emerged over the past generation. Some of those alternative approaches have put the legislature more firmly in control of sentencing. Legislators have decided for themselves the precise sentence that will attach to various types of offenses; other sentencing institutions such as courts are supposed to carry out the choices of the legislature without adding any meaningful choices of their own.

Sentences dominated by legislative choices go back to some of the earliest recorded sources of law. American legislatures during the eighteenth and nineteenth centuries often set specific sentences for designated crimes. Only in the late nineteenth and early twentieth centuries did the state and federal legislatures routinely create more "indeterminate" sentences, authorizing a range of sentences from which a sentencing judge could select a sentence to impose on a particular offender. When legislatures began once again, in the middle of the twentieth century, to designate the specific punishments for certain crimes, they were returning to earlier practices.

■ CODE OF HAMMURABI

(C. H. W. Johns Trans., 1911)

§1: If a man weave a spell and put a ban upon a man, and has not justified himself, he that wove the spell upon him shall be put to death.

§8: If a man has stolen ox or sheep or ass, or pig, or ship, whether from the temple or the palace, he shall pay thirtyfold. If he be a poor man, he shall render tenfold. If the thief has naught to pay, he shall be put to death.

§15: If a man has caused either a palace slave or palace maid, or a slave of a poor man or a poor man's maid, to go out of the gate, he shall be put to death.

§195: If a man has struck his father, his hands one shall cut off.

§196: If a man has caused the loss of a gentleman's eye, his eye one shall cause to be lost.

§197: If he has shattered a gentleman's limb, one shall shatter his limb.

§198: If he has caused a poor man to lose his eye or shattered a poor man's limb, he shall pay one mina of silver.

§209: If a man has struck a gentleman's daughter and caused her to drop what is in her womb, he shall pay ten shekels of silver for what was in her womb.

§210: If that woman has died, one shall put to death his daughter.

§211: If the daughter of a poor man through his blows he has caused to drop that which is in her womb, he shall pay five shekels of silver.

§212: If that woman has died, he shall pay half a mina of silver.

U.S. SENTENCING COMMISSION, MANDATORY MINIMUM PENALTIES IN THE FEDERAL CRIMINAL JUSTICE SYSTEM

i-ix, 5-15, 27-32 (1991)

Mandatory minimum sentences are not new to the federal criminal justice system. As early as 1790, mandatory penalties had been established for capital offenses. In addition, at subsequent intervals throughout the 19th Century, Congress enacted provisions that required definite prison terms, typically quite short, for a variety of other crimes. Until recently, however, the enactment of mandatory minimum provisions was generally an occasional phenomenon that was not comprehensively aimed at whole classes of offenses.

A change in practice occurred with the passage of the Narcotic Control Act of 1956, which mandated minimum sentences of considerable length for most drug importation and distribution offenses. . . . In 1970, Congress drew back from the comprehensive application of mandatory minimum provisions to drug crimes enacted 14 years earlier. Finding that increases in sentence length "had not shown the expected overall reduction in drug law violations," Congress passed [legislation] that repealed virtually all mandatory penalties for drug violations.

[Growing criticism of efforts to rehabilitate inmates led lawmakers] to renew support for mandatory minimum penalties. On the state level this trend began in New York in 1973, with California and Massachusetts following soon thereafter. While the trend toward mandatory minimums in the states was gradual, by 1983, 49 of the 50 states had passed such provisions. . . . On the federal level, a comparable but more comprehensive trend was under way. Beginning in 1984, and every two years thereafter, Congress enacted an array of mandatory minimum penalties specifically targeted at drugs and violent crime. . . . Today there are approximately 100 separate federal mandatory minimum penalty provisions located in 60 different criminal statutes. . . . Of the 59,780 cases sentenced under mandatory minimum statutes [between 1984 and 1990], four statutes account for approximately 94 percent of the cases. These four statutes . . . all involve drugs and weapons violations. . . .

Reasons Cited in Support of Mandatory Minimums

[Field interviews with] judges, assistant United States attorneys, defense attorneys, and probation officers . . . identified six commonly offered rationales for mandatory minimum sentencing provisions.

Retribution or "Just Deserts." Perhaps the most commonly voiced goal of mandatory minimum penalties is the "justness" of long prison terms for particularly serious offenses. Proponents generally agree that longer sentences are deserved and that, absent mandatory penalties, judges would impose sentences more lenient than would be appropriate.

Deterrence. . . . Those supporting mandatory minimums on deterrence grounds point not only to the strong deterrent value of the certainty of substantial punishment these penalties are intended to provide, but also to the deterrent value of sentence severity that these penalties are intended to ensure in the war against crime.

Incapacitation, Especially of the Serious Offender. Mandating increased sentence severity aims to protect the public by incapacitating offenders convicted of serious crimes for definite, and generally substantial, periods of time. Proponents argue that one way to increase public safety, particularly with respect to guns and drugs, is to remove drug dealers and violent offenders from the streets for extended periods of time.

Disparity. Indeterminate sentencing systems permit substantial latitude in setting the sentence, which in turn can mean that defendants convicted of the same offense are sentenced to widely disparate sentences. Supporters of mandatory minimum penalties contend that they greatly reduce judicial discretion and are therefore more fair. Mandatory minimums are meant to ensure that defendants convicted of similar offenses receive penalties that at least begin at the same minimal point.

Inducement of Cooperation. Because they provide specific lengthy sentences, mandatory minimums encourage offenders to assist in the investigation of criminal conduct by others. This is because cooperation — that is, supplying information concerning the activities of other criminally involved individuals — is the only statutorily recognized way to permit the court to impose a sentence below the length of imprisonment required by the mandatory minimum sentence.

Inducement of Pleas. Although infrequently cited by policymakers, prosecutors express the view that mandatory minimum sentences can be valuable tools in obtaining guilty pleas, saving scarce enforcement resources and increasing the certainty of at least some measure of punishment. In this context, the value of a mandatory minimum sentence lies not in its imposition, but in its value as a bargaining chip to be given away in return for the resource-saving plea from the defendant to a more leniently sanctioned charge.

[Now we turn to some of the criticisms of mandatory minimum sentences.]

The "Tariff" Effect of Mandatory Minimums

Years ago, Congress used tariff sentences in sanctioning broad categories of offenses, ranging from quite serious crimes (e.g., homicide) to fairly minor property theft. This tariff approach has been rejected historically primarily because there were too many defendants whose important distinctions were obscured by this single, flat approach to sentencing. A more sophisticated, calibrated approach that takes into account gradations of offense seriousness, criminal record, and level of culpability has long since been recognized as a more appropriate and equitable method of sentencing. . . .

The mandatory minimums set forth in 21 U.S.C. §841(b), applicable to defendants convicted of trafficking in the more common street drugs, are illustrative. For those convicted of drug trafficking under this section, one offense-related factor, and only one, is determinative of whether the mandatory minimum applies: the weight of the drug or drug mixture. Any other sentence-individualizing factors that might pertain in a case are irrelevant as far as the statute is concerned. Thus, for example, whether the defendant was a peripheral participant or the drug ring's kingpin, whether the defendant used a weapon, whether the defendant accepted responsibility or, on the other hand, obstructed justice, have no bearing on the mandatory minimum to which each defendant is exposed. . . .

The "Cliff" Effect of Mandatory Minimums

Related to the proportionality problems posed in mandatory minimums already described are the sharp differences in sentence between defendants who fall just below the threshold of a mandatory minimum compared with those whose criminal conduct just meets the criteria of the mandatory minimum penalty. Just as mandatory minimums fail to distinguish among defendants whose conduct and prior records in fact differ markedly, they distinguish far too greatly among defendants who have committed offense conduct of highly comparable seriousness.

[A] lack of coordination between statutory maximum and mandatory minimum penalties for the same or similar offenses can create dramatic sentencing cliffs among similarly situated defendants. For example, 21 U.S.C. §884 mandates a minimum five-year term of imprisonment for a defendant convicted of first-offense, simple possession of 5.01 or more grams of "crack." . . . However, a first-offender convicted of simple possession of 5.0 grams of crack is subjected to a *maximum* statutory penalty of one year imprisonment. . . .

The "Charge-Specific" Nature of Mandatory Minimums

. . . In general, a mandatory minimum becomes applicable only when the prosecutor elects to *charge* and the defendant is *convicted* of the specific offense carrying the mandatory sentence. . . . Mandatory minimums employ a structure that allows a shifting of discretion and control over the implementation of sentencing policies from courts to prosecutors. [There] is substantial reason to believe that mandatory minimums are not in fact pursued by prosecutors in all instances that the underlying statutes otherwise would require. . . .

Problem 19-1. The Shopaholic

Gary Ewing walked into the pro shop of the El Segundo Golf Course in Los Angeles County on March 12, 2000. He walked out with three golf clubs, priced at $399 apiece, concealed in his pants leg. A shop employee, whose became suspicious when he saw Ewing limp out of the pro shop, telephoned the police. The police apprehended Ewing in the parking lot.

This was not Ewing's first contact with the criminal justice system. In 1984, at the age of 22, he pleaded guilty to theft. The court sentenced him to six months in jail (a suspended term), three years' probation, and a $300 fine. In 1988 he was convicted of felony grand theft auto and sentenced to one year in jail and three years' probation. After Ewing completed probation, however, the sentencing court reduced the crime to a misdemeanor, permitted Ewing to withdraw his guilty plea, and dismissed the case. In 1990 he was convicted of petty theft with a prior conviction, and sentenced to 60 days in the county jail and three years' probation. In 1992 Ewing was convicted of battery and sentenced to 30 days in the county jail and two years' summary probation. One month later, he was convicted of theft and sentenced to 10 days in the county jail and 12 months' probation. In January 1993 Ewing was convicted of burglary and sentenced to 60 days in the county jail and one year's summary probation. In February 1993 he was convicted of possessing drug paraphernalia and sentenced to six months in the county jail and three years' probation. In July 1993 he was convicted of appropriating lost property and sentenced to 10 days in the county jail and two years' summary probation. In September 1993 he was convicted of unlawfully possessing a firearm and trespassing, and was sentenced to 30 days in the county jail and one year's probation.

In October and November 1993 Ewing committed three burglaries and one robbery at a Long Beach, California, apartment complex over a five-week period. During the robbery, Ewing accosted a victim in the mailroom of the apartment complex. Ewing claimed to have a gun and ordered the victim to hand over his wallet. When the victim resisted, Ewing produced a knife and forced the victim back to the apartment itself. While Ewing rifled through the bedroom, the victim fled the apartment screaming for help. Ewing absconded with the victim's money and credit cards. A jury convicted Ewing of first-degree robbery and three counts of residential burglary. The court sentenced him to nine years and eight months in prison, and Ewing was paroled in 1999.

Only 10 months later, while he was still on parole status, Ewing stole the golf clubs at issue in this case. He was convicted of one count of felony grand theft of personal property in excess of $400.

California has a "three strikes and you're out" law that was designed "to ensure longer prison sentences and greater punishment for those who commit a felony and have been previously convicted of serious and/or violent felony offenses." Cal. Penal Code §667(b). When a defendant is convicted of a felony, and has previously been convicted of one or more prior felonies defined as "serious" or "violent" in Cal. Penal Code Ann. §§667.5 and 1192.7, sentencing is conducted pursuant to the three-strikes law. If the defendant has one prior "serious" or "violent" felony conviction, he must be sentenced to twice the term otherwise provided as punishment for the current felony conviction. If the defendant has two or more prior "serious" or "violent" felony convictions, he must receive an indeterminate term of life imprisonment. Defendants sentenced to life under the three-strikes law become eligible for parole on a date calculated by reference to a "minimum term," which is the greater of (a) three times the term otherwise provided for the current conviction, (b) 25 years, or (c) the term determined by the court pursuant to §1170 for the underlying conviction, including any enhancements.

Under California law, certain offenses may be classified as either felonies or misdemeanors. These crimes are known as "wobblers." Some crimes that would otherwise be misdemeanors become "wobblers" because of the defendant's prior record. For example, petty theft, a misdemeanor, becomes a "wobbler" when the defendant has previously served a prison term for committing specified theft-related crimes. Other crimes, such as grand theft, are "wobblers" regardless of the defendant's prior record. Both types of "wobblers" are triggering offenses under the three strikes law only when they are treated as felonies.

In California, prosecutors may exercise their discretion to charge a "wobbler" as either a felony or a misdemeanor. Trial courts may avoid imposing a three-strikes sentence in two ways: first, by reducing "wobblers" to misdemeanors (which do not qualify as triggering offenses), and second, by vacating allegations of prior "serious" or "violent" felony convictions.

In Ewing's case, the prosecutor formally alleged, and the trial court later found, that Ewing had been convicted previously of four serious or violent felonies for the three burglaries and the robbery in the Long Beach apartment complex.

Before sentencing Ewing, the trial court took note of his entire criminal history, including the fact that he was on parole when he committed his latest offense. The judge determined that the grand theft should remain a felony. The court also ruled that the four prior strikes for the three burglaries and the robbery in Long Beach should stand. As a newly convicted felon with two or more "serious" or "violent" felony convictions in his past, Ewing was sentenced under the three strikes law to 25 years to life.

Does this sentence qualify as "cruel and unusual punishment" for purposes of the Eighth Amendment, when the court imposes such a prison term on a repeat offender who stole $1,197 worth of gold clubs? Cf. Ewing v. California, 538 U.S. 11 (2003).

Notes

1. *Federal constitutional limits on legislative choice of sanctions: majority position.* Courts by and large allow legislatures to choose any punishment for a given crime (with the exception of the death penalty) and turn aside most claims that a punishment is "cruel and unusual" or "disproportionate" to the crime. According to the Supreme Court in Ewing v. California, 538 U.S. 11 (2003), the Eighth Amendment does not require strict proportionality between crime and sentence. Instead, it forbids only extreme sentences that are "grossly disproportionate" to the crime. Courts applying this proportionality test engage in three related inquiries. First, the court weighs the crime committed against the sentence imposed. If this "threshold" inquiry leads to an inference of gross disproportionality, the court then compares sentences imposed on other criminals in the same jurisdiction (the "intrajurisdictional analysis") and sentences imposed for commission of the same crime in other jurisdictions (the "interjurisdictional analysis"). How can the Court assess the first prong of its test — the gravity of the offense and the harshness of the penalty — other than by relying on the second and third prongs to provide an answer?

Does the decision in *Ewing* reflect merely the predilections of the majority of the Court rather than a principled assessment of the sentence? Would it have been more honest for the Court to decline proportionality review in imprisonment cases generally? See also Harmelin v. Michigan, 501 U.S. 957 (1991) (because of the severe social harms flowing from illegal drugs, the Court decided that there was no gross disparity between the crime of possession of 650 grams of cocaine and the sentence of life imprisonment); Solem v. Helm, 463 U.S. 277 (1983) (cruel and unusual punishment to impose life imprisonment without possibility of parole on defendant for uttering no-account check for $100; defendant had three prior convictions for third-degree burglary, one prior conviction for obtaining money under false pretenses, one prior conviction of grand larceny, and one prior conviction of third-offense driving while intoxicated).

The Eighth Amendment proportionality of capital punishment for various crimes and types of offenders (such as juveniles and mentally impaired defendants) is a complex topic with its own elaborate jurisprudence. For an overview of these death penalty precedents, go to the web extension for this chapter at *http://www.crimpro.com/extension/ch19*.

2. *Proportionality in the state courts.* State courts have applied the *Ewing* test under the Eighth Amendment to bar some disproportionate sentences. See Bradshaw v. State, 671 S.E.2d 485 (Ga. 2008) (mandatory life sentence for second conviction of failure to register as sex offender violates cruel and unusual punishment ban of the Eighth Amendment; failure to register is a passive felony that causes no harm to society, and crimes such as voluntary manslaughter carry a lighter penalty). It is more common for state courts to uphold a legislative choice of sanctions in the case at hand, even if they recognize that a proportionality challenge might succeed in theory. State v. Moss-Dwyer, 686 N.E.2d 109 (Ind. 1997) (recognizing possible proportionality challenges under state constitution, but refusing to declare a sentence disproportionate where statute made misinformation on a handgun permit application a greater crime than carrying a handgun without a license). A few state courts have been willing to insist, under various provisions of their state constitutions, that the legislature select a punishment that is proportionate to the crime. See State v. Rodriguez, 217 P.3d 659 (Or. 2009) (mandatory 75-month sentence violated state constitutional ban on cruel and unusual punishment when applied to defendants who touched clothed youths with sexual purpose). Whose standards — those of the state, the nation, or the local community — should apply in determining what shocks the conscience?

Nonconstitutional limitations on imprisonment provide more meaningful day-to-day controls than do constitutional limitations. Sentencing guidelines, for example, set out presumptive sentencing ranges for specific offenses. Other limitations may be imposed by state statutes mandating that certain offenders not be sentenced to prison. Among such legislation is a California law requiring drug treatment rather than imprisonment for first-time, nonviolent drug offenders.

3. *Judicial discretion and mandatory penalties.* Many criticisms of mandatory minimum statutes focus on the loss of judicial discretion in sentencing. Consider, for example, the 1970 statement of then-Representative George Bush:

> Federal judges are almost unanimously opposed to mandatory minimums, because they remove a great deal of the court's discretion. In the vast majority of cases which reach the sanctioning stage today, the bare minimum sentence is levied — and in some cases, less than the minimum mandatory is given. . . . Probations and outright dismissals often result. Philosophical differences aside, practicality requires a sentence structure which is generally acceptable to the courts, to prosecutors, and to the general public.

116 Cong. Rec. H33314, Sept. 23, 1970. These criticisms and others have led some state and federal judges to believe that mandatory minimum statutes too often force them to impose a fundamentally unjust sentence. A 1993 survey of judicial opinion found that 90 percent of federal judges and 75 percent of state judges believe that mandatory minimum sentences for drug cases were "a bad idea." More than half of the federal judges believed that mandatory minimums were "too harsh" on first-time offenders. A.B.A. J., October 1993, at 78. Are all mandatory minimums subject to the criticisms about uneven enforcement and loss of judicial discretion?

Can any decisionmaker other than a judge — who decides many individual cases — appreciate the facts about an offender's past that should lead to a lighter sentence? Why do judges sentence below what the legislature might choose as a minimum sentence? Do judges generally share a different political view on crime control?

4. *Mandatory mandatories.* Most mandatory minimum statutes instruct the judge to impose a particular sentence for a particular charge, but they do not require the prosecutor to file a given charge when adequate facts are present. Thus, typical mandatory sentencing statutes give prosecutors considerable bargaining power during plea negotiations; they also offer prosecutors opportunities to avoid mandatory minimum sentences when they believe that such sentences would be unjust or a poor use of resources. Legislatures sometimes constrain this prosecutorial power by passing statutes that require the prosecutor to file charges and that prevent plea bargaining. This sort of "mandatory mandatory" statute, however, is rare. Why do legislators hesitate to pass statutes that remove the prosecutor's discretion to decline charges or to select a charge not subject to the minimum penalty?

5. *Net effects of mandatory minimum penalties.* Studies of mandatory minimum penalties have reached different conclusions about the effect of these laws on the crime rates for the targeted offenses. Some studies have found a deterrent effect for gun crimes and homicides, but other studies have found no such effect on the commission of drug crimes or violent crimes generally. The effects of mandatory minimum penalties on the criminal justice system are clearer. These laws consistently lead to fewer arrests for the designated crimes, fewer charges filed, more dismissals of charges, more trials rather than guilty pleas, and longer sentences imposed and served. See Dale Parent, Terence Dunworth, Douglas McDonald, & William Rhodes, Key Legislative Issues in Criminal Justice: Mandatory Sentencing (National Institute of Justice, Research in Action) (January 1997, NCJ 161839).

6. *Self-correcting democratic process.* If mandatory minimum sentences truly produce the ill effects described by critics, won't the democratically elected legislature recognize these flaws after a time and abandon the experiment? There are a few examples of this happening. In Connecticut in 2001, the legislature granted judges authority to depart from mandatory minimum sentences for certain drug crimes, such as first-time sales or possession within 1,500 feet of a school. What might prevent the legislature from rethinking self-destructive legislation? Is it a lack of information, a lack of time, or something else?

3. *Sentencing Commissions*

While the legislature always sets the upper and lower boundaries on the permissible punishments for a crime, those boundaries can still leave open many choices about the sentence in particular cases. Rather than leaving the remaining sentencing choices to the discretion of judges and parole authorities, some state legislatures have empowered permanent "sentencing commissions" to create additional rules to guide judges as they select sentences within the statutory range. These guidelines (some embodied in statutes and others in administrative rules) are different from statutory maximum and minimum punishments because they allow judges, under some circumstances, to go above or below the recommended range so long as the final sentence remains within the statutorily authorized range. Sentencing guidelines can be binding or merely advisory for the sentencing judge depending on the judge's statutory authority to "depart" from the guidelines without risking reversal on appeal.

What are the effects of creating a sentencing commission and asking it to formulate sentencing rules more specific than the outer bounds of the statutory maximum and minimum sentence? Will sentencing commissions produce rules that look systematically different from the sentencing rules a legislature would adopt on its own? Will those sentencing guidelines produce a different pattern of sentences in individual cases than judges would impose, if left to their own devices? Whatever other effects a sentencing commission may have, it is certainly true that commissions (and the guidelines they create) give sentencing courts a more refined vocabulary for discussing sentencing choices and make more explicit the types of considerations that matter to a sentencing court. Indeed, without sentencing guidelines and the judicial decisions applying them, it would be difficult to study sentencing at all as a topic in a criminal procedure course.

Sentencing commissions have created sentencing rules in almost half of the states. The materials below introduce the basic structure and functions of such commissions, with particular attention paid to the sentencing commission in Minnesota, one of the earliest and most influential of these bodies.

■ ABA STANDARDS FOR CRIMINAL JUSTICE SENTENCING STANDARD 18-1.3(a)

(3d ed. 1994)

The legislature should create or empower a governmental agency to transform legislative policy choices into more particularized sentencing provisions that guide sentencing courts. The agency should also be charged with responsibility to collect, evaluate and disseminate information regarding sentences imposed and carried out within the jurisdiction.

■ DALE PARENT, STRUCTURING CRIMINAL SENTENCING

2-5, 28, 51-53, 57-60 (1988)

For centuries, legislative control over the sentencing process fluctuated between two statutory models of how to formulate punishments for crimes. One model prescribed mandatory penalties, such as capital punishment in nineteenth century England for every theft of fifty shillings or more, or a minimum of two years in prison in twentieth century Michigan for anyone convicted of possessing a gun. The second model prescribed discretionary penalty ranges. [A] person convicted of robbery, for example, could receive probation in the community, or as much as 25 years in prison, or any sanction in between depending on how the facts of the case were assessed in the discretion of the individual judge.

Under the mandatory model, legislatures ousted judges from control over sentencing by stipulating sentences in advance. Every sentencing was required to impose either a stated penalty, or a mandatory minimum sentence, on every offender convicted of the crime, without regard to mitigating circumstances. The judge was permitted no discretion for downward adjustments to reflect either the offender's reduced culpability for the past crime, or his high promise to avoid crime in the future.

The discretionary model exemplified an entirely different approach to the setting of punishment. Under this model, the legislature deferred to the sentencing court's closer opportunity to learn the facts of each crime, to see each offender in person, and to fashion a sentence to fit the particular case. This model left it to the judgment of a single judge to determine how high, or how low, to set the penalty within the authorized sentencing range. The experience or inexperience of the judge, his or her subjective appraisal of the crime's seriousness and the offender's blameworthiness, the decisionmaker's prediction or hunch regarding the offender's likely future conduct — these and similar factors could all influence the discretion to set a severe, moderate, or lenient sentence. . . .

The advantages of each model reflected the disadvantages of the other. By removing all discretion from judges, mandatory sentences sometimes produced punishment that was too severe and disproportionate to the crime. Discretionary sentencing, on the other hand, conferred unguided discretion on judges and inevitably produced unjustifiable discrepancies — unduly lenient sentences for some, undue harshness for others. Whereas mandatory sentences reflected legislative arbitrariness and coerced uniformity, discretionary sentencing power allowed anarchy among judges and produced both arbitrariness and unwarranted disparity.

In at least three major respects, Minnesota's venture altered traditional institutions and concepts in the realm of criminal sentencing:

- It substituted a new system — guided discretion — for the more extreme methods of dividing authority over the punishment process between legislatures and courts.
- It inserted a new governmental entity — the sentencing commission — between the legislature and the judiciary, and authorized the commission to monitor and continuously adjust criminal sentences.
- And it established an unprecedented conceptual connection — known as capacity constraint — between the degree of severity with which guidelines could specify prison sentences and the extent to which state prison resources were available to carry such sentences into effect. . . .

The former system of indeterminate prison sentences set by a judge, subject to the possibility of early release in the discretion of a parole board, was abolished. In its place came a system of determinate sentences, set by the judge under guidance from the sentencing commission, with review by an appellate court. Five key elements were incorporated into this plan:

- First, sentences would be scaled to take account of differences both in the gravity of crimes and the prior records of offenders. Guidance would be specified in the form of sentencing ranges, rather than precise sentences.
- Second, factors relevant to the individualization process would be standardized and weighted in advance. Clear rules would encourage similar outcomes in similar cases. Proportionality among different cases would be facilitated by a carefully constructed hierarchy of offense seriousness.
- Third, a set of departure principles would define the circumstances under which judges could deviate from the guideline sentencing range with good

reasons. Judges would thus retain discretion to set the actual sentence, to do justice on a case-by-case basis.

- Fourth, sentencing judges would be required to state reasons for each sentence that differed from the applicable guideline, to assure accountability and reviewability.
- Fifth, all sentences would be subject to review by an appellate court whose written opinions could, over time, evolve finely tuned principles to guide future sentencers. . . .

The [1988 Minnesota] law created a nine-member Sentencing Guidelines Commission, consisting of the chief justice or his designee, two district court judges appointed by the chief justice, the Commission of Corrections, the chairman of the Minnesota Corrections Board, and four gubernatorial appointees — a prosecutor, a public defender, and two citizens. Commission members would serve four-year terms and be eligible for reappointment. The Commission was authorized to hire a director and other staff. . . .

The guidelines . . . were to recommend when state imprisonment was appropriate and to recommend presumptive sentencing durations. The Commission could set ranges of permissible deviation about the fixed sentence of plus or minus 15 percent, which would not constitute departures. The guidelines were to be based on reasonable combinations of offender and offense characteristics. . . . Judges had to give written reasons for sentences that departed from the guidelines recommendation. The state or the defense could appeal any sentence. On appeal, the Supreme Court was to determine if the sentence was illegal, inappropriate, unjustifiably disparate, or not supported by findings of fact. . . .

The Commission sought to assure that guideline punishments would be proportional to the seriousness of offenders' crimes. To achieve that proportionality, it was necessary for the Commission to rank crimes in the order of their seriousness. The seriousness of a crime varies according to the gravity of the offense and the blameworthiness of the offender. Gravity is determined by the harm caused, directly or as a consequence, by the crime. Blameworthiness is determined by the offender's motivation, intent, and behavior in the crime and is enhanced if the offender previously has been convicted of and sentenced for criminal acts. . . .

In devising an offense seriousness ranking, the Commission had to make . . . relatively broad decisions about elements of behavior and intent as they relate to offense seriousness. For example, most would agree that crimes that involve or threaten physical injury generally are more serious than those that involve the loss of property. Case-level judgments involve finer distinctions and are used to distinguish among offenders convicted of similar crimes who have similar prior records.

Although most of us have an intuitive sense of offense seriousness, the concept is highly complex. Most criminal events consist of an offender and a victim linked by an act defined by law as a crime. Thus, judgments about the seriousness of criminal events may involve facts about offenders, victims, and criminal acts.

Some factors can be dismissed because all would agree they are irrelevant to assessing gravity or ascribing blame — for example, that the victim was a Mason or the offender was a Methodist. Some facts are both irrelevant and invidious — such as that the offender and the victim were of the same or different races. But there is a long list of factors that some would consider relevant to assessing harm or ascribing blame.

Most Frequent Offenses in Seriousness Scale

Seriousness Level	*Most Frequent Offenses*
1	Aggravated forgery, less than $100
	Possession of marijuana (more than 1.5 ounces)
	Unauthorized use of a motor vehicle
2	Aggravated forgery, $150 to $2,500
	Sale of marijuana . . .
3	Aggravated forgery, over $2,500
	Arson, third-degree . . .
	Theft crimes, $150 to $2,500
	Sale of cocaine
	Possession of LSD, PCP
4	Burglary, nondwellings and unoccupied dwellings
	Theft crimes, over $2,500
	Receiving stolen goods, $150 to $2,500
	Criminal sexual conduct, fourth-degree
	Assault, third-degree (injury)
5	Criminal negligence (resulting in death)
	Criminal sexual conduct, third-degree
	Manslaughter, second-degree . . .
	Witness tampering
	Simple (unarmed) robbery . . .
6	Assault, second-degree (weapon)
	Burglary (occupied dwelling) . . .
	Criminal sexual conduct, fourth-degree . . .
	Kidnapping (released in a safe place)
	Sale, LSD or PCP
	Sale, heroin and remaining hard narcotics
	Receiving stolen goods, over $2,500
7	Aggravated (armed) robbery
	Arson, first-degree
	Burglary (victim injured)
	Criminal sexual conduct, second-degree
	Criminal sexual conduct, third-degree
	Kidnapping (not released in a safe place)
	Manslaughter, first-degree
	Manslaughter, second-degree
8	Assault, first-degree (great bodily harm)
	Kidnapping (great bodily harm)
	Criminal sexual conduct, first-degree
	Manslaughter, first-degree
9	Murder, third-degree
10	Murder, second-degree

The victim may be a normal healthy adult or a person who may be especially vulnerable due to age or infirmity. In violent crimes the extent of physical injury may vary from a scratch to death. Some victims may recover fully from physical injuries, while others suffer permanent damage or impairment. In property crimes, the victim's loss could range from a small amount to a fortune. The consequences of property loss may vary greatly with the economic status of the victim. The crime may involve one victim or many. A crime might involve an offender acting alone or in concert with others. The offender might have been immature or mentally impaired and easily induced to participate in a crime. He or she might have been the ringleader who induced others. . . .

The list of factors relevant, or arguably relevant, to assessing offense seriousness is large, and the above variations are a mere sample. Their potential combinations are virtually infinite. Given events as complex and diverse as criminal acts, how was the Commission to go about judging their seriousness?

In the initial unsatisfactory effort [to rank offenses,] each member received a randomly arranged deck of sixty offense cards. Each card listed one offense [and] its statutory maximum sentence. . . . Each member arranged his or her deck in decreasing order of seriousness. [For] the most serious person offenses — homicides — the members' individual ranks clustered together, reflecting a high level of consensus. For less serious person offenses — robberies, sexual assaults, and so forth — consensus declined.

[The] Commission expressed concern about the initial ranking exercise [because it] had overloaded members with information. [The Commission created a subcommittee to divide the task into more manageable components. The subcommittee grouped] crimes into 6 categories — violent, arson, sex, drug, property, and miscellaneous — 5 of which contained 20 or fewer crimes. . . .

The subcommittee instructed the Commission to focus on the usual or typical case in [a] ranking exercise. . . . In phase one individual Commission members ranked crimes within each of the six categories. . . . Phases two, three, and four relied on identification of differences among members, on the articulation of reasons for those differences, and on debate about those reasons. . . . When differences existed it assured that the basis of the differences would be discovered and scrutinized and that the final rankings would reflect a majority opinion.

[The Commission divided the overall ranking into ten seriousness levels. The table reprinted here shows the most common types of offenses within each of the ten seriousness levels.]

■ RICHARD S. FRASE, STATE SENTENCING GUIDELINES: DIVERSITY, CONSENSUS, AND UNRESOLVED POLICY ISSUES

105 Colum. L. Rev. 1190 (2005)

Sentencing guidelines have been adopted in at least eighteen states and the District of Columbia, but the approaches taken are almost as numerous as the jurisdictions adopting them. State guidelines systems differ in their goals, scope of coverage, design, and operation. There are also many similarities, suggesting a substantial degree of consensus on some issues. These similarities also suggest that states can learn and "borrow" from other states; to use a well-worn comparative law metaphor, donor and recipient systems are sufficiently compatible to permit viable "legal transplants."... State guidelines are popular because they have proven more effective than alternative sentencing regimes as a means to promote consistency and fairness, set priorities in the use of limited correctional resources, and manage the growth in prison populations. . . .

SUMMARY OF GUIDELINES SYSTEMS

In 1980 Minnesota became the first jurisdiction to implement sentencing guidelines developed by a permanent sentencing commission, an idea that had been proposed by federal judge Marvin Frankel in the early 1970s. A number of other states had previously experimented with state-wide, judicially enacted, voluntary guidelines. . . .

Where they exist, state sentencing commissions are more widely representative than the federal commission, typically including judges, prosecutors, defense attorneys, correctional officials, public members, and sometimes legislators. There are also major variations in the duties, staffing, and budget of state commissions, and in the role of the commission relative to the legislature. For example, the Minnesota enabling statute gave the commission relatively little guidance and provided that the Commission's initial guidelines would become effective unless the legislature voted otherwise; in later years the legislature reclaimed some of the authority it had delegated, but the Minnesota Commission still retains primary control over the formulation of statewide sentencing policy. In contrast, the Arkansas enabling statute provides a detailed mandate, and in Washington State the legislature has dominated the guidelines revision process. . . .

In all states with permanent sentencing commissions, the commission (or occasionally another state agency) assesses the resource impact of proposed sentencing guidelines and statutes, in particular, the predicted effect on prison populations. The greater uniformity of guidelines sentencing makes such impact assessment more accurate than is possible in an indeterminate sentencing system, and the research and planning capacities of a permanent sentencing commission provide the necessary data and staff. . . .

In seven states (Utah, Maryland, Delaware, Virginia, Arkansas, Missouri, and Wisconsin) and the District of Columbia, guidelines are "voluntary" and not subject to appeal. But there are several varieties of "voluntary" guidelines. In some of these states judges are required to give reasons for departure from the guidelines. Moreover, "compliance rates" in some voluntary guidelines jurisdictions are quite high, which suggests that in some jurisdictions peer pressure or other informal processes may effectively substitute for appellate review. For example, in Virginia, trial court judges must be periodically reappointed by the legislature, and many judges apparently fear that a high departure rate will jeopardize their reappointment.

There are also several varieties of "legally binding" guidelines. In Pennsylvania, sentence appeal is available but the standard of review is highly deferential. However, Pennsylvania may have found another way to encourage judicial compliance with guidelines recommendations: Since 1999, judges' departure rates have been made public, and this change appears to have slightly increased compliance rates. In North Carolina, judges have very broad discretion to sentence within the presumptive, aggravated, or mitigated sentencing ranges and sentences are rarely reversed on appeal. [Other guideline states] have more active appellate review, which, particularly in Kansas, Minnesota, and Washington, has generated a substantial body of substantive appellate case law. But trial courts in these states still retain considerable discretion, as to both the type and the severity of sanctions.

[There is] substantial variation in the decisions each system seeks to regulate, including whether the guidelines abolish parole release discretion, regulate the use of intermediate sanctions, apply to sentencing of misdemeanor crimes, or regulate decisions about the revocation of probation or revocation of postprison parole or supervised release. Eleven guidelines states and the District of Columbia have abolished parole release discretion for all or most felons, usually substituting limited "good time" credits for inmates who obey prison rules. Seven states retain parole for all or most offenses, and use guidelines only to regulate judges' decisions about the imposition and duration of prison sentences. . . .

State guidelines systems also differ somewhat in the nature and priority of their punishment and sentencing reform goals. Adoption of a guidelines system is always motivated at least in part by a desire to make sentencing more uniform and to eliminate unwarranted disparities, but some jurisdictions, especially those with voluntary guidelines or those retaining parole discretion, give this objective much less weight. Another goal inherent in commission-based guidelines sentencing is to promote more rational sentencing policy formulation — decisionmaking that is at least partially insulated from short term political pressures and is comprehensive and informed by data. But states differ substantially in their levels of funding of and deference to the commission. States that abolished parole release discretion and substituted limited "good time" credits were seeking not only to reduce disparity but also to achieve "truth in sentencing," the notion that the length of prison sentences imposed by courts should correspond closely to the amount of time inmates actually serve. [In] the federal system and many states, the sentence reduction for good conduct in prison cannot exceed fifteen percent.

A few jurisdictions have more or less "descriptive," or historically based, guidelines: Recommended sentences reflect existing sentencing norms and the goal is simply to get judges to apply these norms more consistently. But even these states usually make some changes in prior norms — especially to reduce racial disparities. Other states, with "prescriptive" guidelines, usually seek to increase sentence severity for certain offenses, particularly violent and drug crimes. Several states, including Minnesota and Kansas, explicitly based their guidelines on retributive, or just deserts, theories of punishment, with increased emphasis on the severity of the current offense and less on offender characteristics. But these and other guidelines states still leave substantial room for offender-based sentences designed to achieve crime control purposes, applying a "limiting retributive" model. For example, under Minnesota's "modified just deserts" approach, rehabilitation, reintegration, and offender risk management remain very important goals, pursued primarily by varying the conditions of probation. The determination of these conditions is not regulated under the Minnesota guidelines, and almost eighty percent of felony sentences are to probation. . . .

Guidelines systems, once enacted, do not remain static. . . . Utah, Maryland, Michigan, and Virginia began with judicially developed guidelines and later established a permanent, legislatively mandated sentencing commission. Delaware's, Virginia's, and Wisconsin's initial guidelines retained traditional parole release discretion, which was later abolished. Michigan's guidelines were initially voluntary, but became enforceable via sentence appeals in 1999. Several of the earlier guidelines states (Utah, Maryland, Florida, Michigan, and Virginia) began using resource impact assessments in later years. In 1994, Pennsylvania added provisions regulating the use of intermediate sanctions. . . .

Sentencing reform goals have also evolved over time. Although offender risk management has always been at least an implicit goal of most guidelines systems, as is reflected in the substantial weight these systems give to prior criminal record, public safety has come to play an increasingly important role. For example, in 1989 the Minnesota legislature amended the guidelines enabling statute to specify that public safety should be the commission's "primary" consideration. The legislature then also passed numerous laws providing increased penalties for dangerous or repeat offenders. Some of the newer state guidelines systems explicitly include public safety as a goal, or provide for individualized risk assessment procedures for certain offenses.

Another important reform goal that Minnesota recognized at the outset, and that almost all other states have now adopted, is to use guidelines sentencing as a resource management tool — in particular to avoid prison overcrowding, set priorities in the use of limited prison capacity, and gain better control over the growth in prison populations and expenditures. . . . As state prison populations began to shoot up in the 1980s, increasing costs and raising problems of overcrowding and court intervention, resource management became the most important reason for adopting guidelines and a sentencing commission. . . .

Similarities

The discussion above has highlighted the many differences in the designs and aims of state guidelines, but it is important also to note the similarities. There are some matters about which most state systems, especially the ones implemented or revised in recent years, seem to agree. This strong consensus suggests that certain features of guidelines sentencing have proved valuable in practice in multiple jurisdictions. . . .

First, there is broad agreement that sentencing must reflect a wide variety of sentencing theories, reform goals, and systemic needs, and that sentencing and reform purposes must and will evolve over time. Although guidelines are often viewed as deliberately, and perhaps inherently, designed to emphasize retributive goals of proportionality and uniformity, all state guidelines reforms, even at their inception, have also given substantial weight to crime control purposes. As noted above, the latter purposes, along with resource management and truth in sentencing, have received increased emphasis in recent years.

Second, there is strong — but not universal — agreement that sentencing guidelines need to be developed, implemented, monitored, and periodically revised by a permanent, broadly based, independent sentencing commission. One of the most important features of sentencing guidelines reforms is their research component. Most legislatively created guidelines commissions have been charged with the responsibility of collecting and analyzing sentencing data, as background for drafting the initial guidelines and then as a means of monitoring implementation and proposing revisions. This empirical component has become more and more important, as states have begun to focus on resource management goals. Prison and other resource management projections require detailed information on past and current sentencing practices, and the application of sophisticated modeling techniques.

[Another] area of implicit consensus in guidelines states involves the allocation of sentencing authority between various institutions and actors. As Kevin Reitz has shown, sentencing outcomes depend on decisions made both at the systemic level by legislatures and sentencing commissions, and at the case level by the parties, trial and appellate courts, and corrections officials. Kevin R. Reitz, Modeling Discretion in American Sentencing Systems, 20 Law & Pol'y 389 (1998). Reitz argues that the relative influence of these various decisionmakers needs to be kept in balance. He concludes that the federal guidelines have concentrated too much power at the systemic level, both in Congress and the federal sentencing commission, and in the hands of prosecutors. He finds a better balance in state guidelines systems, particularly in Minnesota. State guidelines have generally succeeded in obtaining and preserving broad acceptance by legislators and practitioners; an important reason for this acceptance is that state guidelines allow substantial inputs from all systemic and case-level actors, and avoid concentrations of sentencing power.

A review of state guidelines provisions and their implementation reveals a [final] area of implicit agreement: the importance of keeping guidelines rules relatively simple. Offenders and the public need to be able to understand the rules, and the rules must remain fairly easy for courts and other officials to apply. Complex rules promote errors and disparity; they also waste scarce court and attorney time. . . .

Notes

1. *Sentencing commissions and guidelines: majority position.* Almost half the states use sentencing guidelines created by sentencing commissions. The federal system also operates under sentencing guidelines, created by the U.S. Sentencing Commission. A state sentencing commission typically drafts the initial set of guidelines on behalf of the legislature, which then enacts it as an integrated package of sentencing reforms. In other states, the state judiciary adopts a package of guidelines as procedural rules or as informal guidance to judges. Some guidelines are truly "voluntary": There is no practical consequence for a judge who decides to sentence outside the range recommended in the guidelines, so long as the judge remains within the statutory maximum and minimum for the crime. Other guidelines, to some degree or another, are "presumptive." That is, a judge who sentences outside the presumed range for sentences encounters more risk of reversal. Perhaps a reviewing court will reverse the sentence if the sentencing judge did not write an explanation for the unusual sentence; in other states, a sentence could be reversed if the judge's reason does not satisfy some legal standard (in Minnesota, a "substantial and compelling" reason is necessary). Why would a legislature ask a commission to create a set of sentencing guidelines? Does a commission have any advantages over a legislature in setting specific sentencing ranges for particular types of offenses and offenders? Does it have any advantages over a sentencing court with complete discretion to sentence offenders within statutory boundaries? See Max M. Schanzenbach and Emerson H. Tiller, Reviewing the Sentencing Guidelines: Judicial Politics, Empirical Evidence, and Reform, 75 U. Chi. L. Rev. 715 (2008).

2. *Amending the rules.* The states that have adopted sentencing guidelines have recognized a need to amend the guidelines over time, and they typically give the leading role in the amendment process to a permanent sentencing commission. However, the extent of the commission's power to amend the guidelines varies. In the largest group of states, the commission only recommends changes to the guidelines, and the legislature (and sometimes the state supreme court) must approve the changes before they become law. Elsewhere, amendments to the guidelines take effect at the end of the commission's administrative rulemaking process or after a waiting period that allows the legislature a chance to pass a statute disapproving of the changes. Do these procedural variations make any difference in the content of sentencing guidelines?

3. *Departures from the rules.* Most guidelines allow the judge to depart from the narrow sentence range designated in the guidelines. The departure could affect either the "disposition" of the sentence (active prison term or non-prison sanctions) or the "duration" of the sentence (the number of months to serve). The departure statutes generally require the judge to explain any departure, and an inadequate explanation can lead to reversal on appeal. Appellate courts in these jurisdictions have developed an extensive case law approving or disapproving of various grounds for departure. However, in theory the sentencing court still retains substantial discretion in deciding whether to depart from the guidelines.

In virtually all the guideline systems, departures have remained well below the number of cases sentenced within the guidelines. For instance, in Minnesota "dispositional" departures have occurred in around 10 percent of the total cases sentenced, while "durational" departures have occurred in about 25 percent of the cases involving an active prison term. By what criteria could a sentencing commission decide how many departures are "too many"? A large academic literature explores the departure practices of sentencing judges. To get a sense of these empirical studies, go to the web extension for this chapter at *http://www.crimpro.com/extension/ch19*.

4. *Appellate courts as the source of sentencing guidelines.* Most sentencing statutes provide only the most general guidance to the sentencing court and do not provide for appellate review of any sentence imposed within the broad statutory limits. Indeed, statutes in about half of the states limit appellate courts to the simple task of determining whether the sentence of the trial court fell within the statutory minimum and maximum for the charged crimes. A second, large group of states create a more searching appellate review of sentences, in which the appellate court confirms both the legality and the "reasonableness" or "proportionality" of the sentence. Minn. Stat. §244.11. Given that judges see so many individual cases and develop such expertise in sentencing, shouldn't judges develop sentencing rules rather than just apply rules that others create? Statutes establishing sentencing commissions often reserve some commission posts for judges. Are there other ways to involve judges in the creation of general sentencing rules?

The law in Great Britain enables the appellate courts themselves to develop more specific guidelines for sentencing, announced in decisions of particular cases. Appellate courts in Great Britain have become one of the main institutions for developing sentencing policy. See R. v. Aramah, 76 Crim. App. Rep. 190 (1982) (conviction for importation of herbal cannabis; court establishes benchmark sentences for importation of various drugs in different amounts); Attorney General's Reference (Number 8 of 2004) (Dawson et al.), 2005 NICA 18 (applying *Aramah* guidelines). What might constitute a proper or persuasive reason for an appellate court to change its own sentencing guidelines? R. v. Bilinski, 86 Crim. App. Rep. 146 (1987) (amending the *Aramah* guidelines to reflect new increased statutory maximum sentences). See also State v. Wentz, 805 P.2d 962 (Alaska 1991) (limiting use of judicially created "benchmark" sentence for assault).

5. *Parole and parole guidelines.* Wherever judges or juries exercise great discretion in selecting criminal sentences, states have found it necessary to give parole or corrections authorities the power to review those decisions at some later date. This later review imposes a centralized perspective on the decisions of judges or juries from all over the state, and it coordinates the sentences with the amount of correctional resources actually available. In that way, a parole board performs some of the same functions as a sentencing commission. However, parole boards decide on the actual time an offender will serve *after* the judge has already announced a sentence. Some parole boards decide cases according to formal parole guidelines, while others make more ad hoc decisions, depending on prison capacity and other factors. What are the advantages and disadvantages of selecting the release date later in the process through a parole board rather than through a judge applying up-front sentencing rules?

Prison officials also have some influence over the amount of a prison sentence served. In most states, prison officials have the power to reduce the sentence by up to one-third or one-half of the maximum sentence set by the judge or the parole authority. Prison authorities use this discretion to reward good behavior by inmates: The reductions are known as "good time." Jim Jacobs has pointed out the anomaly of placing legal controls on other sentencing decisions, while leaving good time decisions unregulated. Jacobs, Sentencing by Prison Personnel: Good Time, 30 UCLA L. Rev. 217 (1982). Which institutions would be best suited to create legal constraints on good time decisions?

B. REVISITING INVESTIGATIONS AND CHARGES

The sentencing process reconsiders decisions made earlier in the criminal process, from investigation to adjudication. Sentencing courts never explicitly reverse earlier decisions in the same case, but a sentencing court might allow a close or difficult question decided one way at an earlier stage (for or against the defendant) to influence the sentence. This section evaluates the extent to which courts should reconsider investigative and charging decisions in determining a proper sentence.

1. *Revisiting Investigations*

If some of the defendant's bad acts or statements during investigations are excluded from consideration at a suppression hearing — say because of a *Miranda* violation — should the sentencing judge consider that information after conviction? If some of the government's bad acts during investigations (for example, when government agents propose multiple drug transactions simply to increase the total amount of drugs at issue) do not affect the guilty verdict, should that information nevertheless affect the sentence?

When government agents behave in an outrageous fashion or encourage a person who would not otherwise have committed a crime to do so, the defendant may have a complete defense to the charges, based on entrapment or a due process "outrageous misconduct" claim. See Chapter 10. But entrapment defenses rarely succeed, even when the government agents control the severity of the defendant's crimes. Entrapment, like other complete defenses, is an all-or-nothing doctrine, allowing no subtlety or gradation in the analysis of government behavior or its effect. Sentencing, defendants claim, is a proper time to make more carefully graded judgments about the relative culpability of the offender (compared to offenders not subject to government encouragement). Claims of "sentencing entrapment" or "sentencing manipulation" often arise in drug cases where the amount of drugs in a transaction can have a major impact on the likely sentence.

PEOPLE v. DEON LAMONT CLAYPOOL

684 N.W.2d 278 (Mich. 2004)

TAYLOR, J.

The issue in this case is whether it is permissible for Michigan trial judges, sentencing under the legislative sentencing guidelines pursuant to M.C.L. §769.34, to consider, for the purpose of a downward departure from the guidelines range, police conduct that is described as sentencing manipulation, sentencing entrapment, or sentencing escalation. These doctrines are based on police misconduct, which, alone, is not an appropriate factor to consider at sentencing. Rather, we hold that, pursuant to People v. Babcock, 666 N.W.2d 231 (Mich. 2003), if it can be objectively and verifiably shown that police conduct or some other precipitating cause altered a defendant's intent, that altered intent can be considered by the sentencing judge as a ground for a downward sentence departure. . . .

This case arose from a series of sales of crack cocaine by defendant to an undercover police officer. An acquaintance of defendant's in the drug trade introduced him to an undercover officer as a potential customer. On March 8, 2001, the officer bought 28.35 grams of crack cocaine for $1,100. On March 12, 2001, he bought 49.2 grams for $2,000. Finally, on March 14, 2001, he bought 127.575 grams for $4,000. Defendant was arrested and charged with delivery of 50 or more, but less than 225, grams of cocaine, reflecting the third sale.

Defendant pleaded guilty to this charge.[1] The offense carries a statutorily mandated minimum sentence of ten years of imprisonment. However, according to the legislative sentencing guidelines and the former M.C.L. §333.7401(4), the statutorily mandated minimum ten-year sentence for this offense can be reduced or "departed from," as it is described, if certain conditions set forth in M.C.L. §769.34(3) are met. [The statute provides as follows:

> A court may depart from the appropriate sentence range established under the sentencing guidelines if the court has a substantial and compelling reason for that departure and states on the record the reasons for departure. . . . The court shall not

1. Defendant also pleaded guilty to charges concerning the first and second buys in the series and various other offenses that he committed during the time surrounding the series of buys. However, the present appeal involves only defendant's sentence for the third offense. . . .

> base a departure on an offense characteristic or offender characteristic already taken into account in determining the appropriate sentence range unless the court finds from the facts contained in the court record, including the presentence investigation report, that the characteristic has been given inadequate or disproportionate weight.]

At the sentencing hearing, the defense requested a downward departure from the statutorily mandated ten-year minimum sentence on the bases that defendant has a limited criminal history (only one criminal conviction for misdemeanor retail fraud) for his age of twenty-six and that he has an addiction to cocaine, which was costly and jeopardized his ability to pay for his home. In this case, defense counsel also argued that the police had manipulated defendant by making repeated purchases for increasing quantities of cocaine and that, by doing so, they "escalated" the sentence to which defendant would be subjected. In particular, defense counsel argued that the undercover police officer did not arrest defendant after either of the initial buys, but went back to him repeatedly to purchase cocaine. The defense argued that the officer even paid defendant at least $500 more than the going rate to persuade him to sell a larger quantity of crack cocaine than he otherwise would have sold.

The prosecutor countered that the officer had legitimate law enforcement reasons for the repeated purchases. Those reasons were that many usual sellers of large amounts only will sell small amounts to new buyers, and, thus, it is only by working up to larger amounts that law enforcement can in fact determine what type of seller the suspect is. The prosecutor, however, did not address the defense's distinct claim that no matter what the police motivation may have been, the fact that the police paid defendant $500 over the market price was the sole reason defendant's intent to sell changed from selling a lesser amount to selling a greater amount.

At the conclusion of these arguments, the trial court found substantial and compelling reasons to depart from the mandatory minimum sentence on the basis of defendant's age, minimal criminal history, and stable employment history of approximately two years, and, finally, on the basis of the fact that, in the court's view, defendant had been "escalated" and precluded from getting substance abuse treatment earlier. . . . The court then departed downward two years from the statutorily mandated minimum sentence of ten years and sentenced defendant to eight to twenty years of imprisonment. . . .

'The underlying approach of the guidelines is that the person to be sentenced is first placed in a narrow sentencing compartment based on rigid factors surrounding the offense and offender variable statuses. Then the individual is eligible to be removed from such "default" compartments on the basis of individualized factors. In cases involving controlled substances, however, the Legislature has also established statutorily mandated minimum sentences. Under both provisions, M.C.L. §769.34(3) and the former M.C.L. §333.7401(4), departure from a guidelines range or mandatory sentence is permissible. All these provisions allow a downward departure if the court has a "substantial and compelling reason" for the departure. This Court has determined that this statutory language means that there must be an "objective and verifiable" reason that "keenly or irresistibly grabs our attention"; is of "considerable worth" in determining the appropriate sentence; and "exists only in exceptional cases."

It is clear from the legislative sentencing guidelines that the focus of the guidelines is that the court is to consider *this* criminal and *this* offense. As People v. Babcock, 666 N.W.2d 231 (Mich. 2003), said after discussing the roots of our nation's attachment to the concept of proportionality in criminal sentencing: "The premise of our system of criminal justice is that, everything else being equal, the more egregious the offense, and the more recidivist the criminal, the greater the punishment."

Because of this approach, police misconduct, on which the doctrines of sentencing manipulation, sentencing entrapment, and sentencing escalation are based, is not an appropriate factor to consider at sentencing. Police misconduct, standing alone, tells us nothing about the defendant. However, if the defendant has an enhanced intent that was the product of police conduct or any other precipitating factor, and the enhanced intent can be shown in a manner that satisfies the requirements for a sentencing departure as outlined in *Babcock,* it is permissible for a court to consider that enhanced intent in making a departure.

The trial court in this case concluded, without more, that the defendant was "escalated." It is not clear whether the court was thinking about defendant's intent or the police conduct. Thus, resentencing or rearticulation of the court's reasons for departure on this factor is required because, under M.C.L. §769.34(3), "it is not enough that there *exists* some potentially substantial and compelling reason to depart from the guidelines range. Rather, this reason must be articulated by the trial court on the record." *Babcock,* 666 N.W.2d 231. Moreover, a trial court must articulate on the record a substantial and compelling reason why its *particular* departure was warranted. The trial court is instructed to do this on remand.

Further, we hold that two of the other reasons for departure that the trial court articulated are not substantial and compelling: (1) defendant's employment for two years, and (2) that at defendant's age of twenty-six years he had only one previous criminal conviction. With regard to the employment factor, . . . defendant's employment as a taxi cab driver [for a period of less than two years] does not "keenly" or "irresistibly" grab one's attention and, therefore, does not warrant a downward departure. . . . Nor does the fact that defendant only had one previous criminal conviction (misdemeanor retail fraud) until he reached the age of twenty-six "keenly" or "irresistibly grab" our attention. The trial judge stated that he was "impressed" that defendant had made it to the advanced age of twenty-six with only one previous criminal conviction of a minor nature. We are not. We do not believe that the age of twenty-six is particularly old to not yet have a more lengthy criminal record. Thus, the trial court abused its discretion in this regard.

If a trial court articulates multiple reasons for departure, some of which are substantial and compelling and some of which are not, and the appellate court cannot determine if the sentence departure is sustainable without the offending factors, remand is appropriate. Accordingly, we remand this case for resentencing or rearticulation on the record of the trial court's reasons for departure. . . .

The Chief Justice . . . contends that we are employing the subjective factor of intent to determine whether a sentencing departure is warranted in a particular case. That is, she believes that because intent is subjective, it can never be shown to have been altered in an objective and verifiable way. We disagree. For example, if under surveillance a defendant is importuned to sell more of an illegal substance than he wished and it is clear that he would not have sold it absent the buyer's pleas to do so, the tape of their conversations could well establish in an objective and verifiable fashion the change in the defendant's intent. Similarly, if there is evidence that after a physical assault the assailant helped the victim by securing medical assistance, this could establish objectively and verifiably an immediate repudiation of his previous criminal intent. This is all to say that the trial court cannot depart from the mandatory minimum sentence or guidelines sentence without basing its decision on some actual facts external to the representations of the defendant himself. . . ."

Moreover, we do not consider the intent element of this crime to be "nullified" by allowing a trial judge to consider altered intent as a factor for sentence departure, as the Chief Justice states. The crime of delivery of a controlled substance of a particular amount is a general intent crime. Thus, the only intent required to be convicted of the offense is the intent to deliver a controlled substance. The accused need not have the intent to sell a particular amount of the substance. . . .

We are considering the defendant's intent for the purpose of sentencing. It seems obvious that the sentencing stage is different from the trial stage. Indeed, the latitude for the trial court in sentencing to consider things inadmissible at trial can be found in the Legislature's requirements of what a presentence report can contain. A presentence report . . . can include hearsay, character evidence, prior convictions, and alleged criminal activity for which the defendant was not charged or convicted. Moreover, the sentencing guidelines themselves use this approach by empowering the trial court to consider virtually *any* factor that meets the substantial and compelling standard. . . .

In light of the applicable sentencing statutes and our recent decision in *Babcock,* we . . . remand this case to the trial court for resentencing or rearticulation of the court's reasons for departure, consistent with this opinion.

CORRIGAN, C.J., concurring in part and dissenting in part.

Although I agree with the result of the majority's decision, I cannot agree with its analysis. Any sentencing departure that endorses an inherently subjective factor such as the defendant's intent cannot satisfy our Legislature's requirement that any sentencing departures be based on objective and verifiable factors. I continue to believe that sentencing escalation or entrapment is merely the entrapment defense asserted at sentencing rather than before trial and that these related concepts have no valid legal foundation.

[Sentencing] entrapment or escalation is often used to effectively nullify an element of a crime for which the defendant was convicted by purporting to lessen or eliminate the defendant's intent. This is no different than the application of the entrapment defense before trial. Evidence regarding the nature and extent of defendant's intent is only a proper subject for the case-in-chief, when determining whether the elements of a crime have been established. Reviewing a defendant's subjective intent at sentencing can amount to a nullification of a conviction, or at least an element of a crime, without procedural protections.

In cases in which only a general intent is required, the Legislature has already determined that the specific intent of the individual defendant is irrelevant for the purpose of a conviction. If the intent is irrelevant at the initial stage for the purpose of the conviction, it cannot be used at sentencing as an end-run around the Legislature's decision. Here, the Legislature determined that those who intend to distribute drugs assume the risk of punishment according to the amount distributed. It is not for this Court to make a different policy decision upon sentencing.

[Under the Michigan sentencing guidelines, the trial court is required to choose a sentence within the guidelines range, unless there is a "substantial and compelling" reason for departing from this range.] For a reason to be "substantial and compelling," it must be "objective and verifiable."

Although the majority attempts to conform to the legislative requirements by requiring objective and verifiable proof that police conduct (or any other general cause) influenced the defendant's intent, the fact remains that the departure is, in fact, based on the defendant's intent, which is an inherently *subjective* factor. I cannot fathom how a person's subjective intent can ever be considered objective or verifiable. . . .

CAVANAGH, J., concurring in part and dissenting in part.

[Some courts and scholars] distinguish between sentencing factor manipulation and sentencing entrapment. . . . Under this approach, sentencing factor manipulation may exist regardless of the defendant's predisposition. The doctrine focuses exclusively on the motives of law enforcement authorities in manipulating the sentence, as when an agent delays an arrest with the purpose of increasing the defendant's sentence. An example of "sentencing entrapment" would be when a government agent offers a kilogram of cocaine to a person who has previously purchased only gram or "user" amounts, for the purpose of increasing the amount of drugs for which he ultimately will be held accountable. On the other hand, an example of "sentencing manipulation" would be when an undercover agent continues to engage in undercover drug purchases with a defendant, thereby stretching out an investigation which could have concluded earlier, for the sole purpose of increasing the defendant's sentencing exposure. [The] sentencing entrapment and manipulation doctrines both require a finding of improper motive on the part of the government before a departure is warranted. . . .

The trial court stated on the record that the downward departure was based on substantial and compelling reasons that were objective and verifiable. On appeal, the Court of Appeals [noted], "it objectively appears that the police made additional purchases that resulted in escalating the seriousness of the offenses of which defendant was convicted." . . . Because I believe such determinations to have been proper, . . . I would affirm the decision of the Court of Appeals.

YOUNG, J., concurring in part and dissenting in part.

. . . Although the majority states that police misconduct, standing alone, is not an appropriate factor to consider at sentencing, it nevertheless allows consideration of any police conduct that can be "objectively and verifiably shown" to have "altered a defendant's intent." I believe that this is an internally inconsistent holding and that it constitutes an expansion of the substantive defense of entrapment, a judicially created defense that I believe is violative of the doctrine of separation of powers. . . . Not only does the majority's holding permit the inappropriate extrapolation of the substantive entrapment defense into the sentencing context, it *broadens* the defense in that (1) it permits (indeed, it *requires*) application of a subjective, rather than objective, assessment of the defendant's response to police conduct, and (2) it does not even require *impermissible* or *reprehensible* police conduct, the hallmark of the traditional entrapment defense.

[Consider a hypothetical example, in which there is evidence that a defendant sells more of an illegal substance than he was initially prone to sell because the buyer has pleaded for more. It is entirely beyond me how such evidence demonstrates that the defendant's intent was "altered" by external factors. Rather, the defendant, at the time he committed the offense, *intended* to sell whatever amount of the illegal substance he, in fact, sold; the buyer's pleas simply provided a *motivation* for the defendant's decision to commit the crime of selling a larger amount. Under the majority's view, the defendant's presentation of a videotape depicting him reluctantly pulling the trigger of a gun and killing a victim in response to an accomplice's urgings would presumably support a downward departure from a mandatory sentence or from the sentencing guidelines range.]

A subjective factor such as intent is not somehow transformed into an objective factor simply because it can be supported by evidence other than the defendant's own representations. Although the existence of such external evidence might well render a particular factor *verifiable,* an otherwise subjective factor will remain subjective, even in the face of a mountain of proof. [For example, much like intent, a defendant's *remorse* is a subjective state-of-mind factor that may not be properly considered at sentencing. Remorse would not be somehow transformed into a proper sentencing factor by virtue of tangible or otherwise external evidence, such as testimony that the defendant cries himself to sleep every night or that he wrote apologetic letters to the victim's family. In such a case, the remorse would be *verifiable,* but it would not be *objective*.]

Accordingly, on remand, I would preclude the trial court from considering as a proper sentencing factor defendant's intent.

Problem 19-2. Learning a Lesson

Barbara Graham sold a small amount of cocaine to an undercover police officer. The officer selected the location for this sale, an apartment complex that happened to be approximately 650 feet from a private school. The transaction took place on a Friday night at 11:30 P.M. Graham had no prior drug arrests or convictions. A Florida statute requires a mandatory minimum term of three years' imprisonment for any offender who sells illicit drugs within 1,000 feet of a school. If you were the court, would you nevertheless sentence the defendant to less than three years? How would you explain such a decision? Would you reduce the sentence whenever the government provides the defendant with an opportunity to commit an act (such as selling a larger amount of drugs) that will enhance the punishment under sentencing statutes or guidelines? Compare Graham v. State, 608 So. 2d 123 (Fla. Dist. Ct. App. 1992).

Problem 19-3. Reversing the Exclusion

Juan Guzon Valera shot and killed his wife and another man after he discovered them engaging in sexual activity in a car. After inadequate *Miranda* warnings, Valera told a Hawaii County Police Officer about the events leading up to the killings, and where he had illegally obtained the gun. The statement indicated that Valera did not discover his wife's activities by chance, but followed her car to a parking lot expecting to witness her meeting with another man. The statement also showed that he chased the victims on foot a considerable distance away from their car before shooting them. The jury convicted him of manslaughter (but not second-degree murder) and firearms violations. Although the trial judge suppressed these statements during the jury trial, he relied on them during sentencing to enhance the sentence.

The sentencing judge refused to strike from the pre-sentence investigation report several references to Valera's statement to the police. The judge stated: "I think if the jury had heard the evidence which had to be barred because of the way the police questioned Mr. Valera, a different result would have occurred. I think in sentencing, the Court can consider those items which had to be barred. I think in this case, Mr. Valera acted as an executioner. He stalked his victims and shot them one after the other." He sentenced Valera to serve two 10-year consecutive terms of imprisonment for manslaughter, and lesser, concurrent terms of imprisonment for the firearms violations.

Valera argues on appeal that the sentencing judge violated his constitutional rights to due process and to counsel, and his privilege against self-incrimination as guaranteed by article I, sections 5, 14, and 10 of the Hawaii Constitution, by relying almost exclusively upon his suppressed statements in determining his sentence. How would you rule? Compare State v. Valera, 848 P.2d 376 (Haw. 1993).

Notes

1. *Sentence entrapment and manipulation: majority position.* Indeterminate sentencing statutes do not tell a judge whether to take corrective action if she believes that government agents have attempted to manipulate a sentence. Likewise, most structured sentencing systems have not addressed the issue of "sentencing entrapment" or "manipulation." A few courts have refused to recognize government behavior as a factor at sentencing. More courts have recognized the possibility of taking account of the behavior of government agents but have not found facts that support a departure in a particular case. A few lower state courts in structured sentencing systems, like the trial judge in *Claypool*, have altered sentences because of investigators' choices.

The federal sentencing guidelines have a specific instruction for judges facing a "reverse buy" situation, in which the government agent sells to the target of the investigation: "If, in a reverse sting operation . . . , the court finds that the government agent set a price for the controlled substance that was substantially below the market value of the controlled substance, thereby leading to the defendant's purchase of a significantly greater quantity of the controlled substance than his available resources would have allowed him to purchase . . . , a downward departure may be warranted." U.S.S.G. §2D1.1 (Application Note 17). Is this policy an adequate response to potential government manipulation of the sentence?

2. *Inadequate self-defense and other "partial" substantive criminal law defenses.* Should courts develop refined or modified versions of substantive criminal law defenses other than entrapment, such as self-defense or duress? For instance, a defendant's self-defense argument may not result in an acquittal, but the court may nevertheless rely on the argument to reduce a sentence. Some state sentencing statutes explicitly recognize "partial" or "near-miss" defenses at sentencing: In Tennessee, the court may reduce a sentence if "substantial grounds exist tending to excuse or justify the defendant's criminal conduct, though failing to establish a defense." Tenn. Code

§40-35-113(3). Discussions of criminal law defenses often postpone until sentencing any effort to refine the determination of blameworthiness beyond what is necessary to conclude that a defendant is guilty or not guilty. For additional examples of partial defenses that find some basis in the law of sentencing, go to the web extension for this chapter at *http://www.crimpro.com/extension/ch19*.

3. *Exclusionary rule at the sentencing hearing: majority position.* Most jurisdictions allow sentencing judges to consider evidence obtained in violation of a defendant's constitutional rights, even when that evidence is suppressed at trial. See Smith v. State, 517 A.2d 1081 (Md. 1986). The U.S. Supreme Court held in Estelle v. Smith, 451 U.S. 454 (1981), that a sentencing judge in a capital case could not consider a statement obtained in violation of the Fifth Amendment, but it has never addressed whether the exclusionary rule applies generally in sentencing proceedings. Most lower federal courts have decided that the exclusionary rule does not apply at sentencing in noncapital proceedings, concluding that (1) exclusion would not deter police misconduct because the evidence is already excluded at trial, and (2) the sentencing court needs as much information as possible about the offense and offender to select a proper sanction. See, e.g., United States v. Torres, 926 F.2d 321 (3d Cir. 1991). A smaller group applies the exclusionary rule at sentencing. See Pens v. Bail, 902 F.2d 1464 (9th Cir. 1990). If the application of the exclusionary rule to sentencing depends on whether procedural rules at sentencing can truly influence law enforcement officers, do the "sentencing manipulation" cases throw any light on this question?

2. *Revisiting Charging Decisions: Relevant Conduct*

It might seem obvious that defendants can be punished only for the crimes of which they have been convicted. Obvious, perhaps, but that is not the law in most jurisdictions. To varying degrees, sentencing laws allow defendants to be punished for the "real offense" and not just for the offense of conviction.

How can defendants be punished for acts that are not the basis for a conviction? Under an unstructured sentencing system, the sentencing court can consider any evidence of the offender's wrongdoing, whether or not the conduct formed the basis of the criminal charges. The statutory floor and ceiling for punishing the crime of conviction leave the sentencing judge with plenty of latitude to set a punishment, even if it is based in part on uncharged conduct. It is difficult and perhaps impossible to define offenses with all of the detail necessary to capture facts that affect the assessment of culpability or harm. Even structured sentencing systems tend to allow a *range* of presumptive sentences, and when choosing a sentence within that range, a judge may account for circumstances that the bare bones elements of the crime cannot capture.

Judges receive information about conduct beyond the offense itself from several sources: during trial, from prosecutors, and in pre-sentence investigation reports. Some of this information, although not strictly necessary to establish the elements of the crime of conviction, nonetheless relates directly to the charged offense. The "relevant conduct" might be an element of an offense other than the crime charged, either more or less serious. For instance, the defendant may have used a gun during the robbery, even though the charge was robbery and not armed robbery. Other facts about the offense, such as the defendant's role in a multiparty offense, may receive no mention in the statutory framework.

The extra information could relate to other uncharged offenses committed during the same time period as the charged crime or as part of the same overarching criminal scheme. A court may also consider all suspected criminal conduct in the past, whether or not it led to a conviction. If a prosecutor ignores some wrongdoing, the judge may nevertheless take it into account. Finally, the court might rely on past noncriminal conduct that is nevertheless blameworthy. The sentencing laws allowing the judge to consider uncharged conduct are sometimes called "real offense" systems (as opposed to "charge offense" systems) because the judge sentences based on the "real" criminal behavior, independent of the prosecutor's charging decisions.

Under indeterminate sentencing, it was possible for a judge to consider all of this information, though some judges would reject some or all of it as irrelevant. Structured sentencing has brought the issue of relevant conduct to a more formal and visible level. Legislatures, sentencing commissions, and judges must now decide explicitly which additional facts a sentencing judge may or may not consider and how much impact the uncharged "relevant conduct" should have.

U.S. SENTENCING GUIDELINES §1B1.3(a)

[The seriousness of the offense] shall be determined on the basis of the following:

(1)(A) all acts and omissions committed, aided, abetted, counseled, commanded, induced, procured, or willfully caused by the defendant; and

(B) in the case of a jointly undertaken criminal activity (a criminal plan . . . undertaken by the defendant in concert with others, whether or not charged as a conspiracy), all reasonably foreseeable acts and omissions of others in furtherance of the jointly undertaken criminal activity, that occurred during the commission of the offense of conviction, in preparation for that offense, or in the course of attempting to avoid detection or responsibility for that offense. . . .

(3) all harm that resulted from the acts and omissions specified in [subsection (a)(1)], and all harm that was the object of such acts and omissions. . . .

Illustration of Conduct for Which the Defendant Is Accountable . . .

Defendants F and G, working together, design and execute a scheme to sell fraudulent stocks by telephone. Defendant F fraudulently obtains $20,000. Defendant G fraudulently obtains $35,000. Each is convicted of mail fraud. Defendants F and G each are accountable for the amount he personally obtained under subsection (a)(1)(A). Each defendant is accountable for the amount obtained by his accomplice under subsection (a)(1)(B) because the conduct of each was in furtherance of the jointly undertaken criminal activity and was reasonably foreseeable in connection with that criminal activity.

FLORIDA RULE OF CRIMINAL PROCEDURE 3.701(d)(11)

Departures from the recommended or permitted guideline sentence should be avoided unless there are circumstances or factors that reasonably justify aggravating or mitigating the sentence. Any sentence outside the permitted guideline range must be accompanied by a written statement delineating the reasons for the departure. Reasons for deviating from the guidelines shall not include factors relating to prior arrests without conviction or the instant offenses for which convictions have not been obtained.

STATE v. DOUGLAS McALPIN

740 P.2d 824 (Wash. 1987)

CALLOW, J.

Douglas McAlpin received a sentence of 90 months following his plea of guilty to a charge of first degree robbery. [This sentence] exceeded the presumptive sentence range established under the Sentencing Reform Act of 1981 (SRA). The defendant appealed. . . .

Under the SRA the defendant's presumptive sentence range for first degree robbery was 46 to 61 months. This range, which is based on the seriousness of the crime committed and the offender's "criminal history," accounted for: (1) the defendant's two other current convictions for conspiracy and burglary; and (2) two prior juvenile convictions for second degree theft, both crimes being committed while the defendant was between 15 and 18 years of age and both convictions being entered on the same date.

At the defendant's sentencing hearing, it was revealed that his actual record of juvenile crime far exceeded that which was accounted for in determining the standard sentence range. The presentence report confirmed that the defendant had, in fact, amassed a juvenile record of "three files comprising hundreds of pages." The prosecutor supplemented this report with additional information obtained from juvenile court authorities.

The defendant's juvenile record included the following: (1) prior to reaching his 15th birthday he was convicted four times for second degree burglary, and once for taking a motor vehicle without permission (all felonies); (2) between the ages of 15 and 18, he had been found guilty of false reporting and third degree malicious mischief (both misdemeanors); (3) he had been committed to juvenile institutions on four occasions; and (4) he had had "various additional felony arrests which were handled informally."

The presentence report described the defendant as a "textbook sociopath" who had no remorse for his crimes, a long history of drug abuse as a youth, and two episodes in which he had tortured animals. While in the Kitsap County Corrections Center, sharpened toothbrushes were taken away from him. The report aptly characterized the defendant as an "exceedingly dangerous young man." The defendant's counsel did not object to the introduction of the above record at any time prior to the trial court's oral pronouncement of sentence. . . .

In addition to the juvenile record, it was disclosed that the defendant, in entering his guilty plea to the first degree robbery charge, had also signed a plea bargaining agreement. The prosecutor had agreed not to file charges regarding additional crimes to which the defendant had confessed, and for which he had agreed to make restitution.

The prosecutor recommended a sentence of 61 months, the top of the presumptive range. The trial court, however, imposed a 90-month exceptional sentence. The court cited the following reasons for imposing this sentence:

> That the defendant has an extensive criminal history, as set forth in the presentence report. . . . That such criminal history includes at least five felony convictions as a juvenile prior to the defendant's 15th birthday, four commitments to juvenile institutions and various additional felony arrests which were handled informally. That in the course of the police investigations of the instant offenses the defendant also confessed to his involvement in additional burglaries or criminal trespasses with which he was not charged but for which he agreed to make restitution. That such convictions were not computed as prior criminal history and thus the defendant is not being penalized twice for his behavior. . . .

[According to the statute governing appellate review of exceptional sentences,] we must independently determine, as a matter of law, whether the trial court's reasons justify an exceptional sentence. There must be "substantial and compelling" reasons for imposing such a sentence. RCW 9.94A.120(2). . . .

We turn first to the trial court's consideration of the defendant's lengthy record of juvenile felonies. Generally, "criminal history" may not be used to justify an exceptional sentence, because it is one of two factors (the other being the "seriousness level" of the current offense committed) which is used to compute the presumptive sentence range for a particular crime. A factor used in establishing the presumptive range may not be considered a second time as an "aggravating circumstance" to justify departure from the range.

The term "criminal history" as used in the SRA for purposes of the presumptive range calculation includes only certain types of juvenile crimes. Specifically, it is limited to juvenile felonies committed while the defendant was between 15 and 18 years of age. The trial court, recognizing this limitation, did not rely on the defendant's two prior juvenile convictions for second degree theft, both committed while he was between 15 and 18 years of age, as reasons to impose an exceptional sentence. These crimes had already been considered when computing the presumptive sentence range.

On the other hand, the trial court did cite the defendant's five prior pre-age-15 felony convictions as aggravating factors justifying an exceptional sentence. The defendant asserts that this constituted error; he argues that the Legislature, by excluding such crimes from the presumptive range calculation, intended to exclude consideration of them entirely. We disagree.

One of the overriding purposes of the sentencing reform act is to ensure that sentences are proportionate to the seriousness of the crime committed and the defendant's criminal history. This purpose would be frustrated if a court were required to blind itself to a significant portion of a defendant's juvenile criminal record. . . . The trial court here did not err in concluding that a defendant who has amassed an extensive and recent record of pre-age-15 felonies is significantly different from a defendant who has no record at all. . . .

The trial court cited the following two findings as additional aggravating factors:

> [1] That [the defendant's] criminal history includes . . . various additional [juvenile] felony arrests which were handled informally.
>
> [2] That in the course of the police investigations of the instant offenses the defendant also confessed to his involvement in additional burglaries or criminal trespasses with which he was not charged but for which he agreed to make restitution.

We agree with the defendant that the trial court improperly relied on the above findings. The sentencing reform act bars the court from considering unproven or uncharged crimes as a reason for imposing an exceptional sentence. RCW 9.94A.370, at the time of sentencing, provided inter alia: "Real facts that establish elements of a higher crime, a more serious crime, or additional crimes cannot be used to go outside the presumptive sentence range except upon stipulation." In David Boerner, Sentencing in Washington §9.16, at 9-49 to 9-50 (1985), the author states:

> The policy reasons behind this provision are obvious, and sound. To consider charges that have been dismissed pursuant to plea agreements will inevitably deny defendants the benefit of their bargains. If the state desires to have additional crimes considered in sentencing, it can insure their consideration by refusing to dismiss them and proving their existence. . . .

It is not sufficient that the defendant has a record of arrests which were "handled informally." Nor is it sufficient that the defendant confessed to additional uncharged "burglaries or criminal trespasses." Since these arrests and confessions have not resulted in convictions, they may not be considered at all.

We conclude that some of the trial court's reasons for imposing the exceptional sentence could not be considered as aggravating factors. However, the defendant's lengthy record of pre-age-15 felonies, standing alone, is a substantial and compelling reason and justification for imposing the exceptional sentence. The trial court did not err in deciding to impose a sentence outside the standard range. . . .

Notes

1. *Relevant conduct in state sentencing: majority position.* Sentencing judges in indeterminate sentencing systems have always had the power (but not an obligation) to consider any conduct of the defendant, whether charged or uncharged. This conduct might influence the judge's choice of a maximum or minimum sentence from within the broad statutory range. See People v. Lee, 218 N.W.2d 655 (Mich. 1974) (pending charges mentioned in PSI); People v. Grabowski, 147 N.E.2d 49 (Ill. 1958) (indictments pending for other crimes in same series of events); see also Williams v. New York, 337 U.S. 241 (1949) (death sentence imposed by judge based on pre-sentence report suggesting defendant had been involved in "30 other burglaries" in area of murder).

States with more structured sentencing systems place more restrictions on the use of the defendant's uncharged conduct. Formally, the structured state systems adopt "charge offense" rather than "real offense" sentencing. The charged offense determines a fairly small range of options available to the judge in the normal case. But "real" and "charge" offense concepts define the ends of a spectrum, and all systems allow varying degrees of real offense conduct to affect the sentencing determination. At a minimum, the uncharged conduct is available to influence the judge's selection of a sentence *within* the narrow range that the guidelines designate for typical cases. Some states go further, and allow judges to use uncharged conduct as a basis for a "departure" from the designated normal range of sentences. Other structured sentencing states (like Florida) prevent the judge from using uncharged conduct to depart from the guideline sentence. Commentary to the Minnesota sentencing guidelines states that "departures from the guidelines should not be permitted for elements of alleged offender behavior not within the definition of the offense of conviction." Minn. Sentencing Guidelines cmt. II.D.103.

2. *Relevant conduct in federal sentencing.* In contrast to the states, the federal guidelines create a "modified real offense" system. In a 1995 self-study report, the federal sentencing commission described the tradeoffs at stake in framing a relevant conduct provision:

> If uncharged misconduct is considered, punishment is based on facts proven outside procedural protections constitutionally defined for proving criminal charges, introducing an argument of unfairness. . . . The scope of conduct considered at sentencing will also affect, at least to some extent, the complexity of a sentencing system. The scope can be as limited as the conduct defined by the elements of the offense or as broad as any wrongdoing ever committed by the defendant or the defendant's partners in crime. All things being equal, a large scope of considered conduct will require more fact-finding than a more limited scope. . . . Besides fairness and complexity, the scope of conduct considered at sentencing may have serious implications for the balance between prosecutorial and judicial power in sentencing. For example, if the scope of considered conduct is confined to the offense of conviction, many argue that the sentencing system will provide relatively more power to prosecutors to control sentences. . . . Finding the right balance among fairness, complexity, and the role of the prosecutor has been a struggle for sentencing commissions generally. . . .

Discussion Paper, Relevant Conduct and Real Offense Sentencing (1995). The federal system uses the offense of conviction as a starting point for guidelines calculations, but then calls for adjustments to the "offense level" based on other relevant conduct. The commission explained its support for "real offense" factors on several grounds. First, such a system mirrored prior practices in the indeterminate system. It also gave judges a means to refine and rationalize the chaotic federal criminal code. Finally, the real offense features of the system gave judges a way to check the power of the prosecutor to dictate a sentence based upon the selection of charges.

The use of relevant conduct to enhance sentences in the federal system has come under sharp attack from scholars. See Kate Stith & Jose A. Cabranes, Fear of Judging: Sentencing Guidelines in the Federal Courts 66-77 (1998); Kevin Reitz, Sentencing Facts: Travesties of Real-Offense Sentencing, 45 Stan. L. Rev. 523 (1993); David Yellen, Illusion, Illogic and Injustice: Real-Offense Sentencing and the Federal Sentencing Guidelines, 78 Minn. L. Rev. 403 (1993). Critics have attacked the uses of uncharged or dismissed conduct as bad policy, because of the uncertain proof of the uncharged conduct, and the difficulty of achieving uniform practices in deciding how much uncharged conduct is "relevant." They have also raised constitutional questions about whether reliance on such information violates due process, by punishing a person for conduct without proving it beyond a reasonable doubt. Does real offense sentencing shift power back toward judges? Are there other ways for courts, legislatures, or commissions to respond to potential prosecutorial abuse?

3. *Varieties of uncharged conduct.* In *McAlpin,* what difference is there, if any, between the aspects of the juvenile record that were proper for the sentencing judge to consider and those aspects of McAlpin's prior conduct that were improper for the court to consider? Some wrongdoing by defendants could form the basis for additional criminal charges, or more serious criminal charges. Other conduct, while blameworthy, does not affect the charging options available to the prosecutor. For example, under the federal criminal code, a mail fraud that nets $10,000 is eligible for the same punishment as a mail fraud that nets $100,000; under some state codes, however, the value of stolen property might determine the degree of crime the prosecutor can charge. Should it matter to a sentencing judge (or to a sentencing commission creating sentencing guidelines) whether the conduct in question is an element of some crime for which the defendant was not charged? Consider this approach to the problem in Kansas Statutes §21-4716(c)(3): "If a factual aspect of a crime is a statutory element of the crime . . . , that aspect of the current crime of conviction may be used as an aggravating or mitigating factor only if [it] is significantly different from the usual criminal conduct captured by the aspect of the crime."

4. *Sentencing for multiple counts.* Defendants are often convicted of multiple offenses arising out of the same transaction or course of conduct. The sentencing judge in an indeterminate system has the discretion to impose separate sentences for the multiple convictions and to decide whether those sentences will be served concurrently (all the terms begin at the same time) or consecutively (a second sentence starts after the first one ends). This gives the judge power to limit the effect of a prosecutor's decision to file multiple charges based on the same conduct. Judges with complete power over the concurrent or consecutive nature of sentences have tended to give what might be termed a "volume discount." Additional convictions will increase the total sentence served, but in decreasing amounts for each additional conviction. Some structured systems limit the judge's ability to adjust a sentence based on multiple convictions. The federal sentencing guidelines have intricate rules for the "grouping" of offenses. See U.S. Sentencing Guidelines ch. 3D. More typical is this provision from the Kansas guidelines, codified in Kan. Stat. §21-4720(b):

> When the sentencing judge imposes multiple sentences consecutively, [the] sentencing judge must establish a base sentence for the primary crime. The primary crime is the crime with the highest crime severity ranking. . . . The total prison sentence imposed in a case involving multiple convictions arising from multiple counts within an information, complaint or indictment cannot exceed twice the base sentence. . . .

For instance, if a defendant is convicted of aggravated assault and three counts of burglary in one proceeding, the sentence would be limited to twice the guideline sentence for aggravated assault (the more serious charge).

5. *Prosecutorial motives and control.* Do rules allowing higher punishment for multiple counts than for a single count give too much power to prosecutors? It is often said that structured sentencing systems shift power from judges to prosecutors. Are there avenues other than "real offense" sentencing to limit these types of prosecutorial control over sentences? In this regard, consider the federal "*Petite* policy" governing successive prosecutions in federal court. See Chapter 14.

When sentencing rules place great weight on the charges and criminal history, the prosecutor has greater influence over the sentence to be imposed. Despite the power of prosecutors to influence sentences in structured sentencing states, research suggests they do not tend to change their charging or plea bargaining practices. Structured systems have not produced dramatically longer sentences or changed rates of guilty pleas. See Terance Miethe, Charging and Plea Bargaining Practices Under Determinate Sentencing: An Investigation of the Hydraulic Displacement of Discretion, 78 J. Crim. L. & Criminology 155 (1987). This is not to say that plea bargains have no effect on the viability or uniformity of sentencing rules. Sometimes the prosecutor and defendant agree to charges and to factual and guideline stipulations that place the sentence outside the range that would ordinarily be prescribed by the guidelines — without asking the judge to depart from the guidelines. See Ilene Nagel & Stephen Schulhofer, A Tale of Three Cities: An Empirical Study of Charging and Bargaining Practice Under the Federal Sentencing Guidelines, 66 S. Cal. L. Rev. 501 (1992).

C. REVISITING PLEAS AND TRIALS

Just as sentencing provides an opportunity to reconsider the significance of events during investigations and charge selection, it also provides an opportunity to reconsider choices made during the resolution of charges. This section reviews the interaction between the sentence, guilty pleas, and decisions made at trial.

1. Revisiting Proof at Trial

The prosecution carries the burden of proving all the elements of an offense at trial beyond a reasonable doubt or establishing a factual basis in a guilty plea hearing to show that the government *could have* satisfied this burden. But once the government obtains a conviction, the burden of proving new facts relevant to sentencing becomes easier. Generally, the government need only demonstrate the facts at sentencing by a preponderance of the evidence; there are some sentencing facts for which the *defendant* bears the burden of proof, usually also by a preponderance, such as the facts necessary to justify a downward departure from a presumptive sentence. Hence, it is critical to know which facts must be proven at trial and which can wait until the sentencing hearing.

The U.S. Supreme Court and state supreme courts have held that due process requires the government to prove each element of every offense beyond a reasonable doubt. Sullivan v. Louisiana, 508 U.S. 275 (1993); In re Winship, 397 U.S. 358 (1970). See Chapter 18, section A. The courts have also decided that legislatures are not completely free to shift facts from "element" status to "sentencing" status. In

McMillan v. Pennsylvania, 477 U.S. 79 (1986), the Court held that the government did not violate due process by proving facts supporting a "sentencing enhancement" for visibly possessing a firearm using the lower preponderance standard of proof. The Court recognized, however, that legislatures could not freely convert offense elements into sentencing facts, and that in some situations sentencing facts would have to be treated as if they were elements and would have to be proved to the jury beyond a reasonable doubt. The following case develops further the idea that some factfinding must happen at trial rather than at sentencing, regardless of the label the legislature uses.

■ RALPH BLAKELY v. WASHINGTON

542 U.S. 296 (2004)

SCALIA, J.*

Petitioner Ralph Howard Blakely, Jr., pleaded guilty to the kidnaping of his estranged wife. The facts admitted in his plea, standing alone, supported a maximum sentence of 53 months. Pursuant to state law, the court imposed an "exceptional" sentence of 90 months after making a judicial determination that he had acted with "deliberate cruelty." We consider whether this violated petitioner's Sixth Amendment right to trial by jury.

I.

Petitioner married his wife Yolanda in 1973. He was evidently a difficult man to live with, having been diagnosed at various times with psychological and personality disorders including paranoid schizophrenia. His wife ultimately filed for divorce. In 1998, he abducted her from their orchard home in Grant County, Washington, binding her with duct tape and forcing her at knifepoint into a wooden box in the bed of his pickup truck. In the process, he implored her to dismiss the divorce suit and related trust proceedings.

When the couple's 13-year-old son Ralphy returned home from school, petitioner ordered him to follow in another car, threatening to harm Yolanda with a shotgun if he did not do so. Ralphy escaped and sought help when they stopped at a gas station, but petitioner continued on with Yolanda to a friend's house in Montana. He was finally arrested after the friend called the police.

The State charged petitioner with first-degree kidnaping. Upon reaching a plea agreement, however, it reduced the charge to second-degree kidnaping involving domestic violence and use of a firearm. Petitioner entered a guilty plea admitting the elements of second-degree kidnaping and the domestic-violence and firearm allegations, but no other relevant facts.

The case then proceeded to sentencing. In Washington, second-degree kidnaping is a class B felony. State law provides that [a person convicted of a class B felony faces a maximum punishment of ten years confinement]. Other provisions of state law, however, further limit the range of sentences a judge may impose. Washington's

* [Justices Stevens, Souter, Thomas, and Ginsburg joined this opinion. — EDS.]

Sentencing Reform Act specifies, for petitioner's offense of second-degree kidnaping with a firearm, a "standard range" of 49 to 53 months. A judge may impose a sentence above the standard range if he finds "substantial and compelling reasons justifying an exceptional sentence." The Act lists aggravating factors that justify such a departure, which it recites to be illustrative rather than exhaustive. . . . When a judge imposes an exceptional sentence, he must set forth findings of fact and conclusions of law supporting it. A reviewing court will reverse the sentence if it finds that under a clearly erroneous standard there is insufficient evidence in the record to support the reasons for imposing an exceptional sentence.

Pursuant to the plea agreement, the State recommended a sentence within the standard range of 49 to 53 months. After hearing Yolanda's description of the kidnaping, however, the judge rejected the State's recommendation and imposed an exceptional sentence of 90 months — 37 months beyond the standard maximum. He justified the sentence on the ground that petitioner had acted with "deliberate cruelty," a statutorily enumerated ground for departure in domestic-violence cases.

Faced with an unexpected increase of more than three years in his sentence, petitioner objected. The judge accordingly conducted a 3-day bench hearing featuring testimony from petitioner, Yolanda, Ralphy, a police officer, and medical experts. After the hearing, he issued 32 findings of fact, [and] adhered to his initial determination of deliberate cruelty. Petitioner appealed, arguing that this sentencing procedure deprived him of his federal constitutional right to have a jury determine beyond a reasonable doubt all facts legally essential to his sentence.

II.

This case requires us to apply the rule we expressed in Apprendi v. New Jersey, 530 U.S. 466, 490 (2000): "Other than the fact of a prior conviction, any fact that increases the penalty for a crime beyond the prescribed statutory maximum must be submitted to a jury, and proved beyond a reasonable doubt." This rule reflects two longstanding tenets of common-law criminal jurisprudence: that the "truth of every accusation" against a defendant "should afterwards be confirmed by the unanimous suffrage of twelve of his equals and neighbours," 4 W. Blackstone, Commentaries on the Laws of England 343 (1769), and that "an accusation which lacks any particular fact which the law makes essential to the punishment is . . . no accusation within the requirements of the common law, and it is no accusation in reason," 1 J. Bishop, Criminal Procedure §87, p. 55 (2d ed. 1872). These principles have been acknowledged by courts and treatises since the earliest days of graduated sentencing. . . .

Apprendi involved a New Jersey hate-crime statute that authorized a 20-year sentence, despite the usual 10-year maximum, if the judge found the crime to have been committed "with a purpose to intimidate . . . because of race, color, gender, handicap, religion, sexual orientation or ethnicity." . . .

In this case, petitioner was sentenced to more than three years above the 53-month statutory maximum of the standard range because he had acted with "deliberate cruelty." The facts supporting that finding were neither admitted by petitioner nor found by a jury. The State nevertheless contends that there was no *Apprendi* violation because the relevant "statutory maximum" is not 53 months, but the 10-year maximum for class B felonies in §9A.20.021(1)(b). . . . Our precedents make clear, however, that the "statutory maximum" for *Apprendi* purposes is the maximum sentence a judge may impose solely on the basis of the facts reflected in the jury verdict or admitted by the defendant. In other words, the relevant "statutory maximum" is not the maximum sentence a judge may impose after finding additional facts, but the maximum he may impose without any additional findings. When a judge inflicts punishment that the jury's verdict alone does not allow, the jury has not found all the facts "which the law makes essential to the punishment," Bishop, supra, §87, at 55, and the judge exceeds his proper authority.

The judge in this case could not have imposed the exceptional 90-month sentence solely on the basis of the facts admitted in the guilty plea. Those facts alone were insufficient because, as the Washington Supreme Court has explained, "[a] reason offered to justify an exceptional sentence can be considered only if it takes into account factors other than those which are used in computing the standard range sentence for the offense," State v. Gore, 21 P.3d 262, 277 (Wash. 2001), which in this case included the elements of second-degree kidnaping and the use of a firearm. Had the judge imposed the 90-month sentence solely on the basis of the plea, he would have been reversed. . . .

The State defends the sentence by drawing an analogy to those we upheld in McMillan v. Pennsylvania, 477 U.S. 79 (1986), and Williams v. New York, 337 U.S. 241 (1949). Neither case is on point. *McMillan* involved a sentencing scheme that imposed a statutory minimum if a judge found a particular fact. We specifically noted that the statute "does not authorize a sentence in excess of that otherwise allowed for [the underlying] offense." *Williams* involved an indeterminate-sentencing regime that allowed a judge (but did not compel him) to rely on facts outside the trial record in determining whether to sentence a defendant to death. The judge could have sentenced the defendant to death giving no reason at all. Thus, neither case involved a sentence greater than what state law authorized on the basis of the verdict alone. . . .

III.

Our commitment to *Apprendi* in this context reflects not just respect for longstanding precedent, but the need to give intelligible content to the right of jury trial. That right is no mere procedural formality, but a fundamental reservation of power in our constitutional structure. Just as suffrage ensures the people's ultimate control in the legislative and executive branches, jury trial is meant to ensure their control in the judiciary. *Apprendi* carries out this design by ensuring that the judge's authority to sentence derives wholly from the jury's verdict. Without that restriction, the jury would not exercise the control that the Framers intended.

Those who would reject *Apprendi* are resigned to one of two alternatives. The first is that the jury need only find whatever facts the legislature chooses to label elements of the crime, and that those it labels sentencing factors — no matter how much they may increase the punishment — may be found by the judge. This would mean, for example, that a judge could sentence a man for committing murder even if the jury convicted him only of illegally possessing the firearm used to commit it — or of making an illegal lane change while fleeing the death scene. Not even *Apprendi*'s critics would advocate this absurd result. The jury could not function as circuit-breaker in the State's machinery of justice if it were relegated to making a determination that the defendant at some point did something wrong, a mere preliminary to a judicial inquisition into the facts of the crime the State actually seeks to punish.

The second alternative is that legislatures may establish legally essential sentencing factors within limits — limits crossed when, perhaps, the sentencing factor is a "tail which wags the dog of the substantive offense." *McMillan*, 477 U.S., at 88. What this means in operation is that the law must not go too far — it must not exceed the judicial estimation of the proper role of the judge.

The subjectivity of this standard is obvious. Petitioner argued below that second-degree kidnaping with deliberate cruelty was essentially the same as first-degree kidnaping, the very charge he had avoided by pleading to a lesser offense. . . . Petitioner's 90-month sentence exceeded the 53-month standard maximum by almost 70 percent; the Washington Supreme Court in other cases has upheld exceptional sentences 15 times the standard maximum. Did the court go too far in any of these cases? There is no answer that legal analysis can provide. . . .

Whether the Sixth Amendment incorporates this manipulable standard rather than *Apprendi*'s bright-line rule depends on the plausibility of the claim that the Framers would have left definition of the scope of jury power up to judges' intuitive sense of how far is too far. We think that claim not plausible at all, because the very reason the Framers put a jury-trial guarantee in the Constitution is that they were unwilling to trust government to mark out the role of the jury.

IV.

. . . This case is not about whether determinate sentencing is constitutional, only about how it can be implemented in a way that respects the Sixth Amendment. . . .

Justice O'Connor argues that, because determinate sentencing schemes involving judicial factfinding entail less judicial discretion than indeterminate schemes, the constitutionality of the latter implies the constitutionality of the former. This argument is flawed on a number of levels. First, the Sixth Amendment by its terms is not a limitation on judicial power, but a reservation of jury power. It limits judicial power only to the extent that the claimed judicial power infringes on the province of the jury. Indeterminate sentencing does not do so. It increases judicial discretion, to be sure, but not at the expense of the jury's traditional function of finding the facts essential to lawful imposition of the penalty. . . . In a system that says the judge may punish burglary with 10 to 40 years, every burglar knows he is risking 40 years in jail. In a system that punishes burglary with a 10-year sentence, with another 30 added for use of a gun, the burglar who enters a home unarmed is entitled to no more than a 10-year sentence — and by reason of the Sixth Amendment the facts bearing upon that entitlement must be found by a jury.

But even assuming that restraint of judicial power unrelated to the jury's role is a Sixth Amendment objective, it is far from clear that *Apprendi* disserves that goal. Determinate judicial-factfinding schemes entail less judicial power than indeterminate schemes, but more judicial power than determinate jury-factfinding schemes. Whether *Apprendi* increases judicial power overall depends on what States with determinate judicial-factfinding schemes would do, given the choice between the two alternatives. Justice O'Connor simply assumes that the net effect will favor judges, but she has no empirical basis for that prediction. Indeed, what evidence we have points exactly the other way: When the Kansas Supreme Court found *Apprendi* infirmities in that State's determinate-sentencing regime in State v. Gould, 23 P.3d 801, 809-814 (Kan. 2001), the legislature responded not by reestablishing indeterminate sentencing but by applying *Apprendi*'s requirements to its current regime. The result was less, not more, judicial power.

Justice Breyer argues that *Apprendi* works to the detriment of criminal defendants who plead guilty by depriving them of the opportunity to argue sentencing factors to a judge. But nothing prevents a defendant from waiving his *Apprendi* rights. When a defendant pleads guilty, the State is free to seek judicial sentence enhancements so long as the defendant either stipulates to the relevant facts or consents to judicial factfinding. . . . Even a defendant who stands trial may consent to judicial factfinding as to sentence enhancements, which may well be in his interest if relevant evidence would prejudice him at trial. We do not understand how *Apprendi* can possibly work to the detriment of those who are free, if they think its costs outweigh its benefits, to render it inapplicable.

Nor do we see any merit to Justice Breyer's contention that *Apprendi* is unfair to criminal defendants because, if States respond by enacting "17-element robbery crimes," prosecutors will have more elements with which to bargain. Bargaining already exists with regard to sentencing factors because defendants can either stipulate or contest the facts that make them applicable. If there is any difference between bargaining over sentencing factors and bargaining over elements, the latter probably favors the defendant. Every new element that a prosecutor can threaten to charge is also an element that a defendant can threaten to contest at trial and make the prosecutor prove beyond a reasonable doubt. Moreover, given the sprawling scope of most criminal codes, and the power to affect sentences by making (even nonbinding) sentencing recommendations, there is already no shortage of in terrorem tools at prosecutors' disposal.

Any evaluation of *Apprendi*'s "fairness" to criminal defendants must compare it with the regime it replaced, in which a defendant, with no warning in either his indictment or plea, would routinely see his maximum potential sentence balloon from as little as five years to as much as life imprisonment . . . based not on facts proved to his peers beyond a reasonable doubt, but on facts extracted after trial from a report compiled by a probation officer who the judge thinks more likely got it right than got it wrong. . . .

Justice Breyer's more general argument — that *Apprendi* undermines alternatives to adversarial factfinding — is not so much a criticism of *Apprendi* as an assault on jury trial generally. . . . Ultimately, our decision cannot turn on whether or to what degree trial by jury impairs the efficiency or fairness of criminal justice. One can certainly argue that both these values would be better served by leaving justice entirely in the hands of professionals; many nations of the world, particularly those following civil-law traditions, take just that course. There is not one shred of doubt, however, about the Framers' paradigm for criminal justice: not the civil-law ideal of administrative perfection, but the common-law ideal of limited state power accomplished by strict division of authority between judge and jury. . . .

Petitioner was sentenced to prison for more than three years beyond what the law allowed for the crime to which he confessed, on the basis of a disputed finding that he had acted with "deliberate cruelty." The Framers would not have thought it too much to demand that, before depriving a man of three more years of his liberty, the State should suffer the modest inconvenience of submitting its accusation to "the unanimous suffrage of twelve of his equals and neighbours," 4 Blackstone, Commentaries, at 343, rather than a lone employee of the State. . . .

O'CONNOR, J., dissenting.*

The legacy of today's opinion, whether intended or not, will be the consolidation of sentencing power in the State and Federal Judiciaries. The Court says to Congress and state legislatures: If you want to constrain the sentencing discretion of judges and bring some uniformity to sentencing, it will cost you — dearly. Congress and States, faced with the burdens imposed by the extension of *Apprendi* to the present context, will either trim or eliminate altogether their sentencing guidelines schemes and, with them, 20 years of sentencing reform. . . .

I.

. . . Prior to 1981, Washington, like most other States and the Federal Government, employed an indeterminate sentencing scheme. . . . This system of unguided discretion inevitably resulted in severe disparities in sentences received and served by defendants committing the same offense and having similar criminal histories. . . . To counteract these trends, the state legislature passed the Sentencing Reform Act of 1981. The Act had the laudable purposes of making the criminal justice system "accountable to the public," and ensuring that "the punishment for a criminal offense is proportionate to the seriousness of the offense [and] commensurate with the punishment imposed on others committing similar offenses." Wash. Rev. Code Ann. §9.94A.010. The Act neither increased any of the statutory sentencing ranges for the three types of felonies . . . nor reclassified any substantive offenses. It merely placed meaningful constraints on discretion to sentence offenders within the statutory ranges, and eliminated parole. There is thus no evidence that the legislature was attempting to manipulate the statutory elements of criminal offenses or to circumvent the procedural protections of the Bill of Rights. . . .

II.

Far from disregarding principles of due process and the jury trial right, as the majority today suggests, Washington's reform has served them. Before passage of the Act, a defendant charged with second degree kidnaping, like petitioner, had no idea whether he would receive a 10-year sentence or probation. The ultimate sentencing determination could turn as much on the idiosyncrasies of a particular judge as on the specifics of the defendant's crime or background. A defendant did not know what facts, if any, about his offense or his history would be considered relevant by the sentencing judge or by the parole board. After passage of the Act, a defendant charged with second degree kidnaping knows what his presumptive sentence will be; he has a good idea of the types of factors that a sentencing judge can and will consider when deciding whether to sentence him outside that range; he is guaranteed meaningful appellate review to protect against an arbitrary sentence. . . .

* [Chief Justice Rehnquist and Justices Breyer and Kennedy joined all portions of this opinion reprinted here. — EDS.]

While not a constitutional prohibition on guidelines schemes, the majority's decision today exacts a substantial constitutional tax. [Facts] that historically have been taken into account by sentencing judges to assess a sentence within a broad range — such as drug quantity, role in the offense, risk of bodily harm — all must now be charged in an indictment and submitted to a jury simply because it is the legislature, rather than the judge, that constrains the extent to which such facts may be used to impose a sentence within a pre-existing statutory range. . . . The majority may be correct that States and the Federal Government will be willing to bear some of these costs. But simple economics dictate that they will not, and cannot, bear them all. To the extent that they do not, there will be an inevitable increase in judicial discretion with all of its attendant failings.

[The] guidelines served due process by providing notice to petitioner of the consequences of his acts; they vindicated his jury trial right by informing him of the stakes of risking trial; they served equal protection by ensuring petitioner that invidious characteristics such as race would not impact his sentence. Given these observations, it is difficult for me to discern what principle besides doctrinaire formalism actually motivates today's decision. . . .

The consequences of today's decision will be as far reaching as they are disturbing. Washington's sentencing system is by no means unique. Numerous other States have enacted guidelines systems, as has the Federal Government. Today's decision casts constitutional doubt over them all and, in so doing, threatens an untold number of criminal judgments. Every sentence imposed under such guidelines in cases currently pending on direct appeal is in jeopardy. . . . What I have feared most has now come to pass: Over 20 years of sentencing reform are all but lost, and tens of thousands of criminal judgments are in jeopardy. I respectfully dissent.

KENNEDY, J., dissenting.*

. . . The Court, in my respectful submission, disregards the fundamental principle under our constitutional system that different branches of government converse with each other on matters of vital common interest. . . . Case-by-case judicial determinations often yield intelligible patterns that can be refined by legislatures and codified into statutes or rules as general standards. As these legislative enactments are followed by incremental judicial interpretation, the legislatures may respond again, and the cycle repeats. This recurring dialogue, an essential source for the elaboration and the evolution of the law, is basic constitutional theory in action. . . . Sentencing guidelines are a prime example of this collaborative process. '[Because] the Constitution does not prohibit the dynamic and fruitful dialogue between the judicial and legislative branches of government that has marked sentencing reform on both the state and the federal levels for more than 20 years, I dissent.

BREYER, J., dissenting.**

. . . As a result of the majority's rule, sentencing must now take one of three forms, each of which risks either impracticality, unfairness, or harm to the jury trial

* [Justice Breyer joined this opinion. — EDS.]
** [Justice O'Connor joined this opinion. — EDS.]

right the majority purports to strengthen. This circumstance shows that the majority's Sixth Amendment interpretation cannot be right. . . .

A.

A first option for legislators is to create a simple, pure or nearly pure "charge offense" or "determinate" sentencing system. In such a system, an indictment would charge a few facts which, taken together, constitute a crime, such as robbery. Robbery would carry a single sentence, say, five years' imprisonment. . . .

Such a system assures uniformity, but at intolerable costs. First, simple determinate sentencing systems impose identical punishments on people who committed their crimes in very different ways. When dramatically different conduct ends up being punished the same way, an injustice has taken place. Simple determinate sentencing has the virtue of treating like cases alike, but it simultaneously fails to treat different cases differently. . . .

Second, in a world of statutorily fixed mandatory sentences for many crimes, determinate sentencing gives tremendous power to prosecutors to manipulate sentences through their choice of charges. Prosecutors can simply charge, or threaten to charge, defendants with crimes bearing higher mandatory sentences. Defendants, knowing that they will not have a chance to argue for a lower sentence in front of a judge, may plead to charges that they might otherwise contest. . . .

B.

A second option for legislators is to return to a system of indeterminate sentencing. . . . When such systems were in vogue, they were criticized, and rightly so, for producing unfair disparities, including race-based disparities, in the punishment of similarly situated defendants. [Under] such a system, the judge could vary the sentence greatly based upon his findings about how the defendant had committed the crime — findings that might not have been made by a "preponderance of the evidence," much less "beyond a reasonable doubt." Returning to such a system would . . . do little to ensure the control of what the majority calls "the people," i.e., the jury, "in the judiciary," since "the people" would only decide the defendant's guilt, a finding with no effect on the duration of the sentence. . . .

C.

A third option is that which the Court seems to believe legislators will in fact take. That is the option of retaining structured schemes that attempt to punish similar conduct similarly and different conduct differently, but modifying them to conform to *Apprendi*'s dictates. Judges would be able to depart downward from presumptive sentences upon finding that mitigating factors were present, but would not be able to depart upward unless the prosecutor charged the aggravating fact to a jury and proved it beyond a reasonable doubt. . . .

This option can be implemented in one of two ways. The first way would be for legislatures to subdivide each crime into a list of complex crimes, each of which would be defined to include commonly found sentencing factors such as drug quantity, type of victim, presence of violence, degree of injury, use of gun, and so on. A legislature, for example, might enact a robbery statute, modeled on robbery sentencing guidelines, that increases punishment depending upon (1) the nature of the institution robbed, (2) the (a) presence of, (b) brandishing of, (c) other use of, a firearm, (3) making of a death threat, (4) presence of (a) ordinary, (b) serious, (c) permanent or life threatening, bodily injury, (5) abduction, (6) physical restraint, (7) taking of a firearm, (8) taking of drugs, (9) value of property loss, etc.

[Under this option, the] prosecutor, through control of the precise charge, controls the punishment, thereby marching the sentencing system directly away from, not toward, one important guideline goal: rough uniformity of punishment for those who engage in roughly the same real criminal conduct. . . .

This "complex charge offense" system . . . prejudices defendants who seek trial, for it can put them in the untenable position of contesting material aggravating facts in the guilt phases of their trials. Consider a defendant who is charged, not with mere possession of cocaine, but with the specific offense of possession of more than 500 grams of cocaine. Or consider a defendant charged, not with murder, but with the new crime of murder using a machete. Or consider a defendant whom the prosecution wants to claim was a "supervisor," rather than an ordinary gang member. How can a Constitution that guarantees due process put these defendants, as a matter of course, in the position of arguing, "I did not sell drugs, and if I did, I did not sell more than 500 grams" or, "I did not kill him, and if I did, I did not use a machete," or "I did not engage in gang activity, and certainly not as a supervisor" to a single jury? . . .

The majority announces that there really is no problem here because "States may continue to offer judicial factfinding as a matter of course to all defendants who plead guilty" and defendants may stipulate to the relevant facts or consent to judicial factfinding. [The] fairness problem arises because States may very well decide that they will not permit defendants to carve subsets of facts out of the new, *Apprendi*-required 17-element robbery crime, seeking a judicial determination as to some of those facts and a jury determination as to others. . . .

The second way to make sentencing guidelines *Apprendi*-compliant would be to require at least two juries for each defendant whenever aggravating facts are present: one jury to determine guilt of the crime charged, and an additional jury to try the disputed facts that, if found, would aggravate the sentence. Our experience with bifurcated trials in the capital punishment context suggests that requiring them for run-of-the-mill sentences would be costly, both in money and in judicial time and resources. . . . The Court can announce that the Constitution requires at least two jury trials for each criminal defendant — one for guilt, another for sentencing — but only because it knows full well that more than 90% of defendants will not go to trial even once, much less insist on two or more trials.

What will be the consequences of the Court's holding for the 90% of defendants who do not go to trial? The truthful answer is that we do not know. . . . At the least, the greater expense attached to trials and their greater complexity, taken together in the context of an overworked criminal justice system, will likely mean, other things being equal, fewer trials and a greater reliance upon plea bargaining — a system in which punishment is set not by judges or juries but by advocates acting under bargaining constraints. At the same time, the greater power of the prosecutor to control the punishment through the charge would likely weaken the relation between real conduct and real punishment as well. . . .

For more than a century, questions of punishment (not those of guilt or innocence) have reflected determinations made, not only by juries, but also by judges, probation officers, and executive parole boards. Such truth-seeking determinations have rested upon both adversarial and non-adversarial processes. The Court's holding undermines efforts to reform these processes, for it means that legislatures cannot both permit judges to base sentencing upon real conduct and seek, through guidelines, to make the results more uniform. . . .

Notes

1. *Juries and determinate sentencing laws*. The decision in *Blakely* created a great deal of upheaval in the state and federal courts. Defendants can insist that juries rather than judges find any facts that authorize an increase in the legally available range of sentences. The key appears to be appellate review: if a judge could be overturned on appeal for selecting a given sentence without establishing the existence of a given fact, the jury trial right attaches to that fact. This dynamic affects any "upward departures" from sentences designated in guidelines, if those guidelines have "presumptive" authority and are not simply voluntary for judges.

Within a few months, the Supreme Court ruled in United States v. Booker, 543 U.S. 220 (2005), that the federal sentencing guidelines were unconstitutional because they authorized judges to increase the available range of guideline sentences only after finding various facts about the offense, factual findings that a jury must make. The Court fashioned an unexpected remedy for this Sixth Amendment problem: It severed portions of the statute making the guidelines binding on judges, and thus declared the federal guidelines advisory. In so doing, the Court tried to ensure that the guidelines would continue to operate in a manner as close to the old system as possible: "district courts, while not bound to apply the Guidelines, must consult those Guidelines and take them into account when sentencing." Federal courts of appeals were still authorized by statute to review sentences, overturning any sentences that were not "reasonable."

The Supreme Court has remained active in fleshing out the implications of *Blakely* and *Booker* for the federal sentencing system. For a run-down of those decisions, along with a discussion of doctrinal twists such as the "prior record exception," go to the web extension for this chapter at *http://www.crimpro.com/extension/ch19*.

2. *Other factfinding that affects sentences served*. The effects of *Blakely* might not be limited to determinate sentencing structures. Justice Scalia's bold assertion that "every defendant has the *right* to insist that the prosecutor prove to a jury all facts legally essential to the punishment" could ultimately prove to be far reaching. Restitution orders, revocation of probation and parole, and a host of other punishment decisions that rest on nonjury factfinding may be subject to constitutional challenge. The *Apprendi* ruling also has implications for capital sentencing, which requires that "aggravating factors" be found before a court may impose the death penalty. See Ring v. Arizona, 536 U.S. 584 (2002) (jury rather than judge must find an aggravating circumstance necessary for imposing death penalty).

3. *Translation of jury functions to a new context*. For a judge who interprets the Constitution in light of the historical meaning of the text and historical practices, the right to a jury trial in criminal cases presents several challenges. The criminal system has changed enormously in the past few centuries, most recently in the increased role of guilty pleas and the enormous innovations in sentencing rules.

How can courts in the twenty-first century give meaning to the constitutional vision of a criminal adjudication process that is bounded by the views of juries about reasonable application of the criminal law?

Consider some of the ways that juries' involvement in sentencing might go beyond *Blakely*'s mandate. First, a legislature might require juries to be the finders of all (or at least all significant) sentencing facts. Second, a legislature might want juries not only to find facts but also to advise judges about appropriate punishments or even to impose specific punishments. Suppose you are advising a sentencing commission in a jurisdiction with sentencing guidelines affected by *Apprendi* and *Blakely*. What changes would you advise the commission to make to comply with these cases?

4. *Minimum sentences, discretionary sentencing, and mitigating adjustments*. Despite the breadth of *Blakely*'s holding and dicta, the ruling still allows judicial factfinding in an array of sentencing settings. *Blakely* formally distinguished United States v. Harris, 536 U.S. 545 (2002), which permits judges to find facts that increase *minimum* sentences, and Williams v. New York, 337 U.S. 241 (1949), which permits judges to find facts in the course of making discretionary sentencing determinations. In addition, the *Apprendi* and *Blakely* rulings apply only to facts that increase sentences; judges may still find facts that the law provides as the basis for *decreasing* sentences. Could a jurisdiction, drawing on these gaps in the reach of the *Blakely* rule, construct a sound sentencing system that is still administered principally through judicial factfinding? Should a jurisdiction aspire to do so?

5. *Standard of proof at sentencing: majority position*. In McMillan v. Pennsylvania, 477 U.S. 79 (1986), the Court declared that the federal due process clause allows states to prove some facts affecting the sentence by a preponderance of the evidence. Although *Blakely* changed which facts could be found by a judge at the sentencing hearing rather than by a jury at trial, the Court did not overturn the standard of proof to be used in the sentencing hearing.

Nearly all states have adopted by statute the preponderance standard for facts to be proven at sentencing. Structured sentencing systems in the states typically provide for a presumptive guideline sentence that is set by reference to the facts underlying a conviction, either proven beyond a reasonable doubt at trial or admitted by the defendant in a guilty plea. Yet these guidelines also allow judges, in varying degrees, to depart from the sentence indicated in the guidelines. The departure might be based on facts proven at the sentencing hearing, and most require the prosecution to show these facts only by a preponderance.

6. *Rules of evidence at sentencing*. Williams v. New York established that the rules of evidence for criminal trials need not apply in sentencing hearings. This is true both for indeterminate sentencing systems and for most structured sentencing systems. The Federal Rules of Evidence state this explicitly: "The rules (other than with respect to privileges) do not apply in . . . sentencing." Fed. R. Evid. 1101(d)(3). The federal sentencing guidelines also adopt this position: "any information may be considered, so long as it has sufficient indicia of reliability to support its probable accuracy." U.S. Sentencing Guidelines §6A1.3(a). The rules do not apply because of the perceived burden they would place on sentencing judges, converting the sentencing hearing into a second trial. Should Congress or the U.S. Sentencing Commission change positions and apply the rules of evidence to sentencing hearings?

2. *Revisiting Jury Verdicts and Guilty Pleas*

Because the judge decides the defendant's sentence independently, an opportunity exists to revisit questions that were already answered in the jury's verdict after trial or in the defendant's plea of guilty. To what extent should a sentencing judge fashion a sentence to reward a plea of guilty or to punish a decision to go to trial? What should the sentencing judge do when the jury acquits on some counts and convicts on at least one other count, yet the judge believes that the defendant probably committed all the crimes as charged?

■ UNITED STATES SENTENCING GUIDELINES §3E1.1

(a) If the defendant clearly demonstrates acceptance of responsibility for his offense, decrease the offense level by 2 levels.

(b) If the defendant qualifies for a decrease under subsection (a), the offense [is serious enough to qualify for a level 16 or greater], and the defendant has assisted authorities in the investigation or prosecution of his own misconduct by taking one or more of the following steps:

> (1) timely providing complete information to the government concerning his own involvement in the offense; or
>
> (2) timely notifying authorities of his intention to enter a plea of guilty, thereby permitting the government to avoid preparing for trial and permitting the court to allocate its resources efficiently, decrease the offense level by 1 additional level.

Problem 19-4. Trial Penalty or Reward for Plea?

An experienced police officer watched Milton Coles speak with another person and give that person currency in exchange for a ziplock plastic bag, which the latter retrieved from a hiding place in a nearby tree. A jury found Coles guilty of one count of possessing marijuana. At sentencing, the trial judge made the following statement:

> I never understood why you went to trial in this case, Mr. Coles. Your lawyer did the best he could with no defense at all. I was amazed how successfully he was able to even come up with something plausible. If you had come before the Court and said, "Look, I had a little stuff on me and I needed a little extra money," I would have had some sympathy for you. As it is, though, I don't have any sympathy for you at all. So the Court sentences you to one year.

One year was the maximum available sentence for this offense. Coles has challenged the validity of this sentence, because he claims that the judge penalized him for exercising his constitutional right to stand trial. How would you rule on appeal? Compare Coles v. United States, 682 A.2d 167 (D.C. 1996).

Notes

1. *Sentencing after refusal to plead guilty: majority position.* In a plea agreement a defendant agrees to waive trial, normally in exchange for some perceived advantage at the time of sentencing. In unstructured sentencing systems, judges almost always accept a plea bargain if offered by the parties, but it is not clear what effect the defendant's willingness to plead guilty has on the sentence. Research has shown that defendants pleading guilty tend to receive substantially lower sentences than defendants who go to trial (in some studies the "plea discount" has been one-third or more off post-trial sentences) but that judges tend to sentence based on the original charges filed rather than the charges forming the basis of the guilty plea. A review of this research appears on the web extension for this chapter at *http://www.crimpro.com/extension/ch19*.

Almost all high state courts say that a sentencing court cannot punish a refusal to plead guilty but can enhance a punishment based on "lack of remorse" or failure to "accept responsibility" for a crime. Jennings v. State, 664 A.2d 903 (Md. 1995). Courts routinely treat an agreement to plead guilty as an appropriate reason for imposing a less severe sentence. In practice, is there a difference between "punishing the exercise of trial rights" and "rewarding acceptance of responsibility"? Do these rules encourage judges to do anything more than choose their words carefully?

2. *Plea bargaining and structured sentencing rules.* Section 3E1.1 of the federal sentencing guidelines, reprinted above, allows the sentencing judge to reduce a sentence for "acceptance of responsibility," while commentary to that guideline provision insists that courts should not equate acceptance of responsibility with a decision to plead guilty. Rules in various structured sentencing systems give sentencing judges different instructions about the impact of a plea agreement. The possibilities range from rules saying that plea agreements should not change the sentence at all to rules that allow the judge to accept the sentencing recommendations of the parties within certain broad limits. For instance, under the Minnesota sentencing guidelines, judges must impose the sentence indicated in the guideline grid unless there is a valid ground for departure. A plea agreement, standing alone, is not a sufficient reason to depart from the guidelines. In Washington state, statutory guidelines tell the judge to "determine if the agreement is consistent with the interests of justice and with the [statutory] prosecuting standards" and to reject the agreement if it is not. Wash. Rev. Code §9.94A.431. The federal sentencing guidelines also advise judges to limit the impact of a guilty plea at sentencing. The court may accept sentencing recommendations offered in a plea agreement "if the court is satisfied either that: (1) the recommended sentence is within the applicable guideline range; or (2) the recommended sentence departs from the applicable guideline range for justifiable reasons." U.S. Sentencing Guidelines §6B1.2(b).

3. *Sentence enhancements for perjury and obstruction of justice at trial.* Judges who preside at trial also typically impose the sentence on the same defendant after conviction. In United States v. Dunnigan, 507 U.S. 87 (1993), the Court concluded that a sentencing court can enhance a defendant's sentence by a designated amount under the federal guidelines if the court finds that the defendant committed perjury at trial. A defendant's right to testify "does not include a right to commit perjury." To reduce the risk that a court will wrongfully punish a truthful defendant,

the court must make "findings to support all the elements of a perjury violation in the specific case." Does the sentencing judge's power to punish perjury without a perjury conviction punish the right to trial? Compare Mitchell v. United States, 526 U.S. 314 (1999) (guilty plea does not extinguish the defendant's Fifth Amendment right to remain silent at sentencing).

4. *Acquitted conduct at sentencing*. Although indeterminate sentencing systems typically allow judges to consider prior misconduct when setting a sentence, many states make an exception for acquitted conduct — conduct that formed the basis for a charge resulting in an acquittal at trial. Judges in many states have developed common law rules preventing the use of acquitted conduct at sentencing. See Bishop v. State, 486 S.E.2d 887 (Ga. 1997); State v. Cobb, 732 A.2d 425 (N.H. 1999). On the other hand, a roughly equal number of states approve the use of acquitted conduct. State v. Huey, 505 A.2d 1242 (Conn. 1986); State v. Leiter, 646 N.W.2d 341 (Wis. 2002). Why do so many states limit the use of acquitted conduct but permit sentencing judges to consider prior convictions and prior uncharged conduct more generally?

The Supreme Court in United States v. Watts, 519 U.S. 148 (1997), ruled that neither the Constitution nor the federal sentencing statutes or guidelines bar a judge from considering acquitted conduct at sentencing. In that case, police discovered cocaine in a kitchen cabinet and two loaded guns in a bedroom closet of Watts's house. The jury acquitted Watts of the firearms charge but convicted him of drug possession. The judge increased Watts's sentence on the drug charges after finding by a preponderance of the evidence that Watts had possessed the weapons illegally. The Court explained the use of information underlying acquittals in terms of the different standards of proof at trial and sentencing: Evidence that was insufficient to establish guilt beyond a reasonable doubt might nevertheless be enough to convince the judge to enhance a sentence. In effect, this allows the sentencing judge to ignore the verdict of the jury. See also Edwards v. United States, 523 U.S. 511 (1998) (sentencing judge can determine that defendants were trafficking in both crack and powder, even if jury believed defendants were trafficking only in powder). Do the rulings in *Watts* and *Edwards* survive the later decisions in *Apprendi* and *Blakely*?

5. *"Vindictive" sentencing after retrial.* Just as courts insist that a sentence may not be increased to punish a defendant for exercising the right to trial, federal and state courts say that a trial judge may not punish a defendant for exercising the statutory right to appeal. If a defendant successfully appeals a conviction and is convicted again after retrial, a sentence higher than the original sentence imposed is presumed to be a product of "vindictiveness" by the sentencing judge. A sentence motivated by such vindictiveness violates federal due process. The judge must rebut this presumption by placing on the record his reasons for increasing the sentence after the second conviction. See North Carolina v. Pearce, 395 U.S. 711 (1969). According to *Pearce,* those reasons could be based on "objective information concerning identifiable conduct on the part of the defendant occurring after the time of the original sentence proceeding." Later, the Court said that a court could rebut the presumption of vindictiveness by pointing to any "objective information" that the court did not consider during the first sentencing proceeding. Texas v. McCullough, 475 U.S. 134 (1986).

6. *Probation officers.* Judges who sentence a defendant after a guilty plea have not heard an extensive presentation of the evidence at trial and thus depend heavily on the pre-sentence investigation (PSI) report to inform them about the offender and

the offense. Especially in structured sentencing systems in which particular facts have an identifiable impact on the sentence, probation officers (who create the PSI reports) are critical players in the sentencing process. How might a prosecutor or a defense attorney influence the recommendations of the probation officer? What institutional or individual biases might the probation officer bring to her assessment (and recommendation) of proper sentences? Compare Simon Halliday, et al., Street-Level Bureaucracy, Interprofessional Relations, and Coping Mechanisms: A Study of Criminal Justice Social Workers in the Sentencing Process, 31 Law & Pol'y 405 (2009).

D. NEW INFORMATION ABOUT THE OFFENDER AND THE VICTIM

We have seen how sentencing courts revisit and refine the choices made prior to conviction. But the sentencing judge does more than this; the judge goes on to consider a broader range of information about the offender's past and future, the broader context of the offense, and the viewpoint of the victim.

1. Offender Information

Although the offender's involvement in the crime of conviction is critical to a sentence, judges also consider other aspects of the offender's character and past conduct. In this section, we consider the use at sentencing of the offender's prior criminal record, cooperation with the government in other investigations, and other aspects of an offender's personal history and prospects.

a. Criminal History

At sentencing, the court learns about the defendant's life before the crime of conviction took place. Probation officers collect some of this information; attorneys for either the prosecution or the defense present facts, as well. Often the offender's past will include prior convictions or other encounters with the criminal justice system. Under an unstructured sentencing system, the judge gives the prior criminal record whatever weight she thinks appropriate. Sentencing statutes and guidelines, however, instruct judges in some systems more precisely about the effect that a prior criminal record must have on a sentence.

■ COMMONWEALTH v. ALBERT SHIFFLER

897 A.2d 185 (Pa. 2005)

CASTILLE, J.

. . . On December 26, 2001, at approximately 1:45 A.M., appellant unlawfully entered the home of Robert and Carolyn Wegner in Ephrata Borough, Lancaster

County, Pennsylvania, while the couple was asleep. The Wegners were awakened to find appellant in their bedroom, walking around their bed. When appellant exited the house, the Wegners called emergency services, and Officer Christopher McKim of the Ephrata Borough Police Department was dispatched to the scene of the crime. After arriving at the Wegners' residence, Officer McKim found appellant hiding on the Wegners' porch and ordered him to put his hands up, at which point appellant fled. Officer McKim gave chase and eventually subdued and arrested appellant. During the arrest, appellant caused abrasions to Officer McKim's right eye and left calf and bit the officer's finger, resulting in a puncture wound. While in the Wegners' home, appellant stole approximately $76 in cash and a woman's brassiere.

Appellant was charged with burglary, aggravated assault, theft, and resisting arrest, and on June 25, 2002, entered an open guilty plea to all of the charges. The trial court accepted appellant's plea, and on that same date, the Commonwealth filed its Notice of Intent to Seek Mandatory Sentencing. On September 9, appellant filed a "Motion for the Appropriate Determination of Applicable Prior Offenses."

On October 1, 2002, the trial court held a sentencing hearing, where the Commonwealth introduced evidence that on May 12, 1997, appellant pled guilty in a separate criminal case to three separate charges of burglary.[5] The Commonwealth argued that appellant should be sentenced as a third-time offender under Section 9714(a)(2). Appellant urged that his sentences for those prior convictions were "totally concurrent" and that, therefore, the offenses "should be considered as one conviction" for purposes of Section 9714 and that he was only a second-time offender, pursuant to subsection (a)(1) of the statute. The trial court agreed with appellant and . . . imposed a sentence of five to ten years imprisonment for the burglary charge; a concurrent sentence of two to four years imprisonment for the aggravated assault charge; a consecutive sentence of two years probation for the resisting arrest charge; and restitution in the amount of $12. [The theft charge merged with the burglary charge for sentencing purposes. The government appealed, and the intermediate appellate court ruled in favor of the Commonwealth; the defendant appealed to this court.]

Our task is guided by the sound and settled principles set forth in the Statutory Construction Act, including the primary maxim that the object of statutory construction is to ascertain and effectuate legislative intent. 1 Pa.C.S. §1921(a). In pursuing that end, we are mindful that when the words of a statute are "clear and free from all ambiguity, the letter of it is not to be disregarded under the pretext of pursuing its spirit." 1 Pa.C.S. §1921(b). . . . However, when interpreting non-explicit statutory text, legislative intent may be gleaned from a variety of factors, including, *inter alia:* the occasion and necessity for the statute; the mischief to be remedied; the object to be attained; the consequences of a particular interpretation; and the contemporaneous legislative history. 1 Pa.C.S. §1921(c). Moreover, while statutes generally should be construed liberally, penal statutes are always to be construed strictly, 1 Pa.C.S. §1928(b)(1), and any ambiguity in a penal statute should be interpreted in favor of the defendant. . . .

5. One of the charges stemmed from a burglary committed on October 5, 1996, and the remaining two charges stemmed from two separate burglaries both committed on February 16, 1997. Appellant pleaded guilty to each charge on the same day and was sentenced to three terms of eleven and one half to twenty-three months of imprisonment, to run concurrently.

The three strikes law [at 42 Pa.C.S. §9714(a)] sets forth the mandatory minimum sentences to be imposed upon certain repeat offenders as follows:

> (1) Any person who is convicted in any court of this Commonwealth of a crime of violence shall, if at the time of the commission of the current offense the person had previously been convicted of a crime of violence, be sentenced to a minimum sentence of at least ten years of total confinement, notwithstanding any other provision of this title or other statute to the contrary. Upon a second conviction for a crime of violence, the court shall give the person oral and written notice of the penalties under this section for a third conviction for a crime of violence. . . .
>
> (2) Where the person had at the time of the commission of the current offense previously been convicted of two or more such crimes of violence arising from separate criminal transactions, the person shall be sentenced to a minimum sentence of at least 25 years of total confinement, notwithstanding any other provision of this title or other statute to the contrary. Proof that the offender received notice of or otherwise knew or should have known of the penalties under this paragraph shall not be required. . . .

"Crimes of violence" include only those crimes that are statutorily enumerated in subsection (g), and "burglary of a structure adapted for overnight accommodation in which at the time of the offense any person is present" is one such crime. 42 Pa.C.S. 9714(g). . . .

In Commonwealth v. Dickerson, 621 A.2d 990 (Pa. 1993), this Court was asked to interpret the pre-1995 version of the statute, which defined "previous convictions" for "crimes of violence" as any of a list of enumerated offenses if they had "occurred within seven years of the date of the commission of the instant offense." [The statute set a mandatory minimum prison sentence of five years for all repeat offenders.] There, the defendant raped two women, at 9:45 P.M. and 11:00 P.M. respectively, on December 31, 1986. The two attacks resulted in two separate criminal prosecutions. On February 11, 1988, a jury convicted the defendant of . . . rape and involuntary deviate sexual intercourse (IDSI) arising from the first attack. On September 13, 1988, the defendant was sentenced for those crimes to serve an aggregate term of imprisonment of seven and one-half to fifteen years. On April 4, 1989, the defendant entered a guilty plea to rape, IDSI, and possessing an instrument of crime, each arising from the second attack. [On the basis of the mandatory minimum sentence statute, the trial court sentenced him] to an aggregate term of seven and one half to fifteen years of imprisonment, to run consecutively to his aggregate term for the first set of convictions.

[We vacated the judgment because the defense attorney failed to object to the mandatory minimum sentence, and explained] our reading of the statute, which was consistent with the defendant's position, as follows:

> We understand the . . . language to mean "within seven years *prior to* the date of the commission of the instant offense." The Commonwealth argues that it means "within seven years *before or after* the date of the commission of the instant offense." The dispute arises because the legislature apparently did not consider the anomaly posed by appellee's criminal behavior. In cases of recidivism, we expect the following sequence of events: first offense, first conviction, first sentencing, second offense, second conviction, second sentencing. In such a situation, the legislature provided that the mandatory minimum sentence would be imposed at the second sentencing if the first conviction occurred within seven years before the second offense. If the first conviction

occurred more than seven years before the second offense, the legislature did not consider the criminal sufficiently blameworthy to merit the enhanced minimum sentence. The sequence of events in this case, however, was: first offense, second offense, first conviction, first sentencing, second conviction, second sentencing. We hold that, in this sequence, the mandatory minimum sentencing statute does not apply because the first conviction did not occur within seven years prior to the commission of the second offense.

[We reasoned that the statutory drafters did not intend] that the heavier penalty prescribed for the commission of a second offense should descend upon anyone, "except the incorrigible one, who after being reproved, still hardeneth his neck." If the heavier penalty prescribed for the second violation "is visited upon the one who has not had the benefit of the reproof of a first conviction, then the purpose of the statute is lost." 621 A.2d at 992. Furthermore, the Court commented that the point of sentence enhancement "is to punish more severely offenders who have persevered in criminal activity despite the theoretical effects of penal discipline."

This Court had further occasion to review the current version of the statute in Commonwealth v. Bradley, 834 A.2d 1127 (Pa. 2003). There, the defendant was convicted of . . . aggravated assault in 1997. At his sentencing hearing, the Commonwealth presented evidence of the defendant's two prior convictions for armed robbery in 1991. Specifically, on February 7, 1991, the defendant and two co-defendants robbed a man outside of a restaurant in Harrisburg at around 8:13 P.M. The three men then drove approximately 3 miles and robbed a second victim outside of a different restaurant at around 8:41 P.M. The defendant was eventually convicted of both offenses, but received only a single term of imprisonment. The trial court concluded that the two prior robberies constituted two separate predicate crimes of violence and sentenced the defendant, as a third-time offender, to a mandatory minimum term of twenty-five years of imprisonment. . . . On appeal to this Court, the defendant argued that the 1991 robberies arose from a "single criminal transaction," rather than "separate criminal transactions" as required by the three strikes law.

This Court conducted a statutory interpretation analysis focusing on the meaning of the word "transaction." We found that the word had acquired a "peculiar and appropriate" meaning in the sentencing context and examined its usage in various sections of the Sentencing Guidelines, as well as the usage of the phrase "criminal episode" in the compulsory joinder rule. . . . Ultimately, we rejected the defendant's argument that his 1991 armed robberies were not separate criminal transactions and explained as follows:

> Looking at the temporal and logical relationship between the two 1991 robbery convictions, . . . two separate criminal transactions were involved. The crimes were not committed "at a single time." Nor did the crimes constitute "temporally continuous actions that are part of the same episode, event or incident." Rather, the robberies were discrete criminal incidents occurring at different times and in different locations over three miles apart and involving two victims with no connection to one another. Neither robbery was essential to the successful commission of the other.
>
> Nor does the mere fact that appellant and his confederates committed the same type of crime upon the two victims render them "spree" crimes [that] occurred as continuous actions not separated in time by law abiding behavior. Appellant did not, for example, rob the first victim outside of the [first restaurant] and then immediately rob

> a second victim at the same location. Instead, appellant and his accomplices completed the first robbery, split the proceeds and left the scene of this crime. The trio then drove to a different location three miles away. In another apparent crime of opportunity, the three then robbed their second victim outside a [second restaurant]. Although the offenses were committed in relatively short proximity to one another, they were not part of a single, continuous train of criminal events with no break in criminal activity. Accordingly, we hold that the courts below properly deemed them to be "separate criminal transactions" for purposes of the three strikes provision. . . .

We begin by acknowledging that the narrow text at issue here — *i.e.,* the language in Section 9714(a)(2) which subjects to mandatory minimum sentences those defendants who "at the time of the commission of" their current offense had been "previously convicted" of two or more crimes of violence — seems to apply to appellant's circumstances. There is no dispute that, at the time appellant committed the current burglary offense on December 26, 2001, he had been previously "convicted" of not two, but three, qualifying crimes of violence — *i.e.,* the 1997 trio of burglaries. . . .

However, appellant's statutory ambiguity argument looks beyond the language of subsection (a)(2) to a consideration of the operation of the statute as a whole. Appellant argues that subsection (a)(2), which specifically addresses third-time offenders, is ambiguous precisely because it is silent as to whether convictions for predicate crimes of violence must occur in sequence. He suggests that our holding in *Dickerson,* which recognized that requirement for second-time offender status, logically requires the same sort of "sequentiality" interpretation here. Moreover, appellant generally charges that it would be absurd to construe the statute as intending that he be treated as a third-time offender because, as a matter of fact, he has never been sentenced as a second-time offender under subsection (a)(1). For the following reasons we agree with appellant.

First, this Court is mindful of the requirement to construe penal statutes narrowly and that we are to assume that the General Assembly does not intend an absurd result to flow from the construction of any statute. . . . At the time of his concurrent sentencing for his three prior burglaries in 1997, appellant was not, in fact, sentenced as a second-time offender. . . . The unreasonableness of that result is made more apparent when considering the disparity between the sentence appellant received upon his first sentencing contact with the criminal justice system — an aggregate term of 11.5 to 23 months of imprisonment in a county facility — and [the sentence required here under the recidivist statute], a minimum term of 25 years of imprisonment. . . .

As to the recidivist philosophy, this and other Pennsylvania appellate courts have repeatedly recognized that, the point of sentence enhancement "is to punish more severely offenders who have persevered in criminal activity despite the theoretically beneficial effects of penal discipline," *Dickerson,* 621 A.2d at 992. Particularly salient here is the implicit link between enhanced punishment and behavioral reform, and the notion that the former should correspondingly increase along with a defendant's foregone opportunities for the latter. . . . Just as the second-time offender enhancement under subsection (a)(1) is meant to punish a defendant more severely when that defendant has offended before and has been afforded an opportunity to reform, so too is the third-time offender enhancement under subsection (a)(2), which increases the minimum punishment to twenty-five years, obviously meant to punish a defendant more severely when he has already foregone two opportunities to reform himself. The generally recognized purpose of such graduated sentencing laws is to punish offenses more severely when the defendant has exhibited an unwillingness to reform his miscreant ways and to conform his life according to the law.... We see nothing in the carefully graduated structure of Section 9714 to suggest that the General Assembly intended to require a sentencing court to simply skip a defendant's second strike and proceed to "call him out" by applying three strikes....

Further support for our interpretation of Section 9714 may be found in the General Assembly's 2000 amendment to Section 9714. The General Assembly there deleted former subsection (b) in its entirety. In so doing, the legislature deleted the following qualification of the phrase "previous conviction": "For purposes of this section previous conviction shall include any conviction, whether or not judgment of sentence has been imposed or litigation is pending concerning that conviction." The deleted language, which expressly made enhanced sentencing non-contingent upon prior sentencing — *i.e.*, prior opportunities for reform — is evidence that the General Assembly had previously intended a different understanding of this statute than is directed by the existing language and by our decision and holding today....

Accordingly, we reverse the order of the Superior Court and remand this matter to the trial court for sentencing consistent with Section 9714 (a)(1). Jurisdiction relinquished.

NEWMAN, J., dissenting.

I respectfully dissent from the Opinion of the Majority. I find myself constrained by the clear and unambiguous language of 42 Pa.C.S. §9714. Central to the issue is the language chosen by the legislature in enacting Section 9714.... The exact language at issue provides, "where the person had at the time of the commission of the current offense previously been convicted of two or more such crimes of violence arising from separate criminal transactions, the person shall be sentenced to a minimum sentence of at least 25 years of total confinement." 42 Pa.C.S. §9714(a)(2).... Because there is no question that, at the time of the commission of the current offense, Appellant had three prior convictions, I conclude that, as mandated by the plain language of the statute, the trial court should have imposed the mandatory sentence....

Although this Court [in *Dickerson*] set forth the normal sequence of events, namely, first offense, first conviction, first sentencing, second offense, second conviction, second sentencing, we did not address the present scenario. Instead, *Dickerson* may be differentiated on the basis that the second offense occurred prior to the first conviction. Read within the plain language of Section 9714, at the time of the commission of the second offense, Dickerson had not been convicted for a prior offense.... Thus, clearly, Dickerson could not be sentenced as a second-strike offender pursuant to the plain language of the statute, and not because the Court imposed either an additional requirement that the convictions and sentences be sequential or a recidivist philosophy.

It is certainly the most likely scenario that a chain of events would unfold as: first offense, first conviction, first sentencing, second offense, second conviction, second sentencing, third offense, third conviction, third sentencing. Nevertheless, the legislature could surely foresee other situations, such as this one.

[Even] when considering a recidivist philosophy, it is far from certain that Appellant had not received his two warnings and chances at reform consistent with general recidivist three-strikes policy. Appellant was sentenced for three criminal offenses in one previous proceeding. Appellant received a relatively lenient sentence at that time because the sentences imposed were concurrent. It is more than conceivable that such a situation, in the minds of the legislature, does not deserve to lessen the count of prior convictions for a future offense. [The] Majority reasons that the concurrent nature of the prior sentences resulted in a single opportunity for reform. However, [if] Appellant had been sentenced consecutively, it is asked if a single stretch in prison counts as two opportunities to reform. I believe that the distinction between the two is irrelevant because in both scenarios Appellant has received multiple warnings and opportunities to reform. Presently, the concurrent nature of the sentences for multiple offenses was a benefit and kindness bestowed upon Appellant that he could not have expected. As such, it is illogical to allow the concurrent nature of his convictions to override the plain language of the statute.

Further, the statute is not one that is solely recidivist in nature. Rather, one may interpret the three-strikes law to be partially punitive in nature and thus, to act as a deterrent. Such deterrence is only effective when the punishment for future convictions is clear. Presently, Appellant had reason to know that a conviction subsequent to his prior three would expose him to the three-strikes law mandatory minimum sentence. Moreover, it is possible to interpret the statute as purely punitive in nature, creating a harsher penalty not in the interests of rehabilitation of the offender, but because of a defendant's repeated commissions of criminal acts. . . .

■ WASHINGTON STATE SENTENCING GUIDELINES

Implementation Manual

The offender score is measured on the horizontal axis of the sentencing guidelines grid. An offender can receive anywhere from 0 to 9+ points on that axis. In general terms, the number of points an offender receives depends on four factors: 1) the number of prior felony criminal convictions; 2) the relationship between any prior offenses(s) and the current offense of conviction; 3) the presence of multiple prior or current convictions; and 4) whether the crime was committed while the offender was on community placement. [A higher number of points translates into a longer prison term or a change from nonprison to prison disposition.] RCW 9.94A.030(12) defines criminal history to include the defendant's prior adult convictions in this state, federal court, and elsewhere, as well as [felonies adjudicated] in juvenile court if [they did not result in a diversion].

"Washout" of Certain Prior Felonies

In certain instances, prior felony convictions are not calculated into the offender score. . . . Prior Class A and sex offense felony convictions are always included in the offender score. Prior Class B felony convictions are not included if 1) the offender has spent ten years in the community; and 2) has not been convicted of any felonies since the most recent of either the last date of release from confinement . . . or the day the sentence was entered. Prior Class C felonies are not included if the offender has spent five years in the community and has not been convicted of any felonies since the most recent of either the last date of release from confinement . . . or the day the sentence was entered.

Problem 19-5. Personal History and Prospects

Kelley Grady began a love affair with Brenda Croslin while she was living with her husband, Michael, and their two children. Eventually, Brenda left Michael and began renting a home owned by Kelley's mother.

Michael and Brenda had a violent relationship. On more than one occasion Michael choked and beat Brenda in the presence of their children, and threatened to kill her. On March 7, 1993, Michael and Brenda argued on the telephone, and Michael went to Brenda's house, where Kelley and the children were also present. Michael began yelling for Kelley to come out of the house and threatened to kill him. Kelley telephoned the police, and Michael left after the police arrived.

On July 20, 1993, Brenda went to Michael's house after work to pick up their children. When Brenda arrived, Michael began yelling at her, poking her in the chest, slapping her with his hand, and telling her that she was moving back in with him. Brenda told Michael she was not moving back in with him, and Michael became enraged. Michael called Kelley on the telephone and told him Brenda was moving out of the rental house. Kelley heard Brenda crying in the background. Michael began punching, kicking, and choking Brenda.

After his conversation with Michael, Kelley drove his truck to Brenda's house. Finding nobody there, he drove to Michael's house, parked in front, and honked the horn. Kelley had a cellular telephone, a knife, and a semiautomatic handgun in his car. Brenda went onto the porch and told Kelley to leave. But Kelley began yelling "wife beater" and told Michael to come out of the house and pick on someone his own size. Michael took a butcher knife from the kitchen and jumped off the porch into the yard. Kelley saw Michael come out of the house with what he thought was a gun. Kelley reached into his vehicle, retrieved his gun, and began shooting at Michael and running. There were three initial gunshots, a pause, and then another series of shots. Michael fell to the ground face first. Kelley threw the gun down, told Brenda to call 911, and went to his truck.

The police arrested Kelley when they arrived. Michael was pronounced dead immediately after arriving at the hospital, and an autopsy revealed 11 separate bullet wounds. A toxicology report showed a blood alcohol concentration of .164.

Kelley was charged with one count of first-degree premeditated murder in Michael's death. He claimed self-defense, but the jury found him guilty of voluntary manslaughter. At the sentencing hearing, various witnesses testified that Kelley had a reputation as a peaceful, nonaggressive, nonviolent person who sought to avoid conflict. He had no prior criminal history.

Prior to sentencing, the defendant filed a motion for a "downward departure" sentence. Based on the offense of conviction and the defendant's lack of criminal history, the presumptive sentence under the state sentencing guidelines was a term of incarceration of 46-51 months. The defendant requested a nonprison sentence of 36 months, including up to 30 days in jail, up to 180 days in community corrections, a period of probation, and public and monetary restitution. The trial court sentenced the defendant to 30 days in jail, 180 days in residential Community Corrections, 1 year on electronic surveillance, and 1,000 hours of public restitution.

The judge also ordered the defendant to make no contact with the Croslin children until later review by the Court, and to pay for a psychological evaluation of the Croslin children.

Under the relevant statute, an appellate court may review a "departure" sentence only to determine whether the findings of fact are "supported by evidence in the record" and whether the reasons justifying the departure are "substantial and compelling." As an appellate judge, would you uphold this sentence? Compare State v. Grady, 900 P.2d 227 (Kan. 1995).

Notes

1. *Prior convictions, prior arrests, and pending charges: majority position.* In all U.S. sentencing systems, the prior convictions of an offender are among the most important determinants of the sentence imposed. In jurisdictions with detailed sentencing rules, prior convictions for more serious offenses typically increase the sentence more than prior convictions for less serious offenses. In some systems (such as the Washington system, illustrated above), prior convictions that occurred long ago have less impact on the current sentence. Prior convictions for the same type of crime as the current offense can increase a sentence more than prior convictions for unrelated wrongdoing. What purposes do these provisions serve? Are they designed to deter the offender, or other offenders, from committing future crimes? Are they designed to select a sentence "proportionate" to the crime committed (that is, to give the offender her "just deserts")? Some sentencing judges are more reluctant to increase a sentence based on a prior arrest or a pending unadjudicated criminal charge. Nevertheless, it is highly unusual for sentencing rules to prevent judges from relying on a prior arrest or a pending charge in setting the current sentence. Under the federal sentencing guidelines, a court may depart from the designated range of sentences if the guidelines' calculation of prior criminal record does not adequately account for "similar adult criminal conduct not resulting in a criminal conviction." U.S. Sentencing Guidelines §4A1.3.

2. *Guidelines versus statutes.* The Pennsylvania code section discussed in *Shiffler* provides an example of a "habitual offender" law popularly known as "three strikes and you're out." Almost all states have habitual felon statutes, which increase sentences by designated amounts for offenders with the necessary prior felony record. The "three strikes" variety is distinctive for the type of prior record necessary and the amount of increase in the sentence; about half the states have statutes of this type.

Both the Pennsylvania statute and the Washington guidelines provisions instruct a sentencing judge on the amount to increase a sentence in light of a prior criminal record. Nonetheless, they function quite differently. Under the Washington guidelines, the amount of increase moves up gradually as the prior record becomes more serious. The judge can depart from the guidelines in exceptional cases. Guidelines also do not allow *prosecutors* to choose whether to use the prior record to increase a sentence; most "habitual offender" laws do allow prosecutors to choose whether to charge a defendant as a "habitual offender." Why would a legislature choose a statute (like Pennsylvania's) rather than guidelines (like the Washington provisions) to control the impact of prior criminal record?

3. *Unreliable prior convictions.* The use of prior convictions to enhance the sentence for the current offense becomes more controversial when there are reasons to question the accuracy of the earlier charges. This is true especially when the earlier conviction occurred without the involvement of defense counsel. The federal constitution bars the use at sentencing of uncounseled prior convictions, but only if the government obtained the prior conviction by violating the defendant's constitutional right to counsel. See Nichols v. United States, 511 U.S. 738 (1994) (sentencing court may consider defendant's previous uncounseled misdemeanor conviction in sentencing him for subsequent offense); United States v. Tucker, 404 U.S. 443 (1972) (conviction obtained in violation of Sixth Amendment rights cannot enhance later sentence). These questions often arise when the prior conviction took place in the juvenile system or when the earlier case dealt with charges of driving while intoxicated. See State v. LaMunyon, 911 P.2d 151 (Kan. 1996) (juvenile); State v. Brown, 676 A.2d 350 (Vt. 1996) (DWI).

4. *Offender characteristics at sentencing: majority rule.* A criminal defendant is more than the sum of his contacts with the criminal justice system. The sentencing judge in most cases adjusts the sentence in light of the offender's overall character, including the facts known about his family, physical or mental health, and prospects for rehabilitation. In an unstructured sentencing system, it is difficult to say which personal characteristics of an offender tend to influence the sentence. Most structured systems do not consider such personal characteristics at all in setting the presumptive guideline sentence. Nevertheless, most do allow (and even encourage) the sentencing judge to depart from the guidelines on the basis of personal characteristics. Consider the various grounds the defendant in Problem 19-5 might assert as reasons to reduce his sentence. How could a sentencing court in this system best insulate a departure sentence from reversal on appeal? See People v. Heider, 896 N.E.2d 239 (Ill. 2008) (sentencing statute listed mental retardation as a mitigating factor; sentence here improper because trial court referred to defendant's mental retardation as a factor making him more dangerous to the public but did not make specific findings about nature of future dangerousness).

5. *Family and community.* Sentencing judges also consider the impact of a proposed sentence on the defendant's family and community. The federal sentencing guidelines attempt to limit this practice by declaring that many personal characteristics of the defendant (including the defendant's "family ties and responsibilities") are "not ordinarily relevant" to a sentence. Appellate courts have upheld departure sentences based on such circumstances only when they are present to an "extraordinary" degree. For a review of the empirical research and the complex case law on this issue, go to the web extension for this chapter at *http://www.crimpro.com/extension/ch19*.

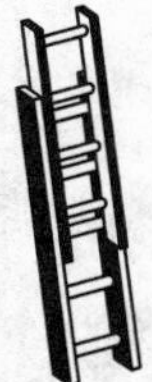

As a staff attorney for a sentencing commission, how would you draft guidance for sentencing courts in identifying the sorts of family circumstances that should lead to a departure up or down from the ordinary sentence? Would one circumstance be the number of children? The likely home for those children if the parent is incarcerated? '

b. Cooperation in Other Investigations

Just as a defendant's past conduct can influence the sentence, so can the defendant's future conduct. Perhaps the most important future conduct for sentencing purposes is the defendant's ability and willingness to help the government investigate other suspects. The defendant can tell investigators about past events or can agree to take part in future "sting" operations. In the federal system, "substantial assistance" to the government is by far the most common reason judges give for "departing" downward to give a sentence lower than the range specified in the guidelines. It is clear that all sentencing systems allow trial judges to reduce a defendant's sentence based on cooperation. What is less clear is exactly who can determine whether the defendant should benefit from an effort to cooperate, and how much the benefit should be.

■ TAGGART PARRISH v. STATE

12 P.3d 953 (Nev. 2000)

AGOSTI, J.

. . . On March 9, 1998, police stopped a vehicle in which the appellant, Taggart Parrish, was riding as a passenger. Parrish attempted to flee on foot from the officers. Immediately, several officers gave chase. During the foot pursuit, Parrish attempted to aim a handgun in one officer's direction. Fortunately, the officer knocked the handgun out of Parrish's hand. A lengthy struggle ensued, during which Parrish attempted to reach the handgun numerous times. Finally, the police subdued and arrested Parrish. The police subsequently discovered methamphetamine in the vehicle in which Parrish had been riding.

After Parrish's arrest, detectives assigned to the Consolidated Narcotics Unit ("CNU") met with Parrish at the jail to discuss the possibility that Parrish would provide "substantial assistance" pursuant to NRS 453.3405(2), [which empowers the sentencing judge to reduce sentences for defendants who qualify under the statutory terms]. The detectives testified that Parrish was very cooperative during this meeting. Parrish, in conjunction with his fiancée, provided information concerning fourteen individuals allegedly involved in drug trafficking. The information was detailed and particular, including names and telephone numbers, maps of areas where police could find drug traffickers, information about surveillance, and how the police could protect themselves during later investigations.

The CNU detectives admitted that it was a "large list" and conceded that Parrish had supplied more information than would normally be provided by others attempting to render substantial assistance. Furthermore, the detectives testified that they recognized three names on the list Parrish provided. One person on the list had already been arrested in California. At the time of Parrish's sentencing hearing, two other individuals on the list had been arrested through means unrelated to the information provided by Parrish. When asked whether he would have liked to have followed up on the information Parrish had provided, one of the CNU detectives responded that he was "definitely interested" in doing so.

However, CNU detectives never investigated the information Parrish gave them. When asked during the sentencing hearing why they had not followed up on these leads, a CNU detective explained:

Caseload and priorities. Priorities of the unit in the last couple of months have not been to respond to these types of leads. I mean, we have been responding to citizens' complaints, and there's an operation that we have been involved with over the last couple of months that has taken all of our time.

Besides a lack of time and other "priorities," CNU detectives testified that because of the events surrounding Parrish's arrest, they would not work with Parrish because Parrish would present a danger to officers. The detectives testified that normally the CNU works with defendants who are attempting to provide substantial assistance by having the defendant participate in a "controlled buy," that is, the police would fit the defendants with a wire, give them money and have them "do a buy for us." However, the detectives admitted that it was possible to investigate the information without involving Parrish and that they were willing to try that approach. Nevertheless, the information Parrish had provided was never investigated in this, or any other, manner.

The detectives also testified that it is the CNU's opinion that lists, like the one provided by Parrish, do not constitute substantial assistance unless "we fully follow it up and it results in arrest." Furthermore, the detectives stated that their supervisors do not like officers testifying at a defendant's sentencing hearing that the defendant provided substantial assistance unless the information provided resulted in "actual bodies and product. That's their policy."[NRS 453.3405(2) requires that the arresting law enforcement agency be given an opportunity to be heard concerning whether the defendant has rendered substantial assistance.]

In addition to a fine of not more than $500,000, the punishment for trafficking in twenty-eight or more grams of a controlled substance is either: (1) life imprisonment, with the possibility of parole after a minimum of ten years has been served; or (2) a definite term of twenty-five years imprisonment, with the possibility of parole after a minimum of ten years has been served. NRS 453.3385(3). Additionally, NRS 453.3405(1) mandates that a defendant convicted of trafficking in a controlled substance is not eligible for a reduced or suspended sentence. . . .

At the sentencing hearing, Parrish moved for a suspended sentence on the trafficking count pursuant to NRS 453.3405(2). Parrish was informed by the written plea memorandum, his attorney and the district court at the time he entered his plea of guilty that he was not eligible for probation on the trafficking count unless the district court determined that he had [rendered] substantial assistance to law enforcement officials. The district court heard evidence on Parrish's motion at the sentencing hearing. However, the district court made no finding concerning whether Parrish had or had not provided substantial assistance. Instead, the district court sentenced Parrish to [life imprisonment], the maximum prison sentence allowed for the crime of trafficking in a controlled substance, [and a fine of $25,000. The district court sentenced Parrish to a consecutive term of twelve to forty-eight months in prison for obstructing and resisting a public officer with the use of a dangerous weapon.] On appeal, Parrish claims that the district court abused its discretion by failing to find that he rendered substantial assistance. . . .

NRS 453.3405(2) allows the district court, upon proper motion, to reduce or suspend the sentence of the defendant when the district court finds the defendant rendered substantial assistance in the identification or apprehension of other drug traffickers. NRS 453.3405(2) reads:

> The judge, upon an appropriate motion, may reduce or suspend the sentence of any person convicted of violating any of the provisions of NRS 453.3385 [or two other drug statutes] if he finds that the convicted person rendered substantial assistance in the identification, arrest or conviction of any of his accomplices, accessories, coconspirators or principals or of any other person involved in trafficking in a controlled substance in violation of NRS 453.3385 [or two other drug statutes]. The arresting agency must be given an opportunity to be heard before the motion is granted. Upon good cause shown, the motion may be heard in camera.

We note that several other states, as well as the federal system, have similar provisions. See, e.g., U.S. Sentencing Commission, Guidelines Manual §5K1.1; Fla. Stat. Ann. §893.135(4); Ga. Code Ann. §16-13-31(f)(2). Such statutes are obviously intended to provide an incentive to drug-trafficking offenders to cooperate with law enforcement in the investigation of other drug traffickers.

Parrish contends that the nature and amount of information he provided to the detectives, information which did identify other drug traffickers, constituted substantial assistance. . . . Parrish further argues that the detectives' failure to follow up on the information he gave them, choosing instead to prioritize other investigations over following up on Parrish's information, should not result in a finding that Parrish had not rendered substantial assistance. Therefore, Parrish contends the district court abused its discretion by failing to find that he rendered substantial assistance. . . .

We begin by noting that the district court is afforded wide discretion when sentencing a defendant. As we have acknowledged, "judges spend much of their professional lives separating the wheat from the chaff and have extensive experience in sentencing, along with the legal training necessary to determine an appropriate sentence." We are also cognizant that in this case the legislature has clearly vested the district court with discretion, by stating that the judge "*may* reduce or suspend the sentence . . . *if* he finds that the convicted person rendered substantial assistance." NRS 453.3405(2) (emphasis added).

Nevertheless, this discretion is not limitless. When imposing a sentence, a district court may not abuse its discretion. Therefore, on appeal, in the absence of a showing of abuse of such discretion, we will not disturb the sentence.

In addition to the "abuse of discretion" standard, we are also mindful of our holding in Matos v. State, 878 P.2d 288 (Nev. 1994). In *Matos*, the defendant, in an effort to reduce his sentence, offered to assist the police pursuant to NRS 453.3405(2). However, because Matos had threatened to kill several members of the Consolidated Narcotics Unit, and had gone so far as to have a "contract" put out on a former police informant, law enforcement officers refused to accept his assistance. Under the facts of *Matos*, we concluded that since the defendant clearly posed a danger to law enforcement officers, those officers could legitimately reject his offer to render substantial assistance. Furthermore, we observed that on appeal this court would imply findings of fact and conclusions of law if the record clearly supports the district court's ruling. Therefore, we held in *Matos* that even if the district court erred in its technical interpretation of the statute, the district court did not err in concluding the defendant had not rendered substantial assistance.

Today's case does not overrule these sound principles. Rather, Parrish's situation does not present the case where law enforcement officers legitimately rejected his offer to assist drug agents. On the contrary, Parrish was approached by CNU officers after he was arrested and was asked if he was willing to provide substantial assistance. Parrish was willing. CNU detectives testified that they were "definitely interested" in following up on the information Parrish provided. One of the detectives further testified that he believed that the information Parrish provided was reliable since two people on Parrish's list had been arrested for drug offenses subsequent to, but not related to, Parrish's disclosure of their identities. Therefore, unlike *Matos,* this is not a case where detectives legitimately refused to work with the defendant. In contrast to *Matos,* detectives in this case seemed quite willing to extract information from Parrish; they simply did not want to work personally with and in close proximity to Parrish.

Parrish correctly argues that nowhere in NRS 453.3405(2) is there a requirement that the police personally work with a defendant who is attempting to provide substantial assistance. While police may legitimately refuse to work closely with a defendant who, in the view of police officers, poses a danger to themselves or the public, substantial assistance, pursuant to the terms of the statute, may be rendered in other ways. We understand the detectives' unwillingness to utilize Parrish in a controlled buy operation after he engaged in a prolonged physical struggle with law enforcement officers during his arrest and had, during the same incident, drawn a weapon on those officers. However, it is clear in this case that the information Parrish provided could have been investigated in a manner that did not personally involve Parrish. The officers themselves evaluated the information positively and thought it was sound enough to warrant further investigation. Therefore, the district court could have found that Parrish rendered substantial assistance even though the detectives refused to work closely with Parrish.[7]

What is so troubling about this case is the district court's apparent acceptance of CNU's "policy" concerning substantial assistance. The CNU detectives testified that in their opinion only arrests, or as they put it, information resulting in "actual bodies and product," constituted substantial assistance. Because the district court did not specifically address this interpretation and sentenced Parrish to the maximum sentence allowed, it seems that the district court may have implicitly accepted CNU's "policy" as a correct statement of the law.

CNU's policy clearly constitutes a misinterpretation of the statute. NRS 453.3405(2) plainly states that the district court may find that the defendant rendered "substantial assistance in the identification, arrest *or* conviction" of other drug traffickers. (Emphasis added.) A plain reading of the statute reveals that an arrest is not a necessary prerequisite to a determination that a defendant has rendered substantial assistance. While CNU is free to develop its own internal policy concerning when the agency, in exercising its opportunity to be heard pursuant to NRS 453.3405(2), will recommend that the court reduce or suspend the sentence of an offender, CNU is not free to represent to the court that substantial assistance has not been rendered simply because their internal requirements have not been met.

Furthermore, we take this opportunity to elaborate on the discretion with which district courts are vested under NRS 453.3405(2). Under this statute, once an

7. From the record, it is unclear whether the police refused to work with Parrish due to the circumstances surrounding his arrest, or whether a lack of time and resources simply prevented the officers from fully investigating the information provided by Parrish. In any event, it is clear that Parrish did provide the police with a large amount of apparently valuable information.

appropriate motion is made, the district court may permissibly exercise its discretion in one of two ways. First, the district court may find that a defendant has not rendered substantial assistance under the statute, and therefore is not eligible for a sentence reduction or suspension. Second, even if the district court finds that a defendant has rendered substantial assistance in accordance with NRS 453.3405(2), the district court is still free in its discretion to reduce or suspend the sentence. The difficulty in this case is that we are unable to ascertain from the record why the district court sentenced Parrish to the maximum sentence allowed.

Our holding today does not require law enforcement to work with every defendant who wishes to render substantial assistance. Neither is law enforcement required to act on every piece of information provided to them by a defendant attempting to render substantial assistance in an attempt to avoid an otherwise harsh, mandatory sentence. Nor do we hold that substantial assistance is rendered as a matter of law whenever a defendant provides law enforcement officers with information. The trial judge is always in the best position to evaluate the sincerity, reliability, quality and value of a defendant's efforts to provide substantial assistance. However, a judicial determination of whether or not substantial assistance has been rendered must be made by application of the statutory requirements to the defendant's efforts. If the district court sets a higher standard than is statutorily required for a finding of substantial assistance, the purpose of the statute is defeated. What is more, offenders who might otherwise be willing to trade information for the possibility of leniency will not do so if the carrot of leniency is illusory.

Those responsible for enforcing the laws of this state, and in turn the public, are benefited when defendants choose to provide the police with information that leads to the "identification, arrest or conviction" of others involved in the drug trade. When offenders perform substantial assistance, it would be unfair to provide no relief under the statute to them unless an articulable reason exists not to reduce or suspend the sentence.

In this case, Parrish provided CNU with a considerable amount of information. The detectives were able to independently corroborate some of that information. It is clear that this information did identify drug traffickers known to law enforcement through its own resources. This enhances the possibility that the rest of the information, if investigated, would have led to the "identification, arrest or conviction" of other drug traffickers. While we are unwilling to hold as a matter of law that Parrish rendered substantial assistance, it is clear to us, based on the nature and amount of information Parrish provided to law enforcement, that the district court could have found that Parrish provided substantial assistance. As we stated in *Matos,* this court may imply factual findings if the record clearly supports the lower court's ruling. Here, we cannot say that the record clearly supports the district court's decision.

Accordingly, we hold that when evidence is presented to the district court concerning whether or not a defendant has rendered substantial assistance pursuant to NRS 453.3405(2), the district court is required to expressly state its finding concerning whether or not substantial assistance has been provided. Because the district court in this case made no such finding, and because the record does not clearly support a finding that there had been no substantial assistance provided to law enforcement, we vacate Parrish's sentence. We cannot determine from the record in this case whether the district court misinterpreted NRS 453.3405(2) since evidence was presented which could support a finding that Parrish had provided substantial assistance. Based on the foregoing, we affirm Parrish's judgment of conviction but vacate his sentence and remand this case for a new sentencing hearing before a different district judge.

U.S. SENTENCING GUIDELINES §5K1.1

Upon motion of the government stating that the defendant has provided substantial assistance in the investigation or prosecution of another person who has committed an offense, the court may depart from the guidelines.

The appropriate reduction shall be determined by the court for reasons stated that may include, but are not limited to, consideration of the following: (1) the court's evaluation of the significance and usefulness of the defendant's assistance, taking into consideration the government's evaluation of the assistance rendered; (2) the truthfulness, completeness, and reliability of any information or testimony provided by the defendant; (3) the nature and extent of the defendant's assistance; (4) any injury suffered, or any danger or risk of injury to the defendant or his family resulting from his assistance; (5) the timeliness of the defendant's assistance.

Notes

1. *Assisting in other investigations: majority position.* In the unstructured sentencing states, cooperation with the government in investigating and trying other criminal cases is generally believed to have some positive effect both on the sentencing court's disposition of the case and on the duration of the sentence imposed. State v. Johnson, 630 N.W.2d 583 (Iowa 2001). Even in highly discretionary sentencing systems, statutes commonly address the sentencing discount a court must give to a defendant who provides assistance to the government. See Brugman v. State, 339 S.E.2d 244 (Ga. 1986) (discussing statute). The more structured sentencing states have followed the same route, instructing the judge that cooperation with the government can serve as a basis for departing from the guideline sentence and imposing some lesser sentence. See Or. Criminal Justice Commission R. 213-008-0002.

2. *Substantial in whose eyes?* There is some variation in the amount of control the prosecution has over the use of the "substantial assistance" sentencing factor. If the prosecution refuses to accept a defendant's offer of cooperation, then the sentence usually will not be affected. But what happens if the government accepts the cooperation and later determines that it was not valuable or complete? Section 5K1.1 of the federal guidelines requires a government motion before the court can reduce the sentence based on the defendant's cooperation, while 18 U.S.C. §3553(e) requires the same before a court can reduce a sentence below a statutory mandatory minimum. Should the court have an independent power to reduce a sentence on these grounds, even in the absence of a government motion? See Wade v. United States, 504 U.S. 181 (1992) (constitution does not preserve for federal judges the power to depart for "substantial assistance" without permission of the government; only when the defendant makes a "substantial threshold showing" of an unconstitutional prosecutorial motive can the court adjust the sentence without a government motion). State legislatures and courts have been debating this issue for years. See State v. Sarabia, 875 P.2d 227 (Idaho 1994) (declaring unconstitutional a statute

allowing sentence below mandatory minimum only when prosecutor moves for reduction based on substantial assistance).

3. *Nonconstitutional controls on assistance discounts.* The real debate over limiting prosecutorial power in this sphere takes place at the non-constitutional level. Legislatures and sentencing commissions must decide whether to make a prosecutor's motion a necessary precondition to this sort of sentence reduction. The concern, of course, is that an unsupervised prosecutor will make the recommendations on arbitrary or inconsistent grounds. In the federal system, prosecutors have attempted to regulate themselves, by creating written policies about which defendants should receive a reduced sentence for substantial assistance. About 80 percent of the federal districts have adopted written guidelines on the subject, and their content is fairly consistent. However, a study sponsored by the U.S. Sentencing Commission found great variety among the 94 federal districts in their granting of substantial assistance motions. The findings of this study and related research receive further attention on the web extension for this chapter at *http://www.crimpro.com/extension/ch19*. As a chief prosecutor, how could you create guidelines within your office that would promote more consistent decisions about sentence discounts for cooperating defendants?

2. *New Information About the Victim and the Community*

What information not related to the offender or the offense may affect the sentence? This section considers two kinds of information beyond the offense and offender: information about the victim and information about the community.

In a traditional indeterminate sentencing system, victims do not formally address the sentencing court. The trial is seen as a process through which the state prosecutes and punishes individuals for violations of collective norms; individuals are compensated through private law (tort) remedies. Of course, the prosecutor attempts in many cases to bring the victim's concerns or information to the court's attention, and the judge may account for this in imposing a sentence. But until recently, the victim has had little opportunity to speak directly to the sentencing court.

In recent decades, through statutes, state constitutional provisions, and procedural rules, most jurisdictions have created a formal role for victims. Many jurisdictions give victims an opportunity to address the court, both to provide information about the harm caused by the crime and to express an opinion about the proper sentence to impose. But what impact should victims have on individual sentences? Should the personal or family circumstances of the victim matter? Will these factors, if considered, become a means for considering invidious factors such as wealth and race?

■ STATE v. ANTWON JOHNSON

873 P.2d 514 (Wash. 1994)

SMITH, J.

Petitioner Antwon Lanell Johnson seeks review of a decision of the Court of Appeals, Division One, affirming the aggravated exceptional sentence imposed upon him by the King County Superior Court following his conviction of one count of assault in the first degree and one count of assault in the second degree. We affirm.

Statement of Facts

On March 13, 1990, Petitioner Antwon Lanell Johnson fired from a handgun several shots at two automobiles driven by Marvin Jones and Taifa Griffith, members of a group called the "Crips", reported to be a rival "gang" to the "Black Gangster Disciples," another "gang" commonly known as "BGD". He fired at another automobile driven by Germaine Scott. The incident occurred in front of John Muir Elementary School in Seattle while school was in session. On March 16, 1990, the King County Prosecuting Attorney filed an information charging Petitioner Johnson with two counts of assault in the first degree, both with deadly weapon allegations. The case proceeded to trial upon a second amended information in the King County Superior Court before a jury. . . .

The information in both counts indicated that assault in the first degree as charged included the lesser offense of assault in the second degree. It further accused Antwon Lanell Johnson "at said time of being armed with a deadly weapon, to-wit; a handgun, under the authority of RCW 9.94A.125."

At trial several eyewitnesses testified that Petitioner Johnson had fired at the automobiles and fled from the scene. These witnesses included William Robbins, a parent picking up his child from school at the time of the shooting; Roy Dunn, a crossing guard who observed the shooting and collected from the street several spent cartridges following the shooting; Germaine Scott, a member of the "Crips" and driver of a third automobile which escaped from the shooting; and Marvin Jones.

Marvin Jones testified that he and Taifi Griffith were members of the "Crips" gang; that they were on "Black Gangster Disciples" (BGD) "turf" on Horton Street near John Muir Elementary School talking to some girls; that four members of the BGD "gang" (Petitioner Johnson was not in the group) saw them and everyone "flashed" their respective "gang signs"; that one of the BGDs ran away from the group; that he and two other "Crips" got into their automobiles to follow the BGD because they believed he had gone to get a gun; that Petitioner Johnson jumped from some bushes and fired at two of the three automobiles driven by the "Crips" in front of John Muir Elementary School; and that all the "Crips" fled from the scene in their automobiles. Germaine Scott testified that during the shooting he observed Petitioner Johnson near the BGD who had earlier run away from the group. . . .

On June 5, 1990, the jury found Petitioner Johnson "guilty" of one count of assault in the first degree and one count of the lesser included offense of assault in the second degree. The jury also found on both counts that Petitioner was armed with a deadly weapon.

At the sentencing hearing on August 13, 1990, Seattle Police Officer Dale Williams related a prior encounter with Petitioner Johnson. He testified that on July 20, 1989 (approximately 9 months prior to the shooting in this case) he arrested two members of the "Crips" gang who were chasing Petitioner Johnson; that Petitioner had not committed any offense and was not arrested; that at the scene of the arrest Petitioner "flashed" what are characterized as "gang signs" at the "Crips," acted in a boastful manner, and told the two "Crips" they should not enter

BGD "turf" in the future; and that later Petitioner told him in a proud manner that he was a member of the BGDs.

Detective Paul Pomerville, a member of the Seattle Police Gang Task Force and an "expert on street gangs", testified at the sentencing proceeding. He stated that in general a "street gang" is a subcultural group with distinct beliefs, values, behavior, art, dress, and written, verbal and nonverbal forms of communication; that the most important value is image or reputation; that reputation is gained by perpetrating acts of violence upon police and rival gangs or through suffering violence during initiation into a gang; and that status and leadership within the group is achieved by committing acts of violence. He also stated that criminal conduct is an integral part of street gang activity; and that its primary focus is to control a geographical area or "turf" where the group can exercise a monopoly control over drug traffic. He also mentioned that one theory explaining the reason for gang membership is breakdown of the family and that the gang becomes a surrogate family providing structure and values. He also testified that he was familiar with Seattle street gangs and that there had been recent violence among them over "turf."

On September 7, 1990, Judge Eberharter signed a judgment and sentence. Petitioner Johnson had an offender score of 3. After determining that "substantial and compelling reasons exist which justify a sentence above/below the Standard range for Counts I and II", the court imposed upon petitioner an exceptional sentence of 170 months' incarceration for assault in the first degree, to run concurrently with an exceptional sentence of 50 months' incarceration for assault in the second degree.[14] The court also entered findings of fact and conclusions of law as follows:

Findings of Fact . . .

5. Antwon Johnson committed these assaults against rival gang members in an attempt to assert BGD dominance over the CRIPS and to advance his own position within the BGD organization.

6. The impact of the defendant's assaults went far beyond the intended victims.

7. The defendant opened fire on gang members immediately next to a public elementary school that was in session.

8. As a result of the defendant's actions, children have become frightened to go to school and parents fearful that their children are not safe while at the school.

9. The defendant invaded the community's zone of safety.

Conclusions of Law . . .

2. These crimes were gang-motivated. The court finds this to be an aggravating factor which justifies going beyond the presumptive standard range.

3. The invasion of the community's zone of safety is an aggravating factor which justifies going beyond the presumptive standard range. . . .

14. The trial court determined that, under the Sentencing Reform Act of 1981 with an offender score of 3 and a deadly weapon finding, assault in the first degree has a seriousness level of XI and a standard range of 85 to 113 months, with a maximum of life; and assault in the second degree has a seriousness level of IV and a standard range of 25 to 29 months, with a maximum of 10 years.

On October 4, 1990, Petitioner Johnson filed a Notice of Appeal, [claiming that] it is "constitutionally impermissible" to punish him "solely based upon his association with" the BGD gang. . . .

Discussion

Review of an exceptional sentence is governed by RCW 9.94A.210(4). An appellate court analyzes the appropriateness of an exceptional sentence by determining (1) whether the reasons given for it are supported by the evidence in the record under a "clearly erroneous" standard of review; (2) whether the reasons given for the exceptional sentence justify departure from the standard range as a "matter of law"; and (3) whether the exceptional sentence is clearly too excessive or too lenient under an "abuse of discretion" standard of review.

RCW 9.94A.390(2) lists several aggravating factors the trial court may consider in imposing an exceptional sentence. They are not exclusive and are illustrative only. None of the factors listed seem to apply in this case. The justification given by the trial court must then be tested against reasons not specified in the illustrations, but allowable under RCW 9.94A.210(4), [which provides]: "(4) To reverse a sentence which is outside the sentence range, the reviewing court must find: (a) Either that the reasons supplied by the sentencing judge are not supported by the record which was before the judge or that those reasons do not justify a sentence outside the standard range for that offense; or (b) that the sentence imposed was clearly excessive or clearly too lenient." Petitioner Johnson challenges only the sentencing court's use of "gang motivation" and "community impact" as justification for the exceptional sentence. He does not claim the exceptional sentence is clearly excessive. . . .

Gang Motivation as Basis for Exceptional Sentence

Petitioner claims an aggravated exceptional sentence was imposed upon him solely because of his association with or membership in the BGD street gang. If that evidence were not relevant to the issues at trial and at sentencing, the punishment would then constitute a violation of the First Amendment right of freedom of association as declared by the United States Supreme Court in Dawson v. Delaware, 503 U.S. 159 (1992). However, the evidence is relevant to the issues in this case.

In *Dawson,* the defendant was sentenced to death, upon a jury verdict, for aggravated murder committed after his escape from a Delaware prison. At sentencing evidence was admitted that he was a member of the Aryan Brotherhood prison gang. The United States Supreme Court concluded: "The Constitution does not erect a *per se* barrier to the admission of evidence concerning one's beliefs and associations at sentencing simply because those beliefs and associations are protected by the First Amendment." Under *Dawson,* then, in general, and as a "matter of law," relevant evidence of a person's beliefs and associations is admissible at a sentencing hearing without amounting to a constitutional violation. Thus, in this case, the trial court did not err in considering Petitioner Johnson's association with a "gang" in determining applicability of an aggravated exceptional sentence.

The court in *Dawson* observed that the "narrowness of the stipulation" made prior to the sentencing hearing allowed only a general statement concerning the nature of the Aryan Brotherhood prison gang. The stipulation provided: "the Aryan Brotherhood refers to a white racist prison gang that began in the 1960's in California in response to other gangs of racial minorities. Separate gangs calling themselves the Aryan Brotherhood now exist in many state prisons including Delaware." The Court noted that the State by stipulation agreed to present no other evidence concerning the Aryan Brotherhood or the chapter in which the defendant held membership. It noted that no evidence was presented to connect general Aryan Brotherhood beliefs with the defendant's motivation for committing the aggravated murder of a woman after his escape from prison. The Court thus concluded that evidence of beliefs and associations of the defendant was irrelevant to his commission of the murder, and remanded to the Supreme Court of Delaware for its consideration whether the error was harmless under Delaware law.

In this case, Detective Pomerville testified at sentencing as an "expert" on "street gangs." He stated that in general the primary activity of a "street gang" is commission of crime and that status and leadership in the group is achieved by committing acts of violence against rival gangs and police. He also stated that the primary focus of a street gang is to control a geographical area "turf" where the group can exercise monopoly control over drug traffic. . . . Detective Pomerville also testified he was familiar with Seattle street gangs and that there had been recent violence among them over "turf." Under *Dawson,* such expert testimony, without more, would not be relevant to commission of an offense even when the defendant acknowledges gang membership. However, it does become relevant when connected to the defendant's motivation for committing a crime.

In this case, the evidence established that Petitioner Johnson's association with the BGD gang was also his motivation for shooting at members of a rival gang. . . . The weight of the evidence supports the conclusion reached by the trial court . . . that the shooting was "gang motivated." The conclusion of the trial court was not "clearly erroneous". . . .

COMMUNITY IMPACT AS BASIS FOR EXCEPTIONAL SENTENCE

Petitioner claims the sentencing court erred in basing his aggravated exceptional sentence upon the community impact of his crimes. . . . Petitioner cites State v. Cuevas-Diaz, 812 P.2d 883 (Wash. App. 1991), for the proposition that impact of a crime on the community at large is not a sufficient basis for an aggravated exceptional sentence. The court in that case stated: . . . "We recognize that the crime victim as well as the community suffer from criminal acts; however, such impact is foreseeable and it exists in any case."

That language would upon first reading seem to eliminate community impact as a basis for an exceptional sentence in any case. However, . . . there is no indication from the *Cuevas-Diaz* opinion as to what evidence, if any, the sentencing court had before it demonstrating actual community impact or fear. In this case, there was evidence of fear in the children and their parents at the John Muir Elementary School because the shooting occurred in front of the school while classes were in session and close to release time for the day. Petitioner lived across the street from the school and foreseeably should have known that school was in session. [In addition to testimony from William Robbins (a parent), the sentencing court was presented with letters from the Mount Baker community near John Muir Elementary School expressing fear and anxiety caused by the shooting. The evidence] of distinctive community impact is simply more compelling here than in *Cuevas-Diaz.*

This court has not previously addressed the issue of community impact of a crime as a basis for imposing an aggravated exceptional sentence. However, it has upheld as constitutional statutes imposing mandatory enhanced sentences for drug offenses committed in specified proximity to schools and school bus stops. The [enhanced sentence] in this case is consistent with our approval of statutory sanctions designed to protect school children from drug trafficking. . . .

The court in *Cuevas-Diaz* affirmed an exceptional sentence for different, but similar, reasons. It stated that "the trial judge's findings relating to the impact of the defendant's activities on others, *i.e.,* the children of the assault victim" provided justification for the exceptional sentence. . . . The Court of Appeals in *Cuevas-Diaz* stated:

> To provide support for an exceptional sentence, the defendant's actions must have had an impact on . . . "other persons" of a destructive nature that is not normally associated with the commission of the offense in question and this impact must be foreseeable to the defendant.

The court in *Cuevas-Diaz* noted the trial court found the victim's children were traumatized by being in the house when their mother was sexually assaulted by the defendant. . . . The court also stated that "such a result is foreseeable to persons who unlawfully enter the private residence of another and commit an assault. Furthermore, the resulting trauma to the children distinguishes this offense from other assaults." The court concluded that "the impact of the offense on the children of the assault victim, alone, supports the exceptional sentence."

In this case, the sentencing court found that the shooting by Petitioner Johnson occurred "immediately next to a public elementary school that was in session". . . . Any person who discharges a deadly weapon at persons fleeing in automobiles in the immediate vicinity of a public elementary school while classes are in session should reasonably foresee that other persons, that is, children and their parents, who are not necessarily the intended victims, would be traumatized by those actions. As in *Cuevas-Diaz,* the resulting trauma to the children and their parents in this case distinguishes the offense from other assaults.

We agree with the reasoning and conclusions of the Court of Appeals in *Cuevas-Diaz,* and conclude in this case that the impact of the shooting by Petitioner Johnson upon the children and their parents at the John Muir Elementary School supports a conclusion that the community impact of petitioner's actions justifies the aggravated exceptional sentence imposed upon him. . . .

MICHIGAN CONSTITUTION ARTICLE I, §24

(1) Crime victims, as defined by law, shall have the following rights, as provided by law:

— The right to be treated with fairness and respect for their dignity and privacy throughout the criminal justice process. . . .

— The right to be reasonably protected from the accused throughout the criminal justice process.

— The right to notification of court proceedings.

— The right to attend trial and all other court proceedings the accused has the right to attend.

— The right to confer with the prosecution.

— The right to make a statement to the court at sentencing.

— The right to restitution.
— The right to information about the conviction, sentence, imprisonment, and release of the accused.
(2) The legislature may provide by law for the enforcement of this section.

Problem 19-6. Vulnerable Victim

Billy Creech obtained from a local newspaper a list of recently married men. From that list, he selected a victim to whom he sent a letter threatening to "torture your family members while you watch, or kill one in front of you," unless the victim periodically sent Creech a money order for $100. The letter ended by saying that "Failure to do this will end in bodily harm to your wife!" Creech was convicted for mailing a letter containing a threat to injure the addressee, a federal crime. Can the court consider this newlywed to be a "vulnerable victim"? Compare United States v. Creech, 913 F.2d 780 (10th Cir. 1990).

Notes

1. *Community views at sentencing: majority position.* Judges do not hand down sentences in a vacuum. Judges may respond implicitly to changing societal conceptions of the seriousness of the offense, or to changes in the prevalence of an offense, or to the particular "message" that a sentence may send to the community. But can judges do so openly? Information about community impact is available much less often than information about the impact on specific victims. One problem with considering community impact is identifying the relevant community. Who should express the community's view? Some courts have allowed victims to offer information about broader community impact. For example, the Pennsylvania Supreme Court in Commonwealth v. Penrod, 578 A.2d 486 (Pa. 1990), allowed victims, family members, and friends to testify at sentencing for drunken-driving defendants "regarding the impact of the offense on the victim, the impact on the community generally, and/or the impact on the family members or friends as members of the community." Should representatives of victims' rights organizations be allowed to speak at every sentencing? Should equal time be given to representatives of those who believe sentences are too severe or that imprisonment harms communities by removing vital members?

2. *Victims' rights at sentencing: majority position.* Over the past 30 years, nearly every state has decided to allow victim involvement at sentencing. It is difficult to capture the depth, range, and impact of this dramatic change in sentencing practice. Almost all states allow victim input through the PSI report. Many allow victims a separate opportunity to make a written or oral statement regarding sentencing, often detailing the kinds of information victims may offer. A few states have retained sharper limits: Several allow judges to choose whether to admit or refuse victim impact information; Texas allows a victim to make a statement only after sentencing, Tex. Code Crim. Proc. art. 42.03.

The rich variety of victim rights statutes has not produced a substantial case law regarding victim impact statements in the noncapital context. When defendants challenge the impact of such statements, they often claim that the judge was biased, or unduly influenced, by the information. See Nichols v. Commonwealth, 839 S.W. 2d 263 (Ky. 1992); People v. Vecchio, 819 P.2d 533 (Colo. Ct. App. 1991) (rejected a claim that the trial judge should have recused himself after the prosecutor filed more than 100 victim impact statements).

3. *Victim impact statements in capital cases.* Courts and legislatures have wrestled with the special problems of integrating victim impact statements with the complex law of capital sentencing. The U.S. Supreme Court limited introduction of victim evidence in capital cases in Booth v. Maryland, 482 U.S. 496 (1987) (victim impact statement in capital cases leads to arbitrary and capricious decisions because sentencing jury's focus would shift away from the defendant and onto the victim and the victim's family), and South Carolina v. Gathers, 490 U.S. 805 (1989) (rejecting prosecutorial argument about victim impact). The Court reversed itself in Payne v. Tennessee, 501 U.S. 808 (1991), holding that the jury could hear victim impact information. In *Payne* the Court upheld admission of testimony from a murder victim's mother, describing the impact of the killing on the victim's three-year-old son. The Court held that the victim impact statements "illustrated quite poignantly some of the harm that Payne's killing had caused." State courts and state legislatures have overwhelmingly followed the invitation in *Payne* to allow victim impact evidence in capital cases. See State v. Muhammad, 678 A.2d 164 (N.J. 1996). A few states still ban victim evidence in capital cases or limit the topics that victims can address. See Bivins v. State, 642 N.E.2d 928 (Ind. 1994); Mack v. State, 650 So. 2d 1289 (Miss.1994).

4. *Implementing victims' rights at sentencing.* As a Michigan legislator, how would you draft legislation to enforce section 24 of the Michigan constitution? Would you provide for victim statements prior to the sentencing hearing, along with any statement at the hearing? If the victim is unwilling to testify, would your statute nevertheless allow the defense or prosecution to subpoena the victim and obtain his evidence under oath? Compare ABA Standards for Criminal Justice: Sentencing §§18-5.9 to 18-5.12.

5. *Vulnerable victims.* Structured sentencing rules often instruct a judge to enhance a sentence if the victim of the crimes was "vulnerable" or otherwise worthy of exceptional protection. The Minnesota Sentencing Guidelines authorize the judge to decrease a sentence if "the victim was an aggressor in the incident," and to increase the sentence if the "victim was particularly vulnerable due to age, infirmity, or reduced physical or mental capacity, which was known or should have been known to the offender" or if the "victim was treated with particular cruelty for which the individual offender should be held responsible." Minn. Sentencing Guidelines II.D.2.a.1, II.D.2.b.1-2. The federal guidelines contain a similar provision for enhancement of the sentence by a designated amount if "the defendant knew or should have known that a victim of the offense was unusually vulnerable due to age, physical or mental condition, or that a victim was otherwise particularly susceptible to criminal conduct." U.S. Sentencing Guidelines §3A1.1. A specified increase is also required when the victim is "a government officer or employee" or a law enforcement officer.

6. *Judicial experience and community priorities.* Is it appropriate for judges in the same jurisdiction to weigh community impact differently? Federal Judge Reena

Raggi argues that federal guidelines should allow local variation among federal districts because particular crimes may create special harms in some localities and because the judges in that area develop special expertise on certain topics:

> I first began to question [the nationally uniform approach of the sentencing guidelines] when I had to impose sentences on a number of defendants who had unlawfully transported firearms into New York from other states. Almost daily my fellow New Yorkers and I would read in the press of the senseless shooting of young children, on the streets, even in their own homes, all victims of random gun fire. . . . Almost invariably the guns used in these crimes, as well as most others unlawfully possessed in this area, had come from out of state. . . . And yet, when it came time for me to impose sentences in my cases . . . I was confronted by a guideline range that rarely exceeded six months' incarceration. . . .
>
> The insight judges have about crimes in their particular districts goes beyond simply recognizing which conduct is more destructive to a community. It also reaches the question of how different levels of conduct contribute to an area's crime problems. For example, despite the fact that no part of the United States is immune from the problem of drugs, few judges have as broad an experience dealing with drug importation and large-scale distribution as my colleagues in the Eastern District of New York. . . . The piers and airports of the district make it, for all intents and purposes, the port of New York and, thus, the entry point for a large percentage of the contraband entering this country. . . . District judges should enjoy more discretion — indeed they should be encouraged — to depart from the guidelines to reflect specific local concerns.

Raggi, Local Concerns, Local Insights, 5 Fed. Sentencing Rep. 306 (1993). Is the idea of community self-defining — a question that also comes up with the idea of "local circumstances"? Consider the following language from a trial judge in a West Virginia case, State v. Broughton, 470 S.E.2d 413 (W.Va. 1996), imposing an unusually severe sentence for delivery of cocaine and marijuana on a Jamaican national who was not a resident of the state:

> We have several convictions of offenses which have caused great difficulty here in this area. We have found ourselves inundated with drugs from outside sources which has created a subculture of crime where there was none before. We even have had a police officer shot and wounded. Sort of things that one would expect in the metropolitan area has come to sleepy little Charles Town. And I don't know if there is any way that we are ever going to be able to stop it, but I do know if the Courts don't lean on these issues when they come up, that we don't have any hope of ever stopping them.

7. *Prosecutorial experience and community priorities.* If judges can adjust sentences to take account of local priorities, should prosecutors also be able to make charging decisions on the basis of local needs? Should prosecutorial needs and resources then be allowed to affect sentences? For instance, the U.S. Attorney's Office in San Diego receives far more immigration cases than it can prosecute. The office prosecutes roughly one percent of the undocumented persons apprehended in the district. Because the San Diego district attorney, as a matter of policy, will not prosecute any cases related to the border, these cases must be prosecuted in federal court or not at all. William Braniff, Local Discretion, Prosecutorial Choices and the Sentencing Guidelines, 5 Fed. Sentencing Rep. 309 (1993). Should the judge enhance a sentence when she knows that an unusually large number of offenders are going

unpunished? Should the judge reduce the sentence out of concern for selective and discriminatory treatment or ignore prosecutorial priorities entirely?

E. RACE AND SENTENCING

Race is an unavoidable part of modern American criminal procedure. Difficult questions arise at all stages of the criminal process: What is the role of race in stops and investigations? Can race be an element in the determination of reasonable suspicion or probable cause? When are racial disparities sufficient to justify challenges to charging practices? What role should race play in jury selection? In arguments at trial?

Previous chapters have explored these and other questions about the role that race plays in decisions throughout the criminal process. But perhaps the most common and visible questions about race arise at the end of the process, in the form of claims that black Americans and other minorities are punished more severely than whites. This section considers the charge that racism is an inherent part of the criminal justice process and that its end product is unequal punishment. In some situations, the responsible decisionmakers may be identifiable; in other situations, the source of racial disparities may be hard to specify even when disparity clearly exists.

Discussion of race and punishment must start with some disquieting facts about prison and jail populations. In June 2009, 39.4 percent of the inmates in state and federal prisons and local jails were African American, although African Americans constitute only about 13 percent of the population. The rate of imprisonment for black males aged 25-29 is about 10.5 percent, while the rate for Hispanic males of the same age group is 4.0 percent, and the comparable rate for white males is 1.6 percent. Bureau of Justice Statistics, Prison and Jail Inmates at Midyear 2009, at tables 16-19 (2010, NCJ 230113). After combining the number of young men on probation or parole with the number in prison or jail, almost a third of young black men are under criminal justice supervision on any given day. African American women remain the fastest growing group in prisons and jails. Drug policies have contributed more than any other crimes to the fast growth in the imprisonment rate for African Americans.

These materials provoke a recurring question: Does the criminal justice system exacerbate or mediate larger social problems? Can criminal justice systems respond to intentional or unintentional racial bias in society? If so, what is the proper role for courts, police, prosecutors, and legislators in crafting such a response?

1. *Race and the Victims of Crime*

The influence of race on punishment has received the most sustained attention in the context of capital punishment. Many facets of the story of race in American capital punishment emerge in the story of Warren McCleskey and his extraordinary trip through the criminal justice system.

On the morning of May 13, 1978, McCleskey drove to pick up Ben Wright, Bernard Dupree, and David Burney. The four men planned to commit a robbery; they drove from Marietta, Georgia, into Atlanta and decided on the Dixie Furniture

Store as a target. McCleskey had a .38 caliber Rossi nickel-plated revolver, which he had stolen in an armed robbery of a grocery store a month earlier. Ben Wright carried a sawed-off shotgun, and the two others had blue steel pistols. McCleskey, who was black, entered the front of the store, and the other three came through the rear by the loading dock. He secured the front of the store by forcing all the customers and employees there to lie on the floor while the other robbers rounded up the employees in the rear and began to bind them with tape. A pistol was taken from George Malcom, an employee, at gunpoint. Before all the employees were tied up, Officer Frank Schlatt, answering a silent alarm, stopped his patrol car in front of the building. Officer Schlatt, who was white, entered the front door and proceeded about 15 feet down the center aisle, where he was shot twice, once in the face and once in the chest. The head wound was fatal. The robbers fled. Sometime later, McCleskey was arrested in Cobb County in connection with another armed robbery. He confessed to the Dixie Furniture Store robbery but denied the shooting. Ballistics showed that Schlatt had been shot by a .38 caliber Rossi revolver. The weapon was never recovered.

McCleskey was convicted in 1978. The jury found two aggravating circumstances that authorized the use of the death penalty: (1) the murder was committed while the offender was committing another capital felony (armed robbery), and (2) the murder was committed against a police officer engaged in the performance of his official duties. The jury sentenced McCleskey to death for murder. Co-defendant Burney was sentenced to life imprisonment, while another co-defendant received a 20-year sentence.

On direct appeal in the Georgia courts, McCleskey first raised the claim that the death penalty violates the due process and equal protection provisions of the federal and state constitutions because prosecutorial discretion permits the government to apply the penalty in a racially discriminatory way. The Georgia Supreme Court rejected this claim as follows: "Appellant's argument is without merit. Gregg v. Georgia, 428 U.S. 153 (1976); Moore v. State, 243 S.E.2d 1 (Ga. 1978)." McCleskey v. State, 263 S.E.2d 146 (Ga. 1980).

Eventually, McCleskey took his claims to federal court: The U.S. district court had the power, under the venerable Habeas Corpus Act of 1867, 28 U.S.C. §2254, to invalidate state convictions obtained in violation of the federal constitution. In federal district court, McCleskey presented the findings of a massive statistical study, dubbed the "Baldus" study (named after its principal author, Professor David Baldus of the University of Iowa). The study analyzed almost 2,500 murder and voluntary manslaughter convictions for crimes committed (or for defendants arrested) between 1973 and 1978 in Georgia. For a random sample of these cases, researchers answered more than 500 questions about each case, such as the defendant's mental and physical condition, the defendant's race and other demographic information, the defendant's prior criminal record, the method of killing, the victim's role in the offense, and so forth. Due to the large number of variables, the researchers could not match many cases that differed in only one respect (for instance, cases that were identical in every respect, except one defendant shot the victim twice while the other defendant shot the victim only once). Thus, they used a statistical technique known as "multivariate regression analysis" to estimate the amount of influence each feature of the case had on the ultimate decision of whether the defendant received the death penalty.

The study concluded that the race of the defendant was not a "statistically significant" factor in the outcome, after "controlling" for all the other factors that could influence the outcome. However, the race of the *victim* remained one of the most important influences on the outcome, even after controlling for other factors.

The district court decided that the study did not establish the intentional discrimination necessary to show a violation of equal protection because the study was flawed. For instance, the court pointed to several errors in the collection of data and noted that "the questionnaire could not capture every nuance of every case." The court also suggested that the study had not successfully isolated the effects of race but instead measured the effects of other permissible factors that were "correlated" with race. McCleskey v. Zant, 580 F. Supp. 338 (N.D. Ga. 1984).

The federal court of appeals took a different approach to the question. It was willing to assume that the study successfully demonstrated "what it purports to prove": Defendants who kill a white victim have a greater chance of receiving the death penalty, and part of that increased risk is based on the race of the victim. Nevertheless, the court of appeals said that this statistical evidence was not enough for McCleskey to prove intentional racial discrimination in his case. When a party relies on statistical patterns of discrimination, the court said, it must show such large racial disparities that the evidence "compels a conclusion that . . . purposeful discrimination . . . can be presumed to permeate the system." The estimated effects of the race of the victim on the death penalty decision were not enough to compel such a conclusion. Indeed, the court said, any statistical study would have difficulty making such a showing about a complex process involving many different decisionmakers. McCleskey v. Kemp, 753 F.2d 877 (11th Cir. 1985). McCleskey then appealed to the U.S. Supreme Court.

WARREN McCLESKEY v. RALPH KEMP

481 U.S. 279 (1987)

POWELL, J.*

This case presents the question whether a complex statistical study that indicates a risk that racial considerations enter into capital sentencing determinations proves that petitioner McCleskey's capital sentence is unconstitutional under the Eighth or Fourteenth Amendment.

I.

[In support of his habeas claim], McCleskey proffered a statistical study performed by Professors David Baldus, Charles Pulaski, and George Woodworth (the Baldus study) that purports to show a disparity in the imposition of the death sentence in Georgia based on the race of the murder victim and, to a lesser extent, the race of the defendant. The Baldus study is actually two sophisticated statistical studies that examine over 2,000 murder cases that occurred in Georgia during the 1970's. The raw numbers collected by Professor Baldus indicate that defendants charged with killing white persons received the death penalty in 11% of the cases,

* [Chief Justice Rehnquist and Justices White, O'Connor, and Scalia joined this opinion. — EDS.]

but defendants charged with killing blacks received the death penalty in only 1% of the cases. . . . Baldus also divided the cases according to the combination of the race of the defendant and the race of the victim. He found that the death penalty was assessed in 22% of the cases involving black defendants and white victims; 8% of the cases involving white defendants and white victims; 1% of the cases involving black defendants and black victims; and 3% of the cases involving white defendants and black victims. . . .

Baldus subjected his data to an extensive analysis, taking account of 230 variables that could have explained the disparities on nonracial grounds. One of his models concludes that, even after taking account of 39 nonracial variables, defendants charged with killing white victims were 4.3 times as likely to receive a death sentence as defendants charged with killing blacks. . . . Thus, the Baldus study indicates that black defendants, such as McCleskey, who kill white victims have the greatest likelihood of receiving the death penalty. . . .

II.

McCleskey's first claim is that the Georgia capital punishment statute violates the Equal Protection Clause of the Fourteenth Amendment.[7] He argues that race has infected the administration of Georgia's statute. . . . McCleskey's claim of discrimination extends to every actor in the Georgia capital sentencing process, from the prosecutor who sought the death penalty and the jury that imposed the sentence, to the State itself that enacted the capital punishment statute and allows it to remain in effect despite its allegedly discriminatory application. [This] claim must fail.

A.

[To] prevail under the Equal Protection Clause, McCleskey must prove that the decisionmakers in his case acted with discriminatory purpose. He offers no evidence specific to his own case that would support an inference that racial considerations played a part in his sentence. Instead, he . . . argues that the Baldus study compels an inference that his sentence rests on purposeful discrimination. McCleskey's claim that these statistics are sufficient proof of discrimination, without regard to the facts of a particular case, would extend to all capital cases in Georgia, at least where the victim was white and the defendant is black.

The Court has accepted statistics as proof of intent to discriminate in certain limited contexts. First, this Court has accepted statistical disparities as proof of an equal protection violation in the selection of the jury venire in a particular district. Although statistical proof normally must present a "stark" pattern to be accepted as the sole proof of discriminatory intent under the Constitution, because of the nature of the jury-selection task, we have permitted a finding of constitutional violation even when the statistical pattern does not approach such extremes. Second, this

7. [We] assume the study is valid statistically without reviewing the factual findings of the District Court. Our assumption that the Baldus study is statistically valid does not include the assumption that the study shows that racial considerations actually enter into any sentencing decisions in Georgia. Even a sophisticated multiple-regression analysis such as the Baldus study can only demonstrate a risk that the factor of race entered into some capital sentencing decisions and a necessarily lesser risk that race entered into any particular sentencing decision.

Court has accepted statistics in the form of multiple-regression analysis to prove statutory violations under Title VII of the Civil Rights Act of 1964.

But the nature of the capital sentencing decision, and the relationship of the statistics to that decision, are fundamentally different from the corresponding elements in the venire-selection or Title VII cases. Most importantly, each particular decision to impose the death penalty is made by a petit jury selected from a properly constituted venire. Each jury is unique in its composition, and the Constitution requires that its decision rest on consideration of innumerable factors that vary according to the characteristics of the individual defendant and the facts of the particular capital offense. Thus, the application of an inference drawn from the general statistics to a specific decision in a trial and sentencing simply is not comparable to the application of an inference drawn from general statistics to a specific venire-selection or Title VII case. In those cases, the statistics relate to fewer entities, and fewer variables are relevant to the challenged decisions.

Another important difference between the cases in which we have accepted statistics as proof of discriminatory intent and this case is that, in the venire-selection and Title VII contexts, the decisionmaker has an opportunity to explain the statistical disparity. Here, the State has no practical opportunity to rebut the Baldus study. Controlling considerations of public policy dictate that jurors cannot be called to testify to the motives and influences that led to their verdict. Similarly, the policy considerations behind a prosecutor's traditionally wide discretion suggest the impropriety of our requiring prosecutors to defend their decisions to seek death penalties, often years after they were made.[17] Moreover, absent far stronger proof, it is unnecessary to seek such a rebuttal, because a legitimate and unchallenged explanation for the decision is apparent from the record: McCleskey committed an act for which the United States Constitution and Georgia laws permit imposition of the death penalty.

Finally, McCleskey's statistical proffer must be viewed in the context of his challenge. McCleskey challenges decisions at the heart of the State's criminal justice system. One of society's most basic tasks is that of protecting the lives of its citizens and one of the most basic ways in which it achieves the task is through criminal laws against murder. Implementation of these laws necessarily requires discretionary judgments. Because discretion is essential to the criminal justice process, we would demand exceptionally clear proof before we would infer that the discretion has been abused. . . . Accordingly, we hold that the Baldus study is clearly insufficient to support an inference that any of the decisionmakers in McCleskey's case acted with discriminatory purpose. . . .

IV. . . .

B.

[McCleskey also] contends that the Georgia capital punishment system is arbitrary and capricious in application, and therefore his sentence is excessive [and contrary to the Eighth Amendment], because racial considerations may influence

17. Requiring a prosecutor to rebut a study that analyzes the past conduct of scores of prosecutors is quite different from requiring a prosecutor to rebut a contemporaneous challenge to his own acts. See Batson v. Kentucky, 476 U.S. 79 (1986).

capital sentencing decisions in Georgia. . . . To evaluate McCleskey's challenge, we must examine exactly what the Baldus study may show. Even Professor Baldus does not contend that his statistics prove that race enters into any capital sentencing decisions or that race was a factor in McCleskey's particular case. Statistics at most may show only a likelihood that a particular factor entered into some decisions. There is, of course, some risk of racial prejudice influencing a jury's decision in a criminal case. There are similar risks that other kinds of prejudice will influence other criminal trials. The question is at what point that risk becomes constitutionally unacceptable. McCleskey asks us to accept the likelihood allegedly shown by the Baldus study as the constitutional measure of an unacceptable risk of racial prejudice influencing capital sentencing decisions. This we decline to do.

Because of the risk that the factor of race may enter the criminal justice process, we have engaged in "unceasing efforts" to eradicate racial prejudice from our criminal justice system.[30] [However,] McCleskey's argument that the Constitution condemns the discretion allowed decisionmakers in the Georgia capital sentencing system is antithetical to the fundamental role of discretion in our criminal justice system. Discretion in the criminal justice system offers substantial benefits to the criminal defendant. Not only can a jury decline to impose the death sentence, it can decline to convict or choose to convict of a lesser offense. Whereas decisions against a defendant's interest may be reversed by the trial judge or on appeal, these discretionary exercises of leniency are final and unreviewable. Similarly, the capacity of prosecutorial discretion to provide individualized justice is firmly entrenched in American law. As we have noted, a prosecutor can decline to charge, offer a plea bargain, or decline to seek a death sentence in any particular case. Of course, the power to be lenient also is the power to discriminate, but a capital punishment system that did not allow for discretionary acts of leniency would be totally alien to our notions of criminal justice. . . .

C.

At most, the Baldus study indicates a discrepancy that appears to correlate with race. Apparent disparities in sentencing are an inevitable part of our criminal justice system. [There] can be no perfect procedure for deciding in which cases governmental authority should be used to impose death. Despite these imperfections, our consistent rule has been that constitutional guarantees are met when the mode for determining guilt or punishment itself has been surrounded with safeguards to make it as fair as possible. Where the discretion that is fundamental to our criminal process is involved, we decline to assume that what is unexplained is invidious. In light of the safeguards designed to minimize racial bias in the process, the fundamental value of jury trial in our criminal justice system, and the benefits that

30. This Court has repeatedly stated that prosecutorial discretion cannot be exercised on the basis of race. Nor can a prosecutor exercise peremptory challenges on the basis of race. More generally, this Court has condemned state efforts to exclude blacks from grand and petit juries. Other protections apply to the trial and jury deliberation process. Widespread bias in the community can make a change of venue constitutionally required. The Constitution prohibits racially biased prosecutorial arguments. If the circumstances of a particular case indicate a significant likelihood that racial bias may influence a jury, the Constitution requires questioning as to such bias. Finally, in a capital sentencing hearing, a defendant convicted of an interracial murder is entitled to such questioning without regard to the circumstances of the particular case.

discretion provides to criminal defendants, we hold that the Baldus study does not demonstrate a constitutionally significant risk of racial bias affecting the Georgia capital sentencing process.

V.

Two additional concerns inform our decision in this case. First, McCleskey's claim, taken to its logical conclusion, throws into serious question the principles that underlie our entire criminal justice system. The Eighth Amendment is not limited in application to capital punishment, but applies to all penalties. Thus, if we accepted McCleskey's claim that racial bias has impermissibly tainted the capital sentencing decision, we could soon be faced with similar claims as to other types of penalty. Moreover, the claim that his sentence rests on the irrelevant factor of race easily could be extended to apply to claims based on unexplained discrepancies that correlate to membership in other minority groups, and even to gender. Similarly, since McCleskey's claim relates to the race of his victim, other claims could apply with equally logical force to statistical disparities that correlate with the race or sex of other actors in the criminal justice system, such as defense attorneys or judges. Also, there is no logical reason that such a claim need be limited to racial or sexual bias. If arbitrary and capricious punishment is the touchstone under the Eighth Amendment, such a claim could — at least in theory — be based upon any arbitrary variable, such as the defendant's facial characteristics, or the physical attractiveness of the defendant or the victim, that some statistical study indicates may be influential in jury decisionmaking. As these examples illustrate, there is no limiting principle to the type of challenge brought by McCleskey. . . .

Second, McCleskey's arguments are best presented to the legislative bodies. It is not the responsibility — or indeed even the right — of this Court to determine the appropriate punishment for particular crimes. It is the legislatures, the elected representatives of the people, that are constituted to respond to the will and consequently the moral values of the people. Legislatures also are better qualified to weigh and evaluate the results of statistical studies in terms of their own local conditions and with a flexibility of approach that is not available to the courts. Capital punishment is now the law in more than two-thirds of our States. It is the ultimate duty of courts to determine on a case-by-case basis whether these laws are applied consistently with the Constitution. Despite McCleskey's wide-ranging arguments that basically challenge the validity of capital punishment in our multiracial society, the only question before us is whether in his case the law of Georgia was properly applied. [This] was carefully and correctly done in this case. . . .

BRENNAN, J., dissenting.*

. . . II.

At some point in this case, Warren McCleskey doubtless asked his lawyer whether a jury was likely to sentence him to die. A candid reply to this question

* [Justices Marshall, Blackmun, and Stevens joined the portions of this opinion reprinted here. — EDS.]

would have been disturbing. First, counsel would have to tell McCleskey that few of the details of the crime or of McCleskey's past criminal conduct were more important than the fact that his victim was white. Furthermore, counsel would feel bound to tell McCleskey that defendants charged with killing white victims in Georgia are 4.3 times as likely to be sentenced to death as defendants charged with killing blacks. In addition, frankness would compel the disclosure that it was more likely than not that the race of McCleskey's victim would determine whether he received a death sentence: 6 of every 11 defendants convicted of killing a white person would not have received the death penalty if their victims had been black, while, among defendants with aggravating and mitigating factors comparable to McCleskey's, 20 of every 34 would not have been sentenced to die if their victims had been black. Finally, the assessment would not be complete without the information that cases involving black defendants and white victims are more likely to result in a death sentence than cases featuring any other racial combination of defendant and victim. The story could be told in a variety of ways, but McCleskey could not fail to grasp its essential narrative line: there was a significant chance that race would play a prominent role in determining if he lived or died. . . .

III. . . .

C.

Evaluation of McCleskey's evidence cannot rest solely on the numbers themselves. We must also ask whether the conclusion suggested by those numbers is consonant with our understanding of history and human experience. Georgia's legacy of a race-conscious criminal justice system, as well as this Court's own recognition of the persistent danger that racial attitudes may affect criminal proceedings, indicates that McCleskey's claim is not a fanciful product of mere statistical artifice.

For many years, Georgia operated openly and formally precisely the type of dual system the evidence shows is still effectively in place. The criminal law expressly differentiated between crimes committed by and against blacks and whites, distinctions whose lineage traced back to the time of slavery. During the colonial period, black slaves who killed whites in Georgia, regardless of whether in self-defense or in defense of another, were automatically executed. A. Higginbotham, In the Matter of Color: Race in the American Legal Process 256 (1978). By the time of the Civil War, a dual system of crime and punishment was well established in Georgia. See Ga. Penal Code (1861). The state criminal code contained separate sections for "Slaves and Free Persons of Color," and for all other persons. . . .

IV.

The Court . . . states that its unwillingness to regard petitioner's evidence as sufficient is based in part on the fear that recognition of McCleskey's claim would open the door to widespread challenges to all aspects of criminal sentencing. Taken on its face, such a statement seems to suggest a fear of too much justice. Yet surely the majority would acknowledge that if striking evidence indicated that other minority groups, or women, or even persons with blond hair, were disproportionately sentenced to death, such a state of affairs would be repugnant to deeply rooted conceptions of fairness. The prospect that there may be more widespread abuse than McCleskey documents may be dismaying, but it does not justify complete abdication of our judicial role. . . .

In fairness, the Court's fear that McCleskey's claim is an invitation to descend a slippery slope also rests on the realization that any humanly imposed system of penalties will exhibit some imperfection. Yet to reject McCleskey's powerful evidence on this basis is to ignore both the qualitatively different character of the death penalty and the particular repugnance of racial discrimination, considerations which may properly be taken into account in determining whether various punishments are "cruel and unusual." Furthermore, it fails to take account of the unprecedented refinement and strength of the Baldus study.

V.

In more recent times, we have sought to free ourselves from the burden of [our history of racial discrimination]. Yet it has been scarcely a generation since this Court's first decision striking down racial segregation, and barely two decades since the legislative prohibition of racial discrimination in major domains of national life. These have been honorable steps, but we cannot pretend that in three decades we have completely escaped the grip of a historical legacy spanning centuries. Warren McCleskey's evidence confronts us with the subtle and persistent influence of the past. His message is a disturbing one to a society that has formally repudiated racism, and a frustrating one to a Nation accustomed to regarding its destiny as the product of its own will. Nonetheless, we ignore him at our peril, for we remain imprisoned by the past as long as we deny its influence in the present. . . .

Notes

1. *Whose race, victim's or defendant's?* Note that the Baldus study found that the race of the *defendant* had no statistically significant effect on the use of capital punishment. In Furman v. Georgia, 408 U.S. 238 (1972), the Supreme Court struck down several capital punishment statutes, declaring that the death penalty (as administered at that time) was "cruel and unusual punishment" and a violation of the Eighth Amendment. Among the many reasons for this decision discussed in the various concurring opinions, several of the justices argued that capital punishment could not stand because it was imposed disproportionately against the poor and racial minorities. Would the Supreme Court have reached a different outcome in *McCleskey* if the Baldus study had pointed to racial discrimination based on the race of the defendant rather than the race of the victim? Can a punishment be racially discriminatory if the government imposes it equally on defendants of all races?

2. *Other venues.* Suppose that on the day after the district court issued its order, the NAACP sends a copy of the Baldus study to a member of the Georgia legislature, and that member distributes copies. As the chair of the senate's committee on criminal justice matters, would you hold hearings? If so, what would be the topic of the hearings — the validity of the study or the most appropriate response to the study? If the Supreme Court had concluded instead that the influence of race in Georgia's

capital punishment system rendered McCleskey's sentence unconstitutional, how would you advise Georgia legislators and prosecutors to respond? Would a victory for McCleskey mean abolition of the death penalty in Georgia?

3. *Adequate proof of discrimination* If racial discrimination does influence some decisionmakers, to some degree, in some cases, how might one demonstrate that fact in a court of law? Both the court of appeals and the Supreme Court concluded that a stronger statistical showing would be necessary before racial influences in sentencing would amount to a constitutional problem. What sort of evidence did the courts have in mind? See State v. Harris, 786 N.W.2d 409 (Wis. 2010) (during sentencing of drug defendant, judge remarked on large number of unemployed and uneducated male defendants who lived with women who were working full time and going to school, and referred to defendant's "baby mama"; in determination of whether judge improperly considered race in sentencing, defendant must prove by clear and convincing evidence that the judge actually relied on race, and not simply whether a reasonable observer might perceive that the judge considered race).

The "race of the victim" effect that appeared in the Baldus study in Georgia has also appeared in statistical studies of other states. These claims have gotten very little serious attention from courts; many simply cite *McCleskey* with no further discussion in refusing to consider the studies as relevant evidence of racial discrimination in the use of capital punishment. See People v. Davis, 518 N.E.2d 78 (Ill.1987). For a review of the most recent statistical studies of the racially disparate impact of capital punishment, go to the web extension for this chapter at *http://www.crimpro.com/extension/ch19*.

2. *Race and Discretionary Decisions Affecting Punishment*

Racial disparities at sentencing can result from decisions made by actors at early stages of the criminal justice process. A strong bias in investigations or arrests may be passed through and perhaps even validated by studies showing unbiased decision making at a later stage of the process. For example, if whites and blacks who are convicted of a particular offense are punished identically, but members of one race are disproportionately investigated, then the sanction will appear neutral but will in fact be highly disparate, because the investigatory practices do not accurately reflect actual underlying behavior. It is not only police decisions that can generate sharp disparities that are passed through the system: Prosecutors may disproportionately direct cases involving members of one race to state court and identical allegations involving another race to federal court, where very different punishments attach to analogous state and federal charges. Or prosecutors may offer pleas in a racially disproportionate fashion.

This section highlights the difficulty of proving the source of discriminatory effects in large, complicated systems with many participants. Discrimination may be especially hard to unearth when it is the product of repeated, low-level behavior of a large group of individuals, and perhaps the result of unconscious influences on decision making. This section also raises questions about the capacity of the law to change group behavior. It is hard enough to alter the behavior of individuals; the challenge of developing effective rules is multiplied when disfavored outcomes reflect complex decisions by large groups of people.

FREDDIE STEPHENS v. STATE

456 S.E.2d 560 (Ga. 1995)

FLETCHER, J.

Freddie Stephens challenges the constitutionality of OCGA §16-13-30(d), which provides for life imprisonment on the second conviction of the sale or possession with intent to distribute a controlled substance. He contends that the provision as applied is irrational and racially discriminatory in violation of the United States and Georgia Constitutions. . . . The challenged statute states:

> [Any] person who violates subsection (b) of this Code section . . . shall be guilty of a felony and, upon conviction thereof, shall be punished by imprisonment for not less than five years nor more than 30 years. Upon conviction of a second or subsequent offense, he shall be imprisoned for life.

Subsection (b) makes it unlawful to "manufacture, deliver, distribute, dispense, administer, sell, or possess with intent to distribute any controlled substance." For a defendant to receive a life sentence for a second conviction, the state must notify the defendant prior to trial that it intends to seek the enhanced punishment based on past convictions.

Stephens contends that the statute as applied discriminates on the basis of race. He argues that this court should infer discriminatory intent from statewide and county-wide statistical data on sentences for drug offenders. In Hall County, where Stephens was convicted, the trial court found that one hundred percent (14 of 14) of the persons serving a life sentence under OCGA §16-13-30(d) are African-American, although African-Americans make up less than ten percent of the county population and approximately fifty to sixty percent of the persons arrested in drug investigations. Relying on evidence provided by the State Board of Pardons and Paroles, the trial court also found that 98.4 percent (369 of 375) of the persons serving life sentences for drug offenses as of May 1, 1994 were African-American, although African-Americans comprise only 27 percent of the state's population. Finally, a 1994 Georgia Department of Corrections study on the persons eligible for a life sentence under subsection (d) shows that less than one percent (1 of 168) of the whites sentenced for two or more convictions for drug sales are serving a life sentence, compared to 16.6 percent (202 of 1219) of the blacks.

In an earlier challenge to death penalty sentencing in Georgia based on statistics showing that persons who murder whites are more likely to be sentenced to death than persons who murder blacks, the United States Supreme Court held that the defendant had the burden of proving the existence of purposeful discrimination and that the purposeful discrimination had a discriminatory effect on him. McCleskey v. Kemp, 481 U.S. 279 (1987). . . .

Stephens concedes that he cannot prove any discriminatory intent by the Georgia General Assembly in enacting the law or by the Hall County district attorney in choosing to seek life imprisonment in this case. His attorney stated at the sentencing hearing: "I cannot prove and I do not feel there is any evidence to show that the district attorney's office is exercising their prosecutorial discretion in a discriminatory manner [and] I don't think I can demonstrate the legislature acted with discriminatory intent in enacting this code section." These concessions preclude this court from finding an equal protection violation under the United States Constitution.

We also conclude that the statistical evidence Stephens presents is insufficient evidence to support his claim of an equal protection violation under the Georgia Constitution. Stephens fails to present the critical evidence by race concerning the number of persons eligible for life sentences under OCGA §16-13-30(d) in Hall County, but against whom the district attorney has failed to seek the aggravated sentence. Because the district attorney in each judicial circuit exercises discretion in determining when to seek a sentence of life imprisonment, a defendant must present some evidence addressing whether the prosecutor handling a particular case engaged in selective prosecution to prove a state equal protection violation. . . .

Stephen's argument about inferring intent from the statistical evidence also ignores that other factors besides race may explain the sentencing disparity. Absent from the statistical analysis is a consideration of relevant factors such as the charges brought, concurrent offenses, prior offenses and sentences, representation by retained or appointed counsel, existence of a guilty plea, circuit where convicted, and the defendant's legal status on probation, in prison, or on parole. Without more adequate information about what is happening both statewide and in Hall County, we defer deciding whether statistical evidence alone can ever be sufficient to prove an allegation of discriminatory intent in sentencing under the Georgia Constitution.

The dissent argues that McCleskey v. Kemp is not the controlling precedent, instead relying on the United States Supreme Court decision on peremptory challenges in jury selections in Batson v. Kentucky, 476 U.S. 79 (1986). We must look to *McCleskey* for a proper analysis of the substantive issue before us, rather than *Batson,* because *McCleskey* dealt with the use of statistical evidence to challenge racial disparity in sentencing, as does this case.

The Supreme Court in *McCleskey* pointed out several problems in requiring a prosecutor to explain the reasons for the statistical disparity in capital sentencing decisions. Many of these same problems exist in requiring district attorneys to justify their decisions in seeking a life sentence for drug offenses based on statewide, and even county-wide, statistics of persons serving life sentences in state prisons for drug offenses.

First, "requiring a prosecutor to rebut a study that analyzes the past conduct of scores of prosecutors is quite different from requiring a prosecutor to rebut a contemporaneous challenge to his own acts. See Batson v. Kentucky, 476 U.S. 79 (1986)." *McCleskey,* 481 U.S. at 296. Second, statewide statistics are not reliable in determining the policy of a particular district attorney. [Even the statistics from Hall County do not accurately reflect the record of the district attorney in this case since she did not assume office until 1993.] Finally, the Court stated that the policy considerations behind a prosecutor's discretion argue against requiring district attorneys to defend their decisions to seek the death penalty. Since district attorneys are elected to represent the state in all criminal cases, it is important that they be able to exercise their discretion in determining who to prosecute, what charges to bring, which sentence to seek, and when to appeal without having to account for each decision in every case. [There] is a rational basis for the sentencing scheme in OCGA §16-13-30(d) and that it does not deprive persons of due process or equal protection under the law.

THOMPSON, J., concurring specially.

[We] are presented once again with the claim that OCGA §16-13-30(d) is being used in a discriminatory fashion. This time, we are introduced to statewide statistical information which must give us pause: From 1990 to 1994, OCGA §16-13-30(d) was used to put 202 out of 1,107 eligible African-Americans in prison for life. During that same period, the statute was used to put 1 out of 167 eligible whites in prison for life. A life eligible African-American had a 1 in 6 chance of receiving a life sentence. A life eligible white had a 1 in 167 chance of receiving a life sentence. An African-American was 2,700 percent more likely to receive a life sentence than a white. . . . These statistics are no doubt as much a surprise to those who work and practice within the judicial system as to those who do not.

Statistical information can inform, not explain. It can tell what has happened, not why. However, only a true cynic can look at these statistics and not be impressed that something is amiss. That something lies in the fact that OCGA §16-13-30(d) has been converted from a mandatory life sentence statute into a statute which imposes a life sentence only in those cases in which a district attorney, in the exercise of his or her discretion, informs a defendant that the State is seeking enhanced punishment.

McCleskey v. Kemp, 481 U.S. 279 (1987), provides a workable test for determining whether the death penalty statute is being applied discriminatorily. *McCleskey* should continue to be applied in death penalty cases where there is a system of checks and balances to ensure that death sentences are not sought and imposed autocratically. Likewise *McCleskey* should be applied in other cases where the courts have discretion to determine the length of time to be served. However, *McCleskey* probably should not be applied where a district attorney has the power to decide whether a defendant is sentenced to life, or a term of years. . . .

I am persuaded that Batson v. Kentucky, 476 U.S. 79 (1986), could be used to supply a general framework in analyzing cases of this kind. . . . Nevertheless, it is my considered view that the judgment in this case must be affirmed because the defendant has failed to meet his burden even under a *Batson*-type analysis.

In order to establish a prima facie case under *Batson,* a defendant must prove systematic discrimination in his particular jurisdiction. Although the statistics presented by defendant are indicative of a statewide pattern of discrimination in the use of OCGA §16-13-30(d), the Hall County statistics are insufficient to make such a case. They simply show that all the persons in Hall County serving a life sentence under OCGA §16-13-30(d) are African-Americans. They do not show how many African-Americans were eligible to receive a life sentence under the statute; nor do they show how many whites were eligible. Moreover, they offer no information concerning the record of the district attorney in this case. Thus, upon careful review, I must conclude that this defendant, in this case and on this record, failed to prove a pattern of systematic discrimination in his jurisdiction. . . .

Statewide, approximately 15 percent of eligible offenders receive a life sentence under OCGA §16-13-30(d). The statistical evidence presented in this case serves as notice to the General Assembly of Georgia that the mandatory life sentence provision of OCGA §16-13-30(d) has been repealed *de facto.* With such notice, there are at least three courses of action the legislature might now choose to pursue.

One. The General Assembly could choose to leave the mandatory life sentence on the books realizing that it is being used in a small percentage of the eligible cases.

Militating against this course of action is the fact that all laws passed by the legislature should be followed. Contempt for and failure to follow any law breeds contempt for and failure to follow other laws.

Two. The General Assembly could reaffirm its commitment to a mandatory life sentence by requiring district attorneys to inform all defendants of prior convictions and thus enforce OCGA §16-13-30(d) with respect to all life eligible offenders. Militating against this course of action is the fact that mandatory life sentences are not favored by the prosecuting bar or by the defense bar. That is evidenced by the fact that from 1990 to 1994 only 203 out of 1,274 life eligible defendants actually received a life sentence under OCGA §16-13-30(d). . . .

Three. The General Assembly could choose to change the mandatory life sentence penalty to one of several sentencing options which the court could impose. For example, the penalty for a second or subsequent sale could be imprisonment for not less than 5 nor more than 30 years, or life. . . . It is my concern that these problems be resolved in whatever way the General Assembly deems best and that, thereafter, the prosecutors and the courts carry out that legislative will.

BENHAM, P.J., dissenting.

Of those persons from Hall County serving life sentences pursuant to OCGA §16-13-30(d), which mandates a life sentence for the second conviction for sale of or possession with intent to distribute certain narcotics, 100 percent are African-American, although African-Americans comprise only approximately 10 percent of Hall County's population. In our state prison system, African-Americans represent 98.4 percent of the 375 persons serving life sentences for violating OCGA §16-13-30(d). These statistics were part of the finding of the trial court in this case. In the face of such numbing and paralyzing statistics, the majority say there is no need for inquiry. It is with this determination that I take issue.

[In Batson v. Kentucky, 476 U.S. 79 (1986), the Supreme Court] installed a system that shifted the burden to the prosecutor to give race-neutral reasons for the peremptory challenges once the defendant established facts supporting an inference that the prosecutor's use of peremptory challenges was racially motivated. [The] court in *Batson* stated that an inference of discriminatory intent could be drawn from certain conduct or statistical data. Beyond its effect on peremptory challenges, the importance of *Batson* was that it significantly reduced the burden on one claiming discrimination, recognizing that under certain circumstances, the crucial information about an allegedly discriminatory decision could only come from the one who made the decision.

This is the course of reasoning we need to follow in analyzing the issue in this case rather than the more restrictive course taken in McCleskey v. Kemp and applied by the majority. . . . I am not unmindful or unappreciative of the vital and taxing role district attorneys are called upon to undertake in the ongoing battle against the blight of illicit drug trafficking. Throughout this state, they shoulder an enormous burden of responsibility for advancing the fight against drugs, and to do so successfully, they must be invested with considerable discretion in making decisions about ongoing prosecutions. However, it is the very breadth of that discretion, concentrated in a single decision-maker, which makes it necessary that the one exercising the discretion be the one, when confronted with facts supporting an inference of discriminatory application, to bear the burden of establishing that the discretion was exercised without racial influence. This case is more like *Batson* than *McCleskey* because all the discretion in the sentencing scheme involved in this case resides in the district attorney, to the exclusion of the trial court, whereas in death penalty cases such as *McCleskey,* the spread of discretion among the prosecutor, the trial court, and the jurors introduces variables which call for more rigorous statistical analysis. In addition, the complexity of the death penalty procedure, with its many safeguards and the recurring necessity of specific findings at every stage from the grand jury to the sentencing jury, differentiates it from the relative simplicity of the sentencing scheme applicable to this case.

[The] U.S. Supreme Court recognized in *McCleskey* itself that statistical proof which presents a "stark pattern" may be accepted as the sole proof of discriminatory intent. In distinguishing *McCleskey* from such a case, the Supreme Court mentioned in a footnote two cases in which "a statistical pattern of discriminatory impact demonstrated a constitutional violation." One was Gomillion v. Lightfoot, 364 U.S. 339 (1960), where a city's boundaries were altered so as to exclude 395 of 400 black voters without excluding a single white voter, and the other was Yick Wo v. Hopkins, 118 U.S. 356 (1886), in which an ordinance requiring permits for the operation of laundries was applied so as to exclude all of the over 200 Chinese applicants and only one white applicant. The statistics in those cases presented a "stark pattern," but no more stark than the pattern presented in this case. In the present case, based on evidence from law enforcement officers who testified as to arrest rates and other relevant statistics,[2] the trial court found that 100% of the people from that county who were serving life sentences pursuant to OCGA §16-13-30(d) were African-Americans and that statewide, 98.4% of all the persons serving life sentences pursuant to OCGA §16-13-30(d) were African-Americans. . . .

In some instances we must lead the way. [This] is the time for this Court to draw from our historical strength and our determination that the citizens of this state be treated fairly before the law, and declare that Georgia's constitutional guarantee of equal protection requires that OCGA §16-13-30(d) be applied evenly, in a race-neutral fashion. . . . I would hold, therefore, as a matter purely of state constitutional law, that equal protection of the law in the context of OCGA §16-13-30(d) requires that the prosecution be required, when a defendant has made a prima facie showing sufficient to raise an inference of unequal application of the statute, to "demonstrate that permissible racially neutral selection criteria and procedures have produced the monochromatic result." *Batson.* . . .

Because appellant has made a sufficient showing of discriminatory application of OCGA §16-13-30(d) that the State should be required to give race-neutral reasons for the "monochromatic" application of that statute in Hall County, this court should vacate the life sentences and remand this case to the trial court for a hearing. At such a hearing, should the trial court find that the prosecution could not provide race-neutral reasons for the "monochromatic result" of the application of OCGA §16-13-30(d) in Hall County, sentencing for the offenses involved would still be permissible, but not with the aggravation of punishment authorized by OCGA §16-13-30(d). On the other hand, should the trial court find that the State has

2. Agent David McIlwraith testified that 50% of the drug investigations involved black males. Investigator Shelly Manny testified that of the 60 drug investigations she conducted in Hall County, only 9 involved blacks and that only 50% of her undercover buys involved black males. Another narcotics investigator testified that since 1989, he had made over 300 cocaine distribution cases in Hall County and only 60% involved black males.

provided appropriate race-neutral reasons, the life sentences would be reimposed, whereupon appellant would be entitled to a new appeal. . . .

The statistics offered in this case show an enormous potential for injustice, and those statistics are just like the tip of an iceberg, with the bulk lying below the surface, yet to be realized. And unless we reveal or expose this massive obstacle that lies in the shipping lanes of justice, it will . . . tear a gaping hole in the ship of state, just as a gaping hole was ripped in the Titanic. . . .

Notes

1. *Who discriminates against whom?* What discrimination does Freddie Stephens claim? Who did Warren McCleskey claim had discriminated against him? Other than the fact that both McCleskey and Stephens asserted that race was the basis for discrimination, were these similar claims?

The racial impact of charges under the Georgia statute described above is not the only example of punishment differences that flow from stark racial differences in charging decisions. In a study of charging for crack cocaine offenses in Los Angeles, Richard Berk and Alex Campbell found that black defendants are more likely than white or Latino defendants to be charged in federal court with sale of crack cocaine (which translates into more severe punishments than for comparable charges in state court). While black defendants represented 58 percent of those arrested by the Sheriff's Department for sale of crack cocaine in Los Angeles between 1990 and 1992, they made up 83 percent of the defendants charged with that crime in federal court. White and Latino defendants arrested for this crime were more likely to be prosecuted in state court. Berk & Campbell, Preliminary Data on Race and Crack Charging Practices in Los Angeles, 6 Fed. Sentencing Rep. 36 (1993). What might be the sources of the racially disparate federal crack prosecutions reported in the Berk and Campbell study?

2. *Competing analogies.* Did the majority in Stephens v. State think that Stephens's claim was the same as McCleskey's? Were you convinced by the competing analogy to discriminatory jury selection in Batson v. Kentucky? Justice Robert Benham, dissenting in *Stephens,* argued that sentencing under the Georgia drug statute was different from capital punishment because it concentrates the decision in the hands of the district attorney. Do you agree? Are there ways a police officer might influence who receives a life sentence under the statute? Do the voters in the county or in the state have some control over this question?

Problem 19-7. The Crack-Powder Differential

In 1986 the United States Congress passed the Anti-Drug Abuse Act to increase the penalties for various drug crimes. The new law imposed heavier penalties on cocaine base (or "crack") than on cocaine powder, a relationship now called the "100 to 1 ratio." An offense involving mixtures weighing 5 grams or more containing cocaine base was subject to the same punishment as an offense involving mixtures weighing 500 grams or more containing cocaine powder. Congress considered crack cocaine to be more dangerous than cocaine powder because of crack's potency, its more highly addictive nature, and its greater accessibility because of its relatively low cost.

Some of the impetus for the federal law came from the news media. Stories associated the use of crack cocaine with social maladies such as gang violence and parental neglect among user groups. Critics of the federal law, however, argued that these social problems did not result from the drug itself, but instead from the disadvantaged social and economic environment in places where the drug often is used.

In practice, the increased penalties for crack meant that African American defendants received heavier penalties than whites for possession and sale of cocaine. Over 90 percent of all people arrested for sale or possession of crack were African American; roughly 80 percent of all people arrested for sale or possession of powder cocaine were white.

By 1989 the Minnesota legislature was debating the same issue. The legislators considered a bill that would make a person guilty of a third-degree offense if he or she possessed 3 or more grams of crack cocaine. Under the same statute, a person who possessed 10 or more grams of cocaine powder would be guilty of the same offense; someone who possesses less than 10 grams of cocaine powder would be guilty of a fifth-degree offense. The bill became known as the "10 to 3 ratio" law.

The sponsors of the bill argued that this structure facilitated prosecution of "street level" drug dealers. Law enforcement officers who testified at legislative hearings suggested that 3 grams of crack and 10 grams of powder indicated a level at which dealing, not merely using, took place. A person convicted of selling 100 grams of crack may often be characterized as a mid-level dealer (someone who provides the drug to street-level retailers). By comparison, 100 grams of powder usually typifies a low-level retailer; 500 grams is more indicative of a mid-level dealer. However, witnesses from the Department of Public Safety Office of Drug Policy contradicted these estimates for the typical amount of drugs carried by dealers, suggesting that most cocaine powder users are dealers as well.

The customary unit of sales for the two drugs were also different. The normal sales unit of crack was a "rock" weighing .1 gram and selling on the street for $20 or $25. On the other hand, the customary unit of sale for powder was the "8-ball," 1/8 ounce or about 3.5 grams, which sold for about $350. Ten grams of powder cocaine could be easily converted into more than 3 grams of crack.

Sponsors of the bill also argued that crack is more addictive and dangerous than cocaine powder. Witnesses at the hearings testified that crack cocaine had a more severe effect on the central nervous system and is more addictive than powder cocaine. Other witnesses pointed out, however, that crack and powder cocaine have the same active ingredient, and both produce the same type of pharmacological effects. The differences in effect between the two drugs were based on the fact that cocaine powder is sniffed through the nostrils, while crack cocaine is smoked. If powder cocaine is dissolved and injected, it is just as addictive as crack.

As a member of the Minnesota legislature, would you support the "10 to 3 ratio" bill? What else would you like to know before you vote? Compare State v. Russell, 477 N.W.2d 886 (Minn. 1991).

Notes

1. *Constitutional challenges to punishment differentials: majority position.* Racial disparities in the application of criminal laws highlight several distinct forms of discrimination. A law could be discriminatory in intent, either at the point of creation or when it is applied. A criminal sanction could also be discriminatory in effect because of uneven (though not intentionally skewed) application of the law. But these are not the only dynamics that create racial differences in criminal punishments. Some laws have racially discriminatory effects, even though the people who create and enforce the law do not intend to burden one racial group more than another and even though they apply the law with complete evenhandedness. These effects occur when the criminal sanctions apply to behavior that people of one race engage in more often than people of other races. Would it ever be unconstitutional for a legislature to criminalize conduct when one racial group is more likely to engage in it?

A number of defendants convicted of trafficking in crack cocaine have argued for a downward departure from the guideline sentence (or an invalidation of the relevant guidelines and statutes) based on an equal protection claim. Federal courts have uniformly rejected this assertion, reasoning that any racial impact of the crack cocaine statutes and guidelines was unintentional. See United States v. Reece, 994 F.2d 277 (6th Cir. 1993) (per curiam). While not often addressing such claims, high state courts have usually rejected the constitutional challenges.

2. *Legislative response.* The Minnesota Supreme Court struck down the legislation described in Problem 19-7 based on the state's equal protection clause in State v. Russell, 477 N.W.2d 886 (Minn. 1991). The legislature responded by increasing the penalties for powder to equal the former penalties for crack. Minn. Stat. §152.021-023. Minnesota's cocaine penalties are now among the toughest in the country — stiffer in some ways than in the federal system.

3. *Crack cocaine in the federal system.* For many years, the federal penalty structure punished cocaine powder and crack offenders equally for amounts that differ by a factor of 100 — the so-called 100-to-1 ratio. Note that this is not a ratio of penalties but of the amounts of drugs generating similar penalties. Proposals to reduce this ratio flared into combustible debates several times over the years. The Sentencing Commission amended the federal sentencing guidelines to reduce the differential between the punishments in 1995, but Congress overturned the amendments. In 2002, the Commission recommended that Congress itself should reduce the ratio, but the legislators took no action.

Then, in May 2007, the U.S. Sentencing Commission took action on its own, amending the crack cocaine guidelines to eliminate any reliance on a 100-to-1 ratio, even though mandatory minimum penalty statutes remained in place to trump the guideline sentences in some cases. After reviewing the statutory purposes of sentencing under 18 U.S.C. §3553(a), the scientific and medical literature, and its own extensive research into sentencing patterns in drug cases, the commission found that the existing crack penalties failed in several respects:

> (1) The current quantity-based penalties overstate the relative harmfulness of crack cocaine compared to powder cocaine.
>
> (2) The current quantity-based penalties sweep too broadly and apply most often to lower level offenders.

(3) The current quantity-based penalties overstate the seriousness of most crack cocaine offenses and fail to provide adequate proportionality.

(4) The current severity of crack cocaine penalties mostly impacts minorities.

Report to the Congress: Cocaine and Federal Sentencing Policy 8 (2007), available at *http://www.ussc.gov/r_congress/cocaine2007.pdf*.

The revised guidelines used different ratios at different offense levels, with higher powder-to-crack ratios operating at higher offense levels. The commission estimated that its modifications to the guidelines would affect 69.7 percent of crack cocaine offenses and would reduce the average sentence of all crack cocaine offenses from 121 months to 106 months.

Congress followed suit with passage of the Fair Sentencing Act of 2010, which adjusted upward the amount of crack needed to trigger mandatory minimum prison terms. Though President Obama's Department of Justice and many public policy groups urged Congress to equalize the sentencing provisions for powder and crack cocaine, Congress settled on a compromise proposal that produced a new 18-to-1 ratio for powder and crack sentences. The Fair Sentencing Act also completely eliminated the mandatory minimum prison term for simple possession of crack cocaine.

What explains the different political outcomes in 1995, 2002, 2007, and 2010? Did the commission manage the 2007 process more effectively, or did an overall change in the political atmosphere or practical experience with drug sentencing make the difference? As for the merits of the proposal, what might explain a ratio between powder and crack that varies, depending on the seriousness of the case?

4. *Race and crack.* Are you persuaded that racial differentials are the central issue in the crack cocaine punishment debate? Do different parts of the criminal world just happen to be controlled by groups of a particular race or ethnicity, as an analogy to the use of racketeering laws against the Mafia suggests? Or do you find convincing the argument that racially disproportionate effects (but not intent) justify reworking the system to start with a 1-to-1 quantity ratio?

Michael Tonry surveyed the various causes of the increasing racial divide in criminal punishments in the United States during the 1980s and 1990s. After tracking the steady increase in the proportion of blacks in the nation's prison population during those years, Tonry notes that the increase did not occur because of increased black participation in serious violent crimes: "The proportions of serious violent crimes committed by blacks have been level for more than a decade. Since the mid-1970s, approximately 45 percent of those arrested for murder, rape, robbery, and aggravated assault have been black (the trend is slightly downward)." Instead, most of the changing racial impact of criminal sentences during this time can be traced to drug law enforcement. According to Tonry, politicians pursued the "War on Drugs" with full knowledge of its likely racial impact. Those policies caused

> the ever harsher treatment of blacks by the criminal justice system, and it was foreseeable that they would do so. Just as the tripling of the American prison population between 1980 and 1993 was the result of conscious policy decisions, so also was the greater burden of punishment borne by blacks. Crime control politicians wanted more people in prison and knew that a larger proportion of them would be black.

Michael Tonry, Malign Neglect: Race, Crime and Punishment in America 52 (1995). Is this the sort of "discriminatory intent" that could form the basis for an equal protection challenge? Does this argument create a politically viable basis for revising penalties for violation of the drug laws?

XX

Appeals

Errors happen in most criminal proceedings. Appellate courts cannot correct every mistake that occurs at the trial level, but they do try to identify and correct the errors that matter most. Depending on the pertinent double jeopardy rules, an appellate court might respond to a trial error by ordering a new trial or a new sentencing proceeding, by remanding the case for further factual findings by the judge (after a bench trial), or by dismissing the charges.

In this chapter, we explore limits on the power or willingness of appellate courts to correct errors in criminal proceedings. The chapter addresses deceptively simple questions: Who should be able to appeal, and when? How much deference should an appellate court show to findings of fact by the trier of fact? When, if ever, should an appellate court allow a judgment to stand even when it believes that an error occurred? What could be more important than getting the right answer in criminal proceedings?

A. WHO APPEALS?

With rare exceptions (notably in capital cases), appeals are not automatic. Cases can be heard on appeal only when at least one of the parties requests an appeal. This section explores the typical legal limits on the power of parties to file an appeal and the circumstances under which parties are willing to do so.

1. *Right to Appeal*

Most federal and state constitutions do not guarantee criminal defendants any "right to appeal." Instead, statutes and rules of appellate procedure determine who can file an appeal and what issues the parties can raise. What limits do legislatures tend to place on the parties' authority to appeal?

■ ARKANSAS STATUTES §16-91-101

(a) Any person convicted of a misdemeanor or a felony by virtue of a trial in any circuit court of this state has the right of appeal to the Supreme Court of Arkansas. . . .

■ ARKANSAS RULE OF CRIMINAL PROCEDURE 24.3(b)

With the approval of the court and the consent of the prosecuting attorney, a defendant may enter a conditional plea of guilty or nolo contendere, reserving in writing the right, on appeal from the judgment, to review of an adverse determination of a pretrial motion to suppress seized evidence or a custodial statement or a pretrial motion to dismiss a charge because not brought to trial within the time provided in [these rules]. If the defendant prevails on appeal, the defendant shall be allowed to withdraw the conditional plea.

■ CALIFORNIA PENAL CODE §1237.5

No appeal shall be taken by the defendant from a judgment of conviction upon a plea of guilty or nolo contendere, or a revocation of probation following an admission of violation, except where both of the following are met:

(a) The defendant has filed with the trial court a written statement, executed under oath or penalty of perjury showing reasonable constitutional, jurisdictional, or other grounds going to the legality of the proceedings.

(b) The trial court has executed and filed a certificate of probable cause for such appeal with the clerk of the court.

■ CALIFORNIA RULE OF COURT 8.304(b)(4)

The defendant need not comply with [the requirement of a written statement under Penal Code §1237.5 if] the appeal is based on [the] denial of a motion to suppress evidence under Penal Code section 1538.5; or [grounds] that arose after entry of the plea and do not affect the plea's validity.

Notes

1. *Nonconstitutional basis for right to appeal.* The Supreme Court held long ago in McKane v. Durston, 153 U.S. 684 (1894), that there is no federal constitutional basis for the right to appeal. That holding still accurately describes the law. State constitutions also do not typically provide for a right to appeal, although there are some exceptions. See Mich. Const. art. I, §20; Wash. Const. art. 1, §22. This is an area dominated by statutes and rules of procedure, which address in some detail the types of cases and claims where appeal is available. All states do provide for at least some appellate review of criminal convictions. If one could demonstrate that appellate review is far more common and important today than it was in 1894, might that convince a court to find a new constitutional basis for appeal?

2. *Appeal after guilty plea: majority position.* Some states allow appeals after guilty pleas only for those issues expressly reserved for appeal in a conditional plea agreement. Others give either the trial court or the appellate court the power to allow the appeal as a completely discretionary matter. Still others (such as California) give the court discretion to allow the appeal only when the defendant meets certain preconditions specified in statute or rule. What variables would be most important in convincing a court to allow an appeal after a plea of guilty? In light of the numbers of appeals and trials occurring each year, how often do you imagine that discretionary appeals after pleas are allowed?

3. *Number of appeals.* The number of defendants who file appeals each year tends to exceed the number of defendants who are convicted at trial. Consider the following statistics for the federal system:

Year	*Criminal Appeals*	*Total Convictions*	*Guilty or Nolo Pleas*	*Convictions After Trial*
1991	9,949	46,768	41,213	5,555
2000	9,162	68,156	64,939	3,217
2008	10,379	82,823	80,184	2,639

To the extent that these numbers are typical of other jurisdictions, they suggest that appeal rights may be important to more defendants than trial rights and that a crucial dimension of appeal rights is the availability of appeals after guilty pleas.

4. *Bail pending appeal.* Most felony defendants, in most places, are released at some point prior to their trials or guilty pleas. See Chapter 12. After conviction, however, statutes and court rules make it far less likely that a trial court will release an offender while the appeal is pending. See 18 U.S.C. §§3143(b)(2), 3145(c); Ex parte Anderer, 61 S.W.3d 398 (Tex. 2001) (condition placed on post-conviction bail — prohibition on operating automobile — was aimed at protecting public and "reasonable" under applicable statute). A convicted person who escapes is ineligible to appeal in most systems, although it may be possible to file an appeal upon recapture. See Ortega-Rodriguez v. United States, 507 U.S. 234 (1993) (nonconstitutional federal law creates no absolute bar to escapee's filing of appeal upon recapture); State v. Troupe, 891 S.W.2d 808 (Mo. 1995) ("escape" rule bars appeal, even for those recaptured).

5. *Motions for new trial.* A defendant may convince a trial judge to reconsider a judgment before taking an appeal to another court. A motion for a new trial is, in

effect, an "appeal" to the trial court. The motion is made routinely after convictions at trial, and trial judges deny the motion in the overwhelming majority of cases. If you were drafting rules of appellate procedure, would you require such a motion before allowing a party to file an appeal with the appellate court? Would you require it for some issues but not for others?

2. *Appeals by Indigent Defendants*

Although defendants have no federal constitutional right to an appeal, the federal equal protection clause does require states to make its chosen appeals process available to all defendants, even those without the financial resources to pay for an appeal. According to Griffin v. Illinois, 351 U.S. 12 (1956), the state must provide a defendant with a free transcript of a trial record, if such a transcript is necessary to file an appeal. In Douglas v. California, 372 U.S. 353 (1963), the Court extended *Griffin* to require the government to provide indigent appellants with an attorney for an initial "appeal as of right." Even when appellate counsel for an indigent defendant believes the defendant could raise only frivolous issues on appeal, she must advise the appellate court of any colorable issue.

■ BRYAN MOSLEY v. STATE

908 N.E.2d 599 (Ind. 2009)

BOEHM, J.

In Anders v. California, 386 U.S. 738 (1967), the Supreme Court of the United States established a procedure permitting appointed counsel to withdraw from "frivolous" criminal appeals. We decline to adopt the *Anders* protocol and hold that in any direct criminal appeal as a matter of right, counsel must submit an advocative brief in accordance with Indiana Appellate Rule 46.

FACTS AND PROCEDURAL HISTORY

Indianapolis Metropolitan Police officers William Flude and Joe Stern responded to a report of an unruly patron at Bubbaz Bar & Grill. After defendant Bryan Mosley refused repeated requests to leave, the officers advised him that he was under arrest. He was told to put his hands behind his back, and Officer Flude placed one handcuff on Mosley's right wrist. Mosley then began to flail his left hand, and Officer Flude thought he was trying to strike Officer Stern. After a "small tussle," Mosley was taken to the ground, where he continued to kick and flail. The officers ultimately restrained Mosley's legs, secured him in handcuffs, and took him into custody.

Mosley was charged with Count I, class A misdemeanor resisting law enforcement, and Count II, class A misdemeanor criminal trespass. Following a bench trial Mosley was acquitted of criminal trespass but convicted of resisting law enforcement. He was sentenced to 363 days probation. Mosley appealed, challenging the sufficiency of the evidence that he resisted arrest. [In particular, he argued that the government did not prove "use of force," a necessary element of resisting law enforcement.]

The Court of Appeals affirmed, finding sufficient evidence to support Mosley's conviction. The Court of Appeals then excerpted Mosley's brief and added:

> We understand that a criminal defendant has a right to an appeal of his conviction. But that does not mean that an appeal should be filed in every case. When it is clear that the trial court did not commit reversible error, it is a waste of the resources of this court and the attorney general's office and, most of all, public defender funds, for an appeal to nonetheless be filed. Trying to create issues where there are none leads to the sort of perfunctory, baseless brief we have before us today. When there are no meritorious arguments to be made, the better approach is to file a brief in accordance with our decision in Packer v. State, 777 N.E.2d 733 (Ind. App. 2002), which outlines the proper procedure for such a situation.

In *Packer,* the Court of Appeals suggested that counsel faced with preparing an appeal in which they had identified no issue of merit should file an "*Anders* brief" using the procedure explained below. We granted transfer to address the points raised by the Court of Appeals in the foregoing paragraph. We summarily affirm the decision of the Court of Appeals that the evidence was sufficient to support Mosley's conviction for resisting arrest. . . .

ANDERS V. CALIFORNIA

The Fourteenth Amendment to the United States Constitution provides that no state shall "deprive any person of life, liberty, or property, without due process of law; nor deny to any person within its jurisdiction the equal protection of the laws." The Sixth Amendment to the United States Constitution provides that in "all criminal prosecutions, the accused shall enjoy the right . . . to have the Assistance of Counsel for his defence." The Sixth Amendment right to counsel applies to the states via the Due Process Clause of the Fourteenth Amendment, and guarantees the assistance of counsel at critical stages of prosecution up through trial, sentencing, and various post-trial matters. However, the Sixth Amendment does not apply to appellate proceedings. Rather, the Equal Protection and Due Process Clauses of the Fourteenth Amendment are the source of the guarantee to indigent defendants of assistance of counsel on appeal. Douglas v. California, 372 U.S. 353 (1963); Halbert v. Michigan, 545 U.S. 605 (2005). That right attaches in any first appeal granted by state law as a matter of right, but not to discretionary review following initial appeals, Ross v. Moffitt, 417 U.S. 600 (1974), state post-conviction proceedings, Pennsylvania v. Finley, 481 U.S. 551 (1987), or habeas corpus actions, Murray v. Giarratano, 492 U.S. 1 (1989).

There is plainly tension between these rights of defendants and the obligation of attorneys not to "bring or defend a proceeding, or assert or controvert an issue therein, unless there is a basis in law and fact for doing so that is not frivolous, which includes a good faith argument for an extension, modification or reversal of existing law." Model Rules of Prof'l Conduct R. 3.1 (2007).

In Anders v. California, 386 U.S. 738 (1967), the Supreme Court of the United States sought to address this issue by proposing the following protocol for counsel to withdraw from nonmeritorious criminal appeals in a manner that is consistent with the requirements of the federal constitution:

> [If] counsel finds his case to be wholly frivolous, after a conscientious examination of it, he should so advise the court and request permission to withdraw. That request must, however, be accompanied by a brief referring to anything in the record that might arguably support the appeal. A copy of counsel's brief should be furnished the indigent and time allowed him to raise any points that he chooses; the court — not counsel — then proceeds, after a full examination of all the proceedings, to decide whether the case is wholly frivolous. If it so finds it may grant counsel's request to withdraw and dismiss the appeal insofar as federal requirements are concerned, or proceed to a decision on the merits, if state law so requires. On the other hand, if it finds any of the legal points arguable on their merits (and therefore not frivolous) it must, prior to decision, afford the indigent the assistance of counsel to argue the appeal.

The *Anders* procedure has been described as a "prophylactic framework" designed to ensure minimum constitutional protection. Pennsylvania v. Finley, 481 U.S. 551 (1987). It is clear, however, that *Anders* represents "merely one method of satisfying the requirements of the Constitution for indigent criminal appeals. States may . . . craft procedures that, in terms of policy, are superior to, or at least as good as, that in *Anders*." Smith v. Robbins, 528 U.S. 259 (2000).

ANDERS IN INDIANA

The first reference to *Anders* in Indiana jurisprudence appears in Justice DeBruler's concurring opinion in Cline v. State, 252 N.E.2d 793 (Ind. 1969). The defendants in *Cline* were convicted of robbing a drugstore and on appeal challenged the sufficiency of the evidence supporting their convictions. "Appellant Covington's sole contention [was] that there was a failure to prove he was the same Covington who participated in the robbery." In light of four positive identifications of Covington as one of the perpetrators, the majority concluded that

> This is one of those cases where the evidence in our opinion is overwhelming in support of the conviction. We realize the appellant's attorney had very little to work with in order to make out a good-faith effort in an appeal, yet the decisions of the United States Supreme Court compels [sic] such an appeal, regardless of merit. In our opinion a great deal of useless effort and work has been expended in this case where there was no real or substantial grounds for an appeal. . . .

Justice DeBruler concurred, but noted that

> No fair and constitutional method for screening out perfunctory appeals in criminal cases has as yet been devised. Any such method would necessarily involve a decision by someone that the proposed appeal being considered has no merit at all. The duty to make this decision properly attaches to the appellate tribunal rather than to the trial court, trial counsel, or appellate counsel. A decision, by an appellate tribunal, that a potential appeal has no merit, would be valid only if it were made after consideration of the occurrences at the trial level and arguments of legally trained personnel in support of both sides of the issue of whether or not a meritorious appeal exists. Anders v. California, 386 U.S. 738 (1967). It would require as much time and effort to effectuate a legally sound screening method as it does to operate our present system of freely taking appeals. . . .

Read in its entirety, *Cline* seems to be Indiana's earliest rejection of the *Anders* protocol.

The Court of Appeals addressed the propriety of *Anders* withdrawals more directly in Dixon v. State, 284 N.E.2d 102 (Ind. App. 1972) (per curiam). In *Dixon,* a public defender filed an *Anders* brief and petitioned to withdraw as counsel from the defendant's appeal from the denial of post-conviction relief. The Court of Appeals denied the request and ordered the public defender to file an amended brief. The court rejected *Anders* and adopted the opinion of the American Bar Association that counsel "should not seek to withdraw because he believes that the contentions of his client lack merit, but should present for consideration such points as the client desires to be raised provided he can do so without compromising professional standards." ABA Standards, *Providing Defense Services* §5.3 (Approved Draft 1968). The *Dixon* court further noted that if it were to allow withdrawal in accordance with *Anders,* "several practical problems would arise, namely; appointment of new counsel should this court find merit to the appeal; representation of the petitioner should he desire to file a petition to transfer, challenging this court's determination of his appeal; and the additional cost of new counsel to the taxpayers." . . .

None of the cases from this Court directly addressed the propriety of an *Anders* brief on direct appeal. In what would serve as the latest major precedent on the subject, the Court of Appeals endorsed *Anders* withdrawals on direct appeal. Packer v. State, 777 N.E.2d 733 (Ind. App. 2002). In *Packer,* the appellant's attorney filed a brief in which counsel repeatedly claimed to be "unable to construct non-frivolous arguments" on the appellant's behalf. There was no indication that counsel had consulted with the appellant or advised her of the positions that would be taken in the brief. The Court of Appeals expressed concern that counsel had provided inadequate representation and explained that a better approach would have been to follow the "dictates" of *Anders.* . . .

Rejecting *Anders*

For the reasons explained below, we disapprove of *Packer* and . . . hold that *Anders* withdrawals are impermissible in Indiana in any direct criminal appeal.

Simply stated, we share the same practical concerns expressed in *Dixon* and Justice DeBruler's concurrence in *Cline.* Several other states have rejected the *Anders* procedure for the same reasons. Overall *Anders* is cumbersome and inefficient. An attorney who withdraws pursuant to *Anders* must still review the record, complete at least some legal research, consult and advise the client, and draft a brief for submission to the Court of Appeals. If all this is done, the attorney "may as well submit it for the purposes of an ordinary appeal." Commonwealth v. Moffett, 418 N.E.2d 585, 590-91 (Mass. 1981). Furthermore, the Court of Appeals must conduct a "full examination of all the proceedings" to determine if there are any meritorious issues. Any saving of time and effort by counsel in preparing an *Anders* brief is offset by increased demands on the judiciary, which is to some extent placed in the precarious role of advocate. See Huguley v. State, 324 S.E.2d 729, 731 (Ga. 1985). And if the reviewing court finds any meritorious issues, even more time and money must be spent in substituting new counsel and starting the appeal all over again. Requiring counsel to submit an ordinary appellate brief the first time — no matter how frivolous counsel regards the claims to be — is quicker, simpler, and places fewer demands on the appellate courts.

An *Anders* brief also raises issues of fairness. An *Anders* withdrawal prejudices an appellant and compromises his appeal by flagging the case as without merit, which invites perfunctory review by the court. State v. Cigic, 639 A.2d 251, 252 (N.H. 1994). The result is to jeopardize receptive and meaningful appellate review. But see People v. Wende, 600 P.2d 1071, 1075 (Calif. 1979) (finding that an *Anders* withdrawal may secure an appellant more comprehensive review by the appellate court). We understand the frustration of the Court of Appeals in receiving underdeveloped briefs and poorly substantiated arguments. We also recognize that our decision to prohibit *Anders* withdrawals may in some cases perpetuate the filing of "perfunctory" appeals. But in a direct appeal a convicted defendant is entitled to a review by the judiciary, not by overworked and underpaid public defenders.

The professional obligation to avoid frivolous contentions is expressly "subordinate to federal or state constitutional law that entitles a defendant in a criminal matter to the assistance of counsel in presenting a claim or contention that otherwise would be prohibited." Ind. Professional Conduct Rule 3.1 cmt. The Indiana Oath of Attorneys expands this to permit a defense that the attorney regards as unjust whether or not constitutional rights are at stake. It provides in relevant part: "I will not counsel or maintain any action, proceeding, or defense which shall appear to me to be unjust, but this obligation shall not prevent me from defending a person charged with crime in any case." Ind. Admission and Discipline Rule 22. [We] ground our opinion in this case on this Court's supervisory authority over matters of appellate procedure and professional responsibility, and do not reach the constitutional claim.

In sum, we believe that disapproving *Anders* is simpler, more effective, fairer, and less taxing on counsel and the courts. Prohibiting *Anders* withdrawals may also force counsel to be more diligent and locate meritorious issues in a seemingly empty record. And in those few cases that offer no colorable argument of trial court error whatsoever, counsel may still be able to solicit a sentence revision or even a change in the law. Prof. Cond. R. 3.1 cmt. ("[The] law is not always clear and never is static. Accordingly, in determining the proper scope of advocacy, account must be taken of the law's ambiguities and potential for change."). We conclude that in any criminal appeal as a matter of right, counsel may neither withdraw on the basis that the appeal is frivolous nor submit an *Anders* brief to the appellate court. . . .

Notes

1. *Counsel for indigent appellants.* The Supreme Court has read the equal protection clause to require equal access to some aspects of the appeals process for both indigent appellants and those who can afford an attorney and various fees. The Court has now expanded the constitutional bases for the right to counsel on appeal. In Halbert v. Michigan, 545 U.S. 605 (2005), the Court declared that the due process and equal protection clauses require appointment of counsel for indigent defendants who pursue first-tier appellate review, even if they were convicted on the basis of a guilty plea. As with the right to appointed counsel at trial, many states use their own constitutions, statutes, or rules of procedure to expand the availability of counsel on appeal beyond what the federal constitution requires. Not every stage of the appeals process is available on equal terms to indigent defendants. Under

Ross v. Moffitt, 417 U.S. 600 (1974), there is no constitutional requirement to provide counsel for preparation of petitions for discretionary appellate review.

2. *Duties of counsel on appeal*. When appellate counsel for an indigent defendant believes the defendant could raise only frivolous issues on appeal, states still must have some mechanism for bringing potential issues to the court's attention. Those mechanisms can take different forms. The Indiana court defended the traditional duties of appellate counsel. It is also possible, consistent with the federal constitution, for appellate counsel to submit an *Anders* brief, or some variation on that model. In Smith v. Robbins, 528 U.S. 259 (2000), the Court approved a California practice allowing counsel to summarize the procedural and factual history of the case, with citations to the record, to attest to a review of the record, to explain his or her evaluation of the case to the client, to provide the client with a copy of the brief, and to inform the client of his right to file a *pro se* supplemental brief. Under this process, the court independently examines the record for arguable issues. See also Commonwealth v. Santiago, 978 A.2d 349 (Pa. 2009) (appellate brief for indigent appellant must refer to anything in record that counsel believes arguably supports appeal, and must specify counsel's reasons for concluding that appeal is frivolous); In re Bailey, 992 A.2d 276 (Vt. 2009) (allowing withdrawal of counsel without brief specifying law or argument that arguably supported each claim, or a statement that counsel did not consider petitioner's claims to be warranted by existing law or by a nonfrivolous argument for modification of existing law).

3. *Self-representation on appeal.* In Martinez v. Court of Appeal of California, 528 U.S. 152 (2000), the Supreme Court refused to extend the right of self-representation at trial — established in Faretta v. California, 422 U.S. 806 (1975) — to a direct appeal. The appellate courts may properly appoint counsel for the appellant, even if the appellant objects. One of the Court's reasons to embrace the right of self-representation at trial was "respect for individual autonomy." Are there any differences between the interests of a defendant at trial and the interests of an appellant when it comes to self-representation?

3. Interlocutory Appeals

Appeals usually take place after a final judgment, but on occasion the rules allow for an "interlocutory" appeal of an issue before the proceedings below have reached an end. These interlocutory appeals are especially important to the government. In general, prosecutors have less access to appellate review than defendants. The U.S. Supreme Court noted the state of the common law on prosecutorial appeals in 1892:

> In a few States, decisions denying a writ of error to the State after judgment for the defendant on a verdict of acquittal have proceeded upon the ground that to grant it would be to put him twice in jeopardy, in violation of a constitutional provision. But the courts of many States, including some of great authority, have denied, upon broader grounds, the right of the State to bring a writ of error in any criminal case whatever, even when the discharge of the defendant was upon the decision of an issue of law by the court, as on demurrer to the indictment, motion to quash, special verdict, or motion in arrest of judgment.

United States v. Sanges, 144 U.S. 310, 312-13 (1892). As the Court suggested in *Sanges,* the double jeopardy clauses of the federal and state constitutions have some bearing on when the prosecutor can appeal: They limit the power of the prosecution to request an appeal after jeopardy "attaches," and they bar virtually any prosecutorial appeal after an acquittal. Against this common law presumption against appeals by the state (bolstered by the constitutional limits on double jeopardy), consider the following statute and judicial decision interpreting a rule of appellate procedure.

■ DELAWARE CODE TIT. 10, §§9902, 9903

§9902

(a) The State shall have an absolute right to appeal to an appellate court a final order of a lower court where the order constitutes a dismissal of an indictment or information or any count thereof, or the granting of any motion vacating any verdict or judgment of conviction where the order of the lower court is based upon the invalidity or construction of the statute upon which the indictment or information is founded or the lack of jurisdiction of the lower court over the person or subject matter.

(b) When any order is entered before trial in any court suppressing or excluding substantial and material evidence, the court, upon certification by the Attorney General that the evidence is essential to the prosecution of the case, shall dismiss the complaint, indictment or information or any count thereof to the proof of which the evidence suppressed or excluded is essential. [The] reasons of the dismissal shall be set forth in the order entered upon the record.

(c) The State shall have an absolute right of appeal to an appellate court from an order entered pursuant to subsection (b) of this section and if the appellate court upon review of the order suppressing evidence shall reverse the dismissal, the defendant may be subjected to trial.

§9903

The State may apply to the appellate court to permit an appeal to determine a substantial question of law or procedure, and the appellate court may permit the appeal in its absolute discretion. The appellate court shall have the power to adopt rules governing the allowance of the appeal; but, in no event of such appeals shall the decision or result of the appeal affect the rights of the defendant and he or she shall not be obligated to defend the appeal, but the court may require the Public Defender of this State to defend the appeal and to argue the cause.

■ STATE v. MATTHEW MEDRANO

67 S.W.3d 892 (Tex. Crim. App. 2002)

COCHRAN, J.

The issue in this case is whether article 44.01(a)(5) of the Texas Code of Criminal Procedure[1] permits the State to bring a pretrial appeal of an adverse

1. Article 44.01(a), in pertinent part, provides:

ruling on a motion to suppress evidence when the trial court does not conclude that the evidence was "illegally obtained." Although this Court, in State v. Roberts, 940 S.W.2d 655 (Tex. Crim. App. 1996), held that the State cannot appeal a pretrial evidentiary ruling unless the defendant claims that the evidence was "illegally obtained," neither the language of the statute nor legislative intent supports this limitation. It is not consistent with the interpretation other state or federal courts have given to the same or similar language in their government-appeal statutes. Moreover, the rule in *Roberts* has proved unworkable in practice. Therefore, we overrule *Roberts* and hold that under article 44.01(a)(5), the State is entitled to appeal any adverse pre-trial ruling which suppresses evidence, a confession, or an admission, regardless of whether the defendant alleges, or the trial court holds, that the evidence was "illegally obtained."

Appellee, Matthew Medrano, was charged with capital murder for the robbery-murder of Benton Smith, a pizza delivery man. The State's only witness to the robbery-murder was Jennifer Erivez, a fourteen-year-old girl, who was standing in the driveway of her home at about 10:00 P.M. waiting for her boyfriend. Jennifer testified that she saw the pizza delivery man drive by and park down the street. Then she saw a maroon car, like a Chrysler LeBaron, drive past slowly and stop under a street light. A man got out of the front passenger side and did something like take the license plate off of the car. Jennifer saw the man's face clearly, but could not recall the car's license plate number. The car then drove further down the street and parked behind the pizza delivery man's truck. The same man got out of the car and walked up to the pizza delivery man. Jennifer heard a gunshot and then saw the man run back to the car. He got in, and the driver sped away.

A few hours later, Jennifer gave police a written description of the person she had seen get out of the car and approach the pizza delivery man. . . . Jennifer also stated that the maroon car contained a total of four people. Because she was unable to recall the car's license plate number, an El Paso police officer, trained in hypnosis, conducted a videotaped hypnotic session the next day. She was still unable to recall the license plate number. About a week later, the police conducted two photo lineups for Jennifer. She did not identify anyone in those lineups, [although Medrano's photo was not in either of those lineups]. After she identified Mr. Medrano as the shooter in a third photo lineup two days later, he was arrested and charged with capital murder.

Defense counsel filed a "Motion to Suppress In Court Identification." . . . After a pretrial suppression hearing, the trial judge orally granted the defense motion. Her written order stated that she granted the motion "for the reasons stated on the record" at the hearing and that she also found "said identification was obtained in violation of the 4th, 5th, 6th and 14th Amendments of the United States Constitution and Article I, sections 9, 10, 13, and 19 of the Texas Constitution." The State certified that it could not prosecute the case without Jennifer's testimony and filed an appeal. . . .

The State is entitled to appeal an order of a court in a criminal case if the order: . . . (5) grants a motion to suppress evidence, a confession, or an admission, if jeopardy has not attached in the case and if the prosecuting attorney certifies to the trial court that the appeal is not taken for the purpose of delay and that the evidence, confession, or admission is of substantial importance to the case.

Article 44.01 was enacted as a vehicle for the State to challenge "questionable legal rulings excluding what may be legally admissible evidence."[5] The purpose of the statute is to permit the pretrial appeal of erroneous legal rulings which eviscerate the State's ability to prove its case. The Texas legislature, in passing Senate Bill 762 in 1987, clearly intended to provide Texas prosecutors with the same vehicle of appeal for pretrial evidentiary rulings as federal prosecutors. . . . There is no question that under 18 U.S.C. §3731, federal prosecutors may appeal a wide variety of pretrial evidentiary rulings — not just those tied to motions to suppress illegally obtained evidence. . . .

All fifty states, as well as the District of Columbia, have provisions permitting the government to appeal adverse rulings of a question of law. Many of those states [at least eighteen of them] use the same or very similar language as that contained in art. 44.01(a)(5), and they permit the State to appeal *any* pretrial ruling suppressing evidence if that evidence is likely to be outcome determinative. [At least thirteen other] states explicitly grant the prosecution a broad right to appeal any pretrial suppression, evidentiary or other legal ruling which is likely to determine the outcome of the case. A few states explicitly permit the State to appeal only orders excluding "seized evidence," "evidence illegally obtained," or "evidence seized in violation of the Constitution." A handful of state courts [four of them] have construed their government-appeal statutes to permit only appeals of constitutionally based pretrial rulings excluding evidence. State v. Shade, 867 P.2d 393 (Nev. 1994); State v. Counts, 472 N.W.2d 756 (N.D. 1991). At least one state, Ohio, has judicially broadened its government-appeal statute to permit pretrial appeals of nonconstitutional trial rulings excluding evidence, despite language to the contrary. O.R.C. §2945.67; Ohio Crim. R. 12. Although a few states apply their government-appeal statutes narrowly, the vast majority of courts and legislatures across the nation broadly construe their state's-right-to-appeal statutes. They focus upon the same major themes: 1) Does this pretrial ruling effectively prevent the government from presenting its case to a jury? And 2) Is the ruling based upon an erroneous interpretation or application of law?

In *Roberts,* this Court followed that handful of states which have very narrowly construed their state's right-to-appeal statutes. This Court ruled that it lacked jurisdiction to consider a State's appeal from a trial court's ruling that civil deposition testimony was inadmissible. We held that the phrase "motion to suppress evidence,"

5. Bill Analysis, S.B. 762, Acts 1987, 70th Leg., ch. 382, §1. The "Background" Section of the bill analysis begins:

> The Texas Constitution provides that the State has no right to appeal in a criminal case, making Texas the only state that bans all prosecution appeals. This prohibition is viewed as a serious problem in the administration of justice for several reasons: (1) On occasion, defendants are released because of questionable legal rulings excluding what may be legally admissible evidence; (2) Legal issues that have been wrongly decided by trial courts nevertheless stand as precedent, albeit unbinding, for police, prosecutors, and courts; and (3) Trial judges may have a tendency to resolve doubtful legal questions in favor of the defendant because such a ruling cannot harm the judge's reversal rate.

as used in article 44.01(a)(5), was limited to motions which sought to suppress evidence on the basis that such evidence was "illegally obtained." The defendant in *Roberts* contended that a videotaped deposition from a civil case was inadmissible hearsay; he did not claim that the deposition testimony was illegally obtained. Because the defendant's motion was not a "motion to suppress evidence" contemplated under art. 44.01(a)(5), went the logic, the order granting the motion was not appealable. [The *Roberts* Court] relied on the fact that the corresponding federal statute authorizes an appeal by the Government, under 18 U.S.C. §3731, "from a decision or order of a district court suppressing or excluding evidence...." Texas article 44.01(a)(5) authorizes an appeal from a motion to suppress evidence, but it does not explicitly authorize an appeal from a motion to *exclude* evidence. In *Roberts,* this Court reasoned, "[B]y using the term 'suppress' alone, not in conjunction with the broader term 'exclude,' the Legislature meant to limit the State's appeal to those instances where evidence is suppressed in the technical sense, not merely excluded."

The legislative history of article 44.01 shows otherwise. The legislative intent, explicitly stated in the Bill Analysis, was to permit the State to appeal any "questionable legal rulings excluding what may be legally admissible evidence." Period.

[The] Texas Legislature was already familiar with the use of the term "motion to suppress evidence" in the context of pretrial hearings. The Texas Legislature apparently chose the term "motion to suppress evidence" in article 44.01(a)(5) because pretrial "motions to suppress evidence" can be heard under article 28.01.... Because the only type of pretrial evidentiary motion mentioned in article 28.01 is a "motion to suppress evidence," it follows that the only type of pretrial evidentiary motion that the State can appeal is the same type that the defendant may file. They are both called a "motion to suppress evidence." Under article 28.01, a motion to suppress evidence is one in which the defendant (or the State) claims that certain evidence should not be admitted at trial for a constitutional, statutory, evidentiary or procedural reason. There is no logical, legal, or linguistic reason that a single phrase concerning the same pretrial evidentiary motion, should bear one meaning for purposes of which pretrial motions a court may consider, but bear a totally different meaning when the State appeals an adverse ruling on that motion. The rule is simple: If the trial court can rule upon a pretrial motion to suppress evidence, the State can appeal it. A motion for the goose is a motion for the gander.

Finally, the rule in *Roberts* is, as this case demonstrates, unworkable. Who decides whether a pretrial motion to suppress evidence is one that seeks to exclude "illegally obtained" evidence? If the defendant labels his motion as one to suppress illegally obtained evidence, is that determinative? If the defendant cites constitutional provisions, is that determinative? If the trial court, in ruling, cites constitutional provisions, is that determinative? Or, as in this case, if the court of appeals determines that, even though both the defendant and trial judge cited constitutional provisions, the motion (and ruling) was not really a motion to suppress illegally obtained evidence? This is a linguistic puzzle that only Humpty Dumpty or a rejection of *Roberts* can resolve....

The trial court's ruling in this case does not involve evidence which would normally be considered "illegally obtained." Still, the ruling excluding Jennifer's identification testimony — which was a legal ruling excluding evidence — is appealable under article 44.01(a)(5) if it could be determined pretrial under article 28.01, §1(6). Relying on the standards concerning the admissibility of post-hypnotic testimony set out in Zani v. State, 758 S.W.2d 233 (Tex. Crim. App. 1988), the trial court orally ruled that Jennifer's identification of Mr. Medrano was inadmissible. After hearing arguments from the prosecutor, the trial court affirmed her oral order with a written ruling that specifically held that the identifications were obtained in violation of the United States and Texas Constitutions. The trial court's written ruling falls squarely within the rulings intended to be appealable under Article 44.01. . . .

WOMACK, J., dissenting.

. . . Today the Court says [our holding in *Roberts*] was wrong because the legislature modeled art. 44.01 after the corresponding federal provision generally, a statute that permits an appeal by the government from suppression or exclusion of evidence. I want to point out four things. First, drafting a statute to apply only to "suppressing" is an odd way of modeling on the federal statute that specifies both "suppressing" and "excluding." Second, our 1996 decision was based on the language of the statute, which is more important than the intentions and interpretations of witnesses who supported the act, which are the primary support for today's decision. "It is the *law* that governs, not the intent of the lawgiver," Antonin Scalia, A Matter of Interpretation 17 (1997), much less the intent of the lawgiver's committee witnesses. But this is only to rehash the 1996 decision of the Court.

In 2002 the more important points are my third and fourth: Today's construction of the ambiguous word increases the scope of the statute, applying it to "excluding" evidence as well as to "suppressing" it. And if that is the correct scope of the statute, the legislature had but to amend the statute by inserting the words "or excluding." Three sessions of the legislature have intervened since our decision, with no action. In this case, that is significant.

If this case were the opposite (if the statute had read "suppressing or excluding evidence," and we had held that it did not apply to the excluding of evidence) legislative inaction might mean little or nothing. What could the legislature do to express more clearly that the statute applied to the excluding of evidence? But when the statute says it applies only to "suppressing" evidence and this Court held that "suppressing" does not mean every "excluding" of evidence, the remedy is quick and easy. If we have misconstrued a statute that is stated clearly, what can the legislature do? Reenact the statute with the additional phrase, "and we really mean it"? When we have misconstrued a criminal-procedure statute that is unambiguous, *stare decisis* has its least force. In such a case we should be more free to overrule our earlier decision. . . .

The Court's other argument that "suppress evidence" means "suppress or exclude evidence" is by reference to Code of Criminal Procedure article 28.01, which provides the procedure for a pretrial hearing like the one that was held in this case. . . . The Court reasons thus: pretrial hearings are to determine motions to suppress evidence; the motion that was filed in this case was decided at a pretrial hearing; therefore it must have been a motion to suppress evidence. . . .

Although pretrial hearings are for motions to suppress evidence (and the other matters that are listed in Article 28.01, section 1), they are not for *only* those matters. There are two reasons. On its face, the statutory list is not exclusive, so the pretrial hearing is not limited to the eleven items on the list. Even if it were exclusive, one item on the list is "(2) Pleadings of the defendant," which include "any other motions or pleadings permitted by law to be filed." Tex. Code Crim. Proc. art. 27.02. It was, therefore, proper for the appellee to file and the court to decide a motion to exclude, not suppress, evidence. So the Court's conclusion that the pretrial motion must be a motion to suppress is invalid.

[There are] strong arguments why the State should be allowed to appeal pretrial rulings excluding evidence. But the statute that was enacted did not allow it, and it still does not. We have no authority to change the statute. I respectfully dissent.

Notes

1. *Appeal of pretrial issues by the government: majority position.* Statutes and procedural rules in most states have now expanded beyond the common law bar on government appeals, granting the government power to appeal certain pretrial rulings. Most of these rules cover a trial judge's decision to dismiss charges before trial or a decision during a suppression hearing to exclude key evidence. See also McCullough v. State, 900 N.E.2d 745 (Ind. 2009) (state constitution allows appellate courts to revise sentences upward or downward, but state has no authority to initiate an appeal of a criminal sentence; prosecutors may urge more severe sentence without filing cross-appeal if defendant seeks a revised sentence). The federal statute, 18 U.S.C. §3731, allows the government to appeal the dismissal of an indictment or information as well as a decision "suppressing or excluding evidence . . . not made after the defendant has been put in jeopardy." Under this statute, the government may also appeal a decision to release a person from pretrial detention. Appeals of pretrial rulings do not create double jeopardy problems because double jeopardy does not "attach" in the lower court until the start of a trial. See Anne Bowen Poulin, Government Appeals in Criminal Cases: The Myth of Asymmetry, 77 U. Cin. L. Rev. 1 (2008) (government access to appellate review in criminal cases is more extensive today than at most times in the history of the country, based on its ability to challenge range of pretrial or postverdict rulings on appeal, or through petitions for writ of mandamus).

2. *Appeal after jeopardy attaches.* Once a trial has begun, the government will have more difficulty obtaining appellate review for any errors of the trial judge. If the judge's error leads to an acquittal or a dismissal of the charges, double jeopardy clearly would prevent a second trial for the same offense. But can the government suspend the proceedings at trial once a major error has occurred and obtain appellate review before an acquittal or dismissal? Most criminal procedure rules and statutes block such appeals; there is, however, a small and growing number of states willing to allow the government to bring an appeal after trial has begun but before an acquittal or a dismissal takes place. See, e.g., State v. Malinovsky, 573 N.E.2d 22 (Ohio 1991) (allowing prosecutorial appeal of midtrial evidentiary ruling, based on procedural rule allowing appeal of "motion to suppress evidence").

Double jeopardy clearly bars government appeals after an acquittal. Ball v. United States, 163 U.S. 662 (1896). However, that limit does not matter in the great majority of cases: Acquittals occur in 1 percent of all felony cases filed. Dismissals of charges after jeopardy attaches are more common than acquittals, and government appeals after dismissals present more complex legal issues. If a dismissal on a legal question occurs after a conviction, an appellate court can reverse the legal ruling and reinstate the fact finder's verdict without requiring a second trial. For dismissals taking place before a verdict, the government may not appeal if the ruling amounts to a resolution, "correct or not, of some or all of the factual elements of the offense charged." United States v. Scott, 437 U.S. 82, 97 (1978); Smith v. Massachusetts, 543 U.S. 462 (2005) (after trial judge granted motion to dismiss one among several charges based on insufficiency of government's evidence, double jeopardy barred any reconsideration by judge on this count). However, if the preverdict dismissal is based on some legal issue not going to the defendant's guilt or innocence (such as pretrial delay), then a reprosecution after a government appeal is consistent with double jeopardy limits.

When *defendants* appeal after conviction and convince the court to overturn the judgment, the government may ordinarily retry the case without violating double jeopardy. One exception occurs when the fact finder at trial is presented with both a greater and lesser included offense and convicts the defendant only of the lesser offense. In that setting, the "implied acquittal" of the defendant prevents the government from retrying the greater charges if the defendant succeeds on appeal. Green v. United States, 355 U.S. 184 (1957). The government also cannot retry a case after a defendant wins an appeal if the error was the government's failure to present legally sufficient facts to support a conviction. For an evaluation of the government's asymmetric appeal rights from an economic perspective, go to the web extension for this chapter at *http://www.crimpro.com/extension/ch20*.

3. *Prosecutorial and appellate court screening of appeals.* Most state statutes leave the chief prosecutor with some control over which issues the government may appeal. The chief prosecutor (or some statewide representative of the government, such as the attorney general) must certify to the appellate court that the trial court's ruling dealt with evidence or some other claim critical to the prosecution of the case and that the appeal is not taken "merely" for purposes of delay. Under what circumstances might the chief prosecutor refuse to certify an issue for appeal? Is this a meaningful limitation on the scope of the government's appeal rights? Should appellate courts themselves sort the important claims from the less important ones? Appellate rules of procedure often give courts the discretion to decline to hear government claims that otherwise qualify for appeal. See State v. Doucette, 544 A.2d 1290, 1293 (Me. 1988).

4. *"Moot" appeals by the prosecution.* A few states, such as Kansas, permit the government to appeal from an acquittal to the state supreme court if the legal issue is of statewide interest and vital to the administration of justice. The appellate decision is only advisory; even if the appellate court sustains the government's position, the trial court acquittal remains final. See Kan. Stat. §22-3602(b)(1)-(3); State v. Martin, 658 P.2d 1024 (Kan. 1983); State v. Viers, 469 P.2d 53 (Nev. 1970) (striking down a provision similar to Kansas statute on the ground that an advisory appeal presents no case or controversy under the state constitution). In Canada, the appellate court has discretionary power to hear government claims of legal error leading to an acquittal. See Alan Mewett, An Introduction to the Criminal Process in Canada 209-12 (1988). Will the defense point of view receive adequate representation in such "moot" appeals?

5. *Interlocutory appeals by the defense.* Defendants may also bring interlocutory appeals, although they can do so for fewer issues than the government. Denials of motions for pretrial release and the trial judge's setting of a bail amount are common grounds for defense interlocutory appeals. See Ill. Supreme Ct. R. 604(c). Why do these decisions receive exceptional treatment? What other choices might a defendant most desire to appeal on an interlocutory basis?

B. APPELLATE REVIEW OF FACTUAL FINDINGS

Appellate courts could take a wide range of approaches in selecting which judgments made at trial to review. They could conceivably engage in complete and new ("de novo") review for all issues of fact and law. But this approach would engender huge administrative costs; in effect, the appellate court would retry the entire case. Alternatively, appellate courts might play an extremely limited role in reviewing verdicts, presuming that all judgments of fact and law are correct and reversing only for fundamental failures in process that would undermine confidence in the fairness of the decisionmakers or the ability of the defendant to put on a case (such as a failure to provide counsel, evident bias on the part of the judge, or jury tampering). An even more extreme system might abolish appellate courts altogether, trusting completely in the trial process.

Appellate courts operate under standards that lie somewhere between these conceivable boundaries. Courts distinguish between review of factual findings and legal judgments at trial. The standards of review for factual findings tend to be more deferential because the factfinder at trial (whether a jury or judge) is in a better position to view and weigh evidence. The standard of review on questions of law is different: Appellate courts often assert the same (or greater) competence in assessing legal issues and tend to review questions of law de novo.

The Supreme Court in Jackson v. Virginia, 443 U.S. 307 (1979), announced the standard that most appellate courts now apply when reviewing the sufficiency of the evidence to support a guilty verdict. James Jackson had been convicted at trial of murdering Mary Cole.

> That the petitioner had shot and killed Mrs. Cole was not in dispute at the trial. The State's evidence established that she had been a member of the staff at the local county jail, that she had befriended him while he was imprisoned there on a disorderly conduct charge, and that when he was released she had arranged for him to live in the home of her son and daughter-in-law. Testimony by her relatives indicated that on the day of the killing the petitioner had been drinking and had spent a great deal of time shooting at targets with his revolver. [That evening, Cole drove Jackson] to a local diner. There the two were observed by several police officers, who testified that both the petitioner and the victim had been drinking. The two were observed by a deputy sheriff as they were preparing to leave the diner in her car. The petitioner was then in possession of his revolver, and the sheriff also observed a kitchen knife in the automobile. The sheriff testified that he had offered to keep the revolver until the petitioner sobered up, but that the latter had indicated that this would be unnecessary since he and the victim were about to engage in sexual activity.
>
> Her body was found in a secluded church parking lot a day and a half later, naked from the waist down, her slacks beneath her body. Uncontradicted medical and expert evidence established that she had been shot twice at close range with the petitioner's gun. She appeared not to have been sexually molested. Six cartridge cases identified as having been fired from the petitioner's gun were found near the body.

443 U.S. at 309-10. Following the common law formula, Virginia defined murder as "the unlawful killing of another with malice aforethought." Premeditation distinguished murder in the first degree from murder in the second degree, and the prosecution bore the burden of proof on this element. Jackson admitted shooting Cole but contended that the shooting had been accidental and that the gun had gone off

while he was resisting her sexual advances, and that in any case he had been too intoxicated to support a finding of premeditation.

The trial judge found Jackson guilty of first-degree murder. Jackson challenged the conviction in both state and federal court on the grounds that the evidence was constitutionally insufficient. Although the Supreme Court announced in its opinion the standard of review for factual judgments on federal collateral review of state convictions, the constitutional standard in *Jackson* has been applied in state and federal courts for almost all review of factual findings, including on direct appeal. The Court held:

> [The] relevant question is whether, after viewing the evidence in the light most favorable to the prosecution, any rational trier of fact could have found the essential elements of the crime beyond a reasonable doubt. This familiar standard gives full play to the responsibility of the trier of fact fairly to resolve conflicts in the testimony, to weigh the evidence, and to draw reasonable inferences from basic facts to ultimate facts. Once a defendant has been found guilty of the crime charged, the factfinder's role as weigher of the evidence is preserved through a legal conclusion that upon judicial review all of the evidence is to be considered in the light most favorable to the prosecution. The criterion thus impinges upon "jury" discretion only to the extent necessary to guarantee the fundamental protection of due process of law.

443 U.S. at 317-20. Applying this new standard, the Court concluded that "a rational factfinder could readily have found the petitioner guilty beyond a reasonable doubt of first-degree murder under Virginia law."

States modify the *Jackson* standards in two ways. First, as with many other broad standards applied throughout the criminal process, different legal cultures and groups of judges will apply similar standards differently and will reach consistently different outcomes. Thus, the flexibility of the *Jackson* standard allows for more aggressive or more deferential review. Second, some states have supplemented the *Jackson* standard to require from appellate courts an additional task when reviewing the factual support for the guilty verdict.

■ KELVIN BROOKS v. STATE

323 S.W.3d 893 (Tex. Crim. App. 2010)

HERVEY, J.

We granted discretionary review in this case to address, among other things, whether there is any meaningful distinction between a legal-sufficiency standard under Jackson v. Virginia, 443 U.S. 307 (1979), and a factual-sufficiency standard under Clewis v. State, 922 S.W.2d 126 (Tex. Crim. App. 1996), and whether there is a need to retain both standards. Under the Jackson v. Virginia legal-sufficiency standard, a reviewing court is required to defer to a jury's credibility and weight determinations. In *Clewis,* this Court adopted a factual-sufficiency standard, which is supposed to be distinguished from a Jackson v. Virginia legal-sufficiency standard primarily by not requiring a reviewing court to defer to a jury's credibility and weight determinations. But then *Clewis* contradicted itself by also requiring a reviewing court to apply this standard with deference to these jury determinations "so as to avoid an appellate court's substituting its judgment for that of the jury." After having made several attempts to "clarify" *Clewis* in part to resolve this fundamental contradiction, we eventually came to realize that the *Clewis* factual-sufficiency standard is "barely distinguishable" from the Jackson v. Virginia legal-sufficiency standard. We now take the next small step in this progression and recognize that these two standards have become essentially the same standard and that there is no meaningful distinction between them that would justify retaining them both. We, therefore, overrule *Clewis* and decide that the Jackson v. Virginia legal-sufficiency standard is the only standard that a reviewing court should apply in determining whether the evidence is sufficient to support each element of a criminal offense that the State is required to prove beyond a reasonable doubt.

[A] jury convicted appellant of possessing with intent to deliver more than four but less than 200 grams of crack cocaine and sentenced him to 25 years in prison. Appellant claimed on direct appeal that the evidence is legally and factually insufficient to support the intent-to-deliver element of this offense.

The evidence shows that two police officers went into a bar to investigate a report that someone matching appellant's description was there with a gun. When the officers asked appellant to step outside, appellant ran and threw two baggies towards a pool table just before one of the officers tased him. One of the baggies contained a small amount (about 3 grams) of marijuana. The other baggie contained one baggie holding 4.72 grams of crack cocaine and another baggie holding six ecstasy tablets that weighed 1.29 grams. Appellant also had a cell phone and, according to one of the officers, "a couple of dollars." Appellant did not appear to be under the influence of narcotics, and he was not in possession of any drug paraphernalia that could have been used for smoking crack cocaine. The police did not find a gun. The police gave appellant's cell phone and money to an acquaintance of appellant's before they took appellant to jail.

An experienced Waco Police Department drug-enforcement investigator (Thompson) testified that the bag containing the 4.72 grams of crack cocaine contained "two larger size rocks and then maybe a smaller one" and a useable amount of "crumbs." He testified that each of the two large rocks weighed at least two grams and the other one weighed "a gram and a half or something like that." Thompson testified that "he would say" that 4.72 grams was a "dealer amount," which could have been cut up into 23 or 24 rocks. He testified that 4.72 grams of crack cocaine is worth about $470.

Thompson stated that a "typical quantity" that a dealer would have would be more than two rocks and that he "would think" that someone with more than a gram would be a dealer. Thompson testified that it is not "typical" for drug users to be in possession of a large amount of drugs and that he has "not run across many people that are [crack cocaine] users that have more than one to two rocks" because they are going to "smoke it as soon as [they] can get it." He also testified that "most" crack cocaine users "typically" would have some type of paraphernalia "to smoke the crack with" and that typically dealers "don't have crack pipes because it's not really common for them to use their product that they are selling." . . .

On cross-examination, Thompson described other factors, none of which are present in the record in this case, indicating that a person could be a dealer: (1) possession of five, ten, or twenty dollar bills; (2) names in the person's cell phone; (3) possession of some document identifying who owes what; (4) possession of a weapon; or (5) others observed the person trying to sell drugs. Thompson also acknowledged that a person could possess 4.72 grams of crack cocaine for personal use.

Appellant testified that he possessed only the baggie containing the small amount of marijuana. He denied possessing the baggies containing the crack cocaine and the ecstasy pills. Appellant also admitted that he has two prior convictions for possession of cocaine and another prior conviction for possession with intent to deliver cocaine. The jury was instructed in the charge that it could have considered these extraneous offenses "in determining the intent, motive, opportunity, preparation, plan, knowledge, identity, or absence of mistake or accident by the Defendant, if any, in connection with the offenses, if any, alleged against him in the indictment in this case, and for no other purpose."

During closing jury arguments, the State relied primarily on Thompson's testimony to argue that appellant possessed the crack cocaine with the intent to deliver it. . . .

The court of appeals decided that "standing alone, 4.72 grams is insufficient evidence of intent [to deliver because this amount is also consistent with personal use], additional evidence is required." The court of appeals decided that the additional evidence is legally sufficient "to establish possession with intent to deliver," but that "viewing the evidence in a neutral light, it is not factually sufficient," [noting that Brooks was not arrested in a high crime or high drug area, the drugs were not packaged in way to suggest that Brooks is a dealer, Brooks was not in possession of any drug paraphernalia for the purpose of dealing, and Brooks did not possess a large amount of cash.]

Is There Any Meaningful Distinction Between Jackson v. Virginia Legal-Sufficiency Review and *Clewis* Factual-Sufficiency Review

We begin the discussion by noting that in Watson v. State, 204 S.W.3d 404 (Tex. Crim. App. 2006), this Court recognized that a factual-sufficiency standard is "barely distinguishable" from a legal-sufficiency standard and that "the only apparent difference" between these two standards is that the appellate court views the evidence in a "neutral light" under a factual-sufficiency standard and "in the light most favorable to the verdict" under a legal-sufficiency standard. It is fair to characterize the Jackson v. Virginia legal-sufficiency standard as: "Considering all of the evidence in the light most favorable to the verdict, was a jury rationally justified in finding guilt beyond a reasonable doubt." Compare this to the *Clewis* factual-sufficiency standard which may fairly be characterized as: "Considering all of the evidence in a neutral light, was a jury rationally justified in finding guilt beyond a reasonable doubt."

Viewing the evidence "in the light most favorable to the verdict" under a legal-sufficiency standard means that the reviewing court is required to defer to the jury's credibility and weight determinations because the jury is the sole judge of the witnesses' credibility and the weight to be given their testimony. Viewing the evidence in a "neutral light" under a factual-sufficiency standard is supposed to mean that the reviewing court is not required to defer to the jury's credibility and weight determinations and that the reviewing court may sit as a "thirteenth juror" and disagree with a jury's resolution of conflicting evidence and with a jury's weighing of the evidence. . . .

The final nail in the coffin that made a legal-sufficiency standard "indistinguishable" from a factual-sufficiency standard came in this Court's decision in Lancon v. State, 253 S.W.3d 699 (Tex. Crim. App. 2008). There this Court decided that the reviewing court cannot decide that the evidence is factually insufficient "solely because [it] would have resolved the conflicting evidence in a different way" since "the jury is the sole judge of a witness's credibility, and the weight to be given the testimony." Our current formulation of a factual-sufficiency standard in *Lancon*, recognizing that the jury is "the sole judge of a witness's credibility, and the weight to be given their testimony," entirely eliminates the viewing the evidence in a "neutral light" component of a factual-sufficiency standard and makes the current factual-sufficiency standard indistinguishable from the Jackson v. Virginia legal-sufficiency standard. . . .

Double-Jeopardy Considerations

The *Clewis* factual-sufficiency standard being "barely distinguishable" (and now indistinguishable) from a legal-sufficiency standard also raises some troubling double-jeopardy questions under the United States Supreme Court's decision in Tibbs v. Florida, 457 U.S. 31 (1982). First, we find it necessary to discuss the proceedings involving Mr. Tibbs in the Florida courts.

In 1976, the Florida Supreme Court reversed Tibbs' convictions for rape of one person and first-degree murder of another person because of the "weakness and inadequacy" of the rape victim's testimony, which was the only testimony that directly connected Tibbs to these crimes. The Florida Supreme Court remanded the case to the trial court for a new trial, which at the time was the remedy provided by Florida law upon a finding that the evidence did not support a defendant's conviction.

Before Tibbs could be retried, the United States Supreme Court decided that double-jeopardy principles prohibit the states from retrying a defendant whose conviction has been reversed on appeal on evidentiary-sufficiency (*i.e.*, legal-sufficiency) grounds essentially because this has the same effect as an acquittal by a jury. After the United States Supreme Court handed down these decisions, the Florida trial court granted Tibbs' motion to dismiss his indictment on the grounds that double-jeopardy principles prohibited his retrial. [The] Florida Supreme Court decided that its 1976 decision reversing Tibbs' convictions was "one of those rare instances in which reversal was based on evidentiary weight."

[The] United States Supreme Court decided that double-jeopardy principles do not bar a retrial when an appellate court sits as a "thirteenth juror" and "disagrees with the jury's resolution of the conflicting testimony." In reaching this decision, the United States Supreme Court noted that a reversal based on "insufficiency of the evidence" has the same effect as a jury acquittal "because it means that no rational factfinder could have voted to convict the defendant" and that "the prosecution has failed to produce sufficient evidence to prove its case." The United States Supreme Court further stated that an appellate reversal based on evidentiary weight "no more signifies acquittal than does a disagreement among the jurors themselves" and that an "appellate court's disagreement with the jurors' weighing of the evidence does not require the special deference accorded verdicts of acquittal." . . .

We believe that the *Clewis* factual-sufficiency standard with its remedy of a new trial could very well violate double-jeopardy principles under *Tibbs* if factual-sufficiency review is "barely distinguishable" from legal-sufficiency review. . . . We also note that, were we to decide that reviewing courts must continue to apply a factual-sufficiency standard with its remedy of a new trial in criminal cases, then we must also be prepared to decide that they should apply this standard as "thirteenth jurors" with no deference at all to a jury's credibility and weight determinations in order to avoid these potential federal constitutional double-jeopardy issues. We must also keep in mind that such a nondeferential standard could violate the right to trial by jury under the Texas Constitution. . . .

We believe that these and the reasons given by the Florida Supreme Court for abandoning its factual-sufficiency standard are good reasons for discarding the confusing and contradictory *Clewis* factual-sufficiency standard. We agree with the Florida Supreme Court that:

> . . . Eliminating reversals for evidentiary weight will avoid disparate appellate results, or alternatively our having to review appellate reversals based on evidentiary shortcomings to determine whether they were based on sufficiency or on weight. Finally, it will eliminate any temptation appellate tribunals might have to direct a retrial merely by styling reversals as based on "weight" when in fact there is a lack of competent substantial evidence to support the verdict or judgment and the double jeopardy clause should operate to bar retrial. . . .

Texas Constitution, Texas Statutes and Case Law Revisited

There is very little to add to what this Court has already extensively written on a direct-appeal court's constitutional and statutory authority to apply this factual-sufficiency standard in criminal cases. Our factual-sufficiency cases decided that Texas direct-appeal courts, which would include this Court in its role as a direct-appeal court in death-penalty cases, are required to apply a civil factual-sufficiency standard under their constitutional grant of general appellate jurisdiction to review "questions of fact," as also codified in Article 44.25, Tex. Code Crim. Proc., which currently states that direct-appeal courts and this Court "may reverse the judgment in a criminal action, as well upon the law as upon the facts." Our factual-sufficiency cases further noted that Articles 36.13 and 38.04, Tex. Code Crim. Proc., and their statutory predecessors, which "reserve the fact-finding function to the jury," have peacefully coexisted with that appellate authority for at least a hundred and twenty-three years and were meant merely to allocate the fact-finding function at the trial level and do not purport to affect appellate review. . . .

The dissenters in this Court's factual-sufficiency cases took the position that, even though direct-appeal courts may have the authority to apply this factual-sufficiency standard under their grant of general appellate jurisdiction, when the courts of appeals acquired criminal jurisdiction in 1981, the Legislature, pursuant to its constitutional authority in Article V, Sections 5(a) and 6(a), to regulate appellate jurisdiction, made significant changes to Article 44.25 that were carefully designed to ensure that direct-appeal courts defer to a jury's credibility and weight determinations. The dissenters considered it significant that in 1981, when Article 44.25 was changed to its current version — permitting a case to be reversed only "upon the law as upon the facts" — its statutory predecessor provided that a case could be reversed "upon the law as upon the facts" and also "because the verdict is contrary to the evidence." . . .

The issue thus becomes whether direct-appeal courts' constitutional jurisdiction to review "questions of fact," as also codified in Article 44.25 authorizing direct-appeal courts to reverse a judgment "upon the facts," should now be construed for the first time to mandate direct-appeal courts to sit as "thirteenth jurors" in criminal cases contrary to 150 years of practice in civil and criminal cases. We decline to question over 150 years of criminal and civil jurisprudence in this State and construe constitutional and statutory mandates to review "questions of fact" to also require direct-appeal courts to sit as "thirteenth jurors" in criminal cases.

As the Court with final appellate jurisdiction in this State, we decide that the Jackson v. Virginia standard is the only standard that a reviewing court should apply in determining whether the evidence is sufficient to support each element of a criminal offense that the State is required to prove beyond a reasonable doubt. All other cases to the contrary, including *Clewis,* are overruled. . . .

We must now decide how to dispose of this case. [Having] decided that there is no meaningful distinction between a *Clewis* factual-sufficiency standard and a Jackson v. Virginia legal-sufficiency standard, we could decide that the court of appeals necessarily found that the evidence is legally insufficient to support appellant's conviction when it decided that the evidence is factually insufficient to support appellant's conviction. However, primarily because the confusing factual-sufficiency standard may have skewed a rigorous application of the Jackson v. Virginia standard by the court of appeals, we believe that it is appropriate to dispose of this case by sending it back to the court of appeals to reconsider the sufficiency of the evidence to support appellant's conviction under a proper application of the Jackson v. Virginia standard. . . .

COCHRAN, J., concurring.

. . . In 1979, the United States Supreme Court delivered its opinion in Jackson v. Virginia, and set the national standard for review of the sufficiency of evidence under the Due Process Clause of the federal constitution. In all criminal trials, state and federal, the government must produce "sufficient evidence to justify a rational trier of the facts to find guilt beyond a reasonable doubt." The Court explicitly rejected the "no evidence" standard of review that it had applied nineteen years earlier in Thompson v. Louisville, 362 U.S. 199 (1960) (stating that the "ultimate question presented to us is whether the charges against petitioner were so totally devoid of evidentiary support as to render his conviction unconstitutional under the Due Process Clause of the Fourteenth Amendment. Decision of this question turns not on the sufficiency of the evidence, but on whether this conviction rests upon any evidence at all."). . . .

A reasonable doubt might arise because the verdict is manifestly against the great weight and preponderance of the credible evidence or because there is nothing more than a mere scintilla of evidence to support some element of the offense. But, of course, the reviewing court does not "ask itself whether *it* believes that the evidence at the trial established guilt beyond a reasonable doubt." Rather, it must give "full play to the responsibility of the trier of fact fairly to resolve conflicts in the testimony, to weigh the evidence, and to draw reasonable inferences from basic facts to ultimate facts." Thus, "*all of the evidence* is to be considered in the light most favorable to the prosecution" because the reviewing court may impinge upon jury discretion only to the extent necessary to guarantee the fundamental protection of due process of law. . . . Legal sufficiency of the evidence is a test of adequacy, not mere quantity. Sufficient evidence is such evidence, in character, weight, or amount, as will legally justify the judicial or official action demanded. . . .

Traditionally, Texas appellate courts have employed a five-zone review of civil verdicts when the burden of proof at trial is that of "preponderance of the evidence." . . . Zone 1 is the "no evidence" zone, similar to the old legal sufficiency standard rejected by the Supreme Court in *Jackson* for criminal cases. . . . If the appellate court finds "no evidence" to support the verdict, the evidence is legally insufficient, and the opponent is entitled to a judgment in his favor as a matter of law. . . .

In zone 2, the party with the burden of proof has offered some evidence in support of his claim or defense and the case is allowed to go to the jury for a verdict. But the evidence supporting the jury's verdict, while more than a "mere scintilla," is slim indeed. . . . The appellate court assumes that the party who had the burden of proof and who originally prevailed may be able to produce additional evidence at a second trial, evidence that he failed to offer at the first trial. . . .

Zone 3, the zone of reasonable disagreement, is the great middle ground, in which a verdict will be upheld for either the party with the burden of proof or the opposing party as there is conflicting evidence or inferences on either side of the vital fact issue or issues, but the jury's verdict is reasonable and does not "shock the conscience," nor it is not so "clearly unjust" to indicate obvious bias.

In zone 4, the party with the burden of proof has offered significant evidence to support the claim or defense; the great weight and preponderance of the credible evidence supports his position. However, the jury has returned a verdict in favor of the opposing party — the party without the burden of proof. [All] of the evidence, both pro and con, is set out, and the appellate court must explain why the verdict is against the great weight and preponderance of the evidence.

At the opposite end of the spectrum from zone 1 is zone 5 — "conclusive evidence" — in which the party with the burden of proof has established conclusively, or as a matter of law, that he is entitled to a judgment in his favor because the opponent has offered no evidence in opposition and the proponent has offered sufficient evidence of the vital fact or claim . . . .

In *Clewis,* this Court attempted to superimpose the five-zone civil standard of review, predicated upon trials in which the burden of proof is by a preponderance of the evidence upon the two-zone criminal standard of review that requires proof beyond a reasonable doubt. Visualizing the five-zone civil standard . . . as a football field with the "no evidence" zone at one end and with each zone comprised of an ever greater quantum of evidence offered by the party with the burden of proof until the "conclusive evidence" zone at the other end, reviewing courts are required to uphold as factually sufficient any verdict in favor of the party with the burden of proof that is at least within the third zone, that of reasonable disagreement. But in assessing the legal sufficiency of evidence in a criminal case, the State's evidence must be persuasive enough to almost make a touchdown; reaching the midfield is never enough to meet the "beyond a reasonable doubt" standard.

In a civil case, if the jury returns a verdict in favor of the party that did not have the burden of proof (usually the defendant), but that verdict is determined by the appellate court to be against the great weight and preponderance of the evidence offered by the party that did have the burden of proof (usually the plaintiff), then the appellate court may reverse the judgment and remand for a new trial. This gives the plaintiff a second opportunity to prove his case before a new jury, after the first jury had rejected his claim although he had originally produced "the great weight and preponderance of the evidence" to support its claim. That scenario would not generally arise in criminal cases because if the jury returns a verdict favoring the party without the burden of proof (the defendant), there will be no appeal because the State may not appeal an acquittal.

Similarly, if the party with the burden of proof in a civil trial (usually the plaintiff) obtains a jury verdict in its favor, but an appellate court determines that there is insufficient evidence, even when viewed in the light most favorable to the verdict, to reach "the zone of reasonable disagreement," then the appellate court may reverse the jury verdict and remand for a new trial. That scenario also would not arise in criminal cases because if the State's evidence is so weak in strength, character, and credibility that it does not reach the level of "the zone of reasonable disagreement," then it most assuredly does not meet the "beyond a reasonable doubt" standard of legal sufficiency required in all criminal cases. Such a lack of evidentiary support is not merely factually insufficient, it is legally insufficient, and the defendant cannot be required to undergo a second trial.

What this Court did in *Clewis* was adopt the language of Texas civil factual sufficiency review without first determining whether there was a proper fit between those civil standards of review and the differing evidentiary standards of proof in civil and criminal cases. . . . These two standards of review depend upon their distinctly different burdens of proof. Like oil and water, they do not mix. They are not logically consistent, and they promote only confusion and conflation of two distinct concepts. We are required to follow the heightened *Jackson* legal sufficiency formulation; we cannot follow a lesser factual sufficiency formulation. I agree that it is time to consign the civil-law concept of factual sufficiency review in criminal cases to the dustbin of history.

PRICE, J., dissenting.

. . . The plurality frames the question as a policy choice, asserting that we granted discretionary review in order to determine whether "there is a need to retain" factual sufficiency review. But as our opinion less than four years ago in *Watson* demonstrated, the authority to reverse a conviction on the basis of factual insufficiency has been recognized from the beginning to be inherent in the appellate jurisdiction of first-tier appellate courts in Texas. . . .

The plurality's primary justification for overruling *Clewis* is that, because the standards for factual sufficiency and legal sufficiency have essentially melded into one, there is no longer any "meaningful distinction between them that would justify retaining them both." But the plurality's premise is flawed. [The] difference is that the [factual sufficiency standard] views all of the evidence in a "neutral" light rather than, as in the [legal sufficiency standard], "in the light most favorable to the verdict." [The] distinction is a real one.

A holding of legally insufficient evidence — that is, that the evidence is so lacking that federal due process will not tolerate a conviction — has double jeopardy implications. Under the standard established by Jackson v. Virginia for deciding whether the evidence satisfies due process, a reviewing court "faced with a record of historical facts that supports conflicting inferences must presume — even if it does not affirmatively appear in the record — that the trier of fact resolved any such conflicts in favor of the prosecution." But this kind of categorical deference is not required of a reviewing court in Texas when conducting a non-due-process review for factual sufficiency. For a reviewing court to view the evidence in a "neutral" light means that it need not resolve every conflict in the evidence, or draw every inference from ambiguous evidence, in favor of the defendant's guilt just because a rational jury *could* have. Rational juries can also choose to acquit a defendant even when presented with legally sufficient evidence. Factual sufficiency review recognizes that there may be rare cases in which, though some jury might convict, and it would not be irrational for it to do so, most juries would almost certainly harbor a reasonable doubt given the tenuousness of the State's evidence or the weight and apparent credibility and/or reliability of the exculpatory evidence. Under these circumstances, factual sufficiency review in Texas permits a first-tier appellate court to reverse a conviction and remand for a new trial, in the interest of justice, to grant the defendant a second chance to obtain a jury acquittal.

The deference required of the appellate court in a factual sufficiency review is of a different kind than that required by legal sufficiency. It is not, as with legal sufficiency analysis, total deference to the jury's prerogative to resolve all conflicts and ambiguities in the record against the defendant. Instead, it is a qualified deference to the jury's apparent assessment of the weight, credibility, or reliability of the (admittedly legally sufficient) evidence. This deference is important because it respects the jury's fact-finding role at the trial court level. But it is not the absolute deference that legal sufficiency review affords to the jury's resolution of conflicts and ambiguities. It demands that, before a first-tier appellate court may reverse a conviction based upon factually insufficient evidence, it must be able to say, with some objective basis in the record, that the jury's verdict, while legally sufficient, is nevertheless against the great weight and preponderance of the evidence, and therefore "manifestly unjust." This does not grant an appellate judge license to declare the evidence to be factually insufficient simply because, on the quantum of evidence admitted, he would have voted to acquit had he been on the jury. . . .

Problem 20-1. Wrong Place, Wrong Time?

An undercover police officer approached an apartment on Sixth Avenue in Saginaw, Michigan, at about 8:30 P.M. on a December evening. He asked a man inside the apartment for a "$10 rock" of crack cocaine and passed two marked $5 bills through an open window. He heard some conversation inside the apartment, then received a small plastic bag containing crack cocaine. Within two hours, the undercover officer returned with a search warrant and several other officers. They found four men inside the apartment: Lemiel Wolfe, Darren Rogers, Alan Wise, and Leonard James.

When the officers entered the apartment, all four of the men in the apartment ran to the back bedroom. The officers found a loaded twelve-gauge shotgun on the floor in the front room. When the police officers entered the back bedroom of the apartment they saw Wise standing over an open vent in the floor, with the grate removed. The officers recovered 27 plastic baggies of crack cocaine from the vent, amounting to less than 50 grams of cocaine. They found no glass pipes or other paraphernalia typically used to smoke cocaine. It appeared to the officers that no one was living in the apartment. The front room contained only a couch, a refrigerator, and a broken television set. The apartment had no running water and the toilet was not in working condition. The bath tub was being used as a toilet.

The officers arrested and searched all four of the men in the apartment. Wolfe was holding $265 in cash, including the two marked $5 bills. In addition, he had a beeper and a key to the back door of the apartment. The search of Rogers revealed a piece of paper with the number of Wolfe's beeper written on it and a shotgun shell of the same type as the shotgun they found in the front room.

The government charged Wolfe and Rogers with possession with intent to deliver less than 50 grams of cocaine, and possession of a firearm during the commission of a felony. Police officers testified at trial to establish the events as described above.

Wolfe testified at trial that he went to Saginaw to visit a friend. He arrived around 6:00 P.M. that evening and went to the Sixth Avenue apartments to visit Sharon Johnson, whose relatives lived in the apartment next to the apartment where the arrest took place. Wolfe visited with her for about five minutes.

Wolfe said that he had invited several friends from Detroit (Rogers, James, and Wise) to visit Johnson. Around 8:00 P.M., he saw his Detroit friends approaching on the street outside the apartments, and he called out to them from the front porch because they were not familiar with the location. Wolfe testified that he left after a few minutes to visit another friend's house. When he returned to Sixth Avenue around 10:00 P.M., Wolfe spoke briefly with the next-door residents, then joined his friends for a party. He went to the local store for food and beer, after collecting money from the others. When Wolfe returned from the store, Leonard James repaid a prior $20 debt with four $5 bills, two of which were the marked bills that James had received earlier that night from the undercover police officer. As the group sat and watched television, Wolfe saw James smoking cocaine, but testified that he saw no other drugs in the apartment. Shortly after his return from the convenience store, the police raided the apartment and arrested Wolfe, along with several others.

Rogers testified as follows:

Q. Wolfe testified that it was about eight o'clock when he saw you. Is he correct?
A. I don't really know what time it was, but when we got there, it was about six when we saw him standing outside. . . .
Q. And how long after Wolfe came back up did he stay upstairs with you?
A. A good little while.
Q. How long is a "good little while"?
A. I'd say an hour, two hours.

Rogers also testified that Leonard James gave Wolfe the marked $5 bills before Wolfe left the Sixth Avenue apartment to visit his other friend.

Wolfe and Rogers were both convicted on both counts; Wolfe appealed. He argues that the government's evidence did not support either of the two charges, because the evidence did not prove that he possessed the cocaine with intent to distribute it, nor did it prove that he possessed a firearm. Under the case law of Michigan, the government can establish possession of cocaine by showing that the defendant physically possessed the cocaine, or that the defendant "had the right to exercise control of the cocaine and knew that it was present." A person's presence, by itself, at a location where drugs are found is insufficient to prove possession. Just as proof of actual possession of narcotics is not necessary to prove possession, actual delivery of narcotics is not required to prove intent to deliver. Intent to deliver has been inferred from the quantity of narcotics in a defendant's possession, from the way in which those narcotics are packaged, and from other circumstances surrounding the arrest.

How would you rule on appeal? Was the evidence sufficient to sustain one or both of the convictions? Was either of the convictions contrary to the weight of the evidence? Would you reach the same outcomes if the police had not found any key on Wolfe when they searched him? Compare People v. Wolfe, 489 N.W.2d 748 (Mich. 1992).

Notes

1. *Sufficiency of the evidence and weight of the evidence.* The federal due process clause, as we have seen, requires a minimum level of evidentiary support for a conviction. Prior to Jackson v. Virginia, 443 U.S. 307 (1979), appellate courts could affirm a conviction so long as there was "some evidence" to support the judgment. In *Jackson,* the Supreme Court decided that a federal court, when reviewing a state court conviction during postconviction habeas corpus proceedings, must confirm that there was sufficient evidence to support a "reasonable trier of fact" in concluding that the government had proven guilt beyond a reasonable doubt. Does this due process standard for the "sufficiency" of the evidence require the appellate court to consider the inculpatory evidence alone, or to consider it in light of the exculpatory evidence?

The "weight of the evidence" inquiry, discussed in *Brooks*, was more common years ago than it is today, but some states still grant their appellate courts this authority. Is it necessary, now that the *Jackson* test has replaced the "some evidence" test? If you were advising legislators or court personnel in a foreign jurisdiction that has recently introduced the criminal jury to its system, what sort of appellate court factual review would you recommend? For a discussion of factual review in systems outside the United States, go to the web extension for this chapter at *http://www.crimpro.com/extension/ch20*.

2. *Evidentiary review and double jeopardy.* The precise type of factual review that an appellate court uses can have double jeopardy consequences. According to Tibbs v. Florida, 457 U.S. 31 (1982), a retrial is possible after an appellate court reverses a conviction because it is contrary to the "weight of the evidence." The prosecution, in such a case, has met the constitutional minimum burden of proof during the first trial, and the defendant's appeal therefore does not bar a second trial. If the prosecution fails to present evidence sufficient to meet the *Jackson* standard in the first trial, it will not receive a second chance. Given this more favorable outcome for the state under the double jeopardy clause, should prosecutors generally favor giving to appellate courts the option of a "weight of the evidence" review? See also State v. Wright, 203 P.3d 1027 (Wash. 2009) (when appellate court reverses conviction under second-degree felony murder statute because statutory scheme did not apply to the conduct at issue, double jeopardy did not bar retrial under second-degree intentional murder statute; because jury was not instructed on intentional murder, conviction for felony murder was not an implicit acquittal on the greater crime).

3. *Video-recording and retrial after reversal*. Suppose all the testimony in a trial were presented to the jury in video-recorded format:

> [The] case would initially be tried as if the jury has been waived. The prosecution and defense would present their cases in open court with the defendant present, but without a jury. All of the proceedings would be taped. At the conclusion of the case, questions leading to sustained objections would be deleted from a copy of the tape as would any statements ruled improper in opening or closing arguments. Testimony could even be taken out of order to meet the convenience of witnesses or attorneys and edited into the tape at the correct place. Sidebars and time intensive nontestimonial activities such as legal arguments and the marking of exhibits would also be eliminated from the final tape. [A jury is impaneled] only at the end of the process to watch the taped trial and deliberate on the verdict.

Ronald Goldstock & James B. Jacobs, A Blockbuster Trial: Catch It All on Tape, Crim. Just. (Spring 1998). How might this innovation at the trial level change practices in the appellate courts? Would appellate judges, after viewing the tapes for themselves, become more willing to question factual findings? Would they become more willing to find reversible error, knowing that an error-free retrial becomes cheaper if the tape is corrected and shown to a new jury?

C. HARMLESS ERROR

"For every wrong there should be a remedy." This notion entered U.S. legal culture through the words of William Blackstone, conveyed by Chief Justice John Marshall. Marbury v. Madison, 5 U.S. (1 Cranch) 137, 163 (1803) ("it is a settled and invariable principle . . . that every right, when withheld, must have a remedy, and every injury its proper redress") (quoting 3 William Blackstone, Commentaries *109). Indeed, this principle has crystallized in many state constitutions, which include language such as Illinois Constitution article I, section 12: "Every person shall find a certain remedy in the laws for all injuries and wrongs which he receives to his person, privacy, property or reputation. He shall obtain justice by law, freely, completely, and promptly." Surely if this principle applies anywhere, it should apply to the operation of the justice system itself. If a defendant's rights are violated during trial on criminal charges, the error should be correctable on appeal.

Yet criminal trials are complex events, and few long trials occur without some error. If the remedy for every error at trial were a new trial, no major trial would ever end. But in cases where the proof is overwhelming, won't the outcome at the retrial be inevitable? Even for substantial errors, if the outcome is inevitable, why drag witnesses, jurors, and judges through a mere charade? Indeed, can there *ever* be reversible error in obvious cases?

The doctrine of harmless error aims to sort out the tension between a desire to be fair to a wronged defendant and the need to have an efficient system that focuses on errors that may have produced a wrong outcome. If stated too broadly, harmless error rules have the capacity to undermine all other procedural rules.

The U.S. Supreme Court took up this challenge in Fahy v. Connecticut, 375 U.S. 85 (1963), where the defendant was charged with willfully injuring a public building by painting swastikas on a synagogue. The Court found that the erroneous admission of an illegally seized can of paint and paintbrush was not harmless because there was "a reasonable possibility that the evidence complained of might have contributed to the conviction."

In Chapman v. California, 386 U.S. 18 (1967), the Court squarely addressed the issue of whether constitutional errors can be considered harmless. Ruth Chapman and Thomas Teale were convicted in a California state court upon a charge that they robbed, kidnapped, and murdered a bartender. At the trial, the prosecutor commented extensively on the decision by both defendants to remain silent; such comments, as we saw in Chapter 18, violate the privilege against self-incrimination. See Griffin v. California, 380 U.S. 609 (1965). In concluding that the denial of the federal rights recognized in *Griffin* amounted to harmless error in Chapman's case, the Court wrote:

> [We] do no more than adhere to the meaning of our *Fahy* case when we hold, as we now do, that before a federal constitutional error can be held harmless, the court must be able to declare a belief that it was harmless beyond a reasonable doubt. While appellate courts do not ordinarily have the original task of applying such a test, it is a familiar standard to all courts, and we believe its adoption will provide a more workable standard, although achieving the same result as that aimed at in our *Fahy* case. [386 U.S. at 22-24.]

While allowing harmless error analysis to apply to some constitutional errors, the *Chapman* Court recognized that other constitutional errors are "so basic to a fair trial that their violation can never be treated as harmless error," and cited Gideon v. Wainwright, 372 U.S. 335 (1963) (right to counsel); Payne v. Arkansas, 356 U.S. 560 (1958) (coerced confession); and Tumey v. Ohio, 273 U.S. 510 (1927) (impartial judge).

In Arizona v. Fulminante, 499 U.S. 279 (1991), the Court reconsidered whether a coerced confession was one of the errors "so basic to a fair trial" that harmless error analysis could not apply. *Fulminante* created a new conceptual divide between "trial errors," which are subject to harmless error analysis, and "structural defects," which are not.

> The admission of an involuntary confession — a classic "trial error" — is markedly different from the other two constitutional violations referred to in the *Chapman* footnote as not being subject to harmless-error analysis. One of those violations, involved in Gideon v. Wainwright, was the total deprivation of the right to counsel at trial. The other violation, involved in Tumey v. Ohio, was a judge who was not impartial. These are structural defects in the constitution of the trial mechanism, which defy analysis by "harmless-error" standards. The entire conduct of the trial from beginning to end is obviously affected by the absence of counsel for a criminal defendant, just as it is by the presence on the bench of a judge who is not impartial. Since our decision in *Chapman,* other cases have added to the category of constitutional errors which are not subject to harmless error the following: unlawful exclusion of members of the defendant's race from a grand jury, see Vasquez v. Hillery, 474 U.S. 254 (1986); the right to self-representation at trial, see McKaskle v. Wiggins, 465 U.S. 168 (1984); and the right to public trial, see Waller v. Georgia, 467 U.S. 39 (1993). Each of these constitutional deprivations is a similar structural defect affecting the framework within which the trial

proceeds, rather than simply an error in the trial process itself. Without these basic protections, a criminal trial cannot reliably serve its function as a vehicle for determination of guilt or innocence, and no criminal punishment may be regarded as fundamentally fair.

It is evident from a comparison of the constitutional violations which we have held subject to harmless error, and those which we have held not, that involuntary statements or confessions belong in the former category. . . .

States have wrestled with their own harmless error standards, which apply to any errors based in state law. Some apply a unitary rule for constitutional and nonconstitutional errors, while others apply a different standard — usually one that makes it harder to find reversible error — for nonconstitutional errors. Most states have procedural rules that limit reversible error to those errors that affect the outcome or the "substantial rights" of the defendant. Does harmless error doctrine quietly overwhelm all the meaningful procedural choices made earlier in the case?

FEDERAL RULE OF CRIMINAL PROCEDURE 52

(a) Harmless Error. Any error, defect, irregularity, or variance that does not affect substantial rights must be disregarded.

(b) Plain Error. A plain error that affects substantial rights may be considered even though it was not brought to the court's attention.

TENNESSEE RULE OF APPELLATE PROCEDURE 36(b)

Effect of Error. A final judgment from which relief is available and otherwise appropriate shall not be set aside unless, considering the whole record, error involving a substantial right more probably than not affected the judgment or would result in prejudice to the judicial process. When necessary to do substantial justice, an appellate court may consider an error that has affected the substantial rights of a party at any time, even though the error was not raised in the motion for a new trial or assigned as error on appeal.

PEOPLE v. WALTER BUDZYN

566 N.W.2d 229 (Mich. 1997)

RILEY, J.

In this appeal, we are asked to review the fairness of the trial for two police officers who were convicted of second-degree murder for killing a suspected drug user while attempting to arrest him while the suspect was holding contraband. We conclude that defendants have demonstrated that their juries were exposed to extrinsic influences that created a real and substantial possibility of prejudice, depriving them of their constitutional rights under the Sixth Amendment. These errors, however, were harmless beyond a reasonable doubt with regard to defendant Larry Nevers. Therefore, we affirm defendant Nevers' conviction. With regard to defendant Walter Budzyn, we conclude that the extrinsic influences were not harmless beyond a reasonable doubt. Accordingly, we vacate defendant Budzyn's conviction and remand for a new trial.

Defendants Budzyn and Nevers were police officers with the Detroit Police Department. They were on duty when the incident occurred that resulted in Malice Green's death. Both were tried at a single criminal proceeding with two different juries.[1]

On November 5, 1992, at approximately 10:15 P.M., defendants were patrolling in the City of Detroit in plain clothes in an unmarked vehicle. They apparently observed a Topaz, driven by Malice Green, with bullet holes in its front passenger door. Defendant Nevers, who only gave testimony before his own jury, testified that he observed the car pull up in front of a house known for its drug activity. Budzyn and Nevers stopped behind the Topaz to investigate. The home, with a storefront attached to it, was occupied by Ralph Fletcher. . . . Robert Hollins and Teresa Pace, witnesses to the event, were present at Fletcher's house and had been smoking cocaine that evening.

Defendant Budzyn, who only testified before his own jury, said that he witnessed Robert Knox running along the building and explained that he chased Knox because, apparently by mistake, he believed that Knox had been in the vehicle with Green. Budzyn caught Knox, brought him around to the front of Fletcher's place, and patted him down for weapons. He also patted down Fletcher, who had been in the car with Green. Manuel Brown, who had been smoking cocaine at Fletcher's place, was walking away from the house, but stopped to watch this activity. Nevers asked Malice Green for his driver's license. Green did not respond to Nevers' request, but walked around to the passenger side of his vehicle and got in. Green was sitting in the passenger seat, with his legs hanging out the open doorway. Budzyn came around to the passenger side, shined his flashlight on him, and asked for his license. Green began to look in the glove compartment, grasped at something that was on the floor, apparently cocaine, and Budzyn asked him to let go of what was in his hand.

At this point, there is substantial disagreement in the testimony given by defendants Budzyn and Nevers and the witnesses to the incident, Brown, Fletcher, Hollins, Knox, and Pace regarding what happened.

The five civilian witnesses testified that after Green refused to open his hand, Budzyn began to hit him repeatedly on the hand with the police flashlight, telling him to open his hand. Budzyn then climbed onto Green, who did not resist but did not comply, straddling him. Brown testified that Budzyn struck Green about ten times on his head with the flashlight. Fletcher, who was only three to five feet away, testified that Budzyn repeatedly hit Green on the hand. Hollins said that he heard Budzyn hit Green six or seven times, and, although he did not see the blows land, that these blows must have landed on Green's head. Knox said that he saw Budzyn hit Green in the hand because Green did not open it when Budzyn asked. Pace testified that from the position on which Budzyn sat on Green, he must have been hitting him on the head.

These five witnesses also said that, while Budzyn was struggling with Green in the Topaz, Nevers struck Green on his knee several times. Brown and Fletcher said

1. There were charges that their crime was racially motivated. Consequently, we note that Budzyn and Nevers are white and Malice Green is black.

that Nevers then went around to the other side of the car, the driver's side, opened the door, and struck Green, who was now lying on the front seat, on the head with his flashlight. Nevers instructed these people to leave the scene.

In contrast to this testimony, Budzyn explained to his jury that while Green was sitting in the passenger side of the vehicle, he suspected that Green was holding narcotics in his fist. He said that he grabbed Green's right arm and that Green kicked him with both his legs. He produced evidence of a small injury to his knee. Budzyn said that he turned and fell backward into the vehicle, dropping his flashlight. Budzyn denied that he ever hit Green at all. Budzyn also said that he only held Green's hands because he suspected that he was holding narcotics. Budzyn called for backup assistance. Budzyn explained that he heard "two hits" after Nevers went around to the driver's door and said that he later was "shocked" to find so much blood on the scene. Budzyn said he retrieved four rocks of cocaine from inside the vehicle.

Like Budzyn, Nevers testified to his jury that he assisted Budzyn when Green resisted Budzyn's efforts to open his hand. Nevers explained that he only hit Green on his knees when Green brought his knees up to stop Nevers from prying open his hand. Nevers then went to the other side of the vehicle because Budzyn told him that Green was attempting to get out of the other side of the car. Nevers then told the people from Fletcher's place to leave. Nevers explained that he hit Green in the head with his flashlight because Green was grabbing for his gun. Nevers said that after he struck him, "[Green] finally let go of my gun and I did not hit him [again]" at that time. Nevers flagged down the EMS medical technicians who had been called to the scene. Green continued to struggle with the officers and Nevers said he saw something "shiny" in Green's right hand and he struck him again, the blow landing on Green's head, because Nevers feared he might be carrying a razor blade or knife. Nevers admitted that, during the course of the incident he hit Green five or six times on the head with his flashlight.

The EMS medical technicians arrived in two vehicles. The first to arrive were Albino Martinez and Mithyim Lewis. The other EMS vehicle soon arrived with two other medical technicians, Lee Hardy and Scott Walsh. Several marked police cars arrived soon after the EMS vehicles. Martinez, Lewis, Hardy, and Walsh all testified that Green was covered with blood and was hanging from the driver's side door when they arrived. There was a pool of blood under his head on the street. These witnesses said that Nevers struck Green in the head with his heavy police flashlight repeatedly even though Green was not offering any significant resistance. Martinez and Walsh said that Nevers told Green to open his hands and hold still, and that, when he did not, Nevers hit him with the flashlight. Martinez and Lewis said that Nevers hit Green four times in the head with the flashlight, while Hardy said he saw Nevers hit Green approximately ten times in the head. Martinez explained that Green was "dazed," and Hardy described him as "stuporous," relating that Green was uttering only a few words like "wait" while Nevers was striking him.

Officer Robert Lessnau, who arrived on the scene in one of the marked police vehicles, pulled Green from the vehicle. The EMS medical technicians testified that Lessnau hit Green with his fists. Martinez and Walsh said that while Lessnau was striking Green, Nevers also hit Green twice in the ribs. Green finally released the car keys he held in one hand and a piece of white paper, apparently for rolling rock cocaine, he held in the other. The uniformed officers, including Sergeant Freddie Douglas, then cuffed Green's hands behind his back as Green struggled. The EMS medical technicians began rendering care to Green. Green suffered a seizure and, soon after, died.

The people presented Dr. Kalil Jiraki, an assistant Wayne County Medical Examiner, as a medical expert to testify regarding the nature of Green's wounds and the cause of his death. Dr. Jiraki testified that Green died from blunt force trauma to his head and that he suffered at least fourteen blows to the head. Dr. Jiraki also explained that Green had 0.5 micrograms of cocaine in his body, indicating that he was under the influence of cocaine at the time of his death. He concluded, however, that it had "no bearing on the cause of his death." In response, defendants presented three pathologists, one of whom, Dr. L. G. Dragovic, testified that he identified eleven blunt-force injuries to Green's head.

Budzyn and Nevers were charged with second-degree murder. Beginning with the first reports of Green's death, the case produced a firestorm of media publicity in the Detroit metropolitan area. The incident occurred soon after the California state courts acquitted four white Los Angeles police officers who had been videotaped beating black motorist Rodney King. The acquittal in the King case resulted in a terrible riot in Los Angeles that drew the attention of the national media. The media reports in Detroit of Green's death included a comparison of the two incidents. Before the trial began, the Detroit Police Department fired defendants. The City of Detroit also agreed to a multimillion dollar settlement with Green's estate. In response to some criticisms of the settlement, a city attorney stated that a generous settlement might spare the city the riotous violence that racked Los Angeles after the acquittal of the police officers. These events occurred during the interval between Green's death in November 1992 and the start of defendants' trial in June 1993, seven months later.

Defendants moved to sever the trials, and the trial court refused to separate the proceedings, but did grant defendants separate juries. Nevers asked for a change of venue because of the extensive pretrial publicity, but the trial court denied this motion. The trial court began the voir dire on June 2, 1993. The people began presenting their case on June 18, 1993. During a recess near the end of trial, on August 5 and 6, 1993, the trial court provided the juries with several film videos to watch to entertain themselves, including a copy of *Malcolm X.* The film begins with a video of the Los Angeles police officers beating Rodney King. Defendants moved for a mistrial on this basis, but this motion was denied.[7]

After approximately seven weeks of trial, the juries began deliberating on August 13, 1993. Budzyn and Nevers were convicted of second-degree murder. The jury in Budzyn's trial deliberated for eight days, and, in Nevers' trial, the jury deliberated for nine days. . . .

[The supreme court held that defendants had been denied their right to a fair and impartial jury because they considered extraneous facts not introduced into evidence. It was undisputed that the jurors watched the film *Malcolm X*; it was also alleged that jurors were made aware of city plans to handle riots after the verdict and that defendants had been involved in a special police anti-drug unit. The film begins with the voice of *Malcolm X*'s character giving a provocative speech charging

7. The trial judge did not select the movies or approve the selections himself, but he took responsibility for the action taken by the employees of the court. The trial judge disqualified himself on ruling on defendants' motion. The Chief Judge of Recorder's Court referred the motion to a third judge who heard the motion and denied it.

"the white man with being the greatest murderer on earth" while the viewer is shown footage of Rodney King being beaten by Los Angeles police officers, interspersed with a picture of an American flag. The Rodney King videotape is shown in slow motion, in eight segments, as the American flag begins to burn. The voiceover makes an explicit reference to Detroit, the location of the incident in the instant case, by stating that the black community has been deprived of democracy in the "streets of Detroit." At another point in the film Malcolm X confronts the police, who finally relent and allow him to call an ambulance and take a bleeding man from the police station to the hospital; Malcolm X says "A hundred years ago, they used to put on white sheets and sic bloodhounds on us. Well, nowadays they've traded in the sheets — well, some of them traded in sheets — . . . they have traded in those white sheets for police uniforms. They've traded in the bloodhounds for the police dogs. . . . You've got these Uncle Tom Negro leaders today that are telling us we ought to pray for our enemy. We ought to love our enemy. We ought to integrate with an enemy who bombs us, who kills and shoots us, who lynches us, who rapes our women and children. No!"]

[We] must decide whether any error was harmless beyond a reasonable doubt. There is no dispute that the extrinsic evidence was not duplicative of other properly admitted evidence for either defendant. Hence, we must determine whether the evidence against defendants was overwhelming. We believe that these extraneous influences were harmless for defendant Nevers in light of the overwhelming evidence of his guilt, but that the errors do require reversal for defendant Budzyn because the evidence against him was not overwhelming.

In the Nevers trial, the four EMS witnesses, who had no apparent motive to lie, provided interlocking testimony that Nevers repeatedly bludgeoned Malice Green in the head with his heavy police flashlight while Green was dazed and not offering significant resistance. The medical testimony of the injuries to Green's head also substantiated this testimony. The people have proven that there was unimpeachable, compelling evidence that defendant Nevers harbored, at the very least, an unjustified intent to commit great bodily harm against Green. Thus, . . . the extraneous influences were harmless. . . . In Budzyn's trial, however, we believe that the evidence against defendant Budzyn, particularly considering he was convicted of second-degree murder, was not overwhelming. The evidence against him was fundamentally weaker than the evidence against Nevers for three reasons.

First, of the three civilian witnesses who testified that defendant Budzyn hit Green in the head with his flashlight (Manuel Brown, Robert Hollins, and Teresa Pace), none was able to see the flashlight actually make contact with Green's head. Unlike the EMS witnesses, they did not have a direct view of the blows. Instead, the three witnesses each inferred the fact that the flashlight hit Green in the head from the positions of the two men in the vehicle and from Budzyn's use of the flashlight to strike Green. Brown, who arguably gave the most damaging testimony of any witness, was the farthest witness away, standing fifteen feet from Fletcher, Hollins, Knox, and Pace.

This testimony also contained some inconsistencies. The three key witnesses who testified that Budzyn hit Green on the head with his flashlight gave conflicting testimony on the nature of the blows that Budzyn administered: Pace and Hollins testified that Budzyn lifted the flashlight above his head or shoulders and brought the flashlight down, while Brown insisted that the blows were horizontal, across his body, and that Budzyn did not lift the flashlight above his head. Also, Fletcher, who was only three to five feet away and was the closest of the witnesses to the incident, testified that Budzyn hit Green's clenched fist with the flashlight, but that he did not see Budzyn hit Green anywhere else on his body.

Second, the civilian witnesses admitted that the altercation occurred after Green refused Budzyn's request that he turn over the incriminating evidence he held in his hand. The civilian witnesses all agreed that Green never complied and that he struggled with Budzyn, although they said he never struck him or kicked him. In fact, Fletcher testified that during the entire episode, Budzyn held onto Green's closed fist, attempting to retrieve the contraband. This is a very different setting from the description the EMS medical technicians gave of the situation in which defendant Nevers was striking Green in the head. Because the exchange occurred in the confined context of the car with the car obscuring the witnesses' view, their testimony that Green did not kick Budzyn does not directly rebut his claim that Green did. The medical evidence also does not necessarily contradict Budzyn's claims, because Nevers hit Green with significant force in the head and these blows may have been the cause of Green's extensive head injuries.

Third, in this credibility contest between Budzyn and these witnesses, the civilian witnesses all had either consumed alcohol or cocaine sometime before witnessing the exchange, three of them were friends with Green (Fletcher, Hollins, and Pace), and there was some suggestion from their testimony that they had reason to dislike these officers. This fact is relevant because an inquiry into whether an error was harmless requires a focus on the nature of the error in light of the weight and strength of the other evidence. People v. Mateo, 551 N.W.2d 891 (Mich. 1996). Defendant Budzyn had searched Fletcher and Knox for weapons before defendant Nevers asked to see Malice Green's driver's license. Defendant Budzyn had also broken into Fletcher's home while Fletcher and Hollins among others were there, a week and a half before this incident, searching the house without warrant, and, on another occasion, had arrested two people outside the house. Thus, these witnesses were not in the same objective position as the EMS medical technicians, who, incidentally, did not offer any testimony regarding Budzyn's actions against Green because they had not yet arrived on the scene.

Even if the jury reasonably believed the testimony of the civilian witnesses, they still might not have concluded that Budzyn was guilty of second-degree murder. The question whether Budzyn's unnecessary use of force as described by the civilian witnesses would be second-degree murder or manslaughter is an issue for the jury. We do not believe that the only, possible reasonable conclusion to draw from this evidence is that it established beyond a reasonable doubt that he harbored an intent to kill, an intent to do great bodily harm, or to commit an act in wanton and wilful disregard that the likelihood that the natural tendency of his conduct was to cause death or great bodily harm. In contrast, the testimony from the EMS medical technicians against Nevers made the conclusion inescapable that he was guilty of second-degree murder. We cannot say that the extraneous factors may not have affected the Budzyn jury's verdict. We, therefore, reverse his conviction and remand for a new trial. . . .

BOYLE, J., concurring in part and dissenting in part.

I agree with the majority's result and rationale with regard to defendant Nevers, and its result in respect to defendant Budzyn. I write separately to explain my disagreement with certain aspects of the rationale in Budzyn.

First, despite differences of origin, history, class, education, race, ethnicity, sex, economic status, or educational level, it is a fundamental presumption of the judicial system that all Americans are equally capable of fairly discharging their public responsibilities. Batson v. Kentucky, 476 U.S. 79 (1986). Therefore, I disagree with the analysis of the opinions of both Chief Justice Mallett and Justice Riley regarding the showing of the movie, *Malcolm X,* to the extent that each employs assumptions about the predispositions of jurors. The system addresses the mind-set of jurors through voir dire, challenges for cause, and motions for change of venue, all of which require a demonstration of reasons why a prospective juror or a given community may be suspect. The approach is both aspirational and pragmatic. The judiciary has no competence to assess the cultural or psychological mind-set of a given jury and assess its reactions in light of its own assumptions. I also agree with the prosecution that the movie was not an extraneous communication, and find no error in this regard. . . .

However, I agree with the majority that the communication of incorrect information to the jurors during deliberations that defendant Budzyn was a member of STRESS [the special police anti-drug unit] was error requiring reversal. . . . Evaluated in the context of the evidence as a whole, the prejudicial significance is that Budzyn's membership in STRESS indicated a propensity for abuse of young black males. By all accounts, Green had what turned out to be cocaine in his hands and refused to surrender it. Thus, Budzyn's initiation of force against Green was lawful, whichever version of the testimony is believed. The issue in Nevers' trial turned on whether the jury believed Nevers' testimony that the deceased was trying to take his gun, thus justifying the life-threatening response. The issue in Budzyn's trial, by contrast, was whether, and at what point, the lawful use of force became unreasonable.

In substance, the jurors were told that Budzyn was a bad actor with a propensity for violence against young black men. Coupled with other evidence admitted at trial, this information could have persuaded the jurors that Budzyn had a man-endangering state of mind. Thus, it is not only the fact, as the majority observes, that this evidence was relevant to besmirching the defendant's character, but the fact that this information supported the prosecution's theory that defendant was guilty of second-degree murder, that is prejudicial.

Our responsibility is not to decide what we would have done or what we think the jury should have done. It is to hypothesize what the jury would have done had it not been exposed to the extrinsic information. Because there was substantial and real prejudice, I cannot conclude that the error was harmless beyond a reasonable doubt. I join in the opinion for reversal of defendant Budzyn's conviction of second-degree murder. I would affirm the conviction of defendant Nevers.

MALLETT, C.J., concurring in part and dissenting in part.

. . . The issues of greatest concern to both the majority and to myself relate to whether defendants were denied their right to a fair trial as a result of exposure to certain extraneous influences. In particular, I am most concerned with the jurors' exposure to the movie *Malcolm X* and to media accounts of contingency plans of suburban law enforcement in case of a riot. . . . Extensive media coverage continued through the trial, including reports speculating on contingency plans in place in the event of postverdict rioting. Jurors on both Budzyn's and Nevers' panels were exposed to portions of these reports.

[Beyond] showing exposure to an extraneous influence, the defendants . . . must make a showing of prejudice reverberating from the extraneous information. The test for determining whether the threshold level of prejudice is met is whether defendants have established a real and substantial possibility that the extraneous matter could have affected the verdict.

The first factor in this threshold inquiry is the nature and source of the extraneous material. The defendants focus their claim of prejudice resulting from the showing of *Malcolm X* on the opening footage of the movie. In an attempt to make his movie more provocative, producer-director Spike Lee presents opening footage of the beating of motorist Rodney King by Los Angeles police officers against the backdrop of a burning American flag. Along with these images, the viewer hears words from a speech by Malcolm X. Virtually every person in America had been exposed to the footage detailing the brutal beating given Mr. King by members of the Los Angeles Police Department. While it was unfortunate that the jurors were perhaps once again confronted with this footage, is it the defendants' position that the jurors became inflamed and were engulfed by emotion and thus rendered incapable of rendering a fair verdict? The possibility that a few police officers will absolutely violate department rules and procedures is never far from the minds of African-Americans, no matter their station in life. The presence of racism in any community can, and sometimes does, cause American citizens to react emotionally and render less than clear judgment. But there is no reasonable probability that the Rodney King footage affected the jurors in this case.

Racism has not and will not quell the desire of African-Americans to fully exercise all the rights and responsibilities associated with democracy. If this were not true, then the four-hundred-year-old struggle for freedom and economic opportunity would have been abandoned long ago. The defendants have not established that the picture of one black man being beaten by police officers could reasonably have prevented the jurors from rendering a fair verdict.

The words of Malcolm X in the opening sequence are indeed provocative.[12] But when these words are taken in the context of the effect of the overall message of the movie, their effect is greatly lessened. Please be clear, I do not dismiss the power of words. I do dismiss the conclusion that there is a real and substantial possibility that conscientious jurors watching this movie, shown during a recess purely for entertainment purposes, would have allowed it to affect their verdict. . . .

Regarding the nature and source of this extraneous influence, the defendants emphasize that the movie was supplied by the court; this factor alone is not determinative. While this fact does tend to bolster the movie's potential prejudicial effect, the nature of this particular extraneous influence weighs heavily against a finding of prejudice. The movie was chosen by the jurors from three others made available to them purely for purposes of entertainment. The jurors should be credited with enough sophistication to separate entertainment from evidence. . . .

I would further find that, even if the defendants had met their initial burden, a reversal is not required here because it can be said, beyond a reasonable doubt, that the other evidence adduced at trial was so overwhelming that there is no real and

12. For example: "Brothers and Sisters, I am here to tell you that I charge the white man, I charge the white man with being the greatest murderer on earth. . . . I charge him with being the greatest kidnapper on earth. . . . We didn't see any democracy on the streets of Harlem . . . on the streets of Detroit. . . . We've experienced only the American nightmare."

substantial possibility that viewing the movie might have contributed to the convictions. I respectfully disagree with the majority's conclusion that the evidence supporting second-degree murder against defendant Budzyn was not overwhelming. [All] five of the eyewitnesses, Fletcher, Pace, Hollins, Brown, and Knox, testified that Budzyn initiated the beating by repeatedly striking Green on the hands. Witnesses Pace and Hollins, who observed the scene from essentially the same vantage point, saw Budzyn swinging his flashlight over his shoulder down toward Green in the direction of Green's head. They both testified that on the basis of the positioning of Budzyn and Green, and the sound of impact, it appeared that Budzyn was repeatedly hitting Green on the head with his flashlight. Further, eye-witness Brown, who observed the scene from a different vantage point, standing on the curb at a slight elevation and to the rear of the car, testified that he actually saw Budzyn strike Green on the head with the flashlight several times. Witness Fletcher's testimony, which did not indicate that Budzyn's blows appeared to land on Green's head, was not necessarily inconsistent with the conclusion of the other witnesses. Fletcher explained that he did not see everything that transpired after observing the blows to Green's hand and after Budzyn positioned himself further into the car on top of Green because Officer Budzyn was positioned in a way that obstructed his view for a period.

I cannot help but conclude that the evidence concerning Budzyn's actions was overwhelming to support the verdict of second-degree murder. This conclusion would not be different even if, as the majority suggests, the injuries actually causing Green's death could have been inflicted solely by Nevers. While Budzyn's actions were perhaps less brutal than Nevers', he initiated the encounter with Green that ultimately resulted in Green's death. His actions went far beyond the level of force necessary in the situation. Rather than calling his partner to assist him in pulling Mr. Green out of the car and handcuffing him, Officer Budzyn exerted excessive force in attempting to get Green to open his clenched fist. Further, Budzyn did not step in to stop Nevers' beating of Green when Nevers continued the beating with actions that were clearly an unjustified and brutal show of force.

The majority attempts to discount the evidence against Budzyn by questioning the credibility of the eyewitnesses. It may or may not be true that because each of these witnesses had been implicated in criminal activity, or because they may have smoked cocaine or consumed alcohol before witnessing the events leading up to Green's death, they were less credible than the EMS witnesses who testified against defendant Nevers. This Court, however, is not in a position to judge the relative credibility of the witnesses against the two officers. The jurors heard the testimony from eyewitnesses Pace, Hollins, Brown, and Fletcher, all of whom were subjected to thorough cross-examination, and evidently found it to be credible. . . .

I recognize that the great majority of police officers conscientiously perform their duties with the utmost regard for the rights of those they seek to protect. However, when police officers cross over the line from keepers of the peace and protectors of lives to aggressors, exerting force far beyond that required in the given situation, the law must treat them no differently than other defendants.

The right to a fair trial by an impartial jury is of paramount importance in securing our liberty. Consequently, this Court has properly taken very seriously the defendants' claims that their juries' exposure to extraneous influences denied them this right. After careful review however, I am left with the distinct and firm impression that the defendants received a fair trial. The potential prejudice from the asserted influences is real. However, it does not rise to a level sufficient to persuade me of a real and substantial possibility that the verdicts were affected. Additionally, given the overwhelming evidence supporting the verdicts, it can be said, beyond a reasonable doubt, that these influences did not contribute to the verdicts.

Problem 20-2. Preserving Error

On an October afternoon, two men wearing dark jeans and hooded pullover sweatshirts entered the lobby of a hotel on South Lake Shore Drive in Chicago. According to Angela Eiland, the hotel's front desk supervisor, one man was around six feet tall, and the other man was shorter, "probably around five-five." Though the hoods covered their foreheads, Eiland observed that the taller man had a missing tooth; the shorter man had a darker complexion and an unshaven face. Eiland asked if she could help them, and the shorter man replied, "Give me the money." He jumped over the counter with a gray cotton bag, while the taller man pointed a gun at her. Eiland opened the register, and the shorter man grabbed the money and turned toward the back office just as Lisa Brooks, hostess of the hotel restaurant, was leaving the office. The shorter man grabbed Brooks and pulled her back into the office. The taller man kept the gun pointed at Eiland.

Robert Comanse, the hotel's front office manager, heard a commotion and left his office, which was adjacent to the back office, to investigate. When he entered the back office, he saw the shorter man holding Brooks' arm. Comanse later described the shorter man as 5 foot 10 or 11 inches tall with spotty facial hair. As Comanse walked by Brooks on his way to the lobby, Brooks told Comanse that the man was a robber. Comanse, close enough to the man to smell his breath, laughed. The man put a gun in his face and said, "This is real. It's a real gun." He ordered Comanse and Brooks to lie face down on the floor. The shorter man demanded, "Where's the money?" Comanse answered that there was no money in the office; the rest of the hotel's money was locked in a safe downstairs.

Outside the lobby Robert Priester, the hotel's director of security, was waiting to accompany Brooks with her "bank" money to open the restaurant. Priester entered the lobby and approached Eiland to determine why Brooks was delayed. The taller man backed away from the desk, and Eiland mouthed the words to Priester that the hotel was being robbed. Priester turned toward the taller man and asked what he was doing. A struggle ensued. The taller man shouted, "They got me, G," and a gunshot rang through the lobby. Priester slumped down, bleeding from his neck. The two men fled. Priester died within hours at Northwestern Memorial Hospital.

Comanse told the police that he had never seen the robbers before, but described the man in the back office as 5 feet, 10 inches or 5 feet, 11 inches tall, wearing a black hooded sweatshirt covering his hair but not his face. Comanse said that he viewed the man's face for approximately 20 to 25 seconds before he laid face down on the floor. He viewed a photo lineup that day, but did not identify anyone.

Fifteen months later, the police investigation of the shooting led to James Brisbon. After interviewing Brisbon, the police started looking for two additional suspects, Nakia Herron and Kenneth Durant. Herron voluntarily came to the police station to participate in several lineups. Though Brooks could not identify anyone, the police still arrested Herron. The next day, Herron spoke with a Chicago police detective on the way to the lockup, saying that he had gone to the hotel with Brisbon and another person, but that he stayed outside while Brisbon and the other person went inside. Two weeks later, in another lineup, Eiland identified Durant as the taller man, but she did not identify Herron as one of the robbers. Comanse identified Herron as the shorter man in the hotel.

After the close of evidence at Herron's trial, the parties discussed jury instructions. The following exchange occurred:

Assistant State's Attorney: No. 10 is IPI Criminal No. 3.15.
The Court: That has all the points in it?
Assistant State's Attorney: Yes.
Defense Counsel: Okay. No objection, judge.

The bulk of the State and defense closing arguments centered around the reliability of eyewitness identifications. In instructing the jury, the trial court recited Illinois Pattern Instruction, Criminal, No. 3.15, as follows:

> When you weigh the identification testimony of a witness, you should consider all the facts and circumstances in evidence, including, but not limited to, the following: The opportunity the witness had to view the offender at the time of the offense *or* the witness's degree of attention at the time of the offense *or* the witness's earlier description of the offender *or* the level of certainty shown by the witness when confronting the defendant *or* the length of time between the offense and the identification confrontation.

The jury found the defendant guilty of first-degree murder and armed robbery. The trial court denied the defendant's motion for a new trial, amended motion for a new trial, and motion to reconsider sentence.

The defendant appealed, arguing that the trial court erred in its reading of the pattern instruction. Specifically, the defendant charged that the trial court's use of the word "or" between the listed factors signaled that the jury could find an eyewitness's testimony reliable based on a single factor. The defendant acknowledged that he did not object to the instruction at trial or in a post trial motion. Instead, he argued that the appellate court should consider this forfeited issue under the plain-error doctrine.

Will the appellate court hear the argument on the merits? Assuming the legal argument about the jury instruction is correct, will the appellate court reverse the conviction? Cf. People v. Herron, 830 N.E.2d 467 (Ill. 2005).

Notes

1. *Harmless error standards: majority position.* State and federal courts vary widely in the details of their harmless error standards, but most courts apply variations on the standards enunciated by the Supreme Court in *Fahy, Chapman*, and *Sullivan*. Was the U.S. Supreme Court correct when it asserted that the *Chapman* standard assessing whether the errors were harmless "beyond a reasonable doubt" was the same as in *Fahy,* where the test of harmless error was "whether there is a reasonable possibility that the evidence complained of might have contributed to the conviction"? Compare the *Chapman* standard to the newer formulation in Sullivan v. Louisiana,

508 U.S. 275 (1993): The inquiry "is not whether, in a trial that occurred without the error, a guilty verdict would surely have been rendered, but whether the guilty verdict actually rendered in this trial was surely unattributable to the error." What other standards might courts use? What factors might argue for a standard even more restrictive than "harmless beyond a reasonable doubt"? See State v. Van Kirk, 32 P.3d 735 (Mont. 2001) (applies "cumulative evidence" approach rather than "overwhelming" weight of evidence approach; question is whether fact finder was presented with admissible evidence that proved same facts as tainted evidence proved).

According to Kotteakos v. United States, 328 U.S. 750 (1946), the "harmless error" standard that applies to nonconstitutional errors is slightly different. Nonconstitutional error is harmless only when "the error did not influence the jury, or had but very slight effect." Some states create separate standards for reviewing constitutional and nonconstitutional errors. See State v. Barr, 210 P.3d 198 (N.M. 2009). Most states, however, apply a single standard to both types of error, following the unitary direction of rules like the federal and Tennessee procedure rules printed above.

2. *Applying the standard.* One striking feature of harmless error review is how often appellate courts apply the concept, without explanation, to affirm judgments after even substantial errors. Even when harmless error is the central question and there is detailed analysis of the facts, as in *Budzyn,* courts treat the standard of review as so well established that it does not require restating.

But we can learn as much from what courts do as from what they say. A study by Landes and Posner, based on a sample of over 1,000 federal appeals, identifies patterns in the outcomes of harmless error cases even if the court opinions do not themselves offer much analysis. Intentional prosecutor and judge errors are more likely than inadvertent errors to be found harmful. Appellate courts are more likely to ignore prosecutor errors than judge errors, possibly because judge errors have a greater influence on jurors. William M. Landes & Richard A. Posner, Harmless Error, 30 J. Legal Stud. 161 (2001).

3. *Structural and trial error.* As we have seen, courts classify errors under two headings: "trial" errors, which are subject to harmless error analysis, and "structural" errors, which call for automatic reversal. See Gonzalez-Lopez v. United States, 548 U.S. 140 (2006) (trial court's violation of a defendant's Sixth Amendment right to be represented by paid counsel of choice amounts to structural error; remedy is reversal of conviction without a showing of prejudice). For a sampling of the state court rulings on this issue, go to the web extension for this chapter at *http://www.crimpro.com/extension/ch20*.

One of the most common and difficult harmless error problems arises in assessing the impact of improper jury instructions. The U.S. Supreme Court has wrestled for at least a decade with whether different kinds of instructional error should be subject to harmless error analysis. In Sullivan v. Louisiana, 508 U.S. 275 (1993), a unanimous Court held that a constitutionally defective reasonable-doubt instruction was a "structural error" not subject to harmless error analysis. Most states, however, continue to apply harmless error analysis to most instructional errors. Compare People v. Harris, 886 P.2d 1193 (Cal. 1994) (misinstruction on elements of robbery harmless error) with Commonwealth v. Conefrey, 650 N.E.2d 1268 (Mass. 1995) (harmless error does not apply to failure to give "unanimity" instruction to jury). Other deviations from the usual procedure for empanelling and instructing a jury are very often deemed to be structural errors in the trial. See

State v. LaMere, 2 P.3d 204 (Mont. 2000) (summoning jurors by telephone rather than by mail in violation of statute governing juror summonses requires automatic reversal).

4. *The capacity of harmless error to make procedure irrelevant.* If a harmless error standard allows many cases with clear trial error to be immune from appellate review, then the justice system may lose the shaping function of appellate courts. See Sam Kamin, Harmless Error and the Rights/Remedies Split, 88 Va. L. Rev. 1 (2002). Are not cases that are obvious most likely to be subject to guilty pleas? Are trials — at least difficult or long ones — ever so obvious that the outcome would be the same regardless of how the evidence was presented or the approach taken by the lawyers?

5. *Procedural forfeiture of error*. The defendant typically must object to an error at trial or raise the objection in a post trial motion for a new trial. If defense counsel fails to take the proper steps at trial (or during pretrial proceedings) to "preserve" the error for appellate review, the appellate courts might never hear the issue. This failure to follow proper procedures at trial can block the appellate court from hearing some errors that could have survived a harmless error test. What purposes could such a limit on appellate review serve? It is commonly justified as a way to give trial judges the chance to correct errors before they become too costly, and to prevent defense counsel from remaining silent about the errors they observe, creating an insurance policy if the jury happens to convict (a strategy known as "sandbagging"). The rules are also said to encourage the creation of complete appellate records. Is this rule about the scope of appellate review too remote from events at trial to have these desired effects?

6. *Plain error.* As Problem 20-2 indicates, an error not brought to the attention of the trial judge for immediate correction usually cannot form the basis for a later appeal. However, appellate courts make an exception for "plain error," as described in the Tennessee rule reprinted above. If the error is plain, the appellate court will ignore the procedural failure of the defense counsel to preserve the error at trial. While the "harmless error" doctrine often involves constitutional arguments, "plain error" is treated as a matter of common law interpretation of the procedural rules. See Puckett v. United States, 129 S. Ct. 1423 (2009) (federal defendant claimed on appeal that government breached plea agreement, but failed to raise issue in district court; defendant must demonstrate plain error under Fed. R. Crim. P. 52); United States v. Cotton, 535 U.S. 625 (2002) (omission from federal indictment of a fact that enhances the statutory maximum sentence does not amount to plain error).

D. RETROACTIVITY

When lower courts violate rules of law announced in later appellate decisions, appellate courts are sometimes willing to ignore those errors by saying that the new rule of law will not receive "retroactive" application. The question of which appellate decisions should receive retroactive application seems simple — and until the middle of this century, it was. Common law systems operated on the assumption that courts "found" the law, and therefore each decision reflected law already in existence. Since the law existed before, during, and after a court's decision, it applied "retroactively" to other active cases, and perhaps (through postconviction review such as habeas corpus) even to defendants who have concluded their direct appeals (sometimes many years ago).

We no longer live in such innocent times. Since the middle of the twentieth century, legal realism has led lawyers and judges to recognize that courts make law, at least interstitially. In light of this honest assessment, some courts have declared that their own rulings will have only prospective application (like statutes) or only limited retroactive effect.

Although the view of judges as law makers has evolved over time, the common law has always recognized legislatures as law "makers" rather than law "finders," and thus statutes were presumed to apply only prospectively. Constitutional doctrine bolstered this assumption: The "ex post facto clause" barred legislation that enhanced the punishment for a prior act.

Compare the two cases below and the retroactivity limits they place on judges and legislatures. Do legislatures think differently about laws because they are limited to prospective application? Do courts think differently about their rulings if decisions are generally applied retroactively?

■ STATE v. CURTIS KNIGHT

678 A.2d 642 (N.J. 1996)

STEIN, J.

After a jury trial, defendant, Curtis Knight, was convicted of first-degree murder, third-degree possession of a weapon for an unlawful purpose, and fourth-degree unlawful possession of a weapon. The Appellate Division reversed defendant's convictions [because] the admission into evidence of defendant's statement to his arresting officer violated defendant's state constitutional right to counsel as construed in State v. Sanchez, 609 A.2d 400 (N.J. 1992). In *Sanchez*, we held that mere recitation of the *Miranda* warnings does not provide an indicted defendant with information sufficient to make a knowing and intelligent waiver of the right to counsel. Recognizing that *Sanchez* was decided after Knight's trial had concluded, the Appellate Division nevertheless determined that the *Sanchez* rule applies retroactively and requires the reversal of Knight's convictions. . . . We affirm.

In March 1990, defendant was tried along with Cesar Glenn for the murder of Glenn Brown, who was also known as Hassan. The State contended that Cesar Glenn held Brown while defendant beat him to death with a pipe. [Because] defendant and his girlfriend, Kathy Capella, had moved to California in October of 1988, New Jersey law enforcement authorities had been unable to find defendant prior to or after his indictment. On October 25, 1989, F.B.I. Agent Mark Wilson and local police officers located and apprehended defendant in Palmdale, California. . . . According to Wilson, defendant waived his *Miranda* rights and stated that while he was living in New Jersey he had been robbed by Brown. After the robbery, defendant learned that someone named Rahaem or Knight had beaten up Brown and inflicted serious injuries in the process. Brown's friends apparently believed that defendant was the culprit, and were looking for defendant to exact revenge for the beating. Defendant thus explained to Wilson that he left New Jersey because he feared for his life and that he did not know that the police were looking for him. Although defendant's explanation was not directly inculpatory, at trial the State used defendant's story to connect him to Brown and to argue that defendant killed Brown to get revenge for the robbery. . . . The jury found defendant guilty of all charged offenses: first-degree murder, fourth-degree unlawful possession of a weapon, and third-degree possession of a weapon for an unlawful purpose.

[Knight] contends that his statement to F.B.I. Agent Wilson should not have been admitted into evidence at trial because defendant had not validly waived his right to counsel before speaking with Wilson. The resolution of that issue turns on whether State v. Sanchez, 609 A.2d 400 (N.J. 1992), which we decided after Knight's trial had concluded but before the Appellate Division had ruled on his appeal, applies retroactively to this case. . . .

This Court has four options in any case in which it must determine the retroactive effect of a new rule of criminal procedure. The Court may decide to apply the new rule purely prospectively, applying it only to cases in which the operative facts arise after the new rule has been announced. Alternatively, the Court may apply the new rule in future cases and in the case in which the rule is announced, but not in any other litigation that is pending or has reached final judgment at the time the new rule is set forth. A third option is to give the new rule "pipeline retroactivity," rendering it applicable in all future cases, the case in which the rule is announced, and any cases still on direct appeal. Finally, the Court may give the new rule complete retroactive effect, applying it to all cases, including those in which final judgments have been entered and all other avenues of appeal have been exhausted.

However, before a court chooses from among those four options, it customarily engages in the threshold inquiry of whether the rule at issue is a "new rule of law" for purposes of retroactivity analysis. Our cases have recognized that if a ruling does not involve a "departure from existing law," the retroactivity question never arises and our power to limit the retroactive effect of a decision is not implicated. That approach apparently stems from the concept, prevalent at common law, that the duty of courts was not to pronounce new law but rather to "maintain and expound" extant judicial rulings. See Linkletter v. Walker, 381 U.S. 618, 622 (1965) (quoting 1 William Blackstone, Commentaries 69 (15th ed. 1809)). A court could "discover" what the law had always been, but it could not create new law. The recognition that the retrospective effect of a judicial ruling could be restricted was unknown to the common-law courts and incompatible with the common-law view that an overruled holding was not bad law, it was simply never the law. In time, however, courts came to accept that some decisions represent a break from prior jurisprudence, and that to apply such new rules retroactively could inflict unjustified burdens on the courts and law enforcement personnel.

In State v. Lark, 567 A.2d 197 (N.J. 1989), we discouraged undue emphasis on the old rule/new rule distinction, and noted our reluctance to decide retroactivity questions on the basis of the now-discredited common-law view of law as "perpetual and immutable." [We] cited approvingly the federal Supreme Court's broad definition of "new rule" that provides that a "case announces a new rule when it breaks new ground or imposes a new obligation on the States or the Federal Government [or] if the result was not dictated by precedent existing at the time the defendant's conviction became final." Teague v. Lane, 489 U.S. 288, 301 (1989). Moreover, we held that a decision involving an "accepted legal principle" announces a new rule for retroactivity purposes so long as the decision's application of that general principle is "sufficiently novel and unanticipated."

If a decision indeed sets forth a "new rule," three factors generally are considered to determine whether the rule is to be applied retroactively: "(1) the purpose of the rule and whether it would be furthered by a retroactive application, (2) the degree of reliance placed on the old rule by those who administered it, and (3) the effect a retroactive application would have on the administration of justice." State v. Nash, 317 A.2d 689 (N.J. 1974). Although those three factors have received detailed attention in our retroactivity case law, our cases also indicate that the retroactivity determination often turns more generally on the court's view of what is just and consonant with public policy in the particular situation presented.

The first factor, the purpose of the new rule, is often the pivotal consideration. For example, if the newly announced rule is an exclusionary rule intended solely to discourage police misconduct, then the rule's purpose would not be served by applying the rule to conduct occurring before the rule was announced. For that reason, exclusionary rules are rarely given retroactive effect. On the other hand, if the old rule was altered because it substantially impaired the reliability of the truth-finding process, the interest in obtaining accurate verdicts may suggest that the new rule be given complete retroactive effect.

The second and third factors come to the forefront of the retroactivity analysis when the inquiry into the purpose of the new rule does not, by itself, reveal whether retroactive application of the new rule would be appropriate. The second factor inquires whether law enforcement agents justifiably relied on the old rule in performing their professional responsibilities. The reasoning underlying this inquiry is that state agents should not be penalized for complying in good faith with prevailing constitutional norms when carrying out their duties. In instances where prior judicial decisions gave state officials reason to question the continued validity of the old rule, the significance of the reliance factor correspondingly decreases.

The third factor in the retroactivity analysis, the effect a retroactive application would have on the administration of justice, recognizes that courts must not impose unjustified burdens on our criminal justice system. Thus, we generally have avoided applying new rules retroactively when such an application would undermine the validity of large numbers of convictions. We have noted our concern about overwhelming courts with retrials, and our awareness of the difficulty in re-prosecuting cases in which the offense took place years in the past.

Our three-pronged retroactivity analysis stems from the test set forth by the United States Supreme Court in Linkletter v. Walker, 381 U.S. 618 (1965). Over the years, however, the federal jurisprudence shifted course, and the federal Supreme Court eventually abandoned the *Linkletter* factors in favor of a more mechanical approach. Under current federal law, new rules based on interpretation of the federal Constitution are to be applied to all cases still on direct appeal, see Griffith v. Kentucky, 479 U.S. 314 (1987), but only in rare circumstances to cases in which all avenues of direct review have been exhausted. Teague v. Lane, 489 U.S. 288 (1989). Although we have noted our agreement with some of the principles underlying *Teague,* we have continued to determine the retroactivity of state rules of law under the *Linkletter* test. See State v. Lark. . . .

The threshold retroactivity issue in this case, whether *Sanchez* announced a new rule of law, is a close question. Our analysis begins with Patterson v. Illinois, 487 U.S. 285 (1988), which was decided four years before *Sanchez.* In *Patterson,* the United States Supreme Court held that reading the *Miranda* rights to an indicted defendant enables that defendant to make an informed and valid waiver of the Sixth Amendment right to counsel. The Court rejected the contention that the Sixth Amendment right to counsel is "more difficult to waive than the Fifth Amendment counterpart." . . .

Four years later, in *Sanchez,* we held that after a defendant has been indicted, administration of *Miranda* warnings during police-initiated interrogation is not adequate to elicit a knowing and voluntary waiver of the right to counsel guaranteed by the State Constitution. We saw *Patterson* as a "change of direction" in the Supreme Court's Sixth Amendment jurisprudence, and found the basis for our decision in "our traditional commitment to the right to counsel." Those observations might imply that the rule set forth in *Sanchez* was not "new," but rather . . . a continuation of traditional adherence to a heightened importance of the right to counsel once the criminal adversarial process has begun. On the other hand, focusing on the period before *Sanchez* was decided, *Patterson* represented the United States Supreme Court's resolution of the question under the federal Constitution, and the *Patterson* Court squarely had rejected the right-to-counsel argument later accepted in *Sanchez*. . . . We therefore conclude that the *Sanchez* rule is "sufficiently novel and unanticipated" to implicate this Court's power to limit the retroactive effect of its decisions. Accordingly, we consider whether retroactive application of the *Sanchez* rule would be appropriate.

To guide us in the inquiry into the purpose of the *Sanchez* rule, we look to the rationale for that rule set forth in *Sanchez* itself:

> The return of an indictment transforms the relationship between the State and the defendant. By obtaining the indictment, the State represents that it has sufficient evidence to establish a prima facie case. Once the indictment is returned, the State is committed to prosecute the defendant. From that moment, if not before, the prosecutor and the defendant are adversaries. . . . Under those circumstances, the perfunctory recitation of the right to counsel and to remain silent may not provide the defendant with sufficient information to make a knowing and intelligent waiver. Such a recitation does not tell the defendant the nature of the charges, the dangers of self-representation, or the steps counsel might take to protect the defendant's interests. [609 A.2d at 408.]

In this case, the inquiry into the purpose of the new rule does not, by itself, reveal whether retroactive application of the rule would be appropriate. Although the *Sanchez* rule is intended, in part, to discourage police interrogation of indicted, unrepresented defendants, it is not solely an exclusionary rule. Similarly, although the rule aims to enhance the reliability of confessions by reducing the inherent coercion of custodial interrogation, it does not replace a rule that substantially impaired the truth-finding function of the criminal trial. Accordingly, we must add to our analysis a consideration of the "reliance" and "administration of justice" factors. Those factors are, to an extent, interrelated in this case.

We fail to discern any appreciable reliance by law enforcement officials on pre-*Sanchez* law. [Only] in exceptional situations would a New Jersey law enforcement officer attempt to interrogate an indicted defendant outside the presence of a defense attorney. We note that in urban counties the first appearance by criminal defendants occurs in Central Judicial Processing (CJP) courts, and in those courts, forms requesting assigned counsel generally are completed by defendants prior to their initial court appearance, and at that court appearance counsel from the public defender's office are generally available to provide representation. . . . Thus, the prevailing practice across much of the State is to provide counsel to defendants immediately after the criminal complaint is filed — even before the grand jury has returned an indictment. . . . Thus, the *Sanchez* rule, which concerns waiver of the right to counsel by indicted yet unrepresented defendants, is implicated only in those unusual cases in which indicted defendants deliberately forgo the right to counsel or absent themselves from their initial court appearance and miss the opportunity to be assigned an attorney. Our assumption is that police do not customarily interrogate indicted and uncounseled defendants.

The third retroactivity factor, the effect retroactive application would have on the administration of justice, militates in favor of limited retroactive application of the *Sanchez* rule. As noted, cases in which the *Sanchez* rule is implicated arise relatively infrequently. Thus, applying *Sanchez* retroactively to cases on direct appeal would neither be chaotic nor overwhelm our courts. However, administration-of-justice considerations counsel against affording *Sanchez* more than "pipeline retroactivity." To accord *Sanchez* complete retroactive effect would impose on the State the burden of reprosecuting some cases in which the offense took place years in the past. Because of failing memories and unavailable witnesses, the problems encountered in prosecuting such cases often are insurmountable.

Based on the three retroactivity factors, we conclude that it would be just and consonant with public policy to apply the *Sanchez* rule in this case. Neither the purpose of the *Sanchez* rule, reliance on pre-*Sanchez* law, nor administration-of-justice considerations justify limiting application of the *Sanchez* rule to cases arising after that decision was announced. Because the pre-*Sanchez* rule did not substantially impair the reliability of the truth-finding process, we will not burden the criminal justice system with the post-conviction-relief applications and retrials that would result from a fully retroactive application of the *Sanchez* decision. *Sanchez* will therefore not apply to those defendants who had exhausted all avenues of direct relief at the time *Sanchez* was decided. . . .

COLEMAN, J., dissenting.

I dissent from the Court's holding that State v. Sanchez should apply retroactively to pipeline cases. The effect of that holding is to require the suppression of an otherwise reliable inculpatory statement by defendant because an F.B.I. Agent in California did not predict that New Jersey would not follow a sixteen-month-old decision of the United States Supreme Court. . . .

As the majority points out, Patterson v. Illinois was consistent with our law and New Jersey did not announce a different rule until nearly four years later when *Sanchez* was decided. Thus, *Sanchez* represented a new rule that could not have been predicted. I fail to see why a rule that served New Jersey well in assuring the reliability of confessions for thirty years under its existing constitution after *Miranda* was decided in 1966 should overnight be found so unreliable as to justify retroactive application of a new rule. The Court rationalizes its conclusion by conjecturing that law enforcement did not rely on *Patterson*. I disagree. It is hard to imagine a rule more deeply etched in the minds of law enforcement agents than the *Miranda* warnings and its progeny, of which *Patterson* is a part. . . . Agent Wilson had every right to rely on the United States Supreme Court's *Patterson* rule when he interrogated defendant only sixteen months after *Patterson* was decided. . . .

MARION REYNOLDS STOGNER v. CALIFORNIA

539 U.S. 607 (2003)

BREYER, J.*

California has brought a criminal prosecution after expiration of the time periods set forth in previously applicable statutes of limitations. California has done so under the authority of a new law that (1) permits resurrection of otherwise time-barred criminal prosecutions, and (2) was itself enacted *after* pre-existing limitations periods had expired. We conclude that the Constitution's Ex Post Facto Clause, Art.I, §10, cl. 1, bars application of this new law to the present case.

I.

In 1993, California enacted a new criminal statute of limitations governing sex-related child abuse crimes. The new statute permits prosecution for those crimes where "the limitation period specified in [a prior statute of limitations] has expired" — provided that (1) a victim has reported an allegation of abuse to the police, (2) "there is independent evidence that clearly and convincingly corroborates the victim's allegation," and (3) the prosecution is begun within one year of the victim's report. Cal. Penal Code §803(g). A related provision, added to the statute in 1996, makes clear that a prosecution satisfying these three conditions "shall revive any cause of action barred by [prior statutes of limitations]." The statute thus authorizes prosecution for criminal acts committed many years beforehand — and where the original limitations period has expired — as long as prosecution begins within a year of a victim's first complaint to the police.

In 1998, a California grand jury indicted Marion Stogner, the petitioner, charging him with sex-related child abuse committed decades earlier — between 1955 and 1973. Without the new statute allowing revival of the State's cause of action, California could not have prosecuted Stogner. The statute of limitations governing prosecutions at the time the crimes were allegedly committed had set forth a 3-year limitations period. And that period had run 22 years or more before the present prosecution was brought. Stogner moved for the complaint's dismissal. He argued that the Federal Constitution's Ex Post Facto Clause, Art. I, §10, cl. 1, forbids revival of a previously time-barred prosecution.

II.

[The] new statute threatens the kinds of harm that, in this Court's view, the Ex Post Facto Clause seeks to avoid. Long ago the Court pointed out that the Clause protects liberty by preventing governments from enacting statutes with "manifestly *unjust and oppressive*" retroactive effects. Calder v. Bull, 3 Dall. 386 (1798). [The] kind of statute at issue falls literally within the categorical descriptions of ex post facto laws set forth by Justice Chase more than 200 years ago in Calder v. Bull. . . . Drawing substantially on Richard Wooddeson's 18th-century commentary on the nature of ex post facto laws and past parliamentary abuses, Chase divided ex post facto laws into categories [as follows]:

* [Justices Stevens, O'Connor, Souter, and Ginsburg joined this opinion.—EDS.]

> I will state what laws I consider ex post facto laws, within the words and the intent of the prohibition. 1st. Every law that makes an action done before the passing of the law, and which was innocent when done, criminal; and punishes such action. *2d. Every law that aggravates a crime, or makes it greater than it was, when committed.* 3d. Every law that changes the punishment, and inflicts a greater punishment, than the law annexed to the crime, when committed. *4th. Every law that alters the legal rules of evidence, and receives less, or different, testimony, than the law required at the time of the commission of the offence, in order to convict the offender.* All these, and similar laws, are manifestly unjust and oppressive. . . . (Emphasis altered from original.)

The second category — including any "law that *aggravates a crime,* or makes it *greater* than it was, when committed" — describes California's statute as long as those words are understood as Justice Chase understood them — i.e., as referring to a statute that "inflicts *punishments,* where the party was not, by *law,* liable to *any punishment.*" After (but not before) the original statute of limitations had expired, a party such as Stogner was not "liable to any punishment." California's new statute therefore "aggravated" Stogner's alleged crime, or made it "greater than it was, when committed," in the sense that, and to the extent that, it "inflicted punishment" for past criminal conduct that (when the new law was enacted) did not trigger any such liability. . . .

So to understand the second category (as applying where a new law inflicts a punishment upon a person not then subject to that punishment, to any degree) explains why and how that category differs from both the first category (making criminal noncriminal behavior) and the third category (aggravating the punishment). . . .

[Numerous] legislators, courts, and commentators have long believed it well settled that the Ex Post Facto Clause forbids resurrection of a time-barred prosecution. Such sentiments appear already to have been widespread when the Reconstruction Congress of 1867 — the Congress that drafted the Fourteenth Amendment — rejected a bill that would have revived time-barred prosecutions for treason that various Congressmen wanted brought against Jefferson Davis and "his coconspirators," Cong. Globe, 39th Cong., 2d Sess., 279 (1866-1867) (comments of Rep. Lawrence). Radical Republicans such as Roscoe Conkling and Thaddeus Stevens, no friends of the South, opposed the bill because, in their minds, it proposed an ex post facto law, and threatened an injustice tantamount to "judicial murder." In this instance, Congress ultimately passed a law extending *unexpired* limitations periods, ch. 236, 15 Stat. 183 — a tailored approach to extending limitations periods that has also been taken in modern statutes. . . .

III.

The dissent . . . emphasizes the harm that child molestation causes, a harm that "will plague the victim for a lifetime," and stresses the need to convict those who abuse children. [We] agree that the State's interest in prosecuting child abuse cases is an important one. But there is also a predominating constitutional interest in forbidding the State to revive a long-forbidden prosecution. And to hold that such a law is ex post facto does not prevent the State from extending time limits for the prosecution of future offenses, or for prosecutions not yet time barred. . . .

KENNEDY, J., dissenting.*

California has enacted a retroactive extension of statutes of limitations for serious sexual offenses committed against minors. The new period includes cases where the limitations period has expired before the effective date of the legislation. To invalidate the statute in the latter circumstance, the Court tries to force it into the second category of Calder v. Bull, which prohibits a retroactive law "that *aggravates a crime,* or makes it *greater* than it was, when committed." These words, in my view, do not permit the Court's holding, but indeed foreclose it. A law which does not alter the definition of the crime but only revives prosecution does not make the crime "greater than it was, when committed." Until today, a plea in bar has not been thought to form any part of the definition of the offense. . . .

The California statute can be explained as motivated by legitimate concerns about the continuing suffering endured by the victims of childhood abuse. The California Legislature noted that young victims often delay reporting sexual abuse because they are easily manipulated by offenders in positions of authority and trust, and because children have difficulty remembering the crime or facing the trauma it can cause. The concern is amply supported by empirical studies.

The problem the legislature sought to address is illustrated well by this case. Petitioner's older daughter testified she did not report the abuse because she was afraid of her father and did not believe anyone would help her. After she left petitioner's home, she tried to forget the abuse. Petitioner's younger daughter did not report the abuse because she was scared. He tried to convince her it was a normal way of life. Even after she moved out of petitioner's house, she was afraid to speak for fear she would not be believed. She tried to pretend she had a normal childhood. It was only her realization that the father continued to abuse other children in the family that led her to disclose the abuse, in order to protect them. . . .

There are two rationales to explain the proposed dichotomy between unexpired and expired statutes, and neither works. The first rationale must be the assumption that if an expired statute is extended, the crime becomes more serious, thereby violating category two; but if an unexpired statute is extended, the crime does not increase in seriousness. . . .

This leaves the second rationale, which must be that an extension of the expired statute destroys a reliance interest. We should consider whether it is warranted to presume that criminals keep calendars so they can mark the day to discard their records or to place a gloating phone call to the victim. The first expectation is minor and likely imaginary; the second is not, but there is no conceivable reason the law should honor it. And either expectation assumes, of course, the very result the Court reaches; for if the law were otherwise, there would be no legitimate expectation. The reliance exists, if at all, because of the circular reason that the Court today says so; it does not exist as part of our traditions or social understanding.

In contrast to the designation of the crime, which carries a certain measure of social opprobrium and presupposes a certain punishment, the statute of limitations has little or no deterrent effect. The Court does not claim a sex offender would desist if he knew he would be liable to prosecution when his offenses were disclosed. . . .

* [Chief Justice Rehnquist and Justices Scalia and Thomas joined this opinion.—EDS.]

The gravity of the crime was known, and is being measured, by its wrongfulness when committed. It is a common policy for States to suspend statutes of limitations for civil harms against minors, in order to protect minors during the period when they are unable to protect themselves. Some States toll the limitations periods for minors even where a guardian is appointed, and even when the tolling conflicts with statutes of repose. The difference between suspension and reactivation is so slight that it is fictional for the Court to say, in the given context, the new policy somehow alters the magnitude of the crime. The wrong was made clear by the law at the time of the crime's commission. The criminal actor knew it, even reveled in it. It is the commission of the then-unlawful act that the State now seeks to punish. The gravity of the crime is left unchanged by altering a statute of limitations of which the actor was likely not at all aware. . . .

Notes

1. *Retroactivity of appellate decisions: majority position.* Historically, appellate courts applied their precedents to all litigants bringing appeals to them, even if the precedents were announced after the proceedings in the trial court were completed. The Warren Court altered the historical approach to retroactivity in Linkletter v. Walker, 381 U.S. 618 (1965), and Stovall v. Denno, 388 U.S. 293 (1967). *Linkletter* dealt with the retroactivity of Mapp v. Ohio, 367 U.S. 643 (1961), which applied the exclusionary rule in state court proceedings for evidence obtained through unconstitutional searches or seizures. Under the new retroactivity doctrine, the appellate court could refuse to give some appellants the benefit of a new constitutional ruling. The defendant in the original appeal would always receive the benefit of the ruling, but other appellants who were complaining on direct appeal about government conduct taking place before the announcement of the new rule might or might not receive the benefit. The answer would depend on the three factors described in the *Knight* decision from New Jersey.

These changes in retroactivity doctrine appeared at a time when the Supreme Court was expanding the influence of the federal constitution in state criminal proceedings. What part did the retroactivity doctrine play in the "activism" of the Warren Court? Imagine yourself as one of the justices who routinely opposed the Court's expansive reading of the constitution. What would be your views about the new retroactivity doctrine? Did it limit the "damage" of wrongheaded decisions, or did it make them possible?

In Griffith v. Kentucky, 479 U.S. 314 (1987), the Supreme Court abandoned the flexible *Linkletter* approach to retroactivity and announced that it would apply its decisions to all cases on direct appeal, even if the new rule of law did not exist at the time of the defendant's trial. In the wake of the *Griffith* case, some state courts have followed suit and have altered their own "retroactivity" standards (which govern the application of state law rulings). See State v. Waters, 987 P.2d 1142 (Mont. 1999) (follows *Griffith*; new rules of criminal procedure are applicable to cases still subject to direct review regardless of whether those rules represent "clear breaks" with the past). It is still common, however, to find decisions such as the New Jersey opinion in *Knight* that retain some discretion on the retroactivity question. When courts insist on some flexibility in deciding retroactivity, are they proclaiming an "activist" posture toward constitutional criminal procedure? Are they suggesting that their decisions in this field are more legislative than judicial, in the traditional senses of those terms?

2. *Retroactivity and plain error*. Recall that appellate courts will normally not hear a claim about legal error at trial if defense counsel failed to preserve that error in the trial court; the only exceptions occur when the legal challenge involves a "plain error." How should courts apply this rule when the legal doctrine involved was not explicitly announced until the time interval between the end of trial and the resolution of the appeal? Won't defendants virtually always fail to object at trial to a failure to observe legal requirements that had not been established at the time of trial? Will defendants actually benefit more if the courts ignore the plain error rule in the context of retroactive changes to the law, but apply the more flexible *Linkletter* approach to retroactivity on direct appeal?

3. *Post-conviction procedural issues*. After a direct appeal is complete, the offender can still challenge the validity of the conviction in court. These postconviction review procedures take a variety of names with somewhat different historical roots; the best-known form, used in both federal and state constitutions, is the writ of habeas corpus. Some states structure their post-conviction processes around a different historical writ — error coram nobis — which focuses more on new evidence. Others have supplanted the traditional postconviction remedies with broader statutes, often simply labeled "postconviction review" acts. These various postconviction review procedures are referred to under the general heading of "collateral" review, and they are nominally civil proceedings. If the judge in a collateral proceeding becomes convinced that the government obtained the conviction illegally, she sometimes has the power to grant relief to the petitioner and overturn the conviction.

The web extension for this casebook contains a chapter dealing with collateral review of convictions. The first section of this chapter considers the history and theory behind the common law writ of habeas corpus. The second section considers some of the basic features of collateral review in the states. Two central questions arise here: What distinguishes collateral review procedures from appeals, and to what extent are such procedures necessary at all? The third section considers the particular and highly political debate about federalism that arises when federal courts review and invalidate convictions obtained in state court. The chapter appears at *http://www.crimpro.com/extension/ch21*.

4. *Retroactivity and collateral review.* Courts usually treat retroactivity questions differently when they arise during post-conviction challenges. Federal courts apply decisions retroactively to cases on direct appeal but not to most defendants who have completed their direct appeals and are bringing a post-conviction collateral attack on the judgment. According to Teague v. Lane, 489 U.S. 288 (1989), new constitutional rules of criminal procedure may not be applied retroactively on federal habeas review unless they place conduct beyond the states' power to criminalize or are "watershed" rules of criminal procedure. State systems, however, are free to give broader retroactive effect during state proceedings to newly announced federal rules of procedure. See Danforth v. Minnesota, 128 S. Ct. 1029 (2008).

If new legal rules were available for post-conviction challenges, would new claims flood the court whenever it announced a new procedural rule? Could this problem be solved by allowing retroactive application of a new rule only for prisoners who have *pending* collateral attacks at the time of the decision? Are there reasons other than sheer numbers of claims to treat those on direct appeal differently from those who have filed (or might file) a collateral attack? See Taylor v. State, 10 S.W.3d 673 (Tex. Crim. App. 2000) (rejects federal retroactivity doctrine and adopts a multifactor approach to determine whether new rules of nonconstitutional state law should be retroactively applied in state post-conviction proceedings).

5. *Ex post facto laws and retroactive statutes.* The ex post facto clause of the federal constitution provides that "[no] state shall . . . pass any . . . ex post facto law." U.S. Const. art. I, §10, cl. 1. In Calder v. Bull, 3 U.S. (3 Dall.) 386, 390 (1798), the Supreme Court explained that the ex post facto clause prohibited the following kinds of laws:

1. Every law that makes an action done before the passing of the law, and which was innocent when done, criminal, and punishes such action.
2. Every law that aggravates a crime, or makes it greater than it was when committed.
3. Every law that changes the punishment, and inflicts a greater punishment than the law annexed to the crime when committed.
4. Every law that alters the legal rules of evidence, and receives less, or different, testimony than the law required at the time of the commission of the offense in order to convict the offender.

In Thompson v. Utah, 170 U.S. 343 (1898), the Court held that a Utah law reducing the size of a criminal jury from 12 to 8 deprived a defendant of "a substantial right involved in his liberty" and thus violated the ex post facto clause. The Court overruled *Thompson* in Collins v. Youngblood, 497 U.S. 37 (1990), concluding that the ex post facto clause does not apply to every change of procedure that "alters the situation of a party to his disadvantage." It upheld a statute allowing an appellate court to reform an unauthorized verdict without having to remand for retrial, even for crimes committed before the passage of the statute. Does *Collins* give a legislature flexibility on the retroactivity question comparable to that of the *Linkletter* rule? Most courts limit application of the ex post facto principle to laws that enhance punishment or are found to be "substantive" rather than "procedural." See also Rogers v. Tennessee, 532 U.S. 451 (2001) (state supreme court abolished common law defense in criminal case and applied new rule retroactively to defendant; due process clause rather than the ex post facto clause controls this situation because it involves judicial rather than legislative action).

6. *Ex post facto and revivification statutes.* In Stogner v. California, 539 U.S. 607 (2003), the Court addressed for the first time the constitutionality of state "revivification" statutes that revive the possibility of prosecution by creating a new and extended statute of limitations after the original time bar has run. Statutes like the one at issue in *Stogner* have been enacted expressly to deal with the psychology that keeps some young offenders from reporting domestic sexual abuse. Both the majority and dissent treat the issue as an easy one under established ex post facto jurisprudence. Do you agree? The majority distinguishes statutes that merely "extend" a prior statute of limitations that has not yet run, saying in dicta that such statutes are constitutional. Can the principles that limit revivification be distinguished from those that allow extension? Does the ex post facto clause have anything to say about how long statutes of limitation can be in the first place?

Table of Cases

Principal Supreme Court cases are in bold. Other principal cases are in italic.

Index